THE ALMANAC OF AMERICAN POLITICS 1994

The Senators, the Representatives and the Governors: Their Records and Election Results, Their States and Districts

Michael Barone and Grant Ujifusa

National Journal

Washington, D.C.

Printed in the United States of America by Arcata Graphics. Composition by Applied Graphics Technologies. Distributed to the trade by Macmillan Publishing Company, 866 Third Avenue, New York, New York 10022.

Photographs by John Eisele, Susan M. Muniak and Bruce Reedy. For information regarding photographs, contact: National Journal, 1730 M Street N.W., Washington, D.C. 20036. Telephone (202) 857-1400. All rights reserved.

ISBN 0-89234-057-6 (Cloth)
ISBN 0-89234-058-4 (Paper)

National Journal Inc.
President: John Fox Sullivan
Vice President, Publishing: Steve Hull
Vice President, Finance: Grace Geisinger
Associate Publisher, Editorial Products: Eleanor D. Evans
Marketing and Circulation Director: Martha Mattare

National Journal Inc. is a wholly-owned subsidiary of the Times Mirror Co.

◥▼ A Times Mirror
◣◢ Company

THE ALMANAC OF AMERICAN POLITICS 1994

Authors: Michael Barone, Grant Ujifusa

Editor: Eleanor Evans

Managing Editor, Research: John Gallagher

Assistant Managing Editor: Cathryn M. Newson

Associate Editor: Tracy McLoone

Contributing Editor: Gary Cohen

Senior Researcher: Eugene Cha

Research Assistants: Doug Adams, Catherine A. Berger, Mary Lou Wendell

Production Assistants: Alida James, Isobel Ellis

Campaign Finance: Dwight Morris, Murielle Gamache

Photographers: John Eisele, Susan Muniak, Bruce Reedy

State Maps: NCEC Services Inc.

Publisher: John Fox Sullivan

The Almanac especially would like to thank the entire staff of *National Journal* for their invaluable support and assistance during the production of this book. Additionally, we would like to acknowledge the following organizations for the services they provided: National Committee for an Effective Congress, Applied Graphics Technologies and Montgomery Data.

CONTENTS

CONGRESS AT-A-GLANCE

GUIDE TO USAGE

The Almanac of American Politics is designed to be self-explanatory. The following guide provides a brief description of each section and a list of sources from which information was derived, both of which serve as a road map to understanding the meaning behind the figures.

The People

Population. All population figures, excluding unemployment rates and voter registration, are from the Bureau of the Census, U.S. Department of Commerce, Washington D.C. 20230, 301-763-4040.

Race and Ethnic Origin. For the 1990 Census, the Census Bureau asked people what their race or ethnic origin was. Race, as defined by the Bureau of the Census, reflects the individual respondents' perception of his or her racial identity and does not reflect any biological or anthropological definition. The basic racial categories are: American Indian or Alaska Native; Asian or Pacific Islander; Black; and White. Hispanic origin is defined as an ethnicity, and includes those who classified themselves in one of three specific Hispanic categories on the census form (Cuban, Mexican, Puerto Rican) or as of "other Spanish/Hispanic origin"; persons of Hispanic origin may be of any race. Origin can be viewed as ancestry, nationality group or country of birth. The "Other" category was intended to include those persons who do not consider themselves to be in the basic racial or ethnic categories.

Households and Housing Information. A Household is defined as including all persons occupying a housing unit; a Married Couple Family is a household of persons related by marriage. Owner occupied housing units include only single-family houses on less than ten acres with no business or medical office on the property. The value of a housing unit is the respondent's estimate of how much the unit would sell for if it were for sale, and determines Median House Value. Monthly rent is defined as the per-month contract rent agreed to for a unit, regardless of any goods or services that may be included (e.g. utilities), and determines Median Monthly Rent.

Age. The Bureau of the Census defines age as based on the number of years a person completed as of April 1, 1990. This definition was used to determine the voting age population, the percentage of population over 65 years of age, and the median age. Many people, however, provided their age as of the date they completed the census form rather than the definition provided by the Bureau of the Census.

Education. The level of higher education is measured by the Census from persons over 25 years of age who have pursued vocational, public, or private forms of college education not necessarily leading to graduation.

Unemployment. All unemployment figures are from the Bureau of Labor Statistics, U.S. Department of Labor, Washington, D.C. 20210, 202-606-7828. These figures represent the average rate of unemployment for each state for 1992.

Registered Voters. Registered voter numbers are from the individual states' election bureaus or political parties, and represent the number of voters officially registered as close as possible to the November, 1992 election. Some states have no voter registration.

Political Lineup. This block includes the names of top state officials as well as a breakdown by party of the state legislative bodies. The names of U.S. senators and a party breakdown of the state's congressional delegation are also provided.

Presidential Vote. The 1988 and 1992 presidential vote is included for each state and congressional district. Presidential vote on the state level was drawn from state election returns. Presidential vote by congressional district was derived from state, county and precinct results as compiled by staff of the National Committee for an Effective Congress (NCEC), 507 Capitol Ct., N.E., Washington, D.C. 20002, 202-547-1151. Discrepancies exist between the state and district figures because of inconsistent reporting methods employed by the counties, the states and the FEC. Results of the presidential primaries were provided by the states and the FEC. Caucus results are not provided.

Biography. This section lists when each governor, senator and representative was elected or appointed, date and place of birth, home, college education and degrees obtained (if any), religion, marital status and, if applicable, spouse's name. Also listed is a brief outline of the politician's career, including military service in the Air Force, Army, Marine Corps, Navy, National Guard, or Reserves, and his or her office addresses and telephone numbers. Committee and subcommittee assignments are provided as well. (Note: On many committees, the chairman and ranking minority member are ex officio members of each subcommittee on which they do not hold a regular assignment.)

Ratings

Rating Groups. The congressional rating statistics of 11 lobby groups provide an idea of a legislator's general ideology and the degree to which the legislator represents different groups' interests. Not just a record of liberal/conservative voting behavior, these ratings come from a range of groups concerned with everything from single issues (environmental concerns) to the political interests of a particular sector (e.g., consumers). The order of the groups is such that the more "liberal" groups are on the left and the more "conservative" are on the right. Three groups, ACLU, NTLC and NSI release ratings only once every two years, the duration of one full congressional session. Following is a general description of each organization, its address and telephone number.

ADA   Americans for Democratic Action
1625 K St., N.W., #210, Washington, D.C. 20006, 202-785-5980.
    Liberal: Since its founding in 1947, ADA members have pushed for legislation designed to reduce inequality, curtail rising defense spending, prevent encroachments on civil liberties and promote international human rights. The ADA uses a broad spectrum of issues for its vote analysis.

ACLU   American Civil Liberties Union
122 Maryland Ave., N.E., Washington, D.C. 20002, 202-544-1681.
    Pro-individual liberties: ACLU seeks to protect individuals from legal, executive and congressional infringement on basic rights guaranteed by the Bill of Rights. The ACLU ratings are published for every Congress; the 1992 ratings include the years 1991 and 1992.

COPE   Committee on Political Education of the AFL-CIO
815 16th St., N.W., 6th Floor, Washington, D.C. 20006, 202-637-5122.
    Liberal-Labor: As the powerful and well-funded arm of the AFL-CIO, COPE is concerned with the economic interests of the American worker. While COPE covers a broad spectrum of issues, it monitors few votes on foreign policy and defense spending. These ratings are based on members' cumulative lifetime records.

CDF   Children's Defense Fund
25 E St., N.W., Washington, D.C. 20001, 202-628-8787
Pro-childrens rights: The Children's Defense Fund is a nonpartisan organization which exists to provide a strong and effective voice for the children of America. The Fund pays particular attention to the needs of poor, minority, and disabled children. CDF is a private nonprofit organization supported by foundations, corporations and individuals.

CFA   Consumer Federation of America
1424 16th St., N.W., #604, Washington, D.C. 20036, 202-387-6121.
Pro-Consumer: CFA is a group spawned in the mid-sixties as a pro-consumer counterweight to various business-oriented lobbies. Their vote ratings concentrate on pocketbook consumer issues and health and safety concerns.

LCV   League of Conservation Voters
1707 L St., N.W., #550, Washington, D.C. 20036, 202-785-8683.
Environmental: Formed in 1970, LCV is the national, non-partisan arm of the environmental movement. LCV works to elect pro-environmental candidates to Congress. LCV ratings are based on key votes concerning energy, environment and natural resource issues, selected by leaders from major national environmental organizations.

ACU   American Conservative Union
38 Ivy St., S.E., Washington, D.C. 20003, 202-546-6555.
Conservative: Since 1971, ACU ratings have provided a means of gauging the conservatism of members of Congress. Foreign policy, social and budget issues are their primary concerns.

NTLC   National Tax-Limitation Committee
201 Massachusetts Ave., N.E., #C-7, Washington, D.C. 20002, 202-547-4196.
Pro-tax limitation: NTLC was organized in 1975 to seek constitutional and other limits on taxes, spending and deficits at the state and federal levels. NTLC actively pursues a balanced budget/tax limitation amendment to the U. S. Constitution. These ratings are based on budget issue votes and bills which would have a major impact on long-term government taxing and spending programs.

NSI   National Security Index of the American Security Council
1155 15th St., N.W., #1101, Washington, D.C. 20005, 202-484-1676.
Pro-strong defense: Founded in 1965, the Council feels that American security is best preserved by developing and maintaining large weapons systems to achieve strategic military superiority. The NSI rates members on their support of defense and foreign policy issues that affect the NSI strategy of peace through strength.

COC   Chamber of Commerce of the United States
1615 H Street, N.W., Washington, D.C. 20062, 202-659-6000.
Pro-business: Founded in 1912 as a voice for organized business, COC represents local, regional and state chambers of commerce in addition to trade and professional organizations.

CEI   Competitive Enterprise Institute
1001 Connecticut Ave., N.W., #1250, Washington, D.C. 20036, 202-331-1010.
Pro-free enterprise: Founded in 1984, CEI's purpose is to advance the principles of free enterprise and limited government. CEI focuses on deficit reduction and tax reform, deregulation and privatization, free market approaches to environmental problems, anti-trust reform and international trade.

National Journal Ratings. *National Journal*'s rating system establishes an objective method of analyzing congressional voting. A panel of *National Journal* editors and staff initially compiled a list of congressional roll call votes and classified them as either economic, social or foreign policy-related. Professor Garrison Nelson of the University of Vermont provided the computerized roll-call data. The interrelationship of these votes was shown by a statistical procedure called "principal components analysis," which revealed which "yea" votes and which "nay" votes fit a liberal or a conservative pattern. The votes in each of the three subject areas were computer-weighted to reflect the degree they fit the common pattern. All members of Congress who participated in at least half of the votes in each area received ratings; those who missed more that half the votes were not scored (shown as *). Absences and abstentions were not counted.

Members of Congress were then ranked according to relative liberalism and conservatism. Finally, they were assigned percentiles showing their rank relative to others in their chamber. Percentile scores range from a minimum of 0 to a maximum of 99. Because some members voted liberal or conservative on every roll call, however, there are ties at the liberal and conservative ends of each scale. For that reason, the maximum percentiles often turn out to be less than 99.

Votes

Key Votes. The Key Votes section attempts to illustrate a legislator's stance on important votes where he or she must vote *for* or *against* a national issue. The process grossly oversimplifies the legislative system where months of debate, amendment, pressure, persuasion, and compromise go into a final floor vote. However, the voting record remains the best indication of a member's general ideologies and position on specific issues.

Following is a list of key votes used. A member who was absent, voted present, or who was not in office at the time of a particular vote receives an asterisk. The votes were drawn from Legi-Slate, a computer system tracking legislation, voting attendance, committee schedules, etc. For information on Legi-Slate or their vote recording process, please contact: Legi-Slate, 777 N. Capitol St., N.E., Ste. 900, Washington, D.C. 20002, 202-898-2300.

Senate Votes, 102d Congress:

1) **$ for Homeownership**   (HR 1281) Transfer $1 billion from public housing programs to new programs, supported by the Bush Administration, to promote homeownership. March 13, 1991. Rejected 40-60. (D:5-51; R:35-9).

2) **Have Cap Gains Debate**   (S 1722) Procedural motion to table a point of order against a capital gains tax cut amendment. September 24, 1991. Rejected 39-60. (D:0-56; R:39-4).

3) **Remove Budget Walls**   (S 2399) Procedural motion on removing the walls barring a shift in funds from defense to domestic programs. March 26, 1992. Passed 50-48. (D:47-8; R:3-40).

4) **Ban Striker Replace**   (S 55) Limit debate on barring employers from hiring workers to replace striking workers. June 16, 1992. Passed 57-42. (D:52-5; R:5-37).

5) **Clarence Thomas Nom.**   Confirm the nomination of Clarence Thomas to be an Associate Justice of the U.S. Supreme Court. October 15, 1991. Passed 52-48. (D:11-46; R:41-2).

6) **Lmt. Death Row Appeal**   (S 1241) Restrict appeals for prisoners on death row. June 26, 1991. Passed 58-40. (D:16-40; R:42-0).

7) **Handgun Wait/5-Day**   (S 1241) Require a five-business-day waiting period for handgun purchases and mandate a criminal background check. June 28, 1991. Passed 67-32. (D:48-8; R:19-24).

8) **Abortion Gag Rule**   (S 323) Prohibit federally financed family planning clinics from counseling pregnant women on abortion. July 16, 1991. Rejected 35-64. (D:8-48; R:27-16).

9) **Use Force in Gulf**   (SJR 2) Authorize the use of United States Armed Forces in the Persian Gulf, pursuant to United Nations Security Council Resolution 678. January 12, 1991. Passed 52-47. (D:10-45; R:42-2)

10) **Keep Salvador Aid**   (S 1435) Table restrictions on military aid to El Salvador. July 25, 1991. Rejected 43-56. (D:5-51; R:38-5).

11) **Cut $1 B from SDI**   (S 1507) Cut $1 billion in funds for the Strategic Defense Initiative. August 1, 1991. Rejected 46-52. (D:41-14; R:5-38).

12) **Override China MFN**   (HR 5318) Override President Bush's veto of a bill granting most-favored-nation trade status to China. October 1, 1992. Rejected 59-40. (D:51-5; R:8-35).

Senate Votes, 103d Congress:

1) **Family Leave**   (HR 1) Require employers with more than 50 employees to provide 12 weeks of unpaid leave to tend to a newborn or an ill family member. February 4, 1993. Passed 71-27. (D:55-2; R:16-25).

2) **HIV Immigrants**   (S 1) Substitute for a separate provision that would prohibit immigration of HIV-infected persons. February 18, 1993. Rejected 52-46. (D:36-19; R:6-37).

3) **Clinton Budget**   (HCR 64) Approve FY94 budget resolution, including instructions to committees to report legislation implementing the Clinton economic program. March 25, 1993. Passed 54-45. (D:54-2; R:0-43).

House Votes, 102d Congress:

1) **Ban Striker Replace**   (HR 5) Bar employers from hiring workers to replace striking workers. July 17, 1991. Passed 247-182. (D:230-33; R:16-149).

2) **$ for Homeownership**   (HR 5679) Recommit a bill to increase funds, backed by the Bush Administration, promoting homeownership. July 29, 1992. Rejected 198-209. (D:39-204; R:159-4).

3) **Tax Rich/Cut Mid Cls.**   (HR 4210) Decrease tax rates for the middle class and raise tax rates for the wealthy. February 27, 1992. Passed 221-209. (D:219-46; R:1-163).

4) **FY93/$15 B Def. Cut**   (HCR 287) Approve the FY93 budget, decreasing by $15 billion the amount of defense funding proposed by President Bush. March 5, 1992. Passed 224-191. (D:219-39; R:5-151).

5) **Handgun Wait/7-Day**   (HR 7) Require a seven-day waiting period for the purchase of handguns. May 8, 1991. Passed 239-186. (D:179-83; R:60-102).

6) **Overseas Mil. Abortion**   (HR 2100) Provide reproductive health services, including abortion, for overseas military personnel and their dependents. May 22, 1991. Passed 220-208. (D:184-79; R:35-129).

7) **Obscn. Art NEA $ Ban**   (HR 2686) Bar the National Endowment for the Arts from funding projects that offensively depict or describe sexual or excretory organs or matter. October 16, 1991. Passed 286-135. (D:140-121; R:146-13).

8) **Death Pen. from Jury**   (HR 3371) Permit juries to impose the death penalty in certain cases where there has been deemed a reckless disregard for life. October 16, 1991. Passed 213-206. (D:63-195; R:150-10).

9) **Use Force in Gulf**   (HJR 77) Authorize the use of force in the Persian Gulf by the U.S. Military. January 12, 1991. Passed 250-183. (D:86-179; R:164-3).

10) **U.S. Mil. Abroad $ Cut**   (HR 5006) Cut $3.5 billion for U.S. troops stationed in Europe and Asia. June 3, 1992. Passed 220-185. (D:180-68; R:39-117).

11) **Limit SDI Funds**   (HR 5504) Limit funding for the Strategic Defense Initiative to $3.6 billion. July 2, 1992. Rejected 201-217. (D:174-82; R:26-135).

12) **Cuba Trade Embargo**   (HR 5323) Strengthen the U.S. trade embargo against Cuba. September 24, 1992. Passed 276-135. (D:139-110; R:137-24).

House Votes, 103d Congress:

1) **Family Leave**   (HR 1) Require employers with more than 50 workers to provide 12 weeks of unpaid leave to tend to a newborn or an ill family member. February 3, 1993. Passed 265-163. (D:224-29; R:40-134).

2) **Deficit Reduction**   (HR 2264) Budget reconciliation for FY94. Includes proposed tax increases and spending cuts to achieve Clinton's deficit reduction goals. March 25, 1993. Passed 219-213. (D:218-39; R:0-175).

3) **Stimulus Plan**   (HR 1335) Pass the Clinton Administration's proposed $16 billion in new spending to stimulate the economy. March 18, 1990. Passed 235-190. (D:231-22; R:3-168).

Election Results

Election Results. Listed for each member of the House are results of the 1992 general, runoff and primary elections, as well as the 1990 general elections (results of any special elections are also listed). Gubernatorial and senatorial results are presented in a like manner. Votes and percentages are included, indicating the margin of victory (due to the process of rounding up and rounding down, some totals may equal more or less than 100%). Candidates receiving less than 4% of the total vote are listed as "Other." Dollar amounts listed to the right of the vote totals are campaign expenditures as reported by the candidate to the Federal Election Commission. Election returns were provided by state Secretaries of State and Boards of Elections.

Campaign Finance

All data are derived from candidates' campaign finance reports and party reports, as well as other official and preliminary studies available from the Federal Election Commission (FEC), 999 E St., NW, Washington, D.C. 20463, 202-219-4140 (toll free, 1-800-424-9530). The figures were compiled by Dwight Morris and Murielle Gamache of the Washington, D.C., bureau of the Los Angeles Times.

Receipts and expenditure activity covers the period beginning January 1, 1991 and ending December 31, 1992 (1991–92 election cycle), for House members. For Senators, these figures represent activity for the 6-year cycle prior to their last election date.

Receipts. Receipts include all incoming funds as reported by the candidate for the 1992 campaign. Candidate committees report all funds received in the form of contributions from individuals, political parties, PACs and the candidate themselves, as well as loans or receipts in the form of earnings on previously received funds (interests, dividends). Refunds have been excluded from the total.

Expenditures (Expend.). Expenditures include all outgoing funds spent by the candidate committees, including loan repayments and contributions by the committee to other candidates or committees. As with Receipts, refunds of contributions have been subtracted from the total.

Cash-on-Hand (C-O-H). This figure refers to a campaign's remaining cash on hand reported as of December 31, 1992. In many cases, this number does not represent the difference between listed receipts and expenditures.

Political Action Committee Contributions (PACS). PACS are defined as organizations not directly affiliated with a candidate or political party, and must be registered as such under the Federal Election Campaign Act. PAC figures represent donations of money, goods or services to a campaign by Political Action Committees. The FEC also treats contributions from one candidate to another as though they are PAC contributions.

Candidate Contributions (Cand.). Candidate Contributions include direct contributions, candidate secured loans and other loans, and transfers from other authorized campaign committees from a candidate to that candidate's campaign committee.

Party Contributions (Party). Party Contributions include contributions from only those organizations registered as party committees under the Federal Election Campaign Act. These contributions can be in the form of funds or of goods and services to a campaign. Independent party expenditures spent on behalf on a candidate but not directly contributed to a candidate committee are not included here.

Out-of-State Contributions (Out of St.). Out-of-State Contributions include all contributions and refunds of $200.00 or more from sources outside of the candidate's home state made during the election cycle. It is impossible to say with any certainty that this figure represents all of a candidates out-of-state contributions since the origin of contributions in increments of less than $200.00 are not necessarily traced by the FEC. Also, Senators were not required to include contributions under $500.00 prior to the 1989-1990 cycle.

Small Individual Contributions (Sm. Indiv.). Small Individual contributions include personal contributions to a candidate committee of less than $200.00.

Large Individual Contributions (Lg. Indiv.). Large Individual contributions include personal contributions to a candidate's committee of $200.00 or more.

Cost-per-Vote (C-P-V). Cost-per-Vote is calculated by dividing total expenditures by the number of votes received by the winning candidate.

Spending Edge (Spnd. Edge). The Spending Edge is the difference between the campaign expenditures of the winning candidate and the losing candidate in each election. Where the winning candidate was outspent by an opponent, the Spending Edge will be a negative number. The FEC does not require candidates raising or spending less than $5000.00 to file, though some do so anyway; if an opponent spent less than $5000.00 and chose not to file, the FEC considers them as having spent $0.00. In these cases, the winning candidate's spending edge will equal their expenditure figure.

Debts. Debts include total debts owed by a campaign following his or her last election cycle.

ABBREVIATIONS

A.A.	Administrative Assistant	AGN	Against
ABC	Americans for Better Childcare Act	AI	Alaska Independent Party
		AI	American Independent Party (CA)
ACLU	American Civil Liberties Union	AME	African Methodist Episcopal
ACP	A Connecticut Party	ANWR	Arctic National Wildlife Refuge
ACU	American Conservative Union	AS	American Samoa
ADA	Americans for Democratic Action, Americans with Disabilities Act	ASI	American Systems Independent Party (PA)

BCCI	Bank of Credit and Commerce International	**ERISA**	Employee Retirement Income Security Act
Bd.	Board	**Expend.**	Expenditure/s
BGH	Bovine Growth Hormone		
Btu	British thermal unit	**FCP**	Free Congress Political Action Committee
BVP	Brooklyn Voters Party (NY)		
		FTP	Free The People Party (CA)
C	Conservative Party (NY)	**FY**	Fiscal Year
CAB	Civil Aeronautics Board		
CAFE	Corporate Average Fuel Economy	**GREEN**	Green Party
Cand.	Candidate	**H**	Capitol Building—House side
CCP	Change Congress Party		
CDF	Children's Defense Fund	**HSOB**	Hart Senate Office Building
CEI	Competitive Enterprise Institute	**I, Ind., Indep.**	Independent
CFA	Consumer Federation of America	**IC**	Independent Conservative
		IMF	International Monetary Fund
CHOB	Cannon House Office Building	**INF**	Independent Fusion Party
		INN	Independent Neighbor's Party (NY)
CIA	Central Intelligence Agency		
COC	Chamber of Commerce of the United States	**IR**	Independent-Republican Party (MN)
COH	Cash-On-Hand	**IRA**	Individual Retirement Account
COLA	Cost of Living Adjustment		
COPE	Committee on Political Education (AFL-CIO)	**ISTEA**	Intermodal Surface Transportation Efficiency Act
CORE	Congress on Racial Equality		
CSP	Common Sense Party (NY)	**IVP**	Independent Voters Party (NY)
D	Democrat		
DCCC	Democratic Congressional Campaign Committee	**JBS**	Jobs Party (NY)
		JWP	Jim Wham Party (IL)
Dem.	Democratic		
DFL	Democratic–Farmer–Labor Party (MN)	**L**	Liberal Party
		LCV	League of Conservation Voters
DLC	Democratic Leadership Council	**LHOB**	Longworth House Office Building
DNC	Democratic National Committee	**LIB**	Libertarian Party
		LIF	Long Island First party (NY)
DOE	U.S. Department of Energy		
DOT	U.S. Department of Transportation	**LWV**	League of Women Voters
DSCC	Democratic Senatorial Campaign Committee	**MFN**	Most Favored Nation
		MTV	Music Television
DSOB	Dirksen Senate Office Building	**NAFTA**	North American Free Trade Agreement
EMILY	Early Money is Like Yeast	**NAP**	New Alliance Party
EPA	U.S. Environmental Protection Agency	**NARAL**	National Abortion Rights Action League

NEA	National Endowment for the Arts	**RSOB**	Russell Senate Office Building
NRCC	National Republican Congressional Committee	**RTL**	Right-to-Life Party (NY)
NRSC	National Republican Senatorial Committee	**S**	Capitol Building—Senate side
NSI	National Security Index of the American Security Council	**S & L**	Savings and Loan
		SDI	Strategic Defense Initiative
		Sen./s	Senator/s
NTLC	National Tax-Limitation Committee	**SIS**	Staten Island Secession Party (NY)
		SOL	Solidarity Party (IL)
PAC	Political Action Committee	**S.U.N.Y.**	State University of New York
P & F	Peace & Freedom Party (CA)	**SWP**	Socialist Workers Party
PDP	Popular Democratic Party (PR)	**TXB**	Tax Break Party (NY)
POP	Populist Party		
PR	Puerto Rico	**UAW**	United Auto Workers
		UDAG	Urban Development Action Grant
R, Repub.	Republican		
RC	Rainbow Coalition		
Rep./s	Representative/s	**VA**	Veterans' Administration
RHOB	Rayburn House Office Building	**VRP**	Voters Rights Party (NY)
RMM	Ranking Minority Member	**WASP**	White, Anglo-Saxon, Protestant
RNC	Republican National Committee	**WIC**	Women and Infant Children

POSTWAR POLITICS

I. THE POSTWAR CONTEXT

The 1990s have been years of peculiar instability in American electoral politics. Any account of these years must explain the wide oscillations in public opinion—how George Bush went from 91% approval in March 1991 to 25% in July 1992, how Ross Perot went from nowhere to first in the presidential race from March to July 1992, how Bill Clinton climbed from 25% in June 1992 to 57% in July 1992, then fell to 43% of the vote, or how he squandered the usual indulgence Americans give to their incoming presidents and fell to a negative job approval rating by May 1993. The best explanation is that the U.S. has been in a period of postwar politics—post-Cold War, post-Gulf war.

For instability of opinion and party preference is characteristic of postwar periods. In June 1945, the British electorate famously rejected Winston Churchill after his five years of magnificent war leadership, ousting his Conservative Party and giving the Labour Party its largest parliamentary majority ever. Similarly, in November 1946, the first general election after the American victory in World War II, the Democrats, for the first time in 16 years, were swept out of control of both houses of Congress, losing 54 seats in the House and 12 in the Senate. Just two years later, in 1948, the Democrats won back control of both houses of Congress by large margins, picking up 75 seats in the House and nine in the Senate, and producing more House freshmen (118) than in any year since, including 1992, and won an upset victory for President Harry Truman. Something similar happened in the United States after World War I. Woodrow Wilson's Democrats in November 1918, just days after the Armistice, lost control of both houses of Congress, losing 26 seats in the House and seven in the Senate; then in November 1920, after the defeat of the Versailles Treaty and Woodrow Wilson's incapacitation, they lost a further 59 seats in the House and 10 in the Senate. Two years later, they snapped back, though not to majorities, with gains of 74 House seats and five in the Senate.

Why these vast shifts in postwar periods? It is as if people come up out of the trenches, after years of bombardment and danger and misery, and suddenly see what Winston Churchill called the "bright, sunlit uplands," with a vast landscape before them. It is exhilarating, but disorienting: people want a road map, a sense of where they are going and how much progress they have made, of what pathways to choose and where each one will lead. Winston Churchill's Conservatives lost because the Labour Party had such a map: the Beveridge Report and other specific plans for the welfare state that the Labour government in fact established in the years just after the war. Robert Taft's Republicans during those same years had a clear domestic program, which in fact they accomplished: dismantle domestic price controls, cut tax rates, limit the power of labor unions. But when voters did not want to take that road any further, they rewarded the Democrats for their programs that encouraged, assisted, subsidized and honored upwardly mobile behavior: the G.I. Bill of Rights, the FHA home mortgage guarantees and the children's allowance created by the combination of generous dependent deductions and a steeply graduated income tax.

It was not so immediately apparent that the United States in the 1990s was in a postwar period. The Cold War ended abruptly, but not with the official suddenness of the Armistice of November 1918 or the unconditional surrenders of May and September 1945. The Berlin Wall came down in October 1989, and Eastern Europe was soon free of the Soviet yoke; but it was not until the failure of the Soviet coup in August 1991 and the abolition of the Soviet Union in December 1991 that the threat to the United States and the free world from Soviet military power clearly had dissipated. In the Gulf war, in contrast, the United States achieved a clear victory in March 1991, but Saddam Hussein remained in power and the war itself, though it momentarily held the nation breathless, was not of the length or magnitude to make Americans feel they had spent long months under siege. Even so, it was plain as these conflicts ended that Americans were living in, and inevitably had special responsibilities in, a new world. Climbing out more slowly, and less surely, we still found that we had emerged from the trenches. We needed a road map. And George Bush, a competent leader in the Cold War and the Gulf war, proved exactly the wrong kind of leader for the postwar period: with his disdain for what he called "the vision thing," his distaste for general principles and abstract concepts, his unwillingness to enunciate and perhaps even envision a long-range strategy, he did not provide his constituents with the one thing they wanted—a road map.

II. THE 1991–92 CAMPAIGN CYCLE

George Bush could have seized the national imagination in his speech to Congress after the Gulf War in March 1991. Instead, he asked for passage of his transportation bill and a routine crime bill. He could have used the occasion of the weakening economy in late 1991 to articulate a vision of America growing with creative private entrepreneurship and empowered personal choice. Instead, he announced that he would delay any economic program until the new year. His plans proved tepid, and lacked the framework—the road map—voters craved. Meanwhile, he was on the defensive politically, not so much from the Democrats as from Pat Buchanan, who abandoned his work as a columnist and television debater to run a feisty campaign in New Hampshire, the state where Bush won his decisive victory over Bob Dole in February 1988 and his second highest percentage in November 1988. But New Hampshire had been intensely afflicted by the unexpected economic downturn, not so much an income recession (for by historic measures this was a shallow recession) but a wealth recession, which attacked not just one year's earnings but seemed to threaten the lifelong accumulation of wealth, in the form of residential real estate and modest investments, the common American experience by the 1990s. More than four-fifths of Americans had accumulated more than $100,000 of wealth in their lifetimes, most of that in their homes; but residential real estate values fell nationally in 1990 and 1991, plummeting sharply in New England and especially New Hampshire, which was hurt by the woes of local high-tech firms. Bush suddenly was forced to defend himself on the most unfriendly of terrain, and in February 1992 Bush won the primary by only 53%–37%. That turned out to be the high-water mark of Buchanan's candidacy, which signalled less the popularity of his eccentric mix of policies (opposition to free trade, immigration, the Gulf war: the old Republicanism of Robert Taft, out of hibernation after 40 years) than Bush's tenuous hold on the public imagination.

At this stage, the best thing going for Bush seemed to be the weakness of the Democrats. Their five candidates were little known or unknown nationally, none had significant foreign policy experience and each seemed to have disqualifying weaknesses. Tom Harkin, senator from Iowa, was a fiery exponent of Democratic old-time religion, a denouncer of trickle-down economics and of George Herbert Walker Bush; but his impressive victory in his home state caucuses was discounted as no one competed against him there. Bob Kerrey, senator from Nebraska, was expected to dazzle voters with inspirational rhetoric and his Congressional Medal of Honor from Vietnam, but, despite his ability to discuss in detail his proposal for national health insurance, he failed to convince voters who saw him up close. Two other candidates found constituencies in New Hampshire and later primaries. Jerry Brown, elected governor of the nation's largest state at 36 and defeated for election to the Senate at 44, abandoned a California Senate race and campaigned as the tribune of outsiders, accepting no contribution higher than $100, giving out his 800 number in television interviews and running against lobbyists and political insiders of both parties. His voters tended to be young and unconnected to existing civic organizations. As odd, in different ways, was the candidacy of Paul Tsongas, lawyer from Lowell, Massachusetts, two-term congressman and one-term senator who retired in 1984 when he found out he had cancer; he underwent bone marrow replacement therapy and, he said, had no recurrence, although after his candidacy was over it was reported that he had indeed had one. Tsongas brandished an 83-page booklet which stated his opinions on many issues, developed over his years in public office and as a Boston lawyer and board member of corporations like Lowell-based Wang. Tsongas focused on the federal budget deficit and called for higher taxes and cuts in spending, including Social Security; his constituency was clustered heavily among the highly educated and affluent, who made up a far larger percentage of Democratic primary voters in 1992 than as recently as 1984 and gave him the New Hampshire primary victory.

But the clear leader in the Democratic field, at least after a December 1991 speech to the Democratic state chairmen, was Bill Clinton, governor of Arkansas. The themes Clinton embraced as head of the moderate Democratic Leadership Council, including welfare reform, national service and a "New Covenant," were attractive, and his abilities and interpersonal skills clearly superior to those of his opponents. This, plus the support of his wife Hillary Clinton (as he then referred to her) on *60 Minutes*, enabled Clinton to survive the charges by Gennifer Flowers in January 1992 of a 12-year affair with her. He was also dogged by stories that he had avoided the military draft, including the release of a letter he wrote to the director of the University of Arkansas ROTC thanking him for "saving me from the draft" and preserving his "political viability"; he promised to enroll in the ROTC, though he was not a student there at the time—an extraordinary circumstance—at a time when he might have been drafted and did not abandon the possibility of joining the ROTC until receiving a high lottery number. As became apparent later, Clinton lied many times about his draft status and concealed the fact that he had received a draft notice. But his genuine strengths as a candidate, his attractive platform, his ability to rally in a crisis and the weakness of his opponents enabled him to finish a solid second in New Hampshire and to win primaries first in Georgia on March 3 and the Super Tuesday South March 10, and then to essentially clinch the Democratic nomination by winning Illinois and Michigan March 17.

But even as Clinton was going through the motions of the Democratic primary, the spotlight was stolen by Texas billionaire Ross Perot, who on *Larry King Live* in February said he would run for president if enough people wanted him to. Perot's crisp certainty and gift for sound bites ("I won't sound bite this") made him popular; his sharp attacks on budget deficits and calls for shared sacrifice struck a chord; his military background and success in business on one hand and his support of abortion rights and even gays in the military on the other made him a bridge between culturally hostile groups in a culturally divided country. Perot's campaign "departisanized the critique of Bush," as Democratic strategist Paul Tully put it, pushing Bush lower and lower in the polls in the spring as a then-wounded and distrusted Bill Clinton could not have done. By June 1992, Perot was running even or ahead in a three-way race in national polls; Clinton was running a poor third and Bush as incumbent president was losing the votes of two of three Americans. The young vote, solidly Republican for a decade, shifted to Perot, and then, especially after his appearance on MTV in June and his selection of Al Gore as vice presidential candidate in July, to Clinton.

Then, on the Thursday of the Democratic convention, Perot withdrew from the race and saluted "revitalization" of the Democratic Party, and Clinton's share of the vote, recently 25%, shot up to 57%. Not a great deal of difference was made by the rest of the campaign. The Bush forces succeeded in the Republican National Convention to reestablish the party's hold on the cultural right, perhaps 20% of the electorate; but the media was outraged by the convention, and so were perhaps 20% on the cultural left. Although Ross Perot reentered the race October 1, he won less support than he had before July 16; yet he was competitive in polls in many states, and ended up finishing second in two (Maine and Utah). Support for Bill Clinton oscillated during the fall debates. After the October 13 debate, in which Dan Quayle beat Al Gore by hammering home his contentions that Clinton would raise taxes and that he had "trouble telling the truth," the Bush-Quayle ticket cut the Clinton-Gore margin in polls to its narrowest until the final week. In the October 15 Oprah Winfrey/Phil Donahue style debate, George Bush seemed bewildered while Bill Clinton shone, and the Clinton-Gore margin widened again. In the final week, Ross Perot made bizarre charges, aired on *60 Minutes*, saying that he had withdrawn from the race because George Bush was threatening to sabotage his daughter's wedding; this, like his other bizarre stories of being shadowed in the streets of Tehran or having commandos attack his house in Dallas, invariably showed him as subjected to the rigors of combat which he, unlike Bush and many other politicians, has never experienced. Perot lost a little support, but most of his voters remained frozen in their commitments. Bush appeared to be closing the gap in the last weekend, but his momentum was slowed by much-ballyhooed but in fact already-told stories about Iran-contra; more likely, a critical quantum of voters decided that, if Bush really had a chance to win, they should vote for Clinton.

III. THE ELECTORAL VERDICT
The dynamic of the election from July on was not in doubt. George Bush was in trouble not so much because of the poor performance of the economy—by historic standards the recession of 1990–91 was not deep and by 1992 it statistically was over—but because of an awareness that he was disengaged from domestic issues. Bush simply would not give voters the domestic policy road map they wanted. The clearest map came from Perot, but he disqualified himself for most voters by his flakiness. Clinton provided a road map of sorts, with lines going off in all directions; but at least he was interested and empathetic. The result was a Democratic victory, with Clinton, "a different kind of Democrat," winning 43% of the vote, to 37% for Bush and 19% for Perot.

Yet for all the wild oscillations in this year of postwar politics, opinion on issues stayed largely the same. Polls showed continued doubts about the efficacy of government as a mechanism to solve domestic problems. There was a call to reform the domestic public sector, just as other sectors had been reformed—the military, heavy industry, the private sector. Those reforms had not been painless: as big units which did not serve consumers, customers or citizens well were broken up, many individuals were hurt; and if small units, capable of supple and rapid adaptation, replaced them, not everyone did well. But the end result was a military capable of the small unit flexibility and high-tech competence seen in the Gulf War, steel and auto industries capable finally of competing with foreign producers, and burgeoning high-tech and service businesses which, without government planning or much assistance, continue to lead the world. On cultural issues, polls showed an American people willing to tolerate behaviors that a generation ago were considered illegitimate; "choice" had become a euphemism for abortion rights, but also for the feeling that people should be left to their own decisions on moral issues. Yet polls also showed a sense that we were neglecting our children, economically by spending less public and private money on them than we ought to, culturally by failing to give them enough time and attention and by neglecting to set moral standards and boundaries. In the campaign, both parties attempted to address these feelings. George Bush, in his speeches to the Detroit Economic Club in September and Denver Ace Hardware owners in October, showed the outlines of a coherent policy, a road map; but voters obviously were skeptical that he would follow it after November 3, and indeed within six weeks his attentions were directed to Somalia. Bill Clinton, in his New Covenant speeches in fall 1991, his convention acceptance speech in July and on the stump, sketched out a new Democratic paradigm with room for reform initiatives and a middle-class tax cut.

It was widely asserted by journalists and Democrats that Americans had undergone a fundamental shift in attitude on economic issues and the place of government, that the recession of the early 1990s caused them to reject the policies of the 1980s and to embrace governmental solutions. This was wishful thinking; polls showed no such thing. Polls did show, as they did in the late 1980s, that voters were prepared to consider mixed government and market proposals for reform. But fundamental attitudes about the place of government are set by sustained and emotionally moving experiences. Most Americans concluded from the Depression of the 1930s that economic markets were not reliable, and from the New Deal and, even more, the victory in World War II and postwar prosperity, that government worked pretty well: hence the political movement away from markets and toward government that prevailed from about 1935 to about

1965. Most Americans concluded from the stagflation and rising taxes of the 1970s that government didn't work very well and from the vibrant economic growth and creativity of the 1980s—seven years of low-inflation economic growth and 18 million new jobs—that markets worked pretty well. Or put more briefly: the breadlines of the 1930s convinced Americans that markets didn't work, and the gas lines of the 1970s convinced Americans that government didn't work. The recession of the early 1990s, thought painful to many, was simply not enough to shift many Americans' underlying attitudes. It may have dented faith in markets, but it did not come close to inspiring faith in government.

Only on foreign policy was a new consensus emerging, primarily because of the sudden extinction of the doves. For a quarter century, from the time a Democratic administration embroiled the nation in a Vietnam war it could not win, until the debate over the Gulf War resolution in January 1991, doves had been among the hardiest and most vocal species in the American political zoo. Their central belief was that the extension of American military power abroad was dangerous and evil—dangerous to us and evil to others. The foreign policy doves, advancing Vietnam as a paradigm for all foreign policy experience, sought to hold down American military expenditures and to prevent American defense technology advances (fearing destabilization of our relations with the Soviet Union). They not only opposed but vilified every American foreign military intervention, so that the relief of Grenada from a bungling dictatorship was portrayed in terms more aptly describing Hitler's takeover of Czechoslovakia.

The doves spoke most eloquently in the three-day congressional debate over the Gulf War resolution, predicting a military war that would be disastrous to us and consequences that would be evil to others. They spoke sincerely, yet their words described not so much the Persian Gulf situation as the dilemma the United States faced in the Gulf of Tonkin when President Johnson asked for a similar resolution in August 1964, as if this were the chance to vote against the resolution they wished more than two members of the Senate had voted against 26 years before. Seldom have so many sincere politicians been so wrong. The first few days of the Gulf War made it apparent that this conflict was neither unduly dangerous to us nor evil to others, and the doves disappeared overnight. The end of the Cold War, many analysts told us, meant the obsolescence of foreign policy hawks, because there was no Soviet Union to defend against any more. It is more apt to say that the beginning of the Gulf War meant the obsolescence of foreign policy doves, because it became apparent that there were circumstances in which the extension of American military power was safe and good. In the years since, former doves have hailed the dispatch of American military forces to Somalia and have called for the involvement of American military forces in Bosnia, disregarding what those on both sides of the Gulf War understood was the tragic potential inherent in any military action and what the denouement of the Gulf War reminded us was the unhappy incompleteness of any military victory.

The 1992 election results showed a country split into fragments. But despite the Clinton headquarters sign that said, "It's the economy, stupid," this was not an electorate split primarily along economic lines. Rather, as is usually the case in American politics, voters were split along cultural lines—by region, race and ethnic group, age, gender and family status, education and religion. The Voter Research Survey (VRS) exit poll figures enable us to chart these divisions.

Age. The baby boomer ticket of Bill Clinton and Al Gore won its largest margins among people old enough to be their parents, those 60 and over (50%–38%). They also turned around the young vote, more favorable than average to George Bush up through May 1992, but in November for Clinton (43%–34%) with a big vote for Perot (22%). Baby boomers, those 30 to 44, voted narrowly for Clinton (41%–38%).

Race and ethnic group. Blacks voted overwhelmingly for Clinton (83%–10%). Hispanics were much less uniform (61%–25%), about midway between blacks and whites (40%–39% for Bush). Asians were for Bush (55%–31%), and one of the few groups that seemed to get more Republican between 1988 and 1992; 40% of Asian-Americans live in California, and perhaps they were reacting to the Los Angeles riots and the lack of concern, especially by liberals, for the Korean and other Asian shopkeepers who had, in Bill Clinton's phrase, worked hard and played by the rules. Irish and Italian Americans, in states like New York where ethnic consciousness remains high, voted less Democratic than average: the Democratic coalition there was blacks, Puerto Ricans, Jews, single women and gays—not the ethnic Catholics, Irish and Italians who delivered the state to John Kennedy in 1960.

Gender. The gender gap after a dozen years seems a permanent part of our politics, with women more strongly for Clinton (45%–37%) than men (41%–38%). But married women and especially married women who had ever had children, voted very much like men, while single and divorced women formed almost a left-wing proletariat. Careless writers and feminist boosters often wrote "women" during the 1991–92 cycle when they meant something more like "those women sympathetic to a broad range of ideas associated with feminism." The latter overwhelmingly believed Anita Hill over Clarence Thomas and supported the much-ballyhooed "year of the woman" Democratic Senate candidates (a similar number of Republican women Senate candidates in 1990 inspired no such ballyhoo). But most American women were only a bit more likely than average to support women Senate candidates.

Education. Some of the most striking differences are along education lines, and not in historically predictable ways. Clinton had his biggest percentage margin among those who never graduated from high school (54%–28%), but they amounted to only 6% of the electorate. In absolute number of votes, he actually got a larger margin from those with a graduate school education (50%–36%), who make up 16% of the electorate. These teachers, social workers, lawyers, nurses and even doctors tend to be young, culturally liberal, and public sector employees—all characteristics that correlate highly with voting Democratic. In contrast, college graduates were, though narrowly, for Bush (41%–39%), and both high school graduates and those with some college voted at about the national average.

Religion. Here is the great divider. In 1960, 78% of Catholics voted for Catholic John Kennedy, 63% of white Protestants for white Protestant Richard Nixon, in a campaign year with undercurrents of religious hostility. In 1992, also a campaign year with undercurrents of religious hostility, white born-again Christians voted very heavily for George Bush (62%–23%) while Jews were even more heavily for Bill Clinton (80%–11%), with non-believers not far behind (62%–18%). White Protestants were for Bush (47%–33%), while Catholics were only narrowly for Clinton (44%–35%), with white Catholics nearly 40 points lower for Clinton than for his hero John Kennedy). But differences today are not just between denominations but also between intensity of religious feeling. The highly observant and traditionally devout voted heavily for Bush. Less observant Catholics and Protestants and those whose religious beliefs tolerate society's liberal ways were more likely to vote for Clinton. Perot, incidentally, did poorly with those of any strong beliefs—born-again Protestants or Jews, traditional Catholics or unbelievers. Instead, he did better with those without deep roots: the young, those living beyond metro area beltways or in new Western or northern New England communities, the middle income and middling educated.

Region. When the country is divided into nine regions, with boundaries determined to reflect similar responses to the Perot candidacy, the biggest margins for Bill Clinton come in the regions containing the nation's two largest metropolitan areas, the Mid-Atlantic (48%–36%) and Pacific (45%–33%); as well as the smallest region, New England (44%–32%). In electoral votes, the big gain here for Democrats from the last three decades was in the Pacific states, where Clinton easily carried all 76 electoral votes; yet the basis for this was established in Michael Dukakis's near-win in the Pacific in 1988. These three regions showed similar collapse in Bush's standings—partly due to the spectacular collapse of residential real estate values in all three areas. Clinton carried three regions with about his national average—the Great Lakes (43%–37%), the Great Plains (40%–36%) and, bolstered by wins in his home state and Al Gore's, barely carried the Mississippi Valley South (45%–43%). George Bush, however, carried the South overall (43%–41% in popular vote, 116 to 52 in electoral votes), and carried three of our regions here as well: the Southwest (41%–37%), the Mountains (38%–35%) and the South Atlantic (43%–41%). Ross Perot's best regions were the Mountains (25%), Great Plains (23%),

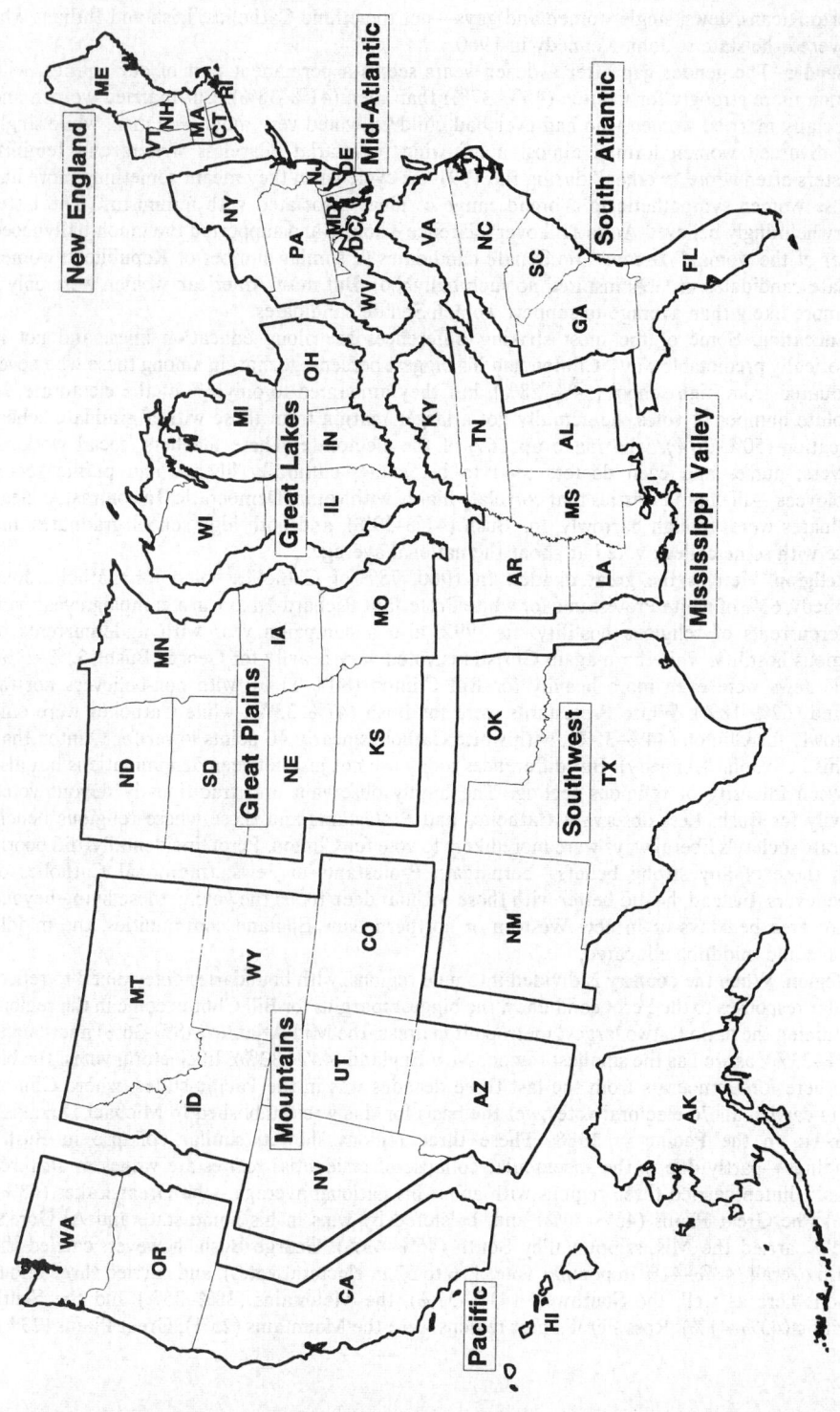

New England (23%), Pacific (21%) and Southwest (22%). He did not do well in the racially polarized South, in heavily black central cities, or in culturally liberal university towns and singles neighborhoods.

Analysis using these same nine regions shows an unexpected phenomenon little discerned in the 1992 election results: straight-ticket voting. It was disguised by the 19% cast for Ross Perot, which left both Bill Clinton and George Bush running behind their parties' congressional candidates' average. But when the Perot vote is allocated as exit polls suggested it should be, split evenly between the two candidates (with perhaps a few more votes for Bush in the South, the Mountain states and Ohio, but this gets us quickly into the realm of spurious precision), the result is a 53%–47% Clinton victory, almost precisely equal to the 52%–46% by which Democratic House candidates beat Republican candidates in preliminary figures. Of course, congressional voting does not follow presidential voting in every congressional district, as examination of the figures in this Almanac will demonstrate. But it is evident that in an uncannily large number of districts, especially those with open seat contests, there was something very much like straight ticket voting. And in seven of our nine regions, the aggregated vote for president and for congress show straight ticket voting, with the two exceptions (the Mississippi Valley, with its many unchallenged Democratic incumbents, and the Mid-Atlantic, with its feisty Republican challengers in terrain where Bush was unpopular) perhaps proving the rule. In seven of nine regions, the Clinton or Bush margin is within 2% of the Democratic or Republican margin in House races.

| | President | | | | U.S. House | | |
	Bush%	Clinton%	Perot%	Clinton+/−	Rep.%	Dem.%	Dem.+/−
United States	37	43	19	+6	46	52	+6
New England	32	44	23	+12	41	53	+12
Mid-Atlantic	36	48	16	+12	48	51	+3
Great Lakes	37	43	19	+6	47	52	+5
Great Plains	36	40	23	+4	47	52	+5
Mountains	38	35	25	−3	52	47	−5
Pacific	33	45	21	+12	41	55	+14
South Atlantic	43	41	16	−2	50	49	−1
Miss. Valley	43	45	11	+2	41	56	+15
Southwest	41	37	22	−4	47	52	+5

This impression of straight ticket voting is strengthened by examination of the campaign promises made by winning Democrats, especially in open seats, echoing the Clinton-Gore campaign promises to end gridlock, revive the economy and reform the healthcare financing system. These are not the small, easy-to-keep promises of past congressional candidates, pledges to attend to local matters and deliver on second-line issues. These are big promises, hard to deliver on, and these candidates, especially the freshman Democrats, may be held accountable for them by voters in 1994 or 1996. The Republicans made big promises too but, their presidential ticket having lost, they will find it easier to deliver on their big one—voting against any new taxes.

If Democrats do deliver, they will be well-rewarded. In 1964, Democrats kept John Kennedy's 1960 campaign promises to revive the economy by cutting taxes and eliminating trade barriers, and won 57% of the House vote and a 2–1 margin in House seats. But the penalties for failure are high: Harry Truman's 1948 Democrats promised labor-law overhaul, national health insurance and federal aid to education, and couldn't pass any of them; they lost House seats in 1950 and control of Congress and the White House in 1952. The 1948 election, as it happens, was the most recent election that produced more than the 110 freshmen members of Congress produced in 1992, and it was the closest thing to a straight-ticket election (it too had a third and even a fourth party presidential candidacy) in the intervening 44 years: the Truman-Barkley ticket beat Dewey-Warren 50%–45%, a 5% margin, while Democratic House candidates beat Republicans 52%–46%, a 6% margin.

It is worth noting too that many Democrats newly elected that year—the most famous of them, Hubert Humphrey—were elected after big campaign promises on major issues. But they couldn't deliver because they were split along cultural lines: federal aid for education, for example, was blocked because southern Protestants wouldn't vote for it if it included Catholic schools and big city Catholics wouldn't vote for it if it didn't. Democrats in the 1990s could have an analogous problem, if feminists refuse to vote for healthcare financing reform unless it covers abortions and cultural conservatives and moderates refuse to vote for it if it does. But such issues of principle, of deeply held personal beliefs, of the cultural divisions which have always been a prime feature of American life since the earliest colonial days, are not trivial and cannot always be swept aside by practical politicians.

IV. THE NEW ADMINISTRATION

The first months of the Clinton Administration were a test of whether the 1992 results represented, as some Democrats argued, a genuine readiness to shift positions on basic economic, foreign and cultural issues, or whether the wild differences in partisan and candidate preference over the period from March 1991 represented the inherent instability of postwar politics, of voters looking for a road map for the future. The initial responses of the voters suggested that postwar politics, not a paradigm shift, was at work. The new president began with an inaugural speech which sounded nationalistic themes and recalled past presidents. But the first issue emphasized in his opening week was removing the ban on gays in the military, something stoutly opposed by the professional military, General Colin Powell and Senate Armed Services Committee Chairman Sam Nunn; the issue arose because of a promise made almost casually in the campaign and on an issue which was not the first demand of many gay rights groups, which had strongly supported the Clinton candidacy. Economically, the candidate who had backed tax cuts for the middle class was transformed into a president who asked for a tax increase for the middle class, and a president-elect who said that he would cut $2 in spending for every dollar in tax increases became a president who increased taxes more than twice as much as he cut spending. The Democratic House in March balked and demanded more spending cuts; the Democratic Senate in April could not pass the short-term stimulus package over a Republican filibuster; in May, House Democratic leaders had to resort to extraordinary arm-twisting to pass by 219–213 the Clinton deficit reduction plan. At every stage, public opinion—longstanding skepticism about the efficacy of government spending and government programs—was felt.

It had been confidently asserted by various political strategists that public support for higher taxes on the rich could be used to rally support for the Clinton package. But, as always in American history, most voters care much less about punishing the rich than about rewarding the middle class and strengthening the entire economy. Support for redistributive economics has never rallied a majority: even in the 1930s, polls showed that Franklin Roosevelt's redistributionism was not a vote-getter, and he won in 1936 as a reward for stopping the downward economic spiral of the Depression, and in 1940 and 1944 on foreign not domestic issues. In American history, increased taxes on the rich have been capable of generating majority support in elections only in times of war. That rule did not change in 1993: none of the Democratic candidates running in the special elections of the first half of the year placed any emphasis on higher taxes on the rich or (with the exception of one who lost his primary) conspicuously supported the Clinton economic plan.

So the search for a road map continues. The initial response to the Clinton plan shows that voters are not ready to repudiate "The Eighties" if that means embracing "The Sixties." If the economic growth of the 1980s is seen to have been uneven and the cultural struggles have left a sense that we have neglected our children, those defects are not enough to make Americans embrace economic redistribution, larger government, and the no-enemies-to-the-left cultural liberalism that many Democrats in the Clinton Administration and Congress seem ready to impose on America. The performance of public sector institutions—education, health care, welfare, the legal system—remains below what it ought to be, and the demand is there for reform. But, at least in mid-1993, no politician had clearly provided a convincing plan for reform, a plausible road map for the future.

THE CLINTON TEAM

William Jefferson Clinton, the 41st American to be president of the United States, is a man of obvious brilliance and important flaws, as gifted a talker and listener as any politician in our times (though his raspy voice would probably have kept him out of politics before the era of electronic amplification) and yet a politician who is sometimes oddly out of touch with opinion and who tells far more than his share of untruths. There are many tensions in him: between the "man from Hope," as he was touted at his Democratic National Convention, after the Arkansas town he spent his first years in, and the boy whose real home town was the gambling resort of Hot Springs; between the charming son of the Bible-believing Baptist South and the product of elite and skeptical Oxford and Yale Law School; between the moderate who ran in 1992 as a "different kind of Democrat" and the liberal who in his first months as president, in 1993, as in his first term as governor, in 1979 and 1980, espoused liberal programs which infuriated many of his supporters.

What is at Bill Clinton's center? If George Bush had few ideas, Bill Clinton has many, some inconsistent and many even in tension with others. In the question, "What does Bill Clinton believe," on a particular issue, it must be understood that the word 'what' is not singular but plural. This is the opposite side of Clinton's ability to listen to others, and empathize with people of all backgrounds and beliefs. No president has entered office with more ideas and proposals about domestic public policy. The good news is that Americans got a president who, unlike George Bush, is engaged in domestic issues and ready to propose serious policy changes. The bad news is that Americans got a president who has difficulty concentrating on priorities or pursuing a consistent course.

It is startling to consider how far Bill Clinton climbed, from a modest though not impoverished life in a back corner of America, and to reflect how long he has been significant in national politics: for 20 years before his election as president at age 46. The teenager who pressed forward to shake hands with President Kennedy in the Rose Garden in 1963 was by 1972 the Texas coordinator for the McGovern campaign; two years later, at 28, he was running for Congress, and almost winning in a heavily Republican district; in 1976, when Jimmy Carter was elected president, Clinton was elected attorney general of Arkansas; in 1978, he was elected governor, at 32. His articulateness made it not farfetched, though it certainly was premature, to speculate then that he might run for president. By June 1987, he was publicly considering, but ruled out in August, a race; in October 1991, he was running.

From the beginning of Clinton's political career, there has been a tension between Arkansas and its common people and the Eastern elite. He knew that political success in Arkansas could only come if he were seen as consistent with traditional values and beliefs. But Arkansas had long shown that it would elect liberal and elitist politicians, like Senator William Fulbright, in whose office Clinton worked, and Governor Winthrop Rockefeller, and impressive credentials certainly helped: Fulbright ran for the Senate after serving as president of the University of Arkansas and Rockefeller was from one of the nation's richest families. So political success, for a politician like Clinton who was never uncomfortable with the national Democratic Party would depend on elite credentials as well: Georgetown University, the Rhodes Scholarship, Yale Law School and all the well-connected friends he met there made him a plausible candidate at 28 and 32 in a way that a locally educated, nationally unconnected 28- or 32-year-old Bill Clinton would not have been.

The confliction of these two sides was most notable during Clinton's struggle to avoid the draft in 1969 and 1970. In his letter to ROTC director Colonel Holmes, he told how "anguished" he was and made it clear he knew that his "political viability" in Arkansas would be threatened if

PRESIDENT

President William Jefferson (Bill) Clinton (D)

Elected 1992, term expires Jan. 1997; born, August 19, 1946, Hope, AR; home, Little Rock, AR; Georgetown University, B.S. 1968; Rhodes Scholar, Oxford University, 1968–70; Yale University, J.D. 1973; Baptist; married (Hillary Rodham).

Career: Professor, University of Arkansas, 1974–76; Democratic Nominee for U.S. House of Representatives, 1974; Arkansas Attorney General, 1976–78; Practicing attorney, 1981–82; Governor of Arkansas, 1978–80, 1982–92.

Office: The White House, 1600 Pennsylvania Ave., NW, Washington, DC 20500, 202-456-1414.

VICE PRESIDENT

Vice President Albert (Al) Gore, Jr. (D)

Elected 1992, term expires, Jan. 1997; born, March 31, 1948, Washington, DC; home, Carthage, TN; Harvard University, B.A. 1969; Vanderbilt School of Religion, 1971–72; Vanderbilt Law School, 1974–76; Baptist; married (Tipper).

Career: Army, 1969–71 (Vietnam); Homebuilding business; Reporter, *Nashville Tennessean*, 1973–76; U.S. House of Representatives, 1976–84; U.S. Senate, 1984–92.

Office: The White House, 1600 Pennsylvania Ave., NW, Washington, DC 20500, 202-456-1414.

1992 Presidential Vote

Clinton (D) 44,908,233 (43%)
Bush (R) 39,102,282 (37%)
Perot (I)................. 19,741,048 (19%)

1988 Presidential Vote

Bush (R) 48,886,097 (53%)
Dukakis (D)............. 41,809,074 (46%)

The People: Est. Pop. 1992: 255,067,000; Pop. 1990: 248,709,873, up 2.5% 1990–1992. 24.8% rural. Median age: 32.9 years. 12.6% 65 years and over. 75.6% White, 12.1% Black, 9% Hispanic origin, 2.9% Asian, .8% American Indian. Households: 55.1% married couple families; 25.6% married couple fams. w. children; 20.3% college educ.; median household income: $30,056; per capita income: $14,420; 64.2% owner occupied housing; median house value: $79,100; median monthly rent: $374. 7.4% Unemployment. Voting age pop.: 185,105,441.

he were seen as dodging the draft. And yet if he were not seen as dodging the draft by his friends in Oxford, he might lose his "political viability" with them. Clinton used his political connections and got Fulbright's and Rockefeller's office to intercede to keep him out of the draft, and to get him the extraordinary deferment for a promise to serve in a ROTC unit in the future in a school he had no apparent intention of attending. With such political influence, he could surely have gotten into a National Guard unit as Dan Quayle did. But that would not have keep him in good stead with the liberal elite.

For most of his career, Clinton has handled the Arkansas-East tension masterfully, and when he has stumbled, he has gotten up and done things better: the Comeback Kid, as he put it when he claimed victory for finishing second in New Hampshire in February 1992. In his first term as Governor, his backing of an increase in license plate fees enraged voters and the housing of Cuban refugees in Fort Chaffee infuriated them: he was defeated in 1980. But he came back; his wife replaced Rodham with Clinton as her last name; he was elected in 1982 and passed a school reform program that included higher taxes; he passed another education reform in 1989, with public school choice, report cards for schools and revocation of driver's licenses for dropouts. In 1990, Clinton had another tough patch in Arkansas; many voters were tired of him, he confessed he had no fire in his belly and he had serious opposition in both primary and general. But he won with 55% and 57%; interestingly, he received a very similar 53% in the presidential race in Arkansas in 1992; a majority of Arkansans are with him, but not a huge majority.

The tension between Bill Clinton's campaign as a "different kind of Democrat" and the initial governing program which looked very much like an old Democratic plan may only be the latest example of the Arkansas-elite story. What cannot be predicted with certainty is how he will resolve the tension, whether he will shift course once again, if his Comeback Kid resiliency will be seen in the White House, or whether it will be as effective when he is in a position as closely scrutinized as the incumbent president of the United States.

THE TOP OF THE CLINTON ADMINISTRATION

It is impossible in the space available here to survey all the individuals who play important roles in the Executive Branch, and unwise in this format: for in every administration there is constant movement and only two members of it, the president and vice president, have fixed terms in office. It is, however, possible to look at those clearly at the top level of the Clinton Administration, with the most serious responsibilities, those of sufficient independent stature that it is unlikely they would be readily replaced.

Vice President Albert Gore, Jr., is the one member of the administration who cannot be fired and is under a special obligation not to disagree publicly with the president. Clinton and Gore had not known each other well before July, but the selection of Al Gore as vice presidential nominee in early July 1992 was one of the galvanizing events of the campaign. The choice of a politician of the same generation, of a similar reputation as a moderate southern Democrat, seemed to show Bill Clinton as confident in who he was, an impression reinforced by the post-convention bus campaigning. Gore, with his greater experience in foreign and defense policy and his interest in the environment, seemed to complement Clinton where his expertise was weakest. If Gore's performance in the vice presidential debate was disappointing—he declined to respond to Dan Quayle's repeated attacks that "Bill Clinton has trouble telling the truth"—he made no serious error in the campaign and was clearly an asset to the ticket.

In Gore's life, much as in Clinton's, there is a tension between Washington and Tennessee, but one more smoothly resolved, and over a much longer time. His father, Albert Gore, Sr., was a school superintendent in Smith County, Tennessee, when he was elected to Congress in 1938: the beginning of the family business. The senior Gore was elected to the Senate in 1952, was a vice presidential candidate when Adlai Stevenson threw the nomination open to the convention in 1956; he showed political courage in voting for civil rights bills and refusing to sign the Southern Manifesto in the 1950s. Al Gore, Jr., grew up living in a Washington hotel and summered in Tennessee, attended Harvard and, despite his antiwar views, served in the Army in

Vietnam. After he returned to Nashville, he became a reporter for *The Tennessean*, went to divinity school at night and jumped at the chance to run for the House when his father's successor, Joe Evins, announced his retirement in 1976. When Senator Howard Baker retired in 1984, Gore ran for the seat and won easily. There he worked on the space program, on new technologies like fiber optics, biotechnology, superconductivity. His father's New Deal heritage showed in his record: more hawkish on military issues than most Democrats, liberal on economic programs, conservative at least originally on some cultural issues. For a time, he shared headlines with his wife Tipper, who lobbied the recording industry to voluntarily rate and label obscene and violent lyrics, to the outrage of many who saw this request for disclosure as an iron hand of censorship.

In April 1987, at 39, Gore announced he was running for president. Sam Nunn and Dale Bumpers had just announced they weren't running, leaving an opening for a southern moderate in a race where almost every southern state was voting on "Super Tuesday," March 8, 1988. Gore was clearly the least dovish of the Democrats, and the only white southerner. But his candidacy got boxed in. He made feints at running hard in Iowa and New Hampshire, and then didn't; he won little noticed caucus victories in Wyoming and Nevada. He carried the South on Super Tuesday, winning 30% to Jesse Jackson's 28% and Michael Dukakis' 23%, finishing first in five states (North Carolina, Kentucky, Tennessee, Arkansas, Oklahoma) and second to Jackson in five more (Virginia, Georgia, Alabama, Mississippi, Louisiana). But he did not get the overwhelming southern victories Bill Clinton won in 1992 when no black candidate was on the ballot; and he was overshadowed in the news by Jackson, Dukakis and George Bush. Gore did poorly in Illinois, Connecticut, Wisconsin and New York, where the anti-Jackson majority coalesced around Dukakis, and Gore may have been hurt as much as helped by his endorsement by New York Mayor Edward Koch.

After the campaign, Gore's career took another course. In 1989, his son was seriously injured in an auto accident, and out of the searing experience of his injury and lengthy recovery, Gore developed an interest in environmental issues of near-religious intensity. His book, *Earth in the Balance*, which insists there is no serious scientific dispute about global warming, became a national bestseller. He was one of the last senators to make up his mind on the Gulf war resolution, voting "yes" only after "excruciating" decision-making; always a strong partisan, he was much quicker to come to the defense of Democrats attacked by Republicans for their "no" votes. Gore decided not to run for president in 1992, just before Clinton decided to run; he must have had some moments of regret as Clinton clinched the nomination; then came the call from Little Rock.

As vice president, most of Gore's work is done out of public sight, and he will surely be attacked by some as ineffective and without influence. The truth is more likely to be the opposite. President Carter's precedent of sharing all top-level papers and information with Vice President Mondale has been followed by Presidents Bush, Reagan and Clinton, and vice presidents have been better informed and a more operative part of government than ever before in our history.

Secretary of State Warren Christopher has never held elective office, but he has held important positions in all the Democratic administrations of the last 30 years. He was born in North Dakota; after his father died, he and his mother moved to Los Angeles in the 1930s, where he grew up poor and did well in school. He became a partner in the big Los Angeles law firm of O'Melveny & Myers, where he was known as a meticulous legal craftsman. In the Johnson Administration, he was deputy attorney general, sent to the scene of urban riots such as Detroit in 1967, to cope with the effects of violence. In the Carter Administration, he was deputy secretary of state, passed over for the top position when Cyrus Vance resigned in May 1980, but praised later for his hard work negotiating the hostage release with the Iranian government. Bill Clinton naturally called on him for counsel in foreign policy and made him the head of his transition staff, then called on him to be secretary of state.

A gift for painstaking negotiation and an abhorrence of violence are two threads of

Christopher's public career. He was criticized for overreliance on negotiation in the Carter years, but he has shown in public statements and writings an appreciation of the gains made in the 1980s due to willingness to use force.

Secretary of Defense Les Aspin is a foreign policy intellectual who moved up through practical politics and elective office—the usual route in Britain and other parliamentary democracies, but not in the United States. His roots are in Wisconsin, long one of our most isolationist and dovish states; his own impulses have been internationalist and increasingly interventionist. Aspin went to Yale and Oxford, and received a Ph.D. in economics from M.I.T. He worked as a staffer for Senator William Proxmire, was part of Robert McNamara's whiz kid operation in the Pentagon when he served in the Army in the late 1960s, but was also detailed to manage Lyndon Johnson's hopeless campaign in the 1968 Wisconsin primary. Aspin shopped around for a congressional district to run in, getting a job teaching at Marquette University in Milwaukee and establishing residence in Racine 25 miles south. He won the seat easily in 1970 and held it without much difficulty through his appointment in 1992.

Early in his House career, Aspin was known for his press releases criticizing the Pentagon, but without the adversary attitude toward American policy and the Pentagon that so many on the left showed. And he was genuinely interested in making defense systems and personnel work, publishing by the late 1970s his own defense strategy. In 1983, he helped save the MX missile; in 1984, he ran in the Democratic Caucus against an elderly chairman of the House Armed Services Committee and won. He was nearly unseated two years later, as liberals were angry with his backing of the Midgetman missile and a vote for aid to the Nicaraguan contras. He maneuvered deftly between a hawkish committee and a dovish House; he supported the Gulf war resolution, and his prediction of the likely military course of the war proved prescient, far more so than Senate Armed Services Chairman Sam Nunn's. Aspin briefed Bill Clinton frequently during the campaign, and these two denizens of Oxford evidently hit it off. Just as in the House he had to move between widely varied views on issues, so in the Pentagon Aspin must move between the career military, with its relatively conservative stands, and the liberalism of the Clinton White House. But this is the sort of challenge Aspin seems to thrive on.

Secretary of the Treasury Lloyd Bentsen, the senior member of the Clinton Administration, has a public career going back 50 years: he was a bomber pilot in World War II and was first elected to Congress in 1948. Bentsen is from the Lower Rio Grande Valley in south Texas, where his father was one of the great landowners of this rough-hewn part of Texas. Bentsen served only six years in the House, enough time for him to be able to claim "I knew Jack Kennedy" in his October 1988 debate with Dan Quayle; then he moved to Houston and spent sixteen years making money. In 1970, he ran for the Senate, and in the primary against liberal incumbent Ralph Yarborough ran footage of the riots outside the 1968 Democratic National Convention in Chicago; in the general, he maneuvered adroitly to win labor and black support and beat a Republican congressman from Houston named George Bush. Bentsen ran for president in 1976 as a southern moderate, but he was a Washington insider in a year when voters wanted someone new from out in the provinces; the southern moderate who won was Jimmy Carter.

From a frontier society, in which there is a huge gulf between Mexico and the United States, between the Mexican-American majority and the Anglo minority, Bentsen has worked hard—earning his own way through school, volunteering to be a bomber pilot—and believes he has a responsibility to use government to help those who don't have his skills, but not to tax individuals and businesses so heavily as to choke off private sector growth. This has made him a moderate, a man in between, and to some extent a politician who oscillates between different views. But he is also a man of careful discipline, considerable foresight and long memory, and in his oscillations he maintains positions that are not just intellectually solid but usually intellectually elegant.

Naturally, he was a defender of Texas's oil and gas interests, and backed price deregulation, and in the late 1970s, as chairman of the Joint Economic Committee, called for major tax cuts to stimulate the economy. He has long been a backer of free trade, and supported the Caribbean Basin Initiative and the North American Free Trade Agreement. But he was willing to play bad cop to the Reagan and Bush Administration's good cop in negotiations with Japan and other trading partners. As chairman of the Senate Finance Committee from 1987 to 1992, Bentsen was an active legislator. He favored cutting the capital gains tax, but also wanted higher taxes on the upper brackets. He backed bigger IRAs for savings, school and first-time home-buying. He used the budget reconciliation process to increase Medicaid coverage, and to influence energy policy. Not always successful, it was nonetheless an impressive record, and one which commended him to Michael Dukakis, who made him his vice presidential candidate in 1988. Bentsen was an effective campaigner and asset to the ticket; this old politician learned some new tricks and produced some of the best sound bites of the campaign. Indeed, if the Democrats had the wit to nominate their ticket in alphabetical order, they might have won; after all, Bentsen had beat Bush in Texas when they went one-on-one. Indeed, the Dukakis-Bentsen ticket got 43% in Texas, a good showing in what is now a heavily Republican state, and on the same day Bentsen was reelected to the Senate by a 59%–40% margin.

Bentsen, who turned 71 in 1992, did not give much serious consideration to running for president again; there was talk in Texas that he would not run for reelection in 1994, and the organization of backers he had carefully nurtured around the state he seemed to be bequeathing to Governor Ann Richards, to whose campaign he gave crucial early behind-the-scenes support in 1990. Bentsen does not recall meeting Bill Clinton when he was Texas coordinator for George McGovern and Bentsen was in his second year in the Senate, in 1972; but he had met him by the late 1970s. Bentsen's nomination to the Treasury gave a signal to financial and currency markets that this would be an administration of gravity and seriousness.

Hillary Rodham Clinton, it is said, is a new kind of First Lady, integrally involved in making public policy, a full working partner of her husband, a political figure on her own. This is not quite right. For past First Ladies have been closely involved in policy decisions—Sarah Childress Polk was her husband's secretary and chief assistant at a time when there was no White House staff—and have been controversially political figures—Eleanor Roosevelt, and to some extent Lady Bird Johnson. Nor were supposedly tradition-minded First Ladies—the most recent being Barbara Bush—the political naifs some supposed. But Hillary Rodham Clinton has moved closer to the rank of political appointee and farther from the category of personal relative than any presidential family member ever, with the exception of Robert Kennedy. An interesting precedent: he was at first the most hated, and ultimately perhaps the most loved person in the Kennedy government, and immensely influential.

Certainly, there were early signs that Hillary Rodham Clinton would be an important part of a Clinton Administration, and not just the "you get me, too," comments she made early in the campaign. In Arkansas, she spearheaded Bill Clinton's education reform package, listening to people statewide (she, like her husband, can be a gifted listener), formulating a package that was intellectually defensible and politically passable. As the 1992 campaign went on, she receded in prominence, (much as she had in his 1982 gubernatorial comeback race, when she added "Clinton" to her name); but she came forward when she was needed most, in the *60 Minutes* appearance following the Gennifer Flowers charges. She slipped twice: her disparaging reference to Tammy Wynette's standing by her man on *60 Minutes*, and her baking-cookies remark in Chicago before the crucial Illinois primary. But she supplied her husband with first class political advice and proved an excellent campaigner.

Clinton campaigns were not Hillary Rodham's first experience with public prominence: she was the student graduation speaker at her 1969 Wellesley commencement; in retrospect, her speech, with its well-meaning, empty phrases, does not read too well. Better are her 1970s articles on children's rights, not so radical as some critics claim, but clearly aimed at expanding legal rights of children regarding their parents. Like many baby boom liberals, Hillary Rodham Clinton started out a Republican, a Goldwater supporter in 1964, but then moved left to the Democratic faith, opposing the Vietnam war and taking liberal stands on cultural issues. This is all modulated by a moral code founded on her long-held religious faith, a shrewd sense of political reality and a keen legal mind. So for most of the 1992 campaign, Hillary Rodham

Clinton stayed out of the center of the spotlight, commenting on public policy, but not presenting herself as a likely Clinton Administration power.

After the inauguration, she moved into greater prominence. When Bill Clinton announced she would head his Health Care Task Force, he referred to her publicly for the first time as Hillary Rodham Clinton; she was now adding back in her maiden name. Clearly, she had much to say about staffing the administration, especially the Justice Department, and in seeing that women and minorities—as termed by affirmative action advocates (an Asian daughter of a millionaire is a minority; Leon Panetta, son of an immigrant from Calabria, Italy, is not)—were well represented, in some cases delaying final appointments for months. Rodham Clinton reportedly opposed the commitment of American troops to Bosnia and opposed the formulation of a welfare reform package before the heathcare financing reform she was working on came forward.

Like Robert Kennedy, and like every vice president since Jimmy Carter invigorated that office, Hillary Rodham Clinton has been influential; but like Kennedy and those four vice presidents, the public can never be sure just how much or with what effect. She is a symbol, positive to some and negative to others, of feminism and the liberal political beliefs that tend to go with it; to others, she is an example of the faith of baby boom liberals with elite education that they, by studying a problem and writing words down on paper, can easily make the world a better and more humane place. That picture, in some ways correct, misses most of the interesting things about this talented person, her original insights and the actions she may bring to bear. But those things can not be known outside the closest circle until memoirs are written, and then will only be known with haziness and uncertainty, as motive flares and memory fades.

THE CONGRESSIONAL STAGE

THE HOUSE OF REPRESENTATIVES

The House of Representatives, intended by the Framers to be the part of government most exquisitely responsive to public opinion, often is that; but it is also controlled by a Democratic majority which has managed to insulate its members from outside political pressures and to embark on unpopular policies. The House is a sort of cocoon, in which the Democratic majority may sometimes be beleaguered but stays together in cooperative camaraderie, and in which the Republican minority remains united in disaffection and rage bordering on the splenetic. House members in many ways are isolated from the rest of Washington. News media pay them little attention, preferring more glamorous and better known (though usually less effective) senators; the Executive Branch and lobbyists concentrate on only those House members who specialize in their areas, ignoring the rest; presidents and cabinet members have little time for probably 400 of the 435 Representatives; and an increasing number of representatives are keeping their families in the district, flying home on Thursday nights and returning Tuesday mornings. The result is that many House members feel little more at home in Washington than the tourists whom they dutifully greet as they are shepherded through the Capitol.

The House Democratic leadership in recent years has often been on the defensive but has always fought back and, in most cases, prevailed. Speaker Thomas Foley, Majority Leader Richard Gephardt and an organization of whips which includes almost half the members of the Democratic Caucus have developed a sense of fellow feeling among House Democrats, a kind of bonding through fire. This is partly due to their individual talents: Foley is intellectually honest and elegant, fair-minded and ready to listen to others; Gephardt is a superb listener and can develop a common course of action to bind together majority. The leadership has taken from Speaker Tip O'Neill the strategy of trying to win with Democratic votes only; the pre-O'Neill days, when liberals and particularly labor lobbyists would try to corral a few crucial Republican votes, are over. In June 1993, with all seats filled, there were 258 Democrats and one Vermont Independent; Foley and Gephardt see their job as winning 218 of those 259 votes. Their communication system is excellent, and they don't buy more than they need: in the May deficit reduction vote, they had exactly 219. From Speaker Jim Wright, the leadership has taken the strategy of utilizing all available resources to win. O'Neill might have beaten the Reagan tax cuts in 1981 had he been willing to employ the weapon that is always the leadership's—delay; but he agreed on a clean, fast vote and lost. Wright did not follow that course, at one point even declaring a new legislative day to get out of a parliamentary knot, and neither do Foley or Gephardt.

The causes for which the leadership has worked have not always been popular. Foley is the son of a judge, and is a man convinced that it is a politician's duty to oppose a momentarily popular but in the long run unwise idea. Early in his speakership, Foley opposed the flag burning constitutional amendments, despite their considerable popularity, arguing that if members stood their ground few if any would be defeated on the issue, which indeed was the case: this strengthened him on other issues. He opposed the balanced budget constitutional amendment, prevailing by just a few votes. He and Gephardt both spoke out strongly against the Gulf war resolution in January 1991, and were almost instantly regarded by a very large majority of Americans as misguided; there was some damage, but not as much as Gulf war proponents expected. Foley has opposed the line-item veto, and prevented the Clinton Administration from endorsing this popular idea. Foley has opposed term limits, and in 1993 went to court in his home state of Washington to get them declared unconstitutional.

But the biggest policy push of Foley and Gephardt since they became speaker and majority leader in June 1989 has been toward higher tax rates. Acting out of patriotic conviction, but also because they favor more federal spending on domestic programs, Foley and Gephardt in the Bush years were the prime movers in the 1990 budget summit for the package that produced higher taxes in October 1990; in the Clinton years they were among the prime supporters of the increased taxes proposed by the president contrary to his campaign promises. House Democrats on both occasions dutifully gave them most of their votes, though not without some hard persuasion.

House Democrats have looked to be in terrific trouble in odd-numbered years, then have recovered at least somewhat in election years. The leadership shakeup in 1989, the Gulf war vote in 1991, the Clinton Administration's unpopularity in 1993—all looked like trouble. But in 1990, the Democrats, aided by their budget summit deal which forced George Bush to break his "read my lips: no new taxes" promise, gained seven seats. In 1992, hurt by redistricting reflecting population increases in the South and West and by the Voting Rights Act interpretation concentrating black voters in a few dozen districts, Democrats seemed doomed to lose one to two dozen seats. But the collapse of the Bush candidacy on the West Coast well before the election helped Democrats win about nine districts there that Republicans expected to take, and overall Republicans picked up only 10 seats. Even so, Republicans remain well-positioned for 1994, for three reasons. The first is that those West Coast seats were looking more vulnerable in early 1993 than Democrats had hoped. The second is that 1992 saw more of what amounted to straight-ticket voting in any election since 1948. On the surface, that was not evident, since Bill Clinton received only 43% of the vote and George Bush only 37%, percentages by definition less than what all but a handful of winning Democrats and Republicans received. But if the Perot votes are distributed as exit polls suggest they would have been, about evenly between the two candidates, the result would have been about 53%–47%, almost precisely the same as the 52%–46% Democratic edge in popular votes cast for the House. Another aspect of the straight ticket phenomenon was that House Democrats, especially freshmen, campaigned on the same macro-issues as Bill Clinton—getting the economy moving, reforming health care—not the sort of local and micro-issues which House members of both parties have used to help them weather difficult years for their parties in marginal districts. These 1992 freshmen Democrats promised great things, and may be held accountable for their promises in 1994. That gives Republicans reason to hope that the advantages of incumbency will prove less in the 1990s than in the 1980s and 1970s.

The third reason, with a qualifying perhaps, that the Democratic majority may prove vulnerable is term limits. Their application to congressional elections has been challenged by Foley on grounds that are by no means trivial, and they may never come into effect. Yet they are already affecting the political calculations of House members and candidates. They are less likely to seek the lifetime political career which was the typical goal of most members elected in the last two decades; they are less likely to move to Washington and become acclimatized to its culture, or the House's; they are more willing to take political risks since they don't expect to stay long anyway. In time, many of these members may change their minds, and try to stay in politics forever; but for the moment, their behavior is more like that of citizen-legislators suspicious of Washington and less like that of the ultra-competent political entrepreneurs who have collectively made the House what it is. The prospect is for more turnover in House membership, less subcommittee chairman expertise and less polished politicking, more party-line voting and more collective party responsibility. There is a case to be made for the House as it has operated over the last two decades. But there is also a case that a House dominated by a term limit rather than a career politician mentality may turn out to be closer to what the Founding Fathers had in mind.

Who are the House Republicans, and how would they wield leadership power? They have been united in the 1990s in fury against the Democrats' increasing manipulations of the rules— the Democrats typically bring up bills on "closed rules," often not allowing Republican amendments—and they have been frustrated by their election year failures to live up to odd-year electoral prospects. They are less skillful politicians on average than the Democrats, less practiced in legislation and less gifted with political instinct. They are also increasingly younger, more conservative, less Washington-oriented. The House Republican leader, Robert Michel, is a man of splendid character from the old Taft Republican Midwestern heartland, inclined to compromise but increasingly feisty, instinctively bipartisan but facing a Democratic leadership uninterested in Republican votes and a Republican Conference full of angry rebels. The number two and three Republicans, Newt Gingrich of Georgia and Dick Armey of Texas, are both professors, of history and economics, both raised in modest surroundings and of northern origin, who represent fast-growing and affluent districts in Southern boom states. They are afraid of almost nothing: Gingrich brought the ethics case against popular Speaker Jim Wright; Armey told President Clinton point-blank that, if he persisted in his economic plan, he would be a one-term president. Gingrich loves to make intellectual arguments against Democrats; they loathe him for his attacks, while trying ignore the intellectual content. Gingrich's narrow election, over Michel's opposition, as Republican whip in March 1989 was a big victory for aggressive conservatives; Armey's ouster of incumbent Jerry Lewis for Republican Conference chair in December 1992 showed the increasing number of conservatives in Republican ranks. Gingrich announced in 1992 that he would not run against Michel for minority leader then, but pointedly left the future open; it is widely assumed that he will run after the 1994 election, and probably win. Gingrich has had plenty of practice now in inspiring and holding together an angry minority. But he has had little practice—no Republican has any in the House—in assembling and holding together a 218-vote majority.

THE SENATE

"The greatest deliberative body in the world," as the United States Senate likes to style itself, is seldom very deliberative these days, and is often scarcely a body at all. This is a legislature where it is every member for him or herself, where the whole is equal to a fair lot less than the sum of its parts, where it is far easier to kill someone else's initiative than it is to get one going. Nominally Democratic, it does not have a working Democratic majority on most issues, and the Democrats with only 56 votes fall well short of the 60 votes needed to shut off a filibuster. Yet the Republicans have schisms too, evident when it is their turn to propose rather than just oppose.

Four senators today tower over the rest of their colleagues, with authority partly from position and seniority, but much more from strength of intellect and character, and especially from a determination to assert their will that others, including Bill Clinton, ignore at their peril. They are, in order of seniority, Robert Byrd, Robert Dole, Sam Nunn and Daniel Patrick Moynihan.

Robert Byrd, the Senate Democratic Leader for 12 years from the 1976 election to 1988, now holds the position he aimed for from his first days in the Senate, when Lyndon Johnson gave him a seat on the committee in return for his fealty, Chairman of the Appropriations Committee. But it is not just the power to dole out money, to fund one program and starve another, that makes Byrd powerful. He is a genuine scholar, and a man determined to maintain the Senate's prerogatives as he understands them. High among them is the appropriating power, and it is Byrd's resistance more than anything else that has killed an effective line-item veto, just as it was Byrd's insistence that maintained plenty of spending flexibility for Congress in the 1990 budget summit package. Ever courteous and proper, never familiar or vulgar, meticulous about detail and willing to visit every colleague's office and wait for an interview to ask for a key vote, Byrd has been called a petty tyrant, though he is not tyrannical and is no more petty than Henry Clay or Daniel Webster or John C. Calhoun. But it is known that he remembers who was for and against him on every important vote.

Bob Dole, in his fourth decade in Congress, emerged as the operative leader of the Republican Party by the fourth week—if not the fourth day—of the Clinton Administration. He brings to the role a background in small town Kansas fully as humble and arguably more typical than Bill Clinton's, plus a record as a war hero and years of painful recovery and a permanent handicap that Clinton, like most products of the elite schools of his generation, can never fully understand.

Dole is one of the last connections with now very old political battles: when he first took the oath of office, Dwight Eisenhower was President and Robert Taft still a vivid inspiration to Midwestern Republicans. Balancing budgets and holding down spending were their main goals in politics, reflecting the orderliness and thrift of the men who ran things in places like Russell, Kansas. Dole consistently in the Reagan and Bush years was a force for raising taxes to reduce the budget deficit, in effect working against the inclinations of the chief executives; in the opening months of the Clinton Administration, he was a force for holding down spending to reduce the budget deficit, again working against the inclination of the President: a balance-wheel both times. Dole won the Republicans' first victory, filibustering the stimulus package in spring 1993, and responded with great zest and considerable grace as the Republicans' lead spokesman on all manner of issues. He could conceivably run for President in 1996, at 73, but for the moment he is one of the leading politicians in America and one of the best.

Sam Nunn is out of a southern tradition, exemplified by his great-uncle Carl Vinson, who served 50 years in the House and chaired the House Armed Services Committee. Nunn was elected to the Senate at 34, in 1972, has concentrated ever since on military issues, and after the 1986 election, at 48, became chairman of the Senate Armed Services Committee. There he has done much to make military policy regardless of who is president. Vinson, the apocryphal story goes, when asked whether he wanted to become Secretary of Defense responded, "I would rather run the Pentagon from up here," and Nunn has followed in those footsteps. When Bill Clinton said he would lift the ban on gays in the military, Nunn announced he was opposed, held hearings and a photo opportunity in a Navy sub, and clearly prevailed with his own "don't ask, don't tell" policy. But Nunn does not always prevail. He was clearly offended when George Bush, immediately after the 1990 elections, doubled the number of American troops in the Persian Gulf and moved toward war; and Nunn's persistent opposition to granting the president authority to militarily enforce the United Nations resolution was defeated. Some critics see Nunn as a vindictive power-grabber; many observers regard his occasional efforts to advance himself as a national candidate as hamhanded. But no one can doubt that the quality of the American military has vastly improved since Nunn began his work on Armed Services, and that he has made considerable contributions to that improvement.

Daniel Patrick Moynihan, erstwhile Harvard professor, member of the Cabinet or subcabinet in the Kennedy, Johnson, Nixon and Ford Administrations, senator from the nation's second largest state for nearly two decades, is now Chairman of the Senate Finance Committee at a moment when some of the most important issues facing government—budget deficits and taxation, healthcare financing, welfare and the underclass it has helped to create and perpetu-ate—come before that body. Moynihan's great gift is to see through the chaff of information in every day's newspapers and magazines, committee reports and lobbyists' briefings, the kernel of wisdom capable of producing a bounteous crop of wheat. It was a common perception when Moynihan succeeded Lloyd Bentsen as Finance Committee chairman in 1993 that he was not a practical politician, not a vote-trader, not a legislative maneuverer. But he had proved himself to be all of those things in passing the Intermodal Surface Transportation Act of 1991, which revolutionized transportation funding and policy, and in June 1993 rallied the Finance Committee to pass a creditable version of Clinton's budget, even on a committee where any Democrat had the ability, in effect, to veto a compromise. Those who think of Moynihan only as an academic who wades into controversy without political calculation should understand that one of his heroes is Charles F. Murphy, head of Tammany Hall from 1902 to 1924, the patron of politicians like Al Smith and Robert Wagner who were the fathers of the New York-style American welfare state that inspired so much of Franklin Roosevelt's New Deal.

Other senators, also men and women of talent and achievement, do not rise as high over the political landscape, partly due to the Senate's rules and traditions. which make it easy to obstruct forward motion. Outriders on the left and right can often defeat a nomination or derail a program, but have trouble assembling a majority on proposals of their own. There are perhaps 25 Democrats who can be counted as solid liberals and perhaps 25 Republicans who can be counted

1994 Senate Elections

State	Senator	Age 11/1/94	Year Apptd. or Elected	Last Elec. %
	Democrats (21)			
HI	Daniel K. Akaka	70	1990	54
NM	Jeff Bingaman	51	1982	63
NV	Richard H. Bryan	57	1988	50
WV	Robert C. Byrd	76	1958	65
ND	Kent Conrad	46	1986	63
AZ	Dennis DeConcini	57	1976	57
CA	Dianne Feinstein	61	1992	54
MA	Edward M. Kennedy	62	1962	65
NE	Robert Kerrey	51	1988	57
WI	Herb Kohl	59	1988	52
NJ	Frank R. Lautenberg	70	1982	54
CT	Joseph I. Lieberman	52	1988	50
TN	Harlan Mathews	67	1992	—
OH	Howard M. Metzenbaum*	77	1976	57
ME	George J. Mitchell	61	1980	81
NY	Daniel Patrick Moynihan	67	1976	67
MI	Donald W. Riegle, Jr.	56	1976	60
VA	Charles S. Robb	55	1988	71
MD	Paul S. Sarbanes	61	1976	62
TN	James R. (Jim) Sasser	58	1976	65
PA	Harris Wofford	68	1991	55
	Republicans (13)			
MT	Conrad Burns	59	1988	52
RI	John H. Chafee	72	1976	55
MO	John C. Danforth*	58	1976	68
MN	Dave Durenberger	60	1978	56
WA	Slade Gorton	66	1988	51
UT	Orrin G. Hatch	60	1976	67
TX	Kay Bailey Hutchison	51	1993	67
VT	James M. Jeffords	60	1988	70
MS	Trent Lott	53	1988	54
IN	Richard G. Lugar	62	1976	68
FL	Connie Mack, III	54	1988	50
DE	William V. Roth, Jr.	73	1970	62
WY	Malcolm Wallop	61	1976	50

*Retiring at the end of the term.

as solid conservatives, leaving half the votes in between—when they are not committed along party lines.

Those lines are at this writing 56 Democrats and 44 Republicans, two fewer seats for the Democrats than they thought they had on election night 1992. But Wyche Fowler of Georgia, ahead 49%–48%, lacked the absolute majority required by state law; in the runoff three weeks later he lost to Republican Paul Coverdell, who though pro-choice had the support of the Christian right, 51%–49%—the third time in a row this seat has changed partisan hands by that margin. And after Lloyd Bentsen resigned to become secretary of the Treasury, appointed Democrat Bob Krueger was unable to hold the seat, finishing second in the May special even though the Republican vote was split between three serious candidates, and losing the June runoff by a spectacular 67%–33% margin to Republican Kay Bailey Hutchison. That seat will be up in 1994 and 33 others, 21 held by Democrats and 13 by Republicans; since the Democrats have more vulnerable seats, the expectation in mid-1993 was that Republicans may have an outside chance at a majority. But it should be added that Senate races sometimes go against the odds. In both 1980 and 1986, almost all the close races went to one party, with the Republicans gaining 12 seats and winning control of the Senate to almost everyone's astonishment in 1980 and the Democrats gaining 8 seats and winning control in something of a surprise in 1986.

ENVOI

Politics is not peopled entirely by elected officials and candidates: there are also professional political operators, practical men and women who work hard to make these most sublime political institutions function. Two major political operators passed from the scene after their party's conventions in 1992.

F. Clifton White, knowing he would die soon, recalled at the Republican Convention in Houston the 1948 convention in Philadelphia where he worked for Thomas E. Dewey. But White left the liberal Deweyites to become one of the fathers of the conservative Republican ascendancy when he started and managed the campaign to nominate Barry Goldwater in 1964. That candidacy failed, of course, and White's effort to nominate Ronald Reagan fell short—by just a few delegates, he insisted—four years later. But for 20 of the next 24 years the Presidency was held by Republicans of one brand of conservatism or another.

Paul Tully, the number two man at the Democratic National Committee, was only 48 and did not know he was dying, though his smoking and diet brought back memories of older pols. But his brilliant demographic insights and organizational work convinced him, even while Bill Clinton languished in third place in polls a few weeks before the Democratic National Convention, that this time the Democrats would win and that his candidate, for the first time since the 1960s, would be elected president. Tully's zest and energy helped make that victory possible, though he died suddenly in September 1992 and did not see final victory.

But others remain, and new people come in every year. Two young operatives, both in their 20s, made a difference in 1992 by bringing humor—barbed, but ultimately good-natured—to a political process that can always use a bit more of it. Corbett O'Meara, a Democrat and graduate student in Detroit, was grousing with friends about George Bush's refusal to accept the Presidential Commission on Debates schedule of joint appearances; "with the aid of some alcohol," they decided to go to Lansing, where Bill Clinton was to visit the site of the first scheduled debate, with one of them dressed in a chicken outfit, suggesting that Bush was "chicken" to debate. This was a brilliant inspiration, for the chicken proved a visual metaphor impossible for the TV camera to resist. At every Bush campaign appearance, there would be another chicken, making the debate issue against him; soon the president of the United States was reduced to arguing with a chicken and trying to make jokes about him; not much later, the Bush forces agreed to debate terms which included the disastrous (for Bush) Oprah Winfrey-style debate in Richmond, Virginia.

Robert McDowell, a Republican and lawyer on K Street in Washington, was angry during fall 1992, as so many Republicans were, over what he regarded as unfairly anti-Bush coverage by TV networks, newspapers and magazines. His inspiration: a bumper sticker that read, "Annoy the Media—Re-Elect Bush." It quickly became the most popular Bush bumper sticker in many areas, and Bush himself was quoting it on the stump; it may even have made some in the media hesitate a moment before accusing Bush of dirty tricks for suggesting that Bill Clinton's spending promises would require him to increase taxes on the middle class. Neither O'Meara nor McDowell achieved great celebrity or made fortunes off their bright ideas, but both can take satisfaction at having contributed wittily and constructively to the political dialogue in the greatest democracy in the history of the world.

ALABAMA

When Alabama's Greek Revival Capitol was reopened in 1993 after seven years of renovation, there was still a controversy over whether the Confederate Stars and Bars should fly over its dome. But what is remarkable is that Alabama has honored the civil rights revolution, so much of which took place, and so much so violently, within its borders. Maya Lin's circular Civil Rights Memorial in Montgomery, the Civil Rights Institute across the street from the 16th Street Baptist Church in Birmingham's Civil Rights District, the Pettus Bridge in Selma and Martin Luther King's Dexter Avenue Baptist Church in Montgomery are among the many sites of civil rights and black history preserved and promoted by the state. To be sure, an aggressive, raw, violent tone still can pervade public life and popular culture; but Alabama, to a greater extent than most states, has come to be at peace with a history that is as difficult, and on occasion as hate-filled, as any state's.

A raucous tone has rung since the first Jacksonian farmers pushed the Indians west and plowed the steeply inclined red clay hills of the Tennessee Valley, and the first plantation owners shipped in hundreds of slaves to grow cotton on the dark Black Belt soil. It was the violent reactions of white Alabamans to desegregation in Tuscaloosa, Freedom Riders in Anniston, schoolchildren on the streets of Birmingham and marchers in Selma that finally prompted national backing for the civil rights revolution. Even in Alabama's peaceful economic development are currents of rawness: the miners hacking away in the 1880s at the solid-iron rock of Red Mountain to feed newly cast steel mills glaring in the valley of Birmingham below; the motorists of the 1980s speeding past exposed red earth of gouged-out hillsides to interchanges where the small factories and Wal-Mart shopping centers have sprout up.

A similar rawness can be seen in Alabama's politics. Fifty years ago, Alabama produced some of the most populist American politicians, crusaders against Wall Street and against the local economic potentates they called the "Big Mules": Hugo Black, a senator until he became a Supreme Court justice in 1937; Lister Hill and John Sparkman young congressmen who went on to the Senate and sponsored landmark health and housing legislation; young politicians who as congressmen in the 1950s—Carl Elliott, Albert Rains, Kenneth Roberts, Robert Jones—gave Alabama arguably the nation's most legislatively productive House delegation. On the state level, the foremost populist was Kissin' Jim Folsom, a huge, oratorically overpowering, personally flawed politician who was elected governor (back when consecutive terms were forbidden) in 1946 and 1954, and whose son became governor in April 1993. He was a serious candidate again in 1962 until he appeared drunk in a late campaign appearance on the new medium of television, and later watched his following taken over by his onetime protege, a young lawyer named George Wallace.

While Wallace was orating in the State Capitol in Montgomery, only a few blocks downhill at the Dexter Avenue Baptist Church, Martin Luther King, Jr., was leading what turned out to be a civil rights revolution. Much of it was spontaneous: seamstress Rosa Parks, tired and footsore, decided one day in 1955 that she was not going to move to the back of the bus as Alabama's segregation laws required. King, a 26-year-old minister from Atlanta with a fancy East Coast education, agreed to lead a seemingly hopeless bus boycott and soon found himself the leader of a national movement whose moral force he was one of the few to comprehend. In the southern standards of the time, what King demanded seemed impossible; it was unthinkable that blacks should even exercise their right to vote. In short-run politics, it helped the politicians who most strongly proclaimed their opposition to desegregation. George Wallace believed he lost the 1958 governor's primary because he was "out-segged," and vowed that he never would be again.

He wasn't, and for most of the 24 years from 1962, when he was first elected governor, until he

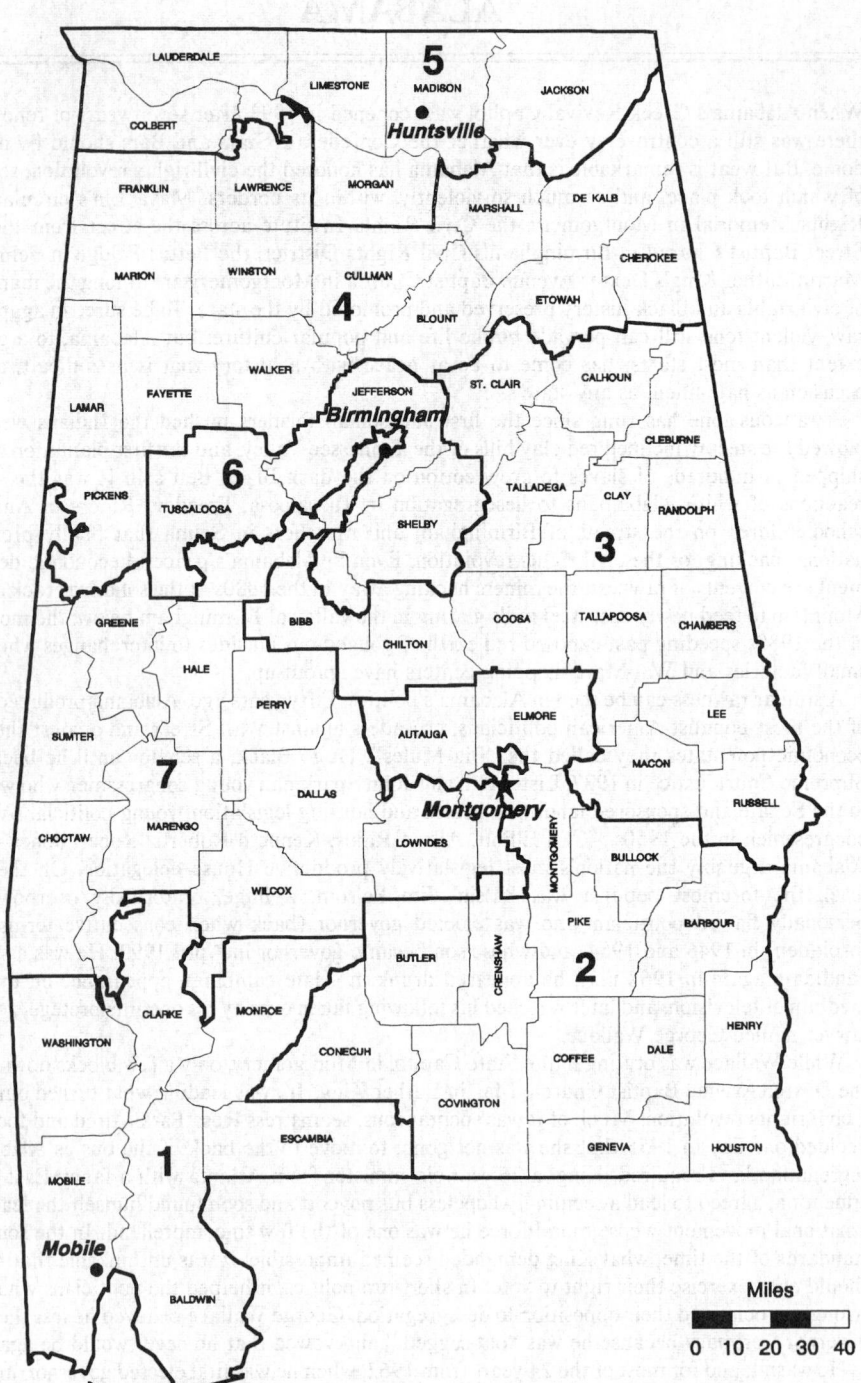

LAUDERDALE

LIMESTONE

5

MADISON

JACKSON

COLBERT

Huntsville

FRANKLIN

LAWRENCE

MORGAN

MARSHALL

DE KALB

MARION

WINSTON

CULLMAN

4

BLOUNT

CHEROKEE

ETOWAH

WALKER

JEFFERSON

ST. CLAIR

CALHOUN

FAYETTE

Birmingham

LAMAR

PICKENS

6

TUSCALOOSA

SHELBY

CLEBURNE

TALLADEGA

CLAY

RANDOLPH

GREENE

BIBB

COOSA

TALLAPOOSA

3

CHAMBERS

HALE

CHILTON

PERRY

ELMORE

LEE

SUMTER

7

DALLAS

AUTAUGA

MACON

MARENGO

Montgomery

RUSSELL

CHOCTAW

LOWNDES

MONTGOMERY

WILCOX

PIKE

BULLOCK

BARBOUR

CLARKE

MONROE

BUTLER

CRENSHAW

2

WASHINGTON

CONECUH

COFFEE

DALE

HENRY

COVINGTON

ESCAMBIA

GENEVA

HOUSTON

MOBILE

1

Mobile

BALDWIN

Miles

0 10 20 30 40

retired from politics in 1986 (although his racial politics had moderated by then), George Wallace set the tone of public life in Alabama. His first and critical term as governor was not only a failure, but a tragedy. His pledge to stand in the schoolhouse door to prevent desegregation was a charade, its only practical effect being to put others' lives at risk. The violent resistance of Alabama officials—Birmingham commissioner Bull Connor's police dogs and fire hoses in 1963, Sheriff Jim Clark's cordons in Selma in 1965—highlighted, as Martin Luther King sensed they would, the unreasonability behind the white South's resistance to desegregation and made possible the passage of the Civil Rights Act of 1964 and the Voting Rights Act of 1965.

Wallace's own career prospered. Sensing how to capitalize on ordinary voters' anger at cultural liberalism, he ran well in the 1964 and 1972 northern Democratic presidential primaries, and as a third-party candidate in the 1968 presidential race won 13.5% of the vote. Crippled by a gunshot wound while running again in May 1972, he lost all force as a national politician when he lost to Jimmy Carter in the March 1976 Florida primary. But he remained the key figure in Alabama, retiring in 1978 but returning to office in 1982 until his final retirement in 1986. In those declining years, Wallace became a sad figure, crippled and unable to hear much, often in dreadful pain, inspiring sympathy by seeking the support of the blacks he had once scorned. This longtime opportunist seemed now to be helping Alabama make peace with its past; "The South has changed," he said, "and for the better."

Alabama has changed. The populism of the 1940s has been transformed, after 40 years of Jim Folsom and George Wallace, into a strident conservatism; a credo that placed Alabama politicians at the fulcrum point of national policy has been shed for one that gives it politicians who stand on the periphery of national debate. While Atlanta was peacefully desegregating and beginning three decades of vibrant white-collar growth, Birmingham was violently resisting the civil rights movement, only to see the shrinkage of its once substantial blue-collar base—the steel industry—and an outflow of talented people of all races. The state's economy, regarded as progressive when manufacturing was the leading edge of growth and after the first big boll weevil infestation of 1915, became positively backward during the Wallace era. The big steel mills of Birmingham, many owned by U.S. Steel, turned cold as demand for steel fell; the shipyards of Mobile scrambled for work; the electric generators of TVA, once hailed as a beacon of progress, were condemned for burning dirty coal or allegedly hazardous nuclear fuel. Alabama lagged behind other southern states in creating service and upscale jobs.

But notable progress has been made in daily life. Legal segregation was ended, and Alabama whites have long since accepted integration in schools, on the job, in restaurants and at the shopping mall. They no longer mind that blacks vote and, since the late 1970s, black support has not cost state candidates all white support. Alabama is a long way from the backward state of the 1930s where most people outside the cities had no paved roads, electricity or indoor plumbing, where children walked barefoot to school and many families never saw $50 in cash over the course of a year. The growth that has transformed so much of the South—the metropolitan expansion as freeways climb over green hills and sprout shopping centers, subdivisions and office complexes—is now visible here, with growth in metro areas, especially space-boosted Huntsville, and in rural counties along the interstates.

But Alabama's politics has produced state and local government that provides little in the way of services. This was the last state without a full kindergarten program, for example, and one with a consistently high infant mortality rate—which prompted even Republican Governor Guy Hunt to support infant and maternal care programs. In the post-Wallace 1980s, Alabama politics was again a battleground between liberal forces (the Alabama Education Association and other unions, trial lawyers and blacks) and various business interests: the special interests and the "Big Mules," as they still call each other, represented pretty openly by Democrats and Republicans. The state's political cleavage runs mostly on corresponding lines, with a Democratic lower-income base—black city neighborhoods, smaller white farm counties, especially near the TVA in the north—and a Republican base in the rising affluent class of whites, not only in country club precincts but in donut-shaped circles around urban centers and in the interstate corridors where young families in search of traditional values and job opportunities have flocked. Each side claims it can produce economic growth—the Republicans by attracting business, the Democrats by pumping money into education. Neither party dominates. Alabama's Democratic base is not firm enough to give the party reliable victories (as in Tennessee), nor has the affluent sector grown fast enough to make the Republican party label an advantage (as in South Carolina).

Democratic primaries still attract the lion's share of voters, though not as many as in the past; the 1990 gubernatorial primary attracted only 742,000 and the runoff only 574,000, compared to 940,000 in 1986 and exactly 1 million in 1982, while the 1992, 1988 and 1984 Democratic presidential primaries drew only 450,000, 405,000 and 428,000 respectively. Democrats still hold most legislative and minor offices, but not as many as in the past. Liberal-backed candidates have an increasing edge in Democratic primaries as turnout declines and blacks cast a larger share of the votes. But then they have more trouble winning general elections. In 1990, Republican Governor Guy Hunt was reelected with 53%, just 3% less than the 56% he won against disastrously split Democratic opposition in 1986. In 1992 George Bush fell far below his 1988 showing of 59% and Ronald Reagan's 61%; but he still came in well ahead of southerner Bill Clinton, 48%–41%. The 1992 redistricting, which produced Alabama's first black congressman since Reconstruction, also produced two new Republicans, leaving Democrats with only a 4–3 edge. The Democrats, by bringing an indictment against Guy Hunt, were able in 1993 to sweep him out of the governorship which he had won in 1986 after a state Democratic Party committee ruled that their number two candidate had actually won the primary. So even with its new-found peace with its past, Alabama can still flare up in angry and unpredictable political fights: don't bet heavy money on any outcome.

Governor. Alabama's tradition of raucous politicking has produced something uncomfortably like banana republic politics. Twice in seven years dominant factions in the Democratic Party have tried to bypass the electoral process and determine the occupant of the governor's office by other means, and twice they have succeeded, though perhaps not with the results intended. The first time came in 1986, when the state Democratic Party committee stripped Attorney General Charlie Graddick, who had won a runoff by 8,756 votes, of the Democratic nomination on the grounds that Republican primary voters had been allowed to vote in the runoff. They gave the nomination instead to former Attorney General Bill Baxley, a flamboyant liberal who had secured convictions in the 1963 Birmingham Sunday school bombing case and who was favored by the teachers' unions and trial lawyers. Baxley lost the general election to Guy Hunt, a Primitive Baptist preacher and former Amway salesman from Holly Pond, who had won 26% of the vote the last time he ran, in 1978. In office Hunt performed above expectations, perhaps because his program—holding down spending, encouraging new business with low taxes—did not require the political maneuvering skills needed for governmental activism; he won reelection in 1990 against Paul Hubbert, former head of the Alabama Education Association and a skilled political operator, with 53% of the vote. Then in December 1992 Hunt, already beset by charges of using the state plane for personal trips, was indicted by Attorney General Jimmy Evans for converting $200,000 from an inaugural fund to personal use. There was little dispute about the facts; Hunt argued that he was advised the transfer was legal. In April 1993 he was convicted by a jury and, under state law, immediately removed from office; he will be reinstated should his conviction be overturned on appeal.

The new governor is Jim Folsom, Jr., who like Hunt has also lost statewide office: he lost 50%–47% to Admiral Jeremiah Denton in the 1980 Senate race. Folsom replaced top Hunt appointees and immediately ordered the Confederate flag to be taken down from atop the Capitol. But he comes in late to affect public policy, and all eyes were already on what was shaping up to be to be a riproaring 1994 race. Paul Hubbert, who had been running hard, was considered likely to challenge Folsom in a primary. Possible Republicans included Charlie Graddick and former Governor Fob James (both party switchers some years back), former Congressman Bill

Dickinson and former Hunt cabinet official Jim Martin. But Spring 1993 polls showed that running ahead of the pack for both the Democratic and Republican nominations was Richard Shelby, even while he remained a senator and a Democrat. Much will obviously depend on Folsom's performance in office, and whether he stays in office; but nothing about Alabama state politics is predictable.

Senators. One result of Alabama's populist tradition is to give the state two Democratic senators, both with solidly conservative voting records on economic, cultural and foreign issues, both with sometimes crucial votes in a closely divided Senate, both with an occasional penchant for the political cheap shot. Neither has become an imposing figure whose opinions command wide influence.

Howell Heflin came to the Senate with a reputation as a judge; "I just try to be the country judge," he says, and in style and temperament that is what he looks to be. Actually, he was a successful trial lawyer in Tuscumbia, in the Tennessee Valley, before being elected in 1970 as the anti-Wallace chief justice of the state Supreme Court; he got a legal reform referendum passed over Wallace's opposition. When Heflin ran for the Senate in 1978, he expected Wallace to be his opponent, but Wallace declined to run. Heflin beat Congressman Walter Flowers in the primary by running against "the Washington crowd"—a slogan used by Alabama candidates of all political stripes. Heflin has a political pedigree: his uncle, "Cotton Tom" Heflin, was a fierce segregationist who served in the Senate from 1920 to 1931. Though he is a huge man with the look of a country storekeeper, he prides himself on being a careful lawyer who picks at the rules of law with the delicate touch of a watch repairman. He is the Senate's chief authority on bankruptcy law, for instance, and produced a 1992 reform package; he is the major technician on the mechanics of the court systems—politically unrewarding work that serves important national purposes.

But in public hearings he has sometimes looked ill-prepared or indecisive. On the Iran-contra committee in 1987, for example, the press expected him, as a folksy backcountry southern lawyer, to be another Sam Ervin. Instead, he seemed maladroit or off the mark, at one point telling reporters that Fawn Hall was putting documents in her undergarments. Weeks later in the Judiciary Committee, he kept observers guessing how he would vote on Judge Robert Bork as he asked Bork why he grew a beard and probed his views on abortion; he voted against Bork for being too unpredictable and having a "proclivity for extremism." In the Clarence Thomas hearings in 1991, Heflin made up his mind early, opposing Thomas before Anita Hill's surprise testimony. But when questioning Thomas, he seemed stunned by Thomas's assertion that he hadn't watched Hill's testimony; and his stumbling attempts to get Thomas to comment on the intricacies of Hill's story elicited instead Thomas's most effective bellows of outrage as he denied her story totally and charged the committee with leaks while likening his situation to a lynching. As chairman of the Senate Ethics Committee during the investigation of the Keating Five, Heflin helped to keep John McCain and John Glenn in the case, though their offenses were much less than those of the other three, presumably because it made this otherwise Democratic scandal bipartisan. He secured approval of the rebukes the committee ultimately agreed on, including the reprimand of Alan Cranston. In May of 1991, Heflin insisted on stepping down as chairman.

Heflin is conservative on many issues, pro-life on abortion, for lower numbers of immigrants, a co-sponsor of the constitutional amendment to require balanced budgets. He provided a key vote for the Gulf war resolution. On the Agriculture Committee, he pushed through a law punishing violence by animal rights advocates against facilities like zoos, aquariums and livestock shows. On economic issues, he speaks in the populist accent of the Tennessee Valley, supporting subsidies to Alabama farm products, championing the economic interests of farmers against environmentalists on pesticides, backing eased restrictions under the Clean Air Act, outspokenly opposing the North American Free Trade Agreement which he fears would negatively impact Alabama's textile industry. Mindful of Huntsville's space industry, he was a leading advocate of funding for the Space Station. Mindful of Alabama's history, he favors civil rights causes, supporting the 1990 Civil Rights Act and the Americans with Disabilities Act. But he strongly supported and pushed through the Senate the nomination of Judge Edward Carnes, who had defended Alabama's death penalty, against liberals angry at his denial of any racial discrimination in its application; he was helped that longtime civil rights advocate and death penalty opponent, Morris Dees of Montgomery, vouched for Carnes.

In partisan contests, Heflin, for all his good-humored folksiness, has tended to campaign negatively, seizing on the weaknesses of his opposition. He won his judgeship in 1970 essentially by campaigning against Wallace; he ran in 1978 against "the Washington crowd"; he won in 1984 against a one-term ex-congressman who had been defeated in his own district. His 1990 opponent, State Senator Bill Cabaniss, who lives in Birmingham's highest income suburb (Mountain Brook), Heflin pilloried as a "Grey Poupon" Republican, "Gucci-clothed, Mercedes-driving, jacuzzi-soaking, Perrier-drinking." Ironically it was Heflin, thanks to a crackerjack fundraising operation that mined liberal money in New York and Beverly Hills, who had by far the richer campaign. Cabaniss billed himself as "a progressive conservative," but his charges that Heflin was too liberal on cultural issues and not strong enough on environmental issues received little attention; his no-new-taxes pledge was undermined by Bush. The result was an easy third term victory for Heflin.

Alabama's junior senator, Richard Shelby, has possibly the most conservative record of any Democratic senator. He voted for the confirmation of Clarence Thomas and for the Gulf war resolution. He voted against the campaign finance bill supported by almost all Democrats and he voted for the Bush crime bill. He was for oil drilling in the Arctic National Wildlife Refuge and against a 4,250-drum limit on nuclear waste stored underground. He backed hefty increases in funding for the Strategic Defense Initiative and its Brilliant Pebbles sensors. He was a major sponsor of a law to enforce court orders on fathers who default on child support payments. And after Thomas Barnes, a young Shelby aide, was murdered a few blocks from the Capitol, Shelby pushed through a law requiring the District of Columbia to hold a referendum on capital punishment (it lost).

But Shelby's independence from his party may cost him now that Democrats control the White House. In February 1993, the Clinton Administration, apparently angered by Shelby's criticism of the president's just released economic plan—"the taxman cometh," ostentatiously decided to make an example of him and Shelby ostentatiously decided to make a display of his independence. At a meeting in which Vice President Al Gore tried to persuade Shelby to support the plan, Shelby turned to the 19 Alabama TV cameras present for the meeting and, to the embarrassment of Gore, further denounced the Clinton program as "high on taxes, low on spending cuts." The punishment for Shelby's apostasy: a multi-million dollar space facility was moved from Alabama to Texas. But, as the Clinton Administration's ratings slid downward, this only raised Shelby's popularity ratings to the highest level in the state, making a politician known more for his suppleness of maneuver appear an embattled defender of principle. Republicans speculated that Shelby would switch parties; analysts wondered whether he would run for governor; Democrats pondered whether there was any way to get him back on the reservation. But Shelby insisted that he would go on as he was, a Democrat but voting blandly against almost all Clinton administration proposals.

In 1992, Shelby broke the political jinx on this seat which, before his election in 1986, had five occupants in ten years. He has certainly shown himself adept at eking out majorities from diverse constituencies. He first won a House seat in 1978 by winning a critical runoff with the support of white conservatives against Chris McNair, a black whose daughter was killed in the 1963 Birmingham church bombings. Despite the large number of blacks in his district, he voted against the Voting Rights Act extension and the Martin Luther King Holiday. In 1986, he got liberal Don Siegelman to drop out of the primary and, with 51% in a five-candidate field, narrowly avoided a runoff. In the general election, his TV ads attacked Republican incumbent Jeremiah Denton—a Vietnam POW for eight years who blinked out "torture" in Morse code when he was interviewed on TV—not only for voting to cut Social Security but for faking invoices to raise campaign money, voting to raise his pay while cutting veterans' benefits, and owning two Mercedes. Shelby won by less than 7,000 votes. In 1992, he had opposition once again from McNair in the primary, but had more money and won 62%–28%. In the general, he attacked Republican Richard Sellers, a political consultant, for being basically unemployed: "he needs a job, but not in the U.S. Senate." Shelby won 65%–33%. The one place he lost was in Shelby County, which includes many new subdivisions outside Birmingham.

Presidential politics. Alabama now seems to be one of the most Republican states in presidential politics. Given George Bush's troubles in 1992, however, the polls were rather close; the Clinton-Gore campaign successfully pressed the Bush-Quayle ticket into spending candidate time and campaign money on a state it would have liked to take for granted. The result of the presidential primary depends on the candidates and turnout: in 1992 it was solidly for Bill Clinton; in 1988 easily for Jesse Jackson; in 1984, voting before Jackson had established himself as a vote-getter, Alabama provided a key victory that kept Walter Mondale in the race.

Congressional districting. The Voting Rights Act, as revised in 1982, was the engine that drove Alabama's congressional redistricting in 1992. The plan adopted was proposed by Republicans and ordered into effect by a federal court. It resulted in the election of a black congressman in the new 68% black 7th District, which stretches from central Birmingham through the Black Belt counties to downtown Montgomery. It also resulted in victories by Republicans in two seats, the 2d and the 6th, from which tens of thousands of blacks had been excluded to raise the black percentage in the 7th. The 6th District ousted 10-year Democratic incumbent Ben Erdreich, who had supported civil rights in Birmingham back when it was not only politically suicidal but also physically dangerous to do so. Meanwhile, Democrat George Wallace, state treasurer and son of the former governor, lost in the 2d District which in its old boundaries had almost ousted veteran Republican Bill Dickinson in 1990.

The People: Est. Pop. 1992: 4,136,000; Pop. 1990: 4,040,587, up 2.3% 1990–1992. 1.6% of U.S. total, 22d largest; 40% rural. Median age: 33.0 years. 12.9% 65 years and over. 73.6% White, 25.3% Black. Households: 57.0% married couple families; 27% married couple fams. w. children; 37% college educ.; median household income: $23,597; per capita income: $11,486; 70.5% owner occupied housing; median house value: $53,700; median monthly rent: $229. 7.3% Unemployment. Voting age pop. (1990): 2,981,799. Registered voters (1992): 2,364,064; no party registration.

Political Lineup: Governor, James E. (Jim) Folsom, Jr. (D); Lt. Gov., vacant; Secy. of State, Billy Joe Camp (D); Atty. Gen., James H. Evans (D); Treasurer, George C. Wallace, Jr. (D); Auditor, Terry Ellis (D); State Senate, 35 (27 D, 8 R); State House of Representatives, 105 (81 D, 23 R, and 1 vacancy). Senators, Howell T. Heflin (D) and Richard C. Shelby (D). Representatives, 7 (4 D and 3 R).

1992 Presidential Vote

Bush (R)	804,283	(48%)
Clinton (D)	690,080	(41%)
Perot (I)	183,109	(11%)

1988 Presidential Vote

Bush (R)	815,576	(59%)
Dukakis (D)	549,506	(40%)

1992 Democratic Presidential Primary

Clinton	307,621	(68%)
Brown	30,626	(7%)
Other	21,789	(5%)
Uncommitted	90,863	(20%)

1992 Republican Presidential Primary

Bush	122,703	(74%)
Buchanan	12,588	(8%)
Uncommitted	29,830	(18%)

GOVERNOR

Gov. James E. (Jim) Folsom, Jr. (D)

Assumed office April, 1993, term expires Jan. 1995; b. May 14, 1949, Montgomery; home, Montgomery; Jacksonville St. U., B.A. 1974; Episcopalian; married (Marsha).

Career: AL Dept. of Industrial Relations, 1974–76; P.R. Rep., Reynolds Aluminum Co., 1976–79; AL Public Service Commissioner, 1979–86; AL Lt. Gov., 1986–93.

Office: Alabama State Capitol, 11 S. Union St., Montgomery 36130, 205-242-7100.

Election Results

1990 gen.	Harold Guy Hunt (R)	663,520	(53%)
	Paul R. Hubbert (D)	582,106	(47%)
1990 prim.	Harold Guy Hunt (R)	119,877	(96%)
	Two Others	5,240	(4%)
1986 gen.	Harold Guy Hunt (R)	696,203	(56%)
	William J. Baxley (D)	537,163	(44%)

SENATORS

Sen. Howell T. Heflin (D)

Elected 1978, seat up 1996; b. June 19, 1921, Poulan, GA; home, Tuscumbia; Birmingham-Southern Col., B.A. 1941, U. of AL, J.D. 1948; United Methodist; married (Elizabeth Ann).

Career: Marine Corps, 1942–46 (WWII); Practicing atty., 1948–71, 1977–79; Chief Justice, AL Supreme Court, 1971–77.

Offices: 728 HSOB 20510, 202-224-4124. Also B-29 Fed. Crthse., 15 Lee St., Montgomery 36104, 205-832-7287; P.O. Box 228, Tuscumbia 35674, 205-381-7060; 316 Fed. Bldg., 1800 5th Ave., N., Birmingham 35203, 205-731-1500; and 437 Fed. Crthse. Bldg., Mobile 36602, 205-690-3167.

Committees: *Agriculture, Nutrition and Forestry* (4th of 10 D): Agricultural Production and Stabilization of Prices; Domestic and Foreign Marketing and Product Promotion; Rural Development and Rural Electrification (Chmn.). *Judiciary* (6th of 10 D): Antitrust, Monopolies and Business Rights; Courts and Administrative Practice (Chmn.); Patents, Copyrights and Trademarks. *Small Business* (9th of 12 D): Innovation, Manufacturing and Technology; Rural Economy and Family Farming.

Group Ratings

	ADA	ACLU	CDF	COPE	CFA	LCV	ACU	NTLC	NSI	COC	CEI
1992	40	27	50	75	75	8	48	33	90	40	44
1991	35	—	64	67	44	7	57	—	—	40	34

National Journal Ratings

	1991 LIB — 1991 CONS		1992 LIB — 1992 CONS	
Economic	39% —	60%	43% —	55%
Social	28% —	69%	42% —	56%
Foreign	37% —	61%	34% —	63%

Key Votes of the 102d Congress

1. $ for Homeownership	AGN	5. Clarence Thomas Nom.	AGN	9. Use Force in Gulf	FOR
2. Have Cap Gains Debate	AGN	6. Lmt Death Row Appeal	FOR	10. Keep Salvador Aid	FOR
3. Remove Budget Walls	AGN	7. Handgun Wait/5-Day	AGN	11. Cut $1B from SDI	AGN
4. Ban Striker Replace	FOR	8. Abortion Gag Rule	FOR	12. Override China MFN	FOR

Key Votes of the 103d Congress

1. Family Leave AGN 2. HIV Immigrants AGN 3. Clinton Budget FOR

Election Results

1990 general	Howell T. Heflin (D)	717,814	(61%)	($3,437,073)
	Bill Cabaniss (R)	467,190	(39%)	($1,853,869)
1990 primary	Howell T. Heflin (D)	540,876	(81%)	
	Mrs. Frank Ross Stewart (D)	123,508	(19%)	
1984 general	Howell T. Heflin (D)	860,535	(63%)	($2,001,386)
	Albert Lee Smith, Jr. (R)	498,508	(36%)	($574,382)

Sen. Richard C. Shelby (D)

Elected 1986, seat up 1998; b. May 6, 1934, Birmingham; home, Tuscaloosa; U. of AL, B.A. 1957, LL.B. 1963; Presbyterian; married (Annette).

Career: Practicing atty., 1963–78; AL Senate, 1970–78; U.S. House of Reps., 1978–1986.

Offices: 509 HSOB 20510, 202-224-5744. Also 113 St. Joseph St., 438 U.S. Crthse., Mobile 36602, 205-694-4164; 1000 Glenn Hearn Blvd., Huntsville 35824, 205-772-0460; 1800 5th Ave., N., 321 Fed. Blvdg., Birmingham 35203, 205-731-1384; 15 Lee St., 828 U.S. Crthse., Montgomery 36104, 205-223-7303; and 118 Greensboro Ave., #240, Tuscaloosa 35401, 205-759-5047.

Committees: *Aging (Special)* (6th of 11 D). *Armed Services* (7th of 11 D): Coalition Defense and Reinforcing Forces; Force Requirements and Personnel (Chmn.); Military Readiness and Defense Infrastructure. *Banking, Housing and Urban Affairs* (5th of 11 D): Economic Stabilization and Rural Development (Chmn.); Securities. *Energy and Natural Resources* (7th of 11 D): Energy Research and Development (Vice Chmn.); Public Lands, National Parks and Forests; Renewable Energy, Energy Efficiency, and Competitiveness.

Group Ratings

	ADA	ACLU	CDF	COPE	CFA	LCV	ACU	NTLC	NSI	COC	CEI
1992	30	41	50	58	58	17	63	33	100	60	50
1991	35	—	55	67	56	13	76	—	—	40	36

National Journal Ratings

	1991 LIB — 1991 CONS		1992 LIB — 1992 CONS	
Economic	38% —	61%	40% —	59%
Social	31% —	66%	39% —	58%
Foreign	33% —	65%	10% —	80%

Key Votes of the 102d Congress

1. $ for Homeownership	FOR	5. Clarence Thomas Nom.	FOR	9. Use Force in Gulf	FOR
2. Have Cap Gains Debate	AGN	6. Lmt Death Row Appeal	FOR	10. Keep Salvador Aid	FOR
3. Remove Budget Walls	AGN	7. Handgun Wait/5-Day	AGN	11. Cut $1B from SDI	AGN
4. Ban Striker Replace	FOR	8. Abortion Gag Rule	AGN	12. Override China MFN	AGN

Key Votes of the 103d Congress

1. Family Leave   FOR   2. HIV Immigrants   AGN   3. Clinton Budget   AGN

Election Results

1992 general	Richard C. Shelby (D)	1,022,698	(65%)	($2,807,764)
	Richard Sellers (R)	522,015	(33%)	($149,578)
	Other	31,811	(2%)	
1992 primary	Richard C. Shelby (D)	304,957	(62%)	
	Chris McNair (D)	136,836	(28%)	
	Bob Miller (D)	28,432	(6%)	
	Mrs. Frank Ross Stewart (D)	25,956	(5%)	
1986 general	Richard C. Shelby (D)	609,360	(50%)	($2,258,547)
	Jeremiah Denton (R)	602,537	(50%)	($4,621,163)

FIRST DISTRICT

Mobile, where the Tombigbee and Alabama Rivers flow into the Gulf of Mexico, was once an American frontier. Held by the Spanish until after the Revolutionary War, it was wrested away by threats of war from Secretary of State John Quincy Adams. During the Civil War, Mobile was one of the blockaded ports of the Confederacy; it was while steaming into Mobile harbor in 1864 that Admiral David Farragut, lashed to his mast, cried, "Damn the torpedoes! Full speed ahead." Today, Mobile is full of graceful signs of its slightly exotic past: behind the docks and rail lines are downtown buildings and old houses with Spanish motifs, French accents, or tropical Art Deco lines. Further inland are neighborhoods with spacious houses, often with double porches, overhung by huge live oaks, graced sometimes with Spanish moss. Mobile is a Gulf Coast version of Charleston or a smaller, perhaps more comfortable, New Orleans, with a taste for shellfish and spicy food. Its economy was based originally on docks and shipyards, factories and terminals, but with a determination to impose touches of beauty on an almost perfectly flat landscape that used to be unhealthy and choked with vegetation.

Mobile is also, as befits a frontier city with a martial past, bristling with arms: one of the proudest possessions of the city is the battleship *U.S.S. Alabama*, moored at the head of Mobile Bay, with its guns aimed out toward the Gulf. Geographically, Mobile lies just about in the middle of America's Gulf Coast. This southern seaboard of the Confederacy, for years afterward a part of the solidly Democratic South, has been one of the most hawkish and often one of the most Republican parts of the nation, from Richard Nixon's reelection in 1972 to George Bush's primaries and general election in 1988. The Mobile area is usually the most Republican part of Alabama and the area most supportive of conservatives in Democratic primaries; blacks vote heavily Democratic, but country club whites are joined in most elections by blue-collar whites whose lives are centered on tradition-minded religions or proud patriotism.

Mobile forms the heart of Alabama's 1st Congressional District, which extends north along the lazily flowing Tombigbee and Alabama rivers, near the old forts and mansions and miles of fields that once grew cotton (more likely now to be producing soybeans or scrub pine). Also here are surviving back country settlements of blacks and Cajans (who may or may not be descended from Louisiana Cajuns). To the south, along the shores of the Gulf of Mexico, are the condominiums which are the final homes of thousands of affluent southerners. Redistricting changed the district only mildly for 1992, slicing off black-majority Wilcox County and northern parts of Clarke County.

The congressman from the 1st District is Sonny Callahan, a Republican with a rags-to-riches biography and a Democrat-to-Republican political history. The oldest boy in a family of nine children whose father died young, Callahan went to work at the age of 12, during World War II; fortunately, the boss was his uncle who owned a warehouse company. After serving in the Navy during Korea, Callahan rose to become president of the company at 32 and expanded into real estate and insurance. Like so many go-getters, he ran for the state legislature and was elected at 38. A Democrat, he ran for lieutenant governor and lost the 1982 Democratic primary to liberal Bill Baxley. Then 1st District Republican Congressman Jack Edwards decided to retire in 1984 after 20 years and asked Callahan to run as a Republican; he did and won, though with smaller margins than expected, 61% in the Republican primary and 51% in the general.

Callahan has boasted one of the most conservative voting records in the House; he wants government spending and revenues to grow no faster than the economy and is solidly anti-abortion. He spent one term on Public Works, where he promoted Mobile area projects, then switched in 1987 to Energy and Commerce, where he pushed to allow more lenient recycling standards for paper manufacturers. He also pushed a bill which directed the Secretary of Agriculture to assist states in developing programs to help forest landowners preserve their property and enhance the multiple-use potential of private forest land. He switched to Appropriations for 1993, where he can continue to pursue projects like replacing the Dog River Bridge (already underway) and securing equal funding for the protection of the Gulf of Mexico at Great Lakes and Chesapeake Bay levels. Interestingly, he is one of the few members of Congress who live on houseboats on the Potomac River (others include Gary Ackerman and James Traficant); he explains that, unlike a Washington house, he can take it back to the district when he retires. He was reelected in 1992 with a solid but not overwhelming margin.

The People: Pop. 1990: 577,375; 34% rural; 13% age 65+; 70% White; 29% Black; 1% Amer. Indian; 1% Asian; 1% Hispanic origin. Voting age pop.: 414,788; 26% Black; 1% Hispanic origin. Households: 57% married couple families; 27% married couple fams. w. children; 36% college educ.; median household income: $22,881; per capita income: $10,961; median gross rent: $322; median house value: $52,600.

1992 Presidential Vote

Bush (R)	118,420	(51%)
Clinton (D)	84,193	(36%)
Perot (I)	26,749	(12%)

1988 Presidential Vote

Bush (R)	119,249	(63%)
Dukakis (D)	69,315	(37%)

Rep. H. L. (Sonny) Callahan (R)

Elected 1984; b. Sept. 11, 1932, Mobile; home, Mobile; U. of AL; Catholic; married (Karen).

Career: Navy, 1952–54; Finch Cos. 1955–85, Pres., 1964–85; AL House of Reps., 1970–78; AL Senate, 1978–82.

Offices: 2418 RHOB 20515, 202-225-4931. Also 2970 Cottage Hill Rd., #126, Mobile 36606, 205-690-2811.

Committees: *Appropriations* (17th of 23 R): Military Construction; Foreign Operations, Export Financing and Related Programs.

Group Ratings

	ADA	ACLU	COPE	CDF	CFA	LCV	ACU	NTLC	NSI	COC	CEI
1992	5	0	27	0	20	0	96	95	100	75	74
1991	0	—	17	20	28	0	100	—	—	90	66

National Journal Ratings

	1991 LIB	—	1991 CONS		1992 LIB	—	1992 CONS
Economic	4%	—	90%		16%	—	80%
Social	0%	—	84%		0%	—	85%
Foreign	0%	—	88%		0%	—	82%

Key Votes of the 102d Congress

1. Ban Striker Replace	AGN	5. Handgun Wait/7-Day	AGN	9. Use Force in Gulf	FOR
2. $ for Homeownership	FOR	6. Overseas Mil. Abortion	AGN	10. US Mil. Abroad $ Cut	AGN
3. Tax Rich/Cut Mid Cls.	AGN	7. Obscn. Art NEA $ Ban	*	11. Limit SDI Funds	AGN
4. FY93/$15B Def. Cut	AGN	8. Death Pen. from Jury	*	12. Cuba Trade Embargo	FOR

Key Votes of the 103d Congress

1. Family Leave	AGN	2. Deficit Reduction	AGN	3. Stimulus Plan	AGN

Election Results

1992 general	H. L. (Sonny) Callahan (R)	128,874	(60%)	($383,760)
	William A. Brewer (D)	78,742	(37%)	($13,297)
	Other.	6,548	(3%)	
1992 primary	H. L. (Sonny) Callahan (R), unopposed			
1990 general	H. L. (Sonny) Callahan (R), unopposed			($183,910)

SECOND DISTRICT

In southern Alabama, the countryside is everywhere apparent. Even in Montgomery, the metropolis of the region, the stone and brick buildings that rise in the irregular downtown grid do not disguise the contours of the hills or mask the lush foliage. You can look downhill from the recently renovated Greek Revival Capitol toward Dexter Avenue Baptist Church where Martin Luther King, Jr., became pastor in 1954, or out toward the newer subdivisions and shopping complexes, and still sense that this was once cottonfields. There is urban development in southeast Alabama's wiregrass region, named for the stiff native grass indigenous to the area: around the town of Dothan, whose major tourist attraction is the Farley Nuclear Visitors Center, past Daleville and the Army's Fort Rucker to Enterprise, site of the Boll Weevil Monument which commemorates the insect that destroyed two-thirds of the cotton crop here in 1915 and then spread throughout the South.

The 2d Congressional District of Alabama covers most of the southeast corner of the state. The 1992 redistricting changed the borders by taking away an 80% black one-third segment of Montgomery County and adding Elmore and Autauga Counties across the river which are 78% white. This vastly altered the political balance, for despite all the changes in daily life, in politics southern Alabama remains racially polarized: blacks vote almost unanimously Democratic, whites in national elections vote very heavily (but not unanimously) Republican, though they often prefer local Democrats. Blacks' party preference is rooted in 1960s era civil rights and in the Kennedy brothers' opposition to Governor George Wallace. The whites' preference has something to do with race but is also linked with foreign and military policy. They want from their leaders not a repudiation of the civil rights laws of the 1960s, but a validation of the proud nationalism and traditional moral values that are so strong here.

Just weeks after redistricting came the announcement of the retirement after 28 years of 2d District Congressman Bill Dickinson. A Republican first elected in Alabama's 1964 Goldwater landslide, he had risen to be ranking Republican on the Armed Services Committee; in leaving, he warned against overlarge cuts, urging that we "maintain the vendor base" for weapons systems like the B-2 and that Democrats not make the defense budget "a bottomless pit" for domestic spending. Had Dickinson run, he might have had trouble; in 1990, he had won by just 51%–49% over Democrat Faye Baggiano, former state Human Resources director, and she was running again. So was George Wallace, Jr., state treasurer and son of the former governor. Also running were two Republicans, Montgomery State Legislator Larry Dixon and Enterprise businessman Terry Everett. Interestingly, Wallace had long won black support; he was endorsed by the New South Coalition and the Alabama Democratic Council; he called his father's standing in the schoolhouse door in 1963 "a bad political stunt." Baggiano won 32% in the primary, but Wallace's 49.7% was not quite enough to avoid a runoff. The runoff campaign was a nasty one and Wallace wasn't helped by a story in *People* magazine in which one of his three former wives claimed he was sometimes violently temperamental. Nonetheless, Wallace pulled off a 57%–43% victory, but ominously did not carry Montgomery County. Meanwhile, there was an upset on the Republican side. Dixon carried Montgomery with 63%, but Everett spent more than $600,000 of his own money and won 84% in the Dothan-Enterprise corridor, for a 58% victory.

The general election got testy. Wallace complained bitterly of "cruel lies" in an Everett ad claiming Wallace had been chauffeured around as a child; just 11 when his father was first elected governor, he was protected by security agents because of frequent death threats. Wallace was also distracted by his father's illness, but he did manage to attack Everett for his high personal campaign spending and for heading a savings and loan (which was profitable and scandal free). Everett called on voters to "Send them a message, not a politician," the first clause recalling Governor Wallace's 1968 and 1972 national campaign themes, the second sounding the anti-incumbent theme of 1992.

The results split the district not so much on racial as on urban-rural lines. Everett carried the Montgomery area 54%–43% and the Dothan-Enterprise corridor 57%–41%. Wallace carried the remaining third of the district 60%–37%, but that wasn't quite enough, as Everett won 49%–48%. This was the first time a Wallace has lost in Alabama since 1958. Redistricting plainly made a difference: subtract Autauga and Elmore Counties and add back the part of Montgomery now in the 7th, and you have a 48%–46% Democratic victory. To be sure, it's not apparent that the race would have taken the same course if it were run in the old district lines, but most likely a Democrat—Baggiano if not Wallace—would have won.

Everett has an interesting background: he served in Air Force Intelligence in Germany in the 1950s, learned Russian, worked as a sports reporter and circulation manager for southern Alabama newspapers, then bought some newspapers himself and sold them for far more, and ended up heading a S&L and owning a large farm and real estate development firm. Though campaigning as an anti-incumbent, he was as slavish a supporter of parochial interests as the most cynical insider: he went to Russia to promote the sale of Alabama peanuts and opposes the North American Free Trade Agreement because it threatens agricultural jobs. He also pledged to get on the Armed Services Committee to protect Fort Rucker and Montgomery's Maxwell Air Force Base. Everett says he is not interested in being a lifetime congressman and his family will stay in Alabama. But he did take care to get a seat on Armed Services and he seems well positioned to hold this new 2d for at least a couple of terms.

The People: Pop. 1990: 577,203; 42% rural; 13% age 65+; 75% White; 24% Black; 1% Asian; 1% Hispanic origin. Voting age pop.: 422,551; 21% Black; 1% Hispanic origin. Households: 59% married couple families; 28% married couple fams. w. children; 40% college educ.; median household income: $24,374; per capita income: $11,636; median gross rent: $329; median house value: $53,700.

1992 Presidential Vote

Bush (R) 123,856 (53%)
Clinton (D) 82,656 (35%)
Perot (I). 27,319 (12%)

1988 Presidential Vote

Bush (R) 133,819 (68%)
Dukakis (D). 62,858 (32%)

Rep. Terry Everett (R)

Elected 1992; b. Feb. 15, 1937, Dothan; home, Enterprise; Baptist; married (Barbara).

Career: Air Force, 1955–59; Businessman; Newspaper reporter, editor and publisher, 1959–88; Real estate developer, 1988–92.

Offices: 208 CHOB 20515, 202-225-2901. Also 3001 Zelda Rd., #100, Montgomery 36106, 205-277-9113; 100 W. Troy St., #101, Dothan 36303, 205-794-9680; 118 S. Main St., #211, Enterprise 36330, 205-393-2996; and City Hall Bldg., Opp 36487, 205-493-9253.

Committees: *Agriculture* (19th of 19R). *Armed Services* (21st of 22 R): Military Installations and Facilities; Oversight and Investigations. *Veterans' Affairs* (8th of 14 R): Compensation, Pension and Insurance; Hospitals and Health Care; Oversight and Investigations.

Group Ratings and 102d Congress Votes: Newly Elected

Key Votes of the 103d Congress

1. Family Leave	AGN	2. Deficit Reduction	AGN	3. Stimulus Plan	AGN

Election Results

1992 general	Terry Everett (R)	112,906	(49%)	($1,042,083)
	George C. Wallace, Jr. (D)	109,335	(48%)	($637,773)
	Three Others........................	5,906	(3%)	
1992 primary	Terry Everett (R)	9,619	(58%)	
	Larry Dixon (R)	6,883	(42%)	
1990 general	William L. Dickinson (R)..............	87,649	(51%)	($596,096)
	Faye Baggiano (D)	83,243	(49%)	($163,663)

THIRD DISTRICT

Fanning out in all directions from Horseshoe Bend, where Andrew Jackson won a climactic battle against the Indians, is the 3d Congressional District of Alabama. It stretches across the central part of the state from the Black Belt in the south to the red clay hills in the north, through land that is densely populated but not much urbanized. In the south is Tuskegee, a black-majority town in a black-majority county, home of Booker T. Washington's Tuskegee Institute. Nearby is Phenix City, a one-time Alabama "sin city" across the Chattahoochee River from Georgia's huge Fort Benning that was cleaned up in the mid-1950s by the young prosecutor John Patterson, who beat George Wallace in the 1958 gubernatorial primary—the one time Wallace let himself be "out-segged." In between is Auburn, home of Auburn University, with its nationally renowned athletic teams and veterinary school. In the northern part of the district is the small industrial city of Anniston and the Army's Fort McClellan. Redistricting changed the boundaries of the 3d slightly for 1992, subtracting two counties just outside Montgomery and adding St. Clair, Bibb and Chilton Counties, heavily white and at the outer edge of greater Birmingham, their red hills increasingly sprouting small subdivisions filled with young families who work farther in but want to raise their children in a country environment.

This is the kind of district which for years has elected conservative southern Democrats who so often have held the balance of power in the House, enabling the increasingly liberal Democratic caucus to hold control but sometimes denying it crucial votes on roll calls. It was represented for 23 years by Bill Nichols, co-author of the 1986 Goldwater-Nichols Act, which strengthened the role of the chairman of the Joint Chiefs of Staff and simplified the military chain of command in a way that paid off, after Nichols's death in 1989, in the Gulf war.

The 1989 special election produced another conservative Democratic congressman with impressive political skills. He is Glen Browder, a two-term legislator elected Alabama secretary of state in 1986, well connected in Montgomery, particularly with the teachers' union and the trial lawyers, the two main Democratic lobbies, but also conservative on issues like the death penalty, school prayer, abortion and gun control. Browder led the six-candidate primary with 25% of the vote and then won the runoff against Tuskegee's black Mayor Johnny Ford by a 63%–37% margin. In the special election, he faced state Senator John Rice, a man of such explosive character that he was nicknamed "Hand Grenade" in the State Capitol, in contrast to Browder's "freckle-faced, aw-shucks, Tom Sawyer approach," as one reporter put it. Rice stressed his support of raising the Confederate flag over the State Capitol, but Browder won an impressive 65%–35% victory.

In the House, Browder joined the Armed Services Committee and the Conservative Democratic Forum. On Armed Services, after he passed an amendment whose practical effect delayed military base closings, he fought to keep Fort McClellan off the base closure list (but it is back on again for 1993); on the Forum, he came forward with a campaign finance reform which instead of public financing would provide a 100% tax credit on contributions of $50 or less—attacked by other Democrats as both too expensive and inadequate. In 1990, he was easily reelected; in 1992, against the same opponent, Browder lost in newly added St. Clair County, but district-wide won a solid—but reduced—60%.

The People: Pop. 1990: 577,116; 47% rural; 13% age 65+; 73% White; 26% Black; 1% Hispanic origin. Voting age pop.: 429,034; 24% Black. Households: 58% married couple families; 27% married couple fams. w. children; 32% college educ.; median household income: $21,594; per capita income: $10,204; median gross rent: $296; median house value: $46,600.

1992 Presidential Vote			1988 Presidential Vote		
Bush (R)	104,928	(47%)	Bush (R)	109,093	(61%)
Clinton (D)	91,983	(41%)	Dukakis (D)	69,634	(39%)
Perot (I)	23,733	(11%)			

Rep. Glen Browder (D)

Elected Apr., 1989; b. Jan. 15, 1943, Sumter, SC; home, Jacksonville; Presbyterian Col., B.A. 1965; Emory U., M.A., Ph.D. 1971; United Methodist; married (Becky).

Career: P.R., Presbyterian Col., 1965; Sportswriter, *Atlanta Journal*, 1966; Investigator, U.S. Civil Service Comm., 1966–68; Asst. Prof., Jacksonville St. U., 1971–1989; AL House of Reps., 1982–86; AL Secy. of St., 1987–89.

Offices: 1221 LHOB, 20515, 202-225-3261. Also, 107 Fed. Bldg., Opelika 36801, 205-745-6221; P.O. Box 2042, Anniston 36202, 205-236-5655; and 115 E. Northside, #205, Tuskegee 36083, 205-727-6490.

Committees: *Armed Services* (18th of 34 D): Military Installations and Facilities; Oversight and Investigations; Readiness. *Budget* (25th of 26 D).

Group Ratings

	ADA	ACLU	COPE	CDF	CFA	LCV	ACU	NTLC	NSI	COC	CEI
1992	45	35	58	60	47	44	48	30	90	50	28
1991	30	—	82	70	67	38	50	—	—	56	22

National Journal Ratings

	1991 LIB — 1991 CONS		1992 LIB — 1992 CONS	
Economic	52%	— 46%	56%	— 42%
Social	37%	— 61%	36%	— 63%
Foreign	38%	— 62%	36%	— 63%

Key Votes of the 102d Congress

1. Ban Striker Replace	FOR	5. Handgun Wait/7-Day AGN	9. Use Force in Gulf FOR
2. $ for Homeownership	AGN	6. Overseas Mil. AbortionAGN	10. US Mil. Abroad $ CutAGN
3. Tax Rich/Cut Mid Cls. FOR		7. Obscn. Art NEA $ Ban FOR	11. Limit SDI Funds AGN
4. FY93/$15B Def. Cut	FOR	8. Death Pen. from Jury FOR	12. Cuba Trade Embargo FOR

Key Votes of the 103d Congress

1. Family Leave	AGN	2. Deficit Reduction AGN	3. Stimulus Plan FOR

Election Results

1992 general	Glen Browder (D)....................	119,175	(60%)	($108,814)
	Don Sledge (R).......................	73,800	(37%)	($22,160)
	Other...............................	4,570	(2%)	
1992 primary	Glen Browder (D), unopposed			
1990 general	Glen Browder (D)....................	101,923	(74%)	($176,550)
	Don Sledge (R).......................	36,317	(26%)	($22,989)

FOURTH DISTRICT

The corduroy ridges of the Appalachian mountains dividing the Atlantic coast from the interior are the nation's coal-and-steel industrial spine, from the black coal country of western Pennsylvania to the red hill country of northern Alabama. Here are America's two premier steel cities, Pittsburgh and Birmingham; around both, and for many miles in between them, is hill country settled by feisty Scotch-Irish farmers in the years between the Revolution and the Civil War. In valley land accessible to railroads are the great steel factories built in the 80 years after the Civil War and the smaller workshops that grew up to serve them. Politically, both regions were not cemented by economic loyalties, but separated by the Civil War: western Pennsylvania was overwhelmingly Republican until the 1930s, while northern Alabama, except for a few mountain communities that remained loyal to the Union during the Civil War, was solidly Democratic through the 1950s. Then both changed. Western Pennsylvania became Democratic during the New Deal years, then more Republican on cultural issues, and then, with the collapse of the steel industry, heavily Democratic again in the 1980s. Northern Alabama left the Democratic Party over civil rights, voting for Goldwater, Wallace and Nixon, then supported Jimmy Carter in 1976, and was split about evenly between Bill Clinton and George Bush. Counties close to Birmingham and along the interstates became Republican in the 1980s, with young families seeking city affluence and country values; more remote hill counties are still voting heavily for populists running against the "Big Mules."

    Alabama's 4th Congressional District covers both areas, from the gritty factory town of Gadsden in the east, across the counties just north of Birmingham, to the hill counties of the west represented by onetime (1937–40) Speaker William Bankhead. Despite the close partisan balance, not all elections are seriously contested here, and there has been no real contest in races for the U.S. House seat since Democrat Tom Bevill won in 1966. What helps Bevill is that he is one of the strongest—and most effective—believers in old-fashioned pork barrel politics. That belief comes from both position and conviction. Bevill chairs the Appropriations Subcommittee on Energy and Water Development—a fancy name for public works. He believes that government should spend generously to build dams and public buildings and, in the process, provide jobs. In northern Alabama 40 years ago, such programs seemed an unalloyed good: local communities desperately needed the facilities, and local people needed the jobs. Later, the need became debatable and the political support less fervent. Bevill had to struggle hard to finish the Tennessee-Tombigbee Waterway project which passes through western Alabama and whose economic justification is pathetically weak.

In the 1980s, Bevill had to fight rear guard actions to protect his appropriations from fiscal conservatives and environmentalists. In the 1990s, he is in better shape. He horse-traded with George Bush, who wanted the hugely expensive Superconducting Supercollider project in Waxahachie, Texas; Bevill supported it and got 30 new water projects in return. Appropriations' Interior Subcommittee Chairman Yates wanted the Chicago area's Fermilab funded; Bevill agreed when Yates agreed to the Supercollider. When Bevill brought his bill forward as the first appropriation of the year in June 1992, he was shocked at the sound defeat of the Supercollider; but in the end, it wound up being included. Though he complained that there was little room for new projects in his 1992 appropriations bill, there was of course something for Alabama—a $2 million environmental research center at the University of Alabama. But Bill Clinton's promises to spend more on infrastructure should give Bevill strong leverage against fiscal conservatives and environmentalists in 1993 and beyond.

Bevill is well liked in Alabama, respected for not retiring and pocketing his campaign treasury as he could have done in 1992, praised for supporting TVA and rural electrification and establishing the Little River Canyon National Preserve as a unit of the National Park System. His 1992 Republican opponent, Martha (Mickey) Strickland, owned acreage in Little River Canyon and protested the preserve; she lost 69%–29%, as Bevill carried every county including Lawrence which he had picked up in redistricting.

The People: Pop. 1990: 577,058; 66% rural; 15% age 65+; 92% White; 7% Black; 1% Amer. Indian. Voting age pop.: 432,040; 6% Black. Households: 65% married couple families; 29% married couple fams. w. children; 26% college educ.; median household income: $20,877; per capita income: $10,170; median gross rent: $262; median house value: $42,800.

1992 Presidential Vote		1988 Presidential Vote	
Bush (R)	107,064 (44%)	Bush (R)	110,149 (57%)
Clinton (D)	104,526 (43%)	Dukakis (D)	83,950 (43%)
Perot (I)	28,558 (12%)		

Rep. Tom Bevill (D)

Elected 1966; b. Mar. 27, 1921, Townley; home, Jasper; U. of AL, B.S. 1943, LL.B. 1948; Baptist; married (Lou).

Career: Army, 1943–46 (WWII); Practicing atty., 1948–66; AL House of Reps., 1958–66.

Offices: 2302 RHOB 20515, 202-225-4876. Also 107 Fed. Bldg., Gadsden 35901, 205-546-0201; 1710 Alabama Ave. #247, Fed. Bldg., Jasper 35501, 205-221-2310; and 102 Fed. Bldg., Cullman 35055, 205-734-6043.

Committees: *Appropriations* (7th of 37 D): Energy and Water Development (Chmn.); Interior; Treasury, Postal Service and General Government.

Group Ratings

	ADA	ACLU	COPE	CDF	CFA	LCV	ACU	NTLC	NSI	COC	CEI
1992	55	43	67	90	60	19	32	10	80	38	17
1991	35	—	92	80	72	23	42	—	—	30	14

National Journal Ratings

	1991 LIB — 1991 CONS		1992 LIB — 1992 CONS	
Economic	51% —	49%	69% —	30%
Social	34% —	65%	46% —	53%
Foreign	40% —	58%	26% —	72%

Key Votes of the 102d Congress

1. Ban Striker Replace	FOR	5. Handgun Wait/7-Day	AGN	9. Use Force in Gulf	FOR
2. $ for Homeownership	AGN	6. Overseas Mil. Abortion	AGN	10. US Mil. Abroad $ Cut	AGN
3. Tax Rich/Cut Mid Cls.	FOR	7. Obscn. Art NEA $ Ban	FOR	11. Limit SDI Funds	AGN
4. FY93/$15B Def. Cut	FOR	8. Death Pen. from Jury	FOR	12. Cuba Trade Embargo	FOR

Key Votes of the 103d Congress

1. Family Leave	FOR	2. Deficit Reduction	FOR	3. Stimulus Plan	FOR

Election Results

1992 general	Tom Bevill (D)	157,907	(69%)	($519,416)
	Mickey Strickland (R)	66,934	(29%)	($20,117)
	Other..............................	5,646	(2%)	
1992 primary	Tom Bevill (D), unopposed			
1990 general	Tom Bevill (D), unopposed			($168,054)

FIFTH DISTRICT

Twice in the last half-century, the northern Alabama counties along the Tennessee River have been transformed by the federal government. The first time was after the Tennessee Valley Authority was created in 1933—an idea prompted by the need to do something with the government's World War I munitions plant at Muscle Shoals, and by Nebraska Senator George Norris's and Franklin Roosevelt's desire to promote public power development. The river then was untamed—unnavigable, with rampaging floods every year—and the hardscrabble farmers and occasional townsmen were poor, without electricity or running water or decent nutrition. The TVA dammed the wild river, controlled flooding, produced cheap electric power and for years was a proud example of what creative government could do. Recently TVA has had problems—plants that don't work, increasing power rates and charges of environmental damage. But for several decades, TVA made northern Alabama voters more favorable to federal government action and more Democratic in elections (even presidential contests) than voters almost anywhere else in the South—despite its relatively low black population.

The second transformation here was wrought by the federal space program. The Redstone Arsenal in Huntsville became a major missile development center after the Soviets put up Sputnik in 1957; NASA built its Marshall Space Flight Center in Huntsville in the 1960s and Huntsville changed from a quaint courthouse town of 14,000 in 1950 to a metropolitan area nearing 250,000 by the 1990s. Huntsville also developed in the 1980s a scientific and technical community of sufficient competence and critical mass to make this the center for much SDI research and development, and one which wants to spend billions on the manned space station. These new professional and technical employees often voted Republican, and for the first time, northern Alabama developed a Republican voting base. The smaller TVA counties voted heavily for Bill Clinton in 1992, but the counties that include Huntsville and Decatur went heavily for George Bush, who carried the area even while losing nationally.

The 5th Congressional District of Alabama includes most of the state's TVA counties, including Huntsville and Decatur; it does not include Guntersville, at the edge of a peninsula in the center of Alabama's largest lake, formed behind a TVA dam, and the 1992 redistricting excluded most of Lawrence County as well. The tradition of representation here, going back to the founding days of the TVA, is Democrats friendly to public works spending: John Sparkman, 1937–46, who then spent 32 years in the Senate; Bob Jones, 1947–77, who eventually chaired Public Works; and Ronnie Flippo, 1977–91, who went to college on workmen's compensation payments after surviving a 55-foot fall while working as an ironworker at a TVA generating plant. When Flippo ran for governor (and lost) in 1990, he was replaced by Democrat Bud Cramer.

But with the new elements in the district, it was not an uncontested race. Cramer had been district attorney for 10 years in Huntsville, and thus was well known throughout the district from Huntsville TV; he was known for setting up the Child Advocacy Center, a shelter for abused children. He won 44% in the primary, and in the runoff faced Public Service Commissioner Lynn Greer, who said Cramer was part of "the country club crowd, and I'm just country." But Cramer won 60%–40%. The Republicans had persuaded 60-year-old state Agricultural Commissioner Al McDonald to switch parties in March 1990; he took conservative stands on cultural traditions and emphasized his rural background. But Cramer whipped him 67%–33% in the general. With his serious, professional manner and his concentration on family problems in an area with many professionals and two-earner families, Cramer seemed a new kind of Democrat.

Once in office, he worked on a National Child Advocacy Center, and concentrated heavily on spending for the TVA counties—and delivered. When a House Appropriations subcommittee zeroed out the space station, he fought back hard, speaking out on the floor and on the Science Committee pushing to secure $260 million for the Advanced Solid Rocket Motor program in Yellow Creek, Mississippi, in Appropriations Chairman Jamie Whitten's district, an obvious effort to get Whitten to oppose any effort of his subcommittee chairmen to cut space station funding. He voted with the House Democratic leadership more than any other Alabama Democrat and fully supported the 5 cent gas tax. He worked overtime to get a Memphis-Atlanta corridor and other highway projects in the district funded, to the tune of $68 million. Cramer's 1992 Republican opponent said he practiced "political, pork-barrel Boss Hogg" politics, and one reporter said he was "on his way to being Alabama's next Tom Bevill," the incumbent in the next-door 4th District. The voters seem to like it: he was reelected with 66% of the vote.

The People: Pop. 1990: 577,235; 39% rural; 11% age 65+; 83% White; 15% Black; 1% Amer. Indian; 1% Asian; 1% Hispanic origin. Voting age pop.: 433,205; 14% Black; 1% Hispanic origin. Households: 62% married couple families; 29% married couple fams. w. children; 44% college educ.; median household income: $28,364; per capita income: $13,268; median gross rent: $361; median house value: $63,000.

1992 Presidential Vote			1988 Presidential Vote		
Bush (R)	110,268	(44%)	Bush (R)	108,499	(60%)
Clinton (D)	102,130	(41%)	Dukakis (D)	73,579	(40%)
Perot (I)	36,921	(15%)			

Rep. Robert E. (Bud) Cramer (D)

Elected 1990; b. Aug. 22, 1947, Huntsville; home, Huntsville; U. of AL, B.S. 1969, J.D. 1972; Methodist; widowed.

Career: Instructor, U. of AL Law Schl., Dir., Clinical Studies Program, 1972–73; Madison Cnty. Asst. Dist. Atty., 1973–75; Practicing atty., 1975–80; Madison Cnty. Dist. Atty., 1981–1990.

Offices: 1318 LHOB 20515, 202-225-4801. Also 301 N. Seminary St., Florence 35631, 205-767-9004; 1000 Glenn Hearn Blvd., P.O. Box 20065, Huntsville 35806, 205-461-9973; and Morgan Cnty. Crthse., P.O. Box 668, Decatur 35602, 205-355-9400.

Committees: *Intelligence (Permanent Select)* (11th of 12 D): Legislation; Program and Budget Authorization. *Public Works and Transportation* (21st of 39 D): Aviation; Surface Transportation. *Science, Space and Technology* (16th of 33 D): Energy; Space.

Group Ratings

	ADA	ACLU	COPE	CDF	CFA	LCV	ACU	NTLC	NSI	COC	CEI
1992	55	43	58	70	60	44	44	20	90	50	29
1991	40	—	83	70	67	46	40	—	—	40	20

National Journal Ratings

	1991 LIB — 1991 CONS		1992 LIB — 1992 CONS	
Economic	52% —	46%	48% —	50%
Social	40% —	58%	42% —	56%
Foreign	40% —	58%	36% —	63%

Key Votes of the 102d Congress

1. Ban Striker Replace	FOR	5. Handgun Wait/7-Day	AGN	9. Use Force in Gulf	FOR
2. $ for Homeownership	AGN	6. Overseas Mil. Abortion	FOR	10. US Mil. Abroad $ Cut	AGN
3. Tax Rich/Cut Mid Cls.	FOR	7. Obscn. Art NEA $ Ban	FOR	11. Limit SDI Funds	AGN
4. FY93/$15B Def. Cut	FOR	8. Death Pen. from Jury	FOR	12. Cuba Trade Embargo	FOR

Key Votes of the 103d Congress

1. Family Leave	FOR	2. Deficit Reduction	FOR	3. Stimulus Plan	FOR

Election Results

1992 general	Robert E. (Bud) Cramer (D)	160,060	(66%)	($389,349)
	Terry Smith (R)	77,951	(32%)	($28,225)
	Other	6,006	(2%)	
1992 primary	Robert E. (Bud) Cramer (D), unopposed			
1990 general	Robert E. (Bud) Cramer (D)	113,047	(67%)	($638,361)
	Albert McDonald (R)	55,326	(33%)	($184,188)

SIXTH DISTRICT

Beyond the statue of Vulcan, beyond the 16th Street Baptist Church bombing: this is metropolitan Birmingham, Alabama, in the 1990s. Birmingham has one of the roughest, in more than one sense of the word, heritages of any big city in the United States. It didn't exist before the Civil War and was a creature entirely made of steel. Built beneath Red Mountain, which is made entirely of iron ore, by 1890 it had the South's biggest steel mills. By the early 20th Century, as the statue of Vulcan, Roman god of fire and metalworking, looked out over the smokestack-rich city in the valley, Birmingham seemed the most up-to-date and progressive city in the South. But worldwide overcapacity in steel and technological obsolescence at home sent the American steel industry into long-term decline starting in the 1950s, and in the years when commercial Atlanta was billing itself as "The City Too Busy to Hate" and building its giant airport, industrial Birmingham's political leaders were plotting to avoid desegregation. Birmingham's violent reaction to civil rights—police commissioner Bull Connor set dogs and firehoses against peaceful demonstrators, and Ku Klux Klansmen bombed the 16th Street Baptist Church killing four young girls in 1963—made a vivid impression over the new medium of television news, helping to pass the Civil Rights Act of 1964, and created a reputation from which Birmingham was still suffering a generation later.

Today, greater Birmingham is a different place. It is still racially polarized, with most blacks living in neighborhoods in the valley corridor between two mountains and most whites on those mountains or in the valleys beyond; and the legal troubles of longtime black Mayor Richard Arrington have not helped. But Birmingham has been transformed economically, with the University of Alabama at Birmingham medical complex now replacing the steel mills as the metro area's biggest employer.

For many years, Alabama's 6th Congressional District consisted of all or most of Birmingham and surrounding Jefferson County, a district that included heavily Democratic black precincts and heavily Republican wealthy and not-so-wealthy white areas. But for 1992, the prevalent interpretation of the Voting Rights Act 1982 revisions, pressed for heavily by blacks and Republicans, required the creation of a new black-majority district. Birmingham's valley areas, 75% black, were appended with rural Black Belt counties to become the new 7th District. This left a restructured 6th District, which included the rest of Birmingham and Jefferson County, all of which was only 8% black, plus all of Shelby County, a rapidly-growing, affluent, very heavily Republican county just to the south. It also stretched out to include a few heavily white rural areas in the university town of Tuscaloosa. The result was one of the biggest political changes in the country. The old 6th District was 37% black, the new 6th District 9% black. The old 6th District went 57% for George Bush in 1988, just 4% more than the national average, making it winnable by either party in House races. The new 6th District went 76% for Bush in 1988, far ahead of any other Alabama district, and one of the most Republican districts in the country.

This spelled trouble, and ultimately defeat, for Democratic Congressman Ben Erdreich. First elected in 1982, Erdreich compiled an economically moderate record that was popular in Birmingham business circles; he and his family were among the few prominent Birmingham whites who supported civil rights at a time when that was not only politically courageous but physically dangerous. What is amazing is not that he lost but that he fought gamely and almost won. The Republican candidate, chosen in a runoff, was former state party chairman and state legislator Spencer Bachus; Erdreich avoided a possible primary when 7th District incumbent Claude Harris retired. Erdreich attacked Bachus for breaking a pledge not to negatively campaign; then he attacked Bachus for missing 3,000 votes during his tenure in the legislature. But this was not enough. Although Erdreich was leading in polls through much of the campaign, Bachus's party identification and his enthusiastic endorsement by the *Birmingham News* helped him win 52%–45%, with 61% in Shelby County and 53% in Jefferson. With any significant number of black voters in the district, it is clear from returns, Erdreich would have won easily: he lost the 6th portion of Jefferson County by 17,000 votes, but the rest of the county went Democratic by 57,000 votes in the 7th District race.

Bachus is a former sawmill owner and lawyer who first was elected to the legislature in 1982 at 35; he was an active legislator for a Republican in a heavily Democratic body. He doesn't look like statewide material yet: he ran for attorney general in 1990 and got 36% of the vote. But, having defeated the strongest possible Democrat, he seems unlikely to lose this district, except in a Republican primary.

The People: Pop. 1990: 577,170; 23% rural; 12% age 65+; 90% White; 9% Black; 1% Asian; 1% Hispanic origin. Voting age pop.: 441,588; 8% Black. Households: 61% married couple families; 28%

married couple fams. w. children; 51% college educ.; median household income: $31,864; per capita income: $16,033; median gross rent: $405; median house value: $72,800.

1992 Presidential Vote			1988 Presidential Vote		
Bush (R)	183,127	(64%)	Bush (R)	170,697	(77%)
Clinton (D)	73,463	(26%)	Dukakis (D)	51,732	(23%)
Perot (I)	28,196	(10%)			

Rep. Spencer Bachus (R)

Elected 1992; b. Dec. 28, 1947, Birmingham; home, Birmingham; Auburn U., B.A. 1969, U. of AL, J.D. 1972; Baptist; divorced.

Career: Natl. Guard, 1969–71; Owner, Lumber Co.; Practicing atty., 1972–92; AL Senate, 1983–84; AL House of Reps., 1984–87; AL Repub. Party Chmn., 1991–92.

Offices: 216 CHOB 20515, 202-225-4921. Also 1900 Intl. Park Dr., #107, Birmingham 35243, 205-969-2296; and 3500 McFarland Blvd., P.O. Drawer 569, Northport 35476, 205-333-9894.

Committees: *Banking, Finance and Urban Affairs* (17th of 20 R): Consumer Credit and Insurance; Financial Institutions Supervision, Regulation and Deposit Insurance; Housing and Community Development. *Veterans' Affairs* (11th of 14 R): Oversight and Investigations.

Group Ratings and 102d Congress Votes: Newly Elected

Key Votes of the 103d Congress

1. Family Leave	AGN	2. Deficit Reduction	AGN	3. Stimulus Plan	AGN

Election Results

1992 general	Spencer Bachus (R)	146,599	(52%)	($502,793)
	Ben Erdreich (D)	126,062	(45%)	($1,015,731)
	Two Others	7,357	(3%)	
1992 runoff	Spencer Bachus (R)	20,114	(59%)	
	Marty Connors (R)	13,856	(41%)	
1992 primary	Spencer Bachus (R)	28,043	(39%)	
	Marty Connors (R)	26,221	(36%)	
	Jim Gunter (R)	11,190	(15%)	
	Mike King (R)	7,075	(10%)	
1990 general	Ben Erdreich (D)	134,412	(93%)	($113,168)
	David A. Alvarez (I)	8,640	(6%)	
	Other	1,745	(1%)	

SEVENTH DISTRICT

As much as any other state, Alabama has taken to celebrating its black heritage, building striking memorials to the civil rights movement in Montgomery and Birmingham, promoting tourism to these and other black history sites, commemorating with dignified restraint a history that was full of raucous hatred and moving sacrifice. Blacks first came to Alabama, as to other states, as slaves; the last slave ship to the United States, the *Clotilde*, docked in Mobile in 1859, where its cargo was then set free. Blacks were part of the great migration into the cottonlands after the Jacksonians swept the Indians out of Georgia, Alabama and Mississippi and sent them on their Trail of Tears to what is now Oklahoma. Today, Alabama's rural blacks are still clustered in the Black Belt of fertile dark soil across the center of the state: around Montgomery, where Rosa Parks refused to move to the back of a city bus in 1955 and a young minister named Martin Luther King, Jr., led a bus boycott; around Selma, founded by Alabama's one vice president, William Rufus King, and the place where Sheriff Jim Clark's troops beat up peaceful marchers on the Edmund Pettus Bridge in demonstrations that led to the march on Montgomery and ultimately the 1965 Voting Rights Act. All 10 of Alabama's majority-black counties are in the Black Belt. But most Alabama blacks now live in urban areas; about one-quarter are in metropolitan Birmingham.

When it came time to create a black-majority congressional district in 1992, it was inevitable that this new 7th District would combine urban black neighborhoods in growing metro areas with declining-population Black Belt counties. Today's 7th has 45% of its population in the narrow valley of Birmingham where the population is 75% black (as compared to 8% black in the rest of Jefferson County). Another 13% are in an 80% black portion Montgomery County (the rest of the county is only 20% black). The rest of the district includes Black Belt counties where the Alabama and Tombigbee Rivers flow lazily past old plantations, plus part of Tuscaloosa, home of the University of Alabama. It thus combines the remnants of Alabama's old cotton economy with neighborhoods built in the shadows of Birmingham's once booming steel mills.

It was obvious from its creation in early 1992 that the new 7th would have a black congressman, the first since Republican Jeremiah Haralson retired in 1876. White incumbent Claude Harris, elected from the old white-majority 7th, retired in 1992 after three terms rather than run here or in the heavily Republican new 6th in suburban Birmingham. In such a geographically disparate district, the Democratic primary was a "friends and neighbors" contest reminiscent of the old days of southern white politics. State Senator Earl Hilliard of Birmingham led the first primary with 31%, winning 58% in Jefferson County but was far behind elsewhere. In second place with 24%, with solid wins in his home area, was State Senator Hank Sanders, who represented eight of the district's 14 counties. Montgomery County Commissioner John Knight, a leader in the Alabama Democratic Conference, got 72% in Montgomery County and finished second in Jefferson, but his 20% overall was good only for third place. Coming in behind him was former Harris aide Sam Taylor, who carried Marengo County in the Black Belt and won 12% districtwide. In the runoff, Jefferson County cast only one-third of the votes, but Hilliard got 71% there, and carried two small rural counties as well. He held Sanders to a 53% edge in Montgomery County, enough for a 50.5%–49.5% victory. Sanders claimed vote fraud but decided not to contest the result.

Hilliard was first elected to the Alabama legislature in 1974 and has a reputation as a politically adept operator. He sponsored fluoride and tax abatement bills, pushed through a horse track for Birmingham and has tried to pump money into schools and scholarships. He voted against a five-cent gas tax increase and once pushed through a controversial pension plan while its opponents were out to dinner. He is pro-choice, favors national health care patterned on the Canadian or Australian model and wants to cut foreign aid. He was criticized by the *Birmingham News* for using state senate campaign funds for business purposes in 1990, but that did not seem to dent his popularity in the 7th District.

The People: Pop. 1990: 577,430; 27% rural; 14% age 65+; 32% White; 67% Black. Voting age pop.: 407,380; 64% Black. Households: 44% married couple families; 20% married couple fams. w. children; 32% college educ.; median household income: $16,560; per capita income: $8,135; median gross rent: $276; median house value: $40,200.

1992 Presidential Vote

Clinton (D) 151,129   (69%)
Bush (R) 56,620   (26%)
Perot (I) 11,633   (5%)

1988 Presidential Vote

Dukakis (D) 138,438   (68%)
Bush (R) 64,070   (32%)

Rep. Earl F. Hilliard (D)

Elected 1992; b. Apr. 9, 1942, Birmingham; home, Birmingham; Morehouse Col., B.A. 1964; Howard U., J.D. 1967; Atlanta U., M.B.A. 1969; Baptist; married (Mary).

Career: Practicing atty., 1972–92; AL House of Reps., 1974–80; AL Senate, 1980–92.

Offices: 1007 LHOB 20515, 202-225-2665. Also Vance Fed. Bldg., #305, 1800 5th Ave., Birmingham 35203, 205-328-2841; P.O. Box 2627, Tuscaloosa 35403, 205-752-3578; Fed. Bldg., #109, Selma 36701, 205-872-2684; and Fed. Bldg., 15 Lee St., #301, Montgomery 36104, 205-262-4724.

Committees: *Agriculture* (17th of 27 D): Environment, Credit and Rural Development; Livestock. *Small Business* (23d of 27 D): Development of Rural Enterprises, Exports and the Environment; Minority Enteprise, Finance and Urban Development; Procurement, Taxation and Tourism; Development of Rural Enterprises, Exports and the Environment.

Group Ratings and 102d Congress Votes: Newly Elected

Key Votes of the 103d Congress

1. Family Leave	FOR	2. Deficit Reduction	FOR	3. Stimulus Plan	FOR

Election Results

1992 general	Earl F. Hilliard (D)	144,320	(70%)	($352,237)
	Kervin Jones (R)	36,086	(17%)	($11,963)
	James Lewis (I)	12,461	(6%)	($58,470)
	James Chambliss (I)	11,466	(6%)	
	Two Others	3,300	(2%)	
1992 runoff	Earl F. Hilliard (D)	35,914	(50%)	
	Hank Sanders (D)	35,244	(50%)	
1992 primary	Earl F. Hilliard (D)	36,005	(31%)	
	Hank Sanders (D)	28,156	(24%)	
	John Knight (D)	23,385	(20%)	
	Sam Taylor (D)	13,595	(12%)	
	Edward B. (E.B.) McClain (D)	8,317	(7%)	
	James Louis Thomas (D)	6,364	(6%)	
1990 general	Claude Harris, Jr. (D)	127,490	(71%)	($238,466)
	Michael D. Barker (R)	53,258	(29%)	($58,952)

ALASKA

In March 1989, the Exxon supertanker *Valdez*, its captain Joseph Hazelwood dozing below deck, ran onto the rocks in Prince William Sound and spilled 11 million gallons of crude oil, killing some 400,000 waterfowl and shore birds, at least 3,500 sea otters and 900 bald eagles, and costing $2.5 billion for Exxon to clean up. Not for the first time, accident had set the course of Alaska: "The purchase of Alaska was not made in any spirit of farsighted policy," wrote historian Henry Clark of William Seward's 1867 agreement, but "by almost stumbling into a treaty." This immense land mass, so remote from the rest of the United States, has puzzled Americans ever since. It has never had a self-sustaining private sector economy, and its growth came almost entirely from government and mineral extraction. It was opened up to settlement by the surprise discovery of gold in Canada's Klondike in 1897. Its interior around Fairbanks was connected to the port of Anchorage by the Alaska Railroad built by the government in the 1920s; it was connected to the rest of North America by the Alcan Highway, built (like most of Alaska's roads) by the Army in eight months during the grim war days of 1942. After a valiant campaign, Alaska was admitted to the Union in 1959 with a statehood act that promised state government a choice of public lands, and for many years afterwards it remained the least populated of American states.

Then, the day after Christmas 1967, at Prudhoe Bay on the Arctic coast, an undulating roar as loud as four jumbo jets directly overhead drew a crowd of 40 men, heavily clothed against the 30-below, 30-knot weather, to an oil rig. Suddenly a natural gas flare shot 30 feet straight up: this was oil, the great 11 billion barrel North Slope oil field. The greatest oil strike ever in the United States, it has made this country a major (though not self-sufficient) producer during the years after the oil shocks of 1973 and 1979, and has made Alaska what it is—and is not—today. It was another accident: oil companies had drilled seven dry wells on Prudhoe Bay, and ARCO chief executive Robert Anderson wouldn't have ordered this one last try, except that he had a drilling rig nearby. Yet this spurting up of the lifeblood of western civilization in the cold darkness of Arctic winter was not the end of the story of this improbable American commonwealth.

Just half a million of 250 million Americans live in this gigantic land mass, larger than all the Northeastern and Great Lakes states put together; almost half are in the Anchorage area, the others scattered in a few small towns and Native settlements over an area so vast that, if superimposed on the Lower 48, it would stretch from Florida to southern California to Lake Superior. Alaska was the only part of the nation occupied by the enemy in World War II (Japan held the Aleutian islands of Attu and Kiska) and is the only part to border Russia, just across the Bering Strait. Alaskans are closer to these Siberian neighbors geographically and, for Natives, ethnically and culturally, than to Americans in the Lower 48. Physically, there is something slapdash about Alaska's civilization: much of the housing is flimsily built, garbage is left outside to freeze in the winter, moose nibble shrubbery in suburban Anchorage backyards, and caribou breed in record numbers near the Trans-Alaska oil pipeline. If a whole town, like Kivalina on the Chukchi Sea, runs out of room, it moves somewhere else. This is still a frontier state with few old people and more males than females. Every American has heard of Alaska, and has some image of its wildness; but less than 10% of Americans have ever been there.

Finding oil in Prudhoe Bay was something like finding it on the moon: it was not clear in 1967 who owned the oil and how it could be taken out. Ownership was in question because the Statehood Act of 1959 provided for the state to choose its own public lands, but only after settling Native land claims. Congress, not Alaska, settled such claims in the 1971 Alaska Native Claims Act which set up 12 regional and 220 village Native corporations, gave them $962 million and time to select their own 44 million acres, and ended the Interior Department's freeze

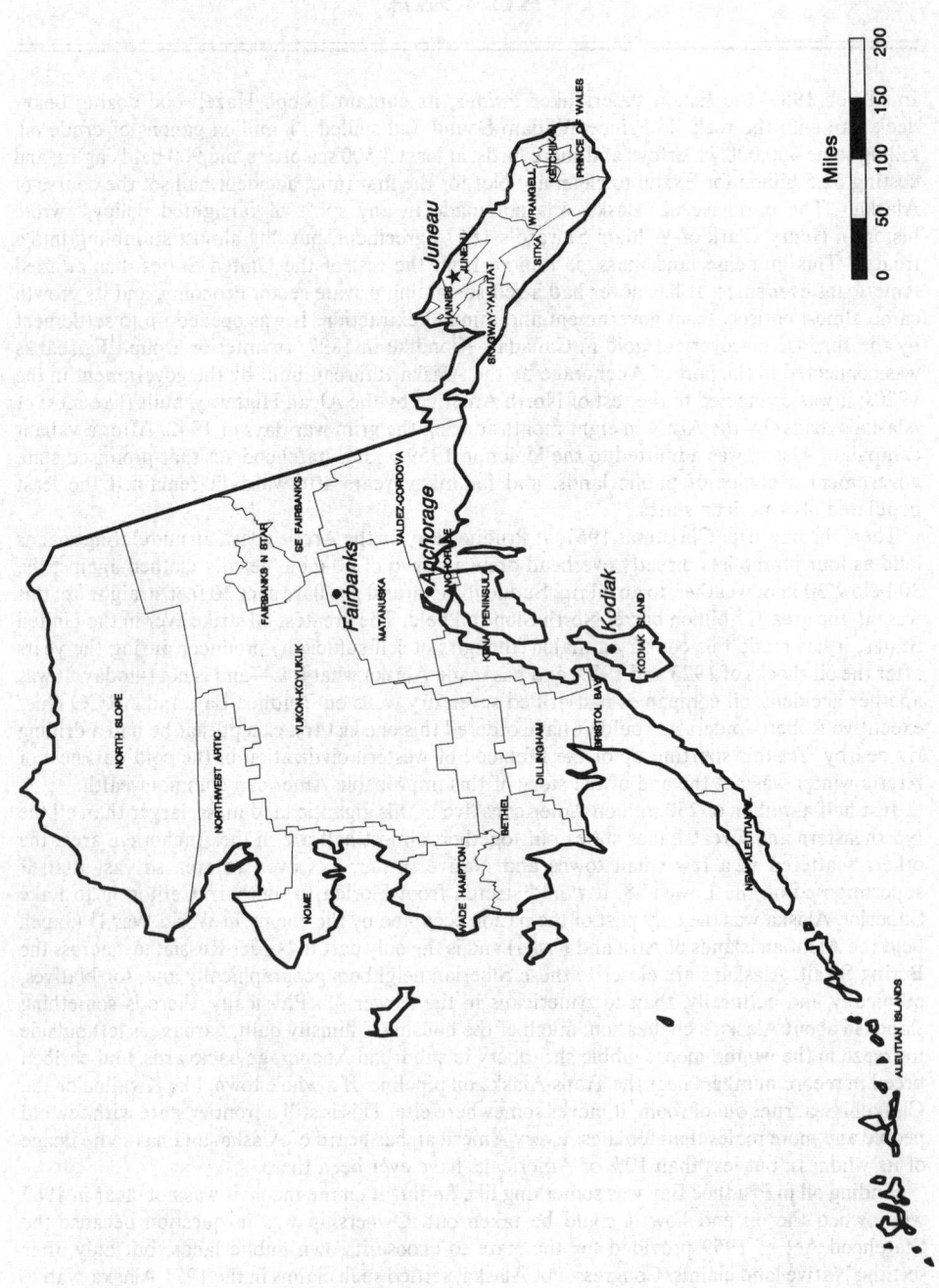

Miles

0 50 100 150 200

that enabled the state to stake claims to mineral-rich acreage. The only feasible way to get the oil out—the waters remain frozen so much of the year—was a pipeline, but that was opposed by environmentalists for fear it would destroy the delicate permafrost and interfere with caribou migrations. Development-minded Alaskans got a pipeline bill through Congress in 1973 by just a one-vote margin in the Senate but the pipeline had to be built on stilts and wasn't opened until 1977, and Congress banned oil exports to Japan and other obvious East Asian markets. Even then, after brilliant lobbying by environmentalists, Congress passed over the objections of Alaska's two senators and in the face of tears from its single Congressman, Don Young, the Alaska Lands Act of 1980, which set aside 159 million acres as wilderness. There were some happy accidents here: the pipeline came on line just as oil prices were approaching their peak, thus generating maximum revenues to the state, which gets 100% of the royalties; the environment was protected and the caribou thrived; the Natives got more autonomy than the non-Native majority of Alaskans would have given them. With oil providing 85% of its revenue, the state abolished its income tax in 1980 and voted lavish benefits, subsidized mortgage interest rates and 25-year residents' housing, granted low-interest college loans and forgave half the debt of students if they would return to Alaska for five years—all for a relatively affluent population, even as the cost-of-living differential from the Lower 48 was being vastly reduced. In the 1970s, Alaska established a Permanent Fund for most of the oil money, totalling $13.2 billion by 1993, and every one-year resident of Alaska gets an annual check—in 1992, $915.84.

Now Alaska is facing other tough decisions—and more control from Congress and the Lower 48. Beyond government, which provides one-third of jobs, the state still doesn't have a self-sustaining private sector, aside from oil. Alaskans, none more than Governor Walter Hickel and two senators and congressman, want oil exploration on a narrow coastal strip of the Arctic National Wildlife Refuge (ANWR), a plot of land they claim is no bigger than the state of Delaware, which may have the potential to be another Prudhoe Bay. Congress seemed about to approve ANWR drilling when the *Valdez* went aground, and then changed its mind; Iraq's seizure of Kuwait raised oil prices and increased pressure for ANWR exploration, but as the war was fought and won, oil prices subsided, and Senator Bennett Johnston's energy bill was defeated in November 1991 by the ANWR provision. Without ANWR, Johnston's bill passed in 1992, even as anti-ANWR drilling Bill Clinton was elected president (with only 30% of Alaskans' votes). Meanwhile, Exxon, which had already spent $2.5 billion in clean-up efforts, agreed in October 1991 to a settlement on various court cases resulting from the disaster. It agreed to pay an additional $900 million over 11 years to restore Prince William Sound, and to pay $100 million in restitution—half to Alaska and half to the federal government, plus a $25 million criminal fine. It has yet to settle cases involving Alaska Natives and other interests.

Most controversies in Alaska end up sounding like arguments between boomers (those who favor development) and greenies (those who call themselves environmentalists). And although the latter are a hardy lot, there is no question where most Alaskans come down. Despite their dependence on government and large corporations for their livelihood, they like to think of themselves as free spirits, adventurers and risk-takers, pioneers on a 21st Century frontier. There is a political streak here which has come out in votes for the Libertarian party, whose 1992 presidential candidate Andre Marrou once served in the Alaska legislature. But the libertarian impulse may be waning: Marrou got only .5% of the vote here, and voters revoked the legislature's 1975 decriminalization of marijuana in 1990. Other institutions remain weak. Unions, which were politically pivotal 20 years ago, aren't any more. The oil companies, while not so unpopular as Lower 48ers thought they would be after the oil spill, were not able to stop higher state oil taxes. Political party organizations have never been strong and voters don't follow party lines—as was shown spectacularly by the election of Walter Hickel as an Independent in 1990. As for the legislature—well, just about any kind of candidate can get elected, and has. In national politics, Alaska is solidly Republican, because national Democrats are seen as wanting to lock up Alaska's resources; no Democrat has been elected to Congress here since 1974, though some contests have been close.

Some regional partisan patterns persist. Greater Anchorage, with about 40% of the state's votes, is affluent and tends to be Republican. The smaller settlements in a 200-mile arc around Anchorage, where boomers from the Lower 48 arrived to seek their fortunes—the Matanuska Valley (one of the few places in Alaska where farming is possible), Seward, the Kenai peninsula, the little port of Valdez at the southern terminus of the pipeline—have been growing more rapidly than any part of the state, attracting people who don't like the big city atmosphere and restrictions of Anchorage; all are heavily Republican, but cast big votes for Ross Perot in 1992. Alaska's second largest city, Fairbanks, a pipeline and mineral service center deep in the interior, unprotected from the Arctic winds in winter and fierce crowds of mosquitoes in its brief but hot summer, once solidly Republican, now seems disgruntled. Older Alaska and Native Alaska, with far fewer people, are Democratic. The old Alaska, first settled by Russians, can be seen in the fishing towns of the Panhandle and in Juneau, located on an inlet of the Pacific up against a steep mountain. Far away to the north and west is the Alaska of the bush, the villages where Natives—Indians, Aleuts, Eskimos—live, often in poverty. Natives make up 16% of Alaska's population and 70% in the vast lands north and west of Anchorage and Fairbanks. But they are only 51,000 people living in an area larger than the northeast United States.

Governor. Accidents of political history: less than an hour before the 1990 filing deadline, 71-year-old real estate developer Walter Hickel filed as a candidate for governor from the Alaskan Independence Party, a group which advocates Alaskan secession from the U.S. Hickel, elected governor back in 1966, became a boomer hero when he ordered highway crew bulldozers to start plowing a road from Fairbanks to the new North Slope oil field. He served less than two years before becoming Richard Nixon's secretary of the interior, then became a hero of the then new environmental movement when he demanded a cleanup of the 1969 Santa Barbara oil spill, and subsequently left office when he opposed Nixon's 1970 Cambodia invasion. Hickel ran unsuccessfully for governor again in 1974, 1978 and 1986. In 1990, he avoided the primaries and ran as the single boomer candidate in the general against two more environmental opponents, Democratic former Anchorage mayor Tony Knowles and Republican legislator Arliss Sturgulewski. Both had only narrowly won their primaries, receiving 25% and 19% respectively of all votes cast. There was a vacuum waiting to be filled and, even though White House Chief of Staff John Sununu called Hickel and urged him not to run, Hickel decided to fill it. At 39%, he came in ahead of Knowles and Sturgulewski who, at 31% and 27% respectively, got little more than they did in the primary.

"We're going to have some fun," Hickel exulted in 1990; critics charge he has made Alaska "Wally's World" or a place as odd as TV's "Northern Exposure." He stirred controversy by supporting the state game board's proposal to shoot 300 gray wolves from planes (there were howls of protest nationwide but Hickel argued it would boost caribou and moose populations—popular targets for hunters) and by his insistence on building a road along the salmon-rich Copper River to the port of Cordova (he threatened to call in the National Guard as a road gang). He wants approval of an $11 billion natural gas pipeline from Prudhoe Bay to Valdez and wants Alaska to be able to sell its oil to East Asia. He has suggested building a water pipeline in the Pacific, to ship plentiful Alaska water to thirsty California. He appointed former oil and mining company employees to regulatory posts and waged a $3 million campaign to open ANWR to drilling. The Alaskan Independence Party, which was Hickel's 1990 vehicle, moved to recall him and Lieutenant Governor Coghill from office, but by early 1993 lacked enough signatures.

Will Hickel run again in 1994, at 75? Can he win? In Alaska's fluid politics, nothing is impossible, but his job rating has been low, and there are a number of candidates ready to take his place. Whatever happens, no one doubts that Alaska is a state still in the making.

Senators. Few senators occupy as central a place in their state's public and economic life as Ted Stevens. "They sent me here," Stevens said in one impassioned debate, "to stand up for the state of Alaska." Alaska's special dependence on the federal government makes Stevens more like an ambassador than a run-of-the-mill legislator. "We ask for special consideration," Stevens is not too shy to say, "because no one else is that far away, no one else has the problems that we have or the potential that we have, and no one else deals with the federal government day in and day out the way we do." Stevens spends plenty of time on national issues, but much of his time and energy over the last quarter century has been necessarily consumed dealing with parochial Alaska issues.

This has often been frustrating work. Stevens could not stop the Alaska Lands Act in 1980 and could not push through ANWR oil drilling in 1989, 1990, 1991 or 1992. He did manage the oil spill bill passed in 1989 in response to the *Valdez* accident, which required double hulls on new tankers and compensation for Alaska. He has worked on fishing legislation: to ban monofilament nets in the high seas, to stop overfishing in international waters in the Bering Sea and to ratify the International Salmon Treaty. He worked for more health and sanitation aid to bush villages and funding for a fetal alcohol syndrome facility important to Natives. He has fought to allow Alaska's oil to be exported to East Asia and, with more success, to allow oil refined in Alaska to be shipped to other countries without first having to go to the Lower 48. On the Clean Air Act, Stevens was quick to object to a provision requiring oxygenated fuel use in America's smoggiest cities in winter months; engines might conk out at 20 or 30 below, he said.

Though Stevens works on non-Alaska issues, as second ranking Republican on Appropriations, and ranking Republican on Defense Appropriations, he is well placed to channel funds into Alaska, from the rocket testing Poker Flats Research Range to a grant for the University of Alaska to harness the energy of the northern lights ("It will cost $10 million or $20 million. But if it is successful, it will change the history of the world."); he backed $13 million to search for extraterrestrial life, but the Senate deleted the funds. After surgery for prostate cancer in 1991, he has pushed for more funding for breast, cervical and prostate cancer research. He has fought against defense cuts, with varying success. On the Commerce Committee, he moved to open up 200 megahertz of the broadcast spectrum to the private sector, with auctions rather than lotteries for frequencies; he played a mediating role between hostile conservatives and supportive Democrats on reauthorization of the Corporation for Public Broadcasting, on which Alaska's rural population is highly dependent. He opposed the Brady bill's handgun purchase waiting period and sponsored the National Rifle Association's instant check proposal instead. As ranking Republican on the Governmental Affairs subcommittee handling civil service and, with the large government work force in high-cost Alaska, he supports increased salaries and benefits for federal workers and argues volubly for higher salaries for senators and Senate staffers.

Stevens served as Republican whip from 1981 to 1984, and was one of four candidates for majority leader in 1984; he lost 28–25 to Bob Dole. He rebounded smartly from that defeat, and seems as busy—sometimes as hassled—as ever. In 1990, he won reelection by a wide margin, while the man who first appointed him, Walter Hickel, was winning the governorship with a plurality; if Stevens's percentage in 1990 was not quite as high as it had been, he still seems to have a safe lifetime seat.

Frank Murkowski, Alaska's junior senator for a dozen years, has mostly followed Stevens's lead. As a member of the Energy Committee, he was the point man on ANWR oil drilling; he also worked hard to preserve logging in the Tongass National Forest even though the wood is uneconomical to harvest. He worked to get funding for patient airplane travel in the bush (commercial travel is costly here), for a Native Languages Preservation Act and bans on driftnets in international waters. In Alaska, he was criticized for his unsuccess on ANWR and for not being a tough enough bargainer in getting $50 million in Exxon funds earmarked for Prince William Sound land acquisition. Murkowski, who once chaired and is now ranking Republican on the Veterans' Affairs Committee, has worked on an Agent Orange compromise and drug discount legislation for veterans. Murkowski served on Intelligence in 1991–92, supporting CIA Director Robert Gates.

Murkowski came to the Senate in 1980 by winning 54% against liberal Democrat Clark Gruening, who had beaten incumbent Mike Gravel in the primary; he was reelected over spirited opposition from Alaska Pacific University president Glenn Olds by 54%–44% in 1986.

In 1992, he attracted strong opposition, from Native leader Willie Hensley, who filed late but got onto the ballot, and former Commissioner of Economic Development Tony Smith, who attacked Murkowski as ineffective on ANWR and the Exxon money. Smith edged Hensley in the primary, 45%–40%, but Murkowski had already run an anti-Smith ad, showing a farmer with a wheelbarrow full of manure, symbolizing the nature of Smith's liberal promises; after the primary, Murkowski hit Smith for accepting a pay raise and taking 58 trips in two years on the public payroll. Smith hit Murkowski for giving none of his substantial honorarium money to charity; Murkowski replied, "Tony is not being straight—again." Also running was a Green Party candidate, who took 8% of the vote; Murkowski, who greatly outspent his rivals, won 53%, essentially the same as 1986, to Smith's 38%.

Back in Washington Murkowski promised to work for ANWR oil drilling, though its prospects are dim, and to allow subsistence hunting and fishing in Glacier Bay park. He ran for Republican conference secretary and finished third, with just 5 votes. For 1993, he rotated off Intelligence and did not get a seat on the Finance Committee as he had hoped.

Representative-At-Large. Alaska's Don Young, onetime tugboat captain on the Yukon and the only licensed mariner in Congress, is, in his words, "not one of these smooth, namby-pamby politicians." He is a hot-tempered, salty-tongued true believer, a development-minded Alaskan, facing off against 432 mostly environment-minded Lower 48ers. Continually frustrated that he cannot make his fellow legislators see reason, back home he is fiercely attacked as ineffective. Young has been ranking Republican on the Natural Resources Committee (formerly Interior) since 1985, but he is heavily outvoted there and does not get along well with its equally hot-tempered chairman, George Miller. Young has lost one battle after another: to open up ANWR to oil drilling, to continue full logging of the Tongass forest, to stop the Alaska Lands Act of 1980. But he can point to some successes, too: the driftnet law which would limit foreign fishing techniques and thereby help Alaska fishermen; blocking reforms to the 1872 Mining Law which, in Young's view, would make it harder to stake a mining claim here than in Russia. But his parlance can get him in trouble. In a campaign debate he suggested that government jobs aren't real jobs at all—although Alaska has the highest percentage of public sector employment in the country.

Young entered election year 1992 as one of the House's most senior Republicans and one of the most endangered. First elected in 1973 after Democratic opponent Nick Begich was killed in a plane crash, his political base has seemed surprisingly weak when he has had significant opposition, in 1978, 1984 and 1986. In 1990, he was held to only 52% by Democrat John Devens, the mayor of Valdez who orchestrated the response to the oil spill and founder of Prince William Sound Community College. He came to the state to run a federal program for the hearing impaired during the Bush Administration; "Alaskans tell me," one Devens brochure read, "they're tired of putting up with a congressman who, at the drop of a hat, shoots his mouth off, or blows up, and then tries to excuse his outburst as 'toughness'."

In 1992, Devens made another run against Young, getting more votes in his 51%–35% primary win over former Young foe Patrick Rodey, than Young got in his 53%–42% primary victory over pro-choice Virginia Collins. In the general, Young trailed in most polls, and ran an ad apologizing for his sometimes volatile behavior. But he also fought back. Young refuted Devens's argument that Congress would listen to him on ANWR by pointing out that even Clinton and Gore opposed it; he pointed to the driftnet bill, the mining bill, COLAs for the government employees he'd called superfluous, the repeal of a small boat recreation fee; he hit Devens for being too pro-environment. The *Anchorage Daily News*'s constant criticisms of Young showed up in the returns, with Young carrying Anchorage by only 47%–44%. But he held even in the Panhandle and won the combined rural and bush vote, 48%–39%, enough for a statewide victory of 47%–43%.

That is not impressive for a longtime incumbent, and there is talk Young may retire or, if Walter Hickel retires, run for governor in 1994. Meanwhile, he remains ranking Republican on Natural Resources, though the six-year cap on such positions Republicans imposed over his objection will force him out in 2001.

Presidential politics. In presidential elections, Alaska votes Alaska issues, but this was not always so: in 1960 and 1968 its vote came eerily close to the national average. Since then, it has voted for development and against the national Democrats: in the year of the Alaska Lands Act, it gave only 26% of its votes to Jimmy Carter, who in some places ran behind Libertarian Ed Clark. In 1988 and 1992, Alaska joined the Pacific Rim shift away from the Republicans, but not necessarily toward the Democrats. In 1992, Bush carried the state with only 40% of the vote, Clinton had only 30% and Ross Perot had 28%, his second best showing after Maine.

Alaska has no presidential primary. Ideologues dominate the caucuses: thin Democratic turnout produced a weak vote for Bill Clinton and Bush maintained the loyalty of state Republicans.

The People: Est. Pop. 1992: 587,000; Pop. 1990: 550,043, up 6.3% 1990–1992. 0.2% of U.S. total, 50th largest; 33% rural. Median age: 29.4 years. 4.1% 65 years and over. 75.5% White, 15.6% American Indian, 4.1% Black, 3.6% Asian, 3.2% Hispanic origin, 1.2% Other. Households: 56.2% married couple families; 34% married couple fams. w. children; 58% college educ.; median household income: $41,408; per capita income: $17,610; 56.1% owner occupied housing; median house value: $94,400; median monthly rent: $503. 9.1% Unemployment. Voting age pop.: 377,699. Registered voters (1992): 306,440; 57,982 D (19%), 66,953 R (22%), 181,505 unaffiliated and minor parties (59%).

Political Lineup: Governor, Walter J. Hickel (AI); Lt. Gov., Jack Coghill (AI); Atty. Gen., Charles E. Cole (R); Commissioner of Revenue, Darrell Rexwinkel (R). State Senate, 20 (10 D and 10 R); State House of Representatives, 40 (22 D, 17 R and 1 I). Senators, Ted Stevens (R) and Frank H. Murkowski (R). Representative, 1 R at large.

1992 Presidential Vote			1988 Presidential Vote		
Bush (R)	102,000	(40%)	Bush (R)	119,251	(60%)
Clinton (D)	78,294	(30%)	Dukakis (D)	72,584	(36%)
Perot (I)	73,481	(28%)	Others	8,281	(4%)

GOVERNOR

Gov. Walter J. Hickel (AI)

Elected 1990, term expires Dec., 1994; b. Aug. 18, 1919, Claflin, KS; home, Juneau; Catholic; married (Ermalee).

Career: Businessman, real estate developer, 1936–66, 1970–90; Civilian aircraft inspector, U.S. Air Force, 1942–46; AK Gov., 1966–69; U.S. Secy. of Interior, 1969–70.

Office: P.O. Box 110001, Juneau 99811, 907-465-3500.

Election Results

1990 gen.	Walter J. Hickel (AI)	68,181	(39%)
	Tony Knowles (D)	53,998	(31%)
	Arliss Sturgulewski (R)	46,553	(27%)
	Other	6,832	(3%)
1990 prim.	Tony Knowles (D)	36,019	(25%)
	Stephen McAlpine (D)	27,656	(19%)
	Arliss Sturgulewski (R)	26,906	(19%)
	Jim Campbell (R)	23,442	(16%)
	Rick Halford (R)	22,466	(16%)
	Four Others	26,935	(4%)
1986 gen.	Steve Cowper (D)	84,943	(47%)
	Arliss Sturgulewski (R)	76,515	(43%)
	Joe Vogler (AI)	10,013	(6%)

SENATORS
Sen. Ted Stevens (R)

Appointed Dec. 1968, seat up 1996; b. Nov. 18, 1923, Indianapolis, IN; home, Girdwood; U.C.L.A., A.B. 1947, Harvard, LL.B. 1950; Episcopalian; married (Catherine).

Career: Army Air Corps, 1943–46 (WWII); Practicing atty., 1950–53, 1961–68; U.S. Atty., 1953–56; U.S. Dept. of Interior, Legis. Cnsl., 1956–58, Asst. to Secy., 1958–60, Solicitor, 1960–61; AK House of Reps., 1964–68.

Offices: 522 HSOB 20510, 202-224-3004. Also Fed. Bldg., Box 4, 101 12th Ave., Fairbanks 99701, 907-456-0261; 222 W. 7th Ave., Anchorage 99513, 907-271-5915; Fed. Bldg., Box 020149, Juneau 99802, 907-586-7400; 120 Trading Bay Rd., #260, Kenai 99611, 907-283-5808; and 109 Main St., Ketchikan 99901, 907-225-6880.

Committees: *Appropriations* (2d of 13 R): Commerce, Justice, State and Judiciary; Defense (RMM); Interior and Related Agencies; Labor, Health and Human Services, and Education; Military Construction. *Commerce, Science and Transportation* (4th of 9 R): Aviation; Communications; Merchant Marine. *Governmental Affairs* (2d of 5 R): Federal Services, Post Office and Civil Service (RMM); General Services, Federalism and the District of Columbia; Oversight of Government Management; Permanent Subcommittee on Investigations. *Intelligence (Select)* (6th of 8 R). *Rules and Administration* (RMM of 7 R). *Joint Committee on the Library* (5th of 5). *Joint Committee on the Organization of Congress* (10th of 12). *Joint Committee on Printing* (4th of 5).

Group Ratings

	ADA	ACLU	CDF	COPE	CFA	LCV	ACU	NTLC	NSI	COC	CEI
1992	20	14	40	33	17	8	74	78	90	80	59
1991	10	—	55	42	33	20	76	—	—	60	56

National Journal Ratings

	1991 LIB — 1991 CONS		1992 LIB — 1992 CONS	
Economic	28%	— 69%	35%	— 64%
Social	37%	— 62%	22%	— 76%
Foreign	0%	— 87%	10%	— 80%

Key Votes of the 102d Congress

1. $ for Homeownership FOR	5. Clarence Thomas Nom. FOR	9. Use Force in Gulf FOR
2. Have Cap Gains Debate FOR	6. Lmt Death Row Appeal FOR	10. Keep Salvador Aid FOR
3. Remove Budget Walls AGN	7. Handgun Wait/5-Day AGN	11. Cut $1B from SDI AGN
4. Ban Striker Replace FOR	8. Abortion Gag Rule AGN	12. Override China MFN AGN

Key Votes of the 103d Congress

1. Family Leave FOR	2. HIV Immigrants AGN	3. Clinton Budget AGN

Election Results

1990 general	Ted Stevens (R) 125,806	(66%)	($1,618,098)
	Michael Beasley (D) 61,115	(32%)	($445)
	Other 2,999	(2%)	
1990 primary	Ted Stevens (R) 81,968	(70%)	
	Bob Bird (R) 34,824	(30%)	
1984 general	Ted Stevens (R) 146,919	(71%)	($1,323,218)
	John E. Havelock (D) 58,804	(29%)	($90,685)

Sen. Frank H. Murkowski (R)

Elected 1980, seat up 1998; b. Mar. 28, 1933, Seattle, WA; home, Fairbanks; U. of Santa Clara, Seattle U., B.A. 1955; Catholic; married (Nancy).

Career: Coast Guard, 1955–56; Pacific Natl. Bank of Seattle, 1957–58; Natl. Bank of AK, 1959–67; Commissioner, AK Dept. of Econ. Devel., 1966–70; Pres., AK Natl. Bank, 1971–80.

Offices: 706 HSOB 20510, 202-224-6665. Also 222 W. 7th Ave., Box 1, Anchorage 99513, 907-271-3735; 101 12th Ave., Fairbanks 99701, 907-456-0233; Box 21647 Fed. Bldg, Juneau 99802, 907-586-7400; 130 Trading Bay Rd., #350, Kenai 99611, 907-283-5808; and 109 Main St., Ketchikan 99901, 907-225-6880.

Committees: *Energy and Natural Resources* (4th of 9 R): Mineral Resources Development and Production; Public Lands, National Parks and Forests (RMM); Renewable Energy, Energy Efficiency, and Competitiveness. *Foreign Relations* (5th of 8 R): East Asian and Pacific Affairs (RMM); International Economic Policy, Trade, Oceans and Environment; Terrorism, Narcotics and International Operations. *Indian Affairs* (2d of 8 R). *Veterans' Affairs* (RMM of 5 R).

Group Ratings

	ADA	ACLU	CDF	COPE	CFA	LCV	ACU	NTLC	NSI	COC	CEI
1992	25	14	40	30	33	8	70	83	90	100	67
1991	5	—	45	42	33	20	86	—	—	60	64

National Journal Ratings

	1991 LIB — 1991 CONS			1992 LIB — 1992 CONS		
Economic	27%	—	72%	27%	—	71%
Social	14%	—	77%	24%	—	75%
Foreign	0%	—	87%	34%	—	63%

Key Votes of the 102d Congress

1. $ for Homeownership	FOR	5. Clarence Thomas Nom.	FOR	9. Use Force in Gulf	FOR
2. Have Cap Gains Debate	FOR	6. Lmt Death Row Appeal	FOR	10. Keep Salvador Aid	FOR
3. Remove Budget Walls	AGN	7. Handgun Wait/5-Day	AGN	11. Cut $1B from SDI	AGN
4. Ban Striker Replace	AGN	8. Abortion Gag Rule	FOR	12. Override China MFN	AGN

Key Votes of the 103d Congress

1. Family Leave	FOR	2. HIV Immigrants	AGN	3. Clinton Budget	AGN

34   ALASKA

REPRESENTATIVE

Rep. Don Young (R)

Elected Mar. 1973; b. June 9, 1933, Meridian, CA; home, Fort Yukon; Yuba Jr. Col., A.A. 1952, Chico St. Col., B.A. 1958; Episcopalian; married (Lula).

Career: Army, 1955–57; Fort Yukon City Cncl., 1960–64; Fort Yukon Mayor, 1964–68; AK House of Reps., 1966–70; AK Senate, 1970–73.

Offices: 2331 RHOB, 202-225-5765. Also 222 W. 7th Ave., #3, Anchorage 99513, 907-271-5978; 401 Fed. Bldg., Box 1247, Juneau 99802, 907-586-7400; Fed. Bldg., Box 10, 101 12th Ave., Fairbanks 99701, 907-456-0210; and 109 Main St., Ketchikan 99901, 907-225-6880.

Committees: *Merchant Marine and Fisheries* (2d of 19 R): Environment and Natural Resources; Fisheries Management (RMM). *Natural Resources* (RMM of 15 R): Native American Affairs (RMM). *Post Office and Civil Service* (3d of 9 R): Compensation and Employee Benefits; Postal Operations and Services (RMM).

Group Ratings

	ADA	ACLU	COPE	CDF	CFA	LCV	ACU	NTLC	NSI	COC	CEI
1992	25	18	67	50	40	0	84	65	100	88	53
1991	10	—	55	30	11	0	67	—	—	67	42

National Journal Ratings

	1991 LIB — 1991 CONS		1992 LIB — 1992 CONS	
Economic	38% —	61%	37% —	62%
Social	0% —	84%	19% —	80%
Foreign	0% —	88%	0% —	82%

Key Votes of the 102d Congress

1. Ban Striker Replace	FOR	5. Handgun Wait/7-Day	AGN	9. Use Force in Gulf	FOR
2. $ for Homeownership	FOR	6. Overseas Mil. Abortion	AGN	10. US Mil. Abroad $ Cut	AGN
3. Tax Rich/Cut Mid Cls.	AGN	7. Obscn. Art NEA $ Ban	FOR	11. Limit SDI Funds	AGN
4. FY93/$15B Def. Cut	AGN	8. Death Pen. from Jury	FOR	12. Cuba Trade Embargo	FOR

Key Votes of the 103d Congress

1. Family Leave	FOR	2. Deficit Reduction	AGN	3. Stimulus Plan	AGN

Election Results

1992 general	Don Young (R)	111,849	(47%)	($873,486)
	John Devens (D)	102,378	(43%)	($469,738)
	Michael States (AI)	15,049	(6%)	($6,835)
	Mike Milligan (Green)	9,529	(4%)	
1992 primary	Don Young (R)	24,869	(53%)	
	Virginia Collins (R)	19,774	(42%)	
	William Holton (R)	1,671	(4%)	
	Other	630	(1%)	
1990 general	Don Young (R)	99,003	(52%)	($564,759)
	John S. Devens (D)	91,677	(48%)	($164,732)

ARIZONA

The desert republic of Arizona, after a roller coaster ride up and down in the late 1980s and early 1990s, seems on the rise, once again one of America's fastest-growing states, rich with innovative technology and creative entrepreneurs. It is recovering from a series of embarrassments: the real estate glut of the late 1980s symbolized by the saga of notorious savings and loan buccaneer Charles Keating; the farce of a governor impeached and removed from office; state politics centered on whether to have a holiday honoring Martin Luther King; the shame of a state legislature laced with corruption. But Arizona seems to continue the breathtaking growth that increased its population from 700,000 at the end of World War II to 3,700,000 in the early 1990s: an almost entirely new society built from scratch on mile-square grids in the desert. This growth has provided a solid basis for a successful society with topnotch big companies and creative small outfits. But it has also left this state with an undernourished public sector and few established community institutions or traditions or standards.

Early Arizona was long on opportunity and thin on preexisting establishment. The first builders of Arizona were copper barons and southern-accented politicians: men like Lewis Douglas, copper heir and congressman, briefly Franklin Roosevelt's budget director and for a longer time Harry Truman's ambassador to Britain; and Carl Hayden, Democratic congressman from statehood in 1912 and senator from 1927 until 1969, whose public works projects watered Arizona's cotton, citrus and cattle farms. The second wave of Arizona's builders were the businessmen, lawyers and developers who shaped the new metropolis of Phoenix and the smaller city of Tucson in the decades after World War II. Free enterprise devotees, they depended little on government and politics. Their major national figure was Barry Goldwater, the Arizona they built was not based on resources (only 1% of the work force is in mining today). Instead, it was a polity based on something like the opposite of New Deal principles, with minimal government and precious little regulation of business, a welcoming of the new ideas of technology and discouragement of the new ideas of cultural liberalism. With the help of Arizona's conservative politicians, typified by businessman-in-politics Goldwater, they built a new America that, like Disneyland, seemed a more gleaming and spotless embodiment of old values than the old America ever was. Goldwater helped to make Arizona a heavily Republican state, the only state to have voted Republican in every presidential election since 1948.

Economically, the mainstay of this Arizona is technology: Phoenix has been attracting high-tech industries since Motorola built a research center for military electronics there in 1948, and big employers now include Motorola's semiconductor operation, Garret aircraft, Honeywell flight systems, and Tucson's Hughes aircraft. Arizona's dry climate is good for precision manufacturing and the cultural environment attracts well-educated technicians, people who like certainty, order and discipline. That is true also of Arizona's retirees, who tend to be affluent—though they do not form an unusually large percentage of the state's population. Phoenix is now the white-collar center of a vast portion of the Southwest, with a well-educated work force.

The result is a state untraditional as much as it is conservative. There is something vibrant and chaotic about Phoenix's explosive growth. This is a city with plenty of money but few standards; plenty of crooked land salesmen, fast-buck artists and drifters who would have been at home in Raymond Chandler's Los Angeles: Charles Keating was not the only one of his kind. And Arizona is still building—the I-10 Freeway, the direct route to Los Angeles, was completed only in 1990—and momentous decisions need to be made, notably on water. "Shadow governments," to use author Joel Garreau's term, have arisen to make many of these decisions. The Salt River Project, for example, has expanded beyond rationing water to provide a sort of regional government; the city of Phoenix under former Mayor Terry Goddard gave different urban cores various powers; private developers, most visibly in the huge Sun City retirement community, make regulations more binding than most governments can. The biggest public policy question facing Arizona, now that the Central Arizona Project is complete, is how to allocate water. The CAP, whose board members are elected, was originally intended to subsidize growers of cotton and other thirsty crops. But these simply don't bring in enough money to pay for the economic value of the water, and in all likelihood the CAP board will let Phoenix and other cities outbid the ag interests: high-tech outbidding cotton. Already, cottonfields are going back to desert; even as metro Phoenix grows outward, especially west along I-10, but also north where it is not hemmed in by Indian reservations, much of the desert will revert to something much like its natural condition when Arizona became a state in 1912. Arizona is not through growing yet, but perhaps now it can avoid some of the corruption apparent in the legislature's Azscam scandal and overreaching that were the unhappy accompaniments of its vitality and spontaneity of recent decades. Some sort of constraint, anyway, was levied in the 1992 elections with the passage of term limits for members of Congress—three terms for House members and two for Senators.

Governor. From the retirement of now Interior Secretary Bruce Babbitt as governor in 1986 until after the 1991 gubernatorial runoff election, Arizona state politics went through a time of troubles, from which it seems to have emerged. The troubles began when Evan Mecham, a perennial political loser, won a three-way race in 1986 with 40% of the vote and immediately raised a national ruckus by rescinding the state's Martin Luther King Holiday, prompting a boycott of the state by various conventioneers; he made enough of a fool of himself that recall petitions were circulated and he was impeached in April 1988, and replaced by Secretary of State Rose Mofford. Then in 1990, a Mecham referendum defeated the King holiday—a move that some say may have cost the state $340 million in lost convention and Super Bowl business—and a Mechamite candidate prevented either major party candidate from getting the absolute majority required by a stop-Mecham law. There was a runoff in February 1991 in which Republican developer (and anti-Mechamite) Fife Symington won 52% to former Phoenix Mayor Terry Goddard's 48%. Meanwhile, it was revealed that sting operators had handed out some $300,000 to Arizona legislators, seven of whom were indicted. "There is not an issue in this world that I [care] about," said one legislator. "I do deals."

Like so many Arizonans, Symington is a migrant, scion of a wealthy Maryland family and distant relative of the late Senator Stuart Symington of Missouri; he made millions as a Phoenix developer, and had a reputation for tasteful work, though some of his projects went under in the real estate glut. Symington has so far weathered any allegations of wrongdoing during his term as director of a failed S&L, but a case brought against him by the RTC in 1991 is still in court. In past two years, he has still been able to achieve many of his goals. He prevented a tax increase and, with the Republican capture of the state Senate in 1992, had hopes of actually cutting taxes, despite severe demands of a growing population for more schools and other services. The

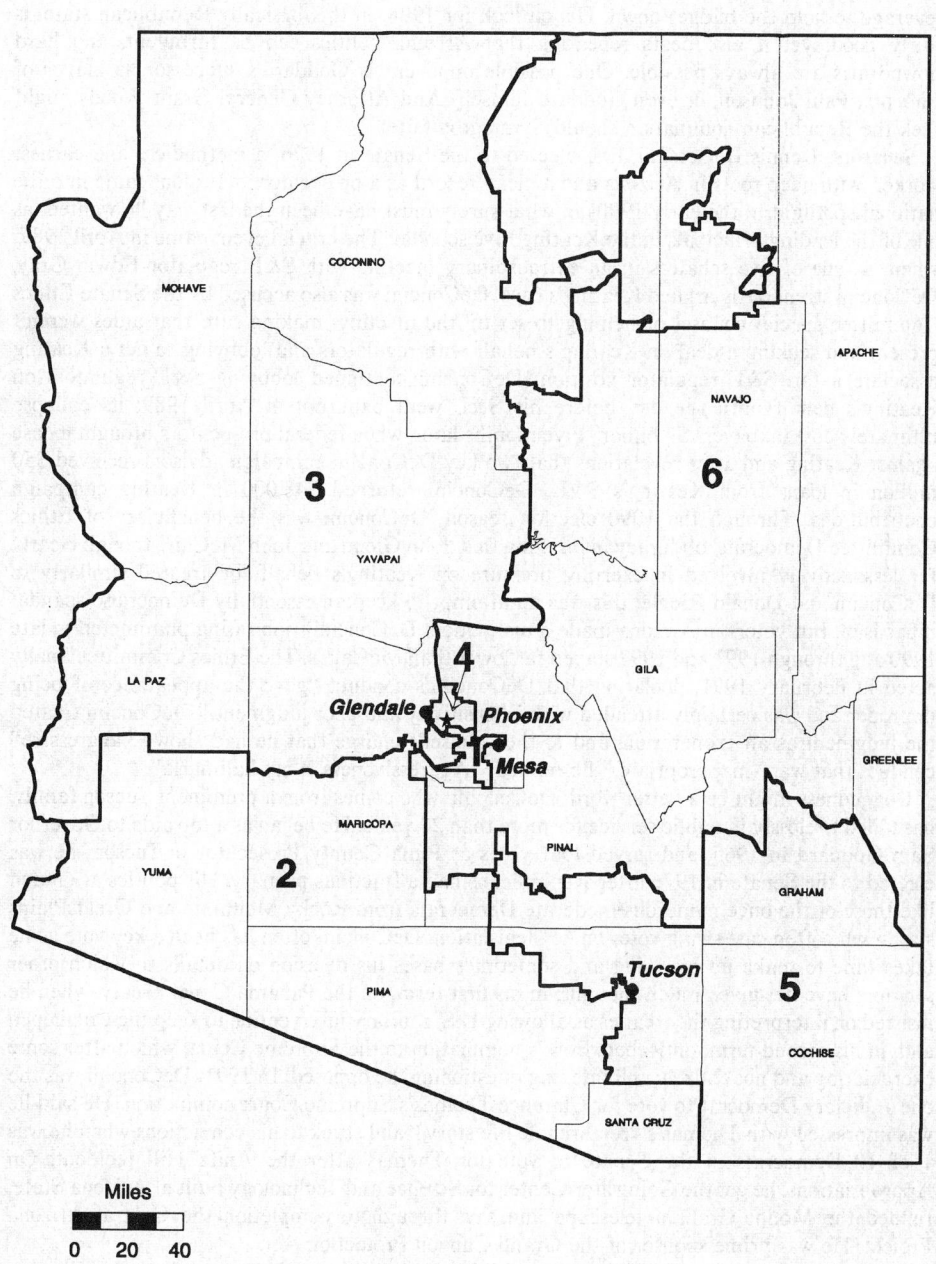

Miles

0   20   40

real estate market seemed to stabilize and small business formations increased. In 1992, voters rejected Mecham, giving him just 11% in his Independent Senate bid, while in referenda approved the King holiday, allowing Arizona to vie for events like the Super Bowl again. They also voted to require a two-thirds vote by the legislature to raise taxes, giving Symington huge leverage to hold the budget down. His outlook for 1994, in this basically Republican state, is fairly good; yet it also bears repeating that Arizona politics can be turbulent, and hard downdrafts are always possible. One possible opponent is Goddard's successor as mayor of Phoenix, Paul Johnson, or even Goddard himself. And Attorney General Grant Woods might seek the Republican nomination should Symington falter.

Senators. Dennis DeConcini, first elected to the Senate in 1976, a methodical and earnest worker, with deep roots in Arizona and a clean record as a prosecutor in Tucson, came into the national spotlight in the early 1990s in what surely must have been the last way he wanted, as one of the leading principals in the Keating Five scandal. The crucial event came in April 1987, when, as one of five senators in an extraordinary meeting with S&L regulator Edwin Gray, DeConcini strenuously argued Keating's case. DeConcini was also accused by the Senate Ethics Committee special counsel of helping to set up the meeting, making sure that aides weren't present and seeking a deal on Keating's behalf with regulators and lobbying to get a Keating associate a top S&L regulator position. DeConcini continued lobbying S&L regulators on Keating's behalf until the day before his S&L went bankrupt in April 1989; its collapse ultimately cost taxpayers $2 billion. Five months later, when federal prosecutors brought a case against Keating and after revelations that two key DeConcini campaign advisors received $50 million in loans from Keating's S&L, DeConcini returned $48,000 in Keating campaign contributions. Through the 1990 election season, DeConcini was the beneficiary of Ethics Committee Democrats' obduracy in insisting that John Glenn and John McCain, though clearly far less actively involved in exerting pressure on Keating's behalf, be treated similarly to DeConcini and Donald Riegle; this was an attempt to keep an essentially Democratic scandal bipartisan. But voters in Arizona made a distinction. DeConcini's job rating plummeted in late 1990 and through 1991 and 1992 stayed far lower than McCain's. The Ethics Committee finally acted in February 1991, declaring that DeConcini's conduct "gave the appearance of being improper and was certainly attended with insensitivity and poor judgment." DeConcini treated the judgment as an exoneration, and to the counsel's charge that he had shown "aggressive" conduct that was "inappropriate," he replied, "Aggressiveness is my hallmark."

Doggedness might be a better word: DeConcini, who comes from a prominent Tucson family, has toiled tirelessly in public service for more than 20 years. He began as a top aide to Governor Sam Goddard in 1965, and served four years as Pima County Prosecutor in Tucson; he was elected to the Senate in 1976 after Republicans had a fractious primary. His politics are much like those of the once numerous moderate Democrats from Rocky Mountain and Great Plains states, who often cast swing votes on key legislation. DeConcini often has been a key vote as he takes time to make up his mind and sometimes bases his decision on details to which other senators have not given much thought: in his first term, on the Panama Canal Treaty, when he insisted on interpreting the treaties as allowing U.S. military intervention to keep the canal open and, in his second term, on Robert Bork's nomination to the Supreme Court, which after some excruciating and not entirely enlightening questioning, he opposed. In 1991, DeConcini was the one Judiciary Democrat to vote for Clarence Thomas's Supreme Court nomination. He said he was impressed with Thomas's "remarkable life story," and stuck to his convictions when he was 1 of 10 Democrats in the Senate to vote for Thomas after the Anita Hill incident. On Appropriations, he got the Goldwater Center for Science and Technology built at Arizona State, funded the Mount Graham telescope and saw through to completion the Central Arizona Project. He was prime sponsor of the Grand Canyon Protection Act.

In 1993 and 1994, DeConcini's most visible role will be as chairman of the Intelligence Committee. He voted against confirmation of Robert Gates as CIA head in 1991, has pushed for greater than proposed intelligence budget cuts, and has made it plain he wants changes in intelligence gathering. Other projects include a bill on sexual harassment in the military and an assault weapons bill; he says his top priorities include a balanced budget amendment, campaign finance reform and the North American Free Trade Agreement.

DeConcini supports term limits, but since Arizona's new law doesn't apply to him yet, he feels free to run, and probably will again in 1994. If so, thanks to the Keating Five scandal, he's likely to face his toughest race ever. In 1982 and 1988, DeConcini beat little-known opponents by 59%–41% and 57%–41% margins. For 1994, there is talk of a primary challenge from Secretary of State Dick Mahoney; Phoenix Congressman Jon Kyl seems likely to run for the Republican nomination, and might have competition from Attorney General Grant Woods.

Arizona's junior senator, John McCain, is a different sort of character than DeConcini—as he will be glad to let you know. Vibrant and outgoing where DeConcini is serious and quizzical, a politician who likes to advance ideas where DeConcini likes to work behind the scenes, they were probably slated never to get along. Then came the Keating Five case. From the start, McCain aggressively distanced himself from the case, despite a personal friendship with Keating which went back to 1981. McCain was vindicated, first when committee counsel Robert Bennett said McCain did nothing more than attend two meetings and exerted no influence on Keating's behalf (thus refuting DeConcini's bitter comment, "He's in it just like I am"), and then when the Ethics Committee found he did no more than "exercise poor judgment." McCain had long admitted making a mistake attending the April 1987 meeting; he did it even though a month earlier he'd had a fierce shouting match with Keating after Keating asked for help and McCain refused. The only reason his case wasn't dismissed earlier was that Senate Democrats wanted to keep at least one Republican involved in the case. McCain's poll ratings did drop substantially, but then rose partway back up, and he attracted only weak opposition—from a retired Air Force general, a liberal activist and Evan Mecham—in 1992.

Actually, McCain was in fairly solid shape for a politician whose roots in the state are not deep. He is the son and grandson of admirals, a Navy fighter pilot and POW, one of the very few career military men in Congress; he spent four years on Capitol Hill as a Navy congressional liaison, and moved to Arizona, his wife's home state, in 1981. As he pointed out when he first ran for Congress in 1982, "the longest place I ever lived in was Hanoi," for five and a half years as a prisoner of war. That was enough for a 32%–26% primary win then; he won the 1982 and 1984 general elections and the 1986 Senate contest easily.

McCain has usually come out on the hawkish side of foreign and military affairs. But he also shows a professional military officer's caution about committing troops and human lives, urging restraint in the 1993 Balkans crisis, and suggesting caution in August 1990 on sending American troops to the Persian Gulf. He didn't hesitate, however, beforehand in threatening a crackdown on Iraq for nuclear proliferation and in January 1991 solidly backed the Gulf war resolution. On the Armed Services Committee, he has called for reduced funding for the B-2 bomber, freezing spending on the Strategic Defense Initiative and fielding lighter ground forces; he has pushed for higher cost of living increases in military pay and against base closings in Arizona. He does not talk much about his years as a prisoner in Vietnam, but served on the special POW/MIA committee and has been a strong supporter of releasing intelligence reports on alleged POW sightings.

Much of McCain's energy on domestic issues has been devoted to the environment, pushing an Arizona wilderness bill, banning flights in the Grand Canyon, and working to stop construction of Cliff Dam. His 1992 campaign ads showed him standing before the Grand Canyon while an announcer described him as "the Grand Canyon's best friend in Congress," but Democrats pointed to his low conservation ratings. McCain's record on most things is conservative: he wants to require a supermajority of 60 votes to increase federal taxes, and he is for a presidential line-item veto.

The 1992 general election proved to be anticlimactic. Claire Sargent, winner of the Democratic primary, said it was the Year of the Woman: "It's time we start electing some Senators with breasts; we've had boobs long enough." She had started a Desert Cities project to design affordable desert urban housing and called for more solar energy research. In typical blundering style, Mecham entered the race in August and made the groundless accusation that McCain was "selling out his fellow POWs" from his seat on the select committee. Mecham was condemned for the remarks and won only 11% of the vote, while McCain won easily with 56%.

Presidential politics. For a few moments in fall 1992, it looked like Arizona might break the longest string of any state in American presidential politics: it had voted Republican in every presidential election since Harry Truman won here in 1948. Bill Clinton was leading George Bush in several Arizona polls; Democrats were optimistic and Republicans, understanding that if they couldn't carry Arizona they couldn't carry much of anything, were in despair. In the end, Bush won, with an anything but smashing 38%–37% margin. In effect, the normal Republican vote—60% for Bush in 1988, for example, was split between Bush and Ross Perot, who got 24%, one of his best showings. Metro Phoenix, where he got 25%, may have been Perot's best million-plus metro area, and he got over 30% in retirement-heavy Mojave and LaPaz Counties along the Colorado River—which is in line with the national pattern of Perot running strongest where voters have the weakest local roots. Clinton's 37%, while almost netting him 8 electoral votes, was in line with other Democratic showings here: Michael Dukakis's 39% or the 40% and 32% John McCain's opponents got in his two Senate elections.

Arizona was nonetheless not heavily contested in fall 1992, and its precinct caucuses late in the spring typically attract little attention. The state is more noteworthy for having produced for its size so many presidential candidates—Barry Goldwater in 1964, Morris Udall in 1976, Bruce Babbitt in 1988. Of different politics and temperament, they are all intellectually honest, personally candid, genuinely engaged in ideas while retaining a lively sense of how the real world works; each has a good sense of humor and is refreshingly unfull of himself; each lost big.

Congressional districting. Arizona gained one congressional district from the 1990 Census, as it did in 1980, 1970 and 1960, increasing its original delegation from two House members to six. The Democratic state Senate and Republican House couldn't agree on a plan, so a federal court drew the lines, with the 2d District continuing to be heavily Hispanic and the new 6th District drawn to maximize the Indian population (though the Hopis, who have had a furious land dispute with the much more numerous Navajo, were carefully placed in the 3d). Democrats, down 4–1 before redistricting, ended up with a 3–3 tie, largely because of the weaknesses of particular Republican candidates. It will be interesting to see whether this closely divided delegation will follow the tradition of bipartisan cooperation pioneered by Republicans Barry Goldwater and John Rhodes, and Democrats Stewart and Morris Udall, 30 and 40 years ago.

The People: Est. Pop. 1992: 3,832,000; Pop. 1990: 3,665,228, up 4.4% 1990–1992. 1.5% of U.S. total, 24th largest; 12% rural. Median age: 32.2 years. 13.1% 65 years and over. 80.8% White, 18.8% Hispanic origin, 5.6% American Indian, 3.0% Black, 1.5% Asian, 9.1% Other. Households: 54.6% married couple families; 25% married couple fams. w. children; 53% college educ.; median household income: $27,540; per capita income: $13,461; 64.4% owner occupied housing; median house value: $80,100; median monthly rent: $370. 7.4% Unemployment. Voting age pop.: 2,684,109. Registered voters (1992): 1,963,492; 833,997 D (43%), 889,644 R (45%), 239,851 unaffiliated and minor parties (12%).

Political Lineup: Governor, J. Fife Symington, III (R); Secy. of State, Richard D. Mahoney (D); Atty. Gen., Grant Woods (R); Treasurer, Tony West (R); Auditor General, Douglas R. Norton (I). State Senate, 30 (18 R and 12 D); State House of Representatives, 60 (35 R and 25 D). Senators, Dennis DeConcini (D) and John McCain (R). Representatives, 6 (3 D and 3 R).

1992 Presidential Vote			1988 Presidential Vote		
Bush (R)	572,086	(38%)	Bush (R)	702,541	(60%)
Clinton (D)	543,050	(37%)	Dukakis (D)	454,029	(39%)
Perot (I)	353,741	(24%)			

GOVERNOR

Gov. Fife Symington, III (R)

Elected Feb., 1991, term expires 1995; b. Aug. 12, 1945, New York, NY; home, Phoenix; Harvard, B.A. 1968; Episcopalian; married (Ann).

Career: Air Force, 1968–71 (Vietnam); Commercial and industrial real estate developer, 1972–91.

Office: Office of the Governor, 1700 W. Washington, 9th Fl., Phoenix 85007, 602-542-4331.

Election Results

1991 runoff	Fife Symington, III (R)	492,569	(52%)
	Terry Goddard (D)	448,168	(48%)
1990 gen.	Fife Symington, III (R)	523,964	(50%)
	Terry Goddard (D)	519,653	(50%)
1990 prim.	Fife Symington, III (R)	163,010	(44%)
	Evan Mecham (R)	91,136	(24%)
	Fred Koory (R).............	61,487	(17%)
	Sam Steiger (R).............	49,019	(13%)
	Other	7,672	(2%)
1986 gen.	Evan Mecham (R)	343,913	(40%)
	Carolyn Warner (D)	298,986	(34%)
	Bill Schulz (I)..............	224,085	(26%)

SENATORS

Sen. Dennis DeConcini (D)

Elected 1976, seat up 1994; b. May 8, 1937, Tucson; home, Tucson; U. of AZ, B.A. 1959, LL.B. 1963; Catholic; married (Susan).

Career: Army, 1959–60, Army Reserves, 1960–67; Practicing atty., 1963–65, 1968–73; Special Cnsl., A.A., Gov. Samuel Goddard, 1965–67; Pima Cnty. Atty., 1973–76.

Offices: 328 HSOB 20510, 202-224-4521. Also 323 W. Roosevelt, #C-100, Phoenix 85003, 602-379-6756; 2730 E. Broadway, #160, Tucson 85716, 602-670-6831; and 40 N. Center St., #110, Mesa 85201.

Committees: *Appropriations* (7th of 16 D): Defense; Energy and Water Development; Foreign Operations; Interior; Treasury, Postal Service and General Government (Chmn.). *Indian Affairs* (2d of 10 D). *Intelligence (Select)* (Chmn. of 9 D). *Judiciary* (4th of 10 D): Antitrust, Monopolies and Business Rights; Constitution; Patents, Copyrights and Trademarks (Chmn.). *Rules and Administration* (5th of 9 D). *Veterans' Affairs* (2d of 7 D). *Joint Committee on the Library* (2d of 5). *Joint Committee on Printing* (2d of 5).

Group Ratings

	ADA	ACLU	CDF	COPE	CFA	LCV	ACU	NTLC	NSI	COC	CEI
1992	75	50	80	64	67	17	20	33	40	10	29
1991	50	—	73	67	67	33	45	—	—	20	38

National Journal Ratings

	1991 LIB — 1991 CONS			1992 LIB — 1992 CONS		
Economic	55%	—	43%	73%	—	25%
Social	39%	—	60%	54%	—	45%
Foreign	78%	—	14%	65%	—	26%

Key Votes of the 102d Congress

1. $ for Homeownership	AGN	5. Clarence Thomas Nom.	FOR	9. Use Force in Gulf	AGN
2. Have Cap Gains Debate	AGN	6. Lmt Death Row Appeal	FOR	10. Keep Salvador Aid	AGN
3. Remove Budget Walls	FOR	7. Handgun Wait/5-Day	AGN	11. Cut $1B from SDI	FOR
4. Ban Striker Replace	FOR	8. Abortion Gag Rule	FOR	12. Override China MFN	FOR

Key Votes of the 103d Congress

1. Family Leave	FOR	2. HIV Immigrants	AGN	3. Clinton Budget	FOR

Election Results

1988 general	Dennis DeConcini (D)................	660,403	(57%)	($2,640,650)
	Keith DeGreen (R)..................	478,060	(41%)	($238,369)
1988 primary	Dennis DeConcini (D)................	195,540	(100%)	
1982 general	Dennis DeConcini (D)................	413,951	(59%)	($2,086,401)
	Pete Dunn (R)......................	292,638	(41%)	($884,517)

Sen. John McCain (R)

Elected 1986, seat up 1998; b. Aug. 29, 1936, Panama Canal Zone; home, Phoenix; U.S. Naval Acad., 1958, Natl. War Col., 1973–74; Episcopalian; married (Cindy).

Career: Navy, 1958–80 (Vietnam); Dir., Navy Senate Liaison Ofc., 1977–81; U.S. House of Reps., 1982–1986.

Offices: 111 RSOB 20510, 202-224-2235. Also 5353 N. 16th St., #190, Phoenix 85016, 602-241-2567; 2675 E. Broadway, Tucson 85716, 602-670-6334; and 151 N. Centennial Way, #1000, Mesa 85201, 602-835-8994.

Committees: *Aging (Special)* (6th of 10 R). *Armed Services* (4th of 9 R): Force Requirements and Personnel; Military Readiness and Defense Infrastructure (RMM); Regional Defense and Contingency Forces. *Commerce, Science and Transportation* (5th of 9 R): Aviation; Communications; Consumer; Surface Transportation (RMM). *Governmental Affairs* (5th of 5 R): General Services, Federalism and the District of Columbia (RMM); Oversight of Government Management; Regulation and Government Information; Permanent Subcommittee on Investigations. *Indian Affairs* (Vice Chmn. of 8 R).

Group Ratings

	ADA	ACLU	CDF	COPE	CFA	LCV	ACU	NTLC	NSI	COC	CEI
1992	20	5	40	33	67	8	85	100	90	90	74
1991	5	—	55	17	39	33	86	—	—	70	71

National Journal Ratings

	1991 LIB — 1991 CONS			1992 LIB — 1992 CONS		
Economic	15%	—	80%	20%	—	79%
Social	0%	—	86%	20%	—	78%
Foreign	27%	—	67%	0%	—	90%

Key Votes of the 102d Congress

1. $ for Homeownership FOR	5. Clarence Thomas Nom. FOR	9. Use Force in Gulf FOR
2. Have Cap Gains Debate FOR	6. Lmt Death Row Appeal FOR	10. Keep Salvador Aid FOR
3. Remove Budget Walls AGN	7. Handgun Wait/5-Day AGN	11. Cut $1B from SDI AGN
4. Ban Striker Replace AGN	8. Abortion Gag Rule FOR	12. Override China MFN AGN

Key Votes of the 103d Congress

1. Family Leave FOR	2. HIV Immigrants AGN	3. Clinton Budget AGN

Election Results

1992 general	John McCain (R)	771,395	(56%)	($3,766,588)
	Claire Sargent (D)	436,321	(32%)	($287,682)
	Evan Mecham (I)	145,361	(11%)	($86,433)
	Three Others........................	28,974	(2%)	
1992 primary	John McCain (R), unopposed			
1986 general	John McCain (R)	521,850	(60%)	($2,228,498)
	Richard Kimball (D).................	340,965	(40%)	($657,908)

FIRST DISTRICT

More than 40 years ago, when Motorola built a research center for military electronics there, almost no one thought Phoenix would become one of America's major metropolises—much less that Motorola's move would be the first in a series of businesses that would make Phoenix one of the nation's important high-tech centers. The 1950 Census counted just 106,000 residents in Phoenix and 331,000 in all of Maricopa County; this was not much more than a local trading post, as it had been since it was founded in 1881 as a haymarket for cavalry horses at Fort McDowell 40 miles northeast. But new businesses symbolized by Motorola changed Phoenix from the sleepy whistlestop of 40 years ago, where the small tufa stone turn-of-the-century Capitol was the most prominent building, to today's high-rise studded metropolis of 2.1 million.

This almost instant city was created not in response to geographical imperative but in spite of it. Neither the copper mines of southern Arizona nor the cotton farms irrigated by the Salt River needed a city the size of Phoenix, nor is there any thickly populated hinterland in the vast land between the Rio Grande and Los Angeles for which this is the natural commercial center. Nor is Phoenix a giant retirement village. Though there are huge retirement developments northwest of town, Phoenix's economic base has been in research and development and high-tech manufacturing, and its population tends to be young and family-oriented, on the way up from whatever level of society they were born into.

Over the years, Phoenix's growth has oozed outward along its mile-square grid streets and its few freeways, blocked off here and there by mountains and Indian reservations. Much of that growth has been to the east, south of the Salt River and east of South Mountain, along today's Superstition Freeway, where metro Phoenix has merged into old towns. One is Tempe, founded as Hayden's Ferry and renamed for an ancient Greek vale, home of Arizona State University and the Fiesta Bowl; it had 7,000 people in 1950 and 142,000 in 1990. Farther east is Mesa, whose central focus is one of the nation's few Mormon temples, and whose Mormon founders used irrigation ditches dug by Indians in 700 A.D.; Mesa had 16,000 people in 1950 and 288,000 in 1990. North of the Salt River, directly east of Phoenix and in the shadows of Camelback Mountain, is Scottsdale, with its trendy shops carefully decked out in Old West style, some even with hitching posts, for this is the site of the annual U.S.-Canada Wrangler Jeans Rodeo Showdown; Scottsdale had no recorded population in 1950, 130,000 in 1990.

The 1st Congressional District of Arizona consists of much of this eastern part of metropolitan Phoenix. Geographically, it is centered on Tempe, and also includes Chandler, once a desert crossroads and now a 91,000-strong suburb. The 1st also includes about half of Mesa, plus the southern portion of Scottsdale and much of the east side of Phoenix, mostly affluent territory south of Camelback Road. These lines are carefully drawn to leave heavily Hispanic and black neighborhoods in the 2d District, and to keep the Salt River and Gila River Indian Reservations in the new 6th District. As a result, the new 1st is 80% non-Hispanic white, mostly affluent, and heavily Republican—65% for George Bush in 1988.

Nevertheless, this district voted for a Democratic congressman in 1992, and in the process rejected the bearer of one of the most respected names in Arizona politics. This was Jay Rhodes, whose father John Rhodes, after settling in Mesa after World War II, represented all or much of Maricopa County from 1952 to 1982 and was House minority leader from 1973 to 1980. The younger Rhodes, a Vietnam veteran and board member of the Central Arizona Project, won a four-way Republican primary here to win the seat in 1986. In the House, he worked constructively on the CAP, the Salt River-Pima-Maricopa Indian water rights and the Arizona wilderness act; on most national issues he had a conservative voting record. Back home, however, he managed to rankle many conservatives—and not just them—with certain actions: one was his support of the 1989 congressional pay raise; another, his support of the 1990 budget summit agreement, complete with the tax increases that broke George Bush's read-my-lips promise. In 1989, he irritated some conservatives in Washington by backing Ed Madigan over Newt Gingrich for Republican whip and he irritated some conservatives in Arizona by being the first Republican to urge Governor Evan Mecham to resign. In 1992, with the additional disadvantage of having had 32 overdrafts at the House bank and a redistricting plan that removed some conservative Republican strongholds to the new 6th District, he attracted four primary opponents, and barely won, squeaking past state legislators Stan Barnes and Bill Mundell by just a 33%–30%–24% margin.

This presented a marvelous opportunity for Sam Coppersmith, who won the Democratic primary with 74%. A native of Pennsylvania, a graduate of Harvard College and Yale Law School who was in the Foreign Service in between, a clarinet player and show tune singer, Coppersmith moved to Arizona in 1982 and soon became involved in civic affairs. He was a top aide to Phoenix Mayor Terry Goddard and head of the local Planned Parenthood chapter. Coppersmith campaigned as a "new-generation Democrat," calling for deficit reduction and public investment, congressional reform and preserving the environment; he is against single-payer national health insurance, preferring to give states more leeway in adopting their own plans; and he is favorable to the North American Free Trade Agreement. He contrasted his pro-choice stand on abortion with Rhodes's pro-life position. Coppersmith's 51% victory in this heavily Republican district was a considerable achievement. But, like many other freshman Democrats, he has set himself a difficult task. "What's vital is the economy, what's vital is health care, and what's vital is getting the deficit under control," he said after winning—thus setting himself a standard that will be tough to meet in 1994. Also, he regards himself as bound by the 3-term limit Arizona voters passed as he was winning in 1992.

The People: Pop. 1990: 610,817; 9% age 65+; 80% White; 3% Black; 2% Amer. Indian; 2% Asian; 6% Other; 13% Hispanic origin. Voting age pop.: 458,227; 3% Black; 11% Hispanic origin. Households: 49% married couple families; 24% married couple fams. w. children; 64% college educ.; median household income: $31,288; per capita income: $15,144; median gross rent: $478; median house value: $88,300.

1992 Presidential Vote			1988 Presidential Vote		
Bush (R)	105,784	(40%)	Bush (R)	131,093	(65%)
Clinton (D)	88,247	(33%)	Dukakis (D)	70,881	(35%)
Perot (I)	68,143	(26%)			

Rep. Sam Coppersmith (D)

Elected 1992; b. May 22, 1955, Johnstown, PA; home, Phoenix; Harvard, A.B. 1976, Yale, J.D. 1982; Jewish; married (Beth).

Career: Clerk, 9th Circ. U.S. Court of Appeals, 1982–83; Asst., Phoenix Mayor Goddard, 1984; Practicing atty., 1984–92; Dir. and Pres., Planned Parenthood of Central/Northern AZ, 1989–92.

Offices: 1607 LHOB 20515, 202-225-2635. Also 404 S. Mill Ave., #201-C, Tempe 85281, 602-921-5500.

Committees: *Public Works and Transportation* (25th of 39 D): Aviation; Economic Development. *Science, Space and Technology* (24th of 33 D): Energy; Investigations and Oversight; Technology, Environment and Aviation.

Group Ratings and 102d Congress Votes: Newly Elected

Key Votes of the 103d Congress

1. Family Leave	FOR	2. Deficit Reduction	AGN	3. Stimulus Plan	AGN

Election Results

1992 general	Sam Coppersmith (D)................	130,715	(51%)	($244,633)
	John J. Rhodes III (R)...............	113,613	(45%)	($336,768)
	Ted Goldstein (Natural Law)...........	10,461	(4%)	
1992 primary	Sam Coppersmith (D)................	17,420	(74%)	
	David J. Sanson III (D)	6,269	(26%)	
1990 general	John J. Rhodes III (R), unopposed			($323,328)

SECOND DISTRICT

Arizona, although technically a part of Mexico for hundreds of years, was not a center of Hispanic civilization like New Mexico; this hot desert land was inhabited mainly by Indians who kept their native ways and language until English-speaking whites came in on cavalry horses, miners' wagons and railroad cars in the late 19th Century. Today's Hispanic Arizonans are mostly descendants of immigrants from Mexico, people who came over the border in the sleepier days before World War II when it was scarcely patrolled, or who have come more recently to take part in the dazzling economic growth which has served as both an attraction and an example to so many *norteno* Mexicans. The 2d District of Arizona was designed to be the state's Hispanic district; its population is 51% Hispanic and includes nearly two-thirds of the state's Hispanic population. On a map, it looks like a regularly-shaped district, but in fact it is a collection of distant communities connected only by many miles of uninhabited desert.

The largest of these communities is central Phoenix, including the old downtown, the state Capitol to the west and the skyscraper districts on North Central Avenue and out toward Camelback Road. The stereotypical Hispanic neighborhood here is a collection of 1940s and 1950s bungalows, unpainted for years and spaced out by empty lots, not far from the railroad or Sky Harbor Airport or nestling within view of South Mountain. In fact, this is a diverse area, with affluent and comfortable neighborhoods, where Hispanics have been moving in scatterings as well as clumps. The west side of Tucson, the next largest gathering of people in the 2d, is similar. The 2d also includes Yuma, at the old crossing of the Colorado River, in the center of an irrigated agricultural valley, often the hottest place in the country (it's the spring training site for the Yakult Swallows, a Japanese baseball team); a desalination plant, proposed to protect Mexican farmlands, was opened here in 1992, 14 years behind schedule. Across the desert, past the Luke Air Force Base shooting range, the Organ Pipe Cactus National Monument, and the Papago Indian Reservation, is the Mexican border town of Nogales.

The 2d is easily the most Democratic district in Arizona. Its predecessor in the 1980s elected Morris Udall to his third decade of service in the House. A major legislator on issues from campaign finance to nuclear waste, presidential candidate in 1976, and chairman of the House Interior Committee from 1977 to 1991, he retired in May 1991 because of illness. In the September 1991 special election, Republicans in the person of car wash owner and Yuma County Supervisor Pat Conner seriously contested the seat, but came up short with 44% of the vote. The winner with 56% was Democrat and career politician, Ed Pastor of Phoenix, since 1976 a Maricopa County Supervisor and, for two years before that, an aide to Governor Raul Castro. "The fact is I am Hispanic, the fact is there is a lot of pride in the Hispanic community," he said on winning. "And I join in that enthusiasm. But as an elected official for 16 years, you represent the entire community." Conner had tried to link Pastor with Keating and a lobbyist in the Azscam scandal, but Pastor said he had returned any donations he had received from the men and touted his pro-choice stance and endorsement from Udall's daughter Anne.

In his first term, Pastor proved to be an active legislator—and fundraiser. By mid-1992, he was one of the top campaign fundraisers in the House. He passed amendments promoting education for the deaf, backed a neighborhood schools improvement act and floor-managed child abuse prevention amendments. He was chief House sponsor of the Morris Udall Scholarship Act, setting up grants at the University of Arizona for the study of natural resources as well as training of professionals for health care for Indians and Alaska Natives—things Udall worked on in the Interior Committee. Pastor strongly backs family medical leave, banning striker replacement and protections against electronic monitoring of employees—the agenda of many union leaders—and had a solid liberal Democratic voting record; that surely helped him win a seat on the Appropriations Committee in late 1992.

Presumably Pastor was raising money to deter strong opposition. If so, he succeeded. He had no primary opposition and was reelected with 66% of the vote over a Yuma farmer. This looks like a safe district for him—for two more elections anyway, if the term limits law is not overturned in court.

The People: Pop. 1990: 610,266; 10% rural; 10% age 65+; 38% White; 7% Black; 5% Amer. Indian; 1% Asian; 27% Other; 50% Hispanic origin. Voting age pop.: 414,274; 6% Black; 45% Hispanic origin. Households: 52% married couple families; 28% married couple fams. w. children; 33% college educ.; median household income: $20,258; per capita income: $8,424; median gross rent: $366; median house value: $54,500.

1992 Presidential Vote			1988 Presidential Vote		
Clinton (D)	74,588	(51%)	Dukakis (D)	70,995	(57%)
Bush (R)	41,757	(28%)	Bush (R)	52,572	(43%)
Perot (I)	28,767	(20%)			

Rep. Ed Pastor (D)

Elected Sept. 1991; b. June 28, 1943, Claypool; home, Phoenix; AZ St. U., B.A. 1966, J.D. 1974; Catholic; married (Verma).

Career: High schl. teacher, 1966–69; Asst., AZ Gov. Castro, 1975; Maricopa Cnty. Bd. of Supervisors, 1976–91.

Offices: 408 CHOB 20515, 202-225-4065. Also 332 E. McDowell, #10, Phoenix 85004, 602-256-0551; 2432 E. Broadway, Tucson 85719, 602-624-9986; and 281 W. 24th St., Yuma 85364, 602-726-2234.

Committees: *Appropriations* (36th of 37 D): Agriculture, Rural Development, Food and Drug Administration and Related Agencies; Energy and Water Development.

Group Ratings

	ADA	ACLU	COPE	CDF	CFA	LCV	ACU	NTLC	NSI	COC	CEI
1992	85	89	83	100	73	56	12	8	20	13	19
1991	83	—	100	100	86	50	0	—	—	25	5

National Journal Ratings

	1991 LIB — 1991 CONS			1992 LIB — 1992 CONS		
Economic	*%	—	*%	66%	—	31%
Social	83%	—	17%	72%	—	24%
Foreign	*%	—	*%	76%	—	19%

Key Votes of the 102d Congress

1. Ban Striker Replace *	5. Handgun Wait/7-Day *	9. Use Force in Gulf *
2. $ for Homeownership AGN	6. Overseas Mil. Abortion *	10. US Mil. Abroad $ Cut FOR
3. Tax Rich/Cut Mid Cls. FOR	7. Obscn. Art NEA $ Ban AGN	11. Limit SDI Funds FOR
4. FY93/$15B Def. Cut FOR	8. Death Pen. from Jury AGN	12. Cuba Trade Embargo AGN

Key Votes of the 103d Congress

1. Family Leave FOR	2. Deficit Reduction FOR	3. Stimulus Plan FOR

Election Results

1992 general	Ed Pastor (D)	90,693	(66%)	($266,660)
	Don Shooter (R)	41,257	(30%)	($27,260)
	Dan Detaranto (L)	5,423	(4%)	
1992 primary	Ed Pastor (D), unopposed			
1991 special	Ed Pastor (D)	32,289	(56%)	($627,840)
	Pat Conner (R)	25,814	(44%)	($186,184)
1991 primary	Ed Pastor (D)	12,374	(37%)	
	Tom Volgy (D)	10,575	(32%)	
	Virginia Yrun (D)	8,874	(27%)	
	Two Others (D)	1,290	(4%)	
1990 general	Morris K. Udall (D)	76,548	(66%)	($112,373)
	Joseph D. Sweeney (R)	39,585	(34%)	($1,445)

THIRD DISTRICT

For all its huge metropolitan growth, the physical landscape of Arizona remains much as it was when white men first settled here more than a century ago. Beneath mountains and along occasionally-running creeks, they built towns that have as Western a look as anywhere in America, like Prescott, originally a gold mining camp, and home since 1888 of America's oldest annual rodeo. The landscape retains a beauty that can overpower mere buildings and parking lots: think of the red rocks of Sedona, an esoteric resort between Prescott and Flagstaff. And some landscape is intentionally preserved, like the sere uplands of the Hopi Indian Reservation. To be sure, some juxtapositions of settlement and nature are abrupt: the real London Bridge transplanted to Lake Havasu City, a retirement community on the Colorado River; or farther north, Bullhead City, one-third of whose people work in "family gambler" casinos in Laughlin, Nevada, just across the bridge over the rock-lined, piping-hot river.

All these areas are part of the 3d Congressional District of Arizona, which stretches from the west side of Phoenix to cover most of the northwest quadrant of the state. Most of the people, however, are clustered in its southeastern corner, in the Phoenix metropolitan area. Here, west of the Black Canyon Freeway, is most of the mushrooming suburb of Glendale, not so long ago a crossroads and now many square miles with 148,000 people; just west is Peoria, as Middle American as its namesake in Illinois, and the huge retirement communities of Sun City and Sun City West, with their dozen or so golf courses and many dozens of shuffleboard courts. The 3d District also includes the corridor along the westbound I-10 Papago Freeway, past Litchfield Park and its Wigwam resort to the now open spaces of Goodyear and Buckeye; this is likely to be the site of Phoenix's fastest growth in the next decade. This is heavily Republican territory: the retirees here remember—and the upwardly-striving, family-oriented young migrants who have populated these new towns in the desert still try to live—the culturally conservative, Ozzie-and-Harriet lifestyle of the 1950s. This more than affluence, which by national standards is not all that striking here, accounts for their political conservatism. Similarly Republican are the Colorado River new cities and Prescott, where Barry Goldwater used to end all his campaigns.

The 3d District's Congressman is Bob Stump, a Republican who quietly and without much notice has become one of the more senior members of the House. He has a political history similar to many older Arizonans': he was a "pinto" (conservative) Democrat, a cotton and grain farmer in the rich irrigated lands west of Phoenix, and a member of the legislature, elected to Congress as a Democrat in 1976. In 1981, after voting for the Reagan budget and tax cuts, he switched parties, to reflect both his constituency and his convictions. It was one of the smoothest party switches of recent times: he won 64% as a Democrat in 1980 and 63% as a Republican in 1982. When Stump switched, Republicans gave him seats on the Armed Services and Veterans' Affairs Committees, whose conservatism was compatible with his own. He is now ranking minority member of Veterans' Affairs, where he works with Chairman Sonny Montgomery getting various bills passed into law and suggests that the VA's "cost-controlled" healthcare system should play a role in any national healthcare reform. He is also second ranking Republican, behind Floyd Spence, on Armed Services. For years, Stump favored high defense spending, and is now cautious about reducing it too steeply. It will be interesting to see how he proceeds with no Republican in charge of the Pentagon. Stump eschews the common course of seeking special benefits for his district or backing publicity-worthy causes; but he returns to the district often, spending only one weekend a year in Washington. He votes a solid conservative line, against big government and spending, for lower taxes and a balanced budget.

If that means running a political risk, he is willing to do it—and anyway the risk does not seem too great. In 1990, Stump saw his percentage decline sharply, to 57% against Roger Hartstone, a Democrat who won his primary as a write-in. But redistricting removed Hartstone's home base of Flagstaff, and when they faced each other again in 1992, Stump won 62%–34%.

The People: Pop. 1990: 610,424; 18% rural; 20% age 65+; 82% White; 2% Black; 3% Amer. Indian;

1% Asian; 6% Other; 12% Hispanic origin. Voting age pop.: 457,328; 2% Black; 9% Hispanic origin. Households: 63% married couple families; 24% married couple fams. w. children; 49% college educ.; median household income: $27,627; per capita income: $13,185; median gross rent: $457; median house value: $79,700.

1992 Presidential Vote			1988 Presidential Vote		
Bush (R)	109,840	(40%)	Bush (R)	132,289	(67%)
Clinton (D)	86,060	(31%)	Dukakis (D)	66,106	(33%)
Perot (I)	73,356	(27%)			

Rep. Bob Stump (R)

Elected 1976; b. Apr. 4, 1927, Phoenix; home, Tolleson; AZ St. U., B.S. 1951; Seventh Day Adventist; divorced.

Career: Navy, 1943–46 (WWII); Cotton and grain farmer; AZ House of Reps., 1959–67; AZ Senate, 1967–76, Senate Pres., 1975–76.

Offices: 211 CHOB 20515, 202-225-4576. Also 230 N. First Ave., #2001, Phoenix 85025, 602-379-6923.

Committees: *Armed Services* (2d of 22 R): Military Installations and Facilities; Research and Technology (RMM). *Veterans' Affairs* (RMM of 14 R): Education, Training and Employment; Hospitals and Health Care.

Group Ratings

	ADA	ACLU	COPE	CDF	CFA	LCV	ACU	NTLC	NSI	COC	CEI
1992	0	0	8	0	0	0	100	100	100	75	96
1991	0	—	0	0	17	0	100	—	—	90	95

National Journal Ratings

	1991 LIB —	1991 CONS		1992 LIB —	1992 CONS
Economic	0%	—	96%	0%	—	91%
Social	0%	—	84%	0%	—	85%
Foreign	0%	—	88%	18%	—	74%

Key Votes of the 102d Congress

1. Ban Striker Replace	AGN	5. Handgun Wait/7-Day	AGN	9. Use Force in Gulf	FOR
2. $ for Homeownership	FOR	6. Overseas Mil. Abortion	AGN	10. US Mil. Abroad $ Cut	AGN
3. Tax Rich/Cut Mid Cls.	AGN	7. Obscn. Art NEA $ Ban	FOR	11. Limit SDI Funds	AGN
4. FY93/$15B Def. Cut	AGN	8. Death Pen. from Jury	FOR	12. Cuba Trade Embargo	FOR

Key Votes of the 103d Congress

1. Family Leave	AGN	2. Deficit Reduction	AGN	3. Stimulus Plan	AGN

Election Results

1992 general	Bob Stump (R)	158,906	(62%)	($303,208)
	Roger Hartstone (D)	88,830	(34%)	($99,133)
	Pamela Volponi (Natural Law)	10,767	(4%)	
1992 primary	Bob Stump (R)	38,634	(67%)	
	Barbara Keough (R)	18,603	(33%)	
1990 general	Bob Stump (R)	134,279	(57%)	($225,149)
	Roger Hartstone (D)	103,017	(43%)	($9,353)

FOURTH DISTRICT

From Camelback Mountain, 1800 feet high above the Valley of the Sun, you can look north over one of America's fastest-growing and most affluent metropolises, spread out over what was clumps of sagebrush three or four decades ago. That was what Frank Lloyd Wright saw from his Taliesin West home and studio when he looked out toward the Biltmore Hotel he designed in the 1930s. Now the same area—northern Scottsdale, the town of Paradise Valley, the northern section of Phoenix between Camelback and Lookout Mountains—includes many of the most upscale parts of fast-growing metropolitan Phoenix. There is still very much of a Western air to these neighborhoods: grass is discouraged, when not prohibited by subdivision covenant; planting anything but desert flora is frowned upon; the architecture of the houses tends toward unadorned stucco with picture windows facing away from the sun; the idea is to suggest that there is a horse corral over in the next lot and sometimes, especially in the northern edges of Phoenix, there is.

The 4th Congressional District of Arizona consists of this northern part of Phoenix, most of Scottsdale and Paradise Valley and part of Glendale, bounded approximately by Camelback Road on the south, Pima Road and the Salt River Indian Reservation on the east, Pinnacle Peak Road on the north and 47th and Grand Avenues on the west. For all its rustic and unplanned air, this is a highly affluent district, and a heavily Republican one; there is scarcely a Democratic precinct to be found.

The congressman from the 4th is Jon Kyl, son of a former Republican congressman from Iowa—the family's migration matching those of so many constituents. Kyl practiced law in Phoenix for 20 years, specializing in water issues. Head of the Phoenix Chamber of Commerce and active in many Republican campaigns, he was a part of the local establishment when he ran for this open seat in 1986 and won it by beating onetime (1973–77) Congressman John Conlan, a religious fundamentalist, 60%–28% in the Republican primary.

In Washington, Kyl has been an active partisan legislator. He was one of the few enthusiasts for the Strategic Defense Initiative on the Armed Services Committee, and was one of three Republicans who blocked the final version of a bill to relax controls of exports of high-tech potential weapons materials. But he was also a major backer of the military base closing law. On domestic issues, he is a vocal supporter of a balanced budget amendment, a line-item veto and a spending limit of 19% of the GNP. With New York's Susan Molinari, he introduced a sexual assault protection act designed to crack down on sexual and domestic violence by shifting focus of the justice system from the criminal to the rights of the victim. From a district where *Arizona Highways* seems to be on every rough-hewn coffee table, he wants to designate more Arizona rivers as Wild and Scenic Rivers and is proud of his work on the San Carlos Indian Water Rights Settlement Act. Kyl became aware of the urge for reform, first as a member of the House Ethics Committee, where he pressed for full disclosure of overdrafts on the House bank, and then back home in Arizona, after it was revealed he had the House's second highest office expenses ($932,000). His argument was that he needed the money to communicate with a remote district; before redistricting, the 4th went all the way up to the Navajo Reservation and the Four Corners, territory now in the new 6th District. He did not draw primary opposition, but evidently noted that two other Arizona Republican incumbents, Jim Kolbe and Bob Stump, saw one-third of their primary votes go to low-funded opponents; Kyl had three opponents in the general causing him to raise and spend one of the larger campaign treasuries in Congress. That enabled him to win with 59%—a solid number, though below the 1988 Bush showing here.

But Kyl may have his eye on more acreage. He is widely assumed to be running for Dennis DeConcini's Senate seat, which is up in 1994. His money-raising capacity and engagement on issues domestic and foreign give him a fair chance of averting, or a good chance of beating, primary opposition. Either against DeConcini, who has been weakened by his part in the Keating Five scandal, or against some other Democrat in this Republican state, he has a fine chance—provided the anti-incumbent mood of the early 1990s doesn't continue.

The People: Pop. 1990: 610,708; 11% age 65+; 87% White; 2% Black; 1% Amer. Indian; 2% Asian; 3% Other; 8% Hispanic origin. Voting age pop.: 465,000; 2% Black; 6% Hispanic origin. Households: 54% married couple families; 24% married couple fams. w. children; 62% college educ.; median household income: $33,681; per capita income: $18,331; median gross rent: $473; median house value: $90,700.

1992 Presidential Vote		
Bush (R)	118,927	(43%)
Clinton (D)	86,922	(31%)
Perot (I)	70,682	(25%)

1988 Presidential Vote		
Bush (R)	154,375	(68%)
Dukakis (D)	72,943	(32%)

Rep. Jon Kyl (R)

Elected 1986; b. Apr. 25, 1942, Oakland, NE; home, Phoenix; U. of AZ, B.A. 1964, LL.B. 1966; Presbyterian; married (Caryll).

Career: Practicing atty., 1966–86; Chmn., Phoenix Chamber of Commerce, 1985–86.

Offices: 2440 RHOB 20515, 202-225-3361. Also 4250 E. Camelback Rd., Phoenix 85018, 602-840-1891.

Committees: *Armed Services* (8th of 22 R): Military Forces and Personnel (RMM); Oversight and Investigations. *Government Operations* (4th of 16 R): Legislation and National Security. *Standards of Official Conduct* (4th of 7 R).

Group Ratings

	ADA	ACLU	COPE	CDF	CFA	LCV	ACU	NTLC	NSI	COC	CEI
1992	5	9	33	10	13	0	92	100	100	75	89
1991	5	—	8	10	17	0	100	—	—	90	89

National Journal Ratings

	1991 LIB — 1991 CONS		1992 LIB — 1992 CONS	
Economic	0% —	96%	0% —	91%
Social	0% —	84%	0% —	85%
Foreign	0% —	88%	0% —	82%

Key Votes of the 102d Congress

1. Ban Striker Replace	AGN	5. Handgun Wait/7-Day	AGN	9. Use Force in Gulf	FOR
2. $ for Homeownership	FOR	6. Overseas Mil. Abortion	AGN	10. US Mil. Abroad $ Cut	AGN
3. Tax Rich/Cut Mid Cls.	AGN	7. Obscn. Art NEA $ Ban	FOR	11. Limit SDI Funds	AGN
4. FY93/$15B Def. Cut	AGN	8. Death Pen. from Jury	FOR	12. Cuba Trade Embargo	FOR

52   ARIZONA

Key Votes of the 103d Congress

1. Family Leave   AGN   2. Deficit Reduction   AGN   3. Stimulus Plan   AGN

Election Results

1992 general	Jon Kyl (R)	156,330	(59%)	($458,358)
	Walter R. Mybeck II (D)	70,572	(27%)	
	Debbie Collings (I)	25,553	(10%)	($14,744)
	Tim McDermott (L)	11,611	(4%)	
1992 primary	Jon Kyl (R), unopposed			
1990 general	Jon Kyl (R)	141,843	(61%)	($442,366)
	Mark Ivey, Jr. (D)	89,395	(39%)	($38,851)

FIFTH DISTRICT

Arizona's first frontier was in the southeastern corner of the state. It was here, just south of today's Tucson, that Franciscan friars built San Xavier del Bac mission in the 18th Century. It was here in the late 19th Century that the mining towns of Tombstone and Bisbee sprang up on desert mountainsides, where miners dug up gold and silver and, for many years, much of America's copper; Cochise County, including those two towns, was the most populous county when Arizona became the 48th state in 1912. It was here that the white man last subdued the Indians, when the Apache leader Geronimo faced the U.S. Army. Southern Arizona remains pioneer country today, too: here is the Biosphere II project, the visionary or addled (you choose) creation of a greenhouse-like structure in the desert in which 8 men and women are living self sufficiently, sealed from outside contact until September 26, 1993. Biosphere has now joined Tombstone as a tourist attraction; but demographically all are within the orbit of Tucson, today Arizona's second metropolis, much smaller, more rough-hewn and more liberal than Phoenix. Tucson is a high-tech city, its economy imperiled by defense cuts; it is the home of the University of Arizona. For nearly 40 years, it was the political base of the brothers Udall: Stewart, congressman in the 1950s, Interior Secretary in the 1960s, now an Arizona lawyer again; Morris, congressman for 30 years, a major legislator and Interior Committee chairman, now sadly retired by Parkinson's disease.

The 5th Congressional District of Arizona includes most, but not all of Tucson and Pima County—the heavily Democratic Hispanic precincts are in the 2d District. It also includes much southeastern Arizona desert real estate: all of Cochise County, including Tombstone and Bisbee and Sierra Vista near Fort Huachuca; some of the small towns of Pinal County between Tucson and Phoenix; and the mining town of Safford. It is smaller than the old 5th District, and designed to be solidly Republican, despite Tucson's historic Democratic preference. The political beneficiary of this is Republican Congressman Jim Kolbe. First elected in 1984, when this was one of the most fiercely contested seats in the country, he has been reelected without difficulty ever since.

Kolbe earned a reputation as a moderate during his six years in the Arizona legislature, spurring Arizona to finally enter the Medicaid program and moving forward groundwater legislation; he is pro-choice on abortion and was against the so-called "gag rule" on abortion counseling. On economic issues, he is an Arizona free marketeer, against tax increases, for the balanced-budget constitutional amendment and line-item veto and in early 1993 was a strong advocate for Republican John Kasich's alternative deficit reduction plan. He is an enthusiast for the maquiladora program, in which U.S. made components shipped to Mexico for assembly can reenter the U.S. without paying full duty, and a strong backer of the North American Free Trade Agreement. On healthcare issues, Kolbe advocates both individual and business tax incentives and calls for malpractice reform. Kolbe has been mentioned as a candidate for statewide office, but his Tucson base might not give him the advantages of a Phoenix candidate.

The People: Pop. 1990: 611,128; 13% rural; 15% age 65+; 78% White; 3% Black; 1% Amer. Indian; 2% Asian; 6% Other; 16% Hispanic origin. Voting age pop.: 466,689; 3% Black; 14% Hispanic origin. Households: 55% married couple families; 23% married couple fams. w. children; 59% college educ.; median household income: $27,047; per capita income: $14,361; median gross rent: $404; median house value: $81,100.

1992 Presidential Vote			1988 Presidential Vote		
Clinton (D)	116,226	(42%)	Bush (R)	127,572	(56%)
Bush (R)	104,509	(37%)	Dukakis (D)	100,900	(44%)
Perot (I)	56,516	(20%)			

Rep. Jim Kolbe (R)

Elected 1984; b. June 28, 1942, Evanston, IL; home, Tucson; Northwestern U., B.A. 1965, Stanford U., M.B.A. 1967; United Methodist; divorced.

Career: Navy, 1967–69 (Vietnam), Naval Reserves, 1970–77; Asst., IL Bldg. Authority Architect, 1970–72; Asst., IL Gov. Ogilvie, 1972–73; Vice Pres., land planning firm; Real estate consultant; AZ Senate, 1977–82.

Offices: 405 CHOB 20515, 202-225-2542. Also 1661 N. Swan Rd., #112, Tucson 85712, 602-881-3588; and 77 Calle Portal, #B-160, Sierra Vista 85635, 602-459-3115.

Committees: *Appropriations* (12th of 23 R): Commerce, Justice, State and Judiciary; Interior. *Budget* (3d of 17 R).

Group Ratings

	ADA	ACLU	COPE	CDF	CFA	LCV	ACU	NTLC	NSI	COC	CEI
1992	25	30	25	20	20	0	76	90	100	88	81
1991	10	—	17	20	28	15	80	—	—	100	76

National Journal Ratings

	1991 LIB — 1991 CONS		1992 LIB — 1992 CONS	
Economic	12% —	86%	0% —	91%
Social	37% —	61%	42% —	56%
Foreign	26% —	70%	30% —	64%

Key Votes of the 102d Congress

1. Ban Striker Replace	AGN	5. Handgun Wait/7-Day	AGN	9. Use Force in Gulf	FOR
2. $ for Homeownership	FOR	6. Overseas Mil. Abortion	FOR	10. US Mil. Abroad $ Cut	AGN
3. Tax Rich/Cut Mid Cls.	AGN	7. Obscn. Art NEA $ Ban	FOR	11. Limit SDI Funds	AGN
4. FY93/$15B Def. Cut	AGN	8. Death Pen. from Jury	FOR	12. Cuba Trade Embargo	AGN

Key Votes of the 103d Congress

1. Family Leave	AGN	2. Deficit Reduction	AGN	3. Stimulus Plan	AGN

Election Results

1992 general	Jim Kolbe (R)	172,867	(67%)	($469,053)
	Jim Toevs (D)	77,256	(30%)	($103,589)
	Perry Willis (L)	9,690	(4%)	
1992 primary	Jim Kolbe (R)	37,140	(65%)	
	Mike Beehler (R)	19,921	(35%)	
1990 general	Jim Kolbe (R)	138,954	(65%)	($250,642)
	Chuck Phillips (D)	75,611	(35%)	

SIXTH DISTRICT

In each of the last three decades, Arizona has created a new congressional district; in each case, the district has stretched from Phoenix and Scottsdale to the Navajo Indian Reservation in the northeast corner of the state. So it is with the new 6th Congressional District of Arizona, whose boundaries are just a bit more irregular than those of its predecessors. The current District includes just the northern edges of Scottsdale and Phoenix, with the suburbs of Carefree and Cave Creek, rustic areas where the mile-square grids are far from filled in and the local stores are more likely to feature horse feed than designer clothes. The 6th also takes in the old mining towns of Globe and Clifton and the sparsely-populated, wind-swept desert up to, and including, the Navajo Reservation. The district takes in seven Indian reservations total, but its erose boundaries exclude the Hopis, who have a longstanding, sometime violent and continuing boundary dispute with the Navajo which is now in federal court. Politically, the 6th's portions of Phoenix and Scottsdale are heavily Republican, but the mining towns and the Navajo Reservation are heavily Democratic, and so sometimes is newly added Flagstaff. The result is a district leaning Republican, but potentially competitive.

So it proved in 1992, when the winner, Karan English, was not only a Democrat, but one from a very small part of the district's vote base. English benefited greatly from the liabilities of her opponents, but also had assets of her own. After working on civic (i.e., water) issues in Flagstaff, she was elected to the Arizona House in 1986 and the Senate in 1990, where she chaired the Environment Committee. She is proud of creating an Arizona Conservation Corps, a law allocating some lottery revenues for small businesses in rural areas, and a waste disposal measure. A Republican colleague claimed, "Karan is a little more interested in owls than people"; but English points to her support of the line-item veto and balanced budget amendment to bolster her image as a moderate Democrat. In early 1992, she was planning to run for Congress in the 3d District against Bob Stump, but when the court plan put Flagstaff in the new 6th, she took on state Senate colleague and Majority Leader Alan Stephens in the primary. Stephens was a power in the Capitol, but he had to move to legally reside in the district and, although the charges had been dropped, he had been indicted in the Azscam scandal. English beat him 44%–30%, with 27% for a candidate based in the Navajo country.

Meanwhile, the Republican primary was won by Doug Wead, an Assemblies of God minister and former Bush White House liaison to the religious right, who moved to Arizona in 1990 to run for Congress and moved four times to stay in the 6th District. Wead was leading in polls and had spearheaded the ultimately successful "It's TIME!" referendum requiring a two-thirds legislative vote for higher taxes. But Wead had some problems: the carpetbagger charge, his frequent past appearances on Jim Bakker's TV show, his aggressive pro-life stand on abortion. That final item was the last straw for Barry Goldwater, who got into conservative politics to keep government taxes low, not to have government regulate personal conduct: Goldwater endorsed pro-choice English, and she took the lead in the polls. English won by the unambiguous margin of 53%–41%, carrying the half of the vote cast in Maricopa County as well as every other county in the district. Given the contingent nature of her victory, plus the Arizona vote for term limits, English doesn't seem to be preparing for a lifetime career in Congress; her husband, whom she married in July 1992, and their five teens-and-up children are staying in Flagstaff.

The People: Pop. 1990: 611,885; 33% rural; 13% age 65+; 64% White; 1% Black; 22% Amer. Indian; 1% Asian; 6% Other; 13% Hispanic origin. Voting age pop.: 424,927; 1% Black; 11% Hispanic origin. Households: 62% married couple families; 28% married couple fams. w. children; 45% college educ.; median household income: $25,710; per capita income: $11,322; median gross rent: $426; median house value: $75,700.

1992 Presidential Vote			1988 Presidential Vote		
Bush (R)	91,269	(38%)	Bush (R)	104,640	(59%)
Clinton (D)	91,007	(37%)	Dukakis (D)	72,204	(41%)
Perot (I)	56,277	(23%)			

Rep. Karan English (D)

Elected 1992; b. March 23, 1949, Berkeley, CA; home, Flagstaff; U. of AZ, B.A. 1975; no religious affiliation; married (Rob Elliot).

Career: Coconino Cnty. Bd. of Supervisors, 1980–86, Chmn., 1983–86; AZ House of Reps., 1986–90; AZ Senate, 1990–92;

Offices: 1024 LHOB 20515, 202-225-2190. Also 117 E. Aspen, Flagstaff 86001, 602-774-1314; 1818 E. Southern, #3-B, Mesa 85240, 602-497-1156.

Committees: *Education and Labor* (23d of 28 D): Elementary, Secondary and Vocational Education; Postsecondary Education and Training. *Natural Resources* (19th of 28 D): National Parks, Forests and Public Lands; Native American Affairs; Oversight and Investigations.

Group Ratings and 102d Congress Votes: Newly Elected

Key Votes of the 103d Congress

1. Family Leave   FOR   2. Deficit Reduction   FOR   3. Stimulus Plan   FOR

Election Results

1992 general	Karan English (D)	124,251	(53%)	($391,015)
	Doug Wead (R)	97,074	(41%)	($667,690)
	Sarah Stannard (I)	13,047	(6%)	($5,785)
1992 primary	Karan English (D)	23,389	(44%)	
	Alan Stephens (D)	15,710	(30%)	
	Albert Hale (D)	14,102	(27%)	
1990 election	Newly created district.			

ARKANSAS

In the 1990s, America is getting to know Arkansas as never before. One view, from a Bush campaign ad, showed a buzzard overlooking a bleak landscape, with an unseen voice reciting that Arkansas ranked at the bottom of the nation in education, health and crime. The brighter view came from Bill Clinton's ceremonial appearances in front of the old State House, whose Greek Revival columns were festooned with flags for his announcement in October 1991, or at the red-brick Governor's Mansion where he and Al Gore baked in the heat as he introduced his running mate in July 1992 and which was bathed in thousands of dollars of lighting arranged by his Hollywood friends for his 1992 election night victory statement. Arkansas took some knocks and a lot of ribbing in the 1992 campaign, but in the end the brighter view prevailed.

Clinton's acceptance speech helped put Arkansas in perspective: the 25th state, like the 42d president, began life without many advantages. In area, it's the smallest state between the Mississippi and the Pacific; in population, it's the smallest state in the South; it has not been blessed with any great natural resource or any growing major industry. Arkansas is the land that was left over when Louisiana and Missouri were carved out of the Louisiana Purchase and what is now Oklahoma was fenced off as Indian Territory. Settled by poor farmers with large families, few slaves and little cash, it has had no Atlanta or Dallas or even Memphis to be a focus of growth. As Arkansas political scientist Diane Blair notes, Arkansas never had a power elite of great plantation owners or economic robber barons. That has left it a heritage without honored traditions or tight standards, but has also made Arkansas a land of great opportunities, where talented young men with original ideas can move upward without limit in politics and business.

This Arkansas has produced old style politicians like John McClellan and William Fulbright, who represented Arkansas in the Senate for a total of 65 years from the 1940s to the 1970s, and Wilbur Mills, chairman of the House Ways and Means Committee from 1958 to 1974; Governor Orval Faubus, who shamed Little Rock and Arkansas around the world by resisting integration at Central High School in 1957, and Governor Winthrop Rockefeller, who steered the state toward integration a dozen years later. It's current politicos include Dale Bumpers and David Pryor, who both served four years as governor before being elected to the Senate in the 1970s, and who both recognized Bill Clinton's talents when he was a youngster; and top Clinton aides Mack McLarty and Bruce Lindsey, as well as politicians whose personal political careers were sidetracked by Clinton's rise, like his successor as governor, Jim Guy Tucker; and, of course, Bill and Hillary Rodham Clinton themselves. Arkansas has also produced men who have made huge fortunes by taking original ideas and making them work: Sam Walton believed that rural and small town America would support a chain of giant discount stores which through tough bargaining with vendors and ultra-quick distribution could undersell competitors, but through demanding management and employee profit-sharing could embody small town friendliness and service; following that vision made him the richest man in America and Wal-Mart the biggest retailer in America at his death in April 1992. Jack Stephens and his late brother Witt started an investment banking house in Little Rock specializing in underwriting municipal bonds and investing in businesses that are a mix of private enterprise, government subsidies and public regulation; their success—and political connections in Arkansas and elsewhere—amassed a billion dollar fortune. Other big Arkansas operations include Tyson Foods, now the biggest chicken producer in America, TCBY (The Country's Best Yogurt) and J.B. Hunt's trucking empire. Yet these business giants, like most of Arkansas's successful politicians, have kept a down home, almost laid-back style. Sam Walton could be seen in Bentonville, driving his pickup truck with cages for his bird dogs in the back, stopping off to eat breakfast in a greasy spoon, just as president-elect Bill Clinton could be seen jogging around Little Rock, on his way to a giant

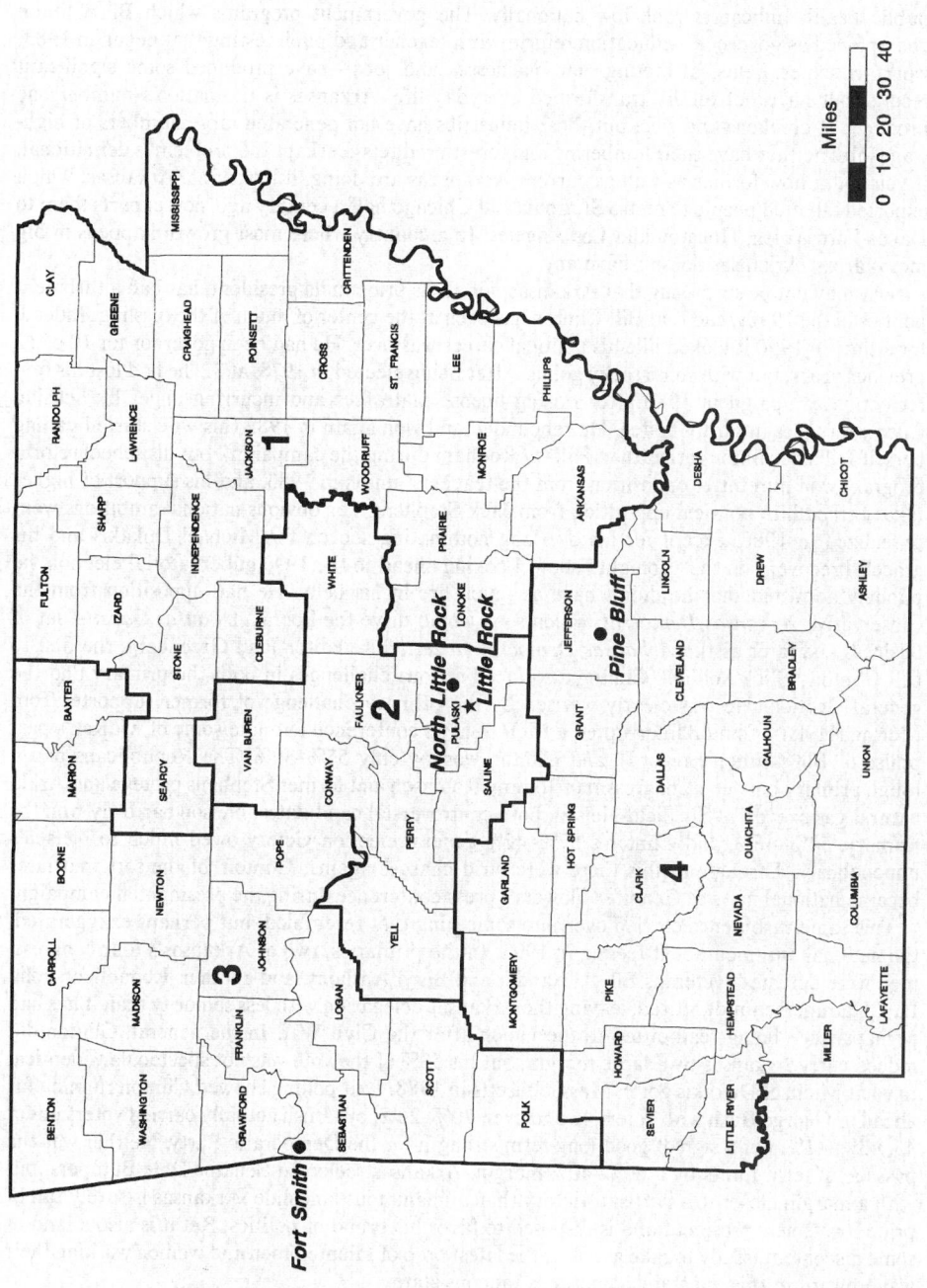

cup of coffee and perhaps a sausage biscuit at McDonald's.

For all these Arkansans' success, there is still an uncomfortable contrast here between billionaires and backwardness, presidents and poverty. Incomes remain stubbornly near the bottom of the states; taxes and spending per capita remain low; achievement in schools and public health indicators rank low nationally. The government programs which Bill Clinton championed as governor—education reform, with teacher and pupil testing that began in 1983, workfare experiments, attracting new businesses and jobs—have produced some significant results, but have not totally transformed everyday life. Arkansas is the nation's number one producer of chickens and rice, but those industries have not generated large numbers of high-wage jobs; neither have their lumbering and forest products. Perhaps the problem is definitional: if you count how former as well as current Arkansans are doing, it looks fine. Arkansas, which exported talented people to metro St. Louis and Chicago half a century ago, now exports them to Dallas-Fort Worth, Houston and Los Angeles. In a country where most growth happens in big metro areas, Arkansas doesn't have any.

So it may not be surprising that Arkansas, for all its pride in its president, has had a turbulent politics in the 1990s, and that Bill Clinton has been at the center of much of the tussling. Indeed, for a time in 1990 it looked like his political career was over. He had been governor for 10 of 12 previous years, but with some rocky going. After being elected in 1978, at 32, he had lost his first reelection campaign in 1980 after raising license plate fees and incurring anger by housing Cuban refugees in Fort Chaffee. He rebounded and won again in 1982 (his wife started calling herself Hillary Clinton rather than Hillary Rodham during the campaign), but his school reform program won him bitter opposition from the teachers' union in 1983, and his support of higher taxes earned him political opposition from Jack Stephens. His obvious national ambitions went unrealized in 1988, except for his overlong nominating speech for Michael Dukakis and his graceful recovery on the "Tonight" show. Looking ahead to the 1990 gubernatorial election, he publicly admitted that he didn't have as much fire in his belly. He had opposition from the conservative *Arkansas Democrat*, which soon would drive the liberal *Arkansas Gazette* out of business and later as the *Arkansas Democrat-Gazette* hire editor Paul Greenberg, the first to call Clinton "Slick Willie." Clinton also faced serious challenges in both the primary and the general election. He was clearly worried by the primary challenge of former supporter Tom McRae (Hillary Clinton interrupted a McRae news conference to quote some of McRae's past praise of Bill Clinton's record), and Clinton won by only 55%–39%. The Republicans had a rough primary between Congressman Tommy Robinson and former Stephens protege and Arkla natural gas executive Sheffield Nelson, both controversial candidates. Nelson narrowly won the primary, 54%–46%, and Clinton's 57%–42% general election victory owed much to Nelson's unpopularity. Through all this there were lurid charges against Clinton, of the sort that later became national news at Gennifer Flowers's press conference during the presidential campaign.

This same turbulence carried over into something that resembled, but perhaps exaggerated, the national anti-incumbent feeling in 1992. In the primaries, two of Arkansas's four congressmen were defeated, veterans Bill Alexander and Beryl Anthony, and another, Republican John Paul Hammerschmidt retired, leaving the Arkansas delegation with less seniority than it has had perhaps since being readmitted to the Union after the Civil War. In the general, Clinton did indeed carry Arkansas by a large margin, but his 53% of the vote was not spectacular, identical to what Michael Dukakis got in Massachusetts in 1988. Exit polling showed Clinton running far ahead of George Bush with voters 45 and over, 70%–26%; but Bush actually carried voters under 45, 43%–41%, not a sign of good long-term strength for the Democratic Party. Neither was the passage of term limits by a 60%–40% margin. Arkansas reelected Senator Dale Bumpers, but with a margin closer to a partisan victory than a unanimous landslide. Arkansas is surely full of pride for its new president and is disposed to favor his brand of politics. But it is also a land of some discontent, ready to take a look at the latest crop of talented men and women working their way upward in this open and sometimes raucous state.

Governor. The transition from Bill Clinton to Arkansas's new Governor, Jim Guy Tucker, was in some ways smooth and some ways rough. Smooth, in that Tucker is bright, articulate and knowledgeable about state government; he spent all or part of 250 days in 1992 as acting governor while Clinton was out of state. And if they were not always friends—they both ran for governor in the 1982 primary, in which Clinton ran first with 42% and Tucker third with 23%—they had become, by 1991, trusted allies. But the transition was a bit untidy, too. Tucker's succession was challenged because of differing sections of the state Constitution; it was settled only in early December 1992, though Tucker let the Clintons live in the Governor's Mansion until they left for Washington in January. And time was lost in the legislative session as most Arkansas Democrats went to Washington for the Inauguration. While Tucker was gone, state Senator Jerry Jewell, as acting governor, ignited a furor when he granted clemency to a murderer sentenced to life in prison and pardoned the son of a friend sentenced to 50 years for cocaine possession with intent to distribute. Jewell's rationale: "The prison population consists primarily of young black males. They're in there primarily because of low achievement in schools, the absence of skills, the flow of drugs." Or, as a resident of his neighborhood told *The New York Times*, "He's black and he let the black boys out."

Tucker does not seem bent on vastly changing Clinton's direction of state government. He is also a liberal who knows he is operating in a not entirely liberal state, and an ambitious politician first elected to Congress in 1976, at 33, who worked in the private sector after losing primaries for senator in 1978 and governor in 1982. Like Clinton, he backs education reforms to which the teachers' union has been reconciled; he looks probably more for economic growth and new jobs than environmental purity; he stands for racial justice, but opposed Jewell's acts and sought curbs on gubernatorial clemency power. His first law to sign made separate categories of residential and commercial burglaries in order to develop tougher penalties for the former. But as the state House rejected the motor voter bill, Bill Clinton's U.S. House was passing it in Washington. Pressed in early 1993 by Republicans, Tucker scheduled the lieutenant governor special election date for July 27, 1993. Their likely candidate was Mike Huckabee, the minister who won 40% against Senator Dale Bumpers in 1992; possible Democrats include Tom McRae, who ran against Clinton in 1990, Little Rock area prosecutor Mark Stodola, and a host of others. For 1994, Tucker could have primary opposition from Attorney General Winston Bryant and state Senator Jay Bradford; possible Republican candidates include 1990 nominee Sheffield Nelson and any Republican who might win the Lieutenant Governor race.

Senators. Dale Bumpers and David Pryor, the two governors who preceded Bill Clinton, have much in common with him. All three grew up in small towns, in successive decades, without any particular political connections; all have always been moderate liberals, notably on race issues; all rose quite quickly in politics, though not without some disappointments.

Dale Bumpers sprang directly from a small-town law practice to statewide office and for a time some thought he was headed to the White House. He was elected governor in 1970, beating Orval Faubus in the primary and Winthrop Rockefeller in the general, and was reelected in 1972; then in 1974, he ran for the Senate and beat 30-year incumbent William Fulbright in the primary. Bumpers has the eloquence and gift for the pungent phrase of a trial lawyer who knows how to sway a jury; he can speak the language of ordinary people, reducing complicated arguments to simple statements. But he is also the town iconoclast, with his idiosyncratic, often unpopular ideas, who is nonetheless respected and even loved by his peers. The Dale Bumpers who served on the committee that quietly integrated the schools in Charleston, Arkansas, is the same Dale Bumpers who loudly proclaimed integration as Arkansas's official state policy, and as senator spoke out for civil rights laws. Bumpers was raised a Franklin Roosevelt liberal Democrat; growing up in the 1930s, he saw FDR's federal government as the one institution working for the common man. But he has bucked organized labor, as when his single vote saved the filibuster that killed the AFL-CIO's labor law reform in 1978.

In the Senate, Bumpers picks and chooses his issues, making him something like a cat: seemingly lazy while he naps but dangerous when he pounces. "Certain senators seem to have an opinion on everything," he says. "I don't like to get involved unless I have very strong feelings and am very prepared." In the 1990s, he has spent much time opposing major federal science and defense projects, leading battles to cut funds for the Strategic Defense Initiative, the Supercollider, new Trident missiles and more intelligence programs. He argues that after the end of the Cold War these are no longer necessary; he had limited success in the Bush years but must hope for more now that Bill Clinton is president. He has led crusades to reform the Mining Act of 1872, to require miners to pay royalties to the government; he has been strongly opposed by senators from the Rocky Mountain states, which are heavily overrepresented in the Senate. He has also tried to reform concessions policy for national parks, again attacking well-entrenched interests. He chairs the mostly unimportant Small Business Committee, from which he passed a law in 1991 authorizing government "micro-loans" of up to $25,000, and he wrote the targeted capital gains tax cut which was part of the first Clinton economic package.

The vagaries of seniority have kept Bumpers from posts of great significance; in 1993 he finally became chairman of Appropriations Agriculture Subcommittee. But Bumpers is probably at his best when he is trying to convey the truth to power. Sometimes he is moved by history, as in 1988 when he made a brilliant speech in favor of preserving the Manassas, Virginia, Civil War battlefield from a shopping center project. He has been early to spot key issues (warning about aerosol cans in 1975, pushing for childhood immunizations in the 1980s) and late in abandoning lost causes (battling long and hard against decontrol of energy prices in the early 1980s). He was one of the three senators (Bradley and Hollings were the others) who voted for the 1981 Reagan budget cuts and against the 1981 tax cuts—a set of positions which, if adopted, would have just about eliminated the budget deficits of the 1980s. Bumpers was urged to run for president twice in the 1980s, but he declined both times, partly because he didn't relish the grueling process and partly because he feared "a total disruption of the closeness my family has cherished."

Bumpers's phenomenal popularity as governor has cooled a bit in his years in Washington but has not burnt out altogether. He was reelected with 59% in 1980, 62% in 1986, 60% in 1992. His opponent the last time was Mike Huckabee, a 36-year-old minister and former president of the Arkansas Baptist Convention, who operates and appears on a community television channel. Huckabee grew up in Hope, the small town where Bill Clinton was born, but has little in common with him on issues. "We need to give the people of Arkansas a senator who does more than talk cornbread and catfish in Arkansas, but votes Kennedy and Cranston in Washington," Huckabee proclaimed, boosting the balanced budget amendment and term limits, and twitting Bumpers for opposing the campaign finance reform measures Clinton backs. Huckabee's showing was significant enough that he has been mentioned as a candidate for lieutenant governor in 1993 or Governor in 1994.

In early 1993, by universal consent, Arkansas's junior Senator David Pryor was christened the new president's "Best Friend in Congress." Pryor first encountered Bill Clinton in 1966 as a teenager handing out political buttons for the democratic gubernatorial candidate that year. Unlike Dale Bumpers, who seems always to have regarded Clinton with the wariness politicians reserve for those who might some day run against them, Pryor regards Clinton warmly and campaigned for him intensely even when his candidacy appeared to be in trouble and Pryor himself was not long removed from a heart attack. They evidently talk frequently, but seem probably more in the nature of congenial political allies than close personal friends. Pryor got his start in politics while Clinton was still in college; he was first elected to the House in 1966 at age 32, and was one of the very few members from the Deep South to support civil rights. He ran for the Senate in 1972 and was only narrowly defeated in the runoff by 76-year-old conservative John McClellan. Pryor was elected governor in 1974 and 1976, where he became known as something of a cost-cutter. In 1978, he won the Senate seat after a close three-way primary contest against House members Jim Guy Tucker and Ray Thornton. Interestingly, the 1990s have been good for all three: Pryor was reelected unopposed in 1990, and can only profit from Clinton's victory; Tucker, long out of office and shy of running against Clinton again, was elected lieutenant governor in 1990 and thus became governor in December 1992; Thornton was elected to the House from the 2d District in 1990 and was the only Arkansas House incumbent reelected in 1992. Pryor has seen many political cycles by now: he left a Washington in 1972 dominated by liberals bent on increasing public spending; he returned in 1979 when pressure was increasing to cut domestic spending and step up defense. In 1993, he has reason to believe that impulses for a more generous, activist government can find expression; and to be sure it would, he used his seat on the Governmental Affairs Committee to try noisily to prevent Republican appointees from cementing themselves into the federal government by placing themselves under civil service.

Indeed, in the first months of the Clinton Administration, Pryor had the pleasure of seeing one of his causes taken up by the White House. Pryor has long been interested in issues concerning the elderly: as a young House member, he staged an investigation of nursing homes by going undercover as an orderly. When the House refused to hold hearings on the elderly, Pryor held his own hearings in a trailer near the Capitol and eventually got established the Select Committee on Aging. With Oregon's Representative Ron Wyden, he pushed through a bill to force drug companies to give their most favorable prices to medicare and medicaid purchasers; in March 1993, he saw President Clinton attack the pharmaceutical industry as greedy and suggest caps on drug price increases. And when Republican Thad Cochran moved to abolish Pryor's Special Committee on Aging, Pryor fought back and won, though its House counterpart was abolished.

Pryor has had some success in his crusades. He has long criticized the IRS for overharsh enforcement methods and in 1988 steered to passage a taxpayer bill of rights. He has run dozens of hearings and demanded more than 40 GAO reports on government use of private consultants, which he sees as a "shadow government," and in 1992 limited consultant payments on the Strategic Defense Initiative. He is attentive to Arkansas interests, holding up the 1986 savings and loan recapitalization bill because of what he regarded as "a deliberate system of harassment" against Arkansas S&Ls, which then had the nation's highest insolvency rate. But he will work against local interests on occasion. As a vocal opponent of chemical weapons, Pryor has fought against production of both the Big-Eye nerve gas bomb and the 155 millimeter artillery shell which can be used to deploy chemical weapons, and was successful in halting construction of the Big-Eye, slated for production in the Arkansas Pine Bluff weapons plant.

Pryor is technically the number three man in the Democratic leadership, as secretary of the Democratic Conference. He got the post because he had been pushing for streamlined Senate procedures, and when he tried to move up to the whip position in November 1990, after Alan Cranston bowed out, he quickly found that Wendell Ford already had the votes. Pryor was sidelined for some months in 1991 after suffering a heart attack. But his hard work in the Senate and on the campaign trail for Bill Clinton signal that he is very much back in business. No one is really speculating on who might oppose him when his seat comes up in 1996: whatever happens elsewhere, a Clinton-Pryor ticket would be strong in Arkansas.

Presidential politics. For Arkansas, presidential politics in 1992 meant the rise and apparent fall and rise again of Bill Clinton. This has long been, in any case, one of the southern states least negatively disposed to national Democratic tickets, and even a northern candidate might have hoped to carry it. It was, as one might expect, Clinton's strongest state, and one of the three places where his percentage most exceeded Michael Dukakis's (the other two: Al Gore's Tennessee and his many appointees' District of Columbia).

For 1992, Arkansas moved its primary from Super Tuesday in March back to May, when state candidates run as well. Its early primary hadn't attracted much attention, since it's the smallest southern state, and neither did the primary in May 1992, since the results were not in doubt. There is no party registration in Arkansas and turnout in the Republican primary was very low.

Congressional districting. Not much to it: six small counties were shifted between districts to meet the equal-population standard.

The People: Est. Pop. 1992: 2,399,000; Pop. 1990: 2,350,725, up 2.0% 1990–1992. 0.9% of U.S. total, 33d largest; 46% rural. Median age: 33.8 years. 14.9% 65 years and over. 82.7% White, 15.9% Black. Households: 59.2% married couple families; 27% married couple fams. w. children; 34% college educ.; median household income: $21,147; per capita income: $10,520; 69.6% owner occupied housing; median house value: $46,300; median monthly rent: $230. 7.2% Unemployment. Voting age pop.: 1,729,594; Registered voters (1992): 1,317,944; no party registration.

Political Lineup: Governor, Jim Guy Tucker (D); Lt. Gov., vacant; Secy. of State, W.J. (Bill) McCuen (D); Atty. Gen., Winston Bryant (D); Treasurer, Jimmie Lou Fisher (D); Auditor, Julia Hughes Jones (D). State Senate, 35 (30 D and 5 R); State House of Representatives, 100 (89 D, 10 R, and 1 I). Senators, Dale Bumpers (D) and David Pryor (D). Representatives, 4 (2 D and 2 R).

1992 Presidential Vote

Clinton (D)	505,823	(53%)
Bush (R)	337,324	(35%)
Perot (I)	99,132	(10%)

1988 Presidential Vote

Bush (R)	466,578	(56%)
Dukakis (D)	349,237	(42%)

1992 Democratic Presidential Primary

Clinton	342,017	(68%)
Brown	55,184	(11%)
Other	14,656	(3%)
Uncommitted	90,710	(18%)

1992 Republican Presidential Primary

Bush	45,590	(83%)
Buchanan	6,551	(12%)
Uncommitted	2,735	(5%)

GOVERNOR

Gov. Jim Guy Tucker (D)

Assumed office Dec. 1992, term expires Jan. 1995; b. June 13, 1943, Oklahoma City, OK; home, Little Rock; Harvard, A.B. 1964, U. of AR, J.D. 1968; Presbyterian; married (Betty).

Career: Marine Corps Reserves, 1962–64; News reporter, Vietnam, 1965, 1967; Teacher, American U. of Beirut, Lebanon, 1966; Practicing atty., 1968–71; Prosecuting Atty., 6th Judicial District of AR, 1971–73; AR Atty. Gen., 1973–77; U.S. House of Reps., 1977–79; Chmn., Cablevision Management Inc., 1982–present; AR Lt. Gov., 1990–92.

Office: State Capitol, #250, Little Rock 72201, 501-682-2345.

Election Results

1990 gen.	Bill Clinton (D)	400,326	(57%)
	Sheffield Nelson (R)	295,883	(42%)
1990 prim.	Bill Clinton (D)	269,329	(55%)
	Tom McRae (D)	190,887	(39%)
	Four Others	30,930	(6%)
1986 gen.	Bill Clinton (D)	439,851	(64%)
	Frank White (R)	248,415	(36%)

SENATORS

Sen. Dale Bumpers (D)

Elected 1974, seat up 1998; b. Aug. 12, 1925, Charleston; home, Charleston; U. of AR, Northwestern U., LL.B. 1951; Methodist; married (Betty).

Career: Marine Corps, 1943–46 (WWII); Practicing atty., 1951–70; AR Gov., 1970–74.

Offices: 229 DSOB 20510, 202-224-4843. Also 2527 Fed. Bldg., 700 W. Capitol, Little Rock 72201, 501-378-6286.

Committees: *Appropriations* (8th of 16 D): Agriculture, Rural Development and Related Agencies (Chmn.); Commerce, Justice, State and Judiciary; Defense; Interior; Labor, Health and Human Services, Education. *Energy and Natural Resources* (2d of 11 D): Energy Research and Development; Mineral Resources Development and Production; Public Lands, National Parks and Forests (Chmn.). *Small Business* (Chmn. of 12 D): Export Expansion and Agricultural Development; Innovation, Manufacturing and Technology; Rural Economy and Family Farming.

Group Ratings

	ADA	ACLU	CDF	COPE	CFA	LCV	ACU	NTLC	NSI	COC	CEI
1992	90	59	80	75	92	50	15	28	40	10	29
1991	70	—	91	67	61	47	24	—	—	20	34

National Journal Ratings

	1991 LIB — 1991 CONS		1992 LIB — 1992 CONS	
Economic	51% —	46%	55% —	43%
Social	53% —	46%	46% —	53%
Foreign	77% —	22%	65% —	26%

Key Votes of the 102d Congress

1. $ for Homeownership	AGN	5. Clarence Thomas Nom.	AGN	9. Use Force in Gulf	AGN
2. Have Cap Gains Debate	AGN	6. Lmt Death Row Appeal	FOR	10. Keep Salvador Aid	AGN
3. Remove Budget Walls	FOR	7. Handgun Wait/5-Day	FOR	11. Cut $1B from SDI	FOR
4. Ban Striker Replace	AGN	8. Abortion Gag Rule	AGN	12. Override China MFN	FOR

Key Votes of the 103d Congress

1. Family Leave	FOR	2. HIV Immigrants	FOR	3. Clinton Budget	FOR

Election Results

1992 general	Dale Bumpers (D)	553,635	(60%)	($2,016,112)
	Mike Huckabee (R)	366,373	(40%)	($910,212)
1992 primary	Dale Bumpers (D)	322,458	(65%)	
	Julia Hughes Jones (D)	177,273	(35%)	
1986 general	Dale Bumpers (D)	433,092	(62%)	($1,797,370)
	Asa Hutchinson (R)	262,300	(38%)	($939,342)

Sen. David Pryor (D)

Elected 1978, seat up 1996; b. Aug. 29, 1934, Camden; home, Little Rock; U. of AR, B.A. 1957, LL.B. 1964; Presbyterian; married (Barbara).

Career: Editor and Publisher, *Ouachita Citizen*, 1957–61; AR House of Reps., 1960–66; Practicing atty., 1964–66, 1972–75; U.S. House of Reps., 1967–72; AR Gov., 1975–79.

Office: 267 RSOB 20510, 202-224-2353. Also 3030 Fed. Bldg., Little Rock 72201, 501-378-6336.

Committees: *Aging (Special)* (Chmn. of 11 D). *Agriculture, Nutrition and Forestry* (2d of 10 D): Agricultural Production and Stabilization of Prices (Chmn.); Domestic and Foreign Marketing and Product Promotion; Nutrition and Investigations. *Finance* (6th of 11 D): Medicare and Long-Term Care; Private Retirement Plans and Oversight of the Internal Revenue Service (Chmn.); Taxation. *Governmental Affairs* (5th of 8 D): Federal Services, Post Office and Civil Service (Chmn.); Oversight of Government Management; Permanent Subcommittee on Investigations. *Joint Committee on the Organization of Congress* (6th of 12).

Group Ratings

	ADA	ACLU	CDF	COPE	CFA	LCV	ACU	NTLC	NSI	COC	CEI
1992	90	64	90	75	92	42	15	10	30	30	24
1991	30	—	64	80	60	27	11	—	—	50	32

National Journal Ratings

	1991 LIB — 1991 CONS		1992 LIB — 1992 CONS	
Economic	54%	— 45%	65%	— 33%
Social	*	— *	58%	— 41%
Foreign	*	— *	86%	— 0%

Key Votes of the 102d Congress

1. $ for Homeownership	AGN	5. Clarence Thomas Nom.	AGN	9. Use Force in Gulf	AGN
2. Have Cap Gains Debate	AGN	6. Lmt Death Row Appeal	*	10. Keep Salvador Aid	*
3. Remove Budget Walls	FOR	7. Handgun Wait/5-Day	*	11. Cut $1B from SDI	*
4. Ban Striker Replace	AGN	8. Abortion Gag Rule	*	12. Override China MFN	FOR

Key Votes of the 103d Congress

1. Family Leave	FOR	2. HIV Immigrants	FOR	3. Clinton Budget	FOR

Election Results

1990 general	David Pryor (D), unopposed			($622,479)
1990 primary	David Pryor (D), unopposed			
1984 general	David Pryor (D)	502,341	(57%)	($1,838,352)
	Ed Bethune (R)	373,615	(43%)	($1,072,879)

FIRST DISTRICT

The flat, mushy lowlands known as the Delta, on both sides of the lower Mississippi River, were some of the country's first industrial farmlands. This land was uncultivated in the 19th Century, when plows were still pulled by mules and muddy flatlands were impassable; then, around 100 years ago, big landowners used machines to drain flat marshlands and used capital to attract poor blacks to tend fields of cotton, rice and later soybeans. The results were a bountiful agriculture and an impoverished people. Around 1940, the Delta began to change slowly: national minimum wage legislation drew young people out of the Delta and mechanization forced many people off the farms. But this land—stretching flat as far as the eye can see, past rows of telephone poles and ribbons of asphalt that shimmer in the heat—remains poor by national standards and the people undereducated and underemployed.

The 1st Congressional District of Arkansas includes most of the state's Delta lands and stretches west to the cool green Ozarks. The Delta started off heavily Democratic, while some of the hill counties are ancestrally Republican. That changed as partisan preferences oscillated wildly just after the civil rights revolution, but the district returned to its historical norm by the late 1980s. Much of the Delta voted for Michael Dukakis in 1988, and in 1990 it provided critical support for, perhaps saving the career of, Bill Clinton. In 1992, Delta counties voted 58% to 69% for Clinton, some of his best county showings anywhere in the United States. And, while the percentages reflect strong support from blacks, few counties this side of the Mississippi have black majorities any more.

The 1st Congressional District was the site in 1992 of one of the many national expressions of anti-incumbent sentiment; it was also the scene of the denouement of a political drama more typically southern. The focus of both was the defeat of Congressman Bill Alexander, first elected in 1968, a member of the Democratic leadership from 1976 to 1986 who probably had hopes of being speaker some day. But Alexander didn't show the political instincts needed to climb to a top job. He did develop a national Democratic voting record and became an impassioned opponent of aid to the Nicaraguan contras, but at times he looked foolish, as when he requisitioned a government plane for a 1985 gasohol inspection trip to Brazil for five lawmakers, when only Alexander ever made the trip. He won the May 1986 primary by just 52%–48%, and that June abandoned the race for majority whip. Even his Appropriations Committee work on district projects was not enough. Alexander won the 1990 primary by only 54%–46%. More trouble followed: he was named in a July 1991 lawsuit to recover a $308,000 debt; he was a business associate in a Florida development with men who ran a research foundation funded by the Appropriations Committee; he had 487 overdrafts totalling $208,000 on the House bank, and was overdrawn in 19 of 39 months studied.

Some thought Alexander would win again because his only primary opponent was 31-year-old Blanche Lambert, who had once been a receptionist in his office. But Lambert knew her way around the 1st District as well as Washington: she grew up in Helena, in the Delta, where her father was a big farmer and her brother the seventh generation to farm their fields, and where she stayed in public schools when they were integrated. "My parents raised independent-minded kids," she said. Lambert worked as a lobbyist in Washington for several years (one employer was Billy Broadhurst, Gary Hart's host on his "Monkey Business" cruise). Lambert hit hard at Alexander's check bouncing: "I'll promise you one thing, I can sure enough balance my checkbook." She called for agricultural enterprise zones, expanding foreign markets (this is America's biggest rice-producing area) and tax credits for medical research. Lambert won by a solid 61%–39% margin, carrying 23 of 25 counties. She raised vast sums more than her Republican opponent and won the general election easily.

In the House, as in Arkansas, she exceeded ordinary expectations, winning a seat on the Energy and Commerce Committee with the help of women allies on the Steering and Policy Committee.

The People: Pop. 1990: 588,588; 53% rural; 15% age 65+; 81% White; 18% Black; 1% Hispanic origin. Voting age pop.: 425,209; 15% Black. Households: 60% married couple families; 28% married couple fams. w. children; 26% college educ.; median household income: $18,180; per capita income: $9,148; median gross rent: $290; median house value: $39,800.

1992 Presidential Vote

Clinton (D) 131,585 (59%)
Bush (R) 71,160 (32%)
Perot (I). 20,116 (9%)

1988 Presidential Vote

Bush (R) 101,784 (51%)
Dukakis (D). 93,331 (47%)

Rep. Blanche M. Lambert (D)

Elected 1992; b. Sept. 30, 1960, Helena; home, Helena; U. of AR, 1979–80, Randolph Macon Col., B.S. 1982; Episcopalian; single.

Career: Staff Asst., U.S. Rep. Bill Alexander, 1982–84; Lobbyist and govt. affairs rep., 1985–91.

Offices: 1204 LHOB 20515, 202-225-4076. Also 615 S. Main, #211, Jonesboro 72401, 501-972-4600.

Committees: *Agriculture* (27th of 28 D): Department Operations and Nutrition. *Energy and Commerce* (27th of 27 D): Energy and Power; Transportation and Hazardous Materials. *Merchant Marine and Fisheries* (22d of 29 D): Coast Guard and Navigation; Environment and Natural Resources.

Group Ratings and 102d Congress Votes: Newly Elected

Key Votes of the 103d Congress

1. Family Leave	FOR	2. Deficit Reduction	FOR	3. Stimulus Plan	FOR

Election Results

1992 general	Blanche M. Lambert (D) 149,558	(70%)	($327,100)
	Terry Hayes (R) 64,618	(30%)	($30,571)
1992 primary	Blanche M. Lambert (D) 86,142	(61%)	
	Bill Alexander (D) 54,686	(39%)	
1990 general	Bill Alexander (D) 101,007	(64%)	($785,626)
	Terry Hayes (R) 56,067	(36%)	($36,731)

SECOND DISTRICT

Little Rock, the central focus of Arkansas for a century and a half, has now become at least momentarily the central focus of the United States and perhaps the world. Television viewers are now familiar with the Old State House and the Governor's Mansion; they have some idea where the major hotels and McDonald's are; they have watched President-elect Bill Clinton choose his Cabinet here and will presumably see President Clinton back here from time to time. Bill Clinton grew up in Hope and Hot Springs, went to school in Washington, D.C., Oxford and New Haven, then lived and ran for Congress in the university town of Fayetteville, in the northwest corner of the state; he has lived in Little Rock only as the official resident of the Governor's Mansion, and in 1981–82 after he was defeated for reelection. Yet in early 1993, he owned no home, and his voting address is a Post Office box in Little Rock.

In any case, Little Rock is and will remain the center of Arkansas, geographically and, even more, politically. It sets the tone of the public life of its state as do only a few other state capitals—Boston, Providence, Atlanta, Denver, Honolulu. Little Rock is home to the *Arkansas Democrat*, the feistily conservative paper that forced the liberal *Arkansas Gazette* out of business in 1991. Its television stations reach to within a few counties of the state's boundaries. It is home to the state government and to Jack Stephens's investment banking firm and Worthen

Bank, to Dillards department stores and the TCBY yogurt chain, and to the Rose Law Firm at which Hillary Rodham Clinton was a partner. Little Rock may not be upscale by national standards, but it is in Arkansas. And the bad name it earned internationally when Governor Orval Faubus forcibly resisted the desegregation of Central High School in 1957 has surely been overshadowed by the good name it has won as Bill Clinton's home.

The 2d Congressional District of Arkansas includes Little Rock, with its large black and affluent white neighborhoods, and North Little Rock, a kind of industrial suburb across the Arkansas River known informally for years as Dog Town. (At the turn of the century, Little Rock officials, peeved that North Little Rock was allowed to incorporate separately, dumped all their stray dogs there.) Politically, Little Rock has been a progressive force in a state with widely divergent political tendencies; it provided key support to Clinton when he was in political trouble in the 1990 primary and general, and again in 1992. The 2d also includes several hill counties to the north and, in the flat southeast, part of the cotton, rice and soybean-growing Mississippi plain. While the 2d has tended to favor moderate establishment politicians—for most of the 1960s and 1970s it was represented by Wilbur Mills, chairman of the House Ways and Means Committee—it also has produced some odd-duck results. In 1958, after the Central High crisis, it elected a segregationist with write-in votes; for three elections starting in 1984 it elected Tommy Robinson, whose antics as sheriff earned him notoriety and popularity, who switched to the Republican Party in 1989 and ran for governor in 1990, and then was identified (he vehemently disputes this) as having 996 overdrafts on the House bank.

The congressman now from the 2d District is Ray Thornton, once president of the University of Arkansas student body and as a nephew of Jack Stephens, a widely respected member of the Arkansas establishment. Thornton was first elected to Congress in 1972 from the 4th District, and served on the Judiciary Committee when it voted for the impeachment of Richard Nixon. He ran for the Senate in 1978 and lost to David Pryor. In 1980, he became president of Arkansas State University, and in 1984 president of the University of Arkansas system. Elected without difficulty in 1990, he is the only recent Arkansas politician, surely, who has lived or worked in all of the state's four congressional districts.

Thornton ran again, he says, to promote his Marshall Plan for America: he would invest 2% of GNP, about $110 billion, in rebuilding the nation's infrastructure and economy. He has served on the Science, Space and Technology Committee, where he worked to promote high-performance computing and maintaining American preeminence in technology. He has a generally moderate voting record, and was the only Arkansas Democrat to vote for the Gulf war resolution (which Bill Clinton at the time said he would have voted for if his vote had made the difference, though he agreed with the opposition arguments). Thornton was embarrassed when it turned out he had one overdraft on the House bank, for $18; it seems not to have diminished the respect he has earned over the years. He was reelected with 74% of the vote—the only Arkansas House incumbent to be reelected in 1992.

The People: Pop. 1990: 587,412; 31% rural; 12% age 65+; 81% White; 18% Black; 1% Asian; 1% Hispanic origin. Voting age pop.: 434,412; 15% Black; 1% Hispanic origin. Households: 58% married couple families; 27% married couple fams. w. children; 43% college educ.; median household income: $25,142; per capita income: $12,334; median gross rent: $383; median house value: $56,300.

1992 Presidential Vote

Clinton (D) 130,435 (55%)
Bush (R) 84,922 (36%)
Perot (I). 19,348 (8%)

1988 Presidential Vote

Bush (R) 117,477 (56%)
Dukakis (D). 89,526 (43%)

Rep. Ray Thornton (D)

Elected 1990; b. July 16, 1928, Conway; home, Little Rock; Yale, B.A. 1950, U. of AR, J.D. 1956; Church of Christ; married (Betty Jo).

Career: Navy, 1951–54 (Korea); Dep. Prosecutor, Pulaski and Perry Cntys., 1956–57; Practicing atty., 1957–71; AR Atty. Gen., 1971–73; U.S. House of Reps., 1973–79; Pres., AR St. U., 1980–84; Pres., U. of AR, 1984–89.

Offices: 1214 LHOB 20515, 202-225-2506. Also 1527 Fed. Bldg., 700 W. Capitol, Little Rock 72201, 501-324-5941.

Committees: *Appropriations* (30th of 37 D): Agriculture, Rural Development, Food and Drug Administration and Related Agencies; VA, HUD and Independent Agencies.

Group Ratings

	ADA	ACLU	COPE	CDF	CFA	LCV	ACU	NTLC	NSI	COC	CEI
1992	85	73	91	80	60	25	8	0	80	38	15
1991	40	—	92	90	67	38	15	—	—	50	13

National Journal Ratings

	1991 LIB — 1991 CONS	1992 LIB — 1992 CONS
Economic	59% — 41%	70% — 29%
Social	54% — 44%	53% — 46%
Foreign	51% — 46%	52% — 46%

Key Votes of the 102d Congress

1. Ban Striker Replace FOR	5. Handgun Wait/7-Day AGN	9. Use Force in Gulf FOR
2. $ for Homeownership AGN	6. Overseas Mil. Abortion AGN	10. US Mil. Abroad $ Cut AGN
3. Tax Rich/Cut Mid Cls. FOR	7. Obscn. Art NEA $ Ban FOR	11. Limit SDI Funds AGN
4. FY93/$15B Def. Cut FOR	8. Death Pen. from Jury AGN	12. Cuba Trade Embargo FOR

Key Votes of the 103d Congress

1. Family Leave FOR	2. Deficit Reduction FOR	3. Stimulus Plan FOR

Election Results

1992 general	Ray Thornton (D)..................	154,946	(74%)	($206,328)
	Dennis Scott (R).....................	53,978	(26%)	($6,212)
1992 primary	Ray Thornton (D), unopposed			
1990 general	Ray Thornton (D)..................	103,455	(60%)	($678,429)
	Jim Keet (R)........................	67,786	(40%)	($430,932)

THIRD DISTRICT

The Ozarks of northwestern Arkansas, once one of the most isolated and backward parts of America, are now in important ways one of the country's leading edges. Much of the scenery remains the same: rounded green mountains spotted with farmhouses, little towns and small cities in valleys, man-made lakes glistening in the sunlight. People are still friendly and lifestyles tradition-minded and family-oriented. These very assets have made the Ozarks one of the nation's favorite retirement areas, a low-cost and safe haven for people who have worked hard and worried much in the suburbs of St. Louis or Chicago. And the Ozarks have also become a center of economic growth. Sam Walton kept the headquarters of his Wal-Mart chain in Bentonville, which has the small town ambience that is so much a part of Wal-Mart's success even though profit-sharing and stock prices have made some Wal-Mart employees millionaires. And down the road near the University of Arkansas in Fayetteville is Don Tyson's Tyson Foods, now the leading chicken producer and processor in the nation: once again, an Arkansas entrepreneur has taken insights gained from his knowledge of Arkansas and enriched the nation as well as the state.

The 3d Congressional District of Arkansas occupies the northwest part of the state, including Bentonville, Fayetteville and the city of Fort Smith on the Oklahoma line, plus several mountain and upcountry counties to the east and south. This is the most Republican part of Arkansas, 2–1 for George Bush in 1988 and for Bill Clinton in 1992 by a bare 42.9%–42.2% margin. The mountain counties have historically been heavily Republican: they had few slaves and were opposed to secession, and remained hostile to the Democratic flatlands. Recently, the Republican trend has been greater around Fort Smith, which dislikes cultural liberalism, and Bentonville, with its many convinced anti-big government entrepreneurs. For 24 years, the 3d District elected John Paul Hammerschmidt, a mountain Republican whose conservatism was joined with a desire to use his Public Works seat for bringing roads and other projects to the district: one such is the soon-to-be-completed U.S. 71 four-lane freeway from Bentonville to Fort Smith. Hammerschmidt was widely popular, and only had one scare since beating an incumbent Democrat in 1966; that was in 1974, when he was opposed by a young law professor living in Fayetteville named Bill Clinton. Hammerschmidt decided to retire in 1992.

The new congressman from the 3d is Tim Hutchinson, a state Representative for eight years called "No-Tax Tim" by Bill Clinton and an ordained Baptist minister, whose brother Asa Hutchinson was the Republican nominee against Senator Dale Bumpers in 1986. Hutchinson was the co-owner of a radio station for seven years in the 1980s, and founder and first administrator of the Benton County Christian School in Rogers. He won the Republican nomination impressively with 53% against a fellow legislator and an investment banker. The Democrats had four serious candidates, and in the runoff Fayetteville auto dealer Don Nelms, who spent $120,000 of his own money, was beaten by Fort Smith lawyer John VanWinkle. VanWinkle spent three years in the 1970s as a social worker for Developmental Disabilities Services, then went to law school; he was chairman of the Sebastian County Democratic Party and Bill Clinton appointed him Sebastian County Chancellor (a judgeship) in 1991. VanWinkle led Nelms 40%–27% in the first primary, then won the runoff 58%–42%. VanWinkle called for government to help those without health insurance, though he worried that "pay or play" would hurt small businesses. He campaigned strongly for Bill Clinton, and had the endorsement of unions and the Arkansas Education Association. Hutchinson said he wanted to ally himself with congressional reformers, backing term limits, the line-item veto and the balanced budget amendment; he called for Dick Armey's process for closing military bases to be applied to cutting waste in all parts of government. He said he would follow Hammerschmidt's voting record, and claimed attacks on him as a religious extremist were "scare tactics" reflecting "a kind of intolerance." In the last week of the campaign, Hutchinson was endorsed by local Perot supporters who dismissed VanWinkle as a "waffler"; this may have made the difference. He won by just 50%–47%, losing most of the smaller counties, but carrying the counties around Bentonville, Fayetteville and Fort Smith.

Hutchinson insists that he is not unwilling to support at least some of Bill Clinton's programs, but is likely to be a solid conservative vote. He got seats on Hammerschmidt's old committees, Public Works and Veterans' Affairs, which should help at election time. VanWinkle is not expected to run again, but Nelms might, and given the close result this could be a seriously contested district in 1994.

The People: Pop. 1990: 589,523; 49% rural; 16% age 65+; 96% White; 2% Black; 1% Amer. Indian; 1% Asian; 1% Hispanic origin. Voting age pop.: 440,426; 1% Black; 1% Hispanic origin. Households: 64% married couple families; 28% married couple fams. w. children; 36% college educ.; median household income: $21,903; per capita income: $10,876; median gross rent: $328; median house value: $48,900.

1992 Presidential Vote			1988 Presidential Vote		
Clinton (D)	109,111	(43%)	Bush (R)	137,239	(66%)
Bush (R)	107,351	(42%)	Dukakis (D)	67,856	(33%)
Perot (I)	35,991	(14%)			

Rep. Tim Hutchinson (R)

Elected 1992; b. Aug. 11, 1949, Gravette; home, Bentonville; Bob Jones U., B.A. 1979, U. of AR, M.A. 1990; Baptist; married (Donna Jean).

Career: Baptist Minister; Founder and Admin., Benton Cnty. Christian Schl., 1975–85; Co-owner and Mgr., KBCV Radio, 1982–89; Prof., John Brown U., 1989–92; AR House of Reps., 1984–92.

Offices: 1541 LHOB 20515, 202-225-4301. Also 248 Fed. Bldg., P.O. Box 1624, Ft. Smith 72902, 501-782-7787; 422 Fed. Bldg., 35 E. Mountain, Fayetteville 72701, 501-442-5258; and 210 Fed. Bldg., 425 N. Walnut, P.O. Box 579, Harrison 72601, 501-741-6900.

Committees: *Public Works and Transportation* (13th of 24 R): Economic Development; Surface Transportation; Water Resources and Environment. *Veterans' Affairs* (7th of 14 R): Education, Training and Employment (RMM); Hospitals and Health Care.

Group Ratings and 102d Congress Votes: Newly Elected

Key Votes of the 103d Congress

1. Family Leave	AGN	2. Deficit Reduction	AGN	3. Stimulus Plan	AGN

Election Results

1992 general	Tim Hutchinson (R)	125,295	(50%)	($339,772)
	John VanWinkle (D)	117,775	(47%)	($489,833)
	Two Others	6,424	(3%)	
1992 primary	Tim Hutchinson (R)	17,380	(53%)	
	Dick Barclay (R)	10,534	(32%)	
	Dryden Pence (R)	4,879	(15%)	
1990 general	John Paul Hammerschmidt (R)	129,850	(71%)	($105,354)
	Dan Ivy (D)	54,330	(30%)	($15,730)

FOURTH DISTRICT

Southern Arkansas runs the gamut of the state, from the Delta flatlands along the Mississippi River, where the water-soaked fields produce America's largest rice crop, passing across small cities with antique pasts like Pine Bluff and El Dorado, west to the Ouachita Mountains and the border town of Texarkana, where the main street divides two states and Texan Ross Perot grew up five blocks west of Arkansas. This is the northwestern corner of the Deep South. There is still a large black population here, a reminder that parts of southern Arkansas were once plantation country; but there is also oil production, a reminder that this is the beginning of the Southwest. There is a big broiler chicken industry in these parts—the business which Perot was wont to condescend to during the 1992 campaign—and the accent is clearly Arkansan: El Dorado, Nevada and Lafayette are all pronounced with long *A*s and penultimate syllable accents, and

Ouachita is, with a bow to the original French, *waSHEEta*. Here is the little railroad-crossing, county seat town of Hope, where President Bill Clinton and White House Chief of Staff Mack McLarty were classmates in kindergarten, and here is Hot Springs, the spa resort and gambling haven where Bill Clinton's stepfather sold cars, his mother bet on the horses and he excelled in high school as he began his climb from southern Arkansas to world eminence.

The 4th Congressional District of Arkansas occupies almost all of the southern geographical half of the state, from the Mississippi River to the Ouachita Mountains, the Delta to Texarkana. It is historically a Democratic district, and one which typically has elected a young man to the House and kept him there as long as he wants, to cut his deals with the Democratic leadership so long as he brings back home benefits for the district. So it has been for the last 50 years, in which the district had only four congressmen: one retired after 25 years to become a federal judge; two others, David Pryor and Ray Thornton, left after six to run for the Senate; the fourth, Beryl Anthony, first elected in 1978, seemed content to remain indefinitely. But in the anti-incumbent year of 1992, voters even in southern Arkansas thought otherwise, defeating Anthony in the Democratic primary runoff and then electing a Republican in an election far out of line with local tradition.

For Anthony had become a symbol of insiders in an outsider year. From 1986 to 1990, he was picked by Speaker Jim Wright to chair the Democratic Congressional Campaign Committee, channeling PAC money to appropriate incumbents and serving as part of the Democratic leadership; he was a member of the Ways and Means Committee, always attentive to the interests of timber producers, which he and many southern Arkansans are. Then it turned out he had 109 overdrafts on the House bank, plus opposition from businessman Pat Pappas and Secretary of State Bill McCuen. In the primary, Anthony won only 40% to 31% for McCuen and 30% for Pappas; as John Brummett wrote in the *Arkansas Democrat-Gazette*, "Against an unknown and a joke, Anthony managed to get four in ten Democrats across southern Arkansas to vote for him." McCuen attacked the overdrafts and the congressional pay raise, and the National Rifle Association chimed in against Anthony; McCuen was attacked for raising his own pay and allegedly taking two female employees on a junket to Las Vegas. It was a battle between, the *Democrat-Gazette* said, "the kind of PACman who has turned a representative system into a sordid contest of monied interests" and "Arkansas's all-too-familiar Secretary of State . . . an appalling pol in his own right." McCuen won 51%–49%, despite Anthony's $1 million campaign chest.

All of which opened the way for Republican Jay Dickey. He is from Pine Bluff, where his uncle and grandfather were both state Senators; he caught polio in 1960, but recovered and became a top college tennis player, and runs 5K races today. Practicing law in Pine Bluff, Dickey represented the Arkansas Fox and Coon Hunters Association challenging state restrictions on running dogs; he won the case in the Arkansas Supreme Court and there are no restrictions on the running of dogs in Arkansas today. In the 1970s and 1980s, Dickey ran Baskin Robbins and Taco Bell franchises and formed an advertising sign company and a travel agency. He won the ordinarily worthless Republican nomination in 1992, and in the general attacked McCuen for his own record, noting a $324,000 no-bid contract on computers for his office. McCuen countered by charging that Dickey's pro-life views meant he condoned incest.

Dickey won with 52% of the vote, at which point McCuen challenged the result as produced by defective voting machinery, but the House Administration Committee dismissed the charges in March 1993. Dickey got seats on the Agriculture and Natural Resources Committees and— good for this franchise owner—a seat on Small Business. Democrats would like to recapture the seat and both McCuen and Pappas are possible candidates. Likelier is state Senator Jay Bradford from Pine Bluff: some Democrats in 1992 said they were voting for "Jay and Jay," Dickey in 1992 and Bradford in 1994. But Dickey has his own positive qualities, and may not be so easy to beat.

The People: Pop. 1990: 585,202; 52% rural; 16% age 65+; 72% White; 27% Black; 1% Hispanic origin. Voting age pop.: 429,410; 24% Black; 1% Hispanic origin. Households: 59% married couple families;

26% married couple fams. w. children; 30% college educ.; median household income: $19,621; per capita income: $9,723; median gross rent: $299; median house value: $39,900.

1992 Presidential Vote		1988 Presidential Vote	
Clinton (D)	134,692 (57%)	Bush (R)	110,078 (52%)
Bush (R)	73,891 (31%)	Dukakis (D)	98,524 (46%)
Perot (I)	23,677 (10%)		

Rep. Jay Dickey (R)

Elected 1992; b. Dec. 14, 1939, Pine Bluff; home, Pine Bluff; U. of AR, B.A. 1961, J.D. 1963; Methodist; divorced.

Career: Practicing atty., 1963–92; Pine Bluff City Atty., 1968–70; Small business and franchise owner, 1982–present.

Offices: 1338 LHOB 20515, 202-225-3772. Also 100 E. 8th St., #2521, Pine Bluff 71601, 501-536-3376; 100 Reserve, #201, Hot Springs 71913, 501-623-5800; and 100 S. Jackson, #201, El Dorado 71730, 501-624-1011.

Committees: *Agriculture* (15th of 19 R): Environment, Credit and Rural Development; General Farm Commodities; Specialty Crops and Natural Resources. *Natural Resources* (15th of 15 R): National Parks, Forests and Public Lands; Oversight and Investigations. *Small Business* (14th of 18 R): Minority Enterprise, Finance and Urban Development; Regulation, Business Opportunities and Technology.

Group Ratings and 102d Congress Votes: Newly Elected

Key Votes of the 103d Congress

1. Family Leave	AGN	2. Deficit Reduction	AGN	3. Stimulus Plan	AGN

Election Results

1992 general	Jay Dickey (R)	113,009	(52%)	($397,841)
	W. J. (Bill) McCuen (D)	102,918	(48%)	($357,911)
1992 primary	Jay Dickey (R), unopposed			
1990 general	Beryl F. Anthony, Jr. (D)	110,352	(72%)	($480,853)
	Roy Rood (R)	42,122	(28%)	($511)

CALIFORNIA

What's wrong with California? What has happened to the state where for so many years everything seemed to be going right? Those were questions almost everyone was asking as the recession of the early 1990s, relatively shallow nationwide, seemed to linger on and even deepen in the nation's most populous state. California, scarcely touched by the deeper recession of 1979–83, and whose economy generated hundreds of thousands of new jobs every year in the 1980s, suddenly found itself losing jobs, with the highest unemployment rate, over 9%, of any megastate; the state which had seen robust, in some areas fabulous, increases in real estate values, suddenly found them plummeting; the place to where so many Americans had come for more than a century seeking their dreams now seemed a nightmare. California has faced economic downturns before, most recently in the early 1970s, and has seen its economic underpinnings more seriously threatened as well: the defense builddown of the 1990s is nothing next to the demobilization that followed victory in the late 1940s, and in a state that seemed then far more dependent on military spending than it does today. But California never before appeared possessed by the sour spirit, the anger, the lack of confidence that is now the oft-articulated tone.

California was leaning toward pessimism even before the recession set in—even as the 1990 Census recorded 30 million Californians, a larger share of the nation's population than any state since 1870, with the highest living standards and highest productivity in the world, and an economy as technically advanced as any that has ever existed. But if its economy was growing, with a gross domestic product that would make it the sixth nation in the world, so also was crime, with the prison inmate population topping 100,000. And if California's growth produced glossy and stylish affluence, it was also based on a continuing flow of immigrants, the most recent living and working in conditions uncomfortably close to Third World levels. If California is famed for its pleasant weather and golden sunlight, its environment was bearing the imprint of rapid growth: air quality in the Los Angeles Basin, while far better than at its worst levels in the late 1960s, was still bad, with angry gray skies and smog obscuring the mountains, while traffic choked up freeways and major arteries not just during rush hour but around the clock.

But the most important cause of California's recent demoralization was the Los Angeles riot following the acquittal in April 1992 of Los Angeles police officers accused of beating Rodney King. America's only major urban riot in nearly a quarter-century, it occurred in a place where it was not supposed to happen—indeed, would not have happened, later analyses made clear, if Police Chief Darryl Gates had prepared his force to contain post-verdict violence and if Gates himself had not spent hours attending a political fundraiser as the riot broke out. And in fact the rioting was stopped rapidly—within 36 hours as compared to the four to seven day duration of late 1960s riots—when Governor Pete Wilson and President George Bush announced they were sending in large numbers of troops.

Blacks in the Los Angeles basin overall have high income levels by national standards, enabling many to move out of low-income South Central long since. The neighborhoods here are integrated—even South Central has large numbers of Hispanics of various origins. And blacks have a share in political power: Los Angeles has had a black mayor, Tom Bradley, since 1973, and many blacks hold high political office in a state that is only 7% black. In 1960s-style, Los Angeles civic leaders and politicians initially responded to the riot with big government and big business solutions, as if the problem were a lack of jobs in what was for a dozen years America's most bounteous local economy, or a lack of government spending in a state where public dollars spent per resident have long been among the nation's highest. But the politicians did the one thing they needed to do to make another riot less likely: hire a new black police chief, Willie Williams, with a mandate to stop the next riot before it starts.

California's economic collapse and moral dismay have been accompanied by a political revolution. From the election of Ronald Reagan as governor in 1966, up through early 1991, California voting behavior was steady and, in retrospect at least, predictable. Voters chose Republicans, usually seemingly boring middle-aged men, for their top political offices, while they chose Democrats, often baby boom liberals for legislature and Congress. In all these elections, voters were in effect ratifying the choices they made in the nation's last economic turmoil, when they passed property-tax-cutting Proposition 13 in 1978, elected Ronald Reagan president with a solid 53%–36% margin in 1980 and sealed their rejection of the politics of Governor Jerry Brown by defeating him 52%–45% when he ran for the Senate in 1982. The top races throughout the 1980s saw only one narrow victory for the Democrats and two landslide reelections of Republican executives. Ronald Reagan was reelected 58%–41% in 1984 and George Bush beat Michael Dukakis 51%–48%; George Deukmejian was elected governor 49%–48% over Tom Bradley in 1982 and reelected 61%–37%; Pete Wilson was elected senator 52%–45% in 1982, reelected 53%–44% in 1988 and then elected governor 49%–46% in 1990. The only statewide Democratic win was Senator Alan Cranston's capture of a fourth term in 1986 by a

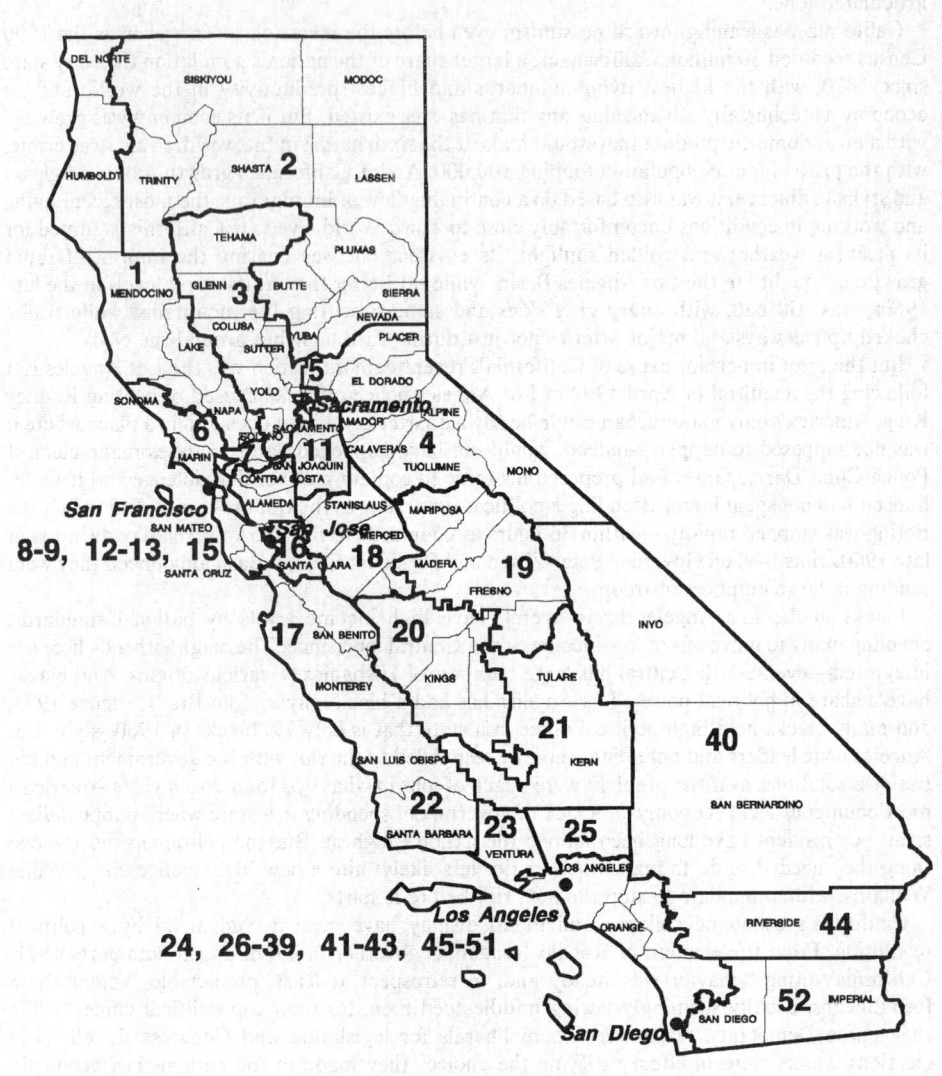

DEL NORTE
SISKIYOU
MODOC
HUMBOLDT
TRINITY
SHASTA
2
LASSEN
TEHAMA
PLUMAS
1
MENDOCINO
GLENN
BUTTE
3
SIERRA
COLUSA
NEVADA
LAKE
SUTTER
YUBA
PLACER
YOLO
5
EL DORADO
SONOMA
NAPA
Sacramento
ALPINE
SACRAMENTO
6
SOLANO
AMADOR
11
CALAVERAS
4
MARIN
SAN JOAQUIN
TUOLUMNE
MONO
CONTRA COSTA
San Francisco
ALAMEDA
STANISLAUS
MARIPOSA
8-9, 12-13, 15
SAN MATEO
San Jose
16
18
MADERA
19
SANTA CLARA
SANTA CRUZ
FRESNO
17
SAN BENITO
20
INYO
MONTEREY
KINGS
TULARE
21
40
SAN LUIS OBISPO
KERN
22
SAN BERNARDINO
SANTA BARBARA
23
25
VENTURA
LOS ANGELES
Los Angeles
24, 26-39, 41-43, 45-51
RIVERSIDE
44
ORANGE
52
IMPERIAL
San Diego
SAN DIEGO

Miles

0 20 40 60 80

50%–47% margin. Trends in party identification and registration worked for Republicans too: the number of registered Republicans rose from 3.4 million in 1978 to 5.1 million in 1990, while registered Democrats grew from 5.7 million to 6.4 million in the same period. Republicans signed up more than 60% of new registrants, while Democratic registration for the first time since 1934 fell below 50% for new voters.

But the congressional and legislative delegations stayed solidly Democratic, thanks largely to the redistricting plans concocted by Congressman Phillip Burton, who died in 1983, and also because of the superior political skills of a small band of Democratic incumbents and staffers and consultants concentrated in a few blocks of Sacramento. The Democrats voted for middle-class spending programs and maintained advantages sought by well-represented groups like labor unions, public employees and trial lawyers. The Republicans reduced or held down overall tax rates and solidly supported the Reagan defense buildup. So long as economic growth continued, the voters were happy. While Californians were busy at work, building new businesses, improvising child care arrangements and maintaining elaborate health regimens, they were assured that their taxes would be held down and government benefits held up. Perceived problems could be attacked, if not solved, by votes in referendums—in 1988 voters passed Proposition 98, which guaranteed 40% of the state budget for education, and Proposition 103, which mandated lower auto insurance rates. That the quality of public services was deteriorating—schools no longer taught the basics, freeways fell into disrepair, universities became playpens for aging 1960s radicals, welfare spawned a criminal underclass—was for a long time not appreciated. Neither was the non-inevitability of economic growth.

Then came the recession of 1990–91, not a massive drop by historic standards, but one which knocked down this state used to bounteous growth. California's population had been rising 2.6% each year in the 1980s, and its work force even faster; suddenly, instead of adding the 300,000 new jobs it needed every year to stay even with its population growth, it found itself losing some 700,000. This juddering shift saw demands on public services rise while state government revenues, contrary to expectations, fell sharply. Policies set by referenda and gridlock between the Republican governor and Democratic legislature prevented speedy governmental response. The state government eventually increased tax rates in 1991, which only deepened the recession and increased budget deficits; it cut spending somewhat in 1992, but only after a monumental months-long wrangle that dismayed a public for once following events in Sacramento.

The political response was a sharp move away from the Republicans and a rather tentative embrace of the Democrats. George Bush's vote collapsed from 51% in 1988 to 33% in 1992. That stunning drop echoed Californian's response to the last incumbent president with no California connections and no apparent feel for the state, Jimmy Carter, whose California vote declined from 48% to 36% in four years; Bill Clinton, perhaps taking a lesson, took his first post-election vacation in California. Bush's drop gave Clinton a solid 13% margin in California, but Ross Perot's 21% kept Clinton's percentage to only 46%, lower than Dukakis's 48% in 1988. Clinton ran even farther behind Dukakis in northern California outside the San Francisco Bay area, the fastest growing part of the state, where he led Bush by just 39%–36%. But Bush's collapse in southern California was devastating: he only barely carried Orange County, lost San Diego County and the fast-growing Inland Empire of San Bernardino-Riverside, and carried by 38%–35% an area he had carried 63%–36% four years earlier.

Democrats—Democratic women—did sweep California's two Senate races in 1992, a clear reversal of the Deukmejian and Wilson victories of 1982–90. Dianne Feinstein, fresh from a narrow loss for governor in 1990, ran far ahead of the man Pete Wilson appointed to fill his old Senate seat, Orange County state Senator John Seymour. Seymour seemed a sort of Wilson clone (personally colorless, pro-choice on abortion, pro-environment on the Coast, pro-agriculture in the Central Valley) but evoked no response, while Feinstein—pro-choice, pro-death penalty—did. Far closer was the battle of the extremes between far left Democrat Barbara Boxer and far right Republican Bruce Herschensohn. Herschensohn carried southern California, which casts 53% of the state's votes, but lost by 2–1 in the San Francisco Bay area, which casts 24%. Democrats also carried California's U.S. House races by a 52%–41%, producing a serious disappointment to Republicans: Wilson had expended much political capital on redistricting plans favorable for Republicans—actually, about equally favorable to both parties—and, with California gaining 7 seats from reapportionment, had fond hopes of converting the Democrats' 26–19 edge in the delegation to an even 26–26. Instead, Democrats gained a net four seats and Republicans a net three. Since the last presidential year, the Republican House vote fell from 44% to 41%; but the Democrats' share also fell, from 53% to 52%. Party registration showed a similar pattern. Republican registration grew from 5.1 million in 1990 to 5.6 million in 1992, but Democratic registration grew from 6.4 million to 7.4 million, the first time since the 1970s Democratic registration had grown at a larger rate. But Democratic registration still remained under the 50% mark, the lowest in 60 years, while Republican registration at 37% was higher than it had been as recently as 1984.

The move against the Republicans may be interpreted in many quarters, not least in Sacramento, as an endorsement of higher tax rates, more active government intervention in the economy and of California's litigation-prone workmen's compensation and tort law. But this is not an endorsement of Democrats' policies but rather a judgment that the Republicans have broken their promises—most of all, the promise of bounteous economic growth. For the Republicans had never carried the San Francisco Bay area nor won significant margins in the increasingly central-city-like Los Angeles County, where the higher than average populations of singles and gays, with their culturally liberal views, have consistently produced a leftish vote even in times of affluence. The biggest Republican losses came in the rest of southern California and in the Central Valley, where economic collapse and the resulting sharp decline in housing prices left voters with negative net worths and shattered dreams. Some may charge that this is a repudiation of Reaganism and the 1980s. But it could just as well be a reaction to the betrayal of Reaganism, to George Bush's and Pete Wilson's support of higher taxes in 1990 and 1991 which was followed by recession and job losses, the precise opposite of what followed Ronald Reagan's lower tax rates in 1980 and 1981. The question for the 1990s is whether the Democrats— President Bill Clinton and in California quite possibly Kathleen Brown, the state treasurer (and sister of Jerry Brown) who in early 1993 was far ahead of Pete Wilson in the 1994 gubernatorial race polls—can produce a governing formula as economically successful as Reagan's and can bridge California's and the nation's wide cultural divides.

For if economic collapse triggered the stampede away from the Republicans, the basic divisions between California's voters are rooted far more often in cultural attitudes than in economic status. This makes sense, in a state and nation where personal beliefs tend to endure while economic conditions change. The cultural division in California today follows a geographical division, not the historic north-south contrast, but the division which developed in the 1970s and 1980s between coast and inland. Coastal California, the big population gainer in the 1970s, tends toward cultural liberalism—the Big Sur coast or the Redwood Empire, San Francisco and Marin County or the west side of Los Angeles; this is the political strength of Jerry Brown (who carried only coastal congressional districts against Bill Clinton in the 1992 presidential primary) and of Democrats in general elections. But go inland, even a few miles, and the cultural climate changes as rapidly as the weather: this California is sunnier in summer, colder in winter, more arid; and from the Central Valley and Sierra Foothills to the San Ramon Valley, or the "Inland Empire" at east end of the Los Angeles basin around San Bernardino, Riverside and the desert beyond, this big growth area of the 1980s has attracted cultural conservatives. While coastal California protected itself from growth with environmental restrictions, new subdivisions and factories and cities proliferated inland. Inland California was the political bedrock for George Deukmejian, Pete Wilson and George Bush in 1988. This cultural politics turns partisan history on its head: the affluent coastal counties were solidly Republican as late as the 1960s while the dusty roads of the Central Valley and the inland industrial suburbs were the heartland of the Democratic Party that carried California for Lyndon Johnson in 1964, when Democrats like Governor Pat Brown stood for building highways and massive water systems and financing universities to uphold American values not deconstruct them.

Culturally, if no state is more diverse than California, no county is more diverse than Los Angeles County, which is to the America of 1990 what New York City was to the America of 1910: the great entry point for immigrants and the venue of their rapid upward mobility. It is also inevitably, as was New York, messy and disorganized, crime-ridden and anxiety-prone. During the 1980s, Los Angeles County's population zoomed upward, not typical behavior for a central city jurisdiction any time after World War II, but exactly what was happening to New York before World War I. Los Angeles now, like New York then, is the starting point not only of the immigrant but of the small-time entrepreneur—often the same person—who starts a small business in a garage, hires people just into town and sells the products out of a van, and makes enough money to expand the business and buy a home. Low-lying stucco buildings all over the Los Angeles basin house these businesses, run and staffed by Mexicans, Koreans, Vietnamese, Soviet Jews, Armenians and Iranians. This Los Angeles, like the great surging cities of the past—Dickens's London, Balzac's Paris or Dreiser's New York and Chicago—is not a comfortable place. Traffic is choking; the air has a sour, burnt look. Housing is cramped, with most people living in stucco houses in tightly-packed subdivisions or garden apartments on tiny plots of land that a midwesterner would find claustrophobic. There is increasingly a New Yorkish surliness and lack of neighborliness in daily life.

Los Angeles was hit badly by the 1990s recession and the 1992 riot, though not as badly as is widely thought. As Californian Joel Kotkin, author of *Tribes*, has pointed out, Los Angeles's boom was based less on big defense contractors than on small factories, less on highly visible tenants of downtown office towers than on the self-employed, who are more numerous than union members. In New York after the panic of 1907 immigration subsided, the pace of business slowed, unemployment and destitution seemed inevitable; yet the economy soon rallied again, and the fabulous, disorderly, clangorous growth continued which soon made New York the largest and richest city in the world. Something very much like that could happen in Los Angeles—and may be happening now. Demographically, the areas where blacks and recent Central American migrants rioted are a small part of LA County, far smaller than heavily Mexican East Los Angeles or affluent black Baldwin Hills where there was no rioting. The entrepreneurial impulse among Koreans, Armenians, Iranians, and many other newcomers remains vibrant; they have not looked to government for aid as Irish-Americans and African-Americans did historically. Indeed, Asians were the one voting bloc which moved toward the Republicans in 1992—perhaps a reaction to the post-riot impulse to provide aid for groups that produced the criminal behavior rather than the Asian-Americans who were often the victims of it. Massive government subsidies could demographically expand a dependent and criminal underclass here, as it has elsewhere. But government assistance could help small businesses in the greater industrial zone that runs from the eastern San Fernando Valley south through East Los Angeles toward Long Beach by, as Kotkin suggests, providing information about technical development and national and international markets.

While Los Angeles fills up with immigrants, the rest of southern California looks more like the Los Angeles of the 1940s: predominantly white, middle class, of midwestern origin, although with more Asians and Hispanics than East Coast experts usually imagine. Essentially, the old Los Angeles has grown out past the freeways into Orange County and the east end of the Los Angeles basin, and out into the desert, past the San Fernando Valley into Ventura County, down south of San Juan Capistrano and Camp Pendleton, where it merges with fast-growing San Diego. This is suburbia, but with 39% growth in the 1980s it had 8.2 million people in 1990, and cast 300,000 more votes than LA County in 1992. Until the early 1990s Southern California radiated the optimism, the somewhat innocent confidence and the know-how of its pioneers, contemporaries of its natural hero Ronald Reagan who came out here in hard times and created a new Middle America more tidy and square and cheerful than the original Middle America ever was. But as real estate prices crashed and two-earner families found themselves with four hour commutes each day to reach houses whose mortgages exceeded their market value, there seemed to be a loss of faith. Culturally, the younger generation here believes less in 1940s traditional values and more in simply leaving people alone; economically, they had lost the policies which produced the growth of the past. Even before the 1990s, the southern Californians who so strongly backed Reagan, like the Yankees who lost their ancient capital of Boston to a majority of Irish Catholics, saw their metropolis of Los Angeles increasingly become the home of people with different backgrounds and values. In 1992, southern California recoiled from George Bush and cast 24% of its votes for Ross Perot, more than any other region in the state. The only Republican with any following was 1992 Senate candidate Bruce Herschensohn, the conservative radio commentator who lives on Hollywood Boulevard but whose natural constituency is now far beyond the Los Angeles city limits; he carried southern California 52%–38% over Barbara Boxer, but that was not enough to win statewide. Southern California, dazed and disoriented, is surely up for grabs in 1994, and is an area where Republicans must reestablish a majority or consign themselves to minority status in the nation's largest state.

A very different cultural atmosphere animates the San Francisco Bay area. Here is an affluent high-tech civilization preoccupied with the physical environment and self-realization. The Bay area is environmentalist and dovish, but not much interested in income redistribution or helping the poor; this fifth largest American metropolitan area provides a conclusive refutation of Karl Marx's or Kevin Phillips's economic theories of politics, since it is arguably the richest of America's great metropolises and also one of the most Democratic. For years, not just San Francisco, but the East Bay and the Peninsula, attracted those who felt their personal lifestyles were not accepted elsewhere or who relished the atmosphere of counter-culture and revolt here that has roots in the turn of the century artists and writers and the Beat Generation of the 1950s—gays and perpetual graduate students, radicals and perennial rebels. Bill Clinton's biggest California margin among voters divided by education, for example, was not among the least educated, or high school graduates who might occupy blue-collar jobs; it was with those holding graduate degrees, who voted for Clinton over Bush by a 55%–27% margin—almost identical to Clinton's Bay area 55%–24% margin. California's Democratic base is made up less of blacks or factory workers than it is of teachers, lawyers, nurses, environmental enthusiasts and public sector administrators. Economic redistribution, however, has a limited appeal here: incomes and wealth, mostly in the form of residential real estate, are by national standards much too high. Also, the Bay Area is aware that its affluence depends heavily on commerce and on continued trade with the nation-states on the other side of the Pacific Rim; one of the complaints against George Bush when he went to Japan in December 1991 was that he took along not Silicon Valley entrepreneurs who have proved they can beat the Japanese but Detroit automakers who for years have sought protection against them. Anti-Japanese appeals may work in the industrial Midwest, but not in California, where trade is important and 10% of the people are of Asian descent.

The Bay Area now has the burden of having its favored politicians prevail in elections. San Francisco's Speaker Willie Brown, though prohibited by the 1990 term limits initiative from running again after 1994, is as strong as ever in Sacramento; while in early 1993 Pete Wilson seemed discredited and likely to lose to Kathleen Brown, who grew up in San Francisco; they too will be judged, as George Bush was, on results. So will Senator Dianne Feinstein, a major figure in San Francisco politics for 20 years, and Senator Barbara Boxer, the personification of Marin County's trendy liberalism. So also will Bill Clinton, about whom the Bay Area seemed just a little standoffish. His 55% of the vote here was lower than Michael Dukakis's 58%, and recalls the fact that Jimmy Carter only barely carried the Bay Area in 1976, before losing it to Ronald Reagan in 1980: this is one part of America where a suburban agnostic is more trusted than a Southern Baptist.

The fastest-growing parts of California in recent years have been the parts least known to most Americans. If Los Angeles is the nation's second largest media market and San Francisco the fourth, the media markets of Sacramento and Fresno in the Central Valley, if added together, would be the ninth; there are as many people in the Central Valley as in Wisconsin or Tennessee.

There is also in inland California some of the cultural conservatism found in those Middle American states. New migrants here tend to be young families fleeing from the smoggy outer reaches of the Los Angeles basin, with its crime-ridden freeways and drug-infested public schools, for the cleaner and culturally more traditional climes of the old Mother Lode country in the foothills of the Sierra, in the growing Sacramento area, and parts of the vast Central Valley. They are pro-choice on abortion but also almost unanimously for capital punishment and strongly against gun control. They provided key votes for Republicans in 1982–90, but gave pluralities to Bill Clinton, Dianne Feinstein and Democrats running for the House in 1992.

Can all these Californias be held together? Can they grow again? If history is any guide, the answer to both questions is yes. For California has always been culturally diverse, since its early pioneer days when its rulers were named Pio Pico and Mariano Vallejo, and 20% of its residents were Chinese indentured servants, and it has always been a place of economic vitality and creativity. Legend has it that California grew because of blind luck, and it was built by big units; it did have its U.S. beginnings in the Gold Rush of 1849 when San Francisco grew from nothing to one of the largest American cities in one year. And California was given its shape by big units: the Southern Pacific Railroad, the giant agribusiness combines who controlled the vast Central Valley acreage, giant engineering projects like the Los Angeles Aqueduct and the California water plan of the 1960s, huge aircraft factories and shipyards and steel plants built to win World War II. These large entities created a framework in which individuals could work, innovate and prosper, inventing their own styles and technologies, new economies and lifestyles. Compare today's California with that of the 1940s, when there were just 7 million Californians, when it was always convertible weather and no one had yet named smog. "California is an island," Carey McWilliams wrote then: America's lightly populated outpost on the Pacific, thousands of miles across plains, mountains and desert from thickly settled parts of the country, separated from hostile Japan only by the open waters of the ocean.

Then came the explosive change of World War II, when California became one of the great defense industry states, making steel and aluminum for the first time, building ships and airplanes by the thousands. Millions of Americans came here and millions stayed. California's economy was expected to collapse when the big firms shut down after the war; instead, as Jane Jacobs points out, one-eighth of all the new jobs in the nation in the late 1940s were created in metro Los Angeles. This small scale growth, multiplied thousands of times over, made California into the nation's most populous state. And so Los Angeles in the 20th Century became a great city, the nation's second greatest, with 14.8 million people, behind New York's 19.3 million but well ahead of Chicago's 8.3 million and Washington/Baltimore's 6.8 million, not so much because of geography (LA has no natural harbor and had to build one) or natural resources (it once exported oil, but has imported it since the 1940s) or its historical eminence (Los Angeles had 102,000 people in 1900), but because people wanted it to be.

The California of the 1940s was a Midwestern Yankee commonwealth: a Mission veneer with a solid Yankee core. The California of the 1990s, in many ways the pacesetter of American culture, is a Pacific nation-state, in some ways resembling that other Pacific nation of similar geographic size and even greater population, in the seismically active interstices between ocean and mountains and wasteland: Japan. Like Japan, California is economically creative, affluent and hard-working, possessing a certain bloodless competence, with an air of nonchalance about its own excellence. Like Japan, California has been a profoundly apolitical commonwealth: Californians, like Japanese, have delegated the conduct of their government to a few faceless leaders and a gaggle of factional politicians who service local constituencies and do their real business largely unnoticed in remote government buildings. After years of growth, in early 1993 California and Japan were both mired in recessions, with unemployment up and real estate prices sharply down, with confidence in the economy low and anger at politicians suddenly high.

But California has strengths Japan cannot claim. Its infrastructure of freeways, water systems and airports are superior to Japan's. Its universities and high-tech firms are far ahead in basic research. Its small business sector is more robust and adaptable. Most important, while Japan believes in racial unity and cultural uniformity, California may well be the most multifaceted society on earth. The 1990 Census recorded that 7% of Californians were black, 10% Asian and 26% Hispanic: huge California is more Hispanic than any state but New Mexico, more Asian than any state but Hawaii. And while some predict a Third World majority in California, what is actually happening is that new migrants are eager to learn American ways even as they, like earlier immigrants, add zest to American culture—fajitas and sashimi and tofu to go with hamburgers and pizza and bagels and bean sprouts. California's openness attracts talented young people without pedigree or privilege, ready to leap to success, and a low-wage labor force ready to produce in America goods and services that high-wage countries like Japan or Germany must purchase from others.

But Californians tend to take this openness, like they do so many of their strengths, for granted, while focusing too intensely on its faults and weaknesses. After the 1989 Loma Prieta earthquake, Californians focused on the deaths on the Nimitz Freeway and the collapse of 1915-era buildings in San Francisco's Marina district; less noted was that the overwhelming majority of buildings and structures withstood the quake, which would have killed hundreds of thousands in a country with Third World construction standards. To grow again, and to live reasonably comfortably together, Californians need more than anything else to appreciate California's strengths and achievements, and the good fortune that places them in arguably the most tolerant and productive society in history; and they need to honor by emulation the many people whose anonymous and unglamorous efforts have built this commonwealth from a wilderness into the most desired destination in the world in just half a dozen generations. It can work again.

Governor. At the pinnacle of California politics, or perhaps it would be better to say at the precipice, is Governor Pete Wilson. In 1991, all seemed before him: if he appeared dull and colorless, "smooth and cool and opaque, like a stone in a river," the *Los Angeles Times*'s Ronald Brownstein says, he was also the man who in two successive election years won the largest number of votes for U.S. senator in history and then was elected governor of the nation's largest state. He seemed well adapted to a state that wanted Republican executives who would not let government grow too much but also a leader who would use government a bit more actively than it had. But when the economic crunch hit, Wilson wound up with the worst of both political worlds—too confrontational and conservative to please most Democrats, too compromising and committed to government action to please many Republicans, too much in the center of controversy and confusion to please most voters. Wilson has made some progress toward his political goals, but at great political cost; he has not made much progress in reforming government, and could be running out of time unless the state's economy perks up and his fortunes rebound.

Wilson, like so many Californians, grew up back east; he came to Camp Pendleton as a Marine and Boalt Hall in Berkeley as a law student, and settled in San Diego. He was elected to the Assembly in 1966 and became mayor of San Diego in 1971; there he was known as a problem solver and moderate, supporting Gerald Ford over Ronald Reagan in 1976, opposing Proposition 13 in 1978. He ran for governor in 1978, and finished fourth in the primary with 9%, about the San Diego media market's share of the statewide vote. In 1982, he ran for senator, beating Jerry Brown in the general, unpopular as he was leaving the governorship amid charges he refused to use harmless pesticides to subdue the citrus-destroying Mediterranean fruit fly. In the Senate Wilson opposed coastal oil drilling, but favored agribusiness positions inland. He enthusiastically backed the Reagan defense buildup, and took up the role of defending California interests Alan Cranston let slip while running for president in 1983. Wilson was reelected rather routinely in 1988, over Lieutenant Governor Leo McCarthy. Then, in early 1989, Governor George Deukmejian announced he was retiring after two tax-cutting, low-headline terms, and Republican leaders, fearful of giving complete redistricting control to the Democrats once again, turned to Wilson as their one proven statewide candidate.

Meanwhile, the Democrats had a primary between Attorney General John Van de Kamp and former San Francisco Mayor Dianne Feinstein. Van de Kamp took the most liberal stands, backing legislator and onetime 1960s radical Tom Hayden's "Big Green" environmental initiative and opposing capital punishment; Feinstein stressed her support of abortion rights and the death penalty. Van de Kamp's support of term limits enraged Speaker Willie Brown, while Feinstein's first 30-second ad recalled how she took charge when Mayor George Moscone and Supervisor Harvey Milk were murdered in 1978; she won 52%–41%, and was immediately hailed as a possible presidential candidate. In the general, Wilson and Feinstein sounded similar: pro-choice and pro-death penalty, pro-defense spending and against offshore oil drilling. Both advanced attractive proposals to do something about the problems of children: Feinstein favored universal pre-kindergarten, Wilson wanted to put social services in the schools. Wilson was helped by backing term limits, which passed 52%–48% on party lines; Feinstein was hurt by backing "Big Green," which lost 64%–36%. In the lowest turnout since 1912, Wilson beat Feinstein 49%–46%, losing 58%–37% in the Bay area but winning 53%–42% in the rest of the state; Feinstein carried counties only in the San Francisco media market and on the coast, losing badly inland. This was Wilson's third solid statewide victory against serious opposition in just eight years, a feat not equalled since Hiram Johnson in the 1910s.

Wilson entered office hoping to mend a public sector in disrepair. California schools, once a national model, were performing poorly, not providing the ladder upward for children of 1980s migrants that they had for those of the 1950s migrants; freeways and transportation systems were jammed and, in the case of the Nimitz Freeway that collapsed in the 1989 earthquake, obsolete; police officers seemed unable to stop gang violence in Los Angeles and other metro areas. Persistent drought from 1990 through 1992 accentuated a mood of discontent, and pointed to the weaknesses of California's water systems. Wilson sought cooperation from the Democratic legislative majorities for his "preventive government" policies—prenatal care, drug treatment for pregnant women, mental health counseling in schools—even as he used his veto to fight the Democrats on redistricting. But with the sharp economic downturn, expected revenues evaporated, producing a $14 billion budget gap. Wilson responded by agreeing with the legislature to raise taxes $7 billion (including a sales tax on snack foods and candy: Californians' faith in health food written into law) and cut spending $4.8 billion. This infuriated conservative Republicans, who booed Wilson at their state convention, without taking the hard edge off Democrats' opposition; the legislature passed a gay rights bill which Wilson vetoed as overly stringent, arousing angry responses from gays, even as he attacked "gay-bashing bigots" which angered many cultural conservatives. Wilson and term limits were threatening the legislative Democrats' hegemony in Sacramento, where they control access to most campaign funds, employ brilliant political consultants and groom staffers to run for vacant seats; they continue despite unpopular policies to control the legislature in large part because they are the voters' only source of information about state politics (no Los Angeles or San Francisco TV station has a Sacramento bureau). But in some ways the Democrats reflect public opinion: veteran legislator John Vasconcellos was ridiculed nationally for starting a task force on "self-esteem," but legislative Democrats' insistence on maintaining a workmen's compensation law which included awards for psychological loss, supported by lawyers who benefit from such cases, is evidence of a sense of entitlement to complete self-esteem—a sort of feel-good guarantee that is very expensive for the private sector but which gives politicians electoral rewards.

Caught between angry conservatives and obdurate liberals, his job rating plunging to a record low, Wilson started California-bashing. Focusing on workmen's compensation, he charged that doing business in California was uneconomic and that immigrants were costing the state increasing amounts for education and welfare. There was force to his argument, but Wilson's pessimistic analysis combined with higher taxes helped dissipate the optimism that had enabled California to respond to economic change in the past. The recession lingered on into 1992, whereupon Wilson admitted that the 1991 tax increase had been a mistake. He fought the legislature into late August, even forcing the state to issue IOUs instead of paychecks, to successfully prevent a tax increase and cut welfare spending by $1.7 billion and education by $2.2 billion. He signed a gay rights bill, without the criminal penalties he criticized before. He modulated his critical rhetoric, and started stressing California's strengths, but he still fared poorly with the voters. His hopes of gains from redistricting were dashed: Democrats gained four seats and Republicans only three in the U.S. House, while Willie Brown's Democrats actually gained a seat in the Assembly by shrewdly exploiting the abortion issue in Wilson's own San Diego. Wilson's hand-picked successor in the Senate, John Seymour, lost by a wide margin to Dianne Feinstein, while the very un-Wilson-like Republican running for the other seat, Bruce Herschensohn, ran better though still lost. Wilson's welfare referendum, considered a sure winner earlier in the year, lost 47%–53%. Hailed as a future presidential candidate when he first took office, Wilson looked very much like a lame duck governor two years later.

For all the discontent, however, there seems little prospect for sharp changes in public policy. Wilson's 1993 budget called for an 11% spending cut and no tax increases; there was still little money left for his positive governmental programs of 1990. His likeliest Democratic opponent, Treasurer Kathleen Brown, decried the 1992 legislative gridlock and criticized Wilson's tactics. But her public policies sound very much like what Wilson (and Feinstein) were calling for in 1990: she sees a need to invest in education, infrastructure, and the environment; from the federal government she wants a short-term economic stimulus, money for retraining defense and other workers, and a targeted capital gains tax cut. She sees California's "sunshine" industries, its position on the Pacific and Latin Rims and its openness to new ideas as its great assets. Like Wilson, she seems to be counting on growth, and hoping she won't have to answer, as he did, the hard question of whether and how much to increase taxes and cut spending if the economy still fails to generate necessary revenues. She surely noted that California voters seemed leery of higher taxes in 1992: by 67%–33% they repealed the snack tax, while by 59%–41% they rejected the Democrats' soak-the-rich tax initiative; by 69%–31% they rejected an initiative to place more healthcare costs on business. Kathleen Brown is, of course, the sister of Jerry Brown and daughter of Pat Brown; members of her family served as governor 16 of the 24 years from 1958 to 1982. But, as she remarks, it is obvious they are different: where Jerry Brown is provocative and angry, Kathleen Brown is agreeable and humorous; though he is a bachelor at 55, she is a grandmother at 47; while he downplayed their father's spending on great water projects, freeways, and universities, she (like Wilson) cites them as guides if not precise prescriptions for the future. As state treasurer, Brown has the power once accumulated by her father's longtime adversary, Speaker and Treasurer Jesse Unruh—control of an investment portfolio of $20 billion—making her a major factor on Wall Street as well as Sacramento's J Street.

Brown's likeliest primary opponent is John Garamendi, longtime state senator elected insurance commissioner in 1990; this is a new post created by Ralph Nader's Proposition 103, and Garamendi has used it to oppose insurance rate increases, and not in total ignorance of the political usefulness of such a record. He chaired the 1992 delegation to the Democratic convention (Kathleen Brown was for her brother Jerry, who lost California narrowly to Bill Clinton); his wife Patty Garamendi has narrowly lost races for the state Senate and for Congress.

Whoever is elected governor, California state government is likely to remain in deadlock. The policies of the Democratic legislature, on tort law, workmen's compensation, education and taxes, will continue to burden the state's private sector economy; and will probably be opposed to some extent by Brown or Garamendi as they were by Wilson. The legislature's Republicans, fractious and untested in power, seem nowhere near able to govern. And any governor's ideas of refurbishing and reforming the public sector may prove too expensive for state government's strained budget. This is in many ways America's ablest state government. But Sacramento's self-perpetuation in power, and the voters' response of policymaking by referendum, have produced this unhappy picture in what should be one of America's happiest states.

Senators. California made some history in 1992, by electing two women to the United States Senate for the first time ever—and, by electing two Democrats, changing its own political preference sharply from 1980–90. That two seats were open was the result of the retirement, under the cloud of the Keating Five scandal, of four-term Democrat Alan Cranston and the replacement of Pete Wilson by his 22-month appointee, Orange County state Senator John

Seymour. For most of two years the nation's largest state was represented by a lame duck and an unelected senator who ranked number 100 in seniority. Now for two years California is represented by two Jewish women from the San Francisco Bay area, from different quarters of the Democratic Party and opposite ends of the Golden Gate Bridge.

Twenty years ago, Dianne Feinstein was a member of the San Francisco County Board of Supervisors, a moderate Democrat whose training was in criminology, appointed by Governor Pat Brown to the women's parole board in 1960; now she is the United States senator elected with the largest vote in American history. In between, her government service has been entirely in San Francisco, the increasingly leftish city where she was a force for moderation, backing more police and the death penalty, vetoing a gay marriage ordinance and opposing commercial rent control. In taking over as mayor after the murders of Mayor George Moscone and Supervisor Harvey Milk in 1978, she showed steadiness and a sense of command that calmed the city. In 1984, Walter Mondale seriously considered her for vice president, passing over her for Geraldine Ferraro because of qualms about her husband Richard Blum's business dealings. Feinstein went on to preside over the San Francisco convention ably, while it was Ferraro who juggled questions about the family business. In fact, Feinstein and Blum's investments have thrived, and *Roll Call* estimated their net worth in 1993 at $40 million, the sixth highest in Congress. Ineligible for a third full term as mayor in 1987, Feinstein looked for an office to run for, running creditably for governor in 1990. When Seymour was appointed by Wilson in January 1991, Feinstein quickly announced for his seat, even though the 1992 race was for only the last two years of the term; evidently she hoped to forestall serious primary competition, and almost did, as most other serious Democrats focused on the race for the six-year seat being vacated by Alan Cranston.

In retrospect, it is hard to see why Wilson appointed Seymour, and passed over interesting possibilities like Condolezza Rice, a black Stanford professor and National Security Council Russia expert, or Hispanic Orange County Supervisor Gaddi Vasquez: probably because Seymour was pro-choice and fiscally conservative, a sort of Wilson clone. But Seymour had a bit of flair—a former mayor of Anaheim, home of Disneyland, he always wore a Mickey Mouse watch. But he had also recently flip-flopped on several issues, inviting charges of opportunism: he switched from pro-life to pro-choice on abortion for his 1990 statewide campaign, he switched to oppose offshore oil drilling after the March 1989 Exxon *Valdez* oil spill, he became fiercely interested in agricultural issues only when he took on statewide office. Also, he had lost the primary for lieutenant governor in 1990—not very auspicious. Seymour was challenged in the 1992 primary by fellow Orange Countian, Congressman William Dannemeyer, a crusader against what he calls the homosexual lobby on AIDS and other issues, who has a sort of crazed look in his eyes even when he says things that turn out to be right; Seymour won by an unimpressive 51%–27% margin, barely carrying Orange County. Meanwhile, Feinstein came in solidly (58%–33%) ahead of state Controller Gray Davis, who ran a spot focusing on her apparent violations of campaign finance laws in 1990 and comparing her to Leona Helmsley. The collapse of Republican support may have hurt Seymour, but the fact is that the standings in Seymour-Feinstein poll pairings scarcely changed during the two years of campaigning. Seymour brought up some tough issues which might have hurt a candidate about whom voters had some hesitation: Feinstein's arguably tricky financing of her 1990 gubernatorial campaign (which resulted in a $190,000 fine), her dodging of many opportunities to debate, alleged conflicts of interests from Blum's investments. Seymour tried to exploit fears of immigration and insisted on an amendment to the anti-riot bill barring aid to those who have committed crimes. He shamelessly carried the ball for big California interests: Central Valley agribusiness, southern California defense contractors, opponents of vast wilderness areas in the desert. But nothing worked. Feinstein's negatives were fairly high, but she won 54%–38%. She carried Los Angeles County (59%–34%) almost as well as the Bay Area (68%–27%) and only barely lost the South (44%–47%), while carrying the rest of the state.

In the Senate, Feinstein got seats on Appropriations, where she can funnel money to

California, and Judiciary, where she is one of the women Chairman Joseph Biden sought to spare him the flak he got for allowing cross-examination of Anita Hill. On Judiciary, Feinstein was among the toughest cross-examiners of Attorney General nominee Zoe Baird. Much has been made of the contrast between left-liberal Barbara Boxer and not-always-liberal Dianne Feinstein, and on criminal law issues and the death penalty Feinstein is not an automatic liberal vote. But she is "100% pro-choice" and a solid backer of the feminist agenda. She opposed the Gulf war resolution; she came out against the North American Free Trade Agreement; she seems to have few qualms about higher taxes; and so on most Senate issues she is likely to be formidably on the left. Formidable: Feinstein has a tough, even prosecutorial demeanor; she is an eloquent and aggressive speaker; she is ready to take on erstwhile allies as well as adversaries. She will certainly be occupied with raising the huge sums needed for her 1994 race for a full six-year term. But Republicans will have a hard time finding a serious opponent unless there is a noted upturn in the party's fortunes, and a revulsion to the Democrats capable of producing victory for quiet Republicans as in 1980–90. Otherwise, Feinstein may break the record, held by Pete Wilson, for the largest number of votes won by a U.S. senator in a non-presidential year.

   California's other Senate seat is held by one of the emblematic figures of American politics of the 1990s, Barbara Boxer. A dozen years ago, she was a member of the Board of Supervisors in Marin County, the terminally trendy suburbs north of San Francisco and the Golden Gate Bridge. Then, in 1982, she won the House seat gerrymandered by Congressman Phillip Burton for his brother John Burton, who then announced he was retiring from Congress because of alcohol and drug problems (Phil Burton died in 1983 and John Burton is now a happy and healthy member of the California Assembly, which he always liked better than Congress). Boxer's record was by some measures the most leftist in the House: she voted for more dollars in federal spending than any other member in the early 1990s, and she denounced the Gulf war resolution with more ardor than probably any other member. She has a flair for the memorable gesture and the unforgettable metaphor: in 1984, as co-chair of a military reform caucus, she disclosed that the Air Force had paid $7,622 for a coffee pot; in 1991, when Senate Judiciary members were reluctant to have Anita Hill testify against the Supreme Court nomination of Clarence Thomas, Boxer led a bipartisan squadron of female House members over to protest, quite against precedent and decorum, on the Senate side of the Capitol. Now, after winning an election that featured heated primaries on both sides and a fiercely fought general election in which no one won an absolute majority, she has a seat in the Senate herself.

   In the process, Barbara Boxer came out ahead of half a dozen of California's leading politicians. Some dropped out early: Sacramento Congressman Robert Matsui decided early in 1991 not to run, and Jerry Brown, after leading in initial polls, decided in late 1991 to run for president instead. That left as the early favorite Lieutenant Governor Leo McCarthy, the nominee against Pete Wilson in 1988, a personable and articulate liberal who was speaker of the Assembly from 1974 to 1980 and counted on positive name identification for a plurality. Another candidate was Congressman Mel Levine, part of the Westside Los Angeles "Berman-Waxman machine"—actually a group of politicians gathered around Congressmen Henry Waxman and Howard Berman who raise large sums of Westside money and spend it on simple TV ads and complexly targeted direct mailings. Levine campaigned as the only Democrat who backed the Gulf war resolution and he took a tough stand after the LA riot, insisting that the first duty of government is to maintain order. But these apparently repelled liberal Westside and Bay Area voters, though Levine did carry the riot areas themselves, where black voters supported not the rioters but those who had tried to stop them. For the women and liberals who make up the majority of Democratic primary voters, 1992 was indeed the year of the woman, and Barbara Boxer did well—despite having 143 overdrafts on the House bank, despite her refusal to appear in debates and her wobbly performance before any but sympathetic audiences. Boxer did not have a majority, but her 44% was enough for a solid win; McCarthy won 31%, with name identification holding him up even in the Inland Empire and Central Valley, where his liberal stands were not popular; Levine had only 22%, running strongest in South Central LA.

The Republican primary was a battle of two very different types. One was Tom Campbell, law professor at Stanford and two-term Congressman from Silicon Valley, free market economist and cultural liberal. The other was Bruce Herschensohn, Los Angeles TV and radio commentator, Nixon speechwriter and Reagan enthusiast, backer of a flat tax and offshore oil drilling and opponent of abortion. To this sublime clash of opposites was added the almost ridiculous candidacy of Sonny Bono, known best from his days in the mid-1960s with Cher, more recently the mayor of Palm Springs. But Bono's liberal stands on cultural issues took votes away from Campbell and his 17% of the vote was decisive: Campbell got 36% to Herschensohn's 38%. This was a reversal of Herschensohn's 1986 37%–30% primary loss to Silicon Valley Congressman Ed Zschau; this time, there were no other strong conservatives in the field, and Herschensohn not only carried Los Angeles and the South but came close to carrying northern California outside the Bay Area. Herschensohn also came fairly close to winning an upset in the general. This was a genuine battle of the extremes—or at least of such extremes as thrive within American electoral politics. Herschensohn ran an effective ad attacking Boxer for charging the government $1,565 for limousine service to the airport; at the same time, his own gentle, friendly persona ("part basset hound, part pixie," in George Will's words) contrasted with Boxer's avoidance of unguarded public appearances. In the end, the race may have been decided by a personal smear: state Democratic political director Bob Mulholland disrupted a Herschensohn campaign appearance and charged that Herschensohn had attended a nude dance club; Mulholland then was suspended without pay until after Boxer won. Herschensohn was the only Republican who rallied a big margin in the South outside LA County, and ran well enough there to carry southern California as a whole; he also carried the North outside the Bay Area. But he lost the Bay Area 61%–30%, and lost statewide 48%–43%.

As a senator, Boxer was reluctant to serve on the Judiciary Committee she had set out to storm, and got seats on Budget, Banking, and Environment and Public Works instead. She can be expected to be as solidly on the left of the Senate as she was in the House. Her strong convictions and flair for the dramatic make her a prime candidate for TV sound bites.

Presidential politics. The nation's largest state likes to be at the center of presidential politics. It likes having a Californian president who seems in touch with the state. These are natural feelings for residents of a state which is conscious of its vast demographic and economic heft and yet somehow, 2,400 miles from the nation's capital and its largest city, senses that its fellow U.S. citizens don't pay it much heed and don't understand the vast changes that have made California so successful and also so stressed. And so California tends to vote for Californians for president: for Richard Nixon three times, for Ronald Reagan twice (three times in Republican primaries). But when California feels it is being ignored by an incumbent president, it reacts with cold fury and unambiguous rejection, regardless of party. In 1980, Jimmy Carter got only 36% of the vote here; in 1992, George Bush got only 33%, the worst for any major party nominee since Alf Landon in 1936.

These are breathtaking results, and had devastating repercussions for California Democrats in 1980 and California Republicans in 1992. They can be explained partly by the recession, and by the shocking drop in real estate values in many parts of the state; they can be explained partly by Bush's cultural conservatism and appeals to the religious right; but they are also the result of a sense of neglect. When Bush went to Japan, Californians complained, he didn't even stop here or take businessmen who know the Pacific Rim and compete there; instead he brought whining auto executives from Detroit! The collapse of support for Bush and Carter in California suggest why Bill Clinton's first post-campaign appearance was in the Glendale Galleria and his first post-election vacation in two Hollywood producers' oceanfront home in Summerland, near Santa Barbara. They suggest why Clinton placed Apple Computer CEO John Sculley prominently at his economic summit and State of the Union address. Clearly Clinton does not want his Arkansas-Tennessee ticket to get rejected in 1996 as his predecessors' were in 1992 and 1980. And he must hope he will not have a California opponent then, as indeed seems unlikely, unless Pete Wilson can rally and win reelection convincingly in 1994.

California also has its nose a bit out of joint about the irrelevance of its last-in-the-nation presidential primary (actually, North Dakota voted a week later in 1992, but who cares?). California's early June primary was critical in the Democrats' 1968 and 1972 contests; since 1976, it has not really mattered on either side. In 1992, George Bush won handily with 74%, but that was evidence only of Pat Buchanan's weakness. Bill Clinton beat Jerry Brown in his home state, 47%–40%, carrying all of inland California and some of the coast; but Clinton would have been nominated easily even if California had gone the other way. Brown's popularity was greatest with the youngest voters, who have little memory of his governorship, which ended in 1982; his alleged flip-flopping on Proposition 13, his refusal to spray pesticides on the citrus-eating medfly, the anti-capital punishment dogmatism of his appointee Chief Justice Rose Bird—all left many voters with a residue of bad feeling for this obviously very talented and able politician. For them, his pose as a root-and-branch reformer, after his governorship and his 1989–90 stint as a Democratic state fundraising chairman, was not convincing.

Congressional districting. Never has more hinged on redistricting than in California in 1992. California now has 52 congressional districts, the most in history (the previous record of 45 was held by New York in 1932–50 and California in 1982–90), and its geography gives great leeway for extracting political advantage. The 1982 plan drawn by Congressman Phillip Burton, revised slightly for 1984–90, had enabled the Democrats to hold firm command of the state delegation (26–19 going into the 1992 elections) despite a shaky hold on state voters. (This was not the first partisan districting plan: California's 1970s and 1960s plans were drawn up to help Democrats, the 1950s and 1940s plans to help Republicans.) And the California House delegation is ideologically split as in no other large state: the Democrats, with few exceptions, are among the most liberal members of their party on all issues; the Republicans, with hardly any exceptions, are among the most conservative on their side.

The key decisions for the 1990s California districting were made by the voters in 1990 and 1986. In 1990 they elected Republican Governor Pete Wilson, thus depriving Democrats of the untrammeled control they had over redistricting in 1982 and 1962. In 1986, they voted out of office Chief Justice Rose Bird and two other Jerry Brown-appointed justices, thus turning over control of the California Supreme Court to Republican appointees. In 1991, there was much huffing and puffing in Sacramento over redistricting, as Speaker Willie Brown put blandishments before Republicans in hopes of winning enough votes to override a Wilson veto; but none prevailed. Meanwhile, Wilson held solid to his plan to appoint a redistricting commission to draw up plans for Congress and the legislature, and then handed them over to the state Supreme Court, which in January 1992 adopted them. In fact, the plan is more evenhanded than a Republican redistricter of, say, Phil Burton's abilities would have concocted. The lines are far more regular than in the ultrapartisan plan passed in Texas by the Democrats (this decade's winner of the Burton award). The districts tend to center around municipalities, with relatively regular boundaries comprehensible to California's not very civic-minded citizens. They include no black-majority districts (California is only 7% black, and the Los Angeles area's former black ghettos are now heavily Hispanic) seven Hispanic-majority districts (though in at least three few Hispanics are registered to vote and the congressmen's names are Dooley, Berman, and Dornan). They include five districts that are 20% or more Asian (but these are not the districts that elect the state's two Japanese American and one Korean-American congressmen).

The People: Est. Pop. 1992: 30,857,000; Pop. 1990: 29,760,021, up 3.6% 1990–1992. 12.0% of U.S. total, 1st largest; 7% rural. Median age: 31.5 years. 10.5% 65 years and over. 69.0% White, 25.8% Hispanic origin, 9.6% Asian, 7.4% Black, 13.2% Other. Households: 52.7% married couple families; 26% married couple fams. w. children; 54% college educ.; median household income: $35,798; per capita income: $16,409; 55.6% owner occupied housing; median house value: $195,500; median monthly rent: $561. 9.1% Unemployment. Voting age pop.: 22,009,296. Registered voters (1992): 15,101,473; 7,410,914 D (49%); 5,593,555 R (37%); 2,097,204 unaffiliated and minor parties (14%).

Political Lineup: Governor, Pete Wilson (R); Lt. Gov., Leo T. McCarthy (D); Secy. of State, March Fong Eu (D); Atty. Gen., Daniel E. Lungren (R); Treasurer, Kathleen Brown (D); Controller, Gray Davis (D). State Senate, 40 (23 D, 15 R, and 2 I); State Assembly, 80 (48 D, 31 R, and 1 vacancy). Senators, Dianne Feinstein (D) and Barbara Boxer (D). Representatives, 52 (30 D and 22 R).

1992 Presidential Vote

Clinton (D)	5,121,249	(46%)
Bush (R)	3,630,566	(33%)
Perot (I)	2,296,004	(21%)

1992 Democratic Presidential Primary

Clinton	1,359,112	(47%)
Brown	1,150,460	(40%)
Tsongas	212,522	(7%)
Other	141,515	(5%)

1988 Presidential Vote

Bush (R)	5,054,917	(51%)
Dukakis (D)	4,702,233	(48%)

1992 Republican Presidential Primary

Bush	1,587,369	(74%)
Buchanan	568,892	(26%)

GOVERNOR

Gov. Pete Wilson (R)

Elected 1990, term expires Jan. 1995; b. Aug. 23, 1933, Lake Forest, IL; home, San Diego; Yale, B.A. 1955, U. of CA at Berkeley, J.D. 1962; Protestant; married (Gayle).

Career: Marine Corps, 1955–58; Practicing atty., 1963–66; CA Assembly, 1966–71, Minority Whip, 1967–69; San Diego Mayor, 1971–83; U.S. Senate, 1983–90.

Office: State Capitol Bldg., Sacramento 95814, 916-445-2841.

Election Results

1990 gen.	Pete Wilson (R)	3,791,904	(49%)
	Dianne Feinstein (D)	3,525,197	(46%)
	Other	383,316	(5%)
1990 prim.	Pete Wilson (R)	1,856,613	(88%)
	David M. Williams (R)	107,397	(5%)
	Jeffrey T. Greene (R)	79,083	(4%)
	Two Others	78,635	(4%)
1986 gen.	George Deukmejian (R)	4,506,601	(61%)
	Tom Bradley (D)	2,781,714	(37%)

SENATORS
Sen. Dianne Feinstein (D)

Elected 1992, seat up 1994; b. June 22, 1933, San Francisco; home, San Francisco; Stanford U., B.A. 1955; Jewish; married (Richard C. Blum).

Career: CA Women's Parole Bd., 1960–66; San Francisco Bd. of Supervisors, 1970–78, Pres., 1970–71, 1974–75, 1978; San Francisco Mayor, 1978–88.

Offices: 331 HSOB 20510, 202-224-3841. Also 1700 Montgomery St., #305, San Francisco 94111, 415-249-4777; 750 B St., #1030, San Diego 92101, 619-231-9712; 11111 Santa Monica Blvd., #915, Los Angeles 90025, 310-914-7300; and 1130 O St., #4015, Fresno 93721, 209-485-7430.

Committees: *Appropriations* (16th of 16 D): Agriculture, Rural Development and Related Agencies; District of Columbia; Foreign Operations; VA, HUD and Independent Agencies. *Judiciary* (9th of 10 D): Patents, Copyrights and Trademarks; Technology and the Law. *Rules and Administration* (8th of 9 D).

Group Ratings and 102d Congress Votes: Newly Elected

Key Votes of the 103d Congress

1. Family Leave	FOR	2. HIV Immigrants	FOR	3. Clinton Budget	FOR

Election Results

1992 general	Dianne Feinstein (D)................	5,853,621	(54%)	($8,054,222)
	John Seymour (R)..................	4,093,488	(38%)	($6,849,805)
	Five Others	832,581	(8%)	
1992 primary	Dianne Feinstein (D)................	1,775,730	(58%)	
	Gray Davis (D)....................	1,009,761	(33%)	
	David Kearns (D)..................	149,918	(5%)	
	Joseph M. Alioto (D)	139,410	(5%)	
1988 general	Pete Wilson (R)....................	5,143,409	(53%)	($12,969,294)
	Leo T. McCarthy (D)	4,287,253	(44%)	($6,986,342)

Sen. Barbara Boxer (D)

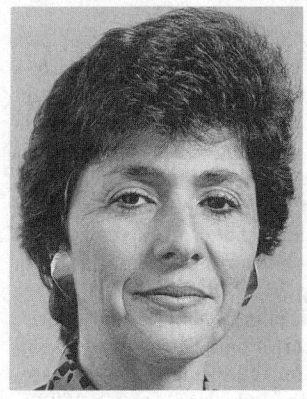

Elected 1992, seat up 1998; b. Nov. 11, 1940, Brooklyn, NY; home, Greenbrae; Brooklyn Col., B.A. 1962; Jewish; married (Stewart).

Career: Stockbroker, researcher, 1962–65; Journalist, *Pacific Sun*, 1972–74; Dist. aide, U.S. Rep. John Burton, 1974–76; Marin Cnty. Bd. of Supervisors, 1976–82; U.S. House of Reps., 1982–92.

Offices: 112 HSOB 20510, 224-3553. Also 1700 Montgomery St., #240, San Francisco 94111, 415-403-0100; and 2250 E. Imperial Hwy., #545, El Segundo 90245, 310-414-5700.

Committees: *Banking, Housing and Urban Affairs* (8th of 11 D): Housing and Urban Affairs; International Finance and Monetary Policy. *Budget* (11th of 12 D). *Environment and Public Works* (10th of 10 D): Superfund, Recycling and Solid Waste Management; Toxic Substances, Research and Development; Water Resources, Transportation, Public Buildings and Economic Development.

Group Ratings (as Member of U.S. House of Representatives)

	ADA	ACLU	COPE	CDF	CFA	LCV	ACU	NTLC	NSI	COC	CEI
1992	60	89	100	70	47	69	0	0	20	33	12
1991	80	—	100	80	50	85	0	—	—	25	7

National Journal Ratings (as Member of U.S. House of Representatives)

	1991 LIB — 1991 CONS		1992 LIB — 1992 CONS	
Economic	88%	0%	91%	0%
Social	84%	16%	92%	0%
Foreign	92%	0%	90%	0%

Key Votes of the 102d Congress (as Member of U.S. House of Representatives)

1. Ban Striker Replace	FOR	5. Handgun Wait/7-Day	FOR	9. Use Force in Gulf	AGN
2. $ for Homeownership	*	6. Overseas Mil. Abortion	FOR	10. US Mil. Abroad $ Cut	*
3. Tax Rich/Cut Mid Cls.	FOR	7. Obscn. Art NEA $ Ban	AGN	11. Limit SDI Funds	FOR
4. FY93/$15B Def. Cut	FOR	8. Death Pen. from Jury	AGN	12. Cuba Trade Embargo	AGN

Key Votes of the 103d Congress

1. Family Leave	FOR	2. HIV Immigrants	FOR	3. Clinton Budget	FOR

Election Results

1992 general	Barbara Boxer (D)	5,173,443	(48%)	($10,415,811)
	Bruce Herschensohn (R).............	4,644,139	(43%)	($7,649,072)
	Six Others.......................	981,781	(9%)	
1992 primary	Barbara Boxer (D)	1,339,126	(44%)	
	Leo McCarthy (D)	935,209	(31%)	
	Mel Levine (D)....................	667,359	(22%)	
	Charles Greene (D).................	122,954	(4%)	
1986 general	Alan Cranston (D)	3,646,672	(50%)	($11,037,707)
	Ed Zschau (R)	3,541,804	(47%)	($11,781,316)

FIRST DISTRICT

No other place in the United States is quite like the North Coast of California. It is the only part of the Lower 48 first settled by Russians, who built Fort Ross in 1812; they sold it in 1841 to a Swiss named John Sutter, whose discovery of gold near Sacramento started the gold rush eight years later. It is the only part of the world with large numbers of redwood trees, shooting up in the moist and drizzly air hundreds of feet toward the sky. It is wet country, and for years has been one of America's prime lumbering areas: Eureka and smaller lumber towns are filled with filigreed Victorian houses and old lumber mills, old saloons and waterfront hotels. It has moved on to other crops: in sunny valleys sealed off the from Coast Range ridges grow some of the nation's premium wine grapes, and Mendocino County has been known from the late 1960s for its premier marijuana fields. Twenty years ago, there were only 20 wineries in Napa Valley; today there are almost 200, with another 100 just west of the ridges in Sonoma County. These valleys were some of California's earliest literary haunts: Robert Louis Stevenson took his honeymoon near Calistoga (named for California plus Saratoga, for the spring water) in Napa, and Jack London owned a giant house in Sonoma which mysteriously burned down in 1913.

California's 1st Congressional District consists of most of the North Coast (though just missing Fort Ross), plus much of the wine-growing area inland and just a bit of the vast Central Valley interior. The North Coast lumbering area from Mendocino on north, once filled with rough-hewn working men, was historically Democratic country, but it backlashed toward the Republicans on cultural issues. As veterans of the counterculture settled in Mendocino County and along the coast it has moved toward the cultural left. Inland, the wine-growing country around Healdsburg and in Napa County is politically more conservative, with neither the blue-collar tradition nor the counterculture past of the coast, though there is often partisan competition. The 1st District's inland portion is around Fairfield, home of Travis Air Force Base. The mix of different economies and cultures, of generations with sharply different experiences and outlooks, makes the 1st District one of California's politically most unstable districts, in which no candidate in either of the last two elections has won an absolute majority of the vote.

It is also a district which has produced increasingly distinctive congressmen. Doug Bosco, a Democrat who held the seat from 1982 to 1990, was a pretty conventional career politician who finally proved unable to balance lumbermen and enviros. Frank Riggs, the Republican who upset Bosco 43%–42% in 1990, was a former policeman who immediately went back on his pledge not to take the "obscene" congressional pay raise. One of three Republicans to vote against the Gulf war resolution, he was a member of the Republican Gang of Seven who insisted on disclosure of the names of House bank check-bouncers only to find he had three overdrafts himself. The congressman now is Dan Hamburg, probably the purest child of the Sixties in Congress today, who beat Riggs 48%–45%.

Hamburg seems miffed by those who call him a counterculture veteran, and the facts of his background are indeed more interesting than the label. He graduated from Stanford in 1970, in a class suffused with opposition to the Vietnam war and devotion to marijuana; the 1967 "summer of love" in San Francisco's Haight-Ashbury was just after his freshman year. After college, Hamburg moved to Mendocino County and founded an "alternative school," which still exists after 22 years; there he met his wife, then the mother of three children at the school. In 1980, he ran for the Mendocino County Board of Supervisors as a "managed growth" candidate and survived a recall by developers. He left office in 1984 and moved with his wife to Taishan, China, near Guangzhou (Canton), where for two years they taught Chinese language and culture to American, European and New Zealander students; this is now the fastest-growing part of China, with a booming free market economy, and it would be interesting to know what Hamburg, given his qualms about market forces at home, thinks of this. Back in the North Coast, he headed the Mendocino antipoverty agency for three years, then earned a masters in philosophy, religion and Chinese at the California Institute for Integral Studies. He made money working for a computer typesetter; when he was laid off from the job while campaigning, he collected $87 a week in unemployment benefits for a period, which led Riggs to call him "Deadbeat Dan." This was not the only clash of lifestyles. Referring to Riggs's former work as a policeman, Hamburg said, "He was a narc. I favor growing your own"—and indeed he favors legalization of marijuana for personal and medicinal use.

Hamburg got an early start raising money and had help from benefit concerts by musicians Bonnie Raitt and Jackson Browne. Riggs had benefited two years before from Bosco's involvement with a local S&L and his vote in the budget summit agreement for a wine tax; now the problems of incumbency hurt him. Hamburg insisted he was a "post-Prop 140 candidate," referring to California's term limits, with a "bigger view of life" than serving in office. In Fairfield Hamburg called for defense reconversion and sustained-yield timbering on the North Coast which he said would result in a sustained job economy: promises which may be tested by reality. With the Peace and Freedom Party vote down from 15% in 1990 to 4% in 1992, Hamburg won 48%, though he reached 50% in only one county.

Immediately this member of the Flower Child generation was tagged as a kind of rebel. He owns no neckties, and wears bolos (as have many westerners) to meet the House dress code. He got seats on the Public Works and Merchant Marine Committees, good places to fulfill his promises to bring "roads, planes and trains"—and boats too—to the North Coast. He called for a millionaire's surtax, evidently unaware of the possibilities of tax avoidance (he could have asked Bonnie Raitt's or Jackson Browne's accountants), and for taxes to encourage investment "in domestic economy and provide worker protections." Hamburg does not, however, seem interested in a lifetime House career and does seem willing to take political risks to advance his convictions in a district where the economic underpinnings and cultural attitudes of many citizens tend to pull politicians in opposite directions. But for 1994, he has as good a chance as anyone to win the first absolute majority in three elections in the North Coast 1st.

The People: Pop. 1990: 572,870; 33% rural; 13% age 65+; 79% White; 4% Black; 3% Amer. Indian; 4% Asian; 5% Other; 11% Hispanic origin. Voting age pop.: 423,536; 4% Black; 10% Hispanic origin. Households: 58% married couple families; 27% married couple fams. w. children; 52% college educ.; median household income: $30,943; per capita income: $14,298; median gross rent: $512; median house value: $136,200.

1992 Presidential Vote		
Clinton (D)	119,491	(46%)
Bush (R)	74,597	(29%)
Perot (I)	61,160	(24%)

1988 Presidential Vote		
Dukakis (D)	110,832	(52%)
Bush (R)	100,825	(48%)

Rep. Dan Hamburg (D)

Elected 1992; b. Oct. 6, 1948, St. Louis, MO; home, Ukiah; Stanford U., B.A. 1970, CA Instit. for Integral Studies, M.A. 1992; Jewish; married (Carrie).

Career: Co-founder, Mariposa Elem. Schl., 1970–76; Ukiah City Plng. Comm. 1976–80, Chmn. 1977; Dir., Ukiah Valley Child Devel. Ctr., 1975–80; Mendocino Cnty. Bd. of Supervisors, 1980–84, Chmn., 1983; Dir., Taishan Educ. Prog., China, 1984–86; Dir., North Coast Opportunities, 1986–89.

Offices: 114 CHOB 20515, 202-225-3311. Also 817 Missouri St., #3, Fairfield 94533, 707-426-0401; 1040 Main St., #103, Napa 94559, 707-254-8508; 910-A Waugh Ln., Ukiah 95482, 707-462-1716; 710 E St., Eureka 95501, 707-441-4949; and 299 I St., #12, Crescent City 95531, 707-465-0112.

Committees: *Merchant Marine and Fisheries* (21st of 29 D): Environment and Natural Resources; Fisheries Management. *Public Works and Transportation* (35th of 39 D): Economic Development; Surface Transportation; Water Resources and Environment.

Group Ratings and 102d Congress Votes: Newly Elected

Key Votes of the 103d Congress

1. Family Leave	FOR	2. Deficit Reduction	FOR	3. Stimulus Plan	FOR

Election Results

1992 general	Dan Hamburg (D)	119,676	(48%)	($647,532)
	Frank Riggs (R)	113,266	(45%)	($716,401)
	Phil Baldwin (P&F)	10,764	(4%)	($10,588)
	Other.............................	7,500	(3%)	
1992 primary	Dan Hamburg (D), unopposed			
1990 general	Frank Riggs (R)	99,782	(43%)	($251,662)
	Douglas H. Bosco (D)................	96,468	(42%)	($413,213)
	Darlene G. Comingore (P&F)...........	34,011	(15%)	($7,291)

SECOND DISTRICT

Rising 14,000 feet over low foothills and the silent Central Valley of California, visible for 100 miles, is the lone snow-capped volcanic cone of Mount Shasta, one of a string of (presumably) burnt-out volcanoes that march up and down the Pacific Coast states. This is the far northern end of California, where truck traffic on Interstate 5 is the only reminder of the choked metropolitan areas where most of the state's people live. It is lumber country mostly, where the mountains that rise on all sides—the Coast Range to the east, the Sierra Nevada to the west, the scattered mountains sealing off the Central Valley north of Redding—are carpeted with trees; rough flannel-shirt, two-lane-road country which was left behind economically when greater Los Angeles and San Francisco were booming following World War II.

In the last dozen years, however, the northern end of California has been attracting young people, mostly young families who come here to raise their children in a small town atmosphere. Overall, the 2d has the highest percentage of non-Hispanic whites of any California district (88%). The political result is that an area which from 1943 to 1980 elected rough-and-ready Democrats who pulled strings in Sacramento and Washington to build roads and dams, now elects abstemious and circumspect Republicans who have solidly conservative voting records and tend to local needs. That is certainly the case in the 2d District of California, which takes in the northern end of California, with two major population areas: one around Redding, just below Mount Shasta, and the other farther south, at the edge of the Sierra foothills, around the Butte County communities of Chico and Paradise.

The congressman from the 2d District is Wally Herger, a solidly conservative Republican, a businessman and rancher first elected to the Assembly in 1980. In 1986 he came to Congress after winning solid margins over the mayor of Redding in the primary and a Shasta County supervisor in the general. In the House he has probably been most vocal as a critic of the Endangered Species Act, which he wants amended to account for economic effects; the spotted owl controversy centers on Oregon, but there are plenty of people here dependent on lumbering whose livelihoods might be endangered by concerns about a species as unmemorable as the spotted owl. Herger also served on the conference committee on the Central Valley Project water bill, the final version of which he opposed saying it "legislates a permanent drought." Redistricting changed the 2d for 1992, subtracting several Central Valley agricultural counties and adding a couple of less-populated counties in the Sierra Nevada. But that posed no problem for Herger, who has raised and spent large sums against hapless and underfinanced Democrats. After the 1992 election, he switched from the Agriculture and Merchant Marine Committees, good for servicing the Valley areas, to Ways and Means and Budget, where he can be a force—a solidly conservative force—on taxes and health care.

The People: Pop. 1990: 573,226; 40% rural; 16% age 65+; 88% White; 1% Black; 3% Amer. Indian; 2% Asian; 2% Other; 6% Hispanic origin. Voting age pop.: 425,392; 1% Black; 5% Hispanic origin. Households: 58% married couple families; 24% married couple fams. w. children; 51% college educ.; median household income: $24,807; per capita income: $12,458; median gross rent: $429; median house value: $94,000.

1992 Presidential Vote			1988 Presidential Vote		
Bush (R)	101,505	(38%)	Bush (R)	125,793	(58%)
Clinton (D)	93,823	(35%)	Dukakis (D)	91,390	(42%)
Perot (I)	67,298	(25%)			

Rep. Wally Herger (R)

Elected 1986; b. May 20, 1945, Yuba City; home, Marysville; American River Comm. Col., A.A. 1967; CA St. U., 1968–69; Mormon; married (Pamela).

Career: Rancher; Owner, Herger Gas Inc. 1969–80; CA Assembly, 1980–86.

Offices: 2433 RHOB 20515, 202-225-3076. Also 55 Independence Cir., #104, Chico 95926, 916-893-8363; and 2400 Washington Ave., #410, Redding 96001, 916-246-5172.

Committees: *Budget* (6th of 17 R). *Ways and Means* (10th of 14 R): Oversight.

Group Ratings

	ADA	ACLU	COPE	CDF	CFA	LCV	ACU	NTLC	NSI	COC	CEI
1992	5	0	25	10	13	6	95	100	100	75	86
1991	5	—	18	20	28	0	100	—	—	89	86

National Journal Ratings

	1991 LIB — 1991 CONS			1992 LIB — 1992 CONS		
Economic	18%	—	82%	0%	—	91%
Social	0%	—	84%	0%	—	85%
Foreign	12%	—	85%	0%	—	82%

Key Votes of the 102d Congress

1. Ban Striker Replace	AGN	5. Handgun Wait/7-Day	AGN	9. Use Force in Gulf	FOR
2. $ for Homeownership	FOR	6. Overseas Mil. Abortion	AGN	10. US Mil. Abroad $ Cut	AGN
3. Tax Rich/Cut Mid Cls.	AGN	7. Obscn. Art NEA $ Ban	FOR	11. Limit SDI Funds	AGN
4. FY93/$15B Def. Cut	AGN	8. Death Pen. from Jury	FOR	12. Cuba Trade Embargo	FOR

Key Votes of the 103d Congress

1. Family Leave	AGN	2. Deficit Reduction	AGN	3. Stimulus Plan	AGN

Election Results

1992 general	Wally Herger (R)	167,247	(65%)	($533,861)
	Elliot Roy Freedman (D)	71,780	(28%)	($4,947)
	Harry H. Pendery (LIB)................	17,529	(7%)	($5,900)
1992 primary	Wally Herger (R)	67,389	(89%)	
	Steve Kunelis (R)	8,467	(11%)	
1990 general	Wally Herger (R)	133,315	(64%)	($515,020)
	Erwin E. (Bill) Rush (D)	65,333	(31%)	($5,951)
	Ross Crain (LIB)	10,753	(5%)	

THIRD DISTRICT

The Sacramento Valley of northern California is one of nature's—and man's—miracles. Nature has sculpted a floor of almost perfectly flat land, surrounded on three sides by mountains, alternately purple and brown in the light. And to this fertile lush black loam, man has added roads and fences as straight as the lines in a geometry text and, most importantly, water. Pacific clouds pour rain into the mountains, which used to run off quickly before it was penned in reservoirs and allocated through a system of canals and aqueducts, levees and pumping plants. The Sacramento and Central Valleys now produce a marvelous variety of crops—rice, plums, almonds, olives, asparagus, pears, hops, beans, celery, onions, potatoes. The Sacramento Valley has always guarded its water jealously and, in the days before one-person-one-vote, it had enough seats in the California Senate to veto water decisions it didn't like; today it must fight to keep enough for its farms against the demands of the cities to the south.

The metropolis of this valley is of course Sacramento. Its historic foundation is apparent coming into town on the West Sacramento Freeway, elevated above utterly flat rice lands painstakingly drained by a network of canals. As you hurtle over the Sacramento River on the M Street Bridge you see, framed perfectly in its arch, California's glorious golden-domed Capitol. On this landing Sacramento was born, and the state government, along with the agriculture symbolized by those rice fields, were for years its lifeblood. Now Sacramento is a major metropolis, spreading far to the south, east and north, with 1.5 million people—one of the fastest-growing major metro areas in the 1980s.

The 3d Congressional District of California includes part of metropolitan Sacramento and much of the Sacramento Valley to the north. It takes in many of the suburbs just north of Sacramento and the American River: all or part of Carmichael, Citrus Heights, North Highlands and Foothills Farms. Although Sacramento is historically Democratic, these suburbs are marginally Republican. The 3d also includes heavily Democratic Yolo County, with industrial West Sacramento just across the Sacramento River from the Capitol and, on the flat farmlands, the tree-shaded, bicycle-pathed town of Davis, with its University of California campus.

Overall, the redistricted 3d probably leans Republican (it gave higher than average percentages to George Bush in 1988 and Pete Wilson in 1990), which is ironic considering that its congressman, Vic Fazio, is part of the House Democratic leadership and was one of his party's chief redistricting operatives. But then 1992 was a difficult year for Fazio in every way: an insider running in an outsider's year, a specialist in Washington politics running in a district one-third of which was new to him, a committed political liberal running in territory increasingly conservative. But he raised and spent vast sums of money—over $1.9 million—and managed to survive. He remains one of the most important members of the House, but whether he will be able to last the decade in this Republican-leaning district and move closer to the speakership to which many think he is headed is unclear.

Fazio has long shown the skills of a political insider, and yet has always been personable and articulate, entirely presentable outside the back rooms and private hallways. This reflects his personality: he is knowledgeable without being cynical, a sharp political operator who keeps score and remembers both friends and enemies, a politician who is anything but an innocent but who retains a certain idealism and a willingness to take serious political risks for what he believes. Fazio got his political start in Sacramento, long California's most political locale, as a staffer in the legislature and a founder of the *California Journal*. He was elected to the Assembly in 1974 and to the House in 1978, replacing an incumbent who had two wives and families, one in California and the other back east. After only two years, he became chairman of the Legislative Appropriations Subcommittee, the panel that handles Congress's own budget—the mayor of Capitol Hill—a position he still holds. In that capacity he handles numerous small requests and vets every committee and subcommittee budget, and he also superintends—and gets a lot of heat for—congressional pay raises, which he sponsored in 1982, 1987 and 1989. As an Appropriations subcommittee chairman, Fazio also gets a certain deference from his fellow members of "the college of cardinals," as when he got $2.8 billion for California after the 1989 Loma Prieta earthquake. Fazio has had other tough insider assignments, including a stint on the Ethics Committee, on which in 1989 he found violations of rules by Speaker Jim Wright—not the stand of a shill for the leadership. After Wright and Tony Coelho resigned in June 1989, Fazio moved into the Democratic leadership as vice-chairman of the Caucus, technically the number five position. After the 1990 elections, he became chairman of the Democratic Congressional Campaign Committee, a post he had sought in 1986 but at the time a perilous position given the odds against Democrats in redistricting; he had been head of the Democrats' IMPAC redistricting operation and was California House Democrats' chief agent in their unsuccessful bid to get a plan passed over Governor Pete Wilson's veto.

Such a concentration of power in one member might invite abuse, but Fazio seems to use his positions straightforwardly to advance the issues in which he believes. He has pet issues: allowing abortions in military medical facilities and funding family planning programs (now both accomplished under Clinton); barring nuclear tests unless the former Soviet republics start testing; seeking approval for the Auburn Dam upriver from Sacramento. On the last he was totally unsuccessful, losing the $698 million project on the House floor 270–140, against a coalition of Republicans opposed to spending and environmentalists opposed to damaging the American Canyon.

Fazio was reelected with just 55% of the vote in 1990, against a crusader against the pay raise. And Governor Wilson's redistricting plan adopted by the state Supreme Court, gave him this 3d District with much new Republican territory. For the first time since 1978, Fazio in 1992 had a well-known and well-financed opponent, Bill Richardson, a state legislator from southern California from 1966–1988 who settled outside Sacramento, a former member of the John Birch Society who started Gun Owners of America and had good access to conservative mailing lists. Richardson seized on a *USA Today* report that Fazio had spent $945,000 in 1991, more than any other member, on office expenses, calling him "the prince of perks." Richardson backed term limits and attacked Fazio for the House bank scandal (though Fazio had no overdrafts) and the pay raise. Fazio responded that Richardson "doesn't want to govern and solve problems," but just wanted attention for his ideological stands. Fazio also stressed local issues, especially in the Sacramento Valley—the threatened loss of Beale Air Force Base, levee protection, keeping the north's water in the Valley (he charged that Richardson voted for 22 years in the legislature to transfer water to southern California). He argued emotionally for the Auburn Dam and said he wanted the Endangered Species Act to take economic factors into account. He maintained defensively that his legislative budget hasn't gone up in real dollars between 1979 and 1993.

Even more important, Fazio used his positions to raise money. Richardson raised $853,000 and, as he neared Fazio in the polls, withheld $234,000 to spend in the last three weeks. But Fazio raised $786,000 from individuals and $1.1 million from PACs and parties, for total spending of $1.9 million, and holding one-fourth of that for the last three weeks—$587,000, more than most incumbents spend in their whole campaign. Concentrated in the Sacramento market and a few small Valley stations, this money helped him win 51%–40%. His biggest margin was in Yolo County, which he carried 64%–30%; he ran unspectacularly ahead in the Sacramento County suburbs, 49%–41%; despite his stress on agriculture and water, he lost, 45%–46%, in the Sacramento Valley. Fazio remains an important and probably busier-than-ever part of the Democratic leadership as chairman of the DCCC. But he seems to have a certain air of fatalism about his own situation. He says he is ready to make tough choices, and cooperate with Bill Clinton, even knowing there may be some political risk. With this district, Fazio knows he could attract serious opposition again; former 1st District Republican Frank Riggs is eying the seat, and more formidable Republicans may be as well.

The People: Pop. 1990: 571,545; 18% rural; 11% age 65+; 76% White; 3% Black; 1% Amer. Indian; 6% Asian; 8% Other; 14% Hispanic origin. Voting age pop.: 418,655; 3% Black; 12% Hispanic origin. Households: 56% married couple families; 27% married couple fams. w. children; 53% college educ.; median household income: $30,296; per capita income: $13,786; median gross rent: $498; median house value: $118,300.

1992 Presidential Vote			1988 Presidential Vote		
Clinton (D)	99,781	(41%)	Bush (R)	110,174	(55%)
Bush (R)	90,799	(37%)	Dukakis (D)	90,437	(45%)
Perot (I)	53,323	(22%)			

Rep. Vic Fazio (D)

Elected 1978; born Oct. 11, 1942, Winchester, MA; home, West Sacramento; Union Col., B.A. 1965, CA St. U., 1969–72; Episcopalian; married (Judy).

Career: Legis. Consult., 1966–75; Co-founder, *The California Journal*; Consult. & Asst., CA Assembly Speaker, 1971–74; CA Assembly, 1975–78.

Offices: 2113 RHOB 20515, 202-225-5716. Also 722-B Main St., Woodland 95695, 916-666-5521; and 322 Pine St., #F, Red Bluff 96080, 916-529-5629.

Committees: *Appropriations* (13th of 37 D): Energy and Water Development; Legislative (Chmn.); Military Construction.

Group Ratings

	ADA	ACLU	COPE	CDF	CFA	LCV	ACU	NTLC	NSI	COC	CEI
1992	90	95	75	100	73	56	8	0	60	50	8
1991	75	—	83	90	56	69	0	—	—	30	7

National Journal Ratings

	1991 LIB	—	1991 CONS	1992 LIB	—	1992 CONS
Economic	61%	—	36%	75%	—	24%
Social	88%	—	0%	84%	—	15%
Foreign	59%	—	39%	51%	—	49%

Key Votes of the 102d Congress

1. Ban Striker Replace	FOR	5. Handgun Wait/7-Day FOR	9. Use Force in Gulf AGN
2. $ for Homeownership	AGN	6. Overseas Mil. Abortion FOR	10. US Mil. Abroad $ Cut AGN
3. Tax Rich/Cut Mid Cls.	FOR	7. Obscn. Art NEA $ Ban AGN	11. Limit SDI Funds FOR
4. FY93/$15B Def. Cut	FOR	8. Death Pen. from Jury AGN	12. Cuba Trade Embargo FOR

Key Votes of the 103d Congress

1. Family Leave   FOR   2. Deficit Reduction   FOR   3. Stimulus Plan   FOR

Election Results

1992 general	Vic Fazio (D) 122,149	(51%)	($1,906,584)
	H. L. (Bill) Richardson (R) 96,092	(40%)	($853,730)
	Ross Crain (LIB) 20,444	(9%)	
1992 primary	Vic Fazio (D), unopposed		
1990 general	Vic Fazio (D) 115,090	(55%)	($1,029,304)
(CA 4)	Mark Baughman (R) 82,738	(39%)	($40,040)
	Bryce Bigwood (LIB) 12,626	(6%)	

FOURTH DISTRICT

With the Gold Rush of 1849, statehood and the creation of the first 27 counties in 1850, California sprang suddenly into existence; and in those years this new state's first boom area was the Mother Lode Country in the Foothills of the Sierras above Sacramento. In what had been vacant valleys locked amid steep hills, there were suddenly mining camps the size of eastern cities, where thousands of would-be millionaires gathered to find gold—though most of those who actually got rich did so by catering to miners' needs. In Placerville, John Studebaker had a buggy shop, Phillip Armour ran a butcher shop and Mark Hopkins had a dry goods store. The biggest mine in California was sunk in Grass Valley in 1857 and worked for half a century. But long before that most of the Mother Lode country emptied out, leaving ghost towns and villages with hundreds of deserted houses—an antique vacation country left behind in time.

Now, in the last 20 years, the Mother Lode country has become a boom area again. Thousands of Californians—many of them families from smog-filled, middle-class suburbs of the Los Angeles basin and the San Francisco Bay area—looking for a more pleasant, small town, tradition-minded environment, found it here along fast-flowing creeks where the '49ers camped. Now for the first time since the 1860 Census, county populations have risen, and old Victorian structures renovated even as new subdivisions are built. Politically, this migration has changed the Mother Lode country from Democrat to Republican. The new migrants are culturally conservative and not economically strained; they reject metropolitan attitudes on issues from gun control to the Gulf war to gay rights. In 1976, the Mother Lode counties from Placer to Tuolumne cast 98,000 votes, 50% for Jimmy Carter and 47% for Gerald Ford—close to the California average. By 1992, they cast 217,000 votes, 40% for George Bush, 34% for Bill Clinton and 25% for Ross Perot—results more like Nevada or Idaho than most of California.

This growth has resulted in the creation, after the 1990 Census, of a new 4th Congressional District of California located almost entirely in the Mother Lode country. Its population is mostly centered near Sacramento; about one-quarter is in the northeast corner of Sacramento County, in middling to upscale suburbs north of the American River—Fair Oaks, Citrus Heights, Orangevale—plus the old town of Folsom. Adjacent to the north is Sacramento overflow into Placer County, running north along I-80 to the old county seat of Roseville. This is where the Mother Lode hills start, where the 4th goes up to the crest of the Sierra Nevada and over to the California shore of Lake Tahoe and the arid salt flats around Mono Lake. Politically, this was a solidly Republican area in the 1980s, but in 1992 Ross Perot cut deeply into the Republican vote, and the 4th District House seat turned out to be more seriously contested than expected.

This was the second tough race, against the same opponent, for John Doolittle, the Republican congressman first elected in 1990 from the old 14th District. Doolittle is from Rocklin, at the edge of the Sacramento metro area where the foothills begin, and for 10 years he represented a state Senate district that stretched up to the Oregon border. His first victory in 1980, when he was 30, was evidence of the area's Republican trend; he made a record against gun control and abortion, and for a crime victims' bill of rights and widespread AIDS testing. Doolittle's conservatism was annealed in the fires of adversity; he graduated from the University of California in Santa Cruz in 1972, when the campus was 97% for George McGovern. Patricia Malberg, who had won only 37% in the old 14th in 1988, came at Doolittle on all fronts in 1990: she was pro-choice on abortion, against offshore oil drilling, against nuclear power and for defense spending cuts. A former ski champion and once a healthcare worker in Africa, she amassed a 2,300-strong volunteer network that contacted some 150,000 households. Doolittle's support for the flag amendment sparked controversy when his first ad talked about the importance of the flag in Vietnam, though he had been in college and Mormon missionary service in Argentina during and after the war. Doolittle won by just 50%–46%.

For 1992 Doolittle was expected to be in stronger shape. He had a perfectly conservative voting record and became California House Republicans' point man on redistricting. But some complained that this was just because he was the only Republican from the Sacramento area and there was much grumbling when he advanced a plan that protected Republican incumbents but gave them little from California's seven new seats. Governor Pete Wilson, in any case, would have no part of such a plan, and Doolittle had little part in shaping the boundaries of the new 4th.

Doolittle was a member of the Gang of Seven freshmen Republicans demanding full disclosure of the House bank scandal. But he also distinguished himself as the House's top user of franked mail and in 1991 joined Maxine Waters in calling for additional staff, a $92 a day expense allowance and more cellular telephones for members, as they had in Sacramento. In 1992, Malberg ran again with considerable enthusiasm. Doolittle won, 50%–46%, a margin close to Bush's over Clinton in the district; he lost two Mother Lode counties and did not show any of the advantage incumbents typically enjoyed in the 1980s. Whether this means continued strong competition depends on whether there are changes in the overall political climate.

The People: Pop. 1990: 571,027; 38% rural; 12% age 65+; 88% White; 2% Black; 1% Amer. Indian; 2% Asian; 2% Other; 7% Hispanic origin. Voting age pop.: 427,008; 2% Black; 7% Hispanic origin. Households: 63% married couple families; 28% married couple fams. w. children; 58% college educ.; median household income: $35,772; per capita income: $16,263; median gross rent: $569; median house value: $152,400.

1992 Presidential Vote

Bush (R) 117,155 (40%)
Clinton (D) 97,501 (34%)
Perot (I) 73,060 (25%)

1988 Presidential Vote

Bush (R) 136,618 (60%)
Dukakis (D) 89,522 (40%)

Rep. John T. Doolittle (R)

Elected 1990; b. Oct. 30, 1950, Glendale; home, Rocklin; U. of CA at Santa Cruz, B.A. 1972, U. of the Pacific, J.D. 1978; Mormon; married (Julia).

Career: CA Senate, 1980–90, Repub. Caucus Chmn., 1987–90.

Offices: 1524 LHOB 20515, 202-225-2511. Also 2130 Professional Dr., Roseville 95661, 916-786-5560.

Committees: *Agriculture* (12th of 19 R): Foreign Agriculture and Hunger; General Farm Commodities; Specialty Crops and Natural Resources. *Natural Resources* (9th of 15 R): Energy and Mineral Resources; National Parks, Forests and Public Lands; Oversight and Investigations.

Group Ratings

	ADA	ACLU	COPE	CDF	CFA	LCV	ACU	NTLC	NSI	COC	CEI
1992	5	0	17	0	13	0	100	89	100	75	91
1991	5	—	9	10	6	0	100	—	—	78	88

National Journal Ratings

	1991 LIB — 1991 CONS	1992 LIB — 1992 CONS
Economic	0% — 96%	0% — 91%
Social	0% — 84%	0% — 85%
Foreign	0% — 88%	0% — 82%

Key Votes of the 102d Congress

1. Ban Striker Replace AGN	5. Handgun Wait/7-Day AGN	9. Use Force in Gulf FOR
2. $ for Homeownership FOR	6. Overseas Mil. Abortion AGN	10. US Mil. Abroad $ Cut AGN
3. Tax Rich/Cut Mid Cls. AGN	7. Obscn. Art NEA $ Ban FOR	11. Limit SDI Funds AGN
4. FY93/$15B Def. Cut AGN	8. Death Pen. from Jury FOR	12. Cuba Trade Embargo FOR

Key Votes of the 103d Congress

1. Family Leave AGN	2. Deficit Reduction AGN	3. Stimulus Plan AGN

Election Results

1992 general	John T. Doolittle (R)................	141,155	(50%)	($622,071)
	Patricia Malberg (D)	129,489	(46%)	($376,190)
	Patrick Lee McHargue (LIB)...........	12,705	(4%)	
1992 primary	John T. Doolittle (R).................	57,631	(71%)	
	Don Brooksher (R)	23,404	(29%)	
1990 general	John T. Doolittle (R)................	128,039	(51%)	($517,668)
(CA 14)	Patricia Malberg (D)	120,742	(49%)	($220,379)

FIFTH DISTRICT

Sacramento, center of California's third-largest media market, home of a national sports franchise (the NBA's Sacramento Kings) and an 18-mile light rail system, capital of the nation's largest state, is no longer just a small city with a lot of civil servants and a vegetable-packing economy. It is now a major American metropolis, with some of the nation's highest job growth in the 1980s, projected to last through the 1990s. Sacramento started as a river port, on the sluggish waters of the Sacramento and American Rivers. It was the destination of many overland migrants, including the ill-fated Donner party in 1846, the site of Sutter's Fort where John Augustus Sutter found the gold that set off the Gold Rush of 1849 and the western terminus of the Pony Express in 1860. It was the natural choice to be California's capital, halfway between the Mother Lode country in the foothills of the Sierras and San Francisco Bay, and in the middle of California's vast valley. Agriculture continues to be important today in Sacra-tomato (as some call it)—it has the world's largest almond processing plant. Government for many years was not a big business here: just a few lobbyists hung out in saloons on K or J Streets; the governor's mansion was a musty antique (Nancy Reagan hated it); and before air conditioning, the 100-plus degree summers emptied out what there was of the city. But now air conditioning has replaced awnings; freeways and shopping malls have followed the city's growth east and north toward the foothills of the Sierras; affluence has made this one of America's higher income metropolitan areas. Government grew, even under conservative Republican governors Ronald Reagan and George Deukmejian, and Sacramento in the 1980s became the home of an army of lobbyists, lawyers and consultants larger than any such group outside Washington. California's cynically competent legislators mostly live year-round in Sacramento, although they usually keep legal residences elsewhere. In the 1980s metropolitan Sacramento grew 35%, more than any other large metro area except that other western capital, Phoenix, to more than 1.5 million.

As Sacramento has grown, it has also become more Republican: this once Democratic, pro-government, working-class bastion has become something very close to an upscale Sun Belt boom town. Sacramento voted against Ronald Reagan for governor in 1966 and 1970, but voted for him for president in 1980 and 1984; it spurned Richard Nixon and Gerald Ford in the 1970s but voted for George Bush in 1988 and gave Bill Clinton only a mediocre 44% plurality in 1992. Civil servants and the *Sacramento Bee* once made Sacramento Democratic, but the increasing strength of the private sector here (even though much of it feeds off government), the growing affluence, immigration and competition from the peppery, conservative *Sacramento Union* all have helped Republicans.

The 5th District of California consists of the center of the Sacramento metropolitan area plus suburbs just northeast of the American River and south along the Sacramento. This is the older core of the metro area, which now extends into four different districts, and is socioeconomically varied, from affluent neighborhoods on older grid streets to scattered low-income black, Mexican-American and Hmong neighborhoods. This is easily the most Democratic of the Sacramento area districts, and indeed is the descendant of districts represented by Democrats continuously since 1952. Its congressman is Robert Matsui, first elected in 1978, and now a Ways and Means member of some influence on a variety of issues.

Born in 1941, the infant Matsui and his family were among the West Coast Japanese Americans forced into internment camps in 1942, and although he has no memory of the experience himself, he does remember the silence his family and others maintained about it. It was Asian shame, when none of the victims had anything to be ashamed about. He was one of the lead sponsors of the 1988 Japanese American Redress law which apologized for the internment policy and provided monetary compensation for every survivor of the camps and for so-called "voluntary evacuees."

Matsui also has worked hard on Ways and Means, where he was a staunch supporter of the 1986 rate-lowering, preference-cutting tax reform. For a time, Matsui showed restiveness and an interest in seeking other office. In 1987, he was the first House member outside Massachusetts to support Michael Dukakis, and at the same time sounded out fundraisers on the possibility of running against then-Senator Pete Wilson. In 1989, Matsui thought briefly about running for attorney general. In early 1991, he expressed interest in running for Alan Cranston's Senate seat. He had fundraising potential among Asian-Americans, and was the only potential candidate from inland California, but in May he dropped out of the race. Always a successful fundraiser, he has served as treasurer of the Democratic National Committee since 1991. But at the same time, he was standoffish from party leaders, criticizing Speaker Tom Foley in March 1992 for not breaking gridlock and not doing enough to forestall anti-incumbent sentiment. He refrained from endorsing Bill Clinton until that summer; even so his wife Doris Matsui became an assistant to the president for public liaison.

In 1987, Harold Ford of Tennessee, pending resolution of his legal troubles, had to relinquish his Ways and Means subcommittee chair. Matsui temporarily ended up with the Human Resources Subcommittee chair with jurisdiction over Social Security, unemployment benefits, welfare reform and child care. The first two issues evoke perfunctory responses from Democrats—no cuts in Social Security, always increase unemployment benefits; but the other two allow room for legislative creativity. Matsui seems to lean against a statist approach to child care and toward a bigger tax credit or earned-income tax credit for families with children. Though Ford, acquitted of all legal charges, is back as chairman, Matsui will continue to be active on child care issues.

Matsui favors targeted capital gains tax cuts and strongly backs free trade and NAFTA, warning against restricting most favored nation status for China. He has tried to encourage mass transit use by attaching to Pat Moynihan's transportation bill a $155 per month limit on tax deductibility of employer-paid parking and a raise to $60 monthly tax-free benefits for public transportation; he also pushed through a tax credit for using energy from wind and crop incineration. But his influence has limits: he and Vic Fazio failed in their attempt to authorize an Auburn Dam upriver from Sacramento.

Matsui has accumulated more than $1.4 million in his campaign treasury and has won reelection easily. It's possible he'd be interested in running for governor in 1994 if no other Democrat does; but that's unlikely, and there are many other attractive statewide slots opening up in 1994.

The People: Pop. 1990: 573,659; 11% age 65+; 59% White; 13% Black; 1% Amer. Indian; 13% Asian; 7% Other; 14% Hispanic origin. Voting age pop.: 421,533; 11% Black; 12% Hispanic origin. Households: 45% married couple families; 21% married couple fams. w. children; 57% college educ.; median household income: $29,974; per capita income: $14,661; median gross rent: $505; median house value: $121,000.

1992 Presidential Vote			1988 Presidential Vote		
Clinton (D)	120,577	(50%)	Dukakis (D)	118,468	(55%)
Bush (R)	73,562	(31%)	Bush (R)	97,313	(45%)
Perot (I)	42,566	(18%)			

Rep. Robert T. Matsui (D)

Elected 1978; b. Sept. 17, 1941, Sacramento; home, Sacramento; U. of CA at Berkeley, A.B. 1963, J.D. 1966; United Methodist; married (Doris).

Career: Practicing atty., 1967–78; Sacramento City Cncl., 1971–78.

Offices: 2311 RHOB 20515, 202-225-7163. Also 8058 Fed. Bldg., 650 Capitol Mall, Sacramento 95814, 916-551-2846.

Committees: *Ways and Means* (8th of 24 D): Human Resources; Trade.

Group Ratings

	ADA	ACLU	COPE	CDF	CFA	LCV	ACU	NTLC	NSI	COC	CEI
1992	80	84	55	90	80	69	8	0	30	29	7
1991	70	—	80	90	67	77	0	—	—	25	7

National Journal Ratings

	1991 LIB	—	1991 CONS		1992 LIB	—	1992 CONS
Economic	55%	—	45%		74%	—	25%
Social	78%	—	22%		76%	—	23%
Foreign	87%	—	13%		65%	—	33%

Key Votes of the 102d Congress

1. Ban Striker Replace	*	5. Handgun Wait/7-Day FOR	9. Use Force in Gulf AGN
2. $ for Homeownership AGN		6. Overseas Mil. Abortion FOR	10. US Mil. Abroad $ Cut FOR
3. Tax Rich/Cut Mid Cls. FOR		7. Obscn. Art NEA $ Ban AGN	11. Limit SDI Funds FOR
4. FY93/$15B Def. Cut FOR		8. Death Pen. from Jury AGN	12. Cuba Trade Embargo FOR

Key Votes of the 103d Congress

1. Family Leave FOR	2. Deficit Reduction FOR	3. Stimulus Plan FOR

Election Results

1992 general	Robert T. Matsui (D)	158,250	(69%)	($1,421,123)
	Robert S. Dinsmore (R)	58,698	(25%)	($32,826)
	Four Others........................	13,612	(6%)	
1992 primary	Robert T. Matsui (D), unopposed			
1990 general	Robert T. Matsui (D)	132,143	(60%)	($734,005)
(CA 3)	Lowell P. Landowski (R)...............	76,148	(35%)	($4,628)
	David M. McCann (LIB)..............	10,797	(5%)	

SIXTH DISTRICT

When the Golden Gate bridge was opened in 1937, San Francisco was one of the nation's best-known cities, but few knew much about the land beyond the bridge's north pierhead. There were less than 50,000 people in Marin County then and, to the north, about 65,000 in Sonoma County. For San Franciscans, Marin was known for the ferry terminus in Sausalito, a fishing village and art colony, and as the beginning of the Redwood Empire, with its giant trees in Muir Woods; near the Bay was the state prison at San Quentin, with its already infamous gas chamber. Farther north, in a sunny valley protected from the fog by the Coast Range, was Santa Rosa, site of agronomist Luther Burbank's laboratory, a California town that looked Middle American enough to be the set for dozens of movies. Politically, this area was then typical of the nation: traditionally Republican, but favoring Franklin Roosevelt in the 1930s.

Today this part of California is far more populous, with 230,000 people in Marin and 388,000 in Sonoma, solidly a part of the San Francisco Bay Area, affluent beyond the dreams of the Americans of 50 years ago and extreme in its cultural attitudes. Trendy Marin, with its hot tubs and its fashionable people getting in touch with themselves, became a national caricature in the late 1970s, and remains one; the interesting question is how such an affluent area could become politically so far to the left. It is an illustration of the primacy of cultural over economic factors and a cultural identity consuming an entire metropolitan area. For even as metro San Francisco's economy has generated increasing numbers of professional jobs, its reputation for cultural tolerance (to the point of absurdity) has attracted many people willing and able to pay its far-above-average real estate prices, and at the same time repelled many others, who are happier in the Central Valley or Sierras or Idaho, where they can live cheaply without civic institutions that insult their values. The result is that affluent Bay Area residents are increasingly self-selected cultural liberals—averse to traditional religion, derisive of traditional sexual and marriage mores, viscerally anti-military. And over the years Marin, with its mountain-bound subdivisions of contemporary houses, and southern Sonoma County, with its rolling countryside and picturesque small towns, have attracted the most liberal of the affluent liberal. Consider the election returns: Marin and Sonoma voted 59% for Michael Dukakis in 1988 and 56% for Bill Clinton in 1992—a dozen points above the national average and perhaps double their percentage in similar income areas nationally.

The 6th Congressional District of California includes all of Marin County and more than half of Sonoma. Its predecessor district was represented for 10 years by Barbara Boxer, now U.S. senator, and the personification of trendy liberalism since she was elected to the Marin County Board of Supervisors in 1976. Boxer's 1992 candidacy for the Senate led to a competitive Democratic primary and even, for a time, a serious Republican challenge. The most talked about candidates initially were J. Bennett Johnston III, son of the Louisiana senator, and Marin Republican Assemblyman Bill Filante. Johnston raised $400,000 with his father's help and stressed his pro-environment stand; but his Oil Patch connection hurt, and he won only 14% in the primary. Two other Democrats tried to build on local bases: former Sonoma Supervisor Eric Koenigshofer won 19% districtwide and former Marin Supervisor Denis Rice won 17%.

But they all were, in California Democrats' year of the woman, bested by Lynn Woolsey, vice-mayor of Petaluma in southern Sonoma, and possessor of a biography that struck a chord: Woolsey was a Marin housewife with three children under the age 6 when her marriage ended in 1968. She went on welfare, got a low-paying job and left her children with 13 different babysitters in a year. Deliverance appeared in the form of a job with a high-tech startup where she rose to become a top executive. She remarried and moved to a house in Petaluma where her mother could live and look after the kids. As she wrote in her campaign literature, "Finally I could concentrate on work. The children had good care at last!" She went on to earn a degree in human resources and started her own personnel service. She won a seat on the Petaluma Council in 1984 and is proud of its record in limiting growth (Marin and Sonoma, with their low-growth policies, are becoming lesser political forces in California), setting up affirmative action programs and a Women of Color Task Force, requiring 15% of new housing reserved for low-income buyers and establishing a voucher system for low-income families' child care. "I know what it means to have an effective safety net to help people get back on their feet," she campaigned. "I know what a bottom line means. I have made the tough decisions to keep our City prosperous in the post-Proposition 13 era."

Woolsey, after winning the June primary, was a formidable general election candidate, and she became unbeatable in September, after Filante had surgery which removed only part of a cancerous brain tumor. He stopped campaigning and although Republicans, including Sonoma Assemblywoman Bev Hansen, stumped for him, Woolsey won with 65% of the vote. She won seats on the Education and Labor Committee, where she vowed to support increased higher education spending, and Budget, where she filled the vacancy created by Leon Panetta's departure. It is possible she will have serious opposition from Hansen or some other Republican, but she appears very strong in this district.

The People: Pop. 1990: 571,360; 19% rural; 13% age 65+; 85% White; 2% Black; 1% Amer. Indian; 3% Asian; 3% Other; 9% Hispanic origin. Voting age pop.: 444,348; 2% Black; 8% Hispanic origin. Households: 53% married couple families; 23% married couple fams. w. children; 67% college educ.; median household income: $40,564; per capita income: $21,603; median gross rent: $709; median house value: $255,900.

1992 Presidential Vote

Clinton (D)	169,301	(56%)
Bush (R)	71,564	(24%)
Perot (I)	60,920	(20%)

1988 Presidential Vote

Dukakis (D)	152,467	(59%)
Bush (R)	107,374	(41%)

Rep. Lynn C. Woolsey (D)

Elected 1992; b. Nov. 3, 1937, Seattle, WA; home, Petaluma; U. of San Francisco, B.A. 1980; Presbyterian; divorced.

Career: Human Resources Mgr., Harris Digital Telephone, 1969–80; Owner, Woolsey Personnel Svc., 1980–92; Petaluma City Cncl., 1985–92, Vice Mayor, 1986, 1991.

Offices: 439 CHOB 20515, 202-225-5161. Also 1301 Redwood Way, #205, Petaluma 94954, 707-795-1462.

Committees: *Education and Labor* (20th of 28 D): Elementary, Secondary and Vocational Education; Human Resources; Labor-Management Relations. *Budget* (26th of 26 D). *Government Operations* (24th of 25 D): Information, Justice, Transportation and Agriculture.

Group Ratings and 102d Congress Votes: Newly Elected

Key Votes of the 103d Congress

1. Family Leave	FOR	2. Deficit Reduction	FOR	3. Stimulus Plan	FOR

Election Results

1992 general	Lynn Woolsey (D).....................	190,322	(65%)	($584,913)
	Bill Filante (R).......................	98,171	(34%)	($436,752)
	Two Others..........................	3,293	(1%)	
1992 primary	Lynn Woolsey (D).....................	25,484	(26%)	
	Eric J. Koenigshofer (D)...............	18,090	(19%)	
	Denis Rice (D).......................	16,979	(17%)	
	J. Bennett Johnston III(D).............	13,202	(14%)	
	Anna Nevenic (D).....................	7,872	(8%)	
	David N. Strand (D)...................	5,666	(6%)	
	William Harrison Morrison (D)...........	4,140	(4%)	
	Joe Nation (D).......................	3,772	(4%)	
	Other...............................	2,565	(3%)	
1990 general	Barbara Boxer (D)....................	137,306	(68%)	($655,402)
	Bill Boerum (R)....................	64,402	(32%)	($32,724)

SEVENTH DISTRICT

The journey inward from the Pacific Ocean to the vast flatness of California's Central Valley passes through wondrous terrain. The traveler starts through the Golden Gate, with the lush green Presidio on one side and the bluff of the Marin mountains on the other; through the waters of San Francisco Bay, looked down upon by ridges above the East Bay on one side and the rising cone of Mount Tamalpais on the other; through the narrow Carquinez Strait to Suisun Bay, with its sloughs and marshes, fed by the sluggish waters of the Sacramento and San Joaquin Delta; finally past the mountains and waters, to the flat, fertile expanse of California's great interior. This is not a journey most tourists make, but it was a familiar route to the first Californians and it passes by much of the industrial base of the Bay Area. On the east side of the Bay is Richmond, developed almost instantaneously during World War I when Henry J. Kaiser built a shipyard in its deep water port and 91,000 people from all over the country were put to work building ships for the Pacific theater; it now has a large black population and is attracting high-tech spinoffs. Across Carquinez Strait is Vallejo, named for an early California Mexican general and member of the first California Senate, the site since 1853 of the giant Mare Island Naval Shipyard. Across the strait are tank farms and factories in Rodeo and Pittsburg and Martinez, the seat of Contra Costa County (literally, the coast opposite San Francisco).

Politically, this industrial area was blue-collar, labor-union Democratic back in the days when San Francisco, with its larger white-collar and professional population, often voted Republican. More recently, as San Francisco has moved to the left on cultural issues, this industrial zone has become a bit more conservative, but by Bay Area rather than national standards. The current 7th Congressional District of California includes most of this area, from Richmond and El Cerrito along both sides of Carquinez Strait and Suisun Bay to include Vallejo, Rodeo, Martinez and Pittsburg. It also proceeds inland through the intermountain interstices of Contra Costa County to include most of the middle-class city of Concord. The district excludes the heavily Republican and higher-income interior Contra Costa communities around Walnut Hill and the San Ramon Valley, a good break for Congressman George Miller.

Miller is one of the products of the Watergate era class of 1974, the first baby boom liberal to chair a House committee. He is also heir to a tradition of Bay Area working-class politics. His father was chairman of the State Senate Finance Committee; when he died in 1969, Miller lost the race to succeed him, but became a staffer for Senate leader (and later San Francisco Mayor) George Moscone. In the House, Miller brings to his work an aggressiveness and zest for political combat, a self-righteousness that is combined with a willingness to dissent from liberal orthodoxy on occasion, a set of convictions not worn down by Capitol Hill clubbiness. Or perhaps he has started his own club: he became famous for sharing a Capitol Hill townhouse with fellow congressmen Charles Schumer, Leon Panetta and Marty Russo, all of whom commuted to families back in their districts; but Panetta was advised to move out and Dick Durbin and Sam Gejdenson took his and Russo's spots.

Since 1991, Miller has chaired the House Natural Resources Committee (he changed the name from Interior and Insular Affairs in 1993) with an aggressive pugnacity that was a sharp change from the courtly humorousness of his predecessor Morris Udall. "People sent me to Congress to kick ass and take names, and I'm not going to roll over," he said. From his Water Subcommittee chairmanship, Miller long crusaded against the big subsidies received by farmers in California's Central Valley and elsewhere in the West. In 1992, using his chairmanship and with extra strength because of the California drought, he passed a major water bill, with projects for most western states and a revision of California's Central Valley Project which channels one-fifth of the state's usable water supply, requires farmers to pay prices closer to those of urban water users and enforces fish and wildlife protection measures; this was passed with the help of Senator Bill Bradley and over furious opposition from Valley politicians Senator John Seymour and Governor Pete Wilson. Miller also stands up for the Endangered Species Act in the controversy over the spotted owl and logging in the Pacific Northwest, and wants to stop logging in a wide swath of land but provide aid to laid-off loggers; here he will be facing strong pressures, some from his usual allies, for change in the law. On the 1992 energy bill, Miller clashed with Energy and Commerce Chairman John Dingell while trying to reclaim jurisdiction Udall had let slip away; Miller wanted to limit nuclear licensing and restrict radioactive storage and hydroelectric dam development.

Miller's great cause in the 103d Congress is likely to be revision of the Mining Act of 1872. He got a revision to the floor of the House in 1992 but it went no further. He argues that miners should pay more for claims staked on government land; many western legislators, including the committee's longtime ranking Republican, Don Young of Alaska, bitterly resent this as confiscation of private property. Another issue that he may face is Puerto Rico. The New Progressive Party's 1992 victory there means there will be renewed pressure for a referendum on statehood, about which Miller's Democratic mentors have tended to be wary; setting the terms for such a referendum is a tricky business, and one for which there are few political rewards for a mainland politician.

Miller also has weighed in on other issues and causes. From his position as chairman of the now abolished Select Committee on Children, Youth and Families, he opposed the ABC bill supported by Marian Wright Edelman's Children's Defense Fund, and, with fellow suburban liberal Tom Downey, he backed an approach that would increase parent choice and give government less supervisory power. That was Miller making trouble on the right; he always does so on the left, as in March 1992 when there was talk as the House bank scandal broke that Miller would run against Speaker Thomas Foley, and when he advised that Democrats should pass redistributive economic legislation to divert attention from their problems. Nothing came of either suggestion.

Miller was one of the big winners out of redistricting. He lost most of his Republican precincts to the new Republican 10th District and gained Vallejo from Vic Fazio. This eliminated the possibility of any serious challenge, at least until 1998, when the California term limits initiative takes effect, which says that incumbents can run again but cannot be listed on the ballot.

The People: Pop. 1990: 572,857; 10% age 65+; 56% White; 17% Black; 1% Amer. Indian; 14% Asian; 6% Other; 13% Hispanic origin. Voting age pop.: 421,835; 15% Black; 11% Hispanic origin. Households: 54% married couple families; 26% married couple fams. w. children; 57% college educ.; median household income: $38,608; per capita income: $16,006; median gross rent: $625; median house value: $167,000.

1992 Presidential Vote			1988 Presidential Vote		
Clinton (D)	140,159	(60%)	Dukakis (D)	126,704	(62%)
Bush (R)	51,356	(22%)	Bush (R)	76,561	(38%)
Perot (I)	39,038	(17%)			

Rep. George Miller (D)

Elected 1974; b. May 17, 1945, Richmond; home, Martinez; San Francisco St. U., B.A. 1968, U. of CA at Davis, J.D. 1972; Catholic; married (Cynthia).

Career: Legis. aide, CA Sen. Majority Ldr., 1969–74; Practicing atty., 1972–74.

Offices: 2205 RHOB 20515, 202-225-2095. Also 367 Civic Dr., #14, Pleasant Hill 94523, 510-602-1880; and 3220 Blume Dr., #281, Richmond 94806, 510-262-6500.

Committees: *Education and Labor* (3d of 27 D): Elementary, Secondary and Vocational Education; Labor-Management Relations; Labor Standards, Occupational Health and Safety. *Natural Resources* (Chmn. of 28 D): Insular and International Affairs; Oversight and Investigations (Chmn.).

Group Ratings

	ADA	ACLU	COPE	CDF	CFA	LCV	ACU	NTLC	NSI	COC	CEI
1992	85	100	92	100	87	75	0	5	10	25	17
1991	95	—	100	100	89	85	0	—	—	20	13

National Journal Ratings

	1991 LIB — 1991 CONS		1992 LIB — 1992 CONS	
Economic	88%	— 0%	69%	— 31%
Social	88%	— 0%	92%	— 0%
Foreign	86%	— 13%	90%	— 0%

Key Votes of the 102d Congress

1. Ban Striker Replace FOR	5. Handgun Wait/7-Day FOR	9. Use Force in Gulf AGN
2. $ for Homeownership AGN	6. Overseas Mil. Abortion FOR	10. US Mil. Abroad $ Cut FOR
3. Tax Rich/Cut Mid Cls. FOR	7. Obscn. Art NEA $ Ban AGN	11. Limit SDI Funds FOR
4. FY93/$15B Def. Cut FOR	8. Death Pen. from Jury AGN	12. Cuba Trade Embargo AGN

Key Votes of the 103d Congress

1. Family Leave FOR	2. Deficit Reduction FOR	3. Stimulus Plan FOR

Election Results

1992 general	George Miller (D)....................	153,320	(70%)	($651,360)
	Dave Scholl (R)	54,822	(25%)	($62,047)
	David L. Franklin (P&F)	9,840	(5%)	
1992 primary	George Miller (D), unopposed			
1990 general	George Miller (D)....................	121,080	(61%)	($448,026)
	Roger A. Payton (R)...................	79,031	(39%)	($47,912)

EIGHTH DISTRICT

Can the future of a city be foreshadowed in the events of a day? On February 20, 1915, Governor Hiram Johnson and Mayor James Rolph led 150,000 people onto the grounds of the Panama-Pacific International Exposition to see the Spanish-Italian baroque style building built on reclaimed land in what became San Francisco's Marina district. The Exposition ostensibly celebrated the completion of the Panama Canal, but was clearly intended to show off San Francisco's recovery from the 1906 earthquake. It also spotlighted San Francisco as the central focus of an America that was becoming, with its acquisition of Hawaii and the Philippines and its interest in an open door policy with China and trade with Japan, a power in what we now call the Pacific Rim.

The Exposition set the physical style of San Francisco: it encouraged the use of Mediterranean color, accent and detail that characterizes most post-Victorian houses and commercial structures in The City (as the *San Francisco Examiner* still calls it). It created the picturesque Marina district, whose old buildings were among the few damaged in the 1989 earthquake, and today's tourist waterfront around Fisherman's Wharf and Ghirardelli Square. This San Francisco has many facets: on a sunny day it looks almost tropical, with brown mountains baking in the sun and light shining off the pastel stucco buildings; when the clouds scud in from the Pacific, it can look sinister, full of dark corners where a private detective's partner might be ambushed by a pretty girl. The buildings can be majestic, like the monumental Beaux Arts City Hall, or tawdry, like the hotels of the Tenderloin; it is a city that looks exotic at first but, when you examine it closely, could only be American.

San Francisco has been a dynamic city, capable of great growth, carrying the American tradition of tolerance of diversity to new lengths; it grew from nothing to a major city in the single year of 1850; its American origins obvious from the regular grids of streets named after politicians and local developers. The San Francisco of 1915 was proud of the writers who had flourished there—Jack London, Ambrose Bierce, Frank Norris—and of the home-town traditions of the arts and crafts movement, just as San Francisco later would have a Herb Caen-ish pride in the beats of the 1950s North Beach, the hippies who thronged Haight-Ashbury in 1967, and the gays of the Castro in the 1970s and 1980s. Over the years, San Francisco's booming economy, based initially on food processing, but now on finance, high-tech and clothing (the Gap, Esprit) has attracted talented newcomers, weighted increasingly toward those who find its liberation-minded cultural attitudes congenial.

Politically, San Francisco was a progressive Republican town, like the two men who led the way into the Exposition. The sour-tempered Hiram Johnson made his name as a reformer throwing out crooked city politicians; his administration gave California primary elections, referenda and recall, and strong civil service laws. "Sunny Jim" Rolph, mayor from 1911 to 1930 and then governor, built the civic center, parks, schools, streetcars and the Hetch Hetchy power lines—the antique infrastructure of San Francisco today. Sympathetic to the conservation movement, willing to deal with labor unions in a union town that had America's only general strike in 1934, tolerant of the diversity of California as the anti-Chinese working class movements of the 19th Century were not, these progressive Republicans were the recognizable ancestors of, though certainly not identical to, the San Franciscans who in the 1970s and 1980s became increasingly culturally liberal—perhaps even radical.

But San Francisco's newest citizens may be moving it in another direction. For if its distinctive style attracted liberal singles and gays in increasing numbers, its economic dynamism on the Pacific Rim has attracted Asians—as indeed San Francisco did from 1850 until immigration was shut off by the Chinese Exclusion Act in 1882. San Francisco's ultraliberal attitudes were symbolized by the election of Mayor George Moscone and openly gay Supervisor Harvey Milk in 1975, and then when they were murdered by a political opponent in 1978, who was let off of murder charges and convicted of the lesser charge of manslaughter by a liberal jury on the theory that he'd been crazed by an addiction to sugary junk food—the Twinkie defense. Over the next ten years, the city's cultural liberalism was tempered by Mayor Dianne Feinstein, who vetoed a gay marriage ordinance and opposed commercial rent control. She was succeeded in 1988 by Art Agnos, elected by a liberal gay-black coalition, who promised shelter to every homeless person in the city and allowed a homeless colony ("Camp Agnos") across from City Hall, and who seemed unable to clamp down on crime as Feinstein had done. But in 1991, the city's usually quiet Asian-American voters joined homeowners in the outer neighborhoods to oust Agnos and elect Frank Jordan, a former police chief, who promised to crack down on crime and the homeless camps but—his campaign manager was gay—supported gay issues.

California's 8th Congressional District takes in four-fifths of San Francisco, all but the southwest corner. It has all of San Francisco's high rise downtown, the increasingly crowded and bustling Chinatown, Telegraph, Nob and Russian Hills, North Beach (which was once really a beach) and Pacific Heights (which is still on heights) and the Marina District (which does not have a very big marina). It extends to the ocean to include Sea Cliff overlooking the Golden Gate Bridge and the Richmond area, with its many Asian-Americans. In the valleys are the mostly black Fillmore and Western Addition areas, but only 13% of the district's residents are black, as compared to 16% Hispanic and 28% Asian—the highest Asian percentage of any district outside Hawaii. The 8th also has the gay Castro district and Noe Valley, Haight-Ashbury, once the bedraggled center of hippiedom and now another yup-and-coming San Francisco neighborhood and, Portrero Hill, with its restored houses overlooking downtown. Farther south are the old residential areas between Candlestick Park, the Cow Palace and I-280, with pastel houses strewn out along grid streets which hug the steep hills.

The 8th District is represented by Nancy Pelosi, a Democrat with deep political roots and a capacity for keeping all parts of her party happy. She has the energy and shrewdness of one who has handled the most delicate political chores and the charm and unflappability of one who has been the parent of five children. Pelosi's father, Thomas D'Alessandro, served in the House from 1939 to 1947 and was mayor of Baltimore for 12 years after that; her brother Thomas D'Alessandro Jr., was mayor from 1967 to 1971. Married to a successful San Francisco businessman, she was California Democratic Party chair in the early 1980s, chaired the their delegate rules Compliance Review Commission for 1984, and served as the Democratic Senatorial Campaign Committee's Finance Chair in 1985. She actually never considered running for the House when San Francisco's congressional politics was dominated by Phillip Burton, congressman since 1965, an old-fashioned labor-liberal Democrat and opponent of the Vietnam war from the beginning. But Burton died in 1983 and his widow Sala, elected to succeed him, died in 1987, at which point Pelosi ran, and won 35%–31% in an April 1987 special primary against gay supervisor Harry Britt.

Pelosi's highest-profile work in the House has come not on left-liberal but on Asian issues. She took the lead, in her first full term, in opposing President Bush's treatment of Chinese students after Tiananmen Square and sponsored the amendment to give them protective immigration status, which passed the House overwhelmingly; foiled when Bush's veto was upheld in the Senate, she continues to pressure the Chinese to observe human rights. In her second full term she was the lead sponsor of the bill to condition China's Most Favored Nation status on human rights reforms. She charged that any Bush Administration pressures on China had been unavailing, and shepherded her bill to passage in the House; after it was vetoed by President Bush, the House voted 345–74 to override (but override failed to get two-thirds in the Senate, 59–50). She continues to try to make MFN status conditional on human rights improvements, acknowledging that others might condition it also on trade and weapons proliferation concessions. Pelosi's other great cause is AIDS funding; she uses the Appropriations seat she won in December 1990 to get research and treatment money, and in late 1992 won $2.5 million for HIV drug treatment programs in San Francisco. She was less successful in keeping San Francisco's Presidio off the base closure list (of course, if the Bay Area delegation had its way, the whole Defense Department might have closed down years ago); although when it closes in 1995, it is slated to become part of the National Park System, thanks to an old provision buried in an Interior bill by Phil Burton.

Pelosi continues to be an important national Democrat. When Mary Rose Oakar was embarrassed by the House bank scandal in April 1992, Pelosi took her place as co-chair of the National Democratic Platform Committee. She was also mentioned as a candidate for vice president. At home, she seems increasingly popular. Redistricting gave her an even more Democratic district, and she was reelected in 1992 with 82% of the vote.

The People: Pop. 1990: 573,192; 14% age 65+; 44% White; 13% Black; 28% Asian; 7% Other; 15% Hispanic origin. Voting age pop.: 481,195; 11% Black; 14% Hispanic origin. Households: 31% married couple families; 12% married couple fams. w. children; 58% college educ.; median household income: $31,659; per capita income: $19,377; median gross rent: $631; median house value: $270,100.

1992 Presidential Vote			1988 Presidential Vote		
Clinton (D)	187,201	(75%)	Dukakis (D)	162,192	(76%)
Bush (R)	39,396	(16%)	Bush (R)	50,277	(24%)
Perot (I)	21,180	(8%)			

Rep. Nancy Pelosi (D)

Elected June, 1987; b. Mar. 26, 1940, Baltimore, MD; home, San Francisco; Trinity College, B.A. 1962; Catholic; married (Paul).

Career: CA Dem. Party, Northern Chmn., 1977–81, St. Chmn., 1981–83; Finance Chmn., DSCC, 1985–87; PR exec., Ogilvy & Mather, 1986–87.

Office: 240 CHOB, 20515, 202-225-4965. Also 450 Golden Gate Ave., #13470, San Francisco 94102, 415-556-4862.

Committees: *Appropriations* (24th of 37 D): District of Columbia; Foreign Operations, Export Financing and Related Programs; Labor, Health and Human Services, and Education. *Intelligence (Permanent Select)* (9th of 12 D): Legislation; Oversight and Evaluation. *Standards of Official Conduct* (4th of 7 D).

Group Ratings

	ADA	ACLU	COPE	CDF	CFA	LCV	ACU	NTLC	NSI	COC	CEI
1992	90	100	92	90	93	100	0	0	30	25	5
1991	90	—	92	90	72	92	0	—	—	20	5

National Journal Ratings

	1991 LIB — 1991 CONS		1992 LIB — 1992 CONS	
Economic	72% —	28%	91% —	0%
Social	88% —	0%	85% —	13%
Foreign	92% —	0%	90% —	0%

Key Votes of the 102d Congress

1. Ban Striker Replace	FOR	5. Handgun Wait/7-Day	FOR	9. Use Force in Gulf	AGN
2. $ for Homeownership	AGN	6. Overseas Mil. Abortion	FOR	10. US Mil. Abroad $ Cut	FOR
3. Tax Rich/Cut Mid Cls.	FOR	7. Obscn. Art NEA $ Ban	AGN	11. Limit SDI Funds	FOR
4. FY93/$15B Def. Cut	FOR	8. Death Pen. from Jury	AGN	12. Cuba Trade Embargo	AGN

Key Votes of the 103d Congress

1. Family Leave	FOR	2. Deficit Reduction	FOR	3. Stimulus Plan	FOR

Election Results

1992 general	Nancy Pelosi (D).....................	191,906	(82%)	($443,238)
	Marc Wolin (R).......................	25,693	(11%)	($49,566)
	Three Others.........................	15,092	(7%)	
1992 primary	Nancy Pelosi (D), unopposed			
1990 general	Nancy Pelosi (D).....................	120,633	(77%)	($440,973)
(CA 5)	Alan Nichols (R).....................	35,671	(23%)	($154,858)

NINTH DISTRICT

Berkeley and Oakland, the two best-known cities on the East Bay opposite San Francisco, stand today on one of the lushest sites in America, overlooking the Bay Bridge and the Golden Gate, basking in the sun which is more common here than across the Bay. Both cities are still the homes of great institutions, but in different ways are also museum pieces, antiques from a moment in the 1960s when both, especially Berkeley, gained an identity that is hard to shake. Berkeley was founded as a university town, named after the 18th Century Irish philosopher Bishop George Berkeley, for his proclamation, "Westward the course of empire takes its way." Famous for years as the home of first-rate scholarship, Berkeley became famous politically in 1964 as the home of student rebellion, when the so-called Free Speech Movement, protesting an administrator's refusal to let students set up a card table to sign up volunteers for Lyndon Johnson's 1964 campaign, led to months of riots, students strikes and classroom confrontation. In 1969, students led protests at "People's Park," a lot owned by the university, and Governor Ronald Reagan sent in the National Guard to protect state property from conversion to a playground: an episode in which both sides relished confrontation more than any outcome. Berkeley in the 1960s gave birth to a street culture that still exists (in 1993 a student went about on campus naked; he was expelled only when administrators had the ingenuity to charge him with sexual harassment); its denizens made common cause with the Black Panthers, a violent quasi-political gang from nearby Oakland and smoked marijuana with the Hell's Angels motorcycle gang, also once based in Oakland. A left group, Berkeley Citizens' Action, took over control of the city council in 1984 (local Democrats, even liberal by California standards, are seen as right-wing opposition) and decreed rent control.

The Berkeley campus, with its view of the Bay, remains beautiful, and old buildings like the shingled Claremont Hotel are grand. Undergraduate students, some 34% of them Asian (a number sharply up after administrators abandoned racial quotas under pressure), are studying hard to get ahead in a high-tech economy. But Berkeley has had little commercial development and its public facilities are taking on a low-maintenance look with not much changed since 1969.

Oakland has a different history, centered around commerce and building its own civic institutions (Gertrude Stein was wrong: there is a there there). It became the western terminus of the transcontinental railroad in 1870 and was connected by ferry to San Francisco; it has always had heavy industry and its port today is the busiest in the Bay. The docks attracted young roustabouts like the writer Jack London, after whom a downtown square is named; civic affairs were run by the local elite, like the Knowland family who owned the *Oakland Tribune*. With the Bay area's largest black community, Oakland spawned the Black Panthers in the 1960s and blacks took control of city government in the 1970s, and through former editor-owner Bob Maynard, the *Tribune* in the 1980s. Oakland has a high crime rate and more than its share of tragedy—notably the firestorm that broke out in the hills in October 1991 which killed 25 people and destroyed 2,500 homes. But Oakland, more than Berkeley, seems to be looking ahead, with Mayor Elihu Harris pledging better law enforcement and local civic leaders trying to spark new businesses.

The 9th Congressional District of California consists of Oakland and Berkeley, plus adjacent towns, notably Alameda, site of an old Navy base on the bay. It has the largest black percentage of any northern California district, but not a majority (32%); it is 16% Asian and 12% Hispanic. Politically, it is leftish Democratic, with the lowest percentage for George Bush in 1988 of any of California's 52 districts.

The congressman from the 9th is Ronald Dellums, a product of the radical politics of the late 1960s, but more than that: he is now chairman of the Armed Services Committee. He won the seat in 1970, criticizing an incumbent who had one of the most liberal voting records in the House, and has lasted far longer than most of his original backers. Dellums has a faith in the domestic public sector which owes something to his background as a social worker; he also has a ramrod-straight bearing and a faithfulness to duty which may owe something to his service as a Marine. He continues to be, as he has been for more than 20 years, a vitriolic critic of current defense policies. But he has also made it clear, in his work as a subcommittee chairman, that he will not use his power to obstruct the will of other elected representatives. On Armed Services, as well as on the Acquisition Subcommittee which he still chairs, he regularly reports bills he voted against and continues to oppose; and, as even his Republican adversaries attested when he was appointed to the Intelligence Committee in 1991, he has kept utterly secure all classified intelligence to which he has access.

It is possible, though not clear yet, that there has been some change in Dellums's substantive views. Dellums came to Congress convinced, as many were at the time, that the extension of U.S. military power was dangerous and evil—dangerous to us and evil to others. He voted against defense budgets, criticized military brass and vocally opposed military actions. He was among the harshest critics of the 1983 Grenada invasion, which he saw as hurting the Grenadans; one of his staffers, it turned out, had close ties with the pro-Communist New Jewel movement there. Dellums brought as much vehemence to his opposition to U.S. military action in the Persian Gulf in 1990 and 1991, leading the lawsuit against President Bush brought by 54 members of Congress to reaffirm that only Congress can declare war. But he did not argue that Saddam Hussein was just progressive and, after the speedy success of U.S. forces, he no longer seems to argue that U.S. military intervention must prove futile. Dellums once told a Berkeley symposium that "We should dismantle every intelligence agency in this country piece by piece, brick by brick, nail by nail." But by 1991, he was saying, "Intelligence acquisition enjoys a rightful place; but responsible agencies must be required to respect both the nation's laws and international laws that we have, by treaty, incorporated into the body of our own jurisprudence"—a statement few would disagree with. Denunciation is a theme that runs through his career, but there are fewer targets now, with South Africa abolishing apartheid, American military action not always objectionable to him and U.S. intelligence agencies no longer seen as the enemy.

Dellums still favors massive defense cuts, $400 billion over five years, and zeroing out the B-2 bomber and Strategic Defense Initiative; he has forged alliances with conservatives to achieve those last two goals. In 1992, he sought to shift $50 billion in military spending to domestic programs "to give our children back their dreams, to give our workers back their work": his faith in the domestic public sector seems undiminished. The year 1993 will see how far Dellums is willing to take the defense cuts: five naval installations in the 9th District were targeted for closure by Defense Secretary Les Aspin. One of them, the Alameda Naval Air Station, employees 11,000 military and civilian personnel.

In some other district, Dellums might have had a problem in 1992: he had 851 overdrafts on the House bank. Indeed, before 1992 his district extended into Contra Costa County suburbs, which he regularly lost to even desultory Republicans, and his overall percentage never rose above 61%. But the creation of the new Republican 10th District meant that Dellums's district is now entirely on the Oakland-Berkeley side of the hills, and he was reelected with 72% in 1992. His only barrier to lifetime tenure is California's term-limits initiative, which says that starting in 1998 his name can no longer appear on the ballot, though he can be elected as a write-in. Will the spirit of the 1960s linger that long, in the voters or in him?

The People: Pop. 1990: 573,669; 12% age 65+; 41% White; 32% Black; 1% Amer. Indian; 16% Asian; 6% Other; 11% Hispanic origin. Voting age pop.: 447,239; 29% Black; 10% Hispanic origin. Households: 37% married couple families; 17% married couple fams. w. children; 62% college educ.; median household income: $30,067; per capita income: $16,833; median gross rent: $538; median house value: $220,200.

1992 Presidential Vote			1988 Presidential Vote		
Clinton (D)	186,714	(78%)	Dukakis (D)	178,152	(80%)
Bush (R)	29,394	(12%)	Bush (R)	44,112	(20%)
Perot (I)	21,207	(9%)			

Rep. Ronald V. Dellums (D)

Elected 1970; b. Nov. 24, 1935, Oakland; home, Oakland; Oakland City Col., A.A. 1958, San Francisco St. Col., B.A. 1960, U. of CA, M.S.W. 1962; Protestant; married (Leola).

Career: Marine Corps, 1954–56; Psychiatric social worker, CA Dept. of Mental Hygiene, 1962–64; Prog. Dir., Bayview Community Ctr., 1964–65; Dir., Hunter's Pt. Bayview Youth Oppor. Ctr., 1965–66; Consultant, Bay Area Social Plng. Cncl., 1966–67; Dir., San Francisco Econ. Oppor. Cncl. Employment Prog., 1967–68; Berkeley City Cncl., 1967–71.

Offices: 2108 RHOB 20515, 202-225-2661. Also 201 13th St., #105, Oakland 94617, 415-763-0370.

Committees: *Armed Services* (Chmn. of 34 D): Military Acquisition (Chmn.). *District of Columbia* (V. Chmn. of 8 D): Fiscal Affairs and Health; Judiciary and Education.

Group Ratings

	ADA	ACLU	COPE	CDF	CFA	LCV	ACU	NTLC	NSI	COC	CEI
1992	95	100	92	100	93	94	0	10	0	25	11
1991	90	—	100	100	94	92	0	—	—	20	8

National Journal Ratings

	1991 LIB	—	1991 CONS	1992 LIB	—	1992 CONS
Economic	88%	—	0%	66%	—	31%
Social	88%	—	0%	92%	—	0%
Foreign	92%	—	0%	90%	—	0%

Key Votes of the 102d Congress

1. Ban Striker Replace FOR	5. Handgun Wait/7-Day FOR	9. Use Force in Gulf AGN
2. $ for Homeownership AGN	6. Overseas Mil. Abortion FOR	10. US Mil. Abroad $ Cut FOR
3. Tax Rich/Cut Mid Cls.AGN	7. Obscn. Art NEA $ BanAGN	11. Limit SDI Funds FOR
4. FY93/$15B Def. Cut FOR	8. Death Pen. from Jury AGN	12. Cuba Trade Embargo AGN

Key Votes of the 103d Congress

1. Family Leave FOR   2. Deficit Reduction FOR   3. Stimulus Plan FOR

Election Results

1992 general	Ronald V. Dellums (D)	164,265	(72%)	($921,771)
	G. William (Billy) Hunter (R)	53,707	(24%)	($73,659)
	Dave Linn (P&F)	10,472	(5%)	
1992 primary	Ronald V. Dellums (D), unopposed			
1990 general	Ronald V. Dellums (D)	119,645	(61%)	($840,029)
(CA 8)	Barbara Galewski (R)	75,544	(39%)	

TENTH DISTRICT

Thirty years ago, when the streets of San Francisco and Oakland were already crowded, the rolling, hill-strewn grasslands on the east of the mountain ridges, over the hill and through the tunnel from Oakland, were largely empty. In the years since, they have started to fill up. Freeways took the first commuters through the Caldecott Tunnel to the woodsy trail-like roads of Orinda and Lafayette; Interstate 580 brought people east from the southern East Bay towns to the Amador Valley and Livermore, site of one of the nation's nuclear laboratories; Interstate 680 running north-south provided a spine for businesses and shopping centers up and down the San Ramon Valley, from the burgeoning town of Concord through Walnut Creek, Danville and Dublin; BART stations in Walnut Creek and Orinda took commuters to downtown San Francisco. Not all this area is filled in yet, and there is much resistance to overdevelopment. But what has evolved in this sunny land, shielded by the mountains from the ocean fogs and rains, is an advanced civilization of high-skill and educated people. Affluent and generally tolerant of— if a little put off by—what happens in San Francisco, they are respectful of economic markets and wary of government, but concerned about preserving a physical environment that can be one of America's most pleasant.

This is the land of the 10th Congressional District, a seat newly created by the court-ordered redistricting of 1992. It consists almost entirely of the interior portion of the Bay Area, with just a few salients beyond—the suburb of Castro Valley on the East Bay, the working class town of Antioch on the San Joaquin River Delta. This area had been voting Republican for years, but was split up between four different Democratic districts. It is easily now the most Republican Bay Area district. Even so, in the political atmosphere of 1992, the Republican widely expected to win this seat, Bill Baker, only barely made it.

Baker entered the race with many assets. He once wrote a newspaper column called "The Angry Taxpayer," and in 12 years in the Assembly he became known as an expert budget-cutter. As one observer wrote, "Baker makes any list of the legislature's quickest minds, tartest tongues and most doctrinaire conservatives." He also helped the city of Oakland, where he like many of his constituents grew up, with its budget problems. But he was attacked for saying, while discussing welfare in a 1980 newspaper interview, that he would tell welfare mothers if they had more children, "If you're going to be a breeder, we're not going to subsidize it." An opponent of abortion rights, Baker hailed a high school delegation in 1991 as "17 survivors of abortion"—a comment for which he later apologized. None of this was helpful in 1992, as Californians, even suburban fiscal conservatives, seemed disgusted with George Bush and the religious right in the Republican Party. Baker beat a weak primary opponent, who tried to portray Baker as an extreme conservative, by only 64%–36%. In the general, he faced Democrat Wendell Williams, who had run against him twice for the Assembly and in 1990 held him to 55%. Williams attacked Baker for being antiabortion and for the "breeder" and "17 survivors" lines; he accused Baker, apparently without evidence, of having ties to the religious right. To head off a near certain Williams attack, Baker, an opponent of some gun control measures, returned a campaign contribution from the National Rifle Association. Baker talked about budget-cutting and called for lower capital gains taxes, measures to spur home construction and "government that is user-friendly to investors." Baker finally won, but with just 52% of the vote—not a stunning showing for a clear favorite in this favorable district.

In the House, Baker serves on the Science Committee, which superintends the Livermore Lab and a branch of the Sandia Lab here, and on Public Works, almost every freshman's choice in an age that celebrates infrastructure. He should be a good bet for reelection, though if the political climate in California doesn't change he could have serious competition again.

The People: Pop. 1990: 571,979; 3% rural; 10% age 65+; 82% White; 2% Black; 1% Amer. Indian; 6% Asian; 3% Other; 9% Hispanic origin. Voting age pop.: 431,696; 2% Black; 8% Hispanic origin. Households: 63% married couple families; 29% married couple fams. w. children; 68% college educ.; median household income: $52,378; per capita income: $23,972; median gross rent: $746; median house value: $273,800.

1992 Presidential Vote			1988 Presidential Vote		
Clinton (D)	127,450	(42%)	Bush (R)	144,386	(58%)
Bush (R)	107,191	(35%)	Dukakis (D)	104,199	(42%)
Perot (I)	66,180	(22%)			

Rep. Bill Baker (R)

Elected 1992; b. June 14, 1940, Oakland; home, Danville; San Jose St. U., B.S. 1963; Catholic; married (Joanne).

Career: Coast Guard Reserves, 1957–65; Budget Analyst, CA Dept. of Finance 1968–72; Exec. V.P., Contra Costa Taxpayers Assn., 1972–78; CA Assembly, 1980–92.

Offices: 1724 LHOB 20515, 202-225-1880. Also 1801 N. California Blvd., Walnut Creek 94596, 510-932-8899; and Dublin City Hall, 100 Civic Plz., Dublin 94568, 510-829-0813.

Committees: *Public Works and Transportation* (14th of 24 R): Economic Development; Investigations and Oversight; Surface Transportation. *Science, Space and Technology* (21st of 22 R): Energy.

Group Ratings and 102d Congress Votes: Newly Elected

Key Votes of the 103d Congress

1. Family Leave	AGN	2. Deficit Reduction	AGN	3. Stimulus Plan	AGN

Election Results

1992 general	Bill Baker (R)	145,702	(52%)	($697,982)
	Wendell H. Williams (D)	134,635	(48%)	($238,906)
1992 primary	Bill Baker (R)	46,786	(64%)	
	Dave Williams (R)	26,387	(36%)	
1990 election	Newly created district.			

ELEVENTH DISTRICT

Journalists from back east looking for clues about California might consider avoiding the premises of Beverly Hills and Nob Hill, might well leave the state's two big metropolitan areas altogether, and examine things around Stockton. For Stockton, just 50 miles south of Sacramento, is in the middle of the Central Valley which saw much of California's most rapid growth in the 1980s and is now subject to some growing problems of it own. This is not a totally new part of California: Stockton was named after Robert Stockton, the second U.S. military governor of California, who captured Santa Barbara and Los Angeles from Mexico and proclaimed California United States territory. Founded in 1847, Stockton was an important trading town during the Gold Rush. The Central Valley, criss-crossed with railroads and canals, became one of the world's greatest agriculture areas; the San Joaquin River channel was deepened to 37 feet and Stockton today is the Central Valley's ocean port. The rich farming attracted immigrants from all over: Mexicans coming up Route 99 joined North Dakotans flocking to the town of Lodi; Italian and Yugoslav immigrants bringing their old world crops; Yankees and Okies bringing their distinct churches and systems of belief; and now Southeast Asian refugees crowd into the older streets of Stockton. The 1980s growth brought traffic congestion and air quality problems to the Central Valley, and some fear that urban development will gobble up the best farmland. It also brought many new voters, and an apparent tilt of a longtime Democratic area slightly to the right.

The new 11th Congressional District of California includes Stockton and most of surrounding San Joaquin County, plus the southern part of Sacramento County, an area of farms and a few subdivisions, dredge tailings and marshy, rich-soiled islands in the delta of the Sacramento and San Joaquin Rivers. The district was widely thought to have been intended by Governor Pete Wilson for former Sacramento County Supervisor Sandy Smoley, like Wilson a moderate and pro-choice Republican, who had lost to Robert Matsui in a Sacramento-based district in 1978. But Smoley lost the Republican primary to Richard Pombo, a 31-year-old rancher and Tracy council member who was known for bringing a Safeway distribution center to town. With his trademark cowboy hat and mustache, he looked the part of the fourth-generation San Joaquin County rancher. Pombo called Smoley "the surefire choice of the hard-line feminists" and attacked her support of Wilson's gay rights bill, calling her "a homosexual rights supporter masquerading as pro-family." When Congressman Barney Frank called Pombo a "low-rent Pat Buchanan," Pombo embraced the label. Smoley had no significant edge in Sacramento County, which cast only 25% of primary votes, and overall Pombo won 36% to Smoley's 27% and 24% for Jack Sieglock, once an aide to former Stockton area Congressman Norman Shumway.

Meanwhile, Democratic primary voters gave a solid 64% victory to Patti Garamendi, onetime Peace Corps volunteer, mother of six, wife of Insurance Commissioner and former state Senator John Garamendi. Garamendi had strong support from women's groups and unions and a well-known name. But she may have suffered from a reputation as a perpetual candidate: she ran unsuccessfully to succeed her husband in the state Senate in 1990, against one of his former aides, and then lost a 1991 special election for the Assembly. And Pombo, far from being defensive about his conservative stands, emblazoned them. He stressed his opposition to abortion, his support of property rights and opposition to the Endangered Species Act. He denounced the lyrics of rap singer Ice-T's song "Cop Killer," and attacked Garamendi when she accused him of racism for it. She said he was a tool of the Christian right; he said that she was just an ambitious liberal politician, a "community activist and socialite." Pombo was not the favorite, but he carried both counties and won 48%–46%.

Pombo predicted "I'm not going to fit in too well [in Congress] because I'm anything but politically correct." He won seats on the Natural Resources and Agriculture Committees, where he seems sure to reflect the outlook of pro-development and property rights-minded landholders. He is as friendly to a multi-purpose as he is hostile to the Endangered Species Act. Given his close margin, he may very well attract serious opposition in 1994, but he is by no means an endangered species himself yet.

The People: Pop. 1990: 571,650; 15% rural; 11% age 65+; 62% White; 6% Black; 1% Amer. Indian; 12% Asian; 7% Other; 20% Hispanic origin. Voting age pop.: 404,873; 5% Black; 18% Hispanic origin. 'Households: 58% married couple families; 29% married couple fams. w. children; 46% college educ.; median household income: $31,605; per capita income: $13,299; median gross rent: $499; median house value: $123,000.

1992 Presidential Vote			1988 Presidential Vote		
Clinton (D)	79,432	(40%)	Bush (R)	97,325	(56%)
Bush (R)	75,319	(38%)	Dukakis (D)	76,929	(44%)
Perot (I)	41,006	(21%)			

Rep. Richard W. Pombo (R)

Elected 1992; b. Jan. 8, 1961, Tracy; home, Tracy; CA Polytechnic Inst., 1979–82; Catholic; married (Annette).

Career: Cattle rancher; Co-founder, Citizens Land Alliance, 1988; Tracy City Cncl., 1990–92.

Offices: 1519 LHOB 20515, 202-225-1947. Also 2321 W. March Ln., #205, Stockton 95207, 209-951-3091.

Committees: *Agriculture* (16th of 19 R): Environment, Credit and Rural Development; Livestock; Specialty Crops and Natural Resources. *Merchant Marine and Fisheries* (16th of 19 R): Coast Guard and Navigation. *Natural Resources* (14th of 15 R): Energy and Mineral Resources; Oversight and Investigations.

Group Ratings and 102d Congress Votes: Newly Elected

Key Votes of the 103d Congress

1. Family Leave	AGN	2. Deficit Reduction	AGN	3. Stimulus Plan	AGN

Election Results

1992 general	Richard W. Pombo (R)	94,453	(48%)	($528,989)
	Patricia Garamendi (D)	90,539	(46%)	($864,411)
	Christine Roberts (LIB)	13,498	(7%)	
1992 primary	Richard W. Pombo (R)	16,704	(36%)	
	Sandy Smoley (R)	12,482	(27%)	
	Jack A. Sieglock (R)	11,029	(24%)	
	Frank W. Hauck (R)	4,455	(9%)	
	Cleo Nichol Robinson (R)	1,703	(4%)	
	Other	341	(1%)	
1990 election	Newly created district.			

TWELFTH DISTRICT

Running south from San Francisco is the Peninsula which connects the city with the mainland of the United States. This is geologically interesting, and active, country: the San Andreas Fault runs just east of the Coast Range, underneath the reservoirs which store San Francisco's water supply. To the west are green mountains splashing down into the foggy ocean. To the east is a zone of flat land between mountain and bay, an unbroken chain of suburbs and urban settlement, with light industry and salt flats along the bay front, and residential neighborhoods and some commercial strips from the Bayshore Freeway up through the Junipero Serra Freeway atop the mountain ridge. Historically, the Peninsula has seemed separate from San Francisco; Dashiell Hammett, writing before the advent of freeways, gets his detective Sam Spade out of the city for most of a day when he follows a false tip down the Peninsula. But today, the Peninsula suburbs are demographically an extension of the city.

The 12th Congressional District of California consists of the northern Peninsula suburbs plus the southwest quadrant of San Francisco—the city's middle-income Sunset district, with older houses amid unburied telephone and electric wires, lying on curving hills that were once sand dunes. Just to the south, across the San Mateo County line at the southern extension of the BART lines, is Daly City with substantial numbers of Mexican-Americans and Asians; nearby, South San Francisco proclaims itself "the industrial city" in big letters on San Bruno Mountain near the Bayshore Freeway; the streets lined with boxy houses in San Bruno and Pacifica wind over sweeping hillsides facing cemeteries where many San Franciscans and veterans of Pacific wars are buried. That is the view from one side of the Junipero Serra Freeway; from the other, the vista is of San Francisco Bay, broader than one might expect, and the airport next door, connecting this metropolis with others on the Pacific Rim; to the south is the neat suburban city of San Mateo and, on twisting streets in the hills above the Burlingame Country Club, the rich suburb of Hillsborough, home to much of the city's WASP elite.

This is an ethnically diverse and economically prosperous constituency. Fully 26% of its residents are Asian—the second highest of any mainland district, after San Francisco's 8th just to the north—and another 14% are Hispanic. Income levels are, if not among the highest in the country, very far above average: one-third of Hispanic households in San Mateo County make over $50,000 a year. The economic orientation here is more toward San Francisco to the north than south to Silicon Valley; the political heritage here is Democratic, from both ethnic heritage or historic labor union ties. The 12th delivered solid margins not just for Bill Clinton in 1992 but for Michael Dukakis in 1988.

The congressman from the 12th District, Tom Lantos, has several distinctions, but none more important than the fact that he is one of the few members of Congress with personal experience living under tyranny. Lantos was born in Hungary and as a teenager fought in the underground against the Nazis, and was one of the Jews saved by Swedish diplomat Raoul Wallenberg. He has the confidence of an intellectual (he taught economics at San Francisco State) who has also shrewdly made some money, and who has moved up politically (he chose to run against a Republican incumbent in the Republican year of 1980 and won), and who has seen first hand in his own lifetime the rise and then the rollback of totalitarianism.

Lantos has spent much of his time in the House on foreign policy. Unlike other Bay Area Democrats, he did not bring to his work an instinctive mistrust of administration policy or doubts of American good intentions. He founded the Congressional Human Rights Caucus, focusing on Communist regimes as well as the right-wing dictatorships other liberal Democrats denounced, although he did vote against contra aid. He is among the most enthusiastic supporters of Israel, and was calling for economic sanctions against Iraq back in 1988 for their gassing of the Kurds. He was an enthusiastic supporter of the Gulf war resolution, and was criticized by some back in his district for holding hearings where an unidentified 15-year-old Kuwaiti girl, identified only as Nayirah, told of Iraqi atrocities; it turned out she was the daughter of the Kuwaiti ambassador, and Lantos was accused of whipping up war fever. But of course Iraqi conduct turned out to be even worse than alleged, and Lantos's judgment that Ambassador April Glaspie's complacent response to Saddam Hussein showed "frightening flawed judgment" seems sound, though it might more fairly be applied to the superiors who gave such instructions than to a career diplomat who carried them out. Lantos has been busy on other foreign fronts as well, keeping in close touch with breaking developments in eastern Europe, especially in Hungary, which he visited in November 1992; in 1990 he was the first American official to visit Albania since 1946. He has strongly advocated a more active American role in the former Yugoslavia.

Lantos has also shown a flair for showmanship with his Government Operations Employment and Housing Subcommittee investigations. His high-publicity hearings on labor law violations by the Food Lion supermarket chain led to legal charges, and he attacked West Coast-based Jack in the Box for child labor law violations. He hopes to get tough OSHA reform legislation passed in the 103d Congress. In 1989 and 1990 he conducted hearings on alleged misconduct under Reagan HUD Secretary Samuel Pierce. Lantos was a founder of the Congressional Friends of Animals Caucus and, like almost all coastal Californians, opposes offshore oil drilling.

Lantos raised and spent a total of $1.7 million on his 1980 and 1982 campaigns; since then, he has been reelected easily. Redistricting only helped in 1992. He had an additional triumph in 1990 when his son-in-law, Dick Swett, upset Republican incumbent Chuck Douglas in the 2d District of New Hampshire.

The People: Pop. 1990: 571,667; 14% age 65+; 56% White; 4% Black; 26% Asian; 5% Other; 14% Hispanic origin. Voting age pop.: 456,457; 4% Black; 13% Hispanic origin. Households: 53% married couple families; 23% married couple fams. w. children; 62% college educ.; median household income: $44,720; per capita income: $20,984; median gross rent: $780; median house value: $320,400.

1992 Presidential Vote			1988 Presidential Vote		
Clinton (D)	139,281	(57%)	Dukakis (D)	127,565	(59%)
Bush (R)	64,984	(27%)	Bush (R)	88,994	(41%)
Perot (I)	38,129	(16%)			

Rep. Tom Lantos (D)

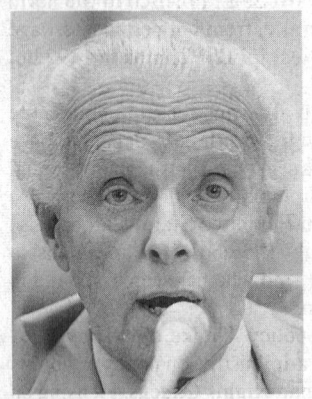

Elected 1980; b. Feb. 1, 1928, Budapest, Hungary; home, Burlingame; U. of WA, B.A. 1949, M.A. 1950, U. of CA, Ph.D. 1953; Jewish; married (Annette).

Career: Economist, Bank of America, 1952–53; TV Commentator, San Francisco, 1955–63; Dir. of Intl. Programs, CA St. U., 1962–71; Advisor, U.S. Sen. Joseph R. Biden Jr., 1978–79; Mbr., Pres. Task Force on Defense & Foreign Policy, 1976; Prof., San Francisco St. U., 1950–80.

Offices: 2182 RHOB 20515, 202-225-3531. Also 400 El Camino Real, #800, San Mateo 94402, 415-342-0300.

Committees: *Government Operations* (7th of 25 D): Employment, Housing and Aviation; Legislation and National Security. *Foreign Affairs* (3d of 27 D): Europe and the Middle East; International Operations; International Security, International Organizations and Human Rights (Chmn.).

Group Ratings

	ADA	ACLU	COPE	CDF	CFA	LCV	ACU	NTLC	NSI	COC	CEI
1992	95	87	92	90	100	94	8	5	50	25	12
1991	75	—	100	100	89	85	11	—	—	11	8

National Journal Ratings

	1991 LIB — 1991 CONS		1992 LIB — 1992 CONS	
Economic	66% —	32%	91% —	0%
Social	78% —	17%	72% —	24%
Foreign	67% —	32%	56% —	40%

Key Votes of the 102d Congress

1. Ban Striker Replace	FOR	5. Handgun Wait/7-Day	FOR	9. Use Force in Gulf	FOR
2. $ for Homeownership	AGN	6. Overseas Mil. Abortion	FOR	10. US Mil. Abroad $ Cut	FOR
3. Tax Rich/Cut Mid Cls.	FOR	7. Obscn. Art NEA $ Ban	FOR	11. Limit SDI Funds	FOR
4. FY93/$15B Def. Cut	FOR	8. Death Pen. from Jury	AGN	12. Cuba Trade Embargo	FOR

Key Votes of the 103d Congress

1. Family Leave	FOR	2. Deficit Reduction	FOR	3. Stimulus Plan	FOR

Election Results

1992 general	Tom Lantos (D)	157,205	(69%)	($600,656)
	Jim Tomlin (R)	53,278	(23%)	($5,554)
	Mary Weldon (P&F)	10,142	(4%)	
	Other	7,782	(3%)	
1992 primary	Tom Lantos (D)	62,397	(82%)	
	Glenn Tenney (D)	8,200	(11%)	
	Jim Dunlap (D)	5,696	(7%)	
1990 general	Tom Lantos (D)	105,029	(66%)	($620,782)
(CA 11)	Bill Quraishi (R)	45,818	(29%)	($97,030)
	June R. Genis (LIB)	8,518	(5%)	

THIRTEENTH DISTRICT

The East Bay is the workaday, unglamorous side of metropolitan San Francisco—the margin of land perhaps five miles wide between San Francisco Bay and the surprisingly high mountains that rise just to the east. The shoreline is not picturesque, with its Navy bases, docks, airports and salt evaporators; the skyscrapers of Oakland are unimpressive compared to those of San Francisco; the Bay Bridge, bisected by Yerba Buena Island cuts an inspiring figure, but the San Mateo Bridge to the south is at best utilitarian. Fifty years ago, when the shipyards of Richmond and the Navy yard in Oakland were buzzing, the East Bay south of Oakland was still largely uninhabited farm fields. In the postwar years, it has filled up, one suburb at a time, along Route 17: San Leandro, originally settled by Portuguese, Castro Valley with its Japanese Gardens, Hayward with its Cal State University campus, Union City with its rail yards, and Fremont with the famous NUMMI auto plant where Chevrolets and Toyotas are produced together and home of the California School for the Deaf.

The 13th Congressional District of California is made up of this string of East Bay towns, somewhat more blue-collar than the Peninsula towns across the Bay. The district is racially and ethnically mixed in the California manner—19% Asian, 18% Hispanic, 7% black—and with a Democratic heritage not yet dampened by high crime (crime rates are much lower here than in Oakland) or revulsion of cultural liberalism (these people are used to TV newscasts from San Francisco). This area looks like much of the Bay Area, with stucco houses and shopping centers, but house prices are below the ridiculously high Bay Area average and the stores are discount chains rather than Saks. Still, income levels are well above the national average.

The row of East Bay districts from Richmond south to San Jose elect four Democratic congressmen with a total of 90 years of seniority, and two major committee and four major subcommittee chairmanships: left-wing power in the 1990s. The congressman from the 13th District is Pete Stark, a Democrat first elected in 1972 when he beat an elderly incumbent who supported the Vietnam war, now a senior member of Ways and Means and chairman of its Health Subcommittee. Stark first attracted attention when he founded a bank in nearby Walnut Creek and attracted deposits from all over the Bay Area by putting a giant peace symbol atop his headquarters and peace symbols on all checks; while other members may use their Banking Committee seats to enrich themselves, he used the riches he got in banking to get to the committee, and from there to Ways and Means. That same puckishness has on occasion gotten Stark into trouble. In 1989, he called HHS Secretary Louis Sullivan "a disgrace to his race" for supporting Bush Administration health policies; in 1991, Stark attacked "Jewish colleagues" for voting for the Gulf war resolution "as a matter of convenience" to help Israel.

Stark has chaired the Health Subcommittee since 1985. It has not always been rewarding work. His major achievement was the Catastrophic Health Care Act of 1988, which was repealed by an overwhelming vote in 1989 after an outpouring of public protest: the problem was that its tax on high-income social security recipients was highly unpopular while the benefits were not appreciated, a reminder that in constructing a healthcare system, even a small mistake can be politically devastating. In the 102d Congress, Stark had a bill providing universal access to long-term care to be paid for by a Social Security-type payroll tax and a 2% gross income tax. For the 103d Congress, he plans to reintroduce a 1992 bill which includes global budgeting, establishing an annual national health budget and then compelling care providers to live within it; this would require close federal regulation, with the government in effect setting maximum prices for drugs and procedures. He sees cost control as the primary goal, with universal access to be phased in over time. On access, he would expand Medicaid to cover everyone with double the poverty income and below, and would establish a "kiddycare" program with insurance for all children under 19 for a premium of $1,250 a year. Where exactly these plans would go is unclear; indeed, although Ways and Means Chairman Dan Rostenkowski has often backed Stark on health issues, he is not interested in lost causes and there could easily be jurisdictional fights with John Dingell and Henry Waxman of Energy and Commerce, not to mention Hillary Rodham Clinton. In early 1993, Stark voiced some skepticism over the administration's proposals on a managed competition approach to health care.

Stark has other items on his agenda. He has succeeded Ron Dellums as chairman of the District of Columbia Committee and may try to achieve statehood for D.C., although it's not clear the House will cast a vote that could make Jesse Jackson and Marion Barry U.S. senators. Stark is an advocate of a carbon tax, to promote energy efficiency and cut the deficit. He has a bill to abolish FEMA and transfer its emergency functions and budget to the Defense Department.

The 1990 election, after the Catastrophic Health Care Act repeal, saw Stark's percentage go down to 58%. But redistricting sheared off some Republican territory for the new 10th District, and Stark's constituents were not troubled in 1992 by his 64 overdrafts on the House bank.

The People: Pop. 1990: 572,333; 9% age 65+; 55% White; 7% Black; 1% Amer. Indian; 19% Asian; 8% Other; 18% Hispanic origin. Voting age pop.: 426,247; 7% Black; 16% Hispanic origin. Households: 59% married couple families; 29% married couple fams. w. children; 55% college educ.; median household income: $43,877; per capita income: $17,335; median gross rent: $726; median house value: $222,700.

1992 Presidential Vote

Clinton (D)	116,829	(54%)
Bush (R)	55,100	(25%)
Perot (I)	43,026	(20%)

1988 Presidential Vote

Dukakis (D)	106,561	(56%)
Bush (R)	83,883	(44%)

Rep. Fortney H. (Pete) Stark (D)

Elected 1972; b. Nov. 11, 1931, Milwaukee, WI; home, Hayward; MIT, B.S. 1953, U. of CA at Berkeley, M.B.A. 1960; Unitarian; married (Carolyn).

Career: Air Force, 1955–57; Founder, Beacon Savings & Loan Assn., 1961; Founder and Pres., Security Natl. Bank, Walnut Creek, 1963–72.

Offices: 239 CHOB 20515, 202-225-5065. Also 22320 Foothill Blvd., Hayward 94541, 415-635-1092.

Committees: *District of Columbia* (Chmn. of 8 D): Government Operations and Metropolitan Affairs; Judiciary and Education. *Ways and Means* (5th of 24 D): Health (Chmn.). *Joint Economic Committee* (3d of 10).

Group Ratings

	ADA	ACLU	COPE	CDF	CFA	LCV	ACU	NTLC	NSI	COC	CEI
1992	95	100	83	100	93	100	4	5	10	13	17
1991	100	—	100	100	89	100	0	—	—	20	11

National Journal Ratings

	1991 LIB — 1991 CONS		1992 LIB — 1992 CONS	
Economic	88%	— 0%	66%	— 31%
Social	88%	— 0%	92%	— 0%
Foreign	86%	— 13%	90%	— 0%

Key Votes of the 102d Congress

1. Ban Striker Replace	FOR	5. Handgun Wait/7-Day FOR	9. Use Force in Gulf AGN
2. $ for Homeownership	AGN	6. Overseas Mil. Abortion FOR	10. US Mil. Abroad $ Cut FOR
3. Tax Rich/Cut Mid Cls.	FOR	7. Obscn. Art NEA $ Ban AGN	11. Limit SDI Funds *
4. FY93/$15B Def. Cut	FOR	8. Death Pen. from Jury AGN	12. Cuba Trade Embargo AGN

Key Votes of the 103d Congress

1. Family Leave	FOR	2. Deficit Reduction FOR	3. Stimulus Plan FOR

Election Results

1992 general	Fortney H. (Pete) Stark (D)	123,795	(60%)	($589,500)
	Verne Teyler (R)	64,953	(32%)	($43,435)
	Roslyn A. Allen (P&F)	16,768	(8%)	
1992 primary	Fortney H. (Pete) Stark (D), unopposed			
1990 general	Fortney H. (Pete) Stark (D)	94,739	(58%)	($300,996)
(CA 9)	Victor Romero (R)	67,412	(42%)	($210,089)

FOURTEENTH DISTRICT

Cupertino, California, hardly seems a place where a revolution began: a suburb between San Jose and Palo Alto, criss-crossed by freeways and mile-square commercial avenues, with the stucco strip malls and subdivisions native to suburban California. Yet here is the center of America's the high-tech computer business: the heart of Silicon Valley, where computer hackers have turned tinkerer's dreams into multi-billion dollar companies and innovators have produced business after business that outthink public planners and out-compete subsidized foreign consortiums. In fact, this area south of San Francisco has long been a land of high-technology startups. William Hewlett and David Packard started their firm in 1939 in a Palo Alto garage, not too many years after Philo Farnsworth invented television in San Francisco. So when Steve Jobs started Apple in Cupertino, less than 20 years ago, or when Andrew Grove started and then reinvented Intel in Santa Clara, they were only the latest in a long tradition. And amid periodic cries for government guidance and subsidies, Silicon Valley has continually proved—most recently in Intel's wresting of the microchip market away from the Japanese—the power of creative individuals. Of course there is much hand-wringing and worrying about the Silicon Valley's future, since rapidly growing businesses are inherently unstable; and there are other nagging problems—traffic is clogged, housing prices remain high, many startups go sour while old businesses fall by the wayside. But the outlook, for this area of such creativity and brains and openness to innovation, must be considered good.

If high-tech business can start anywhere, why are so many of them here? Partly because Stanford University has encouraged its faculty to experiment with—and profit from—high-tech breakthroughs. Partly because of the history of high tech here—Hewlett-Packard and IBM's 1950s San Jose facility. And always experimental San Francisco generates venture capital: old-line WASPs open to new thinking. But mostly, the Silicon Valley is the kind of place where smart young innovators like to live. Counterculture veterans may cluster around the liberal university towns; elite law and medical school graduates head to the prestigious, high salary jobs of central cities; but techies are free to live in this pleasant, healthy environment. Sheltered by hills from coastal fogs and rains, the Silicon Valley boasts a sunny climate with perceptible but gentle seasons, perfect for year-round outdoor sports; there may well be more jogging trails and bicycle paths here than anywhere else in the country. There is a sort of pure Americana here: these communities were rustic but never poor, rural but never bigoted, country-like but still easily accessible to the luxuries of civilization. People here were ahead of the rest of the nation in fighting to preserve the environment, in favoring natural over processed foods, and in indulging in regular exercise. Here live cultural liberals with a respect for market economics, a sense of social responsibility and a certain distrust of the federal government.

Coinciding almost exactly with the boundaries of the Silicon Valley is the current 14th Congressional District of California. Though it includes a stretch of Pacific coast, almost all its people live along San Francisco Bay, in the strip of flat land bounded by the Bayshore and Junipero Serra Freeways, running from Belmont, not far south of San Francisco Airport, through Redwood City, Menlo Park, Palo Alto (home of Stanford), Mountain View, Sunnyvale and Cupertino. Off to one side are a few high-income enclaves: Atherton, with its stone-walled lots; Woodside, with its 1850s country store and mansions dotting the hills; Portola Valley and Los Altos Hills, with stark contemporary homes overlooking the Bay.

While other Bay Area districts reelect members who achieve great power in the House—the four East Bay districts had 90 years' seniority going into 1993—the 14th District and its predecessors have had five members in the last seven elections. One reason is that Republicans elected here tend to be culturally liberal and economically market-oriented, and thus attractive statewide candidates to Silicon Valley fundraisers, as with David Packard. Pete McCloskey left the House in 1982 to run for the Senate, losing the primary 38%–25% to Pete Wilson; so did Ed Zschau in 1986, winning his primary 37%–30% over Bruce Herschensohn but losing the general 50%–47% to Alan Cranston; so did Tom Campbell in 1992, losing his primary to Herschensohn 38%–36%: even a non-techie can see a pattern here. Campbell's candidacy opened up the seat, and for the first time in a year when opinion was swinging very much the Democrats' way; both parties had serious primary contests, and the ultimate winner was Democrat Anna Eshoo.

Eshoo has several distinctions. She is the only member of Congress of Assyrian descent, she is one of several new women members who once were full-time homemakers, she has served both in local government (10 years on the San Mateo County Board of Supervisors) and in national politics (12 years on the Democratic National Committee). Eshoo came back after losing once before, to Campbell by a 52%–46% margin, in the predecessor of this district in 1988. In that campaign, Eshoo originated the technique of distributing videotapes—100,000 copies—complete with hip music, showing her in a postmodern office, telling voters that the Silicon Valley, unlike Orange County or Iowa, should be represented by someone special. It was quite a race: both candidates in that contest could claim to be special (Campbell is a Chicago economics Ph.D. as well as a Stanford law professor, quickly picked by *Roll Call* as one of the 10 brainiest congressmen); and the two spent a total of $2.5 million on the race. For the 1992 primary, Eshoo distributed "First Things First," a 58-page booklet of her issue positions. Assemblyman Ted Lempert, redistricted out of his seat at age 30, had strong backing from environmentalists; but he was hurt when he launched unsubstantiated attacks on Eshoo. A third serious Democrat, who was not able to raise much money, was openly gay San Mateo Supervisor Tom Nolan. Lempert's local support helped him win 36%, but Eshoo had 40% to only 15% for Nolan. On the Republican side, several candidates had serious credentials. Michael Maibach was Intel's chief of governmental affairs; Paul Biddle was the Navy auditor and whistleblower who exposed Stanford University's federal contract overbilling, which brought down its president Donald Kennedy; Dixon Arnett served four terms in the Assembly and was deputy HHS secretary; and Tom Huening was a former airline pilot and San Mateo supervisor whose redistricting initiative came close to passing statewide in 1990. Huening had an additional plus, support from David Packard and other Silicon Valley and Stanford-connected big moneygivers, which helped financially and because of Packard's high reputation. Huening won the primary with 43%, to 17% each for Arnett and Maibach and 14% for Biddle.

In a different year, this would have been a close general election, and Huening acted like a candidate expecting to win; before the November election, he announced a post-election freshman summit in Omaha, which eventually did take place and attracted several Republicans—but not Huening. The collapse of George Bush and the Republican ticket was especially stark in Silicon Valley, and Eshoo had positive things to talk about: her work on setting up a managed-competition health plan for county government (which she touts as a national model), her opposition to coastline developments, her gender in a year when two female Democrats carried this area solidly for senator. Eshoo's victory was an impressive 57%–39%. In the House, she took a seat on the Science, Space and Technology Committee, not normally considered a major assignment, but more sought after than usual for 1993 and potentially important to the Silicon Valley. She got a seat on Merchant Marine and Fisheries as well, where she is likely to be a strong environmentalist; she promises to push for managed-competition health care as well. Eshoo must surely be regarded as a good bet for reelection, though she may be a little nervous about supporting a Clinton economic package that imposes higher taxes on so many of her own voters, especially if the results are not as good as promised. And it is possible that Tom Campbell could run again, though he is more likely to seek statewide office if any.

The People: Pop. 1990: 571,058; 2% rural; 11% age 65+; 69% White; 5% Black; 12% Asian; 4% Other; 13% Hispanic origin. Voting age pop.: 457,209; 4% Black; 12% Hispanic origin. Households: 52% married couple families; 22% married couple fams. w. children; 73% college educ.; median household income: $50,078; per capita income: $26,047; median gross rent: $777; median house value: $401,600.

1992 Presidential Vote

Clinton (D) 143,765 (53%)
Bush (R) 71,754 (26%)
Perot (I). 53,047 (20%)

1988 Presidential Vote

Dukakis (D). 137,090 (55%)
Bush (R) 112,059 (45%)

Rep. Anna G. Eshoo (D)

Elected 1992; b. Dec. 13, 1942, New Britain, CT; home, Atherton; Canada Col., A.A. 1976; Catholic; divorced.

Career: Chmn., San Mateo Cnty Dem. Party, 1980; Chief of Staff, CA Assembly Speaker McCarthy, 1981; San Mateo Cnty. Bd. of Supervisors, 1982–92, Pres., 1986.

Offices: 1505 LHOB 20515, 202-225-8104. Also 698 Emerson St., Palo Alto 94301, 415-323-2984.

Committees: *Merchant Marine and Fisheries* (23d of 29 D): Environment and Natural Resources; Oceanography, Gulf of Mexico and the Outer Continental Shelf. *Science, Space and Technology* (25th of 33 D): Science; Space; Technology, Environment and Aviation.

Group Ratings and 102d Congress Votes: Newly Elected

Key Votes of the 103d Congress

1. Family Leave	FOR	2. Deficit Reduction	FOR	3. Stimulus Plan	FOR

Election Results

1992 general	Anna G. Eshoo (D)	146,873	(57%)	($909,604)
	Tom Huening (R)	101,202	(39%)	($670,277)
	Four Others	11,147	(4%)	
1992 primary	Anna G. Eshoo (D)	32,001	(40%)	
	Ted Lempert (D)	28,858	(36%)	
	Tom Nolan (D)	11,574	(15%)	
	Five Others	6,672	(8%)	
1990 general	Tom Campbell (R)	125,157	(61%)	($685,135)
(CA 12)	Robert Palmer (D)	69,270	(34%)	($103,839)
	Chuck Olson (LIB)	11,271	(5%)	

FIFTEENTH DISTRICT

Within living memory, the broad valley of Santa Clara County around San Jose was planted in orchards and vineyards. Sheltered by mountains from the chilly ocean fogs, with soil incredibly fertile once it was irrigated, this valley produced peaches, plums, prunes, apricots and grapes and made San Jose half a century ago the nation's biggest fruit-packing center. Today, almost all the orchards have been replaced by subdivisions and shopping centers and office buildings, for Santa Clara County has become a metropolitan area of 1.5 million people. San Jose, with a growing downtown, an arena rising for its own major league hockey team (the San Jose Sharks), and a population of 782,000, has become a major American city. Santa Clara County is also the center of Silicon Valley, site of many creative firms that have made the United States the world's computer and microchip industry center, a phenomenon predicted by few if any national policymakers or corporate leaders a quarter-century ago.

The 15th Congressional District of California is made up of the central slice of Santa Clara County plus, over the mountains to the south, a portion of Santa Cruz County. Downtown San Jose is in the 16th District to the east, and Silicon Valley towns like Cupertino and Mountain View are in the 14th District to the west; the 15th District lies in between. At its northern end is Sunnyvale, site of a huge Lockheed plant near the salt evaporators and wetlands at the south end of San Francisco Bay. Just to the south is Santa Clara, with its old mission and Santa Clara

University. The 15th includes much of the upscale and middle-income neighborhoods of San Jose, with over 300,000 people. It also has high-income suburbs nestled in what used to be vineyards beneath the encroaching mountains: Saratoga, Los Gatos, Monte Sereno. After all this settlement, the mountains remain surprisingly wild, a haunt of Ken Kesey's Merry Pranksters in the 1960s, now inhabited with rustic cabins and high-income houses in narrow valleys. Prosperous and pleased with its environment, confident in free market economics and uneasy about the performance of the public sector, people here tend to be more Republican than in other quadrants of the Bay Area. There are fewer singles and gays here than farther north, fewer Mexican-Americans than farther east; the 11% who are Asian-Americans are far likelier to be high-income producers than to be low-income supplicants. But, this being the Bay Area, there are plenty of Democrats here as well; this is a competitive district politically, or would be, if Norman Mineta were not to reelection.

Norman Mineta has been the congressman from the 15th and its predecessor districts, with somewhat different lines but similar socioeconomic makeup, since 1974. He came to Congress from serving as mayor of San Jose, where he called for slowing down development (but not to zero, as in Marin County); when the incumbent Republican retired, Mineta ran and in a Democratic year easily won. He was one of the leaders of the Watergate era class of 1974 Democrats, promoting their House reforms and opposing Republican administrations on foreign and cultural policies.

But Mineta also showed the more practical side suggestive of his service as mayor. He got a seat on the Public Works Committee and, instead of rotating off for a seat on a committee handling high-profile national issues, he chose to stay on and worked his way up to a subcommittee and then the full committee chairmanship. In 1981, he was named chairman of the Aviation Subcommittee, and became an expert on airports and air safety. In 1992, he wrote legislation setting minimum rest periods and maximum work hours for flight attendants, and for 1993 he wants to revise the bankruptcy laws so that airlines in Chapter 11 can't cut fares in ways that bleed money out of otherwise profitable carriers.

In 1989, he switched to chair the Surface Transportation Subcommittee, the key body that authorizes highway projects. Some members would use this seat shamelessly to build four-lane monuments to themselves in impoverished districts; Mineta, from the prosperous Silicon Valley, has tended to local needs but has not needed to overindulge them. Rather, as chairman, he was in charge of the horse trading needed to shepherd through the Surface Transportation Act of 1991. This was more complicated than it might seem, for it authorized states to spend trust fund dollars on subways, light rail and even magnetic levitation systems if they chose; and of course formulas allocating money are always subject to argument. Public Works leaders have long rewarded those who support them, and generally try to amass a solid, even veto-proof majority for the leadership bill. Mineta showed that he could operate this way, but also saw that California got $10.5 billion and 300,000 jobs from the bill, and afterwards grappled, as authorizing chairmen typically do, with Appropriations subcommittee chairmen to get more.

In 1993, Mineta became chairman of the full Public Works Committee. He sought the post in 1990, after the Democratic Caucus voted the aging Glenn Anderson out of the position; but the more senior Robert Roe beat him 121–107 (which meant that George Miller of Contra Costa County, not Mineta, became the first Watergate class member to chair a major committee). Then in 1992 Roe decided to retire, leaving the way entirely open for Mineta. He is probably a shrewd choice for the House: schooled enough in the old pork barrel ways to put together a bill, and articulate enough to defend public works, in the 1990s Clinton-Gore manner, as the infrastructure necessary for continued and robust economic growth. And Mineta had the satisfaction of seeing Public Works be the number one committee choice of incoming House freshmen in 1993—a practical class, with many former local officeholders like himself. The leadership used to have to appoint temporary members to fill all the seats; this time it had to expand the size of the committee.

Mineta has other legislative causes and has served stints on the Budget and Intelligence

Committees, but a great accomplishment was as lead sponsor of the Japanese American redress bill. As a child in World War II, Mineta was shipped off, wearing his cub scout uniform, to one of the internment camps in Wyoming where the government confined West Coast Japanese Americans; his family lost their home and his father's insurance business. While in Wyoming, Mineta met Alan Simpson; later they would work together on the redress bill which officially apologized for the internment and provided a $20,000 payment to each survivor of the camps and to so-called voluntary evacuees. Since then, Mineta has worked to make sure enough money is appropriated for the payments.

Mineta returns often to the 15th District and has continued to run well ahead of party lines there. Redistricting presented no problems, and he won easily. Should he not run, the district would probably be competitive between the parties.

The People: Pop. 1990: 572,360; 4% rural; 9% age 65+; 76% White; 2% Black; 1% Amer. Indian; 11% Asian; 3% Other; 10% Hispanic origin. Voting age pop.: 444,624; 2% Black; 9% Hispanic origin. Households: 57% married couple families; 25% married couple fams. w. children; 68% college educ.; median household income: $50,823; per capita income: $22,833; median gross rent: $794; median house value: $290,200.

1992 Presidential Vote			1988 Presidential Vote		
Clinton (D)	127,060	(46%)	Bush (R)	126,310	(51%)
Bush (R)	83,301	(30%)	Dukakis (D)	119,300	(49%)
Perot (I)	64,192	(23%)			

Rep. Norman Y. Mineta (D)

Elected 1974; b. Nov. 12, 1931, San Jose; home, San Jose; U. of CA at Berkeley, B.S. 1953; United Methodist; married (Danealia).

Career: Army, 1953–56 (Korea); Owner, Mineta Insur. Agcy.; San Jose City Cncl., 1967–71; San Jose Vice Mayor, 1969–71; Mayor, 1971–74.

Offices: 2221 RHOB 20515, 202-225-2631. Also 1245 S. Winchester Blvd., #310, San Jose 95128, 408-984-6045.

Committees: *Public Works and Transportation* (Chmn. of 39 D).

Group Ratings

	ADA	ACLU	COPE	CDF	CFA	LCV	ACU	NTLC	NSI	COC	CEI
1992	100	100	92	100	93	81	0	0	30	25	3
1991	90	—	100	100	78	85	0	—	—	20	6

National Journal Ratings

	1991 LIB	—	1991 CONS		1992 LIB	—	1992 CONS
Economic	84%	—	12%		91%	—	0%
Social	88%	—	0%		85%	—	13%
Foreign	92%	—	0%		90%	—	0%

Key Votes of the 102d Congress

1. Ban Striker Replace FOR	5. Handgun Wait/7-Day FOR	9. Use Force in Gulf AGN
2. $ for Homeownership AGN	6. Overseas Mil. Abortion FOR	10. US Mil. Abroad $ Cut FOR
3. Tax Rich/Cut Mid Cls. FOR	7. Obscn. Art NEA $ Ban AGN	11. Limit SDI Funds FOR
4. FY93/$15B Def. Cut FOR	8. Death Pen. from Jury AGN	12. Cuba Trade Embargo AGN

Key Votes of the 103d Congress

1. Family Leave FOR	2. Deficit Reduction FOR	3. Stimulus Plan FOR

Election Results

1992 general	Norman Y. Mineta (D)	168,617	(64%)	($1,112,414)
	Robert Wick (R)	82,875	(31%)	($62,961)
	Duggan Dieterly (LIB)	13,293	(5%)	
1992 primary	Norman Y. Mineta (D), unopposed			
1990 general	Norman Y. Mineta (D)	97,286	(58%)	($644,962)
(CA 13)	David E. Smith (R)	59,773	(36%)	($624)
	John H. Webster (LIB)	10,587	(6%)	

SIXTEENTH DISTRICT

With more people than San Francisco, higher per capita incomes than San Diego, a tradition of high-tech innovation that rivals any on earth, with a major league sports team and California's biggest indoor arena, with the 11th largest population within city limits in the United States, San Jose has great claims on national attention and respect. Yet San Jose does not yet bulk as large in the national consciousness as it should. At the southern end of the Bay, it remains in the shadow of San Francisco, every tourist's idea of a city: geographically compact, with picturesque public transportation, old-time immigrant groups like Irish Catholics and southern blacks, an economy historically based on heavy industry and sea trade, a large city bureaucracy symbolized by a monumental city hall. San Jose has none of these things. It got its start as a farm-market town, with canneries and fruit-packing operations for the produce from the fertile plains around. It sits not on the Bay, but on the Southern Pacific line above the marshes and salt evaporators; its major transportation arteries are the freeways—U.S. 101, Interstates 280 and 680, California 17—which encircle its old downtown. The main minority group here is Mexican-Americans, who initially came as farm workers but now occupy every occupational niche and, while concentrated on the east side, are also scattered throughout San Jose and adjacent towns; there are also increasing numbers of Asian-Americans. And scattered is the right word to describe San Jose's growth. It has a downtown, now spruced up, and a civic center graced by a cost-overrun indoor arena for the San Jose Sharks hockey team. But starting in the 1950s, San Jose has grown out in every direction, developers hip-hopping across the farmland, putting up subdivisions faster sometimes than the few city employees could update the street map. Economically, San Jose has been sustained by everything from its traditional agriculture to the high-tech businesses centered in Silicon Valley towns just to the west but omnipresent here: an American city, 21st Century style.

The 16th Congressional District of California consists of the larger part of San Jose, plus its urban fringe to the east and the still agricultural Santa Clara Valley to the south, including Gilroy, the garlic capital of the United States. It includes the old and new downtown and the heavily Mexican-American areas to the east. This is the most heavily Hispanic district in the Bay Area (37%) and is also heavily Asian (21%). Politically, it has become solidly Democratic, although its party preference could switch if Hispanics follow the lead of Asians, who were the only demographic group in California—and perhaps the nation—in 1992 to swing toward rather than away from George Bush.

The congressman from the 16th District is Don Edwards, the senior member of the California delegation, first elected in 1962, in what was then a newly created district. He is not, however, a committee chairman, since he sits below the even more senior Jack Brooks on Judiciary and has less seniority on Veterans' Affairs than Sonny Montgomery. Edwards has a conservative background—his family owned the only title company in Santa Clara County during its years of great expansion and he was briefly an FBI agent. Within a few years of serving in Congress, he became one of its most liberal members, an opponent of the Vietnam war from the beginning and a vote for abolishing the House Committee on Un-American Activities when over 400 members were on the other side. He continues, in the 1992 *National Journal* ratings, to have one of the most liberal records in the House.

Since 1971, Edwards has chaired the Judiciary Subcommittee on Civil and Constitutional Rights, working closely with the civil rights lobby on various legislation such as the Voting Rights extensions of 1982, the fair housing law of 1990 and the Civil Rights Restoration Act (which some attacked as a racial quota bill) in 1991. He also spent much time bottling up conservatives' favorite constitutional amendments: to ban abortion, to stop school busing, to require Congress to balance the budget and to permit public school prayer. Edwards has a steadfast majority on his subcommittee and has been entirely unembarrassed about using it to keep these issues off the floor; he may be a bit miffed when the leadership agrees to allow votes on them, though he plays his part. He sometimes has more problems when he takes the initiative. In 1992, he wanted to pass the Freedom of Choice Act, purportedly codifying the *Roe v. Wade* decision on abortion, if only to make an issue of a Bush veto. But he could not get agreement on whether the FOCA should wipe out state laws prohibiting abortion without a parent's consent or with a waiting period; and no bill was passed in 1992. He promised to bring one forward in 1993 with the assurance of Bill Clinton's signature. But a thoroughgoing FOCA would require supporters to go on record against restrictions that have 80% support, while a limited FOCA would enrage feminist groups strongly advocating these bills and, to an increasing extent, the Democratic Party.

Edwards has ventured forward with other controversial measures. After the Rodney King videotape, he sought federal legislation against police brutality. He tried to reverse recent Supreme Court decisions limiting collateral attacks on criminal convictions, even as Republicans were trying to move in the other direction. He has worked long and hard to preserve the wetlands around San Francisco Bay. On the Veterans' Affairs Committee, he has disagreed with Chairman Sonny Montgomery on many issues but they have together been the patrons of oft-embattled VA hospitals. As dean of California's huge delegation, he set up a bi-partisan think tank to provide Golden State members with information and, perhaps, points for agreement. As a former FBI agent, he came to the defense of Judge William Sessions after adverse reports on him, calling him "the best FBI director ever."

Edwards turns 79 in 1994, but appears much younger and gives no sign of retiring. Redistricting has made his district even more Democratic, and he has won with less than 60% of the vote only once since 1962.

The People: Pop. 1990: 571,460; 4% rural; 7% age 65+; 37% White; 5% Black; 1% Amer. Indian; 21% Asian; 18% Other; 36% Hispanic origin. Voting age pop.: 408,987; 5% Black; 33% Hispanic origin. Households: 57% married couple families; 32% married couple fams. w. children; 49% college educ.; median household income: $42,223; per capita income: $14,614; median gross rent: $718; median house value: $233,600.

1992 Presidential Vote

Clinton (D) 86,418 (52%)
Bush (R) 44,693 (27%)
Perot (I).................... 33,882 (20%)

1988 Presidential Vote

Dukakis (D).................. 80,194 (57%)
Bush (R) 60,379 (43%)

Rep. Don Edwards (D)

Elected 1962; b. Jan. 6, 1915, San Jose; home, San Jose; Stanford U., A.B. 1936, Stanford Law, 1936–38; Unitarian; married (Edith).

Career: Navy, 1942–45 (WWII); FBI Agent, 1940–41; Founder & Pres., Valley Title Co., 1950–62.

Offices: 2307 RHOB 20515, 202-225-3072. Also 1042 W. Hedding St., #100, San Jose 95126, 408-345-1711.

Committees: *Foreign Affairs* (24th of 27 D): Africa; International Operations. *Judiciary* (2d of 21 D): Civil and Constitutional Rights (Chmn.); Crime and Criminal Justice; Intellectual Property and Judicial Administration. *Veterans' Affairs* (2d of 21 D).

Group Ratings

	ADA	ACLU	COPE	CDF	CFA	LCV	ACU	NTLC	NSI	COC	CEI
1992	100	100	92	100	93	100	0	0	20	25	6
1991	95	—	100	100	78	92	0	—	—	10	7

National Journal Ratings

	1991 LIB — 1991 CONS		1992 LIB — 1992 CONS	
Economic	84% —	12%	91% —	0%
Social	88% —	0%	92% —	0%
Foreign	87% —	8%	90% —	0%

Key Votes of the 102d Congress

1. Ban Striker Replace	FOR	5. Handgun Wait/7-Day	FOR	9. Use Force in Gulf	AGN
2. $ for Homeownership	AGN	6. Overseas Mil. Abortion	FOR	10. Abroad $ Cut	FOR
3. Tax Rich/Cut Mid Cls.	FOR	7. Obscn. Art NEA $ Ban	AGN	11. Limit SDI Funds	FOR
4. FY93/$15B Def. Cut	FOR	8. Death Pen. from Jury	AGN	12. Cuba Trade Embargo	AGN

Key Votes of the 103d Congress

1. Family Leave	FOR	2. Deficit Reduction	FOR	3. Stimulus Plan	FOR

Election Results

1992 general	Don Edwards (D)	96,661	(62%)	($291,251)
	Ted Bundesen (R)	49,843	(32%)	($505)
	Amani S. Kuumba (P&F)	9,370	(6%)	
1992 primary	Don Edwards (D)	37,833	(71%)	
	Edward R. Dykes (D)	15,105	(29%)	
1990 general	Don Edwards (D)	81,875	(63%)	($209,243)
(CA 10)	Mark Patrosso (R)	48,747	(37%)	($2,581)

SEVENTEENTH DISTRICT

For many Americans, the California coast around Monterey Bay is a working definition of paradise. This kernel of California history where Spanish and then Mexicans governed a virtually empty land and Californians set up their first state capital, still makes a fine living, as it has for nearly 150 years, off the land and sea. The fields around Salinas supply much of the nation's lettuce and cauliflower, the fields around Castroville supply almost all of its artichokes, and the vast greenhouses around Watsonville supply a goodly portion of its strawberries. The fishing fleet and 18 canneries of Monterey are not the major industry they were half a century ago, but they have generated a new industry: Cannery Row is refurbished with upscale shops and hotels, and the Monterey Bay Aquarium has become one of California's top tourist attractions, drawing 1.8 million people a year. There are other tourist attractions on the Monterey peninsula as well, like the Pebble Beach golf courses and the Del Monte Lodge, and Carmel, whose restrictive laws—no house numbers, no door-to-door mail delivery, no live entertainment, no stop lights, no cutting trees without city council permission—try to maintain the atmosphere of 80 years ago, when it really was an artists' colony.

The 17th Congressional District of California includes all the coast of Monterey Bay and then follows the Big Sur coastline south almost to William Randolph Hearst's castle, San Simeon, past perhaps the most beautiful scenery in America. The district extends inland, into sunny valleys sheltered from ocean mists, and covers some of the nation's richest farmland. This area is a prime example of how, while interior California became more Republican, the coast trended Democratic. The older residents—landowners in Salinas and the townspeople who sympathize with them, retirees in Santa Cruz and the Monterey Peninsula—still vote Republican. But an influx of liberation-minded young people now in their prime years, attracted less by the economy (though that was vibrant in the 1980s) than by the atmosphere, moved the coast to the left. Also, the branch of the University of California at Santa Cruz is so liberal (97% for McGovern in 1972) that it has changed the political balance of the whole county. As late as 1980, Monterey and Santa Cruz Counties were voting less Democratic than the country. But in 1984 they were 7% more Democratic, in 1988 9% and in 1992 10% more Democratic.

That trend helps to explain the career of Leon Panetta, the son of Calabrian immigrants, who grew up here as a Republican and made headlines in 1970 when he was fired from the Nixon Administration over disagreements on civil rights enforcement. Panetta switched parties in 1971 and ran for Congress in 1976 against a conservative Republican incumbent. Within two years, he was on the Budget Committee, where he spent most of his House career, being rebuffed for the chairmanship in 1984 but finally getting it in 1989. As a budgeter, he shared an historically Republican preoccupation with the deficit, and was constantly seeking to raise tax rates, a move far more palatable to his fellow Democrats than serious spending cuts. To a considerable extent, he was the architect of the 1990 budget summit agreement as well as the 1993 Clinton economic package, both of which had similar features—higher tax rates, only mild spending cuts, a reliance on low long-term interest rates for economic growth. Panetta also worked on other issues, notably on immigration reform, where he pushed a successful amendment allowing farmers to import otherwise illegal aliens for seasonal work.

The new congressman is Sam Farr, chosen in a June 1993 special election; he entered the race as an overwhelming favorite but, as the reputation of the Clinton Administration was plummeting, ended up winning by a lesser margin than expected. Farr's father, Fred Farr, was a state senator from Monterey County for many years; Sam Farr served as a Monterey County Supervisor and was elected to the California Assembly in 1980. Moderate on economic issues, Farr is very much interested in preserving the environment which is so important here. From his Natural Resources Committee seat in the state legislature, he wrote one of the nation's strictest oil spill liability laws. Close to Panetta in many ways, Farr seemed ideally suited for the 17th District seat. He did have serious competition among Democrats, notably from County Supervisor Barbara Shipnuck and Salinas lawyer Bill Manning. But he raised vastly more money than his opponents and won the all-party primary in April with 26% of the vote. In that contest, Democrats had 58% of the vote, while Republican Bill McCampbell won his party's nomination with just 12%. McCampbell had run weakly against Panetta in 1992, and his work as a Washington lobbyist for the South African homeland of Transkei was not helpful, but he was on stronger ground when he asked voters to send an anti-Clinton message to Washington. Farr won with 52% of the vote to 43% for McCampbell. In the House, Farr sits on the Agriculture and Natural Resources Committees.

The People: Pop. 1990: 571,077; 15% rural; 10% age 65+; 70% White; 4% Black; 1% Amer. Indian; 6% Asian; 19% Other; 31% Hispanic origin. Voting age pop.: 420,688; 4% Black; 26% Hispanic origin. Households: 57% married couple families; 29% married couple fams. w. children; 54% college educ.; median household income: $33,911; per capita income: $15,006; median gross rent: $643; median house value: $219,100.

1992 Presidential Vote			1988 Presidential Vote		
Clinton (D)	111,937	(52%)	Dukakis (D)	103,346	(56%)
Bush (R)	57,990	(27%)	Bush (R)	82,214	(44%)
Perot (I)	42,317	(20%)			

Rep. Sam Farr (D)

Elected June 1993; b. July 4, 1941, San Francisco; home, Carmel; Willamette U., B.S. 1963; Episcopalian; married (Shary).

Career: Peace Corps, Columbia, 1963–65; Staff, CA Assembly, 1965–75; Monterey Cnty. Bd. of Supervisors, 1975–80, Chmn., 1979; CA Assembly, 1980–93.

Offices: 1216 LHOB 20515, 202-225-2861. Also 380 Alvarado St., Monterey 93940, 408-649-3555; 701 Ocean Ave., Santa Cruz 95060, 408-429-1976; and 100 W. Alisal St., Salinas 93901, 408-424-2229.

Committees: *Agriculture* (29th of 29 D). *Natural Resources* (28th of 28 D).

Group Ratings and Key Votes: Newly Elected

Election Results

1993 runoff	Sam Farr (D)	62,864	(54%)	($203,366)
	Bill McCampbell (R)	47,897	(41%)	($93,686)
	Six Others	6,220	(5%)	
1993 special	Sam Farr (D)	23,600	(26%)	
	Bill Manning (D)	17,050	(19%)	
	Barbara Shipnuck (D)	12,982	(14%)	
	Bill McCampbell (R)	10,911	(12%)	
	Bob Ernst (R)	5,126	(6%)	
	Twenty-one Others	12,568	(14%)	
1992 general	Leon E. Panetta (D)	151,565	(72%)	($513,958)
	Bill McCampbell (R)	49,947	(24%)	($77,509)
	Two Others	8,855	(4%)	
1992 primary	Leon E. Panetta (D)	52,580	(86%)	
	Art Dunn (D)	8,631	(14%)	

EIGHTEENTH DISTRICT

The Central Valley of California is a miraculous man-made landscape, a horizontal factory stretching as far as the eye can see. Nature created the vast flatlands, rimmed by mountains rising surreally in the distant haze. But man in the last century has disciplined the land with a remorseless mile-square grid of roads, and the sluggish-flowing California Aqueduct and dozens of arrow-straight canals; pipes fitted with valves and gauges to pump water and fertilizer and pesticides to the fields in measured quantities give an air of industrial precision. The crops grow in carefully spaced rows, filling the fields, for the rich soil and the irrigated water are too precious to waste on decoration or vegetable patches or flower gardens: the Valley is business. Farming here has always been an industrial enterprise; in the 19th Century the land was not given to 160-acre homesteaders but sold to thousands-of-acres capitalist enterprises.

The Central Valley was one of California's surprise boom areas in the 1980s, growing not just crops but people. Middle-wage employees in the San Francisco Bay area drive east at night on I-580, past surreal windmills fluttering on the bare hills of the Altamont pass, across the Westlands fields to modestly priced homes in Modesto, the town immortalized (when it was much smaller) in *American Graffiti*. Water may have become scarce in the recent drought years, and heavily subsidized water may be cut off from cultivators of cotton (which after all can be grown in many states where nature provides the water for free), but the towns and countryside of the Central Valley have been generating a well-rounded economy. On the down side, traffic has become a problem, air pollution on bad days has approached coastal metropolitan levels, the pace of life is getting more hectic and frazzled.

The 18th Congressional District of California includes a large chunk of the Central Valley from Modesto and Stanislaus County south through Merced almost to Fresno. The political tradition here is Democratic: Washington Democrats and Democratic Governor Pat Brown built the irrigation canals and authorized the water subsidies; Democrats own the *Bee* newspapers, the predominant Valley chain; Democrats staffed the Bank of America, long the dominant financial force here; on the walls of insider law firms are signed pictures of Franklin Roosevelt and Pat Brown, not Ronald Reagan and Pete Wilson. Politically, the voters of the 18th District remain fairly heavily Democratic. There are many Hispanics here, and an increasing number of Asians, though neither group produces the overwhelming Democratic majorities blacks do; there are some voters of white southern ancestry, used to voting for local Democrats though happy to vote Republican for president. The Central Valley is the part of California with the highest proportion of families and children, and there is a natural cultural conservatism here, which of course is shared by successful local Democratic politicians. Since 1956 this area has been represented in the House by a Democrat.

The current incumbent is Gary Condit, elected in a September 1989 special election to replace Tony Coelho, the House Majority whip whose sudden resignation in June 1989 stunned most of Washington; Coelho's adroit fundraising and politicking played a major role in keeping the House Democratic in the 1980s. Condit was the Democrats' natural choice for the seat. A native of Oklahoma and son of a Baptist minister, he was elected to the Ceres Council in 1972, the Stanislaus County Board of Supervisors in 1976, and the California Assembly in 1982, where he made an attractive moderate to conservative record on crime and taxes. He was one of the "Gang of Five" Democrats who threatened to topple Speaker Willie Brown in 1988; in retaliation, Condit's chief aide was taken off the state payroll for five months and Condit's Sacramento office was moved every Friday. The Gang of Five's challenge collapsed after the 1988 elections as three new Democrats were elected and Brown didn't need their votes to stay Speaker any more; it was obviously time for Condit to move on. Republicans in the meantime elbowed out pro-choice Modesto Mayor Carol Whiteside for older former state Senator Clare Berryhill, who proved to be a less than vigorous candidate. Condit raised money efficiently and ran an absentee voter drive which essentially won the election before it was held. Some 35% of all votes were cast absentee, the large majority Democratic, and Condit won 57%–35%.

In the House, Condit is the most conservative Democrat of the California delegation and was the only one of them to vote against Clinton's stimulus package. He backs a balanced budget amendment and the line-item veto. His independence irritated Democratic colleagues, probably costing him a seat on the Energy and Commerce Committee, and on the Agriculture Committee he was unable to preserve an advantage California dairy farmers had in subsidies. He came within two votes, 184–186, of passing an amendment, largely backed by Republicans, requiring the federal government to pay for bilingual voting assistance where needed. He was able to pass a bill designating the lower portion of the Merced as a Wild and Scenic River. Condit may be on the Democratic leadership's bad side, but he was reelected in 1990 with 66% of the vote, came out unscathed in redistricting and was unopposed (except by a Libertarian) in 1992.

The People: Pop. 1990: 571,358; 19% rural; 10% age 65+; 65% White; 3% Black; 1% Amer. Indian; 6% Asian; 14% Other; 26% Hispanic origin. Voting age pop.: 391,319; 3% Black; 22% Hispanic origin. Households: 61% married couple families; 33% married couple fams. w. children; 41% college educ.; median household income: $28,324; per capita income: $12,013; median gross rent: $462; median house value: $113,600.

1992 Presidential Vote			1988 Presidential Vote		
Clinton (D)	74,357	(41%)	Bush (R)	75,832	(53%)
Bush (R)	67,898	(37%)	Dukakis (D)	66,366	(47%)
Perot (I)	39,645	(22%)			

Rep. Gary A. Condit (D)

Elected Sept., 1989; b. Apr. 21, 1948, Salina, OK; home, Ceres; Modesto Jr. Col., A.A. 1970, CA St. U., B.A. 1972; Protestant; married (Carolyn).

Career: Ceres City Cncl., 1972–76; Ceres Mayor, 1974–76; Stanislaus Cnty. Bd. of Supervisors, 1976–82; CA Assembly, 1982–89.

Offices: 1123 LHOB 20515, 202-225-6131. Also 415 W. 18th St., Merced 95340, 209-383-4455; and 920 13th St., Modesto 95354, 209-527-1914.

Committees: *Agriculture* (12th of 28 D): General Farm Commodities; Livestock; Specialty Crops and Natural Resources. *Government Operations* (11th of 25 D): Information, Justice, Transportation and Agriculture (Chmn.).

Group Ratings

	ADA	ACLU	COPE	CDF	CFA	LCV	ACU	NTLC	NSI	COC	CEI
1992	55	57	83	40	53	25	48	65	70	75	65
1991	60	—	92	80	50	38	58	—	—	40	51

National Journal Ratings

	1991 LIB — 1991 CONS			1992 LIB — 1992 CONS	
Economic	46%	—	54%	42% —	57%
Social	43%	—	56%	52% —	48%
Foreign	51%	—	46%	76% —	19%

Key Votes of the 102d Congress

1. Ban Striker Replace FOR	5. Handgun Wait/7-Day AGN	9. Use Force in Gulf FOR
2. $ for Homeownership AGN	6. Overseas Mil. Abortion FOR	10. US Mil. Abroad $ Cut FOR
3. Tax Rich/Cut Mid Cls.AGN	7. Obscn. Art NEA $ Ban FOR	11. Limit SDI Funds FOR
4. FY93/$15B Def. Cut FOR	8. Death Pen. from Jury FOR	12. Cuba Trade Embargo AGN

Key Votes of the 103d Congress

1. Family Leave FOR	2. Deficit Reduction AGN	3. Stimulus Plan AGN

Election Results

1992 general	Gary A. Condit (D).................	139,704	(85%)	($311,000)
	Kim R. Almstrom (LIB)...............	25,307	(15%)	
1992 primary	Gary A. Condit (D), unopposed			
1990 general	Gary A. Condit (D)..................	97,147	(66%)	($212,430)
(CA 15)	Cliff Burris (R).....................	49,634	(34%)	($30,963)

NINETEENTH DISTRICT

Fresno, in California's Central Valley, between the flat westlands and the Sierras on the east, is a city agricultural and industrial, middle American and ethnically diverse. It is a creation of the industrial age, founded by the Central Pacific Railroad, and its great city fathers bred the local wine grape, developed the raisin industry and introduced the Smyrna fig. But these are not all of Fresno County's crops, which include cotton, lima beans, tomatoes, cantaloupes, plums, peaches and alfalfa: Fresno produces more dollar value in farm products than any other county in the United States. Central Valley agriculture is industrial in its precision, its thoroughness and its ownership by large corporations: the vineyards outside Fresno radiate in mechanical precision, with vines just 10 feet apart and exposed to the relentless summer sun—nothing romantic or quaint here. The city of Fresno started off as a farm-marketing center, and was Los Angeles tourists' stop-off point on the way to Yosemite. But it has long since grown out north, east and west from its old downtown, and its economy has diversified. Like all the Central Valley, Fresno has always been ethnically diverse, with a telephone book that reads like the United Nations and America's second largest Armenian community, after Los Angeles (Fresno's great chronicler was William Saroyan). In the 1980s its Hispanic population doubled to over 100,000 and its Asian population increased seven-fold to 42,000. In the recession years of the early 1990s, the farmland was gobbled up as subdivisions (though if it wasn't worth more for subdivisions, the farmers wouldn't have sold it), air pollution made the Sierra Nevada invisible on many days and crime rates rose; in March 1993 Fresno voters threw out the mayor, voted term limits for the council after turning out all its members in two years and put in low-tax and pro-growth candidates. But Fresno is also a success story, for many people who would have done far worse if they hadn't moved here.

The 19th Congressional District of California includes most of Fresno, all but the old downtown and a Latino area reserved for the Hispanic-majority 20th District. It spreads with an erose boundary over the farm country below the foothills of the Sierras from Visalia, south of Fresno, to the Mother Lode gold-mining country of Mariposa County. Most of its land mass is part of the Sierra Nevada, and it contains most of three major national parks, Yosemite, Kings Canyon and Sequoia. Strongly Democratic historically, it trended Republican through the 1980s, then swung a bit, but not drastically, toward the Democrats in 1992. The 19th District voted for George Bush and against Senators Barbara Boxer and Dianne Feinstein in 1992. For the Valley is more culturally conservative, more Midwestern in a sense, than California's great coastal areas, and the new migrants have not been heavily Democratic.

The 19th District was the scene of a riproaring battle in 1992 between two candidates who typify partisan culture. The incumbent and eventual winner, Democrat Richard Lehman, comes from a farming family and has spent most of his life in politics. At 20, he was part of Jesse Unruh's Robert Kennedy delegation to the 1968 Chicago convention; he was an aide from 1970 to 1976 to a Fresno state senator; he was elected to the Assembly in 1976, at 28; he became a congressman, unopposed in his first primary, when this district was created in 1982. With a moderate voting record calibrated to local opinion and a sensitivity to farming and water issues, he followed a long tradition of Valley Democrats defending local ag interests in Washington against those like Natural Resources Chairman George Miller who want farm operations to pay the same water rates as city-dwellers. In May 1992, he negotiated a compromise with Miller on the California water bill, but it was opposed by both environmentalists and farming interests, and fell apart—after which Miller rolled over Lehman and other Valley members. Lehman has tried to seek bipartisan, enviro-Valley compromises on other issues including timber rights, the California Desert bill and ranchers' rights. He favors construction of the Mid-Valley Canal and the Auburn Dam. On the Banking Committee he originated the 1987 amendment that created a secondary market for farm real estate loans (Freddie Mac); in 1990 he switched to the pivotal Energy and Commerce Committee.

In vivid contrast to Lehman's local roots and political experience, was his Republican opponent Tal Cloud. Cloud grew up in the Los Angeles area and moved to Fresno only six years before; at 28, he had little political experience and had spent six years as working at his family's paper company. Even so, Lehman considered running in the next-door 20th District, though it might have meant a primary against Democrat Calvin Dooley. With most of the district in the Fresno media market, Cloud ran TV ads there, one of which showed Lehman eating food at a local campaign event with a voiceover recounting Lehman's collection of congressional perks. Lehman, he said, was "a typical career politician who works from a position of weakness," was enamored of perks, and was "dancing" with George Miller. But Lehman, showing his political savvy, vastly outraised Cloud, spending $915,000 to Cloud's $150,000—with and estimated $150,000 to Cloud's $60,000 the last three weeks—the sort of overwhelming edge that may be why the Democrats still control the House. Even at that, Lehman led on election night by only 888 votes, and the final count showed Lehman with a 46.9%–46.4% 1,030-vote lead, less than the 1,098 votes cast for a write-in antiabortion candidate angry at Cloud's pro-choice stand. "No matter what the outcome, this campaign shows that Lehman is finished as a politician," Cloud announced and said he'd run in 1994. Lehman, meanwhile, can be counted on to use all the advantages of incumbency and his political shrewdness to prevent the end of what he must hope will be a lifetime career.

The People: Pop. 1990: 573,077; 20% rural; 11% age 65+; 65% White; 3% Black; 1% Amer. Indian; 7% Asian; 14% Other; 23% Hispanic origin. Voting age pop.: 404,734; 3% Black; 20% Hispanic origin. Households: 57% married couple families; 28% married couple fams. w. children; 52% college educ.; median household income: $29,153; per capita income: $13,516; median gross rent: $450; median house value: $90,200.

1992 Presidential Vote

Bush (R)	97,124	(43%)
Clinton (D)	85,049	(38%)
Perot (I)	41,052	(18%)

1988 Presidential Vote

Bush (R)	103,142	(55%)
Dukakis (D)	83,845	(45%)

Rep. Richard H. Lehman (D)

Elected 1982; b. July 20, 1948, Sanger; home, North Fork; Fresno City Col., A.A. 1968, CA St. U., 1969, U. of CA at Santa Cruz, B.A. 1970; Lutheran; divorced.

Career: CA Natl. Guard, 1970–76; A.A., CA Sen. George N. Zenovich, 1970–76; CA Assembly, 1976–82.

Offices: 1226 LHOB 20515, 202-225-4540. Also 2377 W. Shaw Ave., #105, Fresno 93711, 209-248-0800.

Committees: *Energy and Commerce* (20th of 27 D): Commerce, Consumer Protection and Competitiveness; Energy and Power; Telecommunications and Finance. *Natural Resources* (10th of 28 D): Energy and Mineral Resources (Chmn.); Oversight and Investigations.

Group Ratings

	ADA	ACLU	COPE	CDF	CFA	LCV	ACU	NTLC	NSI	COC	CEI
1992	60	64	83	90	53	38	19	15	40	50	27
1991	60	—	100	100	78	54	25	—	—	30	14

National Journal Ratings

	1991 LIB — 1991 CONS		1992 LIB — 1992 CONS	
Economic	66%	— 32%	50%	— 49%
Social	56%	— 43%	53%	— 47%
Foreign	56%	— 44%	*	— *

Key Votes of the 102d Congress

1. Ban Striker Replace	FOR	5. Handgun Wait/7-Day	FOR	9. Use Force in Gulf	FOR
2. $ for Homeownership	FOR	6. Overseas Mil. Abortion	FOR	10. US Mil. Abroad $ Cut	*
3. Tax Rich/Cut Mid Cls.	AGN	7. Obscn. Art NEA $ Ban	FOR	11. Limit SDI Funds	FOR
4. FY93/$15B Def. Cut	FOR	8. Death Pen. from Jury	AGN	12. Cuba Trade Embargo	FOR

Key Votes of the 103d Congress

1. Family Leave   FOR   2. Deficit Reduction   AGN   3. Stimulus Plan   FOR

Election Results

1992 general	Richard H. Lehman (D)	101,620	(47%)	($915,504)
	Tal L. Cloud (R)	100,590	(46%)	($153,784)
	Dorothy L. Wells (P&F)	13,334	(6%)	
	Other	1,098	(1%)	
1992 primary	Richard H. Lehman (D)	39,846	(76%)	
	Curtis Young (D)	12,728	(24%)	
1990 general (CA 18)	Richard H. Lehman (D), unopposed			($299,728)

TWENTIETH DISTRICT

On the map or from the air it is the most monotonous landscape in America: mile after mile of farmland with mile-square grid roads, cut across by diagonal railroads and canals, with an occasional cluster town. This is California's Central Valley, especially its Westlands, where the land is flatter and the towns scarcer than in the hilly area below the Sierra Nevada. The Westlands is mostly large corporate farm operations; this land was always developed and sold in giant plots. And it produces plenty—alfalfa, cantaloupes, cotton, grapes, lima beans, olives, peaches, plums, raisins, sugar beets, tomatoes, walnuts. The producers pride themselves on their success through free enterprise but, like most entrepreneurs, they are happy to use government safety nets and helping hands, in the form of crop price supports, agricultural research, irrigation systems and (most important) subsidized water. They have fought hard against attempts to change their methods, from Governor Jerry Brown's attempts to encourage Cesar Chavez's United Farm Workers in the 1970s to House Natural Resources Committee Chairman George Miller's attempts to exact market prices for water in the 1990s; technology and mechanization helped them win the first battle but may be causing them to lose the second.

The 20th Congressional District of California includes most of the Westlands of the Central Valley, from south of Bakersfield to north of Fresno. Its irregular boundaries are dictated by a desire to maximize the Hispanic population of the district, so that it takes in the old downtown neighborhoods of both Bakersfield and Fresno, but none of their newer suburbs; it includes heavily Latino towns like Delano, long Chavez's headquarters, but not more Anglo places like Tulare. The 20th's Hispanic percentage is 55%, compared to 20% to 26% in other Central Valley districts; it is also the most Democratic seat between Sacramento and Los Angeles.

This was good political news for Congressman Calvin Dooley, a Democrat who has been the beneficiary of good fortune several times. The first was in 1990, when he ran against incumbent Republican Chip Pashayan, who had received contributions from S&L crook Charles Keating and then interceded with regulators on his behalf, and had switched off the Interior Committee, which handles so many Valley issues, and onto Rules in 1989. Dooley, from an old Valley farming family, won with a solid 55%. Then in 1992, the new district lines were announced and—another break—his fellow and better-known incumbent Democrat Richard Lehman decided to run in the much more Republican 19th District and leave Dooley the 20th. The result was that Dooley won in the fall with 65% of the vote.

Dooley has a moderate voting record on most issues, supporting the balanced budget amendment and the line-item veto, but is more liberal on foreign policy—the only Central Valley vote against the Gulf war resolution. His lobbying efforts against George Miller's water bill were not successful. He and Lehman negotiated a compromise with Miller in May 1992, but it was rejected by both environmental and farming interests, and Miller rolled right over them. Dooley was mentioned as a nominee for secretary of agriculture, but as a white Anglo male didn't fill anyone's quota and did not seem to become a serious contender. But he does appear to have one of the safer Central Valley seats in the House.

The People: Pop. 1990: 573,555; 27% rural; 9% age 65+; 33% White; 6% Black; 1% Amer. Indian; 6% Asian; 38% Other; 55% Hispanic origin. Voting age pop.: 373,437; 7% Black; 50% Hispanic origin. Households: 60% married couple families; 35% married couple fams. w. children; 26% college educ.; median household income: $21,140; per capita income: $8,097; median gross rent: $379; median house value: $63,400.

1992 Presidential Vote

Clinton (D) 55,942 (47%)
Bush (R) 44,674 (37%)
Perot (I). 18,568 (16%)

1988 Presidential Vote

Dukakis (D). 55,851 (53%)
Bush (R) 49,815 (47%)

Rep. Calvin Dooley (D)

Elected 1990; b. Jan. 11, 1954, Visalia; home, Visalia; U. of CA at Davis, B.S. 1977, Stanford U., M.A. 1987; Methodist; married (Linda).

Career: Farmer, 1978–91; A.A., CA Sen. Rose Ann Vuich, 1987–89.

Offices: 1227 LHOB 20515, 202-225-3341. Also 224 W. Lacey Blvd., Hanford 93230, 209-585-8171.

Committees: *Agriculture* (14th of 28 D): Department Operations and Nutrition; General Farm Commodities; Livestock. *Banking, Finance and Urban Affairs* (28th of 30 D): Economic Growth and Credit Formation. *Natural Resources* (17th of 28 D): Oversight and Investigations.

Group Ratings

	ADA	ACLU	COPE	CDF	CFA	LCV	ACU	NTLC	NSI	COC	CEI
1992	75	65	75	50	73	50	20	5	50	50	34
1991	60	—	75	100	50	62	10	—	—	50	26

National Journal Ratings

	1991 LIB — 1991 CONS	1992 LIB — 1992 CONS
Economic	56% — 42%	48% — 50%
Social	53% — 47%	62% — 38%
Foreign	65% — 33%	70% — 29%

Key Votes of the 102d Congress

1. Ban Striker Replace	FOR	5. Handgun Wait/7-Day FOR	9. Use Force in Gulf AGN
2. $ for Homeownership	AGN	6. Overseas Mil. Abortion FOR	10. US Mil. Abroad $ Cut FOR
3. Tax Rich/Cut Mid Cls. FOR		7. Obscn. Art NEA $ Ban FOR	11. Limit SDI Funds FOR
4. FY93/$15B Def. Cut	*	8. Death Pen. from Jury AGN	12. Cuba Trade Embargo AGN

Key Votes of the 103d Congress

1. Family Leave	FOR	2. Deficit Reduction	FOR	3. Stimulus Plan	FOR

Election Results

1992 general	Calvin Dooley (D).....................	72,679	(65%)	($504,352)
	Ed Hunt (R)	39,388	(35%)	($173,744)
1992 primary	Calvin Dooley (D), unopposed			
1990 general	Calvin Dooley (D)....................	82,611	(55%)	($538,354)
(CA 17)	Charles (Chip) Pashayan, Jr. (R)	68,848	(45%)	($622,184)

TWENTY-FIRST DISTRICT

Across the southwest United States on U.S. 66, from the Dust Bowl of Oklahoma and Kansas and Texas they came, in one of the major migrations of the 1930s: the Okies who drove their jalopies laden with all their worldly goods to the Central Valley of California. In a brown decade, the Valley seemed green, with its irrigated fields and its eucalyptus-shaded towns. The Okies drove through the Tehachapi Pass, through the mountains that form a semicircle at the south end of the Valley, and headed toward the oil boom town of Bakersfield and the farm-market center of Fresno, amid pastures, vineyards and orchards. This story was told vividly in John

Steinbeck's *The Grapes of Wrath*, but his vision of the Okies as workers eager to join together with their fellow proletarians and rise up against their bosses did not get the picture quite right. More accurate is Dan Morgan's *Rising in the West*, which shows the strong Pentecostal beliefs which drove many migrants and, unlike Steinbeck, explains how they prospered in California and why they, like the southern Central Valley where their descendants are most often found today, have become politically conservative even in a Democratic year like 1992.

The 21st Congressional District of California is the southernmost district in the Central Valley. It is centered on Bakersfield, home of country singers Buck Owens and Merle Haggard, an oil town where southern accents are still common. It is home to huge Edwards Air Force Base where Chuck Yeager flew the X-1 and where the Space Shuttle ordinarily lands. The district's boundaries are irregular to maximize the Hispanic percentage of the next-door 20th District. As a result, the 21st includes Bakersfield and most of its immediate surroundings, oil fields and high-income subdivisions, and the Kern County desert and mountains communities west and east. It includes the towns of Tulare, Porterville and Visalia in Tulare County and its agricultural area up to the Sierra Nevada. Politically, this was once Democratic territory in the early 1960s, when for that matter so was Oklahoma; by the late 1960s, both had become solidly Republican in national politics, and remain that way today.

The congressman from the 21st District, Bill Thomas, is a senior Republican in the House who has had the task, and sometimes relished it, of leading his party on some very partisan issues and now may be one of its leaders on the high-visibility issue of health care as well. Thomas was first elected in 1978, when Republicans were on the rise, and might have hoped to be in the majority soon. As ranking minority member on House Administration, it has been his lot to defend party positions with arguable merit but with no chance of prevailing, whether on the dispute over who won the Indiana 8th District in 1984 or on the House bank and post office scandals or on campaign finance reform in 1990s. On campaign finance, he has increasingly been more reform-minded than the Democrats, for House Democrats who have benefited handsomely from the current system are loath to give up their advantage. Thomas would restrict PAC contributions and require that a majority of all individual contributions be raised in the district; this would leave many Democrats, financed mainly from Washington, New York and Beverly Hills, bereft of funds. Thomas also passed his bill reducing franked mailings and limiting them to within members' districts. Still, Thomas is seen as too accommodating by conservative House Republican leaders, who tried to replace him with Paul Gillmor of Ohio as ranking member on House Administration in December 1992. But conference members rejected the less senior Gillmor by a 12 vote margin and Thomas got the post again.

On Ways and Means, he backs "Super IRAs" and a $2,500 first-time homebuyer tax credit. He is a free trader, backing the North American Free Trade Agreement, and he opposed the 25% tariff on imported minivans approved in 1992. Some of his proposals have a local angle: he backs geothermal and solar energy tax credits, targeted export assistance for farm products and application of U.S. quality standards to imported pistachios. He was vociferously opposed to George Miller's Central Valley Project water bill, much hated in the Valley, and opposes the Democrats' California Desert bill as too environmentally biased and unbalanced. He successfully blocked what he called a "nightmare" requirement for oil producers to set aside 1% of production for the Strategic Petroleum Reserve.

Thomas was embarrassed to have 119 overdrafts on the House bank totalling $157,000. But he did not have serious competition in this heavily Republican district and won easily.

The People: Pop. 1990: 571,143; 19% rural; 11% age 65+; 71% White; 4% Black; 1% Amer. Indian; 3% Asian; 13% Other; 20% Hispanic origin. Voting age pop.: 398,049; 4% Black; 17% Hispanic origin. Households: 59% married couple families; 30% married couple fams. w. children; 47% college educ.; median household income: $29,943; per capita income: $12,983; median gross rent: $454; median house value: $84,600.

1992 Presidential Vote

Bush (R) 94,727 (46%)
Clinton (D) 66,284 (32%)
Perot (I) 43,016 (21%)

1988 Presidential Vote

Bush (R) 107,624 (64%)
Dukakis (D) 60,740 (36%)

Rep. William M. Thomas (R)

Elected 1978; b. Dec. 6, 1941, Wallace, ID; home, Bakersfield; San Francisco St. U., B.A. 1963, M.A. 1965; Baptist; married (Sharon).

Career: Prof., Bakersfield Comm. Col., 1965–74; CA Assembly, 1974–78.

Offices: 2209 RHOB 20515, 202-225-2915. Also 4100 Truxtun Ave., #200, Bakersfield 93301, 805-327-3611; and 319 W. Murray St., Visalia 93291, 209-627-6549.

Committees: *House Administration* (RMM of 7 R): Administrative Oversight (RMM). *Ways and Means* (3d of 14 R): Health (RMM); Trade.

Group Ratings

	ADA	ACLU	COPE	CDF	CFA	LCV	ACU	NTLC	NSI	COC	CEI
1992	15	17	10	30	20	6	90	83	100	88	74
1991	10	—	18	30	17	15	79	—	—	100	70

National Journal Ratings

	1991 LIB — 1991 CONS		1992 LIB — 1992 CONS	
Economic	0%	— 96%	12%	— 88%
Social	39%	— 60%	31%	— 68%
Foreign	12%	— 85%	28%	— 71%

Key Votes of the 102d Congress

1. Ban Striker Replace	AGN	5. Handgun Wait/7-Day FOR	9. Use Force in Gulf FOR
2. $ for Homeownership	FOR	6. Overseas Mil. Abortion FOR	10. US Mil. Abroad $ Cut *
3. Tax Rich/Cut Mid Cls.	AGN	7. Obscn. Art NEA $ Ban FOR	11. Limit SDI Funds FOR
4. FY93/$15B Def. Cut	AGN	8. Death Pen. from Jury FOR	12. Cuba Trade Embargo FOR

Key Votes of the 103d Congress

1. Family Leave   AGN   2. Deficit Reduction   AGN   3. Stimulus Plan   AGN

Election Results

1992 general	William M. Thomas (R)	127,758	(65%)	($615,587)
	Deborah A. Vollmer (D)	68,058	(35%)	($28,487)
1992 primary	William M. Thomas (R)	37,657	(66%)	
	Carlos Murillo (R)	19,684	(34%)	
1990 general	William M. Thomas (R)	112,962	(60%)	($496,845)
(CA 20)	Michael A. Thomas (D)	65,101	(34%)	($690)
	William H. Dilbeck (LIB)	10,555	(6%)	

TWENTY-SECOND DISTRICT

Santa Barbara is one of California's most paradisical cities, a collection of red tile roofs and leafy live oaks, sheltered by towering mountains just above the sea. The impression is a bit misleading, for Santa Barbara has its problems and its Spanish style is a creation not of 18th Century Mission culture, but of the 20th Century: most of its red-tile-roofed white stucco buildings were put up after a 1925 earthquake leveled much of the town, with the most distinguished of the Spanish Revival buildings designed by an architect with the marvelously un-Latin name of George Washington Smith (though the documents at the Santa Barbara Mission are authentic). Santa Barbara, like Disneyland, does not reproduce the past but presents a bigger, more attractive, cleaner version of it, maintained not by the Disney company but (as in Santa Fe and Nantucket) an Architectural Review Board. But Santa Barbara's affluence isn't ersatz. This has long been one of the nation's richest retirement communities, and one increasingly devoted to preserving its environment and serenity. Both came under threat 20-some years ago. In 1969, an underwater oil well ruptured, coating the beach with oil; pictures of the oil slick in the channel and of volunteers trying to wash oil off grounded birds as Interior Secretary Walter Hickel (now Governor of Alaska) circled in a helicopter above, helped to launch the environmental movement of the 1970s. The wells aren't pumping any more (though some old 19th Century wells send globs of oil to the beach at nearby Summerland, where the Clintons rested in November 1992) but the oil spill did leave a residue in Santa Barbara's politics. This is a Republican community, uninterested in redistribution of wealth, but very concerned about the environment (it has built the nation's largest desalination plant) and liberal on cultural issues like abortion.

The 22d Congressional District of California consists of all of Santa Barbara except the town of Carpinteria at its southeast corner, plus San Luis Obispo County to the north. Not all of this area resembles Santa Barbara. The most notable feature in northern Santa Barbara County, across the Santa Ynez Mountains where Ronald Reagan has his ranch, is Vandenberg Air Force Base, and the nearby town of Santa Maria is pro-military and conservative. San Luis Obispo County is pleasant and as untrendy a place as you could find on this coast; its most notable feature is William Randolph Hearst's castle San Simeon.

Twice in the last three elections, the Santa Barbara district has seen the most expensive House election in the nation. The first was in 1988, when veteran incumbent Republican Robert Lagomarsino was challenged by state Senator Gary K. Hart (no relation to the former Colorado senator). Both candidates raised about $1.5 million, and Lagomarsino won 50%–49%. He bore some wounds, winning against a much less well-financed opponent in 1990 by 55%–44%. Then in 1992, he was whipsawed by redistricting. Both he and fellow Republican incumbent Elton Gallegly lived and had their original political base in the new 23d District, which included almost all of Ventura County. With Gallegly determined to run there, Lagomarsino gallantly agreed to move to Santa Barbara and run in the 22d. But there was already a Republican running there, spending freely, who refused to budge.

This was Michael Huffington, now congressman from the 22d and the highest-spending House candidate. He is the son of Houston oilman and longtime Republican contributor Roy Huffington, appointed by George Bush to be Ambassador to Austria. At Stanford in the late 1960s, Michael Huffington opposed the war in Vietnam, but never became a Democrat. Later he worked at banking and venture capital and in the family business (a joint venture on liquefied natural gas in Indonesia); he started a documentary film company; he was appointed deputy assistant secretary of defense for negotiations policy in 1986. Regarding money, he told a reporter, "Over a certain amount, it becomes meaningless. I'm in that category. I have no financial needs that cannot be met." (*Roll Call* estimates his net worth at $50 million.) Before he ran for Congress, Huffington was anything but famous, though his wife, under her maiden name Arianna Stassinopoulos, is well known and respected for her biographies of Maria Callas and

Pablo Picasso. Huffington bought his Santa Barbara house only in 1988, and didn't start paying California taxes until 1991. Then he decided to run for Congress, and didn't back down for Lagomarsino even when George Bush and Dan Quayle asked him to do so.

Huffington spent some $3 million of his own money on the primary, outspending Lagomarsino 6-1. In an inexpensive media market, he ran saturation TV ads for weeks and sent out at least 15 mailings and numerous videos; and he personally campaigned as well. He shrewdly attacked Lagomarsino for his uses of incumbency, accusing him of helping a constituent sell the Chinese government surveillance cameras it used to track down Tienanmen Square protesters. He even attacked Bush for "trading valueless endorsements for invisible advantages." On issues, Huffington favored tax and spending cuts, but was for abortion rights while the incumbent opposed them; he supported gay rights and opposed the tobacco lobby. Lagomarsino was still able to win in Santa Barbara County, 55%–42%, but he lost in San Luis Obispo 60%–28% and overall 49%–43%. Bitter at seeing his career ended, he threatened to run as a write-in, but did not. Democratic Santa Barbara County Supervisor Gloria Ochoa hoped to capitalize in the general on the Republican split, California's 1992 vogue for women and Santa Barbara's dislike of Texas oil men. But Huffington kept spending, for a total of $5.4 million, and slammed Ochoa for overcharging the state for business expenses and failing to pay property taxes.

Since the election, Huffington has continued to attack Congress. "In business if things weren't going well . . . you'd fire the management." He pledged to serve no more than four terms and called for scrapping the seniority system: "Under term limits, you can't wait to move up." He favors banning PAC contributions. He supported the Clinton Administration on gays in the military, but still directed attacks at Democrats in the House. He may be dismissed by many of his colleagues as a rich dilettante, but he has shown an aggressiveness and an ability to frame issues in a way that advances his cause, suggesting some political shrewdness and toughness behind the hand writing out the check.

The People: Pop. 1990: 572,956; 11% rural; 13% age 65+; 72% White; 3% Black; 1% Amer. Indian; 4% Asian; 11% Other; 21% Hispanic origin. Voting age pop.: 443,156; 3% Black; 18% Hispanic origin. Households: 54% married couple families; 24% married couple fams. w. children; 59% college educ.; median household income: $33,680; per capita income: $16,458; median gross rent: $621; median house value: $229,000.

1992 Presidential Vote			1988 Presidential Vote		
Clinton (D)	106,815	(41%)	Bush (R)	121,486	(56%)
Bush (R)	92,045	(35%)	Dukakis (D)	96,838	(44%)
Perot (I)	61,030	(23%)			

Rep. Michael Huffington (R)

Elected 1992; b. Sept. 3, 1947, Dallas, TX; home, Santa Barbara; Stanford, B.S. 1970, A.B. 1970, Harvard, M.B.A., 1972; Episcopalian; married (Arianna).

Career: Co-founder, Simmons & Huffington Inc., 1974–76; Roy Huffington Inc., 1976–86, Vice Chmn., 1990; Dep. Asst. Secy. of Defense for Negotiations Policy, 1986–87; Chmn., Crest Films Production Co., 1991–92.

Offices: 113 CHOB 20515, 202-225-3601. Also 1819 State St., #D, Santa Barbara 93101, 805-682-6600; 1060 Palm St., #A, San Luis Obispo 93401, 805-542-0426; and 910 E. Stowell Rd., Santa Maria 93454, 805-349-9357.

Committees: *Banking, Finance and Urban Affairs* (18th of 20 R): Financial Institutions Supervision, Regulation and Deposit Insurance; International Development, Finance, Trade and Monetary Policy. *Small Business* (11th of 18 R): Regulation, Business Opportunities and Technology; SBA Legislation and the General Economy.

Group Ratings and 102d Congress Votes: Newly Elected

Key Votes of the 103d Congress

1. Family Leave   FOR   2. Deficit Reduction   AGN   3. Stimulus Plan   AGN

Election Results

1992 general	Michael Huffington (R)	131,242	(53%)	($5,435,177)
	Gloria Ochoa (D)	87,328	(35%)	($663,027)
	Mindy Lorenz (Green)	23,699	(9%)	($18,707)
	Two Others	7,657	(3%)	
1992 primary	Michael Huffington (R)	38,406	(49%)	
	Robert J. Lagomarsino (R)	33,844	(43%)	
	Gordon Klemm (R)	5,570	(7%)	
	Other	1,292	(2%)	
1990 general	Robert J. Lagomarsino (R)	94,599	(55%)	($658,365)
(CA 19)	Anita Perez Ferguson (D)	76,991	(44%)	($241,815)
	Other	1,655	(1%)	

TWENTY-THIRD DISTRICT

On a barren hillside, overlooking a valley hemmed in by mountains north and south, five United States presidents gathered in November 1991 to dedicate the Ronald Reagan Library. It was the first time in 202 years that five presidents had stood together in one place, and in a place the Founding Fathers surely did not imagine would ever be American and yet today seems quintessentially so. The place is Simi Valley, which would become famous five months later as the site of the trial of the four Los Angeles Police Department officers accused of criminally assaulting Rodney King after a high-speed freeway chase. The verdict was criticized as an expression of racism, though given the evidence and argument the jury was presented with, it was a rational response; it was said that Simi Valley was a haven for affluent whites to escape the problems of the city. But Simi Valley is just one of many communities that have grown up outside Los Angeles, where the metropolitan area has grown past geographic barriers which once seemed sure to contain it; in this case, past the mountains that wall in the San Fernando Valley. But of course the San Fernando Valley was once such a community also: it is natural for a metropolitan area to expand, and for younger affluent families to live near its edge.

The interesting thing is not that Simi Valley and other new communities in Ventura County—Moorpark and Thousand Oaks and Camarillo running out toward the industrial port of Oxnard and the county seat of Ventura—have few low-income and black residents, but that they are as diverse as they are. Ventura County in 1990 was 30% Hispanic and 5% Asian; its white Anglo residents include many with names and backgrounds that would have been recognized as ethnic a few years ago. To be sure, here are some of the nation's lowest crime rates, a stark contrast with gang warfare in Los Angeles; also here are some of the highest percentages of intact families in California. And this is car country: Simi Valley claims to have more cars per capita than anywhere in the United States. But after all, these are things most Americans want. Politically, this home of the Reagan Library was strong Reagan country when he was elected governor and president, though it lost some of its cheerful, upbeat optimism in the more downbeat years of his successors, Jerry Brown in California and George Bush in Washington. But the balance toward the Republicans, the yearning for the cheerful order Reagan was able to impart, remains.

California's 23d Congressional District includes almost all of Ventura County (except Thousand Oaks) and just a corner of Santa Barbara County, the town of Carpinteria. Usually strongly Republican, it was anxious and split in 1992. The congressman here is Elton Gallegly, a real estate broker and college dropout from a working-class suburb of Los Angeles. He was elected at 35 to the Simi Valley city council, became mayor in 1980, and ran for Congress in 1986 when the incumbent ran for the Senate. Gallegly's local ties and money prevailed 50%–34% in the 1986 primary over Tony Hope, son of comedian Bob Hope, who had spent the previous decade in Washington. In the next two primaries, Gallegly was opposed by Korean-born entrepreneur Sang Korman who spent over $300,000 each time to win 14% and 32% (in 1992, he ran in the 24th District and finished second in the primary with 24%).

In 1992, Gallegly probably clinched the race when he persuaded fellow incumbent Robert Lagomarsino, from western Ventura County, to run in Santa Barbara instead; Lagomarsino lost the Republican primary to millionaire Michael Huffington, while Gallegly had minimal opposition in June. In November Gallegly had more difficulty. Democrat Anita Perez Ferguson who had run against Lagomarsino in 1990, raised substantial funds in 1992 with support from EMILY's List; she called Gallegly a rubber stamp for Bush and attacked him for noting that her radio ads omitted Perez from her name. He called her a carpetbagger and hit hard on illegal immigration issues. Both candidates sparred on abortion: Gallegly is antiabortion and Ferguson is pro-choice. Gallegly won with a decisive but scarcely overwhelming 54%.

Gallegly might have supposed that his almost perfectly conservative record would make him an easy winner in November. He wants to crack down on illegal immigration, and to counter charges of racism cites polls showing that Latino voters agree; he especially wants to ban welfare aid for illegals. He would give companies a $2,400 tax credit for every laid-off defense worker they hire. He was an original sponsor, before the Bush Administration decided on it, of the resolution authorizing use of American military force against Saddam Hussein, and he also called for recognition of Croatia and Slovenia well before Bush did. He favors a Health Freedoms Act, to ban overregulation of vitamins, herbs and other health foods. He has succeeded in having Port Hueneme near Oxnard designated as a U.S. port of entry. He is the first non-lawyer on the House Judiciary Committee in years, and is ranking Republican on the Insular and International Affairs Subcommittee of Natural Resources, of vast importance to the 4 million Americans in Puerto Rico, Virgin Islands, Guam and American Samoa.

The People: Pop. 1990: 571,562; 5% rural; 9% age 65+; 62% White; 3% Black; 1% Amer. Indian; 5% Asian; 14% Other; 30% Hispanic origin. Voting age pop.: 413,051; 2% Black; 26% Hispanic origin. Households: 63% married couple families; 33% married couple fams. w. children; 54% college educ.; median household income: $42,989; per capita income: $16,617; median gross rent: $733; median house value: $234,200.

1992 Presidential Vote

Clinton (D)	82,613	(38%)
Bush (R)	74,106	(34%)
Perot (I)	58,177	(27%)

1988 Presidential Vote

Bush (R)	115,744	(61%)
Dukakis (D)	75,566	(39%)

Rep. Elton Gallegly (R)

Elected 1986; b. Mar. 7, 1944, Huntington Park; home, Simi Valley; Los Angeles St. Col., 1962–63; Protestant; married (Janice).

Career: Owner, real estate firm; Simi Valley City Cncl., 1979–80; Simi Valley Mayor, 1980–86.

Offices: 2441 RHOB 20515, 202-225-5811. Also 300 Esplanade Dr., #1800, Oxnard 93030, 805-485-2300.

Committees: *Foreign Affairs* (11th of 18 R): Europe and the Middle East; Western Hemisphere Affairs. *Judiciary* (11th of 14 R): Economic and Commercial Law; International Law, Immigration and Refugees. *Natural Resources* (4th of 15 R): Insular and International Affairs (RMM).

Group Ratings

	ADA	ACLU	COPE	CDF	CFA	LCV	ACU	NTLC	NSI	COC	CEI
1992	15	9	50	20	27	6	84	90	100	75	75
1991	10	—	8	30	28	0	85	—	—	90	73

National Journal Ratings

	1991 LIB — 1991 CONS		1992 LIB — 1992 CONS	
Economic	4% —	90%	21% —	76%
Social	16% —	81%	0% —	85%
Foreign	0% —	88%	0% —	82%

Key Votes of the 102d Congress

1. Ban Striker Replace	AGN	5. Handgun Wait/7-Day	FOR	9. Use Force in Gulf	FOR
2. $ for Homeownership	FOR	6. Overseas Mil. Abortion	AGN	10. US Mil. Abroad $ Cut	AGN
3. Tax Rich/Cut Mid Cls.	AGN	7. Obscn. Art NEA $ Ban	FOR	11. Limit SDI Funds	AGN
4. FY93/$15B Def. Cut	AGN	8. Death Pen. from Jury	FOR	12. Cuba Trade Embargo	FOR

Key Votes of the 103d Congress

1. Family Leave	AGN	2. Deficit Reduction	AGN	3. Stimulus Plan	AGN

Election Results

1992 general	Elton Gallegly (R)	115,504	(54%)	($862,061)
	Anita Perez Ferguson (D)	88,225	(41%)	($543,116)
	Jay C. Wood (LIB)	9,091	(4%)	
1992 primary	Elton Gallegly (R)	34,666	(63%)	
	Daphne Becker (R)	15,518	(28%)	
	Robert Shakman (R)	4,597	(8%)	
1990 general	Elton Gallegly (R)	118,326	(58%)	($449,668)
(CA 21)	Richard D. Freiman (D)	68,921	(34%)	($13,147)
	Peggy Christensen (LIB)	15,364	(8%)	

TWENTY-FOURTH DISTRICT

It used to be movie ranch country: when the Hollywood moviemakers of the 1920s and 1930s were looking for filming sites for a western, they only had to drive past the vacant lots of Westwood, up into the Santa Monica Mountains looking out over the empty San Fernando Valley or west to Malibu, where the mountains plunged past the recently built Pacific Coast Highway into the ocean. This was barren land, with few trees, with deep crevasses in which waters rushed down when the rains came. But this area has been transformed. Malibu still cultivates a wild look, but it is famous worldwide as the beach resort of rich showbiz people: small beach houses not five feet removed from the one next door run upward of $1 million. The San Fernando Valley, once mostly uninhabited and then a metaphor for bland suburbia, is now as urbanized in its late 20th Century way as the railroad commuter central cities of the East Coast were in the way of the late 19th. Rich folk live on mountainside homes in Sherman Oaks and Encino, overlooking the Valley on smog-free days. A few blocks away, north of the Ventura Freeway, in post-World War II bungalows in Van Nuys and Reseda and Canoga Park, are people of all manner of ethnic background: Koreans and Filipinos, Salvadorans and Mexicans, Chinese and Iranians, Midwestern Protestants and East Coast Jews. But there are also, especially at the edge of the valley where the mountains rise, high-income subdivisions on curved streets.

The 24th Congressional District of California covers much of this territory: Malibu, the San Fernando Valley west from Sherman Oaks to Woodland Hills and north to Chatsworth; it follows the Ventura Freeway west through the mountains to Agoura Hills, Westlake Village and Thousand Oaks, a mostly new city of 100,000 in Ventura County valleys. Politically, this is a mixed area. Showbiz people, however high-income, are liberal and Democratic, more so indeed than many new ethnic groups; the affluent west end of the Valley and T.O. (as Thousand Oaks is known) are heavily Republican. The result is a district which, when approved by a court in February 1992, seemed Republican, and indeed had performed much like the nation and state as a whole in 1988 and 1990.

It was Republican enough that incumbent Democrat Anthony Beilenson of the old 23d District, who had represented much of the area, considered running instead in the westside 29th District south of the Santa Monica Mountains in a primary against fellow incumbent Henry Waxman. But Waxman, well-financed proprietor of the Waxman-Berman political machine, seemed the clear favorite, so Beilenson decided to take his chances in the new 24th. The race looked tough at first. No less than nine Republicans ran for the nomination. Korean-American businessman Sang Korman had spent $800,000 of his own money running against Elton Gallegly in the old 21st District in 1990; he won 24% this time. Bill Spillane, a retired Thousand Oaks pilot, spent $300,000 in the last three weeks and won 18%. The winner, with 34%, was Ventura County Assemblyman Tom McClintock, a conservative who would privatize street lights and prisons, a fierce critic of Governor Pete Wilson for his 1991 tax increases, antiabortion and anti-gun control. Beilenson stressed the abortion issue (he wrote California's 1967 liberalized abortion law signed by Governor Ronald Reagan) and the environment—his opposition to offshore oil drilling and sponsoring of continuing expansions of the Santa Monica Mountains National Recreation Area. He called for a national health service, with government payment and price-setting. In a year when voters were looking for reform, he stressed his refusal to accept PAC contributions or honoraria—even as he was raising $680,000 from individuals. McClintock's hard-edged conservatism did not go over well as the Bush candidacy was sinking, and the district continued to be a national bellwether, reelecting Beilenson 56%–39% and entitling him to begin his fourth decade as a legislator.

Beilenson had come west after law school, was elected to the Assembly in 1962 (before Willie Brown), to the state Senate in 1966 (the first time Los Angeles County elected more than one senator) and the U.S. House in 1976 (little remembered now, he ran against Alan Cranston for the U.S. Senate nomination in 1968 and lost by a wide margin). For a lifetime professional politician, he sounds oddly like a straight arrow, telling impolitic truths to his colleagues and constituents and—as 1992 showed—being shrewd enough to get away with it. He has been a member of the House Rules Committee since 1978, a body that has been a willing and pliant instrument of the Democratic leadership; but he seems less partisan than his Rules colleagues, and more willing to decide issues on their merits. He appears genuinely concerned about the deficit, for example, but had to watch it expand amid partisan gridlock in the 1980s. He supports a 50 cent gas tax and cuts in Social Security as well as other programs to cut the deficit—politically unpopular stands few other members take. He has spent time and thankless effort on process issues—the budget process, the electoral process, the intelligence process. He chaired the Intelligence Committee for two years and tried unsuccessfully to promote bipartisan cooperation.

Beilenson, once quoted as saying he didn't care much about California issues (though he later said the quote was taken out of context), for years has worked on local environmental matters—preserving the Sepulveda Basin, getting money for the Los Angeles Metro transit system, plus the Mountains Recreation Area—becoming more concerned as local needs escalated with the onset of the southern California recession in 1990. He wants to do more to slow population growth abroad and control immigration at home. He has also taken on the cause, exotic for many districts but perhaps not here, of protecting the African elephant from extinction: his 1988 act prohibits ivory imports into the U.S.; in 1990 and 1991, he secured $8.3 million for projects to prevent the elephants' extinction.

How will Beilenson fare in the 1990s? His big 1992 win may discourage serious competition, but he might be vulnerable if local opinion shifts as hard against the Democrats in 1994 or 1996 as it did against the Republicans in 1992. If he keeps winning, the term limits initiative approved by voters in 1992 bars his name from appearing on the ballot in 1998, though he could be elected as a write-in. But Beilenson, for all the seeming innocence of his politically risky frankness, has shown he can prevail in politically difficult times and should never be counted out.

The People: Pop. 1990: 572,287; 3% rural; 11% age 65+; 78% White; 2% Black; 6% Asian; 7% Other; 13% Hispanic origin. Voting age pop.: 450,914; 2% Black; 12% Hispanic origin. Households: 55% married couple families; 25% married couple fams. w. children; 66% college educ.; median household income: $48,433; per capita income: $25,767; median gross rent: $779; median house value: $304,300.

1992 Presidential Vote

Clinton (D)	128,572	(48%)
Bush (R)	79,728	(30%)
Perot (I)	57,625	(22%)

1988 Presidential Vote

Bush (R)	132,750	(54%)
Dukakis (D)	112,531	(46%)

Rep. Anthony C. Beilenson (D)

Elected 1976; b. Oct. 26, 1932, New Rochelle, NY; home, Los Angeles; Harvard, A.B. 1954, LL.B. 1957; Jewish; married (Dolores).

Career: Practicing atty., 1957–59; Cnsl., CA Assembly Cmte. on Finance & Insurance, 1960; Atty., CA Compensation & Insurance Fund, 1961–62; CA Assembly, 1963–66; CA Senate, 1967–76.

Offices: 2465 RHOB 20515, 202-225-5911. Also 21031 Ventura Blvd., #1010, Woodland Hills 91364, 818-999-1990; and 200 N. Westlake Blvd., #211, Thousand Oaks 91362, 805-496-4333.

Committees: *Budget* (4th of 26 D). *Rules* (3d of 9 D): Rules of the House (Chmn.).

Group Ratings

	ADA	ACLU	COPE	CDF	CFA	LCV	ACU	NTLC	NSI	COC	CEI
1992	85	87	75	90	100	100	9	30	40	38	21
1991	80	—	67	60	72	100	0	—	—	30	31

National Journal Ratings

	1991 LIB — 1991 CONS		1992 LIB — 1992 CONS	
Economic	56%	— 42%	59%	— 41%
Social	78%	— 17%	76%	— 24%
Foreign	92%	— 0%	86%	— 14%

Key Votes of the 102d Congress

1. Ban Striker Replace	FOR	5. Handgun Wait/7-Day	FOR	9. Use Force in Gulf	AGN
2. $ for Homeownership	AGN	6. Overseas Mil. Abortion	FOR	10. US Mil. Abroad $ Cut	FOR
3. Tax Rich/Cut Mid Cls.	AGN	7. Obscn. Art NEA $ Ban	AGN	11. Limit SDI Funds	FOR
4. FY93/$15B Def. Cut	FOR	8. Death Pen. from Jury	AGN	12. Cuba Trade Embargo	AGN

Key Votes of the 103d Congress

1. Family Leave	FOR	2. Deficit Reduction	FOR	3. Stimulus Plan	FOR

Election Results

1992 general	Anthony C. Beilenson (D)	141,742	(56%)	($786,463)
	Tom McClintock (R)	99,835	(39%)	($469,714)
	John Paul Lindblad (P&F)	13,690	(5%)	
1992 primary	Anthony C. Beilenson (D), unopposed			
1990 general	Anthony C. Beilenson (D)	103,141	(62%)	($201,404)
(CA 23)	Jim Salomon (R)	57,118	(34%)	($360,389)
	John Honigsfeld (P&F)	6,834	(4%)	

TWENTY-FIFTH DISTRICT

The edge of the Los Angeles metropolitan area least explored by journalists, travel writers, demographers and psephologists is the north. For years, it was assumed that LA ended at the northern end of the San Fernando Valley, with nothing much beyond the San Gabriel and Santa Susana Mountains; and for years that was true. Not so any more. As Latinos have moved out I-5 into the San Fernando Valley, many whites have moved even further north on I-5 past the rim of mountains to the Santa Clarita Valley, where the old small towns of Newhall and Valencia have been combined into Santa Clarita, with 110,000 people in 1990, and to the smaller towns growing amid forested hills in what is now called Canyon Country. Others have moved even further, out the Route 14 freeway, into the Low Desert around Lancaster and Palmdale, which had nearly 200,000 people in 1990.

California's new 25th Congressional District reflects this population growth. It combines three separate areas, each with about one-third of the population, with three different microclimates, economically linked by heavy dependence on defense industries and politically all very Republican. The oldest is the northwest quadrant of the San Fernando Valley, the still mostly white Anglo areas of Northridge and Granada Hills and Chatsworth; sunny and sheltered from ocean breezes, this is one of the hottest parts of metropolitan LA. Then, north of where I-5 squeezes through the chokepoint of mountain passes, is Santa Clarita and the Canyon Country, fast-growing and with something of an Old West air. Where the mountains stop at the San Andreas Fault, the desert stretches out low and flat, laid out in a Midwestern square-mile grid: dry, exceedingly hot in the summer, occasionally cold in winter. Between Lancaster and Palmdale is the Northrop plant that produces the controversial B-2 Stealth bomber.

It was widely assumed that the election in this new and incumbentless district would be decided in the Republican primary, and it was. The major competitors were Howard "Buck" McKeon, Santa Clarita councilman, and Assemblyman Phil Wyman. Wyman had held office for 14 years and had a solid, even eccentric, conservative record (he once had a bill to ban the allegedly satanic practice of recording certain words into songs backwards). McKeon, Santa Clarita's first mayor, and councilman for five years, had a colorful background as head of Howard and Phil's Western Wear, a family business he helped expand from one store to 52 in three states. Also in the race was John Rousselot, onetime John Birch Society organizer, elected congressman from the old 22d in 1960 and from 1970 to 1980; but with no ties here he got only 7% of the vote. Less than 1,000 votes separated the leaders; McKeon won 40%–38%. In the general, he had spirited competition from a Democrat who was once a Navy pilot, but McKeon won easily.

All politics in such new and fast-growing areas seems to be local. Wyman brought in Oliver North to campaign for him, but McKeon did better with the endorsement of Congressman Bill Thomas who used to represent much of the desert. McKeon talked about cutting taxes and outlawing most abortions, but his chief emphasis seemed to be on stimulating local jobs, especially in defense, and stopping the proposed Elsmere Canyon landfill in the Angeles National Forest. For that, and in recognition of his eight years of service on the William S. Hart School Board, he got seats on the Public Works and Education and Labor Committees, and was elected GOP freshman class president for 1993.

The People: Pop. 1990: 573,189; 10% rural; 8% age 65+; 72% White; 5% Black; 1% Amer. Indian; 6% Asian; 8% Other; 16% Hispanic origin. Voting age pop.: 415,109; 4% Black; 15% Hispanic origin. Households: 63% married couple families; 34% married couple fams. w. children; 59% college educ.; median household income: $46,480; per capita income: $18,849; median gross rent: $690; median house value: $213,000.

1992 Presidential Vote			1988 Presidential Vote		
Bush (R)	89,987	(39%)	Bush (R)	131,044	(67%)
Clinton (D)	83,305	(36%)	Dukakis (D)	64,743	(33%)
Perot (I)	57,398	(25%)			

Rep. Howard P. (Buck) McKeon (R)

Elected 1992; b. Sept. 9, 1939, Los Angeles; home, Santa Clarita; Brigham Young U., B.S. 1985; Mormon; married (Patricia).

Career: Small businessman; Owner, Howard and Phil's Western Wear, 1973–present; William S. Hart School District Bd., 1979–87; Chmn., Valencia Natl. Bank, 1987–88; Santa Clarita Mayor, 1987–88; Santa Clarita City Cncl., 1988–92.

Offices: 307 CHOB 20515, 202-225-1956. Also 23929 W. Valencia Blvd., #410, Santa Clarita 91355, 805-254-2111; and 1008 West Ave., #M-4, Palmdale 93551, 805-948-7833.

Committees: *Education and Labor* (14th of 15 R): Elementary, Secondary and Vocational Education; Labor-Management Relations; Postsecondary Education and Training. *Public Works and Transportation* (21st of 24 R): Aviation; Surface Transportation.

Group Ratings and 102d Congress Votes: Newly Elected

Key Votes of the 103d Congress

1. Family Leave	AGN	2. Deficit Reduction	AGN	3. Stimulus Plan	AGN

Election Results

1992 general	Howard P. (Buck) McKeon (R)	113,611	(52%)		($452,792)
	James H. (Gil) Gilmartin (D)	72,233	(33%)		($168,319)
	Rick Pamplin (I)	13,930	(6%)		($20,178)
	Three Others	18,941	(9%)		
1992 primary	Howard P. (Buck) McKeon (R)	24,509	(40%)		
	Philip D. Wyman (R)	23,804	(38%)		
	Larry Logsdon (R)	4,568	(7%)		
	John H. Rousselot (R)	4,438	(7%)		
	John J. Lynch (R)	3,366	(5%)		
	Other	1,242	(2%)		
1990 election	Newly created district.				

TWENTY-SIXTH DISTRICT

A hiker looking north from the crest of the Santa Monica Mountains in 1910 would have seen spread out, almost totally empty and barren, 20 miles wide and 12 miles deep, the San Fernando Valley. Separated by the Cahuenga Pass from rapidly growing Los Angeles and Hollywood, the Valley was bought up in massive tracts by civic leaders even as they were urging city engineer William Mulholland to build the huge 250-mile aqueduct from the Owens Valley to give Los Angeles water and persuading the city in 1915 to annex 200 square miles of the Valley. In the years after World War II, this was classic suburban territory, filled with *Leave It to Beaver* families.

Now the valley is not 1950s suburban but 1990s urban. It is the place that gave birth to the "Valley girls," who ignore high culture for showbiz and shopping. There are few white Anglo kids on the streets any more, and almost no moms at home; new residents are more likely to be of Mexican rather than Midwestern descent; the freeways are not just jammed with commuters at rush hour but busy at all hours of day and night. Here, in mostly black and Hispanic Pacoima, is where Rodney King was pulled over and beaten and arrested, and where George Holliday took the video 81 seconds of which did so much to change Los Angeles. It should be added that Pacoima and the heavily Hispanic Golden State Freeway corridor in the eastern Valley were not sites of major rioting in April 1992. These are neighborhoods, as they were in the 1950s, where people work hard and try to raise families who will have better chances and make better livings than they have.

The 26th Congressional District of California consists of the Golden State and Hollywood Freeway corridors of the San Fernando Valley—roughly its eastern half—proceeding as far west as Van Nuys on the San Diego Freeway. Some parts remain ethnically similar to 20 years ago: North Hollywood at the southern end of the Valley still has a significant Jewish population. But the northern end, around Pacoima and San Fernando, is one of metro LA's three major Hispanic clusters. The 26th District overall is 53% Hispanic, the sixth highest of any California district, yet they comprise only an estimated 20% of registered voters. Many Central and Mexican-Americans here are not citizens; many more of them are too young to vote; few have developed habits of civic and political participation, and many, working two jobs while raising families, are too busy to do so. The 26th District is solidly Democratic, but less because of its Hispanic voters than because of its Jews.

The congressman from the 26th is Howard Berman, one of the most aggressive and creative members of the House—and one of the most clear-sighted operators in American politics. He is the co-creator of what is known as the Berman-Waxman political machine. Not an organization that staffs precincts and hands out public jobs, it is a small group run by his brother Michael Berman that raises money, endorses candidates and runs campaigns, mainly through direct mail, carefully targeted at the multi-various segments of the southern California electorate. The Berman-Waxman machine had a tough year in 1992: its Senate candidates Mel Levine and Gray Davis lost in what proved to be the year of the woman. Its support of the Gulf war and the hard line it took in response to the Los Angeles riot did not capture the mood of Democratic primary or even general election voters. But the Bermans are smart and motivated by principle, and should not be counted out.

The Bermans showed their political shrewdness back in the McGovern year of 1972, when Howard Berman at 30 challenged and beat the Republican leader in the Assembly in a Hollywood Hills district. Berman had noticed that the Hills, once affluent, WASPy and family-oriented, were increasingly filled with Jews, singles and gays with liberation-minded lifestyles and liberal politics, ready to vote Democratic on cultural issues. Within a year Berman was the Assembly majority leader in Sacramento, the chief drafter of the state's farm labor law. In 1980 he tried to oust Speaker Leo McCarthy, but lost out to an odd alliance of Republicans and old-line Democrats that elected Willie Brown as Speaker. So for 1982, Congressman Phillip Burton and his chief assistant Michael Berman drew a new 26th District for Howard, beginning in the Hollywood Hills and extending to the north end of the Valley. For the 1990s, the new 26th (not drawn by a Berman) no longer includes the Hollywood Hills, but Howard Berman seems strongly entrenched, as comfortable with culturally conservative Mexican-American mothers as he was with culturally liberal Hollywood Hills singles.

There are few House members who have made such an imprint on legislation in so many areas as Howard Berman, and he has done it without any important chairmanship or powerful mentor; he is a close ally of Henry Waxman, but they tend to concentrate on different issues and have even, as on the Gulf war resolution, disagreed. One issue that Berman clearly cares about is Israel, but he doesn't take a narrow role. Since the mid-1980s he has volunteered, from his seat on the Foreign Affairs Committee, to floor manage oft-attacked foreign aid bills, a duty few others seek; eager to maintain aid to Israel, he also defends aid in general by smart political maneuvering. With Republican Henry Hyde wrote a law authorizing embargoes on nations that condone terrorism, and from that Berman became one of the earliest and most prescient critics of American policy toward Iraq. In April 1990, he called for sanctions against the "dangerous and unpredictable" Saddam Hussein. As late as August 1, Berman's bill was stoutly opposed by the Bush Administration—a position Bush himself said later he "absolutely" regretted. Berman was one liberal Democrat who supported the Gulf war resolution, but was understandably critical of the administration—if it had followed his advice there might well have been no need for war. Many liberals were unhappy with Berman, but he was utterly vindicated by events. After the Gulf war, in which Iraq used American weapons and technology, Berman focused increasingly on weapons proliferation. He pushed through an amendment ending subsidies to foreign arms sales and attacked the proposed sale of F-15s to Saudi Arabia; he tried to prevent sales of U.S. weapons to Syria and Iran. He also passed a law banning the double issuing of passports to coddle Arab countries who refuse to honor passports with Israeli marks.

Berman is also interested in immigration. In 1988 he sponsored the provision allowing 20,000 immigrant visas for migrants without close relatives here, to be selected randomly by computer—"Berman visa applications" they are called by those who seek them. In 1990 he worked to provide more family reunification slots, to expedite the immigration of Soviet Jews (a vivid presence in L.A. these days), and to pass amnesty provisions allowing more family members to remain in this country—all incorporated in the 1990 immigration bill, which substantially increased legal immigration—a point not lost on Berman's Hispanic and Asian constituents.

In a totally different area, Berman passed a major amendment to ERISA, the pension law, which would allow states to give workers greater rights than under the federal law—quite an achievement in this highly complex and heavily lobbied area of the law. Berman created a public-private consortium to come up with new transportation alternatives; he wants to see electric cars developed in the Valley and, with Republican David Dreier, encouraged a grant to CALSTART in Burbank to do so. He has passed laws to reward workers who blow the whistle on government fraud and to open up government documents to researchers after 30 years. On the Budget Committee, Berman has not been a major player on key fiscal issues, but his impact in other areas has never been in doubt. He was reelected easily in 1992, and the only threat to his tenure is the California term limits law that bars his name from appearing on the ballot beginning in 1998.

The People: Pop. 1990: 571,538; 8% age 65+; 34% White; 6% Black; 1% Amer. Indian; 7% Asian; 32% Other; 52% Hispanic origin. Voting age pop.: 410,180; 6% Black; 46% Hispanic origin. Households: 50% married couple families; 28% married couple fams. w. children; 40% college educ.; median household income: $32,134; per capita income: $12,198; median gross rent: $624; median house value: $185,300.

1992 Presidential Vote			1988 Presidential Vote		
Clinton (D)	72,673	(56%)	Dukakis (D)	72,596	(56%)
Bush (R)	31,013	(24%)	Bush (R)	56,360	(44%)
Perot (I)	24,167	(19%)			

Rep. Howard L. Berman (D)

Elected 1982; b. Apr. 15, 1941, Los Angeles; home, Sherman Oaks; U.C.L.A., B.A. 1962, LL.B. 1965; Jewish; married (Janis).

Career: Practicing atty., 1967–72; CA Assembly, 1973–82, Majority Ldr., 1974–79.

Offices: 2201 RHOB 20515, 202-225-4695. Also 14600 Roscoe Blvd., #506, Panorama City 91402, 818-891-0543.

Committees: *Budget* (5th of 26 D). *Foreign Affairs* (5th of 27 D): International Operations (Chmn.); International Security, International Organizations and Human Rights. *Judiciary* (11th of 21 D): Administrative Law and Governmental Relations; Economic and Commercial Law; Intellectual Property and Judicial Administration.

Group Ratings

	ADA	ACLU	COPE	CDF	CFA	LCV	ACU	NTLC	NSI	COC	CEI
1992	85	100	73	100	87	100	8	5	50	25	12
1991	85	—	82	100	72	92	11	—	—	22	11

National Journal Ratings

	1991 LIB — 1991 CONS		1992 LIB — 1992 CONS	
Economic	83% —	16%	75% —	25%
Social	88% —	0%	92% —	0%
Foreign	74% —	25%	62% —	35%

Key Votes of the 102d Congress

1. Ban Striker Replace	FOR	5. Handgun Wait/7-Day	FOR
2. $ for Homeownership	AGN	6. Overseas Mil. Abortion	FOR
3. Tax Rich/Cut Mid Cls.	FOR	7. Obscn. Art NEA $ Ban	AGN
4. FY93/$15B Def. Cut	FOR	8. Death Pen. from Jury	AGN

9. Use Force in Gulf	FOR
10. US Mil. Abroad $ Cut	FOR
11. Limit SDI Funds	FOR
12. Cuba Trade Embargo	FOR

Key Votes of the 103d Congress

1. Family Leave	FOR	2. Deficit Reduction	FOR	3. Stimulus Plan	FOR

Election Results

1992 general	Howard L. Berman (D)	73,807	(61%)	($722,606)
	Gary Forsch (R)	36,453	(30%)	($76,667)
	Margery Hinds (P&F)	7,180	(6%)	
	Other	3,468	(3%)	
1992 primary	Howard L. Berman (D), unopposed			
1990 general	Howard L. Berman (D)	78,031	(61%)	($450,401)
	Roy Dahlson (R)	44,492	(35%)	($82,453)
	Bernard Zimring (LIB)	5,268	(4%)	

TWENTY-SEVENTH DISTRICT

In the early years of the 20th Century, when Los Angeles was growing to become one of America's major cities, its richest citizens settled not on the beach (too clammy and cold) or on the west side (too dusty and remote), but in communities they built at the base of the San Gabriel Mountains that rise 10,000 feet above the city, their snow-capped peaks visible most of the year. The premier such community was Pasadena, now with its own institutions of national stature—the Rose Bowl, Cal Tech—and the premier structure was railroader Henry Huntington's house in next-door San Marino, now the Huntington Library, one of the world's great scholarly institutions. Less elite but still comfortable is Glendale, north of downtown Los Angeles, site of Forest Lawn Cemetery; the community's elderly Anglos, legendary for their conservatism, were joined in the 1980s by Iranian and Armenian immigrants who have almost doubled its population. Just west, beneath the Verdugo Mountains, is Burbank (named not for botanist Luther Burbank but for a local dentist-developer), famous now for the NBC Studios and Disney headquarters, as well as the big Lockheed plant.

The 27th Congressional District of California takes in many of these affluent yet yeasty foothill communities, with most of its acreage in the barren mountains. It includes Pasadena and South Pasadena with their turn-of-the-century prairie bungalows, and the black area in Pasadena and Altadena where Jackie Robinson grew up. To the west, connected by a freeway running through the hills, are Burbank and Glendale, now the district's big population center, but still with wildcats in the hills threatening pets and children. Sandwiched between the Verdugo Mountains are La Canada, La Crescenta, Sunland and Tujunga: sunny, affluent suburbs, all Republican areas since they began voting. But the increasing numbers of immigrants and singles, especially in Glendale and Burbank, have been moving the district toward the Democrats.

The congressman from the 27th is Carlos Moorhead, one of Congress's senior Republicans, first elected in 1972 after serving six years in the Assembly. His greatest moment in the national spotlight was in his first term, as one of Richard Nixon's few staunch defenders during the Judiciary Committee impeachment hearings. His greatest moment of potential power, however, began in 1993, when he became ranking Republican on the House Energy and Commerce Committee; he is second ranking Republican on Judiciary. His voting record in 1991 and 1992 was, in *National Journal*'s ratings, tied for the most conservative in the House. He is not abrasive or strident, however; indeed, Tom Bliley of Virginia opposed him for the Energy and Commerce slot on the ground that he is not aggressive enough. Moorhead brings to the House the friendliness and cooperative attitude of civic luncheon clubs, where it is not always reciprocated by the likes of Energy and Commerce Chairman John Dingell or Judiciary Chairman Jack Brooks.

Substantively, Moorhead has worked hard to protect intellectual property rights and copyrights, major United States assets in international trade. As senior California Republican, he worked with Democrat Don Edwards to set up a California Institute for Federal Policy Research—a rare instance of bipartisan cooperation in this delegation. He wants to promote the CALSTART electric vehicle project in Burbank and has proposed using laid-off aerospace workers to build a light-weight, low-floor bus. He amended the 1990 immigration act to add 1,000 border patrol officers. He has worked hard to open up electric transmission grids to independent and renewable energy producers. He got the Santa Fe Railroad to sell 370 miles of track to the LA area transit agency. He backed Hollywood interests opposing the cable TV reregulation bill.

Moorhead, used to winning reelection easily, found 1992 more difficult. He easily beat three opponents in the primary, but with 62%, not a huge percentage for a longtime incumbent. The general election he won by 50%–39% over Doug Kahn, a computer typography business owner, who formerly had lived in Seattle, Miami, and New York—the four corners of the continental United States. With his committee positions, Moorhead can raise unlimited amounts of money, but the numbers indicate that he may have to work the district hard to be assured of winning in 1994, when he turns 72.

The People: Pop. 1990: 572,629; 13% age 65+; 61% White; 8% Black; 1% Amer. Indian; 11% Asian; 10% Other; 20% Hispanic origin. Voting age pop.: 445,763; 8% Black; 18% Hispanic origin. Households: 49% married couple families; 23% married couple fams. w. children; 61% college educ.; median household income: $37,929; per capita income: $20,344; median gross rent: $671; median house value: $293,200.

1992 Presidential Vote

Clinton (D) 98,057 (44%)
Bush (R) 80,986 (36%)
Perot (I)................... 42,071 (19%)

1988 Presidential Vote

Bush (R) 119,543 (57%)
Dukakis (D)................ 89,998 (43%)

Rep. Carlos J. Moorhead (R)

Elected 1972; b. May 5, 1922, Long Beach; home, Glendale; U. of CA, B.A. 1943, U. of Southern CA, J.D. 1949; Presbyterian; married (Valery).

Career: Army, 1942–45 (WWII), Army Reserves, 1945–82; Practicing atty., 1949–72; CA Assembly, 1967–72.

Offices: 2346 RHOB 20515, 202-225-4176. Also 420 N. Brand Blvd., #304, Glendale 91203, 818-247-8445; and 301 E. Colorado Blvd., #618, Pasadena 91101, 818-792-6168.

Committees: *Energy and Commerce* (RMM of 17 R): Oversight and Investigations. *Judiciary* (2d of 14 R): Economic and Commercial Law; Intellectual Property and Judicial Administration (RMM).

Group Ratings

	ADA	ACLU	COPE	CDF	CFA	LCV	ACU	NTLC	NSI	COC	CEI
1992	5	0	25	0	13	13	100	100	100	75	87
1991	5	—	8	10	17	15	100	—	—	90	89

National Journal Ratings

	1991 LIB — 1991 CONS	1992 LIB — 1992 CONS
Economic	0% — 96%	0% — 91%
Social	0% — 84%	0% — 85%
Foreign	0% — 88%	0% — 82%

Key Votes of the 102d Congress

1. Ban Striker Replace AGN	5. Handgun Wait/7-Day AGN	9. Use Force in Gulf FOR
2. $ for Homeownership FOR	6. Overseas Mil. Abortion AGN	10. US Mil. Abroad $ Cut AGN
3. Tax Rich/Cut Mid Cls. AGN	7. Obscn. Art NEA $ Ban FOR	11. Limit SDI Funds AGN
4. FY93/$15B Def. Cut AGN	8. Death Pen. from Jury FOR	12. Cuba Trade Embargo FOR

Key Votes of the 103d Congress

1. Family Leave AGN	2. Deficit Reduction AGN	3. Stimulus Plan AGN

Election Results

1992 general	Carlos J. Moorhead (R)	105,521	(50%)	($705,814)
	Doug Kahn (D)	83,805	(39%)	($167,898)
	Jesse A. Moorman (Green)	11,003	(5%)	($10,097)
	Three Others	12,121	(6%)	
1992 primary	Carlos J. Moorhead (R)	37,172	(62%)	
	Louis Morelli (R)	10,354	(17%)	
	Barry L. Hatch (R)	6,622	(11%)	
	Lionel Allen, Jr. (R)	6,141	(10%)	
1990 general	Carlos J. Moorhead (R)	108,634	(60%)	($400,109)
(CA 22)	David Bayer (D)	61,630	(34%)	($40,303)
	William H. Wilson (LIB)	6,702	(4%)	
	Other	3,963	(2%)	

TWENTY-EIGHTH DISTRICT

It is the great route west to California: passengers on the Santa Fe railroad's Super Chief or motorists on U.S. 66, after hours and days in barren desert, descended through the El Cajon Pass into the Los Angeles Basin, moving in a stately procession, beneath the 10,000-foot snow-capped San Gabriel Mountains, marveling at orange groves and exotic plants. Just beneath the mountains, the Santa Fe and Route 66 ran through a line of towns, built by Midwestern Protestants as independent communities and now mostly high-income suburbs with their own civic institutions. There is Claremont, home of the academically strong Claremont Colleges; La Verne and Glendora; Azusa, named by a Chicago manufacturer for his wife; Duarte, with the City of Hope Medical Center; Monrovia and, just before Pasadena, Arcadia, site of the Santa Anita race track and the Los Angeles County Arboretum.

The 28th Congressional District of California covers much of this territory, with the exception of Azusa, which is part of the Hispanic-majority 31st District. Its eastern end reaches south from Claremont and Glendora to include Covina and West Covina, classic 1950s suburbs now with many Mexican-Americans, where city ordinances require that lawns be kept watered; 1950s homeowner values continue to govern here. The District's western end reaches south from Monrovia and Arcadia to include Temple City. It is far from mono-cultural: 24% Hispanic and 13% Asian in 1990, figures which are likely to rise (though not to the 59% Hispanic of the 31st District). The 28th remains a solidly Republican district, indeed by most measures the most Republican district in Los Angeles County.

David Dreier, the congressman from the 28th, spent most of his life on the Claremont McKenna College campus, as a student and administrator, before he ran for Congress in 1978 and was elected in 1980. He personifies the intellectually rigorous conservatism and free market economics that thrive there. He has become, despite being in the minority party and without a leadership position, an active legislator. On the Rules Committee, he has brought an aggressiveness to the Republicans outnumbered 9–4 there, and he was appointed in 1993 to the new Joint Committee on the Organization of Congress. On issues, he is a firm backer of low taxes and free trade, policies that fueled the Los Angeles Basin 1980s boom and which could well fuel another boom there in the 1990s. Dreier is a strong advocate of NAFTA and has called for free trade with Japan as well. He served on the Banking Committee for a decade and wants to debureaucratize lower-income housing programs, and he swung votes on Rules to allow the House to vote for HUD Secretary Jack Kemp's tenant ownership proposal which passed the House the next day. In response to the Los Angeles riot, he put forth a Minority Employment Empowerment Act to expand job opportunities, and pushed for an urban renewal program that would include enterprise zones, school choice and drug rehabilitation and urban homesteading. He also called for convicted rioters to be sentenced to rebuild the neighborhoods they tore down. He introduced one of the few bills to cut tax rates in the 102d Congress and another to roll back the 1990 budget summit tax increases. He favored increasing the Mexican border patrol and raising the ceiling on FHA mortgages—popular stands in southern California.

Dreier has excelled at electoral politics. He lost his first race for Congress in 1978, at 25, against Democrat Jim Lloyd; but he beat Lloyd in 1980 and then fellow Republican Wayne Grisham after they were redistricted together in 1982. At that point, Dreier decided never to be pressed for funds again and he has raised plenty of money and spent little—something that takes more self-discipline than one would think. At the end of 1992, he had over $2 million cash on hand—the second biggest House treasury in the country. He declined the chance to run for either of California's two Senate seats, though it is conceivable he might run against Dianne Feinstein in 1994 or Barbara Boxer in 1998. He wins reelection in the 28th District easily.

The People: Pop. 1990: 572,189; 11% age 65+; 57% White; 6% Black; 13% Asian; 10% Other; 24% Hispanic origin. Voting age pop.: 423,291; 5% Black; 21% Hispanic origin. Households: 60% married couple families; 30% married couple fams. w. children; 59% college educ.; median household income:

$43,508; per capita income: $18,064; median gross rent: $705; median house value: $231,900.

1992 Presidential Vote			1988 Presidential Vote		
Bush (R)	90,644	(41%)	Bush (R)	135,359	(63%)
Clinton (D)	82,958	(38%)	Dukakis (D)	79,100	(37%)
Perot (I)	45,623	(21%)			

Rep. David Dreier (R)

Elected 1980; b. July 5, 1952, Kansas City, MO; home, La Verne; Claremont McKenna Col., B.A. 1975, M.A. 1976; Christian Scientist; single.

Career: Corp. Relations Dir., Claremont McKenna Col., 1975–78; Mktg. Dir., Industrial Hydrocarbons, 1979–80; Vice Pres., Dreier Development Co., 1985–present.

Offices: 411 CHOB 20515, 202-225-2305. Also 112 N. 2d Ave., Covina 91723, 818-339-9078.

Committees: *Rules* (3d of 4 R): Rules of the House (RMM). *Joint Committee on the Organization of Congress* (V. Chmn. of 12).

Group Ratings

	ADA	ACLU	COPE	CDF	CFA	LCV	ACU	NTLC	NSI	COC	CEI
1992	0	0	8	0	13	6	100	85	100	75	92
1991	0	—	0	10	6	31	100	—	—	90	93

National Journal Ratings

	1991 LIB — 1991 CONS		1992 LIB — 1992 CONS	
Economic	4% —	90%	0% —	91%
Social	0% —	84%	0% —	85%
Foreign	0% —	88%	0% —	82%

Key Votes of the 102d Congress

1. Ban Striker Replace	AGN	5. Handgun Wait/7-Day	AGN	9. Use Force in Gulf	FOR
2. $ for Homeownership	FOR	6. Overseas Mil. Abortion	AGN	10. US Mil. Abroad $ Cut	*
3. Tax Rich/Cut Mid Cls.	AGN	7. Obscn. Art NEA $ Ban	FOR	11. Limit SDI Funds	AGN
4. FY93/$15B Def. Cut	AGN	8. Death Pen. from Jury	FOR	12. Cuba Trade Embargo	FOR

Key Votes of the 103d Congress

1. Family Leave	AGN	2. Deficit Reduction	AGN	3. Stimulus Plan	AGN

Election Results

1992 general	David Dreier (R)	122,353	(58%)	($290,128)
	Al Wachtel (D)	76,525	(37%)	($25,261)
	Two Others	10,504	(5%)	
1992 primary	David Dreier (R), unopposed			
1990 general	David Dreier (R)	101,336	(64%)	($172,451)
(CA 33)	Georgia Houston Webb (D)	49,981	(31%)	($29,177)
	Gail Lightfoot (LIB)	7,840	(5%)	

TWENTY-NINTH DISTRICT

The Westside: the term was not much used 20 years ago, but is now shorthand for what might be the biggest and flashiest concentration of affluence in the world. It is the heartland of one of America's most productive and creative industries—the persistence of the word "industry" here is a charming bit of antiquarianism—and one of the nation's major exports, show business. The first moviemakers came here earlier in the century, looking for a place to shoot silent films where the sunlight was more dependable than Astoria, Queens, or Englewood, New Jersey. They found it in Hollywood, a suburb just annexed by burgeoning Los Angeles when the first movie studio was built in 1911. In 1923 came the Hollywood sign, overlooking the soon-famous intersection of Hollywood and Vine. By the 1930s, the big studio lots were scattered around town, over the mountains in Burbank or out toward the ocean in Westwood and Culver City. The show business elite had moved to Beverly Hills and hills beyond. Show business itself moved far beyond movies, which reached their peak attendance in the early 1950s. It has never regained the gift it had, under the great studio bosses in the 1930s and 1940s, of capturing the American spirit in a way that was universally accessible: commerce and art combining to produce great popular culture.

Now movies are only one part of show business; television programming produces more revenue, and recordings probably even more; all three industries have their business and creative center in the Westside, from Hollywood west to the Ocean. They are immensely profitable, since their products sell worldwide and have no serious international competition: the Westside's superb technical skills are unmatchable and its willingness to exploit appetites for vicarious violence and sex are undisciplined by the restraint to which the great studio bosses of the past heeded. But there is something empty about the Westside's dominance. As new technologies proliferate, its products no longer have a universal appeal. And there is something solipsistic about the Westside: its denizens are increasingly interested in themselves and astonishingly ignorant of the world beyond. The great studio bosses did make some movies about Hollywood and show business, but most of their best work was about America and the world; these men, mostly of Jewish immigrant stock, were acutely aware they could prosper only by touching a chord in the American people. Today's show business people, who have in common no one ethnic origin but rather share values skeptical of tradition and moral restraints, seem increasingly interested in depicting the lives of people like themselves—and of proselytizing others to be more like them. And, while millions of people may seem unaccountably interested in the personal lives of actresses and screenwriters, audiences are declining; network television ratings are sharply down since the early 1980s; the recording industry has long since segmented into a half dozen or more fragments, some of considerable size but headquartered in Nashville or elsewhere. Show business, rich beyond imagination, almost unanimously enthusiastic for liberal Democrats and, by fall 1992, Bill Clinton in particular, has the pleasure of seeing its favored politicians control the White House and Congress, arguably for the first time ever. But this triumph occurred just as show business's hold on American minds seemed to be slipping, partly because of technological change, partly because of Westside self-absorption.

Not everyone on the Westside is in show business, of course. This is also the home of thousands of small entrepreneurs, manufacturers, and inventors and marketers of everything imaginable, who sparked the Los Angeles Basin growth of the 1980s, and there are even traces of pre-show business, old Los Angeles money which is also plentiful. There are large numbers of singles and gays here: apartment-renters provided majorities for Santa Monica's radical city government, which thrived when it imposed rent control but foundered when it invited in more homeless; West Hollywood, which may have a gay majority, is proud of its openly gay mayor. The core of Hollywood itself has gone seedy, and is the home now of many Central American immigrants, a high-crime and riot zone; but the Fairfax neighborhood remains solidly middle-class Jewish and Hancock Park looks as aristocratic as it did when it was built, when Beverly Hills was vacant land. The Westside is the home of a former president who does not at all exemplify its politics, Ronald Reagan; it is also the home, notably on the former Fox lot that is now Century City where Reagan keeps his office, of some of the largest office buildings in the Los Angeles area. It is the center of the second largest Jewish community in the United States, as well as the focus of the 1980s' immigration of Iranians to the United States. It is also the home of some of America's most expensive residential real estate, where people buy houses for $1 million, knock down the structure and build something new for another million or two, and of one of the world's premier high-priced shopping areas, Rodeo Drive, a quite ordinary shopping street 20 years ago.

The 29th Congressional District of California, as drawn for 1992, contains almost all the major elements of Westside Los Angeles, from old, high-income Los Feliz and the gay neighborhood around Silver Lake through Hollywood and Hancock Park, west through Beverly Hills and Westwood, Bel Air and Brentwood, Santa Monica and Pacific Palisades. It is solidly Democratic, and not just in votes: it probably contributes more money to Democratic candidates and liberal causes than any other district with the possible exception of Manhattan's New York 14th. Its boundaries are carefully sculpted to put blacks in the 32d District to the south and Hispanics and Asians in the 30th to the east; far from being racially diverse, it has the highest percentage of non-Hispanic whites (76%) of any Los Angeles Basin district except the 24th on the other side of Mulholland Drive.

The congressman from the 29th, Henry Waxman, is one of the ablest and most powerful members of the House, a shrewd political operator, and a skilled and idealistic policy entrepreneur. There is no Westside glitz about him: he grew up over his family's store in Watts, his personal demeanor is quiet and courteous. He first learned politics at UCLA with the likes of Howard Berman, Willie Brown, David Roberti and John Burton. At each stage of his career, he has seen political openings before others did and gone smartly through them. He ran against Assemblyman Lester McMillan in the mostly Jewish Fairfax area in 1968 and won 64% in the primary. He chaired the redistricting committee in 1971–72, a good place to make friends; and he went to Congress in 1974 in a district designed, he likes to point out, not by his committee, but by a court. Waxman's biggest break came after the 1978 election, when he was elected chairman of the Energy and Commerce Committee's Health and Environment Subcommittee. This was one of the first times House Democrats decided not to observe seniority in handing out subcommittee chairs, and Waxman's opponent, Richardson Preyer, was competent and widely respected. Nevertheless, Waxman argued his case on the issues and—quite unprecedented at the time, though common in Sacramento and now also in Washington—made campaign contributions to other Democrats on the full committee, and won the post, 15–12.

The campaign contributions were no accident. Waxman and his friends Howard Berman and former area congressman Mel Levine, built their own political machine in Los Angeles. Its power comes not from patronage but from fundraising and savvy. Their specialty is targeted direct mail, with hundreds of customized letters and endorsement slates sent out to different lists of people. In the apolitical commonwealth of California, where television advertising is exceedingly expensive and people seem to avoid politics, this has made them critical though not always successful players. 1992 was a tough year for the machine: its U.S. Senate candidates, Mel Levine and Gray Davis, both lost in primaries, as did some of their other notable statewide candidates. The machine also saw state and congressional term limits pass in 1990 and 1992. But it had successes in outlying areas: Yvonne Burke won for county supervisor and Lynn Schenk in the 49th San Diego District for representative.

Waxman has become less involved in local politics as he becomes a major national policymaker. He played a critical role on the Clean Air Act, first in 1981 and 1982 by preventing the Reagan Administration and Energy and Commerce Chairman John Dingell from relaxing the Clean Air Act. After his efforts to tighten it failed, in 1989 and 1990 Waxman and Dingell— frequent shouting match partners who maintained civil if cool relations—worked out a compromise, delaying stricter California-type auto standards until 1994 and moving more aggressively on non-auto issues. In the House and in conference with the Senate, this Waxman-

Dingell alliance, with command over technical detail and parliamentary procedure, largely prevailed and produced a new Clean Air Act which George Bush signed in October 1990. All has not been amity since: Waxman accused the Bush Administration of not enforcing the law, while Dingell seemed to take the other side, and such disputes will likely continue in the Clinton years: as Waxman knows, governance is a process of constant vigilance and diligence, lobbying and noodging.

Health care has naturally been one of Waxman's interests, and he was busy changing the national healthcare system in the 1980s long before the issue was widely debated in the 1990s. His strategy was to expand Medicaid coverage, which he did from 1984 to 1990 by threatening to hold up budget reconciliation bills unless they required states to expand Medicaid eligibility. By 1990, he got coverage for all poor children up to 18, all children under seven and pregnant women in families under 133% of poverty income; he got Medicare to pay deductibles for the poor and for mammograms; he got a health care tax credit, similar to the earned income tax credit, for the working poor. One result was that in the 1980s Medicaid rose from 9% to 14% of state spending, making Waxman hated by many governors, including Bill Clinton, who as governor accused Waxman of plotting to impose federal universal health care and of "using Medicaid as the vehicle and the states' credit cards as the financing mechanism." Which was something like the truth: Waxman's response to the governors was, "These are legitimate expenses. States have objected to mandates to cover some of the most vulnerable population groups, yet they haven't given us any other solution as to how to deal with that overwhelming need. I'm unmoved by their plea." In 1991, Waxman supported the Democrats' play-or-pay bill to insure the uninsured; in 1992, he was one of the Democrats who offered a $45 billion plan for long-term elderly care and who strived unsuccessfully to agree on a total healthcare package. He has said he supports national health insurance, but seems less committed to any particular package than to trying to expand coverage to the maximum extent possible, and remaining Health Subcommittee chairman to continue to fight another day.

Waxman has made a difference on other health issues. He has pushed through billions for AIDS research, a burning issue in the 29th District with its large gay population, and criticized the Bush Administration harshly for neglecting the disease. He has also sought to lessen patent protection for "orphan" drugs (an earlier Waxman measure) used for treating widespread diseases like AIDS. He passed a law providing damages to children injured by required immunizations, sponsored measures to require testing of mammography devices, expanded the availability of generic drugs, extended patent protection for drugs during part of the regulatory process, and tried unsuccessfully to legalize the use of heroin to reduce the pain of terminal cancer patients. He has worked hard to allow fetal tissue research, over the objections of the Bush Administration, and has tried to restrict tobacco advertising by banning cartoon characters like Joe Camel which seem to appeal to children (that will probably be strongly opposed by his new ranking Republican, Thomas Bliley of Virginia).

Waxman, unlike many of his Westside show business constituents, is not at all solipsistic or dilettantish. He has no personal taste for gaudy luxury. He cares about results in the real world and is unmoved by opposition, carefully assessing his colleagues and their motives, gauging their weaknesses and appreciating their strengths, waiting for the right moment to outsmart them and generally unflappable. That was the case in 1992, when for the first time in 20 years he didn't control redistricting. Much of his old district went to make up the new majority-Hispanic 30th, and when colleague Anthony Beilenson said he might run in the new 29th, Waxman coolly said it was a natural constituency for him and that he could win any primary; he offered to help Beilenson if he ran in the much less Democratic 24th, which Beilenson did. In the general election, Waxman had opposition from former Reagan White House aide Mark Robbins, who is openly gay; Robbins attacked Waxman for his 434 overdrafts on the House bank and got support from the vitamin, herb, dietary supplement and alternative healthcare community—this is California—opposed to a Waxman bill for more regulation on their industry. Waxman campaigned little and won by a 61%–26% margin—his lowest percentage ever, but not a danger sign. Waxman will surely become Energy and Commerce chairman if Dingell retires, but that does not seem imminent, and from his subcommittee chair Waxman is about as powerful as a House member can be.

The People: Pop. 1990: 571,386; 16% age 65+; 76% White; 3% Black; 8% Asian; 5% Other; 13% Hispanic origin. Voting age pop.: 497,153; 3% Black; 11% Hispanic origin. Households: 34% married couple families; 12% married couple fams. w. children; 71% college educ.; median household income: $37,540; per capita income: $34,253; median gross rent: $678; median house value: $500,001.

1992 Presidential Vote			1988 Presidential Vote		
Clinton (D)	183,233	(66%)	Dukakis (D)	162,917	(64%)
Bush (R)	55,924	(20%)	Bush (R)	91,595	(36%)
Perot (I)	37,217	(13%)			

Rep. Henry A. Waxman (D)

Elected 1974; b. Sept. 12, 1939, Los Angeles; home, Los Angeles; U.C.L.A., B.A. 1961, J.D. 1964; Jewish; married (Janet).

Career: Practicing atty., 1965–68; CA Assembly, 1968–74.

Offices: 2408 RHOB 20515, 202-225-3976. Also 8425 W. 3d St., #400, Los Angeles 90048, 213-651-1040.

Committees: *Energy and Commerce* (2d of 27 D): Health and the Environment (Chmn.); Oversight and Investigations. *Government Operations* (4th of 25 D): Human Resources and Intergovernmental Relations.

Group Ratings

	ADA	ACLU	COPE	CDF	CFA	LCV	ACU	NTLC	NSI	COC	CEI
1992	95	100	82	100	87	100	0	5	30	25	9
1991	90	—	83	100	83	92	0	—	—	10	10

National Journal Ratings

	1991 LIB — 1991 CONS		1992 LIB — 1992 CONS	
Economic	79% —	18%	83% —	13%
Social	83% —	16%	88% —	8%
Foreign	87% —	8%	82% —	16%

Key Votes of the 102d Congress

1. Ban Striker Replace	FOR	5. Handgun Wait/7-Day	FOR	9. Use Force in Gulf	AGN
2. $ for Homeownership	AGN	6. Overseas Mil. Abortion	FOR	10. US Mil. Abroad $ Cut	*
3. Tax Rich/Cut Mid Cls.	FOR	7. Obscn. Art NEA $ Ban	AGN	11. Limit SDI Funds	FOR
4. FY93/$15B Def. Cut	FOR	8. Death Pen. from Jury	*	12. Cuba Trade Embargo	FOR

Key Votes of the 103d Congress

1. Family Leave	FOR	2. Deficit Reduction	FOR	3. Stimulus Plan	FOR

Election Results

1992 general	Henry A. Waxman (D)	160,312	(61%)	($718,695)
	Mark A. Robbins (R)	67,141	(26%)	($148,274)
	David Davis (I)	15,445	(6%)	($23,849)
	Susan C. Davies (P&F)	13,888	(5%)	
	Two Others	4,700	(2%)	
1992 primary	Henry A. Waxman (D)	72,283	(84%)	
	Scott M. Gaulke (D)	13,350	(16%)	
1990 general	Henry A. Waxman (D)	71,562	(69%)	($287,505)
(CA 24)	John N. Cowles (R)	26,607	(26%)	($1,830)
	Maggie Phair (P&F)	5,706	(5%)	

THIRTIETH DISTRICT

Surrounding downtown Los Angeles are neighborhoods just now becoming antique, as the early 20th Century buildings stop looking familiar and start taking on the patina of the historic. Downtown LA, with its 1980s marble slabs and pink cylinders jutting up to 70 stories from what was once a low-rise business district, seems soulless and detached from the neighborhoods around, which change character with every few years' changes in immigration flow.

Several of these neighborhoods were combined after the 1990 Census to form the new 30th Congressional District, which does not quite include downtown but includes several neighborhoods near it. East of the Los Angeles River it takes in Boyle Heights, once an entry neighborhood for Irish and Jewish immigrants, for the last 30 years predominantly Mexican-American, poor in income terms but with enough community cohesion not to riot in April 1992. To the north of downtown is Lincoln Heights, a heavily Hispanic area centering on the shopping street of North Broadway, plus the LA neighborhoods of Highland Park and Eagle Rock, white middle-class 30 years ago, now mostly Hispanic but with Asians as well. West of downtown, the 30th District takes in lower Sunset Boulevard, the Koreatown strip along Western Avenue, and much of Hollywood and some of South Central. Koreatown was one of the areas worst hurt in the riots and, as elite sympathy is voiced for the rioters more than the hard-working, law-abiding merchants whose property was destroyed, there is residual bitterness here of unknown proportions. Much of Hollywood has become an entry point for Central American migrants, as has the northern edge of South Central; coming from societies where violence is more common and endemic than in Mexico or the United States, they rioted in very substantial numbers. These are all neighborhoods populated more thickly than they were a quarter-century ago, small houses and garden apartments full of large families and many children; new migrants stay with those who have been here a few years, with beds assigned to family members working different shifts so they're slept in 24 hours a day. To most American eyes, these look like poverty neighborhoods, and that is the snapshot view; but if one sees them as part of a longer video, they would appear the first step on the way to prosperity, the first way-station on the Santa Ana and San Bernardino Freeways to middle-income American comfort.

In 1990, the 30th District was recorded as 61% Hispanic and 21% Asian. But many of these are recent immigrants; only 34% of registered voters were Latino and 7% Asian. Indeed, of 572,000 residents, only 32,700 voted in the crucial Democratic primary and 83,000 in the general election; this is arguably a constituency that is way overrepresented. Newly created for the 1992 election, it was expected to reelect Congressman Edward Roybal, an Hispanic with roots in New Mexico, first elected to Congress in 1962, who rose to become chairman of an Appropriations subcommittee and of the Select Committee on Aging; his daughter Lucille Roybal-Allard was elected to the Assembly in 1988 and to the neighboring 33d District seat in 1992. But Roybal announced late in the game he was retiring, and when his former aide Henry Lozano dropped out of the race, Roybal endorsed the Democrat who proved to be his successor,

Xavier Becerra.

Becerra's best-known opponent, Leticia Quezada, had credentials which might have prevailed in a more politics-conscious district. She was a member of the Los Angeles school board, a powerful engine for publicity, and she had the endorsement of Councilman Richard Alatorre and Assemblyman Richard Polanco. Becerra had held elective office as a member of the Assembly for only two years, and from the suburb of Monterey Park which is outside the district. But Becerra had, besides Roybal, endorsements from 34th District incumbent Esteban Torres and County Supervisor Gloria Molina. And he had some impressive credentials: he is a graduate of Stanford Law, worked for state Senator Art Torres and then served on Attorney General John Van de Kamp's staff. He has a liberal record on environment and making AIDS drugs available; he backed campaign finance reform and tougher penalties for gang activities near schools. His supposed carpetbagging evidently didn't matter much; after all, most LA area Latinos are less than a generation away from somewhere else. In this low-turnout primary, Becerra won 32% of the vote, well ahead of Quezada's 22%; trailing were Albert Lum, who is of Asian background, at 16%, businessman Jeff Penichet at 13% and several Latinos who were harshly critical of Becerra at less than 10% each. The general election was less seriously contested: Becerra won 58%–24%. He can be expected to have a fairly solid liberal record in office.

The People: Pop. 1990: 572,604; 8% age 65+; 15% White; 3% Black; 21% Asian; 31% Other; 60% Hispanic origin. Voting age pop.: 415,907; 4% Black; 56% Hispanic origin. Households: 45% married couple families; 27% married couple fams. w. children; 35% college educ.; median household income: $23,435; per capita income: $9,637; median gross rent: $525; median house value: $187,400.

1992 Presidential Vote			1988 Presidential Vote		
Clinton (D)	56,378	(62%)	Dukakis (D)	54,576	(64%)
Bush (R)	21,750	(24%)	Bush (R)	31,250	(36%)
Perot (I)	11,842	(13%)			

Rep. Xavier Becerra (D)

Elected 1992; b. Jan. 26, 1958, Sacramento; home, Los Angeles; Stanford U., B.A. 1980, Stanford Law Schl., J.D. 1984; Catholic; married (Carolina Reyes).

Career: Staff Atty., Legal Assistance Corp. of Central MA; Dist. Dir., CA Sen. Art Torres, 1986; CA Dep. Atty. Gen., 1987–90; CA Assembly, 1990–92.

Offices: 1710 LHOB 20515, 202-225-6235. Also 2435 Colorado Blvd., #200, Los Angeles 90041, 213-550-8962.

Committees: *Education and Labor* (17th of 28 D): Elementary, Secondary and Vocational Education; Labor-Management Relations; Postsecondary Education and Training *Judiciary* (21st of 21 D): Intellectual Property and Judicial Administration; International Law, Immigration and Refugees. *Science, Space and Technology* (31st of 33 D): Technology, Environment and Aviation.

Group Ratings and 102d Congress Votes: Newly Elected

Key Votes of the 103d Congress

1. Family Leave	FOR	2. Deficit Reduction	FOR	3. Stimulus Plan	FOR

Election Results

1992 general	Xavier Becerra (D)	48,800	(58%)	($373,551)
	Morry Waksberg (R)	20,034	(24%)	($57,063)
	Blase Bonpane (Green)	6,315	(8%)	($40,115)
	Elizabeth A. Nakano (P&F)	6,173	(7%)	
	Other	2,221	(3%)	
1992 primary	Xavier Becerra (D)	10,417	(32%)	
	Leticia Quezada (D)	7,089	(22%)	
	Albert C. Lum (D)	5,128	(16%)	
	Jeff J. Penichet (D)	4,136	(13%)	
	Gonzalo Molina (D)	2,320	(7%)	
	Helen Hernandez (D)	1,908	(6%)	
	Four Others	1,716	(5%)	
1990 general	Edward R. Roybal (D)	48,120	(70%)	($190,702)
(CA 25)	Steven J. Renshaw (R)	17,021	(25%)	
	Robert H. Scott (LIB)	3,576	(5%)	

THIRTY-FIRST DISTRICT

Anyone interested in the future of America and today's immigrants should drive straight east from downtown Los Angeles on the San Bernardino Freeway, through the string of suburbs that grew up in the 1940s and 1950s. These were once white middle-class communities, with grids of stucco houses above the dry river beds; they were filled with Midwest and East Coast migrants who had discovered California in World War II and decided to stay, or who had learned of its golden reputation from the new medium of television in the days before smog became part of the language. The atmosphere then was Midwestern, cheerful, busy, with children always under-foot. Over the next generation or so, there has been almost a complete population turnover here, but some things remain the same. Mexican-Americans have spread out from their original East Los Angeles base to become majorities in blue-collar suburbs like El Monte, Baldwin Park and Azusa; all these towns have many more residents than in their Anglo days. But these are not mono-ethnic communities, and East Los Angeles has not become a slum. There are no empty storefronts, but busy shops with new signs; no housing riddled with vandalism and neglect, but newly painted homes with carefully tended gardens; these are neighborhoods still filled with children whose parents believe in traditional values. When blacks and Latinos were rioting in South Central and Hollywood, East Los Angeles was quiet and orderly.

Latinos are not the only migrants here; there are also Asians. Monterey Park and San Gabriel have sprouted Chinese and Korean shopping centers and storefronts, and have become the American center for Taiwanese. In next-door Alhambra, the Asians have made the local high school "an academic giant," reports *The Washington Post*'s Jay Mathews. "Its name is . . . at the top of lists of the leading science and mathematics programs in American education." Sometime in the 21st Century, novels will be written describing the by then vanished atmosphere of these immigrant suburbs, that will surely tell more about the human condition than the 1980s minimalist novels (the eponymous *Less Than Zero*) did about the horrors of growing up rich in Beverly Hills.

In the 1950s, these were Democratic areas—New Dealers bringing their voting habits west—but the new Latinos and Asians seem up for grabs. They voted strongly for Ronald Reagan in 1984, and were only 5% to 8% more Democratic than average in 1988 and 1990 elections; in 1992, Latinos moved toward the Democrats, but Asians, dismayed by responses to the riot, seemed to have trended Republican. The promise of increased government benefits could help the Democrats. But working against them are these new Americans' hard work in building small businesses and their bad experiences with government here and where they came from.

The 31st Congressional District of California covers much of this territory, from the LA city limit through East Los Angeles, Alhambra, San Gabriel, Rosemead, El Monte, Baldwin Park and Azusa; it brushes, but excludes higher-income suburbs, up against the San Gabriel Mountains. It was 59% Hispanic in 1990 and 23% Asian, with one of the lowest percentages of non-Hispanic whites (17%) in California. Its congressman, Marty Martinez, is a Democrat who has been in the right place with the right political patrons at the right time. The owner of an upholstery company, he was elected to the Monterey Park council in 1974. He was tapped in 1980 to run against incumbent Assemblyman Jack Fenton by Howard Berman, who was running for assembly speaker, and the Berman-Waxman machine superintended Martinez's campaign to an eventual win. Their ally Phil Burton in the 1982 redistricting plan forestalled a Republican-Hispanic alliance by creating two Hispanic districts in the eastern Los Angeles Basin. One of them was for Martinez, and after a desultory campaign he beat incumbent Republican and onetime John Birch Society organizer John Rousselot 54%–46%. Despite lackluster showings at the polls over the years, redistricting for 1992 was a boon for him.

Martinez is "one of Congress's lesser lights," says the December 1992 *California Journal*. His attendance rate in 1991, 81%, was the 10th worst in the House, and in 1992 he ran up against three challengers in the primary who garnered 43% of the vote. But as chairman of the Human Resources Subcommittee of Education and Labor, Martinez can now say that he has sponsored legislation that has passed, including reauthorization of the Older Americans Act, new Head Start and juvenile justice laws, and a JEDI bill to place welfare recipients in long-term jobs, all signed by President Bush. He also passed a Native American Languages Act to record these languages before they die out. Faring better with his new district lines in November 1992, Martinez won with 63% to 37% for Reuben Franco.

The People: Pop. 1990: 572,758; 9% age 65+; 18% White; 2% Black; 23% Asian; 27% Other; 58% Hispanic origin. Voting age pop.: 403,292; 2% Black; 53% Hispanic origin. Households: 57% married couple families; 33% married couple fams. w. children; 36% college educ.; median household income: $30,667; per capita income: $10,264; median gross rent: $622; median house value: $178,400.

1992 Presidential Vote		
Clinton (D)	59,616	(51%)
Bush (R)	37,250	(32%)
Perot (I)	18,449	(16%)

1988 Presidential Vote		
Dukakis (D)	61,374	(54%)
Bush (R)	52,500	(46%)

Rep. Matthew G. (Marty) Martinez (D)

Elected 1982; b. Feb. 14, 1929, Walsenburg, CO; home, Monterey Park; Los Angeles Trade Tech. Col., 1950; Catholic; married (Elvira).

Career: Marine Corps, 1947–50; Businessman, 1950–70; Monterey Park Planning Cmte., 1971–74; Monterey Park City Cncl., 1974–80; Monterey Park Mayor, 1976, 1980; CA Assembly, 1980–82.

Offices: 2231 RHOB 20515, 202-225-5464. Also 320 S. Garfield Ave., #214, Alhambra 91801; 818-458-4524.

Committees: *Education and Labor* (7th of 28 D): Human Resources (Chmn.); Labor-Management Relations. *Foreign Affairs* (12th of 27 D): Asia and the Pacific; International Operations; International Security, International Organizations and Human Rights.

Group Ratings

	ADA	ACLU	COPE	CDF	CFA	LCV	ACU	NTLC	NSI	COC	CEI
1992	95	76	91	100	73	69	4	0	50	25	12
1991	65	—	100	80	83	62	11	—	—	20	11

National Journal Ratings

	1991 LIB — 1991 CONS		1992 LIB — 1992 CONS	
Economic	83% —	16%	91% —	0%
Social	60% —	40%	70% —	29%
Foreign	72% —	28%	71% —	26%

Key Votes of the 102d Congress

1. Ban Striker Replace	FOR	5. Handgun Wait/7-Day	FOR	9. Use Force in Gulf	AGN
2. $ for Homeownership	AGN	6. Overseas Mil. Abortion	AGN	10. US Mil. Abroad $ Cut	FOR
3. Tax Rich/Cut Mid Cls.	FOR	7. Obscn. Art NEA $ Ban	AGN	11. Limit SDI Funds	AGN
4. FY93/$15B Def. Cut	FOR	8. Death Pen. from Jury	FOR	12. Cuba Trade Embargo	FOR

Key Votes of the 103d Congress

1. Family Leave FOR   2. Deficit Reduction FOR   3. Stimulus Plan FOR

Election Results

1992 general	Matthew G. (Marty) Martinez (D)	68,324	(63%)	($149,441)
	Reuben D. Franco (R)	40,873	(37%)	($54,817)
1992 primary	Matthew G. (Marty) Martinez (D)	20,248	(57%)	
	Bonifacio (Bonny) Garcia (D)	8,678	(25%)	
	Louis A. M. Ritchie (D)	3,188	(9%)	
	A. Gus Hernandez (D)	3,136	(9%)	
1990 general	Matthew G. (Marty) Martinez (D)	45,456	(58%)	($186,130)
(CA 30)	Reuben D. Franco (R)	28,914	(37%)	($72,867)
	G. Curtis Feger (LIB)	3,713	(5%)	

THIRTY-SECOND DISTRICT

One of the myths engendered by the Los Angeles riot of 1992 is that black Angelenos live in conditions of isolation and poverty. Some do, of course. But in levels of income and in degree of residential integration with non-blacks, Los Angeles blacks rank among the top in the nation; its black-owned businesses have the highest revenues of any city in the nation. Californians have historically shown less prejudice against blacks than most Americans, and job opportunities in Los Angeles—up to and including the office of mayor for the last 20 years—have been plenteous for blacks. This is apparent in the hills just west of Crenshaw, an Art Deco neighborhoods built in the 1920s and 1930s in vacant flat land southwest of downtown LA. Here, in Baldwin Hills, where on clear days you can see the towers of downtown and the snow-capped San Gabriel Mountains beyond, is a high-income black neighborhood, one of the strongest in the country; to the north and west are other comfortable black-majority neighborhoods.; on the flatlands south of Beverly Hills and the Fairfax district not far away, affluent blacks are buying houses as much as anyone else. There was little or no rioting here in April 1992.

This part of Los Angeles is the heart of California's 32d Congressional District, which runs approximately from the Harbor Freeway west past Baldwin Hills to Culver City and almost to the ocean, and south from Olympic Boulevard past the Santa Monica Freeway down almost to Inglewood and the LAX airport. The 32d vies with the Maryland 4th and New York 6th for the largest numbers of affluent blacks. Politically there has been no serious trend toward Republicans, and indeed, affluent, well-educated blacks seem if anything to be culturally more liberal than low-income black voters who may have closer ties to church and tradition, and any affection they have for free market economics is tempered by the knowledge that many of them have profited on the way up by some form of government intervention—a student loan, a public sector job, an affirmative action program. And whites here seem immune to racial backlash. The result is a constituency which elects a hard-working, politically savvy, quietly competent black Democrat, Julian Dixon.

Dixon may have passed his biggest moment in the national spotlight and, if so, is probably glad of it. That came in 1989 when, as chairman of the House Ethics Committee, he had to pass judgment on Speaker Jim Wright. This was as high pressure an assignment as could be imagined: Republicans were baying that the Democrats were going to let their leader off; Wright and his loyalists were pooh-poohing the charges; the press was watching closely for signs of partiality or error. Dixon proceeded deliberately, as he had on other dicey assignments— chairing the District of Columbia Appropriations Subcommittee when Marion Barry was mayor, chairing the Democratic National Convention Rules Committee in 1984 when Jesse Jackson was challenging the legitimacy of party rules—taking time to be sure of the facts and the law, hiring a sharp and unbiased staff, and then moving ahead aggressively when he reached a decision. At times he seemed nervous and all along seemed reluctant; but he did his duty as he saw it—and the speaker of the House was forced to resign.

Dixon's political career goes back 20 years now; he was elected to the California Assembly in 1972 and to the House in 1978, following his 29th District neighbor and ally Henry Waxman by four years in both cases. As an Appropriations subcommittee chairman, he is a member of the House's "college of cardinals," and although his duties often are tedious—defending the D.C. budget against amendments to do away with its domestic partners law, for example—he was well positioned to pass a "dire emergency supplemental" bill with funds for Los Angeles after the riot, or for the city's Metro Rail. Dixon's record on economic and foreign issues is not always as liberal as that of many other black members, perhaps reflecting district opinion or perhaps moderation from laboring on Appropriations, particularly its Defense Subcommittee where he has moved from looking out for Los Angeles area defense contractors to seeking funds for defense conversion and job training. He supports government investment in new rail car technology and (a sign he represents an affluent district) wants unemployed people permitted to withdraw money from their IRAs without penalty. In 1993, he got another challenging, but this time quiet, assignment: a seat on the Intelligence Committee.

Dixon is regularly reelected without significant opposition. He was criticized in 1990 because his wife was part of a joint venture that, on an investment of at most $15,000, won a minority set-aside contract for a Los Angeles Airport duty-free shop that yielded some $150,000 in two years; he resisted an Ethics Committee investigation and was not hurt electorally. But he has passed up chances to run for major local office—the Board of Supervisors seat (America's most populous legislative district) in which former Congresswoman Yvonne Burke barely beat state Senator Diane Watson in 1992 and the Los Angeles mayoralty in 1993.

The People: Pop. 1990: 572,630; 11% age 65+; 24% White; 40% Black; 8% Asian; 19% Other; 30% Hispanic origin. Voting age pop.: 435,528; 40% Black; 26% Hispanic origin. Households: 38% married couple families; 18% married couple fams. w. children; 50% college educ.; median household income: $28,332; per capita income: $14,520; median gross rent: $592; median house value: $231,400.

1992 Presidential Vote			1988 Presidential Vote		
Clinton (D)	147,623	(77%)	Dukakis (D)	146,787	(79%)
Bush (R)	23,956	(13%)	Bush (R)	38,062	(21%)
Perot (I)	17,561	(9%)			

Rep. Julian C. Dixon (D)

Elected 1978; b. Aug. 8, 1934, Washington, D.C.; home, Culver City; CA St. U., B.S. 1962, Southwestern U., LL.B. 1967; Episcopalian; married (Betty).

Career: Army, 1957–60; Practicing atty., 1960–73; CA Assembly, 1972–78.

Offices: 2400 RHOB 20515, 202-225-7084. Also 5100 W. Goldleaf Cir., #208, Los Angeles 90056, 213-678-5424.

Committees: *Appropriations* (12th of 37 D): Defense; District of Columbia (Chmn.); Military Construction. *Intelligence (Permanent Select)* (4th of 12 D): Program and Budget Authorization.

Group Ratings

	ADA	ACLU	COPE	CDF	CFA	LCV	ACU	NTLC	NSI	COC	CEI
1992	80	100	75	100	93	94	4	0	30	13	8
1991	85	—	100	100	78	85	0	—	—	20	4

National Journal Ratings

	1991 LIB — 1991 CONS	1992 LIB — 1992 CONS
Economic	84% — 16%	78% — 18%
Social	88% — 0%	92% — 0%
Foreign	76% — 23%	74% — 25%

Key Votes of the 102d Congress

1. Ban Striker Replace	FOR	5. Handgun Wait/7-Day	FOR	9. Use Force in Gulf	AGN
2. $ for Homeownership	AGN	6. Overseas Mil. Abortion	FOR	10. US Mil. Abroad $ Cut	FOR
3. Tax Rich/Cut Mid Cls.	FOR	7. Obscn. Art NEA $ Ban	AGN	11. Limit SDI Funds	FOR
4. FY93/$15B Def. Cut	FOR	8. Death Pen. from Jury	AGN	12. Cuba Trade Embargo	FOR

Key Votes of the 103d Congress

1. Family Leave   FOR   2. Deficit Reduction   FOR   3. Stimulus Plan   FOR

Election Results

1992 general	Julian C. Dixon (D)	150,644	(87%)	($140,461)
	Bob Weber (LIB)	12,384	(7%)	
	William R. Williams (P&F)	9,782	(6%)	
1992 primary	Julian C. Dixon (D)	59,875	(100%)	
1990 general	Julian C. Dixon (D)	69,482	(73%)	($113,669)
(CA 28)	George Z. Adams (R).................	21,245	(22%)	($3,799)
	Two others..........................	4,873	(5%)	

THIRTY-THIRD DISTRICT

A block from Los Angeles's "modern architecture" City Hall, whose 452-foot white tower, long the symbol of the city, but now dwarfed by 60- and 70-story marble slabs and pink cylinders a few blocks away, is Broadway, America's biggest volume retail shopping street west of Chicago. The sidewalks are thronged, the signs are mostly in Spanish, the merchandise is often strewn on tables: this could be Mexico City or Lima: Latin America transplanted a block from a gleaming symbol of Yankee propriety and gaudy emblems of North American prosperity. Broadway is neither the geographical nor spiritual center of Los Angeles's Latino communities and it is by no means their only major shopping area. But it is an emblem of the entry-level Latino neighborhoods of the nation's second largest city, the places where many immigrants, not so much from Mexico as from Central and South America, come to find a cheap place to live, doubled and tripled up with other families and single newcomers, close enough to drive in an old car to work in factories and warehouses that fill so much of the acreage south and east of downtown.

Broadway and many of these entry-level neighborhoods make up much of California's 33d Congressional District. It includes downtown and the crime-ridden area around once beautiful MacArthur Park; it includes the giant factories south of downtown along the Southern Pacific Railroad and Santa Ana Freeway; it takes in part of East Los Angeles. To the south it includes what were in the 1940s working-class, southern-white suburbs—Huntington Park, South Gate, Bell and Bell Gardens, Commerce and Vernon, Maywood and Cudahy—which in the 1960s were nervously aware that they were separated by just Alameda Street from the black ghettos of Watts and Florence. Today Alameda Street isn't much of an ethnic boundary. Newcomer Latinos have replaced blacks in Florence and Watts, while longer-settled Latinos inhabit the working-class bungalows east of Alameda. The 33d District in 1990 was 84% Hispanic, by far the highest figure of any California district, and the only district that can be truly claimed monocultural; it was only 4% black, 4% Asian and 8% non-Hispanic white. Politically, these neighborhoods are more Democratic than when they were white but less Democratic than when they were black. More important, this is mostly a non-voting constituency: newcomers may not be citizens, workers at two jobs may be too busy to register and Latinos, unlike blacks, tend to see private sector work, not public sector protections, as their way up in the world. As a result, in 1992 only 18,935 people voted in the 33d District's crucial Democratic primary and only 50,779 in the general election, compared to 261,000 in the Westside 29th District and 120,000, 83,000, 109,000 and 149,000 in the Hispanic-majority 26th, 30th, 31st and 34th Districts.

Another possible reason for low turnout is that this new seat was not the scene of a serious contest. Much of its Los Angeles portion had been represented for 30 years by Edward Roybal; he retired from the 30th District seat in 1992, but even before his announcement, his daughter Lucille Roybal-Allard was running in the 33d. Roybal-Allard was elected to the California Assembly in 1986 and there sponsored bills on sexual assault and domestic violence and such causes as requiring more environmental impact reports for toxic waste incinerators, prompted by protests against a proposed incinerator in Vernon. Roybal-Allard won the primary with 75%; in the general election she prevailed with 63%, showing the solidly but not unanimously Democratic leanings of this district. Roybal-Allard's demonstrated faith in public sector programs and regulations suggest she will have a solidly liberal voting record, as her father did.

The People: Pop. 1990: 570,893; 6% age 65+; 8% White; 4% Black; 1% Amer. Indian; 4% Asian; 55% Other; 83% Hispanic origin. Voting age pop.: 384,472; 5% Black; 79% Hispanic origin. Households: 49% married couple families; 34% married couple fams. w. children; 17% college educ.; median household income: $20,708; per capita income: $6,997; median gross rent: $484; median house value: $154,400.

1992 Presidential Vote

Clinton (D)	33,642	(63%)
Bush (R)	12,607	(23%)
Perot (I)	7,149	(13%)

1988 Presidential Vote

Dukakis (D)	34,710	(64%)
Bush (R)	19,706	(36%)

Rep. Lucille Roybal-Allard (D)

Elected 1992; b. June 12, 1941, Los Angeles; home, Los Angeles; CA St. U., B.A. 1965; Catholic; married (Edward Allard).

Career: CA Assembly, 1987–92.

Offices: 324 CHOB 20515, 202-225-1766. Also Edward Roybal Fed. Bldg., 255 E. Temple St., #1860, Los Angeles 90012, 213-628-9230.

Committees: *Banking, Finance and Urban Affairs* (20th of 30 D): Consumer Credit and Insurance; Housing and Community Development. *Small Business* (22d of 27 D): Minority Enterprise, Finance and Urban Development; SBA Legislation and the General Economy.

Group Ratings and 102d Congress Votes: Newly Elected

Key Votes of the 103d Congress

1. Family Leave   FOR   2. Deficit Reduction   FOR   3. Stimulus Plan   FOR

Election Results

1992 general	Lucille Roybal-Allard (D)...............	32,010	(63%)	($264,755)
	Robert Guzman (R)	15,428	(30%)	($166,756)
	Tim Delia (P&F)......................	2,135	(4%)	
	Other................................	1,206	(2%)	
1992 primary	Lucille Roybal-Allard (D)..............	14,112	(75%)	
	Frank Fernandez (D)	3,138	(17%)	
	Lucy F. Kihm (D).....................	1,685	(9%)	
1990 election	Newly created district.			

THIRTY-FOURTH DISTRICT

One of the great population movements in the United States is the upward social and outward geographic movement of the hundreds of thousands of immigrants who have come to the Los Angeles Basin over the last two decades, from crowded entry-level neighborhoods, out the freeways to the suburbs. It is most apparent east and southeast of Los Angeles, in suburbs that a generation ago seemed almost solidly white Anglo and which now have large numbers of Latino residents. Many have made their way up working in small smokeless factories (LA has the world's strictest air pollution controls) along railroad tracks and near river beds, beneath roaring freeways and on grid streets near stucco garden apartment blocks—the factories that have made Los Angeles the nation's number one manufacturing metro area. Others have worked in small business offices and stores. All these people came to the U.S. not to re-create their Third World environment but to get away from it, and see this country not as a land of oppression but of opportunity. Their values resemble those of working class Americans of the pre-Vietnam 1960s: pro-family and respectful of traditional personal morals (LA-area Latinos have lower than average divorce rates and are more likely to raise children in two-parent families), patriotic and pro-military (they are more likely than average to volunteer for military service).

Vast numbers of these new residents, whose rise through hard work has gone shamefully unnoticed in a mainline press which seems convinced that only government can produce upward mobility, live in the 34th Congressional District of California. This is a swatch of suburban Los Angeles County anchored by three different suburbs. On the northwest is Montebello, a working class suburb since the 1940s just beyond East Los Angeles, now heavily Latino. To the east is La Puente, a center of the light-manufacturing economy that created hundreds of thousands of jobs in the Los Angeles Basin in the 1980s, and in which increasing numbers of small businesses are owned by Asians, Latinos and blacks. To the south is Whittier, a town founded by Midwestern Quakers, much of which is in the 34th District, where Richard Nixon grew up and went to Whittier College, and Norwalk, farther south astride the Santa Ana Freeway. The 34th's predecessor district, drawn in 1982, was Phillip Burton's masterpiece; for by creating a second Hispanic-majority seat, he prevented creation of a Republican-Hispanic alliance and assured his own Democratic-leaning redistricting plans must pass. The current 34th has moved, like its people, outward from the central city; it was drawn not for partisan purposes but to maximize the Hispanic percentage, which was 62% in 1990, the second highest figure in California.

The new lines have worked out fine for Democrat Esteban Torres, the 34th District's one and only congressman. Torres rose from working on an auto assembly line through the ranks of the United Auto Workers, to head an antipoverty program in East Los Angeles. He worked in the Carter Administration, and in 1982, with support from the Waxman-Berman machine, he won a solid primary victory against former Congressman Jim Lloyd and won the general election by a 57%–43% margin. On economic issues, Torres is a liberal in the UAW tradition, opposing the North American Free Trade Agreement; on some cultural and foreign issues, notably abortion, his views can be conservative. He represents, after all, the number one family district in Los Angeles, a place where people are committed to family patterns and where high hopes for the future depend on the progress of their children in school and in the workplace. They are interested in having a secure government safety net, but seem to believe that their children will get somewhere—as their parents or grandparents emerged from rural Mexico—largely through their own efforts. Torres has worked to clean up groundwater, especially in the San Gabriel Valley, through both national and local action; he wants to make health insurance more affordable to small business. While on the Banking Committee, he tried to revise the Fair Credit Act to increase credit bureau accuracy and to protect personal privacy, though his effort to allow tougher state laws to prevail was beaten in 1992. He sponsored a truth-in-savings disclosure provision which became law. He has bills to allow more spending to stop gang activity. He successfully knocked out of the 1990 immigration law a pilot program to create a forgery-proof driver's license—a civil rights issue and threat to privacy, Torres felt.

Torres has been reelected with 60% or more since 1984; he had some interest in running for County Board of Supervisors in 1990, but had already filed for reelection when the vacancy came up. In 1992, he faced small businessman Jay Hernandez, who campaigned on traditional values; Torres won 61%–34%, a few points less than other area Latino members. After the election, he won a seat on the Appropriations Committee, a good spot to pursue his groundwater issues and from which he says he will remain interested in fair credit legislation.

The People: Pop. 1990: 573,456; 9% age 65+; 27% White; 2% Black; 1% Amer. Indian; 9% Asian; 31% Other; 62% Hispanic origin. Voting age pop.: 402,525; 2% Black; 57% Hispanic origin. Households: 61% married couple families; 33% married couple fams. w. children; 37% college educ.; median household income: $36,224; per capita income: $12,012; median gross rent: $637; median house value: $172,900.

1992 Presidential Vote		
Clinton (D)	78,889	(51%)
Bush (R)	48,181	(31%)
Perot (I)	27,944	(18%)

1988 Presidential Vote		
Dukakis (D)	79,426	(52%)
Bush (R)	72,423	(48%)

Rep. Esteban E. Torres (D)

Elected 1982; b. Jan. 27, 1930, Miami, AZ; home, West Covina; E. Los Angeles Commun. Col., 1959, CA St. U., 1963, U. of MD, 1965, American U., 1966; No religious affiliation; married (Arcy).

Career: Army, 1949–53; Assembly-line worker, Chrysler Corp., 1953–63; Chief Steward, UAW Local 230, 1961–63; UAW Intl. Rep., Region 6, 1963–64, Inter-Amer. Rep., 1965–68; Dir., E. Los Angeles Commun. Union, 1968–74; UAW Intl. Affairs Dept., 1974–77; U.S. Permanent Rep., UNESCO, 1977–79, Special Asst., Pres. Jimmy Carter, 1979–81; Pres., Intl. Enterprise and Devel. Corp., 1981–82.

Offices: 1740 LHOB 20515, 202-225-5256. Also 8819 Whittier Blvd., #101, Pico Rivera 90660, 310-695-0702.

Committees: *Appropriations* (27th of 37 D): Foreign Operations, Export Financing and Related Programs; VA, HUD and Independent Agencies.

Group Ratings

	ADA	ACLU	COPE	CDF	CFA	LCV	ACU	NTLC	NSI	COC	CEI
1992	85	91	92	90	67	94	4	0	30	29	5
1991	80	—	92	100	89	92	5	—	—	20	6

National Journal Ratings

	1991 LIB — 1991 CONS		1992 LIB — 1992 CONS	
Economic	84% —	12%	91% —	0%
Social	84% —	12%	84% —	16%
Foreign	81% —	18%	74% —	25%

Key Votes of the 102d Congress

1. Ban Striker Replace	FOR	5. Handgun Wait/7-Day	FOR	9. Use Force in Gulf	AGN
2. $ for Homeownership	AGN	6. Overseas Mil. Abortion	FOR	10. US Mil. Abroad $ Cut	FOR
3. Tax Rich/Cut Mid Cls.	FOR	7. Obscn. Art NEA $ Ban	AGN	11. Limit SDI Funds	FOR
4. FY93/$15B Def. Cut	FOR	8. Death Pen. from Jury	AGN	12. Cuba Trade Embargo	AGN

Key Votes of the 103d Congress

1. Family Leave	FOR	2. Deficit Reduction	FOR	3. Stimulus Plan	FOR

Election Results

1992 general	Esteban E. Torres (D)	91,738	(61%)	($254,092)
	J. (Jay) Hernandez (R)	50,907	(34%)	($131,271)
	Carl M. (Marty) Swinney (LIB)	7,072	(5%)	
1992 primary	Esteban E. Torres (D), unopposed			
1990 general	Esteban E. Torres (D)	55,646	(61%)	($217,810)
(CA 34)	John Eastman (R)	36,024	(39%)	($75,123)

THIRTY-FIFTH DISTRICT

In April 1992, the corner of Florence and Normandie in South Central Los Angeles became for a moment the most famous intersection in America: the epicenter of the Los Angeles riot. This was not, as was commonly said, simply an outpouring of anger at the Rodney King verdict; if it were, there would have been rioting everywhere in the Los Angeles Basin, since few citizens agreed with the Simi Valley jury. It was rather, like the urban riots of the 1960s, a result of criminal acts suddenly committed by people in the expectation that so many others would be doing the same thing that all would have impunity; and even so, the rioting this time clearly would have been stopped but for the dereliction of LAPD Chief Darryl Gates, who had prepared no contingency plan and spent hours on his way to and from a political fundraiser as the rioting broke out. The rioting did in fact stop once Governor Pete Wilson and President George Bush announced that some 25,000 troops were being ordered to Los Angeles, eliminating potential rioters' expectation of immunity.

The commitment of troops was much greater than in the big 1960s riots, and this riot ended far sooner. But in the meantime great damage was done. Most visible was the damage to individuals: black and Latino onlookers were killed and injured by rioters and law enforcement personnel; a white truckdriver was viciously beaten at Florence and Normandie; Asian and Latino storeowners were singled out by black and Central American rioters and treated as oppressors when in fact they were providing goods and services which no one else, for reasons now painfully apparent, was willing to provide. Even more harmful may be the damage to Los Angeles's civic culture. For in the aftermath of the riot it was widely repeated that blacks were helpless victims of racism and poverty, when in fact most LA area blacks have moved upward economically and out geographically from the old South Central and Watts ghettos in the 27 years since the 1965 riots, and African-Americans are by quota standards well represented in LA and California politics.

Among those commenting most vociferously on the riot was Congresswoman Maxine Waters, whose 35th Congressional District includes Florence and Normandie as well as much of the South Central and Watts corridors which formed California's first black-majority district 30 years ago. It should be added that the 35th also includes the majority-black middle-income suburb of Inglewood, home of the Los Angeles Forum, Hawthorne, birthplace of the Beach Boys, and Gardena, with California's first licensed poker clubs at which some of the most cutthroat games in the country are played. Latinos have been moving for two decades into South Central and Watts, and the 35th District was 42% Hispanic in 1990; but 43% of its residents and a solid majority of its voters were black, and Waters seems to regard her constituency as essentially black, whatever the Census numbers. Waters came to California in 1961, worked in a garment factory and raised two children, got a sociology degree at California State University and became an assistant Head Start teacher after the Watts riot. A political activist, in 1976 she won a seat in the California Assembly. There she supported Willie Brown and passed minority and women's tenants' rights laws, limits on police strip searches, and a provision mandating divestiture of state pensions funds from South Africa. She was consulted on the 1982 redistricting by Phillip Burton and when Congressman Augustus Hawkins retired in 1990, after 28 years in the House and 28 years in the California Assembly, capped by six years as chairman of the House Education and Labor Committee, Waters was the obvious choice for the seat, and won it easily. She had already made a national name for herself as a vocal supporter of Jesse Jackson in 1984 and 1988 and was probably the most prominent freshman in the 102d Congress.

Waters brings to her work a wrath that is almost palpable, and an insistence that she will assert herself regardless of protocol, partly perhaps a result of anger but also a weapon she uses shrewdly and cynically to get both publicity and results. "I don't have time to be polite," she says, beginning her career by getting herself included in a post-riot White House meeting with George Bush after learning of the meeting on a morning TV show. She told Speaker Foley she was going over there no matter what anyone else did. Sometimes she overblusters: she missed the chance to demand a roll call for one of her amendments, which was beaten, because she was outside the House participating in a press conference; she missed Clark Clifford's BCCI testimony, after announcing at great length how tough she would be, to meet other commitments. But she also succeeded in passing amendments, some of them even making laws more acceptable to conservatives, on Banking, Housing and Urban Affairs. Waters comes from a poor background and believes with fervor in federal aid for the poor and for racial preferences to help blacks overcome years of slavery, segregation and discrimination; she favors drastic reductions in defense spending and was one of six members who voted against supporting the Gulf war once it started and asked how urban gang members could be expected to stop fighting when America's own leaders were waging battles. She was an early but unillusioned supporter of Bill Clinton for the Democratic nomination, and traveled often with Clinton who was happy to have the support of such an outspoken former Jesse Jackson backer. But in fall 1992, she was complaining that Clinton "does not relate to African-Americans in a way we've become accustomed to" and "does not use the term 'affirmative action' and I'm not sure I've ever heard him say 'racism.' There's always the possibility of being double-crossed." At the 1992 Democratic convention, she insisted, "This is the last time I support an all-white anything," and that she would support the Democratic ticket in 2000 only if it has a black or a woman on it.

The Los Angeles riot was occasion for both Water's best and worst moments. She flew home immediately and roused the Department of Water and Power to restore water to the riot area, and was effective in gaining provisions to the post-riot emergency act that eventually made it through Congress and was signed into law. But she also made statements suggesting that the rioters were morally justified and over-emotionally claimed, "Los Angeles is under siege . . . the violence could spill over to many other cities in this country." Which, of course, it never did. Waters was reelected easily in the 35th District and will continue to be, despite her low seniority, a powerful member of Congress. But her statements after the riot leave the question of whether her angry justifications of violence and her faith in increasing government spending and regulation will secure a better life for her constituents.

The People: Pop. 1990: 570,697; 7% age 65+; 10% White; 43% Black; 6% Asian; 30% Other; 42% Hispanic origin. Voting age pop.: 389,120; 44% Black; 37% Hispanic origin. Households: 42% married couple families; 25% married couple fams. w. children; 35% college educ.; median household income: $25,481; per capita income: $9,761; median gross rent: $573; median house value: $148,700.

1992 Presidential Vote		
Clinton (D)	100,432	(77%)
Bush (R)	16,685	(13%)
Perot (I)	11,950	(9%)

1988 Presidential Vote		
Dukakis (D)	101,310	(78%)
Bush (R)	28,119	(22%)

Rep. Maxine Waters (D)

Elected 1990; b. Aug. 31, 1938, St. Louis, MO; home, Los Angeles; CA St. U., B.A. 1970; Christian; married (Sidney).

Career: CA Assembly, 1976–90.

Offices: 1207 LHOB 20515, 202-225-2201. Also 10124 S. Broadway, #1, Los Angeles 90003, 213-757-8900.

Committees: *Banking, Finance and Urban Affairs* (11th of 30 D): Consumer Credit and Insurance; Financial Institutions Supervision, Regulation and Deposit Insurance; Housing and Community Development; International Development, Finance, Trade and Monetary Policy. *Small Business* (26th of 27 D). *Veterans' Affairs* (12th of 21 D): Oversight and Investigations.

Group Ratings

	ADA	ACLU	COPE	CDF	CFA	LCV	ACU	NTLC	NSI	COC	CEI
1992	95	100	92	100	93	75	0	0	20	13	7
1991	90	—	100	100	89	77	0	—	—	11	13

National Journal Ratings

	1991 LIB — 1991 CONS		1992 LIB — 1992 CONS	
Economic	88% —	0%	91% —	0%
Social	88% —	0%	92% —	0%
Foreign	92% —	0%	86% —	10%

Key Votes of the 102d Congress

1. Ban Striker Replace	FOR	5. Handgun Wait/7-Day	FOR	9. Use Force in Gulf	AGN
2. $ for Homeownership	AGN	6. Overseas Mil. Abortion	FOR	10. US Mil. Abroad $ Cut	FOR
3. Tax Rich/Cut Mid Cls.	FOR	7. Obscn. Art NEA $ Ban	AGN	11. Limit SDI Funds	FOR
4. FY93/$15B Def. Cut	FOR	8. Death Pen. from Jury	AGN	12. Cuba Trade Embargo	AGN

Key Votes of the 103d Congress

1. Family Leave	FOR	2. Deficit Reduction	FOR	3. Stimulus Plan	FOR

Election Results

1992 general	Maxine Waters (D)...................	102,941	(83%)	($207,954)
	Nate Truman (R)......................	17,417	(14%)	($7,143)
	Three Others.........................	4,418	(4%)	
1992 primary	Maxine Waters (D)...................	51,534	(89%)	
	Roger A. Young (D)..................	6,252	(11%)	
1990 general	Maxine Waters (D)...................	51,350	(79%)	($759,538)
(CA 29)	Bill DeWitt (R)......................	12,054	(19%)	
	Other................................	2,045	(2%)	

THIRTY-SIXTH DISTRICT

For many southern Californians, there is no better place else to be than the beach. It is not a perfect environment: in the morning there may be mists, the winter air is damp and clammy, even in summer the weather can be chilly, the water is never very warm and is sometimes polluted. But for many this is echt-California, and in this democratic polity there is a beach to suit the taste of just about everyone. The funkiest of all is surely Venice, just south of politically correct Santa Monica, with its beach houses jammed together and the canals dug by a developer in 1904 long stagnant and mudlined but slated to be reconstructed in 1994, with the boardwalk where skateboarding got its start and where the latest crazes are chainsaw juggling and outdoor massages. Right behind is Marina Del Rey, with sleek modern apartment complexes and expensive yacht moorings. Just south, across an inlet, is LAX, the only American airport commonly known by its three-letter code; its theme building, whose swooping arches were intended in 1961 to symbolize the jet era, is now an official historic landmark, like Disneyland's Tomorrowland or the "Jetsons," an antique version of a surpassed future. To the south is El Segundo, named for Socal's second oil refinery, and Manhattan Beach, one of the favorites three decades ago of the original Beach Boys who grew up a couple of miles inland in Hawthorne. Next is tiny Hermosa Beach, with tightly packed frame houses originally the homes of elderly retirees; the current attitude here is suggested by Councilman Robert (Burgie) Benz, who sponsors a beer drinking and vomiting fest every Fourth of July. To the south is more yuppified Redondo Beach and Torrance, whose vast inland expanse is filled with the American headquarters of Japanese companies. The South Bay beaches end where the Palos Verdes Peninsula rises over the ocean; this is also one of the seismically active parts of the LA Basin. Just to the east is the harbor town of San Pedro, once working class, but growing more upscale.

All this beach territory, from Venice south to San Pedro (both of which technically are part of Los Angeles, though the area in between is not), makes up California's 36th District. Historically Republican, this area is still leery of taxes, but culturally it has dabbled with liberal issues since the 1970s. Before redistricting, the 36th's predecessor was solidly Democratic, but only because it bent inland to include enough black voters to elect Waxman-Berman ally Mel Levine, congressman from 1982 until 1992 (Democrats didn't control redistricting and Levine ran for the Senate). In the House, he crusaded against offshore oil drilling, an obvious no-no on the beach, for support of Israel and for public-private investment in high-tech projects like high definition TV; but in the Senate primary he emphasized his support for the Gulf war and the need for order after the LA riot, and finished far behind winner Barbara Boxer.

The new 36th District, only 3% black, had more registered Republicans than Democrats, usually a sure indication of being safe Republican. But cultural issues and the collapse of the Bush candidacy in California made the district competitive, and ultimately Democratic. On the once macho beach, it was the year of the woman, with 73% of Democratic and 68% of Republican primary votes going to female candidates. The best known was undoubtedly Maureen Reagan, who this time, despite her pro-choice stand on abortion, had her father's support, as she did not when she ran for the Senate in 1982 and finished fifth with 5% of the vote. But Reagan was attacked by Los Angeles Councilwoman Joan Milke Flores for carpetbagging and because Reagan's husband lobbied for foreign countries; Flores, though pro-life, won with 34% to Reagan's 31%. Among the Democrats, the best-known name belonged to Ada Unruh, daughter-in-law of the late Speaker and state Treasurer Jesse Unruh, one of the real innovators in California's politics and Ronald Reagan's opponent in the 1970 governor race. But Unruh was outspent by Jane Harman, attorney and onetime Carter Administration official whose husband has made a fortune manufacturing audio equipment, and Harman won 45%–16%.

In the general, Harman campaigned as "pro-choice and pro-change," although she was once a top Washington staffer for Senator John Tunney and made headlines when she quit a White House job to stay home with her children. Shortly afterwards, she divorced her first husband, married Harman and took a job with a Washington, D.C., law firm, and has maintained a Washington residence ever since. She was aided by the abortion issue and by defense cuts which slashed jobs at many of the defense contractors just inland from the beach. Harman stressed her California roots (as a teenager she sat in the gallery at the 1960 Democratic National Convention in Los Angeles) and her moderate, pro-defense stands and called for national health insurance and public investment in high-tech business. She supported a targeted capital gains tax cut and a line-item veto. But the abortion issue probably helped as much as anything, attracting out-of-state money and local votes (the Republican antiabortion mayor of Redondo Beach lost the beach Assembly seat on the issue), and Harman had top-of-the-line consultants. The Republican registration advantage eroded from 5% to 2% during the campaign, an unusual shift in a short time, and Harman ended up winning by an impressive 48%–42% margin.

She has proceeded in office like a politician who wants at least the three terms California law permits before her name can no longer be listed on the ballot. "I don't claim to be an outsider; I claim to be a reformer, and I want to be a bridge builder to the Republicans," she said early; even as she was nailing down seats on the Armed Services and Science Committees with then-Chairmen Les Aspin and fellow Californian George Brown, she was backing southern moderate John Spratt in his strong but unsuccessful caucus race for Budget Committee chairman. She will presumably try to protect South Bay defense industries and promote reconversion of defense businesses and jobs. These are challenging tasks, but she has shown great skill and resources; Republicans will surely contest this seat, but the issue focus must be transformed if they are to have a good chance at winning on the beach.

The People: Pop. 1990: 573,665; 10% age 65+; 69% White; 3% Black; 13% Asian; 6% Other; 15% Hispanic origin. Voting age pop.: 462,697; 3% Black; 13% Hispanic origin. Households: 49% married couple families; 20% married couple fams. w. children; 67% college educ.; median household income: $48,522; per capita income: $25,534; median gross rent: $812; median house value: $369,800.

1992 Presidential Vote			1988 Presidential Vote		
Clinton (D)	111,014	(41%)	Bush (R)	150,984	(60%)
Bush (R)	95,646	(35%)	Dukakis (D)	102,061	(40%)
Perot (I)	62,458	(23%)			

Rep. Jane Harman (D)

Elected 1992; b. June 28, 1945, New York, NY; home, Marina del Rey; Smith Col., B.A. 1966, Harvard, J.D. 1969; Jewish; married (Sidney).

Career: Legis. Dir., U.S. Sen. John Tunney, 1972–73; Chief Cnsl. & Staff Dir., Senate Judiciary Subcmtee., 1973–77; Dep. Cabinet Secy., White House, 1977; Defense Dept. Special Cnsl., 1979; Harman Intl. Industries, Corp. Secy., 1985–92, Dir., 1990–92; Practicing atty., 1987–92.

Offices: 325 CHOB 20515, 202-225-8220. Also 5200 W. Century Blvd., #960, Los Angeles 90045, 310-348-8220.

Committees: *Armed Services* (29th of 34 D): Military Forces and Personnel; Oversight and Investigations; Research and Technology. *Science, Space and Technology* (22d of 33 D): Space; Technology, Environment and Aviation.

Group Ratings and 102d Congress Votes: Newly Elected

Key Votes of the 103d Congress

1. Family Leave	FOR	2. Deficit Reduction	FOR	3. Stimulus Plan	FOR

Election Results

1992 general	Jane Harman (D)	124,751	(48%)	($2,285,356)
	Joan Milke Flores (R)	109,684	(42%)	($811,592)
	Richard H. Greene (Green)	13,297	(5%)	
	Three Others	11,025	(4%)	
1992 primary	Jane Harman (D)	26,812	(45%)	
	Ada Unruh (D)	9,216	(16%)	
	Charlene A. Richards (D)	6,952	(12%)	
	Bryan W. Stevens (D)	5,200	(9%)	
	Paul P. Kamm (D)	4,107	(7%)	
	Gregory Stock (D)	4,027	(7%)	
	Colin Kilpatrick O'Brien (D)	2,940	(5%)	
1990 general	Mel Levine (D)	90,857	(58%)	($587,961)
(CA 27)	David Barrett Cohen (R)	58,140	(37%)	($146,206)
	Edward E. Ferrer (P&F)	7,101	(5%)	

THIRTY-SEVENTH DISTRICT

Los Angeles is the creation not of nature but of man: there is little natural water supply here and no natural port, little in the way of natural resources except for oil which turned out not to be enough for California; it is a place for people who plan big. Nearly a century ago Los Angeles's city fathers decided to build a port where the usually-dry Los Angeles River debouches into the ocean; in 1906 they annexed an eight-mile-long, four-block-wide corridor of land (christened Harbor Gateway in 1984) and the harbor areas of Wilmington and San Pedro, and converted what had been a shallow bay with a few marshy inlets into the biggest port on the West Coast, ahead of San Francisco and San Diego with their splendid natural harbors. Inland from the port, along the rail lines that hug the river bed, grew up heavy and light industry—oil tank farms and big factories, small job shops and warehouses. Interspersed were residential developments, and to the north was Watts, the epicenter of the 1965 riot and also the site of one of the strangest made-by-man structures in this made-by-man city, the 107-foot-high Watts Tower, built from 1921 to 1954 by Simon Rodia out of all manner of salvaged material.

The 37th District of California takes in a swath of low-income industrial suburbs from Watts south to Wilmington. Here are Compton and Lynwood, which switched from all-white to all-black in the 1960s and then in the 1980s became heavily Latino; here is Carson, with recent subdivisions amid freeway interchanges and tank farms; here is Wilmington, an old-fashioned port town facing a spankingly modern port. Overall, the 37th District in 1990 was 34% black and 45% Hispanic, but blacks far outnumber Latinos as registered voters and this is, whatever the Voting Rights Act criteria, essentially a black district.

For 12 years the congressman from the 37th's predecessor district was Mervyn Dymally, a native of Trinidad, elected to the legislature from 1962 to 1970 and lieutenant governor of California from 1974 to 1978. To the surprise of just about everyone, he decided to retire in 1992, and endorsed his daughter Lynn Dymally, a member of the Compton school board, to succeed him. But, unlike another incumbent's daughter, Lucille Roybal-Allard in the 33d District just to the north, Lynn Dymally had serious competition from another political scion, Compton Mayor Walter Tucker. Tucker served as an assistant district attorney from 1984 to 1986, when he was dismissed after changing the date on photographic evidence in a drug case. In 1990, he was a criminal lawyer in Compton and associate pastor of the Bread of Life Christian Center in Carson. Then, his father, the longtime mayor of Compton, suddenly died, and the younger Tucker was elected to take his place in April 1991. The 1992 congressional primary was spirited. A group called Truth in Politics, advised by Mervyn Dymally, accused Tucker of being a convicted felon, when actually he had pleaded no contest to the misdemeanor charge of altering an official document. Tucker said that the slogan "Dymally: a name we can depend on" should be supplemented with "to do nothing." Tucker won 39% of the votes to Dymally's 37%; he got 86% against the Peace & Freedom candidate in the general election. His continued tenure depends on whether he encounters serious primary opposition again, and is presumably limited by California's term limits initiative which bars an incumbent's name from appearing on the ballot after serving three terms.

The People: Pop. 1990: 572,191; 7% age 65+; 12% White; 34% Black; 11% Asian; 29% Other; 44% Hispanic origin. Voting age pop.: 375,081; 34% Black; 40% Hispanic origin. Households: 51% married couple families; 30% married couple fams. w. children; 32% college educ.; median household income: $27,127; per capita income: $9,104; median gross rent: $548; median house value: $140,800.

1992 Presidential Vote			1988 Presidential Vote		
Clinton (D)	90,523	(73%)	Dukakis (D)	94,248	(76%)
Bush (R)	19,299	(16%)	Bush (R)	29,714	(24%)
Perot (I)	12,905	(10%)			

Rep. Walter R. Tucker (D)

Elected 1992; b. May 28, 1957, Compton; home, Compton; Princeton, 1976–78, U. of Southern CA, B.A. 1978, Georgetown Law Schl., J.D. 1981; Baptist; married (Robin).

Career: LA Cnty. Dep. Dist. Atty, 1984–86; Practicing atty., 1986–92; Compton Mayor, 1991–92.

Offices: 419 CHOB 20515, 202-225-7924. Also 145 E. Compton Blvd., Compton 90220, 310-884-9989.

Committees: *Public Works and Transportation* (37th of 39 D): Public Buildings and Grounds; Surface Transportation; Water Resources and Environment. *Small Business* (20th of 27 D): Minority Enterprise, Finance and Urban Development; Regulation, Business Opportunities and Technology.

Group Ratings and 102d Congress Votes: Newly Elected

Key Votes of the 103d Congress

1. Family Leave	FOR	2. Deficit Reduction	FOR	3. Stimulus Plan	FOR

Election Results

1992 general	Walter R. Tucker (D)	97,159	(86%)	($277,586)
	B. Kwaku Duren (P&F)	16,178	(14%)	($4,129)
1992 primary	Walter R. Tucker (D)	22,536	(39%)	
	Lynn Dymally (D).	21,433	(37%)	
	Vera Robles Dewitt (D)	6,491	(11%)	
	Joe Mendez, Jr. (D)	4,804	(8%)	
	Lawrence A. Grigsby (D).	2,307	(4%)	
1990 general	Mervyn M. Dymally (D).	56,394	(67%)	($418,232)
(CA 31)	Eunice N. Sato (R).	27,593	(33%)	

THIRTY-EIGHTH DISTRICT

Long Beach, founded in 1888, with 434,000 people in 1990, would be a major metropolis anywhere but in Los Angeles County where it seems just the largest of many suburbs. But it has an identity of its own. Started as a beach resort, it soon became a port when Los Angeles civic leaders decided that if their town were to be a world-class city it must have a world-class harbor; nature not having provided one, they built it where the Los Angeles River merges into the ocean at Long Beach. By 1909, Los Angeles had annexed the harbor towns of San Pedro and Wilmington next to Long Beach; over the next decades the two cities persuaded the government to dredge channels and build a breakwater and turning basins. Long Beach was developing other businesses as well: it sprouted oil derricks in the 1920s and for a brief while became one of the nation's big oil producers; it was the site of major aircraft plants in the 1940s and after. By the 1980s, the Los Angeles-Long Beach port was the nation's largest, the fastest-growing major cargo center in the world, handling more freight than New York and having long since outhustled San Francisco's complacent merchant class and militant unions. The harbor even acquired the *Queen Mary*, which became the biggest tourist attraction of Long Beach, and, until it was sawed apart and taken to a museum in Oregon, Howard Hughes's "Spruce Goose," the huge cargo seaplane that was piloted just once across this harbor in 1946. Long Beach's downtown, once full of rundown 1920s buildings and pawn shops, was being rebuilt and the Long Beach area was becoming a favorite for Japanese and Asian companies' American headquarters.

The Long Beach area suffered from defense cutbacks and the sag in real estate prices in the early 1990s, but it has come back from setbacks before.

The 38th Congressional District of California includes most of Long Beach, the beachfront and harbor and airport. It extends north and inland to include the post-World War II suburbs of Lakewood, Paramount, Bellflower and Downey. This is middle-class country, but not monochrome; the 38th excludes some black areas of Long Beach but in 1990 was 26% Hispanic and 9% Asian. Long Beach has long leaned mildly to the Republicans, but the incumbent congressman when the 38th was created was Glenn Anderson, a veteran Democrat whose base was originally to the east in the harbor area and just behind the beach towns. He was elected mayor of Hawthorne in 1940, went on to become lieutenant governor of California in 1958, and won a seat in Congress in 1968. He became chairman of the Public Works Committee in March 1988 but was voted out by the Democratic Caucus in December 1990, at age 77; faced with a more Republican district, he decided to retire in 1992.

That set up one of the closest and most narrowly decided primary races in California. The natural Republican advantage was offset by the Democratic trend caused by a sagging economy and sagging Bush candidacy. The Democratic nominee was Evan Anderson Braude, Glenn Anderson's stepson, member of the Long Beach Council since 1986 and something of a political veteran: he was an assistant to the secretary of the California state Senate at age 15 and a Carter Transportation Department appointee from 1977 to 1980. If Braude could have chosen, he would surely have picked as his Republican opponent Dennis Brown, a former assemblyman known as an exceedingly strong conservative, a pro-lifer who habitually cast lone nays on legislation, and who returned from two years of missionary work to enter the race. In an eight-candidate primary Brown won 30% of the vote, but he finished just 105 votes or .2% behind moderate Steve Horn, who had run in 1988 and lost in another district.

Horn came to the race rich in experience. He was an aide to President Eisenhower's labor secretary in the 1950s and to California Senator and Republican Whip Thomas Kuchel in the 1960s; he was in Everett Dirksen's office helping draft the language of the Voting Rights Act in those stirring days of 1965. Horn is also a political scientist scholar, who has written books on question time procedures, the Senate Appropriations Committee and campaign finance; he worked at the Brookings Institute, was a dean at American University, then from 1970 to 1988 was president of Cal State at Long Beach, leaving the job when he first ran for Congress. In 1992 Horn owed much of his moderate label to his pro-choice position on abortion, which he emphasized for all it was worth. But he also took solid Republican stands on a spending freeze, workfare, tort reform and the North American Free Trade Agreement. He accepted no PAC money and ran his campaign out of his son's apartment, sending out 50,000 15-minute videos to voters. After a not particularly acrimonious campaign, Horn won by a 49%–43% margin.

In Washington, Horn, despite his moderate reputation, seems likely to also be a strong party man. He has criticized the Democratic leadership for being too partisan and unfair to Republicans. He is likely to use his Public Works seat to help Long Beach, although he cannot have the clout Anderson had a few years ago. But unless partisan trends go even more harshly against the Republicans, he looks to be in good shape for reelection as long as—two more successful elections—his name can appear on the ballot.

The People: Pop. 1990: 572,676; 12% age 65+; 58% White; 8% Black; 1% Amer. Indian; 9% Asian; 13% Other; 25% Hispanic origin. Voting age pop.: 435,490; 7% Black; 22% Hispanic origin. Households: 46% married couple families; 21% married couple fams. w. children; 53% college educ.; median household income: $34,364; per capita income: $16,497; median gross rent: $636; median house value: $222,700.

1992 Presidential Vote

Clinton (D)	88,728	(44%)
Bush (R)	66,647	(33%)
Perot (I)	43,596	(22%)

1988 Presidential Vote

Bush (R)	108,815	(56%)
Dukakis (D)	85,262	(44%)

Rep. Stephen Horn (R)

Elected 1992; b. May 31, 1931, San Juan Bautista; home, Long Beach; Stanford, A.B. 1953, Harvard, M.P.A. 1955, Stanford, Ph.D. 1958; Protestant; married (Nini).

Career: Army Reserves, Strategic Intelligence, 1954–62; A.A., U.S. Labor Secy. James Mitchell, 1959–60; Legis. Asst., U.S. Sen. Thomas Kuchel, 1960–66; Sr. Fellow, Brookings Inst., 1966–69; Dean, Grad. Studies, American U., 1969–70; Vice Chmn./Mbr., U.S. Commission on Civil Rights, 1969–82; Pres., CA St. U. at Long Beach, 1970–88; Chmn., Amer. Assn. of State Cols. and Universities, 1985–86; Prof., CA St. U. at Long Beach 1988–92.

Offices: 1023 LHOB 20515, 202-225-6676. Also 4010 Watson Plaza Dr., #160, Lakewood 90712, 310-425-1336.

Committees: *Government Operations* (14th of 17 R): Human Resources and Intergovernmental Relations; Information, Justice, Transportation and Agriculture. *Public Works and Transportation* (18th of 24 R): Aviation; Water Resources and Environment.

Group Ratings and 102d Congress Votes: Newly Elected

Key Votes of the 103d Congress

1. Family Leave	AGN	2. Deficit Reduction	AGN	3. Stimulus Plan	AGN

Election Results

1992 general	Stephen Horn (R)	92,038	(49%)	($441,198)
	Evan Anderson Braude (D)	82,108	(43%)	($514,381)
	Paul Burton (P&F)	8,391	(4%)	
	Blake Ashley (LIB)	6,756	(4%)	
1992 primary	Stephen Horn (R)	13,423	(30%)	
	Dennis Brown (R)	13,318	(30%)	
	Tom Poe (R)	5,747	(13%)	
	Andrew J. Hopwood (R)	4,556	(10%)	
	William A. Ward (R)	3,418	(8%)	
	Jerry Bakke (R)	2,177	(5%)	
	Two others	2,460	(6%)	
1990 general	Glenn M. Anderson (D)	68,268	(62%)	($462,503)
(CA 32)	Sanford W. Kahn (R)	42,692	(38%)	($7,579)

THIRTY-NINTH DISTRICT

When Walt Disney began planning Disneyland in the late 1940s, he did not have to drive far southeast of downtown Los Angeles before coming into agricultural land. Dairy farms and orange groves covered most of southeast Los Angeles County and then little-populated Orange County, which had only 216,000 people in 1950, five years before Disneyland opened there in 1955. But even as Disneyland became a vast success, the area around it, a mass of flat land surrounded by mountains and sea, found itself directly in the path of settlement of the most explosively growing metropolitan area in the United States. Orange County's population rose from 216,000 in 1950 to 703,000 in 1960, 1.4 million in 1970, 1.9 in 1980 and 2.4 in 1990.

Always Republican, Orange County became a symbol of conservatism first in California and then nationally; in the 1988 election, only three counties in the nation cast more votes, and Orange County produced the largest plurality, 317,000, for George Bush. Orange County's conservatism reflected a belief in technological progress and traditional values as unyielding as the mile-square grid the county's founders imposed on most of its land, a belief in the market economics that had produced such wonders as Disneyland and the area's advanced military technologies. But these faiths have been tried on occasion. In 1992, with Orange County deep in recession and defense industry layoffs commonplace, Bill Clinton actually led George Bush in some Orange County polls during the summer campaign; and in November Bush won only a 119,000-vote plurality, a disaster not only for him but for Republicans generally in California.

The 39th Congressional District of California consists of area most of which was farmland as Disneyland was being laid out. In Los Angeles County its largest community is Cerritos, once all dairy farms, now a suburb with a marvelous Angeleno mix: 45% Asian, 36% white Anglos, 12% Hispanic. La Mirada to the north is more upscale, as are the La Habra communities which span the LA-Orange County line. The biggest Orange County city here is Fullerton, with its own branch of Cal State University; to the southwest are Buena Park, home of Disneyland competitor Knott's Berry Farm, Cypress, Los Alamitos and Rossmoor. The 39th also pushes east of Fullerton to include, by just a few blocks, the Richard Nixon Library and birthplace in Yorba Linda.

The 39th District's new congressman, Ed Royce, was four years old and growing up in Anaheim when Disneyland opened; his life almost precisely covers the post-World War II growth of Orange County. Like Orange County, he has long been conservative: he was in the Young Americans for Freedom at Cal State Fullerton; he worked several years as a tax and capital projects manager for a cement company. In 1982, a bunch of conservative legislators known as "the Cave Men" took him to a Black Angus restaurant—no avocado and bean sprout sandwiches for them—and after a few beers persuaded him to run for the state Senate. He did, and at age 31 won. The *California Political Almanac* called him "one of the quieter members of the Senate," but he did have an impact. He sponsored a law making "stalking" a crime, now copied in many other states. When the legislature refused to pass his legislation allowing crime victims to object to trial delays, giving grand juries more power and ending shopping for juries, he put it on the ballot as an initiative and it passed by a wide margin in 1990. He helps crime victims get jobs and encourages them to attend Republican fundraisers. Many Vietnamese have moved to Orange County, and Royce passed a law making it easier for University of Saigon graduates to practice medicine in California.

Royce was the natural choice to run for the 39th District seat when its incumbent, William Dannemeyer, a fierce opponent of gay rights and critic of gay activist groups, decided to make what turned out to be a quixotic race against his fellow Orange Countian Senator John Seymour in the 1992 Senate primary. With the blessing of Orange County Republican leaders and his own strength, Royce had no opposition in the decisive Republican primary. Democrat Molly McClanahan ran a spirited campaign, but Royce raised $500,000 and the outcome was never seriously in doubt: in a bad Republican year, Royce won 57%–38%. In the House, he serves on the Science and Foreign Affairs Committees, where he should be a champion of high technology (he looks forward to digital compression technology shrinking the size of telephones) and an assertive American foreign policy. His real goal is probably the Judiciary Committee, where, as in Sacramento, he would face a large and politically wily liberal majority, but where he may hope the strength and popularity of his ideas will enable him in his quiet ways to make some changes nationally as he has in California.

The People: Pop. 1990: 573,941; 9% age 65+; 61% White; 3% Black; 1% Amer. Indian; 14% Asian; 10% Other; 22% Hispanic origin. Voting age pop.: 430,720; 2% Black; 20% Hispanic origin. Households: 62% married couple families; 29% married couple fams. w. children; 58% college educ.; median household income: $46,196; per capita income: $18,190; median gross rent: $736; median house value: $236,600.

1992 Presidential Vote

Bush (R) 100,669 (44%)
Clinton (D) 78,305 (34%)
Perot (I) 50,834 (22%)

1988 Presidential Vote

Bush (R) 149,866 (66%)
Dukakis (D) 76,137 (34%)

Rep. Edward R. Royce (R)

Elected 1992; b. Oct. 12, 1951, Los Angeles; home, Fullerton; CA St. U., B.S. 1977; Catholic; married (Marie).

Career: Accountant, 1978–81; CA Senate, 1982–92.

Offices: 1404 LHOB 20515, 202-225-4111. Also 305 N. Harbor Blvd., #300, Fullerton 92632, 714-992-8081.

Committees: *Foreign Affairs* (18th of 18 R): Africa; Asia and the Pacific. *Science, Space and Technology* (16th of 22 R): Space; Technology, Environment and Aviation.

Group Ratings and 102d Congress Votes: Newly Elected

Key Votes of the 103d Congress

1. Family Leave   AGN   2. Deficit Reduction   AGN   3. Stimulus Plan   AGN

Election Results

1992 general	Edward R. Royce (R)	122,472	(57%)	($529,196)
	Molly McClanahan (D)	81,728	(38%)	($92,510)
	Jack Dean (LIB)	9,484	(4%)	
1992 primary	Edward R. Royce (R), unopposed			
1990 general	William E. Dannemeyer (R)	113,849	(65%)	($627,842)
(CA 39)	Frank X. Hoffman (D)	53,670	(31%)	
	Maxine B. Quirk (P&F)	6,709	(4%)	

FORTIETH DISTRICT

The great American movement west over the last dozen years has turned back east, at least in California. As settlement reached the Pacific Coast, young families looked for affordable houses and neighborhoods and schools, where traditional values are respected, and moved away from the liberation-minded and high-crime coast and toward the sunny, often hot, valleys inland. This impulse can be seen in both southern and northern California, but nowhere it is more apparent than in the eastern end of the Los Angeles Basin, around San Bernardino and Riverside, and east and north past the mountain rims into the desert. This "Inland Empire" of San Bernardino grew so robustly in the 1980s, from 1.56 million to 2.59 million, that it increased from three congressional districts to five.

One of these is the 40th Congressional District, which covers most of the land area of America's physically largest county, San Bernardino, though its population is concentrated in just a few places. About one-third of its people live on the eastern edge of San Bernardino itself, or around Loma Linda, Redlands and Yucaipa—small towns formed by pious Midwesterners at the base of 10,000-foot mountains, now part of the expanding Los Angeles suburban strip. North of the mountains, out beyond the wind-torn El Cajon Pass in the scorching desert, are Victorville and Apple Valley, once tiny gas station stops on the road to Las Vegas; Roy Rogers and Dale Evans have lived for years on a ranch here, with their stuffed Trigger, Buttermilk and Bullett in a nearby museum. Now vast subdivisions and the new city of Hesperia have grown up here, housing more than 150,000 people. The rest of the people of the 40th are scattered across the desert, in ghost towns and weapons testing sites, in Twentynine Palms and its Marine base. The 40th has some of the nation's hottest temperatures and some of its lowest rainfall, the lower 48 states' highest point at Mount Whitney and lowest point in Death Valley.

The congressman from the 40th District is Jerry Lewis, a House member since 1978, an assemblyman for 10 years before that and a House Republican leader until December 1992. Up to that point his career followed the usual path of House Republican leaders of earlier generations. He was an insurance agent in Redlands, a joiner in civic causes, when he was elected to the Assembly at 34. In the House, he got a seat on the Appropriations Committee, where bipartisan cooperation is the norm and enables even a minority member to confer favors on his district. He eventually became ranking Republican on the Legislative Subcommittee, working amicably on Congress's budget with Chairman Vic Fazio, a personable fellow Californian but also a politically adept member of the Democratic leadership. This was Robert Michel's route to the minority leadership, and Lewis seemed to be moving up the ladder: in 1984 he became chairman of the House Republican Research Committee; in 1986 he was chosen chairman of the House Republican Policy Committee; in 1988, he beat Lynn Martin of Illinois by three votes for the Conference chairmanship, technically the number three leadership position.

But even as most House Republicans were becoming hungrier for confrontation with the Democrats, Lewis was becoming more accommodation-minded, and his move up the ladder stalled. In March 1989, he failed to become whip after Dick Cheney left for the Pentagon; he was squeezed between Illinois's Edward Madigan, who had Michel's support, and party rebel Newt Gingrich of Georgia, and decided not to run. In 1990, Lewis loyally supported President Bush's budget summit agreement tax increases, while Gingrich opposed them and backbencher Dick Armey forced a conference vote against them. After the disappointing 1990 Republican elections, Gingrich supported Carl Pursell's race against Lewis for the House Republican Conference chair; Lewis won by a clear but unimpressive 98–64 vote. But shortly thereafter, he was removed by California Republicans as their representative on the party's committee on committees. In the 102d Congress, Lewis seemed actively hostile to the conservatives' new ideas. When Armey introduced Bush's G.I. Bill for Kids, Lewis helped persuade half the House Republicans to vote against it and back a weaker school choice bill instead. He advised Bush not to emulate Truman by campaigning against the imperial Congress; he boasted of how well he got along with House Democrats. So Armey challenged him for the conference chairmanship in December 1992 and won 88–84, taking about 26 of the 30 freshman votes, and soon became the elected Republican most willing to take on President Clinton.

Lewis, surely hurt, returned to his work on Appropriations, shifting ranking minority slots from Legislative, on which he helped trim Congress's budget by 6.5% for FY 1993 (but not as much as fiscal conservatives wanted), to the VA-HUD-Independent Agencies Subcommittee; he also got a seat on the Intelligence Committee. He has paid close attention to local issues, seeking tougher air quality standards (smog accumulates up against the San Bernardino Mountains), opposing what he considers a too restrictive desert protection act (which will probably be enacted now that California has no Republican senator to oppose it), getting $22 million for a school at Fort Irwin and $5 million for a medical test facility at Loma Linda University to assist with defense reconversion. He was reelected easily in 1992 and should have no trouble winning in this district, despite his loss of the leadership post.

The People: Pop. 1990: 573,939; 18% rural; 12% age 65+; 74% White; 5% Black; 2% Amer. Indian; 4% Asian; 7% Other; 16% Hispanic origin. Voting age pop.: 407,775; 5% Black; 13% Hispanic origin. Households: 60% married couple families; 30% married couple fams. w. children; 49% college educ.;

median household income: $30,408; per capita income: $13,568; median gross rent: $507; median house value: $110,300.

1992 Presidential Vote			1988 Presidential Vote		
Bush (R)	86,453	(39%)	Bush (R)	108,755	(64%)
Clinton (D)	76,363	(35%)	Dukakis (D)	60,975	(36%)
Perot (I)	53,955	(25%)			

Rep. Jerry Lewis (R)

Elected 1978; b. Oct. 21, 1934, Seattle, WA; home, Redlands; U. of CA, B.A. 1956; Presbyterian; married (Arlene).

Career: Insurance exec., 1959–78; Field rep., U.S. Rep. Jerry Pettis, 1968; CA Assembly, 1968–78.

Offices: 2312 RHOB 20515, 202-225-5861. Also 1826 Orange Tree Ln., #104, Redlands 92374, 714-862-6030.

Committees: *Appropriations* (6th of 23 R): Defense; VA, HUD and Independent Agencies (RMM). *Intelligence (Permanent Select)* (7th of 7 R): Legislation; Program and Budget Authorization.

Group Ratings

	ADA	ACLU	COPE	CDF	CFA	LCV	ACU	NTLC	NSI	COC	CEI
1992	10	14	17	30	13	0	83	76	100	86	54
1991	0	—	18	30	28	8	83	—	—	100	51

National Journal Ratings

	1991 LIB — 1991 CONS		1992 LIB — 1992 CONS	
Economic	14% —	83%	14% —	86%
Social	22% —	77%	28% —	71%
Foreign	23% —	75%	0% —	82%

Key Votes of the 102d Congress

1. Ban Striker Replace	AGN	5. Handgun Wait/7-Day	AGN	9. Use Force in Gulf	FOR
2. $ for Homeownership	FOR	6. Overseas Mil. Abortion	AGN	10. US Mil. Abroad $ Cut	*
3. Tax Rich/Cut Mid Cls.	AGN	7. Obscn. Art NEA $ Ban	*	11. Limit SDI Funds	AGN
4. FY93/$15B Def. Cut	AGN	8. Death Pen. from Jury	FOR	12. Cuba Trade Embargo	FOR

Key Votes of the 103d Congress

1. Family Leave	AGN	2. Deficit Reduction	AGN	3. Stimulus Plan	AGN

Election Results

1992 general	Jerry Lewis (R)	129,563	(63%)	($546,541)
	Donald M. Rusk (D)	63,881	(31%)	($21,555)
	Margie Akin (P&F)	11,839	(6%)	
1992 primary	Jerry Lewis (R), unopposed			
1990 general	Jerry Lewis (R)	121,602	(61%)	($211,940)
(CA 35)	Barry Norton (D)	66,100	(33%)	($2,371)
	Jerry Johnson (LIB)	13,020	(6%)	

FORTY-FIRST DISTRICT

After the April 1992 riots, many journalists flew to LAX airport and took cabs to nearby South Central and Koreatown to see what went wrong. If they had been interested in finding out what has gone right in the Los Angeles metropolitan area, they might have flown not to LAX but to the airport in Ontario (named for its founder's native province in Canada), and explored the eastern Los Angeles Basin—the Inland Empire, as it is now called. Mostly orange groves a couple of decades ago, this territory now is the site of rapid economic growth, personal upward mobility and ethnic and cultural harmony. The secret of the economic growth is small entrepreneurial businesses, usually started by people with no particular connections or advantages—increasingly, of Asian or Latino immigrant background. California has never been a land of leisure, as stereotype would have it, but rather a place for hard work, where neither the amazing fertility of the soil nor the amazing productivity of the people has happened without a lot of effort first; and, one might add, a tolerant and welcoming attitude toward newcomers. California hasn't always welcomed people from strange places—a strain of anti-Asian feeling reached expression in the Chinese Exclusion Act of 1882 and the Japanese American relocation camps of 1942–44—but certainly since World War II this has been one of the least prejudiced and most welcoming places on earth, a reason why it has been receiving more immigrants than any other American state.

All these trends are apparent in the places that have become California's new 41st Congressional District and the person elected to represent it. The 41st includes most of Ontario and its airport and industrial zone, plus the higher income towns of Montclair and Upland; it includes the old town of Pomona, now much expanded, site of the Los Angeles County Fair; it includes Chino, site of a low security prison, and subdivisions below the Chino Hills; over the hills in Orange County, it includes Yorba Linda, site (just beyond the district line) of the birthplace of Richard Nixon in 1913, when Orange County had 40,000 residents, and the site of the Richard Nixon Library now, when Orange County has 2,400,000 and Yorba Linda 52,000. This was all rapidly growing country in the 1980s, filling up with two-worker households, parents scurrying to get their kids to school and drive dozens of miles on freeways to their jobs; ethnically diverse, in the 1980s it was 32% Hispanic and 10% Asian; believers still in the traditional values scoffed at by the show business Westside, working their way up through the private sector, and mostly strong Republicans.

The new congressman, effectively chosen in the Republican primary, was anything but a political professional. Jay Kim came to California in 1961 from South Korea; he and his wife worked in restaurants and grocery stores. He got engineering degrees at the University of Southern California, and in 1976 he started Jaykim Engineers, designing highways, water reclamation plants and other big projects—mostly government contracts. His electoral career began in 1990, just after he moved into a big house in Diamond Bar, near Pomona, and decided to run for council. He researched the issues and ran first in the nine-candidate race, then was elected mayor. Then he decided to run for the new 41st District, methodically staking out a platform and a strategy. He campaigned for lower taxes and privatizing government services, against illegal immigration and for abortion rights. He loaned his campaign some $169,000 and raised about an equal amount, outspending two seasoned primary opponents, Pomona Assemblyman Charles Bader and former Washington lawyer James Lacy. Kim won the primary with 30% to 28% for Bader and 27% for Lacy; in the general he prevailed 60%–34%.

Kim, the first Korean-American member of Congress, has not been silent. Pledged to observe California's three-term limit, he maintains his big house in California and stays in a studio apartment when in Washington, but he sold his business. He was one of the freshmen Republicans who led the move to abolish the four select committees and got seats on the Public Works and Small Business Committees, but talks more about cutting pork than advancing pet projects. He declined a place on Foreign Affairs and its Asia subcommittee and says he does not have a special agenda as a spokesman for Korean-Americans. He seems likely to speak frequently in debate, and as a member of a racial minority can bring strength to arguments against government regulation and racial and ethnic quotas.

The People: Pop. 1990: 572,529; 1% rural; 6% age 65+; 52% White; 7% Black; 1% Amer. Indian; 10% Asian; 14% Other; 31% Hispanic origin. Voting age pop.: 400,202; 7% Black; 28% Hispanic origin. Households: 65% married couple families; 38% married couple fams. w. children; 55% college educ.; median household income: $44,607; per capita income: $16,002; median gross rent: $656; median house value: $202,700.

1992 Presidential Vote			1988 Presidential Vote		
Bush (R)	78,902	(42%)	Bush (R)	110,058	(66%)
Clinton (D)	64,666	(35%)	Dukakis (D)	55,645	(34%)
Perot (I)	41,112	(22%)			

Rep. Jay Kim (R)

Elected 1992; b. Mar. 27, 1939, Seoul, Korea; home, Diamond Bar; U. of Southern CA, B.S. 1967, M.S., 1973, CA St. U., M.P.A. 1980; Methodist; married (June).

Career: Founder & Pres., Jaykim Engineers, 1977–93; Diamond Bar City Cncl., 1990–91, Diamond Bar Mayor, 1991–92.

Offices: 502 CHOB 20515, 202-225-3201. Also 1131 W. 6th St., #160-A, Ontario 91762, 909-988-1055; and 18200 Yorba Linda Blvd., #203-A, Yorba Linda 92686, 714-572-8574.

Committees: *Public Works and Transportation* (16th of 24 R): Aviation; Economic Development; Surface Transportation. *Small Business* (15th of 18 R): Regulation, Business Opportunities and Technology.

Group Ratings and 102d Congress Votes: Newly Elected

Key Votes of the 103d Congress

1. Family Leave	AGN	2. Deficit Reduction	AGN	3. Stimulus Plan	AGN

Election Results

1992 general	Jay Kim (R)	101,753	(60%)	($764,895)
	Bob Baker (D)	58,777	(34%)	
	Mike Noonan (P&F)	10,136	(6%)	($35)
1992 primary	Jay Kim (R)	13,399	(30%)	
	Charles W. Bader (R)	12,510	(28%)	
	James V. Lacy (R)	12,070	(27%)	
	George Henry Margolis (R)	2,966	(7%)	
	John Hoover (R)	1,868	(4%)	
	James Todhunter (R)	1,753	(4%)	
1990 election	Newly created district.			

FORTY-SECOND DISTRICT

For many years the gateway to the Los Angeles Basin was San Bernardino, situated on flat land where the route through the twisting, windy El Cajon Pass took passengers on the Santa Fe Railroad and motorists on U.S. 66 from the hot and dusty desert to the greener, tree-lined basin. There were orange groves around the little railroad towns and vineyards to the west; this was an agricultural zone until World War II, when Henry J. Kaiser built the West Coast's first major steel mill between the Santa Fe and Southern Pacific lines in Fontana, just west of San Bernardino. Today, these lands have largely filled up. This may be where the smog piles up against the mountains, but it also has some of the lowest real estate prices in the Los Angeles Basin and in the 1980s a thriving small business economy. In this Inland Empire, San Bernardino County grew from 895,000 to 1,418,000 in the 1980s. During much of that time the county, long politically marginal, trended Republican. But it was hard hit by the early 1990s recession and moved sharply away from George Bush and his party, and Bill Clinton carried it in 1992.

The 42d Congressional District of California consists of most of San Bernardino and the towns running west—low-income Rialto, Fontana with many other businesses replacing the closed steel mill, fast-growing Rancho Cucamonga. It is 34% Hispanic, 11% black and only 4% Asian. The district was not drawn in 1992 to be a safe constituency for veteran Congressman George Brown, as were the districts he has represented for all but two years since 1962. Brown was a councilman in Monterey Park, far to the west, in 1958, when he was elected to the California Assembly; he got on the redistricting committee and, lo and behold, he got one of California's eight new districts in 1962. He ran for the Senate in 1970 and almost beat John Tunney in the primary; if he had, this longtime peacenik—a scientist with a Quaker upbringing who cares deeply about arms control issues—might well have won the general. Brown found a new district in 1972 in the Inland Empire and Phillip Burton redrew the lines in 1982 to help him through another decade. But Brown has not won by landslides. Against a religious fundamentalist, a small town businessman and a San Bernardino County Supervisor, Brown won between 53% and 57% in the 1980s.

That evidently suits Brown fine. He started off as one of the House's leading doves, and for years opposed just about any military spending; now he is somewhat more moderate. In 1990, he inherited the chairmanship of the House Science, Space and Technology Committee when the Democratic Caucus voted to oust Glenn Anderson as chairman of Public Works and install Science Chairman Robert Roe in that post instead; at that point Brown won the Science chair by a 166–33 vote. Though still wary of military spending, Brown favors both manned and unmanned space exploration, backing a new space launch vehicle and the Space Shuttle. He wants to restructure the national weapons laboratories and maintain the Landsat remote-sensing system. He supports federal aid for emerging technologies and development of electric vehicles and solar energy. He looks forward to working with Vice President Albert Gore, a former Science Committee member, as "heaven on earth," and he had the pleasure of seeing Science become a sought-after assignment in 1993.

But first he had to win in 1992. The new district was 2% more Republican, he had 26 overdrafts on the House bank and three serious Republicans vied to run against him. Bob Hammock, his 1990 opponent, got 29% of the vote in the primary, 27% went to retired Air Force officer Chuck Williams, and the winner, with 37% was Dick Rutan, the developer and pilot (with partner Jeana Yeager) of the Voyager plane which in 1986 circled the earth without refueling. Rutan was recruited by 28th District Republican David Dreier. Brown raised huge amounts from PACs and sent out mailings proclaiming himself a supporter of business and more jobs, while Rutan was hurt when Yeager switched her support to Brown. Rutan accused Yeager of switching her support in order to get Brown's recommendation for an appointment to NASA's astronaut training program. But Rutan's charge was baseless and Brown won by a 51%–44%

margin. Rutan has promised to run again, and Brown will probably have another serious challenge in 1994; under California's term limits law, his name cannot appear on the ballot after 1996.

The People: Pop. 1990: 571,595; 7% age 65+; 51% White; 11% Black; 1% Amer. Indian; 4% Asian; 18% Other; 34% Hispanic origin. Voting age pop.: 380,921; 10% Black; 30% Hispanic origin. Households: 58% married couple families; 35% married couple fams. w. children; 46% college educ.; median household income: $33,737; per capita income: $12,308; median gross rent: $562; median house value: $125,600.

1992 Presidential Vote			1988 Presidential Vote		
Clinton (D)	76,964	(45%)	Bush (R)	77,923	(54%)
Bush (R)	54,978	(32%)	Dukakis (D)	65,735	(46%)
Perot (I)	35,828	(21%)			

Rep. George E. Brown, Jr. (D)

Elected 1972; b. Mar. 6, 1920, Holtville; home, Riverside; U.C.L.A., B.A. 1946; United Methodist; married (Marta).

Career: Army, 1942–46; Monterey Park City Cncl., 1954–58, Monterey Park Mayor, 1955–56; Personnel, Engineering and Mgmt. Consult., City of Los Angeles, 1957–61; CA Assembly, 1958–62; U.S. House of Reps., 1962–70.

Offices: 2300 RHOB 20515, 202-225-6161. Also 657 La Cadena Dr., Colton 92324, 714-825-2472.

Committees: *Agriculture* (2d of 28 D): Department Operations and Nutrition; Specialty Crops and Natural Resources. *Science, Space and Technology* (Chmn. of 33 D).

Group Ratings

	ADA	ACLU	COPE	CDF	CFA	LCV	ACU	NTLC	NSI	COC	CEI
1992	95	82	91	90	100	81	5	5	50	25	6
1991	70	—	92	100	61	85	15	—	—	20	6

National Journal Ratings

	1991 LIB — 1991 CONS			1992 LIB — 1992 CONS	
Economic	69%	—	31%	78%	—	18%
Social	70%	—	29%	80%	—	20%
Foreign	67%	—	32%	62%	—	38%

Key Votes of the 102d Congress

1. Ban Striker Replace	FOR	5. Handgun Wait/7-Day	FOR	9. Use Force in Gulf	AGN
2. $ for Homeownership	AGN	6. Overseas Mil. Abortion	FOR	10. US Mil. Abroad $ Cut	FOR
3. Tax Rich/Cut Mid Cls.	FOR	7. Obscn. Art NEA $ Ban	AGN	11. Limit SDI Funds	FOR
4. FY93/$15B Def. Cut	FOR	8. Death Pen. from Jury	AGN	12. Cuba Trade Embargo	FOR

Key Votes of the 103d Congress

1. Family Leave	FOR	2. Deficit Reduction	FOR	3. Stimulus Plan	FOR

Election Results

1992 general	George E. Brown, Jr. (D)	79,780	(51%)	($907,227)
	Dick Rutan (R).......................	69,251	(44%)	($443,272)
	Fritz R. Ward (LIB)...................	8,424	(5%)	
1992 primary	George E. Brown, Jr. (D), unopposed			
1990 general	George E. Brown, Jr. (D)	72,409	(53%)	($822,686)
(CA 36)	Bob Hammock (R)....................	64,961	(47%)	($538,156)

FORTY-THIRD DISTRICT

Riverside was a sleepy town of 34,000, a couple hours' drive from Los Angeles, in 1940 when Richard and Pat Nixon were married in the gaudy Mission Inn, with its bell towers, altars, fountains, rotunda, stained-glass windows and wrought-iron grilles. Riverside was not much larger, with 46,000 people, when Ronald and Nancy Reagan spent their honeymoon, also at the Mission Inn, in 1952. Riverside was known then, if at all, as a citrus center, a market town amid orange groves, where the local agricultural college developed among other things the navel orange. Today the Mission Inn is still doing business, but Riverside has changed utterly. The city has expanded to 226,000 people, and Riverside County, which had 105,000 people in 1940, had 663,000 in 1980 and 1,170,000 in 1990—a 76% increase in one decade. Riverside County stretches east to Arizona, so much of this increase was in the desert, but much was in the Inland Empire around Riverside, where the flat Los Angeles Basin plains are interrupted by odd-shaped hills and ridges and the vegetation has an other-worldly air; there are odd by-products from such rapid development, like the dozens of 300-pound pigs that live in the river bed just outside Riverside. This was one of the boom parts of California in the 1980s, where modest-income families found new houses in inexpensive developments and small businesses expanded mightily; it was hit hard by the recession of the early 1990s, when the growth suddenly stopped.

The congressional district which included most of Riverside County was the fastest-growing district in the nation in the 1980s; as a result it was essentially split into two districts for 1992. Eastern Riverside County saw two seriously contested races in a row: in 1990, Republican Al McCandless, now of the 44th District, was challenged by actor Ralph Waite, and in 1992, the newly created 43d District, with no incumbent, saw a race that was finally decided by absentee votes. Such volatility is not accidental in an area where few voters have deep roots, where neither ethnic ties nor economic security produce strong commitment to either party, and where the economy has changed so sharply. The 43d District includes all of Riverside and the towns immediately around; another population node just to the west, around Corona; and also new subdivisions scattered around I-215 and I-15 which run south from Riverside and Corona until they join at Murietta Hot Springs, just north of the utterly new town of Temecula.

No fewer than seven Republicans and seven Democrats ran for this Republican-leaning seat. The Democratic nomination went to Mark Takano, a 33-year-old eighth grade teacher and Harvard graduate. He had institutional support from teachers' unions and financial support from Japanese Americans, and won 29%, enough to beat the one woman and Latino candidate, Raven Workman, who had 20%. The Republican race attracted outsiders, including Claremont Institute president Larry Arnn, a nationally connected conservative endorsed by William Buckley and Senator Orrin Hatch, and business professor Joseph Khoury, who ran ads featuring Milton Berle and "Brooklyn Bridge" star Marion Ross. Khoury won 21% and Arnn 18%, as did locally based conservative Bob Lynn. The winner, with 28%, was Corona developer Ken Calvert, who ran in the old Riverside County district in 1982 and lost the primary to McCandless by a 25%–24% margin: 868 votes kept him out of Congress for 10 years.

Calvert and Takano presented a nice contrast typical of politics in a rapidly-growing area. The Republican was long connected with party politics, married and active in civic affairs, a charter member of the Silver Eagles support group for March Air Force Base personnel, a real estate developer since 1980 and restaurant manager in his 20s. The Democrat, single, was from a family with public sector ties and held a public sector, unionized job himself. He got elected to the community college board of trustees and was active in the Democrats' Asian-Pacific Islander Caucus and an organizer of Save Our Plateau and the Riverside Committee Against Discrimination. Calvert's approach to issues seemed perfunctory, as if he expected the Republican label to prevail easily; he supports lower government spending and holding down taxes and is pro-choice on abortion. Takano seemed to be effervescing with enthusiasm for liberal projects and hoped to take advantage of the recession. At the end Takano charged that Calvert was violating campaign finance laws and then charged him with trying to arrange kickbacks on a homeless shelter he owned; Calvert threatened to sue for libel and Takano admitted some of his details may have been mistaken. Takano led by over 1,000 votes on election night, but "walk-in" absentee votes, legal in California, produced as they usually do a big Republican margin, and Calvert won by 519 votes. He serves on the Science and Natural Resources Committees, probably good assignments for this district, but the narrowness of his win suggests he can not take reelection for granted.

The People: Pop. 1990: 571,090; 14% rural; 8% age 65+; 65% White; 6% Black; 1% Amer. Indian; 4% Asian; 13% Other; 25% Hispanic origin. Voting age pop.: 400,969; 6% Black; 21% Hispanic origin. Households: 63% married couple families; 35% married couple fams. w. children; 50% college educ.; median household income: $37,806; per capita income: $14,449; median gross rent: $595; median house value: $153,200.

1992 Presidential Vote

Bush (R) 76,837 (38%)
Clinton (D) 76,040 (38%)
Perot (I). 48,197 (24%)

1988 Presidential Vote

Bush (R) 97,970 (60%)
Dukakis (D). 64,860 (40%)

Rep. Ken Calvert (R)

Elected 1992; b. June 8, 1953, Corona; home, Corona; San Diego St. U., B.A. 1975; Protestant; married (Robin).

Career: Restaurant Owner, 1975–80; Real estate broker, 1980–92; Chmn, Riverside Cnty. Repub. Party, 1984–88.

Offices: 1523 LHOB 20515, 202-225-1986. Also 3400 Central Ave., #200, Riverside 92506, 909-784-4300.

Committees: *Natural Resources* (12th of 15 R): National Parks, Forests and Public Lands; Native American Affairs; Oversight and Investigations. *Science, Space and Technology* (13th of 22 R): Space; Technology, Environment and Aviation.

Group Ratings and 102d Congress Votes: Newly Elected

Key Votes of the 103d Congress

1. Family Leave   AGN   2. Deficit Reduction   AGN   3. Stimulus Plan   AGN

Election Results

1992 general	Ken Calvert (R)	88,987	(47%)	($422,717)
	Mark A. Takano (D)	88,468	(46%)	($303,691)
	Three Others	13,184	(7%)	
1992 primary	Ken Calvert (R)	13,387	(28%)	
	S. Joseph Khoury (R)	10,624	(22%)	
	Bob Lynn (R)	8,784	(18%)	
	Larry P. Arnn (R)	8,750	(18%)	
	Bill Franklin (R)	2,694	(6%)	
	Daniel Hantman (R)	2,270	(5%)	
	William E. Jones (R)	1,958	(4%)	
1990 election	Newly created district.			

FORTY-FOURTH DISTRICT

From the air a decade ago, a night flight east from Los Angeles showed the lights of 10 million people's streets and houses and then, past the Inland Empire and in the desert, almost perfect darkness: a vast metropolis surrounded by almost uninhabited territory. Today the sprinkled pattern of white lights is more dense in the Inland Empire around Riverside and San Bernardino and has grown as well in the desert. The Inland Empire has filled up with instant towns like Moreno Valley, which did not exist in 1980 and had 118,000 people in 1990. The surreal landscape to the south and east, around the old towns of Perris and Hemet, is filling up with new places like Sun City and Valle Vista. Then, over the 10,000-foot San Jacinto Mountains, desert communities have boomed: Palm Springs, once the lone winter resort for the stars, is now one of a string of communities along Highway 111 and Frank Sinatra and Bob Hope Drives. Among rich retirees, the vogue for the coast lessened as beach cities filled up with enviro-activists and rent control crusaders; the clean, dry, roomy desert, where the days are almost always crystal clear and the sky usually blue and cloudless, became more attractive, and, with everything air conditioned, a comfortable year-round home for more than 150,000 in 1990. That's 200,000 if you count Indio, the heavily Latino center of the Coachella Valley which has 98% of the country's date palms and which features camel races at its annual date festival. Two presidents have retired to the desert, Dwight Eisenhower in Palm Desert for the winters, Gerald Ford in nearby Rancho Mirage, which is also the home of Frank Sinatra and Spiro Agnew.

The fastest-growing congressional district in the United States in the 1980s was the district that included all of the desert and most of the rest of Riverside County, created in 1982 and represented by Republican Al McCandless. For 1992, it was essentially divided into two seats, the new 43d around Riverside and the 44th. The new 44th includes all the desert country and proceeds west to Moreno Valley, including most of the region around Perris and Hemet. It is heavily Republican in most elections, though not in the 1992 presidential contest, and McCandless, a son of the desert born in Imperial County, a successful auto dealer in Palm Desert, would seem ideally suited to it. A Riverside County Board supervisor, McCandless essentially won the seat in 1982 by prevailing in the Republican primary, 25%–24%, over Ken Calvert, now the newly elected congressman from the new 43d. But in the last two elections, McCandless has had to fight hard to hold the seat and his margins have been unimpressive. In 1990, he was challenged by Ralph Waite, an actor who played Pa Walton in the 1970s television series; Waite raised more money than McCandless and accused him of not doing enough to prevent the savings and loan crisis, and lost by only a 50%–45% margin. Then in 1992, McCandless won just 61% against two primary opponents, not an outstanding showing. And in the general, against a geographer who is also a grandmother, he won by only 54%–40%, though he bounced no checks at the House bank and accepted no honoraria.

McCandless is ranking Republican on the Banking Consumer Credit and Insurance Subcommittee which handles credit reporting legislation. He has worked hard on this issue, supporting a bill to give consumers more credit report privacy and protection against false reports but balking at some provisions Democrats wanted in it. He has opposed "unnecessary" coin redesign. He also has worked against the desert protection bill sought by Democrats and some environmentalists as "anti-economy, anti-equitable use"; this will be a harder fight now that there is no California Republican in the Senate to block it and California House Republicans like McCandless can easily be outvoted. He tried for more funds for March Air Force Base, but Ken Calvert will have to take over the struggle since, after redistricting, the base now falls in the 43d District and was targeted for closure in 1993. McCandless argued strongly against the catastrophic health care bill, which passed overwhelmingly in 1988 and then was repealed overwhelmingly in 1989. Given the rapid change in the district and Bush's low percentage, McCandless should look forward to more, and serious, competition.

The People: Pop. 1990: 571,843; 14% rural; 18% age 65+; 64% White; 5% Black; 1% Amer. Indian; 3% Asian; 14% Other; 28% Hispanic origin. Voting age pop.: 417,142; 4% Black; 23% Hispanic origin. Households: 58% married couple families; 25% married couple fams. w. children; 45% college educ.; median household income: $29,049; per capita income: $14,417; median gross rent: $545; median house value: $121,800.

1992 Presidential Vote				1988 Presidential Vote		
Clinton (D)	87,180	(40%)		Bush (R)	97,391	(59%)
Bush (R)	76,772	(36%)		Dukakis (D)	66,685	(41%)
Perot (I)	50,867	(24%)				

Rep. Alfred A. (Al) McCandless (R)

Elected 1982; b. July 23, 1927, Brawley; home, La Quinta; U.C.L.A., B.A. 1953; Protestant; married (Gail).

Career: Marine Corps, 1945–46 (WWII) and 1950–52 (Korea), Marine Reserves, 1947–49; Automobile dealer, 1953–75; Riverside Cnty. Supervisor, 1970–82.

Offices: 2422 RHOB 20515, 202-225-5330. Also 22690 Cactus Ave., #155, Moreno Valley 92553, 909-656-1444; and P.O. Box 14442, Palm Desert 92255, 619-340-2900.

Committees: *Banking, Finance and Urban Affairs* (7th of 20 R): Consumer Credit and Insurance (RMM); International Development, Finance, Trade and Monetary Policy. *Government Operations* (2d of 17 R): Legislation and National Security (RMM).

Group Ratings

	ADA	ACLU	COPE	CDF	CFA	LCV	ACU	NTLC	NSI	COC	CEI
1992	10	13	17	20	27	6	88	95	100	75	79
1991	5	—	8	20	17	8	90	—	—	90	81

National Journal Ratings

	1991 LIB — 1991 CONS		1992 LIB — 1992 CONS	
Economic	4% —	90%	0% —	91%
Social	0% —	84%	26% —	72%
Foreign	25% —	75%	0% —	82%

Key Votes of the 102d Congress

1. Ban Striker Replace AGN	5. Handgun Wait/7-Day AGN	9. Use Force in Gulf FOR
2. $ for Homeownership FOR	6. Overseas Mil. AbortionAGN	10. US Mil. Abroad $ CutAGN
3. Tax Rich/Cut Mid Cls.AGN	7. Obscn. Art NEA $ Ban FOR	11. Limit SDI Funds AGN
4. FY93/$15B Def. Cut AGN	8. Death Pen. from Jury FOR	12. Cuba Trade Embargo FOR

Key Votes of the 103d Congress

1. Family Leave AGN	2. Deficit Reduction AGN	3. Stimulus Plan AGN

Election Results

1992 general	Alfred A. (Al) McCandless (R)	110,333	(54%)	($278,880)
	Georgia Smith (D)	81,693	(40%)	($5,748)
	Phil Turner (LIB)	11,515	(6%)	
1992 primary	Alfred A. (Al) McCandless (R)	33,738	(61%)	
	Bud Mathewson (R)	11,323	(21%)	
	Lewis A. Silva (R)	10,113	(18%)	
1990 general	Alfred A. (Al) McCandless (R)	115,469	(50%)	($602,444)
(CA 37)	Ralph Waite (D).	103,961	(45%)	($624,560)
	Two others.	12,652	(5%)	

FORTY-FIFTH DISTRICT

In the days when the Beach Boys were attending Hawthorne High School and surfboards were unheard of in most of America, one of southern California's best surfing spots was Huntington Beach in Orange County. There wasn't much of a town then, and inland were vegetable fields and orange groves, and nary a freeway in sight. Now, three decades later, the beachfront of Orange County has been filled in. On the coast, Huntington Beach is a city of 181,000, a mixture of family subdivisions and garden apartments. To the north are Stanton and Westminster, the latter the center of the biggest Vietnamese-American community in the nation. South along the San Diego Freeway is Fountain Valley, central focus now of many Asian-owned high-tech businesses, an engine of southern California growth. Near the coast again is Costa Mesa, site of South Coast Plaza, with its luxury stores, America's first mall to offer valet parking, and Newport Beach, with its large harbor and expensive mansions a block or two from the ocean.

All this beachfront segment of Orange County makes up California's 45th Congressional District. When it was created in December 1991, no incumbent lived within the lines, but two tussled over the chance to run there. Republicans Dana Rohrabacher and Robert Dornan were both attracted to this heavily Republican seat. A Rohrabacher aide said he would run there "come hell or high water or Bob Dornan." Dornan insisted that his seniority (he was in his 16th year in Congress, Rohrabacher in his fourth) entitled him to the seat, although he had represented only a little of it before, and that if Rohrabacher took him on he would be "voluntarily ending his congressional career." But after a few days of argument, Dornan conceded and ran in the more politically risky 46th, and Rohrabacher, who used to live in Orange County, returned there to run in the 45th. He persuaded Huntington Beach Mayor Jim Silva not to run, but had two serious opponents, Costa Mesa Councilman Peter Buffa, who got 28% of the vote, and Huntington Beach Councilman Peter Green, who got 24%; Rohrabacher was renominated with less than a majority, 48%. Nor was his 55%–39% showing in the general election spectacular in a district that had voted 68% for George Bush in 1988.

Rohrabacher is something of a free spirit in House Republican ranks, bearded, puckish, with something like a *Saturday Night Live* attitude. He was purged from the Young Americans for Freedom for libertarian stands on the draft and drugs and once had a folk band called The Goldwaters. "There's bureaucracy," ran one of his verses, "It takes a lot of generals to keep us free/With shiny shoes and medals on their chests/They're protecting us from behind their desks." Eventually he calmed down and became an editorial writer for *The Orange County Register*, and later part of the Reagan White House speechwriting shop. He returned to southern California in 1988 when Long Beach-based Congressman Dan Lungren decided not to run again (Lungren went on to be elected attorney general in 1990). Rohrabacher won the three-way primary, with fundraising help from Oliver North, over a county supervisor who had padded her resume, and Steve Horn, now congressman from the Long Beach-based 38th District.

Rohrabacher's biggest headlines in the House came when he led a fight against the National Endowment for the Arts. This debate should have left both him and his opponents more uncomfortable than they seemed: Rohrabacher, because this stuff can't be quite as repugnant to this former rocker and libertarian as it is to Jesse Helms; liberal NEA defenders, because it is scarcely censorship to deny government funding for works like the *Piss Christ* that insult the religious beliefs of many citizens and taxpayers. Rohrabacher has also worked to rescue funding for the 1993 test-flight of the Single Stage to Orbit vehicle, has tried—so far successfully—to prevent the closing of the Long Beach Naval Shipyard (though it is now in the 38th District) and has obtained funds for Santa Ana River flood control. He has started talking ominously about the perils of illegal immigration, but also joined more liberal members to support a bill to halt the forced return of those who have fled Haiti.

The People: Pop. 1990: 570,991; 10% age 65+; 73% White; 1% Black; 1% Amer. Indian; 11% Asian; 5% Other; 15% Hispanic origin. Voting age pop.: 450,774; 1% Black; 13% Hispanic origin. Households: 52% married couple families; 23% married couple fams. w. children; 63% college educ.; median household income: $45,074; per capita income: $21,046; median gross rent: $815; median house value: $264,200.

1992 Presidential Vote			1988 Presidential Vote		
Bush (R)	105,893	(42%)	Bush (R)	148,999	(68%)
Clinton (D)	80,646	(32%)	Dukakis (D)	71,027	(32%)
Perot (I)	63,609	(25%)			

Rep. Dana Rohrabacher (R)

Elected 1988; b. June 21, 1947, Coronado; home, Huntington Beach; Long Beach St. Col. B.A. 1969, U. of Southern CA, M.A. 1971; Baptist; single.

Career: Radio and print journalist, 1970–80; Sr. Speechwriter, Special Asst. to Pres. Reagan, 1981–88.

Offices: 1027 LHOB 20515, 202-225-2415. Also 16162 Beach Blvd., Huntington Beach 92647, 714-847-2433.

Committees: *District of Columbia* (2d of 4 R): Government Operations and Metropolitan Affairs; Judiciary and Education (RMM). *Foreign Affairs* (14th of 18 R): Asia and the Pacific; Economic Policy, Trade and Environment. *Science, Space and Technology* (8th of 22 R): Space; Technology, Environment and Aviation.

Group Ratings

	ADA	ACLU	COPE	CDF	CFA	LCV	ACU	NTLC	NSI	COC	CEI
1992	20	4	25	0	7	6	96	100	90	75	92
1991	15	—	17	10	6	15	100	—	—	90	94

National Journal Ratings

	1991 LIB — 1991 CONS			1992 LIB — 1992 CONS	
Economic	18%	—	79%	9%	— 88%
Social	0%	—	84%	26%	— 72%
Foreign	31%	—	67%	38%	— 56%

Key Votes of the 102d Congress

1. Ban Striker Replace	AGN	5. Handgun Wait/7-Day	AGN	9. Use Force in Gulf	FOR
2. $ for Homeownership	FOR	6. Overseas Mil. Abortion	AGN	10. US Mil. Abroad $ Cut	FOR
3. Tax Rich/Cut Mid Cls.	AGN	7. Obscn. Art NEA $ Ban	FOR	11. Limit SDI Funds	AGN
4. FY93/$15B Def. Cut	AGN	8. Death Pen. from Jury	FOR	12. Cuba Trade Embargo	FOR

Key Votes of the 103d Congress

1. Family Leave	AGN	2. Deficit Reduction	AGN	3. Stimulus Plan	AGN

Election Results

1992 general	Dana Rohrabacher (R)	123,731	(55%)	($321,912)
	Patricia McCabe (D)	88,508	(39%)	($32,473)
	Gary D. Copeland (LIB)	14,777	(7%)	
1992 primary	Dana Rohrabacher (R)	30,649	(48%)	
	Peter Buffa (R)	17,748	(28%)	
	Peter Green (R)	15,592	(24%)	
1990 general	Dana Rohrabacher (R)	109,353	(59%)	($398,963)
(CA 42)	Guy C. Kimbrough (D)	67,189	(36%)	($28,350)
	Richard Gibb Martin (LIB)	7,744	(4%)	

FORTY-SIXTH DISTRICT

Orange County, almost entirely the sparkling new creation of the decades after World War II, is starting to show signs of age. It is still growing, but no longer as it was in the years when Disneyland was new, when it was transforming orange groves, planted in neat rows among mile-square grids into one suburban subdivision and shopping center and office tower after another. The population rose from 130,000 in 1940 to 216,000 in 1950, 703,000 in 1960, 1.4 million in 1970, 1.9 million in 1980, and 2.4 million in 1990. A distinctive civilization was implanted here: mostly white and middle-class, confident of its traditional values and its market capitalism, proud of American principles and American military might.

For critics, Orange County was a symbol of racism and callousness toward the poor. For years it had very few slums and its cultural attitudes were far less liberated than those in Hollywood or the Westside, and its politics were solidly Republican. But as time went on, Orange County turned out to be less homogeneous and more open to change than its critics supposed. Its economy was constantly being transformed by the inevitable upheavals of capitalism: there is no single industry here—not even defense—which is totally responsible for the prosperity of Orange County, and people here must be ready to adapt almost as adeptly as the Taiwanese on the other side of the Pacific Rim. Another kind of change is cultural: Orange County in its restrained way has adapted to changes in family life. There has been ethnic change, as well: Orange County always had a Mexican-American community in Santa Ana, but in the 1970s and 1980s, Hispanics and Asians moved out the freeways, and as Vietnamese refugees began arriving in large numbers after the fall of Saigon, many headed for the county which had always staunchly supported fighting for their freedom from Communism. By 1990 Orange County was about one-quarter Hispanic and one-tenth Asian—scarcely homogeneous.

In the early 1990s, Orange County was also hit hard, for the first time in nearly 20 years, by recession. Defense cutbacks hurt here, as elsewhere in southern California. Higher taxes from George Bush's budget summit agreement of 1990 and Governor Pete Wilson's tax package in

1991 put extra burdens on the small businesses which were the engines of the 1980s California boom; and Republican chief executives seemed to be at blame. At the same time, the cultural conservatism of Orange County in the forms most publically proclaimed, notably the opposition to abortion, came to seem sharply out of line with opinion not only in the rest of California but in Orange County itself. Orange County voters in the presidential race didn't move any great distance toward the Democrats, but they moved sharply away from Bush and the Republicans. Seeking an orderly framework within which to live their lives, Orange Countians old and new seemed to be wandering dispirited, as if their grid streets suddenly were bending unpredictably or running forever skew to each other.

The 46th Congressional District is the geographic and, to the extent there is one, the historic heart of post-World War II Orange County. It consists, with slight variations, of Santa Ana, Garden Grove and the central part of Anaheim: it contains Disneyland and the county courthouse and is just across the freeway or street from Anaheim Stadium, Knott's Berry Farm and John Wayne Airport. Santa Ana, which once had a small Mexican-American neighborhood, is now heavily Latino; Garden Grove has many Latinos and some Vietnamese, though the main Vietnamese shopping area is across the line in Westminster; Anaheim today is mixed as well. Overall, the 46th is 50% Hispanic and 12% Asian. For many years, this corridor has been the most Democratic part of a Republican county, and from 1962 to 1982 districts carefully sculpted in this area elected Democratic congressmen. In the early 1980s the emergence into the electorate of the Vietnamese moved the balance away from the Democrats: these are people who are angry not that the United States got into Vietnam but that it got out. The emergence into the electorate of Latinos may have moved the balance the other way, at least in 1992, when the Latino vote went heavily for Bill Clinton; it should be noted, though, that Pete Wilson ran strongly with Latinos in 1990 and Republicans could do so again.

The congressman from the 46th District is one of the most distinctive politicians in Congress, with his red beard and fiery temperament, his seemingly constant itch for a fight and his strong loyalties and beliefs. He is Robert Dornan, now one of the more senior Republicans in the House, first elected in 1976 in a Westside district and reelected twice there, an unsuccessful candidate for the Senate in 1982 (he finished fourth in the primary with 8% of the vote) and the 1984 upset winner over an incumbent Democrat in the 46th District's predecessor. Dornan is easier to understand if you remember that he was a fighter pilot. He volunteered for pilot training while in college and went on active duty in the Air Force in October 1952; some Democrats attacked him in 1985 for not having served in combat, but he would have if there had not been an armistice nine months after he joined. As it was, he was a fighter pilot until 1958, about as hazardous duty as there is in a peacetime military. Then, with show business connections (his uncle Jack Haley was the Tin Woodsman in *The Wizard of Oz*), he became a TV talk show host in Los Angeles, and was a civilian combat photographer on five of his eight trips to wartime Vietnam. He has a taste for invective: he once called Barbara Boxer's campaign contributors "coke-snorting, wife-swapping, baby-born-out-of-wedlock, radical Hollywood left," and called Governor Pete Wilson's appointment of John Seymour to the U.S. Senate "so unimaginative that I think it begs for a primary challenge." Perhaps this is because this true believer finds himself fighting in hostile arenas: the trendy and often mindless liberalism of the Westside was infuriating to this true believer in the B-1 bomber and bans on abortion, and the political adeptness and verbal cleverness of House liberals seem to enrage him as well. Dornan's temper sometimes enables him to accomplish things others dismiss as impossible. But, whatever the provocation, his ragings often end up ill serving the causes he so fervently stands for.

One of those may have been George Bush. Dornan was the first House member to endorse Bush, in December 1985, and vociferously vouched for his fellow former military pilot to other conservatives during the 1988 primaries. In September 1992, dismayed as Bill Clinton continued to lead Bush in the polls, Dornan began making speeches on the House floor asking pointed questions about Clinton's trip to Moscow and Eastern Europe in 1969 when he was a Rhodes Scholar. In early October, he and three colleagues met with Bush and James Baker and raised the question; two days later on "Larry King Live," Bush called on Clinton to answer questions about the trip. In extended interviews at the time, Dornan made it clear he thought Clinton had not done anything disloyal to the United States but that the ease with which he got a Soviet visa and the fact that he made a visit to Prague, a headquarters of Soviet disinformation operations, suggested that his travels may have been facilitated—as certainly they were monitored—by the KGB. But in an era of sound-bite politics, just raising the point sounded like McCarthyism, as if Dornan were accusing Clinton of pro-Communist behavior. Clinton's denial of specific recollections of his Soviet trip did sound fishy, but for any leading Republican to raise the issue during the fall campaign inevitably sounded much more like an unjust accusation than it was. The questions ought instead to have been asked by the press, not because there was any reason to believe Clinton was pro-Communist, but for the same reason reporters asked him about other early experiences, to understand what he has learned and how his mind works.

This was not the only stormy episode in Dornan's campaign year; indeed, only two of his eight House campaigns have been devoid of turbulence, and in each of those he spent more than $1 million, and only once has he won with as much as 60% of the vote. In 1992, Dornan hoped for an easier race, and in December 1991 threatened to run, even if incumbent Dana Rohrabacher also did so, in the more Republican 45th District on the Orange County beaches. But he backed off, agreed to run in the 46th and had his first primary challenge as an incumbent. His opponent was former Orange County Superior Court Judge Judy Ryan, who is pro-choice and attacked Dornan for his strong opposition to abortion; Dornan charged that Ryan was a creature of her consultant, Eileen Padberg, and lobbied incumbent women Republicans in Congress to not campaign against him. Dornan raised and spent more than $500,000 in the primary; Ryan attacked him for not passing major legislation and the pro-choice group NARAL made $300,000 in independent expenditures against him. Dornan won by a 60%–40% margin, not comforting for an incumbent in a primary. In the general election, he faced a hapless Democrat who raised and spent almost nothing, and only managed a 50%–41% win. Should he wish to run in the next two elections in which his name can appear on the ballot under California's term limits law, Dornan may have to court Orange County's new Latino voters in the 1990s as he courted the Vietnamese in the 1980s.

In the House, Dornan devotes much of his energy to things military, serving on the Armed Services Committee and also on Intelligence. He is proud that he has logged many hours of flying time as a pilot and observer. He has tried to prevent what he considers excessive defense spending cuts, especially in California. But he has also pushed a program to help former military personnel become teachers as well as a ROTC-type program to recruit police officers. He became an enthusiastic supporter of aid to Russia after President Boris Yeltsin addressed Congress. But Dornan is enthusiastic about everything he does and vociferous about everything he opposes, and as he tries to raise objections in a Democratic House or to win reelection in a changing Orange County, or when he substitutes for Rush Limbaugh on his radio program, he will always come out fighting.

The People: Pop. 1990: 570,963; 7% age 65+; 36% White; 2% Black; 1% Amer. Indian; 12% Asian; 18% Other; 49% Hispanic origin. Voting age pop.: 405,366; 2% Black; 45% Hispanic origin. Households: 58% married couple families; 33% married couple fams. w. children; 38% college educ.; median household income: $35,416; per capita income: $11,297; median gross rent: $719; median house value: $187,900.

1992 Presidential Vote		
Bush (R)	47,689	(40%)
Clinton (D)	44,352	(37%)
Perot (I)	27,542	(23%)

1988 Presidential Vote		
Bush (R)	74,822	(62%)
Dukakis (D)	45,162	(38%)

Rep. Robert K. (Bob) Dornan (R)

Elected 1984; b. Apr. 3, 1933, New York, N.Y.; home, Garden Grove; Loyola U.; Catholic; married (Sallie).

Career: Air Force, 1952–58, Air Natl. Guard, 1958–61, Air Force Reserves, 1962–75; Broadcast Journalist, 1965–69; Talk show host, 1969–73; U.S. House of Reps., 1976–82.

Offices: 2402 CHOB 20515, 202-225-2965. Also 300 Plaza Alicante, #360, Garden Grove 92642, 714-971-9292.

Committees: *Armed Services* (10th of 22 R): Military Acquisition; Oversight and Investigations; Readiness. *Intelligence (Permanent Select)* (3d of 7 R): Program and Budget Authorization.

Group Ratings

	ADA	ACLU	COPE	CDF	CFA	LCV	ACU	NTLC	NSI	COC	CEI
1992	5	0	17	0	7	0	100	100	100	71	89
1991	10	—	18	20	22	8	95	—	—	88	85

National Journal Ratings

	1991 LIB — 1991 CONS	1992 LIB — 1992 CONS
Economic	0% — 96%	16% — 80%
Social	16% — 81%	21% — 78%
Foreign	12% — 85%	0% — 82%

Key Votes of the 102d Congress

1. Ban Striker Replace	AGN	5. Handgun Wait/7-Day FOR	9. Use Force in Gulf FOR
2. $ for Homeownership	FOR	6. Overseas Mil. AbortionAGN	10. US Mil. Abroad $ Cut *
3. Tax Rich/Cut Mid Cls.AGN		7. Obscn. Art NEA $ Ban FOR	11. Limit SDI Funds AGN
4. FY93/$15B Def. Cut AGN		8. Death Pen. from Jury FOR	12. Cuba Trade Embargo FOR

Key Votes of the 103d Congress

1. Family Leave	AGN	2. Deficit Reduction	AGN	3. Stimulus Plan	AGN

Election Results

1992 general	Robert K. (Bob) Dornan (R)	55,659	(50%)	($1,581,503)
	Robert John Banuelos (D)	45,435	(41%)	
	Richard G. Newhouse (LIB)	9,712	(9%)	
1992 primary	Robert K. (Bob) Dornan (R)	17,558	(60%)	
	Judith M. Ryan (R)	11,893	(40%)	
1990 general	Robert K. (Bob) Dornan (R)	60,561	(58%)	($1,445,577)
(CA 38)	Barbara Jackson (D)...................	43,693	(42%)	

FORTY-SEVENTH DISTRICT

It is still possible, in crowded metropolitan Orange County, to see what this land looked like before the post-World War II growth. For out the Santa Ana or San Diego Freeways, the vast expanse of the Irvine Ranch has not been entirely developed. The Irvine Ranch was a swath of land extending 10 miles along the Pacific Ocean south from Newport Beach and 22 miles inland, over orange groves and vegetable fields, to the mountains; only in the late 1970s was it sold by its family owners to a billion dollar development consortium. The location was good: near John Wayne Airport and not far from affluent Newport Beach and Costa Mesa's South Costa Plaza, the highest-volume upscale shopping center in southern California, standing in what not too long ago was a lima bean field. The new developers started by donating 1,000 acres for an Irvine branch of the University of California, then devised both conventional and innovative development, with planned communities, handsome clusters of office towers, landscaped shopping plazas, and groups of houses and condominiums (but no cemeteries). Condemned by some urbanologists as monotonous, Irvine, with 110,000 people, actually has lush landscaping and cohesive neighborhoods; one-fifth of its people are Asian and one-eighth of its housing is moderate-income, scattered around the city. It elected a liberal mayor, Larry Agran, who banned ozone-depleting chemicals and invited a Sandinista baseball team to visit; after he was defeated in 1990, he ran for president in 1992, complaining when he was left out of the debates.

The 47th Congressional District of California is centered geographically on the Irvine Ranch lands. On the coast it includes about half of Newport Beach as well as most of Irvine and runs south to the artsy settlement of Laguna Beach. It includes the growing subdivisions of El Toro and Laguna Hills near El Toro Marine Corps Air Station (on the base closure list for 1993). About half its residents live to the north, in and around the city of Orange, an earlier and less systematic but still affluent and orderly Orange County community where even the street signs are orange. Politically, this is a conservative area, one of the most Republican districts in the United States. Its people like the sense of order conveyed by its grid street patterns and the feeling of protection imparted by the subdivision walls and security guards. They feel comfortable as well with the military nearby. Although there are some distinctively rich communities here, the people do not feel that they are some kind of elite; they tend to see themselves as ordinary Americans with classic values who have worked hard and are entitled to enjoy their comfort.

The congressman from the 47th District is Christopher Cox, part of the White House counsel staff in the Reagan years who returned to Orange County, where he had worked for a prestigious law firm, and ran for Congress when an incumbent retired in 1988. He was one of 14 candidates in the Republican primary and, with support from Oliver North and Robert Bork, won with 31%. He has won since without difficulty. Cox is less pugnacious and confrontational than his Orange County colleagues Robert Dornan and Dana Rohrabacher, but just as conservative. His interests have ranged from the former Soviet Union (he and his father published an English translation of *Pravda* from 1984 to 1988) and Lithuanian independence (he supported it in 1990) to lobbying for more local control of highway funds and a proposed monorail system in Orange County. He has a bill to strengthen the budget process by requiring a full budget to be passed before any spending bill can be considered, and a two-thirds vote to exceed budget limits. In 1992 he urged President Bush to veto the legislative budget and insist on deep cuts in congressional staff, and got 143 members to sign a pledge to uphold a veto, just two less than needed: an interesting initiative, now obviously moot. But Cox, with his safe seat and his party totally out of power, will undoubtedly come up with new initiatives that may prove more fruitful in the future and he got a seat on Budget for 1993 which should give him some more leverage.

The People: Pop. 1990: 571,605; 11% age 65+; 75% White; 2% Black; 10% Asian; 5% Other; 13% Hispanic origin. Voting age pop.: 442,117; 2% Black; 12% Hispanic origin. Households: 58% married couple families; 27% married couple fams. w. children; 72% college educ.; median household income: $51,554; per capita income: $25,268; median gross rent: $845; median house value: $279,900.

1992 Presidential Vote			1988 Presidential Vote		
Bush (R)	127,700	(46%)	Bush (R)	162,104	(71%)
Clinton (D)	86,279	(31%)	Dukakis (D)	67,579	(29%)
Perot (I)	64,227	(23%)			

Rep. Christopher Cox (R)

Elected 1988; b. Oct. 16, 1952, St. Paul, MN; home, Newport Beach; U. of Southern CA, B.A. 1973, Harvard, M.B.A., J.D., 1977; Catholic; married (Rebecca).

Career: Practicing atty., 1978–86; Lecturer, Harvard Bus. Schl., 1982–83; Sr. Assoc. Cnsl., White House, 1986–88.

Offices: 206 CHOB 20515, 202-225-5611. Also 4000 MacArthur Blvd., #430, Newport Beach 92660, 714-756-2244.

Committees: *Budget* (9th of 17 R). *Government Operations* (7th of 17 R): Commerce, Consumer and Monetary Affairs (RMM). *Joint Economic Committee* (9th of 10).

Group Ratings

	ADA	ACLU	COPE	CDF	CFA	LCV	ACU	NTLC	NSI	COC	CEI
1992	5	0	17	0	13	0	100	95	100	75	86
1991	10	—	8	10	6	23	100	—	—	80	92

National Journal Ratings

	1991 LIB — 1991 CONS		1992 LIB — 1992 CONS	
Economic	4%	— 90%	0%	— 91%
Social	0%	— 84%	0%	— 85%
Foreign	23%	— 75%	0%	— 82%

Key Votes of the 102d Congress

1. Ban Striker Replace AGN	5. Handgun Wait/7-Day AGN	9. Use Force in Gulf FOR
2. $ for Homeownership FOR	6. Overseas Mil. Abortion AGN	10. US Mil. Abroad $ Cut AGN
3. Tax Rich/Cut Mid Cls. AGN	7. Obscn. Art NEA $ Ban FOR	11. Limit SDI Funds *
4. FY93/$15B Def. Cut AGN	8. Death Pen. from Jury FOR	12. Cuba Trade Embargo FOR

Key Votes of the 103d Congress

1. Family Leave AGN	2. Deficit Reduction AGN	3. Stimulus Plan AGN

Election Results

1992 general	Christopher Cox (R).................	165,004	(65%)	($402,198)
	John F. Anwiler (D)	76,924	(30%)	
	Maxine B. Quirk (P&F)	12,297	(5%)	
1992 primary	Christopher Cox (R)..................	53,628	(68%)	
	Robert L. (Bob) Moore (R)	15,633	(20%)	
	Stephen J. Frogue (R)	9,873	(12%)	
1990 general	Christopher Cox (R)..................	142,299	(68%)	($682,365)
(CA 40)	Eugene C. Gratz (D)	68,087	(32%)	($36,124)

FORTY-EIGHTH DISTRICT

The California coast between Los Angeles and San Diego has never entirely filled up with development, and probably never will as long as the Marine Corps retains custody of Camp Pendleton, its giant training base just south of the Orange-San Diego County line. But on both sides of Pendleton up and down the coast, and for miles inland on the pleasant hills and in sunny valleys, there has been tremendous growth over the past two decades. Little wonder: this area has perhaps the most agreeable climate in the continental United States, beautiful scenery, the physical infrastructure typical of California and low crime rates not seen in Los Angeles or even San Diego. A quarter century ago, this was largely empty territory—never fertile enough to produce a large farm community, never endowed with much manufacturing, never actively promoted as a retirement community. In 1990 there were enough people just north and south of Pendleton to make up a congressional district of 572,000 people, and the Interior Department was struggling to come up with a district plan that would protect the ecosystem of the 4-inch gnatcatcher bird and other endangered species in the area against total subdivization.

The northern part of this 48th District of California includes the Orange County seaside communities of San Clemente, where Richard Nixon lived just after leaving the White House, and San Juan Capistrano, to which the swallows famously return every year. Inland, there are the newer condominium communities of Mission Viejo and Laguna Niguel; just south of Pendleton in San Diego County are Oceanside and Vista. Farther inland amid the hills are Fallbrook and, in Riverside County, Temecula, in the mid-1980s a corner-grocery town serving a vineyard district, now the center of an area with 100,000 people, mostly commuters to Orange County and Riverside attracted by low house prices and traditional values. People in all these areas tend to be Republicans; they are affluent enough to identify with the party of property, conventional enough in their personal lives to identify with what describes itself as the party of the family, unscarred enough by ethnic differences to identify with the party that fancies it is made up of an unethnic majority.

The current congressman from the 48th, Ron Packard, is a Republican who first won when a new district was created for this area in 1982. Packard is a Mormon from Idaho, a dentist who served in the Navy Dental Corps in Camp Pendleton in the 1950s, then moved his growing family (now 7 children and 27 grandchildren) to Carlsbad. There he served on the school board, the Chamber of Commerce, the city council, was a director of the North County Transit District, and mayor: one of the people who keeps things working in these growing communities. He was mayor of Carlsbad in 1982 when he ran for Congress in the new district, and lost the 18-candidate Republican primary by 92 votes to Johnnie Crean, who spent his own money on ads fraudulently claiming President Reagan's endorsement. Packard promptly ran as a write-in and won with 37% to 32% for the Democrat and 31% for Crean. He has been easily reelected since, though with a reduced percentage in anti-Republican 1992.

In the House, Packard has a highly conservative voting record; as you would expect, he's against affluent seniors paying taxes on Social Security benefits. He has passed bills to set up a regional water reuse system in southern California and research on desalinization. He supports a crackdown on illegal immigration and wants Congress to address the problem of unfunded federal mandates that force states to bear the costs for social welfare and health care for both legal and illegal immigrants. All of these reflect a civic-mindedness reminiscent of California's nonpartisan, efficiency-minded municipal politics. But Packard has enough of a partisan edge that his California Republican colleagues in 1990 voted for him to replace the accommodationist Jerry Lewis as their representative on the party Committee on Committees. In 1993 he moved from Public Works to Appropriations, but says he will continue to pursue water and immigration issues.

The People: Pop. 1990: 573,211; 11% rural; 10% age 65+; 74% White; 4% Black; 1% Amer. Indian; 5% Asian; 7% Other; 17% Hispanic origin. Voting age pop.: 426,696; 4% Black; 15% Hispanic origin.

Households: 63% married couple families; 30% married couple fams. w. children; 65% college educ.; median household income: $42,389; per capita income: $19,435; median gross rent: $696; median house value: $237,300.

1992 Presidential Vote

Bush (R) 108,581 (44%)
Clinton (D) 71,621 (29%)
Perot (I). 65,980 (27%)

1988 Presidential Vote

Bush (R) 134,444 (70%)
Dukakis (D). 57,543 (30%)

Rep. Ron Packard (R)

Elected 1982; b. Jan. 19, 1931, Meridian, ID; home, Oceanside; Brigham Young U., Portland St. U., U. of OR, D.M.D. 1957; Mormon; married (Jean).

Career: Navy, 1957–59; Dentist; Carlsbad Sch. Dist. Bd., 1962–74; Carlsbad City Cncl., 1976–78; Carlsbad Mayor, 1978–82.

Offices: 2162 RHOB 20515, 202-225-3906. Also 221 E. Vista Way, #205, Vista 92084, 619-631-1364; and 629 Camino del los Mares, #204, San Clemente 92672, 714-496-2343.

Committees: *Appropriations* (16th of 23 R): Interior; Legislative.

Group Ratings

	ADA	ACLU	COPE	CDF	CFA	LCV	ACU	NTLC	NSI	COC	CEI
1992	0	0	8	0	13	0	100	100	100	71	86
1991	5	—	8	20	22	0	95	—	—	90	82

National Journal Ratings

	1991 LIB — 1991 CONS	1992 LIB — 1992 CONS
Economic	14% — 83%	25% — 74%
Social	16% — 81%	0% — 85%
Foreign	0% — 88%	0% — 82%

Key Votes of the 102d Congress

1. Ban Striker Replace	AGN	5. Handgun Wait/7-Day	FOR	9. Use Force in Gulf	FOR
2. $ for Homeownership	FOR	6. Overseas Mil. Abortion AGN	10. US Mil. Abroad $ Cut AGN
3. Tax Rich/Cut Mid Cls. AGN	7. Obscn. Art NEA $ Ban FOR	11. Limit SDI Funds	AGN
4. FY93/$15B Def. Cut	*	8. Death Pen. from Jury	FOR	12. Cuba Trade Embargo FOR

Key Votes of the 103d Congress

1. Family Leave	AGN	2. Deficit Reduction	AGN	3. Stimulus Plan	AGN

Election Results

1992 general	Ron Packard (R).....................	140,935	(61%)	($363,341)
	Michael Farber (D)...................	67,415	(29%)	($65,944)
	Donna White (P&F).................	13,396	(6%)	
	Ted Lowe (LIB)	8,749	(4%)	
1992 primary	Ron Packard (R).....................	45,217	(64%)	
	Stephen Todd (R)...................	13,632	(19%)	
	Ed Mayerhofer (R)..................	12,077	(17%)	
1990 general	Ron Packard (R)....................	151,206	(68%)	($147,249)
(CA 43)	Doug Hansen (P&F).................	40,212	(18%)	
	Richard L. Arnold (LIB)	30,720	(14%)	

FORTY-NINTH DISTRICT

In 1848, when the United States was dictating the terms of the Treaty of Guadalupe Hidalgo after its successful war with Mexico, it made sure the southern boundary of its new California territory was just south of the port of San Diego. This is one of three splendid natural harbors on the Pacific Coast, and the major West Coast U.S. Navy base for more than 50 years. The port and Navy base in the sheltered harbor are still the central focus of a metropolis which has grown tenfold over that time span and stretches now far inland and to the north. On one side is its downtown, blooming with post-modern buildings like the Horton Plaza amid a few well-preserved early 20th Century relics like the Spreckels Theatre. Across the harbor, on the sand spit that guards it against the ocean, is the white frame castle of the Hotel Del Coronado, with its surprisingly dark wooden interior, the world's largest wooden structure and a favored resort of past American presidents; the town of Coronado has long been a favored retirement place for Navy admirals and captains.

But San Diego is not all harbor and Navy. To the north, the Pacific waves pound against the beach beneath erose cliffs of unique rock formations that stride up and down the coast from La Jolla, on which has been built some of San Diego's great cultural institutions: the Scripps Institute of Oceanography, the University of California San Diego campus, the Salk Institute, and the Torrey Pines reserve, home of this unique, wide-spreading pine tree. They look out over the ocean through clear and gentle air south to La Jolla, the city's highest income neighborhood, north toward Del Mar and the race track that made San Diego a tourist mecca 50 years ago when it was owned by Bing Crosby and friends. The weather—sunny 70% of the time, arguably the most pleasant climate in the continental U.S.—has brought people to San Diego; the informal resort atmosphere of La Jolla and Mission Beach appeal to tourists. But this is a working town as well, a sophisticated high-tech center with nearly 200,000 full- and part-time students at its colleges and universities and growing biotech, electronics and telecommunications industries; someone who looks like a professional surfer may turn out to be a high-tech engineer.

The 49th Congressional District of California, which includes about half the population of San Diego plus Coronado and Imperial Beach, takes in most of the harbor and Navy bases and much of its high-tech businesses and workers. It reaches as far south as the Mexican border and includes most of downtown San Diego and Balboa Park, with the justly famous zoo. It reaches inland where the city's freeway network, denser and more practical than in San Francisco or even Los Angeles, efficiently shuttles commuters from scattered employment centers to their homes on hilltop subdivisions; for San Diego under then-Mayor (1971–82) Pete Wilson wouldn't let developers build on the sides of the hills, so that San Diego doesn't have the picturesque but precarious hillside streets of the Hollywood Hills or Pacific Heights but rather the natural landscape that Cabrillo and Richard Henry Dana saw from the sea, the hills topped unobtrusively by subdivisions. It includes Ocean Beach and Mission Bay and La Jolla and reaches as far north as Torrey Pines and as far inland as the outer boundary of Miramar Naval Air Station.

With its climate, weather, scenery and friendliness, this should be paradise; but politically at least San Diego seems to be in a foul temper—and was even before the recession of the early 1990s kicked in. Voters here tend to be Republican and free market on economics, but liberal on cultural issues like abortion and the environment: the stands of San Diego's Pete Wilson, who was elected to U.S. senator in 1982 and 1988 and governor in 1990. But at the same time, this part of San Diego was rejecting incumbent Republicans—two council members in 1989, two Assembly members in 1990 and two more city council members in 1991. Democratic Congressman Jim Bates lost on the south side of town in 1990, while former mayor and now talk radio show host Roger Hedgecock was sponsoring a DRIP (Don't Reelect Incumbent Politicians) campaign. For 1992 three Republican congressmen had residences within the new 49th District when it was established, but none chose to run here. And Bill Lowery, who had represented most of the district, decided to retire at age 45 after 12 years in Congress, and 300 overdrafts on the House bank and some campaign contributions from unsavory S&L figures. Five Democrats and 10 Republicans ran for the seat in June 1992, with women winning both party's primaries. Democrat Lynn Schenk won 53%–25% over Byron Georgiou, who had spent $400,000 against Bates in the 1990 primary, while Republican Judy Jarvis, a nurse and political novice, won 21%–17% over free-spending dive light entrepreneur Alan Uke.

The nominees presented an interesting contrast, not only on issues (though both were pro-choice) but in background. Schenk became a lawyer in 1970, just as larger numbers of women were entering law school; in 1972 she co-founded the San Diego Lawyers Club to help women attorneys there; in 1973 she co-founded the Women's Bank in San Diego; in 1976 she was a White House fellow; in 1978 she became part of Governor Jerry Brown's cabinet first as deputy secretary and, in 1980, secretary of business, transportation and housing; in 1984, she lost a race for county supervisor, and then won $150,000 in a libel suit against her opponent Susan Golding, now San Diego's mayor; in 1989, she founded a San Diego Urban Corps; in 1990, she became a commissioner of the San Diego Unified Port District. In other words, she became involved in all manner of government and community life. She also became a gifted political fundraiser, and in her 1992 campaign far outraised her rivals. Judy Jarvis had few such contacts. She is a critical care nurse who started the California Nurses' Bureau, turning a $5,000 investment into a $1 million business which she eventually sold to a Fortune 500 company. In 1992, Jarvis ran a door-to-door campaign which essentially won the primary for her and beat nine men in the process. But Jarvis was unable to keep up with Schenk in fundraising for the general, and Schenk won 51%–43%.

Schenk drew good committee assignments: Energy and Commerce and, for this former Port commissioner, Merchant Marine and Fisheries. She certainly has the political skills to hold this district, but they may be tested if the Clinton Administration becomes identified with higher taxes and fails to deliver a vibrant economy.

The People: Pop. 1990: 573,437; 12% age 65+; 75% White; 5% Black; 1% Amer. Indian; 7% Asian; 5% Other; 12% Hispanic origin. Voting age pop.: 479,942; 5% Black; 11% Hispanic origin. Households: 41% married couple families; 16% married couple fams. w. children; 67% college educ.; median household income: $32,562; per capita income: $19,184; median gross rent: $607; median house value: $224,200.

1992 Presidential Vote		
Clinton (D)	114,081	(43%)
Bush (R)	82,834	(31%)
Perot (I)	65,856	(25%)

1988 Presidential Vote		
Bush (R)	147,529	(57%)
Dukakis (D)	113,380	(43%)

Rep. Lynn Schenk (D)

Elected 1992; b. Jan 5, 1945, New York, NY; home, San Diego; U. of CA, B.A. 1967, U. of San Diego, J.D. 1970, London Schl. of Economics, 1970–71; Jewish; married (Hugh Friedman).

Career: CA Dep. Atty. Gen., 1971–74; Cnsl., San Diego Gas & Elec. Co., 1972–78; White House Fellow & Spec. Asst. to V.P., 1976–77; Co-founder, Lawyer's Club 1972, Women's Bank 1973, Urban Corps. 1989; CA Secy. of Business, Transp. & Housing, 1980–83; Practicing atty., 1983–92; San Diego Port Comm., 1990–92, Vice Chmn, 1992.

Offices: 315 CHOB 20515, 202-225-2040. Also 3900 5th Ave., #200, San Diego 92103, 619-291-1430.

Committees: *Energy and Commerce* (23d of 27 D): Telecommunications and Finance; Transportation and Hazardous Materials. *Merchant Marine and Fisheries* (18th of 29 D): Coast Guard and Navigation; Merchant Marine; Oceanography, Gulf of Mexico and the Outer Continental Shelf.

Group Ratings and 102d Congress Votes: Newly Elected

Key Votes of the 103d Congress

1. Family Leave	FOR	2. Deficit Reduction	FOR	3. Stimulus Plan	FOR

Election Results

1992 general	Lynn Schenk (D).....................	127,280	(51%)	($1,131,021)
	Judy Jarvis (R)......................	106,170	(43%)	($433,649)
	John Wallner (LIB)..................	10,706	(4%)	($8,153)
	Two Others	4,742	(2%)	
1992 primary	Lynn Schenk (D).....................	32,303	(53%)	
	Byron Georgiou (D)	14,879	(25%)	
	Bill Winston (D).....................	6,811	(11%)	
	Carol Lucke (D).....................	4,594	(8%)	
	Other...............................	2,066	(3%)	
1990 general	Bill Lowery (R)......................	105,723	(49%)	($575,637)
(CA 41)	Dan Kripke (D)......................	93,586	(44%)	($72,261)
	Karen S. R. Works (P&F).............	15,428	(7%)	

FIFTIETH DISTRICT

San Diego, at one corner of the continental United States, not so long ago a small Navy town known for its good harbor and splendid weather, is now a major metropolis, a city of 1.1 million people and the center of a metro area of 2.5 million. It is also, and is increasingly uncomfortable about it, one of the largest cities anywhere directly on an international border, and between countries with strikingly different economic conditions, political systems and cultural traditions. Affluent San Diego typically faces the ocean or is tucked away in sunny valleys, but lower-income San Diego tends to live in grid streets south of downtown and behind the harbor, between I-5 and I-805, and in industrial National City and Chula Vista; in this zone are most of San Diego's blacks. Latinos are scattered in various parts of the city, in the southern corridor and in Encanto and Chollas Park in the east. Until the early 1980s, San Diego had relatively few Latino residents, evidently because many workers could make high U.S. wages and pay low Mexican living costs; but the 1980s boom changed that. Oddly, there are few evidences of Mexican style in San Diego, fewer even than in Los Angeles, as if the border city was insisting on its Yanqui origins, just as San Diego's civic leaders bridle at the idea of a bi-national airport on the border. Even San Diego's favorite symbol, the red Tijuana Trolley that takes tourists from downtown to the San Ysidro-Tijuana border station, is as resolutely American as Main Street in Disneyland.

The 50th Congressional District of California—the first 50th district in the nation's history—covers the southern and eastern ends of San Diego and includes National City and Chula Vista down toward the border. This district was 41% Hispanic in 1990, and in partisan terms easily the most Democratic district in the San Diego area. Yet even so, districts in this general territory ousted incumbent Democratic congressmen in 1980 and again in 1990, both times electing Republicans who after the ensuing redistricting chose to run in more heavily Republican seats farther from the central city: Duncan Hunter, who now represents the 52d District, and Duke Cunningham, who represents the 51st. It was apparent when the district lines were announced that the new member would likely be chosen in the Democratic primary, and the 1992 race attracted the yeasty cross-section of political operators one might expect in a city where there are few established political organizations or traditions.

The best-known was probably Jim Bates, the four-term Congressman beaten by Cunningham in 1990 after he was disciplined by the House on charges of sexual harassment. Bates had the additional problem of 89 overdrafts at the House bank. With the disadvantages of both incumbency and non-incumbency, he won 20% of the vote. Another well-known candidate was Wadie Deddeh, assemblyman and state senator since 1966. But Deddeh was 71 and had recently had open heart surgery; he got 23%. Juan Carlos Vargas ran primarily as the lone Latino, which was good for 19%.

The winner with 26% was Bob Filner, who had strong support from blacks; he was a Freedom Rider back in 1961 and was imprisoned in Mississippi, and in San Diego was active in civil rights and housing causes. He is hardly a newcomer to politics. A history teacher at San Diego State and director of the Lipinsky Institute for Judaic Studies, he worked on Senator Hubert Humphrey's staff in the 1970s, was elected to the San Diego school board in 1979, to the city council in 1987 and was elected deputy mayor in 1990. Filner is a natural political activist, a backer of defense spending cuts who on the council pushed through a local defense conversion plan, and worked to build more parks and improve police and fire service. During the campaign, Filner was irritated by Republican nominee Tony Valencia's pointed references to his religion before Latino audiences; these seemed, if not instances of bigotry, at least in very poor taste.

Filner won anyway 57%–29%. He was elected treasurer of the freshman class, but was dismayed when the freshmen refused to vote as a bloc on reform proposals. He got seats on Public Works and Veterans' Affairs, and much of his time will doubtless be spent on helping San Diegans adjust to defense cutbacks.

The People: Pop. 1990: 573,244; 1% rural; 8% age 65+; 32% White; 14% Black; 1% Amer. Indian; 15% Asian; 23% Other; 40% Hispanic origin. Voting age pop.: 398,117; 14% Black; 35% Hispanic origin. Households: 54% married couple families; 30% married couple fams. w. children; 44% college educ.; median household income: $27,655; per capita income: $10,577; median gross rent: $540; median house value: $136,200.

1992 Presidential Vote

Clinton (D) 69,546 (48%)
Bush (R) 42,830 (30%)
Perot (I). 30,267 (21%)

1988 Presidential Vote

Dukakis (D). 62,935 (52%)
Bush (R) 57,855 (48%)

Rep. Bob Filner (D)

Elected 1992; b. Sept. 4, 1942, Pittsburgh, PA; home, San Diego; Cornell U., B.A. 1963, U. of DE, M.A. 1969, Cornell U., Ph.D. 1973; Jewish; married (Jane).

Career: Prof., San Diego St. U., 1970-92; Legis. Asst., U.S. Sen. Hubert Humphrey, 1974; Legis. Asst., U.S. Rep. Don Fraser, 1975; San Diego Schl. Bd., 1979–83, Pres., 1982–83; San Diego City Cncl., 1987–92, Dep. Mayor, 1990.

Offices: 504 CHOB 20515, 202-225-8045. Also 333 F St., #A, Chula Vista 91910, 619-422-5963.

Committees: *Public Works and Transportation* (36th of 39 D): Economic Development; Investigations and Oversight; Water Resources and Environment. *Veterans' Affairs* (14th of 21 D): Hospitals and Health Care; Oversight and Investigations.

Group Ratings and 102d Congress Votes: Newly Elected

Key Votes of the 103d Congress

1. Family Leave	FOR	2. Deficit Reduction	FOR	3. Stimulus Plan	FOR

Election Results

1992 general	Bob Filner (D)	77,293	(57%)	($856,046)
	Tony Valencia (R)	39,531	(29%)	($69,936)
	Barbara Hutchinson (LIB)	15,489	(11%)	($19,534)
	Two Others	4,313	(3%)	
1992 primary	Bob Filner (D)	10,932	(26%)	
	Wadie P. Deddeh (D)	9,846	(23%)	
	Jim Bates (D)	8,416	(20%)	
	Juan Carlos Vargas (D)	7,868	(19%)	
	Greg Akili (D)	4,120	(10%)	
	Other	843	(2%)	
1990 election	Newly created district.			

FIFTY-FIRST DISTRICT

Back in the 1950s, when FBI Director J. Edgar Hoover came to the races at Del Mar for two weeks every summer, the rest of north San Diego County, from the track north to the Marine Corps's Camp Pendleton, was mostly uninhabited: there were a few thousand people in the beach towns of Oceanside and Carlsbad and a few thousand more scattered over the dry, brownish hills that rolled inland. Today about 650,000 people live in north San Diego County, and who can blame them? For this is one of America's most beautiful and comfortable environments, with ocean and mountain scenery, sunny and warm weather, with no rural poverty and few (so far) urban problems. Here, amid dry but not desert landscape, you can see miles of rolling hills, with occasional surrealistic trees and sagebrush-like bushes; mountains clump up not in ridges, but here and there, seemingly at random. This land has attracted thousands of new migrants, many but by no means all retirees. Outside the Los Angeles media market, not frequented by many entertainment celebrities, north county does not have a high media profile—which probably suits the quietly successful people who have moved here just fine.

For the second time in two decades, north county grew enough to earn a new congressional seat. This new 51st Congressional District of California includes some 200,000 people in San Diego itself—not in its urbanized core, but in land it annexed during Governor Pete Wilson's long tenure as mayor, including the Rancho Bernardo planned community and Miramar Naval Air Station, whose Navy fliers were made famous in *Top Gun* and infamous in the Tailhook scandal. The 51st also includes the beach communities from Del Mar north to Carlsbad, and the nearby La Costa resort. Inland, with its red-tile roofs filling a sunny valley, is fast-growing Escondido, with 108,000 people in 1990. Overwhelmingly Republican, the 51st District technically didn't have an incumbent when it was created; but soon it nearly had two, as Republicans Bill Lowery from the north side of San Diego and Randy "Duke" Cunningham from the south side, both said they were running here. Cunningham had been expected to run in the 49th District, but he had lived in the 51st before running for Congress in 1990 and knew the environment to be much more Republican than in the culturally liberal 49th, where in fact a Democrat ultimately won. Lowery had 12 years of service to Cunningham's two, but in anti-incumbent 1992 that was not necessarily a help; more relevant numbers may have been Lowery's 300 overdrafts on the House bank to Cunningham's one. Also, after Lowery had been named the number one recipient of S&L contributions in the House and the beneficiary of fundraisers held by S&L operator Donald Dixon, Lowery in 1990 beat by only 49%–44% the same candidate he had whipped 66%–31% two years earlier. In any case, in April 1992 Lowery left the race, though his name remained on the ballot and he got 15% of the vote; Cunningham was renominated with 52%.

Cunningham was a much decorated Navy pilot in Vietnam and an instructor at Miramar afterwards. Derided by the Democrats as not very bright, he is not as verbally adept as many politicians but has demonstrated under trying conditions the kind of non-verbal intelligence necessary for most tasks. In 1990 he set out to run in a district resembling the current 50th against Democratic Congressman Jim Bates, who was charged with sexual harassment. Cunningham had a tough primary against Joe Ghougassian, former U.S. Ambassador to Qatar, whom he accused of being "bankrolled by Arab oil interests"; Cunningham won 46%–30%. In the general, the charges against Bates eroded a Democratic base that in military San Diego, as elsewhere, is increasingly made up of women, and Cunningham won 46%–45%. Now he seems to have a safe seat, for at least as long as the term limits law allows his name on the ballot.

In Washington, Cunningham was something of a celebrity for his military record as Vietnam's first fighter ace, and he was watched carefully in the debate over the Gulf war resolution, which he voted for. After the war he worked with colleague Duncan Hunter to make Filipino Gulf war veterans eligible to apply for U.S. citizenship. He got a seat on the Armed Services Committee and, again with Hunter, lobbied strongly to prevent base closings in the San Diego area. He has called for stricter enforcement of immigration laws and wants a 50-foot easement on the border so property owners can't stop the government from repairing and monitoring its fences. He favors NAFTA and investment tax credits. He was one of the four congressmen who in October 1992 met with George Bush and prompted him to ask questions about Bill Clinton's student trip to Moscow and Eastern Europe, an issue which hurt the Republican ticket. He was more successful when he wrote to Mexico's President Salinas asking him to relax Mexico's strict fishing limits thereby raising the limit on U.S. sport fishermen's take.

The People: Pop. 1990: 572,850; 3% rural; 11% age 65+; 76% White; 2% Black; 1% Amer. Indian; 8% Asian; 5% Other; 13% Hispanic origin. Voting age pop.: 432,607; 2% Black; 12% Hispanic origin. Households: 61% married couple families; 28% married couple fams. w. children; 68% college educ.; median household income: $45,186; per capita income: $20,586; median gross rent: $730; median house value: $230,200.

1992 Presidential Vote

Bush (R) 108,470 (40%)
Clinton (D) 86,870 (32%)
Perot (I).................. 73,580 (27%)

1988 Presidential Vote

Bush (R) 149,926 (67%)
Dukakis (D)............... 72,889 (33%)

Rep. Randy (Duke) Cunningham (R)

Elected 1990; b. Dec. 8, 1941, Los Angeles; home, San Diego; U. of MO, B.A. 1964, M.S. 1966, National U., M.B.A. 1979; Baptist; married (Nancy).

Career: Navy, 1966–87 (Vietnam); Businessman, 1987–90.

Offices: 117 CHOB 20515, 202-225-5452. Also 613 W. Valley Pkwy., #320, Escondido 92025, 619-737-6960.

Committees: *Armed Services* (14th of 22 R): Military Acquisition; Readiness. *Education and Labor* (12th of 15 R): Elementary, Secondary and Vocational Education; Postsecondary Education and Training. *Merchant Marine and Fisheries* (10th of 19 R): Environment and Natural Resources; Merchant Marine.

Group Ratings

	ADA	ACLU	COPE	CDF	CFA	LCV	ACU	NTLC	NSI	COC	CEI
1992	5	0	17	10	13	0	96	95	100	75	82
1991	5	—	17	20	17	0	95	—	—	90	72

National Journal Ratings

	1991 LIB — 1991 CONS	1992 LIB — 1992 CONS
Economic	4% — 90%	21% — 76%
Social	0% — 84%	16% — 82%
Foreign	0% — 88%	0% — 82%

Key Votes of the 102d Congress

1. Ban Striker Replace	AGN	5. Handgun Wait/7-Day AGN	9. Use Force in Gulf	FOR
2. $ for Homeownership	FOR	6. Overseas Mil. Abortion AGN	10. US Mil. Abroad $ Cut AGN
3. Tax Rich/Cut Mid Cls. AGN		7. Obscn. Art NEA $ Ban FOR	11. Limit SDI Funds	AGN
4. FY93/$15B Def. Cut	AGN	8. Death Pen. from Jury	FOR	12. Cuba Trade Embargo FOR

Key Votes of the 103d Congress

1. Family Leave   AGN   2. Deficit Reduction   AGN   3. Stimulus Plan   AGN

Election Results

1992 general	Randy (Duke) Cunningham (R)	141,890	(56%)	($972,606)
	Bea Herbert (D)	85,148	(34%)	($23,315)
	Bill Holmes (LIB)	10,309	(4%)	
	Miriam E. Clark (P&F)	10,307	(4%)	
	Two Others	5,341	(2%)	
1992 primary	Randy (Duke) Cunningham (R)	40,645	(52%)	
	William Davis (R)	14,514	(19%)	
	Bill Lowery (R)	12,039	(15%)	
	Michael Perdue (R)	6,227	(8%)	
	Adelito M. Gale (R)	5,003	(6%)	
1990 general	Randy (Duke) Cunningham (R)	50,377	(46%)	($534,167)
(CA 44)	Jim Bates (D)	48,712	(45%)	($744,463)
	Donna White (P&F)	5,237	(5%)	
	John Wallner (LIB)	4,385	(4%)	

FIFTY-SECOND DISTRICT

San Diego began as a port, but today most of its metropolitan area residents live out of sight of the sea, in hilltop neighborhoods inland that look out over freeways in the valley and distant ridges, or in warm, sunny valleys amid the mountains which become thicker and higher as one travels east from the Pacific. There is a discernible difference in attitudes and values between those who have settled inland and those nearer the ocean, part of the coastal-inland split which became critical in California's political struggles and culture wars in the 1980s. Both groups in San Diego tend to identify as Republicans, and coastal people are if anything somewhat more affluent. But those who settle inland are more likely to be conventionally religious and to have traditional moral values; they tend to be more supportive of the military and for an assertive foreign policy; they are more dubious about the ability of government to shape poor citizens' lives. They are, in a word, more conservative on most of the cultural and foreign issues of recent times, and therefore more reliably Republican: when the voters of oceanfront affluent areas in San Diego shifted sharply toward the Democrats in 1992, those in inland suburbs were generally more faithful to the Republicans.

The 52d Congressional District of California—the highest numbered district in American history—takes in many of these inland San Diego suburbs and proceeds eastward across mountains and desert to the drained-dry Colorado River and the Arizona border. More than half its people are clustered in suburbs directly east of San Diego, off I-8 and Routes 94 and 67— Lemon Grove, La Mesa, Spring Valley, El Cajon, Santee. The rest are scattered in pockets around rural San Diego County and in the Imperial Valley, irrigated desert land where low-paid farm workers harvest some of America's most bounteous crops.

The congressman from the 52d District is Duncan Hunter, who came to the House in 1980 as a brash upset winner in the Reagan landslide and now is one of his party's leaders in the House but nonetheless has been very much on the political defensive at home. He owes his successes as well as his difficulties to the aggressiveness and impulsiveness that he showed as a veteran of helicopter combat assaults in Vietnam and as a poverty lawyer afterwards. Hunter came to Congress brash in the confidence that he had the right answers and that Republicans ought not to compromise with Democrats. On the Armed Services Committee, he was an ardent backer of the Strategic Defense Initiative and of a large Navy, and fought back in 1991 when San Diego Navy bases suddenly were in danger of appearing on shutdown lists; he has worked hard, mostly recently in 1992, to block relaxation of controls on exports of high-technology products. He has called for greater willingness to receive Vietnamese refugees and worked for U.S. citizenship for the 4,000 Filipinos who served with U.S. forces in the Persian Gulf. But he is also a strong backer of measures to crack down on illegal immigration. He backs the 10-foot steel wall being built to replace the chain link fence between San Diego and Tijuana, and he worked to use military personnel to repair border fences and improve border roads; he enacted a "return-to-sender" system, to intercept sewage flows from across the border in Tijuana and return them to Mexico before sewage can enter the Tijuana River and pollute San Diego beaches. And despite his usual support for free market economics, he is not always a free trader: he wants foreign businesses to ante up their fare share of taxes and vociferously opposes NAFTA.

Hunter's biggest wounds in 1992 were self-inflicted. He had 399 overdrafts on the House bank, totalling some $129,000—one of the most egregious records in the House. Yet at first he denied any overdrafts, then said the problem was his charitable contributions, then was reduced to sitting behind a card table for three days in front of the El Cajon courthouse with copies of his checks, ready to explain each one to voters. That fall, Hunter accompanied Bob Dornan and Duke Cunningham on their trip to the Oval Office to urge George Bush to criticize, as they had, Bill Clinton for not revealing the full facts of his trip to the Soviet Union as a student in 1969. Although Hunter did not charge Clinton with misconduct or disloyalty, the mere making of such charges in a campaign sounded like an accusation of something of that order, and was also a violation of the old trial lawyer's rule of never asking a hostile witness a question unless you already know the answer.

At the same time, Hunter was being challenged aggressively at home by Democrat Janet Gastil. A school board member in La Mesa, apple orchard owner and violist, she was neither well-known nor well-financed, but she attacked Hunter for his House overdrafts, for voting for the pay raise and against increasing the minimum wage, for his attacks on Clinton, for being supported by the religious right and for his allegedly false statements during the campaign; Hunter, in turn, sued her (to no avail) for an ad saying he'd "kited" 399 checks. Hunter, who won only 60% against two primary opponents, beat Gastil by an unimpressive 53%–41% margin; Gastil promises to run again and says Hunter is "like a sweater that has begun to unravel, and the House bank scandal was just the first thread." Meanwhile, he continues, as chairman of the Republican Research Committee, to be one of the leaders of the outnumbered Republicans in the House.

The People: Pop. 1990: 573,355; 11% rural; 11% age 65+; 71% White; 3% Black; 1% Amer. Indian; 3% Asian; 9% Other; 22% Hispanic origin. Voting age pop.: 415,404; 3% Black; 19% Hispanic origin. Households: 58% married couple families; 29% married couple fams. w. children; 52% college educ.; median household income: $33,046; per capita income: $14,075; median gross rent: $566; median house value: $155,100.

1992 Presidential Vote			1988 Presidential Vote		
Bush (R)	81,421	(37%)	Bush (R)	120,811	(65%)
Clinton (D)	74,913	(34%)	Dukakis (D)	65,488	(35%)
Perot (I)	63,176	(29%)			

Rep. Duncan Hunter (R)

Elected 1980; b. May 31, 1948, Riverside; home, Coronado; U. of MT, U. of CA, Western St. U., B.S.L & J.D. 1976; Baptist; married (Lynne).

Career: Army, 1969–71 (Vietnam); Practicing atty., 1976–80.

Offices: 133 CHOB 20515, 202-225-5672. Also 366 S. Pierce St., El Cajon 92020, 619-579-3001; and 1101 Airport Rd., #G, Imperial 92251, 619-353-5420.

Committees: *Armed Services* (3d of 22 R): Military Installations and Facilities (RMM); Research and Technology.

Group Ratings

	ADA	ACLU	COPE	CDF	CFA	LCV	ACU	NTLC	NSI	COC	CEI
1992	15	0	27	0	20	0	100	100	100	88	80
1991	5	—	27	20	33	0	100	—	—	78	80

National Journal Ratings

	1991 LIB — 1991 CONS			1992 LIB — 1992 CONS		
Economic	11%	—	89%	28%	—	70%
Social	22%	—	77%	26%	—	72%
Foreign	0%	—	88%	0%	—	82%

Key Votes of the 102d Congress

1. Ban Striker Replace AGN	5. Handgun Wait/7-Day AGN	9. Use Force in Gulf FOR
2. $ for Homeownership FOR	6. Overseas Mil. AbortionAGN	10. US Mil. Abroad $ CutAGN
3. Tax Rich/Cut Mid Cls.AGN	7. Obscn. Art NEA $ Ban FOR	11. Limit SDI Funds AGN
4. FY93/$15B Def. Cut AGN	8. Death Pen. from Jury FOR	12. Cuba Trade Embargo FOR

Key Votes of the 103d Congress

1. Family Leave AGN	2. Deficit Reduction AGN	3. Stimulus Plan AGN

Election Results

1992 general	Duncan Hunter (R)................	112,995	(53%)	($559,970)
	Janet M. Gastil (D).................	88,076	(41%)	($164,480)
	Three Others.......................	12,713	(6%)	
1992 primary	Duncan Hunter (R).................	35,681	(60%)	
	Eric Epifano (R)....................	13,604	(23%)	
	Robert E. Krysak (R)...............	10,337	(17%)	
1990 general	Duncan Hunter (R).................	123,591	(73%)	($376,408)
(CA 45)	Joe Shea (LIB).....................	46,068	(27%)	

COLORADO

Geographically distant from almost every other center of population yet in so many ways quintessentially American, stodgy and set in its ways (author John Gunther said in the 1940s) and a national trendsetter (columnist Joseph Kraft said in the 1970s), Republican mostly in its politics (though it voted for Bill Clinton in 1992) yet the home base of nationally prominent Democrats (Patricia Schroeder, Timothy Wirth, Gary Hart), Colorado is a bit of a puzzle. Think of it as a city-state: for all its expanse of Great Plains and its hundreds of snow-clad peaks, over half its people live in metropolitan Denver and four-fifths in the urban strip paralleling the Front Range, where the Rockies rise suddenly from the mile-high plateau. Colorado started off as a raucous gold-mining camp, and quickly built gaudy cities, with famous theaters not just in Denver but in remote mining towns in the mountains like Cripple Creek and Central City and Aspen and Telluride. For more than half the 20th Century, Colorado grew quietly, living off mining, cattle and farming, and military installations. Then with the giddy growth of the 1950s and 1960s the Denver skyline sprouted new buildings overlooking the Capitol's golden dome and winter sports entrepreneurs started building ski resorts and year-round mountain condominiums. Young people looking for life in a splendid environment settled where the Front Range of the Rockies rears dramatically up over the High Plains, a junction where 2.7 million of Colorado's 3.3 million people now live; for them, Colorado "represented the geography of hope," as newcomer Dick Lamm put it (he went on to be elected governor three times). These newcomers, in what seemed to be the wave of the future, repudiated civic growth-boosters by getting Coloradans in the early 1970s to reject the Winter Olympics and vote out hawkish and pro-development politicians for Vietnam war opponents and environmentalists.

Colorado in the 20 years since has become a laboratory, not only a laboratory of leftish reform but also one of rightish initiatives, a middle American commonwealth where competing visions of the future make gains and suffer setbacks. The antiwar liberals had great success, electing Schroeder and Wirth to the House, Hart to the Senate, and Lamm governor in 1972 and 1974. But their fortunes fell as Republicans took over the legislature in 1976 and a Senate seat in 1978, and Colorado partook thirstily of the gushings of the energy boom of 1974–82. Then came the energy bust, leaving many new soulless Denver skyscrapers empty and oil operators and lenders busted—notably Silverado Savings and Loan, whose demise touched board member and presidential son Neil Bush. Other Colorado businesses encountered trouble: Manville, the state's second biggest company, was tied down by asbestos litigation; the government's plutonium plant at Rocky Flats just north of Denver was shut down in 1989 for numerous safety violations and has ceased any further production of plutonium. Both liberals and conservatives were forced to backtrack. As the anti-Olympics crusaders of the 1970s saw the Los Angeles Olympics of 1984 become a focus of national attention and pride and a local money-maker, Denver played catch-up ball, planning a new convention center, baseball stadium and giant airport and even made a bid for the 1996 Olympics—the kind of boosterish projects they had derided a dozen years before. Free market operators were called on to defend the sleazy operations of outfits like Silverado, which lavished money on its owners with the outcome that the taxpayers would have to pick up the bill.

If Colorado was chastened by the economic shakedown in the late 1980s, by the early 1990s it seemed frisky again and ready for reform—of various kinds. In 1990, for starters, it voted solidly for 12-year term limits, not just on state legislators, but also for the first time in the nation on members of Congress—14 other states followed suit on term limits in 1992. It also voted to allow gambling in old mining towns, with proceeds to go for their historic preservation. In the 1992 primary season, Colorado seemed downright rebellious. Its Democratic primary voters, tilted heavily upscale (45% college graduates) and toward the baby boomers (37% were age 30 to 44), gave Jerry Brown a plurality in early March, and even though he drained off some upscale votes, Paul Tsongas got just about as many votes as Bill Clinton. Meanwhile, one in three Republican primary voters were already willing to vote against George Bush and for Pat Buchanan who never even campaigned in the state. Bush's weakness became even more apparent when Ross Perot entered the race. Colorado was one of Perot's best states in his first campaign; he had a spirited volunteer organization here and seemed to be well ahead of both Bush and Clinton in the state when he left the race July 16.

Over the summer, the chief political action in Colorado was in the Senate primary, made possible by Tim Wirth's surprise retirement. The Republican nomination was clinched by Terry Considine, a former state senator who had started the term limits initiative. The Democratic nomination was fiercely contested. Josie Heath, the nominee two years before against Hank Brown, could not win much support, but she took liberal votes away from Dick Lamm, running on his environmental and restrict-immigration credentials. The winner was Congressman Ben Nighthorse Campbell, part Indian, part-time jewelry-maker, from the Western Slope (i.e., west of the Front Range and not in the "granola belt" of trendy ski resorts). That made for a spirited Senate race, which Campbell won after some ructions. But Considine and conservatives were successful on another referendum, requiring voter approval for state tax increases. Voters also rejected both Democratic Governor Roy Romer's and conservatives' education proposals (Romer wanted more taxes, the conservatives were for school choice).

Much national attention was paid when Colorado voted 53%–47% for Measure 2, which rescinded any state or local ordinances banning discrimination against gays. It was a hot issue: former Republican Senator Bill Armstrong and University of Colorado football coach Bill McCartney issued fiery statements for it; proponents ran TV ads showing graphic sex, while opponents ran TV ads showing parents of gays asking for tolerance—an interesting contrast. The issue sparked a national boycott against Colorado by various organizations, even though the people most directly hurt—in Denver, resorts like Aspen, the university town of Boulder—all voted against Measure 2, as did the Denver metro area as a whole. Nor is it clear that the result signalled anti-gay feeling; many voters said they were just against special treatment or quotas, and in fact a tougher and clearly anti-gay initiative was rejected by voters in the culturally very similar state of Oregon. The tone of daily life in Colorado is friendly; people have the westerner's tolerance of individuality; but there are evidently limits on how far Coloradans will ratify the

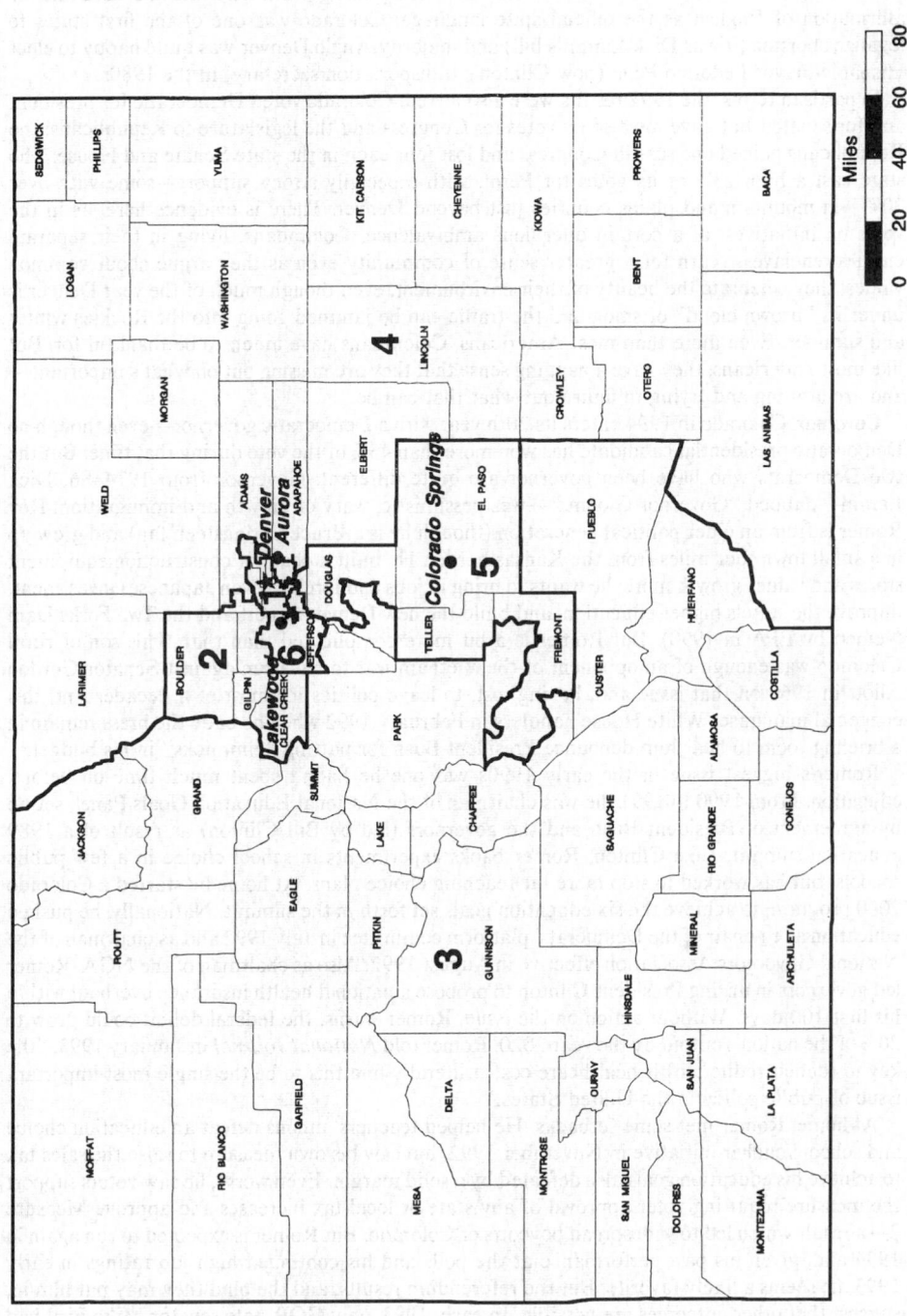

SEDGWICK

PHILLIPS

YUMA

KIT CARSON

CHEYENNE

KIOWA

PROWERS

BACA

LOGAN

WASHINGTON

LINCOLN

4

BENT

LARIMER

WELD

MORGAN

ADAMS

Denver

Aurora

ARAPAHOE

ELBERT

EL PASO

Colorado Springs

5

CROWLEY

OTERO

LAS ANIMAS

BOULDER

2

GILPIN

Lakewood

CLEAR CREEK

DOUGLAS

6

JEFFERSON

TELLER

PUEBLO

HUERFANO

PARK

FREMONT

CUSTER

COSTILLA

JACKSON

GRAND

SUMMIT

LAKE

CHAFFEE

SAGUACHE

ALAMOSA

RIO GRANDE

CONEJOS

ROUTT

EAGLE

PITKIN

GUNNISON

3

HINSDALE

MINERAL

ARCHULETA

MOFFAT

RIO BLANCO

GARFIELD

DELTA

OURAY

SAN JUAN

LA PLATA

MESA

MONTROSE

SAN MIGUEL

DOLORES

MONTEZUMA

Miles

0   20   40   60   80

cultural liberalism which thrives in much of the state. If Measure 2 seemed a failure, so by a larger margin four years before was Coloradans' vote against government-paid abortions and for affirmation of English as the official state language. Colorado was one of the first states to legalize abortion (it was Dick Lamm's bill) and majority-Anglo Denver was quite happy to elect Hispanic mayor Federico Pena (now Clinton's transportation secretary) in the 1980s.

In partisan terms, the 1992 results were also mixed: Colorado voted Democratic for president and for senator, but gave most of its votes for Congress and the legislature to Republicans; the Republicans gained one seat in Congress and lost four each in the state Senate and House. The state cast a high 23% of its votes for Perot, with especially strong support—some with over 30%—in mountain and plains counties just beyond Denver. There is evidence here, as in the votes on initiatives, of a certain querulous ambivalence. Coloradans, living in their separate cultural enclaves, yearn for a greater sense of community even as they argue about common values; they celebrate the beauty of their environment, even though much of the year Denver is under its "brown cloud" of smog and the traffic can be jammed going into the Rockies winter and summer. Even more than most Americans, Coloradans have much to be thankful for. But like most Americans, they have a nagging sense that they are missing out on what's important—and are arguing and trying to figure out what that can be.

Governor. Colorado in 1994 enters its 20th year with a Democratic governor—even though no Democratic presidential candidate has won more than 45% of the vote during that time. But the two Democrats who have been governor are quite different. Governor from 1974–86, Dick Lamm—dubbed "Governor Gloom,"—was pessimistic, wary of growth and immigration. Roy Romer is from an older political generation (though he is a Bruce Springsteen fan) and grew up in a small town four miles from the Kansas border. He built a chain of construction equipment stores and values growth more: he wants to bring in jobs and foreign (even Japanese) investment, improve the state's higher education, and build the new Denver airport and the Two Forks Dam (vetoed by EPA in 1990). But Romer is a bit more complicated than that. This son of rural Colorado was enough of an opponent of the Vietnam war to have run against Senator Gordon Allott in 1966 on that issue and, having lost, to leave politics for most of a decade. And this congenial man upset White House handlers in February 1992 when he bade the press remain in a briefing room to hear him denounce President Bush for putting "gimmicks" in his budget.

Romer's biggest issue in the early 1990s was one he hadn't spent much time on before: education. From 1990 to 1991, he was chairman of the National Education Goals Panel, set up by agreement of President Bush and the governors (led by Bill Clinton) as result of a 1989 education summit. Like Clinton, Romer backs experiments in school choice in a few public schools, but has worked to stop more far-reaching choice plans. At home he started a Colorado 2000 program, to achieve the six education goals set forth in the summit. Nationally, he pushed education as co-chair of the Democrats' platform committee in July 1992 and as chairman of the National Governors Association effective in August 1992. Also as chairman of the NGA, Romer led governors in urging President Clinton to propose a national health insurance overhaul within his first 100 days. Without action on the issue, Romer warns, the federal deficit could grow to 20% of the nation's output by the year 2020. Romer told *National Journal* in January 1993, "the key to [deficit reduction] is healthcare cost. I literally find this to be the single most important issue of public policy in the United States."

At home, Romer met some setbacks. He helped teachers' unions defeat an education choice and school voucher initiative in November 1992, but saw his own measure to raise the sales tax to achieve his education goals also defeated by a solid margin. Even worse, he saw voters support the measure requiring voter approval of any state or local tax increases and approve Measure 2—a result which led to widespread boycotts of Colorado. But Romer is expected to run again in 1994 and, given his past performance at the polls and his continued high job ratings in early 1993, he seems a likely favorite. But the referendum results, and the bind they may put him in, suggest that other outcomes are possible. In early 1993, only GOP state senator Mike Bird had declared his intention to run.

Senators. Hank Brown, the Republican who in two years became Colorado's senior senator thanks to Tim Wirth's unexpected retirement (while Ernest Hollings and Bob Packwood remain junior senators after 26 and 24 years), has the reputation of a practical-minded moderate; but he can also be a tough partisan and has a voting record which is in no danger of being confused for Democratic. He seems quiet yet has excelled in many ways. At the University of Colorado he was a star football player and student body president. He was a Naval aviator and served in Vietnam. After law school, he went to work for Monfort of Colorado, the world's largest cattle feeding operation; Ken Monfort, its head, was an antiwar Democrat at the time. Brown served four years in the Colorado Senate and was elected to Congress in 1980. There he was pro-choice on abortion and sponsored the first wild and scenic river designation for the Cache La Poudre River—not the record of other Colorado Republicans. But he was a sharp critic, on the Ways and Means Committee, of the Democrats' welfare reform package in 1987–88, and got the House to endorse instead the workfare measure that became law; he argued strongly for allowing recipients to take low-paying jobs and he fought hard against efforts to insulate even two-parent families from a work requirement. He was part of the House Ethics Committee that took on Speaker Jim Wright, and was a leader in urging that Congress be covered by the civil rights and labor laws it imposes on others. When Senator Bill Armstrong announced his surprise retirement, Brown clinched the Republican nomination quickly. The upset winner of the Democratic nomination, former Boulder County Commissioner Josie Heath, looked like an attractive candidate. But she turned out to be one of the few 1990 political casualties of the Gulf war; her loud advocacy of a 50% cut in the defense budget rang false when Saddam Hussein invaded Kuwait and hundreds of thousands of American troops were sent to the Gulf. Brown won by a solid 56%–42% margin.

In the Senate, Brown was again not as confrontational as many Republicans. In May 1991 he agreed with Tim Wirth on a 630,000 acre Colorado wilderness bill, blocked for years by Bill Armstrong. He also passed a bill he'd backed since 1981 making the Rocky Mountain Arsenal a national wildlife refuge. Another significant Brown accomplishment was a law to encourage Soviet nuclear scientists to emigrate to the United States, to stop nuclear proliferation. Brown also played a major role in prominent hearings. He was probably the least partisan Republican in the Judiciary Committee hearings on Clarence Thomas; he asked Anita Hill whether she disagreed with Thomas on *Roe v. Wade*, a question Chairman Joseph Biden ruled out of order. As ranking Republican on the committee investigating the BCCI scandal and questioning Clark Clifford, Brown got on amicably with Chairman John Kerry.

But Brown retains his partisan edge. He seems appalled by the level of federal spending and shocked Appropriations Chairman Robert Byrd when he called the Congress and the Appropriations Committee the most irresponsible in history. He has introduced "porkbuster" bills calling for as much as $1.5 billion in cuts; once he and Congressman Joel Hefley appeared publicly with a couple of squealing pigs to make their point. Brown was one of the first to offer an alternative to the Clinton economic plan; his March 1993 proposal would plan to significantly reduce the federal deficit over 5 years without the need of an income tax increase. Brown's seat is up in 1996; from this far vantage point, he seems to have an excellent chance of reelection.

One of the biggest surprises of the 1991–92 campaign cycle was Senator Tim Wirth's announcement in April 1992 that he wouldn't seek a second term. First elected to the House in 1974, Wirth had been an important legislator for almost two decades—a leader of the 1974 Watergate-year freshman Democrats, chairman not so long after of the Energy and Commerce subcommittee regulating telecommunications and the securities industry, the leader with Al Gore in the Senate of those urging action to counter what they argued was global warming. Wirth seemed weary, perhaps because of the time demands of being a major legislator and tending to an always potentially marginal constituency, out of sadness at the death of his longtime friend John Heinz in April 1991, or even out of the gridlock caused by partisan parrying and Senate rules. In early 1993, Wirth was nominated to be undersecretary of State for global affairs after being passed over as secretary of Energy, a post many figured was his after serving as co-chair of the Clinton campaign for much of 1992.

Before Wirth retired, Terry Considine, former state Senator, successful entrepreneur, and promoter of the 1990 term limits initiative, was already running a serious campaign for the seat, though he'd been injured in a September 1991 riding accident. After Wirth's withdrawal, the race became really wild, with a Republican convention contest, a Democratic primary fight, and a seriously contested general election. Considine won the Republican nomination in May with 53%. The Democratic convention was split: 38% for Western Slope Congressman Ben Nighthorse Campbell, 37% for former Governor Dick Lamm, and 25% for Josie Heath. Lamm started off as the best known, but not necessarily favorably: his alarm at population growth, which led him to pioneer abortion rights and environmental issues in the 1960s and 1970s, also led him in 1984 to say that the terminally ill have "a duty to die" rather than pursue elaborate medical treatment. His support of the English language referendum and a book he wrote which opposed further immigration, produced vocal opposition from Hispanic leaders, while one columnist said his comments on the Japanese were subtly reminiscent of "the yellow peril." Lamm attracted some positive attention when he signed the "Lead or Leave" promise to halve the deficit in one term or retire. But his talk about meeting "public needs with evermore limited resources" had a false ring to many at a time when they were more interested in increasing resources than in imposing limits. Heath campaigned largely on her gender, running against a "sea of suits"; her most interesting plank was a National Community Service Corps. But she did not arouse the support her competitors did and was attacked for her millionaire status.

Campbell was a consultant's dream, an interesting candidate (though his temperament made him a consultant's nightmare at times). He is an Indian—only the eighth ever to serve in Congress—of the North Cheyenne tribe, and attends tribal ceremonies every year in Montana. He was captain of the 1964 U.S. Olympic judo team. He was co-grand marshal of the 1992 Rose Bowl parade, called in amid cries that Columbus had massacred the Indians. He wears bolo ties and has his hair in a pony tail; on ceremonial occasions (notably at the 1993 Presidential Inaugural Parade), he rides his horse wearing full Indian headdress. He has taken up Indian causes, passing a law requiring that Indian-labelled arts and crafts must have been made by federally recognized American Indians and trying to rename the Custer Battlefield Monument as Little Big Horn. He had a rough early life, dropping out of high school and joining the Air Force; eventually he built a successful jewelry-making business (he is irked that ethics specialists say he can't have an exemption from congressional income limits on this, as writers in Congress can from book royalties). With a base in the non-trendy Western Slope, he is a moderate Democrat, voting for the Gulf war resolution, winning only a 44% rating from the League of Conservation Voters. He favors term limits and backed the 1990 referendum with a promise to serve no more than four House terms (1992 would have been his last House race) and no more than two in the Senate. Campbell ended up losing Denver and the affluent suburbs of Arapahoe and Jefferson Counties and the granola belt ski counties to Lamm, but not by wide margins. But he carried 54 of 63 counties, and won with 45% to 36% for Lamm and 18% for Heath.

Any other Democrat probably would have lost and all ran much weaker than Campbell in polls. Considine ran an intellectually coherent campaign for reform—of education, taxes, spending, the political process—and he gained steadily in the polls. He hit Campbell for accepting an oil company's plane ride to Alaska (but Campbell disclosed his record of votes unfavorable to oil interests) and for opposing special prosecutors for Congress. The *Rocky Mountain News* reported that Campbell's literature falsely stated he was trapped behind enemy lines for five weeks in Korea; Campbell said the error occurred because his mother was unable to find him for five weeks. But Campbell wasn't the target Considine had expected in Wirth and would have gotten with Lamm or Heath. He was for term limits, favored a capital gains tax cut, was not an extreme environmentalist, and he hardly looked the insider; and he could turn the one liberal issue that clearly worked in Colorado, abortion, against Considine. While complaining about negative campaigning, Campbell was not averse to indulging in it. He attacked Considine because of his indirect ties to the failed Silverado S&L, thought several newspapers pointed out that Considine had done nothing wrong, and for receiving a draft deferment during the Vietnam war (Considine had lower back problems, which were confirmed after his 1991 riding accident). In the end, Campbell won by 55%–45%; it may have helped that the very active Colorado Perot organization endorsed Campbell.

Presidential politics. For three decades, Colorado was not seriously contested in presidential races; it was enough more Republican than the rest of the country that it was in no position to make a difference. Not so now. It was close to the national average in 1988 and was seriously contested enough in 1992 to produce a Democratic victory for the first time since 1964. Both presidential campaigns filled the air with ads—sharing it with Campbell and Considine, various congressional candidates, and proponents and opponents of school choice, gay rights, and tax limits: a rich diet for political junkies. George Bush, Dan Quayle, Bill Clinton, and Al Gore were in Colorado, not just touching down in Stapleton but around the state, almost constantly. Colorado will likely be courted this way in future close contests; it is just different enough, quirky and ready to embrace the latest reform of left or right, to require the individual attention of candidates who want its 8 electoral votes.

Colorado's first ever presidential primaries, as noted, produced victories for Jerry Brown and George Bush, though Pat Buchanan got 30% despite never campaigning in the state.

Congressional districting. For the first time in three decades, Colorado did not gain a House seat out of the decennial census; population growth sagged following the 1980s energy price collapse, and Arizona passed Colorado to become the most populous Mountain state. Governor Roy Romer vetoed two redistricting plans passed by the Republican legislature; then in March 1992, under pressure from a court-appointed master's plan, Romer and the legislature agreed on a plan that didn't greatly change the character of the state's six districts. But the Republicans did end up picking up a seat, the Western Slope 3d District vacated by Ben Campbell when he ran for Senate. The state legislature itself was redistricted by an 11-member commission controlled by Democrats, and they proceeded to gain four seats in both houses, though they're still short of control in each.

The People: Est. Pop. 1992: 3,470,000; Pop. 1990: 3,294,394, up 5.1% 1990–1992. 1.3% of U.S. total, 26th largest; 18% rural. Median age: 32.5 years. 10.0% 65 years and over. 88.0% White, 12.9% Hispanic origin, 4.0% Black, 1.8% Asian, 5.1% Other. Households: 53.8% married couple families; 27% married couple fams. w. children; 58% college educ.; median household income: $30,140; per capita income: $14,821; 62.2% owner occupied housing; median house value: 82,700; median monthly rent: $362. 5.9% Unemployment. Voting age pop.: 2,433,128. Registered voters (1992): 2,003,375; 680,773 D (34%), 668,051 R (33%), 654,551 unaffiliated and minor parties (33%).

Political Lineup: Governor, Roy Romer (D); Lt. Gov., C. Michael Callihan (D); Secy. of State, Natalie Meyer (R); Atty. Gen., Gale A. Norton (R); Treasurer, Gail Schoettler (D). State Senate, 35 (19 R and 16 D); State House of Representatives, 65 (34 R and 31 D). Senators, Hank Brown (R) and Ben Nighthorse Campbell (D). Representatives, 6 (4 R and 2 D).

1992 Presidential Vote

Clinton (D)	629,681	(40%)
Bush (R)	562,850	(36%)
Perot (I)	366,010	(23%)

1992 Democratic Presidential Primary

Brown	69,073	(29%)
Clinton	64,470	(27%)
Tsongas	61,360	(26%)
Kerrey	29,572	(12%)
Other	9,812	(4%)

1988 Presidential Vote

Bush (R)	728,155	(53%)
Dukakis (D)	621,453	(45%)

1992 Republican Presidential Primary

Bush	132,100	(68%)
Buchanan	58,753	(30%)

GOVERNOR

Gov. Roy Romer (D)

Elected 1986, term expires Jan. 1995; b. Oct. 31, 1928, Garden City, KS; home, Denver; CO St. U., B.S. 1950, U. of CO, LL.B. 1952, Yale, 1954; Presbyterian; married (Bea).

Career: Air Force, 1952–53; CO House of Reps., 1958–62; CO Senate, 1962–1966, Asst. Minority Ldr., 1964–66; Practicing atty., businessman, 1966–75; CO Ag. Commissioner, 1975; Chief of Staff, Gov. Richard D. Lamm, 1975–1977, 1982–1983; CO Treasurer, 1977–1986.

Offices: 136 State Capitol, Denver 80203, 303-866-2471.

Election Results

1990 gen.	Roy Romer (D)	626,032	(64%)
	John Andrews (R)	358,403	(36%)
1990 prim.	Roy Romer (D), unopposed		
1986 gen.	Roy Romer (D)	616,325	(58%)
	Ted Strickland (R)	434,420	(41%)

SENATORS

Sen. Hank Brown (R)

Elected 1990, seat up 1996; b. Feb. 12, 1940, Denver; home, Greeley; U. of CO, B.S. 1961, J.D. 1969; George Washington U., LL.M. 1986; C.P.A. accreditation, 1988; Congregationalist; married (Nan).

Career: Navy, 1962–66 (Vietnam); Accountant, 1968–69; Vice Pres., Monfort of CO, Inc., 1969–80; CO Senate, 1972–76, Asst. Majority Ldr., 1974–76; Greeley City Plng. Comm., 1979; U.S. House of Reps., 1980–90.

Offices: 716 HSOB 20510, 202-224-5941. Also 1200 17th St., #2727, Denver 80202, 303-844-2600; 1100 10th St., #201, Greeley 80631, 303-352-4112; 288 N. Cascade, #106, Colorado Springs 80903, 719-634-6071; 411 Thatcher Bldg., 5th and Main Sts., Pueblo 81003, 719-545-9751; and 215 Fed. Bldg., 400 Road Ave., Grand Junction 81501, 303-245-9553.

Committees: *Budget* (7th of 9 R). *Foreign Relations* (6th of 8 R): European Affairs; International Economic Policy, Trade, Oceans and Environment; Near Eastern and South Asian Affairs (RMM). *Judiciary* (6th of 8 R): Constitution (RMM); Patents, Copyrights and Trademarks.

Group Ratings

	ADA	ACLU	CDF	COPE	CFA	LCV	ACU	NTLC	NSI	COC	CEI
1992	20	23	0	25	17	0	89	94	80	100	88
1991	10	—	27	17	28	36	90	—	—	80	76

National Journal Ratings

	1991 LIB — 1991 CONS			1992 LIB — 1992 CONS		
Economic	25%	—	73%	0%	—	89%
Social	31%	—	66%	22%	—	76%
Foreign	27%	—	67%	37%	—	60%

Key Votes of the 102d Congress

1. $ for Homeownership AGN	5. Clarence Thomas Nom. FOR	9. Use Force in Gulf FOR
2. Have Cap Gains Debate FOR	6. Lmt Death Row Appeal FOR	10. Keep Salvador Aid FOR
3. Remove Budget Walls AGN	7. Handgun Wait/5-Day AGN	11. Cut $1B from SDI AGN
4. Ban Striker Replace AGN	8. Abortion Gag Rule AGN	12. Override China MFN FOR

Key Votes of the 103d Congress

1. Family Leave AGN	2. HIV Immigrants AGN	3. Clinton Budget AGN

Election Results

1990 general	Hank Brown (R)	569,048	(56%)	($3,684,020)
	Josie Heath (D)	425,746	(42%)	($1,943,422)
	Two Others	27,233	(3%)	
1990 primary	Hank Brown (R), unopposed			
1984 general	William L. Armstrong (R)	833,821	(64%)	($3,098,129)
	Nancy Dick (D)	449,327	(35%)	($840,595)

Sen. Ben Nighthorse Campbell (D)

Elected 1992, seat up 1998; b. Apr. 13, 1933, Auburn, CA; home, Ignacio; San Jose St. U., B.A. 1957, Meiji U., Japan, 1960–64; no religious affiliation; married (Linda).

Career: Air Force, 1951–53 (Korea); Rancher, horse trainer, jewelry designer; CO House of Reps., 1982–86; U.S. House of Reps, 1987–92.

Offices: 380 RSOB 20510, 202-224-5852. Also 1129 Pennsylvania St., Denver 80203, 303-866-1900; 720 N. Main St., #210, Pueblo 81003, 719-542-6987; 105 E. Vermijo, #600, Colorado Springs 80903, 719-636-9092; 145 Grand Ave., Grand Junction 81501, 303-241-6631; 835 2nd Ave., #228, Durango 81301, 303-247-1609; and 19 Old Town Sq, #238, Ft. Collins 80524, 303-224-1909.

Committees: *Banking, Housing and Urban Affairs* (9th of 11 D): Economic Stabilization and Rural Development; International Finance and Monetary Policy. *Energy and Natural Resources* (9th of 11 D): Mineral Resources Development and Production; Public Lands, National Parks and Forests (Vice Chmn.); Water and Power. *Indian Affairs* (10th of 10 D). *Veterans' Affairs* (7th of 7 D).

Group Ratings (as Member of the U.S. House of Representatives)

	ADA	ACLU	CDF	COPE	CFA	LCV	ACU	NTLC	NSI	COC	CEI
1992	55	72	90	71	53	44	38	11	70	43	32
1991	55	—	40	92	50	38	45	—	—	40	19

National Journal Ratings (as Member of the U.S. House of Representatives)

	1991 LIB	—	1991 CONS	1992 LIB	—	1992 CONS
Economic	58%	—	41%	47%	—	53%
Social	57%	—	42%	64%	—	35%
Foreign	50%	—	50%	60%	—	39%

Key Votes of the 102d Congress (as Member of the U.S. House of Representatives)

1. Ban Striker Replace	FOR	5. Handgun Wait/7-Day AGN	9. Use Force in Gulf FOR
2. $ for Homeownership	*	6. Overseas Mil. Abortion FOR	10. US Mil. Abroad $ Cut FOR
3. Tax Rich/Cut Mid Cls. FOR		7. Obscn. Art NEA $ Ban FOR	11. Limit SDI Funds AGN
4. FY93/$15B Def. Cut AGN		8. Death Pen. from Jury FOR	12. Cuba Trade Embargo *

Key Votes of the 103d Congress

1. Family Leave   FOR   2. HIV Immigrants   AGN   3. Clinton Budget   FOR

Election Results

1992 general	Ben Nighthorse Campbell (D)	803,725	(52%)	($1,561,347)
	Terry Considine (R)	662,893	(43%)	($2,215,791)
	Four Others.........................	85,671	(6%)	
1992 primary	Ben Nighthorse Campbell (D)	117,634	(46%)	
	Richard D. Lamm (D)	93,599	(36%)	
	Josie Heath (D).......................	47,418	(18%)	
1986 general	Timothy E. Wirth (D).................	529,449	(50%)	($3,787,202)
	Ken Kramer (R)......................	512,994	(48%)	($3,785,577)

FIRST DISTRICT

One mile above sea level (as the plaque on the 14th step of the gold-domed Capitol reads), a few miles from where the High Plains yield to the sharp peaks of the Front Range of the Rockies, on no historic trade route and with a fresh water supply adequate for a town one-tenth of its size, sits the great metropolitan center of Denver. With 1.6 million people, it has been the economic and cultural capital for 100 years of the whole Rocky Mountain region that author Joel Garreau called "the Empty Quarter." Denver has a Western air; it hosts the National Western Stock Show every year, and not long ago the May D&F store led a 2,500-pound bull through its china department. But it is not roughneck. Its neat grid of streets, slanted on a 45-degree angle downtown to align with the South Platte River and the railroad lines next to it, its array of parks, the trees which line so many of its streets and are a lush contrast with the sere landscape of the high plains and the Rockies—all these give Denver a burnished, sedate air, despite the unembellished skyscrapers of the 1974–81 energy boom. Most recent growth has been in the suburbs, where three-quarters of the metro area's people now live, but the central city of Denver, though it has its problems, seems to have the yeasty diversity of a central city with little of the social pathology that usually comes with it. The black neighborhoods of northeastern Denver are filled with well maintained 1950s bungalows; the Hispanic quarter northwest of downtown has vitality and sends residents on to upward mobility; gentrified areas south of the Capitol include the elegant elite neighborhood where the Tattered Cover, probably the nation's largest book store, sits opposite posh Cherry Creek Shopping Center. Denver, though it remains majority white Anglo, elected Federico Pena mayor twice in the 1980s; in 1991 it chose between two black candidates, passing over favored District Attorney Norman Early for City Auditor Wellington Webb who, out of funds, campaigned for 41 days without going home or getting into an automobile, walking the streets and staying at homes of supporters.

Denver was skeptical about growth in the early 1970s, when the liberal baby boomers who flocked into politics there assumed economic growth would go on forever; but after the 1980s energy boom collapsed, Denver became boosterish again. Pena built a new convention center downtown and fought against United and Continental, entrenched at Stapleton, to build the new airport 25 miles northeast of downtown; the first plane is scheduled to take off in December 1993 and Stapleton will close shortly afterwards.

Long coterminous with the city of Denver, the 1st Congressional District of Colorado had to spread out to the suburbs to meet the population standard. It now extends northeast toward the new airport, taking in Commerce City and the northern part of Aurora, places with warehouses and trucking terminals on main streets and curved-street subdivisions behind. The 1st remains a heavily Democratic district, including most of metro Denver's blacks and Hispanics, and also many of its singles and gays: the percentage of households with married couples and children is among the lowest in America. In an era when cultural attitudes are a better clue to voting behavior than economic status, this has kept Denver politically liberal since the early 1970s, voting not only for Bill Clinton and Ben Campbell in 1992, but also voting strongly against anti-gay rights Measure 2.

For 20 years, the 1st District has elected Congresswoman Patricia Schroeder, who first ran in 1972 against an incumbent Republican and who is now one of the leading liberal politicians of America. Schroeder sees herself less as a liberal than as part of the vibrant Old West history of skepticism about tradition and authority figures; in Washington, however, and around the country where she has become one of the best-known House members, she is a symbol of feminism and liberalism—a kind of authority figure herself. She still has the breezy air of a midwesterner, the daughter of an aviation insurance adjuster who got his pilot's license and worked her way through school with her own flying service. Her gift for the pithy phrase, unequalled in today's politics—it was she who called Ronald Reagan the "Teflon President"—and her often flip demeanor has put people off and have led some to underestimate her. But she remains an influential officeholder and opinion leader.

Several intellectual strains run clearly through Schroeder's career. One is dovishness. Her candidacy originated when a group of anti-Vietnam war activists caucused in a living room and came up with the then unusual idea of running a woman. Her first act in Washington, getting a seat on the Armed Services Committee over the objections of then-Chairman Edward Hebert, was a sensation (and a harbinger: two years later, Hebert was voted out of the chair). Predictably, she opposed extension of U.S. military power from Vietnam to the Gulf war. "Those certainly aren't my democracies," she said in August 1990. "They aren't big on human rights, for women anyway, or for anybody who doesn't agree with the monarchy." Another thread running through Schroeder's career is thriftiness. She has called for years for greater military burden-sharing by our allies, and has pushed dual-basing—keeping more U.S. troops at domestic bases and ferrying them to South Korea, Japan or Europe if needed; in less elevated tones, she urged colleagues to scuttle foreign bases so they can be sure to save "Camp Swampy" at home. But her cost-consciousness extends across the board and she also votes against many domestic spending bills.

Schroeder has also been persistent in thrusting women's issues forward: she was an early supporter of legalized abortion, and the lead sponsor of the 1992 family and medical leave bill George Bush vetoed and Bill Clinton eventually signed. She has worked hard to get more Democratic women to run for Congress, and to get them elected; one obstacle, up until 1992 anyway, has been that almost no women with young children have been willing to run, as Schroeder did in 1972 (when she thought she wouldn't win). She chaired the Select Committee on Children, Youth and Families, which along with the other select committees was axed in budgetary moves in 1993. Another Schroeder theme is using legal rights and requirements to reshape society: she has supported the Equal Rights Amendment, the Civil Rights Restoration Act, the Freedom of Choice Act. On Post Office and Civil Service she championed whistle-blowers, wanted due process for employees accused of misdeeds and pushed for in-house grievance mechanisms, even on Capitol Hill.

One last apparent strain is her work on Armed Forces: a drive to civilianize the military. Early on, she interested herself in the situation of military families and in the wives of servicemen, passing her Military Family Act in 1985. She has pushed, unsuccessfully until 1993, to allow abortions performed in military hospitals. In 1991 she got the Armed Services Committee to vote to allow women in the military fly combat missions. She has strongly denounced sexual harassment in the military—especially the Tailhook incident; she maintained an icy dignity on reports of military officers' telling dirty jokes about her. She has argued for an end to barring gays from the military. To the Joint Chiefs of Staff she argued that the standards of civilian personnel law should be applied to the military. There are, of course, arguments on both sides here. Most professional military officers argue that military discipline needs to be tighter than in civilian life to build the combat spirit and unit cohesion needed to achieve victory and minimize American casualties. On Schroeder's side it can be said that the most competent American military forces—in World War II—in important ways embodied the values and patterns of the civilian culture of their time; George Marshall and Dwight Eisenhower wanted not a martinet's military but one that partook of the friendly, ordinary-guy atmosphere preserved in the movies of the 1930s and 1940s. Schroeder nicely summarized her thinking when she hailed the 1992 election results as an "American perestroika" that would "restructure government so that it is thoughtful, practical, cost-efficient and people-friendly."

Schroeder is the senior woman in the 103d Congress, always quotable, and likely to be a center of feminist activism: a serious force in Bill Clinton's Washington. She is also, with Les Aspin's elevation to the Pentagon, the number three Democrat on Armed Services, and has a special claim on Aspin's sympathies: she gave him key support when he was nearly booted out of the Armed Services chairmanship in early 1987. She keeps her hand in Colorado politics; she was aggressive in 1990, for instance, in urging a tough approach to the Silverado S&L scandal, arguing for special prosecutors because the U.S. Attorney had received political contributions from Silverado principals and because Neil Bush was on the Silverado board. Schroeder was, briefly, a presidential candidate in 1988. She chaired Gary Hart's campaign until it ended abruptly (ever the family person, she was furious with him); then she was asked to run herself. For three months beginning June 1987, she traveled the country, raised some $787,000, and watched herself rise in the polls to third in a field of unknowns. Then in September 1987, she appeared before supporters in Denver and, choking back a few tears, announced she wouldn't run. "Tears signify compassion, not weakness," she said later—no false male stoicism—but Schroeder did not run again in 1992, even when Democrats were casting about rather desperately for a candidate, and she seems unlikely to run in the future.

In the 1st District, Schroeder still has detractors, but far more supporters. The expansion of the 1st District out into the suburbs didn't hurt her significantly in 1992. The longer-term question is whether Colorado's term limits, passed by the voters in 1990, will be effective in barring her from running in 2002. Breezily, she notes that she will be 62 then, and who knows if she'll want to run? But then who thought in 1972 that this 11-term Congresswoman would win two terms or even one?

The People: Pop. 1990: 549,053; 13% age 65+; 62% White; 13% Black; 1% Amer. Indian; 2% Asian; 10% Other; 22% Hispanic origin. Voting age pop.: 424,850; 11% Black; 18% Hispanic origin. Households: 39% married couple families; 16% married couple fams. w. children; 54% college educ.; median household income: $24,870; per capita income: $14,942; median gross rent: $382; median house value: $74,900.

1992 Presidential Vote

Clinton (D)   135,016   (55%)
Bush (R)   63,283   (26%)
Perot (I).   43,245   (18%)

1988 Presidential Vote

Dukakis (D).   142,535   (61%)
Bush (R)   91,405   (39%)

Rep. Patricia Schroeder (D)

Elected 1972; b. Jul. 30, 1940, Portland, OR; home, Denver; U. of MN, B.A. 1961, Harvard, J.D. 1964; United Church of Christ; married (James).

Career: Field Atty., Natl. Labor Relations Bd., 1964–66; Practicing atty.; Lecturer, Law prof., Commun. Col. of Denver, 1969–70, U. of Denver, Denver Ctr., 1969, Regis Col., 1970–72; Hearing officer, CO Dept. of Personnel, 1971–72; Legal Counsel, CO Planned Parenthood.

Offices: 2208 RHOB 20515, 202-225-4431. Also 1600 Emerson St., Denver 80218, 303-866-1230.

Committees: *Armed Services* (3d of 34 D): Research and Technology (Chmn.). *Judiciary* (7th of 21 D): Civil and Constitutional Rights; Economic and Commercial Law. *Post Office and Civil Service* (2d of 15 D): Civil Service.

Group Ratings

	ADA	ACLU	COPE	CDF	CFA	LCV	ACU	NTLC	NSI	COC	CEI
1992	95	95	80	100	73	94	4	15	40	50	26
1991	90	—	83	100	83	92	0	—	—	30	24

National Journal Ratings

	1991 LIB — 1991 CONS	1992 LIB — 1992 CONS
Economic	72% — 23%	60% — 40%
Social	78% — 17%	76% — 23%
Foreign	78% — 19%	86% — 10%

Key Votes of the 102d Congress

1. Ban Striker Replace FOR	5. Handgun Wait/7-Day FOR	9. Use Force in Gulf AGN
2. $ for Homeownership AGN	6. Overseas Mil. Abortion FOR	10. US Mil. Abroad $ Cut FOR
3. Tax Rich/Cut Mid Cls.AGN	7. Obscn. Art NEA $ BanAGN	11. Limit SDI Funds FOR
4. FY93/$15B Def. Cut FOR	8. Death Pen. from Jury AGN	12. Cuba Trade Embargo FOR

Key Votes of the 103d Congress

1. Family Leave FOR	2. Deficit Reduction FOR	3. Stimulus Plan FOR

Election Results

1992 general	Patricia Schroeder (D)	156,629	(69%)	($398,749)
	Raymond Diaz Aragon (R).	70,902	(31%)	
1992 primary	Patricia Schroeder (D), unopposed			
1990 general	Patricia Schroeder (D)	82,176	(64%)	($521,500)
	Gloria Gonzales Roemer (R)	46,802	(36%)	($161,266)

SECOND DISTRICT

Boulder, Colorado, says the *Rocky Mountain News*'s Clifford May, is an " international mecca for people who thrive on physical challenge and risk," the nation's leading center for bungee jumping, mountain biking, snowshoe running, rock and ice climbing, downhill skiing, land surfing and hot-air ballooning. The terrain and the local mentality both invite this. Boulder is the home of the University of Colorado, full of healthy young people bent on recklessness, many of whom stay on for years to enjoy the granola-liberal atmosphere. And Boulder's site is striking: immediately at the base of the Rockies, looking up to erose rows of peaks rising to 14,000 feet, from a mile-high plain laid out in mile-square grids much farther than the eye can see.

Boulder is the central focus of Colorado's 2d Congressional District. Actually, about half the people in the 2d are clustered in middle-income suburbs north of Denver—Arvada, Wheat Ridge, Westminster, Thornton, Northglenn, Broomfield. Here families of comfortable affluence and struggling finances, of fundamentalist religion and environment-loving liberalism, live in subdivisions with views of the mountains, close to metro Denver's biggest shopping malls—and not far from the much polluted Rocky Flats nuclear plant. This Metro North area is politically marginal, while Boulder is typically heavily Democratic. The 2d District also goes up into the mountains, to include the old mining town of Central City, since 1990 the home of gambling casinos whose proceeds are supposed to go to historic preservation.

The Congressman from the 2d District is David Skaggs, a Democrat who came to Colorado after serving as a Marine in Vietnam and became part of the baby boom liberals who seized control of Colorado Democratic politics in the 1970s and have held it ever since. Like the California Gold Rush generation who held most major offices there from 1850 when they were in their 30s to the 1890s when they were in their 70s, this generation of politicians threatens to hold most of Colorado's top offices for decades. Skaggs served on Congressman Tim Wirth's staff, was elected to the state House in 1980 and became a Democratic leader there. Then in 1986, Skaggs beat Democratic National Committee Vice-chair Polly Baca in the primary and upset hard-campaigning Republican Mike Norton in the general election.

Skaggs has worked hard on many local issues. After Rocky Flats, the district's largest employer, terminated plutonium production in 1992, he secured worker retraining and education programs and insured the continued clean-up of the facility. He has worked to get money for the new Denver airport, scheduled to open in December 1993. With a seat on Appropriations, he has procured federal dollars to preserve the Two Ponds wetland area in Arvada, build a National Oceanic and Atmospheric Agency lab in Boulder and rebuild the I-25 and I-70 "Mousetrap" interchange in Denver. He worked on the Colorado wilderness bill that was killed at the last minute in 1992. One theme he has sounded often is openness: he attacked Dan Quayle's Competitiveness Council for doing its work behind closed doors (of course, so do Skaggs and his colleagues on committees, and they take money from PACs too). Skaggs is a pretty solidly partisan Democrat. He supported the 1990 budget summit and co-sponsored former House Budget Chairman (and now OMB Director) Leon Panetta's 1992 deficit reduction plan.

Skaggs's work on local issues has helped him win by solid margins; redistricting did not appreciably hurt him. His 1992 opponent, Southern Baptist minister Bryan Day, stirred a lot of controversy, but didn't win many hearts; Skaggs, despite 57 overdrafts on the House bank, won by nearly 2–1.

The People: Pop. 1990: 548,953; 8% rural; 8% age 65+; 87% White; 1% Black; 1% Amer. Indian; 2% Asian; 3% Other; 9% Hispanic origin. Voting age pop.: 407,961; 1% Black; 8% Hispanic origin. Households: 56% married couple families; 28% married couple fams. w. children; 61% college educ.; median household income: $35,117; per capita income: $15,823; median gross rent: $477; median house value: $89,700.

1992 Presidential Vote			1988 Presidential Vote		
Clinton (D)	123,144	(45%)	Dukakis (D)	115,446	(51%)
Bush (R)	83,209	(30%)	Bush (R)	110,047	(49%)
Perot (I)	66,678	(24%)			

Rep. David E. Skaggs (D)

Elected 1986; b. Feb. 22, 1943, Cincinnati, OH; home, Boulder; Wesleyan U., B.A. 1964, Yale, LL.B. 1967; Congregationalist; married (Laura).

Career: Marine Corps, 1968–71, Marine Corps Reserves, 1971–77; A.A., Rep. Timothy E. Wirth, 1975–77, Campaign Dir., 1976; Practicing atty., 1977–86; CO House of Reps., 1980–86, Minority Ldr., 1982–85.

Offices: 1124 LHOB 20515, 202-225-2161. Also 9101 Harlan, #130, Westminster 80030, 303-650-7886.

Committees: *Appropriations* (22d of 37 D): Commerce, Justice, State and Judiciary; District of Columbia; Interior. *Intelligence (Permanent Select)* (7th of 12 D): Oversight and Evaluation; Program and Budget Authorization.

Group Ratings

	ADA	ACLU	COPE	CDF	CFA	LCV	ACU	NTLC	NSI	COC	CEI
1992	90	95	82	90	67	69	8	5	30	38	22
1991	85	—	75	90	61	85	0	—	—	40	24

National Journal Ratings

	1991 LIB	—	1991 CONS	1992 LIB	—	1992 CONS
Economic	59%	—	40%	66%	—	31%
Social	74%	—	23%	81%	—	17%
Foreign	82%	—	17%	76%	—	19%

Key Votes of the 102d Congress

1. Ban Striker Replace	FOR	5. Handgun Wait/7-Day	FOR	9. Use Force in Gulf	AGN
2. $ for Homeownership	AGN	6. Overseas Mil. Abortion	FOR	10. US Mil. Abroad $ Cut	AGN
3. Tax Rich/Cut Mid Cls.	FOR	7. Obscn. Art NEA $ Ban	AGN	11. Limit SDI Funds	FOR
4. FY93/$15B Def. Cut	FOR	8. Death Pen. from Jury	AGN	12. Cuba Trade Embargo	AGN

Key Votes of the 103d Congress

1. Family Leave   FOR   2. Deficit Reduction   FOR   3. Stimulus Plan   FOR

Election Results

1992 general	David E. Skaggs (D)	164,790	(61%)	($673,887)
	Bryan Day (R)	88,470	(33%)	($93,577)
	Vern Tharp (Green)	18,101	(6%)	
1992 primary	David E. Skaggs (D)	35,248	(79%)	
	James L. (Flash) Harrington (D)	9,164	(21%)	
1990 general	David E. Skaggs (D)	105,248	(61%)	($396,017)
	Jason Lewis (R)	68,226	(39%)	($49,080)

THIRD DISTRICT

From a plane on a clear night, they look like tiny mottled veins with tiny clots here and there, thicker near Denver but never very bright: the lights of the civilization Americans have built in the Western Slope of the Rockies in Colorado. The lights follow the trails of valley roads and mountainside switchbacks; the nodes mark the dozens of little towns built during mining boom years—the gold rush of the 1870s, the uranium boom of the 1950s, the oil shale boomlet of the

1970s. The Western Slope includes everything west of the Front Range, and with dozens of peaks over 14,000 feet, it has always been a barrier to east-west transportation; except for the mining booms, no one would have settled here. The miners who tracked gold and silver and lead ores also built Victorian towns with opera houses and gingerbread storefronts in valleys and defiles scarcely accessible to the outside world. Now many of these towns have been restored by ski resort operators and joined by dozens of new condominiums and shopping malls.

The political map of the Western Slope is as diverse as its history. Aspen and Telluride, with Victorian houses and counter-cultural substrata, are liberal and Democratic: the "granola belt" they are called. Vail and Crested Butte, with contemporary condominiums and affluent empty-nesters like the Gerald Fords, are conservative and Republican. The rough-handed mining area around Grand Junction, where piles of tailings still crackle with radioactivity and people remember the oil shale boom with nostalgia, is hostile to environmentalists, while the small Hispanic and Indian communities in the south vote heavily Democratic.

The Western Slope forms most of Colorado's 3d Congressional District; the other part is around the small industrial city of Pueblo. There, on the banks of the Arkansas River, are some of the few major steel factories west of the Mississippi, built by the Rockefellers before World War I to make barbed wire and rails. Though many have now shut down, Pueblo has been weathering the decline of the industry better than steel towns back east; McDonnell Douglas, UNISYS and B.F. Goodrich have all opened plants in the area. Pueblo is heavily Democratic and so are the Hispanic counties just to the south. Hispanic, not Mexican-American: the Spanish-speaking people here, as in northern New Mexico, have been living here for 350 years.

The 3d District is politically marginal, for George Bush in 1988, Bill Clinton in 1992. It had three congressmen of two parties in the 1980s; the most successful, Northern Cheyenne Indian Ben Nighthorse Campbell, upset an incumbent in 1986 and won two big margins here before being elected to the Senate in 1992. That opened up a race between two legislators with some similarities. Both Democrat Mike Callihan, the lieutenant governor, and Republican Scott McInnis, the state house majority leader, were in their 40s, were from small towns. McInnis was first elected to the legislature in 1982, and called for cutting entitlements and defense spending. Callihan, with his statewide office and after representing 16 of the district's 36 counties as a state senator, was better known. But he was an unsystematic campaigner, and bemoaned throughout the year the high cost of campaigning; his strategy was "win Pueblo and then hang on."

But Callihan fell off. McInnis campaigned harder and more intensively, with more ads. He promised to have a small staff and to send out no mass mailings; he shied away from George Bush. Yet the basic Republican orientation of the Western Slope helped him, as did a $127,000 independent expenditure by the American Medical Association PAC and the fact that Ben Campbell refused to endorse Callihan. And then there was McInnis's work on an issue always of importance in the West: water. In the legislature, McInnis worked to pass a Basin of Origin bill to protect Colorado's water rights and prevent export of water to other states and he promoted a study of deep groundwater aquifers in the 3d District's Eastern Slope areas. With Callihan having no special appeal in the granola belt, McInnis had some affirmative planks attractive in small towns and won with 55%. In the House, he can be expected to back spending cuts nationally, but to work for programs that help Western Slope communities—and to always protect the Western Slope's water, which he will be well positioned to do from his seat on the Natural Resources Committee. He says he will not present "automatic opposition" to the Clinton Administration, because "I believe in solutions."

The People: Pop. 1990: 549,120; 46% rural; 13% age 65+; 80% White; 1% Black; 1% Amer. Indian; 6% Other; 17% Hispanic origin. Voting age pop.: 403,814; 1% Black; 15% Hispanic origin. Households: 57% married couple families; 27% married couple fams. w. children; 49% college educ.; median household income: $24,521; per capita income: $12,115; median gross rent: $361; median house value: $62,000.

1992 Presidential Vote

Clinton (D) 107,227 (40%)
Bush (R) 92,292 (34%)
Perot (I).................. 67,210 (25%)

1988 Presidential Vote

Bush (R) 120,715 (53%)
Dukakis (D)............... 106,381 (47%)

Rep. Scott McInnis (R)

Elected 1992; b. May 9, 1953, Glenwood Springs; home, Glenwood Springs; Ft. Lewis Col., B.A. 1975, St. Mary's U., J.D. 1980; Catholic; married (Lori).

Career: Glenwood Springs police officer, 1976; Practicing atty., 1980–92; CO House of Reps., 1982–92, Majority Ldr., 1990–92.

Offices: 512 CHOB 20515, 202-225-4761. Also 327 N. 7th St., Grand Junction 81501, 303-245-7107; 134 W. B St., Pueblo 81003, 719-543-8200; 1060 Main Ave., #107, Durango 81301, 303-259-2754; and 526 Pine St., #112, Glenwood Springs 81601, 303-928-0637.

Committees: *Natural Resources* (13th of 15 R): Energy and Mineral Resources. *Small Business* (10th of 18 R).

Group Ratings and 102d Congress Votes: Newly Elected

Key Votes of the 103d Congress

1. Family Leave	AGN	2. Deficit Reduction	AGN	3. Stimulus Plan	AGN

Election Results

1992 general	Scott McInnis (R)....................	143,293	(55%)	($434,449)
	Mike Callihan (D)....................	114,480	(44%)	($326,185)
1992 primary	Scott McInnis (R), unopposed			
1990 general	Ben Nighthorse Campbell (D)	124,487	(70%)	($335,760)
	Bob Ellis (R)........................	49,961	(28%)	($26,917)
	Other.............................	2,859	(2%)	

FOURTH DISTRICT

The High Plains of eastern Colorado are a frustrating place: dusty brown, gently rolling land that seems flat but is actually sloping imperceptibly downward toward the Missouri River. The land is fertile but always needs more water: rainfall is rare, the rivers are just a trickle most of the year, and in many places groundwater is equally scarce. With irrigation, it is fine wheat country, and one of the foremost beef cattle regions. But wheat prices and exports fell in the 1980s and beef consumption is way down from the red-meat days of the middle 1970s. Water prices, thanks to continued growth on the Front Range, are rising beyond what farmers can economically pay; one county is drying up because landowners have sold their water rights to water companies. The free market that once peopled the High Plains with farmers and ranchers and made it the scene of farm protests and revolts is now causing it to empty out, and revert to untamed land, ready again for the buffalo.

The 4th Congressional District of Colorado contains almost all of the state's High Plains plus the medium-sized towns of Greeley, Fort Collins and Loveland—the northern end of the densely populated Front Range. By heritage and usually by inclination, this is Republican territory. The major cities here, Greeley and Fort Collins, have universities, but not liberal student bodies. The only Democratic part of the 4th is its small segment of metro Denver, northern Adams County around Brighton, with large Mexican-American and blue-collar populations.

The congressman from the 4th is Wayne Allard, a Republican who won the seat in a sharp contest in 1990, when incumbent Republican Hank Brown ran for the Senate. Allard by profession is a veterinarian—a big business in an area with some of the largest feedlots in the world—who was elected first to the state Senate; he is a solid conservative, pro-life on abortion. His 1990 Democratic opponent, Dick Bond, was former president of the University of Northern Colorado, a fiscal conservative and pro-choice on abortion, who also served in the state legislature. In that election, Allard carried the Fort Collins-Greeley area and won 61% on the High Plains, for a 54% victory. In 1992, Allard had spirited opposition from state legislator Tom Redder, also fiscally conservative and pro-choice. He tried to capitalize on anti-incumbent feeling by running a TV spot showing pigs at the trough and an old farmer who said he would vote for Allard "when pigs fly." But Allard carried the Fort Collins-Greeley area again and got 66% on the High Plains, for a 58% victory, which he celebrated by showing off inflatable pigs with wings.

In the House, Allard has had a conservative voting record. He serves on the Joint Committee on the Organization of Congress, and specifically recommends term limits, reductions in congressional committees and staff and congressional compliance with the laws Congress imposes on others.

The People: Pop. 1990: 549,216; 35% rural; 11% age 65+; 83% White; 1% Black; 1% Amer. Indian; 1% Asian; 6% Other; 15% Hispanic origin. Voting age pop.: 396,692; 1% Black; 12% Hispanic origin. Households: 60% married couple families; 30% married couple fams. w. children; 50% college educ.; median household income: $26,577; per capita income: $12,387; median gross rent: $379; median house value: $70,100.

1992 Presidential Vote			1988 Presidential Vote		
Bush (R)	96,638	(38%)	Bush (R)	124,253	(56%)
Clinton (D)	94,234	(37%)	Dukakis (D)	99,575	(44%)
Perot (I)	63,203	(25%)			

Rep. Wayne Allard (R)

Elected 1990; b. Dec. 2, 1943, Fort Collins; home, Loveland; CO St. U., D.V.M. 1968; Protestant; married (Joan).

Career: Veterinarian, 1968–69; Owner & veterinarian, Allard Animal Hosp., 1970–90; Loveland City Health Officer, 1970–78; CO Senate, 1982–90.

Offices: 422 CHOB 20515, 202-225-4676. Also Greeley Natl. Plz., #350, 822 7th St., Greeley 80631, 303-351-7582; 315 W. Oak, #307, Ft. Collins 80521, 303-493-9132; 212 E. Kiowa, Ft. Morgan 80701, 303-867-8909; and 19 W. 4th Ave., La Junta 81050, 719-384-7370.

Committees: *Agriculture* (7th of 19 R): Department Operations and Nutrition; Environment, Credit and Rural Development; Foreign Agriculture and Hunger (RMM). *Budget* (10th of 17 R). *Natural Resources* (10th of 15 R): Energy and Mineral Resources; Oversight and Investigations. *Joint Committee on the Organization of Congress* (11th of 12).

Group Ratings

	ADA	ACLU	COPE	CDF	CFA	LCV	ACU	NTLC	NSI	COC	CEI
1992	5	0	10	10	0	0	92	95	100	75	89
1991	0	—	0	20	11	0	95	—	—	100	86

National Journal Ratings

	1991 LIB — 1991 CONS			1992 LIB — 1992 CONS		
Economic	14%	—	83%	0%	—	91%
Social	0%	—	84%	0%	—	85%
Foreign	12%	—	85%	38%	—	56%

Key Votes of the 102d Congress

1. Ban Striker Replace	AGN	5. Handgun Wait/7-Day	AGN	9. Use Force in Gulf	FOR
2. $ for Homeownership	FOR	6. Overseas Mil. Abortion	AGN	10. US Mil. Abroad $ Cut	FOR
3. Tax Rich/Cut Mid Cls.	AGN	7. Obscn. Art NEA $ Ban	FOR	11. Limit SDI Funds	AGN
4. FY93/$15B Def. Cut	AGN	8. Death Pen. from Jury	FOR	12. Cuba Trade Embargo	AGN

Key Votes of the 103d Congress

1. Family Leave	AGN	2. Deficit Reduction	AGN	3. Stimulus Plan	AGN

Election Results

1992 general	Wayne Allard (R)	139,884	(58%)	($551,110)
	Tom Redder (D)	101,957	(42%)	($378,655)
1992 primary	Wayne Allard (R), unopposed			
1990 general	Wayne Allard (R)	89,285	(54%)	($360,206)
	Dick Bond (D)	75,901	(46%)	($481,666)

FIFTH DISTRICT

A century ago, Colorado Springs was already a tourist attraction, as travelers came out on the railroads to stay at the Broadmoor Hotel and see Pike's Peak. In the years since, it has become one of the military fortresses of the United States, safe in the fastness of the continent where the Rockies meet the High Plains, bristling with weapons and highly trained personnel. Here is the Army's Fort Carson; just to the north is the Air Force Academy, its striking modern buildings silhouetted against the mountains. Not far away is Falcon Air Force Base, the central planning site for the Strategic Defense Initiative, and Cheyenne Mountain, where NORAD, from its underground headquarters, patrols the skies for invading planes or missiles. For four decades these have provided one basis for Colorado Spring's growth; now, the end of the Cold War and declining defense budgets put that at risk. The control center for the Space Shuttle may be a casualty, since the Shuttle has never lived up to billings; SDI is without a protector in the Clinton Administration; and who thinks there's much risk of invading planes or missiles arriving soon? Still, Colorado Springs seems to have developed a high-tech economy with some momentum, the area has great attraction for many retirees and the legalization of gambling in Cripple Creek and other nearby mountain towns may help the area's economy.

Colorado Springs is, in any case, the most Republican part of Colorado, and the state's 5th Congressional District, centered here and reaching north to the Denver suburbs of southern Arapahoe County, is the most Republican district in the state and one of the most Republican districts in the country. The 5th District also includes fast-growing Douglas County (8,000 to 60,000 in the 1980s) between the two cities and goes up to Cripple Creek in the mountains.

The 5th District's congressman, Republican Joel Hefley, is in his fourth term but is still very much running against Congress. He is a native of Oklahoma who made his way from the Panhandle of Texas to Colorado Springs in 1965; for 20 years he was a professional civic leader, executive director of the Community Planning and Research Council in Colorado Springs. He served ten years in the state legislature and rose to a leadership post in the state Senate. His major legislative achievements include National Visiting Nurse Association Week and the Leadville Mine Damage Tunnel. Much of his energy is reserved for opposing congressional spending and urging congressional reform. He staunchly backs the line-item veto, calls for reducing federal government overhead by 10% and issues a "Porker of the Week" award.

Hefley's constituents seem to like his approach just fine. His one tough race was the 1986 Republican primary, and he has won easily ever since, and with the best margin of victory of anyone in the Colorado House delegation for 1992.

The People: Pop. 1990: 549,264; 11% rural; 7% age 65+; 85% White; 6% Black; 1% Amer. Indian; 2% Asian; 3% Other; 7% Hispanic origin. Voting age pop.: 394,528; 5% Black; 6% Hispanic origin. Households: 63% married couple families; 33% married couple fams. w. children; 65% college educ.; median household income: $33,348; per capita income: $15,370; median gross rent: $432; median house value: $90,200.

1992 Presidential Vote			1988 Presidential Vote		
Bush (R)	125,749	(49%)	Bush (R)	141,893	(70%)
Clinton (D)	71,185	(28%)	Dukakis (D)	61,038	(30%)
Perot (I)	57,488	(22%)			

Rep. Joel Hefley (R)

Elected 1986; b. Apr. 18, 1935, Ardmore, OK; home, Colorado Springs; OK Baptist U., B.A. 1957, OK St. U., M.S. 1962; Baptist; married (Lynn).

Career: CO House of Reps., 1977–78; CO Senate, 1979–86; Exec. Dir., Community Planning and Research Cncl., 1966–86.

Offices: 2442 RHOB 20515, 202-225-4422. Also 104 S. Cascade Ave., #105, Colorado Springs 80903, 719-520-0055; and 9605 Maroon Cir., #280, Englewood 80112, 303-792-3923.

Committees: *Armed Services* (11th of 22 R): Military Acquisition; Oversight and Investigations. *Natural Resources* (8th of 15 R): National Parks, Forests and Public Lands. *Small Business* (4th of 18 R): Development of Rural Enterprises, Exports and the Environment (RMM).

Group Ratings

	ADA	ACLU	COPE	CDF	CFA	LCV	ACU	NTLC	NSI	COC	CEI
1992	20	0	27	10	7	0	92	95	100	88	85
1991	10	—	25	20	28	0	100	—	—	90	92

National Journal Ratings

	1991 LIB — 1991 CONS		1992 LIB — 1992 CONS	
Economic	0% —	96%	21% —	76%
Social	0% —	84%	0% —	85%
Foreign	17% —	78%	26% —	72%

Key Votes of the 102d Congress

1. Ban Striker Replace	AGN	5. Handgun Wait/7-Day	AGN	9. Use Force in Gulf	FOR
2. $ for Homeownership	FOR	6. Overseas Mil. Abortion	AGN	10. US Mil. Abroad $ Cut	AGN
3. Tax Rich/Cut Mid Cls.	AGN	7. Obscn. Art NEA $ Ban	FOR	11. Limit SDI Funds	AGN
4. FY93/$15B Def. Cut	AGN	8. Death Pen. from Jury	FOR	12. Cuba Trade Embargo	FOR

Key Votes of the 103d Congress

1. Family Leave	AGN	2. Deficit Reduction	AGN	3. Stimulus Plan	AGN

Election Results

1992 general	Joel Hefley (R)	173,096	(71%)	($162,718)
	Charles Oriez (D)	62,550	(26%)	($14,613)
	Other	7,769	(3%)	
1992 primary	Joel Hefley (R), unopposed			
1990 general	Joel Hefley (R)	127,740	(66%)	($111,435)
	Cal Johnston (D)	57,776	(30%)	($15,288)
	Keith L. Hamburger (LIB)	6,761	(4%)	

SIXTH DISTRICT

A generation ago, most people in metro Denver lived in the city itself; at the city limits the tree-shaded sidewalks gave way to the empty High Plains. Today, three-quarters of metro Denver residents live outside the city. Just south of Denver, in Arapahoe County, Englewood, Littleton and Cherry Hills, pioneered in the 1940s and 1950s, are still the homes of much of the city's elite. Aurora, to the east, benefited at first from the growth around Stapleton Airport, now about to be replaced, but has grown big enough—from 50,000 in 1965 to 220,000 in 1990—to support its own regional mall. West, in Jefferson County, which in 1992 cast more votes than Denver, Lakewood and Wheat Ridge are creations of the 1960s and 1970s, affluent but not elite suburbs with winding streets and office complexes, notably Lakewood's gigantic Denver Federal Center.

The 6th Congressional District of Colorado covers this suburban territory, taking in most of Jefferson County, from Denver to Golden, the headquarters of Coors beer, and the mountain suburb of Evergreen, much of the Englewood-Littleton area, and most of Aurora. This is almost entirely Republican domain. The dominant tone is technical and managerial, and people here still yearn for the certainty of traditional limits. They value their environment, but they also see the need for economic growth and scientific innovation—both of which they think liberals tend to underrate. Ronald Reagan's Republicanism touched a chord here, and its appeal persisted even as the Colorado economy sagged, for it proclaimed the virtues of orderliness and predictability to people whose lives have been dominated by change. While Denver voted solidly for Michael Dukakis and Bill Clinton, the 6th District voted in 1988 and 1992 for George Bush.

Dan Schaefer, a Republican who was a public relations consultant and six-year state legislator, has been the only congressman from the 6th District; he was elected in March 1983, after astronaut Jack Swigert, elected in November 1982, died of cancer before he could take office. Schaefer's record in the House is mostly conservative. In 1985, he got a seat on the Energy and Commerce Committee, mostly run by Chairman John Dingell and Democratic titans Henry Waxman and Ed Markey; Schaefer was a strong opponent of cable reregulation, which passed anyway. In late 1992, he was successful in making the Pentagon and Energy Department subject to pollution-control standards (and the fines and penalties) included in the Resource Conservation and Recovery Act.

"Basically, since I've been in Congress, I've been very attentive to my constituents," Schaefer said after another routine reelection in 1992. He kept money coming into Denver's National Veterans Training Institute, got money for renovating Aurora's Fitzsimons Army Medical Center, promoted Golden's National Renewable Energy Laboratory, lobbied for Denver's water rights in the Colorado wilderness bill, and sponsored amendments to reduce carbon monoxide—natural positions in the land of Denver's brown cloud.

The People: Pop. 1990: 548,788; 5% rural; 8% age 65+; 87% White; 3% Black; 1% Amer. Indian; 2% Asian; 2% Other; 6% Hispanic origin. Voting age pop.: 406,563; 3% Black; 6% Hispanic origin. Households: 56% married couple families; 28% married couple fams. w. children; 68% college educ.; median household income: $37,333; per capita income: $18,289; median gross rent: $473; median house value: $92,200.

234   COLORADO

1992 Presidential Vote

Bush (R) 101,679 (38%)
Clinton (D) 98,875 (37%)
Perot (I). 68,186 (25%)

1988 Presidential Vote

Bush (R) 139,864 (59%)
Dukakis (D). 96,478 (41%)

Rep. Dan Schaefer (R)

Elected Mar. 1983; b. Jan. 25, 1936, Guttenberg, IA; home, Lakewood; Niagara U., B.A. 1961, Potsdam U., 1963; Catholic; married (Mary).

Career: Marine Corps, 1955–57; Educator, 1961–67; P.R. consultant, 1967–83; CO House of Reps., 1977–78; CO Senate, 1979–83.

Offices: 2448 RHOB 20515, 202-225-7882. Also 3615 S. Huron, #101, Englewood 80110, 303-762-8890.

Committees: *Energy and Commerce* (6th of 17 R): Oversight and Investigations (RMM); Telecommunications and Finance; Transportation and Hazardous Materials.

Group Ratings

	ADA	ACLU	COPE	CDF	CFA	LCV	ACU	NTLC	NSI	COC	CEI
1992	5	5	27	10	7	0	88	95	100	75	85
1991	5	—	17	30	28	0	95	—	—	90	74

National Journal Ratings

	1991 LIB — 1991 CONS		1992 LIB — 1992 CONS	
Economic	22%	— 77%	0%	— 91%
Social	0%	— 84%	0%	— 85%
Foreign	0%	— 88%	0%	— 82%

Key Votes of the 102d Congress

1. Ban Striker Replace	AGN	5. Handgun Wait/7-Day AGN	9. Use Force in Gulf	FOR
2. $ for Homeownership	FOR	6. Overseas Mil. Abortion AGN	10. US Mil. Abroad $ Cut AGN
3. Tax Rich/Cut Mid Cls. AGN		7. Obscn. Art NEA $ Ban FOR	11. Limit SDI Funds	AGN
4. FY93/$15B Def. Cut AGN		8. Death Pen. from Jury FOR	12. Cuba Trade Embargo FOR

Key Votes of the 103d Congress

1. Family Leave   AGN   2. Deficit Reduction   AGN   3. Stimulus Plan   AGN

Election Results

1992 general	Dan Schaefer (R) 142,021	(61%)	($332,317)
	Thomas A. Kolbe (D) 91,073	(39%)	($9,794)
1992 primary	Dan Schaefer (R), unopposed		
1990 general	Dan Schaefer (R) 105,312	(65%)	($280,103)
	Don Jarrett (D). 57,961	(35%)	($2,958)

CONNECTICUT

Small and isolated, insular throughout much of its history and without significant natural resources, the last state to renounce an established church and one of the last to institute an income tax, Connecticut is America's most affluent state. Its affluence has come, now and in the past, not from any windfall but from its knack for tinkering. In 1831, Alexis de Tocqueville was struck by how this spot on the map gave America "the clock-peddler, the schoolmaster, and the senator. The first gives you time, the second tells you what to do with it, and the third makes your law and civilization." Connecticut made clocks of wood and metal and hats of felt and invented vulcanized rubber; it produced combs, cigars, clocks, silk thread, pins, matches, furniture; it invented and still manufactures Pez candy in Orange, Pepperidge Farm bread and Nivea cream in Norwalk, the Stanley Powerlock tape measure in New Britain and the Wiffle ball in Shelton. Most importantly, Connecticut—one of the least violent parts of America—has always specialized in arms. The quintessential Connecticut Yankee, Eli Whitney, was the inventor not only of the cotton gin—which may have been the proximate cause of the Civil War—but also of the rifles with interchangeable parts with which so many were killed in that tragic conflict. Over the last century, ever since Samuel Colt won a War Department contract to manufacture guns for the Spanish-American War, Connecticut has had a close relationship with the military—and at no time more than during the Reagan defense buildup of the 1980s. United Technologies' various subsidiaries made Air Force jets and the Army's Sikorsky helicopters; General Dynamics's Electric Boat Shipyard in New London made the Navy's nuclear submarines; dozens of other companies made other weaponry.

These arms industries, like Connecticut's civilian manufacturers, depend heavily on precision work. For years, the state was the center of the brass industry, the nation's main producer of precision instruments, a center for machine tools, and the home of Perkin Elmer, which makes the machines that produce semiconductor chips. And if Connecticut workers today are more likely the descendants of Irish and Italian immigrants than of Yankee tinkerers, they have not lost the Yankee knack: Connecticut ranks third in new patents per capita. Connecticut also has the skill of cannily assessing risk: the foundation for its great insurance companies, Aetna, Travelers, Connecticut Mutual and The Hartford. This business requires not just managing money but understanding people: the poet Wallace Stevens, a Hartford resident all his life, worked for The Hartford Company investigating whether claims were valid or bogus.

Then, with the end of the Cold War and the stock market crash of the late 1980s, Connecticut's boom economy went bust. The state lost 142,000 manufacturing jobs, from its 1988 peak of 450,000. United Technologies laid off thousands of workers, and Electric Boat seemed perpetually in danger of being shut down because of opposition to Seawolf submarines. Real estate values, among the highest in the country, fell on the order of 30% to 40%, and homeowners who had borrowed on inflated values suddenly found themselves without their life's savings. Connecticut still had the highest incomes in the nation and the second lowest percentage without health insurance, but in 1991 it had a higher percentage of bad loans than any other state and its wealth—that of ordinary citizens, primarily in residential real estate—was sharply down. Early in the 1990s, Connecticut had the highest sales and corporate taxes in the nation. Fiscal crisis produced, after much controversy, a state income tax in 1991 and a Democratic win for president, for the first time in 24 years, in 1992.

For most of the 20th Century, Connecticut politics was an ethnic struggle between the flinty Connecticut Yankees delineated by Hartford resident Mark Twain, and the ethnics who were already streaming into the state's small industrial cities while Twain was writing *Huckleberry Finn* in his big house on Farmington Avenue. Connecticut Yankees, economically innovative,

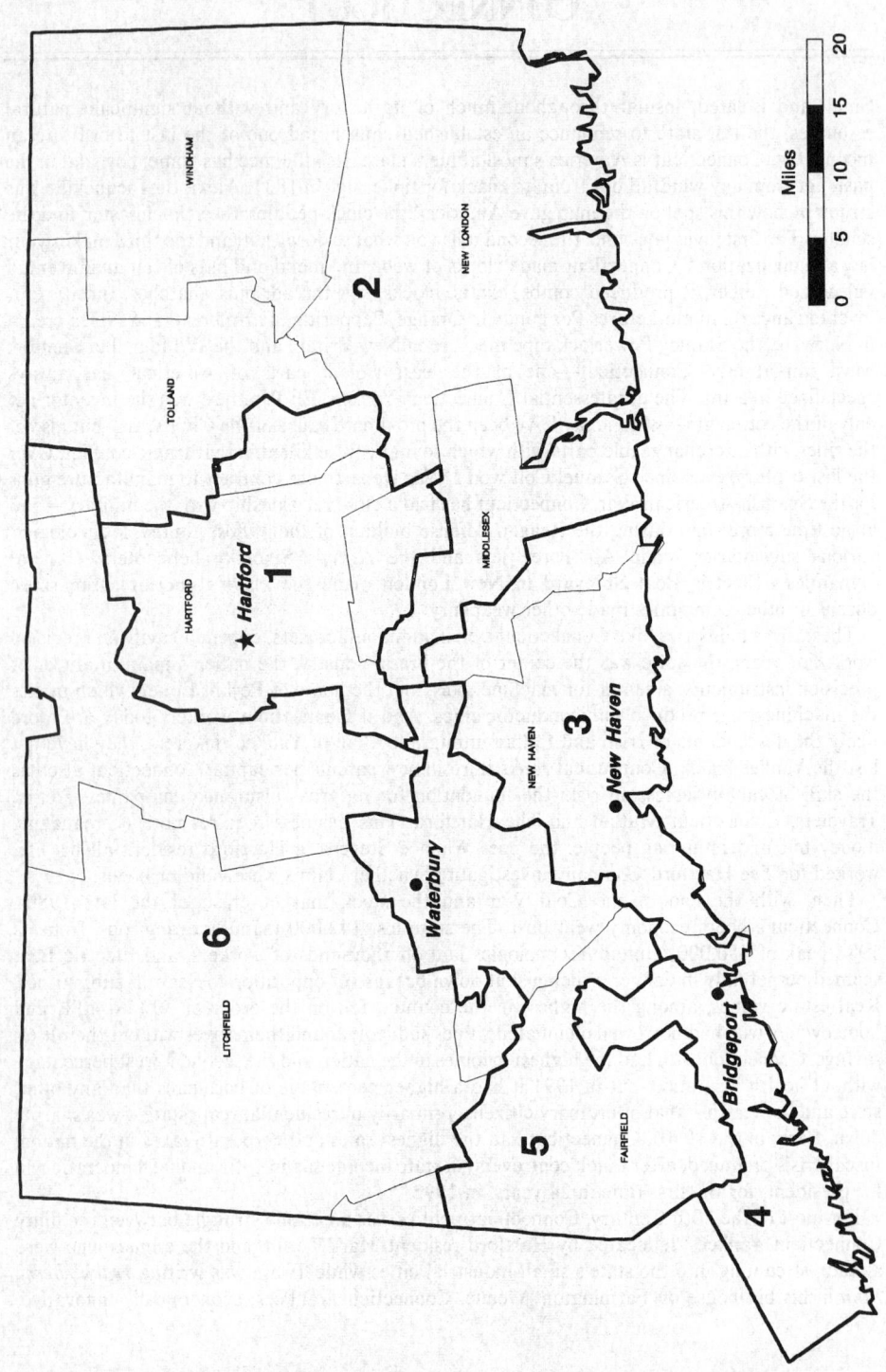

were ornery and reactionary in politics: the last Federalists, loyal enough Republicans to carry the state for Herbert Hoover in 1932. In the years that followed, Connecticut became more Democratic as it grew more affluent—and more Catholic. The key Democratic politician was John Bailey, state party chairman from 1946 to 1975. A master legislative strategist and ticket-balancer, Bailey's power was augmented by Connecticut's strong party and straight ticket voting traditions; he was one of the earliest endorsers of John F. Kennedy, seeing electoral advantage in his Catholicism when most other old-line bosses saw peril. Connecticut also had a vital Republican Party which generated national chairmen, elected senators (including George Bush's father), swept the board when the Democrats were split on Vietnam and cultural issues in 1970 and captured the legislature as recently as 1984. But while Republicans carried the state's electoral votes, Democrats won every senatorial and gubernatorial election but two between 1976 and 1990. The winner each time was Lowell Weicker, who ran as a Republican for the Senate in 1970, 1976 and 1982, and as the candidate of his own A Connecticut Party for governor in 1990.

Governor. Today, Connecticut state politics revolves less around ethnic divisions than around the large—physically and psychically—figure of Lowell Weicker. Weicker has never worn anyone's livery, at least not comfortably; and if he owed his defeat in the 1988 Senate race to opposition from conservatives like Connecticut native William Buckley, he had his revenge two years later when he spied an opening and, as a third-party candidate, was elected governor. In 1989, Democratic Governor William O'Neill was facing a fiscal crisis caused by the economic slowdown after state spending increases of more than 10% a year; he signed a 1989 tax package giving Connecticut one of the highest sales (8%) and corporate tax rates in the nation, plus high taxes on alcohol, tobacco and utilities. After Democratic Congressman Bruce Morrison said he'd oppose O'Neill, and Lowell Weicker entered the race as an Independent, O'Neill prudently decided to retire. The three resulting candidates presented obvious differences on the income tax issue. The Republican nominee, Congressman John Rowland, pledged he'd veto any income tax; Morrison beat a pro-income tax candidate in the Democratic primary and said he'd favor one "only as a last resort"; Weicker refused to rule it out, which is about as close as a politician gets to ruling it in. Weicker won with 40% of the vote, to 37% for Rowland and 21% for Morrison. Morrison carried only New Haven, East Haven and West Haven, while Rowland carried almost the whole western part of the state, the working-class areas around Waterbury and Bridgeport and the high-income suburbs and villages of Fairfield and Litchfield Counties.

Weicker's intentions became clear within days of the election, when he announced that his main tax adviser would be none other than Democrat William Cibes, the income tax advocate Morrison had beaten in the primary. The Democratic legislature resisted Weicker's bills, with stout opposition coming from many Republicans; after a titanic struggle, Weicker won a 4.5% income tax, a 2% reduction in the sales tax and repeal of the 20% corporate tax surcharge. Connecticut's August 1991 income tax didn't produce the furious opposition that greeted New Jersey's 1990 tax rise, perhaps because voters had some notice of Weicker's intentions and because the alternatives were even higher sales and nuisance taxes. A compromise budget was passed in 1992 and pro-income tax candidates did not fare badly in elections that fall, in which the Democrats maintained control. On the other hand, the state's economy seemed not to be recovering, and Weicker's A Connecticut Party, (named so it would fall first alphabetically on the ballot), didn't elect any of its candidates. Its successes did come when, in the 1st, 2d, and 3d Congressional Districts, it nominated Senator Christopher Dodd and three incumbent Democratic House members and saw one of them—Sam Gejdenson of the 2d District—win reelection only with the combined Democratic-ACP total.

Presumably Weicker will run again in 1994 as the ACP candidate; the Republicans will surely run an anti-income tax opponent. Ideologically, they could easily swallow Weicker; but personally is another matter: Weicker is obstreperous, self-righteous, famously difficult to get along with; incorruptible and candid, he is also arrogant and intolerant of dissent. He is inclined to think that the only decent course to be taken is his own, and that only he is courageous enough to take it. Will a majority of voters believe that in 1994, or enough to reelect him with another plurality? Sixth District Representative Nancy Johnson looked to be a frontrunner for the Republican nomination in early 1993, and Democratic state Senator John Larson announced his intention to run.

Senators. Connecticut's two Democratic senators have crossed political paths over the years. Christopher Dodd's father, Senator Thomas Dodd, was notably more conservative on cultural and foreign issues than other Connecticut Democrats; the current Senator Dodd was the leading opponent of efforts to oust Communist-backed forces in Central America and backed programs to accommodate Americans' changing family lifestyles. Joseph Lieberman started off as a liberal reformer, beating the incumbent state senate majority leader in a primary in 1970 (with volunteer help from a freshman Yale Law student named Bill Clinton); but he won his Senate seat in 1988 by running slightly—but noticeably—to the right of Republican Lowell Weicker on cultural issues.

Dodd is one of those liberal baby-boom generation politicians whose formative political experience was service in the Peace Corps. While others were fighting in Vietnam, Chris Dodd was in the Peace Corps in Moncion, Dominican Republic. From his work with poverty-stricken Dominicans, he seems to have absorbed a lesson taught by many Latin American intellectuals, that the United States is responsible for the backwardness of Latin economies, as well as the lesson taught by many Americans, that the hardest task in foreign policy is preventing the United States from supporting repressive right-wing Third World dictators. Elected to the House in the Watergate year of 1974, he moved to the Senate in 1980 after persuading fellow Watergate baby Toby Moffett not to run in the primary and beating former New York Senator James Buckley in the general. As chairman of the Foreign Relations Subcommittee on the Western Hemisphere, he regularly opposed U.S. military aid to El Salvador's government and aid to the Nicaraguan contras; alert to any human rights violations by these forces, he was muted in his criticisms of the pro-Communist Salvador rebels and Sandinistas. Events have not vindicated Dodd's judgment: the El Salvador government has become more observant of human rights than the rebels, and Nicaraguan voters when given the chance voted against the Sandinistas. Latin democracies have chosen not the socialism predicted by the theorists whose advice Dodd followed but free enterprise and the pro-U.S. policies championed by Ronald Reagan.

Dodd's major initiative on domestic policy has also proven unsuccessful: the ABC child care bill, a favorite cause of baby-boom liberals who want a stronger government role in helping individuals adjust to—and perhaps stimulating them to participate in—changing lifestyles. Supported by the AFL-CIO and the Children's Defense Fund, Dodd's version of ABC would have put $2.5 billion into setting federal standards for child health and safety. Its aim seemed to be to institutionalize pre-kindergarten day care on a national basis, and to create a corps of caregivers in the image of the teaching profession, complete with postgraduate training and union representation. Dodd did a good job getting the bill through the Senate, but it was rejected in the House when liberal Democrats George Miller and Tom Downey opposed it. The child care law ultimately passed in 1990 rejected the ABC approach, and it does not seem a live option even with longtime Children's Defense Fund board chairman Hillary Rodham Clinton in the White House.

Dodd is a pleasant man who works hard and, some say, plays hard. Though he was easily reelected in 1986, the national anti-incumbent trend, the unpopularity of Lowell Weicker's income tax and the unsuccess of his two major policy initiatives seemed to make him vulnerable in 1992; his poll ratings showed him hovering at or below the 50% level. But he worked the state hard and fought in spring 1992 to save the Seawolf from extinction, running one of 1992's best fall campaigns. He was helped by weakness in the opposition and by the fact that Nancy Johnson of the 6th District decided not to run. In the Republican primary, wealthy businessman Brook Johnson beat party-endorsed state legislator and Gulf war veteran Chris Burnham. Johnson was attacked for making money through 1980s leveraged buyouts, for investing in jobs overseas, for losing his cool with hecklers and reporters and not voting in local elections. Dodd emphasized his work on child care and support of the family leave bill George Bush vetoed; Johnson, for all the talk of financing his own campaign, was heavily outspent. Dodd, incidentally, also had the ACP line on the ballot, which helped increase his winning margin; overall he won 59%–38%.

In his first years in the Senate, Connecticut's junior senator, Joseph Lieberman, has exerted an influence far out of proportion to his seniority or committee position or political clout, an influence that comes from widespread appreciation of his independence of mind, civility of spirit and fidelity to causes in which he believes. Those qualities were apparent in his 1988 campaign and in a political career that started two decades before. Lieberman hails not from Connecticut's affluent ranks, but is the son of a Stamford liquor store owner. He went to Yale, making his mark there as author of a 1966 biography of that quintessential political boss John Bailey which was both revealing and admiring. He is an Orthodox Jew who observes the Sabbath so rigorously that he declined to appear at the convention that nominated him because it was held on Saturday. (He maintains his Senate voting record by walking to the Capitol on the Sabbath.) He lost a race for Congress in 1980, came back to be elected attorney general in 1982 and 1986, then dared to take on Lowell Weicker who was widely considered unbeatable. On many issues, Lieberman ran to Weicker's right, favoring the death penalty and a moment of silence (but not prayer) in schools, and attacking Weicker's support of a 30-cent gas tax increase. The contest cut across party lines, as many Democrats backed Weicker and many Republicans supported Lieberman. Lieberman ran especially far ahead of Dukakis in the industrialized Waterbury area, in the Naugatuck Valley and around his home base of New Haven. Weicker ran ahead of his ticket in central city Hartford and heavily Jewish Bloomfield, in the college town of Storrs, and in the New York expatriate part of rural Litchfield County.

In the Senate, Lieberman has been distinctive among Democrats on foreign policy: supporting the use of force against Manuel Noriega in Panama before the invasion, calling for recognition of the Lithuanian government and voting against scrapping Trident submarines and M-1 tanks. He was one of very few senators who took the initiative in marshaling arguments and rounding up support for the Gulf war resolution in January 1991; without his vehement but measured support it might not have passed. Presciently, he called for "final victory" over Saddam Hussein after George Bush called off the ground war, and said "We must use all reasonable diplomatic, economic and military means to achieve his removal from power." Remembering the Holocaust, he called for authorizing U.N. use of military force in Bosnia in August 1992. He is a strong supporter of Israel, backing loan guarantees despite Israel's continued construction of settlements in the occupied territories. But he also favored F-15 sales to Saudi Arabia in July 1992 (it meant, he admitted, 2,000 East Hartford jobs) and he interceded with the Clinton campaign to finally get a hearing for Arab-American Institute head James Zogby.

On economics, Lieberman has supported capital gains tax cuts for small and starting businesses and is a major advocate of Jack Kemp's enterprise zones. He opposed the 1990 budget summit agreement because it included gas taxes. But he also favors many regulatory policies; he was a chief sponsor of cable TV reregulation and wants to dismantle the monopoly on airline computer reservation systems; he wants to use tax exemptions and government programs to provide new jobs for laid-off defense workers. A member of the Environment and Public Works Committee, he joined Paul Wellstone and five other senators in a filibuster of the 1991 energy bill and forced backers to abandon oil drilling in the Arctic National Wildlife Reserve: "We have drawn a line in the tundra," as he put it. He was one of three Democrats to back a school choice demonstration project and one of three senators to switch and vote against Clarence Thomas after the testimony of Anita Hill.

Lieberman's influence in Bill Clinton's Washington is great. Perhaps remembering Clinton's help in 1970, Lieberman endorsed Clinton in January 1992, then stuck with him after the Gennifer Flowers story broke while many insiders wrote off his candidacy. For 1994, the question is whether Lieberman will get serious opposition at all. It is possible, but seems highly unlikely, that Lowell Weicker will run to get his old seat back; it is not clear that a conservative

Republican could summon up the enthusiasm and raise the money to make a serious run against a Democrat who supported the Gulf war and wants to cut capital gains taxes.

Presidential politics. Connecticut went Democratic for president in 1992, for the first time since 1968, two years before Bill Clinton arrived at Yale Law School. But Clinton's 1992 victory was less a reversion to the politics of 1960, 1964 and 1968, when Democrats won largely with votes of Catholics and blue-collar workers, than it was an example of the politics of protest in a New England where real estate prices and most voters' personal wealth fell by something like 40% over four years. Clinton's 42% was barely above George McGovern's 40% in 1972 and the 39% Jimmy Carter and Walter Mondale got here in the 1980s. Clinton won only because native son George Bush did poorly with Connecticut's ancestral Republicans, winning just 36%, barely above Barry Goldwater's 32%. The big surprise was the 22% for Ross Perot. His vote was especially heavy in the suburbs and small towns at the far edges of Connecticut's metropolitan areas, where young voters with large families found themselves far behind in their yearly battle with credit card debt and their lifelong quest to build up equity. Here defense cuts and the New England recession struck hard, and many voters struck back with a vote for Perot.

The Connecticut presidential primary, once a vestige of party machine control, has now become a vehicle for similar protest on the Democratic side. The primary was held March 24, a week after Illinois and Michigan had settled both parties' nominations. As usual, only about 100,000 voters showed up for the Republican primary. Democratic primary turnout was also low (173,000 voters), and resulted in an upset victory for Jerry Brown, who had 37% of the vote to 36% for Bill Clinton and 20% for a by-then withdrawn Paul Tsongas. This was less a show of strength for Brown than a sign of Clinton's weakness at that stage of the campaign. It also allowed the New York media, starved for national attention, to claim that their primary could determine the Democratic nomination, which in fact Clinton had all but clinched.

Congressional districting. Connecticut kept six seats in the 1990 Census. A nine-member commission appointed by legislative leaders changed its district boundaries minimally, less than in any similarly sized or larger state, with no discernible political effect. Incidentally, three of Connecticut's six House members are women and one is black—a diversity that arose not from quotas but from candidates making their way up.

The People: Est. Pop. 1992: 3,281,000; Pop. 1990: 3,287,116, down 0.2% 1990–1992. 1.3% of U.S. total, 27th largest; 21% rural. Median age: 34.4 years. 13.6% 65 years and over. 8.3% Black, 6.5% Spanish origin, 1.5% Asian. Households: 55.6% married couple families; 25% married couple fams. w. children; 50% college educ.; median household income: $41,721; per capita income: $20,189; 65.6% owner occupied housing; median house value: $177,800; median median monthly rent: $510. 7.5% Unemployment. Voting age pop.: 2,537,535. Registered voters (1992): 1,955,268; 736,914 D (38%), 506,115 R (26%), 721,239 unaffiliated and minor parties (37%).

Political Lineup: Governor, Lowell P. Weicker, Jr. (ACP); Lt. Gov., Eunice Groark (ACP); Secy. of State, Pauline Kezer (R); Atty. Gen., Richard Blumenthal (D); Treasurer, Francisco Borges (D); Comptroller, William E. Curry, Jr. (D). State Senate, 36 (19 D and 17 R); State House of Representatives, 151 (87 D and 64 R). Senators, Christopher J. Dodd (D) and Joseph I. Lieberman (D). Representatives, 6 (3 D and 3 R).

1992 Presidential Vote

Clinton (D)	682,318	(42%)
Bush (R)	578,313	(36%)
Perot (I)	348,771	(22%)

1988 Presidential Vote

Bush (R)	750,241	(52%)
Dukakis (D)	676,584	(47%)

1992 Democratic Presidential Primary

Brown	64,472	(37%)
Clinton	61,698	(36%)
Tsongas	33,811	(20%)
Other	7,708	(4%)

1992 Republican Presidential Primary

Bush	66,356	(67%)
Buchanan	21,815	(22%)
Uncommitted	9,008	(9%)

GOVERNOR

Gov. Lowell P. Weicker, Jr. (ACP)

Elected 1990, term expires Jan. 1995; b. May 16, 1931, Paris, France; home, Hartford; Yale, B.A. 1953., U. of VA, J.D., 1958; Episcopalian; married (Claudia).

Career: Army, 1953–55; Practicing atty., 1958–68; CT House of Reps., 1962–68; Greenwich Town Selectman, 1964–68; U.S. House of Reps., 1969–71; U.S. Senate, 1971–89; Pres., Research! America, 1989–90.

Office: Executive Chamber, State Capitol, Hartford 06106, 203-566-4840.

Election Results

1990 gen.	Lowell P. Weicker, Jr. (ACP) ...	460,576	(40%)
	John G. Rowland (R)	427,840	(37%)
	Bruce Morrison (D)	236,641	(21%)
	Other	16,044	(1%)
1990 prim.	Lowell P. Weicker, Jr. (ACP), nom. by convention		
1986 gen.	William A. O'Neill (D)	575,638	(58%)
	Julie D. Belaga (R)	408,489	(41%)

SENATORS

Sen. Christopher J. Dodd (D)

Elected 1980, seat up 1998; b. May 27, 1944, Willimantic; home, East Haddam; Providence Col., B.A. 1966, U. of Louisville, J.D. 1972; Catholic; divorced.

Career: Peace Corps, Dominican Republic, 1966–68; Army Reserves, 1969–75; Practicing atty., 1972–74; U.S. House of Reps., 1974–80.

Offices: 444 RSOB 20510, 202-224-2823. Also 100 Great Meadow Rd., Wethersfield 06109, 203-240-3470.

Committees: *Banking, Housing and Urban Affairs* (3d of 11 D): Economic Stabilization and Rural Development; Housing and Urban Affairs; Securities (Chmn.). *Budget* (9th of 12 D). *Foreign Relations* (4th of 11 D): International Economic Policy, Trade, Oceans and Environment; Terrorism, Narcotics and International Operations; Western Hemisphere and Peace Corps Affairs (Chmn.). *Labor and Human Resources* (4th of 10 D): Aging; Children, Family, Drugs and Alcoholism (Chmn.); Education, Arts and Humanities; Labor. *Rules and Administration* (7th of 9 D).

Group Ratings

	ADA	ACLU	CDF	COPE	CFA	LCV	ACU	NTLC	NSI	COC	CEI
1992	75	86	80	92	92	83	11	28	50	30	31
1991	75	—	73	92	83	73	24	—	—	20	20

National Journal Ratings

	1991 LIB	—	1991 CONS	1992 LIB	—	1992 CONS
Economic	65%	—	34%	52%	—	46%
Social	67%	—	32%	69%	—	26%
Foreign	49%	—	46%	56%	—	41%

Key Votes of the 102d Congress

1. $ for Homeownership	FOR	5. Clarence Thomas Nom.	AGN	9. Use Force in Gulf	AGN
2. Have Cap Gains Debate	AGN	6. Lmt Death Row Appeal	AGN	10. Keep Salvador Aid	AGN
3. Remove Budget Walls	AGN	7. Handgun Wait/5-Day	FOR	11. Cut $1B from SDI	AGN
4. Ban Striker Replace	FOR	8. Abortion Gag Rule	AGN	12. Override China MFN	FOR

Key Votes of the 103d Congress

1. Family Leave	FOR	2. HIV Immigrants	FOR	3. Clinton Budget	FOR

Election Results

1992 general	Christopher J. Dodd (D-ACP)	882,569	(59%)	($4,553,792)
	Brook Johnson (R)	572,036	(38%)	($2,395,262)
	Five Others	46,104	(3%)	
1992 primary	Christopher J. Dodd (D-ACP), nom. by convention			
1986 general	Christopher J. Dodd (D)...............	632,695	(65%)	($2,276,764)
	Roger W. Eddy (R)..................	340,438	(35%)	($183,632)

Sen. Joseph I. Lieberman (D)

Elected 1988, seat up 1994; b. Feb. 24, 1942, Stamford; home, New Haven; Yale, B.A. 1964, LL.B. 1967; Jewish; married (Hadassah).

Career: CT Senate, 1970–80, Majority Ldr., 1974–80; CT Atty. Gen., 1983–88.

Offices: 316 HSOB 20510, 202-224-4041. Also One Commercial Plz., #2100, Hartford 06103, 203-240-3566.

Committees: *Armed Services* (11th of 11 D): Defense Technology, Acquisition and Industrial Base; Force Requirements and Personnel; Regional Defense and Contingency Forces. *Environment and Public Works* (7th of 10 D): Clean Air and Nuclear Regulation (Chmn.); Clean Water, Fisheries and Wildlife; Toxic Substances, Research and Development. *Governmental Affairs* (6th of 8 D): General Services, Federalism and the District of Columbia; Oversight of Government Management; Regulation and Government Information (Chmn.); Permanent Subcommittee on Investigations. *Small Business* (6th of 12 D): Competitiveness, Capital Formation and Economic Opportunity (Chmn.); Government Contracting and Paperwork Reduction.

Group Ratings

	ADA	ACLU	CDF	COPE	CFA	LCV	ACU	NTLC	NSI	COC	CEI
1992	70	64	70	83	92	100	22	5	50	50	29
1991	65	—	82	83	89	100	25	—	—	30	18

National Journal Ratings

	1991 LIB	—	1991 CONS	1992 LIB	—	1992 CONS
Economic	66%	—	31%	49%	—	50%
Social	59%	—	38%	44%	—	54%
Foreign	56%	—	42%	54%	—	45%

Key Votes of the 102d Congress

1. $ for Homeownership	FOR	5. Clarence Thomas Nom.	AGN	9. Use Force in Gulf	FOR
2. Have Cap Gains Debate	AGN	6. Lmt Death Row Appeal	FOR	10. Keep Salvador Aid	AGN
3. Remove Budget Walls	AGN	7. Handgun Wait/5-Day	FOR	11. Cut $1B from SDI	FOR
4. Ban Striker Replace	FOR	8. Abortion Gag Rule	AGN	12. Override China MFN	FOR

Key Votes of the 103d Congress

1. Family Leave	FOR	2. HIV Immigrants	FOR	3. Clinton Budget	FOR

Election Results

1988 general	Joseph I. Lieberman (D)...............	688,499	(50%)	($2,570,779)
	Lowell P. Weicker, Jr. (R).............	678,454	(49%)	($2,609,902)
1988 primary	Joseph I. Lieberman (D), nom. by convention			
1982 general	Lowell P. Weicker, Jr. (R).............	545,987	(50%)	($2,306,615)
	Anthony Toby Moffett (D).............	499,146	(46%)	($1,368,147)

FIRST DISTRICT

In 1871, Mark Twain moved to Hartford to become director of an insurance company, and ultimately became the Connecticut capital's most famous citizen. Hartford, already more than two centuries old, was becoming the nation's best-known insurance center. This was not a role envisioned by the harsh Puritans who established Hartford as a haven from backsliding Bostonians, but Connecticut's Yankees turned out to be shrewd businessmen. Thanks to the broad Connecticut River, Hartford became a seaport; its merchants, prevented from trading and writing marine insurance by Thomas Jefferson's Embargo Act of 1807, turned to writing fire insurance and using the capital they'd accumulated in the Napoleonic Wars to finance their ventures. They were also ready to finance tinkerers like Samuel Colt, whose gun factory just south of downtown Hartford became one of the nation's great arms plants—and whose company became a symbol of Connecticut's recession when it went into Chapter 11 in 1992.

Insurance and arms are still economic mainstays of Hartford, Connecticut's capital and the center of its largest metropolitan concentration. Hartford-headquartered Aetna, Travelers, Connecticut Mutual and The Hartford are the biggest names among the state's insurers, with some $200 billion in assets. Just across the river is the Pratt and Whitney jet engine plant in East Hartford, cornerstone of Connecticut-based United Technologies, one of the nation's biggest defense contractors, though painfully downsizing in the 1990s.

In politics, metropolitan Hartford has long been the Democratic stronghold of Connecticut, although in the three-cornered politics of the 1990 governor's race, it went for independent winner Lowell Weicker, the candidate clearly most sympathetic to a state income tax. Hartford's allegiance is not proletarian—this has long been one of the nation's more affluent metro areas—but ethnic: Hartford has many Irish, Italian and French-Canadian Catholics and a fair number of blacks. Most of the immigrants' descendants have moved out of the central city and into the hilly suburbs, but they tend to remain Democratic. One reason was the strength and skill of John Bailey, longtime state (1946–75) and national (1961–68) Democratic chairman, an old-fashioned political boss with a scandal-free career who promoted a raft of first-class candidates. And so the 1st Congressional District, which includes most of metropolitan Hartford, remains a Democratic district, and is represented in Congress by Democrat Barbara Kennelly, John Bailey's daughter and wife of a former speaker of the Connecticut House.

Barbara Kennelly is a former secretary of state who won the 1st in a 1982 special election. She won a seat on the Ways and Means Committee in 1983: Ways and Means' jurisdiction over taxes is vital to the insurance industry, naturally reflected in her work. Her toughest fight, in which she prevailed over Chairman Dan Rostenkowski in committee, was to save single-premium insurance policies from what the insurance companies consider overtaxation. Her 1991 health insurance plan embraced neither the "single payer" or "pay-or-play" approaches, but attempted to fill in the gaps, preserving private medical insurers but requiring some standardization of coverage; she says she is a "scold" to the industry, demanding universal coverage, but she does not want to rule insurers out of the game. She successfully sought to eliminate the taxes on accelerated death benefits, paid under insurance policies to terminally ill people who are expected to die within 12 months. She wants to pay for long-term care by allowing the elderly to insure their assets so they can retain them and still be eligible for Medicaid, and sponsored an Older Women's Breast Cancer Protection Act.

But Kennelly's interests are more varied. She was a lead sponsor of the successful Hate Crimes Statistics Act of 1990, seeking information on those attacked because of race, religion, ethnicity or sexual orientation. She worked hard on the 1988 welfare reform bill to strengthen its child support provisions and to fashion a better dependent care tax credit. On the 1986 tax reform bill, Kennelly concentrated on getting a high deduction for single heads of household and saving the historic preservation and rehabilitation tax credit.

By inheritance and temperament, Kennelly is mostly a team player Democrat, but she has some distinctive positions. She introduced a bill as an alternative to the balanced budget amendment with would require the president and both Budget Committees to submit balanced budgets each year, but it failed 199–220. She backs much of the feminist agenda, opposing caps on punitive damages for sexual harassment and discrimination; she was a booster of Geraldine Ferraro in 1984 and Anita Hill in 1991. She passed up two chances to run for governor in the 1990 cycle, before and after incumbent William O'Neill left the race. Kennelly made a run for Democratic Caucus chair in 1989, but lost to Steny Hoyer 165–82. In 1993, she became the only woman in the Democratic leadership by being chosen one of four deputy whips.

In the 1st District, she has proved a strong vote-getter. In 1992, she had her closest recent race, but won 67%–31% over Philip Steele, son of longtime Hartford radio personality Bob Steele and brother of a onetime (1971–75) 2d District congressman.

The People: Pop. 1990: 547,979; 11% rural; 14% age 65+; 75% White; 14% Black; 2% Asian; 5% Other; 10% Hispanic origin. Voting age pop.: 423,623; 13% Black; 8% Hispanic origin. Households: 51% married couple families; 22% married couple fams. w. children; 49% college educ.; median household income: $39,961; per capita income: $18,644; median gross rent: $572; median house value: $170,700.

1992 Presidential Vote		
Clinton (D)	133,686	(50%)
Bush (R)	82,086	(31%)
Perot (I)	52,154	(19%)

1988 Presidential Vote		
Dukakis (D)	135,387	(55%)
Bush (R)	108,743	(45%)

Rep. Barbara B. Kennelly (D)

Elected 1982; b. Jul. 10, 1936, Hartford; home, Hartford; Trinity Col. (DC), B.A. 1958, Trinity Col. (Hartford), M.A. 1971; Catholic; married (James).

Career: Vice Chmn., Hartford Comm. on Aging, 1971–75; Hartford Court of Common Cncl., 1975–79; CT Secy. of State, 1979–82.

Offices: 201 CHOB 20515, 202-225-2265. Also One Corporate Ctr., Hartford 06103, 203-278-8888.

Committees: *Budget* (14th of 26 D). *House Administration* (11th of 12 D): Accounts; Libraries and Memorials; Office Systems. *Ways and Means* (9th of 24 D): Trade.

Group Ratings

	ADA	ACLU	COPE	CDF	CFA	LCV	ACU	NTLC	NSI	COC	CEI
1992	100	91	92	90	93	88	4	0	40	25	9
1991	80	—	83	100	72	77	0	—	—	20	10

National Journal Ratings

	1991 LIB — 1991 CONS		1992 LIB — 1992 CONS	
Economic	61%	— 36%	66%	— 31%
Social	78%	— 17%	81%	— 19%
Foreign	78%	— 19%	69%	— 30%

Key Votes of the 102d Congress

1. Ban Striker Replace FOR	5. Handgun Wait/7-Day FOR	9. Use Force in Gulf AGN
2. $ for Homeownership FOR	6. Overseas Mil. Abortion FOR	10. US Mil. Abroad $ Cut FOR
3. Tax Rich/Cut Mid Cls. FOR	7. Obscn. Art NEA $ Ban FOR	11. Limit SDI Funds AGN
4. FY93/$15B Def. Cut AGN	8. Death Pen. from Jury AGN	12. Cuba Trade Embargo AGN

Key Votes of the 103d Congress

1. Family Leave FOR	2. Deficit Reduction FOR	3. Stimulus Plan FOR

Election Results

1992 general	Barbara B. Kennelly (D,ACP) 164,735	(67%)	($572,841)
	Philip L. Steele (R)................... 75,113	(31%)	($3,612)
	Two Others 5,582	(2%)	
1992 primary	Barbara B. Kennelly (D), nominated by convention		
1990 general	Barbara B. Kennelly (D).............. 126,566	(71%)	($406,138)
	James P. Garvey (R).................. 50,690	(29%)	

SECOND DISTRICT

One of the most technologically advanced parts of late 20th Century America appears in one of the least likely places—the hilly, wooded land of eastern Connecticut, with its Yankee villages and old mill towns and high-income havens like Old Saybrook. But this was always high-tech country: New London and Norwich were among the 13 colonies' leading workshops and ports, where in the 19th Century, factories sprang up in the little villages on the fast-flowing Quinebaug and Shetucket Rivers that provided waterpower. None became a metropolis, and a sandbar across the mouth of the Connecticut River kept ocean commerce out. But somehow the Yankee technical knack of these towns and rocky hills remained, ever adapting itself to new technology and absorbing the talents of the children and grandchildren of mostly Catholic immigrants. Today, eastern Connecticut, or that large part of it that makes up the 2d Congressional District, has four nuclear power plants, the largest number in any area of similar population in the U.S. In Groton, across the Thames River from New London, is General Dynamics' Electric Boat Company, the major producer of the Seawolf nuclear submarine.

For most of this century, politics in eastern Connecticut was a close battle between Protestant Yankee Republicans and Catholic immigrant-stock Democrats, with the two parties frequently trading control of the district from 1934 to 1974. Then for nearly two decades the seat was held by two baby boom liberal Democrats, opponents of the Vietnam war who benefited from the Watergate scandal and whose ebullient personalities helped them overcome the unpopularity of some of their issue stands: Christopher Dodd, until he ran for the Senate in 1980, and now Sam Gejdenson. With the New England high-tech recession and collapse of real estate values, a new politics surfaced in 1992: an abandonment of party lines, with plurality for Bill Clinton and a big vote for Ross Perot (27% in the 2d District, his highest in the state), in what had been Reagan-Bush territory, and a near-upset of Gejdenson despite, or perhaps because of, all the advantages of incumbency.

Gejdenson was born in a German displaced persons camp, the son of concentration camp inmates, and grew up on a dairy farm in Bozrah; he has a wry sense of humor and styles himself "just a farm boy who spends his week in Washington." His convictions come from the Vietnam era in which he came of political age, and for years he has sought to apply the lessons of Vietnam, even as American ideals inspired democratic upsurges in Eastern Europe, East Asia and Latin America. He makes exceptions to his usual opposition to controversial weapons systems for the nuclear submarines built at Electric Boat, and even tried to mediate a strike there in 1988. In 1992, pressed for reelection, his proudest boast was that he had secured another Seawolf contract over much Washington opposition. He is also one of Congress's most vocal supporters of vast increases in the Coast Guard budget (its academy is in New London). Gejdenson has long championed defense conversion, and introduced a bill to transfer $30 billion from European bases to areas at home most hurt by defense cutbacks; but he admits "there are no silver bullets" and that the Defense budget can't be a jobs program. Gejdenson also made headlines accusing Bush Administration officials of misdeeds in the "Iraqgate" scandal, arguing that they tilted toward Saddam Hussein and let him use agricultural credits to buy weapons before the August 1990 invasion of Kuwait—arguments of some force, though undercut by Gejdenson's vote against the Gulf war resolution.

Gejdenson was suddenly in trouble in 1992 partly because he had always been rather liberal for the district, partly because of general anti-incumbent feeling and in great part because this onetime rebel had become a seemingly complacent Washington insider. On campaign finance, for example, Gejdenson spent much time in 1991 and 1992 on a reform bill; his formula was that one-third of campaign money could come from PACs, one-third from large individual contributors, and one-third from public financing which would be paid for by ending the tax deduction for lobbying expenses and imposing registration fees on PACs. Republicans opposed public financing on principle (though as Gejdenson pointed out their presidential candidates have accepted millions in public money) and argued that spending limits ($600,000 in Gejdenson's plan) usually end up benefiting incumbents. Gejdenson also advocated hiring a House administrator, appointed by the House leadership, and downplayed the House bank scandal; he was also the unofficial manager of Speaker Tom Foley's splendidly successful campaign for reelection to that post.

At home Gejdenson had, as usual, underfinanced opposition, in the person of Pfizer chemist and state Senator Edward Munster; Gejdenson had gobs of PAC money, plus the endorsement of Lowell Weicker's A Connecticut Party. But Munster hit hard, charging Gejdenson with voting "against every weapons system except the bow and arrow" and that "Sam greased the wheels for Saddam" from his work on the Foreign Affairs Subcommittee. Gejdenson, evading early debates, responded by hitting Munster for, among other things, evading $65.37 in property taxes. Munster seemed to ride on the Perot tide, echoing his fiscal ideas, and in the last weeks the perception grew that Gejdenson could lose. He didn't, but it was a close call: this was a 51%–49% race, Gejdenson's closest yet. He lost most of the district's towns and would not have won without his margins in the two university towns, Middletown (Wesleyan) and Storrs (UConn). He can continue to be an influential pillar of the Democratic leadership in Washington, but he may face a tough challenge in the district again, particularly if the Democrats' record does not turn out as well as voters hope.

The People: Pop. 1990: 548,018; 45% rural; 12% age 65+; 92% White; 4% Black; 1% Asian; 1% Other; 3% Hispanic origin. Voting age pop.: 421,275; 3% Black; 2% Hispanic origin. Households: 59% married couple families; 27% married couple fams. w. children; 48% college educ.; median household income: $38,524; per capita income: $16,946; median gross rent: $564; median house value: $150,900.

1992 Presidential Vote			1988 Presidential Vote		
Clinton (D)	113,553	(43%)	Bush (R)	115,314	(51%)
Bush (R)	79,110	(30%)	Dukakis (D)	111,939	(49%)
Perot (I)	72,782	(27%)			

Rep. Samuel Gejdenson (D)

Elected 1980; b. May 20, 1948, Eschwege, Germany; home, Bozrah; Mitchell Col., A.S. 1966, U. of CT, B.A. 1970; Jewish; married (Karen).

Career: CT House of Reps., 1974–78; Legis. Liaison to Gov. Grasso, 1979–80.

Offices: 2416 RHOB 20515, 202-225-2076. Also 74 W. Main, Norwich 06360, 203-886-0139; and 94 Court St., Middletown 06457, 203-346-1123.

Committees: *Foreign Affairs* (2d of 27 D): Economic Policy, Trade and Environment (Chmn.). *House Administration* (4th of 12 D): Accounts; Office Systems (Chmn.). *Natural Resources* (9th of 28 D): Native American Affairs; Oversight and Investigations. *Joint Committee on Printing* (2d of 5). *Joint Committee on the Organization of Congress* (5th of 12).

Group Ratings

	ADA	ACLU	COPE	CDF	CFA	LCV	ACU	NTLC	NSI	COC	CEI
1992	90	100	92	80	100	63	12	5	30	38	6
1991	95	—	100	100	83	54	0	—	—	20	13

National Journal Ratings

	1991 LIB — 1991 CONS		1992 LIB — 1992 CONS	
Economic	84% —	12%	66% —	31%
Social	84% —	12%	88% —	8%
Foreign	92% —	0%	76% —	19%

Key Votes of the 102d Congress

1. Ban Striker Replace	FOR	5. Handgun Wait/7-Day	FOR	9. Use Force in Gulf	AGN
2. $ for Homeownership	AGN	6. Overseas Mil. Abortion	FOR	10. US Mil. Abroad $ Cut	FOR
3. Tax Rich/Cut Mid Cls.	FOR	7. Obscn. Art NEA $ Ban	AGN	11. Limit SDI Funds	FOR
4. FY93/$15B Def. Cut	AGN	8. Death Pen. from Jury	AGN	12. Cuba Trade Embargo	AGN

Key Votes of the 103d Congress

1. Family Leave   FOR   2. Deficit Reduction   FOR   3. Stimulus Plan   FOR

Election Results

1992 general	Samuel Gejdenson (D-ACP)............	123,291	(51%)	($1,019,417)
	Edward W. Munster (R)...............	119,416	(49%)	($140,139)
1992 primary	Samuel Gejdenson (D), nominated by convention			
1990 general	Samuel Gejdenson (D)................	105,085	(60%)	($464,500)
	John M. Ragsdale (R).................	70,922	(40%)	($112,881)

THIRD DISTRICT

Nearly two centuries ago, in 1798, Eli Whitney, a young Yale graduate, won an order from the federal government to produce 10,000 muskets at $13.40 each: the beginning of Connecticut's defense industry. Six years before, Whitney had invented the cotton gin, which revolutionized the South but which for years only embroiled him in a patent suit. On the musket contract, he was determined to make a profit right off, so he set up a system of interchangeable parts and invented a milling machine and gauges: the beginning of standardized American manufacturing. It was also the beginning of New Haven, Connecticut, as a manufacturing center, for Whitney set up his factory along a small, rapidly flowing river just north of this town established more than 150 years before as a religious haven for Puritans. For the next 150 years or so, the town mass-produced rifles, clocks, locks, hardware and toys—anything its tinkerers and entrepreneurs could fashion.

New Haven still bears signs of being a factory town. Yale's gothic spires, redbrick halls and modernist skating rink may be the visual focus of the city, but they are not its economic heart. New Haven is far less dependent on factories than it used to be, but in the 1980s did not develop as big a high-wage white-collar economy as nearby Hartford. Politics in the New Haven area for years was a three-cornered battle, between Yankee Republicans, Irish Democrats and Italians who became its largest ethnic group and usually voted Republican: preferences that go back to the less than warm welcome each group of immigrants received from the last. This has been reflected in the politics of the 3d Congressional District of Connecticut, which coincides essentially with the New Haven metropolitan area, long since spread beyond the narrow city limits over the hills of what were once Yankee villages and countryside. Though often regarded as a Democratic seat, the 3d has been marginal, changing partisan hands several times in the 1980s as well as the 1940s and 1950s.

Representing the district now is Rosa DeLauro, whose roots are in New Haven's Italian-American community and who has high contacts in national politics: she was a top staffer to Senator Christopher Dodd, headed the EMILY's List fundraising group for women candidates and is married to Bill Clinton's 1992 pollster Stan Greenberg. When 3d District incumbent Bruce Morrison ran for governor in 1990, DeLauro won the Democratic nomination here unopposed, and then in a fiery contest narrowly defeated anti-tax and antiabortion state legislator Tom Scott. DeLauro is sympathetic to liberal cultural stands, but is something of a moderate on fiscal issues. The one time she got in trouble in the House was when she was called down for urging that the Senate hold "a full and public" hearing on Anita Hill's charges against Supreme Court nominee Clarence Thomas; it is against House rules to urge the Senate to do anything. In her 1990 campaign, she opposed the budget summit agreement and its tax increases; she was the only Democrat on the Ways and Means Committee to vote against the highway bill with its five cent gas tax and boasted of an amendment to save taxpayers $400 million on bridge repairs; back home in 1991 she opposed a state income tax. DeLauro says she is more interested in avoiding taxes on the middle class than on imposing them on the rich. She pushed a bill to restore pensions for former Raymark employees after their insurer failed.

The 1992 campaign was a rematch, with a different result. Once again DeLauro, with her Washington and national feminist contacts, vastly outraised Scott. Though Scott started the Connecticut Taxpayers Committee and billed himself as "the man Lowell Weicker dislikes" (but surely not the only one?), anti-income tax feeling had cooled by fall 1992; and Scott may have been hurt by the perception he was a negative campaigner. Anyway, DeLauro won 66%–34% in a district carried by Clinton by 44%–35%, in a very good year for the DeLauro-Greenberg household.

The People: Pop. 1990: 547,904; 12% rural; 15% age 65+; 82% White; 12% Black; 1% Asian; 2% Other; 5% Hispanic origin. Voting age pop.: 426,862; 10% Black; 4% Hispanic origin. Households: 54% married couple families; 23% married couple fams. w. children; 48% college educ.; median household income: $39,815; per capita income: $18,243; median gross rent: $623; median house value: $173,300.

1992 Presidential Vote			1988 Presidential Vote		
Clinton (D)	121,163	(44%)	Bush (R)	121,466	(50%)
Bush (R)	96,085	(35%)	Dukakis (D)	119,417	(50%)
Perot (I)	54,147	(20%)			

Rep. Rosa L. DeLauro (D)

Elected 1990; b. Mar. 2, 1943, New Haven; home, New Haven; Marymount Col., B.A. 1964, London Sch. of Economics, 1962–63, Columbia U., M.A. 1966; Catholic; married (Stanley Greenberg).

Career: Exec. Asst., New Haven Mayor Frank Logue, 1976–77; Exec. Asst. and Development Admin., City of New Haven, 1977–79; Chief of Staff, U.S. Sen. Christopher Dodd, 1980–87; Exec. Dir., Countdown '87, 1987–88; Exec. Dir., EMILY's List, 1989.

Offices: 327 CHOB 20515, 202-225-3661. Also 265 Church St., New Haven 06510, 203-562-3718.

Committees: *Appropriations* (32d of 37 D): Agriculture, Rural Development, Food and Drug Administration and Related Agencies; Labor, Health and Human Services, and Education.

Group Ratings

	ADA	ACLU	COPE	CDF	CFA	LCV	ACU	NTLC	NSI	COC	CEI
1992	90	87	92	90	100	94	4	0	20	13	13
1991	95	—	92	100	78	100	0	—	—	20	9

National Journal Ratings

	1991 LIB — 1991 CONS			1992 LIB — 1992 CONS	
Economic	79%	—	18%	78%	—	18%
Social	78%	—	17%	78%	—	21%
Foreign	87%	—	13%	69%	—	30%

Key Votes of the 102d Congress

1. Ban Striker Replace	FOR	5. Handgun Wait/7-Day	FOR	9. Use Force in Gulf	AGN
2. $ for Homeownership	AGN	6. Overseas Mil. Abortion	FOR	10. US Mil. Abroad $ Cut	FOR
3. Tax Rich/Cut Mid Cls.	FOR	7. Obscn. Art NEA $ Ban	AGN	11. Limit SDI Funds	FOR
4. FY93/$15B Def. Cut	AGN	8. Death Pen. from Jury	AGN	12. Cuba Trade Embargo	AGN

Key Votes of the 103d Congress

1. Family Leave	FOR	2. Deficit Reduction	FOR	3. Stimulus Plan	FOR

Election Results

1992 general	Rosa L. DeLauro (D-ACP).............	162,568	(66%)	($1,022,131)
	Thomas Scott (R).....................	84,952	(34%)	($219,786)
1992 primary	Rosa L. DeLauro (D), nominated by convention			
1990 general	Rosa L. DeLauro (D)..................	90,722	(52%)	($957,982)
	Thomas Scott (R).....................	83,440	(48%)	($304,258)

FOURTH DISTRICT

America's most affluent suburbs and some of America's biggest corporate headquarters now share what Americans in earlier centuries would have regarded as unlikely real estate: the hilly land rising from Long Island Sound in the southwest corner of Connecticut. This was lightly populated Yankee farm country in the 17th and 18th Centuries; in the 19th it became industrial as Bridgeport became a factory town, famous as the home of P. T. Barnum; by the early 20th, Greenwich and other Yankee villages clustered around commuter railroad stations became the home of some of New York's elite. Greenwich's beautifully manicured hills, its elaborately simple boat docks, its carefully casual roads, its good manners and dull haircuts, 16 private clubs and 10 private schools, give it a plainly American and understatedly affluent look. But New York's corporate leaders, eager as always to minimize their own commutes, have moved the headquarters of their big firms out of Manhattan, past the Bronx and Westchester, to Greenwich and Stamford and Fairfield and points inland: General Electric, American Brands, Union Carbide, Champion International, Pitney Bowes, United Parcel and Olin are there, to name just the biggest.

The 4th Congressional District of Connecticut covers all of Connecticut along Long Island Sound from Bridgeport to Greenwich, plus several inland towns. It includes Stamford, chock full of office complexes; woodsy Darien and New Canaan; Norwalk has its industrial zone and modest neighborhoods down by the tracks; artsy-craftsy Westport; and Fairfield, home of GE and of affluent overspill from Bridgeport. The basic political balance has been the same since the 1940s, when the heavily affluent suburbs attracted enough people to outvote Bridgeport and elect Clare Boothe Luce as congresswoman in 1942 and 1944. More than the rest of Connecticut, the 4th is oriented to New York rather than Hartford or Boston; people here watch New York TV stations; they are Yankee, not Red Sox, fans; their political attitudes are shaped by what is happening in the City, not in Connecticut. The specter of a state income tax helped Republican John Rowland carry every city and town in the district over its onetime Congressman Lowell Weicker in the 1990 governor's race; the specter of religious right domination of the Republican Party eroded the Episcopalian Republican vote and helped Bill Clinton make a dead heat of the race here against Greenwich native George Bush.

The 4th District's congressman, Christopher Shays, is a product of the upscale towns who sees the district as urban rather than suburban and who has one of the most liberal voting records of House Republicans. Shays volunteered for the Peace Corps with his wife and then served 12 years in the Connecticut House, where he worked with Common Cause on rules reform. He won this seat in 1987 by beating a culturally conservative Democrat from Bridgeport after incumbent Stewart McKinney, a liberal Republican who left his name on an act to help the homeless, died of AIDS. Shays is a pleasant man with a stubborn streak: in 1985, he went to the length of going to jail for seven days to protest judicial system corruption. In Washington, he has been critical of House Republican leaders; he is clearly a party maverick, though, with his plain sincerity, is not disliked.

Shays is somewhat conservative on economic issues; he votes for the balanced budget amendment and is an enthusiastic supporter of the line-item veto. He voted against the ban on striker replacements and unemployment extension bills. But he has been affected by Bridgeport's recent problems—the former mayor tried to declare municipal bankruptcy in 1991, it had a hard time getting rid of 30,000-ton dump "Mount Trashmore," and the University of Bridgeport has been taken over by the Unification Church. So Shays backs an "Urban Marshall Plan" to rebuild central cities, with enterprise zones, economic development block grants, environmental stabilization and payments in lieu of taxes for public housing. He was the lead sponsor for cable TV reregulation and a key voice in getting large cuts in the defense budget for overseas bases.

Shays's toughest contest, in retrospect, was winning the four-way Republican primary nomination by convention in 1987. He has been reelected easily ever since.

The People: Pop. 1990: 547,561; 4% rural; 14% age 65+; 74% White; 13% Black; 2% Asian; 4% Other; 11% Hispanic origin. Voting age pop.: 425,513; 12% Black; 9% Hispanic origin. Households: 55% married couple families; 23% married couple fams. w. children; 54% college educ.; median household income: $47,636; per capita income: $27,130; median gross rent: $706; median house value: $275,500.

1992 Presidential Vote			1988 Presidential Vote		
Bush (R)	110,072	(42%)	Bush (R)	138,369	(58%)
Clinton (D)	109,122	(42%)	Dukakis (D)	101,232	(42%)
Perot (I)	40,802	(16%)			

Rep. Christopher Shays (R)

Elected Aug. 1987; b. Oct. 18, 1945, Stamford; home, Stamford; Principia Col., B.A. 1968, NYU, M.B.A. 1974, M.P.A. 1978; Christian Scientist; married (Betsi).

Career: Peace Corps 1968–70; Aide, Trumbull Mayor, 1971–72; CT House of Reps., 1974–87.

Offices: 1034 LHOB 20515, 202-225-5541. Also 10 Middle St., Bridgeport 06604, 203-579-5870; 888 Washington Blvd., Stamford 06901, 203-357-8277; and 125 East Ave., Norwalk 06851, 203-886-6469.

Committees: *Budget* (4th of 17 R). *Government Operations* (5th of 16 R): Commerce, Consumer and Monetary Affairs; Employment, Housing and Aviation.

Group Ratings

	ADA	ACLU	COPE	CDF	CFA	LCV	ACU	NTLC	NSI	COC	CEI
1992	65	70	67	30	100	100	40	85	70	38	57
1991	60	—	42	50	50	100	50	—	—	70	65

National Journal Ratings

	1991 LIB — 1991 CONS			1992 LIB — 1992 CONS		
Economic	34%	—	65%	41%	—	59%
Social	62%	—	37%	56%	—	43%
Foreign	67%	—	32%	71%	—	26%

Key Votes of the 102d Congress

1. Ban Striker Replace	AGN	5. Handgun Wait/7-Day	FOR	9. Use Force in Gulf	FOR
2. $ for Homeownership	FOR	6. Overseas Mil. Abortion	FOR	10. US Mil. Abroad $ Cut	FOR
3. Tax Rich/Cut Mid Cls.	AGN	7. Obscn. Art NEA $ Ban	FOR	11. Limit SDI Funds	FOR
4. FY93/$15B Def. Cut	FOR	8. Death Pen. from Jury	AGN	12. Cuba Trade Embargo	FOR

Election Results

1992 general	Christopher Shays (R)	147,816	(67%)	($383,207)
	Dave Schropfer (D)	58,666	(27%)	($29,162)
	Al Smith (ACP)	11,679	(5%)	($24,518)
	Two Others	1,454	(1%)	
1992 primary	Christopher Shays (R), nominated by convention			
1990 general	Christopher Shays (R)	105,682	(75%)	($397,417)
	Al Smith (D)	35,352	(25%)	($90,634)

FIFTH DISTRICT

Central Connecticut might be known as the Switzerland of America: its stony hills are physically isolated, the climate is forbidding, local manners are frosty, there is nothing to suggest lavishness. Yet in the last two hundred years, the mountains of Switzerland and the hills of Connecticut have been transformed from subsistence farmland to some of the most productive and affluent places on earth. Their secrets have been thrift, hard work, inventiveness and an intolerance for imprecision. Keeping time is a common motif: Switzerland was long the world's leading watchmaker, and Connecticut has long been America's leading clockmaker. The comparison at some point breaks down: Switzerland has prospered by closing others out, its political neutrality and financial probity reassuring investors and undergirding its banking industry. Connecticut, like the rest of America, is an open society, welcoming newcomers and imbuing immigrants with the Yankee knack for tinkering and precision work. It has also been quick to adapt to market changes: Danbury was once the nation's leading producer of hats; now it cuts almost no felt but is a major corporate headquarters city. Waterbury, once the nation's largest producer of brass, saw the last of its big three brass fabricators shut down in 1985, but has replaced that with health care and now two local hospitals are the city's biggest employers.

An irregularly shaped slice of central Connecticut, all inland from Long Island Sound, from Meriden west to Danbury and the high-income havens of Ridgefield and Wilton, makes up Connecticut's 5th Congressional District. This was the Federalist heartland in the early 19th Century. It voted Republican for nearly a century, then became Democratic as Catholics started outnumbering Protestants. Now, cultural conservatism and economic growth have made it mostly Republican again: it gave George Bush a 7% margin over Bill Clinton in 1992, and has elected only Republican congressmen since 1984.

The current congressmen is one of the most distinctive members of the House, its only black Republican, Gary Franks. He started with an attractive biography: the son of a millworker (all six of whose children went to college), captain of the Yale basketball team, a self-made millionaire in Waterbury real estate, a three-term alderman with the strong support of then-Waterbury Mayor Joe Santopietro. Franks ran for state controller in 1986 and, though he lost, he did carry the 5th District; in 1990, when 5th District incumbent John Rowland ran for governor, Franks took his mostly (he's pro-choice) conservative platform—for the flag amendment, capital gains cuts, for Bush's veto of the 1990 civil rights bill and against racial quotas—into the campaign. He was by no means the party's first pick, finishing last on the first round of balloting at the district convention and being selected as a compromise on the ninth ballot; he was able to win because the rule dropping the low man on each ballot was suspended. In the general, he faced Toby Moffett, one of the first successful baby boomer liberals, who won the 6th District House seat in the Watergate year of 1974, then lost statewide races in 1982 and 1986, and ended up a reporter on Hartford TV. In a result in which race seemed to play little role—the district is only 4% black—Franks won 52%–47%, the first black Republican House victory since Oscar DePriest won his last term on the South Side of Chicago in 1932.

Franks's first term was less auspicious. He did become part of the Congressional Black Caucus, but nonetheless did not seem daunted by being the only black to vote for the Gulf war resolution, to oppose what he regarded as racial quotas and to support Justice Clarence Thomas. At home, he was sued by an S&L for defaulting on loans totalling $471,000, but he settled on repayment terms. He had high staff turnover and routinely ignored many local politicians. Though Connecticut's only Armed Services Committee member, he was not particularly active when the Seawolf, the mainstay of Connecticut's Electric Boat, was at stake—although he did lobby Secretary Dick Cheney personally. In 1991, he hired Mayor Santopietro's brother for what looked like a "no show" job; then both Santopietros were indicted and convicted on federal corruption charges in 1992. In short, Franks gave constituents and colleagues many reasons for believing he was a flake.

All this helped draw serious Democratic opposition. Lynn Taborsak, a plumber, ran as a liberal, who as a state legislator supported the state income tax and proposed including discussion of masturbation in sex education curricula. Probate Judge James Lawlor, more culturally conservative, had a strong base in Waterbury. The charges started flying: Taborsak said Lawlor had "repeatedly shaken down local attorneys" for campaign money; Lawlor attacked Taborsak for collecting unemployment compensation while in the legislature. Lawlor narrowly won the primary, at which point Taborsak ran as the nominee of Governor Lowell Weicker's A Connecticut Party. This was a break for Franks. His vote was down in the Waterbury area, where he is known best and which he lost to Lawlor, who carried the eastern half of the district. But in the affluent towns around Danbury and Weston, which cast 35% of the votes, Taborsak ran ahead of Lawlor; Franks, despite losing many Republican votes and running under 50%, was able to carry the area. Overall, Franks had 44% to 31% for Lawlor and 22% for Taborsak. He is obviously vulnerable to united Democratic opposition, even in this basically Republican seat, unless he is seen to perform better than in his first term.

The People: Pop. 1990: 547,907; 21% rural; 13% age 65+; 88% White; 5% Black; 1% Asian; 2% Other; 6% Hispanic origin. Voting age pop.: 416,500; 4% Black; 5% Hispanic origin. Households: 61% married couple families; 28% married couple fams. w. children; 50% college educ.; median household income: $44,056; per capita income: $20,316; median gross rent: $574; median house value: $182,500.

1992 Presidential Vote			1988 Presidential Vote		
Bush (R)	111,327	(42%)	Bush (R)	137,962	(59%)
Clinton (D)	93,966	(35%)	Dukakis (D)	95,236	(41%)
Perot (I)	60,891	(23%)			

Rep. Gary A. Franks (R)

Elected 1990; b. Feb. 9, 1953, Waterbury; home, Waterbury; Yale, B.A. 1975; Baptist; married (Donna).

Career: Pres., GAF Realty; Waterbury City Alderman, 1985–90.

Offices: 435 CHOB 20515, 202-225-3822. Also 135 Grand St., #210, Waterbury 06701, 203-573-1418; 30 Main St., Danbury 06810, 203-790-1263; 1 First St., Seymour Town Hall, Seymour 06483, 800-556-5089; 142 E. Main St., #204, Meriden City Hall, Meriden 06450, 203-630-4130.

Committees: *Energy and Commerce* (15th of 17 R): Energy and Power; Health and the Environment.

Group Ratings

	ADA	ACLU	COPE	CDF	CFA	LCV	ACU	NTLC	NSI	COC	CEI
1992	20	17	25	30	20	31	88	80	100	88	72
1991	15	—	25	30	22	15	85	—	—	100	75

National Journal Ratings

	1991 LIB — 1991 CONS	1992 LIB — 1992 CONS
Economic	18% — 79%	16% — 80%
Social	40% — 58%	35% — 64%
Foreign	17% — 78%	30% — 64%

Key Votes of the 102d Congress

1. Ban Striker Replace	AGN	5. Handgun Wait/7-Day	AGN	9. Use Force in Gulf	FOR
2. $ for Homeownership	FOR	6. Overseas Mil. Abortion	FOR	10. US Mil. Abroad $ Cut	AGN
3. Tax Rich/Cut Mid Cls.	AGN	7. Obscn. Art NEA $ Ban	FOR	11. Limit SDI Funds	AGN
4. FY93/$15B Def. Cut	AGN	8. Death Pen. from Jury	FOR	12. Cuba Trade Embargo	AGN

Key Votes of the 103d Congress

1. Family Leave	AGN	2. Deficit Reduction	AGN	3. Stimulus Plan	AGN

Election Results

1992 general	Gary A. Franks (R)................	104,891	(44%)	($631,851)
	James J. Lawlor (D)................	74,791	(31%)	($345,164)
	Lynn H. Taborsak (ACP)	54,022	(22%)	($493,563)
	Three Others........................	6,579	(3%)	
1992 primary	Gary A. Franks (R), nominated by convention			
1990 general	Gary A. Franks (R)...................	93,912	(52%)	($581,625)
	Anthony Toby Moffett (D)	85,903	(47%)	($877,116)
	Other................................	1,888	(1%)	

SIXTH DISTRICT

Ball bearings and sports broadcasts: these are some of the things that have made Connecticut, even in recession, the highest income state in the nation. Connecticut, from its Yankee past to its Ellis Islander present and ahead to its third wave of immigrants future, has been a land of tinkerers specializing in precision work; much of the American ball bearing industry is centered around the factory town of New Britain. Connecticut has also lived off ingenuity and adaptability, giving consumers what they want, even when they don't know what that is. As when Bill Rasmussen, a sports announcer in Bristol, down the road from New Britain, had the idea in 1978 to put local sports and UConn games in Connecticut living rooms by transmitting satellite feeds on cable. RCA, eager to unload transponders, convinced him that for the same price he could beam sport broadcasts all over America. So ESPN was born; today it beams sports 24 hours a day up from Bristol.

New Britain and Bristol are the largest cities in the 6th Congressional District of Connecticut, which stretches from the urban corridor alongside the Connecticut River north of Hartford to the tiny Litchfield County towns north and west of industrial Waterbury and Danbury. Its Yankee towns, bearing witness to the prosperity of the Revolutionary era, have now become a country home mecca for ultra-rich New Yorkers. Nonetheless, this once entirely Yankee and Federalist land is now heavily ethnic and politically closely contested. Enfield and Windsor Locks, north of Hartford, are heavily Italian-American; New Britain is heavily Polish-American; the mill towns of Torrington and Winsted, in the clefts of river valleys, are a mixture.

Nancy Johnson, congresswoman from the 6th since 1982, has an interesting resume for a politician: a doctor's wife and a teacher, she raised three children and was active in charitable and community affairs before she was elected to the legislature in 1976 from heavily Democratic New Britain. When 6th District Congressman Toby Moffett ran against Senator Lowell Weicker in 1982, Johnson beat a nuclear freeze organizer for the House seat. Her gender was probably an asset, suggesting more compassion than some voters expect in a Republican; and with her practical experience, she was more woven into the fabric of everyday life than the young campaign organizers who are the Democrats' strongest candidates here.

In the House, Johnson has been an active and effective legislator. Her voting record is mostly market-oriented on economics, fairly liberal on foreign policy and cultural social issues, including abortion. She is pro-choice and has spent much time on child care: she opposed the Democrat's ABC bill and sponsored the Republican substitute giving states $250 million in block grants but without ABC's detailed federal guidelines. She also took the lead on eliminating the old day care tax credit, which tended to help high-income parents, and replaced it with $300 million in vouchers to low-income working mothers. On all these, she has combined genuine concern with the principle that those closest to children, not federal functionaries, can make the best decisions about child care, and that benefits should be targeted toward the needy.

On Ways and Means, Johnson has worked on the unemployment benefits extension, to get states to pay partial benefits for part-time workers and provide for temporary forgiveness of mortgage payments for persons who are "clearly going to regain their footing." She backs a $2,500 tax credit for first-time homebuyers. On health care, she backed the Bush Administration approach of tax credits for low income persons to buy insurance; she seeks federal malpractice protection to doctors and others in federally funded clinics. With Fred Grandy of Iowa, she has introduced a welfare reform package which includes job training. With John Spratt of South Carolina, she founded the Ball Bearing Caucus.

Johnson has been a budget buff, serving on the Budget Committee in 1987–88 and helping to frame the moderate Republican 92 Group budget that included some sharp cuts and some tax increases. She vocally supported President Bush's 1990 budget summit packages, which contained similar features, and was enraged when Minority Whip Newt Gingrich (whose election she supported in March 1989) opposed them. Johnson also decided not to run against Senator Christopher Dodd in 1992, although one poll at the time showed him with an insignificant 35%–32% lead. Perhaps she had her eye on another prize; in early 1993, she seemed the Republican frontrunner to challenge Lowell Weicker for the statehouse in 1994.

The People: Pop. 1990: 547,747; 32% rural; 14% age 65+; 93% White; 2% Black; 1% Asian; 2% Other; 3% Hispanic origin. Voting age pop.: 423,560; 2% Black; 3% Hispanic origin. Households: 60% married couple families; 26% married couple fams. w. children; 49% college educ.; median household income: $42,817; per capita income: $19,863; median gross rent: $571; median house value: $165,900.

1992 Presidential Vote

Clinton (D)	110,828	(40%)
Bush (R)	99,633	(36%)
Perot (I)	67,995	(24%)

1988 Presidential Vote

Bush (R)	128,297	(53%)
Dukakis (D)	113,418	(47%)

Rep. Nancy L. Johnson (R)

Elected 1982; b. Jan. 5, 1935, Chicago, IL; home, New Britain; U. of Chicago, 1951–53, Radcliffe Col., B.A. 1957, U. of London, 1957–58; Unitarian; married (Theodore).

Career: Pres., Sheldon Community Guidance Clinic; Adjunct Prof., Central CT St. Col., 1968–71; CT Senate, 1976–82.

Offices: 343 CHOB 20515, 202-225-4476. Also 480 Myrtle St., #200, New Britain 06051, 203-223-8412.

Committees: *Standards of Official Conduct* (2d of 7 R). *Ways and Means* (6th of 14 R): Health; Trade.

Group Ratings

	ADA	ACLU	COPE	CDF	CFA	LCV	ACU	NTLC	NSI	COC	CEI
1992	40	65	42	50	53	38	58	70	100	75	54
1991	35	—	42	50	33	38	55	—	—	70	47

National Journal Ratings

	1991 LIB — 1991 CONS		1992 LIB — 1992 CONS	
Economic	33%	— 66%	28%	— 70%
Social	54%	— 44%	54%	— 45%
Foreign	38%	— 61%	38%	— 56%

Key Votes of the 102d Congress

1. Ban Striker Replace	AGN	
2. $ for Homeownership	FOR	
3. Tax Rich/Cut Mid Cls.	AGN	
4. FY93/$15B Def. Cut	AGN	

1. Ban Striker Replace　AGN
2. $ for Homeownership　FOR
3. Tax Rich/Cut Mid Cls.AGN
4. FY93/$15B Def. Cut　AGN
5. Handgun Wait/7-Day　FOR
6. Overseas Mil. Abortion FOR
7. Obscn. Art NEA $ Ban FOR
8. Death Pen. from Jury　AGN
9. Use Force in Gulf　FOR
10. US Mil. Abroad $ CutAGN
11. Limit SDI Funds　AGN
12. Cuba Trade Embargo AGN

Key Votes of the 103d Congress

1. Family Leave　FOR　2. Deficit Reduction　AGN　3. Stimulus Plan　AGN

Election Results

1992 general	Nancy L. Johnson (R)................	166,967	(70%)	($570,046)
	Eugene F. Slason (D)	60,373	(25%)	($38,968)
	Daniel W. Plawecki (Concerned Citizens) ...	9,544	(4%)	
	Two Others	2,713	(1%)	
1992 primary	Nancy L. Johnson (R), nominated by convention			
1990 general	Nancy L. Johnson (R)................	141,105	(74%)	($556,718)
	Paul Kulas (D)	48,628	(26%)	($22,211)

DELAWARE

Delaware, second smallest state in area, sixth smallest in population, has a fair claim to being typical of the East Coast and even of the country, despite a peculiar history. These three counties of Delaware owe their separate existence to the politics of the proprietors of William Penn's colony of Pennsylvania, and to Delawareans' own speed in ratifying the Constitution which made it literally the "First State." One might add that over its long history Delaware has been unusually affluent, with some of the nation's highest income levels during the early 20th Century; two-thirds of its people live in the single mostly-wealthy, mostly-suburban county of New Castle; it houses, in beautiful cobblestone mansions in its chateau country, many members of the most extensive wealthy family in America, the du Ponts. Yet the United States today, after all, is mostly suburban and throughout its history has been by world standards affluent, and the du Ponts don't elevate the median income any more than a few hundred more lawyers would. Delaware's ethnic and racial mixture is much like that along the rest of the East Coast, and not that much different than the nation's, though with fewer than average Hispanics and Asians; but there is a mixture here of suburbs, old immigrant neighborhoods, black slums and farmlands. If not all parts of the nation can follow Delaware's exact path to continued prosperity, perhaps they can get an idea of the direction to travel.

Of course, the focus of Delaware's economy during the last two centuries has been the business started when Eleuthere Irenee du Pont, the practical business-minded son of a dreamy, idealistic French immigrant, built a gunpowder mill on the banks of Brandywine Creek in 1802. This was the first enterprise of the family du Pont, and it expanded to become one of America's great munitions and chemical companies. It grew especially rapidly during World War I, generating so much capital that the Du Pont Company bought control of General Motors in the 1920s and held GM for thirty years while it was America's largest corporation. That capital also financed what was arguably the world's finest research and development program. In the years during and after World War II, Du Pont prospered by bringing to the consumer and industrial market new synthetics and plastics like rayon, nylon, cellophane, polyethylene, lucite and teflon: "Better Living Through Chemistry." Delaware's other major business of note has been creating other businesses. In the late 19th Century, it pioneered liberal laws of incorporation, giving more flexibility and power to managers and owners. A large share of the nation's big companies are incorporated in Delaware—their legal births take place in a federal-style building near the Capitol in tiny Dover—which means that much of the nation's corporate law, notably in the 1980s on mergers and acquisitions, is made in Delaware courts.

In the last 20 years, Delaware's job growth, like that of the rest of the country, has been generated less by visible big business units than by the explosive growth of many small ones. Chemical manufacturing, always more capital- than labor-intensive, remains important, but accounts for fewer than 10% of Delaware's jobs. More jobs were created in the 1980s after Governor Pete du Pont's successful fight for liberalizing Delaware's banking laws to encourage out-of-state banks to locate operations here. They did: Chase, Manufacturers Hanover, Morgan and other banks brought 14,000 jobs into Delaware, with the number of finance jobs more than doubling in just over a decade. Delaware has the best business climate of "high intensity" manufacturing states, according to a Grant Thornton study, which credits the rich climate of state-offered incentives for new businesses and the abundance of skilled workers. Delaware had its recession in the early 1990s, though unemployment did not rise or real estate values drop as sharply as elsewhere in the nation. And that should not obscure the robust growth of the previous dozen years, or the fact that Delaware made a mostly comfortable transition from the industrial state it was at the beginning of the 1970s to a 1990s services and professional economy.

258   DELAWARE

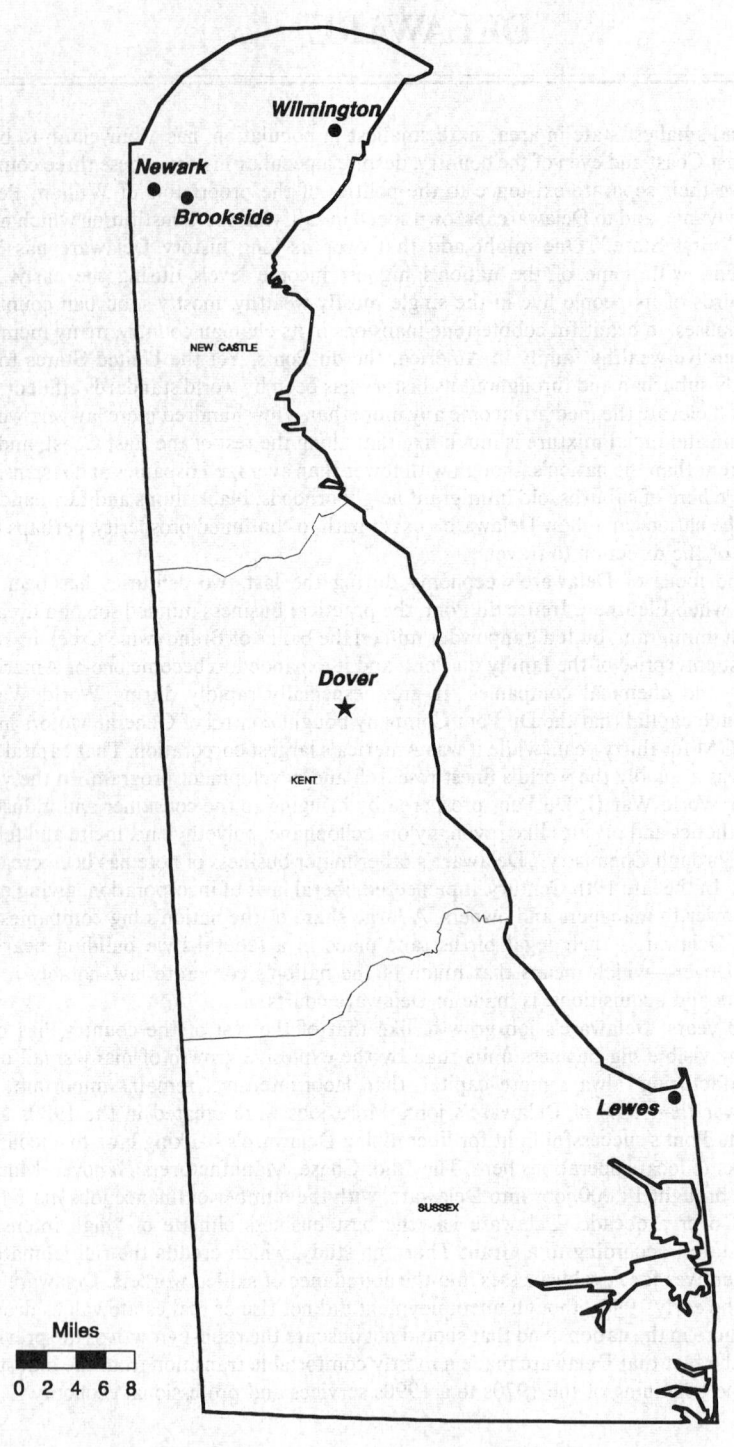

Wilmington

Newark

Brookside

NEW CASTLE

Dover

KENT

Lewes

SUSSEX

Miles

0 2 4 6 8

Despite Delaware's mostly metropolitan character, there is still an intimacy to politics here. Most of Delaware is reached (and politically ignored) by Philadelphia TV, so personal campaigning is still important. The Thursday after the election is "Return Day," when winning and losing candidates—opponents ride in the same car—come back to the downstate town of Georgetown to receive the bipartisan cheers of the voters.

Governor. Tom Carper, the governor of Delaware, grew up in southside Virginia and went to college in Ohio. But out-of-state origins are not uncommon here: the two senators were born in Montana and Pennsylvania. Carper first came to Delaware as an ensign in the Navy, then returned after service in Southeast Asia to get his M.B.A. (He served in the Naval Reserves for nearly 20 years, retiring as a captain in 1991). In 1976, he was elected state treasurer; he ran for Congress in 1982, when incumbent Republican Thomas Evans was in trouble after admitting to an affair with lobbyist Paula Parkinson. In the House, Carper used his seat on the Banking, Finance and Urban Affairs Committee to back bills letting banks into the securities business and eliminating lead paint in public housing, both causes with Delaware constituencies. With a generally moderate voting record, Carper took up other causes such as preventing ocean sludge dumping (Delaware has beach resorts) and giving incentives to subsidized housing owners to continue renting to low-income tenants.

Carper was easily reelected and became the overwhelming choice when he ran for governor in 1992, winning the primary with 89% and the general with 65%. He pledges a partnership with Democratic Lieutenant Governor Ruth Ann Minner, but not a total change in policy. Castle was already increasing spending on education and extending healthcare access to all children, and Carper in addition to supporting these, called for ethics reform (against sexual harassment, for financial disclosure), early childhood education and state standards, and "a vigorous economic development program."

Senators. William Roth, Delaware's senior senator, though his name was attached to one of the major policy changes of the 1980s, is not treated as a major player in Washington. With his trademark toupee and a wife who is a federal judge back in Delaware, he does not cut a social figure nor is he dazzlingly articulate. Yet he has made some significant accomplishments, including winning reelection three times, and backs some powerful political ideas. Roth's political career began almost serendipitously, and his political initiatives, though often expressed in broad principles, seem to have their beginnings in the concrete facts of everyday life in middle-class Delaware. His most famous initiative remains what most people called Kemp-Roth though senators referred to it as Roth-Kemp, the late 1970s proposal to cut federal income tax rates 10% a year for three years, which became the 25% Reagan tax cut enacted in 1981 and took effect in the three grandly prosperous years of 1983, 1984 and 1985. In retrospect, Roth-Kemp was a rational response to bracket creep—the tendency of taxpayers to rise to higher tax brackets because of inflation although real income is stagnating.

Roth's other great economic cause is the promotion of IRAs. The 1986 tax reform cut back on such shelters, and Roth has been trying to extend them ever since. Again, his idea is to let middle-income earners in the high tax brackets hold onto more of their earnings. In 1992, Roth and co-sponsor Lloyd Bentsen introduced a bill which would restore full deductibility of IRAs and expand their availability which was included in the 1992 tax bill later vetoed by President Bush; Roth promises to advance it again. Roth has also been a persistent supporter of creating a Cabinet-level Trade Department, to combine the U.S. Trade Representative, various agencies from the Department of Commerce, the Export-Import Bank and the Overseas Private Investment Corporation to coordinate domestic and international economic policy; he has also advocated a permanent National Economic Council, like President Clinton's. Roth has proposed creating a Mansfield-Roth Fellowship which would give recipients, after language training, one year of experience working for a Japanese government agency in Japan.

Roth is ranking Republican on the Governmental Affairs Committee, where he opposes repeal of the Hatch Act and rides herd on what he feels is the partisan thrust of the General Accounting Office. Since 1981, he has been urging that government bureaucracies undergo performance audits—a cause taken up by the Clinton Administration—and specify strategic goals. In 1993, he introduced legislation to reinvent government, which would create a bipartisan commission to draw up bills, restructure the Executive Branch and overhaul its personnel system. On a few issues Roth tends to be liberal. He opposes ocean dumping and incineration of toxic waste, backs the Coastal Zone Management Act, and wants to protect the striped bass; he is a leading Republican opponent of oil drilling in Alaska's Arctic National Wildlife Refuge coastal plain and of logging in Alaska's Tongass National Forest. He also supported repeal of the ban on women flying combat missions.

Will Roth seek his fifth Senate term in 1994, when he turns 73? His vote-getting record in Delaware has been strong. In 1988, running against then-Lieutenant Governor S. B. Woo, a successful scientist-entrepreneur who raised large sums from Chinese-Americans, Roth was reelected with 62% of the vote, the highest percentage of his career. In early 1993, Roth already had one declared rival, Attorney General Charles Oberly III, and there could well be other Democrats. Should Roth not run, an obvious Republican candidate would be Representative-at-Large and former Governor Mike Castle.

Delaware's junior senator, Joseph Biden, just past 50, ranks 13th in Senate seniority and has already been caught in the national spotlight at moments of controversy and tragedy. If he is not likely to be president, as he was seeking to be in 1987, and if he is not eager to be the center of angry national debate, as he was during the Clarence Thomas hearings in 1991, he can look forward to some not exactly leisurely but at least dignified and stimulating experiences as a senior senator and, he surely hopes, as a longtime chairman of the Senate Foreign Relations Committee, beyond the bitter partisan contests and cultural conflicts played out in the Judiciary Committee he now chairs. To understand Biden it is necessary to look past the caricatures of him that he and, more often, others have put forward, and look to his Delaware roots. He is not a quintessential baby-boom liberal: chronologically, he is just a tad too old and, more importantly, while they were attending elite colleges and marching in protests and organizing in precincts, Biden was winging it through law school and starting a family. Nor is he the son of an impoverished working class family held down for generations, as he suggested when he borrowed words from a speech by the British Labour Party leader Neil Kinnock. Biden grew up in 1950s white collar suburbia (his father was a car salesman and one grandfather was a state Senator in Pennsylvania), a Catholic when it was still assumed that only a Protestant could be president and a teenager with a stutter who taught himself to deliver a speech to his whole school. Biden has kept his roots in Delaware, raising his children there (his first wife and daughter were killed in an auto accident in December 1972, a month after he was elected to the Senate), and commuting still, more than 20 years later, every day on the Metroliner the 80 minutes to Washington.

Biden's great political gift is an articulateness that can verge on the mellifluous; he can inspire, but can also drone on at great length (being elected a senator at 29 does not curb a tendency to verbosity). At his best, he can express vividly the feelings and discontents of middle-class suburbanites. His natural impulse seems to be to reconcile the economic and cultural liberalism which has become his Democratic Party's guiding doctrine, with the economic and cultural conservatism that so many of those he grew up with believe in. The chairmanship of the Judiciary Committee is not an easy place to do this, as the hearings on Robert Bork, Clarence Thomas, Zoe Baird and dozens of less famous others show; it puts Biden in the position of defending the availability of abortion, a practice he was raised to regard as murder. In all these controversies, Biden has tried to maintain an atmosphere of intellectual seriousness and honesty—not easy when most of his colleagues are eager to score points, and the interest groups which orchestrate testimony are in many cases utterly indifferent to the truth. The results are not always happy. The 1987 hearings on Robert Bork set a high intellectual standard for seriousness in much of the questioning, including Biden's, and Bork's responses were a high-level discourse on difficult constitutional issues. But many of Bork's opponents used his candor to vote against him for disgracefully dishonest reasons, from which Biden's attempts to construct an honestly based anti-Bork rationale proved politically indistinguishable. At the same time, Biden used the power of the chair to undermine Bork and helped move critical votes on the committee away from him.

The Bork experience meant that subsequent nominees, of both parties and for at least a generation, will not answer substantive questions candidly or even at all. Clearly Biden was frustrated when nominee David Souter engagingly stonewalled, leaving him in the frustrating position of voting to confirm a nominee who matched him in charm but left him uneasy on merit. Then came the nomination of Clarence Thomas, which seemed to be going through until someone—almost certainly a staffer for Democratic Senator Howard Metzenbaum—leaked charges of sexual harassment by Anita Hill against the nominee. Women members of the House marched over to the Senate in protest, and Biden was bitterly criticized for covering up this information. In fact, Biden had shared it with his Democratic committee colleagues and Republican Strom Thurmond, who agreed that Hill's unwillingness to testify publicly meant that any reference to it would be monstrously unfair to Thomas. Once the story was out though, Hill and then Thomas testified, changing few votes but mesmerizing the country; a majority of voters, and of women, believed Thomas over Hill, despite the strong pro-Hill bias of the press. Biden was criticized by Thomas opponents for not allowing another woman to testify (though there were doubts as to her credibility) and for allowing Republicans to arduously question Hill—a criticism he later agreed with, though it's hard to see how he could have shut them up. Certainly he was trying to make amends later as he insisted on having two new women senators serve on Judiciary in 1993, and advanced as his main legislation a Violence Against Women Act.

Lost in the uproar was Biden's preoccupation with the issue of property rights, which conservative thinkers like Richard Epstein argue should be protected in ways that would overturn most economic legislation. While liberals were trying to justify liberal judicial activism on cultural issues, Biden was trying to support their position and at the same time argue against conservative judicial activism on economic issues. But Judiciary is likely to be less stressful in the Clinton years. Biden helped delay filling some 115 federal judgeships in 1992 so they could be filled by Democrats in 1993. He will surely work again on crime legislation, including his "police officer's bill of rights," which sets standards on the use of force and police misconduct and vetoed by George Bush in the 1991 crime bill. His work in the past has included creating the post of drug czar and inserting capital punishment provisions in earlier crime bills.

During four Congresses, Biden has sat on the Foreign Relations Committee just below Chairman Claiborne Pell, who turns 76 in 1994. In the post-Cold War world, Biden argues, the United States should promote democracy, contain nuclear weapons, rely on multilateral forces like the U.N. and protect the global environment—four goals widely shared by Clinton era Democrats. He criticized the Bush Administration harshly for coddling "the butchers of Beijing" after Tiananmen but still worked closely with the administration on the issue. He strongly urged having a single official in charge of Russian policy—Richard Armitage for Bush, Strobe Talbott for Clinton.

Biden's presidential campaign years are surely in the past. He hoped to inspire a new generation in 1988; instead, he left the race in the fall of 1987, in the midst of the Bork hearings, after charges that he plagiarized the Kinnock speech were made by an "attack video" circulated by a Dukakis staffer. Then in 1988, Biden had a brush with death, suffering two sudden aneurysms. The Democratic nomination is not likely to be up for grabs until 2000, and Biden will presumably confine his campaigning to Delaware, where his admirable personal qualities are well known and his issue positions not unpopular. Biden was first elected in 1972, against a popular incumbent who seemed ready to retire, while this young challenger had energy, an attractive extended family, and an ability to connect with voters' emotions. He still has those assets, as he showed in 1990, when his opponent mailed out 40,000 copies of an 11-minute anti-Biden videotape, but Biden won with 63%—his best showing yet.

Representative-At-Large. The good news for Mike Castle is that after eight years as governor, during which he continued low-tax policies that encouraged business but increased spending on education and extended healthcare access to all children, he retained the popularity that won him reelection with 71% of the vote in 1988. In his race for Delaware's at-large congressional seat, he won the primary by 56%–30% over state Treasurer Janet Rzewnicki in what many called the year of the woman, and he won the general election 55%–43% over former Lieutenant Governor and Senate candidate S. B. Woo, beating the man who raised more in individual contributions (mostly from Chinese-Americans) than any other non-incumbent in 1992, and running 20% ahead of George Bush to do so. The bad news is that, after eight years as the undisputed head of a sovereign if small state government, he is now part of an outnumbered and, for the moment, powerless Republican minority on Capitol Hill. He remains interested in health care, but will have to look carefully to find an opening to influence any bill in 1993 or 1994. He had a friendly and businesslike relationship with Bill Clinton on the National Governors Association, and seemed to welcome his relative obscurity in Washington. But it will be different from Dover. Castle would be an obvious candidate for the Senate should William Roth retire.

Presidential politics. Delaware has had competitive state elections since the Federalists were battling the Jeffersonians, and in Presidential elections over the last 30 years it has come close to matching the national result. Wilmington and the downstate counties, blacks and southern-oriented whites, provide a divided base for the Democrats, counterbalanced by the Republican base in the affluent suburbs. Delaware voted for Kennedy in 1960, Nixon in 1968, Carter in 1976, Bush in 1988, Clinton in 1992, and by no more than a point or two off the national average—as good a barometer as any state. Yet Delaware with its three electoral votes gets little national attention, and other states did not rally to Delaware's two 1988 presidential candidates, Republican Pete du Pont and Democrat Joseph Biden. Delaware chooses its small number of national convention delegates by caucus.

The People: Est. Pop. 1992: 689,000; Pop. 1990: 666,168, up 3.3% 1990–1992. 0.3% of U.S. total, 46th largest; 27% rural. Median age: 32.9. 12.1% 65 years and over. 80.3% White, 16.9% Black, 2.4% Hispanic origin, 1.4% Asian, 1.1% Other. Households: 55.8% married couple families; 26% married couple fams. w. children; 45% college educ.; median household income: $34,875; per capita income: $15,854; median house value: $100,100; median monthly rent: $425. 5.3% Unemployment. Voting age pop.: 502,827. Registered voters (1992): 342,088; 142,542 D (43%), 125,829 R (37%); 67,717 unaffiliated and minor parties (20%).

Political Lineup: Governor, Thomas R. Carper (D); Lt. Gov., Ruth Ann Minner (D); Secy. of State, William T. Quillen (D); Atty. Gen., Charles M. Oberly, III (D); Treasurer, Janet C. Rzewnicki (R); Controller General, Don Dryden (R); Auditor, R. Thomas Wagner, Jr. (R). State Senate, 21 (15 D and 6 R); State House of Representatives, 41 (23 R and 18 D). Senators, William V. Roth, Jr. (R) and Joseph R. Biden, Jr. (D). Representative, 1 R at large.

1992 Presidential Vote

Clinton (D)	126,054	(44%)
Bush (R)	102,313	(35%)
Perot (I)	59,213	(20%)

1988 Presidential Vote

Bush (R)	139,689	(56%)
Dukakis (D)	108,532	(43%)

GOVERNOR
Gov. Thomas R. Carper (D)

Elected 1992, term expires Jan. 1997; b. Jan. 23, 1947, Beckley, WV; home, Wilmington; OH St. U., B.A. 1968, U. of DE, M.B.A. 1975; Presbyterian; married (Martha).

Career: Navy, 1968–73 (Vietnam), Naval Reserves, 1973–91; Industrial Devel. Specialist, DE Div. of Econ. Devel., 1975–76; DE Treas., 1976–82; U.S. House of Reps., 1982–93.

Offices: Legislative Hall, Dover 19901, 302-739-4101; and Carvel State Office Bldg., 12th Fl., 820 N. French St., Wilmington 19801, 302-577-3210.

Election Results

1992 gen.	Thomas R. Carper (D)	179,365	(65%)
	B. Gary Scott (R)	90,725	(33%)
	Two Others	6,944	(3%)
1992 prim.	Thomas R. Carper (D)	36,600	(89%)
	Daniel D. Rappa (D)	4,434	(11%)
1988 gen.	Michael N. Castle (R)	169,733	(71%)
	Jacob Kreshtool (D)	70,236	(29%)

SENATORS
Sen. William V. Roth, Jr. (R)

Elected 1970, seat up 1994; b. July 22, 1921, Great Falls, MT; home, Wilmington; U. of OR, B.A. 1944, Harvard, M.B.A., LL.B. 1947; Episcopalian; married (Jane).

Career: Army, 1943–46 (WWII); Practicing atty., 1950–66; Chmn., DE Repub. State Cmte., 1961–64; U.S. House of Reps., 1967–70.

Offices: 104 HSOB 20510, 202-224-2441. Also 3021 Fed. Bldg., 844 King St., Wilmington 19801, 302-573-6291; 2215 Fed. Bldg., 300 S. New St., Dover 19901, 302-674-3308; and 12 The Circle, Georgetown 19947, 302-856-7690.

Committees: *Banking, Housing and Urban Affairs* (7th of 8 R): Housing and Urban Affairs; International Finance and Monetary Policy; Securities. *Finance* (3d of 9 R): Health for Families and the Uninsured; International Trade; Taxation (RMM). *Governmental Affairs* (RMM of 5 R): Permanent Subcommittee on Investigations (RMM). *Joint Economic Committee* (7th of 10).

Group Ratings

	ADA	ACLU	CDF	COPE	CFA	LCV	ACU	NTLC	NSI	COC	CEI
1992	25	18	20	27	40	42	75	76	60	100	74
1991	20	—	45	25	29	73	81	—	—	60	67

National Journal Ratings

	1991 LIB — 1991 CONS			1992 LIB — 1992 CONS		
Economic	24%	—	75%	30%	—	69%
Social	28%	—	69%	27%	—	72%
Foreign	35%	—	63%	43%	—	55%

Key Votes of the 102d Congress

1. $ for Homeownership	FOR	5. Clarence Thomas Nom.	FOR	9. Use Force in Gulf	FOR
2. Have Cap Gains Debate	FOR	6. Lmt Death Row Appeal	FOR	10. Keep Salvador Aid	FOR
3. Remove Budget Walls	AGN	7. Handgun Wait/5-Day	FOR	11. Cut $1B from SDI	AGN
4. Ban Striker Replace	AGN	8. Abortion Gag Rule	AGN	12. Override China MFN	AGN

Key Votes of the 103d Congress

1. Family Leave	FOR	2. HIV Immigrants	AGN	3. Clinton Budget	AGN

Election Results

1988 general	William V. Roth, Jr. (R)	151,115	(62%)	($1,942,119)
	S.B. Woo (D).......................	92,378	(38%)	($2,235,318)
1988 primary	William V. Roth, Jr. (R), nominated by convention			
1982 general	William V. Roth, Jr. (R)	105,472	(56%)	($797,516)
	David N. Levinson (D)	83,722	(44%)	($777,819)

Sen. Joseph R. Biden, Jr. (D)

Elected 1972, seat up 1996; b. Nov. 20, 1942, Scranton, PA; home, Wilmington; U. of DE, B.A. 1965, Syracuse U., J.D. 1968; Catholic; married (Jill).

Career: Practicing atty., 1968–72; New Castle Cnty. Cncl., 1970–72.

Offices: 221 RSOB 20510, 202-224-5042. Also Fed. Bldg., 844 King St., Wilmington 19801, 302-573-6345; 1101 Fed. Bldg, 300 S. New St., Dover 17901, 302-678-9483; and Box 109, The Circle, Georgetown 19947, 302-856-9275.

Committees: *Foreign Relations* (2d of 11 D): East Asian and Pacific Affairs; European Affairs (Chmn.); International Economic Policy, Trade, Oceans and Environment. *Judiciary* (Chmn. of 10 D): Juvenile Justice.

Group Ratings

	ADA	ACLU	CDF	COPE	CFA	LCV	ACU	NTLC	NSI	COC	CEI
1992	100	86	80	100	75	67	0	17	40	20	23
1991	90	—	91	83	89	93	5	—	—	20	29

National Journal Ratings

	1991 LIB — 1991 CONS			1992 LIB — 1992 CONS		
Economic	85%	—	11%	84%	—	12%
Social	80%	—	17%	89%	—	0%
Foreign	86%	—	0%	86%	—	0%

Key Votes of the 102d Congress

1. $ for Homeownership	AGN	5. Clarence Thomas Nom.	AGN	9. Use Force in Gulf	AGN
2. Have Cap Gains Debate	AGN	6. Lmt Death Row Appeal	AGN	10. Keep Salvador Aid	AGN
3. Remove Budget Walls	FOR	7. Handgun Wait/5-Day	FOR	11. Cut $1B from SDI	FOR
4. Ban Striker Replace	FOR	8. Abortion Gag Rule	AGN	12. Override China MFN	FOR

Key Votes of the 103d Congress

1. Family Leave	FOR	2. HIV Immigrants	FOR	3. Clinton Budget	FOR

Election Results

1990 general	Joseph R. Biden, Jr. (D)	112,918	(63%)	($2,550,061)
	M. Jane Brady (R)	64,554	(36%)	($240,669)
	Other...............................	2,680	(1%)	
1990 primary	Joseph R. Biden, Jr. (D), nominated by convention			
1984 general	Joseph R. Biden, Jr. (D)	147,831	(60%)	($1,602,052)
	John M. Burris (R)	98,101	(40%)	($816,484)

REPRESENTATIVE

Rep. Michael N. Castle (R)

Elected 1992; b. July 2, 1939, Wilmington; home, Wilmington; Hamilton Col., B.A. 1961, Georgetown U., LL.B. 1964; Catholic; married (Jane).

Career: DE Dep. Atty. Gen., 1965–66; DE House of Reps., 1966–68; DE Senate, 1968–76, Minority Ldr., 1975–76; DE Lt. Gov., 1980–84; DE Gov., 1984–92.

Offices: 1205 LHOB 20515, 202-225-4165. Also 3 Christina Ctr., 201 N. Walnut St., #1001, Wilmington 19801, 302-428-1902; and Freer Fed. Bldg., 300 S. New St., Dover 19901, 302-736-1666.

Committees: *Banking, Finance and Urban Affairs* (19th of 20 R): Consumer Credit and Insurance; Housing and Community Development; International Development, Finance, Trade and Monetary Policy. *Merchant Marine and Fisheries* (13th of 19 R): Coast Guard and Navigation; Environment and Natural Resources.

Group Ratings and 102d Congress Votes: Newly Elected

Key Votes of the 103d Congress

1. Family Leave	FOR	2. Deficit Reduction	AGN	3. Stimulus Plan	AGN

Election Results

1992 general	Michael N. Castle (R)	153,037	(55%)	($690,740)
	S.B. Woo (D)........................	117,426	(43%)	($1,017,598)
	Other...............................	5,661	(2%)	
1992 primary	Michael N. Castle (R)	18,377	(56%)	
	Janet C. Rzewnicki (R)	9,812	(30%)	
	Bryant L. Richardson (R).............	4,411	(13%)	
	Other...............................	441	(1%)	
1990 general	Thomas R. Carper (D)	116,274	(66%)	($521,336)
	Ralph O. Williams (R)	58,037	(33%)	($49,770)
	Other...............................	3,121	(2%)	

DISTRICT OF COLUMBIA

It is an irony that the capital city of the world's most successful democracy has a local politics that could charitably be described as dysfunctional. But the problem is not new: the framers of the Constitution, familiar with contemporary London and Paris mobs and remembering how crowds had threatened Congress in Philadelphia, purposely gave the new federal government control of the 10-mile-square enclave that came to be called the District of Columbia. During most of the years since, Congress has kept close control over it, for its own advantage and out of distrust of the city's large black population. For blacks had consistently made up about one-quarter of metropolitan Washington's population since the 1790s, and the city was a center for free blacks before and after the Civil War and Emancipation. Radical Republicans gave the District self-government in the era of Reconstruction in 1871, but Governor Alexander "Boss" Shepherd built great public works and spent the District into bankruptcy, and local self-government ended in 1874. During the civil rights revolution of the 1960s, it began to seem absurd to deny the vote to Washington, which officially became majority-black in 1960. So in 1964, Washingtonians began to cast three electoral votes for president; in 1968 they could vote for school board; in 1971, they finally got to elect a non-voting delegate to Congress; in 1974, they got home rule and could, like residents of every other American city, vote for a mayor and city council.

Washington is now heading toward its third decade of self-government, with little in the way of local political institutions. It has no serious party organizations, being overwhelmingly Democratic—not only more Democratic than any state, but more than any county—so there is not much possibility of party competition. The District voted 85%–9% for Bill Clinton over George Bush in 1992, giving Clinton double his national percentage; 80% of D.C. whites voted for Clinton according to exit polls. Another reason for Washington's political underdevelopment is the sense that not much is at stake. Congress retains, under the Constitution, final authority over the District, which it has used as recently as 1988, forcing repeal of a law requiring Georgetown University to sanction homosexual organizations. And the District's Congressional Delegate Eleanor Holmes Norton thought it wise to ask President Clinton early on to veto any law overturning District home rule. The District's prosecutor and judges are federal appointees, and there are federal police forces that patrol government buildings, embassies, parks and Capitol Hill. The only real political organization assembled in D.C. recently was the coalition of public employee unions and big real estate developers who contributed megabucks to former Mayor Marion Barry. But that fell apart in January 1990, when Barry was arrested in a hotel smoking crack cocaine, a crime for which he was eventually convicted and imprisoned.

A sweeping desire for reform resulted in the victory in 1990 of Mayor Sharon Pratt Kelly (Sharon Pratt Dixon until she remarried in December 1991). A Democratic Party activist and vice president of the local power company, she brought to the race a sharp, almost acerbic edge; when Barry was still flying high, she was sharply criticizing him; when he fell, her attitude fit voters' mood; when *The Washington Post* began arguing vigorously that, for all the other candidates' virtues, Kelly's astringency was what the city needed, voters agreed. Though vastly outspent by Councilman John Ray, she won the Democratic primary in a record turnout with 35% to 25% for Ray, 21% for Councilwoman Charlene Drew Jarvis, 11% for Council President David Clarke, and 7% for Walter Fauntroy, who served 19 years as the District's congressional delegate; against former Police Chief Maurice Turner, running as a Republican, Dixon won with 86%. Then came the hard part. If the District has an underdeveloped politics, it has an overdeveloped government—some 46,000 full-time public employees for a city with a population by 1992 of 589,000. A commission headed by Alice Rivlin, later Clinton's deputy director of

OMB, found that the District had 40% more employees per person than 12 other major cities, even accounting for the fact that it provides both state and city services; and the levels of employee pay and benefits are up toward the top in the country. *The New York Times*, in a story about Chelsea Clinton's school choice, noted without citation that District public schools were "notoriously underfinanced"; in fact, per-pupil spending was higher than that in 97% of over-20,000-pupil systems in the country: the Clintons rejected a public school system that is one of the most generously financed in the country.

The sad fact is that the District has a public sector of Soviet magnitude and social problems of Third World dimensions—two facts that may not be unrelated. The crime rate in the District is very high, and if it is not quite the nation's murder capital as often said—the homicide rate declined in 1992—it is nonetheless the scene of one horrific crime after another. It has a level of infant mortality resembling that of many Third World nations, despite the fact that one-fourth of the city is as affluent as the nation's highest-income suburbs and despite a generous public spending program begun in the Barry Administration. The District has a far lower percentage of people living in families than any state, and the highest percentage of people not covered by health insurance, despite income levels well above the national average. The District government does deliver some services adequately, but most are carried out so poorly as to drive the upwardly mobile middle class, especially upwardly mobile blacks, to the suburban counties (including majority-black Prince Georges County, Maryland) which do a palpably better job. The result is an electorate the affluent minority of which can afford to pay for private schools and other services and the poor near-majority of which lacks the organizational competence to manipulate the system for its benefit. D.C. is in danger instead of manipulation by unscrupulous politicians like Marion Barry, who in 1992 was elected to the Council from Ward 8 east of the Anacostia River, the poorest part of the city, and whose refrain has been to blame all his problems and the city's on white racism.

Against this background, Sharon Pratt Kelly has tried to cut the District payroll and improve services, with limited success. She and Norton managed to lobby for $100 million in emergency funds for the city in 1991—Congress's gesture of good will for newly elected reformers. In May 1991, Dixon responsibly handled a three-day-long riot in the Latino Mount Pleasant neighborhood. Off and on in 1991 and 1992, she spent much effort negotiating with Washington Redskins owner Jack Kent Cooke on a new football stadium—a project not likely to solve the District's basic problems but popular with D.C. voters. In early 1993, she was facing a $1 billion budget gap, with no obvious way of closing it; income taxes are already among the nation's highest, and a suggested commuter tax won't fly in a Congress, where Maryland and Virginia suburbanites are ably represented. The Mayor's inability to meet her own employee-cutting goals will tend to deter even a sympathetic Clinton Administration from handing over more money for a government that is clearly still not functional. Yet even the most orderly of governments would find it hard to improve the moral climate in much of the city, where a young male criminal underclass terrorizes the elderly and single-mother families and their children who cannot afford to escape these neighborhoods, where stray bullets can kill an innocent bystander any day and deliberate murder is common.

At least Kelly, unlike Barry, speaks out against this tragedy, as does the nationally most famous local political figure, Jesse Jackson. Jackson's political missteps may have fumbled away some of his local authority: he moved to Washington after the 1988 presidential election, amid much ballyhoo; registered to vote and suggested that he might run for mayor, at least if his old friend and supporter Marion Barry didn't; then he declined to make the race and ran instead for "shadow senator," a non-paying, non-voting office established purportedly to lobby for statehood. But Jackson, who has a good ear for what is on people's minds, has led campaigns against the violence here instead, insisting, "We can stop the killing. It can save our lives and give us the moral authority to demand statehood." Obviously he recognizes that statehood—a demand subscribed to by Kelly, Norton, the Clinton-Gore ticket and the national Democratic Party—is not likely to be voted by any sane Congress until the District shows that it can govern itself better than it is doing now.

Will Kelly be doing the governing? She has shown a certain competence, but her acerbity has gotten a bit in her way and she has not been able to deliver on her reformist promises. Likely opponents include interim Council President John Ray and councilmen William Lightfoot and, most ominously, Marion Barry, who might hope that his claims of rehabilitation plus support from the public employee unions would give him a large enough vote to prevail in a split field.

The District's representation in the House of Representatives is not so much in doubt. Eleanor Holmes Norton came to office in 1990 under a cloud: her husband hadn't filed their income taxes for several years; she said she wasn't aware of this, an excuse which surely would have opened any male candidate to ridicule. Norton then beat Betty Anne Kane, a reformer and a white who had twice won a city-wide Council seat, by only a 39%–33% margin. (Norton won 62% against her Republican opponent and four minor candidates.) But in the House, Norton proceeded to perform creditably. She got $100 million in emergency funds for the District and established good relations with District of Columbia Committee members, then-Chairman Ronald Dellums as well as ranking Republican Thomas Bliley of Virginia. She kept in close touch with civic groups around the District and was reelected in 1992 by a wide margin. She also got on the good side of Bill Clinton, whose nomination she supported and whom she in turn helped persuade to back a little more money for the District government.

Norton won only a partial victory, however, in her fight for full voting rights on the floor of the House. Delegates from the District and the four other non-states have been allowed to vote in committees but not on the floor since the early 1970s; floor votes, said Thomas Foley and others at the time, would be unconstitutional. But in December 1992, Norton persuaded Foley to switch, and go with the House Democratic Caucus to support votes in the Committee of the Whole for the five delegates, all of them now Democrats. Republicans squawked loudly, quoting Foley against himself and pointing to the fact that the four offshore delegates represent voters who do not pay U.S. taxes. The Democratic leadership retreated and backed an ungainly compromise allowing delegates to vote on the House floor on amendments (but not on final passage of bills), yet permitting a second vote without them should their votes make a difference—a perfectly unsatisfactory arrangement all around. Then a federal judge ruled that giving the delegates any more votes on the floor would be unconstitutional, a refutation of the stand argued by Norton, a law professor herself. The upshot is that if the District wants a vote in Congress, it must do what the other states have done: persuade Congress that it has earned it. And the present District government is very far from doing that.

The People: Est. Pop. 1992: 589,000; Pop. 1990: 606,900, down 3.0% 1990–1992. 0.2% of U.S. total, 48th largest. Median age: 33.5 years. 12.8% 65 years and over. 65.8% Black, 29.0% White, 5.4% Hispanic origin, 1.8% Asian, 2.4% Other. Households: 25.3% married couple families; 10% married couple fams. w. children; 52% college educ.; median household income: $30,727; per capita income: $18,881; 38.9% owner occupied housing; median house value: $123,900; median monthly rent: $441. 8.4% Unemployment. Voting age pop.: 489,808. Registered voters (1992): 340,953; 263,574 D (77%); 28,544 R (8%); 48,835 unaffiliated and minor parties (14%).

Political Lineup: Representative, 1 D at large.

1992 Presidential Vote

Clinton (D)	192,619	(85%)
Bush (R)	20,698	(9%)
Perot (I)	9,681	(4%)

1988 Presidential Vote

Dukakis (D)	159,407	(83%)
Bush (R)	27,590	(14%)

1992 Democratic Presidential Primary

Clinton	45,716	(74%)
Tsongas	6,452	(10%)
Brown	4,444	(7%)
Uncommitted	5,292	(9%)

1992 Republican Presidential Primary

Bush	4,265	(82%)
Buchanan	970	(19%)

REPRESENTATIVE

Rep. Eleanor Holmes Norton (D)

Elected 1990; b. Jun. 13, 1937, Washington, D.C.; home, Washington, D.C.; Antioch Col., B.A. 1960, Yale, M.A. 1963, LL.B. 1964; Episcopalian; divorced.

Career: Asst. Legal Dir., ACLU, 1965–70; New York City Comm. on Human Rights, 1970–77; Equal Empl. Oppor. Comm., 1977–81; Sr. Fellow, The Urban Inst., 1981–82; Prof., Georgetown U. Law Ctr., 1982–90.

Offices: 1415 LHOB 20515, 202-225-8050. Also 815 15th St., NW, #100, Washington 20005, 202-783-5085; and 1151 Chicago St., SE, Washington 20020, 202-678-8900.

Committees: *District of Columbia* (5th of 8 D): Fiscal Affairs and Health; Judiciary and Education (Chmn.). *Post Office and Civil Service* (7th of 15 D): Compensation and Employee Benefits (Chmn.). *Public Works and Transportation* (23d of 39 D): Public Buildings and Grounds (Vice Chmn.); Water Resources and Environment. *Joint Committee on the Organization of Congress* (7th of 12).

Election Results

1992 general	Eleanor Holmes Norton (D)	166,808	(85%)	($143,853)
	Susan Emerson (R)	20,108	(10%)	($11,697)
	Susan Griffin (I)	7,253	(4%)	
	Other	2,585	(1%)	
1992 primary	Eleanor Holmes Norton (D)	51,883	(97%)	
	Other	1,491	(3%)	
1990 general	Eleanor Holmes Norton (D)	98,442	(62%)	($446,856)
	Harry M. Singleton (R)	41,999	(26%)	($85,985)
	George X. Cure (I)	8,156	(5%)	
	Other	11,030	(7%)	

FLORIDA

Florida, of all improbable places, is one of the states where America is meeting its future. Over the years, Florida has been what millions of retirees have looked forward to: the sunny year-round warmth after eternal gray skies over winter factories and rain pounding on office windows. And for millions of young families, from the South and various points north, Florida has been a booming economy, with jobs and opportunities in places that were recently just swampland. For immigrants from Cuba and other parts of Latin America, Florida has been a land of freedom and security from the armed thugs that patrol everyday life in police states. And for Americans and foreigners of all kinds—some 40 million of them in 1992, up from 23 million 10 years before—Florida is a place to travel, with tourist attractions and year-round swimming and restaurants and rooms to suit every taste and pocketbook.

Florida is a creation not of America's elite—though a few millionaires like Henry Flagler and Marcus Plant pioneered tourism here—but a place in which ordinary people have voted with their feet. Half a century ago, it was the least populous state in the South, with 1.4 million people, swampy, isolated, disease-ridden, bigoted, with no mineral resources but phosphate mines, not much agriculture outside its citrus groves and hardly any manufacturing at all. Today it is America's fourth largest state, with 13 million people (it passed Ohio in 1984, Illinois in 1986 and Pennsylvania in 1987). To be sure, Florida is not a replica of the nation; it is rather an exaggeration: a state one-fifth of whose economy is based on tourism in a country where tourism is one of the great growth industries; a state with an economy based on services in a country increasingly service-oriented; the state with the largest proportion of elderly and retired citizens in a country where an increasing percentage will live many years in retirement; a state also with a growing number of school children in a country which replenished by immigration is growing faster and more robustly than any other advanced nation. Florida's architectural style once seemed exotic—Flagler's vast luxury hotels, the pink stucco motels of the 1940s and 1950s, the art deco hotels of Miami Beach—but now they have become leading edge—the Disney World Dolphin Hotel and Arquitectonica's Miami towers. And Florida is becoming a show business center, with actual movie production on the lots at the Universal and Disney World theme parks near Orlando: tourist attractions becoming workplaces, life imitating art imitating life.

Florida, stalling briefly in the early 1990s recession, began growing again in 1992. Jobs were up 174,000, more than in any other state; taxable sales, in a state that depends heavily on the sales tax for government financing, were up 15%; foreign tourism and international trade were up sharply. This last is particularly important. Miami for at least two decades has been the economic and commercial capital of Latin America, and its mecca for political exiles as well; it is the one place from where you can fly nonstop to just about any place in Latin America, and the one place where you can be sure your money and your person are safe from government takeover. With its large Cuban community, Spanish is commonly spoken and understood, a truly international city, and getting more so. Miami and all of Florida are eyeing the North American Free Trade Agreement, and preparing for increased trade with Mexico, especially southern Mexico; Florida will be quick to profit as well from free trade agreements sought by other Latin countries. Florida, jutting south into the Caribbean, has 13 ports, seven international airports, 11 free trade zones and more international banks than any other state but New York.

Yet when Hurricane Andrew's 150-mile-an-hour winds slammed ashore a dozen miles south of Miami in August 1992, it tore apart trailers and subdivision houses causing an estimated $30 billion in damage, and prompted some residents to start looting while others patrolled with guns, guarding their possessions and water supply. Andrew was an exceptional storm, but its damage spotlighted some of Florida's weaknesses. Many of the structures here are flimsily built, and the social bonds that can tie communities together are weak and easily frayed here. Florida is mostly low-lying swampland, and development has ruined much of its unique ecology; only recently, with federal efforts and a compact developed by EPA Administrator Carol Browner when she was Governor Lawton Chiles's top environmental appointee, has there been a move to preserve the Everglades—actually a miles-wide river with millions of little islets—and to restore to natural condition the Kissimmee River which was channelized and straightened.

Florida has little in the way of local elites with traditions of civic responsibility. Many of Florida's great fortunes were made elsewhere, and brought here partly because the state has no income or inheritance taxes. And the real estate developers and trial lawyers who are the main sources of political money may be admirable as smart operators who made fortunes from their wits, but they lack roots and a broad sense of community responsibility. Florida has long been weak in education, with a public school system that is no better than average for the South, and without a first-class research university. And Florida has, in exaggerated form, the American vice of violent crime and the characteristic response of harsh punishment: its combination of white southerners and elderly retirees, both fearful of violent young criminals, make it probably America's most pro-capital punishment state, while statistics show it to be one of the most crime-ridden. Florida's lack of community traditions and mediating institutions are part of the problem—and one that threatens the nation too as it becomes increasingly like Florida.

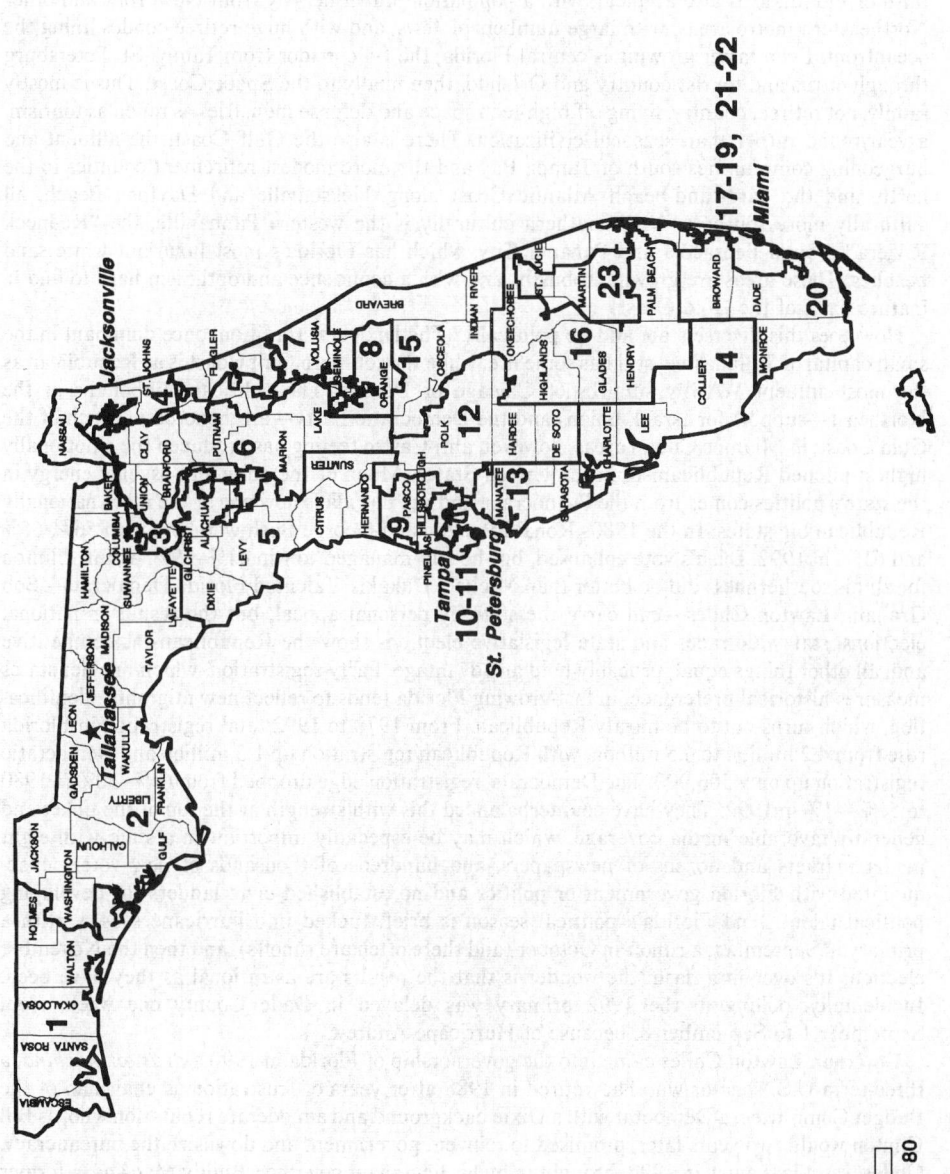

This new Florida, like today's America, has no real center; the state, says Governor Lawton Chiles, is "more of a crowd than a community." Its largest urban center, Miami, is geographically off to one corner and culturally uniquely Cuban and with its eyes increasingly on Latin America. The rest of the Gold Coast, north past West Palm Beach, while containing almost one-third of Floridians is also atypical, with a population drawn heavily from New York and other Northeastern metro areas, with large numbers of Jews, and with huge retiree condos lining the oceanfront. Even faster growing is central Florida, the I-4 corridor from Tampa-St. Petersburg through citrus and tourist country and Orlando, then finally to the Space Coast. This is mostly family, not retiree, country, living off high-tech space and defense industries as much as tourism, a year-round rather than seasonal civilization. There is also the Gulf Coast, the affluent and burgeoning communities south of Tampa Bay and the more modest retirement counties to the north, and the hard-sand-beach Atlantic Coast along Jacksonville and Daytona Beach, all culturally more southern. Very southern culturally is the western Panhandle, the "Redneck Riviera" around Pensacola and Panama City, which has Florida's most luxuriant white sand beaches. These areas are growing robustly, and with a confidence and optimism hard to find in mature parts of the Gold Coast.

How does this diverse state add up politically? The Dixiecrat tradition, once dominant in the small capital of Tallahassee, still has some life, while the southern Gulf Coast is as Republican as the most affluent WASPy suburbs of Chicago or Detroit. The political shibboleths of the Northeast—support for Israel, unions and the Democratic Party—are honored in much of the Gold Coast; in Miami's Cuban areas, however, anti-Castro feeling has produced the emotionally highest-pitched Republicanism in the United States. Much of the noise and psychic energy in the state's politics comes from the Democrats, and yet Florida is now one of the more nationally Republican big states. In the 1980s Ronald Reagan and George Bush won here with 56%, 65% and 61%; in 1992, Bush's vote collapsed, but he still managed to win 41%–39%, as Bill Clinton for all his southernness did no better than Michael Dukakis. Talented Florida Democrats—Bob Graham, Lawton Chiles—can carry the state by personal appeal, but the results in national elections, statewide races and state legislative elections show the Republicans as competitive and, all other things equal, probably hold an advantage. Party registration, which in older states measures historical preference, in fast-growing Florida tends to reflect new migrants' identification, which turns out to be mostly Republican. From 1978 to 1992 total registration in Florida rose from 4.2 million to 6.5 million, with Republican registration up 1.5 million and Democratic registration up only 506,000. The Democrats' registration edge dropped from 64%–30% in 1980 to 51%–41% in 1992. They have counterbalanced this with strength at the top of the ticket and generally favorable media coverage, which may be especially important in a state with eight media markets and dozens of newspapers, and hundreds of thousands of new voters unacquainted with Florida government or politics and no established civic ladders for developing political talent. And Florida's political season is brief, tucked into hurricane season, with a primary in September, a runoff in October (and there often are runoffs), and then the November election. It's over in a flash: the wonder is that the results are as rational as they have been. Incidentally, polling in the 1992 primary was delayed in Dade County one week, from September 1 to September 8, because of Hurricane Andrew.

Governor. Lawton Chiles came into the governorship of Florida in 1990 a *deus ex machina*, a three-term U.S. senator who had retired in 1988 after years of frustration as chairman of the Budget Committee, a Democrat with a Dixie background and a moderate reputation who, as Bill Clinton would two years later, promised to reinvent government and downsize the bureaucracy. Chiles was a late entry in 1990, brought in by his lieutenant governor, Buddy MacKay, a former congressman who nearly won the 1988 Senate race. He was able to beat congressman Bill Nelson in the primary and, by 57%–43%, beat Republican Governor Bob Martinez, elected in 1986 against a death penalty opponent but unpopular since the services tax he got passed in 1987 became a fiasco and had to be repealed. Chiles was hurt by revelations he was taking an anti-depressant drug but was helped by the $100 contribution limit he imposed on his campaign.

Chiles got started right away, tackling the state's $1 billion budget shortfall, cutting projected state spending increases and settling a federal environmental lawsuit by promising to curb development and clean up the Everglades. Despite layoffs of several hundred state employees, voters sensed little impact from Chiles's interesting government reform initiatives. Chiles, clearly influenced by his unhappy experience in Washington trying to get taxes raised to cut the federal deficit, was convinced that taxes needed to be raised to pay for education and infrastructure to make this big state competitive: "The clock is ticking on Florida," he said. The legislature was dubious about Chiles's "right-sizing," and critics noted big increases for education administrators and para-professionals; Chiles was frustrated because an income tax is legally barred here and politically impossible (since non-residents pay one-quarter of sales tax revenues). In June 1992 he proposed a $1.35 billion package extending the sales tax on utilities and various items, including services (which had sunk Martinez), emphasizing that the rich would pay more under his "fair share tax plan." The legislature didn't buy it. After Hurricane Andrew, Chiles predicted more economic troubles. But in fact Florida's economy was reviving, and as reporters wondered whether public agencies were effective, small private businesses rushed in to rebuild houses and commercial buildings, generating a perceptible rise in business activity. In November 1992, Republicans gained in legislative elections, rising to a 20–20 tie in the state Senate (they'll elect a leader in 1993, the Democrats in 1994). Chiles responded with a "smart dollar" budget in January 1993 and a proposed tax increase, this time for only $290 million, as revenues had been rising. In April 1993 he pushed through the legislature a managed competition healthcare plan, creating 11 Community Health Purchasing Alliances to offer universal coverage, with a separate pool for Medicaid recipients.

Chiles's ratings in the polls have been abysmal, lower sometimes than Martinez ever got; voters resent his tax increases and are skeptical that he has improved government. His response is to persevere: "I just go along because I'm so convinced the cause is right." It was not clear in early 1993 whether he would run for reelection in 1994. If he does not, one obvious candidate, unless his policies stay terribly unpopular, would be Buddy MacKay. Other Democrats include Education Commissioner Betty Castor and Orlando Mayor Bill Frederick. Even more Republicans may run. By early 1993 Insurance Commissioner Tom Gallagher and Jeb Bush, son of the former president, a Miami businessman who backs school choice, said they were interested. Other possible Republicans include Senate Republican Leader Ander Crenshaw, Congressmen Bill McCollum and Porter Goss and Secretary of State Jim Smith, a former Democrat who is a familiar name on statewide ballots.

Senators. Florida has two senators neither of whom are well-known nationally, but both popular in Florida though of different parties and both from families that have achieved fame in other fields. The senior Senator, Bob Graham, is careful, methodical, thorough, hard-working, reliable—always wearing his Florida ties, recording every meeting he attends and meal he eats in notebooks he carries everywhere, scheduling meetings with every member of the Florida House delegation and with lobbyists on both sides of environmental, banking and crime issues. He comes from a prominent Florida family: his father started out with a Miami area dairy farm and developed the planned mini-city of Miami Lakes; his half-brother Philip Graham was publisher of *The Washington Post*. He has been in politics almost all his adult life; he was elected to the state House in 1966 at age 30, and to the state Senate in 1970. In 1978, after a come-from-behind win in the Democratic runoff and a solid 56% win in the general, he began the first of two terms as governor. The attention-getting device in that campaign (invented by Senator Tom Harkin for his 1974 House race) was work days: Graham worked one day a week at some local job, from bagging groceries to working construction. He keeps it up still, once a month, and by November 1992 had logged in 265 work days, all of course carefully recorded.

He was a popular governor (one of 15 former governors now in the Senate), backing some tax increases, setting up a water quality trust fund and passing a wetlands protection act, opposing any income tax and, as a capital punishment backer, signing death warrants. His work in the Senate shows the stamp of his Florida experience. On crime and foreign policy, he is a hardliner, leading the opposition to Edward Kennedy's bill that would ban the death penalty where it is imposed disproportionately on blacks; every jury verdict, he said, "is inherently individualized and not necessarily subject to being categorized." A staunch opponent of Fidel Castro, Graham argued for keeping the squeeze on Castro's Cuba after the collapse of the Soviet Union. He was a key backer of the Caribbean Basin Initiative, trying to extend it beyond 1995 and to make more products duty-free. He has worked hard to restore the Kissimmee River to its natural state, to ban oil drilling off the southwest Florida coast and get the federal government to buy up existing leases, to make the Florida Keys a national marine sanctuary and the Suwanee in north Florida a National Wild and Scenic River. He tried to get a baseball team for Tampa Bay and to limit detained aliens' stay at Miami's Krome Avenue Detention Center to 90 days. On national issues, he has been a team player for Democrats, within limits; he voted for the Gulf war resolution and backs the balanced budget amendment. Naturally he has paid heed to issues like drug traffic, health care for elderly, and campaign finance reform (Florida has a tradition of "sunshine laws" requiring full disclosure).

Election year 1992 posed little challenge for Graham. His Republican opponent was Bill Grant, a former Democratic congressman who switched parties in 1989 in a Democratic district, despite a by no means uniformly conservative voting record, and was defeated in 1990. Grant raised little money and had 106 overdrafts on the House bank; that he had promoted Graham for the vice presidential nomination in 1988 was an added irony. Graham got publicity in July for being on Bill Clinton's short list for the vice presidency, and in October he ran workday ads showing him working in a car wash, operating heavy equipment with a road crew and teaching school. Graham won 65%-35%, which made him the first senator reelected to this seat since George Smathers won in 1962 (Lawton Chiles was reelected to the other seat in 1976 and 1982). Graham also helped along underdog Florida Democratic candidates which was one reason— lack of volunteers was another—Senate Democrats made him chairman of their campaign committee for the 1993-1994 cycle. Graham seems unlikely to be a presidential candidate, but is clearly a strong figure in Florida, indeed the strongest thing Florida Democrats have going for them.

A dozen years ago Connie Mack III was a banker in Cape Coral, Florida, with a famous name. Now he is a U.S. senator from the fourth largest state, well-positioned to win a second term in 1994. Mack owes his name to his grandfather, longtime owner and manager of the Philadelphia Athletics (his other grandfather was Morris Sheppard, senator from Texas from 1913 to 1941). He owes his political ascent to good timing, good luck and being on the right side of the issues in an increasingly conservative state. Mack was elected to the House in 1982, chosen in a multi-candidate Republican primary in a newly created Gulf Coast district. In the House he became part of Newt Gingrich's Conservative Opportunity Society and was a supply-sider, though without the angry hard edge of so many of his colleagues. He was lead sponsor in the House of the Gramm-Rudman deficit-cutting measure that originated in the Senate; pro-choice on abortion and for ERA, he switched on both issues when contemplating the 1988 Senate race. He entered that contest in October 1987, prior to Lawton Chiles's decision to retire, then lucked out when former Governor Reubin Askew abruptly left the race in May 1988. The Democrats nominated an attractive candidate, Buddy MacKay, then an articulate and moderate congressman, now Lawton Chiles's lieutenant governor.

But MacKay was vulnerable to Mack's TV spot jibe: "Hey, Buddy, you're liberal," and Mack's calls for "less taxing, less spending, less government, and more freedom." Mack attacked MacKay for opposing contra aid and the balanced budget amendment, and was the beneficiary of $300,000 of TV spots bought by an independent import car dealer PAC. Worries about social security clearly helped MacKay, who carried St. Petersburg and ran far ahead of most Democrats in Mack's own retiree-heavy House district. But Mack ran far ahead of other Republicans in the heavily military Jacksonville area and in the family-oriented I-4 corridor. Mack lost among those who went to the polls on election day, but with a big absentee margin won 50.4%-49.6%. Mack went to bed thinking he had lost and was awakened Wednesday by a call from President Reagan saying he'd won. "I think we just won one more for the Gipper," Mack said, but truthfully it was the other way around.

In the Senate, Mack's record is conservative, but not completely; he has spent considerable effort on the non-ideological subject of cancer legislation, since his mother and wife are cancer survivors and his brother died of the disease. Even though Bob Graham called him an "ideological wacko" in the 1988 campaign, Mack has worked closely with Graham, who in turn seems happy for bipartisan support on state issues in a state that is basically Republican. Mack has some profile on foreign policy issues, as a supporter of Israel and opponent of Fidel Castro, on whose Cuba he has called for tighter trade restrictions. He supported TV Marti strongly. On economics he remains a firm supply-sider; in early 1990 he urged George Bush to stick to his "read my lips" pledge and in early 1992 he called for the resignation of Treasury Secretary Nicholas Brady, all the while demanding lower capital gains taxes. He opposed the catastrophic health care bill in 1988, when almost everyone was for it, and reaped the political benefits in 1989, when almost everyone was against it. He has worked against offshore oil drilling off the Keys and the Gulf Coast; he wants three major league baseball teams in Florida (Orlando, Miami, Tampa-St. Pete) by the year 2000; Miami got the Marlins in July 1991. In 1993, he got a seat on the Appropriations Committee, where he will try to channel more federal money into Florida to help recovery from Hurricane Andrew and for other purposes.

In early 1993, Mack supported term limits, but he is obviously moving ahead to seek a second term in 1994 and did not rule out a third term should the rules allow it. He seems to have insulated himself from attack and to have made a record capable of appealing to most Florida voters. By early 1993 no well-known Democrat had stepped forward to run against him and it was not clear whether he would, as Graham in effect did in 1992, draw a bye.

Presidential politics. Florida leans so heavily away from the national Democrats today that the real question here is only whether (as almost happened in 1992) the Republican nominee can beat himself. The Democrats' weakness is apparent in their percentages of the last four elections: 39%, 35%, 39%, 39%. George Bush's weakness was apparent when he felt obliged to campaign in Florida: any Republican who can't take this state for granted is in deep trouble.

Florida's presidential primary, one of the early March Super Tuesday contests, can be important, though the even larger state of Texas may be voting the same day. In 1992, Florida produced big primary wins for Bill Clinton and George Bush—Patrick Buchanan failed to dent the Gulf Coast and panhandle, perhaps the most hawkish part of America—and in 1988, it produced big wins for Bush and Michael Dukakis. Dukakis's primary victory shows that the conservative southern vote, dominant when George Wallace won his big victory here in 1972 and even when Jimmy Carter beat him narrowly in 1976, is now far less important: registered Democrats have become a smaller part of the electorate, and more liberal.

Is Florida developing a tradition of politically significant presidential relatives? Miami is the home of Jeb Bush, whose wife is Mexican-American and who is fluent in Spanish; he was a cabinet appointee of Governor Bob Martinez, a high honcho in the state Republican Party and in early 1993 said he would run for governor in 1994. The Miami area has also been home to Hillary Rodham Clinton's two brothers, one of whom, Tony, was an attorney for the Dade County Public Defender's Office, where he worked with now Attorney General Janet Reno.

Congressional districting. Florida gained four new House seats from the 1990 Census, going from 19 to 23 representatives, and redistricting was naturally fiercely contested. So great were the rivalries among Democrats—especially between blacks and Senate President Gwen Margolis—that they could not produce a plan despite holding majorities in both houses and the governorship. As a result, a federal court in May 1992 adopted a plan drawn by a Tulane University professor which created three black-majority and two Hispanic-majority districts, some with very peculiar shapes; boundaries of the other 18 districts were not so driven by politics, but sometimes ended up grotesque because of next-door minority districts. As expected, Florida elected three black congressmen, the first here since Reconstruction, and two Cuban-Americans. It also increased the 10–9 Republican edge in the delegation to 13–10, giving

Florida the most Republican delegation of any megastate. At the same time, voters passed overwhelmingly a term limits initiative, which will prohibit House members' names appearing on the ballot after four terms in office.

The People: Est. Pop. 1992: 13,488,000; Pop. 1990: 12,937,926, up 4.1% 1990–1992. 5.2% of U.S. total, 4th largest; 15% rural. Median age: 36.4 years. 18.3% 65 years and over. 83.1% White, 13.6% Black, 12.2% Hispanic origin, 1.2% Asian, 1.8% Other. Households: 54.4% married couple families; 21% married couple fams. w. children; 44% college educ.; median household income: $27,483; per capita income: $14,698; 67.2% owner occupied housing; median house value: $77,100; median monthly rent: $402. 8.2% Unemployment. Voting age pop.: 10,071,689. Registered voters (1992): 6,541,825; 3,318,565 D (51%), 2,672,968 R (41%), 523,292 unaffiliated and minor parties (8%).

Political Lineup: Governor, Lawton Chiles (D); Lt. Gov., Buddy MacKay (D); Secy. of State, Jim Smith (R); Atty. Gen., Robert A. Butterworth (D); Treasurer and Insurance Commissioner, Thomas Gallagher (R); Comptroller, Gerald Lewis (D); Auditor General, Charles L. Lester (D). State Senate, 40 (20 D and 20 R); State House of Representatives, 120 (71 D and 49 R). Senators, Bob Graham (D) and Connie Mack, III (R). Representatives, 23 (13 R, 10 D).

1992 Presidential Vote			**1988 Presidential Vote**		
Bush (R)	2,171,781	(41%)	Bush (R)	2,618,885	(61%)
Clinton (D)	2,071,651	(39%)	Dukakis (D)	1,656,701	(39%)
Perot (I)	1,052,481	(20%)			

1992 Democratic Presidential Primary			**1992 Republican Presidential Primary**		
Clinton	570,566	(51%)	Bush	608,077	(68%)
Tsongas	388,124	(35%)	Buchanan	285,386	(32%)
Brown	139,569	(12%)			
Other	25,598	(2%)			

GOVERNOR

Gov. Lawton Chiles (D)

Elected 1990, term expires Jan. 1995; b. Apr. 3, 1930, Lakeland; home, Tallahassee; U. of FL, B.S. 1952, LL.B. 1955; Presbyterian; married (Rhea).

Career: Army, 1953–54 (Korea); Practicing atty., 1955–71; Instructor, FL Southern Col., 1955–58; FL House of Reps., 1959–66; FL Senate, 1967–70; U.S. Senate, 1971–89; Dir., LeRoy Collins Ctr. for Pub. Policy, 1989–90.

Office: The Capitol, Tallahassee 32399, 904-488-7146.

Election Results

1990 gen.	Lawton Chiles (D)		1,988,341	(57%)
	Bob Martinez (R)		1,526,738	(43%)
1990 prim.	Lawton Chiles (D)		746,325	(69%)
	Bill Nelson (D)		327,731	(31%)
1986 gen.	Bob Martinez (R)		1,847,525	(55%)
	Steve Pajcic (D)		1,538,620	(45%)

SENATORS

Sen. Bob Graham (D)

Elected 1986, seat up 1998; b. Nov. 9, 1936, Coral Gables; home, Miami Lakes; U. of FL, B.A. 1959, Harvard, J.D. 1962; United Church of Christ; married (Adele).

Career: The Graham Cos., Sengra Development Corp., 1962–66; FL House of Reps., 1966–70; FL Senate, 1970–78; FL Gov., 1978–1986.

Offices: 524 HSOB 20510, 202-224-3041. Also 44 W. Flagler St., #1715, Miami 33130, 305-536-7293; and 325 John Knox Rd., Bldg. 600, Tallahassee 32303, 904-681-7726; and 101 E. Kennedy Blvd., #3145, Tampa 33602, 813-228-2476.

Committees: *Aging (Special)* (8th of 11 D). *Armed Services* (9th of 11 D): Coalition Defense and Reinforcing Forces; Defense Technology, Acquisition and Industrial Base; Regional Defense and Contingency Forces. *Environment and Public Works* (6th of 10 D): Clean Air and Nuclear Regulation; Clean Water, Fisheries and Wildlife (Chmn.); Superfund, Recycling and Solid Waste Management. *Intelligence (Select)* (6th of 9 D). *Veterans' Affairs* (4th of 7 D).

Group Ratings

	ADA	ACLU	CDF	COPE	CFA	LCV	ACU	NTLC	NSI	COC	CEI
1992	75	77	60	75	100	75	15	22	100	20	28
1991	65	—	91	75	78	73	38	—	—	20	25

National Journal Ratings

	1991 LIB — 1991 CONS			1992 LIB — 1992 CONS		
Economic	74%	—	25%	52%	—	46%
Social	57%	—	41%	61%	—	38%
Foreign	60%	—	38%	45%	—	54%

Key Votes of the 102d Congress

1. $ for Homeownership	AGN	5. Clarence Thomas Nom. AGN	9. Use Force in Gulf	FOR
2. Have Cap Gains Debate AGN		6. Lmt Death Row Appeal AGN	10. Keep Salvador Aid	FOR
3. Remove Budget Walls	FOR	7. Handgun Wait/5-Day	FOR	11. Cut $1B from SDI	FOR
4. Ban Striker Replace	FOR	8. Abortion Gag Rule	AGN	12. Override China MFN FOR

Key Votes of the 103d Congress

1. Family Leave   FOR   2. HIV Immigrants   AGN   3. Clinton Budget   FOR

Election Results

1992 general	Bob Graham (D)	3,245,565	(65%)	($3,318,473)
	Bill Grant (R)	1,716,505	(35%)	($242,251)
1992 primary	Bob Graham (D)	968,618	(84%)	
	Jim Mahorner (D)	180,405	(16%)	
1986 general	Bob Graham (D)	1,877,231	(55%)	($6,173,663)
	Paula Hawkins (R)	1,551,888	(45%)	($6,723,729)

Sen. Connie Mack III (R)

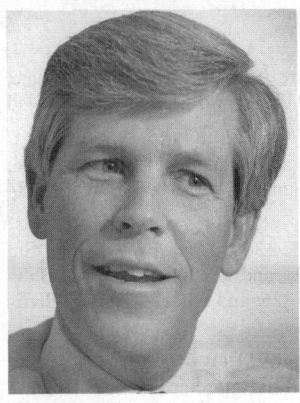

Elected 1988, seat up 1994; b. Oct. 29, 1940, Philadelphia, PA; home, Cape Coral; U. of FL, B.A. 1966; Catholic; married (Priscilla).

Career: Banker, 1966–82; U.S. House of Reps., 1982–88.

Offices: 517 HSOB 20510, 202-224-5274. Also 600 N. Westshore Blvd., #602, Tampa 33609, 813-225-7483.

Committees: *Appropriations* (12th of 13 R): District of Columbia; Foreign Operations; Labor, Health and Human Services, Education; Legislative Branch (RMM). *Banking, Housing and Urban Affairs* (4th of 8 R): Economic Stabilization and Rural Development; Housing and Urban Affairs; International Finance and Monetary Policy (RMM). *Small Business* (5th of 9 R): Competitiveness, Capital Formation and Economic Opportunity (RMM); Urban and Minority-Owned Business Development. *Joint Economic Committee* (8th of 10).

Group Ratings

	ADA	ACLU	CDF	COPE	CFA	LCV	ACU	NTLC	NSI	COC	CEI
1992	10	5	30	18	25	17	96	89	100	100	79
1991	15	—	27	50	22	20	90	—	—	70	78

National Journal Ratings

	1991 LIB — 1991 CONS		1992 LIB — 1992 CONS	
Economic	13% —	86%	11% —	88%
Social	0% —	86%	26% —	73%
Foreign	27% —	67%	21% —	72%

Key Votes of the 102d Congress

1. $ for Homeownership	FOR	5. Clarence Thomas Nom.	FOR	9. Use Force in Gulf	FOR
2. Have Cap Gains Debate	FOR	6. Lmt Death Row Appeal	FOR	10. Keep Salvador Aid	FOR
3. Remove Budget Walls	AGN	7. Handgun Wait/5-Day	AGN	11. Cut $1B from SDI	AGN
4. Ban Striker Replace	AGN	8. Abortion Gag Rule	FOR	12. Override China MFN	FOR

Key Votes of the 103d Congress

1. Family Leave	AGN	2. HIV Immigrants	AGN	3. Clinton Budget	AGN

Election Results

1988 general	Connie Mack III (R)	2,049,329	(50%)	($5,181,639)
	Kenneth H. (Buddy) MacKay (D)	2,015,717	(50%)	($3,714,852)
1988 primary	Connie Mack III (R)	405,296	(62%)	
	Robert W. Merkle (R)................	250,730	(38%)	
1986 general	Lawton Chiles (D)	1,636,857	(62%)	($806,629)
	Van B. Poole (R)....................	1,014,551	(38%)	($472,505)

FIRST DISTRICT

Widely known in the Southeast, scarcely heard of anywhere else, are the Gulf Coast beaches of Florida's Panhandle, from Pensacola east to Destin—the so-called "Redneck Riviera." This area has always been part of Dixie, an expanse of swamp and low farmland, and long heavily dependent on the military. Since John Quincy Adams persuaded Spain to sell Florida to the United States in 1819 to get the port of Pensacola, the United States Navy has had a base there (except during a spot of trouble in the 1860s). This was the site of the nation's first naval aviation training base, the birthplace of carrier aviation and a major base in World War II. Inland to the east is Eglin Air Force Base, which spreads over the lion's share of three counties. In the 1940s and 1950s, these facilities were the main engines of growth; since the 1960s, when the rural South started getting prosperous, this American Riviera has become a major vacation and retirement spot for southerners who enjoy its vast, fine-grained white sand beaches, perhaps the finest in the country, and its pleasant inlet-filled bays.

More than 1,000 miles from Miami, the Panhandle is economically, culturally and politically far from the rest of Florida. Culturally, it is very conservative, an area of large families and traditional churches; Dr. David Gunn, who was murdered by an antiabortion activist in Pensacola in March 1993, was one of the few doctors who performed abortions in the area. The Gulf Coast looks southward toward Castro's Cuba and unruly Caribbean and Latin republics, from a coast bristling with military installations, giant shipyards and huge air bases; George Bush may have been losing in the rest of the country, but even in 1992 he won a majority of the votes here, with Bill Clinton getting about one in four. The Panhandle has become reliably Republican in seriously contested state races now, although it still elects conservative Democrats to the legislature.

The 1st Congressional District of Florida includes the end of the Panhandle, so far west it's in the Central time zone. It stretches from Pensacola and the Alabama border east to include part of Panama City. Historically strongly Democratic, the 1st has continued to elect a Democratic Congressman, Earl Hutto, but with uninspiring majorities and over serious opposition. Hutto first won the district in 1978, after years as a sportscaster and state legislator, beating the Republican mayor of Pensacola. Throughout the 1980s, his concentration on district issues, plus his generally conservative views on national issues, enabled him to win reelection easily. The 1990s have been more difficult. Hutto's record continues to be one of the most conservative of House Democrats, and he has seats on locally important committees—Armed Services and Merchant Marine. Naturally he tends to local needs—benefits for retired military personnel, of whom there are many here; preserving the Pensacola homeport, though he was unable to get the *Forrestal* repaired there; maintaining operations at Eglin. He's chaired a Coast Guard subcommittee, a hot spot with the drug trafficking issue, and now chairs the Armed Services Readiness Subcommittee and is opposed to lifting the ban on gays in the military.

But in 1990 and 1992, Hutto had strenuous opposition from Terry Ketchel, a former House Republican staffer, and won with only 52% each time. In both cases the top of the ticket was heavily Republican here—for Governor Bob Martinez in 1990 and Bush in 1992. In the latter year, as the Defense budget was being cut, Hutto reminded voters that he would be the only Armed Services Committee member left from Florida; but the new base-closing law sharply limits the leverage of even Armed Services members to protect local installations. Ketchel attacked Hutto for voting for an appropriations bill with cuts in Defense administrative positions (as if it were a live option to vote for one with increases) and criticized him both for voting for the Brady bill (one of Hutto's few non-economic liberal votes) and for not opposing Florida offshore oil drilling. Because of a third candidate, Ketchel's share of the vote declined, but Hutto's share suggests continuing vulnerability and future serious contests. This is a part of Florida sure to vote heavily against Governor Lawton Chiles in 1994. Hutto was one of the few House Democrats to vote against the Clinton stimulus package in March 1993; one wonders if he might decide to switch parties.

The People: Pop. 1990: 562,575; 26% rural; 11% age 65+; 83% White; 13% Black; 1% Amer. Indian; 2% Asian; 1% Other; 2% Hispanic origin. Voting age pop.: 419,727; 11% Black; 2% Hispanic origin. Households: 59% married couple families; 26% married couple fams. w. children; 49% college educ.; median household income: $25,866; per capita income: $12,505; median gross rent: $390; median house value: $61,800.

1992 Presidential Vote

Bush (R) 117,809 (51%)
Clinton (D) 59,316 (26%)
Perot (I) 53,250 (23%)

1988 Presidential Vote

Bush (R) 144,294 (73%)
Dukakis (D) 52,230 (27%)

Rep. Earl Hutto (D)

Elected 1978; b. May 12, 1926, Midland City, AL; home, Pensacola; Troy St. U., B.S. 1949, Northwestern U., 1951; Baptist; married (Nancy).

Career: Navy, 1944–46; Pres., Earl Hutto Adv. Agency, 1974–78; Founder and Pres., WPEX Radio, 1960–65; TV Sports Dir., 1954–72; FL House of Reps., 1972–78.

Offices: 2435 RHOB 20515, 202-225-4136. Also 4300 Bayou Blvd., #25-A, Pensacola 32503, 904-478-1123; Cthse. Annex, Shalimar, FL 32579, 904-651-3111; and 5230 W. Hwy. 98, #234, Panama City 32401, 904-872-8813.

Committees: *Armed Services* (4th of 34 D): Readiness (Chmn.); Research and Technology. *Merchant Marine and Fisheries* (3d of 29 D): Coast Guard and Navigation; Environment and Natural Resources; Fisheries Management.

Group Ratings

	ADA	ACLU	COPE	CDF	CFA	LCV	ACU	NTLC	NSI	COC	CEI
1992	15	9	36	20	33	6	83	80	100	88	61
1991	15	—	33	40	44	15	80	—	—	90	50

National Journal Ratings

	1991 LIB — 1991 CONS		1992 LIB — 1992 CONS	
Economic	26%	— 73%	32%	— 68%
Social	16%	— 81%	0%	— 85%
Foreign	31%	— 67%	0%	— 82%

Key Votes of the 102d Congress

1. Ban Striker Replace	AGN	5. Handgun Wait/7-Day	FOR	9. Use Force in Gulf	FOR
2. $ for Homeownership	FOR	6. Overseas Mil. Abortion	AGN	10. US Mil. Abroad $ Cut	AGN
3. Tax Rich/Cut Mid Cls.	AGN	7. Obscn. Art NEA $ Ban	FOR	11. Limit SDI Funds	AGN
4. FY93/$15B Def. Cut	AGN	8. Death Pen. from Jury	FOR	12. Cuba Trade Embargo	FOR

Key Votes of the 103d Congress

1. Family Leave   AGN   2. Deficit Reduction   FOR   3. Stimulus Plan   AGN

Election Results

1992 general	Earl Hutto (D)	118,941	(52%)	($308,621)
	Terry Ketchel (R)	100,349	(44%)	($166,762)
	Barbara Rodgers-Hendricks (Green)	9,342	(4%)	($4,797)
1992 primary	Earl Hutto (D)	60,346	(68%)	
	Ernie Padgett (D)	17,373	(20%)	
	Harry Keller (D)	10,411	(12%)	
1990 general	Earl Hutto (D)	88,416	(52%)	($158,280)
	Terry Ketchel (R)	80,851	(48%)	($182,229)

SECOND DISTRICT

Tallahassee, the small city that is capital of the nation's fourth largest state, was until recently a Spanish-mossed county seat with little to distinguish it but a handsome creole capitol, built in 1845 and preserved opposite its 1977 skyscraper replacement, and two state universities—sited here in the days when almost all Floridians lived along the state's northern edge and Tallahassee was near the population center. Ralph Waldo Emerson, visiting Tallahassee in the 19th Century, said it was a "grotesque place, rapidly settled by public officers, land speculators and desperadoes." The countryside around it is distinctly Dixie: cottonfields, soft pine stands, catfish farms, large families, small towns with big churches, both black and white; Madison County, 50% black, with Florida's lowest per capita income and losing population since 1930, is a noteworthy example. But Tallahassee itself and the subdivisions spreading beyond it are bringing to the state's north end some of the new urbanized Florida, with an additional pro-government tilt: 42% of Tallahassee area jobs are now in city and state government, compared to 15% statewide. Tallahassee has not attained the critical mass of the capitals of the three more populous states (Sacramento, Albany and Austin) but it is on its way.

The 2d Congressional District of Florida is centered on Tallahassee, but extends westward to Panama City and eastward almost to Jacksonville. Historically, this was Democratic country, Jeffersonian and segregationist. Today, it is still Democratic, though for different reasons; there is a large black percentage (23%, the largest in any non-black majority district in Florida) and a strong Democratic preference among state employees and those dependent on them. Tallahassee's Leon County voted 49%–33% for Bill Clinton over George Bush—the highest Clinton percentage in any big Florida county except for heavily Jewish Broward and Alachua, home of the University of Florida. Indeed, this area has supported liberals in Democratic primaries and Democrats in general elections with great consistency even in the Republican 1980s.

The congressman from the 2d District is a Democrat who won the seat in unusual circumstances. Pete Peterson entered the 1990 race as a classic political neophyte. He was a retired Air Force colonel who had spent more than six years as a POW in Vietnam. After he retired from the Air Force, he moved inland from Panama City to Marianna, which is his wife's home town. Peterson knew little about politics, but local Democrats were eager to teach him: the then-congressman, Bill Grant, had switched parties in February 1989, with hoopla from President Bush, Republican National Chairman Lee Atwater and Governor Bob Martinez; the switch was especially startling because, although Grant said he resented the national Democrats' liberalism, he had a rather moderate voting record himself. Some thought Grant was opportunistically angling for a nomination to statewide office; and indeed he turned out to be the nominee against Senator Bob Graham in 1992, whom he had pushed in 1988 for vice president. But if that were so, Grant miscalculated. Democrats hammered at him and Peterson proved to be an appealing candidate, and was elected with 57% of the vote.

As a congressman, Peterson has stressed his many town meetings. As a Public Works Committee member, he co-sponsored the Surface Transportation Act; he supports managed competition healthcare reform. His voting record is middle of the road; he backs term limits and a balanced budget amendment. During his first term he made a trip to Vietnam to urge full access to information about possible Americans left behind. He was reelected with 73% of the vote in 1992 and surely has a safe seat with the added bonus in 1993 of a seat on Appropriations.

The People: Pop. 1990: 562,410; 46% rural; 12% age 65+; 74% White; 23% Black; 1% Amer. Indian; 1% Asian; 1% Other; 2% Hispanic origin. Voting age pop.: 419,263; 21% Black; 2% Hispanic origin. Households: 54% married couple families; 25% married couple fams. w. children; 42% college educ.; median household income: $23,388; per capita income: $11,491; median gross rent: $375; median house value: $57,500.

282   FLORIDA

1992 Presidential Vote

Clinton (D) 100,723 (42%)
Bush (R) 92,805 (38%)
Perot (I). 46,958 (19%)

1988 Presidential Vote

Bush (R) 115,959 (60%)
Dukakis (D). 76,695 (40%)

Rep. Douglas (Pete) Peterson (D)

Elected 1990; b. June 26, 1935, Omaha, NE; home, Marianna; U. of Tampa, B.S. 1976, U. of Central MI, 1977; Catholic; married (Carlotta).

Career: Air Force, 1954–80 (Vietnam); Businessman; Co-owner, CRT Computers, 1984–90; Admin., FL St. U. Dozier Schl. for Boys, 1985–90.

Offices: 426 CHOB 20515, 202-225-5235. 930 Thomasville Rd., #101, Tallahassee 32303, 904-561-3979; 30 W. Government St., #203, Panama City 32401, 904-785-0812.

Committees: *Appropriations* (34th of 37 D): Agriculture, Rural Development, Food and Drug Administration and Related Agencies; Energy and Water Development.

Group Ratings

	ADA	ACLU	COPE	CDF	CFA	LCV	ACU	NTLC	NSI	COC	CEI
1992	75	70	64	80	67	38	19	10	70	38	22
1991	55	—	75	90	67	38	15	—	—	40	22

National Journal Ratings

	1991 LIB — 1991 CONS	1992 LIB — 1992 CONS
Economic	54% — 45%	56% — 42%
Social	56% — 43%	56% — 44%
Foreign	56% — 42%	38% — 56%

Key Votes of the 102d Congress

1. Ban Striker Replace	FOR	5. Handgun Wait/7-Day	AGN	9. Use Force in Gulf	AGN
2. $ for Homeownership	AGN	6. Overseas Mil. Abortion	FOR	10. US Mil. Abroad $ Cut	FOR
3. Tax Rich/Cut Mid Cls.	FOR	7. Obscn. Art NEA $ Ban	FOR	11. Limit SDI Funds	AGN
4. FY93/$15B Def. Cut	FOR	8. Death Pen. from Jury	FOR	12. Cuba Trade Embargo	FOR

Key Votes of the 103d Congress

1. Family Leave   FOR   2. Deficit Reduction   FOR   3. Stimulus Plan   FOR

Election Results

1992 general	Douglas (Pete) Peterson (D)........... 167,215	(73%)	($376,786)
	Ray Wagner (R)...................... 60,425	(27%)	($25,724)
1992 primary	Douglas (Pete) Peterson (D)............ 96,909	(69%)	
	Buster Smith (D) 43,891	(31%)	
1990 general	Douglas (Pete) Peterson (D)........... 103,007	(57%)	($306,104)
	Bill Grant (R)....................... 77,897	(43%)	($839,764)

THIRD DISTRICT

Florida was scarcely settled in the days before the Civil War. There were a few farms and plantations in the northern margin of the state, a few small ports around its periphery, but most of Florida was still a watery, unchartered wilderness, festooned with exotic greenery, inhabited by unusual animals: a part of the United States so far out of the experience of most Americans as to seem foreign. As late as 1940, Florida was the least populous of the southern states, and what population there was tended to be in classic Dixieland, in rural counties with courthouse towns, where the richest white men tended to run civic affairs and blacks lived in flimsy unpainted shotgun houses propped up from the swampy land on blocks, living with little cash and without the vote. This was the Florida, of swamps and lakes and orange groves, of Marjorie Kinnan Rawlings's Cross Creek, where she wrote the great children's classic *The Yearling*, and the Florida of the broad St. Johns River, one of the few rivers in North America that flow (if only sluggishly) north, through the orange grove country to the port of Jacksonville, for many years Florida's largest city.

The 3d Congressional District of Florida occupies much of this old Florida terrain and was drawn for 1992 to have a 55% black majority, in effect collecting together descendants of the slaves who worked the farms and plantations of north Florida over a century ago plus those blacks who have migrated to north Florida since. *The Miami Herald* referred to the 3d as "the ugliest district" in Florida, and its geographical shape is certainly that: it is a long thin chain of land that ties together heavily black neighborhoods in Jacksonville, Gainesville, Daytona Beach and Orlando. Nearly half the population is in Jacksonville, almost one-quarter in and around Orlando (including all-black Eatontown, home of Zora Neale Hurston). Much of it follows Florida watercourses: it touches on Cross Creek, for example, and runs up along the St. Johns River as it makes its way past citrus trees toward Jacksonville. Necessarily, it includes some white areas, particularly around Palatka on the St. Johns.

The campaign for the 3d District had a certain rawness, but in retrospect was a fairly straightforward victory for state legislator Corrine Brown. A state Representative from Jacksonville for 10 years, she had a strong base there, and far outpolled former state Senator Arnett Girardeau; her most spirited competition came from Andy Johnson, a white talk radio host who proclaimed himself "the blackest candidate in the race." Brown led Johnson 43%–31% in the first primary, then polished him off 64%–36% in the runoff. The general election was also seriously contested. There is a Republican base here, and Republican nominee Don Weidner, executive director of the Florida Physicians Association, ran as a fiscal conservative and touted his antiabortion stance. He persuaded a supporter's 12-year old daughter to dress up in a chicken outfit to protest Brown's refusal to take part in several debates, but to no great avail: Brown won 59%–41% in a race that seems to have run pretty much along party lines.

But Brown does not seem to have a monoracial appeal. In the legislature, she sponsored laws to help low-income homeowners weatherize their houses and make emergency repairs, and chaired the Prison Construction Committee. She was a member of Jacksonville's Just Say No to Drugs Committee, and obviously is aware of the toll crime is taking on many of her constituents (Jacksonville was the scene of freeway sniper attacks in November 1992). In the House, she got a seat on the Public Works Committee, plainly to get projects into her district. She is likely to be a solid liberal vote, yet there is something other than a straight 1960s militance in her emphasis: on defense issues, for example, she stresses that the military can be a source of opportunity, a lesson many blacks know from personal experience. Having won the district by a fairly solid margin, Brown can be expected to hold it without great difficulty.

The People: Pop. 1990: 563,079; 16% rural; 12% age 65+; 42% White; 55% Black; 1% Asian; 1% Other; 3% Hispanic origin. Voting age pop.: 400,821; 50% Black; 3% Hispanic origin. Households: 43% married couple families; 19% married couple fams. w. children; 32% college educ.; median household income: $19,780; per capita income: $9,419; median gross rent: $372; median house value: $46,800.

Rep. Corrine Brown (D)

Elected 1992; b. Nov. 11, 1946, Jacksonville; home, Jacksonville; FL A&M, B.A. 1969, M.S., 1974; Baptist; divorced.

Career: Prof., FL Commun. Col., 1977–82, Guidance Counselor, 1982–92; FL House of Reps., 1982–92.

Offices: 1037 LHOB 20515, 202-225-0123. Also 815 S. Main St., Jacksonville 32207, 904-398-8567; 250 N. Beach St., #80-1, Daytona Beach 32114, 904-254-4622; 75 Ivanhoe Blvd., Orlando 32806, 407-872-0656; and 401 SE First Ave., #316, Gainesville 32601, 904-375-6003.

Committees: *Government Operations* (22d of 25 D): Legislation and National Security. *Public Works and Transportation* (32d of 39 D): Aviation; Economic Development; Water Resources and Environment. *Veterans' Affairs* (21st of 21 D): Hospitals and Health Care; Housing and Memorial Affairs.

Group Ratings and 102d Congress Votes: Newly Elected

Key Votes of the 103d Congress

1. Family Leave	FOR	2. Deficit Reduction	FOR	3. Stimulus Plan	FOR

Election Results

1992 general	Corrine Brown (D)	91,918	(59%)	($275,705)
	Don Weidner (R).	63,115	(41%)	($258,394)
1992 runoff	Corrine Brown (D)	29,006	(64%)	
	Andrew Johnson (D).	16,427	(36%)	
1992 primary	Corrine Brown (D)	25,374	(43%)	
	Andrew Johnson (D).	18,209	(31%)	
	Arnett Girardeau (D)	10,746	(18%)	
	Glennie Mills (D)	4,383	(8%)	
1990 election	Newly created district.			

FOURTH DISTRICT

Jacksonville, with nearly one million people in the counties around is north Florida's major city, with bold new skyscrapers looming above a wide river and a fancy shopping mall overshadowing grid streets of tiny shotgun houses; broad freeways leading to vast beachfronts are not far from primeval wetlands and citrus groves. Here is one of Navy's biggest bases at Mayport and other military installations as well. Yet Jacksonville tends to get overlooked in Florida, where its gleaming downtown is just one of a dozen in a state that had no significant commercial office development less than a generation ago; just a decade ago it was known as a smelly, slow-growing paper mill and insurance town. Jacksonville grew in the 1980s as it attracted big installations from AT&T, Brockway International, Prudential, Sears, UPS, American Express and the Mayo Clinic, while maintaining its big military bases and insurance headquarters. Its job base is tilted, more than anywhere else in Florida, toward finance and insurance and transportation and utilities. Jacksonville is culturally part of the South, with a large black population, plenty of blue-collar whites with southern accents, lots of children and relatively few retirees. Its work force is less well educated and its incomes lower than in Florida generally. It has less tourism and less high-tech industry. But, though hurt by base shutdowns in the 1990s, it is economically growing and culturally not on the defensive. Politically, its heritage is Democratic, but it has been trending Republican in state as well as national elections.

The 4th Congressional District of Florida includes most of Jacksonville (minus the areas now in the majority-black 3d District) and beach areas to the north and south to St. Augustine, the oldest European-founded city in the United States, settled by the Spanish in the 16th Century. Farther south is Daytona Beach, with its hard-sand beach, made famous by racing cars. Mostly vacant in the 1940s, when Jacksonville was the largest city in the state, the beaches have now filled up, with giant new subdivisions. For 44 years, since 1948 until his retirement in 1992, Jacksonville was represented by Charles Bennett, a Democrat who contracted polio while in military service in World War II, and a stickler for ethics long before that became fashionable. A backer of an expansive American military policy, he supported the 600-ship Navy in the 1980s on the Armed Services Committee but led fights to cut the Strategic Defense Initiative. Bennett was passed over for Armed Services chairman in December 1984, when Mel Price was ousted by the Democratic Caucus and Les Aspin voted in; his great local achievement for the district was the 35,000-acre Timucuan Historic Preserve. In June 1992, he said he was leaving Congress because of his wife's health; the removal of blacks from his district to the new black-majority 3d District, however, made his reelection chancier, and indeed the new 4th District did choose a Republican in November, after a serious contest.

The Republican was Tillie Fowler, Jacksonville City Council president. She grew up in Milledgeville, Georgia, daughter of a druggist who served in the legislature; she went to law school, worked in Washington for Georgia Senator Robert Stephens and the Nixon Administration. She married a Jacksonville businessman, raised a family there and did volunteer work, and was elected to the Council in 1985. By 1992, she was planning to retire, in line with her belief that "eight is enough"—the theme of Florida's successful 1992 term limits initiative. From there, she decided to run for the House, leaving no doubt of her emphasis: two retired admirals were present at her announcement, and she got House Republican leaders to promise her a seat on the Armed Services Committee if she won. Pro-choice, for a balanced budget amendment, she pledged to make Mayport her top priority. The Democratic candidate, Mattox Hair, from rural Florida, had been student body president at Florida State and served in the Army; he served in the legislature from 1972 to 1988 where he was a major committee chairman; he resigned a judgeship to run for Congress. Hair campaigned as a conservative Democrat; Fowler called him "one of the boys" in Tallahassee and attacked him for voting for a pay raise in 1985. Fowler won with 57%, with her strongest showing in Jacksonville.

In the House, Fowler now sits on Armed Services, long chaired by Carl Vinson who was also from Milledgeville. In her first months she was lobbying for Mayport, objecting to Democratic procedures and arguing against lifting the ban on gays in the military.

The People: Pop. 1990: 562,154; 13% rural; 14% age 65+; 89% White; 6% Black; 2% Asian; 1% Other; 3% Hispanic origin. Voting age pop.: 435,405; 5% Black; 3% Hispanic origin. Households: 58% married couple families; 25% married couple fams. w. children; 53% college educ.; median household income: $31,707; per capita income: $16,845; median gross rent: $483; median house value: $80,700.

1992 Presidential Vote		
Bush (R)	132,023	(53%)
Clinton (D)	75,035	(30%)
Perot (I)	41,075	(17%)

1988 Presidential Vote		
Bush (R)	132,762	(69%)
Dukakis (D)	58,460	(31%)

Rep. Tillie K. Fowler (R)

Elected 1992; b. Dec. 23, 1942, Milledgeville, GA; home, Jacksonville; Emory U., A.B. 1964, J.D. 1967; Episcopalian; married (Buck).

Career: Legis. Asst., U.S. Sen. Robert Stephens, 1967–70; White House Office of Consumer Affairs, 1970–71; Jacksonville City Cncl., 1985–92, Pres., 1989–90.

Offices: 413 CHOB 20515, 202-225-2501. Also 4452 Hendricks Ave., Jacksonville 32207, 904-739-6600; and 533 N. Nova Rd., Ormond Beach 32174, 904-672-0754.

Committees: *Armed Services* (18th of 22 R): Military Forces and Personnel; Military Installations and Facilities. *Merchant Marine and Fisheries* (12th of 19 R): Coast Guard and Navigation; Merchant Marine.

Group Ratings and 102d Congress Votes: Newly Elected

Key Votes of the 103d Congress

1. Family Leave	AGN	2. Deficit Reduction	AGN	3. Stimulus Plan	AGN

Election Results

1992 general	Tillie K. Fowler (R)	135,883	(57%)	($512,267)
	Mattox Hair (D).....................	103,531	(43%)	($427,480)
1992 primary	Tillie K. Fowler (R), unopposed			
1990 general	Charles E. Bennett (D)...............	84,280	(73%)	($108,953)
(FL 3)	Rod Sullivan (R).....................	31,727	(27%)	($13,414)

FIFTH DISTRICT

For the past 25 years, Florida's urban areas have expanded in every unlikely direction, seeking the high ground between the swamps and wetlands that still occupy most of the Florida peninsula. One example is in the Gulf Coast counties north of St. Petersburg and Tampa. Here, in what were sleepy little towns with low brick buildings baking in the Florida sun, sprang up subdivisions and trailer parks and shopping centers with Eckerd drugstores and Winn Dixie markets. Today, more than half a million people live in the towns starting with Clearwater and the northern suburbs of Tampa that run up the spines of U.S. 19 (just off the Gulf Coast), or U.S. 41 and Interstate 75 inland amid the orange groves. This is retirement country, though there are plenty of working people here too. It is mostly comfortable, though far from the most affluent in Florida; and if the existence of such communities is taken for granted by most Americans, their construction—the creation of an infrastructure of water and sewer lines, underground electricity, and phone and TV cables—is the result of the miracles of modern technology.

The 5th Congressional District of Florida, newly created after the 1990 Census, occupies much of this territory; by 1990 there were 562,000 people in land that held perhaps 129,000 in 1960. The 5th swings north to include most of Gainesville, home of the University of Florida, where young people from the more affluent urban corridors of south and central Florida study on a campus surrounded by flimsy houses typical of the impoverished South of 50 years ago; here they can become part of a Florida elite bonded by shared memories of the Gator Growl festivities. It includes still lightly populated Dixie, Gilchrist and Levy Counties (the last named after Florida's first Senator, David Levy Yulee, who was Jewish). And it includes the New Port

Richey area on the Pasco County coast and all of fast-growing Citrus, Hernando and Sumter Counties to the north. Thirty years ago, this area was simply southern Democratic. Now you can see the origins of newcomers in the voting totals. The Gulf Coast counties, with many blue- as well as white-collar retirees, are mixed, while Gainesville is liberal and Democratic. The 5th District also includes, not coincidentally, a small portion of Marion County, notably Dunnellon, home of Karen Thurman, chairwoman of the state Senate Subcommittee on Congressional Reapportionment, who was elected the 5th District's representative in 1992.

Thurman seems to be a hyperactive legislator. She grew up an Air Force brat in Florida and elsewhere; she was a middle school math teacher for nine years, then was elected to the Dunnellon Council and eventually became mayor. In 1982, she was elected to the Florida Senate and was reelected in 1986 with more votes than any other state senator. She sponsored an average of 60 bills a year on subjects like education, the environment and agriculture. In 1992, she easily won the 5th District primary and in the general faced former prosecutor Tom Hogan who called her a "professional, big money politician." Thurman is pro-choice and anti-NAFTA, for fear of Mexican citrus, and wants to get funding for local water and sewer projects. She seems to thrive in the House, enjoying a two-hour working meeting with 14 other freshmen and President Bill Clinton, savoring the possibility (aborted because a more senior Democrat—John Spratt—ended up taking the opening) that she might be the only freshman to chair a subcommittee (on John Conyers's turbulent Government Operations Committee). Thurman shows all the vigor and skills that other Democrats have used to hold onto marginal seats like Florida's 5th.

The People: Pop. 1990: 562,936; 42% rural; 26% age 65+; 90% White; 6% Black; 1% Asian; 1% Other; 3% Hispanic origin. Voting age pop.: 459,932; 5% Black; 3% Hispanic origin. Households: 58% married couple families; 17% married couple fams. w. children; 38% college educ.; median household income: $21,374; per capita income: $11,987; median gross rent: $403; median house value: $62,200.

1992 Presidential Vote

Clinton (D)	110,244	(41%)
Bush (R)	90,656	(34%)
Perot (I)	64,106	(24%)

1988 Presidential Vote

Bush (R)	119,272	(57%)
Dukakis (D)	91,752	(43%)

Rep. Karen L. Thurman (D)

Elected 1992; b. Jan. 12, 1951, Rapid City, SD; home, Dunnellon; U. of FL, B.A. 1973; Episcopalian; married (John).

Career: Middle schl. teacher, 1974–82; Dunnellon City Cncl., 1974–82; Dunnellon Mayor 1979–81; FL Senate 1982–92.

Offices: 130 CHOB 20515, 202-225-1002. Also One Courthouse Sq., #102, Inverness 34450, 904-637-9945; 5700 SW 34th St., #425, Gainesville 32608, 904-336-6614; and 5623 Rte. 19 S., #206, New Port Richey 34652, 813-849-4496.

Committees: *Agriculture* (24th of 28 D): Environment, Credit and Rural Development; Foreign Agriculture and Hunger; Livestock; Specialty Crops and Natural Resources. *Government Operations* (13th of 25 D): Employment, Housing and Aviation; Environment, Energy and Natural Resources; Information, Justice, Transportation and Agriculture.

Group Ratings and 102d Congress Votes: Newly Elected

Key Votes of the 103d Congress

1. Family Leave	FOR	2. Deficit Reduction	FOR	3. Stimulus Plan	FOR

Election Results

1992 general	Karen L. Thurman (D)...............	129,698	(49%)	($352,607)
	Tom Hogan (R).....................	114,356	(43%)	($144,613)
	Cindy Munkittrick (I).................	19,462	(7%)	($14,580)
1992 primary	Karen L. Thurman (D)................	60,144	(76%)	
	Mario F. Rivera (D)	19,141	(24%)	
1990 election	Newly created district.			

SIXTH DISTRICT

The flat rolling grasslands of central Florida, once bypassed by southbound tourists heading for the coast, in the 1980s had become a prime growth areas in the nation's prime growth state. In earlier decades, these areas depended economically on farming, on state institutions (the University of Florida in Gainesville, the big state prison in Raiford) and on passing tourists getting off the interstate to see attractions like Silver Springs, the world's largest formation of clear artesian springs. But as time went on, retirees began settling in places like the bluegrass country around Ocala (one of America's prime horse breeding grounds) and the plenteous lakes in Lake County to the south. These are not necessarily affluent developments: this part of central Florida has the highest percentage of mobile homes in the United States.

The 6th Congressional District of Florida takes up much of this territory. Its boundaries are a bit odd, since it is almost seven-eighths surrounded by the black-majority 3d District. About half of its people live around Ocala or in Lake County. Another one-third live on the west side of Jacksonville or in suburban communities in Clay County just to the south; both areas are heavily Republican. The 6th also includes parts of traditionally Democratic old rural Florida; it no longer, as it did until 1992, includes Gainesville.

The congressman from the 6th District is Cliff Stearns, a Republican first elected in 1988 when Democrat Buddy MacKay ran for the Senate (he lost but in 1990 was elected Lieutenant Governor). Stearns grew up and attended public schools in Washington, D.C., but he is a beyond-the-Beltway conservative, a self-made business success who ended up owning five motels, three restaurants and other real estate—"someone who works in the community, goes to church with his neighbors, and doesn't live in Tallahassee," as he put it in his 1988 campaign, when he beat the favorite, House Speaker Jon Mills, 54%–46%.

In Washington, Stearns became famous—and also hated—on Capitol Hill for his amendment cutting congressional staff pay raises. He worked out a consensus for a return to Florida state government of 77,000 acres set aside for the now-canceled Cross-Florida Barge Canal. Despite his conservative record on spending, he took credit for siting a new federal prison, to be the nation's largest, housing 3,000 inmates, in Sumter County; it's no longer in his district, but a lot of 6th District residents will probably work there. He is proud as well of the new $60 million veterans' psychiatric facility in Gainesville, also outside the lines but not far away. On national issues, he passed an amendment to freeze the National Endowment for the Arts 1993 budget at 1992 levels, backs tax credits for first-time home buyers and IRAs for all, and he supports market-driven healthcare reform.

Stearns easily won in 1990, and by 1992 had conducted 170 town meetings in the district. Redistricting subtracted Gainesville and added half of Duval County and the Jacksonville area, making the 6th 9% more Republican. His 1992 opponent, who operated a diaper service, ran a radio jingle saying "I'm Phil Denton, the diaper man. People tell me I'm prepared for Congress because I've been up to my elbows in it." Denton got 35% of the vote and Stearns 65%.

The People: Pop. 1990: 561,464; 48% rural; 18% age 65+; 89% White; 7% Black; 1% Asian; 1% Other; 3% Hispanic origin. Voting age pop.: 427,270; 6% Black; 3% Hispanic origin. Households: 65% married couple families; 26% married couple fams. w. children; 37% college educ.; median household income: $26,025; per capita income: $12,274; median gross rent: $417; median house value: $66,400.

1992 Presidential Vote

Bush (R) 112,554 (47%)
Clinton (D) 74,328 (31%)
Perot (I). 50,914 (21%)

1988 Presidential Vote

Bush (R) 124,888 (70%)
Dukakis (D). 52,714 (30%)

Rep. Clifford B. Stearns (R)

Elected 1988; b. Apr. 16, 1941, Washington, DC; home, Ocala; George Washington U., B.S. 1963; Presbyterian; married (Joan).

Career: Air Force, 1963–67; Data Control Systems Inc., 1967–68; Negotiator, CBS, 1969–70; Pres., Stearns House Inc., 1972–present.

Offices: 332 CHOB 20515, 202-225-5744. Also 115 S.E. 25th Ave., Ocala 34471, 904-351-8777; 1726 Kingsley Ave., #8, Orange Park 32073, 904-269-3203; and 111 S. 6th St., Leesburg 34748, 904-326-8285.

Committees: *Energy and Commerce* (11th of 17 R): Commerce, Consumer Protection and Competitiveness (RMM); Energy and Power. *Veterans' Affairs* (13th of 14 R): Compensation, Pension and Insurance.

Group Ratings

	ADA	ACLU	COPE	CDF	CFA	LCV	ACU	NTLC	NSI	COC	CEI
1992	5	4	11	20	8	25	92	90	100	75	83
1991	25	—	33	40	39	15	90	—	—	70	80

National Journal Ratings

	1991 LIB — 1991 CONS		1992 LIB — 1992 CONS	
Economic	26%	— 73%	0%	— 91%
Social	16%	— 81%	0%	— 85%
Foreign	17%	— 78%	0%	— 82%

Key Votes of the 102d Congress

1. Ban Striker Replace	AGN	5. Handgun Wait/7-Day FOR	6. Overseas Mil. Abortion AGN	9. Use Force in Gulf FOR

1. Ban Striker Replace   AGN
2. $ for Homeownership   FOR
3. Tax Rich/Cut Mid Cls. AGN
4. FY93/$15B Def. Cut   AGN
5. Handgun Wait/7-Day   FOR
6. Overseas Mil. Abortion AGN
7. Obscn. Art NEA $ Ban FOR
8. Death Pen. from Jury FOR
9. Use Force in Gulf   FOR
10. US Mil. Abroad $ Cut AGN
11. Limit SDI Funds   AGN
12. Cuba Trade Embargo   FOR

Key Votes of the 103d Congress

1. Family Leave   AGN   2. Deficit Reduction   AGN   3. Stimulus Plan   AGN

Election Results

1992 general	Clifford B. Stearns (R) 144,195	(65%)	($309,532)
	Phil Denton (D) 76,419	(35%)	($2,333)
1992 primary	Clifford B. Stearns (R), unopposed		
1990 general	Clifford B. Stearns (R) 138,547	(59%)	($462,925)
	Art Johnson (D) 95,410	(41%)	($26,443)

SEVENTH DISTRICT

New names keep cropping up on the Florida landscape, new communities and towns suddenly spring up and overtake the older town centers with which tourists have been familiar. Just down the road from the hard-sand beach of Daytona, where motorcyclists gather for bikers' Hog Week in late February, is New Smyrna Beach, a new town on the site of an old settlement. Fifteen miles inland, near the old county seat town of Sanford where Amtrak's Auto-Train disembarks its Florida-bound motorists, is Deltona, almost five miles square, a vast development that drained a swatch of Florida swamp and designed a grid of curving streets meandering around small lakes and golf courses, set aside land for shopping centers and office space, and then marketed the place nationwide. Instant city: there were 51,000 people living in Deltona in 1990 where there were 15,000 in 1980 and 4,800 in 1970.

The 7th Congressional District of Florida includes New Smyrna Beach and part of Daytona Beach, most of Sanford and all of Deltona. It stretches from Daytona across the marshy St. Johns River basin to Seminole County, with big Orlando suburbs like Altamonte Springs and small old towns like Oviedo, and goes south to include part of Orlando itself. This is a solidly Republican district in most races, though there is a conservative Democratic heritage here, particularly around Daytona, an area that tended to be central to its predecessor 4th District; but Seminole County tends to be dominated by Orlando media and concerns. Incumbent Republican Craig James, a hard-shell conservative from the Volusia County seat of DeLand, bowed out of the 1992 race early; he had won two heated contests in the old 4th, narrowly ousting 20-year incumbent Bill Chappell in 1988 and beating an environmentalist businessman in 1990. What followed was another serious contest.

The most colorful candidate was John Mica, a political veteran campaigning as an opponent of the status quo. He is from a bipartisan political family: his younger brother Dan Mica was a Democratic congressman from Palm Beach County from 1978 to 1988, when he ran for Senate and lost the primary and is now Clinton's head of the Board for International Broadcasting; another brother is a staffer for Democratic Governor Lawton Chiles. But John Mica has always been a conservative Republican, as state representative from the Orlando area from 1976 to 1980 and then as administrative assistant to U.S. Senator Paula Hawkins from 1981 to 1985. Mica turned 360 feet of New Smyrna beachfront into a real estate business and small fortune, and became a professional lobbyist—and a proud one: "Some of the finest folks I've met are lobbyists." His firm represented American Specialty Chemical, Coopers & Lybrand and Harris (the big Florida computer firm) to mention a few.

In the Republican primary, former legislator Richard Graham attacked Mica as "the ultimate insider, [who] has represented the special interest groups of Washington for the past six years. Can we trust him to make the right decisions for Florida as his former clients keep asking him for favors?" Mica blandly said that all congressmen are lobbyists for their districts, and showed his stuff by lobbying pro bono for the Daytona airport and getting an extension of its runway. Mica won 53%–34%, losing Volusia but carrying Seminole and the Orlando area. Then Democrat Dan Webster attacked Mica as "the epitome of the professional politician." Mica responded fairly accurately that Webster was a liberal backed by trial lawyers and labor unions; Webster's father was a brick mason and he worked his way through college and law school doing construction work in New Smyrna Beach while Mica was a developer there. But this was one Democrat who didn't outhustle the Republican: Mica started his campaign with a $100,000 loan and raised plenty from former clients. Webster carried Volusia with 51%, but Mica got 63% in Seminole and the Orlando area, for a 56%–44% victory.

Mica's agenda, he said, was "No new taxes, less litigation, less regulation." He was one of the Republican freshmen who aggressively urged the abolition of House select committees. To the list of Republican policies he backs—capital gains cut, term limits, antiabortion—he adds support for Head Start. He wants to consolidate federal export programs into a single agency and to require broadcasters to spend 5% of commercial airtime combating drug abuse. He is sponsoring a global environment cleanup act, to monitor other countries' environmental laws and encourage laggards to do better or risk losing U.S. aid. He seems willing to take political risks for his convictions; as he said during the campaign, "I've made a lot of money. I don't need the salary and I don't need the title." He still seems in a strong political position in the 7th District.

The People: Pop. 1990: 563,552; 11% rural; 16% age 65+; 89% White; 4% Black; 1% Asian; 1% Other; 5% Hispanic origin. Voting age pop.: 436,780; 4% Black; 5% Hispanic origin. Households: 60% married couple families; 25% married couple fams. w. children; 51% college educ.; median household income: $30,921; per capita income: $15,132; median gross rent: $529; median house value: $80,400.

1992 Presidential Vote			1988 Presidential Vote		
Bush (R)	105,519	(45%)	Bush (R)	118,214	(67%)
Clinton (D)	81,180	(34%)	Dukakis (D)	58,846	(33%)
Perot (I)	49,588	(21%)			

Rep. John L. Mica (R)

Elected 1992; b. Jan 27, 1943, Binghamton, NY; home, Winter Park; Miami-Dade Comm. Col., A.A. 1965, U. of FL, B.A. 1967; Episcopalian; married (Patricia).

Career: Exec. Dir., Palm Beach & Orange Cnty. Govt. Charter Study Commissions, 1970–74; Pres., MK Development, 1975–92; FL House of Reps., 1976–80; A.A., U.S. Sen. Paula Hawkins, 1981–85; Partner, Mica, Dudinsky & Assoc., 1985–92;

Offices: 427 CHOB 20515, 202-225-4035. Also 237 Fernwood Blvd., Fern Park 32730, 407-339-8080; 840 Deltona Blvd., Deltona 32725, 407-866-1499; and 1396 Dunlawton Blvd., Port Orange 32127, 904-756-9798.

Committees: *Government Operations* (16th of 17 R): Environment, Energy and Natural Resources; Human Resources and Intergovernmental Relations. *Public Works and Transportation* (22d of 24 R): Aviation; Economic Development.

Group Ratings and 102d Congress Votes: Newly Elected

Key Votes of the 103d Congress

1. Family Leave	AGN	2. Deficit Reduction	AGN	3. Stimulus Plan	AGN

Election Results

1992 general	John L. Mica (R)	125,823	(56%)	($459,135)
	Dan Webster (D)	96,945	(44%)	($307,857)
1992 primary	John L. Mica (R)	24,350	(53%)	
	Dick Graham (R)	15,768	(34%)	
	Vaughn S. Forrest (R)	6,073	(13%)	
1990 general	Craig T. James (R)	119,521	(56%)	($634,891)
	Reid Hughes (D)	94,540	(44%)	($1,067,366)

EIGHTH DISTRICT

The center of one of America's, and the world's, great growth industries in the 1980s and surely into the 1990s, is a place few would have picked two decades ago as the center of anything except a bunch of orange groves. The industry is tourism, the place is Orlando and, at least a few people had an idea of its potential. The key decision was made by Walt Disney in the mid-1960s to put his vast theme park near the interchange of Florida's Turnpike and Interstate 4, the "crossroads of Florida," just a few miles west of Orlando. Today Orlando is the world's number one tourist destination, with more hotel rooms (79,000) than anywhere else in the country, attracting people not only to Disney World's Magic Kingdom and EPCOT Center and MGM Studios but also to Sea World and Universal Studios and dozens of other attractions. Orlando is the center of a one million plus metropolitan area, with the biggest job gain, 74%, in the 1980s of any major metro area. And the economy has diversified beyond tourism: Martin Marietta built a big defense plant here way back in 1956, and greater Orlando has a high-tech economy and a population weighted toward young families with children rather than retirees.

The spirit of this place has been set by a man who never lived here but created something now taken for granted. Walt Disney invented the theme park in the flatlands of Orange County, California, but he perfected it in the 17,000 acres of swamp and lakes in Florida's Orange County. And while inventing the theme park, Disney also pioneered in sophisticated communications, utility and waste disposal methods—all out of sight and underground. Yet Disney World does not work just by mechanics; it requires some 34,000 people with know-how and unfailing cheerfulness. Disney's vision of a future that was labor-intensive as well as high-tech, in which the critical ingredient is the provision of services, was a forecast of the service-driven economy that has grown so lustily for decades now. The Orlando metro area, with 32% of its jobs in services, is one of the most service-dominated in the nation.

The 8th Congressional District of Florida includes most of Orlando and surrounding Orange County. It excludes most heavily black neighborhoods and towns now placed in the grotesquely shaped 3d District. It includes central and eastern Orlando and all its suburbs directly to the east, plus most to the south and west. It also takes in most of the Kissimmee area in Osceola County just to the south, and of course, Disney World's Magic Kingdom. Politically, this Orange County, like the Orange County where the original Disneyland was built, is heavily Republican. Occasionally subject to spasms of Democratic sentiment (as California's Orange County was in 1992), it remains heavily leavened to the party which seems friendlier to the wholesome spirit of this service industry and high-tech metropolis.

The congressman from the 8th District is Bill McCollum, one of the most active and aggressive Republicans in the House, involved in one issue after another, regardless of committee jurisdiction. By no means always the winner on roll calls in the Democratic House, he is still a force to be reckoned with. He has generally been wary of increased immigration and eager to enforce existing restrictions; he wants to ensure deportation of criminal aliens and to penalize illegal aliens who enter into fraudulent marriages to remain in the United States. He successfully led the fight against the Brady bill in 1988 by substituting an amendment commanding the government to produce a nationwide list of convicted felons to which all gun dealers would have access; but was on the losing side of the same issue in the 1990s. He has worked with Virginia Democrat Rick Boucher to scale back the harsh RICO law. McCollum has also worked for the long arm statute to authorize FBI investigation of terrorism and other crimes against Americans overseas.

McCollum is a member of the Republican leadership as vice chairman of the House Republican Conference; in December 1992 he beat back a challenge by moderate Nancy Johnson. In the same year he led the fight for a discharge petition to get the issue of congressional term limits to the House floor, which of course failed; he was trying to move term limits again in early 1993, though he said "I don't have any illusions about this." In 1992, he was also busy leading the unsuccessful fight to allow S&Ls to count goodwill as an asset, and blocked the RTC bill for some time. On foreign policy, he was a stern critic of terrorist violence. Placed on the Iran-contra committee by Minority Leader Robert Michel, he was a vocal critic of opponents of the Reagan Administration. On all these controversies, McCollum's attention to detail and bulldog perseverance, even in unfashionable causes, has made him a strong contender. He will need these qualities to fight for the Navy's Orlando Training Installation which employs 17,000 people and which he managed to get removed from the base closing list in 1991 but which got back on the list for 1993.

In 1992, McCollum had spirited competition from Chuck Kovaleski, head of a title insurance fund and a sponsor of the "Eight is Enough" term limit drive. Kovaleski endorsed the "Lead or Leave" pledge and started giving "Silver Swine" awards to perpetrators of government foolishness. But for all Kovaleski's resourcefulness, McCollum won with 69% of the vote.

The People: Pop. 1990: 562,244; 9% rural; 11% age 65+; 81% White; 5% Black; 2% Asian; 3% Other; 11% Hispanic origin. Voting age pop.: 436,385; 5% Black; 10% Hispanic origin. Households: 55% married couple families; 25% married couple fams. w. children; 52% college educ.; median household income: $31,251; per capita income: $15,464; median gross rent: $531; median house value: $84,600.

1992 Presidential Vote			1988 Presidential Vote		
Bush (R)	101,707	(48%)	Bush (R)	108,602	(71%)
Clinton (D)	68,840	(32%)	Dukakis (D)	43,910	(29%)
Perot (I)	42,901	(20%)			

Rep. Bill McCollum (R)

Elected 1980; b. July 12, 1944, Brooksville; home, Altamonte Springs; U. of FL, B.A. 1965, J.D. 1968; Episcopalian; married (Ingrid).

Career: Navy, 1969–72, Naval Reserves, 1972–93; Practicing atty., 1973–81; Chmn., Seminole Cnty. Repub. Cmte., 1976.

Offices: 2266 RHOB 20515, 202-225-2176. Also 605 E. Robinson #650, Orlando 32801, 407-872-1962.

Committees: *Banking, Finance and Urban Affairs* (2d of 20 R): Economic Growth and Credit Formation; Financial Institutions Supervision, Regulation and Deposit Insurance (RMM); International Development, Finance, Trade and Monetary Policy. *Judiciary* (5th of 14 R): Intellectual Property and Judicial Administration; International Law, Immigration and Refugees.

Group Ratings

	ADA	ACLU	COPE	CDF	CFA	LCV	ACU	NTLC	NSI	COC	CEI
1992	15	0	25	0	13	19	92	90	100	86	75
1991	10	—	18	10	17	31	90	—	—	89	71

National Journal Ratings

	1991 LIB — 1991 CONS			1992 LIB — 1992 CONS		
Economic	0%	—	96%	12%	—	86%
Social	0%	—	84%	0%	—	85%
Foreign	30%	—	70%	0%	—	82%

Key Votes of the 102d Congress

1. Ban Striker Replace	AGN	5. Handgun Wait/7-Day	AGN	9. Use Force in Gulf	FOR
2. $ for Homeownership	FOR	6. Overseas Mil. Abortion	AGN	10. US Mil. Abroad $ Cut	AGN
3. Tax Rich/Cut Mid Cls.	AGN	7. Obscn. Art NEA $ Ban	FOR	11. Limit SDI Funds	AGN
4. FY93/$15B Def. Cut	AGN	8. Death Pen. from Jury	FOR	12. Cuba Trade Embargo	FOR

Key Votes of the 103d Congress

1. Family Leave	AGN	2. Deficit Reduction	AGN	3. Stimulus Plan	AGN

Election Results

1992 general	Bill McCollum (R)	141,977	(69%)	($675,211)
	Chuck Kovaleski (D)	65,145	(32%)	($174,940)
1992 primary	Bill McCollum (R)	33,482	(80%)	
	Lew Oliver (R)	8,621	(20%)	
1990 general	Bill McCollum (R)	93,989	(60%)	($564,994)
(FL 5)	Bob Fletcher (D).	63,136	(40%)	($18,635)

NINTH DISTRICT

Half a century ago, the land north of St. Petersburg and Tampa was scarcely inhabited. The Gulf is lined with swamps and inland, the land is spotted with lakes and covered with dense semitropical forests. Over the years, development has moved up the coast and up the major highways inland. Much of this originally was designed for retirees—condominiums, garden apartments, trailer parks. But this is working country as well. Businesses grew up around Clearwater in northern Pinellas County and inland in Pasco County off I-75. And people brought their ancestral political beliefs with them. In the 1950s and 1960s, only white-collar retirees could afford to buy new places in Florida, and retirees were heavily Republican. As blue-collar workers and union members became more affluent in the 1970s and 1980s, they came too, with their traditional Democratic Party identification and cultural conservatism.

The 9th Congressional District of Florida covers much of this area north of St. Petersburg and Tampa. About half its population is in northern Pinellas County around Clearwater and Tarpon Springs, an old resort first settled by Greek sponge divers early in the 20th Century. Another quarter is in northern Hillsborough County, on the suburban fringe of Tampa. The final quarter is the inland portion of Pasco County, north of Tampa, where former crossroads like Zephyrhills have become significant population centers.

The congressman from the 9th District is Michael Bilirakis, a Republican who grew up in Pittsburgh and worked his way through college toiling in a steel mill; he served in the Air Force during the Korean War, and then went to college. He believes strongly that Americans can work their way up, with occasional government assistance (like the G.I. Bill that helped him through school). He favors generous Social Security benefits, government-funded research on Alzheimer's disease and cable reregulation—all issues with local resonance in this elderly and heavily cabled district (the Home Shopping Network is headquartered here). With a seat on Energy and Commerce, he has cast some key votes on regulatory and health issues, against the 1988 Catastrophic Health Care Act, for increased federal elderly home care money, for drug discounts for the VA and other federal purchasers. He has made something of an environmental record, opposing western water subsidies and offshore oil drilling on the Gulf Coast.

Bilirakis, who switched parties in 1980, won the seat in 1982 although it had been designed for a Democrat; tireless constituency service helped him win reelection easily three times. In the last two general elections he had spirited opposition from Cheryl Davis Knapp and, in 1992, tough primary competition as well. Knapp, was a mother at 15 and then worked hard for her education to become a nurse; she had little money in 1990 but in an anti-incumbent year held Bilirakis to a 58%–42% margin. For 1992, Bilirakis lost the Gulf Coast portion of Pasco County in redistricting, which he had always carried. He had primary opposition from state legislator Trish Muscarella, who attacked him for being antiabortion and for continuing to run despite his support for term limits in 1982. Bilirakis won 67%–33%. In the general Knapp called for health care for every citizen and also attacked Bilirakis on abortion. He won 59%–41%, almost the same result as in 1990. Bilirakis has said that he will not run in 1994 unless he has major legislation pending. If he retires, odds will probably favor the Republican nominee, although Democrats have carried this district in seriously contested statewide races.

The People: Pop. 1990: 562,814; 19% rural; 22% age 65+; 91% White; 3% Black; 1% Asian; 1% Other; 4% Hispanic origin. Voting age pop.: 448,534; 3% Black; 4% Hispanic origin. Households: 60% married couple families; 21% married couple fams. w. children; 48% college educ.; median household income: $29,293; per capita income: $15,797; median gross rent: $485; median house value: $84,800.

1992 Presidential Vote			1988 Presidential Vote		
Bush (R)	113,853	(41%)	Bush (R)	136,188	(63%)
Clinton (D)	94,662	(34%)	Dukakis (D)	81,635	(37%)
Perot (I)	68,167	(25%)			

Rep. Michael Bilirakis (R)

Elected 1982; b. July 16, 1930, Tarpon Springs; home, Palm Harbor; U. of Pittsburgh, B.S. 1959, U. of FL, J.D. 1963; Greek Orthodox; married (Evelyn).

Career: Air Force, 1951–55; Steelworker, 1955–59; Govt. contract negotiator, 1959–60; Petroleum engineer, 1960–63; Practicing atty., 1969–83.

Offices: 2240 RHOB 20515, 202-225-5755. Also 1100 Cleveland St., #1600, Clearwater 34615, 813-441-3721.

Committees: *Energy and Commerce* (5th of 17 R): Energy and Power (RMM); Health and the Environment. *Veterans' Affairs* (4th of 14 R): Compensation, Pension and Insurance (RMM); Hospitals and Health Care.

Group Ratings

	ADA	ACLU	COPE	CDF	CFA	LCV	ACU	NTLC	NSI	COC	CEI
1992	20	10	42	30	27	19	80	85	100	75	70
1991	15	—	8	40	28	15	89	—	—	80	73

National Journal Ratings

	1991 LIB — 1991 CONS		1992 LIB — 1992 CONS	
Economic	21% —	78%	31% —	68%
Social	24% —	76%	0% —	85%
Foreign	26% —	70%	18% —	74%

Key Votes of the 102d Congress

1. Ban Striker Replace	AGN	5. Handgun Wait/7-Day	FOR	9. Use Force in Gulf	FOR
2. $ for Homeownership	FOR	6. Overseas Mil. Abortion	AGN	10. US Mil. Abroad $ Cut	AGN
3. Tax Rich/Cut Mid Cls.	AGN	7. Obscn. Art NEA $ Ban	FOR	11. Limit SDI Funds	AGN
4. FY93/$15B Def. Cut	AGN	8. Death Pen. from Jury	FOR	12. Cuba Trade Embargo	FOR

Key Votes of the 103d Congress

1. Family Leave	AGN	2. Deficit Reduction	AGN	3. Stimulus Plan	AGN

Election Results

1992 general	Michael Bilirakis (R)	158,028	(59%)	($779,818)
	Cheryl Davis Knapp (D)	110,135	(41%)	($269,617)
1992 primary	Michael Bilirakis (R)	34,593	(67%)	
	Patricia A. Muscarella (R)	17,295	(33%)	
1990 general	Michael Bilirakis (R)	142,145	(58%)	($815,366)
	Cheryl Davis Knapp (D)	102,495	(42%)	($89,852)

TENTH DISTRICT

Decisions made by pioneers of a community can shape it for decades afterwards: what shaped St. Petersburg, Florida, named after the city then the capital of Russia, was the decision in the early 1900s by *St. Petersburg Times* editor W. L. Straub to stop the industrialization of the waterfront, paving the way for St. Petersburg to become a tourist and, most importantly, a retirement mecca. By the 1950s, its name had become a national cliche, bringing to mind old folks on a park bench trying to get together a game of chess. Starting off on the grid streets facing Tampa Bay, spreading later toward the beaches on the Gulf Coast, St. Petersburg filled up to a greater extent than any other American city with retirees. They were at least modestly affluent and mostly from the North; they adapted easily to a city whose civic tone was set by the *St. Petersburg Times* and its longtime owners Nelson and Henrietta Poynter: sober, good-humored, supportive of clean government and civil rights, but not vociferously liberal.

Like any retirement center, St. Petersburg has had rapid population turnover, reflected in its political trends. White-collar Yankee retirees in the 1940s and 1950s made St. Petersburg the first Republican center in ancestrally Democratic Florida; it voted for Thomas E. Dewey in 1948 and elected a Republican congressman in 1954. Then, as more blue-collar workers could afford Florida retirement and the affluent moved farther down the Gulf Coast, St. Petersburg trended Democratic in the 1970s and 1980s. Pinellas County nearly voted for Jimmy Carter in 1976 and did vote for Bill Clinton in 1992. Also, businesses grew here, and St. Petersburg no longer has as high a percentage of the elderly as the Gulf Coast towns south of the Sunshine Skyway.

St. Petersburg and southern Pinellas County, including Largo and the string of barrier island beach towns from Mullet Key to Belleair Beach, make up the 10th Congressional District of Florida. The congressman here is Bill Young, sixth in seniority among House Republicans, a political insider who has played the Washington game skillfully by the rules. Now that may have become a political liability rather than an asset. He worked in the 1950s for St. Petersburg's first Republican congressman, William Cramer; was elected to the state Senate in 1960, at 29; then when Cramer ran for the Senate in 1970 (and lost to Lawton Chiles), Young ran for the St. Petersburg House seat and won. In the early 1970s, Social Security was vastly increased and indexed to inflation and St. Petersburg basked in prosperity; Young delivered constituency services and was easily reelected.

Early on, Young got a seat on Appropriations, a classic insider's perch, on which he is now third ranking Republican. His special project was the bone marrow donor program, originated by Dr. Robert Good of All Children's Hospital in St. Petersburg. Young was successful in a three-year effort to transfer authority for the program to the National Institutes of Health. He has backed child health research centers, juvenile diabetes centers and more money for pediatric AIDS. In 1980, he got on the Defense Appropriations Subcommittee, where he mostly supported the Reagan and Bush Administrations but had his own pet projects.

From there on, it was smooth political sailing until 1992, when Young suddenly encountered serious opposition and scathing criticism. The criticism came from the *Tampa Tribune*, which called him "a politician who has been in Washington too long and has lost perspective." *The Tribune* started looking at the $166,000 Young had collected in honoraria (all before it was banned in 1991) from defense-related organizations; Young was pressed for details on the trips he'd made for the speeches; he was hit for using political contributions to buy a Lincoln Continental. He was hurt especially by an October 1992 *Tribune* story alleging that he had made inquiries with the Agency for International Development in 1989 on a $25 million contract sought by Geonex, a firm owned by Harry and Judith Flynn which had done only $27.6 million in total business the year before; ten weeks later the Flynns bought Young's North Carolina vacation house, which he had been unable to unload for a higher price, for $165,000, most of it in a promissory note.

For that, Young was hammered hard by Democrat Karen Moffitt, who had interesting credentials. Formerly a special education teacher, she had a Ph.D. and was director of a Diagnostic and Learning Resource System at the University of South Florida; she edited *Special Children, Special Care*, a book for parents and caregivers of children with special health needs. Moffitt was something of a new Democrat, arguing that government programs should be judged on their outcome effects on people, not input of public money; she said the country had neglected education and health care, and supported a capital gains tax cut. Despite St. Petersburg's historical Republicanism, the 10th District is capable of splitting tickets: it voted against Senator Connie Mack in 1988 and by nearly 2–1 against Governor Bob Martinez in 1990. In 1992, Florida elderly voted heavily for Bill Clinton, and Moffitt won 43% of the vote against Young, a considerable achievement against an incumbent who only twice won less than 73% of the vote and never less than 65%. Whether this means Young will be vulnerable in 1994, or whether he will run again, is unclear.

The People: Pop. 1990: 562,301; 26% age 65+; 87% White; 9% Black; 1% Asian; 2% Hispanic origin. Voting age pop.: 462,919; 8% Black; 2% Hispanic origin. Households: 49% married couple families; 15% married couple fams. w. children; 44% college educ.; median household income: $25,145; per capita income: $15,124; median gross rent: $448; median house value: $68,700.

1992 Presidential Vote

Clinton (D)   107,121   (40%)
Bush (R)   96,956   (36%)
Perot (I).   63,765   (24%)

1988 Presidential Vote

Bush (R)   133,151   (56%)
Dukakis (D).   104,686   (44%)

Rep. C. W. (Bill) Young (R)

Elected 1970; b. Dec. 16, 1930, Harmarville, PA; home, Indian Rocks Beach; United Methodist; married (Beverly).

Career: Aide, U.S. Rep. William Cramer, 1957–60; FL Senate, 1960–70, Minority Ldr., 1966–70.

Offices: 2407 RHOB 20515, 202-225-5961. Also 627 Fed. Bldg., St. Petersburg 33701, 813-893-3191.

Committees: *Appropriations* (3d of 23 R): Defense; Labor, Health and Human Services, and Education; Legislative (RMM). *Intelligence (Permanent Select)* (4th of 7 R): Oversight and Evaluation (RMM).

Group Ratings

	ADA	ACLU	COPE	CDF	CFA	LCV	ACU	NTLC	NSI	COC	CEI
1992	15	22	42	20	33	25	76	70	100	63	64
1991	30	—	8	50	28	15	85	—	—	80	61

National Journal Ratings

	1991 LIB — 1991 CONS		1992 LIB — 1992 CONS	
Economic	24%	— 76%	32%	— 68%
Social	27%	— 71%	18%	— 82%
Foreign	22%	— 77%	18%	— 74%

Key Votes of the 102d Congress

1. Ban Striker Replace AGN	5. Handgun Wait/7-Day FOR	9. Use Force in Gulf FOR
2. $ for Homeownership FOR	6. Overseas Mil. Abortion AGN	10. US Mil. Abroad $ Cut AGN
3. Tax Rich/Cut Mid Cls. AGN	7. Obscn. Art NEA $ Ban FOR	11. Limit SDI Funds AGN
4. FY93/$15B Def. Cut AGN	8. Death Pen. from Jury FOR	12. Cuba Trade Embargo FOR

Key Votes of the 103d Congress

1. Family Leave FOR	2. Deficit Reduction AGN	3. Stimulus Plan AGN

Election Results

1992 general	C. W. (Bill) Young (R)	149,606	(57%)	($459,861)
	Karen Moffitt (D)	114,809	(43%)	($202,000)
1992 primary	C. W. (Bill) Young (R), unopposed			
1990 general	C. W. (Bill) Young (R), unopposed			($201,188)
(FL 8)				

ELEVENTH DISTRICT

Tampa, Florida, was one of America's boom towns of the 1980s. Tampa's industrial past goes back to 1886, when Cuban cigar-makers left Key West for what became the Ybor City neighborhood of Tampa; soon after it was the major takeoff spot for U.S. troops in the Spanish-American War of 1898; it also became a major citrus distribution center. The old industrial city developed along the waterfront, where today you can find the world's longest sidewalk (6.5 miles along Bayshore Boulevard) and still see the 13 minarets of Tampa pioneer Henry B. Plant's 1890s Arabian-style Tampa Bay Hotel (long since taken over by the University of Tampa). For a time, Tampa seemed drearily industrial. Now, with a diversified economy, a fast-growing service sector and, not entirely coincidentally, what is quite possibly the nation's most pleasant and convenient major airport, it has moved ahead, with subdivisions and condominiums, office towers and low-rise commercial buildings spreading inland across swamps and lowlands.

Through all this, and in contrast to St. Petersburg with its many retirees, Tampa has remained a city of families and young people, a place with a blue-collar past which is quickly moving upscale as it expands. To be sure, it has had some setbacks: George Steinbrenner's American Ship Building had some rough going with defense contracts in 1992 and the Tampa Bay area didn't get a major league baseball team to fill the Suncoast Dome across Tampa Bay as it had hoped. But the smell of cigars still wafts over Ybor City (though pollution controllers want to get rid of it) and Tampa is still an important military command center: Central Command, which ran the Gulf war, is headquartered at MacDill Air Force Base, and General Norman Schwarzkopf remains a Tampa area resident.

The 11th Congressional District of Florida consists of Tampa and two-thirds of surrounding Hillsborough County. Tampa was historically Democratic as St. Petersburg was Republican, but in fact the two sides of Tampa Bay seem to have come together politically, both voting for George Bush in 1988, both heavily rejecting Governor Bob Martinez, a former Tampa mayor, and both almost evenly split between Bill Clinton and George Bush in 1992. The Tampa area, however, has had the same congressman since its creation in 1962, Democrat Sam Gibbons. He looks like an old-fashioned southern congressman, and has the philosophy of one: specifically, of Cordell Hull, who during decades in Congress and as secretary of state under Franklin Roosevelt championed the cause of free trade. From studying the years before and after World War II, Gibbons carries the conviction that free trade expands every economy and that the ties made by healthy trade relations help prevent the outbreak of war. It has been Sam Gibbons's fate to assert the Cordell Hull free trade tradition in the 1980s and 1990s as politicians generally, and his fellow Democrats in particular, become more beguiled by protectionist and retaliatory trade restrictions. As the American private sector has gone through vast changes, sloughing off 20 million jobs and creating 40 million more, responding to foreign capital and buying foreign products and selling American products and services abroad, demands have naturally arisen from diverse quarters for protection—against foreign competitors and simply against change.

Against these demands Gibbons has usually fought, but not always with great success. For although he has risen to be second ranking Democrat on the Ways and Means Committee, he is without great influence there or on the floor. Ways and Means Chairman Dan Rostenkowski is not a Gibbons fan; he remembers Gibbons's abortive challenge to Tip O'Neill for majority leader in 1972, when Rostenkowski managed O'Neill's campaign, and he knows that Gibbons has not been a team player since Rostenkowski became chairman in 1981. Among House Democrats generally, the great trade strategist has been Dick Gephardt, who has been leaning toward protectionism since spending almost all of 1987 seeking votes in the Iowa caucuses. Against Gephardt's initiatives, Gibbons has tried to use maneuver since outright opposition does not prevail, although he employs that too, as on the bid to raise tariffs on minivans. Gibbons has had more success supporting trade restrictions for political reasons against South Africa, China and the former Soviet Union. He also has shepherded to passage the Caribbean Basin Initiative, and may try to bring CBI nations into a NAFTA-type agreement.

Will Gibbons ever be chairman of Ways and Means? In November 1991, when it looked like Rostenkowski might retire, Gibbons canvassed for votes and appeared to have the support of potential rival Charles Rangel. After the 1992 election, when some thought Rostenkowski might be forced to vacate the chair because of ethics problems, it was widely assumed that Gibbons in that case would replace him: why have an unseemly fight at a difficult time? The likely scenario is that Gibbons would become chairman, but that much of the real power would go to subcommittee chairmen, the House leadership or, on some issues, even Chairman John Dingell of Energy and Commerce.

Gibbons, reelected easily for years, has had some problems in the 1990s. He was criticized by *The Wall Street Journal* for having a business relationship with his lobbyist-campaign fundraiser son Clifford "that's cozy even by the standards of Washington": Sam Gibbons supported mutual insurance companies on taxes, for example, and Clifford Gibbons worked for Mutual of New York. In 1992, he was opposed by Mark Sharpe, a former Navy intelligence officer born at MacDill Air Force Base where his father served in 1960, just two years before Gibbons was first elected; Sharpe was one of four rotating briefers for the chief of Naval Operations until he resigned to run for Congress. A fiscal conservative, Sharpe held Gibbons to a 53%–41% margin—not an outstanding result for a 30-year veteran and perhaps an ominous sign for future elections.

The People: Pop. 1990: 562,293; 1% rural; 12% age 65+; 68% White; 17% Black; 1% Asian; 2% Other; 14% Hispanic origin. Voting age pop.: 430,969; 14% Black; 14% Hispanic origin. Households: 47% married couple families; 20% married couple fams. w. children; 46% college educ.; median household income: $26,166; per capita income: $13,578; median gross rent: $439; median house value: $66,000.

1992 Presidential Vote		1988 Presidential Vote	
Clinton (D)	81,849 (41%)	Bush (R)	95,358 (56%)
Bush (R)	77,942 (39%)	Dukakis (D)	73,836 (44%)
Perot (I)	39,148 (20%)		

Rep. Sam M. Gibbons (D)

Elected 1962; b. Jan. 20, 1920, Tampa; home, Tampa; U. of FL, J.D. 1947; Presbyterian; married (Martha).

Career: Army, 1941–45 (WWII); Practicing atty., 1947–62; FL House of Reps., 1952–58; FL Senate, 1958–62.

Offices: 2204 RHOB 20515, 202-225-3376. Also 2002 N. Lois Ave., #260, Tampa 33607, 813-870-2101; and 201 S. Kings Ave., #6, Brandon 33511, 813-689-2847.

Committees: *Ways and Means* (2d of 24 D): Trade (Chmn.). *Joint Committee on Taxation* (2d of 5).

Group Ratings

	ADA	ACLU	COPE	CDF	CFA	LCV	ACU	NTLC	NSI	COC	CEI
1992	65	77	50	90	87	50	22	0	60	25	18
1991	60	—	58	100	67	62	16	—	—	30	16

National Journal Ratings

	1991 LIB — 1991 CONS		1992 LIB — 1992 CONS	
Economic	59%	— 40%	55%	— 44%
Social	66%	— 33%	66%	— 33%
Foreign	59%	— 39%	44%	— 56%

Key Votes of the 102d Congress

1. Ban Striker Replace	AGN	5. Handgun Wait/7-Day	FOR	9. Use Force in Gulf	AGN
2. $ for Homeownership	FOR	6. Overseas Mil. Abortion	FOR	10. US Mil. Abroad $ Cut	AGN
3. Tax Rich/Cut Mid Cls.	FOR	7. Obscn. Art NEA $ Ban	FOR	11. Limit SDI Funds	FOR
4. FY93/$15B Def. Cut	FOR	8. Death Pen. from Jury	FOR	12. Cuba Trade Embargo	FOR

Key Votes of the 103d Congress

1. Family Leave	FOR	2. Deficit Reduction	FOR	3. Stimulus Plan	FOR

Election Results

1992 general	Sam M. Gibbons (D)	100,984	(53%)	($960,511)
	Mark Sharpe (R)	77,640	(41%)	($51,393)
	Joe DeMinico (I)	12,730	(7%)	($35,534)
1992 primary	Sam M. Gibbons (D), unopposed			
1990 general	Sam M. Gibbons (D)	99,454	(68%)	($825,795)
(FL 7)	Charles Prout (R)	47,754	(32%)	

TWELFTH DISTRICT

The great gleaming cities of Florida, with their skyscrapers rising over bays and rivers, are near the Atlantic or Gulf coasts. But much of the older Florida, the parts of the state most heavily settled half a century ago, is inland. Such is the Florida of Polk County, the biggest inland county south of Orlando, with its many lakes and the small cities of Lakeland, Bartow, Lake Wales and Winter Haven. Orange groves are still plentiful here, and the citrus business is still a mainstay of the local economy; turpentine distilleries, dependent on the big stands of pine, are also found. There are proportionately more manufacturing jobs than almost anywhere else in Florida, and still some phosphate mining, another historic mainstay. The most prominent landmarks here, the gothic Bok Tower and the surrounding Mountain Lake Sanctuary and gardens, were built in the 1920s by retired *Ladies' Home Journal* editor Edward Bok as a monument to himself. But there are relatively few retirees, and almost none of Bok's wealth and prestige, in Polk County today.

Historically, Polk County was as solidly Democratic as the rest of the rural South, and the home of successive Democratic U.S. Senators Spessard Holland (1946–71) and Lawton Chiles (1971–89). Like so many other areas, it trended Republican in the 1970s and 1980s, and at the end of that decade seemed poised for total changeover. It didn't happen in 1990, when Republicans seemed sure to capture two of the three seats they needed for control of the Florida Senate in Polk County; they were foiled when Lawton Chiles unexpectedly ran for governor and, in the process of carrying his home base, helped Democrats to narrow victories in two state Senate races. But it may have happened in 1992, as Chiles's popularity dipped low, and George Bush handily carried Polk County over Bill Clinton. Democrats lost one of the Polk Senate seats, and Republican Charles Canady, loser in one of the 1990 state Senate races, was elected over Democratic legislator Tom Mims in the new 12th Congressional District.

The 12th District as drawn for the 1990s includes all but the northeastern fringe of Polk County plus the western, rapidly suburbanizing edge of Tampa's Hillsborough County. It extends into old-fashioned Florida agricultural country north of Polk County, around Dade City in Pasco County, and to the south, in Hardee, DeSoto and Highlands Counties. Polk County was represented, together with Sarasota and other parts of the Gulf Coast, for 16 years by Andy Ireland, first elected as a Democrat in 1976 and then switching smoothly to the Republican Party in 1984. Ireland was one of the first of many incumbents to announce his retirement in the 1992 cycle. That gave the new 12th District a choice of two candidates with similar backgrounds. Democrat Tom Mims was elected to the Florida House in 1988, where he was an active legislator supported by the teachers' union. Republican Charles T. Canady served in the Florida House from 1984 to 1990, switching to the Republican Party in early 1989 because he had little in common with liberal Democrats. That caused some comment, since his father Charles E. Canady had served for 18 years as Lawton Chiles's top staffer in Washington and Florida; the younger Canady remembers painting the signs for Chiles's walk across Florida in the 1970 campaign. Mims won the Democratic primary 2–1, and had an initial lead in polls; Canady attacked Mims sharply in mailings and in the end with TV spots calling him pro-tax and antibusiness, and won 52%–48%. Feelings between the two remained amicable enough for them to lunch together, as promised, the Friday after the election.

Canady is a believer in term limits, promising to retire in 2000, and supports a balanced budget amendment. He got a seat on the Agriculture Committee and wants to protect local farm producers against foreign competition, and for that reason opposes NAFTA as written in 1992. He appears to have reasonable prospects to hold this district.

The People: Pop. 1990: 562,381; 34% rural; 17% age 65+; 81% White; 13% Black; 1% Asian; 2% Other; 6% Hispanic origin. Voting age pop.: 419,888; 11% Black; 5% Hispanic origin. Households: 62% married couple families; 25% married couple fams. w. children; 35% college educ.; median household income: $25,315; per capita income: $12,277; median gross rent: $381; median house value: $61,800.

1992 Presidential Vote		
Bush (R)	90,694	(45%)
Clinton (D)	68,487	(34%)
Perot (I)	39,770	(20%)

1988 Presidential Vote		
Bush (R)	105,333	(67%)
Dukakis (D)	52,116	(33%)

Rep. Charles T. Canady (R)

Elected 1992; b. June 22, 1954, Lakeland; home, Lakeland; Haverford Col., B.A. 1976, Yale Law Schl., J.D. 1979; Presbyterian; single.

Career: Practicing atty., 1979–92; FL House of Reps., 1984–90.

Offices: 1107 LHOB 20515, 202-225-1252. Also Fed. Bldg., 124 S. Tennessee Ave., Lakeland 33801, 813-863-4453.

Committees: *Agriculture* (17th of 19 R): Department Operations and Nutrition; Foreign Agriculture and Hunger. *Judiciary* (12th of 14 R): Civil and Constitutional Rights; Economic and Commercial Law; International Law, Immigration and Refugees.

Group Ratings and 102d Congress Votes: Newly Elected

Key Votes of the 103d Congress

| 1. Family Leave | AGN | 2. Deficit Reduction | AGN | 3. Stimulus Plan | AGN |

Election Results

1992 general	Charles T. Canady (R)	100,484	(52%)	($156,984)
	Tom Mims (D)	92,346	(48%)	($349,895)
1992 primary	Charles T. Canady (R), unopposed			
1990 general	Andy Ireland (R), unopposed			($384,555)
(FL 10)				

THIRTEENTH DISTRICT

In effect, everyone else followed the circus: when the Ringling Brothers made a going business of the circus they founded in the 1880s, they needed a place for the performers and the animals to rest over the winter. They settled on Sarasota, a bayfront village behind a barrier island on the Gulf of Mexico. It was just far enough north to be reachable by railroad, just far enough south to be semitropical so the elephants would not sicken and die. There John Ringling established the Ringling Museum of Art, with its vast sculpture garden, and built his own Venetian palace, the Ca'd'Zan. In the years after World War II, as it became the custom to retire to a warm climate, the Gulf Coast of Florida started attracting settlers—mostly affluent, WASPy, Republicans from upper crust suburbs of northern cities. The population exploded, with Manatee and Sarasota Counties growing from in 63,000 in 1950 to 489,000 in 1990.

The 13th Congressional District of Florida includes Sarasota County and Manatee County and just to the north, slivers of Tampa's Hillsborough County, and Charlotte County to the south. Essentially, it is a collection of Gulf Coast communities, from Tampa Bay south past Venice (where the circus now has its winter quarters). This is retiree country: 31% of the people here are 65 and over, the second highest percentage of any congressional district in the nation (the highest is the Florida 22d, on the Gold Coast). It is also very heavily Republican, with the second highest Republican registration of any Florida district (the highest is the 14th, just to the south).

For the 1992 election, the 13th District had no incumbent; Andy Ireland, the Democrat-turned-Republican who had represented most of today's 13th and 12th Districts since 1976, decided early in the cycle to retire. The 13th attracted five Republican candidates and two

Democrats. The Republican primary was the noisier, with an expensive campaign by former Bush Administration fellow Brad Baker going into a runoff with Bradenton businessman Dan Miller, who was endorsed by Ireland. The winner in the Democratic primary, in which only about half as many votes were cast, was former Lawton Chiles staffer Rand Snell. The two nominees presented a nice contrast not atypical of their parties. Miller, a native of Michigan with an M.B.A. and Ph.D., was a local businessman and entrepreneur, owner of the Memorial Pier Restaurant, the Suncoast Manor Nursing Center, the Barnett Bank Building and Riverview Center. He served on local commissions, the hospital board of directors and the judicial nominating commission. He was not terribly specific on issues, calling mostly for less government and regulations and lower taxes: "The federal government does not need to solve all our problems." Rand Snell, from a Manatee County family with cattle and agricultural interests, had spent most of his adult life in politics. Out of school, he became a staffer for Lawton Chiles in Washington, then for two years was director for a congressional study on "Biotechnology in a Global Economy." He was Chiles's issues coordinator in the 1990 campaign and then his director of cabinet affairs in Tallahassee in 1991 and 1992. He was more specific on issues, calling for a national healthcare plan, for example. "There are 400 Dan Millers in Washington," Snell said. Miller responded that he was working in Bradenton, while Snell was the real government insider living in Tallahassee and Washington. Snell's political skills helped him break into the Republican vote, but Miller won by a 58%–42% margin.

Miller is not without contacts in the House. Fellow Florida Republican freshman John Mica was his "big brother" at their University of Florida fraternity and another Florida Republican freshman, Tillie Fowler, was in his wife's class at Emory. Miller serves on the Budget Committee and says he wants to use his hospital board experience on health care, starting with fundamental tort reform; he was also appointed to the Minority Leader Michel's Task Force on Health Care Reform.

The People: Pop. 1990: 562,501; 11% rural; 31% age 65+; 90% White; 5% Black; 1% Asian; 1% Other; 4% Hispanic origin. Voting age pop.: 464,980; 4% Black; 3% Hispanic origin. Households: 59% married couple families; 16% married couple fams. w. children; 45% college educ.; median household income: $27,616; per capita income: $16,254; median gross rent: $512; median house value: $81,300.

1992 Presidential Vote			1988 Presidential Vote		
Bush (R)	124,394	(43%)	Bush (R)	153,943	(66%)
Clinton (D)	100,831	(35%)	Dukakis (D)	78,154	(34%)
Perot (I)	65,283	(22%)			

Rep. Dan Miller (R)

Elected 1992; b. May 30, 1942, Highland Park, MI; home, Bradenton; U. of FL, B.S.B.A. 1964, Emory U., M.B.A. 1965, Louisiana St. U., Ph.D. 1970; Episcopalian; married (Glenda).

Career: Businessman, Miller Enterprises, 1973–present; Asst. Prof., Georgia St. U., 1969–73; Adjunct Prof., U. of S. FL, 1975–83.

Offices: 510 CHOB 20515, 202-225-5015. Also 2424 Manatee Ave., #104, Bradenton 34205, 813-747-9081; 1751 Mound St., #A-2, Sarasota 34236, 813-951-6643; and 4000 S. Tamiami, #124-A, Venice 34293, 813-493-2044.

Committees: *Budget* (12th of 17 R). *Education and Labor* (15th of 15 R): Elementary, Secondary and Vocational Education; Human Resources; Postsecondary Education and Training.

Group Ratings and 102d Congress Votes: Newly Elected

Key Votes of the 103d Congress

1. Family Leave   AGN   2. Deficit Reduction   AGN   3. Stimulus Plan   AGN

Election Results

1992 general	Dan Miller (R)	158,881	(58%)	($449,212)
	Rand Snell (D)	115,767	(42%)	($298,309)
1992 runoff	Dan Miller (R)	33,965	(53%)	
	Brad Baker (R).......................	30,527	(47%)	
1992 primary	Brad Baker (R).......................	22,055	(28%)	
	Dan Miller (R)	21,912	(28%)	
	Dave Thomas (R)	15,827	(20%)	
	Rick Louis (R)	13,828	(18%)	
	Jim Thorpe (R)......................	5,127	(7%)	
1990 general (FL 10)	Andy Ireland (R), unopposed			($384,555)

FOURTEENTH DISTRICT

On the edge of the Tropics, in a physical environment teeming with diseases less than a century ago and inhospitable to advanced civilization only a generation ago, Florida's Gulf Coast has sprung up as a model of an America that will be for many when they retire. The wide white sand beaches with gentle breakers, the inlets and broad estuaries that abound for boating, the wetlands filled with exotic birds, eventually made this prime resort country: Thomas Edison had his winter home in Fort Myers, Henry Ford used to visit here, Walter Reuther, after his gunshot wound, recuperated by building a modest house near the Caloosahatchee River. But they were the exceptions: the local economy could not attract many permanent residents, and at the beginning of World War II there were only 68,000 people living on the Gulf Coast from Sarasota south to Naples.

Now there are 1.1 million: the climate and environment attracted affluent suburbanites from the Midwest and Northeast, with the added lure of no state income or inheritance taxes. Developers like Barron Collier, who built the Tamiami Trail across the Everglades and designed Naples with the wealthy in mind (and gave his name to Collier County, the richest in Florida), were determined to avoid the high-rise canyons that line the Atlantic from Miami to Palm Beach. The alternative has been low-rise, city-sized developments like Cape Coral and Port Charlotte, with canals in most backyards, and thinly paved roads along the sand spits next to the sultry, lapping waves of the Gulf, or the luxurious town of Naples set amid preserved coastal islands and interior swamps. This is very much retirement country, with more than one in four residents over 65.

Florida's 14th Congressional District occupies the southern half of this Gulf Coast, from Charlotte County past Cape Coral and Fort Myers south to Naples. This district has the highest Republican registration of any in Florida, and continually casts among the highest Republican percentages. The congressman is Republican Porter Goss, first elected in 1988, who worked 10 years for the CIA and then moved to Sanibel Island and founded a prize-winning local newspaper, served on the city council and passed growth management laws, and was appointed to the Lee County Commission by then-Governor Bob Graham. When incumbent Connie Mack III ran for the Senate in 1988 and won, Goss ran for this seat and effectively won it in the Republican primary, leading 38%–29%–19% former Congressman Skip Bafalis and retired General Jim Dozier (held hostage by Italy's Red Brigade and rescued in 1981); in the runoff Goss won with 72% and in the general beat Jack Conway, onetime top aide to the UAW's Reuther, 71%–29%, winning the largest number of votes of any House candidate in the country.

Goss has a largely conservative voting record in the House and has presented proposals suggesting an active and original mind. When other Republicans were attacking the Clinton budget in early 1993, Goss presented his own list of spending cuts totalling $200 billion over five years. In line with Gulf Coast opinion, he is something of an environmentalist, backing laws which favor states' rights to legislate environmental laws and supporting a continued Coastal Zone Management law. He is something of a reformer too; he proposed charging members $600 from their office accounts for each insertion of extraneous matter into the *Congressional Record*. Naturally, he has been a strong opponent of Castro's Cuba, and as one would expect from a member with a district full of the affluent elderly, he opposed the Catastrophic Health Care Act and wants to repeal the social security earnings tax. In 1993, he left the Foreign Affairs and Merchant Marine Committees to become one of four Republicans on Rules.

The district he represented in 1990 was almost populous enough to be split in half for 1992; the new 14th is now essentially the southern half, and he was reelected easily in 1992, with—as two years before—no Democratic opponent.

The People: Pop. 1990: 562,489; 18% rural; 26% age 65+; 87% White; 6% Black; 2% Other; 6% Hispanic origin. Voting age pop.: 455,734; 4% Black; 5% Hispanic origin. Households: 62% married couple families; 18% married couple fams. w. children; 44% college educ.; median household income: $29,620; per capita income: $17,165; median gross rent: $519; median house value: $90,500.

1992 Presidential Vote			1988 Presidential Vote		
Bush (R)	129,493	(46%)	Bush (R)	146,243	(70%)
Clinton (D)	87,978	(31%)	Dukakis (D)	63,885	(30%)
Perot (I)	63,175	(22%)			

Rep. Porter Johnston Goss (R)

Elected 1988; b. Nov. 26, 1938, Waterbury, CT; home, Sanibel; Yale, B.A. 1960; Presbyterian; married (Mariel).

Career: Army Intelligence, 1960–62; CIA Clandestine Svcs. 1960–71; Businessman, Newspaper publ., 1973–78; Sanibel City Cncl., 1974–82; Sanibel Mayor, 1974–77, 1980; Lee Cnty. Commissioner 1983–88.

Offices: 330 CHOB, 20515, 202-225-2536. Also 2000 Main St., #303, Fort Myers 33901, 813-332-4677; and 3301 Tamiami Trail E., #212, Naples 33962, 813-774-8060.

Committees: *Rules* (4th of 4 R): The Legislative Process. *Standards of Official Conduct* (5th of 7 R).

Group Ratings

	ADA	ACLU	COPE	CDF	CFA	LCV	ACU	NTLC	NSI	COC	CEI
1992	5	0	17	20	33	31	88	95	100	75	79
1991	5	—	8	20	11	46	90	—	—	80	70

National Journal Ratings

	1991 LIB — 1991 CONS		1992 LIB — 1992 CONS	
Economic	12% —	86%	9% —	88%
Social	16% —	81%	25% —	74%
Foreign	17% —	78%	18% —	74%

Key Votes of the 102d Congress

1. Ban Striker Replace AGN	5. Handgun Wait/7-Day FOR	9. Use Force in Gulf FOR
2. $ for Homeownership FOR	6. Overseas Mil. Abortion AGN	10. US Mil. Abroad $ Cut FOR
3. Tax Rich/Cut Mid Cls. AGN	7. Obscn. Art NEA $ Ban FOR	11. Limit SDI Funds AGN
4. FY93/$15B Def. Cut AGN	8. Death Pen. from Jury FOR	12. Cuba Trade Embargo FOR

Key Votes of the 103d Congress

1. Family Leave AGN   2. Deficit Reduction AGN   3. Stimulus Plan AGN

Election Results

1992 general	Porter Johnston Goss (R)	220,351	(82%)	($414,185)
	James King (I)	48,160	(18%)	($18,310)
1992 primary	Porter Johnston Goss (R), unopposed			
1990 general	Porter Johnston Goss (R), unopposed			($244,740)
(FL 13)				

FIFTEENTH DISTRICT

When Cape Canaveral was chosen as the nation's rocket testing site in the 1940s, there were only 20,000 people in all of Brevard County, which stretches along 60 miles of the coast and includes the Cape. It was a backward place with no industry, picked because it was sunny and on the Atlantic coast: rockets have to be launched eastward and spent parts should fall into the ocean. Today, Brevard County north and south of the cape has 400,000 people. It is a prototype of America's future, with no city center but plenty of shopping centers along strip highways, with a white-collar and service economy, knit together by interest in the space program.

The 15th Congressional District of Florida includes all of the Space Coast and Brevard County and extends south into Indian River County and the fast-growing retirement areas around Vero Beach. It continues west past the vast new town of Palm Bay, now the district's largest city, to what is left of primeval Florida. But more may come: the Army Corps of Engineers, which straightened out the Kissimmee River in the early 1970s, is now seeking to restore it to its natural snake-like course, while nearby in the Three Lakes Wildlife Management Area, whooping cranes were released to propagate in the wild. The Space Coast is heavily Republican, distrustful of many national Democrats' disdain for the space program. But since 1978, it has elected Democratic congressmen: for 12 years, until he ran for governor in 1990, Bill Nelson, the first member of the House to go up in space; now Jim Bacchus, onetime speechwriter to former Governor Reubin Askew, who capitalized on Republican splits and his own unique approach to community involvement to win narrow victories in 1990 and 1992.

Bacchus's tactic was called Citizen Saturdays, and his appeal was based on a genuine altruism and community-mindedness which verged on the cloying. Bacchus grew up in the Orlando area, was a reporter for the *Orlando Sentinel* at 20, then worked for Askew in office and in his abortive 1984 presidential campaign. After that, Bacchus returned to the Orlando area, served on the Spaceport Florida Partnership, and became chairman of Goals 2000, a civic action program. Every Saturday, he and his dozens of campaign volunteers took on various civic projects, from calling bingo at retirement homes to planting trees in a crack neighborhood. To this earnestness Bacchus added political skill, raising $350,000 by March 1990 and garnering plenty of free media. The Republicans, in the meantime, had a contested September primary and October runoff, in which party-switcher Jon Vogt, former state Senate president, was upset by Bill Tolley, a longtime Washington lobbyist for Harris Corporation, the computer company based on the Space Coast, who lost 61%–39% to Nelson in 1988. Tolley's conservatism—he was against abortion and against a ban on offshore oil drilling, plus the promise of a seat on the Space Subcommittee helped Bacchus win 52%–48%.

In the House, Bacchus compiled a moderate record, tended to Florida issues and of course promoted the space program. In 1993, he was pushing for legislation which would significantly limit the ability of former members of Congress and top staff to lobby after leaving the Hill. Redistricting eliminated the Orlando portion of the 15th, but could scarcely make the seat more Republican. In 1992, the Republicans once again had a divisive primary between Dixie Sansom, pro-choice and pro-gun control, and Tolley, who argued for term limits and a one-year limit on welfare, and won 54%–46%. Once again, Bacchus raised huge sums, spending heavily in the last two weeks. This turned out to be one of the closest races in the nation, and after a partial recount Bacchus won 51%–49%. It's likely that Bacchus, for all his personal strength, will have serious opposition again in 1994.

The People: Pop. 1990: 562,542; 18% rural; 19% age 65+; 88% White; 8% Black; 1% Asian; 1% Other; 3% Hispanic origin. Voting age pop.: 441,006; 6% Black; 3% Hispanic origin. Households: 61% married couple families; 22% married couple fams. w. children; 49% college educ.; median household income: $29,755; per capita income: $15,225; median gross rent: $485; median house value: $74,800.

1992 Presidential Vote		
Bush (R)	117,206	(43%)
Clinton (D)	83,507	(31%)
Perot (I)	69,605	(26%)

1988 Presidential Vote		
Bush (R)	144,236	(71%)
Dukakis (D)	60,154	(29%)

Rep. James L. Bacchus (D)

Elected 1990; b. June 21, 1949, Nashville, TN; home, Merritt Island; Vanderbilt U., B.A. 1971; Yale, M.A. 1973, FL St. U., J.D. 1978; Presbyterian; married (Rebecca).

Career: Army, 1971–72, Army Reserves, 1973–77; Journalist, *Orlando Sentinel*, 1969–73; Dep. Press Secy. & Chief Speechwriter, FL Gov. Reubin Askew, 1974–76; Special Asst., U.S. Trade Rep. Askew, 1979–81; Gen. Cnsl., FL St. Comprehensive Plan Cmte., 1986–87; Chmn., Orlando Civic Action Campaign, 1987–89.

Offices: 432 CHOB 20515, 202-225-3671. Also 854 Dixon Blvd., Cocoa 32922, 407-632-1776.

Committees: *Banking, Finance and Urban Affairs* (14th of 30 D): Financial Institutions Supervision, Regulation and Deposit Insurance; International Development, Finance, Trade and Monetary Policy. *Science, Space and Technology* (14th of 33 D): Space; Technology, Environment and Aviation.

Group Ratings

	ADA	ACLU	COPE	CDF	CFA	LCV	ACU	NTLC	NSI	COC	CEI
1992	70	68	55	80	87	88	29	10	90	13	22
1991	50	—	83	90	67	77	20	—	—	33	16

National Journal Ratings

	1991 LIB — 1991 CONS			1992 LIB — 1992 CONS		
Economic	68%	—	32%	66%	—	31%
Social	64%	—	35%	60%	—	39%
Foreign	56%	—	42%	44%	—	50%

Key Votes of the 102d Congress

1. Ban Striker Replace FOR	5. Handgun Wait/7-Day FOR	9. Use Force in Gulf FOR
2. $ for Homeownership AGN	6. Overseas Mil. Abortion FOR	10. US Mil. Abroad $ Cut FOR
3. Tax Rich/Cut Mid Cls. FOR	7. Obscn. Art NEA $ Ban AGN	11. Limit SDI Funds AGN
4. FY93/$15B Def. Cut FOR	8. Death Pen. from Jury FOR	12. Cuba Trade Embargo FOR

Key Votes of the 103d Congress

1. Family Leave FOR	2. Deficit Reduction FOR	3. Stimulus Plan FOR

Election Results

1992 general	James L. Bacchus (D)................	132,412	(51%)	($820,388)
	Bill Tolley (R)......................	128,873	(49%)	($215,538)
1992 primary	James L. Bacchus (D)................	31,216	(66%)	
	Larry Bessinger (D)	16,371	(34%)	
1990 general	James L. Bacchus (D)................	120,961	(52%)	($875,386)
(FL 11)	Bill Tolley (R)......................	111,908	(48%)	($364,926)

SIXTEENTH DISTRICT

Spreading outward from its original locus, the ultra-rich resort of Palm Beach, the metropolis at the northern end of Florida's Gold Coast, has become diversified economically and culturally. Northward along the ocean the old elite beach towns of Jupiter and Hobe Sound have become the center of extremely affluent developments stretching up to Stuart in Martin County. Even farther north, around the old city of Fort Pierce, are larger and more modest developments like Port St. Lucie. West and northwest of West Palm Beach, entire square miles have been claimed from swampland, some now with affluent condos surrounded by golf courses, others with space for warehouses and factories. Once confined to a narrow stretch along Lake Worth, metro Palm Beach now runs inland halfway to Lake Okeechobee.

The 16th Congressional District of Florida consists of much of this metro area, though it contains none of city of Palm Beach and only a portion of suburban West Palm. Its boundaries are convoluted to avoid the black-majority 23d District and it includes the beach towns from Jupiter north to St. Lucie. It also takes in much of inland Palm Beach County, with many recently and soon-to-be developed parcels. One-sixth of the district's residents live in citrus and vegetable growing areas around Lake Okeechobee, and as far away as Sebring, site of an auto racing track: here is the source of the Everglades, the 50-mile-wide and six-inch-deep river that flows so slowly to the Gulf of Mexico.

The congressman from the 16th is Tom Lewis, a Republican who served 11 years in the Air Force, worked 17 years for Pratt & Whitney aerospace, and spent seven years on his town council and 10 years in the Florida legislature. With a solidly conservative voting record, he has become something of a local problem-solver. He led the effort to keep the Air Force's hurricane hunter planes flying, which paid off when Florida got advance notice of Hurricane Andrew. He got a veterans' hospital for Palm Beach County, a widening of U.S. 27 south of Lake Okeechobee and expansion by 146,000 acres of the Big Cypress National Preserve. A pilot for 40 years, Lewis sponsored an Aviation Safety Research Act in 1988, the Catastrophic Failure Prevention Research Act of 1990 and a hurricane research act in 1992. His "Name the Orbiter" program got students involved in aerospace and produced for the new space shuttle the name *Endeavour*. He wants protection of Florida citrus, tomatoes, sugar and beef and opposed NAFTA in 1992, but has helped negotiate a GATT agreement. On his agenda for the 103d Congress are such diverse subjects as wind energy research, child pornography crackdown, criminal aliens deportation and encouragement of marine biodiversity.

First elected in a newly created district in 1982, Lewis has had little serious opposition and in 1992 was reelected with 61% of the vote.

The People: Pop. 1990: 561,856; 22% rural; 24% age 65+; 89% White; 4% Black; 1% Asian; 2% Other; 6% Hispanic origin. Voting age pop.: 446,860; 3% Black; 5% Hispanic origin. Households: 62% married couple families; 21% married couple fams. w. children; 45% college educ.; median household income: $30,582; per capita income: $16,952; median gross rent: $575; median house value: $87,900.

1992 Presidential Vote			1988 Presidential Vote		
Bush (R)	108,503	(39%)	Bush (R)	136,565	(65%)
Clinton (D)	98,154	(36%)	Dukakis (D)	74,865	(35%)
Perot (I)	68,543	(25%)			

Rep. Tom Lewis (R)

Elected 1982; b. Oct. 26, 1924, Philadelphia, PA; home, Palm Beach Gardens; Palm Beach Comm. Col., 1956–57, U. of FL, 1958–59; United Methodist; married (Marian).

Career: Air Force, 1943–54 (WWII & Korea); Chief, Jet & Rocket Engine Testing, Pratt & Whitney Aircraft, 1957–73; N. Palm Beach Mayor & City Councilman, 1964–71; FL House of Reps., 1972–80; FL Senate 1980–82.

Offices: 2351 RHOB 20515, 202-225-5792. Also 4440 PGA Blvd. #406, Palm Beach Gardens 33410, 407-627-6192; and 7601 S. U.S. Hwy. 1, #200, Port St. Lucie 34952, 407-283-7989.

Committees: *Agriculture* (4th of 18 R): Foreign Agriculture and Hunger; Livestock; Specialty Crops and Natural Resources (RMM). *Science, Space and Technology* (4th of 22 R): Technology, Environment and Aviation (RMM).

Group Ratings

	ADA	ACLU	COPE	CDF	CFA	LCV	ACU	NTLC	NSI	COC	CEI
1992	10	0	27	0	20	19	96	80	100	83	80
1991	10	—	17	20	17	23	90	—	—	90	76

National Journal Ratings

	1991 LIB — 1991 CONS			1992 LIB — 1992 CONS		
Economic	22%	—	77%	12%	—	86%
Social	0%	—	84%	26%	—	72%
Foreign	0%	—	88%	0%	—	82%

Key Votes of the 102d Congress

1. Ban Striker Replace	AGN	5. Handgun Wait/7-Day	AGN	9. Use Force in Gulf	FOR
2. $ for Homeownership	FOR	6. Overseas Mil. Abortion	AGN	10. US Mil. Abroad $ Cut	AGN
3. Tax Rich/Cut Mid Cls.	AGN	7. Obscn. Art NEA $ Ban	FOR	11. Limit SDI Funds	AGN
4. FY93/$15B Def. Cut	AGN	8. Death Pen. from Jury	FOR	12. Cuba Trade Embargo	FOR

Key Votes of the 103d Congress

1. Family Leave	AGN	2. Deficit Reduction	AGN	3. Stimulus Plan	AGN

Election Results

1992 general	Tom Lewis (R)	157,422	(61%)	($363,795)
	John Comerford (D)	101,237	(39%)	($97,871)
1992 primary	Tom Lewis (R)	29,716	(64%)	
	John Anastasio (R)	16,621	(36%)	
1990 general (FL 12)	Tom Lewis (R), unopposed			($401,225)

SEVENTEENTH DISTRICT

Miami's black neighborhood of Liberty City burst onto national television for a few moments in 1980, when a riot killing 18 people followed the acquittal of a police officer accused of killing a black insurance salesman. It was a first crisis situation for Janet Reno, who had only recently become Dade County Prosecutor, and it spotlighted a continuing tension in Miami between a black community numerically outnumbered and economically outdone by the city's Cuban-Americans. That tension still exists, but may be ebbing. There was a riot again in 1989, after the shooting of a black motorcyclist by a Colombian-born policeman. Originally convicted of manslaughter, the policeman won an acquittal on appeal in May 1993. Minor disturbances were reported, but for the most part, citizens here had no desire to repeat the events of 1989. There remains though a sharp contrast in political preference: blacks are the most Democratic group in Florida, Cuban-Americans the most Republican.

The 17th Congressional District of Florida was created to be a black-majority district. The bulk of the district is on the north side of Miami and its Dade County suburbs, running along the I-95 and 27th Avenue corridors from the Miami River north to the Dade County line. The 17th carefully excludes the mostly white, high-rise condominiums on the shore of Biscayne Bay and heavily Cuban-American Hialeah. It extends south along a narrow corridor on either side of Dixie Highway, expanding here and there to bring in heavily black areas all the way south to Homestead, site of Hurricane Andrew's worst damage.

The 17th as drawn for the 1990s included most of the district represented for 20 years by Bill Lehman, a former used car dealer and liberal Democrat who became an Appropriations subcommittee chairman; in 1992, at 79, and with some decline in his health, he decided to retire. There was little mystery about who would succeed him. State Senator Carrie Meek, first elected to the legislature in 1978, was clearly the best-known and best-liked black politician in the Miami area, and she was elected with 83% of the vote in the primary and with no Republican opposition in the general election.

Meek, the granddaughter of a slave, was born in 1926 in Tallahassee and grew up near the old Capitol in a neighborhood called the Bottom. She attended Florida A&M's lab school where she was a talented athlete; she went to Florida A&M and the University of Michigan (Florida government paid the tuition because its graduate schools were segregated). She came back to Miami to teach physical education at a segregated community college. Here she became active in politics and, when pioneer black legislator Gwen Cherry died in an auto accident, Meek was elected to the Florida House. In the legislature, she was considered highly effective, passing legislation to criminalize stalking, passing a Minority Business Enterprise law, promoting literacy and preventing dropouts. In Washington, she says her first priority is creating jobs through federal programs and private initiatives to help blacks develop their own businesses and banks as, she notes, Cuban-Americans have. She called for letting Haitian refugees into the United States on the same terms as Cubans. But she decries federal programs whose benefits are squandered by "ghetto hustlers," administrators who exploit the system. She showed her own determination and savvy by winning a seat on the Appropriations Committee.

The People: Pop. 1990: 563,284; 10% age 65+; 20% White; 59% Black; 1% Asian; 4% Other; 23% Hispanic origin. Voting age pop.: 391,574; 54% Black; 24% Hispanic origin. Households: 42% married couple families; 21% married couple fams. w. children; 32% college educ.; median household income: $21,899; per capita income: $9,157; median gross rent: $426; median house value: $63,900.

1992 Presidential Vote			1988 Presidential Vote		
Clinton (D)	99,422	(73%)	Dukakis (D).	87,289	(70%)
Bush (R)	25,873	(19%)	Bush (R)	37,800	(30%)
Perot (I).	9,913	(7%)			

Rep. Carrie P. Meek (D)

Elected 1992; b. April 29, 1926, Tallahassee; home, Miami; FL A&M U., B.A. 1946, U. of MI, M.S. 1948; Primitive Baptist; divorced.

Career: Admin., Miami-Dade Comm. Col., 1949–92; FL House of Reps, 1978–82; FL Senate 1982–92.

Offices: 404 CHOB 20515, 202-225-4506. Also 25 W. Flagler St., #1015, Miami 33130, 305-381-9541.

Committees: *Appropriations* (37th of 37 D): Energy and Water Development; Military Construction.

Group Ratings and 102d Congress Votes: Newly Elected

Key Votes of the 103d Congress

1. Family Leave	FOR	2. Deficit Reduction	FOR	3. Stimulus Plan	FOR

Election Results

1992 general	Carrie P. Meek (D)	102,784	(100%)	($461,115)
1992 primary	Carrie P. Meek (D)	31,262	(83%)	
	Darryl Reaves (D).	3,499	(9%)	
	Donald Jones (D)	3,122	(8%)	
1990 election	Newly created district.			

EIGHTEENTH DISTRICT

The *Miami Vice* image of Miami lingers on—the hum of orange and pink neon signs in hot night air, moonlight reflecting off Biscayne Bay onto surrealistic high rises, the pastel, random-shaped, sharp-angled style of clothes and furniture and the air of menace in streets where many are armed and vast quantities of drugs and cash regularly change hands. A resort city known for pseudo-Spanish mansions and art deco beach hotels two generations ago, on its way to becoming a fairly typical American metropolitan area one generation ago, Miami today cannot be mistaken for any other American—or Latin American—city. It lives on the cusp of two civilizations: Anglo and Latino, with different traditions, styles and sensibilities, converging here in Miami, despite some friction, toward an amalgam with many strengths of both. Miami has become commercially and economically the capital of Latin America, the one place from which it is easiest to fly directly to any other part of Latin America, where top business and banking services are available to a sophisticated Spanish-speaking (and usually also English-speaking) clientele. With NAFTA awaiting ratification, and other Latin nations eager to join, Miami stands to be at the center of the largest free-trade zone in the history of mankind, uniquely able to connect all sides.

In the meantime, there are inevitably frictions in a community divided between culturally defined groups with distinct histories and styles. Miami's Dade County in 1990 was 49% Hispanic (almost all Cuban), 32% white Anglo and 19% black. It is a city where you can rise to the top of your profession or business, patronize the best stores and restaurants, live in the best residential areas—all in Spanish, although most Cuban-Americans are fluent in English as well. There is friction on the streets between blacks and Cubans, and a resentment by some blacks of the success the hardworking, anything but fatalistic Cubans have achieved. And there is resentment by many Cuban-Americans of white liberals, reflected in Cuban activist Jorge Mas Canosa's charges that the *Miami Herald* "manipulates information just like *Granma*," the Castro paper in Havana. On its face, the charge is absurd, yet it should be added that many goodhearted liberals, for which the *Herald* is a proxy, have failed to appreciate the totalitarian-ism of Castro's regime, have overpraised its pathetically limited achievements and glossed over the brutality that has been its steady conduct; typical is the liberal Miami politician who calls the city's Cuban-Americans "emigres," the term leftists use to disparage supposedly rich and selfish opponents of supposedly progressive revolutions since the French Revolution 200 years ago. Anglo-Americans, after years of politics in which the shades of difference between candidates are often subtle and in which basic liberties and property are not threatened, have a hard time understanding the enthusiasm of Americans with backgrounds in Latin America, where the differences between political creeds can be enormous and where liberties have frequently been in danger. In U.S. politics, that has led to a friction between the Cuban-Americans, heavily Republican ever since John F. Kennedy refused to send air cover to the Bay of Pigs invasion, and Miami's blacks and Jews, overwhelmingly Democratic since they first came to the city.

The 18th Congressional District of Florida is one of two Hispanic-majority districts in Dade County, about two-thirds Cuban-American, and very heavily Republican. It includes the corridor along Southwest 8th Street—often called Calle Ocho—which was the original Cuban-American commercial strip when the first exiles from Castro's Communist regime came over in the early 1960s. Dade County's Latino population has increased from 50,000 in 1960 to 953,000 in 1990, and Calle Ocho remains a major Cuban-American thoroughfare, humming with commerce and activity. The 18th District spreads south and west toward Miami Airport and the suburb of Kendall; it stretches all the way down to Homestead, site of Hurricane Andrew's worst damage, and then extends back north, around the black-majority 17th, to include the neighbor-hoods of Coconut Grove and Miami Beach's South Beach, the hottest and hippest place in America at the moment, with old art deco hotels that used to house elderly retirees now a temporary home to the world's glitziest celebrities.

The representative from the 18th District is Ileana Ros-Lehtinen, the first Cuban-American elected to Congress. She won the seat in an angry contest after the death in May 1989 of Claude Pepper, one of the most enduring liberals in American politics, who served in the Senate from 1936 to 1950, was defeated in a bitter primary, then served in the House from 1962 and was a major political force, expanding Social Security and Medicare for the elderly, until his death (he was also a staunch opponent of Communism in Latin America). Ileana Ros-Lehtinen, an educator born in Cuba who had served seven years in the legislature and whose husband was then United States Attorney in Miami, was the Republican nominee. Democratic opponent Gerald Richman proclaimed, "This isn't an Anglo seat, it isn't a Jewish seat, it isn't a Cuban-American seat. It's an American seat," which was taken as a challenge to Cuban-Americans. Voting ran almost entirely on ethnic lines: exit polls showed that 96% of blacks and 88% of non-Hispanic whites voted for Richman, while 90% of Hispanics voted for Ros-Lehtinen. Hispanic turnout was 58%, compared to 42% for non-Hispanic whites: this was the difference that enabled Ros-Lehtinen to win with 53%. She was reelected in 1990 by a 60%–40% margin. Then came redistricting, and a much more solidly Cuban-American—and Republican—district.

Ros-Lehtinen is conservative on most but not all issues; she supports federal spending on Miami area projects. She is probably a less controversial local figure than her husband, who sued Florida for violating its own antipollution laws, got major officials convicted on corruption charges, and was not allowed to prosecute the case against Manuel Noriega and left office in 1991. In 1992, Ros-Lehtinen was attacked for her opposition to abortion rights and for voting to relax state housing code requirements; Democrat Magda Montiel Davis was put on the defensive because she favored loosening the trade embargo on Cuba and her husband, lawyer Ira Kurzban, has represented the Cuban government's central bank. They conducted their debates in Spanish. Ros-Lehtinen won 67%–33%.

The People: Pop. 1990: 562,394; 17% age 65+; 29% White; 4% Black; 1% Asian; 6% Other; 67% Hispanic origin. Voting age pop.: 449,992; 3% Black; 67% Hispanic origin. Households: 50% married couple families; 20% married couple fams. w. children; 42% college educ.; median household income: $25,537; per capita income: $14,779; median gross rent: $460; median house value: $95,000.

1992 Presidential Vote		
Bush (R)	93,870	(57%)
Clinton (D)	54,113	(33%)
Perot (I)	16,988	(10%)

1988 Presidential Vote		
Bush (R)	106,697	(69%)
Dukakis (D)	47,975	(31%)

Rep. Ileana Ros-Lehtinen (R)

Elected Aug. 1989; b. July 12, 1952, Havana, Cuba; home, Miami; Miami-Dade Comm. Col., A.A. 1972, FL Intl. U., B.S. 1975, M.S. 1986; Catholic; married (Dexter).

Career: Teacher, Principal & Owner, Eastern Academy Elem. Schl., 1978–85; FL House of Reps., 1982–86; FL Senate, 1986–89.

Offices: 127 CHOB 20515, 202-225-3931. Also 5757 Blue Lagoon Dr., #240, Miami 33126, 305-262-1800.

Committees: *Foreign Affairs* (12th of 18 R): Western Hemisphere Affairs. *Government Operations* (9th of 17 R): Information, Justice, Transportation and Agriculture.

Group Ratings

	ADA	ACLU	COPE	CDF	CFA	LCV	ACU	NTLC	NSI	COC	CEI
1992	25	30	50	50	53	56	78	70	100	57	62
1991	40	—	42	70	28	54	70	—	—	50	52

National Journal Ratings

	1991 LIB — 1991 CONS		1992 LIB — 1992 CONS	
Economic	31% —	69%	26% —	73%
Social	33% —	67%	35% —	65%
Foreign	26% —	70%	18% —	74%

Key Votes of the 102d Congress

1. Ban Striker Replace	AGN	5. Handgun Wait/7-Day	FOR	9. Use Force in Gulf	FOR
2. $ for Homeownership	FOR	6. Overseas Mil. Abortion	AGN	10. US Mil. Abroad $ Cut	AGN
3. Tax Rich/Cut Mid Cls.	AGN	7. Obscn. Art NEA $ Ban	FOR	11. Limit SDI Funds	AGN
4. FY93/$15B Def. Cut	AGN	8. Death Pen. from Jury	FOR	12. Cuba Trade Embargo	FOR

Key Votes of the 103d Congress

1. Family Leave   FOR   2. Deficit Reduction   AGN   3. Stimulus Plan   AGN

Election Results

1992 general	Ileana Ros-Lehtinen (R)	104,755	(67%)	($669,350)
	Magda Montiel Davis (D)	52,142	(33%)	($335,408)
1992 primary	Ileana Ros-Lehtinen (R), unopposed			
1990 general	Ileana Ros-Lehtinen (R)	56,354	(60%)	($560,847)
	Bernard Anscher (D)	36,967	(40%)	($112,071)

NINETEENTH DISTRICT

In the 1920s, when the first millionaires came to Palm Beach to winter in their new Addison Mizner pseudo-Mediterranean mansions, or when the first real estate speculators went to Miami, there was almost nothing man-made between these two tourist cities: Dade, Broward and Palm Beach Counties in 1920 had all together some 66,000 residents. Now, there are more than 4 million, wedged almost entirely in the 5- to 15-mile strip between the Atlantic Ocean and the protected Everglades, whose quiet vastness suggests as forcibly as the loud fury of Hurricane Andrew the ultimate power of nature over man. The contrast between the infant Florida of the 1920s and today's megastate is especially glaring in Boca Raton, where Mizner built in 1926 what is now the Boca Raton Hotel and Club. Its azure-tiled fountains and red-tiled roofs, its pseudo-Moorish columns and pink stucco walls bespeak a vision of a holiday Florida, a bit mannered and antique to today's eye, but still exuberant. Today's Boca Raton, growing inland, is still solidly affluent, but it is also more functional and workaday. In its unadorned high-rise towers live affluent retirees from New York and elsewhere in the Northeast, enjoying Florida's sun and its lack of a state income tax. But also here is the headquarters of W.R. Grace, relocated from 42d Street in Manhattan, and a joint venture between IBM and Intel: high-tech and big money at work in what used to be just paradise.

The 19th Congressional District of Florida occupies some of what used to be swampland and citrus groves when 1920s visitors drove down from Palm Beach to Miami. It touches not at all on the ocean, kept from it by the majority-black 23d District which collects together the black neighborhoods just inland from the Intracoastal Waterway. About half of the 19th's people are in Broward County and half in Palm Beach: it stretches from the edge of West Palm Beach through Lantana (headquarters of the *National Enquirer*) to Boynton Beach, Boca Raton, Deerfield Beach and Sunrise. With the fabulous 1970s and 1980s growth in northern Broward and southern Palm Beach Counties, the district's biggest cities now are not the beach towns, but the new inland communities—Coral Springs, Margate, Tamarac. This is retiree country, with one of the highest elderly percentages in the country; but unlike the Gulf Coast, it is essentially a Democratic area, with a large Jewish population from New York and elsewhere. Condominium associations, typically liberal and Democratic, are important here.

The congressman from the 19th is Harry Johnston, from a civically prominent Palm Beach County family, who served 12 years in the legislature and became state Senate president. In 1986, he ran for governor, finishing third in the primary and thus out of the runoff; in 1988 a Palm Beach County district opened up when incumbent Dan Mica ran for the Senate. Johnston had serious competition in the 1988 general from a Republican county commissioner, but won 55%–45%. In the House, he has had a rather liberal record and has shown legislative skill. He has been busy primarily on the Foreign Affairs Committee, especially on Latin America; he did not take as hard an anti-Communist line as most Florida legislators. He has now inherited the chairmanship of the Africa Subcommittee, which was nearly abolished to meet a six-sub-committee maximum but then preserved after lobbying by the Black Caucus. Johnston also picked up a seat on Budget for 1993 and is one of 11 Democrats involved in Dick Gephardt's healthcare reform advisory board. A man whose career connects the older, southern small town oriented Florida with the gleaming, economically booming, environment-conscious metropolitan Florida of today, Johnston combines a reassuring demeanor with a voting record not far out of the House Democratic mainstream. Redistricting gave Johnston a somewhat more Democratic seat, and he won easily in 1992.

The People: Pop. 1990: 562,978; 2% rural; 28% age 65+; 90% White; 3% Black; 1% Asian; 1% Other; 6% Hispanic origin. Voting age pop.: 462,963; 2% Black; 5% Hispanic origin. Households: 60% married couple families; 19% married couple fams. w. children; 50% college educ.; median household income: $34,396; per capita income: $20,029; median gross rent: $672; median house value: $107,100.

1992 Presidential Vote			1988 Presidential Vote		
Clinton (D)	159,284	(54%)	Dukakis (D)	112,917	(51%)
Bush (R)	89,698	(30%)	Bush (R)	109,234	(49%)
Perot (I)	46,946	(16%)			

Rep. Harry A. Johnston (D)

Elected 1988; b. Dec. 2, 1931, W. Palm Beach; home, W. Palm Beach; VA Military Inst., B.A. 1953; U. of FL, J.D. 1958; Presbyterian, married (Mary).

Career: Army, 1953–55; Practicing atty., 1958–88; FL Senate, 1974–86, Pres., 1985–86.

Offices: 204 CHOB 20515, 202-225-3001. Also Pylon Pk., 1501 Corporate Dr., Boynton Beach 33426, 407-732-4000.

Committees: *Budget* (20th of 26 D). *Foreign Affairs* (7th of 27 D): Africa (Chmn.); Economic Policy, Trade and Environment; International Operations.

Group Ratings

	ADA	ACLU	COPE	CDF	CFA	LCV	ACU	NTLC	NSI	COC	CEI
1992	90	87	67	90	60	94	12	11	30	38	22
1991	80	—	91	80	50	92	11	—	—	22	23

National Journal Ratings

	1991 LIB — 1991 CONS		1992 LIB — 1992 CONS	
Economic	58%	— 41%	66%	— 31%
Social	74%	— 23%	76%	— 23%
Foreign	82%	— 17%	69%	— 30%

Key Votes of the 102d Congress

1. Ban Striker Replace	FOR	5. Handgun Wait/7-Day	FOR	9. Use Force in Gulf	AGN
2. $ for Homeownership	AGN	6. Overseas Mil. Abortion	FOR	10. US Mil. Abroad $ Cut	FOR
3. Tax Rich/Cut Mid Cls.	FOR	7. Obscn. Art NEA $ Ban	AGN	11. Limit SDI Funds	FOR
4. FY93/$15B Def. Cut	FOR	8. Death Pen. from Jury	AGN	12. Cuba Trade Embargo	AGN

Key Votes of the 103d Congress

1. Family Leave	FOR	2. Deficit Reduction	FOR	3. Stimulus Plan	FOR

Election Results

1992 general	Harry A. Johnston (D)	177,423	(63%)	($235,412)
	Larry Metz (R).....................	103,867	(37%)	($63,200)
1992 primary	Harry A. Johnston (D), unopposed			
1990 general	Harry A. Johnston (D)	156,050	(66%)	($469,101)
(FL 14)	Scott Shore (R).....................	80,239	(34%)	($213,139)

TWENTIETH DISTRICT

Over the past three decades, a vast new metropolitan area has grown up in what was the unpopulated hinterland of Fort Lauderdale when it was first made famous as the site of college spring break in the 1961 movie *Where the Boys Are*. Broward County had less than 100,000 people in 1950, but by 1990 it was up to 1.3 million. The land from the strip of beach along the Atlantic Ocean west to the Sawgrass Expressway and the Everglades Wildlife Management Area filled up with subdivisions, shopping centers, office complexes, warehouses and trucking terminals. Broward County is no longer just vacation country; it is also a major business center with high-tech companies and startups that have become national giants, like Blockbuster Video. As it has grown, the ethnic composition of Broward County has changed. In the 1950s, it was understood that Jews couldn't buy houses or rent hotel rooms this far north of Miami. Today, after three decades of Cubans moving into the Miami area and many Jews moving out, Broward County is the most heavily Jewish part of Florida, indeed one of the most heavily Jewish parts of the United States. Nearer the coast, especially in the huge high-rises of Hollywood and Hallandale, most of Broward's Jews are retirees from New York and other northeastern metro areas. But inland, in towns like Pembroke Pines and Davbie, and Plantation and Sunrise that didn't exist a few decades ago, there are many young Jewish parents raising families in communities that pride themselves on fine schools and high property values.

The 20th Congressional District of Florida includes most of southern Broward County, though not the precincts nearest the beach, which are in the 22d and 23d Districts; most of Hollywood, some of Fort Lauderdale, and most of the newer towns are now three-quarters of the district's population. The other quarter is divided between the southern and western parts of Dade County, including some of the neighborhoods hit hardest by Hurricane Andrew, and Monroe County, which includes the Florida Keys from the fishing center of Key Largo to the heavily gay and charmingly restored old city of Key West. Politically, this is a pretty solidly Democratic area, though the Dade portion includes many Republican Cuban-Americans. As drawn by a federal court, the new 20th District contained the homes of two incumbents. But one, Broward-based Larry Smith, had 161 overdrafts on the House bank and faced questions about possible diversion of his campaign funds for personal use; he retired, ending a 10-year career in which he was an impassioned supporter of Israel, and opponent of Castro and drug dealers. The other was Dante Fascell, chairman of the Foreign Affairs Committee for almost 10 years and congressman since 1954 (when Dade County had only one district and the rest of south Florida one other). Fascell was a supporter of the bipartisan foreign policy in the 1950s and early 1960s and of emerging democracy and human rights in the 1980s and early 1990s, and always opposed Castro and other Communists in Latin America. But at 75, he decided to retire rather than seek reelection in a district mostly in Broward County, which he had never represented.

The new representative is Peter Deutsch, a veritable and seemingly unstoppable engine of political ambition. A native of New York, Deutsch graduated from Yale Law School in June 1982, moved to Florida and by November was elected to the state legislature. Two years later, he was reelected with the largest vote in Florida and was unopposed in the next three elections. He started a Medicare Information Program, co-sponsored an Education Quality Act and backed stricter mandatory sentencing, showing he could appeal to both age groups in the area; he passed bills prohibiting nursing home evictions, allowing investment of pension funds in Israeli bonds and expanding grandparents' visitation rights. A *Miami Herald* reporter said Deutsch was "viewed by colleagues as bright but abrasive, and an expert at using procedural rules to advance or torpedo legislation." He supported Governor Lawton Chiles loyally and became chairman of the House Subcommittee on Reapportionment.

A court actually drew the 20th District lines, but could hardly have done better for Deutsch; one wonders whether he moved to Broward calculating (correctly) that this would be the one new heavily Jewish district in the country created after the 1990 Census. He professed to be unafraid of Fascell ("he's going to have to beat me"), became the first congressional candidate in Florida history to get on the ballot by petition, started off his campaign by loaning it $350,000 and allowed himself to be taped making fundraising calls while in the presence of a reporter: "I raise money from special interests because they have a role to play in the process." He is, unsurprisingly, pro-Israel, pro-abortion rights, pro-universal health care. In the Democratic primary, he faced 10-year Broward County Commissioner Nicki Englander Grossman, who was endorsed by Fascell, Smith and retiring Dade County incumbent Bill Lehman as the only candidate with the "knowledge and temperament" for the job. But witty Deutsch mailings implied that Grossman dined lavishly and travelled widely on the public payroll, and he charged that she had backed controversial Republican Sheriff Nick Navarro in 1988. Deutsch won 63%–37% in a primary in which 83% of the votes were cast in Broward and only 4% in Dade. In the general, he faced Beverly Kennedy, a businesswoman whose husband is the only Republican on the Broward County Board of Commissioners and who often ended her speeches with "God bless you." Deutsch beat her 55%–39%, as 80% of the vote was cast in Broward and 8% in Dade.

After the election, Deutsch's campaign still owed $343,000, presumably mostly to him, the third highest debt of any freshman. Deutsch attracted attention when he hired the 20-year-old Harvard student who had managed his campaign as his administrative assistant. He hoped to get on Energy and Commerce, but got Foreign Affairs, Banking, and Merchant Marine instead. Among his first bills were measures to bar members of Hamas, an Islamic resistance movement, from entering the United States and to provide more flood insurance for disasters like Hurricane Andrew. But for Florida's new term limits law, Deutsch would seem on the threshold of a very long congressional career.

The People: Pop. 1990: 562,673; 9% rural; 16% age 65+; 82% White; 4% Black; 2% Asian; 2% Other; 12% Hispanic origin. Voting age pop.: 440,902; 4% Black; 11% Hispanic origin. Households: 59% married couple families; 24% married couple fams. w. children; 51% college educ.; median household income: $35,378; per capita income: $18,285; median gross rent: $624; median house value: $102,300.

1992 Presidential Vote

Clinton (D)	116,568	(47%)
Bush (R)	83,485	(33%)
Perot (I)	48,687	(20%)

1988 Presidential Vote

Bush (R)	106,798	(54%)
Dukakis (D)	92,804	(46%)

Rep. Peter Deutsch (D)

Elected 1992; b. Apr. 1, 1957, New York, NY; home, Lauderhill; Swarthmore Col., B.A. 1979, Yale Law Schl., J.D. 1982; Jewish, married (Lori).

Career: FL House of Reps., 1982–92; Practicing atty., 1983–92.

Offices: 425 CHOB 20515, 202-225-7931. Also 10100 Pines Blvd., Pembroke Pines 33025, 305-437-3936.

Committees: *Banking, Finance and Urban Affairs* (17th of 30 D): Consumer Credit and Insurance; Financial Institutions Supervision, Regulation and Deposit Insurance; Housing and Community Development. *Foreign Affairs* (22d of 27 D): Europe and the Middle East; Western Hemisphere Affairs. *Merchant Marine and Fisheries* (27th of 29 D).

Group Ratings and 102d Congress Votes: Newly Elected

Key Votes of the 103d Congress

1. Family Leave	FOR	2. Deficit Reduction	FOR	3. Stimulus Plan	FOR

Election Results

1992 general	Peter Deutsch (D)....................	130,959	(55%)	($849,785)
	Beverly Kennedy (R)	91,589	(39%)	($88,811)
	James Blackburn (I)	15,341	(6%)	($14,664)
1992 primary	Peter Deutsch (D)....................	28,753	(63%)	
	Nicki Grossman (D)	17,211	(37%)	
1990 general (FL 16)	Lawrence J. Smith (D), unopposed			($275,873)
1990 general (FL 19)	Dante B. Fascell (D)..................	87,677	(62%)	($500,117)
	Bob Allen (R)	53,774	(38%)	($160,220)

TWENTY-FIRST DISTRICT

As Miami and Dade County's Cuban-American and other Latino populations have increased from 50,000 in 1960 to 297,000 in 1970, 580,000 in 1980 and 953,000 in 1990, Cuban-American neighborhoods have pressed outward from the old center of settlement along 8th Street—Calle Ocho—to the southwest, west and northwest. Today, the major city in the Miami area with the highest percentage of Cuban-Americans is Hialeah. The race track here came first, built in the 1920s beyond the edge of urban development. But in the 1960s and 1970s it started filling up as far as the Palmetto Expressway; in the 1980s settlement extended outward to Florida's Turnpike. Now the racetrack is closed, while Hialeah made national headlines when the Supreme Court considered a challenge to its ban on live animal sacrifices for religious purposes. The southwest suburbs with heavy Cuban-American populations—Westwood and Kendall Lakes—also have been growing outwards into what was once swampland. Here planned communities and subdivisions often have just one entrance, and then streets fanning around lakes and golf courses.

The 21st Congressional District of Florida occupies some of these relatively new Cuban-American communities. It includes Hialeah and, just to the north, the planned community of Miami Lakes developed in 1962 by Senator Bob Graham and his father. To the south, it is centered on Kendall Lakes, and its boundaries go out to the Everglades Wildlife Management Area. This is a 70% Hispanic district, almost entirely Cuban-American, and heavily Republican.

Cuban-Americans know first-hand the evils of Communism, appreciate the virtues of free enterprise, cherish traditional moral values, and prefer Republicans to Democrats on all these counts. When the 21st District was created for the 1992 election, it attracted no Democratic candidate at all; the new congressman was chosen in the Republican primary.

He is Lincoln Diaz-Balart, born in Cuba to a prominent family; his aunt was the former wife of Fidel Castro and mother of Castro's only recognized child Fidelito. Diaz-Balart's grandfather was elected to the Cuban Congress in 1936 and his father in 1954; the family left Cuba in 1959, just when Castro took over, and their house was looted and burned. Lincoln Diaz-Balart started off as a poverty lawyer and a Democrat. But he switched parties in 1985 and was elected to the state House as a Republican in 1986, with 78% of the vote; he was elected to the Senate in 1989, with 82%, a year after his younger brother Mario was elected to the state House. In the legislature, Diaz-Balart sponsored laws toughening sentences for crimes against law enforcement officers, increasing penalties for drug money-laundering, providing low-interest home construction loans, creating a statewide substance abuse program, and requiring prospectuses of Florida firms issuing securities to disclose whether they do business with Cuba. His laws legalized federal officials' making arrests for violent felonies and misdemeanors under Florida law and set up the Florida Tourism Commission, with an office in Taiwan.

Diaz-Balart was persuaded by Jorge Mas Canosa's Cuban American National Foundation not to run in 1989 against Ileana Ros-Lehtinen in the then-18th District special election to replace Claude Pepper; in 1992, the Foundation backed Diaz-Balart to run in the new 21st. But he was opposed by fellow Senator Javier Souto, also born in Cuba and a Bay of Pigs veteran, who attacked him for being financed by wealthy contributors and for not being a lifelong Republican. Diaz-Balart won 69%–31%. He is against tax increases and the congressional seniority system. He believes a hemispheric common market is inevitable, but has some problems with parts of the North American Free Trade Agreement. He opposes interdicting Haitian refugees. On spending, "I learned in the legislature you can cut programs. You just have to be careful not to hurt programs for the poor and the elderly."

The People: Pop. 1990: 562,402; 1% rural; 10% age 65+; 26% White; 4% Black; 1% Asian; 7% Other; 70% Hispanic origin. Voting age pop.: 424,125; 4% Black; 70% Hispanic origin. Households: 61% married couple families; 31% married couple fams. w. children; 45% college educ.; median household income: $32,043; per capita income: $13,173; median gross rent: $592; median house value: $91,100.

1992 Presidential Vote
Bush (R) 85,292 (58%)
Clinton (D) 45,778 (31%)
Perot (I)................. 15,545 (11%)

1988 Presidential Vote
Bush (R) 88,119 (72%)
Dukakis (D)............... 34,760 (28%)

Rep. Lincoln Diaz-Balart (R)

Elected 1992; b. Aug. 13, 1954, Havana, Cuba; home, Miami; U. of S. FL, B.S. 1977, Case Western Reserve U., J.D. 1979; Catholic; married (Cristina).

Career: Practicing atty., 1979–92; Asst. St. Atty., 1983–84; FL House of Reps., 1986–89; FL Senate 1990–92.

Offices: 509 CHOB 20515, 202-225-4211. Also 8525 N.W. 53d Terr., #102, Miami 33166, 305-470-8555.

Committees: *Foreign Affairs* (16th of 18 R): Africa; International Operations. *Merchant Marine and Fisheries* (15th of 19 R): Coast Guard and Navigation; Merchant Marine.

Group Ratings and 102d Congress Votes: Newly Elected

Key Votes of the 103d Congress

1. Family Leave   FOR   2. Deficit Reduction   AGN   3. Stimulus Plan   AGN

Election Results

1992 general	Lincoln Diaz-Balart (R), unopposed		($279,481)
1992 primary	Lincoln Diaz-Balart (R) 15,192	(69%)	
	Javier D. Souto (R). 6,941	(31%)	
1990 election	Newly created district.		

TWENTY-SECOND DISTRICT

The barrier islands of Florida's Gold Coast have been developed in spasms of speculative frenzy, not just as vacation places and retirement homes but as embodiments of dreams and fantasies, bearing about the same relation to people's everyday lives as MTV videos. Consider Palm Beach, the great beach resort of the 1920s, where rich WASPs would leave their snow-covered Tudor or Georgian mansions and live in Addison Mizner's pseudo-Mediterranean confections. Or think of Miami Beach, the great resort of the 1950s, where Jews who had grown up amid prejudice and made their fortunes in ebullient postwar America vacationed in surrealistically curved and embellished skyscraper hotels—the Doral, Deauville, Eden Roc, Fontainebleau—giant variations on the themes set out in the much smaller Art Deco hotels at the beach's south end. Or think of the 1970s and 1980s, as the coastline of Dade, Broward and Palm Beach Counties were lined with one high-rise condo after another, a promised land for the retirees of New York and the northeast, free from winter frost and state income tax.

Almost all of this beach area is now gathered together into Florida's 22d Congressional District, entirely different from any previous Florida district, and with the highest percentage of over 65 residents of any in the United States. Its shape was dictated by the governing interpretation of the Voting Rights Act, which required maximizing the black percentage in the 23d and 17th Districts just inland from the coast, sealing the beach towns off by themselves. Actually, the fit is not quite perfect. The 22d starts in the north in Juno Beach, north of Palm Beach, and reaches south to Miami Beach, but there exceeds the population limit and so excludes South Beach, at the moment arguably the trendiest place in North (or South: this is Miami) America. It is 91 miles long and never more than 3 miles wide.

This new 22d became the scene of a battle between two seasoned politicians who had

321

represented parts of it for years but neither of whom seemed wholly comfortable in it. One was Clay Shaw, congressman from Fort Lauderdale, a Republican, native Floridian and Catholic representing increasingly Democratic, Northeastern retiree and Jewish Broward County since 1980. Opposing him was Gwen Margolis, president of the Florida Senate for four years, a Democrat from North Miami Beach who is Jewish and grew up in Philadelphia, an idealistic liberal who has also been a practical politician and a successful real estate investor. The sharp exchanges between the candidates were based on their ideas and records, not their backgrounds. Shaw ran one ad showing a cash register and saying, "We can't afford Gwen Margolis," and another quoting her end-of-session accounts of the state Senate as "fouled up beyond all recognition"; Margolis replied that the quote was taken out of context and mostly she ran things very ably. She ran ads accusing Shaw of voting to decriminalize drug use—he said he was adding civil to existing criminal penalties, and attacking him for opposing the family leave bill and supporting the congressional pay raise. This is a district very much aware that Miami has been a world drug trafficking center and very concerned about drug-related crime. It is highly concerned about receiving Haitian and other refugees, and many residents are opposed to the state's contingency plan to use warehouses in Pompano Beach and other beach towns to house them if they are admitted in large numbers. This was one of the most expensive races in the country, waged mostly over TV on both Miami and West Palm Beach stations. In the end, regional lines held. Margolis carried Dade County 58%–31%. Shaw carried Broward County by the same margin and Palm Beach County by 60%–29%, for a 52%–37% win.

Shaw spent his first eight years in the House on the Judiciary Committee, where he worked on drug and crime bills; he backed ideas like the death penalty for major drug dealers, a federal drug czar, and the use of the military to interdict drug smuggling, which became law in 1988. In July 1988, Shaw switched gears when he won a seat on Ways and Means. There he found himself on the spot while debating the catastrophic health care program, and forced to cast decisive votes in committee; a supporter in 1988, he came out for repeal in 1989. With Democrat Charles Stenholm of Texas, he sponsored the tax credit alternative to the ABC child care bill on the theory that parents, rather than government bureaucrats, can best make decisions on child care; Stenholm-Shaw failed 195–225, but had a major effect on the bill that eventually passed the House. After the 1992 campaign, he came out sharply against allowing more Haitian refugees in south Florida. Most recently, his cause has been welfare reform, coming forward in early 1993 with a bill that would take most people off welfare rolls after two years and require them to work for continued benefits, as Bill Clinton promised to do in the 1992 campaign. He also introduced a bill in March 1993 to make Social Security taxes for domestics "more reasonable and easier to pay."

The People: Pop. 1990: 560,959; 31% age 65+; 83% White; 3% Black; 1% Asian; 2% Other; 13% Hispanic origin. Voting age pop.: 489,631; 2% Black; 11% Hispanic origin. Households: 44% married couple families; 11% married couple fams. w. children; 51% college educ.; median household income: $29,595; per capita income: $24,663; median gross rent: $545; median house value: $117,300.

1992 Presidential Vote

Clinton (D)	115,912	(45%)
Bush (R)	96,986	(38%)
Perot (I)	44,845	(17%)

1988 Presidential Vote

Bush (R)	132,871	(58%)
Dukakis (D)	97,669	(42%)

Rep. E. Clay Shaw, Jr. (R)

Elected 1980; b. Apr. 19, 1939, Miami; home, Ft. Lauderdale; Stetson U., B.A. 1961, U. of AL, M.B.A. 1963, Stetson U., J.D. 1966; Catholic; married (Emilie).

Career: Practicing atty., 1966–68; Ft. Lauderdale Chf. City Prosecutor, 1968–69; Assoc. Municipal Judge, 1969–71; Ft. Lauderdale City Comm., 1971–73; Ft. Lauderdale Vice Mayor, 1973–75, Mayor, 1975–80.

Offices: 2267 RHOB 20515, 202-225-3026. Also 1512 E. Broward Blvd., #101, Ft. Lauderdale 33301, 305-522-1800.

Committees: *Ways and Means* (4th of 14 R): Human Resources; Trade.

Group Ratings

	ADA	ACLU	COPE	CDF	CFA	LCV	ACU	NTLC	NSI	COC	CEI
1992	15	9	25	30	33	19	84	90	100	75	62
1991	0	—	17	10	28	15	90	—	—	100	63

National Journal Ratings

	1991 LIB — 1991 CONS	1992 LIB — 1992 CONS
Economic	18% — 79%	16% — 80%
Social	0% — 84%	29% — 70%
Foreign	16% — 84%	0% — 82%

Key Votes of the 102d Congress

1. Ban Striker Replace	AGN	5. Handgun Wait/7-Day AGN	9. Use Force in Gulf FOR
2. $ for Homeownership	FOR	6. Overseas Mil. AbortionAGN	10. US Mil. Abroad $ CutAGN
3. Tax Rich/Cut Mid Cls.AGN		7. Obscn. Art NEA $ Ban FOR	11. Limit SDI Funds AGN
4. FY93/$15B Def. Cut AGN		8. Death Pen. from Jury FOR	12. Cuba Trade Embargo FOR

Key Votes of the 103d Congress

1. Family Leave   AGN   2. Deficit Reduction   AGN   3. Stimulus Plan   AGN

Election Results

1992 general	E. Clay Shaw, Jr. (R)	128,400	(52%)	($1,138,425)
	Gwen Margolis (D)	91,625	(37%)	($936,960)
	Richard Stephens (I)	15,469	(6%)	($47,234)
	Three Others	11,594	(5%)	
1992 primary	E. Clay Shaw, Jr. (R), unopposed			
1990 general	E. Clay Shaw, Jr. (R)	104,273	(98%)	($120,632)
(FL 15)	Other	2,374	(2%)	

TWENTY-THIRD DISTRICT

Behind the high-rise apartments that seem to line the Atlantic Ocean from Miami Beach to Palm Beach, behind the canals and waterways separating the barrier islands from the mainland, usually a few blocks inland and oftentimes off U.S. 1, the old north-south highway that brought tourists here in the 1940s and 1950s, are the black neighborhoods of south Florida's Gold Coast: gatherings of older stucco houses and commercial storefronts, ranging from dilapidated slums to upper-middle-income enclaves. These are neighborhoods for the most part overlooked by Florida's tourists, nor do they bulk especially large in most resident's minds: the Gold Coast's blacks are heavily outnumbered by whites in Palm Beach and Broward Counties and by Cuban-Americans in Miami's Dade County.

The 23d Congressional District of Florida, created by the May 1992 court redistricting, gathers together many of these black neighborhoods in a constituency that is geographically grotesque but ethnically defined. A little more than half its residents live in Broward County, in and on either side of Fort Lauderdale; a little more than one-third live in Palm Beach County; the rest are scattered, a few in north Dade County, more in a geographically expansive but lightly populated segment that includes migrant worker camps around Lake Okeechobee and the old black neighborhood of Fort Pierce, a small city 120 miles north of Miami.

This new district produced a turbulent political contest. The best known—notorious—candidate was Alcee Hastings, articulate and charming, the son of a hotel maid, and Florida's first black federal judge. He was also impeached by the House of Representatives by a vote of 426–3 in 1988 and convicted and removed from office by the Senate by a vote of 69–26. The impeachment arose out of charges that Hastings conspired with a friend to accept a $150,000 bribe in exchange for giving two convicted swindlers a break in sentencing. The friend, Washington lawyer William Borders, was convicted; Hastings, in a separate criminal trial, was acquitted in 1983, but the House, led on this issue by Congressman John Conyers, senior member of the Congressional Black Caucus, judged the evidence against Hastings strong enough to warrant his removal from office. Hastings was undefensive about all this. He ran an abortive campaign for governor in 1990, then when the 23d was created sprang into the race.

The interesting thing is that he almost lost. In the first Democratic primary, the leader with 35% was Lois Frankel, a white Palm Beach County state Representative with a liberal record; Hastings, with 28%, narrowly edged out Bill Clark, also black, with 27%. In the runoff campaign, Hastings was buoyed by a decision from activist federal Judge Stanley Sporkin that his removal from office was invalid since the charges were not heard by the full Senate; the Supreme Court ruled to the contrary in a case involving another federal judge in January 1993, but by that time, Hastings was in Congress. In the runoff, Frankel continually cited Hastings's impeachment and conviction. His comment on her was, "The bitch is a racist." He won the runoff 58%–42%, with voting evidently closely following racial lines. His stated platform was "the elimination of racism, ageism, anti-Semitism and sexism." In the general election, the result was similar, with Hastings beating Republican Ed Fielding 59%–31%.

After the election, a Florida law student brought suit charging that Hastings was barred from office by his conviction; the suit was dismissed on the grounds that the student did not live in Hasting's district and therefore did not have the standing to file. Hastings entered the House smiling, saying "I'm not a vengeful person. I get on with life. I didn't enter here with my arms and my elbows flying. I came here to work . . . I've met with nothing but pleasant exchanges." He serves on the Foreign Affairs and Merchant Marine Committees.

The People: Pop. 1990: 563,645; 5% rural; 13% age 65+; 39% White; 52% Black; 1% Asian; 2% Other; 9% Hispanic origin. Voting age pop.: 407,766; 46% Black; 9% Hispanic origin. Households: 43% married couple families; 19% married couple fams. w. children; 32% college educ.; median household income: $23,039; per capita income: $10,511; median gross rent: $486; median house value: $67,200.

1992 Presidential Vote

Clinton (D)	94,873	(62%)
Bush (R)	35,265	(23%)
Perot (I)	22,084	(14%)

1988 Presidential Vote

Dukakis (D)	82,738	(59%)
Bush (R)	57,772	(41%)

Rep. Alcee L. Hastings (D)

Elected 1992; b. Sept. 5, 1936, Altamonte Springs; home, Miramar; Fisk U., B.A. 1958, Howard U., 1958–60, FL A&M, J.D. 1963; Methodist; divorced.

Career: Practicing atty., 1964–77; Broward Cnty. Circuit Court Judge, 1977–79; Federal Judge, U.S. District Court, 1979–89.

Offices: 1039 LHOB 20515, 202-225-1313. Also 2701 W. Oakland Park Blvd., Ft. Lauderdale 33311, 305-733-2800.

Committees: *Foreign Affairs* (20th of 27 D): Africa; Europe and the Middle East. *Merchant Marine and Fisheries* (20th of 29 D): Coast Guard and Navigation; Merchant Marine. *Post Office and Civil Service* (15th of 15 D): Oversight and Investigations.

Group Ratings and 102d Congress Votes: Newly Elected

Key Votes of the 103d Congress

1. Family Leave	FOR	2. Deficit Reduction	FOR	3. Stimulus Plan	FOR

Election Results

1992 general	Alcee L. Hastings (D)	84,249	(59%)	($427,931)
	Ed Fielding (R)	44,807	(31%)	($15,622)
	Al Woods (I)	14,879	(10%)	($7,097)
1992 runoff	Alcee L. Hastings (D)	22,046	(58%)	
	Lois Frankel (D)	16,294	(42%)	
1992 primary	Lois Frankel (D)	12,556	(35%)	
	Alcee L. Hastings (D)	10,237	(28%)	
	Bill Clark (D)	9,881	(27%)	
	Kenneth Cooper (D)	1,872	(5%)	
	William Washington (D)	1,711	(5%)	
1990 election	Newly created district.			

GEORGIA

Georgia, in almost every important sense, is the heart of the South. It is only the fourth largest southern state, but Texas and Florida are at the edges of the region and North Carolina off to the side. It was not the South's historic leader: Virginia and South Carolina were the leading southern colonies, and Georgia the last of the 13 to be established. Nor was it the leader of the Confederacy: the first shots were fired in South Carolina and the Confederacy's capitals established in Montgomery and Richmond. But Georgia's position in the South was geographically central, and, after General William Tecumseh Sherman's "march to the sea" from Atlanta, it became a symbol—the worst of the ravaged South determined to rise again. Georgia was the center of Atlanta editor Henry Grady's "New South" in the 1870s and it was the subject of Atlanta writer Margaret Mitchell's *Gone with the Wind*. It was the center as well of the civil rights South: for if the first bus boycott was in Montgomery, Alabama, and the first lunch counter sit-in in Greensboro, North Carolina, the central command post of the civil rights movement, the headquarters in time of Martin Luther King, Jr., and his lieutenants, of black colleges and universities and of most civil rights organizations that sprang up in the 1960s, was Atlanta.

Georgia too was the home base of Jimmy Carter, who first as governor and then as president ratified the reconciliation of black and white, and the white South's acceptance of civil rights. Georgia has been the home base as well for other great institutions: for Coca-Cola, that most southern of great worldwide corporations, for southern regional scholarship, for much of the southern timber and paper industries, for southern banking and legal services, and of course for Atlanta Airport, still the central transportation hub of the South. Ted Turner's Cable News Network has arguably made Atlanta the world's news capital, with Moscow, Baghdad, Washington and Peking all tuned in to watch broadcasts beamed from CNN's Atlanta headquarters. "The World's Next Great City," Atlanta civic boosters used to proclaim; now they drop the "next." Atlanta's selection as the site of the 1996 summer Olympics shows an international appreciation of the strength and success of this multiracial metropolis and of the region of which it is indubitably now the center.

The Atlanta and Georgia that were awarded the Olympics are places of optimism and economic growth. This was not always so. For many years after the Civil War, rural Georgia was a land of poverty and metro Atlanta, for all its showy successes, had a standard of living lower than in big northern metropolises. The industrialized South that Grady proclaimed turned out to be filled with low-wage textile mills. The unionized South that 1940s liberal Governor Ellis Arnall envisioned never materialized. The desegregated South that Martin Luther King and so many others risked their lives for exists today at the ballot box, in public accommodations and at the workplace; but racial divisions and distrust persist. Even so, the overall picture in Georgia is one of great and mostly unpredicted growth. This was one of the fastest-growing states in the 1980s and, after a pause in the early 1990s, started growing robustly again.

In the process, the prosperity of Atlanta has spread into the countryside. But Atlanta is the center of a service economy, while the rest of Georgia remains manufacturing country, with textile mills, apparel factories, carpet mills, paper plants and sawmills generally more important than farming. Economic growth in both regions is uneven. Atlanta's high-crime neighborhoods have, needless to say, added few jobs, and rural counties off the interstates have not grown at the rate of those with interchanges. But people have followed jobs. As low-growth areas shrink in population, there has been a boom in the donut of counties around Atlanta (including majority-black high-income southern DeKalb County) and in small cities on the interstates.

As a result, there has been a narrowing of the once great political chasm between metropolitan Atlanta and the rest of Georgia. During the 1950s and 1960s, Mayors William Hartsfield and Ivan Allen billed Atlanta as "The City Too Busy To Hate," and Atlanta voters, white and black, tended to vote for candidates who favored civil rights. The mayors accepted (but did not initiate) desegregation of schools and public facilities and provided a safer base for civil rights leaders who had to fear for their lives elsewhere in the South. Atlanta blacks were allowed to vote, Atlanta's white congressman voted for the Civil Rights Act of 1964 and Atlanta area voters by wide margins rejected segregationist candidates like Lester Maddox (elected governor in 1966) and George Wallace. In rural Georgia, blacks were barred from the polls and local bosses often manipulated ballots, as Jimmy Carter tells in his recent book *The Turning Point*; white voters strongly favored segregationist candidates and rejected anyone with the tinge of Atlanta. All that ended abruptly in 1970, when Carter was elected governor—the first time a statewide candidate conspicuously supported by blacks still got enough white votes to win. Carter placed a portrait of Martin Luther King in the Capitol, and became one of the first white rural southern politicians to officially accept and honor the civil rights revolution. In the years that followed, the political differences between Atlanta and the rest of the state diminished. The outlying parts of the Atlanta donut counties filled up with affluent young whites, mostly from the South, and increasingly Republican in their politics. In the rural counties, desegregation has long since been accepted and whites no longer see themselves as inevitably in conflict with blacks.

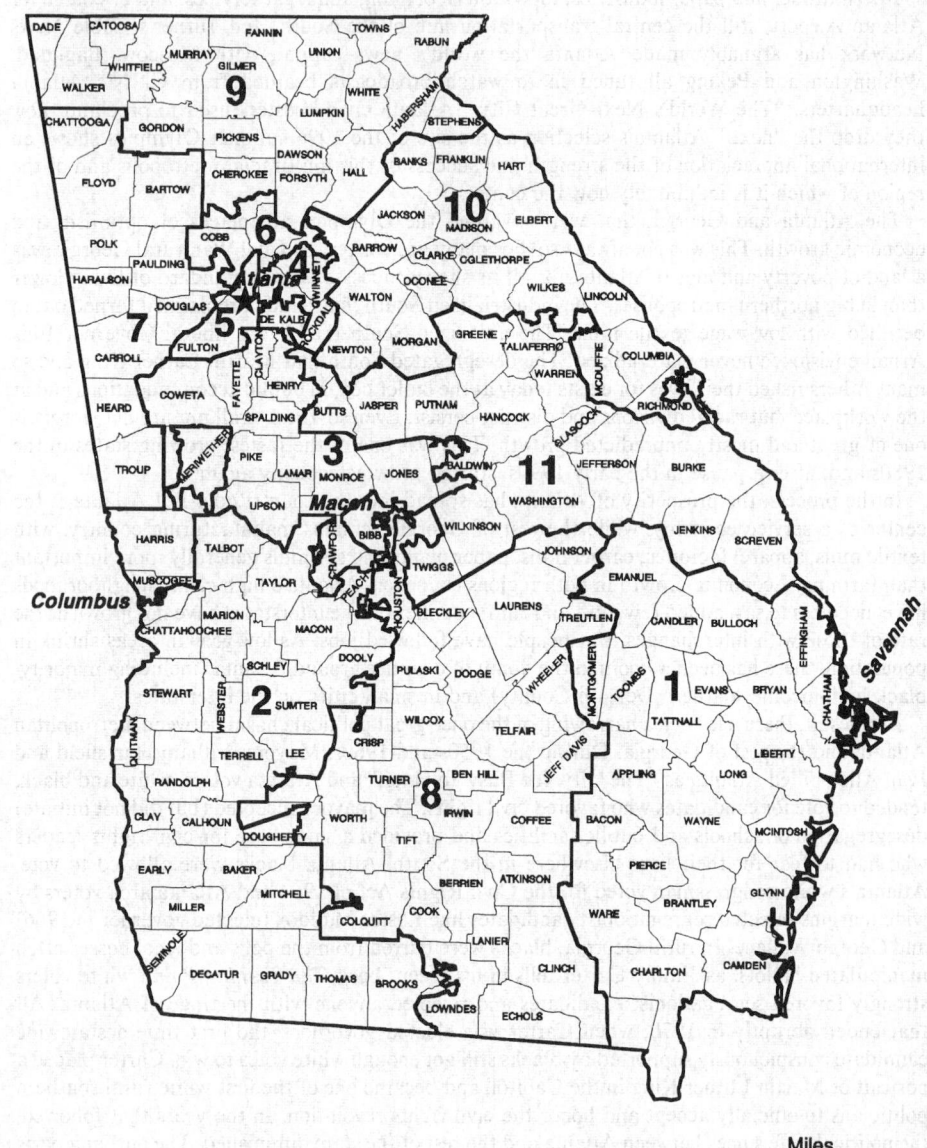

The two regions have not completely converged: metro Atlanta tends to be less tradition-minded on cultural issues and more market-oriented on economics. But the variations within the regions may be as big as those between them. Close in, notably DeKalb County where young people are locating to be close to universities and cultural institutions, the movement is toward the Democrats, while Republicans are making their biggest gains in small counties on the interstates. As politics becomes a matter not just of race and economics, but also values and religion, metro Atlanta and the rest of Georgia have voted within 2% of the state average in the last two presidential and last two contested Senate races, and only a little farther apart in the 1990 gubernatorial race. This has produced some close races. George Bush's 1988 60%–39% margin turned into a 43.4%–42.8% loss in 1992; Democrat Wyche Fowler won the 1986 Senate race 51%–49% and led 49%–48% on Election Day 1992, but, as Georgia law requires a runoff when no one has an absolute majority, had to run again and lost to Republican Paul Coverdell 51%–49%. Governor Zell Miller beat Atlanta area legislator Johnny Isakson in 1990 by just 53%–45%, nothing like the Democratic margins of yore; he carried metro Atlanta 49%–48% and the rest of the state 57%–42%. A serious race cannot be ruled out for 1994, especially if Miller fulfills his one-term pledge and retires. Georgia has become not just the center of the South, but also a center of vibrant, competitive two-party politics in the South, a development that surely would have surprised General Sherman but perhaps not Scarlett O'Hara.

Governor. Few governors have played as pivotal a role in national politics, or have sounded as loud a clarion call of regional leadership, as Zell Miller of Georgia. But Miller did not seem a figure of national proportions when he was elected governor in 1990, after 16 years as lieutenant governor. He won 62%–38% over former Atlanta Mayor Andrew Young in the Democratic runoff, and beat Republican Johnny Isakson, who after 14 years in the legislature ran against the old boys Capitol network, 53%–45% in the general. But Miller was the first governor not supported by legislative insiders like longtime Speaker Tom Murphy since Jimmy Carter won in 1970. Miller won by advocating a state lottery for increased education spending; he spoke in populist tones natural to him but, perhaps, was also inspired by—or helped inspire—consultant James Carville. Young campaigned as the candidate who could bring in jobs from foreign countries and who supported the death penalty for cop-killers; Miller responded by pointing to the underside of Young's record—the "explosion of crime" and drugs in Atlanta. Miller led Young in the first primary 41%–29%, then won the runoff 62%–38%. Young took defeat gracefully, and proceeded to become a full-time and spectacularly successful lobbyist for the Olympics; he had proved not that a black can't win, but that issues besides race could play an important part in such a contest—something that seemed inconceivable 20 or even 10 years ago.

In office, Miller instituted the lottery and increased education spending, appointed the first black woman to the state Supreme Court, strengthened drunk driving laws and started boot camps for first-time offenders. He was an early and effective Bill Clinton supporter. In January 1992, Miller sponsored and pushed through a bill to move the state's presidential primary from March 10 Super Tuesday to March 3. The result was an early contest which Clinton easily won, but also successfully diverted the attention and used up the resources of Paul Tsongas and Bob Kerrey. At the convention in New York, Miller delivered one of the keynotes, a riproaring "Give 'em Hell, Zell" effort; and in the fall campaign, he kept working Georgia hard for Clinton, requiring George Bush to put time and money into a state he must have expected initially to carry easily.

Miller's most dramatic moment came in early 1993, when he urged the legislature to overcome the past and take the Confederate stars and bars off the Georgia state flag; he noted that they were added only in 1956, to express a segregationist faith repugnant to most Georgians today, and there was the suggestion the flag might prove embarrassing in the Olympics. But memories of Sherman's march remain strong; white voters were hostile, and the legislature refused to pass the bill. Miller also tried to move state resources from the elderly (through co-payments by older Medicaid patients) to the young (more pre-school classes). His job rating has been in the mid-range for governors, and he could probably win reelection if he runs. But he pledged in 1990 to serve only one term, and in early 1993 had not made his intentions clear for 1994. Possible GOP candidates include Waycross Mayor John Knox, Senate Minority Leader Arthur "Skin" Edge and Johnny Isakson again. Should Miller keep his pledge, a host of Democrats could line up, including Lieutenant Governor Pierre Howard and Secretary of State Max Cleland.

Senators. Sam Nunn, chairman of the Senate Armed Services Committee, is one of the most powerful senators and one of the few whose word carries genuine political weight beyond Capitol Hill and outside his state. Yet he has not been quite the commanding figure he would probably like to be, either in the Bush years or now under Clinton. For years, Nunn personified the conservative southern Democrat who has backed a strong national defense. And that certainly is his heritage. Nunn comes from the same swath of Georgia where General Sherman's troops marched to the sea, and his grandfather was a Confederate veteran. His great-uncle Carl Vinson, first elected to the House in 1914, served for 50 years and chaired the Naval and then the Armed Services Committee; Nunn's Senate seat was held for nearly 40 years by Richard Russell, an austere chairman of the Senate Armed Services Committee and probably the most powerful member of Congress on war and peace issues in the 1950s. Vinson and Russell used their power to build a strong military, even while most Americans were isolationist. Yet when it came to committing American forces to battle, they were cautious; Russell warned three presidents— Eisenhower, Kennedy and Johnson—against committing American troops to Vietnam. They also carefully hoarded their own power. Vinson was once mentioned as a candidate for secretary of defense; his perhaps apocryphal reply: "I'd rather run the Pentagon from up here." In many ways, he and Russell did, and some think that is Nunn's guiding vision as well.

Nunn's first move, after being elected senator in 1972 at 34 by beating a more liberal Democrat in the primary and a more conservative Republican in the general, was to get a seat on the Armed Services Committee. He studied military issues hard, worked quietly and made a solidly conservative voting record that protected him against criticism in rural Georgia. He chaired the Manpower Subcommittee in the 1970s, where he helped to reform the services and shape the reserve force structure and call-up procedures that proved themselves in the Gulf war in 1991. He supported the Carter defense buildup in 1979 and the vastly bigger Reagan defense buildup beginning in 1981. He became ranking minority member on Armed Services in September 1983, when Henry Jackson died, and seemed content to work on defense issues as part of a bipartisan coalition. But as the 1986 election approached, and it appeared that Democrats might regain a majority, Nunn became more partisan. In 1985, he said he wouldn't campaign against his Georgia Republican colleague Mack Mattingly; in 1986, he did, providing political cover in rural Georgia for Atlanta-based liberal Wyche Fowler, who narrowly beat Mattingly. Nunn did the same for other Democrats running that year, even cutting a spot for fervent disarmer Alan Cranston of California; in 1988, he appeared with Michael Dukakis in Hawkinsville, just down U.S. 341 from Nunn's hometown of Perry. His voting record on non-defense issues moderated somewhat. It was apparent that the only way Nunn could advance to the chair of Armed Services (and perhaps farther) was if the Democrats won a majority in the Senate. The Democrats did win that majority, Nunn became chairman, and in 1987 he made a well-publicized look at running for president in 1988; he might have again in 1991, had not the Gulf war intervened.

Generally, Nunn has supported more defense spending than most Democrats. In the Reagan years, he saved the Strategic Defense Initiative and the B-2 stealth bomber from disabling cuts. But he also enhanced congressional power, by getting the first two-year DOD budget authorization in 1987 and sharply challenging the administration's interpretation of the ABM treaty. In the Bush years, he again prevented deep cuts in the administration budget and provided key support to the 1989 base closing bill. But in 1989, he challenged the nomination of John Tower to be secretary of defense, though Tower had served 23 years in the Senate and had been Armed Services chairman himself for four years. Nunn didn't challenge Tower's competence, but aired stories of drinking and womanizing and declared him unfit. His extraordinary success in persuading almost all Democrats to vote against Tower sealed Nunn's position as a partisan leader, both for his fellow Democrats and for Bush, who mistrusted him deeply ever after. Tower's own comments on Nunn, in the book he was promoting when he died in an April 1991 plane crash, were acid.

Bush's mistrust and Nunn's partisanship form a backdrop to their actions and interactions in the Gulf war. Nunn predicted, the day before Saddam Hussein's August 1990 invasion of Kuwait, that he might act in a way requiring U.S. military action and did in fact support the initial deployment of troops. But he was obviously angry about not being consulted on the November dispatch of 250,000 more troops, two days after the election, which he probably regarded as pushing the U.S. into hostilities, and he shared the caution many military leaders have had about armed conflict since Vietnam. Nunn orchestrated Armed Services hearings in November, clearly stacked against military action and featuring testimony from advocates of caution like former Joint Chiefs Chairmen William Crowe and David Jones, leaving unstated the case for the other side. "The last thing we need," said this son of the land of Sherman's march, "is to have a war over there, a bloody war, and have American boys being sent and brought back in body bags and yet not have the American people behind them." But Nunn's initiative failed to persuade Bush to back off, and Nunn's own leadership of the senators opposing the Gulf war resolution contributed, at least momentarily, to the lack of unanimous support for immediate military action. The Gulf war resolution did pass the Senate 52–47, and the rapid American military victory undermined Nunn's political position at once. He seemed momentarily stunned, and within days declared that he wasn't thinking about running for president in 1992 under any conceivable circumstances—something quite different from what he had said before January 1991 (when political reporters noted that he had switched his position on abortion and resigned from private clubs). One expects Armed Services chairmen to have a good idea of what the armed forces can do, and on this ground, Nunn proved a false prophet. Nunn turned out to have a much less accurate idea of what the American military could do than House Armed Services Chairman Les Aspin who supported the Gulf war resolution before January 12 and presented a fairly accurate prediction of the course of the war. Nunn seemed not to understand the product of the defense buildup and military reform he had worked on for so many years.

The result was a diminution of Nunn's national authority but not in the Senate or in Georgia. Nunn had long been an ally of Bill Clinton in the Democratic Leadership Council, but did not support him strenuously in the 1992 Georgia primary as Governor Zell Miller did; and even before Clinton took office, Nunn fired a shot across his bow by asserting loudly that he opposed Clinton's proposal to end the ban on gays in the military, which he like many military leaders believes will erode unit cohesion and the discipline necessary to weld together troops who must be ready to face combat and death. After Clinton had to backtrack on his promise, Nunn put forth a "Don't Ask, Don't Tell, Don't Investigate" compromise that seemed to assuage some in the administration and Pentagon, but was not enough for some liberals and members of the gay community. Openly gay House Member Barney Frank criticized this as not affording necessary protection during off-duty hours. But Nunn's may be the louder voice, and his high profile, combined with a lack of organized effort supporting Frank, has clearly signalled that Nunn remains an independent and powerful source of authority, not reliably allied to the Democratic administration, and that he will continue in important ways to run the Pentagon "from up here."

On other issues, Nunn takes a lower profile. He worked constructively with Republican Richard Lugar to push through aid to Russia. He moved to curb domestic spending in March 1993, and was opposed by the administration, and he has expressed concern about Clinton's proposed out-year defense cuts. Nunn's position in Georgia remains strong. He has not had a seriously contested campaign since his first election to the Senate in 1972, when southern politics was still roiled by reverberations from the civil rights revolution, and he was unopposed in 1990. While his support from white males dipped a bit after the Gulf war, he still seems likely to be easily reelected in 1996.

Georgia's junior senator, Paul Coverdell, is a Republican who was not widely known despite serving 15 years as state Senate minority leader, two years as state party chairman and two years as director of the Peace Corps. He lost two elections to Wyche Fowler—a 1977 House special election, in which Fowler had 40%, John Lewis 29% and Coverdell 22%, and the 1992 Senate general election, which Fowler led 49%–48%—but beat him 51%–49% in the late November 1992 runoff mandated by the Georgia law requiring an absolute majority to win. But these results indicate not fickleness but steadiness; they are uncannily similar to the 51%–49% margin by which Fowler beat Republican Senator Mack Mattingly in 1986 or the 51%–49% margin by which Mattingly beat Democratic Senator Herman Talmadge in 1980 or, for that matter, the narrow margin by which Bill Clinton edged George Bush here. This is a state that seems closely, perhaps evenly divided, in races between moderate-to-liberal Democrats and conservative but not far right Republicans.

When Coverdell won after Vice President-elect Al Gore and President-elect Clinton campaigned for Fowler, there was talk in Washington that Fowler had run a desultory campaign. Actually, he was in trouble because he was seen for what he was, a national liberal on most issues, with strong convictions and great political skills, blessed with a folksy rural manner, but also one of Majority Leader George Mitchell's chief lieutenants. Two big votes on which he had conspicuously stuck with Sam Nunn were of no great help: his opposition to the Gulf war resolution was a liability, perhaps a crippling one, and he seemed so chagrined by his evident need to vote for the nomination of Georgia native Clarence Thomas that he was unwilling to take advantage of its popularity with both blacks and whites. His support of the 1990 budget resolution, on which he was a key negotiator, was no asset. Fowler was also hurt because, while he was a House member, he told lawyers in his divorce case, "Thankfully we have a bank that doesn't zap me when I bounce a check because we have our own bank"; no one could say from extant records if he had any overdrafts or not.

Coverdell had many obstacles to overcome as well in the race. In the July primary he ran first, with former U.S. Attorney Bob Barr just ahead of Waycross Mayor John Knox, and narrowly won the run-off with Barr by 1,500 votes. In October, Coverdell unveiled his "grandmother" ad, showing 73-year-old Margie Goode Lopp of Cuthbert, Georgia, sitting on a swing and singing a jingle she composed after being repelled by Fowler's ads: "Let's put Paul Coverdell in the Senate and put Wyche Fowler out," it began. Fowler accused Coverdell of mismanaging the Peace Corps and said Coverdell would be part of the obstructionist filibustering minority in the Senate. Coverdell attacked Fowler's votes against the death penalty and the Gulf war resolution, and said Fowler's record was closer to Edward Kennedy than Sam Nunn. Coverdell called for a line-item veto, a balanced budget amendment, a 25% cut in Congress's budget and limiting the legislative session to six months. When the runoff was required, Coverdell got enthusiastic support from national and local Republicans, the Libertarian candidate who had deadlocked the first race, the Georgia Ross Perot organization, and from elite suburban Republicans who liked his pro-choice stand on abortion and the Christian Coalition pleased by his pledge to vote against the federal Freedom of Choice Act. This was a crucial seat, the difference between 56 and 57 Democrats in the Senate, and between 43 and 44 Republicans available to raise the 41 votes needed to filibuster a Democratic measure. National parties poured over $1 million of soft money into the race. Fowler also ran a "grandmother" ad with a grandson in an Atlanta Braves uniform, plus ads criticizing Coverdell for voting for insurance interests when he owned an insurance agency. But Coverdell hammered home his reform agenda, and probably profited from a reduced turnout; very few votes changed, but upscale Republicans were more likely than downscale Democrats to vote, and Coverdell won. He carried the suburban ring around Atlanta and also most of rural north Georgia and the rural counties in the southeast—economically booming areas like next-door South Carolina. He lost in the central and southwest parts of the state, economically ailing like Alabama. The results suggest a good black turnout and that the drop in turnout may have been biggest among downscale whites with only mild support of Fowler.

A Ralph Nader group responded by bringing a lawsuit against the runoff law (on the theory, evidently, that someone has a constitutional right to a Senate seat when the majority of voters who turn out don't want him to have it) and seeking vainly to keep Coverdell from being seated in the Senate. But he was, and got seats on the Foreign Relations, Agriculture and Small Business Committees. Fowler was appointed by George Mitchell as a "special deputy" to the Federal Election Commission, with a senatorial-level salary, though the FEC's biggest pending case concerned the challenges to the election he lost.

Presidential politics. Georgia was in 1992 one of the most closely contested states and had one of the closest popular vote margins in the country. This matches Georgia's close results in the Senate races of 1986 and 1992, when the contrast on issues was much the same as that between Bill Clinton and George Bush. A more liberal Democrat clearly pushes Georgia solidly into the Republican column, where it was in 1988; a Georgia Democrat pushes it solidly into the Democratic column, where it was in 1976 and 1980. George Bush's 1988–92 drop, by the way, was largest in the suburban donut around Atlanta, which he carried by more than 2–1 in 1988 and barely carried in 1992.

Georgia's 1992 presidential primary was scheduled for one week before Super Tuesday at the insistence of Governor Zell Miller, who was intent on helping Bill Clinton. It worked: Clinton had a handsome victory to balance off his defeats the same day in Maryland and Colorado. At the same time, George Bush beat Pat Buchanan 64%–36%, not a great show of strength for Bush, but a clear indication that Buchanan would not be able to carry any southern states. Since there is no party registration, turnout gives some suggestion of each party's strength; the trend clearly favors Republicans. Their presidential primary turnout increased from 200,000 in 1980 to 400,000 in 1988 and 454,000 in 1992. Democratic primary turnout fell from 684,000 in 1984 to 612,000 in 1988 and 454,600 in 1992. That was just 600 more than the Republican turnout, and a good indicator of the close results in the 1992 presidential and senatorial general and runoff elections.

Congressional districting. Georgia's robust growth in the 1980s meant that it gained a House seat for the 1990s, its first gain since 1885. This helped Republicans change the balance of the delegation from 9–1 Democratic to 7–4. One reason was demographics: affluent Atlanta suburbs grew so much that there was no choice but to create two heavily Republican districts there. Another was Speaker Tom Murphy's determination to wreak havoc on the one Republican incumbent, Minority Whip Newt Gingrich; but the district he drew to hurt Gingrich elected another Republican, while Gingrich got a new seat that is likely to be safe. A third factor was the Voting Rights Act, interpreted as requiring a maximum number of majority-black districts. This required the maintenance of the black-majority 5th in Atlanta and the creation of a new black-majority 11th, stretching from Atlanta to Savannah, which diverted Democratic votes from the 1st District, subsequently captured by a Republican. It also required the maximization of the black percentage in the 2d District in southwest Georgia, siphoning off Democratic votes from the 3d District, which went Republican. Of nine Democratic incumbents, only three were reelected, three retired and three were defeated. All eight of the white-majority districts could conceivably be seriously contested by Republicans some time in the decade.

The People: Est. Pop. 1992: 6,751,000; Pop. 1990: 6,478,216, up 4.0% 1990–1992. 2.6% of U.S. total, 11th largest; 37% rural. Median age: 31.6 years. 10.1% 65 years and over. 71.0% White, 27.0% Black, 1.7% Hispanic origin, 1.2% Asian. Households: 55.2% married couple families; 27% married couple fams. w. children; 41% college educ.; median household income: $29,021; per capita income: $13,631; 64.9% owner occupied housing; median house value: $71,300; median monthly rent: $344. 6.9% Unemployment. Voting age pop.: 4,750,913. Registered voters (1992): 3,177,061; no party registration.

Political Lineup: Governor, Zell Miller (D); Lt. Gov., Pierre Howard (D); Secy. of State, Max Cleland (D); Atty. Gen., Michael J. Bowers (D); Auditor, Claude L. Vickers (D). State Senate, 56 (41 D and 15 R); State House of Representatives, 180 (128 D and 52 R). Senators, Sam Nunn (D) and Paul Coverdell (R). Representatives, 11 (7 D and 4 R).

1992 Presidential Vote

Clinton (D)	1,008,966	(43%)
Bush (R)	995,252	(43%)
Perot (I)	309,657	(13%)

1992 Democratic Presidential Primary

Clinton	259,907	(57%)
Tsongas	109,148	(24%)
Brown	36,808	(8%)
Kerrey	22,033	(5%)
Other	9,479	(2%)
Uncommitted	17,256	(4%)

1988 Presidential Vote

Bush (R)	1,081,331	(60%)
Dukakis (D)	714,792	(39%)

1992 Republican Presidential Primary

Bush	291,905	(64%)
Buchanan	162,085	(36%)

GOVERNOR

Gov. Zell Miller (D)

Elected 1990, term expires Jan. 1995; b. Feb. 24, 1932, Young Harris; home, Young Harris; U. of GA, A.B. 1957, M.A. 1958; Methodist; married (Shirley).

Career: Marine Corps, 1953–56; Young Harris Mayor, 1960–64; GA Senate, 1960–64; Dir., St. Board of Probation, Personnel Officer, GA Dept. of Corrections, 1965–66; Exec. Secy., Gov. Lester Maddox, 1969–71; Exec. Dir., GA Dem. Party, 1971–73; GA Lt. Gov., 1974–90.

Offices: 203 State Capitol, Atlanta 30334, 404-656-1776.

Election Results

1990 gen.	Zell Miller (D)	766,662	(53%)
	Johnny Isakson (R)	645,625	(45%)
	Other	37,365	(3%)
1990 runoff	Zell Miller (D)	593,736	(62%)
	Andrew Young (D)	364,416	(38%)
1990 prim.	Zell Miller (D)	434,405	(41%)
	Andrew Young (D)	303,159	(29%)
	Roy E. Barnes (D)	219,136	(21%)
	Lauren (Bubba) McDonald (D)	64,212	(6%)
	Other	31,403	(3%)
1986 gen.	Joe Frank Harris (D)	828,461	(71%)
	Guy Davis (R)	346,508	(29%)

SENATORS

Sen. Sam Nunn (D)

Elected 1972, seat up 1996; b. Sept. 8, 1938, Perry; home, Perry; Emory U., A.B. 1960, LL.B. 1962; United Methodist; married (Colleen).

Career: Coast Guard, 1959–60, Coast Guard Reserves, 1960–68; Farmer; Legal Cnsl., U.S. House Armed Svcs. Cmte., 1962–63; Practicing atty., 1963–72; GA House of Reps., 1968–72.

Offices: 303 DSOB 20510, 202-224-3521. Also 75 Spring St. SW, #1700, Atlanta 30303, 404-331-4811; 915 Main St., Perry 31069, 912-987-1458; 130 Fed. Bldg., Gainesville 30501, 404-532-9976; 600 E. 1st St., Rome 30161, 404-291-5696; and 120 Barnard St., Savannah 31069, 912-944-4300.

Committees: *Armed Services* (Chmn. of 11 D). *Governmental Affairs* (2d of 8 D): Oversight of Government Management; Regulation and Government Information; Permanent Subcommittee on Investigations (Chmn.). *Small Business* (2d of 12 D): Government Contracting and Paperwork Reduction (Chmn.); Rural Economy and Family Farming; Urban and Minority-Owned Business Development.

Group Ratings

	ADA	ACLU	CDF	COPE	CFA	LCV	ACU	NTLC	NSI	COC	CEI
1992	65	55	60	91	75	67	30	39	60	50	31
1991	50	—	64	58	56	40	48	—	—	40	48

National Journal Ratings

	1991 LIB — 1991 CONS		1992 LIB — 1992 CONS	
Economic	44%	— 55%	50%	— 49%
Social	44%	— 53%	42%	— 56%
Foreign	40%	— 59%	29%	— 68%

Key Votes of the 102d Congress

1. $ for Homeownership	AGN	5. Clarence Thomas Nom. FOR	9. Use Force in Gulf	AGN
2. Have Cap Gains Debate	AGN	6. Lmt Death Row Appeal FOR	10. Keep Salvador Aid	FOR
3. Remove Budget Walls	AGN	7. Handgun Wait/5-Day FOR	11. Cut $1B from SDI	AGN
4. Ban Striker Replace	FOR	8. Abortion Gag Rule AGN	12. Override China MFN FOR

Key Votes of the 103d Congress

1. Family Leave　　　FOR　2. HIV Immigrants　　AGN　3. Clinton Budget　　　FOR

Election Results

1990 general	Sam Nunn (D), unopposed			($1,214,695)
1990 primary	Sam Nunn (D), unopposed			
1984 general	Sam Nunn (D)	1,344,104	(80%)	($843,891)
	Mike Hicks (R)	337,196	(20%)	

Sen. Paul Coverdell (R)

Elected 1992, seat up 1998; b. Jan. 20, 1939, Des Moines, IA; home, Atlanta; U. of MO, B.A., 1960; Methodist; married (Nancy).

Career: Army, 1962–64; Businessman, Coverdell & Co. Inc., Chmn., 1991–92; GA Senate, 1971–89, Minority Ldr., 1974–89; Chmn., GA Repub. Party, 1985–87; Dir., Peace Corps, 1989–91.

Offices: 200 RHOB 20515, 202-224-3643. Also 100 Colony Sq., #300, 1175 Peachtree St., NE, Atlanta 30361, 404-347-2202.

Committees: *Agriculture, Nutrition and Forestry* (7th of 8 R): Agricultural Credit; Domestic and Foreign Marketing and Product Promotion; Rural Development and Rural Electrification (RMM). *Foreign Relations* (8th of 8 R): Near Eastern and South Asian Affairs; Terrorism, Narcotics and International Operations; Western Hemisphere and Peace Corps Affairs (RMM). *Small Business* (6th of 9 R): Export Expansion and Agricultural Development (RMM); Rural Economy and Family Farming.

Group Ratings and 102d Congress Votes: Newly Elected

Key Votes of the 103d Congress

1. Family Leave	AGN	2. HIV Immigrants	AGN	3. Clinton Budget	AGN

Election Results

1992 runoff	Paul Coverdell (R)	635,114	(51%)	($3,193,774)
	Wyche Fowler (D)	618,877	(49%)	($4,894,620)
1992 general	Wyche Fowler (D)	1,108,416	(49%)	
	Paul Coverdell (R)	1,073,282	(48%)	
	Three Others	69,889	(3%)	
1992 runoff	Paul Coverdell (R)	80,435	(50%)	
	Bob Barr (R)	78,887	(50%)	
1992 primary	Paul Coverdell (R)	100,016	(37%)	
	Bob Barr (R)	65,471	(24%)	
	John Knox (R)	64,514	(24%)	
	Charles Tanksley (R)	32,590	(12%)	
	Other	7,352	(1%)	
1986 general	Wyche Fowler, Jr. (D)	623,705	(51%)	($2,779,297)
	Mack Mattingly (R)	601,235	(49%)	($5,119,249)

FIRST DISTRICT

Georgia's South Atlantic coast, long one of the poorest parts of the country, has been one of the boom areas of the last dozen years. This was Britain's 13th colony, set up by James Oglethorpe in the 1730s as a refuge and reformatory for convicts. But in quick time the sea islands and lowlands along its wide rivers and inlets became plantation country, and Savannah, Oglethorpe's capital, was by the 19th Century one of America's great cotton ports and, during the Civil War, the site of Confederate forts. After the Civil War, this area was desperately impoverished, with many poor blacks still speaking Gullah dialects, and Savannah languished, living off paper mills and chemical plants. Then, a few decades ago, preservationists started restoring houses and churches on the grid punctuated by 24 squares that Oglethorpe had laid out more than 200 years before; today, Savannah is one of our most graciously preserved cities. On the coast, some of the sea islands were preserved too, from the time they were winter homes of the rich before they discovered Florida, while others filled up with expensive houses and condominiums. Today, prosperity has come rushing down I-95. The ports of Savannah and Brunswick doubled their tonnage, while the resorts of St. Simon's Island and Jekyll Island boomed.

The 1st Congressional District of Georgia includes all the state's Atlantic coast and goes 50 or so miles inland, through cotton and tobacco fields and softwood forests. There are more exotic products here as well: Toombs County is the home of the fragrant Vidalia onion, while tiny Claxton in tiny Evans County has for nearly a century been home to two of the nation's prime fruitcake makers. Not all of Savannah is in the district; black precincts are connected by a narrow corridor along the Savannah River to the black-majority 11th District, which extends all the way to Atlanta. Politically, these counties are ancestrally Democratic, but white voters here—more than 75% after redistricting—are conservative on cultural and military issues. That, plus coastal prosperity, has made this area Republican at the top of the ticket and even in statewide contests; this district went for Republican Paul Coverdell over Democrat Wyche Fowler in the close 1992 Senate contest.

The 1st District, represented by nothing but Democrats since Reconstruction, is now represented by a Republican, Jack Kingston, elected in 1992. That came about for at least three reasons. One was the retirement, at age 49, of Democrat Lindsay Thomas, a farmer and businessman with a moderate record, who left the House to become one of the organizers of Atlanta's 1996 Olympics. The second was redistricting's removal of Savannah blacks. The third was Kingston's strength: he was an incumbent state legislator from Savannah experienced at winning elections. Seven Democrats, all with local bases, ran for the party nomination. Bryan Ginn, son of Thomas's predecessor Bo Ginn and a former aide to Senator Wyche Fowler, with a base in inland rural counties, got 21% of the vote; Buddy DeLoach, former Hinesville mayor, built on a coastal base and got 24%; Barbara Christmas, with a base in Camden County, won 25%. In the runoff, Christmas won 54%–46%. The daughter of a prison warden, she was married to a principal and had served as principal herself in four counties: a public sector career. She called for "programs to help people break the welfare cycle so that we can get them back to work." Kingston was an insurance agent who said he had the idealism of his older hippie siblings and the realism of his younger yuppie siblings; as a legislator, he sponsored an uninsured motorists' act and a bill allowing businesses to buy health insurance and workmen's compensation in a single policy. "We've got to get the government off the back of business," he said. "Business people should proact on the environment instead of react." Kingston, an NRA member and fiscal conservative, called Christmas an "ultraliberal"—against the balanced budget amendment and school prayer.

Kingston won by a 58%–42% margin, carrying Savannah's Chatham County by a 2–1 margin (the results would have been about even if the 11th District portion of Savannah had remained) and carried most of the rural counties as well. He got seats on the Agriculture and Merchant Marine Committees, good assignments for this district.

The People: Pop. 1990: 589,634; 45% rural; 11% age 65+; 75% White; 23% Black; 1% Asian; 1% Other; 2% Hispanic origin. Voting age pop.: 429,159; 20% Black; 1% Hispanic origin. Households: 60% married couple families; 30% married couple fams. w. children; 36% college educ.; median household income: $25,265; per capita income: $11,642; median gross rent: $373; median house value: $58,900.

1992 Presidential Vote

Bush (R) 88,703 (47%)
Clinton (D) 71,770 (38%)
Perot (I) 28,292 (15%)

1988 Presidential Vote

Bush (R) 97,277 (65%)
Dukakis (D) 52,545 (35%)

Rep. Jack Kingston (R)

Elected 1992; b. Apr. 24, 1955, Byron, TX; home, Savannah; U. of GA, B.S. 1978; Episcopalian; married (Libby).

Career: Insurance agent, 1979–92; GA House of Reps., 1984–92.

Offices: 1229 LHOB 20515, 202-225-5831. Also Enterprise Bldg., 6605 Abercorn St., #102, Savannah 31405, 912-352-0101; Statesboro Fed. Bldg., #220, Statesboro 30458, 912-489-8797; Thomas Henry Clarke Bldg., 208 Tebeau St., Waycross 31501, 912-287-1180; and Brunswick Fed. Bldg., 805 Gloucester St., #304, Brunswick 31520, 912-265-9010.

Committees: *Agriculture* (13th of 19 R): Department Operations and Nutrition; Specialty Crops and Natural Resources. *Merchant Marine and Fisheries* (11th of 19 R): Fisheries Management; Merchant Marine.

Group Ratings and 102d Congress Votes: Newly Elected

Key Votes of the 103d Congress

1. Family Leave	AGN	2. Deficit Reduction	AGN	3. Stimulus Plan	AGN

Election Results

1992 general	Jack Kingston (R)................... 103,932	(58%)	($418,883)
	Barbara Christmas (D)............... 75,808	(42%)	($332,319)
1992 primary	Jack Kingston (R)................... 14,799	(81%)	
	William (Bill) Jolley (R)................ 3,401	(19%)	
1990 general	Lindsay Thomas (D).................. 80,515	(71%)	($399,035)
	Chris Meredith (R).................. 32,532	(29%)	($19,130)

SECOND DISTRICT

Southwest Georgia contains much hallowed Democratic ground. Franklin Roosevelt first came here, to the bedraggled resort in Warm Springs 75 miles south of Atlanta, in October 1924, the same month that Jimmy Carter was born in Plains, 75 miles farther south. The Georgia that Roosevelt looked out on from the hilltop of Warm Springs was ragged land, where most people lived in little cabins without electricity or plumbing and scratched out a bare living from overtilled soil. Yet history was made here too, at Fort Benning, where General George Marshall held maneuvers that helped him choose most of the Army's generals in World War II; Benning still remains a giant Army training base, and is one of the big employers in Columbus, as is Warner Robins Air Force Base near Macon.

In the years since Carter went off to Annapolis in 1942 and Roosevelt died at Warm Springs in 1945, economic growth plus government works—rural electrification, the minimum wage, interstate highways, better schools, the military presence—have changed life vastly for the better here in southwest Georgia. Enforced segregation of the races has disappeared, despite predictions that whites would never tolerate integration. But sadly, the economy of southwest Georgia has not taken off. Farmers are hooked on the peanut subsidy, a static system that allows no growth; the big Firestone plant in Americus closed in the 1980s. The paper and lumber businesses are doing somewhat better, fueled by the soft pines that grow so rapidly here, and Jimmy Carter's home town of Plains attracts some visitors, but the Carter Center is on a beautiful site in Atlanta.

The 2d Congressional District of Georgia consists of much of southwest Georgia, including

Warm Springs, Plains and Fort Benning. Its boundaries, however, are erose and convoluted, drawn to maximize the percentage of blacks and make this Georgia's third black majority district. It includes heavily black but not heavily white parts of Columbus, Macon, Albany, Moultrie and Valdosta. This configuration, 40% of it new territory, was bad news for 10-year incumbent Democrat Charles Hatcher, chairman of the Peanuts and Tobacco Subcommittee; this was not his only bad news: it was revealed in April 1992 that Hatcher had 819 overdrafts on the House bank. In the Democratic primary, Hatcher tried to argue that his committee post was necessary to the state's economy. But he got only 40% of the vote, to 21% for black Columbus state Senator and lawyer Sanford Bishop and 19% for Albany state representative and gospel singer Mary Young-Cummings. In the runoff, Hatcher rallied to 47% but Bishop, with 95% in Columbus, won with 53%. In the general, Bishop faced Republican Jim Dudley, a white physician from Americus, who carried surrounding Sumter County (which includes Plains) and the white-majority counties at the southern edge of the district. But Bishop easily crossed racial lines—a majority of registered voters here are white—and won 64%–36%.

Bishop grew up in Mobile, went to Morehouse College and was an award-winning student at Emory Law School. After a year in New York, he began practicing law in Columbus in 1972. He was elected to the state House in 1976 and the state Senate in 1990 and had prime committee positions in both. He authored a tough ethics bill and was appointed to the Southern Growth Policies Board. He had strong support from the business community in Columbus, and his style is not confrontational; he talks of cutting waste and foreign aid as well as increasing aid for schools and Head Start and establishing enterprise zones. He won, as promised by Democratic leaders, a seat on the Agriculture Committee. Bishop appears to be a highly competent legislator and should have little difficulty holding this heavily Democratic seat.

The People: Pop. 1990: 592,011; 37% rural; 12% age 65+; 41% White; 57% Black; 1% Asian; 1% Other; 2% Hispanic origin. Voting age pop.: 415,776; 52% Black; 1% Hispanic origin. Households: 47% married couple families; 23% married couple fams. w. children; 27% college educ.; median household income: $17,942; per capita income: $8,532; median gross rent: $285; median house value: $42,200.

1992 Presidential Vote		
Clinton (D)	96,684	(60%)
Bush (R)	47,692	(29%)
Perot (I)	17,248	(11%)

1988 Presidential Vote		
Dukakis (D)	76,313	(56%)
Bush (R)	59,263	(44%)

Rep. Sanford D. Bishop, Jr. (D)

Elected 1992; b. Feb. 4, 1947, Mobile, AL; home, Columbus; Morehouse Col., B.A. 1968, Emory U., J.D. 1971; Baptist; divorced.

Career: Practicing atty., 1971–92; GA House of Reps., 1976–90; GA Senate, 1990–92.

Offices: 1632 LHOB 20515, 202-225-3631. Also 225 Pine St., Albany 31701, 912-439-8067; 17 10th St., Columbus 31901, 706-323-6894; City Hall, Dawson 31742, 912-995-3991; 682 Cherry St., #1113, Macon 31201, 912-741-2221; and 401 N. Patterson St., #255, Valdosta 31601, 912-247-9705.

Committees: *Agriculture* (25th of 28 D): Department Operations and Nutrition; General Farm Commodities; Specialty Crops and Natural Resources. *Post Office and Civil Service* (13th of 15 D): Postal Operations and Services. *Veterans' Affairs* (18th of 21 D): Hospitals and Health Care; Housing and Memorial Affairs.

Group Ratings and 102d Congress Votes: Newly Elected

Key Votes of the 103d Congress

1. Family Leave	FOR	2. Deficit Reduction	FOR	3. Stimulus Plan	FOR

Election Results

1992 general	Sanford D. Bishop, Jr. (D)	95,789	(64%)	($353,973)
	Jim Dudley (R).......................	54,593	(36%)	($222,806)
1992 runoff	Sanford D. Bishop, Jr. (D)	41,593	(53%)	
	Charles F. Hatcher (D).................	36,778	(47%)	
1992 primary	Charles F. Hatcher (D).................	40,833	(40%)	
	Sanford D. Bishop, Jr. (D)	21,692	(21%)	
	Mary Y. Cummings (D)	19,363	(19%)	
	Lonzy Edwards (D)...................	11,819	(12%)	
	Phil Whigham (D)	4,762	(5%)	
	Stephanie Kaigler (D).................	4,253	(4%)	
1990 general	Charles F. Hatcher (D).................	77,910	(73%)	($296,470)
	Jonathan Perry Waters (R).............	28,781	(27%)	

THIRD DISTRICT

Nearly a century ago, a boy named William Hartsfield, standing in the Candler Racetrack eight miles south of Atlanta's Five Points, spotted his first flying machine. From this moment dates Atlanta's emergence as a world city. Hartsfield went on to become mayor of Atlanta for 24 years, from 1937 to 1961, the builder of the economic capital of the South, and the man who dubbed it "The City Too Busy To Hate"; his two greatest achievements were Atlanta's acceptance of desegregation and the construction of what is now Hartsfield International Airport. By some measures the busiest airport in the world, certainly the busiest in the South and, with Chicago's O'Hare, one of the two busiest in the country, Hartsfield is a direct link between Atlanta, site of the 1996 Olympics, headquarters of Coca-Cola and CNN, and the world.

When Hartsfield saw his first plane, Candler Racetrack was far out in the country. Today, it is at the southern edge of the city limits but near the center of a vast and expanding metropolitan area. But the airport is not without its problems: the demise of Eastern Airlines cost a lot of jobs here, and there are empty terminal gates and an empty maintenance hangar which Atlanta threatened to use to bring a competitor to Atlanta-based Delta, which carries most of the traffic in and out. But the overall trajectory of the economy here is surely upward. The more glitzy, upscale Atlanta is north of downtown, but the airport is by no means in downscale territory. Most people living on the south side of Atlanta and in DeKalb County now are black, and by no means mostly poor; southern DeKalb is one of the nation's two largest concentrations of affluent suburban blacks.

Running along the freeways to the south, southeast and southwest of DeKalb are scores of new communities built in the last 20 years, transforming whole counties from rural outposts—the towns of Jonesboro and Fayetteville here both claim to be the spiritual home of *Gone with the Wind*. These new communities are affluent but not dominated by any establishment, liberation-minded in much of their lifestyles but often tradition-minded in their yearnings. Politically this is conservative country, full of young families, mostly white, who have moved up economically and who like the homier cultural atmosphere of the smaller counties. Their ancestral politics may be Democratic, but their preference in current elections often has been Republican. The 3d Congressional District of Georgia spans much of this territory from the Airport to rural south Georgia. More than 60% of its people are in five Atlanta metropolitan area counties, though back in Hartsfield's time few would have counted even one of them as metropolitan. To the south, the 3d sends two grotesquely shaped salients. One reaches down to the Alabama border and takes in most of the white precincts of Columbus. The other heads toward Macon, but stops just short of it, taking in a series of white-majority rural counties on either side of I-75.

The 3d has an odd political provenance. It includes most of the old 6th District territory represented by House Republican Whip Newt Gingrich in the 1980s, but it was designed by House Speaker Tom Murphy to include enough Democrats, in the rural counties and in black neighborhoods around the airport, to make Gingrich have to fight hard for the seat every two years. It also includes some territory represented by Richard Ray, a conservative Democrat who was Senator Sam Nunn's administrative assistant for 10 years, who spent much time on the Armed Services Committee dealing with the problems of toxic waste from military bases; much of the area was new to Ray, but redistricting left him without any other plausible place to run. Another resident of the new 3d was David Worley, a populist, pro-union Democrat who ran against Gingrich in 1988 and 1990, winning only 41% the first time but, with the help of angry laid-off Eastern workers and ire at the congressional pay raise, coming within 974 votes of beating him in 1990.

But none of these three plausible candidates won the new 3d District in 1992. Instead the winner was Mac Collins, a Republican state senator from Henry County. The Democrats had a bitter primary between Ray, Worley and two other candidates. Worley attacked Ray for opposing abortion and government intervention in the Eastern strike; Ray said Worley "supports billions in foreign aid" and was a career politician, though Worley has never held elective office. Worley carried the Atlanta area counties 49%–31%, but they were outvoted by traditional Democrats in the southern counties who backed Ray 68%–19%; Ray won outright, without a runoff, by 51%–32%. Republicans had a much lower key, lower turnout primary, with the lion's share of votes cast in the Atlanta area; Collins, with a 56%–44% margin in the area he had represented as State senator, won districtwide by 55%–45%. Collins attacked Ray on the congressional pay raise and junketeering, called for less government spending and, in the words of one aide, "ran a 'stealth campaign'—lots of meet and greet and very little campaign dollars." Collins carried only the counties in the Atlanta area, but they cast three-fifths of the district's votes and he won them with 61% of the vote—69% in Fayette. He also ran even in Columbus and got 45% in the rural counties.

Collins grew up in Jackson and owned a trucking company, hauling logs for Georgia-Pacific; he is known, a local paper said, for "his lumbering stature and signature boots." He served as a Democrat on the Butts County Commission in the late 1970s; after he lost in 1980, he went to a Republican Party meeting and was elected chairman; in 1988, he was elected to the state Senate. In the legislature, he worked on welfare and ethics reforms and bills to fight drug dealing. He said that keeping Hartsfield airport humming will be his chief focus in Congress, and he got a seat on the Public Works Committee. With his rural style and Atlanta area partisan appeal, he seems well-positioned to hold this seat.

The People: Pop. 1990: 592,002; 44% rural; 10% age 65+; 80% White; 18% Black; 1% Asian; 1% Hispanic origin. Voting age pop.: 429,264; 16% Black; 1% Hispanic origin. Households: 63% married couple families; 31% married couple fams. w. children; 38% college educ.; median household income: $32,380; per capita income: $13,849; median gross rent: $447; median house value: $70,300.

1992 Presidential Vote

Bush (R)	105,731	(48%)
Clinton (D)	80,628	(37%)
Perot (I)	32,285	(15%)

1988 Presidential Vote

Bush (R)	112,043	(68%)
Dukakis (D)	51,982	(32%)

Rep. Mac Collins (R)

Elected 1992; b. Oct. 15, 1944, Jackson; home, McDonough; Methodist; married (Julie).

Career: Army Natl. Guard, 1964–70; Founder & Pres., Collins Trucking Co., 1965–92; Chmn., Butts Cnty. Comm., 1977–80; Chmn., Butts Cnty. Repub. Party, 1981–82; GA Senate, 1988–92.

Offices: 1118 LHOB 20515, 202-225-5901. Also 173 N. Main St., Jonesboro 30236, 404-603-3395; and 5704 Beallwood Connector, #200, Columbus 31904, 706-327-7728.

Committees: *Public Works and Transportation* (15th of 24 R): Aviation; Economic Development; Surface Transportation. *Small Business* (9th of 18 R): Development of Rural Enterprises, Exports and the Environment; SBA Legislation and the General Economy.

Group Ratings and 102d Congress Votes: Newly Elected

Key Votes of the 103d Congress

1. Family Leave	AGN	2. Deficit Reduction	AGN	3. Stimulus Plan	AGN

Election Results

1992 general	Mac Collins (R)	114,107	(55%)	($246,007)
	Richard Ray (D)	94,271	(45%)	($1,127,731)
1992 primary	Mac Collins (R)	17,484	(55%)	
	Paul Broun (R)	14,546	(45%)	
1990 general	Richard Ray (D)	72,961	(63%)	($378,774)
	Paul Broun (R)	42,561	(37%)	($69,638)

FOURTH DISTRICT

Stone Mountain is a symbol of the southernness of yesterday and today. It is the world's largest mass of exposed granite, and on it was carved the world's largest single piece of sculpture, showing Jefferson Davis, Robert E. Lee and Stonewall Jackson astride their horses: a memorial to the Lost Cause of the Confederacy. Yet even as it was completed in 1972, the South and Atlanta were changing. Stone Mountain, in eastern DeKalb County, is some 15 miles from downtown Atlanta. When Gutzom Borglum began work on the sculpture in 1920, this was a day's drive out to the country from central Atlanta; even when the memorial was completed, suburban development barely reached this far. Today, after two decades of some of the most explosive metropolitan growth in the country, metro Atlanta has extended far past Stone Mountain. Gwinnett County, just past Stone Mountain, cast 21,000 votes in 1972; it cast 150,000 in 1992, a level approaching that of Fulton County, which includes central Atlanta, or DeKalb just to the east. In some ways, DeKalb and the area around Stone Mountain have become centers of the Atlanta metropolitan area. Emory University and the Centers for Disease Control, among the leading intellectual institutions in the South and nation, are in western DeKalb, just beyond the old mansions of Druid Hills, where *Driving Miss Daisy* was filmed. Not far away is Buckhead, the leading retail center of the South. All around are affluent subdivisions and condominiums, places where on the red clay soil of north Georgia styles of living descended from the finest in western tradition are established by the hard working people who have done much to make Atlanta a world-class city.

The 4th Congressional District of Georgia covers much of this territory. It includes the northern half of DeKalb County, mostly affluent, mostly white (the southern, mostly black half is in the black-majority 11th District), with a large Jewish and academic population. It includes Stone Mountain and proceeds out I-85 to include most of Gwinnett County—parts of Lilburn, Snellville, Norcross and Lawrenceville. It moves east to Rockdale County, once clearly rural, now also suburban. The 4th District is very affluent, with a household median income exceeded in the South only by the next-door 6th District, three northern Virginia districts outside Washington, D.C., and five districts in Houston and Dallas-Fort Worth, Texas.

The 4th was, if not an entirely new district, substantially altered in 1992 redistricting: so much so that incumbent Democratic Congressman Ben Jones, who had represented much of it, decided to run in the new 10th District. Actually, his residence was there, and the new 4th, without the black precincts of southern DeKalb, would have been very hard for him to win and hold. At the same time, the 4th was not totally out of reach for a Democrat, particularly given its large Jewish population. Indeed, in its previous boundaries, this had been a district where the cultures of affluent liberals and born-again traditionalists clashed: in the defeat of Democrat Elliott Levitas in 1984 by evangelical Republican Pat Swindall, in Swindall's 1986 and 1988 battles with Jones, then better known as the actor who played Cooter in *The Dukes of Hazzard*, and in the 1992 battle between Republican John Linder and Democrat Cathey Steinberg. Linder had run against Jones in 1990, and lost 52%–48%. In 1992, he was one of six Republicans running here, winning 34% in the first primary to 28% for Gwinnett-based Emory Morsberger; in the runoff, Linder won 62%–38%. DeKalb-based Steinberg won her primary 54%–46% over Bob Wilson.

Both Linder and Steinberg had served in the legislature for all but one term since 1976, and their careers presented a nice contrast. Linder, from a small town in Minnesota, is a dentist and small businessman who served in the Air Force and founded an "I Care" foundation for POW/MIA issues. He is antiabortion: as he said at one temple, "I'm one who happens to believe that the little thing is a baby. I'm prepared to lose the election on that issue." Steinberg, from industrial Pennsylvania, is a counselor and social worker who worked for an international adoption agency and lobbied for senior citizens and dental hygienists in Atlanta. Linder called for campaign finance reform, open meetings and community control of schools. Steinberg wrote domestic violence, family leave and nursing home rights laws. Both had run for office and lost, Linder for Congress in 1990, Steinberg for state Public Service commissioner in 1988. Both could plausibly see themselves as agents of change. Linder backed tort reform, medical savings accounts with a debit card, tax and spending cuts, the line-item veto and making Congress obey the laws it imposes on others. Steinberg backed the Freedom of Choice Act and family and medical leave. In this battle of cultural values and economic views, the front line seemed to be the I-285 Beltway: Steinberg won inside I-285, carrying DeKalb and the district's sliver of Fulton County 60%–40%. Linder did well in the newer areas beyond Stone Mountain, carrying Gwinnett and Rockdale Counties 61%–39%. Four or perhaps two years ago, those figures would have given the victory to Steinberg. But with population growth Linder won 51%–49%.

Linder could scarcely hope to be influential in the heavily Democratic House, yet arguably he was in his first months. Before the Republican Conference he advanced the "Linder rule," requiring ranking Republicans on committees to step down from those positions after three terms. Republicans adopted it 82–44. Democratic leaders naturally brushed aside any term limits for their chairmen, but if Republicans should win a majority in the 1990s, presumably the "Linder rule" would apply to chairmen. Linder also was one of the leaders in the successful fight to abolish the four non-legislative select committees.

The People: Pop. 1990: 589,293; 8% rural; 8% age 65+; 81% White; 12% Black; 4% Asian; 1% Other; 3% Hispanic origin. Voting age pop.: 448,249; 11% Black; 3% Hispanic origin. Households: 56% married couple families; 28% married couple fams. w. children; 64% college educ.; median household income: $40,303; per capita income: $18,607; median gross rent: $566; median house value: $96,600.

342   GEORGIA

Rep. John Linder (R)

Elected 1992; b. Sept. 9, 1942, Deer River, MN; home, Dunwoody; U. of MN, B.S. 1964, D.D.S., 1967; Presbyterian; married (Lynne).

Career: Air Force, 1967–69; Practicing dentist, 1969–82; Founder & Pres., Linder Financial, 1977–92; GA House of Reps., 1976–80, 1982–90.

Offices: 1605 LHOB 20515, 202-225-4272. Also 3003 Chamblee-Tucker Rd., #140, Atlanta 30341, 404-936-9400.

Committees: *Banking, Finance and Urban Affairs* (13th of 20 R): Consumer Credit and Insurance; Financial Institutions Supervision, Regulation and Deposit Insurance. *Science, Space and Technology* (18th of 22 R): Technology, Environment and Aviation. *Veterans' Affairs* (12th of 14 R): Hospitals and Health Care.

Group Ratings and 102d Congress Votes: Newly Elected

Key Votes of the 103d Congress

1. Family Leave	AGN	2. Deficit Reduction	AGN	3. Stimulus Plan	AGN

Election Results

1992 general	John Linder (R) 126,495	(51%)	($542,137)
	Cathey Steinberg (D) 123,819	(49%)	($603,399)
1992 runoff	John Linder (R) 21,807	(62%)	
	Emory Morsberger (R)................. 13,370	(38%)	
1992 primary	John Linder (R) 17,828	(34%)	
	Emory Morsberger (R)................. 14,381	(28%)	
	Jimmy Fisher (R) 5,647	(11%)	
	Richard Robinson (R)................. 5,587	(11%)	
	Tom Phillips (R) 5,455	(11%)	
	Ray Miller (R) 2,480	(5%)	
1990 general	Ben Jones (D) 96,526	(52%)	($711,015)
	John Linder (R) 87,569	(48%)	($696,859)

FIFTH DISTRICT

Venture out of the quiet of the Ebenezer Baptist Church or the shade of Martin Luther King Jr.'s boyhood home two blocks away and into the steam-heat blast of the sun on Auburn Avenue—Sweet Auburn—and you can see, a mile away, downtown Atlanta's atrium-skyscrapers towering in their glory. They are evidence of the wealth and vibrant growth of "The City," as it boasted in the 1960s, "Too Busy To Hate," the commercial capital of the South, the metropolis that has grown up where there was little more than a railroad junction at the time of the War Between the States. But the awesome achievement that is downtown Atlanta is overshadowed by the revolution made in very large part by a man who grew up on Auburn Avenue, where people who never felt air conditioning moved slowly in the sweltering heat, and around Morehouse and Spelman Colleges, where proud professionals worked hard and raised their families and yet never saw more than a few dollars cash at a time. Atlanta's white establishment, led by Mayors William Hartsfield and Ivan Allen and Coca-Cola's Robert Woodruff, deserve some credit for abandoning segregation, but it was King and other civil rights leaders who took the risks that led them to do so. Atlanta's city fathers acted out of good will, but also with an eye for the economic growth of their city, which they knew would be hurt by violent resistance. White Atlanta's decision to desegregate has helped Atlanta prosper, but King's vision and movement to change the way Americans behave have made it possible for a nation to live up to its ideals.

Yet, sadly, not all is entirely well in Atlanta—on Peachtree Street or on Sweet Auburn. Downtown Atlanta's primacy in office buildings was being eclipsed by north side Edge Cities in Buckhead and along I-285. And many of Atlanta's black neighborhoods today have been abandoned by the area's affluent families who have headed to subdivisions in DeKalb County, leaving to the mercies of a criminal underclass, the central city with its high rates of murder and infant mortality, abandoned housing and street crime. But Atlanta still has much to be proud of: the world-wide success of Coca-Cola and CNN, and the securing of the 1996 summer Olympics that was the crowning achievement of former (1981–89) Mayor Andrew Young.

Georgia's 5th Congressional District includes most of Atlanta and a few suburbs, from posh white Sandy Spring in the north to middle-class and increasingly black East Point in the south, plus the rural precincts of southwest Fulton and mostly black southwest DeKalb counties. The congressman is John Lewis, who made history a quarter-century before his election as a hero of the civil rights movement. A sharecropper's son from Troy, Alabama, he was the first in his family to finish high school; he wrote Ralph Abernathy for help in suing for the right to enter Troy State College; he met Martin Luther King when he was 18. In 1959, at age 19, he helped organize the first lunch-counter sit-in, which was received with open hostility hard to imagine today. In 1960, the day after John Kennedy was elected, Lewis sat in at the Krystal Diner in Nashville while a waitress poured cleansing powder down his back and water over his food; after eating, he went to talk to the manager, who turned a fumigating machine on him. In May 1961, he was on the first of the Freedom Rides, riding buses as they were attacked and burned; he was viciously beaten in Rock Hill, South Carolina, and Montgomery, Alabama. He spoke at the 1963 March on Washington. In 1964, he helped coordinate the Mississippi Freedom Project. In 1965, he led the Selma-to-Montgomery march to petition for voting rights and was attacked by policemen. Modestly, quietly, maintaining his poise and good judgment under harsh circumstances, Lewis was one of the people who risked their lives many times to make the civil rights revolution happen.

Lewis responded to these beatings with a stubborn determination to persevere with actions, not just words. His tenure as head of the Voter Education Project in Atlanta and his work at ACTION in the Carter Administration did not give him the publicity and fame, however, that made a national celebrity of Jesse Jackson, whose civil rights movement credentials are much thinner. Lewis's first foray into electoral politics was unsuccessful: he ran in 1977 to replace Andrew Young in the House and was soundly beaten by Wyche Fowler (but ran ahead of Republican Paul Coverdell, who beat Fowler in the 1992 Senate election). After winning a seat on the Atlanta Council in 1981, Lewis ran for Congress in 1986, and trailed Julian Bond 47%–35% in the first primary. But even though Bond won over 60% of the black vote, Lewis won the runoff because, thanks to his hard work on local issues like zoning and city ethics, he drew nearly 90% of the white vote. He has been reelected easily since, with more than 70% in primary and general in 1992.

Lewis describes himself as a coalition-builder: "I don't want to compromise my belief in interracial democracy." He cultivates friendships and alliances with many members, including those who have less faith in government action to solve problems—a path that seems to be followed by many members elected in new black-majority districts. He is now a chief deputy whip, and so is involved in many issues though not usually in a way that gives him publicity. He was instrumental in getting in Atlanta the first federal building in the United States to be named for Martin Luther King, Jr.; he passed a bill to study designating the route from Selma to Montgomery as a national trail, a fitting remembrance of the 1965 march. But while commemorating the civil rights past, Lewis thinks that blacks should run as "mainstream politicians," and was an early supporter of Bill Clinton. Lewis sponsored a bill for tougher billboard control on interstate highways, and in May 1992 cast the key vote on a bill preserving federal forests to save the spotted owl. He got MARTA subway extension financing included in the 1991 transportation bill. Though generally opposed to U.S. military intervention abroad, he applauded the sending of U.S. troops to Somalia in December 1992. In 1993, after election to his fourth term, he won a seat on the Ways and Means Committee.

The People: Pop. 1990: 586,526; 3% rural; 10% age 65+; 35% White; 62% Black; 1% Asian; 1% Other; 2% Hispanic origin. Voting age pop.: 440,803; 57% Black; 2% Hispanic origin. Households: 35% married couple families; 15% married couple fams. w. children; 49% college educ.; median household income: $25,892; per capita income: $15,831; median gross rent: $461; median house value: $74,800.

1992 Presidential Vote			1988 Presidential Vote		
Clinton (D)	140,175	(67%)	Dukakis (D)	117,881	(65%)
Bush (R)	52,191	(25%)	Bush (R)	64,040	(35%)
Perot (I)	15,241	(7%)			

Rep. John Lewis (D)

Elected 1986; b. Feb. 21, 1940, Troy, AL; home, Atlanta; Amer. Baptist Theological Seminary, B.A. 1961, Fisk U., B.A. 1963; Baptist; married (Lillian).

Career: Chmn., Student Nonviolent Coord. Cmte., 1963–66; Field Foundation, 1966–67; Community Organization Dir., Southern Regional Cncl., 1967–70; Exec. Dir., Voter Educ. Project, 1970–76; Assoc. Dir., ACTION, 1977–80; Community Affairs Dir., Natl. Coop. Bank, 1980–82; Atlanta City Cncl., 1981–86.

Offices: 329 CHOB 20515, 202-225-3801. Also Equitable Bldg. #750, 100 Peachtree St., NW, Atlanta 30303, 404-659-0116.

Committees: *District of Columbia* (6th of 8 D): Government Operations and Metropolitan Affairs; Judiciary and Education. *Ways and Means* (16th of 24 D): Health; Oversight.

Group Ratings

	ADA	ACLU	COPE	CDF	CFA	LCV	ACU	NTLC	NSI	COC	CEI
1992	95	100	92	100	100	88	0	5	10	13	8
1991	85	—	92	100	89	85	0	—	—	0	6

National Journal Ratings

	1991 LIB — 1991 CONS		1992 LIB — 1992 CONS	
Economic	79%	— 18%	91%	— 0%
Social	88%	— 0%	92%	— 0%
Foreign	92%	— 0%	90%	— 0%

Key Votes of the 102d Congress

1. Ban Striker Replace	FOR	5. Handgun Wait/7-Day	FOR	9. Use Force in Gulf	AGN
2. $ for Homeownership	AGN	6. Overseas Mil. Abortion	FOR	10. US Mil. Abroad $ Cut	FOR
3. Tax Rich/Cut Mid Cls.	FOR	7. Obscn. Art NEA $ Ban	AGN	11. Limit SDI Funds	FOR
4. FY93/$15B Def. Cut	FOR	8. Death Pen. from Jury	AGN	12. Cuba Trade Embargo	AGN

Key Votes of the 103d Congress

1. Family Leave	FOR	2. Deficit Reduction	FOR	3. Stimulus Plan	FOR

Election Results

1992 general	John Lewis (D)	147,445	(72%)	($246,913)
	Paul Stabler (R)	56,960	(28%)	($59,300)
1992 primary	John Lewis (D)	43,971	(76%)	
	Mable "Able" Thomas (D)	13,686	(24%)	
1990 general	John Lewis (D)	86,037	(76%)	($108,118)
	J. W. Tibbs, Jr. (R)	27,781	(24%)	($7,755)

SIXTH DISTRICT

In the red clay hills north of Atlanta, over the last three decades, an almost wholly new metropolitan quarter has grown up as affluent Atlanta has spread out from Ansley Park just north of downtown and the rolling hills of Buckhead within the city limit past the I-285 Beltway into territory that was once just farms, small towns and little factory cities. Where there were perhaps 100,000 people in the 1950s, there are one million today. No longer is downtown Atlanta the only focus: the Edge Cities of Buckhead, Perimeter Center and Cumberland Mall are now not just shopping but major office centers, rivaling downtown Atlanta in square footage. But in some ways, north Atlanta has not changed greatly: the buildings are tree-shaded and lush foliage and large-lot requirements have given most of the communities a woodsy look; and for all their affluence they still have a folksy atmosphere and at least a hint of a southern accent.

The 6th Congressional District of Georgia occupies a large portion of this new north Atlanta. This is a new district, taking in parts of Fulton, Cobb, DeKalb, Gwinnett and Cherokee Counties and parts of the old 4th, 5th, 7th and 9th Districts (though not the old 6th), and it has as its congressman a politician entirely new to the area, Newt Gingrich, who had represented the old 6th for 14 years. It would surely surprise Georgians a generation or so ago to learn that one of their congressional districts ranks among the nation's richest and best educated, but it does. The 6th ranks 11th of 435 districts in percentage of adults with a college degree, at 40%; it ranks 25th in median household income, at $46,997, behind districts all in larger metro areas. It is easily the most Republican district in Georgia, having voted 75% for George Bush in 1988; indeed, one of the most heavily Republican districts in the country.

Nonetheless, this was not a district easily won by Newt Gingrich, even though as minority whip he ranked second in his party's leadership in the House, and by any measure has been one of the most intellectually creative and politically effective members of Congress, and in directions most 6th District voters approve. But there is something about Gingrich that infuriates most Democrats and puts off many Republicans: his criticisms of things as they are pierce too deeply, wounding their targets' claims to intellectual and moral superiority, while his sloppiness in personal and political matters leaves him open to furious counterattack. Gingrich is still seen as an outside agitator in Congress, though he has served there longer than all but 19 other Republicans, and he does not have deep Georgia roots, though he has been running for office there now for 20 years. Gingrich (like fellow conservative Phil Gramm) is the son of a non-commissioned Army officer. He went to college at Emory and became a history teacher at West Georgia College in Carrollton. After less than four years of teaching, he ran for Congress in 1974, campaigning on ethics issues against an old-line conservative southern Democrat, and lost; he lost again in 1976 but persevered and won in 1978, just as House Republicans were unanimously embracing the Kemp-Roth 30% tax cut. He came to office little affected by what were great struggles for most Democrats of his generation, civil rights and Vietnam; civil rights, because he was raised in the most integrated part of American society, the career military; Vietnam, because as a graduate student who was married with children during the draft years he felt no need to justify his lack of military service. Gingrich has looked back into history for values, and has come out something like an American Gaullist: a nationalist who believes in American exceptionalism and a strong military, a cultural conservative who believes that liberal values are destroying the lives of the poor, a market capitalist who celebrates technological innovation and considers high-tech and traditional values happy companions. All these beliefs run counter to the beliefs of the baby boom liberals who have dominated the thinking of the House for most of the last 20 years and now of the Clinton Administration. And against them Gingrich has been an insistent, impolite and persistent battering ram.

He has also been a partisan Republican who has changed the tone of Republican partisanship. He argued for years that ranking Republicans should fight Democratic bills, not try to compromise with them for a few crumbs in return. He put together in a book the angry comments of Democrats opposed to the 1983 Grenada invasion; in debate, when Gingrich chastised some Democrats for sending a letter to Nicaraguan leader Daniel Ortega, Speaker Tip O'Neill said Gingrich had "challenged the Americanism" of these Democrats and called it "the lowest thing that I've ever seen in my 32 years in Congress." Gingrich challenged him and O'Neill's words were ordered stricken from the record. Gingrich dared to challenge Speaker Jim Wright in December 1987 by bringing the ethics charges against him which, after bitter controversy, brought Wright's resignation in June 1989. In March 1989, after Dick Cheney was appointed secretary of defense, Gingrich ran for whip against Edward Madigan, who as ranking Republican on the Agriculture Committee and the Health Subcommittee worked closely with Democratic chairmen in shaping legislation. Madigan was next in line on the leadership ladder and had the support of his Illinois neighbor, Minority Leader Robert Michel, and of most older Republicans; Gingrich had the support of younger and more conservative members. Gingrich won 87–85, a narrow victory but a decisive one, for the ranks of his opponents started to thin, starting with Madigan himself who pulled strings to become secretary of agriculture, and the numbers of Gingrich's kind increased in Republican ranks.

There were countercurrents. Charges were lodged with the Ethics Committee regarding the financing of Gingrich's book, *Window of Opportunity*, but after some months were thrown out as insubstantial. As a member of the 1990 budget summit, he was purposely derisive, but could not stop the Bush Administration from agreeing to a tax increase; he flinched for a couple of days from taking any position on the increase and only then vociferously opposed it—much to Bob Michel's distress. Gingrich's efforts to recruit stronger Republican challengers produced less than he hoped, as the party lost seats in 1990 and gained only 10 in 1992. And Gingrich himself was heartily challenged. Democrat David Worley, who won 41% against Gingrich in 1988, came back in 1990 with a direct mail campaign excoriating Gingrich for supporting the congressional pay raise and for having a car and driver; his campaign also targeted Eastern Airlines employees reminding them of Gingrich's refusal to support government intervention in their strike. Gingrich spent $1.5 million and won by only 974 votes; he might have lost but for Democrats' adherence to a leadership agreement not to support challengers who attacked the pay raise. Gingrich seemed unabashed, and tried to get George Bush to back sweeping domestic reforms right after the Gulf war; if he had listened, he might have been reelected.

Then came the 1992 contest. Speaker Tom Murphy and the Georgia legislature tried to make things awkward for Gingrich, putting most of his old territory in a new 3d District which reached far into rural Georgia and would be difficult for him to carry. He decided to run in the solidly Republican new 6th. But there he had to face former state Representative Herman Clark in the primary, who attacked him as a carpetbagger and because, after Gingrich demanded disclosure of House bank records, it turned out he had 22 overdrafts on it. Clark ran a low-budget campaign but was the beneficiary of independent expenditures by Democratic lobbies and crossover voting by anti-Gingrich Democrats. Clark carried Cobb County around his home base of Marietta and lost overall by only a 51%–49% margin in a turnout of 70,000 (compared to 15,000 in the Democratic contest). The general election featured personal charges between Gingrich and Democrat Tony Center. Gingrich attacked Center for suing a mother with two children for his legal fee after having won child support payments for her in court; Center attacked Gingrich for allegedly not making alimony payments to his former wife. Party loyalties asserted themselves enough for Gingrich to win a 58%–42% victory. He spent some $1.9 million on the two campaigns.

Can Gingrich after two close shaves be an effective House leader? The increasingly conservative and rebellious tone of House Republicans matches his, and all Republican leadership posts but the top one went to conservatives. Gingrich let it be known that he does not feel bound not to run against Michel for leader in 1994, and it's widely assumed that Gingrich and possibly Dick Armey and Henry Hyde may run for the post. Gingrich must hope that his 1992 victories and his heavily Republican seat will discourage competition at home, and it probably will. But this stormy philosopher may endure still more "perils of Pauline" before— if—he becomes Republican leader in, or speaker of, the House.

The People: Pop. 1990: 586,641; 11% rural; 5% age 65+; 90% White; 6% Black; 2% Asian; 1% Other; 2% Hispanic origin. Voting age pop.: 438,774; 6% Black; 2% Hispanic origin. Households: 62% married couple families; 32% married couple fams. w. children; 70% college educ.; median household income: $46,997; per capita income: $22,181; median gross rent: $600; median house value: $120,500.

1992 Presidential Vote			1988 Presidential Vote		
Bush (R)	155,739	(55%)	Bush (R)	150,405	(75%)
Clinton (D)	82,381	(29%)	Dukakis (D)	50,297	(25%)
Perot (I)	41,874	(15%)			

Rep. Newt Gingrich (R)

Elected 1978; b. June 17, 1943, Harrisburg, PA; home, Marietta; Emory U., B.A. 1965, Tulane U., M.A. 1968, Ph.D. 1971; Baptist; married (Marianne).

Career: Asst. Prof., W. GA Col., 1970–78.

Offices: 2428 RHOB 20515, 202-225-4501. Also 3823 Roswell Rd., #200, Marietta 30062, 404-565-6398.

Committees: *Minority Whip. House Administration* (2d of 7 R): Accounts. *Joint Committee on Printing* (5th of 5).

Group Ratings

	ADA	ACLU	COPE	CDF	CFA	LCV	ACU	NTLC	NSI	COC	CEI
1992	10	0	22	10	20	6	100	100	100	88	76
1991	5	—	17	30	33	8	100	—	—	100	71

National Journal Ratings

	1991 LIB — 1991 CONS			1992 LIB — 1992 CONS		
Economic	12%	—	86%	0%	—	91%
Social	19%	—	78%	0%	—	85%
Foreign	15%	—	84%	0%	—	82%

Key Votes of the 102d Congress

1. Ban Striker Replace AGN	5. Handgun Wait/7-Day AGN	9. Use Force in Gulf FOR
2. $ for Homeownership FOR	6. Overseas Mil. Abortion AGN	10. US Mil. Abroad $ Cut AGN
3. Tax Rich/Cut Mid Cls. AGN	7. Obscn. Art NEA $ Ban FOR	11. Limit SDI Funds AGN
4. FY93/$15B Def. Cut AGN	8. Death Pen. from Jury FOR	12. Cuba Trade Embargo FOR

Key Votes of the 103d Congress

1. Family Leave AGN	2. Deficit Reduction AGN	3. Stimulus Plan AGN

Election Results

1992 general	Newt Gingrich (R)	158,761	(58%)	($1,963,810)
	Tony Center (D)	116,196	(42%)	($411,794)
1992 primary	Newt Gingrich (R)	35,699	(51%)	
	Herman Clark (R)	34,719	(49%)	
1990 general	Newt Gingrich (R)	78,768	(50%)	($1,538,945)
	David Worley (D)	77,794	(50%)	($333,873)

SEVENTH DISTRICT

For 100 years, the red clay hills of north Georgia, once the home of the Cherokee Nation before they were sent west in the 1830s on the Trail of Tears, have been manufacturing country. There are hundreds of textile mills and dozens of carpet mills located near the supply of natural cotton and along the railroad lines heading southwest at the base of the southern Appalachian chain. Factories were hailed as the vanguard of technological progress by the late 19th Century propagandists of the New South, and in fact they produced a higher standard of living than reliance on farming this stubborn land. But there are limits to mill work: it puts little premium on education or the cultivation of civic virtues; it did little to bring in higher-skill white-collar work; because of rigid segregationist hiring practices, it promoted bigotry. North Georgia is now developing a different kind of economy, as the example of Atlanta shines to the south and spreads out interstate highways north into what used to be mill towns. Cobb County, once centered on the Lockheed aircraft factory in Marietta, has already been transformed into an upscale suburb and office center; places like the textile mill town of LaGrange or the carpet mill town of Rome have begun to be affected as well.

The 7th Congressional District of Georgia includes much of this part of north Georgia. It extends along the state's western boundary from LaGrange to Rome, and extends east to Cartersville, where U.S. 41 starts its four-lane roll toward Atlanta, and takes in part of western Cobb County, including the old center of Marietta. This was Democratic territory from the time General Sherman came through in the 1860s until the civil rights revolution of the 1960s. Now in national politics it is Republican, even giving George Bush a hefty majority in 1992, with higher percentages as one gets closer to Atlanta.

Nevertheless, the congressman here is a Democrat, Buddy Darden, one of those talented political entrepreneurs who keep their party the majority in the House. He was a Cobb County legislator when he won the seat in a fall 1983 special election to replace Larry McDonald, the John Birch Society member who was on the Korean Airlines flight 007 shot down by the Soviet Union. Darden has made a middle of the road record in the House and concentrated on projects popular back home. On the Armed Services Committee, he fought hard for Lockheed's Marietta airplane factory and aeronautical center, losing in 1987 when the C-5 military transport plane was zeroed out, winning in 1991 when the Air Force came through with a $64 billion contract to build the F-22 fighters for Lockheed and its partners Boeing and General Dynamics. Darden is likely to continue similar efforts on the Appropriations Committee and its Defense Subcommittee, to which he moved in 1993.

Darden has done well in winning votes here, but this essentially Republican district presents a severe challenge. Redistricting helped him by putting most of Cobb County into the new heavily Republican 6th District, but in 1992, in a rematch against his 1990 opponent, he won with only 57% of the vote, with 56% outside Cobb County—a sharp drop from the last three elections, when he was winning 68% to 74% outside Cobb. Exploring the possibility of running against him in 1994 is Bob Barr, former U.S. Attorney who successfully prosecuted Republican Congressman Pat Swindall, and who came within 1% of winning the 1992 primary runoff for senator against Paul Coverdell, despite low financing and less party support. Barr got 58% of the Senate primary vote in counties in the 7th District and could be a formidable challenger.

The People: Pop. 1990: 587,917; 46% rural; 11% age 65+; 85% White; 13% Black; 1% Hispanic origin. Voting age pop.: 431,636; 12% Black; 1% Hispanic origin. Households: 62% married couple families; 30% married couple fams. w. children; 31% college educ.; median household income: $28,831; per capita income: $12,428; median gross rent: $403; median house value: $64,300.

1992 Presidential Vote			1988 Presidential Vote		
Bush (R)	93,175	(46%)	Bush (R)	101,310	(68%)
Clinton (D)	77,103	(38%)	Dukakis (D)	48,047	(32%)
Perot (I)	30,097	(15%)			

Rep. George (Buddy) Darden (D)

Elected Nov., 1983; b. Nov. 22, 1943, Hancock Cnty.; home, Marietta; N. GA Col., 1961, George Washington U., 1962, U. of GA, B.A. 1965, J.D. 1967; United Methodist; married (Lillian).

Career: Asst. Dist. Atty., Cobb Cnty., 1967–72, Dist. Atty., 1973–77; Practicing atty., 1977–83; GA House of Reps., 1980–83.

Offices: 2303 RHOB 20515, 202-225-2931. Also 376 Powder Springs St., Marietta 30064, 404-422-4480; 301 Fed. Bldg., Rome 30161, 404-291-7777; 315 Bradley St., Carrollton 30117; 404-832-0553; and City Hall, 200 Ridley Ave., LaGrange 30240, 706-882-4578.

Committees: *Appropriations* (28th of 37 D): Defense; Treasury, Postal Service, and General Government. *Standards of Official Conduct* (2d of 7 D).

Group Ratings

	ADA	ACLU	COPE	CDF	CFA	LCV	ACU	NTLC	NSI	COC	CEI
1992	70	39	58	60	60	38	32	15	100	50	24
1991	40	—	58	80	67	69	35	—	—	60	16

National Journal Ratings

	1991 LIB — 1991 CONS			1992 LIB — 1992 CONS	
Economic	47%	—	52%	53% —	46%
Social	46%	—	53%	49% —	50%
Foreign	51%	—	46%	38% —	56%

Key Votes of the 102d Congress

1. Ban Striker Replace	FOR	5. Handgun Wait/7-Day	FOR	9. Use Force in Gulf	FOR
2. $ for Homeownership	AGN	6. Overseas Mil. Abortion	FOR	10. US Mil. Abroad $ Cut	AGN
3. Tax Rich/Cut Mid Cls.	FOR	7. Obscn. Art NEA $ Ban	FOR	11. Limit SDI Funds	AGN
4. FY93/$15B Def. Cut	FOR	8. Death Pen. from Jury	AGN	12. Cuba Trade Embargo	FOR

Key Votes of the 103d Congress

1. Family Leave	AGN	2. Deficit Reduction	FOR	3. Stimulus Plan	FOR

Election Results

1992 general	George (Buddy) Darden (D)............	111,374	(57%)	($510,073)
	Al Beverly (R).......................	82,915	(43%)	($40,778)
1992 primary	George (Buddy) Darden (D), unopposed			
1990 general	George (Buddy) Darden (D)............	95,817	(60%)	($404,874)
	Al Beverly (R).......................	63,588	(40%)	($18,692)

EIGHTH DISTRICT

More than almost any part of America, south Georgia has been under attack and enemy occupation. Most famously, of course, when General William Tecumseh Sherman's troops set out from Atlanta, without supplies or lines of communication, to march through Georgia to the sea. The path they cut through south Georgia has been mostly poor country ever since, its antebellum mansions burned down, its leader captured (the Jefferson Davis Memorial in Ocilla marks the spot where Union troops took him in May 1865), its crops destroyed, and memories of slaves freed handed down as family lore for over a century. But the land bears, if only on its road signs, the memory of another invasion, when the poor white farmers, aided by Andrew Jackson's troops, drove the Cherokees and other Indians off this land west over the Trail of Tears to what is now Oklahoma. Only 50 years ago, archaeologists discovered near Macon a huge Indian earthlodge built nearly 1,000 years ago. And there was the oppression of blacks by whites under the old systems of slavery and legal segregation, the latter dead just one generation now—a past recalled by Macon's new Harriet Tubman Historical and Cultural Museum. More recently, many south Georgians, black and white, find themselves threatened by drug dealers heading north on I-75 from Florida, spreading addiction and AIDS to Macon and smaller towns that thought they were immune to these scourges.

The 8th Congressional District of Georgia runs down the center of the state along these lines of occupation, past immense stands of soft lumber pines, through counties where 60% of the world's kaolin (used for china and ceramics) is mined, all the way from Macon to the Okeefenokee Swamp and the Florida line. To place blacks in the next-door 2d District, the 8th's boundaries twist around Macon, home of music legends Otis Redding, Little Richard and the Allman brothers, a city proud of its restored houses and Japanese cherry trees (it has 20 times as many as Washington); the lines similarly wrap around the south Georgia county seats of Albany, Moultrie and Valdosta. There has been some growth in these towns and along the interstates, but in the more rural counties there is little sign of the Atlantic Coast prosperity apparent just a few miles east. This has been Democratic country since Sherman's troops came through. With high black percentages and relatively little growth, most of the counties in this part of south Georgia have remained some of Georgia's most Democratic, voting only narrowly for Republican presidents in the 1980s, and voting for President Bill Clinton and Senator Wyche Fowler in 1992.

The congressman from the 8th is Roy Rowland, one of very few members of Congress who used to practice medicine. He serves on the Health Subcommittee of Energy and Commerce and chairs the Hospitals and Health Care Subcommittee of Veterans' Affairs. Early on he sponsored laws to ban the tranquilizer Quaalude and to provide cancer treatment for veterans exposed to radiation in the 1940s. He has been a critical voice on several AIDS issues, creating the National AIDS Commission, protecting food handlers with AIDS from discrimination, letting states decide whether to require reporting names of those who test HIV-positive, allowing the entry into the country of HIV-positive visitors but not immigrants. He authored an "anti-hassle" Medicare bill to eliminate burdensome regulations and is sponsoring a product liability bill to establish uniform federal tort standards. He favors a market-based health care system. His views on other issues are rather conservative: he supports a balanced budget amendment and voted against the Clinton economic stimulus package in March 1993, although he did back the Democratic rule that helped it pass.

First elected in 1982, when he beat incumbent Billy Lee Evans who had been fined for accepting illegal campaign contributions, Rowland held the seat without difficulty for eight years. Redistricting caused him some problems by adding new territory and paring off black areas at the edge of the district. He had a primary challenge in 1992, and won over 70% in most parts of the district, but actually lost the areas around Albany, Moultrie and Valdosta. In the general, against Macon-based Republican Bob Cunningham, he also lost those towns 56%–44% and won only 52% in the Macon area. Rowland might have to work these areas hard to avoid another serious challenge in 1994, when he turns 68.

The People: Pop. 1990: 590,835; 51% rural; 12% age 65+; 77% White; 21% Black; 1% Hispanic origin. Voting age pop.: 426,327; 18% Black; 1% Hispanic origin. Households: 60% married couple families; 29% married couple fams. w. children; 34% college educ.; median household income: $25,744; per capita income: $11,958; median gross rent: $341; median house value: $55,800.

1992 Presidential Vote			1988 Presidential Vote		
Bush (R)	93,643	(45%)	Bush (R)	107,034	(64%)
Clinton (D)	83,976	(40%)	Dukakis (D)	59,607	(36%)
Perot (I)	32,068	(15%)			

Rep. J. Roy Rowland (D)

Elected 1982; b. Feb. 3, 1926, Wrightsville; home, Dublin; Emory U., S. GA Col., U. of GA, Medical Col. of GA, M.D. 1952; Methodist; married (Luella).

Career: Army, 1944–46 (WWII); Practicing physician 1952–82; GA House of Reps., 1976–82.

Offices: 2134 RHOB 20515, 202-225-6531. Also P.O. Box 2047, Dublin 31040, 912-275-0024; P.O. Box 6528, Macon 31208, 912-743-0150; and 1810 N. Ashley St., #5, Valdosta 31602, 912-333-0118.

Committees: *Energy and Commerce* (16th of 27 D): Commerce, Consumer Protection and Competitiveness; Health and the Environment; Transportation and Hazardous Materials. *Veterans' Affairs* (6th of 21 D): Education, Training and Employment; Hospitals and Health Care (Chmn.).

Group Ratings

	ADA	ACLU	COPE	CDF	CFA	LCV	ACU	NTLC	NSI	COC	CEI
1992	50	39	58	40	60	19	48	33	100	63	37
1991	35	—	45	70	57	62	42	—	—	67	25

National Journal Ratings

	1991 LIB — 1991 CONS		1992 LIB — 1992 CONS	
Economic	43%	— 57%	41%	— 58%
Social	46%	— 54%	35%	— 65%
Foreign	40%	— 58%	30%	— 64%

Key Votes of the 102d Congress

1. Ban Striker Replace	AGN	5. Handgun Wait/7-Day	FOR	9. Use Force in Gulf	FOR
2. $ for Homeownership	FOR	6. Overseas Mil. Abortion	FOR	10. US Mil. Abroad $ Cut	AGN
3. Tax Rich/Cut Mid Cls.	AGN	7. Obscn. Art NEA $ Ban	FOR	11. Limit SDI Funds	AGN
4. FY93/$15B Def. Cut	AGN	8. Death Pen. from Jury	FOR	12. Cuba Trade Embargo	FOR

Key Votes of the 103d Congress

1. Family Leave	AGN	2. Deficit Reduction	AGN	3. Stimulus Plan	AGN

Election Results

1992 general	J. Roy Rowland (D)	108,472	(56%)	($544,898)
	Bob Cunningham (R)	86,220	(44%)	($201,755)
1992 primary	J. Roy Rowland (D)	85,689	(68%)	
	Bill Lightle (D)........................	41,153	(32%)	
1990 general	J. Roy Rowland (D)	81,344	(69%)	($365,513)
	Bob Cunningham (R)	36,980	(31%)	($105,270)

NINTH DISTRICT

The mountains of north Georgia have become one of the boom areas of the state. This was Indian country once, where the Cherokees devised their own alphabet and printed their own bilingual newspaper and elected their own legislature in a society arguably more civil than the frontier slaveowning Georgia of the day; but they were expelled, sent westward to Oklahoma on the Trail of Tears in the 1830s. One reason for this was greed: the United States had its first gold rush here in 1828 in Dahlonega, where there was a mint until the Civil War. This part of Georgia had virtually no slaves and has few blacks today; after the Civil War it lived in isolation, with some textile mill towns along the railroads, and hairpin curves leading up to remote hills where within living memory moonshine stills were more common than summer cabins. Now the north Georgia mountains, pleasantly cool in the summer when Atlanta swelters, with miles of shoreline on vast lakes formed by dams, are vacation country, popularized by former President Jimmy Carter, connected to the Atlanta area with limited-access highways.

The 9th Congressional District is a swath of north Georgia, from South Carolina west to Alabama, covering most of Georgia's mountains and running south to Forsyth County, once famous for driving all blacks out in 1912, now a fast-growing part of the Atlanta metro area. The 9th contains the Georgia suburbs of Chattanooga, Tennessee, looking out from Lookout Mountain down to the Tennessee River below, and the carpet-making capital of Dalton not far away; it also includes fast-growing Hall County around Gainesville, accessible to Atlanta on I-985 but with huge Lake Sidney Lanier close by. From its Civil War heritage in the hills, from its cultural conservatism in the carpet country, from the economic conservatism of its affluent new migrants in Forsyth County and around Gainesville, the 9th District is heavily Republican in national elections, by some measures second only to the very affluent 6th District. But it has not even come close to electing a Republican congressman in the 20th Century. Traditionally, its congressman was the textile industry's leading backer on the Ways and Means Committee: this was true of Phil Landrum, first elected in 1952, and his successor, Ed Jenkins, first elected in 1976. Jenkins, who passed textile protection bills in the House by wide but not veto-proof margins in 1985, 1986 and 1990, and who pushed a capital gains cut through Ways and Means in 1989, was disappointed in efforts to move up in the party leadership and retired in 1992.

Three Democrats and four Republicans ran for the seat; both parties had runoffs. Much attention was attracted by Republican Daniel Becker, who ran 30-minute infomercials which showed abortions in each trimester from the perspective of a fetus; "abortion stops a beating heart and that is murder," he said. Becker led in the sparse-turnout Republican primary and won the runoff 53%–47%. Meanwhile state Senator Nathan Deal of Gainesville led Tom Ramsey of the Chattanooga area 45%–35% in the Democrats' first primary and carried the eastern and central part of the district in the runoff, winning 55%–45%. Countering Becker, Deal insisted, "Abortion is not in the political arena, it is a personal decision," and stressed his own conservative economic platform—the balanced budget amendment, a congressional pay freeze, the line-item veto, a capital gains tax cut, a law requiring cost assessment of every piece of legislation. A prosecutor and judge in Gainesville in the 1970s, Deal was elected to the state Senate in 1980 and was a committee chairman and leader there. His political skills and perhaps Becker's bizarre appeals enabled Deal to carry a district that went handily for George Bush by a 49%–35% margin. Deal is likely to be one of the more conservative Democrats in the House. He sought a seat on Ways and Means, but Chairman Dan Rostenkowski declined to honor a 9th District tradition, and Deal sits on Public Works, Natural Resources, and Science, Space and Technology instead.

The People: Pop. 1990: 586,310; 78% rural; 12% age 65+; 94% White; 4% Black; 1% Other; 1% Hispanic origin. Voting age pop.: 436,627; 3% Black; 1% Hispanic origin. Households: 66% married couple families; 31% married couple fams. w. children; 30% college educ.; median household income: $26,581; per capita income: $12,027; median gross rent: $365; median house value: $62,200.

1992 Presidential Vote		1988 Presidential Vote	
Bush (R)	98,205 (49%)	Bush (R)	109,872 (70%)
Clinton (D)	70,943 (35%)	Dukakis (D)	46,007 (30%)
Perot (I)	32,808 (16%)		

Rep. Nathan Deal (D)

Elected 1992; b. Aug. 25, 1942, Washington; home, Gainesville; Mercer U., B.A. 1964, J.D. 1966; Baptist; married (Sandra).

Career: Army, 1966–68; Hall Cnty. Atty., 1966–70; Asst. Dist. Atty., NE Judicial Circuit, 1970–71; Hall Cnty. Juvenile Court Judge, 1971–72; Practicing atty., 1971–92; GA Senate, 1980–92, Pres. Pro Tem, 1991–92.

Offices: 1406 LHOB 20515, 202-225-5211. Also 311 Green St., Gainesville 30503, 404-535-2592; 307 Selvidge St., Dalton 30720, 706-226-5320; and 109 N. Main St., LaFayette 30728, 706-638-7042.

Committees: *Natural Resources* (21st of 28 D): Energy and Mineral Resources; Oversight and Investigations. *Public Works and Transportation* (33d of 39 D): Economic Development; Water Resources and Environment. *Science, Space and Technology* (29th of 33 D): Technology, Environment and Aviation.

Group Ratings and 102d Congress Votes: Newly Elected

Key Votes of the 103d Congress

1. Family Leave	AGN	2. Deficit Reduction	AGN	3. Stimulus Plan	FOR

Election Results

1992 general	Nathan Deal (D)...................	113,024	(59%)	($542,479)
	Daniel Becker (R)...................	77,919	(41%)	($161,060)
1992 runoff	Nathan Deal (D)...................	43,275	(55%)	
	Tom Ramsey (D)...................	35,213	(45%)	
1992 primary	Nathan Deal (D)...................	40,634	(45%)	
	Tom Ramsey (D)...................	31,058	(35%)	
	Wyc Orr (D).......................	17,725	(20%)	
1990 general	Ed Jenkins (D)	96,197	(56%)	($318,247)
	Joe Hoffman (R)...................	76,121	(44%)	($134,772)

TENTH DISTRICT

Heading south from Atlanta, General Sherman and his Union troops avoided the towns of central Georgia—fortunately preserving a couple of America's loveliest small cities, Augusta and Athens. Augusta is known for the golf course where the Masters' tournament is held every year; it is proud as well of the antique Medical College of Georgia, dating to 1835, and its new Riverwalk where the old levee used to be. Once a cotton port on the Savannah River with its own Cotton Exchange, Augusta has built a paper industry, stoked by the pines that grow in profusion on the flat Piedmont land, and has grown out into adjoining counties. Athens, on a bluff over a river, is the home of the University of Georgia and site of one of America's finest collection of Greek Revival buildings—gleaming white columns, perfectly proportioned little Parthenons, flat-roofed four square houses surrounded by fluted columns with Corinthian capitals, all dating from the 1830s to the 1850s. Athens too has been spreading outward, another little Atlanta.

The 10th Congressional District of Georgia takes in Athens and the surrounding area and the white precincts of Augusta and its suburbs. It stretches north toward the north Georgia mountains and east to take in the eastern end of fast-growing Gwinnett County, just outside Atlanta. This was once an almost entirely rural expanse, but now is increasingly metropolitan, with subdivisions and shopping centers springing up at interchanges. Politically, this was conservative Democratic country, the home base of longtime (1933–71) Senator Richard Russell. But its fastest-growing areas are affluent and Republican. Gwinnett County is one of the most Republican large counties in the country; the white suburbs of Augusta are heavily Republican; and while Athens, a pale replica of the liberalism of Northeastern university towns, votes Democratic, the two fast-growing counties beyond go Republican. This is a district that, as redistricted for 1992, gave a plurality of votes to George Bush. Yet it voted Democratic in the open seat contest created by the retirement of conservative Democrat and House Banking Committee member Doug Barnard.

The Democratic victory owes much to the political skills and strength of Don Johnson. From rural Hart County where his father prosecuted Ku Klux Klan members in the 1960s, Johnson was a House Ways and Means Committee staffer in the 1970s, then lawyer in a big Atlanta firm, and in 1982 returned home to Royston to practice law with his father. He was elected to the state Senate in 1987 and in 1990 became chairman of the Appropriations Committee. To win the 10th District seat, Johnson first had to beat an incumbent in the Democratic primary: Ben Jones, elected in 1988 and 1990 in a district entirely in the Atlanta suburbs, known nationally as the actor who played Cooter in *The Dukes of Hazzard*. But Jones had no good choices after redistricting, in which Johnson played a major role. Southern DeKalb County, heavily black and Democratic, was taken away from Jones's old 4th District and put in the new black-majority 11th, leaving the new 4th too Republican for his taste; and his residence was in the westernmost end of the new 10th. But metro Atlanta cast few votes in the Democratic primary, and Johnson won without a runoff in a five-candidate field, 53%–30%. (Jones went on to draft a proposal for a TV series based on his first term in Congress.) The Republicans also had a five-candidate primary, with fundamentalist-backed Ralph Hudgens, a former propane business owner and USDA official, leading Augusta area state Senator Frank Albert 32%–27%. In the runoff, Albert won the Augusta area, but Hudgens won by enough in Gwinnett, Athens and the sparse-voting rural counties to win 54%–46%.

In the general, editorial comment heavily favored Johnson, who in the state Senate helped cut the budget while increasing percentages for education and the elderly and expanded toll-free phone service to 129 counties. Despite his political experience, Johnson sounded the note of an outsider, favoring term limits, rotation of leadership positions, supporting ethics legislation and opposing pay increases and special treatment of Congress under the law. But for all his advantages, Johnson did not win by much. The Augusta area, which cast nearly one-third of the vote, went 58% for Hudgens and Gwinnett gave him 57%. Johnson's win of the Athens area with 60% and the rural counties with 62% was enough only for a 54%–46% win. In Washington, Johnson got seats on the Armed Services and Science Committees; he says, "My main interest is technology and technology policy and the role it will play in our economic growth." With his Republican-leaning district and conservative platform, Johnson may prove to be a key vote on many issues in the Clinton years.

The People: Pop. 1990: 591,706; 53% rural; 10% age 65+; 80% White; 18% Black; 1% Asian; 1% Hispanic origin. Voting age pop.: 438,211; 16% Black; 1% Hispanic origin. Households: 60% married couple families; 29% married couple fams. w. children; 37% college educ.; median household income: $27,553; per capita income: $12,550; median gross rent: $390; median house value: $67,200.

1992 Presidential Vote			1988 Presidential Vote		
Bush (R)	99,336	(47%)	Bush (R)	104,251	(66%)
Clinton (D)	81,960	(39%)	Dukakis (D)	53,059	(34%)
Perot (I)	30,662	(14%)			

Rep. Don Johnson (D)

Elected 1992; b. Jan. 30, 1948, Royston; home, Royston; U. of GA, B.A. 1970, U. of GA Law Schl., J.D. 1973, London Schl. of Economics, M.A. 1978; Baptist; married (Suzanne).

Career: Air Force, 1973–77; Staff atty., U.S. House Ways & Means Cmte., 1973; Cnsl., Continental IL Natl. Bank, 1978–80; Practicing atty., 1982–92; GA Senate 1987–92.

Offices: 226 CHOB 20515, 202-225-4101. Also 220 College Ave., #400, Athens 30606, 706-353-6444.

Committees: *Armed Services* (23d of 34 D): Military Installations and Facilities; Oversight and Investigations; Research and Technology. *Science, Space and Technology* (23d of 33 D): Investigations and Oversight; Science; Technology, Environment and Aviation.

Group Ratings and 102d Congress Votes: Newly Elected

Key Votes of the 103d Congress

1. Family Leave	AGN	2. Deficit Reduction	FOR	3. Stimulus Plan	FOR

Election Results

1992 general	Don Johnson (D)........................	108,426	(54%)	($622,590)
	Ralph Hudgens (R).....................	93,059	(46%)	($182,637)
1992 primary	Don Johnson (D)........................	45,891	(53%)	
	Ben Jones (D)	25,924	(30%)	
	Marc Wetherhorn (D)..................	5,250	(6%)	
	Doug Bower (D)	5,018	(6%)	
	Chuck Pardue (D).....................	4,848	(6%)	
1990 general	Doug Barnard, Jr. (D).................	89,683	(58%)	($937,464)
	Sam Jones (R).........................	64,184	(42%)	($154,326)

ELEVENTH DISTRICT

It was the intention of James Oglethorpe, the philanthropist founder of Georgia, that this 13th of the North American colonies do without slaves. It was not to be. The new colony, like all the others, had a hard time attracting labor, and by 1750 slavery was permitted. In antebellum times, after Eli Whitney's cotton gin made cotton a monstrously profitable crop, Georgia's seacoast was settled in slave plantations, and slaves were common in southwest and central Georgia within a triangle formed by the third state capital of Milledgeville, the fourth capital of Atlanta and the second capital, the old cotton town at the fall line of the Savannah River named after King George III's mother, Augusta. For many years after the War Between the States, most freed blacks remained where they were; black immigration to Atlanta was limited and to the North was a trickle until the 1940s. In the next decades, blacks as well as whites flocked to Atlanta and in large numbers worked their way up in the city that was clearly the capital of the South and of the civil rights movement. Atlanta became a black-majority central city, and beginning in the 1970s affluent blacks in very large numbers moved east of the city to comfortable new subdivisions in southern DeKalb County. Interestingly, DeKalb's half-black, half-white schools were the subject of a long busing case which the Supreme Court in 1989 allowed to be dismissed; there does not seem to be great demand for busing students back and forth around the county to seek equal racial numbers in each school.

The 11th Congressional District of Georgia, the state's second black-majority district to be created after the 1990 Census, includes parts of the state recalling all these eras in local black history. Geographically, it is a monstrosity, stretching from Atlanta to Savannah. Its core is the plantation country in the center of the state, lightly populated, but heavily black. It links by narrow corridors the black neighborhoods in Augusta, Savannah and southern DeKalb County. Its population is 64% black and it is heavily Democratic. It elected a new Democratic representative, but its syphoning of blacks from the 1st District in Savannah and the 4th District in DeKalb County helped Republicans gain both of those seats.

The real competition here came in the five-candidate Democratic primary. The initial favorite was DeKalb state Senator Gene Walker, but prior to the primary he was fined for accepting campaign contributions during the legislative session, and his endorsement by Governor Zell Miller was offset by DeKalb state Representative Cynthia McKinney's charge that he was part of a "good ol' boy" network. McKinney led Walker 45%–41% in DeKalb and 31%–22% district-wide. In second place with 25% was George DeLoach, former mayor of Waynesboro, who is white. Another legislator, Michael Thurmond, got one-quarter of the vote in the central part of the district, but almost nothing in DeKalb and finished fourth with 16%. McKinney won the runoff against DeLoach, largely along race lines, 56%–44%; she won the general election with a fair number of whites' votes, 73%–27% and became Georgia's first black woman elected to Congress.

Professionally, McKinney is a political scientist and graduate student (she is working on her Ph.D. at the Fletcher School of Diplomacy at Tufts). But she is also a successful practical politician. Her father J.E. "Billy" McKinney has served in the legislature since 1973 and after she was elected in 1988 they were the only father-daughter legislative team in the country; their one notable fight was over Georgia's sodomy law. She is also a daughter of the civil rights revolution, just 10 when the Voting Rights Act was passed; in the legislature, she criticized Governor Zell Miller for not sending enough contracts to minority business enterprises, and refused to acquiesce in redistricting plans she thought didn't have enough black-majority districts. She got a seat on the redistricting committee and worked long and hard to put together the three black-majority districts. She wanted to increase the state gas tax to fund an urban commuter rail and opposed a major landfill in black-majority Hancock County as "environmental racism"; she took to the state House floor in 1991 to denounce the Gulf war resolution. She carried to Washington a "reputation as a barn burner" and says she admires Maxine Waters and Newt Gingrich—two fighters. She serves on the Agriculture Committee and on Foreign Affairs, and takes an interest in health care issues—her mother was a nurse at Grady Memorial Hospital for almost 40 years.

The People: Pop. 1990: 585,341; 29% rural; 10% age 65+; 34% White; 64% Black; 1% Asian; 1% Hispanic origin. Voting age pop.: 412,740; 60% Black; 1% Hispanic origin. Households: 48% married couple families; 24% married couple fams. w. children; 35% college educ.; median household income: $24,763; per capita income: $10,381; median gross rent: $409; median house value: $58,200.

1992 Presidential Vote			1988 Presidential Vote		
Clinton (D)	121,356	(67%)	Dukakis (D)	92,497	(63%)
Bush (R)	44,419	(24%)	Bush (R)	55,354	(37%)
Perot (I)	15,676	(9%)			

Rep. Cynthia A. McKinney (D)

Elected 1992; b. Mar. 17, 1955, Atlanta; home, Lithonia; U. of Southern CA, B.A. 1978; Catholic; divorced.

Career: Diplomatic Fellow, Spellman Col., 1984; GA House of Reps., 1988–92; Atlanta Bd. of Health Svcs. Plng. Cncl., 1990–92; Adjunct Prof., Agnes Scott Women's Col., 1991–92.

Offices: 124 CHOB 20515, 202-225-1605. Also One S. DeKalb Ctr., #9, 2853 Candler Rd., Decatur 30034,

Committees: *Agriculture* (22d of 28 D): Department Operations and Nutrition; Environment, Credit and Rural Development; Foreign Agriculture and Hunger. *Foreign Affairs* (18th of 27 D): Economic Policy, Trade and Environment; Western Hemisphere Affairs.

Group Ratings and 102d Congress Votes: Newly Elected

Key Votes of the 103d Congress

1. Family Leave	FOR	2. Deficit Reduction	FOR	3. Stimulus Plan	FOR

Election Results

1992 general	Cynthia A. McKinney (D)	120,168	(73%)	($306,978)
	Woodrow Lovett (R)....................	44,221	(27%)	($26,721)
1992 runoff	Cynthia A. McKinney (D)	39,301	(56%)	
	George L. DeLoach (D)	30,389	(44%)	
1992 primary	Cynthia A. McKinney (D)	26,160	(31%)	
	George L. DeLoach (D)	21,122	(25%)	
	Gene Walker (D).......................	18,805	(22%)	
	Mike Thurmond (D)...................	13,313	(16%)	
	Verdree Lockhart (D)..................	4,468	(5%)	
1990 election	Newly created district.			

HAWAII

A century ago, in January 1893, American planters and businessmen, with the help of U.S. Marines, ousted Queen Liliuokalani from the Iolani Palace and overthrew the monarchy established by King Kamehameha to unite the Islands and keep them from western control. These new landlords called on the United States to annex Hawaii, but incoming President Grover Cleveland was appalled at what he called an act of war against this peaceful nation, and Hawaii became a republic until it was annexed by President William McKinley in July 1898. In January 1993, in memory of these events, the Iolani Palace was draped in black and students of Hawaiian descent dressed in white marched beneath the Capitol where only the flag of Hawaii waved. This *Onipa'a* ceremony was arranged by Governor John Waihee, Hawaii's first governor of Hawaiian descent (also Chinese, English, Irish), as an assertion of native Hawaiian pride (tourists were advised to stay away); and as a sentimental gesture to a people whose culture has been transformed, and who now tend to be near the low end of Hawaii's economic ladder, it can be appreciated. But this can go too far: the suggestion by some extremists that Hawaiian Natives be treated like mainland Indians is a suggestion to move from a society that works to one that does not.

For Hawaii, with all its oddness and some of its recent discomforts, is a civilization both American and Pacific which has created a better life for its citizens than almost any of the island and native commonwealths that existed when Queen Liliuokalani was overthrown. Hawaii's diversity comes largely from the years just after annexation, when planters imported thousands of farm workers from the Philippines, Portugal, China, Korea and especially Japan; by 1910, nearly one-third its population was of Japanese descent, about the same figure as today. Hawaii's *Aloha* spirit gave newcomers as warm a welcome as anywhere on earth. Yet the Hawaii Territory was clearly western as well, though only a minority of its people were of European ancestry: when Pearl Harbor was attacked by the Japanese in December 1941, no one in Hawaii or on the mainland doubted that it was America that was attacked; and when the 442d "Go for Broke" Regimental Combat Team was formed, mostly of sons of Japanese immigrants, and soon became the part of the most decorated unit in U.S. military history, no one could doubt that these were Americans fighting. Ironically, it was Hawaii's super-American tolerance that inspired segregationist southern Democrats to block its admission to the Union for years. Today, Hawaiians retain pride in their ethnic heritage—or heritages: for 44% of non-military weddings are "out" marriages and 60% of babies born are of mixed racial background; in 1989, the state gave up trying to tabulate the ethnic origin of its legislators. The sensible future for Hawaii is not to create enclaves or racial preference for the 12% who call themselves Hawaiians or the 21%

who have some Hawaiian ancestry, but to nurture and sustain the special strengths and remember the contributions of all the peoples who have made Hawaii tolerant and affluent—just as Hawaii, to protect the 10,000 species which can be found nowhere else, needs not to put them under glass but to maintain the special environment which has enabled them to flourish.

Hawaii's economy was built first on farming and then on the military, and the Big Five trading companies and big growers like Dole remain important; mid-Pacific, Hawaii remains a key military site, as it has been since Pearl Harbor was built up in 1941. Nearly 10% of paychecks here are issued by the Department of Defense. But the real engine of Hawaii's growth and prosperity is tourism. For a period in the early 1990s, unemployment hovered around just 3% as 1.1 million Hawaiians hosted nearly 7 million tourists every year. In 1992 and 1993, the lingering recessions in California and Japan lead to a decrease in tourism, and Hawaii's unemployment rate edged up to just under 5%. And tourism itself is no cure-all: many tourism jobs are low-wage, and Hawaiians worry that educated young people will go to the mainland to find high-skill work. And there is a certain separatism: visitors from Japan, tourists from the Mainland and residents of Hawaii seem to have little to do with each other. But some problems are in time solved. A few years ago, many were squawking that Japanese investors had bid up real estate prices so high that Hawaiians couldn't afford housing and middle-class tourists couldn't afford rooms. But the Japanese bubble burst and those prices turned out to be unsustainable; real estate is now starting to stabilize, and in the meantime some Hawaiians got nice windfalls. With low unemployment, the tax burden has been dropping despite a welfare-state-minded political leadership, and many small businesses still get started here.

Obvious possibilities for diversification beyond tourism exist: ocean research, on these islands that are the tips of volcanic peaks; astronomy, in this land of clear air; securities markets, in one of the few inhabited places where it's daytime during the four hours when the New York Stock Exchange has closed and Tokyo has not yet opened. After all, Hawaii has American political stability and is sensitive to East Asian ways; it has first-rate transportation and communication facilities. It is a place where you can get Korean *kal bi* ribs on the same menu as hamburgers, where Filipino *lumpia*, Portuguese bread, and *poi* are staples; where Japanese holidays, religions, names and customs are all familiar.

As it seeks new growth, Hawaii needs to avoid being hurt by two special characteristics it shares with no other state. The first is its large landholdings, a product of its native and royal past. Eight public and private entities own 70% of Hawaii's land: the federal government 16%, the state 29%, six private landowners 25%. The Bishop Estate (Mrs. Bishop was the last surviving member of the Hawaiian royal family) owns 8% of the state's land; its five trustees, appointed by the state Supreme Court for life and paid $648,000 a year, are supposed to spend all the Estate's huge income on the Kamehameha School for native Hawaiians. State government has been controlled by essentially the same Democratic machine since 1962, which clinched control of the Bishop Estate board in the 1980s. Most of this land is held on long-term leaseholds; since a state law forcing outright sales was upheld by the U.S. Supreme Court in 1984, the Bishop Estate has sought to diversify, buying a $250 million stake in Goldman Sachs, for example. That presumably will lessen the chance for long-term planning and major developments like the geothermal energy projects on the Big Island.

The second peculiar characteristic of Hawaii is its *Aloha* spirit. Hawaiians want to be Americans—if they didn't, the islands would have become independent, as the Philippines did, or might have sought a separate status, like Puerto Rico. But they have always had, in accentuated form, the tolerance of diversity that is a keynote of the American experience, and each group's traditions still remain distinctive. The Japanese, the largest single migrant group after whites (who are sometimes called *haoles*), are by most measures the most successful, doing well in professions and organizations such as unions, government and the Democratic Party. Whites still tend to have the highest incomes: many came to Hawaii after success on the mainland. Filipinos for some years have tended to fill menial jobs; native Hawaiians have tended to have lower incomes and to have special medical and legal benefits. Politically, the whites have

tended to be Republican, and Japanese and other groups, heavily Democratic.

Hawaii's dominant political institution is the Democratic Party which, under a single chain of leadership, has welded Hawaii's disparate groups together to win elections since territorial days. It had its beginning in the 1950s when returning World War II veterans like Daniel Inouye, Spark Matsunaga and George Ariyoshi joined forces with former mainlander John Burns, who as a policeman during the war helped prevent persecution of Japanese Americans. They allied themselves with the then powerful International Longshoremen's and Warehousemen's Union, and cemented the allegiance of Japanese American voters. In the 1950s, Hawaii, resenting mainland southern Democratic senators, tended to vote Republican. But Inouye was elected to the House as a Democrat in 1959 and the Senate in 1962, and Republicans have won few elections since. Burns was elected governor in 1962 and retired because of illness in 1974; his chosen successor, George Ariyoshi, won in 1974, 1978 and 1982, and retired when he was ineligible for another term. In time, Inouye split with Ariyoshi, and the ILWU's power waned; the machine became centered on the governor's office and the patronage it controlled from state judgeships to the trusteeship of the Bishop Estate. But the succession continued: John Waihee was Ariyoshi's man in 1986, and won after a rough campaign. There are echoes here of a Pacific Rim political style—cool, competent, tough, unsentimental; Hawaii is one of the few states to prohibit write-in votes, a law the Supreme Court upheld in 1992. Republicans have complained about the injustices of one-party rule. This is overblown: there is no threat to political or civil liberties. But in a state where power tends to be centralized, politics is played for keeps.

Governor. John Waihee, the latest in a line of governors from the same Democratic faction going back to 1962, is ineligible to run for another term in 1994. He came to office with elbows out, beating Congressman Cecil Heftel 46%–36% in the primary with some tough negative ads. In the general, he narrowly, 52%–48%, beat Republican Andy Anderson, an ally of longtime Honolulu Mayor Frank Fasi, who has held that office since 1968 except for 1980–84 and has been, first as a Democrat and then as a Republican, a vociferous opponent of the gubernatorial faction. Waihee's 1990 reelection was more placid. As the first governor of Hawaiian descent, his major achievements include, a revival of the Native Hawaiian culture, culminating in *Onipa'a*. He tried to spur building of more housing units, including subsidized rentals and homes for the elderly. He also maintained and extended Hawaii's unique health insurance system, enacted in the mid-1970s: the Hawaiian system requires employers to buy for employees a basic policy, coverage for which is provided by or equal to that of the two big insurers in the state, Blue Cross/Blue Shield and Kaiser Permanente, which compete robustly and between them cover over 75% of the market. The state pays for insurance for the relatively few unemployed. The results have not been entirely satisfactory—costs have been rising at 10% a year and there has been some queuing—and it's not clear that the plan is replicable elsewhere, since few if any other states are such a discrete market and are already nearly universally served by just two big units. But in health care, as in race relations and other areas, Hawaii has things to teach the rest of the country.

The succession to Waihee will probably be fought out in the Democratic primary, with Lieutenant Governor Ben Cayetano, who is of Filipino descent, the clear front-runner. For the Republicans, former Representative Pat Saiki has announced her intention to run and Mayor Frank Fasi is running, though he may do so as an Independent.

Senators. The dominant figure in Hawaii politics for longer than most Hawaii voters can remember has been Senator Daniel Inouye, the only politician who has held major office in Hawaii since statehood in 1960. He was a severely wounded veteran of the 442d Regimental Combat Team, then became a lawyer, and was elected to the state legislature in 1954, the House in 1959 and the Senate in 1962. He has become a nationally visible politician as well, the keynoter at the 1968 Democratic National Convention and a tenacious member of the Senate Watergate committee in 1973-1974. He was the first chairman of the Senate Intelligence Committee, in 1976.

What does he believe in? For one thing, the Senate and its prerogatives. When others have scurried to denounce incumbents accused in scandal, Inouye has stepped forward to defend them, as he did with Senator Harrison Williams, charged in 1982 with bribery in the Abscam scandal. He stood up during the 1990 Keating Five hearings and spoke out for Dennis DeConcini: "What is on trial here is not the five colleagues of mine but the U.S. Senate and for that matter the Congress of the United States." When in 1979 to 1986 he was secretary of the Democratic Conference, the number three position in the party leadership, he seemed headed for the position of Senate majority leader. Indeed, if Robert Byrd could have handed it over to him he might have, since Inouye did not challenge him during his tenure. But Inouye refrained from rounding up votes until Byrd announced in April 1988 he was relinquishing the post, while George Mitchell and Bennett Johnston had already started their campaigns. On the secret ballot, Inouye had only 14 votes, the same as Johnston, while Mitchell had 27, at which point everyone agreed to dispense with a second ballot. The fifth most senior member of the Senate, Inouye has not chaired a major standing committee; as chairman of the Select Committee on Indian Affairs, he was able in 1993 to pass legislation which allowed "Select" to be dropped from the committee name, thus saving it from the demise met by other select committees. He ranks number two on both Appropriations and Commerce and, interestingly, has signed on to Nancy Kassebaum's proposal to abolish the Appropriations Committee and give the appropriating power to the authorizing committees instead.

On foreign policy, Inouye for many years supported an interventionist, even hawkish policy. But by the 1980s, he opposed Republican administrations on Central America, Lebanon and Grenada, and harshly criticized Oliver North and others at the Iran-contra hearings; he also voted against the Gulf war resolution. But as chairman of the Defense Appropriations Subcommittee, he is not as much a defense-cutter as some Democrats would be. He continues to be active on foreign aid, backing larger appropriations than his House counterpart David Obey. He is strongly supportive of Israel and was criticized in 1987 when it was revealed he had inserted in an appropriations bill a small sum (which was later rescinded) to construct schools in France for North African Jewish refugees. For Hawaii, he secured $1.2 billion in aid after Hurricane Iniki struck Kauai in September 1991. He is concerned about NAFTA provisions allowing Mexico to compete with Hawaii on sugar. He wants the island of Kahoolawe, used by the Navy as a target range until 1990, returned to the state and restored to its original pristine condition.

On the Commerce Committee, Inouye backed cable reregulation and is deeply involved in communication issues; he wants to allocate the frequency spectrum by auction. He is deeply concerned about American Indians and, from his chair on Indian Affairs, he pushed hard to get part of the American Indian museum collection, located at three sites in New York City, transferred to a new building on the Smithsonian's Mall. In 1990, he got $2 million for a drug-free schools program for American Indians and Hawaiian natives; in the 1990 crime bill, he also got Indian reservations exempted from the federal death penalty—although individuals there are still subject to tribal law. He is also sympathetic to the claim of Native Hawaiians for some form of sovereignty and sponsored the 1988 Native Hawaiian Health Care Act.

For a time in the early 1990s, Inouye seemed more popular and powerful in Hawaii than ever before. After tiffs with Ariyoshi, he strongly supported John Waihee for governor in 1986, and Waihee won. In 1990, he put all his weight behind Daniel Akaka, appointed to fill the vacancy caused by the death of Senator Spark Matsunaga, when Akaka was trailing in the polls; Akaka won, and by a larger margin than expected. But Inouye did not fare as well in the 1992 campaign as he has in the past. He found himself opposed by brash Republican legislator Rick Reed, who started a newspaper in Maui in the 1970s and defended himself successfully in a libel suit by an alleged organized crime figure. Reed ran against Inouye by characterizing him as a Washington insider and defender of the Keating Five. He also ran an ad with tapes of a woman barber, Lenore Kwock, who had cut Inouye's hair for 20 years, in which she accused Inouye of forcing himself on her sexually some 17 years ago. Kwock did not deny the charges but said she was taped without her consent and demanded the ad be pulled, and it was; Reed was criticized by Fasi and other Republicans. Inouye's poll numbers were far lower than in the past, and on election day he won by a comfortable, though reduced margin, with 57% of the vote, to 27% for Reed and 14% for the Green Party's Linda Martin. After the election, Democratic state Representative Annelle Amaral said she received calls from nine women alleging sexual harassment by Inouye. The issue was referred to the Senate Ethics Committee, but Lenore Kwock opted not to file a complain and none of Amaral's alleged complaintants would come forward; Amaral apologized to Inouye, and the Ethics Committee dropped the case in April 1993.

Daniel Akaka, congressman since 1976, loyal member of the Democratic machine and a Native Hawaiian, was appointed to the Senate by Governor Waihee after the death in April 1990 of Spark Matsunaga. A 442d Regiment veteran, Matsunaga will be remembered for almost single-handedly passing the law to provide redress for the West Coast Japanese Americans interned during World War II, with $20,000 payments to each camp survivor and a formal apology for what was clearly an unjustified violation of constitutional rights. In the House, Akaka had been a quiet member of the Appropriations Committee; in the Senate, looking to the 1990 special election, he managed to halt the use of Kahoolawe Island as a test bombing range. Republican Congresswoman Pat Saiki, also running for the Senate seat, got President Bush to issue an executive order halting the bombing, but Akaka trumped her with a provision in an appropriations bill to ban it. Akaka also introduced two amendments to the crime bill for stiffer penalties for use and distribution of "ice," a drug even more addictive than cocaine that came to Hawaii from Korea and Taiwan. Saiki conceded that Akaka was congenial but suggested he was ineffective and not too bright, a charge that had some credibility since he had served in the House for 13 years without attracting much attention. But Akaka fought back hard, with a media campaign stressing his drug and bombing range amendments, with endorsements from environmental groups, and with a Democratic organizational effort as strong as any Hawaii has seen in years. Akaka won 54%–45%, carrying not just the Democratic Neighbor Islands and poorer areas of Honolulu, but most of Oahu as well.

Since 1990, Akaka has worked on the Energy Committee to pass a Hawaiian tropical forest recovery initiative, a law to stop the introduction of alien species to Hawaii, a law to combat the brown tree snake, and the establishment of the Spark Matsunaga Renewable Energy and Ocean Technology Center at Keahole Point. As chairman of the Mineral Resources Subcommittee, he will have jurisdiction over the hot issue of revising the Mining Act of 1872 to impose mineral royalties. Akaka's seat comes up again in 1994, when he turns 70, and he says he will seek another term. Since Pat Saiki is running for governor, it is unclear who Akaka's general opponent will be, though a Republican is almost always an underdog in Hawaii.

Presidential politics. Two countervailing forces have been at play in presidential elections in Hawaii over the years: a strong Democratic partisan preference, plus an inclination to support incumbents. They help explain why Hawaii went Democratic when most states didn't in 1980 and 1988, but why it supported Presidents Nixon and Reagan solidly in 1972 and 1984 and nearly voted for President Ford in 1976. These tendencies make a certain sense: Hawaii is Democratic because it favors big government on economic issues and tolerance of diversity on cultural issues; it is pro-incumbent because it takes patriotism very seriously, in part because the patriotism of so many of its citizens was once unjustly questioned, and in part because, out here in these heavily fortified Pacific islands, foreign threats seem more menacing. Hawaii's solid 48%–37% vote for Bill Clinton over George Bush would seem to be an exception to the rule. But exit polling indicates that Bush's poor showing was due, as in California and the Pacific Northwest, to a collapse of the Republican vote among affluent whites: the white vote was 48%–32% for Clinton, while it was 42%–41% for Republican Rick Reed over Senator Daniel Inouye. But the Asian vote, which is mostly Japanese American, went only 50%–43% for Clinton, despite its usual strong Democratic preference, apparent in its 77%–17% vote for Inouye; Japanese American support for the commander-in-chief is still strong. Others, mainly Native Hawaiians and Filipinos, were solidly Democratic in both races: 61%–28% for Clinton, 73%–21% for Inouye. In any case, all indicators point to a Clinton victory here in 1996, whatever happens on the Mainland.

Hawaii chooses presidential delegates by caucus. In 1992, they quietly opted for Bill Clinton and George Bush—a contrast from 1988, when the Democrats' choice was Jesse Jackson and the Republican state party establishment, finding its membership ranks swelled by Pat Robertson supporters, canceled a scheduled straw poll for a week, but then let Robertson win.

Congressional districting. Hawaii has two congressional districts: the 1st includes urban Honolulu (city elections now cover all of Oahu) and extends westward to Pearl Harbor and the rural area beyond; the 2d includes the rest of Oahu and the Neighbor Islands. Redistricting by a bipartisan commission changed the lines only slightly. Both districts are represented by liberal Democrats who had served in the past, then lost elections, ran again and won in 1990 and were reelected with 73% of the vote in 1992.

The People: Est. Pop. 1992: 1,160,000; Pop. 1990: 1,108,229, up 4.5% 1990–1992. 0.4% of U.S. total, 41st largest; 11% rural. Median age: 32.6 years. 11.3% 65 years and over. 61.8% Asian, 33.4% White, 7.3% Hispanic origin, 2.5% Black, 1.9% Other. Households: 59.1% married couple families; 29% married couple fams. w. children; 51% college educ.; median household income: $38,829; per capita income: $15,770; 53.9% owner occupied housing; median house value: $245,300; median monthly rent: $599. 4.5% Unemployment. Voting age pop.: 828,103. Registered voters (1992): 464,495; no party registration.

Political Lineup: Governor, John D. Waihee, III (D); Lt. Gov., Benjamin Cayetano (D); Atty. Gen., Robert Marks (D); Comptroller, Robert P. Takushi (D). State Senate, 25 (22 D and 3 R); State House of Representatives, 51 (47 D and 4 R). Senators, Daniel K. Inouye (D) and Daniel K. Akaka (D). Representatives, 2 D.

1992 Presidential Vote

Clinton (D) 179,310 (48%)
Bush (R) 136,822 (37%)
Perot (I) 53,003 (14%)

1988 Presidential Vote

Dukakis (D) 192,364 (54%)
Bush (R) 158,625 (45%)

GOVERNOR

Gov. John D. Waihee III (D)

Elected 1986, term expires Dec. 1994; b. May 19, 1946, Honokaa; home, Honolulu; Andrews U., B.A. 1968, U. of HI, J.D. 1976; no religious affiliation; married (Lynne).

Career: Comm. Educ. Coord. & Dir., Benton Harbor, MI, 1968–71; Program Planner, Honolulu Model Cities, 1971–73; Program Mgr., Honolulu Office of Human Resources, 1973–74; Practicing atty., 1976–82; HI House of Reps., 1980–82; HI Lt. Gov., 1982–86.

Office: State Capitol, Executive Chambers, Honolulu 96813, 808-548-5420.

Election Results

1990 gen.	John D. Waihee III (D)	203,491	(60%)
	Fred Hemmings (R)	131,310	(39%)
	Two Others	5,331	(2%)
1990 prim.	John D. Waihee III (D)	179,383	(88%)
	Benjamin Hopkins (D)	9,735	(5%)
	Robert H. Garner (D)	9,112	(4%)
	Other	4,517	(2%)
1986 gen.	John D. Waihee III (D)	173,655	(52%)
	D.G. Anderson (R)	160,460	(48%)

SENATORS

Sen. Daniel K. Inouye (D)

Elected 1962, seat up 1998; b. Sept. 7, 1924, Honolulu; home, Honolulu; U. of HI, B.A. 1950, George Washington U., J.D. 1952; United Methodist; married (Margaret).

Career: Army, 1943–47 (WWII); Honolulu Dep. Public Prosecutor, 1953–54; HI House of Reps., 1954–58; HI Senate, 1958–59; U.S. House of Reps., 1959–62.

Offices: 722 HSOB 20510, 202-224-3934. Also 7325 Prince Kuhio Fed. Bldg., 300 Ala Moana Blvd., Honolulu 96850, 808-541-2542.

Committees: *Appropriations* (2d of 16 D): Commerce, Justice, State and Judiciary; Defense (Chmn.); Foreign Operations; Labor, Health and Human Services, Education; Military Construction. *Commerce, Science and Transportation* (2d of 11 D): Aviation; Communications (Chmn.); Merchant Marine; Surface Transportation. *Indian Affairs* (Chmn. of 10 D). *Rules and Administration* (4th of 9 D).

Group Ratings

	ADA	ACLU	CDF	COPE	CFA	LCV	ACU	NTLC	NSI	COC	CEI
1992	65	95	80	92	92	42	4	11	50	10	17
1991	80	—	82	92	72	27	14	—	—	20	27

National Journal Ratings

	1991 LIB — 1991 CONS	1992 LIB — 1992 CONS
Economic	50% — 49%	78% — 21%
Social	83% — 16%	77% — 22%
Foreign	46% — 52%	40% — 59%

Key Votes of the 102d Congress

1. $ for Homeownership	AGN	5. Clarence Thomas Nom.	AGN	9. Use Force in Gulf	AGN
2. Have Cap Gains Debate	AGN	6. Lmt Death Row Appeal	AGN	10. Keep Salvador Aid	AGN
3. Remove Budget Walls	FOR	7. Handgun Wait/5-Day	FOR	11. Cut $1B from SDI	AGN
4. Ban Striker Replace	FOR	8. Abortion Gag Rule	AGN	12. Override China MFN	FOR

Key Votes of the 103d Senate

1. Family Leave	FOR	2. HIV Immigrants	FOR	3. Clinton Budget	*

Election Results

1992 general	Daniel K. Inouye (D)	208,266	(57%)	($3,515,722)
	Rick Reed (R)......................	97,928	(27%)	($438,851)
	Linda B. Martin (Green)	49,921	(14%)	($6,687)
	Other................................	7,547	(2%)	
1992 primary	Daniel K. Inouye (D)	94,827	(79%)	
	Wayne K. Nishiki (D)................	25,782	(21%)	
1986 general	Daniel K. Inouye (D)	241,887	(74%)	($1,039,418)
	Frank Hutchinson (R)................	86,910	(26%)	($31,843)

Sen. Daniel K. Akaka (D)

Appointed May, 1990, seat up 1994; b. Sept. 11, 1924, Honolulu; home, Honolulu; U. of HI, B.A. 1953, M.A. 1966; Congregationalist; married (Mary Mildred).

Career: Army Corps of Engineers, 1945–47 (WWII); Public schl. teacher, principal and admin., 1953–71; Dir., HI Office of Econ. Oppor., 1971–74; Asst., HI Gov. Ariyoshi, 1975–76; Dir., Progressive Neighborhoods Program, 1975–76; U.S. House of Reps., 1977–90.

Offices: 720 HSOB 20510, 202-224-6361. Also 3104 Prince Kuhio Fed. Bldg., 300 Ala Moana Blvd., Honolulu 96850, 808-541-2534.

Committees: *Energy and Natural Resources* (6th of 11 D): Mineral Resources Development and Production (Chmn.); Public Lands, National Parks and Forests; Renewable Energy, Energy Efficiency, and Competitiveness. *Governmental Affairs* (7th of 8 D): Federal Services, Post Office and Civil Service; General Services, Federalism and the District of Columbia; Oversight of Government Management. *Indian Affairs* (7th of 10 D). *Veterans' Affairs* (5th of 7 D).

Group Ratings

	ADA	ACLU	CDF	COPE	CFA	LCV	ACU	NTLC	NSI	COC	CEI
1992	90	100	100	92	92	92	0	5	20	20	15
1991	90	—	91	92	83	73	5	—	—	20	18

National Journal Ratings

	1991 LIB — 1991 CONS		1992 LIB — 1992 CONS	
Economic	75% —	21%	84% —	12%
Social	87% —	0%	69% —	26%
Foreign	63% —	33%	62% —	35%

Key Votes of the 102d Congress

1. $ for Homeownership AGN	5. Clarence Thomas Nom. AGN	9. Use Force in Gulf AGN
2. Have Cap Gains Debate AGN	6. Lmt Death Row Appeal AGN	10. Keep Salvador Aid AGN
3. Remove Budget Walls FOR	7. Handgun Wait/5-Day FOR	11. Cut $1B from SDI FOR
4. Ban Striker Replace FOR	8. Abortion Gag Rule AGN	12. Override China MFN FOR

Key Votes of the 103d Senate

1. Family Leave FOR	2. HIV Immigrants FOR	3. Clinton Budget FOR

Election Results

1990 general	Daniel K. Akaka (D)	188,901	(54%)	($1,691,384)
	Patricia Saiki (R)	155,978	(45%)	($2,398,961)
	Other	4,787	(1%)	
1990 primary	Daniel K. Akaka (D)	180,235	(91%)	
	Paul Snider (D)	18,427	(9%)	
1988 general	Spark M. Matsunaga (D)	247,941	(77%)	($494,580)
	Maria M. Hustace (R)	66,987	(21%)	($33,325)

FIRST DISTRICT

In Honolulu, most tourists see the airport and adjacent Hickam Air Force Base, the Arizona monument in Pearl Harbor, perhaps the downtown with its wondrously Victorian Iolani Palace and early 20th Century buildings amid high-rises, and of course Waikiki, with its 40-story hotels rising within a few feet of one another, its restaurants and souvenir shops. But few of Hawaii's 1st District voters live in any of these places. The neighborhoods around Honolulu's downtown and the university campus are lower income and usually Democratic. To the west, around the harbor, are many military families in modest neighborhoods who may vote for Democrats but can be attracted to Republicans. To the east, past Waikiki, around Diamond Head and out to the Kahala and Koko Head beach areas, is higher-income territory, voting for Republicans when they seriously contest a race.

The 1st District is represented by Neil Abercrombie, a Democrat with a distinctive style whose electoral history is a bit complicated. Abercrombie, in his mid 50s, still sports a beard and pony tail and dresses as informally as House rules allow. He would like to take a nation that has moved toward market economics and assertive foreign policies in just the opposite direction, toward a massive welfare state, if not socialism, and dismantle the military ("after a while, they're going to see that there's nowhere to go with all this stuff"); he has arguably the most liberal voting record in Congress. He is proud of passing a Humpback Whale Marine Sanctuary for Hawaii, a plutonium safety act, a renewal of the Native Hawaiian Health Care Act, and obtaining increased money for Child Advocacy Centers. Using his seat on Armed Services, he got authorization for building more military housing on one base, but ultimately wants more military lands turned over to the state.

Abercrombie's first stint in the House came in 1986, when he won a special election for the remainder of gubernatorial candidate Cecil Heftel's House term, and served three months; he lost the primary, after some flimsy charges that he used marijuana, to Mufi Hannemann, a Mormon native of Samoa and Harvard basketball player, who then lost the general election to Republican Pat Saiki. Abercrombie was elected to the Honolulu city council in 1988, and when

Saiki ran for the Senate in 1990, he won a three-way primary against state Senator Norman Mizuguchi and the late senator's son Matt Matsunaga 46%–32%–22%; he won the general 60%–39% against state House Minority Leader Mike Liu. He was easily reelected in 1992.

The People: Pop. 1990: 554,174; 12% age 65+; 29% White; 2% Black; 67% Asian; 1% Other; 5% Hispanic origin. Voting age pop.: 431,736; 2% Black; 4% Hispanic origin. Households: 58% married couple families; 26% married couple fams. w. children; 54% college educ.; median household income: $40,257; per capita income: $17,508; median gross rent: $659; median house value: $307,800.

1992 Presidential Vote			1988 Presidential Vote		
Clinton (D)	87,664	(47%)	Dukakis (D)	99,302	(54%)
Bush (R)	72,182	(39%)	Bush (R)	83,361	(46%)
Perot (I)	23,442	(13%)			

Rep. Neil Abercrombie (D)

Elected 1990; b. June 26, 1938, Buffalo, NY; home, Honolulu; Union Col., B.A. 1959, U. of HI, M.A 1964, Ph.D. 1974; no religious affiliation; married (Nancie Caraway).

Career: Elem. and high schl. teacher, 1959–63; Probation Officer, Marin Cnty., CA, 1964–67; Sociologist, 1967–74; HI House of Reps., 1974–78; HI Senate, 1978–86; Asst. prof., HI Loa Col., 1979–80; Consultant, 1983–87, 1989–90; U.S. House of Reps., 1986–87; Asst., HI Superintendent of Educ., 1987–88; Honolulu City Cncl., 1988–90.

Offices: 1440 LHOB 20515, 202-225-2726. Also 4104 Prince Kuhio Fed. Bldg., 300 Ala Moana Blvd., Honolulu 96850, 808-541-2570.

Committees: *Armed Services* (20th of 34 D): Military Acquisition; Military Installations and Facilities. *Natural Resources* (16th of 28 D): National Parks, Forests and Public Lands; Native American Affairs; Oversight and Investigations.

Group Ratings

	ADA	ACLU	COPE	CDF	CFA	LCV	ACU	NTLC	NSI	COC	CEI
1992	95	100	91	100	100	88	0	0	20	13	7
1991	100	—	100	100	94	77	0	—	—	10	6

National Journal Ratings

	1991 LIB — 1991 CONS		1992 LIB — 1992 CONS	
Economic	88% —	0%	91% —	0%
Social	88% —	0%	92% —	0%
Foreign	83% —	15%	90% —	0%

Key Votes of the 102d Congress

1. Ban Striker Replace	FOR	5. Handgun Wait/7-Day	FOR	9. Use Force in Gulf	AGN
2. $ for Homeownership	AGN	6. Overseas Mil. Abortion	FOR	10. US Mil. Abroad $ Cut	FOR
3. Tax Rich/Cut Mid Cls.	FOR	7. Obscn. Art NEA $ Ban	AGN	11. Limit SDI Funds	FOR
4. FY93/$15B Def. Cut	FOR	8. Death Pen. from Jury	AGN	12. Cuba Trade Embargo	AGN

Key Votes of the 103d Congress

1. Family Leave	FOR	2. Deficit Reduction	FOR	3. Stimulus Plan	FOR

Election Results

1992 general	Neil Abercrombie (D)................	129,332	(73%)	($359,681)
	Warner C. Sutton (R)................	41,575	(23%)	($16,103)
	Rockne Hart Johnson (LIB)............	6,569	(4%)	
1992 primary	Neil Abercrombie (D), unopposed			
1990 general	Neil Abercrombie (D)................	97,622	(60%)	($442,211)
	Mike Liu (R).......................	62,982	(39%)	($267,882)

SECOND DISTRICT

The 2d District of Hawaii includes not only the Neighbor Islands but most of Oahu's acreage except for Honolulu. It has Wheeler Air Force Base, still looking much as it did in December 1941, and the farmlands north of Pearl Harbor, between two jagged chains of mountains that lift the island out of the sea. Over the mountains to the west is the Leeward Coast—calm, sultry and lightly populated; over the mountains to the northeast is the Windward Coast—windy, as its name implies—with many prosperous and Republican subdivisions in and around Kaneohe and Kailua. The Neighbor Islands have distinct personalities. Hawaii, the Big Island, is large enough to boast huge cattle ranches, the active volcano of Kilauea and Mauna Kea, the highest mountain in the world if you count from its base far under the ocean to the peak, rising in a slow slant from Hilo or the Kona (western) Coast. On the north shore, with heavy rainfall and tropical foliage, is the old port of Hilo and Hawaii's macadamia nut industry; this is a blue-collar Democratic area. On the Kona Coast, where there is little rainfall and the landscape is dominated by lava flows, there are retirement condominiums and a higher-income, more Republican population. Maui in recent years has been the fastest-developing island, with dozens of luxury condominiums and vast upscale resorts. Kauai, much of which was devastated by Hurricane Iniki in 1991, is the least-developed and most agricultural of the main islands; parts of it have the nation's highest rainfall, while others seldom get wet. Its large farm work force makes it the most Democratic of the islands.

The 2d District is represented by Patsy Mink, still exuberant and enthusiastically liberal after a long congressional career: she was first elected here in 1964, gave up the seat to run unsuccessfully for the Senate in 1976, then won it again in 1990 after incumbent Daniel Akaka was appointed to the Senate. Mink's support of feminist causes goes back to the days when they were considered laughable rather than fashionable, and she is still looking to batter down barriers to women's advancement. She continues to defend affirmative action programs which many consider quotas, even when they work against Asian-Americans. In early 1993, she turned down a Government Operations subcommittee chair for a seat on the Budget Committee, the better to affect major policy decisions.

Mink has had her political setbacks: she lost the 1976 Senate primary to Spark Matsunaga, and lost races for governor in 1986 and mayor of Honolulu in 1988. In the 1990 special election to fill the 2d District vacancy, she was attacked as an old-fashioned liberal by Mufi Hannemann, who beat Abercrombie in the 1986 1st District primary. But she edged Hannemann 37%–36% in the race for the short term and 40%–37% for the nomination to the full term. The general election and 1992 contests she won easily.

The People: Pop. 1990: 554,055; 22% rural; 10% age 65+; 35% White; 2% Black; 1% Amer. Indian; 57% Asian; 2% Other; 9% Hispanic origin. Voting age pop.: 396,268; 2% Black; 7% Hispanic origin. Households: 64% married couple families; 33% married couple fams. w. children; 48% college educ.; median household income: $37,247; per capita income: $14,032; median gross rent: $633; median house value: $189,700.

1992 Presidential Vote

Clinton (D) 91,646 (49%)
Bush (R) 64,640 (34%)
Perot (I).................... 29,561 (16%)

1988 Presidential Vote

Dukakis (D)................. 93,062 (55%)
Bush (R) 75,264 (45%)

Rep. Patsy T. Mink (D)

Elected Sept., 1990; b. Dec. 6, 1927, Paia, Maui; home, Honolulu; U. of HI, B.A. 1948, U. of Chicago, J.D. 1951; Protestant; married (John Francis).

Career: Practicing atty., 1953–64, 1987–90; HI House of Reps., 1957–59; HI Senate, 1959, 1963–64; U.S. House of Reps., 1965–77; U.S. Asst. Secy. of State for Oceans and Intl. Environment and Scientific Affairs, 1977–78; Pres., Americans for Democratic Action, 1978–81; Honolulu City Cncl., 1983–87.

Offices: 2135 RHOB 20515, 202-225-4906. Also 5104 Prince Kuhio Fed. Bldg., P.O. Box 50124, Honolulu 96850, 808-541-1966.

Committees: *Budget* (21st of 26 D). *Education and Labor* (12th of 28 D): Elementary, Secondary and Vocational Education; Labor-Management Relations; Postsecondary Education and Training. *Natural Resources* (24th of 28 D): National Parks, Forests and Public Lands.

Group Ratings

	ADA	ACLU	COPE	CDF	CFA	LCV	ACU	NTLC	NSI	COC	CEI
1992	100	100	100	90	100	100	0	0	30	25	12
1991	100	—	100	100	100	92	0	—	—	20	7

National Journal Ratings

	1991 LIB — 1991 CONS		1992 LIB — 1992 CONS	
Economic	88%	— 0%	83%	— 13%
Social	88%	— 0%	85%	— 13%
Foreign	92%	— 0%	85%	— 14%

Key Votes of the 102d Congress

1. Ban Striker Replace FOR	5. Handgun Wait/7-Day FOR	9. Use Force in Gulf AGN
2. $ for Homeownership AGN	6. Overseas Mil. Abortion FOR	10. US Mil. Abroad $ Cut FOR
3. Tax Rich/Cut Mid Cls. FOR	7. Obscn. Art NEA $ Ban AGN	11. Limit SDI Funds FOR
4. FY93/$15B Def. Cut FOR	8. Death Pen. from Jury AGN	12. Cuba Trade Embargo AGN

Key Votes of the 103d Congress

1. Family Leave FOR   2. Deficit Reduction FOR   3. Stimulus Plan FOR

Election Results

1992 general	Patsy T. Mink (D).....................	131,454	(73%)	($287,017)
	Kamuela Price (R)	40,070	(22%)	($772)
	Lloyd (Jeff) Mallan (LIB)	9,431	(5%)	
1992 primary	Patsy T. Mink (D).....................	28,512	(82%)	
	David L. Bourgoin (D)	6,063	(18%)	
1990 general	Patsy T. Mink (D).....................	118,155	(66%)	($641,037)
	Andy Poepoe (R)	54,625	(31%)	($204,153)
	Other...............................	5,508	(3%)	

IDAHO

Towering over the state Capitol in Boise is a vast mountain: wilderness is never far away in Idaho, in distance or in time. Idaho ranks third in National Wilderness lands, and easy access to the wild is one of the attractions here. This was the last North American area European pioneers set eyes on—fur traders who wandered here for their yearly rendezvous. The first farmers in Idaho were New England Yankees led by ministers wending their way west on the Oregon Trail in the broad Snake River valley. The northern panhandle, an extension of Washington's Columbia Valley, was first settled by miners seeking gold and silver; loggers followed. Mormons moved north from Utah and settled in eastern Idaho. But what brought the most settlers were federal water reclamation projects first authorized in 1894, four years after statehood, which transformed the barren Snake River Valley into some of the nation's best volcanic soil-enriched farmlands. Many of today's Idahoans knew personally the people who pioneered this state, built the first towns and farms, established the first churches and schools and became its community leaders.

Today, Idaho remains close to its roots and yet is somewhat cosmopolitan. Its economy is still based heavily on agriculture, especially potatoes. That means it uses more water per capita than any other state; it also means this is an exporting state, shipping foodstuffs and lumber to the other side of the Pacific Rim. Idaho's robust economy—employment was up 27% and personal income up 36% from 1987 to 1993—has attracted high-skill workers who like having wilderness so nearby and a family lifestyle where traditional values are respected and traditional rules often enforced. Yet there is also a nonconformity—"unconventional is the Idaho style," as Governor Cecil Andrus put it—and a Western desire to be left alone.

Idaho politics was manipulated for decades by two bosses who could patch together statewide alliances—Democrat Tom Boise from the panhandle and Republican Lloyd Adams from the Mormon east; the regional divisions are still plain today. Overall, Idaho is heavily Republican. Even in 1992, the Boise area and the Magic Valley east along the Snake and Pocatello Rivers voted for George Bush over Bill Clinton and Ross Perot by 44%–28%–26%. But the panhandle voted 37% for Clinton to 33% for Bush and 29% for Perot, a result similar to eastern Washington state. In contrast, the mostly Mormon counties in the east voted 48% for Bush, 28% for Perot and only 18% for Clinton, very much like Utah. A similar pattern, modified by the candidates' regional strengths, prevailed in the 1990 and 1992 Senate races.

Although its first settlers had a Republican heritage, silver-mining Idaho went for William Jennings Bryan and free silver in 1896, and then Wilson and Roosevelt; even as late as 1960, John F. Kennedy won 46% of the vote here. Then, ahead of the national trend, Idaho turned right. Idahoans began to think of themselves less as downtrodden employees of absentee corporations needing a protective federal government, and more as pioneering entrepreneurs who needed to get a bloated, bossy federal government off their backs. The federal government is a real presence here: it owns 65% of Idaho's land; when it blocks exploitation of local resources in order to protect the environment—by vetoing a logging operation or preventing sheep-ranchers from destroying coyotes—Washington arouses strong resentment. And if the Sage-brush Rebellion of the early 1980s fizzled, as voters realized that Idaho does benefit in many ways from federal subsidies, believers in growth still distrust the feds for their restrictions while environmentalists are nervous about radiation releases from federal nuclear plants and overland shipments of nuclear waste.

This temperament is one reason this nationally Republican state has elected nothing but Democratic governors since 1970. Another is the tendency of Democrats—fond of government and politics—to field some of the ablest career-oriented politicians in the state, while many able

Miles

0   20   40

Republicans dislike active government so much that they shun politics and stick with the private sector. Idaho has produced a few politicians of national distinction, notably William Borah, the silver-maned foreign policy expert, and Frank Church, who served 24 years until his defeat in 1980, both of whom chaired the Senate Foreign Relations Committee. It has also produced some highly visible entrepreneurs, like J.R. Simplot, the great processor of potatoes, and J.A. Albertson, proprietor of a major supermarket chain, and Boise is the home of Boise Cascade and of Morrison-Knudsen, the international construction company.

Governor. Cecil Andrus, who has said he will retire in 1994 after four terms as Idaho's governor, is one of the most enduring figures in American public life. He first ran for governor in 1966, when he was chosen to replace the Democratic nominee who died in a plane crash; he lost that year but won in 1970, when he opposed molybdenum mining in the White Clouds Mountains, and then was reelected in 1974. He served four years as Jimmy Carter's secretary of the interior, helping to push through the Alaska Lands Bill and preserving many wilderness areas. "What we want for Idaho," he says, "is a chance to make a living here, then to have a living that is worthwhile." Andrus's gubernatorial comeback race in 1986 was successful by a narrow margin, but he won with 68% in 1990, despite some controversial moments and his March 1990 veto of a tough antiabortion bill although he had long said he was antiabortion. Andrus can be feisty and politically daring: he called the National Rifle Association "the gun nuts of the world" for opposing bans on armor-piercing bullets, noting that, as a lifelong hunter, he had never seen an animal in a bullet-proof vest. One of his great fights has been to stop the Energy Department from shipping nuclear waste to Idaho; he argued this was in violation of state environmental laws, but a federal appeals court ruled otherwise in March 1992. He rallied other governors to fight the federal policy and promises to keep fighting himself. He has complained, like other governors, of federally mandated spending on Medicaid; in response he reduced payments to doctors. He has fought federal agencies to try to get water drawdowns on the Snake and Columbia River dam reservoirs so that young Sockeye and Chinook salmon can make it downriver; in 1992 the salmon count in Salmon, Idaho, 900 miles from the ocean, was exactly one. Idaho's increasing revenues allowed Andrus to seek an expanded school year and more education spending for the talented and gifted, plus property tax relief.

Who will be Andrus's successor? Democrat John Peavey, a state senator from Ketchum, has already announced his bid. Republican possibilities include former Lieutenant Governor Phil Batt, who ran in 1982, and current Lieutenant Governor Butch Otter, also well known as the son-in-law of J.R. Simplot.

Senators. Idaho, like the much more populous western states of Colorado and California, is in the dicey position of being represented in the Senate by two freshmen; but Idaho has only two House members to protect their interests, to California's and Colorado's 52 and six.

Larry Craig, Idaho's senior senator after just two years, is the Republican with the most conservative voting record in the Senate in the 1992 *National Journal* ratings. Born on a farm owned by his family since 1899, he was elected to the state Senate at 29 and to the U.S. House at 35, in 1980. He is a crisp speaker, well-informed, aggressive and tenacious in his advocacy. In the House, he was one of the original movers, with Charles Stenholm of Texas, behind the balanced budget constitutional amendment. In the Senate, he continues the battle, arguing it would create "a fundamental change in the budget environment," and "while not a cure all," is the only way to get the government to balance its books. Craig serves on the Agriculture and Energy Committees and is ranking minority member on two subcommittees with jurisdiction over forestry and mining. He is a staunch opponent of big increases in grazing fees and of revision of the 1872 Mining Act which would impose gross royalties on hard rock minerals, though he concedes that some modest change might be desirable. He wants to change the Endangered Species Act, block gun control measures (he has been on the board of the National Rifle Association) and resist cuts in Forest Service funds. He has also advanced some positive measures: He worked on the successful 1992 energy bill, worked to streamline citizen appeals of government land use decisions, worked on an Idaho-Arkansas land exchange to consolidate federal land management, and added rural health initiatives to the tax bill. Craig also got an expansion of the Nez Perce Historical Park, site of the last official conflict between the U.S. government and Native Americans.

Craig's succession to the Senate was fairly well assured when James McClure announced his retirement after 18 years in the Senate plus six in the House. Craig had primary opposition from Attorney General Jim Jones, and Democrat Ron Twilegar did raise some money and actively campaigned in the general, but Craig won 59% in the primary and seemed well ahead throughout the fall. His one misstep came in a debate with Twilegar when he said that if his wife became pregnant by rape, it would be up to her to decide whether to have an abortion. That was seized on as an evident contradiction to his right-to-life votes, and was certainly an indication that abortion may look different as a personal dilemma than it does as a public policy matter for those on all sides of the issue. Craig still won with a solid 61% of the vote, and at 45 seemed embarked on a long Senate career.

Idaho's other Senate seat changed hands when Steve Symms, also a conservative but with a more slapdash temperament, announced his retirement in August 1991 after two terms, both won by narrow margins, and amid negative publicity about his recent divorce. His achievements included the revival of the 65 mile an hour speed limit; his low point, and that of the 1988 presidential campaign, came when he told national television cameras that he'd heard a rumor that Kitty Dukakis had burned an American flag at an anti-Vietnam war demonstration in college, although he admitted he had no proof and the charge was baseless.

The best known candidate to succeed Symms was Democratic Congressman Richard Stallings, a former professor at Ricks College in Rexburg, whose conservative votes on abortion and gun control, along with his Mormon affiliation, helped him win the heavily Mormon 2d District seat four times. He originally won the seat in 1984 after incumbent George Hansen was convicted for filing false personal financial disclosure forms, by 170 votes of some 202,000 cast. In the House, Stallings amended the 1990 farm bill to increase payments to barley farmers, got the Fort Hall Water Rights Agreement ratified and passed a law allowing states to prohibit export of unprocessed logs from state lands. Although he passed up the 1990 Senate race, Stallings was off and running in spring 1991 for the Symms seat; when Symms withdrew, he spent leftover campaign money on ads attacking Stallings for his vote against the Gulf war resolution. Stallings was challenged in his primary from the left, but was an easy winner.

The easy winner among Republicans, against strong antiabortion opposition, was Boise Mayor Dirk Kempthorne. Like Craig, Kempthorne has spent most of his adult life in politics: as Idaho public affairs director for FMC Corporation, an executive at the Idaho Home Builders Association, manager of Phil Batt's 1982 gubernatorial campaign and mayor of Boise in 1985 and 1989. In that position, Kempthorne rebuilt Boise's downtown and practiced consensus politics in economic boom years. He attacked Stallings for having eight overdrafts on the House bank, pledged never to vote to give away Idaho's water rights, called for a capital gains tax cut and additional compensation to property owners for federal takings. He had solid backing from Symms and McClure and by June 1992 was leading in polls; Stallings's charges that Kempthorne raised taxes in Boise didn't turn it around. Kempthorne won with 57%, barely carrying the panhandle, but running far ahead in the Boise market and carrying the Mormon areas in the east.

Kempthorne wants an across-the-board freeze in federal spending and favors term limits; in early 1993, he proposed an amendment to cut Congress's budget by 25%, but it lost 56–43. He backs the Idaho National Engineering Laboratory's Integral Fast Reactor project and has seats on the Environment and Armed Services Committees.

Presidential politics. George Bush's share of the vote fell 20 points, from 62% to 42%, in four years in Idaho, but it remains one of the most Republican states in the nation. The real race in November was for second place, which Bill Clinton barely won over Ross Perot by 28%–27%. Since 1988, Idaho's presidential primary has been held in late May but is not binding; the contest that counted was the caucus vote for delegates in early March. In May 1992, Bill Clinton won 49%–29% over uncommitted—not an overwhelming endorsement, while George Bush vanquished the same opponent 63%–23%.

Congressional districting. Idaho has two congressional districts; redistricting for 1992 just shuffled nine Boise precincts between them.

The People: Est. Pop. 1992: 1,067,000; Pop. 1990: 1,006,749, up 5.6% 1990–1992. 0.4% of U.S. total, 42nd largest; 43% rural. Median age: 31.5 years. 12.0% 65 years and over. 94.4% White, 5.3% Hispanic origin, 1.4% American Indian, 3.0% Other. Households: 62.2% married couple families; 32% married couple fams. w. children; 49% college educ.; median household income: $25,257; per capita income: $11,457; 70.1% owner occupied housing; median house value: $58,200; median monthly rent: $261. 6.5% Unemployment. Voting age pop.: 698,344. Registered voters (1992): 611,121; no party registration.

Political Lineup: Governor, Cecil D. Andrus (D); Lt. Gov., C. L. (Butch) Otter (R); Secy. of State, Pete T. Cenarrusa (R); Atty. Gen., Larry EchoHawk (D); Treasurer, Lydia Justice Edwards (R); Auditor, J. D. Williams (D). State Senate, 35 (23 R and 12 D); State House of Representatives, 70 (50 R and 20 D). Senators, Larry Craig (R) and Dirk Kempthorne (R). Representatives, 2 (1 D and 1 R).

1992 Presidential Vote			1988 Presidential Vote		
Bush (R)	202,645	(42%)	Bush (R)	253,881	(62%)
Clinton (D)	137,013	(28%)	Dukakis (D)	147,272	(36%)
Perot (I)	130,395	(27%)			

1992 Democratic Presidential Primary			1992 Republican Presidential Primary		
Clinton	27,004	(49%)	Bush	73,297	(63%)
Brown	9,212	(17%)	Buchanan	15,167	(13%)
Other	2,879	(5%)	Uncommitted	27,038	(23%)
Uncommitted	16,029	(29%)			

GOVERNOR

Gov. Cecil D. Andrus (D)

Elected 1986, term expires Jan. 1995; b. Aug. 25, 1931, Hood River, OR; home, Boise; OR St. U., 1948–49; Lutheran; married (Carol).

Career: Navy, 1951–55 (Korea); Lumberjack, 1955–63; ID Senate, 1960–66, 1969–70; ID Gov., 1971–77; U.S. Secy. of Interior, 1977–81; Businessman, 1981–87.

Office: State House, Boise 83720, 208-334-2100.

Election Results

1990 gen.	Cecil D. Andrus (D)	217,801	(68%)
	Roger Fairchild (R)	101,885	(32%)
1990 prim.	Cecil D. Andrus (D), unopposed		
1986 gen.	Cecil D. Andrus (D)	193,429	(50%)
	David Leroy (R)	189,794	(49%)

SENATORS

Sen. Larry Craig (R)

Elected 1990, seat up 1996; b. July 20, 1945, Midvale; home, Payette; U. of ID, B.A. 1969; United Methodist; married (Suzanne).

Career: Army Natl. Guard, 1970–74; Rancher, farmer; ID Senate, 1974–80; U.S. House of Reps., 1980–90.

Offices: 313 HSOB 20510, 202-224-2752. Also 103 N. 4th St., Coeur d'Alene 83814, 208-667-6130; 633 Main St., Lewiston 83501, 208-743-0792; 1292 Addison Ave. E., Twin Falls 83301, 202-734-6780; 250 S. 4th Ave., #216, Pocatello 83201, 208-236-6817; and 2539 Channing Way, Idaho Falls 83404, 208-523-5541.

Committees: *Aging (Special)* (8th of 10 R). *Agriculture, Nutrition and Forestry* (6th of 8 R): Agricultural Credit; Agricultural Production and Stabilization of Prices; Agricultural Research, Conservation, Forestry and General Legislation (RMM). *Energy and Natural Resources* (6th of 9 R): Energy Research and Development; Mineral Resources Development and Production (RMM); Public Lands, National Parks and Forests. *Ethics (Select)* (3d of 3 R). *Joint Economic Committee* (9th of 10).

Group Ratings

	ADA	ACLU	CDF	COPE	CFA	LCV	ACU	NTLC	NSI	COC	CEI
1992	0	5	0	17	0	0	100	89	70	90	93
1991	5	—	27	25	11	14	86	—	—	100	80

National Journal Ratings

	1991 LIB — 1991 CONS		1992 LIB — 1992 CONS	
Economic	0%	— 91%	0%	— 89%
Social	0%	— 86%	0%	— 89%
Foreign	0%	— 87%	0%	— 90%

Key Votes of the 102d Congress

1. $ for Homeownership	FOR	5. Clarence Thomas Nom.	FOR	9. Use Force in Gulf	FOR
2. Have Cap Gains Debate	FOR	6. Lmt Death Row Appeal	FOR	10. Keep Salvador Aid	FOR
3. Remove Budget Walls	AGN	7. Handgun Wait/5-Day	AGN	11. Cut $1B from SDI	AGN
4. Ban Striker Replace	AGN	8. Abortion Gag Rule	FOR	12. Override China MFN	AGN

Key Votes of the 103d Congress

1. Family Leave	AGN	2. HIV Immigrants	AGN	3. Clinton Budget	AGN

376   IDAHO

Election Results

1990 general	Larry Craig (R)............................	193,641	(61%)	($1,620,304)
	Ron J. Twilegar (D)	122,295	(39%)	($544,419)
1990 primary	Larry Craig (R)............................	65,830	(59%)	
	Jim Jones (R)	45,733	(41%)	
1984 general	James A. McClure (R)	293,193	(72%)	($1,016,944)
	Peter Martin Busch (D)	105,591	(26%)	($31,001)

Sen. Dirk Kempthorne (R)

Elected 1992, seat up 1998; b. Oct. 29, 1951, San Diego, CA; home, Boise; U. of ID, B.A. 1975; Methodist; married (Patricia).

Career: Exec. Asst. to the Dir., ID Dept. of Public Lands, 1976–78; Exec. V.P., ID Home Builders Assn., 1978–81; Campaign Mgr., Phil Batt's gubernatorial campaign, 1982; ID Public Affairs Mgr., FMC Corp., 1983–86; Boise Mayor, 1986–93.

Offices: 367 DSOB 20510, 202-224-6142. Also 304 N. 8th St., #338, Boise 83701, 208-334-1776; 118 N. 2d St., Coeur d'Alene 83814, 208-664-5490; 633 Main St., #103, Lewiston 83501, 208-743-1492; 401 2d St. N., #106, Twin Falls 83301, 208-734-2515; 250 S. 4th, #207, Pocatello 83201, 208-236-6775; and 2539 Channing Way, #240, Idaho Falls 83404, 208-522-9779.

Committees: *Armed Services* (8th of 9 R): Coalition Defense and Reinforcing Forces; Defense Techology, Acquisition and Industrial Base; Nuclear Deterrence, Arms Control and Defense Intelligence. *Environment and Public Works* (7th of 7 R): Clean Air and Nuclear Regulation; Clean Water, Fisheries and Wildlife; Water Resources, Transportation, Public Buildings and Economic Development. *Small Business* (7th of 9 R): Innovation, Manufacturing and Technology; Rural Economy and Family Farming.

Group Ratings and 102d Congress Votes: Newly Elected

Key Votes of the 103d Congress

1. Family Leave	AGN	2. HIV Immigrants	AGN	3. Clinton Budget	AGN

Election Results

1992 general	Dirk Kempthorne (R).................	270,468	(57%)	($1,305,338)
	Richard Stallings (D)	208,036	(43%)	($1,222,222)
1992 primary	Dirk Kempthorne (R).................	67,001	(57%)	
	Rod Beck (R)	26,977	(23%)	
	Milton Erhart (R).....................	22,682	(19%)	
1986 general	Steven D. Symms (R).................	196,958	(52%)	($3,229,939)
	John V. Evans (D).....................	185,066	(48%)	($2,135,537)

FIRST DISTRICT

The 1st District, which stretches from the Nevada border to Canada, includes most of usually Republican Boise and the panhandle where the dominant voice is Coeur d'Alene newspaper baron and resort developer Duane Hagadone. In statewide elections, it is the less Republican of the two districts because of the panhandle, yet it has elected nothing but Republican congressmen between 1964 and 1990. But when the 1st's Larry Craig ran for the Senate in 1990, his place was taken by Democrat Larry LaRocco, after a spirited election with contests in both primaries. LaRocco had shown political competence before as Senator Frank Church's local man in Idaho in the late 1970s and as the Democratic challenger who held Craig to 54% in 1982; he played a lead role in the successful push for a state lottery in 1986. LaRocco easily beat two panhandle-based primary opponents. Republican primary winner state Senator Skip Smyser's attempts to paint LaRocco as a liberal misfired as the Democrat came out against the budget summit packages and for a bill to ban oil price increases in times of crises. LaRocco pummeled Smyser for voting in favor of the strict antiabortion law in the legislature and for his votes against issues like education funding, living wills and day care standards—issues that touch Idaho parents' daily lives. LaRocco carried the panhandle with 60% and won 51% in Boise's Ada County as well, for a 53% victory overall.

In the House, LaRocco has a moderately liberal voting record and got a seat on the Natural Resources Committee. He passed a law requiring credit bureaus to report court ordered child support payment delinquencies. He introduced an Idaho wilderness bill in 1993, and has a bill that passed the House in 1992 to protect the raptor dinosaur archaeological site in the Snake River Canyon from development. His Republican opponent in 1992, state Senator Rachel Gilbert, called for electronic devices to allow House members to vote from their districts. Gilbert attacked LaRocco for defending the House as an institution after the bank scandal, but LaRocco won 58%–37%, carrying every county.

The People: Pop. 1990: 503,141; 46% rural; 13% age 65+; 93% White; 1% Amer. Indian; 1% Asian; 2% Other; 5% Hispanic origin. Voting age pop.: 358,572; 4% Hispanic origin. Households: 63% married couple families; 30% married couple fams. w. children; 47% college educ.; median household income: $25,086; per capita income: $11,530; median gross rent: $332; median house value: $60,000.

1992 Presidential Vote			1988 Presidential Vote		
Bush (R)	101,787	(41%)	Bush (R)	120,011	(60%)
Clinton (D)	75,499	(30%)	Dukakis (D)	79,593	(40%)
Perot (I)	67,677	(27%)			

Rep. Larry LaRocco (D)

Elected 1990; b. Aug. 25, 1946, Van Nuys, CA; home, McCall; Stanford U., 1967, U. of Portland, B.A. 1967, Johns Hopkins, 1968–69, Boston U., M.S. 1969; Catholic; married (Chris).

Career: Army Intelligence, 1969–72; Field rep., U.S. Sen. Frank Church, 1975–81; Stockbroker, 1983–90.

Offices: 1117 LHOB 20515, 202-225-6611. Also 304 N. 8th St., #136, Boise 83702, 208-343-4211; 621 Main St., #G, Lewiston, 83501, 208-746-6694; 109 S. Kimball Ave., P.O. Box 67, Caldwell 83606, 208-459-6694; and 408 Sherman Ave., Coeur d'Alene 83814, 208-667-2110.

Committees: *Banking, Finance and Urban Affairs* (12th of 30 D): Consumer Credit and Insurance; Financial Institutions Supervision, Regulation and Deposit Insurance; International Development, Finance, Trade and Monetary Policy. *Natural Resources* (15th of 28 D): Energy and Mineral Resources; National Parks, Forests and Public Lands.

Group Ratings

	ADA	ACLU	COPE	CDF	CFA	LCV	ACU	NTLC	NSI	COC	CEI
1992	80	68	75	70	73	50	24	15	60	50	27
1991	45	—	64	70	44	54	16	—	—	60	26

National Journal Ratings

	1991 LIB — 1991 CONS			1992 LIB — 1992 CONS		
Economic	47%	—	52%	61%	—	38%
Social	62%	—	38%	63%	—	37%
Foreign	56%	—	44%	62%	—	35%

Key Votes of the 102d Congress

1. Ban Striker Replace	FOR	5. Handgun Wait/7-Day	AGN	9. Use Force in Gulf	AGN
2. $ for Homeownership	AGN	6. Overseas Mil. Abortion	FOR	10. US Mil. Abroad $ Cut	FOR
3. Tax Rich/Cut Mid Cls.	FOR	7. Obscn. Art NEA $ Ban	AGN	11. Limit SDI Funds	FOR
4. FY93/$15B Def. Cut	FOR	8. Death Pen. from Jury	AGN	12. Cuba Trade Embargo	FOR

Key Votes of the 103d Congress

1. Family Leave	AGN	2. Deficit Reduction	FOR	3. Stimulus Plan	FOR

Election Results

1992 general	Larry LaRocco (D)...................	140,985	(58%)	($623,327)
	Rachel Gilbert (R)..................	90,983	(37%)	($222,604)
	Two Others	10,822	(5%)	
1992 primary	Larry LaRocco (D), unopposed			
1990 general	Larry LaRocco (D)...................	85,051	(53%)	($447,895)
	C. A. (Skip) Smyser (R)..............	75,397	(47%)	($480,994)

SECOND DISTRICT

The 2d District, from central Boise east to the Utah border, is one of America's most Republican districts in presidential elections but has been competitive in House elections. Richard Stallings, after four wins here, ran unsuccessfully for the Senate in 1992, leading to contests in both primaries. The clear favorite was Republican Mike Crapo, state Senator since 1984 and Senate leader since 1988, a bishop in the Mormon Church at age 31, "intelligent, approachable and even-tempered," said an Idaho Falls *Post Register* reporter. Crapo was attacked from the right but won his primary by a 2–1 margin. The Democratic nominee was state Auditor J. D. Williams, a self-styled "cowboy Democrat," also a Mormon from eastern Idaho, who promised to "put America first" with industrial policy and a tough approach on trade. Crapo opposed all tax increases and favored spending cuts, a balanced budget amendment and the line-item veto; Williams favored higher taxes on the rich and attacked Crapo for opposing a proposal to protect Henry's Fork of the Snake River. Both opposed abortion rights and gun control.

Crapo won 61%–35% and came to Washington with, he said, "a passion for reform." His approach is to set simple, hard-and-fast rules—a balanced budget, term limits, across-the-board spending cuts (excluding social security)—and force tough decisions to adhere to them. Republican leaders evidently recognized him as a comer and freshman members voted him to the new post of new member leader. With a seat on Energy and Commerce and considerable skills, he could be a force in the House.

The People: Pop. 1990: 503,608; 39% rural; 11% age 65+; 92% White; 1% Amer. Indian; 1% Asian; 3% Other; 6% Hispanic origin. Voting age pop.: 340,340; 5% Hispanic origin. Households: 63% married couple families; 33% married couple fams. w. children; 51% college educ.; median household income: $25,446; per capita income: $11,384; median gross rent: $327; median house value: $55,900.

1992 Presidential Vote

Bush (R) 100,858   (43%)
Perot (I). 62,718   (27%)
Clinton (D) 61,514   (26%)
Other 8,925   (4%)

1988 Presidential Vote

Bush (R) 133,870   (66%)
Dukakis (D). 67,679   (34%)

Rep. Michael Crapo (R)

Elected 1992; b. May 20, 1951, Idaho Falls; home, Idaho Falls; Brigham Young U., B.A. 1973, Harvard, J.D. 1977; Mormon; married (Susan).

Career: Practicing atty., 1977–92; ID Senate, 1984–91.

Offices: 437 CHOB 20515, 202-225-5531. Also 304 N. 8th St., #444, Boise 83702, 208-334-1953; 250 S. 4th St., #220, Pocatello 83201, 208-236-6734; 488 Blue Lakes Blvd., #105, Twin Falls 83301, 208-734-7219; and 2539 Channing Way, #330, Idaho Falls 83404, 208-523-6701.

Committees: *Energy and Commerce* (17th of 17 R): Energy and Power; Transportation and Hazardous Materials.

Group Ratings and 102d Congress Votes: Newly Elected

Key Votes of the 103d Congress

1. Family Leave	AGN	2. Deficit Reduction	AGN	3. Stimulus Plan	AGN

Election Results

1992 general	Michael Crapo (R)	139,783	(61%)	($572,532)
	J.D. Williams (D)	81,450	(35%)	($245,954)
	Two Others	8,724	(4%)	
1992 primary	Michael Crapo (R)	45,462	(68%)	
	Gary Glenn (R).	21,443	(32%)	
1990 general	Richard H. Stallings (D)	97,917	(64%)	($406,219)
	Sean McDevitt (R).	56,083	(36%)	($141,681)

ILLINOIS

More than any other state, Illinois has a claim to being central in American politics. Demographically, this is the megastate most like the nation as a whole—with similar percentages of blacks and Hispanics, immigrants and pioneers, city-dwellers and suburbanites and farmers, the affluent and the impoverished, heavy industry and high-tech. Illinois reaches farther south than Richmond, Virginia, and looks north over Lake Michigan frozen in winter; to Westerners it seems like back east and it has long been classified as the gateway to the West by writers on the East Coast. Chicago may no longer be the nation's Second City (greater Los Angeles is), but O'Hare Airport is still the nation's busiest. Chicago may no longer be the hog-butcher of the world, but it remains the central focus of our rail system. Illinois is also a prime producer and processor of corn and soybeans, and the home of the world's greatest commodities exchanges and futures markets. Manufacturing employment may be declining in Illinois, but the white-collar and service economy is larger here than elsewhere between the coasts, and incomes have remained robustly high. But Illinois is not an exact replica of the nation—farm discontent got more amplification in Downstate Illinois in the early 1980s, and Chicago has a yeasty ethnic tradition richer than most other cities—but it comes closer than any other state.

Illinois has always had a robust two-party politics that also has paralleled the nation. In the past century, it has voted for the losing presidential candidate only twice, in 1916 and 1976. The issue of the extension of slavery, which split the nation apart, was most clearly exposed in the seven 1858 debates between Stephen Douglas and Abraham Lincoln. But politics has not always been central to life in Illinois, or America. This was a state of farmers, whose families, communities and churches absorbed more of their energies than politics or government. Chicago was established not by government but by markets; it has always been a free enterprise city, settled by pioneers from New England and Kentucky, by immigrant Irishmen who dug the first canal connecting Lake Michigan and the Illinois River, and by railroad promoters who saw its potential as the great connecting point between East and West and the Great Lakes and the Mississippi Valley. Its factories, built where iron ore from Great Lakes freighters and coal from inland hills came together, attracted migrants from near and far. Its growth was explosive: Chicago did not exist in 1830, boasted 112,000 people as the Civil War began and had 1.2 million when it hosted the World's Fair of 1893. To meet the demands of these masses and referee their cultural struggles, political machines sprang up, allied with the Republicans who predominated in northern Illinois and the Democrats who usually prevailed from Springfield south. Not until the Depression of the 1930s did Chicago become reliably Democratic, and that was in part because so many Republicans had moved to the Cook County suburbs and the Collar Counties surrounding Chicago, still one of America's strongest Republican constituencies, voting for Barry Goldwater in 1964 and George Bush in 1992. Illinois has produced no figures of the stature of Lincoln or Douglas and no presidents since Ulysses S. Grant. But decade after decade, it has given the U.S. important and skillful politicians of both parties—Carter Harrison and Joseph Cannon, Ed Kelly and Harold Ickes, Richard J. Daley and Everett Dirksen, Adlai Stevenson and Charles Percy, and Dan Rostenkowski and Robert Michel.

Over the last quarter-century, Illinois's politics have been the nation's writ amplified (or shouted—for some reason this state has more politicians with booming voices than any other). For the two decades following 1968, when the Democrats held their disastrously violent national convention in Chicago, their party had trouble rallying the middle-class voters who were its historic base, and Democratic presidential candidates failed to win majorities in metro Chicago or Illinois. Chicagoland voters were split along racial lines following the election of Mayor Harold Washington in 1983 and the "council wars" that followed; after Washington's death the atmosphere calmed with the election of Richard M. Daley in 1989.

Illinois has played a pivotal role in at least three of the last four Democratic primary seasons. Its mid-March primary follows Iowa and New Hampshire and is just a week after the southern Super Tuesday contests; it is the first big northern state to vote, and analysts reasonably ask, if a candidate can't carry Illinois, what reason is there to think he can carry any other big state? In 1980 and 1984, big wins in Illinois cinched nominations for Jimmy Carter and Walter Mondale. In 1988, George Bush clinched the Republican nomination here, as Bob Dole left the race in the last week of campaigning. The 1988 Democratic contest seemed inconclusive, since most votes were cast for two local candidates, Downstate-based Senator Paul Simon and then Chicago-based Jesse Jackson; but in fact any other alternative was blocked from emerging, thus winnowing the race down to a contest between Michael Dukakis and Jackson which Dukakis could not help but win. The St. Patrick's Day 1992 Illinois primary clearly decided both parties' contests. George Bush's pulverizing of Pat Buchanan not only clinched the nomination but took Buchanan off the TV news; Bill Clinton's big win over Paul Tsongas and Jerry Brown made his nomination inevitable, although New York-based reporters insisted on treating their state's primary as if it were capable of making a difference. The Illinois primary was also an early

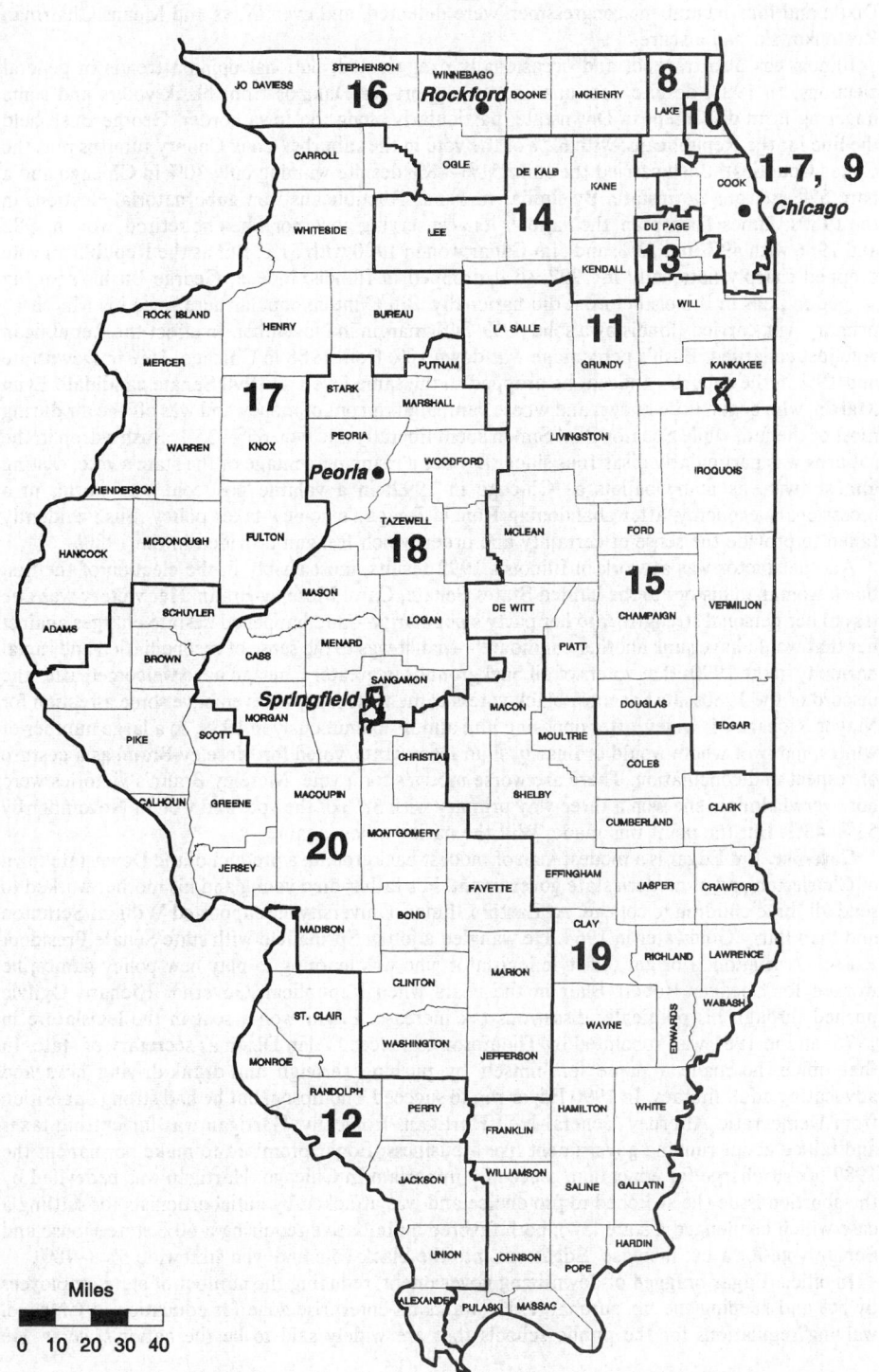

Miles

0 10 20 30 40

warning of the strong anti-incumbent feeling percolating up from the precincts: Senator Alan Dixon and four incumbent congressmen were defeated, and even Ways and Means Chairman Rostenkowski had a scare.

Illinois has also tracked, and occasionally exaggerated, national opinion trends in general elections. In 1988, despite near-unanimous support for Dukakis from black voters and some lingering farm discontent in Downstate, particularly along the Iowa border, George Bush held the line for the Republicans: with 62% of the vote in the suburbs (Cook County suburbs plus the Collar Counties), Bush carried the state 51%–48% despite winning only 30% in Chicago and a bare 52% margin Downstate. By similar margins, Republicans won gubernatorial elections in the 1980s: James Thompson, the nation's longest serving governor when he retired, won in 1982 and 1986 with 49% and 53%, and Jim Edgar won in 1990 with 51%. But as the Republican vote dropped sharply nationally in 1992, so it dropped in Illinois; indeed, George Bush's showing sagged in polls in Illinois before it did nationally. Bill Clinton, popular here since his March 17 primary win, carried Illinois by a solid 49%–34% margin in November. In effect the Republican vote just collapsed: Bush's percentage was down 12% from 1988 in Chicago, 16% in Downstate and 19% in the suburbs. Indeed, he dropped to the same levels as 1990 Senate candidate Lynn Martin, who began little known and whose campaign ran out of money and was off the air during most of the fall, while Senator Paul Simon spent liberally and won 65%–35%. Bush's drop in the suburbs was particularly disastrous since they are a rising percentage of the state's vote, casting almost twice as many ballots as Chicago in 1992; in a volatile post-cold war world, in a recessionary economy, after abandoning Ronald Reagan's no-new-taxes policy, Bush evidently failed to provide the sense of certainty and order which Reagan provided in the 1980s.

Another factor was at work in Illinois's 1992 results, most visibly in the election of the first black woman in history to the United States Senate, Carol Moseley-Braun. Her victory was due less to her personal strength or to her party's popularity—and happened despite charges against her that would have sunk another candidate—than it was to the sense of reconciliation and racial harmony in the 1990s that voters of all backgrounds in greater Chicago have welcomed after the discord of the 1980s. Just as most black voters came to accept and even have some affection for Mayor Richard M. Daley, after opposing him almost unanimously in 1989, so a large number of whites, many of whom would ordinarily shun Democrats, voted for Moseley-Braun as a gesture of respect and conciliation. There are worse motives for a vote. Moseley-Braun's victories were not overwhelming: she won a three-way primary with 38% of the vote and won in November by 53%–43%. But the point was made. Will the nation follow again?

Governor. Jim Edgar is a modest man of modest background, a product of the Downstate town of Charleston and of modern state government. His father died young and his mother worked to send all three children to college. At Eastern Illinois University, he supported William Scranton and then Barry Goldwater in 1964. He wangled a job in Springfield with state Senate President Russell Arrington, a bright old-style legislator who was learning to play new policy games; he worked for Speaker Robert Blair in the years when Republican Governor Richard Ogilvie pushed through his politically disastrous tax increase. Edgar won a seat in the legislature in 1976, and in 1981 was appointed by Thompson to succeed Alan Dixon as secretary of state. In that office, he made a name for himself by pushing through anti-drunk-driving laws and advocating adult literacy. In 1990 Edgar ran to succeed Thompson, but he had strong opposition from Democratic Attorney General Neil Hartigan. Ironically, Hartigan was for cutting taxes and talked about running government like a business; Edgar promised to make permanent the 1989 tax surcharge for education, especially important in Chicago. Hartigan was bedeviled by the abortion issue (he switched to pro-choice and was attacked by antiabortionists for settling a case which challenged a state law); both favored an initiative requiring a 60% state House and Senate vote for a tax increase. Edgar cut into the black vote and won statewide 51%–48%.

In office, Edgar bragged of downsizing government, reducing the number of state employees by 5% and keeping the tax surcharge. He wants an enterprise zone for education in Chicago, waiving regulations for the public schools that are widely said to be the nation's worst. He disagreed with Mayor Daley and Cook County Board President Richard Phelan by deciding to block state collection of sales taxes from the city and county; he opposed Daley's proposal for a gambling casino on the Chicago lakefront and did not support strongly Daley's proposal, now abandoned, for a third Chicago-area airport in the Lake Calumet area. But in early 1993, he got Daley's support for a statewide property tax cap.

Edgar, the first Illinois governor elected since 1924 who had served in the legislature, had the satisfaction of seeing Republicans capture control of the state Senate in 1992. But his own chances in 1994 are unclear. Daley is not likely to run against him, but Phelan, who first gained fame as the special counsel who recommended sanctions against House Speaker Jim Wright, may very well; other possible candidates include State Treasurer Pat Quinn and Attorney General and former Democratic National Committee Vice Chairman Roland Burris and possibly Hartigan again. Also, Edgar had minor heart surgery in 1992 and though he turns just 48 in 1994 has not yet committed himself to the race. This could be one of the nation's most important and seriously contested gubernatorial races.

Senators. Illinois has two Democratic senators, with very different backgrounds but likely to have very similar voting records. Paul Simon has been an important figure in Illinois politics for a quarter century, and was a presidential candidate in 1988; Carol Moseley-Braun was the Cook County Recorder of Deeds, unknown outside Chicago and Springfield inner political circles, until she won an upset victory in the March 1992 Democratic primary and suddenly became a symbolic figure of national importance.

Paul Simon looks the part of the country editor he once was, with his horn-rimmed glasses and bow tie, his extra-flat midwestern accent and his habit of writing his own newsletters and books; his 13th book, *Advice & Consent*, is about the Bork and Thomas confirmation hearings. Simon is an autodidact, with great faith in the ability of government to solve problems, a belief that corruption can be avoided and thrift enforced on government by sheer good will and hard work. He got his start in public life when he bought the *Troy Tribune* at age 19, and crusaded against local gangsters and machine politicians; he was elected to the legislature in 1954; eventually, he owned 14 newspapers and sold the chain in 1966. In 1968, he was elected lieutenant governor, and was prepared to take on politically ailing Republican Governor Richard Ogilvie when he lost the Democratic primary to anti-Daley, anti-spending Daniel Walker. In 1974, when Ken Gray retired from the state's southernmost Downstate congressional district, Simon ran and won; and in 1984, he won a heavily contested Democratic primary for the Senate and then went on to beat Foreign Relations Chairman Charles Percy 50%–48%. The key to this victory was Downstate, which Simon carried heavily in the primary and lost to the Chicago-based Percy by only 50%–49% in November.

Knitting together Simon's record on a miscellany of issues is a sort of perky reformism, which has made him a distinctive member of a party often tarred by corruption in a state where politics is usually a matter of hard-bitten self-interest. He was one of the first American politicians to disclose his personal finances, starting in the 1950s, and is a backer of a balanced budget constitutional amendment (requiring a three-fifths vote of the House and Senate for deficit spending) and presidential line-item veto or reduction authority overridable by majority vote. At the same time, he believes in WPA-type government job training programs and wants to have all student loans disbursed and collected directly by the federal government with an income based repayment schedule. He sponsored a National Literacy Act and an antitrust exemption to allow the television industry to produce joint standards on violence in programming. He has sponsored legislation on missing children, backed tax credits for the purchase of electric cars and pushed for more foreign language requirements in schools. Local issues get his attention too: promoting a St. Louis-to-Chicago-to-Detroit high-speed rail line and the Chicago Underflow Plan. He was for years the one non-lawyer on the Judiciary Committee, where he opposed Judges Bork and Thomas; he has taken relatively few initiatives on the Foreign Relations Committee, where he seemed a bit surprised to find himself backing U.S. military intervention in Somalia.

Simon ran for president in 1988 as an unabashed liberal, despite his stand on the balanced budget amendment, and stressed issues like foreign language education which struck some as peripheral. He finished second in the Iowa caucuses, third in New Hampshire, and out of the running in the South on Super Tuesday; but, at the importuning of Illinois politicos who were on his delegate slates, he stayed in the race and won the Illinois primary a week later. That was testimony to his popularity—and to Chicago media's concentration on home-state candidates (Simon and Jesse Jackson) and lack of interest in out-of-towners.

In 1990, he was expected to have a serious challenge from Congresswoman Lynn Martin, a sharp-tongued partisan widely respected in the House; but her campaign imploded while his thrived. She began with gaffes, while Simon's adeptness at getting media coverage on local newscasts gave him a solid base. Martin's anti-tax stand was undercut by President Bush's budget summit agreement; her attacks on Simon for helping a campaign contributor whose proprietary school had many student loan defaults could not undermine his longtime reputation for integrity. Simon's TV spots hit hard at Martin for voting against education and child care spending, while her campaign ran out of money and was off the air from September 25 to October 25. This was another example of Democrats holding a big state Senate seat through the power of political money: Martin's $4.9 million was dwarfed by Simon's $8.6 million. Simon won a record-smashing victory, with a 979,000-vote margin, carrying even affluent DuPage County outside Chicago; Martin became Bush's secretary of labor and nominated him for reelection at the Republican Convention in Houston.

Carol Moseley-Braun is in some respects the most distinctive member of the Senate; she is in some others the most unlikely—at least if you consider the political odds 11 months before her victory. That was in December 1991, when she was seriously considering bowing out of the race against Senator Alan Dixon. She correctly saw that Dixon, an officeholder for 40 years, a Downstate Democrat with a moderate record not well known in metro Chicago where 70% of primary votes are cast, was vulnerable; but another candidate, businessman Al Hofeld, was spending lavishly of his own money on ads attacking Dixon and seemed to be cornering the anti-incumbent vote. Yet Moseley-Braun (she inserted the hyphen in 1993—in the campaign her last name was Braun) persevered. Her record made her something more than a lightweight candidate: she was first elected to the legislature in 1978 where she performed well even according to Republicans; she was elected Cook County Recorder of Deeds in 1989; she is articulate and possessed of a charming personality. She boasted that she sponsored the state aid bill to Chicago schools for several years to counter any criticism asking what she had done to improve the school system widely described as the nation's worst. She also had solid support from the 20% or so black Democratic primary voters. Meanwhile, Dixon and Hofeld sniped viciously at each other; Moseley-Braun, in Hofeld consultant David Axelrod's words, stayed "really below the fray." In the last week, she started getting free publicity, and won 38% of the vote to 35% for Dixon and 27% for Hofeld.

A few years ago, a supporter of Jesse Jackson and Harold Washington like Moseley-Braun would have been blown away by a respectable Republican like her opponent, former Reagan aide Rich Williamson. But by 1992, Chicago area voters were in a mood for racial reconciliation, and there was no easier way to signal that than to vote for the intelligent, always smiling Moseley-Braun. She benefited also from feminist enthusiasm, and indeed her candidacy may have had its start in her opposition to the confirmation of Clarence Thomas and Dixon's vote for it. And Williamson had some problems: a longtime abortion opponent, he switched to pro-choice just after he filed to run, prompting cries of turncoat from the likes of Illinois resident Phyllis Schlafly. So strong was support for Moseley-Braun that she weathered the storm in September when it was revealed that in 1989 she split among herself and siblings a $28,750 timber royalty inheritance owed to her mother, a nursing home resident who was supposed to have reimbursed Medicaid with the money. Moseley-Braun's explanations were unconvincing at best, and a candidate of other race and gender might have lost the election right there. But Moseley-Braun held on to make a creditable performance in debates, and won.

More controversy arose after the election. She moved into a posh lakefront apartment at below-market rent and was criticized for taking a month-long trip to Africa immediately after the election with her campaign manager and fiance Kgosie Matthews, and was out of touch with Chicago. When Matthews was accused of sexual harassment by some female campaign workers, Moseley-Braun found the charges "groundless" based on an internal investigation. After all her criticism of the Thomas hearings, she bridled at serving on the Judiciary Committee, though she eventually did agree to do so. Her staffers asked the large Chicago commodity exchanges to pay thousands of dollars to host receptions for her even as she was seeking a seat on the Banking Committee. Under criticism from the press, she said, "If this is a honeymoon, I want a divorce." In fact, she was starting to be judged by the standards ordinarily applied to high-level politicians, and the question is whether her considerable talents will enable her to rise above this performance which has disappointed those who, realistically or not, expected so much more from her.

Mayor. Richard M. Daley came to office with a reputation as a pleasant, not particularly articulate man who had inherited the family business. In fact, he has proved to be an innovative, thoughtful and effective politician. His first achievement was to effect a racial reconciliation in a city deeply divided by genuinely seeking out black politicians, community leaders and voters and convincing them of his good faith. He also met with Hispanics, lakefront liberals, gays and members of other voting blocs which, together with tradition-minded whites in the bungalow wards provided the basis for a solid governing majority in a city that is now about 40% black. His second step has been to downsize and privatize city government. Daley's father ran a patronage machine in which city employees were expected to be Democratic precinct and ward committee-men, producing votes for the machine on election day. But a 1970s court case prohibited firing employees for political reasons, and it became obvious that the government bureaucracy was so inefficient that continuing to rely on it would mean ever-higher taxes and municipal ruin. So Daley privatized services from tree trimming to towing abandoned cars.

Daley's big projects have not all come to fruition: he is getting a bigger McCormick Place convention center but still wants permission to build a gambling casino; he is working on reforesting the city by planting half a million trees, but his plans for a new airport around Lake Calumet were abandoned when the legislature would not meet his terms. Chicago has suffered some job losses at big firms—Amoco, United Airlines, Inland Steel, the Sears catalogue division—but Daley is apparently trying to create a climate that will foster small business and job growth. What he hasn't been able to do—neither has anyone else—is dent the pathology of Chicago's black underclass, which lives in violence, has schools that seem totally ineffective and has among the lowest collection rate of child support in the country. He has tried, with black support, police crackdowns in the housing projects and sealing off grid streets to stop drug traffic.

For several years, Daley conspicuously refrained from being a political kingmaker. But in 1992 in Chicago the congressional candidates he conspicuously backed (Dan Rostenkowski, Sidney Yates, Luis Gutierrez) and those he quietly favored (Bobby Rush, Mel Reynolds, Cardiss Collins) all won—probably not a coincidence. Daley was obviously friendly to Bill Clinton's presidential candidacy: his own campaign manager, David Wilhelm, signed on to manage Clinton's campaign, and Daley had a well-publicized meeting with Clinton just before the crucial Illinois primary. Yet after the election, Clinton decided not to appoint—as some thought he would—the mayor's brother, William Daley, a highly competent politician in his own right, as secretary of transportation. But Clinton did appoint Wilhelm to chair the Democratic National Committee and with that a possible consolation prize: the Democratic National Convention in Chicago in 1996.

Presidential politics. Illinois is a presidential bellwether; it has voted for every presidential winner for 100 years except for southerners Jimmy Carter in 1976 and Woodrow Wilson in 1916. Its stubborn divisions and large electoral count make it key in any close election. Illinois's March primary, now one week after Super Tuesday, has been critical and arguably determi-native: it provided key wins for Gerald Ford in 1976, Ronald Reagan and Jimmy Carter in 1980,

Walter Mondale in 1984, George Bush in 1988, and Bill Clinton in 1992. The heavy focus on local politics makes Illinois unrepresentative when an Illinois candidate is in the race, as the 1988 Democratic primary showed.

In 1992, Clinton split the Chicago suburban vote with Bush, each winning 40%. Perot's 20% most likely drew the votes away from Bush. In the Cook County suburbs, Clinton beat Bush 44%–39%; four years ago Bush won the same suburbs with 59% of the vote. Clinton won the suburbs by 55,000 more votes than Dukakis did four years ago while Bush's votes fell by more than 150,000. Bush even won DuPage by only 48%, while in 1988 he won it with 70%.

Congressional districting. A federal court redistricted Illinois's House seats in 1991, choosing a plan favoring Republicans; this was a counterbalance to the court decision 10 years before which favored Democrats. In both cases, Illinois lost two seats; in both cases, but especially in 1992, there was some serious disruption in the delegation. The 1991 plan caused a quick revolution in Illinois politics, for the filing deadline here is in December, the earliest in the nation. It forced two primaries between two Democratic incumbents, one Downstate and one mostly in the Chicago suburbs; it would have forced another, in a mostly Chicago district, if Frank Annunzio had not retired. A new Hispanic-majority seat was created with the resultant effect of giving Dan Rostenkowski a serious battle for the first time in his 34-year House career. Four Democratic incumbents were defeated, two of them by other incumbents.

The People: Est. Pop. 1992: 11,631,000; Pop. 1990: 11,430,602, up 1.7% 1990–1992. 4.6% of U.S. total, 6th largest; 15% rural. Median age: 32.8 years. 12.6% 65 years and over. 78.3% White, 14.8% Black, 7.9% Hispanic origin, 2.5% Asian, 4.2% Other. Households: 54.1% married couple families; 26% married couple fams. w. children; 46% college educ.; median household income: $32,252; per capita income: $15,201; 64.2% owner occupied housing; median house value: $80,900; median monthly rent: $369. 7.5% Unemployment. Voting age pop.: 8,484,236. Registered voters (1992): 6,600,358; no party registration.

Political Lineup: Governor, Jim Edgar (R); Lt. Gov., Bob Kustra (R); Secy. of State, George H. Ryan (R); Atty. Gen., Roland W. Burris (D); Treasurer, Patrick Quinn (D); Comptroller, Dawn C. Netsch (D). State Senate, 59 (32 R and 27 D); State House of Representatives, 118 (67 D and 51 R). Senators, Paul Simon (D) and Carol Moseley-Braun (D). Representatives, 20 (12 D and 8 R).

1992 Presidential Vote

Clinton (D)	2,453,350	(49%)
Bush (R)	1,734,096	(34%)
Perot (I)	840,515	(17%)

1988 Presidential Vote

Bush (R)	2,310,939	(51%)
Dukakis (D)	2,215,940	(49%)

1992 Democratic Presidential Primary

Clinton	776,829	(52%)
Tsongas	387,891	(26%)
Brown	220,346	(15%)
Uncommitted	67,612	(4%)

1992 Republican Presidential Primary

Bush	634,588	(76%)
Buchanan	186,915	(22%)

GOVERNOR

Gov. Jim Edgar (R)

Elected 1990, term expires Jan. 1995; b. July 22, 1946, Vinita, OK; home, Springfield; E. IL U., B.A. 1968; American Baptist; married (Brenda).

Career: Staff Aide, IL House of Reps. & IL Senate, 1968–76; IL House of Reps., 1976–79; Legis. Affairs Dir., IL Gov. Thompson, 1979–81; IL Secy. of St., 1981–90.

Office: 207 State House, Springfield 62706, 217-782-6830.

Election Results

1990 gen.	Jim Edgar (R)	1,653,126	(51%)
	Neil F. Hartigan (D)	1,569,217	(48%)
	Other	35,067	(1%)
1990 prim.	Jim Edgar (R)	482,441	(63%)
	Steven Baer (R)	256,889	(34%)
	Robert Marshall (R)	28,365	(4%)
1986 gen.	James R. Thompson (R)	1,655,849	(53%)
	Adlai E. Stevenson III (SOL)	1,296,626	(40%)
	Other	231,503	(7%)

SENATORS

Sen. Paul Simon (D)

Elected 1984, seat up 1996; b. Nov. 29, 1928, Eugene, OR; home, Makanda; U. of OR, 1945–46, Dana Col., 1946–48; Lutheran; married (Jeanne).

Career: Army, 1951–53; Editor-Publisher, *Troy Tribune*, 1948–66; Owner, weekly newspaper chain, 1948–66; IL House of Reps., 1954–62; IL Senate, 1962–69; IL Lt. Gov., 1969–73; Prof., Sangamon St. U., 1972–73; U.S. House of Reps., 1975–85; Author, 1964-present.

Offices: 462 DSOB 20510, 202-224-2152. Also Kluczynski Bldg., 230 S. Dearborn, #3800, Chicago 60604, 312-353-4952; 3 W. Old Capital Plz., #1, Springfield 62701, 217-492-4960; and 250 W. Cherry, #115B, Carbondale 62901, 618-457-3653.

Committees: *Budget* (7th of 12 D). *Foreign Relations* (6th of 11 D): African Affairs (Chmn.); European Affairs; Terrorism, Narcotics and International Operations. *Indian Affairs* (6th of 10 D). *Judiciary* (7th of 10 D): Antitrust, Monopolies and Business Rights; Constitution (Chmn.); Immigration and Refugee Affairs. *Labor and Human Resources* (5th of 10 D): Disability Policy; Education, Arts and Humanities; Employment and Productivity (Chmn.).

Group Ratings

	ADA	ACLU	CDF	COPE	CFA	LCV	ACU	NTLC	NSI	COC	CEI
1992	95	91	80	92	100	92	7	5	50	10	14
1991	100	—	100	75	100	87	0	—	—	10	18

National Journal Ratings

	1991 LIB — 1991 CONS			1992 LIB — 1992 CONS		
Economic	97%	—	0%	79%	—	20%
Social	84%	—	13%	79%	—	16%
Foreign	86%	—	0%	86%	—	0%

Key Votes of the 102d Congress

1. $ for Homeownership	AGN	5. Clarence Thomas Nom.	AGN	9. Use Force in Gulf	AGN
2. Have Cap Gains Debate	AGN	6. Lmt Death Row Appeal	AGN	10. Keep Salvador Aid	AGN
3. Remove Budget Walls	FOR	7. Handgun Wait/5-Day	FOR	11. Cut $1B from SDI	FOR
4. Ban Striker Replace	FOR	8. Abortion Gag Rule	AGN	12. Override China MFN	FOR

Key Votes of the 103d Congress

1. Family Leave	FOR	2. HIV Immigrants	FOR	3. Clinton Budget	FOR

Election Results

1990 general	Paul Simon (D)................	2,115,377	(65%)	($8,665,789)
	Lynn Martin (R)................	1,135,628	(35%)	($4,921,613)
1990 primary	Paul Simon (D), unopposed			
1984 general	Paul Simon (D)................	2,397,165	(50%)	($4,545,786)
	Charles H. Percy (R)	2,308,039	(48%)	($5,391,567)

Sen. Carol Moseley-Braun (D)

Elected 1992, seat up 1998; b. Aug. 16, 1947, Chicago; home, Chicago; U. of IL, B.A., 1969, U. of Chicago, J.D. 1972; Catholic; divorced.

Career: Asst. U.S. Atty., 1973–77; IL House of Reps., 1978–88, Asst. Majority Ldr.; Cook Cnty. Recorder of Deeds, 1989–92.

Offices: 320 HSOB 20515, 202-224-2854. Also Kluczinski Fed. Bldg., #3996, 230 N. Dearborn, Chicago 60604, 312-353-5420; 117 Fed. Bldg., 600 E. Monroe St., Springfield 62701, 217-492-4126; and Fed. Bldg., 105 S. 6th St., Mt Vernon 62864, 618-383-7920.

Committees: *Banking, Housing and Urban Affairs* (10th of 11 D): Housing and Urban Affairs; Securities. *Judiciary* (10th of 10 D): Courts and Administrative Practice; Juvenile Justice. *Small Business* (12th of 12 D): Export Expansion and Agricultural Development; Urban and Minority-Owned Business Development.

Group Ratings and 102d Congress Votes: Newly Elected

Key Votes of the 103d Congress

1. Family Leave	FOR	2. HIV Immigrants	FOR	3. Clinton Budget	FOR

Election Results

1992 general	Carol Moseley-Braun (D)............	2,631,229	(53%)	($6,699,942)
	Richard S. Williamson (R)............	2,126,833	(43%)	($2,300,924)
	Nine Others........................	181,496	(4%)	
1992 primary	Carol Moseley-Braun (D).............	557,694	(38%)	
	Alan J. Dixon (D)...................	504,077	(35%)	
	Albert F. Hofeld (D).................	394,497	(27%)	
1986 general	Alan J. Dixon (D)...................	2,033,926	(65%)	($1,928,750)
	Judy Koehler (R)	1,053,793	(34%)	($851,305)

FIRST DISTRICT

The South Side of Chicago has been the site of the nation's largest urban black community for nearly a century now. At first it was just a nucleus, a few blocks where black families from the South would settle; it grew rapidly with the first influx of blacks from the Mississippi Delta in the 1910s. By the 1920s, the South Side was well established, a center of blues music in America and of black-owned businesses. Politically, the South Side was a heavily Republican constituency throughout those years; the comfortable white Protestants settled in solid brick houses here believed in the party of Yankee propriety, and the blacks had faith in the party of Lincoln.

This was one of the heartlands of the Republican Party, represented in Congress by House Republican Leader James Mann, and then Appropriations Chairman Martin Madden. After Madden died in the Appropriations Committee room in 1928, the 1st District elected Oscar DePriest, the first black elected to the House in the 20th Century. Blacks remained faithful to the party of Lincoln even during the Depression, voting for Herbert Hoover and DePriest even in 1932. But the New Deal and the racial liberalism of New Dealers like Eleanor Roosevelt and Interior Secretary Harold Ickes (a former Chicago Republican himself) attracted blacks to the Democratic Party, and DePriest was beaten by a black Democrat in 1934. The South Side has been Democratic ever since, a cooperative part of Chicago's Democratic machine and enthusiastically supportive of Mayor Harold Washington in his years in office from 1983–1987.

The years since Washington's death have been a time of disappointment but also a time of renewed energy on the South Side. Disappointment, because no black politician matched Washington's skill while several squabbled to be his successor, the result being the election of Mayor Richard M. Daley in 1989. Advancement through politics has long seemed natural for Chicago ethnic groups, and blacks in the 1970s and 1980s assumed that with their own members in high office there would be patronage jobs and contracts to lift up thousands of lives. But reformers and court decisions virtually outlawed patronage by the 1980s, and the public sector was no longer capable of expanding anyway. At the same time, the heavy manufacturing industries, where jobs could be had by political pressure or union connections, were cutting payrolls by the tens of thousands. Crime and violence, starting with but not limited to gangs that festered in giant housing projects, reduced the value of hard-working residents' homes and made their lives a nightmare. Yet not all South Side neighborhoods have been abandoned. Citizens have banded together to fight crime using high-sodium streetlights and roadblocks. The South Shore Development Bank, much touted by Bill Clinton in 1992, has provided loans to minority businessmen. And many commercial strips on the South Side are full of busy stores and neighborhoods are full of spruced-up houses. The South Side may be showing us that there is no reason declining urban neighborhoods have to go straight down to ruin.

The 1st Congressional District of Illinois includes about half of Chicago's South Side black community within its oddly shaped boundaries. It now extends out into the suburbs, and is no longer the nation's highest percentage black district, but it is by most measures Illinois's most Democratic. It includes the Robert Taylor homes along the Dan Ryan Expressway to the Gothic spires of the University of Chicago, and the mansions of Kenwood, once the home of Chicago's Jewish aristocracy and more recently the headquarters of the Nation of Islam. Miles and miles of the district are made up of bungalow neighborhoods, with single-family houses lining arrow straight streets. The 1st's odd shape follows historic patterns: the eastern half of the district roughly approximate the boundaries of 1st Districts going back to the 1960s; the western half, to which it is connected by a strip a mile wide, has some all-black neighborhoods, but also includes the high-income Irish-American neighborhoods of Morgan Park and Beverly, where the annual South Side Irish St. Patrick's Day Parade is held. It goes as far south as the industrial suburbs of Alsip and Blue Island.

The 1st District was the scene in 1992 of a Democratic primary which suggests the direction of political change in Chicago. The incumbent was Charles Hayes, a union official since the 1940s, first elected in 1983 to replace Harold Washington after he was elected mayor. But it was announced just before the March 1992 primary that Hayes had 716 overdrafts on the House bank. His major challenger was 2d Ward Alderman Bobby Rush, better known as a Black Panther in the late 1960s. But there is more to Rush's background than that: he grew up on the North Side, a Boy Scout whose mother was a Republican precinct captain; in the Army, he became involved in SNCC in the South, then founded the Illinois Black Panthers, where he recruited Fred Hampton, later killed in a raid by police in 1969; Rush served six months in prison for illegal possession of firearms, but also during his time with the Black Panthers he ran a medical clinic which developed the nation's first mass sickle cell anemia testing program. In 1983, he was elected alderman and became a strong Harold Washington supporter; after 1989, he worked amicably with Mayor Richard M. Daley as well. In 1992, Rush acknowledged Hayes's past services but questioned his zeal and effectiveness. In a big primary turnout of 128,000, he beat Hayes 42%–39%, carrying eight of 12 black wards plus Morgan Park and Beverly where many white police veterans live.

Rush's rhetoric today is not what one might expect from his Panther days. On crime, he says, "Blacks are killing blacks. Young blacks are killing other young blacks." and he believes, "We don't need to make excuses for our young people. We need to challenge them." He calls for laws to reduce crime in high schools, increase youth employment and establish community-based organizations: articulating surely the yearnings of his constituents who are struggling to keep their neighborhoods safe so they can raise their families and work their way up in life. "Most African-Americans just want a comfortable, middle-class lifestyle," he says now. "Twenty-five years ago, I didn't know that." He calls for coalition-building with others outside the black community, and he played a supportive role in the Clinton general election campaign. Rush's voting record is likely to be similar to Hayes's or Washington's, but his emphasis is different: while Washington concentrated on getting government jobs and aid programs for blacks even as those were a decreasing part of the economy, and Hayes stood for reinforcing union labor jobs even as they were diminishing, Rush seems to be calling for solutions that require changes in personal values along with government initiatives.

The People: Pop. 1990: 571,908; 14% age 65+; 26% White; 70% Black; 1% Asian; 2% Other; 4% Hispanic origin. Voting age pop.: 418,848; 68% Black; 3% Hispanic origin. Households: 35% married couple families; 15% married couple fams. w. children; 45% college educ.; median household income: $24,140; per capita income: $11,709; median gross rent: $425; median house value: $72,400.

1992 Presidential Vote

Clinton (D) 214,104 (81%)
Bush (R) 32,803 (12%)
Perot (I). 17,355 (7%)

1988 Presidential Vote

Dukakis (D). 202,182 (80%)
Bush (R) 50,575 (20%)

Rep. Bobby Rush (D)

Elected 1992; b. Nov. 23, 1946, Albany, GA; home, Chicago; Roosevelt U., B.A. 1973, U. of IL, 1975–77; Protestant; married (Carolyn).

Career: Army, 1963–68; Student Non-Violent Coor. Cmtee., 1966–68; Co-founder, IL Black Panther Party, 1968; Chicago City Alderman, 1983–92.

Offices: 1725 LHOB 20515, 202-225-4372. Also 655 E. 79th St., Chicago 60619, 312-224-6500; and 9730 S. Western Ave., #237, Evergreen Park 60643, 708-422-4055.

Committees: *Banking, Finance and Urban Affairs* (19th of 30 D): Consumer Credit and Insurance; Housing and Community Development; International Development, Finance, Trade and Monetary Policy. *Government Operations* (14th of 25 D): Commerce, Consumer and Monetary Affairs; Employment, Housing and Aviation.

Group Ratings and 102d Congress Votes: Newly Elected

Key Votes of the 103d Congress

1. Family Leave	FOR	2. Deficit Reduction	FOR	3. Stimulus Plan	FOR

Election Results

1992 general	Bobby Rush (D)	209,258	(83%)	($260,389)
	Jay Walker (R)	43,453	(17%)	($13,740)
1992 primary	Bobby Rush (D)	54,231	(42%)	
	Charles A. Hayes (D)	50,191	(39%)	
	Anna R. Langford (D)	14,094	(11%)	
	Four Others	9,974	(8%)	
1990 general	Charles A. Hayes (D)	100,890	(94%)	($125,509)
	Babette Peyton (R)	6,708	(6%)	($42,901)

SECOND DISTRICT

The Chicago that tourists see, in the Loop and on the Lakefront, is a white-collar city, rich from commerce and trade. But there is also a heavy industry Chicago, diminished in importance economically now, but historically significant and, with the remnants of its great hulking factories around Lake Calumet and the nearby rail yards, with a certain undeniable majesty. Thomas Geoghegan, who writes more poetically than a lawyer ought to be able to, has told in his book, *Whose Side Are You On?*, of the fights to wrest severance benefits and pension rights for the workers whose steel mills shut down, of the decline in the labor movement in a place where it got much of its inspiration (where the Pullman strike of 1894 was broken by federal troops and policemen killed 10 union supporters in the Little Steel strike of 1937). Over the years, Chicago grew around the tight ethnic neighborhoods where workers went home at shift break each afternoon or midnight; today they are mostly empty buildings that suburbanites speed by on the Calumet and Dan Ryan Expressways. Lake Calumet, with so many of its factories idle, was where Mayor Richard M. Daley wanted to build Chicago's third airport.

The 2d Congressional District of Illinois includes much of Chicago's old South Side industrial area plus many suburbs to the south. About two-thirds of its people live in Chicago, in separated neighborhoods: some in the old factory towns around Lake Calumet, some in the once heavily Jewish South Shore neighborhood, some in black wards west of Halsted Street. The Chicago portion of the 2d is overwhelmingly black; many blacks, especially young parents fleeing Chicago public schools, are moving into suburbs directly to the south—Harvey, Dolton, Posen (a reminder of its Polish origin), Markham. Farther south are Homewood and Flossmoor, with significant Jewish populations, high-income Olympia Fields, the planned town of Park Forest, and Chicago Heights, home town of America's premier political reporter for going on three decades now, David Broder. Two-thirds of the 2d's residents are black, and it is heavily Democratic.

The 2d District in 1992 had one of the sharpest changes in representation of any district in the nation, not as much due to the distinction of the current congressman, Mel Reynolds, but because of the disgracefulness of the last, Gus Savage. A self-styled rebel, Savage had a 12-year career in the House riddled with charges of absenteeism, blatantly incomplete campaign finance disclosure statements, nepotism, sexual harassment and, worst of all, bigotry. He welcomed the support of Louis Farrakhan and charged that Reynolds, his primary opponent in 1988 and 1990 as well as 1992, was receiving "pro-Israeli money." He attacked the "suburban Zionist lobby" and refused to talk to white journalists. This conduct never had wide support: Savage never won a primary with more than 52% of the vote and in 1990 beat Reynolds by just 52%–43%. So when more suburbs were added in redistricting, Savage looked like a goner, and Reynolds won by a resounding 63%–37%, carrying seven of the 11 wards in Chicago as well as the suburbs.

Mel Reynolds, like so many black Chicagoans, has roots in Mississippi: he was born in Mound Bayou in the Delta and remembers helping his grandmother pick cotton. He worked his way up through Chicago public schools to the University of Illinois, a Rhodes Scholarship and an Oxford degree and graduate work in the Kennedy School at Harvard; he worked on the presidential campaigns of Edward Kennedy and Jesse Jackson; he was a professor at Roosevelt University. He never closed his campaign headquarters after the 1990 primary and turned it into a service office, holding Halloween parties for kids and securing scholarship money, getting rid of abandoned cars and raising money for ministers' food programs. There was violence: the building which housed Reynolds's headquarters was firebombed and his car was shot at the Thursday before the primary. Reynolds did not try to link Savage to these incidents but did say that Savage's inflammatory and racial rhetoric created a tense and dangerous atmosphere.

In office, he says he wants to use money seized from drug dealers for community services, to build a $2 million jobs program in the 2d District funded by companies and foundations and to start a local scholarship program. Reynolds campaigned hard against fellow Chicago freshmen Bobby Rush and Luis Gutierrez for a seat on the Ways and Means Committee, and by carefully studying Chairman Dan Rostenkowski's 66-page list of committee issues and personally lobbying the 35 members of the Steering and Policy Committee, he won—the first freshman ever picked during Rostenkowski's tenure. He left Christmas Day on a self-financed trip to Somalia to observe the relief effort. He will be an administration stalwart; even before inauguration he promised, "I am inclined to make the case for Governor Clinton and his programs in all circumstances."

The People: Pop. 1990: 572,188; 10% age 65+; 25% White; 68% Black; 1% Asian; 4% Other; 6% Hispanic origin. Voting age pop.: 402,161; 66% Black; 6% Hispanic origin. Households: 46% married couple families; 22% married couple fams. w. children; 42% college educ.; median household income: $30,217; per capita income: $11,468; median gross rent: $449; median house value: $64,200.

1992 Presidential Vote			1988 Presidential Vote		
Clinton (D)	194,639	(80%)	Dukakis (D)	167,574	(78%)
Bush (R)	31,634	(13%)	Bush (R)	48,467	(22%)
Perot (I)	16,950	(7%)			

Rep. Mel Reynolds (D)

Elected 1992; b. Jan. 8, 1952, Mound Bayou, MS; home, Chicago; Chicago City Cols., A.A. 1972; U. of IL, B.A. 1974; Rhodes Scholar, Oxford, Honor Schl. of Jurisprudence, J.D.S. 1976; Harvard JFK Schl. of Govt., 1984–86; Baptist; married (Marisol).

Career: Army Reserves, 1988–present; Founder & Pres., Amer. Scholars Against World Hunger, 1985–87; Asst. Prof., Roosevelt U., 1990–91; Exec. Dir., Community Econ. Devel. Foundation, 1990–91; Radio talk show host, 1990–91.

Offices: 514 CHOB 20515, 202-225-0773. Also 525 E. 103rd St., Chicago 60628, 312-568-7900; and 17926 S. Halsted, #1-W, Homewood 60430, 708-957-9955.

Committees: *Ways and Means* (24th of 24 D): Human Resources; Social Security.

Group Ratings and 102d Congress Votes: Newly Elected

Key Votes of the 103d Congress

1. Family Leave	FOR	2. Deficit Reduction	FOR	3. Stimulus Plan	FOR

Election Results

1992 general	Mel Reynolds (D)	182,614	(78%)	($542,911)
	Ron Blackstone (R)	31,957	(14%)	($35,848)
	Louanner Peters (LPP)	19,293	(8%)	($45,008)
1992 primary	Mel Reynolds (D)	61,450	(63%)	
	Gus Savage (D)	36,865	(37%)	
1990 general	Gus Savage (D)	80,245	(78%)	($190,685)
	William T. Hespel (R)	22,350	(22%)	

THIRD DISTRICT

A century ago, Finley Peter Dunne's fictional Mr. Dooley pontificated on matters political in a saloon on Archery Avenue. This was, and is, Archer Avenue on the South Side of Chicago, one of Chicago's radial streets that cuts across what was once open prairie near the Loop and out the Chicago River and the Chicago and Sanitary Ship Canal. Archer Avenue was one of the paths of outward migration and upward mobility for the children and grandchildren of Chicago's different ethnic and cultural groups. Italians originally living in the river wards along the Canal moved west; the Irish, of course, moved west and south along Cicero Avenue toward Oak Lawn; the Bohemians (as they were called then; now Czechs) were heavily concentrated in the neat bungalows of the industrial suburbs of Berwyn and Cicero, famous as a haven for Al Capone's mobsters in the 1920s.

The 3d Congressional District of Illinois consists of much of this territory, criss-crossed by the Canal, the radial streets and the railroad lines and switching yards so common in this the center of the nation's rail network. It includes the far west edge of Chicago and most of Cicero and Berwyn; Riverside with its early 20th Century prairie-style houses; a few older affluent suburbs like Western Springs and the more recent and middle-income expanses of Oak Lawn and Palos Heights. Politically, this is marginal territory. Ancestral political preferences are mostly Democratic, but this is a culturally conservative area, with a sense of patriotism, although racism here has produced acts of bigotry. It is also economically threatened territory, ready to retaliate against the unconcern of George Bush and to take a chance on Bill Clinton.

The 3d District's congressman, William Lipinski, is an old-line Democrat who started off as a patronage employee, was elected alderman, and in successive decades has beaten incumbent congressmen in races for which he did not initially seem the favorite. His primary function in Congress seems to be as lobbyist for Chicago metropolitan area transportation projects. He has used his seat on the Public Works Committee to get funding for the nearly completed Southwest Rapid Transit Line and $22 million for Midway and O'Hare Airports; in 1990, he passed a passenger facility charge to enable Midway and O'Hare to finance expansion or (as Mayor Daley then hoped) a third airport. He wants to protect the Chicago Transit Authority against expensive federal mandates. On other issues, Lipinski supports greater cooperation between government and business, and industrial policy along Japanese or German lines. He is for a balanced budget amendment and school choice including private as well as public schools. On foreign policy, he was long a supporter of dissidents in the former Soviet Union and Eastern Europe and is a member of the national Democrats' Council on Ethnic Americans.

Lipinski first won this seat in 1982 when he was slated against an aging incumbent and beat him 61%–36% in the primary—a classic example of old-time Chicago politics. He held the seat easily for four more elections, then faced a struggle after 1990s redistricting put him in the same district with fellow Democratic incumbent Marty Russo. Russo had a similar background in Chicago, but had won his seat long before, in the Watergate year of 1974, and had come to be a major legislator on national issues, first on the Energy and Commerce Committee, then on Ways and Means. He played a major role on the 1986 tax reform law and became the chief congressional supporter of a single-payer national health insurance. With more seniority, with much of his old district territory in the new 3d and with far more money—Russo ended up spending $1,075,000, much of it from PACs or colleagues, compared to Lipinski's $375,000—Russo seemed to have the advantage. But Lipinski had the endorsements of the committeemen from Chicago's 13th and 23d Wards: House Speaker Michael Madigan and Lipinski himself. He ran ads attacking Russo for living in a big house outside the district, portrayed himself as "a neighborhood guy" interested in constituency service and Russo as a Washington insider who supported federal funding of obscene art and opposed federal funding of church-run day care. Lipinski recalled Russo's appearance on a 1990 ABC *Prime Time Live* show portraying lobbyists entertaining Ways and Means members in Barbados and enjoyed suggestions that Mayor Richard M. Daley, though officially neutral, valued his committee position and secretly favored him. The *Chicago Tribune* endorsed Lipinski as "more important to the future of Illinois." Russo retaliated by accusing Lipinski of driving a foreign car and of breaking the law by accepting $45,000 in contributions from congressional staffers and their families which a Lipinski aide said was not illegal and wholly voluntary. But this was not enough to prevent a solid 58%–37% Lipinski victory.

In partisan terms, the 3d District leaned Republican in the 1980s. But in November 1992, it went Democratic for president, and Lipinski beat Republican Harry Lepinske 64%–36%. In early 1993 Russo set up a Chicago office for Cassidy & Associates, one of Washington's leading lobbying firms, while Lipinski continued to work for Chicago transportation projects on the Public Works Committee.

The People: Pop. 1990: 570,902; 16% age 65+; 89% White; 2% Black; 1% Asian; 3% Other; 7% Hispanic origin. Voting age pop.: 441,900; 2% Black; 6% Hispanic origin. Households: 58% married couple families; 25% married couple fams. w. children; 40% college educ.; median household income: $36,250; per capita income: $15,854; median gross rent: $489; median house value: $92,100.

1992 Presidential Vote			1988 Presidential Vote		
Clinton (D)	108,342	(41%)	Bush (R)	157,477	(61%)
Bush (R)	102,632	(39%)	Dukakis (D)	100,124	(39%)
Perot (I)	52,905	(20%)			

Rep. William O. Lipinski (D)

Elected 1982; b. Dec. 22, 1937, Chicago; home, Chicago; Loras Col., 1956–57; Catholic; married (Rose Marie).

Career: Army Reserves, 1961–67; Chicago Parks & Recreation Dept., 1958–75; Chicago 23d Ward Committeeman, 1975–present; Chicago City Alderman, 1975–83.

Offices: 1501 LHOB 20515, 202-225-5701. Also 5832 S. Archer Ave., Chicago 60638, 312-886-0481; and 12717 W. Ridgeland Ave., Palos Heights 60463, 708-371-7460.

Committees: *Merchant Marine and Fisheries* (5th of 29 D): Coast Guard and Navigation; Merchant Marine (Chmn.). *Public Works and Transportation* (8th of 39 D): Aviation; Economic Development; Surface Transportation.

Group Ratings

	ADA	ACLU	COPE	CDF	CFA	LCV	ACU	NTLC	NSI	COC	CEI
1992	50	32	67	70	67	38	48	11	40	29	22
1991	45	—	75	60	78	62	30	—	—	20	26

National Journal Ratings

	1991 LIB — 1991 CONS		1992 LIB — 1992 CONS	
Economic	66%	32%	50%	49%
Social	37%	61%	36%	63%
Foreign	48%	51%	54%	45%

Key Votes of the 102d Congress

1. Ban Striker Replace	FOR	5. Handgun Wait/7-Day	FOR	9. Use Force in Gulf	AGN
2. $ for Homeownership	FOR	6. Overseas Mil. Abortion	AGN	10. US Mil. Abroad $ Cut	FOR
3. Tax Rich/Cut Mid Cls.	FOR	7. Obscn. Art NEA $ Ban	FOR	11. Limit SDI Funds	AGN
4. FY93/$15B Def. Cut	*	8. Death Pen. from Jury	AGN	12. Cuba Trade Embargo	FOR

Key Votes of the 103d Congress

1. Family Leave	FOR	2. Deficit Reduction	AGN	3. Stimulus Plan	FOR

Election Results

1992 general	William O. Lipinski (D)	162,165	(64%)	($556,847)
	Harry C. Lepinske (R)	93,128	(36%)	($66,991)
1992 primary	William O. Lipinski (D)	61,124	(58%)	
	Martin A. Russo (D).	38,802	(37%)	
	Two Others	5,324	(5%)	
1990 general	William O. Lipinski (D)	73,805	(66%)	($171,746)
(IL 5)	David J. Shestokas (R)	34,440	(31%)	($42,218)
	Other	3,001	(3%)	

FOURTH DISTRICT

Just beyond the Loop, the Chicago River splits into North and South Branches, both penetrating the heart of old neighborhoods where immigrants fresh off the boat first got their start in Chicago. The South Branch is the guts of Chicago, the site of one of western civilization's astonishing engineering feats: here in 1900 the course of the river was reversed so that sewage flowed Downstate through a canal rather than out into Lake Michigan. Just blocks away was Maxwell Street, thronged with market stalls, long the arrival neighborhood for Chicago's Jews; not far away, in an Italian-American neighborhood on Halsted Street, was Jane Addams's Hull House, the original settlement house, where social workers told new immigrants not how to rebel against middle-class American mores, but how to live them. To the south were Bridgeport, home of the Irish and of the Mayors of Chicago from 1933 to 1979 and again since 1989, and Pilsen, arrival neighborhood for the Bohemians (Czechs). Off the North Branch of the River was Milwaukee Avenue, the main street of Polish-Americans and Ukrainian-Americans for a century now.

Today, many of these places are arrival neighborhoods again, mostly for Chicago's wide variety of Hispanic immigrants. On the South Side, in the old river wards, is Chicago's Mexican-American community, extending west into the heavily Bohemian suburb of Cicero; on the North Side are many Puerto Ricans and other Hispanics. Altogether, the 1990 Census counted 545,000 Hispanics in Chicago, by far the largest Latino concentration north of Texas and Florida and between the two coasts. They have been attracted, as immigrants were 100 years ago, by a vibrant economy that provides opportunity to those who work hard, and by a culture which seems unwelcoming only because of its own high standards.

Under the prevailing interpretation of the Voting Rights Act amendments of 1982, it was considered mandatory to create a new Hispanic-majority congressional district in Illinois. The problem was that the South Side Mexican-American and the North Side Puerto Rican communities were separated by the West Side black ghetto. The solution was today's 4th Congressional District, which has arguably the most convoluted shape of any district in the country: essentially these two Latino communities, defined by erose boundaries to maximize the Hispanic percentage, are connected by a thin line of territory which stretches around the West Side black-majority 7th District to meet at the Cook-DuPage County line. Most of this salient consists of parkland, railroad yards and cemeteries; more than 95% of the votes are in Chicago or Cicero. The 4th's population is about two-thirds Hispanic, with Mexican-Americans outnumbering Puerto Ricans more than 2–1; but eligible voters are 58% white anglo and 39% Latino, with Mexican-Americans and Puerto Ricans about equally split. This is a solidly Democratic district, though by no means as Democratic as the black-majority 1st, 2d or 7th.

The congressman here, Luis Gutierrez, was chosen in the Democratic primary. He is a politician who in his decade-long career has shown some skill at political maneuvering. Gutierrez remembers delivering newspapers to Mayor Richard J. Daley's office at City Hall; he grew up, the son of a cab driver and factory worker, in both Chicago, where he was a social worker, and Puerto Rico, where he taught school. He started off politically as a supporter of Harold Washington by defiantly running—and losing—against Dan Rostenkowski for 32d Ward Committeeman in 1983. Then Washington hired him as a staffer, and backed him in a crucial 1986 special election for Council in one of two new Hispanic seats. Gutierrez won and, with Juan Soliz on the South Side, gave control of the Council to Washington. Then Washington died in 1987 and, in the 1989 election to succeed him, Gutierrez backed (and Soliz opposed) Richard M. Daley. For that, Gutierrez was richly rewarded: he became chairman of the Housing Committee, pushed through his "New Homes for Chicago" plan authorizing the city to sell vacant lots to developers of affordable housing for $1; he was also author of a bill prohibiting discrimination against gays and the disabled. In both cases, he helped Daley cement his support with crucial groups in the middle 20% of the electorate, Latinos and gays; Soliz made a momentary challenge to Daley in 1991, and lost his seat as alderman by 22 votes.

The final "payback," as Gutierrez called it, came in the 4th Congressional District race. Gutierrez and Soliz were again rivals. Gutierrez called crime the number one problem and bragged of his council record; Soliz talked about trade and health care, saying his rival took no stand on these national issues, and called Gutierrez a machine candidate. Certainly Gutierrez seemed a multiethnic candidate: "There is a Hispanic agenda . . . it's the same as the Polish, Irish and Lithuanian agenda. If you work hard, sweat and toil and play by the rules, you will be rewarded . . . with clean streets, safer and better schools, the opportunity to send your kids to college. Tell me who in America and in the 4th Congressional District doesn't want these things?"

Gutierrez beat Soliz by a 60%–40% margin, and went on to an easy victory in the general election. He soon became known as a freshman rebel: when the House leadership came to meet freshmen in Chicago in November, Gutierrez called on the freshmen to organize because "Congress is held in such low esteem." This was not appreciated, and Gutierrez's efforts to get on the Ways and Means Committee did not succeed. In office, Gutierrez persevered, calling for campaign finance reform and, with Eric Fingerhut of Ohio, for a congressional pay freeze. But if he is willing to infuriate the House leadership, he is trying to entrench himself in the 4th District. His family is staying in Chicago; following up on a campaign promise, he has organized a Gutierrez Community Corps to conduct graffiti paintouts and recycling drives. He may be aware that some of the 4th District once was represented by Adolf J. Sabath, a Bohemian immigrant elected to Congress in 1906 who rose to become chairman of the Rules Committee and served until his death in 1952; Gutierrez, though always an American citizen, seems to be trying to follow in the same newcomer tradition.

The People: Pop. 1990: 571,162; 8% age 65+; 27% White; 6% Black; 3% Asian; 42% Other; 64% Hispanic origin. Voting age pop.: 383,285; 6% Black; 58% Hispanic origin. Households: 49% married couple families; 31% married couple fams. w. children; 24% college educ.; median household income: $23,083; per capita income: $8,352; median gross rent: $393; median house value: $64,300.

1992 Presidential Vote			1988 Presidential Vote		
Clinton (D)	82,271	(65%)	Dukakis (D)	79,492	(63%)
Bush (R)	29,093	(23%)	Bush (R)	45,938	(37%)
Perot (I)	15,272	(12%)			

Rep. Luis V. Gutierrez (D)

Elected 1992; b. Dec. 10, 1953, Chicago; home, Chicago; Northeastern IL U., B.A. 1975; Catholic; married (Soraida).

Career: Teacher, Puerto Rico, 1977–78; Social Wkr., Chicago Dept. of Children & Family Svcs., 1979–83; Advisor, Chicago Mayor Harold Washington, 1984–86; Chicago City Alderman, 1986–92, Pres. Pro Tem, 1989–92.

Offices: 1208 LHOB 20515, 202-225-8203. Also 3181 N. Elston Ave., Chicago 60618, 312-509-0999.

Committees: *Banking, Finance and Urban Affairs* (18th of 30 D): Consumer Credit and Insurance; Housing and Community Development. *Veterans' Affairs* (16th of 21 D): Hospitals and Health Care; Oversight and Investigations.

Group Ratings and 102d Congress Votes: Newly Elected

Key Votes of the 103d Congress

1. Family Leave	FOR	2. Deficit Reduction	FOR	3. Stimulus Plan	FOR

Election Results

1992 general	Luis V. Gutierrez (D)	90,452	(78%)	($420,227)
	Hildegarde Rodriguez-Schieman (R)	26,154	(22%)	($3,574)
1992 primary	Luis V. Gutierrez (D)	36,377	(60%)	
	Juan M. Soliz (D)	24,609	(40%)	
1990 election	Newly created district.			

FIFTH DISTRICT

There is scarcely any place in America today with more variety, ethnic and cultural, than the North Side of Chicago. From the air, the geometric grid streets lit by high-sodium lamps seem monotonous; on the ground, on a winter's day with snow swirling, its brick buildings look stolid and forbidding. But this has been the homeland of one immigrant group after another and the chosen neighborhoods of all manner of successful middle-class people. Wooden workingman's cottages from the late 19th Century give way to sturdy huge brick houses of the early 1900s and then to the prairie bungalows of the 1920s and white-shuttered colonials of the 1950s. Chicago was America's number one immigrant destination for Poles, Lithuanians, Czechs, Slovaks, Ukrainians and Romanians; something about the heavy dull clouds of the long winters, the short hot summers, a climate suited to potatoes and cabbage and other earth vegetables, may have reminded them of central and eastern Europe. By the late 1980s, new upwardly mobile immigrants from Mexico and Guatemala, Korea and the Philippines, refugees and recent arrivals from Eastern Europe and the former Soviet Union moved into these melting pot precincts. Family ties, webs of acquaintance that reach back to ancestral villages, have made the North Side of Chicago a natural port of entry for Eastern bloc migrants coming to America.

The 5th Congressional District of Illinois covers an oddly-shaped slice of Chicago's North Side, running from the Lakefront all the way to the suburbs directly south of O'Hare Airport. Its boundaries were carefully drawn to put most Hispanics in the 4th District just to the south, but otherwise it reflects the full variety of the North Side. It includes Chicago's most glamorous lakefront apartments facing the Oak Street beach and the gentrified neighborhoods of New Town, where young families and gays are rehabilitating old houses. It takes in the Polish-American and Ukrainian-American neighborhoods around Milwaukee Avenue, and the old Italian neighborhoods running west on Grand Avenue. Most important politically, it includes, a couple of blocks from the Chicago River, the old church of St. Stanislaus Kostka, a traditional center of the Polish community since the 19th Century, and across Pulaski Park the sturdy and comfortable house where lives one of America's most powerful and capable politicians, Dan Rostenkowski.

A congressman since 1958, Rostenkowski was 32d Ward Democratic committeeman (as his father was before him: between them from 1935 to 1987) and since 1981 has been chairman of the House Ways and Means Committee. But in recent years he has not been allowed to coast. He received the toughest electoral challenge of his life with the redistricting approved in December 1991, just before the filing deadline, and proved that he could win a primary in territory much of which was unfamiliar and some of which was temperamentally hostile to him. And he faced in late 1992 and early 1993 rumors of possible legal action and even an indictment regarding misuse of his office stamp allowance, which could deprive him of his chairmanship; at the same time his committee membership changed sharply and he received new challenges from Bill Clinton's economic and tax proposals. The wonder is not that Rostenkowski looked a bit frazzled in 1992 and 1993, but that he persevered and adapted.

Rostenkowski was first elected to the legislature in 1952, at 24. When the local congressman retired in 1958, Rostenkowski got Mayor Richard J. Daley to back him because Rostenkowski's father had risked detriment in his own Polish ward by backing Daley against Ben Adamowski in the 1955 primary. Daley found young Rostenkowski's ambition odd: in Chicago aldermen were considered the real power and going to Washington was seen as a demotion. In 1968, Rostenkowski became Democratic Caucus chairman, and seemed headed for the speakership. But in 1971, after falling out of favor with Speaker Carl Albert, he was voted out of that post. Then he became chief deputy whip after endorsing long-shot Jim Wright (he won by one vote) for majority leader in 1976. In 1980, after several senior members were defeated, Rostenkowski had the choice of the Ways and Means chairmanship or the post of whip; Rostenkowski took the chair and left the whip's job to Thomas Foley, who in 1989 ascended to speaker.

As Ways and Means chairman, Rostenkowski has been determined to assert that he is not just a political hack but a serious legislator. His 1981 tax bill was loaded up with special provisions to attract support, but was still beaten by Ronald Reagan. But soon Rostenkowski was steering his bills to passage. His great achievement was the tax reform of 1985–86, which flattened rates, eliminated most preferences and generally rationalized the Internal Revenue Code—even though it also eroded his old power base. He played inside politics, keeping control of the Democrats and ignoring the Republicans on his committee, trading for votes on the floor with implied promises of favorable transition rules. He showed he could master the technical details of the tax code and the intellectual policy arguments as well as the politics of the House.

His later experiences as chairman have not all been as happy. The 1988 catastrophic health care law proved a political catastrophe when the affluent elderly rebelled against its tax; it was rapidly repealed in 1989, after Rostenkowski himself was besieged by a group of seniors in Chicago and had to flee in his car. In 1989, the House voted a capital gains rate cut over his opposition, and the 1990 budget summit package raised tax rates on his 1986 reforms against his will. He was rebuffed in late 1990 when the Democratic Caucus voted to make Ways and Means subcommittee chairs elected by the whole caucus rather than by committee members. He was angry when George Bush vetoed tax bills he had shepherded through in March and October 1992. And he aggressively pushed the Democrats' unemployment benefits extension bill and argued for a play-or-pay health care plan. By 1992, he had clearly become a more partisan Democrat, but it is not right to say he has no philosophy; he thinks it part of his duty to advance legislation that can pass in different political circumstances, and so is frustrated when it fails. If he has stuck rather strongly to his belief in free trade, far more than is dictated by his constituency, he has also been willing to move his fulcrum point in balancing the goals of progressive taxation and business incentives.

Rostenkowski's partisan course on taxes was prompted partly by his experience campaigning for reelection. The late 1991 redistricting plan placed Rostenkowski in a district that subtracted many of his former Hispanic constituents and stretched far to the northwest edge of the city, for the first time giving him a lakefront ward. This new 5th District was also the home of 26-year incumbent Frank Annunzio, who talked about running, but was politically wounded: he was one of the leading supporters of savings and loan interests on the Banking Committee in the 1980s, and he was voted out of the Banking chair 127–125 by the Democratic Caucus in December 1990. Redistricted in with Rostenkowski, eligible to transfer his campaign funds to personal use if he retired, he decided after initial hesitation to leave. Rostenkowski, for his part, turned down what would be his last chance to pocket his $1 million-plus campaign treasury. But for the first time, he had serious primary opposition, from former lakefront alderman and University of Illinois professor Dick Simpson, who called him the "arrogant" king of "honorariums and free travel and free lunches and backroom deals and payoffs." Simpson had a clear demographic base on the lakefront and in New Town, plus an opponent that had not campaigned in years. But the old dog learned some new tricks: Rostenkowski boasted of the funds he'd brought in for Chicago, especially for rebuilding the Kennedy Expressway (which bends to avoid his house) and the airline ticket tax he pushed to finance the proposed third airport. Mayor Daley strongly backed the chairman, while Rosty learned to pound the pavement, attend community meetings, deliver stump speeches and shake hands at shopping centers. He needed all his huge funds and new skills to win a 57%–43% victory. He also came out of the March primary even more partisan than before: "The debate on Milwaukee Avenue is over. My middle-class constituents are comfortable with the Democratic plan."

Then in May 1992, the U.S. Attorney in Washington subpoenaed Rostenkowski, evidently because his campaign and government accounts charged $55,000 worth of stamps from the House Post Office. The suggestion, never made directly, was that he or someone on his staff converted the stamps to cash, in effect pocketing taxpayer and contributed funds for personal use. Rostenkowski refused to respond to the subpoena and denied all wrongdoing; his defenders pointed out that he had given up a much larger sum when he ran for reelection. The investigation lingered on into 1993, and further charges were made that Rostenkowski violated House rules on auto leasing and used campaign funds to rent a phantom office in a building he and his sister owned. The lease was a minor matter and the law allows almost total leeway in the use of campaign funds; the nagging question is whether one of America's most talented and durable legislators had violated his constituents' trust for several thousand dollars of cash.

Evidently some constituents and colleagues were troubled. In November 1992, Rostenkowski won by just 57%–39% over Republican Elias R. Non-Incumbent Zenkich (he officially changed his name to this), a native of Bosnia who saw his father shot when he was 10 and who made a fortune as a high-tech engineer in Chicago. In December 1992, 53 House Democrats voted against Rostenkowski for chairman in the secret ballot; and there was speculation that if he were indicted, the rules would force him out of the chair. Rostenkowski promised to work in tandem with Bill Clinton: "You lay out the program, I'm with you," he told him in December, and delivered on the budget and tax package in the spring of 1993. But health care will be a bigger challenge, and Rostenkowski will be called on to work with many other House powers, including John Dingell and Henry Waxman, as well as Daniel Patrick Moynihan, the fourth Senate Finance Chairman he will have worked with. Back in Chicago, where Rostenkowski still spends most of his time, Simpson has kept on campaigning, calling for ethics and FEC investigations of Rostenkowski and calling his contributions to other Democrats "bribes." After a lifetime of politics, Dan Rostenkowski's life is more storm-tossed than ever: even as he continues to shoulder great responsibilities, many of his colleagues wonder whether he is serving his last term. But he has been underestimated before.

The People: Pop. 1990: 571,053; 15% age 65+; 79% White; 1% Black; 6% Asian; 6% Other; 13% Hispanic origin. Voting age pop.: 467,192; 1% Black; 11% Hispanic origin. Households: 44% married couple families; 18% married couple fams. w. children; 47% college educ.; median household income: $33,262; per capita income: $19,242; median gross rent: $514; median house value: $109,200.

1992 Presidential Vote

Clinton (D) 124,273 (51%)
Bush (R) 80,036 (33%)
Perot (I)................... 39,113 (16%)

1988 Presidential Vote

Bush (R) 123,159 (52%)
Dukakis (D)............... 115,011 (48%)

Rep. Dan Rostenkowski (D)

Elected 1958; b. Jan. 2, 1928, Chicago; home, Chicago; Loyola U., 1948–51; Catholic; married (LaVerne).

Career: Army, 1946–48; IL House of Reps., 1952–54; IL Senate, 1954–58; Chicago 32d Ward Committeeman, 1964–87.

Offices: 2111 RHOB 20515, 202-225-4061. Also 4849 N. Milwaukee Ave., #101, Chicago 60630, 312-481-0111; and 818 W. Fullerton, Chicago 60614, 312-276-6000.

Committees: *Ways and Means* (Chmn. of 24 D): Trade. *Joint Committee on Taxation* (Chmn. of 5).

Group Ratings

	ADA	ACLU	COPE	CDF	CFA	LCV	ACU	NTLC	NSI	COC	CEI
1992	95	78	82	90	93	25	0	5	80	38	8
1991	45	—	73	80	67	54	16	—	—	30	16

National Journal Ratings

	1991 LIB — 1991 CONS		1992 LIB — 1992 CONS	
Economic	54%	— 45%	64%	— 36%
Social	53%	— 46%	62%	— 38%
Foreign	61%	— 39%	62%	— 38%

Key Votes of the 102d Congress

1. Ban Striker Replace FOR	5. Handgun Wait/7-Day FOR	9. Use Force in Gulf FOR
2. $ for Homeownership FOR	6. Overseas Mil. Abortion AGN	10. US Mil. Abroad $ Cut FOR
3. Tax Rich/Cut Mid Cls. FOR	7. Obscn. Art NEA $ Ban FOR	11. Limit SDI Funds FOR
4. FY93/$15B Def. Cut FOR	8. Death Pen. from Jury AGN	12. Cuba Trade Embargo FOR

Key Votes of the 103d Congress

1. Family Leave FOR	2. Deficit Reduction FOR	3. Stimulus Plan FOR

Election Results

1992 general	Dan Rostenkowski (D) 132,889	(57%)	($1,455,455)
	Elias R. Non-Incumbent Zenkich (R) 90,738	(39%)	($83,293)
	Blaise C. Grenke (LIB). 8,456	(4%)	
1992 primary	Dan Rostenkowski (D) 56,059	(57%)	
	Dick Simpson (D) 41,956	(43%)	
1990 general	Dan Rostenkowski (D) 70,151	(79%)	($298,653)
(IL 8)	Robert Marshall (R) 18,529	(21%)	

SIXTH DISTRICT

The nation's largest airport was half a century ago an airstrip in an apple orchard (hence its current three-letter code: ORD) and the towns beyond were little suburban villages strung along rail lines, separated by cornfields. But in the 1950s, Mayor Richard J. Daley decided that Chicago needed a new airport, annexed the orchard, and named it after a World War II hero from a good Chicago Irish Catholic Democratic family. Today, O'Hare is surrounded on all sides by suburbs as densely settled as the bungalow wards of the city, with hotels and office buildings clustered near the interchanges in Rosemont and characteristic Chicago yellow-orange brick houses in orderly rows in suburbs like Park Ridge, the childhood home of Hillary Rodham Clinton. Politically, these suburbs have long been solidly Republican, as was the Rodham family, convinced that civic virtues could best be realized by opposing the party of City Hall in Chicago and economic growth could best be assured by opposing the party that backed stifling government regulation. Indeed, Maine Township, which includes Park Ridge, has remained true to the principles which its most famous daughter has renounced, voting for Paul Tsongas over Bill Clinton in the 1992 Illinois primary and for Bush/Quayle over Clinton/Gore in the general election.

The 6th Congressional District of Illinois includes much of this suburban area. It includes Park Ridge and Des Plaines just north of O'Hare and to the west the suburb of Elk Grove Village. The larger part of the district is over the line in DuPage County, including the string of suburbs directly (though far) west of the Loop: Elmhurst, Villa Park, Lombard, Glen Ellyn, Wheaton. It also takes in the newer suburbs along I-290 and Lake Street: Bensenville, Addison, Wood Dale, Bloomingdale. Economically, this is high income territory; culturally, it is cautiously moderate; politically, it is one of the most Republican districts in Illinois.

Its congressman is Henry Hyde, a Republican who is one of the most respected and intellectually honorable members of the House. He comes from hard-bitten Illinois, but acts from deep belief more than political calculation. He first made his name in the House as an opponent of abortion, attaching to Appropriations subcommittee bills his Hyde Amendments prohibiting the use of federal funds to pay for abortions in various circumstances. These were regarded by many as regressive and by others as a time-wasting diversion; for Hyde, who regards abortion as murder, the issue was saving children. Through 1992 Hyde Amendments were passed routinely, but now Clinton has pledged to end the ban on federal funding of abortion and surely there will emotional debate on both sides of this issue for 1993. Hyde will bring the same passion to the Freedom of Choice Act, the attempt to codify *Roe v. Wade*, on which he will presumably argue for the preservation of at least some restrictions on abortion.

Hyde's regard for children and desire to strengthen families takes him well beyond abortion issues. He was one of the few Republicans who supported the family leave bill, and even voted to override President Bush's veto of it in 1992; he felt it was logical to help mothers care for children after they're born. He wants to outlaw commercial surrogate motherhood contracts and he worked to facilitate adoption of Romanian children. He also fashioned legislation to crack down on fathers who fail to pay child support, making crossing state lines to avoid it a felony, and authorizing the FBI to chase them down; Hyde pointed out that less than half of court-ordered child support is ever paid, and the bill passed in 1992. Hyde also proposed that the IRS collect child support through wage withholding. "Denying a little kid food and clothes is like stealing; it's child abuse," Hyde said."Capitalism with a human face isn't such a nutty idea."

Hyde has brought similar passion to other policies. He fatally assaulted the nuclear freeze proposal in 1983, as his incisive questions revealed it for the empty slogan it was; he was a defender of the Reagan Administration in the Iran-contra hearings; on the Intelligence Committee he introduced a bill requiring his fellow members to go through a security clearance. He co-sponsored with California's Howard Berman a ban on arms sales to terrorist-condoning nations including Iraq: pretty good foresight. He is not always partisan. He supported the Brady bill waiting period for gun purchases, opposes term limits on legislators, favors the independent counsel law. His stands seem to stem from deep religious beliefs combined with a trial lawyer's combative instincts, a respect for rules combined with a certain compassion.

Hyde, elected Republican Policy Committee chairman in December 1992, is a member of the House leadership. It was widely expected in early 1993 that he would run for Minority Leader if, as expected, Robert Michel retires from the House or from the post in 1994. If that happens, Hyde will presumably be opposing Newt Gingrich and possibly Dick Armey; he will have the advantage of his reputation for integrity but the disadvantage of being in some eyes insufficiently partisan. Like Ronald Reagan, Hyde grew up an Illinois Democrat and he retains many of the cultural attitudes of New Deal-era Democrats while espousing the views of a Reagan-era Republican: he has something of Reagan's cheery optimism as well as his conservatism, together with a considerably greater capacity for handling legislative detail.

The People: Pop. 1990: 572,268; 12% age 65+; 88% White; 1% Black; 5% Asian; 2% Other; 5% Hispanic origin. Voting age pop.: 437,173; 1% Black; 4% Hispanic origin. Households: 62% married couple families; 29% married couple fams. w. children; 57% college educ.; median household income: $44,216; per capita income: $19,405; median gross rent: $605; median house value: $129,800.

1992 Presidential Vote			1988 Presidential Vote		
Bush (R)	121,868	(47%)	Bush (R)	158,513	(68%)
Clinton (D)	86,448	(33%)	Dukakis (D)	75,931	(32%)
Perot (I)	52,734	(20%)			

Rep. Henry J. Hyde (R)

Elected 1974; b. Apr. 18, 1924, Chicago; home, Bensenville; Georgetown U., B.S. 1947, Loyola U., J.D. 1949; Catholic; widowed.

Career: Navy, 1944–46 (WWII); Naval Reserves, 1946–68; Practicing atty., 1950–75; IL House of Reps., 1967–74, Majority Ldr., 1971–72.

Offices: 2110 RHOB 20515, 202-225-4561. Also 50 E. Oak St., Addison 60101, 312-832-5950.

Committees: *Foreign Affairs* (6th of 18 R): International Operations. *Judiciary* (3d of 14 R): Civil and Constitutional Rights (RMM).

Group Ratings

	ADA	ACLU	COPE	CDF	CFA	LCV	ACU	NTLC	NSI	COC	CEI
1992	15	10	44	20	33	13	94	84	100	75	67
1991	10	—	17	40	44	8	80	—	—	70	71

National Journal Ratings

	1991 LIB — 1991 CONS		1992 LIB — 1992 CONS	
Economic	24% —	74%	21% —	79%
Social	16% —	81%	33% —	67%
Foreign	17% —	78%	0% —	82%

Key Votes of the 102d Congress

1. Ban Striker Replace	AGN	5. Handgun Wait/7-Day	FOR	9. Use Force in Gulf	FOR
2. $ for Homeownership	*	6. Overseas Mil. Abortion	AGN	10. US Mil. Abroad $ Cut	AGN
3. Tax Rich/Cut Mid Cls.	AGN	7. Obscn. Art NEA $ Ban	FOR	11. Limit SDI Funds	AGN
4. FY93/$15B Def. Cut	AGN	8. Death Pen. from Jury	FOR	12. Cuba Trade Embargo	FOR

Key Votes of the 103d Congress

1. Family Leave	FOR	2. Deficit Reduction	AGN	3. Stimulus Plan	AGN

Election Results

1992 general	Henry J. Hyde (R)	165,009	(66%)	($408,987)
	Barry W. Watkins (D)..................	86,891	(34%)	($62,423)
1992 primary	Henry J. Hyde (R), unopposed			
1990 general	Henry J. Hyde (R)	96,410	(67%)	($270,435)
	Robert J. Cassidy (D).................	48,155	(33%)	($1,055)

SEVENTH DISTRICT

The cross-country flyer on a lucky day can get a clear view of the biggest man-made landscape between the Atlantic and Pacific Oceans: Chicago's Loop. High-rise buildings were pioneered in the Loop—named in 1897 for the circle the "El" train forms around the city's center—100 years ago by architects like Louis Sullivan and Daniel Burnham. International School modernists built their most impressive collection of buildings here and along the Lakeshore in the years after World War II; in the last dozen years postmodernists have decorated the Chicago River and reinvented the skyscraper. The Loop now spreads beyond the El, up the wondrous shopping street of North Michigan Avenue with a peak at the John Hancock Tower, and west beyond the commodities exchanges to the Sears Tower on the Chicago River. This is the face Chicago likes to present to the world: giant structures rising where the prairies meet the inland sea, a vast concentration of brains and muscle, the nerve center of the markets of the nation and the world.

Behind the lakefront, where the air traveler sees the grid spread out below with occasional radials, is the muscle and sinew, gristle and fat of the city. And also the parts that do not work so well: houses and apartment buildings are left abandoned; commercial space stands empty and vandalized; giant housing projects, like the Robert Taylor Homes off the Dan Ryan Expressway, rise starkly, their playgrounds empty because of the ever-present threat of gunfire. The West Side of Chicago, the vast acres directly west of the Loop, for years has been a dreadful slum. And the decay has spread west to the Austin neighborhood, just before the border of upper income—and for two decades racially integrated—Oak Park.

The 7th Congressional District of Illinois contains the Loop and most of the North Michigan corridor and the Near North Side, with the infamous Cabrini-Green housing project. It also goes south, past 19th Century Prairie Avenue mansions to the Taylor homes and takes in a few heavily black South Side neighborhoods. Its heart, demographically and spiritually, is the black ghetto of the West Side, far more depopulated and socially disorganized than the South Side. To the west are Oak Park and River Forest, and the much more modest Maywood, which is black-majority, and Broadview and Hillside. About two-thirds of the people here are black; there are few Hispanics since they were confined by painstaking boundary-drawing to the 4th District which practically encircles the 7th on three sides.

Representing the 7th District is Cardiss Collins, a black Democrat first elected in 1973 to replace her husband after he was killed in a plane crash; he had been a routine machine backer and she was expected to be the same. But Chicago politics has changed and Congresswoman Collins has been something more than a cipher. She has a seat on the Energy and Commerce Committee, often the most sought-after assignment for House Democrats, and became chairman of the Commerce, Consumer Protection and Competitiveness Subcommittee in 1991. There she passed laws to clear the way for mass introduction of blank digital audio recording tapes into the U.S. and to probe foreign acquisitions of U.S. firms for danger to national security; she sought to have used oil declared a hazardous waste once it is in transit from a collection center, and to label toys that contain small pieces as "a potential danger" to young children. She plans hearings on the problems of minority-owned franchises and gender equity in college sports. On Henry Waxman's Health Subcommittee, she worked to expand Medicare coverage for Pap smears and mammograms and to establish health clinics in high schools. She has been a supporter of the Chicago futures markets in their fight to be treated equal to and separate from

New York's securities markets.

Collins had serious competition in the mid-1980s, when she twice beat Alderman Danny Davis in primaries, 48%–39% and 60%–40%; she has had no problems since. She got involved in fights over 1990s redistricting and resisted creation of a Hispanic-majority district, arguing correctly that it would either be geographically grotesque or would cut her district in two. She is presumably pleased that, of these two unpleasant alternatives, the first was chosen by the federal court that devised Illinois's final plan.

The People: Pop. 1990: 572,039; 10% age 65+; 27% White; 66% Black; 3% Asian; 2% Other; 4% Hispanic origin. Voting age pop.: 407,120; 60% Black; 4% Hispanic origin. Households: 33% married couple families; 15% married couple fams. w. children; 43% college educ.; median household income: $25,220; per capita income: $13,056; median gross rent: $449; median house value: $89,300.

1992 Presidential Vote			1988 Presidential Vote		
Clinton (D)	184,966	(78%)	Dukakis (D)	166,350	(76%)
Bush (R)	35,530	(15%)	Bush (R)	51,139	(24%)
Perot (I)	15,992	(7%)			

Rep. Cardiss Collins (D)

Elected 1973; b. Sept. 24, 1931, St. Louis, MO; home, Chicago; Northwestern U., B.A. 1967; Baptist; widowed.

Career: Stenographer, IL Dept. of Labor, 1950–58; Secy., accountant and auditor, IL Dept. of Revenue, 1958–72.

Offices: 2308 RHOB 20515, 202-225-5006. Also 230 S. Dearborn St., #3880, Chicago 60604, 312-353-5754; and 328 Lake St., Oak Park 60302, 708-383-1400.

Committees: *Energy and Commerce* (6th of 27 D): Commerce, Consumer Protection and Competitiveness (Chmn.); Oversight and Investigations. *Government Operations* (2d of 25 D): Legislation and National Security.

Group Ratings

	ADA	ACLU	COPE	CDF	CFA	LCV	ACU	NTLC	NSI	COC	CEI
1992	85	100	92	80	93	56	0	0	10	14	11
1991	90	—	100	90	89	69	0	—	—	20	8

National Journal Ratings

	1991 LIB —	1991 CONS	1992 LIB —	1992 CONS
Economic	88% —	0%	91% —	0%
Social	88% —	0%	79% —	20%
Foreign	92% —	0%	90% —	0%

Key Votes of the 102d Congress

1. Ban Striker Replace	FOR	5. Handgun Wait/7-Day	FOR	9. Use Force in Gulf	AGN
2. $ for Homeownership	AGN	6. Overseas Mil. Abortion	FOR	10. US Mil. Abroad $ Cut	FOR
3. Tax Rich/Cut Mid Cls.	FOR	7. Obscn. Art NEA $ Ban	AGN	11. Limit SDI Funds	*
4. FY93/$15B Def. Cut	*	8. Death Pen. from Jury	AGN	12. Cuba Trade Embargo	AGN

Key Votes of the 103d Congress

1. Family Leave	FOR	2. Deficit Reduction	FOR	3. Stimulus Plan	FOR

Election Results

1992 general	Cardiss Collins (D)	182,811	(81%)	($390,942)
	Norman G. Boccio (R)	35,346	(16%)	($6,978)
	Two Others	7,124	(3%)	
1992 primary	Cardiss Collins (D)	66,976	(88%)	
	Clarence Desmond Clemons (D)	8,980	(12%)	
1990 general	Cardiss Collins (D)	80,021	(80%)	($399,748)
	Michael Dooley (R)	20,099	(20%)	

EIGHTH DISTRICT

It is one of America's major headquarters cities, one of the fastest-growing parts of the Midwest in the last dozen years, yet few Americans have heard of it: Schaumburg, Illinois. Half a century ago it was farmland, half a dozen miles beyond O'Hare Field, much of which was an orchard. Today, Schaumburg, near the intersection of the Northwest Tollway and I-290, is one of America's Edge Cities, with lots of office space and miles of subdivisions, with moderately-priced apartments and black residents in some numbers as well. It is the headquarters town of Motorola, one of the most innovative of large corporations, which has done much to wrest the technological edge from the Far East, and Sears, which moved its headquarters to neighboring Hoffman Estates from the Sears Tower in Chicago.

Schaumburg is the biggest city in the 8th Congressional District of Illinois, but not its only Edge City; indeed, there may be more in the 1990s than there were in the 1980s. The 8th sits on prairie and hilly lakelands northwest of Chicago with Schaumburg at its southern end. Around it are Streamwood, Hoffman Estates, Arlington Heights, Rolling Meadows, Palatine: over 60% of the district's population, in the far northwest extremity of Cook County. The 8th also includes the just-filling-up western half of Lake County, with little lake communities being surrounded by new suburbs. The tone of life here is not elite, but it is highly affluent; culturally, this is part of the great rural Midwest as much as it is of yeasty, lusty Chicago; economically, it is suspicious of government spending, which it associates with the corrupt big city of yore. By most measures, this is the most Republican district in Illinois, and one of the most Republican in the nation.

Yet in 1992, this somewhat altered district (it sloughed off heavily Republican McHenry County to the 16th) seemed on the verge of rejecting a Republican who had served 23 years in the House. Philip Crane has supported the ideas which have been on the ascendant in the nation and the world since he first won a special election in 1969—free market economics, a strong national defense, traditional values. Yet his influence has been woefully meager and he continues to languish mostly unnoticed, despite his seniority, on the back benches of the House. It is hard to remember now that in 1980 he was running for president, hoping, as the truer libertarian, to cut in on the elderly Ronald Reagan's support and then take it over when the Reagan candidacy faded.

Now Crane is the second ranking Republican on the Ways and Means Committee, ranking Republican on its Trade Subcommittee—positions of potential leverage on great national issues. But he has been kept out of the loop by Chairman Dan Rostenkowski and other Democrats and he wields little influence on the floor. Crane is a solid free trader and supporter of NAFTA, and his major recent accomplishment was worthy but minor, the Andean Trade Preference Act reducing duties on various legal products of Colombia, Peru, Ecuador and Bolivia, to discourage the drug trade. He has played some role on using trade leverage to punish human rights violations in China, though he disagreed with the approach of the 1992 measure. He worked to get public rail lines excluded from the diesel fuel tax and to get a VA cemetery built in the soon-to-be-closed Fort Sheridan. He helped Motorola get a contract in Taiwan, where he has many contacts. Otherwise, his lack of influence is palpable. His 1992 move to strike funding of the Corporation for Public Broadcasting was defeated by voice vote and his move to zero out the

National Endowment for the Arts lost 329–85. His lone votes against spending measures have helped him win the National Taxpayers Union highest congressional rating.

After nearly a generation of easy elections, Crane found himself challenged seriously in 1992. In the primary, he was opposed by Gary Skoien, onetime aide to former Governor James Thompson, an executive for an international real estate firm. Skoien, a conservative, hit hard at congressional perks and criticized Crane for his antiabortion stand and for voting against the highway bill with its many Illinois projects. He ran a close race but lost 55%–45%. In the general, an early October poll showed the race even between Crane and Democrat Sheila Smith ("Ms. Smith Goes to Washington"), a onetime champion swimmer and owner of a lamp manufacturing company. Smith was endorsed by the *Chicago Tribune*, once (though no longer) the voice of conservative Republicanism, which wrote, "The real question is why Rep. Philip Crane wants to remain in Congress. Once a fairly prominent voice in conservative circles, he has been disengaged from the political process and shown little interest in his district for several years." Crane campaigned desultorily, but in a district which voted more than 70% for George Bush in 1988 he won by the unimpressive margin of 56%–40%. The question now is whether Crane will run again; if so, he seems vulnerable to serious challenge.

The People: Pop. 1990: 571,464; 6% rural; 7% age 65+; 89% White; 2% Black; 4% Asian; 2% Other; 5% Hispanic origin. Voting age pop.: 420,226; 1% Black; 5% Hispanic origin. Households: 65% married couple families; 33% married couple fams. w. children; 61% college educ.; median household income: $47,374; per capita income: $20,488; median gross rent: $667; median house value: $131,900.

1992 Presidential Vote			1988 Presidential Vote		
Bush (R)	118,714	(47%)	Bush (R)	143,724	(71%)
Clinton (D)	76,327	(31%)	Dukakis (D)	59,507	(29%)
Perot (I)	54,269	(22%)			

Rep. Philip M. Crane (R)

Elected Nov., 1969; b. Nov. 3, 1930, Chicago; home, McHenry; DePauw U., Hillsdale Col., B.A. 1952, IN U., M.A. 1961, Ph.D. 1963; Protestant; married (Arlene).

Career: Army, 1954–56; Instructor, IN U., 1960–63; Asst. Prof., Bradley U., 1963–67; Dir., Westminster Academy, 1967–68.

Offices: 233 CHOB 20515, 202-225-3711. Also 1450 S. New Wilke Rd., Arlington Heights 60005, 708-394-0790; and 300 N. Milwaukee Ave., #C, Lake Villa 60046, 708-265-9000.

Committees: *Ways and Means* (2d of 14 R): Social Security; Trade (RMM). *Joint Committee on Taxation* (5th of 5).

Group Ratings

	ADA	ACLU	COPE	CDF	CFA	LCV	ACU	NTLC	NSI	COC	CEI
1992	0	0	8	0	7	0	100	100	90	71	96
1991	0	—	0	0	17	8	100	—	—	89	99

National Journal Ratings

	1991 LIB — 1991 CONS		1992 LIB — 1992 CONS	
Economic	11% —	89%	0% —	91%
Social	0% —	84%	0% —	85%
Foreign	0% —	88%	0% —	82%

Key Votes of the 102d Congress

1. Ban Striker Replace	AGN	5. Handgun Wait/7-Day	AGN
2. $ for Homeownership	FOR	6. Overseas Mil. Abortion	AGN
3. Tax Rich/Cut Mid Cls.	AGN	7. Obscn. Art NEA $ Ban	*
4. FY93/$15B Def. Cut	AGN	8. Death Pen. from Jury	FOR

9. Use Force in Gulf	FOR
10. US Mil. Abroad $ Cut	AGN
11. Limit SDI Funds	AGN
12. Cuba Trade Embargo	FOR

Key Votes of the 103d Congress

1. Family Leave	AGN	2. Deficit Reduction	AGN	3. Stimulus Plan	AGN

Election Results

1992 general	Philip M. Crane (R)	132,887	(56%)	($528,818)
	Sheila A. Smith (D)	96,419	(40%)	($138,921)
	Joe M. Diller (ICP)	9,327	(4%)	
1992 primary	Philip M. Crane (R)	31,396	(55%)	
	Gary J. Skoien (R)	25,296	(45%)	
1990 general	Philip M. Crane (R)	113,081	(82%)	($163,376)
(IL 12)	Steve Pedersen (SOL)	24,450	(18%)	

NINTH DISTRICT

"Make no little plans," said architect Daniel Burnham, and he made no little plans for the Chicago lakefront: the glorious parks he designed are still one of America's urban jewels, and the row of high-rise apartment buildings—some austere works of masters of the international style, some in traditional styles evocative of some other place and time, some sleek Art Deco works of the 1920s and 1930s—are a splendid accompaniment. Behind the lakefront is all the diversity of Chicago. In sturdy brick houses, with scarcely a shoe horn's space between them, or in stubby apartment buildings, are ethnic and racial groups of all sorts, from Argentinians to Slavs, Plains Indians to Indian plainsmen. Two decades ago, the neighborhoods behind the lakefront seemed to be getting grimier and heading downhill; in the past dozen years, they have been busy gentrifying, as young marrieds and gays, professionals and entrepreneurs renovate old houses and open new businesses.

The lakefront has for some years also been the most heavily Jewish part of Chicago. Chicago's Jewish community, prominent more than a century ago, has never been as much a force for increased government responsibility as in New York, nor is it connected as much to a glamorous industry as in Los Angeles. Yet among Jewish voters liberal impulses have been strong: the 19th Century impulse to resist state authority and imposition of cultural uniformity and the 20th Century impulse to increase state responsibility for individuals' lives. Chicago's North Side Jews, on the lakefront or in neighborhoods like Rogers Park and nearby suburbs like Skokie and Niles, have been a solidly Democratic voting bloc, but skeptical of the old Democratic machine. In the biracial city politics of the 1980s or in state politics, Jewish voters and lakefront liberals of all backgrounds have been a key swing group.

The 9th Congressional District of Illinois covers most of Chicago's lakefront, from Diversey Harbor north to Evanston, the home of Northwestern University and a city which has moved from historic Yankee Republican-ness to trendy postgraduate Democratic-ness. The 9th presses inland from the Rogers Park neighborhood at the north end of Chicago west into Polish-American areas at the northwest edge of the city; from Evanston it reaches west through Skokie to Morton Grove and Niles. This is a solidly Democratic district, though some of its inland areas are Republican.

The 9th District's congressman, Sidney Yates, is one of the oldest and most senior members of Congress. Yates started representing Chicago Lakefront wards in 1948, when Harry Truman was president and only Jamie Whitten among current House members was serving; he lost seniority because he ran a nearly successful race against Senator Everett Dirksen in 1962; he was returned to the House in 1964. Yates made a liberal record early on, yet, in the Appropriations manner, he seldom sought national publicity, nor did he seek confrontation with the leaders of Chicago's Democratic machine. Today, Yates ranks second in seniority among the "college of cardinals"—Capitol Hill talk for the 13 House Appropriations subcommittee chairmen—the head of the Appropriations Interior Subcommittee since 1975. This doesn't handle any large percentage of the federal budget, but it does decide issues of importance nationally and in most members' districts: Interior's jurisdiction covers almost one third of the land mass of the U.S.. Yates has long been known as an environmentalist with a detailed knowledge of government land use policy, who has used his appropriating power to create new national parks, wildernesses, seashores, lakeshores, wild and scenic rivers, and the list goes on. Increasingly, such projects are the most politically profitable pork a member can deliver; and members must keep in touch with Yates on them.

Yates has also been the chief congressional nurturer of the National Endowments for the Arts and Humanities and the National Trust for Historic Preservation, a kind of federal Maecenas, again with ramifications in dozens of congressional districts. Preserving our history and cultural institutions has been one kind of socialism that can mostly work, but it has been controversial since 1989, thanks to the fecklessness of NEA administrators, who funded artists like the fabricator of the "Piss Christ," and to the political instincts of Senator Jesse Helms, who found yet another cause on which he could engineer roll calls to embarrass his political opponents. Yates has seen his duty as preserving the NEA budget, and has tried to sidestep both the dubious claims that a denial of grants would restrict artistic freedom (since artists may do whatever they like on their own dollar) and the graceless task of writing a code of conduct for the agency. His strategy in 1990 was to cut the NEA budget by exactly $45,000, the amount of the two most offensive grants; members could claim they were zeroing out the bad art. In 1991, his ploy was "corn for porn": in conference committee he dropped Helms's restriction on using funds for offensive depictions of sexual or excretory organs in return for dropping a provision hated among many Senators raising grazing fees on federal lands. Again he succeeded, using skill and also his popularity among colleagues: Yates is genial, almost never loses his temper, is helpful and courteous and understands the political needs of his colleagues.

For all that, Yates has been challenged in the last two elections, largely because of his age. In 1990, he faced a challenge in the primary from 31-year-old Near North Side Alderman Edwin Eisendrath, a supporter of Mayor Richard M. Daley, with enough personal wealth to finance his own campaign. Eisendrath argued that Yates was out of touch; Yates responded by orchestrating endorsements from Senators Alan Dixon and Paul Simon, Speaker Thomas Foley, and the Sierra Club; Mayor Daley appeared in a photo with Yates and noted that of the $193 million in federal money he sought in 1989, Yates secured every penny. Yates won 70%–27%. In 1992, Yates had opposition again, with similar results. The new district, if anything, was better suited to him than the old. He announced major new grants for using the Chicago River as a national demonstration project for the management of urban watersheds, got more money for the Chicago Cultural Center restoration and a new Navy Pier park. This time he got 65% to 23% for Glenn Sugiyama and 13% for William McTighe.

Yates turns 85 in 1994, but seems to be in fine health and remains active and involved and says he will run again. Sugiyama, in early 1993, said he was running again, but other possible contenders don't seem interested even if Yates retires. Edwin Eisendrath also lives in the 5th District and has said he won't run in the 9th. Other candidates could include state Representatives Jan Schakowsky and Rod Blagojevich and J. B. Pritzker, scion of the Hyatt Hotel family and former aide to Senators Alan Dixon and Terry Sanford.

The People: Pop. 1990: 571,611; 16% age 65+; 68% White; 12% Black; 10% Asian; 4% Other; 9% Hispanic origin. Voting age pop.: 467,183; 11% Black; 8% Hispanic origin. Households: 42% married

couple families; 17% married couple fams. w. children; 60% college educ.; median household income: $32,183; per capita income: $18,691; median gross rent: $508; median house value: $145,000.

1992 Presidential Vote			1988 Presidential Vote		
Clinton (D)	155,446	(61%)	Dukakis (D)	143,120	(58%)
Bush (R)	68,418	(27%)	Bush (R)	102,168	(42%)
Perot (I)	29,294	(12%)			

Rep. Sidney R. Yates (D)

Elected 1964; b. Aug. 27, 1909, Chicago; home, Chicago; U. of Chicago, Ph.D. 1931, J.D. 1933; Jewish; married (Adeline).

Career: Navy, 1944–46; Practicing atty.; Asst. Atty. for IL St. Bank Receiver, 1935–37; Asst. Atty. Gen. for IL Commerce Comm., 1937–40; U.S. House of Reps., 1949–63; U.N. Rep., Trusteeship Council, 1963–64.

Offices: 2109 RHOB 20515, 202-225-2111. Also 230 S. Dearborn St., #3920, Chicago 60604, 312-353-4596; and 2100 Ridge Ave., #2700, Evanston, 60204, 708-328-2610.

Committees: *Appropriations* (4th of 37 D): Foreign Operations, Export Financing and Related Programs; Interior (Chmn.).

Group Ratings

	ADA	ACLU	COPE	CDF	CFA	LCV	ACU	NTLC	NSI	COC	CEI
1992	95	100	100	70	73	88	0	6	20	29	9
1991	95	—	100	90	89	77	6	—	—	22	9

National Journal Ratings

	1991 LIB — 1991 CONS		1992 LIB — 1992 CONS	
Economic	72% —	28%	77% —	23%
Social	88% —	0%	92% —	0%
Foreign	92% —	0%	90% —	0%

Key Votes of the 102d Congress

1. Ban Striker Replace	FOR	5. Handgun Wait/7-Day	FOR	9. Use Force in Gulf	AGN
2. $ for Homeownership	AGN	6. Overseas Mil. Abortion	FOR	10. US Mil. Abroad $ Cut	FOR
3. Tax Rich/Cut Mid Cls.	FOR	7. Obscn. Art NEA $ Ban	AGN	11. Limit SDI Funds	FOR
4. FY93/$15B Def. Cut	*	8. Death Pen. from Jury	AGN	12. Cuba Trade Embargo	AGN

Key Votes of the 103d Congress

1. Family Leave	FOR	2. Deficit Reduction	FOR	3. Stimulus Plan	FOR

Election Results

1992 general	Sidney R. Yates (D)	162,942	(68%)	($228,812)
	Herbert Sohn (R)	64,760	(27%)	($12,599)
	Sheila A. Jones (ERP)	12,001	(5%)	
1992 primary	Sidney R. Yates (D)	63,211	(65%)	
	Glenn M. Sugiyama (D)	22,450	(23%)	
	William M. McTighe, Jr. (D)	12,329	(13%)	
1990 general	Sidney R. Yates (D)	96,557	(71%)	($839,106)
	Herbert Sohn (R)	39,031	(29%)	($15,164)

TENTH DISTRICT

The North Shore suburbs along Lake Michigan have been the favorite residence for Chicago's elite almost since 1855, when the first Chicago & Northwestern opened the railroad line from downtown Chicago north along the lakeshore. The North Shore starts in Evanston, founded by Methodists to promote temperance (a cause that has never prospered in Chicago), and goes on to Wilmette, Winnetka (the home in the *Home Alone* movies), Glencoe, Highland Park, Lake Forest—each with a slightly different personality and character, each long established and with a patina of age 50 years ago, and all similar economically: wealthy. Not far from the gritty, monosyllabic city, these are communities of pleasant, affluent, well-educated people living in an environment whose beautiful natural endowments are kept carefully disciplined.

The 10th Congressional District of Illinois is the North Shore district, starting at the Baha'i Temple on the Wilmette lakefront, just north of Evanston, reaching up past Fort Sheridan (which was closed in May 1993) to the city of Waukegan (once famous as the home of comedian Jack Benny) and the Wisconsin border beyond. The district also goes inland to what for many years was just cornfields (some still are) to Northbrook and Deerfield, just west of Glencoe and Highland Park. Farther inland are suburbs like Arlington Heights, developed in the 1950s and 1960s on the Northwestern railroad line, and Wheeling, developed in the 1960s and 1970s near Interstate 294. To the north is Long Grove and Libertyville, near where the Adlai Stevensons, the late presidential candidate and his son the former senator, have what is now one of the last farms only a few miles from Lake Michigan and the Onwentsia Club.

The congressman from the 10th District is John Porter, a Republican who has long seemed to fit the district well. He is a North Shore native, a graduate of Northwestern, a Republican who is against tax increases and looks with favor on free markets, but who takes liberal stands on some foreign and cultural issues. Porter serves on the Appropriations Committee and on the subcommittees handling labor, health and education and foreign aid issues. His recent top-visibility project was his co-sponsorship of the law to overturn the "gag rule" banning abortion counseling in federally funded health clinics; the rule was lifted soon after Bill Clinton took office. During the transition period, Porter had another success, persuading his fellow Republicans to limit ranking Republican positions on committees to six years; he also joined the newly formed Republican Majority Coalition founded to steer the GOP away from influences of the religious right. Porter is co-chairman of the Congressional Human Rights Caucus; he has proposed establishing a Radio Free Asia and has spoken up for human rights for the Baha'i—the largest religious minority in Iran. He wants the Rio Commission to monitor American and international progress toward the 1992 Earth Summit goals. He has for several years tried to cut the Social Security tax and channel the savings into Individual Social Security Retirement Accounts, without success.

First elected in 1980, Porter had little serious opposition for years. But in 1992, he faced a primary challenge from Phyllis Schlafly ally Kathleen Sullivan, founder of Project Respect, a high school program counseling sexual abstinence. She opposed abortion and National Endowment for the Arts grants to art deemed obscene. The race was closer than many expected: Porter won 60%–40%, not an overwhelming margin in a primary for a 12-year veteran. If a cultural conservative can do so well in such an elite district, it suggests many Republicans thought to be safe in their primaries might be vulnerable. Sullivan said she would run again; Porter claimed she did well because many Republican voters this time crossed over to vote in the Democratic Senate primary. Porter won the general election 65%–35% over a former junior high classmate of his daughter's. In this otherwise safe seat, Porter could have another serious primary challenge.

The People: Pop. 1990: 571,501; 1% rural; 10% age 65+; 82% White; 6% Black; 4% Asian; 3% Other; 7% Hispanic origin. Voting age pop.: 425,723; 6% Black; 6% Hispanic origin. Households: 66% married

couple families; 33% married couple fams. w. children; 66% college educ.; median household income: $50,355; per capita income: $26,405; median gross rent: $605; median house value: $180,200.

1992 Presidential Vote

Bush (R) 112,401 (43%)
Clinton (D) 108,149 (41%)
Perot (I).................. 40,719 (16%)

1988 Presidential Vote

Bush (R) 142,291 (61%)
Dukakis (D)............... 89,696 (39%)

Rep. John E. Porter (R)

Elected 1980; b. June 1, 1935, Evanston; home, Wilmette; M.I.T., 1953–54, Northwestern U., B.S.B.A. 1957, U. of MI, J.D. 1961; Presbyterian; married (Kathryn).

Career: Army Reserves, 1958–64; Atty., U.S. Dept. of Justice, 1961–63; Practicing atty., 1963–80; IL House of Reps., 1973–79.

Offices: 1026 LHOB 20515, 202-225-4835. Also 102 Wilmot Rd., #200, Deerfield 60015, 708-940-0202; and 18 N. County St., #601-A County Bldg., Waukegan 60085, 708-662-0101.

Committees: *Appropriations* (7th of 23 R): Foreign Operations, Export Financing and Related Programs; Labor, Health and Human Services, and Education (RMM).

Group Ratings

	ADA	ACLU	COPE	CDF	CFA	LCV	ACU	NTLC	NSI	COC	CEI
1992	30	30	33	20	40	56	74	90	90	88	70
1991	30	—	17	30	50	62	80	—	—	80	69

National Journal Ratings

	1991 LIB — 1991 CONS	1992 LIB — 1992 CONS
Economic	21% — 79%	24% — 75%
Social	39% — 60%	37% — 63%
Foreign	26% — 70%	54% — 45%

Key Votes of the 102d Congress

1. Ban Striker Replace	AGN	5. Handgun Wait/7-Day FOR	9. Use Force in Gulf FOR
2. $ for Homeownership	FOR	6. Overseas Mil. Abortion FOR	10. US Mil. Abroad $ Cut FOR
3. Tax Rich/Cut Mid Cls.	AGN	7. Obscn. Art NEA $ Ban FOR	11. Limit SDI Funds FOR
4. FY93/$15B Def. Cut	AGN	8. Death Pen. from Jury FOR	12. Cuba Trade Embargo FOR

Key Votes of the 103d Congress

1. Family Leave   AGN   2. Deficit Reduction   AGN   3. Stimulus Plan   AGN

Election Results

1992 general	John E. Porter (R) 155,230	(65%)	($485,778)
	Michael J. Kennedy (D)............... 85,400	(35%)	($34,948)
1992 primary	John E. Porter (R) 32,959	(60%)	
	Kathleen M. Sullivan (R)............... 21,895	(40%)	
1990 general	John E. Porter (R) 104,070	(68%)	($313,498)
	Peg McNamara (D) 47,286	(31%)	
	Other.............................. 2,243	(1%)	

ELEVENTH DISTRICT

When Chicago civic leaders looked around for a site for a third Chicagoland airport, they naturally looked south, to the side of the metropolitan area where growth has not gone as far into the countryside. Chicago Mayor Richard M. Daley favored a site on Lake Calumet, inside the city limits, where steel mills have been closed and neighborhoods are emptying out; Illinois Governor Jim Edgar appeared to favor a "greenfields" site 20 miles farther out near the farm town of Peotone. Other politicians favored sites even farther out: 11th District Congressman George Sangmeister suggested rural Kankakee County, another 20 miles south of Peotone, while his 1992 Republican opponent Robert Herbolsheimer wanted it in the closed arsenal south of Joliet, a small city nearly 50 miles from the Loop. The upshot, so far, is that there are no firm plans to build the airport anywhere; the political vectors have canceled each other out.

The 11th Congressional District of Illinois sits at the southern edge of the Chicago metropolitan area, in or near most of the proposed airport sites, where the subdivisions suddenly thin out and the vast Illinois prairies begin. It also includes a small portion of Chicago and LaSalle County in Downstate Illinois. Its largest city is Joliet, which started off as a canal boat town, has two big prisons, and once produced one-third of America's wallpaper; it includes the old 10th Ward of Chicago, home base of Edward Vrdolyak, Mayor Harold Washington's great adversary in the 1980s "council wars," plus the mostly white suburbs of South Holland, Calumet City and Lansing near the Indiana line. Most of the acreage here is cornfields, but the background of life is industrial; if the great steel mills are closed, there are many small factories still operating, and Joliet and the small towns around Kankakee and the towns of LaSalle County all have their manufacturing base here. Politically, the 11th District is a swing constituency. The Chicago area suburbs are full of ancestral Democrats who trended Republican in the 1980s but turned back to the Democrats in 1992; and if Grundy and Kankakee Counties are heavily Republican historically, LaSalle County has long been evenly balanced between the parties.

The congressman from the 11th District, Democrat George Sangmeister, came to the office through some weird contingencies and has held onto it despite a lackluster legislative record. His father, another George Sangmeister, served 32 years as mayor of Frankfurt, in Will County; the younger Sangmeister was elected county magistrate in 1960, Will County State's Attorney in 1964 and served in the legislature from 1972 to 1986. He was humiliated in 1986 when he lost the lieutenant governor nomination to a follower of Lyndon LaRouche, which probably cost Democrat Adlai Stevenson III the governorship. Then Sangmeister tried to muscle aside a 28-year-old neophyte who had won the Democrats' nomination for Congress, since the incumbent Republican, fatally ill, had withdrawn and the new nominee, Jack Davis, seemed weak. That move failed. But in 1988, Sangmeister came back and in a bitter race beat Davis by just over 1,000 votes. In 1990, Republican Manny Hoffman, mayor of Homewood, outspent Sangmeister, but Sangmeister won handily.

Sangmeister has not, in the words of the *Chicago Tribune*, "shown much evidence he will develop influence on Capitol Hill." He has sponsored routine prosecutorial amendments for tightening habeas corpus procedures and the death penalty, and cheap shots like proposing life sentences for convicted S&L crooks. He had a successful crime bill amendment allowing victims to testify at sentencing hearings. He seems to believe in industrial policy, calling for creation of a Civilian Technology Corporation to invest in new technologies, and promotes the use of ethanol. He hailed the 1991 highway bill and procured a February 1993 GAO study which favored his Kankakee airport site; but negotiations fell apart long before. A Veterans' Affairs subcommittee chairman now, he wants a new outpatient clinic and veterans' cemetery for the Chicago area and calls for establishing December 7 as Remembrance Day.

Redistricting took away many Chicago suburbs and added LaSalle County to the district, although two-thirds of the votes are still in metro Chicago. Six Republicans ran for the 1992 nomination. Vrdolyak protege Sam Panayotovich won 24% of the vote, longtime Will County public defender Sam Andreano won 21%; the winner was Robert Herbolsheimer, with 25% and a big margin in LaSalle County where he grew up. Herbolsheimer spent most of the 1980s as a Reagan appointee and environmental lawyer in Washington; his campaign manager had run Sangmeister's 1990 campaign. Herbolsheimer attacked Sangmeister for favoring excessive defense cutbacks and for supporting a Canadian-style healthcare system, while Sangmeister labeled him as a carpetbagger. The general election results seemed to track closely the presidential race: Herbolsheimer narrowly carried the Downstate counties, but Sangmeister won 59% in Cook and Will Counties for a 56% win. Whether that is testimony to his native strength or to the political winds of 1992, perhaps the 1994 results will tell.

The People: Pop. 1990: 571,050; 20% rural; 13% age 65+; 84% White; 8% Black; 1% Asian; 3% Other; 6% Hispanic origin. Voting age pop.: 417,655; 7% Black; 5% Hispanic origin. Households: 62% married couple families; 30% married couple fams. w. children; 39% college educ.; median household income: $33,632; per capita income: $13,838; median gross rent: $414; median house value: $66,900.

1992 Presidential Vote				1988 Presidential Vote		
Clinton (D)	108,456	(43%)		Bush (R)	125,874	(57%)
Bush (R)	90,058	(36%)		Dukakis (D)	96,131	(43%)
Perot (I)	50,186	(20%)				

Rep. George E. Sangmeister (D)

Elected 1988; b. Feb. 16, 1931, Frankfort; home, Mokena; Elmhurst Col., B.A. 1957, John Marshall Law Schl., J.D. 1960; Lutheran; married (Doris).

Career: Army, 1951–53; Practicing atty., 1960–87; Will Cnty. Justice of the Peace, 1960–63, Magistrate, 1963–64; IL St. Atty., 1964–68; IL House of Reps., 1972–76; IL Senate, 1976–88.

Offices: 1032 LHOB 20515, 202-225-3635. Also 101 N. Joliet St., Joliet 60431, 815-740-2028; 102 W. Madison St., Ottawa 61350, 815-433-0085; and 213 Gold Coast Ln., Calumet City 60409, 708-862-2590.

Committees: *Judiciary* (14th of 21 D): Crime and Criminal Justice; International Law, Immigration and Refugees. *Public Works and Transportation* (18th of 39 D): Aviation; Water Resources and Environment. *Veterans' Affairs* (9th of 21 D): Compensation, Pension and Insurance; Housing and Memorial Affairs (Chmn.).

Group Ratings

	ADA	ACLU	COPE	CDF	CFA	LCV	ACU	NTLC	NSI	COC	CEI
1992	70	61	83	80	80	63	24	5	20	25	23
1991	60	—	82	80	89	85	15	—	—	22	17

National Journal Ratings

	1991 LIB — 1991 CONS		1992 LIB — 1992 CONS	
Economic	88% —	0%	60% —	40%
Social	50% —	48%	47% —	53%
Foreign	65% —	33%	74% —	26%

Key Votes of the 102d Congress

1. Ban Striker Replace FOR	5. Handgun Wait/7-Day FOR	9. Use Force in Gulf AGN
2. $ for Homeownership AGN	6. Overseas Mil. Abortion AGN	10. US Mil. Abroad $ Cut FOR
3. Tax Rich/Cut Mid Cls. FOR	7. Obscn. Art NEA $ Ban FOR	11. Limit SDI Funds FOR
4. FY93/$15B Def. Cut FOR	8. Death Pen. from Jury AGN	12. Cuba Trade Embargo AGN

Key Votes of the 103d Congress

1. Family Leave FOR	2. Deficit Reduction FOR	3. Stimulus Plan FOR

Election Results

1992 general	George E. Sangmeister (D)	135,387	(56%)	($344,786)
	Robert T. Herbolsheimer (R)	107,860	(44%)	($281,243)
1992 primary	George E. Sangmeister (D), unopposed			
1990 general	George E. Sangmeister (D)	77,290	(59%)	($472,757)
(IL 4)	Manny Hoffman (R)	53,258	(41%)	($642,391)

TWELFTH DISTRICT

Their waters swirling together in great roils, the Mississippi and Missouri Rivers, draining a huge watershed in Middle America, join just a few miles above St. Louis and just a few miles down from Alton, Illinois. Most views of this part of the Mississippi focus on the Gateway Arch and the buildings of downtown St. Louis; but the Mississippi shoreline of Illinois is worthy of attention as well. Alton's 19th Century buildings recall its turbulent history, when it was the home of the antislavery agitator Elijah Lovejoy, murdered by a mob; today it is the home of conservative crusader and columnist Phyllis Schlafly. Just across from the Gateway Arch is East St. Louis, where dozens of rail lines and highways funnel into bridges over the river. Once a rail and stockyards center second only to Chicago, East St. Louis is now one of America's poorest and most troubled cities, a half-abandoned slum with one of the nation's highest crime rates and a rapidly declining tax base. Not far away is the relic of another civilization: Cahokia Mounds, where 15,000 people lived between 1050 and 1250 (more than in London or Paris at the time), where huge mounds were built and sun calendars erected by a people whose civilization we know little about. South of East St. Louis and the industrial area around Belleville, the river counties are lightly inhabited, but they were not always unimportant: this was the site of the French Kaskaskia settlement that became Illinois's first capital in 1818. Farther south the river abuts the coal country and the town of Carbondale, once a coal center but now notable as the home of Southern Illinois University. Here also is Egypt, the southern end of Illinois where the Ohio River meets the Mississippi: flat, fertile farmland, protected by giant man-made levees because it is susceptible to yearly floods. There is more than a touch of Dixie here: the unofficial capital of Egypt, Cairo (pronounced *KAYroh*), is a declining town closer to Mississippi than to Chicago and has seen outbreaks of violence between the races.

The 12th Congressional District of Illinois covers all of this riverfront from Alton south to Cairo, with some inland territory as well. Most of its population is in St. Clair (East St. Louis and Belleville) and Madison (Alton) Counties, but as drawn for 1992 the district includes much of an old Egypt-based district that was divided between this and the new 19th District. The congressman from the 12th District is Jerry Costello, a Democrat from an old St. Clair County political family who first won the seat in 1988. For 44 years before that, St. Clair and Madison Counties were represented by Mel Price, chairman of the Armed Services Committee from 1975 to 1985, who stayed in the House well past his prime, announced his retirement in 1988, then died in office. Costello, the St. Clair County board chairman for eight years, son of a former St. Clair County treasurer and sheriff, supported by organized labor, was the obvious favorite and won, but not spectacularly. He won the three-way special primary 46%–27%–25%, then by

53%–47% beat Republican Robert Gaffner.

In the House, Costello has used his seat on Public Works to bring projects to the area—a new bridge and marina for Alton, an extension of the light rail line from St. Louis's Lambert Airport to East St. Louis, rehabilitation of Mississippi River bridges, establishing the Jefferson National Expansion Memorial across the Mississippi, establishing a joint military-civilian use program at Scott Air Force Base near Belleville. Costello has a not entirely liberal voting record, and is rather conservative on cultural issues, but was trusted enough by the leadership to be given a seat on the Budget Committee in 1993. Redistricting extended the district south from the St. Louis area all the way to Cairo, and included incumbent Glenn Poshard's home in the coal country. But Poshard, perhaps realizing that 72% of the new 12th's Democratic primary votes would be cast in St. Clair and Madison Counties, decided to run against fellow incumbent Terry Bruce in the new 19th District, and won, while Costello was reelected easily here.

The People: Pop. 1990: 571,441; 22% rural; 14% age 65+; 82% White; 17% Black; 1% Asian; 1% Hispanic origin. Voting age pop.: 421,266; 15% Black; 1% Hispanic origin. Households: 54% married couple families; 25% married couple fams. w. children; 40% college educ.; median household income: $25,032; per capita income: $11,547; median gross rent: $360; median house value: $47,400.

1992 Presidential Vote				1988 Presidential Vote		
Clinton (D)	132,570	(54%)		Dukakis (D)	124,751	(56%)
Bush (R)	69,829	(28%)		Bush (R)	96,302	(44%)
Perot (I)	42,169	(17%)				

Rep. Jerry F. Costello (D)

Elected Aug. 1988; b. Sept. 25, 1949, East St. Louis; home, Belleville; Belleville Area Col. A.A. 1970, Maryville Col. B.A. 1972; Catholic; married (Georgia).

Career: Dir., IL Court Svcs. & Probation, 1973–80; Chmn., Region's Cncl. of Govts., 1980–84; Chmn., St. Clair Cnty. Bd. of Supervisors, 1980–88.

Offices: 119 CHOB 20515, 202-225-5661. Also 327 W. Main St., Belleville 62221, 618-233-8026.

Committees: *Budget* (19th of 26 D). *Public Works and Transportation* (14th of 39 D): Aviation; Economic Development; Surface Transportation.

Group Ratings

	ADA	ACLU	COPE	CDF	CFA	LCV	ACU	NTLC	NSI	COC	CEI
1992	60	61	83	80	73	56	43	16	60	14	22
1991	55	—	83	80	83	38	15	—	—	30	19

National Journal Ratings

	1991 LIB — 1991 CONS			1992 LIB — 1992 CONS	
Economic	88%	—	0%	63%	— 37%
Social	50%	—	48%	44%	— 56%
Foreign	49%	—	50%	56%	— 40%

Key Votes of the 102d Congress

1. Ban Striker Replace FOR	5. Handgun Wait/7-Day AGN	9. Use Force in Gulf AGN
2. $ for Homeownership AGN	6. Overseas Mil. Abortion AGN	10. US Mil. Abroad $ Cut AGN
3. Tax Rich/Cut Mid Cls. FOR	7. Obscn. Art NEA $ Ban FOR	11. Limit SDI Funds FOR
4. FY93/$15B Def. Cut FOR	8. Death Pen. from Jury AGN	12. Cuba Trade Embargo AGN

Key Votes of the 103d Congress

1. Family Leave FOR	2. Deficit Reduction FOR	3. Stimulus Plan FOR

Election Results

1992 general	Jerry F. Costello (D)	168,762	(71%)	($606,383)
	Mike Starr (R)	68,115	(29%)	($21,024)
1992 primary	Jerry F. Costello (D), unopposed			
1990 general	Jerry F. Costello (D)	95,208	(66%)	($380,559)
(IL 21)	Robert H. (Bob) Gaffner (R)	48,949	(34%)	($26,230)

THIRTEENTH DISTRICT

Not all of the great monuments of Chicagoland are in the Loop or on the Lakefront; some are in the suburbs, out the radial avenues and expressways that fan out from Chicago's Loop. A dozen miles west of the Loop, those lines cross the Tri-State Tollway and reach into DuPage County, once mostly countryside, now mostly suburbia: there were 103,000 people here in 1940 and 781,000 in 1990. But DuPage is not just subdivisions: here in Oak Brook is the headquarters of McDonald's and its Hamburger University, the company which virtually invented fast food and which has reached new heights of fame with Bill Clinton in the White House. One out of eight young Americans has worked at McDonald's, and millions have learned from this corporation the basics of arithmetic and literacy, good work habits and cheerful service, which are not always taught in today's public schools (for examples, look a few miles east to Chicago). Next to Oak Brook are the older railroad commuter towns like Hinsdale and Downers Grove, where subdivisions have grown up on all sides. Commercial development has hop-skipped out to Naperville, once a country village, now itself an Edge City. To the south, on each side of the Sanitary and Ship Canal and the Des Plaines River, are giant public institutions like the Argonne National Laboratory and the Palos Hills Forest Preserve.

The 13th Congressional District of Illinois occupies much of this territory, the southern slice of DuPage County, including Oak Brook, Downers Grove and Naperville, the southwest corner of Cook County around Palos Hills, and the northern slice of Will County north of Joliet. Politically, this is a heavily Republican area, always suspicious of the motives and operations of Chicago's Democrats, devoted to free enterprise and hostile to higher taxes. DuPage County has indeed become Illinois's Republican powerhouse, the source of by far its biggest majorities (63,000 for George Bush even in 1992) and the home base of leading politicians like state Senate President Pate Philip and state House Minority Leader Lee Daniels.

The congressman from the 13th is Harris Fawell, a career politician (he served in the Illinois Senate from 1962 to 1976 and was first elected to the House in 1984) who most recently has been known for opposing the pork barrel measures which help make the careers of so many of his colleagues. He started out on the Education and Labor Committee as a voice for the small businessmen so numerous in this district, opposing increases in the minimum wage and the Democrats' bills requiring plant closing notifications and requiring union representation on pension program boards. He was one of the few consistent opponents of the catastrophic health care program which was repealed in 1990. He took on less familiar issues as well, as with his bill to encourage states to allow termination of parental rights for unfit parents, so boarder babies and the like can be put up for adoption. In 1990, Fawell and several colleagues, including

Democrats Charles Stenholm and Tim Penny, formed a group they called Porkbusters to target pork barrel spending in appropriations bills. Immediately, Fawell was visited with retaliation: after he criticized a 1990 emergency supplemental bill for funding Arkansas fish farms and the D.C. Convention Center, someone moved a $17 million cut in funds for the Argonne Laboratory. But Argonne is too important to be hurt by petty retribution, and quickly received a $456 million project to produce the Advanced Photon Source (high energy X-rays and light sources) by 1996. Fawell persevered in his porkbusting, which he believes sparked some $7 billion in budget cuts in 1992; he claims credit for $26 billion in savings over the years. But he has had time also to sponsor laws promoting various scientific research projects and to speak out for small businesses hurt by soaring healthcare costs.

Fawell essentially won this seat in the 1984 Republican primary, which he won 30%–23%–22%–12%. Like many Chicago area incumbents, he had active primary opposition in 1992, but his porkbusting record in this free enterprise district (not much changed by redistricting) helped him win 73%–27%.

The People: Pop. 1990: 571,344; 4% rural; 8% age 65+; 90% White; 3% Black; 4% Asian; 1% Other; 3% Hispanic origin. Voting age pop.: 412,913; 3% Black; 3% Hispanic origin. Households: 68% married couple families; 37% married couple fams. w. children; 65% college educ.; median household income: $50,087; per capita income: $20,912; median gross rent: $619; median house value: $139,800.

1992 Presidential Vote			1988 Presidential Vote		
Bush (R)	128,612	(47%)	Bush (R)	154,374	(69%)
Clinton (D)	88,314	(32%)	Dukakis (D)	69,949	(31%)
Perot (I)	58,123	(21%)			

Rep. Harris W. Fawell (R)

Elected 1984; b. Mar. 25, 1929, West Chicago; home, Naperville; North Central Col., B.A. 1949, Chicago-Kent Col. of Law, J.D. 1953; United Methodist; married (Ruth).

Career: Practicing atty., 1953–84; IL Senate, 1962–76.

Offices: 2342 RHOB 20515, 202-225-3515. Also 115 W. 55th St., #100, Clarendon Hills 60514, 708-655-2052.

Committees: *Education and Labor* (6th of 15 R): Labor-Management Relations; Labor Standards, Occupational Health and Safety (RMM); Select Education and Civil Rights. *Science, Space and Technology* (6th of 22 R): Energy (RMM).

Group Ratings

	ADA	ACLU	COPE	CDF	CFA	LCV	ACU	NTLC	NSI	COC	CEI
1992	25	26	17	20	27	44	84	90	100	88	83
1991	15	—	8	30	17	62	84	—	—	100	84

National Journal Ratings

	1991 LIB — 1991 CONS			1992 LIB — 1992 CONS		
Economic	14%	—	83%	0%	—	91%
Social	39%	—	60%	38%	—	60%
Foreign	0%	—	88%	56%	—	40%

Key Votes of the 102d Congress

1. Ban Striker Replace AGN	5. Handgun Wait/7-Day FOR	9. Use Force in Gulf FOR
2. $ for Homeownership FOR	6. Overseas Mil. Abortion FOR	10. US Mil. Abroad $ Cut FOR
3. Tax Rich/Cut Mid Cls.AGN	7. Obscn. Art NEA $ Ban FOR	11. Limit SDI Funds FOR
4. FY93/$15B Def. Cut AGN	8. Death Pen. from Jury FOR	12. Cuba Trade Embargo FOR

Key Votes of the 103d Congress

1. Family Leave AGN	2. Deficit Reduction AGN	3. Stimulus Plan AGN

Election Results

1992 general	Harris W. Fawell (R)	179,257	(68%)	($657,908)
	Dennis Michael Temple (D)	82,985	(32%)	($4,327)
1992 primary	Harris W. Fawell (R)	46,417	(73%)	
	Stuart A. (Stu) Wesbury, Jr. (R)	17,202	(27%)	
1990 general	Harris W. Fawell (R)	116,048	(66%)	($271,913)
	Steven K. Thomas (D)	60,305	(34%)	

FOURTEENTH DISTRICT

A dozen or two miles beyond the Loop there is an invisible line marking two different Chicagos. One is the Chicago dominated by blacks and descendants of the vast immigration of 1840–1924, a Chicago where certain loyalties are taken for granted: loyalty to ethnic group, to church (usually the Catholic Church, often with an ethnic prefix), and to party (almost always the Democratic Party, but occasionally, as in Cicero, the Republican). This Chicago is a gritty city, where personal cheerfulness and courtesy lighten up days otherwise as cold and impersonal as the gray Chicago winter sky.

The other Chicago is the beginning of the Great Plains, originally a white Anglo-Saxon Protestant Chicago, a place whose residents are products of the first great wave of immigration to America. The tone of this Chicago is lighter, its streets and highways cleaner and neater, its daily life generally free from evidence of unpleasantness and deprivation. People in this Chicago think of themselves as typical Americans, and their geographical vision takes in the vast plains. This is the Chicago of Colonel McCormick's *Chicago Tribune*, of Paul Harvey and Sears catalogues. Ronald Reagan grew up in Downstate Illinois within the orbit of this Chicago (though he did live in the city briefly), and its spirit helped to characterize his presidency. His migration to southern California, incidentally, is not atypical: you can see in the geometric grids and Republican voting patterns of Orange County or Phoenix almost exact replicas of the grids and patterns in Chicago's suburban "Collar Counties," transported to the once-empty Southwest on the Atchison, Topeka & Santa Fe or U.S. 66 from their beginnings in Chicago's Loop.

The 14th Congressional District of Illinois straddles this line between metropolitan Chicago and Downstate Illinois. It gets as close as 30 miles to Chicago's Loop, in western DuPage County, with two great Chicagoland landmarks: Cantigny, the estate of Colonel Robert McCormick, longtime publisher of the *Chicago Tribune*, and Fermilab, the world's fastest energy particle accelerator: icons of political conservatism and high technology within two miles of each other. The 14th also contains the Fox River Valley, and its industrial cities of Elgin and Aurora, and antique St. Charles in the heart of the "Collar Counties." Farther west, amid what may be the world's richest cornfields, the 14th passes through DeKalb, long the world's leading manufacturer of barbed wire, and goes on to Kendall and Lee Counties, including Reagan's boyhood home in Dixon. This is one of the most heavily Republican belts of territory in the country. Northern Illinois was settled, when Chicago was just a frontier village, by Yankees from Ohio, Indiana, Upstate New York and New England: people who formed the heart of the Republican Party from the year it was founded, in 1854, and who would form the core of the

Grand Army of the Republic a few years later. Their descendants, in this Anglo-Saxon extension of Chicagoland, remain solidly Republican today.

It is often the case that congressmen from high-income districts full of entrepreneurs and professionals are politicians with relatively modest backgrounds. One such is Dennis Hastert, Republican congressman from the 14th, who for 16 years taught government and history and coached at Yorkville High School in Kendall County. Starting in 1980, he served six years in the Illinois Assembly; he was chosen by the party to run for Congress after the March 1986 primary when the incumbent was fatally stricken with cancer. He was attacked by some Republicans as insufficiently conservative and won with only 52% over Kane County Coroner Mary Lou Kearns. But he has won easily since and was strengthened in redistricting. In 1992, he felt secure enough, despite 17 overdrafts on the House bank, not to challenge his Democratic opponent's spot on the ballot for lack of sufficient signatures: "We thought people ought to hear the issues." He won with 67%.

Hastert's great cause in Congress is repeal of the Social Security "earnings tax"—the deduction of benefits among senior citizens who earn over a certain figure. To Hastert this is a "Depression-era fossil"; to many of his constituents it is a big expense and a penalty for being productive; for House members, 268 of whom co-sponsored Hastert's bill in 1992, it's a way of courting the affluent elderly. In 1992, the House did vote to raise the earnings limit $10,200 to $20,000 over a 5-year period, but Hastert is still a long way from his goal (and from finding out how to make up for lost revenue). He voted against the bill which included aid to Chicago after the underground flooding in 1992. His fervor against taxes may have helped get him a seat on the Energy and Commerce Committee in December 1990; but when he was mentioned as a candidate for the National Republican Congressional Committee chairmanship, Minority Leader Robert Michel made it clear he needed more seniority and would not have much support. Michel did however designate Hastert as the GOP House representative to the White House Task Force on Health Care Reform headed by Hillary Rodham Clinton.

The People: Pop. 1990: 571,540; 21% rural; 9% age 65+; 84% White; 4% Black; 2% Asian; 5% Other; 10% Hispanic origin. Voting age pop.: 407,410; 4% Black; 8% Hispanic origin. Households: 65% married couple families; 35% married couple fams. w. children; 50% college educ.; median household income: $39,815; per capita income: $15,769; median gross rent: $484; median house value: $100,100.

1992 Presidential Vote			1988 Presidential Vote		
Bush (R)	105,700	(44%)	Bush (R)	127,399	(65%)
Clinton (D)	83,109	(34%)	Dukakis (D)	67,476	(35%)
Perot (I)	52,914	(22%)			

Rep. Dennis Hastert (R)

Elected 1986; b. Jan. 2, 1942, Aurora, IL; home, Yorkville; Wheaton Col., B.A. 1964, N. IL U., M.S. 1967; Protestant; married (Jean).

Career: High schl. teacher and coach, 1964–80; IL House of Reps., 1980–86.

Offices: 2453 RHOB 20515, 202-225-2976. Also 27 N. River St., Batavia 60510, 708-406-1114; and 1007 Main St., Mendota 61342, 815-538-3322.

Committees: *Energy and Commerce* (9th of 17 R): Energy and Power; Health and the Environment; Telecommunications and Finance. *Government Operations* (3d of 17 R): Environment, Energy and Natural Resources (RMM).

Group Ratings

	ADA	ACLU	COPE	CDF	CFA	LCV	ACU	NTLC	NSI	COC	CEI
1992	5	4	25	20	20	13	92	95	90	75	75
1991	0	—	8	20	28	0	95	—	—	100	77

National Journal Ratings

	1991 LIB — 1991 CONS		1992 LIB — 1992 CONS	
Economic	10%	— 89%	16%	— 80%
Social	0%	— 84%	16%	— 82%
Foreign	22%	— 77%	30%	— 64%

Key Votes of the 102d Congress

1. Ban Striker Replace	AGN	5. Handgun Wait/7-Day AGN	9. Use Force in Gulf FOR
2. $ for Homeownership	FOR	6. Overseas Mil. AbortionAGN	10. US Mil. Abroad $ CutAGN
3. Tax Rich/Cut Mid Cls.AGN		7. Obscn. Art NEA $ Ban FOR	11. Limit SDI Funds AGN
4. FY93/$15B Def. Cut	AGN	8. Death Pen. from Jury FOR	12. Cuba Trade Embargo AGN

Key Votes of the 103d Congress

1. Family Leave   AGN   2. Deficit Reduction   AGN   3. Stimulus Plan   AGN

Election Results

1992 general	Dennis Hastert (R)	155,271	(67%)	($615,535)
	Jonathan Abram Reich (D)	75,294	(33%)	
1992 primary	Dennis Hastert (R), unopposed			
1990 general	Dennis Hastert (R)	112,383	(67%)	($312,555)
	Donald J. Westphal (D)	55,592	(33%)	

FIFTEENTH DISTRICT

The Illinois Central Railroad heads south from Chicago to the city of New Orleans on a railbed elevated a few feet above the rich black soil of the Illinois prairie, topsoil reaching down not just inches but feet. This land dazzled its first settlers, who were used to the land farther east that had to be cleared of trees and stumps before it could be plowed; this treeless prairie could be cultivated almost immediately, and with bounteous results. Today, this remains farming country, made up not of small family farms but of large commercial operations, typically of 1,000 acres or more. Cultivating this soil is a business, requiring informed decisions about crop selection (soybeans and corn are the current favorites), maximizing yields, proper pesticides, marketing decisions, taking advantage of government programs, watching farm export prospects. There is no room here for a little family vegetable garden or a horse corral: this is business. The landscape on the prairies of eastern Illinois is marked by only a few small towns; the largest of which, Champaign-Urbana and Bloomington-Normal, are the sites of universities (the University of Illinois and Illinois Normal). Politically, these prairie lands have been Republican, often very Republican; inclining much more to the politics of former Speaker Joseph Cannon, a Republican from the manufacturing city of Danville east of Urbana, than to that of Vice President Adlai Stevenson, a Democrat from Bloomington, who served under *laissez-faire* Democrat Grover Cleveland and was the grandfather of the Adlai Stevenson nominated by the Democrats for president in 1952 and 1956.

The 15th Congressional District of Illinois occupies much of this prairie, beginning 60 miles from Chicago, where the Illinois Central heads toward Kankakee, and moving over 150 miles of prairie to the courthouse town of Monticello. It includes Bloomington, Champaign-Urbana and Danville, and runs south almost to the National Road and U.S. 40, traditionally the line between northern Republican and southern Democratic Illinois. Today, the area is heavily Republican;

indeed, this was by far George Bush's best Downstate district in 1988, and has been represented for years by Republicans who have been active in local businesses, civic affairs and state legislative politics.

One such Republican is current Congressman Thomas Ewing, a lawyer from Pontiac, between Kankakee and Bloomington, who won nine terms in the state legislature. Ewing's chance for the House came in late 1990 when the 15th District's Congressman Edward Madigan was appointed secretary of agriculture. Madigan was an important legislator on Energy and Commerce and was also chief deputy whip, but was disappointed when in March 1989 he lost the whip race to Newt Gingrich by an 87–85 margin. His path to the leadership blocked, and his accommodationist and compromising style clearly eclipsed by Gingrich's penchant for confrontation, Madigan lobbied personally for the Agriculture job when it opened up, and seemed happy to leave the House. Ewing, the assistant Minority Leader in Springfield from 1982 to 1990 and then deputy minority leader in 1990, quickly became the overwhelming favorite for the seat. In the July 1991 special election, he beat former state representative Gerald Bradley 66%–31%; Bradley had won the Democratic nomination over former Congressman Tim Hall, the only 1974 Watergate-year Democrat to lose his seat in 1976.

Ewing got a seat on the Agriculture Committee, reserved by Illinois's Robert Michel; there he is a promoter of ethanol, produced from Illinois prairie grain and by Decatur-based Archer-Daniels-Midland. He compiled a conservative voting record, except on foreign issues; he called for an extended freeze on federal regulations and voted against the bill which included aid to Chicago after its 1992 floods. Illinois's redistricting plan treated Ewing kindly, and in Democratic 1992 he was reelected with 59% of the vote, though he did lose in Danville. It remains to be seen whether he will be an important force if Republicans should get more leverage in a future Congress.

The People: Pop. 1990: 571,292; 34% rural; 13% age 65+; 89% White; 7% Black; 2% Asian; 1% Other; 1% Hispanic origin. Voting age pop.: 432,983; 7% Black; 1% Hispanic origin. Households: 55% married couple families; 26% married couple fams. w. children; 45% college educ.; median household income: $26,760; per capita income: $12,709; median gross rent: $372; median house value: $52,300.

1992 Presidential Vote			1988 Presidential Vote		
Clinton (D)	107,914	(42%)	Bush (R)	126,872	(57%)
Bush (R)	98,378	(39%)	Dukakis (D)	94,937	(43%)
Perot (I)	47,280	(19%)			

Rep. Thomas W. Ewing (R)

Elected July 1991; b. Sept. 19, 1935, Atlanta, GA; home, Pontiac; Milliken U., B.S. 1957, John Marshall Law Schl., J.D. 1968; Methodist; married (Connie).

Career: Army, 1957–59; Army Reserves, 1959–63; Exec. Dir., Pontiac and Harvey Chambers of Commerce, 1963–68; Asst. State Atty., Livingston Cnty., 1968–73; IL House of Reps., 1974–91.

Offices: 1317 LHOB 20515, 202-225-2371. Also P.O. Box 20, Pontiac 61764, 815-844-7660; 2401 E. Washington St., #201, Bloomington 61704, 309-662-9371; 70 Meadowview Ct., #200, Kankakee 60901, 815-937-0875; 102 E. Madison, #307, Urbana 61801, 217-328-0165; and 4 N. Vermillion, #503-504, Danville 61832, 217-431-8230.

Committees: *Agriculture* (11th of 19 R): Department Operations and Nutrition; Environment, Credit and Rural Development; General Farm Commodities. *Public Works and Transportation* (10th of 24 R): Aviation; Economic Development; Water Resources and Environment.

Group Ratings

	ADA	ACLU	COPE	CDF	CFA	LCV	ACU	NTLC	NSI	COC	CEI
1992	25	5	33	20	40	0	88	93	90	88	80
1991	0	—	13	33	38	0	100	—	—	100	66

National Journal Ratings

	1991 LIB — 1991 CONS		1992 LIB — 1992 CONS	
Economic	*	*	21%	76%
Social	0%	84%	19%	81%
Foreign	*	*	52%	46%

Key Votes of the 102d Congress

1. Ban Striker Replace	AGN	5. Handgun Wait/7-Day *	9. Use Force in Gulf *
2. $ for Homeownership	FOR	6. Overseas Mil. Abortion *	10. US Mil. Abroad $ Cut FOR
3. Tax Rich/Cut Mid Cls.	AGN	7. Obscn. Art NEA $ Ban FOR	11. Limit SDI Funds FOR
4. FY93/$15B Def. Cut	AGN	8. Death Pen. from Jury FOR	12. Cuba Trade Embargo AGN

Key Votes of the 103d Congress

1. Family Leave   AGN   2. Deficit Reduction   AGN   3. Stimulus Plan   AGN

Election Results

1992 general	Thomas W. Ewing (R)	142,167	(59%)	($309,131)
	Charles D. Mattis (D)	97,190	(41%)	($6,328)
1992 primary	Thomas W. Ewing (R), unopposed			
1991 special	Thomas W. Ewing (R)	25,675	(66%)	($268,259)
	Gerald Bradley (D)	13,011	(31%)	($56,099)
1990 general	Edward Madigan (R), unopposed			($277,802)

SIXTEENTH DISTRICT

One of the heartlands of the Republican Party is the far northwest corner of Illinois. Here, in the town square of Freeport, 15,000 people came to hear Abraham Lincoln and Stephen Douglas in one of their seven debates, and the one on terrain most partial to Lincoln. Settled by New England Yankees, northern Illinois was one of the strongest Republican constituencies in 1860 and for years after. Not far away, on a little river once navigable by Mississippi River steamboats, is Galena, one of the earliest settlements in northern Illinois, the home of Ulysses S. Grant before he became general and then president; not far away are Tampico and Dixon, birthplace and boyhood home of Ronald Reagan. Farther up on the Rock River is Rockford, the largest city here beyond Chicagoland, and the home town of John Anderson, a conservative Republican for most of the 20 years he served in Congress before he became known as the liberal reformist independent candidate for president in 1980. During all these years, northern Illinois, perhaps inspired by Democratic Chicago, has remained steadfastly Republican; it backed Herbert Hoover in 1932, Barry Goldwater in 1964 and George Bush in 1992 when most of America and Illinois were going the other way.

The 16th Congressional District consists of much of northwest Illinois. The largest city here is Rockford, famous in conservative circles as headquarters of the paleo-conservative Rockford Institute (they don't like neoconservatives, former Democrats or immigrants). It also extends west to the hilly, almost mountainous country around Galena and the Mississippi River, and east to McHenry County, full of new subdivisions surrounding old towns, where affluent young families make their way up through free enterprise and have conservative cultural values. Over the years, the Republican Party has adapted itself well to trends of opinion here, and has held this congressional seat every year since the Republican Party was founded except for 1912 and

1990. The last two elections, however, have produced results quite different from the elections of moderate Republicans like Anderson from 1960 to 1978 and Lynn Martin, later Bush's secretary of labor, from 1980 to 1988.

Both the 1990 and 1992 elections involved serious Republican primary contests and a strong Democratic candidate; the ultimate winner in 1992 was just the kind of conservative Republican who was supposed to have no chance to win in these enlightened times, Don Manzullo. The 1990 Republican primary produced a 54%–46% victory for John Hallock over Manzullo, a moderate state legislator whose campaign flagged after personal problems were revealed. That opened the way for Democrat John Cox, the state's attorney in Galena, a liberal on most issues who opposed capital punishment and was willing to raise taxes to cut the budget deficit, who won with 55%. In the House, Cox compiled a strongly liberal record on most issues, though bucking local unions by supporting fast track procedure for NAFTA and angering congressional leaders by backing term limits. But he was hurt by redistricting which added heavily Republican McHenry County to the 16th. He was heartened though when the favorite in the 1992 Republican primary, McHenry state Senator Jack Shaffer, was beaten 56%–44% by Manzullo, who attacked him for supporting gasoline, cigarette and computer software tax increases in the legislature.

Manzullo grew up in Rockford, where his family owns Manzullo's Drive-In Restaurant and Italian Villa. In college in Washington in the mid-1960s, he worked for Republican candidates, and he has practiced law in Illinois since 1970. He also lives on a cattle-breeding farm, writes poetry and books on constitutional law, and ran a radio talk show; he and his wife home-school their three young children. Manzullo had backing from many conservative activists but his appeal went further; in the primary he won over 70% in the areas where he is known best. In the general Cox campaigned with a deficit-cutting plan that included higher gas taxes and means-testing Medicare; Manzullo called for a 10% across-the-board income tax cut. Cox barely edged Manzullo in Rockford and Winnebago County and won his home area of Galena. But Manzullo won nearly 2–1 in McHenry County and won overall with 55%. Like Cox, Manzullo seems inclined to stake his congressional future on his principles, and gamble that they will be acceptable in a district where they are not entirely shared; Manzullo has the advantage, however, of the Republican label.

The People: Pop. 1990: 571,488; 26% rural; 12% age 65+; 91% White; 5% Black; 1% Asian; 1% Other; 3% Hispanic origin. Voting age pop.: 415,364; 4% Black; 2% Hispanic origin. Households: 63% married couple families; 31% married couple fams. w. children; 43% college educ.; median household income: $34,668; per capita income: $15,107; median gross rent: $392; median house value: $73,300.

1992 Presidential Vote			1988 Presidential Vote		
Bush (R)	108,949	(42%)	Bush (R)	133,449	(61%)
Clinton (D)	95,103	(36%)	Dukakis (D)	84,349	(39%)
Perot (I)	56,169	(21%)			

Rep. Donald Manzullo (R)

Elected 1992; b. Mar. 24, 1944, Rockford; home, Egan; American U., B.S. 1967, Marquette U. Law Schl., J.D. 1970; Baptist; married (Freda).

Career: Practicing atty., 1970–92; author.

Offices: 506 CHOB 20515, 202-225-5676. Also 3929 Broadway, #1, Rockford 61108, 815-394-1231; and 191 Virginia Ave., Crystal Lake 60014, 815-356-9800.

Committees: *Foreign Affairs* (17th of 18 R): Economic Policy, Trade and Environment; International Operations. *Small Business* (16th of 18 R): Development of Rural Enterprises, Exports and the Environment.

Group Ratings and 102d Congress Votes: Newly Elected

Key Votes of the 103d Congress

1. Family Leave	AGN	2. Deficit Reduction	AGN	3. Stimulus Plan	AGN

Election Results

1992 general	Donald Manzullo (R)	142,388	(56%)	($435,468)
	John W. Cox, Jr. (D)................	113,555	(44%)	($491,002)
1992 primary	Donald Manzullo (R)	41,055	(56%)	
	Jack Schaffer (R)	31,705	(44%)	
1990 general	John W. Cox, Jr. (D)................	83,061	(55%)	($371,114)
	John W. Hallock (R)................	69,105	(45%)	($491,287)

SEVENTEENTH DISTRICT

The western prairies of Illinois are some of America's richest agricultural land—and one of the places that was hardest hit by the early 1980s Farm Belt recession. This land was first settled by Yankees coming overland from northern Indiana and Ohio and Upstate New York. After 1848, Germans, who left their homeland in search of better opportunities, settled this land that in so many ways resembles the flat, orderly plains of northern Germany. All these migrants farmed quarter-sections and built small towns, with banks and stores, community churches and libraries. In time, investors built farm machinery factories, and the Quad Cities of the Mississippi— Davenport, Iowa, and Rock Island, Moline and East Moline, Illinois—became one of the nation's biggest agricultural equipment manufacturing centers. These plants were unionized in the 1930s and 1940s, and in post-World War II America their wages went up as the demand for ever more sophisticated machines rose among the Midwest's government-subsidized farmers. But eventually the cost of subsidies rose too high and the market had its revenge. That was the case in the early 1980s. Farm profits vanished, land values declined and orders for new machinery and equipment dried up. The result was a depression in western Illinois and neighboring Iowa, and a political swing toward the Democrats and away from the Republicans who had been the ancestral party in most of this area. This is one of the few parts of the country where Ronald Reagan's percentage of the vote declined between 1980 and 1984.

That might be ancient history now, except that it still affects the politics of Illinois's 17th Congressional District, which includes most of the state's Mississippi River border with Iowa plus half a dozen more prairie counties to the east. For years, its Democratic base in the Quad Cities was outvoted by Republican counties elsewhere. But in 1982, the longtime Republican congressman here, Tom Railsback, was defeated by a conservative in the primary; ready to take advantage of this opening was Democrat Lane Evans, a local legal services attorney angry at the Reagan recession who took a gamble in running and ended up winning with 53%. By historical standards, Evans should have been a one-term congressman; instead he has thrived. His anti-Reagan voting record helped, and so did his service in the Marine Corps from 1969 to 1971; it helped also that he has a pleasant, boyish demeanor which will never be mistaken for East Coast slick, and that he returns constantly to the district and appears often there on television.

Evans has long called himself a "populist" rather than a liberal, though his voting record is one of the most liberal in the House. He was frustrated in his attempts on the Agriculture Committee and on the floor to steer more money to farmers in the 1980s; subsidies were already dizzyingly high, and there was no hope of getting more. Nor has he been able to turn around the greater trend toward less egalitarian incomes, which began before the Reagan years and is due only in part to tax laws. In recent years, he has concentrated less on economic and more on veterans' issues. On the Veterans' Affairs Committee, he worked hard for years to get compensation for veterans who may have been harmed by their exposure to Agent Orange; despite the Centers for Disease Control study showing no relationship between Agent Orange and cancer, Evans got an amendment for compensation through the previously hostile committee, 16–14, in October 1990. In 1992 he passed measures to provide mental health services for women veterans who are sexually traumatized on active duty, to set up a study of health consequences of Gulf war service and to expand services to homeless veterans. Unhappy with Veterans' Affairs Chairman Sonny Montgomery's lack of sympathy on Agent Orange and other issues, Evans let it be known that he was interested in the chair, but Democrats reelected Montgomery by a 127–123 margin. Evans also serves on Armed Services, where he has concentrated on finding alternatives to tritium production and banning sale of land mines; he tried to require an annual report of weapons in the nuclear stockpile, but it was voted down. Running through much of his work is the motif of protecting workers against possibly dangerous substances, plus a certain appealing earnestness: in the 3d quarter of 1992 he returned a large amount of his personal salary to the treasury requesting that it go towards deficit reduction.

But for all this, Evans did not get an entirely free ride in 1992. Redistricting added several Republican counties to the north and south ends of this population-losing district. He was criticized by the *Chicago Tribune* for opposing NAFTA and by Republican opponent Ken Schloemer for urging an end to the ban on gays in the military. This was attacked by some as a diversionary or irrelevant issue; Schloemer countered by quoting letters Evans sent to the Defense Department protesting the dismissal of a gay serviceman. Evans won with 60% of the vote, a fine showing, but a drop from 1988 and 1990. He won 62% in counties from his old district and 54% in counties added by redistricting. That doesn't necessarily mean trouble, but with the farm recession pretty much over and the prairie economy rising, Evans's formula for winning may need a bit of refiguring.

The People: Pop. 1990: 571,585; 38% rural; 17% age 65+; 93% White; 3% Black; 1% Asian; 1% Other; 3% Hispanic origin. Voting age pop.: 428,001; 3% Black; 2% Hispanic origin. Households: 59% married couple families; 26% married couple fams. w. children; 38% college educ.; median household income: $25,195; per capita income: $12,052; median gross rent: $309; median house value: $41,200.

1992 Presidential Vote

Clinton (D) 124,175 (47%)
Bush (R) 95,554 (36%)
Perot (I). 45,566 (17%)

1988 Presidential Vote

Dukakis (D). 127,357 (51%)
Bush (R) 120,322 (49%)

Rep. Lane Evans (D)

Elected 1982; b. Aug. 4, 1951, Rock Island; home, Rock Island; Augustana Col., B.A. 1974, Georgetown U., J.D. 1978; Catholic; single.

Career: Marine Corps, 1969–71; Practicing atty., 1978–82.

Offices: 2335 RHOB 20515, 202-225-5905. Also 1535 47th Ave., Moline 61265, 309-793-5760; and 1640 N. Henderson St., Galesburg 61401, 309-342-4411.

Committees: *Armed Services* (15th of 34 D): Military Acquisition; Readiness. *Natural Resources* (26th of 28 D): Oversight and Investigations. *Veterans' Affairs* (4th of 21 D): Compensation, Pension and Insurance; Oversight and Investigations (Chmn.).

Group Ratings

	ADA	ACLU	COPE	CDF	CFA	LCV	ACU	NTLC	NSI	COC	CEI
1992	95	100	100	90	100	100	4	0	20	13	12
1991	100	—	100	100	94	85	5	—	—	20	8

National Journal Ratings

	1991 LIB — 1991 CONS		1992 LIB — 1992 CONS	
Economic	88%	0%	89%	9%
Social	88%	0%	92%	0%
Foreign	78%	19%	90%	0%

Key Votes of the 102d Congress

1. Ban Striker Replace	FOR	5. Handgun Wait/7-Day FOR	9. Use Force in Gulf AGN
2. $ for Homeownership	AGN	6. Overseas Mil. Abortion FOR	10. US Mil. Abroad $ Cut FOR
3. Tax Rich/Cut Mid Cls.	FOR	7. Obscn. Art NEA $ Ban AGN	11. Limit SDI Funds FOR
4. FY93/$15B Def. Cut	FOR	8. Death Pen. from Jury AGN	12. Cuba Trade Embargo AGN

Key Votes of the 103d Congress

1. Family Leave   FOR   2. Deficit Reduction   FOR   3. Stimulus Plan   FOR

Election Results

1992 general	Lane Evans (D).....................	156,233	(60%)	($374,415)
	Ken Schloemer (R).................	103,719	(40%)	($117,624)
1992 primary	Lane Evans (D).....................	47,351	(82%)	
	Richard E. Maynard (D)	10,545	(18%)	
1990 general	Lane Evans (D).....................	102,062	(67%)	($390,401)
	Dan Lee (R)	51,380	(33%)	($115,495)

EIGHTEENTH DISTRICT

Vaudeville is the source of the phrase, "Will it play in Peoria?"—an indication of how ancient and possibly how out of date the idea is that Peoria, Illinois, somehow is the quintessence of Middle America. In the middle of Illinois, 154 miles from Chicago and 171 miles from St. Louis, Peoria was the epitome of a hick town. Actually, Peoria has never been entirely typical. Its people are mostly of British or German descent, with some blacks but few of the Asian and Hispanic immigrants common in other parts of America. But in post World War II culturally homogeneous America, Peoria was a fine test market for commercial products; it may have been divided between Democratic union members and white-collar Republicans, but on both sides of the economic line were similar tastes in food, clothes and even cars. In the culturally segmented if not fragmented America of today, Peoria has lost its test market status. Nor is its economy typical. With big farm equipment factories, it suffered terribly in the Farm Belt depression of the early 1980s, losing thousands of jobs. But its biggest employer continues to be Caterpillar, the world standard producer of earth-moving and construction equipment, and one of America's major exporters, with a large blue-collar work force whose United Auto Workers went out on a (mostly unsuccessful) strike in 1992: atypical in a low-strike era. Politically, Peoria leaned Republican in the years after the New Deal, when most of America voted Democratic; in the 1980s, when America was moving to Ronald Reagan (who went to Eureka College, just across the Illinois River), Peoria trended Democratic.

The 18th Congressional District of Illinois, variously configured, has been the Peoria district since the 1940s. It has been represented by such worthies as Everett McKinley Dirksen, who went on to be elected senator in 1950 and was Senate Republican Leader from 1959 to 1969, and Robert Michel, the current House Republican leader, who worked for Dirksen's successor in the House and then won the seat himself in 1956. Michel is a link, the last one in the House, to the days when Republicans were split between followers of Robert Taft and Dwight D. Eisenhower; he combines Taft's skepticism toward federal spending and distaste for federal deficits with Eisenhower's support for an expansive foreign policy. When Michel became leader in 1981, it seemed for a moment that Republicans were on the verge of winning a majority in the House, as they had in the Senate and the Electoral College, and he played a key role in amassing majorities for the Reagan budget and tax cuts in 1981. But Tip O'Neill's Democrats were able to regain control and hold it into the 1990s.

That presented Republicans with a dilemma. Should they try to cooperate with Democrats in the hopes of some concessions, as Michel was inclined to do with Tip O'Neill and Tom Foley (though not Jim Wright) and as many ranking Republicans were inclined to do with their committee chairmen? Or should they fight them aggressively, trying to make a record to take to the voters at the next election, as some younger conservatives argued? Michel's personal inclination is the first of these courses, tempered by an enraged indignation when he thinks the Democrats are playing unfairly (as when Democrats set up an investigation of the absurd "October surprise" charges or when they moved to give increased voting rights to the five Democratic delegates from D.C. and the territories). But as more Republicans come from a new generation, Michel's political incentives have had to move toward the second course; one only need to compare the composition of the Republican Conference in the early 1980s with today. And it was demonstrated in March 1989, when Republican Whip Dick Cheney resigned to become defense secretary and Michel backed his Illinois neighbor Edward Madigan to succeed him against Newt Gingrich, who had brought a complaint (not yet acted upon then) in the Ethics Committee against Speaker Jim Wright. Gingrich won 87–85, setting the direction of the House; Michel intimates like Madigan and fellow Illinois Lynn Martin left to hold or run for other office. By late 1992, after Jerry Lewis was beaten by Dick Armey for Republican Conference chair and Bill Gradison lost to Tom DeLay for Conference secretary, every leadership position but Michel's was won by someone with an approach similar to Gingrich's.

In fact, Michel has been more confrontational since supporting the October 1990 Bush budget summit agreement while Gingrich and nearly half the House Republicans opposed it. Michel supported a Republican campaign finance reform package far more specific and thorough than anything the Democrats could agree on. He told Speaker Tom Foley there would be troubles with the House bank and called for closing it down—which Foley initially resisted—after the GAO released a report on the rampant check kiting there. He backed a subpoena of its records and opposed Foley's plan for creating a CEO for the House, presenting his own reforms eliminating the House doorkeeper and postmaster instead. At the Republican National Convention in Houston, he sharply attacked the House as an institution. Seeing the negative reactions to the 1990 budget summit agreement, he resisted deficit reduction talks in 1992 and stoutly opposed the Clinton economic package in 1993. He called for an Ethics Committee investigation to see whether Banking Committee Chairman Henry Gonzalez violated House rules by disclosing classified information on Iraq. Sometimes Michel's conciliatory side still comes out: when Republicans won a surprise victory on a motion to abolish the Select Committee on Narcotics, Michel joined Democrats in a compromise reauthorizing the nonstanding committees until the end of the year, which he had to withdraw after many freshmen bellowed in fury. After 38 years in the minority, Michel knows a lot about legislative strategy and can still read the mood of the House; his candor, intellectual honesty and basic decency command wide respect on both sides of the aisle—an asset for his party which another leader would take years to build up. There are signs that this may be Michel's last term in the House, or at least as leader. Newt Gingrich, having announced that he would not run against Michel for leader in December 1992, pointedly refrained from discounting 1994; and speculation began that Gingrich, Dick Armey and Henry Hyde might all run then. Whatever the case, it is doubtful that any successor to Michel as minority leader is likely to bring the combinations of combativeness and decency, respect for tradition and willingness to change that he has brought to this largely thankless position over a dozen mostly difficult years.

Another factor Michel must consider is the need to fight for reelection. He won with 58% in the new 18th District in 1992, a considerable drop from his no-opposition 1990 race, but better than his 55% in 1988. But this is a district that cannot be taken entirely for granted. Illinois has the nation's first filing deadline, in December 1993; by that time, it should be plain what Michel's intentions are.

The People: Pop. 1990: 572,238; 37% rural; 14% age 65+; 94% White; 5% Black; 1% Asian; 1% Hispanic origin. Voting age pop.: 422,371; 4% Black; 1% Hispanic origin. Households: 61% married couple families; 28% married couple fams. w. children; 43% college educ.; median household income: $30,189; per capita income: $13,792; median gross rent: $352; median house value: $51,600.

1992 Presidential Vote			1988 Presidential Vote		
Clinton (D)	117,483	(42%)	Bush (R)	141,485	(57%)
Bush (R)	114,090	(41%)	Dukakis (D)	108,191	(43%)
Perot (I)	47,087	(17%)			

Rep. Robert H. Michel (R)

Elected 1956; b. Mar. 2, 1923, Peoria; home, Peoria; Bradley U., B.S. 1948; Apostolic Christian; married (Corinne).

Career: Army, 1942–46 (WWII); A.A., U.S. Rep. Harold Velde, 1949–56.

Offices: 2112 RHOB 20515, 202-225-6201. Also 100 N.E. Monroe, #107, Peoria 61602, 309-671-7027; and 236 W. State St., Jacksonville 62650, 217-245-1431.

Committees: *Minority Leader.*

Group Ratings

	ADA	ACLU	COPE	CDF	CFA	LCV	ACU	NTLC	NSI	COC	CEI
1992	10	0	25	30	33	6	87	95	100	88	64
1991	0	—	10	10	17	0	89	—	—	100	61

National Journal Ratings

	1991 LIB — 1991 CONS	1992 LIB — 1992 CONS
Economic	11% — 88%	9% — 88%
Social	0% — 84%	20% — 80%
Foreign	17% — 78%	0% — 82%

Key Votes of the 102d Congress

1. Ban Striker Replace *	5. Handgun Wait/7-Day *	9. Use Force in Gulf FOR
2. $ for Homeownership FOR	6. Overseas Mil. Abortion AGN	10. US Mil. Abroad $ Cut AGN
3. Tax Rich/Cut Mid Cls. AGN	7. Obscn. Art NEA $ Ban FOR	11. Limit SDI Funds AGN
4. FY93/$15B Def. Cut AGN	8. Death Pen. from Jury FOR	12. Cuba Trade Embargo FOR

Key Votes of the 103d Congress

1. Family Leave AGN	2. Deficit Reduction AGN	3. Stimulus Plan AGN

Election Results

1992 general	Robert H. Michel (R)................	156,533	(58%)	($636,430)
	Ronald C. Hawkins (D)	114,413	(42%)	
1992 primary	Robert H. Michel (R), unopposed			
1990 general	Robert H. Michel (R)................	105,693	(98%)	($579,258)
	Two Others	1,677	(2%)	

NINETEENTH DISTRICT

Southern Illinois is a land of prairies, of land sloping imperceptibly down to the Ohio and Mississippi Rivers. It was settled almost entirely from the south by farmers coming overland from Kentucky and ultimately Virginia, such as Abraham Lincoln's people. In the far southern part of the state, they found hilly terrain, some of which turned out to have coal deposits. To the north they must have been astonished, after miles of thick forest, to see the great American prairie stretch before them, a vast sea of flat treeless land extending past the horizon. For 200 years, settlers had to chop down trees and clear stumps—backbreaking work that slowed the frontier's march forward. The prairie lands proved wondrously rich, and were soon criss-crossed by rail lines taking their produce away and bringing in products of industrial civilization from Chicago and St. Louis and points east. About the same time, vast coal deposits were found in southern Illinois, producing one mining town after another: this was the home turf of John L. Lewis, the imperious leader of the United Mine Workers for half a century and, in the late 1930s and early 1940s, one of the most powerful and eloquent figures in American politics.

The 19th Congressional District of Illinois roughly covers the eastern half of southern Illinois. Most of it is south of the old National Road, which became U.S. 40 and is paralleled by Interstate 70, the traditional boundary between the part of Downstate Illinois settled by southerners and the Downstate settled by Yankees—a boundary also between traditional Democrats and traditional Republicans. North of that line, the 19th includes Decatur, a small city that is home of the giant Archer-Daniels-Midland company, the major producer and promoter of ethanol, and seeker of government subsidy. About a third of the 19th is prairie, straddling or south of the National Road line; the other third is far Downstate, the Egypt region as it is called, where people speak with what Yankees regard as southern accents and southern mores prevail, including an attachment to a conservatively inclined Democratic Party.

In 1992, the 19th was the scene of a contest between two incumbent Democrats, of almost the same age and with similar voting records (interventionist economically and isolationist on foreign policy, but culturally one more liberal than the other), yet with contrasting careers and approaches to politics. The favorite initially was Terry Bruce, first elected in 1984 from a seat including the prairie counties placed in the new 19th. On the December 1991 filing deadline, Bruce seemed to have the advantage for the March 1992 primary: he had represented more of the new district than his rival, Glenn Poshard from the coal-mining country in the south; he had been in Congress 4 years longer; and he had $659,000 in his campaign treasury to Poshard's $600, and the ability to raise lots more from his seat on the Energy and Commerce Committee. Bruce proceeded to run a textbook campaign, emphasizing his powerful Energy and Commerce seat, running TV ads throughout the district, attacking Poshard for supporting the 1990 budget summit agreement.

But in an anti-incumbent year, Poshard's style worked better. He had a more varied background: he joined the Army after high school and served in Korea in the early 1960s; he graduated from Southern Illinois University before the wave of lefty trendiness hit it; he taught history and government and coached high school sports in the coal country towns of Galatia and Thompsonville and got an education Ph.D. He was elected to the state Senate in 1984 and 1986, where he chaired a committee and worked to cut down on pollution from coal use. When longtime (1954–74, 1980–88) and colorful incumbent Ken Gray retired a second time, Poshard was elected to the House in 1988. In the House, he naturally looked after district interests, expanding the Shawnee National Forest and opposing Clean Air Act provisions that would restrict coal use; keeping in close personal touch with the district, he was easily reelected in 1990. He also became something of a reformer, renouncing PAC contributions and backing campaign finance reform; "we ought to get back to the citizen-legislator type of government." Poshard didn't decide to run in the 19th until just before filing deadline—his house was in the new 12th. He eschewed most media ads for lawn signs and personal campaigning, which won him Democratic and newspaper endorsements in Decatur and solid support in his old home area. He called Bruce a "classic Washington insider," and cited a memo Bruce wrote on the House bank ("we need to protect our privacy and wrap up the investigation quickly"). Poshard ran well in the Decatur area with 40%, and cut deeply into Bruce's old district with 44%, mainly by carrying three counties at its southern end. But he won in his own old district areas, carrying its 38,000 votes 90%–10%—quite a testimonial for a candidate outspent more than 4–1.

Poshard, now solidly ensconced, should be a Clinton Democrat: he notes that Clinton understands Delta problems like those of southern Illinois. But he was cautious about some of Clinton's proposed taxes, arguing that the energy tax should exempt ethanol, and he will remain on the lookout for the interests of coal.

The People: Pop. 1990: 571,390; 51% rural; 17% age 65+; 96% White; 4% Black. Voting age pop.: 428,993; 3% Black. Households: 60% married couple families; 27% married couple fams. w. children; 34% college educ.; median household income: $22,979; per capita income: $11,333; median gross rent: $295; median house value: $38,500.

1992 Presidential Vote

Clinton (D)	131,396	(47%)
Bush (R)	95,759	(34%)
Perot (I)	50,706	(18%)

1988 Presidential Vote

Bush (R)	132,401	(52%)
Dukakis (D)	120,078	(48%)

Rep. Glenn Poshard (D)

Elected 1988; b. Oct. 30, 1945, Herald.; home, Carterville; Southern IL U., B.A. 1970, M.S. 1974, Ph.D. 1984; Southern Baptist; married (Jo).

Career: Army, 1962–65; High schl. teacher, 1970–74, Dir., Regional Educ. Svc. Ctr. for Educators of the Gifted, 1974–84; IL Senate 1984–88.

Offices: 107 CHOB 20515, 202-225-5201. Also 201 E. Nolan, W. Frankfort 62896, 618-937-6402; New Rte. #13-W., Marion 62959, 618-953-8532; 363 S. Main St., Decatur 62521, 217-362-9011; 800 Airport Rd., Mattoon 61938, 217-234-7032; 444 S. Willow St., Effingham 62401, 217-342-7220; and 901 W. 9th St., Mt. Carmel 62863, 818-262-7723.

Committees: *Public Works and Transportation* (19th of 39 D): Water Resources and Environment. *Small Business* (12th of 27 D): Development of Rural Enterprises, Exports and the Environment; SBA Legislation and the General Economy.

Group Ratings

	ADA	ACLU	COPE	CDF	CFA	LCV	ACU	NTLC	NSI	COC	CEI
1992	65	61	83	80	80	56	36	20	30	25	28
1991	65	—	75	90	72	54	25	—	—	30	23

National Journal Ratings

	1991 LIB — 1991 CONS	1992 LIB — 1992 CONS
Economic	79% — 18%	61% — 38%
Social	40% — 58%	38% — 60%
Foreign	65% — 33%	82% — 16%

Key Votes of the 102d Congress

1. Ban Striker Replace	FOR	5. Handgun Wait/7-Day AGN	9. Use Force in Gulf AGN
2. $ for Homeownership	AGN	6. Overseas Mil. Abortion AGN	10. US Mil. Abroad $ Cut FOR
3. Tax Rich/Cut Mid Cls.	FOR	7. Obscn. Art NEA $ Ban FOR	11. Limit SDI Funds FOR
4. FY93/$15B Def. Cut	FOR	8. Death Pen. from Jury FOR	12. Cuba Trade Embargo AGN

Key Votes of the 103d Congress

1. Family Leave	FOR	2. Deficit Reduction	FOR	3. Stimulus Plan	FOR

Election Results

1992 general	Glenn Poshard (D)	187,156	(69%)	($312,530)
	Douglas E. Lee (R)...................	83,526	(31%)	($25,303)
1992 primary	Glenn Poshard (D)	57,566	(62%)	
	Terry L. Bruce (D)	35,574	(38%)	
1990 general	Glenn Poshard (D)	138,425	(84%)	($103,396)
(IL 22)	Jim Wham (JWP)...................	26,896	(16%)	($16,737)

TWENTIETH DISTRICT

Is it possible to imagine what Abraham Lincoln's world looked like? Springfield, Illinois, and the area around it gives one a chance. For the prairie countryside of central Illinois is still mostly farmland with few towns; and if farming technology has changed vastly, the patterns of cultivation, the contours of the land, even the shape of the ribbons of back country roads, cannot be so entirely different from what Lincoln saw as a lawyer making his way from one county seat to another on the circuit. On the state historic site at his family's old farmsite near New Salem, one can calibrate the difference. Moreover, Springfield itself has changed relatively little since Lincoln's time. If most of the officefronts and houses captured in the old photographs are gone, some remain; and the scale of Springfield, unlike that of so many small towns which have grown into metropolises, has not changed utterly. Lincoln's clapboard house is still in Springfield, and so is the courtroom where he argued cases before federal judges; the Greek revival downtown bloc where Lincoln & Herndon kept their law offices is open for inspection, as is the state Capitol building built here in 1839. Much of today's Springfield is tawdry, but unlike other state capitals it has not lost its 19th Century scale.

Only 19 congressional districts in the nation can claim to be the lineal descendant of a district whose representative was also a president of the United States. One of them is the 20th Congressional District of Illinois, which includes the southern half of Springfield and much of the Downstate Illinois prairie, which in 1846 elected a 37-year-old railroad lawyer and Whig opponent of the Mexican War named Abraham Lincoln to his single term in the House. Lincoln's denunciation of the Mexican War was so strong that he gave up any chance of a second term, for the countryside south and west of Springfield, straddling the National Road and along the Illinois River, both avenues of migration from the South, were strongly supportive of that war. Those sentiments—a certain hawkishness and predisposition to the Democratic Party—are apparent today. The 20th District, as redistricted for the 1990s, goes well south of the National Road and west to the Mississippi, but includes none of the heavily Republican territory directly north of Springfield.

The congressman from the 20th is, unlike Lincoln, a Democrat and professional politician. Richard Durbin has spent his adult life working in politics: on Paul Simon's staff when he was lieutenant governor (1969–73) and a state Senate staffer in the 1970s; he lost two races for office in the 1970s, but in 1982 won the nomination to oppose incumbent Paul Findley, who had characterized himself as Yasir Arafat's best friend in Congress; that helped Durbin raise large sums from Israel supporters and to attack Findley for concentrating on issues of no importance at home. Durbin won that race, got a seat on Agriculture, and then moved to Appropriations where he works in tandem with senior member Sidney Yates for Illinois projects, for Chicagoland as well as Downstate, including a research center at the Lincoln home. Many other Durbin interests have a local angle, like his efforts to promote ethanol use. But he has national interests too. More than any other House member, he is the author of the smoking ban on flights of two hours or less which, to his surprise, passed in 1987; in 1992 he tried to ban smoking in Head Start and other federally funded child care facilities and in government buildings including the Capitol. He pushed for drug treatment for pregnant women and tried to ban insurance companies from denying coverage because of preexisting conditions.

Redistricting gave Durbin a nearly half-new district, with many Republican-leaning voters in the Madison County suburbs outside St. Louis. He had a serious opponent in 1992, Madison County Treasurer John Shimkus, a West Point graduate and major in the Army Reserves. Shimkus, who refused PAC contributions, ran a serious campaign and held Durbin to 57% of the vote, a sharp drop from earlier years; he only narrowly carried Madison County and lost two others. But in Washington, Durbin grew more powerful as Jamie Whitten was voted out of his Agriculture Appropriations chairmanship by a 29–7 vote because of physical disability and Durbin was voted in 35–0. That makes him one of the "college of cardinals" (the Appropriations subcommittee chairmen), well-positioned to exchange favors and fund local projects, and able to determine funding levels for farm and food programs. It is work that Durbin has shown he can do, and the question at home is whether it is the work his voters want done through the 1990s.

The People: Pop. 1990: 571,138; 48% rural; 16% age 65+; 95% White; 4% Black; 1% Hispanic origin. Voting age pop.: 425,014; 4% Black; 1% Hispanic origin. Households: 60% married couple families; 27% married couple fams. w. children; 36% college educ.; median household income: $26,173; per capita income: $12,289; median gross rent: $337; median house value: $47,000.

1992 Presidential Vote			1988 Presidential Vote		
Clinton (D)	129,865	(46%)	Bush (R)	129,010	(51%)
Bush (R)	94,038	(34%)	Dukakis (D)	123,734	(49%)
Perot (I)	55,712	(20%)			

Rep. Richard J. Durbin (D)

Elected 1982; b. Nov. 21, 1944; East St. Louis; home, Springfield; Georgetown U., B.S. 1966, J.D. 1969; Catholic; married (Loretta).

Career: Staff, Lt. Gov. Paul Simon, 1969–72; Legal Cnsl., IL Sen. Judiciary Cmte., 1972–82; Prof., S. IL Schl. of Medicine, 1978–82.

Offices: 2463 RHOB 20515, 202-225-5271. Also 525 S. 8th St., Springfield 62703, 217-492-4062; 221 E. Broadway, Centralia 62801, 618-532-4265; and 400 St. Louis St., #2, Edwardsville 62025, 618-492-1082.

Committees: *Appropriations* (17th of 37 D): Agriculture, Rural Development, Food and Drug Administration and Related Agencies (Chmn.); District of Columbia; Transportation.

Group Ratings

	ADA	ACLU	COPE	CDF	CFA	LCV	ACU	NTLC	NSI	COC	CEI
1992	90	87	83	100	87	69	4	0	10	13	14
1991	95	—	92	100	89	92	5	—	—	30	11

National Journal Ratings

	1991 LIB — 1991 CONS		1992 LIB — 1992 CONS	
Economic	88%	— 0%	83%	— 13%
Social	78%	— 17%	68%	— 30%
Foreign	73%	— 26%	86%	— 10%

Key Votes of the 102d Congress

1. Ban Striker Replace	FOR	5. Handgun Wait/7-Day	FOR	9. Use Force in Gulf	AGN
2. $ for Homeownership	AGN	6. Overseas Mil. Abortion	FOR	10. US Mil. Abroad $ Cut	FOR
3. Tax Rich/Cut Mid Cls.	FOR	7. Obscn. Art NEA $ Ban	AGN	11. Limit SDI Funds	FOR
4. FY93/$15B Def. Cut	FOR	8. Death Pen. from Jury	AGN	12. Cuba Trade Embargo	AGN

Key Votes of the 103d Congress

1. Family Leave	FOR	2. Deficit Reduction	FOR	3. Stimulus Plan	FOR

Election Results

1992 general	Richard J. Durbin (D)	154,869	(57%)	($921,659)
	John M. Shimkus (R)	119,219	(43%)	($278,357)
1992 primary	Richard J. Durbin (D), unopposed			
1990 general	Richard J. Durbin (D)	130,114	(66%)	($209,360)
	Paul E. Jurgens (R)	66,433	(34%)	($44,861)

INDIANA

Every Memorial Day, the eyes of America turn to Indianapolis, to the center of a state that has the nation's most distinctive nickname and some of its least distinctive borders, for a sports spectacle celebrating the knack for tinkering and taste for powerful machines that made the Midwest the nation's manufacturing center: the Indianapolis 500. This auto race is run on a technologically ancient brick track in a city that is literally the center of American manufacturing: almost precisely half the country's manufacturing jobs are east of the state and the other half west, almost half are north and half south. Indianapolis and Indiana are also the center of an economically, culturally and politically older America. Older economically, because Indiana's employment patterns in the early 1990s resemble those of the United States of the early 1970s: more manufacturing and fewer service and government jobs than average today. On the map, Indiana may look rural, with its large number of small counties and single major metropolitan area of Indianapolis, but it is still a factory state, from the steel mills of Gary and the ring of auto plants 50 or so miles around Indianapolis to the coal-fired power plants in the south. Which is not to say that Indiana is not prosperous: its incomes hover just below the national average, but so does its cost of living; it has a large class of affluent citizens and not much of an urban underclass. It has one of the nation's lower tax levels and some of the most restrictive tort laws.

Indiana also has lower levels of social pathology—violent crime, unwed mothers, and divorce. It retains some of the old norms that in the 1920s and 1930s brought sociologists Robert and Helen Lynd in their search for the typical American place to "Middletown" (actually Muncie). The major metropolitan area, Indianapolis, now has 1.2 million people, but without the extent of single and gay cultures seen in other American metropolises. Ethnically, Indiana seems older too: except for the steel area around Gary—really an extension of the Chicago metropolitan area—Indiana has relatively few descendants from the 1840–1924 wave of immigration, and few recent Hispanic or Asian migrants. Finally, Indiana is transfixed by American sports: Indianapolis's civic leaders have made sports the focus of their development plans, attracting the Colts professional football team to the Hoosier Dome, hosting the Pan-American games in 1987 and the NCAA Final Four in 1991, establishing the Indiana Basketball Hall of Fame, and of course the Indianapolis 500 at the Speedway every Memorial Day.

Politically, Indiana is also typical of an older America, with partisan preferences anchored in the Civil War era and a small overlay of change from the union organizing days of the 1930s. Indiana's cultural conservatism has kept it Republican in presidential elections for the last generation or so, but for many years before it was a fulcrum point in partisan politics, a crucial state from the Civil War to the New Deal in the struggles between Republicans and Democrats. Party identification was handed down with religious affiliation—the Lynds noted that the Presbyterians had little to do with Methodists, but that was nothing next to divisions between Republicans and Democrats—in a state still peopled largely by descendants of its original settlers, Yankees from Ohio and New England and "Butternuts" (as they were called in the Civil

War years) from Kentucky and the South. Most Yankees became Republicans and most Butternuts Democrats, and so the split has remained: a map of the close 1980 Senate campaign results shows liberal Democratic Senator Birch Bayh carrying half the counties south of the old National Road (later U.S. 40) that bisects the state, while conservative Republican Dan Quayle carried all but four of the counties to the north—a result eerily similar to the presidential election of 1868.

In Indiana, as in the Sun Belt, the big city votes more Republican than the rest of the state, at least if you ignore the northwest industrial zone from Gary to South Bend. Greater Indianapolis favored the Bush-Quayle ticket by a solid 48%–32% margin in 1992, as it won statewide 43%–37%; in 1988 Indianapolis and suburbs favored the Republican gubernatorial candidate 55%–45% while almost every other county voted for Governor Evan Bayh. Conversely, the heavily industrial and unionized belt from Gary to South Bend tends to vote Democratic, even against a big winner like Republican Senator Dan Coats. But auto factory towns like Kokomo, Anderson, Muncie and Fort Wayne have mostly stuck with Republicans at the top of the ticket. In the 1920s, the Lynds, liberal academics influenced by Marx's idea of political acts being determined by economic interests, were puzzled as to why the factory workers in "Middletown" didn't vote against the bosses; in the 1930s, they were cheered by signs that they did. But why don't they now? The answer is that cultural identity and personal values have been more important determinants of political allegiance in an America where economic status is so often readily changeable.

But Indiana's strong partisan allegiances seem now to be breaking down. In the late 1980s, the legislature banned the mandatory 2% contributions by state employees to finance whichever party was in power. The Republican machine which had controlled the state government for 20 years, since Dan Quayle was looking for a state job to work his way through law school, lost the governorship in 1988. But in 1992, Democrat Evan Bayh, despite great popularity, wasn't able to sweep in many Democrats, not even his friend Joe Hogsett who was running for the Senate. Instead, Hoosiers split their ticket as never before, with at least 20% splitting between Senate and governor races. This leaves Indiana competitive between the parties, at least if the Democrats stay, as Bayh does, with a relatively conservative platform. Hoosiers' ancestral ties produce rotation in office—but never a revolution in policies or cultural values.

Governor. Evan Bayh in his first term was the nation's youngest and one of its most popular governors. He was reelected in 1992 by a wide margin, running 25% ahead of Bill Clinton. Being elected young is a Hoosier tradition by now: the governor's father Birch Bayh was first elected senator in 1962 at 34, and was beaten in 1980 by Dan Quayle, who was then 33; Evan Bayh was elected at 32. He ran in 1988 as a determined opponent of higher taxes and a less venturesome government activist than his Republican opponent, Lieutenant Governor John Mutz. In office, Bayh abolished the license plate fund, has made no major tax concessions to attract big business and has allowed no state tax increases. He helped attract a 6,300-worker United Airlines repair facility to Indianapolis and pushed for a third Chicago regional airport in Gary, though he was outshoved by Illinois politicians; in 1991 Indiana gained more jobs than all but one other state (Florida). Bayh sponsored some innovative education programs, from adult literacy, to healthcare access and other services for pre-schoolers, to experimental Discovery Schools for high schoolers and college tuition for at-risk youths who pledge to graduate high school and stay off drugs.

Bayh has seen Democrats gain control of the state House in 1989 and 1990 (it was 50–50 and a Republican and Democrat alternated as speaker every other day), his ally Joe Hogsett was elected secretary of state over longtime Indianapolis Mayor William Hudnut in 1990 and Democrat Pam Carter, a black woman, was elected Attorney General in 1992; Bayh himself easily prevailed over outgoing Attorney General Linley Pearson. Bayh cannot seek a third term in 1996, and is not likely to run against Senator Richard Lugar in 1994, but no one would be surprised if he ran for Dan Coats's Senate seat in 1998.

Senators. Richard Lugar has a career in public life going back almost four decades to the late

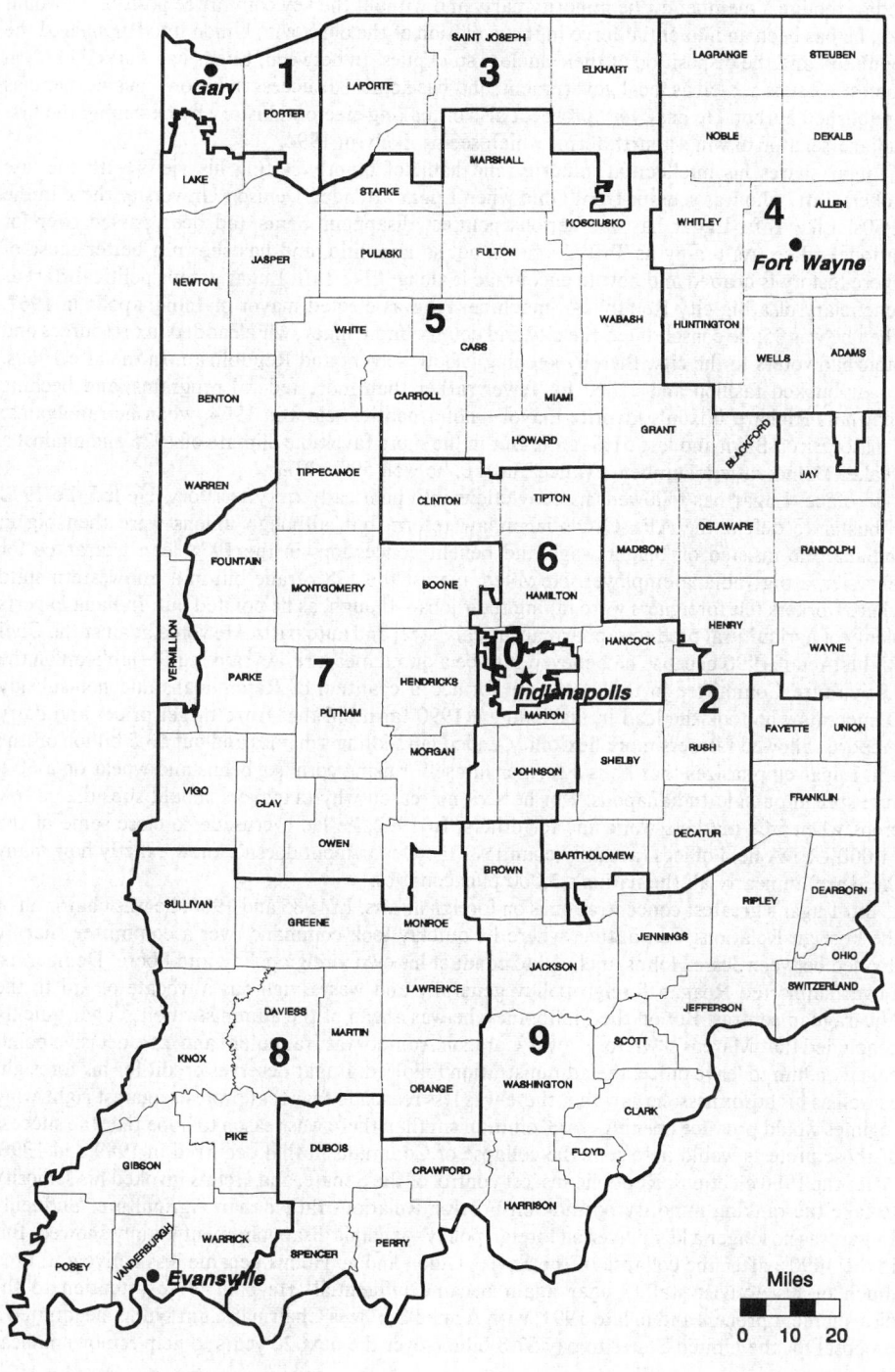

1950s, when as a young Navy officer he prepared intelligence briefings for Chief of Naval Operations Arleigh Burke and briefed President Eisenhower over closed-circuit television. Today, though a member of the minority party and without the key committee position he would like, he has been an influential force in the evolution of the old Soviet Union into Russia and the republics, and the disposition of their nuclear stockpiles. In between, Lugar has worked hard on domestic issues as well as local government, and has achieved success in his own business and as a published author. He has every prospect also of making electoral history by becoming the first Indiana senator to win a fourth term, which seems likely in 1994.

Lugar shares his intellectual integrity and habit of bluntly stating his views with the late Robert Taft, who was senator from Ohio when Lugar attended Denison University there in the 1950s. Like Taft, Lugar has had serious political disappointments and been passed over for national office. As brainy as Taft, Lugar is not so impolitic, and has shown a better sense of where history is headed and how to encourage it along. Like Taft, Lugar got his political start as beneficiary of a big city Republican machine. He was elected mayor of Indianapolis in 1967, when he was 35; he consolidated the city and county into Unigov, which added tax resources and suburban voters to the city, thereby keeping it both solvent and Republican. In the late 1960s, Lugar bucked fashion and called for fewer rather than more federal programs, and became known as Richard Nixon's favorite mayor—not a political asset in 1974, when he ran against Senator Birch Bayh and lost 51%–46%. But in the more favorable climate of 1976 and against a weaker Democratic incumbent, Vance Hartke, he won 59%–40%.

In office, Lugar has followed his convictions into politically risky territory. He led the 1978 filibuster to defeat the AFL-CIO's labor law reform bill, although unions were then big in Indiana. He insisted on bigger wage and benefit concessions in the 1978 loan guarantee for Chrysler, a big Indiana employer. He voted against the 1988 trade bill in a midwestern state where workers felt foreigners were taking their jobs—though, as he pointed out, Indiana exports plenty of agricultural products, pharmaceuticals, steel and auto parts. He voted against the Civil Rights Act of 1990 because he believed it to be a quota measure. As ranking Republican on the Agriculture Committee in the 1990s, he formed a coalition of Republicans and non-subsidy Democrats who took the lead in fashioning a 1990 farm bill that froze target prices and dairy supports, allowed farmers more flexibility, ended land-idling schemes and cut $3.5 billion off the bill. Lugar emphasizes that he is a farmer himself, raising corn, soybeans and wheat on a 600-acre spread outside Indianapolis. But he sees no reason why taxpayers should subsidize a few crops when free markets work fine for others. In 1992, he led a crusade to close some of the 11,000 USDA field offices (actually countless: the Department doesn't know exactly how many there are) in nearly all the nation's 3,000-plus counties.

But Lugar's greatest concentration is on foreign affairs. In 1985 and 1986, he was chairman of the Foreign Relations Committee, where he quickly took command over a committee sharply divided between Jesse Helms, inclined to conduct his own foreign policy, and liberal Democrats. Lugar supported Reagan foreign policy generally and was a vigorous advocate of aid to the Nicaraguan contras. But on the Philippines, he was ahead of the administration: Lugar quickly concluded that Marcos's "victory" over Corazon Aquino was fraudulent and, at a decisive point, called on him to leave office; the administration followed. Lugar deserves credit for his foresight as well as his adroitness: he saw that there was less reason to fear that protests against right-wing regimes would produce openings for Communism than there was reason to hope that the success of those protests would help spur the collapse of Communism that occurred in 1989 and 1990. After the 1986 elections, Republicans lost control of the Senate, and Helms invoked his seniority to take the ranking minority position on Foreign Relations rather than Agriculture. Suddenly Lugar was no longer a key player on foreign policy—and his disappointment plainly showed. But in the 1990s, after the collapse of the Soviet Union and as Helms became less active and fired much of his activist staff, Lugar again became influential. He paid close attention to the disarmament process and in late 1991, with Armed Services Chairman Sam Nunn, negotiated a proposal for the United States to pay $7.8 billion over the next 20 years to help remove nuclear weapons from Russia and other former Soviet republics; Lugar continued to press hard after his bill was passed. Funds from the Lugar-Nunn bill were an essential part of the summer 1992 U.S.-Russia chemical weapons accord. Lugar also called in early 1992 for more U.S. aid to Russia and the republics as "an investment in political, economic and social reform that will pay dividends many times over." Lugar also became involved in the Bosnia crisis, calling in June 1992, long before most others, for use of United Nations and U.S. military force if necessary. His new seat on the Intelligence Committee as of 1993 should make him even more influential.

Lugar has had his disappointments. In 1984, he ran to succeed his friend Howard Baker as Senate majority leader, and finished third behind Bob Dole and Ted Stevens. In 1986, he was elbowed aside in Foreign Relations by Helms, and in August 1988, George Bush picked— instead of Lugar— a junior and less experienced colleague, Dan Quayle, to be his vice president. This was the third time Lugar had been widely mentioned as a possibility for the number two slot—the others were in 1972 and 1980—and probably the last. But Lugar has been well received by Indiana voters. In 1988, he set a record, cutting across all historic lines in Indiana by carrying 91 of 92 counties (he lost Gary's Lake County) and winning 68% of the vote, more than Dan Quayle's 1986 record of 61%. Lugar began the 1993–94 cycle with $1.3 million in the bank and seems prepared to break the Indiana jinx and win a fourth term.

The junior senator from Indiana is Dan Coats, a member of Congress for more than a dozen years who insists politics "is not really what I'd planned to do." He was an aide to Dan Quayle when he served in the House in the 1970s, was elected to succeed him in that seat in 1980, was appointed to succeed him in the Senate in December 1988 and was elected in his own right for the remainder of the term in 1990 and for a full term in 1992. Several themes emerge clearly from Coats's congressional career. One is a devotion to traditional values rooted in religious faith. Coats is strongly against abortion; he backed the ban on fetal tissue research and tried to block research on the abortifacient RU-486—lost causes now in the Clinton years. He backs school prayer and passed a law allowing parents to block dial-a-porn phone numbers. But his views also lead him to positions where he and some liberals agree. He wants to raise the dependent tax exemption from $2,050 to $4,000, and he has led the fight for more money for shelters aiding victims of domestic violence. He has his own health plan, Medisave, which would encourage medical IRAs and, he says, give incentives for healthy lifestyles and preventive care. Another thread in Coats's career is support for the military. In early 1993, he was the lead Republican seeking to block Clinton's plans to end the ban on gays in the military. Coats insisted that he was not anti-gay and that the Clinton plan would, among other things, lead to harm for many gays. Coats is a strong backer of the Strategic Defense Initiative, and he thinks enough of defense needs to have acquiesced when Indiana's only two active bases were included on the 1991 base closing list.

Coats wants to curb the career Congress, calling for term limits (promising to impose them on himself) and backing the line-item veto. Perhaps his most famous cause is allowing states to keep trash from other states outside their borders. In 1992, he got through a bill letting Pennsylvania, Virginia, Ohio and, of course, Indiana ban out-of-state trash; in early 1993, with Oregon liberal Ron Wyden, he was trying to get RCRA changed to give governors the power to freeze trash imports. "We want New Jersey students," he once said in debate. "We want New Jersey residents. We want New Jersey athletes. We want everything from New Jersey but your trash."

Coats has now won two Senate races in two years with increasing margins. In 1990, he was attacked by Democrat Baron Hill for mailing out 13 million franked letters; Hill campaigned by walking the length of the state, but didn't raise the important abortion issue because he had just switched positions on it himself. Hill lost 54%–46%, carrying the northwest industrial corridor from Gary to South Bend, the old Butternut counties along the Ohio River, the Terre Haute area and Bloomington. But Coats carried metro Indianapolis 57%–43% and ran even stronger in his old congressional district. In 1992, the Democrat was Joe Hogsett, who managed Evan Bayh's first two campaigns and succeeded him as secretary of state by beating Indianapolis Mayor William Hudnut in 1990. Hogsett attacked Coats for accepting honoraria from speaking engagements, called for an end to congressional pay raises, perks and privileges, and attacked the North American Free Trade Agreement. But Coats challenged him for breaking his promise to serve a full term in his current office and Hogsett never really caught on. Coats won 57%–41%, only barely losing the northwest industrial corridor and carrying greater Indianapolis 65%–34%.

Presidential politics. In recent presidential elections, Indiana has voted more Republican than any state that is larger, and is larger than any state that has voted more Republican. In the last two elections, this owed something to the local popularity of Dan Quayle, but was more due to the statewide unpopularity of the cultural liberalism which to varying extents has characterized the national Democratic ticket since the late 1960s. Since 1968, Republicans have averaged 56% of Indiana's votes and the Democrats 38%. In 1992, George Bush got fewer votes than any Republican since Barry Goldwater, but even with higher turnout Bill Clinton did not win significantly more votes or a greater share of the vote than Michael Dukakis, Walter Mondale or Jimmy Carter. Indiana once had an influential presidential primary, most recently in 1968, but the May primary date comes so late in the season that it has been unimportant since then.

Congressional districting. Indiana's 1991 districting plan is a mild revision of a 1981 plan enacted by Republicans and defended by them all the way to the Supreme Court in 1986, and which by 1990 was electing two Republicans and eight Democrats to the House. The Court's decision was a classic muddle: it ruled that state legislatures could draw lines for partisan advantage but that courts could overturn them if they were egregious; it then went on to uphold Indiana's lines, although it's not likely that anyone could come up with a clearer case of partisan motivation. Partisan overreaching, actually: Republicans created too many marginal Republican seats, which talented Democrats picked off in favorable circumstances and then held. With control over the process divided, State House politicians in 1991 decided just to leave the lines pretty much alone, which was easy because Indiana didn't lose a seat as it had in 1981 and there were no major population shifts within the state.

The People: Est. Pop. 1992: 5,662,000; Pop. 1990: 5,544,159, up 2.1% 1990–1992. 2.2% of U.S. total, 14th largest; 35% rural. Median age: 32.8 years. 12.6% 65 years and over. 90.6% White, 7.8% Black, 1.8% Hispanic origin. Households: 58.2% married couple families; 28% married couple fams. w. children; 37% college educ.; median household income: $28,797; per capita income: $13,149; 70.2% owner occupied housing; median house value: $53,900; median monthly rent: $291. 6.5% Unemployment. Voting age pop.: 4,088,195. Registered voters (1992): 3,180,157; no party registration.

Political Lineup: Governor, Evan Bayh (D); Lt. Gov., Frank L. O'Bannon (D); Secy. of State, Joseph H. Hogsett (D); Atty. Gen., Pamela Carter (D); Treasurer, Marjorie H. O'Laughlin (R); Auditor, Ann DeVore (R). State Senate, 50 (28 R and 22 D); State House of Representatives, 100 (55 D and 45 R). Senators, Richard G. Lugar (R) and Daniel R. Coats (R). Representatives, 10 (7 D and 3 R).

1992 Presidential Vote

Bush (R)	939,375	(43%)
Clinton (D)	848,420	(37%)
Perot (I)	455,934	(20%)

1992 Democratic Presidential Primary

Clinton	301,905	(63%)
Brown	102,379	(21%)
Tsongas	58,215	(12%)

1988 Presidential Vote

Bush (R)	1,297,763	(60%)
Dukakis (D)	860,643	(39%)

1992 Republican Presidential Primary

Bush	374,666	(80%)
Buchanan	92,949	(20%)

GOVERNOR

Gov. Evan Bayh (D)

Elected 1988, term expires Jan. 1996; b. Dec. 26, 1955, Terre Haute; home, Indianapolis; IN U., B.A. 1978, U. of VA, J.D. 1981; Episcopalian; married (Susan).

Career: Practicing atty., 1981–86; IN Secy. of State, 1986–89.

Office: 206 State House, Indianapolis 46204, 317-232-4567.

Election Results

1992 gen.	Evan Bayh (D)	1,382,151	(62%)
	Linley E. Pearson (R)	822,853	(37%)
1992 prim.	Evan Bayh (D), unopposed		
1988 gen.	Evan Bayh (D)	1,138,574	(53%)
	John Mutz (R)	1,002,207	(47%)

SENATORS

Sen. Richard G. Lugar (R)

Elected 1976, seat up 1994; b. Apr. 4, 1932, Indianapolis; home, Indianapolis; Denison U., B.A. 1954; Rhodes Scholar, Oxford U., M.A. 1956; Methodist; married (Charlene).

Career: Navy, 1957–60; Mgr., family farm; V.P. and Treas., Thomas L. Green & Co., 1960–67; Indianapolis Bd. of Schl. Commissioners, 1964–67; Indianapolis Mayor, 1968–75; Prof., U. of Indianapolis, 1976.

Offices: 306 HSOB 20510, 202-224-4814. Also 1180 Market Tower, 10 W. Market St., Indianapolis 46204, 317-226-5555; Fed. Bldg., 1300 S. Harrison St., #3158, Fort Wayne 46802, 219-422-1505; 122 Fed. Bldg., 101 NW M.L.K. Blvd., Evansville 47708, 812-465-6313; 103 Fed. Ctr., 1201 E. 10th St., Jeffersonville 47132, 812-288-3377; and 5530 Sohl Ave., #103, Hammond 46320, 219-937-5380.

Committees: *Agriculture, Nutrition and Forestry* (RMM of 8 R). *Foreign Relations* (2d of 8 R): East Asian and Pacific Affairs; European Affairs (RMM); Western Hemisphere and Peace Corps Affairs. *Intelligence (Select)* (7th of 8 R). *Joint Committee on the Organization of Congress* (12th of 12).

Group Ratings

	ADA	ACLU	CDF	COPE	CFA	LCV	ACU	NTLC	NSI	COC	CEI
1992	10	14	20	17	17	33	85	82	100	100	78
1991	10	—	36	17	22	27	76	—	—	90	71

National Journal Ratings

	1991 LIB — 1991 CONS		1992 LIB — 1992 CONS	
Economic	15% —	80%	0% —	89%
Social	26% —	72%	25% —	74%
Foreign	26% —	73%	21% —	72%

442　INDIANA

Key Votes of the 102d Congress

1. $ for Homeownership FOR	5. Clarence Thomas Nom. FOR	9. Use Force in Gulf FOR
2. Have Cap Gains Debate FOR	6. Lmt Death Row Appeal FOR	10. Keep Salvador Aid FOR
3. Remove Budget Walls AGN	7. Handgun Wait/5-Day FOR	11. Cut $1B from SDI AGN
4. Ban Striker Replace AGN	8. Abortion Gag Rule FOR	12. Override China MFN AGN

Key Votes of the 103d Congress

1. Family Leave AGN	2. HIV Immigrants AGN	3. Clinton Budget AGN

Election Results

1988 general	Richard G. Lugar (R)................	1,430,525	(68%)	($3,244,601)
	Jack Wickes (D)	668,778	(32%)	($314,233)
1988 primary	Richard G. Lugar (R), unopposed			
1982 general	Richard G. Lugar (R)................	978,301	(54%)	($2,987,573)
	Floyd Fithian (D)	828,400	(46%)	($870,023)

Sen. Daniel R. Coats (R)

Appointed Jan. 1989, seat up 1998; b. May 16, 1943, Jackson, MI; home, Fort Wayne; Wheaton Col., B.A. 1965, IN U., J.D. 1971; Presbyterian; married (Marcia).

Career: Army Corps of Engineers, 1966–68; Asst. V.P. and Cnsl., Mutual Security Life Insurance Co., 1972–76; Dist. Rep. for U.S. Rep. J. Danforth Quayle, 1976–80; U.S. House of Reps., 1980–88.

Offices: 404 RSOB 20515, 202-224-5623. Also 1180 Market Tower, 10 W. Market St., Indianapolis 46204, 317-226-5555; Fed. Bldg., 1300 S. Harrison St., #3158, Fort Wayne 46802, 219-422-1505; 103 Fed. Ctr., 1201 E. 10th St., Jeffersonville 47132, 812-288-3377; 122 Fed. Bldg., 101 NW M.L.K. Blvd., Evansville 47708, 812-465-6313; and 5530 Sohl Ave., #103, Hammond 46320, 219-937-5380.

Committees: *Armed Services* (6th of 9 R): Coalition Defense and Reinforcing Forces; Defense Technology, Acquisition and Industrial Base; Force Requirements and Personnel (RMM). *Labor and Human Resources* (3d of 7 R): Aging; Children, Family, Drugs and Alcoholism (RMM); Education, Arts and Humanities; Employment and Productivity.

Group Ratings

	ADA	ACLU	CDF	COPE	CFA	LCV	ACU	NTLC	NSI	COC	CEI
1992	10	5	40	33	50	17	93	100	90	90	77
1991	5	—	45	25	22	20	100	—	—	80	76

National Journal Ratings

	1991 LIB — 1991 CONS			1992 LIB — 1992 CONS		
Economic	28%	—	69%	29%	—	70%
Social	14%	—	77%	11%	—	86%
Foreign	27%	—	67%	0%	—	90%

Key Votes of the 102d Congress

1. $ for Homeownership FOR	5. Clarence Thomas Nom. FOR	9. Use Force in Gulf FOR
2. Have Cap Gains Debate FOR	6. Lmt Death Row Appeal FOR	10. Keep Salvador Aid FOR
3. Remove Budget Walls AGN	7. Handgun Wait/5-Day FOR	11. Cut $1B from SDI AGN
4. Ban Striker Replace AGN	8. Abortion Gag Rule FOR	12. Override China MFN AGN

Key Votes of the 103d Congress

1. Family Leave   FOR   2. HIV Immigrants   AGN   3. Clinton Budget   AGN

Election Results

1992 general	Daniel R. Coats (R)	1,267,972	(57%)	($3,802,077)
	Joseph H. Hogsett (D)	900,148	(41%)	($1,584,173)
	Four Others	43,306	(2%)	
1992 primary	Daniel R. Coats (R), unopposed			
1990 general	Daniel R. Coats (R)	806,048	(54%)	($3,662,672)
	Baron P. Hill (D)	696,639	(46%)	($1,077,074)

FIRST DISTRICT

At the southernmost point of Lake Michigan is a part of America made by steel. Here, in the northwest corner of Indiana, where the water highway of the Great Lakes comes closest to the steel highway of the transcontinental railroads, America's leading capitalists recognized nearly a century ago the best possible site for manufacturing steel. On empty sand dunes, United States Steel, then the nation's largest corporation, created only a few years before by financier J. P. Morgan, established the city of Gary in 1906 and named it for the company's chairman, Chicago Judge Elbert Gary. For nearly 70 years, the steel mills attracted a diverse work force, much like that in Chicago and quite unlike the rest of Indiana—Irish, Poles, Czechs, Ukrainians and blacks from the American South. Politics here has always been turbulent, from the time Communists led the long and unsuccessful steel strike of 1919 to the racially polarized politics of the 1960s and 1970s. The tone of public life—the clash between union stewards and management foremen, between blacks and eastern European ethnics, between the stalwarts of different factions vying for control of Gary's massive City Hall—was always abrasive, like the clash of steel on steel.

Over all this time, only one thing has brought people here: steel. In the 1920s, the merchants of Gary built massive storefronts along Broadway, looking north to the Gary Works; civic institutions were created and nurtured; nearby Chicago was as culturally and economically diversified as any metropolis in the country. But Gary and Lake County always remained a bit remote, and always lived—and lived well for a time—on and for steel. Over time, steel management and union leaders tried to insulate the industry from the outside world, passing along high wage costs to users, building trade barriers to keep out competition. In the short run, this strategy worked: as late as 1979, steel still employed 70,000 in Gary and northwest Indiana. But then disaster struck. The mills were overmanned and technologically backward; starting in 1980, steel jobs dropped to 35,000 and total jobs dropped by 50,000; few new jobs paid anything like United Steelworkers wages. In time, the steelmakers rebounded: U.S. Steel (renamed USX), Inland, Bethlehem and LTV spent nearly $3 billion modernizing their northwest Indiana plants; the number of man-hours needed to produce a ton of steel was cut by two-thirds; just-in-time methods were introduced; management and high-skill workers cooperated to build higher-quality, less expensive steel to meet customers' needs. By 1989, Indiana was the number one steel producing state in the nation. Unfortunately, Gary has not benefited much from this progress, for the very success of this high-tech production means fewer jobs—7,800 at the Gary Works, for example, compared to 21,000 in 1979.

Nor has politics been Gary's salvation. In the 1970s, racially polarized politics resulted in economic stagnation and flight to the suburbs; Gary's population fell 23% in the 1980s. As long ago as 1967, Gary elected a black mayor, Richard Hatcher; but despite his talents, he was never able to inspire confidence among whites or economic commitment by investors. Blocks of Broadway are now boarded up; there are no hotels or department stores in the city; the publicly financed convention center and airport still do little business.

The Gary area is the one overwhelmingly Democratic part of Indiana, though not out of any Civil War heritage, for this was heavily Republican territory until the United Steelworkers' late 1930s organizing drives. Racial friction in the 1960s and 1970s reduced the appeal of national Democrats, but the decline of the steel industry put Democratic percentages up again. Indiana's 1st Congressional District, stretching from Gary along the Lake Michigan shore east almost to Michigan City, is solidly Democratic; any political battles here are played out in Democratic primaries. Its current congressman, Pete Visclosky, has a career distinguished by earnestness and hard work. From a working class background, he worked for six years on the staff of Congressman Adam Benjamin, who died suddenly in 1982. Visclosky returned to Indiana and in 1984 ran against Katie Hall, a black state senator who had been given the 1982 nomination—and thus the election—by Richard Hatcher, then district party chairman. But Hall was able to win only 33% of the 1984 primary vote; Visclosky had 34% and another white candidate 31%. Visclosky beat Hall 57%–35% in 1986 and 51%–30% in 1990; racial lines seem solid, as does his hold on the district.

Strengthening the northern Indiana economy was Visclosky's obvious priority. He started off working for the misnamed Voluntary Restraint Agreements that had helped delay modernization and protect benefits for employees and retirees of bankrupt steel companies, notably LTV. He tried to strengthen the local economy with a Little Calumet River flood control project, more acreage for the Indiana Dunes National Lakeshore, and transformation of the little-used Gary airport into the Chicago area's third major airport; that last project was stymied when Indiana Governor Evan Bayh supported Chicago Mayor Richard Daley's Lake Calumet site instead, which in turn was defeated by Illinois Senate President Pate Philip. Visclosky finally succeeded in getting a spot on the Appropriations Committee in 1991; there he will be able to work for more local projects. His record on national economic, cultural and foreign issues is rather moderate; he is genuinely concerned about the budget deficit and says he would like to use his Appropriations seat to pare it down. But he has the traditional congressman's belief that the leaders are the key: "In the end, the only people who are going to be able to make the thing work are the chairmen, in conjunction with the leadership."

The 1st District lost population in the 1980s, and 1991 redistricting pared off the industrial town of Michigan City and added inland suburbs in Lake and Porter Counties, making the seat perceptibly less Democratic. Visclosky, however, with his earnest hard work and moderate record, won reelection with 72% in the primary and 69% in the general election.

The People: Pop. 1990: 554,514; 9% rural; 12% age 65+; 70% White; 21% Black; 1% Asian; 4% Other; 8% Hispanic origin. Voting age pop.: 400,694; 19% Black; 7% Hispanic origin. Households: 57% married couple families; 27% married couple fams. w. children; 37% college educ.; median household income: $31,300; per capita income: $13,161; median gross rent: $399; median house value: $56,400.

1992 Presidential Vote

Clinton (D) 117,115 (52%)
Bush (R) 68,392 (31%)
Perot (I)................... 37,129 (17%)

1988 Presidential Vote

Dukakis (D)............... 118,554 (55%)
Bush (R) 98,656 (45%)

Rep. Peter J. Visclosky (D)

Elected 1984; b. Aug. 13, 1949, Gary; home, Merrillville; IN U. Northwest, B.S. 1970, U. of Notre Dame, J.D. 1973, Georgetown U., LL.M. 1982; Catholic; married (Anne Marie).

Career: Practicing atty., 1973–76, 1983–84; Aide, U.S. Rep. Adam Benjamin, 1976–82.

Offices: 2464 RHOB 20515, 202-225-2461. Also 215 W. 35th Ave., Gary 46408, 219-884-1177; City Hall, 6070 Central Ave., Portage 46368, 219-763-2904; and City Hall, 166 Lincolnway, Valparaiso 46383, 219-464-0315.

Committees: *Appropriations* (25th of 37 D): Defense; Treasury, Postal Service, and General Government.

Group Ratings

	ADA	ACLU	COPE	CDF	CFA	LCV	ACU	NTLC	NSI	COC	CEI
1992	85	96	100	60	87	38	16	25	50	50	16
1991	80	—	92	90	78	54	10	—	—	30	17

National Journal Ratings

	1991 LIB — 1991 CONS		1992 LIB — 1992 CONS	
Economic	56%	— 42%	55%	— 45%
Social	78%	— 17%	68%	— 30%
Foreign	62%	— 36%	62%	— 35%

Key Votes of the 102d Congress

1. Ban Striker Replace	FOR	5. Handgun Wait/7-Day	FOR	9. Use Force in Gulf	AGN
2. $ for Homeownership	AGN	6. Overseas Mil. Abortion	FOR	10. US Mil. Abroad $ Cut	FOR
3. Tax Rich/Cut Mid Cls.	FOR	7. Obscn. Art NEA $ Ban	FOR	11. Limit SDI Funds	FOR
4. FY93/$15B Def. Cut	AGN	8. Death Pen. from Jury	AGN	12. Cuba Trade Embargo	FOR

Key Votes of the 103d Congress

1. Family Leave	FOR	2. Deficit Reduction	FOR	3. Stimulus Plan	FOR

Election Results

1992 general	Peter J. Visclosky (D)	147,054	(69%)	($268,786)
	David J. Vucich (R)	64,770	(31%)	
1992 primary	Peter J. Visclosky (D)	53,383	(72%)	
	George T. Jancosek (D)	10,148	(14%)	
	Albert J. La Mere (D)	7,426	(10%)	
	Cyril B. Huerter (D)	3,389	(5%)	
1990 general	Peter J. Visclosky (D)	68,920	(66%)	($299,280)
	William (Bill) Costas (R)	35,450	(34%)	($21,355)

SECOND DISTRICT

Muncie, Indiana, became famous as the "Middletown" that sociologists Robert and Helen Lynd lived in and reported on in 1924–25 and again in 1935, and where a team of sociologists investigated again in 1976–78 (academic research, like so many other things, seems to require more people and take more time than it used to). The Lynds were attracted to Muncie by its typicalness—"every small city from Maine to California," *Life* said—but it wasn't exactly: it was a factory town in a country still almost half rural, it was almost entirely Protestant and northern in a country one-quarter Catholic and one-third southern. It was more typical in being culturally homogeneous but economically riven. In the 1920s, Muncie celebrated its common values and was loath to admit its economic disparities; in the 1930s, the latter came out into the open when Muncie, like most of the industrial Midwest, was unionized in what were sometimes violent uprisings. The business elite—local bankers, merchants, executives at General Motors and the Ball family's glass company—was fiercely opposed by workers who were joining CIO unions and voting Democratic. Partisan politics took on the sharp, bitter tone of a struggle for wealth between two rival classes whose claims seemed irreconcilable.

Now Muncie has changed again. As incomes tripled over 40 years, class antagonisms cooled; it turned out there was plenty for everyone. At the same time, increasing affluence and waning tradition allowed for more variety in personal life. As cultural issues came to the fore, the traditional values shared by the majority of Middletowners of various income levels tended to bring them together. The old factory economy was becoming less important: 35% of Muncie workers were in manufacturing in 1970, less than 20% in 1990. In partisan politics, Muncie was overwhelmingly Republican in the 1920s, voting its Civil War preference as so much of Indiana still does; it shifted toward the Democrats in the 1930s, on economic issues. As economic class conflict became less important, Muncie's cultural traditionalism moved it toward Republicans by the late 1960s. Yet voters were increasingly willing to split tickets, opening opportunities for Democrats—notably, Philip Sharp, Democratic Congressman for Muncie and various parts of central Indiana since 1974.

The 2d Congressional District of Indiana is centered on Muncie and some similar small cities. Anderson, just to the west, has long had big General Motors factories, though some have closed down; Richmond was founded by a major branch of American Quakers, and is the home of their Earlham College; Columbus is the home of Cummins Engine, whose longtime head J. Irwin Miller paid major national architects to design most of the town's important buildings, public and private. All of these have kept their basic national Republican leanings into the 1990s, and the 2d District was carried handily by the Bush-Quayle ticket in 1992.

Philip Sharp, the congressman from the 2d District, has been one of America's busiest politicians for two decades, legislating in Washington and competing in a marginal district back home. His roots are not in Indiana's ancestral parties or in class-conscious labor unions. He is a political scientist who is not a down-the-line labor liberal, as most Democratic members from Indiana were when he started out; he won his seat in 1974 on non-economic as much as economic issues. Once in the House, Sharp opposed the Democratic orthodoxy of oil and gas price controls and, as chairman of a special energy task force in 1978, helped fashion a compromise energy program which phased out price controls over several years. Since 1981, he has chaired the Energy and Power Subcommittee of Energy and Commerce, not always highly visible but making substantial achievements in part by skirting controversy and building consensus.

Over the years, he has been a leader in obtaining natural gas decontrol and wellhead decontrol. In 1987 and 1988, he promoted alternative fuels like ethanol, minimum appliance standards and stopped a $1.75 billion uranium industry bailout. He was lead sponsor of the law to provide better data on foreign investment. He led reauthorization of the Price-Anderson Act, protecting the nuclear power industry from certain liabilities, despite environmentalist opposition, and the setting up of a Defense Nuclear Facilities Safety Board. He played a major role on the 1990 Clean Air Act, co-authoring the provision on ozone and carbon monoxide non-attainment and defraying the cost of scrubbers or new plants for the Midwest's coal-burning utilities. This set up an allowance trading system, in which utilities that exceed new clean air standards could sell their extra "pollution credits" to other utilities, and was a key compromise that made possible passage of the law.

In 1991 and 1992, Sharp's major project was what became the Comprehensive Energy Policy Act of 1992. Sharp kept the issue in subcommittee for a year, while the Senate settled its fractious debates. He then fashioned a bill that restructured the wholesale electricity industry, made it easier to build natural gas pipelines, promoted renewable energy, provided greater energy efficiency standards and further promoted alternate fuels. His bill was passed by the Energy and Commerce Committee 42–1 in March 1992, and a later version passed the House 381–37 in May 1992; finally, after an enormous and turbulent conference committee, it passed both houses in October 1992 and was signed into law. Though he lost one major provision, a setaside for the Strategic Petroleum Reserve, this was quite an achievement for Sharp.

And particularly for a member who cannot take his district for granted. Redistricting added Anderson to the 2d and subtracted one suburban Indianapolis county, making it 4% more Democratic. But in the two decades Sharp has been running for Congress, he has won only twice with more than 60% of the vote, in 1976 and 1986. Sharp naturally tends to local projects, looks out for the interests of the auto industry (he passed a bill requiring car sale stickers to disclose the percentage of U.S.-made parts), and is hawkish on trade. He voted against congressional pay raises and doesn't take honoraria or go on expense-paid foreign travel. He also raises enormous sums of money, outspending his 1992 opponent by nearly 3–1. Sharp's Republican opponents imitate his persistence without being able, at least yet, to duplicate his success. Mike Pence ran against him in 1988 and 1990; William Frazier, his opponent in 1976, 1978 and 1980, tried again and failed in 1992. This was one of Sharp's better years, and he won 57%–40%. But he is still likely to have serious opposition in 1994.

The People: Pop. 1990: 554,321; 43% rural; 14% age 65+; 95% White; 4% Black; 1% Hispanic origin. Voting age pop.: 416,245; 4% Black; 1% Hispanic origin. Households: 60% married couple families; 27% married couple fams. w. children; 32% college educ.; median household income: $26,185; per capita income: $12,311; median gross rent: $331; median house value: $43,000.

1992 Presidential Vote			1988 Presidential Vote		
Bush (R)	101,370	(43%)	Bush (R)	136,021	(61%)
Clinton (D)	82,008	(35%)	Dukakis (D)	88,521	(39%)
Perot (I)	50,458	(22%)			

Rep. Philip R. Sharp (D)

Elected 1974; b. July 15, 1942, Baltimore, MD; home, Muncie; Georgetown U., B.S. 1964, Ph.D. 1974, Oxford U., 1966; United Methodist; married (Marilyn).

Career: Legis. Aide, U.S. Sen. Vance Hartke, 1964–69; Asst. and Assoc. Prof., Ball St. U., 1969–74.

Offices: 2217 RHOB 20515, 202-225-3021. Also 2900 W. Jackson, #101, Muncie 47304, 317-747-5566; P.O. Bldg., Richmond 47374, 317-966-6125; and 331 Franklin St., #A, Columbus 47201, 812-372-3637.

Committees: *Energy and Commerce* (3d of 27 D): Energy and Power (Chmn.); Transportation and Hazardous Materials. *Natural Resources* (2d of 28 D): Energy and Mineral Resources; Oversight and Investigations.

Group Ratings

	ADA	ACLU	COPE	CDF	CFA	LCV	ACU	NTLC	NSI	COC	CEI
1992	85	91	75	80	80	38	25	20	50	38	21
1991	75	—	75	90	78	62	5	—	—	40	31

National Journal Ratings

	1991 LIB — 1991 CONS	1992 LIB — 1992 CONS
Economic	69% — 29%	59% — 41%
Social	68% — 31%	76% — 23%
Foreign	74% — 26%	55% — 44%

Key Votes of the 102d Congress

1. Ban Striker Replace	FOR	5. Handgun Wait/7-Day FOR	9. Use Force in Gulf AGN
2. $ for Homeownership	FOR	6. Overseas Mil. Abortion FOR	10. US Mil. Abroad $ Cut FOR
3. Tax Rich/Cut Mid Cls.	FOR	7. Obscn. Art NEA $ Ban FOR	11. Limit SDI Funds FOR
4. FY93/$15B Def. Cut	FOR	8. Death Pen. from Jury AGN	12. Cuba Trade Embargo FOR

Key Votes of the 103d Congress

1. Family Leave   FOR   2. Deficit Reduction   FOR   3. Stimulus Plan   FOR

Election Results

1992 general	Philip R. Sharp (D)	130,881	(57%)	($623,400)
	William G. Frazier (R)	90,593	(40%)	($176,034)
	Other	7,821	(3%)	
1992 primary	Philip R. Sharp (D), unopposed			
1990 general	Philip R. Sharp (D)	93,495	(59%)	($773,178)
	Mike Pence (R)	63,980	(41%)	($595,457)

THIRD DISTRICT

When Notre Dame University was founded in 1842, Catholics were still a rarity in most of America, and certainly rare on the limestone-bottomed plains of northern Indiana. This was still farm country then and South Bend no more than a crossroads on the St. Joseph River. By the 1920s, both had grown. Notre Dame, thanks to its football team, "the Fighting Irish," was the most famous Catholic university in the land, and South Bend was a significant industrial city, headquarters of Studebaker and dozens of other factories. In the last 50 years, Notre Dame has grown in size and reputation, without giving up football; but South Bend has not done so well. Studebaker went out of business in the 1960s; other major factories closed; high-wage unionized jobs disappeared, replaced by lower-wage jobs with less protection. Elkhart, in the next county to the east, did better, as the nation's largest maker of "manufactured housing," i.e., trailers; and there was growth too in the surrounding agricultural counties. But this part of the United States seems permanently possessed of an economic grievance.

The 3d Congressional District of Indiana has centered for decades on South Bend, which is ordinarily Democratic. Democratic redistricters in 1970 joined it to similarly industrial Michigan City, to the west. The Republican plan of the 1980s excluded Michigan City and helped reelect John Hiler, a Republican congressman often called a "Reagan robot," who lost in 1990. The bipartisan plan of the 1990s added Michigan City back in to the 3d District and reelected Democratic Congressman Tim Roemer in 1992.

Roemer is one of those talented political operators whose numbers explain why the Democrats continue to control the House even in years when opinion favors Republican policies. A South Bend native and Notre Dame graduate, he has genuine local roots. And even before he was elected, he was well-connected in Washington, a veteran of the staffs of former 3d District

Congressman John Brademas and Keating Five Senator Dennis DeConcini, and son-in-law of Senator Bennett Johnston, chairman of the Senate Energy Committee. That helped Roemer raise more PAC money than incumbent Hiler in 1990 and to outspend his Republican challenger by nearly 2–1 in 1992. Roemer has also been adept at sounding outsider themes with insider skill. He calls loudly for reform of the House, though he supports the party that has controlled it for four decades; he opposes aid to Russia and the former Soviet republics; he attacks the space station, though he did vote money for it largely because the bill included $900,000 for Elkhart; he votes against transportation bills containing pork barrel projects. He calls for a "Marshall Plan for America," to promote business, rebuild infrastructure and improve schools; he got the House to pass a resolution favoring this, but not legislation. He managed to attack George Bush for not balancing the budget and for raising taxes in the same breath, and then voted for the similarly structured Clinton economic package. It will be some time, if ever, before Roemer delivers on his promises. What he does do superbly is get around the district and hold constituent meetings.

In 1990, Roemer attacked Hiler for helping to create the S&L crisis, making some misstatements in the process: he accused Hiler of voting for raising S&L deposit insurance to $100,000 in 1980, the year before he came to Congress, and for voting for the Garn-St Germain S&L bill on the Banking Committee in 1982, though he was not on the committee until a year later. But Roemer won a 51% victory. In 1992, although redistricting added Michigan City, two serious Republicans competed to run against him, and the primary winner, Carl Baxmeyer, raised serious money and called Roemer a big spender and said his "Marshall Plan" was fiscally irresponsible. But Roemer won with 57% in 1992—the best percentage for any candidate of either party in the 3d District since 1974, and while George Bush was carrying the district over Bill Clinton. That does not mean that he is guaranteed a safe seat, but it does indicate he will be hard to beat.

The People: Pop. 1990: 554,482; 29% rural; 13% age 65+; 90% White; 7% Black; 1% Asian; 1% Other; 2% Hispanic origin. Voting age pop.: 407,598; 7% Black; 2% Hispanic origin. Households: 59% married couple families; 28% married couple fams. w. children; 37% college educ.; median household income: $29,470; per capita income: $13,385; median gross rent: $395; median house value: $55,000.

1992 Presidential Vote			1988 Presidential Vote		
Bush (R)	91,708	(42%)	Bush (R)	115,955	(58%)
Clinton (D)	82,483	(38%)	Dukakis (D)	83,789	(42%)
Perot (I)	41,358	(19%)			

Rep. Tim Roemer (D)

Elected 1990; b. Oct. 30, 1956, South Bend; home, South Bend; U. of CA at San Diego, B.A. 1979, U. of Notre Dame, M.A., Ph.D. 1985; Catholic; married (Sally).

Career: Staff Asst., U.S. Rep. John Brademas, 1980; Legis. Aide, U.S. Sen. Dennis DeConcini, 1985–89; Instructor, American U., 1989.

Offices: 415 CHOB 20515, 202-225-3915. Also 217 N. Main St., South Bend 46601, 219-288-3301.

Committees: *Education and Labor* (15th of 28 D): Elementary, Secondary and Vocational Education; Postsecondary Education and Training. *Science, Space and Technology* (15th of 33 D): Energy; Space; Technology, Environment and Aviation.

Group Ratings

	ADA	ACLU	COPE	CDF	CFA	LCV	ACU	NTLC	NSI	COC	CEI
1992	55	52	58	30	67	44	40	40	60	63	48
1991	50	—	67	90	50	62	30	—	—	40	37

National Journal Ratings

	1991 LIB — 1991 CONS	1992 LIB — 1992 CONS
Economic	45% — 55%	36% — 63%
Social	37% — 61%	41% — 58%
Foreign	54% — 44%	52% — 46%

Key Votes of the 102d Congress

1. Ban Striker Replace	FOR	5. Handgun Wait/7-Day FOR	9. Use Force in Gulf AGN
2. $ for Homeownership	FOR	6. Overseas Mil. Abortion AGN	10. US Mil. Abroad $ Cut FOR
3. Tax Rich/Cut Mid Cls.	AGN	7. Obscn. Art NEA $ Ban FOR	11. Limit SDI Funds AGN
4. FY93/$15B Def. Cut	AGN	8. Death Pen. from Jury AGN	12. Cuba Trade Embargo FOR

Key Votes of the 103d Congress

1. Family Leave   FOR   2. Deficit Reduction   AGN   3. Stimulus Plan   AGN

Election Results

1992 general	Tim Roemer (D).....................	121,269	(57%)	($416,196)
	Carl H. Baxmeyer (R)	89,834	(43%)	($245,500)
1992 primary	Tim Roemer (D).....................	39,540	(88%)	
	Christopher Alan (D)	3,110	(7%)	
	Anthony Vito Sims (D).................	2,420	(5%)	
1990 general	Tim Roemer (D).....................	80,740	(51%)	($473,055)
	John Hiler (R).......................	77,911	(49%)	($745,145)

FOURTH DISTRICT

The northeast corner of Indiana, in the center of flat agricultural area, can claim to be the center of Middle America. Its first settlers were of New England Yankee stock, establishing orderly communities with public schools and even colleges; they were joined by German immigrants, who built tidy farms and their own civic institutions. In the northern part of the state there are hills and lakes, and the strange swamp that is the central focus of Gene Stratton Porter's children's classic, *Girl of the Limberlost*. The one large city here, Fort Wayne, was built on flatter terrain, along the Maumee River that flows to Toledo, Ohio; it grew as a factory town, surging ahead and then falling back as large factories, often tied to the auto industry, opened and closed over the years. Politically, this area is ancestrally Republican from the Civil War years; since the New Deal, it has sometimes veered to the Democrats in times of economic distress, and the mayoralty of Fort Wayne, the most visible local post, has alternated between the parties. This part of Indiana is also a cradle of vice presidents. Thomas Marshall, Woodrow Wilson's vice president, was born in North Manchester and practiced law in Columbia City; Dan Quayle spent his high school years and later practiced law in Huntington. Both VPs, by the way, moved to the Hoosier metropolis of Indianapolis after their terms were over.

The 4th Congressional District of Indiana consists of nine counties in northeast Indiana, plus a bit of one other; it includes Fort Wayne, Huntington and Columbia City but not North Manchester. This is the district that Dan Quayle won from a Democratic incumbent in 1976 and represented for two terms; he saw, as few did at the time, the potential of the anti-government, lower-taxes trend that dominated the 1980s, but was almost nowhere predicted in the 1970s. In 1980, when Quayle ran for the Senate, the 4th was won by Quayle aide Dan Coats, who in December 1988 succeeded him in the Senate. That set up a March 1989 special election which produced, as special elections early in a president's term often do, a political surprise. The Republican candidate was Dan Heath, public safety director of Fort Wayne, whose Mayor, Paul Helmke, had raised taxes. The Democrat, Jill Long, zeroed in on the tax issue, pledging not to vote to raise them. Long had lost twice, winning 39% in the 1986 Senate race against Quayle and 38% in the 1988 House race against Coats, but she ran dignified campaigns and her serious demeanor and farm background (she grew up on a grain and dairy farm) served her well. She won with 51% and has represented the district ever since.

Long kept her anti-tax pledge in the Bush years and had a moderate economic record. She got a seat on the Agriculture Committee where she worked on the 1990 farm bill and futures regulation; she wants to make sure credit is available to women farmers. She became chairman of the Congressional Rural Caucus in 1993. On the Veterans' Affairs Committee, she passed a hospice care plan. She wants to extend a Hoosier "Buddy Program" for sixth to eighth graders to communicate through computers in their homes. Long's moderate record and serious demeanor have enabled her to win reelection with 61% in 1990 and 62% in 1992, far outpacing the Clinton-Gore ticket's percentage in the district. She was mentioned in December 1992 as a possible agriculture secretary, but does not seem to have been on the short list; she has been mentioned as well for statewide office in Indiana.

The People: Pop. 1990: 554,577; 40% rural; 12% age 65+; 93% White; 5% Black; 1% Asian; 1% Other; 2% Hispanic origin. Voting age pop.: 396,425; 5% Black; 1% Hispanic origin. Households: 62% married couple families; 31% married couple fams. w. children; 40% college educ.; median household income: $30,859; per capita income: $13,436; median gross rent: $373; median house value: $56,200.

1992 Presidential Vote			1988 Presidential Vote		
Bush (R)	102,779	(46%)	Bush (R)	138,954	(67%)
Clinton (D)	69,292	(31%)	Dukakis (D)	68,371	(33%)
Perot (I)	49,565	(22%)			

Rep. Jill Long (D)

Elected Mar. 1989; b. July 15, 1952, Warsaw; home, Larwill; Valparaiso U., B.S. 1974, IN U., M.B.A. 1978, Ph.D. 1984; Methodist; single.

Career: Farmer; Asst. prof., Valparaiso U. 1981–85, 1987–88; Valparaiso City Cncl., 1984–86; Adjunct prof., IN U., 1987–89.

Offices: 1513 LHOB, 20515, 202-225-4436. Also 1300 S. Harrison, #3105, Fort Wayne 46802, 219-424-3041.

Committees: *Agriculture* (11th of 27 D): Environment, Credit and Rural Development; General Farm Commodities; Livestock. *Veterans' Affairs* (10th of 21 D): Hospitals and Health Care.

Group Ratings

	ADA	ACLU	COPE	CDF	CFA	LCV	ACU	NTLC	NSI	COC	CEI
1992	80	78	75	50	80	44	24	30	50	63	27
1991	70	—	75	70	72	46	10	—	—	40	27

National Journal Ratings

	1991 LIB — 1991 CONS			1992 LIB — 1992 CONS		
Economic	59%	—	40%	46%	—	54%
Social	58%	—	40%	72%	—	24%
Foreign	78%	—	19%	71%	—	26%

Key Votes of the 102d Congress

1. Ban Striker Replace	FOR	5. Handgun Wait/7-Day	AGN	9. Use Force in Gulf	AGN
2. $ for Homeownership	AGN	6. Overseas Mil. Abortion	FOR	10. US Mil. Abroad $ Cut	AGN
3. Tax Rich/Cut Mid Cls.	AGN	7. Obscn. Art NEA $ Ban	FOR	11. Limit SDI Funds	FOR
4. FY93/$15B Def. Cut	FOR	8. Death Pen. from Jury	AGN	12. Cuba Trade Embargo	AGN

Key Votes of the 103d Congress

1. Family Leave	FOR	2. Deficit Reduction	AGN	3. Stimulus Plan	FOR

Election Results

1992 general	Jill Long (D).........................	134,907	(62%)	($346,011)
	Charles W. (Chuck) Pierson (R)..........	82,468	(38%)	($6,489)
1992 primary	Jill Long (D)........................	30,603	(87%)	
	J. Carolyn Williams (D)................	4,724	(13%)	
1990 general	Jill Long (D)........................	99,347	(61%)	($752,362)
	Richard Walter Hawks (R)..............	64,415	(39%)	($575,363)

FIFTH DISTRICT

Across the plains of northern Indiana runs the Hoosier Heartland Corridor—the HHC, a publicist's name for U.S. 24 as it runs west from Fort Wayne along the Wabash River through Wabash, Peru and Logansport, and then overland toward the Illinois prairie. Scattered on the major east-west railroad and highway lines that connect the East Coast and Chicago, the Hoosier Heartland's small cities and large towns display a geometric order that bespeaks virtues considered peculiarly American. And if they suffer from layoffs and unemployment, people here remain confident that most Americans are competent, decent, sensible people who will do the right thing in time of crisis. This is a part of America with little immigrant heritage, relatively few blacks, and only a handful of the more recent Latin and Asian immigrants. Basic values have not been shaken so much here as in other parts of the nation: this area has one of the nation's highest percentages of households with families, married couples and children. It is also a place that has given America such icons as James Dean, who grew up in Fairmount (and would be in his 60s today if he had not smashed up his Porsche near the Pacific), and Cole Porter, who grew up in Peru.

The 5th Congressional District of Indiana occupies most of the land on either side of the HHC. There are no big cities within the district: it just skirts Indianapolis, Fort Wayne, South Bend and Gary. And, though farming is important here, it is not altogether a rural area. Factories traditionally have kept most people working here in Marion and Kokomo and along the Wabash. Since the Civil War, this has mostly been Republican country, and the western part of the district was the home base of House Minority Leader (1959–65) Charles Halleck. But it has been willing to elect Democrats to the House, as it did in much of the 1970s and 1980s.

The 5th District was the scene of a serious contest in 1992 between a Democrat who is a master of the political arts responsible for his party's seemingly permanent majority in the House and a Republican who used first one set of issues and then another to defeat him. The Democrat was Jim Jontz, who in 1974 at age 22 defeated by exactly 2 votes the Indiana House majority leader and in 1986 was elected to Congress when the Republican incumbent retired. Single, interested almost exclusively in politics, he had a flair for trademarks: riding his sister's rusty blue Schwinn with mismatched tires in parades, and rotating the same four pairs of shoes in and out of a local shoe repair shop every week for five years. On issues, Jontz voted with other Democrats more than 90% of the time but opposed pay raises and backed the balanced budget amendment, while also increasing spending for college loans and for veterans with Post Traumatic Stress Disorder. He risked controversy only on issues far from the Hoosier Heartland, trying to discourage pesticide use and to stop below-cost timber sales and, most important, he was the driving force in the House for protecting the ancient forests of the Pacific Northwest and the spotted owl thought to be threatened with extinction there, at the cost of many timber industry jobs. Jontz won three times by nonstop campaigning, great fundraising (he was one of the biggest PAC dollar recipients in Washington) and a feel for public opinion: with 52% in 1986, 56% in 1988 and, against a heavy-spending entrepreneur, 53% in 1990.

Stephen Buyer (pronounced *BOOyer*), the Republican who defeated Jontz in 1992, was moved to run by Jontz's first vote in the 102d Congress, against the Gulf war resolution. A graduate of The Citadel and a captain in the Army Reserves on duty in the Persian Gulf, Buyer was enraged that two-thirds of House Democrats voted against the war. After he returned to Indiana, where he was White County Republican chairman, he began appearing in uniform around the Hoosier Heartland, attacking Jontz on his Gulf war stand. In October 1991, Buyer met with all of Jontz's former opponents and launched his campaign. By early 1992, as economic recovery stalled and interest in the Gulf war slackened, Buyer switched attacks to the "corruption" of the House bank and post office, calling for term limits and application of laws passed by Congress to Congress itself. He attacked Jontz for his four overdrafts on the House bank and called for a capital gains tax cut and school choice. Jontz protested that he was anti-incumbent too and kept up his nonstop campaigning. But Buyer zeroed in on the spotted owl issue, and Jontz's switching from Veterans' Affairs to Interior; Buyer brought in union members from the Northwest timber industry to campaign against Jontz and said his stands would raise lumber prices. He also criticized Jontz sharply for not advancing in the House the ban on out-of-state solid waste which Dan Coats had put through the Senate.

Buyer won 51%–49%, carrying the Hoosier Heartland but losing counties at the edge of the district. Redistricting did not affect the result; in fact, Jontz actually carried the counties added to the district. Will he come back? It's not likely that as a non-incumbent he could service the district or raise PAC money as he used to, while Buyer showed tactical flexibility that suggests he should be hard to beat in this usually heavily Republican district. Still a captain in the Army Reserve, Buyer got seats on Armed Services and Veterans' Affairs.

The People: Pop. 1990: 554,240; 58% rural; 13% age 65+; 97% White; 2% Black; 1% Hispanic origin. Voting age pop.: 402,996; 2% Black; 1% Hispanic origin. Households: 64% married couple families; 30% married couple fams. w. children; 31% college educ.; median household income: $27,893; per capita income: $12,252; median gross rent: $335; median house value: $46,400.

1992 Presidential Vote

Bush (R) 103,124 (45%)
Clinton (D) 70,891 (31%)
Perot (I) 52,354 (23%)

1988 Presidential Vote

Bush (R) 138,464 (64%)
Dukakis (D) 77,198 (36%)

Rep. Steve Buyer (R)

Elected 1992; b. Nov. 26, 1958, Rensselaer; home, Monticello; The Citadel, B.S. 1980; Valparaiso U. Law Schl., J.D. 1984; Methodist; married (Joni).

Career: Army, 1984–87, 1990–91 (Persian Gulf); Army Reserves, 1980–84, 1988–present; IN Dep. Atty. Gen., 1987–88; Vice Chmn., White Cnty. Repub. Party, 1988–90; Practicing atty., 1988–92.

Offices: 1419 LHOB 20515, 202-225-5037. Also 120 E. Mulberry St., #106, Kokomo 46901, 317-454-7551.

Committees: *Armed Services* (16th of 22 R): Military Forces and Personnel; Research and Technology. *Veterans' Affairs* (9th of 14 R): Hospitals and Health Care; Housing and Memorial Affairs.

Group Ratings and 102d Congress Votes: Newly Elected

Key Votes of the 103d Congress

1. Family Leave	AGN	2. Deficit Reduction	AGN	3. Stimulus Plan	AGN

Election Results

1992 general	Steve Buyer (R)	111,116	(51%)	($392,922)
	James Jontz (D)	105,209	(49%)	($583,029)
1992 primary	Steve Buyer (R), unopposed			
1990 general	James Jontz (D)	81,373	(53%)	($652,280)
	John Arthur Johnson (R)	71,750	(47%)	($781,224)

SIXTH DISTRICT

Indianapolis is one of America's most symmetric cities, sited in almost the exact center of Indiana, centered on Monument Circle with eight avenues radiating like wheel spokes, with the city occupying most of almost perfectly square Marion County. In the seven surrounding suburban counties, the irregularities of the physical landscape and the asymmetries of the original settlers' boundaries intrude; but a respected order has been established here. The more affluent areas are typically farther out, starting on the north side somewhere north of the home of Benjamin Harrison, Indiana's one president, and the 1920s era Governor's Mansion built on North Meridian Street by the same man who more or less invented the gas station. They include the comfortable in-town neighborhoods built in the 1940s and 1950s, the cul-de-sac subdivisions and condominiums of the 1970s and 1980s, and new developments set out on hills in the once rural counties beyond.

The 6th Congressional District of Indiana includes most of the suburban territory around the core of Indianapolis, which forms the 10th District. The exception is to the west of the city, where most of Hancock and Boone Counties are in the 7th District. But the 6th includes the north side of Indianapolis and the affluent Hamilton County suburbs of Carmel and Fishers; it includes Hancock County to the east and takes in the less affluent but still conservative suburban territory to the south. This is a very heavily Republican area, by far the most Republican in Indiana and indeed one of the most Republican districts in the country.

The congressman from the 6th District is Dan Burton, an active and enthusiastic Republican who has been running for office since he was in his 20s. He had a rough childhood, with an abusive father and some time in the county guardian's home; he enlisted in the Army at 18 and never finished college. A hearty, bluff backslapper, he made his way up selling insurance. He was elected to the Indiana House in 1966, 1976 and 1978 and to the Indiana Senate in 1968 and 1980; he lost races for Congress in 1970 and 1972 and was first elected to the House in 1982 when the legislature created this heavily Republican suburban seat.

Burton is an enthusiastic conservative, confrontation-minded long before most of today's feisty young House Republicans appeared on the scene (or started shaving). He has served on the Foreign Affairs Committee and had the satisfaction of seeing his hard-line opposition to the Soviet Union crowned with success and his critical approach to most sub-Saharan African regimes vindicated. He opposed sanctions on South Africa, and when Nelson Mandela came to the United States questioned why Mandela supported Yasir Arafat, Fidel Castro and Muammar Qaddafi. Burton, now ranking Republican on the Africa Subcommittee, was for years a strong backer of UNITA in Angola and Renamo in Mozambique; he seems to have as much faith in them as the leftish Democrats who have chaired the subcommittee have had in their opponents.

In 1993, Burton was elected chairman of the Republican Study Committee, a group not yet as effective as the Democratic Study Group. Some 130 of the 176 Republicans are members and Burton wants to provide them with a daily "Clinton-Gore" memo. His own judgment on issues has been erratic. If he has been vindicated in many of his foreign policy stands and on the catastrophic health care act, his proposal for universal mandatory AIDS testing is now seen as simply screwy. If he showed political foresight in lambasting George Bush for breaking his no-new-taxes pledge, many of his spending cut amendments lose by overwhelming margins; he has not had as much success choosing targets as some of the less senior porkbusters.

There is no conceivable chance Burton will lose the 6th District seat to a Democrat, nor does there seem to be any chance of serious primary opposition. Redistricting, by removing the industrial town of Anderson, made him even safer. Nevertheless, he has accumulated over $600,000 in his campaign treasury—to run for governor, some Indiana Democrats think, and they have tried to pass a law barring him from using the money in a state race. But the Republican Senate is unlikely to go along; and for that matter it is not at all clear Burton will run for an office that is not up until 1996 anyway.

The People: Pop. 1990: 553,865; 24% rural; 11% age 65+; 98% White; 1% Black; 1% Asian; 1% Hispanic origin. Voting age pop.: 407,482; 1% Black; 1% Hispanic origin. Households: 65% married couple families; 32% married couple fams. w. children; 52% college educ.; median household income: $38,644; per capita income: $17,971; median gross rent: $452; median house value: $81,200.

1992 Presidential Vote			1988 Presidential Vote		
Bush (R)	153,269	(57%)	Bush (R)	183,820	(75%)
Clinton (D)	61,030	(23%)	Dukakis (D)	62,023	(25%)
Perot (I)	54,909	(20%)			

Rep. Dan Burton (R)

Elected 1982; b. June 21, 1938, Indianapolis; home, Indianapolis; IN U., 1956–57, Cincinnati Bible Seminary, 1958–60; Protestant; married (Barbara).

Career: Army, 1956–57, Army Reserves, 1958–63; Founder, Dan Burton Insurance Agency, 1968; IN House of Reps., 1966–68, 1976–80; IN Senate, 1968–70, 1980–82.

Offices: 2411 RHOB 20515, 202-225-2276. Also 8900 Keystone-at-the-Crossing, #1050, Indianapolis 46240, 317-848-0201; and 940 Meridian Plz., Anderson 46016, 317-649-6887.

Committees: *Foreign Affairs* (9th of 18 R): Africa (RMM); International Security, International Organizations and Human Rights. *Post Office and Civil Service* (4th of 9 R): Civil Service (RMM). *Veterans' Affairs* (3d of 14 R): Hospitals and Health Care; Housing and Memorial Affairs (RMM).

Group Ratings

	ADA	ACLU	COPE	CDF	CFA	LCV	ACU	NTLC	NSI	COC	CEI
1992	10	0	25	0	0	13	100	100	100	86	91
1991	5	—	17	10	22	0	100	—	—	80	90

National Journal Ratings

	1991 LIB — 1991 CONS		1992 LIB — 1992 CONS	
Economic	22%	— 77%	21%	— 79%
Social	0%	— 84%	0%	— 85%
Foreign	0%	— 88%	0%	— 82%

Key Votes of the 102d Congress

1. Ban Striker Replace	AGN	5. Handgun Wait/7-Day AGN	9. Use Force in Gulf	FOR
2. $ for Homeownership	FOR	6. Overseas Mil. AbortionAGN	10. US Mil. Abroad $ Cut AGN
3. Tax Rich/Cut Mid Cls.AGN	7. Obscn. Art NEA $ Ban FOR	11. Limit SDI Funds	AGN
4. FY93/$15B Def. Cut	AGN	8. Death Pen. from Jury FOR	12. Cuba Trade Embargo FOR

Key Votes of the 103d Congress

1. Family Leave   AGN   2. Deficit Reduction   AGN   3. Stimulus Plan   AGN

Election Results

1992 general	Dan Burton (R).....................	186,499	(72%)	($407,055)
	Natalie M. Bruner (D)	71,952	(28%)	($32,153)
1992 primary	Dan Burton (R).....................	64,128	(80%)	
	George B. Tintera (R).................	8,700	(11%)	
	William Russell Sparks (R)	6,852	(9%)	
1990 general	Dan Burton (R).....................	116,470	(63%)	($311,727)
	James P. Fadely (D)	67,024	(37%)	($41,180)

SEVENTH DISTRICT

Of the railroad passenger trains that used to run on the lines criss-crossing the township grids of the Midwest, none seemed more romantic than the Wabash Cannonball that ran along the Wabash River, across the rolling farmland of northern Indiana on its way from Detroit to St. Louis, following the curve of the river and then crossing the old National Road, now U.S. 40, which runs in a nearly straight line from Indianapolis to St. Louis. The landscape here is some of the most prosaic in the United States, mostly flat, with neat farms and frame-bungalowed towns, looking unchanged from years ago. But the Cannonball no longer runs; people bounce around the Midwest on commuter airlines or fly from one hub city to another; and the National Road and U.S. 40 have been replaced for through traffic by Interstate 70.

The 7th Congressional District of Indiana covers much of the routes of the Wabash Cannonball and the National Road in western Indiana, starting from the Indianapolis city limits. Its two largest towns are quite different in character. Terre Haute is an old manufacturing town, the boyhood home of Socialist Eugene Debs, which now has a Sony compact disc plant. It has not gained population in years and tends to vote Democratic—a lonely stand in central Indiana. The other major town is Lafayette, where the main business is Purdue University, Indiana's land-grant college, and home base of Nixon-Ford Agriculture Secretary Earl Butz. Growing and prosperous, Lafayette tends to vote Republican.

The congressman from the 7th District is John Myers, one of the most senior House Republicans, who has survived several redistrictings and was in fact first elected in 1966 in a district that was designed to go Democratic. Like most Republican congressmen over the last century, he comes from a small town (Covington, on the Wabash 30 miles north of Terre Haute) where he was a bank officer entwined in local economic and civic affairs. His voting record is solidly conservative; he is proud of having co-sponsored the Mammography Quality Standards Act of 1992, introducing Dan Coats's bill to let states stop out-of-state trash and a bill to lower taxes on capital gains for senior citizens. He ranks fourth in seniority among House Republicans (ahead of him are Robert Michel, elected in 1956, and Jimmy Quillen and Joseph McDade, elected in 1962) and is second ranking on Appropriations, behind Joseph McDade, who in early 1993 was awaiting a likely trial on charges of corruption. Like so many old-time Republicans, and especially those on Appropriations, Myers tends to be accommodationist, ready to cooperate with Democrats in return for some concessions, accepting as his eternal lot the condition of being in the minority.

Myers is ranking Republican on the Energy and Water Development Subcommittee, a key dispenser of public works and dams and other local projects avidly sought by many members. Here he works closely with Chairman Tom Bevill to maintain support for subcommittee bills and priorities. Their enemies include economizers, environmentalists and, sometimes, the authorizing Public Works Committee, the Appropriations subcommittee's rival as proprietor of the pork barrel. Myers also is ranking Republican on Post Office and Civil Service. In the late 1980s, he was the ranking Republican on the House Ethics Committee when it investigated Speaker Jim Wright. Myers was instrumental in hiring as chief counsel Richard Phelan, a Chicago lawyer and a Democrat (and now Cook County board president) who was fiercely critical of Wright; Myers was of the same mind, and showed steely determination to condemn Wright for what he felt were violations of House rules.

In a House less roiled by public discontent, Myers would be nearing the apogee of his power; in fact, he is threatened on a number of fronts. He could easily become ranking Republican on Appropriations, but the younger, more confrontational Republicans now have a clear majority in the Republican Conference, and may demand more partisan positioning than Myers is comfortable with. He might even be opposed for this post, though there are still few confrontation-minded Republicans on Appropriations; his power also could be trimmed if the reformers who want to abolish Appropriations panels altogether somehow succeed. At home, there are mild signs of discontent as well. Myers had 61 overdrafts on the House bank, and in the 1992 primary retired farmer Charles Metzger won 39% of the vote against him—rather high for a challenger to a longtime incumbent. Myers won the general with 59%, a solid but not overwhelming showing, and in May of 1993 was already facing an early challenge from Greencastle Mayor Michael Harmless, a man Myers helped get into West Point years earlier.

The People: Pop. 1990: 554,500; 48% rural; 12% age 65+; 96% White; 2% Black; 1% Asian; 1% Hispanic origin. Voting age pop.: 418,275; 2% Black; 1% Hispanic origin. Households: 62% married

couple families; 29% married couple fams. w. children; 39% college educ.; median household income: $28,080; per capita income: $12,536; median gross rent: $358; median house value: $54,300.

1992 Presidential Vote			1988 Presidential Vote		
Bush (R)	103,801	(46%)	Bush (R)	134,308	(64%)
Clinton (D)	71,273	(32%)	Dukakis (D)	74,254	(36%)
Perot (I)	48,916	(22%)			

Rep. John T. Myers (R)

Elected 1966; b. Feb. 8, 1927, Covington; home, Covington; IN St. U., B.S. 1951; Episcopalian; married (Carol).

Career: Army, 1945–46 (WWII); Cashier and Trust Officer, Foundation Trust Co., 1954–66.

Offices: 2372 RHOB 20515, 202-225-5805. Also 107 Fed. Bldg., Terre Haute 47808, 812-238-1619; and 107 Halleck Fed. Bldg., Lafayette 47901, 317-423-1661.

Committees: *Appropriations* (2d of 23 R): Agriculture, Rural Development, Food and Drug Administration and Related Agencies; Energy and Water Development (RMM). *Post Office and Civil Service* (RMM of 9 R).

Group Ratings

	ADA	ACLU	COPE	CDF	CFA	LCV	ACU	NTLC	NSI	COC	CEI
1992	0	9	17	20	20	6	84	75	100	75	59
1991	0	—	17	30	28	0	70	—	—	90	45

National Journal Ratings

	1991 LIB — 1991 CONS		1992 LIB — 1992 CONS	
Economic	18% —	79%	21% —	76%
Social	25% —	73%	0% —	85%
Foreign	31% —	67%	18% —	74%

Key Votes of the 102d Congress

1. Ban Striker Replace	AGN	5. Handgun Wait/7-Day	AGN	9. Use Force in Gulf	FOR
2. $ for Homeownership	AGN	6. Overseas Mil. Abortion	AGN	10. US Mil. Abroad $ Cut	FOR
3. Tax Rich/Cut Mid Cls.	AGN	7. Obscn. Art NEA $ Ban	FOR	11. Limit SDI Funds	AGN
4. FY93/$15B Def. Cut	AGN	8. Death Pen. from Jury	FOR	12. Cuba Trade Embargo	FOR

Key Votes of the 103d Congress

1. Family Leave	AGN	2. Deficit Reduction	AGN	3. Stimulus Plan	*

Election Results

1992 general	John T. Myers (R)	129,189	(59%)	($369,882)
	Ellen E. Wedum (D)	88,005	(41%)	($51,245)
1992 primary	John T. Myers (R)	32,238	(61%)	
	Charles J. Metzger (R)	20,382	(39%)	
1990 general	John T. Myers (R)	88,598	(58%)	($205,810)
	John William Riley, Sr. (D)	65,248	(42%)	

EIGHTH DISTRICT

"Evansville," wrote John Bartlow Martin earlier in this century, "called the Pocket City (though not by loyal natives), is the capital of a tri-state area comprising the neglected tag ends of Indiana, Kentucky and Illinois." It was a factory town then, building car parts and refrigerators, drawing workers from Kentucky, Tennessee and the picturesque but not very fertile hills of southern Indiana. It is a town of hard-bitten politics, with plenty of partisan conflict; this was the boyhood home of Senator William Jenner, a McCarthy ally who once said General George Marshall would sell out his grandmother to the Communists, and the political base of Senator Vance Hartke, who inspired the not-quite-fair joke that Indiana had two senators, "Bayh and Bought."

Evansville is one of major focuses of the 8th Congressional District of Indiana which, despite its current irregular borders, covers most of the southwest portion of the state. The other is Bloomington, quite a different place, the home of Indiana University and a limestone quarrying center. This southwest corner of Indiana was the first part of the state settled by whites. Vincennes, now a small town on the banks of the Wabash River, was once the metropolis of Indiana, and the Scottish philanthropist and visionary, Robert Owen, established the town of New Harmony downstream. Owen's son was the first congressman from the area, elected in 1842 and 1844. Since then, it has been represented by both parties, at one point in the 1970s electing four different congressmen in four successive elections, the only congressional district to have done so. The overall partisan tradition here has been Democratic since the Civil War, but the Democrats' cultural liberalism can cost them votes.

The congressman from the 8th District for more than a decade now has been Frank McCloskey, a onetime reporter who served as Mayor of Bloomington for 11 years. McCloskey is a man of quiet, earnest, plodding demeanor, but also of perseverance and sincerity. He sees much of his duty as the economic nurturing of Evansville and southwest Indiana. He has long pushed an Evansville-to-Indianapolis highway and got Congress to authorize an I-69 extension from Indianapolis to Memphis for that purpose. He helped arrange small factories to locate in Evansville and Bloomington. For years, he has protected the Navy's Crane Division; he got $1.5 million for it to become a center to study the environmental problems of closing military bases. He set up a FEDCO program which he says increased federal contracts to the area from $7 million in 1987 to $64 million in 1990.

McCloskey chairs the Civil Service Subcommittee, and has sponsored laws to ban the mailing of drugs in non-childproof packages and providing free mail privileges for personnel in the Persian Gulf. He also serves on Armed Services, where he questioned the safety of the military's night vision goggles, which proved to be such a success in the Gulf war. A dove on the Gulf war, he has become a hawk in the Balkans: in April 1993, he wrote a letter, signed by 46 of his colleagues, to President Clinton urging an air campaign against Serbian strongholds in Bosnia and a relaxation of the arms embargo on Bosnia. In February 1993, he opposed the Vance-Owen land division plan "because it rewards genocidal aggression and will lead to an expanded Balkan War," and seemed to favor U.S. military action there.

McCloskey has had a stormy electoral history in this often marginal district. It is still not completely clear who got the most votes in 1984: Republican Rick McIntyre was certified by state officials as winning by 34 votes out of 233,000 cast, a recanvass put McCloskey ahead by 72, the House refused to seat anyone and ran its own investigation; ultimately McCloskey was seated by a House vote largely on party lines. He won the next elections with 53%, 62% and 55%. In 1992, geologist Richard Mourdock (also his opponent in 1990) attacked the congressional pay raise, the budget summit tax increase, and the House bank and Post Office scandals, but still lost by 53%–45%. The 1990s redistricting plan, by putting most of Bloomington back into the district, helped McCloskey, but the numbers suggest he is likely to have serious opposition again.

The People: Pop. 1990: 554,347; 42% rural; 14% age 65+; 96% White; 3% Black; 1% Asian; 1% Hispanic origin. Voting age pop.: 421,666; 3% Black. Households: 58% married couple families; 27% married couple fams. w. children; 37% college educ.; median household income: $25,242; per capita income: $12,153; median gross rent: $341; median house value: $48,800.

1992 Presidential Vote			1988 Presidential Vote		
Clinton (D)	103,844	(42%)	Bush (R)	129,324	(57%)
Bush (R)	97,062	(40%)	Dukakis (D)	98,539	(43%)
Perot (I)	43,177	(18%)			

Rep. Francis X. (Frank) McCloskey (D)

Elected 1982; b. June 12, 1939, Philadelphia, PA; home, Bloomington; IN U., A.B. 1968, J.D. 1971; Catholic; married (Roberta).

Career: Air Force, 1957–61; Journalist, 1961–68; Bloomington Mayor, 1971–82; Pres., IN Assoc. of Cities and Towns, 1981–82.

Offices: 306 CHOB 20515, 202-225-4636. Also 1 City Ctr., #208, 120 W. 7th St., Bloomington 47404, 812-334-1111; and 101 NW M.L.K. Blvd., #124, Evansville 47711, 812-465-6484.

Committees: *Armed Services* (10th of 34 D): Military Acquisition; Military Installations and Facilities. *Foreign Affairs* (25th of 27 D): International Security, International Organizations and Human Rights. *Post Office and Civil Service* (3d of 15 D): Census Statistics and Postal Personnel; Civil Service (Chmn.).

Group Ratings

	ADA	ACLU	COPE	CDF	CFA	LCV	ACU	NTLC	NSI	COC	CEI
1992	95	100	83	90	93	56	12	0	50	25	9
1991	90	—	83	100	83	69	0	—	—	20	9

National Journal Ratings

	1991 LIB — 1991 CONS		1992 LIB — 1992 CONS	
Economic	88% —	0%	75% —	24%
Social	74% —	23%	88% —	8%
Foreign	75% —	25%	69% —	30%

Key Votes of the 102d Congress

1. Ban Striker Replace	FOR	5. Handgun Wait/7-Day	FOR	9. Use Force in Gulf	AGN
2. $ for Homeownership	AGN	6. Overseas Mil. Abortion	FOR	10. US Mil. Abroad $ Cut	FOR
3. Tax Rich/Cut Mid Cls.	FOR	7. Obscn. Art NEA $ Ban	FOR	11. Limit SDI Funds	AGN
4. FY93/$15B Def. Cut	FOR	8. Death Pen. from Jury	AGN	12. Cuba Trade Embargo	AGN

Key Votes of the 103d Congress

1. Family Leave	FOR	2. Deficit Reduction	FOR	3. Stimulus Plan	FOR

Election Results

1992 general	Francis X. (Frank) McCloskey (D)	125,244	(53%)	($512,852)
	Richard Mourdock (R)	108,054	(45%)	($248,152)
	Two Others	5,099	(2%)	
1992 primary	Francis X. (Frank) McCloskey (D)	44,159	(100%)	
1990 general	Francis X. (Frank) McCloskey (D)	97,465	(55%)	($446,040)
	Richard Mourdock (R)	80,645	(45%)	($146,961)

NINTH DISTRICT

The southeastern corner of Indiana, something of a backwater now, was a busy place when white settlers rafted down the Ohio River in the early 19th Century. They were mostly southerners, "Butternuts," from across the river in Kentucky or over the mountains in Virginia, and they built the first large Indiana settlements. Today, you can see their work in the marvelous old buildings of Madison, now quiet but once one of the busiest ports on the Ohio River. Farther down the river is Corydon, from 1816 to 1825 the state capital. The early 19th Century buildings here have been well preserved because these towns were bypassed first by the railroads, then by U.S. routes and interstate highways, and they certainly are remote from major airports. The river is still an artery of commerce, but utilitarian barges have replaced steamers. Butternut Indiana retained its affection for things southern into the Civil War and beyond; local politician Jesse Bright was expelled from the U.S. Senate in 1862 for "supporting the rebellion"; treason presumably being at least as serious an offense in Congress as sexual harassment is today. To this day, the hills along the Ohio River typically vote Democratic. Even more Democratic are the Indiana suburbs of Louisville. Most of Indiana's Ohio River counties and an oddly shaped collection of lightly populated counties inland form Indiana's 9th Congressional District, which has been represented since 1964 by Democrat Lee Hamilton.

Now one of the most senior members of Congress, Hamilton is a man temperamentally attracted to small towns; he started off working for a big Chicago law firm, but decided that he liked small town life and moved to Columbus. It was a good match, for Columbus combines small town tone with intellectual distinction. Thanks to leading citizen J. Irwin Miller, nationally recognized architects have designed most of its buildings. After eight years of law practice, Hamilton ran for Congress in the Democratic year of 1964, and was elected. He has been pretty easily reelected ever since, though most of Columbus was moved to the 2d District.

Hamilton combines a folksiness and lack of urban savvy with a strong intellect, a capacity for hard work and a sense of moral imperative; he is congenial, but don't joke with him about matters he considers serious. Though not well known in some quarters of Washington, he is one of the most respected members of the House and a real power on foreign policy issues. He is chairman of the Foreign Affairs Committee and of its Europe and the Middle East Subcommittee; he chaired the House Intelligence Committee in 1985–87; he was the House chairman of the special Iran-contra investigating committee in 1987–88; he chaired the Joint Economic Committee in 1989–90; with Senator David Boren he was appointed in 1992 co-chairman of the Joint Committee on the Organization of Congress, which he had suggested creating. Until the Iran-contra committee met, Hamilton was little known outside the House. Then his appealing personality and reputation in the House made him something of a national figure. He was seriously considered by both Michael Dukakis and Bill Clinton for the vice presidential nomination and was mentioned as a possible Clinton secretary of state.

The House, in foreign affairs, which Hamilton came to was something like Columbus, Indiana, in commerce: graced with fine architecture, but off the beaten track; with its share of strong intellects, but largely ignored in favor of the more glamorous (and treaty-ratifying and appointment-confirming) Senate. Hamilton thinks the House should be taken more seriously, and his own work has helped. Yet as he has become more visible, he has also attracted criticism. With his steady opposition to contra aid and other aid to anti-Communists in Latin America, and also his strong opposition to the Gulf war resolution, he has arguably overlearned the lessons of Vietnam, the great foreign policy issue of his first few terms in Congress, and one on which he supported Lyndon Johnson's escalations. His dire predictions of the consequences of the Gulf war—massive American casualties, a fracturing of the allied coalition, rising anti-Americanism—almost entirely failed to come true, and he opposed efforts by Howard Berman and Dan Glickman to impose sanctions or cut off credit to Iraq before the invasion of Kuwait. The Iran-contra committee's granting of immunity to Oliver North and John Poindexter (a Hoosier native) destroyed any chance of prosecution, though Hamilton has a strong argument when he says getting the truth out was more important than imposing criminal sanctions. Yet some members argue he wound up the hearings too soon. He continues to be frustrated in writing a foreign aid authorization bill.

In a post-Cold War world, Hamilton sees weapons proliferation as an important foreign policy problem; he is keeping a close eye on nuclear and non-nuclear disarmament in Russia and the former Soviet republics, and favors aid to them as well. He sees support for democracy, free markets and human rights as secondary goals. This may be a bit of a shift: he was not initially a supporter of the National Endowment for Democracy, for example, and has been reluctant to interject human rights objections into Middle East diplomacy. But he can certainly argue that the breakdown of Communism makes advancing democracy worldwide more achievable goal. He has not weighed in heavily on trade issues, but could be a force for the Democratic free trade position that goes back to Cordell Hull. He sees protection of the environment as a major foreign policy goal, and also "the fight against hunger, disease and rapid population growth." He favors U.S. involvement in the former Yugoslavia and in February 1993 called American participation in a multinational peacekeeping force "a prudent commitment of American power." On the Arab-Israeli conflict, he has long been known as genuinely evenhanded, certainly not tilting toward Israel; he believes that U.S. involvement is necessary in reaching any Arab-Israeli agreements. He conducted an investigation of the so-called "October surprise" and in July 1992 exonerated President Bush of all involvement, and after the election reported that the conspiracy theory was unfounded.

How influential will Hamilton and his committee be in the Clinton years? Its powers are limited, constitutionally and otherwise; as he said in the Bush years, "We can modify, we can alter. But the fundamental policy remains the president's policy . . . I think a president can win any foreign policy issue if he fights hard enough for it." His committee has lost the strong voices of Dante Fascell and Stephen Solarz, freshman Democrats shied away—in this domestic era— from it as a first choice assignment and it started off with several vacancies. When House rules required subcommittee cutbacks, Foreign Affairs was compelled to seek an exception to preserve the Africa subcommittee. Hamilton is not likely to spark sudden new initiatives; as he said two months after the fall of Gorbachev, "I guess we've been slow off the mark, but these are momentous events, and you don't want to act abruptly."

On domestic issues, Hamilton is a deficit hawk, urging higher taxes as early as 1989, when he was chairman of the Joint Economic Committee. He co-sponsored a bill to put the Treasury Secretary on the Federal Reserve Board, publish the Fed's budget, and subject it to tough GAO audits—attempts to make the Fed politically more responsive, with possible inflationary effects, and a classic small town cause.

Hamilton has had no difficulty winning reelection in the 9th District for many years. In 1992, the 9th District race got attention when Republican Michael Bailey, a former advertising rep who operates Christian Media Ministries, campaigned by running television ads showing dead fetuses. This did Bailey little good—he lost 70%–30%—but it is a sign of just how uncompetitive many House races generally are that this was the first time in 28 years a Hamilton opponent had run a major TV campaign.

The People: Pop. 1990: 554,516; 59% rural; 13% age 65+; 98% White; 2% Black. Voting age pop.: 404,376; 2% Black. Households: 64% married couple families; 31% married couple fams. w. children; 29% college educ.; median household income: $26,900; per capita income: $11,727; median gross rent: $325; median house value: $49,200.

1992 Presidential Vote			1988 Presidential Vote		
Clinton (D)	97,970	(41%)	Bush (R)	125,439	(58%)
Bush (R)	97,412	(40%)	Dukakis (D)	90,284	(42%)
Perot (I)	44,839	(19%)			

Rep. Lee H. Hamilton (D)

Elected 1964; b. Apr. 20, 1931, Daytona Beach, FL; home, Nashville; DePauw U., B.A. 1952, J.D. 1956, Goethe U., Frankfurt, Germany, 1952–53; United Methodist; married (Nancy).

Career: Practicing atty., 1956–64; Instructor, American Banking Inst. 1960–61.

Offices: 2187 RHOB 20515, 202-225-5315. Also 107 Fed. Ctr., 1201 E. 10th St., Jeffersonville 47130, 812-288-3999.

Committees: *Foreign Affairs* (Chmn. of 27 D): Europe and the Middle East (Chmn.). *Joint Economic Committee* (2d of 10). *Joint Committee on the Organization of Congress* (Co-Chmn. of 12).

Group Ratings

	ADA	ACLU	COPE	CDF	CFA	LCV	ACU	NTLC	NSI	COC	CEI
1992	80	70	75	80	60	44	32	30	70	63	31
1991	65	—	58	80	50	62	15	—	—	50	38

National Journal Ratings

	1991 LIB — 1991 CONS		1992 LIB — 1992 CONS	
Economic	48%	— 51%	53%	— 46%
Social	64%	— 35%	55%	— 44%
Foreign	65%	— 33%	38%	— 56%

Key Votes of the 102d Congress

1. Ban Striker Replace	FOR	5. Handgun Wait/7-Day FOR	9. Use Force in Gulf AGN
2. $ for Homeownership	AGN	6. Overseas Mil. Abortion FOR	10. US Mil. Abroad $ Cut AGN
3. Tax Rich/Cut Mid Cls.	AGN	7. Obscn. Art NEA $ Ban FOR	11. Limit SDI Funds AGN
4. FY93/$15B Def. Cut	FOR	8. Death Pen. from Jury AGN	12. Cuba Trade Embargo FOR

Key Votes of the 103d Congress

1. Family Leave AGN	2. Deficit Reduction FOR	3. Stimulus Plan FOR

Election Results

1992 general	Lee H. Hamilton (D)	160,980	(70%)	($477,591)
	Michael E. Bailey (R).............	70,057	(30%)	($175,013)
1992 primary	Lee H. Hamilton (D), unopposed			
1990 general	Lee H. Hamilton (D)	107,526	(69%)	($392,606)
	Floyd E. Coates (R)	48,325	(31%)	

TENTH DISTRICT

Indianapolis, radiating outward from the Soldiers and Sailors statue in Monument Circle, is precisely at the center of Indiana, dominating it as few other cities do a state. It is the political and governmental capital, industrial and financial center, and the intellectual center of Indiana as well. It is symmetrically laid out: just to the west of the circle is the state Capitol, to the north is the American Legion headquarters, to the east is the City-County building, to the south is the redeveloped Union Station, and Hoosier Dome Stadium. The local papers are owned by former Vice President Dan Quayle's family, the Pulliams. Farther out is the huge and growing Indiana

University Medical Center, and the park and zoo the city is building along the creek-sized White River. Indianapolis has the world's biggest children's museum and has become one of the nation's top centers for religious conventions. In recent years, it has attracted a $1 billion United Airlines repair center and a $67 million Postal Service overnight mail hub—and the Hudson Institute, a leading conservative think tank where Dan Quayle will head a new competitiveness center.

Indianapolis has tried to make itself the amateur sports capital of the United States, and may have succeeded. It showed off its amateur athletic facilities, probably the best in the nation, in the 1987 Pan American Games: a state-of-the-art natatorium, a track and field stadium, a velodrome for cycling, a soccer center, a horse park, plus the Hoosier Dome (built before the city had a football team) and Market Square Arena. And of course Indianapolis has its Basketball Hall of Fame and the Speedway where the Indianapolis 500 is held every Memorial Day weekend. The cheerful, enthusiastic, healthful atmosphere of sports seems very much in tune with the civic tone of a state whose governor is still under 40 and whose best known citizen is a former vice president known for, among other things, his athletic skill.

Politically, Indianapolis has long had robust competition, with Republicans very much ahead in national races but real battles for the offices below—a situation personified today by the eminence of Democratic Governor Evan Bayh and Republican former Vice President Dan Quayle. There is a Democratic core here, made up mostly of blacks in central city neighborhoods; Indianapolis lacks the yeasty ethnic mix of most midwestern cities, and has never had really big CIO unions nor large singles or gay communities. Almost all of this core is in the 10th Congressional District, bounded by an irregular line which runs about five miles out from Monument Circle in all directions; a district represented by one of the nation's quirkier and more distinctive politicians, Democrat Andy Jacobs.

Jacobs is now something of an oldtimer: only 10 Democrats now in the House were there when Jacobs was first elected in 1964. His service was interrupted when he lost to William Hudnut in 1972; but he came back to beat Hudnut in 1974, paving the way for Hudnut's long service as Mayor of Indianapolis. Jacobs is legendarily frugal: in 1974 he refused to board a plane because only first class seats were available; it crashed, killing all aboard. In 1992, he had the fourth lowest staff payroll in the House: "however many people you hire, the work will somehow grow to fit them all." He translates that into policy as well: he has supported a balanced budget constitutional amendment since 1976. He introduces a bill every term to withdraw the perquisites of former presidents. He wrote a law revoking Social Security benefits for prison inmates. He sympathizes with citizens who don't want to part with their money: he wrote a law barring the IRS from garnishing 100% of a taxpayer's salary for delinquent taxes, and one giving volunteer fire departments the right to issue tax-free bonds to buy their equipment. Jacobs worked as a police officer in the Sheriff's Department while in law school and suggested a change in railroad grade crossings which virtually eliminated crossing accidents in Marion County; in Congress he pushed a bill to provide government benefits for widows and children of public safety officers who die in the line of duty. He favors IRAs for health care. On foreign policy, he opposes U.S. military involvements abroad, including the Persian Gulf in 1990 and 1991; as a Marine veteran who sustained a back wound while in combat in Korea (but doesn't accept disability benefits), he coined the term "war wimps" to describe hawks who managed to avoid combat.

Jacobs is a high-ranking member of the Ways and Means Committee, but actually turned down a subcommittee chair in 1985. But since 1987, he has chaired the Social Security Subcommittee, where he has worked to make the Social Security Administration an independent agency and to expedite the process by which women and children with the HIV virus qualify for disability benefits. He conducted a scorching investigation of the SSA in 1992 which revealed numerous processing delays and errors. Jacobs has not been afraid to antagonize Chairman Dan Rostenkowski or various medical lobbies; he is the essence of a non-team player. In December 1990, David Obey sponsored a rules change requiring Ways and Means subcommittee chairmen to be elected by the whole Democratic Caucus; many said this was aimed at Jacobs by Obey and others angry that he had opposed the congressional pay raise. For his own campaigns, he accepts no PAC contributions and raises and spends little money, even when seriously opposed.

By this point he doesn't have to. His early electoral history was like the "Perils of Pauline." (It runs in the family. His father was elected to the House in 1948 and lost in 1950.) He owed his initial election to the Democratic sweep in 1964 and his first reelection to Democratic redistricting in 1966. He lost to William Hudnut after a Republican redistricting in 1972, beat him in the Watergate year of 1974, and has faced little serious challenge since. In 1986, AMPAC spent $300,000 on an independent campaign against him; his percentage fell only to 58%. He has won easily since.

The People: Pop. 1990: 554,797; 11% age 65+; 69% White; 30% Black; 1% Asian; 1% Hispanic origin. Voting age pop.: 410,877; 27% Black; 1% Hispanic origin. Households: 43% married couple families; 20% married couple fams. w. children; 40% college educ.; median household income: $25,304; per capita income: $12,562; median gross rent: $394; median house value: $45,700.

1992 Presidential Vote			1988 Presidential Vote		
Clinton (D)	92,514	(47%)	Dukakis (D)	99,110	(51%)
Bush (R)	70,458	(36%)	Bush (R)	96,822	(49%)
Perot (I)	33,229	(17%)			

Rep. Andy Jacobs, Jr. (D)

Elected 1974; b. Feb. 24, 1932, Indianapolis; home, Indianapolis; Catholic U., 1949, IN U., B.S. 1955, LL.B. 1958; Catholic; married (Kim).

Career: Marine Corps, 1950–52 (Korea); Police Officer, 1954–58; Practicing atty., 1958–65, 1973–74; IN House of Reps., 1959–60; U.S. House of Reps., 1964–72.

Offices: 2313 RHOB 20515, 202-225-4011. Also 441-A Fed. Bldg., 46 E. Ohio St., Indianapolis 46204, 317-226-7331.

Committees: *Ways and Means* (6th of 24 D): Select Revenue Measures; Social Security (Chmn.).

Group Ratings

	ADA	ACLU	COPE	CDF	CFA	LCV	ACU	NTLC	NSI	COC	CEI
1992	85	91	83	70	100	75	20	40	30	25	45
1991	80	—	91	100	78	92	20	—	—	20	41

National Journal Ratings

	1991 LIB — 1991 CONS		1992 LIB — 1992 CONS	
Economic	61%	— 36%	56%	— 42%
Social	71%	— 28%	92%	— 0%
Foreign	67%	— 32%	86%	— 10%

Key Votes of the 102d Congress

1. Ban Striker Replace FOR	5. Handgun Wait/7-Day FOR	9. Use Force in Gulf AGN
2. $ for Homeownership AGN	6. Overseas Mil. Abortion FOR	10. US Mil. Abroad $ Cut FOR
3. Tax Rich/Cut Mid Cls. FOR	7. Obscn. Art NEA $ Ban FOR	11. Limit SDI Funds FOR
4. FY93/$15B Def. Cut AGN	8. Death Pen. from Jury AGN	12. Cuba Trade Embargo FOR

Key Votes of the 103d Congress

1. Family Leave FOR	2. Deficit Reduction FOR	3. Stimulus Plan FOR

Election Results

1992 general	Andy Jacobs, Jr. (D).................	117,604	(64%)	($14,373)
	Janos Horvath (R)...................	64,378	(35%)	($66,727)
	Other...............................	1,849	(1%)	
1992 primary	Andy Jacobs, Jr. (D).................	31,710	(89%)	
	Joe L. Turner (D)	2,349	(7%)	
	Fred Ray (D)	1,551	(4%)	
1990 general	Andy Jacobs, Jr. (D).................	69,362	(66%)	($14,816)
	Janos Horvath (R)...................	35,049	(34%)	($13,201)

IOWA

Iowa, America's most downcast state in the upbeat 1980s, now seems to have turned frisky in the chastened 1990s. In spirit, in temperament, in its preoccupations with issues and its partisan preferences, Iowa seems so often to be going just the other way from the rest of the nation—determinedly, with confidence in its own chipper rectitude, undeterred by being the state out of step. Consider the 1980s, when onetime Des Moines radio announcer Ronald Reagan was president, and Iowa gave him some of his lowest job ratings in the nation. The reason was the stalled economy: in the first seven years of the decade, Iowa saw 7% of its residents leave and its population fall more than any other state but West Virginia. It lost both incomes and wealth, as farmland prices dropped and farm implement factories shut down. These were actually exaggerations of the long-range trend, apparent since 1900, of outmigration. Despite its proximity to major markets, despite its high levels of education—Iowa is dotted with colleges and boasts the nation's highest literacy rates—Iowa by the 1980s was in its ninth straight decade of outmigration; it never generated the new jobs it needed to employ its own young people much less attract others. Iowa's very articulateness may have been working against it. Iowans in the 1980s continually expressed a sense of aggrievement that Iowa's economy, based on the wholesome business of farming, couldn't sustain the desired levels of growth, even though history shows that an essential characteristic of economic growth is long-term decline in basic commodity prices. For half a century, Iowa looked to the federal government to maintain agricultural profits with a fervor that began with Jeffersonian sentimentalism about the moral superiority of farming and ended up as a sense of entitlement and almost greed.

Iowa voters were coddled in these sentiments during ever-lengthier campaigns in this state's first-in-the-nation precinct caucuses. Starting in 1976, when Jimmy Carter's strategist Hamilton Jordan determined that intensive personal campaigning could produce national publicity for a little-known candidate, the Iowa caucuses were a major league event: Ronald Reagan avoided a debate here in 1980, only to be beaten by George Bush, while Carter was overwhelming Edward Kennedy; Walter Mondale won half the votes in an eight-candidate field in 1984, only to see the spotlight fall on the splinter vote for second-place finisher Gary Hart; attention fell for a moment on winners Bob Dole and Dick Gephardt in 1988, as George Bush was humiliated by coming in third in a rush of anti-Reagan feeling, and Michael Dukakis's spinners managed to convince the press that his third-place finish behind Gephardt and Paul Simon still kept him alive. In the 1970s, the Iowa caucuses were scheduled early by Democratic doves who wanted leverage for a dovish constituency (and there was hardly an electorate then more averse to the use of American military power than Iowa Democratic caucus-goers); but while this tended to block hawkish Democrats from the party nomination nationally, the effect in Iowa was to reinforce the state's self-pitying preoccupation with the farm economy.

Now, in the 1990s, Iowa's mentality seems to have changed. The farm bill of 1985 played a part; farm subsidies had been mushrooming, so they were cut way back, and Iowa among other states realized it had to look elsewhere than Washington for growth. At which point, growth happened: starting in 1987, the economy turned upward, and in the recession of the early 1990s, Iowa's unemployment was well below national levels while farmland prices were stable. Moreover, Iowa did not get two years of sick calls from sympathetic-physician presidential candidates in 1990–92, as Iowa Senator Tom Harkin decided to run for president, thus preempting the Democratic side, and Pat Buchanan understood that anti-tax New Hampshire was a much better venue for his Republican candidacy than dovish Iowa. In the vacuum created by the absence of national candidates, Iowans started building their own economy—and getting enthusiastic about it in the process. Governor Terry Branstad proclaimed that Iowa would build a statewide fiber optics network, "the highway of the future," linking Iowa's highly literate and skilled work force, in its growing small cities as well as shrinking small towns, with the world economy. Iowa in 1991 became the first state to legalize modern riverboat gambling, trying to keep the stakes low in a bow to the old-time morality symbolized by Iowa painter Grant Wood's *American Gothic*, but hoping to stimulate some tourist business by competing with Nevada. Riverboat gambling did spruce up the picturesque cities of Dubuque and Davenport. But there is risk in pioneering. By the end of 1992, both Illinois and Missouri also had legalized riverboat gambling; the Dubuque Casino Belle was sold and only two of five original casinos were operating. And there were other losses in Iowa: starting with the city of Marshalltown—home of the writer of *The Music Man*—Iowa cities and state governments invested money with a California-based firm called Iowa Trust which turned out to defraud the state of some $70 million. Dubuque alone lost $23 million; state Senate President Joe Welsh of Dubuque and salesman for Iowa Trust was disciplined by the Senate for his role in the scandal and was forced out of his job as president, though he did retain his seat.

But the very fact that the Iowa Trust scandal shocked Iowans shows that Grant Wood-style rectitude is not at all dead here. For if this is a state that has been more dovish than the nation (from the time of the Vietnam war to 1991, when Iowa's Charles Grassley was one of only two Senate Republicans voting against the Gulf war resolution), it is also culturally more conservative in many ways. Divorce is far less common here than in the rest of the nation; abortion is allowed, but disfavored, and remains unpopular in heavily Catholic communities like Dubuque; people here tend to be older, and so from generations which celebrate traditional morality rather than disdain it. This cultural conservatism is allied to Iowa's aversion to spending, derived from both the New England Yankee and German heritages which are strong cultural forces here; there is something similar in adjacent Minnesota and Wisconsin. Iowa's dovishness, which has roots in this thriftiness and in its large numbers of German-Americans, isolationist before both world wars, made this a more Democratic state than the nation in the 1980s; by 1988, it not only voted for the pacifist-inclined Michael Dukakis, but gave him his second highest percentage of any state, ahead even of Massachusetts. But by 1992, Iowa's cultural conservatism was asserting a stronger force. Iowa did not vote for George Bush, but the drop in his percentage here over his four-year term was only 8%, less than half the national average, and the smallest in the country. To put it another way, this may be one state where questions of Bill Clinton's marital fidelity may have hurt him; for whatever reason, he ran 11% behind Michael Dukakis. This leaves Iowa

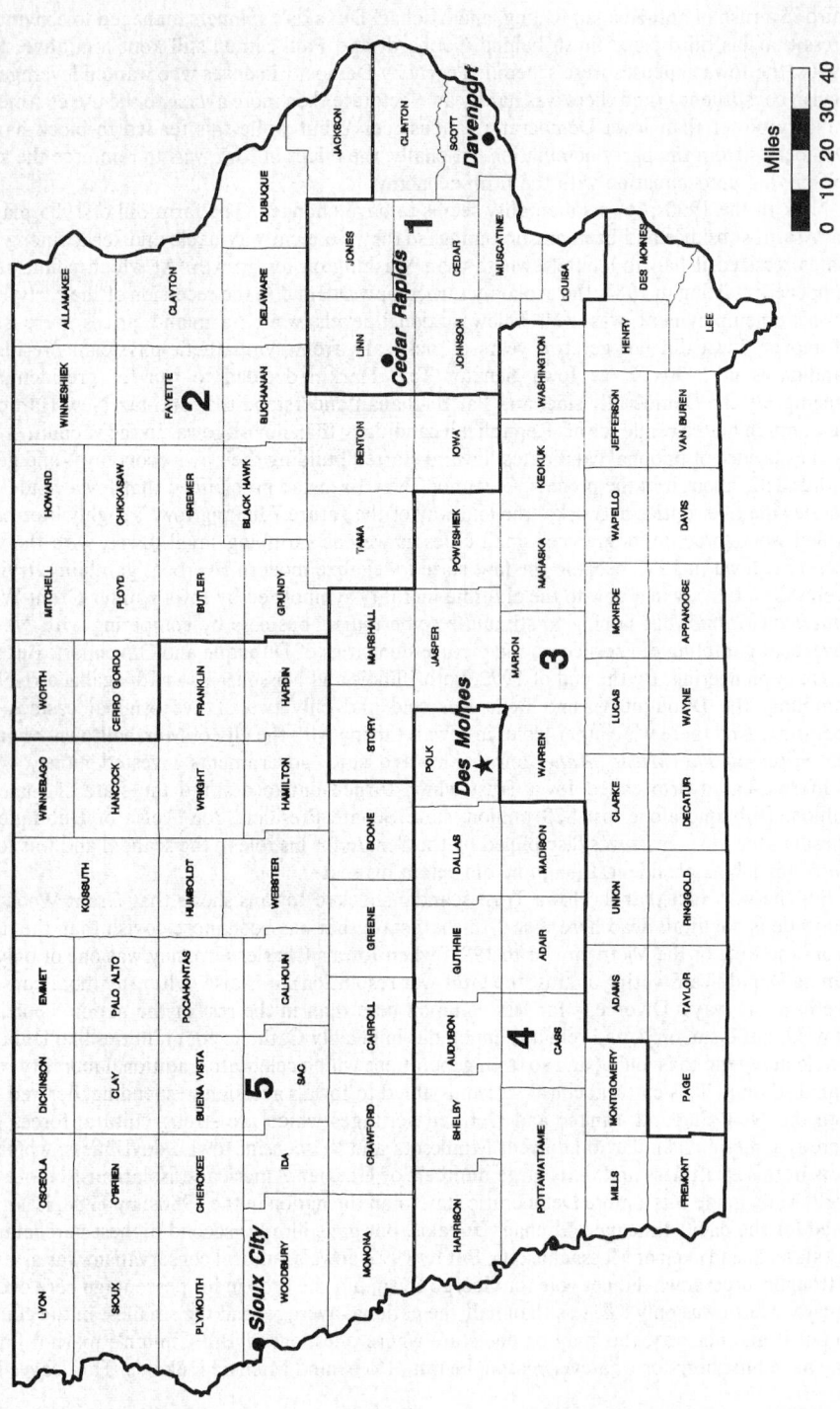

now with a stronger Democratic Party than it had historically and a stronger Republican Party than apparent in the 1992 presidential returns. So Iowa continues its tradition of being politically countercyclical in the 1990s, though in different ways than in the 1980s.

Governor. Iowa's Terry Branstad is now one of the most senior governors in the nation, tied with Mario Cuomo for continuous service; he is, moreover, a Republican in a state that has been favorable to Democrats nationally and in the legislature at home. Yet even as Iowa in some ways is trending Republican in the 1990s, Branstad has found himself on the defensive. One reason is taxes. He cut business taxes in his first term and taxes remained a favorable issue for him in 1986 and 1990. But in 1992, after some maneuvering, he approved a one cent increase in the sales tax and a big increase—7.5% for most employees, 9% for unionized—in state pay; in return he claimed spending reforms, including caps on Medicaid and foster care. This may have contributed to the Republican capture of the state House that fall, for the first time since 1980; the Iowa Trust scandal may have helped too. But raising taxes could be trouble for Branstad in 1994 as it was for George Bush in 1992. Another liability may be abortion: Branstad is antiabortion, and opinion has been moving, slowly, in the pro-choice direction in Iowa, though his support of a parental notification law may prove both effective and popular. On the positive side, Branstad claims to have encouraged job growth, which in fact has occurred since the mid-1980s, and he has championed Iowa's proposed 2,600-mile fiber optics "highway," the Iowa Communications Network, which is scheduled by October 1993 to link hundreds of state government locations, schools and libraries. He says his next priority is education reform, particularly determining criteria for measuring student achievement.

Will Branstad run for a fourth term in 1994? He has expressed no desire to run for the Senate, and he will still be under 50. He has been fortunate in earlier elections in his opponents' weaknesses. His 1982 opponent was hurt because she had legally avoided paying state taxes: Branstad won with 53%. His 1986 opponent, Lowell Junkins, advocated a $400 million bond issue to be paid back from a lottery, a dubious platform: Branstad won with 52%. In 1990, Democrats, after a tough primary and arguments over abortion, chose Don Avenson, who appeared to be a politically unattractive and blatantly unappealing candidate: Branstad won with 61%. The Republican capture of the state House in 1992 may encourage Branstad to run; one declared Republican candidate is 5th District Congressman Fred Grandy.

Senators. "The Eastern snobs of the Republican party don't want someone like Chuck Grassley with a Midwestern twang speaking on national television," he said of the 1992 Republican National Convention, with a straight face. Just a simple Iowa farmer, Charles Grassley might go on to say of himself, who worked as a machinist while serving in the legislature: the picture of a hayseed. But he is also a shrewd and successful Republican politician who has held public office for a third of a century, winning a seat in the Iowa legislature in the Democratic year of 1958, a House seat in the Democratic year of 1974, and a Senate seat by beating a strong incumbent, John Culver, in 1980. Grassley's record in Congress has been guided by three issues: thrift, agriculture and dovishness on defense. He will abandon party lines to vote for higher farm spending and lower defense (the 1990 budget bill), or against extension of U.S. military power (the 1991 Gulf war resolution), or to force a vote on an energy bill with a coal tax (the 1992 energy bill). He stands up for flexibility in planting, as he did by voting against the Senate version of the 1990 farm bill, and also for subsidizing farm products (through export assistance and ethanol programs). He is proud of his work on perpetuating low income "Aggie bonds" for young farmers and plans to push for permanent extension of the program in the 103d Congress.

Grassley also shows his shrewdness on Judiciary, where he is one of the few (4) non-lawyers on that body. He sharply attacked the opponents of Robert Bork's appointment, and appropriately skewered the American Bar Association as blatantly political. But he mostly kept quiet during the Clarence Thomas hearings, asking just one question of Anita Hill. Ironically, in 1991 he was ultimately successful in his three-year crusade to apply civil rights and sexual harassment laws to the Senate; Congress should understand first-hand, he says, the laws it imposes on others. He generally wants to discourage litigiousness, moving to deny attorney's fees to copyright infringement plaintiffs, but he was a major backer of the bill to let victims of rape and families of murder victims sue hard-core pornographers if a connection to the crime can be proved. He succeeded in getting a 25% tax deduction for health insurance for the self-employed; he is seeking 100%. As always, Grassley advances his position soberly, in his own natural style; he is plainly sincere, yet more aware of the political repercussions of his actions than his manner suggests.

Since 1980, Grassley has been the most popular political figure in Iowa, with an appeal that goes far beyond party lines. In 1986, he became the first Iowa senator to win reelection in 20 years; no serious candidate filed to run against him, and he received 66% of the vote—more than any other Iowa senator. In 1988, his support helped Bob Dole win the Iowa presidential caucuses (will there be a reprise in 1996?). His 1992 opponent, Jean Lloyd-Jones, had started a peace institute, but she was an officer in the Iowa Senate which had declined to probe Senate President Joe Walsh's involvement in the Iowa Trust scandal. Grassley carried even her home base, the university town of Iowa City, and all the state's 98 counties, for a 70%–27% victory, a new record; he ran 33 points ahead of George Bush.

Tom Harkin, after years of toiling in Iowa's political vineyards, became a national figure, at least for a moment, in the 1992 presidential race. Few guessed during most of his two-decade career in Iowa politics that he would become a national candidate, and indeed he did so more out of conviction than calculation, because he sensed there was no one in the race who would challenge George Bush as Harkin thought he ought to be. For Harkin is an old-fashioned economic issues liberal, a believer in income redistribution and a vitriolic opponent of "trickle down economics." Harkin is one of the Democrats' Watergate babies, but there is no smooth Ivy League smugness to him. He has a craggy and almost worn look; he grew up poor in a rural town, worked his way through college and law school, spent five years in the Navy during the 1960s, ferrying planes from Vietnam for repair. After a close loss in 1972, Harkin ran for Congress again in 1974 and invented "work days," a campaign technique widely imitated since: he spent a day working at each of a dozen or so local jobs. He won solidly and held the seat with good percentages. Well before the 1984 election, he cornered the Democratic nomination to run against Senator Roger Jepsen, who was gravely weakened by, among other things, insisting he was entitled to commute to work alone in the highway lane reserved for multiple passenger cars. In a tough year for Democrats elsewhere, Harkin was elected to the Senate with 55%.

Harkin styled himself a populist in the Senate; some others, like Bob Dole who was angered by his maneuvering for credit on the 1985 farm bill, called him a demagogue, or worse. In fact, his ag initiatives have fallen flat, notably the 1987 Harkin-Gephardt supply management farm bill, which would have raised overall food costs in order to benefit small farmers with assets of half a million dollars or more; Harkin unavailingly opposed the 1985 and 1990 farm bills that turned the trajectory of farm subsidies downward. Socialism and central planning may be on the way out in the rest of the world, but would stay in American farming if Harkin had his way. Harkin supported, as farm state senators usually do, food aid to the Soviet Union, on whatever terms; interestingly, though representing export-dependent Iowa, he supported the 1990 textile trade restrictions bill and co-sponsored the most stringent of the foreign investment disclosure bills being considered on Capitol Hill.

Harkin has also had legislative success, notably the Americans with Disabilities Act (ADA). Influenced by the plight of his brother who became deaf at age nine, he has long been a champion of the disabled, using his chairmanship of the Labor-HHS Appropriations Subcommittee for that purpose; he has implemented grants for "assistive technology" for the handicapped and a new NIH Institute on Deafness and Other Communications Disorders. The ADA was a great achievement, one that required overcoming resistance based on cost and qualms about the real-world effect of regulations. At Gallaudet University in Washington, D.C., a noted school for the hearing impaired, Harkin gave part of his speech in sign language when he withdrew from the presidential race.

On foreign policy, Harkin is very much a product of the Vietnam experience, an opponent of U.S. military intervention and involvement almost anywhere. He opposed contra aid and verged on being an apologist for the Sandinista government. He obviously was against the dispatch of U.S. troops to the Persian Gulf in 1990, presumably sensing another Vietnam, and filed suit against President Bush to prevent him from using force without congressional approval. That same year, Harkin beat a tough opponent, 2d District Congressman Tom Tauke, a knowledgeable critic of government programs and a smart political operator. But his attacks on Harkin's supposedly luxurious lifestyle fell flat, and Harkin's pro-choice position was an asset. (A dozen years before, the abortion issue defeated pro-choice Senator Dick Clark, as Catholic Democrats deserted his cause; now the leverage was among pro-choice Republicans, and Tauke, who defended his position in a dignified manner under intense pressure, was the net loser.) Harkin won with 54%, carrying all districts but Tauke's and the heavily Republican seat in northwest.

Then came the idea of running for president. In angry phrases, with a Trumanesque zest, Harkin preached that George Bush and the Republicans helped only the rich and that government must get involved to help the poor and middle class. Harkin was not always accurate and didn't play up to the modern media; his style and message came from a time when liberal politicians knew most of the media were against them and were confident that the people would support them if they could only shout their message loud enough. That confidence was not justified by events; Harkin failed to get solid support even from union leaders sympathetic to his positions. The AFL-CIO's decision to withhold any early endorsement of Harkin, who had backed the AFL-CIO on more than 90% of its key votes during his Senate career, was a major blow to Harkin's candidacy and a great tactical victory for Bill Clinton, governor of a right-to-work state. Harkin's sweep of the Iowa caucuses February 10, actually a rather nice testimonial to his home state popularity, was naturally discounted by the media. They also started to point up how Harkin had stretched the truth in past campaigns. But Harkin's greatest problem was that he just didn't strike a chord with many voters. He had a good New Hampshire organization, enough money to run a respectable campaign, and no scandal problems like Bill Clinton or health problems like Paul Tsongas. New Hampshire on February 18, with its mania for low taxes, was not a good Harkin venue: he got only 10% of the vote, a sign that he had essentially no constituency there. Harkin won the Minnesota and Idaho caucuses March 3, but got only 7% in South Carolina March 7 after campaigning there with Jesse Jackson. In debt and ineligible for matching funds, Harkin decided to quit rather than contest Michigan and Illinois on March 17, despite pleas from some union leaders there.

But Harkin didn't entirely vanish from the scene. Within weeks (March 26), he endorsed Bill Clinton, and campaigned gamely for him in primaries and with union audiences, despite the differences between their programs. This brought out the best side of Harkin: he showed none of the defensiveness he does when he's running himself; instead, he was a genuinely happy warrior. He was also a contrast with Paul Tsongas and Jerry Brown, who endorsed Clinton grudgingly and well after the fact; Clinton owes Harkin one. He returned the favor by appointing his wife Ruth Harkin, a Washington lawyer who combines good humor, competence and strong beliefs, to head the Overseas Private Investment Corporation. Meanwhile, Tom Harkin will continue in the Senate, probably still with a poor kid's chip on his shoulder and his sometimes grating self-righteousness that are among his trademarks; generosity and empathy are others. His seat comes up in 1996, and will probably be seriously contested. He is the first Iowa Democrat to win two consecutive six-year Senate terms; none has won a third.

Presidential politics. What if Iowa held precinct caucuses, and nobody came? That's what happened in 1992 and it can be argued that it was a good thing for America and for Iowa. A good thing for America, because Iowa was unable to tilt the Democrats so far to the left, especially on foreign policy, as to make them uncompetitive as candidates and unthinkable as presidents. Good for Iowa, because Iowa voters were not bathed with sympathy for the plight of the farmer and indulged in their self-pity. It is irrational to have a presidential selection system that gives two small and atypical states—Iowa and New Hampshire—such pivotal roles, and since these states' hold on the process depends on Democratic Party rules, and since Democratic Party rules can be recast in just about whatever form President Bill Clinton wants them recast, there is a chance to make the system more rational for 1996.

Congressional districting. In May of 1991, the Democratically controlled Iowa legislature approved a revised congressional district map drawn up by the state's non-partisan Legislative Services Bureau, which Governor Terry Branstad later approved. The state's dramatic population decline in the 1980s necessitated the loss of one of its six congressional seats, and consequently the 2d and 3d Districts in the eastern part of the state were merged, forcing freshman Jim Nussle into a successful contest over Democrat Dave Nagle. No district went untouched: Jim Ross Lightfoot's home town of Shenandoah just narrowly falls in a vastly changed 3d District, and Neal Smith's 4th District was moved westward all the way to the Iowa-Nebraska border.

The People: Est. Pop. 1992: 2,812,000; Pop. 1990: 2,776,755, up 1.3% 1990–1992. 1.1% of U.S. total, 30th largest; 39% rural. Median age: 34.0 years. 15.3% 65 years and over. 96.9% White, 1.7% Black, 1.2% Hispanic origin. Households: 59.2% married couple families; 28% married couple fams. w. children; 42% college educ.; median household income: $26,229; per capita income: $12,422; 70.0% owner occupied housing; median house value: $45,900; median monthly rent: $261. 4.6% Unemployment. Voting age pop.: 2,057,875. Registered voters (1992): 1,703,576; 636,562 D (37%), 532,176 R (31%), 534,836 unaffiliated and minor parties (31%).

Political Lineup: Governor, Terry Branstad (R); Lt. Gov., Joy Corning (R); Secy. of State, Elaine Baxter (D); Atty. Gen., Bonnie Campbell (D); Treasurer, Michael L. Fitzgerald (D); Auditor, Richard D. Johnson (R). State Senate, 50 (27 D and 23 R); State House of Representatives, 100 (51 R and 49 D). Senators, Charles E. Grassley (R) and Tom Harkin (D). Representatives, 5 (4 R and 1 D).

1992 Presidential Vote			1988 Presidential Vote		
Clinton (D)	586,353	(43%)	Dukakis (D)	670,557	(55%)
Bush (R)	504,891	(37%)	Bush (R)	545,355	(44%)
Perot (I)	253,468	(19%)			

GOVERNOR

Gov. Terry E. Branstad (R)

Elected 1982, term expires Jan. 1995; b. Nov. 17, 1946, Leland; home, Des Moines; U. of IA, B.A. 1969, Drake U., J.D. 1974; Catholic; married (Christine).

Career: Army, 1969–71; IA House of Reps., 1973–79; Practicing atty., Farmer, 1974–1982; IA Lt. Gov., 1979–83.

Office: State Capitol, Des Moines 50319, 515-281-5211.

Election Results

1990 gen.	Terry E. Branstad (R)	591,852	(61%)
	Donald D. Avenson (D)	379,372	(39%)
1990 prim.	Terry E. Branstad (R), unopposed		
1986 gen.	Terry E. Branstad (R)	472,712	(52%)
	Lowell L. Junkins (D)	436,924	(48%)

SENATORS

Sen. Charles E. Grassley (R)

Elected 1980, seat up 1998; b. Sep. 17, 1933, New Hartford; home, New Hartford; U. of N. IA, B.A. 1955, M.A. 1956, U. of IA, 1957–58; Baptist; married (Barbara).

Career: Farmer; IA House of Reps., 1958–74; U.S. House of Reps., 1974–80.

Offices: 135 HSOB 20510, 202-224-3744. Also 721 Fed. Bldg., 210 Walnut St., Des Moines 50309, 515-284-4890; 210 Waterloo Bldg., 531 Commercial St., Waterloo 50701, 319-232-6657; 116 Fed. Bldg., 131 E. 4th St., Davenport 52801, 319-322-4331; 103 Fed. Bldg., 320 6th St., Sioux City 51101, 712-233-3331; and 206 Fed. Bldg., 101 1st St., SE, Cedar Rapids 52401, 319-399-2555.

Committees: *Aging (Special)* (3d of 10 R). *Agriculture, Nutrition and Forestry* (8th of 8 R): Agricultural Credit (RMM); Agricultural Production and Stabilization of Prices; Domestic and Foreign Marketing and Product Promotion. *Budget* (2d of 9 R). *Finance* (7th of 9 R): International Trade; Medicare and Long-Term Care; Private Retirement Plans and Oversight of the Internal Revenue Service (RMM). *Judiciary* (4th of 8 R): Courts and Administrative Practice (RMM); Patents, Copyrights and Trademarks.

Group Ratings

	ADA	ACLU	CDF	COPE	CFA	LCV	ACU	NTLC	NSI	COC	CEI
1992	30	0	40	17	50	25	74	83	50	90	62
1991	15	—	45	17	33	33	81	—	—	60	64

National Journal Ratings

	1991 LIB — 1991 CONS		1992 LIB — 1992 CONS	
Economic	0%	— 91%	33%	— 65%
Social	0%	— 86%	0%	— 89%
Foreign	43%	— 55%	56%	— 41%

Key Votes of the 102d Congress

1. $ for Homeownership	FOR	5. Clarence Thomas Nom. FOR	9. Use Force in Gulf	AGN
2. Have Cap Gains Debate FOR		6. Lmt Death Row Appeal FOR	10. Keep Salvador Aid	AGN
3. Remove Budget Walls AGN		7. Handgun Wait/5-Day AGN	11. Cut $1B from SDI	FOR
4. Ban Striker Replace AGN		8. Abortion Gag Rule FOR	12. Override China MFN AGN

Key Votes of the 103d Congress

1. Family Leave	AGN	2. HIV Immigrants	AGN	3. Clinton Budget	AGN

Election Results

1992 general	Charles E. Grassley (R)	899,761	(70%)	($2,486,030)
	Jean Lloyd-Jones (D)	351,561	(27%)	($410,894)
	Others	40,879	(3%)	
1992 primary	Charles E. Grassley (R), unopposed			
1986 general	Charles E. Grassley (R)	588,880	(66%)	($2,513,319)
	John P. Roehrick (D).	299,406	(34%)	($255,673)

Sen. Tom Harkin (D)

Elected 1984, seat up 1996; b. Nov. 19, 1939, Cumming; home, Cumming; IA St. U., B.S. 1962, Catholic U., J.D. 1972; Catholic; married (Ruth).

Career: Navy, 1962–67; Naval Reserves, 1969–72; Practicing atty., 1972–74; Staff Aide, House Select Cmte. on U.S. Involvement in SE Asia, 1973–74; U.S. House of Reps., 1974–84.

Offices: 531 HSOB 20510, 202-224-3254. Also 733 Fed. Bldg., 210 Walnut St., Des Moines 50309, 515-284-4574; Fed. Bldg., Council Bluffs 51501, 712-325-0036; Lindale Mall, #101, 4444 1st Ave. NE, Cedar Rapids 52407, 319-393-6374; 131 E. 4th St., 314B Fed. Bldg., Davenport, 52801, 319-322-1338; 350 W. 6th St., Dubuque 52001, 319-588-2130; and 110 Federal Bldg., 320 6th St., Sioux City 51101, 712-252-1550.

Committees: *Agriculture, Nutrition and Forestry* (5th of 10 D): Agricultural Production and Stabilization of Prices; Agricultural Research, Conservation, Forestry and General Legislation; Nutrition and Investigations (Chmn.). *Appropriations* (10th of 16 D): Agriculture, Rural Development and Related Agencies; Defense; Foreign Operations; Labor, Health and Human Services, Education (Chmn.); Transportation. *Labor and Human Resources* (6th of 10 D): Disability Policy (Chmn.); Education, Arts and Humanities; Employment and Productivity; Labor. *Small Business* (4th of 12 D): Competitiveness, Capital Formation and Economic Opportunity; Export Expansion and Agricultural Development; Government Contracting and Paperwork Reduction.

Group Ratings

	ADA	ACLU	CDF	COPE	CFA	LCV	ACU	NTLC	NSI	COC	CEI
1992	85	88	80	91	75	33	0	0	40	17	13
1991	100	—	82	90	67	73	0	—	—	14	13

National Journal Ratings

	1991 LIB — 1991 CONS		1992 LIB — 1992 CONS	
Economic	89% —	10%	95% —	0%
Social	87% —	0%	76% —	23%
Foreign	86% —	0%	86% —	0%

Key Votes of the 102d Congress

1. $ for Homeownership	AGN	5. Clarence Thomas Nom.AGN	9. Use Force in Gulf	AGN
2. Have Cap Gains Debate	*	6. Lmt Death Row AppealAGN	10. Keep Salvador Aid	AGN
3. Remove Budget Walls	*	7. Handgun Wait/5-Day FOR	11. Cut $1B from SDI	FOR
4. Ban Striker Replace	FOR	8. Abortion Gag Rule AGN	12. Override China MFN FOR

Key Votes of the 103d Congress

1. Family Leave	FOR	2. HIV Immigrants	FOR	3. Clinton Budget	FOR

Election Results

1990 general	Tom Harkin (D)	529,571	(54%)	($5,628,242)
	Thomas J. Tauke (R)	453,273	(46%)	($5,060,104)
1990 primary	Tom Harkin (D), unopposed			
1984 general	Tom Harkin (D)	716,883	(55%)	($2,838,277)
	Roger W. Jepsen (R).................	564,381	(44%)	($3,420,153)

FIRST DISTRICT

New England Yankees, spreading overland to more fertile ground where they could build farms, town halls, church spires and small colleges; Germans, heading west after coming across the ocean and stopping at the river bluffs that recalled their native land; railroad builders, headquartered in Chicago, extending their networks of steel rails over the plains and rivers, to serve fertile farms and pasture lands—these are the people who built eastern Iowa. Today, nearly a century later, the towns and small cities of eastern Iowa are more affluent, but have grown less than the rest of the nation; their ethnic distinctiveness is muted; the old river craft have been replaced by giant barges and a couple of riverboat casinos; the rail lines employ fewer men. Davenport, on the hills over the Mississippi River (which, with Rock Island, Moline and East Moline, Illinois, is part of the Quad Cities) still has the look of the city where Ronald Reagan got his first radio announcing job more than 60 years ago. Cedar Rapids, a couple of counties west of the river, looks more up-to-date, with big high-tech employers (Collins Radio, Kodak bio-research); in 1992, PMX Industries, a metalworking company, opened a plant here, making it the largest single South Korean investment in the U.S. Iowa City, to the south, is a university town complete with trendy bookstores and vegetarian eateries.

Eight counties in eastern Iowa, with Davenport in one corner and Cedar Rapids in another, make up Iowa's 1st Congressional District. Politically, the district is historically Republican; in the 1960s and 1970s, it became marginal, and by the late 1980s had become more Democratic than the state as a whole—though not quite so heavily Democratic as the Quad Cities across the River in Illinois. It became more Democratic also in the 1991 redistricting, which sloughed off several rural southeastern counties and added Cedar Rapids and Iowa City. It is solidly Republican in House elections, however, thanks to Congressman Jim Leach, who was first elected in 1976 and has not had serious opposition since. Leach has generally been styled a liberal Republican, but his background and views are more interesting than that. He was a foreign service officer assigned to the United Nations in 1972 when George Bush was U.S. ambassador there; they became friends and Leach has supported him ever since. In 1973, Leach went back to Iowa to run the family propane business, giving him on-the-ground experience in the state. He is sympathetic to some domestic government programs but frugal, a believer in free enterprise with hands-on experience in a regulated business: all these are reflected in his record in the House. On cultural issues, almost in the tradition of mainline Protestant denominations, he looks with some favor on liberal-minded changes and dislikes the traditional moralism of the religious right. "Most of America," he said at the 1992 Republican National Convention in Houston, "is not in the camp that supports an accelerating socialism of morality." His cultural liberalism comes out in his rejection of limits on the National Endowment of the Arts and his support of international family planning programs.

On economic issues, he is more conservative and market-oriented than the 1940s liberal Republicans who sought support from union leaders. But his chief contribution has been as the Banking Committee member who was closer to being correct about the savings and loan crisis than anyone else in Congress or the White House. In 1980, Leach supported raising the federal deposit insurance limit to $100,000 but understood early that allowing the states to liberate S&Ls from their investment limits without increasing their capital requirements would leave the federal government open to huge losses on deposit insurance. In May 1987, a Leach amendment to limit S&L investments to 100% of capital or 3% of assets was beaten 17–391—a $50 billion blunder, Leach estimates. Leach objected when Speaker Jim Wright stalled the S&L recapitalization bill for two years and blames Congress in general—and House Democrats in particular—for this "congressional Watergate." In 1989, he still found himself voting against the S&L bailout measure because, among other things, the House wouldn't accept his higher capital requirements. He did score a marvelous success in June 1989, however, when he moved to recommit the bill with instructions to delete a list of provisions that helped specific special interests. Usually such motions are easily defeated, and the Democrats considered voting it down; but when they saw the political implications, it passed 412–7. Leach's latest financial crusade was raising the capital standards of Freddie Mac and Fannie Mae, whose collapse could expose the government to harrowing liabilities. In 1993, Leach became the ranking Republican on Banking, but his power comes less from committee position than from the moral authority he has earned from being solitarily right when so many others were expensively wrong.

Leach is also third ranking Republican on Foreign Affairs. He was quick in the past to support South African sanctions, but supported the Bush Administration on some unpopular policies like maintaining ties with China. He chided Democratic opponents of the Gulf war resolution for repudiating their party's historic multilateral internationalism and embracing instead the "flocculent nostrums of George McGovern and Teddy Kennedy," and contrasted the internationalist tradition of Woodrow Wilson and Franklin Roosevelt: "To date the Congress has bellowed and beaten its chest demanding that its counsel be taken, but it has demurred from being held accountable for controversial policies or potentially unfortunate results."

Leach's voting record makes him one of the half-dozen most liberal Republicans in the House. But he sees himself as the "mainstream," a term he revived from Nelson Rockefeller's day to describe an organization of liberal Republicans he formed in 1984, and the various brands of conservatives who now are overwhelmingly the majority in Republican ranks as the interlopers. But when he emerges as chief Republican sponsor of Common Cause's campaign finance reform plan which has very little Republican support, he naturally invites the charge of crypto-Democrat. Leach was very much a George Bush loyalist, chairing his Iowa campaigns in 1980, 1988 and 1992, and pointedly refrained from attacking Bush's 1988 and 1992 platforms. But loyalty to Bush is no longer a litmus test for Republicans; it will be interesting to see to what extent Leach works with other Republicans and to what extent with Democrats.

Before Leach first won this seat in 1976, it had been one of the nation's prime marginal seats for a dozen years. Since then, he has won easily, even while Iowa and the 1st District were trending toward the Democrats. He does not neglect local issues, sponsoring research into scrapie, a so-far incurable disease that attacks the nervous systems of sheep and goats, and promoting ethanol production and tax incentives. Redistricting did not cause him any serious problems.

The People: Pop. 1990: 555,229; 24% rural; 12% age 65+; 95% White; 3% Black; 1% Asian; 1% Other; 2% Hispanic origin. Voting age pop.: 413,406; 2% Black; 1% Hispanic origin. Households: 58% married couple families; 27% married couple fams. w. children; 49% college educ.; median household income: $29,544; per capita income: $13,660; median gross rent: $365; median house value: $55,500.

1992 Presidential Vote

Clinton (D)	128,655	(46%)
Bush (R)	95,660	(34%)
Perot (I)	52,983	(19%)

1988 Presidential Vote

Dukakis (D)	136,716	(56%)
Bush (R)	105,683	(43%)

Rep. James A. Leach (R)

Elected 1976; b. Oct. 15, 1942, Davenport; home, Davenport; Princeton U., B.A. 1964, Johns Hopkins U., M.A. 1966, London Schl. of Econ., 1966–68; Episcopalian; married (Elisabeth).

Career: Staff Asst., U.S. Rep. Donald Rumsfeld, 1965–66; U.S. Foreign Svc., 1968–69, 1971–72; A.A. to Dir. of U.S. Office of Equal Opp., 1969–70; Pres., Flamegas Co., 1973–75; Dir., Fed. Home Loan Bank Bd., Midwest Reg., 1975–76.

Offices: 2186 RHOB 20515, 202-225-6576. Also 209 W. 4th St., Davenport 52801, 319-326-1841; 102 S. Clinton, #505, Iowa City 52240, 319-351-0789; and 309 10th St., SE, Cedar Rapids 52403, 319-363-4773.

Committees: *Banking, Finance and Urban Affairs* (RMM of 20 R): Financial Institutions Supervision, Regulation and Deposit Insurance. *Foreign Affairs* (3d of 18 R): Asia and the Pacific (RMM); Europe and the Middle East.

Group Ratings

	ADA	ACLU	COPE	CDF	CFA	LCV	ACU	NTLC	NSI	COC	CEI
1992	60	70	33	60	67	31	40	70	70	63	66
1991	60	—	42	70	56	46	35	—	—	70	57

National Journal Ratings

	1991 LIB — 1991 CONS		1992 LIB — 1992 CONS	
Economic	31%	— 68%	26%	— 73%
Social	58%	— 40%	59%	— 41%
Foreign	75%	— 24%	71%	— 26%

Key Votes of the 102d Congress

1. Ban Striker Replace	AGN	5. Handgun Wait/7-Day	FOR	9. Use Force in Gulf	FOR
2. $ for Homeownership	FOR	6. Overseas Mil. Abortion	FOR	10. US Mil. Abroad $ Cut	FOR
3. Tax Rich/Cut Mid Cls.	AGN	7. Obscn. Art NEA $ Ban	AGN	11. Limit SDI Funds	FOR
4. FY93/$15B Def. Cut	AGN	8. Death Pen. from Jury	AGN	12. Cuba Trade Embargo	FOR

Key Votes of the 103d Congress

1. Family Leave	FOR	2. Deficit Reduction	AGN	3. Stimulus Plan	AGN

Election Results

1992 general	James A. Leach (R)	178,042	(68%)	($259,804)
	Jan J. Zonneveld (D)	81,600	(31%)	
	Others	1,667	(1%)	
1992 primary	James A. Leach (R), unopposed			
1990 general	James A. Leach (R), unopposed			($87,489)

SECOND DISTRICT

Some of the loveliest landscape in America is hidden away, at least from most tourist eyes, in the northeast corner of Iowa. Here bluffs rise above the Mississippi River, which broadens out in great quiet pools and then flows fast in constricted narrows. Inland from the Mississippi are the rolling hills portrayed with surprisingly little exaggeration in the paintings of Iowa's Grant Wood. These were lands settled by immigrants in the late 19th Century. German Catholics settled Dubuque, whose giant Victorian courthouse looks down on the Mississippi and up at the

Fenelon Place Elevator that rides up the bluff; riverboat gambling came here in 1991, although unhappily the boat was sold a year later. North are the tiny towns of Allamakee County, settled by Swiss Germans, where former Senator John Culver restored his ancestral family home. Just west of Dubuque is Dyersville, where *Field of Dreams* was filmed and to which baseball buffs now repair: "If you build it, they will come." Farther west is Waterloo, which grew rapidly after 1900 as the John Deere tractor factory expanded and the eight-floor Rath factory became the largest meatpacking plant in the world; Rath closed in 1984 and Deere had thousands of layoffs, but Waterloo has rebounded somewhat with 8,000 new jobs and over 120 new businesses—a new greyhound-racing track, two telemarketing companies, and a big technologically advanced Iowa Beef Processing meatpacking operation. To the south are the Amana colonies, settled in the 1850s by the Community of True Inspiration, German pietists, who have retained many of their old customs even as they have built businesses like the Amana appliance firm.

The 2d Congressional District of Iowa covers much of northeastern Iowa, including Dubuque and Waterloo, Allamakee County and Dyersville and the Amana colonies. The current 2d is an amalgam of the old 2d, centered on Dubuque, and the 3d, centered on Waterloo, and its creation in 1991 pitted two incumbents against each other in what both parties thought was a "fair fight." Indeed, both members, three-term Democrat Dave Nagle of the old 3d and freshman Republican Jim Nussle of the old 2d, had won seats that over time have favored the other party.

Dubuque, the focus of the old 2d, for years was Iowa's most Democratic city, and still often is unless abortion is the issue; for the population here is heavily German Catholic and, unlike Catholics many other places, still heavily antiabortion. Nussle won the seat in 1990, when incumbent Republican Tom Tauke ran unsuccessfully for the Senate; it helped that Tauke was carrying the district, but Nussle had his own assets. Nussle grew up in Chicago, attended a Lutheran college (he is Danish-American and speaks Danish) and law school and then moved back to his native Iowa. In the small town way, he soon became Delaware County attorney, known for prosecuting a local day care employee for child abuse. He coupled his antiabortion stance with support for helping expectant mothers with the expenses of parenthood. He emphasized his experience in law enforcement, called for more parental involvement in the drug war as well as in choosing day care, and argued that "People make better decisions about things that affect their lives than does the government." This was enough for him to beat Democrat Eric Tabor in 1990 by one of the closest margins in the country, 50%–49%, and at age 30 Nussle became the youngest member of Congress. Tabor carried his home base but won by just 382 votes out of 63,000 cast in Cedar Rapids's Linn County (no longer in the district), and Nussle's antiabortion stand helped him carry Dubuque County by 483 votes of 31,000 cast.

Waterloo, the focus of the old 3d, was historically Republican, represented for years by politicians whose Iowa-twanged objections to government spending became legendary: H. R. Gross from 1948 to 1974 and Charles Grassley from 1974 to 1980. But in the 1980s, Waterloo and some nearby rural counties trended heavily Democratic as the Rath plant shut down and Deere had big layoffs. And in Democrat David Nagle, the Waterloo area had a canny, sharp-tongued and capable natural politician. He was Democratic state chairman during the 1984 Iowa presidential caucuses and when Republican incumbent Cooper Evans retired in 1986, Nagle won the seat fairly easily. In the House, Nagle focused largely on agricultural issues. His proposals in the 1990 farm bill to turn back the clock and increase farm subsidies above world price levels were voted down in the Agriculture Committee. Nagle had always been a strong partisan, a staunch backer of Speaker Jim Wright in spring 1989 who convened secret strategy meetings for pro-Wright Democrats in his office each morning, and in 1992 he denounced the subpoena of House bank records by special investigator Malcolm Wilkey as a violation of separation of powers.

Nussle's attitude was far different: he was the Republican who, as one of the Gang of Seven (a group of freshman political reformers), entered the House chamber in October 1991 with a paper bag over his head to vocally protest House Democratic leaders' refusal to make full disclosure of House bank overdrafts. Outwardly friendly and pleasant, Nussle seemed disgusted by the House's ways of doing business and violated many taboos—voting against agricultural appropriations, to the dismay of Iowa Democrat Neal Smith, and moving to cut congressional salaries 5% every year the federal budget is not balanced. Nagle conceded that if the issue was congressional reform, he would lose; he hoped to win on the economy and roads. Nussle had substantive issues, too: a health care IRA and national tort reform. But he really made headway with pivotal ads on the House banking scandal. One negative ad barrage highlighted Nagle's "public opinion be damned" response to the Wilkey subpoena; Nagle did not respond for several days, during which he fell sharply in the polls.

Both candidates showed considerable talent, both brought aggressive zest to their work and both took political risks for their principles. The final result could scarcely have been closer. Nagle had a turf advantage, having represented 56% of the new 2d to Nussle's 35%. But Nussle carried his old 2d with 54%, losing Dubuque County by just 18 votes out of 40,000—the abortion issue?—while Nagle carried his old 3d by just 51%–48%; Nussle's denunciations of insiders and deficits may have evoked memories of Grassley and H. R. Gross. Overall, Nussle won 50%–49%. With his political skills, he may continue to be a force for change in the House.

The People: Pop. 1990: 555,494; 49% rural; 16% age 65+; 97% White; 2% Black; 1% Hispanic origin. Voting age pop.: 408,421; 1% Black. Households: 62% married couple families; 28% married couple fams. w. children; 36% college educ.; median household income: $25,010; per capita income: $11,611; median gross rent: $300; median house value: $42,400.

1992 Presidential Vote			1988 Presidential Vote		
Clinton (D)	120,228	(44%)	Dukakis (D)	137,842	(55%)
Bush (R)	95,005	(35%)	Bush (R)	108,563	(44%)
Perot (I)	55,279	(20%)			

Rep. Jim Nussle (R)

Elected 1990; b. June 27, 1960, Des Moines; home, Manchester; Luther Col., B.A. 1983, Drake U., J.D. 1985; Lutheran; married (Leslie).

Career: Delaware Cnty. Atty., 1986–90.

Offices: 308 CHOB 20515, 202-225-2911. Also 2300 JFK Rd., Dubuque 52002, 319-557-7740; 3356 Kimball Ave., Waterloo 50702, 310-235-1109; 1825 4th St., SW, Mason City 50401, 515-423-0303; and 223 W. Main St., Manchester 52057, 319-927-5141.

Committees: *Agriculture* (9th of 19 R): Environment, Credit and Rural Development; General Farm Commodities. *Banking, Finance and Urban Affairs* (9th of 20 R): Economic Growth and Credit Formation; Financial Institutions Supervision, Regulation and Deposit Insurance; International Development, Finance, Trade and Monetary Policy.

Group Ratings

	ADA	ACLU	COPE	CDF	CFA	LCV	ACU	NTLC	NSI	COC	CEI
1992	25	0	25	10	33	6	76	80	90	88	82
1991	20	—	8	10	33	8	85	—	—	90	74

National Journal Ratings

	1991 LIB — 1991 CONS			1992 LIB — 1992 CONS		
Economic	4%	—	90%	26%	—	73%
Social	19%	—	78%	0%	—	85%
Foreign	38%	—	61%	69%	—	30%

Key Votes of the 102d Congress

1. Ban Striker Replace AGN	5. Handgun Wait/7-Day AGN	9. Use Force in Gulf FOR
2. $ for Homeownership FOR	6. Overseas Mil. Abortion AGN	10. US Mil. Abroad $ Cut FOR
3. Tax Rich/Cut Mid Cls. AGN	7. Obscn. Art NEA $ Ban FOR	11. Limit SDI Funds FOR
4. FY93/$15B Def. Cut AGN	8. Death Pen. from Jury FOR	12. Cuba Trade Embargo AGN

Key Votes of the 103d Congress

1. Family Leave AGN	2. Deficit Reduction AGN	3. Stimulus Plan AGN

Election Results

1992 general	Jim Nussle (R)	134,536	(50%)	($865,838)
	David R. Nagle (D)	131,570	(49%)	($853,637)
	Others	1,786	(1%)	
1992 primary	Jim Nussle (R), unopposed			
1990 general	Jim Nussle (R)	82,650	(50%)	($466,259)
	Eric Tabor (D).	81,008	(49%)	($568,659)
	Other................................	2,325	(1%)	

THIRD DISTRICT

From the railroad towns perched below the bluffs on the Mississippi River, the rolling farmland of Iowa heads west, as settlers did more than a century ago, with thick rows of corn increasingly alternating with grazing fields. The southern two tiers of Iowa's counties have none of the state's large cities; the accent here is a bit like that of northern Missouri, with just a touch of the South. Population has been declining for many years, as the numerous children of large farm families seek opportunity elsewhere as mechanization and technology require fewer people on the land. The 3d Congressional District of Iowa covers much of the southern part of the state, including almost all of the southern tier, from the Mississippi River border with Illinois almost to the Missouri River border with Nebraska. The 3d also juts north to include a variety of famous small towns: Pella, home of the Pella window firm; Newton, home of Maytag appliances; Grinnell, with Grinnell College; Marshalltown, memorialized in *The Music Man* and known more recently as the town first involved in the Iowa Trust scandal; and Ames, home of Iowa State University. The historical preference here is Republican, but the trend in the 1980s, when Iowans felt hard pressed by the economy, was toward the Democrats. Michael Dukakis carried the region nicely, but Pella, settled originally by Dutch-Americans, has stayed Republican.

The 3d is the Iowa district most radically redesigned by the 1991 redistricting: incumbent Jim Ross Lightfoot, onetime farm news broadcaster on radio station KMA, whose old 5th District was in southwest Iowa, came from Shenandoah in the far southwest corner of the new district. His Republican status and conservative voting record were scarcely assets in the new seat. After the new district lines were drawn, Democratic Secretary of State Elaine Baxter, based in Burlington on the Mississippi, quickly became a candidate and the favorite. Lightfoot was revealed to have 105 overdrafts on the House bank, and in the June Republican primary, he got only 58% of the vote against a political unknown who said of his showing, "There's only one explanation: God did it." Lightfoot's old district cast only 25% of the primary vote, and he carried the rest of the district by only 53%–47%—a sure sign of trouble. *Roll Call* named him "America's most vulnerable incumbent."

But Lightfoot counterattacked sharply. He defended his overdrafts by saying he was never notified of them and none of his monthly statements showed a negative balance. Baxter was running well ahead in polls (sometimes by double digits) and getting national publicity on the *Today* show and as a feminist favorite at the Democratic National Convention; her pro-choice stance on abortion was also considered a plus in this Democratic majority district. But Lightfoot ran ads attacking her for junkets to Hawaii, redecorating her office (paying $67 for an in-box), and supporting the increase in the sales and gas taxes. A 10-second ad showed a man's hand holding a wallet ("This is your wallet") and then a woman's hands taking the money out ("This is your wallet under Elaine Baxter")—a pungent way to portray the spending issue. Exonerated by the Wilkey Commission of any wrong-doing in the bank scandal, Lightfoot campaigned hard after Congress adjourned, with a bus caravan across the state, and won by a 49%–47% margin. He won 57%–41% in his old 5th District, while Baxter carried the rest of the new 3d by only 49%–46%.

In Washington, Lightfoot has a solidly conservative record, pledging to support no new taxes; he was one of only 28 House members to vote against Senator Tom Harkin's Americans With Disabilities Act. His only liberal votes are those prompted by Iowa's foreign policy isolationism. On the Public Works Subcommittee on Aviation, he worked to require child safety seats on airplanes and to raise the mandatory retirement age for pilots from 60 to 65. He currently sits on the Appropriations Committee and is not averse to steering some spending toward southern Iowa.

The People: Pop. 1990: 555,299; 46% rural; 16% age 65+; 98% White; 1% Black; 1% Asian; 1% Hispanic origin. Voting age pop.: 417,744; 1% Black; 1% Hispanic origin. Households: 61% married couple families; 27% married couple fams. w. children; 39% college educ.; median household income: $24,767; per capita income: $11,567; median gross rent: $315; median house value: $41,200.

1992 Presidential Vote			
Clinton (D)	120,495	(45%)
Bush (R)	96,515	(36%)
Perot (I)	47,028	(18%)

1988 Presidential Vote			
Dukakis (D)	138,616	(56%)
Bush (R)	106,573	(43%)

Rep. Jim Ross Lightfoot (R)

Elected 1984; b. Sept. 27, 1938, Sioux City; home, Shenandoah; Catholic; married (Nancy).

Career: Army, 1956, Army Reserves, 1957–64; Tulsa Police officer, 1959–61; Farm editor, KMA Radio, 1961–70, 1976–84; Mgr., farm equipment manufacturing co., 1970–76; Corsicana City Comm., 1974–76.

Offices: 2444 RHOB 20515, 202-225-3806. Also 501 W. Lowell, Shenandoah 51601, 712-246-1984; 413 Kellogg, Ames 50010, 515-232-1288; 220 W. Salem, Indianola 50125, 515-961-0591; 347 E. 2d St., Ottumwa 52501, 515-683-3551; and 311 N. 3d St., Burlington 52601, 319-753-6415.

Committees: *Appropriations* (15th of 23 R): Foreign Operations, Export Financing and Related Programs; Treasury, Postal Service and General Government (RMM).

Group Ratings

	ADA	ACLU	COPE	CDF	CFA	LCV	ACU	NTLC	NSI	COC	CEI
1992	15	4	25	20	33	0	87	90	100	88	60
1991	0	—	8	10	33	0	100	—	—	100	63

National Journal Ratings

	1991 LIB — 1991 CONS		1992 LIB — 1992 CONS	
Economic	18%	— 79%	27%	— 72%
Social	0%	— 84%	0%	— 85%
Foreign	12%	— 85%	30%	— 64%

482   IOWA

Key Votes of the 102d Congress

1. Ban Striker Replace AGN	5. Handgun Wait/7-Day AGN	9. Use Force in Gulf FOR
2. $ for Homeownership FOR	6. Overseas Mil. AbortionAGN	10. US Mil. Abroad $ CutAGN
3. Tax Rich/Cut Mid Cls.AGN	7. Obscn. Art NEA $ Ban FOR	11. Limit SDI Funds AGN
4. FY93/$15B Def. Cut AGN	8. Death Pen. from Jury FOR	12. Cuba Trade Embargo AGN

Key Votes of the 103d Congress

1. Family Leave AGN	2. Deficit Reduction AGN	3. Stimulus Plan AGN

Election Results

1992 general	Jim Ross Lightfoot (R)	125,931	(49%)	($755,552)
	Elaine Baxter (D)	121,063	(47%)	($645,342)
	Larry Chroman (Natural Law)	10,181	(4%)	($129,096)
1992 primary	Jim Ross Lightfoot (R)	15,757	(58%)	
	Ronald J. Long (R)	11,251	(42%)	
1990 general	Jim Ross Lightfoot (R)	99,978	(68%)	($418,134)
	Rod Powell (D)	47,022	(32%)	($63,591)

FOURTH DISTRICT

Iowa today seems very much in the Middle of America. But once it was part of the West, and then the road to the West: on the route of the first Transcontinental Railroad, a stopping off place for people in a hurry to get to Nebraska and the Rockies and the Pacific, or the Dakotas and the fastness of Montana. At the same time, Iowans were determined to use the wealth accumulated by methodical husbandry of their fertile farmlands to implant firmly the glories of western civilization. You can feel that impulse today in Des Moines when you look across the river from downtown at the Victorian Capitol, its gold dome above a Corinthian pediment, or Terrace Hill, the beautifully restored governor's mansion, atop a hill overlooking the Raccoon River. Take in the nearby Living History Farms, which recreate Indian villages, frontier towns and turn-of-the-century farms, and see what an effort the new settlers made to put their imprint on the environment. The same civilizing impulse can be seen farther west, in the city of Council Bluffs, in the mansion of General Grenville Dodge. Here in 1859, General Dodge lobbied Illinois lawyer Abraham Lincoln on the need for a transcontinental railroad; Lincoln got it through Congress in 1863, Dodge became its chief engineer, and Council Bluffs became its eastern terminus when it was completed in 1869.

Des Moines and Council Bluffs were among the few areas of Iowa which showed growth in the bedraggled 1980s. While small town bankers were foreclosing on farmers' mortgages, main street storefronts were going vacant one by one, and the meatpacking and tractor factories in Iowa's smaller cities were going dark and cold, these and a few other cities were growing. Their tidy shopping centers were gaining businesses that used to go to small towns, as Iowans got into the habit of driving 100 miles for a day's shopping; their office centers were filling up with new service jobs, as manufacturing jobs in other cities were disappearing; their insurance and printing companies were expanding as businesses elsewhere in Iowa were closing down. Now, in the 1990s, as all of Iowa is doing somewhat better, these cities continue to grow—though not as robustly and confidently as they did when they were the gateway to the West.

The 4th Congressional District of Iowa, greatly redesigned in the 1991 redistricting, includes Des Moines and Council Bluffs and their surrounding counties (Polk and Pottawattamie), plus 11 mostly rural counties in between, along the Missouri River. There are different political leanings. Des Moines is in the center of corn and hog country, still hankering for generous farm subsidies; its Iowa-ish cultural liberalism is strengthened by the liberal *Des Moines Register & Tribune*. Council Bluffs is surrounded by beef grazing country, where the federal government is seen as an officious intermeddler; it looks west to Omaha, taking on the culturally more conservative tone of Nebraska and the conservative politics of the *Omaha World-Herald*. The balance is in favor of Des Moines: Polk and next-door Dallas County cast 69% of the 4th District's votes. But the Republican leanings in the west were enough to hold Bill Clinton to a 4% margin.

The congressman from the 4th District since 1958 has been Neal Smith, a Democrat who combines an 1890s Iowan persnickitiness about doing things according to the right procedure with the current Iowan liberal view on most issues. In his early years in the House, he embarked on what seemed quixotic crusades, and had notable successes: passing a tougher meat inspection law and imposing an anti-nepotism rule on Congress. He was the sponsor of the rule requiring committee chairmen to be chosen by votes in the Democratic caucus, rather than by automatic operation of seniority.

Now more than ever, Smith seems determined to do things by the book. He is the third-ranking Democrat on the Appropriations Committee (over 70, but still behind two men in their 80s), and chairman of the Commerce, Justice, State and Judiciary Subcommittee, a body which doesn't disburse much money by federal budget standards but which can impinge on important policy areas. Complicating his task is his insistence on not appropriating money for programs that have not been authorized, although he will compromise in conference committee with his Senate counterparts when they have done so. This was especially troublesome because for years the foreign aid program, always a target for controversial amendments, was not reauthorized. He also superintends funding for the Legal Services Corporation, highly controversial in the Reagan and Bush years, and often unauthorized. Like other Appropriations subcommittee chairmen, he squawks at the low levels of overall spending imposed by the full committee and the budget process, and especially at the unpopularity of foreign aid among the American electorate. He does bring some pork to Iowa, helped by Tom Harkin on the Senate Appropriations Committee, a onetime Smith staffer.

Smith's tendency to be a stickler for doing things right comes out on other issues. He objected to the acceptance of the 27th Amendment, first proposed in 1789, and ultimately ratified by 40 states, to require that Congress can't change its own salary during a term. Smith was troubled by the constitutional implications raised given the long lapses which transpired between state ratifications of the amendment. "The principle of contemporary consensus," he said, "is just too important to ever waive just because it appears popular at the moment." Nor does he take kindly to attacks on Congress as an institution. At an April 1992 Democratic Caucus meeting, he asked Bill Clinton, "Are you going to run with us or against us?" Clinton replied he was "running for change." While he warns against overuse by Congress of "dire emergency" funding, he also fought against allowing OMB to declare when a fiscal emergency exists. On issues generally, Smith's voting record is pretty liberal. But if he becomes chairman of the full Appropriations Committee, he is unlikely to generously accommodate his fellow Democrats if to do so would violate a principle or rule he thinks important.

The 1991 redistricting produced the biggest boundary change Smith had experienced in 34 years. Nonetheless, he won without major difficulty, unopposed in the primary and with 62% in the general election. He carried the Des Moines area with better than 2–1, while winning just 50%–48% in Pottawattamie.

The People: Pop. 1990: 555,276; 26% rural; 14% age 65+; 95% White; 3% Black; 1% Asian; 1% Other; 2% Hispanic origin. Voting age pop.: 412,155; 2% Black; 1% Hispanic origin. Households: 58% married couple families; 27% married couple fams. w. children; 46% college educ.; median household income: $28,591; per capita income: $13,813; median gross rent: $405; median house value: $52,500.

1992 Presidential Vote

Clinton (D) 117,863 (43%)
Bush (R) 107,745 (39%)
Perot (I). 47,835 (17%)

1988 Presidential Vote

Dukakis (D). 131,550 (55%)
Bush (R) 106,044 (44%)

Rep. Neal Smith (D)

Elected 1958; b. Mar. 23, 1920, Hedrick; home, Altoona; MO U., 1945–46, Syracuse U., 1946–48, Drake U., LL.B. 1950; United Methodist; married (Beatrix).

Career: Army Air Corps, 1942–45 (WWII); Farmer; Asst. Polk Cnty. Atty., 1950–52; Practicing atty., 1952–58; Chmn., Polk Cnty. Bd. of Social Welfare, 1956.

Offices: 2373 RHOB 20515, 202-225-4426. Also 544 Insurance Exchange Bldg., Des Moines 50309, 515-284-4634; and 40 Pearl St., Council Bluffs 51502, 712-323-5976.

Committees: *Appropriations* (3d of 37 D): Agriculture, Rural Development, Food and Drug Administration and Related Agencies; Commerce, Justice, State and Judiciary (Chmn.); Labor, Health and Human Services, and Education. *Small Business* (2d of 27 D): SBA Legislation and the General Economy.

Group Ratings

	ADA	ACLU	COPE	CDF	CFA	LCV	ACU	NTLC	NSI	COC	CEI
1992	75	91	75	90	60	25	17	10	60	57	14
1991	55	—	82	70	67	38	11	—	—	40	16

National Journal Ratings

	1991 LIB — 1991 CONS	1992 LIB — 1992 CONS
Economic	50% — 49%	53% — 46%
Social	69% — 30%	72% — 24%
Foreign	68% — 31%	38% — 56%

Key Votes of the 102d Congress

1. Ban Striker Replace	FOR	5. Handgun Wait/7-Day AGN	9. Use Force in Gulf AGN
2. $ for Homeownership AGN		6. Overseas Mil. Abortion FOR	10. US Mil. Abroad $ Cut AGN
3. Tax Rich/Cut Mid Cls. FOR		7. Obscn. Art NEA $ Ban AGN	11. Limit SDI Funds AGN
4. FY93/$15B Def. Cut AGN		8. Death Pen. from Jury AGN	12. Cuba Trade Embargo AGN

Key Votes of the 103d Congress

1. Family Leave   FOR   2. Deficit Reduction   FOR   3. Stimulus Plan   FOR

Election Results

1992 general	Neal Smith (D)	158,610	(62%)	($197,159)
	Paul Lunde (R)	94,045	(37%)	($11,178)
	Others	4,938	(2%)	
1992 primary	Neal Smith (D)	19,285	(99%)	
	Others	291	(1%)	
1990 general	Neal Smith (D)	127,812	(98%)	($56,903)
	Other	2,778	(2%)	

FIFTH DISTRICT

Nestled below and running up the loess bluffs above the Missouri River is one of the oldest market towns on the Great Plains, Sioux City. Although still the largest city on the Plains west of Des Moines and north of Omaha, Sioux City has not grown much in the last five decades. Its traditional economic base has become obsolete, and so has some of the city itself: the waterfront, once raucous with boatmen and stockyard workers, is now quiet; stockyards have been replaced by IBP's modern (and low-wage) beef factory across the river in Nebraska; downtown stores have been replaced by shopping malls at the edge of town where people will still drive for 100 miles to spend a day doing the season's shopping. In different form, Sioux City is still the main commercial center of the fertile plains of northwestern Iowa, and the leading city of Iowa's 5th Congressional District. The district's counties on the gently rolling landscape are an ethnic melange: Irish Catholics in Palo Alto, Dutch in Sioux (the most heavily Republican county in Iowa), and the descendants of the English lords who built huge cattle ranches around Le Mars in Plymouth County. In its newly districted boundaries (and its new number: it used to be the 6th), the 5th District covers most of northern and northwest Iowa, politically an area that, on balance, is a few points more Republican than the rest of the state.

The congressman from the 5th District, Fred Grandy, is known by C-SPAN viewers as an articulate House Republican and by cable rerun viewers as Gopher on "The Love Boat." Grandy is actually from Sioux City; he became friends with David Eisenhower at prep school and then stayed Republican in the hyperliberal environment of late 1960s Harvard; he worked in Washington for Sioux City Republican Congressman Wiley Mayne, defeated after he voted against the impeachment of Richard Nixon; then Grandy became an actor, a smart man who spent 10 years playing a dumb character. "What I really wanted to do was act," he once said, "Eventually, I split the difference and went into politics." Grandy returned to Iowa to run in 1986 for the seat being vacated by the man who had beaten Mayne, Democrat Berkley Bedell. Grandy relied less on celebrity than on hard work, studying the minutiae of farm programs until he could discuss at length farm credit, Payment-In-Kind (PIK), set-asides, target prices, price supports and groundwater contamination. He beat a Bedell protege by a 51%–49% margin.

In the House, Grandy made a record as a Republican partisan but also a "knee-jerk moderate," concentrating heavily on Agriculture Committee work, toiling on the 1987 farm credit bailout and writing a groundwater research program into the 1990 farm bill. But he avoided extremes of Farm Belt demagoguery, insisting on not expanding the cost of the 1990 farm bill lest it be beaten on the floor, even if that meant cutting money from other commodities to pay for soybeans. Grandy pleased Republicans by supporting party positions which went against local inclinations, like voting for contra aid and the Civil Rights Restoration Act, and against mandatory family leave. He won applause from liberals for backing the National Endowment for the Arts and opposing the flag-burning amendment after initially backing it. Grandy was active and vocal on the House bank scandal, calling for early disclosure of overdrafts and pushing for it from his seat on the Ethics Committee where he is now ranking minority member. Grandy insisted that it should be considered "public money" that was involved. In late 1990, he got a seat on the Ways and Means Committee, where he is involved in the details of legislation, working on the unemployment extension bill, talking about the necessity of some day taxing employer-paid benefits as part of a healthcare bill, and proposing with other Republicans a "micro-enterprise" plan to allow welfare recipients to save money to start small businesses. Within his own party, Grandy is a bit to the left; his proposal to elect only the top three Republican leadership positions went nowhere in 1992, largely because of opposition from conservatives.

Grandy's hard work, charm and self-deprecating humor have helped him win reelection easily; he won with 72% in 1990 and was unopposed in 1992. But he does not seem to regard the House as a lifetime career. In 1992, he said he will run for governor and left open the question whether he would challenge Branstad in a primary should Branstad decide to run again; otherwise, he might well run against Senator Tom Harkin in 1996.

The People: Pop. 1990: 555,457; 52% rural; 18% age 65+; 98% White; 1% Black; 1% Asian; 1% Hispanic origin. Voting age pop.: 405,685; 1% Hispanic origin. Households: 62% married couple families; 28% married couple fams. w. children; 38% college educ.; median household income: $24,150; per capita income: $11,461; median gross rent: $285; median house value: $37,000.

1992 Presidential Vote

Bush (R) 109,966 (42%)
Clinton (D) 99,112 (38%)
Perot (I). 50,343 (19%)

1988 Presidential Vote

Dukakis (D). 125,833 (51%)
Bush (R) 118,492 (48%)

Rep. Fred Grandy (R)

Elected 1986; b. June 29, 1948, Sioux City; home, Sioux City; Harvard U., B.A. 1970; Episcopalian; married (Catherine Mann).

Career: Asst., U.S. Rep. Wiley Mayne, 1970–71; Actor, 1971–85.

Offices: 418 CHOB 20515, 202-225-5476. Also 4501 Southern Hills Dr., #21, Sioux City 51106, 712-276-5800; 822 Central Ave., #102, Fort Dodge 50501, 515-573-2738; and 14 W. 5th St., Spencer 51301, 712-262-6480.

Committees: *Standards of Official Conduct* (RMM of 7 R). *Ways and Means* (8th of 14 R): Health; Human Resources.

Group Ratings

	ADA	ACLU	COPE	CDF	CFA	LCV	ACU	NTLC	NSI	COC	CEI
1992	15	13	25	20	27	0	88	75	90	88	76
1991	25	—	17	20	39	8	85	—	—	100	70

National Journal Ratings

	1991 LIB — 1991 CONS		1992 LIB — 1992 CONS	
Economic	18%	— 79%	28%	— 70%
Social	34%	— 65%	23%	— 75%
Foreign	38%	— 61%	52%	— 46%

Key Votes of the 102d Congress

1. Ban Striker Replace	AGN	5. Handgun Wait/7-Day AGN	9. Use Force in Gulf FOR
2. $ for Homeownership	FOR	6. Overseas Mil. AbortionAGN	10. US Mil. Abroad $ Cut FOR
3. Tax Rich/Cut Mid Cls.AGN		7. Obscn. Art NEA $ BanAGN	11. Limit SDI Funds FOR
4. FY93/$15B Def. Cut FOR		8. Death Pen. from Jury FOR	12. Cuba Trade Embargo AGN

Key Votes of the 103d Congress

1. Family Leave	AGN	2. Deficit Reduction	AGN	3. Stimulus Plan	AGN

Election Results

1992 general	Fred Grandy (R)...................	196,942	(99%)	($292,752)
	Others	1,424	(1%)	
1992 primary	Fred Grandy (R), unopposed			
1990 general	Fred Grandy (R)...................	112,333	(72%)	($322,563)
	Mike D. Earll (D).................	44,063	(28%)	($42,597)

KANSAS

In October 1989, when Yevgeny Primakov, then a top deputy to Mikhail Gorbachev, wanted to see "real Americans," he flew out to Dodge City, one of the mythic prairie towns of Kansas. There he visited Boot Hill Museum, saw the reproduction of historic Front Street and the Long Branch Saloon, and was questioned by friendly Kansans who nonetheless asked him about the Soviets' continued occupation of the Baltic States. Primakov chose Dodge City partly because his host was Senate Republican Leader Bob Dole, who was first elected to represent Kansas in the House in 1960, but it was also a choice that was particularly appropriate for a Russian. For Kansas, like so much of Russia, is placid-looking plains country, full of solid farmers who work hard and have deep roots in the soil; wheat-growing country that can feed much of the world, as Kansas does today and as Russia did before it was taken over by the Soviets. But the history of Kansas, like the history of Russia, has also been punctuated by uprisings, intellectual and violent, by moments of anger and rage sweeping through the tall sheaves like a tornado wind. The difference, of course, is that Russian traditions of law and liberty, culture and civility are weak, while in Kansas as in all America they are remarkably strong.

Those roots for Kansas come from one moment of violence, the Bleeding Kansas of the 1850s; violence which broke out when the Kansas-Nebraska Act of 1854 left to local settlers the question of whether this new Kansas Territory would be a free or slave state. Pro-slavery "bushwhackers" rode over the line from Missouri, stealing elections and writing a pro-slavery constitution; but much larger numbers of free-soil "jayhawkers" from New England and the New England-Yankee-settled Great Lakes states put down roots and, despite the massacres of the mad John Brown, prevailed and established their own law and order. The effect on national politics was tumultuous: the Democratic Party was split, the Republican Party was created, the nation was plunged into Civil War. The effect on Kansas was calming: the anti-slavery majority bent the soil to the plow and built small towns thick with schools, churches and colleges, to the point that in the 1939 color movie, *Wizard of Oz*, Kansas was shot in dreary black and white as the image of dull, prim, old-fashioned Middle America. But the rebellious impulse did not totally die out. Kansas lived almost entirely on farming, and its livelihood was always at risk; hailstorms, grasshopper invasions, dry seasons or a drop in world farm prices could mean disaster for thousands of Kansans. The high-rainfall 1880s attracted hundreds of thousands of new settlers to Kansas; the low-rainfall 1890s produced a bust and a populist rebellion. "What you farmers should do," said orator Mary Ellen Lease, "is to raise less corn and more hell." For a few years in the 1890s, and then in farm rebellions of the 1930s, 1950s and 1970s, Kansans did, but afterwards always returned to jayhawker Republicanism.

At least a whiff of rebellion was apparent in the air of 1992. George Bush ended up carrying Kansas, but for much of the campaign he was running behind in polls, and Ross Perot won 27% of the vote here, tying Idaho for his fourth best showing in the nation. Perot did not run that well in any of the five major urban counties, whose recent growth has made Kansas an increasingly urban state despite its wheat-farm image. But most of his strongest showings were not in the wheat country of central Kansas or the grazing lands of the southwest (where seven counties voted 84% to secede from the state in April 1992), either; farm prices and profits have been relatively high and unemployment here very low. Instead, Perot ran best in counties just at the edge of metropolitan expansion and in the sparsely populated Flint Hills, where young families may live on old 80-acre farms but make their living commuting to two jobs in Wichita or Topeka or greater Kansas City, shopping not in the boarded-up county seat storefronts but driving 50 or 100 miles to the nearest mall. Historically, these counties are places where people have deep roots, but many of them have been moving out, and the new residents are oriented to the

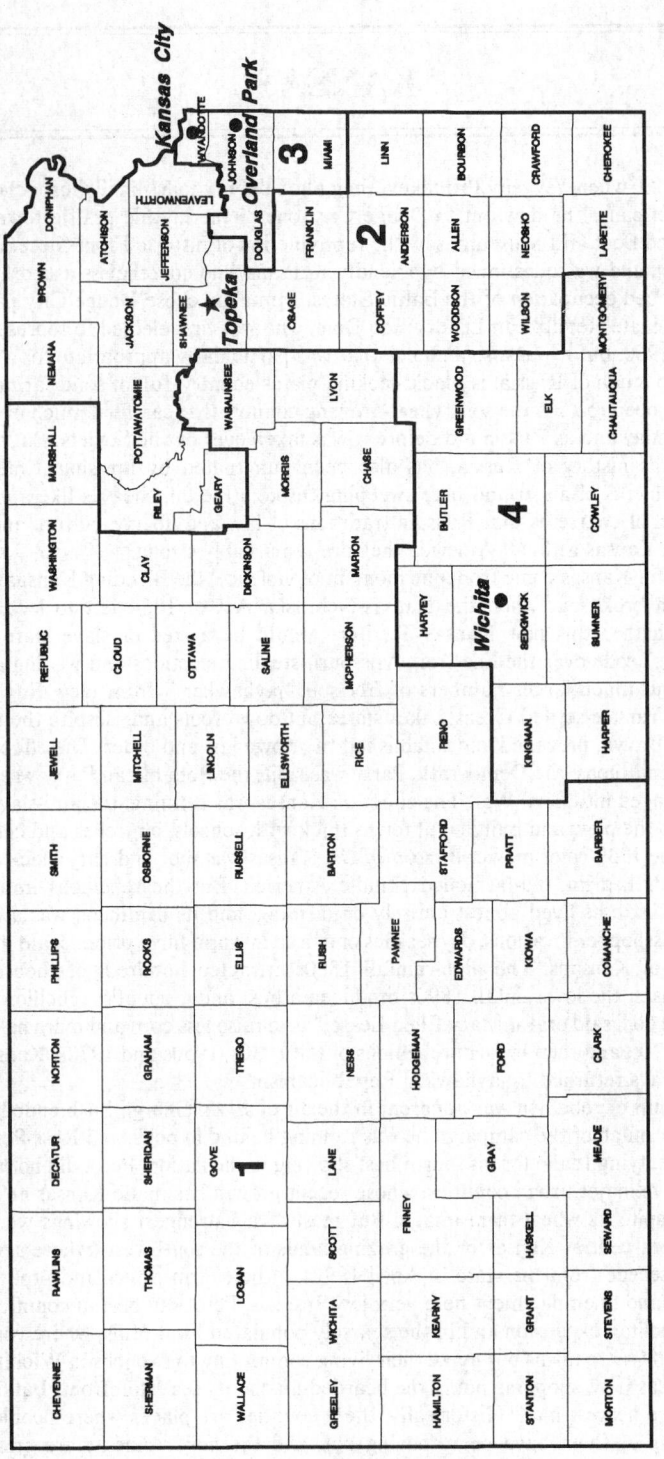

Interstates rather than the courthouse squares. It seems likely that the Perot vote comes in Kansas, as in other states, from the less deeply rooted, from newcomers with a tradition of civic involvement but with none of it in their lives until the Texas billionaire came along.

Governor. One reason for Kansas's sour mood in 1992 was discontent—continued discontent might be a better way to put it—with the leadership of state government. In 1990, the state's voters repudiated both of their last two governors: two-termer John Carlin lost a comeback race in the Democratic primary, and incumbent Republican Mike Hayden, after surviving the primary, lost the general election. The story goes back to 1985, when Carlin as governor and Hayden as state house speaker passed a property tax reform that mandated the first reclassification and reappraisal in more than 20 years and exempted business inventories, farm machinery and livestock—anything with enough money to afford a lobby—from the property tax rolls. When the reform went into effect with so many exemptions, ordinary voters' property taxes suddenly zoomed upward with no new governmental services to show for it.

The winner of the 1990 governor's race, by a 49%–43% margin, was Joan Finney, state treasurer for 16 years, an antiabortion Democrat, a onetime aide to Republican Senator Frank Carlson and an accomplished harpist, characterized by some as refreshingly frank and others as an oddball. Finney carried the urban areas except for Lawrence and Manhattan, two university towns; Hayden carried all of the sparsely populated counties west of Hays. Finney appointed five women to an 11-person cabinet, and worked to cut spending and lower property taxes in almost all the 304 school districts. But her relationship with the legislature has been a fractious one, and her job rating in late 1992 was very low. The 1992 legislative elections came as a jolt: Republicans won control of the state House and Democratic Speaker Marvin Barkis was beaten by 33-year-old carpet layer, Jene Vickrey, who was backed by the Word of Life Fellowship and other Christian conservatives. This was not necessarily a loss for Finney, since Barkis was poised to run against her; it is evidence of a concerted effort by the Christian right to take control of the state Republican Party, an effort evidently to concentrate more on state than on national politics. The governor's race for 1994 must be considered very much up for grabs. By May 1993, Finney already faced primary challenges from state legislator Joan Wagnon, and Barkis was still planning to run; even Finney's Lieutenant Governor, James Francisco, said he was considering a bid against her.

Senators. Senator Bob Dole is one of the towering politicians of his time: chairman of the Senate Finance Committee in the early 1980s, Senate Republican leader since 1984. He emerged from election night 1992 as the most powerful Republican voice in the country, immediately reminding the nation and Bill Clinton that 57% of Americans had voted against Clinton and that he, as leader of 44 Republicans in a Senate whose rules leave them far from powerless, would try to represent all of them. "A little gridlock might be good from time to time," he said. The aggressiveness, the mixture of conciliatory language with clear threats of political hardball, the crisp tongue and sharp humor, are all vintage Bob Dole. Dole is not only one of the most successful politicians of the second half of the 20th century but one of the most enduring. Grievously injured in World War II combat in the first days of Harry Truman's Administration, he took his seat in Congress in the last days of Dwight Eisenhower's. As he ran for his fifth Senate term in 1992, he had served 32 years in Congress, longer than all but three other Senators (Inouye, Thurmond, Byrd), longer as a Republican in Congress than anyone but House Republican Leader Robert Michel. Dole has had his disappointments in national politics. He was the vice presidential candidate on Gerald Ford's losing ticket in 1976, and not an especially popular one. He got little support when he ran for president in 1980. When he did run a serious race in 1988, and seemed on the verge of winning, he lost the New Hampshire primary to George Bush, and then his campaign came apart. Yet by early 1993, Dole was being mentioned again as a presidential candidate, though in 1996 he will turn 73, an age at which only Ronald Reagan has been elected president, and will have to overcome the disadvantages that have prevented Senate leaders as talented as Robert Taft, Lyndon Johnson, and Dole himself from winning presidential nomination. But no one should count him out. How to account for

Dole's endurance? He is a hard worker who still retains an acerbic sense of humor; he has consistently held to certain basic principles, though he is not at all a political theorist; he has earned the respect that a politician can win only by persevering through hard times as well as good, by being bloodied by defeat and coming back to fight against the odds and win a victory.

The son of a cream-and-egg station operator in Russell, Kansas, Dole didn't seem headed for college when he went into the Army during World War II. In Italy in April 1945, just three weeks before V-E Day, he was seriously injured; this strong-bodied high school athlete lost nearly half his weight, almost died, and spent four years in hospital wards. Regarded by some as a hopeless case, he went through largely successful rehabilitation programs, although he does not have use of his right hand and still suffers considerable pain. This may help to explain his sometimes bitter attitude and his support for the handicapped. But it also explains how he advanced himself from county attorney to congressman in a tough 1960 primary, from obscure backbench congressman to a U.S. senator in 1968, from a little-known freshman to Richard Nixon's Republican National Committee chairman in 1971, his first moment of national renown.

One consistent theme of Dole's career has been tough Republican partisanship. He came by it naturally—in Russell, Kansas, not just the banker and the country club member, but the mechanic at the garage and the clerk at the feed store are Republicans—and with no sense that it excludes compassion for the helpless. It was this partisanship that propelled him to volunteer to defend the Nixon Administration when he first came to a very anti-Nixon Senate in 1969, that prompted Nixon to name him Republican National Committee chairman in 1971, and that led Gerald Ford's advisers to believe that Dole's nomination as vice president would propitiate Reagan conservatives in 1976. But Dole also had disappointments. He was shoved out of the RNC when Richard Nixon needed a place for George Bush in 1973, he had his toughest Senate race and was nearly defeated by lawyer-doctor Bill Roy in 1974, and his vice presidential campaign brought him brickbats from the press without convincing Reagan Republicans that he was one of them.

In some important ways, he isn't. He has the old Midwestern Republican's horror of budget deficits, and he is willing to raise taxes to prevent them. As Finance chairman, he loyally floor-managed the Reagan tax cuts of 1981. But, largely on his own hook, he came back in 1982 with the tax-raising TEFRA bill which he passed almost entirely with Republican votes. His disdain for supply-siders in general and for Jack Kemp in particular is legendary. "The good news is that a busload of supply-side economists went off a cliff," he joked. "The bad news is that there were three empty seats." The feeling is mutual: Bob Dole, said Newt Gingrich, is "the tax collector for the welfare state." On other issues, it should be added, Dole is a consistent and hard-fighting conservative. He has always been antiabortion, as indeed every politician was when Dole was first elected to Congress, and he used the abortion issue sharply against Roy in 1974. He has always been a backer of big defense budgets and of an assertive foreign policy, and has thrown scorn on Democrats who in his view would not support U.S. troops. He was the sharpest critic of Bill Clinton's lies about his draft record in the 1992 campaign and led the fight to codify the ban on gays in the military in early 1993. This combination of issue stands, and the knowledge that they are sincerely held, has positioned him well to lead Senate Republicans. He won the party leadership by a narrow margin in 1984, over Ted Stevens, Richard Lugar and James McClure, but his hold on it quickly became secure. His command of Senate procedure is ample, his word is reliable, his relations with different sorts of Republicans and with Democratic leaders amicable enough to keep the flow of business going. He is an old-fashioned politician who does his own work and doesn't delegate much; this hurt his ill-fated 1988 presidential candidacy, but helps his floor leadership.

From his defeat in the 1988 presidential race, he has rebounded as he has before. His bitterness at George Bush after the New Hampshire primary ("stop lying about my record," he said live on NBC) was genuine, but once Bush was in the White House he worked loyally for him. It surely helped that Bush appointed Elizabeth Dole as Secretary of Labor (she later resigned to become head of the American Red Cross in late 1990). He got Republican senators to uphold all but three of Bush's vetoes, even on China (the one Bush veto override came in the House) and provided key votes for Bush's version of the Clean Air Act. A civil rights supporter for years, and the man who fashioned the compromise that got the Voting Rights Act renewed in 1982, Dole followed the administration lead in opposing several civil rights bills as quota measures and then backing a compromise in the fall of 1991. He supported Bush's policies in the Gulf war, despite some personal lobbying against it by Ross Perot. Dole did undercut Bush—or help him abandon his own promise—on taxes when during the 1990 budget summit talks, he helped ditch Bush's capital gains cut and thus increased pressure for income tax rises; Bush ended up repudiating the budget summit agreement in the 1992 campaign, but Dole didn't. Nevertheless, by the end of the Bush term, Dole was a strong Bush partisan, attacking Bill Clinton in the Senate about the explanation of his draft record, and presiding over a tearful after-election dinner for the defeated President.

For the Clinton term, Dole has promised similar partisanship. After the election, he loudly criticized independent counsel Lawrence Walsh's blatantly political Friday-before-election indictment of Caspar Weinberger and called for an investigation of Walsh himself. He opposed the Clinton economic plan without wanting to get into the details of advancing a plan of his own; he has not ruled out a managed competition healthcare reform, but is not open to mandates on business. While his personal relations with Clinton seem pleasant, he is the one man on Capitol Hill whose opposition could threaten any Clinton initiative there, as in early April 1993 when Dole successfuly held together Senate Republicans to filibuster Clinton's economic stimulus plan which the president eventually had to withdraw.

Republicans are excellently positioned to make gains in the Senate in 1994, since 21 of the 34 seats up are held by Democrats. Dole almost surely will be the most visible and articulate Republican in Washington during the Clinton term. Whether he will emerge as a presidential candidate is of course unclear. He does have a deep distrust for Jack Kemp, who some believe will emerge as frontrunner. And he seems to have some affinity with Ross Perot's constituency, which was especially large in Kansas. But he has never run the kind of large organization which seems necessary in a presidential campaign. Dole's standing in Kansas remains strong. For all his national prominence, he stays involved in local issues—the wheat program which he has long supported and ethanol subsidies backed by Dole's friend and contributor Dwayne Andreas. In 1991, there were rumors that Dole was tired of the Senate and might retire, and Congressman Dan Glickman gave serious thought to running for the seat. But Dole decided to run, Glickman backed down, and Dole was easily reelected, even as the Bush ticket was stumbling to a 39% victory in Kansas.

Nancy Kassebaum, first elected in 1978, has little of Dole's strong partisanship or celebrity, but has proved to be a thoughtful legislator to whom colleagues listen and one of steely will to whom they pay respect. She came to the Senate with minimal experience in public office but a fine political legacy as the daughter of 1936 Republican presidential nominee Alf Landon, who died in 1987 at age 100; and she has shown some pretty shrewd political and policy instincts in office. Interestingly, her greatest impact has been on foreign affairs, where she has often proved prescient. She was a major player in the passage of sanctions against South Africa, and has been key in determining the conditions under which they should be scaled back. She came forward in June 1990, with Dan Glickman, to urge a cutoff of $700 million in credit guarantees for Iraq for food purchases, which Saddam Hussein was actually using to acquire arms. This was opposed heartily by the Bush Administration, a monumental blunder in retrospect, since it might have deterred Saddam Hussein from invading Kuwait and would, in any case, have made him militarily weaker. Kassebaum was again far ahead of the curve, calling, after a June 1992 trip there, for United Nations peacekeepers in famine-torn orderless Somalia. Again, the Bush Administration opposed her, and then switched, deciding in November 1992 to send U.S. troops; many lives would have been saved, and U.S. military forces might not have been required in such numbers, if Kassebaum's advice had been taken earlier.

Despite her partisan pedigree, Kassebaum sometimes opposed and has often seemed uncomfortable with some Republican stands in the Reagan and Bush years; she is now ranking Republican on the Labor and Human Resources Committee and a strong supporter of international family planning, which they have opposed, as well as pro-choice at home. On health care, she reintroduced a bill in 1993 calling for an annual limit on insurance premium rate increases and requiring that insurance carriers offer a basic benefits package determined by an independent commission. She has worked for bipartisan budget agreements like the budget summit of 1990, which supply-siders have opposed. She switched her vote to preserve key funding for SDI in fall 1992; she was one of the few Republicans who voted for cable TV reregulation.

After the 1992 election, she wrote in a *Washington Post* op-ed piece that the Republican Party must "reinvent itself," taking its traditional limited government approach to abortion and cutting the federal budget deficit. In December 1992, she co-founded, with former Congressmen Tom Campbell and Warren Rudman, the Republican Majority Coalition to combat the rise of the religious right in Republican politics. Kassebaum's approach is widely popular in Kansas. After winning a relatively close race against Bill Roy in 1978, she was easily reelected in 1984 and 1990, the latter time despite an earlier promise to serve only two terms.

Presidential politics. Kansas, traditionally heavily Republican in presidential politics, was not so in 1992. Ross Perot ran well in spring polls here, and got 27% of the vote, and Bill Clinton led George Bush in some fall polls. The eventual Bush victory here was by an unimpressive margin. The relatively low percentages for Bush in 1992 and 1988 may also reflect an adverse reaction to the man who dispatched Bob Dole's presidential hopes. You can see a similar disappointment factor in Edmund Muskie's Maine in 1972, George Romney's Michigan in 1968, Edward Kennedy's Massachusetts in 1980 and Gary Hart's Colorado in 1984, in all of which the winning nominee did worse than expected in the nomination loser's state.

Congressional districting. Kansas lost one of its five seats in the 1990 Census. The 5th District of freshman Republican Dick Nichols disappeared; he ran in the 4th and lost the primary to a state senator who had already been running hard against incumbent Democrat Dan Glickman.

The People: Est. Pop. 1992: 2,523,000; Pop. 1990: 2,477,574, up 1.8% 1990–1992. 1.0% of U.S. total, 32d largest; 31% rural. Median age: 32.9 years. 13.8% 65 years and over. 90.1% White, 5.8% Black, 3.8% Hispanic origin, 1.3% Asian. Households: 58.5% married couple families; 28% married couple fams. w. children; 48% college educ.; median household income: $27,291; per capita income: $13,300; 67.9% owner occupied housing; median house value: $52,200; median monthly rent: $285. 4.2% Unemployment. Voting age pop.: 1,815,960. Registered voters (1992): 1,365,849; 424,478 D (31%), 587,303 R (43%); 354,068 unaffiliated and minor parties (26%).

Political Lineup: Governor, Joan M. Finney (D); Lt. Gov., James Francisco (D); Secy. of State, Bill Graves (R); Atty. Gen., Robert Stephan (R); Treasurer, Sally Thompson (D); Commissioner of Insurance, Ronald L. Todd (R). State Senate, 40 (27 R and 13 D); State House of Representatives, 125 (66 R and 59 D). Senators, Robert Dole (R) and Nancy Landon Kassebaum (R). Representatives, 4 (2 R and 2 D).

1992 Presidential Vote

Bush (R)	449,469	(39%)
Clinton (D)	389,704	(34%)
Perot (I)	311,316	(27%)

1988 Presidential Vote

Bush (R)	549,049	(56%)
Dukakis (D)	422,636	(43%)

1992 Democratic Presidential Primary

Clinton	82,145	(51%)
Tsongas	24,413	(15%)
Brown	20,811	(13%)
Other	10,723	(7%)
None of the Names Shown	22,159	(14%)

1992 Republican Presidential Primary

Bush	132,131	(62%)
Buchanan	31,494	(15%)
Other	14,121	(7%)
None of the Names Shown	35,450	(17%)

GOVERNOR

Gov. Joan Finney (D)

Elected 1990, term expires Jan. 1995; b. Feb. 12, 1925, Topeka; home, Topeka; Washburn U., B.A. 1982; Catholic; married (Spencer).

Career: A.A., Sen. Frank Carlson, 1953–69; Shawnee Cnty. Election Commissioner, 1970–72; A.A., Mayor of Topeka, 1973–74; KS Treas., 1974–90.

Office: State Capitol, 2d Fl., Topeka 66617, 913-296-3232.

Election Results

1990 gen.	Joan Finney (D)	380,609	(49%)
	Mike Hayden (R)	333,589	(43%)
	Christina Campbell-Cline (I) . . .	69,127	(9%)
1990 prim.	Joan Finney (D)	81,250	(47%)
	John W. Carlin (D)	79,406	(46%)
	Fred Phelps (D)	11,572	(7%)
1986 gen.	Mike Hayden (R)	436,267	(52%)
	Tom Docking (D)	404,338	(48%)

SENATORS

Sen. Robert Dole (R)

Elected 1968, seat up 1998; b. July 22, 1923, Russell; home, Russell; U. of KS, A.B., Washburn U., LL.B. 1952; United Methodist; married (Elizabeth).

Career: Army, 1943–48 (WWII); KS House of Reps., 1951–53; Russell Cnty. Atty., 1953–61; U.S. House of Reps., 1960–68; RNC Chmn., 1971–73; U.S. Senate Majority Ldr., 1984–86; Minority Ldr., 1986–present.

Offices: 141 HSOB 20510, 202-224-6521. Also 636 Minnesota Ave., Kansas City 66101, 913-371-6108; 444 S.E. Quincy, #392, Topeka 66683, 913-295-2745; 100 N. Broadway, Wichita 67202, 316-263-4956; and 310 N. Pine, Pittsburg 66762, 316-232-2030.

Committees: *Minority Leader. Agriculture, Nutrition and Forestry* (2d of 8 R): Agricultural Production and Stabilization of Prices; Nutrition and Investigations; Rural Development and Rural Electrification. *Finance* (2d of 9 R): Energy and Agricultural Taxation; Medicare and Long-Term Care; Social Security and Family Policy (RMM). *Rules and Administration* (5th of 7 R). *Joint Committee on Taxation* (5th of 5).

Group Ratings

	ADA	ACLU	CDF	COPE	CFA	LCV	ACU	NTLC	NSI	COC	CEI
1992	5	5	20	17	25	0	93	72	100	90	75
1991	5	—	45	17	22	13	86	—	—	80	70

494   KANSAS

National Journal Ratings

	1991 LIB — 1991 CONS		1992 LIB — 1992 CONS	
Economic	9%	— 87%	0%	— 89%
Social	14%	— 77%	11%	— 86%
Foreign	0%	— 87%	10%	— 80%

Key Votes of the 102d Congress

1. $ for Homeownership FOR	5. Clarence Thomas Nom. FOR	9. Use Force in Gulf FOR
2. Have Cap Gains Debate FOR	6. Lmt Death Row Appeal FOR	10. Keep Salvador Aid FOR
3. Remove Budget Walls AGN	7. Handgun Wait/5-Day FOR	11. Cut $1B from SDI AGN
4. Ban Striker Replace AGN	8. Abortion Gag Rule FOR	12. Override China MFN AGN

Key Votes of the 103d Congress

1. Family Leave AGN	2. HIV Immigrants AGN	3. Clinton Budget AGN

Election Results

1992 general	Robert Dole (R)	706,246	(63%)	($3,542,989)
	Gloria O'Dell (D)	349,525	(31%)	($249,359)
	Christina Campbell-Cline (I)	45,423	(4%)	
	Other	25,253	(2%)	
1992 primary	Robert Dole (R)	244,480	(80%)	
	Richard Warren Rodewald (R).	59,589	(20%)	
1986 general	Robert Dole (R)	576,902	(70%)	($1,517,585)
	Guy MacDonald (D).	246,664	(30%)	

Sen. Nancy Landon Kassebaum (R)

Elected 1978, seat up 1996; b. July 29, 1932, Topeka; home, Burdick; U. of KS, B.A. 1954, U. of MI, M.A. 1956; Episcopalian; divorced.

Career: Maize Sch. Bd. Mbr., 1972–75; Staff, U.S. Sen. James Pearson, 1975.

Offices: 302 RSOB 20510, 202-224-4774. Also 444 S.E. Quincy, Box 51, Topeka 66683, 913-295-2888; 911 N. Main, Garden City 67846, 316-276-3423; 4200 Somerset, #152, Prairie Village 66208, 913-648-3103; and 111 N. Market, #120, Wichita 67202, 316-269-6251.

Committees: *Foreign Relations* (3d of 8 R): African Affairs; European Affairs; International Economic Policy, Trade, Oceans and Environment (RMM). *Indian Affairs* (6th of 8 R). *Labor and Human Resources* (RMM of 7 R): Children, Family, Drugs and Alcoholism; Education, Arts and Humanities; Labor. *Joint Committee on the Organization of Congress* (8th of 12).

Group Ratings

	ADA	ACLU	CDF	COPE	CFA	LCV	ACU	NTLC	NSI	COC	CEI
1992	25	41	20	25	33	33	67	56	90	100	73
1991	35	—	27	17	28	40	62	—	—	80	58

National Journal Ratings

	1991 LIB — 1991 CONS			1992 LIB — 1992 CONS	
Economic	32%	—	66%	15%	—	80%
Social	48%	—	51%	35%	—	63%
Foreign	41%	—	58%	34%	—	63%

Key Votes of the 102d Congress

1. $ for Homeownership	FOR	5. Clarence Thomas Nom.	FOR	9. Use Force in Gulf	FOR
2. Have Cap Gains Debate	AGN	6. Lmt Death Row Appeal	FOR	10. Keep Salvador Aid	AGN
3. Remove Budget Walls	AGN	7. Handgun Wait/5-Day	FOR	11. Cut $1B from SDI	FOR
4. Ban Striker Replace	AGN	8. Abortion Gag Rule	AGN	12. Override China MFN	AGN

Key Votes of the 103d Congress

1. Family Leave	AGN	2. HIV Immigrants	AGN	3. Clinton Budget	AGN

Election Results

1990 general	Nancy Landon Kassebaum (R)	578,605	(74%)	($521,140)
	Dick Williams (D)...................	207,491	(26%)	($16,627)
1990 primary	Nancy Landon Kassebaum (R)	267,946	(87%)	
	R. Gregory Walstrom (R)..............	39,379	(13%)	
1984 general	Nancy Landon Kassebaum (R)	757,402	(76%)	($355,077)
	James R. Maher (D).................	211,664	(21%)	($30,444)

FIRST DISTRICT

"A prairie is not any old piece of flatland in the Midwest," writes Kansas-born reporter Dennis Farney. "No, a prairie is wine-colored grass, dancing in the wind. A prairie is a sun-splashed hillside, bright with wild flowers. A prairie is a fleeting cloud shadow, the song of the meadowlark. It is the wild land that has never felt the slash of the plow." This prairie once covered almost all of Kansas. Now only a little virgin prairie can still be found, in the Flint Hills region west and south of Topeka, where the waist-deep sea of grass still waves in the wind as it did when the pioneers on the Santa Fe Trail went west through here some 150 years ago; there are proposals to make it a national park. Most of the Kansas prairie has long since been transformed by agriculture. Much of it was grazing land, first for buffalo, then for the cattle driven to Kansas railheads like Abilene and Dodge City in the 1870s and 1880s, a brief moment in history recaptured with varying accuracy in movies over a much longer span, and commemorated in Dodge City's Boot Hill Museum. Then, after the harsh winter of 1886–87 wiped out the cattle herds, came the plow and barbed wire (commemorated in LaCrosse's Barbed Wire Museum), which enabled farmers to keep livestock out of their wheatfields. The farmers also brought to this vacant landscape Yankee civilization, with its schools and churches and colleges, and some foreign traditions as well, like the Cathedral of the Plains built by German Catholics.

Now this farming civilization holds on precariously in much of western Kansas. The 19th Century settlers organized these steppes into the same square townships and counties as their fathers had the heavily watered and forested midwestern states from which they came. The 66 western Kansas counties that make up the state's 1st Congressional District (almost everywhere from the Flint Hills and Abilene west) increased from 76,000 people in 1870 to 570,000 in 1890; then growth slowed to 666,000 in 1940 and dropped to 619,000 in 1990. Since 1980, almost every county here has dropped in population; exceptions are the natural gas exploration areas around Dodge City, Salina and German-Catholic Ellis County, which still has the high birth rates characteristic of most American Catholic communities 30 years ago. Life isn't dismal in the "Big First" (only the Nebraska 3d and the North and South Dakota at-large seats contain more counties), but community institutions are threatened by slow growth, and talented young

496   KANSAS

people move elsewhere to get ahead in life.

Western Kansans know plenty about national and international issues, yet politics here tends to revolve around the details of farm policy and getting the government to help maintain communities as they have grown up over the years. The congressman here, Republican Pat Roberts, spends most of his time on such matters. Roberts comes from a fine Kansas Republican background: his great-grandfather founded Kansas's second oldest newspaper and his father, Wes Roberts, was briefly Republican National Committee chairman in the Eisenhower years. Pat Roberts spent two years as an aide to Senator Frank Carlson and 12 years as chief aide to 1st District Congressman Keith Sebelius. He seems to see himself as protecting Great Plains farmers from outsiders—tax reformers, UN apparatchiks, tax collectors—who ignorantly and carelessly cause them problems while engaged in work of their own. Naturally, he serves on the Agriculture Committee, where he is now ranking Republican. He was a leader in hammering out the 1990 farm bill. Rather than seek ever-higher subsidies, as some Democrats do, Roberts sought to shape programs enabling business-smart farmers to make hay. He sold the Bush Administration on a blueprint for food safety legislation. He opposes Democratic subsidy-hunters who ally with the maritime interests by backing cargo preference, which he attacks as "nothing more than legalized extortion of underdeveloped countries and American agricultural producers."

Roberts serves as co-chairman of the House Rural Health Care Caucus, and has sought to strengthen the National Health Service Corps which attracts health professionals to places like rural Kansas—he's trying to keep hospitals and clinics open in these rural communities. He also gets involved in internal House matters. He was ranking Republican on the task force investigating the House Post Office, where he tried unsuccessfully to get immunity for its chief of staff there whose testimony might have implicated members. He tried to stop members from using public money to join legislative caucuses and publicized the $300,000 owed by members to the House restaurant. He has Kansas's most conservative voting record, except sometimes on foreign policy, where he may be reflecting the area's ancestral isolationism. But mostly he looks after matters relating to the special problems of western Kansas.

For 1992, redistricting predictably added counties to the east, including the home base of 5th District freshman Dick Nichols. But Nichols, his district abolished, didn't relish campaigning against the popular Roberts over the vastness of the 1st and moved into the Wichita-based 4th, where he lost the Republican primary. Roberts was reelected by a huge margin.

The People: Pop. 1990: 619,371; 51% rural; 17% age 65+; 92% White; 1% Black; 1% Asian; 3% Other; 5% Hispanic origin. Voting age pop.: 452,347; 1% Black; 4% Hispanic origin. Households: 62% married couple families; 28% married couple fams. w. children; 43% college educ.; median household income: $23,433; per capita income: $11,328; median gross rent: $297; median house value: $38,000.

1992 Presidential Vote

Bush (R) 122,621   (42%)
Perot (I). 85,004   (29%)
Clinton (D) 81,423   (28%)

1988 Presidential Vote

Bush (R) 157,070   (61%)
Dukakis (D). 101,697   (39%)

Rep. Pat Roberts (R)

Elected 1980; b. Apr. 20, 1936, Topeka; home, Dodge City; KS St. U., B.A. 1958; United Methodist; married (Franki).

Career: Marine Corps, 1958–62; Co-owner, editor, *The Westsider* (AZ newspaper) 1962–67; A.A., U.S. Sen. Frank Carlson, 1967–68; A.A., U.S. Rep. Keith Sebelius, 1968–80.

Offices: 1126 LHOB 20515, 202-225-2715. Also P.O. Box 550, Dodge City 67801, 316-227-2244; P.O. Box 128, Norton 67654, 913-877-2454; P.O. Box 1128, Hutchinson 67502, 316-665-6138; and P.O. Box 1334, Salina 67402, 913-825-5409.

Committees: *Agriculture* (RMM of 19 R). *House Administration* (3d of 7 R): Accounts (RMM); Elections; Libraries and Memorials. *Joint Committee on Printing* (4th of 5). *Joint Committee on the Library* (5th of 5).

Group Ratings

	ADA	ACLU	COPE	CDF	CFA	LCV	ACU	NTLC	NSI	COC	CEI
1992	10	4	17	20	33	0	88	80	100	88	80
1991	5	—	0	10	33	0	83	—	—	90	83

National Journal Ratings

	1991 LIB — 1991 CONS	1992 LIB — 1992 CONS
Economic	0% — 96%	16% — 80%
Social	0% — 84%	0% — 85%
Foreign	36% — 62%	18% — 74%

Key Votes of the 102d Congress

1. Ban Striker Replace AGN	5. Handgun Wait/7-Day AGN	9. Use Force in Gulf FOR
2. $ for Homeownership FOR	6. Overseas Mil. Abortion AGN	10. US Mil. Abroad $ Cut AGN
3. Tax Rich/Cut Mid Cls. AGN	7. Obscn. Art NEA $ Ban FOR	11. Limit SDI Funds AGN
4. FY93/$15B Def. Cut AGN	8. Death Pen. from Jury *	12. Cuba Trade Embargo AGN

Key Votes of the 103d Congress

1. Family Leave AGN	2. Deficit Reduction AGN	3. Stimulus Plan AGN

Election Results

1992 general	Pat Roberts (R)	94,165	(70%)	($601,655)
	Duane West (D)	37,826	(28%)	($64,850)
	Other	3,286	(2%)	
1992 primary	Pat Roberts (R), unopposed			
1990 general	Pat Roberts (R)	102,974	(63%)	($156,356)
	Duane West (D)	61,396	(37%)	($16,701)

SECOND DISTRICT

The green plains of eastern Kansas have seen more than their share of American history. Here, on bluffs above the Missouri River, Fort Leavenworth was built in 1827, famous for years as for its war college and military prison and now the oldest U.S. fort west of the Mississippi. In the 1850s, newly founded towns along the Kansas River and along the Missouri line were the centers of "Bleeding Kansas," where the pro-slavery bushwhackers set up a state capital in tiny Lecompton and anti-slavery New Englanders set up their stronghold down the river at

Lawrence. Farther up the river is Fort Riley, once an outpost against the Indians, now a major Army base threatening, even after the end of the Cold War, to expand into adjacent farm fields, and Manhattan, home of Kansas State University. Topeka, the state capital, sits here on a low bluff above the river: almost 40 years ago it was the city whose system of legal segregation was overturned in the 1954 landmark case, *Brown v. Board of Education.* Farther south, on the Missouri border, are the hills called "the Balkans." Here coal miners, often of Eastern European origin, lived in and near towns like Pittsburg and Girard, once a center of American socialism, where Clarence Darrow and Upton Sinclair made pilgrimages, and its paper, *Appeal to Reason*, had a nationwide 750,000 circulation.

Most of these disparate areas, Topeka and Manhattan, Fort Riley and Fort Leavenworth, wheat-growing counties and the Balkans—most of eastern Kansas except the Kansas City metropolitan area—make up the 2d Congressional District of Kansas. This is the remaining Kansas district most changed by redistricting: it lost Lawrence and the Flint Hills country, and gained the Balkans and much of the now defunct 5th District. The heritage here has been Republican ever since jayhawk Republicans defeated bushwhacker Democrats once the votes were counted honestly in the 1850s. Yet the 2d District and Topeka was the home of Alf Landon, 1936 Republican candidate for president, the only major party nominee in history who lived to be 100. Yet the 2d District has elected Democrats to the House for 20 of the last 24 years—testimony that here, as in so many parts of the country, talented political entrepreneurs are disproportionately Democrats.

One such is the current congressman, Jim Slattery. Born and raised in Atchison County farmland, he won a state legislative seat in 1972 while still in law school in Topeka. He was speaker pro tem of the state House at age 28 in 1976, left the legislature to make money in real estate in 1978, then ran for Congress in the recession year of 1982 against a notably weak Republican incumbent and won. In his first term, Slattery won a seat on the Energy and Commerce Committee—the most coveted committee in the House. In his second term, he won a seat on Budget where he backed the 1990 budget summit and its tax increases. In 1991 and 1992, he pushed to limit production of the B-2 bomber to only 20 units and got the House to zero out the $11 billion Superconducting Supercollider (the Senate put the money back in). He likes to spot loopholes and plug them: one bill eliminated a $67 million windfall that lenders had been receiving from government overpayments for interest on student loans, and another got eligibility for SSI medical benefits extended to families of military personnel overseas. He was an author of a consumer protection provision in the cable TV reregulation law which passed over President Bush's veto. Other Slattery initiatives include an inspector general for the House, whistleblower protection in the nuclear industry, and setting aside radio frequencies for experimental electrical and natural gas meter reading projects. His *National Journal* voting record hovers about 50–50 on economic, cultural and foreign issues.

To some of his colleagues, Slattery must look like an opportunist; he is plainly energetic and engaged, a prime example of the policy entrepreneurs who hold so many historically Republican seats for the Democrats. Slattery's problem is that his hold in recent years, since he supported the 1990 budget summit agreement, has grown perceptibly weaker. His percentage declined to 63% in 1990 and, with the new district lines, to 56% in 1992. That's still an impressive figure, and well ahead of the 50% Bill Clinton would likely have received in a two-candidate race; also, Republican freshman Dick Nichols chose not to run here but in the Wichita-based 4th instead when his 5th District was abolished in redistricting. It will be interesting to see whether Slattery sticks to his sometimes maverick ways or goes down the line for the Clinton Administration, and whether his constituents vote for him for the energetic work he does on a wide variety of second-line issues, or whether they vote him up or down on the performance of the Democratic administration and Congress on first-line issues.

The People: Pop. 1990: 619,385; 41% rural; 14% age 65+; 88% White; 6% Black; 1% Amer. Indian; 1% Asian; 1% Other; 3% Hispanic origin. Voting age pop.: 457,819; 6% Black; 2% Hispanic origin.

Households: 60% married couple families; 29% married couple fams. w. children; 44% college educ.; median household income: $24,903; per capita income: $11,662; median gross rent: $344; median house value: $44,000.

1992 Presidential Vote			1988 Presidential Vote		
Bush (R)	98,884	(36%)	Bush (R)	126,878	(54%)
Clinton (D)	98,457	(36%)	Dukakis (D)	107,003	(46%)
Perot (I)	75,549	(28%)			

Rep. Jim Slattery (D)

Elected 1982; b. Aug. 4, 1948, Good Intent; home, Topeka; Washburn U., B.S. 1970, J.D. 1974, Netherlands Schl. of Intl. Bus. and Econ., 1969–70; Catholic; married (Linda).

Career: Army Natl. Guard, 1970–75; KS House of Reps., 1972–78; Real Estate agent, 1974–78; Pres., Brosius, Slattery & Meyer, Inc., 1979–82;

Offices: 2243 RHOB 20515, 202-225-6601. Also 700 SW Jackson, #803, Topeka 66603, 913-233-2503; and 1001 N. Broadway, P.O. Box 1306, Pittsburg 66762, 316-231-6040.

Committees: *Energy and Commerce* (12th of 27 D): Commerce, Consumer Protection and Competitiveness; Health and the Environment; Telecommunications and Finance. *Veterans' Affairs* (7th of 21 D): Compensation, Pension and Insurance (Chmn.); Education, Training and Employment.

Group Ratings

	ADA	ACLU	COPE	CDF	CFA	LCV	ACU	NTLC	NSI	COC	CEI
1992	75	74	83	60	67	63	28	50	90	50	39
1991	40	—	67	50	67	54	40	—	—	50	39

National Journal Ratings

	1991 LIB — 1991 CONS		1992 LIB — 1992 CONS	
Economic	52% —	46%	55% —	44%
Social	54% —	44%	55% —	44%
Foreign	43% —	55%	52% —	46%

Key Votes of the 102d Congress

1. Ban Striker Replace	FOR	5. Handgun Wait/7-Day	AGN	9. Use Force in Gulf	FOR
2. $ for Homeownership	AGN	6. Overseas Mil. Abortion	FOR	10. US Mil. Abroad $ Cut	AGN
3. Tax Rich/Cut Mid Cls.	FOR	7. Obscn. Art NEA $ Ban	FOR	11. Limit SDI Funds	FOR
4. FY93/$15B Def. Cut	FOR	8. Death Pen. from Jury	AGN	12. Cuba Trade Embargo	FOR

Key Votes of the 103d Congress

1. Family Leave	AGN	2. Deficit Reduction	FOR	3. Stimulus Plan	FOR

Election Results

1992 general	Jim Slattery (D)	151,019	(56%)	($742,215)
	Jim Van Slyke (R)	109,801	(41%)	($36,704)
	Other	7,986	(3%)	
1992 primary	Jim Slattery (D), unopposed			
1990 general	Jim Slattery (D)	99,093	(63%)	($504,861)
	Scott Morgan (R)	58,643	(37%)	($84,568)

THIRD DISTRICT

Kansas City is one of those metro areas that sits astride a state line; more than one-third of its residents live west of the line in Kansas, where the low-lying land near the Missouri River used to house one of the nation's largest stockyards. This is still a working-class town with a few dilapidated looking streets and lots of modest frame houses, and the largest black neighborhood in the state. It is heavily ethnic and Catholic, and supports a Democratic machine politics not found anywhere west of here. To the south, separated from Missouri by just a single small street, is Johnson County, the fastest-growing and highest-income part of Kansas. Adjacent to Kansas City, Missouri's highest income area, starting just a few blocks west of Country Club Plaza (which claims to be the nation's oldest shopping center), Johnson County is a newer version of Kansas City's affluent neighborhoods, with gleaming office parks and burgeoning shopping centers, colonial houses on cul-de-sac streets and upscale condominium units. It is also one of the most Republican parts of a Republican state, and when rural Kansas is upset with farm prices or programs and starts leaning Democratic, Johnson County provides a strong Republican anchor. Yet when an issue pits metropolitan areas against rural—liquor by the drink, the oil severance tax, property tax reassessment—Johnson County votes metropolitan, for bars, for taxing oilmen and against reassessors.

Growth patterns here are a paradigm of those throughout the country: over the last 50 years, working-class Kansas City has hardly grown at all (and cast fewer votes in 1992 than in 1940), while Johnson County has grown, at first steadily, and then in the 1970s and 1980s, explosively. In 1940, Kansas City's Wyandotte County cast 66,000 votes to Johnson's 16,000; in 1960, Wyandotte cast 76,000 to Johnson's 65,000; in 1988, Wyandotte's 61,000 was overwhelmed by Johnson's 195,000. That pattern seemed to guarantee eternal Republican margins here, but suburban disenchantment with George Bush, after four years of falling real estate values and a white-collar recession, produced a small margin for Bill Clinton in 1992.

The 3d Congressional District of Kansas includes both Kansas City and Johnson County, plus most of Douglas County and Lawrence, site of the University of Kansas, to the west and semi-rural Miami County to the south. This has long been a Republican district, electing Republican congressmen who never became well known in Washington but ran well enough in Johnson County to win. The latest in that line is Jan Meyers, who in 1967 became a member of the Overland Park City Council, a part-time body that usually met at night, and in 1972 was elected to the Kansas Senate, also a part-time body, meeting in Topeka 60 miles away. In 1978, she ran for the U.S. Senate and finished fourth in a primary field of 10 with 10% of the vote. In 1984, she gave up her four-year state Senate seat and ran for Congress when the 3d District incumbent retired. This time she won a five-candidate primary with 35% and Johnson County's demographic strength enabled her to beat the mayor of Kansas City in the general 63%–32%.

Meyers is known as a moderate, is pro-choice on abortion, has middle-of-the-road positions on economic, cultural and foreign policy issues. She works on local projects—the I-435-Nall interchange, a $750,000 grant for a neglected and homeless children's center—and worked with other Republicans to develop a health care bill. On Foreign Affairs, she backed the Freedom Support Act providing U.S. aid to Russia. She was hurt a bit by anti-incumbent backlash in 1992. Attacked for using a special House Post Office box for campaign money in the 1980s, she had primary opposition in 1992 from an outspoken conservative state senator, Kerry Patrick; she ran ads the last three weeks calling him a liar and let voters know that she terminated her use of the controversial post office box as soon as she learned of its existence. She won 56%–33% in the four-candidate primary—a decisive margin, but not a stunning victory for an incumbent. Her general election percentages, previously above 70%, fell to a still solid 60% and 58% in 1990 and 1992. In December 1992, Meyers was named ranking Republican on the Small Business Committee, the first time a woman has held a ranking post on a standing committee since Florence Dwyer of New Jersey was ranking Republican on Government Operations in 1972.

The People: Pop. 1990: 619,445; 7% rural; 10% age 65+; 87% White; 9% Black; 1% Amer. Indian; 2% Asian; 1% Other; 3% Hispanic origin. Voting age pop.: 456,132; 8% Black; 3% Hispanic origin. Households: 57% married couple families; 28% married couple fams. w. children; 60% college educ.; median household income: $34,275; per capita income: $16,585; median gross rent: $454; median house value: $75,300.

1992 Presidential Vote			1988 Presidential Vote		
Clinton (D)	116,396	(38%)	Bush (R)	134,809	(54%)
Bush (R)	113,963	(37%)	Dukakis (D)	113,511	(46%)
Perot (I)	75,413	(25%)			

Rep. Jan Meyers (R)

Elected 1984; b. July 20, 1928, Lincoln, NE; home, Overland Park; Williams Wood Col., A.A. 1948, U. of NE, B.A. 1951; United Methodist; married (Louis).

Career: Overland Park City Cncl., 1967–72; KS Senate, 1972–84.

Offices: 2338 RHOB 20515, 202-225-2865. Also 204 Fed. Bldg., Kansas City 66101, 913-621-0832; and 7133 W. 95th St., #217, Overland Park 66212, 913-383-2013.

Committees: *Foreign Affairs* (10th of 18 R): Economic Policy, Trade and Environment; Europe and the Middle East. *Small Business* (RMM of 18 R): SBA Legislation and the General Economy (RMM).

Group Ratings

	ADA	ACLU	COPE	CDF	CFA	LCV	ACU	NTLC	NSI	COC	CEI
1992	30	35	36	20	40	50	72	63	100	88	70
1991	25	—	33	20	44	54	75	—	—	70	60

National Journal Ratings

	1991 LIB — 1991 CONS		1992 LIB — 1992 CONS	
Economic	26% —	73%	21% —	76%
Social	39% —	60%	38% —	60%
Foreign	42% —	57%	38% —	56%

Key Votes of the 102d Congress

1. Ban Striker Replace	AGN	5. Handgun Wait/7-Day	FOR	9. Use Force in Gulf	FOR
2. $ for Homeownership	FOR	6. Overseas Mil. Abortion	FOR	10. US Mil. Abroad $ Cut	AGN
3. Tax Rich/Cut Mid Cls.	AGN	7. Obscn. Art NEA $ Ban	FOR	11. Limit SDI Funds	FOR
4. FY93/$15B Def. Cut	AGN	8. Death Pen. from Jury	FOR	12. Cuba Trade Embargo	FOR

Key Votes of the 103d Congress

1. Family Leave	AGN	2. Deficit Reduction	AGN	3. Stimulus Plan	AGN

Election Results

1992 general	Jan Meyers (R)	169,929	(58%)	($430,833)
	Tom Love (D)	110,076	(38%)	
	Frank Kaul (LIB)	12,791	(4%)	
1992 primary	Jan Meyers (R)	35,911	(56%)	
	Kerry Patrick (R)	20,953	(33%)	
	Jim Hall (R)	3,947	(6%)	
	Gary Adams (R)	3,014	(5%)	
1990 general	Jan Meyers (R)	88,725	(60%)	($209,986)
	Leroy Jones (D)	58,923	(40%)	($76,007)

FOURTH DISTRICT

Wichita is Kansas's largest Kansas-only metropolitan area, smaller than million-plus metro Kansas City, but a Great Plains metropolis of the magnitude of Omaha or Tulsa. Its beginnings were as an agricultural trade center; it grew with local oil and gas discoveries in the 1920s. But its real impetus came during World War II and the years just after, when aircraft factories sprouted up here on the Kansas plains and Wichita suddenly became the nation's major producer of small planes. Today the big three—Cessna, Beechcraft and Learjet—are all located here; so is the bulk of Boeing's military business: this is the general aviation center of America. Wichita has also become a regional health center in the common Great Plains pattern, as rural counties are unable to attract new doctors or maintain hospitals, and people from miles around come to the metropolis for treatment. Wichita has also become a big center for franchising (Pizza Hut and Rent-A-Center are the two largest) and telemarketing. This economic mix has left Wichita vulnerable to the business cycle. General aviation is exquisitely sensitive to fluctuations in business profits: businessmen love buying company planes, but they're easily done without when times get tight or gas prices rise. Low oil prices hurt the Wichita area, with its dozens of stripper wells, and farm prices are notoriously volatile. The national recession of the early 1990s caught up with Wichita later than most states; by 1993, the general aviation industry was reeling here because of record layoffs at Boeing, farm prices were declining and relatively steady oil and health industries could not make up the difference.

Kansas's 4th Congressional District is centered around Wichita, covering wheat-growing areas to the east and west, but with most of its people in Wichita and Sedgwick County. It votes Republican in most statewide elections, and it voted for George Bush again in 1992. But for nearly two decades, it has voted for Democrat Dan Glickman for the House. Glickman is a fine example of how politically adept Democrats, creatively engaged in policy-making and energetic enough to keep in close local touch, can hold otherwise Republican districts in such numbers as to give the Democrats seemingly perpetual control of the House. The 1992 election, though Glickman won by a decisive margin, suggests why that era may be coming to an end. For Glickman, since he was first elected in 1976, has been one of the most creative and effective such Democratic members, with strong local roots; if he can be given a tough race, so can just about any Democrat with a less than entirely safe Democratic district.

But Glickman got something of a reward: quite unexpectedly, in January 1993, Speaker Thomas Foley unseated as chairman of the Intelligence Committee Dave McCurdy of Oklahoma, whom he has long considered overambitious and disloyal, and made Glickman chairman instead, giving him a one-year extension of his six allowed years on the committee so he could serve a full term as chairman. Glickman was not considered an in-depth student of intelligence agencies. Yet he has shown prescience on issues in this area, as in 1990, when he sought an amendment to the farm bill disqualifying Iraq from loan guarantees and other food import assistance. Glickman, with Nancy Kassebaum, fought for this aid cutoff even though it might cost Kansas farmers sales and was opposed vigorously by the Bush Administration, which asserted until July 27 that it would worsen relations between the U.S. and Iraq. It passed anyway, as a provision to the farm bill, 234–175; five days later Saddam Hussein invaded Kuwait. Glickman brings good judgment, a capacity for hard and intellectual curiosity to his work as chairman, as well as, perhaps, a certain geographic kinship: for CIA Director James Woolsey is from Tulsa, Oklahoma, just a few miles down the Arkansas River from Wichita.

Heretofore, Glickman's key committee assignment was as chairman of the Agriculture General Commodities subcommittee (formerly Wheat, Soybeans and Feed Grains), obviously of great interest to Kansas. He was one of the key shapers of the 1990 farm bill, beating back competing demands for higher subsidies (tying grain support prices to fertilizer costs, setting soybeans at $6.25 per bushel) and more limits (no subsidies for producers with incomes over $100,000) to get a bill that could pass on the floor and be signed into law.

Beyond Agriculture, Glickman has a raft of projects. One major item, later endorsed by candidate Bill Clinton, was a lifetime ban on U.S. trade negotiators working for foreign interests. He is seeking revision of the onerous RICO criminal statute and he favors uniform product liability laws, especially for aircraft—putting him on the opposite side of the criminal defense bar and trial lawyers who are usually backed by most Democrats. He harries leaders of the House, urging them to cancel a proposed $70 million U.S. Capitol visitors' center, calling for a House Administrator, in response to the House bank scandal, to oversee day-to-day operations. He is often alert to local interests; he inserted into the vetoed 1992 tax bill a repeal of the luxury tax on general aviation and passed into law a bill allowing sales to schools of fresh food (i.e., by Pizza Hut).

Glickman has considered running for the Senate, most recently in 1991 when it wasn't clear that Bob Dole was running again, but has declined to take on either Bob Dole or Nancy Kassebaum. Instead, he got serious opposition himself in 1992 from Republican state Senator Eric Yost, a conservative who opposes abortion and advocates cuts in Social Security and Medicare entitlements. Then, after the redistricting plan eliminated Republican freshman Dick Nichols' 5th District and placed him in the western plains 1st District of Pat Roberts, Nichols moved into the 4th. Yost squawked and said his move "epitomizes everything the citizens despise in politicians this year" and, with all his spadework, beat Nichols 45%–34% in the primary, with 21% to former Wichita Police Chief Richard LaMunyon. In the general, Glickman was getting whacked from all sides. Yost attacked him vigorously. His record of 105 overdrafts on the House bank put him on the defensive. To protest his vote for cable reregulation, Multimedia Cablevision, the Wichita area cable operator, ran frequent daily ads endorsing Yost and hitting Glickman for the overdrafts and junketeering; Glickman filed complaints, and got to run 600 free editorial responses the last week. The National Rifle Association, angered by his vote for the Brady bill, poured money into anti-Glickman ads attacking him just before the election for voting for higher taxes, including the general aviation luxury tax in the 1990 budget summit agreement. But Glickman vastly outspent Yost and the independent groups combined, lashing Yost as an extremist in his antiabortion views (which may have had special resonance in Wichita, given the August 1991 Operation Rescue demonstrations there). Glickman ended up winning by 52%–42% (with 6% for a Libertarian candidate), well below the 65% he won in 1986 in his toughest challenge of that decade.

For the 103d Congress, Glickman seems likely to shift focus from the many interesting but often second-line issues he has concentrated on and to work more prominently on first-line national issues. In the 102d Congress, he had introduced a healthcare bill with Kassebaum requiring insurance carriers to offer a basic benefits package while establishing annual limits on premium rate increases; he has also been working as part of the House Democratic leadership's small group of legislation shapers. Campaign finance is another preoccupation of Glickman's: he wants a $550,000 per cycle spending limit on House races, a $110,000 aggregate limit on PAC contributions, a 100% tax credit for in-state contributions and reduced broadcast rates. Having survived the toughest challenge he has received since upsetting a Republican incumbent in 1976, Glickman seems to realize that with a Democratic president he will be held to a tough standard on major issues. On election night he said, "I guarantee you ... that if we don't get a national healthcare bill, you deserve to kick us all out." He has indeed set a tough standard.

The People: Pop. 1990: 619,373; 24% rural; 14% age 65+; 87% White; 7% Black; 1% Amer. Indian; 2% Asian; 2% Other; 3% Hispanic origin. Voting age pop.: 449,274; 6% Black; 3% Hispanic origin. Households: 59% married couple families; 28% married couple fams. w. children; 48% college educ.; median household income: $28,308; per capita income: $13,623; median gross rent: $376; median house value: $52,000.

1992 Presidential Vote		
Bush (R)	114,001	(40%)
Clinton (D)	93,428	(33%)
Perot (I)	75,350	(27%)

1988 Presidential Vote		
Bush (R)	135,292	(57%)
Dukakis (D)	100,425	(43%)

Rep. Dan Glickman (D)

Elected 1976; b. Nov. 24, 1944, Wichita; home, Wichita; U. of MI, B.A. 1966; George Washington U., J.D. 1969; Jewish; married (Rhoda).

Career: Practicing atty., 1969–76; Pres., Wichita Bd. of Educ., 1973–76.

Offices: 2371 RHOB 20515, 202-225-6216. Also 401 N. Market, #134, Wichita 67202, 316-262-8396; and 325 N. Penn, Independence 67301, 316-331-8056.

Committees: *Agriculture* (5th of 28 D): Department Operations and Nutrition; General Farm Commodities. *Intelligence (Permanent Select)* (Chmn. of 12 D): Program and Budget Authorization (Chmn.). *Judiciary* (8th of 21 D): Administrative Law and Governmental Relations; Crime and Criminal Justice; Economic and Commercial Law. *Science, Space and Technology* (3d of 33 D): Technology, Environment and Aviation.

Group Ratings

	ADA	ACLU	COPE	CDF	CFA	LCV	ACU	NTLC	NSI	COC	CEI
1992	75	65	64	60	73	50	32	17	100	63	37
1991	50	—	67	70	77	54	32	—	—	33	40

National Journal Ratings

	1991 LIB	—	1991 CONS	1992 LIB	—	1992 CONS
Economic	54%	—	46%	61%	—	38%
Social	60%	—	38%	55%	—	44%
Foreign	43%	—	57%	65%	—	33%

Key Votes of the 102d Congress

1. Ban Striker Replace	FOR	5. Handgun Wait/7-Day	FOR	9. Use Force in Gulf	FOR
2. $ for Homeownership	AGN	6. Overseas Mil. Abortion	FOR	10. US Mil. Abroad $ Cut	FOR
3. Tax Rich/Cut Mid Cls.	FOR	7. Obscn. Art NEA $ Ban	FOR	11. Limit SDI Funds	FOR
4. FY93/$15B Def. Cut	FOR	8. Death Pen. from Jury	AGN	12. Cuba Trade Embargo	FOR

Key Votes of the 103d Congress

1. Family Leave	AGN	2. Deficit Reduction	FOR	3. Stimulus Plan	FOR

Election Results

1992 general	Dan Glickman (D)	143,671	(52%)	($1,046,769)
	Eric R. Yost (R)	117,070	(42%)	($396,254)
	Seth L. Warren (L)	17,275	(6%)	
1992 primary	Dan Glickman (D), unopposed			
1990 general	Dan Glickman (D)	112,015	(71%)	($355,581)
	Roger M. Grund, Sr. (R)	46,283	(29%)	($4,317)

KENTUCKY

In no state has the outward style of life changed as little in the late 20th Century as in Kentucky. Demographically, it is still mostly rural, with well under half its population in the big metropolitan areas of Louisville, Lexington and the Kentucky towns across the Ohio River from Cincinnati. Economically, it still remains heavily dependent on industries important for 100 years: coal, cigarettes, whiskey, heavy manufacturing and auto assembly. Over the last two decades, Kentucky has moved more slowly than the rest of the country in shifting from manufacturing to service jobs. Culturally, Kentucky revels in a southern style that derives more from Virginia cavaliers than from Appalachian mountaineers. But there is a rural tradition still in the rickety cabins in the coal mining Appalachians or in unpainted houses in the soggy lowlands beneath the levees by the Mississippi River. The small-town 19th Century courthouses and the white-fenced bluegrass horse country farms look much the same as they did decades ago, even if fast food restaurants and small shopping centers have sprouted up on roads at the edge of town. Kentucky has splendid civic institutions, the positive side of a deep-rooted people, but there is also a negative side: population growth of just 30% over the past 50 years, reflecting much outmigration and very few outsiders moving in. Kentuckians today are still largely descendants of settlers who poured over the mountains in the 40 years after Daniel Boone made his way through the Cumberland Gap in 1775, raising Kentucky's population from 73,000 at the time of the first census in 1790 to 564,000 in 1820. Satellite dishes and four-lane highways have brought modern civilization into hollows and lowland farms which lacked indoor plumbing and electricity within living memory, but people in this state still have a strong attachment to roots, to place and to family.

Politically, Kentucky seems to have had little outward change. It is a state with hearty partisan competition, where most of the 120 counties vote today as they did in the period just after the Civil War. Most of the hill country was pro-Union and remains Republican today, except for counties where coal miners joined the United Mine Workers in the 1930s and became Democrats. The Bluegrass region and the western Jackson Purchase and Pennyrile areas were more likely to be slaveholding territory and today remain mostly Democratic, though Lexington, as it grows, has become more Republican. Louisville, with many German immigrants, was an anti-slavery town, and for years supported a strong Republican organization. These patterns, which have prevailed now for more than 100 years, are plainly apparent in the returns for senator in 1990, governor in 1991 and president in 1992.

But some change has come into this commonwealth, under its past three governors—and the focus of political attention here is almost always on the governor, because the office confers such patronage and such power—and because Kentucky is one of two states left (the other is Virginia) whose governor is currently ineligible to run for reelection after a single four-year term. (Though in November 1992, voters approved an amendment allowing all statewide officials elected in 1995 to serve a second consecutive term.) Governor Martha Layne Collins, elected in 1983, started a policy of massive tax breaks for new major industries; that attracted Toyota to the antique county seat of Georgetown, just north of Lexington, where it has generated much growth and become one of the state's big employers. Then Governor Wallace Wilkinson, elected in 1987, under pressure for equalizing localities' spending on schools, pushed through a massive education reform, the full effects of which are still to be seen (except for the negative fallout from raising taxes). Most recently, Governor Brereton Jones, elected in 1991, continued Kentucky's tax abatement program (evoking screams—and retaliatory tax breaks—from neighboring states) and sponsored a massive new health program, inspired partly by Humana, the big health services combine headquartered in Louisville.

The surface trappings of Kentucky politics look very much as they did a half century ago, and indeed, the factional fights in Democratic primaries have a lineage that goes back to the 1938 primary, when Senate Majority Leader Alben Barkley was challenged in the primary by Governor Happy Chandler. Chandler became senator, then baseball commissioner, then governor again in 1955, and at 88 supported Wilkinson in the 1987 primary. (Chandler died in June 1991 at the age of 92.) Barkley was later Harry Truman's vice president, then became a senator again and died mid-oration in 1956; his faction was led for years by Bert Combs, who was elected governor in 1959 and supported Jones in the 1991 primary before he died in a December 1991 flood at 80. But Democratic governors, once elected, had to grapple with new problems and have done so in new ways.

Kentucky Republicans also have a political tradition, though not much opportunity to show it recently. From their mountain base, and with strength in Louisville, they are strong enough to win some statewide elections and at one time (1967–71) held the governorship and both Senate seats. For a while, national and state politics diverged: Kentucky became more Republican in national races, becoming competitive only when the Democrats have run a southerner—and more Democratic in state races. The Democrats have won their two of their three highest percentages in history in the last two governor races, and the only Republican wins for senator have been Mitch McConnell's narrow victories in 1984 and 1990.

Governor. There is no question who stands at the apex of Kentucky politics: the governor. The governor's appointment powers are wide; this is not a state with a vibrant civil service tradition. The legislature meets only 60 days every two years; the governor can then shift around line items in the budget as he likes. The governor is also the undisputed leader of his state party. The one-term limit, applied to all statewide officials after Treasurer "Honest Dick" Tate absconded in 1888 with $250,000, has typically limited a governor's time, but not the powers he has within it.

Even so, the substantive reforms of the previous two governors are doing as much to shape life in Kentucky as the work of the incumbent since 1991, Brereton Jones. He and Lieutenant Governor Paul Patton have taken Martha Layne Collins's tax incentive strategy several steps further: "Locate your white-collar jobs in Kentucky, and the state will pay half your rent for 10 years and up to half your startup costs. Locate your manufacturing plant in Kentucky, and the state will reimburse your entire investment," he said in TV ads in 1992. Neighboring Ohio quickly screamed foul, then passed its own incentives in self-defense. Jones has also continued the implementation of Wallace Wilkinson's school reform program mandated by a 1989 state Supreme Court school financing equalization decision. The plan raises the legal dropout age from 16 to 18, increases aid to poorer school districts and rates schools' effectiveness by the achievements of its students with bonuses going to schools that improve and sanctions imposed on those that don't. The reforms also offer extended services and hours for students in need and will institute incentive pay for teachers starting in 1995; Wilkinson and the legislature also raised the sales tax to 6% to help pay for the plan. Jones has also signed a law allowing utilities to impose an "environmental surcharge" to recover the cost of installing scrubbers, and has pushed for a state bottle bill. He wants to expand Medicaid to provide universal healthcare coverage and to set up a health commission able to set rates for care if it exceeds limits set by the state.

Jones has a strange background for a Kentucky Democrat: he was a Republican legislator in

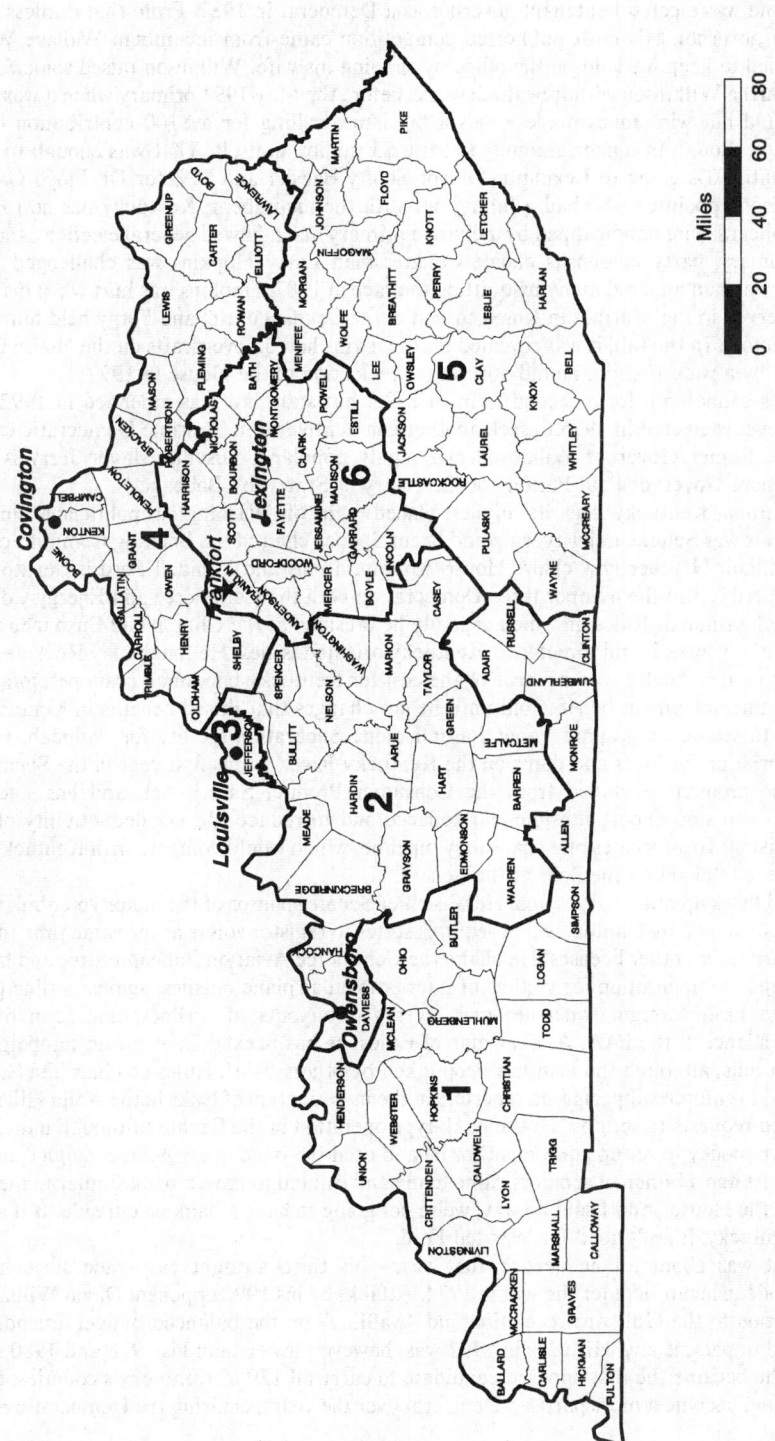

West Virginia in the 1960s, moved to Kentucky in 1972 to take over his wife's family's horse farm and was elected lieutenant governor as a Democrat in 1987. From that dutiless office, he ran for governor. His most publicized competition came from incumbent Wallace Wilkinson, who tried to keep his hold on the office by running his wife. Wilkinson raised some $3 million, but Martha Wilkinson withdrew three weeks before the May 1991 primary when it was apparent she could not win. Jones made ethics a big issue, calling for a $100 contribution limit, but collected enough in higher amounts to raise $3 million himself. That was enough to give him 38%, with 30% going to Lexington Mayor Scotty Baesler and 27% for Dr. Floyd G. Poore, a Wilkinson appointee who had a falling out with the incumbent; Kentucky has no runoff. The Republicans were handicapped by a divisive primary and a flawed general election candidate. In the primary, party consensus choice Congressman Larry Hopkins was challenged by Larry Forgy, who had angered many by quitting the race in 1987. Hopkins was hurt when his claims to have served in the Marines in Korea turned out to be inaccurate, and Forgy held him to a bare 51% victory. In the fall, it was revealed that Hopkins had 32 overdrafts on the House bank, and he lost by a wide margin; he did not run for reelection to the House in 1992.

Jones cannot run for a second term in 1995, but state law was amended in 1992 to allow whomever is elected in 1995 to seek another consecutive term. Possible Democratic candidates include former Governor Wilkinson and highly popular Louisville Mayor Jerry Abramson, Lieutenant Governor Paul Patton and Secretary of State Bob Babbage.

Senators. Kentucky has its highest-placed pair of Washington politicians since Earle Clements was Senate majority whip and Brent Spence chaired the Banking Committee in 1957–58: William Natcher now chairs House Appropriations and Wendell Ford is Senate majority whip. Ford is also the number three Democrat on both the Commerce and Energy Committees and is chairman of Rules, in which capacity he presided at the Clinton and Bush inaugurations. Much of his work is still directed at Kentucky-oriented issues. He fought Jay Rockefeller's coal tax for miners' health care because of the cost for Kentucky non-union coal operators. He held up the unemployment benefits bill until he got changes that raised benefits in Kentucky. He is trying to secure an Atomic Vapor Laser Isotope Separation facility for Paducah. He got an appropriation for locks and dams on the Kentucky River. In his first year in the Senate, he got tobacco products excluded from the Consumer Product Safety Act, and has since beaten attempts to stop export subsidies for tobacco and to reduce the tax deductibility of tobacco advertising. To advocates of a coal slurry pipeline, which would compete with Kentucky coal, he threatened "blood on the floor of the Senate."

Ford takes up other causes, too. He was chief Senate sponsor of the motor voter bill, vetoed by Bush but signed by Clinton, which requires states to register voters at the same time they renew their drivers' or other licenses. He chairs the Commerce Aviation Subcommittee and has fought for higher compensation for victims of international airplane crashes, against airline passenger fees, to limit foreign ownership and leveraged buyouts of airlines, and to maintain the independence of the FAA. As chairman of Rules, he has backed Democratic campaign finance reform bills, although the lead has been taken by others. With Rules co-chair Ted Stevens, he refused to enforce subpoenas on reporters in the investigation of leaks in the Anita Hill affair. He spurned requests to set up a House bank-type operation in the Senate (although initially he did approve money to set up equipment for it) and used the issue in a 1992 campaign spot: "About five years ago a bunch of senators came to me and wanted to have a bank similar to the one they had in the House. And I said no way, we're not going to have a bank on our side. If it ain't good for Kentucky, it ain't good for Wendell Ford."

That was about all he needed that year—his third straight easy race since he beat a Republican incumbent for the seat in 1974. Attacks by his 1992 opponent David Williams on his opposition to the Gulf war resolution and "waffling" on the balanced budget amendment had limited impact, if any. His 63% in 1992 was, however, lower than his 1986 and 1980 showings, when he became the first opposed candidate to carry all 120 of Kentucky's counties. He has, if anything, become a more partisan Democrat over the years, chairing the Democratic Senatorial

Campaign Committee from 1976–82, running for whip unsuccessfully against Alan Cranston in 1988, and seizing the post unopposed when Cranston was hobbled by illness and the Keating Five case in 1990. But with Majority Leader George Mitchell holding the reins pretty closely, Ford is more important on the issues he weighs in on than on Senate procedure generally.

Mitch McConnell, the only Republican to win a statewide race in Kentucky since 1968, is also one of the most partisan Republicans in the Senate. A hard-working defender of Republican causes and an assiduous attacker of Democrats, he had a perfect conservative *National Journal* voting record in 1991. He tends to Kentucky interests—backing tobacco causes, and keeping horse shows operating despite criticism by animal rights activists. On campaign finance reform, he took the lead role for Senate Republicans, killing during the Bush years any chance for the Boren-Byrd bill which would limit PAC contributions and introduce partial public financing. But McConnell was not able to get approval of his own version—no public financing, curbs on union activity, and curtailing out-of-state financing—and in late 1992 said he didn't think he could stop a Democratic plan by filibuster in 1993 or 1994. Nor did his arguments against the motor voter bill—he called it "auto fraudo"—prevent its approval. But sometimes McConnell is vindicated by results: he vitriolically opposed the "October surprise" investigation, and the charges turned out to be as flimsy as he said. Other McConnell crusades are not likely to be successful for a while: his campaign to cap the contingent fees of trial lawyers at 20% and his Pornography Victims Act, which would allow victims of sex crimes to win damages from producers of hard-core pornography that could be proved to have motivated the offender. On this last issue, McConnell is forming an interesting alliance of cultural conservatives and feminists.

McConnell also served on Foreign Relations through 1992. In 1991, in a bipartisan effort, he and Democrat Paul Sarbanes managed the foreign aid authorization, taking over from aging Claiborne Pell and confrontational Jesse Helms; McConnell and Sarbanes piloted the always controversial measure through to approval in the Senate and conference committee, for the first reauthorization since 1985 (though it went nowhere in the House). McConnell got two notable committee assignments for 1993: Appropriations, where he will also be ranking member on the Foreign Operations Subcommittee (he is an avid backer of Israel); and the Ethics Committee, where he will have to deal with the sexual harassment charges against Bob Packwood of Oregon (McConnell was a charter signatory of a sexual harassment guideline policy issued by the Women's Political Caucus in 1991).

Most of McConnell's adult life has been politics. He served on the staff of Senator Marlow Cook in the late 1960s, then moved back to Louisville and in 1977 won the office that had been Cook's political stepping stone, Jefferson County judge executive (the executive position in the county that includes Louisville and most of its suburbs). McConnell ran for the Senate in 1984, highlighting the weakness in incumbent Democrat Dee Huddleston's low profile with ads that showed bloodhounds sniffing for Huddleston in vacation locales where he had collected fees for speeches while the Senate was in session. For the 1990 election, McConnell worked hard, built up chits with the Bush White House, and pounced on the weaknesses of Democrat Harvey Sloane, onetime mayor of Louisville (1973–77, 1981–85) and Jefferson County judge executive (1986–89) and twice unsuccessful candidate for governor (1979, 1983). Sloane was hurt when the *Courier-Journal* (for years a Democratic and pro-Sloane paper) revealed that he had prescribed sleeping pills for himself after his DEA permit expired; McConnell interspersed his positive TV ads about show horses and the like with a spot showing a bottle of pills spilling onto a table as an announcer reminded viewers that Sloane had prescribed drugs for himself. In the end, McConnell's long-accumulated money and political adeptness enabled him to eke out a 52%–48% victory.

McConnell tried to bring his political skills to the chairmanship of the National Republican Senatorial Committee, but lost to Phil Gramm of Texas, 26–17 in 1990 and 20–19 in 1992. The latter time he argued that Gramm's presidential ambitions should preclude the Senate campaign job, but Gramm's record (Republicans thought at the time they had lost only one seat,

510   KENTUCKY

and after the Georgia runoff ended up even) evidently just saved him.

Presidential politics. After the 1988 election, Kentucky withdrew from the southern Super Tuesday primary in early March, and returned to voting in late May, with Arkansas—and was predictably ignored. The state is something of a barometer, however: Bill Clinton won the primary here in 1992, Al Gore in 1988 and George Bush both times. In the general election, Kentucky is competitive when Democrats run a southerner or two, and in 1992 Kentucky saw quite a lot of the national candidates.

Congressional districting. Kentucky lost a district from the 1990 Census and lost three incumbent congressmen to the ravages of House scandals or improprieties in 1992. The new plan sharply changed the 4th District, moving it out of the Jefferson County suburbs and east into the mountains, and in effect merged most of the old 5th and 7th Districts in the mountains, one very Republican and the other very Democratic, into a new 5th. The Republicans won the 5th and held the 4th, but they lost the 6th, when Larry Hopkins retired, to Lexington Mayor Scotty Baesler, the number two finisher in the 1991 Democratic gubernatorial primary.

The People: Est. Pop. 1992: 3,755,000; Pop. 1990: 3,685,296, up 1.9% 1990–1992. 1.5% of U.S. total, 23d largest; 48% rural. Median age: 33.0 years. 12.7% 65 years and over. 92.0% White, 7.1% Black. Households: 59.2% married couple families; 29% married couple fams. w. children; 33% college educ.; median household income: $22,534; per capita income: $11,153; 69.6% owner occupied housing; median house value: $50,500; median monthly rent: $250. 6.9% Unemployment. Voting age pop.: 2,731,202. Registered voters (1992): 2,076,263; 1,374,459 D (72%), 615,732 R (30%), 86,072 unaffiliated and minor parties (4%).

Political Lineup: Governor, Brereton C. Jones (D); Lt. Gov., Paul E. Patton (D); Secy. of State, Bob Babbage (D); Atty. Gen., Chris Gorman (D); Treasurer, Francis Jones Mills (D); Auditor, Ben Chandler (D). State Senate, 38 (25 D and 13 R); State House of Representatives, 100 (72 D and 28 R). Senators, Wendell H. Ford (D) and Mitch McConnell (R). Representatives, 6 (4 D and 2 R).

1992 Presidential Vote

Clinton (D)	665,104	(45%)
Bush (R)	617,178	(41%)
Perot (I)	203,944	(14%)

1992 Democratic Presidential Primary

Clinton	207,804	(56%)
Brown	30,709	(8%)
Tsongas	18,097	(5%)
Uncommitted	103,590	(28%)

1988 Presidential Vote

Bush (R)	734,281	(56%)
Dukakis (D)	580,368	(44%)

1992 Republican Presidential Primary

Bush	75,371	(75%)
Uncommitted	25,748	(25%)

GOVERNOR

Gov. Brereton C. Jones (D)

Elected 1991, term expires, Dec. 1995; b. June 27, 1939, Gallipolis, OH; home, Frankfort; U. of VA, B.S. 1961; Presbyterian; married (Libby).

Career: Real Estate Developer; Horse breeder; KY Lt. Gov., 1987–91.

Office: Office of the Governor, State Capitol, Frankfort 40601, 502-564-2611.

Election Results

1991 gen.	Brereton C. Jones (D)	540,648	(65%)
	Larry J. Hopkins (R)	294,452	(35%)
1991 prim.	Brereton C. Jones (D)	184,703	(38%)
	Scotty Baesler (D)	149,352	(30%)
	Dr. Floyd G. Poore (D)	132,060	(27%)
	Gatewood Galbraith (D)	25,834	(5%)
1987 gen.	Wallace G. Wilkinson (D)	504,674	(65%)
	John Harper (R)	273,141	(35%)

SENATORS

Sen. Wendell H. Ford (D)

Elected 1974, seat up 1998; b. Sep. 8, 1924, Thruston; home, Owensboro; U. of KY, MD Schl. of Insurance; Baptist; married (Jean).

Career: Army, 1944–46 (WWII); Army Natl. Guard 1949–62; Family insur. business; Chief A.A., Gov. Bert Combs, 1959–63; KY Senate, 1965–67; KY Lt. Gov., 1967–71; KY Gov., 1971–74.

Offices: 173-A RSOB 20510, 202-224-4343. Also 1072 New Fed. Bldg., Louisville 40202, 502-582-6251; 305 Fed. Bldg., Owensboro 42301, 502-685-5158; 343 Waller Ave., #204, Lexington 40504, 606-233-2484; and 19 U.S. P.O. and Crthse., Covington 41011, 606-491-7929.

Committees: *Majority Whip. Commerce, Science and Transportation* (3d of 11 D): Aviation (Chmn.); Communications; Consumer. *Energy and Natural Resources* (3d of 11 D): Energy Research and Development (Chmn.); Mineral Resources Development and Production; Water and Power. *Rules and Administration* (Chmn. of 9 D). *Joint Committee on Printing* (Chmn. of 5). *Joint Committee on the Organization of Congress* (3d of 12).

Group Ratings

	ADA	ACLU	CDF	COPE	CFA	LCV	ACU	NTLC	NSI	COC	CEI
1992	75	32	100	92	75	17	15	33	30	10	28
1991	50	—	82	75	65	7	47	—	—	10	33

National Journal Ratings

	1991 LIB — 1991 CONS			1992 LIB — 1992 CONS		
Economic	43%	—	56%	69%	—	27%
Social	28%	—	69%	35%	—	63%
Foreign	56%	—	42%	65%	—	26%

Key Votes of the 102d Congress

1. $ for Homeownership	AGN	5. Clarence Thomas Nom.	AGN	9. Use Force in Gulf	AGN
2. Have Cap Gains Debate	AGN	6. Lmt Death Row Appeal	FOR	10. Keep Salvador Aid	AGN
3. Remove Budget Walls	FOR	7. Handgun Wait/5-Day	FOR	11. Cut $1B from SDI	FOR
4. Ban Striker Replace	FOR	8. Abortion Gag Rule	FOR	12. Override China MFN	FOR

Key Votes of the 103d Congress

1. Family Leave	FOR	2. HIV Immigrants	AGN	3. Clinton Budget	FOR

Election Results

1992 general	Wendell H. Ford (D).................	836,888	(63%)	($2,321,131)
	David L. Williams (R)	476,604	(36%)	($335,304)
	Other............................	17,366	(1%)	
1992 primary	Wendell H. Ford (D), unopposed			
1986 general	Wendell H. Ford (D).................	503,755	(75%)	($1,201,624)
	Jackson M. Andrews (R)	173,330	(25%)	($58,572)

Sen. Mitch McConnell (R)

Elected 1984, seat up 1996; b. Feb. 20, 1942, Sheffield, AL; home, Louisville; U. of Louisville, B.A. 1964, U. of KY, J.D. 1967; Baptist; married (Elaine Chao).

Career: Chief Legis. Asst., U.S. Sen. Marlow Cook, 1967–70; Dep. Asst. Atty. Gen., 1974–75; Jefferson Cnty. Judge Exec., 1977–1984.

Offices: 120 RSOB 20510, 202-224-2541. Also 600 MLK Jr. Pl., #451, Louisville 40202, 502-582-6304; 700 Scott St., Fed. Bldg., #307, Covington 41011, 606-261-6304; Irvin Cobb Bldg., 602 Broadway, Paducah 42001, 502-442-4554; 1501-N S. Main St., London 40741, 606-864-2026; Fed. Bldg., 241 E. Main St., #102, Bowling Green 42101; and 155 E. Main St., #210, Lexington 40508, 606-252-1781.

Committees: *Agriculture, Nutrition and Forestry* (5th of 8 R): Agricultural Production and Stabilization of Prices; Domestic and Foreign Marketing and Product Promotion; Nutrition and Investigations (RMM). *Appropriations* (11th of 13 R): Commerce, Justice, State and Judiciary; Energy and Water Development; Foreign Operations (RMM); Military Construction. *Ethics* (Vice Chmn. of 3 R). *Rules and Administration* (6th of 7 R).

Group Ratings

	ADA	ACLU	CDF	COPE	CFA	LCV	ACU	NTLC	NSI	COC	CEI
1992	15	9	30	18	42	17	89	83	90	100	74
1991	0	—	36	17	11	13	90	—	—	90	70

National Journal Ratings

	1991 LIB — 1991 CONS			1992 LIB — 1992 CONS		
Economic	0%	—	91%	31%	—	68%
Social	0%	—	86%	17%	—	80%
Foreign	0%	—	87%	10%	—	80%

Key Votes of the 102d Congress

1. $ for Homeownership	FOR	5. Clarence Thomas Nom.	FOR	9. Use Force in Gulf	FOR
2. Have Cap Gains Debate	FOR	6. Lmt Death Row Appeal	FOR	10. Keep Salvador Aid	FOR
3. Remove Budget Walls	AGN	7. Handgun Wait/5-Day	AGN	11. Cut $1B from SDI	AGN
4. Ban Striker Replace	AGN	8. Abortion Gag Rule	FOR	12. Override China MFN	AGN

Key Votes of the 103d Congress

1. Family Leave	AGN	2. HIV Immigrants	AGN	3. Clinton Budget	AGN

Election Results

1990 general	Mitch McConnell (R)................	478,034	(52%)	($5,229,296)
	G. Harvey I. Sloane (D)...............	437,976	(48%)	($2,929,641)
1990 primary	Mitch McConnell (R).................	64,063	(89%)	
	Tommy Klein (R)	8,310	(11%)	
1984 general	Mitch McConnell (R)................	644,990	(50%)	($1,767,114)
	Walter D. (Dee) Huddleston (D)	639,721	(49%)	($2,444,091)

FIRST DISTRICT

Where the Ohio River joins the Mississippi—the intersection Huckleberry Finn and Jim missed in the fog—must have struck its early settlers as a site for a great city. But no Pittsburgh or St. Louis grew up on the fertile black soil at this confluence. Instead, the Kentucky land west of the dammed-up Tennessee and Cumberland Rivers was bought from the Chickasaw Indians by General Andrew Jackson and Governor Isaac Shelby in 1818—the Jackson Purchase, it is still called—and settled soon after by farmers. Most people here today are the descendants of these farmers, with memories of the generations that came before retained in family lore. Just to the east of the Tennessee and the Cumberland Rivers is the Pennyrile (after pennyroyal, a common variety of local wild mint), a land of low hills and small farms, where you find the west Kentucky coal fields, the site of much strip mining in recent years.

The 1st Congressional District of Kentucky is made up of the Jackson Purchase and much of the Pennyrile; following the 1992 redistricting, it stretches some 200 miles east of the Mississippi along the Tennessee border. There is a distinctive southern atmosphere here—in the crops that are grown, in the accents of the people, in the large number of blacks and in the fact that the big city people look to is more often Nashville than Louisville. Politically, the southern cultural tradition reinforced by low wage levels and economic growth make the Jackson Purchase and Pennyrile Democratic. Paducah, the largest city in the 1st, produced one of the most enduring Democratic politicians of this century, Alben Barkley, whose career from 1912–1956 included 14 years in the House, 24 in the Senate and four as vice president, and who keynoted four Democratic National Conventions. Since Barkley's time, the 1st District House seat has passed to winners of successive Democratic primaries, usually in upsets. One such was the defeat of Frank Stubblefield by Carroll Hubbard in 1974; another was the defeat of Hubbard by Tom Barlow in 1992.

Hubbard was arguably a victim of the House bank scandal: at first he said he had no overdrafts, then it turned out he had 152. But he had other problems as well. His support was not deep: when he ran for governor in 1979, he won 12% statewide and just 33% in the 1st District. And his position on the Banking Committee afforded him an opportunity to raise campaign contributions and speech honoraria from savings and loans (in mid-1990, he ranked near the top of the list in contributions from S&Ls), banks, home builders and credit bureaus. This ignoble relationship to special interest groups was brought out in lengthy articles in the *Louisville Courier-Journal* just days before the primary. They pointed out that Hubbard was an advocate of relaxed regulation of S&Ls—"He did basically what he thought the industry wanted him to do," former regulator Edwin Gray was quoted as saying. "He was the antithesis of a person who seemed to have the broad public interest at heart." Hubbard was probably not helped by the fact that his wife, Carol Hubbard, was running for the House from the 5th District in eastern Kentucky and was also receiving generous contributions from banking and credit interests. The upshot was that both Hubbards lost. Carol Hubbard won 17% in her primary; Carroll Hubbard won 45% in his, to 48% for opponent Tom Barlow.

By standard criteria, Barlow was one of the unlikelier winners of 1992. Raised and educated in the East, he worked for 11 years for the Natural Resources Defense Council and in the 1980s returned to his ancestral home, the town of Barlow, in Ballard County, just west of Paducah. There he directed sales for a phone equipment company and was Paducah's Kiwanian of the Year in 1991. He ran against Hubbard in 1986 and won 20% of the vote after Hubbard smeared him by saying he was a follower of Lyndon LaRouche. But in 1992 against Hubbard, Barlow carried the Jackson Purchase solidly. In the general, Barlow faced an active campaign from Republican Steve Hamrick who ran a traditional anti-Congress campaign; Barlow actually spoke out in favor of the congressional pay raise, citing the high cost for members to maintain two homes and that it was part of a larger ethics reform package. But Hamrick could only match George Bush's showing in the 1st, and Barlow won 60%–39%. Barlow has some interesting positions: he is antiabortion, in favor of more environmental protections than coal-producing Kentucky might like, favors nuclear power and putting the AVLIS plant in Paducah. He combines a *Mr. Smith Goes to Washington* freshness with some significant experience in Washington, and seems to bring a very different attitude toward representation than the Hubbards.

The People: Pop. 1990: 614,212; 61% rural; 15% age 65+; 91% White; 8% Black; 1% Hispanic origin. Voting age pop.: 460,440; 7% Black; 1% Hispanic origin. Households: 62% married couple families; 29% married couple fams. w. children; 28% college educ.; median household income: $20,331; per capita income: $10,238; median gross rent: $278; median house value: $40,200.

1992 Presidential Vote		
Clinton (D)	116,637	(48%)
Bush (R)	96,602	(39%)
Perot (I)	30,869	(13%)

1988 Presidential Vote		
Bush (R)	120,522	(54%)
Dukakis (D)	101,957	(46%)

Rep. Thomas J. Barlow, III (D)

Elected 1992; b. Aug. 7, 1940, Washington, DC; home, Paducah; Haverford Col., B.A. 1962; Methodist; married (Shirley).

Career: Asst. VP, Philadelphia Fidelity Bank, 1963–68; Rep., Natural Resources Defense Cncl., 1971–82; Sales Dir., Central Service Inc., 1986–92.

Offices: 1533 LHOB 20515, 202-225-3115. Also One Executive Blvd., #LL1, Paducah 42001, 502-444-7216.

Committees: *Agriculture* (19th of 28 D): Environment, Credit and Rural Development; Foreign Agriculture and Hunger; General Farm Commodities. *Merchant Marine and Fisheries* (24th of 29 D): Coast Guard and Navigation. *Natural Resources* (27th of 28 D): Energy and Mineral Resources.

Group Ratings and 102d Congress Votes: Newly Elected

Key Votes of the 103d Congress

1. Family Leave	FOR	2. Deficit Reduction	FOR	3. Stimulus Plan	FOR

Election Results

1992 general	Thomas J. Barlow, III (D)	128,524	(61%)	($209,090)
	Steve Hamrick (R)	83,088	(39%)	($66,705)
1992 primary	Thomas J. Barlow, III (D)	40,014	(48%)	
	Carroll Hubbard, Jr. (D).	37,188	(45%)	
	Charles T. Banken, Jr. (D)	6,019	(7%)	
1990 general	Carroll Hubbard, Jr. (D).	85,323	(87%)	($239,620)
	Marvin Seat (POP)	12,879	(13%)	

SECOND DISTRICT

More than 200 years ago, Americans began settling the limestone-soiled country of central Kentucky. In the 1770s and 1780s, they were staking out towns like Bardstown and starting academies and colleges; they were well-settled when Stephen Collins Foster wrote "My Old Kentucky Home" just before the Civil War. Tourists by the thousands flocked to Mammoth Cave, the world's largest accessible underground cavern, little noticing that the ground above it had given birth to thousands of soldiers for both the Union and the Confederacy. In the Civil War and in the wars of the 20th Century, the area would suffer disproportionate casualties; this is bellicose country. The 2d Congressional District of Kentucky, in its current boundaries, consists of much of the territory south and southwest of Louisville, starting with the southern Jefferson County suburbs and proceeding south to Bowling Green and west to Owensboro. This is rural and small town country, where most people have family roots that go back generations and a connection with the past not often found in big metropolitan areas. Civil War loyalties are reflected in the election returns here; Kentucky cast only 1% of its votes for native son Lincoln, but was deeply split on secession. A color-coded map of the current 2d District would show splotches of counties pro-South and splotches pro-Union, but the bits of color would only hint at the deep and often bitter feelings caused by the splits over the War and the losses people suffered—feelings of which current partisan preferences are a dim but persistent reflection.

William Natcher, chairman of the House Appropriations Committee and one of the House's most hard-working and conscientious members, has represented this district since he won a special election in 1953. He is one-of-a-kind—one of the few who make the House work, a splendid old stickler for doing things the way they are supposed to be done. He is, above all, meticulous and attentive to detail; he abhors waste and disorder; he is appalled by anything that smacks of corruption. He insists on doing what he regards as his duty, even when it means going through perfunctory motions. He has never missed a roll call, answering, by May 1993, some 13,696 roll call votes and 4,228 quorum calls—though he urges new members to miss a roll call early, so they do not become slaves to a record. He maintains a daily journal of his activities, and writes weekly history newsletters to his six grandchildren. He is often called on to take the speaker's chair in House proceedings, especially when a difficult issue is debated. He is the ideal presiding officer: courteous, scrupulously fair, but determined and able to keep the proceedings moving along. Natcher also, in the old-fashioned manner, resists relying on staff; he does his own reading and research and prides himself on being well-prepared. It may be argued that Natcher's punctiliousness wastes much of his time and that his self-reliance reduces the amount of information he can master. But his awesome devotion to duty sets a standard others might well aim for and increases his own power: every House member hesitates before taking on a man so universally esteemed as fair and well-prepared. "It takes someone very rash," says colleague Dale Kildee, "to even offer an amendment to his bill."

Natcher's ascension to the Appropriations chair tells how he does business. For four years, he ranked just behind Jamie Whitten of Mississippi, who set the record for congressional tenure in early 1992, but shortly afterward suffered a stroke which slowed him down perceptibly. Key House Democratic leaders caused Natcher to be made acting chairman in June 1992. He insisted he wanted to do nothing to "hurt my good friend" Whitten, but also insisted, "When my time comes, I want to be chairman of the committee." His time came after the 1992 election. House leaders convinced Whitten to step aside if he wasn't renominated by the Steering and Policy Committee; he wasn't, and Natcher was easily elected chairman. He also retains his chairmanship of the Labor-HHS-Education Subcommittee, which spends more than any other subcommittee except defense; he has been increasingly frustrated with having to make hard choices between education and health spending, and he surely resents being stuck with controversial amendments on abortion, which have led to the demise of some of his bills by presidential veto. Nonetheless, Natcher has an excellent record of managing his bills through the House.

Natcher brings the same hard work to his campaigns. "No campaign contributions were accepted by me from any source," he wrote in 1990, "and this has been my practice all through the years since I have been in politics." He usually spends under $10,000 of his own personal money on his campaign and stays in touch with voters by "graceful stealth," as Francis Clines of *The New York Times* puts it, by making his rounds of courthouse towns on days when Congress is not in session. "I liken running against Bill Natcher to running against God," one chastened opponent said. "He's up there by himself." Natcher has typically been returned to office by overwhelming margins and shows no sign of slowing down even though he turns 84 in 1993. Kentucky redistricters, aware that for all his propriety Natcher is willing to help along what he considers worthy projects in his home state, saw to it that he kept Owensboro and Bowling Green, though he only barely carried the portion of outer suburban Jefferson County they added to the 2d.

The People: Pop. 1990: 615,184; 56% rural; 11% age 65+; 93% White; 5% Black; 1% Asian; 1% Hispanic origin. Voting age pop.: 448,454; 5% Black; 1% Hispanic origin. Households: 65% married couple families; 33% married couple fams. w. children; 30% college educ.; median household income: $23,212; per capita income: $10,609; median gross rent: $310; median house value: $47,900.

1992 Presidential Vote			1988 Presidential Vote		
Bush (R)	107,318	(45%)	Bush (R)	122,880	(60%)
Clinton (D)	99,054	(41%)	Dukakis (D)	83,022	(40%)
Perot (I)	33,187	(14%)			

Rep. William H. Natcher (D)

Elected Aug. 1953; b. Sept. 11, 1909, Bowling Green; home, Bowling Green; W. KY U., A.B. 1930, OH St. U., LL.B. 1933; Baptist; married (Virginia).

Career: Navy, 1942–45 (WWII); Practicing atty., 1934–54; Fed. Conciliation Commissioner, W. Dist. of KY, 1936–37; Warren Cnty. Atty., 1937–49; Commonwealth Atty., 8th Judicial Dist. of KY, 1951–53.

Offices: 2333 RHOB, 202-225-3501. Also 414 E. 10th St., Bowling Green 42101, 502-842-7376; and 312 N. Mulberry St., #4, Elizabethtown 42701, 502-765-4360.

Committees: *Appropriations* (Chmn. of 37 D): Agriculture, Rural Development, Food and Drug Administration and Related Agencies; Commerce, Justice, State and Judiciary; Defense; District of Columbia; Energy and Water Development; Foreign Operations, Export Financing and Related Programs; Interior; Labor, Health and Human Services, and Education (Chmn.); Legislative; Military Construction; Transportation; Treasury, Postal Service, and General Government; VA, HUD, and Independent Agencies.

Group Ratings

	ADA	ACLU	COPE	CDF	CFA	LCV	ACU	NTLC	NSI	COC	CEI
1992	85	70	83	80	80	31	16	0	70	50	12
1991	50	—	100	90	72	46	20	—	—	30	9

National Journal Ratings

	1991 LIB — 1991 CONS		1992 LIB — 1992 CONS	
Economic	66%	— 32%	66%	— 31%
Social	48%	— 51%	66%	— 34%
Foreign	65%	— 33%	44%	— 50%

Key Votes of the 102d Congress

1. Ban Striker Replace	FOR	5. Handgun Wait/7-Day	AGN	9. Use Force in Gulf	AGN
2. $ for Homeownership	AGN	6. Overseas Mil. Abortion	AGN	10. US Mil. Abroad $ Cut	AGN
3. Tax Rich/Cut Mid Cls.	FOR	7. Obscn. Art NEA $ Ban	FOR	11. Limit SDI Funds	AGN
4. FY93/$15B Def. Cut	FOR	8. Death Pen. from Jury	AGN	12. Cuba Trade Embargo	AGN

Key Votes of the 103d Congress

1. Family Leave	FOR	2. Deficit Reduction	FOR	3. Stimulus Plan	FOR

Election Results

1992 general	William H. Natcher (D)	126,894	(61%)	($6,624)
	Bruce R. Bartley (R)	79,684	(39%)	($1,125)
1992 primary	William H. Natcher (D)	35,351	(71%)	
	Bob Evans (D)	10,072	(20%)	
	Paul D. Hamm (D)	4,428	(9%)	
1990 general	William H. Natcher (D)	77,057	(66%)	($6,768)
	Martin A. Tori (R)	39,624	(34%)	($144,315)

THIRD DISTRICT

At the falls of the Ohio River, Americans more than 200 years ago founded one of their first inland metropolises, the river port and industrial city of Louisville (pronounced *LOOuhv'l*). It is one of two major American cities today named for a man who was executed, King Louis XVI of France; the other is St. Paul. Far enough north to enjoy a temperate climate, Louisville nonetheless has always retained an air of the South; when Kentucky decided not to secede in 1861, the decision was not unanimous, and the culture of tidewater Virginia is still visible in the Louisville lawn party. Steamboats are still tied up in front of Louisville's downtown, primed to follow the channel around the falls of the Ohio which prompted George Rogers Clark to found the town in 1778. Mint juleps are served on the verandas of mansions, especially, but not only, during Derby week in May; horse racing is a preoccupation not just then, but throughout the year. Although the Ohio River is crossed with many bridges, and the accent across the river in Indiana may sound the same to outsiders, Louisville partakes of the cavalier culture that second sons of big landowners from the west of England brought to Virginia in the 17th Century and their heirs brought over the Appalachians to the valleys of Kentucky in the 18th Century.

Though Louisville's economy is not particularly southern, tobacco and cigarettes are a major business here, and so is distilling whiskey. Louisville still specializes in assembling large, clunky things like appliances and automobiles (Ford added jobs here in late 1992), and it has one of the nation's major enterprise zones. But its biggest business now is health: Humana, the nation's second-largest operator of for-profit hospitals, has its headquarters here a few blocks from the riverfront, in a Michael Graves building which is one of the monuments of post-modern architecture, and the Humana Festival is a creative mecca for playwrights. Politically, Louisville has always had some un-southern aspects, and has often voted against the rest of Kentucky; if its elite were Virginia cavaliers, many of its burghers were Germans and Pennsylvanians who made this river town a Republican and anti-slavery island in a secessionist and pro-slavery sea. Locally, Louisville and Jefferson County have long had a robust two-party politics, with successive Jefferson County judge executives, Republican Mitch McConnell and Democrat Harvey Sloane, running against each other for the U.S. Senate in 1990.

The 3d Congressional District of Kentucky includes all of Louisville and, after the 1992 redistricting, most of its Jefferson County suburbs—the blue-collar factory zones south of Churchill Downs and the affluent suburbs east of Louisville, running out toward Bluegrass country. Its congressman is Democrat Romano Mazzoli, who won the seat in 1970 by all of 211 votes over a Republican incumbent and has gone through one political peril after another. Mazzoli has, at one time or another, defied almost every rule of House politics, and yet has had some significant achievements. One rule he has violated is: get on a committee that can help you politically. He has spent more than 20 years on Judiciary, where he has supported many liberal causes—the Brady bill, for example, or the bill to ban capital punishment when it is disproportionately imposed on blacks. In 1992, he moved to give all Haitian refugees picked up by the Coast Guard temporary protective status. He spent the years from 1981 to 1986 trying to fashion an immigration reform measure, only to see it whipsawed; then he had the lead taken away from him by Judiciary Chairman Peter Rodino in 1985. That happened because Mazzoli violated another rule: on party issues, support the party line. Instead, he voted against the Democrats on the challenge of the election result in Indiana's 8th District, just across the Ohio River. A third rule: always consult with your colleagues. Known as a loner on his immigration subcommittee, Mazzoli lost his chairmanship in February 1989 to Bruce Morrison, who successfully sponsored a bill vastly expanding legal immigration. Mazzoli got his chair back when Morrison retired in 1991, and started working more closely and voting more often with the Democratic leadership. Rule four: don't antagonize your party's biggest interest groups. Mazzoli has long antagonized feminists by voting antiabortion and has a far from perfect labor voting record. A basic rule says don't vote against your area's major economic interests. But Mazzoli called for a stop to the "Joe Camel" advertising campaign and favored bans on smoking in selected public areas. Still another old rule: bring home the bacon. For years Mazzoli didn't much bother on district projects; only recently has he started plugging projects like the Belvedere Connector and the Louisville Waterfront Development Commission.

Most senior members of Congress pile up big campaign treasuries with money from interests they regulate. Mazzoli has refused to take PAC money since December 1989 when he had limited cash on hand and the prospect of serious opposition; he spends only 10% of his franking allowance. He calls for abolishing PAC contributions and further limits on individual contributions. It would be heartwarming to report that this principled politician has been reelected by the acclamation of a grateful public. But in fact he has had serious opposition in each of the last three elections. In 1988, former TV reporter and Humana executive Jeff Hutter got the AFL-CIO endorsement and held Mazzoli to an unimpressive 61%–39% primary win. Hutter ran again in 1990 along with Paul Bather, a black alderman; Mazzoli won 45% to Hutter's 32% and Bather's 22%—a deciding margin since Kentucky has no runoff. Then in the fall, Mazzoli's opponent, black Republican Al Brown, matched him in money; Mazzoli won with 61%. Redistricting added Republican areas to the district for 1992, and Mazzoli had an attractive opponent in state Representative Susan Stokes, a former teacher, civic volunteer and former mayor of Rolling Fields. Stokes attacked Mazzoli's stand on abortion: this was one of the few seriously contested House races in the country where the Republican was pro-choice and the Democrat pro-life. She ran ads criticizing Mazzoli's votes for the congressional pay raise and for supporting public funding of congressional campaigns; he did not have the money to highlight his reformist credentials and ran no TV ads; this was one of the few races of 1992 where the challenger outspent the incumbent. Stokes tried to dissociate herself from George Bush, who ended up running far behind Bill Clinton in Jefferson County. But, despite strong Mazzoli backing from the *Louisville Courier-Journal*, the incumbent won by just 53%–47%. Mazzoli carried Louisville, especially the black West End, and was running around 55% in middle income neighborhoods along the Watterson Expressway, while Stokes carried the affluent East End suburbs. Mazzoli is an unusually attractive politician, but his narrow win in a good Democratic year suggests he may have serious competition again soon.

The People: Pop. 1990: 613,266; 2% rural; 14% age 65+; 81% White; 18% Black; 1% Asian; 1% Hispanic origin. Voting age pop.: 464,994; 16% Black. Households: 50% married couple families; 22% married couple fams. w. children; 44% college educ.; median household income: $26,614; per capita income: $14,072; median gross rent: $344; median house value: $56,300.

1992 Presidential Vote			1988 Presidential Vote		
Clinton (D)	143,824	(50%)	Bush (R)	128,880	(51%)
Bush (R)	105,520	(37%)	Dukakis (D)	121,917	(49%)
Perot (I)	35,902	(13%)			

Rep. Romano L. Mazzoli (D)

Elected 1970; b. Nov. 2, 1932, Louisville; home, Louisville; U. of Notre Dame, B.S. 1954, U. of Louisville, J.D. 1960; Catholic; married (Helen).

Career: Army, 1954–56; Law Dept., L&N Railroad Co., 1960–62; Practicing atty., 1962–70; Lecturer, Bellarmine Col., 1964–68; KY Senate, 1968–70.

Offices: 2246 RHOB 20515, 202-225-5401. Also Fed. Bldg., #216, 600 MLK Jr. Pl., Louisville 40202, 502-582-5129.

Committees: *Judiciary* (4th of 21 D): Crime and Criminal Justice; Intellectual Property and Judicial Administration; International Law, Immigration and Refugees (Chmn.). *Small Business* (4th of 27 D): SBA Legislation and the General Economy.

Group Ratings

	ADA	ACLU	COPE	CDF	CFA	LCV	ACU	NTLC	NSI	COC	CEI
1992	70	61	75	80	100	56	28	10	60	38	12
1991	65	—	67	90	89	46	10	—	—	20	10

National Journal Ratings

	1991 LIB — 1991 CONS		1992 LIB — 1992 CONS	
Economic	72%	— 23%	66%	— 31%
Social	56%	— 43%	46%	— 53%
Foreign	59%	— 39%	65%	— 33%

Key Votes of the 102d Congress

1. Ban Striker Replace	FOR	5. Handgun Wait/7-Day	FOR	9. Use Force in Gulf	AGN
2. $ for Homeownership	AGN	6. Overseas Mil. Abortion	AGN	10. US Mil. Abroad $ Cut	AGN
3. Tax Rich/Cut Mid Cls.	FOR	7. Obscn. Art NEA $ Ban	AGN	11. Limit SDI Funds	FOR
4. FY93/$15B Def. Cut	FOR	8. Death Pen. from Jury	AGN	12. Cuba Trade Embargo	FOR

Key Votes of the 103d Congress

1. Family Leave	FOR	2. Deficit Reduction	FOR	3. Stimulus Plan	FOR

Election Results

1992 general	Romano L. Mazzoli (D)	148,066	(53%)	($216,638)
	Susan B. Stokes (R)	132,689	(47%)	($364,659)
1992 primary	Romano L. Mazzoli (D)	52,748	(76%)	
	Ron Greene (D)	16,758	(24%)	
1990 general	Romano L. Mazzoli (D)	84,750	(61%)	($303,488)
	Al Brown (R)	55,188	(39%)	($327,390)

FOURTH DISTRICT

The commonwealth of Kentucky has gone to court more than once to establish that the Ohio River up to its northern bank is part of Kentucky: this is, perhaps the northernmost extension of the South. The Ohio sees many different parts of Kentucky. Ashland, near the West Virginia border, is industrial, the home of Ashland Oil, Kentucky's largest corporation; the river here is bound in by tight hills which hold smoke and soot close in the air. Farther down the river, the country is more bucolic: on frozen ice floes in this part of the river, Harriet Beecher Stowe had her readers believe, Eliza fled across the ice in *Uncle Tom's Cabin*. Farther west, between Louisville and Cincinnati, are counties which still look like they're in the 19th Century. But suburban growth obtrudes. Oldham County, just upriver from Louisville, has some of Kentucky's oldest homes, but the horse country is now growing affluent subdivisions. And the northern Kentucky "golden triangle," the three counties across the river from Cincinnati, saw rapid population growth and a sharp rise in incomes in the 1980s. Not far away is Cold Spring, where the predicted midnight appearance of the Virgin Mary brought many Catholics and others in September 1992 (some said they saw her; others did not).

The 4th Congressional District of Kentucky spans all these variations of Ohio River country, from Ashland west to Oldham County; it also includes the typically less populated counties just inland. Economically, it runs the gamut from coal mining towns to rich suburbs. Politically, it runs the gamut from some of the most Democratic counties in America, like Elliott County in the mountains south of Ashland, or the three old counties along the river between Cincinnati and Louisville, some of the most Republican territory, (at least in Kentucky), like Oldham County and the Cincinnati suburbs—not just the spanking-new towns, but the old riverfront cities of Newport, long known for its gambling, and Covington, connected to Cincinnati by a suspension bridge built by John Roebling 16 years before the Brooklyn Bridge. This is a substantially redistricted seat. The old 4th District included most of the Jefferson County suburbs of Louisville; now these heavily Republican areas are gone. Added is all the territory east of the Cincinnati suburbs, in which all but one county voted for Bill Clinton over George Bush. What was once a heavily Republican district has become marginal; Bush carried it in 1992, thanks to big suburban margins, but not by much.

This made life more difficult for Republican Congressman Jim Bunning, though not difficult enough to prompt him to run against Senator Wendell Ford. Bunning is best known around the country as a baseball pitcher, and a fine one. He threw a no-hitter for the Detroit Tigers in 1958 and pitched a perfect game for the Philadelphia Phillies in 1964; he also played for the Pittsburgh Pirates and the Los Angeles Dodgers and retired in 1971 with a 224–184 record, a 3.24 ERA, 2,855 strikeouts and one of the highest totals in baseball history for hitting batters. Bunning also brought that skill and energy to politics in his native northern Kentucky (no, he never played for the Cincinnati Reds). He was elected to the state Senate in 1979, and won a respectable 44% against Martha Layne Collins in 1983 (the best showing for a Republican gubernatorial candidate in the last 20 years). When incumbent 4th District Congressman Gene Snyder retired, Bunning won the seat with 55% of the general election vote.

On Capitol Hill, Bunning has shown much of the assertiveness that he had on the pitching mound and organizing the baseball players' union. Like that other union organizer, Ronald Reagan, Bunning is a solid conservative, and once headed the Conservative Opportunity Society founded by Newt Gingrich. He solidly backed the Gulf war; his son was an airman there, and several of his son's colleagues were killed. In 1990, he got a seat on Ways and Means, where he staunchly opposes outside earning limits on social security beneficiaries—a prime issue in an older, affluent constituency and for this ranking Republican of the Ways and Means Social Security Subcommittee. Bunning crusades against Social Security mail scams and for making Social Security an independent agency. In late 1991 he urged President Bush to address the economy before it was too late—advice Bush must surely wish he had taken. Bunning also has a seat on the Ethics Committee: "it's like permanent jury duty." He was outraged by his colleagues' overdrafts, and led the successful charge against Ethics Chairman Matthew McHugh's proposal to identify only the 24 worst offenders; he was the only Ethics member who wanted to require members to report the interest-free overdrafts as loans.

In 1992 Bunning had serious competition from Dr. Floyd Poore, secretary of Transportation under Governor Martha Layne Collins and public liaison aide for Governor Wallace Wilkinson; Poore finished a respectable third in the 1991 Democratic primary for governor, with 27% to 38% for Brereton Jones and 30% for Scotty Baesler. (Poore is a physician who changed his name legally so that the "Dr." would have to appear on the ballot.) Poore urged pay-or-play healthcare reform, extension of Medicaid to the unemployed and incentives for rural physicians; he attacked Bunning for his franked mail costs. Bunning attacked Poore for taking five-month vacations and for bragging that he drove a Rolls Royce and hit Poore for missing child support payments 20 years ago; Poore accused Bunning of adultery when he was a baseball player (he later apologized to Bunning's wife). Bunning won this nasty race decisively, 62%–38%. The Republican campaign committee gave Bunning the maximum financial assistance allowed; this was one GOP seat they clearly wanted to keep. Poore carried the new counties east of the Cincinnati suburbs, but only with 50.5% of the vote, and they cast only 32% of all votes; Bunning carried the rest of the district with 67%. That seems to indicate he is in strong shape here for the 1990s.

The People: Pop. 1990: 614,410; 46% rural; 12% age 65+; 97% White; 2% Black. Voting age pop.: 449,656; 2% Black. Households: 62% married couple families; 31% married couple fams. w. children; 34% college educ.; median household income: $26,362; per capita income: $11,863; median gross rent: $336; median house value: $56,700.

1992 Presidential Vote			1988 Presidential Vote		
Bush (R)	106,685	(44%)	Bush (R)	125,832	(60%)
Clinton (D)	94,323	(39%)	Dukakis (D)	85,588	(40%)
Perot (I)	40,437	(17%)			

Rep. Jim Bunning (R)

Elected 1986; b. Oct. 23, 1931, Campbell County; home, South-gate; Xavier U., B.S. 1953; Catholic; married (Mary).

Career: Pro baseball player, 1950–71; Investment broker and agent, 1960–86; Ft. Thomas City Cncl., 1977–79; KY Senate, 1979–83.

Offices: 2437 RHOB 20515, 202-225-3465. Also 1717 Dixie Hwy., #160, Ft. Wright 41011, 606-341-2602; 1408 Greenup Ave., #236, Ashland 41101, 606-325-9898; and 704 W. Jefferson St., #219, La Grange 40031, 502-222-2188.

Committees: *Budget* (7th of 17 R). *Standards of Official Conduct* (3d of 7 R). *Ways and Means* (7th of 14 R): Social Security (RMM).

Group Ratings

	ADA	ACLU	COPE	CDF	CFA	LCV	ACU	NTLC	NSI	COC	CEI
1992	10	0	27	20	33	0	90	89	90	71	78
1991	10	—	8	20	28	8	100	—	—	90	86

National Journal Ratings

	1991 LIB — 1991 CONS		1992 LIB — 1992 CONS	
Economic	10% —	89%	20% —	79%
Social	0% —	84%	0% —	85%
Foreign	0% —	88%	0% —	82%

Key Votes of the 102d Congress

1. Ban Striker Replace	AGN	5. Handgun Wait/7-Day	AGN	9. Use Force in Gulf	FOR
2. $ for Homeownership	FOR	6. Overseas Mil. Abortion	AGN	10. US Mil. Abroad $ Cut	AGN
3. Tax Rich/Cut Mid Cls.	AGN	7. Obscn. Art NEA $ Ban	FOR	11. Limit SDI Funds	AGN
4. FY93/$15B Def. Cut	AGN	8. Death Pen. from Jury	FOR	12. Cuba Trade Embargo	FOR

Key Votes of the 103d Congress

1. Family Leave	AGN	2. Deficit Reduction	AGN	3. Stimulus Plan	AGN

Election Results

1992 general	Jim Bunning (R)	139,634	(62%)	($984,180)
	Dr. Floyd Poore (D)	86,890	(38%)	($311,121)
1992 primary	Jim Bunning (R), unopposed			
1990 general	Jim Bunning (R)	101,680	(69%)	($563,409)
	Galen Martin (D)	44,979	(31%)	($76,580)

FIFTH DISTRICT

Since Daniel Boone came through the Cumberland Gap in 1775, the mountains of eastern Kentucky have been a special place. As Virginians poured through and created their version of a Tidewater civilization in the Bluegrass country, the people who settled the counties of the mountains and the Cumberland Plateau, most of them of Irish Protestant or Border Scots descent, brought different values—an assertive egalitarianism, loyalty to family and community and passionate willingness to settle differences by feuds or violence. Most of the people in the mountains today are descendants of families who settled there in the two or three generations after Boone. Handed down are living memories of the old ways of doing things and personal values, from the time not so far distant when there was little contact here with the outside world and the ties to the rest of American civilization were secured mainly by school primers and the King James Bible.

Only when people's lives have been changed and uprooted by outside events and institutions, have their basic political attitudes been changed—and in each case, changed with a lasting imprint. The first agent of such change was the Civil War; the second was the great United Mine Workers organizing drives in the coal mines around the 1930s. The Civil War made the mountains and the Cumberland Plateau a stronghold of the Republican Party. For this was never slave territory—hardly any blacks have ever lived here—and yet communities and families were riven by the rebellion of the South. People have not forgotten: the counties around Somerset and Corbin in south central Kentucky cast some of the highest Republican percentages in the nation in election after election.

Then came coal. Early in this century, vast seams of coal were discovered under the Kentucky mountains; representatives of eastern capitalists began prowling through these hills, hiring courthouse town lawyers to buy up mineral rights from unsuspecting farmers, building tiny industrial slum towns in hollows and creek beds beneath glowering, heavily forested mountainsides. The mines kept mountaineers home, but coal mining is harsh and deadly work: mine accidents, black lung disease and simple exhaustion killed tens of thousands of miners, while low wages and company stores kept them poor. Then John L. Lewis's United Mine Workers came in, and something like open warfare followed, with neither mine operators nor union organizers loath to use violence and threats. The union mostly won in eastern Kentucky, and in the short run raised wages and built hospitals for miners and their families; in the longer run, the UMW phased out many jobs in the mines, in return for job security and health benefits, as coal was replaced by oil as the nation's major fuel. Politically, the UMW counties in the eastern part of the state became heavily Democratic, and have remained so as underground mine jobs have been phased out, during the strip mining boom of the 1970s, and then as UMW members have died out in the 1980s and 1990s.

For half a century, the UMW-Democratic counties in eastern Kentucky were gathered together into the 7th Congressional District, solidly Democratic, represented from 1949 to 1984 by Democrat Carl Perkins, longtime chairman of the House Education and Labor Committee. During the same years, the Cumberland Plateau counties in south central Kentucky, almost as mountainous but without the concentration of underground mines and union organization farther east, were gathered into the 5th Congressional District, one of the most Republican in the country. Then, in redistricting for 1992, the two districts were melded into a new 5th Congressional District, with about half the population from each of the old 5th and 7th. Neither Bill Clinton nor George Bush had a real lock on this new district, but it ended up reelecting 5th District Republican Hal Rogers. Maybe the Civil War is having a more prolonged impact than the New Deal.

The result may also reflect the varying strength of the two parties' candidates. The Democrats were hampered because their 7th District incumbent, Chris Perkins, had never established a firm hold on his father's seat after winning it in 1984. In 1988 and 1990, Perkins was hard pressed by Republican Will Scott's charges of a lavish lifestyle. In December 1991, when the 7th was redistricted in with the 5th, Perkins had already attracted two primary opponents, including Carol Hubbard, wife of 1st District Congressman Carroll Hubbard and a mountain county native. In January 1992 he decided to retire from Congress at 37; though he initially said he had no overdrafts, it was revealed, after his retirement announcement, that he had 514. Perkins's withdrawal attracted six other candidates to the May Democratic primary as well; the winner was not the candidate with the biggest war chest (Hubbard, to whom her husband's Banking Committee lobbyists contributed generously, got only 17% of the vote), but the man with the biggest base, former state Senator John Doug Hays of Pike County, with 30%. Second and third, also with 17% each, were lawyers Ned Pillersdorf of Johnson County and Robert Rowe of Floyd County. But while Hays was getting out votes in his local base, Rogers was all over the old 7th brandishing his seat on the Appropriations Committee and asking how he could help local projects. Hays, whose grandfather Doug "Sawloggin' " Hays was state senator for 13 years, attacked Rogers for supporting trickle-down economics and argued that as a Democrat he could get more money for the district in Bill Clinton's Washington. Rogers countered by pointing to his ongoing efforts to build the $250 million Cumberland Gap twin tunnels and Harlan County flood projects; his speeches and radio ads attacked Hays's Senate attendance record and pro-choice abortion stand while his TV spots were positive and stressed his own record. Rogers bucked local unions by opposing the plant closing bill and favoring U.S.-Mexico free trade, yet his job rating was very high. But, as Democratic state chairman Grady Stumbo said, "If you're asking me which do I think is more important up here, policy or pork barrel, I'll have to admit it's pork barrel."

In November, Rogers won with 55%. He had 71% in his old 5th District, which cast 52% of the new district's votes; he lost 64%–36% in the old 7th District. The returns show the strength of partisan feelings in eastern Kentucky: Owsley County was 78% for Rogers; next-door Breathitt County was 68% for Hays. Democrats may well target this district again, but Rogers will have more time to shower the eastern counties with pork barrel projects, and made a bold move in that direction by being one of three Republicans to vote for Clinton's stimulus package in April 1993. On other issues, he is not necessarily a free marketeer or an internationalist. As ranking Republican on the Appropriations Subcommittee on Commerce, Justice, State and Judiciary, he has complained about its the tight spending leash and has worked closely with Chairman Neal Smith. He is cautious about U.N. intervention in places like Cambodia. He has launched an investigation of the Census, which he thinks is expensive and inaccurate. He is ready to restrict textile imports (there are textile mills in the Cumberlands) and to soften the impact of Clean Air Act regulations on local coal miners. But first comes the pork barrel.

The People: Pop. 1990: 613,979; 87% rural; 12% age 65+; 99% White; 1% Black. Voting age pop.: 441,342; 1% Black. Households: 65% married couple families; 34% married couple fams. w. children; 20% college educ.; median household income: $15,052; per capita income: $7,717; median gross rent: $243; median house value: $35,400.

1992 Presidential Vote

Clinton (D) 109,607 (48%)
Bush (R) 95,843 (42%)
Perot (I)..................... 23,890 (10%)

1988 Presidential Vote

Bush (R) 111,998 (53%)
Dukakis (D)................ 98,058 (47%)

Rep. Harold D. Rogers (R)

Elected 1980; b. Dec. 31, 1937, Barrier; home, Somerset; U. of KY, B.A. 1962, J.D. 1964; Baptist; married (Shirley).

Career: Army Natl. Guard, 1957–64; Practicing atty., 1964–69; Pulaski-Rockcastle Commonwealth Atty., 1969–80.

Offices: 2468 RHOB 20515, 202-225-4601. Also 203 E. Mount Vernon St., Somerset 42501, 606-679-8346; 601 Main St., Hazard 41701, 606-439-0794; and 806 Hambley Blvd., Pikeville 41501, 606-432-4388.

Committees: *Appropriations* (8th of 23 R): Commerce, Justice, State and Judiciary (RMM); Energy and Water Development.

Group Ratings

	ADA	ACLU	COPE	CDF	CFA	LCV	ACU	NTLC	NSI	COC	CEI
1992	25	4	50	40	33	6	80	65	90	88	58
1991	10	—	25	40	39	0	79	—	—	90	43

National Journal Ratings

	1991 LIB — 1991 CONS	1992 LIB — 1992 CONS
Economic	28% — 71%	33% — 67%
Social	0% — 84%	16% — 82%
Foreign	0% — 88%	30% — 64%

Key Votes of the 102d Congress

1. Ban Striker Replace	AGN	5. Handgun Wait/7-Day	AGN	9. Use Force in Gulf	FOR
2. $ for Homeownership	FOR	6. Overseas Mil. Abortion	AGN	10. US Mil. Abroad $ Cut	AGN
3. Tax Rich/Cut Mid Cls.	AGN	7. Obscn. Art NEA $ Ban	FOR	11. Limit SDI Funds	AGN
4. FY93/$15B Def. Cut	AGN	8. Death Pen. from Jury	FOR	12. Cuba Trade Embargo	FOR

Key Votes of the 103d Congress

1. Family Leave   AGN   2. Deficit Reduction   AGN   3. Stimulus Plan   FOR

Election Results

1992 general	Harold D. Rogers (R).................	115,255	(55%)	($885,966)
	John Doug Hays (D)..................	95,760	(45%)	($274,753)
1992 primary	Harold D. Rogers (R), unopposed			
1990 general	Harold D. Rogers (R), unopposed			($111,225)

SIXTH DISTRICT

The Bluegrass country almost plumb in the middle of Kentucky is the most well-settled part of interior America: Lexington was founded in 1779; the town of Hopewell was renamed Paris in 1789 out of gratitude for French help during our Revolution and in a salute to theirs (though the county name remained Bourbon even after Louis XVI was executed). Tobacco farming started here in the 1770s, horse racing in 1787, and the first whiskey distillery, in Bourbon County, was built in 1790. Tobacco, whiskey, and race horses remained the staples of the Bluegrass economy for six generations until 1956, when IBM built its typewriter plant and headquarters in Lexington. IBM's arrival "really was the beginning of Lexington's industrial revolution," as University of Kentucky historian Carl Cone put it. You imagine a Kentucky colonel sitting on the porch, dressed in a white suit and string tie and sipping a mint julep, as IBM engineers in their dark suits and white shirts file into their offices.

In the 1980s, another ingredient was added to the Bluegrass economic mix when Toyota located its $2 billion plant in Georgetown, a town with early 19th Century houses and lush countryside, just one county north of Lexington and west of Paris. Now in the seemingly timeless Bluegrass, economic change seems constant. IBM, finding the Selectric outclassed by the PC, put the business on the block in 1990, threatening all those jobs, while the horse racing industry suffered a slump symbolized by the bankruptcy of the late Leslie Combs's Spendthrift Farm. But just then, Toyota announced a doubling of its plant, so that its projected 4,100 (non-union) workers can keep using innovative methods to build the popular Camry and, when Calumet Farm went up for sale, it was snapped up by a Polish-born investor. From IBM to Toyota to even the Bluegrass horse farms, Lexington seems to be a focus of innovation and certainly of economic growth.

Though the home base of the Whig party's Henry Clay, the Bluegrass country, has been Democratic since his death, and that heritage continues through the late 20th Century. Jimmy Carter twice carried the 6th Congressional District, and it elected Democratic congressmen for years. But Lexington, as it has grown, has become more Republican, and has moved the whole Bluegrass region in that direction. The new 6th District for the 1992 election was designed by a Democratic legislature to elect a Democratic congressman; and it did. But it also narrowly voted for George Bush over Bill Clinton.

Actually, the 1992 House election here was really decided by the 1991 governor's race. That contest eliminated 6th District Republican Congressman Larry Hopkins as a serious political figure here and established Lexington Mayor and new 6th District Democratic Congressman Scotty Baesler as one. Hopkins's race for governor was damaged in the spring of 1991 when it turned out he'd exaggerated his military service and was ruined in the fall when it was revealed he'd had 32 overdrafts on the House bank. Hopkins failed to carry his own district that November, and in January 1992 he announced he was retiring from Congress; he was eligible to convert his $660,000 campaign treasury to personal use. Meanwhile, Baesler, after 10 years as mayor, was running for governor on the Democratic side and, despite a serious funds gap, ran second to Brereton Jones by a 38%–30% margin. Kentucky does not have a runoff, so Baesler's gubernatorial hopes were postponed at least until 1995; but the 6th District seat looked inviting. Baesler, popular from his days as mayor and well known throughout the district from Lexington TV, got 82% in a five-candidate primary and then beat a little-known Republican 61%–39%.

Baesler was well known in these parts even before he became Mayor. He was captain of the University of Kentucky basketball team, class of 1963—the days of the legendary Coach Adolph Rupp. He went on to law school, then became administrator of Fayette County Legal Aid; he was first elected mayor in 1982. As mayor, he created a statewide scholarship program called Sweet 16 Academic Showcase, brought the DARE program into schools to teach kids about drugs, sponsored downtown redevelopment, developed a Family Care Center for poor families, chaired a state commission to develop tourism and the arts and hosted major sports tourneys. His Republican opponent, who served on the council, had never said much in opposition. Baesler claimed some credit for the job growth in the Lexington area and was clearly accorded some; even the U.S. Chamber of Commerce endorsed him. It is widely assumed in Kentucky that Baesler will run for governor again in 1995; what other office would a Kentuckian want? In the meantime, Baesler pledges to stay involved in local issues—which isn't exactly a denial of gubernatorial ambitions. Baesler, a tobacco farmer, has a seat on the Agriculture Subcommittee on Specialty Crops for the 103d Congress.

The People: Pop. 1990: 614,245; 37% rural; 11% age 65+; 90% White; 8% Black; 1% Asian; 1% Hispanic origin. Voting age pop.: 464,792; 8% Black; 1% Hispanic origin. Households: 58% married couple families; 27% married couple fams. w. children; 41% college educ.; median household income: $25,377; per capita income: $12,419; median gross rent: $352; median house value: $61,200.

1992 Presidential Vote			1988 Presidential Vote		
Bush (R)	105,210	(42%)	Bush (R)	124,169	(58%)
Clinton (D)	101,659	(41%)	Dukakis (D)	89,826	(42%)
Perot (I)	39,659	(16%)			

Rep. Scotty Baesler (D)

Elected 1992; b. July 9, 1941, Athens; home, Lexington; U. of KY, B.S. 1963, J.D. 1966; Christian; married (Alice).

Career: Army Reserves, 1966–72; Tobacco farmer; Practicing atty., 1966–67; Fayette Cnty. Legal Aid Admin., 1967–73; Lexington Vice Mayor, 1974–77; Fayette Cnty. District Judge, 1978–81; Lexington Mayor, 1982–92.

Offices: 508 CHOB 20515, 202-225-4706. Also 444 E. Main St., #103, Lexington 40507, 606-253-1124.

Committees: *Agriculture* (23d of 28 D): Environment, Credit and Rural Development; Foreign Agriculture and Hunger; Specialty Crops and Natural Resources. *Education and Labor* (27th of 28 D): Human Resources. *Veterans' Affairs* (17th of 21 D): Hospitals and Health Care.

Group Ratings and 102d Congress Votes: Newly Elected

Key Votes of the 103d Congress

1. Family Leave	FOR	2. Deficit Reduction	AGN	3. Stimulus Plan	FOR

Election Results

1992 general	Scotty Baesler (D)	135,613	(61%)	($273,727)
	Charles W. Ellinger (R)	87,816	(39%)	($65,643)
1992 primary	Scotty Baesler (D)	49,954	(82%)	
	Roy Tudor (D)	4,701	(8%)	
	J.T. Underwood (D)	2,627	(4%)	
	Harvey Carroll, Jr. (D)	2,524	(4%)	
	Other	1,438	(2%)	
1990 general	Larry J. Hopkins (R), unopposed			($120,647)

LOUISIANA

Louisiana is the American state that is most like a Third World republic. For this is a state with an economy uncomfortably like an underdeveloped country, based on pumping minerals out of soggy ground, shipping grain produced in the vast hinterland drained by its great river, and increasingly dependent in recent years on the business typical of picturesque Third World countries—tourism. Its politics too has a third world quality, with its own peculiar election laws and a heritage of no-holds-barred conflict and demagoguery no other state can match: what other state has produced a Huey Long, or a David Duke? With a hereditary rich class and a large low-wage working class, conservative cultural attitudes (Louisiana has the most restrictive abortion law of any state) and a lazy tolerance of rule-breaking, Louisiana feels more like the Caribbean or the Mediterranean than the North Atlantic or the Pacific Rim. This is not an entirely original observation. Three decades ago A. J. Liebling described Louisiana as an outpost of the Levant along the Gulf of Mexico. Most of the United States faces east toward the vast Atlantic Ocean or west toward the even larger Pacific; Louisiana faces south, to the Gulf of Mexico and the steamy heat and volatile societies of Latin America.

New Orleans preserves the look and feel it had as a French and Spanish outpost in the New World. Traditions of centralized control and easygoing corruption—classic traits of colonialism—are part of this heritage. The dirigiste tradition comes from the fact that Louisiana is the only state that operates on the Napoleonic Code of France (which until 1990 required parents to leave a large percentage of their estate to their children), not the common law of England; the concept of civil liberties has shallower roots in Louisiana than in the other 49 states. Here abstract ideals have been overshadowed by the practical need for centralized action. This delta land—much of it below sea level, soggy, swampy, laced with tributaries and offshoots of the Mississippi and other major rivers like the Atchafalaya—requires vast capital expenditures for levees and drainage and causeways. Even today, houses in New Orleans don't have basements, people are buried in above-ground cemeteries (in grandiose crypts), and swamp lands begin abruptly at the edges of subdivisions where people find alligators in their back yards.

The economy that grew up in these rich Delta lands has always been based on raw materials. Antebellum Louisiana produced and exported sugar, rice and cotton in enough abundance to generate the wealth which built grand plantation houses behind alleys of oaks running in from the Mississippi, and to make New Orleans the nation's fifth largest city by the time of the Civil War. Then came oil: the great Spindletop strike just over the Texas line in 1901; oil was found in the salt domes of Louisiana, and Jersey Standard (now Exxon) built the huge Baton Rouge refinery that became the training ground for generations of its top executives. When energy prices boomed after the oil shocks of 1973 and 1981, Louisiana, like an oil-rich Third World country, boomed too, reaching up toward national income levels, generating 500,000 new jobs between 1972 and 1981, only to lose 150,000 in the next six years as oil prices crashed and the rig count dropped from a peak of 455 in 1981 to 88 in 1992. Energy produced 41% of state government revenues in 1982, but only 13% in 1992. That economic turmoil has now abated: Louisiana's unemployment, the highest in the nation in the mid-1980s, was slightly above the national average in the early 1990s. But the instability produced violent tremors in Louisiana politics, with shocks heard around the country and even the world.

The shocks were the greater because Louisiana has greater visible income disparities than almost anywhere else in the United States, an economy more typical of a Caribbean sugar colony than an American state. New Orleans's rich are notoriously unventuresome and tight-knit, determined to hold on to their wealth against the grasp of the impecunious and unlearned masses. They have not hesitated to use the dirigiste tradition in their own interests, though others

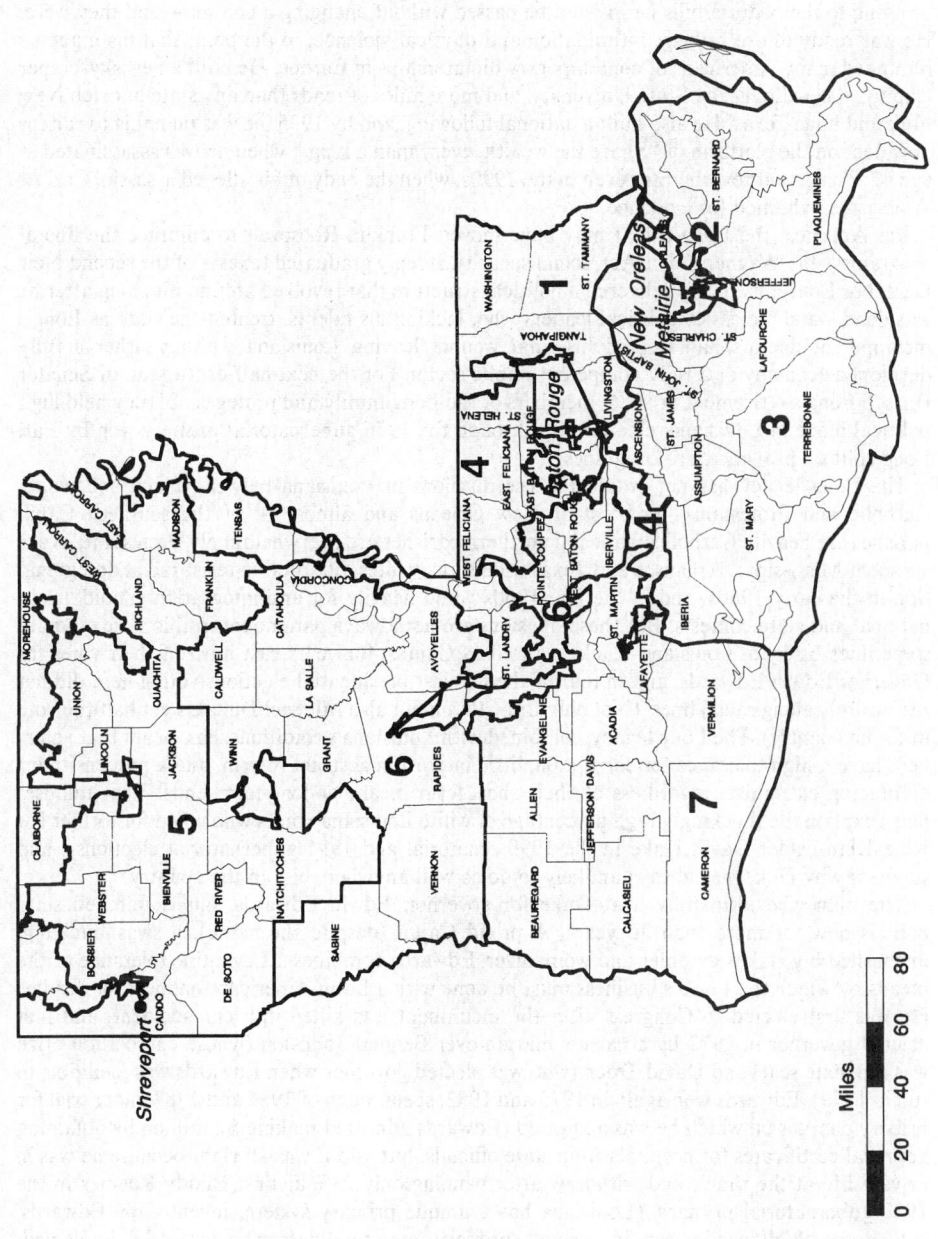

have not hesitated to use it against them. The most enduringly famous, and by far the most talented, was Huey P. Long, who in less than a single term each as governor (1928–32) and senator (1932–35), left an imprint on the state's public life and imposed an organization to its politics that have only in the last decade faded into history. Long's genius was not that he promised to tax the rich to help the poor—hundreds of idealists and demagogues in America have done that—but that, to an amazing extent, he actually delivered. He dominated the legislature so thoroughly that, as governor, he roamed the floors of both chambers at will, bringing to the podium bills he insisted be passed without changing a comma—and they were. He was ready to use bribery, intimidation and physical violence, to the point that his machine reminded many Americans of contemporary dictatorships in Europe. He built a new skyscraper Capitol, a new Louisiana State University, and more miles of roads than any state but rich New York and huge Texas. He also built a national following, and by 1935, he was planning to run for president on the platform of "Share the wealth, every man a king," when he was assassinated at age 42. That event reverberates even in the 1990s, when the body of his alleged assassin, Carl A. Weiss, was exhumed for evidence.

For America, the Long threat may have moved Franklin Roosevelt to embrace the liberal programs—the Wagner Labor Act, social security, steeply graduated taxes—of the second New Deal. For Louisiana, Long delivered a political structure that revolved around him long after he was dead—and a class of political leaders who, lacking his talents, treated the state as Long's incompetent doctors had treated his fatal wound, leaving Louisiana without either a fully developed economy or a fully competent public sector. For the next half-century, until Senator Russell Long's retirement in 1986, members of the Long family and proteges of Huey held high political office in Louisiana; elections up through the 1956 gubernatorial primary won by Earl Long split on pro- and anti-Long lines.

The Long legacy has not eradicated the divisions in Louisiana between black and white, Catholic and Protestant—for most of New Orleans and almost all of the southern Cajun parishes are heavily Catholic, while the northern parishes are overwhelmingly Protestant, as are adjacent Mississippi, Arkansas and Texas. Louisiana whites did forcibly resist racial desegregation in the early 1960s, and in the late 1960s voted heavily for anti-integration candidates in national and state contests. But these divisions are not always paramount in this state, and are sometimes bridged. Louisiana blacks, as well as Cajuns, for years cast most of their votes for Governor Edwin Edwards, and in four of the five last presidential elections voting here did not run entirely along racial lines. (Not only Bill Clinton but also Michael Dukakis got half the vote in Cajun country). The Long legacy, combined with Louisiana's traditions, has meant that voters here have a high tolerance for corruption, little interest in abstract reform, and a propensity for embracing extremists regardless of their short-term means or long-term ends. That mindset helps explain the shockingly high percentage of white Louisiana voters who voted for former Ku Klux Klan leader David Duke in the 1990 senatorial and 1991 gubernatorial elections—and suggests why Duke was always unlikely to do as well anywhere else in the country.

The man who ultimately beat Duke for governor, Edwin Edwards, has dominated state politics now for more than 20 years. A proud Cajun (despite the name), a swashbuckling, unabashed big-stakes gambler and womanizer, Edwards combines a Levantine tolerance of the means by which the world's business must be done with a Latin American fondness for display. He was first elected to Congress after the incumbent was killed in a car accident, and first elected governor in 1972 by a narrow margin over Bennett Johnston (whose consolation prize was a Senate seat) and David Treen (who was elected governor when Edwards was ineligible to run in 1979). Edwards won again in 1975 and 1983, spent much of 1986 and 1987 under trial for bribery charges on which he was acquitted (Edwards admitted making $2 million by obtaining approval certificates for hospitals from state officials, but said it was all right because he was in private life at the time), and withdrew after winning only 28% against Buddy Roemer in the 1987 gubernatorial primary. (Louisiana has a unique primary system, invented by Edwards: candidates of all parties run in a single primary; any candidate who gets 50% is elected;

otherwise, the top two finishers, regardless of party, have a runoff.) Edwards's solutions to the economic crisis of the mid-1980s were characteristic—a state lottery, casino gambling in New Orleans, one-man state budgeting.

Edwards fits naturally in Louisiana's traditional political divides. One divide is between Cajuns and north Louisiana Baptists; the Cajun parishes cast about 30% of the state's vote, the New Orleans area around 25% or so, with about 44% in Protestant parishes from the Baton Rouge area and north. Another divide is by race: blacks are overwhelmingly Democratic, whites typically split. A third divide is by income: with wide economic disparities, Louisiana's low- and high-income whites vote very differently, and are much less influenced than voters in most other states by candidates' cultural values, marital status, lifestyles and the like. As a result, Louisiana politics since Huey Long's time has often been a struggle between reformist and conservative forces on one side and roguish populists on the other, a struggle waged in lavishly financed campaigns and with grandiloquent rhetoric. In that context, Edwards has typically been the roguish populist, while his Republican opponents like Treen and Roemer (though he wasn't a Republican until he switched parties in March 1991) have been reformist conservatives; the sides were pretty closely balanced. That was true also when Senator Russell Long retired in 1986, and Democratic Congressman John Breaux, once a protege of Edwards, beat Republican Congressman Henson Moore by a 53%–47% margin. Blacks, Cajuns, and low income whites dominated one side; well-off whites and northern parish Baptists the other.

Enter David Duke. It should be debated whether his initial rise was abetted by local and national media, ever alert for signs that the American masses are racist or fascist. Duke, it must be added, clearly was: as the *New Orleans Times-Picayune* in time documented better than anyone else, Duke had been an overt Nazi sympathizer since college (selling Nazi literature in his office as late as 1989), a leader of the Ku Klux Klan, founder of the National Association for the Advancement of White People and propagator of racist and anti-semitic messages. Aside from his unpersuasive claims of having changed his mind, there was no reason to think that he had retreated from those views. Unlike most other racist nuts, however, he did have a knack for speaking to mainstream political issues in attractive political language. When he talked about crime and welfare, he left little doubt he hated blacks. Yet he was careful to use words and take stands also used and taken by leading national Republicans and Democrats; he even said he would not repeal the 1964 Civil Rights Act, which was opposed in 1964 by the men who were president, speaker of the House, and Senate majority leader when Duke became a representative in the Louisiana legislature in 1989. After a quixotic run for president in 1988, Duke ran for a state House seat, as a nominal Republican, from a small district in the New Orleans suburb of Metairie; after a highly publicized campaign, he won by a narrow margin. In the legislature, he got publicity for an anti-racial quotas bill. Then he ran for senator in 1990 against incumbent Bennett Johnston, and lost 54%–44%—almost the same margin by which George Bush had beaten Michael Dukakis; Duke clearly made major inroads into the non-affluent white vote, both Cajun and Protestant. Then in 1991, Duke ran for governor, against the Democrat-turned-Republican incumbent Buddy Roemer and the ever-ready Edwin Edwards. Roemer was unpopular because he'd raised taxes after promising not to do so and had failed to get his reforms through the legislature; Edwards was unpopular because many thought he was a crook, and he had few voters except blacks faithful to his populism; Duke, of course, was unpopular too. But in this battle of unpopulars, Duke's core constituency proved larger than Roemer's, as he won 32% to 34% for Edwards and only 27% for Roemer. That eliminated the one acceptable choice to most reformist conservatives; a choice between a crook and a kleagle, as someone said. All articulate opinion in Louisiana moved to Edwards's side, as threats arose of national boycotts of Louisiana tourism if Duke won. President Bush, following the cue of the late Lee Atwater, who had always denounced Duke, urged voters to support the Democrat Edwards; so did Roemer. In a record turnout—as many as voted in the 1992 presidential election—Edwards wrapped up a solid 61%–39% victory. Duke's 39% was an alarming figure, but well under the 48% George Wallace received here in the 1968 presidential election. Duke ran over 60% with middle income whites and white Protestants, but blacks and high-income whites were for Edwards.

And now exit David Duke. Having received more media attention than anyone in history who had won one race for state representative and lost for U.S. senator and governor, Duke ran for president in 1992, and was squashed. Any chance he had of becoming a repository for discontent with George Bush was eliminated when Pat Buchanan ran. Duke did not get on the ballot in the first five primaries, got only 9% in the Louisiana primary, and left the race in soon after (his highest percentage, 11%, was in the March Mississippi primary). It turned out that the demand for a former Klansman outside the peculiar political terrain of Louisiana was about as great as the support for the man in the Uncle Sam suit. Duke fell back into obscurity, was fired from a TV talk show for being too boring, and became an insurance agent.

Governor. Edwards did not cease being uncontroversial as governor. On New Year's Eve 1991, he and a 27-year-old companion were spotted gambling in Las Vegas, and a recall effort was mounted against him in 1992, though it failed to produce the high number of required signatures (Edwards helped draft the recall laws years before). But he did appoint many conservative-reformist to top jobs, and the state's economy rode through the early 1990s recession surprisingly comfortably. Edwards got the legislature to approve casino gambling in New Orleans, after it already allowed riverboat gambling and video poker. But he hasn't been able to get the legislature to change the fiscal system in which residential real estate goes virtually untaxed while the sales tax in New Orleans hit 9%. Facing a budget shortfall in 1993, Edwards announced cuts in higher education. When Hurricane Andrew slammed into the Cajun country in August 1992, causing $1 billion worth of damage, Edwards was highly visible and quick to ask for—and receive—federal disaster assistance.

But only desultory speculation was beginning about the 1995 governor's race. Practically all the well-known candidates have suffered defeats ranging from embarrassing to debilitating: Edwards himself, Roemer, suburban New Orleans Congressman Bob Livingston, Cajun Congressman Billy Tauzin, former Secretary of State Paul Hardy, and former Congressman Clyde Holloway. Notable exceptions are Democrat Mary Landrieu, state treasurer and daughter of former New Orleans Mayor Moon Landrieu, and Republican Fox McKeithen, secretary of state and son of former Governor John McKeithen.

Senators. Bennett Johnston, not widely known nationally, is after 20 years one of the inside powers of the Senate, chairman of the Energy and Natural Resources Committee, a man who has used seniority, charm and, most of all, brainpower to fashion major legislation. Johnston has absorbed setbacks in the Senate and an embarrassingly close reelection race against David Duke in Louisiana to score one of the major legislative triumphs of the 102d Congress, the omnibus energy bill. He is, says *National Journal*'s Margaret Kriz, "an undisputed master of the give and take ... happy to give his adversaries something to take away from the table. But they've learned to read the fine print as carefully as he's composed it." It was natural that Johnston, representing a top oil and gas state, get a seat on Energy when he came to the Senate in 1972. By the late 1970s he was the chief advocate of oil and gas price deregulation: a difficult cause at the time, but one which triumphed in practice and in theory. He was one of the backers of the Strategic Petroleum Reserve, whose salt dome storage areas are in Louisiana; that policy was nicely vindicated in the Gulf war.

But at the same time, he was mastering the policy and politics of other senators and their states; he is knowledgeable about issues as far-ranging as the Tongass National Forest in Alaska and the statehood issue in Puerto Rico. In 1991, he moved a major energy bill, only to be stymied by a filibuster against opening up the Arctic National Wildlife Refuge to oil drilling and opposition to raising the CAFE gas mileage standards on autos. So he dropped those provisions which antagonized respectively the environmental left and heavy industry right, and sculpted a new law before opposition could gather. Its main features were a repeal of Fuel Use Tax restrictions on natural gas, a final end to federal price controls on natural gas, more exploration cost write-offs for independent oil and gas drillers and repeal of the dormant Windfall Profits Tax on domestic oil. Skillfully building support by accepting floor amendments, he inserted at the last minute a measure to ease obstacles in the construction of a nuclear waste dump in Nevada (despite opposition from its two senators) and provision to require more federal purchases of cars that use alternate fuels. Johnston was forthright, however, in his opposition to Bill Clinton's proposed Btu energy tax, and joined David Boren in May 1993 in calling for an outright rejection of it.

Johnston also chairs the Appropriations Subcommittee on Energy and Water Development, which has funding power over many energy and environmental programs. In 1992 he passed the western water bill which included a bounty of water projects throughout the west as well as environmental and water rights compromises in California's Central Valley Project. Although Johnston's relations with full Chairman Robert Byrd must ever be icy—he nearly ran against Byrd for majority leader in 1986—he has channeled much money into the state: five major national research centers for Louisiana universities, the National Wetlands Research Center in Lafayette and a proposed $750 million uranium enrichment plant in Claiborne Parish. At first he opposed the Supercollider project, but switched to strong support after a defense plant in Hammond, Louisiana, got a Supercollider contract. England Air Force Base did have to be closed, but he boasts that Louisiana defense contracts amount to more than $1 billion a year.

Johnston's one conspicuous failure was his drive to become Senate majority leader. He came close to challenging Byrd in 1986—perhaps prompting Byrd's decision to leave the leader post two years later. And in 1989 when he did attempt the race, he had 14 votes to George Mitchell's 27 and another 14 for Daniel Inouye. But Johnston kept his chairs, and took several stands that surely pleased Democratic liberals: he was the first conservative southerner to oppose the nomination of Robert Bork, he led the opposition to funding the Strategic Defense Initiative and he called for unilateral troop reductions in South Korea.

This is a Senate career that almost wasn't. After serving a term as state senator, Johnston ran for governor in 1971 and lost the Democratic nomination by only 4,488 votes to Edwin Edwards—a runoff that started two long and successful political careers. Johnston then entered the August 1972 Democratic Senate primary for a long-shot bid against Allen Ellender, the chairman of the Appropriations Committee; Ellender died after the filing date but three months before the primary, which Johnston then won easily. Reelected easily in 1978 and 1984, Johnston was jerked into the limelight in 1990 as the incumbent targeted by David Duke. In a state with a great weakness for demagogues, at a time when white middle-class voters seemed especially hard pressed and were looking for a vehicle of protest, Duke apparently struck a chord. But Johnston fought back gamely, with some clever ads, and won 54%–44%. It is surely too early to say whether he'll have serious opposition in 1996, or even whether he'll run (Russell Long surprised everyone when he quit in 1986). Footnote: is Johnston starting a political dynasty? His son-in-law Tim Roemer was elected to the House in the Indiana 3d District in 1990 and 1992, and his son Bennett Johnston, Jr., ran in the California 6th in 1992 but lost the primary.

John Breaux, Louisiana's junior senator, is making a name for himself in several quarters, and not just for having been Congress's youngest member, as he was when he was first elected to the House at 28, in 1972, to replace Edwin Edwards. Breaux, like Edwards, is from the county seat of Crowley in Cajun country (it is the birthplace also of Texas Congressman Jack Brooks; what a political town!); he served four years on Edwards's staff, and won the Cajun country House seat when Edwards was elected governor in 1972. Breaux has the politician's affable manner, he is good company and also one of Congress's best tennis players; but he also has serious political skills. In the House he used his seat on Public Works to get $50 million to offset coastal wetlands erosion. He ran for the Senate in 1986, initially trailing his Republican House colleague Henson Moore, who was denouncing the then highly unpopular Edwards. But Breaux nurtured his Cajun base and won 61% in the Cajun parishes, mobilized blacks by attacking a hamhanded national Republican "ballot security" program targeted at black precincts, and won enough low-income whites to carry metro New Orleans and not run far behind in Baton Rouge and Baptist north Louisiana. Breaux held Moore under 50% in the primary and then overtook him by November.

In the Senate, Breaux got on the Environment and Public Works and the Commerce Committees—expanded versions of his House assignments—and managed to support oil company positions while pressing for a wetlands protection bill. In 1990, he backed George Mitchell, Johnston's former rival for the leadership, in his fight with Robert Byrd over benefits for displaced mine workers and, evidently in return, got Mitchell's support on softening oil spill legislation. Later, with Lloyd Bentsen's support, he got a seat on the Finance Committee. He has been active there in helping expand IRAs and repeal the user fee tax on recreational boats. Now a chief deputy whip, Breaux also served as chairman of the Democratic Senatorial Campaign Committee during the 1989–90 cycle; Democrats not only held their own but gained a seat in the person of Paul Wellstone in Minnesota—not exactly a Breaux clone. Breaux identified with the moderate Democratic Leadership Council and replaced Bill Clinton as chairman when Clinton ran for president. He was an active Clinton backer and fundraiser, and exerted pressure for moderate policies: "I worry that people in the interest groups will try to pull him away from the mainstream positions that got him elected."

Breaux bucked the Democratic leadership on some key votes in 1991, supporting the Gulf war resolution in January, voting against the Democratic campaign finance bill in 1992, voting for the confirmation of Clarence Thomas in October. In March 1993, Breaux joined David Boren in proposing an alternative to Bill Clinton's economic stimulus package, postponing about half of Clinton's spending programs until tangible deficit reduction measures had passed. Robert Byrd effectively prevented any vote on Boren/Breaux, but had it been accepted by the administration, the successful GOP filibuster might have been avoided. Later in the year, Breaux also sought to negotiate a compromise with the administration over its proposed Btu energy tax, suggesting greater spending cuts and possible taxes on other energy sources.

In a state most of whose politicians were exhausted after the 1991 gubernatorial race, Breaux did not draw serious competition in 1992. He won a second term in the October primary with 73% of the vote.

Presidential politics. Louisiana came closer than any other southern state to voting for Michael Dukakis in 1988; it was seriously contested by both sides in 1992, and ended up casting the highest percentage for Bill Clinton and Al Gore of any southern state except their own Arkansas and Tennessee. Economic troubles explain the Democrats' strength in 1988. With times better, their strength in 1992 is explained by arithmetic: blacks are about 30% of the electorate; Cajuns and other white Catholics, who are another 30% or so, are open enough to the Democrats to split 50–50; and enough white Protestants voted for the Southern Baptist ticket to get it up near 50% of the total vote. Incidentally, for all Louisiana's taste for demagogues, Ross Perot did not do well here in 1992.

The Louisiana presidential primary, held on southern Super Tuesday in 1992, produced a huge victory for Bill Clinton and a big margin for George Bush.

Congressional districting. Outmigration due to the collapse of oil prices cost Louisiana a House seat for the 1990s. The Voting Rights Act, rather than traditional legislative politics, ended up driving redistricting. The question was how to create two black-majority districts. One, in New Orleans, was easy; the other, as a glance at the districting map makes clear, was hard. The new 4th District is one of the most grotesquely shaped in the country, trekking through bayous and the Atchafalaya swamp from black precincts of Lafayette to Baton Rouge, along the Mississippi and the northern edge of the state, dipping down to black neighborhoods in Monroe and Shreveport. A walk over the boundaries of this district might take as long as Lewis and Clark's journey through the Louisiana Purchase. Politically, the lost seat cost the Republicans.

The People: Est. Pop. 1992: 4,287,000; Pop. 1990: 4,219,973, up 1.6% 1990–1992. 1.7% of U.S. total, 21st largest; 32% rural. Median age: 31.0 years. 11.1% 65 years and over. 67.3% White, 30.8% Black, 2.2% Hispanic origin, 1.0% Asian. Households: 53.6% married couple families; 28% married couple fams. w. children; 37% college educ.; median household income: $21,949; per capita income: $10,635; 65.9% owner occupied housing; median house value: $58,500; median monthly rent: $260. 8.1%

Unemployment. Voting age pop.: 2,992,704. Registered voters (1992): 2,253,888; 1,169,653 D (72%); 424,150 R (19%); 210,085 unaffiliated and minor parties (9%).

Political Lineup: Governor, Edwin W. Edwards (D); Lt. Gov., Melinda Schwegmann (D); Secy. of State, W. Fox McKeithen (R); Atty. Gen., Richard P. Ieyoub (D); Treasurer, Mary L. Landrieu (D). State Senate, 39 (33 D and 6 R); State House of Representatives, 105 (88 D, 16 R, and 1 I). Senators, J. Bennett Johnston (D) and John B. Breaux (D). Representatives, 7 (4 D and 3 R).

1992 Presidential Vote

Clinton (D)	815,971	(46%)
Bush (R)	733,386	(41%)
Perot (I)	211,478	(12%)

1992 Democratic Presidential Primary

Clinton	267,002	(69%)
Tsongas	42,508	(11%)
Brown	25,480	(7%)
McCarthy	15,129	(4%)
Other	34,298	(9%)

1988 Presidential Vote

Bush (R)	883,702	(54%)
Dukakis (D)	717,460	(44%)

1992 Republican Presidential Primary

Bush	83,744	(62%)
Buchanan	36,525	(27%)
Duke	11,955	(9%)

GOVERNOR

Gov. Edwin W. Edwards (D)

Elected 1991, term expires 1996; b. Aug. 7, 1927, Marksville; home, Baton Rouge; LA St. U., 1943–45, LL.B. 1949; Catholic; divorced.

Career: Practicing atty., 1949–64; Crowley City Cncl., 1954–62; LA Senate, 1964–65; U.S. House of Reps., 1965–72; LA Gov., 1972–80, 1984–88; LA Supreme Court, 1980.

Office: State Capitol, P.O. Box 94004, Baton Rouge 70804, 504-342-7015.

Election Results

1991 gen.	Edwin W. Edwards (D)	1,057,031	(61%)
	David Duke (R)	671,009	(39%)
1991 prim.	Edwin W. Edwards (D)	523,195	(34%)
	David Duke (R)	491,342	(32%)
	Buddy Roemer (D)	410,690	(27%)
	Clyde C. Holloway (R)	82,683	(5%)
	Eight Others	41,444	(2%)
1987 gen.	Buddy Roemer (D), unopposed		
1987 prim.	Buddy Roemer (D)	516,078	(33%)
	Edwin Edwards (D)	437,801	(28%)
	Bob Livingston (R)	287,780	(18%)
	Billy Tauzin (D)	154,079	(10%)
	Four Others	162,992	(10%)

SENATORS

Sen. J. Bennett Johnston (D)

Elected 1972, seat up 1996; b. Jun. 10, 1932, Shreveport; home, Shreveport; Washington and Lee U., 1950–53, U.S. Military Acad. at West Point, 1951–52, LA St. U., LL.B. 1956; Baptist; married (Mary).

Career: Army, 1956–59; Practicing atty., 1959–72; LA House of Reps., 1964–68; LA Senate, 1968–72.

Offices: 136 HSOB 20510, 202-224-5824. Also Hale Boggs Fed. Bldg., 500 Camp St., #1010, New Orleans 70130, 504-589-2427; Joe D. Waggonner, Jr. Fed. Bldg., 500 Fannin St., #7A12, Shreveport 71161, 318-226-5085; and 1 American Pl., #1510, Baton Rouge 70825, 504-389-0395.

Committees: *Aging (Special)* (4th of 11 D). *Appropriations* (4th of 16 D): Agriculture, Rural Development and Related Agencies; Defense; Energy and Water Development (Chmn.); Interior; VA, HUD and Independent Agencies. *Budget* (3d of 12 D). *Energy and Natural Resources* (Chmn. of 11 D). *Intelligence (Select)* (9th of 9 D).

Group Ratings

	ADA	ACLU	CDF	COPE	CFA	LCV	ACU	NTLC	NSI	COC	CEI
1992	70	32	90	75	75	25	23	5	60	20	26
1991	40	—	82	75	56	13	52	—	—	40	32

National Journal Ratings

	1991 LIB — 1991 CONS	1992 LIB — 1992 CONS
Economic	46% — 50%	58% — 40%
Social	14% — 77%	39% — 58%
Foreign	63% — 33%	53% — 46%

Key Votes of the 102d Congress

1. $ for Homeownership	AGN	5. Clarence Thomas Nom. FOR	9. Use Force in Gulf FOR
2. Have Cap Gains Debate	AGN	6. Lmt Death Row Appeal FOR	10. Keep Salvador Aid AGN
3. Remove Budget Walls	FOR	7. Handgun Wait/5-Day AGN	11. Cut $1B from SDI FOR
4. Ban Striker Replace	FOR	8. Abortion Gag Rule FOR	12. Override China MFN AGN

Key Votes of the 103d Congress

1. Family Leave FOR	2. HIV Immigrants AGN	3. Clinton Budget FOR

Election Results

1990 primary	J. Bennett Johnston (D)	752,902	(54%)	($5,389,624)
	David Duke (R)	607,391	(44%)	($2,615,267)
	Two Others	35,820	(3%)	
1984 primary	J. Bennett Johnston (D)	838,181	(86%)	($1,046,293)
	Robert M. Ross (R)	86,546	(9%)	
	Larry Napoleon Cooper (R)	52,746	(5%)	

Sen. John B. Breaux (D)

Elected 1986, seat up 1998; b. Mar. 1, 1944, Crowley; home, Lafayette; U. of S.W. LA, B.A. 1964, LA St. U., J.D. 1967; Catholic; married (Lois).

Career: Practicing atty., 1967–68; Legis. Asst. & Dist. Mgr., U.S. Rep. Edwin W. Edwards, 1968–72; U.S. House of Reps., 1972–87.

Offices: 516 HSOB 20510, 202-224-4623. Also 705 Jefferson, #13, Lafayette 70501, 318-264-6871; Hale Boggs Fed. Bldg., #1005, 501 Magazine St., New Orleans 70130, 504-589-2531; and 211 N. 3d St., Monroe 71201, 318-325-3320.

Committees: *Aging (Special)* (5th of 11 D). *Commerce, Science and Transportation* (7th of 11 D): Communications; Merchant Marine (Chmn.); Surface Transportation. *Finance* (10th of 11 D): Energy and Agricultural Taxation; International Trade; Social Security and Family Policy (Chmn.).

Group Ratings

	ADA	ACLU	CDF	COPE	CFA	LCV	ACU	NTLC	NSI	COC	CEI
1992	60	29	80	67	83	25	30	17	60	10	28
1991	30	—	73	67	56	20	57	—	—	40	30

National Journal Ratings

	1991 LIB — 1991 CONS		1992 LIB — 1992 CONS	
Economic	60%	— 35%	55%	— 43%
Social	14%	— 77%	52%	— 46%
Foreign	42%	— 57%	56%	— 41%

Key Votes of the 102d Congress

1. $ for Homeownership	AGN	5. Clarence Thomas Nom. FOR	9. Use Force in Gulf	FOR
2. Have Cap Gains Debate	AGN	6. Lmt Death Row Appeal FOR	10. Keep Salvador Aid	AGN
3. Remove Budget Walls	FOR	7. Handgun Wait/5-Day AGN	11. Cut $1B from SDI	AGN
4. Ban Striker Replace	FOR	8. Abortion Gag Rule FOR	12. Override China MFN FOR

Key Votes of the 103d Congress

1. Family Leave	FOR	2. HIV Immigrants	AGN	3. Clinton Budget	FOR

Election Results

1992 primary	John B. Breaux (D)...................	616,021	(73%)	($2,007,675)
	Jon Khachaturian (I)	74,785	(9%)	($94,919)
	Lyle Stockstill (R)...................	69,986	(8%)	($34,711)
	Nick Accardo (D).....................	45,839	(6%)	
	Fred Clegg Strong (R)	36,406	(4%)	
1986 general	John B. Breaux (D)...................	723,586	(53%)	($2,958,313)
	W. Henson Moore (R).................	646,311	(47%)	($5,986,460)
1986 primary	W. Henson Moore (R).................	529,433	(44%)	
	John B. Breaux (D)...................	447,328	(37%)	
	Samuel B. Nunez (D)..................	73,505	(6%)	
	J.E. Jumonville (D)...................	53,394	(5%)	
	Sherman A. Bernard (D)	52,479	(5%)	

FIRST DISTRICT

New Orleans, sluggishly growing beside the sluggishly flowing Mississippi River, is a unique metropolis, built on unlikely terrain and already a distinctively urban settlement when most of the East Coast cities-to-be were no more than villages. Yet from some vantage points, New Orleans seems scarcely settled today. Climb the levee and look out at the Mississippi and you will see an expanse of water with untidy clumps of trees and disorganized-looking, seemingly abandoned docks—what Mark Twain might have had in his mind's eye when writing *Life on the Mississippi* more than 100 years ago. Or drive just past the last block of a suburban subdivision, and you are in unreclaimed swamp, vegetation and wetness, thick with herons and alligators, extending flatly as far as the eye can see. New Orleans was blessed with a location that funneled all the products of half a continent down a single river to its port and with a history that brought international flair to the Mississippi Valley. It still seems to be living off that history and blessing, with an inward-looking elite preoccupied with who is in which Mardi Gras krewe and interested more in Orleans Parish genealogy than in Oil Patch geology. The old buildings of New Orleans are finely proportioned and its old neighborhoods charming, like those in France; and its early 20th century improvements, like Olmstead's City Park, are grand. But its middle and late 20th century streetscapes and subdivisions, like those of France, are utterly without ornament or charm, utilitarian works of man to master the below-sea-level environment.

The 1st Congressional District of Louisiana includes most of this newer part of the New Orleans metropolitan area, spread over the soggy lands of the lower Mississippi and Lake Pontchartrain. It includes some affluent white neighborhoods—Audubon Park, City Park, Lakeside—and the vast suburb of Metairie in Jefferson Parish, divided by slanting grids and elevated only where bridges jut out over the many canals. The 1st extends across the 26-mile Lake Pontchartrain Causeway (or out eastbound I-10) to include fast-growing St. Tammany Parish, with old towns lush with trees and old houses and clusters of new growth around giant intersections. The 1st also extends north and west, to parts of the Florida Parishes—so called, because even after the United States purchased Louisiana, they were part of the West Florida colony retained by Spain until it was annexed in 1810.

The 1st is a heavily Republican district. Its lines around New Orleans are drawn to maximize the percentage of blacks in the 2d District, and so only 5% of its New Orleans and Jefferson Parish residents are black; overall, the 1st is just 10% black, the lowest percentage in Louisiana. Moreover, the whites here tend to be affluent, highly educated, upscale—which means, in Louisiana, strong for reform and against redistribution, and unabashedly Republican. Like an underdeveloped country, where it seems inconceivable that most people could make decent livings or find anything more than menial jobs, privileged people here are quite unsentimental about maintaining their position, and completely unapologetic about what the guiltily affluent of the Northeast would call their selfishness.

The congressman from this district represents the views and also some of the virtues of this constituency. Bob Livingston bears the name of the New York aristocrat who as chancellor administered the oath of office to George Washington 200 years ago and who as Ambassador to France helped negotiate the Louisiana Purchase. But this Livingston grew up in more modest circumstances, enlisting in the Navy after high school, working his way through school at the Avondale Shipyard. He spent most of his pre-congressional career as a prosecutor and approaches politics with a prosecutorial frame of mind. He won the seat in a 1977 special election, after a Democrat was forced to resign due to fraud and eventually a jail sentence, and Livingston went on to be a tough judge of his colleagues while on the House Ethics Committee during the Abscam investigation.

Livingston is now fifth ranking Republican on the Appropriations Committee, with seats on the Defense and Foreign Operations Subcommittees. He has helped to steer spending to Louisiana defense projects, notably $613 million for Navy sealift vessels, $300 million for a

Navy/Marine amphibious ship, and $325 million for Coast Guard icebreakers, all to be built in Jefferson Parish's Avondale shipyard. He has worked to fund Louisiana projects such as the Harvey Canal flood control levee on the west bank of the Mississippi, and the 12-plane fleet stationed at Keesler Air Force Base for hurricane reconnaissance flights. Livingston was a stout defender of the Reagan and Bush Administrations on issues from Iran-contra to opposing the motor voter bill and gays in the military; he supports the line-item veto, mandatory life sentences for convicted third-time felons and an end to proxy voting in committees. He bitterly attacked the interpretation of the Voting Rights Act (urged by the Republican National Committee and civil rights groups) that resulted in the creation of a grotesquely shaped, black-majority Louisiana 4th District.

Ironically, Livingston is a beneficiary of that implementation, since it kept blacks out of his 1st District and left it overwhelmingly Republican. Despite getting new territory in the Florida Parishes, he was reelected with 73% of the vote in October 1992. Now that David Duke has left politics, Livingston's tenure seems secure. He has been less successful in other efforts. He ran for governor in 1987 and after a poor performance in debate lost his chance to emerge as chief challenger to Edwin Edwards and carried only his home base.

The People: Pop. 1990: 602,848; 28% rural; 12% age 65+; 85% White; 10% Black; 1% Asian; 1% Other; 4% Hispanic origin. Voting age pop.: 444,877; 9% Black; 4% Hispanic origin. Households: 58% married couple families; 28% married couple fams. w. children; 46% college educ.; median household income: $27,877; per capita income: $13,860; median gross rent: $420; median house value: $74,500.

1992 Presidential Vote			1988 Presidential Vote		
Bush (R)	154,584	(56%)	Bush (R)	169,539	(70%)
Clinton (D)	87,429	(31%)	Dukakis (D)	72,424	(30%)
Perot (I)	34,402	(12%)			

Rep. Robert L. (Bob) Livingston (R)

Elected Aug., 1977; b. Apr. 30, 1943, Colorado Springs, CO; home, Metairie; Tulane U., B.A. 1967, J.D. 1968; Episcopalian; married (Bonnie).

Career: Navy, 1961–63; Practicing atty., 1968–70, 1976–77; Asst. U.S. Atty., 1970–73; Chief Special Prosecutor, Orleans Parish Dist. Atty.'s Ofc., 1974–75; Chief Prosecutor, LA Atty. Gen.'s Ofc., Organized Crime Unit, 1975–76.

Offices: 2368 RHOB 20515, 202-225-3015. Also 111 Veterans Blvd., #700, Metairie 70005, 504-589-2753.

Committees: *Appropriations* (5th of 23 R): Defense; Foreign Operations, Export Financing and Related Programs (RMM). *House Administration* (4th of 7 R): Elections (RMM); Personnel and Police.

Group Ratings

	ADA	ACLU	COPE	CDF	CFA	LCV	ACU	NTLC	NSI	COC	CEI
1992	10	0	30	10	20	0	95	84	100	83	58
1991	0	—	8	20	17	0	90	—	—	100	62

National Journal Ratings

	1991 LIB — 1991 CONS			1992 LIB — 1992 CONS		
Economic	10%	—	89%	21%	—	79%
Social	0%	—	84%	0%	—	85%
Foreign	0%	—	88%	0%	—	82%

Key Votes of the 102d Congress

1. Ban Striker Replace AGN	5. Handgun Wait/7-Day AGN	9. Use Force in Gulf FOR
2. $ for Homeownership FOR	6. Overseas Mil. AbortionAGN	10. US Mil. Abroad $ CutAGN
3. Tax Rich/Cut Mid Cls.AGN	7. Obscn. Art NEA $ Ban FOR	11. Limit SDI Funds AGN
4. FY93/$15B Def. Cut *	8. Death Pen. from Jury FOR	12. Cuba Trade Embargo *

Key Votes of the 103d Congress

1. Family Leave AGN	2. Deficit Reduction AGN	3. Stimulus Plan AGN

Election Results

1992 primary	Robert L. (Bob) Livingston (R)	83,685	(73%)	($321,487)
	Anne Thompson (R)	11,620	(10%)	
	Vincent J. Bruno (R)	7,874	(7%)	($7,294)
	Richie Martin (R)	4,789	(4%)	($16,671)
	Jules W. Hillery (I)	4,442	(4%)	
	Other	2,641	(2%)	
1990 primary	Robert L. (Bob) Livingston (R)	132,855	(84%)	($108,207)
	Vincent J. Bruno (R)	25,494	(16%)	

SECOND DISTRICT

Founded by the French in 1718, ruled by the Spanish from 1763 to just days before the French took over to sell it in 1803, New Orleans was a Creole city—part French, a bit Spanish, more than a touch Caribbean—when the American flag was raised over what is now Jackson Square in 1803. The statue of Andrew Jackson still seems an alien intrusion in a square set off by a French Market, the Cabildo, the Presbytere, the Pontalba apartments and Cathedral St. Louis. New Orleans was the fourth largest American city from 1840 until the Civil War and the only sizable city in the South; yet even as it was sending southern cotton out to the mills of Lancashire, it was an alien cultural force in both the nation and region. Urbanized, yet poor and in many ways primitive, New Orleans had yellow fever epidemics late in the 19th Century, even as it was installing electric lights; it had a riot in which Italian immigrants were massacred, even as it was laying streetcar tracks and telephone lines. This was one of the most corrupt American cities during Reconstruction and the Gilded Age, when its votes were regularly bid for and bought; like other southern cities, it became rigidly segregated after 1890. Today, New Orleans remains a major port, but has lost much oil business to Houston and much Latin American trade to Miami and has the second highest poverty rate, 32%, among cities with populations over 90,000.

The 2d Congressional District of Louisiana today includes nine-tenths of the city of New Orleans, everything except the white affluent neighborhoods of Lakeview, City Park, and uptown Audubon Park. It also includes the west bank towns of Jefferson Parish—Gretna, Harvey, Westwego, Waggaman, industrial enclosures between levee and swamp, and a black neighborhood in Kenner, near the airport. But it is New Orleans everyone wants to visit. Here is the French Quarter, its 19th Century homes still intact because the Americans who moved here after 1803 wanted to stay away from the snobbish Creoles and built a new downtown east of Canal Street. Just above the Quarter is the site of Storyville, where prostitution was legal until 1918 and where jazz was probably first played; the old frame houses have long since been torn down and replaced by housing projects. But many similar neighborhoods remain, where blacks and some working-class whites live in rickety frame houses which are not always strong enough to keep the rain out and never tight enough to keep out the summer humidity or the damp winter chill, along the vividly named streets—Elysian Fields, Spain, Desire, Arts—that go north from the river wharves. In the other direction is the downtown flecked with skyscrapers and the ominous Superdome, past the old slum known as the Irish Channel—a reminder that New

Orleans had more foreign immigrants than any other part of the South—to the Garden District. This was the home of the rich, early American settlers, and its antebellum homes are still covered with vines and Spanish moss. Quaintly named trolley cars still roll out St. Charles Avenue to Tulane University and Audubon Park.

New Orleans, for many years a speckled black-and-white city, now has a solid black majority, and the west bank towns have large black minorities; the 2d District is just over 60% black. For nearly 20 years, the district was represented by Lindy Boggs, a charming Louisiana lady with perfect manners and perfect political pitch; she continued winning, even in a black majority seat against respected black opponents, until she decided to retire in 1990. There followed a spirited primary and general battle between several black candidates and one serious white candidate. The winner was 11-year state Senator Bill Jefferson, who twice ran for mayor and lost; he was endorsed by New Orleans Mayor Sidney Barthelemy and in the runoff beat Marc Morial, whose father, the late Dutch Morial, was mayor before Barthelemy. Jefferson had 25% in the primary to 22% for Morial, 19% for state Senator Jon Johnson, 18% for Orleans Parish school board member Woody Koppel, and 7% for city dock board member Edgar "Dooky" Chase III, owner of a well-known soul food restaurant. In the November runoff, charges flew: Jefferson was dogged by reports of defaults on outstanding loans and mortgages, while Morial admitted he was the father of an eight-year-old girl living in the Ivory Coast. Jefferson won with 52% and became the first Louisiana black elected to Congress since Reconstruction.

Jefferson brought political skills to Washington. He was elected freshman Democratic whip and secretary of the Congressional Black Caucus. He was active in the Democratic Leadership Council and got to know its chairman, a young southern governor named Bill Clinton. In November 1991, Jefferson and Mississippi Congressman Mike Espy met with Clinton to talk about a southern strategy, and both started campaigning almost non-stop for Clinton for a year. Jefferson's work paid off in Louisiana, where Clinton won 69% of the primary vote, and his support was helpful to Clinton in many other states as well. In August, Jefferson, Espy, and John Lewis of Georgia arranged a bus tour that rolled through the South. Their efforts for Clinton are landmark: talented southern black politicians helping to build a presidential campaign that can appeal to southern blacks and southern whites.

When he ran for the House, most observers in New Orleans thought Jefferson was just getting ready to run for mayor in 1994. But with his good friend in the White House, and with his own win of a seat on Ways and Means just after the 1992 election, Jefferson looks to be an influential figure on Capitol Hill and in national politics, a potential builder of the biracial coalition the Democrats need. The growth of the 2d District out to the suburbs did not hurt him politically, and he was reelected in October 1992 with 73% of the vote.

The People: Pop. 1990: 602,774; 11% age 65+; 35% White; 61% Black; 2% Asian; 1% Other; 3% Hispanic origin. Voting age pop.: 425,475; 56% Black; 4% Hispanic origin. Households: 38% married couple families; 19% married couple fams. w. children; 40% college educ.; median household income: $18,367; per capita income: $9,790; median gross rent: $372; median house value: $61,800.

1992 Presidential Vote

Clinton (D) 153,134 (68%)
Bush (R) 55,362 (25%)
Perot (I) 13,895 (6%)

1988 Presidential Vote

Dukakis (D) 134,320 (66%)
Bush (R) 68,166 (34%)

Rep. William J. Jefferson (D)

Elected 1990; b. Mar. 14, 1947, Lake Providence; home, New Orleans; Southern U., B.A. 1969, Harvard, J.D. 1972; Baptist; married (Andrea).

Career: Army Reserves, 1969–78, Army Judge Advocate Corps, 1975; Law clerk, U.S. Dist. Judge Alvin Rubin, 1972–73; Legis. aide, U.S. Sen. Bennett Johnston, 1973–75; Practicing atty., 1975–90; LA Senate, 1979–90.

Offices: 428 CHOB 20515, 202-225-6636. Also 501 Magazine St., #1012, New Orleans 70130, 504-589-2274.

Committees: *District of Columbia* (7th of 8 D): Fiscal Affairs and Health; Government Operations and Metropolitan Affairs. *Ways and Means* (22d of 24 D): Oversight; Social Security.

Group Ratings

	ADA	ACLU	COPE	CDF	CFA	LCV	ACU	NTLC	NSI	COC	CEI
1992	85	95	92	100	87	63	0	0	20	29	13
1991	85	—	92	100	78	62	0	—	—	20	4

National Journal Ratings

	1991 LIB — 1991 CONS	1992 LIB — 1992 CONS
Economic	68% — 32%	74% — 26%
Social	84% — 12%	80% — 19%
Foreign	77% — 22%	84% — 16%

Key Votes of the 102d Congress

1. Ban Striker Replace	FOR	5. Handgun Wait/7-Day	FOR	9. Use Force in Gulf	AGN
2. $ for Homeownership	*	6. Overseas Mil. Abortion	FOR	10. US Mil. Abroad $ Cut	FOR
3. Tax Rich/Cut Mid Cls.	FOR	7. Obscn. Art NEA $ Ban	AGN	11. Limit SDI Funds	FOR
4. FY93/$15B Def. Cut	FOR	8. Death Pen. from Jury	AGN	12. Cuba Trade Embargo	AGN

Key Votes of the 103d Congress

1. Family Leave	FOR	2. Deficit Reduction	FOR	3. Stimulus Plan	FOR

Election Results

1992 primary	William J. Jefferson (D)	67,030	(73%)	($352,058)
	Wilma Knox Irvin (D)	14,121	(15%)	($23,640)
	Roger C. Johnson (I)	10,090	(11%)	
1990 general	William J. Jefferson (D)	55,371	(52%)	($446,743)
	Marc H. Morial (D)	50,197	(48%)	($425,391)

THIRD DISTRICT

A few feet below sea level, veined with bayous and creeks and wide streams of water, crossed by only an occasional road or railroad, the wetlands of southern Louisiana is one of America's unique landscapes. Technically, most of this waterlogged land are islands in a broad river mouth, through which the waters of the Mississippi and its tributaries drain into the Gulf of Mexico. It is rich with animal life, herons and egrets, shrimp and crawfish, muskrats and alligators, and supports more people than the casual observer would think. There are cabins along the bayous and crossroad towns where Cajun French remains the first language, and roadside diners feature crawfish etouffe. But the steep-roofed Cajun houses are not the only structures: here and there, jutting out of the swampy land, are huge elaborate metal sculptures—refineries and petrochemical plants, processing the oil and natural gas trapped under these wetlands and the shallow continental shelf of the Gulf, and released through 20th Century oil rig technology. In the 1960s and 1970s, the oil industry, by providing good jobs for young people here, helped preserve Cajun culture and build a Cajun pride that was seldom articulated a generation ago. That pride, and the curiosity of tourists, have helped maintain the way of life in the Cajun parishes in the 1980s and 1990s, as oil payrolls have gone way down and the wetlands seem threatened by coastal erosion—and by Hurricane Andrew, which did $1 billion worth of damage here in August 1992.

The 3d Congressional District of Louisiana includes about half the Cajun country, plus St. Bernard and Plaquemines Parishes downriver from New Orleans. St. Bernard is now working class suburbia and cast among the state's highest percentages in 1990 and 1991 for David Duke's statewide races. The 3d District then spreads west over the swamplands, covering Houma, where seven bayous converge; St. Charles, St. John the Baptist, St. James and Ascension Parishes on both sides of the Mississippi, once the greatest sugar producers in America, are now studded with refineries and petrochemical plants; roughneck Morgan City, services many offshore oil rigs; and Iberia Parish is home to McIlhenny's Tabasco sauce.

The 3d District's congressman is Billy Tauzin, from Thibodaux in Lafourche Parish, who first won the district in a spring 1980 special election and is now one of the top ranking Democrats on the Energy and Commerce Committee and a subcommittee chairman on Merchant Marine and Fisheries. He got the latter seat in early 1989, just in time to be handed the responsibility for legislation inspired by the Exxon *Valdez* oil spill in Alaska; Tauzin took the view that state laws should be preempted by the federal statute, and ultimately got an oil spill prevention and compensation bill through conference committee in August 1990. Tauzin also drew up plans to allow a drawdown of the Strategic Petroleum Reserve (which is mostly in southern Louisiana) to help pay for Persian Gulf troop deployments, and was able to get Congress to build the Reserve back up to one billion barrels. He has led the fight to relax federal wetland regulations, of obvious interest to the 3d District's fishermen, shrimpers and rice farmers, and to compensate those whom the laws blocked from using their land; he has pushed bills to protect the wetlands from coastal erosion, however. On Energy and Commerce, he pushes for more offshore drilling and limits on imported oil. He wants to revise the Endangered Species Act so that it produces results "with the least socioeconomic impact." He was a player on the cable reregulation bill, pushing for more program access, opposed by cable operators and backed by the direct broadcast satellite industry. He also had a bill to allow the Baby Bells to enter the information services business, which he will reintroduce in the 103d Congress.

Tauzin is practically a lifetime politician, first elected to the state legislature at 28. He ran for governor in 1987, but that race was doomed when Edwin Edwards ran, since he and reformist-conservative Buddy Roemer split the Cajun country vote, and Tauzin finished fourth with 10%. He retains local roots—his house was damaged by Hurricane Andrew—but it's not clear he will run statewide again. He didn't make the race in 1991, and by 1995 he may well be loath to give up his seniority and committee positions.

The People: Pop. 1990: 603,258; 34% rural; 9% age 65+; 74% White; 22% Black; 1% Amer. Indian; 1% Asian; 2% Hispanic origin. Voting age pop.: 415,060; 19% Black; 2% Hispanic origin. Households: 63% married couple families; 34% married couple fams. w. children; 27% college educ.; median household income: $23,813; per capita income: $9,911; median gross rent: $338; median house value: $57,900.

1992 Presidential Vote

Clinton (D)	115,063	(44%)
Bush (R)	105,982	(40%)
Perot (I)	36,193	(14%)

1988 Presidential Vote

Bush (R)	128,518	(54%)
Dukakis (D)	108,353	(46%)

Rep. W. J. (Billy) Tauzin (D)

Elected May 1980; b. June 14, 1943, Chackbay; home, Thibodaux; Nicholls St. U., B.A. 1964, LA St. U., J.D. 1967; Catholic; married (Cecile).

Career: Practicing atty., 1968–80; LA House of Reps., 1971–79.

Offices: 2330 RHOB 20515, 202-225-4031. Also 1041 Hale Boggs Bldg., 501 Magazine St., New Orleans 70130, 504-589-6366; 107 Fed. Bldg., Houma 700360, 504-876-3033; 210 E. Main St., New Iberia 70560, 318-367-8231; and 828 S. Irma Blvd., #212-A, Gonzales 70737, 504-621-8490.

Committees: *Energy and Commerce* (8th of 27 D): Energy and Power; Telecommunications and Finance; Transportation and Hazardous Materials. *Merchant Marine and Fisheries* (4th of 29 D): Coast Guard and Navigation (Chmn.); Environment and Natural Resources.

Group Ratings

	ADA	ACLU	COPE	CDF	CFA	LCV	ACU	NTLC	NSI	COC	CEI
1992	40	23	55	40	47	13	71	60	100	75	48
1991	10	—	50	50	44	15	70	—	—	80	44

National Journal Ratings

	1991 LIB — 1991 CONS	1992 LIB — 1992 CONS
Economic	38% — 62%	40% — 59%
Social	25% — 73%	21% — 78%
Foreign	31% — 67%	30% — 64%

Key Votes of the 102d Congress

1. Ban Striker Replace	AGN	5. Handgun Wait/7-Day	AGN	9. Use Force in Gulf	FOR
2. $ for Homeownership	*	6. Overseas Mil. Abortion	AGN	10. US Mil. Abroad $ Cut	FOR
3. Tax Rich/Cut Mid Cls.	AGN	7. Obscn. Art NEA $ Ban	FOR	11. Limit SDI Funds	AGN
4. FY93/$15B Def. Cut	FOR	8. Death Pen. from Jury	FOR	12. Cuba Trade Embargo	FOR

Key Votes of the 103d Congress

1. Family Leave   AGN   2. Deficit Reduction   FOR   3. Stimulus Plan   AGN

Election Results

1992 primary	W. J. (Billy) Tauzin (D)	82,047	(82%)	($311,112)
	Paul I. Boynton (R)	18,402	(18%)	
1990 primary	W. J. (Billy) Tauzin (D)	155,351	(88%)	($474,224)
	Ronald P. Duplantis (I)	14,909	(8%)	
	Millard F. Clement (I)	6,562	(4%)	

FOURTH DISTRICT

Louisiana, founded by the French, ruled for a generation by the Spanish, run for half a century after statehood by a planter and cotton trader elite that included Creoles, Yankees and Jews, was a slave commonwealth. The style of its iron-balconied New Orleans townhouses and the manners of its grand plantation mansions came from the rice and cotton and sugar that were grown in this soggy soil, none of which could have been harvested and processed without the labor of African-American slaves. This is true, of course, of other southern states, but in Louisiana slavery seemed to have a special French rigor and pitilessness; remember that the other French slave commonwealth in the New World became the Republic of Haiti. Louisiana's blacks, enfranchised after the Civil War, for a moment took political power in what was then a black-majority state. But they were soon driven from power—there is a monument in New Orleans to the laws that accomplished this—and left without the vote or any claim on the political system. Louisiana economically was one of the most backward states, with few paved roads and not much electricity until Huey Long became governor in 1928. Yet Louisiana blacks produced some of the nation's most important culture: jazz music may have had its commercial start in the parlors of the legal houses of prostitution in the New Orleans neighborhood of Storyville, but it had deeper roots in the centuries-long experience of black people working hard in the wet soil, under the hot sun of Louisiana.

Today 31% of Louisianans are black and, since the Voting Rights Act of 1965, they have been part of the political culture of the state. And by no means an ignored part: black voters were key in electing Edwin Edwards governor, for example, and black state legislators, which represent more than 20% of the legislature, have become power brokers in Baton Rouge. For a long time there were no Louisiana blacks in Congress, because the black-majority New Orleans district reelected the redoubtable Lindy Boggs. Now, with her retirement in 1990 and the application of the revised Voting Rights Act to the redistricting of 1992, there are two black-majority districts of seven (which between them include almost 60% of Louisiana blacks), and two black congressmen. One of the districts is compact, being made up of most of the city of New Orleans. The other is the new 4th District, one of the most grotesquely shaped in the country.

The 4th has been called a Z-shaped district; actually, it is shaped like a capital Z in cursive writing. It takes in the black precincts, but very few of the white precincts, in most of Louisiana's prominent cities outside New Orleans. The lower end of the cursive Z's tail is in the Cajun country capital of Lafayette; the Z then crosses the trackless Atchafalaya Swamp to include black communities in the "petroleum alley" (which is also old plantation country) along the Mississippi; it curves around to the Florida parishes to reach the black neighborhoods on the north side of Baton Rouge; a side-squiggle of the Z heads up the Red River to include the black parts of Alexandria, while the main diagonal goes up along the Mississippi, where once there were great plantations and now there are black majorities; the top of the Z covers the whole Arkansas border, dipping southward to pick up the black neighborhoods in Monroe and Shreveport and the black college town of Grambling halfway in between.

Such a district might have attracted a free-for-all primary, and in fact eight candidates ran. But one clearly dominated the field: Cleo Fields, a 29-year-old state Senator from Baton Rouge. Fields was the youngest legislator in Louisiana history (how did Huey Long miss that record?) when he was first elected in 1986 at age 23, and he showed great political skills. He championed drug-free zones and encouraged inner city development: more a discipline-oriented than a liberation-oriented agenda. He is pro-environment but remains on good terms with the natural gas industry—always important in Louisiana. A Jesse Jackson supporter in 1988, he is nonetheless not considered a radical. His first race for Congress was unsuccessful when he won 30% against Republican Clyde Holloway in the old 8th District in 1990. As chairman of the redistricting committee in the legislature, Fields announced early for this seat and ran as the favorite. He won 48% in the October primary in an eight-candidate field, winning absolute majorities in such far-flung places as Lafayette, Alexandria and Baton Rouge. In the runoff against state Senator Charles D. Jones, Fields won with a smashing 74%, with 84% in Shreveport and 87% in Lafayette, at opposite ends of the district.

Fields, who turned 30 just after the election, has excelled at every stage of his career. The interesting question now is whether he can transcend the parochial demands of representing a constituency from which white voters have been largely excluded. If so, it seems there is no goal to which he might not reasonably aspire.

The People: Pop. 1990: 603,072; 30% rural; 11% age 65+; 33% White; 67% Black; 1% Hispanic origin. Voting age pop.: 413,858; 63% Black; 1% Hispanic origin. Households: 44% married couple families;

22% married couple fams. w. children; 28% college educ.; median household income: $14,515; per capita income: $7,270; median gross rent: $287; median house value: $40,200.

1992 Presidential Vote			1988 Presidential Vote		
Clinton (D)	150,800	(66%)	Dukakis (D)	139,950	(65%)
Bush (R)	57,286	(25%)	Bush (R)	75,676	(35%)
Perot (I)	17,298	(8%)			

Rep. Cleo Fields (D)

Elected 1992; b. Nov. 22, 1962, Baton Rouge; home, Baton Rouge; Southern U., B.A. 1984; Southern U. Law Schl., J.D. 1987; Baptist; married (Debra).

Career: LA Senate, 1986–92.

Offices: 513 CHOB 20515, 202-225-8490. Also 700 N. 10th St., Baton Rouge 70802, 504-343-9773; 301 N. Main St., Opelousas 70570, 318-942-9691; and 610 Texas St., #201, Shreveport 71101, 318-221-9924.

Committees: *Banking, Finance and Urban Affairs* (25th of 30 D): Consumer Credit and Insurance; Housing and Community Development; International Development, Finance, Trade and Monetary Policy. *Small Business* (18th of 27 D): Minority Enterprise, Finance and Urban Development; SBA Legislation and the General Economy.

Group Ratings and 102d Congress Votes: Newly Elected

Key Votes of the 103d Congress

1. Family Leave	FOR	2. Deficit Reduction	FOR	3. Stimulus Plan	FOR

Election Results

1992 general	Cleo Fields (D)	143,980	(74%)	($305,336)
	Charles Jones (D)	50,851	(26%)	($129,003)
1992 primary	Cleo Fields (D)	62,697	(48%)	
	Charles Jones (D)	18,305	(14%)	
	Joe Shyne (D)	14,157	(11%)	
	Faye Williams (D)	11,264	(9%)	
	Steve Myers (R)	10,275	(8%)	
	Emile K. Ventre (R)	8,982	(7%)	
	Two Others	5,466	(4%)	
1990 election	Newly created district.			

FIFTH DISTRICT

Northern Louisiana, from the low-lying delta lands along the Mississippi River, west toward the Red River and Texas, is part of the Deep South. Most people here are Protestant, not Catholic; they live in small towns or small cities like Shreveport or Monroe; the whites have long stopped believing in racial segregation but are solidly conservative on most cultural issues. This is a part of America where traditional and fundamentalist religion is still strong, where most people still live in traditional two-parent family units, where the wicked ways of New Orleans could be a world away. The countryside is agricultural, though there are few vestiges left of either the large riverfront plantations or backward farm country like Winn Parish, the boyhood home of Huey P. Long. Economically there is some growth: Shreveport, long an oil town, is getting high-tech industry, as General Electric is diverting some electronics manufacturing operations here from another plant in Pittsfield, Massachusetts. Voters here, for more than 100 years, have been voting against cosmopolitan New Orleans and the Catholic Cajun south, sometimes for riproaring populists, and more often, as the economy grows more sophisticated, for market-oriented Republicans.

This is especially true of the new 5th Congressional District of Louisiana, which consists of most of the interior of northern Louisiana; the edges, set off by an incredibly jagged border, are in the new black-majority 4th District which zigzags all the way south to Baton Rouge and Lafayette. As a result, the 5th District is only 22% black, rather than 36% black as it would be if it included all of every parish which it shares with the new 4th. This has great political consequences, since the Louisiana TV network exit polls showed blacks voting for Bill Clinton over George Bush 87%–7% and white Protestants voting for Bush over Clinton 61%–25%. The Republican percentage is especially high in the white areas of Caddo and Bossier (pronounced *bohzh-yer*) Parishes in the Shreveport area, which with a few small rural areas were in the old 4th Congressional District, represented by Republican Jim McCrery. But the white areas of Monroe's Ouachita Parish, like most of affluent urban Louisiana, are also heavily Republican, though this was the largest town in the old 5th District represented for 16 years by Democrat Jerry Huckaby.

The creation of this new district set up a contest between these two incumbents which ultimately turned bitter, even though they had worked with each other for years, going back to the early 1980s when McCrery was a top staffer for old 4th District Congressman Buddy Roemer, before Roemer and McCrery switched parties. Huckaby got a seat on the Agriculture Committee, concentrating largely on keeping cotton subsidies and sugar quotas, with some success; on other issues he was one of the most conservative Democrats in the House. He was reelected easily for years over desultory opposition.

McCrery has had more recent experience of tough competition, in the 1988 special and primary, and the 1990 primary. In the first race, he was helped because the leading Democrat, Foster Campbell, was badly injured while driving illegally on an unopened section of I-49; in 1990, Campbell ran again, raising populist economic issues against McCrery, but McCrery stressed his conservative stands on defense and the budget summit agreement. Attacked for backing the congressional pay raise, McCrery became an exponent of congressional reform—an interesting example of the conservative-reformist combination that has been a steady feature of Louisiana politics since Huey Long. He bounced no checks, refused to take honoraria after pocketing one $300 check which he later gave to charity, backed term limits and the line-item veto.

These stood him in good stead in 1992. Huckaby had 88 overdrafts on the House bank totalling $41,000; he took out newspaper ads apologizing, but was hammered on this and for taking first-class airplane flights back home. A third candidate, Shreveport Democrat Robert Thompson ran some witty black-and-white TV ads inviting voters to vote against not just one but two incumbents. In late August a ruckus erupted when *The Advocate*, a Los Angeles gay and lesbian magazine, ran a cover story "outing" McCrery, charging that he was gay and attacking him for voting against gay rights. McCrery, denied the charges, saying, "The story, contained in an advocacy publication which advances the agenda of radical groups such as Queer Nation, illustrates the base depths to which some will go to advance their own selfish special interests." "Jim McCrery has denied the charges," said Huckaby. "I want to believe him."

Local newspapers strongly supported McCrery, who got married for the first time in 1991 at 42, and the charges did not ruin his chances. He led the October primary with 44% of the vote to 29% for Huckaby; the big surprise was that Thompson got 22%. He cut far deeper into Huckaby's base, holding him to 38% in his old district, than into McCrery's Shreveport base; McCrery got 57% in his old district. In the runoff, McCrery did even better, winning his old district with 72% and even carrying Huckaby's old 5th District by 58%–42%, for a 63%–37% win overall.

McCrery has a solidly conservative record. He likes to point out that he was one of only 72 votes against the catastrophic health care bill which the House rushed to repeal a year after passage. In 1993, he was assigned to Ways and Means where he is likely to pursue a line-item veto and deficit reduction.

The People: Pop. 1990: 603,213; 44% rural; 13% age 65+; 77% White; 22% Black; 1% Hispanic origin. Voting age pop.: 436,413; 19% Black; 1% Hispanic origin. Households: 58% married couple families; 28% married couple fams. w. children; 41% college educ.; median household income: $22,903; per capita income: $11,349; median gross rent: $344; median house value: $54,900.

1992 Presidential Vote			1988 Presidential Vote		
Bush (R)	125,965	(48%)	Bush (R)	162,630	(69%)
Clinton (D)	94,936	(36%)	Dukakis (D)	72,384	(31%)
Perot (I)	36,121	(14%)			

Rep. Jim McCrery (R)

Elected Apr. 1988; b. Sept. 18, 1949, Shreveport; home, Shreveport; LA Tech. U., B.A. 1971, LA St. U., J.D. 1975; Methodist; married (Johnette).

Career: Practicing atty. 1975–78; Asst. Shreveport City Atty., 1979–80; Legis. Dir., U.S. Rep. Buddy Roemer, 1981–84; Regional Mgr., Georgia-Pacific Corp., 1984–88.

Offices: 225 CHOB 20515, 202-225-2777. Also 6425 Youree Dr., #350, Shreveport 71105, 318-798-2254; and 2400 Forsythe, Monroe 71201, 318-388-6105.

Committees: *Ways and Means* (11th of 14 R): Health; Select Revenue Measures.

Group Ratings

	ADA	ACLU	COPE	CDF	CFA	LCV	ACU	NTLC	NSI	COC	CEI
1992	5	0	10	30	20	13	91	74	100	83	76
1991	0	—	8	10	22	8	85	—	—	90	62

National Journal Ratings

	1991 LIB — 1991 CONS			1992 LIB — 1992 CONS		
Economic	24%	—	74%	14%	—	85%
Social	0%	—	84%	0%	—	85%
Foreign	26%	—	70%	0%	—	82%

Key Votes of the 102d Congress

1. Ban Striker Replace	AGN	5. Handgun Wait/7-Day	AGN	9. Use Force in Gulf	FOR
2. $ for Homeownership	FOR	6. Overseas Mil. Abortion	AGN	10. US Mil. Abroad $ Cut	AGN
3. Tax Rich/Cut Mid Cls.	AGN	7. Obscn. Art NEA $ Ban	FOR	11. Limit SDI Funds	AGN
4. FY93/$15B Def. Cut	AGN	8. Death Pen. from Jury	FOR	12. Cuba Trade Embargo	*

Key Votes of the 103d Congress

1. Family Leave	AGN	2. Deficit Reduction	AGN	3. Stimulus Plan	AGN

Election Results

1992 general	Jim McCrery (R)	153,501	(63%)	($743,254)
	Jerry Huckaby (D)	90,079	(37%)	($792,318)
1992 primary	Jim McCrery (R)	69,511	(44%)	
	Jerry Huckaby (D)	46,386	(29%)	
	Robert Thompson (D)	35,306	(22%)	
	Two Others	6,340	(4%)	
1990 primary	Jim McCrery (R)	89,859	(55%)	($481,504)
(LA 4)	Foster L. Campbell (D)	74,388	(45%)	($305,348)

SIXTH DISTRICT

Across the geographic midriff of Louisiana runs an invisible line between Cajun and Catholic southern Louisiana and Anglo-Saxon and Protestant northern Louisiana, a line that separates accents, attitudes and tastes in music and cuisine. It was approximately along that line that the one Louisiana politician who straddled it got his start and met his end: Huey Long, born and raised in Winn Parish north of Alexandria, who became governor at age 36 in the old (and still-standing) Gothic Capitol in Baton Rouge when the city had 30,000 people, and who was shot and killed, allegedly by a young doctor but quite possibly by his own bodyguards, in the 34-story Art Deco Capitol he built, from which you can look south along the Mississippi River to Louisiana State University, which Long also mostly built, and north to the Exxon (once Jersey Standard) refinery, which he taxed to finance his public works. Baton Rouge is now the center of a metro area of half a million, almost all on the east bank of the Mississippi, and reaching far inland to Livingston Parish. Baton Rouge tries to maintain all Louisiana's traditions; according to political consultant James Carville, who comes from nearby Carville in Iberville Parish, it has "the best restaurants per capita of any city in the United States."

About half of the 6th Congressional District of Louisiana, greatly redesigned for the 1990s, consists of Baton Rouge and its suburban fringe, with black neighborhoods shorn off and attached to the black-majority 4th District. The new 6th also includes several Cajun parishes, where the Mississippi, Atchafalaya and Red Rivers make lazy snake-like loops through the flat landscape, and the small city of Alexandria in Rapides Parish; these were in the old 8th Congressional District, abolished since the 1990 Census reduced Louisiana to seven House seats. The new 6th District then includes Winn and several other northern parishes and heads eastward to include two parishes around the Army's Fort Polk; these were in the old 5th and 4th Districts. The political complexion of all this area is historically Democratic, but Republican in national elections. Baton Rouge has become pretty solidly conservative-reformist and therefore usually Republican in other elections as well, and the Republican leanings of the new district are increased because black precincts were systematically snipped away and put in the new 4th.

As might be expected, this new 6th District was the scene of a fight between two incumbents, both Republicans first elected in 1986, plus the Democratic mayor of Alexandria. The most senior Republican was Richard Baker, from Baton Rouge, elected in the old 6th in 1986 when incumbent Republican Henson Moore ran for the Senate and lost to John Breaux. Baker is one of those instinctive politicians whose life work is politics; he was first elected as a Democrat to the Louisiana House from a blue-collar Baton Rouge district at age 24 in 1972, and rose to become chairman of the roads committee. He became a Republican in 1985, and beat a Democratic state senator for the House 51%–46%. He was unopposed in 1988 and 1990; his visible work was primarily on local issues. The new lines were not good news for him. His Baton Rouge base amounted to just 44% of the new district, and he was virtually unknown in the rest. Better known was the other Republican incumbent, Clyde Holloway. He was more of a political accident, a nursery owner and perennial election loser who won the heavily Democratic 8th District in 1986 and 1988 against a black woman with a bizarre personal biography (her estranged husband broke into her house in 1971, beat her, and shot to death the college professor she had been dating). In 1990, he beat Cleo Fields, now the congressman from the new 4th. More important, Holloway ran for governor in 1991, and had the endorsement of the state Republican Party (Buddy Roemer had just switched parties and, with Holloway, wanted to stand opposed to David Duke) and though he finished far out of the money, well behind Edwin Edwards, Duke and Roemer, he did get some publicity outside his old district, only 35% of which was in the new 6th. Though not one of his party's intellectuals, Holloway was lead sponsor of the Republicans' child care tax credit targeted at low-income working families, a version of which became part of the 1990 child care law.

Holloway started off as the favorite, with an endorsement by New Orleans suburban colleague Bob Livingston; Baker, playing off Holloway's tradition of urging squirrel hunters to vote for him absentee because their season starts on primary day, ran an ad showing squirrel hunters ticking off reasons to vote against Holloway. Baker attacked Holloway for getting a disaster loan for his business while on the Agriculture Committee, for not paying withholding taxes to the government and for not donating his salary to a recognized charity as promised. Holloway hit Baker for living outside the district (his house is 200 yards from the line). Baker stressed economic issues—job creation, freeing up credit for businesses, reducing regulation. Holloway stressed cultural issues—abortion, gays, school prayer. In the October primary both had majorities in their old districts; Holloway won 37% to Baker's 33%, and the third candidate, Democrat Ned Randolph, was eliminated with 30%. In the November runoff Baker carried only East Baton Rouge and Livingston Parishes, but got 71% there, for a 51%–49% victory.

Baker serves on the Banking Committee, where the *American Banker* described him as a "flagbearer for deregulation;" he also received a seat on the Natural Resources Committee for 1993. He has been mentioned as a candidate for statewide office, but his close scrape in the new 6th may not embolden him for a statewide race.

The People: Pop. 1990: 602,129; 45% rural; 11% age 65+; 82% White; 14% Black; 1% Amer. Indian; 1% Asian; 2% Hispanic origin. Voting age pop.: 434,108; 13% Black; 2% Hispanic origin. Households: 62% married couple families; 32% married couple fams. w. children; 42% college educ.; median household income: $25,251; per capita income: $12,042; median gross rent: $374; median house value: $63,100.

1992 Presidential Vote

Bush (R)	134,222	(50%)
Clinton (D)	91,273	(34%)
Perot (I)	35,325	(13%)

1988 Presidential Vote

Bush (R)	157,341	(68%)
Dukakis (D)	74,534	(32%)

Rep. Richard H. Baker (R)

Elected 1986; b. May 22, 1948, New Orleans; home, Baton Rouge; LA St. U., B.A. 1971; United Methodist; married (Kay).

Career: Real estate developer, 1972–86; LA House of Reps., 1972–86.

Offices: 434 CHOB 20515, 202-225-3901. Also 5757 Corporate Blvd., #104, Baton Rouge 70808, 504-929-7711; 3406 Rosalino St., Alexandria 71301, 318-445-5504; and 100 E. Texas St., Leesville 71446, 318-238-5443.

Committees: *Banking, Finance and Urban Affairs* (8th of 20 R): Consumer Credit and Insurance; Financial Institutions Supervision, Regulation and Deposit Insurance; Housing and Community Development; Intl. Development, Finance, Trade and Monetary Policy. *Natural Resources* (11th of 15 R): National Parks, Forests and Public Lands; Native American Affairs. *Small Business* (3d of 18 R): Procurement, Taxation and Tourism (RMM).

Group Ratings

	ADA	ACLU	COPE	CDF	CFA	LCV	ACU	NTLC	NSI	COC	CEI
1992	0	0	20	0	20	0	100	89	100	86	81
1991	0	—	8	10	11	0	95	—	—	100	75

National Journal Ratings

	1991 LIB	—	1991 CONS	1992 LIB	—	1992 CONS
Economic	4%	—	90%	14%	—	85%
Social	0%	—	84%	0%	—	85%
Foreign	0%	—	88%	0%	—	82%

Key Votes of the 102d Congress

1. Ban Striker Replace AGN	5. Handgun Wait/7-Day AGN	9. Use Force in Gulf FOR
2. $ for Homeownership FOR	6. Overseas Mil. Abortion AGN	10. US Mil. Abroad $ Cut AGN
3. Tax Rich/Cut Mid Cls. AGN	7. Obscn. Art NEA $ Ban FOR	11. Limit SDI Funds AGN
4. FY93/$15B Def. Cut *	8. Death Pen. from Jury FOR	12. Cuba Trade Embargo FOR

Key Votes of the 103d Congress

1. Family Leave AGN	2. Deficit Reduction AGN	3. Stimulus Plan AGN

Election Results

1992 general	Richard H. Baker (R)................	123,953	(51%)	($770,203)
	Clyde C. Holloway (R)...............	121,225	(49%)	($424,870)
1992 primary	Clyde C. Holloway (R)................	52,012	(37%)	
	Richard H. Baker (R)................	46,990	(33%)	
	Ned Randolph (D)	42,819	(30%)	
1990 primary	Richard H. Baker (R), unopposed			($332,905)

SEVENTH DISTRICT

More than 200 years ago, French-speaking settlers were forced to leave their land of Acadie, which the British had taken over and renamed Nova Scotia, and make their way to the wetlands of southern Louisiana. Here, without much notice, they built steep-roofed houses to slough off nonexistent snow and adapted French cuisine to the crawfish and muskrat they found in abundance in the pelican-tended swamps. The heart of the Cajun country is around Lafayette, just west of the Atchafalaya Basin, where Mississippi waters pour through bayous and canals, with only occasional bits of solid land visible on the 30-mile section of Interstate 10 built on elevated stilts. Over the last half century, the Cajun country has thrived, thanks to oil and gas, which turned out to be plentiful here and just off shore in the Gulf of Mexico; oil rigs are common, and every once in a while the swampy foliage parts to reveal a giant refinery or petrochemical plant. In the past two decades, Cajun pride has grown; Cajun French is being kept alive and Cajun cooking has become a tourist attraction here and, in watered-down form, familiar all over the United States. Both Cajun culture and the oil business are particularly evident in Lafayette, which has rebuilt and Acadian Village and was a major oil exploration center in the late 1970s and early 1980s.

The oil price crash of the middle 1980s hit the Cajun country hard. Rising expectations, the giddy sense that the oil industry promised lasting prosperity, suddenly collapsed, leaving borrowers overextended and ordinary homeowners unable to maintain the standard of living they expected. Politically, the Cajun country seemed to move then toward national Democrats, whom it had shunned because their cultural liberalism seemed alien to the Cajun tradition of respecting the authority of Church and state while tolerating a certain amount of *laissez les bons temps rouler* spirit. The Cajun country delivered above-national-average percentages not only to

Bill Clinton in 1992 but to Michael Dukakis in 1988. And it gave key support to Edwin Edwards, the most famous Cajun politician, in 1991 against David Duke.

The 7th Congressional District of Louisiana covers much of the Cajun country, from Lafayette and the Atchafalaya west along I-10 to Lake Charles and the Texas border. It was represented from 1965 to 1972 by Edwin Edwards, then from 1972 to 1986 by John Breaux, both from Acadia Parish, and now governor and senator, respectively. The current congressman is Jimmy Hayes of Lafayette, a successful real estate developer, prosecutor and Edwards ally. Edwards made him head of the state banking department in 1983, where Hayes rewrote the Louisiana Bank Code and Louisiana Securities law.

In the House, Hayes has won committee assignments which have enabled him to aid Cajun country interests. On the Public Works Committee, he tried to protect the property rights of local wetland owners and rice farmers from what he and they consider overregulation under wetlands laws; he worked to get disaster relief for them after the area was hit by Hurricane Andrew in August 1992. He has in recent years become vociferously opposed to what he considers overspending by the federal government, and in 1993 was one of 22 Democrats to vote against Clinton's stimulus package. He boasts that he had no overdrafts, that he donated his pay raise to local colleges, that he won't collect his federal pension, and that he has one of the lowest franking bills on Capitol Hill.

Hayes won the seat in 1986 by winning 30% in the primary, in which a more liberal candidate was eliminated, then running in tandem with Breaux and beating a pro-business, anti-union state senator in the runoff. The AMA and Realtor PACs made independent expenditures against Hayes, but he was able to outspend them and his opponent out of his own pocket. In 1990, Republican David Thibodaux, who attacked Hayes for his business difficulties, nearly carried Lafayette Parish; Hayes won district-wide 58%–38% in the October primary. The 1992 race was turbulent. Hayes's brother Fredric, who in two terms in the state legislature in 1969–71 tried to ban sex education in Louisiana schools, ran against him as a Republican. Fredric Hayes attacked his brother as "part of the tax-and-spend Democratic elite which has bankrupted this nation," but his real grievance seemed to be a family matter, a dispute over their father's will. Then for a moment, another candidate entered, Paul Hardy, a Cajun politician, who served as lieutenant governor from 1988–92. But Hardy withdrew from the race and Fredric Hayes never was taken seriously: he got 27% in Lafayette Parish, with Jimmy Hayes winning district-wide with 73%.

The People: Pop. 1990: 602,679; 42% rural; 11% age 65+; 79% White; 19% Black; 1% Asian; 1% Hispanic origin. Voting age pop.: 420,905; 18% Black; 1% Hispanic origin. Households: 60% married couple families; 31% married couple fams. w. children; 33% college educ.; median household income: $21,442; per capita income: $10,226; median gross rent: $305; median house value: $49,700.

1992 Presidential Vote

Clinton (D)	123,336	(46%)
Bush (R)	99,985	(38%)
Perot (I)	38,244	(14%)

1988 Presidential Vote

Bush (R)	121,832	(51%)
Dukakis (D)	115,495	(49%)

Rep. James A. (Jimmy) Hayes (D)

Elected 1986; b. Dec. 21, 1946, Lafayette; home, Lafayette; U. of S.W. LA, B.A. 1967, Tulane U., J.D. 1970; Methodist; married (Leslie).

Career: Air Natl. Guard, 1968–74; Asst. Lafayette City Atty., 1971–72; Asst. Dist. Atty., Lafayette Parish, 1974–83; Real estate developer, 1978–86; LA Commissioner of Financial Inst., 1983–85.

Offices: 2432 RHOB, 202-225-2031. Also 109 E. Vermilion, Lafayette 70501, 318-233-4773; and 901 Lake Shore Dr., #402, Lake Charles 70601, 318-433-1613.

Committees: *Government Operations* (19th of 25 D): Environment, Energy and Natural Resources. *Public Works and Transportation* (12th of 39 D): Aviation; Water Resources and Environment (Vice Chmn.). *Science, Space and Technology* (11th of 33 D): Investigations and Oversight (Chmn.); Space.

Group Ratings

	ADA	ACLU	COPE	CDF	CFA	LCV	ACU	NTLC	NSI	COC	CEI
1992	30	26	55	40	47	6	65	53	80	100	46
1991	20	—	50	20	33	23	80	—	—	67	37

National Journal Ratings

	1991 LIB — 1991 CONS	1992 LIB — 1992 CONS
Economic	38% — 62%	37% — 63%
Social	23% — 77%	22% — 77%
Foreign	26% — 70%	38% — 62%

Key Votes of the 102d Congress

1. Ban Striker Replace FOR	5. Handgun Wait/7-Day AGN	9. Use Force in Gulf FOR
2. $ for Homeownership *	6. Overseas Mil. Abortion AGN	10. US Mil. Abroad $ Cut *
3. Tax Rich/Cut Mid Cls. AGN	7. Obscn. Art NEA $ Ban FOR	11. Limit SDI Funds AGN
4. FY93/$15B Def. Cut AGN	8. Death Pen. from Jury FOR	12. Cuba Trade Embargo *

Key Votes of the 103d Congress

1. Family Leave AGN	2. Deficit Reduction AGN	3. Stimulus Plan AGN

Election Results

1992 primary	James A. (Jimmy) Hayes (D)............	84,149	(73%)	($436,331)
	Fredric Hayes (R).....................	23,870	(21%)	($18,675)
	Robert J. (Bob) Nain (R)...............	7,184	(6%)	
1990 primary	James A. (Jimmy) Hayes (D)..........	103,308	(58%)	($309,229)
	David Thibodaux (R)	68,530	(38%)	($157,656)
	Johnny Myers (D).....................	7,369	(4%)	

MAINE

Maine, the land of pointed firs and steady habits, of rock-strewn coast and monosyllabic Yankees, a place for years of seemingly little change, has over the last dozen years gone through dizzying transformations: an up-and-down economic roller coaster ride which has left parts of Maine looking more prosperous than ever before and most state of Mainers feeling they have fallen behind and are worse off than before. Settled by Yankee farmers and fishermen in the mid-19th Century, when it was America's northeastern frontier, Maine grew slowly from 1860, when its population reached 600,000, through the 1970s, when it passed one million. Then, in the 1980s, the New England high-tech boom reached up Interstate 95 and the simple, back-to-nature Yankee style came into vogue, and Maine boomed. The antique dockside buildings on Portland's waterfront were restored and fern-filled; the Mall of Maine expanded and saw office parks spring up nearby, a miniature Edge City; real estate prices rose by hundreds of percents, not just in vacation coves, but in Portland and small towns that had never considered themselves picturesque. The L.L. Bean headquarters in Freeport, open 24 hours a day, 365 days a year, typified the boom: the Anglo-Saxon monosyllable and two chaste initials suggesting the dry understatement of archetypical Down East Yankees; the 24-hour-a-day schedule recalling the hard work needed to eke out a living in this cold soil, between the lobster-filled North Atlantic and the pine-covered north woods; the commercial success of the enterprise a prime example of Maine's unexpected 1980s boom.

That boom had its costs, of course. Maine's manufacturing sector withered as service jobs increased; its main roads were suddenly jammed with cars waiting for the green arrow so they could turn into the mall. Not all of Maine has disappeared into high-tech glitter: farmers, though fewer every year, still try to scratch potatoes out of the far northern fields of Aroostook County, and many of Maine's paper and textile mill towns have the air of neglect and abandonment that comes to places that have been losing jobs and young people for a generation. Not far from neat town squares and picturesque seascapes you can find tarpaper- and plastic-clad homes of poor, uneducated, ill-clothed swamp Yankees.

But most state-of-Mainers were becoming happier and wealthier—until the high-tech boom and New England real estate values crashed sharply after the 1988 election. In three years, Maine lost 40,000 jobs and saw its personal income growth fall from one of the top states to the last. It saw the state budget cut three times, and humiliating stoppages of state services. Increasingly, people wondered if they had let their forest and coast environments and their town Main Streets deteriorate because of development whose benefits seemed ephemeral. And after the Halloween 1991 storm damaged much waterfront property, including George Bush's house in Kennebunkport, people started worrying that the ocean would rise: nothing seemed safe.

Politically, Maine responded with anger and flailing out in all directions. For this state, politically, has always been an odd duck, often running contrary to national cycles. Part of that contrariness comes from the stereotypical state-of-Mainer: a flinty farmer, in plain clothes, speaking in deeply accented monosyllables and occasionally with mordant wit. In the early 20th Century, Maine was the most Yankee state in the nation, stable and conservative but not especially prosperous, a believer in Prohibition and ancestrally Republican since before the Civil War. It held state elections in September, a date originally chosen because it followed the state's early harvest, up through 1958; in the days before polls, the results here were taken as a gauge of national partisan movement—hence the saying, "As Maine goes, so goes the nation." Although in September 1936, Maine voted 56% for Republican Governor Lewis Barrows, and in November only Maine and Vermont voted for Alf Landon over Franklin Roosevelt: "As Maine goes, so goes Vermont," said Roosevelt's campaign manager. Since then, Maine has voted for

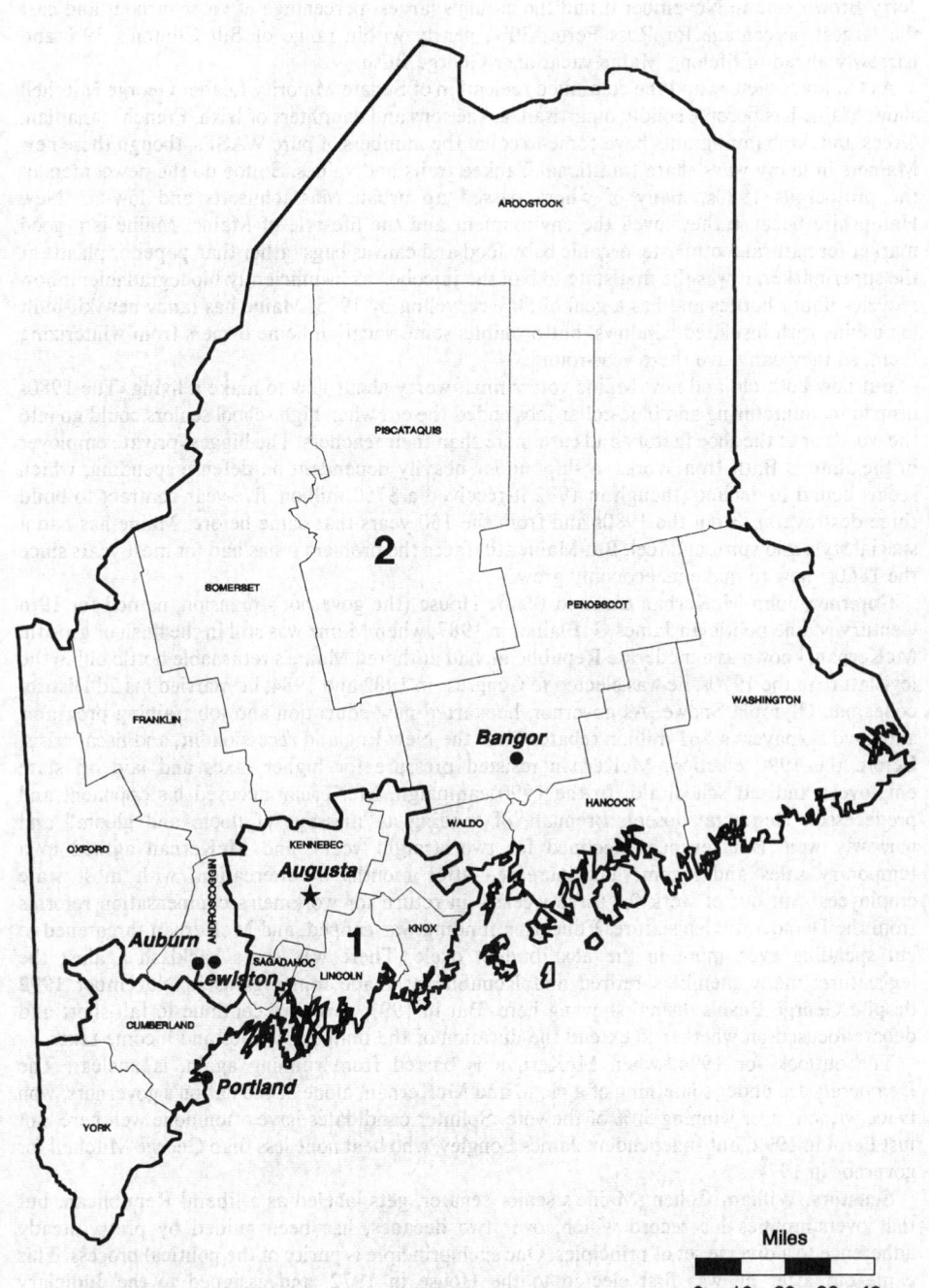

AROOSTOOK

PISCATAQUIS

SOMERSET

2

PENOBSCOT

FRANKLIN

WASHINGTON

Bangor

OXFORD

KENNEBEC

WALDO

HANCOCK

Augusta
★

Auburn

ANDROSCOGGIN

KNOX

SAGADAHOC

Lewiston

1

LINCOLN

CUMBERLAND

Portland

YORK

Miles

0   10   20   30   40

the loser in the close presidential elections of 1948, 1960, 1968 and 1976, and nearly did so again in 1980—a record equalled by no other state. In 1992, its Democratic caucus went narrowly for Jerry Brown, and in November it had the nation's largest percentage of voter turnout and cast the largest percentage for Ross Perot, 30%, nearly within range of Bill Clinton's 39% and narrowly ahead of lifelong Maine vacationer George Bush.

As Clinton's victory and the continued reelection of Senate Majority Leader George Mitchell show, Maine has become solidly bipartisan, as the sons and daughters of Irish, French Canadian, Greek and Arab immigrants have come to equal the numbers of pure WASPs, though these new Mainers in many ways share traditional Yankee traits and values. So too do the newcomers of the prosperous 1980s, many of whom passed up urban Massachusetts and low-tax New Hampshire because they loved the environment and the lifestyle of Maine. Maine is a good market for natural toothpaste, organic baby food and canvas bags rather than paper or plastic at the supermarket; it was the first state to ban the juicebox as insufficiently biodegradable; it now recycles liquor bottles and has a goal of 50% recycling by 1995. Maine has fancy new kit-built log cabins with insulated windows, but prohibits some vacation home owners from winterizing them, so they can't live there year-round.

But now both old and new Maine voters must worry about how to make a living. The 1980s drop in manufacturing and blue-collar jobs ended the era when high school seniors could go into the woods or to the shoe factory and earn more than their teachers. The biggest private employer in the state is Bath Iron Works, a shipbuilder heavily dependent on defense spending, which seems bound to decline (though in 1992 it received a $750 million, five-year contract to build three destroyers). From the 1980s and from the 150 years that came before, Maine has had a special style and spirit and feel. But Maine still faces the problem it has had for most years since the 1860s: how to make its economy grow.

Governor. John McKernan came to Blaine House (the governor's mansion, named for 19th Century Maine politician James G. Blaine) in 1987, when Maine was still in the flush of growth. McKernan, known as a moderate Republican, had authored Maine's returnable bottle bill in the legislature in the 1970s; he was elected to Congress in 1982 and 1984; he married his 2d District colleague, Olympia Snowe. As governor, he started new education and job training programs and gave taxpayers a $61 million rebate. Then the New England recession hit, and fiscal crisis. Before the 1990 election, McKernan resisted pressure for higher taxes and laid off state employees and cut school aid. In the 1990 campaign, McKernan accused his opponent and predecessor, Democrat Joseph Brennan, of sending a "message of doom and gloom" and narrowly won. But revenues declined for two straight years, and McKernan agreed to a temporary sales and income tax increase—after months of altercation, with most state employees shut out of work for three weeks—in return for workmen's compensation reforms from the Democratic legislature. Education funding was capped, and McKernan threatened to cut spending even more in the next budget cycle. There was some backlash against the legislature; many members retired and Republicans made minor gains in November 1992 despite George Bush's dismal showing here. But in 1993, revenues continue to fall short and debate focused on whether to extend the duration of the temporary sales and income taxes.

The outlook for 1994, when McKernan is barred from running again, is unclear. The Democrats are under something of a cloud and McKernan, alone of the nation's governors, won twice without ever winning 50% of the vote. Splinter candidates have often done well here, not just Perot in 1992, but Independent James Longley, who beat none less than George Mitchell for governor in 1974.

Senators. William Cohen, Maine's senior senator, gets labeled as a liberal Republican, but that oversimplifies his record which, over two decades, has been guided by pretty steady adherence to a diverse set of principles. One such principle is purity of the political process. This came out after he was first elected to the House in 1972, and assigned to the Judiciary Committee which had to vote on the impeachment of President Richard Nixon. A former mayor of Bangor with a bent for poetry, Cohen caucused with anti-Nixon Republicans and spoke out with some eloquence for impeachment. In the 1980s, Cohen served on the Iran-contra committee, and again criticized a Republican administration. On contested issues, he supported the Democratic chairmen and wrote a book with George Mitchell, decrying Oliver North and his colleagues as "men of zeal" who undermined the Constitution and the legal process. In the 1990s, Cohen has been a major supporter of renewing the law authorizing independent counsels—the old special prosecutors which proponents think are necessary to ferret out Executive Branch crime and opponents think are irresponsible and oppressive inquisitors.

On another set of issues, Cohen's stands are conservative—the military. When he challenged incumbent Democratic Senator William Hathaway in 1978, Cohen's platform was military preparedness. He has served on Armed Services, where he supported the Reagan defense buildup, opposed the nuclear freeze, backed the MX missile, and backed expansion of the Navy; he looked after the big Navy shipbuilding operations at Bath Iron Works and has recently worked for money for defense reconversion. He argues strongly that the U.S. must not abandon a forward military strategy even after the Cold War, and backs bigger sealift capacity, more mobile forces and missile defense. He urged economic sanctions against Iraq even before Saddam Hussein invaded Kuwait and strongly backed the Gulf war resolution. Cohen doesn't back every weapons system though—he was against the B-2 bomber, but he did make strong partisan defenses in the embattled nominations of John Tower and Robert Gates.

But as Maine went through recession, Cohen spent more time on economic issues, on which he is not always market-oriented. From a state that uses lots of gasoline and home heating oil, he has been willing to back oil price controls and a windfall profits tax. From his position as ranking member on the Aging Committee, he wants to outlaw telemarketing scams against the elderly, protect Medicare against physician overcharges and penalize drug companies whose prices increase more than inflation. He has come up with a healthcare package which includes a refundable tax credit for health insurance premiums and a nationwide low-cost basic benefits package—a response in part, perhaps, to his 1990 opponent's emphasis on the issue. He opposed the U.S.-Canada Free Trade Agreement after attacking Canada for exporting "short" (i.e., underweight) lobsters. On some cultural issues, he sides with liberals. He is pro-choice on abortion and voted to override Bush vetoes of the 1990 civil right bill and the 1992 Family and Medical Leave Act.

Cohen, like many veteran politicians, saw his percentage of the vote decline in the early 1990s. In 1990, his opponent, businessman Neil Rolde, spent more than $1 million of his own money, most of it on TV ads in which he argued effectively for national health insurance: this was one of the few Senate races in which the challenger outspent the incumbent. Cohen spent less, and his percentage fell from 73% in 1984 to a still impressive 61%. In Maine's volatile political environment, it is idle to speculate about 1996, when Cohen's seat comes up, though he seems well positioned to continue to win.

George Mitchell is only the sixth Senate majority leader since Lyndon Johnson turned this formerly perfunctory post into a center of real power in the 1950s. After four years as one of the most important, and on several occasions one of the most effective, Democrats in George Bush's Washington, Mitchell must now adjust to the status of serving in the shadow of a Democratic president and administration. He is from a humble background: his father was an orphan who worked as a janitor at Colby College and his mother was a Lebanese immigrant; he grew up in Waterville, a poor athlete in an athletics-conscious family. After working his way through school, Mitchell got his political start as a protege of another immigrant's son, Senator Edmund Muskie: he became Democratic state chairman in 1966, a dreadful year for Democrats elsewhere but a fine one in contrarian Maine. He then became U.S. attorney for Maine; he had the humiliation of losing a race for governor in the Democratic year of 1974 to an Independent, 40%–37%, but was named federal judge. A chain of events led Mitchell to the Senate: the failed rescue mission in Iran in April 1980, the resignation of Secretary of State Cyrus Vance, the selection of Edmund Muskie to succeed him, and finally the decision by then Governor Joseph Brennan to appoint Mitchell to Muskie's Senate seat in May 1980. It was widely expected that

Mitchell would lose to 1st District Congressman David Emery in 1982. Instead, Mitchell won with 61% of the vote. Mitchell became head of the Democratic Senatorial Campaign Committee in 1985 and had the satisfaction of helping the party to an unexpected majority in 1986, as Democrats won most of the close races. With plenty of support from the class of 1986, Mitchell was elected majority leader in 1988, with 27 votes to 14 each for Daniel Inouye and Bennett Johnston.

To that job, Mitchell has brought a genial temperament and a surprising stubbornness, a patience with the interminably slow pace of Senate floor proceedings and an ability to rip into opponents while sounding unpretentious. Mitchell helped to hand the Bush presidency its first two major setbacks, the defeat of John Tower's nomination to be secretary of defense in March 1991 and the filibuster of the capital gains tax cut in fall 1991. The first was really the initiative of Sam Nunn, with Mitchell soldiering alongside, but the second was all Mitchell's doing; the cut had gone through the House, it had the votes to pass in the Senate, and indeed a more determined administration might have beaten the filibuster. On other issues, as well, Mitchell reached compromises with Bush: the minimum wage (after a Bush veto), the Americans with Disabilities Act, child care, oil spills, the 1991 Civil Rights Act, the major transportation bill.

Indeed, it can be argued that Mitchell pretty much got his way on domestic policy in the first three Bush years: Bush flinched and Mitchell won. The budget summit agreement of 1990 was a great victory for Mitchell, leaving plenty of room for discretionary spending increases by his predecessor and current Appropriations Chairman Robert Byrd, and forcing Bush to break his no-new-taxes promise. This was consistent with Mitchell's strong belief in progressive taxes—he sponsored the leading amendment to more steeply graduate the 1986 tax reform—and may have, as the conservative *Wall Street Journal* charged, produced a "Mitchell recession." Mitchell also played a key role on the Clean Air Act, another longtime Mitchell cause, and a Muskie cause before that; in 1989, Mitchell superintended compromises between the purist Senate committee versions and the Bush Administration, beating by one vote Byrd's amendment to compensate coal miners whose jobs would be lost, and beating the Wirth-Wilson amendment to reduce emissions. By early 1992, Mitchell was calling for deep defense cuts, a middle class tax cut, and higher taxes on the rich, and was decrying the economic slowdown. But it was produced by macroeconomic policies—higher taxes, increased regulations—which he had done as much as anyone else to put in place.

On foreign policy, he differed sharply with Bush, criticizing his conciliatory stand on China, strongly opposing the dispatch of U.S. troops to Saudi Arabia, and leading almost all Senate Democrats in opposition to the Gulf war resolution. But overall, there is a certain irony to Mitchell being a major leader of the party of change. His early agenda for the 103d Congress included such Bush-vetoed measures as early childhood education and family leave; campaign finance and voter registration (which could easily be purely partisan bills); and health care, on which he spent much of 1992 trying to develop a common approach for Senate Democrats, only to see candidate Clinton take a somewhat different tack. The natural role for Mitchell in the Clinton years is to help the administration get its program through the Senate. But there is a tension between Mitchell's down-the-line liberalism and Clinton's "new kind of Democrat," not an unbridgeable gap, but enough of a philosophic difference to make cooperation a matter to be negotiated rather than assumed. And if Mitchell does not have majority support in the Senate or even in the Democratic Caucus for some of his stands, he has shown himself willing to make his case and fight hard for it, using all the Senate's procedural weapons, when he feels strongly about an issue. Mitchell had hoped the Democrats would gain three Senate seats in 1992, to give them 60, enough to overcome any purely partisan Republican filibuster. Instead, they held even at 57 and were further setback in June 1993, when Republican Kay Bailey Hutchison defeated appointed Texas Senator Bob Krueger; and within that number there is considerable ideological variety, as well as a fair amount of fellow feeling and loyalty which Mitchell built up fighting the Republicans and winning when that seemed to be against the odds. The majority leader will be an interesting man to watch.

Mitchell seems extraordinarily popular in Maine; in 1988 he was reelected with 81% of the vote. But since then the state's economy has collapsed, and voters have flailed out against politicians in all directions; so he cannot perhaps take reelection in 1994 entirely for granted. Will Governor John McKernan, barred from a third consecutive term, run? His job ratings have been much lower than Mitchell's, but he might give him a real challenge. Since McKernan is married to 2d District Congresswoman Olympia Snowe, if he were to be elected to the Senate, they would be America's first bicameral couple (although husbands and wives have served in the Senate and House at different times: Republicans Medill McCormick and Ruth Hanna McCormick and Democrats Paul Douglas and Emily Taft Douglas, all from Illinois).

Presidential politics. One of the most stunning rebukes of the 1992 presidential election was the fact that George Bush ran third in Maine, the site of his family summer home in Kennebunkport, where he has spent every summer of his life (except when on wartime duty) and made many of the memorable appearances of his presidency. In York County around Kennebunkport, the home town appeal Bush demonstrated in the 1988 caucuses and in November 1988 evaporated after Maine's economy collapsed. The Kennebunk paper endorsed Clinton, who carried York County. Ross Perot ran ahead of Bush statewide and carried three of Maine's 16 counties.

Maine's caucuses, coming just after the New Hampshire primary, made something of a ruckus in 1992. The state's psychic trauma made it receptive to the message of Jerry Brown, who barnstormed little towns and inspired volunteers, and ended up winning the caucuses. On the Republican side, Bush dominated a caucus process run largely by his supporters—a result that gave little indication of the rebellion which, as November's results showed, was more intense and angry in Maine than just about anywhere else in the United States.

Congressional districting. Maine did not bother redistricting for 1992, but plans to do so by mid-summer 1993. It hardly matters: Maine's district lines have not changed much since the state lost its 3d District in the 1960 Census. The idea then was to split areas of Democratic strength, but now Maine is politically homogeneous enough that party makes less difference than the personal strengths of the candidates. Maine is one of two states (Nebraska is the other) where the electoral vote can be divided if one congressional district votes for a candidate that loses statewide.

The People: Est. Pop. 1992: 1,235,000; Pop. 1990: 1,227,928, up 0.6% 1990–1992. 0.5% of U.S. total, 38th largest; 55% rural. Median age: 33.9 years. 13.3% 65 years and over. 98.4% White. Households: 58.1% married couple families; 28% married couple fams. w. children; 42% college educ.; median household income: $27,854; per capita income: $12,957; 70.5% owner occupied housing median house value: $87,400; median monthly rent: $358. Voting age pop.: 918,926. 7.1% Unemployment. Registered voters (1992): 824,658; 272,089 D (33%), 246,277 R (30%), 306,292 unaffiliated and minor parties (37%).

Political Lineup: Governor, John R. McKernan, Jr. (R); Sec. of State, G. William Diamond (D); Atty. Gen., Michael E. Carpenter (D); Treasurer, Samuel Shapiro (D); Controller, David Bourne (D); Auditor, Rodney L. Scribner (D). State Senate, 35 (20 D and 15 R); State House of Representatives, 151 (90 D and 61 R). Senators, William S. Cohen (R) and George J. Mitchell (D). Representatives, 2 (1 D and 1 R).

1992 Presidential Vote

Clinton (D)	263,420	(39%)
Perot (I)	206,820	(30%)
Bush (R)	206,504	(30%)

1988 Presidential Vote

Bush (R)	307,131	(55%)
Dukakis (D)	243,569	(44%)

GOVERNOR

Gov. John R. McKernan, Jr. (R)

Elected 1986, term expires Jan. 1995; b. May 20, 1948, Bangor; home, Auburn; Dartmouth Col., A.B. 1970, U. of ME, J.D. 1974; Protestant; married (U.S. Rep. Olympia J. Snowe).

Career: Practicing atty., 1977–82; ME House of Reps., 1973–77, Asst. Minority Ldr., 1975–76; U.S. House of Reps., 1982–86.

Office: State House, Sta. 1, Augusta 04333, 207-287-3531.

Election Results

1990 gen.	John R. McKernan, Jr. (R)	243,766	(47%)
	Joseph Brennan (D)	230,038	(44%)
	Andrew Adam (I)............	48,377	(9%)
1990 prim.	John R. McKernan, Jr. (R), unopposed		
1986 gen.	John R. McKernan, Jr. (R)	170,312	(40%)
	James Tierney (D)	128,744	(30%)
	Sherry F. Huber (I)	64,317	(15%)
	John E. Menario (I)	63,474	(15%)

SENATORS

Sen. William S. Cohen (R)

Elected 1978, seat up 1996; b. Aug. 28, 1940, Bangor; home, Bangor; Bowdoin Col., A.B. 1962, Boston U., LL.B. 1965; Unitarian; divorced.

Career: Practicing atty., 1966–72; Asst. Penobscot Cnty. Atty., 1968; Instructor, Husson Col., 1968, U. of ME, 1968–72; Bangor City Cncl., 1969–72, Bangor Mayor, 1971–72; U.S. House of Reps., 1972–78.

Offices: 322 HSOB 20510, 202-224-2523. Also 150 Capitol St., P.O. Box 347, Augusta 04332, 207-622-8414; Fed. Bldg., #204, 202 Harlow St., Bangor 04402, 207-945-0417; 109 Alfred St., Biddeford 04005, 207-283-1101; 11 Lisbon St., Lewiston 04240, 207-784-6969; 10 Moulton St., P.O. Box 1938, Portland 04104, 207-780-3575; and 169 Academy St., Presque Isle 04769, 207-764-3266.

Committees: *Aging (Special)* (RMM of 10 R). *Armed Services* (3d of 9 R): Coalition Defense and Reinforcing Forces; Defense Technology, Acquisition and Industrial Base; Regional Defense and Contingency Forces (RMM). *Governmental Affairs* (3d of 5 R): Oversight of Government Management (RMM); Regulation and Government Information; Permanent Subcommittee on Investigations. *Judiciary* (7th of 8 R): Courts and Administrative Practice; Juvenile Justice (RMM). *Joint Committee on the Organization of Congress* (11th of 12).

Group Ratings

	ADA	ACLU	CDF	COPE	CFA	LCV	ACU	NTLC	NSI	COC	CEI
1992	40	64	50	33	67	67	48	50	80	70	51
1991	65	—	91	42	67	93	43	—	—	40	36

National Journal Ratings

	1991 LIB — 1991 CONS			1992 LIB — 1992 CONS		
Economic	57%	—	40%	37%	—	61%
Social	64%	—	33%	49%	—	49%
Foreign	27%	—	67%	29%	—	68%

Key Votes of the 102d Congress

1. $ for Homeownership	AGN	5. Clarence Thomas Nom.	FOR	9. Use Force in Gulf	FOR
2. Have Cap Gains Debate	FOR	6. Lmt Death Row Appeal	FOR	10. Keep Salvador Aid	FOR
3. Remove Budget Walls	AGN	7. Handgun Wait/5-Day	FOR	11. Cut $1B from SDI	AGN
4. Ban Striker Replace	AGN	8. Abortion Gag Rule	AGN	12. Override China MFN	AGN

Key Votes of the 103d Congress

1. Family Leave	FOR	2. HIV Immigrants	AGN	3. Clinton Budget	AGN

Election Results

1990 general	William S. Cohen (R).................	319,167	(61%)	($1,628,292)
	Neil Rolde (D)	201,053	(39%)	($1,630,894)
1990 primary	William S. Cohen (R), unopposed			
1984 general	William S. Cohen (R).................	404,414	(73%)	($1,063,188)
	Elizabeth H. Mitchell (D).............	142,626	(26%)	($410,611)

Sen. George J. Mitchell (D)

Appointed May, 1980, elected 1982, seat up 1994; b. Aug. 20, 1933, Waterville; home, Portland; Bowdoin Col., B.A. 1954, Georgetown U., LL.B. 1960; Catholic; divorced.

Career: Army counter-intelligence, 1954–56; U.S. Dept. of Justice, 1960–62; Exec. Asst., U.S. Sen. Edmund Muskie, 1962–65; Practicing atty., 1965–77; Chmn., ME St. Dem. Party, 1966–68; Asst. Atty., Cumberland Cnty., 1971; U.S. Atty. for ME, 1977–79; U.S. Dist. Judge for ME, 1979–80.

Offices: 176 RSOB 20510, 202-224-5344. Also Muskie Fed. Bldg., 40 Western Ave., #101-C, Augusta 04332, 207-622-8292; Smith Fed. Bldg., 202 Harlow St., P.O. Box 1237, Bangor 04401, 207-945-0451; 231 Main St., Biddeford 04005, 207-282-4144; 157 Main St., Lewiston 04240, 207-784-0163; J.B. Brown Bldg., #402, 537 Congress St., Portland 04101, 207-874-0883; 541 Main St., #B, Presque Isle 04769, 207-764-5601; Main and Winter Sts., Rockland 04841, 207-596-0311; and 33 College Ave., Waterville 04901, 207-873-3361.

Committees: *Majority Leader. Environment and Public Works* (3d of 10 D): Clean Water, Fisheries and Wildlife; Water Resources, Transportation, Public Buildings and Economic Development. *Finance* (5th of 11 D): Health for Families and the Uninsured; International Trade; Medicare and Long-Term Care. *Veterans' Affairs* (3d of 7 D):

Group Ratings

	ADA	ACLU	CDF	COPE	CFA	LCV	ACU	NTLC	NSI	COC	CEI
1992	95	95	100	83	100	83	0	11	40	20	16
1991	90	—	100	83	72	80	5	—	—	30	22

National Journal Ratings

	1991 LIB — 1991 CONS			1992 LIB — 1992 CONS		
Economic	90%	—	3%	69%	—	27%
Social	87%	—	0%	89%	—	0%
Foreign	86%	—	0%	78%	—	14%

Key Votes of the 102d Congress

1. $ for Homeownership	AGN	5. Clarence Thomas Nom.	AGN	9. Use Force in Gulf	AGN
2. Have Cap Gains Debate	AGN	6. Lmt Death Row Appeal	AGN	10. Keep Salvador Aid	AGN
3. Remove Budget Walls	FOR	7. Handgun Wait/5-Day	FOR	11. Cut $1B from SDI	FOR
4. Ban Striker Replace	FOR	8. Abortion Gag Rule	AGN	12. Override China MFN	FOR

Key Votes of the 103d Congress

1. Family Leave	FOR	2. HIV Immigrants	FOR	3. Clinton Budget	FOR

Election Results

1988 general	George J. Mitchell (D)................	452,590	(81%)	($1,471,426)
	Jasper S. Wyman (R)................	104,758	(19%)	($147,760)
1988 primary	George J. Mitchell (D), unopposed			
1982 general	George J. Mitchell (D)...............	279,819	(61%)	($1,209,599)
	David F. Emery (R)	179,882	(39%)	($1,081,122)

FIRST DISTRICT

The 1st District of Maine stretches from southernmost Kittery and nearby Kennebunkport to the craggy-shored ancestrally Republican counties to the east. The historic center is Portland, revived and renovated during its 1980s boom, with yuppies, bankers and courthouse lawyers; the commercial center now, for shoppers and office employees and drivers, is Maine Mall City, spanning the Portland and Scarborough lines, just off the Maine Turnpike and I-295 and near the airport—the state's heaviest concentration of retail and office space. Most voters in the 1st District, except those far Down East, live within a couple hours drive of this area.

This has been a competitive district in congressional politics, but seems held firmly now by its second-term incumbent, Democrat Tom Andrews. Andrews is a natural organizer who raised $100,000 at age 16 to help disadvantaged children and Central American farmers, rallied students to help Maine's homeless in 1977 and worked against the Seabrook nuclear plant in 1980. He lost a leg to cancer in high school and headed a Maine handicapped organization in the 1980s. He was elected to the Maine House from downtown Portland—revived New England downtowns are great left-wing constituencies—and to the state Senate over an incumbent in 1984. In the 1990 primary, he beat James Tierney, 1986 Democratic candidate for governor; he beat former four-term Congressman David Emery 60%–40% in the general. In Washington, Andrews was elected president of his House freshman class; he wanted to lead a write-in campaign for Mario Cuomo in 1992.

Andrews's positions are down-the-line liberal: for more progressive taxes, alternative energy sources, retraining of laid-off defense workers, national health insurance, a 50% cut in defense spending over 10 years, and mass transit subsidies. He led an unsuccessful effort to cut off funding of the B-2 bomber and voted for a base-closing bill that included Maine's Loring Air Force Base (to be sure, it's in the 2d District), though he favors subsidies and Aegis missile destroyer contracts for Bath Iron Works, which is in the 1st. In 1992, his opponent was Linda Bean, millionaire heiress and granddaughter of L.L. Bean, a staunch conservative on issues from capital gains tax cuts to abortion. She spent $1 million of her own money and ran a barrage of vitriolically negative ads attacking Andrews as a tax-and-spend liberal. The shrillness of her ads, as well as Andrews' skillful efforts challenging their veracity, turned voters against Bean. Her inherited wealth, coupled with George Bush's problems in this economically battered state, helped Andrews to a nearly 2–1 win. Andrews seems solidly entrenched—and a possible Senate candidate sometime in the future, or a gubernatorial candidate in 1994.

The People: Pop. 1990: 636,528; 51% rural; 13% age 65+; 98% White; 1% Asian; 1% Hispanic origin. Voting age pop.: 478,473; 1% Hispanic origin. Households: 59% married couple families; 28% married couple fams. w. children; 47% college educ.; median household income: $30,952; per capita income: $14,362; median gross rent: $474; median house value: $106,400.

1992 Presidential Vote		
Clinton (D)	145,191	(40%)
Bush (R)	115,697	(32%)
Perot (I)	102,828	(28%)

1988 Presidential Vote		
Bush (R)	169,292	(56%)
Dukakis (D)	131,078	(44%)

Rep. Thomas H. Andrews (D)

Elected 1990; b. Mar. 22, 1953, North Easton, MA; home, Portland; Bowdoin Col., B.A. 1976; Unitarian; married (Debra).

Career: Exec. Dir., ME Handicapped Assoc., 1981–87; ME House of Reps., 1982–84; ME Senate, 1985–90; Dir., ME Studies Inst., 1987–90.

Offices: 1530 LHOB 20515, 202-225-6116. Also 135 Commercial St., Portland 04101; 207-772-8240.

Committees: *Armed Services* (21st of 34 D): Military Acquisition. *Merchant Marine and Fisheries* (16th of 29 D): Merchant Marine. *Small Business* (25th of 27 D): Regulation, Business Opportunities and Technology.

Group Ratings

	ADA	ACLU	COPE	CDF	CFA	LCV	ACU	NTLC	NSI	COC	CEI
1992	100	100	92	90	93	100	4	0	30	25	19
1991	100	—	92	100	89	100	0	—	—	20	11

National Journal Ratings

	1991 LIB	—	1991 CONS		1992 LIB	—	1992 CONS
Economic	88%	—	0%		89%	—	9%
Social	88%	—	0%		88%	—	8%
Foreign	83%	—	15%		86%	—	10%

Key Votes of the 102d Congress

1. Ban Striker Replace	FOR	5. Handgun Wait/7-Day	FOR	9. Use Force in Gulf	AGN
2. $ for Homeownership	AGN	6. Overseas Mil. Abortion	FOR	10. US Mil. Abroad $ Cut	FOR
3. Tax Rich/Cut Mid Cls.	FOR	7. Obscn. Art NEA $ Ban	AGN	11. Limit SDI Funds	FOR
4. FY93/$15B Def. Cut	FOR	8. Death Pen. from Jury	AGN	12. Cuba Trade Embargo	AGN

Key Votes of the 103d Congress

1. Family Leave	FOR	2. Deficit Reduction	FOR	3. Stimulus Plan	FOR

Election Results

1992 general	Thomas H. Andrews (D)...............	232,696	(65%)	($850,122)
	Linda Bean (R)......................	125,236	(35%)	($1,464,720)
1992 primary	Thomas H. Andrews (D)................	31,512	(100%)	
1990 general	Thomas H. Andrews (D)...............	167,623	(60%)	($693,165)
	David F. Emery (R)	110,836	(40%)	($463,873)

SECOND DISTRICT

The 2d District covers the northern three-quarters of the state, geographically. In the more thickly populated part of Maine, however, the boundary line is actually rather jagged, and the 2d takes in the traditionally Democratic mill town of Lewiston as well as the traditionally Republican coastal area down east. In contrast to the coastal south, which boomed in the 1980s, much of the north lagged or lost population, especially potato-growing Aroostook County. Anger was strong here in 1992; Ross Perot finished a solid second in the district, with one-third of the votes—his best congressional district in the United States.

The 2d District's Congresswoman Olympia Snowe, first elected in 1978, is now one of the more senior Republicans in the House, and one of the more distinctive, not the least for her personal life: since 1989, she has been married to her former House colleague, Governor John McKernan. But her political longevity and personal connection may nearly have cost her the seat: she won by just 51%–49% in 1990 against underfinanced Democrat Patrick McGowan, while McKernan was winning a three-way race for Governor with less than a majority. McGowan ran again in 1992, hoping that Maine's angry mood would work in his favor. But Snowe succeeded in turning it in the other direction. Her ads attacked McGowan for flip-flopping on Loring Air Force Base, which she had fought hard (though unsuccessfully) to keep out of the base closing bill, and she hit him for not supporting that political outsiders' favorite, the balanced budget amendment. She stressed her own work on women's health issues, including her support of fetal tissue research, which pointed up her pro-choice stand on abortion. And she was the only Republican to vote to override President Bush's veto of a tax bill in early 1992.

Against this, McGowan sounded more generalized "it's time to take care of our own" themes, attacking Snowe for her non-Maine oriented seat on Foreign Affairs, and saying he would serve on Agriculture instead. He took a pro-labor stand but emphasized his own problems, as a country store owner, with government regulators and taxes. And if Snowe was hurt by McKernan's unpopularity, McGowan, as a 10-year legislator, may have been hurt by the unpopularity of Democratic legislative leaders, a couple of whom lost in this Perot-ish district. In any case, Snowe's lead in public polls widened from 40%–36% in September to 48%–34% in late October, and she won by a 49%–42% margin. Nine percent of the vote went to Maine Green Party candidate Jonathan Carter (this district seems to like third party candidates) which may have cost McGowan the election. With under 50% of the vote, Snowe could still be a target in 1994— or perhaps she will take on Senator George Mitchell.

The People: Pop. 1990: 591,400; 60% rural; 13% age 65+; 98% White; 1% Amer. Indian; 1% Hispanic origin. Voting age pop.: 440,155. Households: 60% married couple families; 28% married couple fams. w. children; 36% college educ.; median household income: $24,672; per capita income: $11,446; median gross rent: $365; median house value: $66,500.

1992 Presidential Vote			**1988 Presidential Vote**		
Clinton (D)	118,229	(38%)	Bush (R)	137,839	(55%)
Perot (I)..................	103,992	(33%)	Dukakis (D)...............	112,491	(45%)
Bush (R)	90,807	(29%)			

Rep. Olympia J. Snowe (R)

Elected 1978; b. Feb. 21, 1947, Augusta; home, Auburn; U. of ME, B.A. 1969; Greek Orthodox; married (Gov. John R. McKernan).

Career: Dir., Superior Concrete Co.; Auburn Bd. of Voter Registration, 1971–73; ME House of Reps., 1973–76; ME Senate, 1976–78.

Offices: 2268 RHOB 20515, 202-225-6306. Also 1 Cumberland Place, #306, Bangor 04401, 207-945-0432; 169 Academy St., #306, Presque Isle 04769, 207-764-5124; and 2 Great Falls Plaza, #7B, Auburn 04210, 207-786-2451.

Committees: *Budget* (5th of 17 R). *Foreign Affairs* (5th of 18 R): International Operations (RMM); International Security, International Organizations and Human Rights.

Group Ratings

	ADA	ACLU	COPE	CDF	CFA	LCV	ACU	NTLC	NSI	COC	CEI
1992	50	52	58	50	67	63	60	35	80	50	52
1991	35	—	67	80	39	62	55	—	—	40	45

National Journal Ratings

	1991 LIB — 1991 CONS		1992 LIB — 1992 CONS	
Economic	36%	— 63%	42%	— 57%
Social	43%	— 56%	46%	— 53%
Foreign	40%	— 58%	44%	— 50%

Key Votes of the 102d Congress

1. Ban Striker Replace	AGN	5. Handgun Wait/7-Day	AGN	9. Use Force in Gulf	FOR
2. $ for Homeownership	FOR	6. Overseas Mil. Abortion	FOR	10. US Mil. Abroad $ Cut	FOR
3. Tax Rich/Cut Mid Cls.	FOR	7. Obscn. Art NEA $ Ban	FOR	11. Limit SDI Funds	AGN
4. FY93/$15B Def. Cut	AGN	8. Death Pen. from Jury	FOR	12. Cuba Trade Embargo	FOR

Key Votes of the 103d Congress

1. Family Leave	FOR	2. Deficit Reduction	AGN	3. Stimulus Plan	AGN

Election Results

1992 general	Olympia J. Snowe (R)	153,022	(49%)	($746,611)
	Patrick K. McGowan (D)	130,824	(42%)	($382,410)
	Jonathan K. Carter (Green)	27,526	(9%)	($16,793)
1992 primary	Olympia J. Snowe (R)	25,326	(100%)	
1990 general	Olympia J. Snowe (R)	121,704	(51%)	($306,289)
	Patrick K. McGowan (D)	116,798	(49%)	($228,344)

MARYLAND

Maryland lays claim to being the typical American state, and in many ways is so because of atypicalities that cancel each other out. It was the only one of the 13 colonies founded by Roman Catholics, the Calvert family, and its embrace of religious tolerance came less from abstract principle than from the Calverts' desire to protect their property from Protestant monarchs. It was one of the two big Chesapeake colonies, overshadowed by Virginia, but with the same economy based on tobacco cultivated by slave labor and traded directly with Britain. In time, Virginia and Maryland went their separate ways, Virginia to become the capital of the Confederacy, Maryland to remain part of the Union, though grudgingly (the state song condemns Abraham Lincoln's suppression of pro-Confederate rioters), and to become identified with the North. The puritan impulse was never lively here: Prohibition was enforced only laxly in Baltimore, to the delight of its great journalist-cum-lexicographer, H.L. Mencken; slot machines were legal in the rural counties of the Western Shore; the state's law guaranteeing blacks equal access to public accommodations specifically excluded the Eastern Shore. By not pursuing any one course rigorously, Maryland could be many things at once: northern as well as southern, moralistic as well as libertine, industrial as well as rural, leaving people to their own devices yet with a heavy government presence. Perhaps as a result, much of Maryland's political history reads like a chronicle of rogues, from Luther Martin, the drunken haranguer at the Constitutional Convention, to Spiro Agnew, who took cash bribes as governor and vice president and resigned in 1973 a convicted felon.

Maryland's genial tolerance may have given it a history a little too savory, but this state, perhaps because it is in so many ways typical, cherishes its uniqueness. The Chesapeake Bay, for example, is the nation's largest fresh water estuary, with its unique watermen and shellfish: the terrapin and Chesapeake oyster may be so endangered as to be rare today, but Maryland blue crabs are still common, and the rockfish is coming back. Maryland likes having its state bird (the Baltimore oriole), state flower (the black-eyed Susan), state dog (the Chesapeake Bay retriever), even if today's political correctness has made it convenient to forget the words to "Maryland, My Maryland" and to consider, as the legislature did, a politically correct version of the Calverts' old Italian motto (*fatti maschi, parole femine* which means manly deeds and womanly words).

Maryland also has some reason to be proud of the economy, or economies, it has built over the years. Half a century ago, half the state's population lived in the city of Baltimore and only one-fifth in suburbs; now the proportions are the other way around, and then some: 15% Baltimore, 65% suburbs. And in 1992, the Census Bureau announced that Washington and Baltimore were now a single metropolitan area, the fourth largest in the country, with more than 6 million people. But this is a case of statistical definition at odds with practical reality. Baltimore and Washington are not fraternal, if sometimes quarrelsome, twins like Dallas and Fort Worth or Minneapolis and St. Paul; they are two quite separate cities, with different economic bases, and different attitudes toward public life. Baltimore started off as a port and an industrial city, and has managed to stay diversified and successful as it has spread out into the countryside from its new central core at Harborplace and the solidly built edifices of its downtown grid streets. It makes spices and writes insurance; it headquarters one of the nation's giant power tool makers and one of its great investment banks; it has big government operations, the headquarters of the Social Security Administration and, quietly down the road, the National Security Agency; it is home to the Orioles in their new, intentionally old-fashioned Oriole Park at Camden Yards and is home to Johns Hopkins University in Georgian buildings along the affluent corridor that runs directly north from downtown all the way to the developing edge city of Hunt Valley.

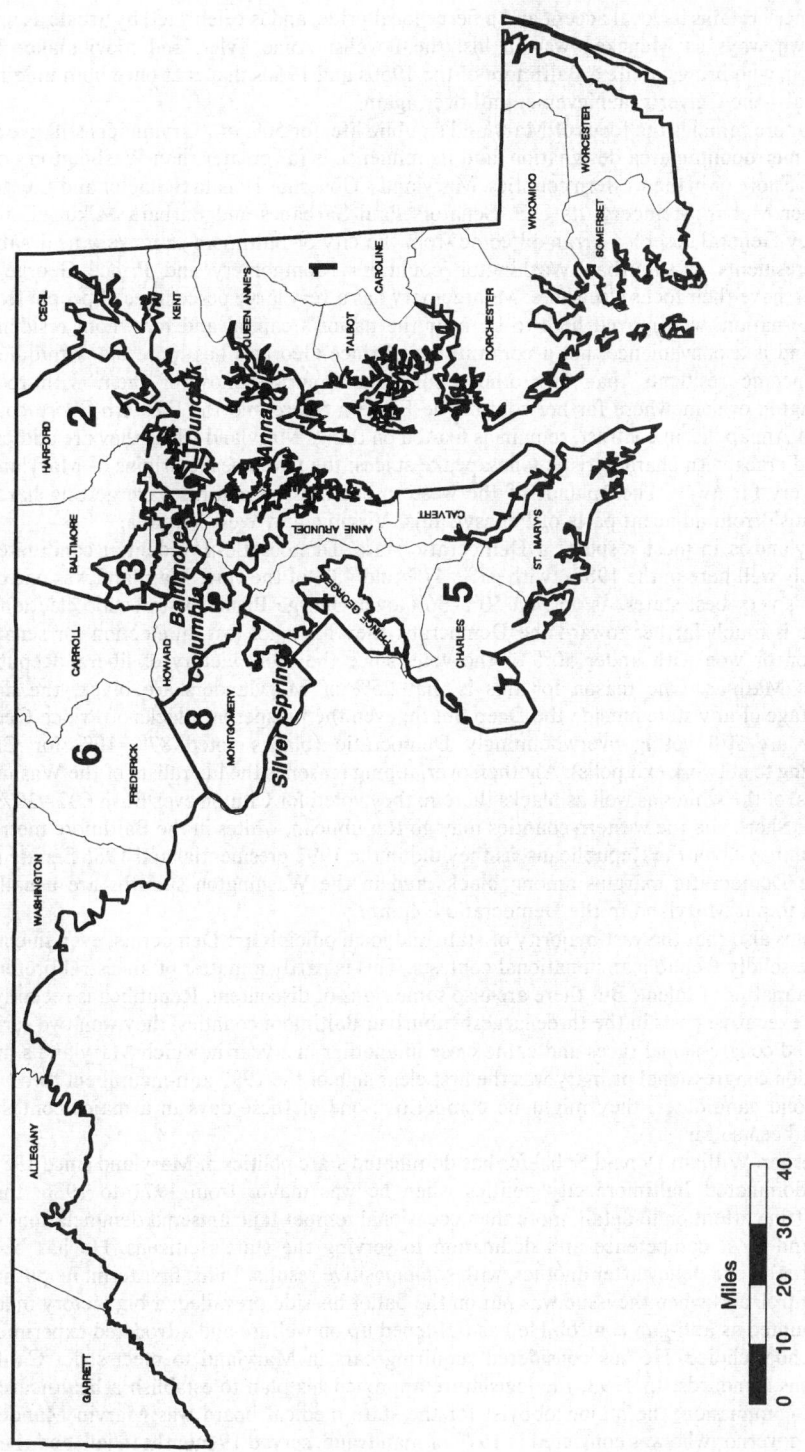

CECL

KENT

QUEEN ANNES

CAROLINE

TALBOT

DORCHESTER

WICOMICO

WORCESTER

SOMERSET

1

HARFORD

2

Dundalk

Annapolis

BALTIMORE

ANNE ARUNDEL

CALVERT

ST. MARYS

Baltimore

3

Columbia

4

PRINCE GEORGE

5

CHARLES

CARROLL

HOWARD

Silver Spring

8

MONTGOMERY

FREDERICK

6

WASHINGTON

ALLEGANY

GARRETT

Miles

0   10   20   30   40

"Bawlmer" retains its local accent and a fierce local pride, and is celebrated by artists as vivid in their own ways as Mencken was in his: the novelist Anne Tyler, and moviemaker Barry Levinson, who brings to life a Baltimore of the 1950s and 1960s that is at once both unique and universal—the Calverts' achievement all over again.

Baltimore remains the focus of Maryland's public life, for 50% of Marylanders still live in the former metropolitan area designation, and its influence is far greater than Washington's on the Eastern Shore or in the western counties. Maryland's Governor Donald Schaefer and Lieutenant Governor Melvin Steinberg, its U.S. Senators Paul Sarbanes and Barbara Mikulski, and its Attorney General Joseph Curran all come from the city of Baltimore or its very near suburbs. Many residents of suburban Washington counties—Montgomery and Prince George's—in contrast, have their focus elsewhere: Montgomery has a very large percentage of people from all over the nation, who moved here to be near the nation's capital and for whom residence in Maryland is a convenience, not a commitment; Prince George's has more black middle- and upper-income residents than any other county in America, most of them with roots in Washington or somewhere farther south. The Eastern Shore and the Western Shore counties south of Annapolis, in contrast, remain as fixated on things Maryland-ish as they are addicted to steamed crabs with characteristic Chesapeake spices: the Chesapeake origins of Maryland are never very far away. The uplands of the western counties, in contrast, are getting harder to distinguish from adjacent parts of Pennsylvania, Virginia and West Virginia.

Maryland is in most respects a Democratic state. Democratic presidential candidates ran relatively well here in the 1980s, with 47%, 47% and 48% of the vote; Maryland was one of Bill Clinton's very best states, as he won 50%–36% over George Bush. In statewide elections, the balance is much farther toward the Democrats; they have not lost an election for senator or governor, or won with under 50% of the vote, since the 1980 victory of liberal Republican Charles Mathias. One reason for this is that 25% of Marylanders are black, the highest percentage of any state outside the Deep South; even the prosperous blacks of Prince George's County are still voting overwhelmingly Democratic (blacks voted 87%–10% for Clinton according to network exit polls). Another, overlapping reason is the liberalism of the Washington suburbs, of the whites as well as blacks therein: they voted for Clinton over Bush 60%–30%. The Eastern Shore and the western counties may go Republican; whites in the Baltimore metropolitan area may favor the Republicans, as they did in the 1992 presidential and 1986 Senate races; but the Democratic margins among blacks and in the Washington suburbs are usually big enough to put Maryland in the Democratic column.

It helps also that the vast majority of state and local officials are Democrats, even in counties that are solidly Republican in national contests. This is partly a matter of ancestral preference, partly a matter of talent. But there are also some signs of discontent. Republicans recently won county executive posts in the three largest suburban Baltimore counties; they won two seriously contested congressional races and came close in another in a year in which Maryland's first-in-the-nation congressional primary was the first clear sign of the 1992 anti-incumbent trend. With some solid candidates, they might be competitive one of these days in a major contest, but haven't been so far.

Governor. William Donald Schaefer has dominated state politics in Maryland since 1986 just as he dominated Baltimore city politics when he was mayor from 1971 to 1986: through unremitting attention to detail, more than occasional temper tantrums and denunciations of the press and by a competence and dedication to serving the state's citizens. He has been an innovator on one policy after another, with some positive results. In his first term, he pushed for gun control, and when the issue was put on the ballot his side prevailed: a big victory in a state long counted as anti-gun control. He has tightened up on welfare and advocated experimenting with school choice. He has considered requiring cars in Maryland to meet strict California emissions standards. In 1993, the legislature approved his plan to establish a healthcare cost-control commission; the major lobbyist for the state medical board was Marvin Mandel, the former governor who was convicted in 1977 of mail fraud, served 19 months in jail, and then had his conviction overturned by the U.S. Supreme Court. On the abortion issue, Schaefer antagonized both sides, but resolved it by putting a referendum on the 1992 ballot: the measure, guaranteeing a right to most abortions but allowing some minor restrictions, passed 62%–38%. Schaefer has been frustrated as revenue overestimates and mandated education and Medicaid spending increases have forced him to cut the budget several times and press for a tax increase once.

Schaefer's roots are in an older Baltimore, and a time when public officials were at least superficially respected more than today. And he may well have the thinnest skin in American politics. He rages at criticism from the press, makes rude calls or sends rude notes to ordinary citizens who criticize him, will scarcely speak the name of Baltimore Mayor Kurt Schmoke, was angry enough at Bill Clinton to go to St. Louis the last week of the 1992 campaign and endorse George Bush. He has antagonized at least some voters: elected with 82% in 1986, he was reelected with 60% in 1990.

Schaefer is not eligible to run for a third consecutive term in 1994. Schmoke is one possible successor, and led in early 1993 polls; some wonder whether a black candidate can win statewide, but his greater problems may be his support of full debates on decriminalizing drugs and his opposition to increased funds for Montgomery County. Other Democrats mentioned are Lieutenant Governor Melvin Steinberg, Attorney General Joseph Curran, Prince George's County Executive Parris Glendening, Montgomery County state Senator Mary Boergers; possible Republicans include Congresswoman Helen Delich Bentley, long close to Schaefer, and Anne Arundel County Executive Robert Neall. Schaefer's 1990 opponent, William Shepard, has also announced he will run again. This much can be said: Maryland will never have another governor with the major strengths and annoying weaknesses of Donald Schaefer.

Senators. First elected to the House in 1970 and to the Senate in 1976, Paul Sarbanes is now one of the senior members of Congress, but he is not much recognized outside official Washington or politically aware Maryland. One reason is that he continues to live in Baltimore (as does his colleague, Barbara Mikulski). Another is that he actively disdains publicity: he sponsors relatively few bills and seldom seeks the limelight. He continues to have one of the most liberal voting records in the Senate. His liberalism is rooted in his experience growing up in Salisbury on the Eastern Shore, the son of a Greek immigrant who owned the Mayflower Grill and taught himself enough on the side to discuss philosophy with his son's Princeton professors. As a big firm lawyer in Baltimore, Sarbanes got started in local politics campaigning in small groups, talking to voters and leaders, listening gravely to what they had to say. Tabbed early as a reformer, in the state legislature he voted against Marvin Mandel to replace Spiro Agnew as governor in 1969—not the most politic move. He beat an incumbent congressman in the 1970 Senate primary and in 1976 defeated former Senator Joseph Tydings in the primary and incumbent Senator Glenn Beall in the general by 59%–41%.

"I have a sense of excitement," Sarbanes said just before the 1992 election, anticipating the result. "We've been through 12 years of sheer torture . . . Now, I think that we can show the country that we can govern." This analysis is arguable—it's not clear that triumph in the Cold War and seven years of low-inflation economic growth qualify as "sheer torture." But Sarbanes was surely right in thinking that, while he has been in the legislative majority most of his congressional career, he has not, with the possible exception of a few Carter years, had the satisfaction of having events go his way and of believing that he would be able to achieve the goals he has earnestly sought. Now is his moment. Indeed, Sarbanes can reasonably claim to have anticipated the February 1993 Clinton economic package. A year earlier, as chairman of the Joint Economic Committee, he joined with Senate Budget Committee Chairman Jim Sasser in backing a package of short-term economic stimulus (he called early for extending unemployment benefits) and long-term government investment. Sarbanes has been using the JEC to argue that the growth in the 1980s was illusory or confined to the rich (Republicans like Dick Armey have sharply disagreed), and he believes that active federal government can do things to reverse this. He also seeks more power by elected politicians over the Federal Reserve: he has a bill to take the 12 regional bank presidents off the Federal Open Market Committee and make them advisors there; and clearly he wants more stimulative monetary policies over time. With a seat on Budget, with a majority in the Senate, with a chance to use his charts—a Sarbanes trademark before Ross Perot ever took them up—to affect national economic policy.

Sarbanes also should be coming into his own on the Foreign Relations Committee. In the Bush years, he blocked appointments of big contributors to ambassadorships, notably Joy Silverman (later the victim in the Sol Wachtler case) to Barbados; it will be interesting to see if he applies similar scrutiny, if not to Pamela Harriman, to those Clinton nominees whose substantive qualifications seem far outweighed by their political contributions. His big project in recent years has been reforming the foreign aid program, which has been carried over year to year without reauthorization until 1991; given foreign aid's current unpopularity, and the particular interests of various countries, this is a tough job. Sarbanes is also likely to work quietly on Maryland projects, including a major Chesapeake Bay Restoration Act and protecting Maryland military bases (which unlike Virginia didn't get much hurt in 1993).

Sarbanes's seat comes up in 1994, and in early 1993 no well-known politician seemed interested in running against him. He won in 1982 and 1988 with 63% and 62%, carrying Baltimore area whites and blacks and running mostly on party lines elsewhere—stronger around his boyhood home of Salisbury. Possible Republican candidates include Senate Minority Leader John Cade and Party Chairwoman Joyce Terhes, neither widely recognized. Sarbanes seems likely to be very strong, unless things turn sour for the Clinton Administration and his confidence that his Democrats can govern becomes unjustified.

Barbara Mikulski came to the Senate with deep roots in immigrant urban America, and more than most there she seems fascinated by the new technology and jobs growing in the outer edges of the urban areas, many of which are held by people with backgrounds like her own. Her roots are in east Baltimore, where her Polish immigrant parents ran a bakery. She got her start in politics as a social worker, organizing Highlandtown to stop a highway from going through; she won, and in the process was elected to the Baltimore City Council in 1971, in time to serve (and spar) with the then new mayor, Donald Schaefer. As a local official with genuine ethnic roots and a woman with genuine liberal impulses, she was chosen head of the Democratic National Committee's Commission on Delegate Selection in 1972. She ran for the Senate in 1974, and got a respectable 43% against Charles Mathias; when Paul Sarbanes ran for the other Senate seat in 1976, Mikulski ran for his 3d District seat and won. Ten years later, she gave up that seat for what seemed like a chancy Senate race, and won handily, with 50% in the primary to 31% for Montgomery County Congressman Michael Barnes and 14% for Governor Harry Hughes. In the general, against former White House aide Linda Chavez, Mikulski won with 61%.

Mikulski is loud and brash, humorous and warm, brusque and aggressive when she feels it is necessary, curious and thoughtful when encountering another new part of the world. She knows Baltimore warp and woof—its neighborhoods and government agencies, charitable institutions and ethnic politicians—and she still lives there, in the Fells Point neighborhood being restored on the waterfront: Fells Point and Don Schaefer's Harborplace, she points out, stand where the highway she opposed was supposed to pass. But she has also become, thanks to an Appropriations subcommittee chairmanship and lots of hard work, the Senate's chief superintendent of the space program and an enthusiast for space exploration. An ardent backer of the manned space station *Freedom* sometimes derided by other liberals, she has found enough money to keep it alive despite her sympathy for veterans' and housing programs also funded by her subcommittee and which, under current budget procedures, tend to be competitors for the same fixed pool of funds. On foreign policy, she usually votes with the doves and opposed the Gulf war resolution, but was attentive even in the Cold War years to human rights violations in left-wing as well as right-wing countries.

On domestic policy, Mikulski is a liberal who insists that "where there are rights there are responsibilities." She surprised many by supporting workfare requirements in 1992. Her biggest domestic initiative is a national service proposal, introduced well before Bill Clinton endorsed the idea in his campaign, in which an adult could perform public services on a National Guard-like schedule and get credits convertible to student loan payments or partial down payment for first-time homebuyers. Mikulski was one of the most vocal defenders of Anita Hill during the Clarence Thomas hearings, and has long denounced sexual harassment. In 1993, she joined the Ethics Committee where she should be a strong voice during the investigation of sexual harassment charges brought against Bob Packwood. She has worked for United Nations family planning funding and more money for Pap smear tests and mammograms; she has sought to exempt from anti-bundling campaign finance laws checks of $50 or less, helpful to EMILY's List, which effectively backed many Democratic women Senate candidates in 1992. Mikulski has not been shy about using her Appropriations seat to help Maryland projects, from the National Institutes of Health in Bethesda to the Baltimore VA program to the Goddard Space Flight Center in Prince George's County to a new $130 million marine biotechnology center in Baltimore. She sponsored a law requiring country of origin disclosure for manufactured car parts. Remembering how she relied on low-cost billboards in her first campaign, she calls anti-billboard proponents "boutique environmentalists."

In 1992, Mikulski was opposed by Alan Keyes, a former Reagan appointee who had run against Sarbanes in 1988. Keyes charged that the national Republican Party was ignoring him because he is black; articulate and angry, he probably hurt himself by any attention he gained from this. Mikulski continued to make a positive impression, and won with 71%.

Presidential politics. Maryland is by any measure now one of the most Democratic states in national elections: it voted for Jimmy Carter in 1980, came close to voting for Walter Mondale and Michael Dukakis in 1984 and 1988 and, with New York, gave Bill Clinton his highest percentage in the country after the District of Columbia and Arkansas. Black voters and liberal Washington suburbanites have provided the key votes for this trend. Yet the Democratic percentages—47%, 47%, 48%, 50%—suggest that there may be a ceiling for national Democrats, or at least one they can't exceed until they win over more Baltimore-area whites.

In 1992, Maryland held its primary a week before Super Tuesday, on March 3, to avoid being ignored as it mostly was on Super Tuesday 1988. Once again, the state Democrats preferred a Massachusetts Greek, this time Paul Tsongas, 41%–33% over Bill Clinton, and registered Republicans opted for George Bush, 70%–30% over Pat Buchanan. Tsongas's victory was suburban, with all his margin and more coming from suburban Baltimore and Montgomery County.

Congressional districting. Population movements to the suburbs and the Voting Rights Act requirement of maximizing the number of black-majority districts made 1992 redistricting a politically wrenching process for Maryland. The legislature wanted to create a new black-majority Prince George's County seat and still leave a Democratic district for House power Steny Hoyer; Governor Schaefer wanted to preserve the Baltimore seat of Republican Helen Bentley, so she could continue her long work for the port of Baltimore—and so that she wouldn't run for the Senate against Barbara Mikulski, as she threatened to do if her district got schmussed. The losers were Republican freshman Wayne Gilchrest and three-term Democrat Tom McMillen, who were put together in a district that combined the Eastern Shore with the Annapolis area. McMillen's loss in November and Beverly Byron's March primary defeat means that there will be no moderate to conservative Democrats in the Maryland delegation for the 103d Congress: the demise of an old breed.

The People: Est. Pop. 1992: 4,906,000; Pop. 1990: 4,781,468, up 2.5% 1990–1992. 1.9% of U.S. total, 19th largest; 19% rural. Median age: 33.0 years. 10.8% 65 years and over. 71.0% White, 24.9% Black, 2.9% Asian, 2.6% Hispanic origin. Households: 54.2% married couple families; 26% married couple fams. w. children; 50% college educ.; median household income: $39,386; per capita income: $17,730; 65.0% owner occupied housing; median house value: $116,500; median monthly rent: $473. 6.6% Unemployment. Voting age pop.: 3,619,227. Registered voters (1992): 2,463,010; 1,506,184 D (61%); 717,963 R (29%); 238,863 unaffiliated and minor parties (10%).

Political Lineup: Governor, William Donald Schaefer (D); Lt. Gov., Melvin A. Steinberg (D); Secy. of State, Winfield M. Kelly, Jr. (D); Atty. Gen., J. Joseph Curran, Jr. (D); Treasurer, Lucille Maurer (D); Comptroller, Louis L. Goldstein (D). State Senate, 47 (38 D and 9 R); State House of Delegates, 141 (116 D and 25 R). Senators, Paul S. Sarbanes (D) and Barbara A. Mikulski (D). Representatives, 8 (4 D and 4 R).

1992 Presidential Vote

Clinton (D)	988,571	(50%)
Bush (R)	707,094	(36%)
Perot (I)	281,414	(14%)

1992 Democratic Presidential Primary

Tsongas	230,490	(41%)
Clinton	189,906	(33%)
Brown	46,480	(8%)
Harkin	32,899	(6%)
Kerrey	27,035	(5%)
Uncommitted	36,155	(6%)

1988 Presidential Vote

Bush (R)	876,167	(51%)
Dukakis (D)	826,304	(48%)

1992 Republican Presidential Primary

Bush	168,364	(70%)
Buchanan	71,647	(30%)

GOVERNOR

Gov. William Donald Schaefer (D)

Elected 1986, term expires Jan. 1995; b. Nov. 2, 1921, Baltimore; home, Annapolis; Baltimore City Col., B.A. 1939, U. of Baltimore, LL.B. 1942, LL.M. 1951; Episcopalian; single.

Career: Army, 1942–45 (WWII), Army Reserves, 1946–79; Practicing atty., 1955–67; Baltimore City Cncl., 1955–71, Pres., 1967–71; Baltimore Mayor, 1971–87.

Office: State House, Annapolis 21401, 410-974-3901.

Election Results

1990 gen.	William Donald Schaefer (D) ..	664,015	(60%)
	William S. Shepard (R)	446,980	(40%)
1990 prim.	William Donald Schaefer (D) ..	358,534	(78%)
	Frederick M. Griisser (D)	100,816	(22%)
1986 gen.	William Donald Schaefer (D) ..	907,291	(82%)
	Thomas J. Mooney (R)	194,185	(18%)

SENATORS

Sen. Paul S. Sarbanes (D)

Elected 1976, seat up 1994; b. Feb. 3, 1933, Salisbury; home, Baltimore; Princeton, A.B. 1954, Rhodes Scholar, Oxford U., B.A. 1957, Harvard, LL.B. 1960; Greek Orthodox; married (Christine).

Career: Law Clerk, Judge Morris A. Soper, U.S. 4th Circuit Crt. of Appeals, 1960–61; Practicing atty., 1961–62, 1965–70; A.A., Pres. Kennedy's Cncl. of Econ. Advisers, 1962–63; Exec. Dir., Baltimore Charter Revision Comm., 1963–64; MD House of Delegates, 1969–70; U.S. House of Reps., 1971–77.

Offices: 309 HSOB 20510, 202-224-4524. Also 1518 Fed. Bldg., 31 Hopkins Plz., Baltimore 21201, 410-962-4436; 1110 Bonifant St., #450, Silver Spring 20910, 301-589-0797; 111 Baptist St., #115, Salisbury 21801, 410-860-2131; 47 S.E. Crain Hwy., Box 331, Cobb Island 20625, 301-259-2404; and 141 Baltimore St., #206, Cumberland 21502, 301-724-4660.

Committees: *Banking, Housing and Urban Affairs* (2d of 11 D): Housing and Urban Affairs (Chmn.); International Finance and Monetary Policy. *Budget* (10th of 12 D). *Foreign Relations* (3d of 11 D): European Affairs; International Economic Policy, Trade, Oceans and Environment (Chmn.); Near Eastern and South Asian Affairs. *Joint Economic Committee* (Vice Chmn. of 10). *Joint Committee on the Organization of Congress* (5th of 12).

Group Ratings

	ADA	ACLU	CDF	COPE	CFA	LCV	ACU	NTLC	NSI	COC	CEI
1992	100	91	100	92	100	92	0	5	40	10	9
1991	100	—	100	92	83	87	0	—	—	10	16

National Journal Ratings

	1991 LIB — 1991 CONS		1992 LIB — 1992 CONS	
Economic	85% —	11%	91% —	5%
Social	87% —	0%	89% —	0%
Foreign	78% —	14%	78% —	14%

Key Votes of the 102d Congress

1. $ for Homeownership	AGN	5. Clarence Thomas Nom.	AGN	9. Use Force in Gulf	AGN
2. Have Cap Gains Debate	AGN	6. Lmt Death Row Appeal	AGN	10. Keep Salvador Aid	AGN
3. Remove Budget Walls	FOR	7. Handgun Wait/5-Day	FOR	11. Cut $1B from SDI	FOR
4. Ban Striker Replace	FOR	8. Abortion Gag Rule	AGN	12. Override China MFN	FOR

Key Votes of the 103d Congress

1. Family Leave	FOR	2. HIV Immigrants	FOR	3. Clinton Budget	FOR

Election Results

1988 general	Paul S. Sarbanes (D)	999,166	(62%)	($1,466,477)
	Alan L. Keyes (R).....................	617,537	(38%)	($662,651)
1988 primary	Paul S. Sarbanes (D)	309,923	(86%)	
	B. Emerson Sweatt (D).................	25,932	(7%)	
	A. Robert Kaufman (D)................	25,450	(7%)	
1982 general	Paul S. Sarbanes (D)	707,356	(63%)	($1,623,533)
	Lawrence J. Hogan (R)	407,334	(37%)	($580,953)

Sen. Barbara A. Mikulski (D)

Elected 1986, seat up 1998; b. July 20, 1936, Baltimore; home, Baltimore; Mt. St. Agnes Col., B.A. 1958, U. of MD, M.S.W. 1965; Catholic; single.

Career: Social worker, admin., Baltimore Dept. of Social Svcs., 1965–70; Baltimore City Cncl., 1971–76; Adjunct prof., Loyola Col., 1972–76; Chmn., DNC Delegate Selection Comm., 1972; U.S. House of Reps., 1976–86.

Offices: 709 HSOB 20510, 202-224-4654. Also 253 World Trade Ctr., Baltimore 21202, 410-962-4510; 60 West St., #202, Annapolis 21401, 410-263-1805; City Ctr. on the Plaza, 213-219 W. Main St., Salisbury 21801, 410-546-7711; 658 Baltimore Ave., #207, College Park 20740, 301-345-5517; and 82 W. Washington St., #402, Hagerstown 21740, 301-797-2826.

Committees: *Appropriations* (11th of 16 D): Foreign Operations; Legislative Branch; Transportation; Treasury, Postal Service and General Government; VA, HUD and Independent Agencies (Chmn.). *Ethics (Select)* (2d of 3 D). *Labor and Human Resources* (7th of 10 D): Aging (Chmn.); Children, Family, Drugs and Alcoholism; Education, Arts and Humanities; Employment and Productivity.

Group Ratings

	ADA	ACLU	CDF	COPE	CFA	LCV	ACU	NTLC	NSI	COC	CEI
1992	100	90	100	92	92	67	0	17	40	0	18
1991	90	—	91	83	78	93	10	—	—	20	20

National Journal Ratings

	1991 LIB — 1991 CONS			1992 LIB — 1992 CONS		
Economic	72%	—	27%	89%	—	9%
Social	70%	—	27%	68%	—	31%
Foreign	75%	—	23%	65%	—	26%

Key Votes of the 102d Congress

1. $ for Homeownership	AGN	5. Clarence Thomas Nom.	AGN	9. Use Force in Gulf	AGN
2. Have Cap Gains Debate	AGN	6. Lmt Death Row Appeal	AGN	10. Keep Salvador Aid	AGN
3. Remove Budget Walls	FOR	7. Handgun Wait/5-Day	FOR	11. Cut $1B from SDI	FOR
4. Ban Striker Replace	FOR	8. Abortion Gag Rule	AGN	12. Override China MFN	FOR

Key Votes of the 103d Congress

1. Family Leave	FOR	2. HIV Immigrants	FOR	3. Clinton Budget	FOR

Election Results

1992 general	Barbara A. Mikulski (D)	1,307,610	(71%)	($3,623,974)
	Alan L. Keyes (R)	533,688	(29%)	($1,175,682)
1992 primary	Barbara A. Mikulski (D)	376,444	(77%)	
	Thomas M. Wheatley (D)	31,214	(6%)	
	Walter Boyd (D)	26,467	(5%)	
	Don Allensworth (D)	19,731	(4%)	
	Three Others	36,621	(8%)	
1986 general	Barbara A. Mikulski (D)	675,225	(61%)	($2,097,216)
	Linda Chavez (R)	437,411	(39%)	($1,699,175)

FIRST DISTRICT

The largest estuary in North America, the Chesapeake Bay, was the central focus of the most thickly settled of the 13 colonies, and today it remains a central focus for much of booming Maryland—and a backwater where remnants of an older civilization live on. The first British here were amazed at the Chesapeake's oysters and terrapin turtles and crabs and rockfish; despite pollution, watermen still make hardy livings bringing them to shore. This was an estuary civilization in colonial days, every little hamlet tied to mother England by the highways of bays and creeks and inlets off the Chesapeake; old settlements like Chestertown, Oxford, St. Michaels and Cambridge don't look much different from when George Washington slept there. On the Western Shore, Annapolis was laid out as a capital in 1694, with one circle planned for the State House and one for the Church; the marble-halled State House, built in 1772, is the oldest U.S. state capitol in continuous use. Annapolis is the home of the United States Naval Academy and its waterfront, though gentrified, is a waterman's as well as a yachter's port.

In post-colonial times, when most Americans were caught up in the romance of westward movement, these estuaries and peninsulas were forgotten, off the main lines of railroads and highways. Some of the Chesapeake has been changed beyond recognition—Baltimore, for instance, or the condominiums and strip malls spread out along Kent Island at the eastern foot of the Bay Bridge. But much has evolved slowly and with a certain continuity. The Eastern Shore counties of Maryland in the 160 years between 1790 and 1950 only doubled in population, perhaps the slowest growth rate on the Eastern Seaboard; and if its towns are industrial today, with little factories and mechanized farms, they still seem antique and the landscape is not vastly different from a century or two ago. There is some change now, as northeastern metropolitan expansion reaches south from the northern end of the Bay or east across the Bridge, and the Eastern Shore becomes increasingly second-home and vacation country, and businesses like Frank Perdue's chicken empire around Salisbury grow. But this is still an old-fashioned America, a country left behind which many would like to find again.

The 1st Congressional District of Maryland includes all of the Eastern Shore and a segment of Maryland west of the Bay, including Annapolis and a strip of four-lane highway suburbs up to the southern row-house tip of Baltimore. In national elections, this is a solidly Republican area—George Bush carried it handily in 1992—and it tends toward the conservative on issues like gun control and abortion. Yet there is a history on both shores of electing local Democrats. The 1st as drawn in 1991 was the home of two incumbents. One was Democrat Tom McMillen, a former University of Maryland and Washington Bullets basketball player and Rhodes Scholar, first elected by a 428 vote margin in 1986 in a district that included Annapolis and extended to the Washington suburbs. The other incumbent was Republican Wayne Gilchrest, a history teacher at Kent County High School and summer housepainter, who beat a beleaguered Democratic incumbent 57%–43% in 1990 in an Eastern Shore district which also included southern Maryland counties now in the 5th District. (The Eastern Shore district has a lurid history: one congressman killed himself amid financial embarrassment; another, Robert Bauman, resigned after charges of soliciting sex from a 16-year-old boy; a third, Roy Dyson, the man Gilchrest ultimately beat, was embarrassed when his top aide, Tom Pappas, committed suicide after *The Washington Post* reported on his questionable personnel hiring practices.)

By many criteria, McMillen should have been the favorite. He had raised huge sums in the past—$757,000 in 1990—and as a member of the Energy and Commerce Committee could easily raise much more; by June 1990, he had $430,000 in cash to Gilchrest's $20,000. He had a moderate record not out of line with the district and his celebrity status was pointed up by a law he passed—the Student-Right-to-Know Act—requiring colleges to disclose graduation rates of student athletes. Gilchrest raised far less and had a penchant for odd remarks; in one debate he began his response, " 'I believe for every drop of rain that falls, a flower grows.' I just had to say that." He won the three-way primary with an unimpressive 47%, running third in the district's western shore. But Gilchrest also had assets. He had represented 53% of the new district, and the Eastern Shore has a certain clannishness, increased when Governor William Donald Schaefer called it a "shit-house." McMillen won only 38% in the primary, over desultory opposition. Gilchrest even had a little legislative accomplishment, a National Academy of Sciences study to define wetlands, a sore subject given varying interpretations of the Wetlands Act, plus the Sierra Club endorsement. Probably decisive was a Gilchrest radio ad accusing McMillen of taking many congressional junkets, including airing one to Japan, with a flight attendant asking, "More sushi, Mr. McMillen?" The ad went on to note that Gilchrest took only one trip, driving his pickup to Ocean City, to address fellow members of the Order of the Purple Heart: "Box of saltwater taffy, Mr. Gilchrest?" McMillen responded with a barrage of negative mailings attacking Gilchrest for stinginess on children's and seniors' issues. But these may have only succeeded in raising Gilchrest's name recognition. The advantages of incumbency have evidently been diminishing since McMillen came to office, and Gilchrest's rumpled, unpolished style seemed to be an advantage rather than a liability. McMillen carried his old district, the Western Shore area, with 58% of the vote; Gilchrest won 60% on the Eastern Shore, and 52% districtwide. He does not have the look of a politician who can hold onto the district indefinitely, but in today's term-limits politics that may not matter.

The People: Pop. 1990: 597,821; 46% rural; 12% age 65+; 83% White; 15% Black; 1% Asian; 1% Hispanic origin. Voting age pop.: 455,221; 14% Black; 1% Hispanic origin. Households: 59% married couple families; 26% married couple fams. w. children; 42% college educ.; median household income: $35,115; per capita income: $16,104; median gross rent: $487; median house value: $100,500.

1992 Presidential Vote		1988 Presidential Vote	
Bush (R)	109,039 (44%)	Bush (R)	132,532 (63%)
Clinton (D)	93,165 (37%)	Dukakis (D)	77,331 (37%)
Perot (I)	47,188 (19%)		

Rep. Wayne T. Gilchrest (R)

Elected 1990; b. Apr. 15, 1946, Rahway, NJ; home, Kennedyville; Wesley Col., A.A. 1971, DE St. Col., B.A. 1973, Loyola Col., 1984; Methodist; married (Barbara).

Career: Marine Corps, 1964–67 (Vietnam); High schl. teacher, 1973–90.

Offices: 412 CHOB 20515, 202-225-5311. Also 1 Plaza E., Salisbury 21801, 410-749-3184; 335 High St., Chestertown 21620, 410-778-9407; and 101 Crain Hwy., NW, #509, Glen Burnie 21061, 410-760-3372.

Committees: *Merchant Marine and Fisheries* (9th of 19 R): Coast Guard and Navigation; Environment and Natural Resources. *Public Works and Transportation* (11th of 24 R): Aviation; Investigations and Oversight; Water Resources and Environment.

Group Ratings

	ADA	ACLU	COPE	CDF	CFA	LCV	ACU	NTLC	NSI	COC	CEI
1992	30	39	36	40	47	88	64	80	100	75	55
1991	20	—	17	50	33	54	70	—	—	90	65

National Journal Ratings

	1991 LIB — 1991 CONS			1992 LIB — 1992 CONS	
Economic	24%	—	74%	30%	—	69%
Social	43%	—	56%	41%	—	58%
Foreign	17%	—	78%	44%	—	50%

Key Votes of the 102d Congress

1. Ban Striker Replace	AGN	5. Handgun Wait/7-Day	FOR	9. Use Force in Gulf	FOR
2. $ for Homeownership	FOR	6. Overseas Mil. Abortion	FOR	10. US Mil. Abroad $ Cut	FOR
3. Tax Rich/Cut Mid Cls.	AGN	7. Obscn. Art NEA $ Ban	FOR	11. Limit SDI Funds	FOR
4. FY93/$15B Def. Cut	AGN	8. Death Pen. from Jury	FOR	12. Cuba Trade Embargo	FOR

Key Votes of the 103d Congress

1. Family Leave	AGN	2. Deficit Reduction	AGN	3. Stimulus Plan	AGN

Election Results

1992 general	Wayne T. Gilchrest (R)...............	120,084	(52%)	($395,104)
	Thomas McMillen (D)	112,771	(48%)	($1,553,849)
1992 primary	Wayne T. Gilchrest (R).................	17,469	(47%)	
	Lisa G. Renshaw (R)	10,933	(30%)	
	Robert P. Duckworth (R)	6,915	(19%)	
	Two Others	1,743	(4%)	
1990 general	Wayne T. Gilchrest (R)...............	88,920	(57%)	($264,932)
	Roy Dyson (D)	67,518	(43%)	($771,809)

SECOND DISTRICT

The spokes of Baltimore's streets spread out in all directions from the downtown centered on the Inner Harbor, connecting the central city with the suburbs where most residents of metropolitan Baltimore now live. The streets reach east to Dundalk and Essex, industrial suburbs where the tone of life was set for years by the giant Sparrows Point steel mill, long the biggest in the country. Northeast they extend to modest working class suburbs and the small towns of the Baltimore and Harford County countryside which are now amid suburban developments—Bel Air, Joppatowne, Aberdeen, Edgewood, the last two near the Aberdeen Proving Grounds and Edgewood Arsenal military installations. Straight north from downtown are the higher-income suburbs, the county seat of Towson, and farther north are Lutherville, Timonium, Cockeysville, Hunt Valley, all flanked by the Baltimore County hunt country. The McCormick food company is headquartered in Hunt Valley, a nascent Edge City; Black and Decker is in Towson.

The 2d Congressional District of Maryland takes up most of this territory. The Sparrows Point area political tradition is union and Democratic, but that has been tempered lately; the northeast suburbs are ancestrally Democratic, but culturally rather conservative; the north suburbs are solidly Republican. Legislative and local offices are mostly held by Democrats, but a Republican won the Baltimore County executive post in 1990, which the party has not held since Spiro Agnew became governor in 1966; and a Republican has represented the 2d in the House since 1984.

This is Helen Delich Bentley, who is not a typical Republican, nor a typical politician of any kind: tough as nails, sentimental as Ronald Reagan, and as dedicated to "Bawlmer" as any politician in the state. The daughter of Serbian immigrants, she grew up in a Nevada mining town where her father died when she was eight and she helped her mother run a boardinghouse. For 24 years, she was a reporter for Baltimore's *The Sun*, specializing in maritime news; for six years she chaired the Federal Maritime Commission. Although much of the port of Baltimore is outside her district, its economic effects are felt everywhere, and nothing seems more important to Bentley. "To me," she says, "the port is Baltimore's economy. It's my child. I feel like the mother of modern Baltimore." It helped her get elected to Congress in 1984 on her third attempt when she defeated incumbent Democrat Clarence Long, who had long opposed dredging the harbor on environmental grounds; Bentley won and got it dredged. "Whenever there is a problem in the port, people turn to her for solutions," *Maryland Business Weekly* writes. In 1989, when the International Longshoremens' Association was threatening to shut down the port, Governor Donald Schaefer asked Bentley to mediate. She walked with union picketers to get their side of the story and stayed up until 3 a.m. going back and forth between the factions. She got a solution, and continues to ballyhoo the port's growth and gains at the expense of its East Coast rivals.

Bentley has other enthusiasms. She is fiercely protectionist, and once smashed with a sledgehammer a TV made by Toshiba, the company which exported secret products to the Soviets. She pushes "buy American" programs and is overtly hostile to NAFTA; she is one of few pro-union Republicans. She is sympathetic to Serbs in the former Yugoslavia, arguing that they have received unfair media coverage and "there's enough blame to go around all over." She has also raised $80,000 from Serbian-Americans in the last five years. Her persistent lobbying got the state of Maryland a $75 million reimbursement from Medicaid, for which Governor Schaefer was grateful. Indeed, Schaefer was her great political protector in redistricting, insisting that he would veto any bill that eliminated her district, while she threatened to run against Senator Barbara Mikulski if one passed. "I think Congress is better off because Helen is there," Schaefer has said. There is even reason to think he would like her to succeed him as governor in 1994, and she has made some moves to run. Well-known in the Baltimore media market, appealing to blue-collar as well as white-collar voters, well-positioned to take advantage of a divisive Democratic primary, she could well win and certainly would be as formidable a candidate as the Republicans have fielded in Maryland in a quarter-century.

In the 2d District, Bentley seems unbeatable. Her toughest challenge came in 1986 from Kathleen Kennedy Townsend, daughter of the late Robert Kennedy; each spent over $1 million, and Bentley won with 59% of the vote. The district lines are favorable to her and probably would be to any serious Republican nominee should Bentley run for governor in 1994.

The People: Pop. 1990: 597,450; 18% rural; 12% age 65+; 92% White; 6% Black; 2% Asian; 1% Hispanic origin. Voting age pop.: 456,798; 5% Black; 1% Hispanic origin. Households: 62% married couple families; 28% married couple fams. w. children; 47% college educ.; median household income: $40,120; per capita income: $17,931; median gross rent: $507; median house value: $110,500.

1992 Presidential Vote

Bush (R)	121,087	(44%)
Clinton (D)	98,267	(36%)
Perot (I)	52,668	(19%)

1988 Presidential Vote

Bush (R)	146,902	(64%)
Dukakis (D)	83,490	(36%)

Rep. Helen Delich Bentley (R)

Elected 1984; b. Nov. 28, 1923, Ely, NV; home, Lutherville; U. of MO, B.A. 1944, U. of NV, George Washington U.; Greek Orthodox; married (William).

Career: Reporter and Maritime Ed., *The Sun*, Baltimore, 1945–69; Chmn., Fed. Maritime Comm., 1969–75; Businesswoman, 1975–85; Columnist and ed., *World Ports Magazine*, 1981–85.

Offices: 1610 LHOB 20515, 202-225-3061. Also 200 E. Joppa Rd., #400, Towson 21204, 301-337-7222; 45 N. Main St., Bel Air 21014, 301-879-2517; 7458 German Hill Rd., Dundalk 21222, 301-285-2747; 4513-R Mountain Rd., Pasadena 21122, 410-437-5817; and 115 W. Bel Air Ave., Aberdeen 21001, 410-272-7099.

Committees: *Appropriations* (18th of 23 R): Labor, Health and Human Services, and Education; Military Construction. *Merchant Marine and Fisheries* (17th of 19 R): Merchant Marine.

Group Ratings

	ADA	ACLU	COPE	CDF	CFA	LCV	ACU	NTLC	NSI	COC	CEI
1992	25	22	50	30	53	6	80	60	100	100	52
1991	25	—	50	50	50	8	60	—	—	40	53

National Journal Ratings

	1991 LIB — 1991 CONS		1992 LIB — 1992 CONS	
Economic	36%	— 63%	37%	— 63%
Social	23%	— 76%	29%	— 71%
Foreign	26%	— 70%	0%	— 82%

Key Votes of the 102d Congress

1. Ban Striker Replace	FOR	5. Handgun Wait/7-Day FOR	9. Use Force in Gulf	FOR
2. $ for Homeownership	FOR	6. Overseas Mil. AbortionAGN	10. US Mil. Abroad $ CutAGN
3. Tax Rich/Cut Mid Cls.	*	7. Obscn. Art NEA $ Ban FOR	11. Limit SDI Funds	AGN
4. FY93/$15B Def. Cut	AGN	8. Death Pen. from Jury FOR	12. Cuba Trade Embargo FOR

Key Votes of the 103d Congress

1. Family Leave   AGN   2. Deficit Reduction   AGN   3. Stimulus Plan   AGN

Election Results

1992 general	Helen Delich Bentley (R)	165,443	(65%)	($956,821)
	Michael C. Hickey (D)	88,658	(35%)	($48,841)
1992 primary	Helen Delich Bentley (R)	29,814	(87%)	
	Robert T. Petr (R)	4,435	(13%)	
1990 general	Helen Delich Bentley (R)	115,398	(74%)	($730,852)
	Ronald P. Bowers (D)	39,785	(26%)	

THIRD DISTRICT

Baltimore is no longer a well-kept secret. Its Harborplace and its new Camden Yards baseball stadium are now national tourist attractions; its charms have been emblazoned on the national consciousness by Anne Tyler's novels and Barry Levinson's and John Waters's movies; even its cuisine—steamed crabs with Baltimore spices, crab cakes—has become known beyond the watershed of the Chesapeake Bay. The central city of Baltimore certainly has its problems—high crime, poor schools, fiscal problems—but the greater Baltimore that slops over both sides of the Baltimore City and County lines retains a distinctive character. There is a patina of age, as on its Washington Monument, built in 1829 and just recently refurbished, and the townhouses of Mount Vernon Square, and an atmosphere of tolerance and diversity nurtured by Maryland's founding Catholics in search of liberty; the nation's first Catholic diocese and cathedral were built here when America was overwhelmingly and militantly Protestant. And this is a city built solidly on commerce which has always known how to reap its pleasures.

The 3d Congressional District of Maryland is centered on Baltimore, and consists of three portions that extend outward like spokes on a wheel from the focus of metropolitan Baltimore at the Inner Harbor. The three spokes are connected by narrow bridges of land, with boundaries designed to build a black-majority 7th District next door. From Harborplace, the 3d extends northeast out into the Polish Highlandtown neighborhood and the mostly white Catholic northeast precincts and close-in suburbs of Overlea and Parkville. It extends northwest to the heavily Jewish suburbs of Pikesville and Owings Mills, past the array of temples and synagogues on Park Heights Avenue to the open subdivisions where the newest Jewish neighborhoods are being built. And it extends southwest, past old rowhouse neighborhoods overlooking Fort McHenry, where Francis Scott Key saw by the dawn's early light the star-spangled banner, out past Arbutus and Lansdowne into Linthicum and Fort Meade in Anne Arundel County and Elkridge and Columbia in Howard County. Here lies the cusp of the Baltimore-Washington boundary; for Columbia, now a 25-year-old "new town" draws from both metro areas. Ancestrally Democratic, this district is now contested territory: Pikesville and Columbia are solidly liberal on most issues; the northeast and close-in southeast areas are culturally more conservative.

The congressman from the 3d is Benjamin Cardin, former speaker of the Maryland House of Delegates and one of the many bright politicos produced by the Jewish neighborhoods of northwest Baltimore. He was first elected to the state legislature in 1966, and after serving there for 20 years, was easily elected to Congress in 1986. In the House, Cardin has been an inside player. He got a seat on Ways and Means in October 1989, with the support of Chairman Dan Rostenkowski; he has worked to revise 401(k) savings plans and to simplify pension rules, as well as developing his own Flexible Medical Access Act healthcare plan, with administrative reform, tort reform and strong cost containment based on Maryland's all-payer rate system. He wants to finance new residential lead abatement programs with a tax on lead production. He is sponsoring a Chesapeake Bay Restoration Act and has sought funding to restore Fort McHenry, expand MARC commuter rail and build a demonstration magnetic levitation train between Baltimore and D.C., and to build the Columbus Biotechnology/Marine Center in Baltimore. Cardin serves on the Ethics Committee and worked to clean up the House bank scandal, but as an insider is leery of some proposed reforms: getting rid of perks, he says, is "nowhere near as important as taking a look at the way Congress does its business."

Cardin is clearly a very able man; former Ohio Republican Congressman Willis Gradison called him "one of the brightest men I've ever worked with." With many friends in Annapolis, Cardin had no problems in redistricting and has been reelected by wide margins. He has been mentioned as a candidate for governor in 1994, and would certainly have considerable support for and serious claims on the office. Otherwise, he stands to be reelected easily.

The People: Pop. 1990: 597,712; 2% rural; 13% age 65+; 80% White; 17% Black; 2% Asian; 2% Hispanic origin. Voting age pop.: 459,046; 16% Black; 2% Hispanic origin. Households: 52% married couple families; 23% married couple fams. w. children; 49% college educ.; median household income: $35,970; per capita income: $17,779; median gross rent: $506; median house value: $90,000.

1992 Presidential Vote			1988 Presidential Vote		
Clinton (D)	136,829	(54%)	Dukakis (D)	116,906	(51%)
Bush (R)	82,494	(32%)	Bush (R)	110,861	(49%)
Perot (I)	34,973	(14%)			

Rep. Benjamin L. Cardin (D)

Elected 1986; b. Oct. 5, 1943, Baltimore; home, Baltimore; U. of Pittsburgh, B.A. 1964, U. of MD, LL.B., J.D. 1967; Jewish; married (Myrna).

Career: MD House of Delegates, 1966–86, Speaker, 1979–86; Practicing atty., 1967–86.

Offices: 227 CHOB 20515, 202-225-4016. Also 540 E. Belvedere Ave., #201, Baltimore 21212, 410-433-8886.

Committees: *House Administration* (12th of 12 D): Accounts; Elections. *Standards of Official Conduct* (3d of 7 D). *Ways and Means* (13th of 24 D): Health; Human Resources.

Group Ratings

	ADA	ACLU	COPE	CDF	CFA	LCV	ACU	NTLC	NSI	COC	CEI
1992	95	96	83	100	100	81	4	10	40	38	7
1991	75	—	92	80	67	62	0	—	—	30	18

National Journal Ratings

	1991 LIB — 1991 CONS		1992 LIB — 1992 CONS	
Economic	56% —	42%	78% —	18%
Social	78% —	17%	88% —	8%
Foreign	75% —	24%	62% —	35%

Key Votes of the 102d Congress

1. Ban Striker Replace	FOR	5. Handgun Wait/7-Day	FOR	9. Use Force in Gulf	AGN
2. $ for Homeownership	AGN	6. Overseas Mil. Abortion	FOR	10. US Mil. Abroad $ Cut	FOR
3. Tax Rich/Cut Mid Cls.	FOR	7. Obscn. Art NEA $ Ban	AGN	11. Limit SDI Funds	FOR
4. FY93/$15B Def. Cut	FOR	8. Death Pen. from Jury	AGN	12. Cuba Trade Embargo	FOR

Key Votes of the 103d Congress

1. Family Leave	FOR	2. Deficit Reduction	FOR	3. Stimulus Plan	FOR

Election Results

1992 general	Benjamin L. Cardin (D)	163,354	(74%)	($646,863)
	William T. S. Bricker (R)	58,869	(26%)	($8,832)
1992 primary	Benjamin L. Cardin (D)	63,793	(84%)	
	Carl A. Mueller (D)	11,707	(16%)	
1990 general	Benjamin L. Cardin (D)	82,545	(70%)	($363,847)
	Harwood Nichols (R)	35,841	(30%)	($4,234)

FOURTH DISTRICT

Prince George's County, Maryland, once tobacco land below the fall line, just north and east of Washington, D.C., is now metropolitan, with tentacles of settlement reaching out from Washington, growing larger and coming together. Today, Prince George's is home to some 729,000 people, a place that gives a hopeful glimpse of the future. This is not official Washington's conventional view, where Prince George's is seen as a working-class haven, overshadowed by faster-growing and higher-income Montgomery to the west and Fairfax

County in Virginia. But Prince George's is by national standards affluent, and the district has the highest percentage of women in the work force in the nation (73%). All this is especially interesting because Prince George's is the nation's biggest black suburban community. The black percentage here increased from 14% in 1970 to 37% in 1980; now it is 50%, as blacks have moved outward from the District of Columbia not only to nearby, modest-income suburbs, but out Routes 450, 214 and 5 to newly-minted, more affluent subdivisions. More than any other place in America, Prince George's County is the home of the black middle class.

The 4th Congressional District includes most of Prince George's County and a portion of Montgomery County to the west; it is mostly, but not entirely, inside the Capital Beltway, though it is not what people usually have in mind when they use the phrase. The biggest industry here is still government: 21.5% of its workers are employed by the federal government, the highest percentage of any congressional district in the nation. The district is 59% black and also 6% Hispanic; it is overwhelmingly Democratic, and its new congressman was effectively chosen in the March 1992 Democratic primary.

The race attracted 13 Democrats and seven Republicans; the two major contenders were state Senator Albert Wynn and Prince George's State Attorney Alex Williams. Williams was probably the best known, from his county-wide state attorney victory; Wynn was the best funded. Wynn ran on a "put America first" platform, emphasizing domestic issues, with ads attacking President Bush; Williams called himself "a strong, independent voice for Congress" in his ads. Wynn spent much effort in Montgomery County, while Williams seemed to be targeting primarily Prince George's blacks. Also, Prince George's County Councilwoman Hilda Pemberton highlighted her pro-abortion rights stand and Montgomery state Delegate Dana Dembrow, one of four white Democrats in the race, attacked the concept of a mandatory black-majority district. Wynn was endorsed by the *Prince George's Journal* and *The Washington Post* and won with 28% of the vote; Williams had 26%, Dembrow 15%, almost all from Montgomery, and Pemberton 13%. The general election was anticlimactic, with Wynn taking 75% of the vote against black businesswoman Michele Dyson. Like many of the blacks elected from new black-majority districts, Wynn seems not to be making a monoracial appeal; he eschews expression of militancy for pronouncements on national issues. He serves on the Banking, Foreign Affairs and Post Office and Civil Service Committees.

The People: Pop. 1990: 597,791; 1% rural; 7% age 65+; 31% White; 58% Black; 5% Asian; 3% Other; 6% Hispanic origin. Voting age pop.: 447,136; 56% Black; 6% Hispanic origin. Households: 47% married couple families; 24% married couple fams. w. children; 56% college educ.; median household income: $41,081; per capita income: $17,251; median gross rent: $643; median house value: $122,600.

1992 Presidential Vote

Clinton (D)	149,262	(74%)
Bush (R)	37,716	(19%)
Perot (I)	14,160	(7%)

1988 Presidential Vote

Dukakis (D)	121,421	(68%)
Bush (R)	56,346	(32%)

Rep. Albert R. Wynn (D)

Elected 1992; b. Sept. 10, 1951, Philadelphia, PA; home, Largo; U. of Pittsburgh, B.S. 1973, Howard U., 1973–74; Georgetown U. Law Schl., J.D. 1977; Baptist; married (Nikki Johnson).

Career: Exec. Dir., PG Cnty. Consumer Protection Comm., 1977–81; Chmn., Metro Washington Cncl. of Consumer Agencies, 1980–81; Practicing atty., 1981–92; MD House of Delegates, 1982–87; MD Senate 1987–92.

Offices: 423 CHOB 20515, 202-225-8699. Also 8700 Central Ave., #306, Landover 20785, 301-350-5055; and 8601 Georgia Ave., #201, Silver Spring 20910, 301-558-7328.

Committees: *Banking, Finance and Urban Affairs* (24th of 30 D): Consumer Credit and Insurance; Housing and Community Development. *Foreign Affairs* (23d of 27 D): Economic Policy, Trade and Environment; Western Hemisphere Affairs. *Post Office and Civil Service* (11th of 15 D): Census Statistics and Postal Personnel.

Group Ratings and 102d Congress Votes: Newly Elected

Key Votes of the 103d Congress

1. Family Leave	FOR	2. Deficit Reduction	FOR	3. Stimulus Plan	FOR

Election Results

1992 general	Albert R. Wynn (D)	136,902	(75%)	($386,186)
	Michele Dyson (R)	45,166	(25%)	($135,945)
1992 primary	Albert R. Wynn (D)	18,353	(28%)	
	Alexander Williams (D)	17,067	(26%)	
	Dana Lee Dembrow (D)	9,928	(15%)	
	Hilda R. Pemberton (D)	8,480	(13%)	
	Francis J. Aluisi (D)	3,774	(6%)	
	Tommie Broadwater (D)	2,564	(4%)	
	Seven Others	5,465	(8%)	
1990 election	Newly created district.			

FIFTH DISTRICT

Southern Maryland is a part of the United States with a distinctive history and not much of a national image. It was first settled by Catholics, the Calvert family of the Lords Baltimore, who founded their capital of St. Marys in 1634, not long after Jamestown and Plymouth Rock. Maryland became one of the two great tobacco colonies, and plantation houses grew up on every inlet off the broad Potomac and Patuxent Rivers, with docks where ships tied up straight from London. For years, none of these towns grew much, and even today many people here are directly descended from the old families; the biggest growth came from government installations like the Point Lookout prisoner of war camp in the Civil War or Patuxent Naval Air Test Center where many astronauts got their first training. This was never puritanical country: liquor flowed even during Prohibition and slot machines were specifically allowed by Maryland law until the 1940s.

The 5th Congressional District of Maryland, with lines redrawn completely in 1991, includes the three counties of southern Maryland, now attracting people who grew up in metro Washington and Baltimore, plus large slices of suburban Prince George's and Anne Arundel Counties between Washington and Annapolis. Its lines are drawn to make the adjacent 4th District in Prince George's majority-black, though with blacks moving outward in Prince

George's and southern Maryland's historic black population, the new 5th is 19% black anyway. Many of its people live north of Washington, in College Park, home of the University of Maryland, and Hyattsville, Greenbelt, Beltsville and Laurel. The 5th also includes southern Prince George's, from Clinton (heavily Democratic, as seems only appropriate) south, and the suburbs of Bowie, Crofton and Davidsonville just west of Annapolis. Historically, this is a Democratic area. But southern Maryland has been conservative on many issues and voted for George Bush over Bill Clinton, and many Prince George's and Anne Arundel whites are Republicans as well.

This new 5th District indeed presented a severe challenge to one of Maryland's shrewdest and most talented politicians, Congressman Steny Hoyer. Hoyer was elected to the Maryland Senate at age 27 and was Senate president from 1975 to 1978; he made a misstep running for lieutenant governor on a losing ticket in 1978. But when the 5th District was declared vacant in 1981, after Representative Gladys Spellman went into an irreversible coma, Hoyer edged out Spellman's husband and several other Democrats in the primary and beat a well-financed, competent Republican candidate in the general.

In the House, Hoyer became an accomplished constituency service politician in the metropolitan Washington tradition, and also a leader of the Democratic Party in the House. He won a seat on the Appropriations Committee, where he is a key man not only for Prince George's County but for Maryland and the overall D.C. metropolitan area, pushing for completion of the Metro system, money for the Baltimore-Washington Parkway reconstruction and the National Archives research center at the University of Maryland. Hoyer also was the chief House sponsor of the Americans with Disabilities Act, skillfully shepherding it through substantive and procedural obstacles in 1989 and 1990. When Whip Tony Coelho and Speaker Jim Wright resigned from Congress in June 1989, Hoyer moved up and won a leadership position as chairman of the Democratic Caucus. In June 1991, when Democratic Whip William Gray retired, Hoyer tried to move up again. But this time he was opposed by Chief Deputy Whip David Bonior and, while Hoyer had the support of many younger members and the Conservative Democratic Forum, Bonior got the backing of most committee chairmen supportive of the seniority system and won the post, 160–109. But Hoyer remains an integral working part of the leadership and, like Bonior, has a district that is less than utterly safe.

In his old district, which nearly had a black majority, Hoyer had a very liberal voting record and courted black constituents ably; opposed by a candidate supported by Louis Farrakhan in the 1990 primary, Hoyer won 79% of the vote and carried every precinct. But the new district moved Hoyer to the right. His *National Journal* voting record was more conservative between 1990–1992, when he voted for the balanced budget amendment. He had serious opposition in 1992 from Lawrence Hogan, Jr., whose father was a Prince George's congressman from 1968 to 1974 and Prince George's County executive, and who himself had chaired the local Reagan campaign. Hogan used Hoyer's leadership position to tie him to the House bank and post office scandals and the federal deficit, and won 50%–45% in the half of the district outside Prince George's. Hoyer had a 60%–38% margin in Prince George's, for a 53%–44% win. But that is not an impressive enough margin to deter competition for a whole decade.

Hoyer's leadership positions will continue to give him great leverage—and great responsibility. He now chairs the Treasury, Postal Service and General Government Appropriations Subcommittee, which oversees several major components of the federal work force and the White House budget. It also enables him to help the 17% of 5th District workers who are federal employees—he has already used the panel to prohibit changes in federal workers' health plans, and he got $5 million for flexiplace telecommuting centers to allow long-commuting feds to work closer to home—but he may be held responsible for layoffs as well. Hoyer has taken on some unpleasant chores for the leadership, enhancing voting status for delegates from D.C. and the territories and helping ease Jamie Whitten aside as Appropriations Chairman. Ultimately, his leadership role will position him to take credit for the successes and be held responsible for the failures of the Clinton Administration, in a district not strongly pro-Clinton in 1992.

Footnote: Hoyer is of Danish descent, like Treasury Secretary Lloyd Bentsen, Attorney General Janet Reno and the original eponym of Prince George's County, Prince George of Denmark, the husband of Queen Anne.

The People: Pop. 1990: 597,573; 30% rural; 8% age 65+; 77% White; 19% Black; 3% Asian; 1% Other; 2% Hispanic origin. Voting age pop.: 449,879; 18% Black; 2% Hispanic origin. Households: 62% married couple families; 31% married couple fams. w. children; 53% college educ.; median household income: $46,936; per capita income: $18,178; median gross rent: $674; median house value: $131,300.

1992 Presidential Vote			1988 Presidential Vote		
Clinton (D)	107,618	(45%)	Bush (R)	115,062	(58%)
Bush (R)	95,356	(39%)	Dukakis (D)	84,162	(42%)
Perot (I)	37,441	(15%)			

Rep. Steny H. Hoyer (D)

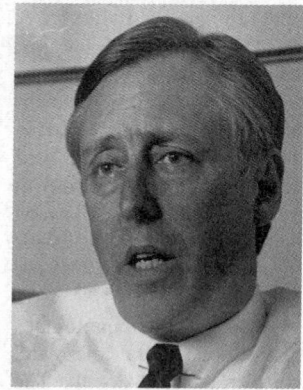

Elected May 1981; b. June 14, 1939, New York, NY; home, Mitchellville; U. of MD, B.S. 1963, Georgetown U., J.D. 1966; Baptist; married (Judith).

Career: Practicing atty., 1966–80; MD Senate, 1966–78, Pres., 1975–78; MD Bd. of Higher Educ., 1978–81.

Offices: 1705 LHOB 20515, 202-225-4131. Also One Town Ctr., #403, 4201 Northview Dr., Bowie 20716, 301-464-6440; and 21-A Industrial Park Dr., #101, Waldorf 20602, 301-843-1577.

Committees: *Appropriations* (15th of 37 D): Labor, Health and Human Services, and Education; Military Construction; Treasury, Postal Service and General Government (Chmn.). *House Administration* (7th of 12 D): Accounts; Elections.

Group Ratings

	ADA	ACLU	COPE	CDF	CFA	LCV	ACU	NTLC	NSI	COC	CEI
1992	90	100	75	90	87	44	17	0	70	38	7
1991	80	—	92	100	72	69	0	—	—	30	9

National Journal Ratings

	1991 LIB — 1991 CONS		1992 LIB — 1992 CONS	
Economic	72% —	23%	71% —	27%
Social	88% —	0%	72% —	24%
Foreign	62% —	36%	38% —	56%

Key Votes of the 102d Congress

1. Ban Striker Replace	FOR	5. Handgun Wait/7-Day	FOR	9. Use Force in Gulf	AGN
2. $ for Homeownership	AGN	6. Overseas Mil. Abortion	FOR	10. US Mil. Abroad $ Cut	AGN
3. Tax Rich/Cut Mid Cls.	FOR	7. Obscn. Art NEA $ Ban	AGN	11. Limit SDI Funds	AGN
4. FY93/$15B Def. Cut	FOR	8. Death Pen. from Jury	AGN	12. Cuba Trade Embargo	FOR

Key Votes of the 103d Congress

1. Family Leave	FOR	2. Deficit Reduction	FOR	3. Stimulus Plan	FOR

Election Results

1992 general	Steny H. Hoyer (D)	118,312	(53%)	($1,584,271)
	Lawrence J. Hogan (R)	97,982	(44%)	($265,065)
	Other.............................	6,990	(3%)	
1992 primary	Steny H. Hoyer (D)	46,400	(84%)	
	Ricardo V. Johnson (D)...............	8,802	(16%)	
1990 general	Steny H. Hoyer (D)	84,747	(81%)	($716,469)
	Lee F. Breuer (R)	20,314	(19%)	($8,709)

SIXTH DISTRICT

The long green sloping fields of western Maryland, cut through by the Appalachian ridges that diagonally cross the state, were America's first western frontier: wheatfields settled first by Pennsylvania Dutch and Scots-Irish hill people, not Chesapeake Bay tobacco growers. Maryland is where the fall line comes closest to an ocean port, and in the 19th Century great paths to the interior were staked out: first the National Road, then the nation's first railroad, the Baltimore & Ohio, crossed the wide valleys of bounteous farms and climbed over the Catoctins Mountains. Towns grew up on single narrow streets lined with rowhouses and today overhung with telephone and streetcar wires, overlooking long vistas of cornfields, pasturelands and mountains of ancient stone rising above the plains. Across this placid land moved vast armies during the Civil War: in Frederick, city officials paid Confederates $200,000 to not burn down the town, and near Sharpsburg, blue- and gray-clad soldiers fought the Battle of Antietam, on the bloodiest day in American military history. Today, there is a new rush of settlement here, in Carroll and Howard Counties, long parts of metro Baltimore, and Frederick County, which grew 31% in the 1980s and is now classified as part of metro Washington; growth remains slow, however, west of the Catoctins.

The 6th Congressional District of Maryland includes all of western Maryland, to mountainous Cumberland and Garrett County, and runs east to Carroll County northwest of Baltimore and the old town of Ellicott City just outside the "new town" of Columbia in Howard County. The political tradition in most of this area, unlike the rest of Maryland, is Republican: this was Union country in the Civil War and has been mostly Republican ever since. The new rush of settlement seems to come from those seeking respite from metropolitan crime and metropolitan values, strengthening the area's conservative leanings.

Despite its bucolic scenery and conservative tenor, or perhaps because of them, the 6th District was the arena in 1992 for two political battles and the first electoral upset that signalled the anti-incumbent mood of the year. The district had seemed content for years to be represented by Beverly Byron, one of the House's most conservative non-southern Democrats, whose father-in-law, mother-in-law and husband had all represented the district in the past. Byron, whose father was one of Dwight D. Eisenhower's top wartime aides, served on the Armed Services Committee, where she supported high defense spending and the Gulf war resolution, but also switched to support women in combat, and was sharply critical of the Tailhook scandal. In the 1992 primary, she was opposed by 10-year Delegate Thomas Hattery, who called for a middle-class tax cut, national health insurance and was pro-choice on abortion; he ran a radio ad based on *Lifestyles of the Rich and Famous* twitting Byron for her travel and the congressional pay raise. Hattery had support from unions and environmental organizations and many liberal Democrats, and won 56%–44%, carrying every county. The March 3 primary was the first congressional primary in the nation, and Hattery's victory signalled accurately that the advantages of incumbency could be outweighed by the liabilities.

But Hattery in turn became the subject of 1992-style attacks in the general, from Republican Roscoe Bartlett. At first glance, Bartlett seemed an odd candidate—a 66-year-old retired University of Maryland physiology professor who won his primary by only a 42%–41% margin.

He is an interesting character, a descendant of a signer of the Declaration of Independence and a Seventh Day Adventist with 10 children. He had invented life support equipment for pilots and astronauts, ran his own business and taught at Frederick Community College—old values and high-tech. Bartlett is solidly conservative, for the line-item veto, and strongly antiabortion; he campaigned with help from Oliver North and Tom Clancy and made attacks on (Rush Limbaugh's term) "feminazis." Most tellingly, Bartlett hit Hattery for his own office perks and accused him of expense account fraud. Hattery unveiled a healthcare plan, called for a federal "job czar," sounded many Clintonesque notes and hit Bartlett for accepting $4,000 in farm subsidies. In a district that gave George Bush a solid margin over Bill Clinton, Bartlett won by a 54%–46% margin, carrying every county but Howard. So at age 66, Bartlett became a member of the Armed Services and Science and Technology Committees, appropriate assignments given his background, and a strong critic of the new administration. He angered some when he told an audience that not more than a third of scholarship winners have "normal American" names; he apologized later, explaining that he should have said "European" and added that he meant to compliment Americans of Asian background.

The People: Pop. 1990: 597,660; 47% rural; 11% age 65+; 94% White; 4% Black; 1% Asian; 1% Hispanic origin. Voting age pop.: 447,554; 4% Black; 1% Hispanic origin. Households: 65% married couple families; 31% married couple fams. w. children; 44% college educ.; median household income: $36,883; per capita income: $15,979; median gross rent: $448; median house value: $113,100.

1992 Presidential Vote

Bush (R) 125,494 (48%)
Clinton (D) 88,196 (34%)
Perot (I). 46,376 (18%)

1988 Presidential Vote

Bush (R) 140,008 (66%)
Dukakis (D). 72,572 (34%)

Rep. Roscoe G. Bartlett (R)

Elected 1992; b. June 3, 1926, Moreland, KY; home, Frederick; Columbia Union Col., B.A. 1947; U. of MD, M.S. 1949, Ph.D. 1952; Seventh Day Adventist; married (Ellen).

Career: Farmer; Prof., U. of MD, 1948–52; Asst. Prof., Loma Linda Schl. of Medicine, 1952–54; Asst. Prof., Howard U. Medical Schl., 1954–56; Research scientist, N.I.H., 1956–58; Research scientist, U.S. Naval Aerospace Medical Inst., 1958–62; Research scientist, Johns Hopkins U., 1962–67; Research Mgr., IBM, 1967–74; Pres., Roscoe Bartlett & Assoc., 1974–86.

Offices: 312 CHOB 20515, 202-225-2721. Also 5831 Buckeystown Pk., Frederick 21701, 301-694-3030; 15 E. Main St., #110, Westminster 21157, 410-857-1115; and 100 W. Franklin St., Hagerstown 21740, 301-797-6043.

Committees: *Armed Services* (22d of 22 R): Military Forces and Personnel; Research and Technology. *Science, Space and Technology* (22d of 22 R): Energy; Technology, Environment and Aviation.

Group Ratings and 102d Congress Votes: Newly Elected

Key Votes of the 103d Congress

1. Family Leave   AGN   2. Deficit Reduction   AGN   3. Stimulus Plan   AGN

Election Results

1992 general	Roscoe G. Bartlett (R)	125,564	(54%)	($307,885)
	Thomas H. Hattery (D)	106,224	(46%)	($596,051)
1992 primary	Roscoe G. Bartlett (R)	15,374	(42%)	
	Michael Downey (R)...................	14,728	(41%)	
	Frank K. Nethken (R)	6,201	(17%)	
1990 general	Beverly B. Byron (D)	106,502	(65%)	($325,997)
	Christopher P. Fiotes (R)	56,479	(35%)	($3,557)

SEVENTH DISTRICT

Baltimore, at the junction of North and South, terminus of America's first railroad and still the East Coast port most closely connected with the great West, is one of the few American cities to have had large numbers of both blacks and European immigrants throughout its history. Its black community has a notable history: the *Afro-American* newspaper has been published here for more than 100 years, there was once a black symphony orchestra, and the city's black neighborhood west of downtown had a vital shopping district before World War II. Baltimore was the home of Clarence Mitchell, for many years the NAACP's lobbyist in Washington, and white Republicans like Mayor and Governor Theodore McKeldin competed zestfully with Democrats for black votes.

Baltimore has been a black-majority city since the late 1970s and most of its west side neighborhoods are heavily black. Black Republicanism has long since died out, and William Donald Schaefer, who carried west Baltimore for mayor as late as 1983, went on to become governor; black Democrats are the key politicians here, notably Mayor Kurt Schmoke, elected in 1987 and 1991. Schmoke's abilities—he is a Rhodes Scholar—and good intentions sparked hopes he has not yet fulfilled, as much of black Baltimore faces the same pathologies of violent crime, single parenthood and labor force non-participation that plague cities elsewhere. Schmoke has made some controversial initiatives: in 1988 he called for a full debate on drug decriminalization and in 1992 the city made available Norplant implants as a contraceptive to public school teenagers. One hopeful initiative was developer James Rouse's 5-year project to rebuild a 72-block area called Sandtown. But in the meantime, middle- and upper-income blacks have left behind the marble-stepped rowhouses of the city and moved to the suburbs.

Maryland's 7th Congressional District includes almost all of Baltimore City's black neighborhoods and extends into the heavily black suburbs running west from the city, Catonsville along the old Baltimore National Pike and Randallstown out Liberty Heights Avenue. The congressman here is Kweisi Mfume, former councilman and radio talk show host, whose name ("Conquering Son of Kings" in Swahili) has echoes of the Black Power 1960s and whose personal history is caught up in the social pathology that is at the root of the problems of the black underclass—and who himself has moved on from these aspects of the past. Mfume's original name was Frizzell Gray; he was 16 when his mother died, at which point he dropped out of school, held low-paying jobs, and fathered five sons out of wedlock. Then he had a conversion-like experience on a Baltimore street corner, took control of his life and moved it in another direction: he adopted his current Ibo name, studied radio broadcasting, eventually graduating from Morgan State, and was elected to the Baltimore City Council at 30; he also helped raise his sons, three of whom have gone on to college. On the council, he was a political critic of Mayor Schaefer, but he was also a stern critic of drug use and destructive behavior. In 1986, when 7th District Congressman Parren Mitchell retired, Mfume won 44% in the crucial Democratic primary, to 23% for Clarence Mitchell III, the retiring incumbent's nephew and a veteran state Senator with many legal problems, and 17% for minister and legislator Wendell Phillips.

Mfume seems to be a classic example of a black politician who has moved from demanding black power to emphasizing the need for individual self-discipline. He frequently presides over the House: "I like to maintain its dignity and decorum," and he does. He has worked on housing, lending and RTC issues on the Banking Committee. With Connecticut Republican Chris Shays, he proposed a bipartisan urban "Marshall Plan," including welfare reform, a national service program and environmental cleanup. In late 1992, he was elected chairman of the Congressional Black Caucus, 27–9, and in that capacity got the leadership to agree to a subcommittee exemption limit to keep a separate Africa Subcommittee on Foreign Affairs; he also maneuvered the Black Caucus into blocking Charles Stenholm's rescission measure, the modified line-item veto, in April 1993 saying it gave up too much congressional authority. "It's a fallacy," Mfume says of the caucus, "for people to assume that there is only one item on our agenda." He has been reelected easily every two years.

The People: Pop. 1990: 597,701; 1% rural; 12% age 65+; 27% White; 71% Black; 1% Asian; 1% Hispanic origin. Voting age pop.: 447,777; 68% Black; 1% Hispanic origin. Households: 34% married couple families; 14% married couple fams. w. children; 37% college educ.; median household income: $25,684; per capita income: $11,718; median gross rent: $432; median house value: $59,400.

1992 Presidential Vote			1988 Presidential Vote		
Clinton (D)	159,191	(77%)	Dukakis (D)	142,381	(77%)
Bush (R)	32,431	(16%)	Bush (R)	43,625	(23%)
Perot (I)	13,009	(6%)			

Rep. Kweisi Mfume (D)

Elected 1986; b. Oct. 24, 1948, Baltimore; home, Baltimore; Morgan St. U., B.S. 1976, Johns Hopkins U., M.A. 1984; Baptist; divorced.

Career: Baltimore City Cncl., 1978–86. Adjunct Prof., Morgan St. U., 1984–85.

Offices: 2419 RHOB 20515, 202-225-4741. Also 3000 Druid Park Dr., Baltimore 21215, 410-367-1900; and 1825 Woodlawn Dr., Baltimore 21207, 410-298-5997.

Committees: *Banking, Finance and Urban Affairs* (10th of 30 D): Financial Institutions Supervision, Regulation and Deposit Insurance; Housing and Community Development. *Small Business* (9th of 27 D): Minority Enterprise, Finance and Urban Development (Chmn.); Procurement, Taxation and Tourism. *Standards of Official Conduct* (5th of 7 D). *Joint Economic Committee* (4th of 10).

Group Ratings

	ADA	ACLU	COPE	CDF	CFA	LCV	ACU	NTLC	NSI	COC	CEI
1992	95	100	92	100	93	75	0	5	10	13	17
1991	100	—	100	100	94	85	5	—	—	20	18

National Journal Ratings

	1991 LIB — 1991 CONS		1992 LIB — 1992 CONS	
Economic	88% —	0%	91% —	0%
Social	88% —	0%	81% —	17%
Foreign	87% —	8%	86% —	10%

Key Votes of the 102d Congress

1. Ban Striker Replace	FOR	5. Handgun Wait/7-Day FOR	9. Use Force in Gulf AGN
2. $ for Homeownership	AGN	6. Overseas Mil. Abortion FOR	10. US Mil. Abroad $ Cut FOR
3. Tax Rich/Cut Mid Cls.	FOR	7. Obscn. Art NEA $ Ban AGN	11. Limit SDI Funds FOR
4. FY93/$15B Def. Cut	FOR	8. Death Pen. from Jury AGN	12. Cuba Trade Embargo AGN

Key Votes of the 103d Congress

1. Family Leave   FOR   2. Deficit Reduction   FOR   3. Stimulus Plan   FOR

Election Results

1992 general	Kweisi Mfume (D)	152,689	(85%)	($216,518)
	Kenneth Kondner (R)	26,304	(15%)	
1992 primary	Kweisi Mfume (D)	55,842	(84%)	
	Michael Vernon Dobson (D)	10,310	(16%)	
1990 general	Kweisi Mfume (D)	59,628	(85%)	($205,671)
	Kenneth Kondner (R)	10,529	(15%)	

EIGHTH DISTRICT

One of America's most affluent and best-educated communities has grown up along an old road down which colonial farmers rolled barrels of tobacco to the port of Georgetown 200 years ago. The old road, now called Wisconsin Avenue and Rockville Pike, is the commercial spine of Montgomery County, Maryland; and this suburban jurisdiction just northwest of Washington, D.C. has for several decades now ranked at the top of the list of counties in income and education. Today's Montgomery County is in large part a creation of the federal government, which has put huge facilities out here—Bethesda Naval Hospital, the National Institutes of Health, the Food and Drug Administration, the National Institute of Standards and Technology—to make it the center of America's fast-growing health industry. But the percentage of workers employed by government has been declining rapidly here, to about one in six in 1990—a figure only a point or two above the national average. In the late 1970s or early 1980s, Montgomery seemed to have reached a critical mass, and started generating thousands of private sector health, high-tech, defense and service-industry jobs.

Wisconsin Avenue and Rockville Pike look like strip highways, with 1950s commercial development and 1960s strip shopping centers like so many in the country. But the stores are upscale, sometimes *very* upscale, the new skyscrapers of downtown Bethesda and the office parks-cum-fitness centers of farther-out Gaithersburg are genuinely impressive. Not all of Montgomery County is exclusively high-income and there are some modest, mostly black and Jewish neighborhoods in Silver Spring and Wheaton. The 1980s saw a significant increase in foreign migration here—the Asian population alone increased 172% from 1980–1990. Fortified by a county government that provides first-rate public services, Montgomery spends more than any other county government in the country except Los Angeles.

Historically, the typical Montgomery County voter was a high-ranking civil servant, but as private employment outpaces government work, the picture is changing; the fastest-growing parts of the county, out past Rockville in Gaithersburg and Germantown, are filling up with Republicans attracted to the politics of Ronald Reagan and George Bush. For nearly two decades, from 1960 to 1978, Montgomery County, most of which makes up Maryland's 8th Congressional District, had a run of liberal Republican congressmen; then, in 1978, it elected liberal Democrat Michael Barnes, who became a leader of his party as chairman of the subcommittee handling Latin American policy. But when Barnes ran for the Senate in 1986, the increasing Republicanness of the newcomers may have tipped the balance back and helped elect the current congresswoman, Connie Morella.

To be sure, Morella is a liberal Republican, one of the three or four most liberal Republicans in the House by any gauge. In the Montgomery County tradition, she takes liberal positions on cultural issues from abortion rights to gun control to contra aid. She was one of three Republicans in the House to vote against the Gulf war resolution (the other two are no longer there: Silvio Conte died and Frank Riggs was defeated). She is more conservative on economic issues: the 8th has the second highest median household income of any district in the country (number one is the New Jersey 11th). Her major legislative interests are original—protecting software produced by federal scientists with limited copyrights, opening more apprenticeships to women. Nevertheless, her Republican colleagues have no desire to disown her. They know a conservative Republican couldn't win in Montgomery County (which gave Bill Clinton a 53%–35% margin over George Bush), and they appreciate her support on some partisan issues. She also has a genuine personal appeal: an ethnic background that not many old-line Republicans, but an increasing number of Montgomery voters, share; a personal history of raising nine children, six of them her late sister's; eight years' experience in the legislature. She is hard-working and cooperative with House colleagues, and presses the flesh in friendly style throughout the district. Her experience raising a large family suggests she has the energy to tend to half a million local constituents who are only a local phone call away, and to make a mark on national issues—a regimen exhausting enough that three of the last four congressmen here relinquished their seats to retire or run for the more restful Senate.

Morella has demonstrated her political strength at the polls, in 1986 beating liberal legislator Stewart Bainum, who spent a total of $1.5 million—much of it his own money—with 53%, and winning by wide margins ever since. Redistricting made the 8th District marginally more Republican, adding high-income Potomac and putting most of Silver Spring and Takoma Park in the black-majority 4th District—but none of this matters as long as Morella runs. She has been mentioned as a candidate for the Senate, but has said she will not run against Senator Paul Sarbanes.

The People: Pop. 1990: 597,760; 6% rural; 10% age 65+; 78% White; 8% Black; 8% Asian; 2% Other; 6% Hispanic origin. Voting age pop.: 455,835; 8% Black; 6% Hispanic origin. Households: 61% married couple families; 30% married couple fams. w. children; 75% college educ.; median household income: $56,789; per capita income: $26,900; median gross rent: $777; median house value: $205,500.

1992 Presidential Vote			1988 Presidential Vote		
Clinton (D)	156,043	(53%)	Bush (R)	130831	(51%)
Bush (R)	103,477	(35%)	Dukakis (D)	128041	(49%)
Perot (I)	35,599	(12%)			

Rep. Constance A. Morella (R)

Elected 1986; b. Feb. 12, 1931, Somerville, MA; home, Bethesda; Boston U., A.B. 1954; American U., M.A. 1967; Catholic; married (Anthony).

Career: Teacher, Montgomery Cnty. Pub. Schls., 1956–60; Instructor, American U., 1968–70; Prof., Montgomery Col., 1970–86; MD House of Delegates, 1979–86.

Offices: 223 CHOB 20515, 202-225-5341. Also 51 Monroe St., #507, Rockville 20850, 301-424-3501.

Committees: *Post Office and Civil Service* (5th of 9 R): Civil Service; Compensation and Employee Benefits (RMM). *Science, Space and Technology* (7th of 22 R): Investigations and Oversight; Technology, Environment and Aviation.

Group Ratings

	ADA	ACLU	COPE	CDF	CFA	LCV	ACU	NTLC	NSI	COC	CEI
1992	70	87	50	70	80	81	35	45	70	38	38
1991	65	—	67	100	50	92	15	—	—	60	39

National Journal Ratings

	1991 LIB — 1991 CONS	1992 LIB — 1992 CONS
Economic	45% — 55%	36% — 64%
Social	74% — 23%	72% — 24%
Foreign	65% — 33%	74% — 26%

Key Votes of the 102d Congress

1. Ban Striker Replace	AGN	5. Handgun Wait/7-Day	FOR	9. Use Force in Gulf	AGN
2. $ for Homeownership	FOR	6. Overseas Mil. Abortion	FOR	10. US Mil. Abroad $ Cut	FOR
3. Tax Rich/Cut Mid Cls.	AGN	7. Obscn. Art NEA $ Ban	AGN	11. Limit SDI Funds	FOR
4. FY93/$15B Def. Cut	FOR	8. Death Pen. from Jury	AGN	12. Cuba Trade Embargo	AGN

Key Votes of the 103d Congress

1. Family Leave	FOR	2. Deficit Reduction	AGN	3. Stimulus Plan	AGN

Election Results

1992 general	Constance A. Morella (R).............	203,377	(73%)	($328,516)
	Edward J. Heffernan (D)	77,042	(27%)	($74,454)
1992 primary	Constance A. Morella (R), unopposed			
1990 general	Constance A. Morella (R).............	130,059	(74%)	($353,659)
	James Walker (D).....................	39,343	(22%)	
	Sidney Altman (I).....................	7,485	(4%)	

MASSACHUSETTS

A city on a hill: that's what John Winthrop thought his Puritans were building in their Massachusetts Bay colony, and Massachusetts in the more than three centuries since has always assumed it has a lot to teach. The Puritans' austere creed taught that only the select would be saved and that they must extirpate the forces of Satan—Indians, Papists, tolerationists. For 150 years, New England was partial to learning, but also insular, hostile to outsiders and economically stagnant. Then, after the American Revolution, the international war between royal Britain and revolutionary and Napoleonic France allowed New England shipowners to cross enemy lines to become the world's leading merchants; they made vast profits in just a few brief years, and plowed them into textile mills, then railroads, then coal-mining and steel-making: this was the capital that made industrial America.

Massachusetts made a new America in other ways. Intellectually, New England flowered: just a few writers from Boston and Concord—Ralph Waldo Emerson, Henry Wadsworth Longfellow, Henry David Thoreau, John Greenleaf Whittier—created an American literary genre and popularized an American philosophy, more than 200 years after Plymouth Rock. Demographically, New Englanders surged through Upstate New York, the Midwest, and across the continent. Long blocked from Upstate New York, they only reached Syracuse in the 1820s; by the 1850s they were in Iowa and Kansas and Oregon's Willamette Valley; by the 1880s they had settled Los Angeles. They built new cities and new colleges in the wilderness; they helped to start the Republican Party and did much to start—and win—the Civil War; they planted their economic system and their values, articulated in the "McGuffey Readers," across the continent: a whole nation looking to Massachusetts for instruction.

But in the meantime Massachusetts itself and Boston, the Hub of the Universe, were being remade. The potato famine of the 1840s and an economy that continued imploding for decades after sent Irishmen across the Atlantic, and many came to Boston, looking for work in the mills, docks and factories. Yankee Protestants had seen Catholics as their great cultural enemy for 200 years and saw their commonwealth as under siege. As the Irish became a majority first in Boston and then statewide, Protestants feared the Irish would use their majorities to ladle out government jobs and benefits to their kind. And the Irish had a much better flair for politics than instinct for commerce; they yearned for the security of a government job, and they encountered such bigotry and rejection by the Yankees that even as successful an Irish Catholic as Joseph Kennedy felt obliged to move to New York in 1927. Politics in Massachusetts for years was a kind of cultural war between Yankee Republicans and Irish Democrats, an argument not so much over the distribution of income or the provision of services as over whose vision of Massachusetts should be honored, whose version of history should be taught.

Sometimes the stakes were concrete—control of patronage jobs, command of the Boston Police Department—but more often they were symbolic. Yankee Republicans tended to back activist government programs: public works and protective tariffs to help business, Civil War and Reconstruction to help suitably distant oppressed people like southern blacks, uplifting (and productivity-enhancing) social movements like temperance. The Irish found 19th Century Democrats—a party promoting laissez-faire—more congenial. They had come from a place where the government was the enemy, and didn't want government spending money to help the rich or to stimulate commerce; they didn't want government to restrict immigration, to advance the blacks who might compete with them in the labor market, or to prohibit the consumption of liquor. So politics in Massachusetts became a conflict whose warriors gird for battle still over cocktails at the Somerset Club or at Billy Bulger's St. Patrick's Day breakfast in South Boston, and then duke it out at the polls and in the gold-domed 1820s State House.

Over the years, the percentage of Irish and Catholics slowly rose. Yankees had smaller families, moved west, intermarried with people of immigrant stock and lost their Yankee identity. The Irish mostly stayed put, raising large families and eventually Massachusetts moved from being one of the most Republican states to one of the most Democratic. Economically Massachusetts did not make much progress. The descendants of the Yankees who had been so venturesome in the early 19th Century became the most cautious investors in the early 20th, while the predominance of the textile mills in their home state meant that for a century beginning in the 1820s Massachusetts imported low-skill labor and exported highly skilled people. As textile mills fled south in the 1920s, Massachusetts started exporting low-skill people as well; and from the waning of Yankee authority until the national rise of the Kennedys, Massachusetts seemed to run out of things to teach the rest of the nation. The state's Yankee Republicans were backward-looking, out of power in Washington, on the defensive at home, without a cause to champion. The Irish Democrats were hostile to Franklin Roosevelt's pro-British internationalism and receptive to the anti-Communism of the very Irish Joe McCarthy.

Then came the Kennedys. Their only residence in Massachusetts after 1927 was their summer home in Hyannis Port. But Rose Kennedy was the daughter of John "Honey Fitz" Fitzgerald, elected to Congress at 31, mayor of Boston in 1906–07 and 1910–14; and her husband Joseph Kennedy, first chairman of the Securities and Exchange Commission in the 1930s and ambassador to the Court of St. James from 1937 to 1940, was perhaps the richest Catholic in the world and a shrewd and ruthless political operator. Joseph Kennedy moved his oldest surviving son, John, to Massachusetts, engineered his election to the House in 1946, the Senate in 1952 and the Presidency in 1960. The Kennedys, with their elegant manners and great achievements, seemed like royalty to the Irish Catholics of Massachusetts and John Kennedy's election in 1960 certified to U.S. Catholics, 78% of whom voted for him, that they too were Americans. Joseph and John Kennedy were, on many issues, conservative or skeptical. But Kennedy's Administration was increasingly, even before his untimely death, identified as liberal, and his example and that of his brother, Edward, elected to the U.S. Senate at 30 in 1962, moved Massachusetts Catholics to the left. At the same time, Massachusetts Protestants were influenced by the leftward direction on the state's great campuses in the 1960s. The universities were also

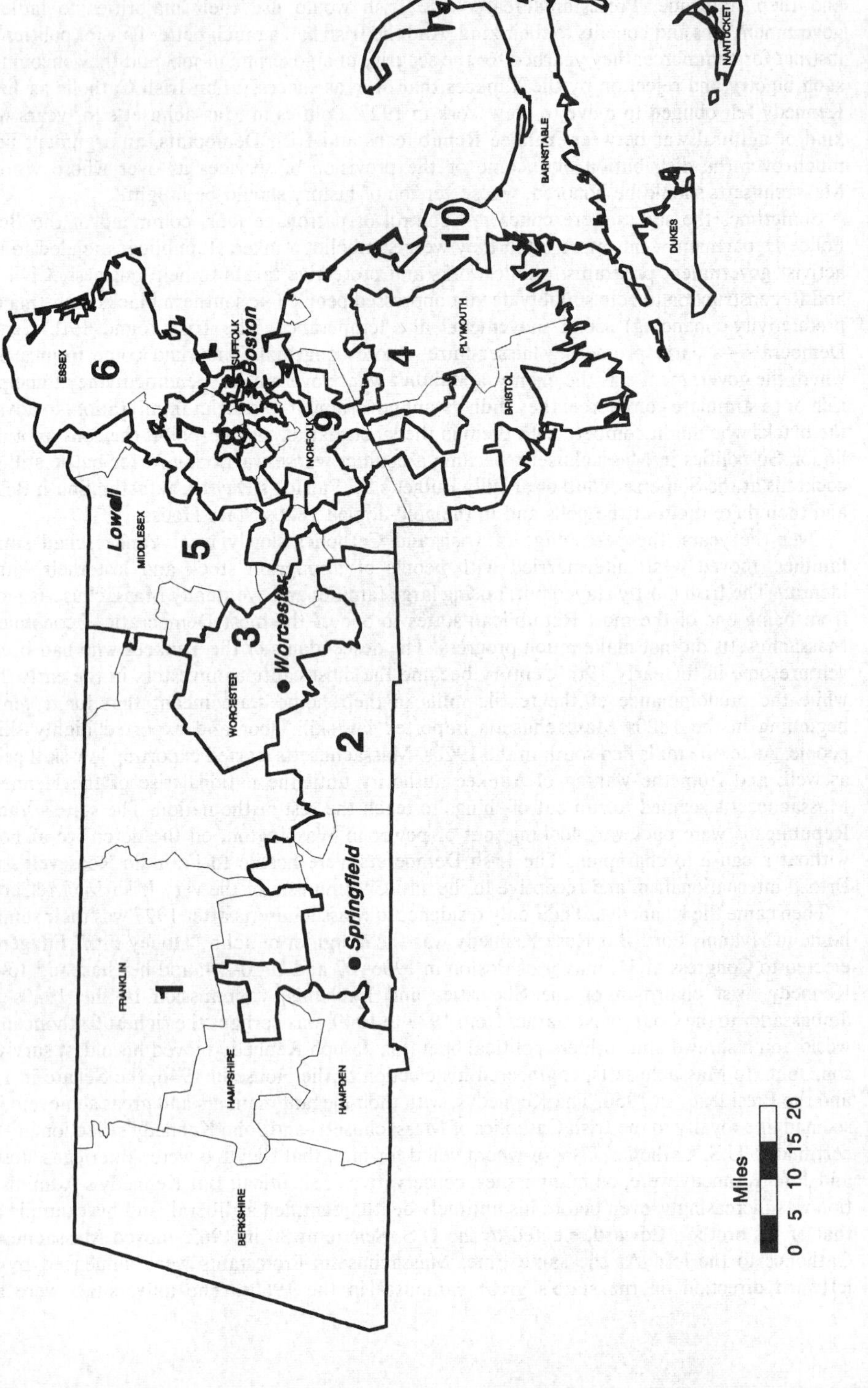

providing the basis for a surging high-tech economy, to the point that Massachusetts started importing high-skill people even as it continued to export those with low skills.

In the 1970s and 1980s Massachusetts, with one interval, had the most liberal governance and national politics of any state in the country. The expanding high-skill population, attracted initially by Massachusetts's many universities and colleges, not obliged to deal with the problems of a vast urban underclass, provided a political base of activists and money; Irish and other Catholic voters, won over by the Kennedys, provided most of the votes. Massachusetts was the only state to vote for George McGovern in 1972 and although it voted twice for Ronald Reagan, the son of an Irish Catholic, its Democratic percentage in other presidential contests from 1968 to 1988 was 53%, just 0.4% behind Rhode Island and well ahead of every other state. The state's Senators included Edward Kennedy, liberal Republican Edward Brooke, and liberal Democrats Paul Tsongas and John Kerry. Its Governors, liberal Republican Francis Sargent and liberal Democrat Michael Dukakis, vastly increased spending and endorsed the lunatic policies Dukakis could not explain in the 1988 presidential campaign: prisoners sentenced to life without parole being given weekend furloughs (the Willie Horton charge—a policy which liberals in the press said it was racist to oppose), prisoners allowed to vote and be registered by state employees sent into prisons for that purpose, government spending that rose 9% a year in the 1980s. An attempted rebellion against this resulted in Dukakis's defeat in 1978 and the election of conservative Democrat Edward King. As historian David Hackett Fischer points out, the mindset of the original settlers remains strong even when the ethnic origin of current residents is far different, and the spirit of the Puritans, the faith that they had much to teach the rest of the world, was strong in Massachusetts liberals: Michael Dukakis is moralistic, humorless, austere, smug and contemptuous of those not sharing his vision.

Today, Massachusetts has largely rejected this politics, and with a suddenness matched in its history by its merchants' sudden emergence as world traders in the 1790s and the appearance of Irish immigrants on Boston docks in the 1840s. When Dukakis announced he was running for president in 1987, his job rating was far above 50%, and the *Boston Globe*, as objective a cheerleader for Massachusetts liberalism as the *Chicago Tribune* was for Midwestern conservatism in the 1940s, was hailing "the Massachusetts miracle." But the state's financial problems were silently worsening as Dukakis campaigned across the country; he won only 53% of the vote in Massachusetts, running strong in the Berkshires and the Pioneer Valley in the west, but only running even in the Boston media market (which includes New Hampshire, a low-tax haven from high-tax Massachusetts since colonial times). Then in 1989 things fell apart. The state economy sagged badly: the slump in minicomputers hurt Massachusetts-based Wang and Digital; Cambridge's Lotus software was outflanked by Seattle's Microsoft; defense spending cutbacks, long sought by Massachusetts politicians, naturally produced job losses. More spectacular was the bursting of the Northeast real estate bubble and the resultant collapse of major New England banks: New Englanders learned anew the old lesson that housing prices don't go up 25% a year indefinitely. The state government essentially went bankrupt: spending had ballooned, revenues were falling and higher tax rates only decreased them more, services were cut, Dukakis was ridiculed and announced his retirement from office. Now it seemed that the rest of the country had something to teach Massachusetts.

The repudiation was complete in the 1990 elections. Liberals like Boston Mayor Raymond Flynn and Congressman Joe Kennedy didn't run for governor; liberal Lieutenant Governor Evelyn Murphy bowed out of the race eight days before the Democratic primary. And former Attorney General Frank Bellotti, in and out of state government since 1962, lost to Boston University President John Silber, a tough-talking critic of liberalism and former Texan who also feels he has much to teach the country. The Republican gubernatorial primary winner was former U.S. Attorney William Weld, pro-choice on abortion and pro-gay rights, but stern on crime and by his own definition reactionary on taxes and spending. After a nasty campaign, Weld beat Silber in November 1990, and Republicans won other races, electing Joe Malone state treasurer and gaining seats in the legislature and that colonial relic, the Governor's

Council. In 1991, Weld actually cut state spending—not projections or current-budget-plus-inflation, but actual spending—privatized services and slashed public payrolls; the state's economy did not start growing much by early 1993 but it was no longer declining. But Democrats remain the hardier party in Massachusetts: they have veto-proof majorities in the legislature; they generate most of the talented young politicos; even as Republicans picked up two congressional seats and seriously contested three others in 1992, Democrats won the total vote cast for Congress by 57%–35%, the largest margin in any big state.

Yet the underlying tectonic plates of Massachusetts politics have shifted. Support for Massachusetts liberalism has slipped among the university elite as they face the limits of government's ability to solve problems and the depressing effects of high taxes. It has slipped as well among the Catholic majority as more exotic policies and effects of cultural liberalism have come out into the open. Edward Kennedy, despite his marriage in 1992, seems less a venerated royal and more a controversial politician. Talk radio hosts like WRKO's Jerry Williams and Howie Carr and the feisty *Boston Herald* have delegitimized Massachusetts liberals' claims to moral superiority, while the *Globe* and other liberal voices are as hollow and unconvincing—nagging and telling others what to do when they haven't a very good idea of what to do themselves. Massachusetts undoubtedly will have more to teach the country, but for the moment it seems to be doing some learning.

Governor. William Weld is the first Yankee Massachusetts Republican governor determined to hold down taxes and government spending since Christian Herter left the State House in 1956; he hangs a picture of James Michael Curley, the scampish mayor of Boston, congressman and one-term governor, in his office. Weld is not technically a Boston Brahmin: he grew up in New York and came to Massachusetts for prep school and college; he still lives in Cambridge (with his wife, a great-granddaughter of Theodore Roosevelt), just off fashionable Brattle Street. As U.S. attorney in Massachusetts, Weld prosecuted many local pols; as an assistant attorney general, he resigned in protest of the controversies surrounding Attorney General Edwin Meese. In the 1990 primary he spent $1.1 million of his own money to overtake party-endorsed antiabortion legislator Steven Pierce, 61%–39%. In the fall he attacked Democratic opponent John Silber for his high salary at Boston University, his close ties to Senate President Billy Bulger and former Boston Mayor Kevin White and his refusal to support a tax-cutting ballot proposition. Silber's bluntness—he said of old people, "When you've had a long time, and you're ripe, then it's time to go"—caused him problems; he finally did in his candidacy when he attacked the "overweening materialism" of many two-career couples and said, "We have a generation of abused children by women who have thought a third-rate day care center was just as good as a first-rate home"—a remark resented not so much by those certain it was wrong as by those who feared it contained an uncomfortable grain of truth. Weld won 50%–47%, with strong votes from women and baby boomers.

Weld amazed Massachusetts his first year by balancing the budget without raising taxes, cutting public spending and payrolls, and repealing Dukakis's increase of estate and state sales taxes. He privatized services, selling state zoos, skating rinks and a reservoir. He expressed liberal stands on abortion, feminism and gay rights—keep the government out of your pocketbook and your bedroom, he told the Republican National Convention in Houston. He held fast on congressional districting and backed the legislature down. Weld had some setbacks in 1992; Democrats gained six seats in the state Senate, enabling them theoretically to override Weld vetoes. He said in May 1992 he would not run against Senator Edward Kennedy in 1994. And Jim Rappaport, John Kerry's 1990 Senate opponent, was elected state party chairman over Weld's opposition.

But in 1993 Weld was working with Bulger on crime and education (Weld was seeking school choice) and was proposing more spending on the environment and a state program to provide seed money for high-tech startups. He pushed for a new cigarette tax and video poker and keno. His job rating remained high and potential opponents kept dropping out. Joe Kennedy said in February 1993 he wasn't running for governor. Boston Mayor Raymond Flynn, after plugging himself for years as an appointee for every post from vice president down, was named ambassador to the Vatican, leading to a special election for mayor of Boston in fall 1993. Paul Tsongas said he would "never" run. John Silber, after articles on his high compensation and investments, seemed unlikely to run. Possible Democratic candidates included Attorney General Scott Harshbarger, and current or former state legislators Patricia McGovern, Mark Roosevelt (a cousin of Weld's wife) and Marjorie Clapprood. Weld is a clear favorite, and a victory could make him a national candidate; his combination of fiscal tightness and cultural liberalism make him appealing to the national press, his high literacy and apparent indifference to unpopularity make him distinctive in any political field.

Senators. Edward Kennedy is now in his fourth decade as a national celebrity. He has had the highs and lows of his personal life followed by millions and criticized vitriolically by many; he has been a presidential candidate and, while still in his 30s, was assumed by many to be the next occupant of the White House. He is now the fourth most senior member of the United States Senate, behind Strom Thurmond, Robert Byrd and Claiborne Pell. His reputation as an idealistic champion of the poor has been burnished by the praise of first-rate celebrators that no American political family has attracted before; to millions of others, he is a symbol of personal immorality and unpunished criminal behavior, a man who has gotten away with things that would have ended anyone else's public career. There is some basis for both views, but neither is an entirely fair picture of this politician who goes before the voters of Massachusetts in 1994 with the outcome for the first time in 32 years not entirely certain.

For the luster of the Kennedys has worn off, in America and even in Massachusetts, and the percentage of Americans who look to the Kennedys for political leadership has grown small; most voters can't remember, or never knew, what made the Kennedys so exciting. Edward Kennedy, elected to the Senate in 1962 when his brother John was president, Senate colleague with his brother Robert in the middle 1960s, was seen as the natural heir after their assassinations in 1963 and 1968. In retrospect, it is plain that Edward Kennedy's presidential chances were ended in July 1969, with the accident at Chappaquiddick, even though the Kennedy family retainers managed to cast a cloud over the specifics in a way that would be considered outrageous if tried by anyone else. Now, after the Good Friday 1991 bar-hopping in Palm Beach and his nephew Willie Smith's trial and acquittal for rape, Kennedy's vote-to-reelect figures in Massachusetts are languishing and his political career may be in some jeopardy.

In fact, Kennedy has been a hardworking and practical politician who, after his brothers' deaths, took up the liberal causes and preoccupation with the poor which had been the focus of Robert Kennedy in the last years of his life. He has worked hard for a quarter century on their behalf—and now, perhaps for the first time in his career, certainly for the first time in 15 years, Kennedy has a friendly Democratic administration to work with. And he was able, as chairman of the Labor and Human Resources Committee, to be legislatively productive in the Bush years. The child care bill passed in 1990, though by no means in the form sponsored by Kennedy's friend Christopher Dodd. A higher minimum wage and the Americans with Disabilities Act, sponsored by Tom Harkin, passed after negotiations with the White House. The Ryan White Comprehensive AIDS Care Act was passed. He played a major role on the Civil Rights Act of 1991, which Bush first opposed as quota legislation, then signed after revisions. Kennedy pushed through a higher education reauthorization bill, and produced a neighborhood schools improvement act that treated the Bush Administration school choice proposals with contempt; he has no truck with the argument that spending more simply rewards teachers and administrators who are not serving children well. Kennedy has played a major role on expanding immigration quotas: the 1965 Immigration Act, which eliminated the quotas of the 1920s, was the first major bill Kennedy floor-managed; but by the early 1980s, he was, like other labor-oriented liberals, hostile to increasing immigration. Heavy illegal Irish immigration to Boston and New York changed his mind, and in 1989 and 1990 he pushed successfully to increase the total number of immigrants.

Where he was frustrated during the Bush years, Kennedy may do better with Clinton. The

Family and Medical Leave Act vetoed by Bush was signed by Clinton in February 1993. National health insurance has long been a Kennedy cause: in the 1970s and 1980s he backed a Canadian-style single-payer government system; he moved toward the Democrats' pay-or-play plan in the 1990s, and is likely to support the Clinton Administration program and to assist in shaping the legislation. As the lead sponsor of many civil rights measures, he may try to raise the cap on punitive damages in sexual harassment suits and ban the death penalty when it is imposed disproportionately on members of different races, an attempt to bring quota legislation to criminal law. He will try to beef up OSHA regulations and reauthorize the Job Training Partnership Act and the Legal Services Corporation. He will be an advocate of the Freedom of Choice Act to provide a statutory guarantee of the right to abortion.

But it should not be assumed that Kennedy will automatically support Clinton programs. In recent years, his record has been increasingly radical, at the farthest left edge of Senate opinion. For example, he helped defeat Judge Robert Bork's nomination in 1987 when, just after the nomination was announced, he shrewdly, though without any fair basis, charged that "Robert Bork's America is a land in which women would be forced into back-alley abortions, blacks would sit at segregated lunch counters." He was precluded from a similarly loud role in the Clarence Thomas hearings in October 1991 because of his role in the Willie Smith case, which reduced to the level of *Saturday Night Live* satire his moral authority to pronounce judgment on sexual harassment. On foreign policy, Kennedy was strongly against any U.S. use of force to back up U.N. resolutions against Iraq in the Persian Gulf; not only did he vote against authorizing military force, he was only one of three senators (Democrat Bob Kerrey and Republican Mark Hatfield were the others) to oppose Bush's seeking the resolutions in the U.N. Here he seems to have moved far from President Kennedy's declaration that America would "bear any burden, pay any price" to advance freedom in the world and more toward Ambassador Joseph Kennedy's isolationism. He has called for deep cuts in the Defense budget, twice as deep as Bush and even deeper than Clinton. It is inconceivable that Kennedy would end up running against President Clinton in 1996 as he did against President Carter in 1980, when he opposed administration policies from the left. He began the race far ahead in the polls, but his inability to articulate his reasons for running, and adverse reaction to him personally and to his policies, resulted in a crushing defeat, relieved only by his stirring speech to the Democratic Convention in New York where he pointedly refused to raise Carter's hand on the podium. But it could be that Kennedy, with less now to lose, will loudly oppose Clinton if he deems his programs a betrayal of liberal principles and of the poor whom he seeks to help.

Since 1980, Kennedy, like the man he succeeded as chairman of the Judiciary Committee in 1979, James Eastland of Mississippi, has had a shrewd political sense and has maintained his popularity in the Senate and in his state, without much regard to how he stands elsewhere. In the Senate, seniority protects his power, and he is a good person-to-person politician as well. In Massachusetts, he was not much in evidence in 1990 and 1991, avoiding the Dukakis debacle as Kennedys have avoided the troubles of other Massachusetts Democrats for years, and ducking from sight pending the Palm Beach trial. He remarried in 1992, which may help him with some voters; yet at a time when feminism is increasingly the energizing force in liberal politics, his past does not ideally position him to be a liberal leader. His strength in Massachusetts depends less every year on the almost religious devotion of the decreasing numbers of Irish and Catholic voters who remember discrimination and loved him as a member of the family that had brought them all into the American mainstream, and more on those who respect him as a hardworking, competent public official. That helped him win with 62% in 1970, the year after Chappaquiddick, and with 69% in 1976, 61% in 1982, 65% in 1988. Governor William Weld has said he won't run against him; neither will Lieutenant Governor Paul Cellucci or his 1988 opponent, Treasurer Joe Malone. Former Bush Transportation Secretary Andrew Card may also be interested. His nephew, Congressman Joe Kennedy, declined to run for governor, which surely helps the Senator: two Kennedys on one ballot might be too many. Ted Kennedy surely will enter 1994 the favorite, but he is not taking his reelection for granted, and no one else should either.

John Kerry, junior Senator from Massachusetts, first won fame as one of the organizers of Vietnam Veterans Against the War in 1971, when he tossed a set of medals over a fence in a rally; Kerry's leadership attracted attention because of his background, unusual for a Vietnam veteran (he went to Yale and his mother is from the Brahmin Forbes family), and because of his record of genuine heroism in combat. "How do you ask a man to be the last to die for a mistake?" he asked in congressional testimony—a good question, and one which also suggested his future political ambitions. Yet his political career did not proceed straight ahead. He ran for Congress in 1972 after some widely observed district-shopping, and lost in a district carried by George McGovern. Chastened, Kerry went to law school, worked for a prosecutor, was elected lieutenant governor on the Dukakis ticket in 1982, and ran for senator in 1984; in both races, he upset a favored rival for the Democratic nomination. In 1982 he won the general as part of a tied ticket with Dukakis; in the 1984 general he beat Raymond Shamie, businessman and state Republican chairman, and onetime member of the John Birch Society, 55%–45%.

Kerry came to the Senate with the reputation of a left liberal, and the similarity of his name to Kennedy's (his initials are J.F.K.) fed an assumption that the two Massachusetts senators would vote alike. They mostly have; but there are notable differences, and on balance Kerry has been significantly more moderate, more respectful of economic free markets and far more willing than ultra-isolationist Kennedy to support an expansive U.S. foreign and military policy. He has worked closely and cordially with William Weld to encourage new businesses in Massachusetts—not a partnership in which one could see Kennedy involved.

In the Senate, Kerry has made his name mainly as an investigator, spending some time up blind alleys with klieg lights but also producing some important information regardless of political fallout. Over four years, though with some fallow intervals, Kerry used his Foreign Relations subcommittee to investigate the Bank of Credit & Commerce International—the now infamous BCCI scandal. His October 1992 report accused the Justice Department, British banking regulators and especially the CIA of "institutional failure" in recognizing the fraudulent nature of BCCI's operations. During that time, he did more than any American official except Manhattan District Attorney Robert Morgenthau to uncover what BCCI was up to. This is not to say that Kerry's operations have been flawless. His subcommittee spent much time investigating charges brought by the thoroughly discredited Christic Institute and tried to pin drug-running charges on Central American rightists—convenient for American politicians supportive of Central American left-wingers, but at best a cartoonish oversimplification of an unhappy part of the world. He was on more solid ground, as later events made clear, in charging Manuel Noriega of Panama with drug-dealing, but failed to deliver on hinted-at revelations that George Bush somehow knew about Noriega's operations; he did support Bush's military action in Panama in December 1989.

Kerry's other great investigation was as chairman of the Select Committee on POW/MIA Affairs, on whether Americans were left behind in Vietnamese hands in 1973. Kerry and Ranking Republican Bob Smith of New Hampshire tended to believe some were; they went to Vietnam and attempted to dig up new evidence. Kerry grilled former Secretary of State Henry Kissinger, bringing to light evidence and testimony showing that he and President Nixon understood that there could possibly be Americans left behind, but giving less credit than due to the defense that it was doves like Kerry himself who, by making American military retaliation impossible, forced Kissinger to negotiate with a very weak hand. But overall this was a serious effort, with an appropriately hedged conclusion: there is evidence "that indicates the possibility of survival, at least for a small number," after 1973, but also said, "there is at this time no compelling evidence that any American remains alive in captivity in southeast Asia."

Kerry has also spoken out interestingly on race issues. In April 1992, just before the Los Angeles riot, he spoke at Yale on affirmative action, arguing that quota programs must be supplemented with initiatives that stress law and order, personal responsibility and the work ethic. "We cannot equate fear of crime or concern about deteriorating schools with racism and then expect those who have been called racists to turn around and invest in the very neighborhoods they have fled." This is not at all Edward Kennedy's line, and it surely irritated many Massachusetts black spokesmen and some white liberals. Similarly, Kerry opposed the Gulf war resolution, but for him it was a close call, and his speech against it was cautious and nuanced. Later he worked to prohibit aid to Azerbaijan until it stopped its fight against Armenia. He is opposed to dolphin-killing drift net fishing, has called for a moratorium on mining in Antarctica and wanted President Bush to take a lead role in the Rio environmental Earth Summit. He has been a campaign finance reformer, refusing PAC money and championing voluntary public financing of congressional races. Echoing his predecessor in the Senate, Paul Tsongas, he insisted, "I have articulated a different kind of Democratic Party for five and a half years."

Kerry came up for reelection in 1990, when voters were reacting against Massachusetts liberalism, and had more opposition than he liked. Republican Jim Rappaport, son of Boston developer and Democratic contributor Jerome Rappaport, spent $4.2 million of his own money on his campaign, and ran one of the most effective ads of the year, showing Michael Dukakis's face turning piece by piece into Kerry's, with an announcer saying ominously, to *Jaws*-like music, "He's back." By mid-September, Rappaport trailed by only 45%–41% in a public poll. Kerry spoke plaintively in debate of his long record in public life, and his first campaign ads featured mostly 20-year-old TV footage showing his opposition to the Vietnam war; he referred to Rappaport as a "chicken hawk," though Rappaport was only 15 when the last U.S. forces left Vietnam. Then Kerry ran what his campaign called the "hot heir" ad, showing a cartoon of Rappaport in a balloon floating to various spots: Jerome Rappaport's government-subsidized Charles River apartments; Rappaport's Vermont farm for which he got a state subsidy intended for needy dairy farmers (he "milked taxpayers for another cash subsidy"); then, to Hawaiian music, a beach scene while the narrator attacked Rappaport for making a profit off a Hawaiian condo complex his partnership bought in 1987 from a failed S&L ("made a fortune on an S&L deal that cost taxpayers millions"). This ridicule helped Kerry to a 57%–43% victory.

Kerry does not seem to have any more, if he ever did, presidential ambitions. While he continues to have an instinct for the sharp jab and cheap shot, he has embarked on projects which have taken original thinking and unusual determination and has produced some intellectually serious work—to the point that it's worth watching what he'll tackle next.

Presidential politics. Massachusetts is the most Democratic state in presidential elections with the arguable exception of Rhode Island. In 1992, it gave Bill Clinton one of his highest percentages in the nation, and his largest percentage margin of any state. Put it another way: Massachusetts, the state where George Bush was born and where his Yankee ancestors lived for generations, was his worst state; Bush's support essentially collapsed here in 1992 and he came within 7% of being outpolled here by Ross Perot. But at this point, Massachusetts's embrace of national Democratic liberalism is less firm than its rejection of Republican cultural conservatism.

Massachusetts's presidential primary has long been in early March and is the leading northern Super Tuesday contest. The Democratic primary in 1992, as in 1988, went to the Greek-ancestry native son: Paul Tsongas this time, Michael Dukakis then. The much smaller Republican primary was won both times by native son George Bush.

Congressional districting. Massachusetts lost one congressional district in each of the last two Censuses, causing a kind of musical chairs. The losers in 1982 were Barney Frank and Margaret Heckler, put into the same district with each other; Frank won and, despite some turbulence, is now in the House and stronger than ever. In 1992, musical chairs was avoided by the early retirement of Brian Donnelly. But Republican Governor William Weld used his veto to force the adoption of a plan, with some of the nation's most grotesquely shaped districts, designed to produce marginal districts Republicans might win; Democrats accepted it because they feared that a Republican federal judge, who had the case if they did not agree, would redistrict incumbents in together (four powerful incumbents—Moakley, Kennedy, Markey, Frank—had residences within five miles of each other in central Boston). Not all members of the all-

Democratic delegation fared well. Joseph Early and Nicholas Mavroules, beset by scandal, both lost to Republicans. Chester Atkins lost some of his favorite territory and lost the Democratic primary. Gerry Studds lost part of his base as well, but with split opposition won handily. Over the decade, six or seven of these seats could be seriously contested by Republicans, a far cry from the 1982–90 cycles, in which there were only five seriously contested races in 11 districts in five elections.

The People: Est. Pop. 1992: 5,996,000; Pop. 1990: 6,016,425, down 0.3% 1990–1992. 2.4% of U.S. total, 13th largest; 16% rural. Median age: 33.6 years. 13.6% 65 years and over. 89.8% White, 5.0% Black, 4.8% Hispanic origin, 2.4% Asian, 2.6% Other. Households: 52.1% married couple families; 24% married couple fams. w. children; 50% college educ.; median household income: $36,952; per capita income: $17,224; 59.3% owner occupied housing; median house value: $162,800; median monthly rent: $506. 8.5% Unemployment. Voting age pop.: 4,663,350. Registered voters (1992): 3,351,918; 1,346,097 D (40%); 447,181 R (13%); 1,558,640 unaffiliated and minor parties (47%).

Political Lineup: Governor, William F. Weld (R); Lt. Gov., Argeo Paul Cellucci (R); Secy. of the Commonwealth, Michael J. Connolly (D); Atty. Gen., L. Scott Harshbarger (D); Treasurer, Joseph Malone (R); Comptroller, William Kilmartin (D); Auditor, A. Joseph DeNucci (D). State Senate, 40 (31 D and 9 R); State House of Representatives, 160 (125 D, 34 R, and 1 I). Senators, Edward M. Kennedy (D) and John F. Kerry (D). Representatives, 10 (8 D and 2 R).

1992 Presidential Vote

Clinton (D)	1,318,639	(48%)
Bush (R)	805,039	(29%)
Perot (I)	630,731	(22%)

1992 Democratic Presidential Primary

Tsongas	526,297	(66%)
Brown	115,746	(15%)
Clinton	86,817	(11%)
Nader	32,881	(4%)

1988 Presidential Vote

Dukakis (D)	1,401,415	(53%)
Bush (R)	1,195,635	(45%)

1992 Republican Presidential Primary

Bush	176,868	(66%)
Buchanan	74,797	(28%)
No Preference	10,132	(4%)

GOVERNOR

Gov. William F. Weld (R)

Elected 1990, term expires Jan. 1995; b. July 31, 1945, Smithtown, NY; home, Cambridge; Harvard, B.A. 1966, J.D. 1970, Oxford U., 1967; Episcopalian; married (Susan).

Career: Practicing atty., 1970–80, 1988–90; U.S. Atty. for MA, 1981–86; U.S. Asst. Atty. Gen., Criminal Div., 1986–88.

Office: State House, Boston 02133, 617-727-9173.

Election Results

1990 gen.	William F. Weld (R)	1,175,817	(50%)
	John Silber (D)	1,099,878	(47%)
	Other	67,167	(3%)
1990 prim.	William F. Weld (R)	270,319	(61%)
	Steven D. Pierce (R)	176,070	(39%)
1986 gen.	Michael S. Dukakis (D)	1,157,786	(69%)
	George S. Kariotis (R)	525,364	(31%)

SENATORS
Sen. Edward M. Kennedy (D)

Elected 1962, seat up 1994; b. Feb. 22, 1932, Boston; home, Hyannis Port; Harvard, B.A. 1956, The Hague Intl. Law Schl., 1958, U. of VA, LL.B. 1959; Catholic; married (Vicki).

Career: Army, 1951–53; Western states coordinator, John F. Kennedy Pres. campaign, 1960; Asst. Dist. Atty., Suffolk Cnty., 1961–62.

Offices: 315 RSOB 20510, 202-224-4543. Also 407 JFK Fed. Bldg., Boston 02203, 617-565-3170.

Committees: *Armed Services* (4th of 11 D): Defense Technology, Acquisition and Industrial Base; Force Requirements and Personnel; Regional Defense and Contingency Forces (Chmn.). *Judiciary* (2d of 10 D): Constitution; Immigration and Refugee Affairs (Chmn.); Patents, Copyrights and Trademarks. *Labor and Human Resources* (Chmn. of 10 D): Children, Family, Drugs and Alcoholism; Education, Arts and Humanities; Labor. *Joint Economic Committee* (2d of 10).

Group Ratings

	ADA	ACLU	CDF	COPE	CFA	LCV	ACU	NTLC	NSI	COC	CEI
1992	100	95	100	92	100	100	0	5	40	20	10
1991	95	—	100	83	82	100	0	—	—	20	20

National Journal Ratings

	1991 LIB — 1991 CONS		1992 LIB — 1992 CONS	
Economic	90%	— 3%	91%	— 5%
Social	87%	— 0%	89%	— 0%
Foreign	86%	— 0%	86%	— 0%

Key Votes of the 102d Congress

1. $ for Homeownership	AGN	5. Clarence Thomas Nom. AGN	9. Use Force in Gulf	AGN
2. Have Cap Gains Debate	AGN	6. Lmt Death Row Appeal AGN	10. Keep Salvador Aid	AGN
3. Remove Budget Walls	FOR	7. Handgun Wait/5-Day FOR	11. Cut $1B from SDI	FOR
4. Ban Striker Replace	FOR	8. Abortion Gag Rule AGN	12. Override China MFN FOR

Key Votes of the 103d Congress

1. Family Leave	FOR	2. HIV Immigrants	FOR	3. Clinton Budget	FOR

Election Results

1988 general	Edward M. Kennedy (D)	1,693,344	(65%)	($2,702,865)
	Joseph D. Malone (R)................	884,267	(34%)	($587,323)
1988 primary	Edward M. Kennedy (D), unopposed			
1982 general	Edward M. Kennedy (D)	1,247,084	(61%)	($2,470,473)
	Raymond Shamie (R).................	784,602	(38%)	($2,305,996)

Sen. John F. Kerry (D)

Elected 1984, seat up 1996; b. Dec. 11, 1943, Denver, CO; home, Boston; Yale, A.B. 1966, Boston Col., LL.B. 1976; Catholic; divorced.

Career: Navy, 1966–70 (Vietnam), Naval Reserves, 1972–78; Organizer, Vietnam Veterans Against the War; Asst. Dist. Atty., Middlesex Cnty., 1976–81; Practicing atty., 1981–82; MA Lt. Gov., 1982–84.

Offices: 421 RSOB 20510, 202-224-2742. Also One Bowdoin Sq., #1000, Boston 02114, 617-565-8519; 222 Milliken Pl., #311, Fall River 02722, 508-677-0522; and 145 State St., #504, Springfield 01103, 413-785-4619.

Committees: *Banking, Housing and Urban Affairs* (6th of 11 D): Economic Stabilization and Rural Development; Housing and Urban Affairs; International Finance and Monetary Policy. *Commerce, Science and Transportation* (6th of 11 D): Aviation; Communications; Foreign Commerce and Tourism (Chmn.); Science, Technology and Space. *Foreign Relations* (5th of 11 D): East Asian and Pacific Affairs; International Economic Policy, Trade, Oceans and Environment; Terrorism, Narcotics and International Operations (Chmn.). *Intelligence (Select)* (7th of 9 D). *Small Business* (5th of 12 D): Innovation, Manufacturing and Technology; Urban and Minority-Owned Business Development (Chmn.).

Group Ratings

	ADA	ACLU	CDF	COPE	CFA	LCV	ACU	NTLC	NSI	COC	CEI
1992	100	91	100	83	92	92	0	11	40	10	13
1991	95	—	100	83	78	93	5	—	—	20	18

National Journal Ratings

	1991 LIB — 1991 CONS	1992 LIB — 1992 CONS
Economic	80% — 16%	84% — 12%
Social	87% — 0%	84% — 11%
Foreign	78% — 14%	65% — 26%

Key Votes of the 102d Congress

1. $ for Homeownership	AGN	5. Clarence Thomas Nom. AGN	9. Use Force in Gulf	AGN
2. Have Cap Gains Debate	AGN	6. Lmt Death Row Appeal AGN	10. Keep Salvador Aid	AGN
3. Remove Budget Walls	FOR	7. Handgun Wait/5-Day	FOR	11. Cut $1B from SDI	FOR
4. Ban Striker Replace	FOR	8. Abortion Gag Rule	AGN	12. Override China MFN FOR

Key Votes of the 103d Congress

1. Family Leave   FOR   2. HIV Immigrants   FOR   3. Clinton Budget   FOR

Election Results

1990 general	John F. Kerry (D)	1,321,712	(57%)	($8,040,970)
	Jim Rappaport (R)	992,917	(43%)	($5,177,801)
1990 primary	John F. Kerry (D), unopposed			
1984 general	John F. Kerry (D)	1,393,150	(55%)	($2,070,004)
	Raymond Shamie (R)	1,139,913	(45%)	($4,180,961)

FIRST DISTRICT

The stony hills and green-clad mountains of western Massachusetts, with more trees today than when Henry David Thoreau was writing in the 1840s, where stone fences passing through thick forest once bounded one working farm from another, probably looks today much like it did 300 years ago. This was the frontier in the 17th Century, where Puritan preachers formed new towns in the wilderness, farming the stony soil and preaching against declension. It was dangerous as well, the site of the Indian uprising known as King Philip's War in 1676, the scene of the Indian raid, supported by the French from Quebec, at Deerfield in 1704. This was Yankee New England's western frontier for nearly 200 years: New York's Dutch and British rulers mollified their Iroquois allies by agreeing to keep out the Yankees, whose reputation as self-righteous Indian killers was well-established; as a result, Yankees did not begin their westward migration along the natural route in Upstate New York until some time after the Revolution. In the 19th Century, western New England was the home of writers and artists, Emily Dickinson living quietly in Amherst, Edith Wharton grandly on her estate in the Berkshires, the sculptor Augustus Saint Gaudens not far from where the Boston Symphony played in the Tanglewood Festival each summer. There were mill towns here as well, jammed in mountain crevasses or along the wide Connecticut River; but as the 20th Century went on, and trees grew up on stony land once farmed, western Massachusetts came to look less settled.

Western Massachusetts has also changed politically. For many years it was one of the heartlands of the Republican Party—flinty, thrifty, chilly just like the area's most famous politician, Calvin Coolidge, who worked his way up from mayor of Northampton to governor and president by lowering taxes and saying no to pleas for government action. But by the 1980s, western Massachusetts was one of the most left-wing parts of America. A town like Stockbridge could attracted liberal artist Norman Rockwell (a solid New Dealer and peacenik) and baby boom radical Arlo Guthrie whose Alice's Restaurant is there. The concentration of colleges and universities in the Pioneer Valley, around Amherst, Northampton and South Hadley, brought together a critical mass of leftist scholars and an even more leftish graduate student proletariat, people defying their Marxist philosophy of economic determinism by remaining in places where they could make little money in order to be surrounded by culturally congenial people and places. The results show up in the election returns: Hampshire County, dominated by Pioneer Valley college towns, voted 61%–37% for Michael Dukakis in 1988 and 54%–22% for Bill Clinton over George Bush in 1992.

The 1st Congressional District of Massachusetts, like all the state's districts, has convoluted boundaries which defy easy description. It includes almost all of the state west of the Connecticut River and the northern half of the state from the Connecticut River east to I-495. But its lines separate close neighbors. The 1st includes Amherst, but not Northampton or South Hadley; it includes West Springfield and Holyoke, but not Springfield just the other side of the Connecticut River; it includes North Brookfield but not Brookfield, and so on. The result is a district that is Democratic, but not overwhelmingly so, and whose Democratic base is split among the Amherst radicals, low-income factory workers of Holyoke and the descendants of ethnic mill and blue-collar workers in factory towns from Pittsfield in the Berkshires to Fitchburg and Leominster in the eastern end of the district. For 32 years, until his death in February 1991, the 1st with somewhat different boundaries was represented by Silvio Conte, a liberal but still partisan Republican who was ranking member of the Appropriations Committee. Conte's death set up a seriously contested Democratic primary plus serious efforts by Republicans of various stripes to capture a seat that for many years Conte was the only Republican capable of winning. The winner of the fragmented Democratic primary was state Senator John Olver of Northampton, whose Pioneer Valley base helped him win 31% of the vote. In the general, Olver faced Steven Pierce, former state House Republican leader, Governor William Weld's conservative opponent in the 1990 primary and a Weld cabinet appointee. With

Massachusetts liberalism in grave disrepute, polls by both parties showed the two candidates virtually even right up to the election. Weld shrewdly scheduled the general for June 4 when, presumably, the more liberal college voting bloc had already left for summer vacation; but it wasn't quite enough to help Pierce, and Olver was able to pull out a close 50%–48% win.

In his first term, Olver had one of the most liberal voting records in the House. He passed a bill creating a network of Manufacturing Outreach Centers to help businesses tap into university resources—a bit of local pork?—and securing two-year funding for the Low-Income Home Energy Assistance Program. He is against NAFTA and for Canadian-style national health insurance. But he had to hustle when Weld insisted on a redistricting plan that took Northampton and South Hadley out of the 1st District and put Fitchburg and Leominster in. Olver was opposed in 1992 by Patrick Larkin, an aide to Conte and supported by his widow; Olver was forced to apologize when he accused Larkin of holding two simultaneous Hill jobs (turns out it was another Patrick Larkin). Olver got help from big name Democrats and ended up winning 52%–43%, carrying Pittsfield and other Berkshire towns narrowly, winning big in the Pioneer Valley and carrying a plurality around Fitchburg. In the 103d Congress, he got a seat on Appropriations with help from Rules Chairman Joe Moakley of Boston. The seat still leans Democratic, but might be seriously contested again.

The People: Pop. 1990: 601,721; 36% rural; 14% age 65+; 92% White; 2% Black; 1% Asian; 3% Other; 5% Hispanic origin. Voting age pop.: 458,088; 1% Black; 4% Hispanic origin. Households: 55% married couple families; 25% married couple fams. w. children; 45% college educ.; median household income: $31,903; per capita income: $14,200; median gross rent: $479; median house value: $123,200.

1992 Presidential Vote

Clinton (D)	130,308	(48%)
Bush (R)	72,238	(26%)
Perot (I)	68,545	(25%)

1988 Presidential Vote

Dukakis (D)	138,999	(56%)
Bush (R)	111,242	(44%)

Rep. John Olver (D)

Elected June 1991; b. Sept. 3, 1936, Homesdale, PA; home, Amherst; Rensselaer Polytechnic Inst., B.S. 1955, Tufts U., M.S. 1956, M.I.T., Ph.D. 1961; No religious affiliation; married (Rose).

Career: Prof., U. of MA, Amherst, 1961–69; MA House of Reps., 1968–72; MA Senate, 1973–91.

Offices: 1323 LHOB 20515, 202-225-5335. Also 78 Center St. Arterial, Pittsfield 02101, 413-442-0946; 881 Main St., Philbin Fed. Bldg., Fitchburg 01420, 508-342-8722; and 187 High St., Holyoke 01040, 413-584-8108.

Committees: *Appropriations* (35th of 37 D): Foreign Operations, Export Financing and Related Programs; Treasury, Postal Service, and General Government.

Group Ratings

	ADA	ACLU	COPE	CDF	CFA	LCV	ACU	NTLC	NSI	COC	CEI
1992	100	100	92	100	100	100	0	0	40	25	11
1991	100	—	100	100	88	89	0	—	—	33	8

National Journal Ratings

	1991 LIB	—	1991 CONS		1992 LIB	—	1992 CONS
Economic	88%	—	0%		91%	—	0%
Social	88%	—	0%		88%	—	8%
Foreign	*	—	*		90%	—	0%

Key Votes of the 102d Congress

1. Ban Striker Replace	FOR	5. Handgun Wait/7-Day	*	9. Use Force in Gulf	*
2. $ for Homeownership	AGN	6. Overseas Mil. Abortion	*	10. US Mil. Abroad $ Cut	FOR
3. Tax Rich/Cut Mid Cls.	FOR	7. Obscn. Art NEA $ Ban	AGN	11. Limit SDI Funds	FOR
4. FY93/$15B Def. Cut	FOR	8. Death Pen. from Jury	AGN	12. Cuba Trade Embargo	AGN

Key Votes of the 103d Congress

1. Family Leave	FOR	2. Deficit Reduction	FOR	3. Stimulus Plan	FOR

Election Results

1992 general	John Olver (D)	135,049	(52%)	($704,238)
	Patrick Larkin (R)	113,828	(43%)	($384,625)
	Others	13,243	(5%)	
1992 primary	John Olver (D), unopposed			
1991 special	John Olver (D)	70,022	(50%)	($757,775)
	Steven D. Pierce (R).................	68,052	(48%)	($882,354)

SECOND DISTRICT

As American as apple pie, the place where basketball was invented, the city where the Webster's unabridged dictionaries (2d and 3d editions) were edited and published, the site of the Armory where M-1 rifles were manufactured in World War II: this is Springfield, Massachusetts, the third largest city in the Bay State, but far from Boston; the second largest city in the Connecticut River Valley, but overshadowed by Hartford; a medium-sized American city built by New England Yankees, where immigrants from a dozen different countries worked their way up.

Springfield is the largest city in the 2d Congressional District of Massachusetts, whose irregular boundaries stretch north to South Hadley and Northampton, college towns of the Pioneer Valley, and east across stony hills to the factory towns of the Blackstone Valley just north of Woonsocket, Rhode Island. Historically, this was a Yankee Republican district for much of the 20th Century, then a solidly Catholic Democratic district while represented by Edward Boland, the longtime Washington roommate of Tip O'Neill, from 1952 to 1988. Now it is perhaps more marginal, but still leans Democratic.

The congressman from the 2d District is Richard Neal, mayor of Springfield from 1984 to 1988. Boland announced his retirement just before the filing deadline, and after Neal had been making the rounds of the district for a year. Unopposed in the Democratic primary, Neal won 80% in the general: in effect he was given the seat. But he has not held it without some tumult, an indication that his tenure may be precarious. Quiet, with a generally liberal record except on some cultural issues (abortion, the flag amendment), he seemed to do nothing politically risky. But he has continued to accrue controversy from his activities as mayor. In 1990, he was opposed in the primary by his predecessor as mayor, Theodore DiMauro, still incensed that Boland's timing had deprived him of a shot at the seat in 1988. DiMauro attacked Neal for overspending as mayor, calling him "the Mike Dukakis of Springfield" and also "a walking photo opportunity, a Ken doll," and hit him for awarding a $2.5 million city health insurance contract to a firm whose chief executive contributed $250 to his campaign. But DiMauro was attacked for saying that the Bank of New England was being liquidated by federal regulators; it was in fact taken over, but not until four months after the primary, which Neal won 64%–36%.

In 1992, Neal again had opposition, this time in a district considerably changed by redistricting: he lost areas around Worcester, and gained the Pioneer Valley towns and the Blackstone Valley. He had another problem: 87 overdrafts on the House bank. He was challenged in the primary by Springfield Councilwoman Kateri Walsh, who attacked him for the overdrafts, and his $400,000 in PAC contributions, and by systems design manager Charles Platten. Walsh won 34% of the vote and Platten 18%; Neal's 48% was good enough for a win, but below the 50% he would need to beat a single opponent and the 60% danger level for an incumbent. Neal won just 42% in the Pioneer Valley and 47% in the Blackstone Valley, and 47% in his home base of Springfield. In the general election, 27-year-old Springfield Councilman Anthony Ravosa again harped on Neal's financial management as mayor. Ravosa won only 31%, but Thomas Sheehan of the For the People Party got 16% and Neal only 53%.

Neal got a break when Joe Moakley of Boston helped him get a seat on the Ways and Means Committee in 1993. There he is likely to support the Clinton tax program but also to increase eligibility for IRAs. But a cloud remains on his horizon: in early 1993 it was reported that a federal prosecutor was investigating whether there were connections between contributions to Neal's 1988 campaign and a no-bid insurance contract he awarded as mayor. Neal denied wrongdoing and claimed he had not been contacted by any federal agents; in February 1993 a state grand jury indicted Charles Kingston, a 1988 Neal campaign aide in 1988 and Springfield deputy tax collector for filing fraudulent income tax returns. Problems connected to his political past may continue to plague Neal, but, like most members with a reasonably safe district and a good committee post, he should be reelected without serious contest.

The People: Pop. 1990: 601,490; 21% rural; 14% age 65+; 88% White; 6% Black; 1% Asian; 4% Other; 6% Hispanic origin. Voting age pop.: 453,960; 5% Black; 4% Hispanic origin. Households: 56% married couple families; 25% married couple fams. w. children; 42% college educ.; median household income: $33,401; per capita income: $14,652; median gross rent: $497; median house value: $128,800.

1992 Presidential Vote			1988 Presidential Vote		
Clinton (D)	121,759	(46%)	Dukakis (D)	132,154	(55%)
Bush (R)	76,277	(29%)	Bush (R)	108,527	(45%)
Perot (I)	65,935	(25%)			

Rep. Richard E. Neal (D)

Elected 1988; b. Feb. 14, 1949, Springfield; home, Springfield; Amer. Intl. Col., B.A. 1972, U. of Hartford, M.A. 1976; Catholic; married (Maureen).

Career: Staff Asst., Springfield Mayor, 1973–78; Springfield City Cncl., 1978–83; Springfield Mayor, 1984–88.

Offices: 131 CHOB 20515, 202-225-5601. Also Fed. Office Bldg., #309, 1550 Main St., Springfield 01103, 413-785-0325; and 4 Congress St., Milford 01757, 508-634-8198.

Committees: *Ways and Means* (18th of 24 D): Select Revenue Measures; Trade.

Group Ratings

	ADA	ACLU	COPE	CDF	CFA	LCV	ACU	NTLC	NSI	COC	CEI
1992	90	91	92	100	100	88	0	0	10	13	9
1991	90	—	100	100	72	69	5	—	—	20	8

National Journal Ratings

	1991 LIB — 1991 CONS			1992 LIB — 1992 CONS		
Economic	84%	—	12%	91%	—	0%
Social	71%	—	28%	66%	—	34%
Foreign	87%	—	8%	90%	—	0%

Key Votes of the 102d Congress

1. Ban Striker Replace	FOR	5. Handgun Wait/7-Day	FOR	9. Use Force in Gulf	AGN
2. $ for Homeownership	AGN	6. Overseas Mil. Abortion	AGN	10. US Mil. Abroad $ Cut	FOR
3. Tax Rich/Cut Mid Cls.	FOR	7. Obscn. Art NEA $ Ban	FOR	11. Limit SDI Funds	FOR
4. FY93/$15B Def. Cut	FOR	8. Death Pen. from Jury	AGN	12. Cuba Trade Embargo	AGN

Key Votes of the 103d Congress

1. Family Leave	FOR	2. Deficit Reduction	FOR	3. Stimulus Plan	FOR

Election Results

1992 general	Richard E. Neal (D).................	131,215	(53%)	($355,367)
	Anthony W. Ravosa, Jr. (R)	76,795	(31%)	($102,179)
	Thomas R. Sheehan (FTP).............	38,963	(16%)	
1992 primary	Richard E. Neal (D)...................	30,370	(48%)	
	Kateri Walsh (D)	21,709	(34%)	
	Charles A. Platten, Jr. (D)	11,513	(18%)	
1990 general	Richard E. Neal (D), unopposed			($534,345)

THIRD DISTRICT

Worcester, Massachusetts, is often overlooked—though it is technically the second largest city in New England, in its city limits. People may drive in for concerts at the Centrum, but otherwise speed by on the Mass Pike or I-495. This is the only major U.S. industrial city not on a river, lake or sea coast, and is far from a commercial airport; and perhaps people here like it that way. Worcester for 200 years now has been one of America's centers of tinkering, contriving and inventing—a high-tech manufacturing center before that term was invented. There have been lurches and pauses in its high-tech growth: 50 years ago, its biggest industries were making wire, textiles, grinding wheels and envelopes—not on the cutting edge. But in the 1970s and 1980s, the electronics and computer industries became well-established in the towns along Interstate 495, the circumferential highway just 20 miles east of Worcester, as they had earlier around Route 128, closer to Boston. The high-tech surge brought prosperity, new residents, a labor shortage and higher housing prices to area towns and suburbs—and then a recession and collapse of real estate values, as the area's minicomputer industry slumped in the late 1980s. But Worcester (its name still pronounced with a particularly pungent Massachusetts accent making it sound as if it had no *R*s) is a metropolitan center with a skilled labor force and ingenious entrepreneurs likely to come up with something to replace minicomputers in the 1990s.

Worcester is the largest city in the 3d Congressional District, but not its geographical center—nothing is, for the bounds of this district are particularly grotesque, to make it serve its political purpose while keeping the population standard. The 3d includes towns north of Worcester up to Rutland and Princeton and east along the I-495 high-tech corridor. Then it is connected by a series of narrow land bridges with Fall River, far to the south, an old textile mill town on an inlet of Narragansett Bay, and to the towns of Westport and Dartmouth fronting on Buzzards Bay, an arm of the Atlantic Ocean. It has been called the Ivy League district (from Princeton to Dartmouth) and the district that now makes inland Worcester a seaport town. Worcester and the Fall River area are heavily Democratic, the area in between is Republican, and the I-495 corridor, once solidly Democratic, trended Republican: techies in Massachusetts tend to be Republican, lawyers and academics Democrats.

The 3d District was a good example of the anti-incumbent trend of 1992: Joe Early, a Worcester Democrat first elected in 1974, a member of the Appropriations Committee with a seemingly safe seat, was beaten after it was revealed he had 140 overdrafts on the House bank. It was more colorful than that: the *Worcester Star-Telegram* called for his resignation; he protested his innocence and in a speech on the floor of the House said of the Ethics Committee members who released the list of violators, "They ran like rats!" He had other problems in 1990—he protested to five judges and 25 lawyers a one-year jail sentence given to a local bookie, and two of his children received scholarships from the head of an aerospace PAC—but was unopposed. But in 1992, (to use a nautical metaphor in this new shore district) the sharks smelled blood in the water, and four Democrats and three Republicans fought to wrest away Early's seat. It was inevitable that one of them should win: Chester Atkins, of the adjoining 5th District, at one point was asking redistricters to put him in with Early, as his one sure way of winning. Instead, they both lost. Early compounded his problems by ducking debates and relying on local politicians he had helped from his seat on the Appropriations Committee. His best-known opponent, former state Senator Gerald D'Amico, had run against him in the primary in 1974, when he was only 25. This time he hit Early for opposing abortion and ran ads showing a red coat hanger outlining Early's face. But D'Amico ran 2–1 behind Early in Worcester, and barely ahead of Worcester School Committee member Brian O'Connell. Former assistant Attorney General Martin Healy had support in the I-495 belt, while UMass professor John Walsh had backing in the Worcester suburbs. Early ran way ahead in the Fall River area and won the primary with 37%, to 20% for D'Amico, 18% for Walsh, 14% for Healy, 12% for O'Connell; a runoff would have finished him.

Meanwhile, there was a Republican primary with state legislator Peter Blute, conservative on spending and antiabortion, coming out ahead of pro-choice colleague David Lionett 49%–37%. In the general, Blute ran ads ridiculing Early for overdrafts, overseas junkets ("Tahiti Joe") and ducking debates; he had a Bart Simpson-like character speaking for Early ("Hey, dude. No big deal"). Early hoped his work on Appropriations aiding district projects and medical institutions would help, but it was not enough. Early carried Worcester with 57% and the Fall River area with 59%. But Blute won the rest of the district 60%–35%, winning overall 50%–44%.

Blute has a political pedigree: his uncle Peter Hines was City Council president in Boston and ran for mayor in 1967; Blute was elected to the legislature in 1986 and made a name as a rabid foe of taxes and supporter of privatization. In the House, he won seats on the Public Works and Science Committees, suggesting he is interested in federal projects that will help the district; but he made a no-new-taxes pledge. For a safe seat, he will have to make further inroads in Worcester and the Fall River area.

The People: Pop. 1990: 601,852; 18% rural; 14% age 65+; 93% White; 2% Black; 2% Asian; 2% Other; 4% Hispanic origin. Voting age pop.: 459,291; 2% Black; 3% Hispanic origin. Households: 58% married couple families; 27% married couple fams. w. children; 48% college educ.; median household income: $36,873; per capita income: $15,917; median gross rent: $515; median house value: $150,500.

1992 Presidential Vote			**1988 Presidential Vote**		
Clinton (D)	123,724	(45%)	Dukakis (D)	127,607	(51%)
Bush (R)	85,047	(31%)	Bush (R)	123,250	(49%)
Perot (I)	62,667	(23%)			

Rep. Peter Blute (R)

Elected 1992; b. Jan. 28, 1956, Boston; home, Shrewsbury; Boston Col., B.A. 1978; Catholic; married (Robi).

Career: P.R., Boston Red Sox, 1979–80; Partner, Sports promotion firm; MA House of Reps., 1987–92.

Offices: 1029 LHOB 20515, 202-225-6101. Also 100 Front St., #1079, Worcester 01608, 508-752-6789; 1039 S. Main St., Fall River 02724, 508-675-3400; and 7 N. Main St., Attleboro 02703, 508-223-3100.

Committees: *Public Works and Transportation* (20th of 24 R): Economic Development; Surface Transportation. *Science, Space and Technology* (19th of 22 R): Science; Technology, Environment and Aviation.

Group Ratings and 102d Congress Votes: Newly Elected

Key Votes of the 103d Congress

| 1. Family Leave | FOR | 2. Deficit Reduction | AGN | 3. Stimulus Plan | AGN |

Election Results

1992 general	Peter Blute (R)	131,473	(50%)	($435,911)
	Joseph D. Early (D)	115,587	(44%)	($924,384)
	Leonard J. Umina (I)	9,691	(4%)	
	Others	4,181	(2%)	
1992 primary	Peter Blute (R)	11,989	(49%)	
	David J. Lionett (R)	8,984	(37%)	
	Michelle Flaherty (R)	3,558	(15%)	
1990 general	Joseph D. Early (D), unopposed			($282,012)

FOURTH DISTRICT

The political transformation of Massachusetts is nowhere better illustrated than in the Boston suburbs of Brookline and Newton. These were Yankee enclaves a century ago, with avenues built by developers to resemble the sweep of Haussmann's Grand Boulevards in Paris, and villages of giant clapboard houses clustering within a few blocks of a commuter railroad station. Brookline was where The Country Club (the very first one) was established in 1882, and where Joseph Kennedy, as an Irish Catholic 20-something banker seeking respectability, moved his family in 1914. Brookline and Newton then were solidly Republican in politics, the political base of leading politicians like Christian Herter, governor of Massachusetts and U.S. secretary of state in the 1950s; as late as 1960, Brookline and Newton and adjacent wards of Boston were electing a Republican congressman. Then came the transformation, personified by the election in 1962 of Michael Dukakis at 29 to the Great and General Court (i.e., the legislature). As Massachusetts's university-educated classes became more liberal, and as Brookline's and Newton's Jewish population grew, and as young liberal-minded families refurbished the graceful old houses, these became liberal Democratic bastions. By the 1970s, the Brookline Town Meeting was opening each year with debates over whether they should recite the Pledge of Allegiance; against that background, it is easier to understand how Dukakis could fail so utterly to understand the cultural attitudes of most Americans. And Brookline and Newton stayed loyal: 69%–29% for Dukakis in 1988, 68%–20% for Clinton in 1992.

The 4th Congressional District of Massachusetts includes Brookline and Newton which form the political home base for its congressman, Barney Frank. But they cast only 25% of the votes, and this grotesquely shaped district is not all of one piece: indeed, one setting out to canvass entirely the district's bounds might have to get off the road and step over fences and trudge through marshes. The shape results from successive redistrictings: in 1982, Frank's district was extended south to the old textile mill city of Fall River, putting him in a race against Republican incumbent Margaret Heckler, which he won 60%–40%; in 1992, the boundaries were adjusted to accommodate adjacent districts, so Frank lost the western half of Fall River and gained New Bedford, a great 19th Century whaling port and still home to one of the largest fishing fleets in the United States. It also curves north to the interior of Plymouth County, around old towns like Bridgewater. This is a Democratic district in national politics, but not nearly so Democratic nor as uniformly culturally liberal as Brookline and Newton; without those two, the district would have voted only about 40% for Dukakis and Clinton. There is a bit of most kinds of America here: high-income WASPy Wellesley, French Canadian mill worker Fall River, Foxboro with its football stadium, Sharon with a middle-income Jewish population, countrified Dover.

Barney Frank, after his moments of notoriety in the national press, has gone back to doing well what he was doing well before: working on legislation, arguing public policy and making political deals, providing constituency service with a thoroughness that produced touching responses when he got in trouble. In May 1987, in a seemingly casual answer to a reporter's question, Frank had admitted he is gay. But in August 1989, the conservative *Washington Times* revealed that Frank had employed as a personal aide a male prostitute and convicted drug possessor, Steve Gobie, and let him live in his apartment where the man was allegedly carrying on his former trade. Frank admitted to paying Gobie, but was careful never to use official or campaign funds; he denied that he tolerated prostitution in his apartment and had thrown the man out when he suspected it was going on. The *Boston Globe* called on him to resign; his picture appeared on the cover of *Newsweek*; he called on the Ethics Committee to investigate. It did, and dismissed all but two minor charges. The committee recommended a reprimand but not censure; Frank agreed in a contrite appearance before the House in July 1990; the House voted 390–38 against expulsion (moved by homophobe William Dannemeyer) and, mostly on party lines, 287–141 against censure (moved by Republican Whip Newt Gingrich); the vote for reprimand was 408–18.

"I think members will agree that I have always had a reputation for honesty, not always tact or tolerance," Frank said to the House, and that reputation was probably one reason he survived. For Frank is one of the smartest members of the House and one of its most gifted legislators; he is also one of the most intellectually honest politicians of his time. At a time when so many members seem to rely on canned speeches produced by staffers and letterhead interest groups, Frank listens to others' arguments and engages them in his rapid-fire delivery. He has made some of the most telling criticisms of conservatism over the years: of opponents of both abortion and child nutrition programs, he said, "Sure, they're pro-life. They believe that life begins at conception and ends at birth."

But he can also direct his fire at his fellow liberals, as in his 1992 book *Speaking Frankly*, which criticizes liberals for their "tyranny of the notsupostas." He has also decried many liberals' unwillingness to criticize people who commit crimes or say that Communism is a terrible system, and chided them as "scolds" for opposing the 65-mile-an-hour speed limit or pursuing an impossible goal like federal gun control. He insists that "Democratic positions are fully consistent with the values of patriotism, free enterprise, working hard for one's self and one's family, and holding people to a standard of behavior fully respectful of the person and property of others." Much of this advice was followed by Bill Clinton in 1992, with obviously positive results. In 1993, Frank's opinion may give the administration some needed political cover to back off on their plan to lift the ban on gays in the military. To the disappointment of many in the gay community, Frank admitted that allowing open homosexuals to serve in the military would not be accepted by most in Congress and the Pentagon. Taking Senator Sam Nunn's "Don't Ask, Don't Tell" compromise a step further, Frank suggested that gays be allowed to conduct an openly gay lifestyle when off-base without fear of reprisal. But the issue of conduct off-base has now become a sticking point between Frank and Nunn; in a newspaper interview, Frank charged that Nunn was obsessed with what happened "in other people's bedrooms." Nunn's reply on *Meet the Press*: "I appreciate Rep. Frank trying to enhance my dull image, but in terms of the obsession with sex, I'm not in Barney's league."

Frank's list of legislative accomplishments is long. He took over the subcommittee handling the bill to provide redress to Japanese Americans interned in World War II and got it through the House and signed into law. He works hard on immigration bills, and pushed for repeal of the silly McCarran-Walter Act provision barring from the United States foreigners deemed subversive by the U.S. In 1990 he expanded immigration limits, adding provisions letting in 1,000 Tibetans, and fought against the provision barring HIV-positive people from entering the country. On housing issues, he pushed successfully for amendments to the fair housing bill for AIDS victims and those with the HIV virus. He passed a bill restructuring HUD programs, limiting prepayment requirements that threatened to expel many tenants, and dealt with the problem of integrating the disabled, the mentally ill, and substance abusers with the elderly in subsidized housing. He is proud of creating the HOME program providing housing block grants to states; on the RTC bill, he inserted affordable housing provisions which he claims will produce more low-income home ownership. He successfully stymied conservative attempts to undermine the Legal Services Corporation, so that it survived into the Clinton years. Frank serves on the Budget Committee and worked to erode the firewalls between defense and domestic spending; he looks forward to using defense savings to pay for domestic programs.

Electorally, Frank has survived nicely into the 1990s. His 1990 opponent demanded that he take an AIDS test; Frank won with 66%. Redistricting didn't hurt him badly, and he won in 1992 with 68% of the vote; even more impressive than the 76% he won in Brookline and Newton was the 59% he won in the rest of the district.

The People: Pop. 1990: 601,392; 27% rural; 14% age 65+; 92% White; 2% Black; 2% Asian; 2% Other; 2% Hispanic origin. Voting age pop.: 461,137; 2% Black; 2% Hispanic origin. Households: 57% married couple families; 27% married couple fams. w. children; 51% college educ.; median household income: $39,005; per capita income: $18,963; median gross rent: $512; median house value: $170,200.

1992 Presidential Vote			1988 Presidential Vote		
Clinton (D)	143,595	(51%)	Dukakis (D)	147,309	(56%)
Bush (R)	74,769	(26%)	Bush (R)	114,414	(44%)
Perot (I)	62,746	(22%)			

Rep. Barney Frank (D)

Elected 1980; b. Mar. 31, 1940, Bayonne, NJ; home, Newton; Harvard, B.A. 1962, J.D. 1977; Jewish; companion, Herb Moses.

Career: Exec. Asst., Boston Mayor Kevin White, 1967–71; A.A., U.S. Rep. Michael Harrington, 1971–72; MA House of Reps., 1973–80; Lecturer, Harvard JFK Schl. of Govt., 1978–80.

Offices: 2404 RHOB 20515, 202-225-5931. Also 29 Crafts St., Newton 02158, 617-332-3920; 558 Pleasant St., #309, New Bedford 02740, 508-999-6462; 222 Milliken St., #300, Fall River 02721, 508-674-3551; and 89 Main St., Bridgewater 02324, 508-697-9403.

Committees: *Banking, Finance and Urban Affairs* (6th of 30 D): Financial Institutions Supervision, Regulation and Deposit Insurance; International Development, Finance, Trade and Monetary Policy (Chmn.). *Budget* (9th of 26 D). *Judiciary* (9th of 21 D): Administrative Law and Governmental Relations; Civil and Constitutional Rights; Intellectual Property and Judicial Administration.

Group Ratings

	ADA	ACLU	COPE	CDF	CFA	LCV	ACU	NTLC	NSI	COC	CEI
1992	100	96	83	100	100	100	0	10	10	25	14
1991	100	—	83	90	56	100	5	—	—	20	18

National Journal Ratings

	1991 LIB — 1991 CONS	1992 LIB — 1992 CONS
Economic	61% — 36%	83% — 13%
Social	84% — 12%	92% — 0%
Foreign	87% — 8%	90% — 0%

Key Votes of the 102d Congress

1. Ban Striker Replace	FOR	5. Handgun Wait/7-Day FOR	9. Use Force in Gulf AGN
2. $ for Homeownership	AGN	6. Overseas Mil. Abortion FOR	10. US Mil. Abroad $ Cut FOR
3. Tax Rich/Cut Mid Cls.	FOR	7. Obscn. Art NEA $ Ban AGN	11. Limit SDI Funds FOR
4. FY93/$15B Def. Cut	FOR	8. Death Pen. from Jury AGN	12. Cuba Trade Embargo AGN

Key Votes of the 103d Congress

1. Family Leave	FOR	2. Deficit Reduction	FOR	3. Stimulus Plan	FOR

Election Results

1992 general	Barney Frank (D)	182,633	(68%)	($376,829)
	Edward J. McCormick, III (R)	70,665	(26%)	($51,350)
	Luke Lumina (I)	13,670	(5%)	
	Others	2,844	(1%)	
1992 primary	Barney Frank (D), unopposed			
1990 general	Barney Frank (D)	143,473	(66%)	($718,160)
	John R. Soto (R)	75,454	(34%)	($31,903)

FIFTH DISTRICT

The history of the Merrimack River Valley at the northern edge of Massachusetts has been one of high-tech boom, bust, boom, bust. In the early 19th Century, when Massachusetts was a kind of maritime republic, with scattered farmers struggling to scratch a living from the stony soil, a few ingenious Yankees flush with profits from the sea trade decided to tame the rapidly flowing Merrimack River and build cotton spinning mills. They created the cities of Lowell and Lawrence and built model dormitories and recreation programs for their female workers. When the maritime trading business faded, Massachusetts continued to grow because of the textile industry which lasted here for nearly 100 years. Then, in the 1920s, the price of labor rose in New England and newly built mills in the Carolinas, nearer the cotton supply, largely ended the businesses Lawrence and Lowell built. Yet many in the work force, by then rather elderly, waited forlornly for some upturn in the local economy.

It came eventually from an unexpected source. Starting in the 1960s in Cambridge, around MIT, moving out to the old Route 128 circumferential highway, and more recently locating along I-495 which passes through Lowell and Lawrence, high tech has powered Massachusetts growth. Wang, headquartered in Lowell, grew prodigiously, and the city was upgraded by the national historical restoration of its old mill area, sparked by former Congressman and Senator Paul Tsongas. In the early 1980s, when the rest of the country was in recession, Massachusetts had one of the nation's lowest unemployment rates; in the middle 1980s, the state surged. Then, in the late 1980s, Wang's minicomputers slumped as businesses bought personal computers and hooked them together, and the payroll fell from 31,500 in 1988 to a restructured 6,300 after declaring bankruptcy in 1992; "now leasing" signs went up on many of Lowell's restored buildings. Yet the overall prospects are surely better than they were in the 1920s. Lowell's new immigrants—mostly from Cambodia and Puerto Rico—provide vitality, and its recent growth shows the power of innovation and adaptability, much weaker ideas in the 1920s or 1950s.

The 5th Congressional District of Massachusetts takes in much of this country, including Lawrence and Lowell, which with surrounding suburbs account for about half its population. Most of the other half is part of the currently troubled high-tech corridor further south on I-495, which runs from the stony hills of Lawrence and Lowell to Maynard (headquarters of Digital) and Marlborough. There are some elite suburbs here like Concord, old mill towns like Ayer, the Army's Fort Devens which is slated to be closed in 1995 (to the wails of many Massachusetts pols who never voted for a defense budget) and the mountains along the New Hampshire line. Most of this area (Lowell and Lawrence are exceptions) is ancestrally Yankee Republican; culturally liberal, it trended toward the Democrats in the early 1970s; booming with high-tech growth, the whole area, including Lawrence and Lowell, trended toward Republicans in national and even statewide contests in the 1980s and 1990; increasingly uneasy about George Bush's evident lack of interest in the domestic economy, it gave a plurality to Bill Clinton in 1992 but his lowest percentage in the state, and the real movement was to that high-tech pioneer Ross Perot. The 5th is by most measures Massachusetts's most Republican district, a kind of Baja New Hampshire; although a better way to put it would be to say it is the least Democratic.

In 1992, the 5th District was the scene of some of the angrier politics of the cycle. Incumbent Chester Atkins was obviously in serious trouble: he won with 52% in 1990 only after smearing his opponent, including attacking his mother's religious beliefs; the very aptitude for politics which made him a lifetime officeholder—he was elected to the state House at 22 in 1970, to the state Senate in 1972, was chairman of the Massachusetts Democratic Party from 1977 to 1990 and was elected to Congress in 1984—hurt him in an anti-incumbent year. Also, he had 127 overdrafts on the House bank and voted for the 1989 pay raise. He angered Cambodians in the district when he called for direct talks with Hun Sen; he infuriated other voters by predicting Fort Devens would be saved (it wasn't); he made public attacks on his old ally, state Senate President Billy Bulger. With no friends left at the State House or in the delegation, he was the obvious man out as Massachusetts was losing a congressional seat; he pleaded publicly to be put in the same district with Worcester's Joe Early, who had ethics problems, but to no avail; when another incumbent retired, he watched Governor Weld and Bulger insist on keeping in the 5th Lawrence and Lowell, where Atkins was unpopular, and throwing out Framingham, which produced all of his majority and more in 1990.

Atkins was dispatched fairly easily, in the Democratic primary, by challenger Martin Meehan who had spent his adult life working for politicians but had never run for office himself. Meehan hit Atkins on the overdrafts and the pay raise, while Republican Michael Conway mocked Atkins by printing rubber checks, and posting a reward for the first person to find Atkins inside the Lawrence city limits. Atkins lost the primary 65%–35%, and lost Lowell and Lawrence and the towns adjoining them by a 75%–25% margin, an astonishing repudiation for an incumbent. Meanwhile, Conway was edged 53%–47% in the Republican primary by Paul Cronin, who was helped by name identification from his one term in the House: he beat John Kerry in 1972, when Kerry faced district-hopping accusations, and lost to Paul Tsongas in 1974. Meehan emerged from the primary with a large debt, but he was able to depict Cronin as a "loser" who had run for a variety of offices since 1974 and frequently lost. Meehan had his own venturesome program—a 50% defense cut, targeted capital gains tax cuts and income tax increases—and backed the balanced budget amendment and term limits. He emphasized his service as a local prosecutor and head of the state securities regulation agency.

Meehan won the general election by 52%–38%, a solid margin but barely over the 50% mark. In the House, he got a seat on the Armed Services Committee. It will be interesting to see whether the high-tech industry revives here, and whether Meehan attracts serious opposition.

The People: Pop. 1990: 601,527; 16% rural; 10% age 65+; 87% White; 2% Black; 4% Asian; 5% Other; 8% Hispanic origin. Voting age pop.: 446,128; 2% Black; 6% Hispanic origin. Households: 60% married

couple families; 30% married couple fams. w. children; 52% college educ.; median household income: $42,701; per capita income: $18,293; median gross rent: $603; median house value: $174,100.

1992 Presidential Vote			1988 Presidential Vote		
Clinton (D)	113,073	(42%)	Bush (R)	131,405	(53%)
Bush (R)	85,366	(32%)	Dukakis (D)	117,137	(47%)
Perot (I)	70,474	(26%)			

Rep. Martin T. (Marty) Meehan (D)

Elected 1992; b. Dec. 30, 1956, Lowell; home, Lowell; U. of MA, B.S. 1978, Suffolk U., M.A. 1981, J.D. 1986; Catholic; divorced.

Career: Staff Asst., U.S. Rep. James Shannon, 1979–81; MA Dep. Secy. of State for Securities & Corps., 1986–90; Middlesex Cnty. 1st Dist. Atty., 1991–92.

Offices: 1223 LHOB 20515, 202-225-3411. Also 11 Kearney Sq., Lowell 01852, 508-459-0101; Bay State Bldg., 11 Lawrence St., #806, Lawrence 01840, 508-681-6200; and Walker Bldg., 255 Main St., #102, Marlborough 01752, 508-460-9292.

Committees: *Armed Services* (27th of 34 D): Military Forces and Personnel; Readiness; Research and Technology. *Small Business* (14th of 27 D): Regulation, Business Opportunities and Technology; SBA Legislation and the General Economy.

Group Ratings and 102d Congress Votes: Newly Elected

Key Votes of the 103d Congress

1. Family Leave	FOR	2. Deficit Reduction	FOR	3. Stimulus Plan	FOR

Election Results

1992 general	Martin T. (Marty) Meehan (D)	133,844	(52%)	($831,544)
	Paul W. Cronin (R)	96,206	(38%)	($551,896)
	Mary J. Farinelli (I)	19,077	(7%)	($224)
	Others	7,437	(3%)	
1992 primary	Martin T. (Marty) Meehan (D)	50,300	(65%)	
	Chester G. Atkins (D)	26,855	(35%)	
1990 general	Chester G. Atkins (D)	110,232	(52%)	($861,333)
	John F. MacGovern (R)	101,017	(48%)	($236,851)

SIXTH DISTRICT

Massachusetts's North Shore, on Massachusetts Bay north of Boston, was once the leading edge of the American economy. It was here in 1640 that the Saugus Iron Works was built—the beginning of American heavy industry. From 1792 to 1815, when Europe's great powers were convulsed in international war, American sea captains suddenly became the busiest shippers in the world. Traders from Boston accumulated the capital which they used to build textile mills and railroads, and financed much of the American industrial revolution; while from the small port of Salem, sailing ships set out for the China trade, bringing back porcelain and artifacts and forever changing American styles. Salem, first settled in 1626, had the country's first millionaire, Elias Hasket Derby, and in 1900, it was the richest city per capita in the United States. The wealth accumulated in those halcyon days spread across America and the world. But the North Shore is a quiet place, from Boston harbor north to the mouth of the Merrimack River, a collection of ethnic factory towns from Lynn on up through next-door Peabody to Newburyport, alternating with the high-income enclaves of Marblehead with its yachts and Beverly with its estates, artsy Rockport and the still-busy fishing port of Gloucester. The largest town is Lynn, whose biggest factory today is the General Electric jet engine plant, which in 1993 employed 6,300, less than half the number of the 1980s buildup.

The North Shore from Lynn onward, plus towns and cities several miles inland, form Massachusetts's 6th Congressional District. This is a varied area demographically and politically. High-income Yankees tend to be Republicans, but liberal ones; Lynn, Salem and Peabody are basically Irish working-class Democratic, as are the Merrimack mill towns. On balance, it is a Democratic district, but Republicans have a base here, and ran even or ahead in 1980s presidential elections. This is, by the way, the site of the original gerrymander, named because its architect, Elbridge Gerry, a Jeffersonian, wanted to corral all the area's Federalist towns into one grotesquely shaped district. Ironically, the current 6th District's boundaries are less grotesque and politically determined than those of any other Massachusetts district.

The 6th District was the scene of anti-incumbent fever in the 1992. The incumbent was Nicholas Mavroules, first elected in 1978 after 11 years as mayor of Peabody. He served on Armed Services and looked after the interests of the GE Lynn plant, but otherwise took mostly liberal stands. But in 1992, there were rumors that federal prosecutors were investigating Mavroules. He was challenged in the primary by state Representative Barbara Hildt, who campaigned against his antiabortion stand. Hildt was helped when Mavroules was indicted in August 1992, less than a month before the primary, for tax evasion, influence peddling and bribery. Hildt didn't mention the indictment, but did talk of the need for "trust." Mavroules's symbol, on many of his signs, was the Energizer bunny, with its slogan, "Still Going," and he won the primary 47%–46%, with 7% going to a third candidate Eric Elbot, considered by some a pro-Mavroules "mole" to take votes from Hildt.

The Energizer bunny kept on going through the fall, but eventually ran into a wall. The Republican primary had been brutal: Alexander Tennant, a former state party executive director, attacked Peter Torkildsen for switching his stand on abortion in April from antiabortion to pro-choice; Torkildsen said he was affected by the case of a 14-year-old rape victim in Ireland. With big margins in North Shore towns, Torkildsen won 56%–44%. Torkildsen brought some fair credentials to the general election: he beat the state House majority leader in 1984, at 26, and in the legislature was instrumental in the fight to repeal Michael Dukakis's services tax; he was the lieutenant governor candidate on Steven Pierce's unsuccessful 1990 ticket and was then appointed Governor William Weld's commissioner of labor and industries. He criticized Mavroules sharply for taking PAC money, refusing to take any himself, and resisted advice to harp on the indictments. Mavroules brought in top Democrats to campaign for him—Senators Edward Kennedy and John Kerry, Congressmen Joe Kennedy, Barney Frank and Les Aspin— but Paul Tsongas declined to campaign for him, and Mavroules fired his campaign manager two weeks before the election. And reports that a tape of his son-in-law would be used against him didn't help. Mavroules carried the biggest towns in the district but lost almost all the rest, and Torkildsen won 55%–45%. (In April 1993, Mavroules plead guilty to 15 of the 17 charges against him.)

On national issues, Torkildsen favors vouchers and tax credits to reform health insurance and will only support a tax increase if it is linked to long-term cuts in spending. Having criticized Democrats for letting Mavroules remain a subcommittee chairman after his indictment, he pressed his fellow Republicans to bar members indicted from serving as ranking minority members. That failed, given opposition from Joseph McDade, the senior Republican and ranking member on Appropriations who is under an indictment himself. Footnote: Torkildsen is an avid collector of political memorabilia, and during the campaign met a great-grandson of James Cox, who showed him one of his rarest buttons: the 1920 Democratic ticket of Cox and Franklin D. Roosevelt.

The People: Pop. 1990: 601,811; 10% rural; 14% age 65+; 95% White; 2% Black; 1% Asian; 1% Other; 3% Hispanic origin. Voting age pop.: 466,764; 2% Black; 2% Hispanic origin. Households: 57% married couple families; 26% married couple fams. w. children; 54% college educ.; median household income: $40,836; per capita income: $18,549; median gross rent: $617; median house value: $181,400.

1992 Presidential Vote			1988 Presidential Vote		
Clinton (D)	134,424	(43%)	Dukakis (D)	144,982	(51%)
Bush (R)	96,857	(31%)	Bush (R)	140,353	(49%)
Perot (I)	75,893	(25%)			

Rep. Peter G. Torkildsen (R)

Elected 1992; b. Jan. 28, 1958, Milwaukee, WI; home, Danvers; U. of MA, B.A. 1982, Harvard JFK Schl. of Govt., M.A. 1990; Catholic; single.

Career: Svc. Coor., Visiting Nurses Assn., 1982–84; MA House of Reps., 1984–90; Commissioner, MA Dept. of Labor and Industry, 1991–92.

Offices: 120 CHOB 20515, 202-225-8020. Also 70 Washington St., Salem 01970, 508-741-1600; 156 Broad St., #106, Lynn 01901, 617-599-2424; 160 Main St., Haverhill 01830, 508-521-0111; and 61 Center St., Burlington 01803, 617-273-4900.

Committees: *Armed Services* (17th of 22 R): Military Installations and Facilities; Research and Technology. *Merchant Marine and Fisheries* (19th of 19 R). *Small Business* (17th of 18 R): Regulation, Business Opportunities and Technology.

Group Ratings and 102d Congress Votes: Newly Elected

Key Votes of the 103d Congress

1. Family Leave	AGN	2. Deficit Reduction	AGN	3. Stimulus Plan	AGN

Election Results

1992 general	Peter G. Torkildsen (R)	159,165	(55%)	($460,934)
	Nicholas Mavroules (D)	130,248	(45%)	($671,110)
1992 primary	Peter G. Torkildsen (R)	16,556	(56%)	
	Alexander T. Tennant (R)	13,043	(44%)	
1990 general	Nicholas Mavroules (D)	149,284	(65%)	($333,912)
	Edgar L. Kelley (R)	80,177	(35%)	($19,771)

SEVENTH DISTRICT

The Yankee Protestants and Irish Catholics who settled Massachusetts arrived by boat, the Yankees to a cold stony land with a few Indians, the Irish to a crowded city with Yankees who seemed even less welcoming. The Yankees whose ancestors once farmed the soil had, by the early 20th Century, founded suburbs filled with solid brick and white frame houses, furnished in Early American furniture, with a view out the paned windows. As the years went on, their local public schools were emptied as young people with children had moved out, and attendance at Protestant churches went down. The Irish, for decades heavily concentrated in the crowded wards of Boston, started moving out into the Yankee suburbs 50 years ago. There were other ethnic groups here and there—Jews, Italians, French Canadians, but the major conflict—fought out in neighborhood playgrounds, in school committee meetings and not least in political campaigns—was between Protestant Yankee Republicans and Catholic Irish Democrats.

The 7th Congressional District of Massachusetts is made up of northern and western suburbs of Boston where vestiges of this conflict can still be seen. Geographically, it forms an arc around Boston, starting with the clapboard beach towns of Winthrop and Revere just beyond Logan Airport, going north as far as Wakefield, whose Lake Quannapowit is home to the nation's oldest inland yacht club, west past working class Woburn and Medford, home of Tufts University, to the patriot town of Lexington that spans Route 128 and Waltham, home of Brandeis University, through high-income Lincoln and Weston to modest-income Natick and Framingham. Most of these towns were Yankee Republican up through the 1950s, but by the 1960s they were pretty solidly Democratic; the high-tech suburbs trended Republican again in the 1980s but swung against George Bush in 1992. The highest income areas seem to run across the grain of their ethnic experience: Weston, with many Catholics, is pretty solidly Republican; Lincoln, with Yankees like Thomas Boylston Adams and George Bush's sister Nancy Ellis, is liberal and perversely countercyclical, voting for George McGovern and Gerald Ford in the 1970s, Walter Mondale and Michael Dukakis in the 1980s, finally striking a national chord with Bill Clinton in 1992.

The congressman in the 7th District is Edward Markey, first elected in 1976 at 30, never having been to Washington before. From a modest economic background, very Irish, Markey is a graduate of Malden Catholic High, Boston College and the Massachusetts legislature. The Capitol he first laid eyes on was full of Democrats for whom Vietnam and Watergate were the paradigmatic events of all world history, a view Markey seemed to share. In his early House years, he was one of the fiercest opponents of nuclear power and a leading political organizer for the nuclear freeze in 1983, as well as a backer of the comprehensive test ban treaty later. Markey's enthusiastic certainty and his thirst for publicity infuriated many colleagues, who saw him as a self-righteous grandstander. But seniority and events have shown Markey to be a productive and creative legislator. He is one of those lucky House members for whom the seniority system has clicked, opening up perhaps the choicest Energy and Commerce sub-committee chair, Telecommunications and Finance, after just 10 years. He got on Energy and Commerce with help from Tip O'Neill because his predecessor had been there; he got on what was then called the Communications Subcommittee early because the high-tech boom on Route 128 convinced him that telecommunications issues would be critical. He met the high standards of Energy and Commerce Chairman John Dingell, who likes aggressive colleagues that are both productive and loyal. The voters of the 7th District also exerted some discipline. Markey started to run for the seat of retiring Senator Paul Tsongas in 1984, but he jumped back into the House race when he failed to raise enough money and had to scramble to win his primary.

The Telecommunications and Finance chairmanship is a juicy position, with fabulous possibilities for campaign fundraising (Markey doesn't take PAC money or accept honoraria, but of course securities and communications executives can make individual contributions, and do) and with subject matter that is intellectually more demanding (and in lobbying terms more fiercely contested) than almost anything else in Congress. Markey's 1988 insider trading bill got near unanimous support and a 1990 law, a response to the 1987 crash, increased the power of the SEC to shut down markets or limit computer program trading in emergencies. Suspicious of junk bonds and other high-risk investments, Markey sought not a complete ban but stronger powers for the regulatory agency. In communications, Markey passed bills slightly reducing commercial time on children's programs, requiring TVs to include decoder circuitry for close-captioned signals for the deaf, and limiting dial-a-porn services. In 1992, he combined his penchant for regulation with political shrewdness to produce the cable TV reregulation bill which passed both houses, was vetoed by President Bush and then in October 1992 was passed over Bush's veto—the only bill passed over his veto in his four-year term. This was very much Markey's project, and he had strong lobbying support (the TV networks) and opposition (most of the cable industry). The law requires the FCC to define reasonable rates for basic cable service, allows consumers and local governments more regulatory power, and gives competitors increased access to programming. In 1993, he was working on a bill to regulate financial planners, requiring a consumer information toll-free number and conflict of interests disclosures—but no new cause of action for trial lawyers to pursue. He is also working on a bill to place greater responsibility on accountants to report fraud and wrongdoing, a measure prompted by the S&L loan scandals.

But Markey's biggest projects, and those most likely to impact American life in the 21st Century, concern telecommunications. In 1993, he passed a bill reallocating, from public to private sector, 200 megahertz of the radio frequency spectrum, four times as much as created the entire cellular phone industry; the computer industry is eying these new frequencies as a way to transmit information. He favors fiberoptic wiring of every household, but sees this as a relatively long-range project, and in the shorter term wants to require phone companies to provide digital service at affordable rates over already existing copper lines; he hopes to create incentives for companies to develop hardware and software for video, data and voice to be transmitted over phone wires. This is likely to be fiercely opposed by newspapers, and financing is still uncertain unless utilities regulators allow the rewiring costs to be depreciated over much longer periods. Markey, once a Watergate-era idealist, is now preoccupied with issues in which regulation and respect for market forces are necessary, and his political skills are directed at stimulating capitalists to create jobs and technology further liberating people from onerous bureaucratic controls.

On issues beyond his committee's ken (there are a few), Markey maintains one of the House's most liberal voting records. He also tends to local issues, making sure the town of Malden keeps the profits from selling urban renewal land, getting more federal funding for cleaning up Boston Harbor, pushing for a $200,000 study on how to save Revere Beach. Incidentally, his wife Susan Blumenthal, a top researcher at the National Institutes of Health, served on Hillary Rodham Clinton's health care task force and was mentioned as a possible head of NIH.

The People: Pop. 1990: 601,476; 1% rural; 15% age 65+; 92% White; 2% Black; 3% Asian; 1% Other; 3% Hispanic origin. Voting age pop.: 485,578; 2% Black; 2% Hispanic origin. Households: 53% married couple families; 22% married couple fams. w. children; 53% college educ.; median household income: $41,318; per capita income: $19,825; median gross rent: $685; median house value: $192,700.

1992 Presidential Vote			**1988 Presidential Vote**		
Clinton (D)	150,073	(50%)	Dukakis (D)	161,506	(55%)
Bush (R)	87,418	(29%)	Bush (R)	129,649	(45%)
Perot (I)	61,963	(21%)			

Rep. Edward J. Markey (D)

Elected 1976; b. July 11, 1946, Malden; home, Malden; Boston Col., B.A. 1968, J.D. 1972; Catholic; married (Susan Blumenthal).

Career: Army Reserves, 1968–73; MA House of Reps., 1973–76.

Offices: 2133 RHOB 20515, 202-225-2836. Also 5 High St., #101, Medford 02155, 617-396-2900.

Committees: *Energy and Commerce* (4th of 27 D): Energy and Power; Telecommunications and Finance (Chmn.); Transportation and Hazardous Materials. *Natural Resources* (3d of 28 D): Energy and Mineral Resources; National Parks, Forests and Public Lands.

Group Ratings

	ADA	ACLU	COPE	CDF	CFA	LCV	ACU	NTLC	NSI	COC	CEI
1992	100	100	83	90	93	88	0	0	30	25	10
1991	100	—	100	100	89	92	0	—	—	20	7

National Journal Ratings

	1991 LIB — 1991 CONS	1992 LIB — 1992 CONS
Economic	88% — 0%	89% — 9%
Social	88% — 0%	92% — 0%
Foreign	87% — 8%	90% — 0%

Key Votes of the 102d Congress

1. Ban Striker Replace	FOR	5. Handgun Wait/7-Day	FOR	9. Use Force in Gulf	AGN
2. $ for Homeownership	AGN	6. Overseas Mil. Abortion	FOR	10. US Mil. Abroad $ Cut	FOR
3. Tax Rich/Cut Mid Cls.	FOR	7. Obscn. Art NEA $ Ban	AGN	11. Limit SDI Funds	FOR
4. FY93/$15B Def. Cut	FOR	8. Death Pen. from Jury	AGN	12. Cuba Trade Embargo	AGN

Key Votes of the 103d Congress

1. Family Leave	FOR	2. Deficit Reduction	FOR	3. Stimulus Plan	FOR

Election Results

1992 general	Edward J. Markey (D)	174,837	(62%)	($928,883)
	Stephen A. Sohn (R)	78,262	(28%)	($290,304)
	Robert B. Antonelli (I)	28,421	(10%)	
1992 primary	Edward J. Markey (D), unopposed			
1990 general	Edward J. Markey (D), unopposed			($207,273)

EIGHTH DISTRICT

A long generation ago, Cambridge, Massachusetts was a plainly aging city, with a grayness in the air matching its gray winter skies. Its two great universities, Harvard and MIT, were closely hemmed in by a not very friendly town of Irish Catholics, Italians and a few Portuguese, living generation after generation in three-decker houses with cracked wood walls letting in the cold or letting out the heat. Boston was the nation's slowest-growing metropolitan area, economically stagnant, still caught in the 17th Century Puritan-Papist rivalry. Students from suburbs across the country exploring Boston from their dormitories and campuses felt they were pawing through the living remnants of 1920s America, a quaint place where people called traffic circles rotaries and milk shakes frappes. Massachusetts has since changed, and nowhere more than in Cambridge. As universities and high-tech have become driving forces of economic growth, Cambridge has gone glitzy, with trendy restaurants and high-priced hotels, boutiques and upscale condominiums. Greater Boston may well have the heaviest concentration of graduate students and post-graduate hangers-on of any major city, and their world is centered on Cambridge, with outposts in low-income Somerville, tenured-faculty haven Belmont, Boston's Back Bay and Allston and Brighton near the Harvard Business School.

Cambridge is the center, and the rest of these communities are part, of Massachusetts's 8th Congressional District, a district with great historic sites from the gold dome of the State House on Beacon Hill to the frigate *Constitution* in the Charlestown docks; a district which, with MIT and the software concentration in Cambridge's once downscale Lechmere Square, is one of the high-tech capitals of America. Redistricting has added the impoverished suburb of Chelsea, whose public schools were taken over by Boston University, and much of the Roxbury black ghetto in Boston; this is by far the most Democratic district in Massachusetts. It has the further distinction of having elected as its two previous congressmen President John F. Kennedy and Speaker Thomas P. O'Neill.

The current congressman is Joseph P. Kennedy II, elected when O'Neill retired in 1986. He is the oldest son of the late Robert Kennedy, and won largely because of affection and veneration for his family. Before 1986, he was living on the South Shore and running the energy corporation he set up which bought oil in bulk and distributed it to low-income citizens. But when O'Neill announced his retirement, and half a dozen leftish candidates with various local bases filed, Kennedy ran, leading some of the other candidates to withdraw. Cambridge state senator George Bachrach made the mistake of charging Kennedy with having ties with Qaddafi's Libya, while O'Neill endorsed Kennedy; before that Kennedy had been running only even in the polls, but he beat Bachrach 52%–30%.

Like his uncle, Senator Edward Kennedy, Joe Kennedy seems to see himself as a tribune of the poor, and three-decker house working-class as well; he was politically adroit enough in the 1986 campaign to temper his liberalism with stands like supporting capital punishment. He oscillates between the boyish impulsiveness of a man who has never had to pay for his mistakes, and a determination to work hard and make a serious record as a mature politician; his admirers insist that he is now very little of the first and much of the second. He has had some disappointments, and perhaps been chastened by them: he lost a seat he expected to win on the Energy and Commerce Committee in 1987. But he has used his Banking Committee seat to some advantage, and in 1993 gave up a chance for a spot on Ways and Means to become Chairman of the Consumer Credit and Insurance Subcommittee. It also helped that he had support from Banking Chairman Henry Gonzalez, grateful that Kennedy warned him of Bruce Vento's last-minute campaign against him for chairman in the December 1990 Democratic Caucus. Kennedy has produced some marginal changes in housing bills, and has spotlighted what he considers "redlining" and racial bias in lending practices (there is some dispute as to whether studies have proven bias exists). Clearly he is setting up a framework for intervention in credit and insurance markets to combat possible racial discrimination. He has also sponsored laws to encourage non-profit groups to build more housing and to increase the pay of nurses in veterans' hospitals. His subcommittee chair gives him jurisdiction over coinage and, as David Warsh of the *Boston Globe* points out, an opportunity to rationalize American money by introducing a usable dollar coin and $2 bill and phase out the penny.

Kennedy has long been seen as a candidate for statewide office. But he made no move to run for governor in 1990 and, after encouraging speculation, announced in February 1993 that he would not run against Governor William Weld in 1994, though polls showed them running about even. Now some speculate on whether he will run for his uncle's Senate seat in 2000, but that is pretty far down the pike. In the meantime, he has a job which suits his advocacy temperament and a committee position where he can do constructive work. It is possible also that he has learned to refrain from the extravagant stances he has taken on some issues. Long critical of British policy in Northern Ireland, he suggested that the British army there is an occupying alien force; in fact, as such Irish-American politicians as Daniel Patrick Moynihan, Tip O'Neill and Edward Kennedy have understood, many residents of Northern Ireland want to stay part of the United Kingdom and want the British Army there for protection against terrorists. Joe Kennedy's boycott of Queen Elizabeth's speech to Congress in 1991 was a childish gesture. So too were Kennedy's words in the Gulf war debate, "Are we to be the international police force, the bully boys of the world?" It is odd for an American leader to suggest, just as the United States has helped overthrow Communism in Eastern Europe and the Soviet Union, that this country is the villain in the world order—a view perhaps still congenial in parts of the 8th District, but not many places elsewhere in the world. His more recent work on foreign policy shows a steadier compass: he has worked to get humanitarian aid to Armenia (there's a big Armenian community in Watertown, west of Cambridge), he has been a supporter of the Aristide government in Haiti, he traveled to Germany in 1992 and urged a crackdown on right-wing violence.

The People: Pop. 1990: 602,396; 11% age 65+; 61% White; 23% Black; 6% Asian; 5% Other; 10% Hispanic origin. Voting age pop.: 495,171; 20% Black; 9% Hispanic origin. Households: 32% married couple families; 13% married couple fams. w. children; 53% college educ.; median household income: $30,417; per capita income: $16,327; median gross rent: $636; median house value: $188,200.

1992 Presidential Vote			1988 Presidential Vote		
Clinton (D)	136,438	(67%)	Dukakis (D)	145,843	(72%)
Bush (R)	39,368	(19%)	Bush (R)	57,591	(28%)
Perot (I)	25,423	(13%)			

Rep. Joseph P. Kennedy, II (D)

Elected 1986; b. Sept. 24, 1952, Brighton; home, Brighton; U. of MA, B.A. 1976; Catholic; divorced.

Career: Community Svcs. Admin., 1977–79; Founder and Pres., Citizens Energy Corp., 1979–86, Citizens Conservation Corp., 1981.

Offices: 1210 LHOB 20515, 202-225-5111. Also Schrafft Ctr., 529 Main St., Charlestown 02129, 617-242-0200.

Committees: *Banking, Finance and Urban Affairs* (8th of 30 D): Consumer Credit and Insurance (Chmn.); Financial Institutions Supervision, Regulation and Deposit Insurance; International Development, Finance, Trade and Monetary Policy. *Veterans' Affairs* (8th of 21 D): Hospitals and Health Care.

Group Ratings

	ADA	ACLU	COPE	CDF	CFA	LCV	ACU	NTLC	NSI	COC	CEI
1992	95	91	83	100	100	100	8	0	50	25	15
1991	95	—	100	90	94	92	0	—	—	20	8

National Journal Ratings

	1991 LIB — 1991 CONS		1992 LIB — 1992 CONS	
Economic	88% —	0%	83% —	13%
Social	78% —	17%	92% —	0%
Foreign	87% —	8%	90% —	0%

Key Votes of the 102d Congress

1. Ban Striker Replace	FOR	5. Handgun Wait/7-Day	FOR	9. Use Force in Gulf	AGN
2. $ for Homeownership	AGN	6. Overseas Mil. Abortion	FOR	10. US Mil. Abroad $ Cut	FOR
3. Tax Rich/Cut Mid Cls.	FOR	7. Obscn. Art NEA $ Ban	FOR	11. Limit SDI Funds	FOR
4. FY93/$15B Def. Cut	FOR	8. Death Pen. from Jury	AGN	12. Cuba Trade Embargo	AGN

Key Votes of the 103d Congress

1. Family Leave	FOR	2. Deficit Reduction	FOR	3. Stimulus Plan	FOR

Election Results

1992 general	Joseph P. Kennedy, II (D)............. 149,903	(83%)	($767,161)
	Alice Harriett Nakash (I)............... 30,402	(17%)	
1992 primary	Joseph P. Kennedy, II (D)............... 45,993	(81%)	
	Charles Calvin Yancey (D).............. 11,005	(19%)	
1990 general	Joseph P. Kennedy, II (D)............. 125,479	(72%)	($832,815)
	Glenn W. Fiscus (R).................. 39,310	(23%)	
	Susan C. Davies (NAP)................ 8,806	(5%)	

NINTH DISTRICT

The "Hub of the Universe," the elder Oliver Wendell Holmes called it in the 19th Century, and it was again for a moment in the 1988 campaign when Michael Dukakis, who prided himself on commuting every day on Boston's T, was running his presidential campaign from a spanking new office building two blocks from Boston Common. Dukakis's Boston was very different from the Boston to which Joseph P. Kennedy, long a resident of New York, sent his sons to run for office in the 1940s. Boston then was a gray city with no new buildings and dust on every windowsill; the sky was dark with pollution and the air was thick with ancient Yankee and Irish animosity. The big office buildings were full of Yankees seeking safe investments for their old family fortunes; the State House and City Hall were full of Irishmen, scampering after good patronage jobs and regaling each other with political battle stories. Today, that Boston is mostly gone. The new skyscrapers are full of venture capitalists and lawyers of every ethnic description, looking for a turn-up in the high-tech economy; the advertising slogans crackle with a sauciness and *double entendre* you can find only here and maybe in New York and Los Angeles.

Most of Boston's neighborhoods have changed. There are still vestiges of the old Irish neighborhoods, as in South Boston, but the central city is increasingly populated by blacks and young singles; its population is down from 801,000 in 1950 to 574,000 in 1990; over 80% of the metropolitan area is in the suburbs. The 9th Congressional District, historically anchored in Boston, has followed the move, and today only one-third of its residents are in Boston, mostly in still-Irish areas of South Boston, Hyde Park and West Roxbury. From there, the 9th heads southwest to Easton and the Patriots Stadium, southeast to Braintree, ancestral home of the Adamses, Brockton, the old shoe manufacturing town, and the old textile mill town of Taunton. Politically, it is Democratic, but not overwhelmingly so for the descendant of a district which for 45 years was represented by Speaker of the House John McCormack.

The current congressman from the 9th is Joe Moakley, chairman of the House Rules Committee, an old Boston Irish pol who grew up in South Boston and still lives there, has an Irish face and a thick accent, shuns publicity for the most part, and remains close to the Catholic Church. Seemingly mild-mannered, he volunteered for the Navy at 15. He served in both houses of the Massachusetts legislature and on the Boston Council; in 1972, after losing the 1970 primary for this seat, he ran in the general as an Independent against anti-busing advocate Louise Day Hicks, and narrowly won. The next term he got a seat on the Rules Committee, where he was clearly Tip O'Neill's man; he is not, however, especially close to the Kennedys (he backed Edward McCormack, the speaker's nephew, against Edward Kennedy in the 1962 Senate primary). On the back benches in the 1970s, he moved up quickly in seniority and became chairman when Claude Pepper died in June 1989. His one great cause has been El Salvador, on which he took the approach of Catholic liberation theologians: acquainted with some of the nuns and priests who were murdered there, he worked to cut off military aid to the Salvadoran government and to grant refugee protection to Salvadorans in the United States. He headed a commission which in 1992 reported that some high-ranking Salvadoran military officials were involved in murder. As Rules chairman, Moakley has worked closely with Speaker Thomas Foley and Majority Leader Dick Gephardt; he helped Whip David Bonior, also a

624   MASSACHUSETTS

Catholic deeply opposed to U.S. Central American policy, win his leadership post. Under their lead, Rules has increasingly limited amendments and debate, to the fury of the outnumbered Republicans.

Moakley also works on more mundane matters, such as channeling federal money to the Central Artery rebuilding (the most expensive highway project in the country), Boston Harbor cleanup and a federal courthouse on Fan Pier. He was especially active in placing Massachusetts members on key committees in 1993. Moakley has been easily reelected every two years and any problems he might have had with redistricting were smoothed out by his longtime South Boston friend, state Senate President Billy Bulger.

The People: Pop. 1990: 601,250; 2% rural; 15% age 65+; 86% White; 7% Black; 3% Asian; 3% Other; 5% Hispanic origin. Voting age pop.: 472,589; 6% Black; 4% Hispanic origin. Households: 51% married couple families; 22% married couple fams. w. children; 50% college educ.; median household income: $38,646; per capita income: $17,980; median gross rent: $616; median house value: $172,000.

1992 Presidential Vote			1988 Presidential Vote		
Clinton (D)	131,644	(48%)	Dukakis (D)	140,852	(52%)
Bush (R)	85,901	(31%)	Bush (R)	127,638	(48%)
Perot (I)	56,431	(21%)			

Rep. John Joseph (Joe) Moakley (D)

Elected 1972; b. Apr. 27, 1927, Boston; home, Boston; U. of Miami, Suffolk U., LL.B. 1956; Catholic; married (Evelyn).

Career: Navy, 1943–46 (WWII); MA House of Reps., 1953–65, Majority Whip, 1957; Practicing atty., 1957–72; MA Senate, 1965–69; Boston City Cncl., 1971.

Offices: 235 CHOB 20515, 202-225-8273. Also 4 Court St., Taunton 02780, 617-824-6676; and World Trade Ctr., #220, Boston 02210, 617-565-2920.

Committees: *Rules* (Chmn. of 9 D): The Legislative Process; Rules of the House.

Group Ratings

	ADA	ACLU	COPE	CDF	CFA	LCV	ACU	NTLC	NSI	COC	CEI
1992	85	82	92	100	93	50	4	5	30	25	6
1991	90	—	100	100	78	54	5	—	—	20	7

National Journal Ratings

	1991 LIB — 1991 CONS		1992 LIB — 1992 CONS	
Economic	88% —	0%	91% —	0%
Social	68% —	31%	72% —	28%
Foreign	92% —	0%	86% —	14%

Key Votes of the 102d Congress

1. Ban Striker Replace	FOR	5. Handgun Wait/7-Day	FOR	9. Use Force in Gulf	AGN
2. $ for Homeownership	AGN	6. Overseas Mil. Abortion	AGN	10. US Mil. Abroad $ Cut	FOR
3. Tax Rich/Cut Mid Cls.	FOR	7. Obscn. Art NEA $ Ban	FOR	11. Limit SDI Funds	FOR
4. FY93/$15B Def. Cut	FOR	8. Death Pen. from Jury	AGN	12. Cuba Trade Embargo	AGN

Key Votes of the 103d Congress

1. Family Leave	FOR	2. Deficit Reduction	FOR	3. Stimulus Plan	FOR

Election Results

1992 general	John Joseph (Joe) Moakley (D)	175,550	(69%)	($1,056,446)
	Martin B. Conboy (R).................	54,291	(21%)	($12,616)
	Lawrence C. Mackin (I)...............	15,637	(6%)	
	Others	8,156	(3%)	
1992 primary	John Joseph (Joe) Moakley (D), unopposed			
1990 general	John Joseph (Joe) Moakley (D)	124,534	(70%)	($318,347)
	Robert W. Horan (R)	52,660	(30%)	

TENTH DISTRICT

The South Shore of Massachusetts Bay, from Boston southward to Plymouth and then down Cape Cod (there is a lot of dispute about which way is up and down on the Cape), is Massachusetts's oldest-settled territory and the site of its fastest-growing new communities. The Pilgrims landed here at Plymouth Rock in 1620; this stony land was farmed by John Adams's father, who was anything but the aristocrat some later members of the Adams family would have you believe. Daniel Webster lived in the South Shore town of Marshfield, today a high-income suburb of Boston far out the usually clogged Southeast Expressway; Joseph P. Kennedy used to summer with his young family on Nantasket Beach in Hull, and then moved out of Massachusetts when the Yankees wouldn't let them into their beach club in Cohasset in the 1920s. The Plymouth area and Cape Cod were originally farming country, with some industry; a railroad, now long-gone, steamed up the middle of the Cape. Provincetown (at the tip of the Cape) was and still is a fishing port, and also one of the major gay vacation areas in the country; the islands of Martha's Vineyard and Nantucket, rich whaling ports in the early 19th Century, are now favored summer resorts for the trendy liberal rich of New York and Washington. Cape Cod is the site of the bogs which still produce half of America's cranberries, but it is also filled increasingly with retirees enjoying the relatively equable year-round climates and, to some longtime residents' dismay, is the fastest-growing part of Massachusetts. The South Shore and the Cape were once exclusively Protestant and Yankee, but in the Massachusetts way it has changed over the years, with Irish and Italian surnames as common as Yankee and the descendants of the Portuguese Azorean fishermen fanning out into the countryside.

Gerry Studds has been congressman from parts of the South Shore and the Cape for more than 20 years. His first name is pronounced Gary, a reminder that he is descended from Elbridge Gerry, fifth vice president of the United States and creator of the original gerrymander; Gerry Studds was a Foreign Service officer who landed a post in the Kennedy White House, then was a New Hampshire prep school teacher and a top volunteer for Eugene McCarthy in 1968, a career path more typical in today's House than imaginable at the time. He returned home and ran for the 10th District seat in 1970 and nearly won; in 1972, to woo the large Portuguese fisherman population in New Bedford, then in the district, he learned Portuguese, and won an ancestrally Republican seat in a nationally Republican year. Studds later got a seat on the Foreign Affairs Committee, where he was one of the most liberal members, convinced that almost any American intervention abroad is dangerous for us and harmful for others. But he started off first on Merchant Marine and Fisheries, a body shunned by most members but of obvious importance to a coastal and fishing district. In his first term, he successfully sponsored legislation to extend U.S. territorial waters out to 200 miles, a great achievement; in the years since, he has taken this seemingly humdrum assignment and made important public policy and immense political capital out of it. The political capital came in handy in 1983, when Studds was censured for having had sex with a 17-year-old page 10 years earlier; under House rules, Studds lost his

Merchant Marine subcommittee chairmanship, and many thought he could not be reelected. With characteristic stubbornness, Studds maintained he had done nothing wrong, and won reelection by beating two serious opponents, Plymouth Sheriff Peter Flynn 61%–34% in the 1984 primary and Republican Lewis Crampton 56%–44% in the general.

Studds became Merchant Marine chairman in 1993, after working on many issues in the intervening years; despite his earlier censure, his succession after the death of Walter Jones was uncontroversial, presumably because of his hard work and competence. Evidently preferring the relative anonymity and local relevance of the committee's work, he had turned down a Foreign Affairs subcommittee chair for one on Merchant Marine in 1987, and in 1993 rotated off Foreign Affairs altogether (though he did pick up a low-seniority post on the important Energy and Commerce Committee). On the Fisheries Subcommittee, he helped shape the oil spill bill passed after the 1989 Exxon *Valdez* disaster in Alaska, and pushed successfully for a moratorium on oil drilling in the Georges Bank along the New England Coast until after 2000. He is tough enough to push a bill halting federal flood insurance of most offshore barrier islands (let them build at their own risk, he says), and idealistic enough to spend time on a bill to preserve the environment in Antarctica. He has passed through the House useful legislation penalizing prank distress calls to the Coast Guard and, working with Alaska Republican Don Young and the maritime industry, for stronger federal inspection of seafood. He pushed through a law to ban from U.S. ports for five years boats that use large-scale drift nets, which kill thousands of dolphins and sea tortoises. He put pressure on the Coast Guard not to allow a speech by cultural conservative Gary Bauer at a Coast Guard prayer breakfast, an unfortunate use of congressional power since Bauer, like Studds, is a public-spirited and principled man who champions causes that are often not popular. Studds wants to protect the Pacific yew, a tree whose bark is the source of a promising anti-cancer drug, and he will be one of the lead forces on reauthorization of the Endangered Species Act; he is strongly for preserving species, even at considerable economic cost. On other issues, for years he pushed to stop U.S. aid to El Salvador; on Energy and Commerce's Health Subcommittee, he has backed single-payer national health insurance.

In the anti-incumbent mood of 1990, Studds suddenly found himself in political trouble. Jon Bryan, an airline pilot and strong conservative whom he had beaten with 67% in 1988, was running hard against the congressional pay raise and contrasting his own support of "family values" with his assertion that Studds is not "an honorable man." And in Massachusetts, the mood was aimed not just at incumbents generally, but specifically at incumbents associated with what most voters considered the dismally failed politics of Michael Dukakis—Studds's percentage fell to 53%. Redistricting was an additional problem in 1992, even though Studds's district grew more than any other. The catalyst for the plan was the retirement of Brian Donnelly of the next-door 11th District; a Boston-based member of Ways and Means, Donnelly had plenty of support in the legislature, but suddenly in March 1992 opted out of the race. As a result, much of the old 11th was appended to Studds's 10th, including the blue-collar cities of Quincy, Weymouth and part of Brockton, while Studds lost New Bedford and the surrounding area, which provided key votes for him in 1990, to Barney Frank's 4th District. But Studds got a break when Bryan decided to run as an Independent while the Republican nomination was won by Dan Daly, an appointee of Governor William Weld. More important than the split opposition was Studds's affirmative strength. He won 61% of the vote district-wide, enough for a solid victory against united opposition, to 24% for Daly and 13% for Bryan. Studds's percentages were over 90% in some towns on the Cape and the Vineyard. With such a splendid showing in one of Massachusetts's more Republican districts, Studds will be hard to beat or even to challenge seriously in the years ahead.

The People: Pop. 1990: 601,510; 27% rural; 16% age 65+; 95% White; 2% Black; 1% Asian; 1% Other; 1% Hispanic origin. Voting age pop.: 466,334; 2% Black; 1% Hispanic origin. Households: 56% married

couple families; 24% married couple fams. w. children; 54% college educ.; median household income: $37,489; per capita income: $17,535; median gross rent: $651; median house value: $163,200.

1992 Presidential Vote			1988 Presidential Vote		
Clinton (D)	133,601	(42%)	Bush (R)	150,566	(51%)
Bush (R)	101,798	(32%)	Dukakis (D)	145,026	(49%)
Perot (I)	80,654	(25%)			

Rep. Gerry E. Studds (D)

Elected 1972; b. May 12, 1937, Mineola, NY; home, Cohasset; Yale, B.A. 1959, M.A. 1961; Episcopalian; single.

Career: U.S. Foreign Svc., 1961–63; Exec. Asst., Domestic Peace Corps, 1963; Legis. Asst., U.S. Sen. Harrison Williams, 1964; High schl. teacher, 1965–69.

Offices: 237 CHOB 20515, 202-225-3111. Also 1212 Hancock St., Quincy 02169, 617-770-3700; 146 Main St., Hyannis 02601, 508-771-0666; 166 Main St., Fed. Bldg., Brockton 02401, 508-584-6666; and 225 Water St., Plymouth 02360, 508-747-5500.

Committees: *Energy and Commerce* (19th of 27 D): Health and the Environment; Transportation and Hazardous Materials. *Merchant Marine and Fisheries* (Chmn. of 29 D): Environment and Natural Resources (Chmn.).

Group Ratings

	ADA	ACLU	COPE	CDF	CFA	LCV	ACU	NTLC	NSI	COC	CEI
1992	100	100	83	100	100	88	0	0	20	25	12
1991	90	—	100	100	89	85	0	—	—	20	11

National Journal Ratings

	1991 LIB — 1991 CONS		1992 LIB — 1992 CONS	
Economic	88%	— 0%	87%	— 12%
Social	88%	— 0%	88%	— 8%
Foreign	85%	— 15%	90%	— 0%

Key Votes of the 102d Congress

1. Ban Striker Replace	FOR	5. Handgun Wait/7-Day	FOR	9. Use Force in Gulf	AGN
2. $ for Homeownership	*	6. Overseas Mil. Abortion	FOR	10. US Mil. Abroad $ Cut	FOR
3. Tax Rich/Cut Mid Cls.	FOR	7. Obscn. Art NEA $ Ban	AGN	11. Limit SDI Funds	FOR
4. FY93/$15B Def. Cut	FOR	8. Death Pen. from Jury	AGN	12. Cuba Trade Embargo	AGN

Key Votes of the 103d Congress

1. Family Leave	FOR	2. Deficit Reduction	FOR	3. Stimulus Plan	FOR

Election Results

1992 general	Gerry E. Studds (D)	189,342	(61%)	($1,440,376)
	Daniel W. Daly (R)	75,887	(24%)	($238,739)
	Jon L. Bryan (I)	39,265	(13%)	($230,617)
	Others	7,156	(2%)	
1992 primary	Gerry E. Studds (D)	576,640	(61%)	
	Paul D. Harold (D)	34,280	(36%)	
	Others	3,320	(3%)	
1990 general	Gerry E. Studds (D)	137,805	(53%)	($620,387)
	Jon L. Bryan (R)	120,217	(47%)	($271,902)

MICHIGAN

Michigan has become a kind of laboratory of reform, a place for testing ways to move from an industrial to a post-industrial economy, from domination by big units—big business, big labor, big government—to learning that growth increasingly comes from small units—small businesses, individual workers, flexible government. It is a laboratory all the more meaningful because Michigan, once a solidly Republican state and then strongly Democratic, has become a political bellwether, voting within 0.8% of the national average in the last three presidential elections. But Michigan did not volunteer for this laboratory role; it was thrust on the state by an economic cataclysm the likes of which few states have suffered. As recently as 15 years ago, this was the Motor State: home of the Big Three auto companies, which had emerged as such in the mid-1920s; headquarters of the United Auto Workers, the bargaining agent for most auto workers and a progressive force in politics since 1937. Only marginal changes—and seemingly never-ending growth—characterized this industry. There had been no major technological changes in American autos from 1940, when the automatic transmission was introduced, until the 1970s, when the companies were forced to invent new technology to meet government anti-pollution standards. And as Americans grew more affluent, as one-car households became two-car households, as consumers had more disposable income and could afford cars that gave them more than basic transportation, the U.S. auto industry prospered, and Michigan along with it. Michigan was the fastest growing state in the Midwest from 1940 to 1965. Michigan incomes grew even faster, and except for Illinois, with its big Chicago white-collar job base, Michigan had the highest incomes in the Midwest. With the Great Lakes and north woods not far away on the freeways, Michigan had developed a comfortable way of life—for many low-skill workers, perhaps as affluent and pleasant a life as any in history.

Then, quite abruptly with the 1979 oil shock, this big-unit economy went bust. It became startlingly clear that the Big Three and the UAW did not have a captive market, that Americans did not *have* to buy a new full-sized, American-made car every two or three years, that foreign competitors were producing better and cheaper cars more responsive to changes in consumer preference. The business and labor big units, so well-adapted for growth in the quarter century after World War II started, proved poorly adapted for the quarter century that followed. Auto employment in Michigan fell from 437,000 in October 1978 to 289,000 in October 1982. Chrysler nearly went bankrupt, Ford was in financial difficulty, General Motors had its first losses in years. Workers came to the end of their 65 weeks of unemployment benefits; housing prices in factory areas plummeted; hundreds of thousands left. As the recession passed, auto employment settled at 280,000, and wages and fringe benefits declined.

Once upon a time, it would have been easy to predict the political effect of such an economic catastrophe: a surge of votes for Michigan's liberal Democrats. For that was the rule of thumb in Michigan's big unit years, from a political history determined by the clashes of two rushes of immigration. The first started in the 1830s with the settlement of what had been a peninsula overgrown with trees (lumber was the first industry on which Michigan over-relied); the second started around 1910 with the growth of the auto industry. The first settlers cut down trees and built farms; Michigan was the prime lumber producing state in the late 19th Century, and Muskegon the "lumber queen of the world"; forests were clear-cut or swept by blazes like the 1881 fire that burned out half the Thumb (look at the map; it's obvious). The farmers, mostly from Upstate New York and New England, proved a taming force: this was part of the vast westward migration of believers in learning and founders of colleges, reformers who hated slavery, manned the underground railroad, and promoted temperance—civilizing influences that in the 1850s made Michigan the first state to ban capital punishment. Michigan was one of the birthplaces of the Republican Party, founded in Jackson in 1854, which swept the state in the elections later that year. Up through the 1920s, Michigan was one of the most Republican states in the nation.

The auto industry drew labor from outstate Michigan and southern Ontario and from the farms of Ohio and Indiana; it brought whites from the Kentucky and Tennessee mountains and (mostly after 1940) blacks from Alabama and Mississippi. But during the three decades when Detroit was a boom town—the nation's fastest growing big city after Los Angeles (the three-county metro area grew from 426,000 to 2.2 million from 1900 to 1930)—it was also a leading immigrant destination. Michigan was mostly a native stock state before 1900, leavened by a Dutch colony (the nation's largest) around Grand Rapids and Holland, and Finns in the mining towns of the Upper Peninsula. But Detroit attracted Poles and Italians, Hungarians and Belgians, Greeks and Jews.

This sudden influx of a polyglot proletariat changed Michigan's politics. The catalyst was the Great Depression of the 1930s, and the impetus came from company managers' desire to use machines efficiently and subsequent treatment of employees mechanically and with great distrust. The result was the 1937 sit-down strikes organized by the new United Auto Workers; management and labor fought, sometimes literally, for shares of what both sides thought was a static-sized pie. The UAW won, and organized most of the companies after Democratic Governor Frank Murphy refused to send in troops to break the illegal strikes. In the years that followed, auto workers became a heavily Democratic voting block.

Michigan politics, during its big-unit years, was a species of class warfare, conducted with a bitterness that split families and neighbors. The union won, but many grew to resent its tactics and success: Murphy's Democrats lost the 1938 elections, not only statewide but in Flint, and Republicans won most contests for nearly 20 years after. But demographics benefited the Democrats: auto workers and post-1900 immigrants produced more children than did outstate Yankees or management. After Walter Reuther's election as UAW president in 1947, voters elected young, liberal G. Mennen Williams governor in 1948; by 1954 the Democrats, closely tied to the UAW, seemed to have become the natural majority in the state. And as growth continued, economic issues became less bitter; by the early 1960s, the class-warfare atmosphere had dissipated. Republican and former auto executive George Romney was narrowly elected governor in 1962, while Henry Ford II joined Walter Reuther in backing Lyndon Johnson in 1964. Romney and his successor, William Milliken, accepted the welfare state policies endorsed by the UAW leadership and the Democrats. The state government was one of the nation's most generous, and not just to the poor and the unemployed: it supported one of the nation's most distinguished and extensive higher education systems, built state parks and recreation areas, and pioneered efforts to end racial discrimination.

The collapse of the big unit economy after 1979 changed all that, and forced the state to change. The first to try to adapt was Governor James Blanchard, a Democrat elected in 1982 with a record of supporting big units: his major achievement in eight years in Congress was managing the Chrysler bailout in the House. Blanchard was elected in a familiar pattern: his

KEWEENAW

ONTONAGON
HOUGHTON
GOGEBIC
BARAGA
IRON
MARQUETTE
DICKINSON
MENOMINEE
DELTA
ALGER
SCHOOLCRAFT
MACKINAC
LUCE
CHIPPEWA

1

EMMET
CHARLEVOIX
CHEBOYGAN
PRESQUE ISLE
ANTRIM
OTSEGO
MONTMORENCY
ALPENA
LEELANAU
GRAND TRAVERSE
KALKASKA
CRAWFORD
OSCODA
ALCONA
BENZIE
MANISTEE
WEXFORD
MISSAUKEE
ROSCOMMON
OGEMAW
IOSCO
MASON
LAKE
OSCEOLA
CLARE
GLADWIN
ARENAC
HURON
OCEANA
NEWAYGO
MECOSTA
ISABELLA
MIDLAND
BAY
TUSCOLA
SANILAC
MUSKEGON
KENT
MONTCALM
GRATIOT
SAGINAW
GENESEE
LAPEER
ST. CLAIR
OTTAWA
IONIA
CLINTON
SHIAWASSEE
Flint 9
OAKLAND
MACOMB
10
Grand Rapids
ALLEGAN
BARRY
EATON
INGHAM
LIVINGSTON
Lansing
8
11
Warren
Detroit
VAN BUREN
CALHOUN
JACKSON
WASHTENAW
Wayne
12, 14-15
KALAMAZOO
7
13
16
6
CASS
ST. JOSEPH
BRANCH
HILLSDALE
LENAWEE
MONROE
BERRIEN

2
3
4
5

Miles

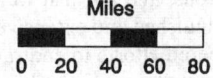

0   20   40   60   80

51% statewide came from 58% in tri-county metro Detroit and 46% in Outstate Michigan, regional differences going back to the era of class-conscious politics, when the UAW and its Democratic allies registered tens of thousands of working-class voters in the Detroit area and carried what was otherwise a Republican state. But cultural differences eroded those patterns in presidential voting in the 1980s, as did Blanchard's experimentation. Blanchard did raise taxes in 1983, but only once, and was chastised by losing the state Senate. But Blanchard worked to build a small unit economy; he was proud of his efforts to stimulate high-skill, capital-intensive, flexible manufacturing, and used $750 million of state pension funds as venture capital for manufacturers of items from tape drives for microcomputers to fiberglass coffins. Dodging his traditional labor allies, Blanchard made it clear that Michigan must learn how to nurture growth and that workers, instead of seeking more vacations and earlier retirements, would have to hustle and work harder than ever before. Yet another approach came from John Engler, the state Senate majority leader who beat Blanchard in 1990. Engler believes in less government activism and industrial policy; he has cut or held the line on every state program but education, and believes in school choice. In early 1993, he advanced a plan to cut property taxes by raising the sales tax, but his basic strategy is to lower taxes and trust markets to produce growth. This view did not prove persuasive to Michigan voters in the 1992 presidential race, when they voted for Bill Clinton, and the tax proposal was defeated in June 1993. But voters also defeated Democratic House Speaker Lew Dodak and deadlocked the once overwhelmingly Democratic House 55–55.

In choosing between these two strategies for small-unit growth, Michigan has not been divided on the old class divisions or metro-Outstate split. In 1988 George Bush carried not only Outstate (56%–43%) but also the Detroit area (50%–49%); in 1992 Bill Clinton carried not only the Detroit area (49%–35%) but Outstate (40%–37%). Engler's defeat of Blanchard did split the regions, but Engler's 53% Outstate was only a few points higher than his metro Detroit 45%. But new divisions have been created. In the Detroit area, the economically growing regions are voting Republican—almost all of Oakland County, about half of Macomb County (no longer as blue-collar as its reputation), and some of western Wayne County; Macomb, once considered the key to Michigan, went for George Bush in 1992 as it did in 1988 and for John Engler in 1990, but Bush lost the state anyway. Only central city Detroit, 70% black and rapidly losing population because of horrifying crime rates, and a few close-in working class suburbs are solidly Democratic. Outstate, there are Democratic belts: old auto factory concentrations (the Flint-Saginaw-Bay City corridor) with sluggish growth; the university town of Ann Arbor; the capital-university town of Lansing—all those state paychecks. More heavily Republican than ever is the western half of the state, especially Grand Rapids and the resort area around Traverse City and Petoskey, which never were all that dependent on autos and have been growing robustly over the last dozen years.

In partisan terms, this means Michigan is neither a Democratic nor a Republican state. It is experimenting. On the bunsen burners right now are a Democratic president and Congress and a Republican governor and legislature. Both could win Michigan's votes again, if their experiments go well; both could be voted out with a switch of not too many votes, if their work turns out to be a botch. This lab bears watching.

Governor. John Engler may be the prototype of a successful Republican politician: not from a corporate or Ivy League background like Michigan's recent Republican governors, but from a small Outstate town and a graduate of Michigan State. He was first elected to the legislature in 1970, at 22, while still a college senior; he has been in politics literally all his adult life. Yet he is no admirer of government's ability to get things done. In his first two years in office, he relentlessly kept his 1990 campaign promises. He cut the state arts budget, especially the Detroit Institute of Arts. He eliminated General Assistance, a welfare program for able-bodied adults maintained in Michigan and a few other states. He amended welfare to allow AFDC recipients to keep more earnings, and was given an election-year waiver of federal regulations by President Bush. He privatized many public services, much to the chagrin of Michigan's strong public employee unions. Democrats yelped and the *Detroit Free Press* habitually called him "mean-spirited," but a 1991 recall effort against him fell flat.

Engler's 1990 victory was a surprise to almost everyone; he lagged far behind in public polls through late October. But his call for increasing education spending and cutting property taxes 20% was popular, and when Blanchard came forward with his own property tax cut, Engler effectively ridiculed it as saving a nickel a week per taxpayer. His 50%–49% victory was attributed by some to low Detroit turnout resulting from Mayor Coleman Young's dislike of Blanchard; but Detroit has been losing population so rapidly—it has half as many residents as 40 years ago—its turnout naturally declines, and Young's popularity was already falling toward the terminal levels it reached in 1993, his 20th year in office. In 1994, Engler will certainly not lack Democratic opposition. Congressman Howard Wolpe, who retired in 1992 when faced with an overwhelmingly Republican district, is running; state Senator Debbie Stabenow in early 1993 already seemed to be running; Wayne County Executive Ed McNamara and former Congressman Bill Brodhead were also possibilities.

Senators. Senator Donald Riegle in early 1993 was entering his 27th year in Congress, with a wildly varied reputation. To detractors, he is a shameless demagogue, gushing with emotional oratory that panders to his constituents' fears and prejudices, besmirched by his involvement in the Keating Five scandal yet shamelessly retaining his chairmanship of the Banking Committee. To admirers, he is a battler for Michigan's beleaguered working class, for American jobs, against the greedy. Cooler minds have seen Riegle as intense and hard-working, capable of managing legislation competently and of carefully assessing political advantage: a professional politician through and through. Riegle started off as one of the youngest members of the class of Republicans elected in 1966 (George Bush, 14 years older, was another) as a reaction against Lyndon Johnson's Great Society. The 28-year-old son of a Flint small businessman, Riegle was an IBM junior manager who returned home, ran against a complacent Democratic congressman and won. But while most of the class of 1966, like Bush, were cheerleaders for Richard Nixon, Riegle went quite the other way, supporting party rebel Pete McCloskey for president in 1972 and becoming a Democrat in 1973. He fiercely criticized the Vietnam war as Nixon was de-escalating it, and he had moved far enough left on economic issues to get the UAW endorsement in Flint even as a Republican. He won the Democratic nomination for senator in 1976 by out-hustling Secretary of State Richard Austin and Congressman Jim O'Hara, and won the general election over another 1966 Republican, Marvin Esch. Once he made the move from businessman Republican to labor-liberal Democrat, Riegle never looked back. He has compiled a strong liberal record and vitriolicly denounces conservatives. He has looked assiduously after Michigan interests, especially those of its big corporations and unions. In the 1970s he managed the Chrysler bailout bill in the Senate, though he'd been against the Lockheed bailout a few years before, and resisted unsuccessfully the provisions Paul Tsongas put in to make sure Chrysler workers and managers made some sacrifices. He has been a protectionist hawk on trade issues, coming up with the Riegle trade amendment of 1988, which aimed to increase American exports to cut the trade deficit—a compromise, worked out with Chrysler and the UAW among others, and endorsed by Michael Dukakis when he was scrambling to win Michigan's delegates. More recently, Riegle has strenuously opposed the North American Free Trade Agreement, calling it "a jobs program for Mexico" which will cost Americans jobs. He failed to preserve the UDAG program, which provided lots of urban development grants for Michigan; he opposed repeal of the Glass-Steagall Act separating commercial banking from the securities business, which helped him raise record sums from the securities industries for his 1988 campaign.

It was the need to raise money for this campaign that linked Riegle with Charles Keating. Keating owned the Pontchartrain Hotel in downtown Detroit when Riegle first met him in March 1986; Riegle helped the city of Detroit get a $6 million UDAG grant to expand the hotel (a project Keating later dropped). In February 1987, Riegle met with an auditor for Keating's Lincoln S&L and was briefed on its troubles with regulators; on March 6, 1987, he met with FHLBB Chairman Edwin Gray and told him that several western senators had questions about regulators' treatment of Keating. On March 7, Riegle flew to Phoenix and toured Keating's headquarters; a Keating lobbyist later testified (but Riegle denies) that Riegle suggested that the two Arizona senators, DeConcini and McCain, meet with Gray. On March 23, Riegle held a fundraiser at the Pontchartrain, collecting $78,000 in legal contributions from people connected to Keating. Though Riegle didn't attend the April 2 meeting with regulators and the four other senators, he was at an April 9 meeting where all five senators met with Gray and San Francisco-based regulators; DeConcini suggested ways to compromise, but the regulators said they were sending a criminal referral on Lincoln to the Justice Department. After that meeting, Riegle, along with McCain and Glenn, did nothing more for Keating or Lincoln. Weeks later, Gray left office, the Lincoln case was sent from San Francisco to Washington, Keating continued operating Lincoln until April 1989, and the taxpayers ultimately got stuck with more than $2 billion in losses. In February 1988, *The Detroit News* printed many of these facts; in March 1988, Riegle announced he was returning the $78,000; in July 1990, he returned another $120,000 he had received from S&L interests since 1983.

Did Riegle do wrong? That was the question the Senate Ethics Committee pondered in early 1991. For Riegle, it could be said that he only questioned the treatment of a businessman with a major interest in his state, and that he quit doing so as soon as the possibility of criminal activity was raised. But the timing of the contributions—money received early in a campaign cycle, as this was, is marvelously useful in deterring serious competition—together with the timing of the intervention, seems a splendid example of a quid pro quo. Ethics Committee counsel Robert Bennett said, "There is substantial evidence that Senator Riegle played a much greater role than he now recalls" in helping Keating. The Ethics Committee concluded that Riegle had broken no laws or Senate rules, but added that his "conduct gave the appearance of being improper and was certainly attended with insensitivity and poor judgment."

Not all of this was known in November 1988, when Riegle beat Jim Dunn, a shopworn and ineffective candidate, 60%–39%. But by early 1989, Riegle was under attack even as he became chairman of the Banking Committee when it was about to consider the savings and loan bailout. *The Detroit News* and *Ann Arbor News* called for him to resign the chairmanship. Ironically, he was performing skillfully, steering the S&L bailout bill to passage in August 1989, staunching S&L losses and giving a new Resolution Trust Corporation power to seize S&L assets and sell them off, and to investigate wrongdoing. Riegle has followed up with investigations of deposit insurance and calls for a higher, 2% equity capital requirement for banks.

But calm leadership on technical issues did not do much for Riegle's sagging Michigan poll ratings. He made well-publicized efforts to defeat the nominations of Timothy Ryan as RTC head and Robert Clarke as Controller of the Currency. He led a successful fight against Richard Bryan's attempt to impose higher gas mileage (CAFE) standards on the auto industry and bludgeoned the Japanese into buying more U.S.-made vehicles for troops in the Gulf. He led the fight in 1993 to raise the tariff on minivans from 2.5% to 25%, a move that would take money out of the pockets of consumers and give it to Michigan automakers. He proposed that the 12 Federal Reserve Bank Presidents be selected by the president and confirmed by the Senate—an attempt to pressure the Fed toward an easier money policy, even at the risk of inflation. Riegle can point to some serious legislation he sponsored: a National Affordable Housing Act, a HUD Reform Act, an energy bill amendment to keep public utilities from raising rates through self-dealing. But despite his long tenure, he does not carry many votes easily. Although he chairs a Finance health subcommittee, he was not expected in early 1993 to be a major player on healthcare reform.

Riegle was obviously in political trouble early in the 1994 cycle, with job ratings well below 50%. Macomb County Prosecutor Carl Marlinga announced in February 1993 he'd challenge him in the primary and state Senator Lana Pollock indicated she may do so as well. Some Democratic leaders have rallied publicly around Riegle, but few seem enthusiastic about his candidacy. Many Republicans have been eyeing the race. Spencer Abraham, former state party chairman and top aide to Vice President Dan Quayle, announced, bringing his dogged persistence and opposition to taxes which have helped Republicans advance in Michigan since he became chairman a decade ago. Peter Secchia, former ambassador to Italy, brings a political mind even sharper than the political tongue that sometimes gets him in to trouble; his admirers include George Bush and liberal columnist (and Italophile) Mary McGrory. Republican Jim Elsman, a Birmingham attorney, has announced, and so might black minister and Detroit City Republican Councilman Keith Butler; former congressman and 1990 nominee Bill Schuette could be another. Other possibilities include western Michigan Congressman Fred Upton, state Senator Vern Ehlers, and Ronna Romney, a talk show host and former daughter-in-law of past-Governor George Romney. No Republican can count on an automatic victory. The same qualities that got Riegle involved in the Keating Five—hard work, a willingness to help Michigan businesses, a fierce desire to win—should also work for him in 1994. (Though perhaps against: *The Wall Street Journal* charged in December 1992 that Riegle may be skirting his post-Keating Five promise not to accept campaign contributions from financial establishments regulated by his committee, by targeting for support the lawyers and lobbyists associated with these industries.) There can be no doubt, after a quarter-century in politics, that Riegle will work hard to win. So look for a tough race, no matter what the odds.

Senator Carl Levin is a politician for whom character has been as great a political asset as his stands on issues. He won his seat in 1978 by beating an incumbent who announced his retirement and then changed his mind, held it narrowly in 1984 against a challenger who had given a public testimonial for his Japanese car, and won a third term in 1990 despite an ad showing him aboard a battleship he had voted not to commission. Levin is rumpled, unfashionable, speaks articulately but without apparent political artifice and takes unpopular stands on issues he cares about, without much regard for the political consequences: for these virtues, Michigan voters are willing to forgive him a few sins. One passionate issue is capital punishment: Levin began his public career as head of Detroit's public defender office, and has not only opposed capital punishment, but many times has led the fight against it in the Senate. This is in line with Michigan tradition—the state constitution has outlawed the death penalty since 1855—but has become a minority stand as Detroit's murder rate has skyrocketed; but no Republican, certainly not 1990 Senate nominee Bill Schuette, has been able to take many votes away from Levin on this issue. Similarly, Levin's identification with the city of Detroit—he was elected to the Council in 1969 and 1973, one of the few candidates with biracial support—and the unpopularity of Mayor Young have not rubbed off on Levin at all. He can support urban spending programs unpopular in the suburbs with impunity; voters know he has convictions on these issues.

Levin has worked hard on political process. He was chief sponsor of the lobbying regulation bill which passed the Senate early in 1993, stipulating that lobbyists disclose the identities of their clients and their income from them and requiring stringent detailing of government officials that are contacted and issues discussed; it broadens the definition of lobbyist to cover those lobbying the Executive Branch as well as Congress. Levin is also the Senate's chief sponsor of the independent counsel law, which Bill Clinton promised to support but may feel less friendly to now that his administration would be the target. On other domestic issues, Levin maintains positions well within the Michigan consensus. He seeks to use trade sanction provision Super 301 on any nation accounting for more than 15% of the US trade deficit, i.e., Japan—a popular stand in a state obsessed with Japan's success in the auto industry, and he is adamantly opposed to NAFTA. He is surely sympathetic to the Clinton Administration, but in its early months questioned some of its policies.

Levin was one of the first Vietnam doves on the Armed Services Committee where he now ranks third behind Chairman Sam Nunn and James Exon. He characterizes his approach as supportive of basic, reliable weapons systems and conventional forces and skeptical of strategic weapons systems, and he is proud of a 1992 law cutting $3 billion in spending on wasteful Defense Department inventory and purchasing practices.

In 1990, two Republicans came forward to oppose Levin: lawyer Clark Durant, former head of the Legal Services Corporation under Reagan, who had privatized and turned a profit on a government-owned Michigan railroad, ran, but without party establishment or Bush Administration support; and Bill Schuette, three-term congressman from Midland and step-son of the former head of Dow Chemical. Schuette lost metro Detroit to Durant but won 60%–40% in the primary, and launched an attack on Levin which misfired: one of his first post-primary ads showed himself, looking much younger than his 37 years, trying to tie Levin to Donald Riegle's involvement in the S&L scandal. This overstretch cost Schuette credibility later when Levin gave him an opening by running an ad showing Levin in the Persian Gulf on the battleship *Wisconsin*. Schuette accurately pointed out that Levin had voted against the ship's recommissioning in 1985, and noted Levin's vote against the Maverick anti-tank missile also being used successfully in the Gulf. Levin responded by pointing out his support of many technologically more simple weapons, notably the M-1 tank produced in Chrysler's plant in Warren, just north of Detroit, and ran an ad showing a retired Reagan Administration Pentagon official saluting Levin for critically assaying defense spending requests. Levin won a comparatively easy 57%–41% victory, carrying outstate Michigan for the first time; his only weak area was the economically vibrant western Michigan region around Grand Rapids.

Presidential politics. Michigan, a bellwether state now for three presidential elections in a row, with 18 electoral votes which, if declining, is still the eighth largest state, and an obvious target for candidates of both parties. Bill Clinton visited Michigan 18 times in 1992 and came back in February 1993 for his much-heralded first television call-in show; its host, Bill Bonds, who over the last 25 years has been the number one anchor in the Detroit media market, is one of the nation's key political journalists. In the campaign, Republicans claimed Al Gore's positions in *Earth in the Balance* would cost thousands of auto jobs (though Bush had pushed the Clean Air Act); Democrats argued that George Bush's NAFTA would hurt Michigan (though Bill Clinton came out for it in September 1992). Campaigns cut special spots, and Macomb County—with frequent campaign appearances and with Detroit television airing every national ad—may have been the best single location from which to witness the campaign.

Having stumbled and tripped and fallen trying different ways of choosing its presidential delegates, Michigan finally opted in 1992 for having both parties run straight primaries, and scheduled them for March 17, the same day as Illinois and a week after Super Tuesday. This was in fact the day both parties' nominations were decided and, if Illinois was more crucial, Michigan was still part of the mix. That was a lot better than 1988, when Michigan was an irrelevant farce: the Republican state convention was controlled by precinct delegates elected in 1986, and the main question was whether Bush strategists could wheedle enough Kemp delegates away from their alliance with Pat Robertson (they could). Democrats held a "firehouse primary," in just few dozen polling places, in which blacks cast some 45% of the votes, many arriving by the dozen in church buses, and Jesse Jackson won a victory misinterpreted by the press as an alliance of white blue-collar workers and blacks.

The Michigan 1992 primary contest was seized upon by underdogs of both parties who found Illinois too daunting. Jerry Brown came to Willow Run, where General Motors had announced the closure of an assembly plant after losing a much publicized contest with another in Arlington, Texas, and donned a UAW jacket, which he wore every time he appeared in Michigan afterwards, hoping to gain some of the union organizers who had earlier backed Tom Harkin. Paul Tsongas came in briefly, hoping to carry the affluent suburbs here. But Bill Clinton was far stronger, and won 51% of the vote to Brown's 26% and Tsongas's 17%; the latter two did best in the Ann Arbor area, home of the University of Michigan, where Brown finished first and Tsongas tied for second.

On the Republican side, Pat Buchanan got it into his head that Michigan's rebellious auto workers were ready to come over to his side. The Sunday before the primary he motorcaded from Bay City to Saginaw to Flint, a hopelessly Democratic area, and then made the mistake of appearing outside UAW Local 599 in Flint, where he was roundly jeered; memories of the sitdown strikes of 1937 are still fresh in these precincts, and there is no place in America more partisanly anti-Republican. Buchanan lost to George Bush 67%–25%.

Congressional districting. Michigan lost one House seat after the 1980 Census and two after the 1990 Census; it is now down to 16, the same as after the 1930 Census. Since control of the legislature was divided, there was a race to the courthouse, and the case was assigned to a federal court panel 2–1 Republican-appointed. Both parties submitted plans, even though for the Democrats that meant resolving the game of musical chairs against some of their own. The court rejected both plans as "excessively partisan" and drew one of its own, with regular-shaped districts and two black-majority seats (which took some doing, because Detroit lost so much population). It was not very polite to incumbents, however, and not just because it renumbered the districts so that only John Dingell had the same number as before (no one messes with John Dingell). Democrat Howard Wolpe, redistricted into the hopelessly Republican 7th District, decided to retire; so did Carl Pursell, who would have had some chance against Democratic incumbent William Ford in the new 13th, but opted out. Democrats Sander Levin and Dennis Hertel were knocked into the same Oakland-Macomb district, as they were in both parties' plans; Hertel decided to retire at 44. Upper Peninsula Republican Bob Davis, with 878 overdrafts on the House bank, decided to retire and Lower Peninsula Republican Guy Vander Jagt, who gamely defended him, was beaten in the 2d District primary. William Broomfield, one of the two most senior Republicans in the House, and Bob Traxler, an Appropriations subcommittee chairman, both decided to retire. And six Democrats won in November with less than 55%. The result is that today five of the 16-member delegation are freshmen, and several veterans are under warning to pay close heed to their districts. Michigan still has some clout, however, with Whip David Bonior and three House Committee chairmen: John Dingell of Energy and Commerce, William Ford of Education and Labor and John Conyers of Government Operations.

The People: Est. Pop. 1992: 9,437,000; Pop. 1990: 9,295,297, up 1.5% 1990–1992. 3.7% of U.S. total, 8th largest; 29% rural. Median age: 32.6 years. 11.9% 65 years and over. 83.4% White, 13.9% Black, 1.1% Asian, 2.2% Other. Households: 55.1% married couple families; 26% married couple fams. w. children; 44% college educ.; median household income: $31,020; per capita income: $14,154; 71.0% owner occupied housing; median house value: $60,600; median monthly rent: $343. 8.8% Unemployment. Voting age pop. (1990): 6,836,532. Registered voters (1992): 4,341,909; no party registration.

Political Lineup: Governor, John M. Engler (R); Lt. Gov., Connie Binsfeld (R); Secy. of State, Richard H. Austin (D); Atty. Gen., Frank J. Kelley (D); Treasurer, Douglas B. Roberts (R). State Senate, 38 (22 R and 16 D); State House of Representatives, 110 (55 D and 55 R). Senators, Donald W. Riegle, Jr. (D) and Carl Levin (D). Representatives, 16 (10 D and 6 R).

1992 Presidential Vote

Clinton (D)	1,871,182	(44%)
Bush (R)	1,554,940	(36%)
Perot (I)	824,813	(19%)

1992 Democratic Presidential Primary

Clinton	297,280	(51%)
Brown	151,400	(26%)
Tsongas	97,017	(17%)
Uncommitted	27,836	(5%)

1988 Presidential Vote

Bush (R)	1,965,485	(54%)
Dukakis (D)	1,675,783	(46%)

1992 Republican Presidential Primary

Bush	301,948	(67%)
Buchanan	112,122	(25%)
Uncommitted	23,809	(5%)

GOVERNOR

Gov. John M. Engler (R)

Elected 1990, term expires Jan. 1995; b. Oct. 12, 1948, Mount Pleasant; home, Mount Pleasant; MI St. U., B.A. 1971, Cooley Law Schl., J.D. 1981; Catholic; married (Michelle).

Career: MI House of Reps., 1970–76; MI Senate, 1978–1990.

Office: Olds Plaza, 111 S. Capitol, Lansing 48953, 517-373-3400.

Election Results

1990 gen.	John M. Engler (R)	1,276,134	(50%)
	James J. (Jim) Blanchard (D) ..	1,258,539	(49%)
	Other	29,890	(1%)
1990 prim.	John M. Engler (R)	409,747	(87%)
	John Laure (R).............	63,457	(13%)
1986 gen.	James J. (Jim) Blanchard (D) ..	1,632,138	(68%)
	William Lucas (R)	753,647	(31%)

SENATORS

Sen. Donald W. Riegle, Jr. (D)

Elected 1976, seat up 1994; b. Feb. 4, 1938, Flint; home, Flint; Flint Jr. Col., 1956–57, W. MI U., 1957–58, U. of MI, B.A. 1960, MI St. U., M.B.A. 1961, Harvard Bus. Schl., 1964–66, St. Benedict's Col., LL.D. 1970; United Methodist; married (Lori).

Career: Consultant, IBM Corp., 1961–64; Faculty, MI St. U., 1962, Boston U., 1965, Harvard, 1965–66; U.S. House of Reps., 1967–77.

Offices: 105 DSOB 20510, 202-224-4822. Also 1155 Brewery Park Blvd., #343, Detroit 48207, 313-226-3188; 30800 Van Dyke, #300, Warren 48093, 313-573-9017; Sabuco Bldg., #910, 352 Saginaw St., Flint 48502, 313-766-5115; Washington Sq. Bldg., #705, 109 W. Michigan Ave., Lansing 48933, 517-377-1713; Fed. Bldg., #716, 110 Michigan Ave., NW, Grand Rapids 49503, 616-456-2592; 309 E. Front St., Traverse City 49884, 616-946-1300; and 200 W. Washington, #323, Marquette 49855, 906-228-7457.

Committees: *Banking, Housing and Urban Affairs* (Chmn. of 11 D). *Budget* (4th of 12 D). *Finance* (7th of 11 D): Deficits, Debt Management and Long-Term Economic Growth; Health for Families and the Uninsured (Chmn.); International Trade.

Group Ratings

	ADA	ACLU	CDF	COPE	CFA	LCV	ACU	NTLC	NSI	COC	CEI
1992	95	86	100	92	83	75	4	11	40	38	16
1991	90	—	100	83	78	67	14	—	—	10	22

National Journal Ratings

	1991 LIB — 1991 CONS			1992 LIB — 1992 CONS		
Economic	85%	—	11%	76%	—	23%
Social	64%	—	33%	79%	—	16%
Foreign	86%	—	0%	78%	—	14%

Key Votes of the 102d Congress

1. $ for Homeownership	AGN	5. Clarence Thomas Nom.	AGN	9. Use Force in Gulf	AGN
2. Have Cap Gains Debate	AGN	6. Lmt Death Row Appeal	AGN	10. Keep Salvador Aid	AGN
3. Remove Budget Walls	FOR	7. Handgun Wait/5-Day	FOR	11. Cut $1B from SDI	FOR
4. Ban Striker Replace	FOR	8. Abortion Gag Rule	AGN	12. Override China MFN	FOR

Key Votes of the 103d Congress

1. Family Leave	FOR	2. HIV Immigrants	*	3. Clinton Budget	FOR

Election Results

1988 general	Donald W. Riegle, Jr. (D)	2,116,865	(60%)	($3,383,849)
	Jim Dunn (R)	1,348,216	(39%)	($442,693)
1988 primary	Donald W. Riegle, Jr. (D), unopposed			
1982 general	Donald W. Riegle, Jr. (D)	1,728,793	(58%)	($1,583,439)
	Philip Ruppe (R)	1,223,286	(41%)	($1,045,545)

Sen. Carl Levin (D)

Elected 1978, seat up 1996; b. June 28, 1934, Detroit; home, Detroit; Swarthmore Col., B.A. 1956, Harvard, LL.B. 1959; Jewish; married (Barbara).

Career: Practicing atty., 1959–64, 1971–73, 1978–79; MI Asst. Atty. Gen. and Gen. Cnsl., MI Civil Rights Comm., 1964–67; Detroit Chief Appellate Defender, 1967–69; Detroit City Cncl., 1969–77, Pres., 1973–77.

Offices: 459 RSOB 20510, 202-224-6221. Also 1860 McNamara Bldg., 477 Michigan Ave., Detroit 48226, 313-226-6020; Fed. Bldg., 145 Water St., #102, Alpena 49707, 517-354-5520; 623 Ludington St., #200, Escanaba 49829, 517-789-0052; Gerald R. Ford Fed. Bldg., 110 Michigan Ave. N.W., #134, Grand Rapids 49503, 616-456-2531; 1810 Michigan Natl. Tower, 124 Allegan St., Lansing 48933, 517-377-1508; P.O. Box 817, Saginaw 48606, 517-754-2494; 15100 Northline Rd., #107-A, Southgate 48195, 313-285-8596; and 24580 Cunningham, #110, Warren 48091, 313-759-0477.

Committees: *Armed Services* (3d of 11 D): Coalition Defense and Reinforcing Forces (Chmn.); Defense Technology, Acquisition and Industrial Base; Nuclear Deterrence, Arms Control and Defense Intelligence. *Governmental Affairs* (3d of 8 D): Oversight of Government Management (Chmn.); Regulation and Government Information; Permanent Subcommittee on Investigations. *Small Business* (3d of 12 D): Innovation, Manufacturing and Technology (Chmn.); Rural Economy and Family Farming.

Group Ratings

	ADA	ACLU	CDF	COPE	CFA	LCV	ACU	NTLC	NSI	COC	CEI
1992	100	95	90	92	100	75	0	11	40	20	19
1991	90	—	82	75	83	73	5	—	—	0	26

National Journal Ratings

	1991 LIB — 1991 CONS		1992 LIB — 1992 CONS	
Economic	90%	— 3%	95%	— 0%
Social	84%	— 13%	84%	— 11%
Foreign	78%	— 14%	86%	— 0%

Key Votes of the 102d Congress

1. $ for Homeownership AGN	5. Clarence Thomas Nom. AGN	9. Use Force in Gulf AGN
2. Have Cap Gains Debate AGN	6. Lmt Death Row Appeal AGN	10. Keep Salvador Aid AGN
3. Remove Budget Walls FOR	7. Handgun Wait/5-Day FOR	11. Cut $1B from SDI FOR
4. Ban Striker Replace FOR	8. Abortion Gag Rule AGN	12. Override China MFN FOR

Key Votes of the 103d Congress

1. Family Leave FOR	2. HIV Immigrants FOR	3. Clinton Budget FOR

Election Results

1990 general	Carl Levin (D)	1,471,753	(57%)	($7,066,832)
	Bill Schuette (R)	1,055,695	(41%)	($2,417,705)
	Other	33,046	(1%)	
1990 primary	Carl Levin (D), unopposed			
1984 general	Carl Levin (D)	1,915,831	(52%)	($3,569,330)
	Jack Lousma (R)	1,745,302	(47%)	($1,765,786)

FIRST DISTRICT

Michigan's Upper Peninsula, commonly known as the UP, is a land apart. Surrounded on three sides by frigid Lake Superior and Lake Michigan, it has its own flora, including the world's largest living object, a giant fungus that lives under 37 acres of a forest floor and is 1,500 years old. Although the UP is no farther north than Montreal or Seattle, it has one of the coldest climates in settled parts of North America. "In October, usually, the first snow falls steady on the northland," writes Dixie Lee Franklin in *A Most Superior Land*, "whispering teasing promises of more to come"—for six months or more. Far away from any major city, with ground too frozen and a growing season too short for most crops, the Upper Peninsula was explored by French voyagers more than 300 years ago but was never thickly settled until prospectors found rich veins of ore here—through 1987 the Keweenaw Peninsula copper veins and immediate surrounding areas produced 13.3 billion pounds of copper; the Marquette, Menominee and Gogebic iron ranges have more than one billion tons of iron ore. Starting in the 1880s, immigrants flocked here to work the mines—Irish, Italians, Swedes, Norwegians, miners' sons from Wales and Cornwall and most prominently Finns, who must have found this cold land with its lakes and hills much like their home. By 1900, the UP was a northern industrial belt, with a few bosses and some absentee overlords, and a work force disposed to radical ideas and union movements.

A major strike in 1913–14, falling ore prices after World War I—events that would be long forgotten elsewhere—are remembered in the UP as the beginning of its decline: the UP's population peaked at 332,000 in 1920. The copper veins were mostly worked out by then, mining iron ore became less labor-intensive, and lumber and farming provided only a few thousand jobs. In the last half-century, there has been great outmigration to Detroit, Chicago and the West Coast; the UP's population has hovered around 300,000, rising to 318,000 in 1980, but dropping back to 313,000 in 1990. But devotion remains high to the UP, which some say has its own dialect, "Yoopanese."

Some 53% of the people in the 1st Congressional District of Michigan live in the Upper Peninsula; the rest are across the breathtaking Mackinac Bridge, in the northern end of the Lower Peninsula (never referred to as the LP). This is a vast area, geographically the second largest district east of the Mississippi, and smaller than only 26 further west; it is a 450-mile drive from Ironwood at the western end of the UP to the Sleeping Bear Dunes overlooking Lake Michigan. The Lower Peninsula counties have two different personalities. On Lake Huron, they are mostly industrial and slow-growing. On Lake Michigan are the affluent resort areas around

Petoskey, Charlevoix and Traverse City, where summer people from Chicago and Detroit have been coming since the 19th Century (this is Ernest Hemingway's "up in Michigan") and which is now filling with affluent retirees and even some Up North-loving entrepreneurs. Politically, the UP has long been Democratic, with a few variations; the Lower Peninsula counties, also with some variation, have long been Republican.

The congressman from the 1st District is Bart Stupak, a freshman Democrat whose career did not lead in a straight line toward Congress—but the 1992 election was odd overall. Stupak is a "Yooper," from Menominee on the Wisconsin border. He was a police officer in Escanaba, then became a Michigan State Police Trooper in 1974, and also got a law degree; in 1984, he was injured in the line of duty and retired from the force. In 1988 he was elected to the Michigan House; in 1990 he lost a race for the state Senate. Stupak got into the race when incumbent Republican Bob Davis decided to drop out in May 1992. Davis's moderate record and concentration on protecting area military bases and bringing in government money had enabled him to hold the district, and carry the UP against some pretty serious Democrats, since 1978. But he had 878 overdrafts on the House bank, totalling some $350,000, and his attempts to explain them fell flat. Stupak faced two Democratic primary opponents from the Lower Peninsula in a district that from July on was clearly in the Clinton column: a favorable position. In the primary Stupak won 58% in the Upper Peninsula and restaurateur Mike McElroy 59% in the Lower Peninsula; but 70% of the votes were cast north of the Bridge, and Stupak won 49%–43%. Meanwhile, the Republican primary was won by former Congressman Philip Ruppe. From a family that owns a brewery on the Keweenaw Peninsula that juts into Lake Superior, Ruppe was part of the class of 1966 Republicans that produced such diverse politicians as George Bush and Michigan Democratic Senator Donald Riegle; he left the seat in 1978 to run for the Senate but was squeezed out when Senator Robert Griffin reentered the race after announcing his retirement; Ruppe then lost to Riegle in 1982, 58%–41%. Ruppe won the primary with 47% to 33% for former Grand Traverse County Commissioner Bill Kurtz and 20% for Keweenaw Peninsula state legislator Stephen Dresch. But in the general Ruppe was attacked for being out of touch with northern Michigan (he had spent many years in Washington, D.C., while his wife was Reagan's Peace Corps director), while Bill Clinton was carrying the UP and margins for George Bush were eroding to almost nothing even in the Traverse City area.

Stupak proclaims himself devoted to creating jobs in northern Michigan and protecting the environment of a district with the longest shoreline in the continental United States; he favors national health insurance and is opposed to abortion and gun control. Upset that K. I. Sawyer Air Force Base near Marquette was on the base closing list, he painfully pondered whether to oppose the Clinton budget resolution in March 1993; after some attention by Whip David Bonior and Bobby Rush, he voted for it. He could easily be a key vote on many issues, as he tries to win voters' longstanding allegiance, as Davis and Ruppe did in their times and as the last Democrat from the UP, elected in 1964 and defeated in 1966, did not.

The People: Pop. 1990: 581,006; 69% rural; 16% age 65+; 96% White; 1% Black; 2% Amer. Indian; 1% Hispanic origin. Voting age pop.: 431,275; 1% Black. Households: 60% married couple families; 27% married couple fams. w. children; 39% college educ.; median household income: $22,788; per capita income: $10,846; median gross rent: $328; median house value: $44,700.

1992 Presidential Vote

Clinton (D) 118,983 (41%)
Bush (R) 101,110 (35%)
Perot (I) 65,402 (23%)

1988 Presidential Vote

Bush (R) 133,946 (54%)
Dukakis (D) 115,350 (46%)

Rep. Bart Stupak (D)

Elected 1992; b. Feb. 29, 1952, Milwaukee, WI; home, Menominee; NW MI Comm. Col., A.A. 1972, Saginaw Valley St. Col., B.S. 1977, Cooley Law Schl., J.D. 1981; Catholic; married (Laurie).

Career: Escanaba Police Officer, 1972–73; MI St. Trooper, 1974–84; Practicing atty., 1981–1992; MI House of Reps., 1989–90.

Offices: 317 CHOB 20515, 202-225-4735. Also 160 E. State St., Traverse City 49684, 616-929-4711; 111 E. Chisholm St., Alpena 49707, 517-356-0690; 1229 W. Washington St., Marquette 49855, 906-228-3700; 2501 14th Ave., Escanaba 49829, 906-786-4504; and 616 Sheldon Ave., #213, Houghton 49931, 906-482-1371.

Committees: *Armed Services* (26th of 34 D): Military Acquisition; Military Forces and Personnel. *Merchant Marine and Fisheries* (25th of 29 D): Coast Guard and Navigation; Merchant Marine.

Group Ratings and 102d Congress Votes: Newly Elected

Key Votes of the 103d Congress

1. Family Leave	FOR	2. Deficit Reduction	FOR	3. Stimulus Plan	FOR

Election Results

1992 general	Bart Stupak (D)	144,857	(54%)	($225,572)
	Philip Ruppe (R)	117,056	(44%)	($449,464)
	Others	6,706	(2%)	
1992 primary	Bart Stupak (D)	24,034	(49%)	
	Mike McElroy (D)	21,304	(43%)	
	Daniel Herringa (D)	4,085	(8%)	
1990 general	Robert W. Davis (R)	94,555	(61%)	($325,232)
(MI 11)	Marcia Gould (D)	59,759	(39%)	($4,072)

SECOND DISTRICT

The shoreline of Lake Michigan, lined with often giant sand dunes, which with the lake winds temper the otherwise frigid Michigan climate, is one of the nation's little-known scenic areas. In the late 19th Century, this was America's greatest lumber country; the ports on the small rivers were choked with logs and full of lumbermen from Norway and Sweden, Ireland and Scotland, Quebec and New England. During the lumber boom, the shoreline just to the south was the locus of America's largest migration from the Netherlands, and today still has the nation's largest concentration of Dutch-Americans. Wooden shoes are seen now only in the Tulip Festival in Holland, but conscientious Dutch work habits have produced some of the most highly skilled workers in America and their innate political conservatism usually produces some of the country's highest Republican percentages.

The 2d Congressional District of Michigan occupies the Lake Michigan shoreline counties, plus a tier of counties inland, from the lumber country around Manistee south to Holland and the resort town of Saugatuck. This was the scene of one of the biggest upsets of upset-heavy 1992, and one with a particular Dutch flavor. The incumbent was Guy Vander Jagt, first elected in 1966, chairman of the National Republican Congressional Committee since 1975, a close second to Robert Michel in the race for minority leader in 1980, second ranking Republican on the Ways and Means Committee. But Vander Jagt was beleaguered in Washington, where he was challenged, but reelected 98–66, as campaign committee chairman, and at home, where against a low-spending Democrat he was reelected with only 55% in 1990. Redistricting gave him the other half of Ottawa County around Holland and Allegan County, both heavily Dutch, but new territory.

The 1992 challenge came from Republican Peter Hoekstra, born in the Netherlands, a graduate of Michigan's Hope College in Holland (he spent a semester in Washington during the Watergate crisis), an executive of Zeeland-based Herman Miller furniture who helped developed the "Equa Chair" in the early 1980s. Hoekstra saved up vacation time and in 1992 took off on a county-by-county bicycle tour of the district. With an earnestness that rang true, Hoekstra called for citizen, not career politicians, refused PAC money and called for abolition of PACs, advocated 12-year term limits, promised to uphold family values and to oppose abortion. He also called for a balanced budget, environmental protection and upholding the Second Amendment. Hoekstra spent only $55,600 to Vander Jagt's $725,000. But on primary day, Hoekstra carried Ottawa and Allegan 53%–31%, while Vander Jagt won just 53%–36% in the rest of the district; since Ottawa and Allegan cast 59% of the primary vote, Hoekstra won 46%–40%.

The general election was anticlimactic. George Bush carried the district handily, and Hoekstra won 63%–35%, even carrying heavy-industrial Muskegon which often goes Democratic. Hoekstra seems to have a safe seat, but like so many new members seems to approach the job with the intention to eventually return home, to Holland and Herman Miller, which may have some effect on his votes and certainly will make him less malleable to the leadership or amenable to political deals.

The People: Pop. 1990: 581,017; 52% rural; 12% age 65+; 91% White; 4% Black; 1% Amer. Indian; 1% Asian; 1% Other; 3% Hispanic origin. Voting age pop.: 414,771; 4% Black; 2% Hispanic origin. Households: 64% married couple families; 31% married couple fams. w. children; 39% college educ.; median household income: $28,905; per capita income: $12,305; median gross rent: $383; median house value: $58,100.

1992 Presidential Vote			1988 Presidential Vote		
Bush (R)	126,969	(45%)	Bush (R)	154,305	(65%)
Clinton (D)	95,351	(34%)	Dukakis (D)	83,237	(35%)
Perot (I)	58,238	(21%)			

Rep. Peter Hoekstra (R)

Elected 1992; b. Oct. 30, 1953, Groningen, Netherlands; home, Holland; Hope Col., B.A. 1975, U. of MI, M.B.A. 1977; Christian Reformed; married (Diane).

Career: Furniture Exec., Herman Miller Co., 1977–92.

Offices: 1319 LHOB 20515, 202-225-4401. Also 42 W. 10th St., Holland 49423, 616-395-0030; 900 Third St., #203, Muskegon 49440, 616-722-8386; and 120 W. Harris St., Cadillac 49601, 616-775-0050.

Committees: *Education and Labor* (13th of 15 R): Labor-Management Relations; Labor Standards, Occupational Health and Safety; Postsecondary Education and Training. *Public Works and Transportation* (23d of 24 R): Economic Development; Water Resources and Environment.

Group Ratings and 102d Congress Votes: Newly Elected

Key Votes of the 103d Congress

1. Family Leave	AGN	2. Deficit Reduction	AGN	3. Stimulus Plan	AGN

Election Results

1992 general	Peter Hoekstra (R)	155,577	(63%)	($100,278)
	John Miltner (D)	86,265	(35%)	($20,518)
	Others	4,919	(2%)	
1992 primary	Peter Hoekstra (R)	34,572	(46%)	
	Guy Vander Jagt (R)	30,203	(40%)	
	Mel De Stigter (R)	10,141	(14%)	
1990 general	Guy Vander Jagt (R)	89,078	(55%)	($452,960)
(MI 9)	Geraldine Greene (D)	73,604	(45%)	($22,155)

THIRD DISTRICT

Grand Rapids today is the center of Michigan's most prosperous and confident metropolitan area. Known since the 19th Century as a major furniture producer, Grand Rapids was left behind in the 20th Century rush to develop Michigan's auto industry; once a demographic competitor of Detroit, it grew much more slowly. But with the decline of the auto industry in the last third of the century, Grand Rapids's slow-but-steady economy has gained speed without losing steadiness. The furniture business, started when Michigan was the nation's number one lumber producer, still booms, with Grand Rapids now specializing in office and luxury residential furniture. And lumber is still important: Peter Secchia, Ambassador to Italy during the Bush years and a possible candidate for Donald Riegle's Senate seat in 1994, made his fortune in that business. Grand Rapids has sprouted other businesses too, the flashiest of them being Amway, the door-to-door cosmetics and cleaning agent empire located in nearby Ada.

Grand Rapids was founded by New England Yankees, but much of its character was set by the Dutch immigrants who began arriving in western Michigan in the 1870s and are still coming today; they include probably one-quarter of Grand Rapids area residents. Politically, the Yankees were the original Republicans, but Dutch-Americans have become the nation's most heavily Republican identifiable ethnic group, except perhaps for Cuban-Americans; they believe strongly in free market economics and the rigorous cultural conservatism exemplified by the Christian Reform churches. Republican Grand Rapids has produced nationally important politicians: Arthur Vandenberg, a newspaper editor who was U.S. senator from 1928 to 1951, and though a onetime isolationist provided key support for the bipartisan internationalist foreign policies of Franklin Roosevelt and Harry Truman; Gerald Ford, backed by Vandenberg in the 1948 primary, who rose to become House Republican leader in 1965, vice president in 1973, and then president of the United States after Nixon resigned in disgrace in 1974. Nixon got a bit of a nudge from the Grand Rapids district, when in an early 1974 special election it voted to replace Ford with a Democrat, a clear sign of the Republican heartland turning on the president.

The 3d Congressional District of Michigan includes all of Grand Rapids and surrounding Kent County, plus one and a half smaller counties east and southeast. It was Michigan's most Republican district in the 1990 governor race. The congressman from the 3d District is Paul Henry, who has a fine Grand Rapids heritage: his father was a noted theologian of modern evangelical Protestantism, and Henry was a political science professor at Calvin College. He served in the Peace Corps, was a staffer for Congressman John Anderson, and served in the Michigan legislature from 1978 to 1984 before his election to Congress. Henry is a moderate Republican with strong religious views, earnest without being preachy, willing to compromise but never abandoning principle. He is an abortion opponent who accepted fetal tissue research; a conservative who opposed the flag-burning amendment and cobbled together a compromise on the National Endowment for the Arts authorization; a free market economist who is lead sponsor of a national bottle deposit bill. He was mentioned by many as a candidate for Donald Riegle's Senate seat in 1994.

In October 1992, after experiencing severe headaches, Henry underwent surgery and doctors removed 90% of a three-inch brain tumor. Surrogates campaigned for him, and he was reelected by a 61%–36% margin. He was sworn into office in the House chamber in a wheelchair in January 1993, and then returned home to Grand Rapids to recuperate. Should Henry decide to retire, Republicans mentioned for the seat include state Senator Vern Ehlers, 1992 term limit referendum chairman Glen Steiles, state Representatives Rick Bandstra and Ken Sikkema, Kent County Commissioners Ken Kuipers and George TerHorst and Henry aide Beth Bandstra, as well as Democratic state Representative Ken Mathieu.

The People: Pop. 1990: 580,874; 24% rural; 11% age 65+; 88% White; 7% Black; 1% Amer. Indian; 1% Asian; 1% Other; 3% Hispanic origin. Voting age pop.: 416,246; 7% Black; 2% Hispanic origin. Households: 59% married couple families; 30% married couple fams. w. children; 47% college educ.; median household income: $31,917; per capita income: $13,924; median gross rent: $425; median house value: $65,600.

1992 Presidential Vote			1988 Presidential Vote		
Bush (R)	128,670	(46%)	Bush (R)	149,772	(64%)
Clinton (D)	94,715	(34%)	Dukakis (D)	85,467	(36%)
Perot (I)	52,773	(19%)			

Rep. Paul B. Henry (R)

Elected 1984; b. July 9, 1942, Chicago, IL; home, Grand Rapids; Wheaton Col., B.A. 1963, Duke U., M.A. 1968, Ph.D. 1970; Christian Reformed; married (Karen).

Career: Peace Corps, Liberia and Ethiopia, 1963–65; Legis. Asst., U.S. Rep. John Anderson, 1968–69; Instructor, Duke U., 1969–70; Prof., Calvin Col., 1970–78; MI Bd. of Educ., 1975–78; MI House of Reps., 1979–82; MI Senate, 1983–84.

Offices: 1526 LHOB 20515, 202-225-3831. Also 166 Fed. Bldg., Grand Rapids 49503, 616-451-8383.

Committees: *Education and Labor* (7th of 15 R): Human Resources (RMM); Postsecondary Education and Training. *Science, Space and Technology* (5th of 22 R): Investigations and Oversight (RMM).

Group Ratings

	ADA	ACLU	COPE	CDF	CFA	LCV	ACU	NTLC	NSI	COC	CEI
1992	35	9	58	20	33	44	80	65	90	88	70
1991	30	—	25	60	33	54	65	—	—	80	62

National Journal Ratings

	1991 LIB — 1991 CONS		1992 LIB — 1992 CONS	
Economic	28% —	71%	31% —	69%
Social	27% —	71%	31% —	69%
Foreign	31% —	67%	62% —	35%

Key Votes of the 102d Congress

1. Ban Striker Replace	AGN	5. Handgun Wait/7-Day	FOR	9. Use Force in Gulf	FOR
2. $ for Homeownership	FOR	6. Overseas Mil. Abortion	AGN	10. US Mil. Abroad $ Cut	FOR
3. Tax Rich/Cut Mid Cls.	AGN	7. Obscn. Art NEA $ Ban	FOR	11. Limit SDI Funds	FOR
4. FY93/$15B Def. Cut	AGN	8. Death Pen. from Jury	FOR	12. Cuba Trade Embargo	FOR

Election Results

1992 general	Paul B. Henry (R)...................	162,451	(61%)	($282,472)
	Carol Kooistra (D)	95,927	(36%)	($44,866)
	Others	6,570	(3%)	
1992 primary	Paul B. Henry (R), unopposed			
1990 general	Paul B. Henry (R)...................	126,308	(75%)	($241,151)
(MI 5)	Thomas Trzybinski (D)................	41,170	(25%)	

FOURTH DISTRICT

The central reaches of Michigan's Lower Peninsula are farm country, flat and treeless for endless miles, exposed to winter winds and snow drifts much of the year. Farms here produce not just wheat or corn but also hardy crops like potatoes, navy beans and sugar beets. The little cities here are often small factory towns, with neat tree-lined streets on a grid layout suddenly ending and turning to bare fields, each with some distinction. Midland in 1891 was a declining lumber town when Herbert Dow perfected an electrolytic process to extract chemicals like bromine from northern Michigan's extensive brine wells; that was the start of Dow Chemical, still headquartered in this now upscale town. Owosso in 1902 was the birthplace of Thomas E. Dewey, Republican candidate for president of the United States in 1944 and 1948; it was also the home of novelist James Oliver Curwood and his "Curwood castle" writing studio, and today's Curwood Festival, lovingly chronicled by Thomas Mallon in *Rockets and Rodeos*. Mount Pleasant, to the north, is the site of Central Michigan University, where parka-clad students stomp through snow to class, and home of Governor John Engler.

The 4th Congressional District of Michigan includes much of this territory north of Lansing and Grand Rapids, and west of Flint and Saginaw. It stretches north up the freeways where thousands drive in fall to hunt and winter to ski, into the rolling country around Houghton Lake, once lumbering country and now a retirement and resort area, with trailers and condominiums in between the knotty pine cottages clustered around icy green lakes. Politically, this is mostly Republican territory, though retirees from the Detroit area and commuters to Flint and Saginaw have brought some Democratic tendencies with them.

The congressman from the 4th District is Dave Camp, a Republican first elected in 1990, when his former boss and predecessor Bill Schuette (now Engler's Agriculture Department director) ran unsuccessfully against Senator Carl Levin. Camp grew up with Schuette in Midland and managed his first successful campaign in 1984. Camp's key victory was in the Republican primary, where he won 33% (62% in Midland County) to 30% for former legislator and Pat Robertson supporter Al Cropsey, 19% for Richard Allen, pro-choice and willing to consider tax increases, and 18% for former Congressman Jim Dunn, a slashingly negative candidate. In the general election, Camp faced an admirer of Lyndon LaRouche.

Camp has compiled a conservative voting record, but is more moderate on foreign affairs issues; he supported the line-item veto and balanced budget amendment and opposed the congressional pay raise. He joined other congressmen in bringing a lawsuit to halt the automatic COLA Congress granted itself in 1989. He served on the Agriculture Committee for two years, then after the 1992 election won a seat on Ways and Means. He tempers his devotion to free enterprise with pleas for aid to farmers whose crops are damaged by this difficult climate. Camp was reelected without difficulty in 1992 and looks to be in strong political shape.

The People: Pop. 1990: 580,890; 72% rural; 12% age 65+; 97% White; 1% Black; 1% Amer. Indian; 1% Other; 2% Hispanic origin. Voting age pop.: 425,582; 1% Black; 1% Hispanic origin. Households: 64% married couple families; 30% married couple fams. w. children; 38% college educ.; median household income: $25,898; per capita income: $11,549; median gross rent: $360; median house value: $49,100.

1992 Presidential Vote

Clinton (D) 104,228 (38%)
Bush (R) 102,284 (37%)
Perot (I). 67,263 (24%)

1988 Presidential Vote

Bush (R) 135,597 (58%)
Dukakis (D). 98,197 (42%)

Rep. Dave Camp (R)

Elected 1990; b. July 9, 1953, Midland; home, Midland; Albion Col., B.A. 1975, U. of San Diego Law Schl., J.D. 1978; Catholic; single.

Career: Practicing atty., 1978–90; MI Special Asst. Atty. Gen., 1980–84; A.A., U.S. Rep. Bill Schuette, 1984–87; MI House of Reps., 1988–90.

Offices: 137 CHOB 20515, 202-225-3561. Also 135 Ashman St., Midland 48640, 517-631-2552; 308 W. Main St., Owosso 48867, 517-723-6759; and 3508 W. Houghton Lake Dr., Houghton Lake 48629, 517-366-4922.

Committees: *Ways and Means* (14th of 14 R): Human Resources; Select Revenue Measures.

Group Ratings

	ADA	ACLU	COPE	CDF	CFA	LCV	ACU	NTLC	NSI	COC	CEI
1992	5	9	25	20	27	13	84	75	100	75	72
1991	15	—	8	30	39	15	80	—	—	100	68

National Journal Ratings

	1991 LIB — 1991 CONS		1992 LIB — 1992 CONS	
Economic	23%	— 76%	0%	— 91%
Social	0%	— 84%	15%	— 85%
Foreign	26%	— 70%	44%	— 50%

Key Votes of the 102d Congress

1. Ban Striker Replace	AGN	5. Handgun Wait/7-Day AGN	9. Use Force in Gulf	FOR
2. $ for Homeownership	FOR	6. Overseas Mil. AbortionAGN	10. US Mil. Abroad $ Cut FOR
3. Tax Rich/Cut Mid Cls.AGN	7. Obscn. Art NEA $ Ban FOR	11. Limit SDI Funds	AGN
4. FY93/$15B Def. Cut	AGN	8. Death Pen. from Jury FOR	12. Cuba Trade Embargo AGN

Key Votes of the 103d Congress

1. Family Leave   AGN   2. Deficit Reduction   AGN   3. Stimulus Plan   AGN

Election Results

1992 general	Dave Camp (R).	157,337	(63%)	($518,118)
	Lisa Donaldson (D).	87,573	(35%)	($15,650)
	Others	6,620	(3%)	
1992 primary	Dave Camp (R), unopposed			
1990 general	Dave Camp (R).	99,952	(65%)	($657,229)
(MI 10)	Joan Dennison (D)	50,923	(33%)	
	Other.	2,841	(2%)	

FIFTH DISTRICT

For a brief moment in the 1870s, the greatest flow of lumber in the United States came through the otherwise obscure waters of Saginaw Bay, the inlet of Lake Huron that separates Michigan's Thumb (which indeed is often called that) and the mitten of its Lower Peninsula. There were 36 sawmills in Bay City then and logs were piled high along both banks of the Saginaw River for miles. Bay City and Saginaw, 15 miles upstream, handled logs from the wide area on both sides of Saginaw Bay drained by the Saginaw River and its tributaries. Neither city has since enjoyed such rapid growth. The automobile industry has also long been an important employer here; a General Motors plant in Saginaw is the world's largest manufacturer of power steering mechanisms. And the flat broad fields around Saginaw Bay which once held so many trees are now the nation's leading producer of navy beans, the raw material of Senate bean soup.

The 5th Congressional District of Michigan includes Saginaw and Bay City and lands on both sides of Saginaw Bay. To the north it goes up past Tawas City and East Tawas to Greenbush on Lake Huron. To the east it includes most of the Thumb. To the south it goes up to the city limits of Flint, including both black and white working-class townships just north of the city. Bay City, with its large Polish population, has long been Democratic; and since the auto industry woes of the 1980s, so are Saginaw and the Flint suburbs. The Thumb historically was among the most Republican parts of Michigan, but that is being eroded by the outward movement of Democrats from Saginaw and Bay City.

In close statewide races, the 5th District is narrowly Democratic, and the area has been represented by Democrats in Congress since April 1974, when Democrat Bob Traxler won a special election to replace Gerald Ford. It was a nationally significant triumph, one of several Democratic victories in districts long held by Republicans (the boundaries and number were different then) that persuaded politicians of both parties that Richard Nixon, reeling from Watergate charges, had no real backing from the voters. Traxler got a seat on Appropriations and rose in 1989 to chair the VA-HUD-Independent Agencies Subcommittee, where his first priority seemed to be getting all manner of projects into his district. Traxler surprised everyone in April 1992 when he announced he was retiring; he probably could have won despite 201 overdrafts on the House bank. A month later, he was robbed and beaten on a Washington street—not a happy good-bye.

It was widely thought that Traxler delayed his announcement until a month before the filing deadline in order to help his district chief of staff Don Hare win the seat. If so, he failed. Two state Senators filed against Hare in the primary and, although he carried Saginaw County with 50%, he finished third. State Senator John Cherry, with strong backing from organized labor, might have won this district, with its still large UAW membership, but although he won 72% in the suburbs around Flint, he did poorly elsewhere, and finished second with 29%. The winner with 46% was state legislator James Barcia. He won an impressive 72% in Bay County and carried the Thumb and northern counties solidly. In the general election, Barcia beat Republican real estate developer Keith Muxlow 60%–38%, running ahead of party lines and carrying two Thumb counties.

Barcia was known in the legislature for his whistleblower protection law, and was not an automatic vote for unions or management. He bucked organized labor by backing a measure to cut the cost of workmen's compensation and bucked feminists by voting pro-life on abortion. In the House he serves on the Public Works and Science Committees, but he will have a hard time funneling as much federal money into the district as Traxler did.

The People: Pop. 1990: 580,981; 51% rural; 13% age 65+; 87% White; 8% Black; 1% Amer. Indian; 2% Other; 3% Hispanic origin. Voting age pop.: 418,692; 7% Black; 3% Hispanic origin. Households: 60% married couple families; 28% married couple fams. w. children; 36% college educ.; median household income: $26,312; per capita income: $11,891; median gross rent: $366; median house value: $47,100.

1992 Presidential Vote

Clinton (D) 119,086 (45%)
Bush (R) 85,603 (32%)
Perot (I) 61,544 (23%)

1988 Presidential Vote

Dukakis (D) 120,804 (51%)
Bush (R) 118,247 (49%)

Rep. James A. Barcia (D)

Elected 1992; b. Feb. 25, 1952, Bay City; home, Bay City; Saginaw Valley St. Col., B.A. 1974; Catholic; married (Vicki).

Career: Staff Asst., U.S. Sen. Philip Hart, 1971; Commun. Svc. Coord., MI Commun. Blood Ctr., 1974–75; A.A., MI Rep. Donald Albosta, 1975–76; MI House of Reps., 1976–82, Majority Whip, 1979–82; MI Senate, 1982–92.

Offices: 1717 LHOB 20515, 202-225-8171. Also 3741 E. Wilder Rd., Bay City 48706, 517-667-0003; 5409 Pierson Rd., Flushing 48433, 313-732-7501; and 301 E. Genessee St., #502, Saginaw 48607, 517-754-6075.

Committees: *Public Works and Transportation* (34th of 39 D): Economic Development; Investigations and Oversight; Water Resources and Environment. *Science, Space and Technology* (18th of 33 D): Science; Space.

Group Ratings and 102d Congress Votes: Newly Elected

Key Votes of the 103d Congress

1. Family Leave	FOR	2. Deficit Reduction	FOR	3. Stimulus Plan	FOR

Election Results

1992 general	James A. Barcia (D) 147,618	(60%)	($288,755)
	Keith Muxlow (R) 93,098	(38%)	($93,557)
	Others 4,276	(2%)	
1992 primary	James A. Barcia (D) 27,138	(46%)	
	John Cherry, Jr. (D) 16,890	(29%)	
	Don Hare (D) 14,761	(25%)	
1990 general	Bob Traxler (D) 98,903	(69%)	($176,815)
(MI 8)	James White (R) 45,259	(31%)	($433)

SIXTH DISTRICT

The southwest corner of Michigan lies at the western end of the overland trail from Detroit, where the state's two southern tiers of counties were settled by New England Yankees and Upstate New Yorkers in the 1830s and 1840s. There they built small towns with schools and churches and colleges, supported temperance and opposed capital punishment, and were original backers of the Republican Party. There are towns in southwest Michigan which still recall proudly their past as termini of the Underground Railroad, and black families who trace their ancestry to slaves who made their way north to freedom. Later, big industries transformed some of the small towns to large cities: Kalamazoo, started by Dutch-Americans who introduced celery to this country, became the home of Upjohn pharmaceuticals; Benton Harbor and St. Joseph, twin towns on Lake Michigan, originally known for cherry and peach orchards, became the home of Whirlpool appliances. But this southwest corner is also where the influence of Michigan recedes: people watch Chicago television and root for the Cubs or White Sox rather than the Tigers.

The 6th Congressional District of Michigan occupies this southwest corner of the state, with

Kalamazoo and Benton Harbor-St. Joseph as its two major urban areas, and three smaller counties besides. This was for many years arch-Republican territory, represented by a succession of congressmen who deplored federal spending and welfare state measures: New Deal opponent Clare Hoffman (1935–63), Nixon defender Edward Hutchinson (1963–77), pork barrel critic and later Reagan OMB Director David Stockman (1977–81). But lately, Kalamazoo has trended toward the Democrats and the 6th actually cast a small plurality for Bill Clinton in 1992.

But that has not affected the Republican congressman from this district. Fred Upton was a staffer for Stockman and a grandson of the founder of Whirlpool, but he did not win the seat by inheritance. In 1986, he challenged Stockman successor Mark Siljander in the primary. Siljander, a conservative and evangelical Christian, sent a tape to ministers on which he said, "We need to break the back of Satan and the lies that are coming our way." Upton won 55%–45%; Siljander stayed in the Virginia suburbs of Washington, D.C., where he ran for the new 11th District seat in 1992 and lost in the primary. Upton is a fiscal conservative, but moderate on some cultural and foreign issues; he has a seat on the Energy and Commerce Committee and on the Health, Transportation and Oversight Subcommittees, where he generally but not always opposes greater regulation. He voted for the Brady bill to delay handgun sales and is promoting a high-speed rail line between Detroit and Chicago. He generally supports space exploration, but opposes the space station; he is for reducing military spending. His first amendment to be passed into law changed federal flood insurance to allow threatened buildings to be demolished before the waters come—a means of cutting government spending; he also passed a $5,000 tax credit for small businesses complying with the Americans with Disabilities Act. He often sponsors across-the-board spending cuts, including limits on congressional mail, and opposed the 1990 budget summit package. But he seems uncomfortable with the cultural conservatism of most House Republican leaders, and quit his deputy whip post in January 1993.

Upton seems to have a good hold on the 6th District. He was challenged in the 1990 primary by pro-life state Senator Ed Fredricks and won 63%–37%. The addition of Kalamazoo to the district bothered him not at all. But he might run for Donald Riegle's Senate seat in 1994; in early 1993 he said he was taking "an honest look" at the race.

The People: Pop. 1990: 580,973; 50% rural; 12% age 65+; 88% White; 10% Black; 1% Amer. Indian; 1% Asian; 1% Other; 2% Hispanic origin. Voting age pop.: 427,134; 8% Black; 1% Hispanic origin. Households: 57% married couple families; 26% married couple fams. w. children; 45% college educ.; median household income: $28,453; per capita income: $13,043; median gross rent: $385; median house value: $54,300.

1992 Presidential Vote

Clinton (D) 100,677 (39%)
Bush (R) 97,234 (38%)
Perot (I). 55,682 (22%)

1988 Presidential Vote

Bush (R) 129,093 (59%)
Dukakis (D). 88,978 (41%)

Rep. Fred Upton (R)

Elected 1986; b. Apr. 23, 1953, St. Joseph; home, St. Joseph; U. of MI, B.A. 1975; Protestant; married (Amey).

Career: Project coord., U.S. Rep. David Stockman, 1975–80; Legis. Affairs, O.M.B., 1981–83, Dir., 1984–85.

Offices: 2439 RHOB 20515, 202-225-3761. Also 421 Main St., St. Joseph 49085, 616-982-1986; and 535 S. Burdick St., #225, Kalamazoo 49007, 616-385-0039.

Committees: *Energy and Commerce* (10th of 17 R): Health and the Environment; Oversight and Investigations; Transportation and Hazardous Materials.

Group Ratings

	ADA	ACLU	COPE	CDF	CFA	LCV	ACU	NTLC	NSI	COC	CEI
1992	30	22	50	60	40	25	72	70	100	88	61
1991	25	—	25	50	28	54	80	—	—	100	67

National Journal Ratings

	1991 LIB — 1991 CONS			1992 LIB — 1992 CONS		
Economic	31%	—	68%	28%	—	70%
Social	32%	—	67%	35%	—	65%
Foreign	23%	—	75%	56%	—	40%

Key Votes of the 102d Congress

1. Ban Striker Replace	AGN	5. Handgun Wait/7-Day FOR	9. Use Force in Gulf FOR
2. $ for Homeownership	FOR	6. Overseas Mil. Abortion AGN	10. US Mil. Abroad $ Cut FOR
3. Tax Rich/Cut Mid Cls.	AGN	7. Obscn. Art NEA $ Ban FOR	11. Limit SDI Funds AGN
4. FY93/$15B Def. Cut	AGN	8. Death Pen. from Jury FOR	12. Cuba Trade Embargo AGN

Key Votes of the 103d Congress

1. Family Leave   AGN   2. Deficit Reduction   AGN   3. Stimulus Plan   AGN

Election Results

1992 general	Fred Upton (R)......................	144,083	(62%)	($367,596)
	Andy Davis (D).......................	89,020	(38%)	($42,769)
1992 primary	Fred Upton (R), unopposed			
1990 general	Fred Upton (R).......................	75,850	(58%)	($503,164)
(MI 4)	JoAnne McFarland (D)................	55,449	(42%)	($78,392)

SEVENTH DISTRICT

The small cities and towns spotting the southern tier farmland counties of Michigan have been incubators of innovation since they were settled by Yankees from New England 150 years ago. The state's public school system was established by two politicians from Marshall, whose dashed hopes to have Marshall become the state capital resulted in the preservation of many of its 19th Century structures whose counterparts in Lansing, which won the contest, have long since been demolished. A few miles away, in Battle Creek, sanitarium operator W.K. Kellogg invented corn flakes as a health food; he and his onetime patient C.W. Post both established factories in the late 19th Century and created the American breakfast cereal industry. Politically, this has ordinarily been Republican territory since 1854, when the party was founded in nearby Jackson as a kind of reformist institution out of the same activist impulse that produced local support for women's rights, Prohibition and opposition to the death penalty. Southern Michigan mostly rejected New Deal tinkering and was hostile to the United Auto Workers, but the people here were receptive to moral claims made by later 20th Century reformers, challenging racial segregation, the Vietnam war and the Watergate coverup: this is one part of the country where such cultural issues helped the Democrats.

The 7th Congressional District of Michigan covers all of six counties and parts of two others in Michigan's southern tier. It was a substantially new district for 1992, taking much territory represented by suburban Detroit Republican Carl Pursell and Lansing Democrat Howard Wolpe, but not including either incumbent's residence. Pursell would have run, if anywhere, in the new 13th District, but instead retired. Wolpe decided against either of two unpalatable alternatives: a primary fight against Democrat Bob Carr in the 8th, or a run in the new 7th, which was at least 5% more Republican than his old seat and in which about half the voters had no acquaintance with the hard-driving constituency service which had offset his liberal voting record. In fact, no Democrat at all filed in the 7th; some Democrats there must be kicking themselves, since Clinton edged Bush out of the district's presidential vote and the Republicans nominated their most conservative candidate, who might conceivably have been vulnerable.

So the new congressman was chosen in the Republican primary, and quite a rough-and-tumble primary it was. Two state senators ran, John Schwarz of Battle Creek and Nick Smith of rural Addison, plus Jackson County Commissioner Thomas Wilson and the 1990 nominee against Wolpe, international lawyer Brad Haskins. Haskins for weeks ran a 15-second radio ad charging that Schwarz, a physician, shouted at and then backed his car into a hospital security officer who had written him a ticket; another local doctor charged that Schwarz had once assaulted him. But Haskins got just 9% of the vote, and Schwarz still carried the Battle Creek area and Eaton County just west of Lansing. There were other issues that may have hurt Schwarz: he raised much money in Washington and from PACs, while Nick Smith boasted of taking no PAC money. Schwarz ended up with 36% to 43% for Smith.

Smith is a dairy farmer whose constant complaints about big government prompted his wife to say he should do something about it or keep quiet. He was elected to the state House in 1978 and the state Senate in 1982. Republicans have controlled the Senate since 1983, and he is proud to claim that he has introduced and passed more tax-cutting legislation than any other Michigan legislator, including a 1992 property tax freeze that he boasts has saved state taxpayers $388 million. He is pro-life on abortion and pushed for arbitration as an alternative to malpractice suits. In 1992 he promised not to vote for any tax increase unless it was offset by a tax cut and promised not to serve more than 12 years. He said his priorities are to reduce the national debt, lower the cost of investing and saving, and cut red tape and regulation; with a seat on the Budget Committee, he will have an opportunity to vote for, if not necessarily accomplish, some of that.

The People: Pop. 1990: 581,005; 52% rural; 12% age 65+; 92% White; 6% Black; 1% Amer. Indian; 1% Asian; 1% Other; 2% Hispanic origin. Voting age pop.: 423,899; 5% Black; 2% Hispanic origin. Households: 60% married couple families; 28% married couple fams. w. children; 43% college educ.; median household income: $29,976; per capita income: $12,900; median gross rent: $382; median house value: $50,500.

1992 Presidential Vote			1988 Presidential Vote		
Clinton (D)	96,872	(38%)	Bush (R)	130,165	(60%)
Bush (R)	96,253	(37%)	Dukakis (D)	87,289	(40%)
Perot (I)	62,657	(24%)			

Rep. Nick Smith (R)

Elected 1992; b. Nov. 5, 1934, Addison; home, Addison; MI St. U., B.A. 1957, U. of DE, M.S. 1959; Congregationalist; married (Bonnalyn).

Career: Air Force Intelligence, 1959–61; Businessman, farmer; Somerset Township Trustee, 1962–66, Supervisor, 1966–68; Hillsdale Cnty Bd. of Supervisors, 1966–68; Hillsdale Cnty. Repub. Chmn., 1966–68; MI Chmn., Agricultural Stabilization and Conservation Svc., 1969–72; Natl. Energy Dir., U.S. Dept. of Agriculture, 1972–74; MI Occup. Safety Standards Comm., 1975; MI House of Reps., 1978–82; MI Senate, 1982–92, Pres. Pro-Tem, 1986–90.

Offices: 1708 LHOB 20515, 202-225-6276. Also 209 E. Washington St., #200-D, Jackson 49201, 517-783-4486; 121 S. Cochran Ave., Charlotte 48813, 517-543-0055; and 118 W. Church St., Adrian 49221, 517-263-5012.

Committees: *Agriculture* (18th of 19 R). *Budget* (15th of 17 R). *Science, Space and Technology* (15th of 22 R): Science; Technology, Environment and Aviation.

Group Ratings and 102d Congress Votes: Newly Elected

Key Votes of the 103d Congress

1. Family Leave	AGN	2. Deficit Reduction	AGN	3. Stimulus Plan	AGN

Election Results

1992 general	Nick Smith (R)........................	133,972	(88%)	($231,043)
	Kenneth Proctor (LIB)................	18,751	(12%)	
1992 primary	Nick Smith (R).......................	26,174	(43%)	
	John Schwarz (R).....................	21,823	(36%)	
	Thomas Wilson (R)....................	7,067	(12%)	
	Brad Haskins (R)	5,598	(9%)	
1990 general	Carl D. Pursell (R)..................	95,962	(64%)	($135,801)
(MI 2)	Elmer White (D)......................	49,678	(33%)	($9,573)
	Other................................	4,126	(3%)	

EIGHTH DISTRICT

Lansing is a state capital chosen because of geographic position, selected in 1847 because it's halfway between Lake Huron and Lake Michigan, and in ignorance of the fact that it has fewer days with sunshine than any place else in the state. It is nonetheless a tidy and pleasant city with more than its share of amenities. It has a beautifully restored Capitol and a fine state history museum; it has Michigan State University, started in 1855 as America's first land-grant college, in next-door East Lansing; its Oldsmobile plant brought in people and stimulated growth in the first half of this century, and state government did the same in the second half. Politically, Lansing has tended to go with the party controlling state government. When the legislature was apportioned to stay Republican, as it was until 1964, the Lansing area was usually Republican; in the years since, Democrats have lost full control of the state House of Representatives only in 1966, and 1992, and Lansing has trended Democratic.

The 8th Congressional District of Michigan includes Lansing and Ingham County, but not the Lansing suburbs just across the line in Clinton and Eaton Counties, which are in the 4th and 7th Districts. It has two other very different population centers. One is the suburban fringe southwest of Flint, an area long Democratic and in deep trouble over the last dozen years with the shutdown of General Motors operations there. This is a solidly Democratic area. The other population center is Livingston County, where I-96 crosses U.S. 23. Strewn with lakes and hills, this has been one of the most rapidly growing counties in Michigan, with many new residents who have left the Detroit area because they dislike its crime, high tax and liberal politics. Livingston is very conservative and Republican; in 1992, only heavily Dutch Ottawa County gave Bill Clinton a lower percentage. But this is an evenly, even precariously balanced district politically. So precarious that incumbent Democrat Howard Wolpe decided to retire rather than run here and incumbent Democrat Bob Carr considered running in the Flint-to-Pontiac 9th District against incumbent Democrat Dale Kildee rather than face a Republican here.

But Carr did decide to run in the 8th and won, narrowly. He now holds one of the classic positions of power in the House: chairman of the Appropriations Transportation Subcommittee, which has the power of the purse over the road, highway and mass transit projects so important to so many members. This is probably not where Carr thought he was headed when he first ran for Congress in 1972. Then he was 29, a resident of Michigan for only four years, but eager to take on a Lansing Republican who had backed Richard Nixon and the Vietnam war. With the help of new 18-year-old voters at Michigan State, he nearly won; two years later the incumbent retired, and Carr became a congressman at 31. He was an outspoken Watergate baby; in his first three months, he called for the resignation of Speaker Carl Albert and got the Democratic Caucus to vote against military aid to Cambodia as the Khmer Rouge were closing in on Phnom Penh. On the Armed Services Committee, he was, with Ron Dellums, Les Aspin and Pat Schroeder, one of the few critics of the military. He lost in the Reagan landslide of 1980, vastly outspent, and with little help from Democrats.

Redistricting put heavily Democratic Pontiac into his old seat, and Carr ran again in 1982 and won. This time he sought not Armed Services but a seat on Appropriations, voted somewhat more conservatively—and, significant here, independent of organized labor—on economics, and emphasized constituency service. He used his seat on the Transportation Subcommittee to aid local projects from the Dixie Highway repaving in Waterford to the new Indian museum in Okemos. In Washington, he irritated colleagues in 1989 when he called for committee chairmen to file written explanations of the cost and purpose of official travel. Nor have his ties with the Michigan legislature been particularly warm; he had few friends in on the redistricting process and, somewhat desperately, at one point proposed expanding the membership of the legislature. Nor was he a team player among Democrats, "I'm in Congress despite being a Democrat," he often said. "There are Democrats who get up every morning and put on little donkey ties and have this barnyard way of doing things between donkeys and elephants. I don't have time for that." In February 1992, Transportation Subcommittee Chairman William Lehman, at 78 and after suffering a stroke in March 1991, announced he was retiring. Carr could see real power tantalizingly close. But he had to wait four months for redistricting and three serious Republicans filed against him. The winner, over Ann Arbor legislator Margaret O'Connor and Lansing-based Sandy Pensler, by a 36%–30%–30% margin was Dick Chrysler, whose slogan was "replace an old Carr with a new Chrysler." An entrepreneur, Chrysler (no relation to *the* Chrysler) started a car customizing company that became Livingston County's largest employer, customizing 95,000 cars a year. Chrysler sold the business and ran for governor in 1986, losing the Republican nomination in a close primary. Chrysler loaned his campaign $1.6 million, took no PAC money and spent $1,762,000, saving $537,000 for the campaign's closing weeks. But Carr retaliated in kind, raising $568,000 from PACs (the 15th highest in the House), spending $1,355,000 altogether and, with steely discipline, $476,000 after October 15. The result was practically a dead heat. Chrysler complained that Carr was a big government spender and an insider politician; Carr claimed credit for creating 10,000 jobs in the district with $200 million in federal road projects. Carr won 48%–46%, carrying Ingham County 50%–42% and Flint's Genesee County 52%–43%; Chrysler carried Livingston 56%–39%. The election returns suggest that Carr could be seriously challenged again. But the campaign finance numbers suggest that will be true only if a challenger can spend the kind of money Chrysler did.

Carr has been acting as if he expects to remain in the House for at least another decade. He says he will not stop earmarking and demonstration projects—subcommittee jargon for district pork, but does promise to show some (not total, but some) respect for the prerogatives of the Public Works Committee that technically should authorize every project before it is funded. He said he was developing a cost-benefit analysis which would provide justification for subcommittee-funded projects: "I'd like to give demonstration projects a respectable name." Carr is skeptical about some spending in Pat Moynihan's 1991 ISTEA law: he is skeptical about magnetic levitation trains, preferring "low-tech, less risky options"; he does not want to build new airports and does not "think we should have built Denver"—the new airport that was the main achievement of Transportation Secretary Federico Pena when he was mayor of Denver. There are other signs of possible friction with the Clinton Administration; when the stimulus package was in trouble, Carr expressed doubt that it would quickly create many jobs, citing the fact that spending formulas aren't proportionate to unemployment and that the state with the lowest ratio of federal dollars to unemployed persons would be Michigan. Carr is a lone wolf, who knows that he must make his own way through the woods.

The People: Pop. 1990: 581,072; 40% rural; 9% age 65+; 90% White; 6% Black; 1% Amer. Indian; 2% Asian; 1% Other; 3% Hispanic origin. Voting age pop.: 431,579; 5% Black; 2% Hispanic origin. Households: 58% married couple families; 29% married couple fams. w. children; 56% college educ.; median household income: $35,911; per capita income: $15,455; median gross rent: $435; median house value: $71,800.

1992 Presidential Vote			1988 Presidential Vote		
Clinton (D)	118,391	(40%)	Bush (R)	132,642	(56%)
Bush (R)	104,437	(36%)	Dukakis (D)	105,153	(44%)
Perot (I)	68,340	(23%)			

Rep. Bob Carr (D)

Elected 1982; b. Mar. 27, 1943, Janesville, WI; home, Okemos; U. of WI, B.S. 1965, J.D. 1968, MI St. U., 1968–69; Baptist; married (Kate).

Career: Staff Asst., MI Senate Minority Ldr., 1968–69; A.A., MI Atty. Gen., 1969–70; MI Asst. Atty. Gen., 1970–72; Cnsl., MI Legislature Cmte. on Legal Educ., 1972; U.S. House of Reps., 1974–80.

Offices: 2347 RHOB 20515, 202-225-4872. Also 2848 E. Grand River, #1, E. Lansing 48823, 517-351-7203; and 3487 S. Linden Rd., Flint 48507, 313-230-0873.

Committees: *Appropriations* (16th of 37 D): Commerce, Justice, State and Judiciary; Legislative; Transportation (Chmn.).

Group Ratings

	ADA	ACLU	COPE	CDF	CFA	LCV	ACU	NTLC	NSI	COC	CEI
1992	70	76	75	40	60	25	22	20	50	57	28
1991	75	—	58	80	72	46	21	—	—	40	17

National Journal Ratings

	1991 LIB — 1991 CONS			1992 LIB — 1992 CONS		
Economic	54%	—	45%	45%	—	55%
Social	67%	—	32%	53%	—	47%
Foreign	69%	—	31%	67%	—	32%

Key Votes of the 102d Congress

1. Ban Striker Replace	FOR	5. Handgun Wait/7-Day AGN	9. Use Force in Gulf AGN
2. $ for Homeownership	AGN	6. Overseas Mil. Abortion FOR	10. US Mil. Abroad $ Cut FOR
3. Tax Rich/Cut Mid Cls.	AGN	7. Obscn. Art NEA $ Ban AGN	11. Limit SDI Funds FOR
4. FY93/$15B Def. Cut	AGN	8. Death Pen. from Jury AGN	12. Cuba Trade Embargo FOR

Key Votes of the 103d Congress

1. Family Leave	AGN	2. Deficit Reduction	FOR	3. Stimulus Plan	FOR

Election Results

1992 general	Bob Carr (D).....................	135,517	(48%)	($1,355,199)
	Dick Chrysler (R).................	131,906	(46%)	($1,762,766)
	Frank McAlpine (NPA)	12,155	(4%)	($21,529)
	Others	5,129	(2%)	
1992 primary	Bob Carr (D), unopposed			
1990 general	Bob Carr (D), unopposed			($223,595)
(MI 6)				

NINTH DISTRICT

General Motors, formed in 1918, was a merger of several smaller car companies; headquartered in Detroit, it had plants in several small cities in Michigan and Ohio. Among them were Flint and Pontiac, two small industrial county seats on the old Woodward Avenue route that led northwest from Detroit. Pontiac, named for the 18th Century Indian chief who sparked a rebellion that spread all the way to what is now Pittsburgh, produced Pontiacs and GMC Trucks; Flint, named for the flint from which Indians made arrowheads, produced Buicks and Chevrolets. For five decades after 1918, Flint and Pontiac grew lustily, attracting new workers from the mountains of Kentucky and Tennessee and the Black Belt of Alabama; country and black music and various southern accents became common in towns first settled by Yankees. There was turmoil too. Flint was the scene in January 1937 of the great sitdown strike that, when Governor Frank Murphy refused to send National Guardsmen to enforce a court order, forced GM to recognize the United Auto Workers as the bargaining agent for all its workers. Yet in many ways these GM company towns built good lives for their citizens. The UAW-GM contracts produced the world's highest wages for industrial workers and lavish fringe benefits, including a healthcare plan as generous as any in the country. The Mott Foundation, started by GM's largest shareholder Charles Stewart Mott, funded schools, historical exhibitions, even a university branch in Flint—an exemplary plowing-back of money into a one-industry town. Workers laid off got 65 weeks of benefits amounting to 90% of regular wages—a real safety net.

Then, starting in the late 1970s, came disaster. Auto sales plummeted with the oil shock of 1979, and imports, especially from Japan, higher in quality and cheaper in price than American makes, were taking an increasing share of the market. The UAW leaders' and GM managers' assumptions that increased labor costs could be passed along to consumers and that they were indifferent to quality proved disastrously wrong: not even the cleverest advertising could force Americans to buy a new American car every two years. In 1979 GM employed more than 70,000 workers in its plants in Flint, a huge share of the labor force in a metro area of 430,000 people; in 1989 the work force was down to 46,000 and, with record losses, GM in 1992 announced it was closing another Flint plant with 4,400 workers by 1995. Thousands have left Flint; those who have stayed have found their real estate values—the store of wealth for most Americans— stagnant; government attempts to finance an upscale shopping mall, a Hyatt hotel and the AutoWorld theme park all went bankrupt. Pontiac was also hurt in the late 1980s when GM closed the Pontiac Fiero plant and foundry and another plant is slated for closing in 1994. But

Pontiac has some advantages. The Detroit metro area has expanded around the city, and surrounding Oakland County gained over 140,000 jobs, mainly in services and retail, in the 1980s. The city may sell the Silverdome where the Detroit Lions play; nearby, in Auburn Hills, is Chrysler's new technical center and, when it moves its offices from crime-plagued Highland Park, headquarters in late 1995.

The 9th Congressional District of Michigan runs from Flint to Pontiac, and has some diverse political territory. It includes the city of Flint and only some of its suburbs to the southeast; this Genesee County portion amounts to 37% of the district and is heavily Democratic. Pontiac, about half black, is heavily Democratic too. But it is only 12% of the district. Lake-strewn Waterford to the west was where many Pontiac whites moved when a school busing plan was ordered in the 1970s and it tends to be Republican. Auburn Hills and Rochester Hills east of Pontiac are high-income and heavily Republican. Clarkston and other burgeoning communities to the north, where hills and lakes and large lots give new residents the advantages of Up North living with an easy commute on I-75, are trending Republican also. Similarly, Lapeer County, north of Pontiac and east of Flint, has been growing and has long been Republican. That means that half the district is solidly Democratic, with a long union heritage; the other half is Republican, in some places very Republican.

The congressman from the 9th District is Dale Kildee, a Democrat first elected in 1976, whose district until 1992 clustered closely around Flint. He is a Democrat who studied for the priesthood, and he brings to politics an intensity of conviction derived from the liberal tradition lively in the American Catholic church—a tradition with little regard for market economics and a strong obligation to care for the needy. He is solidly liberal on economics and always pro-union; he is against abortion and is something of a stickler on ethics. His door-to-door campaigning got him elected to a newly created state legislative seat in 1964 and enabled him to beat a 26-year veteran of the state Senate 10 years later; he won the House seat in 1976, when it was solidly Democratic, without a primary opponent. But the new 9th District boundaries in 1992 presented a difficult challenge. Pontiac and the area around it are in the Detroit media market, and knew nothing of Flint or Kildee, and he had the additional burden of 100 overdrafts on the House bank. The Republicans had four serious candidates, all about half Kildee's age. The primary winner, with 35%, was former Bush/Quayle advance staffer Megan O'Neill, from Clarkston. O'Neill called Kildee a "career politician" who was "beholden to special interest groups" and lambasted him for the overdrafts; Kildee's camp emphasized he had never taken foreign junkets, never voted for a pay raise and had a near-perfect attendance record. "Washington might not be working, but Dale Kildee is," was the tag line on his ads. Money was also a factor: Kildee raised $464,000 from PACs and spent $795,000 altogether; O'Neill spent a total of $129,000. Kildee won 54%–45%, carrying Genesee County 73%–25%, the kind of margin he used to win in his whole district. But O'Neill carried Oakland 57%–42%, despite Kildee's win in Pontiac, and carried Lapeer 51%–47%. Kildee will have an opportunity as an incumbent to ingratiate himself with Oakland voters. But there is a solid Republican base here now, and the Republican areas are growing while the Democratic areas are losing population.

After this close shave, Kildee returned to the House as a major player on important legislation. He is fifth ranking Democrat on the Education and Labor Committee and an ally of Chairman William Ford, also of Michigan. His past achievements include a 1990 bill authorizing funding of Head Start for all eligible children, with a $6 billion increase in funding by 1994, and work on the child care bill of 1990 although the final version was considerably different from his. He is chairman of the Elementary and Secondary Education Subcommittee, a backer of increased federal aid and an opponent of school choice. He is dubious of President Clinton's proposal for national testing standards and proposes instead what he calls the "Opportunity to Learn" funding program to ensure adequate learning resources for all, though he stops at calling for equal funding for all schools. Anyway, research is sparse on the direct relationship between more spending and school performance; the Washington, D.C., public schools have some of the highest per pupil spending in the country, but the Clintons opted not to send their daughter there. Kildee has also taken an interest in trade issues. He was the first House member to argue that imported minivans should be subject not to the 2.5% tariff for cars but to the 25% tariff for trucks. He is also a strong opponent of the North American Free Trade Agreement. And his fastidiousness about ethics raised some hackles when in March 1993, as a newly appointed member of the House Administration Committee, he attacked in public hearings Chairman Charlie Rose for being too heavyhanded and his proposal to hire former Congressman Larry Smith as a consultant on the House restaurants.

The People: Pop. 1990: 580,908; 20% rural; 9% age 65+; 78% White; 18% Black; 1% Amer. Indian; 1% Asian; 1% Other; 3% Hispanic origin. Voting age pop.: 420,631; 16% Black; 2% Hispanic origin. Households: 54% married couple families; 26% married couple fams. w. children; 47% college educ.; median household income: $34,737; per capita income: $15,132; median gross rent: $448; median house value: $64,400.

1992 Presidential Vote			1988 Presidential Vote		
Clinton (D)	117,872	(44%)	Bush (R)	113,351	(51%)
Bush (R)	92,262	(35%)	Dukakis (D)	107,485	(49%)
Perot (I)	55,077	(21%)			

Rep. Dale E. Kildee (D)

Elected 1976; b. Sept. 16, 1929, Flint; home, Flint; Sacred Heart Seminary, B.A. 1952, U. of MI, M.A. 1961, Rotary Fellow, U. of Peshawar, Pakistan; Catholic; married (Gayle).

Career: High schl. teacher, 1954–64; MI House of Reps., 1964–74; MI Senate, 1974–75.

Offices: 2239 RHOB 20515, 202-225-3611. Also 316 W. Water St., Flint 48503, 313-239-1437; and 1829 N. Perry St., Pontiac 48340, 313-373-9337.

Committees: *Budget* (3d of 26 D). *Education and Labor* (5th of 28 D): Elementary, Secondary and Vocational Education (Chmn.); Human Resources; Labor-Management Relations; Postsecondary Education and Training. *House Administration* (9th of 12 D): Accounts.

Group Ratings

	ADA	ACLU	COPE	CDF	CFA	LCV	ACU	NTLC	NSI	COC	CEI
1992	90	83	92	100	93	75	4	0	30	25	7
1991	95	—	92	100	94	77	5	—	—	10	7

National Journal Ratings

	1991 LIB — 1991 CONS			1992 LIB — 1992 CONS		
Economic	88%	—	0%	91%	—	0%
Social	71%	—	28%	68%	—	30%
Foreign	87%	—	8%	82%	—	16%

Key Votes of the 102d Congress

1. Ban Striker Replace	FOR	5. Handgun Wait/7-Day	FOR	9. Use Force in Gulf	AGN
2. $ for Homeownership	AGN	6. Overseas Mil. Abortion	AGN	10. US Mil. Abroad $ Cut	FOR
3. Tax Rich/Cut Mid Cls.	FOR	7. Obscn. Art NEA $ Ban	AGN	11. Limit SDI Funds	FOR
4. FY93/$15B Def. Cut	FOR	8. Death Pen. from Jury	AGN	12. Cuba Trade Embargo	FOR

658   MICHIGAN

Key Votes of the 103d Congress

1. Family Leave   FOR   2. Deficit Reduction   FOR   3. Stimulus Plan   FOR

Election Results

1992 general	Dale E. Kildee (D)	133,956	(54%)	($795,484)
	Megan O'Neill (R)	111,798	(45%)	($129,840)
	Others	3,776	(2%)	($129,840)
1992 primary	Dale E. Kildee (D), unopposed			
1990 general	Dale E. Kildee (D)	90,307	(68%)	($222,531)
(MI 7)	David Morrill (R)	41,759	(32%)	($6,382)

TENTH DISTRICT

Macomb County, Michigan, on the billiard-flat tablelands east of Lake St. Clair and northeast of Detroit, has become in the last several election cycles one of the most closely watched suburban areas in the nation—a political battleground where the electoral fate of Michigan and perhaps the entire country will be determined. Macomb is thought of as the essence of blue-collar ethnic suburbia, and that is certainly its heritage, though today its people have higher incomes and are less likely to be foreign-born than the national average. Macomb is the product of the post-World War II boom: with just over 107,000 people in 1940, many of them in the old sulphur-water spa town of Mount Clemens, Macomb passed the 400,000 mark in 1960 and by 1990 had reached 717,000. Most people came here from Detroit: Polish-Americans marching out Van Dyke from Detroit and Hamtramck to Warren, Italian-Americans heading out Gratiot from Detroit's east side to Roseville and Clinton township, Belgian-Americans from the Mack Avenue corridor moving out farther to St. Clair Shores. These new suburbanites were heavily Catholic, often blue-collar, at least modestly affluent, and ancestrally Democratic. They accepted the New Deal as part of their natural heritage, but resented the efforts of Detroit politicians to tax them to pay for welfare, and were fearful of the high crime rates in Detroit's black neighborhoods; the suburb of East Detroit voted to change its name to Eastpointe, to avoid any implication it is part of the central city.

In 1960, Macomb County was the most Democratic major suburban county in the United States, voting 63% for America's first Catholic president, John F. Kennedy. Since then, Macomb has been moving away from the national Democrats—in 1962, because they would let Detroit tax suburbanites, in 1972, because they didn't vehemently oppose a metropolitan school busing plan. The allegiance finally snapped; Macomb hasn't voted for a Democratic presidential candidate since Hubert Humphrey, and none has gotten more than 40% of its votes since Jimmy Carter in 1976. George Bush carried Macomb solidly in 1988, 60%–39%; his share of the vote dropped drastically in four years, but he still beat Bill Clinton there in 1992, after appearances here by both candidates, 42%–37%. Macomb still elects mostly Republicans to local and state legislative office, though Democrats are competitive and hold some key posts. The Republicans have presented only a few candidates with political skills; the Democrats tend to have candidates with great personal strengths, notably Congressman David Bonior, the House Democratic whip.

The 10th Congressional District of Michigan includes most of Macomb County, everything but Warren, Sterling Heights and tiny Center Line and Utica, and also takes in the much smaller St. Clair County to the northeast. Presidentially, it is a Republican district; it voted for Republican Governor John Engler in 1990; but it continues to reelect Bonior, who brings to his politics the intensity of a former seminarian sympathetic to liberal elements in Catholic thought. One reason Bonior keeps winning is his cultural heritage: he is Polish-American, with roots in Hamtramck and Macomb County; he worked as a probation officer and social worker in Mount Clemens; he served in the military, stateside, in the Vietnam era (and came to oppose the war); and he is pro-life on abortion (though he did vote with most other Democrats against the "gag rule" and ban on fetal tissue research). Bonior also has a knack for identifying with local issues. He was running for the House in 1976 after four years in the legislature, when an ice storm killed many Macomb County trees; in response, he gave out thousands of pine seedlings as a campaign gimmick. This struck a chord with gun-toting sportsmen and baby-boomer environmentalists here, and by now he has handed out more than 400,000 seedlings and featured them in his TV ads. He does conspicuous work as well on local environmental problems—securing funds to study a replacement of the environmentally unsound Clinton River dam, taking credit for provisions in the Oil Spill Liability Act which subjects foreign tanker pilots to the same operating standards as U.S. pilots.

Bonior is interested in both foreign and domestic policy issues; as a member of the Rules Committee, he has been able to take a hand in both. Founder of the Vietnam-era Veterans Caucus in the House, he seems determined to prevent Americans from fighting again. Like many Catholic admirers of liberation theology, he opposed aid to the Nicaraguan contras and El Salvador government. It was Bonior's deep convictions and determination which probably commended him to Speaker Jim Wright, who appointed him chief deputy whip in 1986, an appointment underscoring Wright's sincerity in opposing the administration's Central America policy to House Democrats who shared Bonior's views, and that put Bonior on the leadership ladder. He did not move up immediately: William Gray beat him for whip in June 1989, after Wright and Whip Tony Coelho resigned, 134–97; but when Gray announced his retirement in June 1991, Bonior beat Maryland's Steny Hoyer 160–109.

As whip, Bonior worked hard on extending unemployment benefits, organizing an all-night vigil on the floor in September 1991 and holding up approval of aid to former Soviet republics until President Bush agreed to approve extended domestic jobless benefits and increased public works spending. "I think it's necessary to establish in the minds of House members that we're not letting other people cut in front of our workers." Bonior, in disagreement with Governor Engler as well as President Clinton, is also a strong opponent of NAFTA, "basically the sellout of [American] workers," he says. "We can't let jobs be our number one export." Bonior was a force pushing the Clinton Administration toward crafting the economic stimulus package that Republicans filibustered in the Senate; he differs from administration policy on Israel (of which he is not a strong backer) and abortion.

Redistricting was not a problem for Bonior; he kept most of his old territory and wasn't placed with another incumbent. But he had 76 overdrafts on the House bank, and he drew as his opponent state Senator Doug Carl, who held him to a 54%–45% in 1988, Bonior's closest race since 1976. Carl is a conservative Christian with ties to the evangelical movement who was supported by the National Right to Life Committee, which had backed Bonior in 1988; he attacked Bonior for the overdrafts and congressional perks and pay raises. Bonior responded by attacking Carl's perks and the free life-long health insurance he receives as a legislator when he opposed national health insurance for others. But money was key here. Bonior, who spent $434,000 against Carl in 1988 before he was whip, and $1,188,000 against his 1990 opponent, raised $934,000 from PACs and spent a total of $1,345,000, including a $500,000 October media buy; Carl spent $258,000 total. For all that, Bonior won 53%–44%, actually running better in St. Clair County (56%–41%) than Macomb (52%–45%). Bonior, with his strong convictions, will probably always be vulnerable to a serious challenge in a constituency which is very comfortable with his persona and some of his positions, but quite contrary to others.

The People: Pop. 1990: 580,974; 17% rural; 12% age 65+; 97% White; 2% Black; 1% Asian; 1% Hispanic origin. Voting age pop.: 433,652; 2% Black; 1% Hispanic origin. Households: 62% married couple families; 29% married couple fams. w. children; 42% college educ.; median household income: $36,536; per capita income: $15,603; median gross rent: $471; median house value: $70,900.

1992 Presidential Vote

Bush (R) 115,849 (41%)
Clinton (D) 100,587 (36%)
Perot (I) 60,927 (22%)

1988 Presidential Vote

Bush (R) 136,944 (62%)
Dukakis (D) 85,674 (38%)

Rep. David E. Bonior (D)

Elected 1976; b. June 6, 1945, Detroit; home, Mt. Clemens; U. of IA, B.A. 1967, Chapman Col., M.A. 1972; Catholic; married (Judy).

Career: Air Force, 1968–72; Probation officer, adoption case-worker, 1967–68; MI House of Reps., 1973–76.

Offices: 2207 RHOB 20515, 202-225-2106. Also 59 N. Walnut, #305, Mt. Clemens 48043, 313-469-3232; and 526 Water St., Port Huron 48060, 313-987-8889.

Committees: *Majority Whip. Rules* (5th of 9 D): Rules of the House.

Group Ratings

	ADA	ACLU	COPE	CDF	CFA	LCV	ACU	NTLC	NSI	COC	CEI
1992	80	91	91	90	73	69	0	0	30	29	4
1991	95	—	100	100	83	92	0	—	—	20	5

National Journal Ratings

	1991 LIB — 1991 CONS	1992 LIB — 1992 CONS
Economic	79% — 18%	91% — 0%
Social	78% — 17%	79% — 20%
Foreign	92% — 0%	90% — 0%

Key Votes of the 102d Congress

1. Ban Striker Replace	FOR	5. Handgun Wait/7-Day	FOR	9. Use Force in Gulf	AGN
2. $ for Homeownership	AGN	6. Overseas Mil. Abortion	AGN	10. US Mil. Abroad $ Cut	FOR
3. Tax Rich/Cut Mid Cls.	FOR	7. Obscn. Art NEA $ Ban	AGN	11. Limit SDI Funds	*
4. FY93/$15B Def. Cut	FOR	8. Death Pen. from Jury	AGN	12. Cuba Trade Embargo	AGN

Key Votes of the 103d Congress

1. Family Leave	FOR	2. Deficit Reduction	FOR	3. Stimulus Plan	FOR

Election Results

1992 general	David E. Bonior (D)	138,193	(53%)	($1,345,011)
	Douglas Carl (R)	114,918	(44%)	($258,057)
	Others	7,102	(3%)	
1992 primary	David E. Bonior (D), unopposed			
1990 general	David E. Bonior (D)	96,232	(63%)	($1,188,905)
(MI 12)	Jim Dingeman (R)	51,119	(34%)	($295,184)
	Other	2,474	(2%)	

ELEVENTH DISTRICT

Only minutes on the Lodge Freeway from the empty, abandoned blocks of inner city Detroit is one of the most affluent parts of the nation, with giant office buildings and growing small businesses, expensive houses on large lots and one shopping mall after another. This is southern Oakland County, north of the Eight Mile Road border with Detroit, where most people work in offices or stores and few in factories, and where crime is low and education levels high. Even physically there is a distinction: Detroit is on almost perfectly flat land, while many of the Oakland County suburbs run along a line of hills and lakes that marks the southernmost advance of an Ice Age glacier. Southfield, in southern Oakland County, is Michigan's largest office space center, far ahead of Detroit; Birmingham and Troy have major concentrations of luxury shopping, with other big malls in Troy, Southfield and Novi; Bloomfield Hills has Michigan's highest incomes as well as the Cranbrook institutions with their distinctive architecture. Forty years ago, Detroit had 1.9 million people and Oakland County 396,000; in 1990, Oakland had over one million and Detroit got over that mark only after Mayor Coleman Young pressured Census officials and presented names of people purportedly not counted.

The 11th Congressional District of Michigan includes almost half of Oakland County plus the middle-income suburbs of Redford Township and Livonia west of Detroit. This is mostly high-income and Republican territory, where people tend to believe in free market economics and fiercely oppose higher taxes. But it is also the home to most of the Detroit area's Jews, who have moved out the Lodge first to Southfield and then to West Bloomfield, and indeed are now scattered around most of these suburbs; they tend to remain Democratic, and, together with affluent blacks who have moved to Southfield and other suburbs, form the district's chief Democratic bloc. The congressman from this area when the district lines were drawn in 1992 was William Broomfield, a senior member of the Republican Party in the House, first elected in 1956, ranking minority member of the House Foreign Affairs Committee and always a faithful supporter of bipartisan interventionist foreign policy and Israel. But in April 1992, after 44 years in elective politics, Broomfield decided to retire, setting off a riproaring Republican primary and a serious Democratic challenge as well.

The most colorful candidates were state Senator David Honigman, and former Judge Alice Gilbert, once called "Hanging Alice." Honigman, who had announced even before Broomfield retired, spent $1.3 million of his own money, much of it attacking Gilbert; he ran one ad, a woman dressed in judge's robes doing the wave at a baseball game, mocking Gilbert's opening day attendance at a Detroit Tigers game which she had attended on a day off during a highly publicized murder trial. Gilbert in turn plastered Honigman for taking a squishy, inconsistent position on abortion rights; she was pro-choice, while the third Republican, insurance agent, former Oakland County party chairman and Broomfield campaign chairman Joe Knollenberg, was antiabortion. Knollenberg's ads denounced free-spending millionaire candidates and career politicians. One columnist called the Republican candidates "the Three Stooges." Knollenberg, with less money but with Broomfield's endorsement, won with 43% of the vote to 30% for Honigman and 27% for Gilbert; here, as elsewhere in Michigan, a pro-choice stand was not key in the primary or the general.

Knollenberg is the fifth of 13 children raised on a Downstate Illinois farm. He became an insurance agent after serving in the Army and moved to Oakland County in 1967, where he immediately became involved in Republican Party work from the precinct level up, and served on civic boards; at 58, he jogs several miles a week and his wife Sandie hosts a TV aerobics show. Not dazzlingly articulate, he says of his constituents, "I am one of them . . . I raised a family . . . I built a business . . . I know something about the real world." Knollenberg had game Democratic opposition from Walter Briggs, IV, Broomfield's 1990 opponent and nephew of the late Senator Philip Hart. Briggs, an auditor at Blue Cross/Blue Shield, campaigned on the abortion issue, escorting women past demonstrators into clinics; with a Jewish wife and sons, he campaigned as a strong supporter of Israel. He ran well in Southfield and in heavily Jewish precincts, but Knollenberg won solidly, 58%–40%, in a district long disposed to reelect even quietly self-effacing Republican.

The People: Pop. 1990: 580,934; 5% rural; 12% age 65+; 93% White; 4% Black; 2% Asian; 1% Hispanic origin. Voting age pop.: 444,047; 4% Black; 1% Hispanic origin. Households: 63% married couple families; 28% married couple fams. w. children; 63% college educ.; median household income: $49,021; per capita income: $24,466; median gross rent: $638; median house value: $110,300.

1992 Presidential Vote			1988 Presidential Vote		
Bush (R)	147,786	(47%)	Bush (R)	173,339	(66%)
Clinton (D)	116,266	(37%)	Dukakis (D)	91,266	(34%)
Perot (I)	50,385	(16%)			

Rep. Joe Knollenberg (R)

Elected 1992; b. Nov. 28, 1933, Mattoon, IL; home, Bloomfield Township; E. IL U., B.S. 1955; Catholic; married (Sandie).

Career: Army, 1955–57; Insurance agent, 1958–92.

Offices: 1218 LHOB 20515, 202-225-5802. Also 30833 Northwestern Hwy., #214, Farmington Hills 48334, 313-851-1366; and 15439 Middlebelt St., Livonia 48514, 313-425-7557.

Committees: *Banking, Finance and Urban Affairs* (14th of 20 R): Consumer Credit and Insurance; Housing and Community Development. *Small Business* (13th of 18 R): Minority Enterprise, Finance and Urban Development; Procurement, Taxation and Tourism.

Group Ratings and 102d Congress Votes: Newly Elected

Key Votes of the 103d Congress

1. Family Leave	AGN	2. Deficit Reduction	AGN	3. Stimulus Plan	AGN

Election Results

1992 general	Joe Knollenberg (R)	168,940	(58%)	($490,926)
	Walter Briggs, IV (D)	117,725	(40%)	($272,422)
	Others	6,433	(2%)	
1992 primary	Joe Knollenberg (R)	30,022	(43%)	
	Dave Honigman (R)	20,641	(30%)	
	Alice Gilbert (R)	18,954	(27%)	
1990 general	William S. Broomfield (R)	126,629	(66%)	($78,205)
(MI 18)	Walter Briggs, IV (D)	64,185	(34%)	($78,205)

TWELFTH DISTRICT

The flat expanse of land just north of Eight Mile Road, Detroit's northern city limit was mostly vacant in the years just after World War II. There was a string of suburbs in Oakland County along Woodward Avenue, Detroit's main street, already eight lanes wide, that went out to the Shrine of the Little Flower church in Royal Oak, where in the 1930s Father Coughlin made his radio broadcasts backing, and then opposing, Franklin Roosevelt and denouncing bankers and Jews. In Macomb County to the east, there was some industrial development along Van Dyke, but this was mostly empty land too, while Detroit's population was heading toward two million. Today, these areas are well-settled suburbs, entirely built up, some neighborhoods edging toward seediness, many others continually renovated and restored; while Detroit has been ripped apart by crime, its population falling below one million in 1992.

The 12th Congressional District of Michigan is in this suburban territory, with about half its population in two suburban counties. On the Oakland County side is Royal Oak and other Woodward Avenue suburbs, now attracting singles and gays as well as families; Oak Park, heavily Jewish in the 1950s and now perhaps the only city in America with sizable numbers of Jews, Arabs and blacks; Hazel Park and Madison Heights, mostly peopled with descendants of the Appalachian migrants of a few decades ago; and Troy, once blank fields and now a major office center, with the K-Mart world headquarters across the street from upscale Somerset Mall. On the Macomb County side are Warren and Sterling Heights, the destination often of Polish-Americans moving out from Hamtramck and the East Side of Detroit, and site of the General Motors Technical Center (where CEO Jack Smith is moving his office from Detroit), a big Chrysler plant and the M-1 tank plant where Michael Dukakis took his famous ride in the 1988 campaign. Historically, Macomb County is Democratic, Oakland Republican; but Oak Park and Hazel Park have long been very Democratic, and Macomb has been trending Republican for years; their percentages have been virtually identical in the last three presidential elections.

The 12th District, as created for the 1992 election, contained the homes of two Democratic incumbents; indeed, they were districted together in plans submitted by both parties. Both were from successful political families and had been in politics for many years. Dennis Hertel, originally from the East Side of Detroit, had represented more of the new district, but Sander Levin, originally from the Woodward Avenue suburb of Berkley, had represented south Oakland County in the state Senate as long ago as 1964. Levin raised over $600,000 by the end of 1991, while Hertel was revealed to have 547 overdrafts on the House bank; after 12 years of service as one of Michigan's few members on the Armed Services Committee, Hertel retired at 44. This was a break for Levin, who has not always been so lucky; he ran for governor in 1970 and 1974, both times losing by narrow margins to Republican William Milliken. After heading Agency for International Development population control programs under President Carter, he got lucky in 1982 when James Blanchard left the House to run successfully for governor and William Brodhead retired at 40; their district's were combined and included Levin's home base so he ran and, in a spirited primary, won. He is, by the way, the older brother of Senator Carl Levin, and the two brothers seem to have an entirely comfortable relationship.

Sandy Levin is a hard worker, a detail man, willing to spend endless hours with others working out a solution. He chaired a Democratic task force that helped lay the groundwork for the 1988 workfare law which assisted welfare recipients to get into the work force. In 1987, he got a seat on the Ways and Means Committee, where he has become one of its leading trade hawks; he founded the Congressional Auto Parts Task Force with Marcy Kaptur and chairs the Competitiveness Caucus's Task Force on Japan with Republican Frank Wolf. He campaigned frequently for Richard Gephardt for president in 1987 and 1988, and has remained close to Gephardt ever since. In 1990, he published in the *Congressional Record* the controversial *The Japan That Can Say No*, by Akio Morita and Shintaro Ishihara, when the authors refused to allow it to appear in translation. Levin followed up by inviting Ishihara to a town meeting in the his district, to hear

U.S. workers defend their products, after which he went to Japan to visit Ishihara's constituency. In 1992, he got the House to vote for requiring the United States to negotiate limits on Japanese car and truck sales, including those manufactured in U.S. plants; the Senate wouldn't buy it and President Bush would have vetoed it. He is the House sponsor of the measure to reclassify Japanese minivans from cars with a 2.5% tariff to trucks with a 25% tariff; this would have guaranteed U.S. makers, already with a majority of the minivan market, the whole thing and would have allowed them to raise prices. In 1992 and 1993, Levin has been broadly skeptical, though not explicitly opposed to, the North American Free Trade Agreement; it's likely he has urged or will urge Gephardt to torpedo it, and he openly advocates a strong commission enforcing environmental and workers' rights disputes. He strongly backed extension of unemployment benefits, and wants to reduce the luxury tax which covers some U.S.-made autos. In April 1993, he called for a commission to create an overall U.S. motor vehicle policy: "We have pursued no coherent economic policy for one of the most critical sectors of our economy."

Levin also serves as vice chairman of the Ways and Means Health Subcommittee. He favors increased mental health coverage under Medicare and undoubtedly would push it in a healthcare reform plan. In 1992, he sponsored a plan to cap healthcare spending by state-managed cost containment programs and give any savings to increase Medicaid coverage of children and pregnant teenagers.

Levin was fortunate in 1992 to avoid a primary, but he still had a serious general election. Oakland County Republican Party Chairman John Pappageorge, a retired Army colonel and M-1 tank executive, campaigned civilly but issued strong calls for cutting spending. Most Detroit area Jewish voters, Levin's natural base, were in the new and heavily Republican 11th District; all of Macomb and some of Oakland were new to him. But Levin had a huge money advantage, spending $1,185,000 to Pappageorge's $190,000. Levin carried Macomb by just 51%–47% and was a bit stronger in Oakland, at 54%–44%. He will have more time to get acquainted in new parts of the district, but those numbers could attract serious opposition in 1994, especially if there is a Republican trend.

The People: Pop. 1990: 580,987; 13% age 65+; 93% White; 4% Black; 2% Asian; 1% Hispanic origin. Voting age pop.: 442,555; 3% Black; 1% Hispanic origin. Households: 58% married couple families; 27% married couple fams. w. children; 48% college educ.; median household income: $38,760; per capita income: $16,796; median gross rent: $512; median house value: $75,300.

1992 Presidential Vote

Clinton (D) 119,055 (42%)
Bush (R) 115,065 (40%)
Perot (I). 49,519 (17%)

1988 Presidential Vote

Bush (R) 143,088 (58%)
Dukakis (D). 104,832 (42%)

Rep. Sander M. Levin (D)

Elected 1982; b. Sept. 6, 1931, Detroit; home, Southfield; U. of Chicago, B.A. 1952, Columbia U., M.A. 1954, Harvard, LL.B. 1957; Jewish; married (Victoria).

Career: Practicing atty., 1957–64, 1970–76; Oakland Bd. of Supervisors, 1961–64; MI Senate, 1965–70; Fellow, Harvard JFK Schl. of Govt., 1975; A.A., Agency for Intl. Devel., 1977–81.

Offices: 106 CHOB 20515, 202-225-4961. Also 2107 E. 14 Mile Rd., #130, Sterling Heights 48310, 313-268-4444.

Committees: *Ways and Means* (12th of 24 D): Health; Human Resources.

Group Ratings

	ADA	ACLU	COPE	CDF	CFA	LCV	ACU	NTLC	NSI	COC	CEI
1992	95	96	83	100	93	75	4	0	20	38	13
1991	100	—	100	100	83	77	0	—	—	30	10

National Journal Ratings

	1991 LIB — 1991 CONS		1992 LIB — 1992 CONS	
Economic	79%	— 18%	78%	— 18%
Social	88%	— 0%	72%	— 28%
Foreign	87%	— 8%	65%	— 33%

Key Votes of the 102d Congress

1. Ban Striker Replace	FOR	5. Handgun Wait/7-Day	FOR	9. Use Force in Gulf	AGN
2. $ for Homeownership	AGN	6. Overseas Mil. Abortion	FOR	10. US Mil. Abroad $ Cut	FOR
3. Tax Rich/Cut Mid Cls.	FOR	7. Obscn. Art NEA $ Ban	AGN	11. Limit SDI Funds	FOR
4. FY93/$15B Def. Cut	FOR	8. Death Pen. from Jury	AGN	12. Cuba Trade Embargo	FOR

Key Votes of the 103d Congress

1. Family Leave	FOR	2. Deficit Reduction	FOR	3. Stimulus Plan	FOR

Election Results

1992 general	Sander M. Levin (D)	137,514	(53%)	($1,185,400)
	John Pappageorge (R).	119,357	(46%)	($190,203)
	Others	4,478	(2%)	
1992 primary	Sander M. Levin (D), unopposed			
1990 general	Sander M. Levin (D)	92,205	(70%)	($271,072)
(MI 17)	Blaine Lankford (R)	40,100	(30%)	

THIRTEENTH DISTRICT

From Detroit's Metro Airport west to Ann Arbor runs what was once a key artery in the "arsenal of democracy." Now the I-94 expressway, it was built in 1942 so workers from Detroit could drive to the huge Willow Run bomber plant 30 miles west; later it was known by travelers for its pothole-pocked pavement and the giant Goodyear tire over the billboard with a digital counter showing the year's (American) car production. Today, it is still a key link between factories and suppliers, workers and workplaces, between the blue-collar neighborhoods of southwest Wayne

County and Ann Arbor, home of the University of Michigan. But the expressway symbolizes a shift that has been going on here for at least a dozen years, from many low-skill jobs assembling high-style but low-tech cars, to fewer higher-skill jobs in higher-tech manufacturing, often with smaller firms seeking out market niches. People here like to call I-94 "Automation Alley," and some people have done very well by the changes. But others have been left behind: the 2,460 workers at the General Motors plant in Ypsilanti, where UAW local leaders were so confident that they refused to make concessions when pitted against a plant in Arlington, Texas; the Texas UAW did make concessions, and GM announced that the Ypsilanti plant would close in 1994.

The 13th Congressional District of Michigan covers much of this unpicturesque landscape from the Airport to Ann Arbor. A few of its suburbs are distinctly downscale, like Romulus, where poorer residents have worked a little at a time to build their own houses, on land so flat it oozes water after a rain. Others are proudly middle-income, like Westland, which was named after a shopping center, and Canton Township, which grew robustly in the 1980s; Plymouth and Northville just to the north verge on high-income. Southwest Wayne County has been Democratic since the UAW forced an unwilling Henry Ford to sign a collective bargaining contract in 1941; but as working-class wages went up and working-class consciousness declined it has become less so, and many remaining working-class areas are in the 16th, not the 13th, District. In Washtenaw County, Ann Arbor, the district's largest city, has a Republican history going back to its beginnings as a haven for German veterans of the failed revolutions of 1848; but the student vote in 1970 swung it sharply to the left, and it oscillates now depending on the intellectual fashions of graduate students. Ypsilanti, more working class and also the home of Eastern Michigan University, is more dependably Democratic. Overall, this is a district in which no party has more than a tenuous majority.

The congressman from the 13th District, nonetheless, is one of the most senior Democrats in the House, William Ford, first elected in 1964 and chairman of the House Education and Labor Committee. Ford has a background once typical of liberal politicians but now seldom found in Democratic ranks. He is the son of a Kaiser-Frazer factory worker, who died at 42 in a factory fire; the company at first claimed he had died of a heart attack, and only when Bill Ford, then age 20 and a college freshman, investigated did the facts come out and the company agreed to pay a $5,000 settlement. Ford practiced law in Taylor, and made political and union contacts that got him elected to the legislature in 1962 and, after redistricting, to Congress in 1964 at age 37. "The AFL-CIO sent me to Congress," Ford told a union audience in the 1990s, "the AFL-CIO keeps me in Congress, and the AFL-CIO will tell me when to leave Congress."

From his personal experience, Ford developed a political faith now considered old-fashioned in many quarters: he is a believer in strong labor unions, in active and generous federal government, in the need for Congress to set national priorities and enforce them against often recalcitrant local governments and private companies. He still believes in the Great Society programs he voted for as a freshman and spent the 1980s trying to protect. "I'd like to believe we can convince people that this me-and-me-only crap is over and we've got to make investments in the future generations." The plant closing bill, finally passed in 1988, was something Ford had pushed since 1974. Family and medical leave, a longtime Ford project, was vetoed by President Bush in 1990 and 1992, but signed by President Clinton in February 1993. Ford's longtime goal of overhauling the Hatch Act passed the House in March 1993, thereby allowing federal workers to engage in partisan politics off the job. He is, like so many Michigan Democrats, a trade hawk who backs limits on imported cars and refuses to issue parking passes for staffers with foreign-made cars.

Ford has several other goals for the Clinton years. He wants to pass the striker replacement bill which would increase the leverage unions got in the New Deal's Wagner Act; the bill passed the House in 1991, but Senate Republicans successfully filibustered it in 1992; Clinton's support should help if it comes up again in 1993. Ford has also proposed changes in the OSHA worker safety act, placing more requirements on management and, an interesting innovation, requiring joint management-worker committees to probe plant safety. He passed a Higher Education reauthorization in 1992 which made unsubsidized Stafford loans available to all students regardless of income and increased Pell grant income limits; but he was not able to get Pell grants declared an entitlement, which would have freed them from the appropriations process. He also got a pilot program of direct federal government loans to students, and will undoubtedly push the Clinton Administration plan to eliminate banks from student lending. On elementary and secondary education, Ford is Congress's chief strategist for the National Education Association in torpedoing school choice programs. He is dubious about President Clinton's proposal for national testing standards and proposes instead what he calls "Opportunity to Learn," i.e., more funding, although he does not go so far as to call for equal funding for all schools, and research is sparse on whether there is a direct relationship between more spending and school performance. Here, as on trade and union issues, Ford wants to provide employee security against market pressures.

From 1964 through 1990, Ford had districts which supported without much demur his labor-liberal vision; his 61% in 1990 was on the low side for him. The new 13th District included some solidly Republican territory, and in an anti-incumbent year. Republican incumbent Carl Pursell (of the old 2d), whose home is in Plymouth, decided to retire rather than run against Ford. State Senator Robert Geake, a U of M Ph.D. in psychology and a 20-year legislator with a Plymouth-Northville base, won a six-candidate primary with 48%. Geake attacked Ford for his six overdrafts on the House bank and his frequent first-class air travel. Ford replied, "I may be bragging a little here, but I really believe that you've got to catch me with a smoking gun over a bleeding corpse before people in my district are going to believe I've done something wrong." President Bush came into the district and attacked Ford for opposing school choice. Ford was helped by UAW support—there are probably more auto workers in the 13th than in any other district in America—and by $520,000 in PAC contributions; he spent $872,000 to Geake's $188,000. The election was close. Geake, with big margins in his home area, carried Wayne County 48%–46%. But Ford, with a big margin in his new area of Ann Arbor, carried Washtenaw 61%–35%, and won overall with 52%–43%.

Since his narrow reelection, Ford has become a bit of a congressional reformer: he was one of a handful of senior Democrats to vote for killing the select committees. He also sought a 1% decrease in the Education and Labor Committee budget. But there is no indication that he will trim his sails on the education and labor issues about which he cares so much or abandon the stands he has taken for so many years; he may make some practical-minded compromises, but in early 1993 seemed more to be dominating the Clinton Administration rather than being dominated by it. But the 1992 results suggest there is some risk in this approach, and some possibility of serious opposition in the future.

The People: Pop. 1990: 580,882; 7% rural; 9% age 65+; 85% White; 11% Black; 3% Asian; 2% Hispanic origin. Voting age pop.: 442,363; 10% Black; 1% Hispanic origin. Households: 53% married couple families; 26% married couple fams. w. children; 55% college educ.; median household income: $36,596; per capita income: $16,267; median gross rent: $519; median house value: $76,600.

1992 Presidential Vote

Clinton (D) 129,113 (49%)
Bush (R) 89,040 (34%)
Perot (I). 43,946 (17%)

1988 Presidential Vote

Bush (R) 112,085 (51%)
Dukakis (D). 108,488 (49%)

Rep. William D. Ford (D)

Elected 1964; b. Aug. 6, 1927, Detroit; home, Ypsilanti; Wayne St. U., 1947–48, U. of Denver, B.S. 1949, J.D. 1951; United Church of Christ; married (Mary).

Career: Navy, 1944–46, Air Force Reserves, 1950–58; Practicing atty., 1951–60; Taylor Township Justice of the Peace, 1955–57; Melvindale City Atty., 1957–59; Taylor Township Atty., 1957–64; MI Senate, 1963–65.

Offices: 2107 RHOB 20515, 202-225-6261. Also Fed. Bldg., Wayne 48184, 313-722-1411; 31 S. Huron St., Ypsilanti 48197, 313-482-6636; and 106 E. Washington St., Ann Arbor 48104, 313-471-4210.

Committees: *Education and Labor* (Chmn. of 28 D): Postsecondary Education and Training (Chmn.).

Group Ratings

	ADA	ACLU	COPE	CDF	CFA	LCV	ACU	NTLC	NSI	COC	CEI
1992	95	100	100	80	73	50	0	0	20	25	9
1991	95	—	100	100	78	69	0	—	—	13	9

National Journal Ratings

	1991 LIB — 1991 CONS	1992 LIB — 1992 CONS
Economic	88% — 0%	89% — 9%
Social	84% — 16%	84% — 15%
Foreign	85% — 15%	85% — 14%

Key Votes of the 102d Congress

1. Ban Striker Replace	FOR	5. Handgun Wait/7-Day	FOR	9. Use Force in Gulf	AGN
2. $ for Homeownership	AGN	6. Overseas Mil. Abortion	FOR	10. US Mil. Abroad $ Cut	FOR
3. Tax Rich/Cut Mid Cls.	FOR	7. Obscn. Art NEA $ Ban	AGN	11. Limit SDI Funds	FOR
4. FY93/$15B Def. Cut	FOR	8. Death Pen. from Jury	AGN	12. Cuba Trade Embargo	FOR

Key Votes of the 103d Congress

1. Family Leave   FOR   2. Deficit Reduction   FOR   3. Stimulus Plan   FOR

Election Results

1992 general	William D. Ford (D)................	127,642	(52%)	($872,349)
	Robert Geake (R)....................	105,169	(43%)	($188,138)
	Randall Roe (I)......................	8,626	(4%)	
	Others..............................	4,451	(2%)	
1992 primary	William D. Ford (D), unopposed			
1990 general	William D. Ford (D).................	68,742	(61%)	($354,964)
(MI 15)	Burl Adkins (R)	41,092	(37%)	($42,834)
	Other...............................	2,591	(2%)	

FOURTEENTH DISTRICT

The early auto factories of Detroit—Packard, Hudson, Ford Highland Park, Dodge Main, Briggs, Ford Rouge, Cadillac, Kelsey-Hayes, Chrysler, Plymouth, DeSoto—were built between 1905 and 1925 in an arc about five miles from the city's center, in green fields at what was then the edge of urban development. As they were going up, the flat farmlands all around were platted in grid streets and developed with houses, some wooden bungalows, but many neighborhoods of massive brick one- and two-family houses, often with a driveway at the side and a single elm in front. Commercial developments lined the mile-square and radial main streets, stretching straight as far as the eye could see. Detroit was the nation's second fastest-growing big city in those years, after Los Angeles, and, like Los Angeles, was one of the first American cities built to automobile scale. Its neighborhoods filled up with factory workers and civil servants, professionals and maintenance men, corner store owners and management personnel, Catholics and Protestants and Jews. These outer neighborhoods of Detroit didn't contain every segment of society, but they were a middle-class melting pot. With one exception: Detroit in those days had few blacks, who did not begin their big migrations here from the South, mainly Alabama, until around 1940, when defense plants began hiring in large numbers.

The history of black Detroit is one of conflict and uplift, inspiration and tragedy. The wartime mixture of Appalachian mountain whites and Deep South blacks proved volatile: there was a violent race riot in June 1943. Blacks were pent up in a few terribly overcrowded neighborhoods during the war years, like the Black Bottom which is now the Chrysler Freeway; after 1945, when blacks started moving outward, real estate agents played on racial fears to make sales and in the 1950s whole square miles of Detroit changed racial composition in just a few years. In the 1960s, there was hope that the civil rights movement, encouraged by Walter Reuther's United Auto Workers, and antipoverty programs would improve blacks' lot, and in fact many black Detroiters found good jobs and made good incomes, bought their own houses and built community institutions. Then came the riot of July 1967, followed by vast white flight, a huge proliferation of guns and terrible increases in crime. Detroit's first black mayor, Coleman Young, elected in 1973, responded with policies that may have seemed appropriate in the 1960s but had disastrous results in the 1970s and 1980s: pressuring major employers like the Big Three auto companies to build facilities in Detroit, raising taxes to support a vast army of city employees, and attributing city problems to white racism. But violent crime became a part of everyday life and arson became common, especially on "devil's night" at Halloween, with never a criticism from the mayor—for to criticize blacks who commit crimes would be blaming the victim, playing into the hands of white racists.

Detroit took on a garrison atmosphere. Crime reduced the value of residential real estate to near zero, and the city's population dropped from 1.7 million in 1960 to one million (in probably cooked figures) in 1990. Thousands of houses were abandoned to arsonists and drug dealers; in early 1993, the city's ombudsman proposed that large stretches of property be purchased by the city and fenced off and abandoned. In political dialogue, most black politicians called for, and most black voters seemed to support, an ever-increasing public sector. Yet the existing public sector, which takes a larger share of residents' income than in almost anywhere else in the country, nonetheless serves citizens very poorly. Detroit seemed certain in early 1993 to elect a new mayor in November. But it is a serious question whether its problems are curable.

The 14th Congressional District of Michigan consists of the northern half of Detroit, including most neighborhoods just beyond the auto plants; it also includes adjacent suburbs from high-income Grosse Pointe Woods and defiantly all-white Dearborn Heights to Highland Park, an enclave within the city, which had 52,000 people and fine city services in 1930 and 20,000 people and an essentially defunct government in 1990. To be sure, there are some solid neighborhoods here, including high-income Palmer Woods and Sherwood Forest, and Rosedale Park where many city employees live; but not far away are streets in decay. Politically, this is a solidly Democratic area, one of the most Democratic in the United States; the question in elections here is not percentage but turnout.

The congressman from the 14th District is John Conyers, senior member (and one of the founders) of the Congressional Black Caucus, chairman of the Government Operations Committee. The son of a left-wing operative in the UAW, he was first elected to Congress in 1964—one of six blacks in the House at the time, and the only one to take a militant approach to politics, distancing himself from the Johnson Administration, criticizing the Vietnam war from the beginning, charging that liberals were not doing enough for the poor. His response to the 1967 riot was to introduce the first bill for a guaranteed annual income. He stood by in disgust as his white Michigan Democratic colleagues opposed metropolitan school busing, and in many ways was a bitter bystander to most political fights of the 1970s and 1980s. As a Judiciary subcommittee chairman, he opposed the death penalty in drug bills, the abolition of the insanity defense after the Reagan assassination attempt in 1981 and the revised criminal code—all futilely. He strongly supports the Racial Justice Act (banning executions when the death penalty is imposed disproportionately on blacks) and the Hate Crime Statistics Act. He is a major roadblock to relaxation of the overbroad RICO statute, saying that reform would hinder government efforts to bring S&L crooks to justice. He pushed successfully for the Martin Luther King Holiday, but has made no impact with his proposal for reparations for the descendants of slaves.

But governmental responsibilities—and his own concern about the quality of life in Northwest Detroit—have changed Conyers's emphasis over the years. On Judiciary, he was saddled with the chore of chairing hearings on the impeachment of Florida federal Judge Alcee Hastings, acquitted of criminal bribery but accused by his fellow judges of lying; Conyers recommended impeachment, and the House and Senate followed. Ironically, Hastings was elected to Congress from the new 23d District of Florida. In 1989, Conyers inherited the Government Operations Committee chair from Jack Brooks and took on some new fights, installing chief financial officers in each government department and trying to limit OMB's control over new federal regulations. In January 1993, he introduced a report detailing $300 billion of federal government waste since 1988. He is an advocate of opening up government to full view, from Dan Quayle's now defunct Competitiveness Council to the Kennedy assassination files. He has argued for $3 billion worth of immediate public works projects and, concerned about the effect of alcohol use by pregnant women on their babies, he sponsored the Alcohol Warning Label Act.

Twice in recent years, Conyers has been criticized in the glare of the spotlight. One was in Detroit, when he abruptly ran for mayor against Coleman Young in 1989. His campaign was glitch-ridden and he was light on specifics. But it must have been wrenching for Conyers to take on his old political ally, and to finish a dismal third in the primary; the only reason he could have had for running was a sincere desire to remedy the horrors of living in Detroit today. Conyers's other exposure to the spotlight came in April 1993, when he criticized Attorney General Janet Reno for her decision to storm the Branch Davidian compound in Waco. Reno got great plaudits on network TV for asserting that she felt more strongly about the deaths of 24 children "than you will ever know" and then adding, "I will not engage in recriminations." But the issue of course was not Reno's capacity for sympathy, but the reasons for a decision made which turned out to be hideously wrong; and recriminations, assessments of who erred and why, were entirely in order. If Conyers had been grilling a Republican Attorney General who had made the same decision, the networks probably would have rightly cheered him on.

Neither Conyers's mayoral fiasco nor the revelation of 273 overdrafts on the House bank caused him much damage at the polls. He was reelected in 1990 without serious opposition. In 1992, with more whites added to the district, he was opposed in the primary by Grosse Pointe Woods state Senator John Kelly, but predictably Conyers won 64%–26%.

The People: Pop. 1990: 580,977; 11% age 65+; 29% White; 69% Black; 1% Asian; 1% Hispanic origin. Voting age pop.: 409,188; 65% Black; 1% Hispanic origin. Households: 38% married couple families;

18% married couple fams. w. children; 40% college educ.; median household income: $25,079; per capita income: $11,462; median gross rent: $421; median house value: $29,400.

1992 Presidential Vote			1988 Presidential Vote		
Clinton (D)	165,363	(79%)	Dukakis (D)	144,917	(76%)
Bush (R)	31,360	(15%)	Bush (R)	45,116	(24%)
Perot (I)	11,992	(6%)			

Rep. John Conyers, Jr. (D)

Elected 1964; b. May 16, 1929, Detroit; home, Detroit; Wayne St. U., B.A. 1957, LL.B. 1958; Baptist; single.

Career: Army, 1950–54 (Korea); Legis. Asst., U.S. Rep. John Dingell, 1958–61; Practicing atty., 1959–61; Referee, MI Workmen's Compensation Dept., 1961–63.

Offices: 2426 RHOB 20515, 202-225-5126. Also 669 Fed. Bldg., 231 W. Lafayette St., Detroit 48226, 313-961-5670.

Committees: *Government Operations* (Chmn. of 25 D): Legislation and National Security (Chmn.). *Judiciary* (3d of 21 D): Crime and Criminal Justice; Economic and Commercial Law; Intellectual Property and Judicial Administration. *Small Business* (7th of 27 D): Minority Enterprise, Finance and Urban Development.

Group Ratings

	ADA	ACLU	COPE	CDF	CFA	LCV	ACU	NTLC	NSI	COC	CEI
1992	90	100	89	90	73	81	0	5	10	13	12
1991	95	—	100	100	89	92	0	—	—	20	11

National Journal Ratings

	1991 LIB — 1991 CONS		1992 LIB — 1992 CONS	
Economic	88%	— 0%	76%	— 24%
Social	88%	— 0%	87%	— 13%
Foreign	85%	— 15%	90%	— 0%

Key Votes of the 102d Congress

1. Ban Striker Replace	FOR	5. Handgun Wait/7-Day	FOR	9. Use Force in Gulf	AGN
2. $ for Homeownership	*	6. Overseas Mil. Abortion	FOR	10. US Mil. Abroad $ Cut	FOR
3. Tax Rich/Cut Mid Cls.	FOR	7. Obscn. Art NEA $ Ban	AGN	11. Limit SDI Funds	FOR
4. FY93/$15B Def. Cut	FOR	8. Death Pen. from Jury	AGN	12. Cuba Trade Embargo	AGN

Key Votes of the 103d Congress

1. Family Leave	FOR	2. Deficit Reduction	FOR	3. Stimulus Plan	FOR

Election Results

1992 general	John Conyers, Jr. (D)	165,496	(82%)	($332,818)
	John Gordon (R).....................	32,036	(16%)	
	Others	3,347	(2%)	
1992 primary	John Conyers, Jr. (D)	39,324	(64%)	
	John Kelly (D)	15,780	(26%)	
	Martha Scott (D)	5,281	(9%)	
	Others	1,043	(2%)	
1990 general	John Conyers, Jr. (D)	76,556	(89%)	($288,906)
(MI 1)	Ray Shoulders (R)	7,298	(9%)	($545)
	Two Others	1,898	(1%)	

FIFTEENTH DISTRICT

Few central cities in America have as vibrant a 20th Century history, and as sad a present, as Detroit. This was America's first automobile city, not just for manufacturing most of the nation's cars, but also for being built to automobile scale. Detroit started the century as a second-rank city, no bigger than Milwaukee, with less than half a million people and extending no further than four or five miles out from the site where the French built Fort Pontchartrain on the Detroit River in 1701. As the Motor City boomed, it grew outward along wide avenues and freeways; the auto companies put their factories and headquarters out near the edge of urban settlement; as early as 1954, the nation's first big suburban shopping center, with parking for 10,000 cars, started drawing retail trade from downtown. As metro Detroit expanded to four million, each generation moved out the roadways rapidly in many directions, leaving behind the previous generation's neighborhoods and civic institutions.

Today, that rapid movement has left large parts of Detroit literally empty. The central city, which had nearly 1.9 million people in 1950, barely exceeded one million in 1990, and then only with the help of a city bureaucracy detailed to round up uncounted residents; it had the biggest rate of population loss of any 100,000-plus city in the 1980s except Gary and Newark, and the corresponding congressional district also had the biggest population decline in the 1980s—23%. The reason is obvious: crime. Detroit in 1990 had a murder rate *14 times* that in the suburbs, and over the years, whites and blacks who can afford to leave the city have done so. With more guns than people, personal altercations quickly become homicidal; innocent bystanders are killed by random gunfire. Downtown, the giant Hudson's department store is closed and several skyscrapers are all but empty, while the 70-story Renaissance Center is inaccessible from the sidewalk (you can only get there by car). Vacant fields where there were once five-story apartments or brick houses are populated with pheasants.

Detroit's fate is all the more tragic because it comes in a city where liberal reformers hoped to create model anti-poverty and anti-discrimination programs. Instead, they seem to have undermined the sense of individual responsibility and confidence in the legitimacy of institutions. Nor can the city's problems be blamed entirely on the decline of the auto industry. For most of the 1980s, the number of jobs in metro Detroit rose, from 1.53 million at the trough to 1.91 million seven years later. The response of Detroit's politically talented mayor, Coleman Young, has been anything but helpful. In a time when small economic units have created most new jobs, Young has expended energy courting a few big economic units, bulldozing the viable Poletown neighborhood for a new Cadillac plant. His downtown Peoplemover took years to get into operation, while his efforts to legalize casino gambling were stopped by church-influenced voters. At the same time, he supports higher taxes which have driven out many more jobs than he's brought in.

Young also blames white racism as the proximate cause of black Detroiters' problems. Young opposed gun control on the grounds that city blacks would have no protection against marauding white suburbanites, and he has repeatedly denied that there is anything especially alarming about Detroit's crime rate. He bragged, in his 1989 campaign, of the blacks he has hired as police officers and city employees, but he does little to see that employees actually serve citizens, and in May 1992 his police chief of 15 years was convicted of embezzling $2.3 million from an undercover police operations fund—some of which went to pay rent for his daughter's Beverly Hills, California, house. Young won only 56% of the vote against split opposition in the 1989 mayor race, an indication black voters were beginning to hold him responsible for Detroit's dreadful conditions; by early 1993, he was seldom emerging from the mayor's mansion and had one of the lowest job ratings ever recorded, and he seemed likely to retire in November 1993, voluntarily or otherwise.

The 15th Congressional District of Michigan includes the southern half of Detroit, plus several adjacent suburbs, from Grosse Pointe Farms on Lake St. Clair to industrial Ecorse in the Downriver area, where the whole city government was privatized after it went bankrupt, and including Hamtramck, the Polish-American enclave around the now demolished Dodge Main plant and America's fastest-growing city between 1910–20. The crime rate here is surely among the nation's top three or four districts; median household income, at $15,264, is lower than in all but three other districts. Detroit's ombudsman recently recommended that large parts of the city simply be abandoned and fenced off and its residents consolidated into better areas: this could be, as *Detroit News* editorial page editor Thomas Bray says, "America's first real ex-city."

Representing the 15th District in Congress is Barbara-Rose Collins, a longtime Coleman Young supporter on the Detroit Council until she was elected to the House in 1990. She has an interesting political provenance: she is a member of the Shrine of the Black Madonna, a pan-African Orthodox Christian Church; she was elected to the state House in 1975 and to the Council in 1982; she was a single mother for many years and has been personally affected by crime, since her adult son was convicted of armed robbery. In 1988, she ran against Congressman George Crockett, a 78-year-old former judge and veteran of the labor movement who was general counsel of the UAW as part of its Communist-allied wing in the 1940s, and lost by only 46%–38%; Crockett bowed out of the 1990 race early. In the Democratic primary, Collins led solidly with 34% of the vote.

Collins easily won the general election, but got off to a rocky start in Congress. She filed a complaint against herself with the Federal Election Commission, admitting that her campaign had taken out a $75,000 loan which three persons cosigned, against federal law since cosigning a campaign loan of $1,000 or more is considered a form of contribution; Collins said she was not familiar with federal campaign finance law, which tends to undermine the claim she makes in other contexts that "I've proven that I can work with the big boys." She had unusually high staff turnover and at the same time was the biggest user in 1991 of the congressional franked mail privilege. On the Public Works Committee, she successfully funnelled $58 million in transit projects to the Detroit metro area, including $20 million for a mass transit feasibility study; but anyone who spends 20 minutes in Detroit can tell you for free that mass transit is a money-losing proposition in a city originally built on automobile scale and now half abandoned. Collins's major cause was a bill to order the Bureau of Labor Statistics to develop a measure of the value of non-wage work—i.e., housework. And while it seems unlikely that a measure statistically valid enough to provide a basis for public policy can be developed, this is an interesting idea; it has not come close yet to becoming law.

Because of inner city Detroit's huge population loss, Collins's district was expanded out into the suburbs and new parts of the city for 1992. Primary opponent Thomas Barrow charged that she was "in over her head" and argued that he would provide "responsible representation in Washington." But Collins won 68%–32%. Her sense of the way the political wind is blowing was proved when she appeared with Sharon McPhail, a former Young supporter, as McPhail announced she was running for mayor; clearly Collins has decided Coleman Young is through.

The People: Pop. 1990: 580,933; 14% age 65+; 26% White; 70% Black; 1% Asian; 2% Other; 4% Hispanic origin. Voting age pop.: 417,646; 68% Black; 3% Hispanic origin. Households: 27% married couple families; 11% married couple fams. w. children; 33% college educ.; median household income: $15,264; per capita income: $9,650; median gross rent: $337; median house value: $22,900.

1992 Presidential Vote

Clinton (D) 159,284 (82%)
Bush (R) 24,552 (13%)
Perot (I). 8,998 (5%)

1988 Presidential Vote

Dukakis (D). 143,942 (81%)
Bush (R) 32,722 (19%)

Rep. Barbara-Rose Collins (D)

Elected 1990; b. Apr. 13, 1939, Detroit; home, Detroit; Wayne St. U., 1957; Pan-African Orthodox Christian; widowed.

Career: Detroit Schl. Bd., 1971–73; MI House of Reps., 1975–81; Detroit City Cncl., 1982–90.

Offices: 1108 LHOB 20515, 202-225-2261. Also 1153 Brewery Park Blvd., Detroit 48207, 313-567-2233.

Committees: *Government Operations* (21st of 25 D): Commerce, Consumer and Monetary Affairs; Employment, Housing and Aviation. *Post Office and Civil Service* (8th of 15 D): Postal Operations and Services (Chmn.). *Public Works and Transportation* (22d of 39 D): Aviation; Investigations and Oversight (Vice Chmn.).

Group Ratings

	ADA	ACLU	COPE	CDF	CFA	LCV	ACU	NTLC	NSI	COC	CEI
1992	95	100	90	100	87	63	0	0	10	13	10
1991	100	—	100	100	83	62	0	—	—	20	7

National Journal Ratings

	1991 LIB — 1991 CONS		1992 LIB — 1992 CONS	
Economic	83% —	16%	91% —	0%
Social	88% —	0%	76% —	24%
Foreign	92% —	0%	90% —	0%

Key Votes of the 102d Congress

1. Ban Striker Replace	FOR	5. Handgun Wait/7-Day	FOR	9. Use Force in Gulf	AGN
2. $ for Homeownership	*	6. Overseas Mil. Abortion	FOR	10. US Mil. Abroad $ Cut	FOR
3. Tax Rich/Cut Mid Cls.	FOR	7. Obscn. Art NEA $ Ban	AGN	11. Limit SDI Funds	FOR
4. FY93/$15B Def. Cut	FOR	8. Death Pen. from Jury	AGN	12. Cuba Trade Embargo	AGN

Key Votes of the 103d Congress

1. Family Leave	FOR	2. Deficit Reduction	FOR	3. Stimulus Plan	FOR

Election Results

1992 general	Barbara-Rose Collins (D)	148,908	(81%)	($284,049)
	Charles Vincent (R)	31,849	(17%)	($94,260)
	Others	4,207	(2%)	
1992 primary	Barbara-Rose Collins (D)	37,272	(68%)	
	Tom Barrow (D)	17,728	(32%)	
1990 general	Barbara-Rose Collins (D)	54,345	(80%)	($274,688)
(MI 13)	Carl Edwards, Sr. (R)	11,203	(17%)	
	Three Others	2,269	(3%)	

SIXTEENTH DISTRICT

One of America's great heavy industry corridors is along the Detroit River, the chokepoint of the Great Lakes, in the Downriver communities below Detroit: steel and chemical plants line the water, their dark and rusted hulks glaring across at Canada, while a little ways up the sluggish Rouge River stands the giant Rouge complex, built by Henry Ford in the 1910s for $1 billion to convert Great Lake freighter and railroad car loads of iron ore, coal, limestone and sand into automobiles in 48 hours. This swampy, low-lying land, along the nation's most heavily trafficked waterway and within easy reach of the great east-west rail lines, was a natural place for industry in the early 20th Century. The residential neighborhoods around the older factories and well within range of their sulfurous odors, with their neat, tightly packed houses, were the natural homes of the migrants—Polish, Hungarian, black, Italian, more recently Mexican and Arab (the area has America's largest concentration of Arab-Americans)—who came to work there. This industrial area has seen better times: many of the factories are dormant, and neighborhoods have been abandoned as the original migrants' children have moved outward. But there are also new factories, like Mazda's in Flat Rock, and smaller manufacturers are picking up the slack left by big company layoffs.

The 16th Congressional District of Michigan covers Dearborn and the Downriver communities, plus Monroe County directly to the south. The political tradition here has been Democratic since the New Deal days and, while there is some cultural conservatism seen in top-of-the-ticket races, the basic preference remains much more Democratic here than in increasingly upscale Macomb County. Certainly it remains solidly behind Congressman John Dingell.

John Dingell today by any measure is one of the big men in the House. He was first elected in December 1955, and ranks third in seniority; he has been around so long that one of his former staffers, John Conyers, now chairs a full committee. But he goes back farther. His father, John Dingell, Sr., was elected to the House in 1932, from a new district created as a result of the Detroit area's auto boom. The first Congressman Dingell was one of the most productive urban liberals then, one of the sponsors of Social Security and, starting in 1943, of national health insurance. And the younger John Dingell has been around Capitol Hill almost as long: he was a House page from 1938 to 1943, years when only one current member of Congress—Jamie Whitten, elected in 1941—was there.

But John Dingell is anything but an antique: he is one of the most powerful members of the House, chairman since 1981 of the House Energy and Commerce Committee, chairman of its much-feared Investigations and Oversight Subcommittee, a man who combines seniority and intellect, tradition and conviction. Under Dingell, write *National Journal*'s Richard E. Cohen and Burt Solomon, possibly with understatement, Energy and Commerce "claims jurisdiction over anything that moves, burns or is sold"—clean air and securities markets, telecommunications and energy, railroads and toys, consumer protection and defense contracting. It handles up to 40% of all House bills, it has the largest budget and staff of any House committee, and for a decade it was the House's most sought-after committee assignment. But Dingell's power is as much personal as institutional. He is aggressive, able, hard working and determined to do his duty. His staffers are bright, pit-bull aggressive, committed, and Dingell insists that facts be solidly documented. He gives leeway—and often valuable publicity—to subcommittee chairmen and to junior members, particularly on Oversight and Investigations. But only those he respects and believes get fair play with him; others get nothing.

Dingell and his committee were behind many big stories in the 1980s: the indictment of Reagan White House aide Michael Deaver and the ousting of EPA Administrator Anne Burford, the Pentagon's $640 toilet seat, and General Dynamics' billing the government for dog kennel fees. Dingell and his committee superintended the breakup of AT&T and the sale of Conrail by public offering, studied insider trading, leveraged buyouts and hostile takeovers, stimulated the growth of the generic drug industry and then swooped down to expose its misdeeds.

Dingell's actions have also stimulated some public criticism. Many in the House believe Dingell expands Energy and Commerce's jurisdiction too far. In 1991 and 1992, he clashed repeatedly with Judiciary Chairman Jack Brooks, an old friend and fellow hunter, over cable reregulation, telecommunications and product liability. Dingell won out on cable reregulation; he and subcommittee Chairman Edward Markey shepherded their bill to passage and then passed it into law over President Bush's veto, the only override in his four years. Brooks struck back on Baby Bell legislation, drafting a bill constricting Baby Bell entry into new information systems. Dingell kept that off the floor until it was too late to pass; he is more likely to let the Bells transmit information, which is opposed to the death by the nation's newspapers. These men are not just being petty. All this is part of a bigger battle, in which even free market theorists must admit the government needs a voice, over which of the two wires which go (or will go) into every household in America—the phone wire or the cable TV wire—can be used to transmit information one or both ways. Dingell has also battled Brooks on product liability; Brooks tends to stand with trial lawyers, Dingell is strongly against them (for which he takes his lumps from trial lawyer-financed Ralph Nader). Dingell has also fiercely battled with Henry Gonzalez of Banking: once over a Dingell bill to protect consumers from insolvent insurance companies, another time over a bill to increase SEC oversight of Treasury bond sales after the Salomon Brothers scandal. Lurking behind this is Glass-Steagall, the bar between commercial and investment banking which Dingell wants to maintain—it was one of his father's causes—and others on Banking would like to lower. And, as there are opposing forces in all these battles with huge economic interests in the outcome, these issues are lobbied very heavily and the debate takes place at a high intellectual plane, where Dingell has no difficulty thriving.

The Clean Air Act was another such issue. Dingell was probably the single most critical figure in the passage of the 1990 Clean Air Act. In October 1989, he reached agreement with his longtime adversary on this issue (though ally on many others), Health Subcommittee Chairman Henry Waxman; Dingell has always been wary of piling more costs on heavy industry (like autos), while Waxman, from Los Angeles, has sought maximal reduction of pollutants. Together, for 12 months they worked to compromise on auto industry provisions, smog, acid rain and air toxics, and together—it's hard to think of two tougher negotiators—held the line against the more environment-minded Senate. Dingell and Waxman may also be acting together on health care. Dingell, remembering his father's stand and out of his own conviction and research, supports a single-payer national health insurance system, and he and Waxman have collaborated on their own Health Choice Act. They realize, however, that they may not be able to achieve all their goals, and are ready to work—and also to push hard—for the Clinton Administration; Dingell was one of very few members of Congress with whom Clinton had lengthy one-to-one discussions on the issues, and some speculate that Clinton chose former UAW staffer Howard Paster as his chief congressional liaison as a way to keep in touch with Dingell.

On other issues, Dingell has been a tiger investigating what he considers bogus scientific research—a "university's worst nightmare" says The New York Times. Dingell helped undermine Nobel Prize-winning scientist David Baltimore and oust Stanford President Donald Kennedy when Stanford overcharged the federal government on research grants. But sometimes

Dingell goes too far; in 1989, he was forced to apologize to a New York private investigator after it was disclosed that one of his top staffers had encouraged a lawyer to tape a conversation between the P.I. and the lawyer. He is harshly critical of free traders, who he feels overlook unfair Japanese practices. On gun control, he is a strong opponent of the 1991 Brady Bill; on environmental issues, as a hunter and outdoorsman, he fought to maintain natural habitats and environments long before it was fashionable. In many ways, he is an old-fashioned Franklin Roosevelt Democrat, supporting big government and strenuous regulation, taking a conservative line on some cultural issues, backing an assertive foreign policy: he was the only Michigan Democrat to vote for the Gulf war resolution.

Dingell was first elected at 29, after his father's death, from a district with large Polish, black and Jewish populations. He had one serious fight, because of redistricting, in 1964, beating fellow Democrat John Lesinski, who opposed the Civil Rights Act, even though most of the district was new to Dingell; he has been reelected easily since. He has had an interesting personal life, raising his children after his divorce (his son Christopher was elected to the Michigan Senate in 1986) and marrying in 1981 a granddaughter of one of General Motors's Fisher brothers (Debbie Dingell, active and popular both in Washington and Michigan Democratic circles). For the 1990s, not even the federal judges involved thought to carve up Dingell's district, and he was, without straining, the fifth highest PAC fund recipient in the House, with $767,000 in the 1992 cycle. He outspent his hapless 1992 opponent $1,086,000 to $5,400 and won 65%–31%.

The People: Pop. 1990: 580,884; 13% rural; 13% age 65+; 95% White; 1% Black; 1% Amer. Indian; 1% Asian; 1% Other; 2% Hispanic origin. Voting age pop.: 434,314; 1% Black; 2% Hispanic origin. Households: 60% married couple families; 28% married couple fams. w. children; 39% college educ.; median household income: $35,315; per capita income: $15,175; median gross rent: $456; median house value: $61,700.

1992 Presidential Vote

Clinton (D) 115,339 (43%)
Bush (R) 96,466 (36%)
Perot (I) 52,070 (20%)

1988 Presidential Vote

Bush (R) 125,074 (54%)
Dukakis (D) 104,704 (46%)

Rep. John D. Dingell (D)

Elected Dec. 1955; b. July 8, 1926, Colorado Springs, CO; home, Trenton; Georgetown U., B.S. 1949, J.D. 1952; Catholic; married (Deborah).

Career: Army, 1945–46 (WWII); Practicing atty., 1952–55; Wayne Cnty. Asst. Prosecuting Atty., 1953–55.

Offices: 2328 RHOB 20515, 202-225-4071. Also 5465 Schaefer Rd., Dearborn 48126, 313-846-1276; and 241 E. Elm Ave., #105, Monroe 48161, 313-243-1849.

Committees: *Energy and Commerce* (Chmn. of 27 D): Oversight and Investigations (Chmn.).

Group Ratings

	ADA	ACLU	COPE	CDF	CFA	LCV	ACU	NTLC	NSI	COC	CEI
1992	90	87	83	100	87	38	0	0	50	25	9
1991	65	—	92	90	100	46	22	—	—	22	16

National Journal Ratings

	1991 LIB	—	1991 CONS	1992 LIB	—	1992 CONS
Economic	88%	—	0%	88%	—	11%
Social	64%	—	35%	67%	—	32%
Foreign	59%	—	39%	62%	—	38%

Key Votes of the 102d Congress

1. Ban Striker Replace	FOR	5. Handgun Wait/7-Day	AGN	9. Use Force in Gulf	FOR
2. $ for Homeownership	AGN	6. Overseas Mil. Abortion	FOR	10. US Mil. Abroad $ Cut	FOR
3. Tax Rich/Cut Mid Cls.	FOR	7. Obscn. Art NEA $ Ban	AGN	11. Limit SDI Funds	FOR
4. FY93/$15B Def. Cut	FOR	8. Death Pen. from Jury	FOR	12. Cuba Trade Embargo	FOR

Key Votes of the 103d Congress

1. Family Leave	FOR	2. Deficit Reduction	FOR	3. Stimulus Plan	FOR

Election Results

1992 general	John D. Dingell (D)	156,964	(65%)	($1,086,152)
	Frank Beaumont (R)	75,694	(31%)	($5,401)
	Four Others	8,278	(4%)	
1992 primary	John D. Dingell (D)	50,052	(100%)	
1990 general	John D. Dingell (D)	88,962	(67%)	($602,952)
	Frank Beaumont (R)	42,629	(32%)	($3,774)
	Other	2,023	(2%)	

MINNESOTA

In many ways the model American state, Minnesota has some of the nation's highest voter turnout and lowest crime rates, and is the birthplace of worthy national institutions from Scotch Tape and Betty Crocker to Garrison Keillor and the Mall of America. Improbably situated where the Mississippi and Minnesota Rivers cut gorges through the Great Plains, the Twin Cities of Minneapolis and St. Paul are the center of one of America's 20 largest metropolitan areas, and the one with by far the most frigid weather. Minnesota is a distinctive commonwealth with high traditions of probity and civic-mindedness and a center of innovation in business and government; in many ways it is politically liberal. During the Democrats' quarter-century presidential dry spell, Minnesota was the nation's most Democratic state; it voted for Democrats in five of six elections and nearly voted for George McGovern in 1972. But it also has one of the nation's largest and most active antiabortion movements.

Minnesota's distinctive polity comes from a distinctive history. The far northern states were ignored by most Yankee immigrants, who headed straight west into Iowa, Nebraska and Kansas. But in Minnesota's icy lakes and ferocious winters, other people saw opportunities. James J. Hill, the builder of the Great Northern Railroad ("You can't interest me in any proposition in any place where it doesn't snow"), and others operating out of Minneapolis and St. Paul—already twin cities by 1860—worked to attract Norwegian, Swedish and German migrants who would find the terrain and climate congenial. By 1890, the Twin Cities—rivals that year in a Census competition—were the nerve center of a sprawling and rich agricultural empire stretching west from Minnesota through the Dakotas and eventually into Montana and beyond. Minneapolis and St. Paul became the termini of its rail lines and the site of its grain-milling companies. They also became the center of a three-party politics and an economic radicalism reminiscent of the politics of Scandinavia. For our American regions seem to reflect the geography of Europe, with the East Coast resembling the British Isles and France, the industrial Midwest reminiscent of Germany and Poland, the poor and always hawkish South a Baptist Mediterranean, and the Upper Midwest of Minnesota, Wisconsin and North Dakota as North American versions of Scandinavia. Like Scandinavia, these Upper Midwestern commonwealths pioneered their continent's welfare states, with an effect on public policy far out of proportion to their numbers. Alarmed by the unprecedented concentration of economic power and wealth into the hands of just a few identifiable millionaires who lived on St. Paul's Summit Avenue or the hill above Minneapolis's Hennepin Avenue, the immigrants drew on their native traditions of cooperative activity and bureaucratic socialism. Their rebellion against market capitalism and the magnates' dominance gave the politics of Minnesota its Scandinavian flavor.

As in Wisconsin and North Dakota, a strong third party developed here in the years after the Populist era; this Farmer-Labor Party elected senators in the 1920s and dominated state politics in the 1930s. Hurt by their ties to Communists, the Farmer-Laborites were beaten by Harold Stassen's Republicans in 1938. But this was still a New Deal state and by 1944 the bedraggled local Democrats were merged with the anti-Communist faction of Farmer-Laborites to form the Democratic-Farmer-Labor party. A key role was played by Hubert Humphrey—graduate student in 1940, mayor of Minneapolis in 1945, and the dazzling advocate of the civil rights plank at the 1948 Democratic National Convention. Humphrey's DFL—clean, idealistic, closely tied to labor, backed by many farmers—attracted dozens of talented politicians, including Eugene McCarthy, Orville Freeman, Walter Mondale and Minneapolis's current mayor, Donald Fraser. In 1948, Humphrey's speech helped put the Democrats on record for civil rights, and he was elected to the Senate at age 37.

In the years following, the DFL dominated Minnesota politics, while a series of progressive companies led the development of a strong, diversified economy. The DFL stood for a generous, compassionate federal government, for strong labor unions and high wages, for an expansionist fiscal policy to encourage consumer-led economic growth, for civil rights, and for an anti-Communist but not bombastic foreign policy. Its base was among blue-collar workers in the Twin Cities, in Duluth and the Iron Range, and among farmers of Scandinavian origin. Most of Minnesota's business leaders—executives of the great grain milling companies and the privately held grain traders in particular—were conservative politically. But they were innovation-minded in their work: 3M has been generating new products—more than 60,000 by 1992—since the abrasive material it was founded to sell proved a loser in 1903; Control Data was an early high-tech pioneer; IDS was one of the first mass-marketers of mutual funds; the Dayton retail empire helped invent the shopping mall and the national bookstore chain. Linking DFL political liberalism and business innovation have been a high-skill work force and a squeaky-clean ethic of honesty and integrity, with high wage and salary levels and a high percentage of women working outside the home. Over several decades, Minnesota has grown robustly in prosperous years and has not fallen much behind during recessions.

In effect Minnesota's economy over the past dozen years has been headed where most of the rest of America wanted to go; Minnesota's state government has been headed in directions the country may want to go as well. This is the state that produced the nation's first anti-smoking bill and one of the first public campaign financing schemes. It helped pioneer reduction of state welfare programs, and it passed the nation's first statewide educational choice plan in 1987. It was one of the first states to establish HMOs and in 1992 it passed a HealthRight plan to insure the uninsured, and which encourages insurance pooling for small employers and set targets for reducing healthcare spending. The plan is to be paid for by a higher cigarette tax and a 2% health services tax; some estimates set the cost of the program to the state at $250 million a year. State social services continue to be generous, but are supplemented by the commitment of 78 of Minnesota's biggest companies to donate 5% of their earnings for charity. The state also has pitched in to help business, in November 1991 pledging $840 million of credit and loan guarantees for beleaguered Northwest Airlines, which promised to keep its Twin Cities hub and

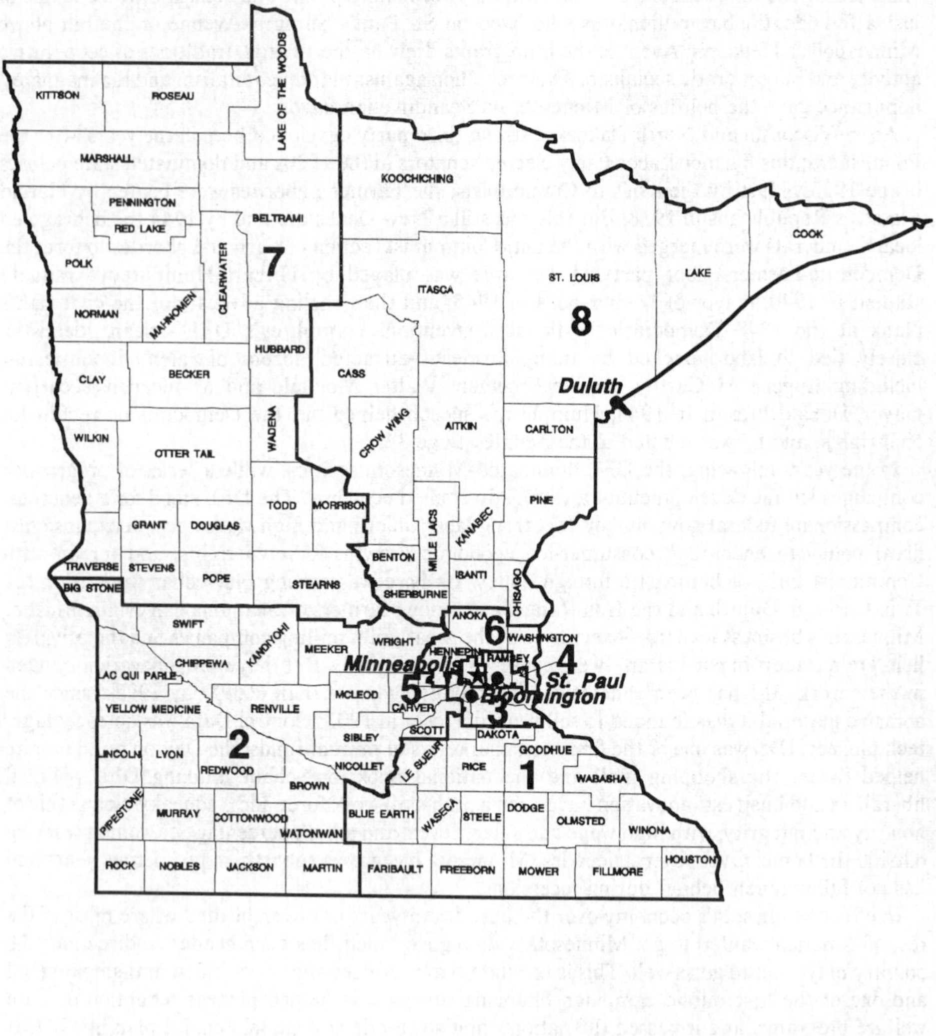

KITTSON

ROSEAU

LAKE OF THE WOODS

MARSHALL

PENNINGTON

RED LAKE

KOOCHICHING

BELTRAMI

COOK

POLK

CLEARWATER

7

ST. LOUIS

LAKE

NORMAN

MAHNOMEN

ITASCA

8

HUBBARD

CLAY

BECKER

CASS

Duluth

WILKIN

WADENA

CROW WING

AITKIN

CARLTON

OTTER TAIL

PINE

TODD

MORRISON

GRANT

DOUGLAS

KANABEC

TRAVERSE

STEVENS

POPE

BENTON

MILLE LACS

ISANTI

BIG STONE

STEARNS

SHERBURNE

CHISAGO

SWIFT

ANOKA

6

WASHINGTON

WRIGHT

KANDIYOHI

MEEKER

HENNEPIN

RAMSEY

4

LAC QUI PARLE

CHIPPEWA

Minneapolis

St. Paul

YELLOW MEDICINE

RENVILLE

MCLEOD

5

CARVER

Bloomington

SIBLEY

SCOTT

LINCOLN

LYON

REDWOOD

NICOLLET

LE SUEUR

DAKOTA

2

GOODHUE

BROWN

RICE

1

PIPESTONE

MURRAY

COTTONWOOD

BLUE EARTH

WASECA

STEELE

DODGE

WABASHA

WATONWAN

OLMSTED

WINONA

ROCK

NOBLES

JACKSON

MARTIN

FARIBAULT

FREEBORN

MOWER

FILLMORE

HOUSTON

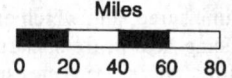

Miles

0   20   40   60   80

build repair facilities in Duluth and the Iron Range. But saddled with huge amounts of debt, Northwest delayed construction plans in December 1992 and some say the state may have squandered millions. So just as Scandinavia is adapting its welfare state by lowering taxes and using market mechanisms, so Minnesota is building on the patchwork American welfare state by adding state protections and regulations: both are continuing their search for a "third way" between unbridled market capitalism and regimented bureaucratic socialism.

Minnesota is well-positioned for that search, because its work ethic has always been strong, its skill levels are high, and it is less troubled by aberrant social behaviors—violent crime, children bearing children, substance abuse—than most of America. So relatively high tax levels here have not choked off economic growth, and government spending on education and social services has tended to upgrade private sector performance rather than just enrich public sector employees and contractors. Higher education levels have helped the Twin Cities develop a diversified economy, with responsive big companies plus entrepreneurial startups and spinoffs and other small firms. Workers and even (the much less numerous) farmers no longer feel at the mercy of a few big milling firms and railroads, young people starting out have many more career choices, and consumers have a much wider range of brand and product choices than they did 50 years ago: the need for New Deal-style intervention and regulation is less. Yet that heritage still counts for something: if Minnesota has an Independent Republican governor and senator (the party renamed itself in the 1970s) and a DFL senator whose election was arguably a fluke, it is still one of the least Republican states in national politics, casting less than one-third of its votes for the incumbent Republican president in 1992.

Governor. Earnest, well-disciplined Minnesota had the wild-and-wooliest governor's race in the country in 1990, and ended up electing the candidate who finished fourth among the four top candidates in the two primaries. He is Arne Carlson, son of Swedish immigrants, a professional politician who served eight years in the legislature and 12 as state auditor, an Independent Republican who boasted of writing day care, rape victim assistance, and handicapped access legislation. None of which helped him in the IR convention, which he bypassed, or in the Republican primary, which he lost 49%–32% to conservative pro-lifer Jon Grunseth. But in mid-October 1990, the *Minneapolis Star-Tribune* charged Grunseth with sexual improprieties with teenage girls; a week later Carlson launched a write-in campaign; the following week the paper printed a woman's charge that she had a nine-year affair with Grunseth while he was married, and he then withdrew from the race. An IR delegation then named Carlson as the nominee, to face the beleaguered and tempestuous DFL incumbent, Rudy Perpich. A dentist from a large Croatian family from the Iron Range, Perpich is a political original, elevated to the governorship in 1976 when incumbent Governor Wendell Anderson appointed himself to the Senate; he lost in 1978 but came back and won in 1982 and 1986. In office, he dubbed Minnesota "the brainpower state" and pioneered educational choice; he also got into controversy and was primaried in 1990 by a former appointee, and won by only 56%–42%. He was clearly in trouble; Citizens' Jury, a Minnesota project in which ordinary citizens exhaustively screened the candidates and their platforms, came out for Carlson.

Carlson's hold on the office must be considered shaky: he won the general by only 51%–47%, and under circumstances that can't be replicated. His job rating, like that of so many incumbents, has sunk well below 50%; he is part, and maybe the minority part, of the minority party. The HealthRight program, even its proponents agree, is going to need some jiggering. Carlson is, he says himself, a shy person uncomfortable with criticism. He did work well with the DFL legislature in 1992, passing HealthRight, and a 7.5 million acre Wetlands Preservation Act; he pushed packages of spending cuts without major tax increases to counter the tendency of spending to rise more rapidly than revenues and was lauded for his fiscal responsibility. He called on citizens to "change their attitudes" to combat violence and held a candlelight vigil during Violence Free Minnesota Week. He has sought the views of Minnesota citizens to establish a "Milestones" program to set effective government goals. That sounds like an attractive record, but Carlson could easily have opposition from the pro-life right; their victories in primaries have already helped the IR win a majority of state legislative seats in the suburbs. And various well-known DFLers could run: state Senate President Roger Moe and Attorney General Skip Humphrey. Any could conceivably win.

Senators. Minnesota has one Independent Republican senator and one leftish DFLer; neither precisely fits the squeaky-clean, anti-Communist DFL profile of Hubert Humphrey or Walter Mondale. David Durenberger is both an attractive senator who has been seriously engaged on difficult issues like health care and a politician whose name has been linked increasingly to tawdriness if not scandal. He was raised in Collegeville, the son of the athletic director at St. Johns College, in a community of Benedictine monks; as a Catholic, he continues to oppose both abortion and capital punishment on pro-life grounds, a common combination in Minnesota if not elsewhere. His specialization in health care also came naturally to one from the leading HMO state who snagged a seat on the Senate Finance Committee. He promoted patient choice and peer review of doctors and encouraged forms of medicare cost control; he tried to salvage elements of the Catastrophic Health Care Act when Congress stampeded to repeal it in 1989; he authored the Small Employer Health Benefit Reform Act of 1990. He supported the long-term health care proposal in the Pepper Commission. He introduced with New Mexico Senator Jeff Bingaman the Health Insurance Purchasing Cooperatives (HICs) Act of 1992 to make affordable coverage available to small businesses; he opposes universal healthcare coverage as too burdensome on businesses. On other issues, he has worked to reform the student loan program and to promote ethanol fuels (very popular with grain farmers). He got an amendment passed to the 1991 Surface Transportation Act to create a 180,000 mile network of interstates and feeder routes available for federal aid.

Quite a contrast with this constructive legislative record are Durenberger's ethical problems. In the mid-1980s, his personal life was in turmoil; he separated from his wife in 1985, amid rumors that he had an affair with a staffer; he got into an altercation with an airport policeman, amid rumors he was drinking too much. In July 1990, the Senate voted 96–0 to denounce (a penalty lighter than censure, harsher than a reprimand) him for improper use of public funds to rent a condominium he partially owned, and for circumventing honoraria limits by accepting expense-paid trips and speaking fees in connection with promoting two books he authored—an offense for which Speaker Jim Wright was forced to resign. More troubles became public in late 1992. Then, just before the November 1992 election, a woman accused Durenberger of raping her and fathering her child in 1963; he denied the charges "with every fiber of my being" and submitted to a paternity test (an issue which still remains in court as of May 1993). Durenberger was then indicted in April 1993 for making false claims to the Senate and for billing the Senate for overnight stays in the condo, after falsifying records that he had sold his interest in it.

November 1992 exit polls showed only 26% of Minnesota voters favored his reelection, while 66% were opposed. Durenberger refused demands he resign; his seat is up in 1994. If he should leave the Senate before August 24, 1993, there would be a special election the next November; after that date, Governor Carlson's appointee would hold the seat until November 1994. Mentioned as IR appointees are former Congressman Vin Weber, former state House Majority Leader Connie Levi, and former state legislator Kathleen Blatz (speculation is that the DFL candidate in 1993 or 1994 will be a woman).

This collection of charges threatens to end what has been a very successful political career. Durenberger jumped into electoral politics in 1978 by running for the Senate seat vacated by the death of Hubert Humphrey and resoundingly beat his opponent. In 1982, Durenberger was opposed by department store heir Mark Dayton, who spent more than $7 million on the race; Durenberger won, 53%–47%, in a recession year. In 1988, he beat one of the great names in Minnesota politics, Hubert Humphrey III, known as Skip, winning 56%–41%. Now the woods are full of potential challengers: Secretary of State Joan Growe, House Speaker Dee Long, and state Senator Ember Reichgott—none of them household names—are mentioned for the DFL nomination, while Connie Levi seems to be the favorite among IRs.

Paul Wellstone, Minnesota's junior senator, is representative of a still-lively impulse in

American politics: the spirit of student protest that blazed out in the late 1960s and, on some campuses at least, lives on in embers. Wellstone himself is a Rip van Winkle, the spirit of Woodstock 1969 come back to earth. As a "rock-the-boat professor" at Carleton College, he taught nothing but the politics of protest and appeared at faculty meetings only when he was leading a group of students to protest something or other; he made a name for himself in local politics by leading protesters in sympathy with the Hormel meatpacker strikers in Austin and getting arrested while picketing a bank that had foreclosed on local farmers; he co-chaired Jesse Jackson's 1988 presidential campaign in Minnesota. His announcement that he was running for the Senate in 1990 attracted little attention: Walter Mondale had still not decided whether to run, Wellstone was opposed by DFL Agriculture Commissioner Jim Nichols, a populist advocate of increasing aid to farmers, and incumbent Republican Senator Rudy Boschwitz had a good job rating and a large campaign treasury. But Mondale chose not to run, Nichols was pro-life on abortion and lost the DFL primary 60%–34%, and Wellstone turned Boschwitz's financial advantage into a disadvantage and put himself in position to benefit from a couple of incredible Boschwitz mistakes.

The Wellstone campaign made shrewd—and in some cases dubious—use of symbolism. Wellstone's TV ads proclaimed that viewers wouldn't be seeing him as often as they saw Boschwitz (because he didn't accept PAC money), but his cute touches ("I'm better looking") guaranteed him more attention. His most-screened ad (often on newscasts) was an obvious takeoff on the movie *Roger and Me*, and like Michael Moore's movie on Flint, Michigan, the Wellstone ad was based on a dishonest premise: the ad purported to show Wellstone in pursuit of a confrontation-shy Boschwitz, even though Boschwitz had already agreed to meet him in debate. But the ad's cleverness and the candidate's charm created an almost cuddly impression—the kind of feel-good, image-heavy politics of which Ronald Reagan was often accused.

Boschwitz responded hamhandedly, needlessly involving himself in the controversy over gubernatorial nominee Jon Grunseth's personal problems, switching his stand on the 1990 civil rights veto override, sending out a letter to a Jewish mailing list suggesting that in this first Senate race between two Jewish candidates Boschwitz was the better Jew because Wellstone took no part in Jewish affairs and had not raised his children as Jews. Wellstone, the only candidate to beat an incumbent in 1990, won 50%–48%, carrying metro Twin Cities 54%–45% while losing outstate Minnesota 51%–47%. Here, as in the governors' race, the Twin Cities were venturesome enough to reject a well-known candidate—the IR's Boschwitz and the DFL's Perpich—for a relatively unknown and culturally liberal challenger—the DFL's Wellstone and the IR's Carlson.

Wellstone got off to a predictably rocky start in the Senate, gratuitously saying he "despised" Jesse Helms, handing Vice President Quayle a videotape of a Minnesota town meeting where people spoke out against war (actually, Wellstone backers stacked the meeting and some participants supported the war policy after Congress voted). Much to his own distress, this opponent of any assertive U.S. foreign policy found that the first issue he had to vote on was the Gulf war, and that the tide of opinion was very much against his own heartfelt views. But this left-wing Democrat of the early 1990s, like some of the right-wing Republicans of the early 1980s, got caught up in the responsibilities of serving as majority party superintendents of complex government programs, working hard trying to master issues and come up with positions that might win majority support. He has put forward a universal single-payer healthcare bill, but with the understanding that it probably won't pass; he skittered back from a purist campaign finance bill to let other Democrats take the lead; he played a skillful role in derailing Bennett Johnston's original energy bill in 1991 because of provisions allowing for oil drilling in Alaska's Arctic National Wildlife Refuge. He has let his pleasant personality prevail and gets along well with colleagues whose views on issues he used to bristlingly oppose, while deftly using senatorial delaying tactics to win points. Wellstone backers see him as a harbinger of a new left politics, brave enough to support major expansions of government responsibility and opposed to U.S. militarism abroad; they point to the 1992 victory of Russ Feingold in Wisconsin as an extension of the trend. But the more evident similarity is that Feingold, like Wellstone, won largely with charming ads almost devoid of issue content: cutie-pie leftism. But Wellstone does evoke some lively Minnesota traditions—the 1960s protesters now grown older but still posing as angry rebels; the Farmer-Laborites of the 1930s, incremental socialists and foreign policy isolationists. His job rating, which hit a low 35% after the Gulf war, rebounded in 1992 and by year's end was as high as any top Minnesota official's. He worked shrewdly and contributed organizational help ("the Wellstone Alliance") to 2d District winner Dave Minge and other DFLers running for the legislature in 1992. Republicans in 1990 may have thought Wellstone would be a one-term fluke, but in this Democratic state he must be regarded as a strong candidate for reelection.

Presidential politics. Minnesota, though still heavily Democratic, in 1992 cast its lowest Democratic presidential percentage in 60 years, just 44% for Bill Clinton; but some of those earlier Democratic percentages may have been enhanced by the Minnesota DFLers Hubert Humphrey and Walter Mondale on the ticket. Minnesota voted an above-average 24% for Ross Perot, who ran especially well in the ring of fast-growing counties just beyond the Twin Cities' and in some farming counties in the southwest part of the state. He did least well in areas where voters tend to be longer settled and have deeper roots: in the Twin Cities core counties, Duluth and the Iron Range, and the wheat farming country of the northwest. And of course Perot may have done well partly because neither Clinton nor Bush seriously contested the state.

Among Minnesota's good government traditions has been a system of caucuses and state party conventions to choose or at least endorse candidates for president and statewide office: the idea is to encourage responsible party organizations. Over the years, though, the idea that only the people can legitimately choose has grown stronger; primary challenges have become common, and often the party endorsement is as much bane as benefit.

For 1992, Minnesota had presidential primaries as well as caucuses. Tom Harkin won the early March Democratic caucuses, largely because of the proximity of his native Iowa. The DFL also held a non-binding "beauty contest" primary in April; Clinton won with 31% and Brown was right behind him with 31%. In the Republican primary, Pat Buchanan got nearly one quarter of the vote—a harbinger of Bush's lackluster performance in November.

Congressional districting. A federal district court redistricted Minnesota's eight House seats in February 1992, in a decision appealed on the grounds a state court was about to act; but the federal plan went into effect for 1992. The plan made no major changes, but did make the suburban 6th District north of Minneapolis and St. Paul a bit more Republican, which contributed to the defeat of the DFL's Gerry Sikorski. In February 1993, the Supreme Court ruled that the federal court should have deferred to the state, and so Minnesota got a new plan in April 1993. Jim Ramstad's 3d District lost the bulk of Dakota County and picked up some suburban areas of Hennepin County; Rod Grams's 6th District picked up parts of Dakota County and lost some of Hennepin.

The People: Est. Pop. 1992: 4,480,000; Pop. 1990: 4,375,099, up 2.3% 1990–1992. 1.8% of U.S. total, 20th largest; 30% rural. Median age: 32.5 years. 12.5% 65 years and over. 94.4% White, 2.2% Black, 1.8% Asian, 1.2% Hispanic origin, 1.1% American Indian. Households: 57.2% married couple families; 29% married couple fams. w. children; 49% college educ.; median household income: $30,909; per capita income: $14,389; 71.8% owner occupied housing; median house value: $74,000; median monthly rent: $384. 5.1% Unemployment. Voting age pop.: 3,208,316. Registered voters (1992): 3,183,901; no party registration.

Political Lineup: Governor, Arne Carlson (IR); Lt. Gov., Joanell Dyrstad (IR); Secy. of State, Joan Anderson Growe (DFL); Atty. Gen., Hubert H. Humphrey, III (DFL); Treasurer, Michael McGrath (DFL); Auditor, Mark B. Dayton (DFL). State Senate, 67 (45 DFL and 22 IR); State House of Representatives, 134 (86 DFL and 48 IR). Senators, Dave Durenberger (IR) and Paul D. Wellstone (DFL). Representatives, 8 (6 DFL and 2 IR).

1992 Presidential Vote

Clinton (D) 1,020,997 (44%)
Bush (R) 747,841 (32%)
Perot (I).................. 562,506 (24%)

1992 Democratic Presidential Primary

Clinton..................... 63,584 (31%)
Brown 62,706 (31%)
Tsongas 43,588 (21%)
Other...................... 22,926 (11%)
Uncommitted 11,366   (6%)

1988 Presidential Vote

Dukakis (D).............. 1,109,471 (53%)
Bush (R) 962,337 (46%)

1992 Republican Presidential Primary

Bush 84,841 (64%)
Buchanan................... 32,094 (24%)
Other...................... 11,723   (9%)

GOVERNOR

Gov. Arne H. Carlson (IR)

Elected 1990, term expires Jan. 1995; b. Sept. 11, 1934, New York, NY; home, St. Paul; Williams Col., B.A. 1957, U. of MN; Protestant; married (Susan).

Career: Control Data Corp., 1962–64; Minneapolis City Cncl., Majority Ldr., 1965–67; MN House of Reps., 1970–78; MN St. Auditor, 1978–90.

Office: 130 State Capitol Bldg., Aurora Ave., St. Paul 55155, 612-296-3391.

Election Results

1990 gen.	Arne H. Carlson (IR).........	895,988	(51%)
	Rudy Perpich (DFL)	836,218	(47%)
	Three Others................	45,016	(2%)
1990 prim.	Jon Grunseth (IR)	169,451	(49%)
	Arne H. Carlson (IR).........	108,446	(32%)
	Doug A. Kelley (IR)	57,872	(17%)
	Three Others................	7,110	(2%)
1986 gen.	Rudy Perpich (DFL)	790,138	(56%)
	Cal R. Ludeman (IR).........	606,755	(43%)

SENATORS

Sen. Dave Durenberger (IR)

Elected 1978, seat up 1994; b. Aug. 19, 1934, Collegeville; home, Minneapolis; St. John's U., B.A. 1955, U. of MN, J.D. 1959; Catholic; separated.

Career: Army Intelligence, 1955–56, Army Reserves, 1956–63; Practicing atty., 1959–66; Exec. Secy., Gov. Harold LeVander, 1967–71; Cnsl. for Legal and Comm. Affairs, Corp. Secy., Intl. Licensing Div. Mgr., H.B. Fuller Co., 1971–78.

Offices: 154 RSOB 20510, 202-224-3244. Also 1020 Plymouth Bldg., 12 S. 6th St., Minneapolis 55402, 612-370-3382.

Committees: *Aging (Special)* (7th of 10 R). *Environment and Public Works* (3d of 7 R): Clean Water, Fisheries and Wildlife; Superfund, Recycling and Solid Waste Management (RMM); Water Resources, Transportation, Public Buildings and Economic Development. *Finance* (6th of 9 R): Health for Families and the Uninsured; Medicare and Long-Term Care (RMM); Social Security and Family Policy. *Labor and Human Resources* (7th of 7 R): Aging; Children, Family, Drugs and Alcoholism; Disability Policy (RMM); Education, Arts and Humanities.

Group Ratings

	ADA	ACLU	CDF	COPE	CFA	LCV	ACU	NTLC	NSI	COC	CEI
1992	25	59	40	50	75	50	42	56	80	60	51
1991	35	—	64	33	50	60	48	—	—	50	48

National Journal Ratings

	1991 LIB — 1991 CONS	1992 LIB — 1992 CONS
Economic	28% — 69%	36% — 63%
Social	54% — 44%	56% — 43%
Foreign	33% — 65%	21% — 72%

Key Votes of the 102d Congress

1. $ for Homeownership FOR	5. Clarence Thomas Nom. FOR	9. Use Force in Gulf FOR
2. Have Cap Gains Debate FOR	6. Lmt Death Row Appeal FOR	10. Keep Salvador Aid FOR
3. Remove Budget Walls AGN	7. Handgun Wait/5-Day FOR	11. Cut $1B from SDI AGN
4. Ban Striker Replace AGN	8. Abortion Gag Rule FOR	12. Override China MFN AGN

Key Votes of the 103d Congress

1. Family Leave FOR	2. HIV Immigrants FOR	3. Clinton Budget AGN

Election Results

1988 general	Dave Durenberger (IR) 1,176,210	(56%)	($5,410,783)
	Hubert H. Humphrey, III (DFL) 856,694	(41%)	($2,477,068)
1988 primary	Dave Durenberger (IR) 112,413	(93%)	
	Sharon Anderson (IR) 5,464	(5%)	
1982 general	Dave Durenberger (IR) 949,207	(53%)	($4,189,619)
	Mark Dayton (DFL)................. 840,401	(47%)	($7,172,312)

Sen. Paul D. Wellstone (DFL)

Elected 1990, seat up 1996; b. July 21, 1944, Washington, D.C.; home, St. Paul; U. of NC, B.A. 1965, Ph.D. 1969; Jewish; married (Sheila).

Career: Prof., Carleton Col., 1969–90.

Offices: 717 HSOB 20510, 202-224-5641. Also 2550 University Ave., St. Paul 55114, 612-645-0323.

Committees: *Energy and Natural Resources* (8th of 11 D): Energy Research and Development; Public Lands, National Parks and Forests; Renewable Energy, Energy Efficiency, and Competitiveness (Vice Chmn.). *Indian Affairs* (8th of 10 D). *Labor and Human Resources* (9th of 10 D): Children, Family, Drugs and Alcoholism; Education, Arts and Humanities; Labor. *Small Business* (7th of 12 D): Rural Economy and Family Farming (Chmn.); Urban and Minority-Owned Business Development.

Group Ratings

	ADA	ACLU	CDF	COPE	CFA	LCV	ACU	NTLC	NSI	COC	CEI
1992	100	95	90	92	100	100	0	11	40	10	12
1991	95	—	100	83	89	93	5	—	—	20	20

National Journal Ratings

	1991 LIB — 1991 CONS		1992 LIB — 1992 CONS	
Economic	97%	0%	95%	0%
Social	87%	0%	89%	0%
Foreign	86%	0%	86%	0%

Key Votes of the 102d Congress

1. $ for Homeownership	AGN	5. Clarence Thomas Nom.	AGN	9. Use Force in Gulf	AGN
2. Have Cap Gains Debate	AGN	6. Lmt Death Row Appeal	AGN	10. Keep Salvador Aid	AGN
3. Remove Budget Walls	FOR	7. Handgun Wait/5-Day	FOR	11. Cut $1B from SDI	FOR
4. Ban Striker Replace	FOR	8. Abortion Gag Rule	AGN	12. Override China MFN	FOR

Key Votes of the 103d Congress

1. Family Leave	FOR	2. HIV Immigrants	FOR	3. Clinton Budget	FOR

Election Results

1990 general	Paul D. Wellstone (DFL)	911,999	(50%)	($1,338,708)
	Rudy Boschwitz (IR)	864,375	(48%)	($6,221,133)
	Other..............................	29,820	(2%)	
1990 primary	Paul D. Wellstone (DFL)	226,306	(60%)	
	James W. Nichols (DFL)	129,302	(34%)	
	Gene Schenk (DFL)..................	19,379	(5%)	
1984 general	Rudy Boschwitz (IR)	1,119,926	(56%)	($6,657,484)
	Joan Anderson Growe (DFL)..........	852,844	(43%)	($1,592,885)

FIRST DISTRICT

Southeast from Minneapolis and St. Paul, the Mississippi River cuts a path through rolling hills and where it widens forms broad calm lakes lapping at the bottomlands: here is one of the finest river landscapes of North America. This far north, the westward tide of Yankee migrants thinned out. In the years after the Civil War, most settlers following the railroads on the floodplains west of the river were Germans and Scandinavians, bringing their families to this terrain so like the Rhine, and to the rolling uplands beyond which resemble the northern European plain. Southeastern Minnesota is a borderland between Yankee and German settlements—politically, between Civil War Republicans and Farmer-Laborites favoring interventionist economic and isolationist foreign policies.

Minnesota's southeastern corner is, today, the state's 1st Congressional District. Within its compact bounds is considerable diversity. Rochester has been home of the Mayo Clinic since it was founded in 1863 when English-born physician William Mayo set up a practice to examine inductees into the Union Army—early involvement of government in medicine; today, Rochester, with its large professional population, is prosperous and growing. Austin, a county away, is headquarters of the Hormel meatpacking firm that beat a bitter strike in 1986; in 1991, Hormel celebrated its 100th birthday with a huge party that included a Spam sculpture contest. Politically, Rochester is an IR stronghold, while Austin, poorer and losing population, is solidly DFL. The 1st District extends north to new subdivisions spreading out from the Twin Cities and to Northfield, home of Carleton College and former professor Senator Paul Wellstone. The 1st also includes the river towns of Red Wing, Wabasha and Winona, with their 19th Century stone storefronts and mountain-like rock outcroppings that overlook the river. There are farms here, but not the big—and troubled—commercial farms you find farther west.

Tim Penny, congressman from the 1st District, transcends some of southeastern Minnesota's divisiveness. A Democrat of Scandinavian descent, he is also an embodiment of Yankee parsimoniousness. Penny is one of those young Democrats with an instinctive feel for politics and vast energy—the reason why Democrats are a majority in most American legislatures. He was elected to the state Senate in 1976 at age 24, after visiting every home in a Republican district; in 1982, he again campaigned door-to-door, while raising $182,000, and won a congressional seat into which two Republican incumbents had been redistricted. In the last four elections, he has received at least 70% of the vote; in 1992, he was endorsed by the Red Wing newspaper, even though his Republican opponent had worked there a few years before.

How does a Democrat win in a usually Republican district? "My fundamental goal," Penny has said, "is to give the Democratic Party a better image on budget issues." In his first term, he chaired a Freshman Budget Group which sought to reduce deficits; ever since, he has compiled a more conservative record on economic issues than most northern, much less Minnesota, Democrats—arousing complaints from Minnesota labor unions and teachers' groups. He supports the line-item veto and the balanced budget amendment. In the late 1980s, he started seeking identical percentage cuts in over-budget appropriations bills. More recently, he has been introducing "Porkbuster" bills cutting specific projects from filbert blight research and Scranton, Pennsylvania's Steamtown theme park, to the space station and Supercollider. His 1992 "Porkbuster" bill would have cut 68 projects for a total of $5.7 billion in savings. Also, in 1992 he took the "Lead or Leave" pledge to retire in 1996 if the budget deficit has not been cut in half; after the 1992 election, he attacked Senator Paul Wellstone for leading the DFL to the left and overreacting to the Democratic victory. Vocal and motivated by convictions, he has been something of a thorn in the side of the Democratic leadership. In 1993, Penny joined Charles Stenholm in calling for greater spending cuts in the Clinton budget, though he voted for it in March, and in May, he joined Stenholm again in calling for consideration of caps on entitlement spending to insure deficit reduction.

Penny has not served on Budget nor has he sought a seat on Appropriations; for the 103d

Congress, he tried unsuccessfully to get a seat on Ways and Means. His committees are Agriculture and Veterans' Affairs where he has addressed concerns of southeastern Minnesota. On Agriculture, he sponsored a Beginning Farmer's Act to subsidize down payments and operating loans for farmers just starting out; Penny has been dismayed at the small number of young Minnesotans going into farming. He has also pushed for export assistance for beef, pork, vegetable oil, and milk products—a Spam subsidy! On Veterans', he has oversight of the more-successful-than-expected G.I. Bill of Rights and has sponsored a law authorizing the military to pay up to $12,000 of a veteran's starting wage, to ease transition to civilian life.

The People: Pop. 1990: 546,909; 48% rural; 14% age 65+; 97% White; 1% Asian; 1% Hispanic origin. Voting age pop.: 398,958; 1% Hispanic origin. Households: 62% married couple families; 30% married couple fams. w. children; 44% college educ.; median household income: $28,371; per capita income: $12,661; median gross rent: $342; median house value: $58,600.

1992 Presidential Vote

Clinton (D)	109,829	(38%)
Bush (R)	98,384	(34%)
Perot (I)	75,227	(26%)

1988 Presidential Vote

Bush (R)	128,191	(51%)
Dukakis (D)	120,933	(49%)

Rep. Timothy J. Penny (DFL)

Elected 1982; b. Nov. 19, 1951, Freeborn Cnty.; home, New Richland; Winona St. U., B.A. 1974; U. of MN, 1975; Lutheran; married (Barbara).

Career: MN Senate, 1976–82.

Offices: 436 CHOB 20515, 202-225-2472. Also 108 West Park Sq., Owatonna, 55060, 507-455-9151.

Committees: *Agriculture* (8th of 28 D): Environment, Credit and Rural Development; Foreign Agriculture and Hunger (Chmn.). *Veterans' Affairs* (5th of 21 D): Education, Training and Employment.

Group Ratings

	ADA	ACLU	COPE	CDF	CFA	LCV	ACU	NTLC	NSI	COC	CEI
1992	45	65	50	30	53	69	52	40	60	50	64
1991	50	—	42	30	44	62	30	—	—	60	67

National Journal Ratings

	1991 LIB — 1991 CONS		1992 LIB — 1992 CONS	
Economic	39% —	60%	47% —	52%
Social	50% —	48%	35% —	64%
Foreign	62% —	36%	76% —	19%

Key Votes of the 102d Congress

1. Ban Striker Replace	FOR	5. Handgun Wait/7-Day	AGN	9. Use Force in Gulf	AGN
2. $ for Homeownership	AGN	6. Overseas Mil. Abortion	AGN	10. US Mil. Abroad $ Cut	FOR
3. Tax Rich/Cut Mid Cls.	FOR	7. Obscn. Art NEA $ Ban	FOR	11. Limit SDI Funds	FOR
4. FY93/$15B Def. Cut	FOR	8. Death Pen. from Jury	AGN	12. Cuba Trade Embargo	AGN

Key Votes of the 103d Congress

1. Family Leave   AGN   3. Deficit Reduction   FOR   3. Stimulus Plan   FOR

Election Results

1992 general	Timothy J. Penny (DFL)	206,369	(74%)	($292,920)
	Timothy Droogsma (IR)	72,367	(26%)	($93,620)
1992 primary	Timothy J. Penny (DFL)	29,816	(92%)	
	E. Douglas (Doug) Anderson (DFL)	1,618	(5%)	
	Joseph B. Campbell (DFL).	1,131	(3%)	
1990 general	Timothy J. Penny (DFL)	156,749	(78%)	($197,442)
	Doug Anderson (IR)	43,856	(22%)	

SECOND DISTRICT

West of the Mississippi and Minnesota Rivers, where the plains rise above the gorges that the rivers have cut through them, is the great farming country of southwestern Minnesota. This is where Laura Ingalls Wilder's family came on the way west from their little house in the big woods in Wisconsin to the "Little House on the Prairie" in South Dakota, and stopped by the shores of Plum Creek, near Walnut Grove, Minnesota, not long after the Indians were forced out by U.S. troops following the Dakota rebellion of 1862. The creeks and rivers cut crevasses into these plains, spotted with occasional hills and towns settled 100 years ago by Yankee, German and Scandinavian farmers. This is a hard place to make a living; Laura's family, after all their struggles, left the farm for town as soon as they could. Even in the 1990s, farmers still struggle against the elements to make a profitable living, and even their successes hurt: with far higher farm productivity, far fewer people live on the land, and even in town, people here have had a hard time developing an economy that can provide jobs for all their children, much less attract newcomers.

The 2d Congressional District of Minnesota takes in roughly the southwestern quadrant of the state. The farm counties over the decades slowly have become depopulated, as young people move off farms into small towns and, more often, to the Twin Cities or other big metro areas. But now there is movement in the other direction. The 2d District's boundaries were shifted eastward after the 1990 Census and now take in outlying counties and townships of the Twin Cities metro area. Some, around Chanhassen and Shakopee southwest of Minneapolis, are relatively high income areas. Others, farther out, like Waverly where Hubert Humphrey had his lakeside home, are more humble—places where modest-income young families are moving into what was once open countryside punctuated by small villages. It is almost as if the southwestern Minnesota farmers who saw their children go off to the big city are now seeing their grandchildren move back out toward the farmlands, or at least into the same political constituency.

By the numbers, this is one of Minnesota's most Republican districts; it gave a majority of its votes to George Bush in 1988. But by 1992, something resembling the old prairie fire farm rebellions had swept through both sections of the district, producing big political changes. First, Congressman Vin Weber, one of the smartest Republican strategists of the Reagan-Bush era, a member of the leadership with strong conservative stands on issues from taxes to abortion and also a shrewd political realist, decided to retire after it was revealed that he had 125 overdrafts at the House bank. Weber says he could have overcome this liability, and might well have; he beat back a strong challenge in 1986. But he sensed that he would have to give up his chance to be a leader on national issues, and he chafed at the pettiness of the issues challengers of both parties were raising: the new members are "not pledging to do anything that addresses any of our nation's problems. We're going to have new members here who are promising not to use a bank that already will have been closed for a year, and to give their parking spot over to a homeless person and not to work out in the House gym. Well, how does that help us resolve our health care problem? How does it help us get a handle on the deficit? How does it restore the economy?" Weber, determined that conservatives should supply answers to these questions, will likely continue to be a force in national politics; in 1993, he formed a conservative think tank "Empower America" with Jack Kemp and Bill Bennett to redefine the conservative agenda.

The race to succeed Weber turned out to be one of the closest House contests of 1992. The IR candidate was state legislator Cal Ludeman, conservative and antiabortion, the unsuccessful nominee against Governor Rudy Perpich in 1986. With more money and name identification, he began the race as the favorite. But the winner turned out to be Dave Minge, a lawyer and school board member in Montevideo, the town where Walter Mondale grew up. Of Norwegian descent, like Mondale, Minge (pronounced with a hard *G*) "redefines the last word in Norwegian stoicism," as *Star Tribune* columnist Jim Klobuchar put it. Minge's father was a small town doctor who left Minnesota to be a medical missionary for five years; Minge practiced law in Minneapolis, taught law for seven years in Wyoming and worked briefly on Capitol Hill. He returned to Minnesota to practice law and to work with community organizations to clean up the Minnesota river and resettle Vietnamese refugees. Minge decided to run for Congress while Weber was still in the race, got the DFL endorsement after he left, then campaigned hard and won the DFL primary against a LaRouche supporter and another underfunded opponent. He attacked Ludeman for legislative votes against minimum wages, drug abuse programs, and federal disaster relief, and wants an end to tobacco subsidies. He called for handling the deficit with a commission like the one Congress used for military base closings and for a "unified" national healthcare plan; he places the deficit ahead of health care and job creation as priorities. He boldly advocated more taxes on "anyone . . . who makes a good income"; Ludeman was against any tax increase.

Minge showed great energy, riding 500 miles on his bicycle (an even more humbling form of campaigning than Paul Wellstone's battered bus of 1990), stopping in 47 towns in nine days, and keeping up a heavy schedule. During the last weekend of the campaign, he appeared with Hillary Clinton in Mankato and then barnstormed 30 cities; Ludeman practically took the weekend off. In the end, it may have mattered that Bill Clinton carried the district, as it had one of the nation's largest Perot percentages. If you split the Perot vote evenly, in line with exit poll questions on voters' second choices, most voters here preferred the DFL to the IR ticket. In 21 of the 27 counties, the DFL-IR margins in presidential and congressional races were very close, diverging only in each candidate's home territory. On election night, Ludeman was called the winner, but Minge, with Norwegian stoicism, went to sleep and woke up to find out he had won by 569 votes. A supporter of term limits, he has promised to serve only 12 years; his challenge in the 103d Congress, however, will be to live up to his earnest promises on the deficit and health care.

The People: Pop. 1990: 546,874; 58% rural; 16% age 65+; 99% White; 1% Hispanic origin. Voting age pop.: 390,233; 1% Hispanic origin. Households: 65% married couple families; 32% married couple fams. w. children; 37% college educ.; median household income: $27,024; per capita income: $12,159; median gross rent: $309; median house value: $55,000.

1992 Presidential Vote			1988 Presidential Vote		
Clinton (D)	103,246	(37%)	Bush (R)	131,863	(52%)
Bush (R)	97,867	(35%)	Dukakis (D)	121,837	(48%)
Perot (I)	79,442	(28%)			

Rep. David Minge (DFL)

Elected 1992; b. Mar. 19, 1942, Clarkfield; home, Montevideo; St. Olaf College, B.A. 1964, U. of Chicago, J.D. 1967; Lutheran; married (Karen).

Career: Practicing atty., 1967–70, 1977–90; Professor, U. of WY Law Schl., 1970–77; Montevideo School Bd., 1990–92.

Offices: 1508 LHOB 20515, 202-225-2331. Also 542 1st St., Montevideo 56265, 612-269-9311; 108 E. 3d St., Chaska 55318, 612-448-6567; and 938 4th Ave., Windom 56101, 507-831-0115.

Committees: *Agriculture* (16th of 28 D): Environment, Credit and Rural Development; General Farm Commodities; Specialty Crops and Natural Resources. *Science, Space and Technology* (28th of 33 D): Science; Technology, Environment and Aviation.

Group Ratings and 102d Congress Votes: Newly Elected

Key Votes of the 103d Congress

1. Family Leave	FOR	3. Deficit Reduction	AGN	3. Stimulus Plan	FOR

Election Results

1992 general	David Minge (DFL)	132,156	(48%)	($355,400)
	Cal Ludeman (IR)	131,587	(48%)	($429,100)
	Stan Bentz (I)	12,146	(4%)	
1992 primary	David Minge (DFL)	13,468	(53%)	
	Pat (Family Farmer) O'Reilly (DFL)	7,465	(30%)	
	Andrew Olson (DFL)	4,282	(17%)	
1990 general	Vin Weber (IR)	126,367	(62%)	($670,606)
	Jim Stone (DFL)	77,935	(38%)	($17,778)

THIRD DISTRICT

Edina, Minnesota, has one of America's great historic sites: here, in the early 1960s, was built Southdale Shopping Center, one of the first major enclosed malls in the United States. The location made sense, for Edina is rich and cold: just southwest of Minneapolis, it is affluent in a modest-looking Minnesota way and freezes throughout the six-month Minnesota winter. Thanks to the concept of the enclosed mall, commerce and civilization have come not only to the once vacant fields and pond-like lakes of Edina but also to the humid swamps of Houston and the oven-hot desert of Arizona. The acme of malls, the Mall of America, stands just a few miles away in Bloomington with 4.2 million square feet, four key tenants, a seven-acre Camp Snoopy theme park and four distinctive shopping "streets."

Shopping malls are not the only example of how the specific gravity of metro areas has shifted toward the suburbs; Minnesota's most publicized business recently has been Northwest Airlines, to which the state has extended $840 million in credit to keep its Minneapolis-St. Paul hub. Edina, the Mall of America, and the airport are all in Minnesota's 3d Congressional District, on the south side of the metro Twin Cities. Its affluent end is in the west, including Edina and lake-strewn Minnetonka; Bloomington and Richfield just south of Minneapolis are older and politically marginal. The 3d also includes fast-growing Eagan and Burnsville across the Minnesota River from the airport and rural-like townships in Dakota and Washington Counties, all the way east to the Mississippi River and the Wisconsin border. This is by a small margin the most Republican district in Minnesota, although it did not have much use for George Bush in 1992.

The congressman from the 3d is Jim Ramstad, a Republican first elected in 1990, who identifies strongly with ideas of new blood and reform in the House. His crucial contest was the 1990 IR convention which he won on the eighth ballot, although he is pro-choice on abortion and most delegates were pro-life. But Ramstad had good endorsements, from then-Senator Rudy Boschwitz and Congressman Vin Weber, both pro-life, and he has natural political instincts. Raised in North Dakota, he used to go with his grandfather to visit Senator Milton Young; he saw President Eisenhower in 1956 and met President Kennedy in 1963 at the same Rose Garden ceremony where a young Bill Clinton was photographed shaking Kennedy's hand (Ramstad is in the background of the now famous photo). He worked as an intern to Young and a staffer to Congressman Tom Kleppe while in his 20s. He beat a Democratic state senator in 1980 (spending a then record-breaking sum of $77,932) and worked on issues like chemical dependency in young people, cocaine babies and the handicapped, while favoring mandatory minimum sentences for drug dealers and boot camps for drug offenders; he used to go around with police on all-night rounds. During this time, he also dealt with a personal alcoholism problem.

In the House, Ramstad has had a similar record on issues: conservative on economics, sympathetic enough to environmentalists to get the Sierra Club endorsement; working to provide legal services for refugees and to help the disabled start businesses; seeking drug tests for released federal prisoners and lengthier terms for repeat offenders. That has proved to be a winning combination in his pioneering suburban district.

The People: Pop. 1990: 546,976; 2% rural; 8% age 65+; 96% White; 1% Black; 2% Asian; 1% Hispanic origin. Voting age pop.: 398,749; 1% Black; 1% Hispanic origin. Households: 63% married couple families; 32% married couple fams. w. children; 66% college educ.; median household income: $43,963; per capita income: $20,067; median gross rent: $577; median house value: $100,500.

1992 Presidential Vote

Clinton (D)	129,171	(39%)
Bush (R)	117,975	(36%)
Perot (I)	79,877	(24%)

1988 Presidential Vote

Bush (R)	146,262	(54%)
Dukakis (D)	125,389	(46%)

Rep. Jim Ramstad (IR)

Elected 1990; b. May 6, 1946, Jamestown, ND; home, Minnetonka; U. of MN, B.A. 1968, George Washington U., J.D. 1973; Protestant; single.

Career: Army Reserves, 1968–74; Research consult., MN House of Reps., 1969; Special Asst., U.S. Rep. Tom Kleppe, 1979; Practicing atty., 1973–80; Adjunct Prof., American U., 1975–78; MN Senate, 1981–90.

Offices: 322 CHOB 20515, 202-225-2871. Also 8120 Penn Ave. S., #152, Bloomington 55431, 612-881-4600.

Committees: *Judiciary* (10th of 14 R): Administrative Law and Governmental Relations; Crime and Criminal Justice. *Small Business* (6th of 18 R): Development of Rural Enterprises, Exports and the Environment; Minority Enterprise, Finance and Urban Development; SBA Legislation and the General Economy. *Joint Economic Committee* (10th of 10).

Group Ratings

	ADA	ACLU	COPE	CDF	CFA	LCV	ACU	NTLC	NSI	COC	CEI
1992	30	43	42	30	53	50	68	75	80	75	76
1991	25	—	33	50	44	62	85	—	—	80	67

National Journal Ratings

	1991 LIB — 1991 CONS	1992 LIB — 1992 CONS
Economic	34% — 65%	9% — 88%
Social	25% — 73%	41% — 58%
Foreign	17% — 78%	56% — 40%

Key Votes of the 102d Congress

1. Ban Striker Replace	AGN	5. Handgun Wait/7-Day AGN	9. Use Force in Gulf FOR
2. $ for Homeownership	FOR	6. Overseas Mil. Abortion FOR	10. US Mil. Abroad $ Cut FOR
3. Tax Rich/Cut Mid Cls.	AGN	7. Obscn. Art NEA $ Ban FOR	11. Limit SDI Funds FOR
4. FY93/$15B Def. Cut	AGN	8. Death Pen. from Jury FOR	12. Cuba Trade Embargo AGN

Key Votes of the 103d Congress

1. Family Leave   FOR   2. Deficit Reduction   AGN   3. Stimulus Plan   AGN

Election Results

1992 general	Jim Ramstad (IR).....................	200,240	(64%)	($695,521)
	Paul Mandell (DFL).................	104,606	(33%)	($18,164)
	Other................................	9,164	(3%)	
1992 primary	Jim Ramstad (IR), unopposed			
1990 general	Jim Ramstad (IR).....................	195,833	(67%)	($935,454)
	Lou DeMars (DFL)	96,395	(33%)	($337,321)

FOURTH DISTRICT

Above the Mississippi River bluffs, forested when the first settlers arrived in the 1850s and one of America's great urban vistas today, stand the two edifices which stamp the character of St. Paul: the Minnesota Capitol and Archbishop Ireland's Cathedral. St. Paul is the older and smaller of the Twin Cities; it was settled mainly by Catholic Irish and German immigrants, while Minneapolis was attracting Protestant Swedes and Yankees. St. Paul became a major transportation hub, a railroad center and river port, while Minneapolis, farther up river at the Falls of St. Anthony, became the nation's largest grain milling center. St. Paul has a vibrant core: beneath the Capitol and the cathedral, its skywalk-linked downtown is home to the Ordway Music Theater, the headquarters of Minnesota Public Radio and an active pop music industry. Inland beyond the cathedral is Summit Avenue, on which capitalists like the Great Northern Railway's James J. Hill built grandiose Romanesque houses, and which, with Monument Avenue in Richmond and Meridian Street in Indianapolis, remains one of America's grand residential boulevards today.

Politically, St. Paul was one of the most Democratic parts of Minnesota even before the Democratic-Farmer-Labor Party was formed in 1944; ever since, St. Paul and Ramsey County have been solid DFL territory. The neighborhoods of St. Paul, soberly lined up on grid streets with solidly built houses, and the close-in suburbs, with their more irregular street patterns and shopping nodes, stayed Democratic in the 1980s, voting solidly in 1984 for Walter Mondale— who announced his candidacy in the State Capitol and lived during the campaign in his house in the woodsy suburb of North Oaks just north of St. Paul—and in 1988 for Michael Dukakis. And this was one part of Minnesota that gave absolute majorities to Bill Clinton in 1992.

Minnesota's 4th Congressional District is made up of St. Paul, the Ramsey County suburbs to the north, West St. Paul and South St. Paul (which are right next to each other) to the south, and Lake Elmo and Woodbury to the east. The 4th District has been held by the DFL since 1948, when Eugene McCarthy won it. The current congressman, Bruce Vento, was first elected in 1976. He came from a blue-collar, union background and a career as a science teacher, was elected to the state House in 1970 and then to a leadership post. He won the party endorsement at the 1976 district DFL convention with union support, and then won the primary easily.

Vento is now one of the senior members of the House, with important committee responsibilities. He chairs the Natural Resources Subcommittee on National Parks and Public Lands, which has one of the busiest schedules in Congress, for national parks seem to have replaced dams and post offices as plums sought by almost every congressman. It must sort through the applications for wilderness areas and national parks, national seashores, lakeshores and historic sites, wild and scenic rivers, and decide which proposals will be sent to the floor, and in what form. Vento favors limiting logging in the Pacific Northwest to save the spotted owl, for example, and has sponsored bills aimed at compromise between environmental absolutists and adamant loggers; but in June 1992, he was foiled by Speaker Tom Foley who convinced members of the committee to abandon support for Vento's compromise of reduced harvests for dollars for job retraining. He pushed a "Keep Pork out of Parks" bill to keep members from using parks as strictly porkbarrel projects. He is, however, proud of the Minnesota Public Lands Act which transferred 8,000 acres to the state for recreation and conservation. He scathingly attacked the Bush Administration for harming the environment; it will be interesting to see whether he and the Clinton Administration work together to create new parks or new environmental restrictions.

Vento ranks 4th in seniority on the Banking Committee, just behind Henry Gonzalez, Stephen Neal, and John LaFalce, but he is still in the chairman's doghouse after an unsuccessful attempt in 1990 to unseat Gonzalez; Vento lost 89–163. In 1992, he criticized the Bush Administration for losing touch with the S&L problem, neglecting the banks, and "jerking around" Congress on the funding of the RTC; his own partisan edge is not in doubt. Vento has also used his Banking slot to be a major force in funding the McKinney Act, a homeless assistance bill reauthorized in 1991.

Vento easily wins reelection every two years. Redistricting did not make major changes in the 4th District, which remains firmly oriented to St. Paul.

The People: Pop. 1990: 546,812; 12% age 65+; 89% White; 4% Black; 1% Amer. Indian; 5% Asian; 1% Other; 3% Hispanic origin. Voting age pop.: 410,506; 3% Black; 2% Hispanic origin. Households: 51% married couple families; 24% married couple fams. w. children; 55% college educ.; median household income: $32,670; per capita income: $15,863; median gross rent: $455; median house value: $83,700. 405,870.

1992 Presidential Vote			1988 Presidential Vote		
Clinton (D)	147,266	(51%)	Dukakis (D)	162,016	(61%)
Bush (R)	79,137	(28%)	Bush (R)	102,725	(39%)
Perot (I)	58,850	(21%)			

Rep. Bruce F. Vento (DFL)

Elected 1976; b. Oct. 7, 1940, St. Paul; home, St. Paul; U. of MN, A.A. 1961; WI St. U., B.S. 1965; Catholic; separated.

Career: Teacher, 1965–76; MN House of Reps., 1971–77, Asst. Majority Ldr., 1974–76.

Offices: 2304 RHOB 20515, 202-225-6631. Also 175 5th St. E., #727, Box 100, St. Paul 55101, 612-224-4503.

Committees: *Banking, Finance and Urban Affairs* (4th of 30 D): Financial Institutions Supervision, Regulation and Deposit Insurance; Housing and Community Development. *Natural Resources* (6th of 28 D): National Parks, Forests and Public Lands (Chmn.); Oversight and Investigations.

Group Ratings

	ADA	ACLU	COPE	CDF	CFA	LCV	ACU	NTLC	NSI	COC	CEI
1992	100	100	92	100	87	94	0	0	30	25	16
1991	90	—	92	100	89	69	0	—	—	10	9

National Journal Ratings

	1991 LIB — 1991 CONS		1992 LIB — 1992 CONS	
Economic	88%	— 0%	91%	— 0%
Social	88%	— 0%	88%	— 8%
Foreign	92%	— 0%	86%	— 10%

Key Votes of the 102d Congress

1. Ban Striker Replace	FOR	5. Handgun Wait/7-Day	FOR	9. Use Force in Gulf	AGN
2. $ for Homeownership	AGN	6. Overseas Mil. Abortion	FOR	10. US Mil. Abroad $ Cut	FOR
3. Tax Rich/Cut Mid Cls.	FOR	7. Obscn. Art NEA $ Ban	AGN	11. Limit SDI Funds	FOR
4. FY93/$15B Def. Cut	FOR	8. Death Pen. from Jury	AGN	12. Cuba Trade Embargo	AGN

Key Votes of the 103d Congress

1. Family Leave	FOR	2. Deficit Reduction	FOR	3. Stimulus Plan	FOR

Election Results

1992 general	Bruce F. Vento (DFL).................	159,796	(57%)	($348,920)
	Ian Maitland (IR)....................	101,744	(37%)	($82,563)
	Four Others.........................	15,988	(6%)	
1992 primary	Bruce F. Vento (DFL), unopposed			
1990 general	Bruce F. Vento (DFL).................	143,353	(65%)	($266,699)
	Ian Maitland (IR)....................	77,639	(35%)	($57,415)

FIFTH DISTRICT

Minneapolis has its origins in a geographical feature scarcely visible today from most of the city and not much noticed, the Falls of St. Anthony, which rush beneath low downtown bridges and mark the head of navigation of the Mississippi River. All riverboats had to stop at the Falls, and waterpower from the Falls was the energy source for the pioneers' grist mills, and later for the giant grain mills that processed the wheat of the northern Great Plains into food for the United States and the world. By 1890, Minneapolis, together with St. Paul, was the center of one of

America's largest urban areas, living mainly off grain. Today Minneapolis is a center of high-tech industry and of banking and finance; it is a regional railroad center, and the headquarters of one the nation's largest airlines, Northwest; it is also the nerve center of an economic area that extends almost 1,000 miles west to the Rocky Mountains in Montana.

The city of Minneapolis itself, together with working-class suburbs to the northwest (Brooklyn Center, Robbinsdale) and upper middle-income suburbs directly to the west (St. Louis Park, Golden Valley), make up Minnesota's 5th Congressional District, whose boundaries were not greatly changed in redistricting. Minneapolis itself has lost population, but increased vigor can be seen in its skywalk-laced downtown skyscrapers and museum quarter. Neighborhoods have grown less populous but haven't decayed: small frame houses on grid streets in the old working-class neighborhoods which once held large families, now typically hold an elderly widow or couple; the large old houses along the chain of lakes which once held the city's elite—home still to Minneapolis's most eminent citizen, Walter Mondale—now hold young double-income couples who like living close-in. North of the Mississippi is the University of Minnesota; to the northeast, behind the railroad and warehouse district along the Mississippi, is an old working-class neighborhood which has become the new home of many Hmongs from Laos. Minneapolis has a political liberalism drawn from its Scandinavian and Yankee heritage, with an impulse for clean government and cultural tolerance that can go to extremes: Minnesota judges overturned a law imposing heavy penalties on crack users on the grounds it was racially discriminatory, since a majority of crack users are blacks.

That same liberal impulse was apparent in the 1992 challenge to DFL Congressman Martin Olav Sabo for the party endorsement. Sabo is one of the most liberal members of the House, but he is also a veteran political insider, elected to the Minnesota legislature at age 22, the minority leader at 30, speaker at 34. In the U.S. House, Sabo got a seat on the Appropriations Committee in his first year, where he now serves on the Defense, Transportation, and Treasury, Postal Service Subcommittees. On the Budget Committee, he was the author of a 1992 move to break down the 1990 budget summit agreement's walls between defense and domestic spending in order to make bigger defense cuts. When Leon Panetta was appointed OMB Director, Sabo was elected Budget chairman. But, as he recognized, he was not in a position to singlehandedly impose his own views on the House or the Democratic Caucus. He won the chairmanship by a solid but not overwhelming margin of 149-112 over John Spratt of South Carolina, who ran as a moderate, and Sabo's first major act in March 1993 was to prepare a resolution increasing the spending cuts in the Clinton economic program in response to complaints from freshmen and other moderates.

Ironically, in 1992 Sabo had problems at home from just the opposite quarter, when he was challenged by Lisa Niebauer-Stall, a financial planner with a theology degree and a feminist activist, who said Democrats don't want "14 more years of do-nothing, tread-softly, make-no-waves, career politicians." With no conventional political credentials beyond a sloganeering liberalism, she was almost able to deny him endorsement in the May 1992 DFL district convention; only Sabo's declaration that he would not run without the endorsement (a stand in line with traditional DFL veneration of party conventions) enabled him to win on the eighth ballot after seven hours of debate. Clearly the center of gravity in internal DFL politics is no longer entirely with unions and the working class but is shifting to feminists and cultural liberals. Sabo won the September primary 63%–28%, an indication of the strength of this left constituency among voters, and of course won the general election easily.

With the Budget Chairmanship, Sabo should have fewer such problems. This son of Norwegian immigrants' Lake Wobegonish taciturnity has long languished in obscurity, whether he was working on local projects—requiring the Pentagon to buy only U.S. supercomputers, commissioning a DOT study on promoting bicycles as an alternative mode of transportation—or cutting military spending on Defense Appropriations. Now on Budget he will be working in broad daylight, in the harsh glare of publicity. In his case and in this district, that should work to his advantage.

The People: Pop. 1990: 546,876; 14% age 65+; 84% White; 10% Black; 2% Amer. Indian; 4% Asian; 1% Other; 2% Hispanic origin. Voting age pop.: 434,447; 7% Black; 1% Hispanic origin. Households: 39% married couple families; 16% married couple fams. w. children; 57% college educ.; median household income: $28,634; per capita income: $15,794; median gross rent: $449; median house value: $77,900.

1992 Presidential Vote			1988 Presidential Vote		
Clinton (D)	167,941	(58%)	Dukakis (D)	181,948	(65%)
Bush (R)	68,072	(23%)	Bush (R)	98,200	(35%)
Perot (I)	52,374	(18%)			

Rep. Martin Olav Sabo (DFL)

Elected 1978; b. Feb. 28, 1938, Crosby, ND; home, Minneapolis; Augsburg Col., B.A. 1959, U. of MN, 1960; Lutheran; married (Sylvia).

Career: MN House of Reps., 1961–78, Minority Ldr., 1969–73, Speaker, 1973–78.

Offices: 2336 RHOB 20515, 202-225-4755. Also 462 Fed. Courts Bldg., 110 S. 4th St., Minneapolis 55401, 612-348-1649.

Committees: *Appropriations* (11th of 37 D): Defense; Transportation; Treasury, Postal Service and General Government. *Budget* (Chmn. of 26 D).

Group Ratings

	ADA	ACLU	COPE	CDF	CFA	LCV	ACU	NTLC	NSI	COC	CEI
1992	100	100	92	100	100	81	0	5	30	25	6
1991	90	—	92	80	78	77	0	—	—	10	8

National Journal Ratings

	1991 LIB — 1991 CONS			1992 LIB — 1992 CONS		
Economic	69%	—	31%	78%	—	18%
Social	88%	—	0%	88%	—	8%
Foreign	78%	—	19%	86%	—	10%

Key Votes of the 102d Congress

1. Ban Striker Replace	FOR	5. Handgun Wait/7-Day	FOR	9. Use Force in Gulf	AGN
2. $ for Homeownership	AGN	6. Overseas Mil. Abortion	FOR	10. US Mil. Abroad $ Cut	FOR
3. Tax Rich/Cut Mid Cls.	AGN	7. Obscn. Art NEA $ Ban	AGN	11. Limit SDI Funds	FOR
4. FY93/$15B Def. Cut	FOR	8. Death Pen. from Jury	AGN	12. Cuba Trade Embargo	AGN

Key Votes of the 103d Congress

1. Family Leave	FOR	2. Deficit Reduction	FOR	3. Stimulus Plan	FOR

Election Results

1992 general	Martin Olav Sabo (DFL)	174,139	(63%)	($585,831)
	Stephen A. Moriarty (IR)	77,093	(28%)	($16,781)
	Five Others	25,083	(9%)	
1992 primary	Martin Olav Sabo (DFL)	35,168	(67%)	
	Lisa Niebauer-Stall (DFL)	14,519	(28%)	
	James W. Therkelsen (DFL)	2,456	(5%)	
1990 general	Martin Olav Sabo (DFL)	144,682	(73%)	($321,644)
	Raymond C. Gilbertson (IR)	53,720	(27%)	($9,497)

SIXTH DISTRICT

North and northwest from Minneapolis and St. Paul, across the oft-frozen Minnesota landscape, run the great lines of transportation which make these Twin Cities the economic and cultural focus of a vast northern Great Plains empire: the rail lines of the Great Northern and Northern Pacific, expansive highways like Interstate 94 and U.S. 10, the invisible air paths by which Northwest Airlines jets fly from Minneapolis-St. Paul to the Pacific Northwest, Alaska, and the Orient. The land is bleak here, though wooded bluffs hover picturesquely over the Mississippi and St. Croix Rivers; the terrain is mostly flat, and many of the famous "thousand" lakes are flanked by swamps. This northern edge of the Twin Cities metro area has mostly been settled by blue-collar workers, moving out from cramped 1920s prairie style homes to plain modern house subdivision clusters just off the main arteries.

This northern suburban fringe and the countryside of lakes and swamps beyond, form the central geographical portion of the 6th Congressional District of Minnesota, the northern suburban Twin Cities district. It runs east of St. Paul and includes Stillwater, facing Wisconsin on hills above the St. Croix River, with Victorian buildings from its days as a lumber port when it nearly became Minnesota's capital. And it extends west of Minneapolis to include upper income Plymouth and several rich suburbs around Lake Minnetonka. The 6th District is not as affluent (or Republican) as the 3d, but by national standards it is quite upscale—one reason being the combination of a low divorce rate and a high percentage of double income families. This as much as any district is where the new American family can be seen: busy at home and busy at the workplace, communicating with each other by Post-it notes (invented at St. Paul's 3M), exhausted at the end of each day, winning through their efforts a material standard of living that would have dazzled their grandparents at a price that might well have appalled them.

The 6th District was the site in 1992 of one of the nation's most seriously contested races, largely because of the personal problems of Congressman Gerry Sikorski. A 10-year veteran of the House at 44, with six more years of experience in the legislature, with a seat on Energy and Commerce, and projects like a garage-door opener safety act (electric door openers are marvelous in Minnesota winters) and gas pipeline safety legislation (after an explosion in Mounds View), Sikorski seemed headed for a lifetime political career. Then in October 1991, it was revealed that Sikorski had 697 overdrafts on the House bank—more than all but eight other members—totalling nearly $120,000. In April 1992, Sikorski showed signs of political panic by switching from pro-life to pro-choice on abortion; this was particularly shocking in a politician with a 16-year record which he said was based on deep moral beliefs, and in a state where antiabortion groups have long been an important force in both parties. Sikorski was opposed in the DFL primary by antiabortion Hennepin County Commissioner Tad Jude, but his switch did provide support from feminists, at the moment the largest and most enthusiastic group of liberal activists. Sikorski also had support from environmentalists. But all that enabled him to win only the narrowest of primary victories.

Meanwhile, the IR nomination was won by Rod Grams, the same age as Sikorski, but with a very different career. From a working class background in Anoka County in the 6th, Grams married early and never graduated from college, became a broadcaster, and in 1983 became an anchor on the Twin Cities' Channel 9; he is also a home builder on the side. Strongly conservative in a mostly liberal business and a mostly liberal metropolis, he quit his job in 1991 to run for office. Antiabortion and an opponent of any new taxes, he launched tough attacks on Sikorski, while his media celebrity and Sikorski's notoriety helped Grams win votes ordinarily unavailable to an IR. Meanwhile, a third candidate, Plymouth lawyer Dean Barkley, attracted more than usual attention by accusing both Grams and Sikorski of not saying where the pain would come in their deficit-cutting plans. He showed where the pain was in his—a one-year freeze on federal spending, a national sales tax, more taxes on Social Security benefits. Barkley ran humorous TV ads, with a close-up shot of his derriere and parts of his face and saying "take a close look at your next congressman," and he got the endorsement of the *Minneapolis Star-Tribune* and the *St. Paul Pioneer Press*. It didn't help Sikorski that he was attacked in October for excessive use of the House franking privilege (1.1 million letters mailed in 1992) and violating House rules by filming a campaign ad in his office.

The winner in the end, by a wider than expected margin, was Grams, with 44% of the vote, to only 33% for Sikorski and a Perot-like 16% for Barkley. Clearly Sikorski's check problems hurt, as he ran well behind Clinton, while Grams showed some affirmative strength, digging into the Perot constituency in recently settled neighborhoods where people have shallow roots. Grams now occupies an interesting position in the House. As a conservative Republican, in the minority, he might seem entitled to sit on the sidelines and carp; but in February 1993 freshmen Republicans elected Grams to one of the two whip positions for their class. Grams also led a group of 40 GOP freshmen in sending a letter to Bill Clinton urging him to cut the budget deficit without raising taxes. Given his media background and quick start in the House, Grams seems likely to lead a group of freshman Republicans that could turn out to be one of the most interesting blocs in the House.

The People: Pop. 1990: 547,055; 10% rural; 6% age 65+; 97% White; 1% Black; 1% Amer. Indian; 1% Asian; 1% Hispanic origin. Voting age pop.: 382,153; 1% Black; 1% Hispanic origin. Households: 67% married couple families; 38% married couple fams. w. children; 56% college educ.; median household income: $42,346; per capita income: $16,970; median gross rent: $513; median house value: $90,900.

1992 Presidential Vote			1988 Presidential Vote		
Clinton (D)	120,759	(39%)	Dukakis (D)	122,032	(50%)
Bush (R)	102,265	(33%)	Bush (R)	120,889	(50%)
Perot (I)	82,587	(27%)			

Rep. Rod Grams (IR)

Elected 1992; b. Feb. 4, 1948, Princeton; home, Ramsey; Brown Inst., 1966–68, Anoka-Ramsey Jr. Col., 1970–72, Carroll Col., 1974–75; Lutheran; married (Laurel).

Career: News Anchor, KMSP-TV, Minneapolis, 1982–91.

Offices: 1713 LHOB 20515, 202-225-2271. Also 2013 2d Ave. N., Anoka 55303, 612-427-5921.

Committees: *Banking, Finance and Urban Affairs* (16th of 20 R): Consumer Credit and Insurance; Financial Institutions Supervision, Regulation and Deposit Insurance; Housing and Community Development. *Science, Space and Technology* (17th of 22 R): Energy; Technology, Environment and Aviation.

Group Ratings and 102d Congress Votes: Newly Elected

Key Votes of the 103d Congress

1. Family Leave AGN 2. Deficit Reduction AGN 3. Stimulus Plan AGN

Election Results

1992 general	Rod Grams (IR)	133,564	(44%)	($439,718)
	Gerry Sikorski (DFL)	100,016	(33%)	($1,217,832)
	Dean Barkley (I)	48,329	(16%)	($64,170)
	James H. Peterson (IFP).	16,411	(6%)	
	Other	2,400	(1%)	
1992 primary	Rod Grams (IR)	11,818	(69%)	
	James C. Hillegass (IR)	5,404	(31%)	
1990 general	Gerry Sikorski (DFL)	164,816	(65%)	($378,087)
	Bruce Anderson (IR)	90,138	(35%)	($16,219)

SEVENTH DISTRICT

The lake-strewn country along the upper stretches of the Mississippi River, settled by Norwegian and German immigrants, may look ordinary, but it is the source of some prime literary and political traditions. Here a century ago in the town of Sauk Centre grew up Sinclair Lewis, whose *Main Street* and *Babbitt* were greeted as the definitive satires of small town life, though on rereading they show affection for their subjects. Not far north of Sauk Centre is Little Falls, the boyhood home of Charles Lindbergh, whose father was a progressive and isolationist congressman who opposed declaring war on Germany in 1917. In those years this seemingly placid country was seething with rage, as WASPy nationalists banned German from schools, renamed sauerkraut liberty cabbage, and boycotted German-American businesses; the rage simmered and became the source of the bitter isolationism of the 1930s and 1940s, of which Lindbergh was the national symbol, and of the bitter anti-Communism of the 1950s. This part of Minnesota is also the home—though the actual location has somehow disappeared from the map—of Garrison Keillor's Lake Wobegon, whose history has an authentic ring: founded by New England Yankees as New Albion in 1852, renamed when Norwegians got a majority on the council in 1880, where the Norwegian flag still flies on holidays but no one has seen a German flag since 1917.

The 7th Congressional District of Minnesota, covering the northwest corner of the state, includes just about all this territory. It takes in the wheat-farming plains up near North Dakota and the German Catholic country, strewn with farm villages named for saints, around Sauk Centre and St. Cloud. This is mixed political country: some wheat counties are heavily DFL; heavily Norwegian Otter Tail County leans Republican; St. Cloud and Stearns County are volatile, dovish and anti-abortion. The 7th's political history reads like something out of "Lake Wobegon Days." Back in 1958, Congresswoman Coya Knutson lost reelection when her husband Andy issued a plaintive statement urging her to come home and make his breakfast again; she was the only Democratic incumbent to lose in heavily Democratic 1958. Other Scandinavian names followed: Odin Langen, Bob Bergland (who became Jimmy Carter's Secretary of Agriculture), and Arlan Stangeland. None except Bergland won by any great margin, and Stangeland finally lost in 1990 after the *St. Cloud Times* reported he made 341 credit card calls to a woman not his wife.

This was political good luck for current congressman Collin Peterson. A former state senator, he had a string of losses: he lost a DFL caucus in 1982, he lost to Stangeland in 1984 and 1986 (by only 121 votes the second time; he declared victory and went to Washington to set up an office), and he lost the DFL primary in 1988; as a DFL consultant said, "He's found ways of alienating a fair number of people in past elections." But with Stangeland's problems, Peterson won in 1990 with a robust 54%. In office, he continued to do things his way, acting as his own press secretary, campaign consultant, and pilot on flights within the district; he says he models himself after veteran Kentucky Congressman William Natcher, who seeks little publicity, has a small office staff and a locker next to Peterson's in the house gym. He got on the Agriculture Committee, pushed bills for rural economic development and wetland preservation and boned up on issues for the next farm bill. He opposed the North America Free Trade Agreement on behalf of local sugar beet growers; in May 1993, he led the effort to form the 24-member Congressional Anti-NAFTA Caucus. He is one of the few Farm Belt members left who favors supply management and wants the government to increase ag subsidies and price supports. On abortion, he opposes the Freedom of Choice Act as going "way too far" and supports Minnesota's parental consent law. In 1992 the IR candidate, 27-year-old state legislator Bernie Omann, ran an energetic campaign with some gutsy stands like supporting NAFTA and hit Peterson for his heavy use of the House franking permit. Omann ran well in his Stearns County base, and ended up losing by just a 51%–49% margin—the narrowness of the margin an eerie echo of Bill Clinton's tiny margin here over George Bush. Peterson's second victory in the 1990s must surely give him satisfaction over scoffers at his electoral performance in the 1980s. But this remains surely one of the most marginal seats in the nation, and likely the site of a serious contest in 1994.

The People: Pop. 1990: 547,021; 62% rural; 15% age 65+; 96% White; 2% Amer. Indian; 1% Hispanic origin. Voting age pop.: 394,259; 1% Hispanic origin. Households: 61% married couple families; 30% married couple fams. w. children; 40% college educ.; median household income: $22,893; per capita income: $10,294; median gross rent: $316; median house value: $50,200.

1992 Presidential Vote		
Clinton (D)	104,359	(38%)
Bush (R)	103,624	(38%)
Perot (I)	63,610	(23%)

1988 Presidential Vote		
Bush (R)	129,301	(52%)
Dukakis (D)	119,049	(48%)

Rep. Collin C. Peterson (DFL)

Elected 1990; b. Jun. 29, 1944, Fargo, ND; home, Detroit Lakes; Moorhead St. U., B.A. 1966; Lutheran; divorced.

Career: Army Natl. Guard, 1963–69; Accountant, 1966–90; MN Senate, 1976–86.

Offices: 1133 LHOB 20515, 202-225-2165. Also 714 Lake Ave., #107, Detroit Lakes 56501, 218-847-5056; Midtown Sq., 3333 W. Division, #210, St. Cloud 56301, 612-259-0559; and MN Wheat Growers Bldg., Rte. 1, Red Lake Falls 56750, 218-253-4356.

Committees: *Agriculture* (13th of 28 D): Environment, Credit and Rural Development; General Farm Commodities; Livestock; Specialty Crops and Natural Resources. *Government Operations* (12th of 25 D): Employment, Housing and Aviation (Chmn.).

Group Ratings

	ADA	ACLU	COPE	CDF	CFA	LCV	ACU	NTLC	NSI	COC	CEI
1992	65	65	75	80	80	63	24	25	60	63	26
1991	65	—	67	80	83	54	15	—	—	40	26

National Journal Ratings

	1991 LIB	—	1991 CONS	1992 LIB	—	1992 CONS
Economic	61%	—	39%	48%	—	50%
Social	48%	—	51%	49%	—	51%
Foreign	67%	—	32%	76%	—	19%

Key Votes of the 102d Congress

1. Ban Striker Replace	FOR	5. Handgun Wait/7-Day	AGN	9. Use Force in Gulf	AGN
2. $ for Homeownership	AGN	6. Overseas Mil. Abortion	AGN	10. US Mil. Abroad $ Cut	FOR
3. Tax Rich/Cut Mid Cls.	AGN	7. Obscn. Art NEA $ Ban	FOR	11. Limit SDI Funds	FOR
4. FY93/$15B Def. Cut	FOR	8. Death Pen. from Jury	AGN	12. Cuba Trade Embargo	AGN

Key Votes of the 103d Congress

1. Family Leave	FOR	2. Deficit Reduction	FOR	3. Stimulus Plan	FOR

Election Results

1992 general	Collin C. Peterson (DFL)	133,886	(51%)	($495,882)
	Bernie Omann (IR)....................	130,396	(49%)	($218,951)
1992 primary	Collin C. Peterson (DFL)	30,917	(71%)	
	Lorelei Kraft (DFL)	12,464	(29%)	
1990 general	Collin C. Peterson (DFL)	107,126	(54%)	($242,364)
	Arlan Stangeland (IR)	92,876	(46%)	($487,224)

EIGHTH DISTRICT

In the 1860s, prospectors in the Arrowhead region of the new state of Minnesota, northwest of Lake Superior in the low hills of the Mesabi Range, happened upon the nation's largest veins of iron ore; they moved on, looking for gold. But in the 1880s, Duluth banker George Stone and Philadelphia financier Charlemagne Tower started mining the Iron Range and created the northern end of the lifeline of American heavy industry. The range runs south alongside rail lines to the port of Duluth nestled on dramatic bluffs over the always cold and every winter frozen waters of Lake Superior—one of the most beautiful settings for a city in North America. Duluth was a grain-shipping rival of Chicago and the premier iron-ore port; its city plan was drawn up by Daniel Burnham and its splendid turn-of-the-century buildings still celebrate the triumph of technology and civilization over wilderness and the elements. Millions of tons of ore have been dug out of the Range, loaded into rail cars for the ride down to Duluth, and into Great Lakes freighters for shipment to Cleveland, Gary, Detroit, Chicago, Pittsburgh and Buffalo.

For most of this century, in this land where the Arctic winds blow down over the Canadian Shield's thousands of inland lakes, about 100,000 people have lived on the Iron Range and another 100,000 in Duluth, most of them the products of America's 1880–1924 wave of immigration—Italians, Poles, Serbs and Croats, Jews, Swedes and Finns. In this punishing environment, they worked to the point of exhaustion, built solid houses with staunch central heating, and bought layers of warm clothing to survive the winter. Life was rough: the work was hard, the hours long, and the pay low; the churches, a separate one for each ethnic group, were the main community institutions. Living conditions improved vastly in the decades of great economic growth after World War II, but life remains rough-hewn today, and there has been continuing economic distress. As the iron and steel industry got more efficient, fewer workers were needed; when the American steel industry collapsed after 1979, they needed even fewer, or none at all. Unemployment topped 20% in the early 1980s; young people have been moving out for years.

The 8th Congressional District of Minnesota includes Duluth and the Iron Range, plus much of the north woods and lake country to the west and south; under the 1990s redistricting, it moves all the way south to the boundaries of the Twin Cities metro area, to Isanti and Sherburne Counties where young families with modest incomes are starting to build new communities. The 8th District has been the bulwark of Minnesota's Democratic-Farmer-Labor Party since it was created in 1944, with turbulent primary and convention politics and solid DFL margins every November. The current congressman, James Oberstar, is from Chisholm in the Iron Range, where his father was a miner and union official. His views are in the liberal Catholic tradition: he believes government has an obligation to help the poor and disadvantaged and to stimulate economic growth, and has little faith in economic markets; he was long dubious about American military involvement abroad, especially in Central America; he is also culturally traditional and an opponent of abortion. After serving in the Navy, he landed a job with Congressman John Blatnik in Washington and became his chief staffer in 1963: he has been working for the 8th District for 30 years. When Blatnik retired in 1974, Oberstar won the seat, beating Tony Perpich, brother of former Governor Rudy Perpich; he won tough primaries in 1980 and 1984, the latter after briefly running for the Senate.

John Blatnik ended his House career as chairman of the Public Works Committee; now Oberstar is the number two Democrat on that committee, and the chairman of its Aviation Subcommittee. For a long time, he has used Public Works to help revive Duluth and the Iron Range economically, backing EDA and UDAG grants before those programs were scaled back or repealed, and pushing for a big public works bill to fight the 1990–91 recession. As Aviation chairman, he pressed to spend more from the federal airport trust fund and moved to help out Minnesota-based Northwest Airlines when its owners had financial trouble. When KLM offered to invest in Northwest, he called for international negotiations between U.S. and foreign airlines to establish equal landing rights. He pushed hard for the big repair facilities Northwest promised to build in Duluth and the Iron Range in return for $840 million of state investment. He tends to be unconfrontational, but as an early supporter of Tom Harkin's presidential candidacy, Oberstar may differ on some Clinton economic proposals.

Oberstar's general election percentage in 1992 was as low as it has ever been. One reason was the year's overall anti-incumbent sentiment; another was the IR nominee's vigorous negative campaigning; another was that Oberstar visited the district infrequently, since his wife died in 1991 and his daughter was finishing high school in the D.C. area. A final reason was redistricting: the new territory added in the west and south is less Democratic than the old 8th (as is indeed almost every part of Minnesota), and Oberstar was little known there. But no major change in Oberstar's career seems pending: he is likely to devote great effort to Public Works and Aviation, especially as they affect northeastern Minnesota, and generally to continue to support major spending programs.

The People: Pop. 1990: 546,576; 60% rural; 15% age 65+; 97% White; 2% Amer. Indian; 1% Hispanic origin. Voting age pop.: 397,885. Households: 61% married couple families; 29% married couple fams. w. children; 40% college educ.; median household income: $24,667; per capita income: $11,302; median gross rent: $308; median house value: $49,000.

1992 Presidential Vote			1988 Presidential Vote		
Clinton (D)	138,426	(48%)	Dukakis (D)	156,267	(60%)
Bush (R)	80,517	(28%)	Bush (R)	104,906	(40%)
Perot (I)	70,539	(24%)			

Rep. James L. Oberstar (DFL)

Elected 1974; b. Sept. 10, 1934, Chisholm; home, Chisholm; St. Thomas Col., B.A. 1956, Col. of Europe, Bruges, Belgium, M.A. 1957; Catholic; widowed.

Career: Navy civilian language teacher, Haiti, 1959–63; A.A., U.S. Rep. John Blatnik, 1963–74; A.A., U.S. House Public Works Cmte., 1971–74.

Offices: 2366 RHOB 20515, 202-225-6211. Also 231 Fed. Bldg., Duluth 55802, 218-727-7474; Chisolm City Hall, 316 Lake St., Chisholm 55719, 218-254-5761; and Brainerd City Hall, 501 Laurel St., Brainerd 56401, 218-828-4400.

Committees: *Foreign Affairs* (10th of 27 D): Economic Policy, Trade and Environment; Western Hemisphere Affairs. *Public Works and Transportation* (2d of 39 D): Aviation (Chmn.); Economic Development; Water Resources and Environment.

Group Ratings

	ADA	ACLU	COPE	CDF	CFA	LCV	ACU	NTLC	NSI	COC	CEI
1992	90	83	92	90	87	88	4	5	20	25	9
1991	85	—	83	80	83	54	11	—	—	20	8

National Journal Ratings

	1991 LIB — 1991 CONS		1992 LIB — 1992 CONS	
Economic	84%	— 12%	89%	— 9%
Social	65%	— 34%	63%	— 37%
Foreign	92%	— 0%	90%	— 0%

Key Votes of the 102d Congress

1. Ban Striker Replace FOR	5. Handgun Wait/7-Day AGN	9. Use Force in Gulf AGN
2. $ for Homeownership AGN	6. Overseas Mil. Abortion AGN	10. US Mil. Abroad $ Cut FOR
3. Tax Rich/Cut Mid Cls. FOR	7. Obscn. Art NEA $ Ban AGN	11. Limit SDI Funds FOR
4. FY93/$15B Def. Cut FOR	8. Death Pen. from Jury AGN	12. Cuba Trade Embargo AGN

Key Votes of the 103d Congress

1. Family Leave FOR	2. Deficit Reduction FOR	3. Stimulus Plan FOR

Election Results

1992 general	James L. Oberstar (DFL).............	167,104	(59%)	($386,646)
	Philip Herwig (IR)	83,823	(30%)	($32,416)
	Harry Robb Welty (PCP)...............	22,619	(8%)	
	Other................................	8,602	(3%)	
1990 general	James L. Oberstar (DFL).............	52,392	(78%)	
	Leonard J. Richards (DFL)	14,535	(22%)	
1990 general	James L. Oberstar (DFL).............	151,145	(73%)	($229,262)
	Jerry Shuster (IR)....................	56,068	(27%)	($16,681)

MISSISSIPPI

Has history cursed Mississippi? Or is Mississippi now, for all its heritage of woes, teaching lessons much of the rest of the nation would do well to learn? No other state had for so many years such a painful contrast between image and reality, between an ideal sincerely strived for and the tawdry facts of everyday life. Magnolia trees on the lawns of antebellum mansions, golden-haired young women in white dresses on the veranda, faithful black servants and retainers: this was once the ideal. And behind it stood loose-jointed frame houses and unpainted back-country stores, cabins without indoor plumbing and poor white crossroads clusters with askew advertising signs. Mississippi, to its embarrassment, still ranks 50th among states in income, literacy and health—despite the best efforts of civic, political and business leaders. As Mississippi's greatest writer, William Faulkner, said of his state, "You don't love because: you love despite."

Why is Mississippi so cursed? History, according to legal historian Frederick Maitland, is the story of the progress from status to contract: in medieval times, you did what you were born to do; in modern times, you do what you agree with others to do. But in Mississippi, status—race— has always mattered more than anything, and contract here has made less progress than in just about any other state. As in rural Britain hundreds of years ago, Mississippi had a few big landowners always ready to lead local men off to fight; but otherwise everyone was expected to stay in his place and do his duty. The one big industrial farming enterprise—the reclaiming of the swampy lands of the Mississippi Delta and their conversion to cotton fields after the Civil War—actually reinforced the status system. For the Delta was worked by black sharecroppers, tied by debt and deference to others' land, working in conditions that resembled slavery until the mechanical cotton picker was developed in 1944.

Yet perhaps the very starkness of the contrast prompts understanding. For Mississippi has changed, materially and in spirit. The task of Mississippi as a polity is to enable two groups with contrasting cultures and political beliefs to live together civilly, with respect and accommodation. And if it has not entirely succeeded, it has made progress. *The Washington Post's* William Raspberry wrote recently that Mississippi "is one of the few places I know where racial relations are actually improving and where continuing the improvement has come to define the way residents think about their state . . . There is an easiness to relationships, a mutual respect and a willingness to move beyond race that, quite frankly, didn't exist during my years in the state. Mississippi," wrote this Mississippi native, "is finally a good place to be."

Materially, that is obvious. Daily life, thanks to cheap gas and air conditioning, national brands and the mechanization of farming, has changed drastically in Mississippi over the last 50 years. Per capita income was 67% of the national average in 1990, but only 36% in 1940. No longer are most Mississippi blacks sharecroppers living without electricity and farming without machines. No longer are the rules of legal segregation or the informal codes of racial behavior enforced with a violence bordering on terrorism. The end of segregation surely helped Mississippi grow economically: it made investment more attractive and elicited a greater quantum of effort and achievement from blacks. Black outmigration, a major fact of Mississippi life for a half-century, has slowed: 36% of Mississippians were black in 1990, up from 35% in 1980, the first uptick since 1900. If Mississippi lagged during the decade of 1980s metropolitan growth, it also doesn't have the horrifying and rising levels of violent crime and family disintegration that are ruining many big cities.

For all its progress, Mississippi still faces difficult tasks. One is how to stimulate growth in a state that still ranks 50th in all too many indicators. For more than a dozen years, Mississippi's leaders have worked to improve its citizens' basic skills, acutely aware that one-third of the

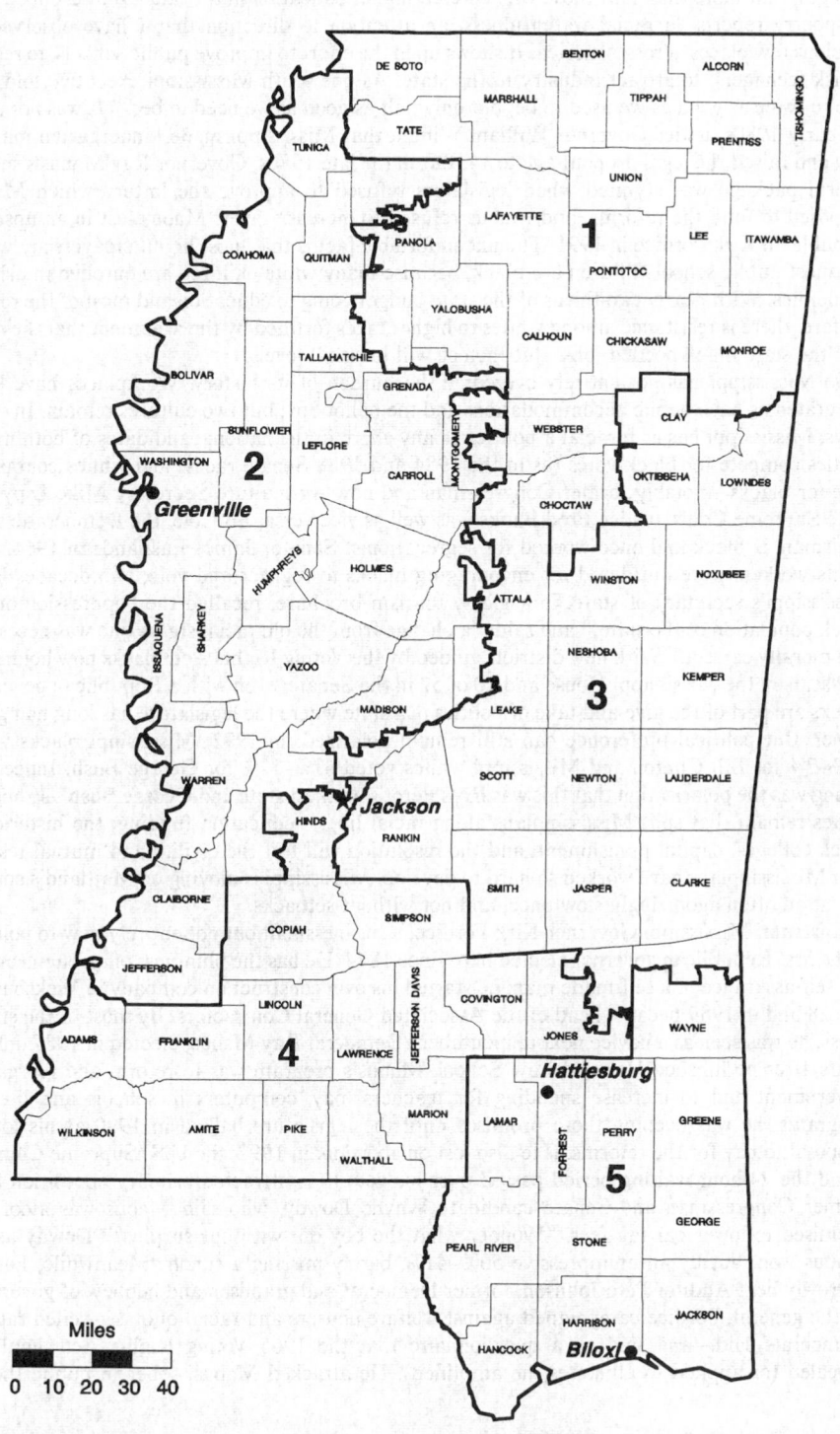

DE SOTO
BENTON
ALCORN
TISHOMINGO
MARSHALL
TIPPAH
TATE
TUNICA
PRENTISS
UNION
1
LAFAYETTE
LEE
ITAWAMBA
COAHOMA
QUITMAN
PANOLA
PONTOTOC
YALOBUSHA
CALHOUN
CHICKASAW
MONROE
TALLAHATCHIE
GRENADA
BOLIVAR
SUNFLOWER
WEBSTER
CLAY
LEFLORE
2
CARROLL
OKTIBBEHA
LOWNDES
WASHINGTON
MONTGOMERY
CHOCTAW
Greenville
HOLMES
WINSTON
NOXUBEE
HUMPHREYS
ATTALA
ISSAQUENA
SHARKEY
NESHOBA
KEMPER
YAZOO
3
MADISON
LEAKE
WARREN
SCOTT
NEWTON
LAUDERDALE
HINDS
Jackson
RANKIN
CLAIBORNE
SMITH
JASPER
CLARKE
COPIAH
SIMPSON
JEFFERSON
JEFFERSON DAVIS
COVINGTON
LINCOLN
JONES
WAYNE
ADAMS
FRANKLIN
4
LAWRENCE
Hattiesburg
WILKINSON
AMITE
PIKE
MARION
LAMAR
FORREST
PERRY
GREENE
WALTHALL
5
GEORGE
PEARL RIVER
STONE
JACKSON
HARRISON
HANCOCK
Biloxi

Miles

0   10 20 30 40

state's adults can't read, that 30% of Mississippians don't qualify for admission to public colleges, that more than half those who entered higher education in the late 1980s dropped out. Raspberry reports "a racial watchfulness, an attention to direction that I have observed in precious few places across America. It shows up in the effort to improve public schools, to rescue at-risk teenagers, to attract industry to the state. As one south Mississippi executive told me, 'We're twice as good as we used to be, but only half as good as we need to be.' " It was not until the early 1980s, under Governor William Winter, that Mississippi made kindergarten mandatory and raised the legal dropout age to 14. But in the late 1980s, Governor Ray Mabus's school reform package was stymied when legislators refused to approve the lottery which Mabus proposed to fund the reforms, and Mabus refused to increase taxes. Mabus lost in an upset to Republican Kirk Fordice in 1991. The uncomfortable fact is that most high taxpayers are white but most public school children are black, because many white children are enrolled in private academies. With nearly two-thirds of the state budget going to education and most of the rest to welfare, there is resistance among whites to higher taxes fortified by the argument that they will cost the state much-needed jobs. But then so will low-skill levels.

So Mississippi has not entirely overcome the burden of its history. Workplaces have been integrated as have public accommodations and the ballot box; but two cultures remain. In some ways, Mississippi has as biracial a politics as anywhere in the nation: candidates of both major parties compete for black votes (as in the 1984 and 1988 Senate races) and whites commonly vote for blacks—notably former Congressman and now Agriculture Secretary Mike Espy and state Supreme Court Justice Fred Banks—as well as vice versa. Ed Cole, the Democratic state chairman, is black and once worked for segregationist Senator James Eastland. In 1964, civil rights workers were murdered for encouraging blacks to register and vote; two decades later, Mississippi's secretary of state, in a glossy tourism brochure, recalled the "oppression of the black population of the state," and said, "a change from the old racial status quo was necessary and morally correct." With new districts guided by the Voting Rights Act, blacks now hold 32 of 122 seats in the Mississippi House and 10 of 52 in the Senate; even with a Republican governor, blacks are part of the give-and-take of politics in a state where the legislature has long had great power. But political preference can still remain polarized: in 1992, Mississippi blacks voted 90%–7% for Bill Clinton and Mississippi whites voted 67%–22% for George Bush. Indeed, so strong was the polarization that this was Ross Perot's weakest state and George Bush's strongest. Issues remain that split Mississippians along racial lines—education funding, the historically black colleges, capital punishment, and the resolution will test the civility and mutual respect that Mississippians have worked so hard to develop. Mississippi is moving on Maitland's course, but at an often agonizingly slow pace, and not without setbacks.

Governor. Mississippi Governor Kirk Fordice, a businessman but not entirely new to politics, is the first Republican governor elected here since 1874. He has the bluntness of an engineer and the self-assurance of a self-made man; he started his own construction company in Vicksburg at age 28 and in 1989 became head of the Associated General Contractors. By most of the state's press, he was seen as a novice next to incumbent Democrat Ray Mabus, elected in 1987 only 11 years after he finished Harvard Law School. Mabus's program was to reform and reorganize government and to increase spending for teachers' pay, computers in schools and literacy programs; he was keeping those promises until the legislature balked in 1990 at his lottery proposal to pay for the reforms. (He also lost on abortion: in 1992, the U.S. Supreme Court let stand the 24-hour waiting period passed over his veto.) He attracted primary opposition from former Congressman and Senate candidate Wayne Dowdy, who said Mabus was aloof and promised to lower car tag fees. "Wonder what the boy did with our surplus?" Dowdy asked. Mabus won, but by an unimpressive 50%–41%, barely missing a runoff. Meanwhile, Fordice narrowly beat Auditor Pete Johnson, former Democrat and grandson and nephew of governors. In the general, Fordice campaigned against welfare abusers and racial quotas—veiled racism, Democrats said—and said on a questionnaire that the 1965 Voting Rights Act should be repealed (or applied to all states, he amplified). He attacked Mabus, sober in public though humorous in private, as aloof: "The problem is that he is a Harvard-educated personality who is not prepared to listen to anybody. He just doesn't do windows." Fordice trailed in polls but won 51%–48%, carrying a large majority of white votes.

Fordice's formula for Mississippi is to attract jobs not by spending on education but by "CEO-to-CEO recruitment"; he claims to have helped produce 17,000 new jobs in 1992. He cut state spending but increased capital investment. He advocates school prayer and term limits, workmen's compensation reform and halving of car tag fees. He installed an "empowerment" interactive telephone line with information on state issues and legislators' positions. A 1% increase in the sales tax was passed over his veto. Fordice got into the national news after the 1992 election when he said "the United States of America is a Christian nation, which does not mean in any way to infer any kind of religious intolerance or any kind of particular dogma that is being forced on anyone." Governor Carroll Campbell of South Carolina stepped forward and added, "The value base of this country comes from the Judeo-Christian heritage we have." A few days later, Fordice apologized and said he only meant "the overwhelming majority of Americans say they are Christians and that Christian values and beliefs should not be denigrated," which would have been unobjectionable if he had said that in the first place.

Mississippi has allowed governors to run for a second consecutive term for a decade now. But Bill Allain, beset by scandal, didn't run in 1987, and Mabus lost in 1991. Will Fordice break the jinx in 1995? Mabus might come back and run, and he surely is aware that Clinton, too, lost his first reelection race and came back. Fordice has said he will decide on whether to seek a second term after giving himself a report card on his promises. In effect, Mississippi has given two very different approaches to its problems a chance to prove themselves. By 1995, voters can make an informed choice between them, or for some other alternative.

Senators. Mississippi, represented in the Senate for 31 years (1947–78) by the same two conservative Democrats, has now been represented since 1988 by the same two conservative Republicans, both politically skilled and popular, both first elected to the House in 1972 when, as in 1992, Mississippi was the most Republican state in the presidential election. Thad Cochran, the senior senator, has managed to amass a solidly conservative record with little controversy or acrimony. He won the House race in 1972 against a white Democrat and a black Independent; he was elected to the Senate in 1978 in a similar three-way contest. In both cases, he won with less than an absolute majority, but was reelected easily. His pleasant personal demeanor, his refusal to engage in racial politics, his conservative stands on almost all issues, and his Republican Party label in a state where most whites have been voting Republican for president for three decades, have made him acceptable to most Mississippi voters.

Cochran is nonetheless a tougher partisan than he looks. In 1990, he challenged John Chafee of Rhode Island for the chairmanship of the Senate Republican Conference, technically the number three leadership position; the leadership at the time seemed overly liberal to many, given Minority Leader Bob Dole's support of higher taxes, Whip Alan Simpson's support of abortion rights and Chafee's liberal leadership on the Clean Air Act. Cochran argued "We need an aggressiveness in defining the differences between the two parties" and won 22–21; he is seen as a possible successor to Dole as Republican leader some day. "We ought not be here just throwing rocks at Democrats," he said in early 1993. But occasionally he will heave one himself, as when he tried to abolish Senator David Pryor's Special Committee on Aging; Senate Democrats, knowing that Pryor is the senator closest to President Bill Clinton, did not go along.

Even in the leadership, Cochran hasn't sought national publicity, and seems to concentrate on Appropriations Committee work and other legislative tasks. He played an active role fashioning the 1990 farm bill; he acted as an advocate for soybean growers, arguing that flexibility programs have provided incentives for overproduction, and he sought to boost exports and provide income protection. He has worked to make educational grants more available to historically black colleges and for vocational training for the disabled; he wants to set up a $1 million prize for school districts with the best "break the mold" education innovations; he successfully sponsored a bill for National Science Foundation technology grants to community colleges. He is a backer of military aid to Greece and Turkey.

Cochran's toughest electoral challenge was in 1984, when he faced former Governor William Winter. But Winter dithered over whether to run, announcing he would become chancellor of Ole Miss, and then weeks later declining the post to make the Senate race. Cochran won 58%–42%, winning white votes by a large margin and making inroads among blacks. In 1990, he attracted no serious opposition; an unknown started to run against him but withdrew before the filing deadline. That leaves him with over $800,000 in his treasury for the 1996 campaign.

Mississippi's junior senator, Trent Lott, may turn out to be the most effective and durable partisan Republican on Capitol Hill. Still in his early 50s, he rose to a leadership position in the House and became an active and visible senator. Starting from a modest background, Lott showed an eye for opportunity but also a steadiness and strength of conviction that led him to take what seemed at the time political risks but which have turned out, in an increasingly Republican state, to have been political masterstrokes. Lott worked his way through law school by running the Ole Miss alumni affairs office, accumulating a stateful of good contacts; he got a job on the staff of Democratic Gulf Coast Congressman William Colmer, and when Colmer retired in 1972, Lott ran for the seat with Colmer's encouragement and endorsement—as a Republican. He was elected with 55% in what was the strongest Nixon district in the country that year. In 1974, Lott was the youngest member of the Judiciary Committee, loyally defending Richard Nixon in the impeachment hearings. In 1980, he was elected Republican whip, and he ran the Republican National Convention's platform committees in 1980 and 1984. He supported Jack Kemp for president in 1987 and 1988, even as he was running for the Senate himself.

Like southerners of another era, Lott can remember in moments of triumph his support for lost causes. He indicated no support for the racial segregation universally accepted in white Mississippi when he came of age, nor does he revisit the cause of Richard Nixon. What he does is advance, with a vehemence born of both aggressiveness and conviction, a coherent set of beliefs. Like many self-made men, he has a visceral dislike for taxes and big government, developed in his case to an articulate belief in supply-side economics and deregulation, though not always free trade. Culturally, he wants to strengthen belief in traditional moral values and the rightness of the existing order: he wants people to believe that America is good to the core, not riddled with rottenness. He believes in an assertive foreign policy and plenty of defense spending. Gregarious and personable, he is on good terms with otherwise feuding conservatives, and has long cultivated his contemporaries among southern Democrats, looking for a vote here and a party switch there. But he can be sharp in debate, aggressively partisan and combative.

Lott seems more comfortable operating as part of a heavily outnumbered minority, as he is in the Clinton years and was in the House, than as one with responsibility for an incumbent administration he cannot control, as he was in the Bush years. Lott jumped ship in 1990 by opposing Bush's budget summit agreement, though he stuck with Bush on tough issues like the FSX and Chinese student visas. On the Senate Ethics Committee, he sat in judgment on the Durenberger, D'Amato and the Keating Five cases, objecting when he felt that committee Democrats were declining to let John McCain and John Glenn off because that would leave only Democrats as miscreants. He proposed in 1991, but later recanted, replacing the committee's senators with six private citizens. In 1993, Bob Dole asked Lott to stay on as vice chairman of Ethics, but he declined and instead joined the Energy and Natural Resources Committee. He also became a member of the Republican leadership by winning the post of conference secretary in December 1992, with 20 votes to 14 for Christopher Bond and five for Frank Murkowski.

In the first months of the Clinton Administration, Lott stepped up as if to be a major critic, then drew back when Bob Dole asked him to be the Republicans' point man to review important Clinton nominations. Lott questioned Commerce Secretary Ron Brown at length about possible conflicts of interest, but thought Zoe Baird's nanny problems would not be a "killer issue," and decided not to raise unsubstantiated allegations brought by opponents against Attorney General Janet Reno. In budget hearings, he pulled a paper out of his pocket which he said had a list of

$216 billion in cuts; when OMB Director Leon Panetta asked him for the list, he put it back in his pocket, which gave the administration a talking point for a week. In March 1993, Lott and Phil Gramm broke with Bob Dole and others in the leadership by offering their own proposal for spending cuts of $178 billion.

Lott gave up a safe seat and the number two Republican leadership post in the House to make the 1988 Senate race, and he had something of a fight for it. Congressman Wayne Dowdy, who beat Secretary of State Dick Molpus in the primary 54%–42%, voiced populist themes and criticized Lott for having a chauffeur. Lott responded with an ad showing the employee in question, a black law enforcement professional named George Awkward, who explained he was guarding Lott because he was a member of the leadership: "I'm nobody's chauffeur, Mr. Dowdy." Lott outraised Dowdy and won a 61%–39% margin in the Jackson area, the Gulf Coast and other counties where turnout had increased 10% since 1980; in the rest of the state, Dowdy prevailed 51%–49%. That suggests which kind of politics represents the future of Mississippi and which the past, and Lott is a strong favorite for reelection in 1994.

Presidential politics. Mississippi was George Bush's number one state in 1992, though he won fractionally less than 50% of the vote, and Ross Perot's worst; just across the river from Bill Clinton's Arkansas, it gave Bush a larger percentage of the vote than did the other five southern states he carried. On balance, it must be regarded as a presidentially Republican state, and not because of race; it is other issues—defense, crime, cultural attitudes, taxes—on which they shunned Walter Mondale and Michael Dukakis and Bill Clinton by decisive margins.

Other evidence of Mississippi's Republican strength is that it is the home of the new Republican National Committee chairman, Haley Barbour. Barbour got his start in Yazoo County and ran Mississippi for Richard Nixon in 1968. He became a leading Republican operative in the 1970s, ran unsuccessfully against Senator John Stennis in 1982 and was Reagan White House political director in 1985 and 1986. His strengths in the 1993 race for chairman were his ties to local politicians across the country and his gift for pungent sound-bites; his first as chairman: "If we make abortion a test of being Republican, we need our heads examined."

Congressional districting. The key player in Mississippi redistricting is the Voting Rights Act, interpreted to mandate the creation of a black-majority district. Ironically, Mike Espy as congressman became so popular with white voters that he wanted to hold down the black percentage in his district to raise it in others; civil rights organization apparatchiks said no. The 1990 districting plan is substantially similar to that of 1980: the 2d District still has a solid black majority. The other four districts voted for George Bush in 1988 and 1992; yet Mississippi, all Republican now at the top of the ticket, elects five Democrats and no Republicans to the House.

The People: Est. Pop. 1992: 2,614,000; Pop. 1990: 2,573,216, up 1.6% 1990–1992. 1.0% of U.S. total, 31st largest; 53% rural. Median age: 31.2 years. 12.5% 65 years and over. 63.5% White, 35.6% Black. Households: 54.7% married couple families; 27% married couple fams. w. children; 37% college educ.; median household income: $20,136; per capita income: $9,648; 71.5% owner occupied housing; median house value: $45,600; median monthly rent: $215. 8.1% Unemployment. Voting age pop.: 1,826,455. Registered voters (1992): 1,640,150; no party registration.

Political Lineup: Governor, Kirk Fordice (R); Lt. Gov., Eddie Briggs (R); Secy. of State, Dick Molpus (D); Atty. Gen., Mike Moore (D); Treasurer, Marshall Bennett (D); Auditor, Steven A. Patterson (D). State Senate, 52 (38 D and 14 R); State House of Representatives, 122 (93 D, 27 R, and 2 I). Senators, Thad Cochran (R) and Trent Lott (R). Representatives, 5 D.

1992 Presidential Vote

Bush (R) 487,793 (50%)
Clinton (D) 400,268 (41%)
Perot (I). 105,045   (9%)

1992 Democratic Presidential Primary

Clinton. 139,893 (73%)
Brown 18,396 (10%)
Tsongas 15,538   (8%)
Uncommitted 11,796   (6%)

1988 Presidential Vote

Bush (R) 557,921 (60%)
Dukakis (D). 363,921 (39%)

1992 Republican Presidential Primary

Bush 111,794 (72%)
Buchanan. 25,891 (17%)
Duke 16,426 (11%)

GOVERNOR

Gov. Kirk Fordice (R)

Elected 1991, term expires Jan. 1996; b. Feb. 10, 1934, Memphis, TN; home, Vicksburg; Purdue U., B.S. 1956, M.S. 1957; Methodist; married (Pat).

Career: Army, 1957–59; Engineer, Exxon Corp., 1956–62; Exec., Fordice Construction Co., 1962–92; Pres., Assoc. General Contractors of Amer., 1989–91.

Office: State Capitol, P.O. Box 139, Jackson 39205, 601-359-3100.

Election Results

1991 gen.	Kirk Fordice (R).	361,500	(51%)
	Ray Mabus (D).	338,459	(48%)
	Other	11,253	(2%)
1991 runoff	Kirk Fordice (R).	31,753	(61%)
	Pete Johnson (R)	20,622	(39%)
1991 prim.	Kirk Fordice (R).	28,411	(45%)
	Pete Johnson (R)	27,561	(43%)
	Bobby Clanton (R).	7,589	(12%)
1987 gen.	Ray Mabus (D).	385,689	(61%)
	Jack Reed (R)	336,006	(39%)

SENATORS
Sen. Thad Cochran (R)

Elected 1978, seat up 1996; b. Dec. 7, 1937, Pontotoc; home, Jackson; U. of MS, B.A. 1959, J.D. 1965, Rotary Fellow, Trinity Col., Ireland, 1963–64; Baptist; married (Rose).

Career: Navy, 1959–61; Practicing atty., 1965–72; U.S. House of Reps., 1972–78.

Offices: 326 RSOB 20510, 202-224-5054. Also 188 E. Capitol St., #164, Jackson 39201, 601-965-4459.

Committees: *Agriculture, Nutrition and Forestry* (4th of 8 R): Agricultural Production and Stabilization of Prices; Agricultural Research, Conservation, Forestry and General Legislation; Domestic and Foreign Marketing and Product Promotion (RMM). *Appropriations* (3d of 13 R): Agriculture, Rural Development and Related Agencies (RMM); Defense; Energy and Water Development; Interior; Labor, Health and Human Services, Education. *Governmental Affairs* (4th of 5 R): Federal Services, Post Office and Civil Service; Oversight of Government Management; Regulation and Government Information (RMM); Permanent Subcommittee on Investigations. *Indian Affairs* (3d of 8 R). *Rules and Administration* (7th of 7 R).

Group Ratings

	ADA	ACLU	CDF	COPE	CFA	LCV	ACU	NTLC	NSI	COC	CEI
1992	10	5	30	17	25	0	85	65	90	100	68
1991	5	—	45	25	28	7	76	—	—	80	61

National Journal Ratings

	1991 LIB — 1991 CONS	1992 LIB — 1992 CONS
Economic	9% — 87%	12% — 86%
Social	23% — 75%	0% — 89%
Foreign	0% — 87%	10% — 80%

Key Votes of the 102d Congress

1. $ for Homeownership	FOR	5. Clarence Thomas Nom. FOR	9. Use Force in Gulf FOR
2. Have Cap Gains Debate	FOR	6. Lmt Death Row Appeal FOR	10. Keep Salvador Aid FOR
3. Remove Budget Walls	AGN	7. Handgun Wait/5-Day AGN	11. Cut $1B from SDI AGN
4. Ban Striker Replace	AGN	8. Abortion Gag Rule FOR	12. Override China MFN AGN

Key Votes of the 103d Congress

1. Family Leave AGN	2. HIV Immigrants AGN	3. Clinton Budget AGN

Election Results

1990 general	Thad Cochran (R), unopposed			($691,865)
1990 primary	Thad Cochran (R), unopposed			
1984 general	Thad Cochran (R)...................	580,314	(61%)	($2,870,894)
	William Winter (D)	371,926	(39%)	($738,739)

Sen. Trent Lott (R)

Elected 1988, seat up 1994; b. Oct. 9, 1941, Grenada; home, Pascagoula; U. of MS, B.A. 1963, J.D. 1967; Baptist; married (Tricia).

Career: Practicing atty., 1967–68; A.A., U.S. Rep. William Colmer, 1968–72; U.S. House of Reps., 1972–1988.

Offices: 487 RSOB 20510, 202-224-6253. Also 1 Gov. Plaza, #428, Gulfport 39501, 601-863-1988; 245 E. Capitol St., #309, Jackson 39201, 601-965-4644; 3100 S. Pascagoula St., Pascagoula 39567, 601-762-5400; 101 S. Lafayette St., Starkville 39759, 601-323-1414; 911 Jackson Ave., Fed. Bldg., #127, Oxford 38655, 601-234-3774; and 200 E. Washington St., #145, Greenwood 38930, 601-453-5681.

Committees: *Armed Services* (5th of 9 R): Defense Technology, Acquisition and Industrial Base; Nuclear Deterrence, Arms Control and Defense Intelligence (RMM); Regional Defense and Contingency Forces. *Budget* (6th of 9 R). *Commerce, Science and Transportation* (8th of 9 R): Merchant Marine (RMM); Science, Technology and Space; Surface Transportation. *Energy and Natural Resources* (9th of 9 R): Energy Research and Development; Public Lands, National Parks and Forests; Renewable Energy, Energy Efficiency, and Competitiveness. *Joint Committee on the Organization of Congress* (9th of 12).

Group Ratings

	ADA	ACLU	CDF	COPE	CFA	LCV	ACU	NTLC	NSI	COC	CEI
1992	10	5	10	17	25	0	100	78	100	90	83
1991	5	—	27	27	17	20	86	—	—	78	65

National Journal Ratings

	1991 LIB — 1991 CONS	1992 LIB — 1992 CONS
Economic	15% — 80%	0% — 89%
Social	0% — 86%	14% — 85%
Foreign	13% — 77%	0% — 90%

Key Votes of the 102d Congress

1. $ for Homeownership FOR	5. Clarence Thomas Nom. FOR	9. Use Force in Gulf FOR
2. Have Cap Gains Debate FOR	6. Lmt Death Row Appeal FOR	10. Keep Salvador Aid FOR
3. Remove Budget Walls AGN	7. Handgun Wait/5-Day AGN	11. Cut $1B from SDI AGN
4. Ban Striker Replace AGN	8. Abortion Gag Rule FOR	12. Override China MFN AGN

Key Votes of the 103d Congress

1. Family Leave AGN	2. HIV Immigrants AGN	3. Clinton Budget AGN

Election Results

1988 general	Trent Lott (R)	510,380	(54%)	($3,405,242)
	Wayne Dowdy (D)	436,339	(46%)	($2,355,957)
1988 primary	Trent Lott (R), unopposed			
1982 general	John C. Stennis (D)	414,099	(64%)	($944,054)
	Haley Barbour (R)	230,927	(36%)	($1,133,384)

FIRST DISTRICT

The keystone of William Faulkner's fictional universe is in the university town of Oxford, situated on a divide between two parts of Mississippi. To the east are the mostly white hill counties, going all the way up to the northeast corner where Mississippi's Tishomingo County meets the Tennessee River. The Tennessee Valley Authority brought electricity here, and the Tennessee-Tombigbee Waterway provided construction jobs for years and a new shipping canal when it was completed in 1985: this is one part of Mississippi where the federal government is regarded as a helper and not a meddling intruder. The metropolis here is Tupelo, home today of the Reverend Donald Wildmon's organization promoting boycotts of products advertised on television shows that he thinks have excessive sex or violence; this was also the boyhood home of Elvis Presley, where he lived until moving to Memphis in the eighth grade. West of Oxford is Mississippi's Delta, the swampy land pioneered by large planters around the turn of the century, with large black work forces little removed—in the conditions of their daily lives or long-term economic chances—from slavery. In the center is Oxford, home of Ole Miss and Faulkner's Jefferson in his fictional Yoknapatawpha County, where he was fired as postmaster for writing novels on the job, and home today of the Center for the Study of Southern Culture.

All this land is part of Mississippi's 1st Congressional District, which also includes the Mississippi suburbs of Memphis. It touches on the river itself and includes half of Tallahatchie County, home of Congressman Jamie Whitten, who has served longer in the House than anyone in American history. He came there first in a November 1941 special election, chosen at age 31 largely because he had prosecuted gamblers that Memphis political boss E. H. Crump had sent scampering over the state line into Mississippi; he took his seat a month before Pearl Harbor. On January 6, 1992, he broke the record for service set by Carl Vinson of Georgia from 1914 to 1965; a month later, at 81, he suffered something in the nature of a stroke, was absent from his duties for more than a month and returned clearly impaired. Whitten was not able to floor-manage the 1992 Appropriations bills like he had for so many years, and in June House Democrats made second-ranking member William Natcher acting chairman. Whitten was first elected chairman in 1978 by 157–88 and last in 1990 by 218–34. His mastery of detail and marbles-in-the-mouth diction made watching him floor manage a bill an awe-inspiring if not informative experience. But in December 1992, the Democratic Steering and Policy Committee unceremoniously voted the chairmanship to Natcher and then Appropriations Democrats voted Whitten by 29–7 out of the chair of its Agriculture Subcommittee, which he had held since 1949 except for one term of Republican control, in favor of Richard Durbin of Illinois.

The capstone of his power was the Agriculture subcommittee, which made him a kind of permanent "Secretary of Agriculture," and his shepherding of emergency farm appropriations enabled him to do favors for dozens of members. Naturally, he used his power to benefit his district and Mississippi; his monuments include the Tennessee-Tombigbee Waterway, which hasn't come close to meeting traffic projections, and an advanced solid rocket motor factory in an abandoned TVA nuclear plant in Yellow Creek. "My district is a part of the nation, and if you handle a national program and leave out your district, you would not want to go home." He has tended to other local interests, especially cotton, and he generally favored expansive federal benefit programs; the continued existence of farm subsidies owes much to him. He was a staunch segregationist for years, but shifted his stance after blacks got the vote. He had a solidly conservative voting record for years, but became more liberal after 1974 when committee chairmen started being elected—or ousted—by the Democratic Caucus. "Conditions change," he told one reporter. "You go with conditions as they are, not like what they used to be."

Whitten's physical and political weakness obviously registered with 1st District voters in November 1992. He won his primary easily, but against a Republican opponent was reelected with 59% of the vote—down from 65% in 1990 and 78% in 1988—and he actually lost in the Memphis suburbs. It is widely expected in Mississippi and Washington that he will not run again in 1994, though he certainly has not said he will step down. In either case, the district may be seriously contested, with both parties and a wide variety of candidates having a chance to win.

The People: Pop. 1990: 515,196; 67% rural; 13% age 65+; 77% White; 23% Black. Voting age pop.: 373,976; 20% Black. Households: 61% married couple families; 30% married couple fams. w. children; 30% college educ.; median household income: $20,867; per capita income: $9,639; median gross rent: $277; median house value: $43,700.

1992 Presidential Vote			1988 Presidential Vote		
Bush (R)	101,252	(50%)	Bush (R)	108,068	(60%)
Clinton (D)	84,765	(42%)	Dukakis (D)	71,167	(40%)
Perot (I)	17,984	(9%)			

Rep. Jamie L. Whitten (D)

Elected Nov. 1941; b. Apr. 18, 1910, Cascilla; home, Charleston; U. of MS, 1927–31; Presbyterian; married (Rebecca).

Career: Schl. principal, 1930–31; Practicing atty., 1931–41; MS House of Reps., 1932–33; Dist. Atty., 1933–41.

Offices: 2314 RHOB 20515, 202-225-4306. Also P.O. Bldg., Charleston 38921, 601-647-2413; P.O. Box 667, Oxford 38655, 601-234-9064; and P.O. Box 1482, Tupelo 38801, 601-844-5437.

Committees: *Appropriations* (Vice Chmn. of 37 D): Agriculture, Rural Development, Food and Drug Administration and Related Agencies.

Group Ratings

	ADA	ACLU	COPE	CDF	CFA	LCV	ACU	NTLC	NSI	COC	CEI
1992	50	47	78	60	67	13	29	7	80	50	9
1991	25	—	75	60	50	46	33	—	—	60	14

National Journal Ratings

	1991 LIB — 1991 CONS			1992 LIB — 1992 CONS		
Economic	43%	—	57%	77%	—	23%
Social	49%	—	51%	*	—	*
Foreign	61%	—	38%	*	—	*

Key Votes of the 102d Congress

1. Ban Striker Replace	AGN	5. Handgun Wait/7-Day	*	9. Use Force in Gulf	FOR
2. $ for Homeownership	AGN	6. Overseas Mil. Abortion	AGN	10. US Mil. Abroad $ Cut	*
3. Tax Rich/Cut Mid Cls.	*	7. Obscn. Art NEA $ Ban	FOR	11. Limit SDI Funds	AGN
4. FY93/$15B Def. Cut	*	8. Death Pen. from Jury	*	12. Cuba Trade Embargo	FOR

Key Votes of the 103d Congress

1. Family Leave	FOR	2. Deficit Reduction	FOR	3. Stimulus Plan	FOR

Election Results

1992 general	Jamie L. Whitten (D)	121,664	(59%)	($267,223)
	Clyde E. Whitaker (R)	82,952	(41%)	($229,004)
1992 primary	Jamie L. Whitten (D)	36,817	(82%)	
	Rex Weathers (D)	8,114	(18%)	
1990 general	Jamie L. Whitten (D)	43,668	(65%)	($96,254)
	Bill Bowlin (R)	23,650	(35%)	($14,750)

SECOND DISTRICT

"The Mississippi Delta," wrote Delta native David Cohn, "begins in the lobby of the Peabody Hotel in Memphis and ends on Catfish Row in Vicksburg." For centuries, the flooding Mississippi and Yazoo Rivers left their sediments in this flat land; "by slow accretion, without foundation of rock or shale, it laid down this land—pure soil endlessly dark, deep and sweet." The irony is that what may well be America's richest agricultural land has been home for more than a century of many of its poorest people. The Delta, criss-crossed by rivers and famously disease-ridden, wasn't much settled until after the Civil War; the tradition here is not of paternal masters and gracious mansions, but of sharp, profit-seeking operators who used 19th Century technology to drain the land, line the river with levees and build railroads on elevated tracks. Black sharecroppers and field hands worked here in conditions reminiscent of Caribbean sugar plantations a century before. From this episode of industrial farming came both great misery and great art: Clarksdale in Coahoma County was the home of W.C. Handy and Muddy Waters, the real birthplace of blues music; Greenville on the Mississippi has produced writers of the caliber of Walker Percy and Shelby Foote; Vicksburg's antebellum mansions, battlefield monuments and riverboat gambling bring in 1.5 million tourists annually from around the country.

Then 20th Century technology changed life in the Delta once again. The mechanical cotton-picking machine, invented in 1944, came along just as northern defense plants were seeking low-wage workers; the great exodus to Chicago and Memphis began, and the Delta's population has been declining ever since. Income levels remain very low, poverty is over 50% in some areas and infant mortality is at Third World levels; the crime and drugs of urban Chicago have been brought back by Delta migrants returning home. There are signs of hope: cotton is being replaced as the Delta's biggest crop by soybeans and catfish (90% of the world's pond-raised catfish come from the Delta); the combined efforts of the Delta regional commission and Delta state governors may also help improve economic conditions. Racial segregation has disappeared from many areas of life to the point that a former head of the state NAACP won two out of every three votes for mayor of Vicksburg, whose population is 50–50, white and black. But still, the Delta has been unable to develop the self-propelling market economy that has brought growth to most of the nation.

Politically, the Delta produced white segregationists as harsh in their own way as the farm operators, notably Delta planter James Eastland, U.S. senator from 1941 to 1979, chairman of the Judiciary Committee from 1955 to 1979, and unrelenting foe of civil rights. But it also produced Mississippi's first post-Reconstruction black congressman, Mike Espy, who in 1993 became U.S. secretary of agriculture. Born the year before *Brown v. Board of Education* and 11 years old when the Voting Rights Act was passed, Espy was able to build on the sacrifices of those who came before and was elected in 1986 in the 2d Congressional District of Mississippi, a seat established in 1982 and then redrawn for 1984 to be a black-majority district. After the 1992 redistricting, it includes all of the not-precisely-defined Delta plus some heavily black areas just to the east, covering all of the Mississippi River almost from Memphis to south of Vicksburg, and sweeping east to include heavily black areas of Jackson and Hinds County. Espy, whose grandfather and father built a chain of funeral homes and were some of the biggest landowners in the state, was educated in northern schools, ran a smart campaign and won 50.1% in the first primary, luckily just avoiding a runoff, won 52% in the general and got a seat on the Agriculture Committee. He actively sought whites' votes, and got them, winning reelection with 65%, 84% and 76%, and he shrewdly endorsed Bill Clinton early in the 1992 cycle and campaigned actively and successfully for the Agriculture appointment.

Succeeding Espy, after a vivid contest, was a different kind of black politician, Bennie Thompson. Espy hails from Yazoo City, Thompson is from Bolton outside of Jackson; Espy quickly made his career on the national stage, Thompson served from 1980–93 on the Hinds County Board of Supervisors. More importantly, Espy actively sought whites' votes, while Thompson appeared clearly interested only in blacks. This proved to be enough, though barely. In the March 1993 all-party first primary, Thompson had 28% of the votes to 20% for Henry Espy, the Agriculture Secretary's older brother and mayor of Clarksdale in the northern Delta. The frontrunner with 34% was Republican Hayes Dent, an aide to Governor Kirk Fordice, just 31 years old and running a feisty campaign seeking black as well as white votes. Late reports of Dent's arrest in a drunken scuffle when he was 22 did not seem to have much effect: voting was mostly along racial lines in the April 1993 runoff, with Thompson prevailing 55%–45%. Most of Thompson's margin came in Jackson and Hinds County, where district lines were drawn to maximize the black percentage; elsewhere Thompson led only 51%–49%. In the House, he serves on the Agriculture and Merchant Marines Committees. It is not clear whether he will have a serious challenge in the primary or general in 1994.

The People: Pop. 1990: 514,469; 55% rural; 13% age 65+; 36% White; 63% Black. Voting age pop.: 345,151; 58% Black. Households: 47% married couple families; 23% married couple fams. w. children; 33% college educ.; median household income: $15,530; per capita income: $7,771; median gross rent: $267; median house value: $39,700.

1992 Presidential Vote			1988 Presidential Vote		
Clinton (D)	105,185	(58%)	Dukakis (D)	101,337	(55%)
Bush (R)	66,905	(37%)	Bush (R)	81,598	(45%)
Perot (I)	9,879	(5%)			

Rep. Bennie G. Thompson (D)

Elected Apr., 1993; b. Jan. 28, 1948, Bolton; home, Bolton; Tougaloo Col., B.A. 1968, Jackson St. U., M.S. 1972; Methodist; married (London).

Career: Bolton Bd. of Aldermen, 1969–73; Bolton Mayor, 1973–79; Hinds Cnty. Supervisor, 1980–93.

Offices: 1408 LHOB 20515, 202-225-5876. Also 137 Madison St., Bolton 39041, 601-859-5555.

Committees: *Agriculture* (26th of 28 D). *Merchant Marine and Fisheries* (26th of 29 D): Environment and Natural Resources; Merchant Marine .

Group Ratings and 102d Congress Votes: Newly Elected

Key Votes of the 103d Congress

1. Family Leave	*	2. Deficit Reduction	FOR	3. Stimulus Plan	*

Election Results

1993 runoff	Bennie G. Thompson (D)	72,561	(55%)	($498,397)
	Hayes Dent (R).......................	58,995	(45%)	($465,485)
1993 special	Hayes Dent (R).......................	34,766	(34%)	
	Bennie G. Thompson (D)	29,041	(29%)	
	Henry Espy (D).......................	20,800	(20%)	
	Unita Blackwell (D)	7,412	(7%)	
	David M. Halbrook (D)	6,027	(6%)	
	Three Others.........................	4,015	(4%)	
1992 general	Mike Espy (D)	133,361	(76%)	($270,710)
	Dorothy (Dot) Benford (R)............	41,248	(24%)	
1990 general	Mike Espy (D)	59,393	(84%)	($365,825)
	Dorothy (Dot) Benford (R)............	11,224	(16%)	

THIRD DISTRICT

Mississippi, old and new: the old Mississippi is the Neshoba County fair, held every August since 1892 in the town of Philadelphia. This is traditionally the place where Mississippi politicians announce their candidacies, with the crowds watching their performance to take measure. It is a mostly white crowd (though Philadelphia is the center of Mississippi's Choctaw Indians). When Ronald Reagan came here in 1980 and Michael Dukakis in 1988, neither mentioned what Philadelphia and Neshoba County are best known for in history, nor is there any memorial except engraved stones at two black churches: it was here in the "Freedom Summer" of 1964 that three civil rights workers, two white and one black, were murdered for the crime of urging black American citizens to register and vote. The new Mississippi is some 80 miles away, in Rankin County just east of Jackson, where subdivisions and shopping centers are sprouting up on the irregular hills and flat lands which only a few years ago seemed well past the zone of urban expansion. This is Mississippi's major patch of metropolitan growth; the only others are DeSoto County outside Memphis, Tennessee, and the Gulf Coast beyond New Orleans.

All of Rankin County and the Madison County suburbs of Jackson and the town of Philadelphia are part of the 3d Congressional District of Mississippi, which stretches north to Starkville, home of Mississippi State University, and south to Laurel, an hour's drive from the Gulf Coast. In the middle is Meridian, a small city that may go down in history as the site of firings of White House Chiefs of Staff: on the last two presidential trips here, first President Nixon informed Bob Haldeman that he was out as Chief of Staff in April 1973 and then in December 1991 John Sununu penned his letter of resignation to President Bush. The political tradition in all these parts is southern Democratic; the political leanings of most of it, especially Rankin County, these days is Republican: Mississippi, old and new.

A living part of the conservative Democratic heritage is 3d District Congressman Sonny Montgomery, first elected in 1966, a gallant and charming storyteller, a veteran of Army service in World War II who concentrates heavily on veterans' and military issues. Montgomery believes strongly in an assertive foreign policy, the all-volunteer military, a large reserve military force and generous veterans' benefits. From his different committee perches, he has made these policies work far better than many thought possible. Chairman of the Veterans' Affairs Committee since 1981, he sponsored the major veterans' legislation of the 1980s, the Montgomery G.I. education bill, passed in 1985 with improvements in 1988, allowing servicemen to put aside $100 a month of their first 12 months pay and receive $300 a month in education aid for 36 months after leaving the service. As intended, this helped military recruitment in addition to providing thousands of servicemen and women with a chance to improve their education, skills and earnings. The first effect was seen plainly in the high quality and performance of military personnel in the Gulf war—a vast improvement from the military of a dozen years before. The second effect, of encouraging young veterans to upgrade their skills, is not as obvious; but if it is even partly as successful as the G.I. Bill of Rights after World War II, it will have vastly improved the American work force in the 2000s and 2010s.

Montgomery can no longer, however, be an old-style autocratic chairman. After years of controversy, he had to accede to some level of compensation for Vietnam veterans exposed to Agent Orange pesticide, even though scientific studies on its ill effects were inconclusive. He was pleased to see the Veterans' Administration raised to Cabinet status in 1988. He passed a package of benefits for Gulf war veterans, extended G.I. bill education benefits, broadened eligibility for VA home loans, expanded service to homeless veterans and improved healthcare programs for women veterans. Veterans' hospitals, poorly equipped and under-used, remain a troubling topic: Montgomery proposed to open them to either veterans' dependents or retired Defense Department employees. On Armed Services, Montgomery has concentrated on strengthening the Reserves and National Guard. In the Vietnam era, the Reserves got much of their power from members of Congress in their ranks, and were never called up for service in the war; military leaders believed they were not anywhere near ready to serve. Not so today: Montgomery was determined that the U.S. have a truly ready reserve, and has made sure that units have necessary training and resources. He urged they be called for service in the Gulf, and they were; he worked hard to make sure they would not lose or be penalized in their jobs, and that their families would not lose medical insurance and other benefits. There are a couple of ironies here: this generally economically conservative Democrat has jurisdiction over the nation's major example of socialized medicine, the VA hospitals; and this representative from a district where history is stained with the murder of civil rights workers has played a major role in creating the most racially integrated institution in American society, the military.

Montgomery's voting record overall is very conservative: he voted against Clinton's stimulus package in March 1993, and he seldom helps the Democratic leadership even on procedural issues. As a result, he has not tried for the Armed Services chairmanship, even though he had more seniority than Les Aspin, who became chairman in 1985, or Ronald Dellums, who succeeded Aspin in 1993. And he nearly lost the Veterans chair after the 1992 election: Lane Evans, who had clashed with him on Agent Orange and other issues, let it be known he was interested in the chair and Montgomery was reelected by the Democratic Caucus by only 127–123. Montgomery has made no secret of his rapport with Republican presidents from Richard Nixon to George Bush, and there has been talk over the years of his switching parties, but he never has. Back home, he is reelected easily by the old and the new Mississippi; his 81% in 1992 was his lowest general election percentage since 1968. If he should retire, this seat could easily go Republican.

The People: Pop. 1990: 515,225; 61% rural; 12% age 65+; 67% White; 31% Black; 1% Amer. Indian. Voting age pop.: 370,288; 28% Black. Households: 57% married couple families; 28% married couple fams. w. children; 39% college educ.; median household income: $21,625; per capita income: $10,303; median gross rent: $324; median house value: $46,800.

1992 Presidential Vote			1988 Presidential Vote		
Bush (R)	116,973	(58%)	Bush (R)	122,510	(67%)
Clinton (D)	67,411	(34%)	Dukakis (D)	60,939	(33%)
Perot (I)	16,049	(8%)			

Rep. G. V. (Sonny) Montgomery (D)

Elected 1966; b. Aug. 5, 1920, Meridian; home, Meridian; MS St. U., B.S. 1943; Episcopalian; single.

Career: Army, 1943–46 (WWII), 1951–52, Army Natl. Guard, 1946–50, 1953–81; Owner, Montgomery Insurance Agency; MS Senate, 1956–66.

Offices: 2184 RHOB 20515, 202-225-5031. Also Fed. Bldg., Meridian 39301, 601-693-6681; 110-D Airport Rd., Pearl 39208, 601-932-2410; and Golden Triangle Airport, Columbus 39701, 601-327-2766.

Committees: *Armed Services* (2d of 34 D): Military Forces and Personnel; Military Installations and Facilities. *Veterans' Affairs* (Chmn. of 21 D): Education, Training and Employment (Chmn.).

Group Ratings

	ADA	ACLU	COPE	CDF	CFA	LCV	ACU	NTLC	NSI	COC	CEI
1992	30	9	25	30	40	6	64	55	100	88	41
1991	5	—	17	30	50	23	70	—	—	90	36

National Journal Ratings

	1991 LIB — 1991 CONS		1992 LIB — 1992 CONS	
Economic	31%	— 68%	40%	— 60%
Social	0%	— 84%	31%	— 68%
Foreign	36%	— 62%	30%	— 64%

Key Votes of the 102d Congress

1. Ban Striker Replace	AGN	5. Handgun Wait/7-Day AGN	9. Use Force in Gulf FOR
2. $ for Homeownership	AGN	6. Overseas Mil. Abortion AGN	10. US Mil. Abroad $ Cut AGN
3. Tax Rich/Cut Mid Cls. AGN		7. Obscn. Art NEA $ Ban FOR	11. Limit SDI Funds AGN
4. FY93/$15B Def. Cut AGN		8. Death Pen. from Jury FOR	12. Cuba Trade Embargo FOR

Key Votes of the 103d Congress

1. Family Leave   AGN   2. Deficit Reduction   FOR   3. Stimulus Plan   AGN

Election Results

1992 general	G. V. (Sonny) Montgomery (D) 162,864	(81%)	($174,165)
	Michael E. Williams (R) 37,710	(19%)	
1992 primary	G. V. (Sonny) Montgomery (D), unopposed		
1990 general	G. V. (Sonny) Montgomery (D), unopposed		($71,181)

FOURTH DISTRICT

Jackson, not much more than a mid-sized county seat a generation ago, is now clearly the metropolis of Mississippi, the pivot point between the Delta and the hills, the rivers flowing sluggishly to New Orleans and the Gulf of Mexico and the highways running north to Memphis and Chicago. Like Mississippi overall, Jackson is racially divided, with a black, not-so-affluent south side and a white affluent north side; in its new subdivisions of pleasant, large colonial houses under huge, overhanging trees, you can get a sense of what growth has meant to Jackson—especially when you consider that at least some of the people in these neighborhoods came from humble rural Mississippi beginnings. This newer Mississippi contrasts with Natchez, where the finest collection of antebellum mansions sit on the bluffs overlooking the Mississippi River. Natchez had white millionaires and half the state's free blacks before the Civil War and was content enough to oppose secession, and was spared major damage in the war because it was of no military importance. Both Jackson and Natchez went through an ugly decade during the civil rights revolution, when Mississippi blacks were murdered for registering to vote or for seeking a higher-paying job; today, the cities are more open, with more social contact between the races than in most northern metropolitan areas, but still yearning for the economic growth and high-skill jobs that seem to have come so naturally to Atlanta, Chicago and Los Angeles, but have so far been scarce in Mississippi.

The 4th Congressional District includes most of Jackson (excluding some black portions, which are in the black-majority 2d) and all of Natchez, it extends east to Laurel and south to the Louisiana line. This is an area that has trended Republican in national and state elections, as newly affluent white Mississippians vote for a party they associate with economic growth and assertive foreign policy, while blacks remain pretty solidly Democratic. But in local contests, Democrats still win many races, even in Jackson, for reasons apparent from 4th District Congressman Mike Parker.

Parker is from Brookhaven, where he owned a funeral home, a business that often provides a base for a political career (Mike Espy, 2d District Congressman until he was appointed Agriculture Secretary, is from a funeral home family too) since everyone in town goes through your doors sooner or later. Parker entered the wide open race here when incumbent Wayne Dowdy ran for the Senate in 1988; Parker ran second in the Democratic primary with 19% and then more than doubling his votes and winning the runoff 61%–39%. Republican nominee Tom Collins, a Jackson-based Vietnam POW, accused Parker of being a Dukakis Democrat; Parker replied in injured tones that he was not endorsing Dukakis and added a criticism of Dukakis' mandatory health insurance proposal in the bargain. Parker mellifluously and in an expensive ad campaign presented himself as backer of family values and believer in things American. The *Jackson Clarion-Ledger* found both candidates so vapid it refused to endorse either one. Parker led smartly for an overall win of 55%–44%—yet another seriously contested election in which the Democrat vastly outspent the Republican. He was reelected with 67% in 1992—this time, with the endorsement of the *Clarion-Ledger*.

Parker has one of the most conservative voting records among House Democrats, often more so than Sonny Montgomery. He says his focus has been "on economic development efforts within my district along with an unequalled devotion to constituent casework rather than legislative initiatives." He says he wants deficit reduction and a balanced budget amendment, plus full funding of the big 1991 transportation bill—priorities that are in tension if not contradiction with each other. But this formula so far has served him well electorally.

The People: Pop. 1990: 513,715; 47% rural; 13% age 65+; 59% White; 41% Black. Voting age pop.: 367,750; 36% Black. Households: 54% married couple families; 26% married couple fams. w. children; 42% college educ.; median household income: $20,234; per capita income: $10,411; median gross rent: $344; median house value: $47,500.

1992 Presidential Vote

Bush (R) 102,666 (50%)
Clinton (D) 84,089 (41%)
Perot (I).................... 16,758   (8%)

1988 Presidential Vote

Bush (R) 124,343 (61%)
Dukakis (D)................ 79,404 (39%)

Rep. Mike Parker (D)

Elected 1988; b. Oct. 31, 1949, Laurel; home, Brookhaven; William Carey Col., B.A. 1970; Presbyterian; married (Rosemary).

Career: Small business owner, 1971–88.

Offices: 1410 LHOB 20515, 202-225-5865. Also 245 E. Capitol, #222, Jackson 39201, 601-965-4085; 230 S. Whitworth St., Brookhaven 39601, 601-835-0707; 521 Main St., Natchez 39120, 601-446-7250; Chancery Ct. Annex, Columbia 39429, 601-731-1622; 728½ Sawmill Rd., Laurel 39440, 601-425-4999; and 150 W. Court Ave., Mendenhall 39114, 601-847-0873.

Committees: *Budget* (12th of 26 D). *Public Works and Transportation* (15th of 39 D): Aviation; Economic Development; Water Resources and Environment.

Group Ratings

	ADA	ACLU	COPE	CDF	CFA	LCV	ACU	NTLC	NSI	COC	CEI
1992	30	17	25	40	33	13	68	60	100	88	45
1991	20	—	33	30	50	23	75	—	—	80	47

National Journal Ratings

	1991 LIB — 1991 CONS		1992 LIB — 1992 CONS	
Economic	34%	— 65%	41%	— 59%
Social	0%	— 84%	16%	— 82%
Foreign	45%	— 55%	30%	— 64%

Key Votes of the 102d Congress

1. Ban Striker Replace	FOR	5. Handgun Wait/7-Day	AGN	9. Use Force in Gulf	FOR
2. $ for Homeownership	AGN	6. Overseas Mil. Abortion	AGN	10. US Mil. Abroad $ Cut	AGN
3. Tax Rich/Cut Mid Cls.	AGN	7. Obscn. Art NEA $ Ban	FOR	11. Limit SDI Funds	AGN
4. FY93/$15B Def. Cut	FOR	8. Death Pen. from Jury	FOR	12. Cuba Trade Embargo	FOR

Key Votes of the 103d Congress

1. Family Leave	AGN	2. Deficit Reduction	AGN	3. Stimulus Plan	AGN

Election Results

1992 general	Mike Parker (D)	130,927	(67%)	($156,969)
	Jack L. McMillan (R)	43,705	(23%)	
	Liz Gilchrist (I)	10,523	(5%)	
	James H. Meredith (I)	9,389	(5%)	
1992 primary	Mike Parker (D), unopposed			
1990 general	Mike Parker (D)	57,137	(81%)	($479,951)
	Jerry (Rev) Parks (R)	13,754	(19%)	

FIFTH DISTRICT

The strand where Mississippi faces the Gulf of Mexico has gone through several transformations. French explorers here founded Biloxi in 1699, before New Orleans or St. Louis, and made it the capital of an empire extending to Yellowstone Park. It was on this strand 150 years later that Jefferson Davis built his "Beauvoir," a raised cottage house with sweeping front stairs, set on a broad lawn and shaded by ancient live oaks. In later decades, rich people from New Orleans came to this Gulf coast in summer to get away from yellow fever and to rest on their Victorian verandas; six American presidents have vacationed here. More recently, almost 150 years after Davis, the Gulf Coast has been booming economically more than any other part of Mississippi. Biloxi and Gulfport, recovered from hurricanes, attract not only vacationers and retirees, but young families and enterprising small businessmen. Pascagoula, once a small town, is now home of the giant Litton Shipyard, whose gray hangar-like buildings and skeletons of ships under construction loom over the flat landscape. Shopping centers and subdivisions are spreading back from the strand into the once lightly-inhabited piney woods.

This is the heart of the 5th Congressional District of Mississippi, some 60% of whose people live on the Gulf Coast. The rest live inland, in farm counties or around the growing medium-sized city of Hattiesburg. This was mostly scrub land, not much good for plantations, and thus has never had many black residents: this southern part of the state is the whitest part of Mississippi. With its low black percentage and mostly booming economy, the 5th District has become prime Republican territory. It went Republican twice against fellow southerner Jimmy Carter, and in 1972 it gave Richard Nixon his highest percentage in any of the 435 congressional districts, a whopping 87%. It was represented for 16 years in the House by Trent Lott, who rose to become Republican whip before he was elected to the Senate in 1988. Since 1989, for the first time since 1972, it is represented by a Democrat, Gene Taylor.

Taylor is a case in point of how the Democrats continue to control the Congress. He was a sales representative for a container company who served on the Bay St. Louis Council for two years and was elected to the state Senate at age 30, in 1983. He ran for Congress in 1988, beating Attorney General Mike Moore in the primary, but losing respectably to Republican Larkin Smith 55%–45%. Then Smith died in an August 1989 plane crash and Trent Lott brushed aside Smith's widow and backed his own longtime aide Tom Anderson, even though Anderson had spent little time in Mississippi and proved to be an arrogant and abrasive candidate. Taylor, in contrast, has some of Lott's qualities, a barely reined-in aggressiveness combined with a down-home manner, and he won resoundingly 65%–35%.

In the House, Taylor has had a mixed record; he is a strong believer in an aggressive trade policy, urging retaliation against unfair trade practices, and more conservative on cultural (e.g., antiabortion) issues. He startled many when he voted against the Gulf war resolution in January 1991, and four Republicans vied for the right to run against him in 1992. But Taylor keeps bucking the Democratic leadership on many if not most votes and plugging away at other issues. He was one of two House Democrats in March 1993 (Ralph Hall of Texas was the other) to vote against all three votes critical to the passage of Clinton's economic package. He wants to eliminate gambling restrictions on U.S.-flag ships "to put Americans in the maritime industry back to work," and he wants to require all NOAA vessels to be built and repaired in U.S. shipyards. He earmarked $70 million for a large helicopter carrier to be built at the Litton Shipyard and was pleased when Litton got a $571 million contract to build two Arleigh Burke class Aegis destroyers by 1997. The 1992 Republican nominee, after a primary and runoff, was retired Air Force General Paul Harvey, and he did cut into Taylor's support. But not nearly enough: Taylor carried every county and won 63%–35%. He seems likely to continue in the House for some time.

The People: Pop. 1990: 514,611; 35% rural; 11% age 65+; 78% White; 20% Black; 1% Asian; 1% Hispanic origin. Voting age pop.: 368,680; 18% Black; 1% Hispanic origin. Households: 59% married couple families; 29% married couple fams. w. children; 41% college educ.; median household income: $21,702; per capita income: $10,116; median gross rent: $329; median house value: $49,200.

1992 Presidential Vote

Bush (R)	99,997	(54%)
Clinton (D)	58,808	(32%)
Perot (I)	24,956	(14%)

1988 Presidential Vote

Bush (R)	121,371	(70%)
Dukakis (D)	51,074	(30%)

Rep. Gene Taylor (D)

Elected Oct., 1989; b. Sep. 17, 1953, New Orleans, LA; home, Bay St. Louis; Tulane U., B.A. 1974; Catholic; married (Margaret).

Career: Coast Guard Reserves, 1971–84; Sales rep., Stone Container Corp., 1977–89; Bay St. Louis City Cncl., 1981–83; MS Senate, 1983–89.

Offices: 215 CHOB 20515, 202-225-5772. Also 2424 14th St., Gulfport 39501, 601-864-7670; 701 Main St., Hattiesburg 39401, 601-582-3246; and 706 Watts Ave., Pascagoula 39567, 601-762-1770.

Committees: *Armed Services* (19th of 34 D): Military Acquisition; Military Installations and Facilities. *Merchant Marine and Fisheries* (13th of 29 D): Coast Guard and Navigation; Fisheries Management; Merchant Marine.

Group Ratings

	ADA	ACLU	COPE	CDF	CFA	LCV	ACU	NTLC	NSI	COC	CEI
1992	30	17	50	20	47	31	76	75	70	50	47
1991	15	—	33	40	44	15	84	—	—	80	52

National Journal Ratings

	1991 LIB — 1991 CONS		1992 LIB — 1992 CONS	
Economic	31%	— 69%	41%	— 59%
Social	0%	— 84%	23%	— 77%
Foreign	48%	— 51%	30%	— 64%

Key Votes of the 102d Congress

1. Ban Striker Replace	AGN	5. Handgun Wait/7-Day	AGN	9. Use Force in Gulf	AGN
2. $ for Homeownership	FOR	6. Overseas Mil. Abortion	AGN	10. US Mil. Abroad $ Cut	AGN
3. Tax Rich/Cut Mid Cls.	AGN	7. Obscn. Art NEA $ Ban	FOR	11. Limit SDI Funds	AGN
4. FY93/$15B Def. Cut	AGN	8. Death Pen. from Jury	FOR	12. Cuba Trade Embargo	FOR

Key Votes of the 103d Congress

1. Family Leave	FOR	2. Deficit Reduction	AGN	3. Stimulus Plan	AGN

Election Results

1992 general	Gene Taylor (D)	120,766	(63%)	($340,311)
	Paul Harvey (R)	67,619	(35%)	($236,140)
1992 primary	Gene Taylor (D), unopposed			
1990 general	Gene Taylor (D)	89,926	(81%)	($322,048)
	Sheila Smith (R)	20,588	(19%)	($210,447)

MISSOURI

Missouri, at the center of America in so many ways, has strong claims to being the typical American state. It is the geographic center of the nation's population—the point has continued to move south and west, from Jefferson County just south of St. Louis in 1980 to central Washington County near the Mark Twain National Forest in 1990. Missouri is at once southern and northern, eastern and western. It is at the confluence of the continent's two greatest rivers, just beyond the boundary of the Louisiana Purchase, the starting point of the Santa Fe Trail, the Transcontinental Railroad and the Pony Express: in the mid-19th Century, it was the exciting frontier. Missouri's most important historical role was as a gateway to the West, an avenue for the great Yankee migrations west from Ohio, Indiana and Illinois and southerners' migration west from Kentucky (Missouri is where Daniel Boone finally stopped looking for elbow room). The northernmost slave state during the civil war, Missouri in the 1850s sent pro-slavery raiders over the border into the Kansas Territory to fight abolitionist settlers, and in the 1860s, it had its own civil war in the hilly counties along the Missouri River. During the 19th Century, Americans turned away from their oceans and headed inward to settle the great interior of the continent, and there was Missouri, at its heart, with farmland and mines, rivers and railroads, a major manufacturing state and in the days before tractors, and the nation's leading breeder and trader of mules.

At the turn of the 20th Century, Missouri was the fifth largest state. St. Louis was the fourth largest city, site of the 1904 World's Fair, and one of the few cities with two major league baseball teams; Missouri, after the 1900 Census, had 16 congressional districts. But as the 20th Century went on, Americans increasingly headed to the coasts, to the big cities of the East and to California, and eventually to Florida and Texas. Missouri has had below-average population growth since 1900, and today it is the 15th largest state, with just 9 congressional districts. This is not to say that Missouri has crumpled up and died. Some of its rural counties, especially in the north near Iowa, have never regained their 1900 populations, but its two big metropolitan areas have grown slowly, adding service and trade jobs to the big manufacturers like Anheuser-Busch beer, Monsanto chemicals, Ralston cereals, Chrysler automobiles and big defense contractors led by McDonnell Douglas.

Even as it has grown slowly, Missouri has moved politically very much in tandem with the rest of the country—not least in expressing anger at politics in 1992. It is one of our best bellwether states, having voted for every presidential winner but one (Eisenhower in 1956) in the 20th Century; from the 1960s to the 1980s it mirrored national trends by moving in its state and congressional politics from pretty solidly Democratic to pretty solidly Republican. In the 1990s, it moved sharply away from a Republican president and took a chance on congenial but little known Democrats in the White House and Governor's Mansion. Missouri also showed sudden new interest in politics. Turnout in presidential elections was stuck between 1.9 million and 2.1 million from 1952 to 1988; in 1992, it was up 14% to 2.4 million. Politicians were energized too: seven Democrats and five Republicans ran for governor, 14 Democrats and two Republicans ran for senator and, in the state's nine House districts, 40 Democrats and 28 Republicans ran for Congress—96 candidates for just 11 major offices. Missouri's ancient Civil War political divisions still hold in some rural areas: Little Dixie in the northeast, first settled by Virginians, is still Democratic; the Ozarks in the southwest, which was pro-Union, is Republican. Metro St. Louis, which had been trending Republican, moved sharply toward the Democrats, and the Kansas City area, always more volatile politically, cast 25% of its votes for Ross Perot and only 29% for George Bush (partly because most of its richest suburbs are across State Line Road in Kansas). Missouri remains culturally more conservative than the rest of the country, indicated

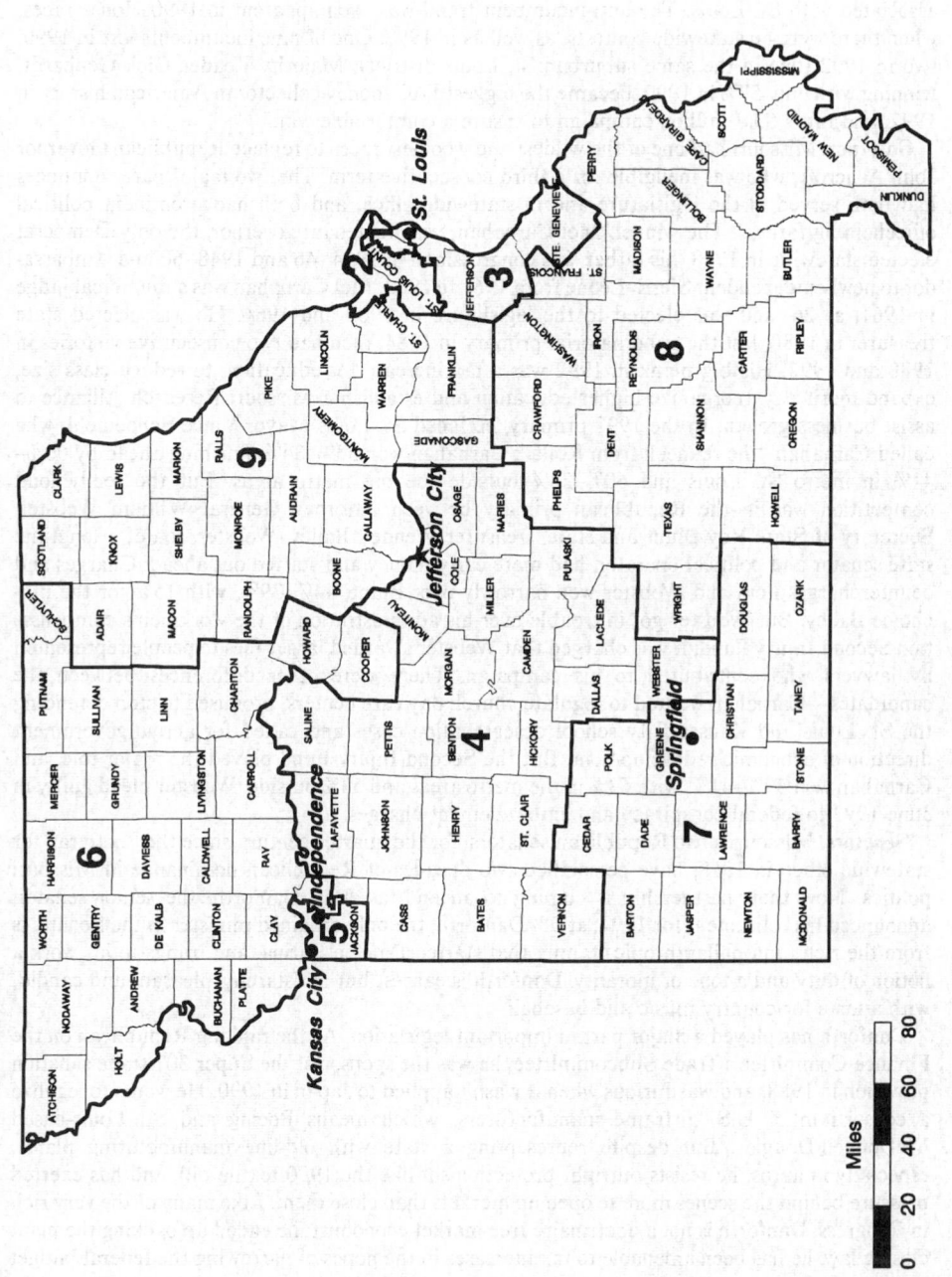

by its restrictions on abortion upheld in the 1989 *Webster* case; but it should be added that William Webster, the attorney general, was beaten soundly in his race for governor, though mostly for reasons other than the abortion issue. The revolution was greatest in this race: Republican Governor John Ashcroft won 64%–35% in 1988, while Democrat Mel Carnahan won 59%–41% in 1992. Meanwhile, Republican Senator Christopher Bond was elected with only 52% of the vote against a Democrat who had what is usually the disadvantage of being associated with St. Louis. The anti-incumbent trend was even apparent in 1990 House races, when there were no statewide contests, as well as in 1992. One of nine incumbents lost in 1990, two in 1992 (one in the same suburban St. Louis district); Majority Leader Dick Gephardt, winning with only 57% in 1990, became the biggest PAC money collector in American history in 1992, and ran a $3.3 million campaign to ensure a comfortable win.

Governor. Missouri had one of the wildest and woolliest races to replace Republican Governor John Ashcroft, who was ineligible for a third consecutive term. The two major party nominees had both served in the legislature and in statewide office, and both had prominent political officeholding fathers. The winner, Mel Carnahan, was lieutenant governor, the only Democrat elected statewide in 1988; his father was congressman in 1944–46 and 1948–60 and Ambassador to newly independent Sierra Leone from 1961 to 1963. Mel Carnahan was a municipal judge in 1961, at 26, and was elected to the legislature in 1962 and 1964. He was elected state treasurer in 1980, lost the gubernatorial primary in 1984, then had two consecutive victories in 1988 and 1992. His big plank in 1992 was a tax increase for education, to reduce class size, expand merit pay, reorganize higher education and establish a Missouri Research Alliance to assist business growth. In the 1992 primary, he faced St. Louis Mayor Vince Schoemehl, who called Carnahan "the redneck from Rolla"; Carnahan won 55%–34%, finishing ahead by 50%–41% in metro St. Louis and 60%–28% outside the big metro areas. But the really loud competition was in the Republican primary between Attorney General William Webster, Secretary of State Roy Blunt and state Treasurer Wendell Bailey. Webster, son of a longtime state senator and political operator, had more early money and started out ahead. Charges and countercharges flew, and Webster won narrowly over Blunt, 44%–39%, with 15% for the pro-choice Bailey. But Webster got in trouble over his administration of the workmen's compensation Second Injury Fund; it was charged that Webster awarded larger fees to people represented by lawyers who contributed to his campaign. There were other differences between the candidates—Carnahan wanted to regulate church day care centers, promised to stop defending the St. Louis and Kansas City school desegregation cases and called for active government direction of economic redevelopment. But the Second Injury Fund played the major role, and Carnahan won 59%–41%, with 63% in the metro areas and 53% outside. Webster plead guilty in June 1993 to federal conspiracy and embezzlement charges.

Senators. Missouri's two Republican senators, for the quarter-century since they both ran for statewide office in 1968, have personified two decades of Republican dominance in Missouri politics. Now their partnership is coming to an end, as John Danforth, the senior senator, announced his retirement for 1994, at 58. Danforth, the only ordained minister in the Senate, is from the rich (and philanthropic) family that started Ralston Purina, and brings to his work a notion of duty and a tone of morality. Danforth is earnest but not starchy, pleasant and candid, with a taste for country music and baseball.

Danforth has played a major part in important legislation. As the ranking Republican on the Finance Committee's Trade Subcommittee, he was the sponsor of the Super 301 trade sanction provision in 1988, and was furious when it wasn't applied to Japan in 1990. He wants to legalize a consortium of U.S. airframe manufacturers, which means Boeing and St. Louis-based McDonnell-Douglas. But despite representing a state with old-line manufacturing plants, especially in autos, he resists outright protectionism like the 1990 textile bill, and has exerted pressure behind the scenes more to open up markets than close them. Like many of the very rich in Congress, Danforth is not a doctrinaire free market economist: he ended up backing the plant closing law, he has been amenable to tax increases in the hopes of narrowing the federal budget deficit; but he opposed the 1986 tax reform because he believed it excessively raised taxes on corporations. With David Boren, he has called for considering a consumption tax, but with other Senate Republicans in early 1993 seemed opposed to a net tax increase. As ranking member on the Commerce Committee, he was a leading backer of the 1992 Cable Reregulation Act, the only law passed over George Bush's veto in four years. He is against both abortion and capital punishment and is interested in legislation recognizing living wills. He visited Cambodia in the 1970s during its troubling period of genocide and moved to cut off military aid to forces including the Khmer Rouge.

Danforth's most wrenching moments in the Senate came in October 1991. He had hired Clarence Thomas in the Missouri attorney general's office, brought him to Washington, sponsored him for jobs in the Reagan and Bush Administrations and was his leading backer in his confirmation hearings for Supreme Court Justice. When Anita Hill's charges were leaked to the press and hearings reopened, Danforth backed Thomas totally, sitting by his side, bringing him over to his house, aggressively advancing his position at every stage. After Thomas was confirmed, Danforth turned around and negotiated with the civil rights lobby (whose opposition to Thomas he considered intellectually dishonest), and a wary Bush Administration, the terms of a compromise that became the Civil Rights Act of 1991. One senses that in both cases Danforth felt obliged to meet his responsibilities however wrenching and distasteful doing so must have been—and that his disgust with some of his colleagues and the political process may have contributed to his announcement in February 1993 that he was retiring.

No one doubts that Danforth could have been reelected easily. Just 32 when he won his first statewide race in 1968, he was elected to the Senate in 1976 by a solid margin, after the original Democratic nominee died in a plane crash; his only close race came in the recession year of 1982, from Democrat Harriett Woods, when Danforth won 51%–49%. In 1988, he won with 68%, carrying all 114 counties and losing only St. Louis City, which now casts only 6% of the state's votes (as compared to 22% half a century ago). Right after Danforth's announcement, Democratic Congressman Alan Wheat and Republican Bill Emerson said they were considering the race; so did Geri Rothman-Serot, who lost 52%–45% to Senator Christopher Bond. Other possible Democrats include Lieutenant Governor Roger Wilson, Attorney General Jay Nixon (Danforth's 1988 opponent) and St. Louis County Executive Buzz Westfall. In April 1993, former Governor John Ashcroft, having lost a race for Republican National Committee chairman, announced he was running. On the basis of past performance, he looks like the strongest candidate: an Assembly of God member and a graduate of Yale and the University of Chicago, an opponent of most taxes and of abortion, he can span divides in the Republican Party, and his 64% victory in 1988 shows he can appeal to the broad electorate. But Missouri has trended sharply Democratic in the 1990s, and no one can take this race for granted.

Senator Christopher Bond has spent most of his adult life in politics. He ran for Congress in 1968 and narrowly lost, was elected state auditor in 1970, was elected governor at 33 in 1972, then lost in an upset to Democrat Joseph Teasdale in 1976 and won a comeback victory against Teasdale in 1980. After two years out of office, he ran for the Senate in 1986 against Danforth's 1982 opponent, Harriett Woods. Woods ran a three-part ad showing a farmer breaking into tears as he and his wife told Woods about their foreclosure, and then named Bond as a board member of the insurance company that foreclosed; evidently this struck voters as either demagoguery or an invasion of privacy, and Woods dropped the ad as she fell in the polls, and Bond won 53%–47%.

Bond's record is mostly, but not entirely conservative. He says he wants to promote programs that involve families in children's lives, and was the chief Senate Republican backer of family and medical leave. He wants to encourage parent involvement in preschool education and pushed to require child safety seats in airplanes. He also draws on his experience as governor to work with local officials, some of whom, like Kansas City Mayor Emanuel Cleaver, appeared in his 1992 fundraising campaign videos. He has pushed for more highway money to Missouri and for banning interstate shipment of solid waste; he won new grants and a rental assistance program to replace long deteriorating St. Louis public housing units. He worked for the sale of F-15s to Saudi Arabia, which would help St. Louis's McDonnell Douglas, and in December 1992 he brokered an agreement between the pension guarantee corporation and TWA to help that St. Louis-hubbed airline out of bankruptcy.

In 1992, 14 Democrats lined up to run against Bond, none of them widely known. The primary winner, with 45% in the St. Louis area and 30% elsewhere, was Geri Rothman-Serot, whose 36% was way ahead of the second-place finisher's 11%. Rothman-Serot's former husband was once lieutenant governor and the 1984 Democratic candidate for governor; in 1990 Rothman-Serot used her own funds to get elected to the St. Louis County Council; she is a cancer survivor, and called for universal health insurance. Rothman-Serot attacked Bond as rich and heartless for his opposition to the Americans with Disabilities Act, the minimum wage increase and plant closing legislation. Bond portrayed himself as a friend of children and local officials, and attacked her for taking contributions from a landfill operator being sued by the state for serious environmental violations. Rothman-Serot made some progress in polls, but in a Democratic year Bond won 52%–45%, running about even in the big metro areas and ahead 56%–41% outside them.

Bond got a seat on Appropriations in 1991, but has failed twice to be elected Republican Conference secretary, losing 26–17 to Bob Kasten in December 1990 and 20–14 (with 5 for another candidate) to Trent Lott in December 1992: he is perceived as a bit moderate by many colleagues. In early 1993, he came out with his own list of spending cuts and supported a targeted investment tax credit, a capital gains tax cut, a permanent R&D credit and IRAs for first-time homebuyers: a solidly Republican platform. With Danforth's retirement Bond is likely to become more prominent in the years ahead.

Presidential politics. Missouri's peculiar balance of northern and southern, urban and rural, has helped to make it a presidential bellwether, and explains its one deviation in the 20th Century: it voted for Adlai Stevenson in 1956, who capitalized on farmer discontent and whose patent lukewarmness about civil rights helped him carry traditional southern Democrats. Discontent in farm counties was helping Democrats in 1988, when Michael Dukakis carried northwest Missouri and lost the state by only 52%–48%. In 1992, George Bush pulled out all the stops, trying to capitalize on outgoing Governor John Ashcroft's popularity, campaigning in the country music center of Branson right after the Houston convention and announcing a $5 billion sale of McDonnell-Douglas F-15s to Saudi Arabia. It was all to little avail. Bill Clinton was always far ahead in polls, and carried Missouri 44%–34%, with big margins in metro St. Louis and Kansas City and a 41%–38% edge in the rest of the state.

Missouri, which joined the Super Tuesday primary for 1988, went back to caucuses for 1992. Bill Clinton was the easy winner in the Democrats' contests, still held on Super Tuesday, with 45% to 39% uncommitted. George Bush, whose grandfather came from St. Louis and who has a brother and cousins living there now, won even more easily on the Republican side.

Congressional districting. Missouri did not lose any seats in the 1990 Census, but with continuing population loss in St. Louis and the northern rural counties (the state's best Democratic areas) the lines had to be redrawn. The incumbent who ended up being hurt was Joan Kelly Horn, a Democrat elected by a 54 vote margin in 1990, whose 2d District lost some heavily Democratic precincts to the majority-black 1st District and expanded farther out into the suburbs; she lost in 1992.

The People: Est. Pop. 1992: 5,193,000; Pop. 1990: 5,117,073, up 1.5% 1990–1992. 2.1% of U.S. total, 15th largest; 31% rural. Median age: 33.5 years. 14.0% 65 years and over. 87.7% White, 10.7% Black, 1.2% Hispanic origin. Households: 56.3% married couple families; 26% married couple fams. w. children; 41% college educ.; median household income: $26,362; per capita income: $12,989; 68.8% owner occupied housing; median house value: $59,800; median monthly rent: $282. 5.7% Unemployment. Voting age pop.: 3,802,247. Registered voters (1992): 3,067,955; no party registration.

Political Lineup: Governor, Mel Carnahan (D); Lt. Gov., Roger B. Wilson (D); Secy. of State, Judith K. Moriarty (D); Atty. Gen., Jay Nixon (D); Treasurer, Bob Holden (D); Auditor, Margaret Kelly (R). State Senate, 34 (19 D and 15 R); State House of Representatives, 163 (98 D, 62 R, and 3 vacancies). Senators, John C. Danforth (R) and Christopher S. (Kit) Bond (R). Representatives, 9 (6 D and 3 R).

1992 Presidential Vote

Clinton (D) 1,053,873 (44%)
Bush (R) 811,159 (34%)
Perot (I). 518,741 (22%)

1988 Presidential Vote

Bush (R) 1,084,953 (52%)
Dukakis (D). 1,001,619 (48%)

GOVERNOR

Gov. Mel Carnahan (D)

Elected 1992, term expires Jan. 1997; b. Feb. 11, 1934, Birchtree; home, Rolla; George Washington U., B.A. 1954, U. of MO, J.D. 1959; Baptist; married (Jean).

Career: Air Force, 1954–56; Practicing atty., 1959–61, 1962–80, 1984–88; Rolla Municipal Judge, 1961–62; MO House of Reps., 1962–66; MO Treasurer, 1980–84; MO Lt. Gov., 1988–92.

Office: State Capitol Bldg., Jefferson City 65101, 314-751-3222.

Election Results

1992 gen.	Mel Carnahan (D)	1,375,425	(59%)
	William B. Webster (R)	968,574	(41%)
1992 prim.	Mel Carnahan (D)	388,098	(55%)
	Vince Schoemehl (D).	235,652	(34%)
	Sharon Rogers (D)	35,104	(5%)
	Four Others	42,134	(4%)
1988 gen.	John Ashcroft (R)	1,339,531	(64%)
	Betty Hearnes (D)	724,919	(35%)

SENATORS

Sen. John C. Danforth (R)

Elected 1976, seat up 1994; b. Sept. 5, 1936, St. Louis; home, Newburg; Princeton, A.B. 1958, Yale, B.D., LL.B. 1963; Episcopalian; married (Sally).

Career: Practicing atty., 1963–68; Ordained clergyman; MO Atty. Gen., 1969–76.

Offices: 249 RSOB 20510, 202-224-6154. Also Fed. Bldg., Cape Giradeau 63701, 314-334-7044; 1735 E. Sunshine, #705, Springfield 65806, 417-881-7068; 8000 Maryland Ave., #440, St. Louis 63105, 314-725-4484; 1233 Jefferson St., Jefferson City 65109, 314-635-7292; and 811 Grand Ave., U.S. Crthse., Kansas City 64106, 816-426-6101.

Committees: *Commerce, Science and Transportation* (RMM of 9 R). *Finance* (4th of 9 R): Health for Families and the Uninsured; International Trade (RMM); Taxation. *Intelligence (Select)* (3d of 8 R).

Group Ratings

	ADA	ACLU	CDF	COPE	CFA	LCV	ACU	NTLC	NSI	COC	CEI
1992	25	27	40	25	58	8	74	67	80	90	64
1991	20	—	55	25	33	27	60	—	—	70	45

National Journal Ratings

	1991 LIB — 1991 CONS	1992 LIB — 1992 CONS
Economic	36% — 62%	33% — 65%
Social	42% — 56%	33% — 66%
Foreign	25% — 74%	29% — 68%

Key Votes of the 102d Senate

1. $ for Homeownership	AGN	5. Clarence Thomas Nom. FOR	9. Use Force in Gulf	FOR
2. Have Cap Gains Debate FOR	6. Lmt Death Row Appeal FOR	10. Keep Salvador Aid	FOR
3. Remove Budget Walls	AGN	7. Handgun Wait/5-Day	AGN	11. Cut $1B from SDI	AGN
4. Ban Striker Replace	AGN	8. Abortion Gag Rule	FOR	12. Override China MFN AGN

Key Votes of the 103d Senate

1. Family Leave	FOR	2. HIV Immigrants	AGN	3. Clinton Budget	AGN

Election Results

1988 general	John C. Danforth (R)	1,407,416	(68%)	($4,060,441)
	Jeremiah W. Nixon (D)	660,045	(32%)	($880,160)
1988 primary	John C. Danforth (R), unopposed			
1982 general	John C. Danforth (R)	784,876	(51%)	($1,849,025)
	Harriett Woods (D)	758,629	(49%)	($1,193,966)

Sen. Christopher S. (Kit) Bond (R)

Elected 1986, seat up 1998; b. Mar. 6, 1939, St. Louis; home, Mexico; Princeton, B.A. 1960, U. of VA, LL.B. 1963; Presbyterian; married (Carolyn).

Career: Practicing atty., 1964–69, 1977–80; MO Asst. Atty. Gen., 1969–70; MO Auditor, 1970–72; MO Gov., 1972–76, 1980–84.

Offices: 293 RSOB 20510, 202-224-5721. Also 1736 Sunshine, #705, Springfield 65804, 417-881-7068; 339 Broadway, #214, Cape Girardeau 63701, 314-334-7044; 600 Broadway, #420, Kansas City 64105, 816-471-7141; 312 Monroe St., Jefferson City 65101, 314-634-2488; and 8000 Maryland Ave., #1050, St. Louis 63105, 314-727-7773.

Committees: *Appropriations* (9th of 13 R): Agriculture, Rural Development and Related Agencies; Defense; Labor, Health and Human Services, Education; Treasury, Postal Service and General Government (RMM); VA, HUD and Independent Agencies. *Banking, Housing and Urban Affairs* (3d of 8 R): Housing and Urban Affairs (RMM); International Finance and Monetary Policy; Securities. *Budget* (5th of 9 R). *Small Business* (3d of 9 R): Competitiveness, Capital Formation and Economic Opportunity; Government Contracting and Paperwork Reduction (RMM).

Group Ratings

	ADA	ACLU	CDF	COPE	CFA	LCV	ACU	NTLC	NSI	COC	CEI
1992	25	25	50	33	50	8	76	76	100	100	69
1991	20	—	64	27	33	13	81	—	—	70	55

National Journal Ratings

	1991 LIB — 1991 CONS	1992 LIB — 1992 CONS
Economic	31% — 68%	27% — 71%
Social	14% — 77%	29% — 70%
Foreign	13% — 77%	32% — 67%

Key Votes of the 102d Senate

1. $ for Homeownership AGN
2. Have Cap Gains Debate FOR
3. Remove Budget Walls AGN
4. Ban Striker Replace AGN
5. Clarence Thomas Nom. FOR
6. Lmt Death Row Appeal FOR
7. Handgun Wait/5-Day AGN
8. Abortion Gag Rule AGN
9. Use Force in Gulf FOR
10. Keep Salvador Aid FOR
11. Cut $1B from SDI AGN
12. Override China MFN AGN

Key Votes of the 103d Senate

1. Family Leave FOR
2. HIV Immigrants AGN
3. Clinton Budget AGN

Election Results

1992 general	Christopher S. (Kit) Bond (R)	1,221,901	(52%)	($5,048,333)
	Geri Rothman-Serot (D)	1,057,967	(45%)	($1,112,187)
	Other	75,048	(3%)	
1992 primary	Christopher S. (Kit) Bond (R)	337,795	(83%)	
	Wes Hummel (R)	70,626	(17%)	
1986 general	Christopher S. (Kit) Bond (R)	777,612	(53%)	($5,376,255)
	Harriet Woods (D)	699,624	(47%)	($4,397,780)

FIRST DISTRICT

St. Louis for years seemed to be the center of America: the starting point for the Lewis and Clark expedition in 1804; the locus half a century later of the Dred Scott case, which produced a Supreme Court case that helped split the nation; the site of the 1904 World's Fair that introduced the hot dog, the ice cream cone and eventually got 19 million people to "Meet Me in St. Louis." Its 630-foot-high Gateway Arch is just below the point where the waters of the Missouri plunge into the Mississippi, about halfway between New Orleans and Lake Superior, the Atlantic and the Pacific. This first major American city west of the Mississippi River was the final resting place of Daniel Boone, and was Chicago's rival as the transportation hub of America. In 1904, St. Louis already had the Wainwright Building, one of Louis Sullivan's first skyscrapers, and Union Station, the world's largest train station when it opened in 1894; some 600,000 people lived in densely-packed brick houses on old street grids radiating outward from downtown. This was a heavily German city, with a teutonic solidity and orderliness which distinguished it from the surrounding southern-accented rural terrain; and from Mitteleuropa came the founders of St. Louis's great businesses—the Anheuser-Busch brewery, May Company department stores, Joseph Pulitzer's *St. Louis Post-Dispatch*—and its first great politician, Senator and Interior Secretary Carl Schurz. And there is almost a European aura to Forest Park, the site of the Fair, and the dozen mansion-lined private streets nearby, like Portland Place.

St. Louis is still one of the 20 largest metro areas in the U.S., but today does not occupy as central a place in the national consciousness, and the central city itself has largely emptied out. The German order that made so many people comfortable in such close quarters and commuting by streetcar seem to have yielded to an American desire for Daniel Boone's wide open (suburban) spaces and the less restrictive automobile. St. Louis's population peaked at 856,000 in 1950; in 1990, it was 396,000, dwarfed by the one million in suburban St. Louis County. Downtown St. Louis has been spruced up admirably: the Gateway Arch was finished in 1965, Union Station has been redeveloped, Laclede's Landing is stocked with shops. But most of St. Louis's old factories have closed and its once tight neighborhoods have emptied out.

Missouri's congressional districts have followed the people out of St. Louis. The 1st District, historically based on the north side of the city, now has more than two-thirds of its votes cast in suburban St. Louis County. It includes most of central and north St. Louis, the affluent and racially integrated suburbs of University City and Clayton just west of Forest Park, and the mostly black and mixed-race suburbs from the city limits north to Bellefontaine Neighbors, Florissant and the airport. In 1990, this district was 52% black, a figure expected to increase over the decade. This is Missouri's most Democratic district, and it has been represented since 1968 by Bill Clay, a union staffer and something of a firebrand civil rights activist in his earlier days (he served 105 days in jail in 1963 for participating in a civil rights demonstration). Now he is one of the leaders of Congress, chairman of the Post Office and Civil Service Committee, second ranking member of Education and Labor, one of the most faithful supporters of organized labor and public employee unions. In the Reagan and Bush years, Clay was able to pass only small items on his agenda: banning U.S. airlines from hiring foreigners as strikebreakers, overturning a Supreme Court decision that allowed age discrimination in employee benefits; he also worked on plant closing and trade adjustment assistance laws. Now the Clinton presidency gives him the opportunity to achieve two major causes, revising the 1938 Hatch Act prohibition on political activity by federal employees and amending the 1935 Wagner Act to prohibit the hiring of permanent replacements for strikers. But neither Hatch Act revisions nor striker replacement is particularly popular with the general public, nor is their purpose of strengthening unions' leverage against employers. Clay failed to get the two-thirds necessary to pass Hatch repeal without amendments in February 1993; in March, however, it passed 333–86. He was also a backer of the family and medical leave bill that passed both houses and became law in February 1993.

Clay has had some serious ethical charges raised against him over the years. In the 1970s, he billed the government for numerous auto trips home though he was apparently traveling on cheaper airline tickets; a year later, he was investigated for tax fraud, and an administrative assistant was sent to jail for falsification of payroll records; in 1992, it was revealed that Clay had 328 overdrafts on the House bank. Such charges along with his liberal record have produced opposition mainly in the suburbs. In 1992, he won 68% in both the primary and general, around 60% in the suburbs but over 80% in the city.

The People: Pop. 1990: 568,472; 1% rural; 14% age 65+; 46% White; 52% Black; 1% Asian; 1% Hispanic origin. Voting age pop.: 418,960; 48% Black; 1% Hispanic origin. Households: 40% married couple families; 17% married couple fams. w. children; 44% college educ.; median household income: $24,963; per capita income: $12,632; median gross rent: $391; median house value: $55,200.

1992 Presidential Vote			1988 Presidential Vote		
Clinton (D)	161,447	(68%)	Dukakis (D)	162,714	(70%)
Bush (R)	45,231	(19%)	Bush (R)	69,059	(30%)
Perot (I)	29,682	(13%)			

Rep. William (Bill) Clay (D)

Elected 1968; b. Apr. 30, 1931, St. Louis; home, St. Louis; St. Louis U., B.S. 1953; Catholic; married (Carol).

Career: Real estate broker; Life insurance business, 1959–61; St. Louis City Alderman, 1959–64.

Offices: 2306 RHOB 20515, 202-225-2406. Also 6197 Delmar Blvd., St. Louis 63112, 314-725-5770; and 49 Central City Shopping Ctr. N., St. Louis 63136, 314-388-0321.

Committees: *Education and Labor* (2d of 28 D): Labor-Management Relations; Labor Standards, Occupational Health and Safety. *House Administration* (3d of 12 D): Administrative Oversight; Libraries and Memorials (Chmn.); Personnel and Police. *Post Office and Civil Service* (Chmn. of 15 D): Oversight and Investigations (Chmn.).

Group Ratings

	ADA	ACLU	COPE	CDF	CFA	LCV	ACU	NTLC	NSI	COC	CEI
1992	95	100	91	100	87	75	0	0	10	13	7
1991	90	—	100	100	94	85	0	—	—	20	6

National Journal Ratings

	1991 LIB — 1991 CONS		1992 LIB — 1992 CONS	
Economic	88%	0%	91%	0%
Social	88%	0%	92%	0%
Foreign	92%	0%	90%	0%

Key Votes of the 102d Congress

1. Ban Striker Replace	FOR	5. Handgun Wait/7-Day	FOR	9. Use Force in Gulf	AGN
2. $ for Homeownership	AGN	6. Overseas Mil. Abortion	FOR	10. US Mil. Abroad $ Cut	FOR
3. Tax Rich/Cut Mid Cls.	FOR	7. Obscn. Art NEA $ Ban	AGN	11. Limit SDI Funds	FOR
4. FY93/$15B Def. Cut	FOR	8. Death Pen. from Jury	AGN	12. Cuba Trade Embargo	AGN

Key Votes of the 103d Congress

1. Family Leave	FOR	2. Deficit Reduction	FOR	3. Stimulus Plan	FOR

Election Results

1992 general	William (Bill) Clay (D)	158,693	(68%)	($297,635)
	Arthur S. Montgomery (R)	74,482	(32%)	($21,862)
1992 primary	William (Bill) Clay (D)	57,242	(68%)	
	Donald (Don) Cross (D)	26,677	(32%)	
1990 general	William (Bill) Clay (D)	62,550	(61%)	($196,909)
	Wayne G. Piotrowski (R)	40,160	(39%)	($12,666)

SECOND DISTRICT

The center of greater St. Louis has been moving west of the Gateway Arch since its construction on the Mississippi River in 1965, out past Forest Park and into St. Louis County, established in 1876 when the city, tired of paying for dusty back roads, separated itself from the sticks; there were about 350,000 people in the city then and 31,000 in the county. In 1990, the city, once at 856,000, was back down to 396,000, while the county was near one million. By the 1960s, the center of office employment had moved from downtown across the county line to Clayton; now even many Clayton office buildings seem half-empty, and the focus is fast moving out the Daniel Boone Expressway (U.S. 40) to Chesterfield, west of the I-270 ring road. Urban problems have headed this way too: McDonnell Douglas's big plant outside the St. Louis airport has been hit hard by defense cutbacks and has laid off thousands, while a local suburban Chrysler assembly plant is joining the old north side Chevrolet plant in mothballs.

The 2d Congressional District of Missouri is made up of central and western St. Louis County, plus some St. Charles County suburbs northwest across the Missouri River. This is the Missouri district most changed by redistricting for 1992; in effect, it has followed its constituents farther out from the city. It covers a sociologically diverse terrain. In north St. Louis County, not far from McDonnell-Douglas and the airport, are blue-collar suburbs, full of white people who grew up on the north side of St. Louis. To the south are comfortable white-collar suburbs like Kirkwood, pleasant but not rich places filled mostly with older whites. In the center of the county, along the Daniel Boone Expressway, are the old high-income suburbs of Ladue, still home to most of St. Louis's elite, and Creve Coeur, and the newer Town and Country, Manchester and Chesterfield.

Politically, the 2d is a mixed bag and an odd duck: one of the few districts that has thrown out three incumbents in the last four elections. The first was Bob Young, a Democrat and former pipefitter and union backer from working-class St. Ann, who lost to Republican Jack Buechner in 1986. Then in 1990, Buechner overconfidently voted for the congressional pay raise and the Bush budget summit package, and was criticized for those votes and a taxpayer-paid trip to Paris while the House was in session. He lost by 54 votes to political consultant Joan Kelly Horn, who ran an ad showing Buechner making statements about how bad it was that people lived off the public trough, then mentioned his travel and honoraria, and ended with a shot of pigs slathering in mud. Horn compiled a generally liberal record and worked the district hard, but fared poorly in redistricting: Bill Clay and Dick Gephardt of the St. Louis-based 1st and 3d Districts insisted on gobbling up many of her most Democratic precincts, while she was given much of Republican-leaning St. Charles County. But Horn fought back doughtily, while the Republicans had their own competitive primary. George Herbert Walker, a cousin of George Bush who had never before run for office, raised more money and got more publicity; but 35-year-old state House Minority Leader Jim Talent put together a countywide organization of "potato salad" volunteers and beat Walker 58%–32%.

Talent grew up in Des Peres and lives in Chesterfield; he was a law clerk to Judge Richard Posner, one of the great free market legal minds, and was a management lawyer in St. Louis; in 1984, at 28, he was elected to the state legislature, where he opposed taxes (even Republican Governor John Ashcroft's road tax) and backed reform of House rules. In the general, Horn attacked Talent as antiabortion; Talent attacked Horn for abandoning the balanced budget amendment at the behest of House Democratic leaders. Horn actually carried St. Charles, but Talent's volunteers helped him exceed Bush's weak showing and win 50%–48%. Talent serves on the Armed Services Committee and is likely to strongly oppose deep defense cuts and tax increases.

The People: Pop. 1990: 568,449; 3% rural; 10% age 65+; 94% White; 4% Black; 2% Asian; 1% Hispanic origin. Voting age pop.: 421,265; 3% Black; 1% Hispanic origin. Households: 65% married couple families; 31% married couple fams. w. children; 61% college educ.; median household income: $43,957; per capita income: $20,654; median gross rent: $519; median house value: $94,900.

1992 Presidential Vote			1988 Presidential Vote		
Bush (R)	126,621	(40%)	Bush (R)	167,072	(63%)
Clinton (D)	114,612	(36%)	Dukakis (D)	99,268	(37%)
Perot (I)	72,885	(23%)			

Rep. Jim Talent (R)

Elected 1992; b. Oct. 18, 1956, Des Peres; home, Chesterfield; Washington U., B.S. 1978, U. of Chicago Law Schl., J.D. 1981; Presbyterian; married (Brenda).

Career: Practicing atty., 1981–92; Law Clerk, 7th Circuit Court of Appeals Judge Richard Posner, 1982–83; MO House of Reps., 1984–92, Minority Ldr., 1989–92.

Offices: 1022 LHOB 20515, 202-225-2561. Also 555 N. New Balas, #315, St. Louis 63141, 314-872-9561; and 820 S. Main St., #206, St. Charles 63301, 314-949-6826.

Committees: *Armed Services* (20th of 22 R): Military Forces and Personnel; Research and Technology. *Small Business* (12th of 18 R): Minority Enterprise, Finance and Urban Development; SBA Legislation and the General Economy.

Group Ratings and 102d Congress Votes: Newly Elected

Key Votes of the 103d Congress

1. Family Leave	AGN	2. Deficit Reduction	AGN	3. Stimulus Plan	AGN

Election Results

1992 general	Jim Talent (R).....................	157,594	(50%)	($910,893)
	Joan Kelly Horn (D).................	148,729	(48%)	($832,813)
	Other..............................	6,119	(2%)	
1992 primary	Jim Talent (R)......................	35,791	(58%)	
	George Herbert (Bert) Walker (R).......	19,555	(32%)	
	Tom McCoy (R)......................	4,322	(7%)	
	Other..............................	1,915	(3%)	
1990 general	Joan Kelly Horn (D).................	94,378	(50%)	($340,390)
	Jack Buechner (R)	94,224	(50%)	($670,758)

THIRD DISTRICT

Middle America, in several senses of the word, lies in the 3d Congressional District of Missouri. The geographical center of the country's population was here in 1980, just south of St. Louis in once rural and now half-suburban Jefferson County; and while that point has moved a few miles southwest, St. Louis is still the metro area nearest the midpoint of a country most of whose people live in million-plus metro areas. Geographically, this is a node where some of the nation's main arteries come together. The Missouri River flows into the Mississippi a few miles north of St. Louis's Gateway Arch, the northern boundary of the 3d; the National Road and its successors, U.S. 40 and Interstate 70, cross the Mississippi just below the Arch. And the great tides of southerners migrating west up the Mississippi and Germans migrating overland met here to create one of the nation's largest and most bustling cities out of a town originally founded by the French in the years after the Civil War. The south side of St. Louis is famous for its tight-knit, neat neighborhoods and pleasant parks; its most famous symbol is the Anheuser-Busch brewery just south of downtown and Grant's Farm, where Ulysses S. Grant lived in the 1850s and where Anheuser-Busch now keeps the Budweiser Clydesdales.

The 3d Congressional District was centered on the south side of St. Louis when its congressman, Dick Gephardt, was growing up there 40 years ago. Now St. Louis City casts only 27% of its votes, and it stretches far south, through modest neighborhoods in the St. Louis County suburbs near the Mississippi River. Here lies the solid middle class of St. Louis, people who keep its offices humming, its stores and warehouses bustling, its schoolchildren instructed and disciplined. In Jefferson County, old towns sitting near the banks of the fast-flowing Mississippi are now receiving an infusion of shopping centers, new subdivisions and apartment complexes. For 1992, the 3d also includes lightly populated Ste. Genevieve County, whose name bespeaks its French origins; it is the site of Missouri's oldest permanent settlement, founded near a salt mine in 1730.

The 3d District is represented in the House by one of America's national political leaders, majority leader and onetime presidential candidate and more recently presidential counselor, Richard Gephardt. Gephardt comes from the south side of St. Louis, from origins not quite so humble as he likes to suggest: his father was a milkman but also a real estate salesman, the family lived comfortably and both sons went to prestigious colleges. A bit too old to be part of the generation of Vietnam-era student rebels, Gephardt returned home from law school in 1965 to work in a large downtown law firm, but was clearly intent on a traditional political career; he moved to the south side and ran for alderman in 1971, and was one of a band of south side reformers on the council. He was thinking about running for mayor when, in 1976, 3d District Congresswoman Leonor Sullivan announced her retirement, and he jumped into the race as an anti-establishment candidate. He beat a labor union official in the 1976 primary and a former board of aldermen president in the general, outspending and outcampaigning both of them.

Gephardt started off in the House as one of the newer breed of Democrats who did not automatically favor big government and higher taxes. With the help of Missouri's Richard Bolling, he got a seat on the Ways and Means Committee, where he was open to arguments for lower tax rates. He voted for the 1981 Reagan tax cut and was the House co-sponsor of Bill Bradley's bill that was the basis of the 1986 tax reform. Gephardt was one of the founders of the moderate Democratic Leadership Council and opposed many popular Democratic causes such as abortion, busing and raising the minimum wage.

Yet around the mid-1980s he began to shift, perhaps after being elected Democratic Caucus chairman in 1984 with an easy victory over the more liberal David Obey; as the 1980s went on the balance of opinion in the Democratic Caucus remained liberal, and Gephardt has always been a superb caucus politician. His ability to work with small universes—caucuses—of colleagues and constituents today is second not even to Bill Clinton's politics. Gephardt is a good listener, ready to sit with colleagues for hours and to digest what they say, to learn not just how to mollify their concerns but to understand what lies beneath them. He is a hard-working detail man, eager to absorb information and willing to spend the time needed to transform agreement in principle into agreement on paper. He has a gift for molding compromises, for coming up with positions and programs that are politically attractive and hold together his caucus while dividing others. So when Gephardt started running for president in 1986, he had the enthusiastic, not just the perfunctory, support of dozens of House colleagues. He started traveling to Iowa to run in the precinct caucuses there, spending 144 days in the state between 1986 and the February 1988 caucuses. Iowa was the biggest population-losing state in the 1980s, bitterly anti-Reagan, and its Democratic activists were unanimously dovish on foreign policy, predominantly liberal on cultural issues like abortion and contemptuous of free market economics. To them, and to many House Democrats in Washington—Gephardt's two arenas at the time—there was a sense the Reagan era was over.

Gephardt adjusted to these new caucuses. He played little role on tax reform in 1985–86 (neither his Iowa schedule nor Dan Rostenkowski would allow it). In 1986, after listening to feminist groups, he dropped his longtime opposition to abortion. In Iowa, he supported mandatory agricultural production controls, a wackily impractical program that would have raised food prices to consumers in order to protect landowners' million-dollar equity. Even more prominently, he went on the offensive on the trade issue. The United Auto Workers are a major factor in Iowa caucuses, and Gephardt, who had opposed the UAW's domestic content bill, came up with his amendment requiring retaliation against countries running large trade surpluses with the United States (read: Japan). It passed the House in late 1987 by a 218–214 margin—a gift to Gephardt's presidential campaign, for the bill clearly was going nowhere in the Senate. Affected by Iowa's woes and Iowa Democrats' articulate bewailing of them, Gephardt proclaimed, "I see a nation beginning to be in a state of decline," a view he has stuck to ever since. "It's your fight too!" voiced his campaign of his trade retaliation, and he won the Iowa caucuses with 31% of the vote, to 27% for Paul Simon and 22% for Michael Dukakis. But he failed to gain momentum in 1988's cluttered media environment, and in New Hampshire found himself under attack for switching positions in a prosperous state that hates taxes and government regulation; he finished second with 20% to Dukakis's 36%. Gephardt won the tiny South Dakota primary February 23 with 44% but the well-financed Dukakis ran a devastating flip-flop ad against him. On Super Tuesday, Gephardt won only Missouri and was effectively out of the race.

Back in the House, Gephardt rebounded from his loss, and in 1989 another House leadership position came his way. With the resignations of Speaker Jim Wright and Majority Whip Tony Coelho, and the succession of Tom Foley to the Speaker's chair, Gephardt ran for majority leader, and in June 1989 beat Georgia's Ed Jenkins 181–76. There he went to work creating a sense of camaraderie in a dispirited Caucus. He attacked the Bush Administration for favoring the rich in seeking to cut capital gains taxes; he criticized Bush for "lack of leadership" on foreign policy and called for major aid to Mikhail Gorbachev's Soviet Union. In the caucus-like setting of the 1990 budget summit talks, Gephardt used OMB Director Richard Darman's desire for agreement to frame the issue as a choice between the Democrats' plan to tax the rich more and Bush's refusal to do so—a contrast that at least momentarily hurt Republican candidates in October 1990 and prevented them from making gains in the November elections. In September 1990, Gephardt supported Bush's dispatch of troops to the Persian Gulf, but in December and into 1991, he led the opposition to the Gulf war resolution and uncharacteristically stumbled by threatening to cut off funds for American troops there: "If Bush decides to use force on his own, Congress has to reach for the only tool left to it, which is to cut off funding for the war." Many thought Gephardt was running for president again. But he decided that it would be impossible to be majority leader and run a long campaign; he did, however, seem ready to run in February 1992 if Bill Clinton had been eliminated in New Hampshire after the Gennifer Flowers incident.

But Clinton remained in the race, Gephardt supported him handsomely and seems happy in his role as a national leader on any number of issues. On trade, his refusal to come out against a North American Free Trade Agreement in spring 1992 helped make NAFTA possible; he was one of the forces urging Clinton to seek new environmental and economic protections in 1992 and 1993; in early 1993, his support seemed essential to getting a treaty through Congress. He continually hits Japan for running a trade surplus with the United States and calls for restrictions on Japanese imports. In early 1993, he was drafting a comprehensive trade package, including an extension of Super 301. In 1992, he maneuvered successfully to avoid passage of a balanced budget amendment, offering his own alternative and then helping to switch votes away at the last minute; he can be expected to oppose it as shrewdly in the future. He also fended off the line-item veto in 1992 and helped reach the enhanced rescission compromise with Bill Clinton that pretty well defanged the proposal. He presented his own healthcare cost containment proposal in 1992 and will likely be key on Clinton's in 1993. Indeed, he has emerged as a close adviser and confidant to Clinton, whose senior advisor, George Stephanopoulos, is only one alumnus of the Gephardt staff in the 1993 White House. Interestingly, Gephardt advanced a proposal for Oxford-style debating in the House.

Gephardt will play a key role also on campaign finance legislation; he is an expert on the subject as the number one PAC fundraiser in both the 1990 and 1992 cycles—$1,241,000 in 1992; his total campaign spending was $1,455,000 in 1990 and $3.3 million in 1992, the second highest in the country after self-financing freshman California Republican Michael Huffington. Gephardt is aware of the demand for congressional reform, yet he is even more acutely aware of the tremendous advantages held by Democratic incumbents under the current scheme. Indeed, in Gephardt's case the money may have been more helpful than one might think necessary: in the anti-incumbent mood of 1990, his percentage was reduced to 57%, dangerously low; the money helped him raise his numbers to 64% in the 1992 general (interestingly, he did best, with 71%, in his new county of Ste. Genevieve). Gephardt can presumably count on reelection, and would certainly be the Democrats' choice for speaker should Foley retire. But Gephardt seems to work well in tandem with Foley now, strengthening rather than undermining him when there was discontent about the House bank and other issues in early 1992, and he already has, because of his talents and drive, a position of vast influence and responsibility.

The People: Pop. 1990: 568,105; 16% rural; 15% age 65+; 96% White; 2% Black; 1% Asian; 1% Hispanic origin. Voting age pop.: 428,707; 2% Black; 1% Hispanic origin. Households: 56% married couple families; 26% married couple fams. w. children; 41% college educ.; median household income: $30,863; per capita income: $14,272; median gross rent: $390; median house value: $71,500.

1992 Presidential Vote			1988 Presidential Vote		
Clinton (D)	121,213	(44%)	Bush (R)	128,331	(53%)
Bush (R)	87,155	(32%)	Dukakis (D)	113,349	(47%)
Perot (I)	64,415	(24%)			

Rep. Richard A. Gephardt (D)

Elected 1976; b. Jan. 31, 1941, St. Louis; home, St. Louis; Northwestern U., B.S. 1962, U. of MI, J.D. 1965; Baptist; married (Jane).

Career: Air Natl. Guard, 1965–71; Practicing atty., 1965–71; St. Louis City Alderman, 1971–76. Dem. Candidate for Pres., 1988.

Offices: 1432 LHOB 20515, 202-225-2671. Also 9959 Gravois, St. Louis 63123, 314-631-9959.

Committees: *Majority Leader. Budget* (2d of 26 D).

Group Ratings

	ADA	ACLU	COPE	CDF	CFA	LCV	ACU	NTLC	NSI	COC	CEI
1992	85	91	78	90	87	44	0	0	40	25	3
1991	75	—	92	100	78	54	0	—	—	30	8

National Journal Ratings

	1991 LIB — 1991 CONS		1992 LIB — 1992 CONS	
Economic	79% —	18%	89% —	9%
Social	74% —	23%	81% —	17%
Foreign	85% —	14%	68% —	32%

Key Votes of the 102d Congress

1. Ban Striker Replace	FOR	5. Handgun Wait/7-Day	FOR	9. Use Force in Gulf	AGN
2. $ for Homeownership	AGN	6. Overseas Mil. Abortion	FOR	10. US Mil. Abroad $ Cut	FOR
3. Tax Rich/Cut Mid Cls.	FOR	7. Obscn. Art NEA $ Ban	FOR	11. Limit SDI Funds	FOR
4. FY93/$15B Def. Cut	FOR	8. Death Pen. from Jury	AGN	12. Cuba Trade Embargo	FOR

Key Votes of the 103d Congress

1. Family Leave   FOR   2. Deficit Reduction   FOR   3. Stimulus Plan   FOR

Election Results

1992 general	Richard A. Gephardt (D)	174,000	(64%)	($3,316,784)
	Mack Holekamp (R)	90,006	(33%)	($425,966)
	Other	7,828	(3%)	
1992 primary	Richard A. Gephardt (D)	71,773	(76%)	
	Leif Johnson (D)	13,433	(14%)	
	Ned L. Abernathy (D)	8,957	(10%)	
1990 general	Richard A. Gephardt (D)	88,950	(57%)	($1,455,794)
	Mack Holekamp (R)	67,659	(43%)	($82,077)

FOURTH DISTRICT

Missouri was the first state settled west of the Mississippi. Pioneers came west on the Missouri River, founding little towns on the bluffs and starting farms on the rolling lands, like those seen in the paintings of Thomas Hart Benton, great-grandnephew of Missouri's first senator, who championed hard money and westward expansion for 30 years and was thrown out of the Senate for opposing the expansion of slavery. Missouri's pioneers were a diverse lot—Virginians and other southerners, making their way to counties north of the Missouri, Germans settling around the still small capital city of Jefferson City. The Capitol boasts a Benton mural, showing dance hall girls, black coal miners, a mother diapering an infant—a reminder that pioneer life was more diverse and certainly less prim than many of its celebrators would have one think.

The 4th Congressional District of Missouri occupies much of this early-settled part of central and western Missouri. It penetrates into Kansas City's Jackson County and its metro overflow in Cass County, but the overall atmosphere here is rural and small town. Political traditions date back to early settlement. The German area around Jefferson City was anti-slavery and remains among the most Republican parts of Missouri. The rural counties around Kansas City were full of pro-slavery-expansion Bushwhackers who rode across the Kansas line to thwart the Yankee Jayhawks, and these areas today vote Democratic. The new resort areas around Lake of the Ozarks tend also to be Republican. But this is Truman country: Harry Truman was born just south of the district and lived just northwest of it, spanning the gaps between country and city, South and North; Truman's mother could remember her house being attacked by Yankee soldiers, and she remained pro-Confederate even when her son was in the White House.

The congressman from the 4th District is Ike Skelton, a Truman Democrat in many ways, a prosecutor and state senator first elected to Congress in 1976. He looks—and votes—the part of an old-fashioned rural Missouri Democrat: his record on economics is in line with his party, but he is more tradition-minded on cultural issues; he supports the same expansive, assertive foreign and defense policies that the preponderance of Democrats supported in the days of Truman. In the Gulf war debate, Skelton was one of the few members to invoke Truman's foreign policy legacy. He serves on the Armed Services Committee and has made great contributions to policy there. In 1986, he was a strong proponent of reorganizing the Pentagon command structure and played a key role in passing the reorganization of the Joint Chiefs of Staff. Since 1987, Skelton has been calling for better strategic training in the services, particularly in the war colleges, and called for improving the higher-level educational programs in the four military branches; in 1993, he became chairman of the Personnel Subcommittee and seems to agree with Joint Chiefs Chairman Colin Powell that allowing open homosexuals to serve in the armed forces would infringe on military effectiveness. Skelton was one of several House members who had a son in the Persian Gulf forces. He is also one of a few whose work over the years has reformed and improved the American military and enabled it to perform so superlatively in the Gulf war.

Skelton also works on local issues, introducing a rural crime bill and blocking reductions in rural mail service, looking after Whiteman Air Force Base (the site for deployment of the B-2 bomber), and expanding the Truman National Historical Site. Skelton's performance at the polls has been impressive. Redistricted in with a Republican incumbent in 1982, Skelton won with 55%; in anti-incumbent 1992, he was reelected with 70%.

The People: Pop. 1990: 569,295; 61% rural; 15% age 65+; 95% White; 3% Black; 1% Amer. Indian; 1% Asian; 1% Hispanic origin. Voting age pop.: 420,487; 3% Black; 1% Hispanic origin. Households: 64% married couple families; 30% married couple fams. w. children; 34% college educ.; median household income: $23,064; per capita income: $10,984; median gross rent: $319; median house value: $49,400.

1992 Presidential Vote			1988 Presidential Vote		
Bush (R)	96,770	(38%)	Bush (R)	130,485	(59%)
Clinton (D)	94,948	(37%)	Dukakis (D)	88,890	(41%)
Perot (I)	65,233	(25%)			

Rep. Ike Skelton (D)

Elected 1976; b. Dec. 20, 1931, Lexington; home, Lexington; Wentworth Military Academy Jr. Col., 1949–51, U. of MO, A.B. 1953, LL.B. 1956; Disciples of Christ; married (Susan).

Career: Lafayette Cnty. Prosecuting atty., 1957–60; MO Special Asst. Atty. Gen., 1961–63; Practicing atty., 1957–76; MO Senate, 1971–76.

Offices: 2227 RHOB 20515, 202-225-2876. Also 1616 Industrial Dr., Jefferson City 65109, 314-635-3499; 514-B N. 7 Hwy., Blue Springs 64014, 816-228-4242; 319 S. Lamine, Sedalia 65301, 816-826-2675; and 219 N. Adams St., Lebanon 65536, 417-532-7964.

Committees: *Armed Services* (5th of 34 D): Military Forces and Personnel (Chmn.). *Small Business* (3d of 27 D): Regulation, Business Opportunities and Technology.

Group Ratings

	ADA	ACLU	COPE	CDF	CFA	LCV	ACU	NTLC	NSI	COC	CEI
1992	45	26	67	40	53	6	65	16	100	86	32
1991	30	—	67	60	50	23	47	—	—	60	34

National Journal Ratings

	1991 LIB —	1991 CONS	1992 LIB —	1992 CONS
Economic	42% —	58%	43% —	56%
Social	34% —	65%	16% —	82%
Foreign	43% —	55%	18% —	74%

Key Votes of the 102d Congress

1. Ban Striker Replace	FOR	5. Handgun Wait/7-Day	AGN	9. Use Force in Gulf	FOR
2. $ for Homeownership	AGN	6. Overseas Mil. Abortion	AGN	10. US Mil. Abroad $ Cut	AGN
3. Tax Rich/Cut Mid Cls.	AGN	7. Obscn. Art NEA $ Ban	FOR	11. Limit SDI Funds	AGN
4. FY93/$15B Def. Cut	AGN	8. Death Pen. from Jury	FOR	12. Cuba Trade Embargo	FOR

Key Votes of the 103d Congress

1. Family Leave	AGN	2. Deficit Reduction	AGN	3. Stimulus Plan	FOR

Election Results

1992 general	Ike Skelton (D)	176,977	(70%)	($426,867)
	John Carney (R)	74,475	(30%)	($4,628)
1992 primary	Ike Skelton (D)	60,347	(79%)	
	Ron Beller (D)	11,540	(15%)	
	Lewis E. Seay (D)	4,638	(6%)	
1990 general	Ike Skelton (D)	105,527	(62%)	($306,485)
	David Eyerly (R)	65,095	(38%)	($7,137)

FIFTH DISTRICT

Named after a state it isn't in and a river that doesn't touch it, Kansas City, Missouri, is the center of one of America's large metro areas, the biggest on the central Great Plains. The first pioneers here started little towns on the bluffs above the Missouri River—Independence, Kansas City, Westport—which coalesced a century later. Here the Santa Fe Trail set out to cross the Sand Hills of Kansas and reach Mexican territory; here Jayhawks and Bushwhackers set out to fight for control of Bleeding Kansas. It was a rail center and had one of the largest stockyards in the country, a major commercial center that built Art Deco skyscrapers and the Country Club Plaza, the first shopping center in America, in the 1920s. It is famous for Harry Truman, whose family lived on a farm now in the suburb of Grandview and who himself lived in Independence, the old county seat just to the east. It is famous also for its black community, and jazz musicians like Scott Joplin, Charlie Parker and Count Basie, and for its much-praised barbecue.

The 5th Congressional District of Missouri includes most of Kansas City in Jackson County, plus Grandview and most of Independence; most of the city's landmarks, including the Truman home, are here. It includes all of Kansas City's black neighborhoods, and is 24% black. Solidly but not overwhelmingly Democratic, for 34 years it was represented by Richard Bolling, one of the real scholars of the House and ultimately chairman of the Rules Committee. When he retired in 1982, he was succeeded by 31-year-old state Representative Alan Wheat. Not terribly remarkable, except that Wheat is black, and has made his political fortune in an overwhelmingly white district—a pattern most political observers would like to see more of in America.

It may help that Wheat grew up in the most integrated segment of American life, the military; his father was a civil engineer in the Air Force, and he lived all over the world. At Grinnell College in Iowa in the early 1970s he protested the Vietnam war, and moved to Kansas City when he was offered a job there by the U.S Department of Housing and Urban Development. After a stint driving a cab, he was an aide to the Jackson County Executive, then at age 25 was endorsed by Harold "Doc" Holliday, Jr., of Freedom, Inc., to succeed Holliday's father in the state House in 1976. When Bolling retired, Wheat decided to run if enough other candidates entered the Democratic primary to split the black vote; in a seven-candidate field, he won with 32%. In the general, he shrewdly made a nonracial appeal and with strong support from Bolling, won with 58%.

In the House, Wheat won Bolling's seat on the Rules Committee in his first term—an unusual achievement for a freshman—and has used it to pass measures like his Parents as Teachers program, based on a Missouri program which helps parents gain an early understanding of children's learning patterns. He is proud of having secured flood control projects for the Blue River and Brush Creek, and funds for the Bruce Watkins Memorial Drive and the Truman Home National Historic Site, the South Riverfront Expressway and a new federal courthouse. He got Congress to ban foreign maintenance of U.S. planes (there's a big TWA repair facility at the Kansas City airport). He worked to get funds for rebuilding historically black colleges and to get the Congressional Black Caucus to accept non-blacks as associate members. He is House sponsor of a constitutional amendment for elimination of the electoral college and direct election of the president.

Wheat has a solidly liberal voting record, which may be risky, including opposition to the Gulf war resolution and backing civil rights bills attacked as quota legislation. His percentage fell to 62% in 1990 and, after it was revealed he had 86 overdrafts on the House bank, he was challenged by county legislator and former football star Fred Arbanas in the primary, but won 58%–37%. Wheat won the 1992 general by a similar margin, 59%–37%. When Senator John Danforth announced he would not run again in 1994, Wheat immediately said he was considering the race, adding his assumption that if former Governor John Ashcroft were to run, it would mean having to beat a Republican who won statewide with 64%. It is said in Missouri, and may well be true, that Wheat's liberal voting record is more of a political problem than his race. Whatever happens in 1994, Wheat has proven that a black can represent a non-majority-black constituency to its satisfaction over a sustained period—a lesson that politicians and voters of all races should remember.

The People: Pop. 1990: 569,289; 1% rural; 14% age 65+; 72% White; 24% Black; 1% Amer. Indian; 1% Asian; 2% Other; 3% Hispanic origin. Voting age pop.: 428,620; 21% Black; 3% Hispanic origin. Households: 47% married couple families; 20% married couple fams. w. children; 46% college educ.; median household income: $26,968; per capita income: $13,650; median gross rent: $398; median house value: $56,300.

1992 Presidential Vote		
Clinton (D)	134,862	(52%)
Bush (R)	67,511	(26%)
Perot (I)	55,799	(22%)

1988 Presidential Vote		
Dukakis (D)	137,016	(60%)
Bush (R)	92,974	(40%)

Rep. Alan Wheat (D)

Elected 1982; b. Oct. 16, 1951, San Antonio, TX; home, Kansas City; Grinnell Col., B.A. 1972; Church of Christ; married (Yolanda).

Career: Economist, U.S. Dept. of HUD, Kansas City and Mid-Amer. Regional Cncl., 1973–74; Aide, Jackson Cnty. Legislature, 1974–75; MO House of Reps., 1977–82.

Offices: 2334 RHOB 20515, 202-225-4535. Also 811 Grand Ave., #935, Kansas City 64106, 816-842-4545; and 301 W. Lexington, #221, Independence 64050, 816-833-4545.

Committees: *District of Columbia* (3d of 8 D): Fiscal Affairs and Health; Government Operations and Metropolitan Affairs (Chmn.). *Rules* (7th of 9 D): The Legislative Process.

Group Ratings

	ADA	ACLU	COPE	CDF	CFA	LCV	ACU	NTLC	NSI	COC	CEI
1992	95	100	91	100	100	88	0	0	20	13	7
1991	100	—	100	100	89	85	0	—	—	10	2

National Journal Ratings

	1991 LIB — 1991 CONS			1992 LIB — 1992 CONS		
Economic	79%	—	18%	91%	—	0%
Social	84%	—	12%	87%	—	13%
Foreign	87%	—	8%	86%	—	10%

Key Votes of the 102d Congress

1. Ban Striker Replace	FOR	5. Handgun Wait/7-Day	FOR	9. Use Force in Gulf	AGN
2. $ for Homeownership	AGN	6. Overseas Mil. Abortion	FOR	10. US Mil. Abroad $ Cut	FOR
3. Tax Rich/Cut Mid Cls.	FOR	7. Obscn. Art NEA $ Ban	FOR	11. Limit SDI Funds	FOR
4. FY93/$15B Def. Cut	FOR	8. Death Pen. from Jury	AGN	12. Cuba Trade Embargo	AGN

Key Votes of the 103d Congress

1. Family Leave	FOR	2. Deficit Reduction	FOR	3. Stimulus Plan	FOR

Election Results

1992 general	Alan Wheat (D)	151,014	(59%)	($673,086)
	Edward (Gomer) Moody (R)	93,562	(37%)	($57,400)
	Two Others	10,736	(4%)	
1992 primary	Alan Wheat (D)	50,873	(58%)	
	Fred Arbanas (D)	32,773	(37%)	
	Three Others	3,890	(4%)	
1990 general	Alan Wheat (D)	71,890	(62%)	($245,132)
	Robert H. Gardner (R)	43,897	(38%)	

SIXTH DISTRICT

The inspiration for Thomas Hart Benton's rolling, surging Missouri fields can be found in the farmland along and behind the bluffs that line the Missouri River in the northwestern part of the state. This part of America was settled in a rush in the late 19th Century, and has been losing people ever since. Fewer hands are now needed on farms than half a century ago, far fewer than at the turn of the century; even the biggest town in northwest Missouri, St. Joseph, has lost people. In 1940, this area had the fifth largest meat-packing industry in the world, but the meat-packing business has generated no more new jobs than farming, and St. Joseph has no more people than it did 50 years ago and fewer than in 1900. The counties of northwest Missouri, aside from those in the Kansas City metro area, had 508,000 people in 1900, 452,000 in 1940 and under 300,000 in 1990.

All these counties, plus Clay and Platte Counties, which include the parts of Kansas City north of the Missouri River, make up Missouri's 6th Congressional District; the two metro counties have gained people almost precisely as the rural counties have declined. The Kansas City area has almost half the district's population, but newly developed, decentralized and without strong political organizations, it cast far less than half of its votes. The historic political tradition here is mostly Democratic, tempered by dislike for national Democrats' cultural liberalism, but strengthened by anger at what people regard as neglect of this salt-of-the-earth farming area—an attitude similar to that found across the border in left-leaning Iowa. Michael Dukakis carried the 6th District's rural counties and lost the Kansas City portions only barely.

The 6th District is represented by Pat Danner, a freshman who but for a few twists of fate might be entering her eighth term. She ran once before for the district, in 1976, and finished second in the primary, behind a man named Morgan Maxfield who, it was discovered during the campaign, had falsified his life story; Maxfield lost to 33-year-old Republican Tom Coleman. Despite some close races, Coleman became one of the senior members of the Agriculture and the Education and Labor Committees and held the district until 1992. In 1990, Coleman had won just 52% against a Democrat who spent only $22,000. Naturally there was a seriously contested Democratic primary in 1992.

In this Danner was clearly the frontrunner candidate. She had been a staffer for Congressman Jerry Litton, whose race for the Senate opened up the seat in 1976 (and ended tragically when he died in a plane crash primary night after winning the Democratic nomination); she was co-chair of the Ozark Regional Planning Commission during the Carter Administration; in 1982 she was elected to the state Senate. In 1990, her son Stephen was elected in an adjoining district, and they became the only mother-son team in a state Senate in America. In Jefferson City, Danner supported ratification of the Madison Amendment, pending since the 1790s, which prohibits Congress from changing its pay during a session; she also worked on day care and vocational-technical education bills. Danner won the eight-candidate Democratic primary with 52% of the vote, and tore into Coleman for voting for the congressional pay raise and for support of an economy in which children did not seem likely to do as well as their parents. Coleman retaliated by attacking Danner for accepting state Senate pay raises, voting her son a $27,000 pay raise when he became deputy lieutenant governor and voting against "buy American" legislation. Despite that, Danner won by a solid 55%–45% margin.

In some respects, Danner is a moderate: she does not favor nationalized health care; she is willing to back some components of the Freedom of Choice Act, but she voted for the Missouri abortion law upheld in the 1989 *Webster* case; she backs a trust fund for receipts from new taxes, so they will be used to cut the deficit; she is contributing her pay raise to 6th District scholarships. She failed to get the seat on Agriculture she wanted, and settled for Public Works instead.

The People: Pop. 1990: 568,823; 37% rural; 14% age 65+; 96% White; 2% Black; 1% Asian; 1% Other; 2% Hispanic origin. Voting age pop.: 420,360; 2% Black; 1% Hispanic origin. Households: 62% married couple families; 29% married couple fams. w. children; 40% college educ.; median household income: $27,165; per capita income: $12,641; median gross rent: $362; median house value: $54,900.

1992 Presidential Vote			1988 Presidential Vote		
Clinton (D)	110,137	(40%)	Bush (R)	119,494	(51%)
Bush (R)	88,980	(32%)	Dukakis (D)	116,582	(49%)
Perot (I)	75,150	(27%)			

Rep. Pat Danner (D)

Elected 1992; b. Jan. 13, 1934, Louisville, KY; home, Smithville; NE MO St. U., B.A. 1973; Catholic; married (Markt Meyer).

Career: Dist. Asst., U.S. Rep. Jerry Litton, 1973–76; Co-Chmn., Ozarks Regional Plng. Comm., 1977–81; MO Senate, 1982–92.

Offices: 1217 LHOB 20515, 202-225-7041. Also 5754 N. Broadway, Bldg. 3, Kansas City 64118, 816-455-2256; and 201 S. 8th St., #330, St. Joseph 64501, 816-233-9818.

Committees: *Public Works and Transportation* (28th of 39 D): Aviation; Economic Development; Surface Transportation. *Small Business* (15th of 27 D): Development of Rural Enterprises, Exports and the Environment.

Group Ratings and 102d Congress Votes: Newly Elected

Key Votes of the 103d Congress

1. Family Leave		FOR	2. Deficit Reduction		AGN	3. Stimulus Plan	FOR

Election Results

1992 general	Pat Danner (D)	148,887	(55%)	($482,984)
	Tom Coleman (R)	119,637	(45%)	($533,305)
1992 primary	Pat Danner (D)	43,821	(52%)	
	Sandra Lee Reeves (D)	20,842	(25%)	
	John J. Kauffman (D)	6,795	(8%)	
	John Gallagher (D)	4,671	(6%)	
	Jeff Bailey (D)	3,327	(4%)	
	Three Others	4,389	(5%)	
1990 general	Tom Coleman (R)	78,956	(52%)	($315,922)
	Bob McClure (D)	73,093	(48%)	($22,428)

SEVENTH DISTRICT

The fastest-growing region of Missouri in the 1980s was neither of its big metropolitan areas, but the Ozarks region around Springfield. Filled with green hills sometimes labelled mountains and dam-made lakes sporting boats of all kinds, with small towns and the small city of Springfield, home of the fast-growing Assemblies of God, the Ozarks region is the kind of place in which many Americans would like to live—and more do every day. New subdivisions pop up around Springfield, as do retirement developments and condominiums in the mountains to the south around the country music center of Branson, the fastest growing tourist spot in the U.S. and where George Bush made his first post-convention campaign stop. Incomes are below average, but so is the cost of living and the crime rate. The climate here is relatively temperate and the cultural tone distinctly traditional. Historically, southwestern Missouri is Republican—against secession in 1861 and, though Springfield changed hands several times during Missouri's Civil War, its sympathies stayed pro-Union. Its conservative response to the big-spending government of the 1960s and cultural liberalism of the 1970s reinforced its Republicanism, but in 1988 it became closely contested after a longtime Republican incumbent retired and as Farm Belt discontent and anti-incumbent fever swept most of Missouri.

The 7th Congressional District of Missouri covers most of the southwest corner of the state, centered on Springfield. It is a solidly Republican district and is held, sometimes less than solidly, by a very solid conservative, Mel Hancock. Hancock seems to care less about winning personally than about advancing his principles: he promoted a successful anti-tax referendum in 1980 but lost races for senator in 1982 and lieutenant governor in 1984. He won the seat in 1988, when incumbent Gene Taylor retired, by winning the primary by a 39%–36% margin, then beating a former Springfield judge 53%–46%. He has one of the most conservative voting records in the House, and abstains from introducing his own legislation; most bills introduced by junior members of the minority, he points out, go nowhere anyway. He favors term limits, opposes NAFTA and believes television corrupts moral values. In a district long hungry for public works, he makes a point of voting against pork barrel spending, but also works to fund local projects. In 1990, Hancock was surprised when Democratic Springfield lawyer Pat Deaton spent only $103,000 but won 48% of the vote against him. Deaton ran again in 1992, but this time had a divisive primary which he won by only 50%–38% and then lost the general 62%–38%. Even though Arkansas is next door, this is a district which George Bush carried 45%–36%.

The People: Pop. 1990: 568,017; 48% rural; 16% age 65+; 97% White; 1% Black; 1% Amer. Indian; 1% Hispanic origin. Voting age pop.: 428,507; 1% Black; 1% Hispanic origin. Households: 61% married couple families; 27% married couple fams. w. children; 38% college educ.; median household income: $21,712; per capita income: $11,029; median gross rent: $315; median house value: $48,200.

748   MISSOURI

1992 Presidential Vote			1988 Presidential Vote		
Bush (R)	118,817	(45%)	Bush (R)	139,627	(62%)
Clinton (D)	96,621	(36%)	Dukakis (D)	86,049	(38%)
Perot (I)	48,824	(18%)			

Rep. Mel Hancock (R)

Elected 1988; b. Sept. 19, 1929, Cape Fair; home, Springfield; SW MO St. Col., B.S. 1951; Church of Christ; married ("Sug").

Career: Air Force, 1951–53, Air Force Reserves, 1953–65; Intl. Harvester Co., 1947–51, 1953–59; Hardware Mutual Insurance, 1960–67; Owner & Pres., Federal Protection Inc., 1969–89.

Offices: 129 CHOB 20515, 202-225-6536. Also 2840 E. Chestnut Expwy., Springfield 65802, 417-862-4317; and 302 Fed. Bldg., Joplin 64801, 417-781-1041.

Committees: *Ways and Means* (12th of 14 R): Oversight; Select Revenue Measures (RMM).

Group Ratings

	ADA	ACLU	COPE	CDF	CFA	LCV	ACU	NTLC	NSI	COC	CEI
1992	10	0	25	0	7	0	96	100	100	75	93
1991	5	—	8	10	28	0	100	—	—	90	95

National Journal Ratings

	1991 LIB — 1991 CONS		1992 LIB — 1992 CONS	
Economic	12% —	86%	9% —	88%
Social	0% —	84%	0% —	85%
Foreign	0% —	88%	0% —	82%

Key Votes of the 102d Congress

1. Ban Striker Replace	AGN	5. Handgun Wait/7-Day	AGN	9. Use Force in Gulf	FOR
2. $ for Homeownership	FOR	6. Overseas Mil. Abortion	AGN	10. US Mil. Abroad $ Cut	AGN
3. Tax Rich/Cut Mid Cls.	AGN	7. Obscn. Art NEA $ Ban	FOR	11. Limit SDI Funds	AGN
4. FY93/$15B Def. Cut	AGN	8. Death Pen. from Jury	FOR	12. Cuba Trade Embargo	FOR

Key Votes of the 103d Congress

1. Family Leave	AGN	2. Deficit Reduction	AGN	3. Stimulus Plan	AGN

Election Results

1992 general	Mel Hancock (R)	160,303	(62%)	($426,525)
	Thomas Patrick (Pat) Deaton (D)	99,762	(38%)	($310,658)
1992 primary	Mel Hancock (R)	66,667	(77%)	
	Ron Houseman (R)	13,469	(16%)	
	Stephen Keith Pennington (R)	6,304	(7%)	
1990 general	Mel Hancock (R)	83,609	(52%)	($182,474)
	Thomas Patrick (Pat) Deaton (D)	76,725	(48%)	($103,265)

EIGHTH DISTRICT

Mark Twain might not recognize life on the Mississippi below St. Louis today, where the land flattens out and the river is hidden behind levees, screening small towns and river roads from the sight of rows of barges tethered together, full of coal or soybeans. The Mississippi today is an industrial waterway; but it was never really all that romantic, for Twain's steamboats, as he is at pains to point out, were dangerous, noisy contraptions, forever blowing up or getting embedded in roots and branches in the swirling river currents. This is one of the older-settled parts of the United States: French settlers founded Missouri towns like Cape Girardeau in the late 1700s. But the big influx started just a few years after the 1811 earthquake centered on New Madrid; the spongy Mississippi valley land is also seismically very active, and this was the site of one of the most devastating earthquakes in U.S. history. When an earthquake prognosticator predicted another big one here for December 3, 1990, townsfolk left, schools closed and tourists and media flocked in: "Visit New Madrid while it's still here," signs said. (It is.)

Outwardly, the southeast quadrant of Missouri—the river valley and the hills to the west, with coal and lead mines with their miles of tunnels, plus the Bootheel that hangs down in the far southeast—hasn't changed much in 50 years. The only big growth here in that time has been around Cape Girardeau and along the route of Interstate 44; there has been a big population outflow from the Bootheel, as machines replace low-wage farm workers, and from some mining communities, as ores give out or become uneconomical to extract. Politically, the heritage here is mostly Democratic, although with a strong southern accent. But Cape Girardeau is Republican and most counties have trended that way over time, reflected in presidential contests and in elections in the 8th Congressional District of Missouri, which covers most of the southeast quadrant of the state, and which since 1980 has elected Republican Bill Emerson.

Emerson has natural political instincts not often found in Republicans. He was a congressional page in 1954, on the floor of the House when it was fired upon by Puerto Rican terrorists; in the 1970s, he was a Washington lobbyist, who upon spotting the personal vulnerability of the Democratic incumbent back home in southeast Missouri, went back to the state to run, and won with 55%. Emerson got a seat on the Agriculture Committee (he's now on Public Works as well) enabling him to make a popular record in this agricultural district. Chubby, pleasant, Emerson is ready to vote for attractive economic programs, especially those purported to help farmers: higher soybean supports, and food stamp and other nutrition programs. Opposed to creating the Select Committee on Hunger in the early 1980s, he became its ranking Republican and fought to save it from abolition, unsuccessfully, in 1993. He spends much time on highway and water projects for the district; he pushed for funding for the Mississippi Delta commission and for the Ozarks National Scenic Riverways visitors' center. He is a co-sponsor of the "microenterprise" bill to help welfare recipients start small businesses. He was named to the Joint Committee on the Organization of Congress in 1992.

Emerson has generally won reelection by decisive but not huge margins; the 8th is Democratic enough to have voted for Bill Clinton in 1992. Emerson won with only 53% in 1986; in 1988 and 1990 he had 58% and 57%, the latter time against Governor Mel Carnahan's son; in 1992 he won with 63%. When Senator John Danforth announced his retirement in February 1993, Emerson immediately expressed interest in running for Senate; it remains to be seen whether he will challenge in the primary former Governor John Ashcroft, who has run very strong in rural Missouri.

The People: Pop. 1990: 568,385; 63% rural; 16% age 65+; 94% White; 4% Black; 1% Hispanic origin. Voting age pop.: 417,903; 4% Black. Households: 61% married couple families; 28% married couple fams. w. children; 25% college educ.; median household income: $18,207; per capita income: $9,300; median gross rent: $268; median house value: $37,500.

1992 Presidential Vote

Clinton (D) 109,858 (46%)
Bush (R) 89,238 (37%)
Perot (I) 41,558 (17%)

1988 Presidential Vote

Bush (R) 116,668 (56%)
Dukakis (D) 92,880 (44%)

Rep. Bill Emerson (R)

Elected 1980; b. Jan. 1, 1938, Hillsboro; home, Cape Girardeau; Westminster Col., B.A. 1959, U. of Baltimore, LL.B. 1964; Presbyterian; married (Jo Ann).

Career: Air Force Reserves, 1963–92; A.A., U.S. Rep. Bob Ellsworth, 1961–65; A.A., U.S. Sen. Charles Mathias, 1965–70; Govt. Affairs Dir., Fairchild Ind., 1970–73; Pub. Affairs Dir., Interstate Natural Gas Assn., 1974–75; Exec. Asst., FEC Chmn., 1975; Fed. Relations Dir., TRW Inc., 1975–79; Consultant, 1979–80.

Offices: 2454 RHOB, 202-225-4404. Also 339 Broadway, Cape Girardeau 63701, 314-335-0101; and 612 Pine, Rolla 65401, 314-364-2455.

Committees: *Agriculture* (2d of 19 R): Department Operations and Nutrition; General Farm Commodities (RMM); Specialty Crops and Natural Resources. *Public Works and Transportation* (6th of 24 R): Public Bldgs. and Grounds; Surface Transportation; Water Resources and Environment. *Joint Committee on the Organization of Congress* (10th of 12).

Group Ratings

	ADA	ACLU	COPE	CDF	CFA	LCV	ACU	NTLC	NSI	COC	CEI
1992	20	9	42	10	33	6	92	65	100	88	59
1991	15	—	25	50	39	0	85	—	—	90	47

National Journal Ratings

	1991 LIB — 1991 CONS	1992 LIB — 1992 CONS
Economic	32% — 67%	28% — 72%
Social	0% — 84%	0% — 85%
Foreign	17% — 78%	0% — 82%

Key Votes of the 102d Congress

1. Ban Striker Replace	AGN	5. Handgun Wait/7-Day	AGN	9. Use Force in Gulf	FOR
2. $ for Homeownership	FOR	6. Overseas Mil. Abortion	AGN	10. US Mil. Abroad $ Cut	AGN
3. Tax Rich/Cut Mid Cls.	AGN	7. Obscn. Art NEA $ Ban	FOR	11. Limit SDI Funds	AGN
4. FY93/$15B Def. Cut	AGN	8. Death Pen. from Jury	FOR	12. Cuba Trade Embargo	FOR

Key Votes of the 103d Congress

1. Family Leave   AGN   2. Deficit Reduction   AGN   3. Stimulus Plan   AGN

Election Results

1992 general	Bill Emerson (R) 147,398	(63%)	($488,949)
	Thad Bullock (D) 86,730	(37%)	($11,974)
1992 primary	Bill Emerson (R) 28,973	(69%)	
	E. Earl Durnell (R) 12,807	(31%)	
1990 general	Bill Emerson (R) 81,452	(57%)	($704,447)
	Russ Carnahan (D) 60,751	(43%)	($246,595)

NINTH DISTRICT

Hannibal, the little town perched above the Mississippi River in northern Missouri, is famed as the all-American home of Tom Sawyer and Huckleberry Finn, and of Mark Twain who created them. Actually, as those who read the books as adults know, Hannibal was not really typical and Twain's view of it was anything but sentimental. For Hannibal is smack in the middle of Little Dixie, the section of northeastern Missouri which was settled by southerners and was pro-slavery and Democratic, while Twain himself came to abhor slavery and became close friends with Union General and Republican President Ulysses S. Grant. Hannibal and Little Dixie remain fervently Democratic and culturally conservative. Over the years, Little Dixie has produced such notable Democratic politicians as Champ Clark, speaker of the House from 1911 to 1919 and presidential candidate in 1912, and Clarence Cannon, author of the definitive text on the House's parliamentary procedure and the curmudgeonly chairman of the House Appropriations Committee until his death in 1963.

The 9th Congressional District of Missouri includes Little Dixie and goes as far south as Franklin and outer St. Charles Counties in metro St. Louis. It has Columbia, home of the University of Missouri, and Fulton, home of Westminster College, where in 1946 Winston Churchill, accompanied by President Harry Truman, told the world that "from Stettin on the Baltic to Trieste on the Adriatic, an iron curtain has descended across the continent." It also includes the old German town of Hermann, laid out by members of the German settlement, Society of Philadelphia, who hoped to preserve the customs of their homeland in the isolation of the wilderness. Hermann and, to a lesser extent, the St. Louis exurbs tend to vote Republican, while the Democratic sentiments of Little Dixie are sometimes shaky.

The congressman from the 9th District is Harold Volkmer, a middle-of-the-road Democrat first elected in 1976, whose biggest achievement was passage in 1986 of the McClure-Volkmer amendments weakening federal gun control laws. Volkmer was a tireless proponent of this, getting the signatures of a majority of members to pry the measure out of the Judiciary Committee, pressing the issue when many others would rather leave it to campaign rhetoric. As chairman of the Agriculture Subcommittee on Forests, Family Farms and Energy, he worked on the tricky issue of whether forests should be cut or left standing to preserve arguably endangered species like the spotted owl. This is of great importance to members from Oregon and Washington, and much less to Volkmer, whose instinct over the years has been to oppose environmentalists; but in 1992 he pushed a bill setting aside some 6.8 million acres of old-growth forest, less than the nine million in the Natural Resources Committee's bill but enough to cost an estimated 22,000-plus jobs. Volkmer also sponsored a bill to protect the Pacific yew, whose bark contains a cancer-fighting chemical.

Volkmer, persistent and mettlesome, is not particularly popular in the House. In the 9th District, he has generally won by good margins, but has long had trouble in Columbia and surrounding Boone County: his style does not suit a college town. In 1992, he was opposed by Republican Rick Hardy, a political science professor at the University of Missouri who was active in party politics. Hardy waged a vigorous campaign and apparently caught Volkmer, perhaps distracted by all his forestry hearings, unaware. Hardy carried Boone County 55%–29% (there were Green and Independent candidates on the ballot), a stunning blow to the incumbent. Volkmer carried the rural counties in Little Dixie and elsewhere by only 51%–44%, unimpressive given Bill Clinton's lead over George Bush there; he was saved by his 56%–39% win in Franklin and St. Charles Counties. These results may prove to be a wakeup call for Volkmer, but they could also inspire a strong candidacy by Hardy or some other Republican here in 1994.

The People: Pop. 1990: 568,238; 51% rural; 13% age 65+; 95% White; 4% Black; 1% Asian; 1% Hispanic origin. Voting age pop.: 416,794; 3% Black; 1% Hispanic origin. Households: 62% married couple families; 30% married couple fams. w. children; 38% college educ.; median household income: $26,055; per capita income: $11,741; median gross rent: $338; median house value: $55,200.

1992 Presidential Vote

Clinton (D) 110,175 (41%)
Bush (R) 90,836 (34%)
Perot (I). 65,195 (24%)

1988 Presidential Vote

Bush (R) 121,243 (54%)
Dukakis (D). 104,871 (46%)

Rep. Harold L. Volkmer (D)

Elected 1976; b. Apr. 4, 1931, Jefferson City; home, Hannibal; Jefferson City Jr. Col., St. Louis U., U. of MO, LL.B. 1955; Catholic; married (Shirley).

Career: Army, 1955–57; Practicing atty., 1957–60; Marion Cnty. Prosecuting Atty., 1960–66; MO House of Reps., 1967–76.

Offices: 2409 RHOB 20515, 202-225-2956. Also 370 Fed. Bldg., Hannibal 63401, 314-221-1200.

Committees: *Agriculture* (7th of 28 D): Department Operations and Nutrition; General Farm Commodities; Livestock (Chmn.). *Science, Space and Technology* (4th of 33 D): Space.

Group Ratings

	ADA	ACLU	COPE	CDF	CFA	LCV	ACU	NTLC	NSI	COC	CEI
1992	50	35	91	60	73	19	40	21	80	50	26
1991	35	—	75	90	78	23	42	—	—	40	22

National Journal Ratings

	1991 LIB — 1991 CONS		1992 LIB — 1992 CONS	
Economic	59%	— 40%	51%	— 48%
Social	30%	— 68%	28%	— 72%
Foreign	43%	— 55%	38%	— 56%

Key Votes of the 102d Congress

1. Ban Striker Replace	FOR	5. Handgun Wait/7-Day	AGN
2. $ for Homeownership	FOR	6. Overseas Mil. Abortion	AGN
3. Tax Rich/Cut Mid Cls.	FOR	7. Obscn. Art NEA $ Ban	FOR
4. FY93/$15B Def. Cut	FOR	8. Death Pen. from Jury	FOR

9. Use Force in Gulf	FOR
10. US Mil. Abroad $ Cut	AGN
11. Limit SDI Funds	AGN
12. Cuba Trade Embargo	FOR

Key Votes of the 103d Congress

1. Family Leave	FOR	2. Deficit Reduction	FOR	3. Stimulus Plan	FOR

Election Results

1992 general	Harold L. Volkmer (D)...............	124,694	(48%)	($511,550)
	Rick Hardy (R).....................	118,811	(46%)	($139,860)
	Jeff Barrow (Green)	10,565	(4%)	($8,395)
	Other.............................	7,265	(3%)	
1992 primary	Harold L. Volkmer (D)...............	45,899	(57%)	
	Justus D. Griffin (D).................	16,785	(21%)	
	Joseph P. Caulfield (D)................	9,124	(11%)	
	Anthony DeFranco (D)................	3,567	(4%)	
	Two Others	4,970	(6%)	
1990 general	Harold L. Volkmer (D)...............	94,156	(57%)	($238,679)
	Don Curtis (R)	69,514	(43%)	($36,045)

MONTANA

A river runs through it—many rivers actually: the pristine trout stream of Norman MacLean's story and Robert Redford's film may be the most famous and beautifully rendered, but Montana also has the headwaters of the Missouri, from its source in Beaverhead County to its mouth in the Gulf of Mexico, the longest river in North America; and the Clark Fork which flows into the Columbia and eventually the Pacific. This is a vast and empty land, sitting atop America, spanning the Rockies so that on Interstate 15 you can cross the Continental Divide three times. Not far away, at Egg Mountain near Choteau on the Deep Teton River, is the world's most plenteous source of dinosaur remains. But Montana's recorded history is recent: at its 1989 centennial, the son of one of its original cattleman-settlers watched 105 cowboys drive 4,000 cattle with 300 covered wagons trailing behind. Montana has had some development lately: it has seen Ted Turner and Jane Fonda hang out in Bozeman with its new health food stores; Hollywood types, like "Brat Pack" stars Charlie Sheen and Kiefer Sutherland, buy spreads near Flathead Lake or Big Timber or the ski resort of Whitefish, where grizzlies come down to forage and the bars hold mouse races. It has ranchers practicing "holistic resource management" (which means moving livestock around the same property more often to mimic the old bison migrations); it has ghost towns no one has lived in for more than 100 years. The city of Butte, where stone temples of commerce and grim looming mineheads are now being restored to a cleanliness they seldom had when this was the Richest Hill on Earth, was once the only real city between Minneapolis and Seattle, full of company "goons" and IWW organizers, with a Socialist mayor and millionaires who bought seats in the U.S. Senate.

For all that, Montana is still Big Sky country, a land of great empty vistas, with mountains in the west and hundreds of miles of plateaus and plains in the east—the 4th largest state in area and 44th in population, with 800,000 people in an area larger than Michigan, Indiana and Illinois put together. This is still small-town America: voter turnout exceeded 20,000 in only five counties, centered on Billings in the east, the university town of Missoula, Great Falls just east of the Rockies, Kalispell near Lake Flathead, Bozeman (also a university and resort town), and the state capital of Helena. Its economy is still commodity-based—wheat-raising and cattle-grazing in the east, mining here and there in the west. The first white Americans came here as agents of the government—the Lewis and Clark expedition in 1805. Next came the mountain men, seeking the natural resource of fur, and then came the miners seeking gold, silver and copper—sudden riches that would make them kings not of this barren land but of the metropolis back East. Raucous mining towns sprang up, complete with outlaws and vigilantes. The mining economy gave Montana a radical, class warfare politics. On one side was the Anaconda Mining Company, which from about 1900 to the 1940s bought up almost all of Montana's newspapers, many of its utilities, many of its politicians, and had strong allies in the Stockmen's Association and the Farm Bureau. On the other side were progressives like Senators Thomas Walsh, who exposed the Teapot Dome scandal, and Burton Wheeler, who backed the New Deal but broke with Franklin Roosevelt over court packing and isolationism, the labor unions (Montana has no right-to-work law and is the most pro-union state in the Rockies), and pork barrel beneficiaries (for a while in the 1930s, Montana received more federal money per capita than almost any other state). The echoes of class warfare have grown dimmer over the years; Anaconda sold its newspapers in 1959, and closed its big Montana smelter in the 1970s. Only a few extremes of partisan division remain: Missoula, Great Falls, depopulated Butte and the Indian reservations are Democratic; the rest of the state is Republican in varying degrees.

What remains is the sense of space. Hunting and fishing, as in *A River Runs Through It*, are never far away; if development has centered in a few small cities and resort areas, none has grown large enough to drive the game away. The muscular tone of a land settled by ranch hands, miners and railroad workers, of cowboy hats, boots and blue jeans, of men who do hard physical work and relax hard afterwards, remains a link with Montanans going back to the mountain men, miners and cowboys who drove herds of cattle across the open range. And it is an attraction to tourists, to buyers of second homes, and even to the Japanese, who look from their crowded cities across the Pacific and see an almost empty treasure trove, rich with minerals and timber so needed in East Asia. With a boost from Mike Mansfield, senator from Montana for 24 years and ambassador to Japan for 12, Montana sells everything from dog sleds to dandelion extract to Helena's Kessler Beer to Japan. The Japanese, in turn, have invested in Montana mines and land, and have come over as tourists, attracted, as are Montanans, to what makes it American.

Governor. Montana's governorship race was blown wide open in January 1992, when incumbent Stan Stephens, the first Republican elected in 20 years, retired after collapsing from a blood clot in his brain, and as the state was about to face a $1 billion budget gap. Democrats, who then held both houses of the legislature by wide margins, had a spirited primary contest, with state Representative Dorothy Bradley a 41%–34% winner over lawyer Mike McGrath. Republican Auditor Andrea Bennett was already challenging Stephens, but Attorney General Marc Racicot (pronounced like *roscoe*) had both Stephens's nod and his own assets and won 69%–31%. Bradley was pro-choice, Racicot pro-life. Both advocated a 4% sales tax, to be voted on in referendum, but Bradley's plan became known as "tax and spend" while Racicot's tax reduction plan promised to downsize government. After a campaign conducted with a specificity and civility that would do honor to any larger state—although to be sure there were some negative charges—Racicot won by a 51%–49% margin. That, plus a Republican turnaround of a 39–61 deficit in the state House to a 53–47 majority, must be taken as a narrow vote for a smaller public sector. Now, and with a still Democratic state Senate, Racicot and the state House must deliver the services voters want at a price they're willing to pay.

Senators. For only the second time in its history, Montana has senators of both major parties; since direct election of senators began, it has only elected Republicans twice, in 1946 and 1988.

Max Baucus, the Democratic senator, in his early 50s is already one of the more senior members of the Senate, and the Democrat positioned to take a lead on two important issues: trade and infrastructure. Baucus is from a well-known ranching family (they own property seen in *A River Runs Through It*), who returned home from Stanford and Washington in 1971, was elected to the legislature in 1972 and then in 1974, at 32, won the 1st District House seat by beating three other past or future holders of it (current Congressman Pat Williams and former Congressman Arnold Olsen in the primary and Republican incumbent Richard Shoup in the general). In 1978, Baucus won his Senate seat by beating an appointed senator easily in the primary and a conservative Republican investment adviser in the general. Now, starting in 1993, he chairs the Environment and Public Works Committee, and ranks just behind Chairman Daniel Patrick Moynihan on Finance and chairs its Trade Subcommittee.

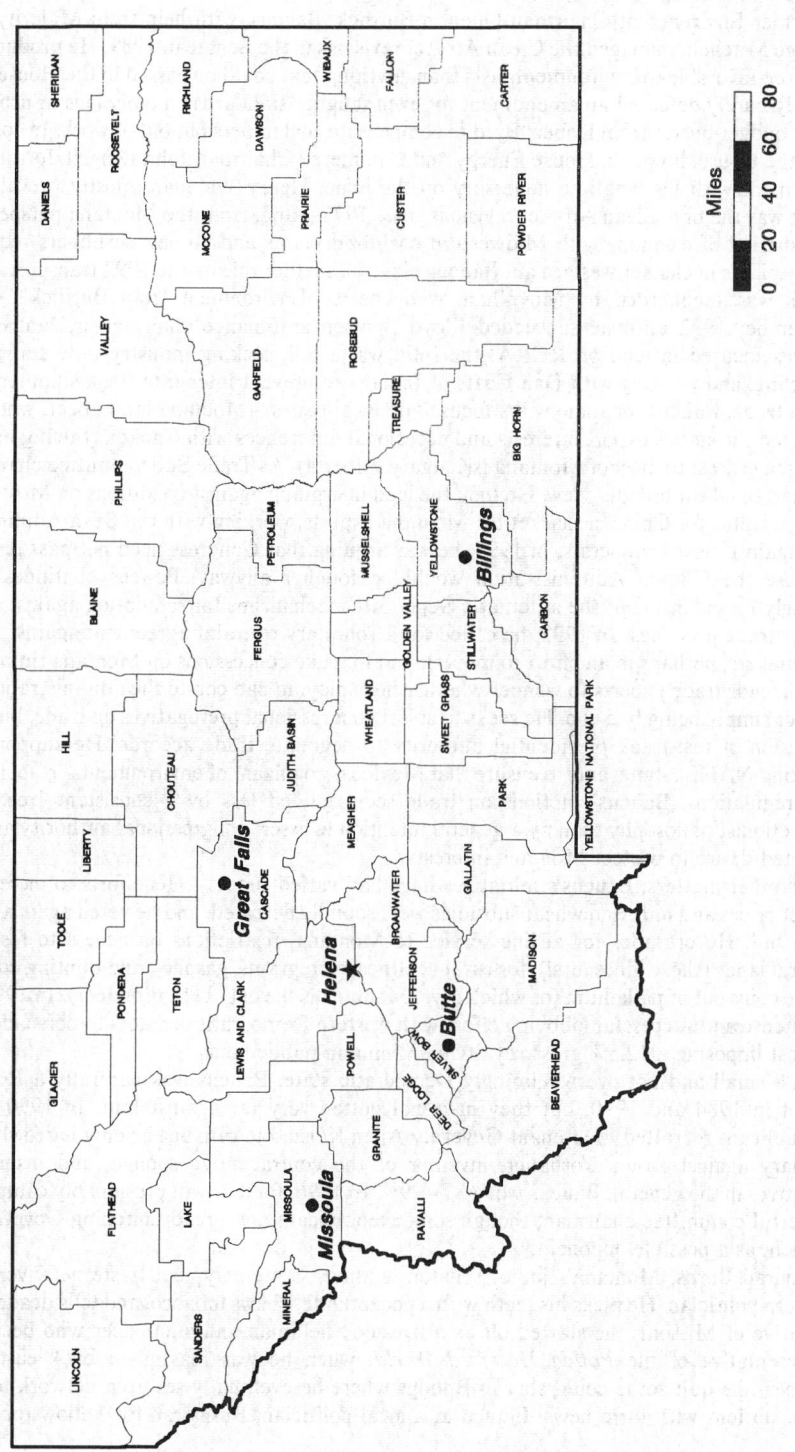

SHERIDAN

RICHLAND

WIBAUX

FALLON

CARTER

ROOSEVELT

DANIELS

DAWSON

MCCONE

PRAIRIE

CUSTER

POWDER RIVER

VALLEY

GARFIELD

ROSEBUD

TREASURE

BIG HORN

PHILLIPS

PETROLEUM

MUSSELSHELL

YELLOWSTONE

Billings

BLAINE

FERGUS

GOLDEN VALLEY

STILLWATER

CARBON

SWEET GRASS

YELLOWSTONE NATIONAL PARK

HILL

CHOUTEAU

JUDITH BASIN

WHEATLAND

LIBERTY

MEAGHER

PARK

GALLATIN

TOOLE

Great Falls

CASCADE

BROADWATER

MADISON

PONDERA

TETON

LEWIS AND CLARK

Helena

JEFFERSON

Butte

SILVER BOW

BEAVERHEAD

GLACIER

POWELL

DEER LODGE

GRANITE

FLATHEAD

LAKE

MISSOULA

Missoula

RAVALLI

MINERAL

SANDERS

LINCOLN

Miles

0 20 40 60 80

These are not the first major responsibilities Baucus has had in the Senate. In the quiescence of former Environment Chairman Quentin Burdick, Baucus, with help from Majority Leader George Mitchell, managed the Clean Air Act revisions in the Senate in 1989. He produced a bill far more favorable to environmentalists than anything that could be passed in the House, though he only barely defeated an amendment for even tougher standards on emissions in urban areas and a budget-buster from Robert Byrd to compensate coal miners put out of work. In conference with the House, however, House Energy and Commerce Chairman John Dingell, fortified by an agreement with his longtime adversary on the issue, Henry Waxman, mostly prevailed. The result was the first Clean Air Act revisions since 1977—and, from the Montana perspective, no cost-sharing of cleanups with Midwestern coal-fired plants and no new scrubbers required on utility plants in cleaner western air. Baucus played a smaller role on the 1992 transportation bill, which was shepherded by Moynihan, who chaired Environment from Burdick's death in September 1992 until he succeeded Lloyd Bentsen as Finance chairman in January 1993. Baucus focused instead on RCRA, the solid waste bill, seeking industry-wide standards for recycling, and working with Dan Coats of Indiana to prevent interstate trash shipments.

On trade, Baucus for some years focused on local issues—Montana lamb, beef, wheat—and reflected the state's export interests and occasional differences with Canada (the big metropolitan area nearest to most of Montana is Calgary, Alberta). As Trade Subcommittee chairman, he has had to take a broader view. He took the lead in arguing against conditions on Most Favored Nation status for China, a market for Montana exports, working with the Bush Administration and against most Democrats; in 1993, he was arguing that Congress need not pass restrictions because the Clinton Administration would be tougher anyway. Baucus continues to push strongly for extension of the automatic Super 301 mechanisms for retaliation against allegedly unfair trade practices. In 1992, he called for a voluntary restraint agreement against Japanese automakers, perhaps in an effort to move Japan to make concessions on Montana timber. All of which leads trade experts to wonder whether he is playing bad cop to the administration's good cop, or simply being bad cop. He seeks to assert congressional prerogatives on trade, but also for extension of fast-track presidential authority to negotiate trade accords. He supported fast-tracking NAFTA, but wants to ensure that Mexico is cognizant of environmental responsibilities and regulations. Baucus's actions on trade seem guided less by a consistent free trade or protectionist philosophy than by a general intention to assert congressional authority and a very directed desire to protect Montana interests.

On other matters, Baucus's initiatives have had varied success. His efforts to increase farm target prices and milk and wheat subsidies were soundly defeated, and he voted against the 1990 farm bill. He crusades for airline service to Montana, restrictions on access to fossils from federal lands (those dinosaurs!), for rural healthcare programs, gasohol, and minting commemorative coins out of palladium (of which Nye, Montana is the only U.S. producer). In 1993, he led an intense and successful lobbying effort with western Democratic senators to persuade Clinton against imposing a 12.5% gross royalty on mining in public lands.

In a small and not overwhelmingly Democratic state, Baucus was naturally a Republican target in 1984 and 1990, but they have not gotten very far against him. In 1990, national Republicans recruited Lieutenant Governor Allen Kolstad to run, but he only narrowly won his primary against Bruce Vorhauer, inventor of the contraceptive sponge, and inspired high negatives in the general. Baucus won 68%–29%. In 1996, Baucus will presumably campaign as a powerful committee chairman, though some Republicans are already pitching Governor Marc Racicot as a possible opponent.

Conrad Burns, Montana's junior senator, is almost a stereotypical Easterners' version of a western politician. He picks his teeth with a pocketknife, chews tobacco, and tells deadpan jokes. A native of Missouri, he started off as a livestock fieldman and auctioneer who became field representative of the *Polled Hereford World*; when he was reassigned back east (to Des Moines), he quit so he could stay in Billings where he eventually set up a network to provide radio stations with farm news. Piqued at a local politician, Burns ran for Yellowstone County

Commissioner in 1986 and won; two years later, he ran against Democratic Senator John Melcher. This was a long-shot race: Melcher had been senator for 12 years and congressman for seven before that, and still seemed a rumpled veterinarian in touch with Montanans; he had a moderate voting record and a deserved reputation as a party maverick. As so many Republicans do, Burns attacked his opponent as "a liberal who is soft on drugs, soft on defense and very high on social programs," adding that Melcher had backed ousted Philippine President Ferdinand Marcos. Melcher responded with tactics that had worked in the past, including a reprise of his talking cow ads of 1982. But Burns's attractive radio delivery plus President Reagan's veto of a wilderness bill that Melcher supported (and Burns opposed) hurt the incumbent, as did public opposition to the "let-it-burn" policy that resulted in the huge Yellowstone fires of summer 1988. Burns, who ended every speech with a Western "You bet!" won 52% of the vote.

In the Senate, Burns's main issue is telecommunications—not so un-Montanan a cause when you think about it. He sponsored, with Al Gore, a bill to let telephone companies offer cable services, a move opposed by the cable and broadcasting industries, which was effectively stalled by Commerce Committee Chairman Ernest Hollings. He also has a bill to let phone companies into video programming, to establish by 2015 a two-way interactive telecommunications network available to every home, school and business. In November 1991, Burns finally reached agreement with Baucus on a Montana wilderness bill, with neutral language on water rights; but the bill was liberalized and then stalled in the House in 1992. He has a pretty solidly conservative voting record on other issues and became chairman of the Republicans' Committee on Committees in 1993 and got a seat on Appropriations as well. He remains ready with quips: "We all do dumb things 15 minutes a day. The key is not to go over your quota!"

Montana has never reelected a Republican senator (Mansfield beat the last one in the Republican year of 1952), and Burns's job rating in 1992 was not particularly high. Many Democrats hoped Representative-at-Large Pat Williams would run against Burns in 1994, but citing his desire to hold on to his House seniority, Williams decided not to run. Other possible candidates are former Senator John Melcher, 1992 gubernatorial candidate Dorothy Bradley, Billings businessman Mike Gustafson and Secretary of State Mike Cooney.

Representative-At-Large. Montana's 1992 race between two incumbents for representative-at-large was a classic contest of opposites. Pat Williams, from Butte and Helena, with roots in the labor movement, former teacher, state legislator and Capitol Hill staffer, is an old-fashioned liberal Democrat, close to organized labor, supportive of teachers' groups and, from his subcommittee chair, chief patron of federal aid to the arts. He comes from a district with a history of purists and radicals: half a century ago, it elected Communist party-liner Jerry O'Connell, vicious anti-Semite Jacob Thorkelson, Jeanette Rankin, who voted against the declaration of war in 1941 as she had in 1917, and Mike Mansfield. Williams is a believer in redistributive economics, has a lyric sense that Montana is the last state "in the lower 48 to have an opportunity to set our destiny in major and meaningful ways." On the Education and Labor Committee, he has been the staunchest opponent of aid to church schools, raising that issue with regards to child care when others wanted to slough over it, since so many existing day care centers and preschools are run by churches. He has defended the National Endowment of the Arts despite its grant for art as offensive as a crucifix submerged in the urine of the artist, fashioning a compromise directing the NEA not to fund obscene projects and empowering it to order the return of federal grant money, if courts decided the art was obscene.

From the eastern district, with its vast plains overlooked by giant buttes, came Ron Marlenee, a rancher who loves to drive pickup trucks, sputtering often with rage at the intrusions of government bureaucrats and liberal cultural mores. He called Washington, D.C., a "work-free drug place" that "has a homicide rate so high its tourism promotion should issue every visitor a handgun." On the Interior Committee, he sat on the National Parks and Public Lands Subcommittee, and for years blocked Montana wilderness bills sought by Williams and Baucus because they would limit mineral exploration and grazing. He is not quite an ideological conservative; as a senior member of the Agriculture Committee, he was one of the few

Republicans for higher target prices for farmers. But he was angry at Montana's new glitterati liberals: "A lot of people are coming into the state of Montana who want to take your jobs and your businesses."

This was a battle between two philosophies, between those who would use the federal government to limit and regulate land use and those who want private sector economic development. Both candidates were proven vote-getters: since 1978, Williams had won 61% of the votes in the 1st District; Marlenee (who had well-financed opponents more often) 58% in the 2d. The campaign posters reflected the personal nature of Montana politics, where voters expect to talk with candidates in person: "Montana's Pat" versus "Ron: Putting Montanans First." Polls in 1991 and 1992 tended to rise and fall with national events: Williams led at first, Marlenee went up after Williams's reservations about the Gulf war proved unfounded and the Republican ran issue radio ads about the Democrat, then Williams rose as George Bush's fortunes foundered in the fall. In the end, the partisan margin was the same in the House as in the presidential race here: 3 points Democratic. Williams won 50%–47%, carrying his old 1st District 55%–42%; Marlenee carried his old 2d, which cast slightly fewer votes, 53%–45%. Williams carried Missoula, Helena and Butte by wide margins, and cut into the urban vote in the old 2d, narrowly holding Billings and Great Falls.

Williams is likely to continue to be an active legislator on Education and Labor and Natural Resources; and, with Marlenee's old seat on Agriculture, he is likely to have more running room on Montana issues. In 1993, Williams disappointed many Democrats by announcing he would not run against Senator Conrad Burns in 1994. There could be another seriously contested race for the at-large House seat though: the 1992 race, featuring two strong candidates with deep roots in the state's different traditions, came close enough to a dead heat to suggest the possibility of more fights and a different outcome.

Presidential politics. Montana, with only 3 electoral votes now, can't expect to see much of presidential candidates, particularly because its presidential primary is in early June, the same day as California's and New Jersey's. Only Alaska, Idaho, Utah and North Dakota are farther out of the national political jetlanes. Yet this was the closest Rocky Mountain state in 1988, and one of the closest in 1992, and actually got visits from Bill Clinton and Dan Quayle, plus a Clinton TV buy. Clinton carried the state with 38% to George Bush's 35%, with a sizable 26% for Ross Perot, who ran second in 20 counties and got 36% in Phillips County on the Canadian border. Most of the Clinton margin came from Missoula, Butte, Great Falls and the reservations; most outer counties went for Bush.

Congressional districting. Montana, which had two congressional districts for 80 years, lost one in the reapportionment following the 1990 Census. At which point the state did what so many Americans do: it filed a lawsuit. Montana challenged the reapportionment formula, pointing out that with a population of almost 800,000, the Montana at-large district would be 40% larger than average. In October 1991, two Montana federal judges agreed, and for a time threatened the national apportionment. But the Supreme Court took the case and in March 1992 made the common sense observation that since states can't have fractional congressmen, any apportionment formula will give some states larger than average districts. The political result was that the long-expected battle went forward between Democrat Pat Williams of the western 1st District and Republican Ron Marlenee of the eastern 2d District.

The People: Est. Pop. 1992: 824,000; Pop. 1990: 799,065, up 3.0% 1990–1992. 0.3% of U.S. total, 44th largest; 47% rural. Median age 33.8 years. 13.3% 65 years and over. 92.7% White, 6.0% American Indian, 1.5% Hispanic origin. Households: 57.7% married couple families; 28% married couple fams. w. children; 48% college educ.; median household income: $22,988; per capita income: $11,213; 67.3% owner occupied housing; median house value: $56,600; median monthly rent: $251. 6.7% Unemployment. Voting age pop.: 576,961. Registered voters (1992): 529,822; no party registration.

Political Lineup: Governor, Marc Racicot (R); Lt. Gov., Dennis Rehberg (R); Secy. of State, Mike Cooney (D); Atty. Gen., Joseph Mazurek (D); Auditor, Mark O'Keefe (D). State Senate, 50 (30 D and 20 R); State House of Representatives, 100 (53 R and 47 D). Senators, Max Baucus (D) and Conrad Burns (R). Representative, 1 D at large.

1992 Presidential Vote

Clinton (D)	154,507	(38%)
Bush (R)	144,207	(35%)
Perot (I)	107,225	(26%)

1992 Democratic Presidential Primary

Clinton	54,989	(47%)
Brown	21,704	(18%)
Tsongas	12,614	(11%)
No Preference	28,164	(24%)

1988 Presidential Vote

Bush (R)	190,412	(52%)
Dukakis (D)	168,956	(46%)

1992 Republican Presidential Primary

Bush	65,176	(72%)
Buchanan	10,701	(12%)
No Preference	15,098	(17%)

GOVERNOR

Gov. Marc Racicot (R)

Elected 1992, term expires Jan. 1997; b. July 24, 1948, Thompson Falls; home, Helena; Carroll Col., B.A. 1970, U. of MT Law Schl., J.D. 1973; Catholic; married (Theresa).

Career: Army, 1973–76; Dep. Missoula Cnty. Atty., 1976-77; Asst. MT Atty. Gen., 1977–88; MT Atty. Gen., 1988–92.

Office: Office of the Governor, State Capitol, Helena 59620, 406-444-3111.

Election Results

1992 gen.	Marc Racicot (R)	209,401	(51%)
	Dorothy Bradley (D)	198,421	(49%)
1992 prim.	Marc Racicot (R)	68,103	(69%)
	Andrea (Andy) Bennett (R)	31,038	(31%)
1988 gen.	Stan Stephens (R)	190,604	(53%)
	Tom Judge (D)	169,313	(47%)

SENATORS
Sen. Max Baucus (D)

Elected 1978, seat up 1996; b. Dec. 11, 1941, Helena; home, Helena; Stanford U., B.A. 1964, LL.B. 1967; Protestant; married (Wanda).

Career: Staff atty., Civil Aeronautics Bd., 1967–69; Legal Asst., Securities and Exchange Comm., 1969–71; Practicing atty., 1971–74; MT House of Reps., 1973–74; U.S. House of Reps., 1975–78.

Offices: 511 HSOB 20510, 202-224-2651. Also Granite Bldg., 23 S. Last Chance Gulch, Helena 59601, 406-449-5480; 202 Fratt Bldg., 2817 2d Ave. N., Billings 59101, 406-657-6970; Fed. Bldg., 32 E. Babcock, #114, P.O. Box 1689, Bozeman 59715, 406-586-6104; Silver Bow Ctr., 125 W. Granite, Butte 59701, 406-782-8700; 107 5th St. N., Great Falls 59401, 406-761-1574; 715 Main St., Kalispell 59901; and 211 N. Higgins, #102, Missoula 59802, 406-329-3123.

Committees: *Agriculture, Nutrition and Forestry* (8th of 10 D): Agricultural Credit; Agricultural Production and Stabilization of Prices; Domestic and Foreign Marketing and Product Promotion. *Environment and Public Works* (Chmn. of 10 D). *Finance* (2d of 11 D): International Trade (Chmn.); Medicare and Long-Term Care; Taxation. *Intelligence (Select)* (8th of 9 D). *Joint Committee on Taxation* (2d of 5).

Group Ratings

	ADA	ACLU	CDF	COPE	CFA	LCV	ACU	NTLC	NSI	COC	CEI
1992	95	73	80	75	100	58	4	5	50	20	18
1991	70	—	91	58	78	80	24	—	—	20	22

National Journal Ratings

	1991 LIB	—	1991 CONS	1992 LIB	—	1992 CONS
Economic	57%	—	40%	73%	—	25%
Social	59%	—	38%	64%	—	34%
Foreign	71%	—	27%	76%	—	22%

Key Votes of the 102d Congress

1. $ for Homeownership	AGN	5. Clarence Thomas Nom. AGN	9. Use Force in Gulf	AGN
2. Have Cap Gains Debate	AGN	6. Lmt Death Row Appeal AGN	10. Keep Salvador Aid	AGN
3. Remove Budget Walls	FOR	7. Handgun Wait/5-Day AGN	11. Cut $1B from SDI	FOR
4. Ban Striker Replace	FOR	8. Abortion Gag Rule AGN	12. Override China MFN AGN

Key Votes of the 103d Congress

1. Family Leave   FOR   2. HIV Immigrants   FOR   3. Clinton Budget   FOR

Election Results

1990 general	Max Baucus (D)	217,563	(68%)	($2,568,899)
	Allen C. Kolstad (R)	93,836	(29%)	($747,661)
	Other	7,937	(2%)	
1990 primary	Max Baucus (D)	81,687	(83%)	
	John Driscoll (D)	12,622	(13%)	
	Emmett (Curly) Thornton (D)	4,367	(4%)	
1984 general	Max Baucus (D)	215,704	(57%)	($1,386,561)
	Chuck Cozzens (R)	154,308	(41%)	($492,391)

Sen. Conrad Burns (R)

Elected 1988, seat up 1994; b. Jan. 25, 1935, Gallatin, MO; home, Billings; U. of MO, 1952–54; Lutheran; married (Phyllis).

Career: Marine Corps, 1955–57; TWA and Ozark Airlines, 1958–61; Field rep., *Polled Hereford World*, 1962; Mgr., Billings Livestock Show, 1968; Radio & TV broadcaster, 1968–86; Yellowstone Cnty. Commissioner, 1986–88.

Offices: 183 DSOB 20510, 202-224-2644. Also 2708 First Ave. N., Billings 59101, 406-252-0550; 208 N. Montana Ave., #202-A, Helena 59601, 406-449-5401; 415 N. Higgins, Missoula 59802, 406-329-3528; 104 4th St. N., Great Falls 59401, 406-252-9585; 324 W. Towne, Glendive 59330, 406-365-2391; 10 E. Babcock, Fed. Bldg. #106, Bozeman 59715, 406-586-4450; 125 W. Granite, #211, Butte 59701, 406-723-3277; and 575 Sunset Blvd., #101, Kalispell 59901, 406-257-3360.

Committees: *Aging (Special)* (9th of 10 R). *Appropriations* (13th of 13 R): District of Columbia (RMM); Interior; Legislative Branch; VA, HUD and Independent Agencies. *Commerce, Science and Transportation* (6th of 9 R): Communications; Consumer; Science, Technology and Space (RMM); Surface Transportation. *Small Business* (4th of 9 R): Innovation, Manufacturing and Technology (RMM); Rural Economy and Family Farming.

Group Ratings

	ADA	ACLU	CDF	COPE	CFA	LCV	ACU	NTLC	NSI	COC	CEI
1992	5	9	30	25	8	0	89	83	90	100	77
1991	5	—	36	17	22	13	86	—	—	90	70

National Journal Ratings

	1991 LIB — 1991 CONS	1992 LIB — 1992 CONS
Economic	15% — 80%	15% — 80%
Social	0% — 86%	16% — 83%
Foreign	0% — 87%	0% — 90%

Key Votes of the 102d Congress

1. $ for Homeownership FOR	5. Clarence Thomas Nom. FOR	9. Use Force in Gulf FOR
2. Have Cap Gains Debate FOR	6. Lmt Death Row Appeal FOR	10. Keep Salvador Aid FOR
3. Remove Budget Walls AGN	7. Handgun Wait/5-Day AGN	11. Cut $1B from SDI AGN
4. Ban Striker Replace AGN	8. Abortion Gag Rule FOR	12. Override China MFN AGN

Key Votes of the 103d Congress

1. Family Leave FOR	2. HIV Immigrants AGN	3. Clinton Budget AGN

Election Results

1988 general	Conrad Burns (R)	189,445	(52%)	($1,076,010)
	John Melcher (D)	175,809	(48%)	($1,338,622)
1988 primary	Conrad Burns (R)	63,330	(85%)	
	Tom Faranda (R)	11,427	(15%)	
1982 general	John Melcher (D)	174,861	(54%)	($830,892)
	Larry Williams (R)	133,789	(42%)	($708,286)

REPRESENTATIVE

Rep. Pat Williams (D)

Elected 1978; b. Oct. 30, 1937, Helena; home, Helena; U. of MT, 1956–57, U. of Denver, B.A. 1961; Catholic; married (Carol).

Career: Army, 1960–61, Army Natl. Guard, 1962–69; Public schl. teacher; MT House of Reps., 1967, 1969; Reg. Dir., Humphrey Pres. campaign, 1968; Exec. Asst., U.S. Rep. John Melcher, 1969–71; MT Coord., Family Educ. Prog., 1971–78.

Offices: 2457 RHOB 20515, 202-225-3211. Also 316 N. Park Ave., #443, Helena 59624, 406-443-7878; 305 W. Mercury, #306, Butte 59701, 406-723-4404; 302 W. Broadway, Missoula 59802, 406-549-5550; 216 N. 29th St., Billings 59101, 406-256-1019; and 325 2nd Ave. N., #101, Great Falls 59401, 406-771-1242.

Committees: *Agriculture* (26th of 28 D): General Farm Commodities. *Education and Labor* (6th of 28 D): Labor-Management Relations (Chmn.); Postsecondary Education and Training. *Natural Resources* (7th of 28 D): National Parks, Forests and Public Lands; Native American Affairs.

Group Ratings

	ADA	ACLU	COPE	CDF	CFA	LCV	ACU	NTLC	NSI	COC	CEI
1992	85	83	92	90	67	38	8	0	20	50	26
1991	65	—	73	80	67	54	20	—	—	44	19

National Journal Ratings

	1991 LIB — 1991 CONS	1992 LIB — 1992 CONS
Economic	51% — 49%	63% — 36%
Social	73% — 26%	71% — 28%
Foreign	69% — 31%	74% — 25%

Key Votes of the 102d Congress

1. Ban Striker Replace	FOR	5. Handgun Wait/7-Day	AGN	9. Use Force in Gulf	AGN
2. $ for Homeownership	AGN	6. Overseas Mil. Abortion	FOR	10. US Mil. Abroad $ Cut	FOR
3. Tax Rich/Cut Mid Cls.	FOR	7. Obscn. Art NEA $ Ban	AGN	11. Limit SDI Funds	FOR
4. FY93/$15B Def. Cut	AGN	8. Death Pen. from Jury	AGN	12. Cuba Trade Embargo	FOR

Key Votes of the 103d Congress

1. Family Leave	FOR	2. Deficit Reduction	FOR	3. Stimulus Plan	FOR

Election Results

1992 general	Pat Williams (D)	203,711	(50%)	($1,336,673)
	Ron Marlenee (R)	189,570	(47%)	($1,292,583)
	Other	10,454	(3%)	
1992 primary	Pat Williams (D), unopposed			
1990 general	Pat Williams (D)	100,409	(61%)	($345,258)
	Brad Johnson (R)	63,837	(39%)	($90,238)

NEBRASKA

The first settlers coming west called the Platte River "the sea of Nebraska." Actually, it's not a single river but a braid of streams that weave a silver chain around sandbars and islands, flooding the level floor of the great plain; a mile wide, as the saying goes, and six inches deep. Nebraska was formed in one rush of settlement in the 1880s, when its population increased from 452,000 to 1,062,000, more than it has increased in the century since (it was 1,578,000 in 1990). That same decade Omaha became a major railroad center and Lincoln the state capital. Today, Nebraska remains heavily dependent on farming and related industries, and Omaha and Lincoln are still its only significant cities. This is a state that sprang suddenly into existence and has changed strikingly little since.

That is not what its founders intended: they hoped Nebraska would develop diversified farming, industrial and commercial centers like those in Ohio, Illinois, Missouri or Minnesota. But while the 1880s were a time of plentiful rain here, the 1890s were a decade of drought, and Nebraska stopped growing. Many rural counties, and even Omaha, lost population, and have been exporting people ever since; the creative energies in the economy seem to have skipped over the Great Plains and moved far to the West. Nebraska's settlers, like most migrants, were young people, optimistic and motivated, in search of opportunity, with families full of children. Some 48% of Nebraskans in 1890 were children; in 1990, only 27% were—which means there are actually 60,000 fewer children in this state than there were 100 years ago.

The sudden boom of the 1880s and the bust of the 1890s produced the most colorful—and atypical—politics of Nebraska's history: the populist movement and William Jennings Bryan, the "silver tongued orator of the Platte." Bryan was only 36 when he delivered the famous Cross of Gold speech at the 1896 Democratic National Convention and was swept to the Democratic nomination; he was thought so radical that Democratic President Grover Cleveland wouldn't support him, but he still won 47% of the vote in the first of three attempts. Nebraskans supported Bryan, whose program may have been forward-looking, but whose purpose was retrograde: to restore Nebraska to the prosperity it had enjoyed a few years before. Since Bryan's time, Nebraska's most notable politician has been George Norris, who led the House rebellion against Speaker Joseph Cannon in 1911, and in the 1930s pushed through the Norris-LaGuardia Anti-Injunction Act, the first national pro-union legislation, and the Tennessee Valley Authority. But most Nebraskans were repelled by the New Deal, which seemed to threaten their stable society, and for half a century Nebraska has been among the most Republican of states in national elections.

But Nebraska has not been stagnant. Economically, it has shown some dynamism. Omaha is the home base of the fast-growing ConAgra food combine and of mega-investor Warren Buffett, whose corny humor complements his knack for picking stocks that go up hundreds of percents. And after the nearby Strategic Air Command base brought the world's most advanced phone system to the Omaha area 40-odd years ago, hotel chains, credit card companies and telemarketers set up operations, making this the world's leading place to make a living by talking on the phone. Politically, Nebraska has some pizzazz too. Nebraska's nonpartisan unicameral legislature provides a forum for politicians of all beliefs to become well known and, if only to ensure variety and competition, voters will consider Democrats as well as Republicans for high partisan office. So Nebraska has elected Democratic governors for all but 12 years since 1960; it now has two Democratic senators and one Democratic congressman out of three.

Governor. Governor Ben Nelson, elected in 1990, was the third Democrat in a row to beat an incumbent Republican associated with tax increases; the other two have gone on to become senators. His victory was narrow and his course in office has been cautious. He beat Republican

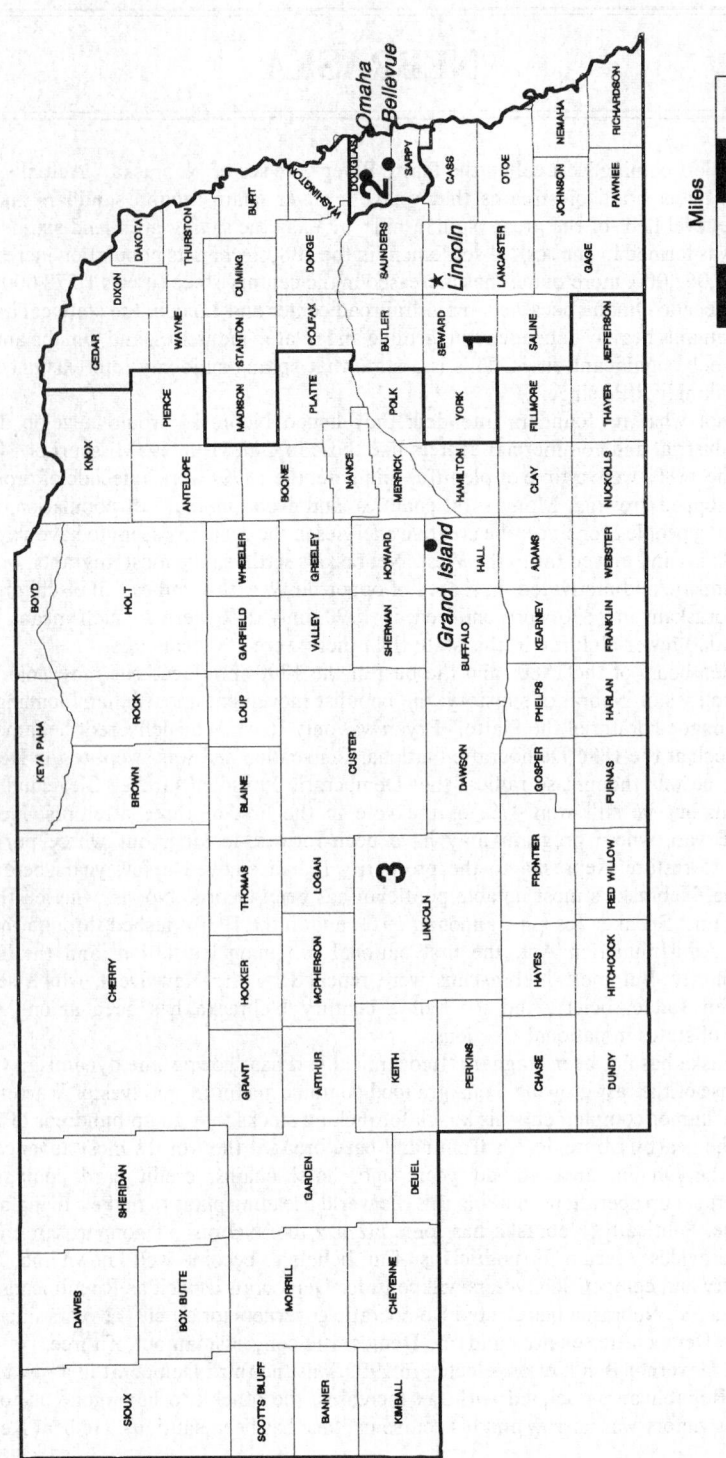

Miles

80
60
40
20
0

incumbent Kay Orr by 4,030 votes in 1990 largely because her 1987 tax reform raised taxes on some voters; also, her political consultants failed to place many of her scheduled TV spots in October, even though she had paid for the time. Nelson had been lucky too in his primary, when he beat Bill Hoppner, who was supported by former boss Senator Bob Kerrey, by a 42-vote margin after a 48-day recount. In a pattern also seen in Senate contests, Nelson ran strongest in the eastern part of the state (though he lost Omaha's Douglas County—the only governor in the history of Nebraska to so do) and in the southern tier, while Orr ran strongest in the Platte Valley, the sparsely populated central and western counties, and around heavily Republican Madison. Nelson, who had criticized Orr for "sitting in Lincoln and looking east," noted the population decline in 83 of 93 counties and pledged to serve "one Nebraska," spreading economic growth outward from Omaha and Lincoln. In office, he has made periodic budget cuts and has cut taxes a bit for many voters; he has pushed through cuts in Aid to Families with Dependent Children (AFDC) programs, but proposed increases in his 1993 budget. His job rating in late 1992 seemed solid.

Senators. Jim Exon is now in his third decade as a major figure in Nebraska politics: he was a popular pinchpenny governor elected in 1970 and 1974 and was elected to the Senate in 1978. Coming to the Senate with a reputation as an economizer, he has spent most of his career as a team-playing Democrat—not a down-the-line liberal vote by any means, but almost always sticking with his party on tough issues and when his vote is needed. His voting record is just about at the Senate midpoint on economic, cultural and foreign issues and he has pursued several issues with some legislative success. One was foreign investment in the United States: his Exon-Florio bill lets the president stop foreign takeovers that threaten national security. Another is trucking. From his chair of the Surface Transportation Subcommittee, he has tried to settle disputes regarding undercharges between trucking firms and shippers and has attempted to increase penalties for drug sales near truck stops. He has worked to keep Amtrak running and to make it safer. A critical vote sometimes on the Armed Services Committee, where he would cut defense more than Republicans but less than many Democrats, he co-sponsored a 1992 law allowing only five more underground nuclear tests in Nevada through 1996, then banning them if other nuclear nations agree to ban theirs too. He is Congress's leading proponent of barter arrangements, especially with the former Soviet republics, and creating an Office of Barter in the Commerce Department; this sparked the Clinton Administration to consider a proposal to send petroleum engineers to Siberia in return for oil for the Strategic Petroleum Reserve. On environmental issues, he successfully opposed the Two Forks Dam in Colorado which would block the flow of the South Platte and supported the Niobrara Wild and Scenic River Act.

Exon has not been cowed by new administrations. In 1989, he was the first senator to oppose the nomination of former colleague John Tower for secretary of defense, saying the evidence showed a pattern of problems with alcohol; in October 1990, Tower came to Nebraska to support Exon's opponent, former Congressman Hal Daub, and accused Exon of being "a big boozer" himself, which Exon denied. In 1993, Exon was quick to say that Clinton's economic package contained much "investment" that wasn't investment, was cautious about the Democrat's campaign finance reform and objected to farm program cuts in the first Clinton package.

Exon won reelection in 1984 by only 52%–48% and attracted a well-known opponent, Hal Daub, in 1990. Daub, once dubbed the "pit bull" of Nebraska Republicans, pledged not to accept PAC money, but had taken $1 million of it in the 1980s; Exon won 59%–41%. The outlook for 1996 is not clear.

Nebraska's junior senator, Bob Kerrey, is the fifth Congressional Medal of Honor holder to serve in the Senate. (Kerrey's was from service in Vietnam; the other four received their medals for service in the Civil War.) He is an attractive figure, capable of inspiring an audience and plainly sincere in his stands on issues. He is a relative newcomer who has already reached the national spotlight. He served one term as a governor of this sparsely populated state to voters' satisfaction, and was handily elected to the Senate in 1988; three years later, he was running for president, campaigning all over New Hampshire and winning the South Dakota primary, but not doing much elsewhere. Now he is back in the Senate, and the issue he emphasized, healthcare reform, is at the top of the national agenda.

Kerrey's biography shows a man of great determination. After graduating from the University of Nebraska with a pharmacy degree in 1966, he volunteered for the Navy SEALs. After three months in Vietnam in March 1969, a grenade exploded at his feet (he lost his right leg below the knee, but still jogs six miles a day), but he kept directing his platoon's fire until his men were able to escape. He was awarded the Medal of Honor by President Nixon, and later became an avid opponent of the war he had so honorably served. Back in Lincoln, he started a chain of restaurants, then ran for governor in 1982 as a Democrat, even though he had been a Republican not long before; he beat incumbent Charles Thone. In office, he made some tough budget cuts and settled water rights disputes. His one blotch came when state insurance failed to pay off depositors of two failed state-chartered S&Ls, and Kerrey was partner in a real estate deal with the principal owner of one of them, although there was no evidence of any wrongdoing on Kerrey's part. In 1986, Kerrey shocked most politicians by deciding not to seek reelection, despite 70%-plus job approval ratings; in 1988, he surprised very few by winning 57%–42% the Senate seat held by appointee David Karnes after the death of Edward Zorinsky.

In the Senate, Kerrey attracted more attention than most freshmen, though did not get more results. On the Agriculture Committee, he set himself the task of increasing farm price supports and took on fellow Nebraskan and Agriculture Secretary Clayton Yeutter and Indiana Republican Richard Lugar—and was defeated. He had more success—and of course his record as a war hero gave him more credibility—when he spoke out against the constitutional amendment to allow state bans on flag burning. Kerrey's great crusade, though, was against the Gulf war. Although he supported the initial deployment of troops to the Gulf, he vocally opposed military action, taking to the floor often with Terry Sanford of North Carolina to predict that there would be many casualties and that Bush's threats to Saddam Hussein was more the language of "a little league football coach than a commander in chief"—not prognostications of great foresight. In July 1991, with little publicity, he introduced his national healthcare bill, a publicly financed system with total spending and minimum benefits determined by the federal government. States would set physician fees and spending targets and negotiate hospital budgets; funds would come from a 5% payroll tax, cigarette and alcohol taxes and a new top-bracket income tax.

Through much of 1991, Kerrey was rumored to be considering a presidential run. In September, he abruptly entered the race, announcing on a brilliant day outside the skyscraper Capitol in Lincoln that he wanted to "lead America's fearless, restless voyage of generational progress." The press corps followed him closely, recognizing his capacity for inspiring speeches and speculating on how Democrats might be united by a Medal of Honor winner who was also antiwar. But on the stump in New Hampshire, Kerrey's candidacy languished. He spoke knowledgeably of health issues, but his inspiring speeches evidently did not convince voters; the one-sixth of Democratic primary voters who met one or more candidates in person far preferred Bill Clinton. Kerrey finished third in New Hampshire, with only 11%, just barely ahead of Tom Harkin and Jerry Brown. Then, despite his 40%–25% win over Harkin in South Dakota and his harsh attacks in Georgia on Bill Clinton's lack of candor on his experiences with the draft—he said of Clinton that Bush would "open him up like a soft peanut"—he finished fourth or fifth in five states a week later, and "I just woke up Wednesday and said it was over." Unlike Tom Harkin, he did not endorse Clinton early or campaign for him, and Clinton never really seriously considered him for vice president, even though many Democrats relished the picture of a Medal of Honor winner debating former National Guardsman Dan Quayle.

Back in the Senate, Kerrey has continued working on health care, calling in April 1993 for a healthcare trust fund, a pay-as-you-go mechanism, to finance federal health programs. Also in 1993 he introduced, with Connecticut's Joseph Lieberman, a government restructuring bill to "do more with less," setting up a bipartisan commission to streamline the federal government. On Agriculture, he worked on export assistance, crop insurance and wetlands laws and successfully got President Clinton to exclude ethanol from his energy tax. He has a bill to establish a network of state-based electronic libraries.

Kerrey comes up for reelection in 1994. His election in 1988 came after a long campaign which featured a nasty fight in the Republican Party between Omaha Congressman Hal Daub and David Karnes, the Omaha lawyer appointed when Democratic Senator Edward Zorinsky died in March 1987. Karnes won the primary, but his statement that "We need fewer farmers at this point in time" went over poorly in agriculture-transfixed Nebraska, and Kerrey won the general 57%–42%. Kerrey seems to remain well-regarded, even loved, in Nebraska, and seems sure to be reelected if he runs.

Presidential politics. Over the last 50 years, Nebraska has voted more Republican in presidential elections than any other state—61% to Kansas's second place 57%. It was not the number one Bush state in 1992, but was his best state outside the South, and it was Bill Clinton's third worst, after Utah and Idaho. There is an urban-rural split, with greater Lincoln and Omaha more Democratic; elsewhere in the state, Ross Perot outpolled Bill Clinton in 1992.

Nebraska has a presidential primary in May which once attracted attention; the whole national press followed Robert Kennedy and Eugene McCarthy out here in 1968 and took note when Frank Church won in 1976. No more: nominations are now sewn up long before May, and Nebraska has gone unnoticed. In 1992, its native son, Kerrey, was out of the running by then.

Congressional districting. Nebraska hasn't lost a House seat since the Census of 1960. The June 1991 redistricting plan switched all or part of seven counties between districts—marginal changes, but ones which might have made the difference in the close 2d District race in November 1992.

The People: Est. Pop. 1992: 1,606,000; Pop. 1990: 1,578,385, up 1.7% 1990–1992. 0.6% of U.S. total, 36th largest; 34% rural. Median age: 33.0 years. 14.1% 65 years and over. 93.8% White 3.6% Black, 2.3% Hispanic origin. Households: 58.2% married couple families; 28% married couple fams. w. children; 47% college educ.; median household income: $26,016; per capita income: $12,452; 66.5% owner occupied housing; median house value: $50,400; median monthly rent: $282. 3.0% Unemployment. Voting age pop.: 1,149,373. Registered voters (1992): 951,395; 389,102 D (41%), 464,955 R (49%), 97,338 unaffiliated and minor parties (10%).

Political Lineup: Governor, E. Benjamin Nelson (D); Lt. Gov., Maxine Moul (D); Secy. of State, Allen J. Beermann (R); Atty. Gen., Donald Stenberg (R); Treasurer, Dawn Rockey (D); Auditor, John Breslow (D). Unicameral Legislature, 49 (no party affiliation). Senators, J. James Exon (D) and Robert Kerrey (D). Representatives, 3 (2 R and 1 D).

1992 Presidential Vote

Bush (R)	343,678	(47%)
Clinton (D)	216,864	(29%)
Perot (I)	174,104	(24%)

1992 Democratic Presidential Primary

Clinton	68,562	(46%)
Brown	31,673	(21%)
Tsongas	10,707	(7%)
Other	14,931	(10%)
Uncommitted	24,714	(16%)

1988 Presidential Vote

Bush (R)	397,956	(60%)
Dukakis (D)	259,235	(39%)

1992 Republican Presidential Primary

Bush	156,346	(81%)
Buchanan	25,847	(13%)
Other	9,905	(5%)

GOVERNOR

Gov. E. Benjamin Nelson (D)

Elected 1990, term expires Jan. 1995; b. May 17, 1941, McCook; home, Lincoln; U. of NE, B.A. 1963, M.A. 1965, LL.B. 1970; Methodist; married (Diane).

Career: Gen. Cnsl., Central Natl. Group Insurance, 1972–74, Pres. & CEO, 1977–81; NE Dir. of Insurance, 1975–76; Exec. V.P., Natl. Assn. of Insurance Commissioners, 1982–85; Practicing atty., 1985–90.

Office: State Capitol, P.O. Box 94848, Lincoln 68509, 402-471-2244.

Election Results

1990 gen.	E. Benjamin Nelson (D)	292,771	(50%)
	Kay A. Orr (R)	288,741	(49%)
	Other	5,030	(1%)
1990 prim.	E. Benjamin Nelson (D)	44,721	(27%)
	Bill Hoppner (D)	44,679	(27%)
	Mike Boyle (D)	41,227	(25%)
	Bill Harris (D)	31,527	(19%)
	Three Others	4,805	(3%)
1986 gen.	Kay A. Orr (R)	298,325	(53%)
	Helen Boosalis (D)	265,156	(47%)

SENATORS

Sen. J. James Exon (D)

Elected 1978, seat up 1996; b. Aug. 9, 1921, Geddes, SD; home, Lincoln; U. of Omaha, 1939–41; Episcopalian; married (Patricia).

Career: Army, 1941–45 (WWII); Branch mgr., Universal Finance Corp., 1946–54; Pres., Exon's Inc. office equip., 1954–70; NE Gov., 1970–78.

Offices: 528 HSOB 20510, 202-224-4224. Also 1623 Farnam St., #700, Omaha 68102, 402-341-1776; 287 Fed. Bldg., 100 Centennial Mall N., Lincoln 68508, 402-437-5591; 2106 1st St., Scottsbluff 69361, 308-632-3595; and 275 Fed. Bldg., North Platte 69101, 308-534-2006.

Committees: *Armed Services* (2d of 11 D): Coalition Defense and Reinforcing Forces; Nuclear Deterrence, Arms Control and Defense Intelligence (Chmn.); Regional Defense and Contingency Forces. *Budget* (5th of 12 D). *Commerce, Science and Transportation* (4th of 11 D): Aviation; Communications; Surface Transportation (Chmn.).

Group Ratings

	ADA	ACLU	CDF	COPE	CFA	LCV	ACU	NTLC	NSI	COC	CEI
1992	75	45	80	83	75	42	26	17	60	30	26
1991	50	—	82	67	78	53	38	—	—	20	36

National Journal Ratings

	1991 LIB — 1991 CONS		1992 LIB — 1992 CONS	
Economic	60% —	35%	51% —	48%
Social	35% —	63%	52% —	46%
Foreign	46% —	52%	52% —	47%

Key Votes of the 102d Congress

1. $ for Homeownership	AGN	5. Clarence Thomas Nom.	FOR	9. Use Force in Gulf	AGN
2. Have Cap Gains Debate	AGN	6. Lmt Death Row Appeal	AGN	10. Keep Salvador Aid	AGN
3. Remove Budget Walls	AGN	7. Handgun Wait/5-Day	FOR	11. Cut $1B from SDI	AGN
4. Ban Striker Replace	FOR	8. Abortion Gag Rule	FOR	12. Override China MFN	AGN

Key Votes of the 103d Senate

1. Family Leave	FOR	2. HIV Immigrants	AGN	3. Clinton Budget	FOR

Election Results

1990 general	J. James Exon (D)	349,779	(59%)	($2,410,097)
	Hal Daub (R)	243,013	(41%)	($1,452,681)
1990 primary	J. James Exon (D)	157,959	(99%)	
	Other	2,006	(1%)	
1984 general	J. James Exon (D)	332,217	(52%)	($886,760)
	Nancy Hoch (R)	307,147	(48%)	($583,632)

Sen. Robert Kerrey (D)

Elected 1988, seat up 1994; b. Aug. 27, 1943, Lincoln; home, Omaha; U of NE, M.S. 1966; Congregationalist; divorced.

Career: Navy, 1966–69 (Vietnam); Businessman, Restaurant owner, 1972–81; NE Gov., 1983–87.

Offices: 303 HSOB 20510, 202-224-6551. Also 7602 Pacific St. Omaha 68114, 402-391-3411; and 100 Centennial Mall N., #294, Fed. Bldg, Lincoln 68508, 402-437-5246.

Committees: *Agriculture, Nutrition and Forestry* (9th of 10 D): Agricultural Production and Stabilization of Prices; Agricultural Research, Conservation, Forestry and General Legislation; Nutrition and Investigations. *Appropriations* (13th of 16 D): Agriculture, Rural Development and Related Agencies; Commerce, Justice, State and Judiciary; Energy and Water Development; Treasury, Postal Service and General Government; VA, HUD and Independent Agencies. *Intelligence (Select)* (4th of 9 D).

Group Ratings

	ADA	ACLU	CDF	COPE	CFA	LCV	ACU	NTLC	NSI	COC	CEI
1992	90	78	80	91	75	50	0	17	30	25	18
1991	75	—	55	78	50	80	5	—	—	29	30

National Journal Ratings

	1991 LIB — 1991 CONS		1992 LIB — 1992 CONS	
Economic	55% —	43%	60% —	39%
Social	63% —	36%	89% —	0%
Foreign	70% —	29%	74% —	24%

Key Votes of the 102d Congress

1. $ for Homeownership AGN	5. Clarence Thomas Nom.AGN	9. Use Force in Gulf AGN
2. Have Cap Gains Debate AGN	6. Lmt Death Row Appeal AGN	10. Keep Salvador Aid AGN
3. Remove Budget Walls FOR	7. Handgun Wait/5-Day FOR	11. Cut $1B from SDI FOR
4. Ban Striker Replace FOR	8. Abortion Gag Rule AGN	12. Override China MFN FOR

Key Votes of the 103d Senate

1. Family Leave FOR	2. HIV Immigrants FOR	3. Clinton Budget FOR

Election Results

1988 general	Robert Kerrey (D)	378,717	(57%)	($3,461,148)
	David Karnes (R)	278,250	(42%)	($3,411,361)
1988 primary	Robert Kerrey (D)	156,498	(91%)	
	Ken L. Michaelis (D)	14,248	(8%)	
1982 general	Edward Zorinsky (D)	363,350	(67%)	($523,141)
	Jim Keck (R)	155,760	(29%)	($489,186)

FIRST DISTRICT

The eastern half of Nebraska, between the Missouri River and the 98th parallel, was laid out in remorseless Midwestern mile-square grids and became some of America's prime farmland in the single decade of the 1880s. The land here has contours just regular enough and weather just favorable enough to make farming economically viable. The plains here have completed most of their gentle decline from the Rockies to sea level; above the river bottoms the land is open to the winds. This land was settled by Yankee-descended Midwestern farmers and German immigrants; politically it has long been Republican in national elections, but votes Democratic in seriously contested state races.

The 1st Congressional District of Nebraska includes 25 counties in eastern Nebraska. It does not include Omaha and its suburbs, which form the 2d District, but does take in Lincoln, the state capital and home of the University of Nebraska Cornhuskers. Lincoln is the single fast-growing part of the district; almost every other place lost population in the 1980s. Lincoln is also singular politically: more hospitable to Democrats, fond of moderate-toned Republicans; evenly split between Bill Clinton and George Bush in 1992, when most of the rest of Nebraska gave Bush many more votes and was split between Clinton and Ross Perot for second place.

The congressman from the 1st District is Douglas Bereuter (pronounced *BEEwriter*), a Republican first elected in 1978. His background is unusual for a Republican, or even a Democratic, politician: he was educated and made his living as a city and regional planner; he was a member of Nebraska's unicameral and nonpartisan legislature. Bereuter's voting record is generally conservative, but he focuses on legislating, which means cooperating with the majority Democrats. "I work as effectively with people across party lines as any Republican. I think I'm far less partisan than almost any member of any party." He is part of the Society of Statesman, a two-dozen-member group of nonconfrontational Republicans; he was the one Republican to vote against George Bush's capital gains tax cut in 1989. On the Foreign Affairs Committee, he works hard on foreign policy issues, particularly on encouraging exports. Nebraska is a major exporter of farm products, and Bereuter has written bills to facilitate such exports and has put pressure against other countries' agricultural subsidies; he played a part in the U.S. threat to retaliate against European oilseed subsidies, on which the Europeans finally agreed to compromise. On the Banking Committee, he is proud of the new Section 502 home-loan guarantees for low- and moderate-income homebuyers in small towns and rural areas. He has worked hard on Indian housing issues in several housing bills. With Nebraska Democrats and against 3d District Republican Bill Barrett, he worked on the Niobrara Wild and Scenic River bill. He helped write the flood control bill in a way to reduce incentives for building in inherently unsafe coastal and shoreline areas. He worked on getting $3.2 million for the Missouri River bridge at Niobrara and $1.6 million for a Lewis and Clark museum.

Bereuter has been reelected with solid percentages, 65% in 1990 and 60% in 1992. In early 1993, he was hinting he might run for senator or governor in 1994, but he has had opportunities to run statewide before and chose not to do so.

The People: Pop. 1990: 526,291; 39% rural; 15% age 65+; 96% White; 1% Black; 1% Amer. Indian; 1% Asian; 1% Other; 1% Hispanic origin. Voting age pop.: 389,907; 1% Black; 1% Hispanic origin. Households: 59% married couple families; 28% married couple fams. w. children; 46% college educ.; median household income: $25,763; per capita income: $12,088; median gross rent: $338; median house value: $49,700.

1992 Presidential Vote			**1988 Presidential Vote**		
Bush (R)	107,081	(43%)	Bush (R)	122,890	(56%)
Clinton (D)	80,696	(32%)	Dukakis (D)	96,015	(44%)
Perot (I)	59,974	(24%)			

Rep. Doug Bereuter (R)

Elected 1978; b. Oct. 6, 1939, York; home, Lincoln; U of NE, B.A. 1961, Harvard, M.C.P. 1966, M.P.A. 1973; Lutheran; married (Louise).

Career: Army, 1963–65; Urban planner, U.S. Dept. of HUD, 1965–66; Div. Dir., NE Econ. Devel. Dept., 1967–68; Dir., NE Office of Planning, 1968–70; NE Senate, 1974–78.

Offices: 2348 RHOB 20515, 202-225-4806. Also 1045 K St., Lincoln 68508, 402-438-1598; and 502 N. Broad St., Freemont 68025, 402-727-0888.

Committees: *Banking, Finance and Urban Affairs* (4th of 20 R): Consumer Credit and Insurance; Housing and Community Development; International Development, Finance, Trade and Monetary Policy (RMM). *Foreign Affairs* (7th of 18 R): Economic Policy, Trade and Environment; International Security, International Organizations and Human Rights (RMM). *Intelligence (Permanent Select)* (2d of 7 R): Oversight and Evaluation; Program and Budget Authorization.

Group Ratings

	ADA	ACLU	COPE	CDF	CFA	LCV	ACU	NTLC	NSI	COC	CEI
1992	20	23	33	30	47	25	79	70	90	88	61
1991	10	—	17	10	33	46	85	—	—	100	56

National Journal Ratings

	1991 LIB — 1991 CONS		1992 LIB — 1992 CONS	
Economic	12% —	86%	9% —	88%
Social	30% —	68%	28% —	71%
Foreign	26% —	70%	30% —	64%

Key Votes of the 102d Congress

1. Ban Striker Replace	AGN	5. Handgun Wait/7-Day	AGN	9. Use Force in Gulf	FOR
2. $ for Homeownership	FOR	6. Overseas Mil. Abortion	AGN	10. US Mil. Abroad $ Cut	AGN
3. Tax Rich/Cut Mid Cls.	AGN	7. Obscn. Art NEA $ Ban	FOR	11. Limit SDI Funds	AGN
4. FY93/$15B Def. Cut	AGN	8. Death Pen. from Jury	FOR	12. Cuba Trade Embargo	AGN

Key Votes of the 103d Congress

1. Family Leave	AGN	2. Deficit Reduction	AGN	3. Stimulus Plan	AGN

Election Results

1992 general	Doug Bereuter (R)	142,713	(60%)	($365,386)
	Gerry Finnegan (D)	96,309	(40%)	($84,533)
1992 primary	Doug Bereuter (R)	58,005	(99%)	
	Others	875	(1%)	
1990 general	Doug Bereuter (R)	129,654	(65%)	($223,898)
	Larry Hall (D)	70,587	(35%)	($65,064)

SECOND DISTRICT

Omaha, the commercial metropolis of Nebraska, the largest city on the Great Plains north of Kansas City and west of Minneapolis, the city that still produces one out of five American steaks, got its start from government: Abraham Lincoln picked it as the eastern terminus of the Union Pacific railroad, from which emerged the stockyards and livestock exchange that made it a top livestock town. Over the years, Omaha filled up with cattle hands from the West and European immigrants, especially Germans and Czechs; it developed fine civic institutions from the Joslyn Art Museum to the Ak-Sar-Ben (spell it backwards) Exhibition to its refurbished old theaters. Though a major city by the 1880s, Omaha has remained small enough (though famous on Wall Street as the place where Warren Buffett lives and works) to be readily comprehensible; you don't feel distant, physically or psychologically, from the other side of town, and you usually know people from a broader range of backgrounds than you would in a large homogeneous neighborhood within a big metropolitan area. The older, less affluent part of Omaha is near the river and Iowa; to the west, the city has been quietly booming, with affluent neighborhoods and new shopping areas. All over, Omaha's economy has been changing. It still has many processors of food products, like the hard-charging ConAgra company, and the giant Peter Kiewit construction firm; but it is also the nation's telecommunications center, handling 100 million '800' and '900' calls annually and employing 10,000 people in 24 telemarketing centers.

The 2d Congressional District of Nebraska is metropolitan Omaha: Douglas County with Omaha and its western suburbs; Sarpy County with suburbs to the south and the old Strategic Air Command headquarters at Offutt Air Force Base; and a sliver of Cass County just to the south. Politically, Omaha has long had a competitive politics, with Democrats strong on the south side around the stockyards and northeast, and Republicans strong in the area west of 72d Street; and the 2d District has been competitive more often than not over the last two decades.

The current congressman is Democrat Peter Hoagland, a former state legislator and lawyer from an old-line Omaha Republican family, who has won three seriously contested races, in the course of which his campaigns have spent almost $2.5 million and his three Republican opponents almost $2.2 million. Hoagland is a moderate with a middle-of-the-road stand on economics and more conservative views on foreign and defense issues, a supporter of the Gulf war resolution. He was a voice on the Banking Committee for higher capital requirements on S&Ls and tougher regulation of credit unions; when criticized for backing, with Republican Doug Bereuter, an amendment to allow limited partnerships (including one headed by a prominent Omaha businessman) to buy up ailing S&Ls, he rewrote it so that it was praised by the S&L's sternest critic, Iowa Republican Jim Leach. On the housing bill, Hoagland worked to increase funds for public housing, to make it easier to evict drug dealers, and to give incentives to owners of subsidized housing to continue renting to low-income tenants. With Omaha now hit by drugs, murders and Los Angeles gangs, Hoagland worked with state legislators to get federal funds for anti-drug programs and proposed legislation to establish boot camps for drug offenders. He backed some popular measures at home (the Niobrara Wild and Scenic River

Act) and took some risks on others (coming out early against high-stakes gambling across the Missouri in Council Bluffs, Iowa). He favors interstate branch banking and a targeted capital gains cut. Hoagland was the subject of the book *House Rules*, in which reporter Robert Cwiklik, after being granted insider access by Hoagland, criticized him for accommodating political realities and spending much time raising money for reelection. But such criticisms could be leveled against almost any incumbent in a marginal district. In effect, Cwiklik was complaining because Hoagland is competent at what he does.

Hoagland first won the seat in 1988, when Republican incumbent Hal Daub ran for the Senate. In the primary, he beat Cece Zorinsky, wife of former Omaha Mayor and Senator Edward Zorinsky who died in March 1987, by a 51%–44% margin, after she refused to debate. Hoagland won the general 51%–49%, although he was outspent by physician Jerry Schenken. He hit Hoagland for backing higher taxes and voting against tough crime laws; Hoagland hit Schenken for opposing plant closings and a waiting period for handgun purchases. In 1990, Hoagland had spirited opposition from former Senate staffer and Union Pacific Railroad lobbyist Ally Milder, who was hurt in September when Veterans' Affairs Secretary Ed Derwinski came to town and said, "These drug lords even use wetbacks to carry drugs across the borders," and undercut in October when Hoagland voted against the budget summit package. Hoagland won 58%–42%.

In 1992, Hoagland was opposed by another Republican who had lost his first primary, former Douglas County Attorney and bar owner Ron Staskiewicz. They aired some genuine differences on issues: Hoagland was for family and medical leave and gun control; Staskiewicz was against federal intervention to control healthcare costs while Hoagland favored standardizing forms and regulations to stop "the medical arms race." But much of the campaigning was more negative. Staskiewicz hit the congressional pay raise and House bank scandal, though Hoagland voted against the pay raise and had no overdrafts; Staskiewicz declined a no-new-taxes pledge. Staskiewicz was hurt by news reports of people being arrested outside his bar, Don't Drink the Water, which drew huge and uncontrollable crowds to its after hours dance club: "if we're concerned about gun control, you could do more by cleaning up your bar," Hoagland said in debate. Hoagland also attacked him for not paying $5,000 in debts incurred in the mid-1980s in South Dakota, and hit Staskiewicz for charging his campaign $21,000 for rent of a campaign headquarters above the bar. Hoagland spent $699,000 and Staskiewicz $378,000, and as George Bush was carrying the district Hoagland was barely reelected, 51%–49%; indeed, if one adds in the votes cast in former 2d District counties now in the 1st District, more were cast for Republicans (including popular 1st District incumbent Doug Bereuter) than Democrats. Hoagland is a hard-working, competent, personally attractive legislator, but there is every sign that this is likely to be a seriously contested district in 1994.

The People: Pop. 1990: 526,573; 6% rural; 10% age 65+; 86% White; 10% Black; 1% Amer. Indian; 1% Asian; 1% Other; 3% Hispanic origin. Voting age pop.: 379,295; 8% Black; 2% Hispanic origin. Households: 55% married couple families; 28% married couple fams. w. children; 56% college educ.; median household income: $30,889; per capita income: $14,322; median gross rent: $405; median house value: $60,700.

1992 Presidential Vote

Bush (R)	115,255	(47%)
Clinton (D)	78,701	(32%)
Perot (I)	48,657	(20%)

1988 Presidential Vote

Bush (R)	121,437	(58%)
Dukakis (D)	88,547	(42%)

Rep. Peter Hoagland (D)

Elected 1988; b. Nov. 17, 1941, Omaha; home, Omaha; Stanford, A.B. 1963, Yale, LL.B. 1968; Episcopalian; married (Barbara).

Career: Army, 1964–65; Practicing atty., 1968–88; NE Legislature, 1979–87.

Offices: 1113 LHOB, 20515, 202-225-4155. Also 8424 Zorinsky Fed. Bldg., 215 N. 17th St., Omaha 68102, 402-344-8701.

Committees: *Ways and Means* (19th of 24 D): Select Revenue Measures; Trade.

Group Ratings

	ADA	ACLU	COPE	CDF	CFA	LCV	ACU	NTLC	NSI	COC	CEI
1992	85	78	75	80	87	63	24	10	100	50	19
1991	50	—	83	80	50	85	15	—	—	10	24

National Journal Ratings

	1991 LIB —	1991 CONS	1992 LIB —	1992 CONS
Economic	56%	42%	62%	37%
Social	62%	37%	72%	24%
Foreign	56%	42%	44%	50%

Key Votes of the 102d Congress

1. Ban Striker Replace FOR	5. Handgun Wait/7-Day FOR	9. Use Force in Gulf FOR
2. $ for Homeownership AGN	6. Overseas Mil. Abortion FOR	10. US Mil. Abroad $ Cut AGN
3. Tax Rich/Cut Mid Cls. FOR	7. Obscn. Art NEA $ Ban FOR	11. Limit SDI Funds AGN
4. FY93/$15B Def. Cut FOR	8. Death Pen. from Jury AGN	12. Cuba Trade Embargo AGN

Key Votes of the 103d Congress

1. Family Leave FOR	2. Deficit Reduction FOR	3. Stimulus Plan FOR

Election Results

1992 general	Peter Hoagland (D)................	119,512	(51%)	($699,387)
	Ronald L. Staskiewicz (R)	113,828	(49%)	($378,721)
1992 primary	Peter Hoagland (D)................	42,825	(85%)	
	Jess M. Pritchett (D)	7,501	(15%)	
1990 general	Peter Hoagland (D)................	111,903	(58%)	($929,247)
	Ally Milder (R)......................	80,845	(42%)	($625,716)

THIRD DISTRICT

West of Grand Island, Nebraska is wheat and livestock country. For miles on end you can see nothing but rolling brown fields, sectioned off here and there by barbed wire fences, and in the distance a grain elevator towering over a tiny town and its miniature railroad depot. The winds and rain and tornadoes that come suddenly out of the sky remind you that the original settlers likened this part of the country to an ocean and thought themselves in their wooden wagons almost as helpless as passengers at sea in a wooden rowboat. Settlers passed through here on the

Oregon Trail in the 1840s, then set down roots in the 1880s, but the rain they hoped for fell too unreliably, and wheatlands gave way to pasture and open range. It is a beautiful but hard land, exacting much from its people, as the novels of western Nebraska's Willa Cather make poignantly clear.

The 3d Congressional District of Nebraska has 33% of its people spread out over 82% of its acreage. And the land is emptying out: except along the interstate, the 3d has been losing population for decades; these 66 counties had 608,000 people in 1940, 525,000 in 1990. Geographically and politically, the 3d District is where the Midwest becomes the West. It has a Farm Belt demand for subsidies and the West's angry opposition to federal interference. In presidential elections, it is perhaps more Republican than the Rockies: 67% for George Bush in 1988, and even in 1992, 49% for Bush, 27% for Ross Perot and only 23% for Bill Clinton. In congressional elections, it has long been Republican, but is seriously contested when an incumbent retires. Republican Virginia Smith won it only narrowly in 1974, then held it by wide margins; when she retired in 1990, it was the scene of another serious battle, with a narrow win for Republican Bill Barrett.

Barrett is a mainstream Nebraska Republican, a real estate and insurance man from the Platte River town of Lexington, who served in Nebraska's unicameral legislature for 12 years and as speaker for four. In 1990 he won the five-candidate Republican primary with 30%, running well in his home area and in the eastern end of the district, in the Lincoln media market. Democrat Sandra Scofield, a former Omaha professional who returned to her family farm and was elected to the legislature, hammered at Barrett for supporting Governor Kay Orr's 1987 tax package and for his antiabortion stand. Barrett charged that Scofield had missed the tax vote and, with vigorous campaigning from Smith, won what proved to be a friends-and-neighbors contest, losing most of the western area, and carrying his home area in the southern tier of counties, with 51% of the vote.

Barrett had an active first term, working on the Agriculture Committee promoting planting flexibility and helping first-time farmers, and pushing for rural health care and against the gas tax; he wrote amendments to prevent farm property from counting against student loan eligibility and reducing estate taxes on farms. He was president of the Republican freshman class in 1990 and was part of the six-member panel investigating the House post office. Following the usual pattern in this district, he was reelected in 1992 with 72% of the vote.

The People: Pop. 1990: 525,521; 56% rural; 18% age 65+; 96% White; 1% Amer. Indian; 1% Other; 3% Hispanic origin. Voting age pop.: 379,996; 2% Hispanic origin. Households: 62% married couple families; 29% married couple fams. w. children; 40% college educ.; median household income: $22,344; per capita income: $10,942; median gross rent: $284; median house value: $38,000.

1992 Presidential Vote

Bush (R) 121,342 (49%)
Perot (I).................... 65,473 (27%)
Clinton (D) 57,467 (23%)

1988 Presidential Vote

Bush (R) 153,629 (67%)
Dukakis (D)................ 74,673 (33%)

Rep. William (Bill) Barrett (R)

Elected 1990; b. Feb. 9, 1929, Lexington; home, Lexington; Hastings Col., B.A. 1951; Presbyterian; married (Elsie).

Career: Navy, 1951–52; Businessman, real estate and insurance, 1956–90; NE Legislature, 1978–90, Speaker, 1986–90.

Offices: 1213 LHOB 20515, 202-225-6435. Also 312 W. 3d St., Grand Island 68801, 308-381-5555; and 1502 2d Ave., #2, Scottsbluff 69361, 307-632-3333.

Committees: *Agriculture* (8th of 19 R): Department Operations and Nutrition; Environment, Credit and Rural Development; General Farm Commodities. *Education and Labor* (10th of 15 R): Human Resources; Labor-Management Relations; Select Education and Civil Rights. *House Administration* (5th of 7 R): Administrative Oversight; Libraries and Memorials (RMM); Office Systems. *Joint Committee on the Library* (4th of 5).

Group Ratings

	ADA	ACLU	COPE	CDF	CFA	LCV	ACU	NTLC	NSI	COC	CEI
1992	10	4	25	20	27	0	84	65	100	88	78
1991	0	—	8	10	33	0	89	—	—	90	73

National Journal Ratings

	1991 LIB — 1991 CONS			1992 LIB — 1992 CONS		
Economic	0%	—	96%	9%	—	88%
Social	0%	—	84%	0%	—	85%
Foreign	0%	—	88%	30%	—	64%

Key Votes of the 102d Congress

1. Ban Striker Replace	AGN	5. Handgun Wait/7-Day AGN	9. Use Force in Gulf	FOR
2. $ for Homeownership	FOR	6. Overseas Mil. AbortionAGN	10. US Mil. Abroad $ CutAGN
3. Tax Rich/Cut Mid Cls.AGN		7. Obscn. Art NEA $ Ban FOR	11. Limit SDI Funds	AGN
4. FY93/$15B Def. Cut	AGN	8. Death Pen. from Jury FOR	12. Cuba Trade Embargo AGN

Key Votes of the 103d Congress

1. Family Leave   AGN   2. Deficit Reduction   AGN   3. Stimulus Plan   AGN

Election Results

1992 general	William (Bill) Barrett (R)	170,857	(72%)	($487,992)
	Lowell Fisher (D)	67,457	(28%)	($91,170)
1992 primary	William (Bill) Barrett (R), unopposed			
1990 general	William (Bill) Barrett (R)	98,607	(51%)	($624,575)
	Sandra K. Scofield (D)	94,234	(49%)	($457,655)

NEVADA

Creating modern Nevada was a gamble, but there was little to lose and the odds were with the house. It was the early 1930s; there were only 91,000 Nevadans, many of them ancient denizens of mining ghost towns; the country was in Depression; the state government was about to go bankrupt. Nevada's vast riches—$500 million taken out of the Comstock Lode silver mine in the 20 years after 1859—were long gone. So Nevada reduced its residency requirement for divorce to six weeks and legalized gambling. Catering to what most Americans considered sin—casinos, pawnshops, divorce mills, quick wedding chapels, even legal brothels—has turned out to be good business. Nevada has been America's fastest growing state since 1960; in the 1980s its population rose 50%, from 800,000 to 1.2 million, adding 6,000 new residents every week; from April 1990 to July 1992, it added another 125,000, growing 10% in just two years.

Las Vegas, a mere spot on the map when gambling was legalized, is now a metro area of 925,000 and Reno, in the 1940s the divorce capital of America, has 250,000. Gaming—the Nevada word for gambling—generates most of this growth: Las Vegas's 22 million tourists spend $14 billion a year, Reno's five million spend almost $4 billion; almost half Nevada's jobs are in services some way related to gambling or tourism. The 6.4% gambling receipts tax generates enough revenue so that Nevada has no income, corporate or inheritance tax, and the cost of living is low; half the houses in Las Vegas are valued at under $100,000 and many migrants from California can not find a house that costs as much as the one they sold. Nevada's growth slowed just a bit during the early 1990s recession, and individual operators sometimes go under. But the new 3,000-room Mirage and 4,000-room Excalibur hotels have been attracting such non-racy crowds as the American Booksellers and Southern Baptist conventions, while providing attractions that new gambling operations elsewhere can't match. The longer term problems are those of growth: Las Vegas is gobbling up water to keep all those lawns, golf courses and waterfalls moist, just yards away from the bleakest desert in North America.

From mining to gaming, Nevada has been a second chance state, a place for outcasts and losers from the outer world to recoup. The four owners of the Comstock Lode—MacKay, Fair, Flood, O'Brien—were Irishmen; the first big hotel on the Las Vegas strip, the Flamingo, was built in 1946 by Jewish gangster Bugsy Siegel, later gunned down in his Beverly Hills home; most of the big casinos were owned by mobsters until Howard Hughes—a different kind of outcast—bought them up in the late 1960s. Nearly one out of six adults here is divorced or separated—the highest rate in the nation. Nevada today strives for respectability, pointing out that its casinos are now owned by publicly traded companies—Hilton is probably the state's largest private employer. Its low taxes have also made it a regional distribution and credit card operations center. There is still some mining, a little gold and silver, plus less glamorous diatomaceous earth, used for swimming pool filters and kitty litter. But even where there is growth—the sudden rise of Laughlin as a big casino center on the Colorado River (some 15,000 people live in the Pahrump Valley)—there is still a Wild West atmosphere.

Nevada has had a volatile politics of late. Historically, it was Democratic, sending politically shrewd Democrats to Washington to protect the interests of a state always heavily dependent on the federal government. The most powerful were Key Pittman, chairman of the Senate Foreign Relations Committee, who backed FDR's foreign policy only after Roosevelt agreed to buy absurdly large amounts of silver, and penny-pinching Pat McCarran, author of the repressive McCarran Act, who shamelessly pushed aid for Reno and Las Vegas (the airport there is named for him) and became suddenly solicitous of civil liberties when mobsters and casino owners were called to testify before the Kefauver committee investigating crime and racketeering. But in the 1980s, Nevada trended sharply Republican, primarily because of its newcomers. This came not

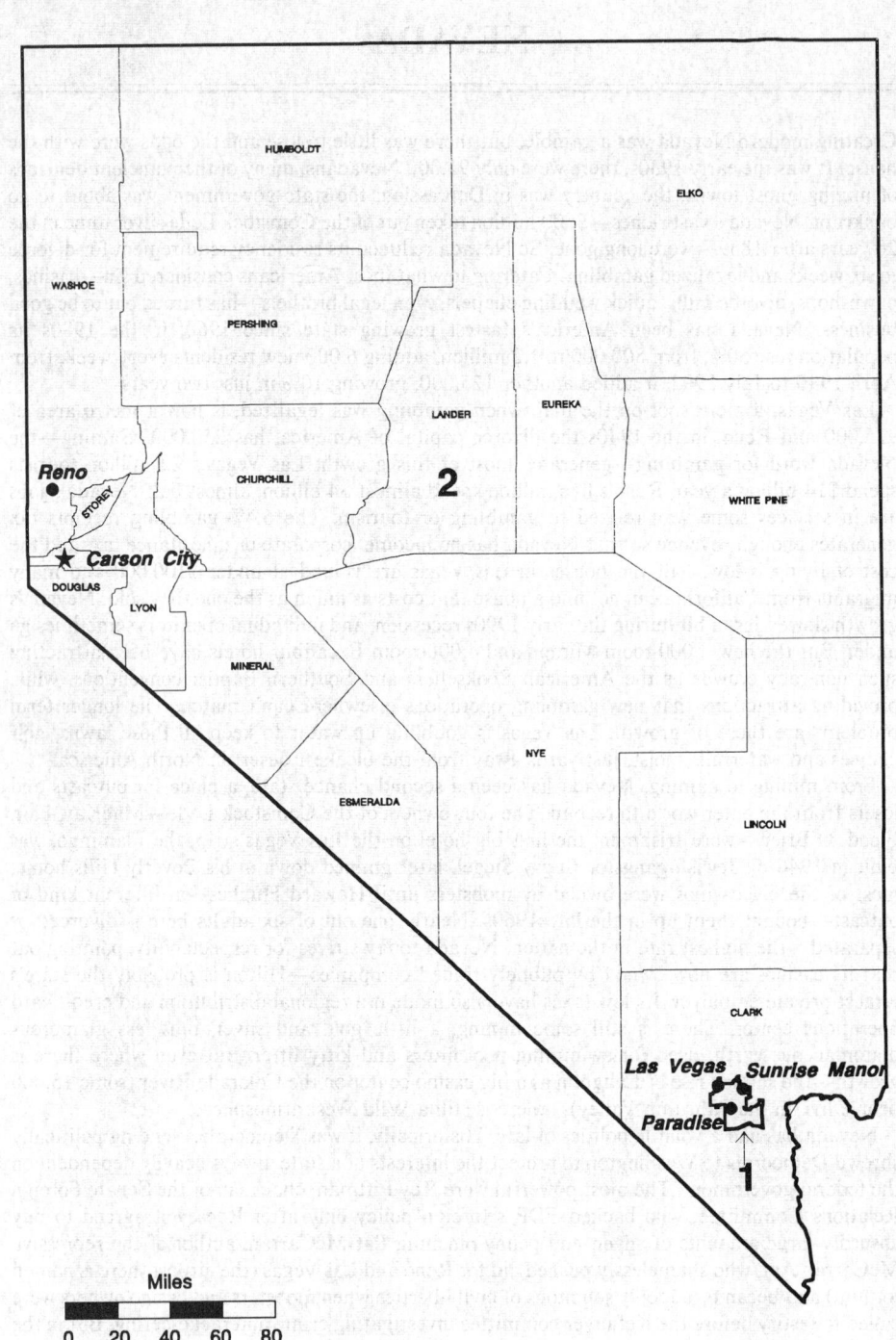

Miles

0   20   40   60   80

out of devotion to family values, for Nevada is the least family-oriented state, with the nation's largest percentage of non-family households. Nevada's conservatism comes from a population who thinks it is sharper than others, has a special angle, is always a step ahead of the market, that they can and will beat the odds. In 1992, evidently, the odds shifted. The Democrats ran a crackerjack registration drive in Las Vegas's Clark County, where turnout rose 56% from 1988 and which Bill Clinton carried 40%–32% and Senator Harry Reid carried 55%–36%. The Democrats hold three of Nevada's four seats in Congress and a big margin in the state Assembly; but Republicans control the state Senate 11–10, after winning one race by 32 votes. Nevada may be vastly more populous than it used to be, but a few votes can still make a difference.

Politics can also make a difference, Nevadans have discovered, as they worry over the federal government's choice of Yucca Mountain, at the edge of the old Yucca Flats nuclear test site, as the nation's single high-level nuclear waste disposal site. This "Screw Nevada" law, as it is known locally, passed on the last day of the session in 1987, when Nevada was politically weak: Harry Reid was in his first year in the Senate, his colleague Chic Hecht seemed headed for sure defeat, and the House delegation had little seniority. The plan is to bury the waste deep within the mountain, 1,000 feet above the water table, in reinforced steel containers in a 1,400-acre maze of storage tunnels, where they will rest undisturbed for presumably eternity, in all likelihood safe from contact with water. Nevada opinion is strongly opposed and Nevadans in Congress have tried to stop it. The state delayed issuing drilling permits for the Energy Department to make necessary tests, and Senators Harry Reid and Richard Bryan threatened to filibuster the energy bill if it preempted state regulations. But the Nevada delegation didn't have the votes and in March 1992 Governor Bob Miller reluctantly issued permits for the studies. Congresswoman Barbara Vucanovich tried to block federal preemption in the Natural Resources Committee, while Bryan held up the appointment of Deputy Energy Secretary Linda Stuntz to put pressure on DOE. With Reid and Bryan threatening to block the energy bill, Energy and Natural Resources Chairman Bennett Johnston promised them he would keep federal preemption out of the bill in conference committee, though House Energy and Commerce Chairman John Dingell, angry at Bryan's push for higher mileage standards on U.S.-made cars, insisted on including it. Johnston agreed instead to a National Academy of Sciences study of the site, on which EPA would issue new radiation disposal standards. At the end of session in October 1992, Vucanovich tried to strip that language also from the energy bill, and lost 323–102; Reid and Bryan tried to filibuster but lost 84–8. "We face this every time there is an opportunity to screw Nevada, there is an appetite to do so," Bryan said, but added, "I remain confident we will not have a nuclear waste dump at Yucca Mountain." At the earliest the depository won't be ready until 2010; given the slow pace of government, and the likelihood of continued resistance from a Nevada delegation growing in seniority, it may not ever be.

Governor. Nevada Governor Bob Miller's biography tracks much of the state's recent history. His father, Ross Miller, was a bookmaker in Chicago and owner of the Slots-A-Fun casino in Las Vegas. Bob Miller was elected Las Vegas district attorney—a delicate position indeed—in 1978 and reelected in 1982; charges were made against him but nothing came close to sticking; he was elected lieutenant governor in 1986 and became governor after Richard Bryan was elected senator in 1988. If Miller represents a second generation in Nevada public life—knowledgeable about the gaming industry, but utterly clean ethically—he has been concerned with a second generation of issues: improving public education, reforming workmen's compensation and welfare; with a rising population, new schools must be built, and the workmen's compensation fund has been bankrupt for some time. Despite Nevada's robust growth, Miller had to cut spending sharply in 1991 and recommended few increases in 1993. He called for no new taxes and group health insurance to help small businesses, and warned that, given the proliferation of gambling elsewhere in the country, Nevada cannot necessarily count on that for continued growth. And of course he has tried to stop the nuclear waste depository in Yucca Mountain, holding up permits for federal testing until March 1992, and continuing to oppose it thereafter.

Miller was elected to a full term by a robust margin in 1990, and saw Nevada Democrats do well, except in the state Senate, in 1992. He has been ruled eligible for a second full term by the state attorney general, but Republicans say they will challenge the ruling. If Miller does decide to run in 1994, he will likely be a strong candidate but should expect spirited GOP opposition from either Lieutenant Governor Sue Ellen Wagner or Secretary of State Cheryl Lau.

Senators. Senator Harry Reid, who has held high office in Nevada for most of the last 25 years, looks mild-mannered but has proved he can be tough. He was elected lieutenant governor in 1970, came within 624 votes of beating Paul Laxalt in the 1974 Senate race, lost for Las Vegas mayor in 1976, and then became head of the Gaming Commission from 1977 to 1981—as sensitive a post as any in Nevada. When Jim Santini, then a Democratic congressman, ran for the Senate, Reid ran for the new 1st District seat that covers most of Las Vegas and its suburbs—the 1980 Census had given Nevada a second district for the first time—and won in 1982 and 1984. When Laxalt retired, Reid ran for the Senate again; his opponent turned out to be Santini, who had opportunistically switched parties at the last minute and ran as a Republican. Reid's ads depicted him as David to Santini's Goliath, and he won 50%–45%.

On many national issues, Reid tends toward the more conservative side of Senate Democrats. He is antiabortion and was the first Democratic senator to support President Bush on the Gulf war resolution. He was prepared to vote for the Clarence Thomas nomination but changed his mind after the testimony of Anita Hill. At the same time, he has long been an ally of organized labor, which is strong in Las Vegas. On Nevada issues, Reid's greatest success came in 1990 when he produced an agreement on water allocation, from Lake Tahoe and the Truckee River, between Nevada and California. Reid persevered through two years of negotiations, getting the Pyramid Lake Paiute Indians to agree to return their fisheries to the state for $25 million, plus $40 million in economic aid. He has been less successful on stopping the Yucca Mountain nuclear waste depository. He pushed through a Nevada Wilderness Protection Act in 1990, over the objections of Republican Barbara Vucanovich; he has managed to stop a moratorium on all mining claims, but at the price of accepting higher fees for those making claims, and worked to stop increases in grazing fees as well. He pushed through an amendment in the 1992 tax bill prohibiting states from taxing pension income of non-residents.

In 1992, Reid looked to be an easy winner when Republican Brian McKay passed up the race. But in the September primary, Reid was pressed by Charles Woods, a businessman seriously scarred in World War II, who had run for governor of Alabama and other offices there in the 1960s and 70s. Woods's TV ads helped him win 39% to only 53% for Reid, who lost most of the Cow Counties (counties outside Las Vegas and Reno). In the general, Republicans had hopes that rancher Demar Dahl could win an upset. But Reid won 51%–40%, and came out of it feistier than ever. Back in Washington, Reid moved to phase out the Special Committee on Aging chaired by Bill Clinton's best friend in the Senate, David Pryor, but lost 43–56 (but then Reid has opposed another presidential best friend before—Paul Laxalt). When Ross Perot appeared before the Joint Committee on the Organization of Congress, Reid admonished him, "I think you should start checking your facts a little more and stop listening to the applause as much." As chairman of the Appropriations Legislative Branch Subcommittee, he promised to cut congressional administrative spending 14% by 1997, but strongly opposed proposals to do away with the Appropriations Committee altogether. In a Senate not Democratic by a wide margin, Reid remains a vital and much sought-after vote for the Clinton Administration.

Senator Richard Bryan has been a statewide figure for more than a decade: elected attorney general in 1978, governor in 1982 and 1986, then senator in 1988 by beating malapropism-prone Republican incumbent Chic Hecht, 50%–46%. Bryan attacked Hecht for not fighting hard enough against the nuclear waste disposal site designation; Hecht attacked Bryan for creating zero-population Bullfrog County around the site (it was thrown out by the state Supreme Court) and because Michael Dukakis supported putting the site in Nevada.

Bryan's number one cause in the Senate (after the Yucca Mountain waste disposal site, of course) has been CAFE—increasing the Corporate Average Fuel Economy standards. For the big U.S. automakers, that would mean an increase to 40 miles per gallon on fuel economy standards by the year 2001; foreign manufacturers, because they already get higher mileage, would have to improve even more. Automakers argue, as they did in 1974 against the original CAFE, that the goal is technologically impossible without building smaller, less safe cars; Bryan says the measure will summon up creative responses, as it did before. Bryan has not succeeded: his CAFE bill lost on the Senate floor in September 1990, passed the Commerce Committee in March 1991 but was not included in the 1992 Comprehensive Energy Act. It did incur, however, the wrath of House Energy and Commerce Chairman John Dingell, who said that the siting of a "high-level repository of nuclear waste," i.e., the Yucca Mountain depository, "has greatly elevated in importance from my viewpoint in light of the great interest shown by the junior senator from Nevada in increasing CAFE standards." On another local issue, Bryan has fought against massive rewriting of the Mining Act of 1872, so far with success. Other Bryan causes include a bill protecting consumers against unfair credit reports and successful opposition to a NASA appropriation for investigating the possibility of extraterrestrial life.

On many issues, Bryan's moderate stance makes him a crucial vote in the Senate: he was for the Gulf war resolution and, after Anita Hill's testimony, against the Clarence Thomas nomination. Much of his energy in the 103d Congress is likely to be spent on the Ethics Committee which he now chairs. He accepted the assignment with some reluctance, but his record suggests that he should be a stickler for propriety, and willing to risk the anger of his colleagues. He will also be running for reelection, and by mid-1993 had no strong opponent. Nevada's Democratic trend must be heartening for him; but there are no sure things in such a fast-changing state.

Presidential politics. In the 1940s, Nevada was a Democratic state; in the 1960s, it was divided much as the nation was, voting narrowly for John Kennedy in 1960 and Richard Nixon in 1968. In the 1980s, it was heavily Republican, over 60% for Ronald Reagan and 59%–38% for George Bush in 1988. In 1992, it surprised just about everyone, including strategists for both candidates, by voting for Bill Clinton. But he won only a 37%–35% margin, with a thumping 26% for Ross Perot. Nevada at one time had a presidential primary, predictably ignored by the candidates, but now has caucuses.

Congressional districting. With a population increase of 50%, Nevada was the fastest growing state in the nation during the 1980s. It did not gain another seat, however, and the district lines were marginally redrawn, with little political effect.

The People: Est. Pop. 1992: 1,327,000; Pop. 1990: 1,201,833, up 9.4% 1990–1992. 0.5% of U.S. total, 39th largest; 12% rural. Median age: 33.3 years. 10.6% 65 years and over. 84.3% White, 10.4% Hispanic origin, 6.6% Black, 3.2% Asian, 1.6% American Indian, 4.4% Other. Households: 51.4% married couple families; 23% married couple fams. w. children; 47% college educ.; median household income: $31,011; per capita income: $15,214; 54.8% owner occupied housing; median house value: $95,700; median monthly rent: $445. 6.6% Unemployment. Voting age pop.: 904,885. Registered voters (1992): 649,905; 295,111 D (45%), 255,897 R (39%), 98,897 unaffiliated and minor parties (15%).

Political Lineup: Governor, Bob Miller (D); Lt. Gov., Sue Wagner (R); Secy. of State, Cheryl A. Lau (R); Atty. Gen., Frankie Sue Del Papa (D); Treasurer, Robert L. Seale (R); Controller, Darrell Daines (R). State Senate, 21 (11 R and 10 D); State Assembly, 42 (29 D and 13 R). Senators, Harry Reid (D) and Richard H. Bryan (D). Representatives, 2 (1 D and 1 R).

1992 Presidential Vote

Clinton (D)	189,148	(37%)
Bush (R)	175,828	(35%)
Perot (I)	132,580	(26%)

1988 Presidential Vote

Bush (R)	206,040	(59%)
Dukakis (D)	132,738	(38%)

GOVERNOR
Gov. Bob Miller (D)

Assumed office Jan. 1989, term expires Jan. 1995; b. Mar. 30, 1945, Chicago, IL; home, Carson City; U. of Santa Clara, B.A. 1967, Loyola U. Law Schl., J.D. 1971; Catholic; married (Sandy).

Career: Practicing atty., 1971–87; Clark Cnty. Dep. Dist. Atty., 1971–73; Legal advisor, Las Vegas Metro. Police Dept., 1973–75; Justice of the Peace, Las Vegas Township, 1975–78; Clark Cnty. Dist. Atty., 1979–86; NV Lt. Gov., 1987–88; Chmn., Western Govs. Assn., 1992–present.

Office: Executive Chambers, Capitol Bldg., Carson City 89710, 702-687-5670.

Election Results

1990 gen.	Bob Miller (D)	207,878	(66%)
	Jim Gallaway (R)	95,789	(31%)
	Other	8,984	(3%)
1990 prim.	Bob Miller (D)	71,537	(81%)
	Other	16,760	(19%)
1986 gen.	Richard H. Bryan (D)	187,268	(72%)
	Patty Cafferata (R)	65,081	(25%)

SENATORS
Sen. Harry Reid (D)

Elected 1986, seat up 1998; b. Dec. 2, 1939, Searchlight; home, Searchlight; Southern UT St. Col., A.S. 1959; UT St. U., B.S. 1961, George Washington U., J.D. 1964; U. of NV, 1969–70; Mormon; married (Landra).

Career: Practicing atty., 1969–82; Henderson City Atty., 1964–66; NV Assembly, 1969–70; NV Lt. Gov., 1970–74; Chmn., NV Gaming Comm., 1977–81; U.S. House of Reps., 1982–86.

Offices: 324 HSOB 20510, 202-224-3542. Also 245 E. Liberty St., #102, Reno 89501, 702-784-5568; 500 E. Charleston Blvd., Las Vegas 89104, 702-474-0041; and 600 E. Williams St., #302, Carson City 89701, 702-882-7343.

Committees: *Aging (Special)* (7th of 11 D). *Appropriations* (12th of 16 D): Energy and Water Development; Interior; Labor, Health and Human Services, Education; Legislative Branch (Chmn.); Military Construction. *Environment and Public Works* (5th of 10 D): Clean Water, Fisheries and Wildlife; Toxic Substances, Research and Development (Chmn.); Water Resources, Transportation, Public Buildings and Economic Development. *Indian Affairs* (5th of 10 D). *Joint Committee on the Organization of Congress* (4th of 12).

Group Ratings

	ADA	ACLU	CDF	COPE	CFA	LCV	ACU	NTLC	NSI	COC	CEI
1992	80	45	70	73	75	67	23	22	70	10	25
1991	65	—	91	92	72	53	33	—	—	10	36

National Journal Ratings

	1991 LIB — 1991 CONS	1992 LIB — 1992 CONS
Economic	46% — 50%	68% — 31%
Social	35% — 63%	38% — 61%
Foreign	58% — 41%	65% — 26%

Key Votes of the 102d Congress

1. $ for Homeownership AGN	5. Clarence Thomas Nom. AGN	9. Use Force in Gulf FOR
2. Have Cap Gains Debate AGN	6. Lmt Death Row Appeal FOR	10. Keep Salvador Aid AGN
3. Remove Budget Walls FOR	7. Handgun Wait/5-Day FOR	11. Cut $1B from SDI FOR
4. Ban Striker Replace FOR	8. Abortion Gag Rule FOR	12. Override China MFN FOR

Key Votes of the 103d Congress

1. Family Leave FOR	2. HIV Immigrants AGN	3. Clinton Budget FOR

Election Results

1992 general	Harry Reid (D).....................	253,150	(51%)	($3,259,802)
	Demar Dahl (R)....................	199,413	(40%)	($471,371)
	Others	43,333	(9%)	
1992 primary	Harry Reid (D).....................	64,828	(53%)	
	Charles Woods (D).................	48,364	(39%)	
	Others	9,551	(8%)	
1986 general	Harry Reid (D).....................	130,955	(50%)	($2,055,756)
	Jim Santini (R).....................	116,606	(45%)	($2,656,747)
	Others	14,271	(5%)	

Sen. Richard H. Bryan (D)

Elected 1988, seat up 1994; b. July 16, 1937, Washington, D.C.; home, Carson City; U. of NV, B.A. 1959, U. of CA, Hastings Col. of Law., LL.B. 1963; Episcopalian; married (Bonnie).

Career: Army, 1959–60; Clark Cnty. Dep. Dist. Atty., 1964–66; Clark Cnty. Public Defender, 1966–68; Cnsl., Clark Cnty. Juvenile Court, 1968–69; NV Assembly, 1968–72; NV Senate, 1972–78; NV Atty. Gen., 1978–82; NV Gov., 1982–1988.

Offices: 364 RSOB 20510, 202-224-6244. Also 300 Las Vegas Blvd. S., #1110, Las Vegas 89101, 702-388-6605; 300 Booth St., #2014, Reno 89509, 702-784-5007; and 600 E. William St., #304, Carson City 89701, 702-885-9111.

Committees: *Banking, Housing and Urban Affairs* (7th of 11 D): Economic Stabilization and Rural Development; Housing and Urban Affairs; Securities. *Commerce, Science and Transportation* (8th of 11 D): Aviation; Consumer (Chmn.); Foreign Commerce and Tourism; Science, Technology and Space. *Ethics (Select)* (Chmn. of 3 D). *Intelligence (Select)* (5th of 9 D). *Joint Economic Committee* (4th of 10).

Group Ratings

	ADA	ACLU	CDF	COPE	CFA	LCV	ACU	NTLC	NSI	COC	CEI
1992	80	68	80	67	83	67	19	28	70	10	27
1991	70	—	91	83	67	67	38	—	—	20	38

National Journal Ratings

	1991 LIB — 1991 CONS			1992 LIB — 1992 CONS		
Economic	66%	—	31%	61%	—	37%
Social	57%	—	41%	57%	—	42%
Foreign	63%	—	33%	65%	—	26%

Key Votes of the 102d Congress

1. $ for Homeownership	AGN	5. Clarence Thomas Nom.	AGN	9. Use Force in Gulf	FOR
2. Have Cap Gains Debate	AGN	6. Lmt Death Row Appeal	AGN	10. Keep Salvador Aid	AGN
3. Remove Budget Walls	FOR	7. Handgun Wait/5-Day	FOR	11. Cut $1B from SDI	FOR
4. Ban Striker Replace	FOR	8. Abortion Gag Rule	AGN	12. Override China MFN	FOR

Key Votes of the 103d Congress

1. Family Leave	FOR	2. HIV Immigrants	AGN	3. Clinton Budget	FOR

Election Results

1988 general	Richard H. Bryan (D)	175,548	(50%)	($2,957,789)
	Jacob (Chic) Hecht (R)	161,336	(46%)	($3,007,864)
	Others	12,765	(4%)	
1988 primary	Richard H. Bryan (D)	62,278	(79%)	
	Patrick Fitzpatrick (D)	4,721	(6%)	
	Others	11,346	(14%)	
1982 general	Jacob (Chic) Hecht (R)	120,377	(50%)	($1,657,070)
	Howard W. Cannon (D)	114,720	(48%)	($1,592,094)

FIRST DISTRICT

Nevada's congressional districts vastly differ in physical size; the 1st consists of the greater part of Las Vegas and its close-in suburbs; the 2d is the whole rest of the state. The 1st, something like a nervously drawn circle in the center of Clark County, takes in all of Las Vegas, most of Henderson, part of North Las Vegas and just a bit of the Las Vegas Colony Indian Reservation—.2% of the state's land mass when you add it all up. It is also the most Democratic part of the state.

Congressman James Bilbray is a Democrat from a well-connected Las Vegas family (his father was Clark County assessor). A state legislator for six years, he made a second attempt (the first was in 1972) for the House in 1986 when Harry Reid left the 1st to run for the Senate. Reid won and so did Bilbray, 54%–44%. Mostly quiet on national issues, Bilbray has made a record on local matters. Using his seat on Armed Services, he has worked to get new facilities and projects for Nellis Air Force Base. He backed the 1990 Nevada Wilderness Act and sponsored the Red Rock National Conservation Act; he wants to create a Spring Mountains National Recreation Area. Of course, he has vehemently opposed the nuclear waste disposal site at Yucca Mountain.

On national issues, Bilbray votes near the ideological midpoint in the House. He supported the Gulf war resolution as well as several challenged weapons systems, and recently joined the moderate Democratic Leadership Council. He has switched from opposing to supporting federal abortion funding, a decision he says he made after discussion with his family. In 1992, he was opposed by retired Air Force General Coy Pettyjohn; with a big Democratic registration drive, Bilbray won 58%–38%. Without any higher office to run for, he seems well ensconced in the House.

The People: Pop. 1990: 601,042; 11% age 65+; 73% White; 10% Black; 1% Amer. Indian; 4% Asian; 5% Other; 12% Hispanic origin. Voting age pop.: 457,378; 9% Black; 11% Hispanic origin. Households:

49% married couple families; 21% married couple fams. w. children; 44% college educ.; median household income: $29,611; per capita income: $14,837; median gross rent: $505; median house value: $88,900.

1992 Presidential Vote

Clinton (D) 98,700 (43%)
Bush (R) 70,440 (31%)
Perot (I). 55,964 (24%)

1988 Presidential Vote

Bush (R) 86,736 (56%)
Dukakis (D). 67,413 (44%)

Rep. James H. Bilbray (D)

Elected 1986; b. May 19, 1938, Las Vegas; home, Las Vegas; U. of NV at Las Vegas, B.A. 1962, American U., J.D. 1964; Catholic; married (Michaelene).

Career: Army, 1955–56, Reserves, 1957–60; U. of NV Regent, 1968–72; Clark Cnty. Dep. Dist. Atty., 1964–68; Practicing atty., 1968–86; Las Vegas Municipal Judge, 1978–80; NV Senate, 1980–86.

Offices: 2431 RHOB 20515, 202-225-5965. Also 1785 E. Sahara Ave., Las Vegas 89104, 702-792-2424; and 240 Water St., Henderson 89015, 702-565-4788.

Committees: *Armed Services* (16th of 34 D): Military Forces and Personnel; Military Installations and Facilities; Research and Technology. *Intelligence (Permanent Select)* (8th of 12 D): Legislation; Program and Budget Authorization. *Small Business* (8th of 27 D): Procurement, Taxation and Tourism (Chmn.); Regulation, Business Opportunities and Technology.

Group Ratings

	ADA	ACLU	COPE	CDF	CFA	LCV	ACU	NTLC	NSI	COC	CEI
1992	70	57	75	70	67	56	33	5	100	63	22
1991	35	—	100	90	78	54	40	—	—	20	13

National Journal Ratings

	1991 LIB — 1991 CONS		1992 LIB — 1992 CONS	
Economic	83%	— 16%	59%	— 40%
Social	42%	— 58%	52%	— 48%
Foreign	51%	— 46%	38%	— 56%

Key Votes of the 102d Congress

1. Ban Striker Replace	FOR	5. Handgun Wait/7-Day AGN	9. Use Force in Gulf	FOR
2. $ for Homeownership	AGN	6. Overseas Mil. Abortion AGN	10. US Mil. Abroad $ Cut AGN
3. Tax Rich/Cut Mid Cls.	FOR	7. Obscn. Art NEA $ Ban FOR	11. Limit SDI Funds	AGN
4. FY93/$15B Def. Cut	FOR	8. Death Pen. from Jury FOR	12. Cuba Trade Embargo FOR

Key Votes of the 103d Congress

1. Family Leave	FOR	2. Deficit Reduction	FOR	3. Stimulus Plan	FOR

Election Results

1992 general	James H. Bilbray (D)	128,278	(58%)	($667,018)
	J. Coy Pettyjohn (R)	84,217	(38%)	($113,776)
	Scott A. Kjar (LIB)	8,993	(4%)	
1992 primary	James H. Bilbray (D), unopposed			
1990 general	James H. Bilbray (D)	84,650	(61%)	($705,037)
	Bob Dickinson (R)	47,377	(34%)	($149,778)
	William Moore (LIB)	5,825	(4%)	

SECOND DISTRICT

The 2d District is the more Republican of Nevada's two districts, and includes 99.8% of the state's land area. Reno, a smaller and more gracious gambling metropolis than Las Vegas, set amid wooded mountains and with a somewhat diversified economy, is the 2d's largest city, but 26% of the district's votes are cast in Las Vegas suburbs.

Representative Barbara Vucanovich, first elected in 1982, is the only Republican in the Nevada delegation. Widowed in her forties, she owned a speed reading school and a travel agency while raising five children. The daughter of a Catholic Democrat who was New York state's chief engineer under Al Smith and FDR, she has one of the most conservative voting records in Congress. She has some affirmative causes, the most prominent of which is breast cancer research and prevention, which she has pushed with some success. Vucanovich serves on both the Appropriations and Natural Resources Committees, and is ranking Republican on subcommittees overseeing military construction and mining, both of clear importance to her district. It is on the latter that she has been most active. She strongly opposed Mining and Natural Resources Subcommittee Chairman Nick Joe Rahall's rewrite of the Mining Act of 1872, which she thought favored eastern coal; she proposed 150 amendments to stall its passage, and indeed it lapsed unpassed at the end of the 102d Congress. She sharply opposed Bill Clinton's proposed 12.5% gross royalty on mining and invited him to Elko to see mining operations; cornering him at a meeting she asked if 12.5% was his final decision ("Well, I don't know yet," was his response). She also fought hard against the Yucca Mountain nuclear waste depository. She is not always effective—the 1990 Nevada Wilderness Act was passed over her opposition—but she keeps on fighting.

Vucanovich had serious opposition in 1992 from Reno Mayor Pete Sferrazza, who had to hustle in the Democratic primary to beat a teacher who carried the Las Vegas area. Sferrazza campaigned against the congressional pay raise and against Vucanovich's opposition to abortion. Vucanovich only narrowly carried the Las Vegas area (48%–46%) and Reno's Washoe County (44.8%–44.6%); her big margin in the Cow Counties (52%–40%) gave her only a 48%–43% victory. That suggests she may have serious opposition in the future.

The People: Pop. 1990: 600,791; 23% rural; 10% age 65+; 84% White; 3% Black; 3% Amer. Indian; 3% Asian; 3% Other; 8% Hispanic origin. Voting age pop.: 449,696; 2% Black; 7% Hispanic origin. Households: 56% married couple families; 26% married couple fams. w. children; 51% college educ.; median household income: $32,413; per capita income: $15,592; median gross rent: $515; median house value: $103,900.

1992 Presidential Vote

Bush (R)	105,388	(38%)
Clinton (D)	90,448	(33%)
Perot (I)	76,616	(28%)

1988 Presidential Vote

Bush (R)	119,304	(65%)
Dukakis (D)	65,325	(35%)

Rep. Barbara F. Vucanovich (R)

Elected 1982; b. June 22, 1921, Camp Dix, NJ; home, Reno; Manhattanville Col., 1938–39; Catholic; married (George).

Career: NV franchise owner, Evelyn Wood Speed Reading Co., 1964–68; Owner, travel agcy., 1968–74; Dist. Rep., U.S. Sen. Paul Laxalt, 1974–81.

Offices: 2202 RHOB 20515, 202-225-6155. Also 300 Booth St., Reno 89509, 702-784-5003; 700 Idaho St., Elko 89801, 702-738-4064; and 6900 Westcliff St., #509, Las Vegas 89128, 702-255-6470.

Committees: *Appropriations* (14th of 23 R): Agriculture, Rural Development, Food and Drug Administration and Related Agencies; Military Construction (RMM). *Natural Resources* (3d of 15 R): Energy and Mineral Resources (RMM); Insular and International Affairs; Oversight and Investigations.

Group Ratings

	ADA	ACLU	COPE	CDF	CFA	LCV	ACU	NTLC	NSI	COC	CEI
1992	5	9	17	20	20	19	96	90	100	75	68
1991	0	—	9	30	22	0	100	—	—	78	66

National Journal Ratings

	1991 LIB — 1991 CONS	1992 LIB — 1992 CONS
Economic	10% — 90%	0% — 91%
Social	0% — 84%	16% — 82%
Foreign	12% — 85%	0% — 82%

Key Votes of the 102d Congress

1. Ban Striker Replace AGN	5. Handgun Wait/7-Day AGN	9. Use Force in Gulf FOR
2. $ for Homeownership FOR	6. Overseas Mil. Abortion AGN	10. US Mil. Abroad $ Cut AGN
3. Tax Rich/Cut Mid Cls. AGN	7. Obscn. Art NEA $ Ban FOR	11. Limit SDI Funds AGN
4. FY93/$15B Def. Cut AGN	8. Death Pen. from Jury FOR	12. Cuba Trade Embargo FOR

Key Votes of the 103d Congress

1. Family Leave AGN	2. Deficit Reduction AGN	3. Stimulus Plan AGN

Election Results

1992 general	Barbara F. Vucanovich (R)	129,575	(48%)	($688,379)
	Pete Sferrazza (D)	117,198	(43%)	($202,888)
	Daniel M. Hansen (IA)	13,285	(5%)	($17,015)
	Two Others	10,522	(4%)	
1992 primary	Barbara F. Vucanovich (R)	45,792	(69%)	
	Don Hensley (R)	9,843	(15%)	
	Dick Baker (R)	5,697	(9%)	
	Terry L. Flower (R)	4,583	(7%)	
1990 general	Barbara F. Vucanovich (R)	103,508	(59%)	($441,075)
	Jane Wisdom (D)	59,581	(34%)	($41,287)
	Dan Becan (LIB)	12,120	(7%)	

NEW HAMPSHIRE

New Hampshire, with four-tenths of 1% of the nation's population, in an odd corner of the country and with some of its most unusual public policies, has nonetheless set the nation's political course over the last two decades. The mechanism of this influence is New Hampshire's first-in-the-nation presidential primary, a device specifically sanctioned by the Democratic rules reformers of the 1970s which did much to defeat the Democratic presidential candidates of the 1980s. For good reason, George Bush ended his victory speech in November 1988 by saying, "Thank you, New Hampshire." But by 1992, he too was in political trouble here, and his rather narrow primary victory over Pat Buchanan was the earliest clear sign of the trouble that moved him from 63% of New Hampshire's votes in November 1988 to 38% four years later, and defeat in his campaign for reelection.

In a country that prides itself on its feistiness and freedom from outside direction, New Hampshire has always been even feistier and less fettered by authority. Before the Revolution, New Hampshire was almost an outlaw colony, its great fortunes made by poachers in the king's forests and smugglers avoiding taxes. In this free environment, 19th Century entrepreneurs built textile mills along fast-flowing rivers; the Amoskeag Mills in Manchester, lining the Merrimack River for a mile, were once the largest cotton mills on the globe, employing 17,000 and producing enough cloth every two months to put a band around the world. Around the mills grew a city of red brick dormitories and three-family frame houses filled with immigrants from Quebec, Ireland, Poland and Greece, set down amid dirt-roaded villages of flinty Yankee farmers and mechanics. New Hampshire held to its traditions of local government and little external control, and its refusal to join most other states and enact an income or sales tax or provide statewide guidance of schools and social services seemed to doom it to continued backwardness.

But low taxes proved to be New Hampshire's fortune. Starting in the 1960s, New Hampshire for 30 years had the fastest growth on the East Coast, attracting businesses from Massachusetts and other high-tax states. It became a location of choice for entrepreneurs and high-tech innovators, attracting an increasing number of people skeptical of government programs—like John Sununu, who grew up in New York and worked in Massachusetts but lived and made his political career in New Hampshire. From 1965 to 1990, Massachusetts grew from 5.5 million to 6.0 million, up 9%; New Hampshire grew from 676,000 to 1,109,000, up 64%. The bedraggled New Hampshire of 50 years ago, of poor Yankee farmers and French Canadian mill hands, largely disappeared, and in its place arose one of the nation's most prosperous economic communities. This "Nouvelle Hampshire," to use Henry Allen's term, has none of the architectural purity of Amoskeag: its shopping centers and new subdivisions have a slap-dash, half-built look, as if there were no time for details in the hurry to build. The boom was feverish in the late 1980s, producing more jobs per capita than any other state and fabulous increases in real estate value; descendants of Amoskeag mill hands and stone-poor farmers found themselves with high-income jobs and even substantial wealth, property and perhaps interests in business worth hundreds of thousands of dollars.

The low taxes that spurred this growth, making New Hampshire a tax haven in Governor John Sununu's 1980s as it was in Governor Benning Wentworth's 1760s, would probably have been raised in the late 1960s or early 1970s, as they were in so many states at the time, but for the far from gentle advocacy of the *Manchester Union Leader* and its owner William Loeb. The *Union Leader* insisted that governors and legislators "take the pledge" to vote for no sales or income tax, and from 1972 on, all did. That meant keeping education and welfare as local responsibilities and holding down spending. At the same time, New Hampshire boasted the highest SAT

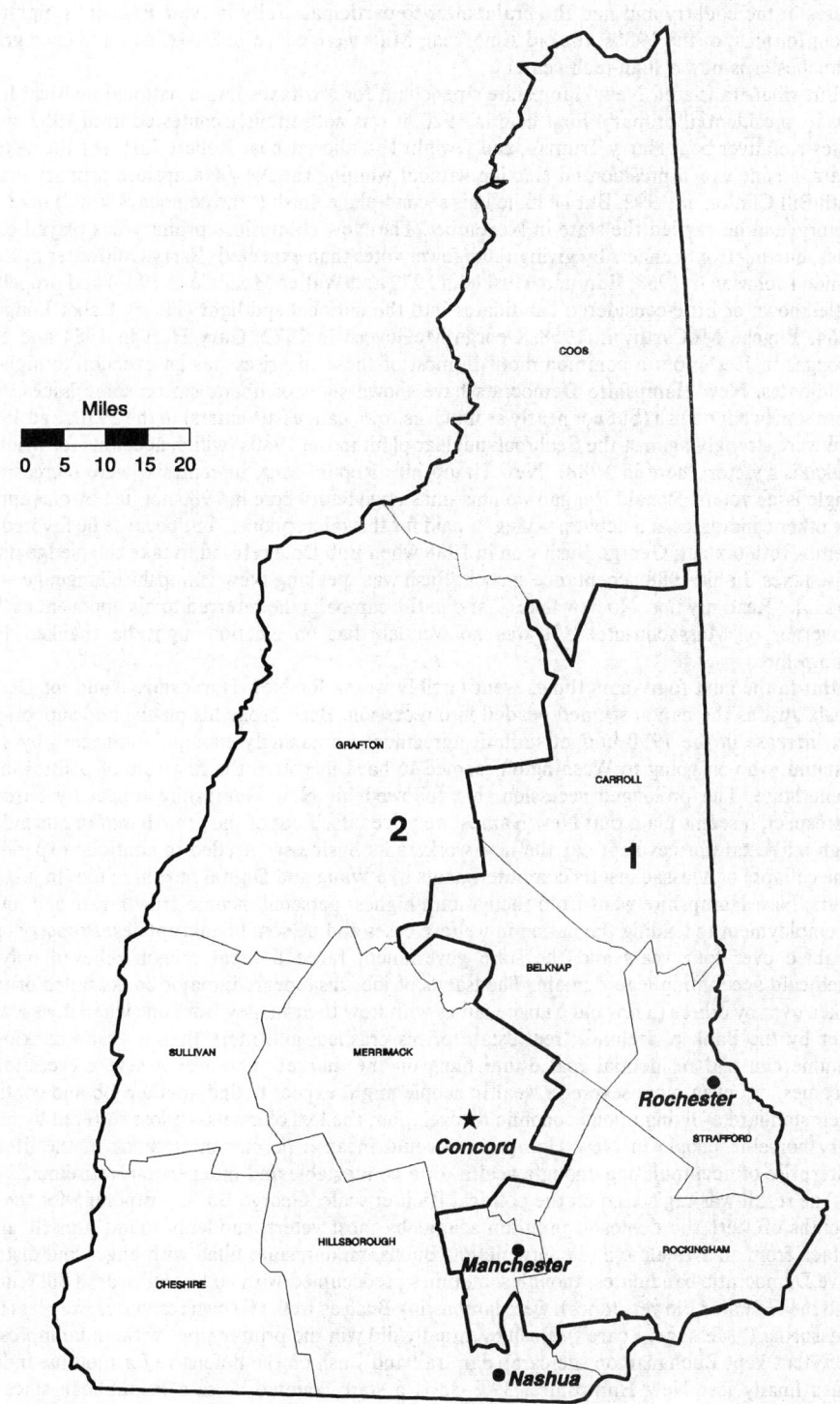

Miles

0   5   10   15   20

COOS

GRAFTON

CARROLL

2

1

BELKNAP

SULLIVAN

MERRIMACK

Rochester ●

STRAFFORD

★
Concord

HILLSBOROUGH

ROCKINGHAM

CHESHIRE

Manchester ●

● Nashua

scores in the country and had the brainpower to participate fully in New England's high-tech boom for most of the 1980s: the old Amoskeag Mills were converted to offices, and once grimy Manchester is now a high-tech center.

But what translated New Hampshire's penchant for low taxes into a national political force was its presidential primary. First held in 1920, it was not seriously contested until 1952, when Estes Kefauver beat Harry Truman, and Dwight Eisenhower beat Robert Taft. For the next 40 years, no one won a presidential election without winning the New Hampshire primary first—until Bill Clinton, in 1992. But he hailed his second-place finish ("the comeback kid!") here as a victory, and he carried the state in November. The New Hampshire primary has played other roles, hurting front-runners by giving them fewer votes than expected (Barry Goldwater in 1964, Lyndon Johnson in 1968, Edmund Muskie in 1972 and Walter Mondale in 1984) and propelling little-known or little-considered candidates into the national spotlight (Henry Cabot Lodge in 1964, Eugene McCarthy in 1968, George McGovern in 1972, Gary Hart in 1984 and Paul Tsongas in 1992): but a common motif in most of these surprises was an aversion to high-tax candidates. New Hampshire Democrats have shown signs of liberalism on some issues: they were somewhat dovish (but not nearly as much as Iowa caucus attenders) in the 1970s and 1980s and were strongly against the Seabrook nuclear plant in the 1980s (which accounts for Michael Dukakis's victory here in 1988). New Hampshire Republicans, in contrast, were increasingly single-issue voters. Ronald Reagan won his smashing victory here in 1980 not just by one-upping the other candidates at a debate, saying "I paid for this microphone," but because he favored the Kemp-Roth tax cut; George Bush won in 1988 when Bob Dole refused to take the pledge not to raise taxes. In his 1988 acceptance speech, Bush was speaking New Hampshire language when he said, "Read my lips. No new taxes," and in the campaign he referred to his opponent as "the Governor of Massachusetts." It was no wonder that on election night he thanked New Hampshire.

But in the next four years things went terribly wrong for New Hampshire—and for George Bush. Just as the nation seemed headed into recession, Bush broke his pledge and supported a tax increase in the 1990 budget summit agreement—amazingly enough, engineered by John Sununu, who on going to Washington seemed to have forgotten the first rule of politics in his home state. The prolonged recession that followed hit New Hampshire especially hard. In retrospect, it seems plain that New Hampshire priced itself out of the growth market: its giddily high real estate prices kept out the new workers its businesses needed to continue expanding. The collapse of Massachusetts computer giants like Wang and Digital hurt here too. In just two years, New Hampshire went from the nation's highest personal income growth rate and lowest unemployment to leading the nation in welfare cases and personal bankruptcies. Property taxes doubled over four years and the state government faced a fiscal crunch relieved only by Medicaid accounting legerdemain. Thousands of jobs disappeared; major banks failed or were taken over by others (a few old Yankee ladies withdrew their money from one when it was taken over by the Bank of Ireland); real estate prices crashed, and more than a year's backlog of commercial and residential real estate hung on the market. This was a severe recession in incomes, but even more severe in wealth; people might expect to find another job and continue their standard of living upon economic recovery, but the loss of assets—a loss suffered by many very non-elite people in New Hampshire—could mean a permanent setback in the lifelong enterprise of accumulating enough wealth for a comfortable and independent retirement.

The result was registered on the political Richter scale. George Bush, postponing for the last months of 1991 the domestic program sought by most voters, suddenly found himself under attack from an articulate and energetic Pat Buchanan in a state filled with anger and distress. Five Democratic candidates, though sometimes preoccupied with collateral issues (Bill Clinton and the Gennifer Flowers tapes), were lambasting Bush as well. His own responses were less than reassuring ("Message: I care"). Bush eventually did win the primary, but with an unimpressive 53% that kept Buchanan on the campaign trail and Bush on the defensive for months. Indeed, Bush finally lost New Hampshire, 39%–38%, a state counted as safe Republican since the

1960s, and where he won his second highest percentage in 1988. The political earthquake did not level every candidate: Republican Governor Judd Gregg was elected senator, though by a narrow 48%–45% margin, and Democrat Deborah Arnesen, who advocated a broad-based tax and challenged the *Union Leader*'s low tax orthodoxy, lost the governor's race decisively, 56%–40%, to Republican Stephen Merrill.

Governor. In late February, within 24 hours after the primary returns are in, the national politicians and the press switch off Channel 9, stuff the *Union Leader* into the wastebasket and clear out of the Sheraton Wayfarer parking lot not to be seen again for at least three years. New Hampshire then has its politics to itself. Its key issue—taxes—was raised bluntly in the 1992 gubernatorial campaign. State Representative Deborah "Arnie" Arnesen campaigned cheerfully as the "Tax Lady," called the *Union Leader*'s pledge a "pledge to fail," arguing that it robs the state of revenues necessary for education and economic development, and called for a 6% state income tax. It was a message that resonated with the 33% of New Hampshire voters who are registered Democrats: she won the primary with 48% to 27% for former Congressman Norman D'Amours and 23% for former state Democratic Chairman Ned Helms. Against this, former Attorney General Stephen Merrill, the 53% winner of a five-candidate Republican primary, asserted New Hampshire orthodoxy, adapted to current economic conditions. Breaking the pledge, he said, would slow down the economy even more, and increase bankruptcies and foreclosures, while schools would be better if the people who know them firsthand pay for them. Merrill instead called for further government spending cuts and for sale of some of the state's recently closed military bases. Arnesen campaigned gamely, but her race, even as the top of the Republican ticket was in trouble, seemed to run counter to her intent, and she lost 56%–40%. But she may try again; New Hampshire is one of two states that elects its governor every two years.

Senators. New Hampshire has two freshman Republican Senators, and a look at the percentages by which they won shows the change in New Hampshire politics: Bob Smith was elected in 1990 by a 65%–32% margin while Judd Gregg was elected in 1992 by 48%–45%.

Ten years ago, Bob Smith was a real estate agent in Tuftonboro; now his conservative principles have made him senior senator from one of the nation's political trend-setting states: "Mr. Smith goes to Washington," as his campaign slogan put it. Smith ran for the House and lost the primary in 1980, lost the general in 1982, and finally won the seat in 1984. In 1990, when Senator Gordon Humphrey honored a promise to retire after 12 years, Smith won the Republican nomination over a pro-choicer, 65%–29%, and in the general faced feisty former (1975–80) Senator John Durkin. Durkin attacked Smith for opposing abortion, and (this worked better in the 1970s) supporting big oil companies, and called for $10 billion in new spending programs. Smith won overwhelmingly and went on to compile one of the most conservative voting records in the Senate.

Smith has done other things as well. His concerns that the U.S. left POWs and MIAs in Vietnam, prompted him in March 1991 to call for a special committee to investigate; in September 1991, Bob Dole named him vice chairman of the new Select Committee on POW/MIA Affairs, chaired by Massachusetts Democrat John Kerry. In June 1992, Smith concluded that the Pentagon was aware of scores left behind, and later attacked the Defense Intelligence Agency's debunking of evidence to that effect. He opposed reestablishing relations with Vietnam pending a full accounting. In January 1993, the committee's final report concluded there was "no compelling evidence" that POWs or MIAs are now in Southeast Asia, but the investigation brought to light disturbing evidence that some may have been left behind, and could not rule out the possibility that some are still there against their will.

Smith has been one of the Republicans' "porkbusters," opposing projects added without authorization in the appropriations process; he is the Senate sponsor of Pennsylvania Congressman Bob Walker's bill, supported by George Bush at the Republican Convention in Houston, to let taxpayers designate 10% of their taxes for deficit reduction; he seeks to bind Congress to the rules and regulations it imposes on others. In January 1993, while driving from suburban

Virginia to work, Smith witnessed the murders outside CIA headquarters: "Coolly and methodically, with no emotion, no expression and no words, he simply walked up to the automobiles and fired at point-blank range into the windows at these people. It was a pretty horrifying experience to witness." He was criticized for opposing bans on the assault weapon used; his response is that the man, not the gun, did the killing. Smith's race for reelection in 1996 will be a good measure of how much New Hampshire politics has been altered by the early 1990s recession. By pre-1990s standards, he would win easily; Democrats may hope that times have changed and try to give him a battle.

New Hampshire's other Senate seat came up in 1992 because of the retirement after two terms of Warren Rudman. He left behind several achievements: he was co-author of the Gramm-Rudman Act, which reduced budget deficits for several years; he was co-chairman of the Iran-contra investigating committee; he was chief sponsor of the nomination of that quintessential, taciturn New Hampshire Yankee, Justice David Souter. Rudman first won the seat in 1980 after leading in the Republican primary, by a 20%–17% margin, a Tufts University professor named John Sununu, who of course went on to be elected governor three times and George Bush's chief of staff for three years. Rudman announced his retirement in March 1992, saying the government "is not functioning"; he went on to form, with Paul Tsongas, the Concord Coalition seeking budget deficit reduction.

Judd Gregg, in his second two-year term as governor after four terms as 2d District congressman, was the clear favorite for the seat. Gregg is the son of former Governor Hugh Gregg, whose backing of Ronald Reagan in 1976 and George Bush in 1980 helped both men to crucial primary victories. Judd Gregg, who was a junior at Columbia during the student riots of 1968, is a man of great certainty and few words: a tax increase is "an absurd idea," the state's banking industry "is going down the drain," "there is no magic wand" to cure the state's economy, but "sure," he will win the Senate election. The last proved not quite that simple. In the September primary, Gregg was challenged by construction company owner Hal Eckman, and won by just a 50%–38% margin, losing the state capital of Concord. Meanwhile, businessman John Rauh won the six-candidate Democratic primary with 51% of the vote. Rauh, a nephew of the great Washington liberal advocate Joseph Rauh, made money in Cincinnati with a plastic film business, then moved to New Hampshire in 1986. In the primary, he beat Franklin Mayor Brenda Elias and Terry Bennett, a physician who called for dismantling Russian submarines in the Portsmouth Naval Shipyard as a way to keep the base running. Rauh called for a line-item veto and balanced budget amendment, said he would produce "a prosperous economy, not legislative tinkering" and attacked Gregg for opposing abortion. Gregg was also attacked for having been deferred from the draft in 1969 for bad knees, sleepwalking and severe acne, and his father said the family doctor may have "exaggerated" his physical problems. (Gregg later said his father had been misquoted.) Gregg actually ran behind in some polls, and his victory was by an unimpressive 48%–45% margin. In the Senate, he can be expected to be a solid conservative vote. He serves on the Commerce, Labor and Budget Committees.

Presidential politics. New Hampshire's first-in-the-nation primary status remains enshrined in Democratic Party rules and Republican tax-hater hearts: it is a fact of late 20th Century political life which our descendants in the 23d Century will puzzle to understand. One argument for it seems to have grown stronger in 1992, the idea that this small state provides a venue for "retail politics"—the candidates meeting in person with voters, exchanging ideas and allowing them to gauge their character. In-person contact was one of the things that saved Bill Clinton: his poll numbers fell dizzyingly from the mid-30s to the low 20s after the Gennifer Flowers charges, but then they plateaued, and the network exit polls suggested that people who had seen him in person decided to vote for him much more than those who saw other candidates, and stuck with him when he was in trouble. The *Union Leader* helped spark the Buchanan candidacy, supporting it with its sharply-worded editorials, though its news coverage was more objective than that of many liberal-leaning national media outlets. Even more important, Manchester's WMUR-TV, Channel 9, provided thorough and fair-minded coverage of the primary and the candidates from the beginning. Channel 9's rule was to cover every candidate every day he was in New Hampshire, and it did, allowing them to present their views and make their arguments without the overlay of smirky, opinionated commentary that national network reporters use to promote the superiority of their intellects and moral character. Channel 9 just showed the candidates and the state, and let voters make their own decisions. New Hampshire was not heavily contested in the general election, even though polls showed a close race, often with Clinton ahead; both sides reasoned, correctly, that if Bush lost New Hampshire he was in far more trouble than its four electoral votes could get him out of.

A word may be in order about New Hampshire's electoral geography. New Hampshire is one of the few states which has more registered Republicans (39%) than Democrats (33%). The Republican heart of the state is the Merrimack Valley, with the two biggest cities of Manchester and Nashua; old Yankee towns farther north are also heavily Republican, and so are the once-booming suburbs just north of the Massachusetts line. More Democratic is the western edge of the state along the Connecticut River, which partakes a bit of the Ben & Jerry's Vermont liberalism, and Portsmouth and smaller old mill towns along the Maine border. The highest Democratic percentages in New Hampshire often come from Hanover, home of Dartmouth University; the highest Republican percentages from Dixville Notch in the far north, whose 30 voters, led in 1992 by 93-year-old Town Moderator Neil Tillotson, troop in at one minute after midnight and cast the nation's first recorded votes every presidential year.

Congressional districting. With only slight changes, New Hampshire's two congressional districts have had the same boundaries since 1881, neatly separating the Merrimack River mill towns of Manchester and Nashua, the state's largest cities. That was done originally to split the Catholic Democratic vote; but now both cities are high-tech Republican towns. So the split has the same political effect, giving Democrats a chance for upset victories in either seat.

The People: Est. Pop. 1992: 1,111,000; Pop. 1990: 1,109,252, up 0.2% 1990–1992. 0.4% of U.S. total, 40th largest; 49% rural. Median age: 32.8 years. 11.3% 65 years and over. 98.0% White, 1.0% Hispanic origin. Households: 59.7% married couple families; 30% married couple fams. w. children; 50% college educ.; median household income: $36,329; per capita income: $15,959; 68.2% owner occupied housing; median house value: $129,400; median monthly rent: $479. 7.5% Unemployment. Voting age pop.: 830,497. Registered voters (1992): 660,995; 219,773 D (33%), 257,317 R (39%), 183,905 unaffiliated and minor parties (28%).

Political Lineup: Governor, Stephen E. Merrill (R); Lt. Gov., Ralph D. Hough (R); Secy. of State, William M. Gardner (D); Atty. Gen., Jeffrey R. Howard (R); Treasurer, Georgie A. Thomas (R); State Senate, 24 (13 R and 11 D); State House of Representatives, 400 (257 R, 138 D, 4 L, and 1 I). Senators, Bob Smith (R) and Judd Gregg (R). Representatives 2 (1 D and 1 R).

1992 Presidential Vote

Clinton (D)	209,040	(39%)
Bush (R)	202,484	(38%)
Perot (I)	121,337	(23%)

1992 Democratic Presidential Primary

Tsongas	55,638	(33%)
Clinton	41,522	(25%)
Kerrey	18,575	(11%)
Harkin	17,057	(10%)
Brown	13,654	(8%)
Cuomo	6,577	(4%)
Other	14,460	(9%)

1988 Presidential Vote

Bush (R)	281,537	(63%)
Dukakis (D)	163,696	(36%)

1992 Republican Presidential Primary

Bush	92,233	(53%)
Buchanan	65,087	(37%)
Other	16,845	(10%)

GOVERNOR

Gov. Stephen E. Merrill (R)

Elected 1992, term expires Jan. 1995; b. June 21, 1946, Hampton; home, Manchester; U. of NH, B.A. 1969, Georgetown U., J.D. 1972; Episcopalian; married (Heather).

Career: Air Force, 1973–76; Practicing atty., 1976–82, 1989–92; Cnsl. & Chief of Staff, NH Gov. John Sununu, 1982–85; NH Atty. Gen., 1985–89.

Office: State House, Concord 03301, 603-271-2121.

Election Results

1992 gen.	Stephen E. Merrill (R)	289,170	(56%)
	Deborah Arnesen (D)	206,232	(40%)
	Miriam Luce (LIB)	20,663	(4%)
1992 prim.	Stephen E. Merrill (R)	60,809	(53%)
	Edward C. Dupont, Jr. (R)	15,207	(22%)
	Elizabeth Hager (R)	15,207	(21%)
	Other	15,207	(4%)
1990 gen.	Judd Gregg (R)	177,773	(60%)
	J. Joseph Grandmaison (D)	101,923	(35%)
	Miriam F. Luce (LIB)	14,343	(5%)

SENATORS

Sen. Bob Smith (R)

Elected 1990, seat up 1996; b. Mar. 30, 1941, Trenton, NJ; home, Tuftonboro; Trenton Jr. Col., A.A. 1963, Lafayette Col., B.A. 1965, Long Beach St. Col., 1968–69; Catholic; married (Mary Jo).

Career: Navy, 1965–67 (Vietnam), Naval Reserves, 1962–65, 1967–69; High schl. teacher, 1975–84; Real Estate agent, 1975–84; Chmn., Gov. Wentworth Schl. Bd., 1978–83; U.S. House of Reps., 1984–90.

Offices: 332 DSOB 20510, 202-224-2841. Also 50 Phillippe Cote St., #200, Manchester 03101, 603-634-5000; 46 S. Main St., Concord 03301, 603-228-0453; and 1 Harbour Pl., Portsmouth 03801, 603-433-1667.

Committees: *Armed Services* (7th of 9 R): Coalition Defense and Reinforcing Forces; Defense Technology, Acquisition and Industrial Base (RMM); Military Readiness and Defense Infrastructure. *Environment and Public Works* (5th of 7 R): Superfund, Recycling and Solid Waste Management; Toxic Substances, Research and Development (RMM); Water Resources, Transportation, Public Buildings and Economic Development. *Ethics (Select)* (3d of 3 R).

Group Ratings

	ADA	ACLU	CDF	COPE	CFA	LCV	ACU	NTLC	NSI	COC	CEI
1992	5	5	10	25	17	25	96	94	70	90	93
1991	10	—	18	17	22	50	90	—	—	70	84

National Journal Ratings

	1991 LIB	—	1991 CONS	1992 LIB	—	1992 CONS
Economic	9%	—	87%	0%	—	89%
Social	0%	—	86%	0%	—	89%
Foreign	13%	—	77%	21%	—	72%

Key Votes of the 102d Congress

1. $ for Homeownership	FOR	5. Clarence Thomas Nom. FOR	9. Use Force in Gulf FOR
2. Have Cap Gains Debate FOR		6. Lmt Death Row Appeal FOR	10. Keep Salvador Aid FOR
3. Remove Budget Walls	AGN	7. Handgun Wait/5-Day AGN	11. Cut $1B from SDI AGN
4. Ban Striker Replace	AGN	8. Abortion Gag Rule FOR	12. Override China MFN FOR

Key Votes of the 103d Congress

1. Family Leave   AGN   2. HIV Immigrants   AGN   3. Clinton Budget   AGN

Election Results

1990 general	Bob Smith (R)......................	189,792	(65%)	($1,419,127)
	John A. Durkin (D)..................	91,299	(32%)	($319,879)
	Other.............................	10,302	(3%)	
1990 primary	Bob Smith (R)......................	56,215	(65%)	
	Tom Christo (R)	25,286	(29%)	
	Two Others	4,777	(6%)	
1984 general	Gordon J. Humphrey (R).............	225,828	(59%)	($1,806,653)
	Norman E. D'Amours (D)	157,447	(41%)	($1,066,485)

Sen. Judd Gregg (R)

Elected 1992, seat up 1998; b. Feb. 14, 1947, Nashua; home, Greenfield; Columbia U., A.B. 1969, Boston U., J.D. 1972, LL.M. 1975; Protestant; married (Kathleen).

Career: Practicing atty., 1976–80; NH Exec. Cncl., 1978–80; U.S. House of Reps., 1980–88; NH Gov., 1988–92.

Offices: 393 RSOB 20510, 202-224-3324. Also 125 N. Main St., Concord 03301, 603-225-7115; 28 Webster St., Manchester 03104, 603-622-7979; 136 Pleasant St., Berlin 03570, 603-752-2604; and 99 Pease Blvd., Portsmouth 03801, 603-431-2171.

Committees: *Budget* (9th of 9 R). *Foreign Relations* (9th of 9 R): European Affairs; Near Eastern and South Asian Affairs. *Labor and Human Resources* (4th of 7 R): Aging (RMM); Children, Family, Drugs and Alcoholism; Education, Arts and Humanities; Employment and Productivity.

Group Ratings and 102d Congress Votes: Newly Elected

Key Votes of the 103d Congress

1. Family Leave   AGN   2. HIV Immigrants   AGN   3. Clinton Budget   AGN

Election Results

1992 general	Judd Gregg (R)...................	249,591	(48%)	($875,675)
	John Rauh (D).....................	234,982	(45%)	($1,109,467)
	Katherine Alexander (LIB).............	18,214	(4%)	
	Others............................	15,629	(3%)	
1992 primary	Judd Gregg (R).....................	57,141	(50%)	
	Harold Eckman (R)	43,264	(38%)	
	Jean T. White (R).....................	10,642	(9%)	
	Others.............................	3,690	(3%)	
1986 general	Warren Rudman (R).................	154,090	(63%)	($831,098)
	Endicott Peabody (D)................	79,222	(32%)	($307,760)

FIRST DISTRICT

The 1st Congressional District of New Hampshire includes Manchester, its suburbs and the seacoast. Manchester was once a heavily French Canadian textile mill town; in the 1980s it became a fast-growing high-tech city. There are new shopping malls here and in towns on the Massachusetts border; Portsmouth has restored its downtown to some of its historic splendor; Wal-Mart, drawn by the combination of new affluence and down-home tastes, built its first New England stores in this area. There is a Democratic heritage here, especially in Manchester, but in general elections this is usually Republican territory.

The congressman is Bill Zeliff, a Republican first elected in 1990 when incumbent Bob Smith was elected to the Senate. Zeliff has been something of a stormy petrel, blown and tossed by the hard and unpredictable winds of New Hampshire politics. An innkeeper from the north country, he won the 1990 primary by 314 votes in an eight-candidate race. Zeliff had the endorsement of John Sununu, but second-place finisher and Reagan appointee Larry Brady had the endorsement of the *Manchester Union Leader*, although both Sununu and the paper seemed to focus their attacks on the perceived favorite, state legislator Douglas Scamman, accusing him of being soft on taxes. Zeliff carried the north country, Scamman the coastal regions, Brady the Manchester area—the three basic voting blocs here. In the general, Zeliff won with an unimpressive 55% of the vote, after outspending Democrat Joseph Keefe by more than 2–1, and not complying with New Hampshire's voluntary $400,000 campaign spending limit. For this, he was $375,000 in debt at the end of 1990, the number one freshman debtor in the House; he was still raising money from PACs to pay it off in early 1993.

In the House, Zeliff's record was generally conservative, but he is pro-choice on abortion, and for that reason was sharply opposed by the *Union Leader* in both the primary and general elections. In 1992, he won the primary unimpressively, by a 50%–35% margin over Manchester lawyer Ovide Lamontagne, this time carrying the coast as well as the north country, but losing the Manchester area. In the general, Zeliff faced antiabortion Democrat Bill Preston, whose endorsement by the *Union Leader* shook Zeliff's already shaky political firmament. Zeliff won, but by only a 53%–43% margin—a sign of possible serious opposition in 1994.

The People: Pop. 1990: 554,303; 45% rural; 11% age 65+; 97% White; 1% Black; 1% Asian; 1% Hispanic origin. Voting age pop.: 415,779; 1% Black; 1% Hispanic origin. Households: 60% married couple families; 29% married couple fams. w. children; 51% college educ.; median household income: $36,511; per capita income: $16,044; median gross rent: $555; median house value: $132,600.

1992 Presidential Vote

Bush (R)	104,653	(39%)
Clinton (D)	101,415	(38%)
Perot (I)....................	61,571	(23%)

1988 Presidential Vote

Bush (R)	141,952	(64%)
Dukakis (D).................	78,235	(36%)

Rep. William H. Zeliff, Jr. (R)

Elected 1990; b. June 12, 1936, East Orange, NJ; home, Jackson; U. of CT, B.S. 1958; Protestant; married (Sydna).

Career: Army Natl. Guard, 1958–64; Sales/Mktg. mgr., DuPont Co., 1961–76; Innkeeper, small business owner.

Offices: 224 CHOB 20515, 202-225-5456. Also 340 Commercial St., Manchester 03101, 603-669-6330; and 601 Spaulding Tnpk., #28, Portsmouth 03801, 603-433-1601.

Committees: *Government Operations* (12th of 17 R): Commerce, Consumer, and Monetary Affairs. *Public Works and Transportation* (9th of 24 R): Investigations and Oversight; Surface Transportation; Water Resources and Environment. *Small Business* (8th of 18 R): SBA Legislation and the General Economy.

Group Ratings

	ADA	ACLU	COPE	CDF	CFA	LCV	ACU	NTLC	NSI	COC	CEI
1992	20	17	25	10	13	6	92	85	100	88	84
1991	10	—	8	10	6	23	80	—	—	100	85

National Journal Ratings

	1991 LIB — 1991 CONS		1992 LIB — 1992 CONS	
Economic	4%	— 90%	0%	— 91%
Social	30%	— 68%	23%	— 75%
Foreign	17%	— 78%	18%	— 74%

Key Votes of the 102d Congress

1. Ban Striker Replace	AGN	5. Handgun Wait/7-Day AGN	9. Use Force in Gulf FOR
2. $ for Homeownership	FOR	6. Overseas Mil. Abortion FOR	10. US Mil. Abroad $ Cut FOR
3. Tax Rich/Cut Mid Cls.	AGN	7. Obscn. Art NEA $ Ban FOR	11. Limit SDI Funds AGN
4. FY93/$15B Def. Cut	AGN	8. Death Pen. from Jury FOR	12. Cuba Trade Embargo FOR

Key Votes of the 103d Congress

1. Family Leave   AGN   2. Deficit Reduction   AGN   3. Stimulus Plan   AGN

Election Results

1992 general	William H. Zeliff, Jr. (R)	135,396	(53%)	($778,358)
	Bob Preston (D)	108,578	(43%)	($174,565)
	Others	11,339	(4%)	
1992 primary	William H. Zeliff, Jr. (R)	28,877	(50%)	
	Ovide Lamontagne (R)	20,493	(35%)	
	Maureen E. Barrows (R)	8,447	(15%)	
1990 general	William H. Zeliff, Jr. (R)	81,684	(55%)	($924,367)
	Joseph F. Keefe (D)	66,176	(45%)	($377,993)

SECOND DISTRICT

The 2d Congressional District includes Nashua, the state's second largest city, and Salem, both right on the Massachusetts line and solidly conservative—people came here to leave "Taxachusetts." It also includes, farther from Boston and readier for taxes and government services, the state capital of Concord and the towns in the Connecticut River Valley, from Keene near Mount Monadnock north to Hanover, home of Dartmouth University, an area of artist retreats from the sculptor August Saint Gaudens a century ago to writer J. D. Salinger today. The 2d runs to the farthest north country: Dixville Notch and the paper mill town of Berlin, the Mount Washington Hotel and cog railway and the resort of Bretton Woods where the world monetary system, and the basis for post-World War II prosperity, were established in a conference in 1944.

The congressman from the 2d District is Dick Swett, a Democrat first elected in a 1990 upset. The upset was the result of ideological infighting common among New Hampshire Republicans and the negative reactions of some, including Nancy Sununu, whose husband was then White House chief of staff, to the personal life of Chuck Douglas, the one-term congressman and former state Supreme Court Justice. Douglas had won the seat narrowly in the 1988 primary, 47%–41%, and in the general beat Nashua Mayor Jim Donchess by just 57%–43%. In 1990, his private life, punctuated by several divorces, contrasted with that of Swett, former Yale football star, son-in-law of California Congressman Tom Lantos, architect and father of five. "Three wives versus five children," as someone put it. Mrs. Sununu was quoted in a Swett brochure: "I have known Chuck Douglas for over 15 years and I've never appreciated his values and his morals." Swett was also helped by money raised by his father-in-law; he eventually paid a fine of $20,000 for exceeding New Hampshire's voluntary spending limit, but he argued that the state statute was unclear, that federal regulations should govern and that he was singled out for selective prosecution, presumably because he is a Democrat. Charges that some contributors tried to wiggle around federal contribution limits are still pending.

Swett won 53%–47%, and has proved considerably more conservative than most House Democrats (including his father-in-law): around the House midpoint on economic, cultural and foreign issues. He serves on the Public Works Committee, and put some imprint on the 1991 ISTEA landmark transportation act and, from the Science Committee, on paper and pulp mill energy efficiency provisions of the 1992 energy law; he also sponsored an interstate compact to allow a North Country school district straddling the New Hampshire-Maine state line. He has called for Congress to submit to the rules and regulations it imposes on others and, against some pressure, voted for the balanced budget amendment.

In 1992, five Republicans lined up to run against him, and had a riproaring primary. The primary winner, by a 34%–31%–26% margin, Nashua state Representative Bill Hatch, charged that Swett campaign workers had carried signs calling both Pat Buchanan and Hatch Nazis. But he made little impact and Swett won with 62% of the vote.

The People: Pop. 1990: 554,949; 53% rural; 11% age 65+; 97% White; 1% Black; 1% Asian; 1% Hispanic origin. Voting age pop.: 414,350; 1% Black; 1% Hispanic origin. Households: 61% married couple families; 30% married couple fams. w. children; 50% college educ.; median household income: $36,145; per capita income: $15,874; median gross rent: $541; median house value: $125,500.

1992 Presidential Vote

Clinton (D) 107,625 (40%)
Bush (R) 97,831 (37%)
Perot (I) 59,766 (22%)

1988 Presidential Vote

Bush (R) 139,585 (62%)
Dukakis (D) 85,461 (38%)

Rep. Dick Swett (D)

Elected 1990; b. May 1, 1957, Bryn Mawr, PA; home, Bow; Yale, B.A. 1979; Mormon; married (Katrina).

Career: Alternative energy developer, architect; Pres., Veritas Group Inc., 1987–90.

Offices: 230 CHOB 20515, 202-225-5206. Also 18 N. Main St., Concord 03301, 603-224-6621.

Committees: *Public Works and Transportation* (20th of 39 D): Aviation; Economic Development; Surface Transportation. *Science, Space and Technology* (17th of 33 D): Energy; Technology, Environment and Aviation.

Group Ratings

	ADA	ACLU	COPE	CDF	CFA	LCV	ACU	NTLC	NSI	COC	CEI
1992	85	70	83	70	80	94	32	50	60	38	38
1991	45	—	92	60	61	77	40	—	—	30	33

National Journal Ratings

	1991 LIB — 1991 CONS		1992 LIB — 1992 CONS	
Economic	46%	— 54%	53%	— 46%
Social	43%	— 56%	61%	— 38%
Foreign	54%	— 44%	56%	— 40%

Key Votes of the 102d Congress

1. Ban Striker Replace	FOR	5. Handgun Wait/7-Day FOR	9. Use Force in Gulf FOR
2. $ for Homeownership	AGN	6. Overseas Mil. Abortion FOR	10. US Mil. Abroad $ Cut FOR
3. Tax Rich/Cut Mid Cls.	AGN	7. Obscn. Art NEA $ Ban FOR	11. Limit SDI Funds AGN
4. FY93/$15B Def. Cut	FOR	8. Death Pen. from Jury FOR	12. Cuba Trade Embargo FOR

Key Votes of the 103d Congress

1. Family Leave	FOR	2. Deficit Reduction	AGN	3. Stimulus Plan	FOR

Election Results

1992 general	Dick Swett (D)	157,328	(62%)	($785,452)
	Bill Hatch (R)	91,126	(36%)	($232,617)
	Others	6,731	(2%)	
1992 primary	Dick Swett (D)	27,552	(65%)	
	Emily Northrup (D)	14,543	(34%)	
	Others	425	(1%)	
1990 general	Dick Swett (D)	74,866	(53%)	($465,160)
	Chuck Douglas (R)	67,225	(47%)	($540,605)

NEW JERSEY

Named by the Duke of York for the Channel Island on which he was sheltered during the English Civil War, plagued in its early years with rival claims from its neighbors, New Jersey has spent much of its history betwixt and between, its major cities on the swampy sides of America's two greatest harbor rivers, overshadowed for years by the metropolises of New York and Philadelphia—"a valley of humility between two mountains of conceit," its neighbor Benjamin Franklin called it. But New Jersey has much to say for itself. It is "a sort of laboratory in which the best blood is prepared for other communities to thrive on," Woodrow Wilson said when he was governor of New Jersey, just a tad defensively; it is "the fighting center of the most important social questions of our time." Today, New Jersey is the nation's ninth most populous state, one which fully enjoyed the 1980s boom and suffered more than most from the 1990s wealth recession. It is among the top half-dozen states in high-tech businesses and Hispanic population, in toxic waste sites and in tourism. Within its close boundaries is an astonishing diversity, geographically from beaches to mountains, demographically from old Quaker stock to new immigrants, economically from inner city slums to hunt country mansions. New York writers are inclined to look on New Jersey as something quaint, but New Jersey comes far closer to resembling America than does Manhattan, even if its traffic signals are arrayed horizontally rather than vertically and its accents can be impossible for outsiders to understand. The row houses seen on emerging from the Holland Tunnel, many renovated by Wall Street commuters and Latin immigrants, give way within a few miles to the skyscrapers of Newark and middle-income suburbs. Not far is the horse country around Far Hills, the university town of Princeton and old industrial towns like Paterson, and dozens of suburban towns and small factory cities where people work hard and raise their families over generations.

In the last 20 years, a new New Jersey has sprouted up, and can be seen even from Manhattan: the oil tank farms and swamplands of the Jersey Meadows have become sports palaces and office complexes; the intersection of I-78 and I-287 has become a major shopping and office center, one of the "edge cities" which grow up on the far sides of urban settlement; U.S. 1 north of Princeton has become one of the nation's high-tech centers; the flat vegetable fields once dotted with gas station junctions now have tourist attractions like Great Adventure park. For the first census year since 1840, New Jersey in 1990 had more people (7.7 million) than New York City (7.3 million), and far more than metropolitan Philadelphia (5.9 million); it was generating more new jobs than either New York or Pennsylvania: the row of books is finally becoming more prominent than the bookends. For many years, New Jersey's growth was essentially suburban, an economic and cultural extension of the two big cities across the harbor-rivers. Now New Jersey, with its greatest growth in the interior and along the shore, while the cities and towns within a dozen miles of Manhattan and half a dozen of Center City Philadelphia lose population, is taking on an identity of its own. It is the home of Bruce Springsteen and of big league football, basketball and hockey franchises; Atlantic City has America's biggest gambling casinos outside Nevada; the world's longest expanse of boardwalks lies on the Jersey Shore almost from Cape May to Sandy Hook.

Not that New Jersey hasn't had its problems, sometimes even leading the nation in those. Waste disposal is one: this most densely populated of states is struggling to find ways to dispose sanitarily of its wastes, including pollutants left behind by its chemical industries. Another is the early 1990s recession: the reversals of the financial services industry hurt New Jersey, cutting job growth to zero and below, depressing commercial and residential real estate markets, playing havoc with the state government budget. The state government had played an important role in building state pride: Governor Brendan Byrne in the 1970s started the Meadowlands complex

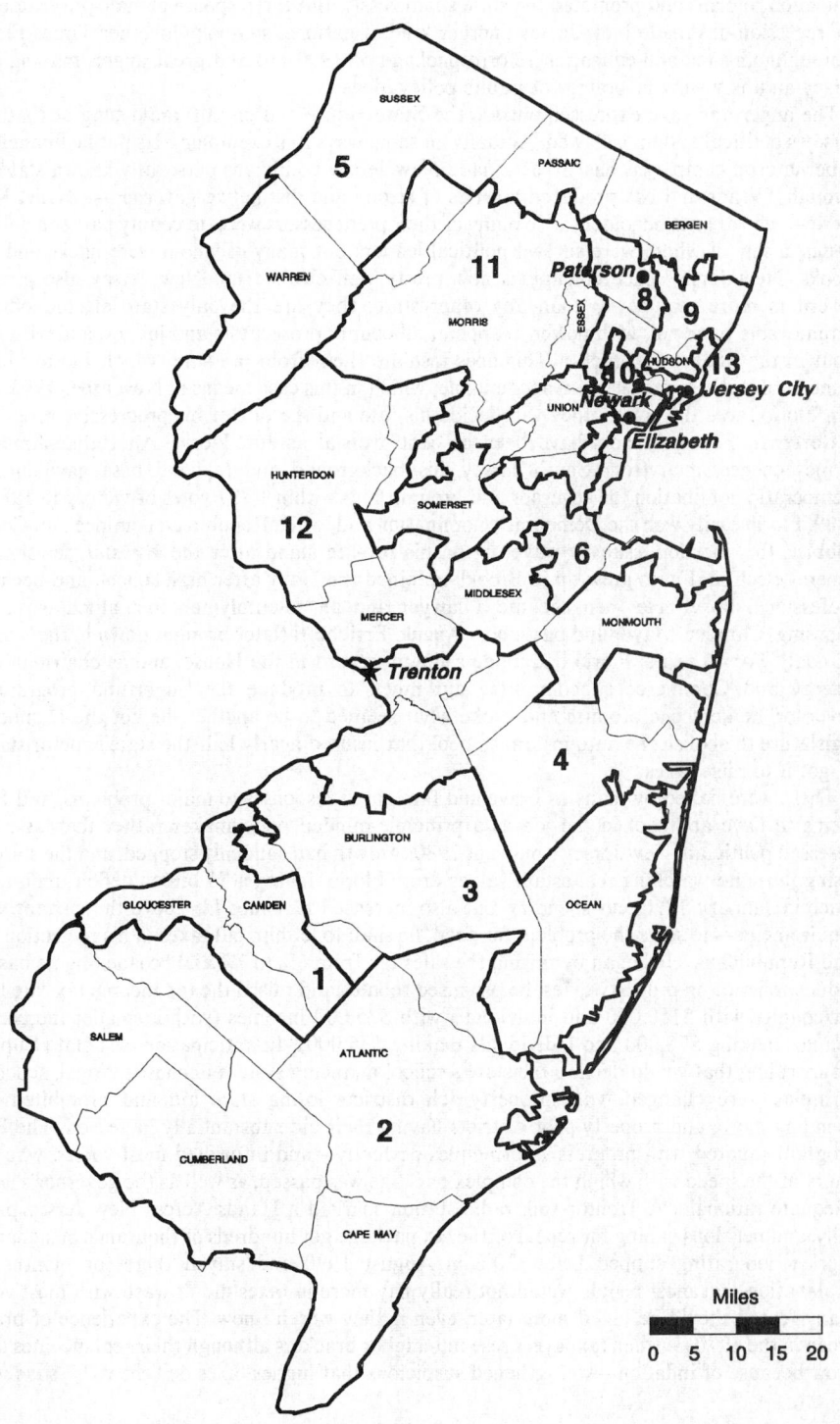

SUSSEX

5

PASSAIC

WARREN

BERGEN

11

MORRIS

Paterson

8

9

ESSEX

HUDSON

13

10

Jersey City

UNION

Newark

HUNTERDON

7

Elizabeth

SOMERSET

12

6

MIDDLESEX

MERCER

MONMOUTH

★ *Trenton*

4

BURLINGTON

3

GLOUCESTER   CAMDEN

OCEAN

1

SALEM

ATLANTIC

2

CUMBERLAND

CAPE MAY

Miles

0   5   10   15   20

and got casino gambling legalized in Atlantic City; in the 1980s, Governor Tom Kean started education reforms and promoted the state shamelessly. But the response of state government to the recession has made New Jersey another kind of national symbol: Governor James Florio's thoroughgoing tax-and-education reform package of 1990 aroused great anger, making New Jersey an unknowing laboratory of public policy ideas.

The anger and rage expressed outside the State House and on talk radio suggest that New Jersey's political system is flawed. Actually, in some ways it is exemplary. Its public financing of gubernatorial campaigns has, at last, made New Jersey politicians personally known statewide through TV ads and has produced a series of strong and distinctive governors—Byrne, Kean, Florio—who are not beholden, as so many of their predecessors were, to county partisan political bosses, a few of whom were shrewd political leaders but many of whom were hacks and even crooks. New Jersey, once corrupt, is now pretty well cleaned up. New Jersey also gives its governors more real power than any other state: they are the only state elected officials, unremovable by recall, with power to appoint all county prosecutors and judges, and with great clout in the budgetary process. This does insulate them from pressure, which Florio's critics bemoan. But it also makes them accountable, which in this case means in November 1993 when Jim Florio faces the voters, they will decide his fate and the fate of his progressive program.

Governor. Few governors have been as controversial as Jim Florio. An Italian-American former congressman from South Jersey, his background and regional base gave him the Democratic nomination for governor and brought him within 1,797 votes of victory in 1981. In 1989, Florio easily won the Democratic nomination and, when Republican nominee Jim Courter bobbled the abortion issue by wavering on his pro-life stand after the *Webster* decision, the general election. Florio grew up in Brooklyn, joined the Navy after high school, and became a professional boxer. He then became a lawyer and an assemblyman first allied with, then opposing, Camden Mayor and party boss Angelo Errichetti (later brought down in the Abscam scandal). For 15 years, Florio had made a liberal record in the House, and as chairman of an Energy and Commerce subcommittee did much to produce the Superfund program. As governor, he kept one promise and broke what seemed to be another: he got the Democratic legislature to abolish the auto insurance pool that insured nearly half the state's motorists, and he got it to raise taxes.

These were hailed by many as brave and farsighted responses to major problems, and Florio seems to have approached the job as a principle-minded policymaker rather than as a poll-obsessed politician. New Jersey's buoyant 1980s growth had suddenly stopped, and the state was losing jobs and watching real estate values drop. Florio, facing a $3 billion deficit upon taking office in January 1990, cut spending but also increased revenues far above the current year's requirements—to solve the problem for good, he said; to let him cut taxes in his reelection year, said Republicans. He began by raising the sales tax from 6% to 7% and broadening its base. To reduce reliance on property taxes, he promised rebates and raised the top income tax rate to 7% for couples with $150,000 and individuals with $75,000 incomes (with a smaller increase for couples making $70,000 and individuals making $35,000). In anticipation of a state Supreme Court ruling that would declare the state's school financing system unconstitutional, school aid formulas were changed, with property-rich districts losing state aid and prohibited from spending more, and property-poor districts having their aid substantially increased. The Florio program squared with progressive principles perfectly—and infuriated most voters, who were angry at the speed with which the complex package was passed, as well as the governor's lack of adequate rationale. A Trenton talk radio station sparked a Hands Across New Jersey protest rally, and petitions calling for repeal of the tax package got hundreds of thousands of signatures; Florio's job rating slipped below 20% in August 1990 and stayed there for months. His explanation that most people would not really pay more in taxes didn't wash with most voters; many feared they'd be taxed more later, even if they weren't now. The experience of bracket creep in the 1970s—when taxpayers rose into higher brackets although their real incomes didn't grow because of inflation—strengthened suspicions that higher taxes on "the rich" soon would mean higher taxes on most people. Moreover, the taxes covered large numbers of voters, many of whom are hard-working and hard-pressed and don't consider themselves rich at all; couples living on $70,000 in Jersey suburbs shop at K-Mart, not Saks Fifth Avenue. And while some of the feeling against spending more on inner city schools can be traced to racism, some reflects a judgment that spending more on ineffective school systems (Jersey City's and Patterson's had to be taken over by the state) would not do any good.

The political fallout stayed negative for some time. Every member of the New Jersey House delegation except Jim Courter, who was leaving office, voted against the 1990 budget summit packages with their new taxes; even so, Democrats did poorly in the fall elections, nearly losing three congressional seats plus Bill Bradley's supposedly safe Senate seat, dropping the one state legislative seat up that year, and trailing 55%–42% in the 12 seats with two-party contests. "I got the message; the results were really directed at me and the policies of my administration," Florio said. In 1991, the Republicans won control of both houses of the legislature, perhaps getting more than they wanted; with more than two-thirds of the seats in both houses, they could override Florio's vetoes, passing not only their own congressional and legislative redistricting plans but forced to put up or shut up on their promises to lower taxes. They put up, a little: they lowered the sales tax 1%. That left Florio room to argue that no one could lower taxes or spending, and his job rating did creep upward slowly in 1992 and early 1993; he also pushed through a healthcare reform program, an assault weapons ban and a state jobs czar.

But as campaigning started in spring 1993, Florio's job rating was still well under 50%, and he was running behind Republican Christine Todd Whitman, the former county officeholder who nearly beat Bill Bradley in 1990, and who won the Republican primary with 40% of the vote in June 1993. In the heated race, former Attorney General Cary Edwards won 33%, and former state Senator James Wallwork won 24%. Florio took heart from the Clinton economic package, which in some ways resembled his own; and Democratic National Chairman David Wilhelm said that the race "will be a referendum on the type of leadership" both Florio and Clinton have provided. But in early 1993, the political viability of both these Democrats was still in doubt.

Senators. Bill Bradley, senior Senator from New Jersey, is a politician and public policy maker of national stature, undeniably able, a student of and original thinker on major issues of economics and foreign policy, not far out of line with public opinion but often far ahead of conventional wisdom. Careful and deliberate in his judgments, he has been a celebrity since he was old enough to vote, when he was a star basketball player at Princeton. He showed even in those years a steely self-discipline, passing up two years of lucrative pro basketball for a Rhodes Scholarship and foregoing millions by refusing to make commercial endorsements; instead he wrote a thoughtful memoir, *Life on the Run.* Bradley also, unusual for a politician, listens closely to others, even opponents, engaging their ideas, and in response developing and sometimes even changing his own. When he first ran for the Senate in 1978, his Republican opponent, Jeffrey Bell, was championing the 30% Kemp-Roth federal income tax cut; Bradley, unlike most Democrats at the time, did not airily dismiss it but struggled to come up with an original response. He won with 55% of the vote, less than expected given Bradley's celebrity as a Princeton and New York Knicks basketball player. In the Senate, with Dale Bumpers and Ernest Hollings, he was one of three Democrats who voted for the Reagan budget and against the 1981 tax cuts, both of which would have eliminated most of the 1980s deficit. Bradley, not satisfied with traditional Democratic economics, by 1982 came up with a proposal to cut tax rates sharply and eliminate most preferences and tax shelters. That led directly to the 1986 tax reform, which would surely never have happened without Bradley—a stunning achievement for a politician with little seniority on the minority side of the aisle at the time, and freighted with the kind of celebrity status other politicians usually resent. At each stage of the tax reform debate Bradley was there, quietly encouraging others, avoiding the spotlight but offering advice and lobbying key members.

Bradley has taken a similar approach—intensive study, original proposals supported by facts and strong argument, a willingness to fight for his goals—to other issues. One is the former

Soviet Union: Bradley traveled extensively in Russia and the Republics, and had probably more first-hand knowledge of the region than any other senator; he was skeptical about direct aid to Gorbachev's Soviet Union but after the breakup called for technical aid to the Republics and for a Freedom Exchange of students, which could ultimately number 70,000 people per year, with Russia and the Republics. Another Bradley issue has been the related problems of race and crime in inner cities; Bradley scathingly criticized George Bush for using race issues in campaigns, and called for major aid to cities in 1992 and proposed an urban community building initiative in 1993. From there, it is a long jump to California water, but Bradley, as chairman of the Water and Power Subcommittee, gained jurisdiction over this subject in which he has been long interested. He bored in hard and relentlessly, insisting that California farmers pay something closer to market prices for their heavily subsidized water; in 1992, he shrewdly included in his bill on California's Central Valley Water Project projects in other Western states and eventually passed something like his own version over the powerless objection of appointed California Senator John Seymour. Earlier, he had sponsored the Student Right-to-Know act requiring publication of college graduation rates. On most other issues, Bradley's record tends to be fairly liberal and partisan Democratic.

In early 1990, there was plenty of speculation about Bradley running for president; in late 1990, he nearly lost his seat in the Senate. He won by only 50%–47% over Christine Todd Whitman, who started out almost totally unknown; Bradley ran only even in north Jersey, served by New York TV, while in south Jersey, served by Philadelphia TV, he won 54%–43%. His major problem was the issue on which he made his greatest achievement: taxes. This usually frank politician would not take a stand on the issue that was energizing Jersey voters, the Florio tax plan. Probably Bradley was in conflict: the progressive Florio plan went against the thrust of his own 1986 tax reform, and yet to come out against it would be to abandon a loyal ally under fire, and most active New Jersey Democrats as well. So Bradley ran ads showing him playing basketball, while Whitman argued reasonably, "He is a tax expert . . . this is the biggest tax increase in New Jersey history. I'd like to know what he thinks, how he differs from the governor, if at all." Or, as a Whitman bumper sticker put it, "Get Florio, Dump Bradley." Only Bradley's vast fundraising advantage (he has much support in Hollywood entertainment circles) and a flurry of last-minute campaigning enabled him to win.

Bradley did not run for president in 1992 and, with a younger Democrat elected, is unlikely to have another chance at least until 2000, when he turns 57. Bradley's poor showing in 1990 did not take him completely out of the speculation in 1991 as much as his own lack of interest in running did. He was mentioned prominently as a vice presidential nominee, but was not chosen; he was one of three keynoters at the Democratic National Convention, in the same Madison Square Garden where he had played so many basketball games. In November and December 1992, he was mentioned as a possible secretary of state, and might well have wanted the job; it went to Warren Christopher, but Bradley is a plausible candidate should it open up again.

But it may well be that Bradley is happy working as a senator. In early 1993, he was taking his own stands on economic issues, breaking with many Democrats to support the line-item veto. And the tension between Bradley's approach on taxes and Florio's was again apparent when Bradley responded coolly to the Clinton economic package's high tax rates and targeted exemptions, which looked like a revival of the tax avoidance and bracket creep Bradley had been at pains to do away with. As fourth in rank on the Finance Committee, Bradley's voice remains respected and his vote, with Democrats controlling the committee by only 11–9, could be crucial.

Frank Lautenberg is one of a species common for the last century and still today—the millionaire who becomes a senator. A dozen years ago, he was a Democratic moneygiver and member of the board of the New York & New Jersey Port Authority; now he is heading for his twelfth year in the U.S. Senate. He has shown he knows how to play the game—and that it helps to come in with a large pile of chips. Lautenberg grew up poor, the son of an immigrant silk worker in Paterson who died young, and was a World War II veteran who would never have gone to college without the G.I. Bill of Rights. In 1952, he started a company called Automatic Data Processing, which by 1990 employed 20,000 people and processed the payroll for one of every 14 non-government workers in the U.S.. With an open Senate seat in New Jersey in 1982, the nation's second most expensive state to campaign in (because you have to buy New York and Philadelphia TV), Lautenberg decided to run, spending $5 million of his own money and spotlighting his high-tech experience. He beat several professional politicians in the primary and upset Republican Congresswoman Millicent Fenwick, 51%–48%, in the general. In 1988, he again showed good campaign skills, including hiring James Carville and Paul Begala, now famous for their 1992 work for Bill Clinton. He was opposed by Republican Pete Dawkins, a Heisman Trophy winner from West Point, a Rhodes Scholar, a brigadier general and a celebrity Wall Street executive. Dawkins had moved to New Jersey the year before and started running, and was hurt by his own statements (he'd "blow his brains out" if he had to live in a small town) and a *Manhattan, inc.* profile calling him essentially a phony. Dawkins raised $7.6 million, but Lautenberg held his fire until October, when he ran an ad showing Dawkins's announcement speech, while a voice said, "Be real, Pete." Dawkins responded with negative ads, but Lautenberg pummeled him and then turned positive, winning 54%–46%.

Lautenberg believes that government helped him and many others work their way up, and has a solid liberal voting record—the most anti-Bush record in 1992. He chairs the Appropriations Subcommittee on Transportation, where he sponsored the laws which banned smoking first on two-hour flights and then on all domestic flights, and now wants to ban smoking in federal facilities including the Capitol. He is a big booster of money for Amtrak and mass transit, and has promoted high-speed rail and smart highway research and development. He passed a radon bill that developed control standards and has backed the Superfund (which pays to rehabilitate polluted areas), but opposes Indiana Senator Dan Coats's bill to let states block interstate shipments of solid waste (guess whose state sends solid waste to whose).

Will Lautenberg run again in 1994? He turns 70 then and still does not have universal name identification. But he is a tough and aggressive man who does not wilt in competition, and with an estimated $45 million net worth, he has proven a willingness to spend his own money and an ability to win. Others who might be interested in the seat include the congressmen most often mentioned as running for the vacancy that would have been created had Bradley been appointed to the Cabinet: Republican Richard Zimmer and Democrat Bob Torricelli. Both are brainy and smart political operators, with quite different convictions.

Presidential politics. New Jersey has become a pivotal state in presidential politics, one that both Democrats and Republicans consider essential for victory. It is the one state that keeps presidential and vice presidential candidates in the northeast metropolitan corridor, hoping for New York and Philadelphia TV coverage no matter how safe for one party New York or Pennsylvania appear. New Jersey voted for Kennedy in 1960, Nixon in 1968, Reagan in 1980, Bush in 1988, Clinton in 1992; in close elections over the last 50 years, it has voted for the loser only in 1948 and 1976. Mostly suburban, New Jersey has never had the urban Democratic base of New York, nor does it have the mass of unattached singles who move New York and California to the left. In 1988, it rejected the liberalism of Michael Dukakis and voted solidly for George Bush. In 1992, after three years of recession that lowered incomes and, even more, lowered housing values which are most voters' store of wealth, New Jersey deserted Bush, toyed with the idea of Ross Perot and finally gave Bill Clinton a 43%–41% victory.

New Jersey's presidential primary in early June is usually overshadowed by California's held on the same day. Before 1992, New Jersey Democrats chose delegate slates by congressional districts, which produced almost unanimous delegations and gave the state greater clout; Jesse Jackson got Michael Dukakis to agree to prohibit these rules, however, and so New Jersey is of little importance in the primary season.

Congressional districting. New Jersey grew 5% in the 1980s, well below the national average, and lost a congressional district in the 1990 Census. The Democrats had full control of the process, with the governor and legislature, in calendar year 1991, but could not reach agreement.

When the Republicans, much to everyone's surprise, won veto-proof control of the legislature, the Democrats realized that any plan they drew as lame ducks could be repealed by the Republicans. So they established a bipartisan commission, similar to the one which draws legislative district lines; the Republicans, confident that their population-gaining districts would fare better than the Democrats' population-losing ones, acquiesced. The commission plan joined the Jersey Shore and Middlesex County districts represented by Democrats into a new 6th District and created a new 41% Hispanic district linking parts of Jersey City, Newark and other cities facing New York City.

The People: Est. Pop. 1992: 7,789,000; Pop. 1990: 7,730,188, up 0.8% 1990–1992. 3.1% of U.S. total, 9th largest; 11% rural. Median age: 34.5 years. 13.4% 65 years and over. 79.3% White, 13.4% Black, 9.6% Hispanic origin, 3.5% Asian, 3.5% Other. Households: 56.5% married couple families; 26% married couple fams. w. children; 46% college educ.; median household income: $40,927; per capita income: $18,714; 64.9% owner occupied housing; median house value: $162,300; median monthly rent: $521. 8.4% Unemployment. Voting age pop.: 5,930,726. Registered voters (1992): 4,060,337; 1,175,041 D (29%), 817,837 R (20%), 2,067,459 unaffiliated and minor parties (51%).

Political Lineup: Governor, Jim Florio (D); Lt. Gov., Donald T. DiFrancesco (R); Secy. of State, Daniel J. Dalton (D); Atty. Gen., Robert J. Del Tufo (D); Treasurer, Samuel Crane (D); Auditor, Richard L. Fair (D). State Senate, 40 (27 R and 13 D); General Assembly, 80 (58 R and 22 D). Senators, Bill Bradley (D) and Frank R. Lautenberg (D). Representatives, 13 (7 D and 6 R).

1992 Presidential Vote			1988 Presidential Vote		
Clinton (D)	1,436,206	(43%)	Bush (R)	1,743,192	(56%)
Bush (R)	1,356,865	(41%)	Dukakis (D)	1,320,352	(42%)
Perot (I)	521,829	(16%)			

1992 Democratic Presidential Primary			1992 Republican Presidential Primary		
Clinton	256,337	(63%)	Bush	240,535	(78%)
Brown	79,877	(20%)	Buchanan	46,432	(15%)
Tsongas	45,191	(11%)	Write-In (Perot)	23,303	(8%)
Other	23,817	(6%)			

GOVERNOR

Gov. Jim Florio (D)

Elected 1989, term expires Jan. 1994; b. Aug. 29, 1937, Brooklyn, NY; home, Princeton; Trenton St. Col., B.A. 1962, Columbia U., 1962–63, Rutgers U., J.D., 1967; Catholic; married (Lucinda).

Career: Navy, 1955–58; Practicing atty., 1967–74; NJ Assembly, 1970–74, U.S. House of Reps., 1974–90.

Office: State House, 125 W. State St., CN-001, Trenton 08625, 609-292-6000.

Election Results

1989 gen.	Jim Florio (D)	1,379,937	(61%)
	Jim Courter (R)	838,553	(37%)
	Four Others	34,563	(2%)
1989 prim.	Jim Florio (D)	248,398	(68%)
	Barbara Boggs Sigmund (D)	60,541	(17%)
	Alan J. Karcher (D)	56,143	(15%)
1985 gen.	Thomas H. Kean (R)	1,372,631	(70%)
	Peter Shapiro (D)	578,402	(30%)

SENATORS
Sen. Bill Bradley (D)

Elected 1978, seat up 1996; b. July 28, 1943, Crystal City, MO; home, Denville; Princeton, B.A. 1965, Rhodes Scholar, Oxford U., M.A. 1968; Presbyterian; married (Ernestine).

Career: Air Force Reserves, 1967–78; U.S. Olympic Team, 1964; Pro basketball player, New York Knicks, 1967–77.

Offices: 731 HSOB, 202-224-3224. Also PO. Box 1720, 1609 Vauxhall Rd., Union 07083, 201-688-0960; and One Greentree Ctr., #303, Rte. 73, Marlton 08053, 609-983-4143.

Committee: *Aging (Special)* (3d of 11 D). *Energy and Natural Resources* (4th of 11 D): Public Lands, National Parks and Forests; Renewable Energy, Energy Efficiency and Competitiveness; Water and Power (Chmn.). *Finance* (4th of 11 D): Deficits, Debt Management and Long-Term Economic Growth (Chmn.); Health for Families and the Uninsured; International Trade.

Group Ratings

	ADA	ACLU	CDF	COPE	CFA	LCV	ACU	NTLC	NSI	COC	CEI
1992	85	82	60	91	75	83	4	19	40	22	28
1991	90	—	100	75	72	87	10	—	—	10	36

National Journal Ratings

	1991 LIB — 1991 CONS	1992 LIB — 1992 CONS
Economic	73% — 26%	63% — 36%
Social	73% — 23%	74% — 25%
Foreign	86% — 0%	65% — 26%

Key Votes of the 102d Congress

1. $ for Homeownership	AGN	5. Clarence Thomas Nom. AGN	9. Use Force in Gulf	AGN
2. Have Cap Gains Debate AGN	6. Lmt Death Row Appeal AGN	10. Keep Salvador Aid	AGN
3. Remove Budget Walls	FOR	7. Handgun Wait/5-Day	FOR	11. Cut $1B from SDI	FOR
4. Ban Striker Replace	FOR	8. Abortion Gag Rule	AGN	12. Override China MFN FOR

Key Votes of the 103d Congress

1. Family Leave	FOR	2. HIV Immigrants	FOR	3. Clinton Budget	FOR

Election Results

1990 general	Bill Bradley (D) 977,810	(50%)	($12,444,283)
	Christine Todd Whitman (R) 918,874	(47%)	($801,660)
	Three Others 41,770	(2%)	
1990 primary	Bill Bradley (D) 197,454	(92%)	
	Daniel Z. Seyler (D) 16,287	(8%)	
1984 general	Bill Bradley (D) 1,986,644	(64%)	($5,142,316)
	Mary V. Mochary (R) 1,080,100	(35%)	($956,398)

Sen. Frank R. Lautenberg (D)

Elected 1982, seat up 1994; b. Jan. 23, 1924, Paterson; home, Montclair; Columbia U., B.S. 1949; Jewish; separated.

Career: Army Signal Corps, 1942–46 (WWII); Co-founder, Automatic Data Processing, 1952–82; NY & NJ Port Authority Comm., 1978–82.

Offices: 506 HSOB 20510, 202-224-4744. Also Barrington Commons, 208 Whitehorse Pk., #1819, Barrington 08007, 609-757-5353; and Gateway 1, Gateway Ctr., Newark 07102, 201-645-3030.

Committees: *Appropriations* (9th of 16 D): Commerce, Justice, State and Judiciary; Defense; Foreign Operations; Transportation (Chmn.); VA, HUD and Independent Agencies. *Budget* (6th of 12 D). *Environment and Public Works* (4th of 10 D): Clean Water, Fisheries and Wildlife; Superfund, Recycling and Solid Waste Management (Chmn.); Toxic Substances, Research and Development. *Small Business* (10th of 12 D): Competitiveness, Capital Formation and Economic Opportunity; Export Expansion and Agricultural Development.

Group Ratings

	ADA	ACLU	CDF	COPE	CFA	LCV	ACU	NTLC	NSI	COC	CEI
1992	100	91	100	92	83	92	4	17	40	30	21
1991	95	—	100	67	83	100	5	—	—	10	28

National Journal Ratings

	1991 LIB — 1991 CONS		1992 LIB — 1992 CONS	
Economic	90%	— 3%	69%	— 27%
Social	87%	— 0%	84%	— 11%
Foreign	86%	— 0%	78%	— 14%

Key Votes of the 102d Congress

1. $ for Homeownership	AGN	5. Clarence Thomas Nom.	AGN	9. Use Force in Gulf	AGN
2. Have Cap Gains Debate	AGN	6. Lmt Death Row Appeal	AGN	10. Keep Salvador Aid	AGN
3. Remove Budget Walls	FOR	7. Handgun Wait/5-Day	FOR	11. Cut $1B from SDI	FOR
4. Ban Striker Replace	FOR	8. Abortion Gag Rule	AGN	12. Override China MFN	FOR

Key Votes of the 103d Congress

1. Family Leave	FOR	2. HIV Immigrants	FOR	3. Clinton Budget	FOR

Election Results

1988 general	Frank R. Lautenberg (D)	1,599,905	(54%)	($7,298,663)
	Peter M. Dawkins (R)	1,349,937	(46%)	($7,616,249)
1988 primary	Frank R. Lautenberg (D)	326,072	(78%)	
	Elnardo Webster (D)	51,938	(12%)	
	Harold Young (D)	41,303	(10%)	
1982 general	Frank R. Lautenberg (D)	1,117,549	(51%)	($6,435,743)
	Millicent Fenwick (R)	1,047,626	(48%)	($2,606,633)

FIRST DISTRICT

There is scarcely now a sadder place in America than Camden, New Jersey. Across the Delaware River from Philadelphia's lively Society Hill, it was once a locus of innovation and art. In 1894, a machinist here named Eldridge Johnson produced the Victor Talking Machine—the birth of the company that became RCA Victor in 1929. In 1897, Camden was the site of the invention of condensed soup, and the Campbell Soup Company was founded soon afterwards. Camden was also the longtime home of poet Walt Whitman. Camden was then the landmark on the Jersey side of the Delaware River, not the broadest and certainly not the most picturesque of the estuaries along the Atlantic, but probably the East Coast's premier industrial waterway, with a concentration of steel factories, chemical plants and oil tank farms equal to any in the country. The flat lands of South Jersey all around, ignored in the 19th Century, with easy access to cheap water transport and plenty of skilled labor from the Philadelphia area, were one of the country's fastest-growing industrial areas for a quarter-century starting in the 1940s. Today, Camden is a dismal slum, laid waste by crime and with few jobs left, and much of South Jersey lives with the residue of 1940s industrial growth—a high concentration of toxic waste, malodorous fumes, high cancer rates.

The 1st Congressional District of New Jersey is, more or less, greater Camden, the Delaware riverfront from Riverton south to a point across from the Delaware state line, and suburbs running southeast to the flat vegetable fields of South Jersey. Its boroughs and townships retain their separate identities, and next to rundown Camden is Collingswood, with its middle-class porches still freshly painted and its shops prosperous. The district includes some underclass poor, but most people here are at some level of upward mobility from the grinding working-class life of 50 years ago, living in comfortable communities, worried that the petrochemical plants which have helped many of them move up may also be poisoning their land, water and air. Politically, this is an area with a Democratic heritage, the home base of Governor Jim Florio (though not happy with his 1990 tax increases), an area that solidly supported Bill Bradley in 1990 and Bill Clinton in 1992.

The congressman from the 1st District is Rob Andrews, a Democrat who started off as a protege of Florio's local machine, but who quickly developed into a formidable politician in his own right. Andrews grew up in a modest home in Bellmawr, made a splendid record in college and law school, returned home and with Florio's support was elected to the Camden County Board of Chosen Freeholders (what a wonderful name!) before he was 30. There he reduced taxes to their lowest level since 1970, passed a recycling program that exceeded state requirements and established a Camden Alliance to replace welfare with jobs. When Florio resigned from Congress, he put off the election to replace him until November 1990; he supported Andrews though Andrews was silent on his tax increase. Andrews had other help. He spent $541,000 on his campaign, and had a Republican opponent who claimed to have attended a college he hadn't and switched positions on abortion. Even so, in the anti-Florio climate, Andrews won by only 54%–43%.

He entered Congress as the youngest Democrat there, and one of the more unconventional. Though he voted against the Gulf war resolution, he otherwise had a conservative record on foreign issues and was only moderate on economics; he charged that many federal programs spend too much money on administrators, clerical staff and conferences, without helping ordinary people. He introduced legislation allowing the government to make direct loans to college students, instead of guaranteeing loans by banks; he managed to get the House to approve direct loan demonstration projects, and got Bill Clinton to propose the idea on the campaign trail and then in the White House. Andrews fought hard to save jobs at the Philadelphia Navy Yard, just across the Walt Whitman Bridge, and he made quite a flurry by accusing the Navy of illegally diverting repair work to foreign shipyards. He steadfastly voted against tax increases and against fast track for the North American Free Trade Agreement.

Andrews's political acumen was shown in the 1992 election, when he outspent his opponent $762,000 to $176,000 and won 67%–29%. He is a politician to watch.

The People: Pop. 1990: 594,494; 4% rural; 12% age 65+; 77% White; 16% Black; 2% Asian; 4% Other; 6% Hispanic origin. Voting age pop.: 435,926; 14% Black; 5% Hispanic origin. Households: 55% married couple families; 27% married couple fams. w. children; 38% college educ.; median household income: $35,250; per capita income: $14,502; median gross rent: $514; median house value: $93,700.

1992 Presidential Vote			1988 Presidential Vote		
Clinton (D)	118,060	(48%)	Bush (R)	115,528	(53%)
Bush (R)	78,095	(32%)	Dukakis (D)	102,356	(47%)
Perot (I)	48,252	(20%)			

Rep. Robert E. Andrews (D)

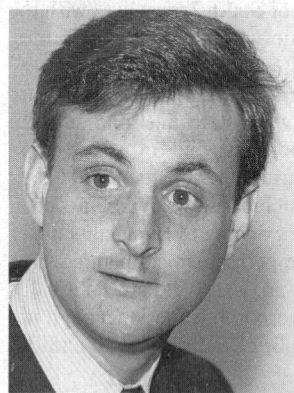

Elected 1990; b. Aug. 4, 1957, Camden; home, Bellmawr; Bucknell U., B.A. 1979, Cornell U., J.D. 1982; Episcopalian; single.

Career: Practicing atty., 1982–87; Adjunct Prof., Rutgers Col. of Law, 1985–86, 1989–90; Dir., Camden Cnty. Bd. of Chosen Freeholders, 1987–90.

Offices: 1005 LHOB 20515, 202-225-6501. Also 16 Somerdale Sq., Somerdale 08063, 609-627-9000; and 63 N. Broad St., Woodbury 08096, 609-848-3900.

Committees: *Education and Labor* (13th of 28 D): Human Resources; Labor Standards, Occupational Health and Safety; Postsecondary Education and Training. *Foreign Affairs* (15th of 27 D): Europe and the Middle East; International Operations.

Group Ratings

	ADA	ACLU	COPE	CDF	CFA	LCV	ACU	NTLC	NSI	COC	CEI
1992	70	87	83	60	73	69	32	15	70	38	26
1991	70	—	92	90	67	62	15	—	—	10	26

National Journal Ratings

	1991 LIB — 1991 CONS			1992 LIB — 1992 CONS		
Economic	50%	—	49%	43%	—	57%
Social	60%	—	38%	78%	—	21%
Foreign	56%	—	42%	0%	—	82%

Key Votes of the 102d Congress

1. Ban Striker Replace	FOR	5. Handgun Wait/7-Day	FOR	9. Use Force in Gulf	AGN
2. $ for Homeownership	FOR	6. Overseas Mil. Abortion	FOR	10. US Mil. Abroad $ Cut	*
3. Tax Rich/Cut Mid Cls.	AGN	7. Obscn. Art NEA $ Ban	AGN	11. Limit SDI Funds	AGN
4. FY93/$15B Def. Cut	AGN	8. Death Pen. from Jury	FOR	12. Cuba Trade Embargo	FOR

Key Votes of the 103d Congress

1. Family Leave	FOR	2. Deficit Reduction	AGN	3. Stimulus Plan	FOR

Election Results

1992 general	Robert E. Andrews (D)................	153,525	(67%)	($762,588)
	Lee A. Solomon (R)...................	65,123	(29%)	($176,586)
	Four Others..........................	9,424	(4%)	
1992 primary	Robert E. Andrews (D), unopposed			
1990 general	Robert E. Andrews (D)................	72,415	(54%)	($541,960)
	Daniel J. Mangini (R).................	57,299	(43%)	($79,662)
	Three others	4,080	(3%)	

SECOND DISTRICT

The builders of the Camden & Atlantic Railroad in 1852 may not have known it, but when they extended their line to the little inlet town of Absecon, they were starting America's biggest beach resort, Atlantic City. Like all resorts, it was a product of developments elsewhere: of industrialization and spreading affluence, of railroad technology and the conquest of diseases which used to make summer a time of terror for parents and doctors. In the years after the Civil War, first Atlantic City and then the whole oceanfront strand from Brigantine to Cape May became America's first seaside resort, and Atlantic City developed its characteristic features: the Boardwalk in 1870, the amusement pier in 1882, the rolling chair in 1884, salt water taffy in the 1890s, Miss America in 1921. By 1940, when 16 million Americans visited every summer, Atlantic City was a common man's resort of old traditions, but declined in the years after World War II as people could afford nicer vacations. By the early 1970s, Atlantic City was grim, with a bedraggled Convention Hall (site of the 1964 Democratic National Convention), empty hotels, gritty streets of rowhouses built in the ugliest Philadelphia style. Then in 1977, New Jersey voters legalized casino gambling in Atlantic City and gleaming new hotels sprang up, big name entertainers came in and Atlantic City became more glamorous than it had been in 90 years. But not for many of its residents: casino and hotel jobs tend to be low-wage, and the slums begin just feet from the massive parking lots of the casinos. Four of the last seven mayors have been charged with misconduct; and by 1990, as the Taj Mahal opened, it became plain that casino owners had overbuilt. Will these new jewels some day seem as begrimed as the old?

The Jersey Shore south of Atlantic City is a string of different resorts. There is the old Methodist town of Ocean City, where Gae Talese grew up the son of Italian immigrants, as he tells movingly in *Unto the Sons*. There is Wildwood, with its gritty boardwalk, and Cape May, with its beautifully preserved Victorian houses. Behind the Shore are swamp and flatland, the Pine Barrens and vegetable fields that gave New Jersey the name "Garden State." Growth has been slow in these small towns and gas station intersections, communities in whose eerie calmness in the summer you can hear mosquitoes whining. In the flatness, you can also find towns clustered around low-wage apparel factories or petrochemical plants on the Delaware estuary: the Northeast high-tech service economy has not reached this far south in Jersey yet.

This part of South Jersey makes up New Jersey's 2d Congressional District. Politically, it was long marginal country, with strong Democratic presences in the chemical industry towns across from Wilmington, Delaware and in Atlantic City, and a strong Republican presence in Cape May. In the 1990s, Democrats have been dominant, with Bill Bradley carrying the area nicely in 1990 and Bill Clinton almost as well in 1992. In congressional elections, it has voted for nearly 20 years for William Hughes, a moderate Democrat who as an Ocean City lawyer and prosecutor beat Nixon defender Charles Sandman in 1974. Hughes got a seat on the Judiciary Committee, where for most of the 1980s he chaired the Subcommittee on Crime, giving him the duty of shepherding the House biennial crime and drug bills which inevitably attracted controversial amendments. He drafted the 1984 and 1990 crime acts, and the 1986 and 1988 drug bills. Subject matter included bans on child pornography, boot camps for drug offenders, limits on steroid use, and the Brady bill's waiting period on handgun sales. Then in 1991, Hughes switched to chair the Subcommittee on Courts, Intellectual Property and Judicial Administration, the panel that handles federal courts and RICO, patents and copyrights. Arcane stuff, of vast importance to moneyed interests, especially in the entertainment industry: Hughes worked on the law preventing digital audio tapes from being copiable, hence opening the way for this technology; and he established felony penalties for theft of copyrighted material, including computer software. He also worked on patent legislation, court reform and prison conditions. Looking ahead, he wants to reform cable TV copyright laws to repair what he considers the damage done in the 1992 Cable Reregulation Law passed over George Bush's veto (he wants cable companies to pay program originators), and to reverse a Supreme Court ruling allowing employers to change the terms of health insurance contracts retroactively. Hughes was a sponsor of the 1988 ocean dumping ban, passed after Jersey Shore beaches were fouled by waste; the last garbage barge set out from New York in June 1992. He was disappointed in early 1993 when the Select Aging Committee he was in line to chair was abolished, along with other non-legislative committees.

Hughes is an able and busy legislator who won reelection easily in the 1980s and had no major party opponent in 1990. But in 1992, he had a serious challenge from Vineland Assemblyman Frank LoBiondo, who had strong support from the National Rifle Association and held Hughes to a 56%–42% victory, his lowest margin ever.

The People: Pop. 1990: 594,723; 30% rural; 15% age 65+; 78% White; 14% Black; 1% Asian; 4% Other; 6% Hispanic origin. Voting age pop.: 450,845; 13% Black; 5% Hispanic origin. Households: 54% married couple families; 24% married couple fams. w. children; 36% college educ.; median household income: $32,410; per capita income: $14,732; median gross rent: $525; median house value: $93,400.

1992 Presidential Vote		1988 Presidential Vote	
Clinton (D)	101,718 (40%)	Bush (R)	130,627 (59%)
Bush (R)	97,696 (39%)	Dukakis (D)	91,402 (41%)
Perot (I)	50,773 (20%)		

Rep. William J. Hughes (D)

Elected 1974; b. Oct. 17, 1932, Salem; home, Ocean City; Rutgers U., A.B. 1955, J.D. 1958; Episcopalian; married (Nancy).

Career: Practicing atty., 1959–74; Cape May Cnty. First Asst. Prosecutor, 1960–70.

Offices: 241 CHOB 20515, 202-225-6572. Also Central Park E., Bldg. 4, #5, 222 New Rd., Linwood, 08221, 609-927-9063; and 151 N. Broadway, P.O. Box 248, Pennsville 08070, 609-678-3333.

Committees: *Judiciary* (5th of 21 D): Intellectual Property and Judicial Administration (Chmn.). *Merchant Marine and Fisheries* (2d of 29 D): Coast Guard and Navigation; Fisheries Management.

Group Ratings

	ADA	ACLU	COPE	CDF	CFA	LCV	ACU	NTLC	NSI	COC	CEI
1992	80	91	83	70	93	88	20	38	60	25	30
1991	70	—	92	70	61	92	26	—	—	33	36

National Journal Ratings

	1991 LIB — 1991 CONS		1992 LIB — 1992 CONS	
Economic	55% —	44%	55% —	45%
Social	68% —	31%	68% —	30%
Foreign	54% —	44%	67% —	32%

Key Votes of the 102d Congress

1. Ban Striker Replace	FOR	5. Handgun Wait/7-Day	FOR
2. $ for Homeownership	AGN	6. Overseas Mil. Abortion	FOR
3. Tax Rich/Cut Mid Cls.	AGN	7. Obscn. Art NEA $ Ban	AGN
4. FY93/$15B Def. Cut	AGN	8. Death Pen. from Jury	AGN

9. Use Force in Gulf	FOR
10. US Mil. Abroad $ Cut	FOR
11. Limit SDI Funds	FOR
12. Cuba Trade Embargo	*

Key Votes of the 103d Congress

1. Family Leave	FOR	2. Deficit Reduction	FOR	3. Stimulus Plan	FOR

Election Results

1992 general	William J. Hughes (D) 132,465	(56%)	($608,150)
	Frank A. LoBiondo (R). 98,315	(42%)	($284,773)
	Three Others. 6,247	(3%)	
1992 primary	William J. Hughes (D), unopposed		
1990 general	William J. Hughes (D) 97,698	(88%)	($211,686)
	William A. Kanengiser (POP) 13,120	(12%)	

THIRD DISTRICT

The Pine Barrens of New Jersey are one of the last vacant spots on the Eastern seaboard; not quite *terra incognita*, but still not thickly populated. Encroached by the Philadelphia suburbs of South Jersey on the west and the burgeoning retirement developments of the Jersey Shore on the east, they are crossed even today mostly by narrow two-lane roads and are the site of the Army's Fort Dix and the Great Adventure theme park. For years, the Barrens were seen as a barrier to civilization; only recently have environmentally-minded Jerseyites decided that their natural ecology should be preserved.

The 3d Congressional District of New Jersey spans the Pine Barrens. Most of its residents live in the South Jersey suburbs of Philadelphia, in the spread-out suburb of Cherry Hill with its 1960s and 1970s shopping centers, or in the older towns along the Delaware River and newer ones inland toward Fort Dix. This is comfortable, but not hugely affluent, suburban country. East of the Pine Barrens is Ocean County, including the barrier islands from Normandy Beach south to Little Egg Harbor, with older beachfront communities and larger clusters of new subdivisions and condominium complexes inland. Ocean County has been one of the fastest-growing areas in the Northeast, its population up 25% in the 1980s. It resembles much of Florida, in its large and relatively affluent elderly population disgusted with the conditions of life in New York and other big cities, determined to extract the largest possible social security benefits, and concerned about the local environment. This was designed to be a Republican district: both the west and east ends are solidly Republican.

The congressman is Republican James Saxton, a former teacher and real estate broker who served nine years in the legislature, the kind of locally connected politician who is cautiously conservative about most national issues but cares about the home district first. He was one of the Republicans who opposed the budget summit package in 1990—no surprise, given the froth of anger at Governor Jim Florio's tax package at home. He was also one of the original sponsors of the 1988 ocean dumping law, which bans plastics dumping and requires tracing of medical waste—the hottest issue on the Shore that year. In 1992, he sponsored a bill requiring uniform testing of ocean waters. His chief causes for the 1990s are establishing a National Institute for the Environment, somewhat akin to the National Institutes of Health; and preserving Fort Dix, long one of the Army's basic training sites. Saxton got a seat on the Armed Services Committee in 1991 specifically to preserve Fort Dix. In 1991, the Department of Defense recommended that all but a small National Guard and Reserve unit there be done away with—a loss of about 800 jobs. By 1993, Saxton succeeded in turning much of the base into a federal prison and state police training center. But now Saxton must also deal with McGuire Air Force Base which was on the 1993 list of base closures; job losses here could affect 3,000 people.

Saxton first won the seat in 1984 with support from his home area outside Philadelphia. He has been reelected comfortably.

The People: Pop. 1990: 594,667; 18% rural; 15% age 65+; 87% White; 8% Black; 2% Asian; 1% Other; 3% Hispanic origin. Voting age pop.: 451,844; 7% Black; 2% Hispanic origin. Households: 66% married couple families; 29% married couple fams. w. children; 47% college educ.; median household income: $41,257; per capita income: $18,138; median gross rent: $651; median house value: $128,300.

1992 Presidential Vote			1988 Presidential Vote		
Clinton (D)	114,503	(40%)	Bush (R)	154,804	(62%)
Bush (R)	113,583	(40%)	Dukakis (D)	94,963	(38%)
Perot (I)	54,996	(19%)			

Rep. H. James Saxton (R)

Elected 1984; b. Jan. 22, 1943, Scranton, PA; home, Vincentown; E. Stroudsburg St. Col., B.A. 1965, Temple U., 1967–68; United Methodist; married (Helen).

Career: Jr. High Schl. Teacher, 1965–68; Real estate broker, 1968–84; NJ Assembly, 1975–82; NJ Senate, 1982–84.

Offices: 438 CHOB 20515, 202-225-4765. Also 100 High St., Mt. Holly 08060, 609-261-5800; 1 Maine Ave., Cherry Hill 08002, 609-428-0520; and 7 Hadley Ave., Toms River 08753, 908-914-2020.

Committees: *Armed Services* (13th of 22 R): Military Acquisition; Military Installations and Facilities. *District of Columbia* (3d of 4 R): Fiscal Affairs and Health; Government Operations and Metropolitan Affairs (RMM). *Merchant Marine and Fisheries* (4th of 19 R): Environment and Natural Resources (RMM); Oceanography, Gulf of Mexico and the Outer Continental Shelf. *Post Office and Civil Service* (9th of 9 R): Oversight and Investigations. *Joint Economic Committee.*

Group Ratings

	ADA	ACLU	COPE	CDF	CFA	LCV	ACU	NTLC	NSI	COC	CEI
1992	15	13	50	30	33	38	80	68	100	75	54
1991	10	—	27	40	28	54	74	—	—	67	51

National Journal Ratings

	1991 LIB — 1991 CONS		1992 LIB — 1992 CONS	
Economic	26%	— 74%	31%	— 68%
Social	16%	— 81%	23%	— 77%
Foreign	17%	— 78%	0%	— 82%

Key Votes of the 102d Congress

1. Ban Striker Replace AGN	5. Handgun Wait/7-Day FOR	9. Use Force in Gulf FOR
2. $ for Homeownership FOR	6. Overseas Mil. Abortion AGN	10. US Mil. Abroad $ Cut AGN
3. Tax Rich/Cut Mid Cls. AGN	7. Obscn. Art NEA $ Ban FOR	11. Limit SDI Funds AGN
4. FY93/$15B Def. Cut AGN	8. Death Pen. from Jury FOR	12. Cuba Trade Embargo FOR

Key Votes of the 103d Congress

1. Family Leave FOR	2. Deficit Reduction AGN	3. Stimulus Plan AGN

Election Results

1992 general	H. James Saxton (R)	151,368	(59%)	($416,807)
	Timothy E. Ryan (D)	94,012	(37%)	($30,015)
	Eight Others	10,418	(4%)	
1992 primary	H. James Saxton (R)	25,388	(89%)	
	Frank W. Drake (R)	3,044	(11%)	
1990 general	H. James Saxton (R)	99,688	(58%)	($730,989)
(NJ 13)	John H. Adler (D)	67,587	(39%)	($203,147)
	Other	4,131	(2%)	

FOURTH DISTRICT

New Jersey, a state long thought to be split between a North Jersey that is an appanage of New York City and a South Jersey that has the distinctive accent of Philadelphia, is becoming a state with its own identity. In the 1980s, it bubbled over with pride at its growth and new civic institutions; in 1990, it raged with anger at Governor Jim Florio's tax increases. This shows a new unity: for the great medium of protest was the first New Jersey-oriented talk radio station, started in Trenton in 1989, and the symbolic event was the Hands Across New Jersey demonstration on a route approximating I-195, from the Jersey Shore west to the State House in Trenton overlooking the Delaware River. Trenton itself, an old manufacturing city ("Trenton makes, the world takes," the sign proclaims over the rooftops), where John Roebling of Brooklyn Bridge fame started making wire in 1848, and Walter Scott Lenox started making dishes in 1889, is now the anomalous capital of a mostly white-collar state.

The 4th Congressional District of New Jersey covers approximately the same span as Hands Across New Jersey, from Trenton to the Jersey Shore, roughly following I-195 to the Shore communities of Manasquan and Point Pleasant and Mantoloking. It includes the old colonial town of Burlington on the Delaware River and the Great Adventure Safari and Entertainment Park in the Pine Barrens. This is one part of America where the population movement has been eastward, from the old neighborhoods of Trenton and its close-in suburbs to the new subdivisions of Ocean County and Wall Township. Trenton has long been a solidly Democratic town, but its suburbs are much less so, with the Jersey Shore parts of the district solidly Republican.

The congressman from the 4th District is Christopher Smith, a Republican who originally seemed a fluke but who has proved durable, a serious legislator and popular politician. Smith won in 1980, at 27, by beating convicted Abscam defendant Frank Thompson, in a district then much more centered on Trenton; his main credential was as executive director of the New Jersey Right to Life Committee. But he beat a series of serious opponents—a longtime Trenton state senator in 1982, the head of New Jersey's AFSCME in 1984, an experienced young liberal in 1986, Trenton mayor Arthur Holland's wife Betty in 1988, the Trenton Democratic chairman in 1990—with over 60% of the vote, and has passed some legislation as well. His motivation comes from religion: "Christ said it in Matthew 25: 'Whatsoever you do to the least of my brethren, you do likewise to me.' That was my motivating scripture through all of my years in Right to Life, and it continues to be," he said in 1992. He is concerned as well about children and victims of human rights violations; if his antiabortion stance comes from his Catholicism, his concern for victims also is part of a lively Catholic tradition which does not count everything by its marketplace value.

On the abortion issue, Smith has worked to cut off federal funding and opposes the Freedom of Choice Act; he also opposed aid to China's one-infant-per-family policy which has fostered coerced abortion and sterilization. On children's issues, he saved the Child Survival Fund, which immunizes Third World children against disease, from the budget ax and increased spending from $25 million to $245 million; he also pushed for money for pregnant women and neonatal care in the developing world. He has backed tax credits for adoptive parents and has an omnibus bill to promote adoption. He serves on the Foreign Affairs Committee, and was pushing for trade sanctions against Romania for human rights abuses back in 1985. In 1989, he was one of the first two congressmen to visit political prisoners in the last known Soviet political prisoner camp.

Locally, Smith has worked very hard. He has used his Veterans' Committee seat to help open a VA outpatient clinic in Ocean County. Interested in the environment, he advocates a wildlife refuge in Manasquan Cove. He has worked for senior citizens' housing projects, a housing rehab program, homeless shelters and the "weed and seed" anti-crime experiment in Trenton. In 1992, challenged by Brian Hughes, son of former Governor Richard Hughes, Smith carried all parts of the district, winning with 62% of the vote.

The People: Pop. 1990: 594,673; 16% rural; 17% age 65+; 81% White; 12% Black; 1% Asian; 2% Other; 5% Hispanic origin. Voting age pop.: 452,119; 11% Black; 4% Hispanic origin. Households: 58% married couple families; 26% married couple fams. w. children; 41% college educ.; median household income: $36,888; per capita income: $16,107; median gross rent: $583; median house value: $129,800.

1992 Presidential Vote			1988 Presidential Vote		
Bush (R)	109,907	(41%)	Bush (R)	140,170	(59%)
Clinton (D)	105,335	(39%)	Dukakis (D)	97,182	(41%)
Perot (I)	50,721	(19%)			

Rep. Christopher H. Smith (R)

Elected 1980; b. Mar. 4, 1953, Rahway; home, Washington Township; Trenton St. Col., B.S. 1975; Catholic; married (Marie).

Career: Sales exec., family-owned sporting goods business, 1975–80; Exec. Dir., NJ Right to Life, 1976–78.

Offices: 2353 RHOB 20515, 202-225-3765. Also 1720 Greenwood, Trenton 08609, 609-890-2800; 427 High St., #1, Burlington City 08016, 609-386-5534; and 100 Lacey Rd., #38-A, Whiting 08759, 908-350-2300.

Committees: *Foreign Affairs* (8th of 18 R): International Security, International Organizations and Human Rights; Western Hemisphere Affairs. *Veterans' Affairs* (2d of 14 R): Hospitals and Health Care (RMM).

Group Ratings

	ADA	ACLU	COPE	CDF	CFA	LCV	ACU	NTLC	NSI	COC	CEI
1992	40	43	67	60	60	44	68	55	100	75	38
1991	45	—	75	70	50	62	60	—	—	40	38

National Journal Ratings

	1991 LIB — 1991 CONS			1992 LIB — 1992 CONS		
Economic	47%	—	52%	37%	—	62%
Social	34%	—	65%	33%	—	66%
Foreign	33%	—	66%	30%	—	64%

Key Votes of the 102d Congress

1. Ban Striker Replace	FOR	5. Handgun Wait/7-Day	FOR	9. Use Force in Gulf	FOR
2. $ for Homeownership	FOR	6. Overseas Mil. Abortion	AGN	10. US Mil. Abroad $ Cut	AGN
3. Tax Rich/Cut Mid Cls.	AGN	7. Obscn. Art NEA $ Ban	FOR	11. Limit SDI Funds	AGN
4. FY93/$15B Def. Cut	AGN	8. Death Pen. from Jury	AGN	12. Cuba Trade Embargo	FOR

Key Votes of the 103d Congress

1. Family Leave	FOR	2. Deficit Reduction	AGN	3. Stimulus Plan	AGN

Election Results

1992 general	Christopher H. Smith (R)................	149,095	(62%)	($413,493)
	Brian M. Hughes (D)....................	84,514	(35%)	($164,038)
	Four Others...........................	7,616	(3%)	
1992 primary	Christopher H. Smith (R), unopposed			
1990 general	Christopher H. Smith (R)................	99,920	(63%)	($292,826)
	Mark Setaro (D).......................	54,961	(35%)	($55,772)
	Three others	4,418	(3%)	

FIFTH DISTRICT

The northern edge of New Jersey was first settled three centuries ago by the Dutch, for whom this plateau of land behind the Hudson River Palisades seemed a natural part of Nieuw Amsterdam and New York. The Dutch influence is still apparent in old steep-roofed farmhouses and in many of the place names—Bergen County, Cresskill, Closter. But overall, northernmost New Jersey has the well-settled look of so many Northeastern suburbs, with touches both of affluence and small town hominess, criss-crossed at its edges with limited access highways lined with shopping centers, five million square feet in the town of Paramus alone, which houses greater New York's first Nordstrom. Not far away is Saddle River, with million-dollar houses on multi-acre lots, for a while the retirement home of President Richard Nixon until he moved to a condominium in nearby Park Ridge. This area may look like WASP suburbia on the surface, but in fact is home to successful people of all ethnic groups, many descended by two or three generations from those who first saw the Statue of Liberty from the steerage deck and passed through the inspection queues at Ellis Island.

The 5th Congressional District consists of most of northern Bergen County, plus a swath of North Jersey stretching west to the hill-enclosed upper reaches of the Delaware, crossing one ridge of mountains after another, running south along Delaware I-78. Three-fifths of its population is clustered in Bergen; to the west, little subdivisions set amid the lakes of western Passaic County are filling up with young families; farther west are once rural, now fast-growing Sussex and Warren Counties. Politically, this area is solidly Republican; indeed the fast-growing areas to the west are probably more heavily Republican than the older settled area within 30 minutes of the George Washington Bridge.

Since 1980, the congresswoman from this district has been Marge Roukema, a Republican whose Dutch name and Italian descent tell much of the district's ethnic history. She was a teacher who gave up her job to raise her children and was involved in community activities before becoming a political candidate—founding a senior citizens' housing corporation and serving on a local school board. Like some other Republican congresswomen, she brings to politics maturity and experience in the actual workings of civic institutions. She tends to be market-oriented on economics but rather dovish on foreign policy. She has also staked out some important issues and made them her own.

The most important of these is family leave; she was the lead Republican sponsor, and often the key spokesperson for, the Family and Medical Leave Act which passed Congress in 1990 and 1992 and was vetoed by President Bush, and then was passed again and signed by President Clinton in February 1993. As finally passed, it covers employers with 50 or more employees, requiring them to give permanent workers 12 weeks unpaid leave per year for medical emergencies—the birth of a child, the serious illness of an immediate family member. Opponents charged that it imposed too great a cost on business; Roukema argued passionately that it provided a decent level of protection at affordable cost and, after much travail, prevailed. Roukema's other great crusade is against student loan program defaults. When they reached $2 billion in 1990, she worked on the House floor for reforms to make lenders and borrowers more accountable, and to crack down on for-profit trade schools that were generating many defaulted loans and in effect living off government guarantees. She failed to persuade Education and Labor Committee leaders or the House, but in 1992, when defaults reached the $3 billion level, she persevered. She also got a change in loan rules so that home equity is not counted in determining loan eligibility; this helps in northern New Jersey where, even despite 1990s drops, housing prices are among the highest in the country. She is opposed to Clinton's proposed direct government loan program, suspicious that it would produce any cost savings. On other issues, she is at odds with labor-liberals on Education and Labor; on housing, she favors penalty-free IRA withdrawals for first-time homebuyers and supported Jack Kemp's push for tenant management and ownership of public housing. In 1990, she tried to find a middle ground on the age discrimination bill. She is active, in other words, on a wide variety of legislation, with views that are not readily pigeonholed and convictions that reflect close study of the issues.

When Republicans gained veto-proof control of the New Jersey legislature, Roukema was spared a major crunch in redistricting. The real struggle in the 5th District comes, if anywhere, in the Republican primary; in 1992, Roukema had articulate opposition from Lou Sette, who criticized her for favoring abortion rights and supporting too much government spending. Roukema won by a 62%–24% margin; she ran strongest in Bergen County and weaker in the western part of the district. Her November victory was anticlimactic.

The People: Pop. 1990: 594,581; 19% rural; 13% age 65+; 91% White; 1% Black; 4% Asian; 3% Hispanic origin. Voting age pop.: 452,561; 1% Black; 3% Hispanic origin. Households: 69% married couple families; 33% married couple fams. w. children; 55% college educ.; median household income: $53,433; per capita income: $23,942; median gross rent: $717; median house value: $213,100.

1992 Presidential Vote			1988 Presidential Vote		
Bush (R)	146,004	(49%)	Bush (R)	178,419	(66%)
Clinton (D)	99,733	(34%)	Dukakis (D)	91,227	(34%)
Perot (I)	48,661	(16%)			

Rep. Marge Roukema (R)

Elected 1980; b. Sept. 19, 1929, W. Orange; home, Ridgewood; Montclair St. Col., B.A. 1951, Rutgers U.; Protestant; married (Richard).

Career: High schl. teacher, 1951–55; Ridgewood Board of Educ., 1970–73; Co-founder, Ridgewood Sr. Citizens Housing Corp., 1973.

Offices: 2244 RHOB 20515, 202-225-4465. Also 1200 E. Ridgewood Ave., Ridgewood 07450, 201-447-3900; and 1500 Rte. 517, #105, Hackettstown 07840, 908-850-4747.

Committees: *Banking, Finance and Urban Affairs* (3d of 20 R): Economic Growth and Credit Formation; Housing and Community Development (RMM); International Development, Finance, Trade and Monetary Policy. *Education and Labor* (3d of 15 R): Elementary, Secondary and Vocational Education; Labor-Management Relations (RMM); Postsecondary Education and Training.

Group Ratings

	ADA	ACLU	COPE	CDF	CFA	LCV	ACU	NTLC	NSI	COC	CEI
1992	50	35	42	60	47	38	68	53	90	71	51
1991	35	—	55	60	44	54	50	—	—	67	45

National Journal Ratings

	1991 LIB — 1991 CONS	1992 LIB — 1992 CONS
Economic	46% — 53%	37% — 62%
Social	43% — 56%	38% — 62%
Foreign	47% — 52%	56% — 40%

Key Votes of the 102d Congress

1. Ban Striker Replace	AGN	5. Handgun Wait/7-Day FOR	9. Use Force in Gulf	FOR
2. $ for Homeownership	FOR	6. Overseas Mil. Abortion FOR	10. US Mil. Abroad $ Cut FOR
3. Tax Rich/Cut Mid Cls.AGN	7. Obscn. Art NEA $ Ban FOR	11. Limit SDI Funds	FOR
4. FY93/$15B Def. Cut	AGN	8. Death Pen. from Jury AGN	12. Cuba Trade Embargo FOR

Key Votes of the 103d Congress

1. Family Leave	FOR	2. Deficit Reduction	AGN	3. Stimulus Plan	AGN

Election Results

1992 general	Marge Roukema (R)	196,198	(72%)	($504,596)
	Frank R. Lucas (D)	67,579	(25%)	($2,117)
	Four Others	10,594	(4%)	
1992 primary	Marge Roukema (R)	27,030	(62%)	
	Lou Sette (R)	10,243	(24%)	
	Ira M. Marlowe (R)	4,839	(11%)	
	Other	1,372	(3%)	
1990 general	Marge Roukema (R)	118,101	(76%)	($443,540)
	Lawrence Wayne Olsen (D)	35,010	(22%)	
	Other	2,998	(2%)	

SIXTH DISTRICT

For several generations, great transportation arteries have brought people out of the huge central cities of New York and Philadelphia and into the long-empty flatlands and hills of New Jersey—to vacation, to raise families, and to work toward affluence and build communities. The railroads of the late 19th Century created the towns of the Jersey Shore, from 1874, when the first train from New York City reached Long Branch, which quickly became the summer home of presidents from Grant to Wilson (Garfield, convalescing after he was shot, died there in 1881) and of New York race horse owners and socialites. The great freight rail lines in the New York-Philadelphia corridor sparked big electrical and chemical industries here, building on the inventions of Thomas Edison, many produced in his Menlo Park laboratory, just off the rail lines. The same corridor was also the site of America's first cloverleaf intersection, at the junction of U.S. 1 and U.S. 9, and the intersection of two of America's great post-World War II highways, the New Jersey Turnpike and the Garden State Parkway. The Turnpike now 12 lanes wide, roars past oil tank farms and petrochemical plants, major rail lines and Newark Airport and the oily waters of Raritan Bay; the Parkway links leafy affluent suburbs a dozen miles west of the Hudson with the Jersey Shore.

The 6th Congressional District of New Jersey ties together these great transportation nodes, and the upward mobility and economic progress that have taken place around them. It includes the central core of Middlesex County—New Brunswick and Edison Township and the surrounding communities—a heavy industry area that also, since the time of Thomas Edison, has housed some of America's great research and development facilities. Here, immigrant factory workers in small frame houses have raised their families in small towns that seem as far removed from Manhattan as any place in the Midwest. The 6th District includes a strip of territory overlooking Lower New York Bay, with spacious estates on highlands above little port towns. It takes in a strip of beach towns from Sandy Hook south to Sea Girt: Long Branch, with its seedy boardwalk amusements; Deal's grand mansions, windows always closed to save the air conditioning, are being bought up by Syrian Jews; Allenhurst, with its renovated clapboard Victorians; Asbury Park, once the vital center of this beachfront; Irish-American Spring Lake, with streets of neat houses; Ocean Grove, founded in 1869 as a Methodist resort "free from the dissipation and follies of fashionable watering places," still for teetotalers, who throng to its 10,000-seat, 1894 Great Hall. The Shore is still a vacation area that attracts millions, but these are also year-round communities, with their own upward-striving families, whose teenage energies have been given expression by the Shore's biggest celebrity, singer Bruce Springsteen.

The 6th District as redrawn in 1992 combined the larger parts of two older districts, placing together two incumbents. Bernard Dwyer, whose political roots were in the long-powerful Middlesex County Democratic machine and who after a lifetime in politics was rewarded with a House seat in 1980 at age 59, had represented three-fifths of the new district. But, despite bringing new projects into the district, in 1990 he won only 51% of the vote, losing Middlesex County. Dwyer announced his retirement the day after the districting plan was announced. That left the way open, though not entirely clear, for Jersey Shore incumbent Frank Pallone. Pallone is the son of a disabled Long Branch policeman, an environmentalist since entering college in Vermont in 1969, where he worked for the state's first-in-the-nation bottle deposit law, and a professional politician who had run for office since law school. He was elected to the New Jersey Senate in 1983, where he did not always follow party lines and concentrated on environmental issues. When Congressman Jim Howard, chairman of the Public Works Committee and father of the 55-mile-per-hour speed limit and many highway projects, died in March 1988, Pallone ran for Congress. Although the district leaned Republican, it was also angry about the untreated sludge, plastic containers and medical waste that was washing up on the beach in 1987 and 1988. This was not only unsightly and unhealthy; it was ruining the Jersey Shore economy, and Pallone's bumper sticker, instead of naming his party, read "Stop Ocean Dumping." Combined with his conservative stands on taxes and crime, his environmental emphasis helped him win 52%–48% over state legislator Joseph Azzolina. In the House, Pallone got seats on the Public Works and Merchant Marine Committees and continued to be a maverick, speaking out against the congressional pay raise and distancing himself from Governor Jim Florio's 1990 tax increase. Still, in 1990 he beat Asbury Park Councilman Paul Kapalko by only 49%–46%. Pallone was clearly the target of Republican redistricters; but he retained much of his Shore base, and had a slightly more Democratic district overall.

But he had some trouble getting known in the new areas; he won only 55% in a primary against a Middlesex opponent. And in the general, he was opposed by Republican state Legislator Joseph Kyrillos. Pallone campaigned for a single-payer government health insurance system; Kyrillos, an executive for a healthcare service organization, wanted more marginal reforms. Kyrillos ran against Congress, but Pallone had some advantages: he vastly outspent Kyrillos, $929,000 to $403,000; Bill Clinton finished ahead of George Bush in the district; and Pallone had pulled in much federal money for district projects. Pallone won by 52%–45%, with nearly identical margins in both counties. So he will continue to work for environmental causes and be a potentially critical vote on Clinton economic programs. But the 6th District is likely to remain marginal, and quite possibly seriously contested again.

The People: Pop. 1990: 594,650; 12% age 65+; 78% White; 11% Black; 5% Asian; 2% Other; 6% Hispanic origin. Voting age pop.: 465,588; 10% Black; 5% Hispanic origin. Households: 57% married couple families; 26% married couple fams. w. children; 47% college educ.; median household income: $42,309; per capita income: $18,135; median gross rent: $645; median house value: $159,500.

1992 Presidential Vote		
Clinton (D)	110,821	(44%)
Bush (R)	98,397	(39%)
Perot (I)	41,867	(17%)

1988 Presidential Vote		
Bush (R)	132,480	(56%)
Dukakis (D)	105,023	(44%)

Rep. Frank Pallone, Jr. (D)

Elected 1988; b. Oct. 30, 1951, Long Branch; home, Long Branch; Middlebury Col., B.A. 1973, Fletcher Schl. of Law and Diplomacy, M.A. 1974, Rutgers U., J.D. 1978; Catholic; married (Sarah).

Career: Asst. prof., Rutgers U., 1979–80; Practicing atty., 1981–83; Long Branch City Cncl., 1982–88; NJ Senate, 1983–88; Instructor, Monmouth Col., 1984–86.

Offices: 420 CHOB 20515, 202-225-4671. Also IEI Airport Plz., #18, Hazlet 07703, 908-264-9104; 1174 Fischer Blvd., Toms River 08753, 201-929-1400; and 540 Broadway Ave., #119, Long Branch 07740, 201-571-1140.

Committees: *Energy and Commerce* (21st of 27 D): Commerce, Consumer Protection and Competitiveness; Health and the Environment; Transportation and Hazardous Materials. *Merchant Marine and Fisheries* (10th of 29 D): Coast Guard and Navigation; Environment and Natural Resources.

Group Ratings

	ADA	ACLU	COPE	CDF	CFA	LCV	ACU	NTLC	NSI	COC	CEI
1992	90	78	83	60	87	88	28	40	80	38	27
1991	60	—	92	80	83	85	30	—	—	10	34

National Journal Ratings

	1991 LIB — 1991 CONS			1992 LIB — 1992 CONS		
Economic	56%	—	42%	45%	—	55%
Social	62%	—	37%	78%	—	21%
Foreign	51%	—	46%	56%	—	40%

Key Votes of the 102d Congress

1. Ban Striker Replace	FOR	5. Handgun Wait/7-Day	FOR	9. Use Force in Gulf	FOR
2. $ for Homeownership	FOR	6. Overseas Mil. Abortion	FOR	10. US Mil. Abroad $ Cut	FOR
3. Tax Rich/Cut Mid Cls.	AGN	7. Obscn. Art NEA $ Ban	FOR	11. Limit SDI Funds	FOR
4. FY93/$15B Def. Cut	AGN	8. Death Pen. from Jury	FOR	12. Cuba Trade Embargo	FOR

Key Votes of the 103d Congress

1. Family Leave	FOR	2. Deficit Reduction	AGN	3. Stimulus Plan	FOR

Election Results

1992 general	Frank Pallone, Jr. (D)	118,266	(52%)	($929,541)
	Joseph M. Kyrillos (R)	100,949	(45%)	($403,153)
	Seven Others	6,878	(3%)	
1992 primary	Frank Pallone, Jr. (D)	19,087	(55%)	
	Bob Smith (D)	12,769	(37%)	
	Barbara Jensen (D)	1,784	(5%)	
	Jeffrey R. Gorman (D)	1,286	(4%)	
1990 general	Frank Pallone, Jr. (D)	77,866	(49%)	($634,109)
(NJ 3)	Paul A. Kapalko (R)	73,696	(46%)	($115,202)
	Three Others	7,081	(5%)	

SEVENTH DISTRICT

The arteries beneath the curve of the First Watchung Mountain are one of New Jersey's historic lines of development—the old rail lines of the late 19th Century opened up commuter suburbs, then in the 1940s the four lanes of U.S. 22 created an automobile civilization, and finally Interstate 78, not completed until the mid-1980s, put Newark only an hour's distance from the Pennsylvania line. This newest road stimulated the development of an Edge City called Bridgewater Commons, where a huge shopping mall and office developments that included the new headquarters of AT&T rose up amid the horse country around Far Hills and Bernardsville where the likes of Malcolm Forbes and Charles Engelhard owned huge estates.

The 7th Congressional District of New Jersey covers these several generations of suburban development. After the 1992 redistricting, the 7th no longer includes any of industrial Elizabeth, but begins just to the west, taking in affluent railroad commuter towns like Short Hills and Summit. It also includes more modest suburbs along U.S. 22 like Union and Westfield and the old city of Plainfield, plus the working class suburbs of Woodbridge and South Plainfield in Middlesex County. It then follows I-78 and the Watchung Mountains far into the countryside to the fields of Somerset County. Once this was all solidly Republican; now the closer-in suburbs are more mixed, though sharply averse to Governor Jim Florio's tax increase. The farther-out Edge City areas are, if anything, increasingly Republican. In the House, this area has been represented by Republicans for many years.

The congressman is Bob Franks, who came to the office rather suddenly, after 13 years in the New Jersey Assembly and stints as state Republican chairman. For 20 years before him, the district was represented by Matthew Rinaldo, a seasoned local politician and generally liberal Republican, with a penchant for taking popular stands on issues and amassing campaign contributions, for which his position as ranking Republican on the Energy and Commerce Subcommittee on Telecommunications and Finance must have helped. Rinaldo was renominated in June 1992 and was headed for easy reelection when he announced on September 11 that he was leaving Congress to accept a private business opportunity; he also had, provided he left that year, a chance to convert his $900,000 campaign treasury to personal use, though he said he would use it for political and charitable contributions.

To fill the vacant Republican nomination, the organization chose Franks, who was not only state party chairman but also a protege of former Governor Tom Kean and campaign manager for two other New Jersey congressmen. Franks had helped lead vocal opposition to the Florio tax increases and helped produce the two-thirds-plus Republican majorities in the 1991 legislative elections; he is pro-choice on abortion and called for a "bold new approach" to Congress. But Franks had serious competition from Democrat Leonard Sendelsky, a well-known local builder active in civic organizations. The two ran even in Middlesex, while Franks won 55% in the rest of the district, for a 53%–43% win.

With smart political instinct, an anti-tax record and seats on the Budget Committee and Public Works (1993's number one choice), Franks has good prospects to hold onto the seat for years as Rinaldo did.

The People: Pop. 1990: 594,844; 4% rural; 14% age 65+; 80% White; 10% Black; 5% Asian; 1% Other; 5% Hispanic origin. Voting age pop.: 467,739; 9% Black; 4% Hispanic origin. Households: 64% married couple families; 27% married couple fams. w. children; 53% college educ.; median household income: $50,996; per capita income: $23,253; median gross rent: $699; median house value: $186,200.

1992 Presidential Vote			1988 Presidential Vote		
Bush (R)	125,592	(44%)	Bush (R)	160,286	(60%)
Clinton (D)	115,846	(41%)	Dukakis (D)	106,975	(40%)
Perot (I)	40,690	(14%)			

Rep. Bob Franks (R)

Elected 1992; b. Sept. 21, 1951, Hackensack; home, New Providence; DePauw U., B.A. 1973, S. Methodist U., J.D. 1976; Methodist; single.

Career: Political consultant, 1976–79; Med Data Inc., 1979–81; NJ Assembly, 1979–92; Co-owner, *County News*, 1982–84; NJ Repub. St. Chmn., 1988–89, 1990–92.

Offices: 429 CHOB 20515, 202-225-5361. Also 2333 Morris Ave., #B-17, Union 07083, 908-686-5576.

Committees: *Budget* (14th of 17 R). *Public Works and Transportation* (19th of 24 R): Economic Development; Surface Transportation.

Group Ratings and 102d Congress Votes: Newly Elected

Key Votes of the 103d Congress

1. Family Leave	FOR	2. Deficit Reduction	AGN	3. Stimulus Plan	AGN

Election Results

1992 general	Bob Franks (R)...................	132,174	(53%)	($453,991)
	Leonard Sendelsky (D)...............	105,761	(43%)	($223,704)
	Five Others.....................	6,104	(3%)	
1992 primary	Bob Franks (R), nominated by convention			
1990 general	Matthew J. Rinaldo (R).............	100,066	(75%)	($405,355)
	Bruce Bergen (D).................	31,099	(23%)	
	Other.........................	2,907	(2%)	

EIGHTH DISTRICT

Paterson, New Jersey, is one of few American cities that has turned out exactly as its original planner intended some 200 years ago. The planner was Alexander Hamilton, who in the 1790s journeyed 20 miles from Manhattan into the interior of New Jersey to the Great Falls of the Passaic River. Watching the water surge down 72 feet—the highest falls along the East Coast— he predicted that an industrial city would rise at this place, and he formed the Society for Establishing Useful Manufactures, which opened a calico factory in 1794 and got Pierre L'Enfant, the designer of Washington, D.C., to design Paterson (named after then-Governor William Paterson). In 1836, Samuel Colt began manufacturing revolvers here and the first locomotive, the Sandusky, was built here in 1837; a walkout of Paterson cottonworkers in 1828 was America's first factory strike. Paterson ultimately became America's "Silk City," employing 25,000 silk mill workers before the great strike of 1913 led by the radical Industrial Workers of the World, at a time when the city fathers were erecting imposing public buildings and the narrow streets were buzzing with rumors of anarchist plots. Paterson kept producing locomotives and, after the silk mills started closing down following another unsuccessful strike in 1924, became a cloth-dying center. Throughout, it attracted immigrants from England, Ireland and, after 1890, Italy and Poland. But now Paterson is a kind of misfit in time and place: still a manufacturing center at a time when manufacturing is no longer considered the nation's prime work, still an old fashioned central city, though it is surrounded by suburbs of New York and Newark and is an easy freeway ride away from the George Washington Bridge.

The 8th Congressional District of New Jersey includes Paterson as its largest city, plus much suburban territory west and south of Paterson and north and west of Newark. It includes the mixed factory and middle-class towns south of Paterson on the Passaic River—Clifton, Passaic, Nutley, Belleville. On higher ground are Bloomfield and, up on a ridge with views of New York City, part of Montclair. Part of the affluent Oranges are also included, as well as Wayne Township west of Paterson. The political heritage of the 8th District is Democratic, less because of its radical past than because of the allegiances of its immigrant groups. But recently, the central cities have been outvoted by increasingly Republican suburbs, and the 8th District voted Republican for president in the 1980s.

In 1992, with even more suburbs added to the district, incumbent Robert Roe, the hardworking chairman of Public Works, decided to retire after 23 years; as chairman of the Water Resources Subcommittee for many years, he pasted together the 1977 and 1987 water power projects bills; he also chaired the Science Committee from 1987 to 1990. Roe's successor is another Democrat, Herb Klein, an Adlai Stevenson volunteer in his youth and an assemblyman for two terms in the early 1970s who in 1992 had the political skill to win a seriously contested primary and then beat a well-known Republican in a Republican-leaning district. In the Assembly, Klein helped establish the state Economic Development Authority and wrote generic drug legislation; he is a believer in close government regulation of the economy. Klein lost his Assembly seat in 1975 after supporting Governor Brendan Byrne's income tax proposal; he remained a member of many civic boards and an active Democratic fundraiser.

In the Democratic primary, Klein beat two candidates from the southern part of the district;

in the general, he spent much of his own money, and was owed $580,000 by his campaign in November, the most of any House freshman. Klein charged that the Republican economic policies of 1981–92 had failed, and he opposed NAFTA, but his most telling attacks were on his opponent's ethics. Republican state Senator Joseph Bubba was a strong opponent of higher taxes; he also backed the controversial $2 billion Passaic River flood tunnel plan. Klein hit Bubba for not paying overdue property taxes until he ran for Congress, for keeping $43,000 in contributions from a contractor who admitted bribing the mayor of Passaic with another $25,000, and for taking $1,500 from a video gambling promoter charged with illegal kickbacks. Bubba called Klein an out-of-touch millionaire and accused him of compromising wetlands for profit when Klein's law firm represented a developer. Neither candidate ended up winning a majority. Klein won with 47%, Bubba had 41% and "Independent for Change" candidate Gloria Kolodziej won 8%.

Klein can be expected to be a solid vote for progressive taxation and government health insurance; he is willing to take political risks to back his convictions that government should do more to help ordinary people. He has also shown the ability to run an effective campaign, though the closeness of the 1992 race may mean another serious contest here in 1994.

The People: Pop. 1990: 594,912; 15% age 65+; 67% White; 13% Black; 4% Asian; 8% Other; 17% Hispanic origin. Voting age pop.: 461,626; 12% Black; 15% Hispanic origin. Households: 55% married couple families; 24% married couple fams. w. children; 42% college educ.; median household income: $39,944; per capita income: $18,527; median gross rent: $595; median house value: $192,900.

1992 Presidential Vote

Clinton (D)	107,304	(45%)
Bush (R)	99,974	(42%)
Perot (I)	27,703	(12%)

1988 Presidential Vote

Bush (R)	123,358	(55%)
Dukakis (D)	101,357	(45%)

Rep. Herb Klein (D)

Elected 1992; b. June 24, 1930, Newark; home, Clifton; Rutgers U., B.A. 1950, Harvard Law Schl., J.D. 1953, NYU, LL.M. 1958; Jewish; married (Jacqueline).

Career: Air Force, 1954–56; Practicing atty., 1956–92; NJ Assembly, 1971–75.

Offices: 1728 LHOB 20515, 202-225-5751. Also 200 Fed. Plz., #500, Paterson 07505, 201-523-5152.

Committees: *Banking, Finance and Urban Affairs* (15th of 30 D): Economic Growth and Credit Formation; Financial Institutions Supervision, Regulation and Deposit Insurance; Housing and Community Development. *Science, Space and Technology* (19th of 33 D): Energy; Technology, Environment and Aviation.

Group Ratings and 102d Congress Votes: Newly Elected

Key Votes of the 103d Congress

1. Family Leave	FOR	2. Deficit Reduction	AGN	3. Stimulus Plan	FOR

Election Results

1992 general	Herb Klein (D)	96,742	(47%)	($1,249,023)
	Joseph L. Bubba (R)	84,674	(41%)	($432,784)
	Gloria J. Kolodziej (IFC)	16,170	(8%)	($3,850)
	Seven Others	8,242	(4%)	
1992 primary	Herb Klein (D)	9,456	(39%)	
	Harry A. McEnroe (D)	6,786	(28%)	
	Clare I. Lagermasini (D)	6,510	(27%)	
	Joseph C. Iozia (D)	1,127	(5%)	
	Other	502	(2%)	
1990 general	Robert A. Roe (D)	55,797	(77%)	($558,625)
	Stephen Sibilia (IC)	13,180	(18%)	
	Bruce Eden (POP)	3,563	(5%)	

NINTH DISTRICT

The George Washington Bridge, one of America's several wondrous suspension bridges completed in the 1930s, strides across the Hudson, its western tower almost up against the green cliff of New Jersey's Palisades. It is one of the glories of modern engineering which enable people and goods to be transported through the irregular terrain of metropolitan New York— tidal rivers and cliffs and broad expanses of swamp. The dramatic beauty of the Palisades contrasts with the ugly sprawl of the Hackensack River Valley and the Jersey Meadowlands. For a century or more, this giant swamp on both sides of the Hackensack River was the image of New Jersey for many New Yorkers, a landscape of giant gas station signs, oil tank farms, truck terminals and 12 lanes of New Jersey Turnpike, a smelly, ugly place that meant that you were still not where you wanted to go, full of garbage and pig farms, briefly famous when Secaucus tavern owner Henry Krajewski ran for president in 1956 and commemorated in today's New Jersey Garbage Museum. But the Meadowlands were also the largest hunk of empty real estate near such a huge city center, and eventually they were developed. In the 1970s, the state built the Meadowlands Sports Complex—Giants Stadium (Giants and Jets now), the Meadowlands Racetrack, the Brendan Byrne Arena (Nets and Devils). Private development followed—hotels, warehouses, light industry, whole small cities.

The 9th Congressional District of New Jersey includes much of the Palisades and the Meadowlands. It runs from the high-rise towers of Fort Lee and Cliffside Park, where apartment houses brag how close they are to New York City, and to the west and north the leafy suburbs of Englewood and Teaneck, and southwest to the high land overlooking the Meadowlands and the Passaic River in old small towns like Rutherford, with Polish, German and Italian-Americans. Hackensack, an old industrial town that is the Bergen County seat, and much of Fair Lawn, a planned town with a large Jewish population, are also in the 9th. This area was growing in the 1950s and 1960s, as New Yorkers moved out of the City; it lost population in the 1970s and 1980s, as young people moved elsewhere and left empty nesters, despite the Meadowlands growth.

This was Republican country in the New Deal years, white-collar enclaves where people struggled to get by on their paychecks and resented the idea of their taxes going to the political machines of Hudson County and New York City. Englewood, Teaneck and other towns near the Bridge have since become more Democratic as they have become extensions of the Upper West Side, while the old ethnic towns have trended Republican. This district, with its almost New Yorky atypicality, voted exactly the national average in the 1988 presidential election.

Bob Torricelli, congressman from the 9th, is an articulate and ambitious—over ambitious in the eyes of some—Democrat who started his political career while in his 20s. He was an aide to Governor Brendan Byrne and Walter Mondale in the 1970s and helped manage the Carter-

Mondale victory over Edward Kennedy in Illinois. In 1982, he returned home to New Jersey, raised lots of money and beat an incumbent Republican congressman. In the House, he took politically beneficial committee assignments: Foreign Affairs (many of his ethnic constituents have particular interest in Israel, Greece, Korea, the Philippines and Cuba) and Science and Technology (North Jersey is one of the biggest high-tech areas in the country).

In 1989, Torricelli was one of the strongest defenders of Speaker Jim Wright and bluntly opposed campaign finance reform that he thought would work against Democrats. But he broke with Speaker Tom Foley and Majority Leader Dick Gephardt on the Gulf war resolution in January 1991, and the strength of his advocacy upset the leadership which felt he was giving the Republicans campaign ammunition. Already passed over for Democratic Congressional Campaign Committee chairman, he then was not assigned a seat on the Intelligence Committee, which he had expected. By early 1992, Torricelli was critical of Foley on the House banking scandal (he was embarrassed to find he had 27 overdrafts himself), and was clearly no longer on the leadership team. This is not the first time Torricelli has criticized those he has served ably and aggressively: he was harshly critical of his former boss Walter Mondale in 1984, of New Jersey Democratic gubernatorial candidate Peter Shapiro in 1985, and of Governor Florio on his tax package—particularly its effect on the public school system. Some thought Torricelli wanted to run for governor himself in 1989 and would have but for Florio's strength; but his political judgment on the Florio tax plan and the Gulf war has proven sound.

But Torricelli has other causes. In 1991, he inherited the chairmanship of the Western Hemisphere Subcommittee, held for a decade by Democrats of liberal or leftish sympathies. Torricelli went the other way, backing new trade sanctions on Castro's Cuba "to shorten the suffering of the Cuban people by isolating Castro and forcing him out." His bill imposed penalties on U.S. companies that use subsidiaries in third countries to trade with Cuba, and was initially opposed by the Bush Administration. But Torricelli lobbied Bill Clinton, who endorsed it while campaigning in the Florida primary; Cuban-American leader Jorge Mas Canosa allowed that a Clinton Administration would not be a threat, at which point the Bush Administration sought a compromise. They got it—companies would not have to abrogate existing contracts— but Torricelli's bill went through with a new $50,000 fine for violators of the ban on travel and new restrictions on trade to Cuba. He also blocked the sale of medicine to Cuba. On other Latin issues, Torricelli had long warned of the danger of the Sendero Luminoso, even beyond Peru. And he was willing to use U.S. military force in Haiti but also wanted to see President Aristide compromise and supported screening Haitians who want asylum in the U.S. in Haiti, not Florida or Guantanamo Bay. Torricelli was attacked by some who wanted conciliation with Castro—he argued, why conciliate with an evil dictator who is on the way out?—and others suggested he was courting Cuban-Americans who are numerous just outside the 9th District in Hudson County and might help him if he runs statewide.

That is not a terribly big if: he is interested in issues with statewide appeal. It was widely reported in late 1992 that if Senator Bill Bradley had been appointed secretary of state, Torricelli wanted Florio to appoint him to the seat, or otherwise might have run for it in 1993; he is not an implausible candidate if Senator Frank Lautenberg does not run for reelection in 1994; he could easily become a candidate for governor in 1997. His campaign treasury is already over $1 million, and he has won handily in the 9th District, which with the Cuban-American vote gives him a good statewide base.

The People: Pop. 1990: 594,790; 16% age 65+; 76% White; 6% Black; 7% Asian; 3% Other; 11% Hispanic origin. Voting age pop.: 481,031; 6% Black; 10% Hispanic origin. Households: 54% married couple families; 22% married couple fams. w. children; 44% college educ.; median household income: $40,816; per capita income: $20,012; median gross rent: $640; median house value: $194,500.

1992 Presidential Vote

Clinton (D) 122,676 (47%)
Bush (R) 102,578 (40%)
Perot (I).................... 31,534 (12%)

1988 Presidential Vote

Bush (R) 134,923 (53%)
Dukakis (D)................. 117,314 (47%)

Rep. Robert G. Torricelli (D)

Elected 1982; b. Aug. 26, 1951, Paterson; home, Englewood; Rutgers U., B.A. 1974, J.D. 1977, Harvard JFK Schl. of Govt., M.P.A. 1980; United Methodist; married (Susan).

Career: Asst., NJ Gov. Brendan Byrne, 1975–77; Cnsl., Vice Pres. Walter Mondale, 1978–81; Practicing atty., 1981–82.

Offices: 2159 RHOB 20515, 202-225-5061. Also 25 Main St., Court Plz., Hackensack 07601, 201-646-1111.

Committees: *Foreign Affairs* (4th of 27 D): Africa; Asia and the Pacific; Western Hemisphere Affairs (Chmn.). *Intelligence (Permanent Select)* (5th of 12 D): Oversight and Evaluation; Program and Budget Authorization. *Science, Space and Technology* (8th of 33 D): Space; Technology, Environment and Aviation.

Group Ratings

	ADA	ACLU	COPE	CDF	CFA	LCV	ACU	NTLC	NSI	COC	CEI
1992	85	83	83	90	87	63	16	5	90	33	13
1991	60	—	92	90	83	69	20	—	—	30	12

National Journal Ratings

	1991 LIB — 1991 CONS	1992 LIB — 1992 CONS
Economic	69% — 29%	69% — 30%
Social	74% — 23%	70% — 30%
Foreign	50% — 49%	44% — 50%

Key Votes of the 102d Congress

1. Ban Striker Replace	FOR	5. Handgun Wait/7-Day FOR	9. Use Force in Gulf FOR
2. $ for Homeownership	AGN	6. Overseas Mil. Abortion FOR	10. US Mil. Abroad $ Cut FOR
3. Tax Rich/Cut Mid Cls.	AGN	7. Obscn. Art NEA $ Ban FOR	11. Limit SDI Funds FOR
4. FY93/$15B Def. Cut	FOR	8. Death Pen. from Jury AGN	12. Cuba Trade Embargo FOR

Key Votes of the 103d Congress

1. Family Leave   FOR   2. Deficit Reduction   FOR   3. Stimulus Plan   FOR

Election Results

1992 general	Robert G. Torricelli (D)	139,188	(58%)	($1,001,343)
	Patrick J. Roma (R)	88,179	(37%)	($172,946)
	Six Others	11,337	(5%)	
1992 primary	Robert G. Torricelli (D)	24,010	(80%)	
	Nancy Harrigan (D)...................	4,733	(16%)	
	Matthew C. Guice (D)	1,429	(5%)	
1990 general	Robert G. Torricelli (D)	82,535	(53%)	($495,219)
	Peter J. Russo (R)....................	69,658	(45%)	($34,513)
	Other...............................	2,573	(2%)	

TENTH DISTRICT

Newark is the hollow core of New Jersey, the city to which main transportation arteries once led and whose corporate headquarters buildings were the tallest in the state. In 1930, 442,000 people lived here, one of every nine in the state; in 1990, 275,000 did, one of every 28. Downtown Newark still has the Prudential and Public Service headquarters, there are still factories in the Ironbound district, the area around Newark airport has some industrial development; but big corporation leaders and small businessmen alike have not put new jobs here since the 1967 riot. The reason is obvious: high crime. Some neighborhoods of Newark have retained their vitality, but very large parts are dominated by criminals and deserted by most law-abiding residents who can get out. Newark has its assets—the Newark Museum with its Tibetan art, the 775 banners on downtown lampposts bearing civic messages—but overall conditions are grim.

Most of Newark—the Central, South and West Wards—plus Irvington, most of the Oranges and part of Montclair to the west, and much of Elizabeth, Rahway and Linden to the south, make up New Jersey's 10th Congressional District. As redrawn in 1992, the 10th is 60% black, and overwhelmingly Democratic; its boundary lines wiggle around to include blacks in Jersey City, Montclair and Elizabeth and leave Hispanics in the next-door 13th. The congressman from the 10th is Donald Payne. Payne had run against incumbent Peter Rodino, chairman of the House Judiciary Committee when it voted to impeach President Richard Nixon, in 1980 and 1986 and lost, though he is black and the district had a black majority. When Rodino retired in 1988, Payne got 73% in the Democratic primary and easily won the general, and has been returned easily ever since.

Payne, the first black member of Congress from New Jersey, is a member of the Education and Labor, Foreign Affairs and Government Operations Committees—an unusually heavy workload. His first bill, to declare a National Literacy Day, was signed into law. He has worked on national issues such as AIDS babies, and wants tougher sentencing of convicted drug pushers. With his political ally Newark Mayor Sharpe James, he has encouraged a "Newark Fighting Back" program. He was among those who filed suit against President Bush to bar him from attacking Iraq without congressional approval; after the Gulf war, Payne pushed for minority-owned businesses to be included in the bidding for contracts rebuilding Kuwait. On the Higher Education bill, he pushed for more scholarships and grants for students who want to become teachers in areas with large numbers of minorities.

The People: Pop. 1990: 593,876; 12% age 65+; 26% White; 60% Black; 2% Asian; 5% Other; 12% Hispanic origin. Voting age pop.: 444,082; 57% Black; 11% Hispanic origin. Households: 39% married couple families; 18% married couple fams. w. children; 34% college educ.; median household income: $28,849; per capita income: $12,833; median gross rent: $520; median house value: $136,100.

1992 Presidential Vote

Clinton (D) 126,415 (70%)
Bush (R) 36,299 (20%)
Perot (I). 14,887 (8%)

1988 Presidential Vote

Dukakis (D). 128297 (72%)
Bush (R) 49043 (28%)

Rep. Donald M. Payne (D)

Elected 1988; b. July 16, 1934, Newark; home, Newark; Seton Hall, B.A. 1957; Baptist; widowed.

Career: Elem. & High Schl. teacher, 1957–64; Exec., Prudential Insurance Co., 1964–72; Pres., YMCAs of the U.S., 1970; Essex Cnty. Board of Freeholders, 1972–78, Dir. 1977–78; Vice Pres., Urban Data Systems Inc., 1975–88; Newark Municipal Cncl., 1982–89.

Offices: 417 CHOB 20515, 202-225-3436. Also Fed. Bldg., 970 Broad St., #1435-B, Newark 07102, 201-645-3213.

Committees: *Education and Labor* (10th of 28 D): Elementary, Secondary and Vocational Education; Labor-Management Relations; Select Education and Civil Rights. *Foreign Affairs* (14th of 27 D): Africa. *Government Operations* (17th of 25 D): Human Resources and Intergovernmental Relations.

Group Ratings

	ADA	ACLU	COPE	CDF	CFA	LCV	ACU	NTLC	NSI	COC	CEI
1992	95	100	91	90	93	81	0	0	10	13	9
1991	95	—	100	100	89	92	0	—	—	20	6

National Journal Ratings

	1991 LIB — 1991 CONS	1992 LIB — 1992 CONS
Economic	88% — 0%	91% — 0%
Social	88% — 0%	92% — 0%
Foreign	92% — 0%	90% — 0%

Key Votes of the 102d Congress

1. Ban Striker Replace	FOR	5. Handgun Wait/7-Day FOR	9. Use Force in Gulf AGN
2. $ for Homeownership	AGN	6. Overseas Mil. Abortion FOR	10. US Mil. Abroad $ Cut FOR
3. Tax Rich/Cut Mid Cls.	FOR	7. Obscn. Art NEA $ Ban AGN	11. Limit SDI Funds FOR
4. FY93/$15B Def. Cut	FOR	8. Death Pen. from Jury AGN	12. Cuba Trade Embargo AGN

Key Votes of the 103d Congress

1. Family Leave	FOR	2. Deficit Reduction	FOR	3. Stimulus Plan	FOR

Election Results

1992 general	Donald M. Payne (D)	117,287	(78%)	($285,455)
	Alfred D. Palermo (R)	30,160	(20%)	($26,276)
	Two Others	2,185	(2%)	
1992 primary	Donald M. Payne (D)	31,846	(74%)	
	Willie L. Flood (D)	4,167	(10%)	
	Brian Connors (D)	3,601	(8%)	
	Stanley J. Moskal (D)	3,502	(8%)	
1990 general	Donald M. Payne (D)	42,106	(81%)	($168,522)
	Howard E. Berkeley (R)	8,954	(17%)	
	Other	643	(1%)	

ELEVENTH DISTRICT

New Jersey's Morris County, west of the Watchung Mountain ridges, was one of the first settled interior parts of the United States west of the Hudson. Morris County has long been a place of comparative affluence, the home of skilled craftsmen in the Revolutionary War, with plenty of water mills and iron forges by the 19th Century. But only in the late 20th Century has it comes into its own, as one of the most affluent quarters of the United States. And it is not just a collection of country estates with huddled small towns for the servants to live in, but a well-rounded community with all the appurtenances of urbanity except the high crime and poverty rates which city-lovers in places like Manhattan congratulate themselves for tolerating. The very rich have lived here for some time, connected to Manhattan by commuter rail lines; but in the 1970s and 1980s more rushed out the newly completed I-80 and I-280 or the ring road I-287. Today, more than 20 Fortune 500 companies are headquartered in Morris County, and the area has generated thousands of small businesses, filling new office parks and starting up in home offices, with business often conducted over car phones.

The 11th Congressional District of New Jersey includes all of Morris County plus similar adjacent areas. It is one of the wealthiest districts in the country: number one in median household income in 1990, at $57,219, with the highest median housing value in New Jersey, $214,600, exceeded by four districts in the New York area, 25 in California and one in Hawaii. It is family territory, with relatively few singles; not a strongly culturally conservative area, but much more so than Manhattan. Politically, it is heavily Republican, the most Republican district in New Jersey, and one of the most in the Northeast.

The congressman from the 11th is Dean Gallo, a Republican who grew up in the old mill town of Boonton. He became a real estate agent and served on the Parsippany-Troy Hills Council, on the Morris County Board of Freeholders and in the New Jersey Assembly. There he was a Republican leader working closely with Governor Thomas Kean, and shared Kean's liking for positive governmental action and low tax rates. He was first elected to the House in 1984. On the Public Works Committee, he worked on national and local issues with Robert Roe from the next-door 8th District, who ultimately became chairman, and took a stand supporting proposals to get rid of acid rain. Gallo's idea of using tax incentives to encourage mass transit and van pooling resulted in a $75 monthly tax exemption for allowances for employees who use those forms of commuting. In 1989, Gallo moved to the Appropriations Committee and in 1991 to its Energy and Water Subcommittee, a good place for the practical-minded. In early 1992, he became co-chairman of the Northeast-Midwest Coalition. He has strongly supported the Picatinny Arsenal and wants to keep work going forward on the Passaic River flood tunnel project. He decries Washington bureaucratic gridlock, but has pointed out that it occurs partly because of voters' decisions; he opposed the Clinton economic package, with its Florio-like higher taxes.

The 11th District used to be closer-in toward Newark, but has now followed the people out to Morris County. Gallo won this seat in 1984 by beating a quiet Democratic incumbent, and has held it easily ever since.

The People: Pop. 1990: 594,526; 13% rural; 11% age 65+; 89% White; 3% Black; 4% Asian; 1% Other; 4% Hispanic origin. Voting age pop.: 458,318; 3% Black; 4% Hispanic origin. Households: 67% married couple families; 31% married couple fams. w. children; 60% college educ.; median household income: $57,219; per capita income: $25,454; median gross rent: $730; median house value: $214,600.

1992 Presidential Vote			1988 Presidential Vote		
Bush (R)	153,731	(51%)	Bush (R)	182,282	(68%)
Clinton (D)	97,697	(33%)	Dukakis (D)	85,514	(32%)
Perot (I)	46,407	(16%)			

Rep. Dean A. Gallo (R)

Elected 1984; b. Nov. 23, 1935, Hackensack; home, Parsippany; Protestant; divorced.

Career: Realtor, 1968–84; Parsippany-Troy Hills Cncl., 1968–71, Pres., 1970–71; Morris Cnty. Board of Freeholders, 1971–1975, Dir., 1973–75; NJ Assembly, 1975–84.

Offices: 2447 RHOB 20515, 202-225-5035. Also 22 N. Sussex St., Dover 07801, 201-328-7413; 1 Morris St., Morristown 07960, 201-984-0711; and 3 Fairfield Ave., W. Caldwell 07006, 201-228-9262.

Committees: *Appropriations* (13th of 23 R): Energy and Water Development; VA, HUD and Independent Agencies.

Group Ratings

	ADA	ACLU	COPE	CDF	CFA	LCV	ACU	NTLC	NSI	COC	CEI
1992	25	26	33	40	27	19	76	60	100	75	47
1991	20	—	42	50	22	38	60	—	—	90	49

National Journal Ratings

	1991 LIB — 1991 CONS		1992 LIB — 1992 CONS	
Economic	27%	— 73%	26%	— 73%
Social	35%	— 63%	42%	— 56%
Foreign	23%	— 75%	0%	— 82%

Key Votes of the 102d Congress

1. Ban Striker Replace	AGN	5. Handgun Wait/7-Day FOR	9. Use Force in Gulf FOR
2. $ for Homeownership	FOR	6. Overseas Mil. Abortion FOR	10. US Mil. Abroad $ Cut AGN
3. Tax Rich/Cut Mid Cls.	AGN	7. Obscn. Art NEA $ Ban FOR	11. Limit SDI Funds AGN
4. FY93/$15B Def. Cut	AGN	8. Death Pen. from Jury FOR	12. Cuba Trade Embargo FOR

Key Votes of the 103d Congress

1. Family Leave	AGN	2. Deficit Reduction	AGN	3. Stimulus Plan	AGN

Election Results

1992 general	Dean A. Gallo (R)	188,165	(70%)	($618,448)
	Ona Spiridellis (D)	68,871	(26%)	($132,520)
	Five Others	11,400	(4%)	
1992 primary	Dean A. Gallo (R), unopposed			
1990 general	Dean A. Gallo (R)	92,681	(65%)	($694,735)
	Michael Gordon (D)	47,414	(33%)	($105,031)
	Other...............................	3,591	(2%)	

TWELFTH DISTRICT

It was once the main East Coast arterial highway, carrying the nation's highest volume of truck traffic; today it is crowded with cars taking high-salary workers and clerical help to one of the East Coast's thickest concentrations of office buildings in one of the bigger Edge Cities spawned in the 1980s. This is U.S. 1, which once just connected the industrial cities of Trenton and New Brunswick on its way from Philadelphia to New York; now it is better thought of as connecting the university towns around Princeton and Rutgers, and is a locus of telecommunications and pharmaceutical research. This had been empty bucolic country, looked out on by Scott Fitzgerald's undergraduates from their gothic Princeton towers; now it is filled with postmodern office campuses and hotels and restaurants clamoring for attention.

The 12th Congressional District of New Jersey extends several dozen miles on either side of this stretch of U.S. 1. To the west, it takes in the rolling country of Hunterdon County, around the old county seat town of Flemington, where the Lindbergh kidnapping trial attracted many of the nation's top reporters nearly 60 years ago. This is one of the fastest-growing parts of New Jersey, filling up with affluent if not elite young families. On the other side of U.S. 1, the 12th takes in modest-income suburbs like East Brunswick in Middlesex County and much of Monmouth County, almost to the beach resorts of the Jersey Shore. Some of these communities are long-settled, others are spanking new. What most of the district has in common politically is a Republican preference. Princeton, like so many university towns, is now leftish politically, and southern Middlesex County has vestiges of working class Democratic sentiment. But Hunterdon in the west and Monmouth in the east are solidly Republican.

The congressman from the 12th District is Richard Zimmer, a Republican raised in a garden apartment, "the New Jersey equivalent of a log cabin," he said, who worked his way through Yale. He was head of New Jersey Common Cause in the 1970s and was elected to the legislature in 1981; there he was a stickler for ethics and a fierce opponent of higher government spending, opposing not only Governor Jim Florio's tax program in 1990 but the last budget of Republican Governor Thomas Kean in the 1989. In 1990, an off-year in state politics, the 12th District seat opened when incumbent Jim Courter announced his retirement after being soundly beaten by Jim Florio in the 1989 governor race. The two Republicans who vied with Zimmer had more celebrity: Rodney Frelinghuysen, scion of a New Jersey family that has been in politics since colonial times, and whose father represented much of the area for 22 years in the House; and former New York Giants football player Phil McConkey, who ran an anti-tax, anti-abortion campaign. But Zimmer's fiscal austerity (Frelinghuysen voted for Kean's budget), his pro-choice stand on abortion (McConkey was pro-life) and environmental record evidently helped him to a 38% win, to 29% and 31% for his rivals. The general election was the most expensive in the nation, with $2.9 million in spending because Democrat Marguerite Chandler spent liberally of her own money. But Zimmer's abortion rights stand deprived her of one major talking point, and she carried only Princeton.

Zimmer has carried his views to Washington. He has one of the most conservative records on economics and spending, and opposes not only Democratic projects but the Space Station ("in its current scaled-down configuration, Space Station Freedom could better be called Space Station Lite—one-third of the mission for nearly four times the price") and a new nuclear submarine. He is pushing a one-subject-one-bill measure to stop the "Christmas tree bills" that are now seemingly unstoppable. After Bill Clinton was elected, Zimmer circulated a letter assuring the new president that signers were "ready to make the tough decisions on spending cuts to help you deliver on your pledge to cut the deficit in half"; Democrats were chary, because it contained a no-new-taxes pledge. On the environment, Zimmer had passed a farmland preservation act in the legislature; he got an expansion of the Morristown National Historic Park and is working on protection for the Morris and Delaware & Raritan Canals. He has a bill to reduce aircraft noise in residential areas and to halt oil and gas drilling up to 100 miles off the Jersey Shore. He brings to the House a market approach, calling for EPA to establish risk ratings to allow rational rather than emotive environmental decisions.

In 1991, it looked like Zimmer, a Republican in the center of the state, would be the odd man out in redistricting. But when Republicans won a veto-proof majority in the 1991 legislative elections, Zimmer was suddenly given a new lease on political life. More than half the 12th District was new to him in 1992, but much of that was in Monmouth County and was safely Republican. Zimmer, whose home is on the Delaware River side of the district, works on Shore issues, and though a Monmouth Republican dubbed him the "coastal congressman," he does not totally pander to local opinion: he is reluctant to back federal subsidies of flood insurance and has questioned whether just pumping in more sand works to maintain the Shore beaches.

Zimmer was easily reelected in 1992, and was considered likely to run for the Senate in 1993 if Bill Bradley had been appointed to the Cabinet and there had been a special election to fill the seat. He wasn't and there wasn't, but there still is the possibility that Zimmer will run for Senator Frank Lautenberg's seat in 1994.

The People: Pop. 1990: 594,577; 34% rural; 11% age 65+; 88% White; 5% Black; 4% Asian; 1% Other; 3% Hispanic origin. Voting age pop.: 455,866; 5% Black; 2% Hispanic origin. Households: 67% married couple families; 32% married couple fams. w. children; 62% college educ.; median household income: $54,630; per capita income: $24,615; median gross rent: $696; median house value: $205,200.

1992 Presidential Vote		1988 Presidential Vote	
Bush (R)	130,651 (43%)	Bush (R)	157,907 (61%)
Clinton (D)	121,447 (40%)	Dukakis (D)	102,805 (39%)
Perot (I)	50,357 (17%)		

Rep. Dick Zimmer (R)

Elected 1990; b. Aug. 16, 1944, Newark; home, Delaware Township; Yale, B.A. 1966, LL.B. 1969; Jewish; married (Marfy).

Career: Practicing atty., 1969–90; Chmn., NJ Common Cause, 1974–77; NJ Assembly, 1981–87; NJ Senate 1987–91; Chmn., NJ Repub. Platform Cmtee., 1989.

Offices: 228 CHOB, 202-225-5801. Also 133 Franklin Corner Rd., Lawrenceville 08648, 609-895-1559; 36 W. Main St., #201, Freehold 07728, 908-303-9116; and 1119 Main St., Flemington 09922, 908-788-1952.

Committees: *Government Operations* (11th of 17 R): Legislation and National Security. *Science, Space and Technology* (11th of 22 R): Space; Technology, Environment and Aviation.

Group Ratings

	ADA	ACLU	COPE	CDF	CFA	LCV	ACU	NTLC	NSI	COC	CEI
1992	40	43	42	20	40	50	76	80	90	63	85
1991	20	—	42	40	11	85	70	—	—	70	80

National Journal Ratings

	1991 LIB — 1991 CONS			1992 LIB — 1992 CONS	
Economic	28%	—	71%	0% — 91%	
Social	37%	—	61%	37% — 63%	
Foreign	23%	—	75%	44% — 50%	

Key Votes of the 102d Congress

1. Ban Striker Replace	AGN	5. Handgun Wait/7-Day	AGN	9. Use Force in Gulf	FOR
2. $ for Homeownership	FOR	6. Overseas Mil. Abortion	FOR	10. US Mil. Abroad $ Cut	FOR
3. Tax Rich/Cut Mid Cls.	AGN	7. Obscn. Art NEA $ Ban	FOR	11. Limit SDI Funds	AGN
4. FY93/$15B Def. Cut	AGN	8. Death Pen. from Jury	FOR	12. Cuba Trade Embargo	FOR

Key Votes of the 103d Congress

1. Family Leave	FOR	2. Deficit Reduction	AGN	3. Stimulus Plan	AGN

Election Results

1992 general	Dick Zimmer (R)	174,216	(64%)	($911,638)
	Frank Abate (D)	83,035	(30%)	($62,937)
	Carl J. Mayer (I)	11,051	(4%)	($105,182)
	Three Others	4,455	(2%)	
1992 primary	Dick Zimmer (R), unopposed			
1990 general	Dick Zimmer (R)	107,851	(64%)	($1,224,626)
	Marguerite Chandler (D)	52,256	(31%)	($1,707,539)
	Three others	8,193	(5%)	

THIRTEENTH DISTRICT

The Statue of Liberty, standing in New York Harbor since 1886, has been the great symbol of America welcoming immigrants to its shores. Actually, the Statue is on the New Jersey side of the Harbor; and the shore on which many immigrants first settle, in the old days when they got off the boat and today when they are more likely to disembark at Kennedy or Newark Airport, is in New Jersey. The towns sitting on the granite and gneiss ridge of Hudson County, New Jersey, overlooking the Harbor, have in particular been immigrant territory. Today they are, as they were a century ago, the most densely populated part of urban America except for Manhattan and with one of the largest percentages of immigrants. This was not always so during the years in between. After immigration was shut off by the laws of 1921 and 1924, many children and grandchildren of the Irish and Italian immigrants stayed in Hudson County, living in the same neighborhoods, working on the same docks or the same big factories—Maxwell House and Palmolive were here—and voting the dictates of the same political machine.

Hudson County was the setting of one of America's classic political machines, undisciplined by any metropolitan elite. From 1917 to 1949, the boss of Hudson County was Frank ("I am the law") Hague; his machine chose governors and U.S. senators, prosecutors and judges, and had influence in the White House of Franklin D. Roosevelt. He collected high taxes from the industries clustered here—who then passed them on to consumers everywhere—and in return gave them an orderly city, free of most crime and vice, and a work force insulated against racketeers and militant unions. Hague's successor, John V. Kenny, was boss from 1949 to 1971—continuous power for 54 years, a record beaten only in Albany.

But by the early 1970s, unnoticed by a media focusing on black-white relations, change was coming again to Hudson County in the form of new immigrants. The 1965 immigration law changed the rules, and the influx of refugees from Communist Cuba reached Hudson County not long after arriving in Miami. Hudson County was 34% Hispanic in 1990; Union City has become mostly Cuban and West New York, Latino. Hoboken has filled with Manhattan types looking for lower rents in the five-story Victorian apartments that sparkle with light off the Hudson, and a quick commute through the PATH tubes to Wall Street or Greenwich Village (an estimated 85% of Hoboken adults work in Manhattan). The Jersey City waterfront is the scene of huge new condominium developments—Port Liberte, opposite the Statue of Liberty; Newport, with thousands of housing units and hundreds of thousands of square feet of office space; Liberty Place on the site of the old Colgate-Palmolive factory; Weehawken, with its substantial 1920s houses overlooking Manhattan on the site where Aaron Burr shot Alexander Hamilton in 1804, and Lincoln Harbor, filled with New York bank employees overlooking the traffic waiting to go through the Lincoln Tunnel.

The 13th Congressional District of New Jersey includes most of Hudson County plus most of the immigrant entry ports along the water, from the Hackensack River and Newark Bay to Arthur Kill and Raritan Bay. It was designed to be an "Hispanic influence" district; 41% of its residents in 1990 were Hispanic and 14% black. With most of Jersey City and all of Union City and West New York and Weehawken, it includes 105,000 people in the old Ironbound area and

North Ward of Newark, half of them Hispanic, and takes in the industrial city waterfront areas of Elizabeth, Linden, Carteret and Perth Amboy. It is ordinarily a Democratic district, but not overwhelmingly; many Cuban-Americans are Republicans, and Republicans have carried the area on occasion. Cultural conservatism is no disadvantage with an immigrant population that is highly religious, anti-Communist, family-oriented and economically upwardly mobile.

When the new district boundaries were announced, Frank Guarini, Hudson County congressman for 14 years, decided to retire at 68; a successful lawyer and member of the Ways and Means Committee, he became president of the National Italian-American Foundation. There followed a race with a clear favorite, state Senator Robert Menendez. The son of Cuban immigrants, Menendez was born in New York, elected to the Union City school board in 1974 at 20, worked for Union City Mayor William Musto in the 1970s, but quit and testified against him in a corruption trial, and ran against him and lost in 1982. In 1986, Menendez was elected mayor of Union City (New Jersey's most densely populated community: 58,012 people in 1.3 square miles); he became an assemblyman in 1987 and state Senator in 1991 (New Jersey allows double officeholding). As mayor of Union City, he developed a drug education program bringing police into the schools for both education and enforcement, an innovative child care program, and a topnotch recycling effort; and, in Trenton, the anti-hate crime Ethnic Intimidation Act of 1990 and the Green Acres Bond Act of 1991. Menendez was challenged in the primary by Robert Haney, who called him a machine politician; Menendez did have most politicians' support, plus that of Miami-based Cuban-American leader Jorge Mas Canosa, though Haney had some backing in Jersey City. But Menendez won 68%–32%. In the general, against Guarini's 1990 opponent, Fred Theemling, he won 64%–31%.

In Washington, Menendez promises to seek targeted tax incentives and enterprise zones (there are state enterprise zones in the 13th District); he serves on the Public Works Committee, where he will likely work for district projects, and on Foreign Affairs, where he will surely be a strong opponent of Fidel Castro.

The People: Pop. 1990: 594,875; 12% age 65+; 42% White; 14% Black; 5% Asian; 14% Other; 41% Hispanic origin. Voting age pop.: 453,979; 12% Black; 38% Hispanic origin. Households: 45% married couple families; 21% married couple fams. w. children; 31% college educ.; median household income: $28,721; per capita income: $13,028; median gross rent: $505; median house value: $142,700.

1992 Presidential Vote			1988 Presidential Vote		
Clinton (D)	94,651	(53%)	Dukakis (D)	95,237	(54%)
Bush (R)	64,358	(36%)	Bush (R)	80,681	(46%)
Perot (I)	14,981	(8%)			

Rep. Robert Menendez (D)

Elected 1992; b. Jan. 1, 1954, New York, NY; home, Union City; St. Peter's Col., B.A. 1976, Rutgers Law Schl., J.D. 1979; Catholic; married (Jane Jacobsen-Menendez)

Career: Union City Board of Educ., 1974–82; Union City Mayor, 1986–92; NJ Assembly, 1987–91; NJ Senate 1991–92.

Offices: 1531 LHOB 20515, 202-225-7919. Also 911 Bergen Ave., Jersey City 07306, 201-222-2828; and 654 Ave. C, Bayonne 07002, 201-823-2900.

Committees: *Foreign Affairs* (16th of 27 D): International Operations; Western Hemisphere Affairs. *Public Works and Transportation* (30th of 39 D): Economic Development; Surface Transportation; Water Resources and Environment.

Group Ratings and 102d Congress Votes: Newly Elected

Key Votes of the 103d Congress

1. Family Leave   FOR   2. Deficit Reduction   FOR   3. Stimulus Plan   FOR

Election Results

1992 general	Robert Menendez (D).................	93,670	(64%)	($645,640)
	Fred J. Theemling, Jr. (R)	44,529	(31%)	($7,499)
	Five Others	7,515	(5%)	
1992 primary	Robert Menendez (D).................	24,245	(68%)	
	Robert P. Haney, Jr. (D)...............	11,409	(32%)	
1990 general	Frank J. Guarini (D).................	56,455	(66%)	($316,782)
(NJ 14)	Fred. J. Theemling, Jr. (R).............	24,870	(29%)	
	Four others	3,951	(5%)	

NEW MEXICO

America, from its oldest settlement to its newest technology, can be found, in unusual and even surrealistic form, in New Mexico. For the oldest permanently inhabited city in the United States is not Plymouth, Massachusetts, or Jamestown, Virginia, or even St. Augustine, Florida; it is probably Acoma, New Mexico. Probably, because Acoma, inhabited by the Anasazi, "an agricultural, settled and architecturally sophisticated people," said historian Roger Kennedy in *Rediscovering America*, had perhaps 1,000 years of unrecorded history before Spanish conquistadors came upon it in 1540. Some 450 years later, much of what makes New Mexico distinctive still recalls the people found here by the first European explorers—something true of no other state but Hawaii. While the Pilgrims built flimsy wood houses, the Indians in New Mexico were living in extensive dwellings hundreds of years old, made with the adobe that is still the characteristic building material here. Other state cultures are generally based on what early white settlers brought to the land; natives, except in Hawaii and Alaska, have mostly disappeared. Not in New Mexico. The English-speaking culture here is superimposed, at times rather lightly, on a society whose written history dates back to the Spanish settlement of Santa Fe in 1609, and to centuries long past when the Pueblo Indians set up stable agricultural societies on the sandy, rocky lands of northern New Mexico, using small pebbles as mulch to retain scarce moisture. Pueblo culture is still celebrated in the Indian pottery that commands premium prices in Santa Fe and in the annual Gathering of Nations pow-wow in Albuquerque which attracts 30,000 Indians. Today, a very substantial minority of New Mexicans are descendants of these Indians or the Spanish, or both. New Mexico had the highest percentage of Hispanics (38%) in the U.S. after the 1990 Census. Nearly one-third of the people in this state speak Spanish in everyday life, and only a few are recent migrants from Mexico. The Hispanic roots go very deep, as witnessed by the recent discovery of Hebrew symbols left on Christian gravestones by the *conversos*, Jews who hid their religion after it was outlawed by the Spanish in 1492; there are families here who have secretly maintained Jewish practices for centuries. New Mexico is the northernmost salient of the great Indian-Spanish civilizations of the Cordillera, which extend along the mountain chain through Mexico and Central America to South America, as far away as Chile and Argentina.

Yet New Mexico also is a civilization built on the highest of technologies. It was to a remote mesa called Los Alamos that General Leslie Groves brought his Manhattan Project scientists during World War II to build a secret town and develop a secret weapon that would in one explosion win World War II and change the course of history. Los Alamos remains a government high-tech laboratory, and New Mexico has others as well—the White Sands Missile Range near Alamogordo, where the first atomic bomb was detonated, and the Sandia Laboratories near Albuquerque, run by AT&T for the government, a non-nuclear high-tech weapons research facility. And if New Mexico was in on the takeoff of nuclear power, it has also come in for part of the landing. Near Carlsbad, New Mexico, is the site of the federal Waste Isolation Pilot Plant (WIPP), where the Energy Department wants to conduct a seven-year test of radioactive waste storage; the Energy Department wanted to use 1% of WIPP's capacity, while some of the state's congressional delegation held out for .5% and ultimately prevailed in 1992 legislation.

These two kinds of New Mexicos, very old and very young, intermingle with others of intermediate age in different proportions in this land of majestically vast vistas. The Hispanic-Indian culture predominates north and west of Albuquerque, with picturesque old towns and some still-functioning pueblos. "Little Texas," in the south and east, has small cities, plenty of oil wells, vast cattle ranches and desolate military bases and resembles, economically and culturally, the adjacent west Texas High Plains. Here, as everywhere in New Mexico, government is a prime employer (accounting for 27% of jobs, one of the highest figures in the country) and often the moving force in the local economy. In the middle is Albuquerque which, with the arrival of air conditioning, grew from a small desert town of 35,000 in 1940 into a Sun Belt metropolis of 602,400 today. Albuquerque has a large Hispanic minority, as do many fast-growing U.S. cities; its economy is based heavily on high tech, especially nuclear power; but it has relatively low income and education levels—the downscale Sun Belt. Each of these three areas has about one-third of the state's population, and their necessarily impressionistic boundaries are followed pretty closely by the boundaries of New Mexico's three congressional districts.

For many years, New Mexico politics was a somnolent business. Local bosses—first Republican, later Democratic—controlled the large Hispanic vote. Elections in many counties featured irregularities that would have made a Chicago ward committeeman blush. New Mexico also had for years another feature of boss-controlled politics, the balanced ticket: one Spanish and one Anglo senator, with the offices of governor and lieutenant governor split as well. But for all its distinctiveness, in national politics New Mexico was a bellwether, never voting for a losing presidential candidate from 1912, when it became a state, until 1976 when it backed Gerald Ford. In 1988 it voted 52%–47% for George Bush, close to the national average; in 1992, 46% for Bill Clinton, 37% for Bush and 16% for Ross Perot, 3% more for Clinton and less for Perot than the nation. Democrats usually have a solid base in the Hispanic areas, but there is little harsh ethnic polarization. New Mexico's relatively downscale newcomers—low-skill laborers and retirees who can afford a trailer but not a Scottsdale condominium—are culturally conservative, and if anything lean a bit Republican. Of all the border states, New Mexico has the least immigration from Mexico and Latin America; most Hispanic growth is from high birth and low death rates. But the Cordillera civilization not so far away is never entirely out of the minds of New Mexicans.

A footnote: for a state with such visually dazzling scenery, New Mexico has not been an environmentalist stronghold—not affluent enough, perhaps. It has lagged behind in wilderness areas and national parks; the 500 square mile Gray Ranch near the Mexican border was preserved not by the government, but by the private Nature Conservancy; former Congressman Manuel Lujan, a Bush appointee, was one of the less environment-minded Interior secretaries.

Governor. The single constant in New Mexico politics, it seems, is Governor Bruce King. New Mexico allows its governors a second consecutive four-year term for the first time in 1994, so King has been in and out—elected in 1970, elected again in 1978, elected a third time in 1990, sometimes winning by narrow margins, but never losing. He was succeeded twice by more liberal Hispanic Democrats, Jerry Apodaca in 1974 and Toney Anaya in 1982, and most recently replaced a conservative Republican, Garrey Carruthers, elected in 1986. King, a rancher from Santa Fe County in the Hispanic north, has a cowboy walk and a Little Texas malaprop-prone

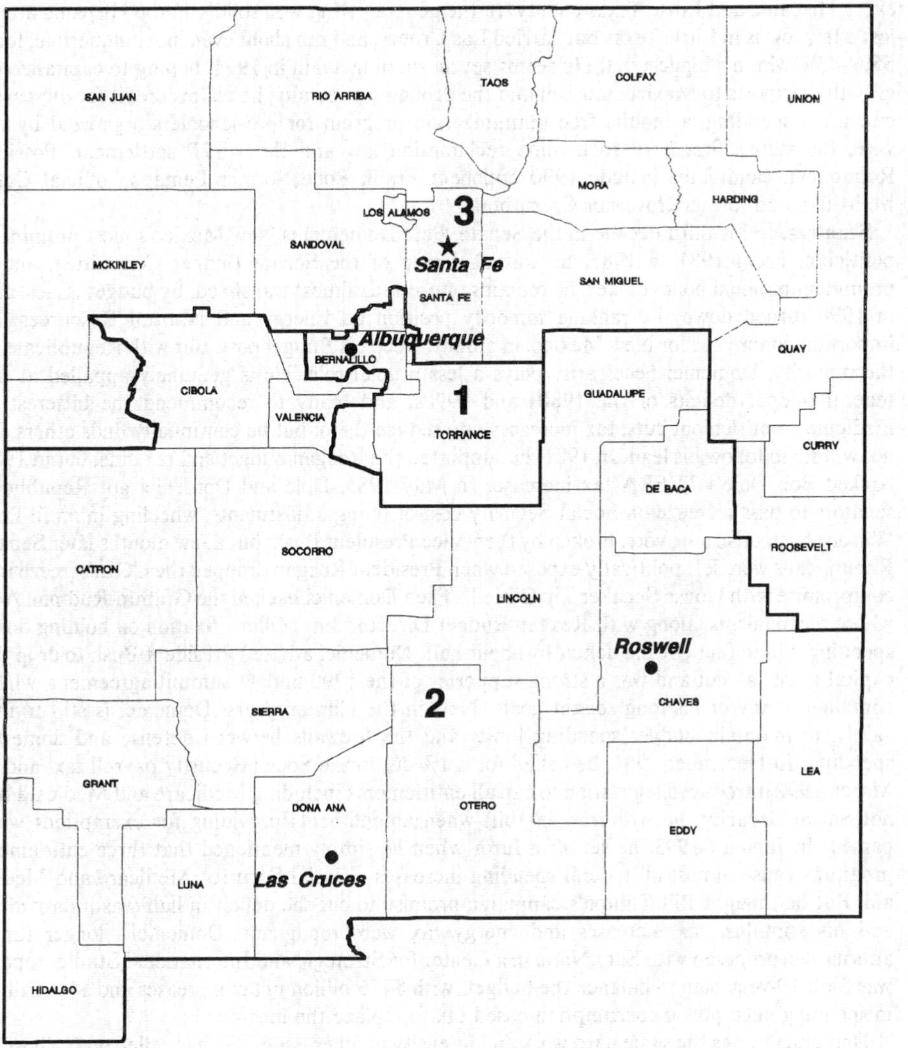

TAOS

COLFAX

SAN JUAN

RIO ARRIBA

UNION

MORA

HARDING

LOS ALAMOS

3

SANDOVAL

MCKINLEY

★ **Santa Fe**

SAN MIGUEL

SANTA FE

QUAY

Albuquerque

BERNALILLO

CIBOLA

1

GUADALUPE

VALENCIA

TORRANCE

CURRY

DE BACA

SOCORRO

ROOSEVELT

CATRON

LINCOLN

Roswell ●

2

CHAVES

SIERRA

LEA

GRANT

OTERO

DONA ANA

EDDY

LUNA

Las Cruces ●

HIDALGO

Miles

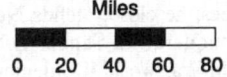

0   20   40   60   80

personality; he is bilingual and a teetotaler with a popular wife (one King campaign ad said, "Get two for the price of one!"). A few of his appointees had ethics problems, and in 1980 there was a nasty prison riot in Santa Fe; but those issues, brought up in the 1990 Democratic primary, did not prevent him from winning 53%–39% over former Attorney General Paul Bardacke. King ran barely ahead in Albuquerque and behind in fast-growing Las Cruces, but carried almost every Hispanic and Little Texas county. In the general, King won solidly in the Hispanic areas, lost a few towns in Little Texas but carried Las Cruces, and ran about even in Albuquerque, for a 55%–45% win, his biggest yet. He seems set on running again in 1994, hoping to capitalize on growth in exports to Mexico, tourism and the economy generally; he claims credit for increased education spending, a mobile free immunization program for pre-schoolers organized by his wife, the state's first hard rock mine reclamation law and the WIPP settlement. Possible Republican candidates include 1990 opponent Frank Bond, former Pentagon official Colin McMillan and former Governor Carruthers.

Senators. In his third decade in the Senate, Pete Domenici is New Mexico's most prominent politician. From 1981 to 1987, he was chairman of the Senate Budget Committee, and a prominent national policymaker; he remains interested, almost transfixed, by budget issues, and in 1990 turned down the ranking minority position on Energy and Natural Resources, an important committee for New Mexico, in order to keep his Budget post. But with Republicans in the minority, Domenici necessarily plays a less crucial role. He is genuinely appalled at the federal budget deficits of the 1980s and 1990s, and ready to recommend the bitterest of medicine—entitlement cuts, tax increases—to reduce them; but he continually finds others are not willing to follow his lead. In 1981, he supported the Reagan budget and tax cuts, but in 1982 backed Bob Dole's TEFRA tax increase. In May 1985, Dole and Domenici got Republican senators to pass a freeze on Social Security cost of living adjustments, wheeling in an ill Pete Wilson to establish a tie vote, broken by then-Vice President Bush; but a few months later Senate Republicans were left politically exposed when President Reagan dropped the COLA freeze in a compromise with House Speaker Tip O'Neill. Then Domenici backed the Gramm-Rudman Act, whose mechanisms, along with Reagan Budget Director Jim Miller's fixation on holding down spending, did in fact cut the deficit by about half. Domenici advised President Bush to drop the capital gains tax cut and was a strong supporter of the 1990 budget summit agreement, which contained many of his long sought goals. Now in the Clinton years, Domenici is still trying, vainly, to maintain budget spending limits and the firewalls between defense and domestic spending. In December 1991, he called for a 1% cut in the Social Security payroll tax, and in March 1992 introduced legislation to cap all entitlements including Medicare and Medicaid but not Social Security; he withdrew his bill when amendments providing for exemptions were passed. In January 1993, he set off a furor when he simply mentioned that three entitlement programs cause almost all federal spending increases—Social Security, Medicare and Medicaid. But he thought Bill Clinton's campaign promise to cut the deficit in half was improvident and his stimulus, tax increases and energy tax were repugnant. Domenici's longer range alternative, proposed with Sam Nunn in a Center for Strategic and International Studies report, was for a 10-year plan to balance the budget, with $476 billion in tax increases and $1.4 trillion in spending cuts, plus a consumption-based tax to replace the income tax.

Domenici brings the same hard work and intensity to other issues. He has called on Hollywood and other business executives to take responsibility for the morality of their products. He favors malpractice insurance reform, with a limit on jury awards for pain and suffering. He supported President Bush's veto of the Hatch Act, though New Mexico has a high percentage of federal employees; he closely tends New Mexico's two big federal research laboratories, Los Alamos and Albuquerque's Sandia Labs, making sure their research work continues, adapted to the post-Cold War world. Domenici's budget frustrations over the years have undoubtedly strengthened his reform impulses. A member of the Appropriations Committee, he favors two-year appropriation cycles. And he was one of the four members of the Senate and House to conceive the Joint Committee on the Organization of Congress, taking on another often thankless task of reforming the committees and procedures in which almost every member has such a stake. Domenici's principles have cost him a chance at the Republican leadership. His willingness to back higher taxes (*The Wall Street Journal* once headlined an editorial John Maynard Domenici) helps explain why in December 1990 he lost his race for head of the Senate Republican Policy Committee to Don Nickles 23–20.

Domenici's political position in New Mexico seems exceedingly strong. His only electoral loss was in 1970, when he lost the gubernatorial race to Bruce King who, after hiatuses, still holds the office. In his last two Senate races, Domenici set New Mexico records, winning 72% of the vote in 1984 and 73% in 1990. His 1990 opponent, Tom Benavides, was distinguished by his eye patch, his proposal to name a region Benavides County, and his bill to legalize pari-mutuel betting on ostrich racing.

New Mexico's junior senator, Jeff Bingaman, is a Democrat with good political lineage: his father was a professor at Western New Mexico University in Silver City, and his uncle was campaign manager for Senator Clinton Anderson, one of the savviest politicians of his generation. A year out of law school, Bingaman was counsel to the state constitutional convention; a few years later, he went into law practice in Santa Fe with former Governor Jack Campbell; Bingaman's wife, Anne, started a highly successful law practice of her own that helped finance his first campaigns (she is now assistant U.S. attorney general for antitrust). In a small state, bright young people are not nearly as numerous as they are in New York or Washington or Los Angeles, and Bingaman rose fast. He ran for attorney general in 1978 and won; in 1982, he ran against Senator Harrison Schmitt, the former astronaut, also from Silver City, and won with 54%, partly because it was a recession year, but also because of Schmitt's misleading and negative ads.

Bingaman became a member of the Armed Services Committee and a protege of Chairman Sam Nunn, who created a subcommittee tailored to his interests, now called Defense Technology, Acquisition and Industrial Base. This gives Bingaman lots of say over New Mexico's Los Alamos and Sandia labs; he also has worked on superconductivity research and chartering the semi-conductor consortium, Sematech. He sponsored a $1.6 billion defense conversion package which passed in 1992 and $100 million in seed money for regional partnerships of small technology firms. He wants to make government research more accessible to the private sector and wants to expedite the process for government labs to enter into partnerships with private companies to develop new technologies; he has proposed a Critical Technologies Institute think tank to focus on civilian R&D and manufacturing. He wants to pass a law providing an education technology infrastructure program, involving computers, interactive television and information networks. Much of his work anticipated the Clinton Administration technology thrust; "it is a pleasure," he said, "to work with an administration that is proud to have a stated technology policy."

Bingaman also serves on the Energy Committee, where he has worked to protect the archaeological sites of the Mimbres Indians and the Glorieta battlefield. He opposed raising federal grazing fees but pledged to work with Interior Secretary Bruce Babbitt on revising the 1872 Mining Act. He managed to get out of an unpleasant assignment ruling on the Keating Five, when he recused himself from the Ethics Committee because his wife's law firm had represented aides to Alan Cranston. He earnestly takes lessons to learn Spanish, tries to stop cut-rate cigarette sales to soldiers, fights bubonic and pneumonic plague (most U.S. cases are in New Mexico), and promotes physical fitness through his HealthNet state fitness encouragement program.

Bingaman has had good job ratings at home, and in 1988, campaigning as "serious about New Mexico," he won 63%–37%, the best showing by a Democratic Senate candidate in New Mexico since Clinton Anderson won his third term in 1960. But this is a seat Republicans have their eyes on, and if the Clinton Administration should get into trouble, Bingaman might also; he has never had to run carrying the baggage of a Democratic administration, which can get awfully heavy in the Rocky Mountains.

Presidential politics. New Mexico, the most Democratic of the Rocky Mountain states and seriously contested in 1988, went for Bill Clinton in 1992. Its bellwether status—it has voted for the winner in every presidential election since statehood in 1912, except for 1976—seems more accidental than anything else; it's hard to think of a state more atypical of the nation.

Congressional districting. The boundaries of New Mexico's three congressional districts were slightly redesigned for 1992, with the apparent aim of making the Republican-held 1st and 2d both marginally more Democratic.

The People: Est. Pop. 1992: 1,581,000; Pop. 1990: 1,515,069, up 4.2% 1990–1992. 0.6% of U.S. total, 37th largest; 27% rural. Median age: 31.3 years. 10.8% 65 years and over. 75.6% White, 38.2% Hispanic origin, 8.9% American Indian, 2.0% Black, 12.6% Other. Households: 56.0% married couple families; 29% married couple fams. w. children; 46% college educ.; median household income: $24,087; per capita income: $11,246; 67.4% owner occupied housing; median house value: $70,100; median monthly rent: $312. 6.8% Unemployment. Voting age pop.:1,068,328. Registered voters (1992): 707,586; 412,023 D (58%), 239,736 R (34%), 55,827 unaffiliated and minor parties (8%).

Political Lineup: Governor, Bruce King (D); Lt. Gov., Casey Luna (D); Secy. of State, Stephanie Gonzales (D); Atty. Gen., Thomas Udall (D); Treasurer, David W. King (D); Auditor, Robert E. Vigil (D). State Senate, 42 (27 D and 15 R); State House of Representatives, 70 (56 D and 14 R). Senators, Pete V. Domenici (R) and Jeff Bingaman (D). Representatives, 3 (2 R and 1 D).

1992 Presidential Vote		
Clinton (D)	261,617	(46%)
Bush (R)	212,824	(37%)
Perot (I)	91,895	(16%)

1988 Presidential Vote		
Bush (R)	270,341	(52%)
Dukakis (D)	244,497	(47%)

1992 Democratic Presidential Primary		
Clinton	95,933	(53%)
Brown	30,705	(17%)
Tsongas	11,315	(6%)
Other	8,221	(5%)
Uncommitted	35,269	(19%)

1992 Republican Presidential Primary		
Bush	55,522	(64%)
Buchanan	7,871	(9%)
Uncommitted	23,574	(27%)

GOVERNOR

Gov. Bruce King (D)

Elected 1990, term expires Jan. 1995; b. Apr. 6, 1924, Stanley; home, Santa Fe; U. of NM, 1943–44; Baptist; married (Alice).

Career: Army, 1945–47 (WWII); Rancher; Cnty. Commissioner, 1954–58; NM House of Reps., 1959–68; NM Gov., 1971–74, 1979–82; Chmn., Western Govs. Conference, 1973–74.

Office: State Capitol, #417, Santa Fe 87503, 505-827-3000.

Election Results

1990 gen.	Bruce King (D)	224,564	(55%)
	Frank M. Bond (R)	185,692	(45%)
1990 prim.	Bruce King (D)	95,884	(53%)
	Paul Bardacke (D)	70,169	(39%)
	Tony Scarborough (D)	8,931	(5%)
	Bob Gold (D)	6,256	(4%)
1986 gen.	Garrey E. Carruthers (R)	209,455	(53%)
	Ray B. Powell (D)	185,378	(47%)

SENATORS
Sen. Pete V. Domenici (R)

Elected 1972, seat up 1996; b. May 7, 1932, Albuquerque; home, Albuquerque; U. of NM, B.S. 1954, Denver U., LL.B. 1958; Catholic; married (Nancy).

Career: Practicing atty., 1958–72; Albuquerque City Comm., 1966–70, Mayor Ex-Officio, 1967–70.

Offices: 427 DSOB 20510, 202-224-6621. Also 625 Silver SW, #120, Albuquerque 87102, 505-766-3481; New Postal Bldg., 120 S. Federal Pl., Santa Fe 87501, 505-988-6511; Sun Belt Plz., 1065 S. Main St., Bldg. #D-13, Las Cruces 88005, 505-526-5475; and Fed. Bldg. #140, Roswell 88201, 505-623-6170.

Committees: *Appropriations* (6th of 13 R): Commerce, Justice, State and Judiciary (RMM); Defense; Energy and Water Development; Interior; Transportation. *Banking, Housing and Urban Affairs* (8th of 8 R): Housing and Urban Affairs; Securities. *Budget* (RMM of 9 R). *Energy and Natural Resources* (3d of 9 R): Energy Research and Development (RMM); Public Lands, National Parks and Forests; Renewable Energy, Energy Efficiency, and Competitiveness. *Indian Affairs* (5th of 8 R). *Joint Committee on the Organization of Congress* (7th of 12).

Group Ratings

	ADA	ACLU	CDF	COPE	CFA	LCV	ACU	NTLC	NSI	COC	CEI
1992	15	0	30	17	33	0	78	72	100	78	61
1991	10	—	45	17	28	13	76	—	—	90	61

National Journal Ratings

	1991 LIB — 1991 CONS		1992 LIB — 1992 CONS	
Economic	20%	— 78%	22%	— 76%
Social	23%	— 75%	17%	— 80%
Foreign	13%	— 77%	10%	— 80%

Key Votes of the 102d Congress

1. $ for Homeownership	FOR	5. Clarence Thomas Nom.	FOR	9. Use Force in Gulf	FOR
2. Have Cap Gains Debate	FOR	6. Lmt Death Row Appeal	FOR	10. Keep Salvador Aid	FOR
3. Remove Budget Walls	AGN	7. Handgun Wait/5-Day	FOR	11. Cut $1B from SDI	AGN
4. Ban Striker Replace	AGN	8. Abortion Gag Rule	FOR	12. Override China MFN	AGN

Key Votes of the 103d Congress

1. Family Leave	AGN	2. HIV Immigrants	AGN	3. Clinton Budget	AGN

Election Results

1990 general	Pete V. Domenici (R)	296,712	(73%)	($2,250,086)
	Tom R. Benavides (D)	110,033	(27%)	($38,510)
1990 primary	Pete V. Domenici (R), unopposed			
1984 general	Pete V. Domenici (R)	361,371	(72%)	($2,658,008)
	Judith A. Pratt (D)....................	141,253	(28%)	($301,661)

844 NEW MEXICO

Sen. Jeff Bingaman (D)

Elected 1982, seat up 1994; b. Oct. 3, 1943, El Paso, TX; home, Santa Fe; Harvard, B.A. 1965, Stanford, LL.B. 1968; United Methodist; married (Anne).

Career: Army Reserves, 1968–74; NM Asst. Atty. Gen., 1969; Practicing atty., 1970–78; NM Atty. Gen., 1979–82.

Offices: 110 HSOB 20510, 202-224-5521. Also 119 E. Marcy St., #101, Santa Fe 87501, 505-988-6647; 625 Wilver Ave., SW, #130, Albuquerque 87102, 505-766-3636; 505 S. Main St., Las Cruces 88001, 505-523-6561; and 114 E. 4th St., #103, Roswell 88201, 505-622-7113.

Committees: *Armed Services* (5th of 11 D): Defense Technology, Acquisition and Industrial Base (Chmn.); Military Readiness and Defense Infrastructure; Nuclear Deterrence, Arms Control and Defense Intelligence. *Energy and Natural Resources* (5th of 11 D): Energy Research and Development; Public Lands, National Parks and Forests; Renewable Energy, Energy Efficiency, and Competitiveness (Chmn.). *Labor and Human Resources* (8th of 10 D): Children, Family, Drugs and Alcoholism; Disability Policy; Education, Arts and Humanities; Employment and Productivity. *Joint Economic Committee* (3d of 10).

Group Ratings

	ADA	ACLU	CDF	COPE	CFA	LCV	ACU	NTLC	NSI	COC	CEI
1992	75	76	80	92	75	58	4	17	40	20	28
1991	65	—	82	67	61	40	19	—	—	20	29

National Journal Ratings

	1991 LIB — 1991 CONS	1992 LIB — 1992 CONS
Economic	46% — 50%	58% — 40%
Social	68% — 30%	66% — 32%
Foreign	62% — 37%	55% — 44%

Key Votes of the 102d Congress

1. $ for Homeownership	AGN	5. Clarence Thomas Nom.	AGN	9. Use Force in Gulf	AGN
2. Have Cap Gains Debate	AGN	6. Lmt Death Row Appeal	AGN	10. Keep Salvador Aid	AGN
3. Remove Budget Walls	FOR	7. Handgun Wait/5-Day	FOR	11. Cut $1B from SDI	AGN
4. Ban Striker Replace	FOR	8. Abortion Gag Rule	AGN	12. Override China MFN	FOR

Key Votes of the 103d Congress

1. Family Leave	FOR	2. HIV Immigrants	AGN	3. Clinton Budget	FOR

Election Results

1988 general	Jeff Bingaman (D)...................	321,983	(63%)	($2,808,659)
	Bill Valentine (R)	186,579	(37%)	($659,624)
1988 primary	Jeff Bingaman (D), unopposed			
1982 general	Jeff Bingaman (D)...................	217,682	(54%)	($1,586,245)
	Harrison H. (Jack) Schmitt (R).........	187,682	(46%)	($1,692,204)

FIRST DISTRICT

The future and the past of New Mexico come together in its single metropolis, Albuquerque. Its Spanish and Indian past is memorialized in its name (for a 17th Century Spanish grandee) and age (founded in 1706) and its quaint Old Town; its high-tech future is symbolized by Sandia Laboratories and Kirtland Air Force Base, the government installations that are the city's biggest employers. When rocket scientist Robert Goddard moved here in 1930 and nuclear scientist J. Robert Oppenheimer reconnoitered the site in 1940, Albuquerque was still a town of 35,000 sitting at the junction of the Rio Grande and the old U.S. 66 that paralleled the Santa Fe Railroad. Since then, Albuquerque has grown more than any place in New Mexico and, with a metro population of 600,000, has as many people as all New Mexico did when the scientists first arrived. Albuquerque's prosperous neighborhoods have climbed the gently rising heights to the east, and its poorer residents have spread north and south of downtown in the Rio Grande Valley. Albuquerque is counted as part of the Sun Belt, but its climate is closer to that of the High Plains of west Texas: hot in the summer, sometimes very cold in the winter, with high winds most of the time. Nor is its economy like that of other Sun Belt cities: it owes more to government; it has lower income levels; its 16% growth in the 1980s was well below that of Phoenix, Los Angeles, Dallas or even El Paso. It has some white-collar job growth and diversification and has become something of a tourist center (it is home of the International Balloon Fiesta). But it still depends primarily on government, which fortunately has come through, as with the 1990 designation of Kirtland Air Base as site of one of four "superlabs."

The 1st Congressional District of New Mexico is, for all practical purposes, the city of Albuquerque and its suburbs; it also includes largely empty Torrance County and communities north and south along the Rio Grande. Albuquerque is one Sun Belt city which is not solidly Republican, and in 1992 it went by a decisive margin for Bill Clinton after voting Republican for president in the 1980s—not far off the national average. The 1st District in 1990 was 38% Hispanic, a mixture of the descendants of longtime New Mexicans and recent immigrants.

The congressman from the 1st District is Steven Schiff, a Republican first elected in 1988 on the retirement of 20-year incumbent Republican Manuel Lujan, Jr., who became Bush's secretary of the interior. Schiff is an unusual New Mexico figure, as he points out. He is a native of Chicago who came to Albuquerque to attend law school; he is Jewish in a state made up mostly of Anglo Protestants and Hispanic Catholics; he is aggressive and a stickler for doing things by the book in a state often tolerant of lax practices. Since coming to the state, Schiff has served in the New Mexico Air National Guard, and is now a lieutenant colonel in the Air Force Reserves. After law school, he became a prosecutor and, after a few years of private practice, in 1980 was elected district attorney of Albuquerque's Bernalillo County, where he was proud of the death penalty convictions he obtained.

Schiff is the sort of man who goes where his sense of right and wrong take him, regardless of politics. He is pro-choice on abortion but believes the Freedom of Choice Act goes too far; he opposed a bill allowing military personnel to sue military physicians for malpractice, because they may already qualify for disability; he opposed a bill to criminalize animal rights terrorism; he voted against the flag amendment because of its technical language. He worked to create the Petroglyph National Monument on the west side of Albuquerque and to buy land for the Tres Pistolas animal preserve. He wrote an amendment barring criminals from evading obligations to repay their victims by filing for bankruptcy, and an amendment allowing 16- and 17-year-olds accused of violent federal crimes to be tried as adults. He refuses to accept honoraria and in 1993 was put on the Ethics Committee. He also sits on the Science and Judiciary Committees.

Schiff's toughest race was his first, when he beat two big names in 1988. In the primary, he edged his predecessor's brother, Edward Lujan, by a 41%–37% margin; in the general, he beat Tom Udall, son of former Interior Secretary Stewart Udall and nephew of former House Interior Committee Chairman Morris Udall, winner of a 10-candidate Democratic primary, by

51%–47%. He won much more easily in 1990 against a candidate with fraudulent credentials, and comfortably in 1992 against respectable but underfinanced state legislator Robert Aragon.

The People: Pop. 1990: 505,329; 8% rural; 10% age 65+; 56% White; 3% Black; 3% Amer. Indian; 1% Asian; 15% Other; 38% Hispanic origin. Voting age pop.: 371,549; 2% Black; 34% Hispanic origin. Households: 53% married couple families; 26% married couple fams. w. children; 54% college educ.; median household income: $27,074; per capita income: $13,373; median gross rent: $400; median house value: $83,800.

1992 Presidential Vote			1988 Presidential Vote		
Clinton (D)	95,754	(45%)	Bush (R)	97,414	(54%)
Bush (R)	81,038	(38%)	Dukakis (D)	82,867	(46%)
Perot (I)	33,034	(16%)			

Rep. Steven H. Schiff (R)

Elected 1988; b. Mar. 18, 1947, Chicago, IL; home, Albuquerque; U. of IL, B.A. 1968, U. of NM, J.D. 1972; Jewish; married (Marcia).

Career: Air Natl. Guard, 1969–91; Air Force Reserves, 1991–present; Asst. Dist. Atty., Bernalillo Cnty., 1972–77; Practicing atty., 1977–79; Asst. City Atty. and Cnsl., Albuquerque Police Dept., 1979–81; Dist. Atty., Bernalillo Cnty., 1981–89.

Offices: 1009 LHOB, 202-225-6316. Also 625 Silver Ave. SW, #140, Albuquerque 87102, 505-766-2538.

Committees: *Government Operations* (6th of 17 R): Human Resources and Intergovernmental Relations (RMM). *Judiciary* (9th of 14 R): Crime and Criminal Justice; Intellectual Property and Judicial Administration. *Science, Space and Technology* (9th of 22 R): Energy; Space. *Standards of Official Conduct* (7th of 7 R).

Group Ratings

	ADA	ACLU	COPE	CDF	CFA	LCV	ACU	NTLC	NSI	COC	CEI
1992	25	43	58	30	20	13	72	70	90	88	60
1991	20	—	33	40	28	23	65	—	—	80	49

National Journal Ratings

	1991 LIB — 1991 CONS			1992 LIB — 1992 CONS		
Economic	14%	—	83%	26%	—	73%
Social	48%	—	51%	32%	—	67%
Foreign	17%	—	78%	30%	—	64%

Key Votes of the 102d Congress

1. Ban Striker Replace	AGN	5. Handgun Wait/7-Day	AGN	9. Use Force in Gulf	FOR
2. $ for Homeownership	FOR	6. Overseas Mil. Abortion	FOR	10. US Mil. Abroad $ Cut	FOR
3. Tax Rich/Cut Mid Cls.	AGN	7. Obscn. Art NEA $ Ban	FOR	11. Limit SDI Funds	AGN
4. FY93/$15B Def. Cut	AGN	8. Death Pen. from Jury	FOR	12. Cuba Trade Embargo	FOR

Key Votes of the 103d Congress

1. Family Leave	AGN	2. Deficit Reduction	AGN	3. Stimulus Plan	AGN

Election Results

1992 general	Steven H. Schiff (R).................	128,426	(63%)	($589,743)
	Robert J. Aragon (D).................	76,600	(38%)	($81,541)
1992 primary	Steven H. Schiff (R), unopposed			
1990 general	Steven H. Schiff (R)..................	97,375	(70%)	($538,273)
	Rebecca Vigil-Giron (D)...............	41,306	(30%)	($123,215)

SECOND DISTRICT

The plains of southern and eastern New Mexico are about as disparate a landscape as can be imagined: miles of sagebrush-strewn acreage, and then, suddenly, 9,000-foot mountain peaks rising in the distance. The eastern part of this region, Little Texas, is an extension of the Texas civilization that filled up empty counties when irrigation was developed. Oil has long been the economic mainstay here; cattle ranching is common; cotton is grown on irrigated land. The little cities are full of people with Texas twangs, not the lilt of northern New Mexico. West from Clovis and Portales, Lovington and Hobbs, the towns become fewer and farming mostly disappears. The scrub land shades into desert, and people in the area are crammed into small cities, protected from an environment that is burning hot in the summer and sometimes deathly cold in winter.

The 2d Congressional District of New Mexico includes the entire southern half of the state geographically—most of Little Texas, plus the desert on either side of the Rio Grande and the mining territory in the mountains just north of the Mexican border and just short of the Arizona line. The largest city here is Las Cruces, home of New Mexico State University and only 45 miles north of the million-plus metropolis of El Paso, Texas, and Chihuahua, Mexico. These places today vote the opposite of their partisan tradition: Little Texas, settled by yellow dog Democrats from the Lone Star state, is now solidly Republican; Las Cruces, long leaning Republican, has become Democratic. In most recent elections, the 2d District has gone Republican. But redistricting subtracted Republican and added Democratic counties, and in 1992 the district was rather evenly split in the presidential election.

The congressman from the 2d District is Joe Skeen, a sheep rancher and Republican who represents the district's conservative leanings on most issues. Generally opposed to high government spending, he is happy to make exceptions for defense, science and agriculture; he is well positioned to do so, as a member of the Appropriations Agriculture and Defense Subcommittees. He is a staunch opponent of raising federal grazing fees for livestock producers, and battled Mike Synar of Oklahoma hard on this issue in 1992; in 1993, he must battle the Clinton Administration as well, and Interior Secretary Bruce Babbitt has already claimed authority to raise the fees. Skeen worked diligently to bring the WIPP nuclear waste disposal site to a salt cavern near Carlsbad, helping it pass through Congress in 1992. On occasion, he cooperates with Democrats on Appropriations, and in 1991 backed the "corn for porn" swap— killing the grazing fee increase in return for killing Senate limitations on federal funding for obscene and sacrilegious art. He brought the F-117A Stealth fighter plane base from Tonopah, Nevada, to Holloman AFB near Alamogordo.

Skeen was first elected to the House in 1980, after narrowly losing the gubernatorial races in 1974 and 1978. He won the hard way, as a write-in, when Democratic incumbent Harold "Mud" Runnels died and the Democrats put Governor Bruce King's nephew on the ballot. Skeen got 38% of the vote to 34% for King and 28% for Runnels's widow, also a write-in. In 1986, Skeen beat Runnels's son Mike 63%–37%; unopposed in 1988 and 1990, he won by just 56%–44% in 1992. His opponent, a former state Supreme Court justice, hit Skeen for opposing an increase in the minimum wage and unemployment benefits extension, given the district's higher than average unemployment. Skeen won the one-sixth of the district that was new with just 51%, and the part he had previously represented with 57%.

The People: Pop. 1990: 504,767; 33% rural; 12% age 65+; 52% White; 2% Black; 4% Amer. Indian; 1% Asian; 9% Other; 42% Hispanic origin. Voting age pop.: 350,322; 2% Black; 37% Hispanic origin. Households: 61% married couple families; 31% married couple fams. w. children; 40% college educ.; median household income: $21,456; per capita income: $9,672; median gross rent: $325; median house value: $52,200.

1992 Presidential Vote			1988 Presidential Vote		
Clinton (D)	70,630	(41%)	Bush (R)	94,585	(57%)
Bush (R)	68,754	(40%)	Dukakis (D)	72,760	(43%)
Perot (I)	31,780	(18%)			

Rep. Joe Skeen (R)

Elected 1980; b. June 30, 1927, Roswell; home, Picacho; TX A&M U., B.S. 1950; Catholic; married (Mary).

Career: Navy, 1945–46 (WWII), Air Force Reserves, 1949–52; Engineer, Zuni and Ramah Navajo Indian Reservations, 1950–51; Sheep rancher, 1951–present; NM Senate, 1960–70, Minority Ldr., 1965–70.

Offices: 2367 RHOB 20515, 202-225-2365. Also 1065 S. Main St., #A, Las Cruces 88005, 505-527-1771; and 257 Fed. Bldg., Roswell 88201, 505-622-0055.

Committees: *Appropriations* (9th of 23 R): Agriculture, Rural Development, Food and Drug Administration and Related Agencies (RMM); Defense.

Group Ratings

	ADA	ACLU	COPE	CDF	CFA	LCV	ACU	NTLC	NSI	COC	CEI
1992	20	22	42	30	27	6	76	60	100	88	50
1991	0	—	17	30	39	0	85	—	—	90	47

National Journal Ratings

	1991 LIB — 1991 CONS		1992 LIB — 1992 CONS	
Economic	14% —	83%	16% —	80%
Social	25% —	73%	34% —	66%
Foreign	0% —	88%	0% —	82%

Key Votes of the 102d Congress

1. Ban Striker Replace	AGN	5. Handgun Wait/7-Day	AGN	9. Use Force in Gulf	FOR
2. $ for Homeownership	FOR	6. Overseas Mil. Abortion	AGN	10. US Mil. Abroad $ Cut	AGN
3. Tax Rich/Cut Mid Cls.	AGN	7. Obscn. Art NEA $ Ban	FOR	11. Limit SDI Funds	AGN
4. FY93/$15B Def. Cut	AGN	8. Death Pen. from Jury	FOR	12. Cuba Trade Embargo	FOR

Key Votes of the 103d Congress

1. Family Leave	AGN	2. Deficit Reduction	AGN	3. Stimulus Plan	AGN

Election Results

1992 general	Joe Skeen (R)	94,838	(56%)	($493,406)
	Dan Sosa, Jr. (D)	73,157	(44%)	($40,973)
1992 primary	Joe Skeen (R), unopposed			
1990 general	Joe Skeen (R), unopposed			($80,737)

THIRD DISTRICT

"The dancing ground of the sun" the Pueblo Indians called the land of northern New Mexico, where the long, empty vistas stretch for miles, detailed in pinpoint clarity in the cold light and clear air. For 100 years, artists have been coming here, attracted by the scenery and by a unique civilization that is part Indian, part Spanish, only a little Mexican (for northern New Mexico was Mexican only briefly, from 1821 to 1846), part Anglo-American. The Spanish language, Indian pottery and dances, the adobe pueblos give the impression that life has gone on for centuries on this rocky desert soil in much the same way. Actually, the civilization hasn't been so stable. The pueblos were built in sudden spurts; the Spanish conquistadors and priests brought the Catholic religion, the baroque accents of the adobe buildings and the Spanish language in a rush; successive waves of American settlement have changed New Mexico in different ways. The Indian crafts which are thriving today nearly died out in the 1880s, and the Palace of the Governors, built in 1610, had its Victorian balustrade torn off in 1913 to restore its original appearance; the unchanged look is carefully maintained. Yet up the back roads in Rio Arriba or Taos Counties, one can find a religion that mixes Catholicism with adaptations of Indian festivals, buildings not that much different from the old pueblos, and a standard of living reminiscent of the Indian past—quite a contrast to Santa Fe, with its thousands of affluent, bohemian migrants, its 300 restaurants and the second-largest art market in the country.

The politics of northern New Mexico is a unique blend. For years, debate was conducted and votes bartered in Spanish, not by separatists, but by Republican and Democratic politicos, often cynically, sometimes corruptly; loyalties ran to families and communities more than to principles or parties. In the back country, you can still find more than just vestiges of the old communities and the old politics—though no one is going to let you in on them, even if you speak good Spanish—while in Santa Fe and Los Alamos, or in the new subdivisions along the Rio Grande north of Albuquerque, voters put a premium on environmentalism.

The 3d Congressional District of New Mexico contains most of the state's historic Spanish-speaking and Indian parts. Its largest and most dominant city is Santa Fe, which grew lustily in the 1980s, but the district runs from the High Plains along the Texas border, past the haunting Sangre de Cristo Mountains, through the vast ridges and isolated buttes in the center (on one of which the government built Los Alamos in World War II to create the atomic bomb), to the windy and dusty desert-like plains, dotted occasionally by mountains, with Indian reservations in the west. The population is 34% Hispanic origin and 20% Indian (with at least 6% overlap between the categories). Politically, it is heavily Democratic, with 1980s newcomers to Santa Fe and Taos moving it farther in that direction.

The congressman from the 3d District is Bill Richardson, a political dynamo who plays important roles on major legislation. Richardson is a political anomaly: an Hispanic with an Anglo name, a relative newcomer to New Mexico who carries towns where families go back 300 years, an ambitious politician who has sometimes taken impolitic stands apparently just because he thought they were right. Born in California and raised by his Mexican mother in Mexico City, Richardson has always been bilingual. He moved to New Mexico in 1978 after holding staff jobs on Capitol Hill, worked as executive director of the state Democratic Party for a month and started running against Republican Congressman Manuel Lujan in a district that then included Albuquerque and most of northern New Mexico, raising $200,000 and winning 49% in Republican 1980. New Mexico gained a seat in 1982 and Lujan was quite happy to give up the Hispanic counties to the new 3d; Richardson beat former Lieutenant Governor Roberto Mondragon 36%–31% in the primary and clobbered a Republican with 64% to become, in just four years, New Mexico's only Democrat in the House. Richardson has worked his district hard and has been reelected without difficulty.

In the House, Richardson is a chief deputy whip with important committee posts. He is a member of the Energy and Commerce Committee, where he has voted both with and against

Chairman John Dingell. Richardson bucked Dingell and lost 22–21 on a clean fuel amendment to the Clean Air Act, but succeeded in promoting reformulated gasoline; he wrote amendments on accidental release of air toxins and established an environmental entity to study pollution on the U.S.-Mexican border. Despite a generally liberal record, he takes some pro-business stands: he would grandfather protection for existing "orphan" drugs and backs a national bill limiting product liability suits (opposed by Ralph Nader and trial lawyers). He has supported some immigration reform bills, but opposed employer sanctions. He opposed 1992 cable reregulation, and was criticized harshly by most Energy and Commerce Democrats and in local editorials for his heavy receipt of cable PAC contributions. But he said the bill did not toughen equal opportunity hiring requirements, and so opposed the one bill passed over President Bush's veto. Richardson had greater success on the Waste Isolation Pilot Project, which he has long opposed; he insisted on strong environmental standards, invoking an obscure law to block a shipment of nuclear waste at one point, and in October 1992 eventually agreed with 2d District Republican Joe Skeen and others in the delegation on opening WIPP with half the waste requested by the DOE and under EPA standards.

Richardson has taken a lead role on one issue outside his committee purview, the North American Free Trade Agreement with Mexico. He has pushed the idea at every opportunity and spent much time keeping the Bush Administration in touch with House Democrats; he has lobbied Majority Leader Dick Gephardt and Hispanic Caucus members, bucked organized labor and other Democratic lobbies and emerged as a genuine leader. He understands well the downside potential—how negatively Mexico would react were it to feel rejected, and what could be more threatening to the quality of life in the United States than a hostile and increasingly impoverished Mexico? He knows that Mexico has moved far toward an advanced economy and an embrace of many American values, and that it can move much further with NAFTA.

1992 was a busy time for Richardson. He chaired the platform drafting committee for the Democratic National Convention. In December, he was named the House Democrats' fourth chief deputy whip, and he was almost named secretary of the interior; Bill Clinton was apparently close set on him, until environmentalist group leaders objected on the grounds of Richardson's less than purist record on their issues. But he recovered gamely, and was named chairman of a new Natural Resources Subcommittee on Native American Affairs—not a bad post for the member with the second highest percentage of Indian constituents.

Richardson has been mentioned from time to time as a candidate for statewide office, and as district boundaries change has represented most of the state at one time or another. He certainly would not run against Senator Jeff Bingaman or Governor Bruce King, both Democrats, in 1994, but he might take a look at the Senate seat held by Republican Pete Domenici when it comes up in 1996.

The People: Pop. 1990: 504,973; 40% rural; 10% age 65+; 44% White; 1% Black; 20% Amer. Indian; 1% Asian; 13% Other; 34% Hispanic origin. Voting age pop.: 346,759; 1% Black; 33% Hispanic origin. Households: 58% married couple families; 31% married couple fams. w. children; 45% college educ.; median household income: $23,610; per capita income: $10,689; median gross rent: $372; median house value: $68,400.

1992 Presidential Vote

Clinton (D)	95,233	(51%)
Bush (R)	63,032	(34%)
Perot (I)	27,081	(15%)

1988 Presidential Vote

Dukakis (D)	88,870	(53%)
Bush (R)	78,342	(47%)

Rep. Bill Richardson (D)

Elected 1982; b. Nov. 15, 1947, Pasadena, CA; home, Santa Fe; Tufts U., B.A. 1970, Fletcher Schl. of Law and Diplomacy, M.A. 1971; Catholic; married (Barbara).

Career: Congressional rel., U.S. Dept. of State, 1973–75; Staff, Senate Foreign Relations Subcmte., 1975–78; Exec. Dir., NM Dem. Party, 1978; Pres., Richardson Trade Group, 1978–82.

Offices: 2349 RHOB 20515, 202-225-6190. Also 411 Paseo de Peralta, Santa Fe 87501, 505-988-7230; Gallup City Hall, 2d and Aztec, Gallup 87301, 505-722-6522; San Miguel Cnty. Crthse., P.O. Box 1805, Las Vegas 87701, 505-425-7270; and 602 Mitchell, Clovis 88101, 505-769-3380.

Committees: *Energy and Commerce* (11th of 27 D): Health and the Environment; Telecommunications and Finance; Transportation and Hazardous Materials. *Intelligence (Permanent Select)* (2d of 12 D): Program and Budget Authorization. *Natural Resources* (11th of 28 D): National Parks, Forests and Public Lands; Native American Affairs (Chmn.).

Group Ratings

	ADA	ACLU	COPE	CDF	CFA	LCV	ACU	NTLC	NSI	COC	CEI
1992	75	74	73	80	67	63	33	0	80	57	14
1991	50	—	92	90	83	69	20	—	—	30	7

National Journal Ratings

	1991 LIB — 1991 CONS		1992 LIB — 1992 CONS	
Economic	72%	— 23%	56%	— 44%
Social	62%	— 37%	76%	— 23%
Foreign	56%	— 42%	36%	— 63%

Key Votes of the 102d Congress

1. Ban Striker Replace	FOR	5. Handgun Wait/7-Day	AGN	9. Use Force in Gulf	AGN
2. $ for Homeownership	FOR	6. Overseas Mil. Abortion	FOR	10. US Mil. Abroad $ Cut	AGN
3. Tax Rich/Cut Mid Cls.	FOR	7. Obscn. Art NEA $ Ban	AGN	11. Limit SDI Funds	AGN
4. FY93/$15B Def. Cut	FOR	8. Death Pen. from Jury	FOR	12. Cuba Trade Embargo	*

Key Votes of the 103d Congress

1. Family Leave	FOR	2. Deficit Reduction	FOR	3. Stimulus Plan	FOR

Election Results

1992 general	Bill Richardson (D)................... 122,850	(67%)	($600,683)
	F. Gregg Bemis (R)................... 54,569	(30%)	($48,064)
	Other............................... 4,798	(3%)	
1992 primary	Bill Richardson (D), unopposed		
1990 general	Bill Richardson (D)................... 104,225	(74%)	($420,907)
	Phil T. Archuletta (R)............... 35,751	(26%)	($20,902)

NEW YORK

There is nothing inevitable about New York; nothing inevitable about its successes or failures. There was nothing foreordained about New York's becoming America's largest city, its financial capital, the center of arts and letters and entertainment, the number one immigrant destination for more than 100 years. These things happened because New Yorkers—and not least those people from elsewhere who opted to become New Yorkers—chose to make them happen, worked to make sure they would happen. And they built institutions allowing New York to continue to excel, to make sure good things would continue to happen—something more difficult than they imagined.

Yet if there is nothing inevitable about New York, there is a certain enduring character to the place which in its earliest incarnation was the 17th Century Dutch colony of Nieuw Amsterdam. Simon Schama's *The Embarrassment of Riches* paints a picture of the old world Amsterdam: the richest city in the world; full of people who work hard all day and stay up late partying, smoke too much tobacco and drink too much coffee and gin, and curse and gossip and insult from morning to night, but are dazzlingly smart and shrewd; people who know their way around every corner of the globe and can make fine aesthetic discriminations, but are attached to their uncomfortable, crowded, bad-smelling city; merchants and manipulators with no aristocratic pedigree, welcoming any religious or ethnic group who can achieve and accumulate and show good taste, cherishing education and culture but indifferent to credentials. This could be a portrait of the New York of today, of Tom Wolfe and Tina Brown, or the New York of Alexander Hamilton and Aaron Burr, or the New York of Edith Wharton and Theodore Dreiser, or the New York of the Algonquin Round Table and Henry Luce's early *Time*. Probably fewer than 2% of today's New Yorkers are descended from the Dutch of Nieuw Amsterdam, but the character of the place endures in daily life and in the workings of its great institutions, and helps explain its miraculous and entirely uninevitable growth. Combine Amsterdam and America: Dutch character with British-born political freedoms and American military invulnerability— something the Dutch have never enjoyed except perhaps in the last few years—and you have the opportunity to build a city-state that can lead the world.

But New York was not always the nation's leader. In 1776, New York was the seventh most populous colony; only in the 19th Century did the descendants of Dutch patroons, Huguenot refugees, British West Indies traders and Yankee farmers become the nation's most successful merchants and capitalists, forging the first routes to the great American interior through the valleys of the Hudson and the Mohawk, over the Finger Lakes and the Great Lakes, and building grand brownstone mansions on broad midtown Manhattan avenues. That early diversity provides one clue to New York's success: if New York has been cynical, ready to cooperate with Loyalists and Revolutionaries, depending on who was ahead, it has also been tolerant, ready to accept anyone smart or rich enough to be counted a success. It has been propelled upward at each stage—forging ahead of London as a financial and manufacturing center by the First World War, and staying ahead of surging Chicago—by incorporating every wave of immigrants and consistently rewarding intelligence and hard work, unconcerned about preserving hierarchies.

New York's success has been a product not only of market economics, but of government— and politics. The Iroquois, the most deeply-rooted and militarily strong Native Americans, kept in place for 100 years by an alliance with British troops, were driven out of New York by the Revolution; the Erie Canal, which connected western New York state with he Hudson River, was the project of Governor DeWitt Clinton's state government; the railroads were subsidized by land grants and favorable laws. And New York led the nation in political innovation: Martin

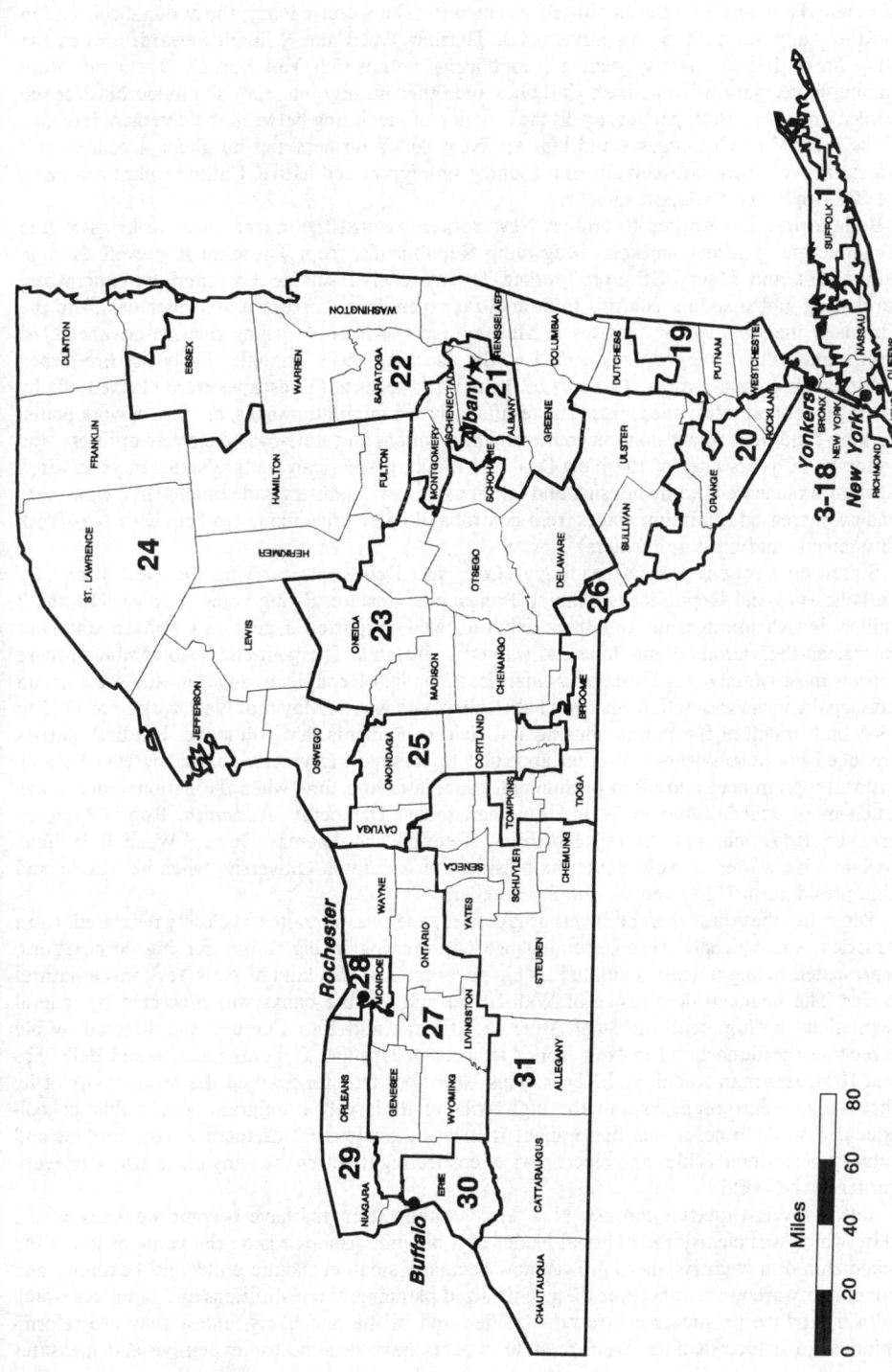

Van Buren's Albany Regency was the first state political machine, an ally of New York City's Tammany Hall, and Van Buren himself invented the Democratic Party, the national convention and the inaugural parade. His adversaries, Thurlow Weed and William Seward, formed the Whig Party and ultimately became Republicans; noting that Van Buren's Democrats were winning large margins from Irish Catholics and other immigrants, they too made bids for the newcomers' votes. Both parties served the function of mediating between the divergent interests of the New York City masses and Upstate New York's farmers and burghers, a conflict still evident in New York between city and country, immigrant and native, Catholic and Protestant, the Big Apple and the apple-knockers.

Both parties also worked to protect New Yorkers against the untramelled workings of free economic and political markets. Mugwump Republicans, from Theodore Roosevelt through Elihu Root and Henry Stimson, worked to create civil service laws and bureaucratized purchasing and spending controls to protect taxpayers from corrupt party machines. And the Tammany machine led by Charles F. Murphy and the talented young men he advanced, Al Smith and Robert Wagner, responded to the shocking 1911 Triangle Shirtwaist fire (when hundreds of women jumped 11 floors to their death because fire escapes were blocked off) by passing labor and safety measures. The results included minimum wages, maximum work hours, working-conditions regulations, encouragement of unions and state-owned electric utilities—the prototype 20 years later of the New Deal and the first American welfare state. In years after, New York pioneered public housing and fair housing laws, industry-wide unions (in the garment trades), increased minimum wages, rent control and dairy price fixing (to help both New York City tenants and Upstate farmers).

Statewide elections were exceedingly close, with Democrats carrying the New York City Catholic vote and Republicans winning Protestants Upstate. Swing votes were cast by the 2 million Jewish immigrants and their children, who supported a generous welfare state but mistrusted the Tammany machine and wanted civil rights. The politician who combined these appeals most cannily was Fiorello LaGuardia: a nominal Republican and almost a socialist, an Episcopalian who was half-Jewish and half-Italian, and who as Mayor of New York from 1933 to 1945 built much of the public housing and civic monuments that still stand. But both parties produced politicians whose position appealed to these swing voters, politicians who became nationally prominent and often presidential candidates at a time when the national media was much more concentrated in Manhattan than today: Democrats Al Smith, Robert Wagner, Franklin Roosevelt and Averell Harriman; Republicans Thomas Dewey, Wendell Willkie, Dwight Eisenhower (a New Yorker as president of Columbia University when he was elected U.S. president in 1952) and Nelson Rockefeller.

The polity that these men built was productive, generous, tolerant and closely regulated. In an America where people were becoming used to working in big units—for big corporations, represented by big unions, regulated by big government—this kind of New York was a natural leader. The financial dominance of Wall Street and the big banks was protected by federal regulation; the high-tech thrust of America after the mid-20th Century was directed by big companies headquartered in New York's suburbs or Upstate: General Electric and Bell Labs and IBM, Eastman Kodak and Xerox. This New York took for granted the productivity of its thousands of entrepreneurs and the high skills of its largely immigrant-born, public school-educated work force; it was blase about its own miraculous infrastructure—the bridges and subways, electronic cables and electric wires connecting it better than any place else with every corner of the world.

But in the last quarter-century, New York's public strengths have become weaknesses: the state which was clearly the national leader of a big-unit America is on the verge of losing the leadership of a country where growth now occurs in small economic units, and flexibility and adaptability are more important than centralized planning; the institutions and practices which helped produce its successes are now ossified and brittle and likely, unless they are reform-minded, to induce decline. Welfare state benefits have become too expensive and measures meant to protect against corruption stifle innovation, and both have failed to achieve their objectives—ghettos throb with the pains of disorganization, and payoffs and rackets are part of the everyday cost of doing business in New York as in no other place in the country. The noble aim of creating a public sector which would guarantee cheap rents, topnotch public schools and colleges, public hospitals, instead guarantees that none of these will be available: rent control keeps housing scarce, school bureaucracies stifle good teaching, public hospitals ration care down to nothing. The attempt to create a fail-safe society has produced a sure-to-fail government. The government intended to aid growth now seemed to be cutting it off—not completely, but enough to explain why New York state, which grew 32% in population from 1940 to 1965, grew only 1% from 1965 to 1990, while California was growing 60%. People and businesses started voting with their feet, especially during the terms of Mayor John Lindsay, a liberal Republican hailed when he was elected in 1965 by the powerful New York-based liberal Republican media of the day as the next John Kennedy, though about all he shared with Kennedy was good looks. Lindsay denounced Democrats for being too cozy with municipal unions, but gave up more to them than any mayor before or since; he institutionalized the practice of borrowing against next year's revenues to pay this year's bills, bringing city government to the brink of bankruptcy two years after he left office. He skillfully convinced New York's blacks that he cared about them, while allowing the institutions which had taught previous generations' immigrants to embrace middle-class values, to now scorn those values. "The confluence of radical spite, absurd legal extrapolations, and liberal disdain for white ethnics that led to forced busing, the bloating of welfare rolls, and the mau-mauing of white teachers broke the spine of New York's civic culture," writes liberal Jim Sleeper in *The Closest of Strangers*. Antagonized middle-class New Yorkers fled not just to the suburbs, but by the hundreds of thousands to (then) low-tax New Jersey, Connecticut and Florida. In the 1970s, the population of New York, city and state, dropped by 1 million—an unprecedented hemorrhage of talent and productivity, a flight of the middle class away from a polity that seemed to be dying.

Retrenchment followed the mid-1970s bankruptcy crisis. Private financiers and the state government took control of city government, cut spending and negotiated cutbacks in jobs and salaries with public employees' unions; citizens endured the loss of services and deterioration of streets, bridges and subways; even renters lost some of their advantages as stringent rent control left many city neighborhoods devastated by forcing landlords to abandon buildings. With the financial boom of 1981–87, New York once again brimmed with confidence, and the buzzing of economic growth and cultural innovation could again be heard over the never-ending blare of car horns. Manhattan boomed as an office center and remained the center of America's financial, clothing, entertainment, media and publishing industries. Its population was rising and it was attracting immigrants once again. The outer boroughs attracted migrants from Latin America, the eastern Mediterranean, Asia, even Russia, injecting youth and vitality into what had been aging, listless communities.

Yet all was not well. New York's old welfare state measures left clever members of the middle class in comfortable niches, on public payrolls protected from accountability, in rent-controlled apartments paying a fraction of market rent. These same measures left newcomers and the lower classes out in the cold (literally, in the case of the homeless, because of rent control's incentives for tearing down buildings). Through these years New York has had two bright and original-minded governmental leaders: the first, Edward Koch, mayor for 12 years, from 1977 to 1989; the second, Mario Cuomo, elected in 1982 to be governor for 12 years. Both have made genuine contributions: Koch rationalized and disciplined city government in many ways, Cuomo appointed some fine administrators and cut taxes. But neither reformed the civic culture created to discipline market capitalism and prevent political corruption, but which instead now stifles economic creativity.

Cuomo gave strong rhetorical endorsement to that culture, even as he has cut taxes and spending. Mayor David Dinkins, who beat Koch in the 1989 primary, 51%–42%, and in November narrowly prevailed over Republican former U.S. Attorney Rudolph Giuliani, 50%–

48%, is a true believer in the current liberalism of racial preferences for blacks and perhaps others and ever-greater increases in pay for municipal union members. Dinkins won in spite of these beliefs, and because New Yorkers were tired of racial tension, highlighted by the beatings of blacks in Howard Beach in 1986, the Tawana Brawley hoax of 1987, and the 1989 murder of a black by white thugs in Brooklyn's Bensonhurst neighborhood. This tension was apparent in 1988, when Jesse Jackson carried the city in the presidential primary, though it is only 25% black, by maximizing black turnout in the Democratic primary and carrying the Hispanic vote and some of white Manhattan as well, despite Koch's attacks on Jackson's anti-semitic statements ("Hymietown") made in 1984, his coolness toward Israel and (literally) embrace of Yasir Arafat, and his support of racial quotas and preferences. But both Jackson and Koch spoke out against the epidemic of drugs that was ripping apart so many ghetto neighborhoods in moral tones that Dinkins seldom summoned regarding crime: his primary objective was for conciliation over anger, and votes critical to his victory over Giuliani probably came from Koch's enthusiastic endorsement. In early 1993, it was not clear whether such factors would work for Dinkins in the fall. He gained some control over city spending, disappointing his public employee union supporters, but he hesitated for weeks before denouncing a boycott by blacks of a Korean-owned grocery in Brooklyn and sparked a police protest rally on the grounds of City Hall after he comforted relatives of a suspected drug dealer shot by a policeman: incidents that led many New Yorkers to believe he practices a racial double standard. In May 1993, City Council President Andrew Stein, lagging in polls and having spent almost $3 million, was pressured by party leaders to drop his bid for the mayor's race; that left Dinkins with only minor opposition for the September 14 primary. But by mid-1993, Dinkins was running in a dead heat in polls with Giuliani, who announced just prior to Memorial Day that he would run on a Liberal-Republican ticket with Democrats Herman Badillo for city comptroller and Susan Alter for public advocate. The public employee unions, black politicians and gay activists are backing Dinkins. Giuliani's backing is not well-organized, but the source of its strength is suggested by the successful effort of a Queens local school board to prevent School Chancellor Joseph Fernandez from foisting a controversial curriculum for first to third graders which would include books like *Heather Has Two Mommies*.

But the vitality of New York has not been entirely quenched. The city's population rose 3.5% in the 1980s, the first significant rise in a decade since the 1940s, as immigrants streamed in, reviving sagging neighborhoods in the outer boroughs and creating new businesses; some 28% of New York City residents are foreign born. The Caribbean blacks of Brooklyn, the Hispanics of Jackson Heights, Corona and Queens, the Koreans of Flushing, the Greeks of Astoria are living the American dream; even that sore spot, the South Bronx, is filling in, thanks to some innovative Koch housing programs. There are still horrifying problem neighborhoods—much of Harlem and Brownsville in Brooklyn, but it no longer seems likely, as it did in the late 1970s, that these sources of blight would spread over the city. Even as faith in government's ability to change lives is declining, the evidence that ordinary people, mostly on their own and with very few advantages, can not only cope but rise and prosper is increasingly apparent in New York.

Not all of New York state is New York City, by any means; but the city's strengths and its problems flow beyond its limits. New York suburbs are still outvoted by the City, because so much suburban overflow is in New Jersey or Connecticut. The suburbs have by national standards very large and well-paid local governments, with high property taxes (the City's are low, on residences) and a hunger for state school aid that keeps the suburban-dominated Republican state Senate a faithful ally in maintaining New York's big government apparatus. Beyond the New York City orbit is Upstate, with 36% of the state's residents and a larger share of its voters, historically Protestant and Republican, now heavily Catholic and sometimes Democratic. Upstate no longer has central transportation arteries as in the days of the New York Central's water level route, and so is off the beaten path: passenger trains seldom run, freight lines are long bankrupt and airports here are not very busy. Its population has not risen much since the 1950s. The largest city, Buffalo, is one of those Great Lakes factory cities where old steel mills have closed and the economy has continued to sag after the recession of 1973–74; Upstate's biggest employer, IBM, is in trouble and has been making its first-ever layoffs, while healthier big Upstate companies—General Electric, Kodak, Xerox—have not been hiring in large numbers. Upstate has great assets: a fine physical environment—green hills, majestic mountains, glistening lakes, a plentiful water supply—and winters are no colder than those in booming Minnesota or New Hampshire. It has a highly-skilled labor force and high-tech experience. It has the North American Free Trade Agreement, which puts Upstate on the doorstep of the most prosperous part of Canada: the Golden Horseshoe of Ontario from St. Catharines to Hamilton and Toronto is just across the river from Buffalo's Niagara Frontier, and Interstate 87 runs straight from Albany to Montreal. This was one of America's first frontiers, with fine colleges and cultural institutions going back to the early 1800s wave of Yankee settlements; it set the dominant cultural tone of the Yankee America that won the Civil War, settled the West and stretched the United States all the way to the Pacific Ocean. But now Upstate is struggling to adapt to a new economy, freighted with New York's high tax structure and an economy based on big-unit companies in a small-unit age.

Politically, New York is inevitably counted as a Democratic state. For the last 20 years, it has elected only Democratic governors, and has tended to favor Democratic senators (Republican Alfonse D'Amato has been elected three times, but twice by the narrowest of pluralities) and House members; in presidential contests it has been the most Democratic of the 10 big states ever since Massachusetts fell off that list (actually, Pennsylvania was 0.2% more for Walter Mondale). But there is a certain shakiness in the standing of the Democrats, with the exception of Senator Daniel Patrick Moynihan. Cuomo was reelected with only 53% of the vote against split opposition in 1990, and his job rating has fallen as the state's practice of borrowing to balance its budget becomes more well-known. Bill Clinton's 50% of the vote here was exceeded only in Arkansas and Washington, D.C., but this was due to his 69% in New York City; he won just 44% in the suburbs and 40% Upstate, the latter a sharp drop from Michael Dukakis's 47%. Republicans, to be sure, have run far worse, notably George Bush in 1992. But Al D'Amato's 49%–48% victory in 1992, coupled with Mario Cuomo's first win in 1982 over Lewis Lehrman by a 51%–47% margin, suggests that Democrats have been skating close to thin ice.

Governor. Mario Cuomo, governor of New York, is one of the largest figures in American politics. This is not just because of what he has done, though he can claim to have led the state ably and creatively, nor what he says, which is not usually original; it is mostly his forcefulness, his insistent strength, that makes him a leader. He appears decisive even when being pettily argumentative, and farsighted even though this son of New York, who does not often travel outside the state, is markedly parochial. No Democrat more eloquently denounced the Reagan policies of the 1980s than Cuomo in his 1984 Democratic National Convention keynote speech; yet it can be argued that he did something similar in New York by cutting tax rates to stimulate economic growth and by allowing the functional equivalent of deficits, heavy borrowing to meet current expenses while sloughing state responsibilities off onto local governments. But Cuomo could respond that one state can't let its tax rates get way out of line with others without paying a price much of which will inevitably come from the poor.

All of this is delivered in a voice that is authentically New York. Cuomo grew up in South Jamaica, Queens, a rough neighborhood even then, the son of a hard-working immigrant grocer, speaking only Italian until he entered school. Cuomo has always been competitive: he got top grades at St. John's University and law school, clerked for a judge on New York's highest court and even had a tryout for baseball's minor leagues. He had a successful law practice in Brooklyn, just one of thousands of outer borough lawyers when he was appointed by Mayor John Lindsay in 1972 as a mediator between advocates and opponents of a low-income housing project in middle-income Forest Hills. His political rise was choppy: he lost a primary for lieutenant governor in 1974, was appointed secretary of state, ran for mayor and lost to Ed Koch in 1977, was elected lieutenant governor in 1978, and ran for governor as an underfinanced-underdog in 1982. He beat Koch, 52%–48%, in the primary, and Rite-Aid entrepreneur Lew Lehrman, 51%–

47%, in the general—and soon became one of the most popular New York politicians.

As governor, Cuomo increased education spending sharply and cut New York state's top income tax rates from 10% to 7% in 1990. He vetoed capital punishment and doubled the number of prison beds. With billion dollar bond issues, he pushed $25 billion in infrastructure programs to rebuild roads, clean up the environment and rebuild New York City's crumbling transportation system. He appointed topnotch administrative heads who helped develop an innovative Child Assistance Program, which he claims is a model for welfare reform. He is proud of his Liberty Scholarships, of his programs to combat AIDS, of his acid rain legislation. He has also taken some unpopular steps, as when he tried to shift school aid away from rich suburban districts—a source of continuing tension with the Republican state Senate.

Cuomo's reforms go only so far. Interestingly for a man who represents the site of the world's greatest financial markets, Cuomo seems to profoundly mistrust economic markets and to feel, in line with some Catholic tradition, that they are inherently unjust. Yet he finds himself under a practical constraint that Catholic tradition also understands (as did Abraham Lincoln, a volume of whose writings Cuomo edited) the need to reconcile moral ideals with reality. In practice, Cuomo has innovated but has also worked to maintain a public sector that is far larger and more expensive than that of any other state, without producing better results, and in some respects clearly producing worse ones. Cuomo's fiscal problems eased by early 1993, and New York seemed to be growing again, though not at the bounteous rates of the 1980s.

From 1984 to 1992, national reporters enjoyed speculating whether Cuomo was going to run for president, and he enjoyed teasing them with equivocal comments and sly hints. But for the most part he has confounded everyone by doing what he stated he would. In February 1987, he announced in a radio interview he wasn't running, and in fact he never did, though the Democrats were ready (as demonstrated) to nominate an ethnic northeast governor and it seemed possible their nominee could win. In November 1990, Cuomo blundered badly when asked about Iraq's seizure of Kuwait: "You could negotiate something that gets them out of Kuwait for the most part, leaves them maybe a little bit on the water, leaves them a little bit of the oil"—a comment which he said just laid out a possible option, but which amounted to appeasement of aggression. In January 1991, more coyly, he told reporters, "I would prefer the position advocated by Senator Sam Nunn," i.e., vote against the Gulf war resolution. In spring 1991, he said he was unlikely to run unless he solved New York state's fiscal problems; plausibly, since the existence of such problems undermined any claims of achievement. Then in October 1991, as Bill Clinton was making his New Covenant speeches, Cuomo made it plain he really was thinking about running, throwing in a couple of good jabs at Clinton. But he deliberately left himself hostage to the Republican state Senate by saying he wouldn't run if he couldn't get a fiscal package through; predictably, he couldn't, and even as Democratic state Chairman John Marino had a plane idling at Albany Airport ready to fly Cuomo to New Hampshire to file nominating papers, the governor was holding an angry press conference telling why he wouldn't run. His relations with Clinton got no warmer. He didn't endorse him in the New York primary (though did anyone but reporters care?) and he was obviously (and understandably) miffed when, on the famous tapes, Gennifer Flowers said that Cuomo appeared like a "Mafioso " and Clinton said, "Well, he acts like one." One reason Cuomo never ran for president may be fear of smears linking him to organized crime, for which there is no scintilla of evidence; and perhaps he simply doesn't want the job. He seldom leaves New York and his foreign experience is limited to just a few trips. He turns 68 in 2000, the next time the nomination is likely to be open, and is as unlikely as ever to run.

Clinton made sure to reconcile with Cuomo, who in turn delivered a handsome (and not overlong) nominating speech at Madison Square Garden. During the fall campaign, when Clinton was asked on MTV whom he might name to the Supreme Court, he named Cuomo, although Cuomo does not in fact meet Clinton's litmus test: while Cuomo favors allowing abortion as public policy, and in a major speech at Notre Dame defended this policy as consistent with his Catholic faith, he has never said whether he agrees with the *Roe v. Wade* decision. When Supreme Court Justice Byron White announced his retirement in March 1993, Cuomo was mentioned as a possible nominee; in April he asked Clinton that he not be considered.

Meanwhile, Cuomo moved ahead to run for a fourth term in 1994; if he wins and serves, he will have been governor in New York longer than anyone since DeWitt Clinton, who served 1777–95 and 1801–04, when he was elected vice president of the United States. Cuomo won his second term in 1986, at the height of his popularity and in the glow of the Statue of Liberty celebrations that commemorated the immigrant experience, by a record 65%–32% margin. In 1990, Republicans rejected New York University Dean Herbert London, who had the Conservative Party nomination, because he was antiabortion; but party leaders could only come up with economic consultant Pierre Rinfret, who sounded like an ignorant blowhard, while London was knowledgeable and competent. Rinfret won only 21%, to London's 20%; the headline was that Cuomo won only 53%, far less than expected. With Cuomo's job rating down, many Republicans think they can beat him in 1994, and in early 1993 more than half a dozen figures were pondering the race. They include well-known names like D'Amato, Lehrman, London, Assembly Republican Leader Clarence Rappleyea, plus former party chairmen Patrick Barrett and Richard Rosenbaum, former Ambassador to France Evan Galbraith, and former Manhattan Congressman Bill Green. Republican primaries, by the way, are heavily tilted toward Upstate New York and the Italian-Americans who form practically the entire Republican primary electorate in New York City and much of it in the suburbs and Upstate, and who have been strongly anti-Cuomo in recent years. The most disappointed potential contender in early 1993 was surely Lieutenant Governor Stan Lundine, a former Upstate congressman, who would have become governor had Cuomo moved to the Supreme Court; now he waits, in an office that gives him less publicity than Attorney General Robert Abrams, who lost to D'Amato in 1992. Both of them could be candidates should Cuomo surprise everyone and retire; so also might former Congresswoman and 1984 Vice Presidential Nominee Geraldine Ferraro, who lost the close and bitter 1992 Senate primary to Abrams, and Congressman Charles Schumer.

Senators. Daniel Patrick Moynihan, the nation's best thinker among politicians since Lincoln and its best politician among thinkers since Jefferson, stands at the summit of a long career in public life. He is New York's senior senator, chairman of the Senate Finance Committee, crucially positioned to influence key Clinton Administration programs and to advance his own proposals and ideas. And for all his academic credentials, Moynihan has a range of experience in American government as broad as any member of Congress. He worked for Governor Averell Harriman in the 1950s, served as assistant secretary of labor in the Kennedy and Johnson Administrations, was chief domestic adviser to President Nixon and was his ambassador to India, and ambassador to the United Nations under President Ford—the only person in American history, he likes to note, who has served in the cabinet or subcabinet of four successive presidents.

Moynihan is known rightly for his ability to spot emerging issues long before anyone else, qualities that were apparent at least as early as 1965, when he wrote "The Negro Family: The Case for National Action." But the long expanse of his career has only underlined the consistency of his ideas and interests and the persistence with which he has kept at his causes. To be sure, he picks his moments to come forward to fight and to retire from the fray, and he learns from the flow of history; but since he has anticipated so often the direction things are going, he has more to teach and less to learn. Every summer Moynihan spends several weeks in an old one-room schoolhouse in Pindars Corners, deep in the hills of Upstate New York, writing in distinctive prose another book on any one of a dozen subjects; then he returns to Washington, to converse with colleagues in the peculiar languid atmosphere of the Senate floor and then rise in anger to challenge a bad idea. This is the kind of philosopher-politician who the Founding Fathers hoped would people the Senate—although they would have been surprised to see one spring, as Moynihan did, from the Manhattan slum of Hell's Kitchen.

Moynihan's preoccupations are many and enduring, and traceable through his career. Start, because it begins with A, with architecture. Three decades ago, he bemoaned the dilapidated state of Pennsylvania Avenue; a redevelopment corporation was set up, and now it is a splendid boulevard, with buildings restored and new, in one of which he keeps an apartment. He is also the father of the graceful new Thurgood Marshall Federal Judiciary Center, next door to Union Station, and has set his eye on the Capitol employees' parking lots, with a view to putting gardens or parks there. From 1973 to 1975, Moynihan was ambassador to India and he is an expert on things Indian. He got a special exemption from Senate Rules to chair the Near Eastern and South Asian Affairs Subcommittee in 1993. Tying these two subjects together is his wife Elizabeth Moynihan's scholarly work on the gardens of the great Moguls; she has also managed his campaigns in New York: a true Renaissance woman.

In the early 1960s, before Ralph Nader, Moynihan was arguing that traffic deaths could be reduced by redesigning car interiors. Today, he is something like the nation's transportation czar. He combined his chairmanship of the Water Resources, Transportation and Infrastructure Subcommittee and the need to reauthorize the highway bill to produce "Ice Tea," insider language for the Intermodal Surface Transportation Efficiency Act of 1991, which provided vast new sums for transportation and gave states the choice of whether to use money for highways or mass transit. It made funding formulas more favorable to New York—a pet Moynihan cause on which he publishes yearly data to show New York is shortchanged—and funded magnetic levitation or maglev trains, also a favorite cause. He put in money to rebuild a Brooklyn courthouse (he can recite the history of all of New York's courthouses), which he was forced to drop, but got back in 1992, and got New York reimbursed for building its Thruway, as he argued should have been done by the Interstate Highway Act of 1957.

In *The Politics of a Guaranteed Income*, Moynihan describes how the Senate Finance Committee defeated the Family Assistance Plan he produced for Richard Nixon in 1970 and 1971. Now he is that committee's chairman. He helped to pass the Clinton budget resolution in early 1993, probably out of party loyalty; like British politicians he has studied, he seems to believe that you should routinely support your party on issues in which you aren't much interested, and save your originality for the things you really care about. But there are clearly some areas of possible clash. Clinton proposed to raise tax rates and use the tax code to provide incentives; Moynihan told *National Journal*, "You want to keep to an absolute minimum the amount of economic behavior that is tax-driven." He did, after all, support the 1986 tax reform, after preserving deductibility of state taxes (worth more in New York than anywhere else) and helped get rid of passive loss deductions for real estate. He is wary of raising the marginal tax rate above 36%, as Clinton's super-tax would do (New York has many very high income voters), and he put a quick stop to talk about delaying Social Security COLAs, calling it a "death wish" for Democrats—just as in early 1981 he got the Senate on record 96–0 against cutting Social Security benefits and in early 1990 he had both Republicans and Democrats in a tizzy with his "Moyniplan" proposal to cut the Social Security payroll tax 1% (he points out that it takes in much more than Social Security is paying out now). He has said he does not particularly favor a VAT, that it is not needed here, as it was in Europe to prevent tax evasion. In early 1993 in *Time* magazine, an unnamed Clinton source said of Moynihan, "He's not one of us. He can't control Finance like Bentsen did. He's cantankerous, but . . . we'll roll right over him if we have to." But in fact Moynihan is a more capable steerer of the committee than some think, and it's not clear who will roll whom. Finance's ranking Republican Bob Packwood and House Ways and Means Chairman Dan Rostenkowski in early 1993 were preoccupied by ethics investigations, and the administration cannot drop many Democratic votes on a committee they control by only 11–9. Moynihan said he'd work for Clinton's investment tax credit, but insisted first on a solid concession. That was preserving the deductibility of gifts of appreciated property to non-profit entities such as universities and museums; here Moynihan was using taxes to affect behavior, and channeling more money to America's Tocquevillian cultural institutions than the National Endowments for the Humanities and Arts will ever give.

But what Moynihan really wants to do on Finance is to make progress on a problem he spotted in 1965, for which he was harshly criticized for decades by black leaders and liberals, only a few now with the good grace to admit, in the face of overwhelming evidence, that they were wrong and he is right. Family breakdown among blacks has reached harrowing proportions, and has hurt children grievously; and family breakdown overall is now about as common as it was among blacks in 1965. "We have eliminated poverty for the elderly," Moynihan said in *Family and Nation* in 1985, "only to see it burgeon for children." He translated this insight into legislation that became the 1988 Welfare Reform Act, which recognized, for the first time, the responsibilities of fathers to provide for their children, and fosters the idea that those who receive benefits have responsibilities in return, encouraging workfare experiments. Now Moynihan wants to do more. He sharply criticized HHS Secretary Donna Shalala at her first hearings for only perfunctorily mentioning welfare and reminded her that the Children's Defense Fund, on whose board both she and Hillary Rodham Clinton used to sit, had opposed the 1988 welfare reform act because of workfare. Here Moynihan will be pressing the Clinton Administration hard, in a direction it may not want to go. "It is the policy of the United States to strengthen families," says a phrase Moynihan inserted into the 1992 tax bill.

Moynihan has also been a force in foreign policy. In 1975 and 1976, he was ambassador to the United Nations, where he denounced the Soviet Union and some Third World nations, opposing their resolution declaring Zionism as racism. Moynihan was criticized harshly by liberals for not being more conciliatory toward Communists and their allies; he argued that he was only taking international law seriously. International law is a constant Moynihan theme, which he addressed in his 1990 book *On The Law of Nations*. Once considered a foreign policy hawk, in the late 1970s Moynihan became convinced that the Soviet Union was not a strong enemy and would come apart through ethnic conflict. Moynihan believes ethnic allegiances and rivalries are more important in politics than economic differences: it is the theme of his and Nathan Glazer's *Beyond the Melting Pot*, a description of New York's ethnic groups which was published in 1963 and still rings true today, and it is the theme of his 1993 book *Pandemonium*, which describes how ethnic conflicts produce war and genocide. In the 1980s, Moynihan continued to denounce the Soviet Union though not always in agreement with the Reagan Administration. Generally classed now with foreign policy doves, there is a great difference between them and Moynihan: most doves believed that the Soviet Union was dangerous but not evil, dangerous because it was militarily powerful and on the rise in the world because of the attractiveness of socialism, not evil because our system and theirs were converging. Moynihan believed the opposite, that the Soviet Union was evil but not dangerous: evil because totalitarian systems by nature do evil things, not dangerous because it was economically weak. Indeed, Moynihan and Ronald Reagan are the only two American leaders who explicitly predicted, in 1979 and 1982, the demise of the Soviet Union. Today, Moynihan believes the United States should have a far smaller military and basically abolish the CIA. He calls for greater reliance on international law, understanding that it is not self-executing but can be a powerful tool in the hands of a country which has a vested interest in maintaining law and order. Electoral politics has proved surprisingly congenial to Moynihan. After beating Bella Abzug in the 1976 primary, Moynihan won a party-line victory against incumbent James Buckley in a year when Republicans were hurt by President Ford's opposition to federal loan guarantees for New York City. For 1982, Moynihan's opposition to Reagan programs prevented the emergence of opposition from the left, and he eliminated the main Republican candidate, Bruce Caputo, when it became known the man had falsified his military record. Moynihan won 65%–34% in 1982 and 67%–31% in 1988, both records for New York. He is a partisan Democrat with an affection for old-time party bosses but also many ties with reformers; he is dismayed by his party's lack of success with working-class Catholics and ethnics, though he has carried them by large margins. He has insisted the 1994 Democratic state convention not give perennial candidate Al Sharpton the 25% of its votes it did in 1992 to put him on the ballot; in that race, there was no Democratic incumbent, but for the next, there most emphatically is. It's an interesting question whether a serious Republican, like former Congressman Bill Green, will take on the difficult challenge of running a race against Pat Moynihan.

Alfonse D'Amato, New York's junior senator, is nobody's idea of a philosopher in politics. He is loud, persistent, he pinches cheeks and puts his arms around shoulders and stands just a little too close when he speaks, he uses lushly vulgar expressions and is utterly shameless in his bids for popularity. Yet he gets along well enough with Pat Moynihan, and their interests overlap more than one might think: Moynihan really does care about getting New York reimbursed for the Thruway and D'Amato really does care about human rights in Lithuania. Most of all though, D'Amato seems to believe in helping people in New York, in manically aggressive constituency service that has gotten him labeled "Senator Pothole." He is shamelessly devoted to causes popular with New York constituencies—mass transit, AIDS funding, Israel, the death penalty for drug dealers, Wall Street brokerages in their fights against the big banks. He came to office as the lucky beneficiary of splits in the opposition; his major experience was as a wheelhorse in Nassau County Republican machine politics; his personal manner does not especially inspire confidence or arouse enthusiasm.

So he stays in favor by doing favors. This can cause trouble if he does the wrong favors for the wrong people; the Senate Ethics Committee in 1991, after a two-year investigation, rebuked him for letting his brother use his office while representing a defense contractor, and in May 1993 the brother was convicted of mail fraud for taking a $120,000 concealed payment from a defense contractor in exchange for lobbying D'Amato. And D'Amato sometimes carries things too far, as when he recommended the Congressional Medal of Honor for a victim of the *Achille Lauro* terrorists. But he was also prescient in condemning Saddam Hussein, and his stands, sometimes with cameras rolling, for human rights in the former Soviet Union have been vindicated by history. His middle-of-the-road voting record contains few positions that are obnoxious to a majority of New Yorkers.

D'Amato's first victory, in 1980, he owed to the insight that he could win the Republican primary against Senator Jacob Javits, who was, as D'Amato's ads bluntly pointed out, 76, ailing and liberal, and that he could beat a liberal Democrat in a year when voters were turning against liberals. That is what happened, as D'Amato first beat Javits and then beat Elizabeth Holtzman, now New York City Comptroller, by a 45%–44% margin. In 1986, at the peak of Ronald Reagan's popularity, D'Amato beat Mark Green, New York City Consumer Commissioner, by a solid 57%–41% margin; it was Green who afterward brought the Ethics Committee complaint against D'Amato.

Running for his third term in 1992, D'Amato seemed vulnerable and Democrats fought for the nomination to oppose him. The leading Democrats were Holtzman, Robert Abrams, the state attorney general, Geraldine Ferraro and Al Sharpton. There was a clear issues difference: Ferraro was notably more moderate on health care (against single-payer national health insurance), crime (for the death penalty), defense (only $100 billion in cuts). And as the first woman nominated on a major party ticket, she was well-positioned to take advantage of the feminist enthusiasm that prompted so many journalists to label 1992 "the year of the woman." But she also had problems left over from charges made during the 1984 presidential campaign. Holtzman attacked Ferraro for not throwing out a pornography distributor tenant from a building she and her husband owned in 1985, as they had promised; she was criticized for having had a convicted labor racketeer as a fundraiser in her first congressional campaign in 1978. A Holtzman ad showed a Village Voice headline, "What You Don't Know About Ferraro And The Mob." Ferraro attacked this as "ethnic slurs" and Mario Cuomo said he was "disappointed" with Abrams and Holtzman. But Ferraro was clearly hurt and hired a retired federal judge to clear her finances and ran ads showing her as a teacher and comparing herself to the embattled Anita Hill. Holtzman was attacked by some leading feminists (and backed by others), but insisted Ferraro couldn't beat D'Amato. Meanwhile, D'Amato mostly was quiet. Lawrence Rockefeller, nephew of the late Governor and a liberal and environmentalist, filed to run against him in the primary; but he had not taken care to hire professional signature-gatherers, and his petitions were thrown out as invalid. Abrams won the September primary by some 11,000 votes, 37%, to 36% for Ferraro; Holtzman had 12% and Sharpton 14%.

D'Amato immediately pounced on Abrams for making anti-Italian slurs, and wrote a verse: "Lizzie Holtzman took an axe/She gave Geraldine 40 whacks/When Bobby Abrams saw what she done/He took the axe and gave her 41." Ferraro, clearly bitter, refused to concede the race for two weeks, awaiting absentee votes. D'Amato, vastly better financed, attacked Abrams as "hopelessly liberal." Certainly Abrams was proud of his record fighting toxic polluters and consumer fraud, in favor of national health insurance and huge defense cuts to finance new programs, although in 1991 he wouldn't say how he would have voted on the Gulf war resolution. D'Amato touted his constituency service with ads saying "Gettin' it done. Makin' waves. Takin' 'em on," and to pound home the point, staged a 14-hour filibuster in mid-October to save 875 jobs at a Smith-Corona factory in the Upstate town of Cortland. Mid-October is also when Abrams made the mistake that cost him the election: after being heckled by D'Amato supporters in Binghamton, Abrams called D'Amato a "fascist." D'Amato demanded an apology; Abrams said his remark was "unfortunate" but for several days refused to apologize for calling D'Amato one of the few bad things he clearly is not. D'Amato took this, with some basis, as an anti-Italian slur and ran an ad attacking Abrams, showing Mussolini. Cuomo evidently took umbrage, saying "Bobby's race is all negative." D'Amato called Abrams "Mudslide Bob" and a "sleazebag," citing a commission that criticized him for taking money from developers whom he regulated. He said Abrams's national health insurance plan would raise New Yorkers' taxes by an average of $4,500 a year and, when it was revealed that Abrams was late in paying taxes on a $400,000 country home, D'Amato said, "He wants to raise other people's taxes ... Let him pay his own." Meanwhile, he highlighted issues—defense cuts, health insurance—where he was closer to Bill Clinton's positions than Abrams was.

This was another squeaker: D'Amato 49%, Abrams 48%. Exit polls showed D'Amato with high percentages among Italian descent voters (66%, 25% ahead of George Bush: the fascist slur hurt), Irish descent (63%) and white Protestants (62%); Abrams did well with blacks (84%) and those with no religious affiliation (74%), but not as well with Jews (59%). D'Amato is now ranking Republican on the Banking Committee. He said during the campaign that he would not run again in 1998, but added, D'Amato-like, "I have no intention of running—but I never say never." And in June 1993, he said the odds that he would run for governor were "at least 50–50."

Presidential politics. For more than 100 years, New York was a pivotal state in presidential politics: it was the nation's largest state and closely divided first between Whigs and Jacksonians, then between Democrats and Republicans. But now California, with 54 electoral votes, is much larger than New York, with 33. It is also much more changeable, thus attracting candidates' attention, while New York typically is the most Democratic large state. Back in the 1960s New York's Democratic margins came from middle-income Jews and Catholics in the outer boroughs of New York City; today they come primarily from blacks and Puerto Ricans in the outer boroughs and liberal whites in Manhattan. Manhattan liberals tend to be young singles, affluent childless couples, feminists, gays and lesbians, the often underpaid highly-educated people who flock to this center of arts and letters—the nation's prime leftish voting bloc. Bill Clinton's 69%–24% margin over George Bush in New York City gave him an insurmountable lead; and he carried the suburbs (44%–40%) and Upstate (40%–37%) as well. His 50% total was not impressive, but Bush's 34% total was, in a negative sense—almost as low a percentage as Barry Goldwater got in 1964, at the high water mark of faith and smug confidence in the New York welfare state.

New York has had fireworks in its last three Democratic presidential primaries which have produced more heat than light on the course of the campaign. (The Republicans have had little fuss and in 1992 had no primary at all, because Pat Buchanan didn't satisfy New York's convoluted ballot requirements.) New York didn't have primaries at all before 1968, and turnout is low—about 1.0 million in 1980 and 1992, 1.3 million in 1984 and 1.5 million 1988. The New York press hypes the primaries as if they mattered, and perhaps they do locally: in 1984 Jesse Jackson's anti-semitic remarks ("Hymietown") and Mayor Edward Koch's attacks ("Jews and others who care about Israel would be crazy" to vote for Jackson) set the tone for much angry rhetoric in New York City politics. Walter Mondale won with 45% to 27% for Gary Hart and 26% for Jackson. And in 1988, Koch seized the spotlight away from the candidate he endorsed, Al Gore, destroying any small chance Gore had of emerging as an alternative to Michael Dukakis, who won 51%, and Jackson, who won 37%.

In 1992, the New York press called the New York primary a major test of Bill Clinton, and it was, in the sense that he had to show he could carry on gracefully under pressure from a hostile press, which he did, showing up on "Imus in the Morning" and parrying questions from Gabe Pressman. But nothing that could have happened in the primary—except some extraneous revelation—could have pried away from Clinton the nomination he had effectively clinched in Illinois and Michigan on March 17. The Democrats were certainly not going to nominate Jerry Brown, the only alternative still left in the race, or Paul Tsongas, who was on later ballots though he had withdrawn from competition March 19, or Mario Cuomo, who had never actually run. Clinton scarcely ran ahead of the competition in the suburbs and Upstate, but won New York City with strong support from blacks and carried the state with 41% of the vote to 26% for third-place Brown and 29% for the withdrawn Tsongas. An unimpressive victory, but in a non-crucial primary.

For years, one of the distinctive features of New York politics was the existence of minor parties. Today they don't much matter. The Liberal Party and its predecessor, the American Labor Party, were founded to give Jewish garment workers a line on which they could vote for Roosevelt for president and against Tammany Hall for other offices; the Conservative Party was founded to withhold votes from liberal Republicans like Nelson Rockefeller or John Lindsay and encourage the Republican Party to nominate more conservative candidates. Both have long outlived their *raisons d'etre*. In 1992, Bill Clinton received 97,500 votes on the Liberal line, which gave 406,000 votes to John Kennedy in 1960: those old garment workers are dying off. The minor parties matter now only when they put on the ballot a candidate with specific appeal or when they nominate a separate candidate to hurt a major party candidate. But the first hasn't happened since 1969 and 1970 and the second doesn't make much difference any more.

Congressional districting. When John Kennedy was elected president in 1960, New York elected 43 congressmen and California 30. When Bill Clinton was elected in 1992, New York elected 31 congressmen and California 52: this is what happens when one state grows rapidly and another grows not at all. New York lost three districts in the 1990 Census, not as traumatic as the five seats it lost in 1980, but bad enough. Other factors complicated matters—the need for compromise between the Democratic Assembly and Republican Senate, the new interpretation of the Voting Rights Act requiring a maximum number of black and Hispanic districts, the ouster of Speaker Mel Miller in December 1991 after a criminal conviction—and Governor Cuomo did not sign the redistricting plan until June 1992, the latest of any state but Massachusetts and two-district Maine. Some carnage was avoided when Long Island Democrat Robert Mrazek ran for the Senate and when, after the plan was announced, outer borough Democrat James Scheuer and Rochester area Republican Frank Horton retired after congressional careers spanning three decades. There were two other notable casualties: Brooklyn Democrat Stephen Solarz ran in a Hispanic-majority district, where he narrowly lost the primary; Manhattan Republican Bill Green, a knowledgeable and thoughtful liberal, also lost in the general as portions of Brooklyn and Queens were added to his district. The plan, it should be added, has many grotesquely-shaped districts, some with weird salients crossing over bodies of water into other boroughs. It makes one wonder what New York's congressional districts would have looked like if lines were drawn under the same rules in 1910, when there were nearly one million more people in Manhattan than there are today, and ethnic groups were scrambled together block by block.

The People: Est. Pop. 1992: 18,119,000; Pop. 1990: 17,990,455, up 0.7% 1990–1992. 7.2% of U.S. total, 2d largest; 16% rural. Median age: 33.9 years. 13.1% 65 years and over. 74.4% White, 15.9% Black, 12.3% Hispanic origin, 3.9% Asian, 5.5% Other. Households: 49.9% married couple families; 23% married couple fams. w. children; 45% college educ.; median household income: $32,965; per capita income: $16,501; 52.2% owner occupied housing; median house value: $131,600; median monthly rent: $428. 8.5% Unemployment. Voting age pop.: 13,730,906. Registered voters (1992): 9,033,094; 4,256,952 D (47%); 2,776,954 R (31%); 1,999,188 unaffiliated and minor parties (22%).

Political Lineup: Governor, Mario M. Cuomo (D); Lt. Gov., Stan Lundine (D); Secy. of State, Gail S. Shaffer (D); Atty. Gen., Robert Abrams (D). State Senate, 61 (35 R and 26 D); State Assembly, 150 (101 D and 49 R). Senators, Daniel Patrick Moynihan (D) and Alfonse M. D'Amato (R). Representatives, 31 (18 D and 13 R).

1992 Presidential Vote

Clinton (D)	3,444,450	(50%)
Bush (R)	2,346,649	(34%)
Perot (I)	1,090,721	(16%)

1992 Democratic Presidential Primary

Clinton	412,349	(41%)
Tsongas	288,330	(29%)
Brown	264,278	(26%)
Other	42,769	(4%)

1988 Presidential Vote

Dukakis (D)	3,347,882	(51%)
Bush (R)	3,081,871	(48%)

GOVERNOR

Gov. Mario M. Cuomo (D)

Elected 1982, term expires Jan. 1995; b. June 15, 1932, Queens; home, Queens; St. John's U., B.A. 1953, LL.B. 1956; Catholic; married (Matilda).

Career: Legal Asst., Judge Adrian Burke, NY St. Court of Appeals, 1956–58; Practicing atty., 1958–74; Prof., St. John's Law Schl., 1958–74; NY Secy. of St., 1975–78; NY Lt. Gov., 1978–82.

Office: Executive Chamber, State Capitol, Albany 12224, 518-474-8390.

Election Results

1990 gen.	Mario M. Cuomo (D-L)	2,157,087	(53%)
	Pierre A. Rinfret (R)	865,948	(21%)
	Herbert I. London (C)	827,614	(20%)
	Four Others	206,247	(5%)
1990 prim.	Mario M. Cuomo (D) unopposed		
1986 gen.	Mario M. Cuomo (D)	2,775,229	(65%)
	Andrew J. O'Rourke (R)	1,363,810	(32%)
	Dennis Dillon (RTL)	130,802	(3%)

SENATORS

Sen. Daniel Patrick Moynihan (D)

Elected 1976, seat up 1994; b. Mar. 16, 1927, Tulsa, OK; home, Pindars Corners; City Col. of NY, 1943, Tufts U., B.A. 1948, M.A. 1949, Ph.D. 1961; Catholic; married (Elizabeth).

Career: Navy, 1944–47; Aide, NY Gov. Averell Harriman, 1955–58; U.S. Asst. Secy. of Labor, 1963–65; Dir., Joint Ctr. for Urban Studies, MIT and Harvard, 1966–69; Asst. to Pres. Nixon, Urban Affairs, 1969–71; Prof., Harvard, 1971–73; U.S. Ambassador to India, 1973–75; Ambassador to the U.N., 1975–76.

Offices: 464 RSOB 20510, 202-224-4451. Also 405 Lexington Ave., #4101, New York 10174, 212-661-5150; Guaranty Bldg., 28 Church St., Buffalo 14202, 716-846-4097; and 214 Main St., Oneonta 13820, 607-433-2310.

Committees: *Environment and Public Works* (2d of 10 D): Clean Air and Nuclear Regulation; Superfund, Recycling and Solid Waste Management; Water Resources, Transportation, Public Buildings and Economic Development (Chmn.); *Finance* (Chmn. of 11 D): International Trade; Private Retirement Plans and Oversight of the Internal Revenue Service; Social Security and Family Policy. *Foreign Relations* (7th of 11 D): African Affairs; Near Eastern and South Asian Affairs (Chmn.); Terrorism, Narcotics and International Operations. *Rules and Administration* (6th of 9 D). *Joint Committee on the Library* (3d of 5). *Joint Committee on Taxation* (Vice Chmn. of 5).

Group Ratings

	ADA	ACLU	CDF	COPE	CFA	LCV	ACU	NTLC	NSI	COC	CEI
1992	100	95	90	83	92	67	0	11	40	10	23
1991	95	—	82	92	89	93	0	—	—	10	22

National Journal Ratings

	1991 LIB — 1991 CONS		1992 LIB — 1992 CONS	
Economic	75% —	21%	61% —	37%
Social	87% —	0%	89% —	0%
Foreign	78% —	14%	86% —	0%

Key Votes of the 102d Congress

1. $ for Homeownership	FOR	5. Clarence Thomas Nom.	AGN	9. Use Force in Gulf	AGN
2. Have Cap Gains Debate	AGN	6. Lmt Death Row Appeal	AGN	10. Keep Salvador Aid	AGN
3. Remove Budget Walls	FOR	7. Handgun Wait/5-Day	FOR	11. Cut $1B from SDI	FOR
4. Ban Striker Replace	FOR	8. Abortion Gag Rule	AGN	12. Override China MFN	FOR

Key Votes of the 103d Congress

1. Family Leave	FOR	2. HIV Immigrants	FOR	3. Clinton Budget	FOR

Election Results

1988 general	Daniel Patrick Moynihan (D-L)	4,048,649	(67%)	($4,809,810)
	Robert R. McMillan (R-C)	1,875,784	(31%)	($528,989)
1988 primary	Daniel Patrick Moynihan (D), unopposed			
1982 general	Daniel Patrick Moynihan (D-L)	3,232,146	(65%)	($2,708,660)
	Florence Sullivan (R-C-RTL)	1,696,766	(34%)	($117,875)

Sen. Alfonse M. D'Amato (R)

Elected 1980, seat up 1998; b. Aug. 1, 1937, Brooklyn; home, Island Park; Syracuse U., B.S. 1959, J.D. 1961; Catholic; separated.

Career: Practicing atty., 1962–65; Nassau Cnty. Public Admin., 1965–68; Hempstead Town Receiver of Taxes, 1969; Hempstead Supervisor, 1971–77; Vice Chmn., Nassau Cnty. Bd. of Supervisors, 1977–80.

Offices: 520 HSOB 20510, 202-224-6542. Also 420 Leo O'Brien Fed. Bldg., Albany 12207, 518-463-2244; Fed. Bldg., 111 W. Huron, #620, Buffalo 14202, 716-846-4111; 7 Penn Plz., 7th Ave., #600, New York 10001, 212-947-7390; 1259 Fed. Bldg., 100 S. Clinton St., Syracuse 13260, 315-423-5471; and 100 State St., 304 Fed. Bldg., Rochester 14614, 716-263-5866.

Committees: *Appropriations* (4th of 13 R): Defense; Foreign Operations; Transportation (RMM); Treasury, Postal Service and General Government; VA, HUD and Independent Agencies. *Banking, Housing and Urban Affairs* (RMM of 8 R). *Intelligence (Select)* (2d of 8 R).

Group Ratings

	ADA	ACLU	CDF	COPE	CFA	LCV	ACU	NTLC	NSI	COC	CEI
1992	30	24	70	70	67	58	52	78	100	60	46
1991	15	—	64	67	39	40	86	—	—	50	48

National Journal Ratings

	1991 LIB — 1991 CONS	1992 LIB — 1992 CONS
Economic	36% — 62%	39% — 60%
Social	26% — 72%	31% — 68%
Foreign	35% — 63%	41% — 57%

Key Votes of the 102d Congress

1. $ for Homeownership FOR	5. Clarence Thomas Nom. FOR	9. Use Force in Gulf FOR
2. Have Cap Gains Debate FOR	6. Lmt Death Row Appeal FOR	10. Keep Salvador Aid FOR
3. Remove Budget Walls AGN	7. Handgun Wait/5-Day FOR	11. Cut $1B from SDI AGN
4. Ban Striker Replace FOR	8. Abortion Gag Rule FOR	12. Override China MFN FOR

Key Votes of the 103d Congress

1. Family Leave FOR	2. HIV Immigrants AGN	3. Clinton Budget AGN

Election Results

1992 general	Alfonse M. D'Amato (R-C-RTL)	3,166,994	(49%)	($11,550,958)
	Robert Abrams (D-L)	3,086,200	(48%)	($6,408,981)
	Four Others	205,632	(3%)	
1992 primary	Alfonse M. D'Amato (R), unopposed			
1986 general	Alfonse M. D'Amato (R-C-RTL)	2,378,197	(57%)	($12,914,822)
	Mark Green (D)	1,723,216	(41%)	($1,635,676)

FIRST DISTRICT

Long Island—the Island to most New Yorkers—is America's largest, most populous and in some ways most troubled island: 103 miles long, 12 to 20 miles wide, with sandspit beaches fronting the Atlantic Ocean and gentle hills and cliffs above Long Island Sound. Nearly 7 million people live here, more than in all but nine states, 4.3 million in the New York City boroughs of Brooklyn and Queens and 2.6 million in the suburban counties of Nassau and Suffolk. Brooklyn, at the western end of the island, is urban and thickly settled, while the Hamptons at the east end are carefully manicured countryside, preserved by a stylish New York elite. The Hamptons and the old whaling village of Sag Harbor, originally settled by New Englanders, were left behind in the rush of westward migration; today they appear more comfortable than grand, a shingled and windmilled portion of middle America kept more pristine than workaday middle America ever was.

But demographically, the Hamptons are only a small (though growing) part of Long Island; more important are the (no longer growing) suburbs created in the rush eastward after World War II. Developers looked for cheaper land for aircraft factories and shopping centers, subdivisions and office parks, and found them first in Nassau County just east of Queens and then in Suffolk County even farther east. Suffolk attracted young families, of Irish and Italian descent rather than Jewish or black, looking for more ground and trees and less crime and tension than in their City neighborhoods. Politically, Suffolk County is one of the most conservative parts of New York. It also became turbulent political territory, as life in Long Island has turned sour in the last decade: defense plants shut down and jobs evaporated as the defense buildup and then the Cold War ended; Lilco, the local utility, had cost overruns on its nuclear plant in Shoreham, and then went into bankruptcy after Governor Mario Cuomo shut the plant down for safety reasons, giving Long Island the nation's highest electric rates.

The 1st District of New York covers eastern Suffolk County, running east from Smithtown on the North Shore and Patchogue on the South Shore. It includes the Hamptons but, more important politically, the Brookhaven National Laboratory and the defense plants in the center of the Island. This was a heavily pro-Bush constituency in 1988 and a disenchanted-with-Bush constituency in 1992; yet for Congress, voting did not change much. The congressman here is Democrat George Hochbrueckner, an engineer who worked his way up in the aerospace industry without a college degree (he helped design the black box on Grumman's F-14) and then became a professional politician. He served in the New York Assembly for ten years and ran for Congress in 1984. He lost that time, but in 1986 won against a Republican who backed the Shoreham plant. Hochbrueckner got a seat on the Armed Services Committee, where he has been a backer of Grumman and other Long Island contractors; lately he has been touting plans for economic reconversion. He became known as "Compost Man" for his attempts to encourage composting in the 1990 farm bill and is a big booster of recycling. He has worked on funding to combat Lyme disease, a real menace in this area.

In such a heavily Republican area, Hochbrueckner has naturally had serious challenges. In 1988 Edward Romaine, a teacher and county legislator, called for lower spending and attacked his support of Mario Cuomo's shutdown of Shoreham, and Hochbrueckner won by only 51%–49%. In 1990, he had an easier time and won 57%–35% over a 28-year-old Army officer. In 1992, he had more troubles—49 overdrafts on the House bank, more defense shutdowns, demands for congressional reform. Romaine ran again, calling for lower spending, and nearly won; Hochbrueckner led 52%–48%. With retirements and defeats, Hochbrueckner is now the only one of the five Long Island members who has ever before represented the Island in Congress; Gary Ackerman of the 5th District has more seniority in the House, but his district never included Nassau or Suffolk. The Island delegation reportedly is inclined to cooperate on a bipartisan basis. Given Long Island's special needs, this allows Hochbrueckner an important opportunity and puts him in some peril—opportunity to produce some tangible gains for this troubled suburbia, peril if he conspicuously fails to do so.

The People: Pop. 1990: 580,076; 8% rural; 12% age 65+; 89% White; 4% Black; 2% Asian; 1% Other; 4% Hispanic origin. Voting age pop.: 433,094; 4% Black; 4% Hispanic origin. Households: 67% married couple families; 33% married couple fams. w. children; 49% college educ.; median household income: $45,464; per capita income: $17,614; median gross rent: $782; median house value: $158,400.

1992 Presidential Vote

Bush (R)	101,160	(40%)
Clinton (D)	96,890	(38%)
Perot (I)	54,128	(21%)

1988 Presidential Vote

Bush (R)	134,518	(61%)
Dukakis (D)	87,389	(39%)

Rep. George Hochbrueckner (D)

Elected 1986; b. Sept. 20, 1938, Jamaica, Queens; home, Coram; S.U.N.Y., 1959–60, Hofstra U., 1960–61, Pierce Col., 1961–62, U. of CA at Northridge, 1962–63; Catholic; married (Carol Ann).

Career: Navy, 1956–59; Engineer, 1961–75; NY Assembly, 1974–84.

Offices: 229 CHOB 20515, 202-225-3826. Also 3771 Nesconset Hwy., #213, Centereach 11720, 516-689-6767.

Committees: *Armed Services* (12th of 34 D): Military Installations and Facilities; Research and Technology. *Merchant Marine and Fisheries* (9th of 29 D): Coast Guard and Navigation; Environment and Natural Resources.

Group Ratings

	ADA	ACLU	COPE	CDF	CFA	LCV	ACU	NTLC	NSI	COC	CEI
1992	95	91	92	100	93	75	4	0	50	25	5
1991	75	—	100	100	89	62	0	—	—	20	8

National Journal Ratings

	1991 LIB — 1991 CONS		1992 LIB — 1992 CONS	
Economic	72% —	23%	91% —	0%
Social	71% —	28%	71% —	28%
Foreign	73% —	26%	76% —	19%

Key Votes of the 102d Congress

1. Ban Striker Replace	FOR	5. Handgun Wait/7-Day	FOR	9. Use Force in Gulf	AGN
2. $ for Homeownership	AGN	6. Overseas Mil. Abortion	FOR	10. US Mil. Abroad $ Cut	FOR
3. Tax Rich/Cut Mid Cls.	FOR	7. Obscn. Art NEA $ Ban	FOR	11. Limit SDI Funds	FOR
4. FY93/$15B Def. Cut	FOR	8. Death Pen. from Jury	AGN	12. Cuba Trade Embargo	AGN

Key Votes of the 103d Congress

1. Family Leave	FOR	2. Deficit Reduction	FOR	3. Stimulus Plan	FOR

Election Results

1992 general	George Hockbrueckner (D-LIF).........	117,940	(52%)	($606,190)
	Edward P. Romaine (R-C-RTL).........	110,043	(48%)	($226,283)
1992 primary	George Hockbrueckner (D), unopposed			
1990 general	George Hockbrueckner (D-TXB).........	75,211	(57%)	($638,635)
	Francis W. Creighton (R)..............	46,380	(35%)	($45,544)
	Clayton Baldwin, Jr. (C)...............	6,883	(5%)	
	Peter J. O'Hara (RTL).................	5,111	(4%)	

SECOND DISTRICT

In one of the vast migrations of the years after World War II, hundreds of thousands of New Yorkers—mostly people who had trouble imagining they'd live anywhere but the close-packed streets of the City—moved to what had been the potato fields of central Long Island. The highways that Robert Moses built to connect Jones Beach with the masses of Queens and Brooklyn suddenly became routes of migration, commuter paths, as young veterans and their families found they could afford to leave the row-house neighborhoods where they had grown up for the comparatively spacious lots and single-family houses of Levittown and other Long Island subdivisions. The first wave of postwar migration moved into Nassau County, and it was a pretty accurate cross-section of all but the poorest New Yorkers: almost half Catholic, about one-fourth Jewish and one-fourth Protestant. Then, as Long Island developed its own employment base, another wave moved farther east into Suffolk County—more Catholic and less Jewish, more blue-collar (aircraft manufacturers have long been Suffolk County's biggest employers) and less white-collar, more ancestrally Democratic, but firmly traditional and culturally conservative.

The 2d Congressional District of New York includes a large hunk of central Long Island—technically, most of western Suffolk County, the South Shore towns of Babylon and Islip, which within them contain dozens of suburbs separated only by name. There are some spacious houses here with views of Great South Bay, but mostly this is the lower-income part of Long Island, situated past the fashionable and expensive suburbs, far from the picturesque North Shore and separated by the Great South Bay from the beaches of Fire Island. This area filled up with people in the 1950s and 1960s and has grown little since, but with some of the lowest-priced housing on the Island, it continues to attract young families. Its minority neighborhoods are concentrated in North Amityville and Wyandanch, but blacks and Hispanics throughout the area make the district 9% black and 9% Hispanic origin.

The 2d District, created after the 1960 Census, has had just three congressmen, switching from Republican to Democrat in 1974 and back again in 1992. The Democrat was Tom Downey, one of the quintessential members of the Watergate class of 1974, elected at the constitutionally minimum age of 25. He was a leader in shaping the 1988 welfare reform and 1990 child care reform bills, both of which sought to strengthen community institutions rather than bureaucracies, and promote middle-class values of hard work and family cohesion rather than personal liberation: impressive achievements. But for all his legislative success and hard work back home, Downey could never take the seat entirely for granted, and in 1992 he had the additional problems of 151 overdrafts on the House bank and the fact that his wife worked as House bank auditor from 1988 to 1991.

This opened the way for Rick Lazio, a young member of the Suffolk County Legislature (as Downey was in 1974). He criticized Downey for the overdrafts and for his junkets, called for congressional reform, urged a capital gains tax cut and a tax credit for first-time home-buyers. He stressed his work in Suffolk on law enforcement issues. Downey campaigned hard, and spent $1.4 million to Lazio's $276,000. But the basically Republican character of the district and the anti-incumbent impulse swept him out as his predecessor had been swept out by Watergate and the turbulent economy of the oil crunch years 18 years earlier. Lazio won 53%–47% and promises to serve no more than six consecutive terms. He is a member of the Banking and Budget Committees, and seems to be one of the freshman Republicans most open to some tax and spending increases.

The People: Pop. 1990: 580,303; 10% age 65+; 79% White; 10% Black; 2% Asian; 3% Other; 9% Hispanic origin. Voting age pop.: 437,905; 9% Black; 9% Hispanic origin. Households: 68% married couple families; 33% married couple fams. w. children; 45% college educ.; median household income: $50,076; per capita income: $17,515; median gross rent: $817; median house value: $158,600.

1992 Presidential Vote			1988 Presidential Vote		
Bush (R)	92,762	(40%)	Bush (R)	128,359	(61%)
Clinton (D)	91,430	(40%)	Dukakis (D)	82,713	(39%)
Perot (I)	44,603	(19%)			

Rep. Rick A. Lazio (R)

Elected 1992; b. Mar. 13, 1958, West Islip; home, Brightwaters; Vassar Col., B.A. 1980, American U., J.D. 1983; Catholic; married (Patricia Moriarty).

Career: Asst. Dist. Atty., Suffolk Cnty., 1983–88; Suffolk Cnty. legislator, 1989–92; Practicing atty., 1989–92.

Offices: 314 CHOB 20515, 202-225-3335. Also 126 W. Main St., Babylon 11702, 516-893-9010.

Committees: *Banking, Finance and Urban Affairs* (15th of 20 R): Consumer Credit and Insurance; Financial Institutions Supervision, Regulation and Deposit Insurance; Housing and Community Development. *Budget* (13th of 17 R).

Group Ratings and 102d Congress Votes: Newly Elected

Key Votes of the 103d Congress

1. Family Leave	FOR	2. Deficit Reduction	AGN	3. Stimulus Plan	AGN

Election Results

1992 general	Rick A. Lazio (R-C)	109,386	(53%)	($276,191)
	Thomas J. Downey (D-L)	96,328	(47%)	($1,446,911)
1992 primary	Rick A. Lazio (R), unopposed			
1990 general	Thomas J. Downey (D)	56,722	(56%)	($635,392)
	John W. Bugler (R-RTL)	36,859	(36%)	
	Dominic A. Curcio (C)	8,150	(8%)	

THIRD DISTRICT

It was a pivotal moment in American suburban history: in September 1947, families moved into 300 tiny 750-square-foot houses, built in record time by mass production, which sold for $6,990, with no down payment for veterans. This was Levittown, and by the time the last new house was sold for $9,500 in November 1951, the name had become a synonym for rapid suburban development. Developer William Levitt recognized that many young veterans and their families were eager to move out of crowded New York City neighborhoods, so he bought a Nassau County potato field, planted trees, designed floor plans to allow easy additions and built a community of 65,000 people. Four decades later, Levittown houses, with much added on, sell for well into six figures. The postwar surge and then the trend toward empty nesters can be seen in Nassau County population figures: 450,000 in 1940, 1.3 million in 1960, 1.4 million in 1970, then back to around 1.3 million in 1980 and 1990 as youngsters moved out.

Nassau County is the home of what may be the nation's premier county Republican machine. It was the creation of Nassau Republican Chairman J. Russell Sprague, who managed to carry the county for Alf Landon in 1936 and that same year persuaded the voters to adopt a county executive form of government, in which control of political patronage would center in one man, responsible to the Nassau County Republican chairman. Nassau's Republican machine, often attacked, has mostly provided competent local government and candidates who are returned to office by an intelligent and well-informed electorate.

The 3d Congressional District of New York includes nearly half of Nassau County, made up of two distinct areas. Most people here live in towns strung out on either side of Sunrise Highway or just off the Southern or Northern State Parkways from Levittown and Hicksville, east to the county line. About one-fifth of the 3d's population lives in its northern geographic half, in the less densely populated old estate areas around Oyster Bay, Old Westbury and Manhasset. Relatively few of greater New York's very richest people live in the 3d District, but the overall level of affluence is high, and the district has the third highest median income of any in the nation, just behind one in northern New Jersey and another in the Maryland suburbs of Washington. Politically, the 3d tends to be pretty solidly Republican, though in 1992 that didn't mean very solidly at all.

Two weeks after the district lines became official, Congressman Norman Lent announced his retirement; a longtime supporter of the Nassau County Republican machine, he could probably have won easily but decided not to adapt to so much new territory. Lent started his congressional career in 1970 by beating Allard Lowenstein, the famed antiwar activist; he ended it as ranking Republican on John Dingell's Energy and Commerce Committee. To succeed Lent, there were serious contests in both the Republican primary and the general election.

The favorite in both, and ultimate winner, was County Comptroller Peter King. His primary opponent, Robert Previdi, who had run in 1988 and 1990 and lost to North Shore Democrat Robert Mrazek, complained that the Republican organization tried to throw out his petitions; King replied, "He wrote a book a few years ago that he dedicated to his wife and to Joe Mondello," the county Republican chairman. King emphasized his record of holding down spending and his spotting in early 1991 the county government's fiscal crisis, and won 68%–32%. The general election was tougher. Democrat Steve Orlins grew up in Nassau County and then went far afield, studying in Taiwan as well as at Harvard, establishing a law firm in Beijing in 1979, starting his own Asian trading company and then selling it to Lehman Brothers. He moved back to Long Island and ran for Congress in 1992, spending over $700,000 of his own money. King campaigned as a political insider and fiscal conservative, Orlins as a reformer and supporter of abortion rights. King won, but by only 50%–47%, "a rejection of out-of-town bosses and liberal money," he said. He is expected to be the most conservative of the new Long Island members; he wants to cut taxes and expand health coverage, with tax credits for companies that provide health insurance for their employees. He is also a strong supporter of the Irish Republic Army, a factional terrorist group which wants to separate Northern Ireland from Britain.

The People: Pop. 1990: 580,468; 13% age 65+; 91% White; 2% Black; 3% Asian; 1% Other; 4% Hispanic origin. Voting age pop.: 455,852; 2% Black; 4% Hispanic origin. Households: 70% married couple families; 30% married couple fams. w. children; 55% college educ.; median household income: $56,060; per capita income: $23,702; median gross rent: $811; median house value: $204,900.

1992 Presidential Vote			1988 Presidential Vote		
Clinton (D)	126,112	(44%)	Bush (R)	164,426	(60%)
Bush (R)	121,176	(42%)	Dukakis (D)	111,286	(40%)
Perot (I)	40,450	(14%)			

Rep. Peter T. King (R)

Elected 1992; b. Apr. 5, 1944, Manhattan; home, Seaford; St. Francis Col., B.A. 1965, U. of Notre Dame, J.A. 1968; Catholic; married (Rosemary).

Career: Army Natl. Guard, 1968–73; Practicing atty., 1968–72, 1978–81; Dep. Atty., Nassau Cnty., 1972–74; Exec. Asst., Nassau Cnty. Exec., 1974–76, Gen. Cnsl., 1977; Hempstead Town Cncl., 1977–81; Nassau Cnty. Comptroller, 1981–92.

Offices: 118 CHOB 20515, 202-225-7896. Also 1003 Park Blvd., Massapequa Park 11762, 516-541-4225.

Committees: *Banking, Finance and Urban Affairs* (20th of 20 R): Consumer Credit and Insurance; Economic Growth and Credit Formation; International Development, Finance, Trade and Monetary Policy. *Merchant Marine and Fisheries* (14th of 19 R): Coast Guard and Navigation; Merchant Marine. *Veterans' Affairs* (14th of 14 R): Compensation, Pension and Insurance.

Group Ratings and 102d Congress Votes: Newly Elected

Key Votes of the 103d Congress

1. Family Leave	AGN	2. Deficit Reduction	AGN	3. Stimulus Plan	AGN

Election Results

1992 general	Peter T. King (R-C)	124,727	(50%)	($263,345)
	Steve A. Orlins (D).................	116,915	(46%)	($1,127,239)
	Two Others	9,980	(4%)	
1992 primary	Peter T. King (R)	8,346	(68%)	
	Robert Previdi (R)	3,853	(32%)	
1990 general	Norman F. Lent (R-C)	79,304	(61%)	($398,706)
(NY 4)	Francis T. Goban (D)	41,308	(32%)	($125)
	John J. Dunkle (RTL)................	6,706	(5%)	
	Other..............................	2,343	(2%)	

FOURTH DISTRICT

Garden City is one of America's first suburbs, created more than a century ago by New York retailer A. T. Stewart at a time when reformers wanted to maintain the commercial vitality and social interaction of the city but in a setting that preserved the healthful openness of the countryside. Garden City's wide avenues and single-family homes, connected to New York City by the Long Island Railroad, were intended to be middle-income territory; but Garden City's amenities have made it one of the highest-income parts of Long Island. In the century after its founding, the rest of Nassau County has changed from almost entirely rural to suburban. The big rush came after World War II, as one town ran into another (though most did not lose their separate identities), freeways replaced strip highways, shopping centers sprang up at intersections and schools and places of worship dotted the landscape. Garden City now sits amid Nassau County's civic institutions, just south of Mineola, with the county government and the site of Roosevelt Field where Charles Lindbergh took off for Paris, west of Nassau Coliseum and Eisenhower Memorial Park and Nassau County Medical Center.

The 4th Congressional District includes all of these communities. It also takes in half of Levittown, all of the neat and conservative suburbs along the Queens line from New Hyde Park to Valley Stream and the Five Towns, Lawrence, Inwood, Cedarhurst, Hewlett and Woodmere, affluent and comfortable though near Kennedy Airport's flight paths. Politically, this is mostly

874   NEW YORK

Republican territory, though political preference tends to go with ethnic background: black and Jewish areas, like West Hempstead and the Five Towns respectively, tend to be Democratic; Irish and Italian Catholic areas, like East Meadow and Elmont, heavily Republican. Though the balance usually remains on the Republican side, in 1992 Nassau County voted for Bill Clinton over George Bush.

The 4th District also had a close congressional race, prompted by the retirement of Raymond McGrath, a backer of the Nassau County Republican organization and a fierce fighter for New York interests, like deductibility of state and local taxes, on the House Ways and Means Committee. In 1992, the 4th had serious contests in both the primary and the general election. The Republican organization's choice and ultimate winner was Town of Hempstead Councilman David Levy, a close ally of County Chairman Joseph Mondello. Levy was challenged in the primary by Assemblyman Daniel Frisa, emboldened by discontent with the organization and high local taxes and, according to Mondello, supported by his predecessor as chairman, Joseph Margiotta, who had been convicted of extortion in 1982. It got pretty heavy: Levy distributed a *Newsday* editorial accusing Frisa of falsely reporting that Levy stole $56,000 from HUD. Levy won, but by only 53%–41%. Meanwhile, Democrats had a close primary too, between candidates who spent considerably more than the Republicans. Joan Axinn, a philanthropist from the North Shore, lent her campaign $338,000; Phil Schiliro, a Long Island native who spent 10 years as a top aide to California Congressman Henry Waxman, raised money as only someone connected with the Energy and Commerce Committee can do. Schiliro won, but by only 51%–49%.

In the general, Schiliro attacked Levy as a party hack and claimed credit for his work on the Clean Air Act and other legislation for Waxman. Levy criticized Schiliro for moving back to the district after 12 years and bragged that the Town of Hempstead had held taxes down. Schiliro spotlighted Long Island's higher than average rates of breast cancer and promised to back extra research; Levy was happy to echo this. This was one of two contests in which local politicians backed by the Republican machine were opposed by lavishly funded Long Island natives who had returned to the area after many years; in both cases the Republicans won, narrowly. Levy's victory was by 50%–46%, not much in this area. In Congress, Levy calls for tax relief, including indexing federal income taxes to the local standard of living. He has seats on the Foreign Affairs and Public Works Committees.

The People: Pop. 1990: 580,492; 15% age 65+; 74% White; 16% Black; 3% Asian; 2% Other; 7% Hispanic origin. Voting age pop.: 451,532; 15% Black; 7% Hispanic origin. Households: 65% married couple families; 28% married couple fams. w. children; 50% college educ.; median household income: $50,887; per capita income: $20,349; median gross rent: $705; median house value: $197,000.

1992 Presidential Vote

Clinton (D) 119,947 (47%)
Bush (R) 106,016 (41%)
Perot (I) 30,476 (12%)

1988 Presidential Vote

Bush (R) 144,338 (57%)
Dukakis (D) 106,968 (43%)

Rep. David A. Levy (R)

Elected 1992; b. Dec. 18, 1953, Johnson Cnty., IN; home, Baldwin; Hofstra U., B.A. 1974, J.D. 1979; Jewish; married (Tracy).

Career: Radio news reporter, 1974–81; Press Secy., Town of Hempstead, 1981–82; Assoc. Public Affairs Dir., Long Island Lighting Co., 1982–84; Cnsl., Nausau Cnty. Republican Cmte., 1984–87, 1989–92; Minority Special Cnsl., NY St. Assembly, 1985–86; Exec. Asst., Hempstead Town Supervisor, 1987–92; Hempstead Town Cncl., 1989–92.

Offices: 116 CHOB 20515, 202-225-5516. Also 203 Rockaway Ave., Valley Stream 11580, 516-872-9550.

Committees: *Foreign Affairs* (15th of 18 R): Europe and the Middle East; International Operations. *Public Works and Transportation* (17th of 24 R): Aviation; Surface Transportation.

Group Ratings and 102d Congress Votes: Newly Elected

Key Votes of the 103d Congress

1. Family Leave	AGN	2. Deficit Reduction	AGN	3. Stimulus Plan	AGN

Election Results

1992 general	David A. Levy (R-C)	110,710	(50%)	($209,225)
	Philip Schiliro (D-L).................	100,386	(46%)	($502,513)
	Vincent Garbitelli (RTL)	9,548	(4%)	
1992 primary	David A. Levy (R)	12,646	(53%)	
	Daniel Frisa (R)	8,890	(41%)	
	Francis Lees (R)......................	1,410	(6%)	
1990 general	Raymond J. McGrath (R-C)	71,948	(55%)	($618,882)
(NY 5)	Mark S. Epstein (D-L)	53,920	(41%)	($291,412)
	Edward K. Kitt (RTL)	6,000	(5%)	

FIFTH DISTRICT

The North Shore of Long Island is "Gatsby country," where peninsulas jutting out into the Sound are covered with vast green lawns leading to the mansions of America's great capitalists. Nineteenth century millionaires commuted by steam yacht from Manhattan to their estates in what now is Queens or Nassau County; in the early 20th Century the richest people in business and show business spent their leisure time here, playing croquet while their servants unloaded bootleggers' boats at their private docks during Prohibition. Inland, behind the expansive lawns, Long Island was still farm country, with little villages clustered at railroad stations, occasional colonial era houses, and acres of billboard-strewn wasteland on the highways to New York City. But the City grew out: affluent neighborhoods developed in Douglaston and Bayside on the water, just beyond the middle-class Flushing area of Queens inland; the Great Neck peninsula became a very affluent, mostly Jewish suburb; farther out, on Sands Point and Oyster Bay, old estates alternated with more modest homes originally built for servants and newer subdivision mansions; further east, in Suffolk County, affluent subdivisions grew up on hilly land above the bays and points.

The 5th Congressional District of New York ties together a disparate collection of New York City neighborhoods and suburbs on or within a few miles of the North Shore; at several points the district is connected across open water, and anyone wishing to go from one end of it to the other must be a good swimmer. About one-third of its votes are cast in Suffolk County, where the political leanings are conservative on cultural and economic issues. In the middle, with about one-quarter of the votes, are the North Shore communities of Nassau, the Jewish areas Democratic and liberal, the WASPy areas Republican but rather culturally liberal also. Half the district's population and about 40% of its voters are in the borough of Queens. Here along the Sound are the affluent double-house Bayside neighborhood, and higher-income Douglaston and Little Neck, next to the Nassau border—all Republican territory. A few blocks inland is Flushing, an old Dutch settlement from the 17th Century, with the Queens numbered-street grid superimposed on old Dutch trails; its newer apartment buildings, mostly Jewish since the 1950s, by the 1980s were becoming heavily Asian, especially Chinese and Korean, though the Democratic preference of earlier residents prevails. The 5th also goes south almost to the Long Island Expressway, to pleasant home-owner neighborhoods like Fresh Meadows and Oakland Gardens. But even here, far from Manhattan and in relatively affluent areas, there are plenty of high-rises, with a population density usually approached only in metropolitan areas.

The 5th District as drawn in June 1992 was the only possible district in which three incumbent congressmen could run. One was Robert Mrazek, a Democrat who had represented a suburban North Shore district for 10 years, but who started running for the Senate early in 1991; then in April 1992 it was revealed he had 920 overdrafts on the House bank, which ended his candidacy. Another was James Scheuer, the Flying Dutchman of New York politics, who for all but two years from 1964 to 1992 represented districts including parts of the Bronx, Brooklyn, Queens and Nassau, though his original residence was in Manhattan; but in 1992, either because he had 133 overdrafts or simply because at 72 he did not want to learn another district and run against another incumbent, he decided to retire. That left one, Gary Ackerman, who didn't live in the 5th and had represented only 9% of the district; but the heart of his home turf, the heavily Jewish apartment complexes of central Queens, had been attached to districts dominated by Brooklyn (over Jamaica Bay) and (over the Throgs Neck Bridge) Westchester. Ackerman had 111 overdrafts himself, but had not been on the list of worst abusers which had been leaked in March 1992, as Mrazek and Scheuer were; Ackerman was the Ethics Committee member widely assumed to have leaked the original list of the 24 worst abusers, and resigned from the committee in July 1992 before an investigation could be launched.

A colorful character, Ackerman always wears a white carnation and lives on a boat in Washington. He was a teacher who started the *Queens Tribune* and sold it to publisher Jerry Finkelstein, father of City Council President Andrew Stein. Ackerman won his seat in Congress in a March 1983 special election. His great cause in Congress has been the rescue of Ethiopian Jews and relieving government-caused famine in Ethiopia and Sudan. He has voted faithfully for the interests of public employees, of whom there are many in Queens. Acerbic but humorous, he is a pungent speaker: his comment on the Gulf war resolution (on which he voted yes) was "Slam, bam, thanks Saddam. You should have took the letter. Now take the loss, reverse the course, 'cause it ain't going to get no better."

In 1992 Ackerman did not get a free ride in either the primary or the general election; instead he had tough competition from an old liberal and a young conservative (none of the three had a residence in the district). The liberal was Rita Morris, a retired librarian from Nassau County (and mother of Democratic campaign consultant Hank Morris), who was furious that there were not more women in Congress when Anita Hill's charges against Clarence Thomas surfaced. She decided to spend her life savings of $500,000 on the race. Just before the primary, *Newsday* reported that Ackerman had negotiated a $45,000 yearly consulting contract for his wife with Finkelstein, which Morris said was an attempt to evade outside income restrictions; Ackerman charged that Morris's son had turned her into a "mud wrestler." Ackerman won by 60%–40%. The Republican candidate was Allan Binder, 31, who grew up in Suffolk County, worked for Texas Congressman Tom DeLay and was elected to the Legislature in 1990. He had passed a lockout law requiring cigarette machines to be activated only by tokens to be sold only to those 18 and over. Binder called Ackerman a "typical tax and spend" liberal and called for tax cuts. Binder won in Suffolk 58%–38%, but Ackerman won Nassau 59%–40% and Queens 61%–38%.

Ackerman continues to serve on the Post Office and Civil Service Committee, where he can support public employees, and Merchant Marine and Fisheries, where he works to clean up Long Island Sound. He is also on Foreign Affairs, where he chairs the Asian and Pacific Affairs Subcommittee; he sought the post, according to *CongressDaily*, because "I love Asian food. That's probably the overriding reason for becoming chairman. Lots of good restaurants." Whether he will have serious competition in this basically but not overwhelmingly Democratic district is not clear.

The People: Pop. 1990: 581,073; 1% rural; 15% age 65+; 79% White; 3% Black; 11% Asian; 2% Other; 7% Hispanic origin. Voting age pop.: 462,648; 3% Black; 7% Hispanic origin. Households: 63% married couple families; 27% married couple fams. w. children; 58% college educ.; median household income: $50,103; per capita income: $24,296; median gross rent: $660; median house value: $255,000.

1992 Presidential Vote			1988 Presidential Vote		
Clinton (D)	131,042	(52%)	Bush (R)	123,097	(51%)
Bush (R)	88,505	(35%)	Dukakis (D)	119,339	(49%)
Perot (I)	30,459	(12%)			

Rep. Gary L. Ackerman (D)

Elected Mar., 1983; b. Nov. 19, 1942, Brooklyn; home, Queens; Queens Col., B.A. 1965; Jewish; married (Rita).

Career: Jr. high schl. teacher, 1966–70; Editor and publisher, *Queens Tribune*, 1970–78; Pres, advertising agcy., 1972–78; NY Senate, 1979–83.

Offices: 2445 RHOB, 202-225-2601. Also 218–14 Northern Blvd., Bayside 11361, 718-423-2154; and 229 Main St., Huntington 11743, 516-423-2154.

Committees: *Foreign Affairs* (6th of 27 D): Asia and the Pacific (Chmn.); International Security, International Organizations and Human Rights. *Merchant Marine and Fisheries* (28th of 29 D): Merchant Marine. *Post Office and Civil Service* (4th of 15 D): Compensation and Employee Benefits.

Group Ratings

	ADA	ACLU	COPE	CDF	CFA	LCV	ACU	NTLC	NSI	COC	CEI
1992	70	100	91	100	67	75	0	0	40	33	11
1991	85	—	100	90	78	77	10	—	—	20	7

National Journal Ratings

	1991 LIB — 1991 CONS			1992 LIB — 1992 CONS		
Economic	88%	—	0%	91%	—	0%
Social	88%	—	0%	84%	—	16%
Foreign	74%	—	25%	75%	—	25%

Key Votes of the 102d Congress

1. Ban Striker Replace	FOR	5. Handgun Wait/7-Day	FOR	9. Use Force in Gulf	FOR
2. $ for Homeownership	AGN	6. Overseas Mil. Abortion	FOR	10. US Mil. Abroad $ Cut	FOR
3. Tax Rich/Cut Mid Cls.	FOR	7. Obscn. Art NEA $ Ban	AGN	11. Limit SDI Funds	FOR
4. FY93/$15B Def. Cut	FOR	8. Death Pen. from Jury	AGN	12. Cuba Trade Embargo	*

Key Votes of the 103d Congress

1. Family Leave	FOR	2. Deficit Reduction	FOR	3. Stimulus Plan	FOR

Election Results

1992 general	Gary L. Ackerman (D-L) 110,476	(52%)	($917,483)
	Allan E. Binder (R-C). 94,907	(45%)	($123,206)
	Other. 5,448	(3%)	
1992 primary	Gary L. Ackerman (D). 34,337	(60%)	
	Rita A. Morris (D) 22,819	(40%)	
1990 general	Gary L. Ackerman (D-L), unopposed		($272,549)
(NY 7)			

SIXTH DISTRICT

New York City's largest black middle-class areas are not in Harlem or Brooklyn, but far out in the southeast corner of Queens, in the "architectural monotony of block upon block of boxlike frame and brick houses," as one critic described them, built mostly from the 1920s to the 1950s in the neighborhoods of Springfield, Laurelton, St. Albans and Rosedale, near Kennedy Airport and the tidal marsh of Jamaica Bay, just before the Nassau County line. There was a small black community in South Jamaica when Mario Cuomo was growing up there in the 1930s and 1940s, and over the years blacks who have accumulated savings have bought houses and raised their families in neighborhoods on the streets fanning east from Jamaica. Here they have fought to maintain the relatively spacious streets, relishing unrefracted light in their windows, enjoying safe schools and parks and good neighborhood stores: people who have, in Bill Clinton's felicitous phrase, "worked hard and played by the rules."

Such neighborhoods form most of the 6th Congressional District of New York, a district of (for New York) uncharacteristic geographic compactness, taking up almost all of southern Queens, roughly south of the Interborough and Grand Central Parkways, including half of the Rockaway Peninsula across Jamaica Bay. It includes the heavily black neighborhoods in the southeast and white ethnic Richmond Hill and Ozone Park. In 1990, 56% of the people here were black, 16% Hispanic, 6% Asian and 23% non-Hispanic white. There are some pockets of poverty here, but mostly it is middle-class country: the district's median income was $36,200, far ahead of the $23,000 to $26,000 of New York's other black-majority districts, indeed ahead of the $30,300 of Queens's white-majority 7th District.

The congressman from the 6th District is Floyd Flake, a black leader who has moved up by a different route than the City's other black congressmen (though one similar to its first, Adam Clayton Powell). Flake, the son of a janitor and one of 13 children, went to college and then divinity school. In 1976, at 31, he became minister at Allen A.M.E. Church in Queens, and in 10 years built it up from 1,400 to 6,000 members and 3 to 743 employees, built a $12 million housing project for the elderly, built a private school for 480 students, and handled a budget with annual revenues over $17 million. At a time when public institutions were not serving middle-class blacks well, Flake created an institution that did. In 1986, after Congressman Joseph Addabbo died, Flake ran against the Queens Democratic organization choice, Alton Waldon; Flake lost the special primary by 276 votes even though he won by 167 at the polls, because his name had been kept off the absentee ballots by one of New York's endless election law technicalities. Flake understandably felt cheated and, with the endorsement of Mayor Edward Koch as well as of many local blacks, beat Waldon in the September primary for the next full term and was elected without difficulty in this overwhelmingly Democratic district.

In the House, Flake has worked on housing issues, on which he has some expertise, from his seat on the Banking, Housing and Urban Affairs Committee. But his major travail during the last Congress was a federal prosecution on charges that he embezzled funds from a church-sponsored housing project and from the church itself, charges evidently first made by a disgruntled former church employee. In April 1991, mid-trial, the judge suggested to the prosecutors that their evidence was shaky; the prosecution moved that charges be dismissed, and they were. While there is no warrant supporting Flake's charge that this was a racially motivated case, the dismissal is strong evidence that the case never should have been prosecuted, a conclusion widely shared. In 1992 Flake ran a slate of his own candidates for elective and party office; Flake withdrew most of his candidates when the Queens Democratic organization withdrew a challenge to his own ballot status. But the organization had already retaliated by endorsing a primary opponent, Simeon Golar, against Flake. Golar came originally from the Liberal Party, and had headed housing programs under Mayor John Lindsay—a time when the City lost one million residents. In 1982 and 1984, he ran serious races against Addabbo in this district; in 1986 he filed late and in 1990 he got only negligible percentages in a Bronx congressional district. Golar charged that Flake possessed by "arrogance and egomania" and was using his church as a "political machine" that "evokes scary reminders of Jonestown." Flake insisted the real issue "is one of a community in transition that has responded to my leadership in a way it has not responded to the majority of the elected officials' leadership in the district, which causes a natural degree of tension and in some instances fear." He added of Golar, "the most he can do is besmirch character because he has nothing to offer the community." Evidently most local voters agreed: Flake won the primary 77%–23%. In the 103d Congress Flake became chairman of Banking's General Oversight and Investigations Subcommittee.

The People: Pop. 1990: 581,812; 11% age 65+; 23% White; 56% Black; 1% Amer. Indian; 6% Asian; 7% Other; 16% Hispanic origin. Voting age pop.: 433,982; 54% Black; 15% Hispanic origin. Households: 52% married couple families; 25% married couple fams. w. children; 38% college educ.; median household income: $36,223; per capita income: $13,150; median gross rent: $565; median house value: $157,900.

1992 Presidential Vote			1988 Presidential Vote		
Clinton (D)	115,526	(75%)	Dukakis (D)	105,816	(73%)
Bush (R)	28,033	(18%)	Bush (R)	39,511	(27%)
Perot (I)	9,380	(6%)			

Rep. Floyd H. Flake (D)

Elected 1986; b. Jan. 30, 1945, Los Angeles, CA; home, Rosedale; Wilberforce U., B.A., 1967, Payne Theological Seminary, M.A. 1970, Northeastern U., 1974–76; African Methodist Episcopal; married (Elaine).

Career: Social worker, Head Start, 1968–69; Mktg. analyst, Xerox Corp., 1969–70; Assoc. Dean of Students, Lincoln U. 1970–73; Boston U., Dean of Students and Chaplain, Dir., MLK Afro-American Ctr., 1973–76; Pastor, Allen A.M.E. Church, 1976–present; Founder and Chmn., Allen Christian Schl., 1982–present, Allen Home Care Agcy., 1983–present.

Offices: 1035 LHOB, 202-225-3461. Also 196-06 Linden Blvd., St. Albans 11412, 718-849-5600; and 20-80 Seagirt Blvd., Far Rockaway 11691, 718-327-9791.

Committees: *Banking, Finance and Urban Affairs* (9th of 30 D): Consumer Credit and Insurance; Financial Institutions Supervision, Regulation and Deposit Insurance; General Oversight, Investigations, and the Resolution of Failed Financial Institutions (Chmn.). *Government Operations* (18th of 25 D): Employment, Housing and Aviation. *Small Business* (10th of 27 D): Minority Enterprise, Finance and Urban Development.

Group Ratings

	ADA	ACLU	COPE	CDF	CFA	LCV	ACU	NTLC	NSI	COC	CEI
1992	90	100	92	90	93	75	0	0	20	13	8
1991	100	—	100	90	67	69	0	—	—	20	10

National Journal Ratings

	1991 LIB	—	1991 CONS	1992 LIB	—	1992 CONS
Economic	79%	—	21%	91%	—	0%
Social	88%	—	0%	92%	—	0%
Foreign	92%	—	0%	85%	—	14%

Key Votes of the 102d Congress

1. Ban Striker Replace	FOR	5. Handgun Wait/7-Day	FOR	9. Use Force in Gulf	AGN
2. $ for Homeownership	AGN	6. Overseas Mil. Abortion	FOR	10. US Mil. Abroad $ Cut	FOR
3. Tax Rich/Cut Mid Cls.	FOR	7. Obscn. Art NEA $ Ban	AGN	11. Limit SDI Funds	FOR
4. FY93/$15B Def. Cut	FOR	8. Death Pen. from Jury	AGN	12. Cuba Trade Embargo	AGN

Key Votes of the 103d Congress

1. Family Leave	FOR	2. Deficit Reduction	FOR	3. Stimulus Plan	FOR

Election Results

1992 general	Floyd H. Flake (D)	96,972	(81%)	($281,172)
	Dianand D. Bhagwandin (R-C)	22,687	(19%)	($45,015)
1992 primary	Floyd H. Flake (D)	36,343	(77%)	
	Simeon Golar (D)	11,036	(23%)	
1990 general	Floyd H. Flake (D, L)	44,306	(73%)	($205,031)
	William Sampol (R)	13,224	(22%)	
	John Cronin (RTL)	3,111	(5%)	

SEVENTH DISTRICT

The Borough of Queens, home of Mario Cuomo and Geraldine Ferraro, of Shea Stadium and the 1939 and 1964 World's Fairs, the National Tennis Center and the West Side Tennis Club in Forest Hills, of St. John's University and the Steinway piano factory, of LaGuardia and Kennedy Airports, home to nearly 2 million people, is a place that still doesn't get much attention or much respect. Its history is little-known: from the 17th Century most of Queens was nondescript farmland with little villages becoming urban nodes, which then grew rapidly when the subways got out this far. There is no obvious center to Queens, like downtown Brooklyn or the Grand Concourse in the Bronx; even Queens Boulevard is just another arterial street, starting in the industrial mishmash around the Queensborough Bridge (usually referred to by its Manhattan name, 59th Street) and ending near the unimpressive brick Borough Hall, sited by the Grand Central Parkway overpass, across from the Pastrami King and Crossroads Drugs.

Queens has grown not from a central point outward or directly from Manhattan, but around dozens of nodes; more than any other part of New York, this is a borough of neighborhoods. Some are of genuine distinction, like the old Tudor-mansioned Forest Hills; others bear the stamp of immigrant origins: Irish Sunnyside or College Point; Astoria, on the tip of Queens near the Triborough Bridge, is Greek-American and effervescently prosperous; Jackson Heights and Corona are the homes of today's Colombian and Dominican immigrants. Back before World War II, Queens was mostly made up of one- and two-family frame house neighborhoods that were Yankee, German or Irish; it looked upon Manhattan as the City (a locution still used in many Queens neighborhoods) and voted defiantly Republican. Then, after World War II, as new subway lines were built out farther, Queens became a borough of high-rise apartments, like giant Lefrak City near the intersection of Queens Boulevard and the Long Island Expressway. An airier place to live and raise a family than Manhattan, with good public schools, low rents and easy access to Manhattan, central Queens became heavily settled and heavily Jewish.

The 7th Congressional District of New York is a collection of Queens neighborhoods, loosely connected by narrow corridors, plus, over the Bronx-Whitestone Bridge, a salient of land running far into the Bronx. To describe the erose boundaries here would take the rest of this book. The major neighborhoods are Long Island City, just across from Manhattan, its single Citicorp tower contrasting with warehouses and housing projects, peopled by many ethnic groups; Sunnyside, Maspeth and Middle Village, working class neighborhoods off the Long Island Expressway; the (as of 1990) non-Hispanic parts of Corona, Elmhurst and Jackson Heights, three-story apartment neighborhoods; the expanse of Flushing Meadow, site of the still-remembered Trylon and Perisphere rising over the 1939 World's Fair; and Whitestone and College Point, working class villages on Long Island Sound. In the Bronx it includes Italian East Bronx neighborhoods, the giant Parkchester apartment complex and the area around Yeshiva University: mostly white ethnics between the Hispanic South Bronx and black Williamsbridge. The 7th is about one-fifth Hispanic, only about one-tenth black; it is the one district in New York City that can be called predominantly white working class, and is fairly solidly Democratic.

The congressman here is Thomas Manton, a son of Irish immigrants, former policeman and IBM salesman who worked his way up in politics to Congress, and the Queens Democratic Party chair. Elected to the City Council in 1969, Manton represented a conservative district opposed to liberal Mayor John Lindsay; in 1972 he unsuccessfully ran against conservative Democratic Congressman James Delaney in the primary; in 1978, when Delaney retired, he ran and lost to Geraldine Ferraro. Ferraro's plan to represent Queens until she ran against Senator Alfonse D'Amato in 1986 was upset when she became the 1984 Democratic nominee for vice president and then when her husband had legal problems in 1985; she eventually ran for the Senate in 1992, but narrowly lost the primary. Manton was well prepared to move up when Ferraro moved out: he ran in the 1984 primary, and won with 30% of the vote for 27%, 22% and 21% to three others. In the general he beat Conservative Party stalwart Serphin Maltese 53%–47%.

Manton now seems comfortably ensconced in the House, a member of the Energy and Commerce Committee and a formidable PAC fundraiser. His legislative initiatives seemed geared to local problems: an amendment to the hazardous waste law designed to stymie the Long Island Railroad's plans to build a Long Island City waste transfer site; prohibition of sewage sludge composting plants in New York City, in opposition to a plan by Mayor Dinkins; Clean Air Act amendments to help New York businesses. On the Telecommunications Subcommittee, he opposed cable reregulation—Time Warner is a big employer of people here. This former cop moved to ensure that disability payments to law enforcement personnel injured in the line of duty were on a par with those killed on duty. Usually reelected easily, in 1992 Manton got a spirited challenge from Senator Bob Dole aide Dennis Shea, who returned to the district, attacked Manton's 17 overdrafts on the House bank totaling $22,000 and hit him for his liberalism. Manton won 59%–41% in Queens but only 52%–48% in the Bronx, for a total 57%–43% win. Though decisive, that may not be enough to deter competition in a district which, while carefully designed by Manton, still contains many pockets of Republicanism and discontent with liberal policies.

The People: Pop. 1990: 580,116; 17% age 65+; 58% White; 10% Black; 12% Asian; 8% Other; 21% Hispanic origin. Voting age pop.: 473,059; 9% Black; 19% Hispanic origin. Households: 46% married couple families; 19% married couple fams. w. children; 36% college educ.; median household income: $30,324; per capita income: $14,905; median gross rent: $520; median house value: $205,900.

1992 Presidential Vote

Clinton (D)	91,319	(56%)
Bush (R)	57,343	(35%)
Perot (I)	14,979	(9%)

1988 Presidential Vote

Dukakis (D)	87,565	(54%)
Bush (R)	75,069	(46%)

Rep. Thomas J. Manton (D)

Elected 1984; b. Nov. 3, 1932, New York City; home, Sunnyside; St. John's U., B.B.A. 1958, LL.B. 1962; Catholic; married (Diane).

Career: Marine Corps, 1951–53; NYC Police Officer, 1955–60; IBM salesman, 1960–64; Practicing atty., 1964–84; NYC Cncl., 1969–84.

Offices: 203 CHOB 20515, 202-225-3965. Also 46–12 Queens Blvd., Sunnyside 11104, 718-706-1400; and 2114 Williamsbridge Rd., Bronx 10461, 718-931-1400.

Committees: *Energy and Commerce* (17th of 27 D): Commerce, Consumer Protection and Competitiveness; Telecommunications and Finance; Transportation and Hazardous Materials. *House Administration* (6th of 12 D): Personnel and Police (Chmn.). *Merchant Marine and Fisheries* (7th of 29 D): Fisheries Management (Chmn.); Merchant Marine. *Joint Committee on the Library* (3d of 5).

Group Ratings

	ADA	ACLU	COPE	CDF	CFA	LCV	ACU	NTLC	NSI	COC	CEI
1992	85	73	83	100	80	38	8	5	60	29	10
1991	80	—	92	90	78	62	10	—	—	20	6

National Journal Ratings

	1991 LIB — 1991 CONS	1992 LIB — 1992 CONS
Economic	78% — 22%	88% — 11%
Social	66% — 33%	52% — 47%
Foreign	70% — 29%	62% — 35%

Key Votes of the 102d Congress

1. Ban Striker Replace FOR	5. Handgun Wait/7-Day FOR	9. Use Force in Gulf AGN
2. $ for Homeownership AGN	6. Overseas Mil. Abortion AGN	10. US Mil. Abroad $ Cut FOR
3. Tax Rich/Cut Mid Cls. FOR	7. Obscn. Art NEA $ Ban AGN	11. Limit SDI Funds FOR
4. FY93/$15B Def. Cut FOR	8. Death Pen. from Jury FOR	12. Cuba Trade Embargo AGN

Key Votes of the 103d Congress

1. Family Leave FOR	2. Deficit Reduction FOR	3. Stimulus Plan FOR

Election Results

1992 general	Thomas J. Manton (D)	72,280	(57%)	($1,013,635)
	Dennis C. Shea (R-C)	54,639	(43%)	($182,737)
1992 primary	Thomas J. Manton (D), unopposed			
1990 general	Thomas J. Manton (D)	35,177	(64%)	($316,301)
(NY 9)	Ann Pfoser Darby (R)	13,330	(24%)	
	Thomas V. Ognibene (C)	6,137	(11%)	

EIGHTH DISTRICT

It makes little sense to talk of the New York Jewish "community"; there are many Jewish communities, some would say as many as there are Jews. The Dutch founders of New York came from the European country then most tolerant of Judaism, and there have been Jews in New York since colonial days. The 19th Century brought many German Jews, some insisting they were more German than Jewish, and some who founded great merchant banking dynasties.

Then, starting around 1890, Ashkenazi Jews from Eastern Europe—from what were then the Romanov and Hapsburg Empires and are now Poland, Lithuania, Belarus, Ukraine, Hungary and Romania—began arriving in very large numbers. Persecuted in the wake of World War I, as many as 400,000 Jews came past the Statue of Liberty to Ellis Island every year in the early 1920s, until a 1924 law virtually shut down immigration; had a malapportioned, rural-dominated, nativist Congress not done that, perhaps 2 million of the 6 million who perished in the Holocaust would instead have become Americans.

The Ashkenazi Jews first settled in the Lower East Side, moving out the subways to Brooklyn and the Bronx almost as soon as they were built. They raised children who moved up faster and farther in this society than any new group in memorable history, rising despite prejudice to the top of almost every profession, virtually inventing vast new businesses from the rag trade to show biz: second-caste people from third rate countries almost immediately becoming elite in the world's foremost country. The descendants of New York's Jews live all over the country, yet New York remains America's most heavily Jewish city and metropolitan New York contains more Jews than any metropolis outside of Tel Aviv.

The 8th Congressional District of New York may be—there are no reliable figures as the Census does not distinguish religion—the nation's most heavily Jewish congressional district. About three-fifths of it is in Manhattan, two-fifths in Brooklyn; odd boundaries isolate blacks and Hispanics in nearby majority-minority districts. As drawn, it included at its extremes, it includes the homes of then-incumbent Congressmen Ted Weiss on the Upper West Side of Manhattan and Stephen Solarz in Brighton Beach, Brooklyn. The Upper West Side from 59th Street north to Morningside Heights and Columbia University is one of the heavy voting areas here: the venerable apartments along Central Park West and West End Avenue and Riverside Drive, and the brownstones on the cross streets which house some of America's most idealistic and dedicated liberal to radical voters. These are professional people, some rich, some struggling, who like the grittiness of the Upper West Side, the almost European atmosphere of boulevarded upper Broadway and the fierce struggle that is daily life in New York. In the 1950s, the West Side's cause was reform, the evisceration of the old Tammany Hall Democratic machine; by the late 1960s, the cause was peace, the ending of United States involvement in Vietnam; by the late 1980s, the cause was feminism, the ending of gender-incorrect speech and the preservation of abortion rights. Another big voting area is Greenwich Village, America's original Bohemia in the 1910s, now a neighborhood of expensive apartments and houses interlaced with much cheaper dwellings, and New York's most conspicuously gay center; politically the Village has long had a taste for what it regards as radical. Then there are new Village-type residential areas to the south: SoHo, where old factory buildings have been refurbished as lofts; TriBeCa, where commercial space now houses artists; Battery Park City, the attractive modern apartments built on a landfill west of the now-crumbled West Side Highway.

In Brooklyn, the 8th District includes two major neighborhoods: Brighton Beach and Coney Island, long gone to seed but spruced up by the Russian Jewish immigrants who flocked here in the 1980s; and Borough Park, with many Orthodox Jews, militantly pro-Israel, the New York neighborhood with the lowest share of votes (3%) for Jesse Jackson in the 1988 presidential primary. These areas are politically different from the heavily Jewish Manhattan places, to which they are connected by a narrow land bridge running along the Brooklyn waterfront and the massive Bush Terminal buildings. The Russians are anti-socialist and pro-free enterprise and Borough Park is extremely hostile to racial preferences and favors tough police treatment of crime; they are ready to vote Republican and look askance at liberal Democrats. This was Stephen Solarz's constituency and his foreign policy stands—strongly pro-Israel, leading the Gulf war resolution against Iraq, backing Cold War defense spending—suited them well. But Solarz, bereft of friends in the New York legislature when Brooklyn-based Speaker Mel Miller was ousted from office, and in trouble himself because of 743 overdrafts on the House bank, could see that his Brooklyn base would be outvoted by Manhattan. Voters there would hate his defense positions and were loyal to their hard-working incumbent, Ted Weiss, the most leftish and dovish of House members. So Solarz ran in the Hispanic-majority 12th District and lost; Weiss was heading for certain victory when he died of heart disease the day before the September primary.

Weiss still won 89% of the vote; but the new congressman would be chosen by a convention of almost 1,000 county Democratic committee members. Six candidates ran—Weiss's widow Sonya Weiss, Assemblymen Jerrold Nadler and Richard Gottfried, state Senator Franz Leichter, Councilwoman Ronnie Eldridge and former Congresswoman (1970–76) Bella Abzug. The convention was as tumultuous as can be imagined. Abzug withdrew in favor of Eldridge, the wife of columnist Jimmy Breslin; Leichter, who had expressed doubt about whether he had the energy for the job, and Gottfried, who was elected to the Assembly in 1968 at 21 and has been there ever since, had few votes. The key vote was procedural, for a system of weighted voting under which Nadler won 62% of the votes and Eldridge 21%; opponents decried this system, perhaps with some reason. Nadler became the Democratic nominee for the 8th District and for the last two months of Weiss's term represented his old Manhattan-Bronx 17th District; Nadler's general election was automatic.

The product of a New York education and of the late 1960's antiwar movement, Nadler was a junior at Columbia during the 1968 campus riots. He worked as a legislative staffer (at one point for Gottfried), then was elected to the Assembly himself in 1976. There he was known as a noodge, an expert on mass transit who worked to keep blue-collar port and freight rail jobs (opponents might call that featherbedding); he voted against the big tax cut of 1987. Entering the House, with a leg up in seniority over other freshmen, he called for a comprehensive transportation bill, though Congress had just passed that in the form of Senator Pat Moynihan's ISTEA in 1991. Nadler wants large cuts in the defense budget coupled with military conversion job retraining; a lesbian and gay civil rights activist, he is strongly in favor of lifting the ban on gays in the military. He maneuvered well, becoming second vice president of the Democrats' freshman class and getting a coveted seat on Public Works. He sponsored in the 103d Congress Stephen Solarz's Religious Freedom Restoration Act, to reverse a Supreme Court decision allowing the Army to bar the wearing of yarmulkes. He is likely to have one of the House's most liberal voting records.

The People: Pop. 1990: 581,453; 15% age 65+; 74% White; 8% Black; 6% Asian; 5% Other; 12% Hispanic origin. Voting age pop.: 486,890; 8% Black; 11% Hispanic origin. Households: 32% married couple families; 13% married couple fams. w. children; 59% college educ.; median household income: $32,784; per capita income: $26,168; median gross rent: $544; median house value: $223,100.

1992 Presidential Vote		
Clinton (D)	168,838	(77%)
Bush (R)	37,558	(17%)
Perot (I)	12,197	(6%)

1988 Presidential Vote		
Dukakis (D)	147,922	(73%)
Bush (R)	55,239	(27%)

Rep. Jerrold Nadler (D)

Elected 1992; b. June 13, 1947, Brooklyn; home, New York City; Columbia U., B.A. 1970, Fordham U., J.D. 1978; Jewish; married (Joyce Miller).

Career: Legislative asst. and law clerk, NY Assembly, 1970–76; NY Assembly, 1976–92.

Offices: 424 CHOB 20515, 202-225-5635. Also 1841 Broadway, #800, New York 10023.

Committees: *Judiciary* (17th of 21 D): Civil and Constitutional Rights; International Law, Immigration and Refugees. *Public Works and Transportation* (24th of 39 D): Economic Development; Surface Transportation; Water Resources and Environment.

Group Ratings and 102d Congress Votes: Newly Elected

Key Votes of the 103d Congress

1. Family Leave	FOR	2. Deficit Reduction	FOR	3. Stimulus Plan	FOR

Election Results

1992 general	Jerrold Nadler (D-L)	138,296	(81%)	($45,505)
	David L. Askren (R).................	25,548	(15%)	($2,150)
	Two Others	6,404	(4%)	
1992 special	Jerrold Nadler (D), nominated by convention			
1992 primary	Theodore S. Weiss (D)	58,115	(89%)	
	Arthur R. Block (D).................	7,026	(11%)	
1990 general	Theodore S. Weiss (D-L)	79,161	(80%)	($112,722)
(NY 17)	William W. Koeppel (R)..............	15,219	(15%)	($431,513)
	Two others.........................	4,015	(4%)	

NINTH DISTRICT

Brooklyn: the single word used to arouse laughter in a comedian's monologue, applause when someone said they were from there; it evoked an accent that twisted the English language almost to non-recognition, a raucous and brusque confrontational style, a sense of humor with an edge, the chip-on-the-shoulder assertiveness of those sure they will always be in second place. Brooklyn would never be more important than Manhattan; the Dodgers would always lose the series to the Yankees or the playoff to the Giants, and when they finally did win, in 1955, they moved to Los Angeles two years later. Brooklyn, as its Dutch name testifies, was a separate community from the 17th Century on, one of the largest cities in the country in the 19th Century with its own celebrities (Henry Ward Beecher, Walt Whitman, John Roebling). By 1898, when the five boroughs were welded into Greater New York, 1 million people lived in Brooklyn, but the Brooklyn of the comedians really came into being as the subways were built in the early 20th Century. Suddenly workers in all the little Manhattan factories no longer had to live in Lower East Side tenements. They moved out the subway lines, into neighborhoods of three- to five-story apartments and four-family houses. Brooklyn grew from 1.1 million in 1900 to 1.6 million in 1910 to 2.0 million in 1920 and 2.6 million in 1930. The old Brooklynites were mostly Protestant—Dutch, Yankee, German—plus some Catholic Irish. The new Brooklynites were heavily Italian and Jewish, the people who peopled sports and entertainment for a long generation, making their home town and its impenetrable accent nationally famous. In 1940, as the nation was about to go to war, Brooklyn had 2.7 million people: one in every 49 Americans lived in Brooklyn.

Today, 2.3 million people, one in every 108 Americans, live in Brooklyn, and it is no longer a staple of national comedy. Some of its old neighborhoods—Jewish Brownsville, Italian East New York—have been ravaged by crime and stand empty and toothless, but there is great vitality in most of Brooklyn, among upwardly mobile Hispanic immigrants and a hard-working black middle class, and in neighborhoods of the grandchildren of the earlier Jews and Italians. The farther reaches of Ocean Parkway and the expanse of Flatlands and Canarsie, the quiet corners of Sheepshead Bay and Gerritsen are such places. Here young Orthodox Jews raise families within walking distance of school, and neighbors patrol the streets at night to keep down the crime which has wrecked neighborhoods just a few miles away.

The 9th Congressional District of New York includes many such neighborhoods in Brooklyn and in the borough of Queens as well. Its geography is grotesque; its demography more comprehensible: this is where descendants of the 1890–1924 migrations live. In Brooklyn it extends from Prospect Park south along Ocean Parkway to Coney Island and Sheepshead Bay: still one of the most Jewish areas in the United States. It extends east over Flatlands and much of Canarsie and then across Jamaica Bay south to the Rockaway Peninsula and north to a collection of Queens neighborhoods: Howard Beach, next to Kennedy Airport; the old German neighborhoods of Glendale and Ridgewood, still orderly and spotlessly clean; Italian Woodhaven and Tudor-trimmed Forest Hills; much of the heavily Jewish high-rise area along Queens Boulevard. The balance here is Democratic but not overwhelmingly: Jewish portions of the 9th are heavily Democratic, though troubled by crime and not warm to Mayor David Dinkins; the other ethnic areas are mostly Republican.

The congressman from the 9th District is Charles Schumer, one of the most creative and active—if not hyperactive—members of the House, who has made important contributions to public policy without traditional House power, through energy, imagination, good humor and, not least, a certain amount of *chutzpah*: the old Brooklynite, derumpled a bit at Harvard. He seems well aware that there is a country west of the Brooklyn Bridge, optimistic but tempered by the memories of one just barely old enough to recall the Dodgers leaving town, with the brains and creativity that have enabled so many Brooklyn-born people to institute change.

The year he graduated from Harvard Law, 1974, Schumer was elected to the New York Assembly; in 1980, just before he turned 30, he was elected to the House. Immediately he raised a campaign treasury of over $1 million, lest he and Brooklyn neighbor Stephen Solarz be redistricted together in 1982; they weren't, and Schumer went on to concentrate on legislation. From the unlikely venue of the Banking Committee, a panel most talented members lobby to get off of, Schumer spotted the perverse incentives set up by the combination of deposit insurance and letting S&Ls make risky investments; he fought Banking Chairman Fernand St Germain, calling early on for higher capital requirements, and helped shape the 1989 S&L bailout bill. After that, he proposed a sweeping reform to split banks into the insured (core banks) and uninsured, which was not adopted, but helped focus attention on the risks of unlimited bank deposit insurance. He has also worked on housing programs, building on the success of the Nehemiah projects in Brooklyn.

Schumer's other big committee is Judiciary. He chairs the Crime and Criminal Justice Subcommittee which handles the biennial crime bills, and floor-managed House passage of the Brady bill requiring a delay in handgun purchases; unlike many Democrats, he backs the death penalty. He wrote an auto theft law to reduce the market for resale of stolen parts. He slipped a provision in the cable reregulation bill allowing franchisers to shop around for the least expensive service. He came up with a key compromise regarding farm laborers in the immigration reform law of 1986, and another in 1990 on employment-sponsored immigration. With free marketeer Dick Armey of Texas, he launched an unsuccessful 1990 effort to prohibit subsidy payments to farmers with adjusted gross incomes over $100,000. In 1992, he worked hard to increase funding for tuberculosis control, and amended the energy bill to phase out exports of highly enriched nuclear fuel. Other causes include reducing credit card interest rates, cracking the Arab economic boycott of Israel, and a federal law against impeding access to abortion clinics.

With redistricting looming again in 1992, Schumer accumulated $2.1 million. It turned out he didn't need it: Solarz was forced to run in the majority-Hispanic 12th District, and Schumer had no primary competition. Speculation focuses on statewide office: he would be an obvious candidate for the Senate in 1994, but only in the unlikely event that Daniel Patrick Moynihan retires; he could conceivably run for governor as well, in the somewhat less unlikely event that Mario Cuomo retires. In the meantime, he seems busy and happy in his work.

The People: Pop. 1990: 579,876; 20% age 65+; 82% White; 3% Black; 6% Asian; 3% Other; 8% Hispanic origin. Voting age pop.: 469,387; 3% Black; 7% Hispanic origin. Households: 52% married couple families; 21% married couple fams. w. children; 44% college educ.; median household income: $34,758; per capita income: $17,918; median gross rent: $534; median house value: $208,300.

1992 Presidential Vote			1988 Presidential Vote		
Clinton (D)	121,361	(59%)	Dukakis (D)	105,372	(52%)
Bush (R)	67,034	(32%)	Bush (R)	95,705	(48%)
Perot (I)	17,606	(9%)			

Rep. Charles E. Schumer (D)

Elected 1980; b. Nov. 23, 1950, Brooklyn; home, Brooklyn; Harvard, B.A. 1971, J.D. 1974; Jewish; married (Iris).

Career: NY Assembly, 1974–80.

Offices: 2412 RHOB 20515, 202-225-6616. Also 1628 Kings Hwy., Brooklyn 11229, 718-965-5400.

Committees: *Banking, Finance and Urban Affairs* (5th of 30 D): Financial Institutions Supervision, Regulation and Deposit Insurance; Housing and Community Development. *Foreign Affairs* (11th of 27 D): Economic Policy, Trade and Environment; Europe and the Middle East. *Judiciary* (10th of 21 D): Crime and Criminal Justice (Chmn.); International Law, Immigration and Refugees.

Group Ratings

	ADA	ACLU	COPE	CDF	CFA	LCV	ACU	NTLC	NSI	COC	CEI
1992	95	91	82	90	100	88	0	5	30	25	16
1991	85	—	92	100	67	92	0	—	—	20	13

National Journal Ratings

	1991 LIB — 1991 CONS		1992 LIB — 1992 CONS	
Economic	72%	— 23%	78%	— 22%
Social	78%	— 17%	92%	— 0%
Foreign	77%	— 23%	82%	— 16%

Key Votes of the 102d Congress

1. Ban Striker Replace	FOR	5. Handgun Wait/7-Day	FOR	9. Use Force in Gulf	AGN
2. $ for Homeownership	AGN	6. Overseas Mil. Abortion	FOR	10. US Mil. Abroad $ Cut	FOR
3. Tax Rich/Cut Mid Cls.	FOR	7. Obscn. Art NEA $ Ban	AGN	11. Limit SDI Funds	FOR
4. FY93/$15B Def. Cut	FOR	8. Death Pen. from Jury	AGN	12. Cuba Trade Embargo	AGN

Key Votes of the 103d Congress

1. Family Leave	FOR	2. Deficit Reduction	FOR	3. Stimulus Plan	FOR

Election Results

1992 general	Charles E. Schumer (D-L) 116,545	(89%)	($387,059)
	Alice G. Gaffrey (C). 14,985	(11%)	
1992 primary	Charles E. Schumer (D), unopposed		
1990 general	Charles E. Schumer (D-L) 61,468	(80%)	($93,863)
(NY 10)	Patrick Kinsella (R-C) 14,963	(20%)	

TENTH DISTRICT

Bedford, a century ago one of Brooklyn's fashionable neighborhoods, has given its name to half of what was in the 1960s reputed to be Brooklyn's most downtrodden black ghetto. The reputation was never entirely correct: if Bedford's and Stuyvesant's brownstones looked bedraggled even before modern urban decay, they also remain solid and, on many streets, well-tended. The black community settled here well before World War II, but was then one of the smaller of dozens of Brooklyn ethnic enclaves; it grew in the years after World War II as crime and crowdedness moved people out of Harlem and busloads of blacks came north from the Carolinas in the 1950s and early 1960s. Sluggish job growth has meant less migration, but Brooklyn's black community with some of New York's highest birth rates has grown rapidly, and far beyond the original bounds of Bedford-Stuyvesant.

The 10th Congressional District of New York is centered on Bedford-Stuyvesant and is entirely contained within Brooklyn; there regularity ends. It is shaped something like a set of barbells, with one end including gentrified Brooklyn Heights and downtown Brooklyn, plus part of the mixed Fort Greene and Williamsburg neighborhoods. To the east it extends to Jamaica Bay, including much of East New York and Canarsie and Brownsville: a wide variety here, from utterly bombed out blocks to secure and hardy blocks of rowhouses or high-rise rent-supplemented apartments. The district in 1990 was 61% black and 19% Hispanic, with some blocks of Italians and Hasidic Jews. Politically, it is overwhelmingly Democratic.

The congressman from the 10th District is Ed Towns, a black Democrat from East New York as experienced in government as in politics. Towns has been a teacher, social worker and hospital administrator, and is active in the civic affairs of this racially changing community. He served as Brooklyn's deputy borough president for six years and evidently succeeded in making himself uncontroversially popular. Towns's two best known legislative initiatives are the Student Athlete Right-to-Know Act, which requires colleges to report the graduation rates of student athletes, and strengthening the National Health Service Corps and the Minority Health Initiative, especially for Native Americans (not too many of them in Brooklyn!). He won a seat in 1990 on Energy and Commerce Committee, where he votes usually with Chairman John Dingell, and was key on the Clean Air Act 22–21 vote; born in North Carolina, like many New York blacks, he also votes with tobacco interests as part of an informal tobacco inner city alliance.

Redistricting and the revelation that he had 408 overdrafts on the House bank sparked some opposition in the 1992 primary. City Councilwoman Susan Alter attacked Towns's undistinguished record and challenged the idea, defended explicitly by some blacks, that only a black can fairly represent a black-majority district. Alter got 28% of the votes, a Canarsie lawyer 9% and Towns 63%. In 1993 he succeeded the late Ted Weiss of Manhattan as chairman of the Human Resources and Intergovernmental Affairs Subcommittee of Government Operations. This panel has a long history of superintending the Food and Drug Administration, pressuring for more stringent enforcement of drug laws and regulations; there was a story that Towns had been asked by Weiss to leave the subcommittee in 1983 after a Towns aide allegedly passed a draft of a subcommittee report to a drug company lobbyist. But Towns denies he was ever asked to leave and he pledges to follow the subcommittee's aggressive regulatory tradition.

The People: Pop. 1990: 581,311; 10% age 65+; 21% White; 61% Black; 2% Asian; 10% Other; 19% Hispanic origin. Voting age pop.: 416,561; 60% Black; 18% Hispanic origin. Households: 34% married couple families; 16% married couple fams. w. children; 35% college educ.; median household income: $23,164; per capita income: $11,479; median gross rent: $441; median house value: $165,200.

1992 Presidential Vote		
Clinton (D)	125,300	(83%)
Bush (R)	19,200	(13%)
Perot (I)	5,720	(4%)

1988 Presidential Vote		
Dukakis (D)	113,210	(82%)
Bush (R)	24,620	(18%)

Rep. Edolphus Towns (D)

Elected 1982; b. July 21, 1934, Chadbourn, NC; home, Brooklyn; NC A&T U., B.S. 1956, Adelphi U., M.S.W. 1973; Presbyterian; married (Gwendolyn).

Career: Army, 1956–58; Prof., Medgar Evers Col.; NY public schl. teacher; Dep. hospital admin., 1965–71; Brooklyn Dep. Borough Pres., 1976–82.

Offices: 2232 RHOB 20515, 202-225-5936. Also 545 Broadway, #200, Brooklyn 11206, 718-387-8696.

Committees: *Energy and Commerce* (18th of 27 D): Commerce, Consumer Protection and Competitiveness; Health and the Environment. *Government Operations* (9th of 25 D): Environment, Energy and Natural Resources; Human Resources and Intergovernmental Relations (Chmn.)

Group Ratings

	ADA	ACLU	COPE	CDF	CFA	LCV	ACU	NTLC	NSI	COC	CEI
1992	80	100	82	80	80	69	0	0	10	14	10
1991	90	—	100	90	78	85	0	—	—	13	6

National Journal Ratings

	1991 LIB — 1991 CONS			1992 LIB — 1992 CONS		
Economic	88%	—	0%	87%	—	13%
Social	88%	—	0%	81%	—	19%
Foreign	92%	—	0%	90%	—	0%

Key Votes of the 102d Congress

1. Ban Striker Replace	FOR	5. Handgun Wait/7-Day	FOR	9. Use Force in Gulf	AGN
2. $ for Homeownership	*	6. Overseas Mil. Abortion	FOR	10. US Mil. Abroad $ Cut	*
3. Tax Rich/Cut Mid Cls.	FOR	7. Obscn. Art NEA $ Ban	AGN	11. Limit SDI Funds	FOR
4. FY93/$15B Def. Cut	FOR	8. Death Pen. from Jury	*	12. Cuba Trade Embargo	AGN

Key Votes of the 103d Congress

1. Family Leave	FOR	2. Deficit Reduction	FOR	3. Stimulus Plan	FOR

Election Results

1992 general	Edolphus Towns (D-L) 97,509	(96%)	($699,589)
	Owen Augustin (C)..................... 4,315	(4%)	
1992 primary	Edolphus Towns (D) 34,734	(63%)	
	Susan Alter (D)..................... 15,407	(28%)	
	Frank Seddio (D) 5,042	(9%)	
1990 general	Edolphus Towns (D-L) 36,286	(93%)	($282,933)
(NY 11)	Ernest Johnson (C) 1,676	(4%)	
	Other............................. 1,094	(3%)	

ELEVENTH DISTRICT

In 1947, when Jackie Robinson suited up for the Brooklyn Dodgers and became the first black major league baseball player, there weren't that many blacks in Brooklyn. New York's large black ghetto was Manhattan's Harlem, with only a scattering of blacks at the southern edge of Brooklyn's Bedford-Stuyvesant, where landlords would rent cheap apartments to blacks. An IND subway, built to replace the El, connected Bedford-Stuyvesant blacks with the center of black life and entertainment in Harlem, and in 1941, as the El was being demolished, inspired Duke Ellington's "Take the A Train."

In the years since, Harlem has lost population, and large parts of the South Bronx have become vacant as landlords abandon rent controlled apartments. But Brooklyn's black neighborhoods have grown and, to some extent, prospered. Many New York blacks are from families originally from seaboard southern states. But large numbers, especially in Flatbush, south of the Hasidic Jewish outposts in Crown Heights, come from what New Yorkers called "the Islands"—Haiti, Dominican Republic, Jamaica, Barbados, Guyana, Trinidad and Tobago. They speak deeply accented English or French or Spanish, and various forms of creole; they bring spiced bread, peanut punch, Matouk's Special Hot Calypso Sauce, reggae and calypso music. These Caribbean immigrants work hard, tend to stay in families more often than low-income American-born blacks, are commercially and civically inclined; they come from places where life and property are not always respected by governments and are working, like so many other immigrants to America, to build new communities.

The 11th Congressional District of New York, in central Brooklyn, extends from downtown Brooklyn and Prospect Park across Crown Heights—the scene of terrible violence between blacks and Hasidic Jews—and covers most of Flatbush, East Flatbush and Brownsville. Most of this area was once heavily Jewish, the largest concentration of Jews in America from the 1920s to the 1960s; today the 11th District is 74% black, the highest percentage of any district in the country, with probably as many blacks with roots in the Islands as in the American South. Some neighborhoods here are in dreadful shape, like depopulated Brownsville, while others, like much of Flatbush, seem to have considerable strength.

The congressman from the 12th District, Major Owens, has had a long career in New York politics and government. He started out as a librarian, worked in the Brownsville Community Council and with CORE, was commissioner of New York City's Community Development Agency under Mayor John Lindsay from 1968 to 1973, and was called by critic Charles Morris "the most capable and canny" of New York's anti-poverty program directors. That was a high-pressure job, with few guidelines to draw on, and Owens may have been relieved when he was elected to serve in the antique chamber of the New York Senate in 1974. In 1982, when Congresswoman Shirley Chisholm, immigrant from Barbados and presidential candidate in 1972, announced her retirement, Owens entered the primary to succeed her and beat Chisholm's choice.

Owens now chairs the Education and Labor Committee Subcommittee on Select Education and Civil Rights. He worked on the Americans With Disabilities Act and, fittingly for a librarian, the Literacy Corps and library funding in the child care bill. He seems not to dissent from committee Democrats' consensus to give more money to education without demanding specific results. He resisted giving the Bush Education Department more money for research, evidently fearful of the results, and criticized the incoming Clinton Administration for their early spending initiatives on infrastructure rather than programs like Head Start.

Owens has had only nominal opposition; 48 overdrafts on the House bank hurt not at all in 1992.

The People: Pop. 1990: 582,332; 9% age 65+; 16% White; 74% Black; 3% Asian; 4% Other; 11% Hispanic origin. Voting age pop.: 416,159; 72% Black; 11% Hispanic origin. Households: 36% married couple families; 20% married couple fams. w. children; 40% college educ.; median household income: $26,148; per capita income: $11,706; median gross rent: $482; median house value: $181,100.

1992 Presidential Vote			1988 Presidential Vote		
Clinton (D)	104,584	(86%)	Dukakis (D)	88,925	(83%)
Bush (R)	11,686	(10%)	Bush (R)	18,265	(17%)
Perot (I)	3,907	(3%)			

Rep. Major R. Owens (D)

Elected 1982; b. June 28, 1936, Memphis, TN; home, Brooklyn; Morehouse Col., B.A. 1956, Atlanta U., M.S. 1957; Baptist; married (Maria).

Career: V.P., Metro. Cncl. of Housing, 1964; Brooklyn Public Library, 1958–65, Community Coord., 1964–65; Chmn., Brooklyn Congress on Racial Equality; Exec. Dir., Brownsville Community Cncl., 1966–68; NYC Community Devel. Commissioner, 1968–73, Dep. Admin., 1972–74; Dir., Community Media Library Program, Columbia U., 1973–74; NY Senate, 1974–82.

Offices: 2305 RHOB 20515, 202-225-6231. Also 289 Utica Ave., Brooklyn 11213, 718-773-3100.

Committees: *Education and Labor* (8th of 28 D): Elementary, Secondary and Vocational Education; Human Resources; Labor-Management Relations; Select Education and Civil Rights (Chmn.). *Government Operations* (8th of 25 D): Information, Justice, Transportation and Agriculture.

Group Ratings

	ADA	ACLU	COPE	CDF	CFA	LCV	ACU	NTLC	NSI	COC	CEI
1992	85	100	92	90	93	94	0	5	10	13	14
1991	100	—	100	100	78	77	0	—	—	11	7

National Journal Ratings

	1991 LIB — 1991 CONS			1992 LIB — 1992 CONS	
Economic	88%	—	0%	74%	—	25%
Social	88%	—	0%	92%	—	0%
Foreign	92%	—	0%	90%	—	0%

Key Votes of the 102d Congress

1. Ban Striker Replace	FOR	5. Handgun Wait/7-Day	FOR	9. Use Force in Gulf	AGN
2. $ for Homeownership	AGN	6. Overseas Mil. Abortion	FOR	10. US Mil. Abroad $ Cut	FOR
3. Tax Rich/Cut Mid Cls.	FOR	7. Obscn. Art NEA $ Ban	AGN	11. Limit SDI Funds	FOR
4. FY93/$15B Def. Cut	FOR	8. Death Pen. from Jury	AGN	12. Cuba Trade Embargo	AGN

Key Votes of the 103d Congress

1. Family Leave	FOR	2. Deficit Reduction	FOR	3. Stimulus Plan	FOR

Election Results

1992 general	Major R. Owens (D-L).................	80,028	(94%)	($177,235)
	Michael Gaffney (C)...................	4,287	(5%)	
	Other..............................	1,179	(1%)	
1992 primary	Major R. Owens (D), unopposed			
1990 general	Major R. Owens (D-L).................	40,570	(95%)	($172,498)
(NY 12)	Two Others.........................	2,180	(5%)	

TWELFTH DISTRICT

West Side Story, Leonard Bernstein's musical with Romeo as an Italian-American and Juliet as a Manhattan Puerto Rican, was written in 1957, amid a vast wave of migration that seemed likely to make Puerto Ricans the majority in New York. Actually, since that time the flow of Puerto Ricans in either direction has balanced out; but since the 1965 immigration act opened the way, New York has had a vast influx of Hispanics from places not under the U.S. flag. They include Dominicans, most of whom are black, and Colombians, largely of Indian ancestry, Panamanians, which like Puerto Ricans are a polyglot society, and those from other parts of South and Central America and Mexico.

The 12th Congressional District of New York is a serpentine-shaped entity designed to join these diverse peoples together to form a single constituency in which, by Census definition, 57% of residents are Hispanic. Stitched together, often by the thinnest of threads, are the Sunset Park neighborhood in Brooklyn, now heavily Puerto Rican and, on the other side of the borough, Bushwick, once German, now with mixed Latins and a political machine run by Assemblyman Vito Lopez. It takes in the Dominican neighborhood in East Elmhurst and Corona, Queens, and the Colombian blocks a few miles west in Jackson Heights, plus some black neighborhoods in East New York. It includes the Puerto Rican parts of Williamsburg in Brooklyn and, across the bridges in Manhattan, Puerto Rican blocks in the Lower East Side. In at least three places the district is connected only by cemeteries or parks.

The 12th District primary attracted attention largely because this is the district incumbent Stephen Solarz chose to run in. By any measure Solarz was one of the most effective leaders in the 102d Congress. He was the lead sponsor of the Gulf war resolution, marshaling agreements and assembling support in a masterful way. Solarz chaired the Foreign Affairs Asia Subcommittee, traveled widely, and took a deep interest in, and contributed importantly to, the emergence of democracy around the world. But Solarz had two problems for 1992. One was checks: he had 743 overdrafts on the House bank. The other was redistricting. Assembly Speaker Mel Miller, a Brooklynite determined to preserve Brooklyn districts for both Solarz and Charles Schumer, was convicted of a crime in December 1991 and removed from office; the new speaker, Saul Weprin, is from Queens and didn't care. The June 1992 plan included a Brooklyn-Queens mostly Jewish district where Schumer had the clear advantage, while Solarz's Brighton Beach home base, with its many Russian Jewish immigrants and the Orthodox community in Borough Park, was tied to Greenwich Village and the West Side of Manhattan; in this new 8th District, the clear advantage belonged to Ted Weiss, whose leftish foreign policy was far more to Manhattanites' taste than Solarz's support of American military efforts. Solarz did have an advantage in his $2 million warchest, the largest of any House member, accumulated in anticipation of a possible race against Schumer, and he decided to run and use it in the majority-Hispanic 12th.

It was not such a bad decision: he almost won. There was something a little ludicrous about this international-minded congressman posing as a constituency problem-solver; his slogan was "Paying attention. Taking action," and a Spanish radio ad, translated, said, "New Yorkers count on Congressman Solarz to create jobs, and he has. He is committed to using his experience and his power to do even more." He was helped by the multi-candidate field. Elizabeth Colon, Executive Director of the Association of Puerto Rican Executive Directors, had a base in the Lower East Side and was endorsed by the *New York Times*. Ruben Franco stepped down as president of the Puerto Rican Legal Defense and Education Fund to run; unfortunately, his residence was in the South Bronx, even farther afield than Solarz's. From Jackson Heights was Eric Ruano Melendez, a city employee and real estate broker, and from the South Bronx Rafael Mendez, a follower of the crazed New Alliance Party. The leading candidate was Nydia Velazquez, former City Council member from Williamsburg and head of Puerto Rico's community affairs office in New York. Solarz was attacked for being white and running in an Hispanic district, on the flawed theory that it could only fairly be represented by a Hispanic. As if in reply, Mayor David Dinkins and Jesse Jackson endorsed Velazquez, who came out slightly ahead of Solarz, 34%–28%. In the general election confidential hospital records were leaked to a New York tabloid showing that in September 1991 Velazquez had attempted suicide, was hospitalized and later underwent counseling. She went on to win the general election with 77% of the vote, and her success in winning in this challenging district must be taken as strong evidence that she is not incapacitated from meeting her responsibilities. She serves on the Banking Committee and seems likely to be a strong liberal vote. Incidentally, her connections in Puerto Rico are to the Popular Democratic Party, which is against statehood and her party was defeated in 1992 local elections; Puerto Rico's representative in the House, Carlos Romero Barcelo, is from the rival New Progressive Party and is likely to be on heated rather than warm terms with a *Populara* like Velazquez.

The People: Pop. 1990: 577,757; 8% age 65+; 14% White; 14% Black; 20% Asian; 32% Other; 57% Hispanic origin. Voting age pop.: 416,223; 13% Black; 54% Hispanic origin. Households: 42% married couple families; 23% married couple fams. w. children; 25% college educ.; median household income: $20,444; per capita income: $8,534; median gross rent: $454; median house value: $175,100.

1992 Presidential Vote			**1988 Presidential Vote**		
Clinton (D)	67,274	(68%)	Dukakis (D)	66,079	(71%)
Bush (R)	25,664	(26%)	Bush (R)	27,587	(29%)
Perot (I)	5,133	(5%)			

Rep. Nydia M. Velazquez (D)

Elected 1992; b. Mar. 28, 1953, Yabucoa, PR; home, Brooklyn; U. of PR, B.A. 1974, N.Y.U., M.A. 1976; Catholic; divorced.

Career: Instructor, U. of PR, 1976–81; Adjunct prof., Hunter Col., 1981–83; Special Asst., U.S. Rep. Edolphus Towns, 1983; NYC Cncl., 1984; Migration Dir., PR Dept. of Labor and Human Resources, 1986–89; Secy., Dept. of PR Community Affairs in the U.S., 1989–92.

Offices: 132 CHOB 20515, 202-225-2361. Also 815 Broadway, Brooklyn 11206, 718-599-3658.

Committees: *Banking, Finance and Urban Affairs* (23d of 30 D): Consumer Credit and Insurance; Economic Growth and Credit Formation; General Oversight, Investigations, and the Resolution of Failed Financial Institutions; Housing and Community Development. *Small Business* (17th of 27 D): Minority Enterprise, Finance and Urban Development.

Group Ratings and 102d Congress Votes: Newly Elected

Key Votes of the 103d Congress

1. Family Leave	FOR	2. Deficit Reduction	FOR	3. Stimulus Plan	FOR

Election Results

1992 general	Nydia Velazquez (D)	55,926	(77%)	($461,749)
	Angel Diaz (R-C-RTL)................	14,976	(20%)	($5,390)
	Two Others	2,165	(3%)	
1992 primary	Nydia Velazquez (D)	11,508	(34%)	
	Stephen Solarz (D)...................	9,581	(28%)	
	Elizabeth Colon (D)	8,839	(26%)	
	Ruben Franco (D)....................	2,499	(7%)	
	Two Others	1,701	(5%)	
1990 election	Newly created district.			

THIRTEENTH DISTRICT

One corner of America pondering secession—not from the United States, but from New York City—is Staten Island. Geographically, Staten Island has always been closer to New Jersey than New York, though it became part of New York City in 1898. For two-thirds of a century it was connected to the rest of the City only by ferry (5-cent toll for many years) or through Bayonne, New Jersey, until the 5-mile-long Verrazano Narrows Bridge was finished in 1965. It is far less densely populated than the rest of New York: with about as much acreage as Brooklyn has for 2.3 million people, Staten Island has 379,000—and that's after recent robust population growth. Some of Staten Island is almost rural, though not bucolic; if it has the highest point on the eastern seaboard, Todt Hill, it also has the Fresh Kills dump. Culturally, Staten Islanders are tradition-minded and conservative—more so than in perhaps most New York's suburbs—quite a contrast from Manhattan at the other end of the ferry. Home values rose rapidly in the 1980s, then fell in the 1990s; New York City income taxes, the highest in the nation, went to pay for many programs opposed by most Staten Islanders. In November 1990, voters agreed to form a commission to study the feasibility of secession; in November 1993, they vote on secession, though their choice is not binding. But there's some reason for caution. Experts say that Staten Island would have to pay even higher taxes for the services it now gets from New York City, whose residential property taxes are relatively low.

The 13th Congressional District of New York is made up of Staten Island plus a couple of adjacent neighborhoods over the Verrazano Narrows Bridge in Brooklyn. The largest neighborhood is Bay Ridge, heavily Catholic and Italian, mostly middle-class, with thick New York accents and resentment of high New York taxes and welfare payments: large single-family houses and small apartment buildings by the looming towers of the Bridge. The 13th also includes most of heavily Italian Bensonhurst, where in 1989 the murder of a black youth transfixed the city and altered its politics. This district may have more Italian-Americans and may also be home to more police officers than any other district in America.

The 13th is represented by Susan Molinari, the youngest member of Congress when she was chosen in a March 1990 special election. She had an advantage: her father Guy Molinari had represented the district from 1980 until he was elected Staten Island Borough president in November 1989, and her grandfather S. Robert Molinari was an Assemblyman from Staten Island in the 1940s. Susan Molinari, a member of the New York City Council since 1985, indeed the minority leader (she was the only Republican), beat a loud but ineffectual Democratic opponent Robert Gigante, 59%–35%.

Molinari brought to the House her father's determination to concentrate on local issues, along with a zest and energy that few members can match. But unlike her father and George Bush, who campaigned for her, and like so many younger voters of the type the Times Mirror poll calls "upbeats," Susan Molinari is pro-choice on abortion. She also opposed Bush on the child care bill and parted with many Republicans on the Americans with Disabilities Act; she had a less conservative record on cultural issues than on economics and foreign and defense policy. Her biggest achievement was on defense, and came almost immediately, when she bucked senior Armed Services Committee members and senior New York delegation liberals and got the House to vote 230–188 to designate Staten Island as a Navy homeport. (Liberals seemed to think that if New York could bar nuclear weapons from its harbor, it might somehow convince the Soviets the City was neutral and should not be a target in a nuclear war.) She continued to fight for the homeport in early 1993, when it again appeared on the base closings list.

Molinari has been active as well on other issues, sponsoring "glass ceiling" and sexual assault prevention laws. In early 1993 she chaired a Republican Balkan Crisis Task Force to present policy alternatives in the former Yugoslavia. She did not get the seat she sought on Appropriations, but came forward with a plan to improve Head Start and fought the Triborough Bridge and Tunnel Authority on the Verrazano's high tolls.

Redistricting changed the district's Brooklyn lines and gave Molinari a serious Brooklyn opponent, Assemblyman Sal Albanese. He carried Brooklyn 51%–44% but Molinari carried Staten Island 64%–32% and won comfortably. As a woman and young baby boomer, she has become a nationally prominent Republican and has been on many talk shows; some think she may be a candidate for statewide office some day, though not likely in 1994.

The People: Pop. 1990: 579,521; 14% age 65+; 82% White; 6% Black; 6% Asian; 2% Other; 7% Hispanic origin. Voting age pop.: 449,131; 5% Black; 6% Hispanic origin. Households: 57% married couple families; 26% married couple fams. w. children; 40% college educ.; median household income: $38,437; per capita income: $17,143; median gross rent: $553; median house value: $188,800.

1992 Presidential Vote			1988 Presidential Vote		
Bush (R)	100,761	(48%)	Bush (R)	113,701	(60%)
Clinton (D)	82,796	(39%)	Dukakis (D)	74,642	(40%)
Perot (I)	26,317	(12%)			

Rep. Susan Molinari (R)

Elected Mar. 1990; b. Mar. 27, 1958, Staten Island; home, Staten Island; S.U.N.Y., B.A. 1980, M.A. 1981; Catholic; divorced.

Career: Finance asst., Natl. Repub. Govs. Assn. 1981–82; Ethnic Liaison, RNC, 1983–84; NYC Cncl., 1985–90.

Offices: 123 CHOB 20515, 202-225-3371. Also 14 New Dorp Ln., Staten Island 10306, 718-987-8400; and 9818 4th Ave., Brooklyn 11209, 718-630-5277.

Committees: *Education and Labor* (9th of 15 R): Elementary, Secondary and Vocational Education; Human Resources. *Public Works and Transportation* (8th of 24 R): Economic Development (RMM); Investigations and Oversight; Water Resources and Environment.

Group Ratings

	ADA	ACLU	COPE	CDF	CFA	LCV	ACU	NTLC	NSI	COC	CEI
1992	35	39	58	30	47	44	64	65	100	88	69
1991	30	—	58	70	44	38	70	—	—	70	44

National Journal Ratings

	1991 LIB — 1991 CONS			1992 LIB — 1992 CONS	
Economic	34%	—	65%	16%	—	80%
Social	35%	—	63%	46%	—	53%
Foreign	26%	—	70%	0%	—	82%

Key Votes of the 102d Congress

1. Ban Striker Replace	AGN	5. Handgun Wait/7-Day	FOR	9. Use Force in Gulf	FOR
2. $ for Homeownership	FOR	6. Overseas Mil. Abortion	FOR	10. US Mil. Abroad $ Cut	AGN
3. Tax Rich/Cut Mid Cls.	AGN	7. Obscn. Art NEA $ Ban	FOR	11. Limit SDI Funds	AGN
4. FY93/$15B Def. Cut	AGN	8. Death Pen. from Jury	FOR	12. Cuba Trade Embargo	FOR

Key Votes of the 103d Congress

1. Family Leave	FOR	2. Deficit Reduction	AGN	3. Stimulus Plan	AGN

Election Results

1992 general	Susan Molinari (R-C)	107,903	(56%)	($507,962)
	Sal F. Albanese (D-L)	73,520	(38%)	($247,739)
	Kathleen M. Murphy (RTL)	10,825	(6%)	($24,514)
1992 primary	Susan Molinari (R)	9,110	(71%)	
	Kathleen M. Murphy (R)	3,731	(29%)	
1990 general	Susan Molinari (R-C)	58,616	(60%)	($141,216)
(NY 14)	Anthony J. Pocchia (D-L-SIS)	34,625	(35%)	($35,052)
	Christine Sacchi (RTL)	4,370	(4%)	

FOURTEENTH DISTRICT

It's hard to find any remnants of early 19th Century New York, the city that diarists Philip Hone and George Templeton Strong described with such zest; this is a city continually being torn down and rebuilt, its earlier structures expendable after a generation or so on the high-priced real estate of this tight little island. Yet the mayor of this quintessentially 20th Century city lives and works in two buildings of 19th Century scale: City Hall, built in 1803–11, where his ground floor office, dwarfed by the Municipal and Woolworth Buildings, overlooks City Hall Park; and Gracie Mansion, built in 1799, which looks across East End Avenue to 1950s high-rise apartments.

The 14th Congressional District of New York covers most of the East Side of Manhattan, from 14th Street north to 96th Street, though its actual boundaries are more irregular than that. The district also has small salients on Manhattan's Lower East Side and Upper West Side; 10% of its population is in the Brooklyn neighborhood of Greenpoint and 12% in the Queens neighborhood of Astoria, areas quite different in atmosphere from Manhattan: Astoria is mostly Greek, boisterous and prosperous, with a festive air about its business streets; Greenpoint is industrial and polyglot, quietly hard-working, one of the homes of the archetypical Brooklynese accent.

The 14th is the lineal descendant of the Silk Stocking District, based originally in the few blocks east of Fifth Avenue along Central Park and set apart as a separate House seat in 1918. In decades since, affluent Manhattan, thriving in its securities, publishing, advertising, entertainment, broadcasting, and communications industries, has spread from this narrow enclave and taken over the greater part of the island, and the political attitudes of this much-broadened upper class—defined partly by income, but also by tastes in the arts, fashion, letters, all the things in which New York remains clearly the nation's capital—have changed.

Historically, the Silk Stocking district was more Republican and more tolerant than the rest of the nation, or for that matter the rest of New York City: the politics of Theodore Roosevelt and the old *New York Herald-Tribune* and Henry Luce's *Time* magazine. It accepted many New Deal programs but distrusted union leaders and Democratic Party politicians. It felt that the nation's natural leaders were the well-educated Protestant gentlemen one saw strolling down Madison Avenue to their clubs, who in fact have continued to hold high government posts, though not the presidency, since the era of Franklin D. Roosevelt. But Silk Stocking politics took a turn during the tenure of John Lindsay, congressman from 1958 to 1965, mayor from 1965 to 1973. Lindsay moved from liberal Republican to radical Democrat, from an elite who felt themselves the natural leaders of society to a rebellious vanguard who opposed society's basic values. As mayor, Lindsay ran up the huge debts that nearly bankrupted the city in 1975, while neighborhoods deteriorated so badly that New York lost 1 million people in the 1970s: a horrifying statistic. His successor as congressman and ultimately as mayor was Edward Koch, who moved in the other direction, and in the process lost the support of Manhattan by backing capital punishment, opposing racial quotas and questioning poverty programs.

Those who think economics is the basis of American politics should come to the East Side, where the 14th has the highest average household income in America, $74,780, and is also solidly Democratic (2–1 against George Bush in *1988*). If it is affluent, it is also full of singles, gays and others who see anything past the canyons of Manhattan's east-west grid streets, New Jersey and America beyond, as hostile country. Indeed, it is Democratic enough that in 1992 it rejected incumbent Bill Green, a liberal Republican whose record on issues fit the district closely, for Democrat Carolyn Maloney. Elected in 1978 because of feuds among Democrats, Green was a moderate on economics and thoroughgoing liberal (but not radical) on cultural and foreign issues; he also showed a quiet effectiveness at solving problems and was reelected with 61% in 1988 and 1990. But he 1992 he had two special problems. One was redistricting: he was totally unknown in Astoria and Greenpoint, and exactly the opposite kind of Republican that voters there are attracted to (conservative on culture, perhaps liberal on economics). The other was the enthusiasm for feminism and women candidates among the liberal Democrats of the Upper East Side.

Carolyn Maloney brought to the race more political savvy than Green's recent opponents. Born and educated in the South, she came on a summer trip to New York in 1970, when she was 22, loved it, and "just stayed." In the early 1970s she worked on welfare education programs; from 1977 to 1982 she was a legislative staffer. In 1982 she was elected to the City Council from an East Side-West Side district; one observer described her as "a little spacey" until she found a cause, but then "a pit bull." The 1991 state redistricting gave her an all-East Side district entirely within the 14th District; that helped her win the Democratic House primary easily, vanquishing among others Abe Hirschfeld who made a complete fool of himself in early 1993 when he briefly owned but did not run the *New York Post*. Maloney's campaign had little money and she talked of running against millionaires, though her own net worth is well into seven figures; she campaigned personally with brio, sampling baklava in Astoria, accusing Green in Greenpoint, where residents were opposed to a new trash incinerator, of being part owner of a company that owns an incinerator. Green won the Manhattan part of the district, but only by 50%–44%, below his previous showings; Maloney carried Greenpoint 60%–34% and Astoria 64%–35%, for a 50%–48% upset victory.

"Usually when I come to Washington," Maloney said, "it's to march." She showed a certain naivete, insisting that she had no second choice to a seat on Appropriations, ending up on Banking and Government Operations. She is for deeper defense cuts than almost any other member, wants more opportunities for women and minorities and supports the balanced budget amendment. In this taxi-riding district she is for a higher gas tax, which shouldn't hurt, but she also favors higher taxes on the rich, which could be a problem in arguably the richest district in the country. But it's not clear whether Republicans will be competitive here as Green was.

The People: Pop. 1990: 578,639; 16% age 65+; 80% White; 5% Black; 6% Asian; 4% Other; 11% Hispanic origin. Voting age pop.: 514,290; 4% Black; 10% Hispanic origin. Households: 30% married

couple families; 10% married couple fams. w. children; 69% college educ.; median household income: $42,184; per capita income: $41,151; median gross rent: $678; median house value: $242,500.

1992 Presidential Vote			1988 Presidential Vote		
Clinton (D)	160,596	(69%)	Dukakis (D)	144,657	(65%)
Bush (R)	53,830	(23%)	Bush (R)	76,527	(35%)
Perot (I)	16,467	(7%)			

Rep. Carolyn B. Maloney (D)

Elected 1992; b. Feb. 19, 1948, Greensboro, NC; home, Manhattan; Greensboro Col, A.B. 1968; Presbyterian; married (Clifton).

Career: NYC Bd. of Educ., 1970–77; Legis. aide, NY Assembly, NY Senate, 1977–82; NYC Cncl., 1982–92.

Offices: 1504 LHOB 20515, 202-225-7944. Also 950 Third Ave., 19th Fl., New York 10022, 212-832-6531; 28–11 Astoria Blvd., Long Island City 11102, 718-932-1804; and 619 Lorimer St., Brooklyn 11211, 718-349-1260.

Committees: *Banking, Finance and Urban Affairs* (16th of 30 D): Consumer Credit and Insurance; Financial Institutions Supervision, Regulation and Deposit Insurance; Housing and Community Development. *Government Operations* (15th of 25 D): Environment, Energy and Natural Resources; Legislation and National Security.

Group Ratings and 102d Congress Votes: Newly Elected

Key Votes of the 103d Congress

1. Family Leave	FOR	2. Deficit Reduction	AGN	3. Stimulus Plan	FOR

Election Results

1992 general	Carolyn B. Maloney (D-L)	101,652	(50%)	($277,223)
	Bill Green (R-INN)	97,215	(48%)	($1,141,470)
	Other	2,970	(2%)	
1992 primary	Carolyn B. Maloney (D)	37,415	(66%)	
	Abraham J. Hirschfeld (D)	12,864	(23%)	
	Charles W. Juntikka (D)	3,521	(6%)	
	Frederick D. Newman (D)	2,534	(5%)	
1990 general	Bill Green (R-BVP)	52,919	(61%)	($458,486)
(NY 15)	Frances L. Reiter (D-LIB)	33,464	(39%)	($19,403)

FIFTEENTH DISTRICT

Harlem, for many years America's most famous black ghetto, has fallen on grim times. Actually, Harlem as the central focus of black America was only a moment in black history, and Harlem itself has not always been black. Its five-story tenements were built almost 100 years ago for working-class whites, and central Harlem became all black only around 1920—the beginning of the decade when black entertainers and night clubs on 125th Street became world-famous. This Harlem was a wondrous place as the *WPA Guide* described 50 years ago: "To whites seeking amusement, it is an exuberant, original and unconventional entertainment center; to Negro college graduates, it is an opportunity to practice a profession among their own people; to those aspiring to racial leadership, it is a domain where they may advocate their theories unmolested; to artists, writers and sociologists, it is a mine of rich material; to the mass of Negro people, it is the spiritual capital of Black America." It was around this time, in 1944, that

Harlem first got its own congressional district and a congressman, Adam Clayton Powell, Jr., who won national fame for his Powell Amendments banning racial discrimination in government programs.

Harlem has been in decline for decades now. Its brownstones are often abandoned and empty, if they haven't been pulled down; family structure has deteriorated until the father-and-mother household is a rarity; drugs and crime and AIDS infection and infant mortality are at horrifying levels. Its population is down more than 200,000 since the 1940s. The boom in jobs and economic growth in the rest of Manhattan has hardly touched Harlem; its high school graduates may get into City College because of its open admissions policy, but sadly seldom have the basic skills needed for white-collar work; to the burgeoning number of blue-collar jobs in the outer boroughs and the suburbs, Harlemites do not seem able to make their way. The entrepreneurial impulse which spurs Koreans to open greengroceries and Haitians to buy cab medallions is scarce in Harlem. The big state office building on 125th Street faces on a street scene with the disorder of a Third World capital.

The 15th Congressional District of New York includes all of Harlem, indeed almost all of northern Manhattan, (approximately) from East 96th Street and West 91st Street on up. That means the district takes in some of the white liberal Upper West Side and the precincts around Columbia University; it includes the once Irish and now Dominican Inwood neighborhood at the north tip of Manhattan; it includes Washington Heights, with many Puerto Ricans and other Latinos, where Mayor David Dinkins enraged many New Yorkers by paying a condolence call on the family of a drug dealer shot by police. Overall the district is 47% black and 45% Hispanic—figures testifying to black flight from Harlem and the continuing rush of Western Hemisphere immigrants to fill it in.

The congressman from the 15th District is Charles Rangel, first elected in 1970 when he narrowly beat the legendary but fading Adam Clayton Powell. Rangel is the senior member of the New York delegation and fourth ranking Democrat on Ways and Means. Like most Harlem politicians, he began his career calling on government to give money and social guidance to Harlemites, to enable them to work their way upward; that call is still echoed today, but as an incantation in which no one has much faith. Rangel's main emphasis for at least ten years has been denunciation of the drug trade. From 1983 until it was abolished in 1993 with the other House select committees, Rangel chaired the Select Committee on Narcotics Abuse and Control, and seldom missed a chance to relate other problems to drugs; after all, he has seen how it can destroy a community. Rangel wants money spent on rehabilitation programs as much as interdiction and police work, and was a scathing critic of Republican Administrations' anti-drug efforts. But he also worked with the Bush Justice Department to create the Weed and Seed program, combining intensive law enforcement with social services. He also takes sharp issue with liberals who call for legalization of marijuana and provision of free needles to curtail AIDS. He denounces professional sports leagues for letting drug users return to play. In response to the abolition of the Select Narcotics Committee, Rangel formed a drugs caucus to continue work on the issue. He speaks out strongly against letting doctors give heroin to terminal cancer patients. Everything is refracted through drugs: but for a congressman who is not cynical about his responsibilities and not just interested in making a comfortable place for himself, as many other Harlem politicians are, everything is refracted through drugs.

On Ways and Means, Rangel worked to protect state and local tax deductibility in the 1986 tax reform, and can be counted on to continue; he does not think enterprise zones are a panacea, but pushed them even before the Los Angeles riot. He is a prime defender of Section 936, the tax exemption that has created many jobs in Puerto Rico. Representing one of the lowest income districts in New York and the nation, Rangel has not been averse to income tax increases or considering a value added tax. He was strongly critical of the Bush Administration's policy toward Haiti and Haitian refugees.

Rangel is smart, articulate in a wonderful New Yorkish way and usually upbeat. Nevertheless, notes of anger entered into his feuds with Mayor Edward Koch in the 1980s and his support of Jesse Jackson in the 1988 presidential primary and of Mayor David Dinkins in 1989 and 1993. At one point he called on Hasidic Jews to stop criticizing Dinkins lest they provoke "a backlash . . . tragically and anti-semitically." As the *New York Post*'s Eric Breindel pointed out, "This is not a caution; this is a threat. And backlash can have but one meaning here—violence." None of this, nor his 64 overdrafts on the House bank, cause Rangel problems at the polls; he is reelected without serious opposition.

The People: Pop. 1990: 580,354; 12% age 65+; 14% White; 47% Black; 1% Amer. Indian; 2% Asian; 22% Other; 45% Hispanic origin. Voting age pop.: 437,373; 47% Black; 42% Hispanic origin. Households: 26% married couple families; 12% married couple fams. w. children; 35% college educ.; median household income: $19,238; per capita income: $10,367; median gross rent: $402; median house value: $162,600.

1992 Presidential Vote			1988 Presidential Vote		
Clinton (D)	123,846	(85%)	Dukakis (D)	122,071	(87%)
Bush (R)	15,505	(11%)	Bush (R)	18,860	(13%)
Perot (I)	4,700	(3%)			

Rep. Charles B. Rangel (D)

Elected 1970; b. June 11, 1930, New York City; home, New York City; N.Y.U., B.S. 1957, St. John's U., LL.B. 1960; Catholic; married (Alma).

Career: Army, 1948–52 (Korea); Asst. U.S. Atty., S. Dist. of NY, 1961; Legal Cnsl., NYC Housing and Redevel. Bd., Neighborhood Conservation Bureau, 1963–68; Gen. Cnsl., Natl. Advisory Comm. on Selective Svc., 1966; NY Assembly, 1966–70.

Offices: 2252 RHOB 20515, 202-225-4365. Also 163 W. 125th St., New York 10027, 212-663-3900; 601 W. 181st St., New York 10033, 212-927-5333; and 2110 1st Ave., New York 10029, 212-348-9830.

Committees: *Ways and Means* (4th of 24 D): Oversight; Select Revenue Measures (Chmn.).

Group Ratings

	ADA	ACLU	COPE	CDF	CFA	LCV	ACU	NTLC	NSI	COC	CEI
1992	95	100	92	100	93	69	0	0	20	25	10
1991	95	—	100	100	83	77	0	—	—	20	8

National Journal Ratings

	1991 LIB — 1991 CONS			1992 LIB — 1992 CONS	
Economic	88%	—	0%	83%	—	13%
Social	88%	—	0%	80%	—	19%
Foreign	92%	—	0%	90%	—	0%

Key Votes of the 102d Congress

1. Ban Striker Replace	FOR	5. Handgun Wait/7-Day	FOR	9. Use Force in Gulf	AGN
2. $ for Homeownership	AGN	6. Overseas Mil. Abortion	FOR	10. US Mil. Abroad $ Cut	FOR
3. Tax Rich/Cut Mid Cls.	FOR	7. Obscn. Art NEA $ Ban	AGN	11. Limit SDI Funds	FOR
4. FY93/$15B Def. Cut	FOR	8. Death Pen. from Jury	AGN	12. Cuba Trade Embargo	AGN

Key Votes of the 103d Congress

1. Family Leave	FOR	2. Deficit Reduction	FOR	3. Stimulus Plan	FOR

Election Results

1992 general	Charles B. Rangel (D-L)............... 105,011	(95%)	($669,095)
	Jose A. Suero (C-INF)................. 4,345	(4%)	
	Other............................. 1,337	(1%)	
1992 primary	Charles B. Rangel (D) 41,391	(82%)	
	Jessie Fields (D) 4,984	(10%)	
	Harry C. Fotopoulos (D)................ 4,219	(8%)	
1990 general	Charles B. Rangel (D-R-L)............. 55,882	(97%)	($601,550)
(NY 16)	Other............................. 1,592	(3%)	

SIXTEENTH DISTRICT

It may not quite be "the beautiful Bronx," as borough historian Lloyd Utlan calls it, but the Bronx seems to be coming back. The beautiful days were in the 1930s and 1940s, when Presidents Roosevelt and Truman rode down 138th Street, when Babe Ruth hit home runs out of Yankee Stadium, when Art Deco apartment buildings went up along the Grand Concourse, when shoppers thronged Tremont Avenue stores and New Yorkers from all over flocked to the Bronx Zoo. This Bronx was built in a trice, starting in 1906 when the first subway came in, enabling the sons and daughters of immigrants to move from dimly lit Lower East Side tenements to comparatively spacious quarters; the Bronx's population grew from 200,000 in 1900 to 430,000 in 1910, 732,000 in 1920, and 1.3 million in 1930—more than the 1.2 million of 1990.

The Bronx fell rapidly in the dozen years after John Lindsay was elected mayor in 1965. One reason was rent control, insisted on by New York tenants, which guarantees that owners of low-rent property won't maintain it: the result is empty vandalized shells and venues for drug deals. Another was the drop in low-income, low-skill jobs in Manhattan and the Bronx, abetted by high union and minimum wages, restrictive work rules and the tolls exacted by organized crime. A third reason was the disintegration of family structure: stable, law-abiding males became scarce in these parts. But most important was crime. With no community institutions and little parental supervision, poor minority teenagers here committed an alarming number of crimes, with seeming impunity. Arson became increasingly common, perpetrated by kids for kicks or on behalf of landlords who wanted to get insurance money for rent controlled buildings. A vicious cycle was created: crime drove away jobs, which drove away fathers, which produced more crime. A section of the South Bronx with 476,000 people in 1960 and 460,000 in 1970 dropped to 233,000 in 1980, a stunning change. As people left, presidential candidates came in—Jimmy Carter in 1977, Ronald Reagan in 1980—promising help.

Now the South Bronx seems to have turned around. It is still one of the lowest income parts of America, and still is high crime; but it is beginning to be possible for low-income families here to work their way up. Government has helped, particularly the city government under Mayor Edward Koch, which provided more intensive police patrols and housing subsidies. Rent control was phased out, criminals held in prison longer, pocket parks were built and graffiti painted over. But citizens here did much of the work, forming community groups called Banana Kelly or Mid-Bronx Desperadoes (now MBD Housing) to build single-family pastel bungalows and small-scale apartment projects for the elderly, single-parent families and former homeless. Local institutions, notably Bronx-Lebanon Hospital, remained in operation, employing area residents and becoming a strong force for neighborhood stability; warehousing and truck terminals opened up as the streets became safer. Population rose in the South Bronx in the 1980s more than almost anywhere else in New York City; there are now $150,000 ranch houses on Charlotte Street, where Jimmy Carter went in 1977.

The 16th Congressional District of New York includes most of the Bronx south of the Bronx Zoo. It includes the Art Deco apartments of the Grand Concourse and the narrow commercial strips of Westchester Avenue, Boston Road and the Hub. It includes the industrial flatlands of Bruckner Boulevard and Hunts Point and the hard-rock ridges through which the original subways bore. This is still a low-income district, with 42% of residents below the poverty line, the most in the country, the lowest median family income, the second lowest per capita income, the third lowest median household income of any congressional district. The people here are 59% Hispanic, and though not entirely Puerto Rican, it is New York City's largest Puerto Rican community, and 43% black (the categories aren't mutually exclusive). Politically, this is quite possibly the most heavily Democratic district in the country.

The congressman from the 16th is Jose Serrano, chosen in a March 1990 special election. A native of Mayaguez, Puerto Rico, who grew up in the Millbrook project in the South Bronx, Serrano has moved up while other Bronx politicians have fallen by the wayside due to corruption. He was elected to the New York Assembly in 1974 and chaired the Education Committee beginning in 1983; in 1985, he ran for Bronx Borough president, bucking the Bronx Democratic organization, and nearly won. His disparaging remarks about corruption in the Bronx were remembered in 1987 when the man who beat him for borough president had to be replaced after a criminal conviction in the Wedtech scandal. Then, Congressman Robert Garcia, long the co-sponsor of Jack Kemp's enterprise zones, was also convicted of accepting a payment disguised as a consulting fee to his wife from Wedtech, the corrupt affirmative action defense contractor, ; he resigned in January 1990 (the convictions were later reversed but far too late to help him politically). Serrano was the obvious choice for the Democratic nomination and won the seat easily.

In the House, Serrano has a liberal voting record, and has a seat on the Appropriations Labor, HHS and Education Subcommittee. One of his great causes is the Classroom Safety Act, aimed at an obvious problem, but with an interesting approach: he urges federal money for victim counseling, conflict resolution and peer mediation, as well as the more obvious metal detectors and video-surveillance devices. Another cause is pediatric AIDS, also depressingly common in the South Bronx.

The People: Pop. 1990: 581,053; 7% age 65+; 4% White; 43% Black; 1% Amer. Indian; 2% Asian; 35% Other; 59% Hispanic origin. Voting age pop.: 385,226; 43% Black; 57% Hispanic origin. Households: 28% married couple families; 15% married couple fams. w. children; 22% college educ.; median household income: $15,060; per capita income: $7,102; median gross rent: $398; median house value: $148,000.

1992 Presidential Vote			1988 Presidential Vote		
Clinton (D)	101,195	(81%)	Dukakis (D)	98,339	(85%)
Bush (R)	19,029	(15%)	Bush (R)	17,534	(15%)
Perot (I)	4,123	(3%)			

Rep. Jose E. Serrano (D)

Elected Mar. 1990; b. Oct. 24, 1943, Mayaguez, PR; home, Bronx; Lehman Col.; Catholic; married (Mary).

Career: Army Medical Corps, 1964–66; Banker 1961–69; Dist. 7 Schl. Bd., 1969–74; NY Assembly, 1974–90.

Offices: 336 CHOB 20515, 202-225-4361. Also 890 Grand Concourse, Bronx 10451, 718-538-5400.

Committees: *Appropriations* (31st of 37 D): Foreign Operations, Export Financing and Related Programs; Labor, Health and Human Services, and Education.

Group Ratings

	ADA	ACLU	COPE	CDF	CFA	LCV	ACU	NTLC	NSI	COC	CEI
1992	95	100	91	100	93	88	0	0	10	13	9
1991	100	—	100	100	89	85	0	—	—	10	2

National Journal Ratings

	1991 LIB — 1991 CONS		1992 LIB — 1992 CONS	
Economic	88%	— 0%	91%	— 0%
Social	88%	— 0%	81%	— 17%
Foreign	85%	— 15%	90%	— 0%

Key Votes of the 102d Congress

1. Ban Striker Replace	FOR	5. Handgun Wait/7-Day	FOR	9. Use Force in Gulf	AGN
2. $ for Homeownership	*	6. Overseas Mil. Abortion	FOR	10. US Mil. Abroad $ Cut	FOR
3. Tax Rich/Cut Mid Cls.	FOR	7. Obscn. Art NEA $ Ban	AGN	11. Limit SDI Funds	FOR
4. FY93/$15B Def. Cut	FOR	8. Death Pen. from Jury	AGN	12. Cuba Trade Embargo	AGN

Key Votes of the 103d Congress

1. Family Leave	FOR	2. Deficit Reduction	FOR	3. Stimulus Plan	FOR

Election Results

1992 general	Jose E. Serrano (D-L).................	85,222	(91%)	($96,339)
	Michael Walters (R-C).................	7,975	(9%)	
1992 primary	Jose E. Serrano (D), unopposed			
1990 general	Jose E. Serrano (D-L).................	38,024	(93%)	($132,359)
(NY 18)	Three Others........................	2,772	(7%)	

SEVENTEENTH DISTRICT

The Bronx, a product almost entirely of the first half of the 20th Century, was originally a collection of middle-class neighborhoods clustered around subway stops; a borough where children of immigrants left gloomy Manhattan for the sunlight of wide Bronx avenues and the vistas of a city where the street grid bent to adapt to nature's ridges and hills. Different ethnic groups were clustered here and there: Irish in Kingsbridge, in the valley between Riverdale and the Grand Concourse; Italians in Bedford Park, north of Fordham University and Bronx Park; well-to-do WASPs and Jews in Riverdale, on the palisades above the Hudson River; Jews with less education and advantages originally in the Art Deco apartments on the Grand Concourse, who in a rush moved to Co-op City, the giant union-built apartment complex, with 35 35-story buildings, built in 1965 on marshland between the Hutchinson River Parkway and I-95.

The 17th Congressional District of New York includes much of these Bronx neighborhoods plus several in the Westchester County suburbs just to the north. Co-op City is one anchor, and perhaps the largest political bloc in the district; just to the west is the heavily black, middle-income neighborhood of Williamsbridge. The 17th's portions of Yonkers, Mount Vernon and New Rochelle in Westchester are carefully drawn to include most blacks there. The district also dips south along the Harlem River to take in some housing projects in the South Bronx. The 17th is, in Voting Rights Act argot, a minority-influence district, 42% black and 28% Hispanic.

Eliot Engel, the congressman from the 17th District, is a son of the Bronx and resident of Co-op City, a teacher and guidance counselor who got elected to the New York Assembly in 1976, at 29. He was elected to the House in 1988 to replace Democrat Mario Biaggi, once the most decorated member of the New York police department, after he was convicted in two tawdry bribery cases. (Engel replaced a convicted incumbent in the Assembly, too; like Jose Serrano of the next-door 16th, he has gotten big political breaks from the downfall of others.) Engel filed to run against Biaggi in June, giving up his Assembly seat; he won 48% of the primary vote to Biaggi's 26% and Vincent Marchiselli's 26%; in November, Biaggi was on the ballot again, but as the Republican nominee, and Engel beat him 56%–27%. Biaggi tried a comeback again in 1992, but Engel beat him in the Democratic primary 74%–26%.

Engel has a seat on the Foreign Affairs Committee, a political advantage in polyglot metro New York. He is a firm supporter of Israel, sponsor of a successful resolution to declare that Jerusalem "is and should remain" the capital of Israel; he also supported of the Gulf war resolution and is somewhat more hawkish than most New York Democrats. He has introduced a bill to ban sales of weapons to the Royal Ulster Constabulary in Northern Ireland and keeps an eye on African issues: covering all the bases for the 17th District. Engel has worked conscientiously on his Subcommittee on Economic Policy, Trade and Environment fashioning new export legislation to reduce red tape but still control export of strategic materials. His record on economic and cultural issues is solidly liberal. He also has bills to establish a clearinghouse for complaints of unfair depiction of minorities on television and radio, to subsidize energy co-generation (Co-op City is interested) and to make airplane noise a priority when considering changes in routes. He wants to help discharged veterans by retraining them to help communities fight crime and restore housing.

Engel survived the 1992 redistricting comfortably, though if the black population increases in the district, he may face a black challenger later in the decade.

The People: Pop. 1990: 578,424; 14% age 65+; 29% White; 42% Black; 4% Asian; 14% Other; 28% Hispanic origin. Voting age pop.: 437,836; 40% Black; 25% Hispanic origin. Households: 38% married couple families; 18% married couple fams. w. children; 38% college educ.; median household income: $27,227; per capita income: $13,155; median gross rent: $483; median house value: $174,200.

1992 Presidential Vote

Clinton (D)	119,964	(75%)
Bush (R)	30,215	(19%)
Perot (I)	7,961	(5%)

1988 Presidential Vote

Dukakis (D)	117,153	(73%)
Bush (R)	42,546	(27%)

Rep. Eliot L. Engel (D)

Elected 1988; b. Feb. 18, 1947, Bronx; home, Bronx; Hunter-Lehman Col., B.A. 1969; City U. of NY, Lehman Col., M.A. 1973; NY Law Schl., J.D. 1987; Jewish, married (Patricia).

Career: Teacher, guidance counselor, NYC public schl., 1969–77; NY Assembly, 1977–88.

Offices: 1433 LHOB, 20515, 202-225-2464. Also 3655 Johnson Ave., Bronx 10463, 718-796-9700.

Committees: *Education and Labor* (16th of 28 D): Elementary, Secondary and Vocational Education; Labor-Management Relations. *Foreign Affairs* (8th of 27 D): Africa; Economic Policy, Trade and Environment; Europe and the Middle East.

Group Ratings

	ADA	ACLU	COPE	CDF	CFA	LCV	ACU	NTLC	NSI	COC	CEI
1992	95	100	91	90	93	94	4	0	50	25	6
1991	90	—	100	100	78	85	15	—	—	30	9

National Journal Ratings

	1991 LIB — 1991 CONS		1992 LIB — 1992 CONS	
Economic	66%	— 32%	91%	— 0%
Social	84%	— 12%	85%	— 13%
Foreign	70%	— 29%	65%	— 33%

Key Votes of the 102d Congress

1. Ban Striker Replace	FOR	5. Handgun Wait/7-Day	FOR	9. Use Force in Gulf	FOR
2. $ for Homeownership	AGN	6. Overseas Mil. Abortion	FOR	10. US Mil. Abroad $ Cut	FOR
3. Tax Rich/Cut Mid Cls.	FOR	7. Obscn. Art NEA $ Ban	AGN	11. Limit SDI Funds	FOR
4. FY93/$15B Def. Cut	FOR	8. Death Pen. from Jury	AGN	12. Cuba Trade Embargo	FOR

Key Votes of the 103d Congress

1. Family Leave	FOR	2. Deficit Reduction	FOR	3. Stimulus Plan	FOR

Election Results

1992 general	Eliot L. Engel (D-L)	98,068	(80%)	($469,220)
	Martin Richman (R)	16,511	(14%)	
	Three others	7,802	(6%)	
1992 primary	Eliot L. Engel (D)	35,859	(74%)	
	Mario Biaggi (D)	12,680	(26%)	
1990 general	Eliot L. Engel (D-L)	45,758	(61%)	($389,698)
(NY 19)	William J. Gouldman (R)	17,135	(23%)	
	Kevin Brawley (C-RTL)	11,868	(16%)	

EIGHTEENTH DISTRICT

The great granite ridges that form the spine of Manhattan and the Bronx move north into the thin peninsula of land between Long Island Sound and the Hudson River that is lower Westchester County. Blessed with some of America's loveliest scenery, easily accessible to Manhattan by train since the mid-19th Century, this became some of the country's first suburban terrain, with grand estates built by great millionaires, like Jay Gould's Gothic revival Lyndhurst or John D. Rockefeller's spectacular Kykuit, and with villages for retainers clustered around the railroad stations.

Today Westchester County still looks suburban, perhaps more than ever before, now that it has a nice patina of age. It has little commuter railroad stations across from faux Tudor drugstores, soda fountains and cobblestone post offices; and it also has shopping malls and gallerias and corporate headquarters. Westchester does have its share of homeless and racial ghettos, its seedy neighborhoods if not slums. Intensive development has not proceeded too far north of White Plains, for just to the north Westchester is crossed by the first of several mountain ridges—the closest the Appalachians come to the ocean. Historically Republican, Westchester is now intensely marginal political territory. More than Nassau or Suffolk County or northern New Jersey, it has attracted liberal-minded professionals, often Jews, who have made very high income places like Scarsdale Democratic strongholds. In addition, blue-collar voters and blacks in places like Mount Vernon make this a mixed constituency. Westchester votes a lot like the comfortable central city neighborhoods it physically resembles—Cambridge's Brattle Street, Washington's Cleveland Park, Philadelphia's Chestnut Hill.

The 18th Congressional District of New York contains the heart of suburban Westchester County, but actually has less than half the county's population, and also includes a little territory in the Bronx and widely scattered areas in Queens. Politics, as one might expect, is at work here; this is a district designed for Congresswoman Nita Lowey, a Democrat first elected in 1988 and a favorite of Governor Mario Cuomo. The 18th includes most of southern Westchester, but not most of the black neighborhoods of Yonkers, Mount Vernon and New Rochelle, which are in the minority-influence 17th District. It includes the rich, Catholic and conservative suburbs of Pelham, Eastchester and Bronxville, and the more Jewish and liberal Scarsdale, plus some of the Long Island Sound towns. The 18th also contains the southern half of White Plains, the county seat-corporate headquarters-shopping mall center. From there the 18th goes on its odyssey, picking up a few thousand people in Bronx communities facing the Sound and the urban resort of City Island. Then it crosses the Throgs Neck Bridge and is connected by a block-wide land-bridge through Flushing to two distinct areas of Queens. One is Lefrak City and other high-rise apartments in Rego Park, along Queens Boulevard where the first condominium conversion in New York took place in 1966; this area is heavily Jewish and very Democratic. The other is the heavily Italian neighborhoods around St. John's University, including the home of its most famous alumnus, Mario Cuomo, in the pleasant winding streets of Hollis Wood, a more politically mixed area.

Nita Lowey was born in the Bronx, raised her family in Queens, and now lives in upper-crust Harrison in Westchester. She went to work for Mario Cuomo in 1975, after he was appointed secretary of state by Governor Hugh Carey; she was an assistant secretary of state when she decided to run for Congress in 1988. She had serious competition. In the primary, she beat Hamilton Fish III, son and grandson of Republican Hudson River congressmen, and as a former publisher of the *Nation*, considerably more radical than Lowey; she won 44%–36%. Then she beat by 50%–47% Joseph DioGuardi, a two-term incumbent who trumpeted his experience as a CPA and argued that government should be run like a business; she was helped by charges that a car dealer involved in DioGuardi's campaign had been promising to reimburse his employees for $1,000 contributions. This was a race in which both candidates spent over $1 million, Lowey spending $657,000 in personal funds. Lowey has made a liberal record in the House, pushing through bills to expand preventive health care for the elderly and to deter on student loan defaults. She won reelection easily in 1990 against an underfinanced opponent. In 1992, DioGuardi ran again, preaching congressional reform and citing his book *Unaccountable Congress*. Lowey won by just 53%–47% in Westchester and lost the Bronx 64%–36%. But she carried the new Queens portion of the district by 71%–29% for a 56%–44% win, thanks to redistricting.

Lowey has been a team player and a minor part of the Democratic leadership in the House. After the 1992 election she won a seat on the Appropriations Committee.

The People: Pop. 1990: 581,021; 17% age 65+; 74% White; 7% Black; 8% Asian; 3% Other; 10% Hispanic origin. Voting age pop.: 469,196; 7% Black; 10% Hispanic origin. Households: 56% married couple families; 23% married couple fams. w. children; 54% college educ.; median household income: $43,754; per capita income: $24,392; median gross rent: $594; median house value: $286,000.

1992 Presidential Vote			1988 Presidential Vote		
Clinton (D)	117,572	(50%)	Bush (R)	123,526	(53%)
Bush (R)	94,652	(40%)	Dukakis (D)	107,548	(47%)
Perot (I)	21,986	(9%)			

Rep. Nita M. Lowey (D)

Elected 1988; b. July 5, 1937, New York City; home, Harrison; Mt. Holyoke Col., B.A. 1959; Jewish, married (Stephen).

Career: Asst. for Econ. Devel. and Neighborhood Preservation, NY Secy. of St., and Dep. Dir., Division of Econ. Opportunity, 1975–85; NY Asst. Secy. of St., 1985–87.

Offices: 1424 LHOB 20515, 202-225-6506. Also 222 Mamaroneck Ave., White Plains 10605, 914-428-1707; and 97–45 Queens Blvd., #505, Rego Park 11374, 718-897-3602.

Committees: *Appropriations* (29th of 37 D): Foreign Operations, Export Financing and Related Programs; Labor, Health and Human Services, and Education.

Group Ratings

	ADA	ACLU	COPE	CDF	CFA	LCV	ACU	NTLC	NSI	COC	CEI
1992	100	100	92	100	93	88	0	0	30	25	10
1991	100	—	100	100	78	85	0	—	—	20	10

National Journal Ratings

	1991 LIB — 1991 CONS		1992 LIB — 1992 CONS	
Economic	88% —	0%	89% —	9%
Social	88% —	0%	81% —	17%
Foreign	92% —	0%	82% —	16%

Key Votes of the 102d Congress

1. Ban Striker Replace	FOR	5. Handgun Wait/7-Day FOR	9. Use Force in Gulf AGN
2. $ for Homeownership	AGN	6. Overseas Mil. Abortion FOR	10. US Mil. Abroad $ Cut FOR
3. Tax Rich/Cut Mid Cls.	FOR	7. Obscn. Art NEA $ Ban AGN	11. Limit SDI Funds FOR
4. FY93/$15B Def. Cut	FOR	8. Death Pen. from Jury AGN	12. Cuba Trade Embargo AGN

Key Votes of the 103d Congress

1. Family Leave   FOR   2. Deficit Reduction   FOR   3. Stimulus Plan   FOR

Election Results

1992 general	Nita M. Lowey (D)...................	115,841	(56%)	($1,277,433)
	Joseph J. DioGuardi (R-C-RTL)	92,687	(44%)	($583,905)
1992 primary	Nita M. Lowey (D), unopposed			
1990 general	Nita M. Lowey (D)....................	82,203	(63%)	($911,766)
(NY 20)	Glenn D. Bellitto (R)	35,575	(27%)	($15,356)
	John M. Schafer (C-RTL)	13,030	(10%)	

NINETEENTH DISTRICT

The great interior of America can be said to begin where the Hudson River squeezes through the chain of Appalachian ridges at the Hudson Highlands. This chokepoint was the barrier to British military power during the Revolutionary War, when American forces built a chain across the river to keep the British from sailing north; it was over control of this part of the Hudson that Benedict Arnold betrayed his country, and it was here that the new nation built its Military Academy high on the cliffs at West Point. The Hudson was the impetus for the builders of the Erie Canal and the water-level New York Central, the great projects that made New York City the port of the American interior, as well as the builders of the Croton Aqueduct not far away, which provided the water without which New York could not grow—and also provided a way for the first cockroaches to reach the city.

The lower Hudson was Dutch country, with ancient estates like now restored Philipsburg Manor and Washington Irving country in Tarrytown. In the late 19th Century, the ridges east of the Lower Hudson were first the site of great estates of New York's very rich and then became high-income suburbs: colonial-style Bedford, woodsy Chappaqua, John Cheever's Ossining. And in the mid-20th Century, these hills became home to some of America's leading corporations. *Reader's Digest* had built its colonial-style campus north of Pleasantville as early as the 1930s; General Foods moved to the north side of White Plains in the 1950s; soon after, not far from the Cross-Westchester Expressway, IBM and Pepsico and Texaco built headquarters.

The 19th Congressional District of New York covers much of the lower Hudson. It reaches south to take in part of White Plains and the corporate territory nearby, and includes northern Westchester County—now, for all its rural look, with almost as many people as the population-losing suburbs nearer New York City. The 19th runs north across towns filling up with middle-income public and corporate employees seeking reasonably priced housing in safe areas, up to the old city of Poughkeepsie on the Hudson and the valleys of Millbrook and Amenia inland. The 19th crosses the Hudson where the rebels' chain did, by West Point and the Storm King Highway, and runs inland in Orange County. IBM, with its headquarters in Armonk, a research center in Yorktown Heights, and major operations in Wappingers Falls, has been a major area employer, and its growth and policy of lifetime employment have contributed greatly to local prosperity; now, with IBM threatened by losses and cutting its payroll, times may be tougher. Politically, sentiments here run counter to what might be expected. The older communities, with their well-educated and liberally inclined residents, have been historically Republican but are more inclined now to the Democrats. The newer communities, with upwardly striving people often disgusted by the crime and cultural disorder of New York City, may be filled with ancestral Democrats but are trending Republican.

Hamilton Fish, the congressman from the 19th District, bears a fine old political name made famous by two of his ancestors. One Hamilton Fish was a governor and senator, and Ulysses S. Grant's secretary of state. Another, the current incumbent's father, represented much of this area in the House from 1920 to 1944 and was a bitter critic and enemy of the Hudson Valley's

Franklin D. Roosevelt, who would not allow him in the White House, even when he was ranking Republican on the Foreign Affairs Committee; he died in January 1991 at age 102, missing by five days the longevity record for members of Congress set by California Senator Cornelius Cole (1822–1924). And another Hamilton Fish, the current 19th's congressman's son, ran for the House in Westchester as a Democrat in 1988 and lost the primary to Nita Lowey.

Today's Congressman Fish is now one of the more senior Republicans in the House, first elected in 1968 when he beat none other than future Watergate burglar G. Gordon Liddy by 8,000 votes in the Republican primary, and John Dyson, later originator of the "I Love New York" ads, 48%–46% in the general. Rather market-oriented on economics, more liberal on cultural matters, Fish's main role in the House is as ranking Republican on the House Judiciary Committee. Fish is notably less conservative than most other committee Republicans, and has played a pivotal role in reaching compromises that can get some crucial Republican support. Examples include the Fair Housing Act of 1988 and the Americans With Disabilities Act in 1990; probably neither would have passed without Fish's work. He also supported the Civil Rights Act of 1991, denounced by many Republicans as encouraging racial quotas. With a Democratic president and congressional majorities, Fish's compromise role may be less crucial, but he continues to be a workhorse on legal issues. He has expressed skepticism about major league baseball's antitrust exemption, has supported reauthorization of the independent counsel law but with new safeguards, has worked for civil justice reform. He opposed many restraints proposed by Chairman Jack Brooks on the Baby Bells, has worked to preserve most of the insurance industry's antitrust exemptions and wants to allow public pension fund managers to serve on creditors' committees in bankruptcy proceedings.

Fish has long been reelected easily. In 1992, his margin was narrower than usual, 60%–40%. Much of Westchester had been added to the 19th by redistricting, parts hard hit by IBM's troubles. Fish carried Westchester by only 54%–46%, while winning with 66% in the rest of the district. He could conceivably have serious competition in the future or could decide, as he approaches 70, to retire.

The People: Pop. 1990: 580,386; 30% rural; 11% age 65+; 86% White; 7% Black; 2% Asian; 1% Other; 5% Hispanic origin. Voting age pop.: 444,175; 7% Black; 5% Hispanic origin. Households: 64% married couple families; 31% married couple fams. w. children; 57% college educ.; median household income: $50,239; per capita income: $22,458; median gross rent: $653; median house value: $198,300.

1992 Presidential Vote

Bush (R) 109,965 (42%)
Clinton (D) 104,949 (40%)
Perot (I) 45,088 (17%)

1988 Presidential Vote

Bush (R) 142,996 (60%)
Dukakis (D) 94,387 (40%)

Rep. Hamilton Fish, Jr. (R)

Elected 1968; b. June 3, 1926, Washington, D.C.; home, Millbrook; Harvard, A.B. 1949, N.Y.U., LL.B. 1957; Episcopalian; married (Mary Ann).

Career: Naval Reserves 1944–46 (WWII); Vice Consul, U.S. Foreign Svc., Ireland, 1951–53; Practicing atty. 1957–68; Cnsl., NY Assembly Judiciary Cmte., 1961; Dutchess Cnty. Civil Defense Dir., 1967–68.

Offices: 2354 RHOB 20515, 202-225-5441. Also 70 Gleneida Ave., Carmel 10512, 914-225-5200; 2 Church St., Ossining 10562, 914-762-7561; and 1440 Rte. 9, Wappingers Falls 12590, 914-297-5711.

Committees: *Judiciary* (RMM of 14 R): Economic and Commercial Law (RMM); Intellectual Property and Judicial Administration.

Group Ratings

	ADA	ACLU	COPE	CDF	CFA	LCV	ACU	NTLC	NSI	COC	CEI
1992	40	74	58	60	60	81	48	55	100	43	54
1991	45	—	75	70	50	85	35	—	—	40	34

National Journal Ratings

	1991 LIB — 1991 CONS		1992 LIB — 1992 CONS	
Economic	44%	— 56%	33%	— 67%
Social	56%	— 43%	50%	— 50%
Foreign	26%	— 70%	38%	— 56%

Key Votes of the 102d Congress

1. Ban Striker Replace	FOR	5. Handgun Wait/7-Day	FOR	9. Use Force in Gulf	FOR
2. $ for Homeownership	FOR	6. Overseas Mil. Abortion	AGN	10. US Mil. Abroad $ Cut	AGN
3. Tax Rich/Cut Mid Cls.	AGN	7. Obscn. Art NEA $ Ban	AGN	11. Limit SDI Funds	FOR
4. FY93/$15B Def. Cut	AGN	8. Death Pen. from Jury	AGN	12. Cuba Trade Embargo	FOR

Key Votes of the 103d Congress

1. Family Leave	FOR	2. Deficit Reduction	AGN	3. Stimulus Plan	AGN

Election Results

1992 general	Hamilton Fish, Jr. (R-C)	139,610	(60%)	($617,832)
	Neil McCarthy (D)	92,854	(40%)	($132,279)
1992 primary	Hamilton Fish, Jr. (R), unopposed			
1990 general	Hamilton Fish, Jr. (R-C)	99,866	(71%)	($411,614)
(NY 21)	Richard L. Barbuto (D)	34,128	(24%)	($729)
	Richard S. Curtin (RTL)	5,925	(4%)	

TWENTIETH DISTRICT

From Sunnyside, the whimsical house Washington Irving built in Tarrytown near the country he immortalized as Sleepy Hollow, you can see across the waters of the Tappan Zee, the widest point of the Hudson, and get a sense of how the land looked when first settled by Dutchmen. All around is Irving country—the old towns of Tarrytown, Irvington, Dobbs Ferry and Hastings-on-Hudson, now comfortably affluent suburbs. On the other side of the Tappan Zee is Rockland County, a stretch of suburbs between the Hudson and the Ramapos, the first Appalachian chain west of New York. First settled by Dutchmen, Rockland then was studded by little towns that grew up as if 1,000 miles from Gotham, but have thrived on the actual proximity: the town of Nyack here was the home of the actress Helen Hayes, and James A. Farley, Franklin Roosevelt's chief political major domo and Democratic National chairman, was from Stony Point just below the Hudson Highlands.

The 20th Congressional District of New York spans the Tappan Zee, connecting most of the Irving suburbs with Rockland County and stepping over the Ramapos 120 miles inland to the border of Pennsylvania. Past the Ramapos is most of Orange County, New York's second fastest-growing county in the 1980s, where old villages between mountains and farms on the nation's biggest deposit of muck soil outside the Everglades have been flanked with new modest income subdivisions. Farther out, past the Shawangunk Mountains, is Sullivan County and the Catskills Borscht Belt resort district, a Jewish resort area with huge kosher hotels since the late 19th Century. Politically, this area has been trending Republican, as old Upstate-minded residents are joined by newcomers fleeing the city, though Westchester has been leaning somewhat Democratic.

The 20th's congressman, Republican Benjamin Gilman, is a professional politician who served six years in the Assembly before he was elected to the House in 1972. Gilman is moderate on economics and foreign policy, rather liberal on cultural issues; he is pleasant and seems to arouse little animosity. In 1993, Gilman became the ranking Republican on the Foreign Affairs Committee, and potentially a member of considerable influence, in position with a few others to bestow or withhold the label of "bipartisan" on the foreign initiatives of a Democratic administration. Gilman has long been known as a strong supporter of Israel and an opponent of most Arab arms deals. He was stoutly in favor of the Gulf war resolution. He has championed minority religious believers' rights in the former Soviet Union and in June 1993, co-sponsored a foreign aid amendment to end the arms embargo against Bosnia. The proposal, Gilman said, "signals President Clinton that he must . . . live up to his pledge to help the Bosnian Muslims defend themselves against the Serbian onslaughts." He is working with Chairman Lee Hamilton on reauthorizing the foreign aid law. He has had a hand in recent drug legislation, advocating, for example, a coordinated anti-drug effort between the U.S. and the U.N. or O.A.S. and, on a local level, getting Westchester County designated as a target drug area. He is author of a bill allowing federal agencies to pay back student loans for students that agree to work at the agency for a specific length of time.

Gilman first won the seat in 1972, beating ultra-liberal John Dow. Redistricting in 1982 gave Gilman his one difficult race, when the Irving country was connected to Rockland and he faced Republican-turned-Democrat Peter Peyser; Gilman won 53%–42%. More recently he has won easily without serious opposition.

The People: Pop. 1990: 580,025; 23% rural; 11% age 65+; 83% White; 8% Black; 3% Asian; 2% Other; 6% Hispanic origin. Voting age pop.: 428,788; 8% Black; 6% Hispanic origin. Households: 65% married couple families; 32% married couple fams. w. children; 54% college educ.; median household income: $47,107; per capita income: $19,680; median gross rent: $659; median house value: $193,500.

1992 Presidential Vote

Clinton (D)	116,694	(45%)
Bush (R)	107,107	(41%)
Perot (I)	37,014	(14%)

1988 Presidential Vote

Bush (R)	135,464	(58%)
Dukakis (D)	99,201	(42%)

Rep. Benjamin A. Gilman (R)

Elected 1972; b. Dec. 6, 1922, Poughkeepsie; home, Middletown; U. of PA, B.S. 1946, NY Law Schl., LL.B. 1950; Jewish; married (Rita Gail).

Career: Army Air Corps, 1942–45 (WWII); NY Asst. Atty. Gen., 1953–55; Practicing atty., 1955–72; Atty., NY Temporary Comm. on the Courts; NY Assembly, 1967–72.

Offices: 2185 RHOB 20515, 202-225-3776. Also 407 E. Main St., P.O. Box 358, Middletown 10940, 914-343-6666; 377 Rte. 59, Monsey 10952, 914-357-9000; and 32 Main St., Hastings-on-Hudson 10706, 914-478-5550.

Committees: *Foreign Affairs* (RMM of 18 R): Europe and the Middle East (RMM). *Post Office and Civil Service* (2d of 15 D): Postal Operations and Services.

Group Ratings

	ADA	ACLU	COPE	CDF	CFA	LCV	ACU	NTLC	NSI	COC	CEI
1992	75	78	92	80	100	81	32	50	90	50	37
1991	60	—	92	90	61	54	30	—	—	20	26

National Journal Ratings

	1991 LIB — 1991 CONS	1992 LIB — 1992 CONS
Economic	61% — 36%	43% — 57%
Social	58% — 40%	71% — 28%
Foreign	33% — 66%	38% — 56%

Key Votes of the 102d Congress

1. Ban Striker Replace	FOR	5. Handgun Wait/7-Day	FOR	9. Use Force in Gulf	FOR
2. $ for Homeownership	FOR	6. Overseas Mil. Abortion	FOR	10. US Mil. Abroad $ Cut	AGN
3. Tax Rich/Cut Mid Cls.	AGN	7. Obscn. Art NEA $ Ban	AGN	11. Limit SDI Funds	FOR
4. FY93/$15B Def. Cut	AGN	8. Death Pen. from Jury	FOR	12. Cuba Trade Embargo	FOR

Key Votes of the 103d Congress

1. Family Leave   FOR   2. Deficit Reduction   AGN   3. Stimulus Plan   AGN

Election Results

1992 general	Benjamin A. Gilman (R)	150,301	(66%)	($576,538)
	Jonathan L. Levine (D)	66,826	(29%)	($27,833)
	Robert F. Garrison (RTL)	10,204	(5%)	
1992 primary	Benjamin A. Gilman (R), unopposed			
1990 general	Benjamin A. Gilman (R)	95,495	(69%)	($497,635)
(NY 22)	John G. Dow (D)	37,034	(27%)	($3,473)
	Margaret M. Beirne (RTL)	6,656	(5%)	

TWENTY-FIRST DISTRICT

Albany, as readers of its novelist laureate William Kennedy know, is within living memory an antique city. Its solid rowhouses show its 19th Century prosperity; its once teeming lumberyards and railroad car shops, old restaurants and hotels have the patina of age and the accumulated grime of decades of coal smoke burned during six-month-long winters. Its history is traceable back to 1624, when the Dutch built Fort Orange on the banks of the Hudson so seagoing ships could dock at the edge of the great gloomy forests near the confluence of the Hudson and the Mohawk—the natural crossroads of Upstate New York even before the building of the Erie Canal and the New York Central Railroad. This was one of America's early industrial centers. Troy, a few miles up river, was a steel town rivaling Pittsburgh in the 1840s, and later the leading producer of detachable collars; Cohoes, at the junction of the Hudson and the Mohawk, became a leading textile producer; Schenectady, a few miles up the Mohawk, was the site of Charles Steinmetz's fabled General Electric laboratories and has been a big GE town ever since. Albany was one of America's biggest lumber towns as well as the state capital.

Albany continues to have one of the nation's most famed Democratic political machines, dating back to 1921, when Daniel O'Connell and his brothers and local aristocrat Edwin Corning took control of City Hall. They never really relinquished it: Daniel O'Connell died in 1977 at age 91, still boss after 56 years, and his early partner's son, Erastus Corning II, was mayor from 1942 until his death in 1983. The machine was sustained by legions of city and county employees, by a certain creativity when it came to counting votes, by the raffish atmosphere found in the speakeasies of so many cities during Prohibition and which lingered in Albany for decades after. Curiously, the machine made possible the transformation of antique Albany into the shiny new metropolis it is today: Mayor Corning provided financing for Nelson Rockefeller's monumental South Mall, expressways were built, the old Union Station was spruced up, and yuppies began buying and renovating old townhouses. These days, the Albany machine is battered in some elections and can't always control the suburbs as it once could Albany; but it clings to power in the H. H. Richardson City Hall facing the gaudy State House.

The 21st Congressional District of New York includes all of Albany and Schenectady Counties, plus Troy on the Hudson's east bank, and the carpet-making town of Amsterdam and Montgomery County on the Mohawk. More than half its votes are cast in Albany County, and it is a solidly Democratic district. It has also been a Democratic machine district, as was shown in 1988, the last time the seat changed hands. Four days after the July filing deadline and on the last day for withdrawal, 30-year incumbent Democrat Samuel Stratton announced he was retiring for health reasons, giving the Democratic machine a chance to name a replacement. It promptly picked Assemblyman Michael McNulty, whose roots in Albany politics go back to his grandfather, who served as Albany County sheriff, as did his father, who was also mayor. Michael McNulty was first elected to office in 1969, at 22, and served 13 years as town supervisor and mayor in the industrial suburb of Green Island; he was elected to the New York Assembly in 1982; being in Congress is a fulfillment of his family's and his own ambition. McNulty won the 1988 general election by 62%–38% against a venture capital specialist who attacked him for avoiding the issues and for having been chosen by party bosses rather than primary voters. He has not been seriously challenged since.

McNulty is hard-working, serious, abstemious, pleasant to his staff, a conscientious campaigner, one of those members who likes to preside over the House and does so with ascetic rigor. He is liberal on economics, pro-life on abortion, tends to support defense spending and an internationalist foreign policy. He served for four years on the Armed Services Committee, but in 1993, with defense spending down, shifted to Ways and Means.

The People: Pop. 1990: 580,320; 15% rural; 15% age 65+; 90% White; 6% Black; 2% Asian; 1% Other; 2% Hispanic origin. Voting age pop.: 451,451; 5% Black; 2% Hispanic origin. Households: 50% married couple families; 22% married couple fams. w. children; 48% college educ.; median household income: $31,489; per capita income: $15,304; median gross rent: $453; median house value: $98,800.

1992 Presidential Vote			**1988 Presidential Vote**		
Clinton (D)	140,251	(48%)	Dukakis (D)	154,308	(56%)
Bush (R)	99,094	(34%)	Bush (R)	121,617	(44%)
Perot (I)	51,086	(17%)			

Rep. Michael R. McNulty (D)

Elected 1988; b. Sept. 16, 1947, Troy; home, Green Island; Holy Cross Col., B.A. 1969; Catholic; married (Nancy Ann).

Career: Green Island Supervisor, 1969–77; Green Island Mayor, 1977–83; NY Assembly, 1983–88.

Offices: 217 CHOB 20515, 202-225-5076. Also U.S. Post Office, Jay St., Schenectady 12305, 518-374-4547; O'Brien Fed. Bldg., #827; Albany 12207, 518-465-0700; 9 Market St., Amsterdam 12010, 518-843-3400; and 33 2d St., Troy 12180, 518-271-0822.

Committees: *Ways and Means* (20th of 24 D): Select Revenue Measures; Trade.

Group Ratings

	ADA	ACLU	COPE	CDF	CFA	LCV	ACU	NTLC	NSI	COC	CEI
1992	90	87	91	100	80	25	13	15	70	38	9
1991	80	—	100	100	78	54	10	—	—	10	9

National Journal Ratings

	1991 LIB — 1991 CONS		1992 LIB — 1992 CONS	
Economic	88%	— 0%	83%	— 13%
Social	71%	— 28%	60%	— 40%
Foreign	62%	— 36%	44%	— 50%

Key Votes of the 102d Congress

1. Ban Striker Replace	FOR	5. Handgun Wait/7-Day	FOR	9. Use Force in Gulf	FOR
2. $ for Homeownership	AGN	6. Overseas Mil. Abortion	AGN	10. US Mil. Abroad $ Cut	FOR
3. Tax Rich/Cut Mid Cls.	FOR	7. Obscn. Art NEA $ Ban	FOR	11. Limit SDI Funds	AGN
4. FY93/$15B Def. Cut	FOR	8. Death Pen. from Jury	AGN	12. Cuba Trade Embargo	FOR

Key Votes of the 103d Congress

1. Family Leave	FOR	2. Deficit Reduction	FOR	3. Stimulus Plan	FOR

Election Results

1992 general	Michael R. McNulty (D-C)	166,371	(63%)	($252,821)
	Nancy Norman (R-L)	91,184	(34%)	
	Other	7,723	(3%)	
1992 primary	Michael R. McNulty (D), unopposed			
1990 general	Michael R. McNulty (D-C)	117,239	(64%)	($149,204)
(NY 23)	Margaret B. Buhrmaster (R)	65,760	(36%)	($23,299)

TWENTY-SECOND DISTRICT

The Hudson River, an arm of the ocean and an avenue of commerce in colonial days, an inspiration to artists, is still one of America's great sights, though it is no longer central, as it was until not so long ago, in the nation's consciousness and politics. The classic mansions overlooking the River, like Clermont, whose builder Robert Livingston financed Robert Fulton's first steamboat, and Montgomery Place, built by Janet Livingston Montgomery, the widow of the general who captured Quebec in 1775, are reminders of the cool serenity of the 18th Century mind and the daring nature of its spirit. Robert Livingston administered the first oath of office to George Washington in 1789 and helped negotiate the Louisiana Purchase in 1803; it was on a visit to his lands in the 1790s that James Madison and Aaron Burr welded the Virginia-New York alliance that set the course of American political history. The Hudson was also a center of America in the romantic era: from Frederick Church's Moorish mansion, Olana, you can see the still unspoiled river landscape that inspired his art and that of others of the Hudson River school of painters. The Hudson gave birth also to our passionate party politics: nearby is Kinderhook, home of Martin Van Buren, the innkeeper's son who in alliance with Andrew Jackson invented the torchlight parade, the national party convention and, some argue, the Democratic Party itself. Later in the 19th Century the Hudson was also lined with the palaces of the nation's first great millionaires and the comfortable country houses of New York's gentry. In one of the latter, Springwood in Hyde Park, Franklin Roosevelt was born and lived; this politician, who expanded government at home and was the victorious Commander-in-Chief of American military forces throughout the world, was most comfortable looking out over his sloping lawn down to the river that he remembered iceboating on in the winters of the 1880s.

The 22d Congressional District of New York includes much of the Hudson Valley, the grand river south of Albany and the smaller river, freshly fed by the Adirondacks, to the north; for 1992 it extends even further north to include most of Essex County and Lake Placid. Much of the district, just outside the old manufacturing city of Troy and the still grandly 19th Century racing center Saratoga Springs, is essentially suburban Albany, and has been heavily Republican since the late 19th Century (Roosevelt never carried his home territory except when he ran for state Senate in 1910). The congressman from the 22d, Gerald Solomon, is a strong partisan Republican, a veteran of the Marine Corps and insurance businessman in Glens Falls who was elected Township Supervisor in 1966, New York assemblyman in 1972 and congressman in 1978. Since 1991 Solomon has been ranking Republican on the Rules Committee and so plays a role in practically every issue that comes before the House. He has a solidly conservative voting record, except occasionally on economic issues (in March 1993 he introduced a plan for higher taxes on $200,000 incomes plus $190 billion in new spending cuts), and can be an acerbic partisan on procedure. Solomon, who left college and then enlisted in the Marines when the Korean War began, has sponsored a number of measures cracking down on college students: his Solomon Amendment in the early 1980s cut off college aid for young men who had not registered for the draft; a 1990 amendment cut off highway funding for states that don't suspend drug offenders' driver's licenses; a 1992 measure cut off college aid for first-time drug offenders who don't attend drug counseling and second-time drug offenders for two years. Why should people who break laws get government subsidies? he argues. Solomon can also be generous to those who do right; as ranking Republican on Veterans' Affairs he helped pass the 1984 G.I. Bill of Rights, which creatively increased veterans' benefits and helped attract good-quality recruits to the volunteer military that performed so well in the Gulf war.

With Bill Clinton in the White House and Democrats in firm control of the House, Solomon was a lead spokesman for Republicans in early 1993. He denounced the Democrats' plan to give floor votes to the five representatives of the territories and District of Columbia, and got a partial retreat; he pressed loudly for a line-item veto, denouncing the Democrats' version as insufficient. In March 1993 he objected vehemently on the floor when Rules Committee Democrat Louise Slaughter made an unusual parliamentary motion to cut off a colloquy between Solomon and Republican Robert Walker. "You had better not do that, ma'am," he said, in words he later edited out of the *Congressional Record*. "You will regret that as long as you live." A later statement out of his office said, "Mr. Solomon doesn't take that kind of treatment from anybody, and lets them know about it." It is not likely to be the last fiery exchange between Solomon and Rules Committee Democrats. Of course, if Republicans ever win a majority in the House, Solomon would become Rules Chairman, with interesting results. He is reelected every two years routinely.

The People: Pop. 1990: 580,522; 67% rural; 13% age 65+; 96% White; 2% Black; 1% Asian; 2% Hispanic origin. Voting age pop.: 434,410; 2% Black; 2% Hispanic origin. Households: 62% married couple families; 30% married couple fams. w. children; 46% college educ.; median household income: $33,306; per capita income: $14,646; median gross rent: $465; median house value: $99,600.

1992 Presidential Vote		
Bush (R)	116,283	(41%)
Clinton (D)	99,984	(36%)
Perot (I)	62,533	(22%)

1988 Presidential Vote		
Bush (R)	146,610	(60%)
Dukakis (D)	98,001	(40%)

Rep. Gerald B. H. Solomon (R)

Elected 1978; b. Aug. 14, 1930, Okeechobee, FL; home, Queensbury; Siena Col., 1948–49, St. Lawrence U., 1953–54; Presbyterian; married (Freda).

Career: Marine Corps, 1951–52; Founding partner, Assoc. of Glens Falls Insurance co., 1964–78; Queensbury Town Supervisor, 1966–77; NY Assembly, 1972–78.

Offices: 2265 RHOB 20515, 202-225-5614. Also Gaslight Sq., Saratoga Springs 12866, 518-587-9800; 419 Warren St., Hudson 12534, 518-828-1657; and 21 Bay St., Glens Falls 12801, 518-792-3031.

Committees: *Rules* (RMM of 4 R): Rules of the House. *Joint Committee on the Organization of Congress* (9th of 12).

Group Ratings

	ADA	ACLU	COPE	CDF	CFA	LCV	ACU	NTLC	NSI	COC	CEI
1992	15	19	58	20	20	19	96	90	100	63	82
1991	15	—	45	30	33	8	90	—	—	56	84

National Journal Ratings

	1991 LIB — 1991 CONS		1992 LIB — 1992 CONS	
Economic	32% —	67%	31% —	68%
Social	0% —	84%	18% —	81%
Foreign	0% —	88%	0% —	82%

Key Votes of the 102d Congress

1. Ban Striker Replace	FOR	5. Handgun Wait/7-Day	AGN	9. Use Force in Gulf	FOR
2. $ for Homeownership	FOR	6. Overseas Mil. Abortion	AGN	10. US Mil. Abroad $ Cut	AGN
3. Tax Rich/Cut Mid Cls.	AGN	7. Obscn. Art NEA $ Ban	FOR	11. Limit SDI Funds	AGN
4. FY93/$15B Def. Cut	AGN	8. Death Pen. from Jury	FOR	12. Cuba Trade Embargo	FOR

Key Votes of the 103d Congress

1. Family Leave	FOR	2. Deficit Reduction	AGN	3. Stimulus Plan	AGN

Election Results

1992 general	Gerald B. H. Solomon (R-C-RTL)	164,436	(65%)	($286,286)
	David Roberts (D)	86,896	(35%)	($32,189)
1992 primary	Gerald B. H. Solomon (R), unopposed			
1990 general	Gerald B. H. Solomon (R-C-RTL)	121,206	(68%)	($240,615)
(NY 24)	Bob Lawrence (D)	56,671	(32%)	($95,100)

TWENTY-THIRD DISTRICT

One of the first American frontiers was the Mohawk River Valley of Upstate New York, which remained static for 150 years: from the establishment of Fort Orange in 1624 in what now is Albany until the Revolutionary War, white settlers did not dare move west along the Mohawk. The British used their Iroquois allies as a buffer against the French and in return kept New England Yankees from moving westward. Only after the French were driven from the colonies in 1759 did the pressures for westward settlement prevail; the British tried to keep their word to the Indians, but once the Revolutionary War started, the Iroquois dominion ended.

This is the background of *Drums Along the Mohawk* and of James Fenimore Cooper's Leatherstocking Tales. But there is little in these rolling hills today to evoke the bloody violence whose conclusion made possible the digging of the Erie Canal and the building of the New York Central. As migration slowed and trade increased, the Mohawk Valley became one of the nation's early industrial centers. The little Oneida County hamlets of Utica and Rome, where the canal builders had to dig through the route's highest ground, became sizable factory towns; even the utopian Oneida Community, believers in plural marriage and communal ownership, kept open a stainless steel factory. First settled by New England Yankees, these towns attracted a new wave of immigration from the Atlantic coast in the early 20th Century. Today they are the most heavily Italian and Polish-American communities between Albany and Buffalo; politically, they are marginally Republican, nearly voting for Bill Clinton in 1992.

The 23d Congressional District of New York, in the Mohawk Valley, is centered on Utica and Rome in Oneida County and includes a row of more sparsely settled counties to the south. Here the hilly land has an early 19th Century cast, in places like Cooperstown, the supposed birthplace of baseball in 1839 and certainly one of the loveliest and best-preserved small towns in America, and Pindars Corners, the crossroads where Senator Daniel Patrick Moynihan has a farm and a 19th Century schoolhouse to which he repairs periodically and writes books and articles. The 23d District is ancestrally Republican; indeed, Madison County here was one of the hotbeds of abolitionism in the 1850s. But it is also an area that feels bypassed by more recent economic growth and in need of government assistance and sustenance.

The congressman from the 23d is Sherwood Boehlert, a Republican with deep roots in Oneida County and a distinctive figure on Capitol Hill. Boehlert worked for his two predecessors in Congress, then was elected Oneida County Executive in 1978 and won the House seat in 1982. He has worked in government as much as politics, and does not share the free market economists' disdain for its works. His record is moderate on economics and foreign policy, downright liberal on some cultural issues. He has labored to maintain subsidies to dairy farmers and got equal treatment with California dairy farmers in the 1990 farm bill. He wrote tough acid rain provisions into the 1990 Clean Air Act. He has taken liberal stands on civil rights, abortion and gun control, but voted for the Gulf war resolution and the flag amendment and sponsored Pledge of Allegiance Day (the Pledge was written by Francis Bellamy in Rome, New York, in 1892). But he is revolted by the cultural and religious right: "I wanted to throw up about every five minutes in Houston," was his reaction to the 1992 Republican National Convention. He often decries House Republicans' confrontational tactics and occasionally gets them to back off, as when some wanted to walk out rather than vote on Democrats' proposal for a House administrator.

But Boehlert is not one of those Republicans, once common in the Northeast, who are crypto-Democrats. He warned against overzealous defense cuts and domestic spending increases by the Clinton Administration, but was one of three Republicans to vote for the Clinton economic stimulus plan in March 1993. And he is likely to go his own way, as on his latest great crusade: opposition to the Superconducting Supercollider. From his seat on the Science Committee and on the floor, he has attacked the Supercollider for "siphoning money from the bulk of American science" for a project of marginal worth, taking on both the Bush and Clinton Administrations and powerful Texas politicians of both parties. Boehlert sometimes ranges far afield, trying to stop the Energy Department from making sole-source contracts overseas; he looks very carefully after Griffiss Air Force Base, Rome's largest employer, which he saved from closure in 1991 but which was targeted again in 1993.

Boehlert is usually reelected easily. Nothing was noteworthy about the 1992 election except the identity of the Right To Life Party nominee, Randall Terry, head of Operation Rescue. Terry got 4% of the votes, the Democrat got 28% and Boehlert won with 64%.

The People: Pop. 1990: 580,259; 55% rural; 15% age 65+; 95% White; 3% Black; 1% Asian; 1% Other; 1% Hispanic origin. Voting age pop.: 435,794; 3% Black; 1% Hispanic origin. Households: 58% married couple families; 27% married couple fams. w. children; 40% college educ.; median household income: $26,155; per capita income: $11,792; median gross rent: $366; median house value: $67,800.

1992 Presidential Vote			1988 Presidential Vote		
Bush (R)	99,495	(40%)	Bush (R)	128,287	(55%)
Clinton (D)	92,554	(37%)	Dukakis (D)	103,327	(45%)
Perot (I)	55,887	(22%)			

Rep. Sherwood Boehlert (R)

Elected 1982; b. Sept. 28, 1936, Utica; home, New Hartford; Utica Col., B.A. 1961; Catholic; married (Marianne).

Career: Army, 1956–58; P.R. Mgr., Wyandotte Chemicals Corp., 1961–64; A.A., U.S. Rep. Alexander Pirnie, 1964–72; A.A., U.S. Rep. Donald Mitchell, 1973–79; Oneida Cnty. Exec., 1978–82.

Offices: 1127 LHOB, 202-225-3665. Also 10 Broad St., #200, Utica 13501, 315-793-8146; 41 S. Main St., Oneonta 13820, 607-432-5524; and 42 S. Broad St., Norwich 13815 607-336-7160.

Committees: *Post Office and Civil Service* (8th of 9 R): Oversight and Investigations (RMM). *Public Works and Transportation* (4th of 24 R): Aviation; Economic Development; Water Resources and Environment (RMM). *Science, Space and Technology* (3d of 22 R): Science (RMM).

Group Ratings

	ADA	ACLU	COPE	CDF	CFA	LCV	ACU	NTLC	NSI	COC	CEI
1992	75	70	75	60	80	88	40	45	100	50	34
1991	45	—	75	90	56	77	40	—	—	40	26

National Journal Ratings

	1991 LIB — 1991 CONS		1992 LIB — 1992 CONS	
Economic	48% —	51%	39% —	61%
Social	50% —	48%	63% —	37%
Foreign	46% —	53%	44% —	50%

Key Votes of the 102d Congress

1. Ban Striker Replace	FOR	5. Handgun Wait/7-Day	FOR	9. Use Force in Gulf	FOR
2. $ for Homeownership	FOR	6. Overseas Mil. Abortion	FOR	10. US Mil. Abroad $ Cut	AGN
3. Tax Rich/Cut Mid Cls.	AGN	7. Obscn. Art NEA $ Ban	AGN	11. Limit SDI Funds	AGN
4. FY93/$15B Def. Cut	AGN	8. Death Pen. from Jury	FOR	12. Cuba Trade Embargo	FOR

Key Votes of the 103d Congress

1. Family Leave	FOR	2. Deficit Reduction	AGN	3. Stimulus Plan	FOR

Election Results

1992 general	Sherwood Boehlert (R)................ 139,774	(64%)	($372,109)
	Paula DiPerna (D) 61,835	(28%)	($63,220)
	Randall A. Terry (RTL) 8,688	(4%)	
	Geoffrey Grace (C).................... 8,011	(4%)	
	Other................................ 1,354	(1%)	
1992 primary	Sherwood Boehlert (R), unopposed		
1990 general	Sherwood Boehlert (R)................ 91,348	(84%)	($272,533)
(NY 25)	William L. Griffen (L) 17,481	(16%)	($10,577)

TWENTY-FOURTH DISTRICT

The North Country of Upstate New York, thought some early 19th Century visionaries, was the land of the future. Financier Gouveneur Morris, French slave trader James Leray, and Dutch silver speculator David Parish bought up thousands of acres between the Adirondacks and the St. Lawrence River and tried to unload them on farmers unaware of the shortness of the growing season and the unnavigability of the river. They left behind grand mansions, but their hopes for huge profits were frustrated when the Erie Canal turned the stream of settlement westward, and Canadians built their new capital far north of the river and away from the Americans. Northern New York still had its cultural institutions—churches, colleges, public schools—and was not without its business innovations: it was in Watertown in 1878 that 26-year-old Frank Woolworth put a sign over a table of odds and ends that read "Any Article 5 cents," starting America's first retail chain and inventing the concept of discount stores.

More recently, the North Country has looked to government for help. The St. Lawrence Seaway proved too small for most ocean-going freighters and remains frozen three months of the year; the locks are slow and icebreakers would wreck the shoreline. The state government has built prisons in Ogdensburg and Cape Vincent, and private developers have built big malls in Watertown and Massena (attracting Canadians, as New York now has lower taxes). The state maintains Indian reservations, which allow gambling prohibited elsewhere. But the biggest initiative has been the enlargement of Fort Drum, near Watertown, where at the behest of Congressman David Martin the Army in 1985 stationed a new 10,000-person light infantry division and began a $1.3 billion construction program. The Army has long preferred warm weather training sites, but Martin and others pointed out that many potential U.S. adversaries (including the major one at the time) are not located in the tropics.

The 24th Congressional District of New York occupies most of the North Country, from Plattsburgh on Lake Champlain along the St. Lawrence Seaway and over the Adirondacks Forest Preserve to Watertown and Oswego on Lake Ontario. Redistricting added Oswego County and removed part of Herkimer County on the Mohawk River. Just as the lines were being fixed in June 1992, incumbent David Martin announced his retirement. It quickly became apparent that his successor would be John McHugh, a Republican state Senator whose district included most of the 24th District, and who had plenty of financing plus Martin's endorsement. His primary opponent, Morrison Hosley, owned two general stores deep in the Adirondacks and was a strong opponent of abortion. McHugh, who was a staffer for his predecessor in the state Senate for nine years, specialized in dairy issues (New York has long price-fixed dairy products to help farmers) and military bases—both part of the North Country's economic lifeblood. He won the primary 70%–30% and beat his Democratic opponent 61%–24%, with Hosley taking 13% as the Conservative and Right To Life nominee.

In Washington, McHugh retained Martin's administrative assistant and hired Martin himself to monitor the Defense Base Closure and Realignment Commission, obviously to look after Fort

Drum. McHugh got his wish for a seat on the Armed Services Committee, plus one on Government Operations. He seems to be a pragmatic sort of Republican, generally conservative but willing to spend money and ready to deal to help North Country interests.

The People: Pop. 1990: 580,376; 65% rural; 12% age 65+; 95% White; 3% Black; 1% Amer. Indian; 1% Asian; 1% Other; 2% Hispanic origin. Voting age pop.: 426,600; 3% Black; 2% Hispanic origin. Households: 60% married couple families; 31% married couple fams. w. children; 36% college educ.; median household income: $25,687; per capita income: $11,060; median gross rent: $368; median house value: $56,700.

1992 Presidential Vote			1988 Presidential Vote		
Bush (R)	86,311	(38%)	Bush (R)	114,754	(56%)
Clinton (D)	85,078	(37%)	Dukakis (D)	89,384	(44%)
Perot (I)	54,537	(24%)			

Rep. John M. McHugh (R)

Elected 1992; b. Sept. 29, 1948, Watertown; home, Pierrepont Manor; Syracuse U., B.A. 1970, S.U.N.Y., M.S. 1977; Catholic; married (Katharine).

Career: Confidential Asst., Watertown City Mgr., 1971–76; Research and Liaison Chief, NY Sen. Douglas Barclay, 1976–84; NY Senate, 1984–92.

Offices: 416 CHOB 20515, 202-225-4611. Also 404 Key Bank Bldg., 200 Washington St., Watertown 13601, 315-782-3150; 104 W. Utica St., Oswego 13126, 315-342-5664; and 104 Fed. Bldg., Plattsburgh 12901, 518-563-1406.

Committees: *Armed Services* (19th of 22 R): Military Installations and Facilities; Oversight and Investigations. *Government Operations* (13th of 17 R): Employment, Housing and Aviation; Environment, Energy and Natural Resources.

Group Ratings and 102d Congress Votes: Newly Elected

Key Votes of the 103d Congress

1. Family Leave	FOR	2. Deficit Reduction	AGN	3. Stimulus Plan	AGN

Election Results

1992 general	John M. McHugh (R-VRP)	122,257	(61%)	($170,749)
	Margaret M. Ravenscroft (D)	47,675	(24%)	
	Morrison J. Hosley, Jr. (C-RTL)	26,763	(13%)	($149,493)
	Other	4,374	(2%)	
1992 primary	John M. McHugh (R)	21,452	(70%)	
	Morrison J. Hosley, Jr. (R)	9,320	(30%)	
1990 general (NY 26)	David Martin (R-C), unopposed			($59,112)

TWENTY-FIFTH DISTRICT

Syracuse is a middle American city in the middle of Upstate New York, halfway between Albany and Buffalo on the Erie Canal and the old New York Central Railroad, for years the nation's major east-west transportation routes. Built on a swamp that was a salt spring, Syracuse is the home of many inventions: the dental chair, Stickley mission furniture, the drive-in bank teller, the foot measuring devices used in shoe stores. It was one of the first big manufacturers of typewriters and is the site of the New York State Fair. Its agricultural hinterland is rich with specialty crops like wine grapes, and its industrial jobs are mostly high-skill. Syracuse has spread out slowly across the countryside, but there is redevelopment of the Erie Canal waterfront where the city got its start.

The 25th Congressional District of New York includes all of Syracuse and Onondaga County. It goes west to include part of Auburn, the home town of Governor, Senator and Secretary of State William Seward, and south to Cortland County and almost to Binghamton. Seward was the first great Republican politician of Upstate New York, and historically Syracuse is heavily Republican, partly out of antipathy to New York City. But it is also one of the most heavily Catholic cities in the United States and very ethnic, and will at least consider Democrats: Onondaga County gave a plurality to Bill Clinton in 1992 and gave 46% of the its votes to Mario Cuomo in 1990.

The congressman from the 25th District is James Walsh, son of a Syracuse mayor and former congressman. Like other Republicans from economically sluggish Upstate areas, he is open to government intervention in the economy and is proud of his support of the Clean Air Act, the Americans with Disabilities Act and the Civil Rights Act of 1992. He was one of only three House Republicans to support the Clinton stimulus package in March 1993 (a second was Sherwood Boehlert of the next-door 23d District). But he also supports the balanced budget amendment and the line-item veto. Walsh came to the House as almost a professional civic activist: he was a Peace Corps volunteer, a social worker, then worked for New York Telephone and Nynex, who detailed him to a local university, and was elected five times to the Syracuse Common Council. He ran for Congress in 1988 when a Republican incumbent nearly beaten two years earlier decided to retire; in the general Walsh beat Democrat Rosemary Pooler by a solid 57%–42%.

Walsh had a somewhat tougher than expected contest in 1992. Democrat Rhea Jezer, a music teacher and Democratic Party activist, criticized him as a product of nepotism who did "diddly squat" in Washington, attacked his opposition to abortion and, appealing to UAW and other local union members, hit him for voting against plant closing notification and striker replacement laws. Walsh won 56%–44%. In Washington, he campaigned for an Appropriations Committee seat, and prevailed over Susan Molinari of Staten Island; he also got his first choice subcommittee, Agriculture.

The People: Pop. 1990: 580,233; 26% rural; 13% age 65+; 90% White; 7% Black; 1% Amer. Indian; 1% Asian; 1% Hispanic origin. Voting age pop.: 435,738; 5% Black; 1% Hispanic origin. Households: 54% married couple families; 25% married couple fams. w. children; 48% college educ.; median household income: $31,080; per capita income: $14,148; median gross rent: $433; median house value: $77,600.

1992 Presidential Vote

Clinton (D)	108,335	(41%)
Bush (R)	95,476	(36%)
Perot (I)	58,232	(22%)

1988 Presidential Vote

Bush (R)	128,873	(53%)
Dukakis (D)	113,625	(47%)

Rep. James T. Walsh (R)

Elected 1988; b. June 19, 1947, Syracuse; home, Syracuse; St. Bonaventure U., B.A. 1970; Catholic; married (Diane).

Career: Peace Corps, 1970–72; Social worker, Onondaga Cnty. Dept. of Social Svcs., 1972–74; Marketing exec., NYNEX, 1974–88; Syracuse Common Cncl., 1978–88, Pres. 1986–88.

Offices: 1330 LHOB 20515, 202-225-3701. Also P.O. Box 7306, Syracuse 13261, 315-423-5657; and 1 Lincoln St., Auburn 13021, 315-255-0649.

Committees: *Appropriations* (19th of 23 R): Agriculture, Rural Development, Food and Drug Administration and Related Agencies; District of Columbia (RMM).

Group Ratings

	ADA	ACLU	COPE	CDF	CFA	LCV	ACU	NTLC	NSI	COC	CEI
1992	25	26	75	40	53	50	72	80	100	75	47
1991	25	—	50	80	33	31	63	—	—	70	51

National Journal Ratings

	1991 LIB — 1991 CONS		1992 LIB — 1992 CONS	
Economic	33%	— 66%	34%	— 66%
Social	29%	— 70%	25%	— 75%
Foreign	33%	— 67%	30%	— 64%

Key Votes of the 102d Congress

1. Ban Striker Replace AGN	5. Handgun Wait/7-Day FOR	9. Use Force in Gulf FOR
2. $ for Homeownership FOR	6. Overseas Mil. Abortion AGN	10. US Mil. Abroad $ Cut AGN
3. Tax Rich/Cut Mid Cls. AGN	7. Obscn. Art NEA $ Ban FOR	11. Limit SDI Funds AGN
4. FY93/$15B Def. Cut AGN	8. Death Pen. from Jury FOR	12. Cuba Trade Embargo FOR

Key Votes of the 103d Congress

1. Family Leave FOR	2. Deficit Reduction AGN	3. Stimulus Plan FOR

Election Results

1992 general	James T. Walsh (R-C)................	135,076	(56%)	($294,850)
	Rhea Jezer (D-CSP)................	107,310	(44%)	($96,083)
1992 primary	James T. Walsh (R), unopposed			
1990 general	James T. Walsh (R-C)................	95,220	(63%)	($340,553)
(NY 27)	Peggy L. Murray (D-L)	52,438	(35%)	($11,779)

TWENTY-SIXTH DISTRICT

The southern tier of Upstate New York is territory not often explored by today's Americans. In colonial days the Catskills looming over the Hudson were a great barrier, a mysterious zone in which phantom Dutchmen played ten pins and Indians still lurked in the days of James Fenimore Cooper. Then this became part of a great pathway west, along the Erie Lackawanna and Delaware & Hudson Railroad lines that steamed over giant viaducts and along narrow river valleys through these hills and mountains. Now this quarter of Upstate New York is bypassed by major air travel networks, it has little passenger rail service, its interstate highways are lightly traveled; the one big employer in the area, IBM, is in financial trouble.

The 26th Congressional District of New York includes much of this southern tier, from the antique small cities of Kingston and Beacon on the Hudson River, west across the still-mysterious Catskills to the industrial city of Binghamton on the upper Susquehanna River and the university town of Ithaca looming high over Cayuga Lake's waters. Kingston, settled by Dutchmen more than 300 years ago, was Rip van Winkle country, and in the 19th Century was the political base of Governor and Vice President DeWitt Clinton. The Catskills, once as Dutch as their name, became a Jewish resort area in the late 19th Century, with the kosher resorts of the Borscht Belt; more recently they were known for Woodstock, the eponymous non-site of the much-remembered 1969 music festival. Politically, the heritage here is Republican, but much of this region has trended Democratic: Ithaca and Tompkins County, like so many university areas, are heavily Democratic; Binghamton and Broome County voted for Bill Clinton in 1992 and strongly for Mario Cuomo in 1990; the Borscht Belt has long been Democratic and the Catskills seem to be moving that way.

The 26th District, in slightly different form, was represented for 18 years by Democrat Matthew McHugh, a Democrat who headed the Ethics Committee panel investigating the House bank scandal. Earnest and hard-working, when McHugh announced his retirement in May 1992, regrets came from Republicans as well as Democrats, and Speaker Tom Foley took the unusual step of praising him as "a member who was the watchword for decency, honesty and all that is best in the concept of public service." McHugh's retirement set off contests for both parties' nominations even before the district boundaries were established. Interestingly, there were more votes cast in and more attention focused on the Democratic primary—an indication of which way the political wind was blowing here. The two main Democrats were both experienced politicians: Maurice Hinchey, assemblyman from Ulster County since 1974, and Juanita Crabb, mayor of Binghamton since 1982. Hinchey stressed his activist legislative record, particularly on solid and toxic waste disposal; Crabb argued that she had more hands-on experience and represented the trend of the "year of the woman." Hinchey responded with endorsements from female legislators and TV and radio spots featuring actress Mary Tyler Moore. Hinchey carried Ulster County 80%–18% and held Crabb to a 54%–39% lead in Broome; critically, he carried Tompkins 58%–37%. Meanwhile, Republicans chose their candidate, Bob Moppert, by a 70%–30% margin. Moppert owned a moving company in Binghamton and was a Mayflower van lines agent. He was involved in civic activities and was elected a Broome County legislator in 1986 and became majority leader his first term.

Both candidates came from humble backgrounds; both enlisted in the Navy in the 1950s, right after high school; then their paths diverged, Moppert to small businesses and civic involvement, Hinchey to graduate school and politics. Hinchey worked his way through SUNY New Paltz as a night-shift toll collector on the New York Thruway, got a master's degree in 1969 and then did more graduate study in Albany while a state legislator. In the campaign. Moppert called for less government spending and bureaucracy; Hinchey again talked about his legislative record—he had more than 600 bills passed—on areas including acid rain, toxic waste, illegal dumping (and organized crime influence), groundwater and wetlands protection. Moppert's platform struck local editorialists as dull, Hinchey's as dazzling. With an assurance that may derive from his successful establishment of a family medical practice center in Ulster County, an urban cultural parks program in Kingston and other Upstate towns, and his sponsorship of cleanups of the Hudson, he called for national health insurance, a repeal of Reagan-Bush tax cuts for the rich and corporations and return of money to the ordinary citizen via domestic programs (no one seems to have challenged his arithmetic on this), and "reindustrializating America." He put forth a 29-page "demilitarization" plan that would eliminate 2.6 million military and defense jobs and create 3.4 million civilian jobs, with new spending on housing, education, infrastructure, radioactive and toxic waste cleanup, rail improvements, industrial reorganization, regional assistance and worker retraining.

In a contest that was not only partisan but geographic, Hinchey beat Moppert 50%–47%.

Hinchey carried Ulster 58%–39% and Moppert carried the Binghamton area 57%–41%; Ithaca and Tompkins County again decided it, going 64%–34% for Hinchey. So Hinchey brings his activism to the Banking and Natural Resources Committees. Will his obvious energy and legislative skill enable him to keep his ambitious 1992 campaign promises as he was able to keep smaller promises in Albany?

The People: Pop. 1990: 580,540; 43% rural; 13% age 65+; 88% White; 6% Black; 2% Asian; 1% Other; 4% Hispanic origin. Voting age pop.: 446,955; 5% Black; 4% Hispanic origin. Households: 54% married couple families; 25% married couple fams. w. children; 47% college educ.; median household income: $30,335; per capita income: $13,786; median gross rent: $449; median house value: $94,400.

1992 Presidential Vote			1988 Presidential Vote		
Clinton (D)	116,450	(44%)	Bush (R)	125,479	(52%)
Bush (R)	91,462	(35%)	Dukakis (D)	114,749	(48%)
Perot (I)	53,675	(20%)			

Rep. Maurice D. Hinchey (D)

Elected 1992; b. Oct. 27, 1938, New York City; home, Saugerties; S.U.N.Y., B.S. 1968, M.A. 1969; Catholic; married (Ilene).

Career: Navy, 1956–59; Cement plant worker, 1959–1964; NY St. Thruway toll collector, 1959–68; Analyst, NY St. Dept of Educ., 1971–74; NY Assembly, 1974–92.

Offices: 1313 LHOB 20515, 202-225-6335. Also 291 Wall St., Kingston 12401, 914-331-4466; 100A Fed. Bldg., Binghamton 13901, 607-773-2768; and Carriage House-Terrace Hill, Ithaca 14850, 607-273-1388.

Committees: *Banking, Finance and Urban Affairs* (27th of 30 D): Consumer Credit and Insurance; Financial Institutions Supervision, Regulation and Deposit Insurance; General Oversight, Investigations, and the Resolution of Failed Financial Institutions. *Natural Resources* (22d of 28 D): National Parks, Forests and Public Lands; Oversight and Investigations.

Group Ratings and 102d Congress Votes: Newly Elected

Key Votes of the 103d Congress

1. Family Leave	FOR	2. Deficit Reduction	FOR	3. Stimulus Plan	FOR

Election Results

1992 general	Maurice D. Hinchey (D-L)	119,557	(50%)	($368,777)
	Bob Moppert (R-C)	110,738	(47%)	($203,274)
	Other	6,821	(3%)	
1992 primary	Maurice D. Hinchey (D)	19,426	(54%)	
	Juanita M. Crabb (D)	14,226	(40%)	
	Barbara A. Wolfson (D)	2,002	(6%)	
1990 general	Matthew F. McHugh (D)	97,815	(65%)	($200,047)
(NY 28)	Seymour Krieger (R)	53,077	(35%)	($23,766)

TWENTY-SEVENTH DISTRICT

Across the Finger Lakes of New York, the long, thin, deep-blue lakes in folds between the rolling hillsides thick with grapevines, ran one of the first paths of westward migration. Cut off from white settlement by the British and Iroquois, Upstate New York opened up after the Revolution, and streams of New England Yankees moved west along the Mohawk River and the Erie Canal, dug by hand labor and finished in 1825, connecting the Hudson River and Lake Erie, the East Coast and the vast interior of America. The Finger Lakes region became one of the fastest-growing and most dynamic parts of America; town squares here today have monuments to the enthusiasms of the 1830s and 1840s, when these new communities were full of young families on the rise, and religious revivals were so fervent that the area was known as the Burnt-Over district. Here in the village of Palmyra, near the Erie Canal, Joseph Smith had his vision of the angel Moroni and saw the golden tablets which led him to found the Mormon Church. Preachers fanned the local enthusiasm for abolition of slavery, greater here than anywhere else in the country. This was the birthplace of the women's movement: in Seneca Falls in 1848, Elizabeth Cady Stanton and Lucretia Mott produced a Declaration of Sentiments that started the women's suffrage movement. Upstate was also the birthplace of the temperance movement, another women's cause in those days.

The 27th Congressional District of New York covers much of this territory, now economically less dynamic and politically calmer than in its heyday. After the 1992 redistricting, the 27th starts at Aurelius, one of the many Upstate towns with classical names, and includes Seneca Falls and Palmyra, then passes south of Rochester and through Batavia and Attica to the Buffalo suburb of Amherst. Most of this is part of America's Republican heartland, though the Buffalo area, with its historic heavy industry base, has tended to be Democratic.

The congressman from the 27th is Bill Paxon, a Republican who is one of his party's few natural politicians. Paxon's roots are in Buffalo's Erie County, where his father was a family judge. Paxon volunteered at 15 in the first congressional campaign of Jack Kemp, then famous as a quarterback for the Buffalo Bills in the 1960s and not yet known as an advocate of sweeping tax cuts. In 1977, the same year he graduated from Canisius College (almost a prerequisite for a political career here), Paxon was elected to the Erie County legislature at 23, the youngest member ever. In 1982, at 28, he was elected to the New York Assembly. In 1988, when Kemp ran for president and left the seat open, Paxon won the Republican nomination without opposition and then spent $688,000 and won the general election with 53%. He was reelected in 1990 with 57%.

Paxon has played relatively little part in legislation in the House, amassing a conservative voting record except on some economic issues, fighting against the gas tax increase in the 1991 energy bill and trying to stop imports of solid waste from Canada; he started off with a seat on Banking and in 1993 moved to the plummier Energy and Commerce Committee. But what really seems to energize him is campaigning. As a bachelor, he uses practically all his spare time to campaign in his district and for Republicans around the country. He even loves to raise money; Paxon, says one Republican staffer, is "an animal. You never see him without his phone." In 1991, he made contributions to members of the Republican majority in the state Senate who would be making redistricting decisions, and was reported to have promised $10,000 a year for state Senate Republicans as long as he held his seat. It was money well-spent: western New York had been losing population and had to lose a seat, and his district would have been easy to carve up among the others. Instead, Paxon's district gained territory from 30-year veteran Republican Frank Horton, who decided in June 1992 to retire. That meant easy renomination for Paxon and a solid 63% victory in a district more Republican than before.

But reelection was not the only thing on Paxon's mind in 1992. He was running hard for the chairmanship of the National Republican Congressional Committee, which was certain to be vacated after the August 1992 primary defeat of 18-year Chairman Guy Vander Jagt. Paxon was not the only member interested; Don Sundquist of Tennessee had run a close race against Vander Jagt two years before and other senior members were eyeing the spot. Paxon lobbied hard, campaigned and raised money for other members, sketched out his plans for change and, when the Republican Conference met in December 1992, he was chosen unanimously. He quickly installed as leading vice-chairmen Susan Molinari, Rick Santorum and Jim Saxton—a youth movement—and fired 25 staffers and reexamined the consulting contracts. He made it plain that he had no litmus tests for Republican candidates and promised to serve as chairman only two terms. His success or failure will probably be due to factors outside his control—the fate of the Clinton Administration, in particular. But, with many Republicans still running behind their issue positions because they lack political skills, Paxon's own abilities may enable him to make a difference that could propel him to a position of party leadership.

The People: Pop. 1990: 580,317; 55% rural; 13% age 65+; 92% White; 2% Black; 1% Asian; 1% Hispanic origin. Voting age pop.: 433,859; 2% Black; 1% Hispanic origin. Households: 63% married couple families; 30% married couple fams. w. children; 48% college educ.; median household income: $34,573; per capita income: $14,934; median gross rent: $434; median house value: $81,100.

1992 Presidential Vote			1988 Presidential Vote		
Bush (R)	115,432	(42%)	Bush (R)	142,464	(59%)
Clinton (D)	90,194	(33%)	Dukakis (D)	100,338	(41%)
Perot (I)	67,721	(25%)			

Rep. Bill Paxon (R)

Elected 1988; b. Apr. 29, 1954, Buffalo; home, Amherst; Canisius Col., B.A. 1977; Catholic; single.

Career: Erie Cnty. Legislature, 1978–82; NY Assembly, 1982–88.

Offices: 1314 LHOB 20515, 202-225-5265. Also 5500 Main St., Williamsville, 14221, 716-634-2324; and 10 E. Main St., Victor 14564, 716-742-1600, 800-453-8330.

Committees: *Energy and Commerce* (12th of 17 R): Commerce, Consumer Protection and Competitiveness; Health and the Environment; Transportation and Hazardous Materials.

Group Ratings

	ADA	ACLU	COPE	CDF	CFA	LCV	ACU	NTLC	NSI	COC	CEI
1992	10	0	33	30	20	6	92	75	100	75	74
1991	10	—	17	30	28	15	85	—	—	80	72

National Journal Ratings

	1991 LIB — 1991 CONS		1992 LIB — 1992 CONS	
Economic	23% —	76%	28% —	70%
Social	0% —	84%	0% —	85%
Foreign	0% —	88%	0% —	82%

Key Votes of the 102d Congress

1. Ban Striker Replace AGN	5. Handgun Wait/7-Day AGN	9. Use Force in Gulf FOR
2. $ for Homeownership FOR	6. Overseas Mil. Abortion AGN	10. US Mil. Abroad $ Cut AGN
3. Tax Rich/Cut Mid Cls. AGN	7. Obscn. Art NEA $ Ban FOR	11. Limit SDI Funds AGN
4. FY93/$15B Def. Cut AGN	8. Death Pen. from Jury FOR	12. Cuba Trade Embargo FOR

Key Votes of the 103d Congress

1. Family Leave AGN   2. Deficit Reduction AGN   3. Stimulus Plan AGN

Election Results

1992 general	Bill Paxon (R-C-RTL)	156,596	(63%)	($1,017,327)
	W. Douglas Call (D)	89,906	(37%)	($71,370)
1992 primary	Bill Paxon (R), unopposed			
1990 general	Bill Paxon (R-C-RTL)	90,237	(57%)	($506,343)
(NY 31)	Kevin P. Gaughan (D-L)	69,328	(43%)	($100,353)

TWENTY-EIGHTH DISTRICT

Rochester, New York, with a metro area just over one million, is one of the major cities of Upstate New York strung out along the man-made artery that made the region's fortune: the Erie Canal. Located where the Erie Canal crosses the Genesee River, Rochester became a major industrial city, the "Flour City" in the 1830s, as it milled the wheat produced by western New York farmers, and then a high-tech city, when a bank clerk named George Eastman began making photographic dry plates and marketed the first still camera and film for Thomas Edison's motion picture camera in 1888 and 1889. Later, Bausch & Lomb developed their lens business here. Rochester, the home of Susan B. Anthony and Frederick Douglass, has lived on high-tech versions of the eye. Its great industries—Bausch & Lomb, Eastman Kodak, and Xerox, which started here as Haloid—have thrived on technical innovation, precision workmanship, high reliability, and customer service, which have given Rochester an affluent and well-educated population which maintains fine civic institutions and provides a more elevated tone of life than found in many 20th Century American cities.

The 28th Congressional District of New York includes Rochester and most of its Monroe County suburbs—a compact district in a state whose redistricting produced a dozen grotesqueries, and the first time in 50 years that the heart of Monroe County hasn't been separated into two districts. The original idea was to split the Democratic city so it would be outvoted by the Republican countryside; with the election of a Democrat in 1986 that purpose became moot, and the 1992 plan placed two incumbents together in a district that gave a plurality to Bill Clinton. Republican Frank Horton, with 30 years in the House, was the more senior; he had sponsored the Inspector General, Whistleblower Protection and Paperwork Reduction Acts, but as one of the last Rockefeller-liberal Republicans faced the threat not only of a tough general election but also a primary challenge from the right, and he retired.

That leaves as congresswoman from the 28th Democrat Louise Slaughter. With an accent and occasional fieriness that are evidence of her roots in the Kentucky mountains, Slaughter has become a seasoned political professional. She worked as a local staffer for Mario Cuomo when he was lieutenant governor in the 1970s and won a seat on the Monroe County Legislature; she was elected to the New York Assembly in 1982 and 1984. In 1986, she took on one-term Republican Fred Eckert, an abrasive conservative, calling him "Congressman No" and attacking him for doing nothing to free hostage Terry Anderson, a reporter and native of Rochester, from captivity in Lebanon. Outraising Eckert, she won 51%–49%.

Slaughter has worked on health programs, like her successful 1992 awareness law for DES, the anti-miscarriage drug which has caused serious birth defects, and her flu vaccine demonstration program for senior citizens. She worked on funding for the Rochester-Monroe County Airport. She worked well with the Democratic leadership, winning a seat on the Rules Committee in 1989 and on Budget in 1991. She became chairman of the Congressional Arts Caucus in 1993. On foreign policy, she pressed for direct negotiations with Terry Anderson's captors and opposed the Gulf war resolution. She is often outraged when she feels women's concerns are slighted: she was one of seven women House members who marched on the Senate, demanding that Anita Hill testify against Clarence Thomas; she was furious when George Bush vetoed an NIH authorization for fetal tissue research; she has even criticized William Natcher, octogenarian Appropriations chairman, for his attitude toward some women's issues.

On Rules, Slaughter has been a strong Democratic partisan—strong enough to arouse anger in Republicans, as in March 1993 when she made an unusual parliamentary motion to cut off a colloquy between Gerald Solomon and Robert Walker, prompting Solomon to threaten, in words he later deleted from the *Congressional Record*, "You had better not do that, ma'am. You will regret that as long as you live." In 1992 Slaughter became head of the Democratic Caucus's reorganization committee, with a goal of enabling the House to act more expeditiously and cost effectively. It sought to split the functions of the Steering and Policy Committee, and to create a 20-member Speaker's Working Group on Policy Development, all appointed by the speaker. The committee declined to recommend abolition of select committees, but was outflanked in early 1993 when freshmen Republicans forced their demise. It did recommend that delegates be given enhanced voting status, despite the apparently contrary Constitutional language and the fact that four out of five delegates represent constituents who don't pay federal taxes; it tried to cut the time for "special orders" speeches used by Republicans and by some Democrats like Henry Gonzalez to speak directly to voters via C-SPAN; Republicans objected so vociferously that Democrats had to retreat. Essentially, Slaughter's package was an attempt to centralize control of the House at a time when it contained a record number of new, independent-minded members and when voters wanted a change from politics as usual.

At home, Slaughter had more trouble than usual in 1992. Although her district became approximately 6% more Democratic in redistricting, her share of the vote fell from 59% in 1990 to 55% in 1992—the equivalent of a 10-point drop.

The People: Pop. 1990: 580,347; 4% rural; 13% age 65+; 80% White; 14% Black; 2% Asian; 2% Other; 4% Hispanic origin. Voting age pop.: 439,077; 12% Black; 3% Hispanic origin. Households: 50% married couple families; 23% married couple fams. w. children; 53% college educ.; median household income: $33,899; per capita income: $16,205; median gross rent: $477; median house value: $90,000.

1992 Presidential Vote

Clinton (D) 119,055 (44%)
Bush (R) 103,544 (38%)
Perot (I)....................... 48,467 (18%)

1988 Presidential Vote

Dukakis (D)................. 128,982 (52%)
Bush (R) 121,214 (48%)

Rep. Louise M. Slaughter (D)

Elected 1986; b. Aug. 14, 1929, Harlan Cnty., KY; home, Fairport; U. of KY, B.S. 1951, M.S. 1953; Episcopalian; married (Robert).

Career: Monroe Cnty. Legislature, 1976–79; Regional Coord., Lt. Gov. Mario Cuomo, 1976–79; NY Assembly, 1982–86.

Offices: 2421 RHOB 20515, 202-225-3615. Also 311 Fed. Bldg., 100 State St., Rochester 14614, 716-232-4850.

Committees: *Budget* (11th of 26 D). *Rules* (9th of 9 D): Rules of the House.

Group Ratings

	ADA	ACLU	COPE	CDF	CFA	LCV	ACU	NTLC	NSI	COC	CEI
1992	95	96	92	100	93	100	4	15	30	25	16
1991	95	—	100	100	78	92	5	—	—	20	12

National Journal Ratings

	1991 LIB	—	1991 CONS	1992 LIB	—	1992 CONS
Economic	78%	—	21%	91%	—	0%
Social	84%	—	12%	88%	—	8%
Foreign	78%	—	19%	76%	—	19%

Key Votes of the 102d Congress

1. Ban Striker Replace FOR	5. Handgun Wait/7-Day FOR	9. Use Force in Gulf AGN
2. $ for Homeownership AGN	6. Overseas Mil. Abortion FOR	10. US Mil. Abroad $ Cut FOR
3. Tax Rich/Cut Mid Cls. FOR	7. Obscn. Art NEA $ Ban AGN	11. Limit SDI Funds FOR
4. FY93/$15B Def. Cut FOR	8. Death Pen. from Jury AGN	12. Cuba Trade Embargo FOR

Key Votes of the 103d Congress

1. Family Leave FOR	2. Deficit Reduction FOR	3. Stimulus Plan FOR

Election Results

1992 general	Louise M. Slaughter (D).............	140,908	(55%)	($526,345)
	William P. Polito (R-C)...............	112,273	(44%)	($245,526)
	Other................................	1,897	(1%)	
1992 primary	Louise M. Slaughter (D), unopposed			
1990 general	Louise M. Slaughter (D)..............	97,280	(59%)	($322,216)
(NY 30)	John M. Regan, Jr. (R-C-RTL)	67,534	(41%)	($24,712)

TWENTY-NINTH DISTRICT

The Niagara Frontier is the romantic name for the Buffalo metropolitan area and the northwest corner of Upstate New York facing Lake Ontario. This really was the frontier once, between the United States and British-held Upper Canada, when American troops crossed the raging Niagara River in the War of 1812 to fight the Battle of Lundys Lane. Not many years later, Niagara Falls became a prime North American vacation spot, a must-see sight for European tourists and American honeymooners. By the mid-20th Century, Niagara Falls vacations had

930   NEW YORK

become routine, and few tourists took notice of the huge water intakes farther up the river, the hydroelectric power lines strung out on giant pylons fanning out in every direction, providing cheap public power for the chemical and steel factories that made the Niagara Frontier one of the heavy industry capitals of America. Nor did they notice the school and the 200 frame houses which had been built on a toxic waste dump near Love Canal, land sold by Hooker Chemical to the city of Niagara Falls with a warning that no one should live there—and where children developed horrifying birth defects and some died.

The 29th Congressional District of New York includes the heart of the Niagara Frontier: the Falls; the Buffalo suburbs of Tonawanda and Kenmore; and the northwest one-third of Buffalo itself, with the city's downtown and its cultural institutions. To meet the equal population standard, the 29th goes east to include towns and farm country along the southern shore of Lake Ontario to the Rochester suburb of Gates. Like most of Upstate New York this was once Republican territory; as heavy industries declined, it trended Democratic. Its most famous congressman was William Miller, Republican National Committee chairman in 1961–64 and Barry Goldwater's 1964 vice presidential nominee; but it hasn't elected a Republican since Democrat John LaFalce was elected in 1974.

LaFalce, temperamentally an activist, has used his committee posts to find policy innovations to help the Niagara Frontier and similar areas. In 1983 and 1984, LaFalce used his Banking subcommittee chair to champion industrial policy—a hot subject of discussion among Democrats for a time, but shot down by skepticism of Republicans and some Democrats as well. Next, LaFalce took up the banner of promoting competitiveness, and inserted a provision in the 1988 trade bill. He came up with his own proposal for Third World debt in 1987, calling for an intermediary agency to buy debt with backing from the IMF's gold fund. He wants to create a government sponsored entity like Fannie Mae to provide a secondary market for small business loans. He strongly backed the U.S.-Canada Free Trade Agreement, which enabled the Niagara Frontier, with its low land costs and rents, to partake of the prosperity of Ontario's Toronto-based Golden Horseshoe, but he voted against fast-tracking of the NAFTA agreement with Mexico, saying it would cost American jobs.

As chairman of the Small Business Committee since 1987, LaFalce has dissented from Democratic orthodoxy on occasion, taking account of small business fears of overregulation in his own versions of family and medical leave, the Americans with Disabilities Act and civil rights bills, and he was the leader in the successful fight to repeal high-red-tape Section 89. He has been less influential on the Banking Committee; he was not close to former Chairman Fernand St Germain, nor is he to current Chairman Henry Gonzalez. He does, however, rank third in seniority now, behind Gonzalez, who turns 78 in 1994, and Stephen Neal, who has close elections every two years in North Carolina.

Despite his energy and his moderate record on small business and cultural issues, LaFalce has been closely pressed in the two elections in the 1990s. In 1990 he was held to 55% of the vote, though the Republican had only 31% and a Conservative 14%. In 1992 he managed to dodge redistricting bullets but was opposed by William Miller, Jr., son of the former congressman. Adding part of Buffalo helped: LaFalce carried Erie County 60%–36% and the rest of the district by only 50%–45%. In the politically volatile Niagara Frontier, he may face a serious challenge again.

The People: Pop. 1990: 579,831; 23% rural; 15% age 65+; 91% White; 4% Black; 1% Amer. Indian; 1% Asian; 1% Other; 3% Hispanic origin. Voting age pop.: 441,240; 4% Black; 2% Hispanic origin. Households: 54% married couple families; 24% married couple fams. w. children; 43% college educ.; median household income: $28,951; per capita income: $13,350; median gross rent: $383; median house value: $71,200.

1992 Presidential Vote

Clinton (D) 103,528 (40%)
Bush (R) 86,730 (33%)
Perot (I) 70,231 (27%)

1988 Presidential Vote

Dukakis (D) 123,639 (51%)
Bush (R) 117,293 (49%)

Rep. John J. LaFalce (D)

Elected 1974; b. Oct. 6, 1939, Buffalo; home, Tonawanda; Canisius Col., B.S. 1961, Villanova U., J.D. 1964; Catholic; married (Patricia).

Career: Army, 1965–67; Law Clerk, U.S. Navy Gen. Cnsl., 1963; Lecturer, George Washington U., 1965–66; Practicing atty., 1967–74; NY Senate, 1971–72; NY Assembly, 1973–74.

Offices: 2310 RHOB 20515, 202-225-3231. Also Fed. Bldg., 111 W. Huron St., Buffalo 14202, 716-846-4056; Main P.O. Bldg., 615 Main St., Niagara Falls 14302, 716-284-9976; and Fed. Bldg., 100 State St., Rochester 14614, 716-263-6424.

Committees: *Banking, Finance and Urban Affairs* (3d of 30 D): Economic Growth and Credit Formation; Financial Institutions Supervision, Regulation and Deposit Insurance; Housing and Community Development; International Development, Finance, Trade and Monetary Policy. *Small Business* (Chmn. of 27 D): SBA Legislation and the General Economy (Chmn.).

Group Ratings

	ADA	ACLU	COPE	CDF	CFA	LCV	ACU	NTLC	NSI	COC	CEI
1992	85	83	100	90	87	44	12	5	20	25	13
1991	90	—	83	100	78	46	10	—	—	30	14

National Journal Ratings

	1991 LIB — 1991 CONS		1992 LIB — 1992 CONS	
Economic	88%	— 0%	83%	— 13%
Social	64%	— 35%	50%	— 49%
Foreign	73%	— 26%	65%	— 33%

Key Votes of the 102d Congress

1. Ban Striker Replace	FOR	5. Handgun Wait/7-Day FOR	9. Use Force in Gulf AGN
2. $ for Homeownership	AGN	6. Overseas Mil. AbortionAGN	10. US Mil. Abroad $ Cut FOR
3. Tax Rich/Cut Mid Cls.	FOR	7. Obscn. Art NEA $ BanAGN	11. Limit SDI Funds FOR
4. FY93/$15B Def. Cut	FOR	8. Death Pen. from Jury AGN	12. Cuba Trade Embargo FOR

Key Votes of the 103d Congress

1. Family Leave	FOR	2. Deficit Reduction	FOR	3. Stimulus Plan	FOR

Election Results

1992 general	John J. LaFalce (D-L)	128,230	(55%)	($467,841)
	William E. Miller, Jr. (R-C)	98,031	(42%)	($83,110)
	Two Others	9,197	(4%)	
1992 primary	John J. LaFalce (D), unopposed			
1990 general	John J. LaFalce (D-L)	68,367	(55%)	($145,079)
(NY 32)	Michael T. Waring (R)	39,053	(31%)	
	Kenneth J. Kowalski (C-RTL)	16,853	(14%)	($231)

THIRTIETH DISTRICT

Buffalo, New York is primed to be one of America's success stories of the 1990s—not its most glamorous or dazzling, but of the modest sort of so many American communities. Buffalo has had its successes before. For if it is famous for the snow piled up at the eastern end of Lake Erie which supposedly keep it immobilized half the year, it should also be credited with building a heavy industrial base in the late 19th and early 20th Centuries, as America's number one grain milling center and major steel producers. Today, the Lackawanna mills are cold, grain milling waned when the St. Lawrence Seaway opened in the 1950s; Buffalo is eclipsed in state politics by New York City and Albany and economically by the bigger Great Lakes industrial cities of Cleveland, Detroit and Chicago, and its architecturally bold 1920s City Hall and downtown skyscrapers are far overshadowed by the high-rise horizon of Toronto, not many miles away. But Buffalo has considerable assets which went unnoticed until the late 1980s. It has a high-skill labor force that works at reasonably low-wage rates; it has cheap real estate; it has spruced up and gentrified its rather handsome waterfront on what is now a fairly clean Lake Erie; it even has an interesting history, as the western terminus of the Erie Canal and as home of two Presidents (Fillmore and Cleveland) and the place where another (McKinley) was fatally shot and a fourth (Theodore Roosevelt) sworn in to replace him.

The key to Buffalo's recent resurgence can be summed up in one word: Canada. Canada is literally right across the Peace Bridge, and Buffalo is the major metropolitan area on the doorstep of the richest part of Canada, whose Free Trade Agreement with the United States was signed in late 1988. Toronto's wages, real estate prices and taxes are much higher than Buffalo's, and since Ontario elected a quasi-socialist provincial government, its taxes have gone up again; meanwhile, its labor market is much tighter and its unions more militant. Canadian investment has been flowing into Buffalo and if Ontario, now more sluggish than Upstate New York, can resume its economic growth, benefits will ooze south of the border.

The 30th Congressional District of New York consists of the eastern and southern two-thirds of Buffalo, plus most of the Erie County suburbs east and south of the city, from working-class Cheektowaga and the steel-mill town of Lackawanna to higher-income Hamburg on Lake Erie and East Aurora, home of turn of the century writer Elbert Hubbard, to the southeast. This is a solidly Democratic district, by any measure the most Democratic in Upstate New York, although some of the suburbs are Republican; but as Buffalo has fitfully revived in the late 1980s and early 1990s, it has been politically volatile, lashing out against some usual favorites. Such was the case in 1992, when 18-year incumbent Henry Nowak suddenly announced his retirement.

This set up a contest between two politicians with bases not in Buffalo but in the suburbs—changing demographics. Erie County Executive Dennis Gorski, a Democrat, was the favorite. Gorski returned from service in Vietnam to be elected to the County Legislature here in 1971, the New York Assembly in 1974 and County Executive in 1987. There he narrowed the county deficit, worked on developing the shoreline, and claims to have taken 7,000 people off welfare. Gorski had primary competition from Erie County Sheriff Thomas Higgins, who called him aloof and held him to a solid but not overwhelming 62%-38% victory.

Republicans recruited a strong candidate, Town of Hamburg Supervisor Jack Quinn, a native of south Buffalo, former teacher and coach, elected to the Hamburg Council in 1981 and the full-time job of town supervisor in 1983. There he was proud of bringing in new jobs and starting an anti-drugs program. Quinn was nominated by Republicans but also created his own Change Congress Party (his name appeared on the ballot under both labels) and, in anti-incumbent 1992, ran on an 11-point program of congressional reform, including term limits and a reduction in House staff. Quinn called on Gorski to release the 1993 county budget and attacked him for receiving contributions from public employees. These were winning themes: Erie County went nationally Democratic, as usual, but Bill Clinton had only 43% of the vote here, and George

Bush only 29%; Ross Perot won 27%, his best showing in a major central-city metropolitan county. In a stunning upset, Quinn won 52%–46%. He brands himself a moderate and suggests he looks favorably on government spending; he also promised, as so many freshmen have, to continue living in his home district and to spend as little time in Washington as possible.

The People: Pop. 1990: 580,818; 13% rural; 15% age 65+; 81% White; 17% Black; 1% Amer. Indian; 1% Asian; 1% Other; 1% Hispanic origin. Voting age pop.: 441,257; 15% Black; 1% Hispanic origin. Households: 51% married couple families; 22% married couple fams. w. children; 39% college educ.; median household income: $26,263; per capita income: $12,176; median gross rent: $374; median house value: $68,000.

1992 Presidential Vote			1988 Presidential Vote		
Clinton (D)	119,115	(45%)	Dukakis (D)	149,485	(60%)
Perot (I)	73,333	(28%)	Bush (R)	100,470	(40%)
Bush (R)	68,174	(26%)			

Rep. Jack Quinn (R)

Elected 1992; b. Apr. 13, 1951, Buffalo; home, Hamburg; Siena Col., B.A. 1969, S.U.N.Y., M.A. 1973; Catholic; married (Mary Beth).

Career: Teacher and coach, Orchard Park Central Schl., 1973–83; Hamburg Town Supervisor, 1984–92.

Offices: 331 CHOB 20515, 202-225-3306. Also 403 Main St., #501, Buffalo 14203, 716-845-5257.

Committees: *Public Works and Transportation* (24th of 24 R): Economic Development; Water Resources and Environment. *Veterans' Affairs* (10th of 14 R): Education, Training and Employment; Oversight and Investigations.

Group Ratings and 102d Congress Votes: Newly Elected

Key Votes of the 103d Congress

1. Family Leave	FOR	2. Deficit Reduction	AGN	3. Stimulus Plan	AGN

Election Results

1992 general	Jack Quinn (R-CCP)	125,734	(52%)	($199,257)
	Dennis T. Gorski (D-C)	111,445	(46%)	($459,349)
	Other	6,025	(3%)	
1992 primary	Jack Quinn (R), unopposed			
1990 general	Henry J. Nowak (D-L)	84,905	(78%)	($93,158)
(NY 33)	Thomas K. Kepfer (R)	18,181	(17%)	
	Louis P. Corrigan, Jr. (C)	6,460	(6%)	

THIRTY-FIRST DISTRICT

The Southern Tier of New York is one of the nation's forgotten stretches of territory; yet it has an interesting and distinctive history. Elmira was once the home of Mark Twain and, though far from the Mississippi, was where he wrote *Huckleberry Finn.* On Lake Chautauqua, not far from Lake Erie, a training camp for Methodist Sunday school teachers was founded in 1874, where in summers, on wide green lawns and on porches and in gazebos decorated with ornate Victorian gingerbread, some 25,000 people heard educational talks and inspirational lectures from the likes of William Jennings Bryan. Corning is the headquarters of Corning Glass Works, one of America's long-successful and also artistically distinguished manufacturing companies. In between are two small Indian reservations, miles and miles of dairy farms, and much of New York's wine country; sheltered by hills, the lands at the edge of Upstate's deep lakes are the largest grape-growing area outside California, and the leader in concord grapes, with headquarters of prime New York State wineries and Welch's grape juice.

The Southern Tier's western half forms the 31st Congressional District of New York. Politically, this was Republican country since the party's founding. The towns and countryside are no longer homogeneously Protestant, but remain solidly Republican in most elections, though occasionally willing to consider a Democrat. In fact, the area was represented by Democrat Stan Lundine, onetime mayor of Jamestown, from 1976 until he was tapped to become Mario Cuomo's lieutenant governor 10 years later. The current Republican congressman carries a familiar name, and with considerable grace: he is Amory Houghton, scion of the very rich family that owns the Corning Glass Works and a top executive at Corning for 25 years, who had considered retiring to be a missionary in Africa, but instead ran for Congress. The Houghtons are not just rich folks in a small town, they are charter members of the American establishment: Houghton's father was an ambassador to France; his grandfather, a congressman in the 1920s, built one of the biggest mansions on Washington's Embassy Row, his family endowed the rare books library at Harvard, and this latest Houghton sat on boards of companies like IBM, Citicorp and Procter and Gamble. Cheerful, articulate, used to being in comfortable command, Amo Houghton ran a chipper and well-financed campaign in 1986, chatted with voters, competed with a serious Democratic opponent, outpolling him with 77% in his home county of Steuben and 60% in the district. In the 1988 campaign, opposed only by a Liberal Party candidate who at 24 was too young to serve, Houghton did "work days" as a disc jockey at Elmira's WENY, as a cook at the Texas Hots restaurant in Wellsville, and as a man-on-the-street reporter for the *Olean Times-Herald*. He won with 70% and 71% in 1990 and 1992.

By one estimate, he is the richest member of Congress, with $420 million, although most of that may represent the wealth of many family members; anyway, he is clearly rich, the only member of Congress who pays for his foreign travel out of personal funds, and who gave $27,000 to colleagues' campaigns in 1992. He is the only former CEO of a Fortune 500 company currently in Congress, and only the second in the last 50 years (the other was Illinois Senator Charles Percy, once of Bell & Howell). If he was not a typical freshman congressman when elected, he may well be more what the Founding Fathers had in mind than the politically adept youngsters with few local ties who win in so many districts. He seems to have the cheerful unassuming nature of one to whom much is given, who has been living up to his responsibilities and has enjoyed himself in the process. With the same good will his company used to enhance life in Corning, and for blacks and women in management, he produced a bill settling a Seneca Indian land dispute. He is not unwilling to put burdens on the rest of society which he is ready for his own interests to shoulder: he backed the plant closing law, spoke out for the beleaguered catastrophic health care program and was one of two Republicans who in the party conference in early 1993 refused to say they would back no new taxes. He was repelled by the 1992 Republican National Convention and said its "harsher and more belligerent voices do not represent, at least for me, either an appealing or enduring base for growth in coming years."

The People: Pop. 1990: 580,400; 60% rural; 15% age 65+; 95% White; 2% Black; 1% Amer. Indian; 1% Asian; 1% Other; 1% Hispanic origin. Voting age pop.: 428,466; 2% Black; 1% Hispanic origin. Households: 58% married couple families; 27% married couple fams. w. children; 39% college educ.; median household income: $25,124; per capita income: $11,382; median gross rent: $341; median house value: $48,300.

1992 Presidential Vote

Bush (R) 97,447 (40%)
Clinton (D) 82,671 (34%)
Perot (I). 62,325 (25%)

1988 Presidential Vote

Bush (R) 132,922 (59%)
Dukakis (D). 91,462 (41%)

Rep. Amo Houghton (R)

Elected 1986; b. Aug. 7, 1926, Corning; home, Corning; Harvard, B.A. 1950, M.B.A. 1952; Episcopalian; married (Priscilla).

Career: Marine Corps, 1945–46 (WWII); Corning Glass Works, 1951–86, Chmn. and CEO, 1964–86.

Offices: 1110 LHOB 20515, 202-225-3161. Also 700 W. Gate Plz., W. State St., Olean 14760, 716-372-2127; 32 Denison Pkwy. W., Corning 14830, 607-937-3333; and Fed. Bldg., #122, Prendergast & 3d Sts., Jamestown 14701, 716-484-0252.

Committees: *Ways and Means* (9th of 14 R): Oversight (RMM); Social Security.

Group Ratings

	ADA	ACLU	COPE	CDF	CFA	LCV	ACU	NTLC	NSI	COC	CEI
1992	30	43	50	40	27	13	68	90	100	88	53
1991	20	—	50	50	28	8	70	—	—	70	53

National Journal Ratings

	1991 LIB — 1991 CONS		1992 LIB — 1992 CONS	
Economic	28%	— 71%	28%	— 70%
Social	43%	— 56%	52%	— 48%
Foreign	34%	— 65%	18%	— 74%

Key Votes of the 102d Congress

1. Ban Striker Replace	AGN	5. Handgun Wait/7-Day AGN	9. Use Force in Gulf	FOR
2. $ for Homeownership	FOR	6. Overseas Mil. Abortion FOR	10. US Mil. Abroad $ Cut AGN
3. Tax Rich/Cut Mid Cls. AGN	7. Obscn. Art NEA $ Ban AGN	11. Limit SDI Funds	AGN
4. FY93/$15B Def. Cut	AGN	8. Death Pen. from Jury FOR	12. Cuba Trade Embargo AGN

Key Votes of the 103d Congress

1. Family Leave   AGN   2. Deficit Reduction   AGN   3. Stimulus Plan   AGN

Election Results

1992 general	Amo Houghton (R-C).................	150,696	(71%)	($444,296)
	Joseph P. Leahey (D)	52,010	(24%)	($5,850)
	Gretchen S. McManus (RTL)	10,848	(5%)	
1992 primary	Amo Houghton (R), unopposed			
1990 general	Amo Houghton (R-C).................	89,831	(70%)	($178,401)
(NY 34)	Joseph P. Leahey (D)	37,421	(29%)	($6,462)
	Other............................	1,807	(1%)	

NORTH CAROLINA

North Carolina, which for years was joined by few others in fancying itself the leader of the South, now has some entitlement to regard itself as a leader of the nation, a state whose growing economy, booming demography and vibrant culture are in many ways typical of the way the nation is going—or would like to go. This was mostly unanticipated. Few people 20 years ago picked North Carolina as a state that would chart a path to the future. It had no great central city, no Atlanta primed to become another Chicago or Los Angeles, but rather a series of small metropolitan areas spaced out over thickly-settled countryside. It did not have what seemed to be cutting-edge industries; the biggest employer was textiles, typically an underdeveloped nation's first industry, and the other two were stolid furniture and soon-to-be-disfavored tobacco. It seemed to be off the nation's main lines of commerce; a south Atlantic state, too steamy to be businesslike in the summer and too cold to be a resort in the winter. It did not seem socially advanced, with a population made up almost entirely of native-born Anglo-Saxons and blacks and with an attachment to traditional and sometimes fundamentalist religion.

Yet North Carolina has emerged as one of America's leading growth states. It grew 13% in the 1980s, to become the tenth largest state, and continues to grow robustly in the 1990s, with one of the nation's lowest unemployment rates. That happened even though the number of textile and tobacco jobs have declined. North Carolina's economy has diversified, with huge job growth around the two metro areas whose airports became major airline hubs in the 1980s, Charlotte and Raleigh-Durham. North Carolina firms have become national leaders: headquartered in Charlotte are NationsBank, formerly NCNB, the nation's fourth largest bank, and Nucor, the nation's leading minimill steelmaker; in the midst of Raleigh-Durham is Research Triangle park. Professional and high-tech job sectors have been growing rapidly. While Carolina politicians were seeking protection for textiles, this more advanced economy was coming into being so quietly and quickly that one of its biggest problems was a labor shortage: not enough people were migrating to the state.

But not everything is changed. There is still a low-wage economy here, with old factories and almost no unions and little regulation: this dark side of North Carolina was revealed when the chicken plant in Hamlet caught fire in 1991 due to lax safety standards and 25 workers died. North Carolina still has problems with infant mortality and one of the nation's largest percentage of trailers as housing units. Plenty of green space and reminders of rural roots, from barbecue stands to country Baptist churches, remain in North Carolina's "countrified cities." And that is what most Tarheels like: they can live surrounded by forests or farms and yet be within an hour's drive of huge shopping centers and thousands of workplaces.

The change has not been directed from any single establishment; the forces that have produced it are decentralized—and sometimes hostile. North Carolina does have a small and articulate elite, which looks for guidance to the University of North Carolina at Chapel Hill and the resolutely progressive editors of the state's newspapers; the most prominent are the *Raleigh News & Observer* and the *Charlotte Observer*, which helped expose Jim and Tammy Fae Bakker. Quite different attitudes are nurtured by tradition-minded churches in a state where churchgoing is deeply ingrained, endorsed for years in Sunday blue laws and strengthened periodically by religious revivals; if Bakker was discredited, North Carolina's Billy Graham remains a strong voice for revealed religion, appearing in Bill Clinton's inauguration as he had in Dwight Eisenhower's 40 years before. In the economically backward state North Carolina was when infant mortality was common and indoor plumbing was not, religion was a fountain of hope and a source of discipline; and is still for a great many, in this now economically bustling state.

North Carolina has grown with the aid of both its progressive and tradition-minded citizens,

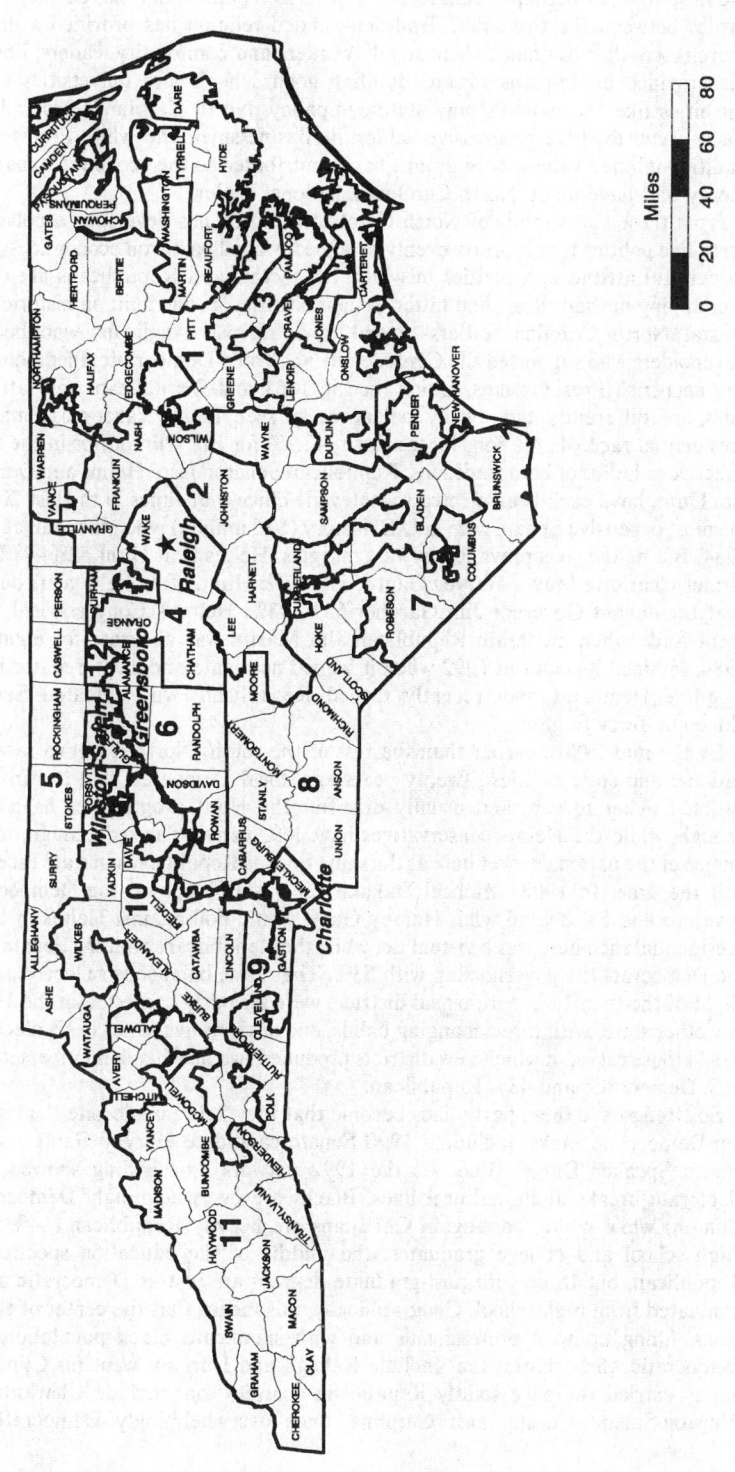

and in spite of, or perhaps because of, the polarized politics that has developed out of a series of battles between the two sides. Tradition-minded religion has provided a discipline for many churchgoers that has made them steady workers and community leaders; liberal progressivism has provided an impetus toward building good schools and universities and highways and amenities like the nation's only state symphony. North Carolina's professionals—white and black—tend to share progressive values; its businessmen and white Protestants tend to share tradition-minded values; both groups have contributed to the economic dynamism and cultural energy that have made North Carolina a national leader.

From these two strands of North Carolina tradition has developed a polarized, increasingly party-line politics that is pretty evenly balanced, waged partly on economic issues but even more on cultural attitudes; a politics in which Democrats and Republicans are distinctive, seldom overlapping in their ideas, and bitter in their rivalries. It has built on historic partisan patterns: coastal North Carolina settlers tended to be British Anglicans who became Methodists, slaveholders who supported the Confederacy and voted Democratic; Piedmont settlers tended to be Scots-Irish Presbyterians, Union men in 1861 and Republicans ever after. Today the two sides are differently but evenly balanced, as seen in the razor-close margin of the 1992 presidential race (43.4% for George Bush, 42.7% for Bill Clinton) or in the fact that the most effective paladins of both traditions, Republican Senator Jesse Helms and Democratic Governor Jim Hunt, have each been elected to statewide office four times in the last 20 years, and waged the most expensive Senate race in U.S. history ($26 million) when they ran against each other in 1984. But neither has prevailed by vast margins. Helms beat Hunt 52%–48% and in 1990 beat former Charlotte Mayor Harvey Gantt 53%–47%; Hunt, after eight years out of office, in 1992 beat Lieutenant Governor Jim Gardner 53%–43%. Helms's Congressional Club, seemingly a spent force when moderate Republican Jim Martin was governor for eight years starting in 1984, retained its clout in 1992 when it helped nominate and elect Senator Lauch Faircloth, a longtime Democrat only recently turned Republican, who defeated Senator and former Governor Terry Sanford.

By the mid-1980s, earlier than the rest of the south, North Carolina saw a convergence of national and state politics. Twenty years ago, local Democrats had to run far ahead of their national ticket to win, and usually did. But the Hunt progressives have changed attitudes enough, while the Helms conservatives have left many polarized enough, to boost the performance of the national ticket here at the same time as Republicans in state races now to win about half the time. In 1988, Michael Dukakis ran just 2% behind the Democratic candidate for governor and 5% behind what Harvey Gantt would poll against Helms in 1990; by 1992, the presidential race here was a virtual tie, while the Republicans won the Senate seat with 50% and the Democrats the governorship with 53%. That close balance is reflected also in House races. Eight of the then 11 congressional districts were seriously contested in the 1980s, more than in any other state, with three changing hands, one of them five times in six elections; in the twelve 1992 House races, in which new districts produced two new black members, the overall vote was 51% Democratic and 48% Republican.

So strong have these party lines become that they held fast despite the visibility of blacks in top Democratic ranks, including 1990 Senate candidate Harvey Gantt and since 1991 state House Speaker Daniel Blue. As the 1992 network exit polling showed, North Carolina's electorate breaks along cultural lines. Blacks are overwhelmingly Democratic (91% for Bill Clinton) while white, born-again Christians are heavily Republican (64% for George Bush). High school and college graduates, the middle of the education spectrum, generally vote Republican, but those with post-graduate degrees are just as Democratic as those who never graduated from high school. Geographically, this means that the center of the Piedmont urban areas, filling up with professionals and with significant black populations, are increasingly Democratic: the counties that include Raleigh and Durham went for Clinton, and Bush only barely carried the once solidly Republican counties that include Charlotte, Greensboro and Winston-Salem. Coastal east Carolina, once overwhelmingly Democratic, is now mixed, depending on the balance between blacks and white born-agains; non-metropolitan Piedmont counties are heavily Republican. The result is an exquisite balance between two cultural and political blocs which have contributed to North Carolina's unanticipated growth—though neither is inclined to give the other much credit.

Governor. Governor Jim Hunt of North Carolina might be where Bill Clinton is now, if a few things in recent history had happened differently. Hunt was first elected governor in 1976 two years prior to Clinton, but was successful much sooner than Clinton: with education reform that included student and teacher competency tests as well as higher teacher pay, an effort to attract high-tech jobs to Research Triangle Park and elsewhere, and a stern backing of capital punishment. Hunt persuaded voters to repeal the ban on serving a second consecutive term and probably could have won a third if that were allowed. But then he lost the monumental race against Jesse Helms for an office voters see more as a place for the principled advocacy in which Helms specializes rather than the pragmatic problem-solving which is Hunt's forte. Hunt missed his chance to run for the Democratic presidential nomination in 1988 or 1992. He also passed up a Senate race in 1986 and in 1988 did not challenge his successor, Republican Jim Martin, who reduced business taxes, recruited out-of-state companies, started a highway improvement program and followed through on Hunt's education program with his "career ladder" $397 million merit pay program. Martin seized control of the state Republican Party from Helms's Congressional Club in 1987 and, with Republican Lieutenant Governor Jim Gardner, secured a usually winning coalition in the state Senate and House in 1989. But then he proposed a tax increase, saw it beaten and, after bitter newspaper attacks, announced he wasn't running for office again.

Hunt's decision to run again for governor in 1992 was no surprise. He had to beat two older rivals. One was Attorney General Lacy Thornburg, who argued for even more education spending and stronger backing of the death penalty; but he fell far short in the primary, losing 65%–27%, and carried only four of 100 counties. The Republican candidate was Lieutenant Governor Jim Gardner, who has had a long and colorful career. He was elected to Congress in 1966 at 33, beating House Agriculture Chairman Harold Cooley; he ran for governor in 1968 and won 43%, losing to Bob Scott. Gardner ran again in 1972, losing the runoff by 1,782 votes in a year the Republican ticket swept the top offices. He founded the Hardees hamburger chain and made a fortune, then lost it, then started several more companies some of which went bankrupt (one bumper sticker read, "Honk if Jim Gardner owes you money"). In 1988, Gardner was elected Lieutenant Governor and became head of the "Drug Cabinet." He opposed Martin's tax increase proposals and concentrated on attacking Hunt as soft on crime; Hunt called for school-based apprenticeship programs and more spending on day care and education reform, and said he would apply ideas from David Osborne's *Reinventing Government*. Hunt won by a 53%–43% margin.

Senators. Jesse Helms, after a public career of 20 years in Washington and 40 years in North Carolina, is one of America's most hated and most fervently supported politicians. He grew up the son of the police chief of Monroe, North Carolina, 15 miles from the birthplace of Andrew Jackson—a breeding ground, it seems, for true-believing, contentious leaders. With Jacksonian tenacity he has stuck to his early convictions—respect for elders and law and order, traditional religious faith and moral principles, patriotism, the order imposed by racial segregation—with the exception of the last, and his abandonment of it has often seemed grudging and halfhearted. In a time of relativism and ambiguity, Jesse Helms stands out for the clarity of his views and his steadfast insistence on articulating them. Helms has always been an advocate, not a principal; a talker rather than a doer. He has never held or sought executive office: before he ran for the Senate in 1972, his only political office was a seat on the Raleigh city council in the 1950s. When Senate Republicans were in the majority, he had little success managing legislation. Helms's percentages in his four races have been in a narrow range—54%, 55%, 52%, 53%—and he makes no attempt to mollify voters who disagree with him. "The other side," he says quite accurately, "could nominate Mortimer Snerd and he'd get 40% to 45% of the vote in November, right off the top." Few other senators would be comfortable with such a large percentage against them; Helms evidently is.

Helms believes in free market economics, but has never much emphasized economic issues. On the Agriculture Committee, his support of textile import limits, pretty much a necessity in North Carolina, seems perfunctory, and he didn't relish managing farm bills. What energizes him are foreign and cultural issues—wars and culture wars. He takes the tone of a Jeremiah who believes that doom is just around the corner, but can be delayed a little longer, and who in the meantime wants to identify all those who insist on the wrong path. His characteristic legislative technique is to craft amendments designed less to pass than to embarrass those who vote against them—legislating with an eye on the next election. That is what he has done on issues he opposes such as abortion and the fetal tissue research ban, school busing, Japanese American redress, AIDS funding and, perhaps with greatest visibility, on the National Endowment of the Arts. His causes are by no means all loony—why should the government finance a crucifix submerged in the urine of the artist or Robert Mapplethorpe's highly erotic photographs?—but he manages often to offend colleagues who want to mask unpopular positions or smooth over conflicts between different groups of supporters.

On foreign policy, this Jeremiah has had to deal with the consequences of success. His mistrust of Third World governments, often justified by events, produced his opposition to the Panama Canal Treaties—electorally a splendidly successful stand, helping to defeat perhaps a dozen liberal senators in 1978 and 1980 and keeping alive Ronald Reagan's presidential candidacy when it threatened to die in the North Carolina primary in 1976. Helms has proven a better prophet than many of his critics, decrying the Ceausescu dictatorship in Romania when most mainstreamers wanted to overlook it; arguing against low-interest loans to the foundering Soviet republics and arming the Iraqis; opposing the Sandinistas in Nicaragua long before free elections belied congressional Democrats' assurance that they were the people's choice; backing freedom in Eastern Europe and the Baltic States when others said it was an impossible dream. But Helms's exertions of power have been more negative than positive, even since 1987, when he became ranking Republican on the Foreign Relations Committee. (He had pledged in the 1984 campaign not to take the chairmanship, and to remain chairman of Agriculture; but when Republicans lost their majority he considered himself no longer bound by that promise, and got fellow Republicans to follow seniority and place him ahead of former committee Chairman Richard Lugar.) There he was able to hold up ambassadorial nominees and to exert pressure on policy toward regimes from Nicaragua to Lebanon. It helped Helms that Claiborne Pell was a largely passive chairman and that Helms concentrated all the Republican staff at his level. But then Democrats gave more staff to subcommittee chairmen and ran rings around Helms and his staffers. In January 1992, Helms shocked almost everyone when he fired nine top staffers, and let other Republicans influence staff hiring. "I gather from the nature of the changes that he is no longer interested in political battle," a former staffer said. Helms was slowed down by illness—prostate cancer treatments and open heart surgery—and perhaps disheartened by the seemingly endless Keating Five case that closed his ten-year tenure on the Ethics Committee. But even there he was characteristically confrontational, publishing special counsel Robert Bennett's tough recommendations when Democrats wanted to slide them under the table. Even after his surgery, he kept close watch on Nicaragua and the former Soviet Union, trying to prevent a Sandinista resurgence in the former and insisting on collateral for loans and economic guarantees in the latter.

This may be Helms's last term. But the force and vigor with which he came back to beat Harvey Gantt in 1990, after running behind in the polls for months and being scorned by local media (a former journalist himself, Helms refused to talk to reporters and his campaign staff communicated with them only by fax), came back to win. This was probably the most watched Senate race in the country, a contest between an obdurate opponent of the Martin Luther King holiday and a black liberal who refused to trim on issues, proclaiming his support of more federal spending in TV spots and in personal appearances on the steps of each of North Carolina's 100 county courthouses. Rather than attack runoff primaries and suggest that white voters are racists, as Jesse Jackson has, Gantt played by the rules and cheerily asked whites for their votes. His personal story was an inspiring example of hopeful developments in the South: Gantt was educated in segregated schools and was admitted to Clemson University by court order; he made a successful living as an architect; he was twice elected mayor of Charlotte; far from harboring resentments or seeking reparations, he seemed exuberant and optimistic. He was the top vote-getter in the first primary, but didn't get the required 40% of the vote; in the runoff he beat an east Carolina district attorney 57%–43%. In the general, he did a superb job of framing the issues, dismissing Helms's preoccupation with the NEA and abortion as unimportant.

Armed with money raised by nationwide direct mail, Helms seized the initiative in mid-October with three ads. One attacked racial quotas by showing white hands crumpling a rejection slip while the announcer said the man had lost his job to a minority though he was better qualified, and then accused Gantt of supporting quotas. A radio spot attacked Gantt for "secret" campaigning because he ran ads on black radio stations (a similar charge could be made against Helms and most other candidates in this segmented society). The third attacked Gantt for using "his office and minority status" to make a $450,000 profit on a $679 investment in a TV station license which was then sold to a white corporation—a charge Democrats and journalists cried was racist but which was in fact true: Gantt had not resisted the temptation to take financial advantage of a law providing for racial preference for blacks. Gantt fell in the polls, and there was reason all along to think some of the Helms vote was hidden, concealed by conservative voters who would not speak openly to pollsters of the hated liberal media. Gantt carried young voters and Helms the elderly—the opposite of partisan patterns elsewhere in the nation that year—and Gantt won solidly in Charlotte but ran behind in much of east Carolina. It was said by some that Gantt lost because of racism. But what is remarkable is that North Carolina's polarized politics has developed to the point that a black candidate can compete on an equal basis with a white—something that would have been astonishing 20 years ago.

Helms's philosophy and political organization showed strength again in reclaiming North Carolina's other Senate seat in 1992. The incumbent, Terry Sanford, was in obvious trouble. He had only narrowly beaten moderate Republican James Broyhill in 1986, when he was 69 years old. He had good credentials—governor from 1960 to 1964, president of Duke University from 1969 to 1985, unsuccessful presidential candidate in 1972 and 1976—but proved either politically inept or, much like Helms, indifferent to the political effect of his convictions. In 1990 and early 1991, he took the floor often in opposition to U.S. military action to enforce the United Nations resolutions against Iraq and he voted against the Gulf war resolution, a highly unpopular stand in traditionally hawkish North Carolina with its six military bases. As a member of the Senate Ethics Committee, he was clearly reluctant to condemn any of the Keating Five. Sanford raised little early money, and two serious Republican opponents emerged, former Charlotte Mayor Sue Myrick and former Democrat Lauch Faircloth (his name is short for McLauchlin and pronounced *lock*). Myrick had conservative stands on abortion and gun control and some popularity in Charlotte. But Faircloth had substantial amounts of his own money and support of the Congressional Club. There was irony here: Faircloth, who switched parties in February 1991, had been appointed to the state highway commission by Sanford, served as highway commissioner for four years and then secretary of commerce under Jim Hunt. In 1984, he ran third in the Democratic gubernatorial primary; there was talk he'd wanted the 1986 Senate nomination and resented that Sanford got it. Myrick attacked Faircloth for his millionaire status and as a two-timer who backed both Helms and Hunt in 1984, but Faircloth won the primary by a 48%–30% margin (40% is enough to win), carrying even Charlotte. Faircloth was a stealth candidate in the general, making few appearances but running lots of ads, accusing Sanford of voting like Ted Kennedy, for supporting welfare over workfare and funding for a Boston harbor tunnel.

Then in early October, Sanford had heart surgery. Though he was back on the campaign trail by late October, that obviously raised the age issue against the 75-year-old incumbent, and

Faircloth won 50%–46%; Sanford was one of two anti-Gulf war resolution senators from the South who lost in 1992 (the other was Wyche Fowler of Georgia). Faircloth promised to push spending cuts. "One man can't turn the Senate around," he said, "but they'll flat know I was there." Reporters may not, however: in Helms style, he was totally inaccessible to them on swearing-in day. He seems likely to have a solidly Helmsish voting record.

Presidential politics. North Carolina was as competitive as any state in the country in the 1992 general election: polls showed the race close all fall and Ross Perot was a less serious factor than almost anywhere else in the country. George Bush ended up winning by the narrowest of edges, a result similar to the 1992 and 1990 Senate races and not so different from the governor and House races. North Carolina's straight-ticket politics shows great durability.

North Carolina, which switched its primary to Super Tuesday in 1988, switched it back to May in 1992. Bill Clinton and George Bush, two southerners who had already clinched their parties' nominations, won overwhelmingly. Clinton's victory recalled Albert Gore's win here in 1988; Bush's recalled his narrow win over Bob Dole. North Carolina has been really crucial only once: in 1976, when after five straight losses, Ronald Reagan started denouncing the Panama Canal Treaty and won his first victory over Gerald Ford. That kept Reagan's candidacy alive not just for 1976 but for 1980; what would history have done without North Carolina?

Congressional districting. North Carolina's robust growth in the 1980s gave it a new 12th congressional district in the 1990 Census, its first new seat in 60 years. It had one of the most turbulent districting processes in the nation, thanks to application of the Voting Rights Act, whose 1982 amendments were interpreted by the Justice Department as requiring the creation of not one but two black-majority districts in a state that had none before. Thus in December 1991 was struck down the first Democratic plan, which would have created a new black-majority 1st District in east Carolina, but would have left Charlie Rose's 7th District with a large number of blacks and created a Republican-leaning new seat in the central Piedmont.

Republicans chortled, hoping for the creation of a black-Lumbee Indian majority district that would cost Rose his majority, but the last laugh was on them. Clever Democratic districters drew up a plan with a second black district consisting of a thin line of territory, in some places no wider than I-85, linking black precincts from Durham west to Charlotte; the new Republican 12th District disappeared, and the marginal 5th and 8th Districts were made more Democratic—pretty ingenious work. It violated the age-old principle of contiguity, but it was accepted by the Justice Department in 1992. Nevertheless, it was widely attacked for its extremely irregular district lines (its only competitor for this was Texas, a plan also drawn by Democrats to preserve their own seats while complying with the Voting Rights Act), and in June 1993, a case was pending in the U.S. Supreme Court on the future of the plan.

The People: Est. Pop. 1992: 6,843,000; Pop. 1990: 6,628,637, up 3.1% 1990–1992. 2.6% of U.S. total, 10th largest; 50% rural. Median age: 33.1 years. 12.1% 65 years and over. 75.6% White, 22.0% Black, 1.2% American Indian, 1.2% Hispanic origin. Households: 56.6% married couple families; 26% married couple fams. w. children; 41% college educ.; median household income: $26,647; per capita income: $12,885; 68.0% owner occupied housing; median house value: $65,800; median monthly rent: $284. 5.9% Unemployment. Voting age pop.: 5,022,488. Registered voters (1992): 3,817,380; 2,313,520 D (61%), 1,217,114 R (32%), 286,746 unaffiliated and minor parties (8%).

Political Lineup: Governor, James B. Hunt, Jr. (D); Lt. Gov., Dennis A. Wicker (D); Secy. of State, Rufus L. Edmisten (D); Atty. Gen., Michael F. Easley (D); Treasurer, Harlan E. Boyles (D); Auditor, Ralph Campbell (D). State Senate, 50 (39 D and 11 R); State House of Representatives, 120 (78 D and 42 R). Senators, Jesse A. Helms (R) and Lauch Faircloth (R). Representatives, 12 (8 D and 4 R).

1992 Presidential Vote

Bush (R) 1,134,661 (43%)
Clinton (D) 1,114,042 (43%)
Perot (I). 357,864 (14%)

1992 Democratic Presidential Primary

Clinton. 443,498 (64%)
Brown 71,984 (10%)
Tsongas 57,589   (8%)
No Preference 106,697 (15%)

1988 Presidential Vote

Bush (R) 1,237,258 (58%)
Dukakis (D). 890,167 (42%)

1992 Republican Presidential Primary

Bush 200,387 (71%)
Buchanan. 55,420 (20%)
No Preference 27,764 (10%)

GOVERNOR

Gov. James B. Hunt, Jr. (D)

Elected 1992, term expires Jan. 1997; b. May 16, 1937, Greensboro; home, Lucama; NC St., B.S. 1959, M.S. 1962, U. of NC at Chapel Hill, J.D. 1964; Presbyterian; married (Carolyn).

Career: Cattle rancher; Ford Foundation Econ. Advisor to Nepal, 1964–66; Practicing atty., 1966–92; NC Lt. Gov., 1972–76; NC Gov., 1976–84.

Office: State Capitol, Raleigh 27603, 919-733-4240.

Election Results

1992 gen.	James B. Hunt, Jr. (D)	1,368,246	(53%)
	Jim Gardner (R).	1,121,955	(43%)
	Scott McLaughlin (LIB)	104,983	(4%)
1992 prim.	James B. Hunt, Jr. (D)	459,300	(65%)
	Lacy H. Thornburg (D)	188,806	(27%)
	Marcus W. Williams (D)	25,660	(4%)
	Two Others	27,840	(4%)
1988 gen.	James G. Martin (R)	1,222,338	(56%)
	Robert G. Jordan III (D)	957,687	(44%)

SENATORS

Sen. Jesse A. Helms (R)

Elected 1972, seat up 1996; b. Oct. 18, 1921, Monroe; home, Raleigh; Wingate Col., Wake Forest U.; Baptist; married (Dorothy).

Career: Navy, 1942–45; City Editor, *Raleigh Times*; A.A., U.S. Sens. Willis Smith, 1951–53 and Alton Lennon, 1953; Exec. Dir., NC Bankers Assn., 1953–60; Raleigh City Cncl., 1957–61; Exec. V.P., WRAL-TV and Tobacco Radio Network, 1960–72.

Offices: 403 DSOB 20510, 202-224-6342. Also P.O. Box 2888, Raleigh 27602, 919-856-4630; and P.O. Box 2944, Hickory 28601, 704-322-5170.

Committees: *Agriculture, Nutrition and Forestry* (3d of 8 R): Agricultural Production and Stabilization of Prices (RMM); Domestic and Foreign Marketing and Product Promotion; Nutrition and Investigations. *Foreign Relations* (RMM of 8 R): International Economic Policy, Trade, Oceans and Environment; Terrorism, Narcotics and International Operations; Western Hemisphere and Peace Corps Affairs. *Rules and Administration* (3d of 7 R).

Group Ratings

	ADA	ACLU	CDF	COPE	CFA	LCV	ACU	NTLC	NSI	COC	CEI
1992	5	5	0	13	0	0	100	100	80	100	99
1991	5	—	9	20	6	7	100	—	—	88	82

National Journal Ratings

	1991 LIB — 1991 CONS	1992 LIB — 1992 CONS
Economic	22% — 77%	0% — 89%
Social	0% — 86%	0% — 89%
Foreign	13% — 77%	28% — 71%

Key Votes of the 102d Congress

1. $ for Homeownership	FOR	5. Clarence Thomas Nom. FOR	9. Use Force in Gulf	FOR
2. Have Cap Gains Debate FOR		6. Lmt Death Row Appeal FOR	10. Keep Salvador Aid	FOR
3. Remove Budget Walls AGN		7. Handgun Wait/5-Day AGN	11. Cut $1B from SDI	AGN
4. Ban Striker Replace	*	8. Abortion Gag Rule FOR	12. Override China MFN FOR

Key Votes of the 103d Congress

1. Family Leave	AGN	2. HIV Immigrants	AGN	3. Clinton Budget	AGN

Election Results

1990 general	Jesse A. Helms (R).................	1,088,331	(53%)	($17,761,579)
	Harvey B. Gantt (D).................	981,573	(47%)	($7,811,520)
1990 primary	Jesse A. Helms (R).................	157,345	(84%)	
	L. C. Nixon (R)	15,355	(8%)	
	George Wimbish (R).................	13,895	(8%)	
1984 general	Jesse A. Helms (R).................	1,156,768	(52%)	($16,917,559)
	James B. Hunt, Jr. (D)	1,070,488	(48%)	($9,461,924)

Sen. Lauch Faircloth (R)

Elected 1992, seat up 1998; b. Jan. 14, 1928, Concord; home, Clinton; Presbyterian; divorced.

Career: Army, 1954–55; Farmer, businessman; Owner, Faircloth Farms, Coharie Mills, Coharie Farms; NC Highway Commissioner, 1961–64, Chmn., 1967–73; NC Secy. of Commerce, 1977–83.

Offices: 702 HSOB 20515, 202-224-3154. Also Fed. Bldg., #366, 310 New Bern Ave., Raleigh 27601, 919-856-4791; Fed. Bldg., #219, 401 W. Trade St., Charlotte 28202, 704-375-1993; Fed. Bldg., #16, 37 Battery Pk., Asheville 28801, 704-254-3079; and Fed. Bldg., #422, 251 Main St., Winston-Salem 27101, 919-631-5313.

Committees: *Armed Services* (9th of 9 R): Defense Technology, Acquisition and Industrial Base; Force Requirements and Personnel; Military Readiness and Defense Infrastructure. *Banking, Housing and Urban Affairs* (5th of 8 R): Economic Stabilization and Rural Development (RMM); Housing and Urban Affairs; Securities. *Environment and Public Works* (6th of 7 R): Clean Air and Nuclear Regulation; Clean Water, Fisheries and Wildlife; Toxic Substances, Research and Development.

Group Ratings and 102d Congress Votes: Newly Elected

Key Votes of the 103d Congress

1. Family Leave	AGN	2. HIV Immigrants	AGN	3. Clinton Budget	AGN

Election Results

1992 general	Lauch Faircloth (R)	1,297,892	(50%)	($2,952,102)
	Terry Sanford (D)..................	1,194,015	(46%)	($2,486,380)
	Three Others........................	85,984	(3%)	
1992 primary	Lauch Faircloth (R)	129,159	(48%)	
	Sue Myrick (R)......................	81,801	(30%)	
	Eugene (Gene) Johnston (R)	46,112	(17%)	
	Larry E. Harrington (R)...............	13,496	(5%)	
1986 general	Terry Sanford (D)...................	823,662	(52%)	($4,168,509)
	James T. Broyhill (R)	767,668	(48%)	($5,188,244)

FIRST DISTRICT

Eastern North Carolina in colonial days was a smaller version of the Chesapeake Bay colonies of Virginia and Maryland—a fertile land intersected by dozens of rivers and inlets, with tobacco plantations and farms with docks on the water accessible to the ocean and so to London. North Carolina was settled later than the Chesapeake colonies, and was poorer, with smaller landholdings; but vestiges of its 18th Century past can still be seen in New Bern with its Tryon Palace, the governor's house when this was the capital, and the tiny well-preserved town of Edenton on Albemarle Sound. Today, east Carolina, the North is usually omitted—it's understood you couldn't possibly be talking about South Carolina, which anyway is west of here—is still tobacco country, indeed the major tobacco producing land in the United States. It is also a place inhabited almost entirely by the descendants of the original white settlers and black slaves of 200 years ago. They live in small towns and cities and in some of the most thickly-settled rural land in the United States. For tobacco is a labor-intensive crop which produces great yields; a family can make a living off 40 acres of tobacco land; with a tobacco allotment, part of a government program dating back 60 years, many here do. To be sure, there has been outmigration, of whites especially to the North Carolina Piedmont, of blacks especially to the end of bus lines in New York and Philadelphia. But there are still many Tarheels around.

Enough, for example, to create the 57% black 1st Congressional District of North Carolina, a newly drawn seat for 1992. Its wildly erose lines take in some 28 different counties, though only nine in their entirety. It would take pages to describe this 2,039-mile journey, so suffice it to say that most areas of concentrated black population in east Carolina are in this seat. Some are urban—black ghettos of Fayetteville, Rocky Mount, New Bern—but more are probably rural, and there are plenty of black tobacco farmers here. The largest city here is Greenville, home of East Carolina University, but the surrounding county has only 11% of the district's population. This is ancestral Democratic country, and though many whites have become Jesse Helms Republicans, the new 1st District is solidly Democratic.

When the new district lines were approved, Congressman Walter Jones, 78 and often wheelchair-bound, announced his retirement. First elected in 1966, he had chaired the Merchant Marine and Fisheries Committee since 1980 after chairing the Peanuts and Tobacco Subcommittee of Agriculture. He was the first retiree to announce he'd take advantage of the law allowing him to pocket his campaign treasury; he died in September, and presumably the money goes to his heirs. His seat did not, however, even though his son Walter Jones, Jr., a state legislator ran for it and won 38% in the first Democratic primary—just 2% away from the 40% which under North Carolina law would have given him the nomination. In second place, with 31%, was Eva Clayton. In the mid-1970s, she was director of the Soul City Foundation, civil rights leader Floyd McKissick's attempt to form a black "new town." That foundered, but

Clayton backed Jim Hunt in 1976 and became an assistant secretary for community development in his first term as governor. She was elected to the Warren County Board of Commissioners and chaired it from 1984 to 1991. She then started her own consulting firm and ran for the 1st District seat when it opened up. Clayton is part of the black middle class who have worked their way up in government or worked closely with it. In the campaign, she backed more public investment and job training and lower defense spending to cut the deficit; she had the backing of the state AFL-CIO and fundraising support from EMILY's List.

Clayton far outpaced the other black candidates, and in the June runoff beat Jones by a 55%–45% margin. That guaranteed her victory on November 3, and that same day she won a special election to fill the duration of Jones's term. Thus she became the first black member of Congress from North Carolina since George White served in the late 1890s, and the first woman to serve a full term. In Washington, she was elected chairman of the freshman class, another first for a woman. She missed her first choice committee, Energy and Commerce, but did get Agriculture instead.

The People: Pop. 1990: 553,426; 58% rural; 14% age 65+; 41% White; 57% Black; 1% Amer. Indian; 1% Hispanic origin. Voting age pop.: 399,949; 53% Black; 1% Hispanic origin. Households: 48% married couple families; 21% married couple fams. w. children; 28% college educ.; median household income: $18,226; per capita income: $8,918; median gross rent: $290; median house value: $45,600.

1992 Presidential Vote			**1988 Presidential Vote**		
Clinton (D)	109,657	(61%)	Dukakis (D)	96,501	(61%)
Bush (R)	53,019	(29%)	Bush (R)	62,023	(39%)
Perot (I)	18,266	(10%)			

Rep. Eva M. Clayton (D)

Elected 1992; b. Sept. 16, 1934, Savannah, GA; home, Littleton; Johnson C. Smith U., B.S. 1955, NC Central U., M.S. 1962, U. of NC Law Schl., 1967–69; Presbyterian; married (Theaoseus).

Career: Exec. Dir., Soul City Foundation, 1974–76; NC Asst. Secy., Community Development, 1977–81; Pres., & Owner, Technical Resources Intl. Inc., 1981–92; Warren Cnty. Commissioner, 1983–91, Chmn., 1982–90.

Offices: 222 CHOB 20515, 202-225-3101. Also 400 W. 5th St., Greenville 27834, 800-274-8672; and P.O. Box 676, Warrenton 27589, 919-257-4800.

Committees: *Agriculture* (15th of 28 D): Department Operations and Nutrition; Environment, Credit and Rural Development; Specialty Crops and Natural Resources. *Small Business* (13th of 27 D): Development of Rural Enterprises, Exports and the Environment; Procurement, Taxation and Tourism.

Group Ratings and 102d Congress Votes: Newly Elected

Key Votes of the 103d Congress

1. Family Leave	FOR	2. Deficit Reduction	FOR	3. Stimulus Plan	FOR

Election Results

1992 general	Eva M. Clayton (D)	116,078	(67%)	($551,028)
	Ted Tyler (R)	54,457	(31%)	($6,131)
	Other	2,727	(2%)	
1992 runoff	Eva M. Clayton (D)	43,210	(55%)	
	Walter B. Jones, Jr. (D)	35,729	(45%)	
1992 primary	Walter B. Jones, Jr. (D)	33,634	(38%)	
	Eva M. Clayton (D)	27,477	(31%)	
	Willie D. Riddick (D)	9,112	(10%)	
	Staccato Powell (D)	5,893	(7%)	
	Thomas C. Hardaway (D)	5,771	(7%)	
	Thomas B. Brandon, III (D)	5,085	(6%)	
	Other	1,227	(1%)	
1990 election	Newly created district.			

SECOND DISTRICT

The coastal plain of North Carolina was long bypassed by history. It was settled after Virginia and South Carolina, and only filled in with English settlers as Scots-Irish families were streaming down the valley of Virginia to the western Piedmont. This has always been tobacco country, with life organized around a crop high-yield enough that a 40-acre plot of land can support a family (if it has a tobacco allotment). Tobacco was an important colonial crop, even more so after James B. Duke, a farmer from Durham County, created Bull Durham tobacco and Lucky Strike cigarettes. Cigarette factories grew up in Durham and eventually, from Duke's fortune, so did the gothic buildings of Duke University. But otherwise this was a backward area for years. Its small farms and little cities were homes mainly to tenant farmers and mill hands, people raising families in thin-walled frame houses often with no electricity or running water, in an economy where most people didn't handle much paper money and had no reason to have bank accounts.

Today, life is much better in the coastal plain. Not just because incomes are up, but because this is now one of America's fastest-growing metropolitan areas; Raleigh-Durham, with a dynamic economy, provides many counties around it with jobs. Most farmers here now own their own land, textile workers are better paid, and the four-lane roads and interstates enable people to live where they have family roots and church affiliations, where traditional moral principles are valued and where traditional religion remains strong, and at the same time partake of one of the nation's boom economies. Yet there is still a cultural divide. The Research Triangle area anchored by Durham, Raleigh and Chapel Hill has more Ph.D.s than any other area in the nation, and has been moving left politically despite rising incomes. The once rural counties all around, whose people are prosperous beyond their dreams but not highly educated, are moving to the right.

North Carolina's 2d Congressional District, as it was drastically redrawn for the 1992 election, consists of about three-quarters of a circle of rural counties, centered around Raleigh, in the state's coastal plain. It includes about half of Durham, a slice of Chapel Hill, but none of Raleigh; its other metropolises are Rocky Mount, Wilson, Sanford and Roanoke Rapids. Its oddly shaped boundaries are designed in part to maximize the black population in the 1st District just to the east. As a result, the 2d District has a far lower black percentage than in the 1980s (22% versus 40%), and is much less Democratic. While the Research Triangle counties have long voted solidly against Jesse Helms, these outer counties give him 60% of their votes.

This provided a quite different, and probably more difficult, political terrain for 2d District Congressman Tim Valentine. Valentine started off between North Carolina's progressive Democratic and conservative Republican blocs; an adviser to conservative Democratic Governor Dan Moore in the mid-1960s, he ran for Congress in 1982 as a conservative against black former legislator and U.S. Attorney Mickey Michaux. Valentine won the first primary, but Michaux had 46% in the runoff; in 1984, another black, Durham legislator Ken Spaulding, won 48% against Valentine. Since then, Valentine has not had primary opposition; the 1992 redistricting meant that Valentine, once vulnerable in the Democratic primary, became vulnerable instead in the general election.

Valentine's opponent in the new 2d District was the Republican who won 41% in the old 3d District in 1990, Don Davis, a retired Army quartermaster who made a fortune selling food for 25 manufacturers at 130 military bases. Davis campaigned as a Helms conservative and in this Helms country held Valentine to a 54%–44% margin. Valentine carried Durham and the heavily black counties north of Raleigh, but lost the fast-growing counties to the east and south.

Valentine's voting record has been smack at the midpoint of the House on most issues though he voted against the House version of Clinton's stimulus plan. But, if he has often voted for the balanced budget amendment, and backed the Gulf war resolution, the B-2 and SDI, he has also often cooperated, in North Carolina fashion, with the House Democratic leadership. Naturally, he has used the advantages of incumbency to build support. Chairman of the Science Subcommittee on Technology, Environment and Aviation, Valentine has cosponsored legislation to increase science and technology literacy, and works for Research Triangle projects. He worked to stop the proposed Lake Gaston pipeline to Virginia Beach and to maintain peanut and tobacco programs. He plugs grants for Duke University and money for research on tornadoes. He has attacked foreign aid programs on the grounds that they are "out of control." Valentine has a couple of bigger projects. He would tax corporations to fund a $1.4 billion Advanced Technology Program, to give grants to develop new manufacturing technologies; his bill passed the House in September 1992. He has written of the need to have alternate routes to technical education apart from college. And his bill to encourage energy-efficient lighting technologies was included in the October 1992 energy law. Valentine's future, however remains uncertain in this rapidly changing district.

The People: Pop. 1990: 552,529; 58% rural; 13% age 65+; 77% White; 22% Black; 1% Amer. Indian; 1% Asian; 1% Hispanic origin. Voting age pop.: 420,023; 20% Black; 1% Hispanic origin. Households: 58% married couple families; 26% married couple fams. w. children; 41% college educ.; median household income: $27,271; per capita income: $13,172; median gross rent: $376; median house value: $67,000.

1992 Presidential Vote			1988 Presidential Vote		
Bush (R)	99,256	(45%)	Bush (R)	106,485	(61%)
Clinton (D)	88,141	(40%)	Dukakis (D)	67,661	(39%)
Perot (I)	30,669	(14%)			

Rep. Tim Valentine (D)

Elected 1982; b. Mar. 15, 1926, Nash County; home, Nashville; The Citadel, A.B. 1948, U. of NC, LL.B., 1952; Baptist; married (Barbara).

Career: Air Force, 1944–46 (WWII); NC House of Reps., 1955–60; Legal Advisor, NC Gov. Dan Moore, 1965, Cnsl., 1967; Chmn., NC Dem. Exec. Cmte., 1966–68; Practicing atty., 1952–82.

Offices: 2229 RHOB 20515, 202-225-4531. Also 3310 Croasdaile Dr., #302, Durham 27705, 919-383-9404; and 101 Triangle Ct., Nashville 27856, 919-459-8881.

Committees: *Public Works and Transportation* (7th of 39 D): Aviation; Surface Transportation (Vice Chmn.); Water Resources and Environment. *Science, Space and Technology* (7th of 33 D): Science; Technology, Environment and Aviation (Chmn.).

Group Ratings

	ADA	ACLU	COPE	CDF	CFA	LCV	ACU	NTLC	NSI	COC	CEI
1992	45	38	42	20	40	38	48	37	80	29	47
1991	25	—	58	50	44	69	55	—	—	70	44

National Journal Ratings

	1991 LIB — 1991 CONS		1992 LIB — 1992 CONS	
Economic	34%	— 65%	41%	— 58%
Social	42%	— 58%	36%	— 63%
Foreign	33%	— 67%	69%	— 30%

Key Votes of the 102d Congress

1. Ban Striker Replace AGN	5. Handgun Wait/7-Day FOR	9. Use Force in Gulf FOR
2. $ for Homeownership AGN	6. Overseas Mil. Abortion FOR	10. US Mil. Abroad $ Cut FOR
3. Tax Rich/Cut Mid Cls. FOR	7. Obscn. Art NEA $ Ban FOR	11. Limit SDI Funds FOR
4. FY93/$15B Def. Cut FOR	8. Death Pen. from Jury FOR	12. Cuba Trade Embargo AGN

Key Votes of the 103d Congress

1. Family Leave AGN	2. Deficit Reduction FOR	3. Stimulus Plan AGN

Election Results

1992 general	Tim Valentine (D).....................	113,693	(54%)	($457,958)
	Don Davis (R)........................	93,893	(44%)	($180,484)
	Other................................	3,983	(2%)	
1992 primary	Tim Valentine (D), unopposed			
1990 general	Tim Valentine (D)...................	130,979	(75%)	($286,351)
	Hal C. Sharpe (R)	44,263	(25%)	($56,842)

THIRD DISTRICT

Nearly 500 years ago, Giovanni de Verrazano sailed past the Gulf Stream and landed on a sandspit island he thought was the outer edge of China. He was wrong: it was the Outer Banks of North Carolina. These are probably America's most unstable barrier islands, constantly changing shape and cut by new inlets as they are battered by the ocean currents and storm winds. They were settled early by Europeans: Sir Walter Raleigh's Roanoke colony was founded here in 1587 then vanished shortly thereafter; pirates rested in Pamlico and Albemarle Sounds behind the inlets. History is still much with the Outer Banks: an antique form of English is spoken on Ocracoke Island, reachable only by ferry; the 208-foot lighthouse on Cape Hatteras looks out on some of the most treacherous currents in the Atlantic which have claimed a hundred ships; the sands along Kitty Hawk, with their constant winds, are where the Wright Brothers made mankind's first heavier-than-air flight in 1903.

Today, the Outer Banks have become vacation and retirement country, with affluent beachfront communities around Nags Head and Duck, near Kitty Hawk, and, much farther south, around Beaufort (*BOWfort*, not *BEWfort* as in South Carolina) and Morehead City. Inland, amid swamps, are some of America's biggest military bases, the Marine Corps's Camp Lejeune, the Army's Fort Bragg and Seymour Johnson Air Force Base. The sight of servicemen with their short haircuts cruising on one of the garish strip highways outside the bases is not an exotic one here. The flat lands of east Carolina have long been tobacco- and peanut-raising country; in recent years they have also taken to raising hogs, and Sampson County is now America's number one hog county. And hogs are of course the basis of North Carolina's famous barbecue—now an export item, from an operation called Carolina Oink Express.

The 3d Congressional District of North Carolina covers the Outer Banks and much of the coastal plain. This is one of the state's irregularly shaped districts, with boundaries designed to put heavily black areas in the 1st District and leave mostly white territory in the 3d. This means that Fort Bragg and Camp Lejeune are outside the 3d, and Seymour Johnson is inside; it means the 3d shares the towns of Greenville, Elizabeth City, Kinston and New Bern with the 1st. It also means the 3d is not really contiguous: Wayne and Sampson Counties are connected to the rest only by a line. This made for a more Republican district than the old 3d, and one in which about half the territory was new to Democratic Congressman Martin Lancaster, who had to fight to hold the seat in 1992.

Lancaster grew up on a tobacco farm, was North Carolina's Outstanding 4-H Club alumnus, served in the Navy during the Vietnam war, and served eight years in the legislature. He was an ally of Governor Jim Hunt and other progressives, and shepherded through the legislature major bills like a tough drunk driving measure. In Congress, he has had a voting record roughly at the midpoint of the House on economic, cultural and foreign policy issues. He serves on Armed Services, where he stoutly defended the Marine Corps's Osprey aircraft and serves on the panel on Morale, Welfare and Recreation (MWR); MWR is of great concern to service personnel, and Lancaster was called "Mr. MWR" by one trade journal. He has moved to keep PXs open even if bases are shut down (many retirees and families remain in the area). He co-sponsored the bill giving free mail privileges to Persian Gulf troops. He got a seat on the Merchant Marine and Fisheries Committee, chaired by 1st District Congressman Walter Jones from 1980 until his death in September 1992. Lancaster keeps tabs on local projects, getting $10 million for a new Lawson bridge over the Neuse River and $150,000 for a Corolla-Currituck County bridge study; he has tried to ban natural gas exploration off the Carolina coast.

Lancaster won his seat in 1986 in a classic friends-and-neighbors primary, winning 85% in a big turnout in his home county. In anti-incumbent 1990, after voting for the budget summit bill, he was held to 59% by Republican Don Davis (who had beaten a 100-year-old opthamologist in the primary). In 1992, Davis ran in the 2d District and Lancaster was opposed by state Senator Tommy Pollard, whom Democrats had redistricted out of his legislature seat; Pollard has the odd distinction of having been convicted of shooting his ex-wife's husband in a truck stop brawl in 1975, but was pardoned (and endorsed in a TV spot by the victim). Pollard criticized Lancaster for having five overdrafts at the House bank and bragged of his ability to bring in highway money. The result was Lancaster's closest election yet: he won 54%–43%, and would obviously have benefited by retaining some of the black constituents he lost to the 1st District.

The People: Pop. 1990: 551,918; 62% rural; 12% age 65+; 76% White; 22% Black; 1% Amer. Indian; 1% Asian; 1% Other; 1% Hispanic origin. Voting age pop.: 412,775; 20% Black; 1% Hispanic origin.

Households: 61% married couple families; 28% married couple fams. w. children; 40% college educ.; median household income: $24,553; per capita income: $11,567; median gross rent: $359; median house value: $62,600.

1992 Presidential Vote			1988 Presidential Vote		
Bush (R)	89,877	(47%)	Bush (R)	98,397	(61%)
Clinton (D)	74,702	(39%)	Dukakis (D)	62,412	(39%)
Perot (I)	28,195	(15%)			

Rep. H. Martin Lancaster (D)

Elected 1986; b. Mar. 24, 1943, Wayne Cnty.; home, Goldsboro; U. of NC, A.B. 1965, J.D. 1967; Presbyterian; married (Alice).

Career: Navy, 1967–70 (Vietnam), Naval Reserves, 1970–present; Research asst., U.S. Sen. Constitutional Rights Subcmte., 1966; Practicing atty., 1970–86; NC House of Reps., 1978–86.

Offices: 2436 RHOB 20515, 202-225-3415. Also 103 Fed. Bldg., 134 N. John St., Goldsboro 27330, 919-736-1844.

Committees: *Armed Services* (14th of 34 D): Military Forces and Personnel; Readiness; Research and Technology. *Merchant Marine and Fisheries* (15th of 29 D): Coast Guard and Navigation; Fisheries Management. *Small Business* (24th of 27 D).

Group Ratings

	ADA	ACLU	COPE	CDF	CFA	LCV	ACU	NTLC	NSI	COC	CEI
1992	45	48	50	50	60	25	58	10	90	75	34
1991	40	—	58	70	61	69	40	—	—	60	30

National Journal Ratings

	1991 LIB — 1991 CONS			1992 LIB — 1992 CONS		
Economic	45%	—	55%	42%	—	57%
Social	46%	—	53%	53%	—	47%
Foreign	43%	—	55%	18%	—	74%

Key Votes of the 102d Congress

1. Ban Striker Replace	AGN	5. Handgun Wait/7-Day	FOR	9. Use Force in Gulf	FOR
2. $ for Homeownership	AGN	6. Overseas Mil. Abortion	FOR	10. US Mil. Abroad $ Cut	AGN
3. Tax Rich/Cut Mid Cls.	AGN	7. Obscn. Art NEA $ Ban	FOR	11. Limit SDI Funds	AGN
4. FY93/$15B Def. Cut	AGN	8. Death Pen. from Jury	FOR	12. Cuba Trade Embargo	FOR

Key Votes of the 103d Congress

1. Family Leave	AGN	2. Deficit Reduction	FOR	3. Stimulus Plan	FOR

Election Results

1992 general	H. Martin Lancaster (D)	101,739	(54%)	($548,584)
	Tommy Pollard (R)	80,759	(43%)	($236,233)
	Other	4,552	(2%)	
1992 primary	H. Martin Lancaster (D), unopposed			
1990 general	H. Martin Lancaster (D)	83,930	(59%)	($499,436)
	Don Davis (R)	57,605	(41%)	($84,160)

FOURTH DISTRICT

One of the boom areas of the 1980s, and one which refutes both the "age of greed" stereotype of liberal Reagan haters and the free market determinism of conservative Reagan lovers, is the Research Triangle area of North Carolina. Research Triangle was established in the mid-1950s by Governor Luther Hodges as an R&D industrial park located between three small cities—the musty state capital of Raleigh, the Lucky Strike-manufacturing city of Durham, and the tiny university town of Chapel Hill. With the drawing power of three universities (North Carolina State in Raleigh, Duke in Durham and the University of North Carolina in Chapel Hill), Research Triangle slowly began attracting big research outfits like Burroughs-Wellcome, Glaxo and the Environmental Protection Agency; by the late 1980s it was booming, with over 34,000 people working for more than 65 major companies, stimulating hundreds of small startups and service businesses. Raleigh-Durham airport, which had four gates in the early 1970s, became a major national hub; its metro area grew by more than 30% in the 1980s, the fastest metropolitan growth north and east of Atlanta, and had one of the lowest unemployment rates, under 4%, in the nation.

The 4th Congressional District of North Carolina encompasses most of the Research Triangle area—it has grown too big for one district—including Raleigh, all but one Wake County precinct, and most of Chapel Hill and surrounding Orange County; Durham County is outside the district, but the 4th includes still largely rural Chatham County to the west. Politics here revolves around cultural issues; economic issues play little role in this booming environment where both tradition-minded and liberal-minded cultural views are vividly articulated, by Jesse Helms and his Congressional Club and by university liberals and progressives like Jim Hunt. In the early 1980s, it seemed that the traditionalists might win over the often technical-minded newcomers. But Jesse Helms's vitriolic and confrontational style repelled young voters, especially those with graduate degrees, and the Research Triangle, with perhaps the nation's highest percentage of Ph.D.s, tilted toward the Democrats. Hunt beat Helms here 58%–41% in their great Senate race in 1984; Bill Clinton beat George Bush here 47%–39%, possibly his best showing in any majority white southern metro area.

That has been good news for Congressman David Price, who first won the district by beating a Republican incumbent in 1986, and won by a nearly 2–1 margin in 1992. Price has a background that seems perfectly suited for what the Research Triangle has become: from rural Tennessee, he was a Morehead Scholar at UNC-Chapel Hill, earned a Ph.D. in political science and became a professor at Duke. In a state where traditional religion is strong, Price also has an authentic religious background; he graduated from divinity school at Yale and has been active as a lay Baptist preacher. He is also an able and practical politician—state Democratic chairman when Jim Hunt was first governor, executive director of the 1984 Hunt Commission that revised the national Democratic Party's rules and brought party and elected officials back into the process.

Price has a fairly, but not entirely, liberal voting record. Early on, he showed political entrepreneurship, passing a Home Equity Loan Consumer Protection Act and a bill raising home mortgage insurance limits (real estate values in the Research Triangle have been zooming, and people want to capitalize on this new wealth). After the 1990 election, he won a seat on Appropriations and funneled money to the Triangle Transit Authority, a joint UNC-EPA lab, Raleigh's Textile and Clothing Technology center, the Research Triangle Biotech Center and to a tornado research study. He co-sponsored a science and technical education bill and an energy-efficient lighting program. After the 1992 election, he won one of the three seats on the Budget Committee reserved for members also on Appropriations.

Redistricting greatly benefited Price, and not just because he lost Republican Randolph County; he kept all of Raleigh and, unlike other Democrats, has a large black urban base to boost his percentage. Predictably, he went up from 56% in 1986 and 58% in 1988 and 1990, to 65% in 1992. Price has already written one book on his work in office, *The Congressional*

Experience: A View from the Hill; the political science profession and the nation will evidently have more opportunity to learn what legislative politics is like from an academic political scientist who is also a successful political operator.

The People: Pop. 1990: 552,441; 31% rural; 8% age 65+; 77% White; 20% Black; 2% Asian; 1% Hispanic origin. Voting age pop.: 429,326; 19% Black; 1% Hispanic origin. Households: 54% married couple families; 26% married couple fams. w. children; 62% college educ.; median household income: $34,569; per capita income: $16,708; median gross rent: $477; median house value: $95,500.

1992 Presidential Vote			1988 Presidential Vote		
Clinton (D)	126,577	(47%)	Bush (R)	102,372	(53%)
Bush (R)	105,612	(39%)	Dukakis (D)	90,808	(47%)
Perot (I)	38,878	(14%)			

Rep. David E. Price (D)

Elected 1986; b. Aug. 17, 1940, Erwin, TN; home, Chapel Hill; U. of NC, B.A. 1961, Yale, B.D. 1964, Ph.D. 1969; Baptist; married (Lisa).

Career: Legis. Aide, U.S. Sen. Bartlett, 1963–67; Asst. Prof., Yale U., 1967–73; Prof., Duke U., 1973–86; Exec. Dir., NC Dem. Party, 1979–80, Chmn., 1983–84; Staff Dir., DNC Comm. on Pres. Nominations, 1981–82.

Offices: 2458 RHOB 20515, 202-225-1784. Also 225 Hillsborough St., #330 Raleigh 27603, 919-857-8611; 1777 Chapel Hill-Durham Blvd., #202, Chapel Hill 27514, 919-967-8500; and 101 Fed. Bldg., Sunset Ave., Asheboro 27203, 919-625-3060.

Committees: *Appropriations* (23d of 37 D): Commerce, Justice, State and Judiciary; Transportation. *Budget* (18th of 26 D).

Group Ratings

	ADA	ACLU	COPE	CDF	CFA	LCV	ACU	NTLC	NSI	COC	CEI
1992	85	70	67	90	80	56	13	0	60	25	13
1991	60	—	83	100	67	92	10	—	—	50	15

National Journal Ratings

	1991 LIB	—	1991 CONS	1992 LIB	—	1992 CONS
Economic	61%	—	36%	64%	—	35%
Social	58%	—	40%	64%	—	36%
Foreign	62%	—	36%	56%	—	40%

Key Votes of the 102d Congress

1. Ban Striker Replace	FOR	5. Handgun Wait/7-Day	FOR	9. Use Force in Gulf	AGN
2. $ for Homeownership	AGN	6. Overseas Mil. Abortion	FOR	10. US Mil. Abroad $ Cut	FOR
3. Tax Rich/Cut Mid Cls.	FOR	7. Obscn. Art NEA $ Ban	FOR	11. Limit SDI Funds	FOR
4. FY93/$15B Def. Cut	FOR	8. Death Pen. from Jury	AGN	12. Cuba Trade Embargo	FOR

Key Votes of the 103d Congress

1. Family Leave	FOR	2. Deficit Reduction	FOR	3. Stimulus Plan	FOR

Election Results

1992 general	David E. Price (D)	171,299	(65%)	($444,259)
	Lavinia (Vicky) Goudie (R)	89,345	(34%)	($12,270)
	Other................................	4,416	(2%)	
1992 primary	David E. Price (D), unopposed			
1990 general	David E. Price (D)	139,396	(58%)	($793,291)
	John Carrington (R)	100,661	(42%)	($890,838)

FIFTH DISTRICT

From the coastal plain of North Carolina, the terrain rises slowly through modest hills cut by rivers in the Piedmont, until finally the first mountain ridges appear, their mysterious blue haze filling the crevasse valleys or clinging to the steep hillsides. The Piedmont, in between the plain and the mountains, was first settled by independent-minded Scots-Irish farmers and by followers of British and German sects like the Moravians. This was hardscrabble farm country during the Civil War, with few slaves; by the late 19th Century, it was becoming industrialized, with textile mills alongside streams, furniture factories not far from hardwood forests and the R. J. Reynolds cigarette factories in Winston-Salem (the latter was named by the Moravians; both gave their names to popular cigarette brands). This Piedmont economy was hailed as the basis of a progressive New South, although textile mills paid low wages and tobacco employed few workers; in fact, only in the last dozen years has the North Carolina economy taken off and grown substantially more affluent. Some successes are notorious: the RJR Nabisco merger cost Winston-Salem a corporate headquarters but made many local millionaires. Other successes are less obvious: the country's most advanced tire recycling plant in Winston-Salem, a custom furniture making operation in Kernersville, the Hanes family's Moravian cookie business in Clemmons.

All these are within or just outside the new boundaries of the 5th Congressional District of North Carolina, which sweeps along the northern edge of the state from the coastal plain to the main Appalachian chain, stopping along the way to include a little more than half of the Winston-Salem area. That metro area casts only 30% of the district's votes, however; the rest are sprinkled across the countryside and in small industrial cities like Reidsville, Eden and Mt. Airy. With jagged lines drawn to maximize its Democratic vote, the 5th also takes in some mountain country around Boone and Morganton.

The congressman from the 5th District since 1974 has been Steve Neal, a quiet, unoratorical small newspaper publisher who is, among other things, a grandnephew of R. J. Reynolds—part of the elite in this stratified society. Neal upset a Republican incumbent in the Watergate year of 1974, and has held the district by narrow margins in every year but 1982. Like other North Carolina Democrats, he has a middle of the road voting record in the House. He is interested in environmental matters, early in his career working to stop a power plant and saving the New River, more recently working to revive the Solar Energy and Energy Conservation Bank and preserve land near Nags Head from development. He has worked long and hard to get funds for the nutrition program at Wake Forest University's Bowman Gray medical school in Winston-Salem. He has opposed higher cigarette taxes and restrictions on cigarette ads, and backed textile import restrictions. He voted against the flag amendment and the Gulf war resolution, but also against Clinton's stimulus package.

But by far Neal's most important role is as second ranking Democrat on the Banking Committee and chairman of its Financial Institutions Supervision Subcommittee. There, he played a major role on the S&L issue, sponsoring the 1987 amendment to recapitalize the S&Ls with the $5 billion sought by S&L lobbyists, rather than the $15 billion sought by the administration in conference; the amount was changed to $10.8 billion but Neal's figure as well as others turned out to be gross underestimates of the problem. Neal's approach seems to have been motivated by principle, not, as in the case of Speaker Jim Wright, by a desire to please generous constituents: in general, Neal has been a deregulator, voting to break down the barriers that exist in financial services, whether they affect S&Ls or banks. He has favored allowing banks to have branches in other states; North Carolina has long had statewide branch banking, and now has some of the nation's largest banks, Charlotte-based NationsBank and Winston-Salem-based Wachovia. Neal has also pushed for a "zero inflation" policy requiring the Federal Reserve to eliminate inflation in five years, which Congress has declined to adopt but which Federal Reserve Chairman Alan Greenspan has, with some changes, endorsed. Neal has resolutely opposed attempts to reduce the independence of the Fed, which surely would result in more inflation over time.

Neal has won only one election with 60% of the vote; he had 59% in 1990, a rise from the 54% and 53% in 1988 and 1986; but redistricting took black constituents away to create the new black-majority 12th District, although the legislature tried to compensate elsewhere. In 1992, he faced strenuous competition from Republican Richard Burr, a onetime Wake Forest football player and successful Winston-Salem businessman. Burr ran an anti-incumbent race, citing Neal's seven overdrafts on the House bank; Neal, after 18 years in Congress, ran "to change the way our country is headed." Neal carried every county, running essentially dead even in Winston-Salem's Forsyth County, and won overall 53%–46%. He now holds one of the House's most important chairmanships, but could easily have a serious fight again in 1994.

The People: Pop. 1990: 552,337; 60% rural; 14% age 65+; 84% White; 15% Black; 1% Hispanic origin. Voting age pop.: 428,296; 14% Black; 1% Hispanic origin. Households: 58% married couple families; 25% married couple fams. w. children; 36% college educ.; median household income: $25,543; per capita income: $12,716; median gross rent: $348; median house value: $59,000.

1992 Presidential Vote		1988 Presidential Vote	
Bush (R)	99,408 (43%)	Bush (R)	112,259 (58%)
Clinton (D)	98,056 (43%)	Dukakis (D)	82,564 (42%)
Perot (I)	30,631 (13%)		

Rep. Stephen L. Neal (D)

Elected 1974; b. Nov. 7, 1934, Winston-Salem; home, Winston-Salem; U. of CA, U. of HI, A.B. 1963; Presbyterian; married (Landis).

Career: Small businessman, mortgage banker, 1959–66; Newspaper publisher, Community Press Inc., 1966–74.

Offices: 2469 RHOB 20515, 202-225-2071. Also 2000 W. First St., #508, Winston-Salem 27104, 919-631-5125.

Committees: *Banking, Finance and Urban Affairs* (2d of 30 D): Economic Growth and Credit Formation; Financial Institutions Supervision, Regulation and Deposit Insurance (Chmn.); General Oversight, Investigations, and the Resolution of Failed Financial Institutions; International Development, Finance, Trade and Monetary Policy. *Government Operations* (6th of 25 D): Legislation and National Security.

Group Ratings

	ADA	ACLU	COPE	CDF	CFA	LCV	ACU	NTLC	NSI	COC	CEI
1992	65	52	50	50	73	81	27	10	70	29	35
1991	55	—	64	80	44	100	30	—	—	50	35

National Journal Ratings

	1991 LIB — 1991 CONS		1992 LIB — 1992 CONS	
Economic	42% —	58%	48% —	52%
Social	56% —	44%	63% —	37%
Foreign	58% —	41%	56% —	40%

Key Votes of the 102d Congress

1. Ban Striker Replace	AGN	5. Handgun Wait/7-Day	FOR	9. Use Force in Gulf	AGN
2. $ for Homeownership	AGN	6. Overseas Mil. Abortion	FOR	10. US Mil. Abroad $ Cut	FOR
3. Tax Rich/Cut Mid Cls.	FOR	7. Obscn. Art NEA $ Ban	FOR	11. Limit SDI Funds	FOR
4. FY93/$15B Def. Cut	FOR	8. Death Pen. from Jury	AGN	12. Cuba Trade Embargo	FOR

Key Votes of the 103d Congress

1. Family Leave	FOR	2. Deficit Reduction	FOR	3. Stimulus Plan	AGN

Election Results

1992 general	Stephen L. Neal (D).................	117,835	(53%)	($517,594)
	Richard M. Burr (R)	102,086	(46%)	($188,130)
	Two Others	3,762	(2%)	
1992 primary	Stephen L. Neal (D), unopposed			
1990 general	Stephen L. Neal (D).................	113,814	(59%)	($647,331)
	Ken Bell (R)	78,747	(41%)	($174,574)

SIXTH DISTRICT

For more than 50 years, furniture store managers and owners from all over the country have gathered in the huge Furniture Mart in High Point, the center of the U.S. furniture business, for the giant trade show put on by manufacturers. This had been rolling farmland settled by Quakers, the site of the Battle of Guilford Courthouse in the Revolutionary War, then slaveholding country in the years before the Civil War. The furniture business grew here early in the 20th Century because of the proximity of hardwoods in the mountains not far west and the abundance of low-wage labor in the flatlands not far east. Soon it was said of High Point that there were so many factories, "only a wise man knows his own factory whistle." Today, employment in furniture continues to grow, unlike employment in North Carolina's other basic industries of textiles and tobacco, and wages have risen. Race relations are now outwardly pleasant in the city where in 1960 black students at North Carolina A&T started the first lunch counter sit-in at a local Greensboro five-and-dime.

The 6th Congressional District of North Carolina in its new bounds is a relatively regularly shaped seat—except that the threadlike 12th District slices it in half in order to pick up black-majority precincts from Durham to Charlotte. It includes most of Guilford County, furniture-manufacturing Davidson County to the west, textile-producing Alamance County to the east and Quaker-settled Randolph County to the south. This area has enjoyed solid economic growth, but many here still feel dependent on textiles which, as the classic cheap-labor industry, is always vulnerable to competition from abroad.

The congressman from the 6th District, Howard Coble, is a Republican who expresses his constituents' anxieties with some force. A Coble priority for 1991 was opposition to fast-tracking NAFTA; he will oppose GATT as well if the textile industry gets used as a bargaining chip. He also opposes expansion of the Federal Prison Industries program, which has federal prisoners producing 20% of federal government furniture; he wants the furniture priced as if its workers were paid North Carolina wages. Coble is also a near-fanatic on the congressional pension, which he calls "lavish" and which he alone of congressmen in 1992 was swearing he would decline. He wants to require a three-fifths majority in both the House and Senate to raise taxes, he supports term limits and is proud he didn't have a single overdraft on the House bank; "I'll wear a suit two years too long. I'll drive a car 10 years too long. I'm also very fastidious when it comes to maintaining my check balance."

With most black voters in the central Piedmont removed to the 12th District, Coble had easy sledding in 1992, beating Democrat Robin Hood (she filed under that name to make a point) by 71%–29%. It was not always so: he won the seat in 1984 by beating Democratic incumbent Robin Britt and in 1986, in a $1.1 million race, Coble beat Britt again by exactly 79 votes. Since 1988 he has won with at least 62%.

The People: Pop. 1990: 552,663; 53% rural; 12% age 65+; 91% White; 7% Black; 1% Asian; 1% Hispanic origin. Voting age pop.: 427,871; 7% Black; 1% Hispanic origin. Households: 62% married couple families; 27% married couple fams. w. children; 42% college educ.; median household income: $30,628; per capita income: $14,942; median gross rent: $403; median house value: $72,900.

1992 Presidential Vote			1988 Presidential Vote		
Bush (R)	119,874	(51%)	Bush (R)	133,247	(70%)
Clinton (D)	75,651	(32%)	Dukakis (D)	56,511	(30%)
Perot (I)	38,180	(16%)			

Rep. Howard Coble (R)

Elected 1984; b. Mar. 18, 1931, Greensboro; home, Greensboro; Appalachian St. U., 1949–50; Guilford Col., A.B. 1958, U. of NC, J.D. 1962; Presbyterian; single.

Career: Coast Guard, 1952–56, 1977–78, Coast Guard Reserves, 1960–82; NC House of Reps., 1969, 1978–84; Asst. U.S. Atty., NC Middle Dist., 1969–73; Commissioner, NC Dept. of Revenue, 1973–77; Practicing atty., 1979–83.

Offices: 403 CHOB 20515, 202-225-3065. Also P.O. Box 299, 324 W. Market St., Greensboro 27402, 919-333-5005; P.O. Box 1813, #A, 1404 Piedmont Dr., Lexington 27293, 704-246-8230; P.O. Box 814, 124 W. Elm St., Graham 27253, 919-229-0159; 241 Sunset Ave., #101, Asheboro 27203, 919-626-3060; and 510 Ferndale Blvd., High Point 27262, 919-886-5106.

Committees: *Judiciary* (7th of 14 R): Civil and Constitutional Rights; Intellectual Property and Judicial Admin. *Merchant Marine and Fisheries* (5th of 19 R): Coast Guard and Navigation (RMM); Fisheries Management.

Group Ratings

	ADA	ACLU	COPE	CDF	CFA	LCV	ACU	NTLC	NSI	COC	CEI
1992	10	0	25	20	27	6	92	90	90	75	86
1991	15	—	25	10	17	15	90	—	—	80	85

National Journal Ratings

	1991 LIB — 1991 CONS		1992 LIB — 1992 CONS	
Economic	12% —	86%	16% —	80%
Social	0% —	84%	0% —	85%
Foreign	17% —	78%	38% —	56%

Key Votes of the 102d Congress

1. Ban Striker Replace	AGN	5. Handgun Wait/7-Day	AGN	9. Use Force in Gulf	FOR
2. $ for Homeownership	FOR	6. Overseas Mil. Abortion	AGN	10. US Mil. Abroad $ Cut	FOR
3. Tax Rich/Cut Mid Cls.	AGN	7. Obscn. Art NEA $ Ban	FOR	11. Limit SDI Funds	AGN
4. FY93/$15B Def. Cut	AGN	8. Death Pen. from Jury	FOR	12. Cuba Trade Embargo	FOR

Key Votes of the 103d Congress

1. Family Leave	AGN	2. Deficit Reduction	AGN	3. Stimulus Plan	AGN

Election Results

1992 general	Howard Coble (R)	162,822	(71%)	($435,093)
	Robin Hood (D)	67,200	(29%)	($27,822)
1992 primary	Howard Coble (R), unopposed			
1990 general	Howard Coble (R)	125,392	(67%)	($572,846)
	Helen R. Allegrone (D)	62,913	(33%)	($33,135)

SEVENTH DISTRICT

Southernmost North Carolina, where the state boundary dips down along the Atlantic coast, is tobacco country, economically dependent on this crop for more than 200 years. Tobacco can be cultivated profitably in only a few places in the world; it is labor-intensive, requiring close tending and serial picking (one leaf on a stalk matures before the one above it); and it is valuable enough that North Carolina farmers today, if they have one of the tobacco allotments handed out in the 1930s or have bought the rights to one, can make a living off 40 acres. Tobacco produces more voters per federally assisted acre than any other crop. This tobacco country, it should be added, is racially diverse, the home of many blacks as well as the Lumbee Indians, whose origins have been lost in antiquity, but who are treated by state segregation laws and by continuing custom as a race distinct from whites and blacks; each race makes up about one-third of the population of Robeson County around Lumberton.

Southernmost North Carolina is also military country. The port city of Wilmington is home of the World War II battleship U.S.S. *North Carolina*, which runs a 70-minute show on its history every night during the summer. Eastward, in swampland, is Camp Lejeune, home base of one-fifth of the Marine Corps. Inland, near Fayetteville, is the huge complex of Fort Bragg and Pope Air Force Base, whence 39,000 troops left for the Persian Gulf in 1990. As the site of one of the biggest bases in the country, Fayetteville has developed the strip highway to an art form, with strip joints, fast food galore and the world's first Putt-Putt golf course.

North Carolina's 7th Congressional District covers much of this territory, from Camp Lejeune to Wilmington to Fayetteville; many black areas are cordoned off in the black-majority 1st District, but the 7th still includes some 100,000 blacks and almost all of Robeson County's Lumbees. This is an ancestrally Democratic area, and its boundaries were carefully sculpted to protect Democratic Congressman Charlie Rose, whose seat the Republicans had hoped to obliterate. Rose was hurt by the removal of many blacks, but he still retains the Lumbees, and redistricters avoided expanding the 7th to Republican coastal areas by including the big military bases, which swell its population but don't contain many voters (this is by far the lowest turnout district in the state).

Charlie Rose is a politically adept veteran who, as it happens, was in need of political help. He first ran for the seat in 1970, nearly beating the incumbent in the primary, and then won it in 1972, and was not seriously challenged for 20 years. Rose has been a talented inside player in the House. From his seat on the House Administration Committee, he directed the design of the House's computer systems, telephone system upgrades and the House TV system installation. (He is an avid video-taker and electronic gadget lover himself.) After the Democratic Caucus in December 1990 voted out Chairman Frank Annunzio, one of the S&Ls' great friends for years, by 127–125, Rose ran and won 158–64 over the more senior Joseph Gaydos (who retired in 1992). There Rose passed the motor-voter bill, supported the opening of Kennedy assassination documents and urged reform of the Capitol Police and campaign finance. He replaced the contractor at the House restaurants, to whom members owed $250,000, and superintended the investigation of the House Post Office on charges of embezzlement and drug dealing among its employees and mysterious massive stamp sales to certain members; in the course of the probe, the Postmaster resigned, as did task force member Mary Rose Oakar from the committee. Republicans blamed Democrats for the problems; Democrats blamed a few Post Office employees. The Post Office controversy dragged on into the 103d Congress, in which Rose will also have to manage a campaign finance bill. He is likely to be a reliable team player for House Democrats.

If Rose's House Administration work is important to the House, his Agriculture seat is important to his constituents. He rose to chair the Tobacco and Peanuts Subcommittee by 1990, and helped preserve the tobacco allotment system, which props up prices by letting only allotment holders produce these crops, by convincing the Democratic leadership that changes in tobacco supports could defeat every member of the cohesive and leadership-supporting North Carolina Democratic delegation. Rose now chairs the Specialty Crops and Natural Resources Subcommittee (House Administration counts as a minor committee, so Rose can keep this Agriculture chair); he wants to rewrite the FIFRA pesticide legislation somewhere between the environmentalist and conservative approaches. Rose could some day be chairman of Agriculture; he ranks third on the committee and is a dozen years younger than Chairman Kika de la Garza. But Rose has other causes as well. He has since 1986 been investigating what is now called Iraqgate, the misuse of agricultural loans by Saddam Hussein's regime to pay for arms. He promises to continue working for Tibetan independence (he has known the Dalai Lama for years) and to get federal recognition of the Lumbees.

For all his surefootedness in the House, Rose has shown some clumsiness (to put it kindly) on his campaign and personal finances. During the 1986 campaign, it was announced that between 1978 and 1985 he had diverted $64,000 of campaign funds for personal use; the House Ethics Committee, acting with typical speed and rigor, ruled in March 1988 that he had violated the law, but recommended no disciplinary action because of mitigating circumstances. Rose's ethics problems resurfaced in May 1989, when the Justice Department filed a civil lawsuit that charged him with failing to report over $138,000 in personal loans from his campaign on disclosure forms. In April 1992, a federal judge upheld the $30,000 in fines the Justice Department sought and rejected Rose's and Speaker Tom Foley's claim that the executive branch had no right to go beyond Congress's own discipline.

Redistricting and charges of scandal caused Rose problems in the 1992 election. Against the same Republican, Robert Anderson, he had beaten 66%–34% in 1990, he won only 57%–41%; Rose actually lost the areas around Wilmington and Camp Lejeune on the coast and most of his winning margin came from Robeson County (saved by the Lumbees!). Unless House Democrats generally and Rose in particular grasp the reform mantle successfully, he could face a serious challenge even in this Democratic area in 1994.

The People: Pop. 1990: 552,037; 41% rural; 9% age 65+; 70% White; 19% Black; 7% Amer. Indian; 1% Asian; 1% Other; 3% Hispanic origin. Voting age pop.: 414,739; 17% Black; 3% Hispanic origin. Households: 61% married couple families; 31% married couple fams. w. children; 43% college educ.; median household income: $24,708; per capita income: $11,663; median gross rent: $391; median house value: $63,600.

1992 Presidential Vote			1988 Presidential Vote		
Clinton (D)	71,334	(43%)	Bush (R)	74,456	(56%)
Bush (R)	70,159	(43%)	Dukakis (D)	57,660	(44%)
Perot (I)	22,194	(14%)			

Rep. Charlie Rose (D)

Elected 1972; b. Aug. 10, 1939, Fayetteville; home, Fayetteville; Davidson Col., A.B. 1961, U. of NC, LL.B. 1964; Presbyterian; married (Joan).

Career: Practicing atty., 1964–72; Chief 12th Dist. Court Prosecutor, 1967–70.

Offices: 2230 RHOB 20515, 202-225-2731. Also 208 P.O. Bldg., Wilmington 28401, 919-343-4959; and 218 Fed. Bldg., Fayetteville 28301, 919-323-0260.

Committees: *Agriculture* (3d of 28 D): Department Operations and Nutrition; Foreign Agriculture and Hunger; General Farm Commodities; Livestock; Specialty Crops and Natural Resources (Chmn.). *House Administration* (Chmn. of 12 D): Administrative Oversight (Chmn.). *Joint Committee on the Library* (Chmn. of 5). *Joint Committee on Printing* (Vice Chmn. of 5).

Group Ratings

	ADA	ACLU	COPE	CDF	CFA	LCV	ACU	NTLC	NSI	COC	CEI
1992	95	73	83	100	67	50	4	0	40	38	9
1991	70	—	92	100	72	54	0	—	—	40	13

National Journal Ratings

	1991 LIB — 1991 CONS		1992 LIB — 1992 CONS	
Economic	60% —	39%	83% —	13%
Social	64% —	35%	64% —	35%
Foreign	76% —	24%	51% —	48%

Key Votes of the 102d Congress

1. Ban Striker Replace	FOR	5. Handgun Wait/7-Day	FOR	9. Use Force in Gulf	AGN
2. $ for Homeownership	AGN	6. Overseas Mil. Abortion	AGN	10. US Mil. Abroad $ Cut	FOR
3. Tax Rich/Cut Mid Cls.	FOR	7. Obscn. Art NEA $ Ban	FOR	11. Limit SDI Funds	AGN
4. FY93/$15B Def. Cut	FOR	8. Death Pen. from Jury	AGN	12. Cuba Trade Embargo	FOR

Key Votes of the 103d Congress

1. Family Leave	FOR	2. Deficit Reduction	FOR	3. Stimulus Plan	FOR

Election Results

1992 general	Charlie Rose (D).....................	92,414	(57%)	($254,579)
	Robert C. Anderson (R)..............	66,536	(41%)	($17,374)
	Other.............................	4,151	(3%)	
1992 primary	Charlie Rose (D), unopposed			
1990 general	Charlie Rose (D).....................	94,946	(66%)	($153,315)
	Robert C. Anderson (R)..............	49,681	(34%)	($21,131)

EIGHTH DISTRICT

From Atlanta to Durham in the Carolina Piedmont, along Interstate 85, is the thickest concentration of America's textile industry—the mills are so thick you can almost see the lint. Within North Carolina, I-85 passes through the nation's leading textile-producing area, past Salisbury, Concord and Kannapolis, for years the eponymous company headquarters of Cannon Mills. Eastern North Carolina was settled by English coming up the rivers or overland from the coast; but the Piedmont land along Interstate 85 was settled primarily by Scots and diverse groups like Quakers and Moravian sects, coming down the Blue Ridge from Pennsylvania through Virginia. These migratory patterns were reflected in Civil War divisions and continue in current voting habits. The coastal counties all the way up through the Sand Hills were Confederate and are now Democratic. The textile mill towns along I-85 were anti-secession and are now Republican.

The 8th Congressional District of North Carolina, as redistricted, combines the area around Kannapolis with Sand Hill counties extending east almost to Fayetteville. About two-thirds of the people are in the textile areas, including some urban overflow from Charlotte; except on the very west, the 8th is not bordered by one of North Carolina's two black-majority districts, and Democratic legislators were careful to maximize the number of blacks here, which is the highest of any non-black majority seat in the state. The intended beneficiary, Bill Hefner, congressman since 1974, is an adept Democratic politico who has operated shrewdly in the Democratic Caucus in Washington and also kept happy the folks back home. When Hefner first ran in the Watergate year of 1974, voters here were hungry for reform but not liberalism; Hefner promised to "help restore Christian morality in the federal government" and to protect "human-oriented programs," and excoriated congressmen who "arranged for themselves an increase in salary in the form of a $9,000 per year expense fund." A gospel singer, with a Winston-Salem TV and Kannapolis radio program, his campaign rallies included country music as well as politics.

Once in the House, Hefner did become more supportive of people programs, but less interested in imposing tradition-minded values. With other North Carolina Democrats, he stuck with the House Democratic leadership on the Reagan budget and tax votes in 1981, and became a team player, though his voting record is by no means uniformly liberal. In return, he and other North Carolinians got leadership support on local issues like textile restrictions—Hefner is a NAFTA opponent—and tobacco subsidies. He also got a seat on Appropriations, which he unabashedly used to help the district; in 1982, after only eight years in the House, he became chairman of the Military Construction Subcommittee, a key pork barrel panel which determines spending on military bases. Hefner is proud of his work on the Carolinas Medical Center, Fort Bragg, the Uwharrie National Forest and four different airport projects; in a time of shrinking military budgets, his impulse now is to question the need for bases abroad. Hefner has been less successful in his own leadership aspirations. In 1986, unable to win much support beyond his North Carolina base, he ran a distant third for whip.

With the large Republican vote in the textile counties, Hefner has only once, in 1976, won more than 60% of the vote; he came close to losing in 1984 and 1988. In 1992, he had primary opposition from Sand Hills state legislator Don Dawkins, who carried his home county and held Hefner to a 67%–33% win. In the general, Hefner was opposed by Coy Privette, who had been his pastor back in 1974. Privette since formed the Christian Action League to fight abortion and (a hot issue in North Carolina) liquor by the drink, and won a seat in the legislature in 1984. Though in 1974 he had called Hefner a "people's candidate, and he will be a people's congressman," by 1992 he was echoing Hefner's 1974 themes and criticizing Hefner's votes for the $35,000 pay increase and against the Gulf war resolution. Hefner was a feisty campaigner; after open heart surgery in the summer, he had a tussle off the House floor with Republican Robert Dornan, whom Privette later brought in to campaign. Hefner won by the comfortable margin of 58%–37%, but that was largely due to his 67% in Sand Hills; he had just 54% in the textile counties. There is some speculation that Hefner, in his 60s, will retire soon.

The People: Pop. 1990: 552,039; 55% rural; 12% age 65+; 72% White; 23% Black; 3% Amer. Indian; 1% Asian; 1% Other; 1% Hispanic origin. Voting age pop.: 403,584; 21% Black; 1% Hispanic origin. Households: 61% married couple families; 29% married couple fams. w. children; 34% college educ.; median household income: $26,180; per capita income: $11,462; median gross rent: $359; median house value: $56,700.

1992 Presidential Vote

Bush (R) 86,493 (44%)
Clinton (D) 81,736 (42%)
Perot (I). 27,296 (14%)

1988 Presidential Vote

Bush (R) 93,130 (58%)
Dukakis (D). 66,494 (42%)

Rep. W. G. (Bill) Hefner (D)

Elected 1974; b. Apr. 11, 1930, Elora, TN; home, Concord; Baptist; married (Nancy).

Career: Entertainer, radio business, 1954–74.

Offices: 2470 RHOB 20515, 202-225-3715. Also P.O. Box 385, 101 Union St. S., Concord 28025, 704-786-1612; P.O. Box 4220, 507 W. Innes St., #225, Salisbury 28144, 704-636-0635; and P.O. Box 1503, 202 E. Franklin St., Rockingham 28379, 919-997-2070.

Committees: *Appropriations* (14th of 37 D): Defense; Military Construction (Chmn.).

Group Ratings

	ADA	ACLU	COPE	CDF	CFA	LCV	ACU	NTLC	NSI	COC	CEI
1992	40	62	88	60	83	13	6	0	50	17	19
1991	55	—	91	90	67	54	10	—	—	40	17

National Journal Ratings

	1991 LIB — 1991 CONS		1992 LIB — 1992 CONS	
Economic	64%	— 35%	60%	— 40%
Social	47%	— 52%	47%	— 52%
Foreign	49%	— 50%	*	— *

Key Votes of the 102d Congress

1. Ban Striker Replace	FOR	5. Handgun Wait/7-Day	FOR	9. Use Force in Gulf	AGN
2. $ for Homeownership	*	6. Overseas Mil. Abortion	FOR	10. US Mil. Abroad $ Cut	*
3. Tax Rich/Cut Mid Cls.	FOR	7. Obscn. Art NEA $ Ban	FOR	11. Limit SDI Funds	*
4. FY93/$15B Def. Cut	FOR	8. Death Pen. from Jury	AGN	12. Cuba Trade Embargo	FOR

Key Votes of the 103d Congress

1. Family Leave   FOR   2. Deficit Reduction   FOR   3. Stimulus Plan   FOR

Election Results

1992 general	W. G. (Bill) Hefner (D)	113,162	(58%)	($594,617)
	Coy C. Privette (R).	71,842	(37%)	($108,332)
	J. Wendell Drye (L)	10,447	(5%)	
1992 primary	W. G. (Bill) Hefner (D)	32,790	(67%)	
	Don (D. D.) Dawkins (D)	16,373	(33%)	
1990 general	W. G. (Bill) Hefner (D)	98,700	(55%)	($656,383)
	Ted Blanton (R)	80,852	(45%)	($300,893)

NINTH DISTRICT

"An agreeable village but in a damn rebellious country," recorded General Cornwallis when, before the unpleasantness at Yorktown, he visited Charlotte, North Carolina: "A veritable nest of hornets." This town, settled by Scots-Irish who came down the Blue Ridge from Pennsylvania, with 1.2 million people is now the biggest metro area between Washington and Atlanta. Charlotte has grown as a banking and distribution center for much of the Piedmont South, as the center of the nation's biggest textile manufacturing region and as an airline hub for USAir; the 60-story tower of NationsBank, the nation's fourth largest bank, sits next to a $50 million performing arts center. The rebelliousness Cornwallis noted can still be seen in this home of one of the nation's biggest stock car race tracks. And the pro-business boosterism which once made Charlotte the most Republican part of North Carolina has changed to a pride in overcoming cultural divisions, which has made Charlotte in many elections favor progressive Democrats. The city is proud that it responded amicably to a busing order approved in a landmark Supreme Court case in 1971; it is proud that it uncovered the shenanigans of its nearby South Carolina neighbors Jim and Tammy Fae Bakker; and, it is proud that it elected Harvey Gantt, who is black, mayor several times and then replaced him with Sue Myrick, a Republican woman whose grievance wasn't race but traffic.

The 9th Congressional District of North Carolina includes most of Charlotte and Mecklenburg Counties—its black precincts are gathered into the black-majority 12th District—and then extends west to include most of Gaston and Cleveland Counties. If the 9th included whole counties, it would be politically marginal and in fact with different boundaries came close to electing Democrat D. G. Martin in 1984 and 1986. But with few (less than 10%) blacks, the 9th is heavily Republican.

The 9th's congressman is Alex McMillan, a Republican first elected in 1984, and since 1988 reelected by wide margins. McMillan is "the personification of the city's leadership core," said *The Leader*, a Charlotte weekly. McMillan was CEO of Harris-Teeter Supermarkets, a longtime civic activist, a moderate Republican who beat a candidate supported by Jesse Helms's Congressional Club 58%–42% in the 1984 primary. McMillan's record breathes the spirit of civic activism; "a frustrated doer amid spinning wheels," the *Charlotte Observer* wrote. Speaking of his new black Democratic colleague Melvin Watt, McMillan said, "We both represent a city and a county that have a history of overcoming differences." Like some suburban Republicans, McMillan voted for the Brady bill for a waiting period for handgun purchases and supports abortion rights. From his seat on Energy and Commerce, he has put forth bills to help solve the nation's scrap tire problem and one to reduce medical liability. As one might expect, he favors textile import restrictions and opposes anti-tobacco bills.

McMillan seems to concentrate most of his energy on the budget, attending Budget Committee hearings endlessly, lucidly explaining hard budget choices to colleagues, constituents and reporters, pushing measures to cap federal spending while holding himself open to consider tax increases. But in 1992, he lost a fight in the Republican conference to succeed Ohio's Willis Gradison as ranking Republican on Budget; he was beaten by John Kasich, who had more seniority in Congress though less on the committee, and seems more likely to oppose tax increases and less likely to consider collaboration with Democrats.

The People: Pop. 1990: 552,490; 24% rural; 10% age 65+; 88% White; 9% Black; 1% Asian; 1% Hispanic origin. Voting age pop.: 421,244; 8% Black; 1% Hispanic origin. Households: 60% married couple families; 28% married couple fams. w. children; 55% college educ.; median household income: $35,346; per capita income: $17,234; median gross rent: $472; median house value: $83,200.

1992 Presidential Vote

Bush (R)	130,798	(52%)
Clinton (D)	81,731	(33%)
Perot (I)	36,454	(15%)

1988 Presidential Vote

Bush (R)	134,304	(69%)
Dukakis (D)	59,191	(31%)

Rep. Alex McMillan (R)

Elected 1984; b. May 9, 1932, Charlotte; home, Charlotte; U. of NC, B.A. 1954, U. of VA, M.B.A. 1958; Presbyterian; married (Caroline).

Career: Army Intelligence, 1954–56; Salesman, Carolina Paper Board Corp., 1958–83; V.P., R.S. Dickson & Co., 1963–70; Treas. & V.P., Ruddick Corp., 1968–83; Mecklenburg Cnty. Bd. of Commissioners, 1973; Pres., CEO, Harris-Teeter Supermarkets, 1976–83.

Offices: 401 CHOB 20515, 202-225-1976. Also 401 W. Trade St., Charlotte 28202, 704-372-1976; and 224 S. New Hope Rd., #H, Gastonia 28054, 704-861-1976.

Committees: *Budget* (2d of 17 R). *Energy and Commerce* (8th of 17 R): Commerce, Consumer Protection and Competitiveness; Health and the Environment; Telecommunications and Finance.

Group Ratings

	ADA	ACLU	COPE	CDF	CFA	LCV	ACU	NTLC	NSI	COC	CEI
1992	15	4	33	20	27	19	84	90	100	88	76
1991	15	—	25	20	11	15	85	—	—	100	70

National Journal Ratings

	1991 LIB — 1991 CONS	1992 LIB — 1992 CONS
Economic	12% — 86%	9% — 88%
Social	16% — 81%	25% — 74%
Foreign	0% — 88%	0% — 82%

Key Votes of the 102d Congress

1. Ban Striker Replace	AGN	5. Handgun Wait/7-Day	FOR	9. Use Force in Gulf	FOR
2. $ for Homeownership	FOR	6. Overseas Mil. Abortion	AGN	10. US Mil. Abroad $ Cut	AGN
3. Tax Rich/Cut Mid Cls.	AGN	7. Obscn. Art NEA $ Ban	FOR	11. Limit SDI Funds	AGN
4. FY93/$15B Def. Cut	AGN	8. Death Pen. from Jury	FOR	12. Cuba Trade Embargo	FOR

Key Votes of the 103d Congress

1. Family Leave	AGN	2. Deficit Reduction	AGN	3. Stimulus Plan	AGN

Election Results

1992 general	Alex McMillan (R)	153,650	(67%)	($236,315)
	Rory Blake (D)	74,583	(33%)	($30,914)
1992 primary	Alex McMillan (R), unopposed			
1990 general	Alex McMillan (R)	131,936	(62%)	($385,183)
	David P. McKnight (D)	80,802	(38%)	

TENTH DISTRICT

Wreathed in the haze that gave them the name "Smoky," the heavily wooded mountains of North Carolina seem placid and ancient. Geologically, they are some of the oldest ranges in the world; economically, they are churning with activity. The North Carolina counties where the hills of the Appalachians rise from the Piedmont are not just countryside; nestled in their valleys is perhaps the largest concentration of furniture factories in the world, where skilled craftsmen create from the hardwoods of Carolina forests both high quality and mass market furniture. Other industries are here as well—textiles, though not as much as in the I-85 corridor in the Piedmont, and chickens in the Holly Farms complex (acquired by Tyson) in Wilkes County.

The 10th Congressional District of North Carolina covers much of this hill and mountain country, roughly between I-85 and the Blue Ridge Parkway. Very roughly, in fact, for the Democratic legislators drew the lines carefully to connect various cities' black communities in the next-door 12th District and to maximize the vote for Democrats in the 5th District to the north and the 11th District to the west. As a result, the 10th wiggles around Democratic strongholds such as the late Senator Sam Ervin's hometown of Morganton and the college town of Boone, and instead includes heavily Republican areas deep in the hills. The result is a district that is by most measures the most Republican in North Carolina, although the Republicans here tend not to be Jesse Helms fans, but rough-hewn hill Republicans, unsympathetic to government regulators, from factory inspectors to revenuers on the lookout for illegal stills.

The congressman from this district is Cass Ballenger, a Republican who started his own business in 1957 making plastic wrappings for J.C. Penney underwear. Ballenger served on the Catawba County Board of Commissioners for eight years and in the state legislature for 12. He ran for Congress in 1986 after James Broyhill, scion of a furniture family and congressman for 24 years, was appointed to the Senate. In the House primary, Ballenger promised to be a "Broyhill Republican" and beat an opponent backed by Helms's Congressional Club. He has won general elections without difficulty.

Ballenger has one of the most conservative voting records in the House. He has fought the Democrats' on family leave and the ban on striker replacement, and amended an OSHA law by exempting employers when violations are caused by employees breaking company work rules. But he also intervened actively to close down a hazardous waste incinerator in Lenoir where workers were suffering nerve damage; he personally lobbied then-EPA head William Reilly and senior Democrats Henry Waxman and John Dingell to shut the plant and investigate what went wrong. On foreign policy, Ballenger and his wife have organized humanitarian trips to Central and South America, delivering donated medical supplies and other necessities. Reelected by a sizeable margin in 1992, Ballenger was a leading contributor among House incumbents to other campaigns, giving about $17,000 to mostly conservative Republicans.

The People: Pop. 1990: 552,303; 71% rural; 12% age 65+; 93% White; 5% Black; 1% Hispanic origin. Voting age pop.: 421,043; 5% Black; 1% Hispanic origin. Households: 65% married couple families; 29% married couple fams. w. children; 35% college educ.; median household income: $28,511; per capita income: $13,434; median gross rent: $352; median house value: $63,700.

1992 Presidential Vote

Bush (R) 127,910 (53%)
Clinton (D) 76,262 (32%)
Perot (I) 35,572 (15%)

1988 Presidential Vote

Bush (R) 142,283 (70%)
Dukakis (D) 61,070 (30%)

Rep. Cass Ballenger (R)

Elected 1986; b. Dec. 6, 1926, Hickory; home, Hickory; U. of NC, Amherst Col., B.A. 1948; Episcopalian; married (Donna).

Career: Naval Air Corps, 1944–45; Businessman; Pres., Hickory Paper Box Co., 1948–70; Founder & Pres., Plastic Packaging Inc., 1957–present; Catawba Cnty. Bd. of Commissioners, 1966–74, Chmn. 1970–74; NC House of Reps., 1974–76; NC Senate, 1976–86.

Offices: 2238 RHOB 20515, 202-225-2576. Also P.O. Box 1830, Hickory 28603, 704-327-6100; and P.O. Box 1881, Clemmons 27012, 919-766-9455.

Committees: *District of Columbia* (4th of 4 R): Fiscal Affairs and Health (RMM); Judiciary and Education. *Education and Labor* (8th of 15 R): Labor-Management Relations; Labor Standards, Occupational Health and Safety; Select Education and Civil Rights (RMM). *Foreign Affairs* (13th of 18 R): Economic Policy, Trade and Environment; Western Hemisphere Affairs.

Group Ratings

	ADA	ACLU	COPE	CDF	CFA	LCV	ACU	NTLC	NSI	COC	CEI
1992	10	4	25	0	27	6	92	95	100	75	82
1991	10	—	17	10	17	0	95	—	—	90	93

National Journal Ratings

	1991 LIB — 1991 CONS		1992 LIB — 1992 CONS	
Economic	4%	— 90%	0%	— 91%
Social	0%	— 84%	19%	— 81%
Foreign	0%	— 88%	18%	— 74%

Key Votes of the 102d Congress

1. Ban Striker Replace	AGN	5. Handgun Wait/7-Day	AGN	9. Use Force in Gulf	FOR
2. $ for Homeownership	FOR	6. Overseas Mil. Abortion	AGN	10. US Mil. Abroad $ Cut	FOR
3. Tax Rich/Cut Mid Cls.	AGN	7. Obscn. Art NEA $ Ban	FOR	11. Limit SDI Funds	*
4. FY93/$15B Def. Cut	AGN	8. Death Pen. from Jury	FOR	12. Cuba Trade Embargo	FOR

Key Votes of the 103d Congress

1. Family Leave	AGN	2. Deficit Reduction	AGN	3. Stimulus Plan	AGN

Election Results

1992 general	Cass Ballenger (R)	149,033	(63%)	($278,963)
	Ben Neill (D)	79,206	(34%)	($23,101)
	Other	6,888	(3%)	
1992 primary	Cass Ballenger (R), unopposed			
1990 general	Cass Ballenger (R)	106,400	(62%)	($302,006)
	Daniel R. Green, Jr. (D)	65,710	(38%)	($37,846)

ELEVENTH DISTRICT

Western North Carolina, the protrusion of the Tarheel state deep into the fastness of the eastern United States' highest and oldest mountains, is a land of long and ornery traditions. First settled by whites not long after the Revolutionary War, it still has tiny Indian communities and hollow towns where people are descended from the first white settlers. Its biggest city, Asheville, is memorialized in Thomas Wolfe's novels and was a retreat for lung patients in the early 20th Century. It was also the home of the eccentric George Vanderbilt, who built the chateau-like Biltmore mansion, now a tourist attraction. Over a ridge is the Smoky Mountains National Park, the nation's most heavily visited, 20 degrees cooler in the summer than the lowland towns nearby. The climate and the forested, green, fog-wisped mountains have attracted millions of tourists, thousands of retirees, including those who could afford to live anywhere—like Carl Sandburg and Billy Graham—to this area.

The orneriness of the mountains has come out in its politics. During the Civil War, it was the part of the state most reluctant to secede. There were few slaves (only 7% of the people here today are black) and many small farmers loyal to the Union, and those who took up the Confederate cause did so largely because of the efforts of Governor Zebulon Vance, an Asheville native and reluctant secessionist himself. Ancestral party loyalties remain strong and evenly balanced; the retirees who have come to the mountains south of Asheville haven't tipped things much. This western end of the state, with erose boundaries drawn by legislators for 1992, makes up the 11th Congressional District of North Carolina. It is one of the most closely contested in the nation: it threw out incumbents in five of the six elections between 1980 and 1990.

The current congressman is Charles Taylor, a Republican tree farmer and one of the biggest private landholders in the area, who served in the legislature from 1966 to 1974 and ran for Congress the first time in 1988. He barely lost then, and in 1990 won when incumbent James McClure Clarke voted for the unpopular budget summit agreement. On the House Interior Committee, Taylor worked to delay drawdowns of area lakes each year by the TVA until August 1, to keep waters high for tourist season; he worked to get the Asheville veterans' hospital refurbished and funding for I-26, which funnels tourists through these mountains. Taylor was also one of the Gang of Seven, the Republican freshmen who pushed for full disclosure of overdrafts on the House bank and other major congressional reforms.

The 11th was expected to have a close race in 1992. Redistricting was supposed to help Democrats; if the new district lines had been in effect in 1990, Taylor would have lost by 931 votes. But Democrat John Stevens proved to be a diffident candidate while Taylor was personable; and Taylor was able to sound anti-incumbent themes in an anti-incumbent year. The Clinton-Gore ticket just carried this district, but Taylor, who outspent his opponent by almost 3–1, ran much better than George Bush, winning 55%–45%, the biggest margin for anyone in this seat since 1974. Taylor got a seat on the Appropriations Committee, an excellent place for him to pursue local projects—extending the drawdown delay to October 1 and getting $37 million to compensate TVA for its losses—while voting for reduced federal spending.

The People: Pop. 1990: 552,497; 69% rural; 18% age 65+; 90% White; 7% Black; 1% Amer. Indian; 1% Hispanic origin. Voting age pop.: 430,423; 6% Black; 1% Hispanic origin. Households: 60% married couple families; 24% married couple fams. w. children; 38% college educ.; median household income: $23,564; per capita income: $11,923; median gross rent: $333; median house value: $59,500.

1992 Presidential Vote

Clinton (D) 105,006 (43%)
Bush (R) 103,849 (43%)
Perot (I). 34,643 (14%)

1988 Presidential Vote

Bush (R) 119,845 (58%)
Dukakis (D). 87,880 (42%)

Rep. Charles H. Taylor (R)

Elected 1990; b. Jan. 23, 1941, Brevard; home, Brevard; Wake Forest U., B.A. 1963, J.D. 1966; Baptist; married (Elizabeth).

Career: Tree farmer; NC House of Reps., 1966–72, Minority Ldr., 1968–72; NC Senate, 1972–74, Minority Ldr., 1972–74.

Offices: 516 CHOB 20515, 202-225-6401. Also 22 S. Pack Sq., #330, Asheville 28801, 704-251-1988; Cherokee Cnty. Cthse., 201 Peachtree St., Murphy 28906, 704-837-3249; and 200 S. Lafayette St., Shelby 28150, 704-484-6971.

Committees: *Appropriations* (20th of 23 R): Commerce, Justice, State and Judiciary; Legislative. *Merchant Marine and Fisheries* (18th of 19 R): Environment and Natural Resources.

Group Ratings

	ADA	ACLU	COPE	CDF	CFA	LCV	ACU	NTLC	NSI	COC	CEI
1992	15	4	25	30	27	6	87	95	100	86	78
1991	10	—	17	20	11	0	90	—	—	90	83

National Journal Ratings

	1991 LIB — 1991 CONS	1992 LIB — 1992 CONS
Economic	23% — 76%	25% — 75%
Social	19% — 78%	0% — 85%
Foreign	17% — 78%	30% — 64%

Key Votes of the 102d Congress

1. Ban Striker Replace	AGN	5. Handgun Wait/7-Day AGN	9. Use Force in Gulf FOR
2. $ for Homeownership	FOR	6. Overseas Mil. Abortion AGN	10. US Mil. Abroad $ Cut AGN
3. Tax Rich/Cut Mid Cls. AGN		7. Obscn. Art NEA $ Ban FOR	11. Limit SDI Funds AGN
4. FY93/$15B Def. Cut	AGN	8. Death Pen. from Jury FOR	12. Cuba Trade Embargo FOR

Key Votes of the 103d Congress

1. Family Leave　　AGN　　2. Deficit Reduction　　AGN　　3. Stimulus Plan　　AGN

Election Results

1992 general	Charles H. Taylor (R)................	130,158	(55%)	($1,212,765)
	John S. Stevens (D)	108,003	(45%)	($431,722)
1992 primary	Charles H. Taylor (R), unopposed			
1990 general	Charles H. Taylor (R)................	101,991	(51%)	($523,867)
	James McClure Clarke (D)	99,318	(49%)	($499,869)

TWELFTH DISTRICT

"This is perhaps the Negros' temporary farewell to Congress," said George White, a Tarboro, North Carolina lawyer and Republican, in his last days in the House of Representatives in 1901. Segregation was being imposed by law, and blacks informally but effectively were being stricken from the voting rolls in the rural South. But White was confident that "Phoenix-like he will rise up some day and come again." It was 28 years until another black was elected to Congress and

70 years until another black won in the South; in North Carolina, although blacks have been politically influential since the Voting Rights Act of 1965, George White's prediction did not come true until 1992, when two blacks were elected. One, Eva Clayton, was from the mostly rural and small town 1st District—the kind of country where most blacks lived in George White's day. The other, Melvin Watt, represents the new 12th District, whose notorious boundaries connect several of North Carolina's urban centers, like those where most American blacks live today.

The 12th District is the most egregious example in the nation of the application, urged by blacks and Republicans, that the 1982 revisions of the Voting Rights Act require the maximization of black percentages in certain districts. It is called the I-85 district, because it consists of a series of urban black areas, many of them poor, mostly connected by a line sometimes no wider than I-85, splitting adjacent districts in two. "I love the district because I can drive down I-85 with both car doors open and hit every person in the district," said candidate Mickey Michaux. "In one county, northbound drivers on I-85 would be in the 12th District, but southbound drivers would be in another," harrumphed *The Wall Street Journal*. "The next county over, the district would 'change lanes,' and southbound drivers would be in the 12th District." There is an argument for connecting together voters with some sense of affinity and common interest. But there is also an argument that such districts amount to a form of apartheid, and their shape eerily resembles those of some of South Africa's homelands.

The contest for the new seat turned out to be the kind of friends-and-neighbors Democratic primary common in the old segregated South. Michaux, a former state legislator who won 46% in the runoff in the old 2d District in 1982, got 76% in Durham County, which had 17% of the district's residents and cast 28% of Democratic primary votes. But he won no more than 22% elsewhere, for 29% district-wide. Larry Little, based in Winston-Salem, won 66% there but no more than 20% elsewhere, for 15%. The winner was Melvin Watt of Charlotte. He won 86% of the vote in Mecklenburg County, where 27% of the votes were cast, plus 59% in Greensboro-High Point, which had no strong favorite son, and carried most of the small counties. Overall, he won 47%, well over the 40% which in North Carolina gives victory without a runoff. He won the general election easily over Barbara Gore Washington, a black lawyer from Greensboro.

Watt had served only two years in the state Senate, but was rich in experience. He grew up in a place called Dixie outside Charlotte, now overgrown with woods, in a tin-roofed house with no electricity or running water. His dream was to attend the University of North Carolina, and he was one of the first black students there; he went on to Yale Law School and then a civil rights law practice in Charlotte. He managed Harvey Gantt's campaigns for city council and mayor in the 1980s and for U.S. Senate in 1990; in the latter race, against Jesse Helms, he and Gantt pursued their strategy with a steely consistency and good humor under fierce pressure.

Watt's views on issues are fairly standard liberal Democratic fare: lower defense spending, universal health insurance, investment in job training, pro-choice on abortion, increased Head Start funding and prenatal care. He calls for a "drug-free society." He took care in his campaign to appeal to white voters and civic leaders, and in the general election ran far ahead of racial lines, winning 70% of the vote in a district where 53% of adults are black. He showed a moving respect also for those who have come before, saying on election night, "I'm proud to be a part of George Henry White's prophecy. But I am saddened that it took 92 years. And I'm disappointed, because I know that thousands and thousands of people, but for the color of their skin, would have been just as qualified to fill this office." In Washington, he was one of three freshmen appointed to the Democratic Steering and Policy Committee and seems headed for an influential House career. He is a prime example of one of 1992's paradoxes, how the new Voting Rights districts, which seemed to promote mono-racial politics, have instead produced several talented black politicians with rich experience in local life and civic affairs and a determination to represent their entire communities. Watt's political future, however, may be predicated on maintenance of the district's lines. Should the U.S. Supreme Court strike them down (a case was pending there in June 1993), his ability to forge multi-racial support will be all the more critical.

970 NORTH CAROLINA

The People: Pop. 1990: 551,957; 14% rural; 12% age 65+; 41% White; 57% Black; 1% Asian; 1% Hispanic origin. Voting age pop.: 410,871; 53% Black; 1% Hispanic origin. Households: 43% married couple families; 19% married couple fams. w. children; 37% college educ.; median household income: $23,068; per capita income: $10,878; median gross rent: $381; median house value: $57,800.

1992 Presidential Vote			1988 Presidential Vote		
Clinton (D)	125,189	(66%)	Bush (R)	58,457	(37%)
Bush (R)	48,406	(25%)	Dukakis (D)	101,415	(63%)
Perot (I)	16,886	(9%)			

Rep. Melvin L. Watt (D)

Elected 1992; b. Aug. 26, 1945, Mecklenburg; home, Charlotte; U. of NC, Chapel Hill, B.S. 1967, Yale, J.D. 1970; Presbyterian; married (Eulada).

Career: NC Senate, 1985–86; Campaign Mgr., Harvey Gantt for Senate, 1990; Practicing atty., 1971-92; Co-developer, co-owner, East Town Manor nursing home, 1989-present.

Offices: 1232 LHOB 20515, 202-225-1510. Also 214 N. Church St., #130, Charlotte 28202, 704-344-9950; 315 E. Chapel Hill, #202, Durham 27702, 919-688-3004; 301 S. Green St., #210, Greensboro 27402, 919-375-9402.

Committees: *Banking, Finance and Urban Affairs* (26th of 30 D): Consumer Credit and Insurance; Housing and Community Development; International Development, Finance, Trade and Monetary Policy. *Judiciary* (20th of 21 D): Administrative Law and Governmental Relations; Economic and Commercial Law. *Post Office and Civil Service* (10th of 15 D): Postal Operations and Services.

Group Ratings and 102d Congress Votes: Newly Elected

Key Votes of the 103d Congress

1. Family Leave	FOR	2. Deficit Reduction	FOR	3. Stimulus Plan	FOR

Election Results

1992 general	Melvin L. Watt (D)	127,262	(70%)	($480,713)
	Barbara Gore Washington (R)	49,402	(27%)	($22,761)
	Other	4,160	(2%)	
1992 primary	Melvin L. Watt (D)	26,495	(47%)	
	Mickey Michaux (D)	16,187	(29%)	
	Larry D. Little (D)	8,298	(15%)	
	Earl Jones (D)	5,338	(9%)	
1990 election	Newly created district.			

NORTH DAKOTA

No state is closer to its roots than North Dakota. There are North Dakotans alive today who knew the men and women that settled this land and saw the state enter the Union in 1889, just a little more than 100 years ago. As children, they walked in the ruts left by the early settlers' wagon trains; they saw the Indians, recently defeated, herded off onto reservations; they saw still shining new the rails that brought the world's commerce to these desolate prairies. This was the frontier to which Teddy Roosevelt came in 1884, determined to shoot one of the fast-disappearing buffalo, a place where settlers were only then breaking the sod and plowing under the natural prairies that some eco-theorists, much to North Dakotans' disgust, want to restore. In those days, the land was rich with promise. Once the soil was broken, this was some of the best wheat land in the world, empty by then of Indians and buffalo, connected to markets by rail, ready to become a cog in the industrial world being created by entrepreneurs and to raise its living standards to unparalleled heights.

And so, in a sudden rush of settlement during the 20 years before World War I, North Dakota filled up to pretty much its present population; there were 632,000 people here in 1920 and in counts since, the number has fluctuated between 617,000 and 680,000; in 1990 it was 639,000 (cumulatively, the state with the lowest growth rate since 1950). Wheat is not the only crop here; as the plains become more arid in the west, ranching and livestock grazing—along with strip mining and oil production—are important, and hardy root crops like potatoes and sugar beets grow as well. But wheat is still number one. Typically the state produces about one-tenth of the U.S. crop, and a fair percentage of the world's; its durum wheat is the main ingredient of American pasta. At the same time, wondrous increases in productivity have meant that it takes far fewer farmers to produce far more crops, and so over the years North Dakotans have moved off farms and into towns or, more often, to other states altogether. Its four biggest counties, containing Fargo, Grand Forks, Bismarck and Minot, grew from 134,000 in 1930 to 291,000 in 1990, while the state's other 48 counties dropped from 546,000 to 347,000. Farming is still important: nearly one-quarter of North Dakotans still live on farms and ranches, and many living in town own land or depend on farming for their livelihood.

Naturally this has affected politics. Historically, North Dakota's economy has depended not on wages but, because farmers are small businessmen, on profits; its whole economy has been in effect heavily leveraged. And because farmers and those dependent on them, while they may gain from upswings in the market, want to be protected against the downswings, there has been a cry reverberating with varying intensity throughout North Dakota's history for government protection against market forces. Since commodity prices tend to fall over long periods of economic growth, there has been a countercyclical element in North Dakota politics, a tendency to vote against the national trends, and a radical strain going back nearly a century and still lively today. That radical strain also owes much to the immigrant origins of so many of North Dakota's early settlers: Norwegians in the eastern part of the state, Canadians along the northern border, Volga Germans in the west, colonies of Poles and Czechs and Icelanders, and native Germans throughout the state. (Volga Germans are descendants of early 19th Century German migrants to Russia who kept their German language and character.) Yet there is also an orderliness to North Dakota's small cities, a communitarian tradition of cooperative action, that can also be traced back to this German and Scandinavian heritage.

Another product of the radical tradition, chronicled colorfully and with unusual frankness in the North Dakota Heritage Museum in Bismarck, was the Non-Partisan League (NPL) formed in 1915. Its constituency was lonely marginal farmers, cut off in many cases from the wider American culture by language barriers and seemingly at the mercy of the grain millers of

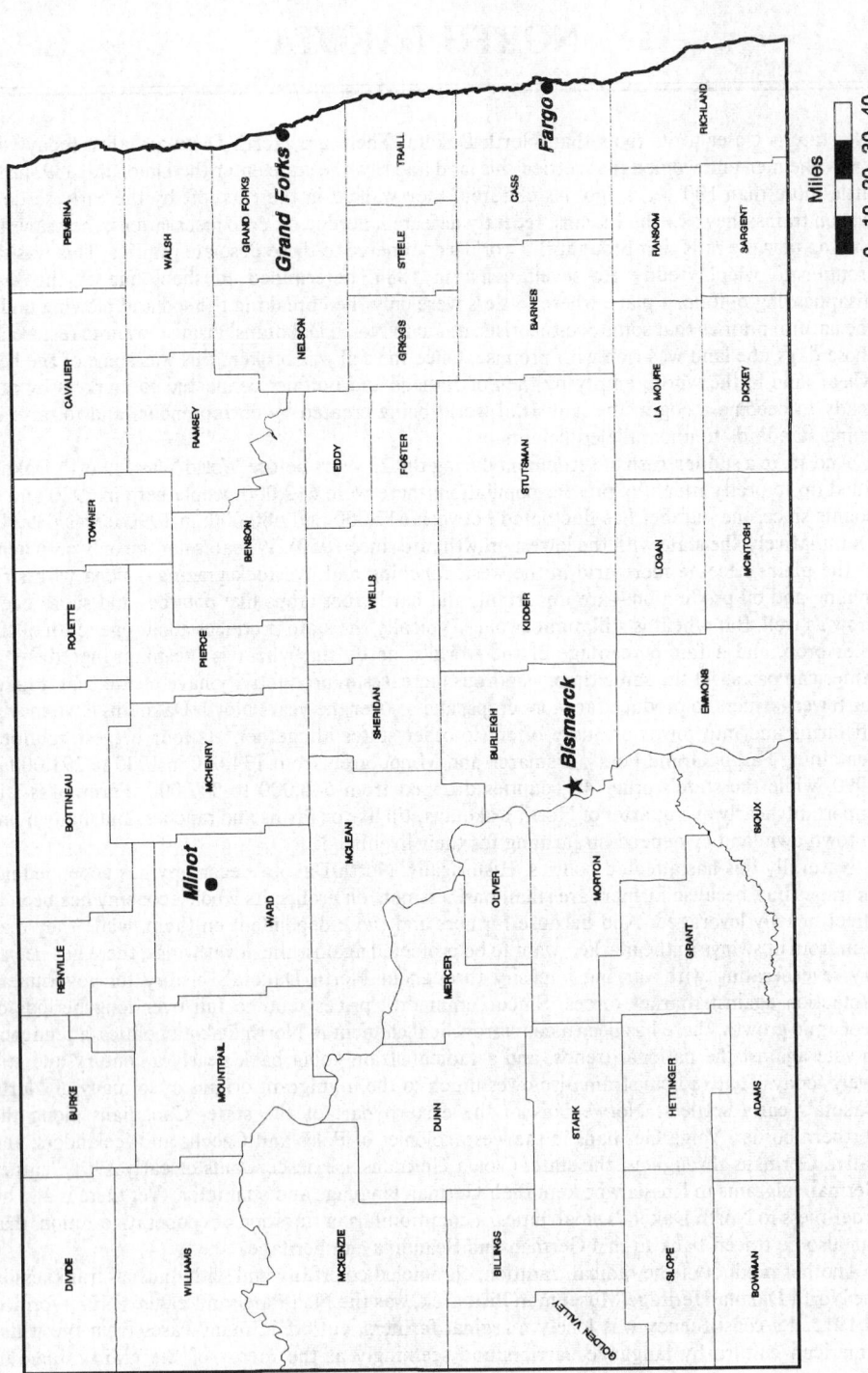

Minneapolis, the railroads of St. Paul, the banks of New York and the commodity traders of Chicago. The NPL's program was socialistic—government ownership of railroads and grain elevators—and, like most North Dakota ethnics, opposed going to war with Germany. The NPL often determined the outcome of the usually decisive Republican primary and sometimes swung its support to the otherwise heavily outnumbered Democrats, instituting reforms and creating a state-owned bank. A particular NPL favorite was "Wild Bill" Langer, governor intermittently in the 1930s, elected to the Senate in 1940 but allowed to take his seat only after a lengthy investigation of campaign irregularities. By 1960, the NPL had more or less merged into the Democratic Party, a merger symbolized by the election of the late Democratic Senator Quentin Burdick, whose father, Usher Burdick, served 20 years in the House as an NPL-endorsed Republican. "Young Burdick," as he was long known, continued NPL tradition, supporting wheat subsidies and pork barrel projects and avoiding controversial cultural issues. Today, North Dakota's leading Democrats, Senators Kent Conrad and Byron Dorgan, champion a politics clearly of NPL lineage: for government farm programs, and government intervention in the economy generally, wary if not hostile to American military involvement abroad, cheerfully championing the little guy from North Dakota against out-of-state corporations.

But the radical strain is not the only political product of North Dakota's heritage. For the orderliness and closeness of life in small communities nurtures a conservative strain. This is a place where everyone knows everyone else, where divorce is as uncommon as anywhere in the United States and the two-parent family is still very much the norm, where abortions are available in only one clinic in the whole state. There is no voter registration because poll watchers would obviously spot anyone not eligible to vote (and hence it has one of the nation's highest voter turnouts). North Dakota is proud that its students achieve some of the nation's highest math scores, even though its teacher pay is 49th in the country—parents and neighbors make sure students work hard and teachers are able to keep track of students from kindergarten to high school.

Politics is personal too, in this small state where every politician is personally known to many, perhaps most, voters. North Dakotans did not much cotton to Bill Clinton in 1992: his southernness, the charges of womanizing and evading the draft, did not go over well, and he got only 32% of the vote here—lower than in any other state but Alaska, Nebraska, Idaho and Utah, and less than half of what some state Democrats were winning the same day. North Dakota is a sort of Ireland in America—well-educated but economically behind, geographically remote from great booming metropolises. If the typical elderly North Dakotan is a hard-working retired farmer, with fond memories of NPL agitation and a belief in government programs, the typical young North Dakotan is a family person with a college education (49% of the state's parents are college graduates) alternatively open to government intervention and encouraging free enterprise. Older North Dakotans in 1992 heavily favored the Democrats in the one House and two Senate races; young North Dakotans voted Republican generally and provided the nucleus for the statewide margins of George Bush and the new Republican Governor, Gold Star wax scion Edward Schafer. The impulse of older North Dakota, personified by 80-plus Senator Quentin Burdick, when the idea was floated of a museum near Lawrence Welk's birthplace in Strasburg, was to seek a $500,000 federal grant; but when the idea was unjustly ridiculed (for maintaining ties with a part of our American heritage such as Welk's Volga German community is a valid national purpose), the townsfolk went about raising the money privately, as they had for the Welk property. It's too soon to say that North Dakota has moved away from its radical political roots. But the conservative strain in its heritage is asserting itself as well.

Governor. North Dakota's skyscraper Capitol, towering over neatly-kept Bismarck and the rolling plains beyond, has held a Republican governor for only four of the 32 years from 1960 to 1992. Indeed, six of the other 12 statewide elected offices are held by Democrats, many of them exceedingly popular. But in November 1991, two-term Democratic incumbent George Sinner decided, a few months after heart bypass surgery, to retire; a father of 10 who vetoed a law which would have made most abortions illegal, he was mentioned for secretary of agriculture in the Clinton Administration but not tapped. His retirement left the way open to a clear favorite on the Republican side and a fight among hitherto dominant Democrats.

The Republican favorite was Ed Schafer, bearer of a famous name in North Dakota: his father founded the Gold Seal company, makers of Gold Seal glass wax, Snowy Bleach and Mr. Bubble; Schafer heads a classic car dealership, Dakota Classics, and an aquaculture fish farm, Fish 'N Dakota, and ran for Congress in 1990. The Democrats had a battle between Attorney General Nick Spaeth and state Senate leader Bill Heigaard. Heigaard, pro-choice and well wired into the party, won the state convention endorsement in April, but Spaeth, antiabortion and a backer of state investment in economic development (the "Growing North Dakota" plan), waged a tough campaign and won the June primary 65%–35%. In the fall, Spaeth attacked Schafer for his denunciation of the "Growing North Dakota" plan which Schafer's business had taken advantage of for tax breaks and loan assistance. Spaeth also questioned whether Schafer, who had run Gold Seal from New Jersey for years, met North Dakota's five-year residency requirement. Schafer boosted his own plan for development which leaves the initiative with local communities, and charged that the Democrats' state agencies were hard to deal with. Both candidates were appealing to the yearning North Dakotans have for new businesses and jobs; evidently Schafer's sojourn out of state did not much trouble them and his local-oriented plan for economic development proved more attractive. Or, with an eye on the state's budget pinch, they may have felt that a Republican would be less likely to raise taxes. Schafer won, 58%–41%, carrying all the major towns and all but seven counties, winning over 60% with voters under 60, while Spaeth got 55% from those 60 and over.

Senators. North Dakota has two Democratic senators, one of whom once worked for the other and then succeeded him in elective office. Interestingly, it is the subordinate of the two who is now the senior senator: Kent Conrad was elected to the Senate in 1986, upsetting a Republican incumbent in a race Byron Dorgan declined to make. Now Dorgan holds the seat Conrad initially won, because Conrad decided to honor a campaign pledge and not run again in 1992; but Conrad then was persuaded to run for the seat made vacant by the death in September 1992 of Senator Quentin Burdick—a fellow Democrat but no political friend of either Conrad or Dorgan. But all this seat swapping is less important than the philosophical and biographical common ground of the two current incumbents. Both served as state tax commissioner, and used the office to seek greater revenues from out-of-state corporations. Both are direct heirs of the state's radical economic tradition, its faith that North Dakotans need government protection from the vagaries of farm prices and that government regulations and subsidies can help ordinary people. Neither has yet become a power in the Senate. But together, and with help from other prairie populists like Tom Daschle of South Dakota, Tom Harkin of Iowa and Paul Wellstone of Minnesota, they can be a formidable bloc.

The central point of Kent Conrad's Senate career so far has been the pledge he made in the 1986 campaign that "the federal deficit, the trade deficit and real interest rates will be brought under control or I will not seek this office again." At the time, with the Gramm-Rudman law just enacted, it seemed like a keepable promise, and in fact interest rates and the trade deficit did fall. Moreover, North Dakotans did not seem to be holding him to it: in March 1992 polls showed him with more than 60% when paired against Republicans. But in April 1992, after ruminating on the issue and after his wife had been mugged and dragged down the street near their Capitol Hill home, Conrad rose and shocked the Senate by saying that he was not running because he had not kept his pledge. He could have argued that he had tried. He has favored crackdowns on tax cheats, higher taxes on the top income brackets and across-the-board freezes in some discretionary spending. He had also advocated the repeal of income tax indexing (giving government a nice windfall from inflation). On the Budget Committee, he put forward deficit-cutting amendments, losing only 11–10 in 1991 when he excepted education, agriculture, health care and veterans' benefits and offered a $51 billion cut in 1992 with spending cuts, entitlement restraints and tax increases. To be sure, he did cast pro-spending votes on notch babies and the honeybee program, both of which benefit North Dakota.

On other issues, Conrad showed sensitivity to North Dakota opinion. He was one of the few Democrats to support most favored nation status for China, a major buyer of North Dakota wheat. He backed more coal and alternative fuels research; North Dakota has lignite deposits and grain that can be used for gasohol. On the Agriculture Committee, he has backed far more expensive farm bills than most other senators have been willing to support, and he has opposed NAFTA because he fears inroads by Mexican and Canadian agricultural products.

At home, Conrad held more than 1,000 public meetings, keeping in touch with the rural counties where he had won his highest margin of victory in 1986 against Republican Mark Andrews. Though he decided to step down, the evidence suggested that Conrad surely could have won again in 1992, and, indeed he did just that when Senator Burdick died in September 1992. Under state law, the special election could not be held in November but had to be held before January, so Conrad had to run for this seat while still serving the last month of his first term in the other. But he overcame this awkwardness, and that of running at all after saying he would quit, by explaining, "When I decided not to seek reelection to my seat five months ago, I kept my pledge to the people of North Dakota. Now, with the death of Senator Burdick, we face a new situation." At home, he was nominated unanimously at a Democratic convention. His Republican opponent was Jack Dalrymple, chairman of the Dakota Growers Pasta cooperative, whose great-grandfather started one of the first bonanza farms, and who called for a vastly expensive new ($5 per bushel) wheat program, which even Conrad called unrealistic. Dalrymple attacked Conrad for broken promises, but Conrad's credit with voters, in a state where he was personally known to many, remained strong; also, Democrats argued that North Dakota shouldn't be represented by two freshman senators. Conrad was attacked strongly by Darold Larsen, an antiabortion candidate, but had far more money and won by a 63%–34% margin. "I think that this election proved that hard work and straight talk still matter in North Dakota," was Conrad's verdict. Interestingly, for a few hours in December 1992, Conrad was technically the holder of both Senate seats: he was sworn in December 14 to fill the remainder of Burdick's term; then a few hours later Dorgan was sworn in to fill the remainder of Conrad's seat, giving him a jumpstart in seniority on his fellow freshman Senators.

Byron Dorgan has been one of the most popular politicians in North Dakota for a quarter-century, but it has taken him some time to finally make it to the Senate. He declined to challenge Mark Andrews in 1986 or to take on Quentin Burdick in the 1988 primary; then in 1992, his former assistant Kent Conrad's decision to retire opened the way for him. Dorgan made his reputation after he was appointed state tax commissioner in 1969, and brought highly publicized actions to get out-of-state corporations to pay more state taxes. He was elected to the House in 1980; his toughest race came in 1990, when he faced current Governor Edward Schafer and won 65% of the vote. He approaches issues with zest and has the kind of cornball good humor that New Deal enthusiasts liked to summon up when liberals thought they represented the ordinary, inarticulate little guy, in contrast to the conservatives seen as old stuffed shirts.

Dorgan served on the House Ways and Means Committee for 10 years and left some marks—adding rural enterprise zones to the urban aid package responding to the 1992 Los Angeles riots, channeling more audits to high-income taxpayers, killing an intangibles write-off provision that would benefit corporate takeovers. He also passed some amendments chipping away at defense construction, spare parts and consultant spending. He would cap pharmaceutical price increases at the rate of inflation and wants self-employed business owners (like farmers) to have a bigger deduction for health insurance. He opposes gas tax increases and NAFTA, and was one of the leading and most vocal opponents of fast tracking the trade pact. An M.B.A., he chaired a House Democrats' task force on government waste, and co-sponsored several overhead-trimming amendments to appropriations bills. In the Senate, he has promised to be a deficit-cutter and can be expected to continue the North Dakota tradition of progressive attacks on corporations' "Wall Street speculation and greed," to be for rural enterprise zones at home, and suspicious of trade agreements or military involvement abroad.

Dorgan's election to the Senate was not quite automatic. Though he claimed only four overdrafts on the House bank, he actually had 98. His Republican opponent, Fargo city commissioner Steve Sydness had an interesting background: he used to work for Henry Kissinger's political and economics consulting firm; he had lost to Dorgan 71%–28% in 1988. Sydness favored SDI and the B-2; both candidates were for most favored nation status for China and were wary of free trade, and favored relaxation of the wetlands law (which has classified hundreds of seasonal puddles in North Dakota as protected wetlands). Dorgan got most editorial endorsements; here, as elsewhere in America, editorials are no longer written by crusty old conservatives but by baby boom liberals. Dorgan won by a solid but not overwhelming 59%–39% margin.

Representative-At-Large. In early 1992, North Dakota Insurance Commissioner Earl Pomeroy was planning to retire at 40 from a long career in politics and serve in the Peace Corps in Russia. Back in 1974, when Byron Dorgan challenged Congressman Mark Andrews and Kent Conrad managed his campaign, Pomeroy was Dorgan's driver; in 1980, at 28, he won a seat in the legislature, and in 1984 and 1988 he was elected insurance commissioner. Articulate, cheerful, a critic of insurance companies, he was the obvious choice for the House seat, when Conrad announced he was retiring and Dorgan ran for Conrad's seat in the Senate; he was nominated unanimously by the Democratic convention and his plans for Russia were set aside. Republican John Korsmo, known as the father of a child actor who appeared in *Dick Tracy* and *Hook*, who had planned to run against Dorgan, never made much headway against Pomeroy. Pomeroy won by a 57%–39% margin, almost a carbon copy of Dorgan's margin in the Senate race. In the House, Pomeroy was one of only two freshman Democrats assigned to the Budget Committee, and like Conrad and Dorgan he promised to be a "deficit hawk," calling for "a greater handle on soaring healthcare costs."

Presidential politics. North Dakota's cultural conservatism seemed to have overcome its economic radicalism in the 1992 presidential race. It gave Bill Clinton only 32% of its votes, ahead of Ross Perot's 23% by a smaller margin than it was behind George Bush's 44%. In the pattern of many other states, Perot ran perceptibly stronger in some media markets (Bismarck, Minot) than others (Fargo, Grand Forks), suggesting a selective market-by-market time buy.

Over two weeks in March, about 5,000 North Dakotans voted in Democratic party caucuses and gave Bill Clinton, supported by Governor George Sinner, a solid margin. The Republicans had a primary June 9, which George Bush handily won.

The People: Est. Pop. 1992: 638,800; Pop. 1990: 638,800, down 0.4% 1990–1992. 0.3% of U.S. total, 47th largest; 47% rural. Median age: 32.4 years. 14.3% 65 years and over. 94.6% White, 4.1% American Indian. Households: 59.1% married couple families; 30% married couple fams. w. children; 49% college educ.; median household income: $23,213; per capita income: $11,051; 65.6% owner occupied housing; median house value: $50,800; median monthly rent: $266. 4.9% Unemployment. Voting age pop.: 463,415. No state voter registration.

Political Lineup: Governor, Edward T. Schafer (R); Lt. Gov., Rosemarie Myrdal (R); Secy. of State, Al Jaeger (R); Atty. Gen., Heidi Heitkamp (D); Treasurer, Kathi Gilmore (D); Auditor, Robert W. Peterson (R). State Senate, 49 (25 D and 24 R); State House of Representatives, 98 (65 R and 33 D). Senators, Kent Conrad (D) and Byron L. Dorgan (D). Representative, 1 D at large.

1992 Presidential Vote			1988 Presidential Vote		
Bush (R)	136,244	(44%)	Bush (R)	166,559	(56%)
Clinton (D)	99,168	(32%)	Dukakis (D)	127,739	(43%)
Perot (I)	71,084	(23%)			

1992 Republican Presidential Primary

Bush	39,863	(83%)
Paulsen	4,093	(9%)
Perot (write-in)	3,852	(8%)

GOVERNOR

Gov. Edward T. Schafer (R)

Elected 1992, term expires Dec. 1996; b. August 8, 1946, Bismarck; home, Bismarck; U. of ND, B.A. 1969, U. of Denver, M.B.A. 1970; Episcopalian; married (Nancy).

Career: Gold Seal Co., 1971–86, Pres., 1978–86; Pres. & owner, Dakota Classics auto dealership, and TRIESCO Properties real estate, 1986–present; Pres. & owner, Fish 'N Dakota aquaculture, 1990–present.

Office: State Capitol, 600 E. Boulevard, Bismarck 58505, 701-224-2200.

Election Results

1992 gen.	Edward T. Schafer (R)........	176,398	(58%)
	Nicholas Spaeth (D)..........	123,845	(41%)
1992 prim.	Edward T. Schafer (R), unopposed		
1988 gen.	George A. Sinner (D).........	179,094	(60%)
	Arthur A. Link (R)	119,986	(40%)

SENATORS

Sen. Kent Conrad (D)

Elected 1986, seat up 1994; b. Mar. 12, 1948, Bismarck; home, Bismarck; Stanford U., B.A. 1971; George Washington U., M.B.A. 1975; Unitarian; married (Lucy Calautti).

Career: Asst., ND Tax Commissioner, 1974–80; Dir., Mgmt. Planning and Personnel, ND Tax Dept., 1980; ND Tax Commissioner, 1981–86.

Offices: 724 HSOB 20510, 202-224-2043. Also Fed. Bldg., #228, 3d & Rosser Ave., Bismarck 58501, 701-258-4648; 657 2d Ave. N., Fargo 58102, 701-232-8030; 100 1st St. SW, #105, Minot 58701, 701-852-0703; and Fed. Bldg., 102 N. 4th St., #104, Grand Forks 58201, 701-775-9601.

Committees: *Agriculture, Nutrition and Forestry* (6th of 10 D): Agricultural Credit (Chmn.); Domestic and Foreign Marketing and Product Promotion; Rural Development and Rural Electrification. *Budget* (8th of 12 D). *Finance* (11th of 11 D): International Trade; Medicare and Long-Term Care; Taxation. *Indian Affairs* (4th of 10 D).

Group Ratings

	ADA	ACLU	CDF	COPE	CFA	LCV	ACU	NTLC	NSI	COC	CEI
1992	90	67	80	75	75	17	12	39	60	20	31
1991	75	—	91	75	72	47	43	—	—	20	30

National Journal Ratings

	1991 LIB	—	1991 CONS	1992 LIB	—	1992 CONS
Economic	51%	—	46%	91%	—	5%
Social	59%	—	38%	47%	—	52%
Foreign	68%	—	31%	62%	—	35%

Key Votes of the 102d Congress

1. $ for Homeownership AGN	5. Clarence Thomas Nom.AGN	9. Use Force in Gulf AGN
2. Have Cap Gains DebateAGN	6. Lmt Death Row AppealAGN	10. Keep Salvador Aid AGN
3. Remove Budget Walls FOR	7. Handgun Wait/5-Day FOR	11. Cut $1B from SDI AGN
4. Ban Striker Replace FOR	8. Abortion Gag Rule AGN	12. Override China MFN AGN

Key Votes of the 103d Congress

1. Family Leave FOR	2. HIV Immigrants AGN	3. Clinton Budget FOR

Election Results

1992 special	Kent Conrad (D).....................	103,246	(63%)	($2,479,021)
	Jack Dalrymple (R)	55,194	(34%)	($282,104)
	Other...............................	4,871	(3%)	
1992 primary	Kent Conrad (D), nominated by convention			
1988 general	Quentin N. Burdick (D)..............	171,899	(59%)	($2,026,617)
	Earl Strinden (R)	112,937	(39%)	($906,807)

Sen. Byron L. Dorgan (D)

Elected 1992, seat up 1998; b. May 14, 1942, Dickinson; home, Bismarck; U. of ND, B.S. 1965, U. of Denver, M.B.A. 1966; Lutheran; married (Kimberly).

Career: Martin-Marietta Exec. Develop. Prog., 1966–68; ND Dep. Tax Commissioner, 1968–69, Tax Commissioner, 1969–80; U.S. House of Reps., 1980–92.

Offices: 713 HSOB 20510, 202-224-2551. Also 312 Fed. Bldg., 3rd & Rosser Ave., Bismarck 58502, 701-250-4618; 112 Robert St., Fargo 58107, 701-239-5389.

Committees: *Commerce, Science and Transportation* (10th of 11 D): Consumer; Foreign Commerce and Tourism; Surface Transportation. *Governmental Affairs* (8th of 8 D): Oversight of Government Management; Regulation and Government Information; Permanent Subcommittee on Investigations. *Indian Affairs* (9th of 9 D). *Joint Economic Committee* (6th of 10).

Group Ratings (as Member of the U.S. House of Representatives)

	ADA	ACLU	COPE	CDF	CFA	LCV	ACU	NTLC	NSI	COC	CEI
1992	70	91	83	60	87	56	28	30	40	38	34
1991	75	—	75	70	78	15	25	—	—	40	37

National Journal Ratings (as Member of the U.S. House of Representatives)

	1991 LIB — 1991 CONS		1992 LIB — 1992 CONS	
Economic	54% —	45%	51% —	48%
Social	57% —	42%	66% —	34%
Foreign	75% —	24%	75% —	24%

Key Votes of the 102d Congress (as Member of the U.S. House of Representatives)

1. Ban Striker Replace FOR	5. Handgun Wait/7-Day AGN	9. Use Force in Gulf AGN
2. $ for Homeownership AGN	6. Overseas Mil. AbortionAGN	10. US Mil. Abroad $ Cut FOR
3. Tax Rich/Cut Mid Cls. FOR	7. Obscn. Art NEA $ Ban FOR	11. Limit SDI Funds FOR
4. FY93/$15B Def. Cut AGN	8. Death Pen. from Jury AGN	12. Cuba Trade Embargo FOR

Key Votes of the 103d Congress

1. Family Leave	FOR	2. HIV Immigrants	FOR	3. Clinton Budget	FOR

Election Results

1992 general	Byron L. Dorgan (D)	179,347	(59%)	($1,124,512)
	Steve Sydness (R)....................	118,162	(39%)	($498,107)
	Other...............................	6,448	(2%)	
1992 primary	Byron L. Dorgan (D), unopposed			
1986 general	Kent Conrad (D)....................	143,932	(50%)	($908,374)
	Mark Andrews (R)	141,797	(49%)	($2,270,557)

REPRESENTATIVE

Rep. Earl Pomeroy (D)

Elected 1992; b. Sept. 2, 1952, Valley City; home, Valley City; U. of ND, B.A. 1974, J.D., 1979; Presbyterian; married (Laurie Kirby).

Career: Practicing atty., 1979–84; ND House of Reps., 1980–84; ND Insurance Commissioner, 1984–92; VP, Natl. Assn. of Insurance Commissioners, 1989, Pres., 1990.

Offices: 318 CHOB 20515, 202-225-2611. Also Fed. Bldg., 657 2nd Ave., #266, Fargo 58102, 701-235-9760; Fed. Bldg., 304 E. Broadway Ave., #337, Bismarck 58501, 701-224-0355.

Committees: *Agriculture* (20th of 28 D): Environment, Credit and Rural Development; Foreign Agriculture and Hunger; General Farm Commodities; Specialty Crops and Natural Resources. *Budget* (24th of 26 D).

Group Ratings and 102d Congress Votes: Newly Elected

Key Votes of the 103d Congress

1. Family Leave	FOR	2. Deficit Reduction	FOR	3. Stimulus Plan	FOR

Election Results

1992 general	Earl Pomeroy (D)....................	169,273	(57%)	($430,228)
	John T. Korsmo (R)	117,442	(39%)	($150,639)
	Two Others	11,183	(4%)	
1992 primary	Earl Pomeroy (D), unopposed			
1990 general	Byron L. Dorgan (D)	152,530	(65%)	($504,800)
	Edward T. Schafer (R)...............	81,443	(35%)	($284,855)

OHIO

Ohio, arguably the most pivotal state in U.S. politics, the site of so much campaigning by national candidates in 1992 that it seemed there were few fall days when at least one presidential or vice presidential candidate was not there, is in many ways the essence of Middle America. It is the first state across the Appalachians, its flat plains and gently rolling hills are the threshold of the great American heartland, and it was the first Midwestern state admitted to the Union. Settled by Virginians in its southwest corner around Cincinnati, settled by New Englanders in its northeast corner around what became Cleveland, Ohio has always been regionally split between cultures: between the southern-accented counties south of the National Road and U.S. 40 and the northern-accented cities and towns to the north; between Butternut and Copperhead territory that didn't want to fight the Civil War and Yankee territory that fiercely prosecuted the War and Reconstruction afterwards. That heritage left Ohio narrowly divided between the two major parties, and a state that produced presidential candidates and presidents—Hayes, Garfield, McKinley, Taft and Harding. Ohio, in the years after the Civil War, became one of the great industrial states, the long time headquarters of John D. Rockefeller's Standard Oil, the site of major steel mills along the narrow and languidly flowing Cuyahoga and Mahoning Rivers, and home of the biggest soap companies, machine tool makers, tire manufacturers and producers of safety glass.

With the Depression of the 1930s, Ohio became the scene of something like class warfare, with sitdown strikes and victories for the CIO industrial unions in autos, steel and tires—industries people thought would never have unions—and of strikers killed in riots when National Guard troops were called in. Again, Ohio became a microcosm of national politics, where the antagonisms that fueled national party politics came out with special vehemence and force. On top of its Civil War divisions was superimposed a politics of union-management struggle; the cities which moved toward the Democrats—Cleveland, Akron, Youngstown, Toledo—were strongly CIO, while those which remained heavily Republican—Cincinnati, Columbus, the dozens of small factory towns dotting the flat limestone plains of northern and central Ohio—were by and large not union strongholds. The stakes seemed big. The CIO leaders wanted to organize all of American industry and build a Scandinavian-style welfare state; Republican leaders like Ohio Senator Robert Taft feared socialism and involvement in European wars, which he thought would dragoon Americans and erode their freedoms. These battles were fought in Ohio, a state then and (in most respects) now typical of the nation, with income levels, urban-rural balance, ethnic mix near the national average.

First regional and then economic politics left Ohio deeply divided. Its electoral votes have long been a fiercely contested prize; its governors and senators often become presidential candidates or national figures. It is the only megastate with Republican House delegations for most of the last 40 years and the only one not to have voted for a Republican senator for the last 20. It has oscillated fairly regularly between Democratic and Republican governors. In effect, politics in Ohio has become two very different contests—the heavy-industry, CIO-dominated north-and-east, and the rest of the state.

The industrial north-and-east includes the coal strip-mining counties across the Ohio River from Wheeling, West Virginia, which were strong United Mine Workers' territory in their day; it includes the steel mill corridors of the Mahoning Valley in Youngstown and Warren and the Cuyahoga River corridor in Cleveland, a center of the national strength of the United Steelworkers for years; it includes Akron which, in the days when the big American rubber companies had factories operating there (none do today), was the center of the United Rubber Workers. It passes along the shore of Lake Erie (much less polluted now than 15 years ago, and

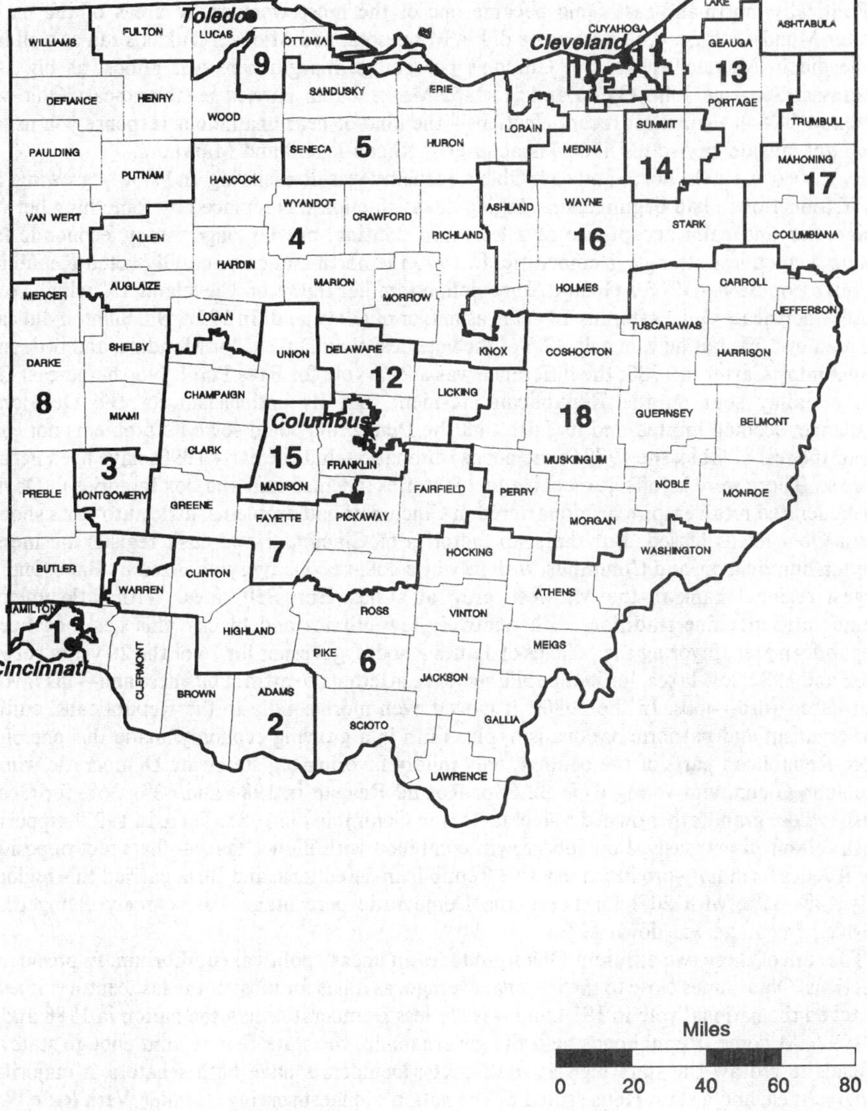

Toledo

Cleveland

WILLIAMS   FULTON   LUCAS   OTTAWA   CUYAHOGA   LAKE   19   ASHTABULA

9   GEAUGA   13

DEFIANCE   HENRY   SANDUSKY   ERIE   PORTAGE

WOOD   SUMMIT   TRUMBULL

PAULDING   PUTNAM   SENECA   5   HURON   LORAIN   MEDINA   14   MAHONING   17

HANCOCK   ASHLAND   WAYNE

VAN WERT   WYANDOT   CRAWFORD   RICHLAND   16   STARK   COLUMBIANA

ALLEN   4

HARDIN   CARROLL

MERCER   AUGLAIZE   MARION   MORROW   HOLMES   JEFFERSON

LOGAN   TUSCARAWAS   HARRISON

DARKE   SHELBY   UNION   DELAWARE   KNOX   COSHOCTON

8   MIAMI   CHAMPAIGN   12   LICKING   18   GUERNSEY   BELMONT

3   CLARK   Columbus   15   FRANKLIN   MUSKINGUM   NOBLE   MONROE

PREBLE   MONTGOMERY   GREENE   MADISON   FAIRFIELD   PERRY   MORGAN

FAYETTE   PICKAWAY   WASHINGTON

BUTLER   CLINTON   7   HOCKING

WARREN   ROSS   VINTON   ATHENS

HAMILTON   1   HIGHLAND   PIKE   6   MEIGS

Cincinnati   CLERMONT   BROWN   ADAMS   JACKSON   GALLIA

2   SCIOTO

LAWRENCE

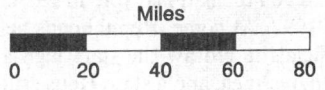

Miles

0   20   40   60   80

even swimmable) to Toledo, with its glass and auto plants which were organized by the United Auto Workers. North-and-east Ohio was hurt badly by the collapse of the auto-steel-coal economy following the oil shock of 1979: the great steel factories along the Mahoning and Cuyahoga became cold, black hulks; the tire factories of Akron emptied out. People who had counted on making well-above-average wages even for low-skill work, and who were looking forward to an early and comfortable retirement, suddenly found themselves facing the end of their unemployment benefits in communities where the traditional big employers had pretty much shut down and there were no visible job openings in new firms. Hundreds of thousands of people moved out, and the area's population declined by 4% in the 1980s.

Politically, north-and-east Ohio became one of the most Democratic areas of the nation. Walter Mondale ran as well here as he did in Minnesota, and Michael Dukakis ran as well here as he did in Massachusetts; Bill Clinton's percentage margin here was almost as big as in Arkansas. Senators John Glenn and Howard Metzenbaum carried north-and-east Ohio with 58% and 64% in their most recent elections—the kind of near-unanimous response you usually don't get outside city-states like Massachusetts, Rhode Island and Maryland.

By the early 1990s, north-and-east Ohio's economy was diversifying and slowly growing, and population growth had begun again. Raging dissatisfaction was replaced by something between resignation and calm acceptance of a less than exciting, but no longer scary, economic fate. Voters seemed less strongly Democratic. In 1990 the north-and-east actually voted Republican for governor, 55%–45% for George Voinovich, a familiar figure on Cleveland TV, which covers most of northeast Ohio, after his 10 years as mayor of Cleveland. In 1992, Bill Clinton did carry the area by 16%, but he won only 47% of the vote, less than Dukakis or Mondale, and little more than Jimmy Carter in 1980; the difference was a 22% vote for Ross Perot. North-and-east Ohio was certainly sour on the Republican president, but its enthusiasm for the Democratic challenger seemed limited and its faith that the Democrats could solve its problems not clear.

For the rest of Ohio, the 1980s were not as traumatic—but the early 1990s have been perhaps more so. There were layoffs at machine tool factories in Cincinnati and box factories in Dayton, the Federated retail empire headquartered in Cincinnati had problems, little auto parts shops in north Ohio towns closed. But the soap factories of Cincinnati and cash register business in Dayton hummed on, and Columbus, with its white-collar economy symbolized by Banc One, the largest regional bank in the Midwest, grew at almost Sun Belt rates. With little union or Democratic machine tradition, with relatively few ethnics and blacks, this has long been a Republican area, favoring the policies of James Rhodes, governor for 16 of the 20 years between 1962 and 1982: low taxes, limited public services, attempts to attract business and—his favorite four-letter word—jobs. In the 1980s, it moved even more solidly to the Republicans: cultural conservatism and patriotic nationalism, plus faith in a growing economy, made this one of the more Republican parts of the country, only mildly favoring big statewide Democratic winners like John Glenn, and voting 67%–32% for Ronald Reagan in 1984 and 63%–36% for George Bush (whose grandfather owned a steel factory in Columbus) in 1988. Then, in 1992, support for Bush fell off disastrously. Low job growth combined with higher taxes—the exact opposite of the Rhodes formula—produced massive Republican defections, and Bush carried this region by only 44%–35%, with 20% for Perot; the Democratic percentage was scarcely changed, but Bush's percentage was down 19%.

The sum of these two different Ohios produces an uneasy political equilibrium. In presidential elections, Ohio comes close to the national average, as it has for most of the last century: it nearly matched the national vote in 1984 and was 2% less Democratic than the nation in 1988 and 3% in 1992. At home, Republicans held the governorship, the state Senate, and enough statewide officials to redraw the state legislative districts; Democrats have both senators, a majority of congressmen, and a state House ruled by the nation's longest-serving Speaker, Vern Riffe. What neither side has been able to do—nor have business and labor—is capture people's imagination or attract them with a vision of a better tomorrow. The turn of the century Ohio that produced Thomas Edison and the Wright brothers, the cash register and auto safety glass, showed its citizens that a more comfortable and more exciting future was possible through mechanical technology and business organization; the 1940s Ohio that produced the big CIO unions, showed Americans that mass production and job security could win a war and create an affluent life. The Ohio of today has 250,000 fewer manufacturing jobs than 20 years ago but is still a manufacturing state, though an increasingly skilled and supple one; but it lacks a guiding vision and sense of where it is going.

Governor. George Voinovich is a Republican governor whose victories have mostly come from Democratic constituencies, a career politician who cast himself successfully as a reformer while mayor of Cleveland and an adversary of the insiders in Columbus, a pleasant man who has not been averse to some pretty aggressive politicking on occasion. He has worked to hold down taxes and has fought for new incentives and tax credits to keep business from moving to tax-cutting Indiana or Kentucky. As Republican governor of a critical state, he gave strong support to George Bush in 1992, though not without some critical asides on the Bush campaign strategy.

Voinovich is an example of what has become a rule in Ohio politics: before you can win an election for senator or governor, you must run once and lose. It applies to Voinovich and to Celeste, Rhodes, Glenn, Metzenbaum and every senator and governor but one for the last 30 years. Voinovich's first and losing race was for senator against Metzenbaum in 1988. When Voinovich ran for governor in 1990, deft intervention from Republican National Chairman Lee Atwater—just about Atwater's last political initiative—persuaded Republican rival Robert Taft II to run for secretary of state instead of governor. Democratic gubernatorial rival Anthony Celebrezze, Jr., attorney general and son of a longtime Cleveland mayor and judge, was hurt after switching from pro-life to pro-choice on abortion in late 1989, and never dented Voinovich's support in the Cleveland market.

Voinovich's job rating has been passable, but faced with a large budget shortfall, he's likely to have serious opposition. The run-once-and-lose rule is good news for him: none of the conceivable Democratic nominees—state Senator Robert Burch, who has announced his intention to run, or state Treasurer Mary Ellen Withrow and Attorney General Lee Fisher—has run for senator or governor yet, but there is speculation by some that former Governor Celeste may run.

Senators. Two Democrats have dominated Ohio's senatorial politics for a quarter century: John Glenn and Howard Metzenbaum, once bitter enemies with sharply contrasting views on issues, now are both partisan Democratic bulwarks, allies and even friends. Both are also almost surely serving their last terms: Glenn's seat comes up in 1998, Metzenbaum's in 1994.

John Glenn, the focus of national attention when he was the first American to orbit the earth, has had a political career which soared above the reach of gravity for a while, but now seems headed gently downward, and for a while in October 1992 looked like it was about to hit splashdown. Once regarded as a national hero seemingly above partisan politics, he was the embodiment of the small town virtues of family, God-fearing religion, duty, patriotism and hard work typical of his home town of New Concord, Ohio. But by the early 1990s he had become an officeholder with few known achievements and an increasingly partisan record; once respected as a likely presidential candidate, he found the overhanging debt from his failed presidential campaign and role in the Keating Five scandal as grave political liabilities. Both images draw from genuine elements in Glenn's character. He really does believe in traditional small town values, and in the early 1970s, when George McGovern was the standard of comparison and liberal activists seemed adverse to them, Glenn stood out as a moderate Democrat. But Glenn also brings to politics the aggressiveness that enabled him to become a brilliant fighter pilot and astronaut and a successful investor and Senate candidate; in Ronald Reagan's 1980s, when he was running for president and seeking influence in the Senate, that drive brought him closer to liberal Democrats.

That process, if obscure in Washington, was clearer to Ohio voters. In his first full Senate race in 1970 (he withdrew his candidacy in 1964 after injuring himself in a household accident), Glenn lost industrial north-and-east Ohio and was upset in the primary by Howard Metzenbaum, who lost the general election to Robert Taft, Jr. In 1974, Glenn came back and beat

Metzenbaum in the primary and in the general election carried practically every county in the state—a kind of nonpartisan victory. He was reelected with 69% of the vote in 1980. Then came his 1983–84 presidential candidacy, greeted as coolly by the voters as his 1976 keynote speech had been greeted by Democratic convention delegates, who were wowed by Barbara Jordan's much less substantive oration. Glenn did not shine in the 1984 campaign debates, and his decision to stay in one more week to contest southern primaries helped pile up a current debt of $3.1 million, which he has never been able to pay off—and which became a liability in his 1992 election. He also skirted around the edge of the campaign finance law, another example of how aggressive politicking brought this straight arrow into questionable ethical territory.

But the 1984 campaign produced a reconciliation with Metzenbaum and Glenn's withdrawal from celebrity status into the work of the Senate. As chairman of the Governmental Affairs Committee, he naturally became an adversary of the Republican administration. For example, his pointed delay in confirming anyone as head of OMB's regulatory office prompted Vice President Dan Quayle's Competitiveness Council to overrule regulations, prompting other members of Congress to retaliate: a fine example of early 1990s gridlock. Glenn is solidly pro-choice on abortion and was reflexively dovish on the Gulf war resolution—the former stand being of great importance to Democratic primary voters these days. He sponsored the Democratic campaign finance bill vetoed by Bush and wants healthcare reform but is concerned about the effect on small business. Less visible but arguably more important has been the detailed work Glenn has done on two issues most politicians now consign to the back burner. For more than a decade, Glenn has been Congress's chief watchdog on nuclear proliferation, criticizing particularly U.S. exports of nuclear technology and materials to Pakistan and to Iraq; now that the Cold War is over, it's clear that Glenn was attacking the greatest threat of nuclear warfare in the 21st century. Similarly, Glenn weighed in early and often on the need to clean up government nuclear materials plants, notably the Fernald plant just outside Cincinnati. In 1993, Glenn was leading the effort to elevate the Environmental Protection Agency to Cabinet-level status.

Unfortunately for Glenn, most of this work hasn't made headlines, and some of the time he has become bogged down in trivia (does it really matter much if the Federal Protective Service in New York was chauffeuring heads of state and congressmen?). That gave an opening to his 1992 opponent, Michael DeWine, to ask continually, "What on earth has John Glenn done?" The one answer that did occur to many voters was not helpful to Glenn: his involvement in the Keating Five scandal. Glenn had known Charles Keating, once a prominent Cincinnatian, for years, and was one of five senators present at the extraordinary meeting with federal regulators in the spring of 1987. After regulators told Glenn they were referring the case against Keating to the Justice Department for criminal investigation, Glenn turned down a Keating aide's offer to raise any further money for his PAC; but he did set up a January 1988 meeting between Keating and House Speaker Jim Wright, after which Glenn said he had no further contact with Keating. Many thought the Senate Ethics Committee should have dismissed Glenn's case and John McCain's altogether; but committee Democrats, apparently to keep McCain, the lone Republican in the case, refused to do so. They ultimately recommended the same lack of punishment for Glenn and McCain as for the more culpable Dennis DeConcini and Donald Riegle, although specifying that Glenn was guilty only of poor judgment and not of any impropriety.

Armed with the Keating Five issue and with discontent with Washington, DeWine was holding Glenn under 50% in polls in September 1992. But Glenn rallied and DeWine turned out to have problems of his own. Elected lieutenant governor in 1990, he had served five terms in Congress, where he had 31 overdrafts at the House bank and became momentarily famous for falling asleep during the Iran-contra hearings (at which he was one of the most pro-Reagan Administration members). Glenn, testy in personal appearances, hired media consultants who ticked off some of his achievements in government, thus answering DeWine's question, and ripped into DeWine on his overdrafts and antiabortion stance. DeWine, looking and sounding younger than his age, could not beat the lose-once-before-you-win rule, and Glenn won 51%–

42%. For the first time, Glenn was dependent on his 58%–35% margin in north-and-east Ohio and lost the rest of the state 47%–45%, which he once carried 65%–32%.

Howard Metzenbaum has been heavily involved in Ohio politics for more than half a century. He spent many of his adult years in Cleveland in business, making his fortune by owning airport parking lots (not a business one enters for love). He served in the Ohio legislature from 1943 to 1950, and managed Senator Stephen Young's upset victories in 1958 and 1964, over John Bricker and Robert Taft, Jr. Then Metzenbaum ran himself, beat Glenn and almost beat Taft in 1970; appointed to fill a vacancy in 1974, he lost the primary to Glenn for the full term; he finally won in 1976, beating Cleveland Congressman James Stanton in the primary and Taft in the general. Winning reelection by handsome margins in 1982 and 1988, Metzenbaum has now had a hand in winning elections for this Senate seat, in one of the nation's largest states, for terms totalling 30 years. He shows great political skills and an ambition inextricably linked to strong convictions. A staunch New Dealer 50 years ago, attacked for having joined the leftish National Lawyers Guild, he has one of the most liberal records in the Senate today and formed the Coalition for Democratic Values to champion liberal ideas when they seemed nationally to be in eclipse.

Having fought uphill and come so far, Metzenbaum is an indefatigable and cheerful worker, undeterred by setbacks and incapable of embarrassment. In the early 1980s, when Republicans controlled the Senate, he mastered the rules and used the threat of delaying amendments and filibusters to kill legislation he opposed. After the Democrats regained control in 1986, he used committee positions to embarrass the Republicans, assailing S&L regulators for selling a package of failed thrifts too cheaply and persistently questioning the role played by Republican gubernatorial candidate, Fife Symington, in a failed Arizona S&L. Never mind that Metzenbaum himself in 1983 accepted a $250,000 "finder's fee" for making a phone call putting a prospective buyer in touch with the owner of Washington's Hay-Adams hotel, returning the money only after the transaction was revealed, or that he lobbied the Senate Finance chairman on a tax break for companies that pay for employees' legal services while his son-in-law Joel Hyatt heads the nation's largest legal services firm. His most spectacular moment came in the Clarence Thomas hearings where he doggedly pursued Thomas to articulate his personal views on abortion. Moreover, it was Metzenbaum staffers who first learned about and contacted Anita Hill and the Senate special counsel's report on the matter implied that they may have had a hand in leaking the story to the press.

Metzenbaum has also passed major legislation. He is lead sponsor of Senate gun control bills, including the Brady bill handgun purchase waiting period and bans on automatic rifles and plastic weapons. He was one of the leaders in framing a tough savings and loan bill in early 1989. He was lead sponsor of the plant-closing notification legislation enacted after the fight over the 1988 trade bill. He is probably the Senate's strongest backer of organized labor, and his ties to unions go back 40 or 50 years, but he is also a backer of trial lawyers and an admirer of their friend Ralph Nader. He backs high auto gas mileage standards, despite claims they would cost Ohio auto workers jobs, and scuttled the nomination of one Bush appointee for arguing that higher mileage would mean flimsier cars and more traffic deaths. He has attacked life insurance companies for misleading marketing, backed reregulation of cable TV and has severe qualms about the U.S.-Mexico free trade agreement.

Long a critic of Republican administrations, Metzenbaum could be a gadfly of Clinton's. Although he supported Clinton in 1992, Metzenbaum created his Coalition for Democratic Values as a counterweight to the Democratic Leadership Council once headed by Clinton, and he could easily criticize the Democratic president for not being liberal enough. His 1988 campaign, Metzenbaum said at the time, would be his last; it was plenty nasty, with Republican George Voinovich attacking him for opposing "laws that will put child pornographers out of business," but Metzenbaum won with 57%, about two-thirds of the vote in north-and-east Ohio and a slight majority in the rest of the state in both races. But Metzenbaum will probably try to extend his influence over this seat into the 21st century: he has said it's his "objective" for son-in-law Hyatt to win the seat, and by early 1991 Hyatt was already travelling around the state. Should Metzenbaum not run again, there is speculation that Marcy Kaptur and Louis Stokes may take up the race. Among Republicans, state Senator Eugene Watts has announced, and Lieutenant Governor Mike DeWine may make the race. Congressman John Kasich may run should his friend DeWine opt not to.

Presidential politics. Ohio with 21 electoral votes is a crucial state in presidential politics, essential for both parties, a roadblock for the side that can't carry it. Of the seven non-southern megastates, it was the closest in 1992; it received the most visits from the Bushes and Quayles (28) and Clintons and Gores (45) in the fall. Campaigns, starting with Republicans in 1984 and Democrats in 1988, have cut special TV spots for Ohio. No Republican has ever been elected president without carrying Ohio; no Democrat, at least in the electoral vote arithmetic of the 1980s, could hope to win without it. When California and the South seemed solidly Republican in the 1980s, Republican campaign managers Ed Rollins and Lee Atwater put great effort into Ohio, on the theory (originally Richard Nixon's) that if Democrats lost here there was no way they could get 270 electoral votes. In 1992, with the West Coast suddenly solidly Democratic and the South split, the arithmetic worked the other way: if the Clinton campaign could carry Ohio, 270 electoral votes for Bush seemed impossible. It helped Clinton that race relations had eased in the Cleveland media market after the 1989 election of Mayor Michael White, a black Democrat who eschewed divisive politics, backed a reform school board slate and welcomed the Democratic Leadership Council convention to town; it also helped Clinton that voters of Lithuanian and other Baltic and Eastern European descent were unhappy at George Bush's hesitation in recognizing Baltic independence and his overlong backing of Mikhail Gorbachev over more democratic forces in the former Soviet Union. Hurting Clinton were Al Gore's remarks, in his book *Earth in the Balance*, about doing away with the internal combustion engine and Clinton's own advocacy of a 40 mile per gallon CAFE standard, which the Bush campaign charged would cost Ohio thousands of jobs. The lead appeared to see-saw in the last two weeks, and Clinton finally won 40%–38%, with a bigger than expected 21% for Ross Perot. Clinton did not run as strongly in southern-accented Ohio as Jimmy Carter had in 1976, when he carried Ohio by an even narrower margin, but Clinton's margins in the north-and-east were larger. This is one state (Georgia is another) which analysts of both parties agree probably would have switched to Bush if somehow Perot had vanished from the ballot just before election day; Clinton of course still would have had a comfortable electoral vote majority.

Ohio's presidential primary, ordinarily held in May but rescheduled for June in 1992 because of redistricting delays, hasn't been important since 1972. In 1992, Clinton and Bush won big victories here that were scarcely noticed anywhere else.

Congressional districting. Ohio lost two districts in the 1990 Census; this state that elected 24 congressmen in 1970 elected 19 in 1992. With a Republican Senate and Democratic House, the legislature drew new lines so late, in March 1992, that the primary had to be delayed from May to June. The plan was designed to eliminate a Republican seat in south Ohio and a Democratic seat in the northeast, and did so, though Republicans lost the new 6th where two Republican incumbents had to run. To accommodate all these political imperatives, the district lines are convoluted; there are at least three grotesque U- or barbell-shaped districts. In 1992, Ohio voters overwhelmingly passed term limits of four consecutive 2-year terms for U.S. House members and two 6-year terms for U.S. Senators, effective January 1993.

The People: Est. Pop. 1992: 11,016,000; Pop. 1990: 10,847,115, up 1.5% 1990–1992. 4.4% of U.S. total, 7th largest; 26% rural. Median age: 33.3 years. 13.0% 65 years and over. 87.8% White, 10.6% Black, 1.3% Hispanic origin. Households: 56.1% married couple families; 27% married couple fams. w. children; 39% college educ.; median household income: $28,706; per capita income: $13,461; 67.5% owner occupied housing; median house value: $63,500; median monthly rent: $296. 7.2% Unemployment. Voting age pop.: 8,047,371. Registered voters (1992): 6,542,931; no party registration.

Political Lineup: Governor, George V. Voinovich (R); Lt. Gov., Mike DeWine (R); Secy. of State, Robert Taft (R); Atty. Gen., Lee Fisher (D); Treasurer, Mary Ellen Withrow (D); Auditor, Thomas E. Ferguson (D). State Senate, 33 (20 R and 13 D); State House of Representatives, 99 (53 D and 46 R). Senators, John H. Glenn, Jr. (D) and Howard M. Metzenbaum (D). Representatives, 19 (10 D, 8 R, and 1 vacancy).

1992 Presidential Vote

Clinton (D)	1,984,942	(40%)
Bush (R)	1,894,310	(38%)
Perot (I)	1,036,426	(21%)

1992 Democratic Presidential Primary

Clinton	638,347	(61%)
Brown	197,449	(19%)
Tsongas	110,773	(11%)
Other	95,765	(9%)

1988 Presidential Vote

Bush (R)	2,416,549	(55%)
Dukakis (D)	1,939,629	(44%)

1992 Republican Presidential Primary

Bush	716,766	(83%)
Buchanan	143,687	(17%)

GOVERNOR

Gov. George V. Voinovich (R)

Elected 1990, term expires Jan. 1995; b. July 15, 1936, Cleveland; home, Columbus; Ohio U., B.A. 1958, Ohio State U., J.D. 1961; Catholic; married (Janet).

Career: OH Asst. Atty. Gen., 1963–64; OH House of Reps., 1967–71; Cuyahoga Cnty. Auditor, 1971–76; Cuyahoga Cnty. Commissioner, 1977–78; OH Lt. Gov., 1979; Cleveland Mayor, 1979–89.

Office: Office of the Governor, 77 S. High St., 30th Fl., Columbus 43266, 614-466-3555.

Election Results

1990 gen.	George V. Voinovich (R)	1,938,103	(56%)
	Anthony J. Celebrezze, Jr. (D)	1,539,416	(44%)
1990 prim.	George V. Voinovich (R), unopposed		
1986 gen.	Richard F. Celeste (D)	1,858,372	(61%)
	James A. Rhodes (R)	1,207,264	(39%)

SENATORS

Sen. John H. Glenn Jr. (D)

Elected 1974, seat up 1998; b. July 18, 1921, Cambridge; home, Columbus; Muskingum Col., B.S. 1943; Presbyterian; married (Annie).

Career: Marine Corps, 1943–65 (WWII & Korea); NASA astronaut, 1959–65, first American to orbit the Earth, 1962; V.P., Royal Crown Cola Co., 1966–68, Pres., Royal Crown Intl., 1967–69.

Offices: 503 HSOB 20510, 202-224-3353. Also 200 N. High St., #600, Columbus 43215, 614-469-6697; 201 Superior Ave., Cleveland 44114, 216-522-7095; 550 Main St., #10407, Cincinnati 45202, 513-684-3265; and 234 N. Summit St., #726, Toledo 43604, 419-259-7592.

Committees: *Aging (Special)* (2d of 11 D). *Armed Services* (6th of 11 D): Coalition Defense and Reinforcing Forces; Military Readiness and Defense Infrastructure (Chmn.); Nuclear Deterrence, Arms Control and Defense Intelligence. *Governmental Affairs* (Chmn. of 8 D): Permanent Subcommittee on Investigations (Vice Chmn.). *Intelligence (Select)* (3d of 9 D).

Group Ratings

	ADA	ACLU	CDF	COPE	CFA	LCV	ACU	NTLC	NSI	COC	CEI
1992	80	82	80	75	92	75	11	22	50	10	22
1991	90	—	91	75	78	73	10	—	—	0	29

National Journal Ratings

	1991 LIB — 1991 CONS		1992 LIB — 1992 CONS	
Economic	80%	— 16%	54%	— 45%
Social	78%	— 20%	79%	— 16%
Foreign	67%	— 32%	49%	— 48%

Key Votes of the 102d Congress

1. $ for Homeownership	AGN	5. Clarence Thomas Nom.	AGN	9. Use Force in Gulf	AGN
2. Have Cap Gains Debate	AGN	6. Lmt Death Row Appeal	AGN	10. Keep Salvador Aid	AGN
3. Remove Budget Walls	FOR	7. Handgun Wait/5-Day	FOR	11. Cut $1B from SDI	FOR
4. Ban Striker Replace	FOR	8. Abortion Gag Rule	AGN	12. Override China MFN	FOR

Key Votes of the 103d Congress

1. Family Leave	FOR	2. HIV Immigrants	FOR	3. Clinton Budget	FOR

Election Results

1992 general	John H. Glenn, Jr. (D)	2,444,419	(51%)	($4,974,109)
	Michael DeWine (R)	2,028,300	(42%)	($3,053,156)
	Martha Kathryn Grevatt (I)............	321,670	(7%)	
1992 primary	John H. Glenn, Jr. (D), unopposed			
1986 general	John H. Glenn, Jr. (D)	1,949,208	(62%)	($1,319,026)
	Thomas N. Kindness (R)	1,171,893	(38%)	($657,908)

Sen. Howard M. Metzenbaum (D)

Elected 1976, seat up 1994; b. June 4, 1917, Cleveland; home, Lyndhurst; Ohio State U., B.A. 1939, LL.B. 1941; Jewish; married (Shirley).

Career: Practicing atty., businessman; OH House of Reps., 1943–46; OH Senate, 1947–50; Co-founder, Airport Parking Co. of Amer., Chmn., 1958–66.; Chmn. of the Bd., ITT Consumer Svs. Corp., 1966–68.

Offices: 140 RSOB 20510, 202-224-2315. Also 200 N. High St., #405, Columbus 43215, 614-469-6774; 1240 E. 9th St., #2919, Cleveland 44114, 216-544-7272; City Ctr. One, 100 Fed. Plaza E., #510, Youngstown 44503, 216-746-1132; 10411 Fed. Bldg., Cincinnati 45202, 513-684-3894; and 234 Summit St., Toledo 43603, 419-259-7536.

Committees: *Environment and Public Works* (8th of 10 D): Clean Air and Nuclear Regulation; Superfund, Recycling and Solid Waste Management; Water Resources, Transportation, Public Buildings and Economic Development. *Intelligence (Select)* (2d of 9 D). *Judiciary* (3d of 10 D): Antitrust, Monopolies and Business Rights (Chmn.); Constitution; Courts and Administrative Practice. *Labor and Human Resources* (3d of 10 D): Aging; Disability Policy; Education, Arts and Humanities; Labor (Chmn.).

Group Ratings

	ADA	ACLU	CDF	COPE	CFA	LCV	ACU	NTLC	NSI	COC	CEI
1992	90	91	90	100	92	100	0	22	40	11	21
1991	100	—	100	83	100	93	0	—	—	10	24

National Journal Ratings

	1991 LIB — 1991 CONS		1992 LIB — 1992 CONS	
Economic	97%	— 0%	84%	— 12%
Social	87%	— 0%	84%	— 11%
Foreign	86%	— 0%	86%	— 0%

Key Votes of the 102d Congress

1. $ for Homeownership	AGN	5. Clarence Thomas Nom. AGN	9. Use Force in Gulf	AGN
2. Have Cap Gains Debate AGN		6. Lmt Death Row Appeal AGN	10. Keep Salvador Aid	AGN
3. Remove Budget Walls	FOR	7. Handgun Wait/5-Day	FOR	11. Cut $1B from SDI	FOR
4. Ban Striker Replace	FOR	8. Abortion Gag Rule	AGN	12. Override China MFN FOR

Key Votes of the 103d Congress

1. Family Leave	FOR	2. HIV Immigrants	FOR	3. Clinton Budget	FOR

Election Results

1988 general	Howard M. Metzenbaum (D)	2,480,038	(57%)	($8,547,545)
	George V. Voinovich (R)	1,872,716	(43%)	($8,233,859)
1988 primary	Howard M. Metzenbaum (D)	1,070,934	(83%)	
	Ralph A. Applegate (D)	210,508	(17%)	
1982 general	Howard M. Metzenbaum (D)	1,923,767	(57%)	($2,794,172)
	Paul E. Pfeifer (R)	1,396,790	(41%)	($1,025,595)

FIRST DISTRICT

Looking down on the curves of the Ohio River from its seven hills is Cincinnati, the Queen City of the West in the 19th Century, the nation's fourth largest city at the outbreak of the Civil War, a heavily German beehive of riverboats and sausage factories, known as Porkopolis (it celebrated its bicentennial in 1988 with a sculpture topped by four flying pigs). For years, Cincinnati has given off an air of the recent past; Mark Twain said he'd like to be in Cincinnati when the apocalypse came because everything there is 20 years behind, and now the city seems to be stepping, stylishly and gracefully, into the 1970s. Growing slowly over many decades, Cincinnati has long-settled good looks and an urbanity that is somehow consistent with its natural terrain: the bottomlands along the river, the hills and rolling terrain above. In the middle of Cincinnati is Mill Creek, lined with factories; on the hills to the west are the modest streetcar suburbs of the last century and the early years of this one. On Mount Adams and toward the northeast, fall a string of affluent neighborhoods, with stately mansions like the William Howard Taft house, and comfortable Tudors and colonials where the 20th Century bourgeoisie—Reform Jewish as well as WASP and German—have lived.

Cincinnati was the site of great innovation: the first iron suspension bridge, in 1867, connected Cincinnati to northern Kentucky and was designed by John Roebling who later built the Brooklyn Bridge; the first baseball team, the Red Stockings, in 1869; the country's leading Reform Jewish seminary, Hebrew Union College, in 1875. Over the past century, Cincinnati has not had the growth spurts of cities like Cleveland or Houston, but neither has it had their sharp contractions. It has spawned not flashy but solid industries, like the Procter & Gamble soap business, now headquartered in a striking two-towered office complex at the edge of downtown; it has America's biggest concentration of machine tool makers. Its Cincinnati Reds have been one of America's most exciting teams in some years, but have also been hurt by the gambling of star Pete Rose and the racist ravings of owner Marge Schott. Downtown Cincinnati's spruced-up Fountain Square shows off the well-maintained skyscrapers of the past, its first class restaurants still attract a dressy clientele. Old ethnic neighborhoods, crowded with brick row houses on steep hills, keep their thick local accent and special local foods, from German sauerbrauten to Cincinnati chili (served with spaghetti and grated cheese).

Ohio's 1st Congressional District includes almost all of Cincinnati, except for its affluent eastern edge, plus the middle-class suburbs that cling to the woody hills north and east, all the way along to the Indiana border and North Bend, the home of President William Henry Harrison. Ancestrally Republican, when it was a German anti-slavery island in a southern-stock pro-Confederate sea, this is territory that is now competitive between the parties, as Cincinnati's affluent population moves east and northeast. City elections here have long been competitive between the old line Republicans and a combination of Democrats and Charterites (the latter started by Charles Taft, liberal brother of Senator Robert Taft, Sr.) and are so highly publicized that council members become celebrities in this media market. As a result, one or both Cincinnati area congressional districts have been seriously contested in almost every election back to 1964, and both have been represented by nothing but former Cincinnati council members since 1950 with the understandable exception of Robert Taft, Jr. (One former council member and mayor, Jerry Springer, has even become a national talk show host.)

That record was kept intact, through a bizarre series of events, in 1992. The first of these was the failure of Republican Steve Grote to get enough signatures to get on the ballot. The second was the June 29 decision by incumbent Democrat Charles Luken to retire at age 41 after one term—nearly one month after he had won the June 2 primary and with no overdrafts or other scandal to his name. "Basically, I just feel I belong at home," said this man whose father had served in the seat, except for one term, from 1974 to 1990. Under Ohio law, the Democrats had a special primary in August to choose a new nominee, and the Republicans were left without a candidate, even in a district where their 1990 nominee, black council member Kenneth

Blackwell, lost to Luken by only 51%–49%. So they backed Grote, who had managed to secure a spot on the ballot as an Independent, while the Democrats split, and chose former Cincinnati Mayor and Councilman David Mann over black state Senator William Bowman by a 33%–32% margin in an eight candidate field. Mann had twice been mayor and was first elected to the council in 1974: he is a professional politician with a flair for the business. He is a bit of a ham and once made TV news when—as a symbolic protest—he worked in a soup kitchen while Reagan was visiting the area; but he was also principled enough to vote against an ordinance aimed narrowly at abortion protesters even though he is pro-choice. Mann supports federal aid to cities and government assistance for jobs and housing, but also backs the balanced budget amendment and says he need not decide on term limits, since Ohio passed term limits in a 1992 referendum.

Despite all these assets, Mann won in November by only 51%–43% over the Independent Grote. This is not an overwhelming margin, and suggests that a vigorous Republican candidacy or a national sag in Democratic fortunes could make this a seriously contested race in 1994.

The People: Pop. 1990: 571,052; 1% rural; 13% age 65+; 68% White; 30% Black; 1% Asian; 1% Hispanic origin. Voting age pop.: 420,762; 27% Black; 1% Hispanic origin. Households: 44% married couple families; 20% married couple fams. w. children; 43% college educ.; median household income: $25,405; per capita income: $12,616; median gross rent: $336; median house value: $64,300.

1992 Presidential Vote			1988 Presidential Vote		
Clinton (D)	104,494	(43%)	Bush (R)	126,174	(55%)
Bush (R)	104,339	(43%)	Dukakis (D)	101,336	(45%)
Perot (I)	34,531	(14%)			

Rep. David Mann (D)

Elected 1992; b. Sept. 25, 1939, Cincinnati; home, Cincinnati; Harvard, A.B. 1961, LL.B. 1968; Methodist; married (Elizabeth).

Career: Navy, 1961–65; Practicing atty., 1968–92; Cincinnati City Cncl., 1974–92; Cininnati Mayor, 1980–82, 1991.

Offices: 503 CHOB 20515, 202-225-2216. Also 2210 Kroger Bldg., 1014 Vine St., Cincinnati 45202, 513-683-2723.

Committees: *Armed Services* (25th of 34 D): Military Acquisition; Oversight and Investigations. *Judiciary* (19th of 21 D): Administrative Law and Governmental Relations; Crime and Criminal Justice; Economic and Commercial Law.

Group Ratings and 102d Congress Votes: Newly Elected

Key Votes of the 103d Congress

1. Family Leave	FOR	2. Deficit Reduction	AGN	3. Stimulus Plan	AGN

Election Results

1992 general	David Mann (D)...............	120,190	(51%)	($278,294)
	Stephen Grote (I).............	101,498	(43%)	($83,038)
	Jim Berns (I)................	12,734	(5%)	($1,817)
1992 special	David Mann (D)...............	14,794	(33%)	
	William Bowman (D)...........	14,378	(32%)	
	Virginia Rhodes (D)...........	6,387	(14%)	
	Mary Ann Boyd (D)...........	3,638	(8%)	
	Steven Reece (D).............	1,929	(4%)	
	Others......................	3,637	(9%)	
1992 primary	Charles J. Luken (D), unopposed			
1990 general	Charles J. Luken (D)...........	89,932	(51%)	($651,544)
	J. Kenneth Blackwell (R).......	80,362	(49%)	($670,640)

SECOND DISTRICT

Cincinnati is one of the most Republican metropolitan areas in the nation. Its tradition has been Republican since the 1850s, when Harriet Beecher Stowe composed her novel, *Uncle Tom's Cabin*, here in this island of German, pro-Union, Republican sentiment in a southern, Democratic, pro-slavery sea. In later years, Cincinnati did not attract as many southern and eastern European immigrants as did Great Lakes industrial cities like Cleveland, Detroit and Chicago; its ethnic character (like its physical appearance) and its political preference have remained pretty well fixed. Even many of the Appalachians here are Republicans, from Civil War Republican counties in the hills. Democratic constituencies here never got very large: economically, it was never a strong CIO town; culturally, it is home to a strong anti-pornography movement that, among other things, canceled a Robert Mapplethorpe exhibit here. Cincinnati kept up that record into George Bush's time: in 1988 it gave Bush his highest percentage in a million-plus metro area except for Phoenix, Arizona; in 1992, it was the best Bush million-plus metro area, and the only one where he got an absolute majority.

For 140 years after 1852, Cincinnati and surrounding Hamilton County were divided by a north-south line into two congressional districts. After the 1990 Census, redistricters created one mostly city district which leaned a bit to the Democrats and a mostly suburban district that contained much of the territory that has made the metro area so heavily Republican. This 2d Congressional District of Ohio includes the affluent eastern suburbs around elite Indian Hill and newer Montgomery, plus a few affluent precincts of Cincinnati itself; it includes recent growth areas like northeastern Hamilton County and Anderson Township south of the Little Miami River, both heavily Republican; it heads east along the Ohio River to include Clermont County, a fast-growth area for 20 years, plus two rural counties facing north; and takes in an oddly-shaped sliver of Warren County between Cincinnati and Dayton.

Altogether, the 2d is a very Republican district, and the congressman for nearly 20 years was a Republican out of the Cincinnati tradition that includes Salmon P. Chase (Lincoln's Treasury Secretary and Chief Justice), President and Chief Justice William Howard Taft, Speaker of the House Nicholas Longworth (who married Teddy Roosevelt's daughter Alice), and the late Senator Robert Taft, Sr., men of probity and learning, conservatives who sought to maintain the values and the political system that produced the prosperity and urbanity of ordered communities like Cincinnati. A recent product of this tradition was Bill Gradison, first elected in 1974, a leading Republican authority on budget and healthcare issues. But his bid for a leadership position failed in December 1992, and Gradison in January 1993 announced he was resigning from Congress to become head of the Health Insurance Association of America, a post from which he would likely be a major player on any health care finance reform.

The new congressman, Rob Portman, was for all practical purposes chosen in the March 1993

Republican primary. He entered with advantages and disadvantages. He campaigned for Gradison before he was 21, worked for a major Washington lobbying law firm, then practiced law in Cincinnati and worked in the Bush White House. One serious opponent, former Cincinnati Mayor Ken Blackwell, dropped out of the race, disappointing Republicans who wanted to elect another black to their ranks. But two candidates remained with serious credentials. Jay Buchert, president of the National Association of Homebuilders, campaigned as "not a politician" and sniped at Portman and the other major contender, former Congressman Bob McEwen. McEwen was a juicy target: he had 166 overdrafts on the House bank, and he had lost in 1992 to a Democrat in the next-door 6th District; he had represented some of Clermont County before, though, and emphasized his proven conservative record. But Portman had the biggest advantages: an excellent local financial base and Hamilton County party support, plus national endorsements from his Bush White House days, as well as from Gradison and Blackwell. He fended off charges that he was an insider and a lobbyist for foreign interests. Portman, with solid support in Cincinnati, won 36% of the vote; McEwen, carrying counties he had once represented, had 30%; Buchert had 25%. The general election was anticlimactic: Portman won 70%–30%. By most standards, this is one of the safest Republican districts in the nation.

The People: Pop. 1990: 570,779; 29% rural; 11% age 65+; 96% White; 2% Black; 1% Asian. Voting age pop.: 417,438; 2% Black. Households: 63% married couple families; 31% married couple fams. w. children; 46% college educ.; median household income: $34,688; per capita income: $16,813; median gross rent: $409; median house value: $79,000.

1992 Presidential Vote		1988 Presidential Vote		
Bush (R)	143,964 (52%)	Bush (R)	167,011	(71%)
Clinton (D)	78,117 (28%)	Dukakis (D)	69,311	(29%)
Perot (I)	51,356 (19%)			

Rep. Rob Portman (R)

Elected May, 1993; b. Dec. 19, 1955, Cincinatti; home, Cincinatti; Dartmouth Col., B.A. 1979, U. of MI Law Schl., J.D. 1984; Methodist; married (Jane).

Career: Practicing atty., 1984–88; Hamilton Cnty. Repub. Cmte., 1984–present; Assoc. Cnsl., Pres. Bush, 1989; Dep. Asst. and White House Legis. Affairs Dir., 1990–91; Alternate U.S. Rep. to UN Human Rights Comm., 1992.

Offices: 238 CHOB 20515, 202-225-3164. Also 8010 Fed. Bldg., 550 Main St., Cincinatti 45202, 513-684-2456.

Committees: *Government Operations* (17th of 17 R). *Small Business* (18th of 18 R).

Group Ratings and 102d Congress Votes: Newly Elected

Key Votes of the 103d Congress

| 1. Family Leave | * | 2. Deficit Reduction | AGN | 3. Stimulus Plan | * |

Election Results

1993 special	Rob Portman (R)	53,020	(70%)	($775,587)
	Lee Hornberger (D)	22,652	(30%)	($21,652)
1993 primary	Rob Portman (R)	17,432	(36%)	
	Bob McEwen (R)	14,495	(30%)	
	Jay Buchert (R)	12,441	(25%)	
	Robert Dorsey (R)	2,939	(6%)	
	Three Others.........................	1,714	(4%)	
1992 general	Willis D. (Bill) Gradison (R)	177,720	(70%)	($96,108)
	Thomas R. Chandler (D)	75,924	(30%)	($105)

THIRD DISTRICT

Dayton, Ohio, just south of the old National Road that spans the Midwest, is one of the unsung centers of American technological innovation. This was the home of James Ritty, who in 1879 invented the cash register—that indispensable instrument of mass retail trade—and of John Henry Patterson, who bought it from Ritty for $6,500 in 1884 and established the National Cash Register company (NCR). It was home for a while of a former Patterson subordinate Tom Watson, Sr., who feuded with him and went off and founded IBM. It was in Dayton in the 1890s that Wilbur and Orville Wright, tinkering in their bicycle shop and observing the horseless carriages driven through Dayton's streets, experimented with kites and gliders and constructed the first wind tunnel in the world and the first heavier-than-air flying machine which they took to ever-windy Kitty Hawk, North Carolina, to fly in 1903. A century ago Dayton was a town buzzing with mechanical innovations, with inventors like Charles Kettering who invented the automatic starter for cars, practical enough to turn them into profitable businesses.

More recently Dayton has been grappling with new technologies. NCR has been buffeted by the volatility of the office and personal computer markets, and by an unsought takeover bid from IBM in 1991. The Big Three auto firms and their suppliers have gone through a decade of downsizing their work forces, adapting technologies and work patterns to supply products just in time—and GM is downsizing more. The Dayton area has Wright-Patterson Air Force Base—the largest Air Force base in the world, with 28,000 workers on 8,000 acres, but defense also has been in decline. By the late 1980s, outmigration had slowed, and metro Dayton was growing enough to show a slight gain for the decade, but in the early 1990s the town was hit by more layoffs in old industries. Dayton's spirit of tinkering and innovation, of practical organization and mechanical dreaming, has not entirely vanished, but it's not clear if it can produce enough new industry growth to balance job losses in the old.

Dayton has been known as a bellwether since Richard Scammon and Ben Wattenberg's *The Real Majority* of 1970. In the 1980s and 1990s Dayton's Montgomery County has tracked the nation fairly well, voting Democratic in state and congressional races until it voted 55%–45% (1% off the state average) for Governor George Voinovich in 1990, and Republican for president until it voted 41%–40% for Bill Clinton in 1992. The 3d Congressional District of Ohio includes Dayton and all but a small corner of Montgomery County. Its congressman, Tony Hall, is a Democrat with a distinctive approach to issues. In many of the causes he has undertaken, he has seemed good-hearted and guileless to the point of naivete—and yet he has been as successful in public life as the craftiest politico. Hall comes by his interest in politics partly through family—his father was once mayor of Dayton—but his views also owe much, as do those of many elected officials of his generation, to his service in the Peace Corps. He was in the by-no-means-primitive, but also rather cynical, country of Thailand in 1966 and 1967, when the Vietnam war was raging not far away. When he returned to Dayton, he was elected to the state House of Representatives, evidently without much struggle, in the otherwise hideously turbulent political year of 1968. He advanced to the Ohio Senate in 1972, and to the U.S. House in 1978 when liberal Republican Charles Whalen retired. He won 55% that year and has won easily ever since. In the House, he acquired a seat on Rules in his second term.

Hall became a born-again Christian in the early 1980s, and is antiabortion. But his number one cause has been to alleviate world hunger. He succeeded Mickey Leland, who died in a plane crash in Ethiopia, as chairman of the Select Committee on Hunger, and decried the civil wars and infrastructural deficiencies that obstructed food delivery in so much of Africa (although he glosses over how African socialism has reduced food supplies). Early on he was working to send food and medical help to Somalia and Haiti; in February 1992 he called for UN intervention in Somalia. In Dayton, he called for unused hotel and restaurant food to be used to feed the poor and, in Washington, launched Operation Food Share, based on the same principle, in a shelter near the Capitol. In April 1993, Hall embarked on a 21-day fast in response to the House's decision not to reauthorize his Select Hunger Committee. After losing over 20 pounds, he relented when the World Bank and Mike Espy's Agriculture Department agreed to take additional steps to reduce world hunger.

He tends to Dayton area problems and to Wright-Patterson Air Force Base (though only a small part is actually in the district). He has been working for funding for the new Dayton Aviation Heritage National Historic Park, to save the Air Force Museum, to stop the transfer of the Mound Plant nuclear power work to Washington state, and to get immunizations for local children. With Republican David Hobson he is working to protect the innovative but controversial Dayton Area Health Plan which emphasizes preventive health care and conducts outreach programs for the disadvantaged.

In anti-incumbent 1992, Hall got his toughest challenge since 1978. Pete Davis, an NCR attorney and lieutenant commander in the Navy Reserve who was sent to Tel Aviv during the Gulf war, ran a harsh negative campaign against Hall, attacking his vote against the Gulf war resolution, pounding on him for taking special interest contributions (from Waste Management, which was planning a big landfill in west Dayton), and for living in a custom-built house in Virginia. Hall responded by running a witty ad stating he'd never bounced a check at the House bank and had only "one bad haircut" at the House barber shop. Hall won by 60%, running well ahead of where Clinton would have finished even in a two-way race.

The People: Pop. 1990: 570,913; 5% rural; 13% age 65+; 80% White; 18% Black; 1% Asian; 1% Hispanic origin. Voting age pop.: 428,764; 16% Black; 1% Hispanic origin. Households: 53% married couple families; 23% married couple fams. w. children; 47% college educ.; median household income: $30,083; per capita income: $14,500; median gross rent: $403; median house value: $64,200.

1992 Presidential Vote			1988 Presidential Vote		
Clinton (D)	107,659	(41%)	Bush (R)	131,119	(58%)
Bush (R)	104,215	(40%)	Dukakis (D)	95,502	(42%)
Perot (I)	47,465	(18%)			

Rep. Tony P. Hall (D)

Elected 1978; b. Jan. 16, 1942, Dayton; home, Dayton; Denison U., A.B. 1964; Presbyterian; married (Janet).

Career: Peace Corps, Thailand, 1966–67; Real estate broker, 1968–78; OH House of Reps., 1969–72; OH Senate, 1973–78.

Offices: 2264 RHOB 20515, 202-225-6465. Also 501 Fed. Bldg., 200 W. 2d St., Dayton 45402, 513-225-2843.

Committees: *Rules* (6th of 9 D): Rules of the House.

Group Ratings

	ADA	ACLU	COPE	CDF	CFA	LCV	ACU	NTLC	NSI	COC	CEI
1992	60	64	67	90	67	44	25	5	40	25	14
1991	75	—	75	100	67	46	10	—	—	30	17

National Journal Ratings

	1991 LIB	—	1991 CONS	1992 LIB	—	1992 CONS
Economic	61%	—	36%	63%	—	36%
Social	60%	—	38%	38%	—	60%
Foreign	78%	—	19%	71%	—	26%

Key Votes of the 102d Congress

1. Ban Striker Replace	FOR	5. Handgun Wait/7-Day	FOR	9. Use Force in Gulf	AGN
2. $ for Homeownership	FOR	6. Overseas Mil. Abortion	AGN	10. US Mil. Abroad $ Cut	FOR
3. Tax Rich/Cut Mid Cls.	FOR	7. Obscn. Art NEA $ Ban	FOR	11. Limit SDI Funds	FOR
4. FY93/$15B Def. Cut	FOR	8. Death Pen. from Jury	AGN	12. Cuba Trade Embargo	FOR

Key Votes of the 103d Congress

1. Family Leave	FOR	2. Deficit Reduction	FOR	3. Stimulus Plan	FOR

Election Results

1992 general	Tony P. Hall (D)	146,072	(60%)	($596,272)
	Pete Davis (R).......................	98,733	(40%)	($174,058)
1992 primary	Tony P. Hall (D), unopposed			
1990 general	Tony P. Hall (D), unopposed			($133,861)

FOURTH DISTRICT

Central Ohio is hard to categorize: driving through, it looks like mostly farm fields, yet it makes most of its living off factories in small towns and on rural highways; it seems far from anywhere important, yet is on one of the great east-west routes—the old rail lines and newer highways—that cross the country; it seems old-fashioned and rooted in an older technological time, yet it (more precisely, the town of Wapakoneta, a typically Ohioan-Indian name) is the home town of Neil Armstrong, first man on the moon. Not far away, in Lima, Abrams M-1 tanks continue to roll off the assembly line—one instance of continuing defense production after the Cold War. Politically, this crossroads on the flat limestone plains of northern Ohio is one of the Republican heartlands of the United States. On the B&O tracks from Dayton to Toledo that intersect the east-west rail lines used by Richard Nixon in 1968, Ronald Reagan in 1984 and George Bush in 1992 to make whistle-stop campaign tours, one can summon up memories of past campaign styles and loyalties.

Much of central Ohio makes up the 4th Congressional District, one seat that thanks to redistricting was made more geographically regular; it is now less U-shaped and more rectangular. It includes Wapakoneta; Lima, which got its name when it was pulled from a hat, and famous when John Dillinger's gang murdered the sheriff in 1933; Bucyrus, which gave its name to a company producing giant earth-moving equipment; Marion, where young Socialist-to-be Norman Thomas delivered newspapers edited by President-to-be Warren Harding; and Mansfield, home of John Sherman, one of Ohio's great 19th Century Republican statesmen, and his brother General William Tecumseh Sherman, who marched through Georgia for the Union and refused to be considered for president. This has been a Republican stronghold since the Civil War, industrial since the late 19th Century, quietly prosperous over most of the years since World War II though shaken by the collapse of the auto-steel-coal industries after the oil shock of 1979. Through all this, it has remained mostly Republican, giving George Bush a solid margin and Bill Clinton less than one-third of its votes in 1992.

Mike Oxley, congressman from the 4th District, is one of several Baby Boomers among the Ohio Republican delegation; he was first elected in a 1981 special election by the surprisingly narrow margin of 378 votes, but has won easily ever since. He brought to the office a small city background, a stint as an FBI agent, work for previous local Republican congressmen and a reputation as a moderate—he supported George Bush over Ronald Reagan in 1980. In the House he seems to be a partisan and almost always conservative Republican. He served on the now-defunct Select Committee on Narcotics Abuse and Control, where he urged more sting operations; he also wants federal criminals required to make full restitution to their victims as part of any plea bargain or release program.

Much of his time and energy seem devoted to work on the Energy and Commerce Committee, where he is a reliable opponent of regulation and control. He was a player on the 1990 Clean Air Act, working with Ohioans of both parties to protect that state's high-sulfur power plants and big factories from being saddled with high costs; he was skeptical about whether data provided by environmental organizations and Canadians proved the dangerous effects of acid rain. He successfully pushed his "auction" proposal, a market approach to pollution reduction, which, by allowing firms to sell polluting rights, lets supple and adaptive firms rather than rule-bound federal bureaucrats figure out how to best reduce pollution. In 1991 and 1992, he concentrated on legislation to permit the Baby Bells to provide information services, something sharply opposed by newspapers. None of these causes was successful, but Oxley seems to be a key man for the Baby Bells in the future.

Unlike current Ohio Democrats and historic Ohio Republicans, Oxley has been a free trader: factories in small towns surprisingly are often exporters. He is happy to promote the cause of leading employers, hailing orders of Abrams tanks by Saudi Arabia and Kuwait. Oxley has been reelected routinely with percentages in the low 60s.

The People: Pop. 1990: 570,917; 46% rural; 13% age 65+; 94% White; 5% Black; 1% Hispanic origin. Voting age pop.: 417,175; 4% Black; 1% Hispanic origin. Households: 63% married couple families; 30% married couple fams. w. children; 31% college educ.; median household income: $27,312; per capita income: $12,009; median gross rent: $337; median house value: $50,300.

1992 Presidential Vote		
Bush (R)	118,142	(46%)
Clinton (D)	77,975	(30%)
Perot (I)	58,900	(23%)

1988 Presidential Vote		
Bush (R)	150,999	(66%)
Dukakis (D)	76,200	(34%)

Rep. Michael G. Oxley (R)

Elected June 1981; b. Feb. 11, 1944, Findlay; home, Findlay; Miami U. of OH, B.A. 1966, OH St. U., J.D. 1969; Lutheran; married (Patricia).

Career: FBI Spec. Agent, 1969–72; OH House of Reps., 1973–81; Practicing atty., 1972–1981.

Offices: 2233 RHOB 20515, 202-225-2676. Also 3121 W. Elm Plz., Lima 45805, 419-999-6455; 24 W. 3d St., #314, Mansfield 44902, 419-522-5757; and 100 E. Main Cross St., Findlay 45840, 419-423-3210.

Committees: *Energy and Commerce* (4th of 17 R): Telecommunications and Finance; Transportation and Hazardous Materials (RMM).

Group Ratings

	ADA	ACLU	COPE	CDF	CFA	LCV	ACU	NTLC	NSI	COC	CEI
1992	5	0	17	20	20	0	96	95	100	86	81
1991	5	—	8	30	17	0	80	—	—	100	82

National Journal Ratings

	1991 LIB — 1991 CONS		1992 LIB — 1992 CONS	
Economic	4%	— 90%	0%	— 91%
Social	16%	— 81%	16%	— 82%
Foreign	22%	— 77%	0%	— 82%

Key Votes of the 102d Congress

1. Ban Striker Replace	AGN	5. Handgun Wait/7-Day	FOR	9. Use Force in Gulf	FOR
2. $ for Homeownership	FOR	6. Overseas Mil. Abortion	AGN	10. US Mil. Abroad $ Cut	AGN
3. Tax Rich/Cut Mid Cls.	AGN	7. Obscn. Art NEA $ Ban	FOR	11. Limit SDI Funds	AGN
4. FY93/$15B Def. Cut	AGN	8. Death Pen. from Jury	FOR	12. Cuba Trade Embargo	FOR

Key Votes of the 103d Congress

1. Family Leave   AGN   2. Deficit Reduction   AGN   3. Stimulus Plan   AGN

Election Results

1992 general	Michael G. Oxley (R)	147,346	(61%)	($648,337)
	Raymond Ball (D)	92,608	(39%)	($68,324)
1992 primary	Michael G. Oxley (R), unopposed			
1990 general	Michael G. Oxley (R)	103,897	(62%)	($330,272)
	Thomas E. Burkhart (D)	64,467	(38%)	($19,102)

FIFTH DISTRICT

Undergirded by limestone, as flat and fertile as any part of the country, astride the land routes from the parts of the country which were economically the most productive in the years they were settled, northern Ohio has been blessed with a favorable location since its New England Yankees (who first settled the "Firelands," land reserved for Connecticut Yankees whose farms were burned in the Revolution) were joined by German Protestants around the middle of the 19th Century. Northwest Ohio is the beginning of the great corn and hog belt that stretches into Illinois and Iowa, and was long one of the heartlands of the Republican Party. Fremont, settled by abstemious Yankees, was the home of President Rutherford B. Hayes, whose wife Lucy served only lemonade in the White House; nearby Sandusky was settled by Germans who built big wineries and breweries. Not far away is Milan, birthplace of the great inventor and capitalist Thomas Edison.

This is prime industrial country: its limestone, rail connections and location near the Great Lakes have spurred the growth of a factory economy which in dollar terms is far more important than agriculture. Since the first settlement, northern Ohio hasn't had spectacular population growth, but it grew steadily for many decades, surging ahead in the 1950s and 1960s as its small factories supplied the big auto plants in Detroit and Ohio cities. Growth lagged noticeably in the early 1980s as the collapse of the auto industry cast a pall over the whole area. Northern Ohio, with low labor costs, lower taxes, and less racial tension, is competitive with Detroit or Cleveland. But the whole Great Lakes area is worried that the job losses of its big and highly visible companies won't be offset by new jobs created by smaller and less visible firms.

Ohio's 5th Congressional District sweeps across the northwest corner of the state, from the town of Grafton, just beyond the westward expansion of metropolitan Cleveland, across the limestone plains through Sandusky, its harbor on Lake Erie, home of the giant Cedar Point amusement park. It continues through Milan and Fremont, past part of the university town of Bowling Green and the Toledo suburb of Perrysburg, to the western Ohio towns of Defiance and Napoleon (wonderful names!). It avoids Toledo and the overflow directly east and west. Historically, this was a solidly Republican district from the Civil War through the New Deal and up through the 1970s. But in the wake of the collapse of the auto-steel economy, Democrats have been competitive in statewide and national races here, though not yet for the 5th District.

The current congressman from the 5th is Paul Gillmor, now in his third term, a 22-year veteran of the Ohio legislature, a professional though not especially provocative politician. Gillmor had been long eying the seat, but had to win it over the wishes of his predecessor, Delbert Latta, who wanted to pass it along to his son. Gillmor passed a state law blocking Latta from resigning to have his son designated the party nominee; then Gillmor beat the junior Latta in the 1988 primary by exactly 27 votes out of 63,000 cast. Now Gillmor may be creating a family dynasty of his own. In 1992 his wife Karen was elected to the state Senate from the 26th District, which overlaps the 5th Congressional in Sandusky and Seneca Counties; all the more strikingly, she had a baby (Paul Michael, known as Little P.M.) just before the primary, and went on to win the general with 61%. Paul Gillmor had an easier year: he did not give birth, he did not have an opponent in the general election, and he had no overdrafts at the House bank.

In the House, Gillmor managed to freeze 1992 funding for House committees at 1991 levels, proposed tax incentives like George Bush's before Bush did and criticized the handling of the House Post Office scandal. He got a repeal of Coast Guard recreational boating user fees (important on Lake Erie), prevented a funding cutoff of the Army Division of Civilian Marksmanship which holds national matches at Camp Perry in the 5th District, and boasts that he made Ohio the number one loan recipient of a rural housing loan program. Gillmor's most original idea is to repeal the 12th Amendment which provides that the House, with each state casting just one vote, choose the president if there is no electoral college majority; he would have a runoff instead. It's a cumbersome solution, but the 12th Amendment, as speculation during Ross Perot's candidacy made clear, is an absurdity; it would be nice if Congress acted on this before another Perot or third party candidacy makes it necessary—too late for Congress and the state legislatures to act. Gillmor landed a spot on the Energy and Commerce Committee after the GOP leadership failed in its attempt to oust House Administration Ranking Member William Thomas in favor of Gillmor.

The People: Pop. 1990: 570,946; 54% rural; 13% age 65+; 94% White; 2% Black; 1% Other; 3% Hispanic origin. Voting age pop.: 410,950; 2% Black; 2% Hispanic origin. Households: 65% married couple families; 32% married couple fams. w. children; 32% college educ.; median household income: $30,117; per capita income: $12,755; median gross rent: $351; median house value: $57,800.

1000   OHIO

1992 Presidential Vote

Bush (R) 108,421 (41%)
Clinton (D) 88,773 (34%)
Perot (I). 66,051 (25%)

1988 Presidential Vote

Bush (R) 143,846 (62%)
Dukakis (D). 87,268 (38%)

Rep. Paul E. Gillmor (R)

Elected 1988; b. Feb. 1, 1939, Tiffin; home, Old Fort; Ohio Wesleyan U., B.A. 1961, U. of MI, J.D. 1964; Lutheran; married (Karen).

Career: Air Force, 1965–66; OH Senate, 1966–88.

Offices: 1203 LHOB 20515, 202-225-6405. Also 120 Jefferson St., #200, Port Clinton 43452, 800-541-6446; and 148 E. South Boundary St., Perrysburg 43551, 419-872-2500.

Committees: *Energy and Commerce* (13th of 17 R): Oversight and Investigations; Telecommunications and Finance; Transportation and Hazardous Materials.

Group Ratings

	ADA	ACLU	COPE	CDF	CFA	LCV	ACU	NTLC	NSI	COC	CEI
1992	20	17	50	30	33	19	80	60	100	75	61
1991	10	—	25	50	50	23	65	—	—	70	49

National Journal Ratings

	1991 LIB — 1991 CONS		1992 LIB — 1992 CONS	
Economic	32%	— 67%	28%	— 70%
Social	19%	— 78%	29%	— 70%
Foreign	17%	— 78%	18%	— 74%

Key Votes of the 102d Congress

1. Ban Striker Replace	AGN	5. Handgun Wait/7-Day	AGN	9. Use Force in Gulf	FOR
2. $ for Homeownership	FOR	6. Overseas Mil. Abortion	AGN	10. US Mil. Abroad $ Cut	AGN
3. Tax Rich/Cut Mid Cls.	AGN	7. Obscn. Art NEA $ Ban	FOR	11. Limit SDI Funds	AGN
4. FY93/$15B Def. Cut	AGN	8. Death Pen. from Jury	FOR	12. Cuba Trade Embargo	FOR

Key Votes of the 103d Congress

1. Family Leave	FOR	2. Deficit Reduction	AGN	3. Stimulus Plan	AGN

Election Results

1992 general	Paul E. Gillmor (R), unopposed			($254,988)
1992 primary	Paul E. Gillmor (R), unopposed			
1990 general	Paul E. Gillmor (R)	113,615	(68%)	($254,688)
	P. Scott Mange (D)	41,693	(25%)	($248)
	John E. Jackson (I)	10,612	(6%)	($4,650)

SIXTH DISTRICT

Ohio was settled from the south, where the Ohio River and its tributaries made the hills of inland America permeable to coastal Americans. Yankee settlers came down the Ohio from Pittsburgh and founded Marietta in 1788 as Ohio's first town. Around the same time George Washington procured for his Revolutionary War veterans bounty lands in the Virginia Military District of Ohio between the Scioto and Miami Rivers, centered on Chillicothe. In Marietta the Yankees built New England style churches; in Chillicothe the young Virginian Thomas Worthington who became governor of Ohio built his home, Adena, designed by architect Benjamin Latrobe. Virginians soon outnumbered New Englanders, and their traces remain on the landscape, laid out in irregular-shaped parcels as in Virginia, not the Northwest Ordinance's checkerboard grid imposed on most of the Midwest. There have been lasting political effects too. These rolling lands south of U.S. 40 have never attracted much industry; most people here speak with an accent that sounds southern to northern Ohioans; they retain, with conservative cultural attitudes, a Democratic heritage that manifests itself as a willingness to vote Democratic on occasion (it elects Vern Riffe, the senior state House Speaker in the nation). It was one sign of the shrewdness of Bill Clinton's campaign that the Clinton-Gore bus trip out of the New York convention went through just this part of Ohio, and that Clinton ultimately carried the state in part by running just about even here. Clinton returned to the area in early 1993 to sell his economic package to the middle-class voters.

The 6th Congressional District of Ohio covers most of southern Ohio, from Marietta down the Ohio River to the gritty industrial towns of Ironton and Portsmouth; it runs across the hilly landscape to include part of Chillicothe and all of Piketon (site of a bitter year-long strike, starting in June 1991, over work rules at a nuclear materials plant), and west over to Warren County between Dayton and Cincinnati. It has no large central cities and almost entirely avoids metropolitan areas. As of 1992, this is a combination of two old districts: the 6th, which extended farther north toward Columbus and west toward Cincinnati, and the 10th, which extended from Ironton and Marietta north to Lancaster and Zanesville, east of Columbus. Both were represented for many years by Republicans; the new 6th is represented by a Democrat. Therein lies a tale of how two Republicans of very different generations and temperaments fought each other in a bitter primary, opening the way for a Democrat who had lost races for Congress three times before.

The two Republicans were Clarence Miller, representative from the 10th since 1966, and Bob McEwen, representative from the 6th since 1980. Miller brings to mind the days when Robert Taft conservatives dominated the midwestern delegations: he is an engineer, precise and orderly, who prided himself on never missing roll call votes and, as a member of the Appropriations Committee, introduced amendments for precise percentage spending cuts. Bob McEwen's life has been politics: after college and two years in the real estate business, he was elected to the legislature in 1974 at age 24; in 1980 he was elected to Congress; in 1988 he made a well-publicized feint at running against Senator Howard Metzenbaum, and then left the race to George Voinovich; in 1990 he was mentioned as a possible candidate for lieutenant governor, but his House colleague Mike DeWine got that. McEwen was a Reagan-era Republican, not much concerned about budget deficits, an enthusiast for assertive foreign policy, without the single-minded devotion to bringing home pork barrel projects of his Republican predecessor. During redistricting it was assumed Miller would retire if the old 10th was merged into the 6th. When the plan came out, he filed to run in the June primary here, though he was 74 and had an injured hip; he came close to withdrawing in May, but stayed in out of distaste for his opponent. When the House bank scandal broke, McEwen first told reporters he had no overdrafts, then that he had only a few; it turned out he had 166. The primary was bitter and close. McEwen, who had represented most of the new district, won after a recount and a lawsuit by Miller by 33,194 votes to 32,908.

That gave a fine opening for Democrat Ted Strickland, son of a steelworker and eighth of nine children, Methodist minister, former director of a children's home, a prison psychologist and psychology professor at Shawnee State College, candidate for Congress three times before and winner of 46% against McEwen in 1980. In the 1992 primary, Strickland emphasized his pro-choice stance and less rigid opposition to gun control and beat Chillicothe mayor Joseph Sulzer by a 2–1 margin. In the general, Strickland campaigned for more highways and school spending and for countering alcohol and drug abuse, school dropouts and teen pregnancy: "building communities where children are nurtured and educated and protected and cared for," he said. He and his wife (author of a kindergarten screening test and a children's book on former Kentucky Governor Martha Layne Collins) have made their way up as counseling professionals. Strickland attacked House procedures and hit McEwen for missing 25 roll call votes on days he received honoraria for speeches; McEwen hit Strickland for getting paid $35 an hour to conduct prison encounter groups and for not saying he'd vote against gun control.

Strickland won a general election that turned out to be almost as close as the Republican primary: 51%–49%. This was all the more a stinging rebuke of McEwen since George Bush carried the district. McEwen carried the 59% of the district he used to represent, but by only 55%–45%; Strickland carried the old Miller areas 59%–41%. McEwen got a second chance in early 1993 when he decided to run for the 2d District seat being vacated by Bill Gradsion, but he lost in the March primary to Rob Portman. Strickland's challenge now is to deliver, both on his promises to shape new national programs and on the old-fashioned work of delivering projects to southern Ohio. He got a good start on "delivering" when, in April 1993, he was back in the district helping to mediate a riot at the maximum-security Lucasville prison where he had previously worked as a psychologist.

The People: Pop. 1990: 570,804; 60% rural; 13% age 65+; 97% White; 2% Black. Voting age pop.: 420,945; 2% Black. Households: 61% married couple families; 29% married couple fams. w. children; 30% college educ.; median household income: $21,761; per capita income: $10,349; median gross rent: $315; median house value: $46,200.

1992 Presidential Vote		1988 Presidential Vote	
Bush (R)	102,481 (40%)	Bush (R)	128,989 (59%)
Clinton (D)	99,761 (39%)	Dukakis (D)	90,322 (41%)
Perot (I)	50,532 (20%)		

Rep. Ted Strickland (D)

Elected 1992; b. Aug. 4, 1941, Portsmouth; home, Lucasville; Ashbury College, B.A. 1963, Ashbury Theological Seminary, M.Div. 1967, U. of KY, Ph.D. 1980; Methodist; married (Frances).

Career: Methodist Children's Home advisor, 1968–76, Asst. Dir., 1974–76; Prof., Shawnee State, 1986–92; Consulting psychologist, Southern Ohio Correctional facility, 1986–92.

Offices: 1429 LHOB 20515, 202-225-5705. Also 1236 Gallia St., Portsmouth 45662, 614-353-5171.

Committees: *Education and Labor* (24th of 28 D): Elementary, Secondary and Vocational Education; Labor Standards, Occupational Health and Safety; Postsecondary Education and Training. *Small Business* (16th of 27 D): Development of Rural Enterprises, Exports and the Environment; Regulation, Business Opportunities and Technology.

Group Ratings and 102d Congress Votes: Newly Elected

Key Votes of the 103d Congress

1. Family Leave   FOR   2. Deficit Reduction   FOR   3. Stimulus Plan   FOR

Election Results

1992 general	Ted Strickland (D)	122,720	(51%)	($237,082)
	Bob McEwen (R)	119,252	(49%)	($716,672)
1992 primary	Ted Strickland (D)	23,339	(55%)	
	Joseph P. Sulzer (D)	11,015	(26%)	
	Bob Smith (D)	8,427	(20%)	
1990 general	Bob McEwen (R)	117,220	(71%)	($196,934)
	Raymond S. Mitchell (D)...............	47,415	(29%)	($11,171)

SEVENTH DISTRICT

The hills and plains of central Ohio are dotted with towns and small cities that have been manufacturing centers almost since they were settled in the early 19th Century, when the dominant technologies were the waterwheel and the open forge. In the 15 decades since, they have been replaced by one after another new technology, and the local manufacturing economy, sometimes with uncomfortable fits and starts, has adjusted and advanced. Such has been the case with the capital G-shaped slice of central Ohio that makes up the state's 7th Congressional District. Its largest city is Springfield, where International Harvester was the biggest employer for years; in the 1980s the firm went bankrupt, downsized drastically, and is now named Navistar. To the south are the eastern suburbs of Dayton around Wright-Patterson Air Force Base, whose name recalls the Dayton-based fathers of the airplane and the cash register.

The Dayton area suffered from job losses in the early 1980s and 1990s, but there is some small business growth, less visible than elsewhere in Ohio but with long-term impact. Reminders of technological advances past and future exist in smaller places too. In the northern end of the 7th District are Bellefontaine, site of the first concrete street in America. Marysville, not far away, is the site of Honda's first U.S. plant, where its best-selling car model, the Accord, is assembled by American workers with mostly American managers at a level of quality that most observers not long ago thought Americans could not achieve. Even as old factories are shut down, new ones open that are more productive; the result is higher incomes and, though not often remembered, far less of the backbreaking hard work and drudgery that were the lot of almost everyone in supposedly better times.

The 7th District has always been Republican territory. It backed the policies of Ohio Republicans William McKinley—tariff protection, railroad regulation, antitrust suits against monopolies, discouragement of labor unions—and James Rhodes—low taxes, encouragement of new businesses and jobs. It is culturally conservative and economically non-interventionist, but without ideological fervor. It was one of the few Ohio districts to stick with and give a good margin to George Bush in 1992.

The 7th District's current congressman is David Hobson, a Republican from Springfield, first elected in 1990 after eight years in the state Senate. Hobson has been in real estate and owned until 1993 two Japanese steakhouses. In the House his first bill was the National Child Abuse Registration Act which established a registered network of convicted child abusers; he is obviously interested in the kind of programs which engage many local civic leaders. He is fiscally conservative on most national issues, voting against most spending issues and backing the balanced budget amendment; he worked with Ohio colleagues Bill Gradison and John Kasich to sculpt a Republican healthcare bill which would set up tax free health savings accounts for companies with health plans. But this hasn't stopped him from working with Dayton Democrat Tony Hall to secure a federal waiver for the Dayton Area Health Plan and to build Dayton's national aviation historic park. Hobson is not a partisan firebrand like his Ohio colleague John

Boehner or predecessor Mike DeWine; he serves on the Ethics Committee, and did not make a loud issue of House perquisites or scandals, though he was one of the four Republicans who dissented from its March 1992 report which called for only limited disclosure of the worst abusers of the House bank.

Previous holders of this seat have run for statewide office, Clarence Brown for governor in 1982, DeWine for lieutenant governor in 1990. Hobson seems to have no such ambition, but he has proved very strong in the district. He was unopposed in the 1992 primary and won the general with 71%. Redistricting for 1992 shifted the 7th south and east and added the home town of 10th District incumbent Clarence Miller, but Miller chose to go with most of his old base and run against Bob McEwen in the new 6th, and Hobson ran about 25% ahead of George Bush. Hobson received two key assignments for the 103d Congress—Budget and Appropriations, and can be expected to continue his role as a Republican voice on health care.

The People: Pop. 1990: 570,939; 43% rural; 12% age 65+; 93% White; 5% Black; 1% Asian; 1% Hispanic origin. Voting age pop.: 421,434; 5% Black; 1% Hispanic origin. Households: 64% married couple families; 30% married couple fams. w. children; 37% college educ.; median household income: $30,364; per capita income: $12,919; median gross rent: $376; median house value: $62,400.

1992 Presidential Vote			1988 Presidential Vote		
Bush (R)	112,701	(45%)	Bush (R)	141,450	(66%)
Clinton (D)	84,098	(33%)	Dukakis (D)	73,604	(34%)
Perot (I)	54,307	(22%)			

Rep. David L. Hobson (R)

Elected 1990; b. Oct. 17, 1936, Cincinnati; home, Springfield; OH Wesleyan U., B.A. 1958, OH St. Col. of Law, J.D. 1963; Methodist; married (Carolyn).

Career: OH Natl. Guard, 1958–63; Real estate agent; Restaurant owner; OH Senate, 1982–90, Majority Whip, 1986–88, Pres. Pro Tem, 1988–90.

Offices: 1507 LHOB 20515, 202-225-4324. Also 220 P.O. Bldg., 150 N. Limestone St., Springfield 45501, 513-325-0474; and 212 S. Broad St., Lancaster 43130, 614-654-5149.

Committees: *Appropriations* (21st of 23 R): Military Construction. *Budget* (11th of 17 R). *Standards of Official Conduct* (6th of 7 R).

Group Ratings

	ADA	ACLU	COPE	CDF	CFA	LCV	ACU	NTLC	NSI	COC	CEI
1992	15	26	33	30	33	13	80	80	100	88	63
1991	10	—	25	30	28	8	80	—	—	80	68

National Journal Ratings

	1991 LIB — 1991 CONS			1992 LIB — 1992 CONS		
Economic	14%	—	83%	16%	—	80%
Social	37%	—	61%	30%	—	69%
Foreign	17%	—	78%	38%	—	56%

Key Votes of the 102d Congress

1. Ban Striker Replace AGN	5. Handgun Wait/7-Day AGN	9. Use Force in Gulf FOR
2. $ for Homeownership FOR	6. Overseas Mil. Abortion AGN	10. US Mil. Abroad $ Cut FOR
3. Tax Rich/Cut Mid Cls. AGN	7. Obscn. Art NEA $ Ban FOR	11. Limit SDI Funds AGN
4. FY93/$15B Def. Cut AGN	8. Death Pen. from Jury FOR	12. Cuba Trade Embargo FOR

Key Votes of the 103d Congress

1. Family Leave AGN	2. Deficit Reduction AGN	3. Stimulus Plan AGN

Election Results

1992 general	David L. Hobson (R)	164,195	(71%)	($298,896)
	Clifford S. Heskett (D)...............	66,237	(29%)	
1992 primary	David L. Hobson (R), unopposed			
1990 general	David L. Hobson (R)	97,123	(62%)	($389,136)
	Jack Schira (D).....................	59,349	(38%)	($89,019)

EIGHTH DISTRICT

Some of the prime industrial country of the early 20th Century sits in the far west end of Ohio, where U.S. 40, the old National Road, heads straight as an arrow in its last miles across Ohio to Indiana, and the rail lines criss-cross the land from Cincinnati to Dayton. Here the Great and Little Miami Rivers drain south into the Ohio where U.S. 40 jogs southward twice to go over the Miami and Stillwater River dams, built after the great flood of 1913 that killed 361 people in Dayton and caused $1 billion in damage. Between Dayton and Cincinnati grew up large factory towns like Middletown and Hamilton, as well as smaller ones. Now, in the late 20th Century, these have adapted better than the huge factory cities of the Great Lakes region, while comfortable suburban tracts have grown up in what were once open fields.

The 8th Congressional District of Ohio covers much of this territory, including most of four counties north of Dayton and U.S. 40, Preble County west of Dayton, and Butler County between Dayton and Cincinnati. About half its people live in Butler, around Hamilton and Middletown, which has become part of what is essentially a single metropolitan strip from northern Kentucky to U.S. 40 north of Dayton. Politically, this is solidly Republican territory, with its representative selected in the Republican primary.

The current congressman, John Boehner (pronounced *bayner*), won the seat by beating not just one but two of his predecessors in 1990, and in his first term made far more impact than just about any minority party freshman in memory. The two eliminated were Buz Lukens, elected in 1966, 1968, 1986 and 1988, and convicted in May 1989 of having sex with a 16-year-old girl whose mother accused him of offering her a government job to keep her silent. The other was Thomas Kindness, who held the seat from 1974 until he ran for the Senate in 1986. Boehner, a plastics company president and three-term Ohio legislator, attacked Kindness for deserting his constituents to become a Washington lobbyist after losing his Senate bid, and won 49%–32%, with 17% for Lukens.

Boehner quickly became part of the Gang of Seven, young freshman Republicans who joined together to insist that House leaders reveal the names of all the 355 members who had overdrafts at the House bank and then went on to assail Democratic leaders and Republican go-alongers on the pay raise, the House Post Office scandal and what they called the speaker's "slush fund." They also argued that members of Congress should be subject to regulatory laws they impose on other citizens, and in May 1992 Boehner invited OSHA inspectors to his office, where they found what would have been 15 violations if Congress were covered by the OSHA regulations. That same month Boehner took the lead in resurrecting the 27th Amendment to the Constitution, proposed by James Madison with the original Bill of Rights in 1789, to prohibit Congress

1006 OHIO

from varying its pay during its current term. Six states ratified it between 1789 and 1791, Ohio did so in 1873, and from 1978 to 1992, 32 more states followed suit. The 39 state mark should count as the three-quarters needed, Boehner argued; the U.S. archivist certified the amendment ratified and Congress voted nearly unanimously to accept the amendment. What's amazing, of course, is that politicians as seasoned as members of Congress didn't observe this rule even without the amendment, since it provides them with a fine defense to charges they have raised their own pay: they can't collect the raise without the voters' permission. Yet in Boehner's view Congress is still in violation: in October 1992 he sued to void the January 1993 cost-of-living increase made automatic in the 1989 pay raise bill as a violation of the 27th Amendment.

The Gang of Seven's work evidently struck a chord around the nation. Six of the seven, all except Boehner, had serious challenges in the 1992 general election; six out of the seven won, Boehner with 74%. Can he have as much impact in his second term as his first? He will certainly try to keep his reforms going from his new seat on the House Administration Committee and his voice heard as the new chairman of the Conservative Opportunity Society.

The People: Pop. 1990: 570,837; 38% rural; 12% age 65+; 96% White; 3% Black; 1% Asian. Voting age pop.: 415,686; 3% Black. Households: 65% married couple families; 32% married couple fams. w. children; 36% college educ.; median household income: $31,171; per capita income: $13,355; median gross rent: $389; median house value: $65,900.

1992 Presidential Vote

Bush (R) 121,174 (47%)
Clinton (D) 75,375 (29%)
Perot (I). 60,172 (23%)

1988 Presidential Vote

Bush (R) 151,025 (69%)
Dukakis (D)............... 67,060 (31%)

Rep. John A. Boehner (R)

Elected 1990; b. Nov. 17, 1949, Cincinnati; home, West Chester; Xavier U., B.S. 1977; Catholic; married (Debbie).

Career: Navy, 1969; Pres., Nucite Sales, Inc., 1976–90; Union Township Bd. of Trustees, 1981–85, Pres., 1984; OH House of Reps., 1985–90.

Offices: 1020 LHOB 20515, 202-225-6205. Also 5617 Liberty-Fairfield Rd., Hamilton 45011, 513-894-6003; and 12 S. Plum St., Troy 45373, 513-339-1524.

Committees: *Agriculture* (10th of 19 R): General Farm Commodities; Livestock. *Education and Labor* (11th of 15 R): Elementary, Secondary and Vocational Education; Labor-Management Relations. *House Administration* (6th of 7 R): Accounts; Office Systems (RMM).

Group Ratings

	ADA	ACLU	COPE	CDF	CFA	LCV	ACU	NTLC	NSI	COC	CEI
1992	5	0	17	10	13	0	96	95	100	88	82
1991	0	—	0	20	11	0	95	—	—	100	85

National Journal Ratings

	1991 LIB — 1991 CONS		1992 LIB — 1992 CONS	
Economic	4%	— 90%	9%	— 88%
Social	0%	— 84%	0%	— 85%
Foreign	0%	— 88%	18%	— 74%

Key Votes of the 102d Congress

1. Ban Striker Replace AGN	5. Handgun Wait/7-Day AGN	9. Use Force in Gulf FOR
2. $ for Homeownership FOR	6. Overseas Mil. Abortion AGN	10. US Mil. Abroad $ Cut AGN
3. Tax Rich/Cut Mid Cls. AGN	7. Obscn. Art NEA $ Ban FOR	11. Limit SDI Funds AGN
4. FY93/$15B Def. Cut AGN	8. Death Pen. from Jury FOR	12. Cuba Trade Embargo AGN

Key Votes of the 103d Congress

1. Family Leave AGN	2. Deficit Reduction AGN	3. Stimulus Plan AGN

Election Results

1992 general	John A. Boehner (R).................	176,362	(74%)	($530,835)
	Fred Sennet (D)	62,033	(26%)	($6,730)
1992 primary	John A. Boehner (R), unopposed			
1990 general	John A. Boehner (R).................	99,955	(61%)	($732,765)
	Gregory V. Jolivette (D)	63,584	(39%)	($114,852)

NINTH DISTRICT

Seventy years ago Toledo was one of America's boom towns. The 1920s here was "a decade of fabulous figures," Harlan Hatcher wrote: the Willys-Overland plant employed 25,000 workers and turned out an auto every 30 seconds; the city built $20 million coal and iron ore docks; the Libbey-Owens-Ford merger made Toledo, with good local supplies of natural gas and sand, the nation's biggest glass manufacturer; the city built a new museum and transcontinental airport. Toledo had long been well-situated, where the Maumee River empties into Lake Erie, where two dozen rail lines connected it with the East Coast and Chicago and the coal fields of Kentucky and West Virginia. It was well-positioned to be one of the centers of the brash rising auto industry, a national leader when it produced the Jeep in the 1940s. But in the late 1970s and early 1980s, auto company management allowed the union to bid wages and benefits too high while the union allowed management to let quality get too low, to the point that consumers would not buy enough American-made cars for the industry to survive without vast subsidy or major shrinkage. Subsidy, beyond the temporary Chrysler loan and a few small trade barriers, was not forthcoming, and so Toledo and other auto-dependent cities went through tough times: contrast the confident, growing city of the 1920s with the Toledo that sadly saw the tasteful Portside Festival Marketplace close in 1990.

Ohio's 9th Congressional District is centered on Toledo; as the city's population has stagnated, it has spread east to the flatlands of Ottawa County, south to Bowling Green State University, and west to rural Fulton County. Toledo has been heavily Democratic since CIO unions organized the plants in the late 1930s; the collapse of the auto industry so unnerved the district that in 1980 it voted for Ronald Reagan and elected a Republican congressman, but in 1982 it became solidly Democratic again, electing Democrat Marcy Kaptur, who has held the seat ever since.

Kaptur spent eight years as an urban planner in Toledo, then got a job in the Carter White House; she was shrewd enough to return to Toledo in 1982 when no one else wanted to run for the House seat. She has been fixated continually on trade issues especially those regarding the Japanese; from her planning days she seems to assume that if government could just set down enough rules, Toledo and similar areas could go back to the days before the late 1970s shakeout. She has been a leader in prohibiting top government officials from representing foreign interests for a year after they leave government, and in 1993 will introduce measures to cover more government officials with even tougher restrictions—a 5-year ban on representing any foreign interest and a permanent ban on representing any foreign government or political party. She has pressured the Japanese to buy more American auto parts and at the same time is leery of

1008   OHIO

Japanese investment in the United States; she worked to stop the Library of Congress from accepting a $1.5 million Japanese grant in 1992. She co-chairs the Competitiveness Caucus and the Congressional Auto Parts Caucus. She has proposed a "Trade Corps" to encourage Foreign Service officer-like professionalism and training among government officials dealing with trade issues. "When you are dealing in important international economic areas, you need people as sophisticated as our foreign service officers. It shouldn't be left to amateurs." She is, predictably, an opponent of the North American Free Trade Agreement and says that 100,000 Ohio jobs have already been lost to Mexico.

With a seat on Appropriations, Kaptur is able to work on local projects such as securing funds to restore Toledo's Farmers' Market and the Central Union Terminal. She took a lead initiative on building a World War II Memorial in Washington and minting 50th anniversary coins to pay for it. She is reelected every two years with huge majorities, and in 1993 was being touted as a possible candidate for the Senate in 1994, should Metzenbaum decide to retire.

The People: Pop. 1990: 570,911; 14% rural; 13% age 65+; 83% White; 12% Black· 1% Asian; 2% Other; 3% Hispanic origin. Voting age pop.: 421,038; 11% Black; 2% Hispanic origin. Households: 53% married couple families; 25% married couple fams. w. children; 42% college educ.; median household income: $28,856; per capita income: $13,477; median gross rent: $392; median house value: $58,000.

1992 Presidential Vote			1988 Presidential Vote		
Clinton (D)	118,713	(47%)	Dukakis (D)	117,368	(52%)
Bush (R)	81,784	(32%)	Bush (R)	107,658	(48%)
Perot (I)	50,151	(20%)			

Rep. Marcy Kaptur (D)

Elected 1982; b. June 17, 1946, Toledo; home, Toledo; U. of WI, B.A. 1968, U. of MI, M.A. 1974; Catholic; single.

Career: Urban planner, Toledo, Lucas Cnty. Planning Comm., 1969–75; Urban planning consultant, 1975–77; Asst. Dir. for Urban Affairs, Pres. Carter, 1977–80; Dep. Secy., Natl. Consumer Coop. Bank, 1980–81.

Offices: 2104 RHOB 20515, 202-225-4146. Also Fed. Bldg., 234 Summit St., #719, Toledo 43604, 419-259-7500.

Committees: *Appropriations* (21st of 37 D): Agriculture, Rural Development, Food and Drug Administration and Related Agencies; District of Columbia; VA, HUD and Independent Agencies.

Group Ratings

	ADA	ACLU	COPE	CDF	CFA	LCV	ACU	NTLC	NSI	COC	CEI
1992	75	70	100	70	87	56	8	0	40	14	14
1991	85	—	82	100	78	62	5	—	—	30	15

National Journal Ratings

	1991 LIB — 1991 CONS			1992 LIB — 1992 CONS		
Economic	88%	—	0%	74%	—	25%
Social	67%	—	33%	59%	—	40%
Foreign	62%	—	36%	52%	—	46%

Key Votes of the 102d Congress

1. Ban Striker Replace FOR	5. Handgun Wait/7-Day FOR	9. Use Force in Gulf AGN
2. $ for Homeownership AGN	6. Overseas Mil. AbortionAGN	10. US Mil. Abroad $ Cut FOR
3. Tax Rich/Cut Mid Cls. FOR	7. Obscn. Art NEA $ Ban FOR	11. Limit SDI Funds FOR
4. FY93/$15B Def. Cut FOR	8. Death Pen. from Jury AGN	12. Cuba Trade Embargo FOR

Key Votes of the 103d Congress

1. Family Leave FOR	2. Deficit Reduction FOR	3. Stimulus Plan FOR

Election Results

1992 general	Marcy Kaptur (D)	178,879	(74%)	($335,095)
	Kenny Brown (R)	53,011	(22%)	($43,930)
	Ed Howard (I)	11,162	(5%)	
1992 primary	Marcy Kaptur (D), unopposed			
1990 general	Marcy Kaptur (D)	117,681	(78%)	($211,524)
	Jerry D. Lammers (R)	33,791	(22%)	($200)

TENTH DISTRICT

Cleveland, on America's North Coast—as local promotional materials call Lake Erie—is one of America's great 20th Century cities. It owes its rapid growth early in this century to heavy industry: this was the original home base of John D. Rockefeller's Standard Oil; the city's twisting and deep Cuyahoga River was the site of several of the nation's largest steel mills; great industrial fortunes here built civic institutions like the museums in Wade Park, Case Western University and the Cleveland Symphony, and financed the campaigns of northeast Ohio Republican Presidents James Garfield and William McKinley. On the old Public Square, designed like a New England town green by the Yankees who settled this Western Reserve (the northeast corner of Ohio) in the early 19th Century, the two eccentric Van Sweringen brothers, trolley magnates of the early 20th, built the Terminal Tower, the highest skyscraper for years in interior America. This yeasty, ethnic city, with more than 40 nationalities—Czechs, Hungarians, Poles, Italians, Germans: the Hapsburg Empire and more—and with many distinct ethnic neighborhoods, produced a robust two-party politics. In the 1930s, after the New Deal and when CIO unions organized the steel factories and auto assembly plants, Cleveland became pretty solidly Democratic, though with some affluent Republican suburbs (notably Shaker Heights, laid out by the Van Sweringens).

But Cleveland never grew as much as it hoped: the nation's fourth largest city in 1910, it was overtaken in size first by Detroit, then by Los Angeles, eventually by the likes of Houston and Dallas; today it's the center of the nation's 14th largest metropolitan area. The central city declined from 914,000 in 1950 to 506,000 in 1990, as the children who grew up in those tightly-packed neighborhoods made more money and moved to the suburbs; movement was especially great in wards east of the Cuyahoga River, which were almost entirely ethnic in 1950 and almost entirely black by 1970. The 1970s were a bad decade for Cleveland, which became an object of ridicule by national sophisticates. Its heavy industries were fast declining, Lake Erie and the Cuyahoga River were badly polluted (yes, the river did actually catch fire in June 1969, as did Mayor Ralph Perk's hair as he wielded an acetylene torch at a bridge opening). City politics became racially polarized with the election of black Mayor Carl Stokes in 1967 and 1969, and was dominated in the late 1970s by Mayor Dennis Kucinich, a neighborhood-based demagogue whose fiscal policies seriously undermined the city government's economy. But the city's economy has revived, and the city government rescued by George Voinovich, elected mayor in 1979 and governor in 1990. Cleveland sprouted a new downtown headquarters for British Petroleum (here because it bought Standard of Ohio), the second-largest performing arts center in the nation at Playhouse Square, and a downtown baseball stadium and basketball arena (funded by an increase in liquor and cigarette taxes). Cleveland continues to be headquarters of several of the nation's largest law firms, some of its businesses like iron-ore giant Cleveland-Cliffs have sharply revived; the city's number one employer is now health services, and the Cleveland Clinic handles 700,000 outpatients a year. The Rock and Roll Hall of Fame will be completed in 1994 just north of downtown along the Lake.

The 10th Congressional District of Ohio includes most of the west side of Cleveland and most of the western suburbs in Cuyahoga County. Excluded is one salient of mostly black Cleveland precincts attached to the 11th District across the Cuyahoga; also several western suburbs— Brook Park, Middleburg Heights, are in the convoluted suburban 19th District. Suburbs include Lakewood, built up by the 1920s but still comfortable middle-class territory, and Rocky River and Bay Village, growing more affluent as one moves westward along the lake. Inland is Parma, a creation of the 1950s, when second- and third-generation ethnics moved out to subdivision houses set amid what was once calculated to be America's densest concentration of bowling alleys. The political tradition here is almost entirely Democratic, but in the 1980s Republican national candidates ran well in the suburbs and some city wards; George Voinovich, popular from his decade as mayor, carried the area for in his 1990 governor's race.

Despite its heritage, the 10th District elected a Republican congressman in 1992, and one who outwardly seems to have little in common with west side Cleveland's yeasty traditions: Martin Hoke, cellular telephone entrepreneur. Hoke made a serious candidate, but clearly could not have won if not for the problems of incumbent Congresswoman Mary Rose Oakar—problems which nearly defeated her in the primary and resulted in a humiliating repudiation in the general election. For Oakar in many ways seemed to personify the district: she was a city councilwoman elected to the House in 1976, ethnic (Arab-American) and antiabortion, a member of the Democratic leadership who by incredible persistence made mammography a Medicare benefit. But Oakar also had 213 overdrafts on the House bank, and this was not the first of her problems. In 1987, it was revealed that she'd kept a former aide and housemate on salary for two years after the woman moved to New York and that she'd given another woman staffer a $10,000 raise one month after she and Oakar bought a house together. In 1992, the *Cleveland Plain Dealer* said she had been pressured to resign from the House Administration Committee task force investigating the House Post Office after allegations arose that she put "ghost employees" on the Post Office payroll; she called the allegations "damnable lies" and sued the *Plain Dealer*. The allegations were later disproved, but in April 1992, Oakar also resigned as co-chair of the Democratic National Platform Committee.

Oakar was challenged in the primary by County Commissioner Tim Hagan, who has the appearance of a hard-shelled politician but actually may be one of the last true-believing white liberal Democrats in the country. Hagan has taken on cynical politicoes of both races, and suffered for it; in the brief House primary, he declined to attack Oakar on her overdrafts or the 1987 charges until she ran an ad that seemed to accuse him of overlooking corruption while county commissioner. A third candidate filed—encouraged by Oakar?—who siphoned off protest votes, while the *Plain Dealer* for unknown reasons endorsed an unknown, William Green, and Oakar, who stressed her constituency services, won 39% to 30% for Hagan.

That set up a marvelous opportunity for Hoke, who lived outside the district in Shaker Heights but nonetheless beat the mayor of Rocky River in the five-candidate primary. Hoke called Oakar "the most persuasive argument for term limits" and handed out matchbooks with aspirins attached saying, "Congress giving you a headache? Take two of these and vote for Martin R. Hoke." He battered her in an appearance on *This Week with David Brinkley* and led in the October polls; the final result was a 57%–43% Hoke victory. Hoke will have an opportunity as a minority member to cast votes against the congressional establishment: he's for term limits, eliminating congressional pensions, reduced franked mailings, less staff and banning PAC contributions. But the key question for 1992 may turn out to be whether he can establish a record that will reelect him in a basically Democratic district. Hoke is more interesting than he first appears, however: he is the descendant both of colonial era German ministers and of a Romanian immigrant who opened a west side restaurant; he is an accomplished pianist; he started his law practice in his basement; he started a business providing auto repair service for travelers flying out of Cleveland-Hopkins airport and then started Red Carpet Cellular in 1985. This adaptability and his skillful and aggressive campaign against Oakar suggest he may have some political lasting power.

The People: Pop. 1990: 570,530; 15% age 65+; 92% White; 2% Black; 1% Asian; 2% Other; 4% Hispanic origin. Voting age pop.: 435,093; 2% Black; 3% Hispanic origin. Households: 52% married couple families; 23% married couple fams. w. children; 43% college educ.; median household income: $30,323; per capita income: $14,813; median gross rent: $388; median house value: $72,600.

1992 Presidential Vote			1988 Presidential Vote		
Clinton (D)	107,465	(41%)	Bush (R)	131,372	(52%)
Bush (R)	92,846	(36%)	Dukakis (D)	119,818	(48%)
Perot (I)	58,092	(22%)			

Rep. Martin R. Hoke (R)

Elected 1992; b. May 18, 1952, Lakewood; home, Cleveland; Amherst Col., B.A. 1973, Case Western Reserve U., J.D. 1980; Presbyterian; divorced.

Career: Founder & Pres., Red Carpet Car Care, 1980–present, Red Carpet Cellular, 1985–present; Practicing atty., 1982–92.

Offices: 212 CHOB 20515, 202-225-5871. Also 21270 Lorain Rd., Fairview Park 44126, 216-356-2010.

Committees: *Budget* (17th of 17 R). *Science, Space and Technology* (14th of 22 R): Space; Technology, Environment and Aviation.

Group Ratings and 102d Congress Votes: Newly Elected

Key Votes of the 103d Congress

1. Family Leave	FOR	2. Deficit Reduction	AGN	3. Stimulus Plan	AGN

Election Results

1992 general	Martin R. Hoke (R)	136,433	(57%)	($682,166)
	Mary Rose Oakar (D)	103,788	(43%)	($1,292,286)
1992 primary	Martin R. Hoke (R)	13,119	(33%)	
	Earl Martin (R)	11,016	(28%)	
	Sally Conway Kilbane (R)	9,744	(25%)	
	Carol Fedor (R)	3,621	(9%)	
	Bill Smith (R)	1,704	(4%)	
1990 general	Mary Rose Oakar (D)	109,390	(73%)	($284,053)
	Bill Smith (R)	39,749	(27%)	

ELEVENTH DISTRICT

Cleveland, like most great American cities, has grown in great bursts of migration, when capitalists' investments suddenly were paying off beyond their wildest dreams and low-wage workers were attracted from ready corners of the country and the world. Cleveland's first great surge of growth started in the 1890s and lasted through the 1920s, as tens of thousands of immigrants from central and southern Europe arrived here, looking for jobs in steel and auto and other factories. Bohemians came to the tight-packed neighborhoods along Broadway, Hungarians a bit to the northeast, Jews north of University Circle along East 105th Street, Italians to Little Italy south of Mayfield Road.

As the nation's heavy industries geared up for World War II and enjoyed years of unexpected prosperous growth afterward, a second surge of immigrants came, this time blacks from the American South. From Cleveland's old black ghetto, south of Carnegie Avenue downtown to East 105th, the rapidly increasing number of blacks covered most of the east side by the middle 1960s, with only a few Bohemian and Italian enclaves left east of the Cuyahoga and west of the city limits. Migration stopped around 1965, but blacks have continued to move out beyond the city limits to the east side suburbs, including modest East Cleveland and Warrensville Heights and upper-income Shaker Heights, laid out on broad boulevards by streetcar magnates, the Van Sweringen brothers, in 1905. These surges of migration led to political changes. A succession of ethnic mayors—Anthony Celebrezze, Ralph Locher—was followed by the election in 1967 and 1969 of Carl Stokes, the nation's first big city black mayor, and Cleveland had racially polarized city politics for much of the 1970s. Ironically, Cleveland has never had a black majority and elected its second black mayor, Michael White, in 1989, in large part because the electorate as a whole preferred his accommodating politics to the plainly more polarizing and reputedly more unprincipled ways of longtime city Council Chairman George Forbes.

The 11th Congressional District of Ohio includes most of the east side of Cleveland, plus the suburbs just to the east, which together have about as many people as the city now. Some of these—East Cleveland, Warrensville Heights—are mostly black; some—Shaker Heights is the most notable—have stable black percentages with carefully maintained neighborhoods. Others are the natural destination of blacks seeking low-crime neighborhoods and middle-class schools not often found on the city side of Cleveland's impressive set of museums and medical centers. This is, of course, a heavily Democratic district, with a solid black majority, and it has been represented since 1968 by Louis Stokes, Carl Stokes's brother. The Stokeses come from a humble background. "I want you to study and get an education," their mother said. "Get something in your head so you will never have to work with your hands the way I have." Louis Stokes served in the segregated Army in World War II, got a law degree when practically no law firm would hire blacks, and challenged the Ohio congressional district lines when it was considered unthinkable that a black could be elected to Congress.

Able and not afraid of controversy, plagued by his own foibles but so far not mortally, Stokes has taken on tough assignments in the House. In 1977, after Henry Gonzalez resigned the post in fury, Stokes became chairman of the Select Committee on Presidential Assassinations, on which he supervised responsible hearings and the production of a report that disputed the Warren Commission findings and concluded that Kennedy "was probably assassinated as a result of a conspiracy." Following the chagrin caused by the film *J.F.K.*, he returned to the subject in 1992, setting up a special commission to look into the matter, and despite Justice Department objections was able to secure release of most of the still secret files on the assassination. In 1980, as the Abscam scandal was breaking, Stokes was called on to chair the Committee on Standards of Official Conduct, the official name of the House Ethics Committee. He held that hot potato for four years, handling Abscam, the abuse of congressional pages and the charges made against Geraldine Ferraro when she was nominated for vice president in 1984. In 1987 and 1988, he chaired of the House Intelligence Committee and a member of the special committee investigating the Iran-contra scandal. In 1991, as all but one other member rotated off, Stokes was called again to head up Ethics—just in time for the House bank and Post Office scandals. He was not unsinged himself. He recused himself from investigating the bank and admitted he'd overdrawn his account "on occasion"; it turned out he had 551 overdrafts. He did, however, look into who was leaking lists of violators; presumably he saw to it, though he's not saying so, that Gary Ackerman of New York, widely suspected by other members of being the leaker, resigned from the committee rather than force an inquiry.

Stokes gave up the Ethics Committee chair in 1993 and is now the sixth ranking Democrat on the Appropriations Committee and chairman of the VA-HUD-Independent Agencies Subcommittee. This covers an odd hybrid of agencies, which tend to get played off against one another: Stokes is likely to increase housing money at the expense of space, for example, and to argue with his Senate counterpart Barbara Mikulski and Vice President Al Gore, who are more space-minded. He can be counted on to shepherd minority set-aside programs, like his minority scholarship program for the CIA and NSA, and a 10% minority set-aside for Supercollider contracts. Of course he works to get projects and money into Cleveland. The irony would come if the set-aside and race-conscious programs Stokes has concentrated on are ruled unconstitutional by the courts as the redistricting law was when he challenged it a quarter-century ago. It is not clear if Stokes, a founder of the Congressional Black Caucus, has left behind a paradigmatic solution to the problems of black Americans which are still apparent in parts of the 11th District. But he has over a long haul established a record of honorable and competent public service and met difficult challenges—an achievement that was in no way guaranteed him when he entered politics and public life. He has expressed an interest in running for the Senate in 1994, should Metzenbaum retire.

The People: Pop. 1990: 571,295; 15% age 65+; 39% White; 59% Black; 1% Asian; 1% Other; 1% Hispanic origin. Voting age pop.: 424,100; 55% Black; 1% Hispanic origin. Households: 38% married couple families; 16% married couple fams. w. children; 41% college educ.; median household income: $22,459; per capita income: $12,629; median gross rent: $376; median house value: $58,100.

1992 Presidential Vote			1988 Presidential Vote		
Clinton (D)	169,870	(73%)	Dukakis (D)	176,683	(78%)
Bush (R)	37,886	(16%)	Bush (R)	48,767	(22%)
Perot (I)	23,428	(10%)			

Rep. Louis Stokes (D)

Elected 1968; b. Feb. 23, 1925, Cleveland; home, Shaker Heights; Western Reserve U., 1946–48, Cleveland Marshall Law Schl., J.D. 1953; African Methodist Episcopal Zion; married (Jeanette).

Career: Army, 1943–46 (WWII); Practicing atty., 1954–68.

Offices: 2365 RHOB 20515, 202-225-7032. Also New Fed. Ofc. Bldg., 1240 E. 9th St., #2947, Cleveland 44199, 216-522-4900; and 2140 Lee Rd., #211, Cleveland Heights 44118, 216-522-4907.

Committees: *Appropriations* (6th of 37 D): District of Columbia; Labor, Health and Human Services, and Education; VA, HUD and Independent Agencies (Chmn.).

Group Ratings

	ADA	ACLU	COPE	CDF	CFA	LCV	ACU	NTLC	NSI	COC	CEI
1992	95	100	92	100	100	81	0	0	10	14	4
1991	100	—	100	90	78	77	0	—	—	22	6

National Journal Ratings

	1991 LIB — 1991 CONS		1992 LIB — 1992 CONS	
Economic	88% —	0%	78% —	18%
Social	88% —	0%	92% —	0%
Foreign	92% —	0%	90% —	0%

Key Votes of the 102d Congress

1. Ban Striker Replace	FOR	5. Handgun Wait/7-Day	FOR	9. Use Force in Gulf	AGN
2. $ for Homeownership	AGN	6. Overseas Mil. Abortion	FOR	10. US Mil. Abroad $ Cut	FOR
3. Tax Rich/Cut Mid Cls.	FOR	7. Obscn. Art NEA $ Ban	AGN	11. Limit SDI Funds	FOR
4. FY93/$15B Def. Cut	FOR	8. Death Pen. from Jury	AGN	12. Cuba Trade Embargo	AGN

Key Votes of the 103d Congress

1. Family Leave	FOR	2. Deficit Reduction	FOR	3. Stimulus Plan	FOR

Election Results

1992 general	Louis Stokes (D)	154,718	(69%)	($449,248)
	Beryl E. Rothschild (R)	43,866	(20%)	($79,232)
	Ed Gudenas (I)	19,773	(9%)	($15,102)
	Two Others	5,267	(2%)	
1992 primary	Louis Stokes (D), unopposed			
1990 general	Louis Stokes (D)	103,338	(80%)	($198,984)
	Franklin H. Roski (R)	25,906	(20%)	

TWELFTH DISTRICT

Five hundred years after its namesake discovered North America (or stumbled on San Salvador Island), Columbus, Ohio, is approaching big league status. With its city limits stretching out toward farmland at each point of the compass, Columbus is geographically the largest city in Ohio; its metropolitan area, though far smaller than Cleveland's and a bit smaller than Cincinnati's, is growing more rapidly and has some time since passed the magic million mark. Columbus has the advantages of being a state capital, the home of Ohio State University, and a major white-collar employment town: its big employers include Nationwide Insurance and multistate giant Banc One. This does not make Columbus quite recession-proof (state government, Ohio State and local defense contractors all shed jobs in 1992), but it has attracted the kind of upscale, enterprising people who produced most of America's growth in the 1970s and 1980s. It is now the home base of The Limited's Leslie Wexner, and the headquarters of Wendy's. Columbus does have some heavy industry, and watching the 'pork queens' at the Ohio State Fair recalls its beginnings as a farm market town. But Columbus would rather visitors see the new $43 million Wexner Center for the Visual Arts, a post-post-modern structure that has evoked vast architectural controversy, or, while it was on, Ameriflora '92, the extravagant flower show put on to celebrate the 500th anniversary of Columbus's voyage.

Columbus politically has always been a Republican city, with an even more Republican hinterland. It had few of the Eastern European immigrants and CIO unions that made Cleveland so Democratic; for most of the last 30 years, its mayor has been a Republican with support from a machine redolent of the era of William McKinley (whose statue sits in front of the flat-domed Capitol). Recently, local Republicans have had spirited competition from Democrats, but this was a metro area that preferred George Bush to Bill Clinton in 1992. The

Columbus area dominates two of Ohio's congressional districts: the 12th extends east to the small industrial town of Newark and north to bucolic Delaware County and includes the affluent east side of the city; the 15th includes most of the territory within the city limits and extends south and west to include Madison County. The 12th includes some of the city's black neighborhoods but more of the affluent east side around Bexley.

The congressman from the 12th District is a Republican, but not an old-fashioned machine Republican: John Kasich. Kasich, a self-starter, was a 26-year-old former Ohio State student from McKees Rocks, Pennsylvania, when he ran a strenuous door-to-door campaign and beat a Democratic state senator in 1978. In 1982, he ran for the House and, with the help of a favorable districting plan, beat a Democrat who had upset an incumbent in 1980. Kasich is peppery and brash, self-confident and aggressive, spewing forth ideas, a fair percentage of which are good and some of which even get enacted into law. But he has not been a loner; he has worked with other Republicans, and sometimes with Democrats, and now, just past 40, is a genuine leader of his party.

Kasich made his first commotion on Armed Services, where he was the leading Republican opponent of the B-2 bomber and succeeded in drastically limiting its production to 20 new planes from Bush's request of 132 in 1989. He also succeeded in stopping a $110 million expansion of the Pentagon building just after the end of the Cold War. He was one of the tigers who pushed through the military base closing bill (chief sponsor Dick Armey wasn't on Armed Services). With Jon Kyl and Duncan Hunter, he stopped a bill weakening restrictions of high-tech defense exports—which threatened, he said, nuclear proliferation. Kasich has also been active on the Budget Committee. He pushed through with then-Budget Chairman Leon Panetta an amendment requiring more burden-sharing by European and other allies. And in late 1992 he successfully bucked seniority to become ranking Republican on Budget after the departure of Bill Gradison. Kasich led aggressive challenges against the Clinton budget proposals in 1993, and can be expected to continue articulating a conservative fiscal voice.

Kasich seems widely popular at home, and has carried the solidly Republican 12th District by solid margins. He has been mentioned as a candidate for statewide office, and said he might consider a run for Metzenbaum's seat in 1994, should his friend Lieutenant Governor Mike DeWine decline to run.

The People: Pop. 1990: 571,341; 15% rural; 9% age 65+; 74% White; 23% Black; 1% Asian; 1% Hispanic origin. Voting age pop.: 416,926; 21% Black; 1% Hispanic origin. Households: 52% married couple families; 26% married couple fams. w. children; 49% college educ.; median household income: $30,859; per capita income: $14,723; median gross rent: $417; median house value: $74,700.

1992 Presidential Vote

Bush (R)	108,359	(41%)
Clinton (D)	105,852	(40%)
Perot (I)	47,080	(18%)

1988 Presidential Vote

Bush (R)	129,438	(59%)
Dukakis (D)	90,077	(41%)

Rep. John R. Kasich (R)

Elected 1982; b. May 13, 1952, McKees Rocks, PA; home, Westerville; OH St. U., B.A. 1974; Christian; divorced.

Career: A.A., OH Sen. Donald Lukens, 1975–77; OH Senate, 1978–82.

Offices: 1131 LHOB 20515, 202-225-5355. Also Fed. Bldg., 200 N. High St., Columbus 43215, 614-469-7318.

Committees: *Armed Services* (4th of 22 R): Readiness (RMM); Research and Technology. *Budget* (RMM of 17 R).

Group Ratings

	ADA	ACLU	COPE	CDF	CFA	LCV	ACU	NTLC	NSI	COC	CEI
1992	15	5	42	30	33	25	84	75	100	86	68
1991	15	—	8	20	28	23	85	—	—	100	82

National Journal Ratings

	1991 LIB — 1991 CONS	1992 LIB — 1992 CONS
Economic	22% — 77%	21% — 76%
Social	25% — 73%	23% — 75%
Foreign	26% — 70%	30% — 64%

Key Votes of the 102d Congress

1. Ban Striker Replace	AGN	5. Handgun Wait/7-Day	AGN	9. Use Force in Gulf	FOR
2. $ for Homeownership	FOR	6. Overseas Mil. Abortion	AGN	10. US Mil. Abroad $ Cut	AGN
3. Tax Rich/Cut Mid Cls.	AGN	7. Obscn. Art NEA $ Ban	FOR	11. Limit SDI Funds	AGN
4. FY93/$15B Def. Cut	AGN	8. Death Pen. from Jury	FOR	12. Cuba Trade Embargo	FOR

Key Votes of the 103d Congress

1. Family Leave	AGN	2. Deficit Reduction	AGN	3. Stimulus Plan	AGN

Election Results

1992 general	John R. Kasich (R)...................	170,297	(71%)	($242,096)
	Bob Fitrakis (D)	68,761	(29%)	($44,659)
1992 primary	John R. Kasich (R), unopposed			
1990 general	John R. Kasich (R)....................	130,495	(72%)	($278,977)
	Michael A. Gelpi (D)	50,784	(28%)	($47,815)

THIRTEENTH DISTRICT

One part of America where the imprint of the westward track of New England Yankee migration is most apparent is on the southern shore of Lake Erie in northern Ohio. The Yankees, cooped up in New England for 200 years, shot across the country through Upstate New York, west across Ohio and Michigan to Chicago, and then to Kansas and southern California in just two or three generations, providing inspiration, manpower and technical might for the Union victory in the Civil War, and leaving a deep imprint in many places along the way. One of those places was the Western Reserve, the northeast corner of Ohio along Lake Erie, created for the excess population of Connecticut, whose towns, colleges and cultural institutions were mostly established by Yankees. Consider Oberlin College, founded in 1832 as the first co-educational college in the world, though no women dared apply till 1837; it accepted black students a few years later, and the town became a center of the Underground Railroad. Or consider Hiram, home of another college and of James Garfield, who once represented the area in Congress when it was the most Republican part of Ohio, and who is the only president elected directly from the House, in 1880. Or look in between the subdivisions for old white New England farmhouses or in little community centers for the buildings where hard-working citizens built communities with, above all, good schools and, with their accumulated savings, invested in what became some of the nation's leading industries.

In partisan terms, the area was naturally Republican territory. The Yankees, with their reformist ideas and dislike of slavery and the South, were a natural Republican base wherever they moved in the young nation, and the area remained heavily Republican for years. But the great masses of immigrants lured to Cleveland and the smaller industrial cities built by Yankee capital provided a base for labor unions and Progressive politics. After the New Deal and the bloody CIO organizing drives of the late 1930s, the Western Reserve had something like class-warfare politics for 30 years, with the Democrats usually winning. Northern Ohio, like New England, moved away from the Republicans and toward the Democrats. Now the Western Reserve may be moving toward a post-industrial economy like Connecticut or Massachusetts. Factory employment has been falling, but total jobs are rising again; small, adaptive business units with highly skilled workers are the growth sectors. That leaves the Western Reserve, like New England, generally Democratic—but not reliably so. Michael Dukakis carried the area in 1988, but not by a huge margin; Republican George Voinovich, former mayor of Cleveland, carried it solidly in 1990; Bill Clinton carried it by a wide margin in 1992, but with less than an absolute majority.

The 13th Congressional District of Ohio is grotesquely-shaped—something like a barbell—with two large segments of Western Reserve lands connected by a sort of land bridge between Cleveland and Akron. The western end includes the factory towns of Lorain and Elyria plus Oberlin and Medina County, once a rural area, now filling up with outmigrants from Cleveland along I-71. The eastern, less heavily populated area, includes all of Geauga County, high-income hilly townships with many reminders of New England origins, and rural parts of Trumbull and Portage Counties. This end of the district tends to vote Republican, while on the west end Lorain County is Democratic and Medina County Republican. The easy winner of the district, had he run, would have been Don Pease, congressman since 1976, a Democrat who was once editor of the Oberlin *News-Tribune* and state senator. Pease was a thoughtful and innovative legislator, whose limitation on $100,000-plus earners' tax deductions was incorporated into the 1990 budget summit tax increase and whose wage standards provisions were included in the 1988 trade law. But in October 1991 Pease said he would retire, leading to a wild and woolly race in the redistricted 13th.

The two leading candidates were both known quantities. Republican Margaret Mueller, a millionaire social worker from Geauga County, had run three times against Dennis Eckart in the old 11th District; she spent as much as $860,000, mostly her own money, in 1988, but never topped 40% of the vote. Mueller is pro-life, for eight-year term limits, for across-the-board cuts in spending; she beat former legislator and son of Cleveland Indians co-owner Jeffrey Jacobs in the six candidate primary by a 37%-27% margin. The well-known Democrat was Sherrod Brown, momentarily out of office, but literally a career politician: he was the youngest Ohioan ever elected to the state House, at age 21, just after graduating from Yale in 1974; in 1982, he was elected secretary of state (while his brother, Charlie Brown, was elected attorney general of West Virginia), and worked hard to increase voter registration and turnout. He lost that office to Robert Taft in 1990, and Republican redistricters took care to keep Brown's home town of Mansfield outside the 13th. But Brown moved into a rented lake cottage in Medina County and in the primary beat Margaret Mathna, a former aide to Cleveland Congresswoman Mary Rose

Oakar, by 45%–22%. Brown showed great flair in the general election campaign, taking a 200-mile bicycle tour; with solid labor support, he campaigned loud and hard against the North American Free Trade Agreement and championed universal health care. Mueller defended NAFTA, attacked Brown's record as secretary of state, and pointed out that his ex-wife had accused him of abuse in her divorce papers. There were also three Independents in the race, but the result was unambiguous. Brown won 53%–35%, winning 61% in Lorain County and majorities or near-majorities in most of the rest of the district; Mueller carried Geauga by only 100 votes.

After skillful lobbying of the members of the Democratic Steering and Policy Committee, Brown was one of only five freshman to land a seat on Chairman John Dingell's powerful Energy and Commerce Committee. Profiled as one of *National Journal*'s "Up and Comers" in 1993 ("How do I make sure I'm on the final list?" he asked when told he was a candidate for the series), Brown will likely be a solid liberal vote in the House, though with special emphasis on protectionist trade policy. He can be expected to work hard to maintain his popularity in this weirdly-shaped district.

The People: Pop. 1990: 570,838; 36% rural; 11% age 65+; 92% White; 4% Black; 1% Other; 3% Hispanic origin. Voting age pop.: 412,451; 4% Black; 2% Hispanic origin. Households: 66% married couple families; 32% married couple fams. w. children; 41% college educ.; median household income: $34,725; per capita income: $14,307; median gross rent: $403; median house value: $76,700.

1992 Presidential Vote			1988 Presidential Vote		
Clinton (D)	101,854	(38%)	Bush (R)	122,863	(54%)
Bush (R)	96,037	(35%)	Dukakis (D)	106,085	(46%)
Perot (I)	72,038	(27%)			

Rep. Sherrod Brown (D)

Elected 1992; b. Nov. 9, 1952, Mansfield; home, Lorain; Yale U., B.A. 1974, OH St. U., M.A. 1979, M.A. 1981; Presbyterian; divorced.

Career: OH House of Reps. 1975–83; Prof., Ohio State U. Mansfield, 1979–81; OH Secy. of State 1983–91.

Offices: 1407 LHOB 20515, 202-225-3401. Also 1936 Cooper Foster Pk., Lorain 44053, 216-282-5100.

Committees: *Energy and Commerce* (24th of 27 D): Health and the Environment; Oversight and Investigations. *Foreign Affairs* (17th of 27 D): Asia and the Pacific; Europe and the Middle East. *Post Office and Civil Service* (14th of 15 D).

Group Ratings and 102d Congress Votes: Newly Elected

Key Votes of the 103d Congress

1. Family Leave	FOR	2. Deficit Reduction	FOR	3. Stimulus Plan	FOR

Election Results

1992 general	Sherrod Brown (D)	134,486	(53%)	($486,354)
	Margaret R. Mueller (R)	88,889	(35%)	($864,338)
	Mark Miller (I)......................	20,320	(8%)	
	Two Others	8,563	(3%)	
1992 primary	Sherrod Brown (D)	30,820	(45%)	
	Margaret Rose Mathna (D)	15,234	(22%)	
	Christopher Rothgery (D).	4,825	(7%)	
	Thomas Muzilla (D)	4,237	(6%)	
	Ed Boyle (D)........................	3,968	(6%)	
	Bernice Kammiller (D).................	3,394	(5%)	
	William VanderWyden, III (D)	3,054	(5%)	
	Other..............................	2,317	(3%)	
1990 general	Donald J. (Don) Pease (D)	93,431	(57%)	($348,032)
	William D. Nielsen (R).................	60,925	(37%)	($124,483)
	John M. Ryan (I)	10,506	(6%)	

FOURTEENTH DISTRICT

Polymer Valley—the name doesn't appear on many maps, but it is being used by at least some Ohioans today for an area that was known not so long ago as Rubber Town: Akron. (The name is from the Greek word for high, the same root as Acropolis, because Akron sits on a ridge between the Great Lakes and Mississippi watersheds.) Twenty years ago, Akron was as synonymous to tires as Detroit was to cars: Firestone, Goodyear, General Tire, and B. F. Goodrich all had their headquarters and big tire factories here; the United Rubber Workers had been the big union since the 1930s. The Akron area's population was heavily descended from migrants, some from Eastern Europe but more from West Virginia, who thronged here in the 1910s and 1920s to snap up jobs in the tire factories for 10 or 12 hours a day at the price of smelling burning rubber for 24. But by the early 1990s, the smell of rubber had long since passed from Akron's air, and the language of class conflict had mostly passed from its politics. At first the rubber companies started decentralizing their plants; then the European competitors they scorned started making money on radials; then, after the oil shock of 1979, the auto market collapsed. The Akron plants were antiquated, and the last auto tire plant here was shut down in the 1970s, the last truck and airplane tire plants in 1984 and 1985. General Tire was bought by a German firm, and Firestone merged with Bridgestone and its headquarters moved to Nashville.

Enter polymers: plastics and other hydrocarbons that can be formed or shaped like rubber into useful industrial products. The first polymer, polyvinyl chloride (PVC), was invented in 1926 when B. F. Goodrich chemist Waldo Semon, looking to make synthetic rubber, found a mysterious goo in the bottom of his test tube; the company did not bother to patent it till 1933, but now PVC is everywhere, in pipes and siding and shoes and toys and cartops and stadium covers. Polymers were a natural extension of the rubber companies' business, and now the Akron area and the Cuyahoga Valley north to Cleveland are called Polymer Valley. Ohio now ships more plastic resins than any other state but Texas and employs more people in the field than any other state but California. What Akron doesn't have is the large number of high-wage, low-skill, unionized jobs it did in the rubber companies' heyday. What it does have is a more upscale work force and the basis for growth in the future.

Akron's political heritage has been Democratic since the CIO organizing days, modulated by the skills of longtime Akron and also National Republican chairman Ray Bliss in the 1950s and 1960s. Akron and surrounding Summit County, with some variation in district boundaries, have long made up Ohio's 14th Congressional District, represented by a Republican from 1950 to 1970 and by Democrats since 1970. The 14th includes all of Summit County, except the northern tier of townships, plus the area around Kent (and Kent State University, site of the

1970 shooting of four students by National Guard troops) just to the east. The current congressman, Tom Sawyer, was first elected in 1986, after serving as mayor of Akron. Sawyer seized on one issue in the House as he had polymers as mayor of Akron: the Census. In his second term he inherited the chair of the Post Office Subcommittee on the Census and Population (now Census, Statistics and Postal Personnel)—a post that seems inevitably to go to members from population-losing districts—just in time for the 1990 count. Sawyer has been in the forefront of those who criticize the Census Bureau for doing a worse job than in 1980 and for massive undercounts; "The 1990 census may be the first in modern history that is less accurate than the one before it," he said. Sawyer argued strongly for adjusting the Census results, to the point of subpoenaing and threatening court action against Commerce Secretary Robert Mosbacher for not divulging adjusted figures for local census divisions. Sawyer's case is politically driven: central cities and industrial areas that have been losing population, like Akron which lost 6% in the 1980s, fear the loss of political representation and formula-apportioned government funds that results from publication of the Census counts. The problem is that, while there are statistically valid arguments for adjusting the count, there is no single argument that all the experts insist is statistically valid: it is an issue on which experts can reasonably differ. Given the inevitability of such disagreement, politicians are obviously going to select the expert opinion that promotes their partisan and parochial interests. In the end, members of Congress were apportioned to the states according to the unadjusted Census counts; the steam went out of Sawyer's demands to use the adjusted count when it became clear that adjustments would give the biggest boost to areas with large numbers of immigrants and underclass minorities—the portion of the population most likely to have been undercounted. California and New York would be the beneficiaries, not Akron or Erie, Pennsylvania, the home of ranking Republican Tom Ridge. Sawyer has called for broad Census reform, and for hearings on increasing the House from the 435 members it has had since 1913, which would reduce the political pressure for adjusting the Census numbers.

Sawyer has worked on other legislation, using his seat on Education and Labor to promote the National Literacy Act of 1991 to increase adult literacy, and the Dwight D. Eisenhower Mathematics and Science Education bill which provides technical assistance to schools that revise their science and math programs. Sawyer wants to amend RCRA to allow states to charge fees for importers of out-of-state solid waste. His interest in this area goes back to his tenure as mayor, when three men at a local company were killed by the explosion of 80,000 pounds of solvents from New Jersey. Unsuccessful in a bid for a seat on Ways and Means in 1993, Sawyer instead got assigned to the less politically popular but, perhaps, ultimately career rewarding Ethics Committee.

The People: Pop. 1990: 570,987; 8% rural; 13% age 65+; 87% White; 11% Black; 1% Asian; 1% Hispanic origin. Voting age pop.: 433,109; 10% Black; 1% Hispanic origin. Households: 55% married couple families; 24% married couple fams. w. children; 44% college educ.; median household income: $28,184; per capita income: $13,931; median gross rent: $394; median house value: $59,800.

1992 Presidential Vote

Clinton (D)	118,715	(45%)
Bush (R)	81,232	(31%)
Perot (I)	60,000	(23%)

1988 Presidential Vote

Dukakis (D)	122,836	(53%)
Bush (R)	108,364	(47%)

Rep. Tom Sawyer (D)

Elected 1986; b. Aug. 15, 1945, Akron; home, Akron; U. of Akron, B.A. 1968, M.A. 1970; Presbyterian; married (Joyce).

Career: OH House of Reps., 1977–83; Akron Mayor, 1984–86.

Offices: 1414 LHOB 20515, 202-225-5231. Also 411 Wolf Ledges Pkwy., #105, Akron 44311, 216-375-5710.

Committees: *Education and Labor* (9th of 28 D): Elementary, Secondary and Vocational Education; Postsecondary Education and Training; Select Education and Civil Rights. *Foreign Affairs* (26th of 27 D): International Security, International Organizations and Human Rights. *Post Office and Civil Service* (5th of 15 D): Census Statistics and Postal Personnel (Chmn.). *Standards of Official Conduct* (7th of 7 D).

Group Ratings

	ADA	ACLU	COPE	CDF	CFA	LCV	ACU	NTLC	NSI	COC	CEI
1992	95	100	83	100	100	63	4	0	30	38	10
1991	90	—	92	100	72	62	0	—	—	30	14

National Journal Ratings

	1991 LIB — 1991 CONS		1992 LIB — 1992 CONS	
Economic	78% —	21%	78% —	18%
Social	84% —	12%	88% —	8%
Foreign	87% —	8%	76% —	19%

Key Votes of the 102d Congress

1. Ban Striker Replace	FOR	5. Handgun Wait/7-Day	FOR	9. Use Force in Gulf	AGN
2. $ for Homeownership	AGN	6. Overseas Mil. Abortion	FOR	10. US Mil. Abroad $ Cut	FOR
3. Tax Rich/Cut Mid Cls.	FOR	7. Obscn. Art NEA $ Ban	AGN	11. Limit SDI Funds	FOR
4. FY93/$15B Def. Cut	FOR	8. Death Pen. from Jury	AGN	12. Cuba Trade Embargo	AGN

Key Votes of the 103d Congress

1. Family Leave	FOR	2. Deficit Reduction	FOR	3. Stimulus Plan	FOR

Election Results

1992 general	Tom Sawyer (D)	165,335	(68%)	($209,155)
	Robert Morgan	78,659	(32%)	
1992 primary	Tom Sawyer (D)	54,933	(75%)	
	Jack Resnick (D)	13,109	(18%)	
	Dennis Chrobak (D)	4,786	(7%)	
1990 general	Tom Sawyer (D)	97,875	(60%)	($264,793)
	Jean E. Bender (R)	66,460	(40%)	($3,021)

FIFTEENTH DISTRICT

Columbus, the capital of Ohio, is no longer a regional mid-sized city, the place where the bed fell on James Thurber's father, the town *My Sister Eileen* left behind for New York, the college town to which Philip Roth's Newark-born hero was finally able to say goodbye. Columbus is now the center of a metropolitan area of more than 1 million people, the headquarters of major research centers, of financial powers like Nationwide Insurance and Banc One, and of retailers

1022   OHIO

from The Limited to Wendy's and the home of Ohio State University.

The 15th Congressional District of Ohio is made up of most of Columbus, all but the east side, plus southern and western Franklin County and rural Madison County directly to the west. The 15th includes most of Columbus's black population, some white working-class areas on the south side of the city and in nearby Grove City, and the Ohio State University campus area. Politically, these Democratic areas are more than balanced by the heavily Republican suburb of Upper Arlington, across the Olentangy River from Ohio State, and by the Republican subdivisions that seem to be sprouting up in rural land and between the old villages.

For 26 years, since it was first created, the 15th District had the same congressman, Chalmers Wylie, a Republican who was a much decorated veteran and 33d degree Mason, the ranking Republican for 10 years on the Banking Committee. Honest and careful in his work, he was embarrassed by the S&L debacle the committee's longtime chairman, Fernand St Germain, helped to create, and embarrassed in 1991 when it was revealed he had 515 overdrafts on the House bank. His decision to retire in 1992 set up a serious three-way contest which resulted in a Republican victory but may not be the last time this district is heartily contested this decade.

The Democrats had a strong candidate, Richard Cordray, a Marshall Scholar at Oxford and Supreme Court law clerk, a winner of $45,000 on *Jeopardy*, who grew up in Grove City and returned to live with his father and, in 1990 at 31, beat a six-term state representative. Cordray showed the political smarts of many Watergate-era Democrats before him, but was notably more conservative on issues, supporting term limits and opposing most new taxes. The Republicans nominated Deborah Pryce, who quickly ran into a problem. Elected twice to a countywide judgeship, she quit the bench to run and got the party endorsement. But her easy nomination gave abortion opponents the impression she agreed with them; actually, she said, after she won the primary without opposition, she was against abortion herself (she has an adopted daughter), but she would vote for a Freedom of Choice Act which would restrict states' power to limit abortions. That prompted pro-lifer Linda Reidelbach to run a spirited campaign as an Independent. Pryce talked much about congressional reform—term limits, rotating chairmanships, line-item veto—and called for limiting spending increases to 3%.

In the end, Pryce's money and party identification advantages evidently made the difference. She won 44% of the vote to Cordray's 38%; Reidelbach had a surprisingly large 18%. Pryce's emphasis on congressional reform was matched by her freshman activities; she attended the Omaha meeting of Republicans in November and was elected interim-president of the freshman Republican class. It will be interesting to see which side of her—the pro-choic reformer, or the tough-on-crime prosecutor and judge—dominates in her House career.

The People: Pop. 1990: 570,740; 10% rural; 10% age 65+; 92% White; 5% Black; 2% Asian; 1% Hispanic origin. Voting age pop.: 442,506; 5% Black; 1% Hispanic origin. Households: 52% married couple families; 24% married couple fams. w. children; 51% college educ.; median household income: $31,020; per capita income: $15,076; median gross rent: $438; median house value: $73,000.

1992 Presidential Vote

Bush (R)	119,588	(45%)
Clinton (D)	94,232	(35%)
Perot (I)	52,316	(20%)

1988 Presidential Vote

Bush (R)	147,250	(66%)
Dukakis (D)	77,393	(34%)

Rep. Deborah Pryce (R)

Elected 1992; b. July 29, 1951, Warren; home, Columbus; Ohio State U., B.A. 1973, Capital U. Law Schl., J.D. 1976; Presbyterian; married (Randy Walker).

Career: Admin. Law Judge, OH Dept. of Insurance, 1976; Sr. Asst. Columbus City Prosecutor, 1978; Franklin Cnty. Munic. Court Judge, 1985–1992; Practicing atty., 1992.

Offices: 128 CHOB 20515, 202-225-2015. Also 200 N. High St., #400, Columbus, OH 43215, 614-469-5614.

Committees: *Banking, Finance and Urban Affairs* (12th of 20 R): Consumer Credit and Insurance; Financial Institutions Supervision, Regulation and Deposit Insurance; Housing and Community Development. *Government Operations* (15th of 17 R): Environment, Energy and Natural Resources.

Group Ratings and 102d Congress Votes: Newly Elected

Key Votes of the 103d Congress

1. Family Leave	AGN	2. Deficit Reduction	AGN	3. Stimulus Plan	AGN

Election Results

1992 general	Deborah Pryce (R)	110,390	(44%)	($556,741)
	Richard Cordray (D)	94,907	(38%)	($312,366)
	Linda Reidelbach (I)	44,906	(18%)	($41,841)
1992 primary	Deborah Pryce (R), unopposed			
1990 general	Chalmers P. Wylie (R)	99,251	(59%)	($242,592)
	Thomas V. Erney (D)	68,510	(41%)	($15,977)

SIXTEENTH DISTRICT

Canton, Ohio, is an industrial city, but different from huge factory towns like Youngstown and Akron. It has many employers, not just a few, and its work has typically been high-skill not low-skill; it was fashioning new kinds of plows and reapers and making watches in the 19th Century, and has been making roller bearings since 1899. Canton did not attract masses of immigrants; its factories did not run on harsh stopwatch discipline. The class-warfare politics created during the CIO union organizing drives and sitdown strikes of the late 1930s did not really take here; its politics remains closer to that of its president, William McKinley. Although later his name was synonymous with outmoded, standpat politics, McKinley was in his time a very successful politician, who won two elections by decisive margins and began a period of three decades in which the Republican Party, with scarce support in the one-third of the nation that was the South, was the clear majority party in the United States—the only time it has been so. His policies—the protective tariff, the gold standard, the enforcement of law and order in labor relations—were summed up in the phrase, the "full dinner pail," and for many years produced economic growth and technological progress that improved the quality of life.

The 16th Congressional District of Ohio includes Canton and surrounding Stark County, plus three-and-a-half counties to the west: Wayne, site of the College of Wooster, Holmes with its Amish communities, and Ashland and part of Knox, both new territory in 1992. Stark, usually Republican, voted for Bill Clinton in 1992, but the other counties tilted the 16th District back into the Bush column. And it was carried easily, as usual, by Congressman Ralph Regula, who is fittingly a graduate of the William McKinley School of Law. First elected in 1972, Regula is one of the senior Republicans in the House; ABC reporter Cokie Roberts once said "in terms of straight legislative ability, he's one of the most effective people in Congress." An old-fashioned Republican, Regula likes to work with Democrats to craft legislation and avoid ideological confrontations; during the debate on the "gag rule" on abortion counseling, he offered an amendment to establish abortion counseling only if the patient requested it. He is the fourth ranking Republican on the Appropriations Committee and as ranking Republican on its Interior Subcommittee, he worked through most of the 1980s to stop bans on offshore oil drilling, though with little success. As ranking Republican on the now defunct Select Aging Committee, he advocated more preventive care, including Medicare coverage for influenza shots. He wrote a 1992 law to provide technical assistance to small firms for teaching employees basic skills.

Regula was more comfortable with George Bush than with Ronald Reagan, but passed up the 1992 Republican National Convention to stay home, and ran far ahead of the ticket in November—indeed, as well as Bush and Ross Perot put together.

The People: Pop. 1990: 570,705; 37% rural; 14% age 65+; 94% White; 5% Black; 1% Hispanic origin. Voting age pop.: 419,413; 4% Black; 1% Hispanic origin. Households: 62% married couple families; 29% married couple fams. w. children; 33% college educ.; median household income: $27,524; per capita income: $12,413; median gross rent: $353; median house value: $58,000.

1992 Presidential Vote		
Bush (R)	98,824	(39%)
Clinton (D)	95,157	(37%)
Perot (I)	60,639	(24%)

1988 Presidential Vote		
Bush (R)	131,961	(58%)
Dukakis (D)	94,491	(42%)

Rep. Ralph S. Regula (R)

Elected 1972; b. Dec. 3, 1924, Beach City; home, Navarre; Mt. Union Col., B.A. 1948, William McKinley Schl. of Law, LL.B. 1952; Episcopalian; married (Mary).

Career: Navy, 1944–46 (WWII); Teacher and schl. principal, 1948–52; Practicing atty., 1952–73; OH Bd. of Educ., 1960–64; OH House of Reps., 1965–66; OH Senate, 1967–72.

Offices: 2309 RHOB 20515, 202-225-3876. Also 4150 Belden Village St., NW, Canton 44718, 216-489-4414.

Committees: *Appropriations* (4th of 23 R): Interior (RMM); Transportation.

Group Ratings

	ADA	ACLU	COPE	CDF	CFA	LCV	ACU	NTLC	NSI	COC	CEI
1992	35	35	67	50	33	25	72	60	100	100	46
1991	20	—	58	50	44	8	55	—	—	60	44

National Journal Ratings

	1991 LIB — 1991 CONS		1992 LIB — 1992 CONS	
Economic	38% —	62%	39% —	60%
Social	27% —	71%	25% —	74%
Foreign	26% —	70%	44% —	50%

Key Votes of the 102d Congress

1. Ban Striker Replace FOR	5. Handgun Wait/7-Day FOR	9. Use Force in Gulf FOR
2. $ for Homeownership FOR	6. Overseas Mil. AbortionAGN	10. US Mil. Abroad $ Cut FOR
3. Tax Rich/Cut Mid Cls.AGN	7. Obscn. Art NEA $ Ban FOR	11. Limit SDI Funds AGN
4. FY93/$15B Def. Cut *	8. Death Pen. from Jury FOR	12. Cuba Trade Embargo FOR

Key Votes of the 103d Congress

1. Family Leave FOR	2. Deficit Reduction AGN	3. Stimulus Plan AGN

Election Results

1992 general	Ralph S. Regula (R).................	158,489	(64%)	($209,305)
	Warner Mendenhall (D)...............	90,224	(36%)	($105,293)
1992 primary	Ralph S. Regula (R), unopposed			
1990 general	Ralph S. Regula (R).................	101,097	(59%)	($156,205)
	Warner D. Mendenhall (D)	70,516	(41%)	($68,021)

SEVENTEENTH DISTRICT

Where the hills of western Pennsylvania fade into the plains of northern Ohio, the tiny Mahoning River flows east and south. The first coal mine along the river opened in 1826, canals followed, and in 1892 the first steel mill was built in Youngstown. "Soon," writes historian Harlan Hatcher, "the banks of the river were lined with Bessemer converters, open-hearth furnaces, strip and rolling mills, pipe plants, and manufacturers of steel accessories and products." For nearly a century the Mahoning Valley, centered on Youngstown, between the Lake Erie docks that unload iron ore from Great Lakes freighters and the coalfields of western Pennsylvania and West Virginia, was one of the steel capitals of the United States. Now, in the late 20th Century, the steel mills stand empty and smokeless and silent—except those that have been dynamited and torn down. Big steel management allowed foreign producers to gain a technological edge back in the 1950s and 1960s; worldwide overcapacity in steel grew as almost every developing country decided it needed its own steel mills, while cooperation between the United Steelworkers and management after the 119-day strike in 1959 boosted wages and fringe benefits to price domestic steel out of the market. Import restrictions kept the furnaces hot for a while, but the oil shock of 1979 produced sharply higher energy prices and a collapse in U.S. autos and steel. Every plant in Youngstown and the Mahoning Valley closed and in the early 1980s metro Youngstown—Mahoning and Trumbull Counties—had one of the nation's highest unemployment rates.

Steel has since revived, but elsewhere, in decentralized minimills or in huge new rolling plants in northern Indiana. The biggest business headquartered in Youngstown is not steel, but the shopping center empire of Edward DeBartolo. The high-wage standard of living of the 1970s has vanished; young people looking for opportunities routinely leave; population has declined. Politically, the Mahoning Valley writhed in anger. Republican in the 1920s, the area was solidly Democratic for years after the United Steelworkers organized the plants following sometimes bloody skirmishes in the late 1930s. But as the steel industry collapsed, the district flirted again with Republicans, electing a Republican congressman in 1978, 1980 and 1982, and voting less than 50% for Jimmy Carter in 1980. Then, when the Mahoning Valley failed to share in the national recovery, it trended back toward the Democrats, and is now again one of the more Democratic parts of the country, and full of anger: Bill Clinton carried the area 2–1, while Ross Perot got nearly as many votes as George Bush.

Mahoning and most of Trumbull County plus, following the 1992 redistricting, Columbiana County which runs south to the Ohio River and the West Virginia border, form the 17th Congressional District of Ohio, whose congressman reflects the angry, anti-establishment mood of the Mahoning Valley. He is James Traficant, first elected in 1984. Controversy has always surrounded Traficant, and much of it goes back to his campaign for Mahoning County sheriff in 1980. He admitted taking large bribes from mobsters to overlook gambling, loan-sharking, drug trafficking and prostitution in Mahoning County and argued, when presented with tapes of some of these transactions, that this was part of his own sting operation (the man he said he returned the money to had, however, disappeared). The charges did not come out during the 1980 campaign, which Traficant won, and when he was tried on criminal charges in 1983 he acted as his own lawyer and persuaded the jury to find him not guilty. In 1984 he ran for the House and won a seven-candidate Democratic congressional primary with 56% of the vote and beat the Republican incumbent 53%–46%.

Traficant hasn't calmed down in Congress. "People see me as having a set of testicles—excuse my mouth," he told *The Washington Post*; in 1992, he said "It's time for Congress to tell the president to shove his veto pen up his deficit." Traficant loves to engage in one-minute tirades, so vivid they're often shown on evening news broadcasts; one netted him an hour on Phil Donahue. He takes particular aim at foreign aid, seeking across-the-board cuts, and tries to cut aid to Israel, to which he seems especially hostile; he was a particularly vitriolic opponent of the Gulf war. He passionately backs measures to help the Mahoning Valley, and is in policy terms one of Congress's most flamboyant protectionist and isolationist members (positions held by Republicans who represented the area in the 1920s). After a couple of terms, he seems to be learning to direct his rage into legislation. He passed a law declaring any company that falsely labels a product "Made in America" ineligible for defense contracts. He pressured the Ways and Means Committee into considering his taxpayer's rights amendments by standing on the floor for 10 hours and raising points of order against every section of the Treasury bill. He pushed a law creating 435 college scholarships, one in each congressional district, to be repaid by four years of service to the federal government—a forerunner of Bill Clinton's national service proposal. In early 1993, from his newly acquired chair of the Public Works Subcommittee on Public Buildings and Grounds, Traficant introduced a bill which would ban smoking in all federal buildings—including the House and Senate offices; it seems, on this issue at least, Traficant shares policy ground with none other than Hillary Rodham Clinton.

Traficant survived redistricting nicely in 1992. His colleagues might have tried to eliminate his district, but someone would have had to run against him and he seems very popular indeed in the Mahoning Valley. Not without limit, however: when he put himself on the ballot for president in 1988, he won 18% in his District, just behind Jesse Jackson.

The People: Pop. 1990: 570,963; 26% rural; 16% age 65+; 88% White; 10% Black; 1% Other; 1% Hispanic origin. Voting age pop.: 427,856; 8% Black; 1% Hispanic origin. Households: 58% married couple families; 25% married couple fams. w. children; 33% college educ.; median household income: $25,220; per capita income: $11,938; median gross rent: $337; median house value: $48,400.

1992 Presidential Vote

Clinton (D) 131,983 (50%)
Bush (R) 67,858 (26%)
Perot (I) 64,339 (24%)

1988 Presidential Vote

Dukakis (D) 148,987 (60%)
Bush (R) 98,250 (40%)

Rep. James A. Traficant, Jr. (D)

Elected 1984; b. May 8, 1941, Youngstown; home, Poland; U. of Pittsburgh, B.S. 1963; Youngstown St. U., M.S. 1973, M.S. 1976; Catholic; married (Patricia).

Career: Dir., Mahoning Cnty. Drug Program, 1971–81; Mahoning Cnty. Sheriff, 1980–84.

Offices: 2446 RHOB 20515, 202-225-5261. Also 11 Overhill Rd., Boardman 44512, 216-788-2414; 555 Youngstown-Warren Rd., Niles 44406, 216-652-5649; and 109 W. 3d St., E. Liverpool 43920, 216-385-5921.

Committees: *Public Works and Transportation* (10th of 39 D): Economic Development; Public Buildings and Grounds (Chmn.); Surface Transportation. *Science, Space and Technology* (10th of 33 D): Space.

Group Ratings

	ADA	ACLU	COPE	CDF	CFA	LCV	ACU	NTLC	NSI	COC	CEI
1992	85	77	90	100	93	50	8	15	20	50	14
1991	85	—	100	100	78	62	15	—	—	20	15

National Journal Ratings

	1991 LIB — 1991 CONS			1992 LIB — 1992 CONS		
Economic	69%	—	29%	56%	—	42%
Social	69%	—	30%	67%	—	32%
Foreign	62%	—	36%	82%	—	16%

Key Votes of the 102d Congress

1. Ban Striker Replace	FOR	5. Handgun Wait/7-Day FOR	9. Use Force in Gulf AGN
2. $ for Homeownership	AGN	6. Overseas Mil. Abortion FOR	10. US Mil. Abroad $ Cut FOR
3. Tax Rich/Cut Mid Cls.	AGN	7. Obscn. Art NEA $ Ban FOR	11. Limit SDI Funds AGN
4. FY93/$15B Def. Cut	FOR	8. Death Pen. from Jury FOR	12. Cuba Trade Embargo FOR

Key Votes of the 103d Congress

1. Family Leave   FOR   2. Deficit Reduction   AGN   3. Stimulus Plan   FOR

Election Results

1992 general	James A. Traficant, Jr. (D)	216,503	(84%)	($98,740)
	Salvatore Pansino (R)	40,743	(16%)	($3,488)
1992 primary	James A. Traficant, Jr. (D)	108,658	(92%)	
	M. Ross Norris (D)	10,054	(8%)	
1990 general	James A. Traficant, Jr. (D)	133,207	(78%)	($79,064)
	Robert R. DeJulio (R)	38,199	(22%)	($1,700)

EIGHTEENTH DISTRICT

The hilly land of east central Ohio has been industrial country from its earliest settlement in the 1790s. The local clay was used to make pottery, the coal that lies near the surface was dug up, a green vitriol works was built, and a nail factory went into operation, all before 1814. For more than 100 years this area has been part of the great coal and steel belt that centers on Pittsburgh and Cleveland and stretches from the coal mines of West Virginia to Lake Erie, the destination of the once common freighters filled with iron ore from Minnesota's Mesabi Range. This area is filled with small cities, each with its little steel mill or factory, most of them old towns whose storefronts and wooden, working-class houses bear the unmistakable imprint of the early 20th Century. For a time the pay was good, but after the oil shock of 1979, the coal and steel economy went into collapse; the impact here was cushioned by continuing demand for coal from electric utilities, but that will be reduced by the 1990 Clean Air Act. Wage levels have sagged and the hopes many had of getting ahead have been disappointed.

Ohio's 18th Congressional District covers much of this land along the Ohio River, just west of West Virginia, and spreads west over hilly farmland pockmarked by strip mines, from Steubenville on the Ohio, which used to have the nation's worst air quality, to New Rumley, the birthplace of General Custer. The 1992 redistricting extended it farther west, to include Zanesville, the birthplace of writer Zane Grey and architect Cass Gilbert and home of a famous Y-shaped bridge, and Newark—almost all the way across the old National Road and U.S. 40 to Columbus. As one goes west, the territory is less industrial, but overall the 18th is, sociologically and politically, a kind of ethnic working-class neighborhood. Politically, it is Democratic, though less so after redistricting.

The congressman from this district since 1976 is Democrat Douglas Applegate. First elected to the Ohio legislature in 1960, Applegate serves on practical-minded committees—Public Works and Transportation and Veterans' Affairs—that help him do something concrete for his district. He chaired the Veterans' Affairs Subcommittee on Compensation, Pension and Insurance, and worked to increase benefits for survivors of veterans who died of combat-related injuries. While previous benefits to surviving spouses had been paid based on a veteran's rank, Applegate has tried to pursue a more equitable payment structure. Another major cause has been to establish a national tracking system for hazardous waste shipments so the contents of any truck or rail car could be instantly traced in case of accident; he got language in the Hazardous Materials Transportation Act which called for a study of his proposal.

Applegate has been routinely reelected. In 1992, he won just 54% of the vote in the 30% of the district that was new to him, but won 74% in the rest, for an overall vote of 68%.

The People: Pop. 1990: 570,784; 60% rural; 15% age 65+; 97% White; 2% Black. Voting age pop.: 421,278; 2% Black. Households: 61% married couple families; 28% married couple fams. w. children; 25% college educ.; median household income: $22,808; per capita income: $10,531; median gross rent: $298; median house value: $44,000.

1992 Presidential Vote			1988 Presidential Vote		
Clinton (D)	110,491	(43%)	Bush (R)	120,109	(52%)
Bush (R)	87,512	(34%)	Dukakis (D)	110,141	(48%)
Perot (I)	58,605	(23%)			

Rep. Douglas Applegate (D)

Elected 1976; b. Mar. 27, 1928, Steubenville; home, Steubenville; Presbyterian; married (Betty).

Career: Real estate agent, 1950–76; OH House of Reps., 1960–68; OH Senate, 1968–76.

Offices: 2183 RHOB 20515, 202-225-6265. Also 46060 National Rd. W., St. Clairsville 43950, 614-695-4600; Ohio Valley Tower, #610, Steubenville 43952, 614-283-3716; 225 Underwood St., Zanesville 43701, 614-452-7023; and 1330 4th St., NW, New Philadelphia 44663, 216-343-9112.

Committees: *Public Works and Transportation* (4th of 39 D): Public Buildings and Grounds; Surface Transportation; Water Resources and Environment (Chmn.). *Veterans' Affairs* (3d of 21 D): Compensation, Pension and Insurance; Hospitals and Health Care.

Group Ratings

	ADA	ACLU	COPE	CDF	CFA	LCV	ACU	NTLC	NSI	COC	CEI
1992	70	48	92	70	80	44	12	15	30	38	20
1991	45	—	92	80	78	31	45	—	—	20	20

National Journal Ratings

	1991 LIB — 1991 CONS	1992 LIB — 1992 CONS
Economic	52% — 46%	61% — 38%
Social	25% — 73%	49% — 50%
Foreign	50% — 49%	76% — 19%

Key Votes of the 102d Congress

1. Ban Striker Replace FOR	5. Handgun Wait/7-Day AGN	9. Use Force in Gulf AGN
2. $ for Homeownership AGN	6. Overseas Mil. Abortion AGN	10. US Mil. Abroad $ Cut FOR
3. Tax Rich/Cut Mid Cls. FOR	7. Obscn. Art NEA $ Ban FOR	11. Limit SDI Funds FOR
4. FY93/$15B Def. Cut AGN	8. Death Pen. from Jury FOR	12. Cuba Trade Embargo FOR

Key Votes of the 103d Congress

1. Family Leave FOR	2. Deficit Reduction FOR	3. Stimulus Plan FOR

Election Results

1992 general	Douglas Applegate (D)	166,189	(68%)	($102,335)
	Bill Ress (R)	77,229	(32%)	($26,810)
1992 primary	Douglas Applegate (D), unopposed			
1990 general	Douglas Applegate (D)	120,782	(74%)	($94,754)
	John Hales (R)	41,823	(26%)	

NINETEENTH DISTRICT

Ohio's Western Reserve—the northeast corner of the state that belonged to Connecticut until 1800—still has something of the Yankee imprint on it. Along the shore of Lake Erie, east of Cleveland where the hills rise which produce the steel streams of the Cuyahoga and the Mahoning, is land settled by Yankees in the years before the Civil War. This area produced some of the strongest opposition to slavery and support of the Union armies and the Republican Party in the nation. Its thrifty, hard-working, well-educated citizens built communities with fine schools and, with their accumulated savings, invested in what became some of the nation's leading industries. That brought great masses of immigrants to Cleveland and the other cities of northeast Ohio, which remained solidly Republican until the Great Depression and the bloody CIO organizing drives of the late 1930s; then, for 30 years, the Western Reserve was Democratic during Ohio's class-warfare politics. In the early 1980s, when the auto and steel industries lost thousands of jobs, northeast Ohio went heavily Democratic; in the early 1990s, as the economy has diversified and recovered, it has been willing to vote Republican: Lake County, suburban territory northeast of Cleveland, voted for Governor George Voinovich in 1990 and, narrowly, for George Bush in 1992.

The 19th Congressional District of Ohio takes in an irregularly-shaped hunk—a very irregularly-shaped hunk—of northeast Ohio and the old Western Reserve. It includes all of Lake County, with mixed middling-to-affluent suburbs and industrial Ashtabula County in the northeast corner of the state. It also includes a motley collection of the Cuyahoga County suburbs of Cleveland. East of Cleveland are affluent Italian, Jewish and WASP suburbs, Beachwood, Pepper Pike and Chagrin Falls. Directly south of Cleveland are more working-class suburbs on either side of the Cuyahoga River gorge and west to Brook Park around the convention center and airport.

This district included most of the home bases of two talented young Cleveland area congressmen, though not the home suburbs, Euclid and Lakewood, of either one. But neither chose to run in 1992. Dennis Eckart's October 1991 announcement that he was retiring was especially shocking: he was 41, with 12 years seniority in the old 11th District (plus six years in the Ohio legislature), a seat on Energy and Commerce and a good relationship with its chairman, John Dingell, a knack for politics (he played Dan Quayle in practice debates with Lloyd Bentsen in 1988 and Al Gore in 1992) and for public policy (he wrote a major urban smog section of the 1990 Clean Air Act). It was less surprising that Ed Feighan of the old 19th District retired in March 1992: he had 397 overdrafts on the House bank. Feighan is another political prodigy, elected to the state House at 25 and running (unsuccessfully) for mayor of Cleveland in 1977 at 29; in the House, he was the lead sponsor of the Brady bill, which would impose a seven-day waiting period on the sale of handguns and was also the first political employer of Clinton aide George Stephanopoulos.

The race attracted nine Democrats and five Republicans, and the winner was the youngest of the candidates, 33-year-old state Senator Eric Fingerhut. He is one of the many natural Democratic politicians with marvelous political skills and unstoppable drive: from law school to Congress in seven years. He was chairman of Common Cause Ohio, headed Cleveland Works (a welfare recipients job training program), headed a local group trying to close a toxic waste facility, managed Michael White's successful (and biracially supported) campaign for mayor of Cleveland in 1989, then was elected to the state Senate in 1990. There he helped oust the oldtime Democratic leader, wrote a recycling bill, created an Ohio Energy Strategy Task Force and advanced a gun safety bill.

In the 1992 primary, though his residence in Cleveland was outside the district, he won 24% of the vote to 19% for Cuyahoga Auditor Tim McCormack, 18% for former Cleveland Mayor Dennis Kucinich, 17% for union official Frank Valenta and 13% for Brook Park Mayor Thomas Coyne, Jr. The Republican winner, in something of an upset, was Lake County Commissioner Robert Gardner, with 34%, to 29% for businessman Tucker Marston and 27% for 1984 nominee Matthew Hatchadorian. Gardner is a teacher and counselor who was elected to his township board in 1981 and the county commission in 1986; less articulate and polished than Fingerhut, and, he lamented, far less well-financed, he took unpopular stands like a balanced policy in the Middle East and most favored nation status for China. Fingerhut echoed the job creation and healthcare themes of the Clinton campaign, and added a strong emphasis on campaign finance reform. On some foreign issues, he avoided cheap shots, backing NAFTA with some changes and saying that Israel must become self-sufficient economically.

Fingerhut won by a less than overwhelming margin. In the House, he became one of two chairmen of the freshman class task force on reform, and surprised some older members, not pleasantly, with his straight arrow zeal. They might agree with a Republican state Senate colleague who found him "arrogant and pompous. He likes to think he's the moral conscience and the only one who knows what's right." But he has shown the political skills and adaptability to the times that suggest he will be hard, in any political circumstances, to beat.

The People: Pop. 1990: 570,834; 12% rural; 15% age 65+; 96% White; 2% Black; 1% Asian; 1% Hispanic origin. Voting age pop.: 436,395; 2% Black; 1% Hispanic origin. Households: 62% married couple families; 26% married couple fams. w. children; 43% college educ.; median household income: $34,385; per capita income: $16,609; median gross rent: $464; median house value: $77,200.

1992 Presidential Vote			1988 Presidential Vote		
Clinton (D)	114,358	(40%)	Bush (R)	129,904	(53%)
Bush (R)	106,947	(37%)	Dukakis (D)	115,147	(47%)
Perot (I)	66,424	(23%)			

Rep. Eric D. Fingerhut (D)

Elected 1992; b. May 6, 1959, Cleveland; home, Mayfield Heights; Northwestern U., B.A. 1981, Stanford, J.D. 1984; Jewish; single.

Career: Staff Atty., Cleveland Legal Aid Society, 1984–85; Practicing atty., 1985–87; Chmn., Common Cause Ohio, 1986–88; Assoc. Dir., Cleveland Works, 1987–1989; Special Asst., Cleveland Mayor White, 1989–90; OH Senate 1990–92.

Offices: 431 CHOB 20515, 202-225-5731. Also 2550 SOM Center Rd., #385, Willoughby Hills 44094, 216-943-1919.

Committees: *Banking, Finance and Urban Affairs* (30th of 30 D): Economic Growth and Credit Formation; International Development, Finance, Trade and Monetary Policy. *Foreign Affairs* (21st of 27 D): Asia and the Pacific; Economic Policy, Trade and Environment. *Science, Space and Technology* (20th of 33 D): Space.

Group Ratings and 102d Congress Votes: Newly Elected

Key Votes of the 103d Congress

1. Family Leave	FOR	2. Deficit Reduction	FOR	3. Stimulus Plan	FOR

Election Results

1992 general	Eric D. Fingerhut (D)	138,465	(53%)	($611,478)	
	Robert A. Gardner (R)	124,606	(47%)	($450,117)	
1992 primary	Eric D. Fingerhut (D)	20,929	(24%)		
	Tim McCormack (D)	16,053	(19%)		
	Dennis J. Kucinich (D)	15,453	(18%)		
	Frank J. Valenta (D)	14,254	(17%)		
	Thomas J. Coyne, Jr. (D)	11,258	(13%)		
	Kathleen Cotter (D)	4,407	(5%)		
	Three Others	3,924	(5%)		
1990 general	Dennis E. Eckart (D)	111,923	(66%)	($453,883)	
	Margaret R. Mueller (R)	58,372	(34%)	($72,686)	

OKLAHOMA

The history of Oklahoma has been one of sudden exhilarating boom and protracted sickening bust. It was settled in a rush, first by the Five Civilized Tribes driven west by Andrew Jackson's troops over the Cherokees' Trail of Tears in the 1830s, then by white settlers one morning in April 1889, when, in the great land rush memorialized in an Edna Ferber novel, the Rodgers and Hammerstein musical and half a dozen Hollywood movies, thousands of would-be homesteaders drove their wagons across the territorial line at the sound of a gunshot, the most adventurous or unscrupulous of them literally jumping the gun—the Sooners. The heritage of these rushes remains. Oklahoma celebrated the Year of the Indian in 1992, honoring the state's 67 tribes and spotlighting their council houses, historic sites and festivals. Oklahoma has the second largest Indian population of any state, 253,000 in the 1990 Census, though there are no reservations; but there has been much intermarriage over the years, and many Oklahomans proudly claim some Indian blood; assimilation into everyday life plus commemoration of historic traditions seem to have provided a better life for Native Americans here than approaches elsewhere.

Statehood came to Oklahoma late, in 1907, at which point it filled up with farmers, rising from 1.5 million people in 1907 to 2.4 million in 1930. Then, a decade of bust. Oklahoma literally went up in smoke, or rather dust, as soil loosened by erosion was whipped into giant dust clouds: the Dust Bowl. "On a single day, I heard, 50 million tons of soil were blown away," John Gunther reported later. "People sat in Oklahoma City, with the sky invisible for three days in a row, holding dust masks over their faces and wet towels to protect their mouths at night, while the farms blew by." Okies headed in droves west out U.S. 66 to the green land of California and Oklahoma's population sank to 2.3 million in 1940 and 2.2 million in 1950, not to reach its 1930 level again until 1970.

Then another boom—this time from oil. As the oil shocks of 1973 and 1979 sent oil prices up, Oklahoma's population rose from 2.5 million in 1970 to 3 million in 1980 and 3.3 million in 1983. Then, with the collapse of oil prices and of Oklahoma's farm economy as well, bust again. A giddy rise was followed by a giddier fall: the rig count fell from 882 in January 1982 to 232 in February 1983, 128 in 1986 and 93 in 1989. Just as the dust cloud symbolized Oklahoma's 1930s bust, so the auction of oil drilling equipment was a symbol of the 1980s calamity. The 1990 Census reported just 3.1 million Oklahomans. The nation's lowest unemployment state in the early 1980s recession, Oklahoma suffered during the late 1980s boom, but it was hurting less than most states by the early 1990s recession and the unemployment rate actually declined in 1992.

But in the meantime, Oklahoma has been going through extraordinary political turbulence. Its partisan patterns had seemed well-set: most of its early settlers were southerners, and historically it has been Democratic. But the Oklahoma City and Tulsa metropolitan areas, which now contain more than half the state's people, have been trending Republican since the 1950s; Little Dixie in the south remains Democratic, while the northern wheat counties are Republican. The post-oil boom years saw the election of a Republican governor in 1986 and a Democrat in 1990; Oklahoma voters were disgusted by a stubborn budgetary crisis and were among the first in the nation to impose term limits on their state legislators in 1990. Then they saw their governor afflicted by bizarre personal tragedy and charges of tawdry corruption. Amidst all this, it was probably a good idea to focus on Oklahoma's not too lengthy history and on its Indian heritage, and to build an appreciation of enduring strengths.

Governor. The governor of Oklahoma, Democrat David Walters, has had one of the most turbulent terms of any governor in the land. He came to office after an eight-year career as a real estate developer and a 1990 campaign in which wild charges were hurled, and which has

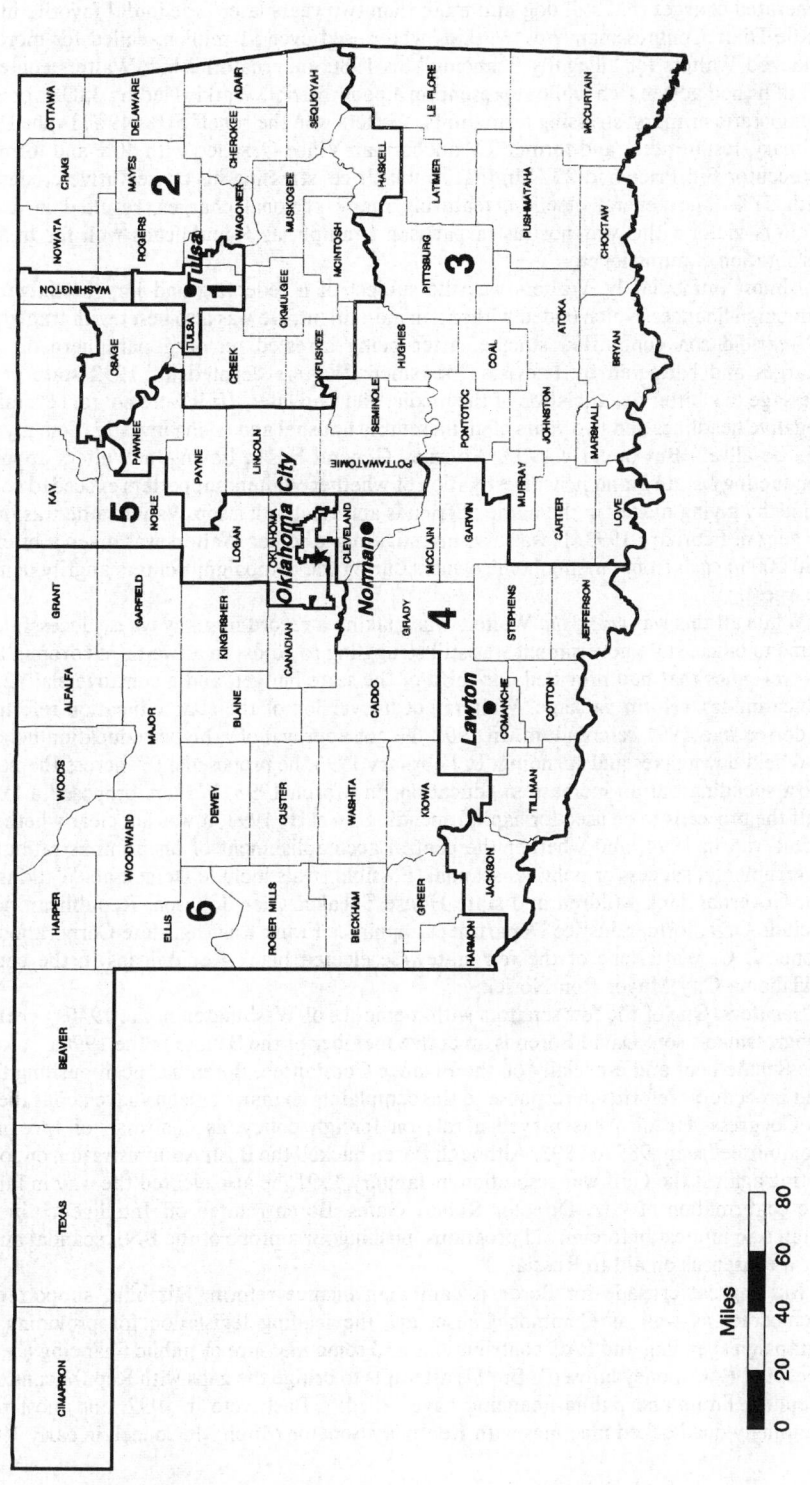

generated charges that still dog him more than two years later. The initial favorite in 1990 was Little Dixie Congressman Wes Watkins who raised over $1 million, called for more jobs and attacked Walters for "illegally financing" his 1986 gubernatorial bid; Walters contended that Watkins had gotten rich while representing a poor district. Watkins led by 3,838 votes after the Democratic primary; stressing term limits, Walters won the runoff 51%–49%. In the Republican primary, restaurateur and former TV anchorman Vince Orza led with 40% and former federal prosecutor Bill Price had 27%; in that runoff Price, stressing his conservative credentials, won with 51%. The general election, featuring many personal charges, resulted in a 57%–33% Walters victory; this was not just a partisan triumph, as Republicans won for treasurer and corporation commissioner.

Almost immediately, Walters was the subject of a federal grand jury investigation of his campaign finances, which ended without an indictment. He was also beset with tragedy when his 19-year-old son committed suicide, after being arrested on drug paraphernalia possession charges and badgered by television newsmen; Walters devoted his 1992 state of the state message to a bitter denunciation of the media, and said later, "If it were not for several thousand negative headlines and two years of an incredibly unusual and trying investigation, my son would still be alive." But in early 1993, Attorney General Susan Loving, a Walters appointee, was conducting a state grand jury investigation of whether Walters supporters exceeded contribution limits by giving money in the name of friends and relatives; a top Walters aide was indicted for forgery in February 1993. It was also investigating whether Walters was given a briefcase with $30,000 in cash from nursing home owners during the campaign; Walters angrily denied all the charges.

While all this was going on, Walters was making a record in many ways successful. When he came to office, state government was still struggling to adjust to a two-thirds drop in the oil and gas revenues that had provided one-third of the state budget, and a controversial $230 million education-tax reform package. Walters got his version of the state education reform package endorsed in a 1991 referendum. In 1992, he got approval of a higher education bond package and held down taxes and spending. In February 1993, he proposed a 9% across-the-board cut in most spending but an increase in education. In March 1993, Walters proposed a lottery, with half the proceeds to be used for capital spending. In early 1993, it was not clear whether Walters would run in 1994, and whether the central accomplishment of his administration would be governmental success or political scandal. Possible rivals include Democrats Watkins, Lieutenant Governor Jack Mildren and state House Speaker Glen Johnson; Republican possibilities include Orza, former Justice Department appointee Frank Keating, state Corporation Commissioner J. C. Watts, one of the few statewide elected black Republicans in the country, and Oklahoma City Mayor Ron Norick.

Senators. One of the few senators with memories of Washington in the 1940s, when he was a congressman's son, David Boren is an active member of the Senate in the 1990s. A key vote on the Senate floor and especially on the Finance Committee, Boren has been pushing for process and procedural reforms in response to the complaints so many citizens have about the workings of Congress. He also has played a role on foreign policy, as chairman of the Intelligence Committee from 1987 to 1993. Although Boren bucked the Bush Administration on some issues, voting against the Gulf war resolution in January 1991, he also cleared the way in fall 1991 for the confirmation of CIA Director Robert Gates. Boren rotated off Intelligence in 1993, but retains an interest in foreign aid programs, pushing for a probe of the BNL scandal and working for a consensus on aid to Russia.

But a great crusade for Boren is campaign finance reform. His bills, supported by most Democrats as well as Common Cause, are the leading legislation for providing limits on campaign spending and PAC contributions and some measure of public financing (he has never accepted PAC money himself). But his attempts to bridge the gaps with Republicans opposed to spending limits and public financing have failed: a Bush veto in 1992, and most recently in seemingly deadlocked meetings with Kentucky Senator Mitch McConnell in early 1993. Boren still has hopes to win enough votes to get cloture, and passage of a bill through the Senate. His greater problem may be the House, where Democrats are loath to give up the enormous financial advantages they enjoy under the current system. Boren would also further restrict lobbying by ex-officials, in agreement with President Clinton (although Clinton aide George Stephanopoulos appears to have trespassed on the existing law when he met with his former House bosses during the 1992 campaign). Now co-chairman, with Congressman Lee Hamilton, of the Joint Committee on the Organization of Congress, Boren has promised to come out with reform proposals by late 1993.

As a moderate to even conservative Democrat, Boren started off 1993 as a thorn in the Democrats' side. He and John Breaux of Louisiana pushed in early 1993 for cuts and delays in spending in the Clinton economic stimulus package until deficit reduction measures had actually been passed. Robert Byrd used parliamentary procedures to prevent any vote on Boren-Breaux, which had it been accepted might have prevented the successful Republican filibuster. On the Finance Committee, which Democrats control only 11–9, Boren, always hostile to energy taxes and regulation, quickly opposed the Clinton energy tax and threatened to use his swing vote against any type of Btu tax.

Boren has long been a popular figure in Oklahoma politics. He was elected governor in 1974 as a reformer, with 64% of the vote against current 1st District Congressman James Inhofe. He has won 65%, 76% and 83% in successive elections for senator—the last two are Oklahoma records. In 1990, against a candidate who filed at the last minute, he carried 2,352 of 2,354 precincts.

In 1980, Don Nickles was a 31-year-old small businessman from Ponca City, a Catholic running for the Senate with the support of Protestant evangelicals—a strong base in the home state of Oral Roberts. Since that time, he has been a U.S. senator of strong convictions and durable political strength and one of the most conservative members. Several threads run through his record. One is opposition to energy taxes and regulations; he backed the successful fights to deregulate oil and natural gas prices, to repeal the windfall profits tax and to repeal the 55-mile-per-hour speed limit. He supported drilling in the Arctic National Wildlife Refuge and opposed increasing CAFE standards for cars. He put into the 1992 energy bill measures changing the alternative minimum tax for oil and natural gas and strongly opposed the Clinton Btu tax. Another thread is protection against the AIDS virus: he legislated a procedure for AIDS testing of convicted rapists and sex offenders and got the Senate on record during the first Clinton months, 76–23, against allowing HIV-positive immigrants into the U.S. Nickles favors internal reforms like limiting congressional franking and applying to Congress the laws it applies to others; he was one of the backers of the 203-year old Madison amendment which banned mid-term changes in congressional pay. He is strongly supportive of Israel, and passed a bill to stop military and economic aid to Jordan. He advocates judicial changes such as blocking criminals from using bankruptcy to avoid paying restitution to victims, and linking recipients welfare payments with their children's school attendance. He wants to shore up the Pension Benefit Guaranty Corporation to prevent savings and loan-type losses.

Nickles is solidly partisan and headed the National Republican Senatorial Committee during the 1989–90 cycle, when Republicans lost one seat with the upset victory of radical Democrat Paul Wellstone in Minnesota. In December 1990, Nickles ran for Republican Policy Committee chairman, and beat Pete Domenici 23–20 on the second ballot. Domenici backed the 1990 budget summit tax increases while Nickles opposed them insisting, "You are going to see a Republican Party that is unified against tax increases." Evidently so: in December 1992 Nickles kept the post without opposition. In Oklahoma, Nickles has run stronger than many in Washington expected. In 1986, he faced Jim Jones, Ways and Means member and Budget chairman in the first Reagan term. But Jones ran some smirky ads, and Nickles's sincerity seemed to strike a chord with voters; he won 55%–45%. In 1992, his Democratic opponent was Steve Lewis, who had worked his way up from poverty to become speaker of the state House, and had run unsuccessfully for governor in 1990. Nickles attacked him as a Ted Kennedy clone who would raise taxes, and won 59%–38%, the best showing for a Republican Senator in Oklahoma since 1924.

Presidential politics. Oklahoma in many elections has been the most Republican of southern states; in 1992 it was the least Democratic, casting 34% for next-door neighbor Bill Clinton (but then, George Bush and Ross Perot are neighbors as well). There are relatively few blacks here, no large quarter of urban singles, not many Mexican-Americans and no liberal-inclined Native American voting bloc; Oklahomans with a Democratic heritage tend to be conservative on cultural, foreign and some economic issues, and find national Democrats unappealing, even southerners like Bill Clinton and Jimmy Carter.

Oklahoma was not on anyone's list of target states in 1992. Nor was it the subject of much attention as one of the southern Super Tuesday primaries, when it voted overwhelmingly for Clinton and Bush. It was more interesting in 1988, when it voted solidly for Al Gore (a very distant relation of onetime Oklahoma Senator Thomas Gore, grandfather of writer Gore Vidal) and by the narrowest of margins for George Bush over Kansas neighbor Bob Dole.

Congressional districting. For the 1990s, Oklahoma was fortunate not to lose a congressional district. Control was in Democrats' hands, and in May 1991 the Governor signed the legislature's "incumbent protection plan," as one state legislator called it. The plan strengthened Democrat Mike Synar in the 2d District and Republican Jim Inhofe in the 1st by slicing heavily Republican southeast Tulsa from the 2d and restoring it to the 1st.

The People: Est. Pop. 1992: 3,212,000; Pop. 1990: 3,145,585, up 2.1% 1990–1992. 1.3% of U.S. total, 28th largest; 32% rural. Median age: 33.2 years. 13.5% 65 years and over. 82.1% White, 8.0% American Indian, 7.4% Black, 2.7% Hispanic origin, 1.1% Asian, 1.3% Other. Households: 57.7% married couple families; 28% married couple fams. w. children; 44% college educ.; median household income: $23,577; per capita income: $11,893; 68.1% owner occupied housing; median house value: $48,100; median monthly rent: $259. 5.7% Unemployment. Voting age pop.: 2,308,578. Registered voters (1992): 2,302,279; 1,452,949 D (63%), 775,754 R (34%), 73,576 unaffiliated and minor parties (3%).

Political Lineup: Governor, David Walters (D); Lt. Gov., Jack Mildren (D); Secy. of State, John Kennedy (D); Atty. Gen., Susan Loving (D); Treasurer, Claudette Henry (R); Auditor, Clifton Scott (D). State Senate, 48 (37 D and 11 R); State House of Representatives, 101 (68 D and 33 R). Senators, David Lyle Boren (D) and Don Nickles (R). Representatives, 6 (4 D and 2 R).

1992 Presidential Vote

Bush (R)	592,929	(43%)
Clinton (D)	473,066	(34%)
Perot (I)	319,878	(23%)

1988 Presidential Vote

Bush (R)	678,367	(58%)
Dukakis (D)	483,423	(41%)

1992 Democratic Presidential Primary

Clinton	293,266	(70%)
Brown	69,624	(17%)
Woods	16,828	(4%)
Other	36,411	(9%)

1992 Republican Presidential Primary

Bush	151,612	(70%)
Buchanan	57,933	(27%)
Other	8,176	(4%)

GOVERNOR

Gov. David Walters (D)

Elected 1990, term expires Jan. 1995; b. Nov. 20, 1951, Elk City; home, Oklahoma City; U. of OK, B.A. 1973, Harvard, M.B.A. 1977; Catholic; married (Rhonda).

Career: Asst. Provost, U. of OK Health Sci. Ctr., 1977–80, Assoc. Provost, 1980–82; Real estate developer and investor 1982–90; OK Human Svcs. Comm., 1983–86, Chmn., 1985–86.

Office: State Capitol Bldg., #212, Oklahoma City 73105, 405-521-2342.

Election Results

1990 gen.	David Walters (D)	523,196	(57%)
	Bill Price (R)	297,584	(33%)
	Thomas Ledgerwood (I).......	90,534	(10%)
1990 runoff	David Walters (D)	243,252	(51%)
	Wes Watkins (D)	236,597	(49%)
1990 prim.	Wes Watkins (D)	175,568	(32%)
	David Walters (D)	171,730	(32%)
	Steve Lewis (D)	160,455	(30%)
	John (Shorty) Barnett (D)	23,648	(4%)
	Other	11,605	(2%)
1986 gen.	Henry Bellmon (R)..........	431,762	(47%)
	David Walters (D)	405,295	(45%)
	Jerry Brown (I).............	60,115	(7%)

SENATORS

Sen. David Lyle Boren (D)

Elected 1978, seat up 1996; b. Apr. 21, 1941, Washington, D.C.; home, Seminole; Yale, B.A. 1963, Rhodes Scholar, Oxford U., 1965, U. of OK, J.D. 1968; United Methodist; married (Molly).

Career: OK Natl. Guard, 1968–74; OK House of Reps., 1968–74; Prof. and Chmn., Dept. of Govt., OK Baptist U., 1968–74; Practicing atty.; OK Gov., 1974–78.

Offices: 453 RSOB 20510, 202-224-4721. Also 621 N. Robinson, #350, Oklahoma City 73102, 405-231-4381; 409 S. Boston, #1820, Tulsa 74103, 918-581-7785; and 211 Oak St., Seminole 74868, 405-382-6480.

Committees: *Agriculture, Nutrition and Forestry* (3d of 10 D): Agricultural Credit; Agricultural Production and Stabilization of Prices; Domestic and Foreign Marketing and Product Promotion (Chmn.). *Finance* (3d of 11 D): Energy and Agricultural Taxation; International Trade; Taxation (Chmn.). *Joint Committee on the Organization of Congress* (Chmn. of 12). *Joint Committee on Taxation* (3d of 5).

Group Ratings

	ADA	ACLU	CDF	COPE	CFA	LCV	ACU	NTLC	NSI	COC	CEI
1992	60	55	60	50	67	42	35	29	80	50	35
1991	45	—	55	42	50	33	45	—	—	56	38

National Journal Ratings

	1991 LIB	—	1991 CONS	1992 LIB	—	1992 CONS
Economic	34%	—	64%	48%	—	51%
Social	38%	—	61%	51%	—	48%
Foreign	54%	—	44%	41%	—	57%

Key Votes of the 102d Congress

1. $ for Homeownership	FOR	5. Clarence Thomas Nom. FOR	9. Use Force in Gulf	AGN
2. Have Cap Gains Debate AGN		6. Lmt Death Row Appeal FOR	10. Keep Salvador Aid	AGN
3. Remove Budget Walls	FOR	7. Handgun Wait/5-Day FOR	11. Cut $1B from SDI	FOR
4. Ban Striker Replace	AGN	8. Abortion Gag Rule FOR	12. Override China MFN FOR

Key Votes of the 103d Congress

1. Family Leave	FOR	2. HIV Immigrants	FOR	3. Clinton Budget	FOR

Election Results

1990 general	David Lyle Boren (D)	735,684	(83%)	($1,591,093)
	Stephen Jones (R)	148,814	(17%)	($140,912)
1990 primary	David Lyle Boren (D)	445,969	(84%)	
	Virginia Jenner (D)	57,909	(11%)	
	Manuel Ybarra (D)	25,169	(5%)	
1984 general	David Lyle Boren (D)	906,131	(76%)	($1,192,026)
	William E. (Bill) Crozier (R)	280,638	(23%)	($6,925)

Sen. Don Nickles (R)

Elected 1980, seat up 1998; b. Dec. 6, 1948, Ponca City; home, Ponca City; OK St. U., B.A. 1971; Catholic; married (Linda).

Career: OK Natl. Guard, 1970–76; Vice Pres. and Gen. Mgr., Nickles Machine Co., 1976–80; OK Senate, 1979–80.

Offices: 133 HSOB 20510, 202-224-5754. Also 1820 Liberty Tower, 100 N. Broadway, Oklahoma City 73102, 405-231-4941; 3310 Mid-Continent Tower, 401 S. Boston, Tulsa 74103, 918-581-7651; 1916 Lake Rd., Ponca City 74601, 405-767-1270; and Fed. Bldg., 5th and D Ave., #115, Lawton 73501, 405-357-9878.

Committees: *Appropriations* (7th of 13 R): Defense; Energy and Water Development; Foreign Operations; Interior (RMM); VA, HUD and Independent Agencies. *Budget* (3d of 9 R). *Energy and Natural Resources* (5th of 9 R): Energy Research and Development; Mineral Resources Development and Production; Renewable Energy, Energy Efficiency, and Competitiveness (RMM). *Indian Affairs* (7th of 8 R):

Group Ratings

	ADA	ACLU	CDF	COPE	CFA	LCV	ACU	NTLC	NSI	COC	CEI
1992	0	5	30	8	8	0	96	100	80	89	77
1991	0	—	18	25	17	7	95	—	—	100	82

National Journal Ratings

	1991 LIB	—	1991 CONS	1992 LIB	—	1992 CONS
Economic	0%	—	91%	21%	—	78%
Social	0%	—	86%	0%	—	89%
Foreign	13%	—	77%	10%	—	80%

Key Votes of the 102d Congress

1. $ for Homeownership FOR	5. Clarence Thomas Nom. FOR	9. Use Force in Gulf FOR
2. Have Cap Gains Debate FOR	6. Lmt Death Row Appeal FOR	10. Keep Salvador Aid FOR
3. Remove Budget Walls AGN	7. Handgun Wait/5-Day AGN	11. Cut $1B from SDI AGN
4. Ban Striker Replace AGN	8. Abortion Gag Rule FOR	12. Override China MFN AGN

Key Votes of the 103d Congress

1. Family Leave AGN	2. HIV Immigrants AGN	3. Clinton Budget AGN

Election Results

1992 general	Don Nickles (R)	757,876	(59%)	($3,492,603)
	Steve Lewis (D)	494,350	(38%)	($1,455,848)
	Two Others	42,197	(3%)	
1992 primary	Don Nickles (R), unopposed			
1986 general	Don Nickles (R)	493,436	(55%)	($3,252,965)
	James R. Jones (D)...................	400,230	(45%)	($2,564,982)

FIRST DISTRICT

Tulsa, Oklahoma, founded in the 20th Century, with skyscrapers going up in the 1920s, is one of the American cities made by oil. Its character was set from the start: raw, but intent on culture; optimistic and ready to seek economic change, yet culturally and politically conservative; predominantly WASP, yet with an Indian heritage recalled today in the Gilcrease Museum left by one-eighth Creek Indian oil millionaire Thomas Gilcrease, and an ethnic heritage suggested by the Gershon & Rebecca Fenster Museum of Jewish Art. Tulsa's buildings then may not have been air-conditioned, but its economy already was based on oil; Oral Roberts had not yet built his church headquarters, his university, or his 60-story City of Faith hospital, but Tulsa was inspired by enthusiastic religion. Its leading citizens did not shop in galleries, but they already had pretensions of culture and looked down on the mud-on-their-boots sorts of Oklahoma City.

Politically, Tulsa was and still is one of America's most conservative cities, heavily Republican in presidential elections, devout in its belief in free markets and traditional moral values. Despite the collapse of oil prices in the 1980s, Tulsa is still full of a contagious enthusiasm for new business enterprises and innovations. Ordinary people here do not resent and attack the oil companies or the new rich; they identify with them. They see not class conflict, but a coincidence of economic interests. They see government as interfering with efforts to produce desired goods and services and are ready to pay for them—although Tulsans are pleased that the federal government built the McClellan-Kerr Waterway that has made the Catoosa suburb a seaport.

Oklahoma's 1st Congressional District consists of Tulsa County, plus a small part of Wagoner County to the east; for the 1990s it gained back the parts of Republican south Tulsa which were in the 2d District from 1982 to 1990. This should be a solidly Republican district; it has voted for nothing but Republican presidential candidates over the last 50 years. Yet no Republican has had a firm hold on the Tulsa seat since the 1960s. One reason is that Tulsa Democrats, like longtime (1972–86) Congressman Jim Jones, tend to reflect the city's conservatism. Another is that the Republican congressman, James Inhofe, had an up-and-down political (and business) career. He lost the governor's race to David Boren in 1974 and the 1st District race to Jim Jones in 1976; he was elected mayor of Tulsa in 1978, 1980 and 1982, but lost in 1984. He was heavily outspent in 1986, but won the House seat with 55%. In 1988, publicity about a lawsuit he brought against his brother over the family business hurt him, as did charges of campaign finance irregularities; he won with 52%. The family lawsuit was then settled and Inhofe received some $3.6 million from his brother; in 1990, he won with 56%.

In Washington, Inhofe has a very conservative voting record and opposes tax increases. He specializes in aviation issues: he pushes for bills to preserve American Airlines's Tulsa-based SABRE reservations system, wants to have the NTSB rather than the FAA judge cases brought by the FAA, wants the FAA to establish visual flight rule routes in crowded airspace and favors F-15 sales to Saudi Arabia. Inhofe had yet another business problem in 1991: a federal court ordered him to pay the FDIC $588,000 on promissory notes he'd given to a failed insurance company. In 1992, after winning his primary 2–1, he was opposed in the general by Tulsa County Commissioner John Selph, a former social worker and director of the Tulsa Boys' Home. Each claimed to be an "outsider," Selph because he was a challenger, Inhofe because he bucked his own party leadership, as on the 1990 budget summit package. Selph ran very strong in the district and got 47%; but Inhofe won with 53%, suggesting he might have lost without redistricting changes that made the area 4% more Republican. It is certainly possible he will have serious opposition again.

The People: Pop. 1990: 524,135; 6% rural; 11% age 65+; 82% White; 10% Black; 5% Amer. Indian; 1% Asian; 1% Other; 2% Hispanic origin. Voting age pop.: 386,430; 8% Black; 2% Hispanic origin. Households: 55% married couple families; 26% married couple fams. w. children; 54% college educ.; median household income: $27,472; per capita income: $14,695; median gross rent: $366; median house value: $60,700.

1992 Presidential Vote

Bush (R)   122,137   (49%)
Clinton (D)   73,509   (30%)
Perot (I).   52,077   (21%)

1988 Presidential Vote

Bush (R)   131,350   (65%)
Dukakis (D).   71,086   (35%)

Rep. James M. Inhofe (R)

Elected 1986; b. Nov. 17, 1934, Des Moines, IA; home, Tulsa; U. of Tulsa, B.A. 1961; Presbyterian; married (Kay).

Career: Army, 1955–56; businessman, land developer, 1962–86; OK House of Reps., 1968–69; OK Senate, 1969–77, Repub. Ldr., 1975–77; Tulsa Mayor, 1978–84.

Offices: 442 CHOB 20515, 202-225-2211. Also 1924 Utica St., #530, Tulsa 74104, 918-581-7111.

Committees: *Armed Services* (15th of 22 R): Military Acquisition; Readiness. *Merchant Marine and Fisheries* (7th of 19 R): Coast Guard and Navigation; Merchant Marine. *Public Works and Transportation* (5th of 24 R): Aviation; Investigations and Oversight (RMM); Water Resources and Environment.

Group Ratings

	ADA	ACLU	COPE	CDF	CFA	LCV	ACU	NTLC	NSI	COC	CEI
1992	10	0	36	0	27	0	96	100	100	75	81
1991	5	—	9	20	39	0	100	—	—	90	85

National Journal Ratings

	1991 LIB — 1991 CONS		1992 LIB — 1992 CONS	
Economic	14%	— 86%	9%	— 88%
Social	0%	— 84%	0%	— 85%
Foreign	17%	— 78%	0%	— 82%

Key Votes of the 102d Congress

1. Ban Striker Replace AGN	5. Handgun Wait/7-Day AGN	9. Use Force in Gulf FOR
2. $ for Homeownership FOR	6. Overseas Mil. Abortion AGN	10. US Mil. Abroad $ Cut AGN
3. Tax Rich/Cut Mid Cls. AGN	7. Obscn. Art NEA $ Ban FOR	11. Limit SDI Funds AGN
4. FY93/$15B Def. Cut AGN	8. Death Pen. from Jury FOR	12. Cuba Trade Embargo FOR

Key Votes of the 103d Congress

1. Family Leave AGN	2. Deficit Reduction AGN	3. Stimulus Plan AGN

Election Results

1992 general	James M. Inhofe (R).................	119,211	(53%)	($418,928)
	John Selph (D)	106,619	(47%)	($328,960)
1992 primary	James M. Inhofe (R)..................	36,354	(68%)	
	Richard L. Bunn (R).................	17,339	(32%)	
1990 general	James M. Inhofe (R).................	75,618	(56%)	($612,116)
	Kurt Glassco (D).....................	59,521	(44%)	($406,280)

SECOND DISTRICT

Less than a century ago, what is now northeast Oklahoma was officially Indian Territory, the place where in the 1830s the Five Civilized Tribes were driven from Georgia and Alabama over the Trail of Tears. More than one in seven people here report their race as American Indian, and many more claim some Indian blood. The Indian percentage is highest in the hilly counties just west of the Ozarks of Arkansas, where county names—Cherokee, Delaware, Sequoyah—recall the Civilized Tribes. Much national attention is focused on the problems of Indians in states where there are large reservations. But no one seems to be asking if the experience of the Indians in Oklahoma—where they are now relatively prosperous and living comfortably as part of a larger community—has any useful lessons for Native Americans elsewhere.

Northeastern Oklahoma of the 1980s grew out of overspill from the Tulsa metropolitan area, from developments around the man-made lakes that have become focuses for recreation, and from growth around towns like Tahlequah in these pleasant green hills, so unlike the brown plains farther west. The 2d Congressional District of Oklahoma is made up of the northeast corner of the state, minus Tulsa County. It includes Muskogee, the patriotic subject of the 1969 song "Okie from Muskogee." It is ancestrally Democratic, from the time it was settled overland from the South. It is also hawkish, devoted to tradition-minded religion, increasingly unhappy with higher taxes. The congressman from the 2d District, Mike Synar, is a native of Muskogee who does not share most of these attitudes. Synar was a classmate of the 4th District's Dave McCurdy at Oklahoma University; in 1978, a year after graduating from law school, he ran for Congress against an incumbent who recently had been divorced and was rumored to have a heart-shaped waterbed. Synar won the primary 54%–46%, the general 55%–45%. On that shaky base, he constructed a distinctive career.

Synar has a liberal voting record, by far the most liberal of any white member from the South, more liberal than most Democrats from the North. He is also, though from a state legendary for its corrupt county governments, temperamentally a reformer, independent to the point of cursedness, eager to upset cozy ways of doing things if he thinks they are wrong. He has spent some effort on Oklahoma issues, using his Energy and Commerce seat to help deregulate natural gas and to exempt oil wells from toxic pollutant limits. But he also runs some breathtaking political risks. From a mostly rural Oklahoma district, he voted for the Brady bill waiting period on handgun purchases. In his first term, he sponsored a key amendment to the Fair Housing Act that passed by one vote, and supported the civil rights bill attacked as quota legislation in his sixth and seventh terms. He voted against the flag-burning amendment and against the Gulf war resolution.

Synar also takes on causes that are unpopular with key lobbies and opposed by many Democrats. Among them is his effort to raise from $1.86 per animal unit to $5.36 by 1997 the monthly grazing fees charged cattle ranchers on 174 million acres of public rangeland in the West; this passed the House in 1990 and 1992, but not the Senate where cattlemen have greater leverage and representation. Synar has fought for restrictions on tobacco advertising and regulations on tobacco by the FDA—measures that infuriate colleagues from the Carolinas, Virginia and Kentucky. For nearly a decade, he has been lead House sponsor of Common Cause-supported campaign finance reform bills to limit PAC contributions (he accepts none himself), lower individual contributions and lower voluntary spending limits: an attempt to upset the system which has done well for so many Democratic incumbents. Synar brought the 1986 lawsuit in which the Supreme Court declared unconstitutional the Gramm-Rudman trigger mechanism, thereby undercutting colleagues' claim to have provided an automatic budget-balancing mechanism. Not surprisingly, he lost badly in a 1988 race for caucus chairman.

This record has inspired opposition at home; against a political unknown, he won the 1990 Democratic primary by only 56%–44%. That inspired the candidacy in 1992 of Drew Edmondson, former Muskogee County District Attorney, son of 20-year 2d District Congressman Ed Edmondson and nephew of former Governor and Senator Howard Edmondson. Drew Edmondson grew up only three blocks from Synar, and had run unsuccessfully for the seat himself in 1976, but has quite different politics: he opposes gun control, is against fast-tracking NAFTA, opposes the ban on cigarette ads. He attracted plenty of financial support from tobacco interests, cattlemen and the National Rifle Association and spent $850,000. Two nuisance candidates prevented either man from getting a majority in the August primary: Synar led 43%–38%. Usually such a showing would be fatal for an incumbent. But Synar struck back: "This is not a contest between two men. This is a battle between me and the special interests I have been opposing." Synar raised plenty of money and won the runoff 53%–47%. The general election was anticlimactic; redistricting, by removing south Tulsa precincts from the 2d, made the district 4% more Democratic, and Synar won easily.

Synar must surely feel vindicated in his willingness to take political risks for principle. But it's unclear whether he can translate those principles into action. His campaign finance reform will have hard going in a House whose Democrats don't want to give away their majority. President Bill Clinton, after embracing grazing fee increases, pulled back, at least temporarily, at the behest of western senators, in an action that dismayed Synar as bad policy and bad politics. The liberalism Synar has championed will surely do better under Clinton than Bush, but the causes he has taken on will continue to be politically difficult—and competition back home, given the closeness of the 1992 results, can't be entirely ruled out.

The People: Pop. 1990: 524,389; 63% rural; 15% age 65+; 77% White; 5% Black; 17% Amer. Indian; 1% Hispanic origin. Voting age pop.: 381,772; 5% Black; 1% Hispanic origin. Households: 63% married couple families; 29% married couple fams. w. children; 35% college educ.; median household income: $20,633; per capita income: $9,914; median gross rent: $289; median house value: $40,800.

1992 Presidential Vote			1988 Presidential Vote		
Clinton (D)	96,486	(42%)	Dukakis (D)	98,940	(51%)
Bush (R)	81,432	(36%)	Bush (R)	95,865	(49%)
Perot (I)	49,124	(22%)			

Rep. Michael L. (Mike) Synar (D)

Elected 1978; b. Oct. 17, 1950, Vinita; home, Muskogee; U. of OK, B.A. 1972, J.D. 1977, Northwestern U., M.S. 1973, U. of Edinburgh, Rotary Scholar, 1974; Episcopalian; single.

Career: Rancher, 1956–present; Real estate broker, 1967–present; Practicing atty., 1977–78.

Offices: 2329 RHOB 20515, 202-225-2701. Also Fed. Bldg., 125 S. Main, #2B22, Muskogee 74401, 918-687-2533.

Committees: *Energy and Commerce* (7th of 27 D): Energy and Power; Health and the Environment; Telecommunications and Finance. *Government Operations* (5th of 25 D): Environment, Energy and Natural Resources (Chmn.). *Judiciary* (6th of 21 D): Economic and Commercial Law; Intellectual Property and Judicial Administration.

Group Ratings

	ADA	ACLU	COPE	CDF	CFA	LCV	ACU	NTLC	NSI	COC	CEI
1992	95	91	83	90	87	81	0	0	30	25	18
1991	90	—	75	100	83	77	0	—	—	30	17

National Journal Ratings

	1991 LIB	—	1991 CONS	1992 LIB	—	1992 CONS
Economic	72%	—	23%	71%	—	27%
Social	78%	—	17%	81%	—	17%
Foreign	87%	—	13%	86%	—	10%

Key Votes of the 102d Congress

1. Ban Striker Replace	FOR	5. Handgun Wait/7-Day	FOR	9. Use Force in Gulf	AGN
2. $ for Homeownership	AGN	6. Overseas Mil. Abortion	FOR	10. US Mil. Abroad $ Cut	FOR
3. Tax Rich/Cut Mid Cls.	FOR	7. Obscn. Art NEA $ Ban	AGN	11. Limit SDI Funds	FOR
4. FY93/$15B Def. Cut	FOR	8. Death Pen. from Jury	AGN	12. Cuba Trade Embargo	AGN

Key Votes of the 103d Congress

1. Family Leave	FOR	2. Deficit Reduction	FOR	3. Stimulus Plan	FOR

Election Results

1992 general	Michael L. (Mike) Synar (D)	118,542	(56%)	($1,190,197)
	Jerry Hill (R)	87,657	(41%)	($30,312)
	Other	7,314	(3%)	
1992 runoff	Michael L. (Mike) Synar (D)	56,662	(53%)	
	Drew Edmondson (D)	50,084	(47%)	
1992 primary	Michael L. (Mike) Synar (D)	47,562	(43%)	
	Drew Edmondson (D)	42,080	(38%)	
	Robert W. (Bob) Blackstock (D)	15,446	(14%)	
	Charles Lee Kilgore (D)	5,059	(5%)	
1990 general	Michael L. (Mike) Synar (D)	90,820	(61%)	($631,839)
	Terry M. Gorham (R)	57,331	(39%)	($62,793)

THIRD DISTRICT

West of Arkansas and just north of Texas, Little Dixie is the most recognizably southern part of Oklahoma. It was settled between 1889 and 1907 by white southerners, most of them poor; some county names (Leflore, Pontotoc) were taken directly from Mississippi. It remains mostly rural today and, like the rural Deep South, by no means as poor or bedeviled by racial tension as it was three decades ago. A private economy that has produced jobs is one reason; another is government, which built interstate highways and turnpikes connecting many people to jobs in more vibrant metropolitan areas, and dam-made lakes have spurred the creation of resort and retirement communities.

The 3d Congressional District of Oklahoma includes most of the Little Dixie counties, and juts up into the center of the state into the old university town of Stillwater, which is Republican territory, to include enough people to meet the population standard. It remains a solidly Democratic constituency, delivering a solid plurality for Arkansas neighbor Bill Clinton in 1992 and, except for a few peripheral counties, has never had a Republican representative. For 30 years, until his retirement in 1976, it was represented by Carl Albert, speaker of the House his last six years and majority leader for nine years before that.

The current congressman, Bill Brewster, was chosen in an old-fashioned, multi-candidate primary when incumbent Wes Watkins ran for governor (and lost) in 1990. The candidates relied less on television than on personal campaigning and local support networks. One candidate was Lieutenant Governor Robert Kerr III, grandson of Senator Robert Kerr (1949–63) who was legendary for his political clout and boldness in using his position to enrich himself and his Kerr-McGee company. Establishing residence in the hills near the Arkansas border, he got former Speaker Albert's endorsement. The other main contender was Brewster, a registered pharmacist, Angus cattle raiser, and an accomplished state legislator whose campaign was struck by tragedy when two of his children died in a plane crash the same day he announced his candidacy. Brewster won the August primary 51%–41%, and won in November with ease. In the House he has had a fairly moderate record, and was one of 22 Democrats to vote against the Clinton stimulus package in March 1993. He got a seat on Ways and Means in 1993 and scored an early victory there when President Clinton agreed to move the collection point for his proposed Btu tax from utilities to customers' actual bills. As the only pharmacist in the House (Bob Kerrey is one in the Senate, and of course Hubert Humphrey was too), he hopes to play a part in the healthcare debate. He favors the balanced budget amendment and tax incentives for new jobs. Against 25-year old teaching assistant Robert Stokes, Brewster won with 75% in 1992.

The People: Pop. 1990: 524,287; 56% rural; 16% age 65+; 83% White; 4% Black; 11% Amer. Indian; 1% Asian; 1% Other; 1% Hispanic origin. Voting age pop.: 388,151; 4% Black; 1% Hispanic origin. Households: 60% married couple families; 27% married couple fams. w. children; 35% college educ.; median household income: $18,394; per capita income: $9,635; median gross rent: $294; median house value: $35,800.

1992 Presidential Vote		
Clinton (D)	94,753	(41%)
Bush (R)	77,040	(34%)
Perot (I)	55,973	(24%)

1988 Presidential Vote		
Bush (R)	98,425	(50%)
Dukakis (D)	97,357	(50%)

Rep. Bill Brewster (D)

Elected 1990; b. Nov. 8, 1941, Ardmore; home, Marietta; Southwestern OK St. U., B.S. 1964; Baptist; married (Mary Sue).

Career: Army Reserves, 1968–71; Co-owner, Brewster Angus Farms, 1968–present; Pharmacist, Owner, Colleyville Drug Inc., 1964–77; OK House of Reps., 1982–90.

Offices: 1727 LHOB 20515, 202-225-4565. Also 900 N. Mississippi, #B, Ada 74820, 405-436-1980; 118 Fed. Bldg., McAlester 74501, 918-423-5951; and 123 W. 7th Ave., #206, Stillwater 74074, 405-743-1400.

Committees: *Ways and Means* (23d of 24 D): Oversight; Social Security.

Group Ratings

	ADA	ACLU	COPE	CDF	CFA	LCV	ACU	NTLC	NSI	COC	CEI
1992	60	35	50	50	47	25	48	0	100	75	33
1991	20	—	67	60	56	23	45	—	—	60	28

National Journal Ratings

	1991 LIB — 1991 CONS	1992 LIB — 1992 CONS
Economic	41% — 58%	46% — 54%
Social	44% — 55%	49% — 50%
Foreign	38% — 62%	44% — 50%

Key Votes of the 102d Congress

1. Ban Striker Replace	AGN	5. Handgun Wait/7-Day	AGN	9. Use Force in Gulf	FOR
2. $ for Homeownership	FOR	6. Overseas Mil. Abortion	FOR	10. US Mil. Abroad $ Cut	FOR
3. Tax Rich/Cut Mid Cls.	FOR	7. Obscn. Art NEA $ Ban	FOR	11. Limit SDI Funds	AGN
4. FY93/$15B Def. Cut	FOR	8. Death Pen. from Jury	AGN	12. Cuba Trade Embargo	FOR

Key Votes of the 103d Congress

1. Family Leave	AGN	2. Deficit Reduction	FOR	3. Stimulus Plan	AGN

Election Results

1992 general	Bill Brewster (D)	155,934	(75%)	($386,144)
	Robert W. Stokes (R)	51,725	(25%)	($6,338)
1992 primary	Bill Brewster (D), unopposed			
1990 general	Bill Brewster (D)	107,641	(80%)	($446,766)
	Patrick K. Miller (R)	26,261	(20%)	

FOURTH DISTRICT

The very lightly treed hills west of Oklahoma City and north of the Red River filled up rapidly with farmers in the early years of this century, filtering north from Texas, past the well-watered green lands of the east toward the bare brown pasturelands of the southwest. These were young people with large families, and in the years since this land has emptied out, as children have grown up and moved elsewhere and fewer hands are needed for farming. People in southwest Oklahoma instead have accumulated around major government institutions: the state capital of Oklahoma City; Norman, home of the University of Oklahoma; Lawton, to the southwest, home of the Army's Fort Sill.

These are major landmarks for the 4th Congressional District of Oklahoma, which begins a few miles from the oil-derrick-surrounded state Capitol in Oklahoma City, smack dab in the middle of the state, and proceeds south and west to cover half of Oklahoma's Red River Valley. Demographically, this seat is becoming more suburban, but the cultural tone remains rural. That's so even in the actual suburbs, stretching out over the midwestern mile grid roads, where in new subdivisions dust still gets tracked indoors, and people still prefer chicken-fried steak to stir-fried chicken (though they eat both). Politically, this country is ancestrally Democratic, but Norman, Lawton and the Oklahoma City fringe now tend to vote Republican, and George Bush carried this district not only in 1988 but in 1992, though he lost a lot of votes to Ross Perot.

The congressman from the 4th District, Dave McCurdy, in ten years has moved from a freshman with a marginal district to a national party leader. He grew up in a family of modest income, graduated from the University of Oklahoma in 1972 (a classmate of the 2d District's Mike Synar and like Synar a Rotary scholar at the University of Edinburgh), and briefly practiced law before running in 1980. With a moderate voting record on economic and cultural issues, and considerable foreign policy expertise, McCurdy has made himself an important leader—or would-be leader—in the House. Instinctively, he is both conservative and insurrectionary, not an unnatural combination in a liberal Democratic House, and also ambitious. He got a seat on Armed Services and voted for the Reagan tax cuts, and was for much of the Reagan military buildup (he is in the Air Force Reserve, and spent a week with the Reserves in December 1990 in the Persian Gulf). His first move forward was to support Les Aspin's campaign for chairman of Armed Services in 1984. The next year he worked with Aspin on an MX missile compromise, opposed by most House Democrats but adopted by Congress. He also led compromise efforts to give the Nicaraguan contras humanitarian aid, switching to a tougher position when Daniel Ortega flew to Moscow, then supporting the Arias peace plan and Speaker Jim Wright's mediation efforts. As a moderate Democrat, willing to work with both wings of his party and with Republicans, well-informed and confident of his own abilities, this rather junior member of the House became an important national policymaker.

His alliance with Wright enabled him to become chairman of the Intelligence Committee; he avoided the six-year limit on service by resigning from the Committee in December 1987, then was appointed by Wright for another six-year term in December 1988; even though Wright was forced to resign from the House in June 1989, Speaker Thomas Foley honored Wright's promise and made McCurdy chairman in January 1991. McCurdy let it be known that he thought the intelligence agencies had been performing poorly, failing to inform the government of Saddam Hussein's aggression in the Middle East or the economic collapse of the Soviet Union. He promised a "thorough look at organization and management and operation of the agencies" and pledged that the committee would be more aggressive in overseeing the agencies. He kept a considerable profile on other issues as well, sponsoring the Democratic Leadership Council's national service plan, under which volunteers could serve in the military or in civilian service jobs to earn vouchers toward college expenses, job training or down payments on a home. He strongly supported the Gulf war resolution and backs free trade. He proposed a Citizen Democracy Corps to aid fledgling political institutions in Russia and saw the Bush Administration, after criticizing it, come up with a similar proposal. He was active in the DLC and formed a "Mainstream Forum" for moderate House Democrats in 1990.

McCurdy thought out loud about running for president in September 1991, but took himself out of the race in October, and actively campaigned for Bill Clinton in New Hampshire, when he needed help the most. At the 1992 Democratic National Convention, he was sharply critical of Speaker Foley and said Democrats suffered from "lack of a clear agenda" and was mentioned as a replacement for Foley; he was one of the last committee chairmen to endorse Foley for reelection. In 1993, some of McCurdy's maneuvering began to catch up with him. Foley abruptly stripped him of the Intelligence Committee chairmanship, by not waiving the six-year requirement—a pretty sharp slap in the face. (Ironically, McCurdy had called in 1991 for more leadership control of chairmen.) Mentioned as a possible secretary of defense, he was rumored to have told Clinton (McCurdy denies it) that choosing Aspin would leave the radical Ron Dellums chairing Armed Services. McCurdy did get an Armed Services subcommittee chair, and remains vocal and well-informed. But he is not one of the leaders of the House fighting for the Clinton program, nor is he well-positioned (it would cut off his partisan advancement) to be one of the leaders of a bipartisan coalition against it.

McCurdy has been very strong in the 4th District. In 1992, he carried the Oklahoma City portion 67%–33% and the more rural portion 74%–25%.

The People: Pop. 1990: 524,407; 26% rural; 11% age 65+; 83% White; 7% Black; 5% Amer. Indian; 2% Asian; 2% Other; 4% Hispanic origin. Voting age pop.: 382,399; 6% Black; 3% Hispanic origin. Households: 62% married couple families; 31% married couple fams. w. children; 47% college educ.; median household income: $25,391; per capita income: $11,554; median gross rent: $364; median house value: $50,800.

1992 Presidential Vote			1988 Presidential Vote		
Bush (R)	90,975	(42%)	Bush (R)	99,336	(59%)
Clinton (D)	72,551	(33%)	Dukakis (D)	70,080	(41%)
Perot (I)	53,894	(25%)			

Rep. Dave McCurdy (D)

Elected 1980; b. Mar. 30, 1950, Canadian, TX; home, Norman; U. of OK, B.A. 1972, J.D. 1975, U. of Edinburgh, Rotary Scholar, 1977–78; Lutheran; married (Pam).

Career: Air Force Reserves, 1970–72, 1985-present (Persian Gulf, 1990); OK Asst. Atty. Gen., 1975–77; Practicing atty., 1978–80.

Offices: 2344 RHOB 20515, 202-225-6165. Also P.O. Box 1265, Norman 73070, 405-329-6500; 103 Fed. Bldg., Lawton 73501, 405-357-2131; and 805 Main St., Duncan 73533, 405-252-1434.

Committees: *Armed Services* (6th of 34 D): Military Installations and Facilities (Chmn.); Readiness; Research and Technology. *Science, Space and Technology* (6th of 33 D): Energy; Space.

Group Ratings

	ADA	ACLU	COPE	CDF	CFA	LCV	ACU	NTLC	NSI	COC	CEI
1992	70	55	64	70	60	38	32	25	90	75	37
1991	30	—	64	70	67	54	26	—	—	60	35

National Journal Ratings

	1991 LIB — 1991 CONS		1992 LIB — 1992 CONS	
Economic	48% —	52%	41% —	58%
Social	50% —	50%	59% —	41%
Foreign	43% —	55%	44% —	50%

Key Votes of the 102d Congress

1. Ban Striker Replace	AGN	5. Handgun Wait/7-Day	FOR	9. Use Force in Gulf	FOR
2. $ for Homeownership	FOR	6. Overseas Mil. Abortion	FOR	10. US Mil. Abroad $ Cut	FOR
3. Tax Rich/Cut Mid Cls.	AGN	7. Obscn. Art NEA $ Ban	FOR	11. Limit SDI Funds	AGN
4. FY93/$15B Def. Cut	FOR	8. Death Pen. from Jury	AGN	12. Cuba Trade Embargo	FOR

Key Votes of the 103d Congress

| 1. Family Leave | FOR | 2. Deficit Reduction | FOR | 3. Stimulus Plan | FOR |

Election Results

1992 general	Dave McCurdy (D)................... 140,841	(71%)	($584,409)
	Howard Bell (R).................... 58,235	(29%)	
1992 primary	Dave McCurdy (D), unopposed		
1990 general	Dave McCurdy (D)................... 100,879	(74%)	($357,531)
	Howard Bell (R)..................... 36,232	(26%)	($2,923)

FIFTH DISTRICT

Oklahoma City, as befits the capital and largest city of a state built in sudden booms and languished in long busts, still has an unfinished look about it. The Capitol, surrounded by oil rigs which were pumping crude until 1989, was opened in 1917 without a dome because money ran out, and only recently a local group called the Capitol Domers started a campaign to raise $14 million to finish the dome. The city and the building are situated almost precisely in the middle of the state and the middle of the continent. Oklahoma City, like many state capitals, was not the spontaneous creation of commerce but the deliberate creation of government, built on land that is browner and more eroded by creeks than the greener, rolling Oklahoma farther east. During the 1960s, the city fathers decided not to let the old city limits fence them in, so Oklahoma City started annexing land, and now spills out into farm and grazing land in five counties and four congressional districts, covering 624 square miles.

The 5th Congressional District of Oklahoma includes most of Oklahoma City, but it is a carefully chosen part: the most Democratic sections of the city, including its black areas, are chopped off and included in Democratic districts. This is a solidly Republican area as a result. The 5th proceeds north through wheat country, to the onetime state capital of Guthrie and the market town of Ponca City, areas as Republican as any similar place in nearby Kansas. Connected by a strip of mostly uninhabited Osage County is Bartlesville, headquarters of Phillips Petroleum, solidly conservative in the Oil Patch manner. The 5th District is by far Oklahoma's most Republican district: a constituency created by Democratic legislatures to corral solidly Republican precincts and give Democrats a chance to win the five other districts, as they have at one time or another over the past decade.

The 5th District, formerly a safe seat, was the scene in 1992 of one of the most striking expressions of anti-incumbent sentiment in the country. The incumbent was Mickey Edwards, a Republican first elected in 1976 when the district was entirely in Oklahoma County and was hotly contested. Edwards had one of the most conservative voting records in the House, but was also an opponent of institutional change: he was against the line-item veto, defended the War Powers Acts, tried to rein in young Republicans attacking House procedures. He had some stake in this, with a seat on Appropriations and as fourth-ranking member of the Republican leadership. But in April 1992, it was revealed that Edwards had 386 overdrafts on the House bank and was often overdrawn by an amount that exceeded his next paycheck; the total amount was relatively low ($54,000), but he was named as one of the leading offenders. Edwards apologized and said, "I stand here humiliated because the Ethics Committee was not willing to reconsider the definition of a net deposit." He was obviously in trouble; the fact that his fourth marriage, to a former Miss Oklahoma, had ended didn't help.

Two strong Republicans opposed him in the primary. One, 1990 gubernatorial nominee Bill Price, hit Edwards hard; another, state legislator Ernest Istook, called for less pork barrel spending. In the August primary, Price won 37% of the vote, Istook 32% and Edwards only 26%. In the September runoff, Istook won 56%–44%, probably picking up many Edwards supporters irritated by Price's intense criticism of the incumbent. Highly favored in the general election, he won by only 53%–47% over oil and gas lawyer Laurie Williams who attacked Istook for his antiabortion stance. The grandson of Hungarian immigrants, a former radio reporter and lawyer, Istook first attracted attention as Governor David Boren's head of the alcohol control board; his refusal to stop an investigation of illegal connections between wholesale and retail liquor distributors eventually denied him Senate confirmation for that post. He promises to keep his family in Oklahoma and has Edwards's old seat on Appropriations.

The People: Pop. 1990: 523,729; 13% rural; 13% age 65+; 85% White; 6% Black; 5% Amer. Indian; 2% Asian; 2% Other; 3% Hispanic origin. Voting age pop.: 387,789; 5% Black; 2% Hispanic origin. Households: 57% married couple families; 26% married couple fams. w. children; 56% college educ.; median household income: $28,348; per capita income: $15,024; median gross rent: $370; median house value: $58,200.

1992 Presidential Vote			1988 Presidential Vote		
Bush (R)	129,379	(51%)	Bush (R)	134,015	(65%)
Clinton (D)	62,251	(25%)	Dukakis (D)	70,918	(35%)
Perot (I)	59,542	(24%)			

Rep. Ernest J. Istook, Jr. (R)

Elected 1992; b. Feb. 11, 1950, Ft. Worth, TX; home, Oklahoma City; Baylor U., B.A. 1971, Oklahoma City U. Law Schl., J.D. 1976; Mormon; married (Judy).

Career: Political reporter, Oklahoma City KOMA-radio, 1972–73, WKY-radio, 1973–76; Dir., OK Alcohol Beverage Control Bd., 1977; Practicing atty., 1977–92; OK House of Reps., 1986–92.

Offices: 1116 LHOB 20515, 202-225-2132. Also 5400 N. Grand Blvd., #505, Oklahoma City 73112, 405-942-3636; First Court Pl., #205, Bartlesville 74003, 918-336-5546; and 5th and Grand Sts., Ponca City 74601, 405-762-6778.

Committees: *Appropriations* (22d of 23 R): District of Columbia; Treasury, Postal Service, and General Government.

Group Ratings and 102d Congress Votes: Newly Elected

Key Votes of the 103d Congress

1. Family Leave	AGN	2. Deficit Reduction	AGN	3. Stimulus Plan	AGN

Election Results

1992 general	Ernest J. Istook, Jr. (R)	123,237	(53%)	($364,915)
	Laurie Williams (D)	107,579	(47%)	($336,418)
1992 runoff	Ernest J. Istook, Jr. (R)	26,659	(56%)	
	Bill Price (R)	20,679	(44%)	
1992 primary	Bill Price (R)	20,485	(37%)	
	Ernest J. Istook, Jr. (R)	17,975	(32%)	
	Mickey Edwards (R)	14,519	(26%)	
	John David Hershberger (R)	2,294	(4%)	
	Other	659	(1%)	
1990 general	Mickey Edwards (R)	114,608	(70%)	($373,414)
	Bryce Baggett (D)	50,086	(30%)	($6,277)

SIXTH DISTRICT

First settled less than a century ago, western Oklahoma is a fertile land forever at the mercy of the elements. The western plains are scorching hot under the summer sun and snow-blown in winter; this is one of the windiest parts of America. The rural counties here have far fewer people than before the dust bowl of the 1930s, and the once booming oil and natural gas exploration here in the Anadarko Basin and other fields has in recent years done little for the region.

The 6th Congressional District of Oklahoma is made up of the western plains of Oklahoma, plus blue-collar and black neighborhoods in Oklahoma City. This land was settled by farmers moving south from Kansas, starting when the gun went off the morning of the great land rush in 1889. A few of its counties in the south have always been heavily Democratic; most of the rest are heavily Republican, and always have been: these divisions are as permanent as if Oklahoma had been split down the middle during the Civil War, except that of course there were no whites in the state at the time. The bigger fact here is depopulation: counties wholly within the 6th Congressional District had 423,000 people in 1930 and 282,000 in 1990. Forty percent of the district's votes in 1992 were cast in metropolitan Oklahoma City.

By most measures, the 6th should be a Republican district, yet its congressman since 1974 has been Democrat Glenn English. The inclusion of Democratic parts of Oklahoma City since 1982 have helped him, but are not critical to his success; in 1992, against a strong candidate, state Corporation Commissioner Bob Anthony, well-known for his family chain of clothing stores, English won 69% in the rural counties and 66% in the Oklahoma City areas. English's political formula is to vote conservative on most issues and support generous aid for farm areas and western Oklahoma. Although he once left Oklahoma to be an aide to the California Assembly's liberal Democrats, he has the most conservative voting record of Oklahoma Democrats. He can be a tough negotiator: in 1981, just four days before the showdown on the 1981 Reagan tax cut, he extracted a written promise from Ronald Reagan to veto "with pleasure" any windfall profits tax on natural gas. That promise effectively protected this otherwise vulnerable revenue source in 1982, when Republicans were scrambling for politically painless ways to, in the phrase of the day, "enhance revenues." In a similar spirit, in 1991, just before the vote on the Gulf war resolution, he asked George Bush whether we would fight until the removal of Saddam Hussein. When Bush could not provide that assurance, English voted no saying, "If history has taught us anything, it's that war is an all or nothing business"—advice Bush today may wish he had taken.

As chairman of the Agriculture Committee and the Conservation, Credit and Rural Development Subcommittee, he put together a reauthorization of the Commodities Future Trading Commission in 1992 and has sought to give rural communities more funds and more flexibility in spending them. He negotiated conservation sections of the 1990 farm bill, bringing together environmentalists and commodity groups, and getting them to agree on swampbuster, water quality, and conservation easements provisions. He seeks to beef up the farm credit system, the FmHA and REA. He favors the balanced budget amendment, and WPA-style work projects and youth work camps for welfare recipients. A tough bargainer and infighter, English is one of those members who keeps the House working and at the same time keeps his constituents happy.

The People: Pop. 1990: 524,638; 30% rural; 15% age 65+; 77% White; 13% Black; 5% Amer. Indian; 1% Asian; 2% Other; 4% Hispanic origin. Voting age pop.: 382,199; 12% Black; 3% Hispanic origin. Households: 57% married couple families; 26% married couple fams. w. children; 38% college educ.; median household income: $21,797; per capita income: $10,540; median gross rent: $323; median house value: $39,500.

1992 Presidential Vote

Bush (R) 91,966 (43%)
Clinton (D) 73,516 (34%)
Perot (I). 49,268 (23%)

1988 Presidential Vote

Bush (R) 119,376 (61%)
Dukakis (D). 75,042 (39%)

Rep. Glenn English (D)

Elected 1974; b. Nov. 30, 1940, Cordell; home, Cordell; Southwestern St. Col., B.A. 1964; United Methodist; married (Jan).

Career: Army Reserves, 1965–71; Chief Asst., Majority Caucus, CA Assembly, 1967–68; Exec. Dir., OK Dem. Party, 1969–73; Petroleum landman, 1973–74.

Offices: 2206 RHOB 20515, 202-225-5565. Also 109 Old P.O. Bldg., 215 Dean A. McGee Ave., Oklahoma City 73102, 405-231-5511; Fed. Bldg., P.O. Box 3612, Enid 73702, 405-233-9224; and 1120 9th St., Woodward 73801, 405-256-5752.

Committees: *Agriculture* (4th of 28 D): Department Operations and Nutrition; Environment, Credit and Rural Development (Chmn.); General Farm Commodities; Specialty Crops and Natural Resources. *Government Operations* (3d of 25 D): Legislation and National Security.

Group Ratings

	ADA	ACLU	COPE	CDF	CFA	LCV	ACU	NTLC	NSI	COC	CEI
1992	55	48	67	40	47	38	56	45	60	75	44
1991	35	—	67	50	61	31	50	—	—	40	36

National Journal Ratings

	1991 LIB — 1991 CONS	1992 LIB — 1992 CONS
Economic	38% — 62%	28% — 70%
Social	35% — 63%	33% — 67%
Foreign	49% — 50%	44% — 50%

Key Votes of the 102d Congress

1. Ban Striker Replace	AGN	5. Handgun Wait/7-Day AGN	9. Use Force in Gulf AGN
2. $ for Homeownership	FOR	6. Overseas Mil. AbortionAGN	10. US Mil. Abroad $ CutAGN
3. Tax Rich/Cut Mid Cls.AGN		7. Obscn. Art NEA $ Ban FOR	11. Limit SDI Funds AGN
4. FY93/$15B Def. Cut AGN		8. Death Pen. from Jury FOR	12. Cuba Trade Embargo AGN

Key Votes of the 103d Congress

1. Family Leave   FOR   2. Deficit Reduction   AGN   3. Stimulus Plan   AGN

Election Results

1992 general	Glenn English (D)....................	134,734	(68%)	($553,316)
	Bob Anthony (R)	64,068	(32%)	($375,794)
1992 primary	Glenn English (D), unopposed			
1990 general	Glenn English (D)....................	110,100	(80%)	($157,414)
	Robert Burns (R)	27,540	(20%)	

OREGON

New England on the Pacific Rim, a quintessentially American state thousands of miles from where most Americans live, an experimental commonwealth and laboratory of reform, home of angry owl-hating loggers and crusaders against homosexuality: all these things are Oregon. This is an affluent high-tech civilization where one can still see much the same land and water that Lewis and Clark saw in 1805 when they came down the Columbia River gorge, past what is now Portland, to the Pacific Coast port of Astoria. This Oregon was settled by Americans when John Jacob Astor set up his fur trading post at Astoria in 1811 and when New England Yankees rode the Oregon Trail and down the Columbia to the well-watered Willamette Valley. In this remote land, nearly 2,000 miles from the Mississippi River frontier and 700 miles from the small settlements of California, the orderly, productive society of Oregon was established. It grew steadily over the years, with a few booms—when timber, always its first industry, surged in 1900–10, during the war and after in the 1940s, and in the 1970s when homebuilding boomed and the mountains, waters and empty spaces of Oregon's natural environment began to be widely appreciated. Too widely for some, like Governor Tom McCall (1966–74), who used to urge people to visit Oregon, "but for heaven's sake don't come to live here," while others made rueful jokes about the endless rain.

Since McCall's time, Oregon, like the New England from which most of its original settlers came, has moved sharply left on cultural issues, creatively pioneering new public policies but also sparking some antagonistic backlash. Its economy, like those of the other two West Coast states, has grown robustly, but has suffered some sharp setbacks as well. The political result in the late 1980s was a confident and thoughtful liberalism; in the early 1990s it has been flailing about in every direction, with mixed results.

One reason Oregon was able to adopt pioneer liberal stands on cultural issues was the lack of countervailing institutions. This is the state with the lowest rate of church membership, with large numbers of believers in astrology, New Age lore, and the like; the public voices of its big institutions have been friendly to almost any kind of innovation. So Oregon was among the first states to outlaw throwaway bottles. By the early 1970s, it had decriminalized marijuana and legalized most abortions—daring moves in those times. Early on it was ready to back limits on development and use of property. A gun control law passed which banned semiautomatic weapons, and weekly betting on professional sports games was legalized. In 1990 its voters passed a workfare referendum, but it could not be implemented because of federal regulations. Led by state Representative Vera Katz, Oregon approved a school reform package with ungraded classes up to third grade and statewide apprenticeship programs, letting students choose job training or college prep after tenth grade. Led by state Senate President John Kitzhaber, an emergency room physician, the legislature passed healthcare reform that uses Medicaid to produce universal health access but cuts back coverage for medical procedures below a certain point on a rank-order list of some 700. This is the closest thing an American state has come to explicit rationing of health care, and has the cool rationality one might expect from America's most secular state; it would be interesting to see if Americans overall would accept this rationing, but the Bush Administration ruled that it violated the Americans With Disabilities Act and refused a federal waiver. In March 1993, however, Clinton approved the Oregon plan with some minor revisions; the state embarked on developing a funding mechanism to phase in the plan by January 1, 1994.

But sometimes there have been unanticipated costs—or opposition to Oregon's pioneering. In June 1990, the Fish and Wildlife Service declared that the spotted owl was an endangered species, and a series of court rulings resulted in a ban against further logging in much of the

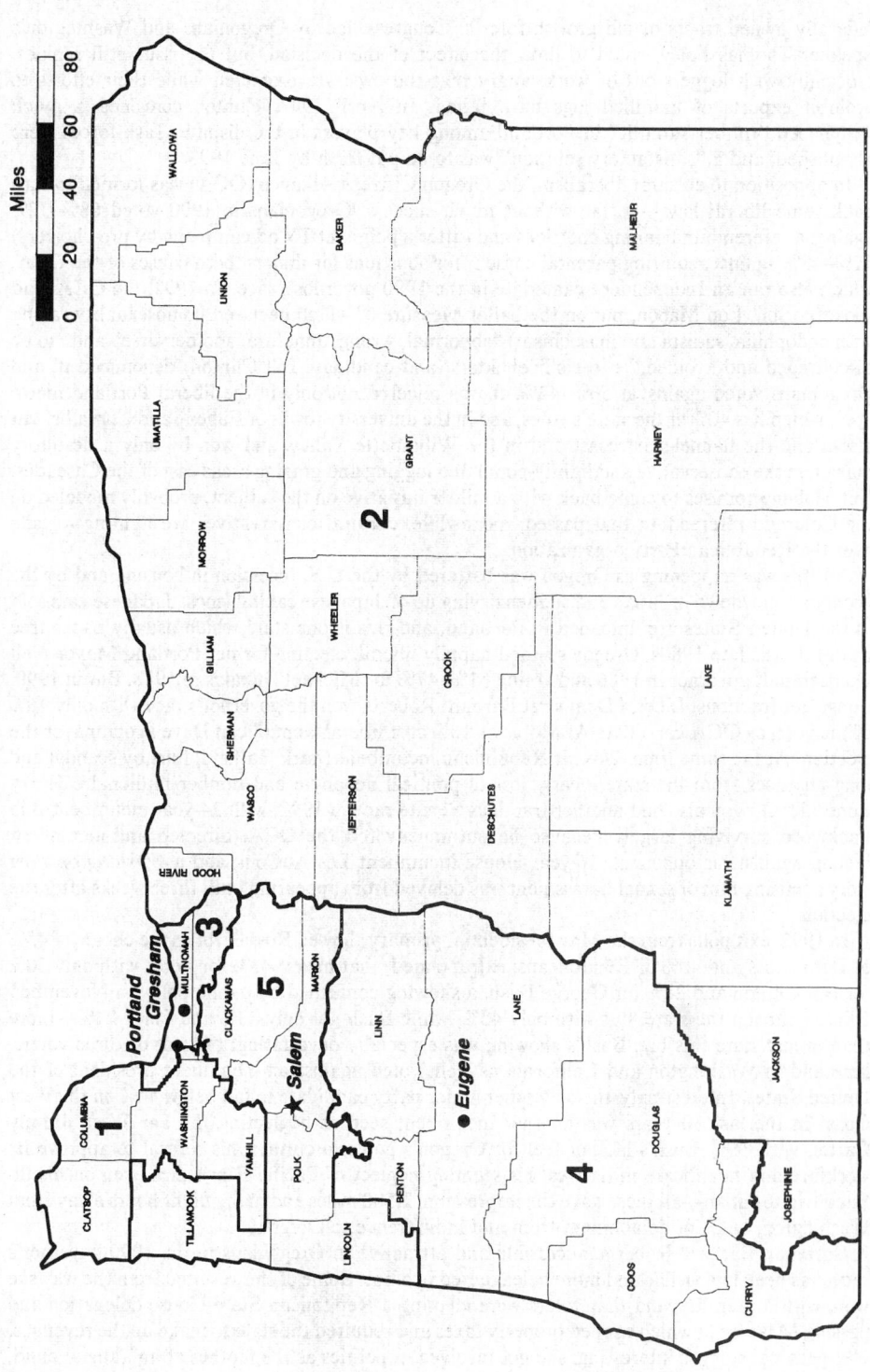

federally owned tracts of old growth forests. Congress, led by Oregonians and Washington's Speaker Thomas Foley, voted to limit the effect of the decision, but the issue still rankles, especially with loggers out of work, angry that the owls are protected while their efforts to prohibit exports of unmilled logs have failed. In April 1993, Clinton convened a much ballyhooed "timber summit" in Portland among key players in the dispute. Task forces were established, and a "satisfactory solution" was to be put forth by June 1993.

In opposition to cultural liberalism, the Oregon Citizens Alliance (OCA) was formed to turn back some liberal laws—so far without much success. Oregonians in 1990 voted 68%–32% against a referendum banning abortions and (after a poignant TV ad campaign by pro-choicers) 52%–48% against requiring parental consent for abortions for minors, both causes of the OCA, which also ran an Independent candidate in the 1990 governor's race. In 1992, the OCA lead spokesperson, Lon Mabon, put on the ballot Measure 9, which declared homosexuality (along with pedophilia, sadism and masochism) "abnormal, wrong, unnatural and perverse" and "to be discouraged and avoided." Most officeholders (and candidate Bill Clinton) denounced it, and Oregonians voted against it 56%–44%. It was rejected not only in the liberal Portland metro area, which has 40% of the state's votes, and in the university towns of Eugene and Corvallis, but also along the flannel-shirt coast and in the Willamette Valley, and won by only a desultory margin in the conservative and lightly-populated logging and grazing areas east of the Cascades. But Mabon promises to come back with a milder initiative on the subject, probably modeled on the Colorado referendum that passed; meanwhile, cultural conservatives are fighting to take over the Republican Party organization.

All this was happening as Oregon was battered by the U.S. recession in housing and by the economic slowdown in Japan and sudden drying up of Japanese capital (most Japanese cars sold in the United States are unloaded in Portland, and this is one state which usually backs free trade). In the late 1980s, Oregon seemed happily liberal, electing former Portland Mayor Neil Goldschmidt governor in 1986 and voting 51%–47% for Michael Dukakis in 1988. But in 1990, things got fractious. Liberal Democrat Barbara Roberts won the governor's race with only 46% of the vote, as OCA candidate Al Mobley's 13% cost liberal Republican Dave Frohnmayer the election. At the same time, 24-year Republican incumbent Mark Hatfield, hurt by scandal and long absences from the state, nearly lost to political neophyte and lumber millionaire Harry Lonsdale. Oregon also had another fractious Senate race in 1992, with 24-year incumbent Bob Packwood surviving largely because he outmaneuvered the OCA, directed anti-incumbent feeling against his opponent, 16-year House incumbent Les AuCoin, and a *Washington Post* story accusing him of sexual harassment was delayed from appearing until three weeks after the election.

In 1992, exit polls from the May presidential primary showed Ross Perot as the choice of 45% of Democrats and 40% of Republicans; extrapolated, that meant 43% for Perot with only 30% for Bill Clinton and 28% for George Bush, a showing confirmed by public polls. In November, Clinton carried the state, but with only 43%, while Bush got only 33% and Perot 24%—more than in any state this big. Bush's showing was especially devastating: two out of three voters, here and in Washington and California as well, voted against an incumbent president of the United States. Interestingly, the only other major party candidate to fall below 40% on the West Coast in the last 50 years was another incumbent seen as neglecting the Far West, Jimmy Carter, with 36%. Bush's lack of feel for Oregon's political culture, his refusal to approve its workfare and healthcare initiatives, his seeming neglect of Pacific Rim states even on his ill-fated trip to Japan—all these gave the impression, 2,500 miles and many flight hours away from Washington, D.C., of detachment from and indifference to Oregon.

Governor. Barbara Roberts, accessible and attractive to Oregonians in the 1990 governor's race, has been less visible and more beleaguered in office. Some of this resulted from the way she won, with a plurality, and that voters were electing a Republican State House delegation and passing Measure 5, which capped property taxes and required the state to make up the revenues. Her personal story is interesting: she got involved in politics as the mother of an autistic child, seeking to focus attention on their needs. Later, she was elected to the school board and the legislature, became House majority leader and was elected secretary of state in 1984 and 1988; her husband Frank Roberts is the Oregon legislature's senior member (no separation of powers here). Once in office, Barbara Roberts went beyond Salem, in a "Conversation with Oregon" program asking 80,000 voters to come to one of 30 teleconferencing sites and comment on state government—an exercise in civic participation foreshadowing Ross Perot. She hoped they would identify areas for cuts and back a tax increase, but they didn't, leaving her exposed as a likely tax-raiser (Oregon has never had a sales tax, and has voted down several).

Taxes are not the only issue on which Roberts has taken liberal stands, and she remains controversial. Two attempts have been made to recall her, both of which fell short of signatures. But her job rating in 1993 was 2–1 negative, and Republicans gained a seat in the state House they already controlled and nearly won control of the state Senate; Roberts once quipped that no one could get away with her policies but "a one-term liberal Democratic governor." She will surely have competition when she tries for a second term in 1994. Possible Republicans include Superintendent of Public Instruction Norma Paulus (the 1986 nominee), former Congressman Denny Smith, and former state GOP chairman, Craig Berkman. And then there is the possibility of a Democratic primary challenge or an OCA-backed or other third party candidate such as Herschel Taylor, who led the two efforts to recall Roberts and may run as an independent.

Senators. Oregon has two of the senior Republicans in the Senate, both former chairmen and now ranking members of major committees (Appropriations and Finance), both of considerable intellect, character and distinctive views, and both almost certainly serving their last terms: Mark Hatfield and Bob Packwood. (If they serve them out, they will have been colleagues for 28 years, the same as Warren Magnuson and Henry Jackson of Washington, and only two years behind the record of John McClellan and William Fulbright of Arkansas.) They have known each other for years, but on many issues they differ, and each is now under a different kind of political cloud.

The senior senator is Mark Hatfield, one of the Senate's most deeply religious members, and also one found to have violated ethics laws and Senate rules. He was elected Oregon's secretary of state at age 34 in 1956, and in 1958 was elected governor and served for eight years; in 1966, he was elected to the Senate and has been there ever since. As a young serviceman, he was one of the first Americans to see Hiroshima after it was bombed, and for years has been the most dovish senator. He was the cosponsor of the McGovern-Hatfield amendment to end the Vietnam war in the early 1970s; he was an enthusiastic backer of the nuclear freeze in the 1980s; he has never voted for a defense authorization bill, though while Appropriations chairman, he presided over the huge defense buildup of the 1980s. He voted against the Gulf war resolution (one of two GOP senators to do so) and against the alternative measure of economic sanctions. He is dovish as well on other foreign issues, and skeptical about, if not hostile to, Israel. He opposes the death penalty, even against terrorists, and calls for life imprisonment instead. In 1992, he had the satisfaction of seeing the Senate finally adopt a moratorium on nuclear testing for one year, something he had been seeking for years.

Much of Hatfield's work is done on Appropriations. He put together various "court-stripping" measures to prevent or nullify court decisions unfavorable to the lumber industry on the spotted owl issue; he consistently backs more roads in federal forests to benefit of loggers. Though antiabortion, he has backed amendments to allow family planning counseling (including counseling on abortion) at Title X clinics. He has procured money for Portland's popular light rail, for a downtown Portland courthouse, for "urban-grants" for Portland State University, for Columbia River projects, for Oregon Indian tribes, as well as for national causes like Alzheimer's research, and boasts of his own Math and Science Enhancement law.

Hatfield also got money for Oregon Health Sciences University (whose president, it turned out, personally admitted Hatfield's daughter to medical school), and for the University of South Carolina (which, it was revealed, granted a full scholarship to his son). Hatfield was politically embarrassed in 1984 when it was revealed his wife had received $55,000 from developer Basil Tsakos as a real estate fee (though no property changed hands) while Hatfield was promoting Tsakos's plan for a $15 billion trans-Africa oil pipeline. That year, as it happened, Hatfield had only nuisance opposition; he was lucky that the two stories about his children did not surface until after the 1990 election. He was lucky also that it was not until spring 1991 that FBI and Senate investigations began of his failure to list on disclosure statements the gifts of $9,000 in artwork and $5,000 in air travel he received from the University of South Carolina president, who resigned his post because of criticism over spending university funds on lavish travel expenses. In August 1992, the Senate Ethics Committee formally rebuked Hatfield for accepting and failing to report nearly $43,000 in gifts from 1983 to 1988. The committee found no link between the gifts and Hatfield's role in legislation, but Hatfield admitted, "my mistakes were many and my omissions serious."

Hatfield's opponent for 1990 was Harry Lonsdale, a businessman from eastern Oregon who self-financed much of his campaign; his lack of political experience helped in an anti-incumbent year, and Lonsdale shrewdly played to that feeling by declaring that "24 years in Washington has changed Mark Hatfield." Lonsdale was free to make unrealistic promises (ban log exports), to attack Hatfield on abortion (a highly visible issue because of the ballot referendum), for opposing a state anti-gay discrimination law, and as a "timber beast" because of his pro-lumber stance in the owl dispute. He ran spots set in the Gould Battery dump in Portland, hitting Hatfield for taking money from polluters. A late September poll showed Hatfield leading by only 49%–43%. Suddenly, Senate business became less pressing and Hatfield returned home: he hit Lonsdale as an environmental zealot whose policies would cost hundreds of jobs; a Hatfield ad charged that Lonsdale's company had dumped waste water with toxic chemicals. The final issue revolved around cult leader Bhagwan Shree Rajneesh, whose takeover of an eastern Oregon town led to a federal prosecution of his commune. Hatfield ran an ad quoting a letter Lonsdale wrote in 1984, after charges that Rajneesh followers poisoned a U.S. attorney, to Attorney General Frohnmayer: "I conclude that Rajneeshpuram just may be the happiest town in America. They must be doing something right!" Hatfield won 54%–46%, carrying most parts of the state, and cutting into the cultural liberal vote in the Portland area. That left Hatfield with another six-year term; cries that he should be recalled after the ethics charges came to nothing.

Bob Packwood is one of the most politically shrewd and legislatively accomplished of senators, with a distinctive and consistent set of principles he's backed for over a quarter-century now. He is also, in the view of many, one of the most cynical operators in national politics, and his long career came under a very dark cloud in late November 1992, just after he had been elected to a fifth six-year term, when *The Washington Post* ran an article accusing him of numerous incidents of sexual harassment.

Even so, it was not surprising that some women's groups backed him in 1992 against a strong pro-choice Democrat, and despite rumors prevalent even then of womanizing. One of his principle crusades has been abortion rights: in the early 1970s, he championed zero population growth; in the late 1970s, he was the Senate's leading opponent of abortion bans; in 1980 most of his campaign money came from pro-abortion rights contributors. In the 1980s, he led fights to fund Title X family planning programs and to write *Roe v. Wade* into federal law; he was the first Senate Republican to oppose Robert Bork and only one of two Senate Republicans to oppose Clarence Thomas (Jeffords of Vermont was the other).

On foreign policy, Packwood has long been a staunch supporter of Israel and opponent of Arab arms sales, and quietly supported the Gulf war resolution. He has been more pro-environment than Hatfield, though he came down pretty harshly against the spotted owl. On economics, he tends to oppose regulations, favors free trade and wants to lower taxes, and played a key role on one of the key laws of the 1980s, the 1986 tax reform. As chairman of the Finance Committee, he started off with a bill that catered to Oregon interests—Packwood, as his support by pro-choice and pro-Israel lobbies shows, is not indifferent to the views of big contributors—but when he got in trouble at home, opposed in the May 20 primary by a young conservative, he found himself ridiculed as "Senator Hackwood" and "H & R Packwood with another of my 17 versions of tax reform." In late April, over a pitcher of beer with an aide, he started pencilling figures and came up with a bill that stripped away most tax preferences and lowered the top rate all the way to 27%—an approach that, with changes in details and some "perils of Pauline" maneuvering, carried the Finance Committee, the Senate and the conference committee and became law. In the meantime, Packwood won renomination by the none too huge margin of 58%–42%. No longer chairman in his fourth term, he fought against tax increases and for a capital gains cut, backed free trade (but got concessions to protect Oregon plywood), opposed reregulation of cable TV, and continued to back feminist causes. He tends to local issues, passing legislation to ban driftnet fishing and defeating the import tariff on sport utility vehicles and mini-vans.

One consistent thread going through Packwood's career is his partisan skill, which he played to the hilt in 1992. First, he persuaded the OCA not to support a primary opponent like the one who had nearly beaten him in 1986 or an independent candidate like the one who helped beat Dave Frohnmayer in the 1990 gubernatorial race. With help from Senate Republican campaign chairman Phil Gramm, Packwood stressed how his defeat would only hurt Republicans. He muted—but did not retract—his pro-choice stands and avoided any stand on anti-gay Measure 9 until after he had no opposition from the right. Meanwhile, Congressman Les AuCoin, popular in the Portland area, was hurt when it was revealed he had 83 overdrafts on the House bank, not seven as he first indicated; he was attacked as a Washington insider by Harry Lonsdale, fresh from his near-victory over Hatfield, for "perks, PACs and payraise." Packwood joined in, taking the unusual step of running an anti-AuCoin ad before the primary; it hurt AuCoin, who won by only 330 votes out of 362,000 cast, 42.2%–42.1%. After the primary, Packwood, with a huge campaign warchest raised from his Finance Committee perch and from feminists and Israel supporters, really hit AuCoin, with an ad showing a TV game show called "Hypocrisy." (Contestant: Congressional Hypocrites for $200. Host: This Oregon congressman voted himself a $30,000 pay raise after he said he wouldn't. Contestant: Who is Les AuCoin?) Packwood also hit AuCoin for protecting "bugs and birds," for opposing NAFTA, and for not saying how he would raise taxes to pay for his national healthcare plan. Packwood pinned the burdens of incumbency on AuCoin in an anti-incumbent year, and led throughout October; meanwhile, AuCoin's message was mostly negative, never sounding a hopeful note as Bill Clinton's did.

On October 29, Packwood coolly denied six women's charges of sexual harassment to *The Washington Post*, and asked for time to review records and gather information about the charges; on October 31, the *Post* told Packwood it wouldn't run a story before election day. Packwood won 52%–47%, losing metro Portland 54%–46% but carrying the rest of the state 56%–44%. Three weeks later the *Post* story ran, with the suggestion that it was odd that a supporter of feminist stands should be a sexual harasser; it might have easily argued that one opposed to enforcement of some traditional sexual mores might violate others. Packwood no longer denied the charges, asked for an Ethics Committee investigation and sought alcohol counseling. The Portland *Oregonian*, which had endorsed Packwood for reelection, called for his resignation; oddly, it turned out that he had kissed an *Oregonian* reporter during the campaign but that never came up in the story the *Post* published.

But Packwood remains resolute about staying in the Senate, despite grass-roots movements in Oregon calling for his resignation. In February 1993, more women came forward with charges of unsolicited advances on Packwood's part, and the case was referred to the Ethics Committee. In May 1993, the Senate Rules Committee voted unanimously to dismiss petitions brought by Oregonians to unseat Packwood. In any case, Packwood's clout will be diminished and it's hard to imagine he will run again or be elected in 1998. If he does leave the Senate, an Oregon law passed by referendum in 1986 requires an election and bars the governor from appointing a successor; if scheduled more than 80 days in advance, party primaries are held, otherwise candidates are nominated by party caucus. This could draw almost any famous and some non-famous names in Oregon politics—AuCoin or Portland Congressmen Ron Wyden or former

1058   OREGON

Governor Neil Goldschmidt or Portland's incoming Mayor Vera Katz among Democrats, or Republicans Dave Frohnmayer or Norma Paulus.

Presidential politics. Oregon, with its seven electoral votes, seemed an irrelevancy in presidential politics in the early 1980s. Now, as part of a 72-electoral-vote Pacific Coast bloc that gave George Bush less than one-third of its votes in 1992, it bulks rather large.

The halcyon days of Oregon's presidential primary are gone. This late May contest ended Harold Stassen's career as a serious presidential candidate in 1948, when he lost 52%–48% to Thomas Dewey, and it gave Robert Kennedy his only defeat in 1968. Oregon in those days was part of a West Coast campaign swing, just before the California primary; at a time when campaigners were not yet used to flying all over the country they, like National Football League teams in the 1950s, scheduled West Coast contests together to minimize travel time.

Important note: Crook County, a sparsely populated lumbering area east of the Cascades, was up through November 1992 the nation's bellwether county; the only county to vote through all its legal existence only for winning presidential candidates, it went for George Bush on November 3. Another victim of the spotted owl? Anyway, there won't be any national political reporters poking around Prineville in 1996.

Congressional districting. Oregon's divided legislature sought a bipartisan approach to redistricting, but a smoothing out of the lines necessarily had a partisan effect, reducing the Democratic percentage in the 1st District—which may have helped persuade Congressman Les AuCoin to run against Bob Packwood. Congressional politics here has a certain volatility, because distance and the lack of nonstop flights make it hard for even the most conscientious congressman to get back to the district very often. The Oregon House delegation averaged only six years of seniority as the 103d Congress convened.

The People: Est. Pop. 1992: 2,977,000; Pop. 1990: 2,842,321, up 4.5% 1990–1992. 1.1% of U.S. total, 29th largest; 30% rural. Median age: 34.5 years. 13.8% 65 years and over. 92.8% White, 4.0% Hispanic origin, 2.4% Asian, 1.6% Black, 1.4% American Indian, 1.8% Other. Households (1980): 55.6% married couple families; 25% married couple fams. w. children; 53% college educ.; median household income: $27,250; per capita income: $13,418; 63.1% owner occupied housing; median house value: $67,100; median monthly rent: $344. 7.5% Unemployment. Voting age pop.: 2,118,191; Registered voters (1992): 1,774,449; 792,115 D (45%); 641,914 R (36%); 340,420 unaffiliated and minor parties (19%).

Political Lineup: Governor, Barbara Roberts (D); Secy. of State, Phil Keisling (D); Atty. Gen., Ted Kulongoski (D); Treasurer, Jim Hill (D). State Senate, 30 (16 D and 14 R); State House of Representatives, 60 (32 R and 28 D). Senators, Mark O. Hatfield (R) and Bob Packwood (R). Representatives, 5 (4 D and 1 R).

1992 Presidential Vote

Clinton (D)	621,314	(43%)
Bush (R)	475,757	(33%)
Perot (I)	354,091	(24%)

1992 Democratic Presidential Primary

Clinton	159,802	(45%)
Brown	110,494	(31%)
Tsongas	37,139	(10%)
Other	13,357	(4%)
Miscellaneous	33,540	(9%)

1988 Presidential Vote

Dukakis (D)	616,206	(51%)
Bush (R)	560,126	(47%)

1992 Republican Presidential Primary

Bush	203,957	(67%)
Buchanan	57,730	(19%)
Miscellaneous	35,805	(12%)

GOVERNOR

Gov. Barbara Roberts (D)

Elected 1990, term expires Jan. 1995; b. Dec. 21, 1936, Corvallis; home, Salem; Portland St. U. 1961–64, Marylhurst Col., 1989–present; no religious affiliation; married (Frank).

Career: Accountant, office mgr., 1965–75; Parkrose Schl. Bd., 1973–83; Multnomah Cnty. Commissioner, 1978; OR House of Reps., 1981–85, Majority Ldr., 1983–84; OR Secy. of State, 1985–90.

Office: State Capitol, #254, Salem 97310, 503-378-3111.

Election Results

1990 gen.	Barbara Roberts (D)	508,749	(46%)
	Dave Frohnmayer (R)	444,646	(40%)
	Al Mobley (I)...............	144,062	(13%)
	Other	14,583	(1%)
1990 prim.	Barbara Roberts (D), unopposed		
1986 gen.	Neil Goldschmidt (D)	549,456	(52%)
	Norma Paulus (R)	506,989	(48%)

SENATORS

Sen. Mark O. Hatfield (R)

Elected 1966, seat up 1996; b. July 12, 1922, Dallas; home, Portland; Willamette U., B.A. 1943, Stanford, M.A. 1948; Baptist; married (Antoinette).

Career: Navy, 1943–46 (WWII); Prof., Willamette U., 1949–57; OR House of Reps., 1951–55; OR Senate, 1955–57; OR Secy. of State, 1956–58; OR Gov., 1958–66.

Offices: 711 HSOB 20510, 202-224-3753. Also 727 Center St., NE, #305, Salem 97301; and One World Trade Ctr., 121 SW Salmon St., #1420, Portland 97204.

Committees: *Appropriations* (RMM of 13 R): Commerce, Justice, State and Judiciary; Energy and Water Development (RMM); Interior; Labor, Health and Human Services, Education; Transportation. *Energy and Natural Resources* (2d of 9 R): Public Lands, National Parks and Forests; Renewable Energy, Energy Efficiency and Competitiveness; Water and Power. *Indian Affairs* (8th of 8 R). *Rules and Administration* (2d of 7 R). *Joint Committee on Printing* (5th of 5). *Joint Committee on the Library* (4th of 5).

Group Ratings

	ADA	ACLU	CDF	COPE	CFA	LCV	ACU	NTLC	NSI	COC	CEI
1992	70	68	80	75	67	42	23	44	40	56	37
1991	60	—	100	58	61	27	24	—	—	50	36

National Journal Ratings

	1991 LIB — 1991 CONS			1992 LIB — 1992 CONS		
Economic	42%	—	57%	41%	—	58%
Social	54%	—	44%	62%	—	36%
Foreign	60%	—	38%	60%.	—	38%

Key Votes of the 102d Congress

1. $ for Homeownership	AGN	5. Clarence Thomas Nom.	FOR	9. Use Force in Gulf	AGN
2. Have Cap Gains Debate	FOR	6. Lmt Death Row Appeal	FOR	10. Keep Salvador Aid	AGN
3. Remove Budget Walls	FOR	7. Handgun Wait/5-Day	FOR	11. Cut $1B from SDI	FOR
4. Ban Striker Replace	FOR	8. Abortion Gag Rule	AGN	12. Override China MFN	AGN

Key Votes of the 103d Congress

1. Family Leave	FOR	2. HIV Immigrants	FOR	3. Clinton Budget	AGN

Election Results

1990 general	Mark O. Hatfield (R)	590,095	(54%)	($2,714,661)
	Harry Lonsdale (D)	507,743	(46%)	($1,479,099)
1990 primary	Mark O. Hatfield (R)	220,449	(78%)	
	Randy Prince (R)	59,970	(21%)	
1984 general	Mark O. Hatfield (R)	808,152	(67%)	($671,167)
	Margie Hendriksen (D).	406,122	(33%)	($257,512)

Sen. Bob Packwood (R)

Elected 1968, seat up 1998; b. Sept 11, 1932, Portland; home, Portland; Willamette U., B.A. 1954, NY U., LL.B. 1957; Unitarian; divorced.

Career: Law Clerk, OR Supreme Court, 1957–58; Practicing atty., 1958–68; OR House of Reps., 1963–69.

Offices: 259 RSOB 20510, 202-224-5244. Also 101 SW Main St., #240, Portland 97204-3210, 503-294-3448.

Committees: *Commerce, Science and Transportation* (2d of 9 R): Communications (RMM); Foreign Commerce and Tourism; Surface Transportation. *Finance* (RMM of 9 R): International Trade; Medicare and Long-Term Care; Taxation. *Joint Committee on Taxation* (4th of 5).

Group Ratings

	ADA	ACLU	CDF	COPE	CFA	LCV	ACU	NTLC	NSI	COC	CEI
1992	60	67	90	50	50	25	33	56	90	30	40
1991	50	—	100	67	33	13	43	—	—	60	45

National Journal Ratings

	1991 LIB — 1991 CONS			1992 LIB — 1992 CONS		
Economic	41%	—	58%	45%	—	54%
Social	56%	—	43%	44%	—	54%
Foreign	39%	—	60%	47%	—	51%

Key Votes of the 102d Congress

1. $ for Homeownership	AGN	5. Clarence Thomas Nom.	AGN	9. Use Force in Gulf	FOR
2. Have Cap Gains Debate	FOR	6. Lmt Death Row Appeal	FOR	10. Keep Salvador Aid	FOR
3. Remove Budget Walls	FOR	7. Handgun Wait/5-Day	FOR	11. Cut $1B from SDI	AGN
4. Ban Striker Replace	FOR	8. Abortion Gag Rule	AGN	12. Override China MFN	AGN

Key Votes of the 103d Congress

1. Family Leave	FOR	2. HIV Immigrants	FOR	3. Clinton Budget	AGN

Election Results

1992 general	Bob Packwood (R)	717,455	(52%)	($8,034,249)
	Les AuCoin (D)	639,851	(47%)	($2,629,397)
	Others	18,727	(1%)	
1992 primary	Bob Packwood (R)	176,939	(59%)	
	John De Zell (R)	61,128	(20%)	
	Stephanie Jones Salvey (R)	27,088	(9%)	
	Randy Prince (R)	20,358	(7%)	
	Valentine Christian (R)	10,501	(4%)	
	Others	3,397	(1%)	
1986 general	Bob Packwood (R)	656,317	(63%)	($6,523,492)
	Rick Bauman (D)	375,735	(36%)	($64,139)

FIRST DISTRICT

Postmodern skyscrapers rising above the riverfront and below a range of hills: this is downtown Portland. The city started here, along the Willamette River just before it flows into the Columbia, and downtown was built on the narrow margin of land west of the river and below the hills, not on the flat expanse that stretches east to the snow-capped peak of Mount Hood. Downtown Portland was once a dowdy place, proper in a New Englandish way, with a few formal buildings above the warehouses and factories. But in the last decade there has been an explosion of creativity here, symbolized by handsome postmodern high-rises—the pyramid-crested brick KOIN Tower, the wedge-shaped Justice Center—and restored Victorian store-fronts and a downtown transit trolley, the new light rail line know as MAX (Metropolitan Area Express), and just across the river the new Oregon Museum of Science and Industry. Portland is the proud home of Nike athletic shoes, and of the Wieden and Kennedy advertising firm that created the "Just Do It" campaign.

Similarly, the affluent neighborhoods in the hills overlooking downtown are full of old lumber barons' mansions with splendid views, as well as postmodern houses with hot tubs. Just over the hills are the valleys and interstices between green mountains of suburban Washington County. Not so long ago this was a farm county, with 39,000 people in 1940; now it has 311,000 and is an integral part of metro Portland. This is an affluent area with a high-tech aura; computer and high-tech companies have been flocking to what some call Silicon Forest, attracted by an environment—at the foot of mountains, woodsy and even rustic but outfitted with all the comforts and services of modern civilization—that appeals to a high-skill work force.

Downtown Portland and its western hills, plus a bit of the residential areas east of the Willamette, and Washington County make up the bulk of Oregon's 1st Congressional District. The 1st also proceeds northwest along the Columbia to Astoria and the Pacific Coast, and southwest to Yamhill County, where metro growth is spreading. Like Oregon, the 1st District is historically New England Republican, electing only Republican congressmen from 1892 to 1972; like New England, it then trended sharply left on cultural issues, even as its high-tech economy brought new affluence, and since 1974 it has been Democratic. For 18 years, it was represented by Les AuCoin, a quintessential Watergate-era Democrat, a state legislator at 28 and congressman at 32, consistently dovish on foreign policy and inclined to liberal cultural stands, concerned about the environment and a proud champion of legalized abortion. AuCoin ended up a power in the House and ran for the Senate in 1992; he lost 52%–47% to Bob Packwood, in large part because he had 83 overdrafts on the House bank—an example perhaps of his political skill catching up on him. AuCoin surely would have won if *The Washington Post* had printed charges of sexual harassment against Senator Bob Packwood just before, rather than just after, the election, and he remains a viable statewide candidate.

One reason AuCoin opted for the Senate race is that two heavily Democratic coastal counties were removed from the 1st, and remaining Washington County often votes Republican. But while AuCoin broke only even here, the 1st voted for Bill Clinton and stayed Democratic in the House race, indeed voted for one of the leftmost new Democrats in the country. By conventional reckoning, Elizabeth Furse was the underdog in both the primary and general elections. Her primary opponent, Gary Conkling, used to work for AuCoin and the 3rd District's Ron Wyden, and was an advocate of such Oregon initiatives as the healthcare rationing program and Portland's light rail. But Furse's credentials as founder of the Oregon Peace Institute and her attacks on Conkling as a lobbyist, the funds she raised from EMILY's List and women generally, propelled her to a 60%–40% win. Her general election opponent was also, by past standards, well suited to the district. State Treasurer Tony Meeker, as a Republican legislator, sponsored Oregon's successful bottle bill; he was endorsed by the *Oregonian* and led in most polls. But voters did not take to Meeker's antiabortion position and Furse made her pro-choice policy a cornerstone of her campaign. Moreover, Meeker was whipsawed on anti-gay Measure 9: he was against it, as were a large majority of 1st District voters, but the OCA phone banks encouraged conservatives to vote against him. Furse outorganized Meeker and, echoing Clinton's jobs and change themes, won 52%–48%.

Furse comes to Washington with an unusual background. She was born a colonist, the daughter of British parents in Kenya; at 15 she marched as a member of Black Sash, an anti-apartheid group, in South Africa; she became a U.S. citizen in 1972 and taught self-sufficiency to women in Watts, California, volunteered for the United Farm Workers, and became an advocate for American Indian treaty rights in Washington. She moved to Oregon in 1978 and worked to restore rights of Indians and managed the successful 1982 state nuclear freeze referendum. With her husband, she owns a vineyard in Washington County. She can be expected to be a solid liberal vote in the House, voting mostly as AuCoin would have, but more ideology-driven. It will be interesting to see whether she can maintain and increase her support in this primarily suburban and upscale district.

The People: Pop. 1990: 568,501; 18% rural; 12% age 65+; 91% White; 1% Black; 1% American Indian; 3% Asian; 2% Other; 4% Hispanic origin. Voting age pop.: 425,759; 1% Black; 3% Hispanic origin. Households: 56% married couple families; 26% married couple fams. w. children; 64% college educ.; median household income: $33,227; per capita income: $17,120; median gross rent: $453; median house value: $84,500.

1992 Presidential Vote		1988 Presidential Vote	
Clinton (D)	136,630 (44%)	Dukakis (D)	119,198 (50%)
Bush (R)	99,304 (32%)	Bush (R)	116,864 (50%)
Perot (I)	73,134 (24%)		

Rep. Elizabeth Furse (D)

Elected 1992; b. Oct. 13, 1936, Nairobi, Kenya; home, Hillsboro; Evergreen St. Col., B.A. 1974; Protestant; married (John Platt).

Career: Owner, Helvetia Vineyards, 1983-present; Founder & Dir., Oregon Peace Instit., 1985–1991; Dir., Restoration Prog. for Native American Tribes, 1980–86.

Offices: 316 CHOB 20515, 202-225-0855. Also 2701 NW Vaughn, #860, Portland 97210, 503-326-2901.

Committees: *Armed Services* (33d of 34 D): Research and Technology. *Banking, Finance and Urban Affairs* (22d of 30 D): Consumer Credit and Insurance; Housing and Community Development; International Development, Finance, Trade and Monetary Policy. *Merchant Marine and Fisheries* (17th of 29 D): Environment and Natural Resources; Merchant Marine.

Group Ratings and 102d Congress Votes: Newly Elected

Key Votes of the 103d Congress

1. Family Leave	FOR	2. Deficit Reduction	FOR	3. Stimulus Plan	FOR

Election Results

1992 general	Elizabeth Furse (D).................	152,917	(52%)	($778,290)
	Tony Meeker (R)...................	140,986	(48%)	($719,611)
1992 primary	Elizabeth Furse (D).................	38,600	(60%)	
	Gary Conkling (D)	25,684	(40%)	
1990 general	Les AuCoin (D)	150,292	(63%)	($445,342)
	Earl Molander (R)	72,382	(30%)	($2,024)
	Rick Livingston (I).................	15,585	(7%)	($32,309)

SECOND DISTRICT

Walling eastern Oregon off from the rest of the state are the Cascades, the magnificent chain of once (quite possibly still) volcanic mountains that drain almost every drop of moisture out of the air coming in from the Pacific and that separate green, wet western Oregon from the brown, parched east. Eastern Oregon has 70% of the state's land, but only 365,000 of its 2.8 million people, most of whom still make their living off the land: beef and dairy cattle, timber and lumber, fish from the Columbia River and wheat from the irrigated plains. The effect of the Cascades can be tactilely gauged in the one place they are breached—by the Columbia River Gorge. Here, surrounded by brown hills on both sides, funneled winds pound in steadily from the west, making the Columbia the best windsurfing site in the United States.

This mostly skipped-over land has—or, rather, had—one political distinction. For in the heart of eastern Oregon, amid forested slopes and bare plateaus, is Crook County, which, after Palo Alto County, Iowa, voted for Walter Mondale in 1984, stood as the only county of the nation's 3,143 that had voted for the popular vote winner in every presidential election since its creation (in 1882). Crook County is lumber country, almost entirely white Protestants, "a red-neck, white-sock county," Jay Mathews, of *The Washington Post*, quoted a school librarian as saying; Mathews was one of several national reporters who flocked to the county seat of Prineville in the 1988 and 1992 cycles to see where the country was going. Alas, these reporters did not get a very good idea in 1992. For Prineville and Crook County were furious that the spotted owl was threatening their lumber livelihood and they angrily rejected (voting 63% for Measure 9) the

1064   OREGON

cultural liberalism of metro Portland, Governor Barbara Roberts and Bill Clinton. Crook County voted a second time for George Bush, and now the nation and its political reporters must make do without a bellwether county.

The 2d Congressional District of Oregon covers all of the state east of the Cascades and the southernmost valley between the Cascades and the Coast Range. Population concentrations here are far apart: Pendleton in the northeastern wheat fields; La Grande in the rich Grande Ronde Valley; The Dalles where the Columbia River Gorge begins; Bend in the center of the state, near Crook County. In the southwestern corner, separated from other areas by the Cascades and the once huge volcano whose blown-off cone is now 2,000-foot deep Crater Lake, is the lumber and pear orchard country around Medford, Ashland, Klamath Falls and Grants Pass. Like most of the intermountain west, the 2d District is mostly Republican, and voted for George Bush, though by smaller than usual margins, in 1992.

The 2d is represented in the House by Bob Smith, a cattle rancher and 22-year veteran of the Oregon legislature who led the Republicans in both houses. He looks rough-hewn in his cowboy boots and western shirts, but he is also a skilled legislator. One proud accomplishment was an amendment to the 1988 Drought Relief Act, limiting feed grain aid to only those farmers who grow their own feed grain. Another was a rural healthcare law, co-sponsored with Portland Democrat Ron Wyden, which provides tax credits and educational benefits to attract medical personnel to underserved areas. Smith personally negotiated a $105 million wheat sale to Turkey and is critical of European farm subsidies and trade barriers. He has been less successful in his fight to eviscerate the Endangered Species Act before it (in his view) eviscerates the Pacific Northwest lumber industry; he has opposed the limited measures supported by Oregon Democrats ("the largest legislative lockup of public lands in the history of the lower 48 states") and is death on the spotted owl. He has been odd man out before, opposing the 1984 Oregon Wilderness law and the 1988 Wild and Scenic Rivers Act which passed anyway with support from other Oregon members. Now, as ranking member on the Natural Resources Oversight and Investigations Subcommittee, he will have to match his political skill against subcommittee chairman George Miller from neighboring California, a strong environmentalist and architect of many pro-environment laws affecting Oregon.

Smith won this seat in 1982 when then-incumbent Denny Smith (no relation) decided to run in the newly created Willamette Valley 5th District, a much more marginal seat (he lost it in 1990). Bob Smith won the 1982 Republican primary with 63% and the general with 56% and has had no trouble holding the seat since; he won by 2–1 margins in anti-incumbent 1990 and 1992. Redistricting did not affect the district's boundaries much. Smith may consider a run for governor in 1994.

The People: Pop. 1990: 568,437; 50% rural; 16% age 65+; 91% White; 2% American Indian; 1% Asian; 3% Other; 5% Hispanic origin. Voting age pop.: 417,866; 4% Hispanic origin. Households: 61% married couple families; 26% married couple fams. w. children; 44% college educ.; median household income: $23,949; per capita income: $11,704; median gross rent: $363; median house value: $62,400.

1992 Presidential Vote			1988 Presidential Vote		
Bush (R)	106,696	(38%)	Bush (R)	126,631	(56%)
Clinton (D)	97,458	(35%)	Dukakis (D)	100,624	(44%)
Perot (I)	74,346	(27%)			

Rep. Robert F. (Bob) Smith (R)

Elected 1982; b. June 16, 1931, Portland; home, Burns; Willamette U., B.A. 1953; Presbyterian; married (Kaye).

Career: Cattle rancher; OR House of Reps., 1960–72, Speaker 1968–72; OR Senate, 1972–82.

Offices: 108 CHOB 20515, 202-225-6730. Also 771 Ponderosa Village, Burns 97720, 800-533-3303; and 259 Barrett Rd., Medford 97501, 503-776-4646.

Committees: *Agriculture* (5th of 19 R): Department Operations and Nutrition (RMM); General Farm Commodities; Livestock. *Natural Resources* (5th of 15 R): National Parks, Forests and Public Lands; Oversight and Investigations (RMM).

Group Ratings

	ADA	ACLU	COPE	CDF	CFA	LCV	ACU	NTLC	NSI	COC	CEI
1992	5	4	25	30	13	0	92	75	100	75	82
1991	5	—	17	20	22	0	85	—	—	90	68

National Journal Ratings

	1991 LIB — 1991 CONS		1992 LIB — 1992 CONS	
Economic	18%	— 79%	21%	— 76%
Social	6%	— 84%	0%	— 85%
Foreign	0%	— 88%	18%	— 74%

Key Votes of the 102d Congress

1. Ban Striker Replace	AGN	5. Handgun Wait/7-Day	AGN	9. Use Force in Gulf	FOR
2. $ for Homeownership	FOR	6. Overseas Mil. Abortion	AGN	10. US Mil. Abroad $ Cut	AGN
3. Tax Rich/Cut Mid Cls.	AGN	7. Obscn. Art NEA $ Ban	FOR	11. Limit SDI Funds	AGN
4. FY93/$15B Def. Cut	AGN	8. Death Pen. from Jury	FOR	12. Cuba Trade Embargo	FOR

Key Votes of the 103d Congress

1. Family Leave	AGN	2. Deficit Reduction	AGN	3. Stimulus Plan	AGN

Election Results

1992 general	Robert F. (Bob) Smith (R)	184,163	(67%)	($401,670)
	Denzel Ferguson (D)	90,036	(33%)	($87,361)
1992 primary	Robert F. (Bob) Smith (R)	63,213	(99%)	
	Other	897	(1%)	
1990 general	Robert F. (Bob) Smith (R)	127,998	(68%)	($284,700)
	Jim Smiley (D)	60,131	(32%)	

THIRD DISTRICT

Portland, Oregon, is one of the least known of America's great metropolises, with a spirit all its own. This is one of the few American cities with a new light rail system which runs a line down the middle of the Banfield Freeway, and a free transit system for the downtown shopping district. It has a rare collection of post-modern architecture downtown, and when the clouds dissipate, views of the glorious peak of Mount Hood from almost every quarter. It has a Metropolitan Greenspaces program, which is expanding its inventory of natural areas. Portland is proud of its New England beginnings (had a coin toss come up heads, it would have been called Boston) and its traditional Rose Festival. It also boasts of its local breweries (the most in the country, it is said) and its bicycle paths.

Portland's economy, to be sure, is more basic than boutique: it is in many ways a muscular, blue-collar town where Oregon unloaded its supplies from the east on the docks or in the railroad yards, and where it shipped out Oregon's products, mainly lumber and fruit. But Portland has also generated high-tech companies and businesses like Nike athletic shoes, which attract younger people with white-collar jobs and liberal cultural attitudes. Portland has been particularly conscious for the last two decades that it is on the Pacific Rim, living more and more on foreign trade, seeing East Asians as customers rather than competitors: this is the one major U.S. metro area from which you cannot fly nonstop to Washington, D.C., but you can to Tokyo.

The 3d Congressional District of Oregon takes in most of Portland and Multnomah County east of the Willamette River, extending over suburban plains and hills to the splendid scenery of the Bonneville Dam in the Columbia River Gorge and Mount Hood high in the Cascades. It is a middle-class, largely white district that voted solidly Democratic in national and state elections throughout the 1980s and was strongly for Bill Clinton in 1992.

The 3rd District's Ron Wyden, after a dozen years in the House, is poised to be a key player on the key issue of health care in the 103d Congress. Wyden first became well-known in Portland as director of the Oregon Gray Panthers, an advocacy group for the elderly; he was the spark behind the referendum to reduce the price of dentures. In 1980, he beat an incumbent congressman in the Democratic primary 60%–40%, and has held onto the district without trouble, indeed by impressive margins, ever since.

Wyden came to Washington just as Ronald Reagan was becoming president and John Dingell chairman of the Energy and Commerce Committee. Wyden has a friendly style, but also the political shrewdness to get a seat on Energy and Commerce, and on Henry Waxman's Health and the Environment Subcommittee and Dingell's Investigations panel—and to remain on excellent terms with both even as they fought for years over the Clean Air Act. Working closely under Dingell's direction on Investigations, Wyden sponsored health measures that were not Waxman's prime concern and used his Small Business subcommittee chair to spotlight some issues. He has a genius for coming up with sensible-sounding ideas no one else has thought of and a knack for making the counter-intuitive political alliances which are so helpful in passing unfamiliar measures through the House.

Wyden's most recent bill, sponsored with Connecticut Republican Nancy Johnson, provides federal payment of malpractice premiums for doctors working in federally funded clinics—a practical way to get more care for the poor. He also passed a law to conserve the Pacific yew, a rare tree needed to produce a cancer-fighting drug, and a WIC Infant Formula Act to prohibit manufacturers from engaging in anti-competitive bidding practices. He got a Fertility Clinic Success Rate and Certification Act through the House in 1992, and has argued that the French abortifacient drug RU-486 should no longer be banned in the U.S. because similar multi-hormonal drugs have been useful in treating cancer. He strongly supported Oregon's innovative health plan that rations coverage by treatment, and decried President Bush for vetoing it, though he acknowledged that Bush's concerns about the Americans with Disabilities Act were not frivolous. Wyden was part of an informal group of House Democrats, convened by Richard Gephardt in 1992, to come up with legislative options for a passable healthcare plan, and will likely be involved in any major healthcare legislation in 1993. His own approach to hold down healthcare costs is to set up a managed competition system but have overall caps on spending if costs get too high. He has become involved in trade issues, generally favoring free trade, but calling for an environmental commission before the Mexico free trade agreement is implemented.

With a safe district and a busy workload in the House, Wyden passed up chances to run against Senators Bob Packwood and Mark Hatfield in 1986, 1990 and 1992. He could be a candidate, however, if Packwood's seat opens up midterm.

The People: Pop. 1990: 568,276; 6% rural; 13% age 65+; 86% White; 6% Black; 1% Amer. Indian; 4% Asian; 1% Other; 3% Hispanic origin. Voting age pop.: 427,976; 5% Black; 3% Hispanic origin. Households: 49% married couple families; 22% married couple fams. w. children; 53% college educ.; median household income: $27,150; per capita income: $13,167; median gross rent: $414; median house value: $59,300.

1992 Presidential Vote

Clinton (D)	146,835	(53%)
Bush (R)	72,338	(26%)
Perot (I)	58,900	(21%)

1988 Presidential Vote

Dukakis (D)	151,683	(62%)
Bush (R)	93,690	(38%)

Rep. Ron Wyden (D)

Elected 1980; b. May 3, 1949, Wichita, KS; home, Portland; Stanford U., B.A. 1971, U. of OR, J.D. 1974; Jewish; married (Laurie).

Career: Co-Dir. and Co-Founder, OR Gray Panthers, 1974–80; Dir., OR Legal Svcs. for the Elderly, 1977–79; Prof. of Gerontology, U. of OR, 1976, Portland St. U., 1979, U. of Portland, 1980.

Offices: 1111 LHOB 20515, 202-225-4811. Also 500 NE Multnomah, #250, Portland 97232, 503-231-2300.

Committees: *Energy and Commerce* (9th of 27 D): Health and the Environment; Oversight and Investigations; Telecommunications and Finance. *Small Business* (5th of 27 D): Regulation, Business Opportunities and Technology (Chmn.). *Joint Economic Committee* (5th of 10).

Group Ratings

	ADA	ACLU	COPE	CDF	CFA	LCV	ACU	NTLC	NSI	COC	CEI
1992	95	87	73	100	100	81	0	0	30	25	13
1991	85	—	83	100	83	77	5	—	—	30	11

National Journal Ratings

	1991 LIB — 1991 CONS		1992 LIB — 1992 CONS	
Economic	72%	— 23%	78%	— 18%
Social	73%	— 26%	88%	— 8%
Foreign	92%	— 0%	90%	— 0%

Key Votes of the 102d Congress

1. Ban Striker Replace	FOR	5. Handgun Wait/7-Day	FOR	9. Use Force in Gulf	AGN
2. $ for Homeownership	AGN	6. Overseas Mil. Abortion	FOR	10. US Mil. Abroad $ Cut	FOR
3. Tax Rich/Cut Mid Cls.	FOR	7. Obscn. Art NEA $ Ban	AGN	11. Limit SDI Funds	FOR
4. FY93/$15B Def. Cut	FOR	8. Death Pen. from Jury	FOR	12. Cuba Trade Embargo	AGN

Key Votes of the 103d Congress

1. Family Leave	FOR	2. Deficit Reduction	FOR	3. Stimulus Plan	FOR

FOURTH DISTRICT

Eugene sits in the last bit of lowland at the south end of Oregon's Willamette Valley, beset by mountains on three sides; it is a farming center, lumber metropolis and, most notably, university town. Settlers first arrived here in 1846, farming in the valley and cutting timber in the hills. In 1876, the University of Oregon was established, a symbol of Oregon's strong Yankee cultural ethic and sparse settlement: its first graduating class had just five students. Thousands of miles from most Americans, Eugene and next-door Springfield have grown steadily into the comfortable middle-sized towns in which many Americans would like to live. The university gives this part of Oregon a special bean-sprout tone. Eugene has bicycle paths along the river banks and on main streets and likes to bill itself as the Running Capital of the Universe.

Beyond the Eugene city limits is a different atmosphere. This is timber country: surrounded by green-clad mountains, southwestern Oregon around Eugene and the southwest coast cuts more timber than any place else in the country. But demand for wood is volatile, dependent on the vagaries of interest rates; and the demand from East Asia is increasingly for unprocessed logs rather than milled lumber, which means fewer jobs for Oregon. The early 1980s, when recession reduced the demand for housing, were tough on southern Oregon; the late 1980s, when cutting of old-growth forests was banned to protect the endangered spotted owl, was even worse. In between, many big lumber companies switched their major operations to the pinelands of the Southeastern U.S., while sawmills ran short of work because of log exports to the Far East. Voters in the timber areas are culturally conservative and economically interventionist, seeking bans on export of unprocessed logs and revision of the Endangered Species Act to allow logging to go on despite the spotted owl.

The congressman from the 4th Congressional District of Oregon, Peter DeFazio, is a Watergate-era liberal Democrat who worked as a staffer for Congressman James Weaver; in 1982, he moved to Springfield and won a seat on the county commission, and then his House seat in a 1986 three-way race. In Congress, DeFazio has compiled a record that seems to satisfy both Eugene and the rest of the district. He is liberal on many issues, sometimes stridently so; he was one of the congressmen who brought suit against U.S. intervention in the Persian gulf, and responded to the Gulf war almost hysterically, calling for both a cease-fire and use of nuclear weapons—bad judgment in both directions. He held up passage of an Urban Aid bill for two days in an effort to increase Social Security spending for "notch babies." His persistence on the issue surely irritated some of his colleagues and may have cost him a seat on the Appropriations Committee in 1993. His most pressing issue, of course, was the federal court ruling that old-growth forests cannot be logged in order to preserve the spotted owl (almost no one has ever seen a spotted owl, by the way; they're very shy). DeFazio, representing the nation's number one timbering and one of its most enviro-conscious districts, has produced a middle position which would reduce the no-logging buffer zone in return for what he calls "a much more sensitive form of management." For his pains, he was attacked by timber interests and portrayed as Smokey the Bear with a chain saw by one environmental group.

The 4th District used to be a marginal district, because it is farther in flight time from the U.S. Capitol than any other in the continental United States. To get back to Washington, D.C.

takes an eleven hour flight that includes a stop and change of planes. (Now at least you can fly out of Eugene instead of having to drive two hours to the Portland airport.) But DeFazio has put much effort into tending to the district and tries to get back three weekends a month and has put much of his staff into district offices. DeFazio thought about making the 1992 Senate race against Bob Packwood, but deferred to Les AuCoin; it's possible he may run for the Senate some time in the future.

The People: Pop. 1990: 568,395; 39% rural; 15% age 65+; 95% White; 1% American Indian; 1% Asian; 1% Other; 2% Hispanic origin. Voting age pop.: 425,193; 2% Hispanic origin. Households: 58% married couple families; 25% married couple fams. w. children; 49% college educ.; median household income: $24,593; per capita income: $11,919; median gross rent: $390; median house value: $60,400.

1992 Presidential Vote			1988 Presidential Vote		
Clinton (D)	123,593	(42%)	Dukakis (D)	126,545	(55%)
Bush (R)	94,032	(32%)	Bush (R)	105,487	(45%)
Perot (I)	74,640	(25%)			

Rep. Peter A. DeFazio (D)

Elected 1986; b. May 27, 1947, Needham, MA; home, Springfield; Tufts U., B.A. 1969, U. of OR, M.S. 1977; Catholic; married (Myrnie).

Career: Air Force, 1967–71; Dist. Office Dir., U.S. Rep. James Weaver, 1977–82; Lane Cnty. Bd. of Commissioners, 1982–86.

Offices: 1233 LHOB 20515, 202-225-6416. Also 215 S. 2d St., Coos Bay 97420, 503-269-2609; 211 E. 7th Ave., Eugene 97401, 503-465-6732; and 621 W. Madrone, #406, P.O. Box 126, Roseburg 97470, 503-440-3523.

Committees: *Natural Resources* (12th of 28 D): Energy and Mineral Resources; National Parks, Forests and Public Lands; Oversight and Investigations. *Public Works and Transportation* (11th of 39 D): Aviation; Surface Transportation.

Group Ratings

	ADA	ACLU	COPE	CDF	CFA	LCV	ACU	NTLC	NSI	COC	CEI
1992	90	95	82	80	87	75	9	0	30	25	16
1991	80	—	100	90	72	77	11	—	—	20	13

National Journal Ratings

	1991 LIB — 1991 CONS		1992 LIB — 1992 CONS	
Economic	56% —	42%	71% —	27%
Social	77% —	22%	87% —	13%
Foreign	72% —	28%	90% —	0%

Key Votes of the 102d Congress

1. Ban Striker Replace	FOR	5. Handgun Wait/7-Day	AGN	9. Use Force in Gulf	AGN
2. $ for Homeownership	AGN	6. Overseas Mil. Abortion	FOR	10. US Mil. Abroad $ Cut	FOR
3. Tax Rich/Cut Mid Cls.	FOR	7. Obscn. Art NEA $ Ban	AGN	11. Limit SDI Funds	FOR
4. FY93/$15B Def. Cut	FOR	8. Death Pen. from Jury	AGN	12. Cuba Trade Embargo	AGN

Key Votes of the 103d Congress

1. Family Leave	FOR	2. Deficit Reduction	FOR	3. Stimulus Plan	FOR

Election Results

1992 general	Peter A. DeFazio (D)	199,372	(71%)	($301,116)
	Richard L. Schulz (R)	79,733	(29%)	($6,348)
1992 primary	Peter A. DeFazio (D), unopposed			
1990 general	Peter A. DeFazio (D)	162,494	(86%)	($217,527)
	Tonie Nathan (LIB)	26,432	(14%)	($3,343)

FIFTH DISTRICT

The Willamette Valley was the great promised land at the end of the Oregon Trail, one of America's most fertile valleys, shielded by the Coast Range from the cold storms of the Pacific but squeezing most of the moisture out of the clouds in the form of rain, fog, and persistent mist. Here, New England Yankees planted small towns they called Salem and Albany and Oregon City, founded schools and colleges, built high-spired churches and eventually Salem's cylindrical-domed Art Deco state Capitol. This was one of the few valleys in the West which settlers found readily suitable for agriculture. California's great valleys depend on irrigation as does the cultivation of wheat in eastern Washington. But in the Willamette Valley the soil is fertile, the plain created by the waters of the Willamette sweeping down from the mountains is broad, and the rains everyone hears about in Oregon are dependable. But this is not only farming country now: metro Portland is spreading south and young people seeking a pleasant environment are moving into the neat little cities and towns between the two mountain ranges.

The 5th Congressional District of Oregon includes much of the northern Willamette Valley. Near Portland it has the old pioneer town of Oregon City, and spreads south to the state capital of Salem (rather conservative) and Corvallis (home of Oregon State University and quite liberal). Then the district hops over the Coast Range to take in Lincoln and Tillamook Counties, fishing and logging and cheesemaking communities (strongly Democratic) and now also includes all of Polk County. Historically, the Willamette Valley was Republican, like the New England whence most of its settlers came, but, also like New England, it has been trending Democratic on cultural issues. The 5th voted for Bill Clinton in 1992, crossed over for Bob Packwood, but voted against the anti-gay Measure 9 and, by nearly a 2–1 margin, to reelect its freshman Democratic congressman, Mike Kopetski.

Kopetski won the seat in 1990 by beating Republican Denny Smith, who in turn had beaten House Ways and Means Chairman Al Ullman in 1980 and had beaten Kopetski by only 707 votes in 1988. Kopetski is a classic Watergate era liberal Democrat—he was a staffer on the Senate Watergate committee—who served two years in the Oregon House; he ran as a strong pro-choicer on abortion but took a middle-ground position on the spotted owl issue. In the House and on the Agriculture Committee, he spent much time on the issue, getting it to approve in June 1992 his owl preservation plan (Alternative 8A of 14 plans) developed by a congressionally appointed "Gang of Four" scientists. Though Kopetski was lauded for passing a plan on such a heated issue, it came under attack by many Republicans, including the 2d District's Bob Smith, and by Democrats, like Indiana's Jim Jontz, who wanted less logging—and Kopetski got PAC contributions from both the Sierra Club and Weyerhaeuser. Kopetski's other big achievement was getting the House to place a one-year moratorium on nuclear test explosions; he argued that the tests aren't scientifically needed, but he admitted the reason it passed was the collapse of the Soviet Union. On other issues, he mostly voted a partisan line, breaking notably by voting to uphold President Bush's vetoes of cable reregulation and the bill conditioning extension of most favored nation status to China.

Kopetski's legislative and electoral prowess payed off in December 1992 when he received a seat on the Ways and Means Committee.

The People: Pop. 1990: 568,712; 35% rural; 13% age 65+; 91% White; 1% Black; 1% American Indian; 2% Asian; 2% Other; 5% Hispanic origin. Voting age pop.: 421,120; 1% Black; 4% Hispanic origin. Households: 60% married couple families; 27% married couple fams. w. children; 53% college educ.; median household income: $28,608; per capita income: $13,180; median gross rent: $403; median house value: $69,100.

1992 Presidential Vote			1988 Presidential Vote		
Clinton (D)	116,798	(40%)	Dukakis (D)	118,156	(50%)
Bush (R)	103,387	(35%)	Bush (R)	117,454	(50%)
Perot (I)	73,071	(25%)			

Rep. Mike Kopetski (D)

Elected 1990; b. Oct. 27, 1949, Pendleton; home, Salem; American U., B.A. 1971, Lewis & Clark Col., J.D. 1978; no religious affiliation; divorced.

Career: Staff Aide, Senate Watergate Cmte., 1973–74; Cmte. admin., OR House of Reps., 1977–79, 1981; Labor-mgmt., educ. consultant, 1981–84; OR House of Reps., 1984–88; Vice Pres., Currier-McCormick Communications, 1989–90.

Offices: 218 CHOB 20515, 202-225-5711. Also Equitable Ctr. Bldg., #340, 530 Center St., NE, Salem 97301, 503-588-9100.

Committees: *Ways and Means* (21st of 24 D): Human Resources; Select Revenue Measures.

Group Ratings

	ADA	ACLU	COPE	CDF	CFA	LCV	ACU	NTLC	NSI	COC	CEI
1992	85	96	67	100	67	63	4	0	30	38	13
1991	75	—	83	90	56	54	5	—	—	20	13

National Journal Ratings

	1991 LIB — 1991 CONS		1992 LIB — 1992 CONS	
Economic	59%	— 40%	71%	— 27%
Social	73%	— 26%	85%	— 13%
Foreign	78%	— 19%	90%	— 0%

Key Votes of the 102d Congress

1. Ban Striker Replace	FOR	5. Handgun Wait/7-Day	AGN	9. Use Force in Gulf	AGN
2. $ for Homeownership	AGN	6. Overseas Mil. Abortion	FOR	10. US Mil. Abroad $ Cut	FOR
3. Tax Rich/Cut Mid Cls.	FOR	7. Obscn. Art NEA $ Ban	AGN	11. Limit SDI Funds	FOR
4. FY93/$15B Def. Cut	FOR	8. Death Pen. from Jury	AGN	12. Cuba Trade Embargo	AGN

Key Votes of the 103d Congress

1. Family Leave	FOR	2. Deficit Reduction	FOR	3. Stimulus Plan	FOR

Election Results

1992 general	Mike Kopetski (D)	174,443	(64%)	($325,620)
	Jim Seagraves (R)	97,984	(36%)	($39,612)
1992 primary	Mike Kopetski (D)	55,461	(99%)	
	Other	495	(1%)	
1990 general	Mike Kopetski (D)	124,610	(55%)	($844,797)
	Denny Smith (R)	101,650	(45%)	($884,828)

PENNSYLVANIA

Pennsylvania, long a backwater in American politics, the megastate least transformed economically and culturally over the last half-century, emerged in the 1992 electoral cycle not once but several times as the central focus of American politics. In 1991, the special Senate election made necessary by the tragic death of Senator John Heinz produced an upset victory for Democrat Harris Wofford that in important ways presaged the presidential result of 1992: spotlighting the healthcare issue and showing severe Republican losses in the suburbs. Then Pennsylvania became the venue for struggles over cultural issues. Governor Robert Casey's limited abortion restrictions were upheld by the Supreme Court in June 1992, but in this *Casey* decision, three Republican appointees refused to overturn *Roe v. Wade*. Meanwhile, the 1992 Pennsylvania Senate race was heralded as a test of opinion on the charges made by Anita Hill against Justice Clarence Thomas the year before. The Democratic nomination to oppose incumbent Arlen Specter, who had questioned Hill persistently and charged at one point that she had committed perjury, was won by Lynn Yeakel, a political neophyte whose ads featured Specter questioning Hill. Pennsylvania was important in other respects: for incumbent defeats in the April congressional primary; as the site of Jerry Brown's presidential campaign announcement in front of Independence Hall; its large poll margins for Bill Clinton which meant that George Bush would have had to carry almost every conceivable state to win. But if Pennsylvania was the setting for many political arguments, it did not settle them. Wofford won solidly, 55%–45%, in 1991, but could not immediately enact one of his primary objectives, national health insurance. Bill Clinton carried the state, but with a 45%–36% plurality—lower shares of the vote than Michael Dukakis or Walter Mondale. Pennsylvania has not obviously become a solidly Democratic state, as it seemed to in the New Deal years. Lynn Yeakel's much-ballyhooed campaign fell short, with Arlen Specter winning 49%–46%. Perhaps 1994, when Wofford's seat is up again, and when Casey must step down, will see more conclusive results in the Keystone state.

Pennsylvania started off as the center of America. Philadelphia was the 13 colonies' largest city when it hosted the Continental Congress in 1776 and the Constitutional Convention in 1787. This was one of the newer colonies, founded 50 years after Massachusetts and 70 years after Virginia. Under the benevolent rule of the Penns and with its Quaker traditions, Pennsylvania soon became the major settlement in the Middle Colonies: its tolerance attracted Englishmen of all religious sects as well as Germans. The rich green farmlands west to the first Appalachian chain filled rapidly. Bordermen from Scotland, Yorkshire and Northern Ireland crossed the corduroy-like ridges and settled the mountainous interior where General Braddock had been beaten by the French and Indians not long before, and where a decade later George Washington would again lead troops when the Whiskey Rebellion flared up. On the banks of a wide estuary, with its thriving commerce and rich hinterland, Philadelphia seemed destined to be the London of America, the capital and metropolis and academy all rolled into one. But Philadelphia, and Pennsylvania, failed to hold the central position the Founders had expected. The nation's capital was sited on the Potomac rather than the Delaware as part of a political deal, and the Erie Canal and the water-level railroad from the Hudson to Lake Erie channeled trade away from Philadelphia to New York. Philadelphia's Quaker tradition, tolerant of diversity and indifferent to others' behavior, was overshadowed in intellectual life by New England's Puritan tradition, angrily intolerant and always ready to use the state to impose cultural values from abolitionism to prohibition and women's rights. So, in antebellum America, Philadelphia was eclipsed by Washington in government, New York in commerce and Boston in culture.

Instead, Pennsylvania became America's energy and heavy industry capital. The key was coal. Northeast Pennsylvania became the nation's primary source of anthracite, the hard coal used for home heating, and western Pennsylvania became a major source of bituminous coal, the soft coal used in steel production. Connected with Philadelphia by the Pennsylvania Railroad, the area around Pittsburgh, where the Allegheny and Monongahela rivers join to become the Ohio, was the center of the nation's steel industry by 1890. Immigrants poured in from Europe and from the surrounding hills to work in the mines and factories. Pittsburgh became synonymous with industrial prosperity, the inspiration behind the civic pride that celebrated chuffing smokestacks. In 1900, Pennsylvania was the nation's second largest state and growing rapidly. The boom ended conclusively with the Depression of the 1930s, and in parts of Pennsylvania has never returned. After World War II, both home heating and industry switched away from coal; John L. Lewis's United Mine Workers traded higher pay and benefits for payroll cuts. Even when coal prices boomed in the 1970s, strip mining created relatively few new jobs. Similarly, Pennsylvania steel ceased to be a growth industry three decades ago, when big company managers made some bad technological decisions acceding to big wage and benefit increases with the mistaken confidence that they could always pass the costs along. Big steel got import quotas in 1969—Pennsylvania has been the nation's most protectionist state since the first Bessemer converter furnaces were lit—but this has not revived employment. By the time quotas lapsed in the 1990s, the industry had modernized, but mostly in huge new Indiana mills and other mini-mills scattered far from the cold or bulldozed factories that had lined the Monongahela.

The result has been the slowest population growth in the nation: there were 9.5 million Pennsylvanians in 1930, 11.9 million in 1990. Pennsylvania cast 36 electoral votes for Franklin Roosevelt in 1940 and 23 for Bill Clinton in 1992; it had as many congressmen (30) as California in 1960, and now has 21 while California has 52. People growing up here are as likely to leave the state as stay, and few out-of-staters have moved in. Pennsylvania looks and sounds today more like it did in the 1940s than any other major state. But the 1980s boom saw some new Pennsylvania growth. Southeast of the first Appalachian ridge, the Philadelphia metro area partook of the upscale boom that was even more spectacular up and down the East Coast. Center City Philadelphia sprouted new office towers, the edge city around King of Prussia blossomed, and pharmaceutical and biotech jobs replaced those of the Fairless steel plant. Outlet stores proliferated around Reading and new jobs sprung up in the Dutch country. West of the first mountain ridge, growth was slower and spottier, radiating outward from Pittsburgh, where a high-tech, research-oriented economy was growing. But in mill towns tucked in river valleys between mountains farther from the Golden Triangle, there was little growth, and overall population loss continued. Then the white-collar recession of 1990–91 attacked real estate values and suburbanites' jobs, sharply changing the economic picture in eastern Pennsylvania; the change was less sharp in western Pennsylvania, but optimism was about as scarce.

Traditionally, Pennsylvania was the most Republican of the mega-states—for Lincoln and the Union, for the steel industry and the high tariff. Its malodorous Republican machines built parties which were not representative of one ethnic segment but organizations with places for just about everyone: in Philadelphia's huge City Hall, a knockoff of Paris's Hotel de Ville; in Pittsburgh's massive, Roman-columned City-County Building; in Harrisburg's grandiose Capi-

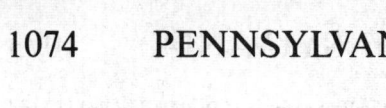

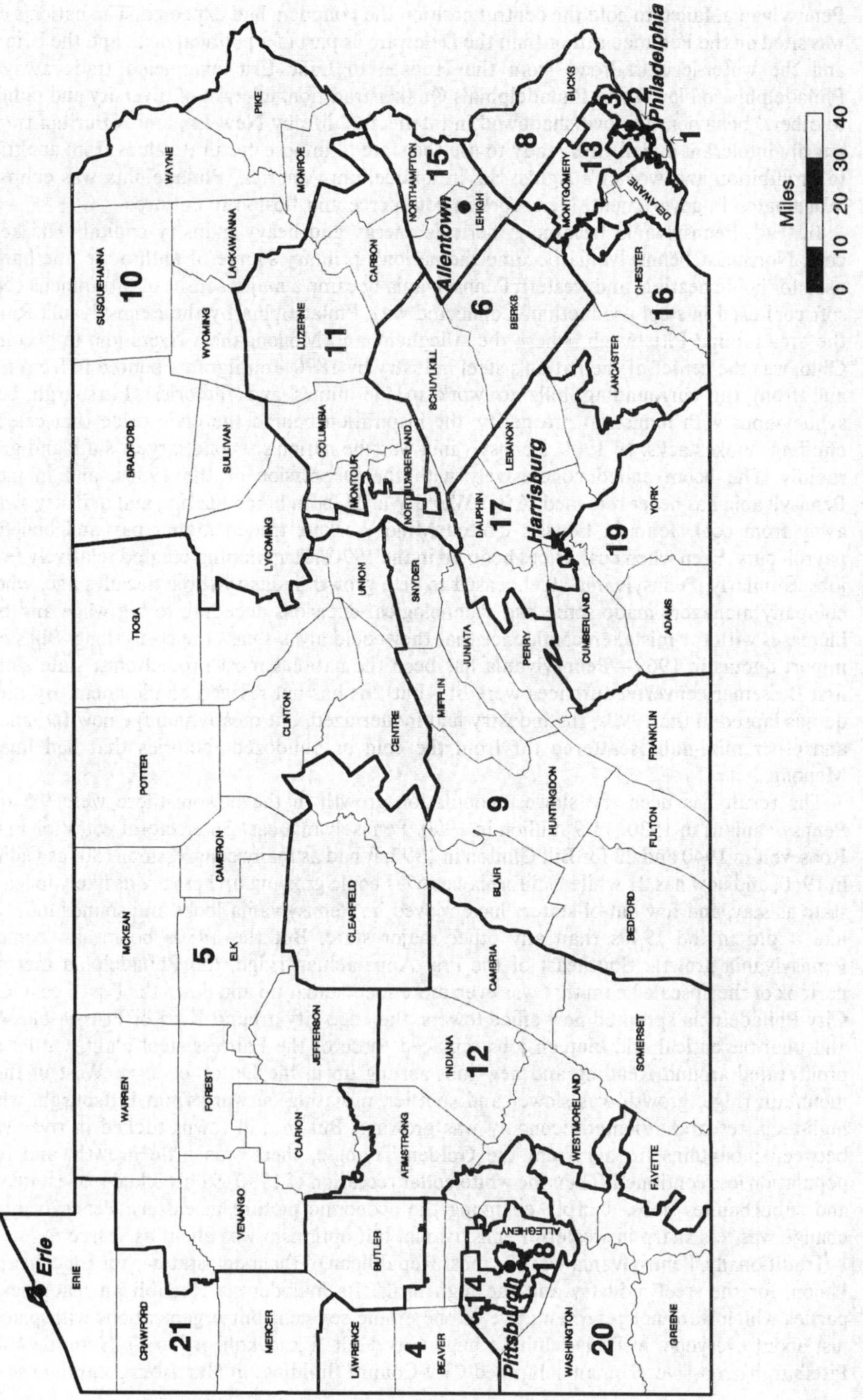
Erie
Pittsburgh
Harrisburg
Allentown
Philadelphia
Miles
0 10 20 30 40
1
2
3
4
5
6
7
8
9
10
11
12
13
14
15
16
17
18
19
20
21
ERIE
CRAWFORD
MERCER
LAWRENCE
BEAVER
WASHINGTON
GREENE
ALLEGHENY
BUTLER
VENANGO
WARREN
FOREST
CLARION
ARMSTRONG
WESTMORELAND
FAYETTE
INDIANA
JEFFERSON
CLEARFIELD
ELK
MCKEAN
CAMERON
POTTER
CAMBRIA
SOMERSET
BLAIR
BEDFORD
HUNTINGDON
FULTON
CENTRE
CLINTON
MIFFLIN
JUNIATA
FRANKLIN
PERRY
CUMBERLAND
ADAMS
YORK
TIOGA
LYCOMING
UNION
SNYDER
BRADFORD
SULLIVAN
MONTOUR
NORTHUMBERLAND
COLUMBIA
DAUPHIN
LEBANON
LANCASTER
SCHUYLKILL
SUSQUEHANNA
WYOMING
LUZERNE
LACKAWANNA
CARBON
BERKS
CHESTER
WAYNE
PIKE
MONROE
NORTHAMPTON
LEHIGH
MONTGOMERY
BUCKS
DELAWARE

tol with its rotunda modeled on St. Peter's in London and staircase modeled on the Paris Opera. In 1932, Pennsylvania was the only big state that stuck with Herbert Hoover and voted against Franklin Roosevelt. But the New Deal, John L. Lewis's United Steelworkers and CIO industrial union movement, and a series of bloody strikes made industrial Pennsylvania almost as Democratic in the 1930s and 1940s as it had been Republican from the 1860s to the 1920s. Even then parts of Pennsylvania not heavy with big steel factories and coal mines—the northern tier of counties along the New York border, the central part of the state around the Welsh railroad town of Altoona, and the Pennsylvania Dutch country around Lancaster—remained the strongest Republican voting bloc in the East. Philadelphia became a mostly Democratic city, but in the suburban counties the antique Republican machines, anchored in old courthouse and railroad station towns, stayed in control. The result was a key marginal state in presidential elections from the 1950s to the 1980s.

Diverse economic trends divided Pennsylvania politically in the 1980s; now it is voting as one state again. Western Pennsylvania voted for Michael Dukakis and almost for Walter Mondale in the 1980s, while the east—with the Philadelphia machine in tatters and the suburbs booming—gave decisive margins for Ronald Reagan and George Bush. But in 1992, Bill Clinton got the same 45% on both sides of the Appalachians. East of the mountains his liberal cultural stands—emphasized by Lynn Yeakel's assaults on Arlen Specter—may have been an asset; Clinton carried three of four suburban Philadelphia counties. West of the mountains, in culturally little-changed factory towns and mountainous countryside, they probably held his vote down; he ran well behind Mondale and Dukakis there. Either party, to win a majority here, must move against the grain of its national appeal: for Pennsylvania, with its continued support for anti-abortion laws, is culturally more tradition-minded than most of America, while on economic issues it is more favorably disposed to government intervention. The Democrats will be tested in 1994 on whether their approach can command majority support, just as the Republicans were tested with mixed results, in 1991 and 1992. Pennsylvania may not be ready yet to cede center stage.

Governor. Governors of Pennsylvania have seldom bulked large on the national scene. Yet Bob Casey, in his last two years in office (he cannot run again in 1994), is worthy of national attention—more certainly than he was granted during the 1992 Democratic National Convention where, at the behest of feminist leaders, he was not allowed to speak at all. For Casey, with his deep Catholic beliefs, his roots in the coal town of Scranton and his confidence that government can make the lives of ordinary people better, is the lineal descendant of those practical New Dealers who believed in a government compassionate to the helpless and supportive of traditional values. Casey ran for governor three times, in 1966, 1970 and 1978, before finally winning in 1986; he beat Ed Rendell, now mayor of Philadelphia, in the primary and beat baby boomer William Scranton, son of a former governor, in the general with the help of an ad showing Scranton years before with long hair and beads. In office, Casey programmed billions for new water and sewer systems, an aggressive recycling program and tough landfill regulations. He has taken pride in his measures helping children, from health care to enforcing child support decrees, and in his appointments of many women to high office. His Industrial Resource Center has used public seed money to spur private investments of $140 million in small manufacturers, and the state's Ben Franklin Partnership has provided over $100 million funding for high-tech R&D; many new small businesses have generated more new jobs than troubled big firms have lost.

But he is known best nationally as an opponent of abortion. He is the sponsor of the actually rather limited abortion restrictions—a 24-hour waiting period, parental or judicial consent, no abortions for sex selection or after 24 weeks of pregnancy—mostly upheld by the Supreme Court in the 1992 *Planned Parenthood v. Casey* case, in which the majority pointedly refrained from reversing *Roe v. Wade*. For that role as well as his openly voiced skepticism about Bill Clinton, he was denied a chance to speak at the Democrats' convention, and subjected to the indignity of watching a pro-choice Pennsylvania Republican take the podium instead. His backing of the Clinton-Gore ticket in the fall could not have been more lukewarm; the whole episode shows how lockstep the Democrats have become on abortion, insisting not only on endorsing one extreme position (as the Republicans have, on the other side) but on silencing those who disagree (as the Republicans have not).

Casey's ire may be all the greater in that he was reelected in 1990 with 68% over a pro-choice Republican Auditor General Barbara Hafer. Unhappily, the 1990s slowdown left the state unable to pay for Casey's investments, and he proposed higher taxes early in 1991 and saw his popularity plummet. And Casey's role for the end of his term has been further diminished: suffering from a seriously debilitating hereditary disease, Casey underwent a heart and liver transplant in June 1993.

Casey is ineligible to run for a second term, but has left no political heir. Lieutenant Governor Mark Singel switched from pro-life to pro-choice while running for the Senate in 1992, forfeiting Casey's support, and lost, but his obvious goal is the governorship. Democratic insurance man Charles Volpe has already announced and State Treasurer Catherine Baker Knoll, who led the ticket in 1992, might run, as might state representatives Bob O'Donnell (though he was ousted as speaker in 1993) or Dwight Evans, a black from Philadelphia. But the Republicans are probably the favorites. As analyst David Buffington points out, Pennsylvanians have alternated the parties in the governorship every eight years since World War II. One likely candidate is Attorney General Ernie Preate, who argued the *Casey* case in the Supreme Court, but he won the A.G. position by only 50%–48% against big-spending Democrat Joe Kohn in 1990. And Barbara Hafer, who led the Republican ticket in 1990, may feel vindicated enough by her 1990 warning of fiscal troubles to run again. Congressman Tom Ridge, who has already announced his intention to run, will have to become known beyond his base in Erie.

Senators. Pennsylvania's senior Senator is one of the nation's most durable "career politicians"—a characterization he accepts, even in an anti-incumbent year like 1992. Specter has held public office and been an important national figure off and on for more than a quarter-century, from his service as a top staffer to the Warren Commission in 1964, when he helped develop the single assassin theory, up through 1991, when he was attacked by Oliver Stone for that theory in Stone's fantasy movie *J.F.K.* and by feminists for his questioning of Anita Hill in the Clarence Thomas hearings. Challenged fiercely by pro-life Stephen Freind in the 1992 primary and pro-choice Lynn Yeakel in the general, he won the first handily and survived the second. His roots go back to Kansas, where, astonishingly enough, he grew up in the same small town as Bob Dole. After the Warren Commission, he came back to Philadelphia, where he had gone to college, switched parties and was elected District Attorney as a Republican in 1965 and 1969. He then lost for D.A. in 1973, for the Senate in 1976, and for governor in 1978, before narrowly edging a former state Republican chairman in the 1980 primary and beating a low-spending Democrat 50%–48% in the general for his Senate seat. In 1986, he won reelection by a 56%–43% margin against a low-profile Democrat. His assets have always been brains and hard work; he is respected by colleagues and constituents, but not especially well-liked. He sides with conservatives on some divisive issues, with liberals on others, building up no permanent credit with either; he is aggressive and prosecutorial once he takes a stand. These traits are both his strength and weakness; they explain why he was vulnerable in 1992, and why he won.

It is against that background that the uproar over his questioning of Anita Hill must be considered. Specter has been anything but a hard right member of the Judiciary Committee. He stands solidly on the pro-choice side of the abortion issue, and his vote as much as anyone else's is what sunk Judge Robert Bork's nomination to the Supreme Court in 1987. Yet he does not line up automatically with the liberal legal lobbies, as they would like. He has sponsored one tough anti-crime bill after another and backs capital punishment. He supported Judge David Souter's nomination and Judge Clarence Thomas's, and when Anita Hill came before the committee with charges against Thomas that were both serious and unsubstantiated, he questioned her with the rigor that senators skeptical or disbelieving of the truth of testimony are ordinarily entitled to use. Politically, this evoked a firestorm from people enraged that Hill's testimony had not been earlier received and was not being accepted without demur—responses that are emotionally understandable but which were blithely ignorant of the lessons taught by the history of Joe McCarthy and Titus Oates. Specter's most aggressive moment in the hearings came when he accused Hill of contradicting herself and committing perjury; examination of the record shows there was a basis for his charge.

Under attack from two sides, Specter did not retreat in 1992. He weathered a vitriolic primary assault from pro-life legislator Stephen Freind, and won 65%–35%. He watched Lynn Yeakel, daughter of a former Virginia congressman and head of a charity called Women's Way, upset the lieutenant governor in the Democratic primary after she aired a videoclip of Specter questioning Hill which asked, "Did this make you as mad as it made me?" In the general the previously untested Yeakel had some problems. She forked over $17,000 in back income taxes to Philadelphia just before she filed to run. She attacked Republicans for the demise of an Erie department store that closed back in the Carter years. She performed poorly in the initial debate, and Specter was given a boost when the AFL-CIO decided not to endorse her. In the Citizens Jury process, in which randomly selected citizens hear both candidates' positions in detail, she came in behind Specter on almost all issues in both eastern and western Pennsylvania. Specter's in-depth knowledge of national issues, plus his assiduous constituency service, his years of courtship of blacks and Jews (he is very pro-Israel), and his visits to all 67 counties, paid off. Despite a late surge by Yeakel, Specter won 49%–46%, winning both sides of the state, and running far ahead of the Republican ticket in metropolitan Pittsburgh and Philadelphia.

What will Specter do in his third term? As a Republican in Bill Clinton's Washington, he is suddenly no longer a crucial vote on most issues, though Clinton did target him—to no avail—in early 1993 as a possible swing vote in favor of his stimulus plan. On Appropriations, he can be counted on to push Pennsylvania projects. And on major issues, he is capable of playing an important role as he did, with his sharp intellect and character, on the Gulf war resolution in January 1991. Specter underwent surgery in June 1993 for a non-malignant brain tumor; but this durable politician will, no doubt, soon return to the fray.

From former college president and state Labor and Industry secretary to United States senator and the short list for vice president, Harris Wofford came a long way in little more than a year's time. But he had spent most of a lifetime doing things that gave him unique preparation for the national spotlight. From an affluent background, he was the first white student in years at Howard Law School in Washington, D.C.; he was active in the civil rights movement back in the 1950s, and Martin Luther King, Jr., drew on his writings on non-violence in India. It was Wofford who persuaded John Kennedy to call Coretta Scott King in October 1960 after Dr. King had been jailed in rural Georgia where his life seemed in danger—a call that helped Kennedy win many black votes in the November election. Wofford helped Sargent Shriver set up the Peace Corps, one of the all-time successful government agency starts. While college president at Bryn Mawr, he wrote a book called *Of Kennedys and Kings: Making Sense of the Sixties*, an account that is both admiring and without illusions, appreciative but without the saccharine tone of so many New Frontier memoirs.

Wofford came to the Senate through tragedy and connections and won his seat through perseverance and convictions. After John Heinz's death in a plane crash in April 1991, Governor Casey waited weeks to fill the vacancy, seeking out Pennsylvania native Lee Iacocca, but finally settling on Wofford, whom he had known since 1954 and who shared his support of liberal economic programs and some abortion restrictions. Little known, not well financed, forced to run in November 1991 in a state which had not elected a Democratic senator since 1962, Wofford started out far behind. In July 1991, he trailed the obvious Republican candidate, U.S. Attorney General and former Governor Richard Thornburgh, by 65%–21%. But Thornburgh had his own problems: a crackpot court decision delayed the nominating process, and Thornburgh seemed a reluctant candidate. He obviously enjoyed being in the Cabinet and had never shown an iota of interest in serving in the Senate. When he did start running, he talked much about his record as governor (though he had last been elected in 1982 with 51% of the vote) and his contacts in Washington. This was precisely the wrong tack for a Republican when voters were growing increasingly angry with George Bush's disengagement from domestic issues. Meanwhile, Wofford started running a spot calling for national health insurance. "If criminals have the right to a lawyer," he said, in a line suggested by a local doctor, "I think working Americans should have the right to a doctor." Never mind that the line conflates two notions of rights; the ad had greater political power than Thornburgh's assurances that holding down taxes would produce economic growth, and by the end of September Thornburgh was down to a 50%–38% lead. In October, Wofford picked up votes of the elderly and reduced 1988's big Republican margins in the suburbs to a dead heat, as Bill Clinton would do a year later, and won the special by a 55%–45% margin. It was a wakeup call for George Bush, but he pushed the snooze button and put off talk of any new economic programs until the State of the Union address two months later.

Wofford instantly became a national celebrity and a participant in the presidential race. Paul Tsongas had been his star Peace Corps volunteer in Ethiopia, and he gave him some aid; but once Tsongas was out, Wofford gave greater help to Bill Clinton, with whom he'd worked on his national service proposal idea with its Peace Corps echoes. In July, Wofford emerged on the short list for vice president; passed over, he still supported Clinton strongly, while his old ally Casey, snubbed because of his abortion stand, was conspicuously cool to the national ticket. His first legislative move was to reduce government health care (by stopping free care for members of Congress) rather than expand it (by the national health service he has promised). He has also put in a bill for a national service program which he hopes would evoke the Peace Corps spirit and help young people afford college. Great success and celebrity came to Wofford in 1991 and 1992; in 1993 and 1994 he will be tested on policy and politics. Can he and the Clinton Administration produce a workable national healthcare reform? Can the massive highway and infrastructure program he supported jump-start the economy? Will the Republicans seriously challenge him, or will he be reelected easily as John Heinz once was? Among Republicans, Representative Rick Santorum and businessman Bob Monahan were said to be seriously interested in a Senate bid, and 1990 gubernatorial nominee Barbara Hafer had formed an exploratory committee for this senate seat in the spring of 1993.

Presidential politics. In 1992, Pennsylvania voted Democratic for president as it did in 1948, 1960, 1968 and 1976, and came close to doing in 1984 and 1988: it now seems one of the more Democratic states but not necessarily willing to give up its swing state status. With its older, deeply-rooted population, it tends to be culturally conservative; with its long-dying blue-collar communities, it tends to be economically more liberal—though both tendencies are being muted with time. Pennsylvania's late April presidential primary has not been crucial since the 1976 Democratic race, when Jimmy Carter clinched the Democratic nomination by beating Henry Jackson and Morris Udall here.

Congressional districting. Pennsylvania lost three congressional districts in the 1950 Census, and two in each of the following four decades reducing its delegation to 21. Control of redistricting was split between the parties, but the plan seemed to eliminate two Republican seats, one in metro Philadelphia and one in metro Pittsburgh. The latter actually stayed Republican, but Democrats gained two previously Republican seats in the east and lost only one, ending up with an 11–10 edge in the delegation.

The People: Est. Pop. 1992: 12,009,000; Pop. 1990: 11,881,643, up 1.1% 1990–1992. 4.8% of U.S. total, 5th largest; 31% rural. Median age: 35.0 years. 15.4% 65 years and over. 88.5% White, 9.2% Black, 2.0% Hispanic origin, 1.2% Asian, 1.0% Other. Households: 55.7% married couple families; 25% married couple fams. w. children; 36% college educ.; median household income: $29,069; per capita income: $14,068; 70.6% owner occupied housing; median house value: $69,700; median monthly rent: $322. 7.5% Unemployment. Voting age pop.: 9,086,833. Registered voters (1992): 5,993,002; 3,043,757 D (51%), 2,567,643 R (43%), 381,602 unaffiliated and minor parties (6%).

Political Lineup: Governor, Robert P. Casey (D); Lt. Gov., Mark S. Singel (D); Secy. of Commonwealth, Brenda K. Mitchell (D); Atty. Gen., Ernie Preate (R); Treasurer, Catherine Baker Knoll (D); Auditor General, Barbara Hafer (R). State Senate, 50 (25 D, 24 R, and 1 vacancy); State House of Representatives, 203 (105 D and 98 R). Senators, Arlen Specter (R) and Harris Wofford (D). Representatives, 21 (11 D and 10 R).

1992 Presidential Vote

Clinton (D)	2,239,164	(45%)
Bush (R)	1,791,841	(36%)
Perot (I)	902,667	(18%)

1992 Democratic Presidential Primary

Clinton	715,031	(57%)
Brown	325,543	(26%)
Tsongas	161,572	(13%)
Other	63,349	(5%)

1988 Presidential Vote

Bush (R)	2,300,087	(51%)
Dukakis (D)	2,194,944	(48%)

1992 Republican Presidential Primary

Bush	774,865	(77%)
Buchanan	233,912	(23%)

GOVERNOR

Gov. Robert P. Casey (D)

Elected 1986, term expires Jan. 1995; b. Jan. 9, 1932, Jackson Heights, NY; home, Scranton; Holy Cross Col., A.B. 1953, George Washington U., J.D. 1956; Catholic; married (Ellen).

Career: Practicing atty., 1957–69, 1979–87; PA Senate, 1963–67; PA Auditor Gen., 1969–77.

Office: 225 Capitol Bldg., Harrisburg 17120, 717-787-2500.

Election Results

1990 gen.	Robert P. Casey (D)	2,065,244	(68%)
	Barbara Hafer (R)	987,516	(32%)
1990 prim.	Robert P. Casey (D)	636,594	(78%)
	Philip J. Berg (D)	184,365	(22%)
1986 gen.	Robert P. Casey (D)	1,717,484	(51%)
	William W. Scranton (R)	1,638,268	(48%)

SENATORS

Sen. Arlen Specter (R)

Elected 1980, seat up 1998; b. Feb. 12, 1930, Wichita, KS; home, Philadelphia; U. of PA, B.A. 1951, Yale, LL.B. 1956; Jewish; married (Joan).

Career: Air Force, 1951–53; Practicing atty., 1955–56, 1974–80; Asst. Cnsl., Warren Comm., 1964; PA Asst. Atty. Gen., 1964–65; Philadelphia Dist. Atty., 1966–74.

Offices: 530 HSOB, 202-224-4254. Also 600 Arch Street, #9400, Philadelphia 19106, 215-597-7200; Fed. Bldg., #2031, Liberty Ave. & Grant St., Pittsburgh 15222, 412-644-3400; 1159 Fed. Bldg., 6th & State Sts., Erie 16501, 814-453-3010; 1159 Fed. Bldg, Harrisburg 17101, 717-782-3951; Park Plaza, #503, Scranton 18503, 717-346-2006; and P.O. Bldg., #201, 5th & Hamilton Sts., Allentown 18101, 215-434-1444.

Committees: *Aging (Special)* (10th of 10 R). *Appropriations* (5th of 13 R): Agriculture, Rural Development and Related Agencies; Defense; Foreign Operations; Labor, Health and Human Services, Education (RMM); Transportation. *Energy and Natural Resources* (8th of 9 R): Energy Research and Development; Public Lands, National Parks and Forests; Renewable Energy, Energy Efficiency and Competitiveness. *Judiciary* (5th of 8 R): Antitrust, Monopolies and Business Rights; Technology and the Law (RMM). *Veterans' Affairs* (4th of 5 R).

Group Ratings

	ADA	ACLU	CDF	COPE	CFA	LCV	ACU	NTLC	NSI	COC	CEI
1992	65	59	90	83	75	50	30	50	90	60	35
1991	40	—	64	58	61	40	71	—	—	50	44

National Journal Ratings

	1991 LIB — 1991 CONS		1992 LIB — 1992 CONS	
Economic	40%	— 59%	42%	— 57%
Social	52%	— 47%	55%	— 44%
Foreign	37%	— 61%	46%	— 53%

Key Votes of the 102d Congress

1. $ for Homeownership	FOR	5. Clarence Thomas Nom.	FOR	9. Use Force in Gulf	FOR
2. Have Cap Gains Debate	FOR	6. Lmt Death Row Appeal	FOR	10. Keep Salvador Aid	AGN
3. Remove Budget Walls	FOR	7. Handgun Wait/5-Day	AGN	11. Cut $1B from SDI	AGN
4. Ban Striker Replace	FOR	8. Abortion Gag Rule	AGN	12. Override China MFN	FOR

Key Votes of the 103d Congress

1. Family Leave	FOR	2. HIV Immigrants	FOR	3. Clinton Budget	AGN

Election Results

1992 general	Arlen Specter (R)...................	2,358,125	(49%)	($10,454,793)
	Lynn Yeakel (D)...................	2,224,966	(46%)	($5,028,669)
	John F. Perry (LIB).................	219,319	(5%)	($53,690)
1992 primary	Arlen Specter (R)...................	683,118	(65%)	
	Stephen F. Freind (R)...............	366,608	(35%)	
1986 general	Arlen Specter (R)...................	1,906,537	(56%)	($5,993,230)
	Robert W. Edgar (D)	1,448,219	(43%)	($3,968,994)

Sen. Harris Wofford (D)

Appointed May, 1991, seat up 1994; b. Apr. 26, 1926, New York, NY; home, Bryn Mawr; U. of Chicago, B.A. 1948, Yale, LL.B. 1954, Howard U., J.D. 1954; Catholic; married (Clare).

Career: Army 1944–45; Advisor, J.F. Kennedy Pres. campaign, 1960; Spec. Asst., Pres. Kennedy, 1960–63; Peace Corps, 1963–66; Pres., S.U.N.Y. Westbury, 1966–70; Pres., Bryn Mawr Col., 1970–78; Practicing atty., 1978–86; PA Dem. St. Chmn., 1986; PA Secy. of Labor and Industry, 1986–91.

Offices: 521 DSOB 20510, 202-224-6324. Also 9456 Green Fed. Bldg., 600 Arch St., Philadelphia 19106, 215-597-9914; 1306 Liberty Ctr., 1001 Liberty Ave., Pittsburgh 15222, 412-562-0533; Fed. Square Sta., P.O. Box 55, Harrisburg 17108, 717-233-5849; 130 Fed. Square, Erie 16501, 814-454-7114; and 116 N. Washington Ave., Kane Bldg., #3K, Scranton 18503, 717-347-2341.

Committees: *Environment and Public Works* (9th of 10 D): Clean Water, Fisheries and Wildlife; Superfund, Recycling and Solid Waste Management; Toxic Substances, Research and Development. *Foreign Relations* (9th of 11 D): International Economic Policy, Trade, Oceans and Environment; Near Eastern and South Asian Affairs; Western Hemisphere and Peace Corps Affairs. *Labor and Human Resources* (10th of 10 D): Aging; Children, Family, Drugs and Alcoholism; Education, Arts and Humanities; Employment and Productivity. *Small Business* (8th of 12 D): Export Expansion and Agricultural Development (Chmn.); Urban and Minority-Owned Business Development.

Group Ratings

	ADA	ACLU	CDF	COPE	CFA	LCV	ACU	NTLC	NSI	COC	CEI
1992	100	82	100	92	83	67	0	25	60	20	18
1991	79	—	88	89	87	86	22	—	—	0	11

National Journal Ratings

	1991 LIB — 1991 CONS		1992 LIB — 1992 CONS	
Economic	84%	— 15%	95%	— 0%
Social	77%	— 22%	84%	— 11%
Foreign	86%	— 0%	86%	— 0%

Key Votes of the 102d Congress

1. $ for Homeownership	*	5. Clarence Thomas Nom. AGN	9. Use Force in Gulf	*
2. Have Cap Gains Debate	AGN	6. Lmt Death Row Appeal AGN	10. Keep Salvador Aid	AGN
3. Remove Budget Walls	FOR	7. Handgun Wait/5-Day FOR	11. Cut $1B from SDI	FOR
4. Ban Striker Replace	FOR	8. Abortion Gag Rule AGN	12. Override China MFN FOR

Key Votes of the 103d Congress

1. Family Leave   FOR   2. HIV Immigrants   FOR   3. Clinton Budget   FOR

Election Results

1991 special	Harris Wofford (D)	1,860,760	(55%)	($3,241,556)
	Dick Thornburgh (R)	1,521,986	(45%)	($3,993,070)
1988 general	H. John Heinz III (R)	2,901,715	(67%)	($5,151,512)
	Joe Vignola (D)	1,416,764	(32%)	($544,137)

FIRST DISTRICT

In the center of Center City Philadelphia, the 1680s look out on the 1780s, 1880s and 1980s: the statute of William Penn, who founded the city in 1682, stands 37 feet high atop the 548-foot tower of the 1880s Second Empire-style City Hall at Market and Broad; east is Independence Hall where Americans in the 1780s drew up the nation's Constitution; west is the tower of One Liberty Place, with its "romantic modernist" spire, the 1980s building that broke tradition to rise above City Hall. Philadelphia is built on a certain order: earlier American colonies were settled by practical men, out to make money or replicate a farm settlement back home; but Penn was a Quaker, a member of one of those rationalizing sects of the 17th Century, who intended to impose order on his new environment, and did. Hence Philadelphia was designed not with the cowpath street patterns of Boston or Charleston, but with a grid of numbered and named streets, with occasional open squares, replicated in dozens of American cities.

Penn's city of brotherly love has turned out to be a commercial and industrial metropolis that has grown steadily over the years, spreading out over the countryside and becoming the nation's fifth largest, if never one of its most visible, cities. Yet there are still places in which you can see the distant past: in the restored townhouses of Society Hill and the tree-shaded public buildings around Independence Hall, and, on the way to the ornate City Hall, the Federal and Greek Revival buildings, little temples of commerce, built when Philadelphia was the nation's largest city. Interspersed are I.M. Pei's modernist Society Hill Towers (though the rich in Philadelphia, unlike New York or Chicago, don't much like apartments) and the 1920s masonry-faced skyscrapers and 1970s glass-and-steel towers built around City Hall and in Center City farther west.

The bulky prominence of City Hall is a metaphor for Philadelphia's recent economic troubles, or rather those of the municipality: for metro Philadelphia, with a diversified economy, grew comfortably during the 1980s and was set back less by the early 1990s recession than glitzier metro areas. Center City remains vibrant and industries from insurance (Cigna, Aetna, Metropolitan Life) to biotechnology (SmithKline Beckman, Sterling, Pennwalt) grow here even as older industries (the Navy's Philadelphia Shipyard) wind down. What has come skidding close to bankruptcy is the city government, swollen with overpaid employees, committed to a costly, union-run health plan and mismanaged with ferocious incompetence by Mayor Wilson Goode from 1983 to 1991. The city government's credit was about to be cut off during the 1991 mayoral campaign, which resembled a Philadelphia cheesesteak food fight, with former Mayor Frank Rizzo as the Republican nominee. But Rizzo died during the campaign and the easy winner was former District Attorney Ed Rendell, a liberal Democrat determined to confront the unions and privatize city services, much as Democrat Richard M. Daley was doing in Chicago. Rendell put together a package of cuts and privatizations and faced down the unions' strike threat in September 1992. Involved, ebullient and with a reservoir of trust from both blacks and whites, he is engaged in one of America's most difficult tasks of reinventing government.

City Hall lies at the geographic center of Pennsylvania's 1st Congressional District. The 1st runs north on both sides of the Broad Street corridor to include much of black North Philadelphia and south through most of heavily Italian South Philadelphia, where Italian families, groceries and restaurants have been pressed tightly into narrow English and Indian-named streets under a tangle of overhead wires: the neighborhood where the various "*Rockys*" were filmed and the original Philadelphia cheesesteaks are sold. The district also includes the oil tank farms where the Schuylkill flows into the Delaware, Philadelphia airport, and a swath of industrial suburbs along the river to the black-majority city of Chester. This was created as a black-majority district, in the argot of the Voting Rights Act, but also includes many Hispanics; it is heavily Democratic, and may well have racially polarized primaries before the year 2000.

For now, the 1st is represented by Thomas Foglietta, whose long career embodies Philadelphia's traditions of family politics and party switching. Foglietta, whose father was a Republican politician, was once a Republican himself during the 20 years he served as councilman from South Philadelphia. He first won his house seat in 1980 as an Independent, beating convicted Abscam defendant Ozzie Myers (one of Frank Rizzo's gifts to Congress) 38%–34%; he held the seat as a Democrat in the 1982 primary against another incumbent, Joseph Smith, 52%–48%. (Party switching is common here: Rizzo, elected mayor twice as a Democrat, became a Republican by 1987; Rendell's 1991 Republican opponent was a former Democratic hack.) Foglietta had serious primary challenges in 1982 and 1984 from South Philadelphia politico James Tayoun, but held on by 52%–45% and 62%–38%. He has won by large margins since: in 1992 he had no primary opposition even though the district became majority-black and in the general beat a Republican who compared him to "a street thug" because of his support of the pay raise, special interest contributions, and using government funds to rent a Lincoln Town Car.

Foglietta's record is staunchly liberal—pro-choice, pro-labor and dovish on foreign policy. Prior to his appointment to the Appropriations Committee in 1993, he served on the Armed Services Committee, and spent much effort trying to come up with work for the Philadelphia Navy Yard (which is still targeted for closure). He blocked the *Forrestal* overhaul from going to Pensacola, Florida; got the overhaul of the *Kennedy*; and argued that the Navy Yard should be a prototype for military-to-civilian conversion. In a classic camel's-nose-under-the-tent maneuver, he got $5 million in 1992 to begin a $70 million hazardous waste removal at Independence Park. He has worked to funnel federal money to Philadelphia city government and the SEPTA mass transit agency. He helped found and is chairman of the Congressional Urban Caucus, a body that once was not needed (because most northern Democrats represented central cities) but became useful with the growth of the suburbs.

The People: Pop. 1990: 566,133; 13% age 65+; 36% White; 52% Black; 2% Asian; 7% Other; 9% Hispanic origin. Voting age pop.: 413,321; 50% Black; 7% Hispanic origin. Households: 35% married couple families; 15% married couple fams. w. children; 25% college educ.; median household income: $20,372; per capita income: $9,703; median gross rent: $404; median house value: $36,700.

1992 Presidential Vote			1988 Presidential Vote		
Clinton (D)	150,091	(72%)	Dukakis (D)	158,262	(73%)
Bush (R)	39,086	(19%)	Bush (R)	59,095	(27%)
Perot (I)	17,052	(8%)			

Rep. Thomas M. Foglietta (D)

Elected 1980; b. Dec. 3, 1928, Philadelphia; home, Philadelphia; St. Joseph's Col., B.A. 1949, Temple U., J.D. 1952; Catholic; single.

Career: Practicing atty., 1952–80; Philadelphia City Cncl., 1955–75; Reg. Dir., U.S. Dept. of Labor, 1976.

Offices: 341 CHOB 20515, 202-225-4731. Also Green Fed. Bldg., 600 Arch St., #10402, Philadelphia 19106, 215-925-6840; 1806 S. Broad St., Philadelphia 19125, 215-463-8702; and 2630 Memphis St., Philadelphia 19125, 215-426-4616.

Committees: *Appropriations* (26th of 37 D): Military Construction; Transportation.

1084   PENNSYLVANIA

Group Ratings

	ADA	ACLU	COPE	CDF	CFA	LCV	ACU	NTLC	NSI	COC	CEI
1992	80	100	91	100	100	56	0	0	20	33	9
1991	95	—	100	100	78	62	0	—	—	11	6

National Journal Ratings

	1991 LIB — 1991 CONS	1992 LIB — 1992 CONS
Economic	88% — 0%	83% — 17%
Social	88% — 0%	79% — 21%
Foreign	86% — 13%	81% — 18%

Key Votes of the 102d Congress

1. Ban Striker Replace	FOR	5. Handgun Wait/7-Day	FOR	9. Use Force in Gulf	AGN
2. $ for Homeownership	AGN	6. Overseas Mil. Abortion	FOR	10. US Mil. Abroad $ Cut	AGN
3. Tax Rich/Cut Mid Cls.	FOR	7. Obscn. Art NEA $ Ban	AGN	11. Limit SDI Funds	FOR
4. FY93/$15B Def. Cut	FOR	8. Death Pen. from Jury	AGN	12. Cuba Trade Embargo	*

Key Votes of the 103d Congress

1. Family Leave   FOR   2. Deficit Reduction   FOR   3. Stimulus Plan   FOR

Election Results

1992 general	Thomas M. Foglietta (D) 150,172	(81%)	($366,203)
	Craig Snyder (R) 35,419	(19%)	($41,210)
1992 primary	Thomas M. Foglietta (D), unopposed		
1990 general	Thomas M. Foglietta (D) 73,423	(79%)	($234,057)
	James Love Jackson (R)............... 19,018	(21%)	($5,969)

SECOND DISTRICT

Tightly-packed but formidable rowhouses, the old fieldstone houses of Germantown, the Schuylkill River quietly flowing past boat houses below the small Greek temples of the Water Works, with the larger temple of the Museum of Art and the skyscraper towers behind: most of this was the Philadelphia of Thomas Eakins, memorialized in his 19th Century paintings. This is also much of black Philadelphia today. Concentrated in neighborhoods radiating outward from Center City, Philadelphia's black communities lie in West Philadelphia, across the Schuylkill on either side of Market Street; in North Philadelphia, on either side of Broad Street; and to the northwest, off the ancient and narrow diagonal of Germantown Avenue that ran through open fields in Benjamin Franklin's time and was still not entirely settled in Eakins's. Much of this area forms the heart of Pennsylvania's 2d Congressional District, which also includes many Center City skyscrapers, the leafy and cobblestoned lanes of Chestnut Hill, and a couple of suburbs just west of the city. The black percentage of the district was reduced in redistricting, but is still well over 50%, and the story of politics here is essentially the story of black Philadelphia politics.

That story goes back a long way, and has moments of glory as well as (like that of every other American ethnic group) tawdriness. Pennsylvania never had slavery—part of William Penn's Quaker legacy—and Philadelphia had a large black community before the Civil War. Vestiges of its Lincoln Republican heritage are still apparent, most recently in the 1992 reelection of Senator Arlen Specter, who has a long record of support for civil rights, and his supporters pointed out that his opponent Lynn Yeakel's father had been a southern segregationist congressman and her husband belonged to an all-white country club. Specter won a large enough percentage of black votes to make the difference in his 49%–46% statewide win. Philadelphia's best known black politicians have included somnolent hacks and noisy militants, with a few notable stars. One such star was William Gray: pastor (like his father and grandfather) of the

Bright Hope Baptist Church, elected congressman from the 2d District in 1978, chairman of the House Budget Committee from 1982 to 1988, House majority whip from 1989 to 1991, when he surprised just about everyone by resigning to become president of the United Negro College Fund. Not a star was Wilson Goode, a former bureaucrat elected mayor in 1983 and 1987, who presided over the MOVE bombing in 1985 and the effective bankruptcy of city government by the time his second term ended in 1991.

Gray's resignation was seemingly timed to block the election of a longtime political rival, but in vain: Lucien Blackwell won the seat in November 1991 and held it in 1992. Blackwell is part of an older generation, a former longshoreman and boxer, a labor union stalwart who has lived in the same house in West Philadelphia for decades. A longtime city councilman, he attended to parochial neighborhood and racial concerns when leaders like Gray and Goode were also concerned with the world beyond. Blackwell finished second in the spring 1991 mayoral primary, behind Ed Rendell but ahead of George Burrell, who is also black and was Gray's choice for mayor. In the special House race, ward leaders gave Blackwell the Democratic nomination, and he won with 39% to 28% for state Senator Chaka Fattah and 27% for former state welfare secretary John White, who were running under other party labels. Blackwell had to run again, in the April 1992 Democratic primary, where he was opposed by C. Delores Tucker, former secretary of the commonwealth, who had wanted the Democratic nomination in 1991. The primary was held within the newly redistricted boundaries, with more white voters, but also with more of the blacks in Blackwell's West Philadelphia base. Just before the primary Tucker and Senate candidate Lynn Yeakel endorsed each other with Gloria Steinem looking on; but Blackwell won by a narrow 54%–46% margin.

On national issues, Blackwell can be expected to be a solid labor-liberal, and his tendency is to be outspoken in his constituents' interests; whether a sixty-something backbencher will be much heard is another question. He has fought hard for the seat, but may have to fight again; there are other ambitious black politicians here, with contrasting styles and conflicting ambitions, and Blackwell's margins have not been large enough to scare everyone off.

The People: Pop. 1990: 565,242; 15% age 65+; 34% White; 62% Black; 2% Asian; 1% Other; 1% Hispanic origin. Voting age pop.: 438,250; 58% Black; 1% Hispanic origin. Households: 32% married couple families; 12% married couple fams. w. children; 40% college educ.; median household income: $24,880; per capita income: $13,121; median gross rent: $479; median house value: $42,300.

1992 Presidential Vote

Clinton (D)	183,758	(79%)
Bush (R)	31,878	(14%)
Perot (I)	14,514	(6%)

1988 Presidential Vote

Dukakis (D)	192,671	(79%)
Bush (R)	51,458	(21%)

Rep. Lucien E. Blackwell (D)

Elected Nov. 1991; b. Aug. 1, 1931, Whitset; home, Philadelphia; Baptist; married (Jannie).

Career: Army, 1952–54 (Korea); Pres., Local #1332 Intl. Longshoreman's Union, 1973–91; PA House of Reps., 1973–75; Philadelphia City Cncl., 1975–91.

Offices: 410 CHOB 20515, 202-225-4001. Also 3901 Market St., Philadelphia 19104, 215-387-2543.

Committees: *Budget* (23d of 26 D). *Public Works and Transportation* (24th of 39 D): Aviation; Economic Development (Vice Chmn.); Investigations and Oversight.

Group Ratings

	ADA	ACLU	COPE	CDF	CFA	LCV	ACU	NTLC	NSI	COC	CEI
1992	90	100	100	90	100	69	0	0	20	29	10
1991	*	—	100	100	83	57	0	—	—	*	8

National Journal Ratings

	1991 LIB — 1991 CONS		1992 LIB — 1992 CONS	
Economic	*%	*%	78%	18%
Social	*%	*%	81%	17%
Foreign	*%	*%	90%	0%

Key Votes of the 102d Congress

1. Ban Striker Replace	*	5. Handgun Wait/7-Day	*	9. Use Force in Gulf	*
2. $ for Homeownership	AGN	6. Overseas Mil. Abortion	*	10. US Mil. Abroad $ Cut FOR
3. Tax Rich/Cut Mid Cls.	FOR	7. Obscn. Art NEA $ Ban	*	11. Limit SDI Funds	FOR
4. FY93/$15B Def. Cut	FOR	8. Death Pen. from Jury	*	12. Cuba Trade Embargo AGN

Key Votes of the 103d Congress

1. Family Leave   FOR   2. Deficit Reduction   FOR   3. Stimulus Plan   FOR

Election Results

1992 general	Lucien E. Blackwell (D)	164,355	(77%)	($228,229)
	Larry Hollin (R)	47,906	(22%)	($170,007)
	Other	1,666	(1%)	
1992 primary	Lucien E. Blackwell (D)	48,299	(54%)	
	C. Delores Tucker (D)	41,528	(46%)	
1991 special	Lucien E. Blackwell (D)	51,820	(39%)	($68,823)
	Chaka Fattah (Consumer)	37,068	(28%)	($180,221)
	John F. White (I)	36,469	(28%)	($219,903)
	Nadine G. Smith Bulford (R)	6,928	(5%)	
1990 general	William H. Gray III (D)	94,584	(92%)	($814,125)
	Donald Bakove (R)	8,118	(8%)	($506)

THIRD DISTRICT

North and east of Center City Philadelphia, stretching more than a dozen miles along the Delaware River and back along the parklands by Frankford, Tacony and Pennypack Creeks, are most of the white residential neighborhoods of Philadelphia. They start off in the closely packed 19th Century houses of Kensington, where people of Irish and Italian descent live in rude frame houses and income levels are lower than in most black neighborhoods—a part of the city in which you could (if you blot out the cars) easily imagine yourself on some 1930s movie set. Farther out is northeast Philadelphia, a suburban-like expanse the size of a major city itself. Here, when the alley-wide streets of North and South Philadelphia and the river wards were already teeming with houses and people, and the Main Line suburbs were already well-settled, the workers of Philadelphia's docks and factories and Center City offices were just starting to move out and fill up vacant land. They established places like the little neighborhood near Pennypack Park where, on Mower Street, the man who has become a kind of symbol of Philadelphia, Sylvester Stallone, grew up. For all of Philadelphia's high crime and bankrupt city government, northeast Philadelphia, with about one-third of the city's population, is still new urban territory (more than half its dwelling units were built after 1950) and is still growing.

Politically this is lively country. Along the Delaware River in Kensington and Frankford, in blocks of closely packed brick row houses and neighborhood bars with neon lights, reside mostly Irish and Italians with their pungent accents. You expect to see a ward leader knocking on the doors and distributing coal for the winter. Most people here are Catholic, but there are many Jews, living in neighborhoods like neither Brooklyn nor Scarsdale. The houses are pleasant, but modest; the politics Democratic, but conservative on cultural issues and many residents are part of the hard-pressed lower-middle class. Northeast Philadelphia recoiled from the national Democrats in the 1970s, voted for Reagan and Bush in the 1980s, and then returned to give Bill Clinton an absolute majority in 1992.

The congressman from the 3d District is Robert Borski, who like many politicians got his start as an athlete: captain of the Frankford High basketball and baseball teams in 1966, a coach after graduating from college with an athletic scholarship. His athletic contacts surely helped him get a job as a floor manager at the Philadelphia Stock Exchange. Borski was the political beneficiary of a chain of events: the indictment of northeast Philadelphia Democratic Congressman Joshua Eilberg in 1978, the election of Republican Charles Dougherty in 1980, the lack of interest by other politicians in the race against Dougherty in 1982. Borski ran and won, and won the next four times easily. Redistricting added Kensington to the district and a bit of gentrified Society Hill and Center City, which didn't hurt Borski. Dougherty returned and ran an aggressive race in 1992, but in that Democratic year, and despite 33 bad checks at the House bank, Borski won 59%–39%.

Borski has a low profile and a labor-liberal voting record in the House. He seems to concentrate heavily on transportation and on the Public Works Committee, where he chairs the Investigations and Oversight Subcommittee. He wants the federal government to spend lots more on highways and mass transit, especially greater Philadelphia's SEPTA. In 1992, he introduced the Infrastructure Reinvestment and Economic Revitalization Act which calls for bonds to finance a one-time nationwide investment in infrastructure construction. He has also sponsored bills to ban backhauling of garbage in food trucks and specifying Coast Guard responsibilities in oil spills.

The People: Pop. 1990: 565,884; 18% age 65+; 87% White; 5% Black; 3% Asian; 3% Other; 4% Hispanic origin. Voting age pop.: 437,308; 4% Black; 4% Hispanic origin. Households: 51% married couple families; 22% married couple fams. w. children; 29% college educ.; median household income: $29,157; per capita income: $13,429; median gross rent: $472; median house value: $64,900.

1992 Presidential Vote

Clinton (D)	125,078	(52%)
Bush (R)	75,388	(31%)
Perot (I)	39,582	(16%)

1988 Presidential Vote

Bush (R)	127,736	(52%)
Dukakis (D)	119,379	(48%)

Rep. Robert A. Borski (D)

Elected 1982; b. Oct. 20, 1948, Philadelphia; home, Philadelphia; U. of Baltimore, B.A. 1972; Catholic; married (Karen).

Career: Stockbroker, 1972–76; PA House of Reps., 1976–82.

Offices: 2161 RHOB 20515, 202-225-8251. Also 7137 Frankford Ave., Philadelphia 19135, 215-335-3355; and 2630 Memphis St., Philadelphia 19125, 215-426-4616.

Committees: *Foreign Affairs* (13th of 27 D): Europe and the Middle East. *Public Works and Transportation* (6th of 39 D): Aviation; Investigations and Oversight (Chmn.); Water Resources and Environment. *Standards of Official Conduct* (6th of 7 D).

Group Ratings

	ADA	ACLU	COPE	CDF	CFA	LCV	ACU	NTLC	NSI	COC	CEI
1992	80	52	83	100	87	56	16	5	70	29	10
1991	60	—	91	100	89	46	30	—	—	10	2

National Journal Ratings

	1991 LIB — 1991 CONS		1992 LIB — 1992 CONS	
Economic	88% —	0%	78% —	18%
Social	42% —	57%	57% —	41%
Foreign	65% —	33%	52% —	46%

Key Votes of the 102d Congress

1. Ban Striker Replace	FOR	5. Handgun Wait/7-Day	FOR	9. Use Force in Gulf	FOR
2. $ for Homeownership	AGN	6. Overseas Mil. Abortion	AGN	10. US Mil. Abroad $ Cut	FOR
3. Tax Rich/Cut Mid Cls.	FOR	7. Obscn. Art NEA $ Ban	FOR	11. Limit SDI Funds	AGN
4. FY93/$15B Def. Cut	FOR	8. Death Pen. from Jury	FOR	12. Cuba Trade Embargo	FOR

Key Votes of the 103d Congress

1. Family Leave	FOR	2. Deficit Reduction	FOR	3. Stimulus Plan	FOR

Election Results

1992 general	Robert A. Borski (D)	130,828	(59%)	($664,231)
	Charles F. Dougherty (R)	86,787	(39%)	($215,321)
	Other	4,356	(2%)	
1992 primary	Robert A. Borski (D), unopposed			
1990 general	Robert A. Borski (D)	89,908	(60%)	($277,011)
	Joseph M. McColgan (R)	59,901	(40%)	($74,417)

FOURTH DISTRICT

On the banks of the Beaver and Ohio Rivers, near where they join in westernmost Pennsylvania, is—or was—one of America's great heavy industrial zones. For 100 years, this was steel country, with mills rising black and brooding from the bottomlands and filling the narrow river valleys with smoke. The immigrant families and their sinewy sons, except those who became some of America's great football players, worked hard in the hot mills. The families in little frame houses on the hillsides above looked down on a riverscape lined with piles of iron ore, limestone and coal, littered with cranes, stocks and furnaces. But, however unpicturesque, this was a land of opportunity for thousands whose lives before coming here were far worse. For a few heady years, the high union wages and early retirement plans seemed to make working in the mills the way to affluence. But after the oil shock of 1979 when the industry crashed, whole mills were closed and thousands of jobs vanished. Today, the Beaver and Ohio valleys have lost population as thousands of workers who have long since exhausted their unemployment benefits finally have given up and moved elsewhere.

The western Pennsylvania steel country now has six congressional districts; four decades ago, before the decline of the steel industry and resulting outmigration, it had 11. The 4th Congressional District of Pennsylvania, as redrawn after the 1990 Census, contains much of the classic steel country: Beaver and Lawrence Counties; the northern tier of townships in Pittsburgh's Allegheny County, suburban territory with a rough, rural air to it; and western Westmoreland County, with affluent suburbs on the hills between more steel towns. This is a heavily Democratic seat, though its 1980s predecessor, with rather different boundaries but with more than half the same territory, was intended to tilt Republican. What the district has tilted to, at least up to 1992, is electing a melancholy string of incompetent congressmen. For 20 years, the area was represented by Frank Clark, a Democrat who lost in the ultra-Democratic Watergate year of 1974; His conqueror was Gary Myers, a Republican who after four years in Congress decided to go back to being a foreman in a steel mill. Democrat Eugene Atkinson, who had lost to Myers in 1976, won unimpressively in 1978, then switched to the Republican Party just as the steel industry headed for its worst tailspin and the steel country was about to be the one part of the country trending Democratic: bad political moves every one. The craziest district lines in the world couldn't save a politician like this, and didn't. In 1982, Atkinson lost 60%–39% to Joe Kolter, a 13-year veteran of the legislature. A solid labor-liberal, he is a pleasant man given to malapropisms ("some of the people taking over defunct S&Ls are people who have defuncted themselves") and worse. He drew three serious primary opponents in 1992 and in March lost the AFL-CIO endorsement after he missed a key vote on unemployment benefits.

The best came in March 1992, a month before the primary, when the *Pittsburgh Press* printed excerpts from an audiotape of a Kolter strategy meeting. Kolter called himself a "political whore" and said that at funeral homes he would "just walk in and, if I faintly remember who these people are, just walk in a shed a little tear and sign my name and take off." The big surprise of the primary was not that Kolter lost—he got only 20%, a devastating result for an incumbent—but that so did two other state representatives, one of whom had labor endorsement. The easy winner, with 45%, was Ron Klink, a reporter and anchor for KDKA-TV, who issued a 39-page "Ron Klink Plan for Jobs." His non-political background and his promise to create industrial jobs in this area where their lack is so painfully obvious gave him 79% of the vote in the general election against a Republican who had held Kolter to 56% in 1990. Now the question is whether he can live up to his promise. He can try to make waves in Washington, but his fate may hinge on the macroeconomy, and on whether an economic revival will have visible impact on the Beaver and Allegheny valleys.

The People: Pop. 1990: 565,809; 33% rural; 16% age 65+; 96% White; 3% Black. Voting age pop.: 431,775; 3% Black. Households: 63% married couple families; 27% married couple fams. w. children;

36% college educ.; median household income: $26,792; per capita income: $12,684; median gross rent: $332; median house value: $55,400.

1992 Presidential Vote			1988 Presidential Vote		
Clinton (D)	118,701	(48%)	Dukakis (D)	128,445	(59%)
Bush (R)	76,291	(31%)	Bush (R)	90,923	(41%)
Perot (I)	50,654	(21%)			

Rep. Ron Klink (D)

Elected 1992; b. Sept. 23, 1951, Canton, OH; home, Jeannette; Protestant; married (Linda).

Career: Businessman, Restaurant Owner; Reporter and Anchor, KDKA-TV, Pittsburgh, 1978–92.

Offices: 1130 LHOB 20515, 202-225-2565. Also 11279 Center Hwy., N. Huntingdon 15642, 412-864-8681; Beaver Trust Bldg., #305, 250 Insurance St., Beaver 15009, 412-728-3005; 2700 Rochester Rd., Mars 16046, 412-772-6080; and 304 E. North St., New Castle 16101, 412-654-9036.

Committees: *Banking, Finance and Urban Affairs* (29th of 30 D): Economic Growth and Credit Formation. *Education and Labor* (22d of 28 D): Labor-Management Relations; Postsecondary Education and Training. *Small Business* (21st of 27 D): Procurement, Taxation and Tourism; SBA Legislation and the General Economy.

Group Ratings and 102d Congress Votes: Newly Elected

Key Votes of the 103d Congress

1. Family Leave	FOR	2. Deficit Reduction	FOR	3. Stimulus Plan	FOR

Election Results

1992 general	Ron Klink (D)	186,684	(79%)	($240,419)
	Gordon R. Johnston (R)	48,484	(20%)	($13,993)
	Other	2,754	(1%)	
1992 primary	Ron Klink (D)	45,884	(45%)	
	Mike Veon (D)	22,379	(22%)	
	Joseph P. Kolter (D)	19,683	(20%)	
	Frank LaGrotta (D)	13,153	(13%)	
1990 general	Joseph P. Kolter (D)	74,114	(56%)	($132,920)
	Gordon R. Johnston (R)	58,469	(44%)	($8,837)

FIFTH DISTRICT

North central Pennsylvania, isolated from the rest of the country by chains of mountains, off the main east-west rail and highway lines until the 1970s, is one of those empty spaces that make even the Northeastern states seem lightly populated to someone used to the densely packed terrain of Western Europe or East Asia. In narrow valleys, pressed tightly by mountains and fast-flowing rivers, connected by roads that switch back and wind precariously over mountains, are a few population concentrations. The largest is in the Nittany Valley, the home of Pennsylvania State University, long known for its powerful football teams coached by Joe Paterno. This is one major node of Pennsylvania's 5th Congressional District (the redistricted descendant of the 23d, extended a bit east), which includes the geographically largest swath of this empty quarter. Another is to the west, around Oil City, where Colonel Edwin Drake sunk the first successful oil well in 1859, and where Pennsylvania crude is still an economic asset; and

Lewisburg, home of Bucknell University and one of the more famous federal prisons, Allenwood. The solidly built courthouses and banks in the center of each county seat testify to the long history of prosperity in this part of the country; yet today, even with the main east-west truck line, Interstate 80, it is a low-wage area. The 5th remains a rural and small-town district, populated mainly by descendants of the English stock farmers who moved here in the early 19th Century; it is one part of America that no later wave of immigration has reached.

Pennsylvania's Republican tradition goes back to the Civil War, and that tradition is strong here. State College has sometimes trended Democratic (despite Paterno's Republicanism) and Bill Clinton did not run far behind George Bush here in 1992. In congressional races, the district was seriously contested from the mid-1970s through the 1980s, but in 1992 it reelected Republican Bill Clinger without opposition.

By now, Clinger is one of the more senior House Republicans. He is generally rated a party moderate, though his recent vote ratings definitely put him in the conservative camp. He is willing to reconsider tradition-minded positions on cultural issues and convince liberal journalists he shares their views. He comes up with original, thought-provoking causes. He got the upper Allegheny designated a Wild and Scenic River. He wants to install a clock in the Capitol to keep track of the national debt. His biggest legislative triumph was passage of an anti-backhauling bill, barring trucks from using the same containers to carry garbage in one direction and food in the other. He wants to require "rural community impact statements" for proposed hazardous waste landfills and incinerators: waste-choked East Coast metro areas look to the empty hills of central Pennsylvania as disposal sites. He has risked some anger back home by continuing to support a levee on the Susquehanna in Lock Haven, even though the locals no longer want it. But supporting construction projects is not alien to Clinger, who is the second ranking Republican on the Public Works Committee, behind fellow Pennsylvanian (and shameless pork barreler) Bud Shuster, and for 1993 ranking Republican on the Government Operations Committee. From that venue, Clinger criticized Hillary Rodham Clinton's healthcare task force for holding its meetings behind closed doors; Clinger believes all advisory meetings should be public, and will try to amend the Federal Advisory Committee Act to reflect that.

The People: Pop. 1990: 565,736; 66% rural; 14% age 65+; 97% White; 1% Black; 1% Asian; 1% Hispanic origin. Voting age pop.: 431,401; 1% Black; 1% Hispanic origin. Households: 60% married couple families; 27% married couple fams. w. children; 31% college educ.; median household income: $23,934; per capita income: $10,946; median gross rent: $334; median house value: $47,800.

1992 Presidential Vote			1988 Presidential Vote		
Bush (R)	89,385	(41%)	Bush (R)	113,978	(60%)
Clinton (D)	78,057	(36%)	Dukakis (D)	76,882	(40%)
Perot (I)	48,100	(22%)			

Rep. William F. (Bill) Clinger, Jr. (R)

Elected 1978; b. Apr. 4, 1929, Warren; home, Warren; Johns Hopkins U., B.A. 1951, U. of VA, LL.B. 1965; Presbyterian; married (Julia).

Career: Navy, 1951–55; Marketing, Blair Co., 1955–62; Practicing atty., 1965–75, 1977–78; Chief Cnsl., Econ. Devel. Admin., U.S. Dept. of Commerce, 1975–77.

Offices: 2160 RHOB 20515, 202-225-5121. Also 315 S. Allen St., #219, State College 16801, 814-238-1776; and 605 Pennbank Bldg., Warren 16365, 814-726-3910.

Committees: *Government Operations* (RMM of 17 R): Legislation and National Security. *Public Works and Transportation* (2d of 24 R): Aviation (RMM); Surface Transportation; Water Resources and Environment.

Group Ratings

	ADA	ACLU	COPE	CDF	CFA	LCV	ACU	NTLC	NSI	COC	CEI
1992	10	13	8	30	27	13	90	60	100	88	60
1991	15	—	42	30	28	15	70	—	—	90	52

National Journal Ratings

	1991 LIB — 1991 CONS	1992 LIB — 1992 CONS
Economic	30% — 69%	12% — 86%
Social	30% — 68%	25% — 74%
Foreign	33% — 67%	0% — 82%

Key Votes of the 102d Congress

1. Ban Striker Replace	AGN	5. Handgun Wait/7-Day AGN	9. Use Force in Gulf	FOR
2. $ for Homeownership	FOR	6. Overseas Mil. AbortionAGN	10. US Mil. Abroad $ CutAGN
3. Tax Rich/Cut Mid Cls.AGN	7. Obscn. Art NEA $ BanAGN	11. Limit SDI Funds	AGN
4. FY93/$15B Def. Cut AGN	8. Death Pen. from Jury FOR	12. Cuba Trade Embargo FOR

Key Votes of the 103d Congress

1. Family Leave	AGN	2. Deficit Reduction	AGN	3. Stimulus Plan	AGN

Election Results

1992 general	William F. (Bill) Clinger, Jr. (D), unopposed			($266,090)
1992 primary	William F. (Bill) Clinger, Jr. (D), unopposed			
1990 general	William F. (Bill) Clinger, Jr. (R)	78,189	(59%)	($338,431)
	Daniel J. Shannon (D)	53,465	(41%)	($6,765)

SIXTH DISTRICT

The gentle hills of southeastern Pennsylvania, above Philadelphia and the Delaware River and below the first chains of the Appalachians, were America's first polyglot interior. It was largely settled in the 18th Century by Quaker townsmen, Welsh farmers, German peasants and members of pietistic sects, who came to be known as Pennsylvania Dutch. They were a diverse lot looking for tolerance in William Penn's commonwealth who found a land that yielded up riches, first in crops, then in ironworking and other industry. In time this civilization poured over the mountain chains, where the farmers were rougher and more violent, and where the towns existed solely to mine rich veins of anthracite and bituminous coal, the primary energy source of late 19th and early 20th Century America. These mountain communities were less orderly; tough-talking miners and factory workers stayed menacingly in the background unless a character stumbled into the wrong roadhouse at night or wrong diner at dawn: this was the Pennsylvania John O'Hara grew up in and described in his 1930s and 1940s novels and stories.

Linked together by the Reading Railroad in 1842, and one of America's prime industrial sites for a century after, the anthracite country around Pottsville and the hat and textile mills of Reading were left behind by the economic growth of the late 20th Century. The anthracite country, nestled amid mountains, has never rebounded from the switch from coal to oil for home heating: Schuylkill County around Pottsville had 228,000 people in 1940 and 153,000 in 1990. But Reading has come back, starting in 1970, when a company called Vanity Fair began selling seconds and overruns of stockings and lingerie at wholesale prices in what had been the Berkshire Knitting Mills; this was the first of the factory outlets. By 1992, Reading was home to some 300 outlets, selling deep-discounted goods on the polished wood floors of converted brick mills, bringing in more than half a billion dollars a year, generating 5,000 jobs and 2,000 motel rooms.

The 6th Congressional District of Pennsylvania includes Berks and Schuylkill Counties centered on Reading and Pottsville, plus an almost unconnected sliver of Northumberland County, industrial area between mountains and the upper Susquehanna River. Politically, it is split between the rough mining tradition of the anthracite country and the quietism of the Pennsylvania Dutch. For three decades, this has been a potentially marginal district, but it was represented for 24 years by Democrat Gus Yatron, who as Foreign Affairs Human Rights Subcommittee chairman condemned abuses in Nicaragua, Chile, the Philippines, China and Iraq. But his percentage in the 6th dropped to 57% in 1990, and a former aide accused him of salary kickbacks. The aide ended up being indicted for skimming off campaign money, but Yatron decided to retire in 1992.

The obvious successor, state Senator Michael O'Pake, who kept Berks and Schuylkill together during redistricting, decided not to run, which led to a free-for-all for the district. Both parties' primaries featured two candidates from Berks County and one each from Schuylkill; both Schuylkill men, Republican John Jones III and Democrat Tim Holden, won. They could both be characters out of O'Hara. Jones is from one of those families who seem to have been running things since O'Hara's times, keeping the mines open and unstruck and keeping Schuylkill County Republican in most elections. He went to boarding school, became a lawyer, and runs a family business operating public golf courses. Holden comes from a political family from the coal mining hamlet of St. Clair; his great-grandfather was a coal miner (who founded the forerunner to the UMW) and his father Joseph "Socks" Holden served four terms as Schuylkill County Commissioner. Holden was a football player who says he has been around athletics all his life and has always gone to church and fire company block parties. He became the first Democrat elected Schuylkill County Sheriff in 75 years, in 1985, at 28, and was reelected with 75%. Jones called Holden "an idealess, clueless candidate," who was simply not competent to be congressman. Holden said the race was Main Street versus Wall Street and that he represented "the hardworking men and women" of the district. Jones backed term limits and congressional salary cuts and raised more money than Holden; when Holden endorsed magnetic levitation trains, Jones attacked him constantly for backing bullet trains and wondered caustically who would ride on them. Holden got help from out-of-district Democrats, including Hillary Rodham Clinton's brothers Anthony and Hugh Rodham, who were stumping in the region for their brother-in-law.

By all indicators, this district should have gone Republican. Dick Thornburgh carried it in his losing race for senator, and George Bush carried it over Bill Clinton, though his vote was down more than 20% from his 1988 62% level. This seems to be one of those culturally conservative areas, with relatively few of the singles and working wives who cast such large Clinton margins elsewhere. But, apparently helped by the class contrast, Tim Holden won 52%–48%. He pledged to work for his "campaign cornerstones—jobs, healthcare, the economy and the environment."

He opposes national health insurance as "socialized medicine," but favors a national board of health care professionals to set rates for medical care and drugs. His hostility to market economics is apparent in his strong opposition to NAFTA. He successfully sought a seat on the Agriculture Committee, even though local farmers get little benefit from subsidies. Holden has made some difficult challenges for himself, and has set himself up to be held accountable in 1994 for the Clinton Administration's and Democratic Congress's success, or lack of it, in reviving the economy and reforming the health care system.

The People: Pop. 1990: 565,923; 44% rural; 17% age 65+; 92% White; 2% Black; 1% Asian; 2% Other; 3% Hispanic origin. Voting age pop.: 435,058; 2% Black; 2% Hispanic origin. Households: 59% married couple families; 25% married couple fams. w. children; 28% college educ.; median household income: $28,766; per capita income: $13,349; median gross rent: $367; median house value: $65,900.

1992 Presidential Vote			1988 Presidential Vote		
Bush (R)	90,140	(41%)	Bush (R)	117,434	(62%)
Clinton (D)	78,776	(36%)	Dukakis (D)	73,464	(38%)
Perot (I)	50,333	(23%)			

Rep. Tim Holden (D)

Elected 1992; b. Mar. 5, 1957, Pottsville; home, St. Clair; U. of Richmond, 1976–78, Bloomsburg St. U., B.A. 1980; Catholic; separated.

Career: Insurance broker/real estate agent, Holden Insurance Agency, 1980–85; Schuylkill Cnty. Sheriff, 1985–92.

Offices: 1421 LHOB 20515, 202-225-5546. Also Berks Cnty. Ctr., 633 Court St., Reading 19801, 215-371-9931; Meridian Bank Bldg., #303, 101 N. Centre St., Pottsville 17901, 717-662-4212; and Northumberland Cnty. Cthse., Market Sq., Sunbury 17801, 717-988-1902.

Committees: *Agriculture* (21st of 28 D): Department Operations and Nutrition; Environment, Credit and Rural Development; Livestock. *Armed Services* (31st of 34 D): Military Acquisition; Oversight and Investigations.

Group Ratings and 102d Congress Votes: Newly Elected

Key Votes of the 103d Congress

1. Family Leave	FOR	2. Deficit Reduction	AGN	3. Stimulus Plan	FOR

Election Results

1992 general	Tim Holden (D)	108,312	(52%)	($284,349)
	John E. Jones III (R)	99,694	(48%)	($442,058)
1992 primary	Tim Holden (D)	20,057	(39%)	
	Warren H. Haggerty, Jr. (D)	16,647	(33%)	
	John A. Reusing (D)	14,193	(28%)	
1990 general	Gus Yatron (D)	74,394	(57%)	($191,512)
	John F. Hicks (R)	56,093	(43%)	($71,317)

SEVENTH DISTRICT

The close-in suburbs of the great Eastern cities are homes to some of the most curious, and most long-lasting, political machines in America. They are Republican; they conduct business in the accents of ordinary people, ethnic as well as WASP; they have a tolerance for patronage, and for what city reform liberals would call corruption, that is sharply at odds with their embodiment of middle-class morality; they are old, going back to the days when political machines were as much part of the urban landscape as trolley lines or overhead electrical wires; and, unlike most big city Democratic machines, they are still in business. One such machine is the War Board of Pennsylvania's Delaware County. This is a diverse area, mostly but not entirely white, predominantly Catholic where it was predominantly Protestant two generations ago. Its housing stock and population are aging but still well-maintained, above average in income but varying widely from the affluent Main Line commuter towns. People here treasure traditional cultural values but also feel pinched by recession and worry about retirement; they have deep roots in greater Philadelphia, but also deep fears about crime in nearby city neighborhoods.

The 7th Congressional District includes almost all of Delaware County, except for a few towns appended to Philadelphia districts, and extends north to include Main Line suburbs and King of Prussia, the edge city where the Schuylkill Expressway intersects the Pennsylvania Turnpike. As redistricted, the 7th had two Republican incumbents, but Richard Schulze decided to retire after 18 years in office. That left the district for Curt Weldon, a Republican backed by the War Board and with anything but an aristocratic pedigree. He first came to public attention as mayor of Marcus Hook, Pennsylvania's southernmost town on the Delaware River, the home of oil tank farms and a rusty-looking old steel mill; he went on the county council, ran in 1984 against liberal Democrat Bob Edgar (who got to Congress when the War Board split 10 years before), lost by 412 votes, and ran again (with no primary opposition) in 1986 when Edgar ran unsuccessfully for the Senate.

Tip O'Neill once said that all politics is local, and Weldon's politics certainly is: he prides himself on attending every Eagle Scout induction in the district. He has worked hard to keep the Philadelphia Navy Yard open, and to find new uses for it. He has been a big cheerleader for the V-22 Osprey tilt-rotor aircraft, one of whose major contractors, Boeing Vertol, is in the district. Weldon has achieved a certain fame as founder of the Congressional Fire Services Caucus, which most members laughed at at first but then joined; it sponsored measures calling for new alarm systems in congressional offices and a new Fire Training Center in Illinois. Weldon personally helped to put out a fire in former Speaker Jim Wright's office, and he had the satisfaction of seeing George Bush come to Delaware County in October 1992 to sign Weldon's Fire Service bill into law.

On national issues, Weldon has a rather high union voting record, and favors protectionist-minded measures like domestic content labeling of autos. He took the lead in November 1991 in getting 82 House Republicans to write President Bush asking him to make Jack Kemp his domestic policy czar (Bush could have done worse, and did). Weldon's formula worked well in the new 7th District. In 1992, opposition came from Montgomery County lawyer Fiorindo Vagnozzi in the primary; with War Board support, Weldon won with 77%. In the general, against the former mayor of Media, the Chester County seat, Weldon won by nearly 2–1, running far ahead of Bush.

The People: Pop. 1990: 565,815; 5% rural; 15% age 65+; 93% White; 4% Black; 2% Asian; 1% Hispanic origin. Voting age pop.: 440,656; 4% Black; 1% Hispanic origin. Households: 60% married couple families; 26% married couple fams. w. children; 53% college educ.; median household income: $41,710; per capita income: $20,175; median gross rent: $568; median house value: $133,000.

1992 Presidential Vote

Bush (R) 124,751 (43%)
Clinton (D) 111,511 (39%)
Perot (I). 49,798 (17%)

1988 Presidential Vote

Bush (R) 167,029 (64%)
Dukakis (D). 94,532 (36%)

Rep. Curt Weldon (R)

Elected 1986; b. July 22, 1947, Marcus Hook; home, Aston; West Chester St. Col., B.A. 1969; Protestant; married (Mary).

Career: Elem. schl. teacher, vice principal, 1969–76; Dir., Training and Manpower Devel., CIGNA Corp., 1976–81; Marcus Hook Mayor, 1977–82; Delaware Cnty. Cncl., 1984–86, Chmn. 1985–86.

Offices: 2452 RHOB 20515, 202-225-2011. Also 1554 Garrett Rd., Upper Darby 19082, 215-259-0700.

Committees: *Armed Services* (7th of 22 R): Military Acquisition; Readiness. *Merchant Marine and Fisheries* (6th of 19 R): Environment and Natural Resources; Oceanography, Gulf of Mexico and the Outer Continental Shelf (RMM).

Group Ratings

	ADA	ACLU	COPE	CDF	CFA	LCV	ACU	NTLC	NSI	COC	CEI
1992	25	26	83	40	33	38	80	75	100	88	66
1991	30	—	55	60	39	46	65	—	—	60	61

National Journal Ratings

	1991 LIB — 1991 CONS		1992 LIB — 1992 CONS	
Economic	40%	— 59%	36%	— 63%
Social	24%	— 75%	16%	— 82%
Foreign	33%	— 67%	18%	— 74%

Key Votes of the 102d Congress

1. Ban Striker Replace	FOR	5. Handgun Wait/7-Day	FOR	9. Use Force in Gulf	FOR
2. $ for Homeownership	FOR	6. Overseas Mil. Abortion	AGN	10. US Mil. Abroad $ Cut	AGN
3. Tax Rich/Cut Mid Cls.	AGN	7. Obscn. Art NEA $ Ban	FOR	11. Limit SDI Funds	AGN
4. FY93/$15B Def. Cut	AGN	8. Death Pen. from Jury	FOR	12. Cuba Trade Embargo	FOR

Key Votes of the 103d Congress

1. Family Leave	FOR	2. Deficit Reduction	AGN	3. Stimulus Plan	AGN

Election Results

1992 general	Curt Weldon (R).	180,648	(66%)	($565,974)
	Frank Daly (D).	91,623	(34%)	($173,865)
	Other.	1,627	(1%)	
1992 primary	Curt Weldon (R).	73,304	(77%)	
	Fiorindo Vagnozzi (R).	21,413	(23%)	
1990 general	Curt Weldon (R).	105,868	(65%)	($480,165)
	John Innelli (D).	56,292	(35%)	($109,618)

EIGHTH DISTRICT

Bucks County, one of William Penn's three original counties, had a dual nature from the beginning: it was a paradise of bucolic hills and creeks running into the Delaware, and then in 1727 James Logan, Penn's secretary, established the Durham Furnace iron works there. Bucolic Bucks, mellow and well-settled farmland with old fieldstone houses and covered bridges, captured the imagination of writers and artists back in the 1920s, attracting a theatrical crowd—Oscar Hammerstein, Moss Hart, Dorothy Parker, S. J. Perelman—who gave it a certain celebrity status. Then in the years after World War II, industrial Bucks came to the fore. Its location directly between Philadelphia and industrial Trenton, New Jersey, along the ocean-navigable Delaware River and several rail lines, led to huge new developments: U.S. Steel's Fairless Works, one of the few big postwar steel plants, down by the river, and the Levitt organization's second Levittown, in what had been farmland and swamp between U.S. 13 and U.S. 1.

Politically, Bucks County, like all of Pennsylvania, was solidly Republican: it was the home of Senator Joseph Grundy, longtime head of the Pennsylvania Manufacturers Association, who opposed the 1930 Smoot-Hawley tariff on the grounds that it was not protectionist enough. But unlike other suburban Philadelphia counties, where most blue-collar immigration took place years ago when the county machines were ready to enroll new residents in their party, development came after the New Deal in Bucks. So lower Bucks, around the Fairless Works and Levittown, is fairly solidly Democratic, while upper Bucks, fast-growing in the 1980s, and once again attracting trendy New Yorkers such as Calvin Klein and Billy Joel, is Republican but environment-conscious. Perkasie, for example, encourages recycling by requiring residents to pay $1.50 for every 40-pounds of trash picked up from their homes.

The 8th Congressional District of Pennsylvania includes all of Bucks County plus Horsham Township in Montgomery County. With only slightly different boundaries, it has been one of the nation's prime marginal districts for much of the last two decades. The main reason was Democrat Peter Kostmayer, an environment-minded, defense-cutting liberal, who first won the seat in 1976 at age 30, lost it in 1980 but won it back two years later, and held it with varying margins through 1990. Kostmayer worked hard on local environmental issues, raised national money with his liberal environmental and foreign policy stands, and ran an amazingly good constituency service operation. But in 1992, he was plainly in trouble. He attracted strong opposition in state Senator Jim Greenwood, and he had House check problems—at least 50 overdrafts in recent years and charges of many more overdrafts earlier in the 1980s, including a $23,000 check to his father. Kostmayer still raised $1.2 million, most of it from outside the district, some from the likes of Jack Lemmon and Abby Rockefeller. But he was embarrassed when his former wife contributed $500 to Greenwood with a warm endorsement, noting that she was prohibited by court order after a nasty divorce from talking about their personal life.

Greenwood came to the race with an unusual background for a Republican. He was a social worker who in the 1970s supervised emotionally troubled youths at a school in Langhorne in Lower Bucks, and as a county children and youth agency caseworker helped decide when to place abused children with foster families. Greenwood went on to be elected to the state House in 1980 and the state Senate in 1986; there he sponsored a Family Preservation Act, calling for intensive intervention by social workers to keep children with their families if possible rather than place them in foster care. Greenwood also sponsored bills to limit teacher strikes and to mandate statewide solid waste recycling—popular causes in Bucks. In his 1992 campaign, he issued detailed proposals to shrink the federal budget (he is avidly anti-tax) and create a healthcare system. His campaign was not entirely positive: most of the fall he ran a TV spot citing Kostmayer's 50 overdrafts and calling him out of touch, and intoned the usual challenger's mantra—term limits, line-item veto, congressional reform. Kostmayer, in turn, while stressing the environment, ran mostly negative spots, attacking Greenwood for accepting contributions from polluters. Kostmayer's attempts to identify with attacks on incumbents were deft—he was one of the first incumbents to support ending many perks in 1991, and he endorsed Lynn Yeakel before her primary victory in the Senate race—but he did not overcome the check problem.

Greenwood in the end proved the shrewder campaigner, gambling by spending most of his money on early September TV and then, when an October poll showed him behind by only 41%–39%, raising much more, for a total exceeding $725,000—one of the best showings of any challenger. He stayed calm and collected when Kostmayer launched vitriolic attacks on him in debate. He did not get dragged down by the national ticket; George Bush ended up losing Bucks by only a 39%–38% margin. The result was a 52%–46% Greenwood victory, and Peter Kostmayer, the same age as Bill Clinton, left national office just as Clinton came in.

Greenwood comes to Washington an experienced legislator, with a deliberate approach to the job: "You do it by paying attention to detail. You do it by amendments in committee . . . And you do it by offering good ideas that are hard to resist." His real life experience working with troubled families should make him distinctive in Republican ranks, and perhaps capable of influencing Democrats as well, and his seat on the highly coveted Energy and Commerce Committee should serve him well. With Bucks's mild Republican leanings, and without the problems that troubled Kostmayer in 1992, Greenwood seems a good bet to hold this seat—though it still has the capacity to give an incumbent a real challenge.

The People: Pop. 1990: 565,820; 18% rural; 11% age 65+; 94% White; 3% Black; 2% Asian; 1% Other; 2% Hispanic origin. Voting age pop.: 421,289; 3% Black; 1% Hispanic origin. Households: 66% married couple families; 32% married couple fams. w. children; 49% college educ.; median household income: $43,483; per capita income: $18,374; median gross rent: $608; median house value: $139,700.

1992 Presidential Vote			1988 Presidential Vote		
Clinton (D)	101,630	(39%)	Bush (R)	133,893	(61%)
Bush (R)	99,269	(38%)	Dukakis (D)	85,452	(39%)
Perot (I)	56,261	(22%)			

Rep. Jim Greenwood (R)

Elected 1992; b. May 4, 1951, Philadelphia; home, Erwinna; Dickinson Col., B.A. 1973; Protestant; married (Christina).

Career: Legis. Asst., PA Rep. John Renninger, 1972–76; Caseworker, Bucks Cnty. Child & Youth Social Svcs., 1977–80; PA House of Reps., 1980–86; PA Senate, 1986–93.

Offices: 515 CHOB 20515, 202-225-4276. Also 69 E. Oxford Ave., Doylestown 18901, 215-348-7511; and One Oxford Valley, #800, Langhorne 19047, 215-752-7711.

Committees: *Energy and Commerce* (16th of 17 R): Commerce, Consumer Protection and Competitiveness; Health and the Environment.

Group Ratings and 102d Congress Votes: Newly Elected

Key Votes of the 103d Congress

1. Family Leave	AGN	2. Deficit Reduction	AGN	3. Stimulus Plan	AGN

Election Results

1992 general	Jim Greenwood (R)	129,593	(52%)	($717,249)
	Peter H. Kostmayer (D)	114,095	(46%)	($1,242,355)
	Other	5,850	(2%)	
1992 primary	Jim Greenwood (R)	36,394	(81%)	
	Joseph P. Schiaffino (R)	9,472	(19%)	
1990 general	Peter H. Kostmayer (D)	85,015	(57%)	($826,742)
	Audrie Zettick Schaller (R)	65,100	(43%)	($142,957)

NINTH DISTRICT

Like a series of vertebrae through central Pennsylvania, the Appalachian mountain chain has been a formidable barrier through most of Pennsylvania's history. Up close the mountains look tantalizingly low: you imagine that you could hike over them in an hour or so. But they are much more daunting than they seem. The colonials and British regulars led by General Braddock to defeat near Pittsburgh in 1754 found it hard going, despite their guidance from George Washington; 19th Century pioneers in Conestoga wagons found it not much easier, for there are few gaps in the ridges and unless you build a tunnel you have to climb over the top.

During the 18th Century, the mountains provided Quaker Pennsylvania with a rampart against Indian attacks, and allowed the commonwealth to become the richest and most populous of the colonies. But in the 19th Century, when people wanted to open up and trade with the vast interior, the mountains provided a barrier, so they went over New York's Erie Canal and New York Central Railroad instead. It took the aggressive capitalists who built the Pennsylvania Railroad to get trains over these ridges, and a nation facing war in 1940 to build the first highway, the Pennsylvania Turnpike, that could dependably get trucks over them. Today, the old towns look much as they did 60 years ago; the farmhouses and red barns still sit on rolling hills in the shadow of the ridges, isolated and out of touch with the pulsing rhythms of the America of the early 1990s.

Pennsylvania's 9th Congressional District lies wholly within these mountains. This part of the Alleghenies (the term is often used interchangeably with Appalachians in Pennsylvania), was settled by poor Scottish and Ulster Irish farmers just after the Revolutionary War. They were fiercely independent and proud, as the Whiskey Rebellion demonstrated—corn was not an article of commerce out here unless distilled into easily portable, if not very potable, alcohol. The settlers worked their hardscrabble farms and built little towns; the 9th is mostly not coal country, and was spared the boom-bust cycles of northeastern Pennsylvania and West Virginia. This was an important area for the Pennsylvania Railroad, however. Near Altoona was the Pennsylvania Railroad's famous Horseshoe Curve, and in Altoona the railroad built the nation's largest car yards. As rail transportation became less important, and the prosperous Pennsylvania Railroad became the bankrupt Penn Central, Altoona's population fell from 82,000 in 1930 to 52,000 in 1990. Redistricting for 1992 changed the 9th's boundaries only marginally, and left the district with substantially the same political balance.

This part of Pennsylvania has been solidly Republican since the election of 1860, and has not come close to electing a Democrat to Congress for years. The current incumbent, E. G. (Bud) Shuster made his fortune building a computer business then settled in the southern Pennsylvania mountains. He became interested in local affairs, ran for Congress and beat the favorite, a local state senator, in the 1972 Republican primary; he is now one of the senior Republicans in Congress. In the 1970s, Shuster was a hard-driving Republican partisan and conservative firebrand, the House's most vociferous opponent of the automobile air bag, and chairman of the Republican Policy Committee until 1980. Then he ran for minority whip against Trent Lott and lost. Since then, he has concentrated almost all his efforts on the Public Works Committee, where he is now ranking Republican, working with Democrats to craft bipartisan highway and water projects bills with national scope—and with plenty of pork for the 9th District. Shuster has obviously taken a long journey from his earlier conservatism, although his work is arguably in line with the 19th Century Republican tradition of subsidizing canals and railroads and the World War II subsidies for the Pennsylvania Turnpike—transportation arteries that made most commerce possible in these mountains.

Shuster is anything but bashful about bringing home the bacon, and may indeed be the most successful pork barreler in Congress. He is proud that U.S. 220 between Altoona and the Turnpike at Bedford was completed in 1989, as a "demonstration project" with 100% federal financing, and that Democratic Governor Bob Casey, named part of it the Bud Shuster Highway. He says his most significant accomplishment in the 102d Congress was passing his Intermodal Surface Transportation Act of 1991 which promises to complete the interstate highway program in 1993. He is proud that Pennsylvania came away with $934 million in new projects, the most of any state, including $287 million for 13 projects in the 9th District. He is pleased that the nation's first federally funded bus testing center is in Blair County, Pennsylvania. Anyone wondering why Republicans had so little success cutting back government spending during the Reagan and Bush years should contemplate Bud Shuster's career.

On other issues, Shuster does have a conservative record. In 1991, he was ranking Republican on the Intelligence Committee, where he called Chairman Dave McCurdy's plan to overhaul and reduce the size of the CIA as "very premature." In 1993, as ranking member of Public Works, Shuster called Clinton's proposed Btu tax "a bad idea," and asserted that it would devastate some air carriers by escalating costs and undermining the nation's highway transportation system, thus inhibiting Clinton's goal of improving the nation's infrastructure. Redistricting did not change the district much and Shuster ran unopposed in 1992.

The People: Pop. 1990: 565,858; 70% rural; 15% age 65+; 98% White; 1% Black. Voting age pop.: 425,141; 1% Black. Households: 63% married couple families; 28% married couple fams. w. children; 23% college educ.; median household income: $24,309; per capita income: $11,229; median gross rent: $305; median house value: $49,200.

1992 Presidential Vote			1988 Presidential Vote		
Bush (R)	97,764	(48%)	Bush (R)	117,717	(64%)
Clinton (D)	66,923	(33%)	Dukakis (D)	65,663	(36%)
Perot (I)	40,200	(20%)			

Rep. E. G. (Bud) Shuster (R)

Elected 1972; b. Jan. 23, 1932, Glassport; home, Everett; U. of Pittsburgh, B.S. 1954, Duquesne U., M.B.A. 1960, American U., Ph.D. 1967; United Church of Christ; married (Patricia).

Career: Army, 1954–56; Vice Pres., Electronic Computer Div., RCA; Founder and chmn., computer software co.

Offices: 2188 RHOB 20515, 202-225-2431. Also RD 2, Box 711, Altoona 16601, 814-946-1653; and 179 E. Queen St., Chambersburg 17201, 717-264-8308.

Committees: *Public Works and Transportation* (RMM of 24 R).

Group Ratings

	ADA	ACLU	COPE	CDF	CFA	LCV	ACU	NTLC	NSI	COC	CEI
1992	5	0	17	0	13	0	100	95	90	88	77
1991	15	—	42	20	28	0	95	—	—	90	71

National Journal Ratings

	1991 LIB	—	1991 CONS	1992 LIB	—	1992 CONS
Economic	26%	—	74%	16%	—	80%
Social	0%	—	84%	26%	—	72%
Foreign	0%	—	88%	18%	—	74%

Key Votes of the 102d Congress

1. Ban Striker Replace AGN	5. Handgun Wait/7-Day AGN	9. Use Force in Gulf FOR
2. $ for Homeownership FOR	6. Overseas Mil. AbortionAGN	10. US Mil. Abroad $ CutAGN
3. Tax Rich/Cut Mid Cls.AGN	7. Obscn. Art NEA $ Ban FOR	11. Limit SDI Funds AGN
4. FY93/$15B Def. Cut AGN	8. Death Pen. from Jury FOR	12. Cuba Trade Embargo FOR

Key Votes of the 103d Congress

1. Family Leave AGN	2. Deficit Reduction AGN	3. Stimulus Plan AGN

Election Results

1992 general	E. G. (Bud) Shuster (R), unopposed	($556,385)
1992 primary	E. G. (Bud) Shuster (R), unopposed	
1990 general	E. G. (Bud) Shuster (R), unopposed	($429,942)

TENTH DISTRICT

"Coal is the theme song of this city in the hills," wrote the *WPA Guide* of Scranton 50 years ago. But as those words were written, the anthracite kingdom was dying, or dead. Demand for hard coal as a home heating fuel started to decline in the 1920s and plummeted in the 1940s; the three major anthracite counties fell in population from 991,000 in 1930 to 699,000 in 1990, and Scranton's Lackawanna County fell from 310,000 to 219,000. In the process, the coal dust and air pollution vanished, the ethnic groups became less distinctive, and what had been communities of young families became communities of old people. In the 1960s and 1970s, there was an influx of textile and apparel mills, bringing low-wage, non-union jobs to what had once been a high-wage, unionized area. But the anthracite kingdom, created by unbridled free enterprise, has become used to looking to government for sustenance.

That is the basis of the politics of Pennsylvania's 10th Congressional District, which is centered on Scranton and includes most of the northeast corner of Pennsylvania—green hills with little towns in crevassed river valleys, criss-crossed by giant viaducts built for the railroads linking coal and iron mines with great cities' factories, the outer borough New Yorkers' resorts of the Poconos and new condominiums and vacation homes springing up on inexpensive real estate. Historically, this is very Republican territory; the anthracite mines brought some Democrats, but their numbers are declining; the 10th went narrowly for George Bush in 1992. But congressional politics here depends less on party than on pork. For years the great benefactor of the anthracite kingdom was Daniel Flood of neighboring Wilkes-Barre and the 11th District, and Appropriations subcommittee chairman. When scandal forced him to resign in 1980, the new great benefactor was Joseph McDade, a Republican first elected in the 10th in 1962, and ranking minority member of the Appropriations Defense Subcommittee. Now McDade has scandal problems himself, and the district must be wondering if he can survive them and keep the federal money pouring in.

McDade is short, chunky, white-haired, Irish, good-humored, a get-along guy whose legal defense fund is chaired by none less than Tip O'Neill; he has many friends on the Democratic side and his liberal voting record has not prevented him from keeping many on the Republican. He and fellow Pennsylvanian John Murtha now have the top two seats on Defense Appropriations and they continue Flood's law requiring the military to buy tons of unneeded and expensive Pennsylvania coal. McDade is proud of channeling funds to Steamtown, a failed commercial railroad theme park, which he snuck into the huge 1986 omnibus appropriations bill and has nursed along ever since, even though the park is dilapidated, polluted, and its two restored locomotives are from Canada; a former Smithsonian curator calls it "a third-rate collection in a place to which it has no relevance." But the Park Service is commanded to spend money on it even while park rangers are laid off and Independence Hall is structurally imperiled—and while McDade's fellow Scrantonite, Governor Bob Casey, pushes a proposal to tear down nearby historic structures and railbeds for what is almost surely a commercially unviable shopping mall. Scrantonites are grateful though: before death and even with indictment, they established McDade Park with an Anthracite Museum and the McDade Technology Center at the University of Scranton.

The indictment came after a long investigation, beginning in December 1988 when *The Wall Street Journal* detailed that McDade had received $45,000 in campaign contributions and speaking fees from officials involved in United ChemCon, a company with a plant in his district, for which he arranged a Defense Department minority set-aside contract; it was charged that some of the employees were reimbursed by the company for their contributions—which would make them illegal. Only in May 1992 was McDade indicted on these charges and for allegedly accepting $100,000 in bribes and illegal gratuities—Lear jet trips to Florida, expense-paid vacations at posh resorts, sham "scholarships" for his son—from six defense contractors and lobbyists in the 1980s. McDade accused the prosecutor, a protege of Senator Arlen Specter, of being politically biased; he attacked the RICO law under which he was indicted and said he was unaware of illegal contributions and reimbursed donors for any questionable expenditures. The indictment has not forced him to resign any position, including the ranking Republican slot on the full Appropriations Committee (the Democrats have a rule requiring indicted chairmen to step down; Republicans don't). In the April 1992 primary, he was not only renominated, but won the Democratic nomination with 1,518 write-ins. "There's no question I'm very fortunate," McDade said; Ed Mitchell, a Democrat who in 1976 gave him his toughest race said, "He does a good job. He brings home the bacon." For 1993, the question is whether Republicans will remove him from his committee and subcommittee posts, and whether his clout will be reduced; already in late 1991, the House sought to rein in Steamtown's ever increasing costs, but similar efforts went nowhere in the Senate. McDade's future and that of 10th District politics depend on how his legal case comes out, and whether he retains the Appropriations clout which has made him unbeatable for 30 years.

The People: Pop. 1990: 565,777; 54% rural; 17% age 65+; 98% White; 1% Black; 1% Hispanic origin. Voting age pop.: 428,610; 1% Black; 1% Hispanic origin. Households: 60% married couple families; 26% married couple fams. w. children; 33% college educ.; median household income: $25,648; per capita income: $12,005; median gross rent: $339; median house value: $70,100.

1992 Presidential Vote			1988 Presidential Vote		
Bush (R)	95,803	(41%)	Bush (R)	118,139	(59%)
Clinton (D)	88,193	(38%)	Dukakis (D)	83,728	(41%)
Perot (I)	46,881	(20%)			

Rep. Joseph M. McDade (R)

Elected 1962; b. Sept. 29, 1931, Scranton; home, Clarks Summit; U. of Notre Dame, B.A. 1953, U. of PA, LL.B. 1956; Catholic; married (Sarah).

Career: Clerk, Chief Fed. Judge John W. Murphy, 1956–57; Practicing atty., 1957–62; Scranton City Solicitor, 1962.

Offices: 2370 RHOB 20515, 202-225-3731. Also 514 Scranton Life Bldg., Scranton 18503, 717-346-3834.

Committees: *Appropriations* (RMM of 23 R): Defense (RMM); Interior.

Group Ratings

	ADA	ACLU	COPE	CDF	CFA	LCV	ACU	NTLC	NSI	COC	CEI
1992	15	35	75	30	47	13	76	75	100	86	38
1991	30	—	56	70	61	23	65	—	—	44	30

National Journal Ratings

	1991 LIB — 1991 CONS	1992 LIB — 1992 CONS
Economic	41% — 59%	35% — 65%
Social	29% — 70%	28% — 72%
Foreign	16% — 84%	29% — 71%

Key Votes of the 102d Congress

1. Ban Striker Replace FOR	5. Handgun Wait/7-Day FOR	9. Use Force in Gulf FOR
2. $ for Homeownership FOR	6. Overseas Mil. Abortion AGN	10. US Mil. Abroad $ Cut *
3. Tax Rich/Cut Mid Cls. AGN	7. Obscn. Art NEA $ Ban FOR	11. Limit SDI Funds AGN
4. FY93/$15B Def. Cut AGN	8. Death Pen. from Jury FOR	12. Cuba Trade Embargo FOR

Key Votes of the 103d Congress

1. Family Leave FOR	2. Deficit Reduction AGN	3. Stimulus Plan AGN

Election Results

1992 general	Joseph M. McDade (R)	189,414	(90%)	($343,892)
	Albert A. Smith (LIB)	20,134	(10%)	
1992 primary	Joseph M. McDade (R), unopposed			
1990 general	Joseph M. McDade (R), unopposed			($373,388)

ELEVENTH DISTRICT

Nestled in the valley of the East Branch of the Susquehanna River, surrounded by mountain ridges, grew up one of the major industrial centers of America in the late 19th Century: the mountains were laced with veins of anthracite coal, the main home-heating fuel of the era. To this valley, in the chain of little cities north and south of Wilkes-Barre, named for two backers of the American Revolution, came thousands of immigrants, attracted by the high wages they were paid to scrape out the coal needed to heat the houses and smudge the skies of America. The supply was endless—the area produced 40% of the world's hard coal—but demand was not; the peak year of anthracite production was 1917, and long strikes in 1922 and 1925 hastened conversion to oil and gas heat. By the 1930s, the valley around Wilkes-Barre was in decline; surrounding Luzerne County's population, 445,000 in 1930, was 328,000 in 1990.

This is the land of Pennsylvania's 11th Congressional District, which includes all of Luzerne County and similar territory east to the town of Jim Thorpe and the Poconos and west almost to the Susquehanna. The miners have been a Democratic voting bloc since the 1930s, but there were also a lot of Republicans here, people in white-collar occupations as well as ancestral Pennsylvania Republicans from all walks of life. For more than 30 years, the district was represented by Daniel Flood, a mustached Democrat who, from his perch on the Appropriations Committee, brought millions in federal dollars to the anthracite country. But in 1980, he resigned amid scandal, and over next six years the 11th District had a series of bizarre elections and no less than four different congressmen of both parties, who served in their order of finish in the 1980 special election.

Now the seemingly safe incumbent is Democrat Paul Kanjorski. He has deep roots in the Wilkes-Barre area, serving nine years as a workmen's compensation administrative law judge and 12 years as Nanticoke City Solicitor. He effectively won the seat in the 1984 primary by noting that the then-incumbent was travelling in Central America while Wilkes-Barre area residents had to boil their tap water because it was contaminated; he held it in 1986 against a 25-year-old former Reagan White House aide who raised $1.3 million from Reagan connections but won only 29% of the vote. With an economically liberal and culturally moderate record, skepticism about foreign commitments and Washington lobbyists, Kanjorski is one of those congressmen always looking to benefit local areas and who seems suspicious of the outside. While chairing the Post Office and Civil Service Subcommittee on Human Resources, he sharply attacked White House perquisites and expenses and called for full public disclosure of all tax-payer based White House spending; President Bush once apologized at a breakfast meeting for the skimpy meal and blamed Kanjorski's investigations. He anticipated candidate Bill Clinton's call for higher taxes on foreign corporations (with revenue estimates no experts think can be met), and has introduced legislation closing foreign corporation tax loopholes. He wants tougher environmental and labor standards on foreign aid projects, which would of course zero many out. He has proposed a special senior citizens COLA, to be based on their cost of living. His major project is the Earth Conservancy Applied Research Center, a public-private combined project for developing new technologies to reclaim the environment of mine-ravaged northeastern Pennsylvania; he got $20 million for it in 1991. The Conservancy is also seeking to buy the bankrupt Blue Coal Company's extensive surface landholdings.

Untouched by scandal, with only 7 overdrafts on the House bank, Kanjorski seems widely popular in the 11th, and was reelected easily in 1992 in a district whose presidential vote just about replicated the national average.

The People:　Pop. 1990: 565,802; 40% rural; 19% age 65+; 98% White; 1% Black; 1% Hispanic origin. Voting age pop.: 441,019; 1% Black; 1% Hispanic origin. Households: 57% married couple families; 24% married couple fams. w. children; 29% college educ.; median household income: $24,310; per capita income: $11,937; median gross rent: $327; median house value: $57,600.

1992 Presidential Vote		1988 Presidential Vote	
Clinton (D)	91,616 (42%)	Bush (R)	104,667 (53%)
Bush (R)	84,199 (38%)	Dukakis (D)	92,717 (47%)
Perot (I)	42,950 (20%)		

Rep. Paul E. Kanjorski (D)

Elected 1984; b. Apr. 2, 1937, Nanticoke; home, Nanticoke; Temple U., 1957–61, Dickinson U., 1962–65; Catholic; married (Nancy).

Career: Army Reserves, 1960–61; Practicing atty., 1966–85; Nanticoke City Solicitor, 1969–81; Admin. Law Judge, 1971–80.

Offices: 2429 RHOB 20515, 202-225-6511. Also 10 E. South St., Wilkes-Barre 18701, 717-825-2200.

Committees: *Banking, Finance and Urban Affairs* (7th of 30 D): Consumer Credit and Insurance; Economic Growth and Credit Formation (Chmn.); Financial Institutions Supervision, Regulation and Deposit Insurance; International Development, Finance, Trade and Monetary Policy. *Post Office and Civil Service* (6th of 15 D): Civil Service.

Group Ratings

	ADA	ACLU	COPE	CDF	CFA	LCV	ACU	NTLC	NSI	COC	CEI
1992	80	48	83	90	67	50	16	5	40	25	21
1991	50	—	92	90	78	62	25	—	—	10	14

National Journal Ratings

	1991 LIB — 1991 CONS		1992 LIB — 1992 CONS	
Economic	88%	— 0%	83%	— 13%
Social	40%	— 58%	38%	— 60%
Foreign	51%	— 46%	71%	— 26%

Key Votes of the 102d Congress

1. Ban Striker Replace	FOR	5. Handgun Wait/7-Day	AGN	9. Use Force in Gulf	AGN
2. $ for Homeownership	AGN	6. Overseas Mil. Abortion	AGN	10. US Mil. Abroad $ Cut	FOR
3. Tax Rich/Cut Mid Cls.	FOR	7. Obscn. Art NEA $ Ban	FOR	11. Limit SDI Funds	AGN
4. FY93/$15B Def. Cut	FOR	8. Death Pen. from Jury	AGN	12. Cuba Trade Embargo	AGN

Key Votes of the 103d Congress

1. Family Leave   FOR   2. Deficit Reduction   FOR   3. Stimulus Plan   FOR

Election Results

1992 general	Paul E. Kanjorski (D)................ 138,875	(67%)	($342,314)
	Michael A. Fescina (R) 68,112	(33%)	($54,724)
1992 primary	Paul E. Kanjorski (D), unopposed		
1990 general	Paul E. Kanjorski (D), unopposed		($405,630)

TWELFTH DISTRICT

The steel and coal country of southwestern Pennsylvania, northern West Virginia and eastern Ohio, within a 100-mile ring of Pittsburgh, is one of America's most troubled industrial regions. Even as central Pittsburgh upgrades its economy, the small factory towns and mining villages know that steel and coal are no longer job-growth industries. This area was first settled by Scots-Irish farmers in the 1790s; in the 19th Century bituminous coal was discovered here, and immigrants from other parts of Europe were attracted to work the mines and the blast furnaces. It has long been a land of economic class conflict, but up through the 1920s it was one of the most Republican parts of America, and Republican policies—high tariffs, discouragement of labor unions—were thought to have contributed greatly to steel's growth. Now people in these parts seem to see the Democrats with their support for unions, for trade restrictions and perhaps for industrial policy, as their tribunes: the steel and coal country is one part of America where Republican policies grew steadily more unpopular during the 1980s and where deeply embedded cultural conservatism did not produce many votes for George Bush in recessionary 1992. This is pretty solidly Democratic territory now.

The 12th Congressional District of Pennsylvania includes much of this coal and steel country. Its best known community is Johnstown, the steel town whose disastrous flood of May 31, 1889, when a dam broke and a 75-foot wall of water half a mile wide swept through the town killing more than 2,200 people, is still remembered. Johnstown had 67,000 people in 1920, 28,000 in 1990. From Johnstown, the redistricted 12th reaches south to the West Virginia border and west to take in Armstrong and Indiana Counties northeast of Pittsburgh. It also includes the hills around Ligonier, Pennsylvania, green with prosperity, where Mellons and others of Pittsburgh's elite have vast estates.

For all its distinctiveness, the 12th proved in 1990 to be an distant early warning—the canary in the coal mine, to use a local image—of the discontent with incumbents in Congress expressed so sharply in 1992. The local congressman, John Murtha, seemed well in line with district opinion and he undeniably occupies a position where he can help an economically ailing district. First elected in one of those 1974 special elections that helped topple Richard Nixon, Murtha was a Marine who reenlisted to fight in Vietnam. He is a member of the Appropriations Committee and chairman of the Defense Subcommittee, the undisputed power broker of the Pennsylvania delegation, a politician whose voting record—hawkish and patriotic on foreign policy, interventionist on economics and usually tradition-minded on cultural issues—seemed perfectly suited to the steel and coal country. But Murtha is also one of those old-time politicians who operate best in secret, standing at the back of the House chamber and trading gossip and votes, avoiding national and local reporters and appearing on television only when he is presiding over the chamber. He has depended on fellow members, not the press, to transmit his messages; his audience was the House Democratic Caucus, nothing wider, though he would work with administration lobbyists from time to time.

All of which left him vulnerable to the primary challenge in April 1990 of Westmoreland County lawyer Kenneth Burkley. Relying mostly on free media, Burkley charged that Murtha was using his position to benefit himself more than his constituents: "Murtha continues to line his pockets—and you pay for the fabulous prizes." He was helped by articles in the long pro-Murtha *Johnstown Tribune-Democrat* pointing out that in 1989 only $1,000 of Murtha's first $200,000 in contributions came from the district. Murtha admitted that his new duties as head of the Defense Appropriations panel kept him from returning to the district much in 1989; but by early 1990 he was there often, and won the May primary by a meager 51%–43%, a split eerily similar to his 1982 race against another incumbent. But it did change some of Murtha's ways. He started visiting the district more, spending whole days in single communities, stressing local issues like his bill which exempted Rolling Rock brewery in Latrobe from having to label its recyclable bottles with alcohol health warnings. He hired a press secretary and if he still remains secluded from national reporters he is now courting the local press. He did not quit using his skills as an insider: redistricting removed most of Westmoreland County, which Burkley had carried, from the district and added Armstrong and Indiana, which have much in common with the Johnstown area. In 1992, he had no opposition in the primary or the general election.

Murtha is now in his third term, under his second president, as Defense Appropriations chairman. His inclinations are hawkish—he was one of two Pennsylvania Democrats to vote for the Gulf war resolution, though he opposes intervention in Bosnia. But now all the pressures are for defense cuts and, reflecting his district, he says he wants to shift more federal spending to domestic issues. He is proud of having reduced foreign military aid by $1 billion and the Bush defense budget request by $7 billion. He led a move to slash 10,000 Navy jobs as punishment for the Tailhook scandal, spoke out against a Navy plan to build a $250 million office building in northern Virginia, and would rather cut out a third Seawolf submarine than stop work on the B-2 or the Strategic Defense Initiative: this Marine is no patsy for the Navy. Nor is this hawk always for military intervention; his first reaction to the dispatch of troops to Somalia in November 1992 was to "challenge the mission" and saying it would be "costly and unwise." He sees that the military continues to be required to buy uneconomic Pennsylvania coal. He was against rebuilding Homestead Air Force Base after Hurricane Andrew which was already targeted for closure before the storm. On trade, he is an opponent of NAFTA and supporter of steel import quotas. On health care, he backs what he calls the CHAMPUS reform, a managed care system that he says has been effective in holding down costs in the military; he opposes efforts to decentralize military health care programs and as an abortion opponent, he is against allowing abortions in military hospitals.

After Jamie Whitten's 1992 illness, it was rumored that Murtha would seek the full Appropriations chairmanship for 1993. But he seemed content to wait behind the six more senior Democrats.

The People: Pop. 1990: 565,760; 70% rural; 17% age 65+; 98% White; 1% Black. Voting age pop.: 431,625; 1% Black. Households: 61% married couple families; 27% married couple fams. w. children; 25% college educ.; median household income: $22,024; per capita income: $10,586; median gross rent: $293; median house value: $44,300.

1992 Presidential Vote

Clinton (D) 102,768 (47%)
Bush (R) 72,664 (33%)
Perot (I)................... 44,846 (20%)

1988 Presidential Vote

Dukakis (D)................ 112,739 (55%)
Bush (R) 92,372 (45%)

Rep. John P. Murtha (D)

Elected Feb., 1974; b. June 17, 1932, New Martinsville, WV; home, Johnstown; U. of Pittsburgh, B.A. 1962, Indiana U. of PA, 1963–64; Catholic; married (Joyce).

Career: Marine Corps, 1952–55, 1966–67 (Vietnam), Marine Corps Reserves, 1955–65, 1968–90; Owner, Johnstown Minute Car Wash; PA House of Reps., 1969–74.

Offices: 2423 RHOB 20515, 202-225-2065. Also Vine and Walnut Sts., #200, Center Town Mall, Johnstown 15907, 814-535-2642; and P.O. Bldg., 201 N. Center St., Somerset 15501, 814-445-6041.

Committees: *Appropriations* (8th of 37 D): Defense (Chmn.); Interior; Legislative.

Group Ratings

	ADA	ACLU	COPE	CDF	CFA	LCV	ACU	NTLC	NSI	COC	CEI
1992	65	57	92	90	73	25	24	10	90	63	9
1991	40	—	92	80	67	54	26	—	—	30	9

National Journal Ratings

	1991 LIB	—	1991 CONS	1992 LIB	—	1992 CONS
Economic	69%	—	29%	69%	—	30%
Social	50%	—	48%	54%	—	46%
Foreign	48%	—	51%	18%	—	74%

Key Votes of the 102d Congress

1. Ban Striker Replace FOR	5. Handgun Wait/7-Day AGN	9. Use Force in Gulf FOR
2. $ for Homeownership AGN	6. Overseas Mil. Abortion AGN	10. US Mil. Abroad $ Cut AGN
3. Tax Rich/Cut Mid Cls. FOR	7. Obscn. Art NEA $ Ban AGN	11. Limit SDI Funds AGN
4. FY93/$15B Def. Cut FOR	8. Death Pen. from Jury AGN	12. Cuba Trade Embargo FOR

Key Votes of the 103d Congress

1. Family Leave FOR	2. Deficit Reduction FOR	3. Stimulus Plan FOR

Election Results

1992 general	John P. Murtha (D), unopposed			($794,097)
1992 primary	John P. Murtha (D), unopposed			
1990 general	John P. Murtha (D)...................	80,686	(62%)	($1,097,107)
	Willeam A. Choby (R).................	50,007	(38%)	($5,951)

THIRTEENTH DISTRICT

Montgomery County, Pennsylvania, is the hinterland of Philadelphia: rolling hills cut on one side by the Schuylkill River and at intervals by the Pennsylvania and Reading Railroad lines radiating outward from Center City. Older suburbs, the rich Main Line towns and more modest places like Glenside and Ambler, grew up around rail stations, with comfortable houses within walking distance for commuters. Here and there are the old Schuylkill River factory towns, Conshohocken and Norristown and towns established 200 years ago by German sects. Farther out are 18th and 19th Century villages, once surrounded by farm fields, now encroached on by subdivisions where people depend on cars not rail lines to get to work, and office complexes in places like Blue Bell, the headquarters of Unisys. Statistically, Montgomery County is the most affluent part of metro Philadelphia, but as in most suburban counties there is much variety here—economically, with high income enclaves like Gladwyne, and ethnically, with Jewish suburbs out York Road.

Most of Montgomery County makes up Pennsylvania's 13th Congressional District; parts of the county are nibbled off by the 6th, 7th, 8th and 15th Districts. It is one of those quintessentially Republican seats, where the style of politics was set for years by Ivy-educated Republican men, and where Republicans with more modest and sometimes ethnic backgrounds manned the local precincts and staffed local offices. But the suburbs were a land of discontent in the recession of the early 1990s, which hit harder at residential real estate and other forms of wealth than at incomes, and which saw permanent layoffs of white-collar and professional workers more than temporary layoffs of blue-collar and factory workers. And that discontent had political effects. For 24 years the 13th District was represented by Lawrence Coughlin, a Republican and a Yale contemporary of George Bush, who carried Montgomery County 60%–39% in 1988. But in 1992 Bush's support fell to 39% and Bill Clinton carried the county with 44%. Meanwhile, Coughlin chose to retire, and in the race between Republican Jon Fox, a longtime local officeholder, and Democrat Marjorie Margolies-Mezvinsky, a longtime television news reporter and (this is not a misprint) mother of 11, it was the Democrat who came out, barely, ahead.

Mezvinsky is not at all a political outsider, but she is *sui generis*, a person who makes sudden decisions on impulse and then follows through with great effort over long periods of time. She grew up in Philadelphia, an energetic do-everything girl; she went into television news just when stations suddenly wanted to put women on the air. Covering a story on Korean adoptions in Philadelphia, she decided at 28 to adopt a Korean 6-year-old; four years later, she adopted a Vietnamese child. In 1975, on assignment in Washington, she met and married Iowa Congressman Edward Mezvinsky. When he was defeated in 1976, they moved to Montgomery County, with her two children and his four, two they had together, plus three other refugee children of which they were legal guardians. Marjorie Mezvinsky commuted for years to Washington to work at NBC affiliate Channel 4, then she switched to part-time assignments in 1990. After the Clarence Thomas-Anita Hill hearings, and after Coughlin announced his retirement, she decided to run for Congress.

Naturally, there was more competition in the Republican than in the Democratic primary. Fox, after seven years as a state representative and one as a county commissioner, had solid support from the local Republican machine and was called a "zen master of constituency service" by the *Philadelphia Inquirer*; but two little-known candidates held him to 52% in the primary, and Mezvinsky immediately attacked him as "a political animal [who] runs and runs and runs from political feeding to political feeding." Fox boasted of sponsoring job fairs and putting up traffic lights, while Mezvinsky attacked him for waffling ("pro-choice, that's me; multiple choice, that's Jon Fox") and campaigned effervescently while maintaining a hectic personal life (her house burned down and her oldest daughter had a wedding during the summer). Mezvinsky called for jump-starting the economy and supported family leave—the standard Clinton platform—and in the "year of the woman" ran well ahead of ticket-mate Lynn Yeakel, especially in Jewish areas. The result was a razor-thin margin for Mezvinsky.

In Washington, Mezvinsky's energy, articulateness and good sense of humor did not go unnoticed; she was one of five freshman Democrats named to the powerful Energy and Commerce Committee. It is less clear whether she will change Congress as much as her rhetoric suggests; after all, the Democratic majority there already favors most of her platform and shares much of her liberalism. The 13th District could prove one of the important suburban bellwethers for 1994; no Democrat has represented this area since 1916. Mezvinsky is an attractive incumbent, but her constituents may ask her some angry questions if she does not prove as distinctive, and her Democratic majority does not prove as productive, as her aggressive campaign suggested.

The People: Pop. 1990: 565,663; 8% rural; 15% age 65+; 90% White; 6% Black; 2% Asian; 1% Hispanic origin. Voting age pop.: 439,398; 6% Black; 1% Hispanic origin. Households: 61% married couple families; 27% married couple fams. w. children; 55% college educ.; median household income: $44,764; per capita income: $22,786; median gross rent: $600; median house value: $146,600.

1992 Presidential Vote			1988 Presidential Vote		
Clinton (D)	118,579	(44%)	Bush (R)	145,609	(60%)
Bush (R)	107,439	(39%)	Dukakis (D)	95,710	(40%)
Perot (I)	44,148	(16%)			

Rep. Marjorie Margolies-Mezvinsky (D)

Elected 1992; b. June 21, 1942, Philadelphia; home, Narberth; U. of PA, B.A. 1963; Columbia U., 1969–70; Jewish; married (Edward Mezvinsky).

Career: Broadcast journalist, WCAU-TV, Philadelphia, 1967–71; WNBC-TV, NYC, 1971–75; WRC-TV, Washington, DC, 1975–90; NBC contributing corresp., 1990–92.

Offices: 1516 LHOB 20515, 202-225-6111. Also One Presidential Blvd., #200, Bala Cynwyd 19004, 215-667-3666.

Committees: *Energy and Commerce* (26th of 27 D): Oversight and Investigations; Telecommunications and Finance. *Government Operations* (23d of 25 D): Commerce, Consumer and Monetary Affairs. *Small Business* (19th of 27 D): SBA Legislation and the General Economy.

Group Ratings and 102d Congress Votes: Newly Elected

Key Votes of the 103d Congress

1. Family Leave	FOR	2. Deficit Reduction	AGN	3. Stimulus Plan	AGN

Election Results

1992 general	Marjorie Margolies-Mezvinsky (D)	127,685	(50%)	($559,060)
	Jon D. Fox (R)	126,312	(49%)	($719,618)
	Other.................................	3,513	(1%)	
1992 primary	Marjorie Margolies-Mezvinsky (D)	28,095	(79%)	
	Bernard Tomkin (D)	7,318	(21%)	
1990 general	Lawrence Coughlin (R)	89,577	(60%)	($235,766)
	Bernard Tomkin (D)	58,967	(40%)	($39,173)

FOURTEENTH DISTRICT

The Golden Triangle that is the inevitable center of Pittsburgh, the tip of land where the Allegheny and Monongahela Rivers come together to form the Ohio, has been a strategic site for more than 200 years. It was there, to Fort Duquesne, that Braddock's army was headed (with George Washington helping lead the way) when it was ambushed and defeated in 1754. A few years later, trees were felled, and a city was carved out of the wilderness here and named after the English statesman William Pitt—the first urban center in the American interior. Pittsburgh grew rapidly in those days when most of the nation's commerce moved over water; when traffic switched to railroads, Pittsburgh still did nicely, since rail lines had to run at riverside rather than scale the mountains. Then came Andrew Carnegie—and steel. A Scottish immigrant working as a telegrapher for the Pennsylvania Railroad, he saw that steel would replace iron for railroad bridges and built a steel factory in Pittsburgh—then a rail junction with large deposits of coal nearby and ready access to iron ore from the Great Lakes. With associates like Henry Clay Frick and Henry Phipps, Carnegie built his capacity to the point that when he sold out in 1901, the resulting U.S. Steel Corporation had a near-monopoly of the business.

The Pittsburgh that Carnegie and his steel men built is one of giant mills in the bottomlands along the rivers and massive buildings downtown like the classic City-County Building next to the Richardsonian jail. There were 12 cable cars going up the Duquesne Incline and other routes, connecting mills with the neighborhoods above, and the ever-present grime of coal smoke in the air. The Pittsburgh smog—a word used here before it was in Los Angeles—was so bad that street lights stayed on all day downtown, and photographs circa 1947 show a midnight-like darkness at nine in the morning. In the years after World War II, Pittsburgh's business leaders and Mayor David Lawrence were determined to clean up the smog and did so: Pittsburgh is one of our cleaner-aired cities today. They cleaned up the riverfront and created a grand park at the junction of the three rivers. It also ranks high, though not as high as it used to, as a headquarters of major corporations (USX, Westinghouse, Heinz, Alcoa, Koppers, PPG) and has fine cultural institutions from Carnegie-Mellon University and the University of Pittsburgh with its "cathedral of learning" to its public television station (home of "Mr. Rogers' Neighborhood"). In the early 1980s, Pittsburgh formed a high-tech council to encourage start-up businesses. By the early 1990s, it had a robust high-tech, white-collar sector, replacing the manufacturing jobs which in the metropolitan area had declined from 265,000 in the mid-1970s to 112,500 by late 1992. The old millworker towns in the outer metro ring continued to lose population and jobs, but much of the central city is vital, with yuppie-like growth in Mount Washington and Manchester and fine homes still maintained in Shadyside and Squirrel Hill.

The 14th Congressional District of Pennsylvania includes all of the city of Pittsburgh plus suburban territory to the west and north. It takes in the city's black neighborhoods and Shadyside, and its depopulated white working class areas. To the west it goes out along a new expressway to (but does not include) the airport, which is USAir's major hub (Bill Clinton's opposition to the USAir-British Airways merger cost him some votes here in 1992), to the north through middle income townships, and northeast along the Ohio River, to some of the hilly high-income precincts of Sewickley. The 14th has its Republican neighborhoods and a Republican heritage; but that has not been very lively since the New Deal, and this is a solidly Democratic district today. Though unhappy with the Democrats' cultural liberalism in the 1970s, it became more Democratic in the years of the steel industry's collapse in the 1980s.

Democrat William Coyne has been the 14th's congressman since 1980. With a characteristic Irish-American knack for politics, this onetime accountant has moved up; he was elected to the legislature at age 34 in 1970, to the city council, to the chairmanship of the Democratic Party in Pittsburgh in 1978, and then to Congress in 1980 when he beat the son of his predecessor in the Democratic primary by a 65%–35% margin. After the 1984 election, he won a seat on the Ways and Means Committee. Philosophically, Coyne wants the government to spend more on transportation, education and energy conservation, which he sees as producing economic growth. Legislatively, he produced funds for home dialysis treatments and more medicare reimbursement. He lobbied and got $17 million for the Pittsburgh airport expansion, worked to extend unemployment compensation benefits, and sponsored legislation to make small-issue tax-exempt Industrial Development Bonds a permanent part of the tax code. He secured funding for the Software Engineering Institute and the Children's Hospital. Coyne has also procured funding to study restructuring the former Hays Ammunition Plant; with Pittsburgh's recent popularity among film producers (*Lorenzo's Oil* and *Hoffa* were filmed here), one idea is to turn the old structure into a film and sound studio.

Coyne is, in short, a locally oriented congressman who seldom, if ever, attracts national attention, the tenth ranking member of Ways and Means who could escape notice at a Washington cocktail party. He has been reelected easily every two years.

The People: Pop. 1990: 565,838; 17% age 65+; 80% White; 18% Black; 1% Asian; 1% Hispanic origin. Voting age pop.: 449,679; 16% Black; 1% Hispanic origin. Households: 44% married couple families; 17% married couple fams. w. children; 42% college educ.; median household income: $24,751; per capita income: $14,255; median gross rent: $379; median house value: $50,900.

1992 Presidential Vote			1988 Presidential Vote		
Clinton (D)	145,419	(58%)	Dukakis (D)	160,379	(66%)
Bush (R)	66,016	(26%)	Bush (R)	84,066	(34%)
Perot (I)	38,460	(15%)			

Rep. William J. Coyne (D)

Elected 1980; b. Aug. 24, 1936, Pittsburgh; home, Pittsburgh; Robert Morris Col., B.S. 1965; Catholic; single.

Career: Army, 1955–57; Accountant, 1957–70; PA House of Reps., 1971–72; Pittsburgh City Cncl., 1974–80.

Offices: 2455 RHOB 20515, 202-225-2301. Also 2009 Fed. Bldg., 1000 Liberty Ave., Pittsburgh 15222, 412-644-2870.

Committees: *Budget* (13th of 26 D). *Ways and Means* (10th of 24 D): Trade.

Group Ratings

	ADA	ACLU	COPE	CDF	CFA	LCV	ACU	NTLC	NSI	COC	CEI
1992	95	96	92	100	93	63	4	5	30	50	6
1991	80	—	83	100	78	77	0	—	—	20	6

National Journal Ratings

	1991 LIB — 1991 CONS	1992 LIB — 1992 CONS
Economic	84% — 12%	83% — 13%
Social	84% — 12%	88% — 8%
Foreign	81% — 18%	82% — 16%

Key Votes of the 102d Congress

1. Ban Striker Replace	FOR	5. Handgun Wait/7-Day FOR	9. Use Force in Gulf AGN
2. $ for Homeownership AGN	6. Overseas Mil. Abortion FOR	10. US Mil. Abroad $ Cut FOR
3. Tax Rich/Cut Mid Cls. FOR	7. Obscn. Art NEA $ Ban AGN	11. Limit SDI Funds AGN
4. FY93/$15B Def. Cut FOR	8. Death Pen. from Jury AGN	12. Cuba Trade Embargo AGN

Key Votes of the 103d Congress

1. Family Leave   FOR   2. Deficit Reduction   FOR   3. Stimulus Plan   FOR

Election Results

1992 general	William J. Coyne (D)	165,633	(72%)	($323,937)
	Byron W. King (R)	61,311	(27%)	($73,936)
	Two Others	2,094	(1%)	
1992 primary	William J. Coyne (D)	70,162	(77%)	
	Al Guttman (D)	21,607	(24%)	
1990 general	William J. Coyne (D)	77,636	(72%)	($130,904)
	Richard E. Caligiuri (R)	30,497	(28%)	

FIFTEENTH DISTRICT

Tucked among the rolling hills of eastern Pennsylvania, little known to the rest of America, the Lehigh Valley was long one of America's major heavy industrial areas and at the end of the 1980s was poised on the way to the post-industrial future. All farmland in the early 1800s, its dependable labor force and location on a river emptying into the Delaware made it a natural site for early industries. For most of the 20th Century, the Lehigh Valley was the source of some of America's best-known products: Easton produced Crayola crayons and Dixie cups, Allentown made Mack trucks, and Bethlehem was the home base of the nation's number two steelmaker, Bethlehem Steel. Recent years brought troubles for Mack and near-bankruptcy for Bethlehem Steel, yet the Lehigh Valley, far from withering, grew smartly during the 1980s. It has major appliance factories, cement operations, and a big AT&T facility in Allentown. More important, Interstate 78, finally completed in 1990, puts the Lehigh Valley just 90 minutes straight west of New York City. Growth seemed on the way, with the Lehigh Valley's low cost of living, relatively high skill levels, and (compared to New York and post-Florio New Jersey) low taxes. But the early 1990s recession which hit the big East Coast metropolises hard had impact here too.

The 15th Congressional District of Pennsylvania consists of the Lehigh Valley plus a small adjacent portion of Montgomery County. A solidly Democratic constituency in its heavy industrial days, it turned pretty solidly Republican in the 1980s, then gave Bill Clinton a 41%–37% plurality and Ross Perot a rather high 21% in 1992. From 1978 through 1990, it elected a Republican congressman, Don Ritter, an engineer and believer in the free market system, an opponent of tax increases and backer of diversifying government research and development spending. For a dozen years, the success of Ritter's policies and his local achievements—the

Delaware-Lehigh Canal Heritage Corridor, Allentown's Basin Street project—helped him win reelection against a series of mostly uninteresting local politicoes. But 1992 brought more difficult economic times and a more interesting opponent, and the result was the election of Democrat Paul McHale, former state legislator and Marine Corps veteran of Operation Desert Storm.

McHale is a Lehigh Valley native who volunteered for the Marine Corps after graduating from college in 1972. He got a law degree and hung out his shingle in Bethlehem in 1977, and was elected to the state House in 1982. There he worked on child passenger safety, a tough juvenile sentencing law, and getting a tunnel for the Pennsylvania Turnpike Northeast Extension. But in August 1990, he volunteered for active duty in the Marines, and by August 16 was in Saudi Arabia. In October, he came home but returned to the Gulf in November and served through the war; he resigned from the legislature, and his wife won his seat. McHale's campaign sounded some familiar themes. He attacked Ritter for accepting $162,000 in honoraria and free trips to Las Vegas and Palm Springs, for introducing as original a bill nearly identical to one sponsored by another Republican, for accepting $2,700 from owners of a Pen Argyl landfill. He attacked Ritter's proposed 800 "Jobline" as a "Band-Aid." He supported the line-item veto, a phased-in balanced budget amendment, universal access to health insurance with managed competition, and the Brady Bill. He called for national extension of Pennsylvania's Ben Franklin partnerships and an R&D investment tax credit. McHale's campaign started a Citizen Saturday program working on a volunteer project once a month, and he said he would continue it once in office.

Though considerably outspent, McHale won by a 52%–47% margin. His stated goals for his first term are not immodest: to play a role in shaping economic legislation, to help produce a new health care system, to produce congressional reform. These are big promises and, as he said just after the election, "There will be no excuse for inaction." As Ritter showed, a congressman who emphasizes second-priority stands and constituency service can hold onto a district for more than a decade, until unpropitious economic times and an attractive opponent combine to defeat him. McHale is taking a course more like that of politicians in the 1940s and 1950s, promising to deliver on first-line issues, staking his incumbency in a marginal district on the success of the macroeconomy and the Clinton Administration.

The People: Pop. 1990: 565,818; 26% rural; 15% age 65+; 92% White; 2% Black; 1% Asian; 3% Other; 5% Hispanic origin. Voting age pop.: 434,459; 2% Black; 4% Hispanic origin. Households: 61% married couple families; 26% married couple fams. w. children; 37% college educ.; median household income: $33,049; per capita income: $15,073; median gross rent: $458; median house value: $101,400.

1992 Presidential Vote

Clinton (D) 92,363 (41%)
Bush (R) 81,349 (37%)
Perot (I). 47,740 (21%)

1988 Presidential Vote

Bush (R) 104,773 (55%)
Dukakis (D). 84,834 (45%)

1114   PENNSYLVANIA

Rep. Paul McHale (D)

Elected 1992; b. July 26, 1950, Bethlehem; home, Bethlehem; Lehigh U., B.A. 1972, Georgetown U. Law Sch., J.D. 1977; Catholic; married (Katherine).

Career: Marine Corps, 1972–74, 1990–91 (Persian Gulf); Marine Reserves, 1974–80, 1984–present; Practicing atty., 1977–92; PA House of Reps., 1982–91.

Offices: 511 CHOB 20515, 202-225-6411. Also 26 E. 3d St., Bethlehem 18015, 215-866-0916; Hamilton Financial Ctr., One Center Sq., #203, Allentown 18101, 215-439-8861; and 168 Main St., Pennsburg 18073, 215-541-0614.

Committees: *Armed Services* (30th of 34 D): Military Acquisition; Readiness. *Science, Space and Technology* (21st of 33 D): Energy; Technology, Environment and Aviation.

Group Ratings and 102d Congress Votes: Newly Elected

Key Votes of the 103d Congress

1. Family Leave   FOR   2. Deficit Reduction   AGN   3. Stimulus Plan   FOR

Election Results

1992 general	Paul McHale (D)	111,419	(52%)	($221,935)
	Don Ritter (R)	99,520	(47%)	($865,974)
	Other	2,385	(1%)	
1992 primary	Paul McHale (D)	30,818	(74%)	
	Dave Clark (D)	10,891	(26%)	
1990 general	Don Ritter (R)	77,178	(61%)	($577,790)
	Richard J. Orloski (D)	50,233	(39%)	($102,312)

SIXTEENTH DISTRICT

The Pennsylvania Dutch country, settled by Germans in the 18th Century when it was Pennsylvania's frontier, remains a distinctive part of America. These Germans were Amish, Mennonites, members of pietistic sects and cults seeking religious liberty and determined to farm their rich lands in the same intensive way they had in Germany. Today, many of their descendants—the Eisenhower family is the most famous example—have blended into the broader America, but in the Dutch country around Lancaster, many "Plain People" still live. Tourists can still see Amish families clad in black, clattering over the back roads in horse-drawn carriages, with scrupulously tended farms set amid rolling hills, the barns decorated with hex signs. Farmers here continue to produce some of the highest per-acre yields on earth, with simple equipment and limited use of chemical fertilizers. But efficient farming is not all that is happening here economically. Lancaster is the headquarters of Armstrong, and nearby Hershey is where Milton Hershey built his chocolate firm back in 1903—the main street is Chocolate Avenue and the lampposts are topped with ceramic Hershey Kisses. But the Dutch area also has many small firms; new startups prosper, profiting from the skills and work habits of the labor force. Lancaster County grew robustly in the 1980s, so much so that some began to worry that the Dutch farm areas would be spoiled by overdevelopment; it has not been hit as badly by the early 1990s recession as many other areas.

The 16th Congressional District of Pennsylvania includes most of Lancaster County and part of Chester County, ranging east from the Dutch country through the small towns and spreading suburbs of greater Philadelphia, including America's leading mushroom-growing center around Kennett Square (fragrant with the compost needed for the crop) and on to the Wyeth country around Chadds Ford. The latter area is new, resulting from the collapse of three Republican districts into two, but the new 16th, like the old, is by most measures the most Republican district in Pennsylvania and the whole Northeast; it has favored the party of Lincoln since it abandoned the party of Pennsylvania's only president, Lancaster native James Buchanan, in the years just before the Civil War.

The 16th's Congressman, Robert Walker, is one of the House's more senior Republicans, the chief deputy republican whip, though there is still something boyish about him—scrappy, good-humored, ready to push his principles forward even at the cost of being mocked. Walker got his start as one of the young Republicans who used the "special orders" procedure, which allows speechmaking after the legislative business of the day, to present their views to a wide public on C-SPAN; he was also the one caught at the podium, gesturing and asking rhetorical questions, when Speaker Tip O'Neill ordered the C-SPAN cameras to show that the Republicans were speaking to an empty House. His leadership post formalizes what he has long done: staying on the floor, good-humored but vigilant, willing to let the majority make him look ridiculous (as it often does) and ready to pounce on their mistakes and make them look bad in turn (this often happens too). His quiver is full of amendments to cut spending and he is willing to use irritating tactics, objecting to unanimous consent requests for one-minute speeches, demanding roll calls and even teller votes on routine matters, when he thinks the Democratic leadership has gone too far.

Walker has on occasion been a substantive legislator, though his adversaries charge that some of his initiatives—the 1988 drug-free workplace law, his debt-buydown plan—are cheap shots. The debt-buydown got national notice when George Bush endorsed it in his 1992 convention speech. It would allow taxpayers to designate up to 10% of their income tax for deficit reduction and require all spending except Social Security and debt service to be cut by that percentage. It's an appealing gimmick, with one obvious but remediable flaw (it gives taxpayers votes in proportion to their taxes paid, which gives the rich far more than a one-person-one-vote share); it does give taxpayers a direct say in spending, and if adopted would probably reduce the deficit very substantially, with hard decisions on 'how' left to Walker's colleagues.

Walker is ranking Republican on the Science, Space and Technology Committee, where he supports the space program, including the controversial Space Station. He wrote the law establishing the National Space Council, which gave Vice Presidents Quayle and Gore (both space buffs, with surprisingly similar views on space) superintendency over the space program, and he has sharply opposed the accretion of power over the space program by the Appropriations subcommittees. Walker came out with a budget reform bill which would enact the presidential line-item veto and eliminate the Appropriations Committee's process altogether; authorizing committees would both write laws and ante up the money to pay for them. He objects to some science spending as pork barrel, but he wants to spend more on hydrogen energy, rural growth research, earthquake R&D, and research about possible global weather changes, and has proposed a Cabinet-level Department of Science, Space, Energy and Technology.

In his by now long congressional career, Walker has seen his ideas gain more ascendancy than most pundits would have thought, but has mostly been frustrated in advancing them in the seemingly ever-Democratic House. Will he plug on chipperly in a Washington wholly controlled by Democrats and full of enthusiasm for Bill Clinton and his new way? Probably: certainly he has a safe seat in the 16th District, one of the few Eastern districts where George Bush did well in 1992.

The People: Pop. 1990: 565,908; 44% rural; 12% age 65+; 90% White; 5% Black; 1% Asian; 4% Hispanic origin. Voting age pop.: 417,051; 5% Black; 3% Hispanic origin. Households: 64% married couple families; 31% married couple fams. w. children; 42% college educ.; median household income: $37,553; per capita income: $16,321; median gross rent: $500; median house value: $115,300.

1992 Presidential Vote

Bush (R) 109,019 (48%)
Clinton (D) 72,724 (32%)
Perot (I) 43,271 (19%)

1988 Presidential Vote

Bush (R) 128,968 (69%)
Dukakis (D) 58,526 (31%)

Rep. Robert S. Walker (R)

Elected 1976; b. Dec. 23, 1942, Bradford; home, East Petersburg; Millersville U., B.S. 1964, U. of DE, M.A. 1968; Presbyterian; married (Sue).

Career: PA Natl. Guard, 1967–73; High schl. teacher, 1964–67; A.A., U.S. Rep. Edwin D. Eshleman, 1967–77.

Offices: 2369 RHOB 20515, 202-225-2411. Also Lancaster Cnty. Crthse., 50 N. Duke St., Lancaster 17603, 717-393-0666; Exton Commons, #595, Exton 19341, 215-363-8409.

Committees: *Science, Space and Technology* (RMM of 22 R). *Joint Committee on the Organization of Congress* (8th of 12).

Group Ratings

	ADA	ACLU	COPE	CDF	CFA	LCV	ACU	NTLC	NSI	COC	CEI
1992	10	5	25	0	7	6	96	100	100	88	89
1991	5	—	8	0	17	8	100	—	—	90	91

National Journal Ratings

	1991 LIB — 1991 CONS		1992 LIB — 1992 CONS	
Economic	4%	— 90%	0%	— 91%
Social	19%	— 78%	15%	— 85%
Foreign	12%	— 85%	18%	— 74%

Key Votes of the 102d Congress

1. Ban Striker Replace	AGN	5. Handgun Wait/7-Day	AGN	9. Use Force in Gulf	FOR
2. $ for Homeownership	FOR	6. Overseas Mil. Abortion	AGN	10. US Mil. Abroad $ Cut	FOR
3. Tax Rich/Cut Mid Cls.	AGN	7. Obscn. Art NEA $ Ban	FOR	11. Limit SDI Funds	AGN
4. FY93/$15B Def. Cut	AGN	8. Death Pen. from Jury	FOR	12. Cuba Trade Embargo	FOR

Key Votes of the 103d Congress

1. Family Leave	AGN	2. Deficit Reduction	AGN	3. Stimulus Plan	AGN

Election Results

1992 general	Robert S. Walker (R)	137,823	(65%)	($158,564)
	Robert Peters (D)	74,741	(35%)	($10,507)
1992 primary	Robert S. Walker (R), unopposed			
1990 general	Robert S. Walker (R)	85,596	(66%)	($98,284)
	Ernest E. Guyll (D)	43,849	(34%)	

SEVENTEENTH DISTRICT

Through the center of Pennsylvania flows the Susquehanna, the longest river in the East if you include the Chesapeake Bay, which is actually the flooded lower Susquehanna valley. Starting in the mountain fastness of central Pennsylvania, emptying next to the antique town of Havre de Grace into the Chesapeake, the Susquehanna is the one river strong enough to break through the Appalachian chains of central Pennsylvania. But few songs are written to celebrate the Susquehanna, it occupies nothing like the place of the Hudson or even the Schuylkill in art, it has not given a name to a fever (Potomac), a school of painting (Hudson) or economics (Charles), or to a state (Delaware, Connecticut, Ohio, Mississippi, Alabama, Illinois, Missouri, Colorado).

The 17th Congressional District of Pennsylvania covers much of the lower Susquehanna valley, where it breaks through the mountains and drains the fertile plains of the Pennsylvania Dutch Country, one of colonial America's great frontiers. Its big population center is Harrisburg, the central city huddled around the distinctive Capitol building, the metro area spreading over various valleys, not far upstream from the Three Mile Island nuclear power plant. From there the district spreads east to the Pennsylvania Dutch country, including Lebanon County and part of Lancaster County. Here the black buggies of the "Plain People" click-clack over the roads of some of the most fertile farmland in the world.

This is a solidly Republican area. Harrisburg has been a Republican town from the days when the party seemed to conquer all in Pennsylvania; Republicans held the governorship for all but eight years from 1860 to 1934, and filled the ornate halls of the Capitol—its dome is modeled after London's St. Paul's, the stairway on the Paris Opera—with Republican patronage hacks. The Pennsylvania Dutch country is even more Republican. The 17th District had elected a Democratic congressman as recently as 1980, when it stretched north from Harrisburg along the Susquehanna; now it is a safe Republican seat.

The congressman is George Gekas who, as state senator from Harrisburg, helped draw the district boundaries and won the seat easily in 1982. Conservative in fiscal impulse and on crime issues, Gekas has been an active legislator, leading the Republican ranks on some issues, starting his own crusades on others. In the legislature, Gekas had sponsored the state's mandatory sentencing and child abuse laws, and in the House Judiciary Committee he sponsored the death penalty for drug dealers convicted of murder and has backed tough anti-crime laws. He unsuccessfully tried to prohibit Legal Services lawyers from taking any abortion cases and to bar congressmen elected before 1980 from converting leftover campaign funds to personal use. He is a supporter of biomedical research and has sought to protect labs from "animal rights terrorists" (not as much an overstatement as it sounds) and secured passage of a Farm Animal and Research Facilities Protection Act. He was the lead Republican backing application of independent counsel act procedures to members of Congress. He introduced his own healthcare reform bill, designed to subsidize education of primary care doctors, encourage innovation among states in testing alternate delivery and finance systems, reform medical malpractice and restructure Medicaid. With his activist record and Republican constituency, Gekas seems to have a safe seat.

The People: Pop. 1990: 565,702; 39% rural; 13% age 65+; 90% White; 7% Black; 1% Asian; 1% Other; 2% Hispanic origin. Voting age pop.: 427,392; 6% Black; 1% Hispanic origin. Households: 59% married couple families; 27% married couple fams. w. children; 33% college educ.; median household income: $31,841; per capita income: $14,434; median gross rent: $415; median house value: $76,500.

1992 Presidential Vote

Bush (R) 114,245 (50%)
Clinton (D) 72,594 (32%)
Perot (I).................... 40,495 (18%)

1988 Presidential Vote

Bush (R) 122,558 (64%)
Dukakis (D)................ 67,751 (36%)

Rep. George W. Gekas (R)

Elected 1982; b. Apr. 14, 1930, Harrisburg; home, Harrisburg; Dickinson Col., B.A. 1952, Dickinson Law Sch., J.D. 1958; Greek Orthodox; married (Evangeline).

Career: Army, 1953–55; Asst. Dist. Atty., Dauphin Cnty., 1960–66; PA House of Reps., 1967–75; PA Senate, 1977–83.

Offices: 2410 RHOB 20515, 202-225-4315. Also 2101 N. Front St., #302, Harrisburg 17110, 717-232-5123; 222 S. Market St., #102-A, Elizabethtown 17022, 717-367-6669; and 400 S. 8th St., Lebanon 17042, 717-273-1451.

Committees: *Intelligence (Permanent Select)* (5th of 7 R): Legislation (RMM). *Judiciary* (6th of 14 R): Administrative Law and Governmental Relations (RMM); Crime and Criminal Justice.

Group Ratings

	ADA	ACLU	COPE	CDF	CFA	LCV	ACU	NTLC	NSI	COC	CEI
1992	15	13	18	30	20	19	88	85	100	88	74
1991	5	—	25	30	28	8	90	—	—	100	72

National Journal Ratings

	1991 LIB — 1991 CONS		1992 LIB — 1992 CONS	
Economic	23%	— 76%	28%	— 72%
Social	30%	— 68%	28%	— 72%
Foreign	0%	— 88%	18%	— 74%

Key Votes of the 102d Congress

1. Ban Striker Replace	AGN	5. Handgun Wait/7-Day	AGN	9. Use Force in Gulf	FOR
2. $ for Homeownership	FOR	6. Overseas Mil. Abortion	AGN	10. US Mil. Abroad $ Cut	AGN
3. Tax Rich/Cut Mid Cls.	AGN	7. Obscn. Art NEA $ Ban	FOR	11. Limit SDI Funds	AGN
4. FY93/$15B Def. Cut	AGN	8. Death Pen. from Jury	FOR	12. Cuba Trade Embargo	FOR

Key Votes of the 103d Congress

1. Family Leave   AGN   2. Deficit Reduction   AGN   3. Stimulus Plan   AGN

Election Results

1992 general	George W. Gekas (R)	150,158	(70%)	($190,885)
	Bill Sturges (D)	65,881	(30%)	($47,217)
1992 primary	George W. Gekas (R), unopposed			
1990 general	George W. Gekas (R), unopposed			($93,331)

EIGHTEENTH DISTRICT

Pittsburgh is surely the hilliest of the large metropolitan areas of the United States; not the least indicator of the nerve of its founders is that they were willing to build on such steep terrain. In its years of great growth, from the mid-1800s to the early 1900s, with the steel mills lining the riverbanks, Pittsburgh and its suburbs spread up and down hills, through the interstices of river valleys and over gaps to the next nearly level spot. Then, as growth resumed in mid-20th century, the spreading out process continued. One result is that there are no clusters of rich and poor suburbs, no one middle-class zone: they are spread out around the irregular terrain. The richest Pittsburghers, for example, live in Fox Chapel and Sewickley to the northeast and northwest; there are upper-middle-income suburbs like Mount Lebanon south of the Golden Triangle, but also some north of the Allegheny; working class enclaves, now vastly depopulated, are strung along the Monongahela River, near the mostly cold steel mills, but are found in other pockets as well. Pittsburgh does not yet have an edge city, though there are new housing and a few office developments to the north and to the west around the airport, now a major hub for USAir.

When John Kennedy was elected president, there were four congressional districts in Pittsburgh's Allegheny County, numbered 27th through 30th; now all of Pennsylvania has only 21, and there are only two fully in Allegheny County. One, the 14th, is made up primarily of the city of Pittsburgh; the other, the 18th, includes suburbs to the north, south and east, plus most of the industrial Mon Valley to the southeast. This is a new creation of redistricting, containing most of the Republican-leaning suburban 18th and most of the heavily Democratic Mon Valley 20th. It was expected to be a Democratic district, and as recently as 1988, both of the old districts elected Democrats. But instead it was won by a Republican: the 20th District's Joseph Gaydos, a solid labor-liberal, retired after 24 years, and the new seat was won by Rick Santorum, a one-term Republican who has twice in a row won in great political upsets.

Santorum is one of those natural politicoes, of whom the Republicans have so few and the Democrats so many. He is the son of an Italian immigrant who was a clinical psychologist for the Veterans' Administration, and he has long been involved in politics, working on campaigns while at Penn State, working for a state senator while getting his law degree at Dickinson, joining after graduation the blue chip Pittsburgh law firm that included former Governor Dick Thornburgh, active in Pittsburgh Republican politics, and then taking on Congressman Doug Walgren in 1990. Walgren had a seat on Energy and Commerce and thus the ability to raise money, but Santorum went out and knocked on 25,000 doors, amassed an army of volunteers including many right-to-lifers, attacked Walgren for voting "for a pay raise seven times" and saying he spent only 29 days in the district. On issues, Santorum opposed the congressional pay raise, backed the line-item veto, came out for limits on PAC contributions. National Republicans gave Santorum no help—the first time he heard from the campaign committee was on election night—but the national anti-incumbent mood was especially strong in western Pennsylvania.

In the House, Santorum was one of the "Gang of Seven" freshman Republicans who lobbed one attack after another on the ways of the House, helping to expose the House bank scandal and obtaining full disclosure of overdrafts, seeking an outside audit of a $46 million House contingency fund, trying to cut the House franked mail budget. He put forward a budget plan to set performance goals, not just spending limits, for government agencies. On health care, he said companies should give employees $3,000 cash for deductibles and then let insurance cover the rest. He certainly angered Democratic leaders in Washington; he must have riled legislators of both parties in Harrisburg, too, for they gave him this solidly Democratic district (though the 70% Democratic registration figure he used overstates its voting habits). Not surprisingly, the 1992 Democratic primary attracted 12 candidates. Surprisingly, the winner by a fairly large margin (19%–13% over the runner-up) was a former Republican, state Senator Frank Pecora, who switched party registration and sought to switch offices after redistricting transferred his district from the Penn Hills area east of Pittsburgh to the Philadelphia suburbs. Also the son of Italian immigrants, but 28 years older than Santorum, Pecora was not able to cast himself as much of a reformer, while Santorum could continue his door-knocking campaign plus raise enough money for TV ads. The result was a 61%–38% Santorum victory; as many as half his voters may have been at least nominal Democrats.

Can Santorum hold this district forever? Quite possibly: some Democrats consistently win in heavily Republican seats. But it's not clear he'll want to. He supports term limits, though he has not committed himself to any set date for retirement. He may continue bomb-throwing in the House, but he probably hopes for big Republican gains soon or will look for something else to do.

He has been mentioned as an opponent for Senator Harris Wofford in 1994, and his western Pennsylvania base and his reformist style could make him formidable—if Wofford is in trouble for failing to keep his promises on healthcare reform. In the meantime, Santorum should continue to be part of the noisy opposition in the House.

The People: Pop. 1990: 565,771; 2% rural; 19% age 65+; 91% White; 8% Black; 1% Asian. Voting age pop.: 447,649; 7% Black. Households: 55% married couple families; 21% married couple fams. w. children; 43% college educ.; median household income: $29,003; per capita income: $15,251; median gross rent: $394; median house value: $55,000.

1992 Presidential Vote

Clinton (D)	137,507	(52%)
Bush (R)	80,795	(30%)
Perot (I)	46,754	(18%)

1988 Presidential Vote

Dukakis (D)	147,588	(58%)
Bush (R)	104,800	(42%)

Rep. Rick Santorum (R)

Elected 1990; b. May 10, 1958, Winchester, VA; home, Pittsburgh; PA St. U., B.A. 1980, U. of Pittsburgh, M.B.A. 1981, Dickinson Law Sch., J.D. 1986; Catholic; married (Karen).

Career: A.A., PA Sen. J. Doyle 1981–86; Dir., PA Senate Local Govt. Cmte., 1981–84; Dir., PA Senate Transportation Cmte., 1984–86; Practicing atty., 1986–89.

Offices: 1222 LHOB 20515, 202-225-2135. Also 606 Weyman Rd., Pittsburgh 15236, 412-882-3205; 541 5th Ave., McKeesport 15132, 412-664-4049.

Committees: *Ways and Means* (13th of 14 R): Human Resources (RMM); Oversight.

Group Ratings

	ADA	ACLU	COPE	CDF	CFA	LCV	ACU	NTLC	NSI	COC	CEI
1992	20	17	58	20	33	19	83	90	90	88	69
1991	15	—	42	30	28	0	80	—	—	80	75

National Journal Ratings

	1991 LIB — 1991 CONS		1992 LIB — 1992 CONS	
Economic	30% —	69%	35% —	64%
Social	0% —	84%	0% —	85%
Foreign	23% —	75%	52% —	46%

Key Votes of the 102d Congress

1. Ban Striker Replace	FOR	5. Handgun Wait/7-Day	AGN	9. Use Force in Gulf	FOR
2. $ for Homeownership	FOR	6. Overseas Mil. Abortion	AGN	10. US Mil. Abroad $ Cut	AGN
3. Tax Rich/Cut Mid Cls.	AGN	7. Obscn. Art NEA $ Ban	FOR	11. Limit SDI Funds	FOR
4. FY93/$15B Def. Cut	FOR	8. Death Pen. from Jury	FOR	12. Cuba Trade Embargo	AGN

Key Votes of the 103d Congress

1. Family Leave	AGN	2. Deficit Reduction	AGN	3. Stimulus Plan	AGN

Election Results

1992 general	Rick Santorum (R)	154,024	(61%)	($626,793)
	Frank A. Pecora (D)	96,655	(38%)	($284,757)
	Other	3,650	(1%)	
1992 primary	Rick Santorum (R), unopposed			
1990 general	Rick Santorum (R)	85,697	(51%)	($251,496)
	Douglas (Doug) Walgren (D)	80,880	(49%)	($717,124)

NINETEENTH DISTRICT

The Mason-Dixon Line, the historic boundary between Maryland and Pennsylvania, runs through some of the country's most pleasant rolling farmlands west of the Susquehanna River up through the first of the Appalachian chains. It was over this invisible line that Robert E. Lee's Confederate troops crossed and were then repulsed in the Confederacy's northernmost advance in the Battle of Gettysburg in July 1863. Nearby was the westernmost capital of the United States during the Revolutionary War, the small city of York, capital from September 1777 to June 1778. This is where the Continental Congress passed the Articles of Confederation, received word from Benjamin Franklin in Paris that the French would help the colonies with money and ships, and issued the first proclamation calling for a national day of thanksgiving. Little today reminds you that it was once the frontier and later fiercely fought over: the rolling green farmland looks peaceful, prosperous and mostly undisturbed by the commercial trappings and stylistic excesses of the late 20th Century.

Some 50 miles of the Mason-Dixon Line is the southern boundary of the 19th Congressional District of Pennsylvania, which is centered on York, including the suburbs of Harrisburg across the Susquehanna, the old town of Carlisle with Dickinson College and Carlisle Barracks, and President Eisenhower's retirement home near Gettysburg. Eisenhower was of Pennsylvania Dutch stock himself; his father migrated in the late 19th Century, with a group of Mennonite brethren, to Kansas and then Texas. The district has the look of a deeply contented land and is ordinarily heavily Republican. But there was enough of a Democratic heritage here to elect Democrats in 1954, 1958 and 1964, and enough discontent in 1992 to produce not one but two serious opponents to Republican Congressman Bill Goodling. A moderate Republican, with an active record of supporting bipartisan education measures, well rooted in the district (Goodling was a teacher, coach and principal in a small town in York County and his father served as congressman from the area for 12 years), he seemed well suited to the district.

Then, in October 1991, came the House bank scandal. Goodling turned out to be one of the worst abusers of the bank, with 430 overdrafts totalling $188,000. Goodling said he would take no questions from reporters on the subject, and was cleared of any criminal wrongdoing, but the facts cast him in a new and unfavorable light. And they aroused serious opposition where little had been forthcoming before. In one corner was Democrat Paul Kilker, a businessman whose graphics company in York created 100 new jobs in three years and started an on-site day care center. In another was Tom Humbert, whose family started the Snyder's of Hanover pretzel company, and who resigned as an aide to HUD Secretary Jack Kemp to run as an Independent after missing the GOP filing deadline. Kilker campaigned as a moderate Democrat against an incumbent he believed was out of touch with the district and who "lives by a different set of rules." Humbert campaigned as a conservative, against an incumbent who on the Education and Labor Committee cooperated with Democrats in supporting measures sought by teachers' unions and opposing education reforms. In both sets of charges there was some truth. Goodling's check overdraft record was disturbing, and in fall 1992 came other evidence that he felt he was above the rules: charges that he violated a "Clean and Green" land preservation law when he sold most of his York area horse farm in 1991. And as ranking Republican on Education and Labor, Goodling did work to protect the basic structure of federal aid to education (a structure that requires armies of bureaucrats to enforce it) and vocational education, although he did fight the Democrats when they opposed Bush's education reforms in the 1990s. Interestingly, Kemp avoided any endorsement of Humbert, while reform-minded Republicans like Newt Gingrich, Dan Quayle and Lynn Martin trooped in to support Goodling.

In this negative environment, Goodling ended up with only a plurality of the votes, 45%. His opponents split the majority: 34% went to Kilker, 20% to Humbert. Curiously, the percentages are within 2% of the Bush-Clinton-Perot numbers in the district. Goodling was not the only senior member of Education and Labor to have trouble at the polls: Chairman William Ford was reelected with the lowest margin of his career, high-ranking Democrats Austin Murphy and Dale Kildee came close to defeat, and Republican Tom Coleman, who like Goodling often fashioned bipartisan legislation, lost. The question now is whether Goodling will continue what he once called "our usual bipartisan bit" on many issues, or indeed whether Democrats will even seek his support now that they control the Executive Branch as well as both houses of Congress. Education and Labor has worked on chummily and smugly for years, with general public approval for more education spending giving way to dissatisfaction and even dismay at the end result of the system.

The People: Pop. 1990: 565,789; 50% rural; 13% age 65+; 95% White; 3% Black; 1% Asian; 1% Other; 1% Hispanic origin. Voting age pop.: 431,983; 2% Black; 1% Hispanic origin. Households: 63% married couple families; 28% married couple fams. w. children; 33% college educ.; median household income: $32,424; per capita income: $14,539; median gross rent: $416; median house value: $80,200.

1992 Presidential Vote			1988 Presidential Vote		
Bush (R)	105,647	(47%)	Bush (R)	123,621	(66%)
Clinton (D)	75,515	(33%)	Dukakis (D)	64,277	(34%)
Perot (I)	44,373	(20%)			

Rep. Bill Goodling (R)

Elected 1974; b. Dec. 5, 1927, Loganville; home, Jacobus; U. of MD, B.S. 1953, Western MD Col., M.A. 1957; Methodist; married (Hilda).

Career: Army, 1946–48; Public schl. teacher, admin., 1952–74; Pres., Dallastown School Bd., 1966–67.

Offices: 2263 RHOB 20515, 202-225-5836. Also Fed. Bldg., 200 S. George St., York 17405, 717-843-8887; 212 N. Hanover St., Carlisle 17013, 717-243-5432; 140 Baltimore St., Gettysburg 17325, 717-334-3430; 2020 Yale Ave., Camp Hill 17011, 717-763-1988; and 44 Frederick St., Hanover 17331, 717-632-7855, 800-631-1811.

Committees: *Education and Labor* (RMM of 15 R): Elementary, Secondary and Vocational Education (RMM). *Foreign Affairs* (2d of 18 R): Europe and the Middle East.

Group Ratings

	ADA	ACLU	COPE	CDF	CFA	LCV	ACU	NTLC	NSI	COC	CEI
1992	10	22	33	20	27	19	83	74	100	75	69
1991	20	—	25	60	22	0	73	—	—	70	64

National Journal Ratings

	1991 LIB — 1991 CONS			1992 LIB — 1992 CONS		
Economic	21%	—	78%	35%	—	65%
Social	33%	—	67%	22%	—	78%
Foreign	35%	—	65%	18%	—	74%

Key Votes of the 102d Congress

1. Ban Striker Replace AGN	5. Handgun Wait/7-Day FOR	9. Use Force in Gulf FOR
2. $ for Homeownership AGN	6. Overseas Mil. AbortionAGN	10. US Mil. Abroad $ CutAGN
3. Tax Rich/Cut Mid Cls.AGN	7. Obscn. Art NEA $ Ban FOR	11. Limit SDI Funds AGN
4. FY93/$15B Def. Cut AGN	8. Death Pen. from Jury *	12. Cuba Trade Embargo FOR

Key Votes of the 103d Congress

1. Family Leave AGN	2. Deficit Reduction AGN	3. Stimulus Plan AGN

Election Results

1992 general	Bill Goodling (R)	98,599	(45%)	($201,951)
	Paul V. Kilker (D).....................	74,798	(34%)	($238,346)
	Thomas M. Humbert (I)...............	44,190	(20%)	($122,486)
1992 primary	Bill Goodling (R), unopposed			
1990 general	Bill Goodling (R), unopposed			($40,698)

TWENTIETH DISTRICT

Southwest Pennsylvania, south of Pittsburgh and next to the deceptively straight-edged West Virginia state line, is one of the industrial backlands of America. Into these hills 200 years ago came Scots and Irish bordermen, wild settlers never entirely tamed by townsmen in their own native countries or here: this was the land of the Whiskey Rebellion of 1794. Then in the 19th Century, it was discovered that under these never-ending ridges were more or less never-ending seams of bituminous coal, the great industrial fuel of steel age factories. The offspring of the original settlers were joined by immigrants from Italy, Poland and Czechoslovakia, living in little frame houses packed into the towns on interstices between hills and rivers, within walking distance of steel factories, foundries and coal mine shafts. Life was never easy here, and in the last two decades it seems to have gotten harder. The local steel industry has never recovered the huge number of jobs lost in the recession after the 1979 oil price rise; coal has never recovered from the battering it took after oil prices fell in 1982–83. Young people had been moving out for years; now, so do people in their prime family years; the elderly stay on often only because there is no market for their houses. Living standards and working conditions are much better than a generation ago, but there is less work and less hope for the advancement that makes the burdens of everyday living more bearable. In the 1980s, the population of the three counties in the southwest corner of Pennsylvania, which together make up most of the state's 20th Congressional District, fell 7%.

The 20th District was slightly altered by redistricting, losing its part of Beaver County and part of Fayette, and extending up to Greensburg in Westmoreland County and the Pittsburgh suburbs around Bethel Park and Moon Township. The political complexion is little changed: this has been Democratic territory since the United Mine Workers backed the New Deal and established the United Steelworkers as the bargaining agent in the steel mills. Recent decades made the 20th even more Democratic, more than almost any other non-central city district. Yet the 20th saw an exceedingly close congressional race in 1992, and almost a Republican pickup. The reason: the scandals that keep accumulating around Congressman Austin Murphy.

In outward appearance, Murphy is a conventional labor-liberal Democrat, with local roots and a Marine Corps record. First elected in 1976, he sits on Natural Resources, where he supports coal interests and pushed for the Southwestern Pennsylvania Industrial Heritage Commission, and on Education and Labor, where he is a rock-solid labor vote. Since 1985, he has chaired the Labor Standards Subcommittee and was the lead sponsor of the minimum wage bills of 1989 and 1991. He backs only minor weakening of the Davis-Bacon Act (requiring high construction wages on government projects) and laws discouraging industrial homework (which undercuts unions). He is co-chairman of the Mining Caucus, a backer of generous black lung compensation, and introduced a Black Lung Benefits Restoration Act in 1991. Murphy complained that many of the bill's more generous provisions were blocked by "the scourge of budgetary impact" upon enactment.

His ethics problems first became public in 1987, when he was reprimanded by the House, 324–68, for letting someone else cast his vote on the floor, for diverting supplies to his former law firm and for paying a staffer for work not done; the latter two offenses seem petty, but the first was unnervingly fundamental. He still won reelection in 1988 with 73% in the primary and 72% in the general. Then in 1990, primary opponent William Nicolella charged that Murphy, who has a wife and family in the 20th District, also had a woman friend and teenage son in the northern Virginia suburbs of Washington. Murphy's response was, "I have never abandoned my responsibility to any of my children," and called the charges "slanderous." In the anti-incumbent climate of the year, his percentages fell only to 70% in the primary and 63% in the general. 1992 proved more difficult. In the April primary, he had serious opposition from Washington County Commissioner Frank Mascara, who won 34% and held Murphy to 36%; in third and fourth places were Ken Burkley, who ran against John Murtha in the 12th District primary in 1990, and Nicolella, Murphy's 1990 primary opponent. It was a result reminiscent of Murphy's first primary, in 1976, when he won with 29% in a 12-candidate field: he is lucky Pennsylvania has no runoff. Murphy had only 6 overdrafts at the House bank. But right after the primary in April, he was the subject of a subpoena of expense account records because of his extensive purchases of stamps at the House Post Office. Through the fall campaign 27-year-old ad agency executive Bill Townsend, though outfunded almost 6–1, ran "scandal of the week" news releases that bit hard into Murphy's support. Endorsed by Perot, Townsend, a Republican, waged a grass roots campaign and knocked on thousands of doors. Ultimately, Murphy won by only a 51%–49% margin. These are dreadful showings for a longtime incumbent, and suggest that Murphy could easily lose in 1994, if he runs; if he doesn't, the Democratic nominee would be the overwhelming favorite.

The People: Pop. 1990: 565,789; 40% rural; 17% age 65+; 96% White; 3% Black. Voting age pop.: 436,821; 3% Black. Households: 61% married couple families; 26% married couple fams. w. children; 36% college educ.; median household income: $26,294; per capita income: $13,349; median gross rent: $332; median house value: $56,600.

1992 Presidential Vote

Clinton (D)	121,823	(51%)
Bush (R)	69,811	(29%)
Perot (I)	48,251	(20%)

1988 Presidential Vote

Dukakis (D)	127,283	(59%)
Bush (R)	89,992	(41%)

Rep. Austin J. Murphy (D)

Elected 1976; b. June 17, 1927, Speers; home, Monongahela; Duquesne U., B.A. 1949, U. of Pittsburgh, LL.B. 1952; Catholic; married (Ramona).

Career: Marine Corps, 1944–46 (WWII); Practicing atty., 1953–76; Washington Cnty. Asst. Dist. Atty., 1956–57; PA House of Reps., 1958–70; PA Senate, 1970–76.

Offices: 2210 RHOB 20515, 202-225-4665. Also 306 Fallowfield Ave., Charleroi 15022, 412-489-4217; 96 N. Main St., Washington 15301, 412-228-2777; Rt. 21 S., Uniontown 15401, 412-438-1490; 93 High St., Waynesburg 15370, 412-627-7611; 260 Miller's Run Rd., Bridgeville 15017, 412-221-2129; and 8 S. 4th St., Youngwood 15697, 412-925-1370.

Committees: *Education and Labor* (4th of 28 D): Labor-Management Relations; Labor Standards, Occupational Health and Safety (Chmn.). *Natural Resources* (4th of 28 D): Energy and Mineral Resources; Insular and International Affairs; National Parks, Forests and Public Lands.

Group Ratings

	ADA	ACLU	COPE	CDF	CFA	LCV	ACU	NTLC	NSI	COC	CEI
1992	65	39	83	80	53	50	33	10	30	38	25
1991	50	—	82	80	83	46	39	—	—	33	27

National Journal Ratings

	1991 LIB — 1991 CONS		1992 LIB — 1992 CONS	
Economic	64%	— 36%	83%	— 13%
Social	35%	— 65%	31%	— 69%
Foreign	64%	— 35%	75%	— 24%

Key Votes of the 102d Congress

1. Ban Striker Replace	FOR	5. Handgun Wait/7-Day	AGN	9. Use Force in Gulf	AGN
2. $ for Homeownership	AGN	6. Overseas Mil. Abortion	AGN	10. US Mil. Abroad $ Cut	FOR
3. Tax Rich/Cut Mid Cls.	FOR	7. Obscn. Art NEA $ Ban	FOR	11. Limit SDI Funds	FOR
4. FY93/$15B Def. Cut	FOR	8. Death Pen. from Jury	*	12. Cuba Trade Embargo	FOR

Key Votes of the 103d Congress

1. Family Leave	FOR	2. Deficit Reduction	FOR	3. Stimulus Plan	FOR

Election Results

1992 general	Austin J. Murphy (D)................	114,898	(51%)	($309,425)
	Bill Townsend (R)...................	111,591	(49%)	($51,775)
1992 primary	Austin J. Murphy (D)................	36,585	(36%)	
	Frank R. Mascara (D)	33,942	(34%)	
	Kenneth B. Burkley (D)	14,422	(14%)	
	William A. Nicolella (D)	8,520	(8%)	
	Eugene G. Saloom (D)	7,755	(8%)	
1990 general	Austin J. Murphy (D)................	78,375	(63%)	($191,739)
	Suzanne Hayden (R)	45,509	(37%)	($3,258)

TWENTY-FIRST DISTRICT

Where is the best natural harbor on Lake Erie? This is a trivia question few will get right: it is in Erie, Pennsylvania, protected by the Presque Isle peninsula, up in the remotest corner of Pennsylvania, 428 miles from Center City Philadelphia. Erie is the largest city in Pennsylvania's 21st Congressional District, about half of which is in Erie County. The rest of the district is to the south, including Sharon, on the Ohio border and part of the Youngstown-Warren area, long a major steel-producing town, and Butler County, suburban and country area directly north of Pittsburgh. There is farm country here and even some woods, but heavy industry, or its demise, sets the dominant tone of the district. This combination has produced a close political balance, with Democratic Erie and Sharon areas balanced by Republican Butler and Crawford Counties; for years, this was one of the classic marginal seats in the nation.

Now, however, it is the political property—as long as he runs—of Tom Ridge, a Republican who comes from a somewhat un-Republican background. He is from a Catholic, Slovak-Irish, working-class family in Erie and once lived in a housing project; he went to Harvard and—an unusual combination—served in Vietnam. He has a mixed voting record by the lights of almost every rating group. He is not always market-oriented on economics, is sometimes dovish on defense and foreign policy, is liberal on some cultural issues and tradition-minded on others. On the Banking Committee, he has passed bills to extend more credit to low-income neighborhoods by discounting deposit insurance premiums for certain banks and to expand Section 108 loans for infrastructure development to small cities and rural communities. He also introduced the Vento-Ridge FHA reform measure that passed the House; it called for tougher capital standards and was designed to ensure the future actuarial solvency of the FHA fund. He called for having the Secret Service investigate S&L fraud and for an inspector general ("a pit bull not a lap dog") to oversee Congress. During the Gulf war, he introduced the bill to pay for mail service for Desert Storm personnel out of the congressional franking funds. Ranking Republican on the Census and Population Subcommittee in the 102d Congress, he pushed successfully to have armed services personnel counted as residents of their home towns, which cost Massachusetts and gained for Washington state a seat in the House, but failed in his efforts to have illegal aliens excluded from the count. He favors increased spending on veterans' homelessness and Post Traumatic Stress Disorder treatment.

Ridge announced in February 1993 that he will run for governor in 1994, when incumbent Bob Casey will be ineligible to run. Ridge's biggest problem is that he is from Erie, and hence unknown in the 20 other districts. The addition of Butler County to the 21st in 1992 gave him an excuse to run ads on Pittsburgh TV stations, and gave him at least a little head start toward statewide name identification; but he has a long way to go. He may have some ways to go too in building up knowledge of state government, with which he has had little direct experience, while possible primary opponents, Attorney General Ernie Preate and Auditor Barbara Hafer, have years of Harrisburg experience.

The People: Pop. 1990: 565,806; 44% rural; 15% age 65+; 95% White; 4% Black; 1% Hispanic origin. Voting age pop.: 424,816; 3% Black; 1% Hispanic origin. Households: 58% married couple families; 26% married couple fams. w. children; 33% college educ.; median household income: $25,845; per capita income: $11,884; median gross rent: $326; median house value: $50,200.

1992 Presidential Vote			1988 Presidential Vote		
Clinton (D)	105,538	(45%)	Dukakis (D)	104,662	(51%)
Bush (R)	80,902	(34%)	Bush (R)	101,259	(49%)
Perot (I)	48,004	(20%)			

Rep. Tom Ridge (R)

Elected 1982; b. Aug. 26, 1945, Munhall; home, Erie; Harvard, B.A. 1967, Dickinson Law Sch., J.D. 1972; Catholic; married (Michele).

Career: Army, 1968–70 (Vietnam); Practicing atty., 1972–82.

Offices: 1714 LHOB 20515, 202-225-5406. Also 108 Fed. Bldg., Erie 16501, 814-456-2038; 305 Chestnut St., Meadville 16335, 814-724-8414; 91 E. State St., Sharon 16146, 412-981-8440; and 327 N. Main St., Butler 16001, 412-285-7005.

Committees: *Banking, Finance and Urban Affairs* (5th of 20 R): Economic Growth and Credit Formation (RMM); General Oversight, Investigations, and the Resolution of Failed Financial Institutions; Housing and Community Development. *Post Office and Civil Service* (6th of 9 R): Census Statistics and Postal Personnel. *Veterans' Affairs* (5th of 14 R): Education, Training and Employment; Oversight and Investigations (RMM).

Group Ratings

	ADA	ACLU	COPE	CDF	CFA	LCV	ACU	NTLC	NSI	COC	CEI
1992	30	35	50	30	40	19	68	65	80	63	61
1991	15	—	58	30	33	8	70	—	—	90	54

National Journal Ratings

	1991 LIB — 1991 CONS		1992 LIB — 1992 CONS	
Economic	36%	— 64%	38%	— 61%
Social	37%	— 61%	38%	— 60%
Foreign	30%	— 69%	44%	— 50%

Key Votes of the 102d Congress

1. Ban Striker Replace	AGN	5. Handgun Wait/7-Day	AGN	9. Use Force in Gulf	FOR
2. $ for Homeownership	FOR	6. Overseas Mil. Abortion	FOR	10. US Mil. Abroad $ Cut	FOR
3. Tax Rich/Cut Mid Cls.	AGN	7. Obscn. Art NEA $ Ban	FOR	11. Limit SDI Funds	FOR
4. FY93/$15B Def. Cut	AGN	8. Death Pen. from Jury	FOR	12. Cuba Trade Embargo	FOR

Key Votes of the 103d Congress

1. Family Leave	AGN	2. Deficit Reduction	AGN	3. Stimulus Plan	AGN

Election Results

1992 general	Tom Ridge (R)	150,729	(68%)	($705,861)
	John C. Harkins (D)	70,802	(32%)	($15,800)
1992 primary	Tom Ridge (R), unopposed			
1990 general	Tom Ridge (R), unopposed			($361,712)

RHODE ISLAND

The tiny little city-state with a mouthful of an official name, Rhode Island and Providence Plantations, has as turbulent a political history as any state in the Union. A successful trading community since the 1600s, a leader in manufacturing since Samuel Slater replicated from memory an English water-powered cotton textile mill in Pawtucket in 1791, Rhode Island also had its beginning as an upstart community, a refuge for religious dissenters, "the sewer of New England," as the orthodox Cotton Mather put it. Rhode Island profited from slavery (two-thirds of America's slaves arrived on ships owned by Rhode Islanders) and war (the state boomed during the Civil War), and carried its tradition of tolerating just about anything into politics. Rhode Island refused to pay for the Revolutionary War, declined to send delegates to the 1787 Constitutional Convention, and delayed joining the Union until the other 12 states had, prompting George Washington to say, "Rhode Island still perseveres in that impolitic, unjust—and one might add without much impropriety—scandalous conduct, which seems to have marked all her public counsels of late." The new nation's first bank failure occurred in Rhode Island in 1809, when a bank capitalized at $45 issued $800,000 in bank notes. In the 1840s, conflict between hard money merchants and soft money farmers resulted in two state governments and a conflict known as Dorr's War, with the outcome determined when merchant Dorr's two ancient cannons failed to fire.

Then, in the 1930s, Rhode Island had something resembling a political revolution. Thousands of immigrants from French Canada, Ireland and Italy had come to Rhode Island to work in the textile mills; by the early 1900s, this colony of dissident Protestants had become the most heavily Catholic state in the nation. Yankee Republicans were able to appeal to Catholics by running French Canadians for high office for example; but national events—Al Smith's candidacy in 1928, when he carried Rhode Island, and Franklin Roosevelt's New Deal—moved the Catholics toward the Democrats. Then came the revolution: in 1935, the Democrats under Governor Theodore Green, although they had won only 20 of the 42 state Senate seats, refused to seat two Republicans. With the lieutenant governor's tie-breaker they voted Democrats into the seats, and proceeded in 14 minutes to declare the state Supreme Court seats vacant, abolish state boards that controlled Democratic cities, strengthen the power of the governor and reorganize state government to get rid of Republicans. This ended the direct political control by Rhode Island's "Five Families"—the Browns, Metcalfs, Goddards, Lippitts and Chafees—who owned or ran many of the textile mills, the Rhode Island Hospital Trust (long the largest bank), the *Providence Journal*, the Rhode Island School of Design and the state Republican Party—and ultimately lost the leadership of Rhode Island politics to the heirs of the 1935 Green revolution. The Democrats have won most elections with the lion's share of votes from Rhode Island's 64% Catholic majority, starting with Green's election in 1936 at age 69 to the first of his four terms as U.S. senator. From 1940 to 1980, Democrats won every election for the U.S. House seat; its Democratic percentages in presidential elections from 1968 to 1992 were among the highest in the country, rivalled only by Massachusetts. Republicans have won when they've been able to capitalize on scandal or Democratic disarray. The only really durable Republican politician has been John Chafee, elected governor in 1962, 1964 and 1966, senator in 1976, 1982 and 1988; but even he has lost twice statewide.

But Rhode Island political patterns were destabilized by economic transformation in the 1970s and 1980s. Manufacturing was reduced from almost half of Rhode Island jobs to one-quarter, with twice as many jobs in services, trade and finance. For years, the unions remained politically powerful, though representing fewer and fewer workers; the state economy was quietly upgraded from blue-collar to white-collar, from textiles to high tech; the electorate,

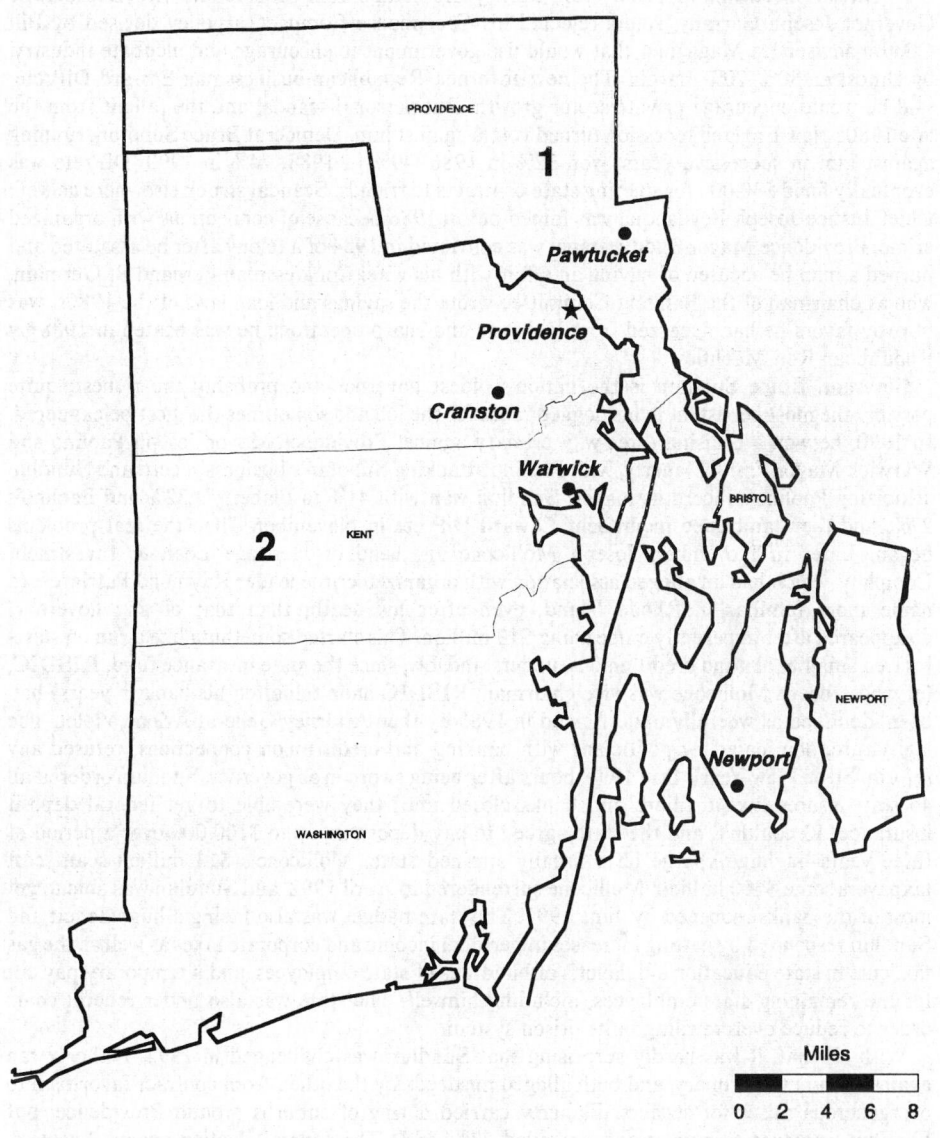

PROVIDENCE

1

Pawtucket

Providence

Cranston

Warwick

BRISTOL

2

KENT

NEWPORT

Newport

WASHINGTON

Miles

0   2   4   6   8

instead of being a mass of Catholic factory workers pressed into neighborhoods of three-story three-family houses, became comfortably affluent and suburban. Old political ties frayed, tolerance of scandal and sleaze diminished, and in the 1980s there were wild oscillations around the political spectrum. In 1984, after eight years of apparent satisfaction with Democratic Governor Joseph Garrahy, voters rejected his Greenhouse Compact, a policy devised by Bill Clinton adviser Ira Magaziner that would use government to encourage and incubate industry, by almost an 80%–20% margin. The new governor, Republican businessman Edward DiPrete, said he would encourage private sector growth. But personal scandal and the fallout from the late 1980s New England recession turned voters against him. Democrat Bruce Sundlun, running against him in successive years, won 32% in 1986, 49% in 1988, 74% in 1990. DiPrete was eventually fined $30,000 for steering state contracts to friends. Scandal struck elsewhere as well: Chief Justice Joseph Bevilacqua was forced out in 1986 because of connections with organized crime; Providence Mayor Buddy Cianci was convicted in 1984 of a felony after he assaulted and burned a man he accused of having an affair with his wife; Congressman Fernand St Germain, who as chairman of the Banking Committee wrote the savings and loan laws of the 1980s, was hurt by favors he had accepted from lobbyists and sharp operators; he was beaten in 1988 by Republican Ron Machtley.

Governor. Bruce Sundlun is the nation's oldest governor and probably the richest; quite possibly the most persistent in his dogged races for the job and sometimes the most beleaguered. In 1990, he won a bruising three-way primary against Providence Mayor Joseph Paolino and Warwick Mayor Frank Flaherty, with Paolino attacking Sundlun's business record and Sundlun criticizing Paolino's record as mayor; Sundlun won with 41% to Flaherty's 32% and Paolino's 27%, and then lambasted incumbent Edward DiPrete in November. Then the real problems began. Later in November, Joseph Mollicone Jr., head of Heritage Loan & Investment Company, which had an alleged association with organized crime leader Raymond Patriarca, (a name more familiar in Rhode Island, even after his death, than that of any governor) disappeared after apparently embezzling $13 million. This started something like a run on state-insured small banks and credit unions, understandably, since the state insurance fund, RISDIC, (of whose board Mollicone was vice chairman; RISDIC hadn't audited his bank in years) had been identified as woefully underfunded in 1985 by then-Attorney General Arlene Violet. The legislature, dominated by politicians with banking and credit union connections, refused any reform. So on New Year's Day 1991, hours after being sworn in as governor, Sundlun ordered all 45 state-insured credit unions and banks closed until they were able to get federal deposit insurance; 13 couldn't, and the state agreed to pay depositors up to $100,000 over a period of three years—a huge charge on a fiscally strained state. Mollicone's $13 million scam cost taxpayers some $500 million; Mollicone surrendered in April 1992, and Sundlun was able to get most of the banks reopened by June 1991. The state budget was also facing a huge deficit and Sundlun responded by getting increases in personal income and corporate taxes as well as the gas tax, cuts in state education aid, layoffs of hundreds of state employees, and a temporary pay cut for the remaining state employees, including himself. The state was also under federal court order to reduce overcrowding in its prison system.

With all that, it was hardly surprising that Sundlun was challenged in 1992. Flaherty ran against him in the primary, and both alleged misdeeds by the other, from contract favoritism to overgenerous raises for staffers. Flaherty carried a ring of suburbs around Providence, but Sundlun won everything else and prevailed 52%–48%. The general election against business-woman Betty Leonard proved easier; Sundlun won 62%–34%. And Rhode Island, once one of three states that elected governors every two years, will begin four year terms with a two term limit in 1994.

Senators. Ethnic Catholic Rhode Island has two blue-blooded WASPs as U.S. senators, both enduring political figures of great popularity. Claiborne Pell, first elected to the Senate in 1960, is now not only Rhode Island's senior politician, but one of the nation's: in the Senate, only Strom Thurmond and Robert Byrd have served longer. Pell's father was a one-term congressman from

New York, a friend of Franklin Roosevelt and minister to Portugal and Hungary. Pell himself served as a foreign service officer for several years, then settled on Bellevue Avenue in Newport, where you find the Vanderbilt and Auchincloss "cottages." (Rhode Island's Five Families tend to live on Providence's College Hill, with comfy summer places on Rhode Island Sound; the oceanfront palaces of Newport were built mostly by New Yorkers.) Pell has been what he long wanted to be, chairman of the Senate Foreign Relations Committee, since 1987, in title, anyway.

But Pell has been an increasingly inactive, passive chairman—diffident, polite, but often tongue-tied—of a committee that wields much less influence than it once did. Some might call that an improvement. The ranking Republican, Jesse Helms, has spent much of his time monitoring Bush and Clinton Administration appointments, keeping track of policy in peripheral areas in which he is interested. Most committee Democrats were longtime doves, reflexively opposed to the exertion of American military power almost anywhere, up through and including the Gulf war, whose outcome they spectacularly failed to foresee. Then, as if to make up for this staggering mistake, some, notably second ranking Joseph Biden, vehemently backed U.S. military intervention in Bosnia in 1993. In all these debates, Pell has been a kind of footnote. In fall 1990, Pell called for the War Powers Act to be invoked during the Persian Gulf crisis, but did not pursue the point; almost entirely ignored, this legacy of the Vietnam era has become effectively a dead letter. Pell propitiated the erstwhile doves in 1991 by backing their requests for bigger subcommittee budgets and allowing them greater visibility—Joseph Biden on European Affairs, Paul Sarbanes on International Economic Policy, Christopher Dodd on Western Hemisphere and, in 1993, Daniel Patrick Moynihan on South Asia and the Middle East. In June 1992, Pell called for consideration of military action to enforce UN sanctions in Bosnia; in early 1993, he was almost entirely silent on the issue. He and Helms did have one achievement, a 1992 bill penalizing countries trading in chemical weapons, but with a provision allowing the president to waive the penalties. Pell does have his interests: banning nuclear weapons on the ocean floor and banning environmental alteration (the burning oilfields in Kuwait?) as a weapon of war. But he has done nothing remotely comparable to William Fulbrights's hearings on Vietnam or Richard Lugar's work on the Philippines in 1986.

Over the years, Pell has accomplished more on education. He is the second ranking Democrat on Labor and Human Resources, and for years has chaired the subcommittee on Education, Arts and the Humanities. His Pell grants for needy college and university students have become a household word over a generation; they have never been fully funded over the current $2,400 per year level, however, and Pell has backed off from attempts to make them an entitlement not subject to annual appropriations. He has also worked on a teacher training act. Pell was for many years the congressional father of the National Endowment for the Arts, but has played little role in the controversy over its funding in the 1990s. He has also been one of the main promoters of ocean research (Rhode Island's license plates call it the "Ocean State").

For all of Pell's oddness, he is a formidable figure in Rhode Island, an iron fist in a velvet glove. He has received everything he wanted in politics, and by whipping the toughest competition this little state could offer. In the 1960 Democratic primary, he beat former Governor Dennis Roberts and former Governor, Senator and U.S. Attorney General J. Howard McGrath; this was the first time since Theodore Green's governorship that a candidate endorsed by the Democratic organization was beaten. In 1972, when Rhode Island was going Republican for president, Pell faced John Chafee, then a popular former governor and secretary of the navy, and beat him decisively. Reelected with 75% in 1978 and 73% in 1984, he faced another tough challenge in 1990 from Congresswoman Claudine Schneider. She had a strong environmental record and a great deal of energy; her popularity ratings were as high as Pell's, and she shared most of his issue positions and a bit of his oddity (she cut a TV ad for an inspirational audio tape which promoted weight loss, a more passionate life and financial independence). At a Pell-Schneider forum televised in August, Pell was asked to identify a piece of legislation he'd sponsored recently to help people in Rhode Island; he replied, "I couldn't give you a specific answer. My memory's not as good as it should be." The next day, however, Iraq invaded Kuwait, and Pell was soon getting coverage, on Rhode Island TV if not so much nationally, opining on the crisis and visiting the Persian Gulf. It was an exquisitely polite race, with Pell praising Schneider ("You've done a fine job . . . in the Congress, and I would congratulate you") and Schneider ads conceding Pell's strong points ("We all love Claiborne Pell," she said). "Quiet accomplishments that make a world of difference," Pell's ads proclaimed, and Rhode Islanders apparently agreed, giving him a 62%–38% victory. Pell holds, it may be worth noting, the seat won by Theodore Green in 1936 at 69, a seat that a generation of Rhode Island politicians assumed would soon become open; to stay in the Senate until the age Green retired at (93), Pell (now 75) would have to win three more terms and serve until 2012.

Senator John Chafee, a scion of one of Rhode Island's Five Families and a Marine veteran of World War II and Korea, has been a statewide elected official for most of the last three decades. He is usually counted as a liberal Republican, perhaps the most liberal in the Senate, because of the cumulation of individual stands on various issues; but he can also be a stubborn and angry Republican partisan. From a state where labor unions were politically dominant when he started off in politics, if not today, where he could not have hoped to rise without some sympathy for union positions, he tends to be liberal and interventionist on economics. He was a strong supporter of family and medical leave and opposed President Bush's school choice plan. But he bucks unions and many Democrats by backing the North American Free Trade Agreement, the investment tax credit and reducing regulation to make more credit available by banks. He sided with the Clinton Administration on three of eight early budget votes, but he joined with relish the Republican filibuster against the Clinton stimulus package. "The American people will come to see gridlock as a pretty good thing," he said, if it's over this. He came to the Senate well after the Vietnam war, but shares some of the caution about American military intervention of post-Vietnam doves and was cautious in 1992 and early 1993 about going into Bosnia. He also came out for repealing the ban on gays in the military. From a part of the country where Catholics had large families and Protestants preached birth control, he is pro-choice and was a vehement opponent of the "gag rule." He does not leave Rhode Island issues unaddressed. He worked to save the Seawolf submarine, produced just over the line in Connecticut, and to repeal the luxury tax which has destroyed Rhode Island's boat-building industry (boatbuilders are not themselves rich: see John Casey's Rhode Island novel *Spartina*). He inserted into the 1991 banking bill a provision helping Rhode Island finance the RISDIC payouts and favors not only highway (there's room for only so many in this small state) but other forms of infrastructure spending.

Chafee is a Republican in the conservationist tradition that goes back to Theodore Roosevelt. He is ranking Republican on the Environment and Public Works Committee, and played an unusually large role for a minority member on the 1987 water projects bill passed over President Reagan's veto, the 1988 ocean dumping law, the 1989 oil spill law and, especially, the 1990 Clean Air Act, on which he was often the effective manager of the bill in the Senate. He has also worked on smaller bills, on barrier islands, billboard control, commercial fishing safety, wetlands, and state partnerships for wildlife preservation. He strongly backed the Rio treaties on global climate change and biodiversity. On gun control, he favors a ban on the manufacture, sale and possession of handguns.

Chafee's other great specialty is health: he is chairman of the Republican Task Force on Health Care, and is designated by Senate Republicans as their lead man on the issue. That leaves some uncomfortable, since he has backed managed competition, though as he added in an early 1993 letter to President Clinton, "Refining this theory so that it will work in practice will take much thought and creativity." He says that managed competition would set boundaries of benefits and standards for insurance, which would mean reduced benefits and service for some. In November 1991, Chafee came up with a Republican healthcare package, with tax incentives for workers and employers, beefed-up preventive care, and overhaul of medical malpractice. In September 1992, he prepared a compromise with Senate Finance Chairman Lloyd Bentsen on a bill setting up group purchasing cooperatives and trying to reform small group insurance without totally eliminating insurers' discretion; it set up a cost containment commission, encouraged portability and managed care and provided for 100% tax deductibility for self-employed. But it was attached to the urban aid bill, and was defeated. In January 1993, Chafee began work on a new healthcare proposal, and cited his skepticism of global budgeting saying, "Global budgeting means a cap . . . By mid-November, if you've exceeded your cap, what do you do?"

Chafee's liberal positions cost him the post of Republican Conference chairman, which he won by a 28–25 margin over the abrasive Jake Garn in December 1984 and lost to the personable Thad Cochran in December 1990, 22–21. And, for all his popularity, this Republican has had electoral setbacks in this Democratic state: he was defeated when he sought a fourth term as governor in 1968 and he lost the 1972 Senate race to Pell. He came back, however, winning an open Senate seat in 1976. He had a close race in the recession year of 1982, winning just 51% against former Attorney General Julius Michaelson; in 1988, against Lieutenant Governor Richard Licht, whose uncle had beaten him 20 years before, he won with 55% while Michael Dukakis was carrying the state with 56%. In the last two races, Chafee got strong financial support from environmentalists. Chafee turns 72 in 1994, but will be the clear favorite if he runs; the Democratic nominee—just who is too hard to predict in this volatile state—will be favored if he doesn't.

Presidential politics. Rhode Island is always among the most Democratic states in presidential elections—over the last generation, the most Democratic on average. The ancestral Democratic preference of the nearly two-thirds of Rhode Islanders who are Catholic has played a role. It should be added that abortion is not a big issue here, and Rhode Island overall is pro-choice: in states where Catholics are beleaguered minorities they may stand together and strongly oppose abortion; in Rhode Island, where they're the strong majority and where the mostly Italian Catholics have never paid much attention to the mostly Irish priests anyway, they come out on this issue like Americans generally.

Rhode Island holds a presidential primary the same day as Massachusetts and has the lowest turnout in the nation, a vestige of the days when Democratic Party bosses had sway. Massachusetts neighbor Paul Tsongas and Maine neighbor George Bush won their primaries in 1992, but Bill Clinton carried the state in November.

Congressional Districting. The boundaries of Rhode Island's two congressional districts have never changed much, and were altered only slightly for 1992. Providence is split and both districts are overwhelmingly Democratic. Interestingly, this ultrapolitical state is currently represented in the House by two men who graduated from Annapolis and West Point—perhaps voters' way of finding squeaky-clean representatives in a state with more than its share of crooked politicians.

The People: Est. Pop. 1992: 1,005,000; Pop. 1990: 1,003,464, up 0.2% 1990–1992. 0.4% of U.S. total, 43d largest; 14% rural. Median age: 34.0 years. 15.0% 65 years and over. 91.4% White, 4.6% Hispanic origin, 3.9% Black, 1.8% Asian, 2.5% Other. Households: 53.5% married couple families; 24% married couple fams. w. children; 43% college educ.; median household income: $32,181; per capita income: $14,981; 59.5% owner occupied housing; median house value: $133,500; median monthly rent: $416. 8.9% Unemployment. Voting age pop.: 777,774. Registered voters (1992): 554,081; no party registration.

Political Lineup: Governor, Bruce Sundlun (D); Lt. Gov., Robert A. Weygand (D); Secy. of State, Barbara Leonard (R); Atty. Gen., Jeffrey B. Pina (R); General Treasurer, Nancy J. Mayer (R). State Senate, 50 (39 D and 11 R); State House of Representatives, 100 (89 D and 11 R). Senators, Claiborne Pell (D) and John H. Chafee (R). Representatives, 2 (1 D and 1 R).

1134   RHODE ISLAND

GOVERNOR

Gov. Bruce Sundlun (D)

Elected 1990, term expires Jan. 1995; b. Jan. 21, 1920 Providence; home, Providence; Williams Col., B.A. 1946, Harvard, LL.B. 1949; Jewish; married (Marjorie).

Career: Army Air Corps, 1942–45 (WWII); Air Force Reserves, 1945–66; Dir., COMSAT Corp., 1963-91; Pres., Exec. Jet, 1970–76; Pres., Outlet Communications, 1976–84, Chmn. & CEO, 1984–88; Chmn., Sundlun & Co., 1988–91.

Office: The State House, #222, Providence 02903, 401-277-2080.

Election Results

1992 gen.	Bruce Syndlun (D)	261,484	(62%)
	Betty Leonard (R)	145,590	(34%)
	Three Others	17,744	(4%)
1992 prim.	Bruce Sundlun (D)	78,735	(52%)
	Francis X. Flaherty (D)	72,011	(48%)
1990 gen.	Bruce Sundlun (D)	264,411	(74%)
	Edward D. DiPrete (R)	92,177	(26%)

SENATORS

Sen. Claiborne Pell (D)

Elected 1960, seat up 1996; b. Nov. 22, 1918, New York, NY; home, Newport; Princeton, A.B. 1940, Columbia U., A.M. 1946; Episcopalian; married (Nuala).

Career: Coast Guard, 1941–45 (WWII), Coast Guard Reserves, 1945–78; Foreign Svc., U.S. Dept. of State, Czechoslovakia and Italy, 1945–52; Exec. Asst., RI Dem. St. Chmn., 1952, 1954; Consultant, DNC, 1953–60.

Offices: 335 RSOB 20510, 202-224-4642. Also 418 Fed. Bldg., Providence 02903, 401-528-5456.

Committees: *Foreign Relations* (Chmn. of 11 D): Terrorism, Narcotics and International Operations. *Labor and Human Resources* (2d of 10 D): Aging; Children, Family, Drugs and Alcoholism; Education, Arts and Humanities (Chmn.). *Rules and Administration* (2d of 9 D). *Joint Committee on the Library* (Vice Chmn. of 5).

Group Ratings

	ADA	ACLU	CDF	COPE	CFA	LCV	ACU	NTLC	NSI	COC	CEI
1992	80	91	90	82	92	83	8	17	50	30	12
1991	90	—	100	83	72	100	0	—	—	22	22

National Journal Ratings

	1991 LIB — 1991 CONS		1992 LIB — 1992 CONS	
Economic	90% —	3%	67% —	32%
Social	87% —	0%	89% —	0%
Foreign	78% —	14%	65% —	26%

Key Votes of the 102d Congress

1. $ for Homeownership	AGN	5. Clarence Thomas Nom.	AGN	9. Use Force in Gulf	AGN
2. Have Cap Gains Debate	AGN	6. Lmt Death Row Appeal	AGN	10. Keep Salvador Aid	AGN
3. Remove Budget Walls	FOR	7. Handgun Wait/5-Day	FOR	11. Cut $1B from SDI	FOR
4. Ban Striker Replace	FOR	8. Abortion Gag Rule	AGN	12. Override China MFN	FOR

Key Votes of the 103d Congress

1. Family Leave	FOR	2. HIV Immigrants	FOR	3. Clinton Budget	FOR

Election Results

1990 general	Claiborne Pell (D)...................	225,105	(62%)	($2,363,904)
	Claudine Schneider (R)	138,947	(38%)	($2,056,923)
1990 primary	Claiborne Pell (D), unopposed			
1984 general	Claiborne Pell (D)...................	286,780	(73%)	($430,739)
	Barbara M. Leonard (R)..............	108,492	(27%)	($143,842)

Sen. John H. Chafee (R)

Elected 1976, seat up 1994; b. Oct. 22, 1922, Providence; home, Warwick; Yale, B.A. 1947, Harvard, LL.B. 1950; Episcopalian; married (Virginia).

Career: Marine Corps, 1942–45 (WWII), 1951–53 (Korea); Practicing atty., 1952–63, 1973–75; RI House of Reps., 1957–63, Minority Ldr., 1959–63; RI Gov., 1963–69; Secy. of the Navy, 1969–72.

Offices: 567 DSOB 20510, 202-224-2921. Also 301 John Pastore Fed. Bldg., 2 Exchange Terr., Providence 02903, 401-528-5294.

Committees: *Environment and Public Works* (RMM of 7 R): Clean Water, Fisheries and Wildlife (RMM). *Finance* (5th of 9 R): Health for Families and the Uninsured (RMM); International Trade; Medicare and Long-Term Care. *Intelligence (Select)* (5th of 8 R). *Small Business* (9th of 9 R): Export Expansion and Agricultural Development; Urban and Minority-Owned Business Development (RMM).

Group Ratings

	ADA	ACLU	CDF	COPE	CFA	LCV	ACU	NTLC	NSI	COC	CEI
1992	40	77	50	17	33	67	44	33	90	80	53
1991	60	—	82	45	61	80	24	—	—	40	40

National Journal Ratings

	1991 LIB	—	1991 CONS	1992 LIB	—	1992 CONS
Economic	69%	—	29%	25%	—	73%
Social	78%	—	20%	69%	—	26%
Foreign	43%	—	55%	49%	—	48%

Key Votes of the 102d Congress

1. $ for Homeownership	AGN	5. Clarence Thomas Nom. FOR	9. Use Force in Gulf FOR
2. Have Cap Gains Debate AGN		6. Lmt Death Row Appeal FOR	10. Keep Salvador Aid FOR
3. Remove Budget Walls	AGN	7. Handgun Wait/5-Day FOR	11. Cut $1B from SDI FOR
4. Ban Striker Replace	AGN	8. Abortion Gag Rule AGN	12. Override China MFN AGN

Key Votes of the 103d Congress

1. Family Leave FOR	2. HIV Immigrants FOR	3. Clinton Budget AGN

Election Results

1988 general	John H. Chafee (R)	217,273	(55%)	($2,841,985)
	Richard A. Licht (D)	180,717	(45%)	($2,735,917)
1988 primary	John H. Chafee (R), unopposed			
1982 general	John H. Chafee (R)	175,248	(51%)	($1,065,627)
	Julius C. Michaelson (D)	167,283	(49%)	($438,630)

FIRST DISTRICT

The 1st Congressional District is the eastern half of Rhode Island, east of Narragansett Bay, a line that cuts through Providence and then proceeds west and north to the Massachusetts-Connecticut-Rhode Island border. It includes much of Providence (elite College Hill around Brown University) and all of next-door Pawtucket; the onetime textile mill towns of the Blackstone Valley, Woonsocket and Central Falls; high income Barrington and Bristol and, south on the ocean, the old city of Newport, with its restored 18th Century houses and the "cottages" that are really palaces. Ethnically, this is the more French Canadian and less Italian of the two Rhode Island districts; politically, it is strongly Democratic in most elections.

Nevertheless, the congressman from the 1st is Republican Ron Machtley, who has an unusual background for a Rhode Island politician: he grew up in Pennsylvania, graduated from the Naval Academy, and was home-ported in Rhode Island; he returned there after leaving the Navy, and became a fishing and admiralty lawyer in Newport County. In 1988, he got it into his head to run against Congressman Fernand St Germain, chairman of the House Banking Committee since 1981 and the architect, with the help of some lobbyists (one of whom bought him dinner every night of the week) of the savings and loan legislation that produced half a trillion dollars in losses for the taxpayers. First elected in 1960, always funneling senior citizen housing into eastern Rhode Island, St Germain had long been invulnerable. But in the 1988 primary, political consultant Scott Wolf won 45% against him, though Wolf's chances had been heavily discounted by Washington PAC operatives. Machtley meanwhile was parading a 250-pound hog named Lester H. Pork ("Les Pork") to symbolize his opposition to St Germain's big spending policies; in the last week of October, an internal Justice Department report was leaked finding "substantial evidence of serious and sustained misconduct" by St Germain. Machtley won with 56%.

Machtley sits on the House Armed Services Committee, where he looks after Rhode Island interests, including the Newport Naval Base and the nuclear submarine contracts for Electric Boat in eastern Connecticut. His voting record is quite liberal on cultural issues, more conservative on defense and economic issues; he pushed for housing and child care for military personnel, military energy conservation and funds for a Blackstone Valley Heritage Corridor around Central Falls and Woonsocket. He got some good press when he attacked NASA's Search for Extraterrestrial Intelligence program. On environmental issues, he made a liberal enough record to get the endorsement of the League of Conservation Voters. In 1990, he had serious opposition from Wolf, who called for bigger defense cuts and opposing "established interests" like oil companies, the AMA and insurance companies. But Machtley responded that Wolf's proposed defense cut would cost the state 13,000 jobs and won with 55% in a Democratic year. In 1992, he was easily reelected against weak opposition. He has been mentioned as a candidate for senator or governor, but has made no serious moves yet to run.

The People: Pop. 1990: 501,696; 9% rural; 16% age 65+; 91% White; 3% Black; 1% Asian; 2% Other; 4% Hispanic origin. Voting age pop.: 393,122; 3% Black; 3% Hispanic origin. Households: 55% married couple families; 24% married couple fams. w. children; 42% college educ.; median household income: $31,675; per capita income: $15,224; median gross rent: $482; median house value: $136,400.

1992 Presidential Vote			1988 Presidential Vote		
Clinton (D)	107,141	(48%)	Dukakis (D)	115,562	(57%)
Bush (R)	62,758	(28%)	Bush (R)	85,619	(43%)
Perot (I)	50,842	(23%)			

Rep. Ronald K. Machtley (R)

Elected 1988; b. July 13, 1948, Johnstown, PA; home, Portsmouth; U.S. Naval Acad., Annapolis, B.S. 1970, Suffolk U. J.D., 1978; Protestant; married (Kati).

Career: Navy, 1970–75, Naval Reserves, 1975–present; Practicing atty. 1978–88.

Offices: 326 CHOB 20515, 202-225-4911. Also 200 Main St., #200, Pawtucket 02860, 401-725-9400; 127 Social St., #172, Woonsocket 02895, 401-762-4052; and 320 Thames St., Newport 02840, 401-848-7920.

Committees: *Armed Services* (12th of 22 R): Military Acquisition; Military Installations and Facilities. *Government Operations* (10th of 17 R): Employment, Housing and Aviation (RMM). *Small Business* (5th of 18 R): Minority Enterprise, Finance and Urban Development (RMM).

Group Ratings

	ADA	ACLU	COPE	CDF	CFA	LCV	ACU	NTLC	NSI	COC	CEI
1992	55	68	50	60	80	88	44	60	100	38	53
1991	45	—	58	80	39	77	47	—	—	50	44

National Journal Ratings

	1991 LIB — 1991 CONS			1992 LIB — 1992 CONS		
Economic	39%	—	60%	34%	—	66%
Social	50%	—	48%	67%	—	32%
Foreign	39%	—	60%	18%	—	74%

Key Votes of the 102d Congress

1. Ban Striker Replace	AGN	5. Handgun Wait/7-Day	FOR	9. Use Force in Gulf	FOR
2. $ for Homeownership	FOR	6. Overseas Mil. Abortion	FOR	10. US Mil. Abroad $ Cut	AGN
3. Tax Rich/Cut Mid Cls.	AGN	7. Obscn. Art NEA $ Ban	AGN	11. Limit SDI Funds	AGN
4. FY93/$15B Def. Cut	AGN	8. Death Pen. from Jury	FOR	12. Cuba Trade Embargo	FOR

1138   RHODE ISLAND

Key Votes of the 103d Congress

1. Family Leave   FOR   2. Deficit Reduction   AGN   3. Stimulus Plan   AGN

Election Results

1992 general	Ronald K. Machtley (R)	135,982	(70%)	($564,588)
	David R. Carlin, Jr. (D)	48,092	(25%)	($90,459)
	Two Others	9,801	(5%)	
1992 primary	Ronald K. Machtley (R), unopposed			
1990 general	Ronald K. Machtley (R)	89,963	(55%)	($879,464)
	Scott Wolf (D)	73,131	(45%)	($370,118)

SECOND DISTRICT

The 2d Congressional District is the western half of Rhode Island. While the 1st includes many mill towns, the 2d has most of its population in working and middle-class towns like Cranston and Warwick which, despite their Anglo-Saxon names, are inhabited mostly by people with Irish, Italian, French and Portuguese surnames. The 2d also has the affluent suburbs to the south along Narragansett Bay and the area around Westerly, where many residents work at the Electric Boat shipyards in Groton, Connecticut. For 10 years, the 2d was represented by Republican Claudine Schneider, whose environmentalism, almost frenetic hard work, and cheerful personality made her popular statewide.

The current congressman from the 2d is Jack Reed, a Democrat who won the seat in 1990 against some expectations when Schneider ran against Senator Claiborne Pell and lost. Reed is from working-class Cranston, a graduate of West Point who served in the 82d Airborne and then went to Harvard Law School. He served in the state Senate for six years, where he was close to the party leadership while building a good reputation. In the 1990 primary, he beat several better known Democrats, with the help of the state party endorsement and $350,000, much of which he held back for a TV barrage in the last three weeks; he won 49%–27% over Edward Beard, the incumbent Schneider beat in 1980. In the general, he faced Republican Trudy Coxe, executive director of Save the Bay. Reed talked in idealistic terms of the laws he pushed helping children, and of the volunteer work he did for the homeless, and played up his military background, though he seemed to favor substantial defense cuts. He was also helped by the revelation that Coxe's husband, who was unpopular Governor Edward DiPrete's 1988 campaign director, had used a state computer to work on Coxe's campaign. Reed won with 59%.

Reed has seats on four committees, Education and Labor, Judiciary, Merchant Marine and Intelligence. He has pushed bills to exclude home equity from calculations for eligibility for financial aid. A major achievement for 1991 was Reed's successful effort to get the House to agree to a $180 million loan guarantee package for Rhode Island. Reed actively lobbied his Democratic colleagues on the issue and even got Banking Chairman Henry Gonzalez and other members of the committee to hold a hearing in Providence. Reed also pushed a bill to extend the two-year limit for realizing capital gains on home sales for those who lost access to their money because of Rhode Island's banking crisis. He has fought defense cuts in Rhode Island, especially at the Electric Boat shipyard, but also supports defense conversion. Reed was predictably reelected by a wide margin in 1992.

The People: Pop. 1990: 501,768; 19% rural; 14% age 65+; 88% White; 4% Black; 1% Amer. Indian; 2% Asian; 3% Other; 5% Hispanic origin. Voting age pop.: 384,337; 4% Black; 4% Hispanic origin. Households: 55% married couple families; 25% married couple fams. w. children; 43% college educ.; median household income: $32,729; per capita income: $14,739; median gross rent: $498; median house value: $129,500.

1992 Presidential Vote

Clinton (D)	106,158	(46%)
Bush (R)	68,843	(30%)
Perot (I)	54,203	(23%)

1988 Presidential Vote

Dukakis (D)	109,561	(54%)
Bush (R)	92,142	(46%)

Rep. Jack Reed (D)

Elected 1990; b. Nov. 12, 1949, Cranston; home, Cranston; U.S. Military Acad., West Point, B.S. 1971, Harvard, M.P.P. 1973, J.D. 1982; Catholic; single.

Career: Army, 1967–79; Assoc. Prof., U.S. Military Acad. Dept. of Soc. Sciences, 1978–79; Practicing atty., 1982–90; RI Senate, 1984–90.

Offices: 1510 LHOB 20515, 202-225-2735. Also Garden City Ctr., 100 Midway Place, #5, Cranston 02920, 401-943-3100.

Committees: *Education and Labor* (14th of 28 D): Elementary, Secondary and Vocational Education; Postsecondary Education and Training. *Intelligence (Permanent Select)* (12th of 12 D): Oversight and Evaluation. *Judiciary* (16th of 21 D): Intellectual Property and Judicial Administration. *Merchant Marine and Fisheries* (14th of 29 D): Environment and Natural Resources; Merchant Marine.

Group Ratings

	ADA	ACLU	COPE	CDF	CFA	LCV	ACU	NTLC	NSI	COC	CEI
1992	90	83	92	90	100	94	4	0	20	13	15
1991	95	—	92	90	78	92	0	—	—	20	17

National Journal Ratings

	1991 LIB — 1991 CONS		1992 LIB — 1992 CONS	
Economic	72% —	23%	78% —	18%
Social	74% —	23%	78% —	21%
Foreign	87% —	8%	76% —	19%

Key Votes of the 102d Congress

1. Ban Striker Replace	FOR	5. Handgun Wait/7-Day	FOR	9. Use Force in Gulf	AGN
2. $ for Homeownership	AGN	6. Overseas Mil. Abortion	FOR	10. US Mil. Abroad $ Cut	FOR
3. Tax Rich/Cut Mid Cls.	FOR	7. Obscn. Art NEA $ Ban	AGN	11. Limit SDI Funds	FOR
4. FY93/$15B Def. Cut	AGN	8. Death Pen. from Jury	AGN	12. Cuba Trade Embargo	AGN

Key Votes of the 103d Congress

1. Family Leave	FOR	2. Deficit Reduction	FOR	3. Stimulus Plan	FOR

Election Results

1992 general	Jack Reed (D)	144,450	(71%)	($815,622)
	James W. Bell (R)	49,998	(24%)	($39,260)
	Two Others	9,965	(5%)	
1992 primary	Jack Reed (D)	50,518	(76%)	
	Spencer Dickinson (D)	15,592	(24%)	
1990 general	Jack Reed (D)	108,818	(59%)	($897,224)
	Gertrude M. (Trudy) Coxe (R)	74,953	(41%)	($571,643)

SOUTH CAROLINA

South Carolina stands as one of America's great success stories. Two generations ago, it looked like an underdeveloped country: beneath a thin veneer of rich people, this was among the poorest of states in the union, with income levels less than half the national average and with high levels of illiteracy and disease. Even today South Carolina, founded by planters from Barbados, can still suggest the West Indies. Physically, its semitropical climate, lush foliage and trademark palmettos, and the $4 billion of destruction wreaked by Hurricane Hugo's 135 mile-per-hour winds in September 1989 are reminiscent of the Caribbean. But economically and culturally, South Carolina is part of the booming South Atlantic seaboard and Piedmont, from Baltimore and Washington south into Florida, filling up with new retirement condominiums, factories and office buildings, giant airports and shopping centers, and leading the nation's economic growth.

In South Carolina, this growth lies atop the plantation economy built on the swampy lowlands below the Fall Line, where the great 18th and 19th Century planters built rice paddies and cultivated exotic crops like indigo in the days before cotton was king. The great wealth of these low-country planters was destroyed by the Civil War which they, more than any other southerners, provoked. But their pride and way of life continued as did that of former slaves. As late as 1940, 43% of South Carolinians were black, most living in conditions that would be incomprehensible today. New economic growth started here in the 1920s, with that lowest-wage of industries, textiles. Mills were built in the up country above Columbia, hiring poor whites (never blacks) from the hardscrabble farms in the area. Politics here was a rough business, with harsh appeals to racial fear and economic envy, and with limited participation: in 1940, just 99,000 South Carolinians voted for president, 96% of them Democratic—the highest Democratic percentage in the nation. In the Democratic primary the year Strom Thurmond ran for governor, 1946, only 271,000 people voted in this state of more than 2 million.

Now this once underdeveloped country has joined the First World. Personal incomes, discounted for a somewhat lower cost of living, are now close to national levels; health standards are similar to those in the rest of the nation; education levels have been rising toward the national average. South Carolina was helped for some years by the military bases clustered around Charleston, by the big textile mills around Greenville and Spartanburg, and by the outmigration of low-country blacks to big cities of the Northeast. Then, starting in the 1970s, South Carolina became the most aggressive state in the South in attracting new industry. It enticed French and German firms to set up major operations in the Piedmont and the lowlands. It advertised its business climate (one of the lowest rates of unionization), its taxes (low), and its willingness to meet local employers' needs (very high). But it also used some of its new affluence to upgrade the quality of its local work force through public expenditures on schools as well as highways, teachers as well as police. Capping its success symbolically was German car manufacturer BMW's decision in June 1992 to build its U.S. assembly plant off I-85 in Spartanburg County, a decision prompted in part by $130 million in incentives from Governor Carroll Campbell. But even more typical are the decisions of hundreds of small employers to open plants, rent offices and create jobs in what has become one of America's more vibrant economic environments.

Much of this was possible because South Carolina was relieved, quite against the will of its white majority, of the burdens and stigma of racial segregation. Beginning in the 1950s, fewer people were kept from the polls by the poll tax, and turnout surged as South Carolina became competitive in the presidential elections of 1952, 1956 and 1960. Then the Civil Rights Act of 1964 and the Voting Rights Act of 1965 ended segregation of public accommodations and the workplace, bringing blacks suddenly into the electorate.

Politically, this new South Carolina has been moving, more than any other state in the South,

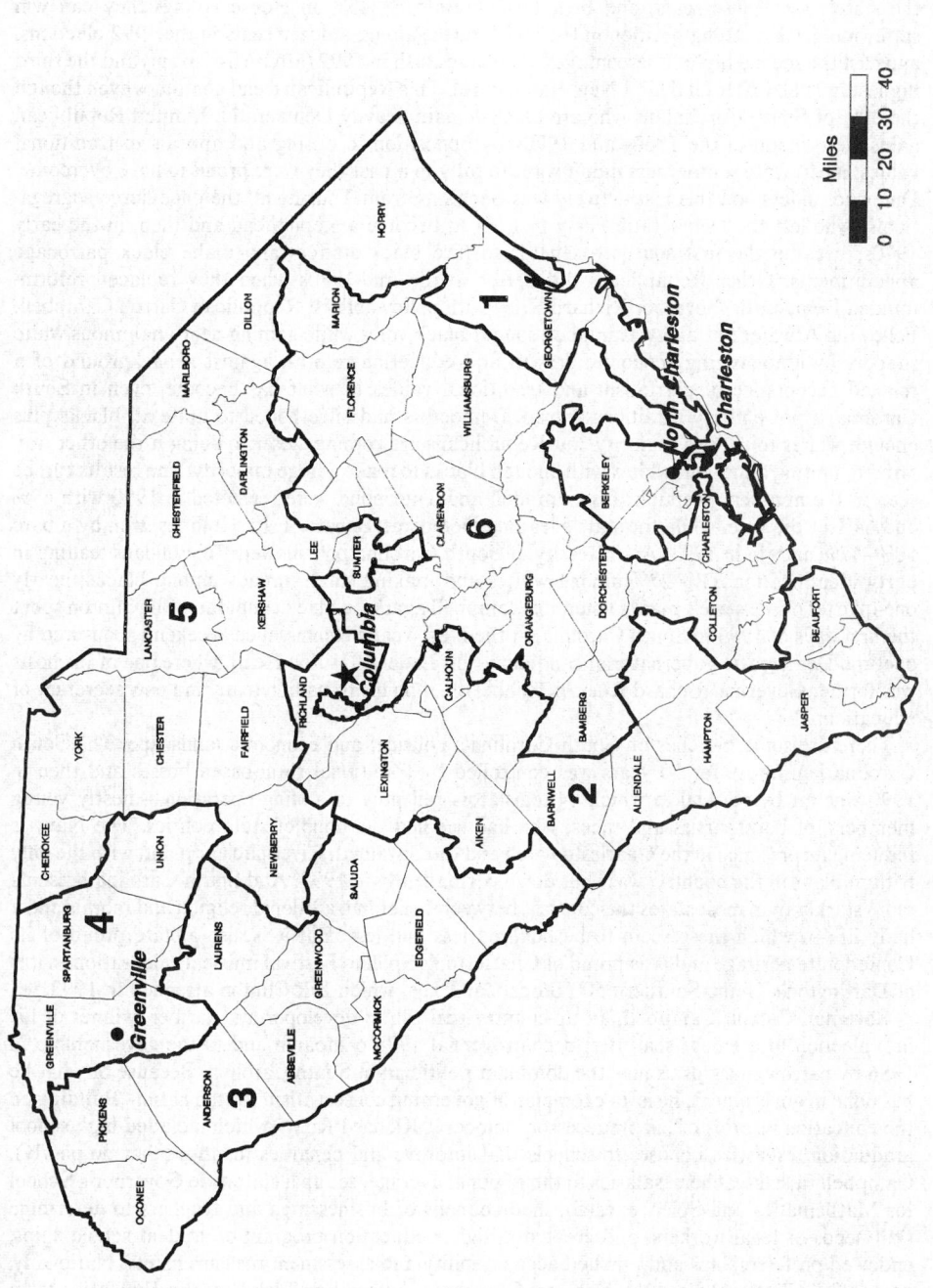

toward the Republicanism exemplified by its native son, the late Republican National Committee chairman and 1988 Bush campaign manager Lee Atwater. Republicans hold the governorship and one Senate seat and came close to winning the other in 1992; they hold three of the state's six House seats, and beat Democrats 52%–45% in House voting; they can win statewide, have a strong position in the legislature, gaining a dozen seats in the 1992 elections, and cast the second highest percentage for George Bush in 1992 (after Mississippi) and the third highest in 1988 (after Utah and New Hampshire). This Republican trend continues even though the 30% of South Carolinians who are black remain heavily Democratic. Limited Republican gains were made in the 1960s and 1970s by opposition to busing and appeals to traditional values; most white southerners didn't want to rally to a past they were proud to have overcome. One who understood this instinctively was Senator Strom Thurmond, the once fierce segregationist who left the Democratic Party in 1964 to become a Republican and then, in the early 1970s, became the first southern senator to hire black staffers and make black patronage appointments. Other Republicans did better in the mid-1980s when they replaced reform-minded Democratic Governor Richard Riley with policy-activist Republican Carroll Campbell. Following Atwater's strategy, Campbell sought black votes while gaining near-unanimous white support by emphasizing economic growth and education reform, against a background of a relaxed acceptance of patriotism and traditional values in what has become, even in South Carolina, a not entirely traditional world. Democrats had once hoped to unite all blacks plus enough whites to make a majority, but Republicans are coming closer to doing it the other way around, uniting almost all whites with enough blacks to make a huge majority. The results can be seen in the numbers: Republicans Campbell and Thurmond were reelected in 1990 with 69% and 64% of the vote, while the state's leading Democrat, Senator Fritz Hollings, won by a bare 50%–47% margin in 1992. A University of South Carolina poll showed Republicans leading in party identification 63%–27% among whites and making small inroads among blacks; nearly one-quarter of the state's blacks voted for Campbell against a black candidate. Bill Clinton spent the first days of 1993 in South Carolina, at the New Year's Renaissance Weekend sponsored by onetime Democratic gubernatorial candidate Phil Lader at Hilton Head, where one of his hosts was former Governor Richard Riley, personnel chief on his transition team and now secretary of education.

There are some blotches on South Carolina's political and economic landscape. The South Carolina legislature for 50 years was controlled by traditional rural-based bosses and then in 1990 was hit by scandal in which 14 legislators fell prey to a sting operation—mostly young members, of both parties and races, who had seemed the hope of state politics. The Navy is reducing its presence in the Charleston area and the Savannah River nuclear plant, with the only tritium plant in the country, was shut down permanently in 1993. And South Carolina presents more starkly than most states the contrast between belief in traditional religion and morals and a daily life in which these seem to be honored less and less. But it is also a state proud of its Confederate heritage and is as proud of Charleston's Spoleto Festival musical celebration as it is of Darlington's Heinz Southern 500 Stock Car Race, which Bill Clinton attended in 1992.

Governor. Carroll Campbell, an up-country real estate developer and farmer, winner of his first election to a House seat after a controversial 1978 campaign and to the governorship in 1986 by narrow margins, is now the dominant politician in South Carolina. Because of what he has done in government, he is an exemplar of governing conservatism for the nation. Building on the education reforms of his predecessor Democrat Richard Riley (which included high school graduation tests with bonuses to schools that improve and penalties for those that do poorly), Campbell raised teachers' salaries to the regional average, set up a statewide Governor's School for Mathematics and Science, established councils of businessmen and teachers to determine skill needs of local workers, and created a higher education program of student scholarships, endowed professorships and pursued accountability and assessment measurements. Nationally, he and Bill Clinton chaired the National Governor's Association Task Force on Education from 1989–90 that set national goals for achievement. (In 1991, Clinton told *The Wall Street Journal* that Campbell was the conservative he admired most.) On the environment, Campbell worked to get a compromise between competing interests regarding South Carolina's many wetlands and blocked shipments of out-of-state waste until neighboring states adopted their own treatment plans. He is proud of programs to reduce infant mortality. With all that, he cut income taxes and, when a tax rise seemed necessary in 1992, cut the state budget 4% across the board instead.

Politically, Campbell was an ally of Lee Atwater's and provided key help for George Bush in 1988 when he moved the South Carolina primary to the Saturday before Super Tuesday and gave Bush strong backing in his 49%–21% victory over Bob Dole. At home, Campbell was winning 70% job ratings from blacks as well as whites. In 1990, his opponent was black state Senator Theo Mitchell, who called black leaders supporting Campbell "house niggers," "Uncle Toms," and "black prostitutes who have sold out their race, their dignity, their honor and their integrity"; Campbell still won some 25% of the black vote. Campbell has not yet succeeded in his plan to reorganize government and centralize power in the governor's office, but he did cut spending sharply and attain his major goal of attracting the BMW plant to the state after a three-year effort.

Campbell's ambitions are not limited to state politics. On education reform, he took a national role and as head of the Republican Governors Association won midterm victories by backing Fife Symington in the 1991 Arizona special election and persuading Buddy Roemer of Louisiana to switch parties in 1991. He so far has shown no interest in running against Senators Thurmond or Hollings, though it is possible he may run for one of their seats when they come up in 1996 and 1998. He is surely interested in who succeeds him (he is barred from seeking a third term), and neither of the two immediately obvious contenders, Democratic Lieutenant Governor Nick Theodore and Republican Congressman Arthur Ravenel, seems exactly in his mold. Whatever the outcome of the 1994 governor's race, no one in South Carolina would be surprised to see Campbell run for president in 1996. As of August 1993, he becomes head of the National Governors Association, a national platform Bill Clinton used well; as for Clinton, Campbell told George Will in early 1993, "If he becomes a Democrat, he's in trouble," referring to tax and spend liberal Democrats.

Senators. The most enduring figure in today's American politics is Strom Thurmond: first elected to the legislature in 1932 and governor in 1946, he ran for president as a "States' Rights Democrat" and won 39 electoral votes in 1948; he was elected senator as a write-in candidate in 1954, resigned and ran for the seat again in 1956; he has served as both a Democrat and a Republican, and was elected in 1990 to a seventh term which, if he serves it out, will make him the oldest person ever to serve in Congress. He switched to the Republican Party to support Barry Goldwater in 1964, a move that seemed unwise at the time but proved sentient about the direction of opinion; in 1968, Thurmond provided key backing to hold the South for Richard Nixon at the Republican National Convention. Thurmond has combined a reputation for steadfastness with a flexibility and adroitness that have enabled this onetime symbol of racial segregation to prosper politically in an era of integration. In 1957, he set a record, filibustering for over 24 hours against a fair housing bill. But when South Carolina blacks started voting in large numbers after the Voting Rights Act of 1965, Thurmond shifted gears and became the first Southern senator to hire black staffers and appoint blacks to high positions (including a federal judgeship). He voted for renewal of the Voting Rights Act and the Martin Luther King Holiday. He probably gets few black votes, but the few that are adamantly against him don't form a strong political base for a possible opponent.

Thurmond's party switch was an example of his mind at work; there are no baroque embellishments to his thoughts and he is not interested in nuance or qualification. His intellect is simple but strong: he decides where he wants to go, figures out how to get there, and then does it. His health seems fine. He has been a proud teetotaler and physical fitness buff all his life, and always an appreciator of beautiful women. His first wife was 23 years younger than he; after she died, he married a South Carolina beauty queen 44 years younger; the first of his four children was born when he was 69; he is now seeing them through college. In hearings and on the Senate floor, Thurmond usually seems heavily scripted, but he responds aptly to arguments and interjections and is always polite and courtly.

Thurmond, the senior member of the Senate, was president pro tempore when Republicans were in the majority, and thus in line of succession to the presidency; he may be again. For a dozen years, he chaired or was ranking minority member on Judiciary, which put him at the center of the hot fights over Supreme Court nominees Robert Bork, David Souter and Clarence Thomas. He has sponsored many bills to extend the death penalty and reduce federal courts' jurisdiction over collateral attacks on state criminal convictions. He has supported gun control measures endorsed by police, such as bans on cop-killer bullets and plastic guns. He is a stickler for ethics, supporting outside income limits for senators, bans on lobbying for federal projects on a contingent fee basis and lobbying for foreign countries by former federal officials.

In 1993, Thurmond exercised his option to switch to the ranking position on Armed Services, replacing John Warner there and elevating Orrin Hatch on Judiciary. Thurmond landed in Normandy on D-Day and had served on Armed Services for 34 years. He clearly wants to hold down cuts in military spending and opposes lifting the ban on gays in the military; he wants to look after South Carolina's military bases. He is also a member of Veterans' Affairs and Labor and Human Resources. He backs the use of fetal tissue in research; one of his daughters has diabetes, research on which requires such material.

Thurmond's almost non-stop politicking in South Carolina has helped keep his popularity exceedingly high. His last tough challenge was from businessman Charles Ravenel in 1978, when he got 56%; he won with 67% and 64% in 1984 and 1990. He says that if he stays healthy he will run again in 1996, for a term that would take him to 2002, when he turns 100. He continues to raise campaign money, although he has also donated $733,000 to scholarships and endowed chairs in South Carolina. His longevity is breathtaking: this is a man whose children will likely live into the 2050s; a senator ready to become the oldest member of Congress ever in February 1996.

Taking the oath of office for his sixth term in January 1993 was Ernest (Fritz) Hollings, still South Carolina's junior senator after 26 years of service at age 71. But Hollings has always done things at unusual ages. He was first elected to the legislature in 1948, at 26, was a member of the leadership two years later, was elected governor in 1958 at 36, serving as South Carolina first faced school desegregation, and then spent four years out of office until he beat another former governor in the 1966 Senate race. Hollings may look like an aristocrat, but he is from a middle-class family, got his education at Charleston's The Citadel and made his living as a trial lawyer; he has one of the quickest and sharpest tongues in the Senate. He is "the Senate bully," wrote his former colleague the late John Tower, and his instinct for zeroing in on others' weaknesses can be directed at the strong as well as the weak. Hollings has had his disappointments. His campaign for president fell flat in 1984, and after he was the only South Carolinian to vote against the Gulf war, he suddenly found himself supported by far less than half his state's voters after enjoying years of top-level visibility.

Hollings has also been disappointed in his work on the budget. He became chairman of the Senate Budget Committee in May 1980 when Edmund Muskie became secretary of state; then he was ranking minority member in 1981 and 1982, when the groundwork for the huge deficits of the 1980s was laid by the Reagan budget and tax cuts. His response was to suggest a budget freeze, a proposal which others quickly thawed with loopholes until there was little freeze left. In 1985, he joined forces with Phil Gramm of Texas and Warren Rudman of New Hampshire to co-sponsor the Gramm-Rudman-Hollings deficit-cutting bill, which had some effect but didn't prove to be the autopilot some hoped: the S&L bailout and the Gulf war, inconveniently expensive, could not have been included in its calculations of the deficit. In 1993, he advocated replacing the proposed energy tax and the tax increase on social security benefits favored by Clinton with a value-added tax; the VAT revenue would go to reduce the deficit. This is typical Hollings: he believes in an activist federal government, but one subject to strict discipline; his frustration is that the dominant political forces for a dozen years believed in neither.

As chairman of the Commerce, Science and Transportation Committee, Hollings is an activist and a regulator, the major opponent of deregulating broadcasting and a major proponent of the cable reregulation bill; he wants to stop the FCC from reassigning low-frequency users to high frequencies, but he would allow the Baby Bells to manufacture phone equipment and to enter joint ventures, though not with each other. He has worked on various ocean issues on the committee, including the 1988 ocean dumping law, and has championed a National Global Climate Change Research Act. He is pushing constitutional amendments for a line-item veto and to limit campaign spending. On trade issues, he proudly proclaims himself a "hawk," shepherding the textile trade bill to passage in 1990, but President Bush's veto was sustained. In early 1991, he led opposition to fast-tracking the U.S.-Mexico Free Trade Agreement. His response to Japanese criticism of American workers was to tell workers in Hartsville they "should draw a mushroom cloud and put underneath it: 'Made in America by lazy and illiterate Americans and tested in Japan.'"

Hollings's vote against the Gulf war resolution was a break from his usual hawkish record on foreign and military issues (though he did lead opposition to the MX missile in the early 1980s); he seemed guided by his disgust with the rulers of Kuwait. Fully 70% of voters disagreed with Hollings, who led former GOP Congressman (and 1986 loser for lieutenant governor) Tommy Hartnett by only 39%–30% at the time. But, as a former congressman himself, Hartnett had a hard time sounding the anti-incumbent theme. Hollings raised more money, argued he was the true "outsider," and ran an ad showing himself being praised at a White House ceremony by President Reagan. Hartnett called for term limits and the line-item veto, charged Hollings with supporting hiring quotas for gays, and hit Hollings for inspecting his own beachfront property while on a helicopter surveying wreckage from Hurricane Hugo. Hollings won by the unimpressive margin of 50%–47%, while the Democrats from the two adjoining states who also voted against the Gulf war resolution, Terry Sanford and Wyche Fowler, were defeated. This was Hollings's closest margin by far since 1966 and suggests that he may not run for reelection in 1998. Meanwhile, in a Democratic Senate, with his committee positions and strong views, he remains a major force.

Presidential politics. South Carolina is one of the top three Republican states, with Utah and Idaho, to judge from the 1992 and 1988 presidential vote—a tribute to the late Lee Atwater. This is also evidence of the expanding South Carolina private sector economy, the strength of its traditional cultural values and the fact that so much of its growth has been in Hilton Head-style condominium communities on the coast and suburban areas well away from the cities.

It is also interesting that South Carolina's Republican primary has become more important than its Democratic contest. Atwater purposefully scheduled the Republican primary here on the Saturday before Super Tuesday, and in 1988 George Bush won a smashing victory over Bob Dole and Pat Robertson, forecasting the southern sweep that clinched his nomination. In 1992, Bush won with two-thirds of the vote, squashing Pat Buchanan's claims to represent the South and reducing David Duke to the single-digit crank candidate he had been before winning a Louisiana legislative seat by a few dozen votes. The Democrats, in contrast, scheduled their 1988 caucus after Super Tuesday, to deflect attention; it was won by Jesse Jackson, who was born in South Carolina, and was briefly registered to vote there after his 1984 campaign. In 1992, they switched timing to vote the same day as the Republicans, with a huge victory for Bill Clinton over the several Yankees in the race.

Congressional districting. The Voting Rights Act amendments of 1982 were interpreted to require creation of a black-majority district in South Carolina, and the plan adopted in May 1992 stitches together black majority areas in the lowlands (but not the condominium-glutted coast) and in Columbia and Charleston to create the new 6th District. Incumbent Democrat Robin Tallon, who had long won black votes, announced he was running, but withdrew on filing day in June. By taking away blacks, the new plan made the 1st and 2d Districts safer for Republicans, and the largely unchanged 4th District surprisingly went Republican too.

1146   SOUTH CAROLINA

The People: Est. Pop. 1992: 3,603,000; Pop. 1990: 3,486,703, up 3.2% 1990–1992. 1.4% of U.S. total, 25th largest; 45% rural. Median age: 32.0 years. 11.4% 65 years and over. 69.0% White, 29.8% Black. Households: 56.4% married couple families; 27% married couple fams. w. children; 39% college educ.; median household income: $26,256; per capita income: $11,897; 69.8% owner occupied housing; median house value: $61,100; median monthly rent: $276. 6.2% Unemployment. Voting age pop.: 2,566,496. Registered voters (1992): 1,537,140; no party registration.

Political Lineup: Governor, Carroll A. Campbell, Jr. (R); Lt. Gov., Nick A. Theodore (D); Secy. of State, Jim Miles (R); Atty. Gen., T. Travis Medlock (D); Treasurer, Grady L. Patterson, Jr. (D); Comptroller General, Earle E. Morris, Jr. (D). State Senate, 46 (30 D and 16 R); State House of Representatives, 124 (73 D, 50 R, and 1 I). Senators, Strom Thurmond (R) and Ernest F. (Fritz) Hollings (D). Representatives, 6 (3 D and 3 R).

1992 Presidential Vote

Bush (R)	577,508	(48%)
Clinton (D)	479,514	(40%)
Perot (I)	138,782	(12%)

1992 Democratic Presidential Primary

Clinton	73,221	(63%)
Tsongas	21,338	(18%)
Harkin	7,657	(7%)
Brown	6,961	(6%)
Other	7,237	(6%)

1988 Presidential Vote

Bush (R)	606,443	(62%)
Dukakis (D)	370,554	(38%)

1992 Republican Presidential Primary

Bush	99,558	(67%)
Buchanan	38,247	(26%)
Duke	10,553	(7%)

GOVERNOR

Gov. Carroll A. Campbell, Jr. (R)

Elected 1986, term expires Jan. 1995; b. July 24, 1940, Greenville; home, Greenville; American U., M.A. 1985; Episcopalian; married (Iris).

Career: Real estate developer; farmer; SC House of Reps., 1970–74; Exec. Asst., SC Gov. James B. Edwards, 1975–76; SC Senate, 1976–78; U.S. House of Reps., 1978–86.

Office: P.O. Box 11369, The State House, Columbia 29211, 803-734-9818.

Election Results

1990 gen.	Carroll A. Campbell, Jr. (R)	528,831	(69%)
	Theo Mitchell (D)	212,034	(27%)
	Others	20,100	(3%)
1990 prim.	Carroll A. Campbell, Jr. (R), unopposed		
1986 gen.	Carroll A. Campbell, Jr. (R)	384,565	(51%)
	Mike Daniel (D)	361,325	(49%)

SENATORS
Sen. Strom Thurmond (R)

Elected 1956, seat up 1996; b. Dec. 5, 1902, Edgefield; home, Aiken; Clemson U., B.S. 1923; Baptist; separated.

Career: Army, 1942–46 (WWII); Teacher and coach, 1923–29; Edgefield Cnty. Supervisor of Educ., 1929–33; Practicing atty., 1930–38, 1951–55; SC Senate, 1933–38; Circuit Judge, 1938–42; SC Gov., 1947–51; States' Rights candidate for U.S. Pres., 1948; U.S. Senate, 1954–56; Pres. Pro Tem, U.S. Senate, 1981–87.

Offices: 217 RSOB 20510, 202-224-5972. Also 1835 Assembly St., #1558, Columbia 29201, 803-765-5496; 334 Meeting St., #600, Charleston 29493, 803-724-4282; 211 York St. NE, #29, Aiken 29801, 803-649-2591; and 401 W. Evans St., Florence 29501, 803-662-8873.

Committees: *Armed Services* (RMM of 9 R). *Judiciary* (2d of 8 R): Antitrust, Monopolies and Business Rights (RMM); Courts and Administrative Practice. *Labor and Human Resources* (5th of 7 R): Children, Family, Drugs and Alcoholism; Education, Arts and Humanities; Employment and Productivity (RMM); Labor. *Veterans' Affairs* (2d of 5 R).

Group Ratings

	ADA	ACLU	CDF	COPE	CFA	LCV	ACU	NTLC	NSI	COC	CEI
1992	10	9	40	25	33	0	89	83	90	100	73
1991	10	—	36	25	22	7	90	—	—	70	66

National Journal Ratings

	1991 LIB — 1991 CONS	1992 LIB — 1992 CONS
Economic	20% — 78%	15% — 80%
Social	14% — 77%	17% — 80%
Foreign	0% — 87%	21% — 72%

Key Votes of the 102d Congress

1. $ for Homeownership FOR	5. Clarence Thomas Nom. FOR	9. Use Force in Gulf FOR
2. Have Cap Gains Debate FOR	6. Lmt Death Row Appeal FOR	10. Keep Salvador Aid FOR
3. Remove Budget Walls AGN	7. Handgun Wait/5-Day FOR	11. Cut $1B from SDI AGN
4. Ban Striker Replace AGN	8. Abortion Gag Rule FOR	12. Override China MFN FOR

Key Votes of the 103d Congress

1. Family Leave ∗	2. HIV Immigrants AGN	3. Clinton Budget AGN

Election Results

1990 general	Strom Thurmond (R)	482,032	(64%)	($2,333,689)
	Robert H. Cunningham (D)	244,112	(33%)	($6,232)
	Two Others	24,122	(3%)	
1990 primary	Strom Thurmond (R), unopposed			
1984 general	Strom Thurmond (R)	644,815	(67%)	($1,682,962)
	Melvin Purvis (D)....................	306,982	(32%)	($9,023)

Sen. Ernest F. (Fritz) Hollings (D)

Elected 1966, seat up 1998; b. Jan. 1, 1922, Charleston; home, Charleston; The Citadel, B.A. 1942, U. of SC, LL.B. 1947; Lutheran; married (Peatsy).

Career: Army, 1942–45 (WWII); Practicing atty., 1947–55, 1963–66; SC House of Reps., 1948–54, Speaker Pro Tem, 1951–54; SC Lt. Gov., 1954–58; SC Gov., 1958–62.

Offices: 125 RSOB 20510, 202-224-6121. Also 1835 Assembly St., Columbia 29201, 803-765-5731; 112 Custom House, 200 E. Bay St., Charleston 29401, 803-727-4525; and 126 Fed. Bldg., Greenville 29304, 803-233-5366; 103 Fed. Bldg., Spartanburg 29301, 803-585-3702.

Committees: *Appropriations* (3d of 16 D): Commerce, Justice, State and Judiciary (Chmn.); Defense; Energy and Water Development; Interior; Labor, Health and Human Services, Education. *Budget* (2d of 12 D). *Commerce, Science and Transportation* (Chmn. of 11 D): Communications; Foreign Commerce and Tourism; Science, Technology and Space.

Group Ratings

	ADA	ACLU	CDF	COPE	CFA	LCV	ACU	NTLC	NSI	COC	CEI
1992	35	41	70	50	58	42	63	39	60	60	38
1991	55	—	73	75	67	67	62	—	—	40	34

National Journal Ratings

	1991 LIB — 1991 CONS	1992 LIB — 1992 CONS
Economic	57% — 40%	43% — 55%
Social	42% — 56%	37% — 62%
Foreign	49% — 46%	47% — 51%

Key Votes of the 102d Congress

1. $ for Homeownership	AGN	5. Clarence Thomas Nom. FOR	9. Use Force in Gulf	AGN
2. Have Cap Gains Debate	AGN	6. Lmt Death Row Appeal FOR	10. Keep Salvador Aid	AGN
3. Remove Budget Walls	AGN	7. Handgun Wait/5-Day	AGN	11. Cut $1B from SDI	AGN
4. Ban Striker Replace	AGN	8. Abortion Gag Rule	AGN	12. Override China MFN FOR

Key Votes of the 103d Congress

1. Family Leave   AGN   2. HIV Immigrants   AGN   3. Clinton Budget   FOR

Election Results

1992 general	Ernest F. (Fritz) Hollings (D)	591,030	(50%)	($4,188,829)
	Tommy Hartnett (R)	554,175	(47%)	($886,816)
	Other	35,233	(3%)	
1992 primary	Ernest F. (Fritz) Hollings (D), unopposed			
1986 general	Ernest F. (Fritz) Hollings (D)	456,500	(63%)	($2,233,843)
	Henry D. McMaster (R)	262,886	(36%)	($584,288)

FIRST DISTRICT

Looking out across the harbor to Fort Sumter are the glorious mansions of the Battery, gazing on the same view that the hot-blooded young swells of Charleston saw in 1861 when they fired the shots that began the Civil War. Today there are few more beautiful urban scenes in America than the pastel "single houses" of Charleston, built flush with the sidewalk, turning their shoulders to the streets, with open piazzas inside their gateways facing south to catch the breeze, lovingly restored and maintained. Charleston, founded in 1670 and blessed with one of the finest harbors on the Atlantic, was one of the South's two leading cities through the Civil War. Across its docks went cargoes of rice, indigo and cotton—all cultivated by black slaves, enriching the white planters and merchants who dominated the state's economic and political life. In the years following the Civil War, Charleston became an economic backwater, enabling the old buildings to survive; now the prosperity of recent years—metropolitan Charleston grew 18% in the 1980s—has financed its restoration. Charlestonians are proud that after Hurricane Hugo swept ashore at 135 miles an hour, they repaired the damage so rapidly and so faithfully that little of it was noticeable a year later.

This is an old society, descended from Barbados planters and French Huguenots, Sephardic Jews and English gentry second sons, and was once a leading force in American political life. The hotheads in the gallery disrupted the 1860 Democratic National Convention here so boisterously that it was adjourned and reconvened in Baltimore, while southern Democrats split off and nominated their own candidate, enabling Abraham Lincoln to win with 38% of the popular vote. South Carolina's blacks also have a lively history. There were free blacks here before the Civil War (some even owned slaves themselves), and Charleston's black culture was memorialized in George Gershwin's *Porgy and Bess*. The local accent, which seems to outsiders to have a touch of New Jersey and which can be incomprehensible when rapidly spoken, is best appreciated in the speech of Charleston native Ernest Hollings.

Charleston and the lowland country along the coast have been accelerating from the economic somnolence of a few decades ago. The big Navy and Air Force bases where the Ashley and Cooper Rivers meet (as Charleston tradition has it) to form the Atlantic Ocean, provided an initial impetus, 20 years ago comprising one-third of payrolls in the Charleston area. Then came beachfront development, of several kinds. East of Charleston are old beach lowland communities like Pawleys Island, home of hammocks. Farther north, toward North Carolina, is the Grand Strand on either side of Myrtle Beach, one of the South's favorite vacation and second home areas. South of Charleston are higher-income condominium communities, of which Hilton Head, started by Charles Fraser in 1957, was the prototype, built then in one of the poorest areas in the United States. The 1980s saw a boom here beyond the military and the condominiums, and jobs increased nearly 50% in a decade: Charleston and the lowlands have moved into what development experts used to call "takeoff."

The 1st Congressional District of South Carolina, as redesigned in 1992, is the Charleston and lowlands district, drawn to maximize the black population of the next-door 6th but, given the plantation heritage here, is still 20% black. It includes the old houses of the Battery of Charleston and the beachfront and affluent suburbs strung out on high ground in all directions. It proceeds north past Pawleys Island to the Grand Strand; it runs south to Kiawah Island, but stops short of Hilton Head. About two-thirds of the voters are in metropolitan Charleston, which has produced notable Democrats—Hollings, Mayor Joe Riley, Jr., Police Chief Reuben Greenberg, who is both black and Jewish—but votes mostly Republican.

The congressman from the district is a Republican, Arthur Ravenel, an experienced Charleston politician with a fine old South Carolina Huguenot name. He is folksy and has, unusual for a Republican, significant support from black voters. Ravenel has a fairly conservative record, but makes a point of being something of an environmentalist—a plus in an increasingly affluent district many of whose residents came here because of the environment. He worked on Coastal Zones reauthorization; he wants to prohibit drilling in the Arctic National Wildlife Refuge and preserve the ecosystems in the ancient forests of the Pacific Northwest. Locally, he was concerned about acid rain because of damage to the Medway Plantation. He supported the Americans with Disabilities Act and the Family and Medical Leave Act, and backed cable TV reregulation over a Bush veto. He has a vivid approach to drug smugglers: "What we need to do, upon positive identification, which is very important, is begin shooting down the drug-carrying planes and machine-gunning any survivors. I believe that very quickly these tough measures will put an end to drug smuggling." He conceded that "maybe a mistake will be made" and a family flying back from the Bahamas might be shot down, but "you have to weigh that tragedy with the tens of thousand of lives lost to drugs."

Ravenel has also worked on local projects, to get funding for a Charleston bridge replacement and military health care. In 1993, the Defense Department announced that five facilities in this district were targeted for closing. Ravenel, who sits on Armed Services, has promised to fight to save these bases, working in tandem with both Thurmond and Hollings. Ravenel won this district by only 52%–48% in 1986, when it included more Charleston area blacks; he won in 1990 and 1992 with nearly two-thirds of the vote. He announced in early 1993 that he will run for governor in 1994. This maverick's campaign is not likely to win party organization support, but will surely be pungent. Barring a very strong Democratic candidate, the 1st District is likely to remain Republican, and the likely GOP candidates for 1994 are former Pentagon official Van Hipp, state highway commissioner Bob Harrell, and Mendel Rivers, son of a previous congressman from this district.

The People: Pop. 1990: 581,445; 25% rural; 9% age 65+; 77% White; 20% Black; 1% Asian; 1% Hispanic origin. Voting age pop.: 427,621; 18% Black; 1% Hispanic origin. Households: 60% married couple families; 30% married couple fams. w. children; 48% college educ.; median household income: $28,705; per capita income: $13,112; median gross rent: $441; median house value: $75,400.

1992 Presidential Vote			1988 Presidential Vote		
Bush (R)	101,830	(53%)	Bush (R)	102,935	(69%)
Clinton (D)	63,318	(33%)	Dukakis (D)	46,787	(31%)
Perot (I)	26,620	(14%)			

Rep. Arthur Ravenel, Jr. (R)

Elected 1986; b. Mar. 29, 1927, St. Andrews Parish; home, Mt. Pleasant; Col. of Charleston, B.A. 1950; French Huguenot; married (Jean).

Career: Marine Corps, 1945–46; Realtor, gen. contractor; cattleman; SC House of Reps., 1952–58; SC Senate, 1980–86.

Offices: 231 CHOB 20515, 202-225-3176. Also 640 Fed. Bldg., #640, Charleston 29403, 803-724-4175; 263 Hampton St., Walterboro 29488, 803-549-5395; P.O. Box 550, Estill 29918, 803-625-3177; and P.O. Box 1538, Beaufort 29902, 803-524-2166.

Committees: *Armed Services* (9th of 22 R): Military Acquisition; Military Forces and Personnel. *Merchant Marine and Fisheries* (8th of 19 R): Environment and Natural Resources; Fisheries Management.

Group Ratings

	ADA	ACLU	COPE	CDF	CFA	LCV	ACU	NTLC	NSI	COC	CEI
1992	40	26	42	30	47	69	80	100	100	75	55
1991	25	—	58	50	50	100	75	—	—	70	47

National Journal Ratings

	1991 LIB — 1991 CONS			1992 LIB — 1992 CONS	
Economic	34%	—	65%	31%	—	69%
Social	30%	—	68%	42%	—	56%
Foreign	26%	—	70%	30%	—	64%

Key Votes of the 102d Congress

1. Ban Striker Replace	AGN	5. Handgun Wait/7-Day AGN	9. Use Force in Gulf FOR
2. $ for Homeownership	FOR	6. Overseas Mil. AbortionAGN	10. US Mil. Abroad $ CutAGN
3. Tax Rich/Cut Mid Cls.AGN		7. Obscn. Art NEA $ Ban FOR	11. Limit SDI Funds AGN
4. FY93/$15B Def. Cut AGN		8. Death Pen. from Jury FOR	12. Cuba Trade Embargo FOR

Key Votes of the 103d Congress

1. Family Leave FOR	2. Deficit Reduction AGN	3. Stimulus Plan AGN

Election Results

1992 general	Arthur Ravenel, Jr. (R)................	121,938	(66%)	($561,793)
	Bill Oberst, Jr. (D)	59,908	(33%)	($56,902)
	Other................................	2,703	(1%)	
1992 primary	Arthur Ravenel, Jr. (R), unopposed			
1990 general	Arthur Ravenel, Jr. (R)................	80,839	(66%)	($99,261)
	Eugene Platt (D)......................	42,555	(34%)	($14,040)

SECOND DISTRICT

In 1786, just after the Revolutionary War, the South Carolina legislature decided to move the state's capital away from the Charleston aristocracy and into the up-country interior, away from a city named after a king to a new city named after a discoverer of America: so began Columbia. The State House was built on high ground above the Congaree River in a town of one-and-a-half story houses with first floor porticoes, dormers and raised brick basements—"Columbia cottages." The major event in Columbia's later history was the arrival in 1865 of Sherman's Army, which burned everything but the State House. In the post-Sherman years, Columbia grew slowly, with state government and the university, the Army's Fort Jackson and local insurance companies proving steady employers. In the 1970s and 1980s, it started to boom, attracting plants such as Michelin, Allied Chemical, United Technologies, FN of Belgium, Du Pont and Square D. Approaching half a million in metro area population, Columbia is becoming a true city, and not just a village-capital.

The Columbia to which Jimmy Byrnes, after years in top posts in Democratic Washington, returned as governor to lament the *Brown v. Board of Education* decision in 1954, has trended Republican in the years since. Upwardly mobile South Carolinians, transplanted from underdeveloped rural areas to comfortable subdivisions with two-car garages, preferred Republicans first in national and then in state and local elections. The Columbia area went for Eisenhower in the 1950s; and when blacks got the vote in 1965, they were usually outnumbered by increasingly Republican whites—particularly if you count not just Columbia's Richland County, but also the once rural and now mostly suburban Lexington County across the river.

South Carolina's 2d Congressional District includes most of metropolitan Columbia, except for black neighborhoods lopped off to create the new black-majority 6th District. It contains the city's affluent white neighborhoods and the spread-out towns of Richland and Lexington Counties, with their shopping centers and many churches and the Army's huge training center, Fort Jackson. The district extends south through the horse-farm area around Aiken and several lightly-populated black-majority rural counties, and then includes Beaufort and Hilton Head on the coast—the former is an old town, with wonderful mansions and a history intertwined with slave plantations and the Marine Corps's Parris Island training base; the latter has been developed with much meticulous attention to its natural environment, a model now for Atlantic coast condominium and vacation communities. This is a heavily Republican district: blacks provide most of the Democratic votes in these parts, and since this new 2d is only 25% black, Republicans carry almost every election here.

The congressman from the 2d District is Republican Floyd Spence, who has been around almost as long, it seems, as Strom Thurmond. Spence started running for office in the Columbia area in 1956, became a Republican in 1962, two years before Thurmond, narrowly lost a House race that year to Democrat-later-turned-Republican Albert Watson and, when Watson ran for governor in 1970, ran again for the House seat and won. He has been easily reelected ever since, by pluralities that are not always huge but which, because of racial polarization, are secure; after redistricting, the seat is even safer.

Spence can claim a number of distinctions in the House. In 1971, he became the first member to sponsor the balanced budget constitutional amendment. In 1988, he became the first House member to have and survive a double-lung transplant. He served for many years on the House Ethics Committee. In 1993, he became ranking Republican on the House Armed Services Committee—a double coup for South Carolina, as Strom Thurmond took the same spot in the Senate at the same time. Spence has worked on veterans' hospital and healthcare legislation and on local projects like a resolution honoring historically black colleges and expanding the Congaree Swamp National Monument. But his main work now is to limit proposed defense spending cuts—"responsible downsizing of defense expenditures rather than drastic cuts," he says. In the process, he will surely look after huge Fort Jackson just outside Columbia and other local bases that have already been put on the Defense Department's 1993 hit list.

The 2d District is now so heavily Republican that Spence should be able to win reelection with no difficulty at all.

The People: Pop. 1990: 580,624; 40% rural; 10% age 65+; 72% White; 25% Black; 1% Asian; 1% Other; 1% Hispanic origin. Voting age pop.: 430,168; 23% Black; 1% Hispanic origin. Households: 59% married couple families; 28% married couple fams. w. children; 50% college educ.; median household income: $30,500; per capita income: $13,807; median gross rent: $435; median house value: $73,400.

1992 Presidential Vote			1988 Presidential Vote		
Bush (R)	119,658	(52%)	Bush (R)	122,981	(69%)
Clinton (D)	82,652	(36%)	Dukakis (D)	56,205	(31%)
Perot (I)	25,853	(11%)			

Rep. Floyd D. Spence (R)

Elected 1970; b. Apr. 9, 1928, Columbia; home, Lexington; U. of SC, A.B. 1952, LL.B. 1956; Lutheran; married (Deborah).

Career: Navy, 1952–54, Naval Reserves, 1947–52, 1954–85; SC House of Reps., 1956–62; Practicing atty., 1956–69; SC Senate, 1966–70, Minority Ldr., 1966–70.

Offices: 2405 RHOB 20515, 202-225-2452. Also 5000 Thurmond Mall, The Pavilion, #106, Columbia 29201, 803-254-5120; and 1681 Chestnut St., P.O. Box 1609, NE Orangeburg 29115, 803-536-4641.

Committees: *Armed Services* (RMM of 22 R): Military Acquisition (RMM); *Veterans' Affairs* (6th of 14 R): Housing and Memorial Affairs.

Group Ratings

	ADA	ACLU	COPE	CDF	CFA	LCV	ACU	NTLC	NSI	COC	CEI
1992	15	0	42	10	27	6	92	95	100	75	69
1991	10	—	25	20	28	8	95	—	—	80	62

National Journal Ratings

	1991 LIB — 1991 CONS		1992 LIB — 1992 CONS	
Economic	4%	— 90%	28%	— 70%
Social	19%	— 78%	21%	— 78%
Foreign	0%	— 88%	0%	— 82%

Key Votes of the 102d Congress

1. Ban Striker Replace	AGN	5. Handgun Wait/7-Day AGN	9. Use Force in Gulf FOR
2. $ for Homeownership	FOR	6. Overseas Mil. Abortion AGN	10. US Mil. Abroad $ Cut AGN
3. Tax Rich/Cut Mid Cls. AGN		7. Obscn. Art NEA $ Ban FOR	11. Limit SDI Funds AGN
4. FY93/$15B Def. Cut AGN		8. Death Pen. from Jury FOR	12. Cuba Trade Embargo FOR

Key Votes of the 103d Congress

1. Family Leave   AGN   2. Deficit Reduction   AGN   3. Stimulus Plan   AGN

Election Results

1992 general	Floyd D. Spence (R)................	148,667	(88%)	($179,539)
	Gebhard Sommer (LIB)...............	20,816	(12%)	
1992 primary	Floyd D. Spence (R), unopposed			
1990 general	Floyd D. Spence (R)................	90,054	(89%)	($130,173)
	Gebhard Sommer (LIB)...............	11,101	(11%)	

THIRD DISTRICT

The South Carolina up country, many days' travel by wagon from the low-country plantations owned by Charleston aristocrats, was first settled by Scots-Irish farmers, like the family of John C. Calhoun in the years just before and after the Revolutionary War. The pioneers wanted to make big plantations of these forests, but the land did not always cooperate: it was too hilly for the labor-intensive rice crop grown in the lowlands and sometimes too cold for cotton. So while the coastal plantations were tended by thousands of slaves, relatively few were brought here, and the land went mostly to small farms owned by whites. Today the racial and cultural tone of up-country South Carolina shows traces of these roots: this is a mostly white part of the South, with a hell-of-a-fella tone to daily life, an economically growing and culturally tradition-minded slice of Middle America.

The 3d Congressional District of South Carolina covers much of this territory, following the Georgia border from the government's troubled Savannah River Plant all the way north to the North Carolina border. In the southern part of the 3d are a few heavily black communities, like Edgefield, where Strom Thurmond grew up and first won public office in the 1930s. But the major population center here is the increasingly affluent suburban strip linking Aiken and Augusta, Georgia. In the northern part of this district Calhoun had his mansion and his son-in-law created Clemson University nearby. Here today, the Savannah River intersects Interstate 85, the main street of America's textile belt, in what has in recent years been one of the nation's prime economic growth areas. The politics of this area, ancestrally Democratic, has been trending Republican for years. Yankified Aiken started voting Republican for Dwight Eisenhower in the 1950s, well before Thurmond switched parties in 1964; Anderson skittered around, supporting Jimmy Carter for a while but then veering Republican again; the textile mill counties from Clemson to the mountains are heavily Republican. What had been a Jimmy Carter district in 1976 and 1980 became a George Bush district in 1988 and 1992; in 1992 it was even carried by Tommy Hartnett, Republican challenger to Senator Fritz Hollings.

The congressman from the 3d District, however, is Democrat Butler Derrick, who as the second ranking Democrat on the Rules Committee and as one of four chief deputy whips is a member of the House Democratic leadership. Derrick was part of the Democrats' Watergate class, first elected to the House in 1974. The national Democratic strength here early in Derrick's career gave him leeway to fashion a distinctive record, while working in tandem with the Democratic leadership. He did well enough on the Budget Committee in his first four years that he got a seat on the Rules Committee in 1979 (he served again on Budget in 1983–89). Rules's work is mostly technical, uninteresting if not meaningless to most citizens: scheduling legislation on the floor, deciding what amendments can be offered, setting time limits on debate. On such issues, Derrick is, as expected, mostly faithful to the leadership, which uses its procedural powers as leaders have always done to help achieve the substantive outcomes it wants.

At the same time, a seat on Rules gives a politically adept legislator a platform to advance ideas and projects of every kind. Derrick has pursued some procedural issues: he is the House's leading advocate of its position on the pocket veto, a stand it asserted against President Bush but will probably be of little importance in the Clinton years. He worked on campaign finance reform, and was assigned a seat on House Administration in 1993 for that purpose, helping to frame the Democratic leadership bill. He proposes a system of voluntary spending limits and a restriction of PAC contributions. Derrick supports tougher restrictions on prisoners' use of habeas corpus and in 1991 he switched to support the Brady bill waiting period for handgun purchases. In disagreement with the leadership, he supports the balanced budget amendment and the line-item veto.

The 3d District was not much changed by the 1992 redistricting. Despite the anti-incumbent mood, Derrick was reelected in 1992 with his best margin since 1986. He ran weakest in the two ends of the 3d, in Aiken and Pickens County, but boosted his percentage in Anderson to 65%, running well ahead of the Democratic ticket. He promised to work hard on health care reform and to convert the Savannah River facility to commercial energy production.

The People: Pop. 1990: 580,873; 58% rural; 13% age 65+; 78% White; 21% Black. Voting age pop.: 434,796; 19% Black. Households: 60% married couple families; 27% married couple fams. w. children; 34% college educ.; median household income: $25,897; per capita income: $11,813; median gross rent: $326; median house value: $54,100.

1992 Presidential Vote			1988 Presidential Vote		
Bush (R)	101,962	(51%)	Bush (R)	107,999	(67%)
Clinton (D)	69,161	(35%)	Dukakis (D)	54,344	(33%)
Perot (I)	26,424	(13%)			

Rep. Butler C. Derrick (D)

Elected 1974; b. Sep. 30, 1936, Springfield, MA; home, Edgefield; U. of SC, 1954–58, U. of GA, LL.B. 1965; Episcopalian; married (Beverly).

Career: Practicing atty., 1965–74; SC House of Reps., 1969–74.

Offices: 221 CHOB 20515, 202-225-5301. Also 101 Fed. Bldg., Anderson 29622, 803-224-7401; 211 York St. NE, #5, Aiken 29801, 803-649-5571; and 129 Fed. Bldg., Greenwood 29646, 803-223-8251.

Committees: *House Administration* (10th of 12 D): Libraries and Memorials; Personnel and Police. *Rules* (2d of 9 D): The Legislative Process (Chmn.).

Group Ratings

	ADA	ACLU	COPE	CDF	CFA	LCV	ACU	NTLC	NSI	COC	CEI
1992	80	65	58	80	80	44	28	5	80	63	20
1991	70	—	75	90	61	77	37	—	—	70	23

National Journal Ratings

	1991 LIB — 1991 CONS		1992 LIB — 1992 CONS	
Economic	48% —	51%	53% —	46%
Social	68% —	31%	61% —	38%
Foreign	51% —	46%	56% —	40%

Key Votes of the 102d Congress

1. Ban Striker Replace	AGN	5. Handgun Wait/7-Day	FOR	9. Use Force in Gulf	FOR
2. $ for Homeownership	AGN	6. Overseas Mil. Abortion	FOR	10. US Mil. Abroad $ Cut	FOR
3. Tax Rich/Cut Mid Cls.	FOR	7. Obscn. Art NEA $ Ban	AGN	11. Limit SDI Funds	FOR
4. FY93/$15B Def. Cut	FOR	8. Death Pen. from Jury	AGN	12. Cuba Trade Embargo	FOR

Key Votes of the 103d Congress

1. Family Leave	FOR	2. Deficit Reduction	FOR	3. Stimulus Plan	FOR

Election Results

1992 general	Butler C. Derrick (D)	119,119	(61%)	($673,677)
	Jim Bland (R)	75,660	(39%)	($17,339)
1992 primary	Butler C. Derrick (D), unopposed			
1990 general	Butler C. Derrick (D)	72,561	(58%)	($907,179)
	Ray Haskett (R)	52,419	(42%)	($74,264)

FOURTH DISTRICT

When northern investors sought sites for textile mills as long ago as the 1880s, they looked to the up country of South Carolina where, one chronicler wrote, they "were attracted by the mild climate, abundant water power, proximity to the cotton fields and plenty of native [white] labor already accustomed to a low standard of living." And so by 1900 the textile industry of the South became centered along the Southern Railway and Seaboard Coast Line tracks between Charlotte and Atlanta, especially in the Piedmont of South Carolina. As mills fled New England and the Northeast in the 1920s, the concentration here became even thicker. The textile country could look bucolic, but Greenville, Spartanburg and the dozens of mill towns thick in the surrounding countryside were as industrial as Lancashire or the Ruhr, with mills rising up on what were once twisting woodland paths.

Today, this same stretch of land along South Carolina's Interstate 85, which parallels the Southern Railway, remains the number one textile-producing area in the United States. But it is much more than that. Greenville and Spartanburg Counties now have a diversified manufacturing economy, and have excelled in attracting foreign companies. The number of textile and apparel jobs declined from 57,000 in the early 1970s to 42,000 in the late 1980s, from 27% of all jobs to 14%, but new businesses include domestic companies like Stouffer's Lean Cuisine, Digital Computer, Procter & Gamble and Wal-Mart, which has its largest distribution center here. Foreign companies include Adidas, Hitachi and, part of the largest concentration of German investment in the United States, Hoechst. Michelin's North American headquarters is near Greenville and BMW is building its North American plant next to the Greenville-Spartanburg Airport just off I-85, on a site assembled by Governor Carroll Campbell with a $130 million package of tax incentives he put together; he claims the plant will generate 2,000 jobs and $1 billion in revenue. The airport will expand by 1995 to include runways, capable of accommodating 747s loaded with autoparts, within taxiing distance of the new BMW factory.

What attracts all these businesses? Sometimes big tax concessions, as with BMW. More important, overall tax levels are low, while state government has built infrastructure—the airport, the Interstate highways, the port of Charleston which is now one of the busiest on the East Coast. Unions are not a problem: South Carolina has the lowest rate of unionization in the United States. The work ethic seems strong. As public schools in northern metropolises seem more interested in teaching children peripheral subjects and schooling them in self-esteem, public schools in South Carolina strive to teach the basics of reading, mathematics and good work habits. Culturally this area ranges from conservative to very conservative, with a strong influence by Greenville's Bob Jones University and many evangelical and fundamentalist churches. But the culture of mainstream churches and civic boosters has a certain bedrock conservatism to it as well. Politics here can be a battle between these two strains, religious right Republicans versus more commerce-minded Republicans and moderate Democrats. The latter two groups, with their greater political adeptness tend to win most of the time, producing among others the last two governors of the state, Democrat Richard Riley and Republican Carroll Campbell. But the other side can also be victorious, as it was in the 1992 House race.

South Carolina's 4th Congressional District, only slightly revised by redistricting, fits almost perfectly around the Greenville-Spartanburg area. It has been seriously contested when politically skillful local Democrats have risen to challenge the Republicans whose party carries the area, sometimes by vast margins in races not only for president but statewide. One such Democrat was Liz Patterson, state senator from Spartanburg, the daughter of Olin Johnston (South Carolina governor from 1935–39 and 1943–45, and senator 1945–65), and a civic activist who won the seat when Campbell was elected governor in 1986. Patterson usually voted with the Democratic leadership and crafted the kind of interstitial government programs—child care centers in Veterans' Administration medical facilities, credit for early payment of low income mortgages by developers—that have helped many Democrats win reelection. She became head of the Textile Caucus in 1992. But she won only 52% in her first two elections and, in 1990, 61% after opposing the budget summit agreement tax increase package.

But in 1992 the 4th District elected Republican Bob Inglis, in what was treated as an upset but should have been predictable. Inglis is a young lawyer, a graduate of elite schools (Duke, Virginia Law), who campaigned hard for term limits and against PAC contributions; he refused the latter and promised to serve only three terms. Inglis ran a huge door-to-door effort, targeting key precincts with many volunteers; they hung tens of thousands of doorknobs fliers attacking the House bank, post office and other scandals, and charging Patterson with doing nothing about them. Inglis benefited as well from a 200,000-person mailing of comparative issue stands by the Christian Coalition. Inglis won 57% in Greenville County and 43% in Spartanburg County, for a

50%–48% district-wide victory.

In office, Inglis pledged again to pass term limits legislation and ban PAC contributions. He confounded predictions that he would be co-opted by opposing additional funding for the Southern Connector road Patterson had backed to link I-85 and I-385 because of its inclusion in a pork laden bill. His reelection in 1994 cannot be considered certain, but he seems more in tune with the district's partisan leanings than his predecessor.

The People: Pop. 1990: 581,385; 36% rural; 12% age 65+; 79% White; 20% Black; 1% Asian; 1% Hispanic origin. Voting age pop.: 437,750; 18% Black; 1% Hispanic origin. Households: 58% married couple families; 26% married couple fams. w. children; 39% college educ.; median household income: $27,703; per capita income: $13,011; median gross rent: $367; median house value: $58,900.

1992 Presidential Vote			1988 Presidential Vote		
Bush (R)	107,970	(54%)	Bush (R)	114,778	(68%)
Clinton (D)	65,106	(33%)	Dukakis (D)	54,814	(32%)
Perot (I)	24,131	(12%)			

Rep. Bob Inglis (R)

Elected 1992; b. Oct. 11, 1959, Savannah, GA; home, Greenville; Duke U., B.A. 1981, U. of VA Law Schl., J.D. 1984; Presbyterian; married (Mary Anne).

Career: Practicing atty., 1984–92.

Offices: 1237 LHOB 20515, 202-225-6030. Also 201 Magnolia St., #108, Spartanburg 29301, 803-582-6422; 300 E. Washington St., #101, Greenville 29601, 803-232-1141; and 405 W. Main St., Union 29379, 803-427-2205.

Committees: *Budget* (16th of 17 R). *Judiciary* (13th of 14 R): Administrative Law and Governmental Relations; Economic and Commercial Law.

Group Ratings and 102d Congress Votes: Newly Elected

Key Votes of the 103d Congress

1. Family Leave	AGN	2. Deficit Reduction	AGN	3. Stimulus Plan	AGN

Election Results

1992 general	Bob Inglis (R)	99,879	(50%)	($215,364)
	Liz Patterson (D)	94,182	(48%)	($348,528)
	Others	4,349	(2%)	
1992 primary	Bob Inglis (R)	21,301	(71%)	
	Bill McCuen (R)	4,760	(16%)	
	Jerry L. Fowler (R)	4,029	(13%)	
1990 general	Liz Patterson (D)	81,927	(61%)	($485,095)
	Terry Haskins (R)	51,338	(38%)	($144,353)

FIFTH DISTRICT

Some of the fiercest battles of the Revolutionary War were fought in up-country South Carolina, on hilly lands just being settled by Scots-Irish farmers moving up the sluggish rivers of the lowlands or down the Virginia Piedmont valley. This was a country of violent passions and unclear lines; Carolinians have long argued over which side of the North and South Carolina boundary Andrew Jackson was born in 1767. In the years since, the fighting spirit and Calvinist faith of up-country Carolinians have never wavered; this remains one of the most intensely religious and pro-military sections of the country. But it is no longer one of the most impoverished. For many years, the dominant industry here was textiles, traditionally the first factory enterprise of industrializing countries, with low pay and poor working conditions. But in the 1980s the number of textile jobs declined, and small business prosperity more recently has been barreling out the interstates from Greenville-Spartanburg and Columbia and Charlotte, to transform counties once dependent on tobacco fields and textile mills.

The 5th Congressional District of South Carolina consists of all or part of 13 counties, mostly in the up country. They include none of the three area metropolitan centers, but much of their growing fringe. In the east, they verge on lowland tobacco country, including Marlboro and Chesterfield Counties, although heavily black areas here have been lopped off and placed in the new black-majority 6th District. In the west, they include Rock Hill and York County, just south of Charlotte, and a segment of the I-85 textile corridor. Politically, this remains Democratic territory; while the fast-growing metro areas tend to go Republican, the smaller counties in the white up country and black lowlands have stayed Democratic.

John Spratt, the congressman from the 5th District, has in a decade become one of the most respected if not the best known members of the House; early on he made *Roll Call's* list of the 20 smartest members of Congress. He comes from a prominent York County family, just south of Charlotte, and has degrees from Davidson, Yale Law and Oxford; he first got involved in politics in Charles Ravenel's unsuccessful 1974 campaign for governor. Spratt was elected to the House in 1982, when the incumbent retired a week before the filing deadline; Spratt put a campaign together fast and won 38% in the primary, 55% in the runoff against a candidate who spent $929,000, and 68% in the general. He has been reelected easily, without opposition in 1990.

In his first term Spratt, who had served in the Pentagon after law school, got a seat on the Armed Services Committee, and became an ally of Les Aspin in his battle over the MX missile. Spratt nominated Aspin at the 1984 Democratic Caucus after none less than Speaker Tip O'Neill got up and spoke for elderly Chairman Mel Price. Aspin won and Spratt became, according to *National Journal*, "one of the House's more influential members on matters military." Spratt's low-key demeanor and, to outsiders, thick Carolina accent do not long mask his first-rate mind and impressive knowledge of details. In the late 1980s, Spratt stitched together compromises on binary nerve gas weapons, the Strategic Defense Initiative, and the Savannah River and other nuclear plants—keeping military projects flowing through a House many of whose members were temperamentally inclined to zero out military spending.

Frustrated by "our feckless inability to do something about the deficit," Spratt passed through the House in 1990 a bill that would require the administration and both houses of Congress to submit balanced budgets. In 1991, he got on the Budget Committee, and after the 1992 election ran for chairman. He presented himself as a somewhat more conservative alternative to Minnesotan Martin Sabo and, in a campaign that stayed on the issues and avoided rancor, he lost by a perhaps surprisingly close vote of 149-112. Spratt left Budget after his loss to Sabo and assumed the chair of the Commerce, Consumer and Monetary Affairs Subcommittee on Government Operations; he still plans to introduce a modified line-item veto proposal in 1993. Spratt was also one of the six Democrats appointed by Speaker Foley in late 1992 to the Joint Committee on the Organization of Congress. He is currently head of the Congressional Textile Caucus and co-chairs the Ball Bearing Caucus, representing two longtime local industries which have often sought protection from imports.

Spratt has been involved in other local issues as well. He got disaster relief for the up country after Hurricane Hugo and special aid to Sumter schools after hundreds of pupils were transferred there from Florida after Hurricane Andrew. He got permission for an Air Force-state land swap between Shaw Air Force Base and Myrtle Beach Air Force Base which is to be converted. For 15 years, he spent much time dealing with Catawba Indian Tribe land claims in York, Lancaster and Chester Counties, and in 1992 succeeded in brokering a settlement hailed by all sides and by Republicans like Governor Carroll Campbell as well as Democrats.

Metropolitan Charlotte's expansion into York County and the conservative impulse symbolized by Jim Bakker, the jailed televangelist whose Heritage USA theme park was located in York County, may produce a long-term Republican trend in the district. But against his toughest opponent since 1982, Spratt won in 1992 with 61%. He survived redistricting without major changes and without, as seemed possible at one point, a primary against 6th District incumbent Robin Tallon who opted to retire. Spratt has shown scant interest in statewide office, though he would certainly be a plausible candidate for a Senate seat if either should ever come open.

The People: Pop. 1990: 581,174; 63% rural; 12% age 65+; 68% White; 31% Black. Voting age pop.: 422,161; 28% Black. Households: 59% married couple families; 28% married couple fams. w. children; 32% college educ.; median household income: $25,215; per capita income: $11,009; median gross rent: $327; median house value: $52,800.

1992 Presidential Vote			1988 Presidential Vote		
Bush (R)	86,118	(45%)	Bush (R)	92,919	(61%)
Clinton (D)	81,192	(42%)	Dukakis (D)	60,559	(39%)
Perot (I)	23,462	(12%)			

Rep. John M. Spratt, Jr. (D)

Elected 1982; b. Nov. 1, 1942, Charlotte, NC; home, York; Davidson Col., A.B. 1964, Oxford U., M.A. 1966, Yale, LL.B. 1969; Presbyterian; married (Jane).

Career: Army Operations, U.S. Dept. of Defense, 1969–71; Practicing atty., 1971–82; Pres., Bank of Ft. Mill, 1973–82; Pres., Spratt Insurance Agcy., 1973–82.

Offices: 1536 LHOB 20515, 202-225-5501. Also 305 Fed. Bldg., Rock Hill 29731, 803-327-1114; 39 E. Calhoun St., Sumter 29150, 803-773-3362; and 88 Public Sq., Darlington 29532, 803-393-3998.

Committees: *Armed Services* (9th of 34 D): Military Acquisition; Oversight and Investigations. *Government Operations* (10th of 25 D): Commerce, Consumer and Monetary Affairs (Chmn.). *Joint Committee on the Organization of Congress* (5th of 12).

Group Ratings

	ADA	ACLU	COPE	CDF	CFA	LCV	ACU	NTLC	NSI	COC	CEI
1992	75	74	67	80	100	56	28	0	100	50	24
1991	50	—	83	90	56	92	21	—	—	30	21

National Journal Ratings

	1991 LIB — 1991 CONS			1992 LIB — 1992 CONS	
Economic	54%	—	45%	56%	—	42%
Social	60%	—	38%	57%	—	43%
Foreign	49%	—	50%	38%	—	56%

Key Votes of the 102d Congress

1. Ban Striker Replace AGN	5. Handgun Wait/7-Day FOR	9. Use Force in Gulf FOR
2. $ for Homeownership AGN	6. Overseas Mil. Abortion FOR	10. US Mil. Abroad $ Cut AGN
3. Tax Rich/Cut Mid Cls. FOR	7. Obscn. Art NEA $ Ban FOR	11. Limit SDI Funds AGN
4. FY93/$15B Def. Cut FOR	8. Death Pen. from Jury AGN	12. Cuba Trade Embargo FOR

Key Votes of the 103d Congress

1. Family Leave FOR	2. Deficit Reduction FOR	3. Stimulus Plan FOR

Election Results

1992 general	John M. Spratt, Jr. (D)................	112,031	(61%)	($381,942)
	Bill Horne (R).......................	70,866	(39%)	($102,728)
1992 primary	John M. Spratt, Jr. (D), unopposed			
1990 general	John M. Spratt, Jr. (D), unopposed			($173,157)

SIXTH DISTRICT

South Carolina was first settled by planters from Barbados, bringing with them a tropical plantation economy, which they transferred to the not quite tropical climate of the Carolina coastal lowlands. Here the flat mainland and many islands are laced with sluggish-flowing rivers and swamps, and here the planters brought thousands of slaves directly from Africa. Colonial South Carolina was one of the richest parts of North America, with dazzling Georgian architecture in Charleston and classic plantation gardens; the planters built great irrigation systems and grew rice and cotton and the dye-plant indigo, all heavily in demand in Britain and elsewhere. And of course all this wealth was built on the slave labor of thousands of African-Americans, many of them still speaking their ancestral languages, or a patois mixing them with English. A majority of colonial South Carolinians were black slaves; so were most residents of the lowlands when the Civil War started with the bombardment of Fort Sumter in Charleston Harbor, although by that time there were also many free blacks in Charleston, some of whom owned slaves themselves.

South Carolina's African-American heritage has left an imprint on American culture, still apparent in the lowlands today. The special accents and dialects of lowland blacks were long retained: traces of Gullah and others still can be found on lowland islands and the Charleston accent, which to outsiders seems often incomprehensible (should C-SPAN run subtitles when Senator Hollings speaks?). The poverty that was the almost universal lot of lowland blacks after the Civil War has only in the last generation been alleviated, as development comes to the coast and the long cultural isolation of people here is dissipated. But many blacks who grew up here have long since left, leaving after high school graduation on the bus for New York, nicknamed "the chicken-bone special" because of the fried chicken their families packed for the journey.

The new 6th Congressional District of South Carolina, created for 1992 to have a black majority, actually includes very little of the coast, now mostly lined with affluent condominium communities; but it does include most of the geographic expanse of lowland South Carolina. Its erose and irregular boundaries are designed to include the black central city neighborhoods of Charleston and Columbia but leave in the adjacent 1st and 2d Districts their affluent white city and suburban areas. The 6th district includes much of Orangeburg, home of the historically black South Carolina State University, and Florence, at the center of the Pee Dee tobacco-growing country in eastern South Carolina. This last area was the center of the old, 39% black 6th District, represented for 10 years by Democrat Robin Tallon, a genial clothing store owner who won mostly black votes in the general and courted tobacco farmers on the Agriculture Committee. Tallon filed to run for reelection in 1992, and might have prevailed in a multi-candidate primary; but on the last possible day he withdrew, saying that he wanted to avoid what might be a racially divisive contest in this new black majority district.

The new congressman is James Clyburn, former state human affairs commissioner, who won the seat effectively in the Democratic primary, with 56% of the vote against four black opponents all with serious claims for the nomination. One was Charleston state Senator Herbert Fielding, one of the first black South Carolina legislators of this century and at 69 the oldest candidate in the 1992 race here. He carried Charleston County, but it cast only 10% of primary votes, and he had only 12% districtwide. The youngest candidate, at 43, was Ken Mosely, professor at South Carolina State, who ran well against Republican Floyd Spence in the 2d District in 1982 and 1984 and was critical of the welfare system; he got 41% in Orangeburg County but only 13% districtwide. From Florence came state Senator Frank Gilbert, who billed himself as a "hell-raiser" and ran strongly in the Florence area. But Clyburn, well known from nearly two decades as human rights commissioner and two nearly-successful statewide races for secretary of state, ran first or second in all these areas and piled up huge margins in others (88% in his home county of Sumter).

In November, Clyburn won 65% of the vote and became the first black to represent South Carolina in Congress since 1897. He has been active in the civil rights movement since his youth and also has good working relationships with leading businessmen and Republicans; he has a knack for accommodating people of different backgrounds and at the same time a successful record of lobbying the legislature for civil rights laws. He supports additional government spending programs but is by no means scornful of the need to nurture family values. His strong performance in 1992 indicates that he has a safe seat.

The People: Pop. 1990: 581,202; 51% rural; 12% age 65+; 37% White; 62% Black; 1% Hispanic origin. Voting age pop.: 412,159; 58% Black. Households: 49% married couple families; 24% married couple fams. w. children; 30% college educ.; median household income: $19,254; per capita income: $8,628; median gross rent: $314; median house value: $47,900.

1992 Presidential Vote			1988 Presidential Vote		
Clinton (D)	118,085	(62%)	Dukakis (D)	97,845	(60%)
Bush (R)	59,970	(31%)	Bush (R)	64,831	(40%)
Perot (I)	12,292	(6%)			

Rep. James E. Clyburn (D)

Elected 1992; b. July 21, 1940, Sumter; home, Columbia; SC St. U., B.A. 1962; African Methodist Episcopal; married (Emily).

Career: Teacher, 1962–66; Dir., Charleston Neighborhood Youth Corps, 1966–68; Exec. Dir., SC Commission for Farm Workers, 1968–71; Asst., SC Gov. West, 1971–74; SC Human Affairs Commissioner, 1974–92.

Offices: 319 CHOB 20515, 202-225-3315. Also 1703 Gervais St., Columbia 29201, 803-799-1100; 181 E. Evans St., Florence 29502, 803-622-1212; and 4900 LaCrosse Rd., N. Charleston 29418, 803-747-9660.

Committees: *Public Works and Transportation* (31st of 39 D): Economic Development; Public Buildings and Grounds; Surface Transportation. *Veterans' Affairs* (19th of 21 D): Education, Training and Employment; Oversight and Investigations.

Group Ratings and 102d Congress Votes: Newly Elected

Key Votes of the 103d Congress

1. Family Leave	FOR	2. Deficit Reduction	FOR	3. Stimulus Plan	FOR

Election Results

1992 general	James E. Clyburn (D)...............	120,647	(65%)	($324,379)
	John Chase (R)......................	64,149	(35%)	($114,289)
1992 primary	James E. Clyburn (D)...............	41,415	(56%)	
	Frank Gilbert (D)....................	11,089	(15%)	
	Ken Mosely (D).....................	9,494	(13%)	
	Herbert U. Fielding(D)..............	9,130	(12%)	
	John Roy Harper, III (D)............	2,680	(4%)	
1990 general	Robin M. Tallon (D), unopposed			($95,350)

SOUTH DAKOTA

A century ago, the Census Bureau and the historian Frederick Jackson Turner proclaimed the closing of the American frontier. One of the last places closed was what had been the Dakota Territory until it was admitted to the Union as South Dakota and North Dakota in 1889. South Dakota in particular was the home of the Oglala Sioux, one of the largest Native American tribes who had built a herding and buffalo hunting civilization by becoming masters of the horses the Spaniards had imported to North America 350 years earlier. It was the Sioux warrior chief Sitting Bull, now buried on a bluff above the Missouri River, who destroyed Custer at Little Big Horn in 1876; it was Oglala Sioux who were the victims at the massacre of Wounded Knee in 1890. Today, the Oglala Sioux on the reservations of South Dakota are among the poorest Americans, trying to stay in touch with their culture but so traumatized by defeat and disease (which wiped out many other tribes altogether) that they have difficulty adapting to the new. In 1989, legislators, while voting a Martin Luther King Holiday, renamed Pioneer Day (which had been Columbus Day) in October as Native American Day, and Governor George Mickelson, in response to publisher Tim Giago of the Indian *Lakota Times*, declared 1990 (the centennial of Wounded Knee and Sitting Bull's death), a Year of Reconciliation, with a peace pipe ceremony at the Capitol involving leaders of nine Sioux nations. Mickelson also proclaimed 1991 the beginning of a Century of Reconciliation, and Indian history is now taught in the state high schools. But penned off in reservations, Indians are far from mainstsream economic participation, while alcoholism and suicide, surely in some way the after-effects of wounds suffered 100 years ago, continue. There is still healing to do.

The settlement of South Dakota a century ago was a rapid and sometimes violent process. The first gold strikes in the Black Hills came in 1876, and soon the mountains swarmed with settlers; Deadwood became a city of 20,000 where Calamity Jane ruled the saloons and Wild Bill Hickock was shot in the back while holding two pair—aces and eights. (Deadwood today has legalized gambling, with proceeds used for historic preservation). Hunters, knowing that the buffalo could not be contained by barbed wire fences, massacred them so thoroughly that when Teddy Roosevelt got to the Dakota Territory in 1885, he had a hard time finding one to shoot. It was not long before the railroad came through, and before enough settlers, many of them German and Scandinavian immigrants recruited by the railroads and land speculators, had built sodhouses, broken the land and set down enough roots to justify making two Dakota states.

Today, the buffalo are long gone, but South Dakota has never quite filled up. In the 25 years between statehood and World War I, the eastern third of the state, sectioned off Midwestern style into 640 acre square miles, filled up with farmers. But moving westward, before you get to the Missouri River in the middle of the state, green turns to brown, cultivation grows sparse and then stops; the plains are open grazing land, scarcely touched by the white men who were so eager to establish dominion over them a century ago. The land is punctuated not by roads meeting every mile at precise angles but by buttes, gullies and grasslands sweeping to the horizon with no sign of human habitation. By 1910, South Dakota's settlement patterns were established—with patches of frontier left here and there—and the state's political character was pretty well set. During the 1890s, voters here flirted briefly with the Populists and William Jennings Bryan; but by the 1920s, South Dakota had become almost as monolithically Republican as Nebraska. Voters in South Dakota never had much use for the Non-Partisan League, which caught on in the more Scandinavian soil of North Dakota, and there was never anything here comparable to the Farmer-Labor Party of Minnesota. As in most Great Plains states, there have been periodic farm revolts against incumbent administrations. But South Dakota began with a large enough Republican base that, despite such revolts, the state between 1936 and 1970 had a Democratic governor for only two years and elected only one Democrat to the Senate, George McGovern.

The last two decades have seen political and economic fluctuations aplenty. Most of these came in the 1970s, with the rise of McGovern's Democrats, who captured at various times the governorship, the legislature, both Senate seats and both House seats. Like other upper Midwest states, South Dakota tends to be dovish on foreign policy (as it was isolationist before Pearl Harbor) and sternly intolerant of corruption: Vietnam and Watergate hurt Republicans. But, in response to Indian militancy at Wounded Knee and after, there was a sharp Republican shift by the late 1970s. An economic shift started in 1981, when Citicorp moved credit card operations to Sioux Falls to escape New York's usury laws and high wages. The Citicorp operation here grew from 50 employees to 2,700; other banks followed; shopping centers burgeoned as Sioux Falls grew and shoppers started driving more than 200 miles on freeways for the selection a big mall could provide; medical centers grew, as South Dakotans sought the better care large hospitals could provide. As a result, metro Sioux Falls grew 13% in the 1980s; Rapid City, which served a similar function for the western part of the state, grew 16%; Watertown and Brookings, mid-sized freeway towns, grew as well, while almost every other county in the state lost population. There are still some 35,000 farms in South Dakota, but population patterns here on the Plains now look more like those in the Rockies, with most people concentrated in a few areas, while vast acreage remains vacant, punctuated with infrequent ranches and resort areas—a landscape that would not have been totally alien to Sitting Bull.

South Dakota's low taxes helped attract new white-collar jobs, and it still has no state income tax. Happy to send Democrats to Washington to vote for more spending, it keeps Republicans in control in Pierre to hold down taxes. It is experimenting with gambling, allowing slot machines and $5 per hand blackjack in Deadwood. Casino-style gambling was legalized in 1989, with over $500 million bet the first two years; gambling is legal on Indian reservations as well. These are just some of South Dakota's many attempts to attract tourists; there is also Mount Rushmore and the Crazy Horse Memorial, the gold panning creeks and tourist attractions of the Black Hills, and Wall Drug, the 46,000-square foot emporium between the Badlands and Rapid City which snares three-quarters of the freeway traffic.

Governor. Rounding out his second term was George Mickelson, who had set a tone of reconciliation in a state more familiar with angry frontier faceoffs. But in April 1993, Mickelson, two cabinet officials and five prominent South Dakota businessmen were killed in an Iowa plane crash. Mickelson was something of a government reformer, willing to raise taxes, which still remain among the lowest in the nation. He was proud of his revolving economic development fund, financed by a temporary one-cent sales tax increase, which he said attracted jobs and industry. He and the others in the fatal crash had in fact been on a lobbying mission in Cincinnati to protect jobs at a Sioux Falls meatpacking plant.

The new governor is Walter Dale Miller, a rancher who lives near Rapid City. Picked by Mickelson to be lieutenant governor in 1986 and 1990, Miller became one of Mickelson's senior advisors and technically the state's first full time lieutenant governor. Miller spent 20 years in

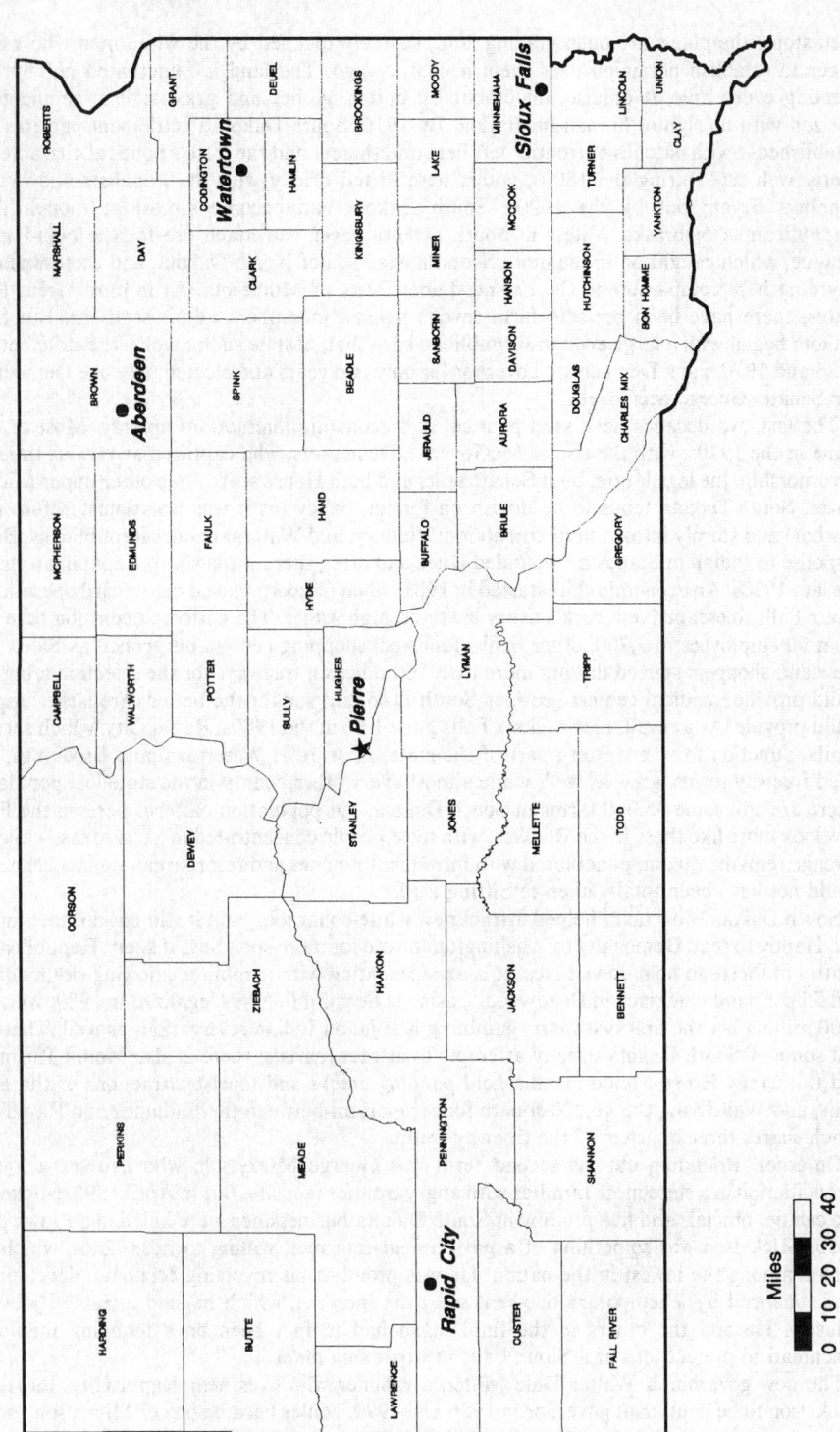

Miles

0 10 20 30 40

the South Dakota legislature where he compiled a purely conservative record. Like Mickelson, he is antiabortion, and he pledges to carry on Mickelson's economic initiatives but with his own stamp.

Miller has all but announced he will run for the seat in 1994 and former Governor William Janklow seems likely to take him on in the primary. Ted Muenster, the 1990 Senate nominee, could be a possible Democratic opponent as well as state Senator Lars Herseth, Mickelson's 1986 opponent.

Senators. Larry Pressler is now one of the more senior senators (only 13 Republicans have served more years in the Senate), and one with impressive credentials: Vietnam veteran (the first elected to the Senate), Rhodes scholar, Harvard lawyer. He was first elected to the House by beating an incumbent Democrat in the Democratic year of 1974, easily elected to the Senate in 1978, and reelected by the widest margin in South Dakota history in 1984. But he is only now beginning to be taken seriously by his colleagues, even while, as the 1990 election results showed, he has become more critically regarded by his constituents. Pressler was a classic example of the 1970s congressman who wanted to please the folks back home, opposing every congressional pay raise and voting for farm price supports and export subsidies galore. His positive accomplishments were sparser, partly because colleagues saw him as a cheap-shot artist: short-line railroads, Continental Scientific Drilling. Pressler has always been earnest and his integrity is unquestioned: he immediately refused a bribe from FBI agents disguised as Arab sheiks during the 1979 Abscam sting. But he did not hew faithfully to any perceptible system of beliefs. He went from being one of the most dovish Republicans to having the most hawkish record in the Senate; he moved sharply to the right on cultural issues; his *National Journal* economic ratings oscillated from 60% liberal to the 36% range to 5% in five years. His record was the most conservative in 1988, when there was talk he would be challenged in the primary by former Governor Bill Janklow; then he switched to much more liberal records on foreign and economic issues in 1989, when it became clear his chief opponent would be a Democrat.

The 1990 opponent was Ted Muenster, top aide to Governor Richard Kneip in the 1970s, spurred on by the *Sioux Falls Argus-Leader* whose coverage of Pressler was almost as critical and hostile as Ted Kennedy's from the *Boston Herald* or Jesse Helms's from the *Raleigh News & Observer*. Pressler's Democratic South Dakota colleague Tom Daschle went well beyond usual partisan rhetoric when he said of Pressler, "A Senate seat is a terrible thing to waste." Muenster and Pressler both raised money in Washington and nationally, and fought it out in cheap South Dakota TV time. Pressler won by just 52%–45%, running weaker in fast-growing Sioux Falls and Watertown; he was helped by Muenster's poor showing among Indians. Pressler carried, in effect, the old South Dakota; with the new South Dakota, it is plain, he could be in trouble.

Since 1990, Pressler's voting record has settled into a more rational pattern and he began to build on some of his initiatives, especially in foreign affairs. In 1985, he authored an amendment barring non-humanitarian aid to Pakistan in the cause of nuclear non-proliferation, and Pressler continues to be the chief congressional monitor of Pakistan's nuclear arsenal. Similarly, in 1992, he wrote an amendment conditioning aid to Russia on withdrawal of former Soviet troops from the Baltic States and Moldova; he unsuccessfully tried to kill a provision for a year's grace period. He has worked for more allied and U.N. burden sharing on Somalia and has called for U.S. recognition of Vietnam. If Pressler sometimes seems naive on foreign affairs, he conscientiously raises basic human rights issues which reflect core American values. He works on domestic issues as well. On the Commerce Committee, he successfully got an outage prevention agency for telecommunications networks, an AM stereo standard, a law to let citizens stop telephone solicitations and a Landsat law. He encourages farm product exports and improved rural medical care, and complains about excessive Common Market subsidies. With John Danforth retiring, he is slated to become ranking member (or if Republicans gain seven seats, chairman) of the Commerce Committee, a position of great leverage on regulatory issues. He will have to face off against some pretty tough operators (Ernest Hollings, Daniel Inouye,

Wendell Ford) and will be hard to figure out by many lobbyists (hint: put some rural aid in your package).

Pressler would probably never have been an influential member of the House, but in the Senate, with its obstruction-loving rules and respect for seniority, and Pressler's own earnest study of issues, he could be a force. He is willing to use his senatorial prerogatives as stiffneckedly as anyone: in August 1992, just before recess, he held up 31 judicial appointments to get White House action on several South Dakota nominations; for this he was chastised furiously by Bob Dole and Alan Simpson. Later, he staunchly opposed Zoe Baird's nomination for attorney general when many Republicans wanted to let her through, but was quickly mollified by Ron Brown.

Junior Senator Tom Daschle is one of those baby boomers who has spent almost all his adult life in politics: when he returned from service in the Air Force in 1972, at the high point of South Dakota Democratic fortune, he became a Washington staffer to Senator James Abourezk; in 1978, as Abourezk was about to retire, Daschle returned to South Dakota, ran for the eastern House district that Larry Pressler was vacating, and won by exactly 139 votes over the former P.O.W. who had come close to beating George McGovern in 1974. Daschle beat fellow incumbent Clint Roberts in 1982 as South Dakota returned to a single at-large district. In 1986, he was elected to the Senate by 52%–48% over incumbent James Abdnor, who was hurt by primary competition from then Governor Bill Janklow. Two years later, in January 1989, new Senate Majority Leader George Mitchell named Daschle co-chairman of the Senate Democratic Policy Committee—in effect, though not in title, the number two man in the Senate leadership. Daschle rose by standing for a set of principles and campaigning effectively for them, although his record did get somewhat more conservative in the year he first ran for the Senate.

Daschle stands at the upper quadrant of liberal senators, especially on foreign policy issues; his record is more mixed on cultural issues. With North Dakota's two Democrats, Tom Harkin of Iowa and perhaps Paul Wellstone of Minnesota, he is a "prairie populist," resisting cuts in farm subsidies. This effort mostly failed in the 1990 farm bill, which Daschle decried, "amounts to a slow economic death sentence for the nation's family farmers." But in 1993, these five, plus Nebraska's two Democratic senators, can cost the Democrats 7 of their 56 Senate votes, and obviously have real leverage with the Clinton Administration. But Daschle, however, did get a reformulated gasoline amendment into the 1990 Clean Air Act and bigger tax breaks for ethanol in the 1992 energy bill—both attempts to promote use of Dakota grain. Despite a Centers for Disease Control study showing no connection between exposure and cancer, Daschle was the leader in getting the Senate to agree to compensation for Vietnam veterans exposed to Agent Orange.

Daschle seems to be operating as a ground-tester for Mitchell on sensitive issues. He brings a tough-on-sexual-harassment attitude to the Ethics Committee. He has co-sponsored Harris Wofford's tax-financed universal long-term and acute healthcare bill that would call for administration by an independent agency. In 1993, he sponsored a measure to abolish the Appropriations Committee—the stronghold of Mitchell's predecessor Robert Byrd—and transfer its function to the individual committees instead.

Daschle's brand of prairie populism isn't sweeping America; if it were, Richard Gephardt, whom he supported in 1988, would be serving his second term as president. But Daschle's politics has done very well in South Dakota. The state's Republicans tried to give him a fight in 1992, when they hatched a plot to get former Governor Bill Janklow to run. But Janklow refused and a memo about this move was leaked. The result probably diminished the stature of Charlene Haar, a teacher long active in Republican affairs, who got the nomination unopposed. She was ignored or scorned by feminists and reporters busy proclaiming "the year of the woman" elsewhere, and was vastly outspent by Daschle who skillfully mined Washington PACs and national liberal groups. Daschle won with 65% of the vote—not quite up to Pressler's best, but an outstanding result nonetheless.

Representative-at-Large. The House member representing the nation's second most populous district is South Dakota's Representative-at-Large Tim Johnson. Johnson has a more moderate record than Daschle, and is rather conservative on cultural issues. When national Democrats were making support for abortion rights a litmus test, Johnson was one of 50 House Democrats to write DNC Chairman Ron Brown in April 1989 saying, "The principle and practice of abortion on demand is dead wrong." Given the importance of feminist groups in Democratic circles today, he is unlikely to be able to raise enough money to be a viable Senate candidate. Johnson is also an enthusiastic backer of the line-item veto and in October 1992 helped pass presidential line-item rescission authority 312–97 in the House (it died in the Senate). On the Agriculture Committee, he is more to the left, claiming credit for passing legislation including price supports for sunflowers and other oilseeds. He voted against the 1990 farm bill, but may have an opportunity to fashion a 1995 bill more to his liking from his new chair of the Agriculture Subcommittee on General Farm Commodities. On the Natural Resources Committee, he backed the two big South Dakota water projects which passed the House in 1992, the $100 million Mid-Dakota Project and the $230 million Lake Andes-Wagner irrigation project. He has been busy trying to build a bridge across the Missouri River to Nebraska in his home town of Vermillion.

Johnson first won the seat in 1986 by beating fellow state Senator Jim Burg in the Democratic primary, 48%–45%, with big margins in his southeastern home area and in Sioux Falls and Rapid City, and in the general winning 59%. He has not had tough competition since. While South Dakota Senate races tend to be fiercely and expensively contested—if only because a relatively small expenditure can affect 1% of the seats in the Senate—races for this seat, which is 0.23% of House seats, attract much less money and weaker competition. With an attractive family and with frequent visits back to the state, Johnson has built up high popularity, winning with 72%, 68% and 69%.

Presidential politics. With only three electoral votes, South Dakota is not a glittering prize in presidential contests. Nevertheless, it has been close in four of the last six elections. With typical Farm Belt contrariness, it has tilted against the party in power, giving good, though losing, votes to Democrats in 1972, 1976, 1988 and 1992 and going heavily Republican in 1980. George Bush won in 1988, 53%–47%, his national average; in 1992, he won 41%–37%, better than his national average. Both times he lost booming Sioux Falls but won heavily in the west.

For years, South Dakota's presidential primary was eclipsed by California's, held on the same day. In 1988 and 1992, it was held in February, just one week after New Hampshire. Far from becoming a trendsetter, it has become a Great Plains booster. In 1988, its winners were Bob Dole of Kansas and Dick Gephardt of Missouri, neither of whom remained in the race a month later. In 1992 its top two Democrats were Bob Kerrey of Nebraska and Tom Harkin of Iowa, both of whom were out of the race a month later. Among the Republicans, Pat Buchanan missed the filing deadline, and George Bush won 69% against an uncommitted slate.

The People: Est. Pop. 1992: 711,000; Pop. 1990: 696,004, up 2.1% 1990–1992. 0.3% of U.S. total, 45th largest; 50% rural. Median age: 32.5 years. 14.7% 65 years and over. 91.6% White, 7.3% American Indian. Households (1980): 58.9% married couple families; 29% married couple fams. w. children; 43% college educ.; median household income: $22,503; per capita income: $10,661; 66.1% owner occupied housing; median house value: $45,200; median monthly rent: $242. 3.1% Unemployment. Voting age pop.: 497,542. Registered voters (1992): 448,292; 189,935 D (42%); 215,285 R (48%); 43,072 unaffiliated and minor parties (10%).

Political Lineup: Governor, Walter D. Miller (R); Lt. Gov., vacant; Secy. of State, Joyce Hazeltine (R); Atty. Gen., Mark Barnett (R); Treasurer, G. Homer Harding (R); Auditor, Vernon L. Larson (R). State Senate, 35 (20 D and 15 R); State House of Representatives, 70 (41 R and 29 D). Senators, Larry Pressler (R) and Thomas A. Daschle (D). Representative, 1 D at large.

1992 Presidential Vote		
Bush (R)	136,718	(41%)
Clinton (D)	124,888	(37%)
Perot (I)	73,295	(22%)

1988 Presidential Vote		
Bush (R)	165,415	(53%)
Dukakis (D)	145,560	(47%)

1992 Democratic Presidential Primary		
Kerrey	23,892	(40%)
Harkin	15,023	(25%)
Clinton	11,375	(19%)
Tsongas	5,729	(10%)
Brown	2,300	(4%)

1992 Republican Presidential Primary		
Bush	30,964	(69%)
Uncommitted	13,707	(31%)

GOVERNOR

Gov. Walter D. Miller (R)

Assumed office Apr. 1993, term expires Jan. 1995; b. Oct. 5, 1925, New Underwood; home, New Underwood; Methodist; widowed.

Career: Rancher; SD House of Reps., 1967–86; Pres., Dakota National Life Insurance Co., 1970–85; SD Lt. Gov., 1986–93.

Office: Executive Office, State Capitol, Pierre 57501, 605-773-3212.

Election Results

1990 gen.	George S. Mickelson (R)	151,198	(59%)
	Bob L. Samuelson (D)	105,525	(41%)
1990 prim.	George S. Mickelson (R), unopposed		
1986 gen.	George S. Mickelson (R)	152,543	(52%)
	R. Lars Herseth (D)	141,898	(48%)

SENATORS

Sen. Larry Pressler (R)

Elected 1978, seat up 1996; b. Mar. 29, 1942, Humboldt; home, Humboldt; U. of SD, B.A. 1964, Rhodes Scholar, Oxford U., 1966, Harvard, M.A., J.D. 1971; Catholic; married (Harriet).

Career: Army, 1966–68 (Vietnam); U.S. House of Reps., 1974–78.

Offices: 283 RSOB 20510, 202-224-5842. Also 1923 6th Ave., #105-A, Aberdeen 57402, 605-226-7471; 112 Rushmore Mall, Rapid City 57701, 605-341-1185; and 309 Minnesota Ave., Sioux Falls 57102, 605-335-1990.

Committees: *Aging (Special)* (2d of 10 R). *Commerce, Science and Transportation* (3d of 9 R): Aviation (RMM); Communications; Foreign Commerce and Tourism; Science, Technology and Space. *Foreign Relations* (4th of 8 R): East Asian and Pacific Affairs; Near Eastern and South Asian Affairs; Terrorism, Narcotics and International Operations (RMM). *Judiciary* (8th of 8 R): Juvenile Justice; Technology and the Law. *Small Business* (RMM of 9 R): Export Expansion and Agricultural Development; Rural Economy and Family Farming (RMM); Urban and Minority-Owned Business Development.

Group Ratings

	ADA	ACLU	CDF	COPE	CFA	LCV	ACU	NTLC	NSI	COC	CEI
1992	20	5	20	17	33	8	85	83	100	90	71
1991	5	—	36	8	22	20	86	—	—	80	66

National Journal Ratings

	1991 LIB — 1991 CONS		1992 LIB — 1992 CONS	
Economic	15%	— 80%	15%	— 80%
Social	0%	— 86%	0%	— 89%
Foreign	13%	— 77%	43%	— 55%

Key Votes of the 102d Congress

1. $ for Homeownership	FOR	5. Clarence Thomas Nom. FOR	9. Use Force in Gulf	FOR
2. Have Cap Gains Debate FOR	6. Lmt Death Row Appeal FOR	10. Keep Salvador Aid	FOR
3. Remove Budget Walls AGN	7. Handgun Wait/5-Day AGN	11. Cut $1B from SDI	AGN
4. Ban Striker Replace AGN	8. Abortion Gag Rule FOR	12. Override China MFN AGN

1. $ for Homeownership FOR   5. Clarence Thomas Nom. FOR   9. Use Force in Gulf   FOR
2. Have Cap Gains Debate FOR   6. Lmt Death Row Appeal FOR   10. Keep Salvador Aid   FOR
3. Remove Budget Walls AGN   7. Handgun Wait/5-Day AGN   11. Cut $1B from SDI   AGN
4. Ban Striker Replace AGN   8. Abortion Gag Rule   FOR   12. Override China MFN AGN

Key Votes of the 103d Congress

1. Family Leave   AGN   2. HIV Immigrants   AGN   3. Clinton Budget   AGN

Election Results

1990 general	Larry Pressler (R)	135,682	(52%)	($2,124,359)
	Ted Muenster (D)	116,727	(45%)	($1,323,770)
	Other	6,567	(3%)	
1990 primary	Larry Pressler (R), unopposed			
1984 general	Larry Pressler (R)	235,176	(74%)	($1,155,683)
	George V. Cunningham (D)	80,537	(26%)	($166,426)

Sen. Thomas A. Daschle (D)

Elected 1986, seat up 1998; b. Dec. 9, 1947, Aberdeen; home, Aberdeen; SD St. U., B.A. 1969; Catholic; married (Linda).

Career: Air Force, 1969–72, Air Force Reserves, 1975–78; Legis. Asst., U.S. Sen. James Abourezk, 1972–77; U.S. House of Reps., 1978–86.

Offices: 317 HSOB 20510, 202-224-2321. Also P.O. Box 1274, Sioux Falls 57101, 605-334-9596; P.O. Box 1536, Aberdeen 57401, 605-225-8823; and P.O. Box 8168, Rapid City 57709, 605-348-3551.

Committees: *Agriculture, Nutrition and Forestry* (7th of 10 D): Agricultural Credit; Agricultural Research, Conservation, Forestry and General Legislation (Chmn.); Rural Development and Rural Electrification. *Ethics (Select)* (3d of 3 D). *Finance* (9th of 11 D): Energy and Agricultural Taxation (Chmn.); International Trade; Medicare and Long-Term Care. *Indian Affairs* (3d of 10 D). *Veterans' Affairs* (6th of 7 D).

Group Ratings

	ADA	ACLU	CDF	COPE	CFA	LCV	ACU	NTLC	NSI	COC	CEI
1992	95	73	90	75	92	58	22	22	60	20	16
1991	85	—	91	83	67	53	24	—	—	10	22

National Journal Ratings

	1991 LIB — 1991 CONS		1992 LIB — 1992 CONS	
Economic	75% —	21%	69% —	27%
Social	70% —	27%	64% —	34%
Foreign	86% —	0%	78% —	14%

Key Votes of the 102d Congress

1. $ for Homeownership	AGN	5. Clarence Thomas Nom.	AGN	9. Use Force in Gulf	AGN
2. Have Cap Gains Debate	AGN	6. Lmt Death Row Appeal	AGN	10. Keep Salvador Aid	AGN
3. Remove Budget Walls	FOR	7. Handgun Wait/5-Day	FOR	11. Cut $1B from SDI	FOR
4. Ban Striker Replace	FOR	8. Abortion Gag Rule	AGN	12. Override China MFN	FOR

Key Votes of the 103d Congress

1. Family Leave	FOR	2. HIV Immigrants	FOR	3. Clinton Budget	FOR

Election Results

1992 general	Thomas A. Daschle (D)	217,095	(65%)	($3,981,548)
	Charlene Haar (R)	108,733	(33%)	($478,421)
	Two Others	8,667	(3%)	
1992 primary	Thomas A. Daschle (D), unopposed			
1986 general	Thomas A. Daschle (D)	152,657	(52%)	($3,485,870)
	James Abnor (R).	143,173	(48%)	($3,410,387)

REPRESENTATIVE

Rep. Tim Johnson (D)

Elected 1986; b. Dec. 28, 1946, Canton; home, Vermillion; U. of SD, B.A. 1969, M.A. 1970, J.D. 1975; Lutheran; married (Barbara).

Career: Practicing atty., 1975–85; Clay Cnty. Dep. State Atty., 1985; SD House of Reps., 1978–82; SD Senate, 1982–86.

Offices: 2438 RHOB 20515, 202-225-2801. Also 1610 S. Dakota Ave., Sioux Falls 57102, 605-332-8896; 809 South St., #104, Rapid City 57709, 605-341-3990; and 615 S. Main, Aberdeen 57401, 605-226-3440.

Committees: *Agriculture* (9th of 28 D): Environment, Credit and Rural Development; General Farm Commodities (Chmn.). *Natural Resources* (14th of 28 D): National Parks, Forests and Public Lands; Native American Affairs.

Group Ratings

	ADA	ACLU	COPE	CDF	CFA	LCV	ACU	NTLC	NSI	COC	CEI
1992	70	61	67	80	80	69	32	5	50	50	22
1991	65	—	83	90	67	69	20	—	—	40	30

National Journal Ratings

	1991 LIB — 1991 CONS			1992 LIB — 1992 CONS		
Economic	56%	—	42%	64%	—	35%
Social	53%	—	47%	48%	—	51%
Foreign	56%	—	42%	69%	—	30%

Key Votes of the 102d Congress

1. Ban Striker Replace	FOR	5. Handgun Wait/7-Day	AGN	9. Use Force in Gulf	AGN
2. $ for Homeownership	FOR	6. Overseas Mil. Abortion	AGN	10. US Mil. Abroad $ Cut	FOR
3. Tax Rich/Cut Mid Cls.	FOR	7. Obscn. Art NEA $ Ban	FOR	11. Limit SDI Funds	FOR
4. FY93/$15B Def. Cut	FOR	8. Death Pen. from Jury	AGN	12. Cuba Trade Embargo	AGN

Key Votes of the 103d Congress

1. Family Leave	FOR	2. Deficit Reduction	AGN	3. Stimulus Plan	FOR

Election Results

1992 general	Tim Johnson (D).....................	230,070	(69%)	($376,741)
	John Timmer (R)	89,375	(27%)	($170,143)
	Three Others.........................	13,457	(4%)	
1992 primary	Tim Johnson (D), unopposed			
1990 general	Tim Johnson (D).....................	173,814	(68%)	($463,625)
	Don Frankenfeld (R).................	83,484	(32%)	($211,617)

TENNESSEE

Tennessee is economically the fastest-growing state in the Mississippi Valley South, yet the imprint of the past remains evident on the lives of ordinary people, and in the state's politics. Tennessee has four sizable metropolitan areas, but nearly half its people still live scattered in 79 mostly rural counties stretching 500 miles from Bristol to Memphis—often in the same counties where their ancestors settled in the years from 1796, when Tennessee was admitted to the Union, to 1829, when its first president, Andrew Jackson, rode off from the Hermitage on his way to the White House. The state was as feisty and quick to take umbrage as Old Hickory; it peopled the armies of our early wars so eagerly it became known as The Volunteer State; and it took sides so strongly in the Civil War that most of its counties today still vote their 1860s loyalties: the Union counties, mainly in the east but with a scattering to the west, vote solidly Republican, while the Confederate counties in middle and west Tennessee are heavily Democratic.

Within the limits of these enduring party loyalties, political entrepreneurs have set the tone for the state. From the 1920s to 1948, Edward Crump, longtime mayor of Memphis, used his total control of Democratic primary votes there to elect governors and senators. But the Tennessee Valley Authority and the cheap electric power it generated provided an institutional base for reform liberal Democrats Estes Kefauver and Albert Gore, Sr., elected to the Senate in 1948 and 1952. They were soon national figures, with reliable enough backing from Tennessee's yellow-dog Democratic majority to vote for civil rights bills and to refuse to sign the segregationist Southern Manifesto, and still thrive electorally.

Tennessee has never had a large black population—16% in 1990, half of whom live in and around Memphis—and the state was not riven by the racial animosity that seared so much of the South in the 1950s and 1960s, thanks in large part to the actions of its leading politicians, but also to the continuing hold of ancestral partisan preferences. Eventually, the Democrats' cultural liberalism on issues other than race moved west Tennessee voters away from their ancestral party, and moderate east Tennessee Republicans Howard Baker and Bill Brock, elected to the Senate in 1966 and 1970, set the state's tone; Baker protege Lamar Alexander, elected governor in 1978, instituted education reforms and attracted Japanese investment that have changed and strengthened the state over the last dozen or so years. But in the 1980s, the state reverted to its old basic divisions, and Tennessee Democrats now hold the governorship, both Senate seats, six of nine House seats and solid majorities in the state legislature—not to mention the vice presidency of the United States.

Tennessee's regional personalities remain distinct: the east is feisty and Republican, middle Tennessee has been devoutly Democratic since the days of Nashville's Andrew Jackson, the west is the one part that has long been racially polarized. The persistence of these differences is matched by the musical traditions which have made Tennessee, for many Americans, the music capital of the nation. Tennessee is associated with country music, but there are several strains to it. East Tennessee country music has been influenced by bluegrass and the mountain fiddling tradition, with string bands and vocal harmony. The country music first developed in Nashville 50 years ago, featuring solo singers in bands, seems rooted in the gospel music also centered in that city—which, as it happens, is also the nation's leading center of religious publishing. (Nashville's Grand Ole Opry, broadcast since 1925, and Knoxville's Tennessee Barn Dance, broadcast since 1942, have names suggesting the difference.) West Tennessee, the Mississippi lowlands around Memphis, is a northern extension of the Mississippi Delta, the part of America that gave birth to the blues in the 1890–1920 period. Memphis produced many musicians who drew on the blues tradition, from the jazz musicians of Beale Street in the 1920s, to Elvis Presley of Graceland mansion in the 1950s and 1960s.

Those traditions have remained as Tennessee has grown and prospered. While other states in the Mississippi Valley barely grew or even lost population, Tennessee gained 8.3% in the 1980s, and its boom town, metro Nashville, gained 16%, the biggest major metro growth between Atlanta and Dallas-Fort Worth. Tennessee has attracted more Japanese investment than any other state but California—starting in 1977 with a Nissan forklift distribution center, including the big Nissan pickup plant in Smyrna, amounting by 1990 to 56 factories and 34 distribution centers. The Japanese were attracted to Tennessee not just by financial concessions, but by its respect for tradition and hard work, its lack of strong unions and state corporate income taxes and (though they won't say so) its lack of minorities. They like the fact that Tennesseans do business with less lawyering and more ceremony than Americans in bigger states, and they were impressed when Lamar Alexander showed them satellite photos of the U.S. taken at night, indicating how many Americans live within a day's drive of Tennessee. It was Tennessee's lack of change—its absence of the institutions that sprang from the labor strife of the 1930s and the civil rights strife of the 1960s—that attracted the Japanese, and they in turn helped to attract General Motors' Saturn project to Spring Hill near Nashville.

The election of Vice President Albert Gore, Jr., elevates to national prominence the success of Democrats—and of scions of famous families—in Tennessee politics. Democrats now hold most of the top state posts, and many are the sons of prominent politicians: Congressmen Jimmy Duncan, Jim Cooper and Bob Clement, among others. But Tennessee has also generated ideas. Lamar Alexander enacted education reforms in Tennessee, primarily merit pay for teachers and teacher competency tests, and amplified these into a broader agenda as chairman of the National Governors Association in 1986 and as George Bush's hard-charging secretary of education in 1991. Governor Ned McWherter's proposed healthcare plan has made Tennessee an interesting laboratory of reform on that issue. And Albert Gore's concern about environmental trends, demonstrated in his book *Earth in the Balance*, shows a visionary quality not seen in many politicians. From a state where the American past is vividly present may come harbingers of the American future.

Governor. Completing more than two decades at the top of Tennessee politics, 14 years as speaker of the House and two four-year terms as governor, Ned McWherter, son of a west

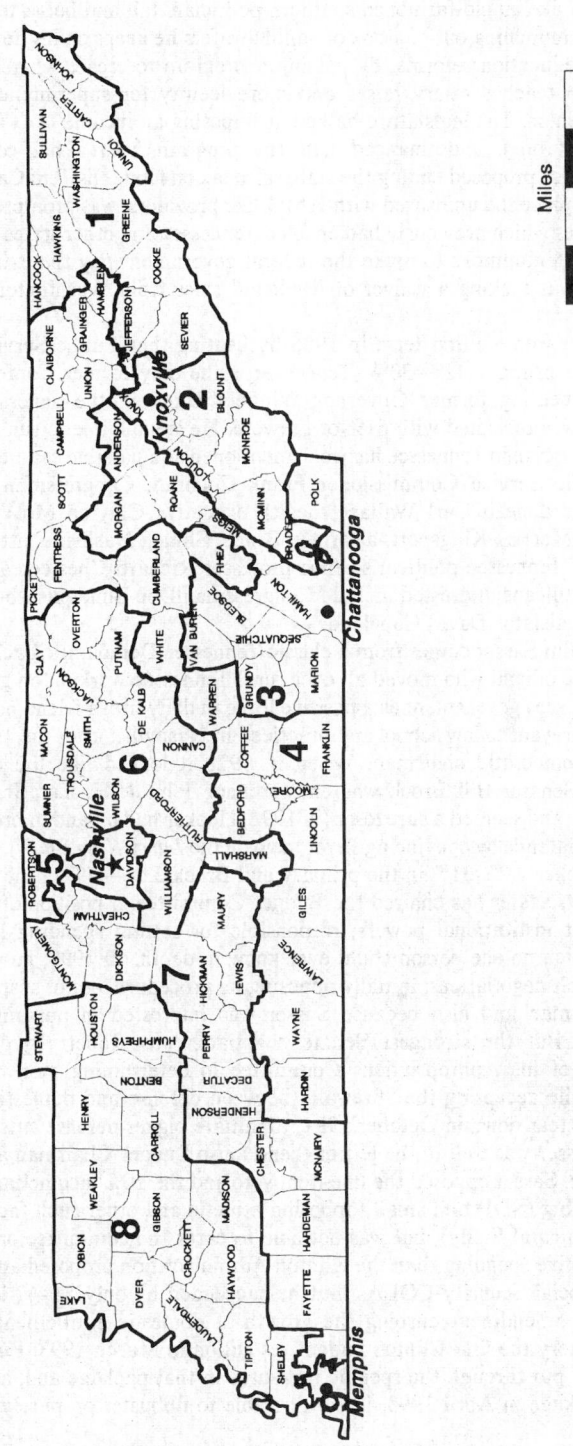

Tennessee sharecropper, has left a notable record. McWherter, who never graduated from college, looks like an old-fashioned southern politician: tall and hefty, telling droll stories in his thick accent, munching out of a box of vanilla wafers he keeps on his desk. McWherter built on Alexander's education reforms, by passing a program to create what he called 21st Century Schools, with teacher salary raises and more leeway for superintendents and principals in choosing teachers. The legislature balked at imposing an income tax (Tennessee is one of nine states without one), and financed half the program with a half-cent sales tax increase. McWherter also proposed ending the state sales tax on food. His TennCare healthcare program, which would place the uninsured with HMO-like providers, was prompted by abrupt changes in Medicaid rules which previously had enabled Tennessee and other states to increase benefits and use accounting gimmicks to make the federal government pay the extra costs. In June 1993, McWherter was seeking a waiver of Medicaid rules from Washington to go ahead with the program.

McWherter won his first term in 1986 by beating then-Public Service Commissioner Jane Eskind in the primary 42%–30% (Tennessee is the only former Confederate state without a runoff) and beating former Governor Winfield Dunn in the general 54%–46%. In 1990, McWherter was reelected with 61% of the vote. He is ineligible to run in 1994, and just about every live politician in Tennessee has been mentioned as a possible candidate. Democratic names include Public Service Commissioner Frank Cochran, Congressman Bob Clement, former National Guard head Carl Wallace, health executive Clayton McWhorter, Shelby County Mayor Bill Morris, Kingsport attorney Bruce Shine, Nashville attorney Walter Bussart, University of Tennessee political science professor Richard Chesteen and state Senator Steve Cohen. Republicans interested include Congressman Don Sundquist, businessman Bob Corker and former legislator David Copeland.

Senators. Jim Sasser comes from a classic Tennessee Democratic background; his father was an agriculture official who moved all over rural Tennessee working on government programs, a tradition that sees government as a positive force in daily life, a friend not an enemy of ordinary people. Sasser went to law school and practiced in Nashville; after the 1972 election he became Tennessee Democratic chairman. When in 1976 it looked like the only candidate against Republican Senator Bill Brock was entrepreneur John J. Hooker, Jr., who had lost a 1970 governor race and seemed a sure loser (in 1992, Hooker had a hand in propelling Ross Perot into the presidential race by convincing Perot to go on the *Larry King Show*), Sasser entered the race and beat Hooker 44%–31% in the primary and Brock 52%–47% in the general.

Since 1989, Sasser has chaired the Budget Committee, a position often in the spotlight but without great institutional powers, responsible for setting spending levels for thousands of programs which no one person could ever know in depth. In 1990, he was part of the lengthy budget summit negotiations, initially opposing its procedure, out of suspicion of OMB Director Richard Darman and also because Sasser was interested in pursuing other deficit-cutting mechanisms. But the strongest Senate negotiator was Robert Byrd, who insisted on the prerogatives of his Appropriations Committee in determining more discretionary domestic spending, while accepting the "firewall" between defense and domestic spending that Sasser was trying to tear down in October 1991, to initiate bigger defense cuts and a middle-class tax cut. Here Sasser was well to the left of then-House Budget Chairman and now OMB Director Leon Panetta. Sasser opposed the line-item veto and the 10% income tax checkoff; he proposed defense cuts big (SDI) and small (opposing athletic and other such facilities at a planned Air Force base in rural Sicily), but was not able to carry the committee or the Senate. He favors more stimulative spending than the Clinton Administration proposed and is absolutely opposed to cutting Social Security COLAs, but he succeeded by only 51–47 in beating Sam Nunn's March 1993 amendment curbing the growth of domestic entitlement programs. Sasser did propel to victory the first Clinton budget resolution in March 1993. But it's not clear that the votes exist to put through the specific measures in that package and, as shown on the Clinton stimulus package in April 1993, it is vulnerable to filibuster on purely partisan issues. Sasser seems aware of the problem: in January 1993 he said Clinton will "have a very difficult, if not an impossible, task in cutting the deficit in half by 1997."

Over the years, Sasser has kept in touch with Tennessee, visiting each of the state's 95 counties once a year, hiking through the Cherokee National Forest to see how much timber is harvested, boating over Kentucky Lake to see how the fish are affected by water pollution. He has done well at the ballot box. In 1982, against a hawkish congressman, and in 1988, against an east Tennessee lawyer, Sasser won with more than 60% of the vote, carrying 94 of 95 counties the second time—an almost unheard of feat in a state where partisan loyalties run so deep. In 1994, with both of Tennessee's Senate seats up, Sasser's will presumably be the less attractive target for Republicans, and so his reelection prospects look good.

Tennessee's junior senator until January 1993 was Albert Gore, Jr., scion of a great political family and an important force in his own right even before his selection in July 1992 as Bill Clinton's running mate. His father Albert Gore, Sr., was a county school superintendent who was elected to the House in 1938 from a yellow-dog Democratic district in middle Tennessee; he went on to the Senate in 1952, beating a crusty conservative incumbent, and was a leading liberal there, supporting civil rights bills, opposing the Vietnam war and voting against Nixon Supreme Court appointees; his narrow defeat by Republican Bill Brock in 1970 came after one of the hardest-fought and most colorful campaigns of our times. Al Gore, Jr., served in the Army in Vietnam, went to divinity school and became a reporter for the *Nashville Tennessean*; when an incumbent retired in 1976, he was easily elected to the House and easily won the Senate seat when Howard Baker retired in 1984. He supported traditional Democratic positions on economics, took a harder line than most Democrats on foreign policy and developed the interest in science and the environment which, together with his articulateness, made him such a popular vice presidential candidate.

The choice to succeed Gore belonged to Governor Ned McWherter. His first choice, Congressman John Tanner, from just a county over from McWherter in west Tennessee, turned the job down. Many then expected McWherter to name Congressman Jim Cooper, who was plainly interested in the seat. Instead, McWherter chose Harlan Mathews, who at 65 had been his top aide and closest friend for many years. Mathews was elected state treasurer by the legislature in 1974, managed McWherter's 1986 campaign and then became his cabinet secretary in 1987. He was criticized, but never charged with wrongdoing, for depositing state funds in banks controlled by the Butcher brothers, big Democratic contributors later convicted of fraud. Mathews said he would only serve for two years and would not run in the November 1994 special election for the last two years of Gore's term. On issues, he described himself as a "fiscal conservative" and said he would vote as Gore did—though there is a bit of tension between the two. He serves on the Foreign Relations, Energy and Rules Committees.

The 1994 race for this seat began even before it was filled in 1993. Congressman Jim Cooper, son of former Governor Prentice Cooper and an active member of the Energy and Commerce Committee, seemed a sure candidate; former Public Services Commissioner Jane Eskind is another possibility; Republican Fred Thompson, Howard Baker's chief aide on the Senate Watergate committee and later a movie actor as well as a Nashville lawyer, was said to be interested, while former Governor Lamar Alexander, pondering a national candidacy in 1996, was not. In May 1993, Mathews startled everyone by registering a campaign committee; McWherter, who had endorsed Cooper, advised Mathews to "go home and get a good night's sleep." Mathews's intent may just be to use the campaign committee as a source of funds for expenses not reimbursable by the government, but he left the door open to running; perhaps this is leverage to get what he has been rumored to want all along, a seat on the TVA board in 1995. In any case, there should be a riproaring Senate race in Tennessee in 1994, the most wide open at least since 1984 or maybe even 1976.

Presidential politics. The unique continuity in Tennessee politics comes out in presidential elections. Tennessee gave George Bush in 1988 the same 58% it gave Ronald Reagan in 1984; it went for Ronald Reagan over Jimmy Carter in 1980 by almost exactly the same small margin—

not just statewide, but in almost every county—that it gave Dwight Eisenhower over Adlai Stevenson in 1952 and 1956. The margin for the Bill Clinton-Al Gore ticket, 47%–42%, was just a bit better—which would be expected with a Tennessean on the ticket. Indeed, Al Gore's Tennessee was one of three jurisdictions—Bill Clinton's Arkansas and the federal government's District of Columbia were the other two—where the Democratic percentage for president in 1992's three-candidate race was notably higher than in 1988's two-party race. Tennessee's presidential primary is held on Super Tuesday; the easy winners in 1992 were those two southern moderates, Bill Clinton and George Bush.

Congressional districting. Tennessee needed only minor changes to get its districts back to equal population after the 1990 Census. Democrats controlled the process, and the new map increased their percentages in Democrat Marilyn Lloyd's 3d District and the 7th District seat Republican Don Sundquist seems likely to vacate to run for governor in 1994. Tennessee was the largest state to reelect all its House members in anti-incumbent 1992; that won't happen in 1994, since Jim Cooper seems sure to run for senator, and Don Sundquist and Bob Clement may well run for governor.

The People: Est. Pop. 1992: 5,024,000; Pop. 1990: 4,877,185, up 2.9% 1990–1992. 2.0% of U.S. total, 17th largest; 39% rural. Median age: 33.6 years. 12.7% 65 years and over. 83.0% White, 16.0% Black. Households: 57.2% married couple families; 26% married couple fams. w. children; 37% college educ.; median household income: $24,807; per capita income: $12,255; 68.0% owner occupied housing; median house value: $58,400; median monthly rent: $273. 6.4% Unemployment. Voting age pop.: 3,660,581. Registered voters (1992): 2,726,449; no party registration.

Political Lineup: Governor, Ned McWherter (D); Lt. Gov., John S. Wilder (D); Secy. of State, Riley C. Darnell (D); Atty. Gen., Charles W. Burson (D); Treasurer, Steve Adams (D); Comptroller, William Snodgrass (D). State Senate, 33 (19 D and 14 R); State House of Representatives, 99 (63 D and 36 R). Senators, James R. (Jim) Sasser (D) and Harlan Mathews (D). Representatives, 9 (6 D and 3 R).

1992 Presidential Vote			1988 Presidential Vote		
Clinton (D)	933,521	(47%)	Bush (R)	947,233	(58%)
Bush (R)	841,300	(42%)	Dukakis (D)	679,794	(42%)
Perot (I)	199,968	(10%)			

1992 Democratic Presidential Primary			1992 Republican Presidential Primary		
Clinton	214,485	(67%)	Bush	178,219	(73%)
Tsongas	61,717	(19%)	Buchanan	54,585	(22%)
Brown	25,560	(8%)	Other, Uncommitted	12,849	(5%)
Uncommitted	12,551	(4%)			

GOVERNOR

Gov. Ned McWherter (D)

Elected 1986, term expires Jan. 1995; b. Oct. 15, 1930, Palmersville; home, Nashville; United Methodist; single.

Career: Farmer, businessman; TN House of Reps., 1969–86, Speaker, 1973–86.

Office: State Capitol, 7th Ave. & Charlotte, Nashville 37243, 615-741-2001.

Election Results

1990 gen.	Ned McWherter (D)	480,885	(61%)
	Dwight Henry (R)	289,348	(37%)
	Other	20,148	(3%)
1990 prim.	Ned McWherter (D), unopposed		
1986 gen.	Ned McWherter (D)	656,602	(54%)
	Winfield Dunn (R)	553,449	(46%)

SENATORS

Sen. James R. (Jim) Sasser (D)

Elected 1976, seat up 1994; b. Sept. 30, 1936, Memphis; home, Nashville; Vanderbilt U., B.A. 1958, J.D. 1961; United Methodist; married (Mary).

Career: Marine Corps Reserves, 1957–63; Practicing atty., 1961–76; Chmn., TN St. Dem. Party, 1973–76.

Offices: 363 RSOB 20510, 202-224-3344. Also 569 U.S. Crthse., Nashville 37203, 615-736-7353; 239 Fed. Bldg., Chattanooga 37402, 615-756-8836; 320 P.O. Bldg., Knoxville 37902, 615-545-4264; 390 Fed. Bldg., 167 N. Main, Memphis 38103, 901-544-4187; U.S. P.O. Bldg., B-8, Jackson 38301, 901-424-6600; and Tri-City Airport, Blountville 37617, 615-323-6207.

Committees: *Appropriations* (6th of 16 D): Commerce, Justice, State and Judiciary; Defense; Energy and Water Development; Military Construction (Chmn.); Transportation. *Banking, Housing and Urban Affairs* (4th of 11 D): International Finance and Monetary Policy (Chmn.); Securities. *Budget* (Chmn. of 12 D). *Governmental Affairs* (4th of 8 D): Federal Services, Post Office and Civil Service; General Services, Federalism and the District of Columbia (Chmn.); Permanent Subcommittee on Investigations. *Joint Committee on the Organization of Congress* (2d of 12).

Group Ratings

	ADA	ACLU	CDF	COPE	CFA	LCV	ACU	NTLC	NSI	COC	CEI
1992	95	77	90	83	92	50	7	11	40	10	19
1991	90	—	91	83	83	53	5	—	—	0	22

National Journal Ratings

	1991 LIB — 1991 CONS		1992 LIB — 1992 CONS	
Economic	90% —	3%	80% —	17%
Social	73% —	23%	62% —	36%
Foreign	78% —	14%	86% —	0%

Key Votes of the 102d Congress

1. $ for Homeownership	AGN	5. Clarence Thomas Nom. AGN	9. Use Force in Gulf AGN
2. Have Cap Gains Debate AGN		6. Lmt Death Row Appeal AGN	10. Keep Salvador Aid AGN
3. Remove Budget Walls	FOR	7. Handgun Wait/5-Day FOR	11. Cut $1B from SDI FOR
4. Ban Striker Replace	FOR	8. Abortion Gag Rule AGN	12. Override China MFN FOR

Key Votes of the 103d Congress

1. Family Leave	FOR	2. HIV Immigrants	AGN	3. Clinton Budget	FOR

Election Results

1988 general	James R. (Jim) Sasser (D) 1,020,061	(65%)	($3,069,615)
	Bill Andersen (R) 541,033	(35%)	($612,421)
1988 primary	James R. (Jim) Sasser (D), unopposed		
1982 general	James R. (Jim) Sasser (D) 780,113	(62%)	($2,091,872)
	Robin L. Beard (R)................... 479,642	(38%)	($1,639,858)

Sen. Harlan Mathews (D)

Appointed Jan. 1993, seat up 1994; b. Jan. 17, 1927, Sumiton, AL; home, Nashville; Jacksonville St. Col., B.A. 1949, Vanderbilt U., M.A. 1950, Nashville Schl. of Law, J.D. 1962; Baptist; married (Patsy).

Career: Navy, 1944–46 (WWII); TN Comm. of Finance, 1961–71; Sr. V.P., Amcon Intl. Inc., 1971–73; TN St. Treasurer, 1974–87; Dep. & Cabinet Secy., Gov. McWherter, 1987-93.

Offices: 505 DSOB 20515, 202-224-1036. Also 403 Fed. Bldg., 167 N. Main St., Memphis 38103, 901-544-4224; B-9 Fed. Bldg., 109 S. Highland St., Jackson 38301, 901-424-0505; 3322 West Ends Ave., #120, Nashville 37203, 615-736-5129; 315 P.O. Bldg., Knoxville 37902, 615-545-4253; 256 Fed. Bldg., 900 Georgia Ave., Chattanooga 37402, 615-756-1328; and Tri-City Airport, Blountville 37616, 615-323-6217.

Committees: *Energy and Natural Resources* (10th of 11 D): Energy Research and Development; Mineral Resources Development and Production (Vice Chmn.); Renewable Energy, Energy Efficiency, and Competitiveness. *Foreign Relations* (11th of 11 D): East Asian and Pacific Affairs; Near Eastern and South Asian Affairs; Western Hemisphere and Peace Corps Affairs. *Rules and Administration* (9th of 9 D). *Joint Committee on Printing* (3d of 5).

Group Ratings and 102d Congress Votes: Newly Appointed

Key Votes of the 103d Congress

1. Family Leave	FOR	2. HIV Immigrants	AGN	3. Clinton Budget	FOR

Election Results

1990 general	Albert Gore, Jr. (D)	530,898	(68%)	($1,905,865)
	William R. Hawkins (R)...............	233,703	(30%)	($6,510)
	Other.................................	19,321	(2%)	
1990 primary	Albert Gore, Jr. (D), unopposed			
1984 general	Albert Gore, Jr. (D)	1,000,607	(61%)	($3,035,498)
	Victor Ashe (R)......................	557,016	(34%)	($1,777,581)
	Ed McAteer (I).......................	87,234	(5%)	

FIRST DISTRICT

Between the corduroy-like ridges of the Appalachian chains, as they bend west and then south, the valley of Virginia extends far into northeastern Tennessee. Two great movements have made its history. The first, right after the Revolutionary War, was the rush of settlers over the mountains and through these valleys; here in tiny Jonesborough the early settlers established the free state of Franklin in 1784, and many pioneer cabins, federal mansions and Greek Revival churches are lovingly preserved. The second movement was the building of the railroads in the 1850s. Other Appalachian areas were cut off from the rest of America, with railroads serving only coal mines. But the small industrial cities that had grown up here—Johnson City, Kingsport, Bristol—were on the main lines of national commerce even before the Civil War. The War had a different political effect here than in most of the South: northeast Tennessee, the home of wartime Governor and then Vice President Andrew Johnson, had few slaves and with its connection to northern industry was Union territory; it remains heavily Republican to this day.

The political continuity is all the more surprising because this area has had continuous economic growth and has developed the sort of industrial economy which produced unions and Democrats in the North. Its growth has been helped by modest wage levels, a skilled and hard-working labor force, low electric power rates because of the TVA and good transportation routes (rail lines and now Interstate 81). Its small cities boast major paper and printing plants, and have the look of comfortable, clean, 1920s factory towns. Growth has been rapid only in Sevier County, where Gatlinburg and Pigeon Forge are the main tourist centers—5,000 motel rooms, dozens of tourist attractions—for travelers to the Great Smoky Mountains National Park.

The far northeastern end of the state forms the 1st Congressional District of Tennessee, a district so heavily Republican that it has not elected a Democrat to the House for more than 100 years. Nonetheless, it has had turbulent politics on occasion. For almost 40 years (1921–61, with one two-year hiatus), the seat was held by B. Carroll Reece, a fierce mountain politician who was once Republican National Committee chairman. After Reece died in 1961, and his widow was elected to fill out his term, there was a hotly contested primary here, the winner of which, Jimmy Quillen, has held the seat ever since. Quillen is a bread-and-butter politician, a former owner of the *Johnson City Times* interested in doing things for his district. He takes great pride in the establishment of what now is the James H. Quillen College of Medicine at East Tennessee State University and in the James H. and Cecile C. Quillen Center for Rehabilitative Medicine, both in Johnson City. The medical school seems to be his pride and joy: Quillen remembered that the 1986 Republican gubernatorial nominee, Winfield Dunn, had vetoed the College of Medicine when he was governor in the early 1970s, and his conspicuous coolness toward Dunn helped Democrat Ned McWherter carry the 1st District, a key to his 54% statewide victory. Quillen also maintained a good relationship with Democratic Senator Jim Sasser in 1988, when Sasser was opposed by a Kingsport lawyer who had earlier been thinking about taking on Quillen; Sasser carried the 1st too. Quillen prides himself on keeping in touch, and on his "open door" policy of taking his entire district staff to each county in the district during off-election years.

Most of Quillen's contemporaries have long left the House. He was persuaded, by his wife's illness he said, to give up his ranking minority position on the Rules Committee in 1991 to the more partisanly combative Gerald Solomon. But he did not retire, as some expected, in 1992, though he could have converted over $1 million in campaign money to personal funds had he done so. He won reelection, as usual, by a wide margin, in a district every county of which voted for George Bush over Bill Clinton. In March 1993, Quillen had heart bypass surgery at 77, but seemed to recover quickly. "I'm anxious to get back in harness again, to control our runaway president," he said. "I have no plans not to run again."

The People: Pop. 1990: 541,978; 53% rural; 14% age 65+; 97% White; 2% Black. Voting age pop.: 419,046; 2% Black. Households: 63% married couple families; 27% married couple fams. w. children; 31% college educ.; median household income: $21,952; per capita income: $11,024; median gross rent: $295; median house value: $51,200.

1992 Presidential Vote			1988 Presidential Vote		
Bush (R)	107,515	(51%)	Bush (R)	120,132	(68%)
Clinton (D)	76,113	(36%)	Dukakis (D)	55,907	(32%)
Perot (I)	24,358	(12%)			

Rep. James H. (Jimmy) Quillen (R)

Elected 1962; b. Jan. 11, 1916, Wayland, VA; home, Kingsport; United Methodist; married (Cecile).

Career: Navy, 1942–46 (WWII); *Kingsport Press*, 1934–35; *Kingsport Times*, 1935–36; Founder, publ., *Johnson City Times*, 1939–44; TN House of Reps., 1955–62, Minority Ldr., 1959–60.

Offices: 102 CHOB 20515, 202-225-6356. Also Fed. P.O. Bldg., #157, Kingsport 37662, 615-247-8161.

Committees: *Rules* (2d of 4 R): The Legislative Process (RMM).

Group Ratings

	ADA	ACLU	COPE	CDF	CFA	LCV	ACU	NTLC	NSI	COC	CEI
1992	5	4	33	10	27	6	92	84	90	75	61
1991	5	—	33	40	44	0	90	—	—	80	46

National Journal Ratings

	1991 LIB — 1991 CONS		1992 LIB — 1992 CONS	
Economic	18% —	79%	16% —	80%
Social	0% —	84%	21% —	78%
Foreign	31% —	67%	26% —	72%

Key Votes of the 102d Congress

1. Ban Striker Replace	AGN	5. Handgun Wait/7-Day	AGN	9. Use Force in Gulf	FOR
2. $ for Homeownership	FOR	6. Overseas Mil. Abortion	AGN	10. US Mil. Abroad $ Cut	AGN
3. Tax Rich/Cut Mid Cls.	AGN	7. Obscn. Art NEA $ Ban	FOR	11. Limit SDI Funds	AGN
4. FY93/$15B Def. Cut	*	8. Death Pen. from Jury	FOR	12. Cuba Trade Embargo	FOR

Key Votes of the 103d Congress

1. Family Leave	AGN	2. Deficit Reduction	AGN	3. Stimulus Plan	*

Election Results

1992 general	James H. (Jimmy) Quillen (R)	114,797	(68%)	($325,383)
	J. Carr (Jack) Christian (D)	47,809	(28%)	
	Two Others	7,552	(4%)	
1992 primary	James H. (Jimmy) Quillen (R), unopposed			
1990 general	James H. (Jimmy) Quillen (R), unopposed			($263,291)

SECOND DISTRICT

Knoxville, the largest city in east Tennessee, is nestled between mountain ridges where the Holston and French Broad Rivers join to form the Tennessee. It was established not long after the first wave of pioneers came through the gaps and down between the mountains of the Appalachian chain. During the Civil War it was Union territory, and has remained Republican in allegiance ever since: the ancestral tug of Tennessee politics. But its Republican heritage is tempered by another tradition, that of the Tennessee Valley Authority. A venturesome program when created in the 1930s, it is now part of the fabric of life in east Tennessee, sometimes criticized as its cheap hydroelectric power capacity was filled and more of its production came from expensive and sometimes poorly functioning nuclear plants. But TVA cut its payroll from 35,000 to 21,000 from 1988 to 1992 and hasn't raised rates since 1987: a big organization reformed at the command of the marketplace.

The 2d Congressional District of Tennessee, which includes Knoxville and several mountainous counties to the south, is one of the most reliably Republican districts in the nation—but also one of the more practical-minded. The congressman, Jimmy Duncan, is similarly inclined; his father represented the district from 1964 until his death in 1988. Jimmy Duncan, Jr., then a criminal court judge, had fierce competition in Democrat Dudley Taylor, from a family long prominent in east Tennessee politics, and a wounded Vietnam veteran. Taylor attacked Duncan, a contemporary of Dan Quayle, for signing up with the National Guard after drawing a low draft number. He also attacked Duncan for his ties to convicted banker Jake Butcher. But Duncan won with 57% in the special election to fill out his father's term and 56% in the election for the 101st Congress—well below usual Republican showings here, but an unambiguous victory.

Duncan's main work in the House has been to oppose what he considers ridiculous federal spending. He claimed to identify $78 million of unnecessary spending on the new Secret Service headquarters. He got the House to approve his amendment to eliminate $12 million from NASA's budget earmarked for the search for extraterrestrial intelligence, "a project which has spent millions of dollars with little or no results," he says leaving a loophole open. He has crusaded against the Corps of Engineers' plan to restore Florida's Kissimmee River to its original shape after spending millions to straighten it out. Duncan has, however, obtained money for local projects like resurfacing the Foothills Parkway in the Great Smoky Park, a $40 million federal judicial center in Knoxville, a $1.25 million grant to help Kimberly-Clark expand its operation in Loudon County and a $1 million grant to help put local public TV Channel 15 on the air. He has won reelection easily and in 1993 he became ranking Republican on the Public Buildings and Grounds Subcommittee of Public Works.

The People: Pop. 1990: 541,780; 36% rural; 13% age 65+; 92% White; 6% Black; 1% Asian; 1% Hispanic origin. Voting age pop.: 416,979; 6% Black. Households: 59% married couple families; 26% married couple fams. w. children; 41% college educ.; median household income: $25,267; per capita income: $13,118; median gross rent: $337; median house value: $59,400.

1992 Presidential Vote

Bush (R) 107,920 (48%)
Clinton (D) 92,752 (41%)
Perot (I) 25,157 (11%)

1988 Presidential Vote

Bush (R) 118,578 (65%)
Dukakis (D) 64,249 (35%)

Rep. John J. Duncan, Jr. (R)

Elected 1988; b. July 21, 1947, Lebanon; home, Knoxville; U. of TN, B.S. 1969, George Washington U., J.D. 1973; Presbyterian; married (Lynn).

Career: Army Natl. Guard & Army Reserves, 1970–87; Practicing atty., 1973–81; St. Trial Judge, 1981–88.

Offices: 115 CHOB 20515, 202-225-5435. Also 318 P.O. Bldg., Knoxville 37902, 615-523-3772; 200 E. Broadway, #419, Maryville 37801, 615-984-5464; and Crthse., Athens 37303, 615-745-4671.

Committees: *Natural Resources* (7th of 15 R): National Parks, Forests and Public Lands; Oversight and Investigations. *Public Works and Transportation* (7th of 24 R): Aviation; Investigations and Oversight; Public Buildings and Grounds (RMM).

Group Ratings

	ADA	ACLU	COPE	CDF	CFA	LCV	ACU	NTLC	NSI	COC	CEI
1992	25	9	42	20	33	6	84	100	70	63	87
1991	20	—	33	30	56	8	100	—	—	80	84

National Journal Ratings

	1991 LIB — 1991 CONS		1992 LIB — 1992 CONS	
Economic	23%	— 76%	26%	— 73%
Social	0%	— 84%	0%	— 85%
Foreign	26%	— 74%	44%	— 50%

Key Votes of the 102d Congress

1. Ban Striker Replace	AGN	5. Handgun Wait/7-Day	AGN	9. Use Force in Gulf	FOR
2. $ for Homeownership	FOR	6. Overseas Mil. Abortion	AGN	10. US Mil. Abroad $ Cut	FOR
3. Tax Rich/Cut Mid Cls.	AGN	7. Obscn. Art NEA $ Ban	FOR	11. Limit SDI Funds	FOR
4. FY93/$15B Def. Cut	AGN	8. Death Pen. from Jury	FOR	12. Cuba Trade Embargo	FOR

Key Votes of the 103d Congress

1. Family Leave	AGN	2. Deficit Reduction	AGN	3. Stimulus Plan	AGN

Election Results

1992 general	John J. Duncan, Jr. (R)	148,377	(72%)	($170,836)
	Troy Goodale (D)	52,887	(26%)	($6,471)
	Other	4,137	(2%)	
1992 primary	John J. Duncan, Jr. (R), unopposed			
1990 general	John J. Duncan, Jr. (R)	62,797	(81%)	($200,935)
	Peter Hebert (I)	15,127	(19%)	

THIRD DISTRICT

Through some of the most vivid scenery of the Appalachian chain, etching its way through the serrated ridges of east Tennessee, is the river that gave Tennessee its name. From Knoxville, the river cuts through a ridge and then plunges down a long valley to the city of Chattanooga at the Georgia line. There it switches course again, winding around the table-top Lookout Mountain and then moving into northern Alabama. This is the land of the 3d Congressional District of Tennessee. Chattanooga, its largest city, was just a village when it was a Civil War battlefield; it grew into an industrial city after the War. It is now trying to revive its riverfront with the 12-story-high Tennessee Aquarium, the world's largest fresh water aquarium which opened in April 1992; it includes an exhibit in which you can follow the course of a drop of rain from the headwaters of the Tennessee until it flows out the Mississippi River into the ocean.

The 3d Congressional District of Tennessee is centered on Chattanooga, with an irregular shape that has a political provenance. It reaches far north to take in the Democratic area around Oak Ridge, site of the nuclear laboratory, but avoids heavily Republican counties on either side of this salient; it reaches east to the North Carolina line and west to the Cumberland Plateau to take in more Democratic areas. All this is necessary because Chattanooga has been trending Republican in recent years, evidently pinning its hopes for growth more on the private sector, which developed the Aquarium among other attractions, and less on public sector institutions like the Tennessee Valley Authority, which has laid off more than a third of its work force.

The congresswoman from the 3d District is Marilyn Lloyd. First elected in 1974, she has been through a harrowing set of experiences in her two decades in congressional politics. She won in the Watergate year of 1974 after her husband, the Democratic nominee, died in a plane crash; she was named to replace him on the ballot and beat a shaky Republican incumbent. She got in trouble in the early 1980s when she was unable to deliver on a major district project, the Clinch River breeder reactor, a TVA cause that struck most members as wildly uneconomic. Lloyd won with only 52% and 54% in her next two elections, thanks to big margins in Oak Ridge. In 1987, she announced she was retiring, but ran again in 1988.

Lloyd now has a voting record moderate on economics and cultural issues and very hawkish on defense and foreign policy; but she also told military leaders in debate following the Tailhook scandal that "Men must accept women as human beings, not as sex objects." She switched to pro-choice on abortion in 1992. She is the second ranking Democrat on the Science Committee and has worked on nuclear research and cleanup, technology transfer and the role of the national laboratories. She had a brush with breast cancer, and has worked on the Breast Cancer Screening Safety Act and introduced a Breast Implant Informed Decision Act; she wants to create a housing ombudsmen program to assist the elderly in public housing. In 1992, Lloyd was clearly aided by redistricting, but faced an aggressive challenge from 34-year-old Republican Zach Wamp, a real estate broker who campaigned for spending cuts, term limits and against the Democratic Congress. At the beginning of the campaign, Wamp revealed that he had once had a cocaine problem and he had undergone treatment for it 10 years ago. Lloyd said she wanted to reform Congress too, and brought up Wamp's "criminal" past (two bad checks for $20 written while he was in college) and litigation against his real estate firm; he called these "vicious, personal attacks." Democrats had hoped that the Clinton-Gore ticket would help, but it ran even with Bush-Quayle in the district. Wamp carried Chattanooga and Hamilton County 51%–44%, but lost the area around Oak Ridge 60%–36%; overall Lloyd won by just 49%–47%, the closest margin of her career. She was running almost precisely even with Clinton, which suggests that she may well have serious opposition in 1994, and that her fate may depend on the popularity of the administration. Wamp has announced he will run again in 1994.

The People: Pop. 1990: 542,065; 35% rural; 14% age 65+; 87% White; 12% Black; 1% Asian; 1% Hispanic origin. Voting age pop.: 410,463; 11% Black; 1% Hispanic origin. Households: 59% married

1184   TENNESSEE

couple families; 26% married couple fams. w. children; 38% college educ.; median household income: $24,687; per capita income: $12,338; median gross rent: $348; median house value: $55,000.

1992 Presidential Vote

Clinton (D)	97,112	(44%)
Bush (R)	97,073	(44%)
Perot (I)	25,719	(12%)

1988 Presidential Vote

Bush (R)	119,222	(61%)
Dukakis (D)	75,533	(39%)

Rep. Marilyn Lloyd (D)

Elected 1974; b. Jan. 3, 1929, Ft. Smith, AR; home, Chattanooga; U. of AL, 1953; Shorter Col., 1958–60; Church of Christ; married (Robert Fowler).

Career: Co-owner and mgr., WTTI Radio, Dalton, GA, 1965–72.

Offices: 2406 RHOB 20515, 202-225-3271. Also 253 Jay Solomon Fed. Bldg., Chattanooga 37401, 615-267-9108; and 1211 Joe L. Evins Fed. Bldg., Oak Ridge 37830, 615-576-1977.

Committees: *Armed Services* (7th of 34 D): Military Acquisition. *Science, Space and Technology* (2d of 33 D): Energy (Chmn.); Investigations and Oversight.

Group Ratings

	ADA	ACLU	COPE	CDF	CFA	LCV	ACU	NTLC	NSI	COC	CEI
1992	45	41	64	50	67	25	50	63	80	63	39
1991	30	—	82	70	56	38	50	—	—	33	26

National Journal Ratings

	1991 LIB — 1991 CONS		1992 LIB — 1992 CONS	
Economic	49%	— 50%	44%	— 55%
Social	29%	— 70%	45%	— 55%
Foreign	39%	— 60%	0%	— 82%

Key Votes of the 102d Congress

1. Ban Striker Replace	FOR	5. Handgun Wait/7-Day	FOR	9. Use Force in Gulf	FOR
2. $ for Homeownership	AGN	6. Overseas Mil. Abortion	AGN	10. US Mil. Abroad $ Cut	AGN
3. Tax Rich/Cut Mid Cls.	AGN	7. Obscn. Art NEA $ Ban	FOR	11. Limit SDI Funds	AGN
4. FY93/$15B Def. Cut	FOR	8. Death Pen. from Jury	FOR	12. Cuba Trade Embargo	FOR

Key Votes of the 103d Congress

1. Family Leave	FOR	2. Deficit Reduction	FOR	3. Stimulus Plan	FOR

Election Results

1992 general	Marilyn Lloyd (D)	105,693	(49%)	($637,790)
	Zach Wamp (R)	102,763	(47%)	($267,844)
	Other	8,077	(4%)	
1992 primary	Marilyn Lloyd (D)	29,895	(81%)	
	David Stacy (D)	6,974	(19%)	
1990 general	Marilyn Lloyd (D)	49,662	(53%)	($234,107)
	Grady L. Rhoden (R)	36,855	(39%)	($1,414)
	Peter T. Melcher (I)	5,598	(6%)	
	Other	1,550	(2%)	

FOURTH DISTRICT

The invisible line between Civil War Republican and Civil War Democratic territory runs along the Cumberland Plateau, the westernmost upswelling of the Appalachians, west of the valley where the Tennessee River runs south from Knoxville to Chattanooga. It separates the Tennessee valley, which had few slaves and whose economic ties were with the North, from the rolling farmlands of middle Tennessee, first settled by Andrew Jackson in the 1790s and resolutely Democratic from the time he became the first president to call himself a Democrat in the 1830s. And not only is this line invisible, it is also irregular: some counties in west Tennessee, where the Tennessee River runs north from Alabama to Kentucky, are Union Republican.

The 4th Congressional District of Tennessee runs across this line and crosses the state northeast to southwest, from Lee County, Virginia, all the way to Tishomingo County, Mississippi. It is some 300 miles long, yet seldom more than one county wide, and contains such spots as Lynchburg, home of the Jack Daniels distillery since 1860. It was created after the 1980 Census as an entirely rural district, with boundaries slightly modified for the 1990s. The northeastern counties are Civil War Republican to this day; the central and western counties, except for the two westernmost which are Republican, are Civil War Democratic.

The congressman from the 4th District, since its first election in 1982, is Jim Cooper, one of several Tennessee politicians who come from successful political families; his father, Prentice Cooper, was three times elected governor of Tennessee and ran for the Senate against Albert Gore, Sr., in 1958. Jim Cooper graduated from the University of North Carolina in three years, was a Rhodes Scholar, and went on to Harvard Law; after practicing in Nashville for a couple years, he returned home to Shelbyville and ran for the new 4th District seat. He had a tough opponent, Cissy Baker, whose father Howard Baker was then Senate majority leader; but Cooper raised $905,000, won 66% of the vote and became the youngest member of Congress for 1983 and 1984. He tends to be middle-of-the-road on economic issues, fairly liberal on cultural issues, more conservative on foreign issues—stands not too far out of line with Tennessee opinion. But he is willing to risk some unpopular stands. He has spoken out against tobacco use, opposed the National Rifle Association and opposed the flag burning constitutional amendment. Cooper is brainy and hard-working—and also ambitious. He made no secret of the fact that he was interested in the Senate seat vacated when Al Gore was elected vice president, that he wanted to be appointed by Governor Ned McWherter, which he wasn't, and that he would run for it in 1994, which he surely will.

And he will run with a serious record on major issues. On the Energy and Commerce Committee, he was one of the prime backers of the 1992 cable TV reregulation bill, the one bill passed over George Bush's veto in four years. Earlier, he was part of the "group of nine" which helped get a compromise on Clean Air between committee Chairman John Dingell and Health Subcommittee Chairman Henry Waxman—the key to the 1990 Clean Air Act. He has been a prime sponsor of measures to discourage the Baby Bells—former AT&T subsidiaries—from getting into the information services market; they want to use their telephone wires to provide computerized services, while newspapers are deathly afraid this would destroy advertising business. Cooper's drafts require the Baby Bells to demonstrate "no substantial possibility" that their position will impede competition. He can be a bit of a populist, opposing corporate writeoffs for intangibles in mergers and favoring more refunds to natural gas customers overcharged by pipeline companies. But he is a leader of the Conservative Democratic Forum, backing the budget firewalls between defense and domestic spending, a backer of Bill Clinton, but also an early admirer of Paul Tsongas. He is a bit of a stickler, turning down all PAC money since April 1991 after accepting it in his early years.

Cooper's biggest issue is health care. He is probably the House's biggest proponent of managed competition, an approach encouraged by Bill Clinton among others. Cooper was in touch early with the Jackson Hole group of healthcare professionals and advisors that devised managed competition, and knows the issue well. He put off introducing his own bill in early 1993 in deference to Clinton, but sharply criticized the global budgeting approach when it was considered; he said he hoped the president would delegate the definition of a national basic benefits package to an appointed board. Highly respected by a key segment of Democrats and even Republicans, Cooper should be a critical voice on health care.

Cooper has not neglected home issues. He championed the Tennessee Walker Horse industry, centered in his home town of Shelbyville, and he secured money for the Big South Fork National River and Recreation Area. Among possible candidates to succeed him in this district seat are state Representatives Gary Johnson, Larry Curlee and Les Winningham, and Pulaski lawyer Andy Hoover, all Democrats, and Republican state Representatives Shirley Duer and Mike Williams and Tennessee Women's Political Caucus head Sharon Bell.

The People: Pop. 1990: 541,650; 74% rural; 14% age 65+; 96% White; 4% Black. Voting age pop.: 405,647; 3% Black. Households: 65% married couple families; 29% married couple fams. w. children; 24% college educ.; median household income: $20,685; per capita income: $9,886; median gross rent: $277; median house value: $44,400.

1992 Presidential Vote			1988 Presidential Vote		
Clinton (D)	100,292	(48%)	Bush (R)	94,190	(58%)
Bush (R)	83,923	(40%)	Dukakis (D)	66,940	(42%)
Perot (I)	23,838	(11%)			

Rep. Jim Cooper (D)

Elected 1982; b. June 19, 1954, Nashville; home, Shelbyville; U. of NC, B.A. 1975, Rhodes Scholar, Oxford U., M.A. 1977, Harvard, J.D. 1980; Episcopalian; married (Martha).

Career: Practicing atty., 1980–82.

Offices: 125 CHOB 20515, 202-225-6831. Also 116 Depot St., Shelbyville 37160, 615-684-1114; City Hall, 7 S. High St., Winchester 37398, 615-967-4150; 208 E. 1st North St., P.O. Box 2025, Morristown 37814, 615-587-9000; and 215 Lantana Rd., P.O. Box 845, Crossville 38555, 615-484-1864.

Committees: *Budget* (10th of 26 D). *Energy and Commerce* (15th of 27 D): Energy and Power; Health and the Environment; Telecommunications and Finance.

Group Ratings

	ADA	ACLU	COPE	CDF	CFA	LCV	ACU	NTLC	NSI	COC	CEI
1992	70	65	67	70	80	63	32	50	100	63	34
1991	35	—	42	60	64	77	40	—	—	70	37

National Journal Ratings

	1991 LIB — 1991 CONS		1992 LIB — 1992 CONS	
Economic	39% —	61%	47% —	52%
Social	57% —	42%	71% —	28%
Foreign	51% —	46%	30% —	64%

Key Votes of the 102d Congress

1. Ban Striker Replace	AGN	5. Handgun Wait/7-Day	FOR	9. Use Force in Gulf	FOR
2. $ for Homeownership	AGN	6. Overseas Mil. Abortion	FOR	10. US Mil. Abroad $ Cut	FOR
3. Tax Rich/Cut Mid Cls.	AGN	7. Obscn. Art NEA $ Ban	FOR	11. Limit SDI Funds	AGN
4. FY93/$15B Def. Cut	FOR	8. Death Pen. from Jury	FOR	12. Cuba Trade Embargo	FOR

Key Votes of the 103d Congress

1. Family Leave	FOR	2. Deficit Reduction	FOR	3. Stimulus Plan	FOR

Election Results

1992 general	Jim Cooper (D)......................	98,984	(64%)	($195,279)
	Dale Johnson (R)	50,340	(33%)	
	Other................................	5,187	(3%)	
1992 primary	Jim Cooper (D)......................	52,281	(85%)	
	John Dooley (D)	6,370	(10%)	
	J. Patrick Lyons (D)	3,025	(5%)	
1990 general	Jim Cooper (D)......................	52,101	(67%)	($56,922)
	Claiborne (Clay) Sanders (R)...........	22,890	(30%)	($12,588)
	Other................................	2,285	(3%)	

FIFTH DISTRICT

By common consent, Nashville is the heart of Tennessee, the center of its biggest metropolitan area, the middle of middle Tennessee. Nashville was one of the first American cities established west of the Appalachians; Andrew Jackson built his Hermitage nearby above the banks of the Cumberland River, and this was always his political home base—and has remained Democratic ever since. It was the capital of Tennessee early on, just as it was—and still is—the center of its political life and discourse: the *Tennessean* and the *Nashville Banner* still present Democratic and Republican views of Tennessee politics, and Nashville is the biggest television market in the state. Nashville is proud of its universities and of its very own Parthenon; it is firmly established as the religious publishing center of the country, producing more Bibles probably than any city in the world—the buckle on the Bible Belt. And of course, Nashville is the home of country music, a $6 billion industry centered on the Country Music Hall of Fame at the north end of Music Row, and the Grand Ole Opry, first aired on radio in 1925, now broadcast from the giant theme park on the banks of the Cumberland in Opryland U.S.A. Country music has boomed in recent years, doubling in recording sales and taking 34% of the nationwide radio audience, more than any other format.

Nashville was also the boom city of Tennessee in the 1980s, with metropolitan growth of 16%, the highest of any major metro area between Atlanta and Dallas-Fort Worth. Country music and Bible publishing flourished, Ingram grew as the nation's largest book wholesaler and the Goo-Goo Cluster candy factory churned out its product, Nissan built a big plant in nearby Smyrna and General Motors set its Saturn plant in nearby Spring Hill, and many smaller businesses started up. Nashville also had commercial and apartment real estate booms, followed by busts in the early 1990s. But the overall picture is of growth and, for those who can remember back more than a generation, a lifestyle of comfort mostly undreamed of—air conditioning everywhere, shopping malls and supermarkets overflowing with affordable goods. An agreeable quality of life, plenty of medium-wage, high-skill labor, a central location, and absence of urban strife and militant unions have all helped make Nashville a boom town.

The 5th Congressional District of Tennessee includes all but one precinct of Nashville and Davidson County plus the bulk of increasingly suburban Robertson County to the north—but this is not all of metropolitan Nashville now that development has spread into once rural areas. The 5th is usually a reliably Democratic district in statewide elections, and it has long elected liberals who generally vote with their co-partisans from the North; this is, after all, the home of the first Democratic president. It was also for several years the home of Al Gore, when he was a divinity student at Vanderbilt and reporter for the *Tennessean*, and the Clinton-Gore ticket carried Davidson County 52%–38% in 1992.

The congressman from the 5th District is Bob Clement, a Democrat whose father was elected governor of Tennessee in 1952, 1954 and 1962 and memorably keynoted the 1956 Democratic National Convention. Bob Clement won the seat after the incumbent, Bill Boner, resigned in October 1987 just ahead of an ethics investigation to begin a tumultuous term as mayor of Nashville. The special election to succeed Boner was a multi-million dollar contest between failed candidates for other offices. In the December 1987 primary, the winner with 40% was Clement, former public service commissioner and candidate for governor in 1978 and for the 7th District House seat in 1982, followed by Phil Bredesen, who had lost the mayoral race to Boner (but ultimately succeeded him), with 36%, and Jane Eskind, public service commissioner and candidate for senator in 1978 and governor in 1986, with 15%; Tennessee has no runoff. In the January 1988 general, Clement easily beat the Republican who had lost to Boner in 1986.

In the House, Clement sought a seat on Appropriations, without success; but his Public Works assignment turned out to be one of the most popular among freshmen in 1993. Clement has worked on airport noise abatement and on obtaining improvements for Nashville's airport; he pushed to study the New Madrid Fault earthquake zone near the Mississippi River and to finish the Natchez Trace Parkway into Nashville; he has worked hard on nuclear plant design standards and increasing penalties for drug sales at truck stops.

Clement has been reelected fairly easily. In 1992, he had primary opposition from Chip Forrester, a former Al Gore state director and state Democratic Party executive director, who charged that Clement had accomplished little; but Clement, who had Al Gore's endorsement, won 66%–24%. He may run for governor in 1994 and, with a well-known name and Nashville base, could win a multicandidate Democratic primary and perhaps the general election as well.

The People: Pop. 1990: 541,878; 5% rural; 12% age 65+; 75% White; 23% Black; 1% Asian; 1% Hispanic origin. Voting age pop.: 416,608; 21% Black; 1% Hispanic origin. Households: 48% married couple families; 21% married couple fams. w. children; 47% college educ.; median household income: $28,208; per capita income: $14,874; median gross rent: $430; median house value: $74,200.

1992 Presidential Vote			1988 Presidential Vote		
Clinton (D)	112,795	(53%)	Bush (R)	100,268	(52%)
Bush (R)	79,398	(37%)	Dukakis (D)	93,139	(48%)
Perot (I)	21,531	(10%)			

Rep. Bob Clement (D)

Elected Jan. 1988; b. Sept. 23, 1943, Nashville; home, Nashville; U. of TN, B.S. 1967, Memphis St. U., M.B.A. 1968; United Methodist; married (Mary).

Career: Army, 1969–71, Army Natl. Guard, 1971–present; TN Public Svc. Comm., 1973–79; Bd. of Dir., TN Valley Authority, 1979–81; Founder and owner, Bob Clement & Assoc., 1981–83; Owner and partner, Charter Equities real estate, 1981–83; Pres., Cumberland U., 1983–87.

Offices: 1230 LHOB 20515, 202-225-4311. Also 552 U.S. Crthse., Nashville 37203, 615-736-5295; 2701 Jefferson St., N. Nashville 37208, 615-320-1363; and 101 5th Ave. W., Springfield 37172, 615-384-6600.

Committees: *Public Works and Transportation* (13th of 39 D): Aviation; Economic Development; Surface Transportation. *Veterans' Affairs* (13th of 21 D): Education, Training and Employment; Hospitals and Health Care.

Group Ratings

	ADA	ACLU	COPE	CDF	CFA	LCV	ACU	NTLC	NSI	COC	CEI
1992	65	59	75	60	53	38	39	15	90	63	30
1991	50	—	75	90	67	54	20	—	—	40	21

National Journal Ratings

	1991 LIB — 1991 CONS		1992 LIB — 1992 CONS	
Economic	66%	— 32%	54%	— 46%
Social	48%	— 51%	54%	— 46%
Foreign	54%	— 44%	62%	— 35%

Key Votes of the 102d Congress

1. Ban Striker Replace	FOR	5. Handgun Wait/7-Day FOR	9. Use Force in Gulf FOR
2. $ for Homeownership	AGN	6. Overseas Mil. Abortion FOR	10. US Mil. Abroad $ Cut FOR
3. Tax Rich/Cut Mid Cls.	FOR	7. Obscn. Art NEA $ Ban FOR	11. Limit SDI Funds FOR
4. FY93/$15B Def. Cut	FOR	8. Death Pen. from Jury AGN	12. Cuba Trade Embargo FOR

Key Votes of the 103d Congress

1. Family Leave   FOR   2. Deficit Reduction   AGN   3. Stimulus Plan   FOR

Election Results

1992 general	Bob Clement (D)....................	125,233	(67%)	($600,244)
	Tom Stone (R)	49,417	(26%)	($10,590)
	Steven L. Edmondson (I)	6,724	(4%)	($122)
	Other................................	6,216	(3%)	
1992 primary	Bob Clement (D).....................	42,794	(66%)	
	Chip Forrester (D)	15,724	(24%)	
	David Mills (D).......................	6,043	(9%)	
1990 general	Bob Clement (D).....................	55,607	(72%)	($298,005)
	Tom Stone (I)	13,577	(18%)	
	Al Borgman (I).......................	5,383	(7%)	
	Two Others	2,193	(3%)	

SIXTH DISTRICT

West of the Cumberland Plateau and the last chain of Appalachians is the rolling countryside of middle Tennessee, "the dimple of the universe" in one felicitous saying. This is hilly and fertile land, cut by deep rivers ambling along in S-curves. The terrain here was never much suited for plantation crops, and there were few big landholdings; this has long been a land of small farmers and small county seat towns, nestled amid what people here regard as some of the loveliest scenery on earth. Middle Tennessee has also been one of the heartlands of the Democratic Party. It was the political home base of Andrew Jackson and supported him nearly unanimously; during the Civil War, though it had very few slaves, it resisted the invading Union armies. For 140 years after Jackson, it voted solidly Democratic and elected as its congressmen some of the luminaries of the national Democratic Party: James K. Polk (1825–39), speaker of the House and later president; Cordell Hull (1907–21, 1923–31), later senator and secretary of State; Albert Gore Sr., (1939–53), later senator; and Albert Gore Jr., (1977–85), later senator and now vice president.

The 6th Congressional District of Tennessee includes 14 middle Tennessee counties east and south of Nashville, plus a bit of Nashville itself. The heritage here is old and rural, but economic growth has fanned out into the farmland from Nashville—symbolized most vividly by the big Nissan plant in Smyrna and General Motors's Saturn plant in Spring Hill (actually a mile outside the district), but also evident in thousands of jobs created by Japanese companies and American startups, firms fleeing the North and entrepreneurs fleeing Texas. Many new voters here are Republican, not only in the affluent suburbs of Williamson County just south of Nashville, but in the more modest suburbs spreading to the east. In 1976, the counties that made up the 6th District voted 65%–34% for Jimmy Carter over Gerald Ford: Civil War Democrats. In 1992, although Al Gore's farm on the Caney Fork outside Carthage is in the district, the 6th District counties voted only 47%–40% for Bill Clinton over George Bush. The 6th is now competitive in national elections, and Republicans have won seats in the legislature from Williamson, Sumner and Rutherford Counties in the ring around Nashville.

The congressman from the 6th District is Bart Gordon, a Democrat first elected in 1984 when Gore left the House seat to run for the Senate. Gordon was Democratic State Chairman from the large base of Murfreesboro and Rutherford County. He ran a computerized fundraising operation and voter contact system—then a novelty in this district where a personal handshake from a candidate was the norm. He won a multicandidate primary with 28% of the vote—there is no runoff in Tennessee—and won the general election 63%–37%.

In the House, Gordon used his insider skills to build a close relationship with Speaker Jim Wright and Majority Whip Tony Coelho, and got a seat on the Rules Committee in 1987, giving him an opportunity to concentrate on diverse issues. He advanced a bill, much of which became law, requiring telephone 900-number businesses to state costs and billing procedures, allow refunds on disputed calls, require beeps to indicate passage of time for billings and adhere to strict advertising guidelines. Gordon went after trade schools with high student loan default rates and even posed in 1991 as a student (though he was 42 at the time) with an NBC investigative unit. He passed new accountability provisions for the federal financial aid system in 1992 which are intended to eliminate almost $1 billion in losses. He offered a substitute amendment to the 1990 Family and Medical Leave Act which limited the scope of the bill and some of its effects on small business; it passed 259–157 in 1992, and was the basis of the bill vetoed by President Bush that year and signed by President Clinton in February 1993. He has argued against spending programs like the B-2 Stealth bomber and opposed construction of a temporary nuclear waste dump in middle Tennessee. In 1993, he became a member of the Budget Committee, and urged President Clinton to rely more heavily on spending cuts in his budget plan.

That emphasis may have owed something to the fact that Gordon had serious opposition in

1992 for the first time in eight years. Williamson County businesswoman Marsha Blackburn ran a vigorous campaign, attacking Gordon's spending record and the congressional pay raise. She carried Williamson County and the Nashville portion of the district, but Gordon carried the other 13 counties and won 57%–41%—a solid margin, although subject to erosion should current demographic trends continue.

The People: Pop. 1990: 542,002; 54% rural; 11% age 65+; 93% White; 6% Black; 1% Asian; 1% Hispanic origin. Voting age pop.: 399,552; 5% Black; 1% Hispanic origin. Households: 66% married couple families; 33% married couple fams. w. children; 38% college educ.; median household income: $29,234; per capita income: $13,286; median gross rent: $378; median house value: $71,300.

1992 Presidential Vote			1988 Presidential Vote		
Clinton (D)	109,895	(47%)	Bush (R)	103,630	(61%)
Bush (R)	93,036	(40%)	Dukakis (D)	65,686	(39%)
Perot (I)	28,151	(12%)			

Rep. Bart Gordon (D)

Elected 1984; b. Jan. 24, 1949, Murfreesboro; home, Murfreesboro; Middle TN St. U., B.S. 1971, U. of TN, J.D. 1973; United Methodist; single.

Career: Practicing atty., 1974–84; Chmn., TN St. Dem. Party, 1981–83.

Offices: 103 CHOB 20515, 202-225-4231. Also P.O. Box 1986, 106 S. Maple St., Murfreesboro 37133, 615-896-1986; and 17 S. Jefferson, Cookeville 38501, 615-528-5907.

Committees: *Budget* (17th of 26 D). *Rules* (8th of 9 D): The Legislative Process.

Group Ratings

	ADA	ACLU	COPE	CDF	CFA	LCV	ACU	NTLC	NSI	COC	CEI
1992	70	68	67	60	67	56	25	5	70	50	22
1991	60	—	92	100	72	54	15	—	—	40	15

National Journal Ratings

	1991 LIB — 1991 CONS			1992 LIB — 1992 CONS		
Economic	79%	—	18%	59%	—	41%
Social	60%	—	38%	57%	—	41%
Foreign	54%	—	44%	56%	—	40%

Key Votes of the 102d Congress

1. Ban Striker Replace	FOR	5. Handgun Wait/7-Day	FOR	9. Use Force in Gulf	FOR
2. $ for Homeownership	AGN	6. Overseas Mil. Abortion	FOR	10. US Mil. Abroad $ Cut	FOR
3. Tax Rich/Cut Mid Cls.	FOR	7. Obscn. Art NEA $ Ban	FOR	11. Limit SDI Funds	FOR
4. FY93/$15B Def. Cut	FOR	8. Death Pen. from Jury	AGN	12. Cuba Trade Embargo	FOR

Key Votes of the 103d Congress

1. Family Leave	FOR	2. Deficit Reduction	FOR	3. Stimulus Plan	FOR

Election Results

1992 general	Bart Gordon (D)	120,777	(57%)	($988,920)
	Marsha Blackburn (R)	86,289	(41%)	($181,515)
	Other	5,962	(3%)	
1992 primary	Bart Gordon (D)	45,576	(83%)	
	Bob Ries (D)	4,912	(9%)	
	Don Schneller (D)	4,371	(8%)	
1990 general	Bart Gordon (D)	60,538	(67%)	($367,090)
	Gregory Cochran (R)	26,424	(29%)	($8,996)
	Ken Brown (I)	3,793	(4%)	

SEVENTH DISTRICT

Rural Tennessee north of Mississippi is one of the most sparsely settled areas in the state. Along each side of the Tennessee River as it flows north and widens out into Kentucky Lake amid heavy forests are small rural communities that go back to pre-Civil War days and have not grown much since. Farther west the land is flatter and more open, a northward extension economically and demographically of the northern Mississippi farmlands, with cotton fields and a large black rural population. This mostly empty land is bounded on two sides by large metropolitan areas, Nashville to the east and Memphis to the west.

The 7th Congressional District of Tennessee spans this territory, from the Cheatham County suburban fringe of Nashville, west across the Tennessee River and south to the Mississippi border and finally to the white neighborhoods on the east side of Memphis. It is a mixed district politically. Most of the rural counties are heavily Democratic, with a few Republican exceptions, while the fringe of Nashville is mixed and the 7th District's portion of Memphis is, like all white parts of Memphis, heavily Republican. The balance has usually tipped toward Republicans, though the lines in Memphis and Shelby County were altered by 1990s redistricting to help the Democrats.

The congressman from the 7th District is Don Sundquist, a self-made man from Moline, Illinois, who made his way up through Republican politics (he beat Frank Fahrenkopf for president of the Young Republicans in 1971 and became acquainted with the young National Chairman George Bush). He became a plant manager in Shelbyville, Tennessee, then went to work for a Memphis printing and marketing firm. For a time in 1979, he was manager of Howard Baker's 1980 presidential campaign. In 1982, when Republican incumbent Robin Beard ran against Senator Jim Sasser, Sundquist ran in the 7th District and won 51%–49% against Democrat Bob Clement, now congressman from Nashville's 5th District. (They may face each other again in the 1994 governor's race.) Sundquist won 75% in Memphis and Shelby County and 35% in the rural counties.

In the House, Sundquist serves on the Ways and Means Committee. He worked out a compromise to refinance TVA's long-term loans in 1989, won special tax accounting rules to benefit cotton warehouse owners, got proposed tariff penalties removed on typewriters made by Brother International in Bartlett, Tennessee, and backed wider use of tax-exempt bonds. He has opposed tax increases, including President Bush's 1990 budget summit agreement, and backed bans of honoraria for House members and restrictions on franked mail. He made his biggest splash in October 1990, when he challenged longtime chairman of the National Republican Congressional Committee Guy Vander Jagt. Sundquist was enraged by top staffer Ed Rollins's letter to Republican candidates advising them to trumpet any opposition they had to the budget summit tax increases, and he complained that the committee had little success for all the money it spent. But Vander Jagt had support from Whip Newt Gingrich and most party conservatives, and Sundquist lost 98–66.

For more than a decade, Sundquist has worked the rural counties in his district hard, with 100 "community days" a year. He was reelected easily in the 1980s and won 62% in 1990 and 1992, in the latter case even though 80,000 residents of Shelby County were removed from the 7th District and placed in the 9th or 8th. Shelby still cast 42% of the district's votes, and Sundquist's 76% there, together with 55% in the rural counties, was enough to assure a solid victory.

In 1994, Sundquist, who spends most of his time in Tennessee rather than Washington, is expected to run for governor. Among possible Republican candidates for the 7th District are former U.S. Attorney Ed Bryant, Shelby County Election Commissioner Gerald Gaia, Germantown Mayor Charles Salvaggio, and Shelby County Republican Chairman Maida Pearson. Among possible Democrats are former state Representative Harold Byrd, Clarksville Mayor Don Trotter and 1992 primary loser Guthrie Castle and primary winner David Davis.

The People: Pop. 1990: 542,270; 43% rural; 10% age 65+; 86% White; 12% Black; 1% Asian; 1% Hispanic origin. Voting age pop.: 397,089; 12% Black; 1% Hispanic origin. Households: 65% married couple families; 32% married couple fams. w. children; 42% college educ.; median household income: $29,242; per capita income: $13,758; median gross rent: $412; median house value: $69,500.

1992 Presidential Vote			1988 Presidential Vote		
Bush (R)	114,544	(50%)	Bush (R)	109,719	(65%)
Clinton (D)	91,644	(40%)	Dukakis (D)	57,919	(35%)
Perot (I)	22,486	(10%)			

Rep. Don Sundquist (R)

Elected 1982; b. Mar. 15, 1936, Moline, IL; home, Memphis; Augustana Col., B.A. 1957; Lutheran; married (Martha).

Career: Navy, 1957–59; Jostens, Inc., 1961–72; Partner, Graphic Sales of Amer., 1972, Pres., 1973–82.

Offices: 339 CHOB 20515, 202-225-2811. Also 5909 Shelby Oaks Dr., #213, Memphis 38134, 901-382-5811; 117 S. 2d St., Clarksville 37040, 615-552-4406; and 149 Cypress St., Selmer 38375, 901-645-4402.

Committees: *Ways and Means* (5th of 14 R): Select Revenue Measures; Trade.

Group Ratings

	ADA	ACLU	COPE	CDF	CFA	LCV	ACU	NTLC	NSI	COC	CEI
1992	5	0	18	10	27	6	96	100	90	75	73
1991	0	—	17	20	39	8	90	—	—	100	67

National Journal Ratings

	1991 LIB — 1991 CONS		1992 LIB — 1992 CONS	
Economic	14%	— 83%	20%	— 79%
Social	0%	— 84%	15%	— 85%
Foreign	0%	— 88%	26%	— 72%

Key Votes of the 102d Congress

1. Ban Striker Replace	AGN	5. Handgun Wait/7-Day	AGN	9. Use Force in Gulf	FOR
2. $ for Homeownership	FOR	6. Overseas Mil. Abortion	AGN	10. US Mil. Abroad $ Cut	AGN
3. Tax Rich/Cut Mid Cls.	AGN	7. Obscn. Art NEA $ Ban	FOR	11. Limit SDI Funds	AGN
4. FY93/$15B Def. Cut	*	8. Death Pen. from Jury	FOR	12. Cuba Trade Embargo	FOR

Key Votes of the 103d Congress

1. Family Leave	AGN	2. Deficit Reduction	AGN	3. Stimulus Plan	AGN

Election Results

1992 general	Don Sundquist (R)	125,101	(62%)	($1,001,217)
	David R. Davis (D)	72,062	(36%)	($106,774)
	Others	5,685	(3%)	
1992 primary	Don Sundquist (R), unopposed			
1990 general	Don Sundquist (R)	66,141	(62%)	($451,944)
	Kenneth Bloodworth (D).	40,516	(38%)	

EIGHTH DISTRICT

West of Nashville and the TVA lakes, north of Memphis, rivers roll lazily through flat to gently rolling land that could almost be the northern end of Mississippi. Cotton and soybeans are the main crops; more blacks remain in rural areas here than in any other part of Tennessee, a reminder of its old plantation economy. The towns here are small, edged in by farm fields; the river bottoms, often flooded, are heavily forested. The big city in these parts is Memphis, with its large black population and orientation toward Mississippi.

The 8th Congressional District of Tennessee includes much of this west Tennessee farmland, from the TVA lakes west to the Mississippi; its largest city is Jackson, but it includes the northern suburban fringe of Memphis. Historically this is Democratic country, although there are a few Republican counties which had favored the Union in the Civil War; it trended Republican in national races in the 1960s and 1970s, but has turned back toward the Democrats with the help of some smart local politicians. One of them is Ned McWherter, first elected to the legislature from Weakley County in 1968 and speaker from 1973 to 1986, and governor since 1986. Another is Congressman John Tanner who, when 19-year incumbent Ed Jones retired in 1988, won the seat with a whopping 66% in a four-candidate primary and 62% against a Republican Pat Robertson backer in the general.

Tanner is a banker and lawyer from Obion County, exactly the sort of local notable who traditionally runs things in southern politics; after law school and service in the Judge Advocate Corps, he came back to west Tennessee, was elected to the legislature in 1976 and became chairman of the Commerce Committee. Like McWherter, he combines political shrewdness with a country demeanor; many stops on his 1988 campaign schedule were listed as "Tanner handshakin' and good ol' boyin'." At the same time, he raised over $800,000. When his Republican opponent said Tanner would be a liberal national Democrat, his reply was, "Bull. Ed Jones has been his own man and John Tanner will be his own man." Tanner has a moderate to conservative voting record. But he has not been an automatic vote for the Pentagon on the Armed Services Committee, questioning the C-17 transport for example; and he came up with a "MediGuard" program to have National Guard personnel provide medical services in underserved urban and rural areas, and wants to continue to use the military to counter drug trafficking. On the Science Committee, he probed the alleged environmental mismanagement at the Rocky Flats nuclear weapons factory near Denver. He also directed attention to the New Madrid Fault, which produced a three great earthquakes from 1811–12, and got $2 million for a silt retention basin in Reelfoot Lake, created by the New Madrid quake. He backs the line-item veto and a balanced budget amendment.

Tanner seems happy in his work. Or so one must conclude from the fact that he could have been a United States senator for the asking: Governor McWherter was ready in November 1992 to appoint him to succeed Al Gore, but he refused the post, presumably because he did not relish campaigning statewide in 1994 and 1996 for the seat. In the 8th District, he has held 530 public meetings in his first two terms and was reelected in 1990 and 1992 without major party opposition.

The People: Pop. 1990: 541,852; 52% rural; 14% age 65+; 79% White; 20% Black; 1% Hispanic origin. Voting age pop.: 402,271; 17% Black; 1% Hispanic origin. Households: 60% married couple families; 27% married couple fams. w. children; 30% college educ.; median household income: $22,622; per capita income: $10,712; median gross rent: $311; median house value: $47,200.

1992 Presidential Vote		
Clinton (D)	101,328	(48%)
Bush (R)	89,533	(42%)
Perot (I)	19,328	(9%)

1988 Presidential Vote		
Bush (R)	101,448	(58%)
Dukakis (D)	74,249	(42%)

Rep. John Tanner (D)

Elected 1988; b. Sept. 22, 1944, Halls; home, Union City; U. of TN, B.S. 1966, J.D. 1969; Disciples of Christ; married (Betty Ann).

Career: Navy, 1968–72; TN Natl. Guard, 1974–present; Practicing atty., 1973–88; Dir., Sr. V.P., Metro. Fed. Savings & Loan; TN House of Reps., 1976–88.

Offices: 1427 LHOB 20515, 202-225-4714. Also 203 W. Church St., Union City 38261, 901-885-7070; Fed. Bldg., #B-7, Jackson 38301, 901-423-4848; and 2836 Coleman Rd., Memphis 38128, 901-382-3220.

Committees: *Armed Services* (17th of 34 D): Military Acquisition; Oversight and Investigations. *Science, Space and Technology* (12th of 33 D): Investigations and Oversight; Space.

Group Ratings

	ADA	ACLU	COPE	CDF	CFA	LCV	ACU	NTLC	NSI	COC	CEI
1992	65	55	58	70	53	25	50	35	90	38	39
1991	30	—	42	50	33	31	50	—	—	67	30

National Journal Ratings

	1991 LIB — 1991 CONS			1992 LIB — 1992 CONS	
Economic	36%	—	64%	46% — 53%	
Social	53%	—	46%	44% — 55%	
Foreign	46%	—	53%	38% — 56%	

Key Votes of the 102d Congress

1. Ban Striker Replace	FOR	5. Handgun Wait/7-Day	AGN	9. Use Force in Gulf	FOR
2. $ for Homeownership	FOR	6. Overseas Mil. Abortion	FOR	10. US Mil. Abroad $ Cut	AGN
3. Tax Rich/Cut Mid Cls.	FOR	7. Obscn. Art NEA $ Ban	FOR	11. Limit SDI Funds	AGN
4. FY93/$15B Def. Cut	FOR	8. Death Pen. from Jury	FOR	12. Cuba Trade Embargo	FOR

Key Votes of the 103d Congress

1. Family Leave	FOR	2. Deficit Reduction	FOR	3. Stimulus Plan	FOR

Election Results

1992 general	John Tanner (D)	136,852	(84%)	($167,669)
	Lawrence J. Barnes (I)	9,605	(6%)	
	David L. Ward (I).....................	6,930	(4%)	
	Other............................	10,045	(6%)	
1992 primary	John Tanner (D), unopposed			
1990 general	John Tanner (D), unopposed			($153,941)

NINTH DISTRICT

Memphis, the largest city in Tennessee, is in the far southwestern corner of the state, 500 miles from Tennessee's Appalachian border with Virginia and only 20 miles from a Mississippi cotton field. Memphis is symbolized by its musical tradition, entirely separate from Nashville's country music: Beale Street, near downtown Memphis, gave birth to jazz in the 1920s, rooted in the blues music of the lower Mississippi Valley, particularly the Delta; Elvis Presley, Mississippi-born but living in Memphis most of his adult life, drew on the blues and black music generally to produce the rock-and-roll which made him a star in his lifetime and a strong presence years after his death. Memphis's large black population is evidence of the city's economic heritage as a capital of the Cotton Kingdom; today it still has the world's largest spot cotton market. For some years Memphis tried to live this heritage down, redeveloping Beale Street; now it recognizes its history as an asset, and is proud of its old fountains and the courtyard of the Peabody Hotel, where you can get a sense of the days when big Mississippi planters came north to sell their crop and make financial arrangements for the next season. Memphis's heritage also includes the Lorraine Motel, where Martin Luther King was assassinated in 1968, now site of a civil rights museum, and Graceland, the grandiosely decorated mansion where Elvis Presley lived and, contrary to sightings, died August 16, 1977, and which is now one of the nation's biggest tourist attractions.

Memphis has become more than a cotton center and it has more than just history. Geographically central in the U.S., it is the home of the first supermarket (Piggly Wiggly) and the first Holiday Inn. It calls itself "America's distribution center"; one of its biggest businesses is Federal Express, which ships all of its U.S. packages in and out of Memphis Airport every night. Just north of Mud Island in the Mississippi, near the old downtown, is the 32-story Great American Pyramid arena, for sports events and conventions.

Like Mississippi, Memphis has not had an entirely happy political life. The hard edge of racial animosity may have now worn off, but racial polarization, to most people's discomfort, remains. Blacks still vote almost unanimously Democratic; whites vote by percentages almost as high for Republicans, at least in seriously contested races. The 9th Congressional District of Tennessee consists of most of the city of Memphis and a bit of its suburban fringe; in 1990, 59% of its residents were black.

The congressman from the 9th District, Harold Ford, has been in office for two decades and has had a career full of ups and downs. The ups included his election to the House in 1974, at 29, after four years in the state legislature; he is part of a politically prominent Memphis family, well-established as morticians, and came of age just as black majority districts were first being created. Ford moved up quickly in the House, winning a seat on the Ways and Means Committee and in 1981 becoming chairman of the subcommittee handling welfare programs, Public Assistance and Unemployment Compensation. But he did relatively little with this assignment until early 1987, when it marked up a welfare reform bill. Then—here was one of his downs—Ford was indicted in April 1987 and automatically lost his chairmanship.

Ford's indictment was on federal charges of bank and tax fraud stemming from money he had received from C.H. Butcher, Jr., an east Tennessee banker and brother and partner of Jake Butcher, the 1982 Democratic candidate for governor; the Butchers' banking empire collapsed in 1983 and in 1985 C.H. Butcher was sentenced to 20 years in jail for defrauding depositors of $20 million. The indictment said that more than $1 million in sham loans were made by a C.H. Butcher firm to a corporation controlled by Ford, who then used the money for personal reasons. Ford said he expected to repay the loans when he sold his interest in the family funeral home to Butcher. Ford charged that the assistant U.S. attorney bringing the case was politically motivated and certainly the initial proceedings seemed stacked: a trial judge in Knoxville imposed a gag order on Ford, which was overturned as "blatantly unconstitutional," and the case was ordered transferred to Memphis. Trial there resulted in a hung jury in April 1990, with the jury split along racial lines 8–4 for acquittal. Charges of alleged jury misconduct prompted black Judge Odell Horton to pick jurors for the second trial from mostly white Jackson; Ford appealed that to the Supreme Court and lost in October 1992. A second judge, Jerome Turner, then presided over a jury selection that resulted in 11 whites and one black; then in February 1993, Bush holdover acting Attorney General Stuart Gerson backed Ford's request for a Memphis jury, at which point the U.S. attorney in Memphis resigned; Judge Turner angrily denied the request for a new jury, and Ford left the court complaining of chest pains.

It turned out that Gerson and White House liaison Webster Hubbell, a former law partner of Hillary Rodham Clinton, had met with 26 members of the Congressional Black Caucus delegation the day before Gerson's decision. Republican leaders called for an investigation of this obvious political pressure. Then, to the surprise of many in Washington, Ford was acquitted in April 1993. Overall, this six-year episode reflects discredit on just about everyone. Butcher was a crook. Ford was extravagant in his personal life and foolish to take money from the Butchers; he indulged in shameless political posturing and incendiary racial appeals. The prosecutors were surely not motivated by racial prejudice nor did the Reagan and Bush Administrations have a political vendetta (Ford was not that big a political fish), but why did they pursue a bribery case so doggedly when there was never any hard evidence that Ford did anything, or was asked to do anything, in return for the money? Stuart Gerson, Webster Hubbell and (quite possibly) the Clinton White House clearly succumbed to political pressure to help a political ally of the latter two. It is hard to resist the conclusion that the "loans" should never have been offered or else repaid, and that the case quite possibly never should have been brought; only the judges and the members of the second jury seem to have acted responsibly.

Ford returned to his Human Resources Subcommittee chair after a six-year hiatus. He had remained active on some issues in the meantime, working for special accounting rules for cotton warehouse owners and for allowing public housing residents to qualify for jobs programs currently limited to welfare recipients; he has one of the most liberal voting records in the House. The 1988 welfare reform contained few of Ford's initiatives, and he does not seem to favor the kind of workfare suggested by Bill Clinton during the 1992 campaign. Meanwhile, Ford is in another kind of trouble. It was revealed in April 1992 that he had 388 overdrafts on the House bank, and he loaned some $18,000 to his campaign—not, he says, from the House bank. But in early 1993, he was the only sitting member not to have received a letter of exoneration from legal liability from special investigator Malcolm Wilkey, and Ford's office was not commenting on the matter. Can one hope there will not be another indictment or trial?

In Memphis's racially polarized atmosphere, Ford is reelected every November pretty much along racial lines—58%–31% in 1990, 58%–29% in 1992. Against primary opponent Larry Patterson in 1992 he won 65%–32%.

The People: Pop. 1990: 541,710; 12% age 65+; 39% White; 59% Black; 1% Asian; 1% Hispanic origin. Voting age pop.: 393,874; 54% Black; 1% Hispanic origin. Households: 40% married couple families; 18% married couple fams. w. children; 42% college educ.; median household income: $22,117; per capita income: $11,296; median gross rent: $362; median house value: $54,900.

1198   TENNESSEE

1992 Presidential Vote

Clinton (D) 151,590 (66%)
Bush (R) 68,358 (30%)
Perot (I)................. 9,400 (4%)

1988 Presidential Vote

Dukakis (D)............... 126,171 (61%)
Bush (R) 80,047 (39%)

Rep. Harold E. Ford (D)

Elected 1974; b. May 20, 1945, Memphis; home, Memphis; TN St. U., B.S. 1967, John Gupten Col., A.A. 1969; Howard U., M.P.A. 1982; Baptist; married (Dorothy).

Career: Mortician, 1969–75; TN House of Reps., 1971–75.

Offices: 2211 RHOB 20515, 202-225-3265. Also 369 Fed. Bldg., 167 N. Main St., Memphis 38103, 901-544-4131.

Committees: *Ways and Means* (7th of 24 D): Human Resources (Chmn.); Oversight.

Group Ratings

	ADA	ACLU	COPE	CDF	CFA	LCV	ACU	NTLC	NSI	COC	CEI
1992	85	100	86	80	73	63	5	0	10	29	11
1991	80	—	100	80	50	77	0	—	—	14	12

National Journal Ratings

	1991 LIB — 1991 CONS		1992 LIB — 1992 CONS	
Economic	65%	34%	65%	35%
Social	88%	0%	92%	0%
Foreign	78%	19%	86%	14%

Key Votes of the 102d Congress

1. Ban Striker Replace	FOR	5. Handgun Wait/7-Day FOR	9. Use Force in Gulf AGN
2. $ for Homeownership	FOR	6. Overseas Mil. Abortion FOR	10. US Mil. Abroad $ Cut FOR
3. Tax Rich/Cut Mid Cls. FOR		7. Obscn. Art NEA $ Ban AGN	11. Limit SDI Funds FOR
4. FY93/$15B Def. Cut FOR		8. Death Pen. from Jury AGN	12. Cuba Trade Embargo AGN

Key Votes of the 103d Congress

1. Family Leave   *   2. Deficit Reduction   FOR   3. Stimulus Plan   *

Election Results

1992 general	Harold E. Ford (D).................	123,276	(58%)	($194,631)
	Charles L. Black (R)................	60,606	(29%)	
	Richard Lipstock (I)...............	14,075	(7%)	
	James Vandergriff (I)...............	12,265	(6%)	
	Other............................	2,533	(1%)	
1992 primary	Harold E. Ford (D).................	74,145	(65%)	
	Larry S. Patterson (D).............	36,321	(32%)	
	Two Others........................	4,271	(4%)	
1990 general	Harold E. Ford (D).................	48,629	(58%)	($284,282)
	Aaron C. Davis (R)................	25,730	(31%)	
	Thomas M. Davidson (I).............	7,249	(9%)	
	Other............................	2,149	(2%)	

TEXAS

Texas, the second largest state in size, third and soon to be second largest in population, already second largest in number of schoolchildren and persons with drivers' licenses, is one of two states that was once an independent republic and, like the other, California, continues to be a sort of empire in its own right. It has personality, or rather is a caricature that like any good political cartoon has large elements of truth to it: this was a state settled by dirt farmers, without lineage or much in the way of manners; it provided only a chance to scratch a hard living out of soil and then, with the discovery of oil, the chance, and the risks, of sudden riches. Yet it has become one of the most productive and creative commonwealths in the world. Nowhere is this more apparent than in its political strength. Forty years ago, the two Democratic Party congressional leaders were Texans: Sam Rayburn and Lyndon Johnson; today, Texans are disproportionately at the top of both parties and national leadership. Two of the three candidates for president in November 1992 were Texans, and the other was from next-door Arkansas; and if George Bush and Ross Perot lost, together they won 56% of the nation's votes to Bill Clinton's 43%. The outgoing secretary of state in 1992 was a Texan, James Baker, as was the incoming secretary of the treasury in 1993, Lloyd Bentsen—both of whose appointments soothed nervous leaders all over the world. Bentsen and his former Senate colleague (and onetime opponent) Phil Gramm are both impressive leaders of their parties, strong in intellect and with shrewd political sense. Governor Ann Richards is a political figure of national stature and, at least through early 1993, local popularity.

Texas has had disappointments. The late John Tower was rejected for secretary of defense and Speaker Jim Wright was forced to resign in 1989; and Bush was beaten when he certainly wanted to win in 1992. The Texas economy crashed when oil prices dived in the mid-1980s, the savings and loan scandal had its epicenter and more than half its losses here, and the $8 billion Superconducting Supercollider, located by George Bush in Waxahachie, was nearly zeroed out in 1992 and is still in jeopardy. But Texas rebounds. High school students here must take Texas history, so they will remember the Alamo, the nine years of the independent Texas Republic, the Confederate veterans who returned from the war to scratch a living out of the hard soil or headed west to be cowboys. They may notice that the Alamo was not a victory, the Republic did not last, the Confederacy was a lost cause, and the *Lonesome Dove* cattle drives lasted only a few years; but they also learn that the Alamo was the beginning of a war that resulted in victory, and that Texas, after all its defeats, has come back to win great success. The same is true of its leading politicians: Lyndon Johnson lost his first Senate election, as did George Bush, John Tower and Phil Gramm. Johnson and Bentsen both suffered humiliating defeats (in 1960 and 1976 respectively) as presidential candidates only to emerge later as popular national candidates and key policymakers; Bush lost two statewide races before carrying Texas four times on national tickets; Ann Richards won her upset victory to become governor by maintaining a steely discipline under harsh attack even while trailing far behind in the polls. The lesson is that in Texas defeat is never final and it is always worth making the fight. "That spirit of fighting against adversity," Richards says, "gives us a certain spark. And we are far more sophisticated than anyone gives us credit for. Texas is rushing into the 21st Century."

Texas started off as a marchland on the border of the Third World, with an economy based on commodities, mainly cotton, whose prices were in long-term decline. Its farmers felt like part of a colonial economy controlled by bankers and Wall Street financiers. But with the Spindletop well in 1901, Texas became the nation's—and for a time the world's—leading producer of oil. But oil prices, too, fell in free markets, and were propped up by politicians—the 1936 "hot oil" act that Rayburn, as chairman of the Commerce Committee, pushed through and the oil depletion allowance maintained for years by Rayburn, Johnson, Bentsen and others. These politicians also got subsidies for cotton growers and defense plants and space facilities in World War II and through the long years of the Cold War; these were in effect a windfall of the New Deal and Democrats' continuing control of Congress. Texans, with their memories of the Confederacy, voted heavily Democratic for years and Texas often had the largest Democratic delegation in Congress. At the same time, Texas remained culturally conservative—raucously patriotic and hawkish on defense spending and foreign policy, churchgoing and upholding traditional moral values (Texas didn't allow liquor by the drink until 1970 and only recently allowed horse racing and a lottery), hating socialists and one-worlders with a special fervor on display in the 1960 presidential campaign, when right-wing protesters battered Lyndon and Lady Bird Johnson with signs in the ornate lobby of the Adolphus Hotel.

Texas's economy and culture have been transformed in the decades since then. It is less dependent on raw commodities. Even the "awl bidness" has grown more sophisticated: finding and extracting oil is now high-skill work, and by the 1970s Texas was less the place where oil was found and more the place where you found people who could locate, drill, store and refine it. These skills led naturally to high tech, and starting in the 1960s Texas was building the critical mass of knowledge and finance needed to produce firms like Texas Instruments and Ross Perot's Electronic Data Systems (EDS). At the same time, the University of Texas and Texas A&M—helped by the huge income from their oil lands—were providing a superb university infrastructure to go with the highway system that tied this state together. When the 1980s began, Texas state government drew 28% of revenues from energy; by 1990, only 8%. The Dallas-Fort Worth Metroplex is rich with defense contractors, big and small; Houston is home to firms like Compaq, the sudden computer giant, and to the enormous Texas Medical Center; San Antonio, with the Air Force's prime hospital, has big medical technology and biotech industries; Austin, as UT doubled its number of engineering professors, had high-tech growth rivaling Route 128 in Massachusetts and Silicon Valley in California. The space program gave a boost to Houston's high tech in the 1960s and 1970s; the Supercollider in Waxahachie is expected to expand the Metroplex economy through the 2000s. Texas's low taxes (and lack of income tax) helped attract corporate headquarters like American Airlines in the 1970s and GTE, J.C. Penney and Exxon in the 1980s. The result has been to put Dallas-Fort Worth and Houston solidly on the list of the top ten metro areas, ahead of old industrial centers like Cleveland, Pittsburgh and St. Louis, and threatening to overtake Washington/Baltimore, Boston and Detroit.

This economy was troubled in the early 1990s. The real estate market remained soft, still suffering from overbuilding generated by crooked S&Ls in the 1980s. Oil prices remained stubbornly low, and energy employment has fallen by 400,000 over the last dozen years, with much new effort directed to complying with environmental restrictions. High-tech business had sharps downs as well as ups. Defense spending cuts hurt, especially in Dallas-Fort Worth. Texas

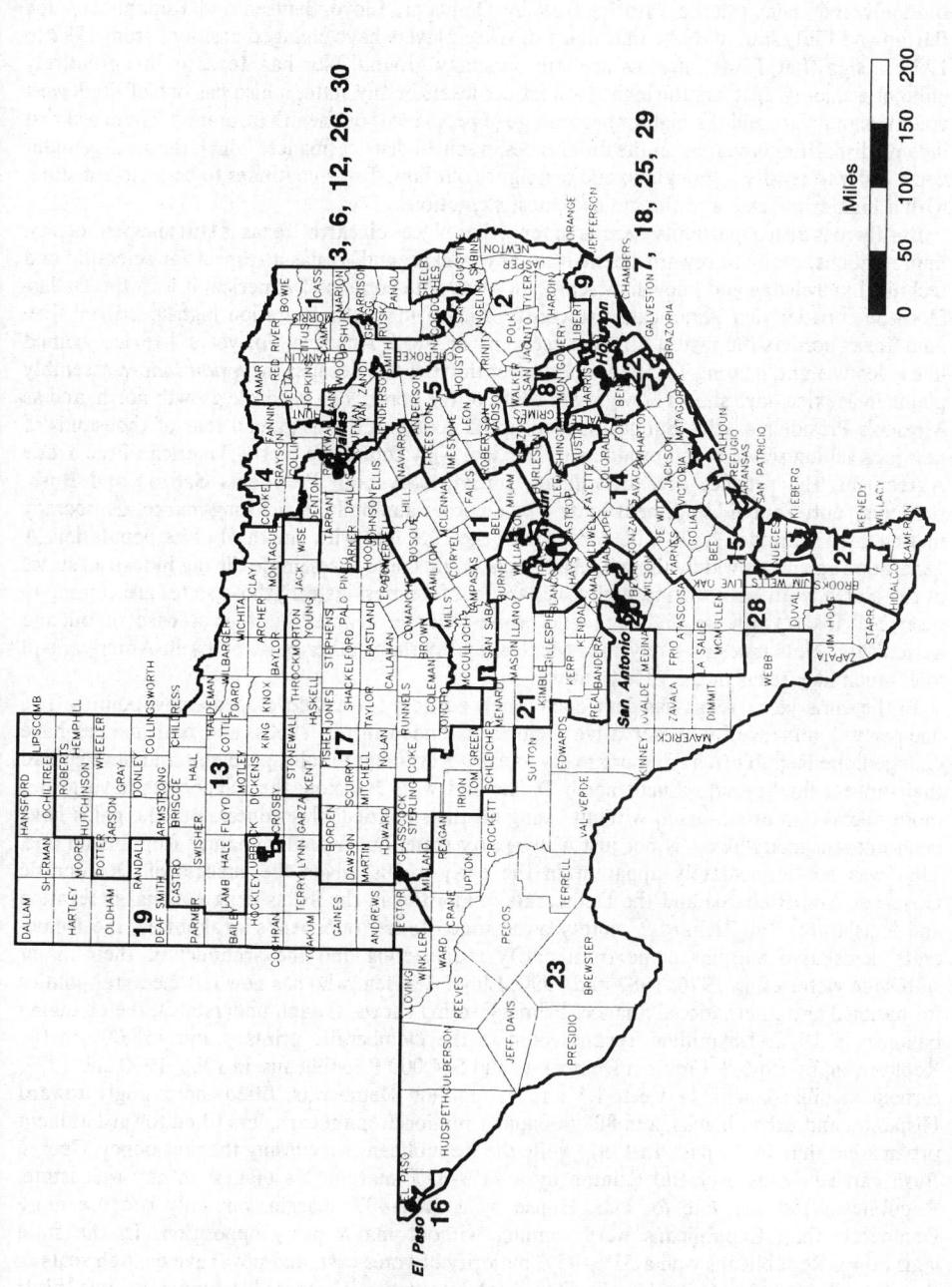

Miles

0 50 100 150 200

still found itself embarrassingly dependent on its political clout to keep government support for projects its economy depended on—the V-22 Osprey plane, rescued from Defense Secretary Dick Cheney's cut list by Congress; the Space Station Freedom, canceled in one 1992 vote only to be resurrected by a squad including Dan Quayle and Al Gore; the Supercollider, zeroed out suddenly and then restored with legwork by Democrat Lloyd Bentsen and Republicans Joe Barton and Phil Gramm. Note that many of these players have changed positions from 1992 to 1993: a sign that Texas interests are still on shaky ground. Nor has Texas built an entirely affluent economy. If it has the eighth lowest tax levels of any state, it also has one of the lowest voter turnout rates and the highest percentage of people without health insurance. There are vast income disparities, apparent in the differences in school district finances which the state is under court order to rectify—though no one can figure out how. Texas continues to be a violent state, with a high crime rate and the nation's most executions.

But there is also opportunity here as in few other places on earth. Texas is still an open society, unpretentious, ready to reward talent from any background. It has a respect for scientific and technical knowledge and know-how scarce in some elite corners of America: it is in the Dallas-Houston corridor that Americans are constructing a magnetic levitation high-speed rail line. And Texas borders the fastest growing economy in North America. For years, Mexico seemed like a deadweight, holding Texas back. But over the past two decades the *maquiladora* assembly plants in Mexico have shown how growth south of the border can generate growth north, and as Mexico's President Carlos Salinas opened up its economy, Texas gained tens of thousands of new jobs selling services and products to Mexico. Now comes the North American Free Trade Agreement, the product of extraordinary initiative by both Presidents Salinas and Bush, reducing "anti-Yanqui" sentiment south of the border and building a strong market democracy in a country sharing a 2,500-mile border with the U.S. and with one-third of its population. A generation ago it was widely thought that Texas would come to resemble the big industrial states of the North, with labor unions, high taxes and big factories; instead, those states are coming to resemble Texas, with its high-tech and white-collar economies built on a base of oil and agriculture. Now it seems likely that Mexico, and perhaps other parts of Latin America, will look much like Texas in the 21st Century.

In the same years Texas has developed a new economy, it has developed a new politics. The one-party dominance by conservative Democrats ended in the 1960s, and both parties have changed: the Republicans are more ready to use government to solve problems and have spread their appeal far beyond affluent north Dallas and west Houston; the Democrats have grown more liberal and urban-based without losing all their political shrewdness. But the gains have been uneven: today Texas is not just a two-party state, but a predominantly Republican one. That was not immediately apparent in the early 1990s, given the success of Democratic Governor Ann Richards and the Democrats' majorities in the Texas congressional delegation and legislature. But Richards's victory owed much to her opponent's weaknesses, the Democrats' legislative margins come from crafty redistricting and the architect of their major statewide victories, in 1976, 1982 and 1990, Lloyd Bentsen, who has now left electoral politics for national and international finance. Primary voting shows, though understates, the changing balance: in 1978, 1.8 million Texans voted in the Democratic primary and 158,000 in the Republican; by 1986, 1.1 million Democrats and 544,000 Republicans; in 1988, 1990 and 1992, turnout stabilized, with between 1.5 and 1.7 million Democrats, tilted increasingly toward Hispanics and urban blacks, and 800,000 and 1 million Republicans, less tilted toward affluent urban areas than in the past. In 1992, while the Republicans were losing the presidency, George Bush carried Texas over Bill Clinton by a 41%–37% margin, his biggest in any megastate. Republicans lost the vote for U.S. House by a 50%–48% margin, but only because more Democrats than Republicans were running without major party opposition. In the state legislature, Republicans won a 51%–45% majority of votes cast, and now have enough seats in the state Senate (13, to 18 for the Democrats) to make it impossible, under its two-thirds majority rules for Democrats to pass their programs without Republican support. Republican

Barry Williamson won the seat for chairman of the Railroad Commission (which regulates oil, among other things), to be sure because Democrat Lena Guerrero, a Richards appointee, was caught lying about her college record; but Williamson's victory was by a wide 54%–39% margin, and echoed statewide victories by Republicans for treasurer, agriculture commissioner and Supreme Court seats in 1990 and 1988. And now, of course, Texas has two Republican senators. When Lloyd Bentsen's seat came up, Ann Richards had a hard time finding a politician who would take the job. Democratic incumbents in other offices evidently didn't want to give up their current jobs and take a chance on this risky race.

The Senate race was a test between the Democrats trained and promoted by Bentsen and the Republicans whose untiring leader is Phil Gramm. For much of the last decade Texas politics has been a duel between these two: Democrats won when Bentsen was on the statewide ticket and put together an effective statewide campaign for the whole ticket, as in 1982 and 1988, or when he helped pick Richards as a Democratic ticket-leader whom he made acceptable to conservative powers, as in 1990. Republicans have won when Gramm led the ticket, in 1984, and in the absence of other factors, as in 1986 and 1992. Bentsen's weapon was an in-depth organization, with business leaders and lawyers in every county, in alliance with the liberals whom he has effectively courted since he beat their paladin, Senator Ralph Yarborough, in the bitter 1970 primary; with their help he beat the favorite in the general election, a Houston oil man named George Bush. Gramm's weapon has been surprise political initiative—resigning his seat and running for reelection in 1983 when he switched parties, engineering a special election in 1985 in the rural 1st District to break open the rural South for Republicans, sponsoring the Gramm-Rudman deficit reduction law later that year.

The patterns of support for the two parties are different in Texas than in major states of the North; the state's response to economic conditions is, if anything, the precise opposite of that of industrial states with a New Deal heritage. Texas's Democratic bastion now is the Border area, which casts about 8% of the state's votes: it was 58%–42% for Dukakis-Bentsen (the first presidential ticket whose members both spoke Spanish), 60%–38% for Ann Richards, 53%–33% for Clinton-Gore. Yet it should be added that Mexican-Americans are not unanimously Democratic, and if they are manipulated by traditional bosses in some Border counties, they are increasingly independent-minded in urban areas. Another Democratic area, but not as strong as liberals have hoped, is the urban strip from San Antonio to Austin; it went 57%–40% for Richards, who served as a county commissioner in Austin before she was state treasurer, and just 42%–38% for Clinton. Austin's cultural liberals are not as dominant as they once were: this is now a high-tech town, with lots of free market enthusiasts in new subdivisions running north of the pink marble Capitol and the UT campus. And San Antonio has a large, heavily Republican Anglo minority. Historically, the other strong Democratic area was rural Texas, which carried the state for Kennedy in 1960 and Humphrey in 1968. But Ann Richards lost to oilman Clayton Williams outside the big metro areas by 51%–46%, and Bush carried them with 42% to 35% for Clinton and 22% for Ross Perot. Cultural attitudes remain conservative in the rural counties, many of which have only been lightly touched by the 1980s Texas booms and some of which, in the western plains where the aquifers are giving out, shared in the Great Plains depopulation.

But 45% of Texas's votes are cast in the two big metro areas. Both Dallas-Fort Worth and Houston now lean Republican but are competitive between the parties. Both have large black communities that are almost unanimously Democratic and Houston has a large Hispanic population as well. But more importantly, these are fast-growing areas where the old economic lines that seemed to dictate voting behavior are breaking down. The startling 1980s growth in these metro areas—33% in the Metroplex, 20% in greater Houston—included a lot of Yankees and baby boomer techies; they now have some of the nation's highest percentages of working women, in vivid contrast to rural Texas, and there are increasingly large numbers of singles and culturally liberal professionals. In Dallas-Fort Worth, a lot of voters, especially affluent women, bridled at Republican gubernatorial candidate Clayton Williams's cowboy image and patently offensive comments, and the Metroplex voted 48%–47% for Ann Richards.

Texas breaks the old political rules in yet another way: it seems to lean Republican in times of economic trouble and Democratic in prosperity. The Democrats' two recent big victories have come in 1982, while Texas was enjoying the oil price boom, and in 1990, when its economy was perceptibly rebounding; in 1984, 1986 and 1992, when oil prices were low, Republicans were victorious. Texas voters in the 1980s have tended to call in Phil Gramm's Republicans to deal with a weak economy; they see the free market, not government intervention, as more likely to produce economic growth. In other times, or when looking for practical men or women of action to run the everyday business of government, they may still indulge their historic preference and call in Lloyd Bentsen's Democrats. This is one tension which Texans must keep resolving. Then there is the tension between the traditional culture of the rural South and the self-consciously modern culture of the rapidly growing cities; and there is tension between Texas's traditional image of white Anglo uniformity and suspicion of outsiders, and its increasingly heterogeneous population and natural friendliness. And so the struggles between Texas's leading politicians and between Texans' warring natures continue, with no end result clearly in sight, but a sense that this nation-state is setting the mold for much of the country and perhaps beyond.

Governor. Ann Richards is a national-rank politician though she seems to have no presidential ambitions, the most popular governor after her first two years of any in the large states, a liberal Democrat thriving in an increasingly Republican and, on many issues, solidly conservative state. She has a wonderful gift for a phrase, as she showed when she first made the national news with her 1988 Democratic National Convention keynote speech ("Poor George. He just can't help it. He was born with a silver foot in his mouth."). Richards is a recovering alcoholic who has not taken a drink for more than a decade and who persevered during a campaign as lengthy and stressful as any non-presidential campaign in recent memory. She has roots in the feminist movement, as a supporter in the 1970s of Sarah Weddington, the lawyer who brought the *Roe v. Wade* case; but her great political benefactor, an unseen but powerful force behind her race for state treasurer in 1982 and governor in 1990 was Lloyd Bentsen, and to her now goes Bentsen's mantle as chief strategist and financier of the Texas Democratic Party.

When Richards began her campaign for governor, the Democrats were definitely the underdogs, even though Republican Bill Clements was leaving office unpopular. In addition, the Republican primary was easily won by Clayton Williams, a rancher and oilman whose brilliant TV ads showed him in a cowboy hat calling for boot camps for teenage drug offenders ("I'll introduce 'em to the joys of busting rocks"); he had 61% to 15% for former Congressman Kent Hance, 14% for Ross Perot lawyer and school reformer Tom Luce (who worked for Perot in 1992 but is now a Republican again) and 10% for Clements protege Jack Rains. Meanwhile, the Democratic primary was nasty even by Texas standards. Attorney General Jim Mattox, a self-styled populist, attacked Richards for allegedly using cocaine; she refused to answer the charges specifically and responded that she had used no mind-altering drugs in 10 years; Richards in turn infuriated former Governor Mark White by accusing him of unethical business practices and made similar comments questioning Mattox's integrity. Richards led Mattox in the first primary 39%–37%, with 19% for White; in the runoff, with strong support in cities where liberal women cast far more votes than ever before in Texas, she won 57%–43%. In the long general election campaign, Williams made gaffes ("if it's inevitable, just relax and enjoy it," he joked about rape) and crumpled under pressure (after a rough debate with Richards, he refused to shake her hand, a moment replayed many times on TV). Williams seemed to stand for an old-fashioned cowboy stereotype of Texas; Richards, though her Waco accent is as thickly Texan as anyone's, seemed modern and appealed especially to upscale metropolitan women. Richards actually carried the normally Republican big metro areas, Houston by 49%–48% and Dallas-Fort Worth by 48%–47%; she won big on the Border, 60%–38%, and San Antonio-Austin, 57%–40%. Despite losing rural Texas 50%–46%, she won statewide, 49%–47%. This was all the more impressive because other results were split: Republican Senator Phil Gramm won easily, Democrats Bob Bullock and Dan Morales won with just 52% for lieutenant governor and attorney general, respectively, and Republican Kay Bailey Hutchison, now senator, was elected treasurer, and Republican Rick Perry upset populist Jim Hightower for agriculture commissioner.

In office, Richards worked with the same steely discipline she showed in the campaign. She pushed through a state lottery, insurance reform, a corporate income tax, a minimum 35-year capital murder sentence, caps on lobbyist spending and stricter limits on toxic waste dumping. She was careful to avoid raising cultural hackles: "I try very hard not to be front and center on every feminist issue." She hosted visits by Queen Elizabeth II and Mexico's President Carlos Salinas. Most importantly, she avoided a major tax increase and pointedly disagreed with Bullock who backed a state income tax. She was proud of her appointments—in the first two years 46% were women, 20% Hispanic, 15% black. But her two most visible appointments were disasters—Railroad Commission member Lena Guerrero and Senate appointee Bob Krueger. With roots and a legislative seat in the Lower Rio Grande Valley, Guerrero had dazzling credentials—until it was revealed during the fall 1992 campaign that they were almost all false: she was not Phi Beta Kappa, had not even graduated from college, had flunked six courses, including some on Mexican-American history and the Texas legislature. Richards's instinct was to stand by Guerrero and urge her to tell the truth; but her candidacy collapsed and she lost to Republican Barry Williamson 54%–39%. And Krueger was resoundingly defeated by Republican state Treasurer Kay Bailey Hutchison in the 1993 special election to fill Lloyd Bentsen's Senate seat.

Richards's other big problem, heading into 1993, was education reform. She and the legislature had been forced to respond to court decisions declaring Texas's current school financing system unconstitutional and requiring a new system. The new plan, passed in June 1993, gives Texas's 101 richest school districts five options for reducing their wealth so that it may be redistributed to poorer districts. It can be argued that this court action is a clumsy tool, that money alone does not produce good schools (indeed, the Washington, D.C., public schools are among the most lavishly funded in the country); it is also obvious that rich urban school districts will react in rage to what the courts seem to want: mandatory transfers of money from them to poorer districts. The school financing plan will test Richards's surefootedness and political sense as much as any she has dealt with before. Dealt with effectively, it could guarantee her a second term. If not, the signs are ominous: Texas increasingly seems Republican, and no governor has won a second consecutive term since 1974.

Senators. To the list of Texas giants in the Senate—Sam Houston, the first president of the Republic, Tom Connally, chairman of the Foreign Relations Committee when the United States rescued most of Europe from Communism, Lyndon Johnson, master of the Senate in the 1950s and 1960s—now must be added the name of Lloyd Bentsen, who in his 23d year in the Senate, 44 years after he was first elected to the House, resigned to become Bill Clinton's secretary of the treasury. For a decade, Bentsen has been one of the few giants in a Senate below its historic peak, chairman of the Senate Finance Committee, unsuccessful candidate for president in 1976 but an impressive success as the Democratic nominee for vice president in 1988, a leader who managed to exert greater influence on state politics and do more for his party politically than even Johnson had, even as he was crafting complex and politically sensitive legislation in Washington. A politician whose career began in the age of radio, Bentsen has learned the art of the sound bite: in 1988, he delivered to Dan Quayle the single most devastating putdown of the decade ("Senator, you're no Jack Kennedy"). He is the one Clinton appointee whose resignation the President probably could not politically afford.

Texas's senior senator now, and a politician of presidential stature in his own eyes and those of some others as well, is Phil Gramm. The son of an Army sergeant who flunked third, seventh and ninth grades and then went on to get a Ph.D., Gramm was an economics professor at Texas A&M in the mid-1970s. A man seething with energy and conviction and ambition, he started giving speeches around the state, boosting free market economics and decrying the grasping hand of government. One of his first fans was Dicky Flatt, a print shop owner in Mexia who became a perennial volunteer and a staple in Gramm speeches, the hard-working American whose money the government is taking away to spend on someone else. In 1976, at 34, after only seven years in Texas, Gramm ran against Lloyd Bentsen and lost the primary 64%–28%. Undaunted, he ran for an open House seat in 1978, making the runoff by 115 votes over current Congressman Chet Edwards, and then winning the primary runoff 53%–47% and easily beating the Republican in the general. Within three years, Gramm was a major national figure. He got a seat on the Budget Committee, promising Majority Leader Jim Wright to be a team player. But, while he kept attending Democratic strategy meetings, he became co-sponsor of the Gramm-Latta budget resolution, the 1981 Reagan budget cuts, which passed the House over the opposition of the Democratic leadership.

For that apostasy, Speaker Tip O'Neill kicked Gramm off the Budget Committee in 1983. But Gramm turned that to his advantage by switching parties, resigning and running for triumphant reelection in a special election campaign that gave him exposure in both the Houston and Dallas-Fort Worth media markets. "I had to choose between Tip O'Neill and y'all," he said, showing his capacity for attractively framing issues, "and I decided to stand with y'all." He won with 55% and a year later easily won the Republican Senate nomination when John Tower announced retirement from Congress. The Democratic winner in an epic three-way primary was Lloyd Doggett, a liberal state senator from Austin, whom Gramm attacked for holding a fundraiser at a gay male strip joint in San Antonio. Gramm won 59%–41%. Then, in his first year in the Senate, ranking 99th in seniority, Gramm came forth a bold initiative: the Gramm-Rudman deficit reduction law. Gramm-Rudman budget initiatives swept all before it, became the law of the land, and was followed by substantial declines in the deficit in 1987 and 1988. Gramm has remained loyal to this handiwork, even against conservative opposition.

Appointed to the 1990 budget summit, he did not resist a tax increase, as some conservatives hoped, but, after George Bush caved in on the issue, ended up negotiating the final packages. The reason, some cynics said, was that he did not want to be associated with any chaos that might occur by shutting down the government per the sequestration provisions of his own Gramm-Rudman law. "I have always felt on budget issues the party that defines the parameters of the debate almost always wins the debate," he later said. Then in 1991 he opposed the social security payroll tax cut proposed by Democrat Pat Moynihan as well as a similar bill, which also included a cut in capital gains taxes, by Republican Senator Malcolm Wallop and suburban Houston congressman Tom DeLay. Gramm insisted that it would lead to higher rates for middle income taxpayers and that voters would recoil against anything that seemed to undermine the long-term strength of the social security system. In both cases Gramm remained loyal to Bush, for whom he made the nominating speech in New Orleans in 1988 and the keynote speech in Houston in 1992. Gramm has long backed zero-based budgeting and opposes the idea that government departments are entitled to continued spending plus inflation, and then can argue more—a view that keeps government growing faster than the economy. But he hasn't been successful in getting others to act on that argument.

In 1991, he joined Newt Gingrich in backing a series of growth incentives (mostly tax cuts); in 1992 he proposed a 5% defense spending cut with the money going to increase personal exemptions on the income tax. In June 1992, he held up Senate business by pushing for the balanced budget constitutional amendment. On other issues, he is a strong and vehement free trader, supportive of the North American Free Trade Agreement, popular in Texas where trade with Mexico is creating many jobs. He is tough on crime, favoring the death penalty for drug-related murders and no federal judicial review for death row prisoners who got a fair hearing in state courts.

Gramm makes little effort to hide his national ambitions. "I think anybody who's ever been a city councilman, much less a United States senator, is interested in being president of the United States," he said in 1992. It was not apparent from the first pages of text just which Texas Republican he was nominating in the 1988 speech, and at the 1992 convention keynote there was considerable mention of Dicky Flatt as well as of George Bush. It is an unkept secret that Gramm hopes to run for president in 1996. He would bring to that race a bullish aggressiveness, a strong and well-disciplined mind, a gift for the pungent phrase, a folksy southernness which comes from being raised near Fort Benning, Georgia. He knows how to frame issues to make them work for him. But Gramm has made enemies along the way, and not just among Democrats. He has decried pork barrel spending, but has been un-shy about seeking money for Waxahachie's Supercollider, Austin's Sematech research center, Ingleside's Navy homeport and research on mesquite and the prickly pear; he threatened to "get" North Dakota's Kent Conrad when Conrad accused him of hypocrisy on pork barrel spending. He was criticized by some for going all out to keep the Bush Administration from transferring some regulatory authority to the SEC from the Commodity Futures Trading Commission, whose chairman at the time was his wife, also a Ph.D. economist, Wendy Lee Gramm. He was elected chairman of the National Republican Senatorial Committee in 1991 by a 26–17 vote; he hoped initially to gain seats, but watched in 1992 as the press ballyhooed "the year of the woman" (there were no such articles when most of the women candidates were Republicans in 1990), then ended up seeing Republicans gain just one seat. Fundamentals came through: two of the three southeastern Democrats who had voted against the Gulf war resolution were defeated, Terry Sanford in North Carolina and Wyche Fowler in the late November runoff in Georgia. Gramm then sought, despite the usual practice, to win a second term at NRSC, and was opposed by Mitch McConnell of Kentucky; Gramm won by 20–19, with key support from megastate incumbents who narrowly won their races and four grateful freshmen. "I did not come to Washington to be loved, and I have not been disappointed," Gramm says.

What is likely to come of Gramm's presidential ambitions? His 1992 keynote was widely recorded as a bust, and certainly it was not lofty or lyrical; but his main message, that Republicans will hold your taxes down, has strength. Gramm sees himself as a man with a mission to change the role of government in American life and as the logical successor to fellow party-switcher Ronald Reagan. But he does not have Reagan's geniality; there is a note of anger to him—a sharp edge of hostility toward those whose view of America is quite different. In this friendly country, angry candidates—Pat Buchanan, Jerry Brown are 1992's examples—do not wear well. It is also not clear that Gramm has a core constituency outside of Texas. The religious right, which finds his views acceptable, can't help noticing that most issues that engage this economist are economic; his Senate colleagues' affections for him are limited, as his one-vote margin showed; the economic right of the Republican Party that felt betrayed by George Bush's breaking his read-my-lips promise cannot help noticing Gramm's support of that move; the remnants of the cultural left in the Republican Party find nothing congenial about him at all. But Gramm has traveled a long way from the economics department at A&M, and in the process has left by the wayside some who thought he wouldn't get very far.

In Texas Gramm should have nothing to worry about in 1996 if he does not run for president, or probably even if he does. Democrats in the state House voted to repeal the law that let Bentsen run both on the national ticket and for reelection to Senate in 1988, but it remains on the books (though efforts to repeal it continue) and so Gramm could run for both. He won 60% of the vote in 1990, the best in Texas since 1958, raising $15 million and ending the campaign with a $4 million surplus. He carried rural Texas and the two big metro areas with more than 60%, and he ran ahead even in the Border counties; only inner city districts and Austin rejected him.

Texas's junior senator is Kay Bailey Hutchison, a Republican and a woman chosen in a stunning June 1993 victory over the man Governor Ann Richards appointed to fill Lloyd Bentsen's seat. Hutchison's victory echoed with greater resonance the defeat of the last Texas senator appointed by a Democratic governor to replace a Texan taking a high position in Washington: the 1961 loss of conservative Democrat "Dollar Bill" Blakeley to Republican John Tower, replacing then-Vice President Lyndon Johnson. Tower's victory was a sign that Republicans could be competitive in Texas; Hutchison's victory was a sign that Republican policies were in the ascendant nationally. That was true even though the appointed Democrat, Bob Krueger, assiduously avoided supporting the Clinton program, and was the one member of the Senate to vote for no budget plan at all. Democrats tried to excuse Krueger's loss by saying he was a poor politician—he took up that refrain himself. But in fact Krueger was a skilled politician. He was a two-term congressman in the 1970s who did much to deregulate energy prices, and a Senate candidate who won 49% of the vote against John Tower in 1978, when Jimmy Carter was president. Krueger finished a close third in a three-way Senate primary in 1984, and ran toward the top of the ticket as a candidate for Railroad Commissioner (an oil-regulating job) in 1990. But Texas is increasingly Republican, and in the May 1993 open general Krueger won only 29% of the vote, finishing second to Hutchison, who also had 29%, while two other Republicans, Congressmen Joe Barton and Jack Fields, had 14% each. Krueger's cause was obviously doomed, and his campaign flailed around, running absurd ads in which Krueger said he was a lousy politician, and dressed up in an Arnold Schwarznegger Terminator outfit, and made fun of his own expertise on Shakespeare.

Hutchison also had affirmative strengths as a candidate. Her background was varied. After graduating from UT Law School in 1967, she could not get a job as a lawyer because of her gender; she worked instead as a reporter for a Houston TV station, covering the legislature in Austin. Then in 1972, she was elected to the legislature herself and served two terms. In 1982, she ran for Congress from the north Dallas district, and lost a close runoff to Steve Bartlett, now Dallas's mayor. In 1984, she opened a candy-making business, then in 1990 was elected Texas state treasurer, succeeding Ann Richards. Articulate and pleasant but willing to be partisan, pro-choice on abortion but opposing a Freedom of Choice Act that would wipe out state parental consent laws, Hutchison in some ways reflected affluent north Dallas and west Houston, an impression enforced by her strong opposition to higher federal taxes. But she worked hard to cultivate support in small towns and rural areas, campaigning in county courthouse towns and through east Texas, which paid off in 1993.

And Hutchison in 1993, like Richards in 1990, showed that she was tough enough to withstand aggressive personal criticism, to maintain her poise and self-command when others lost theirs. Hutchison was accused of having hit an employee, a daughter of the late former Governor and Treasury Secretary John Connally, in charges that were trumpeted across the state; she calmly denied them, and in a debate announced she had passed a lie detector test on the subject and called on her opponents to move on to other things. That helped her surpass Fields and Barton—and Krueger—in the general. In the June runoff, she kept her focus sharply on Bill Clinton and his tax program, telling Texans that they could send a message to Washington. Clinton had lost Texas to George Bush 40%–37%; from the opening weeks of his administration, after he promised to end the ban on gays in the military, his poll numbers had plummeted in Texas; just before the June 5 runoff, his job rating in Texas was 73% negative.

The depth and breadth of Hutchison's victory was astonishing. Statewide she won 67%–33%—better than Gramm or Bentsen had ever run, ahead of any Senate candidate since the 1950s, when Republicans did not put up serious candidates. She won the Dallas-Fort Worth Metroplex 71%–29% and greater Houston 70%–30%, amazing margins in two of the nation's ten largest metropolitan areas; she also carried the usually Democratic San Antonio-Austin corridor and south Texas; and she carried the rest of Texas, once heavily Democratic, 68%-32%. Yellow dog Democratic counties went Republican in droves: Krueger carried 15 counties, Hutchison 239. Hutchison promised to oppose Clinton's tax increases any way she could; she will also have to fend off Democrats' desire to retaliate at Texas by cutting spending on the space station and Supercollider. But her prospects for reelection to a full term in 1994, after this demonstration of personal and party strength, seemed excellent.

Presidential politics. Texas is now a major player in presidential politics, a source of candidates, a fount of campaign funds and a dynamo in the electoral college with 32 electoral votes, more than any state except California or New York, with more national candidates than both put together. George Bush, Ross Perot, Lloyd Bentsen, Phil Gramm—all have run in the last dozen years or may well in 1996, or both. The most stereotypically Texan of them is the billionaire Perot, though the stereotype is not precise. Perot is indeed a billionaire, with a deep east Texas accent and a Texas gift for the memorable sound bite ("I'm not gonna sound bite this"). But he is also a rebel against some things Texan, a school reformer who imposed a no-pass-no-play rule regarding school athletics. A seeming traditionalist (he used to insist that his employees cut their hair and marry their girlfriends), he sent signals that he was the most secular of the fall 1992 candidates. A man of proud military bearing, his oft-articulated fantasies—Vietnamese terrorists stalking his house and being repelled by the dog, the delusion that the Bush campaign was going to sabotage his daughter's wedding—portray him as being subjected to the rigors of combat which, as it happened, he never saw in his military career. Perot's penchant for conspiracy was especially obvious in his persuading the FBI in Dallas to approach Bush state chairman Jim Oberwetter and offer to sell him wiretaps of Perot; Oberwetter of course would have no part of it, though no one asked why the FBI initiated a sting that involved it in a political campaign and was based on a charge relayed by Perot that originated with an obvious crank. Perot did run a strong 28% in the Dallas-Fort Worth Metroplex, his home since leaving the Navy. But in Bowie County, which includes his home town of Texarkana, perhaps the single jurisdiction in which all three candidates were best known—it is Perot's boyhood home, right next door to Clinton's Arkansas and has voted yes or no on Bush in six elections—Perot got just 22% of the vote, to 39% each for Bush and Clinton.

For all the ruckus and commotion, Texas remained a Republican state presidentially, as it did in 1988 when Lloyd Bentsen's presence on the Democratic ticket got its percentage up to only 43%. Bill Clinton stumped Texas in his bus and on LBJ's birthday, and George Bush had to campaign in his home state and had trouble raising money there. But Clinton's cultural liberalism and Bush's opposition to trial lawyers (an issue familiar because it dominates state Supreme Court races, which trial lawyer candidates mostly lose) helped Bush carry his home state by 4%. No Democratic candidate has carried the Dallas-Fort Worth Metroplex or greater Houston since LBJ, and no Democratic candidate has carried rural and small town Texas since Jimmy Carter in 1976. The good news for the Democrats is that they no longer need Texas to win. For nearly 150 years, since Texas was admitted to the Union in 1845, Democrats never won the presidency without carrying Texas. In 1992 they did.

The Texas 1992 March Super Tuesday primary produced big victories for Bill Clinton and George Bush. Both are the kind of moderate, southern-based candidates the Super Tuesday contests were concocted to nominate, at least on the Democratic side.

Congressional districting. Texas's 1991 redistricting plan wins the Phil Burton Award for the decade—for its creatively drawn lines in unlikely places; for the convoluted boundaries of its districts which, snakelike, seem to be threatening to swallow each other; for the partisan effrontery which enabled the Democrats to protect all but one of their incumbents and to capture the state's three new seats as well; for the ingenuity with which white urban Democrats, long dependent on black votes, were given districts where Democratic rural counties were substituted for urban black neighborhoods. The plan was the product of Bob Mansker, political aide at the time to Metroplex Congressman Martin Frost, who was terribly at risk; Frost's old district was 29% black and 21% Hispanic, and the chairman of the state Senate redistricting panel, Eddie Bernice Johnson, had her eye on just about every one of his black and Hispanic areas to create a new district for herself. That she got—there was no way Frost could prevent it—nor was he able to pry Waxahachie away from Republican Joe Barton; but the new plan gave Frost a safe district anyway. What remains to be seen is whether this plan can stand the legal and political tests of the decade. At least half a dozen seats Democratic now might see challenges to an incumbent or a turnover if the seat becomes open, while all of the Republican seats seem solid (each voted at least 68% for Bush in 1988).

Thanks to Frost's plan the Texas delegation is 21–9 Democratic, giving it as many Democrats as it had in the days of Sam Rayburn when it was all but unanimously Democratic and mostly conservative, with rural bases, oil money connections and loyalty to their leadership. Now there is more diversity, with five Hispanics (one of them a Republican), two blacks and several white liberals, as well as nine Republicans, eight more than ever in Mr. Sam's day; while the Texas delegation is not as fractious as California's, it's nowhere near as united as it was in Mr. Sam's day.

The People: Est. Pop. 1992: 17,656,000; Pop. 1990: 16,986,510, up 3.8% 1990–1992. 6.8% of U.S. total, 3d largest; 20% rural. Median age: 30.8 years. 10.1% 65 years and over. 75.2% White, 25.5% Hispanic origin, 11.9% Black, 1.9% Asian, 10.6% Other. Households: 56.6% married couple families; 30% married couple fams. w. children; 47% college educ.; median household income: $27,016; per capita income: $12,904; 60.9% owner occupied housing; median house value: $59,600; median monthly rent: $328. 7.5% Unemployment. Voting age pop.: 12,150,671. Registered voters (1992): 8,439,874; no party registration.

Political Lineup: Governor, Ann W. Richards (D); Lt. Gov., Bob Bullock (D); Secy. of State, John Hannah, Jr. (D); Atty. Gen., Dan Morales (D); Acting Treasurer, John Bell (D); Comptroller of Public Accounts, John Sharp (D); Auditor, Lawrence Alwin (D). State Senate, 31 (18 D and 13 R); State House of Representatives, 150 (91 D and 59 R). Senators, Phil Gramm (R) and Kay Bailey Hutchison (R). Representatives, 30 (21 D and 9 R).

1992 Presidential Vote

Bush (R)	2,496,071	(41%)
Clinton (D)	2,281,815	(37%)
Perot (I)	1,354,781	(22%)

1992 Democratic Presidential Primary

Clinton	972,151	(66%)
Tsongas	285,191	(19%)
Brown	118,923	(8%)
Other	106,710	(7%)

1988 Presidential Vote

Bush (R)	3,036,829	(56%)
Dukakis (D)	2,352,748	(43%)

1992 Republican Presidential Primary

Bush	556,280	(70%)
Buchanan	190,572	(24%)
Uncommitted	27,936	(4%)

GOVERNOR

Gov. Ann W. Richards (D)

Elected 1990, term expires Jan. 1995; b. Sept. 1, 1933, Lakeview; home, Austin; Baylor U., B.A. 1954; Methodist; divorced.

Career: Jr. high schl. teacher, 1956; Travis Cnty. Commissioner, 1976–82; TX Treasurer, 1982–90.

Office: State Capitol, P.O. Box 12428, Austin 78711, 512-463-2000.

Election Results

1990 gen.	Ann W. Richards (D)	1,925,670	(49%)
	Clayton Williams (R)	1,826,431	(47%)
	Twenty Others	140,645	(4%)
1990 runoff	Ann W. Richards (D)	640,995	(57%)
	Jim Mattox (D)	481,739	(43%)
1990 prim.	Ann W. Richards (D)	580,191	(39%)
	Jim Mattox (D)	546,103	(37%)
	Mark W. White (D)	286,161	(19%)
	Four Others	74,805	(4%)
1986 gen.	William (Bill) Clements (R)	1,813,779	(53%)
	Mark W. White (D)	1,584,515	(46%)

SENATORS

Sen. Phil Gramm (R)

Elected 1984, seat up 1996; b. July 8, 1942, Ft. Benning, GA; home, College Station; U. of GA, B.A. 1964, Ph.D. 1967; Episcopalian; married (Wendy).

Career: Prof., TX A&M U., 1967–78; U.S. House of Reps., 1978–84.

Offices: 370 RSOB 20510, 202-224-2934. Also 2323 Bryan, Dallas 75201, 214-767-3000; 222 E. Van Buren., #404, Harlingen 78550, 512-423-6118; 712 Main, Houston 77002, 713-229-2766; 113 Fed. Bldg., 1205 Texas Ave., Lubbock 79401, 806-743-7533; 123 Pioneer Plz., #665, El Paso 79901, 915-534-6896; 9311 San Pedro, #565, San Antonio 78216, and InterFirst Plz., 102 N. College St., #201, Tyler 75702, 903-593-0902.

Committees: *Appropriations* (8th of 13 R): Agriculture, Rural Development and Related Agencies; Commerce, Justice, State and Judiciary; Defense; Foreign Operations; VA, HUD and Independent Agencies (RMM). *Banking, Housing and Urban Affairs* (2d of 8 R): Economic Stabilization and Rural Development; Intl. Finance and Monetary Policy; Securities (RMM). *Budget* (4th of 9 R).

Group Ratings

	ADA	ACLU	CDF	COPE	CFA	LCV	ACU	NTLC	NSI	COC	CEI
1992	0	5	20	8	17	0	93	94	80	100	82
1991	0	—	27	17	12	20	95	—	—	89	84

National Journal Ratings

	1991 LIB — 1991 CONS	1992 LIB — 1992 CONS
Economic	0% — 91%	0% — 89%
Social	0% — 86%	0% — 89%
Foreign	0% — 87%	10% — 80%

Key Votes of the 102d Congress

1. $ for Homeownership FOR	5. Clarence Thomas Nom. FOR	9. Use Force in Gulf FOR
2. Have Cap Gains Debate FOR	6. Lmt Death Row Appeal FOR	10. Keep Salvador Aid FOR
3. Remove Budget Walls AGN	7. Handgun Wait/5-Day AGN	11. Cut $1B from SDI AGN
4. Ban Striker Replace AGN	8. Abortion Gag Rule FOR	12. Override China MFN AGN

Key Votes of the 103d Congress

1. Family Leave AGN	2. HIV Immigrants AGN	3. Clinton Budget AGN

Election Results

1990 general	Phil Gramm (R) 2,302,357	(60%)	($12,349,397)
	Hugh Parmer (D) 1,429,986	(37%)	($1,677,087)
	Other............................ 89,814	(2%)	
1990 primary	Phil Gramm (R), unopposed		
1984 general	Phil Gramm (R) 3,111,348	(59%)	($9,452,360)
	Lloyd Doggett (D) 2,202,557	(41%)	($5,887,858)

Sen. Kay Bailey Hutchison (R)

Elected June 1993, seat up 1994; b. July 22, 1943, Galveston; home, Dallas; U of TX, B.A. 1992, J.D. 1967; Episcopalian; married (Ray).

Career: Political & legal corresp., KPRC-TV, 1967–70; TX House of Reps., 1972–76; Vice Chmn., Natl. Transp. Safety Bd., 1976–78; V.P. & Gen. Cnsl., RepublicBank Corp., 1978–82; Owner, McCraw Candies, 1984–88; TX Treasurer, 1990–93.

Offices: 703 HSOB 20510, 202-224-5922. Also 961 Fed. Bldg., 300 E. 8th St., Austin 78701, 512-482-5834; 1919 Smith St., #800, Houston 77002, 713-653-3456; and Earle Cabell Bldg., 1100 Commerce St., #7C14, Dallas 75242, 214-767-0577.

Committees: *Armed Services* (10th of 10 R). *Commerce, Science and Transportation* (9th of 9 R). *Small Business* (10th of 10 R).

Group Ratings and Key Votes: Newly Elected

Election Results

1993 runoff	Kay Bailey Hutchison (R) 1,188,716	(67%)	($3,785,382)
	Bob Krueger (D) 576,538	(33%)	($3,194,086)
1993 special	Kay Bailey Hutchison (R)............. 593,479	(29%)	
	Bob Krueger (D)..................... 592,982	(29%)	
	Joe L. Barton (R) 284,135	(14%)	
	Jack M. Fields, Jr. (R) 277,560	(14%)	
	Richard Fisher (D)................... 165,564	(8%)	
	Nineteen Others..................... 131,923	(6%)	
1988 general	Lloyd Bentsen (D)................... 3,149,806	(59%)	($8,829,361)
	Beau Boulter (R).................... 2,129,228	(40%)	($1,353,345)

FIRST DISTRICT

Texarkana doesn't look like the political center of anywhere. It is an old city, with a population of 50,000 and a rural and small town hinterland somewhat larger. Its neat grid streets are noteworthy chiefly because the city, as its name suggests, crosses the Texas-Arkansas state line; the downtown post office straddles the boundary, with the west wing serving Texarkana, Texas, and the east wing Texarkana, Arkansas. Yet this small city and its surroundings produced not one but two presidential candidates in 1992: Ross Perot grew up in Texarkana, while Bill Clinton's boyhood home of Hope, Arkansas, is only 30 miles east on Interstate 30. Both men grew up in comfortable but not lavish circumstances: Perot's father was a cotton broker, Clinton's stepfather a Buick dealer; both lived in town, where the houses were shaded by trees from the pounding summer sun and most people had electricity and indoor plumbing—a vivid contrast with the countryside when Perot was growing up in the 1930s and even when Clinton was young in the late 1940s.

Did the particular atmosphere of the Texarkana area have an effect on these men's politics? One can guess that it did. For both, by their own accounts, were taught to believe that they had obligations to those less fortunate, even while they were obliged themselves to work hard and achieve in school to get ahead. Texarkana was populist country then, a place where farmers producing cotton and crops felt themselves at the mercy of Dallas cotton brokers, Wall Street financiers and railroad magnates who were grabbing all the gains of their hard work. Outside Texarkana, in landscape littered with small houses amid lazily winding rivers, there was little protection from the sun and wind, and precious little ornament; the reservoirs and motels and shopping centers one sees there now are signs of an affluence still only beginning to penetrate what was a zone of subsistence if not poverty. The politics here was always Democratic: Clinton, who remembers his grandfather as a Franklin Roosevelt fan, has certainly never been anything else, while Perot seems more at ease with moderate Democrats like Lloyd Bentsen than with other politicians. And in Texarkana this politics was surely affected by Wright Patman, congressman from the 1st District of Texas from 1928 until his death in 1976, a populist who began his career in the House by moving to impeach Treasury Secretary Andrew Mellon, punctuated it by calling constantly for low interest rates and ended it by being ousted as Banking Committee chairman. But culture here was always traditional: this is an area of heavy churchgoing and proud patriotism. Traces of that can be seen in Perot's military bearing and Clinton's religious cadences.

The 1st Congressional District of Texas includes most of the northeastern corner of the state—east Texas from Texarkana west to within two counties of Dallas and south almost to Lufkin; its boundaries actually became less irregular in the 1991 redistricting. In 1985, the 1st was the scene of one of the pivotal political battles of the decade. To shake the Democrats' hold on rural southern districts, Republican Senator Phil Gramm contrived a special election in the Texas 1st by getting Democratic incumbent Sam Hall appointed to a federal judgeship and recruiting former Texas A&M and pro quarterback Edd Hargett to run as a Republican. Both national and Texas Democrats responded by pouring in money—some raised by Speaker Jim Wright from unscrupulous S&L operators. It was a battle of giants, with Gramm and Lee Atwater on one side, Wright, Senator Lloyd Bentsen and Democratic Congressional Campaign Committee chairman Tony Coelho on the other. The Republicans just missed a breakthrough, as Hargett failed in the first contest to win the 50% needed to avoid a runoff. Hargett's verbal gaffe on trade issues and a relentless emphasis on Social Security helped Democrat Jim Chapman to a 51%–49% win. Gramm's gambit lost, but the Democrats paid a price. It was only after the S&L operators made their crucial contributions here that Jim Wright began intervening with federal regulatory agencies and bottling up reform bills on their behalf, at an ultimate cost to the taxpayer of over $100 billion.

In the House, Chapman was a slavish follower of Wright and for his loyalty Chapman got a seat on Appropriations in 1989. Since Wright's demise, Chapman has made a name on his own. On Appropriations, he is a big backer of Texas's Supercollider and the Space Station Freedom, and works to fund east Texas highway projects, disaster relief and a new supply facility in the Red River Army Depot. On the floor, he successfully pushed through an amendment to the Americans with Disabilities Act allowing restaurants to transfer workers with AIDS from food handling jobs, though there is no proof the disease can be spread this way; it won 199–187 but was later stricken from the bill.

His record has made him popular in the 1st District but may have cost him a seat in the Senate. Republicans touted Chapman's opponents in 1988 and 1990 but he won over 60% both times. In 1992, civic leader Robert E. (Swede) Lee raised $100,000 and decided to run as a Republican; but after winning the March 10 primary, he dropped out of the race April 6, letting Chapman win unopposed (Texas law prohibits write-ins from being counted). But Chapman's ADA amendments sparked bitter opposition from gay rights leaders, who protested vigorously in January 1993 when Chapman was seeking the appointment to Bentsen's Senate seat.

The People: Pop. 1990: 565,594; 56% rural; 16% age 65+; 78% White; 18% Black; 1% Amer. Indian; 2% Other; 3% Hispanic origin. Voting age pop.: 415,855; 16% Black; 3% Hispanic origin. Households: 60% married couple families; 27% married couple fams. w. children; 37% college educ.; median household income: $21,697; per capita income: $10,785; median gross rent: $334; median house value: $43,600.

1992 Presidential Vote

Clinton (D) 85,771 (39%)
Bush (R) 84,545 (38%)
Perot (I). 50,567 (23%)

1988 Presidential Vote

Bush (R) 110,323 (55%)
Dukakis (D). 92,008 (45%)

Rep. Jim Chapman, Jr. (D)

Elected Aug. 1985; b. Mar. 8, 1945, Washington, D.C.; home, Sulphur Springs; U. of TX, B.A. 1968, Southern Methodist U., J.D. 1970; United Methodist; married (Betty).

Career: Practicing atty., 1970–76, 1984–85; Dist. Atty., 8th TX Judicial Dist., 1976–84.

Offices: 2417 RHOB, 202-225-3035. Also P.O. Box 538, Sulphur Springs 75482, 903-885-8682; Fed. Bldg., #G-15, 100 E. Houston St., Marshall 75670, 903-938-8386; and P.O. Box 248, New Boston 75510, 903-628-5594.

Committees: *Appropriations* (20th of 37 D): Energy and Water Development; Legislative; VA, HUD and Independent Agencies.

Group Ratings

	ADA	ACLU	COPE	CDF	CFA	LCV	ACU	NTLC	NSI	COC	CEI
1992	75	64	75	60	80	13	24	5	70	25	22
1991	30	—	67	90	44	0	26	—	—	44	23

National Journal Ratings

	1991 LIB — 1991 CONS	1992 LIB — 1992 CONS
Economic	51% — 49%	48% — 50%
Social	49% — 51%	51% — 49%
Foreign	43% — 57%	36% — 63%

Key Votes of the 102d Congress

1. Ban Striker Replace	FOR	5. Handgun Wait/7-Day	FOR
2. $ for Homeownership	AGN	6. Overseas Mil. Abortion	FOR
3. Tax Rich/Cut Mid Cls.	FOR	7. Obscn. Art NEA $ Ban	FOR
4. FY93/$15B Def. Cut	AGN	8. Death Pen. from Jury	AGN

9. Use Force in Gulf	FOR
10. US Mil. Abroad $ Cut	FOR
11. Limit SDI Funds	*
12. Cuba Trade Embargo	FOR

Key Votes of the 103d Congress

1. Family Leave   FOR   2. Deficit Reduction   AGN   3. Stimulus Plan   FOR

Election Results

1992 general	Jim Chapman, Jr. (D), unopposed			($208,815)
1992 primary	Jim Chapman, Jr. (D), unopposed			
1990 general	Jim Chapman, Jr. (D).................	89,241	(61%)	($463,377)
	Hamp Hodges (R).....................	56,954	(39%)	($408,677)

SECOND DISTRICT

The landmarks of Lone Star history are particularly thick in east Texas, where this giant state was first settled. There's still an Indian reservation in Polk County and the Big Thicket National Preserve to remind you of what this land once looked like. Over near Beaumont is the site of Spindletop, where the world's first gusher spewed out in 1901 and started the Texas oil boom; not far away is the huge oil field that wildcatter H. L. Hunt found in 1931, the foundation for a billion dollar fortune. Much of east Texas looks little different from the wildcat days of 50 years ago: the town squares with courthouses and churches; the stands of cheap, quick-growing pine; plus the strip highway culture of the 1950s. Yet much has changed. Real incomes have tripled over 50 years, endemic diseases have been wiped out, racial segregation has been abolished and the isolation of the small town has been ended by television, the interstate highway and the regional shopping mall. And metropolitan growth, sprinting outward from Houston's loop freeways, is spreading in between the pine forests and reservoirs, creating a new Texas.

The 2d Congressional District of Texas includes all or part of 19 east Texas counties, most of them still seemingly rural; it runs from the oil port of Orange past Lufkin and Nacogodoches to Jacksonville. The political tradition here is Democratic and populist, devoted to traditional values but with a taste for military posture and a certain Texas rowdiness. It delivered solid margins for Ann Richards in 1990 and Bill Clinton in 1992.

The 2d District's congressman is Charlie Wilson—his campaign signs just say "Charlie," with a Texas lone star dotting the 'i'—one of the genuine characters in the House. He is tall, almost spectrally thin, with an aggressive military bearing, flamboyant and pleasure-loving, always ready with a wisecrack or quip, yet also serious-minded when he wants to be and even idealistic. He graduated from the Naval Academy, served four years in the Navy, then got elected to the legislature upon returning to east Texas. He made a record in the Texas Senate that got him classed as a liberal—a high-risk label in the civil rights era—and won the House seat of a scandal-plagued conservative in the 1972 Democratic primary; a term later, he shoved aside a fellow Texan for a seat on Appropriations. Though somewhat liberal on economic issues, he is a hawk on matters military. He now sits on the Appropriations Defense Subcommittee, the small and pro-military panel that often has the House's final say on the defense budget. Wilson made his mark in American, perhaps in world, history as a champion of the Afghan rebels, the man who probably more than any other member of Congress is responsible for U.S. aid to the *mujaheddin*, which helped them to force the Soviets out of their country. He traveled 14 times to Afghanistan, Pakistan and South Asia in the 1980s, started sponsoring secret appropriations for the Afghans in 1982 and kept close relations with Pakistan's leaders. Wilson also serves on the foreign aid subcommittee; he backed debt relief for Egypt because of its role in the Gulf war, and pushed for arms export control in the Middle East.

Wilson's much publicized high living (at least one trip to Afghanistan was with an aide who was a former Miss World) sparked challenges in 1990 and 1992 from Donna Peterson, herself a West Point graduate returned to east Texas. In her first race, she championed traditional values, attacked Wilson for not voting to censure Barney Frank, capitalized on local opposition to Wilson's backing for expansion of the Big Thicket National Preserve and was photographed castrating a calf whom she named Charlie. She held Wilson to a not very impressive 56% of the vote. In 1992, Wilson had an additional problem, 81 overdrafts on the House bank totalling $143,000, and did not receive a letter of exoneration from special counsel Malcolm Wilkey until well after the election. Wilson said he would donate $25 to charity for each check and added, "If my constituents didn't forgive sloppiness and a certain amount of eccentricity, I wouldn't be here in the first place." Peterson's campaign was well-financed and publicized, and a poll Peterson commissioned showed her ahead. Wilson called for a ban on ads and for a series of debates; "he does retail better than Wal-Mart," one observer said. Peterson accused Wilson of failing to respect women and Wilson accused her of being removed from her first military flight class for

1216   TEXAS

misconduct. Redistricting had made the district mildly less Democratic, but the final result was the same as in 1990, a 56% victory for Wilson; he won 61% in the counties from Lufkin to Orange closer to Louisiana and just 52% in the western counties closer to Houston. It was not an overwhelming margin—and he spent more than $1 million with half of that coming from PACs, but it's hard to see how a stronger campaign could be waged against him and in more adverse circumstances than in 1992.

The People: Pop. 1990: 565,906; 61% rural; 14% age 65+; 77% White; 17% Black; 3% Other; 5% Hispanic origin. Voting age pop.: 413,391; 15% Black; 5% Hispanic origin. Households: 61% married couple families; 28% married couple fams. w. children; 32% college educ.; median household income: $21,216; per capita income: $10,113; median gross rent: $333; median house value: $41,800.

1992 Presidential Vote			1988 Presidential Vote		
Clinton (D)	91,731	(43%)	Dukakis (D)	101,986	(52%)
Bush (R)	76,365	(35%)	Bush (R)	95,806	(48%)
Perot (I)	47,157	(22%)			

Rep. Charles Wilson (D)

Elected 1972; b. June 1, 1933, Trinity; home, Lufkin; Sam Houston St. U., 1950–51, U. of TX, 1951–52, U.S. Naval Acad., Annapolis, B.S. 1956; United Methodist; divorced.

Career: Navy, 1956–60; Mgr., lumber store & building co., 1961–71; TX House of Reps., 1960–66; TX Senate, 1966–72.

Offices: 2256 RHOB 20515, 202-225-2401. Also 701 N. 1st St., #201, Lufkin 75901, 409-637-1770.

Committees: *Appropriations* (9th of 37 D): Defense; Foreign Operations, Export Financing and Related Programs.

Group Ratings

	ADA	ACLU	COPE	CDF	CFA	LCV	ACU	NTLC	NSI	COC	CEI
1992	65	57	82	80	53	31	45	10	100	71	19
1991	25	—	82	70	50	46	30	—	—	50	24

National Journal Ratings

	1991 LIB — 1991 CONS		1992 LIB — 1992 CONS	
Economic	52% —	48%	56% —	42%
Social	50% —	48%	49% —	51%
Foreign	35% —	64%	30% —	64%

Key Votes of the 102d Congress

1. Ban Striker Replace	FOR	5. Handgun Wait/7-Day	AGN	9. Use Force in Gulf	FOR
2. $ for Homeownership	FOR	6. Overseas Mil. Abortion	FOR	10. US Mil. Abroad $ Cut	FOR
3. Tax Rich/Cut Mid Cls.	FOR	7. Obscn. Art NEA $ Ban	FOR	11. Limit SDI Funds	AGN
4. FY93/$15B Def. Cut	FOR	8. Death Pen. from Jury	AGN	12. Cuba Trade Embargo	FOR

Key Votes of the 103d Congress

1. Family Leave	FOR	2. Deficit Reduction	AGN	3. Stimulus Plan	FOR

Election Results

1992 general	Charles Wilson (D)......................	118,625	(56%)	($1,193,599)
	Donna Peterson (R)	92,176	(44%)	($344,065)
1992 primary	Charles Wilson (D)......................	74,674	(71%)	
	Stuart Williamson (D)	16,938	(16%)	
	Edgar (Bubba) Groce (D)...............	13,912	(13%)	
1990 general	Charles Wilson (D)......................	76,974	(56%)	($740,342)
	Donna Peterson (R)	61,555	(44%)	($124,884)

THIRD DISTRICT

North Dallas is known all over the world now, the locus of the most successful television program of the 1980s and of the eponymous football novel of the 1970s. The north side of Dallas is in fact one of the nation's most affluent, educated and Republican places. That's ironic, because this part of north Texas started off as one of the poorest, least educated and most Democratic places in the nation. Dallas, named for James K. Polk's vice president, got its commercial start as the place where the first railroad in Texas stopped at the three forks of the Trinity River. By the 1940s, John Gunther wrote, "Its wealth originally came from cotton . . . but primarily it is a banking and jobbing and distributing center, the headquarters of railroads and utilities." On that base, Dallas became one of the nation's leading high-tech cities, the home of Texas Instruments and Ross Perot's EDS, and one of the nation's major defense contracting centers. Increasingly Dallas business has demanded and rewarded expertise, and the city has attracted high-skill people from all over the world, but especially from rural Texas and the rural South.

In the rolling, scrub-covered hills north of downtown Dallas, this growth has built a vast affluent metropolis, extending now 30 miles out into the countryside, defining the mansion-lined streets of Highland Park, building Southern Methodist University as a larger-than-life copy of Thomas Jefferson's University of Virginia. One of the nation's first upscale shopping centers was built here, around the Neiman Marcus store in North Park, as was the nation's first cluster of singles apartments (The Village) along Greenville Avenue. Alongside the Central Expressway, now so choked it may be double-decked, is the office tower where Ross Perot's on-and-off presidential campaign and post-campaign, United We Stand America, have been conducted. North Dallas has long since spread east to White Rock Lake (where Stanley Marcus, the genius of Neiman Marcus, lived for years) and north far past the LBJ Freeway; it has moved north beyond fast-growing Plano in Collin County. With its giant modernist office towers looming over freeways, north Dallas has become the business center of the Dallas-Fort Worth Metroplex, and indeed of a much larger territory: for this is the big city nearest to the population center of the North American free trade area. With its huge airport, and its well-developed business services, north Dallas is poised to be the center of a continent.

Politically, north Dallas has moved about as far from the area's traditional populist Democrats as it could. In 1944, it backed the Texas Regular campaign against Franklin Roosevelt; in 1954 Dallas County elected Republican Bruce Alger to Congress; in 1960 its bitter, angry conservatism became notorious when Alger and others manhandled Lyndon and Lady Bird Johnson in the lobby of the Adolphus Hotel. Unanchored to traditional politics, angry that their money was being taken away by political fixers in Washington, north Dallas millionaires financed odd ducks and fanatics and made laughingstocks of themselves. The raucousness of Dallas politics changed to remorse after President Kennedy was shot there in 1963; and today north Dallas is no longer so alienated. Its continued economic optimism, its belief in old-fashioned hard work and new-fangled technological competence, and its entrepreneurialism have spread outward toward large parts of the rest of the nation.

The 3d Congressional District of Texas is—as much as any—north Dallas's district, though its boundaries are so convoluted as to defy easy description. It includes the Park Cities, Highland

Park and University Park, the home of Ross Perot and Bill Clements and much of the Dallas elite, and the affluent north Dallas neighborhoods that fan out from the Dallas North Tollway. Across town it includes the affluent area around White Rock Lake to the east. A narrow corridor connects most of the upscale suburbs of Garland and Richardson; from there one salient heads south and takes in the eastern Dallas County suburbs of Mesquite and Sunnyvale while another heads north to add Plano and other fast-growing, affluent communities that make up about half the population of Collin County to the north. Politically, all these areas have one thing in common: they are among the most heavily Republican territory in the U.S. This is a district that voted 74% for George Bush in 1988.

The congressman from the 3d District is Sam Johnson, former Air Force fighter pilot and prisoner of war in Vietnam for seven years. The seat came up in a May 1991 special election when incumbent Steve Bartlett, a frustrated political entrepreneur, resigned to run for mayor of Dallas (he won that fall). Johnson had served in the Texas state house since 1984, and he ran second in the primary, with 20%, to 28% for two-time 5th District House candidate and former Peace Corps head Tom Pauken. Pauken, criticized by the *Dallas Morning News* for a TV ad saying he "stood up" to a black politician, ran only a soft ad against Johnson's vote in the legislature for an education reform package diverting money from rich to poor districts. Johnson emphasized his war record, tended to stay above the fray and, although he showed limited knowledge of issues in debate, beat Pauken 53%–47%. His biggest margin was in Collin County, the most newly-settled part of the district.

In the House, Johnson has had a perfectly conservative record, opposing, as the representative of an affluent area, pork barrel projects of all kinds, voting for more IRAs and against extending unemployment benefits. He was one of four congressmen who met with President Bush in October 1992 and urged him to ask for details on Bill Clinton's 1969 trip to Moscow and Eastern Europe—legitimate questions, but which implied a charge that Johnson and the others didn't make and which backfired politically against Bush. Johnson was opposed only by a Libertarian candidate in 1992 and obviously has a safe seat.

The People: Pop. 1990: 565,581; 2% rural; 8% age 65+; 86% White; 4% Black; 3% Asian; 2% Other; 6% Hispanic origin. Voting age pop.: 420,115; 4% Black; 5% Hispanic origin. Households: 61% married couple families; 31% married couple fams. w. children; 72% college educ.; median household income: $45,232; per capita income: $22,946; median gross rent: $534; median house value: $100,100.

1992 Presidential Vote			1988 Presidential Vote		
Bush (R)	133,834	(48%)	Bush (R)	169,019	(74%)
Perot (I)	84,097	(30%)	Dukakis (D)	58,077	(26%)
Clinton (D)	58,398	(21%)			

Rep. Sam Johnson (R)

Elected May 1991; b. Oct. 11, 1930, San Antonio; home, Dallas; Southern Methodist U., B.A. 1951, George Washington U., M.S. 1974; Methodist; married (Shirley).

Career: Air Force, 1951–79 (Korea & Vietnam); Builder; TX House of Reps., 1984–91.

Offices: 1030 LHOB 20515, 202-225-4201. Also 6600 LBJ Freeway, #190, Dallas 75240, 214-767-4848.

Committees: *Banking, Finance and Urban Affairs* (11th of 20 R): Financial Institutions Supervision, Regulation and Deposit Insurance; Housing and Community Development; International Development, Finance, Trade and Monetary Policy. *Science, Space and Technology* (12th of 22 R): Science; Space. *Small Business* (7th of 18 R): Regulation, Business Opportunities and Technology.

Group Ratings

	ADA	ACLU	COPE	CDF	CFA	LCV	ACU	NTLC	NSI	COC	CEI
1992	10	0	25	0	13	0	100	100	100	88	86
1991	0	—	0	29	18	9	100	—	—	100	92

National Journal Ratings

	1991 LIB — 1991 CONS		1992 LIB — 1992 CONS	
Economic	0% —	96%	0% —	91%
Social	0% —	84%	0% —	85%
Foreign	17% —	83%	0% —	82%

Key Votes of the 102d Congress

1. Ban Striker Replace	AGN	5. Handgun Wait/7-Day	*	9. Use Force in Gulf	*
2. $ for Homeownership	FOR	6. Overseas Mil. Abortion	AGN	10. US Mil. Abroad $ Cut	AGN
3. Tax Rich/Cut Mid Cls.	AGN	7. Obscn. Art NEA $ Ban	FOR	11. Limit SDI Funds	AGN
4. FY93/$15B Def. Cut	AGN	8. Death Pen. from Jury	FOR	12. Cuba Trade Embargo	FOR

Key Votes of the 103d Congress

1. Family Leave	AGN	2. Deficit Reduction	AGN	3. Stimulus Plan	AGN

Election Results

1992 general	Sam Johnson (R).....................	201,569	(86%)	($481,802)
	Noel Kopala (LIB)	32,570	(14%)	
1992 primary	Sam Johnson (R).....................	44,920	(83%)	
	David Corley (R)	9,107	(17%)	
1991 runoff	Sam Johnson (R).....................	23,999	(53%)	($291,656)
	Tom Pauken (R)	21,643	(47%)	($426,525)

FOURTH DISTRICT

The Red River Valley, the rural area settled early in Texas's history as a republic, today remains mostly rural in tone. The hardscrabble farm country above this unnavigable river reached its peak population in many counties more than 70 years ago, when large families lived in small houses without electricity and tilled the land with backbreaking labor. This was the part of Texas that first sent Speaker Sam Rayburn to Congress in 1912. The Red River then was one of the strongest Democratic parts of the country, with a sentimental regard for Confederate veterans and a seething hatred of Wall Street bankers; today, that economic populism is muted, but traditional religious values remain strong, even as people head for work on the interstate, listen to country music on their Walkmans and shop at Wal-Marts.

The 4th Congressional District of Texas is the lineal descendant of the seat which was represented by Sam Rayburn for 49 years. In 1940, when Rayburn first became speaker, his 4th Congressional District voted 90% for Franklin Roosevelt; the 4th District of 1988, with one-quarter of its people part of the Dallas-Fort Worth Metroplex overspill and one-third in the oil towns of Tyler and Longview, voted 63% for George Bush. Redistricting subtracted blacks in Tyler and some new Metroplex spillover in Kaufman County and added more Red River areas, which made the 4th more conservative in primaries and Democratic, though for a conservative Democrat, in the general.

And that is the kind of congressman the 4th District has. Ralph Hall was elected to the House in 1980 after a 30-year career in local politics and business. He has a more conservative than liberal voting record, and once declined to vote for Tip O'Neill for speaker. He was one of two Democrats voting to expel Barney Frank on ethics charges in 1990, and in 1993 opposed both President Clinton's budget resolution and his stimulus package. Why does he stay a Democrat? Probably because of his seats on Energy and Commerce and Science, Space and Technology. During reauthorization of the 1990 Clean Air Act, he put together an alternative fuels package with Houston area Republican Jack Fields emphasizing greater use of reformulated gasoline, which by requirement will be sold in the nation's smoggiest cities by the mid-1990s, and denied non-petroleum fuels what Hall regarded as an unfair advantage. Hall had also worked for '900' number regulation, and cable TV reregulation, but he is skeptical of expansion of the Baby Bells into other industries. He chairs the Space Subcommittee on Science, Space and Technology, where he is a big booster of the Supercollider and the Space Shuttle and promotes expansion of a commercial space industry. Hall sees no limit to the possibilities of space: "I fully and firmly believe that we're going to find some cures for the dreaded diseases, cancer and diabetes, there because we can't find them on Earth."

Hall at 69 had more competition in 1992 than he has been used to, and survived handily, with 66% in his first primary challenge since 1980 and a 58%–38% margin in November. But this is a district which could change hands or see a serious contest sometime between now and 2000.

The People: Pop. 1990: 567,231; 49% rural; 14% age 65+; 86% White; 8% Black; 1% Amer. Indian; 2% Other; 4% Hispanic origin. Voting age pop.: 414,229; 8% Black; 3% Hispanic origin. Households: 63% married couple families; 30% married couple fams. w. children; 45% college educ.; median household income: $26,974; per capita income: $12,724; median gross rent: $385; median house value: $57,100.

1992 Presidential Vote

Bush (R)	95,182	(41%)
Perot (I)	69,648	(30%)
Clinton (D)	65,522	(28%)

1988 Presidential Vote

Bush (R)	122,019	(63%)
Dukakis (D)	71,887	(37%)

Rep. Ralph M. Hall (D)

Elected 1980; b. May 3, 1923, Fate; home, Rockwall; U. of TX, TX Christian U., Southern Methodist U., LL.B. 1951; United Methodist; married (Mary Ellen).

Career: Navy, 1942–45 (WWII); Rockwall Cnty. Judge, 1950–62; TX Senate, 1962–72; Practicing atty.; Pres. and CEO, TX Aluminum Corp.; Gen. Cnsl., TX Extrusion Co. Inc.

Offices: 2236 RHOB 20515, 202-225-6673. Also 104 N. San Jacinto St., Rockwall 75087, 214-771-9118; 119 N. Fed. Bldg., Sherman 75090, 214-892-1112; and 211 Fed. Bldg., Tyler 75702, 214-597-3729.

Committees: *Energy and Commerce* (10th of 27 D): Energy and Power; Health and the Environment; Telecommunications and Finance. *Science, Space and Technology* (5th of 33 D): Science; Space (Chmn.).

Group Ratings

	ADA	ACLU	COPE	CDF	CFA	LCV	ACU	NTLC	NSI	COC	CEI
1992	40	22	50	30	47	0	76	63	100	63	58
1991	5	—	17	40	50	0	90	—	—	80	46

National Journal Ratings

	1991 LIB — 1991 CONS		1992 LIB — 1992 CONS	
Economic	33% —	66%	35% —	65%
Social	0% —	84%	26% —	72%
Foreign	31% —	67%	30% —	64%

Key Votes of the 102d Congress

1. Ban Striker Replace	AGN	5. Handgun Wait/7-Day	AGN	9. Use Force in Gulf	FOR
2. $ for Homeownership	FOR	6. Overseas Mil. Abortion	AGN	10. US Mil. Abroad $ Cut	AGN
3. Tax Rich/Cut Mid Cls.	AGN	7. Obscn. Art NEA $ Ban	FOR	11. Limit SDI Funds	FOR
4. FY93/$15B Def. Cut	FOR	8. Death Pen. from Jury	FOR	12. Cuba Trade Embargo	FOR

Key Votes of the 103d Congress

1. Family Leave	AGN	2. Deficit Reduction	AGN	3. Stimulus Plan	AGN

Election Results

1992 general	Ralph M. Hall (D)	128,008	(58%)	($739,979)
	David L. Bridges (R)	83,875	(38%)	($34,412)
	Steven Rothacker (LIB)................	8,450	(4%)	($6,283)
1992 primary	Ralph M. Hall (D)	36,837	(66%)	
	Roger Sanders (D)	18,833	(34%)	
1990 general	Ralph M. Hall (D), unopposed			($210,585)

FIFTH DISTRICT

Dallas is not all glitz and postmodern marble. From each side of downtown, on one of the three street grids that run skew to each other, is an older Dallas, with neighborhoods of high-ceiling old mansions, modest bungalows and shotgun houses running out toward the old airport at Love Field or the State Fair Grounds and the Cotton Bowl in east Dallas or south to the desolate

1222   TEXAS

treeless parks along the cement-lined Trinity River. Some of this older Dallas is being renovated and rebuilt, with chic cafes and trendy stores serving those who make their livings catering to the rich farther north. Other once middle-class neighborhoods are filling up with immigrants from Mexico and other parts of Latin America, once again noisy with children as they were in the 1950s when their parents were migrants not from Mexico or Central America but from the almost all-anglo counties of north and central Texas.

Texas's 5th Congressional District, thanks to imaginative redistricting, now combines east Dallas and rural central Texas, into a constituency designed to reelect Democrat John Bryant, yet give most of his black and Hispanic precincts to the new majority-black 30th District. In Dallas the 5th includes part of the singles neighborhood of Oak Lawn, much of the eastern edge of the city and parts of the suburbs of Garland, Mesquite and Seagoville; 56% of the district's population is in Dallas County. Then, through a narrow corridor which avoids many new subdivisions, the district goes southeast to include seven rural and small town counties, about halfway between Dallas and Houston. It also reaches out to bring in black neighborhoods in Tyler and Bryan. The Dallas County precincts were chosen because they are reliably, though not overwhelmingly, Democratic; the central Texas counties have a strong enough Democratic tradition to have voted for Ann Richards over Clayton Williams for governor in 1990.

The congressman from the 5th is John Bryant, an old-fashioned Democrat from Dallas who was born in small town Texas. He is a career politician, elected to the Texas House in 1974 two years after finishing law school; he was elected to the U.S. House in 1982 with 65% against a well-known opponent in the Democratic primary. In his first term, Bryant won a seat on the most coveted legislative committee, Energy and Commerce. In his work can be discerned a reasonably consistent set of values. He sees government as a protector of children and young people: he pushed for the Children's Television Act which limits the amount of advertising time on children's programming and passed a Children of Substance Abusers Act. He believes in greater federal regulation: of stock trading, of Baby Bell long distance market access, of network syndication rules, though—this is Texas—he is opposed to regulation of oil and natural gas prices. He is a work horse, serving on Judiciary as well as Energy and Commerce and Budget.

Bryant also shares the desire rural Texans felt for years to insulate themselves against the outside world. He is hostile to immigration, doubtful that the country can produce enough jobs for its citizens if more immigrants are allowed in (although it has produced nearly 40 million jobs in the last 20 years); he fought the 1990 immigration bill. He was chief sponsor of a bill to require foreign owners of U.S. companies to disclose assets—a bill attacked as a know-nothing attempt to discourage foreign investment but which has passed the House twice; in 1989–90 a more moderate measure sponsored by Philip Sharp passed the House and became law. Bryant has sponsored bills to require U.S. allies to bear a larger share of defense costs and boasts of his efforts to transfer foreign aid funding to domestic job creation. On both immigration and foreign investment, Bryant seems a tribune of a native-born working class that sees demographic and economic change as a threat and that wants to maintain its current place rather than take chances on economic growth.

Bryant made national headlines in April 1992 when, after the House bank scandal broke, he called for Speaker Thomas Foley to step aside. "For Tom Foley," he argued, "political leadership is not a responsibility he relishes. For him, political leadership is painful, and political combat, even when absolutely necessary in order to present the nation with a Democratic alternative, is to be avoided if at all possible." Bryant seems to have acted out of conviction not ambition, for he was not seeking any leadership post and had 55 overdrafts himself; and it can be argued that Foley took some of this criticism to heart. Even so, Bryant clearly is not on Foley's good side. Meanwhile, Bryant remains busy at home, tending his new counties, saving the Mexia State School, the largest employer in Limestone County, and getting books from the Library of Congress when the school library in Buffalo burned down. Bryant was reelected by a 59%–37% margin, actually running better in the new parts of the district (61%–36%) than in Dallas County (56%–39%).

The People: Pop. 1990: 565,916; 25% rural; 12% age 65+; 64% White; 16% Black; 1% Asian; 10% Other; 17% Hispanic origin. Voting age pop.: 414,120; 15% Black; 15% Hispanic origin. Households: 53% married couple families; 26% married couple fams. w. children; 38% college educ.; median household income: $24,045; per capita income: $11,219; median gross rent: $401; median house value: $52,900.

1992 Presidential Vote		
Clinton (D)	70,298	(40%)
Bush (R)	59,588	(34%)
Perot (I)	45,131	(26%)

1988 Presidential Vote		
Bush (R)	89,284	(53%)
Dukakis (D)	80,495	(47%)

Rep. John Bryant (D)

Elected 1982; b. Feb. 22, 1947, Lake Jackson; home, Dallas; Southern Methodist U., B.A. 1969, J.D. 1972; United Methodist; married (Janet).

Career: Practicing atty., 1972–82; Chief Cnsl., TX Senate Consumer Affairs Subcmte., 1973; TX House of Reps., 1974–82.

Offices: 205 CHOB 20515, 202-225-2231. Also 8035 E. R.L.Thornton Freeway, #518, Dallas 75228, 214-767-6554.

Committees: *Budget* (7th of 26 D). *Energy and Commerce* (13th of 27 D): Health and the Environment; Oversight and Investigations; Telecommunications and Finance. *Judiciary* (13th of 21 D): Administrative Law and Governmental Relations (Chmn.); International Law, Immigration and Refugees.

Group Ratings

	ADA	ACLU	COPE	CDF	CFA	LCV	ACU	NTLC	NSI	COC	CEI
1992	80	80	82	90	73	75	14	13	40	38	14
1991	80	—	92	90	72	77	11	—	—	33	5

National Journal Ratings

	1991 LIB — 1991 CONS			1992 LIB — 1992 CONS		
Economic	64%	—	35%	65%	—	34%
Social	74%	—	26%	57%	—	41%
Foreign	78%	—	19%	65%	—	35%

Key Votes of the 102d Congress

1. Ban Striker Replace	FOR	5. Handgun Wait/7-Day	FOR	9. Use Force in Gulf	AGN
2. $ for Homeownership	AGN	6. Overseas Mil. Abortion	FOR	10. US Mil. Abroad $ Cut	FOR
3. Tax Rich/Cut Mid Cls.	FOR	7. Obscn. Art NEA $ Ban	FOR	11. Limit SDI Funds	FOR
4. FY93/$15B Def. Cut	FOR	8. Death Pen. from Jury	AGN	12. Cuba Trade Embargo	FOR

Key Votes of the 103d Congress

1. Family Leave	FOR	2. Deficit Reduction	FOR	3. Stimulus Plan	FOR

Election Results

1992 general	John Bryant (D)	98,567	(59%)	($795,462)
	Richard Stokley (R)	62,419	(37%)	($44,542)
	William H. Walker (LIB)...............	6,344	(4%)	
1992 primary	John Bryant (D), unopposed			
1990 general	John Bryant (D)	65,228	(60%)	($1,034,491)
	Jerry Rucker (R).....................	41,307	(38%)	($453,165)
	Other................................	2,939	(3%)	

SIXTH DISTRICT

Waxahachie, Texas, in Ellis County just south of Dallas, was once cottonfield country; Ellis County in the 1880s boasted it was the "Queen Cotton County of the world." Well into the 20th Century, Waxahachie remained one of the largest primary cotton markets in Texas, the site of a textile mill that produced heavy materials and home of two cottonseed oil mills. That meant Waxahachie and Ellis County were at the low end of the national economy, with most of its rural people working in back-breaking drudgery under the broiling Texas sun, and people in town concentrated in low-tech, low-skill operations. Waxahachie in the 1990s may be at the other end of the national economy, for it is slated to be literally the center of the Supercollider being built by the Energy Department—"the greatest basic science facility," in one booster's words, "of the latter 20th Century." The accelerator, designed to probe the material origins of the universe, is being built like a 54-mile race track, centered on Waxahachie; it is supposed to cost some $8 billion to build and $270 million a year to run. More than 30 states competed for the SSC; Texas won, publicized in an announcement made shortly after the 1988 election. If politics played a role in giving George Bush's home state a major high-tech facility, then surely politics played a role in 1993 in saving the Supercollider from demise. Originally on Clinton's budget hit list, the Supercollider avoided the ax—and got a 24% increase in funding—most assuredly to strengthen the hold of Bentsen replacement Bob Krueger for the Senate special election. But Krueger's loss to Republican Kay Bailey Hutchison may put the Supercollider in jeopardy once again.

Anyway, thanks to the Supercollider, Waxahachie, with only 18,500 people, is the political linchpin of Texas's 6th Congressional District. The 6th is the descendant of a district that stretched across rural territory from Houston to Dallas-Fort Worth, and was represented from 1978 to 1984 by Phil Gramm, who switched from Boll Weevil Democrat to Republican, even as the balance of population in the 6th shifted from rural to metropolitan. Now, after the 1991 redistricting, it is entirely contained in the Dallas-Fort Worth Metroplex. Its convoluted boundaries were drawn by Democrat Martin Frost, but to accommodate Republican Congressman Joe Barton, who won the 6th District in 1984 when Gramm ran for the Senate. Barton promised that he would stick with Waxahachie and the Supercollider however the lines were drawn; Frost did not relish fighting a Republican incumbent in Republican-leaning territory, and so drew a new 6th District which in effect is a collection of Republican neighborhoods and suburbs south of Dallas and almost entirely surrounding Fort Worth. It starts with parts of Waxahachie and Ennis, then goes north through a narrow corridor to include the bulk of Arlington, its largest community and one with many defense engineers; it includes an affluent area on the east side of Fort Worth and the Bible Belt suburbs north of Fort Worth and west of DFW Airport—Bedford, Euless, Grapevine, Colleyville. The new 6th then crosses a couple of reservoirs to bypass Fort Worth on the west, except for its most affluent neighborhood around Texas Christian University, to include the rural country around Joshua. Almost every precinct is heavily Republican; the district voted 72% for George Bush in 1988, making it one of the dozen or two most Republican in the nation.

Joe Barton is a feisty, aggressive, true-believing conservative who had to fight hard for this seat: he won his 1984 Republican runoff by only 10 votes, got 57% in the general election, then won with 56% in 1986 against the well-financed Democrat Pete Geren, who since 1989 has represented the Fort Worth-based 12th District. Barton has two great causes. One is the Supercollider, of which he is surely the House's most enthusiastic advocate: on it he has centered his whole career. The other is the constitutional balanced budget amendment, of which he is chief House sponsor; he wants to require a three-fifths vote for a tax increase if government spending grows at a faster rate than the economy. He has also pushed hard to allow sales of the F-16 (made in Fort Worth) to Taiwan. He has a seat on the Energy and Commerce Committee, where he opposed cable reregulation (and got many cable contributions); he opposed a 100% Medicaid buy-in for the low-income elderly because it would leave no incentive to hold costs down.

In December 1992, just after Lloyd Bentsen's appointment as treasury secretary, Barton announced he was running for the Senate. Looking younger than his years, he stressed that he has represented all or part of Texas counties with 45% of the state's population (the 6th once extended to Houston's Harris County), that he is in line with majority Texas opinion on the balanced budget amendment and keeping the ban on gays in the military, and that on the Supercollider and F-16 he has shown he can get results. In the multi-candidate field, his chance of finishing in the top two was not trivial; but his 14% win was not enough to get him there and he finished third out of 24.

The People: Pop. 1990: 566,256; 9% rural; 6% age 65+; 88% White; 5% Black; 2% Asian; 2% Other; 5% Hispanic origin. Voting age pop.: 412,594; 4% Black; 5% Hispanic origin. Households: 64% married couple families; 34% married couple fams. w. children; 67% college educ.; median household income: $41,697; per capita income: $18,824; median gross rent: $470; median house value: $92,300.

1992 Presidential Vote			1988 Presidential Vote		
Bush (R)	127,158	(46%)	Bush (R)	150,576	(72%)
Perot (I)	83,633	(30%)	Dukakis (D)	58,345	(28%)
Clinton (D)	65,846	(24%)			

Rep. Joe L. Barton (R)

Elected 1984; b. Sept. 15, 1949, Waco; home, Ennis; Texas A&M U., B.S. 1972, Purdue U., M.S. 1973; United Methodist; married (Janet).

Career: Asst. to V.P., Ennis Business Forms, 1973–81; White House Fellow, U.S. Dept. of Energy, 1981–82; Consultant, Atlantic Richfield Co., 1982–84.

Offices: 1514 LHOB 20515, 202-225-2002. Also InterFirst Tower, #507, Conroe 77301, 409-760-2291; 809 University Ave., #222 Creekwide Plz., Bryan 77840, 409-846-9791; InterFirst Bank Bldg., #101, Ennis 75119, 214-875-8488; and 3509 Hulen, #110, Ft. Worth 76107, 817-737-7737.

Committees: *Energy and Commerce* (7th of 17 R): Energy and Power; Telecommunications and Finance. *Science, Space and Technology* (10th of 22 R): Investigations and Oversight; Science.

Group Ratings

	ADA	ACLU	COPE	CDF	CFA	LCV	ACU	NTLC	NSI	COC	CEI
1992	5	0	27	0	13	0	100	90	100	75	85
1991	10	—	8	20	39	0	90	—	—	90	79

National Journal Ratings

	1991 LIB — 1991 CONS		1992 LIB — 1992 CONS	
Economic	17% —	82%	0% —	91%
Social	25% —	73%	0% —	85%
Foreign	17% —	78%	0% —	82%

Key Votes of the 102d Congress

1. Ban Striker Replace	AGN	5. Handgun Wait/7-Day	AGN	9. Use Force in Gulf	FOR
2. $ for Homeownership	FOR	6. Overseas Mil. Abortion	AGN	10. US Mil. Abroad $ Cut	AGN
3. Tax Rich/Cut Mid Cls.	AGN	7. Obscn. Art NEA $ Ban	FOR	11. Limit SDI Funds	AGN
4. FY93/$15B Def. Cut	AGN	8. Death Pen. from Jury	FOR	12. Cuba Trade Embargo	FOR

Key Votes of the 103d Congress

1. Family Leave	AGN	2. Deficit Reduction	AGN	3. Stimulus Plan	*

Election Results

1992 general	Joe L. Barton (R)	189,140	(72%)	($1,423,644)
	John Dietrich (D)	73,933	(28%)	($13,751)
1992 primary	Joe L. Barton (R)	34,366	(79%)	
	Mike McGinn (R).....................	9,089	(21%)	
1990 general	Joe L. Barton (R)	125,049	(67%)	($458,346)
	John E. Welch (D)	62,344	(33%)	($6,568)

SEVENTH DISTRICT

Memorial Park, the largest greensward in greater Houston, is in many ways the epicenter of the whole metropolitan area. In a city proud of its lack of zoning laws, where Taco Bells sit next to gleaming high rises a block away from exquisite maisonettes and down the road from a galleria, Memorial Park is a planned enterprise that works, funneling traffic slowly past joggers, rich with trees and with views of the high-rises a few miles east in downtown and closer by in the Post Oak-Westheimer area. This is the home—he proved it by moving back here when he lost—of President George Bush; his old Houston homes and his new planned one are within a mile west of the park, just south of Buffalo Bayou; his favorite shopping mall is nearby on Sage and San Felipe and his favorite barbecue joint a mile east on Memorial; his new office is atop the Park Laureate building at 10000 Memorial before it hits Chimney Rock. When the young Bush family moved to Houston in 1960, this was, if not quite the frontier, at least the outer edge of urban settlement, a new zone of affluent houses on comfortable wooded acreage, before upscale shopping malls and office buildings sprang up. Now Memorial Park and George Bush's Houston are part of the interior of the metropolitan area, probably its retail and not far from its commercial center of gravity, though the industrial center of gravity remains far to the east, near the Ship Channel.

Today's 7th Congressional District of Texas is the lineal descendant of the district that elected George Bush its first member of the House in 1966 and 1968. First created for those elections, it has been much pared back since, as the population of the west side of Houston has skyrocketed; there are probably more than 1.5 million people today in the area that had 350,000 when Bush was first elected. Indeed, the 1980s 7th District had 784,000 people in 1990, the second most in Texas, and had to be pared back again, to the point that Memorial Park now sits just outside the far eastern edge of the district, which then extends west on Westheimer and the Katy Freeway and occupies part of Harris County west of Hillcroft and Bingle. It remains hyper-Republican, quite possibly the most Republican district in the country; folks may have been unhappy with some aspects of Bush's presidency, but few voted for Bill Clinton or Ross Perot.

Bill Archer, the congressman from the 7th District, was elected in 1970 when Bush ran for the

Senate (and lost to Lloyd Bentsen). Archer is now ranking Republican on the House Ways and Means Committee. He started off in politics as a Democrat, but his devotion to free market economics, cultural conservatism and an assertive foreign policy are not in doubt; he has one of the most conservative voting records in Congress. Moreover, he can argue his positions ably and with plenty of facts and figures. But his work, in the minority for more than 22 years, must be frustrating; one can understand why Bush took the risks of a statewide candidacy rather than become the guy who is beaten by, or on occasion totally ignored by, someone like Dan Rostenkowski. Archer, with his strong convictions and secure political base, has been willing to be in an even smaller minority: he opposed the 1984 Social Security bailout and was one of the Republicans who nearly scuttled the 1986 tax reform in December 1985. He is not afraid to call Democratic tactics for extending unemployment benefits "ridiculous," as he did in 1992 and came fairly close to getting the bill recommitted to Ways and Means (losing 219–191).

Archer does have an effect at times. In 1992, he got the House to adopt his provision extending the alternate minimum tax to independent oil and gas producers, and he worked to let homeowners who sell their homes at a loss to deduct that against a future gain from a home sale. He has been less successful on eliminating capital gains taxes for those who invest in enterprise zones, a proposal squelched for years by Rostenkowski. Archer's relationship with the chairman has remained pleasant, but of course Rostenkowski has held just about all the cards; should someone else become chairman, Archer might gain influence.

The People: Pop. 1990: 566,440; 4% rural; 6% age 65+; 77% White; 6% Black; 6% Asian; 5% Other; 12% Hispanic origin. Voting age pop.: 413,369; 5% Black; 11% Hispanic origin. Households: 57% married couple families; 31% married couple fams. w. children; 71% college educ.; median household income: $42,157; per capita income: $23,171; median gross rent: $475; median house value: $88,000.

1992 Presidential Vote			1988 Presidential Vote		
Bush (R)	137,541	(57%)	Bush (R)	150,889	(78%)
Clinton (D)	52,501	(22%)	Dukakis (D)	41,363	(22%)
Perot (I)	49,201	(21%)			

Rep. Bill Archer (R)

Elected 1970; b. Mar. 22, 1928, Houston; home, Houston; Rice U., 1945–46, U. of TX, B.B.A. 1949, LL.B. 1951; Catholic; married (Sharon).

Career: Air Force, 1951–53; Pres., Uncle Johnny Mills Inc., 1953–61; Hunters Creek Village Cncl., Mayor Pro Tem, 1955–62; TX House of Reps., 1966–70; Dir., Heights State Bank, Houston, 1967–70; Practicing atty., 1968–71.

Offices: 1236 LHOB 20515, 202-225-2571. Also 1003 Wirt Rd., #311, Houston 77055, 713-467-7493.

Committees: *Ways and Means* (RMM of 14 R). *Joint Committee on Taxation* (4th of 5).

Group Ratings

	ADA	ACLU	COPE	CDF	CFA	LCV	ACU	NTLC	NSI	COC	CEI
1992	0	0	17	0	13	13	100	89	100	75	92
1991	0	—	0	20	17	23	95	—	—	100	93

National Journal Ratings

	1991 LIB — 1991 CONS			1992 LIB — 1992 CONS		
Economic	4%	—	90%	0%	—	91%
Social	0%	—	84%	0%	—	85%
Foreign	0%	—	88%	0%	—	82%

Key Votes of the 102d Congress

1. Ban Striker Replace	AGN	5. Handgun Wait/7-Day	AGN	9. Use Force in Gulf	FOR
2. $ for Homeownership	FOR	6. Overseas Mil. Abortion	AGN	10. US Mil. Abroad $ Cut	AGN
3. Tax Rich/Cut Mid Cls.	AGN	7. Obscn. Art NEA $ Ban	FOR	11. Limit SDI Funds	AGN
4. FY93/$15B Def. Cut	AGN	8. Death Pen. from Jury	FOR	12. Cuba Trade Embargo	FOR

Key Votes of the 103d Congress

1. Family Leave	AGN	2. Deficit Reduction	AGN	3. Stimulus Plan	AGN

Election Results

1992 general	Bill Archer (R), unopposed	($121,751)
1992 primary	Bill Archer (R), unopposed	
1990 general	Bill Archer (R), unopposed	($200,871)

EIGHTH DISTRICT

When Houston Intercontinental Airport opened in 1969, it was located far north of the city, in vacant ground near the small town of Humble (named for the oil company that was the predecessor of Exxon)—much too far, said many, from downtown Houston or from just about any other concentration of population. Today Intercontinental is still a long way from downtown Houston—traffic jams on the way to the airport have only started to abate after it has spent $7 billion on infrastructure since 1985—but it is no longer in the middle of nowhere. It's in the middle of a zone of rapid metropolitan expansion and growth, of commercial office space and upscale residential subdivisions rising on land that once held roadside stands and barbecues and unpainted farmhouses with water pooling on low swampy fields. Greater Houston has spread far out into the countryside, past Loop 610 in the inner city, past the Sam Houston Beltway, past the now mislabeled Farm-Market 1960, out beyond once rural Montgomery County.

So also has moved the 8th Congressional District of Texas. A district that once covered the docks along the Houston Ship Channel has moved out with the people, so that its southern boundary runs roughly along the Sam Houston Parkway. It includes almost all of Montgomery County and two still mostly rural counties to the west and takes in College Station, home of Texas A&M University. This institution deserves more notice than it usually gets: it is one of Texas's two major state universities, with quite a different atmosphere from the University of Texas at Austin. A&M specializes in technical subjects, though it has other topnotch departments; it has a military lineage, though students are no longer required to serve in the cadet corps; it attracts a student body with strong credentials that is much more conservative culturally and politically than UT's. Senator Phil Gramm used to teach economics at A&M and HUD Secretary Henry Cisneros graduated from there and served on the board until 1993; A&M is also the site of the George Bush Presidential Library. College Station, and almost all the rest of the 8th District, is staunchly Republican: defiantly free market on economics, respectful of tradition on cultural issues, firmly hawkish on military policy.

The congressman from the 8th District is Jack Fields, who first won the seat when he upset a liberal Democratic incumbent in 1980; now he has turned out to be one of the more active and experienced legislators in conservative Republican ranks—and a contender for Lloyd Bentsen's Senate seat in the spring 1993 special election. Fields has kept his roots in this area even as it has changed. He lives on land his family has owned since the 1860s; he returns home every weekend where his family still has its business, the Rosewood Cemetery and Funeral Home, in Humble; he has held more than 500 town meetings in 12 years and had the satisfaction of seeing his constituency share his opinions increasingly over time. Fields has served on the Energy and Commerce Committee since his second term, and is now third ranking Republican. He supported decontrol of oil and natural gas prices and sponsored the Hall-Fields alternate fuels amendment to the clean air bill to encourage the use of reformulated gasoline and required its use by 1995 in the nine smoggiest cities. Fields showed considerable skill in compromising Hall-Fields to keep it alive and protecting it on the floor and in conference; now he is moving to help school buses convert to alternative fuels. His current energy proposals include incentives for energy-efficient appliances and tax credits for use of renewable energy sources. His efforts to open up oil exploration in the Arctic National Wildlife Refuge or the coastal shelf in the Gulf of Mexico have not been successful. He used some fancy footwork to kill a measure allowing tax-exempt bond financing for a Dallas-Houston bullet train he opposes. On Energy and Commerce, Fields has tended to go where the action is, shifting from the Clean Air Act panel in 1989–90 to become ranking Republican on Telecommunications and Finance in 1993.

Fields is also ranking minority member on the Merchant Marine and Fisheries Committee. He has worked there on Coast Guard oil spill response efforts, on getting funds to clean up Galveston Bay and the Houston Ship Channel, on his abandoned barge act and a bill to transfer a Navy vessel to Texas A&M at Galveston.

Fields, with his perfectly conservative voting record on just about every issue, is an example of activist conservatism: against federal spending and government regulations, but willing and able to work within the system. He has proved widely popular in the 8th District, but was unable to expand that popularity statewide in a run for Lloyd Bentsen's vacated Senate seat. Fields finished 4th with 14% in the 24-field open primary on May 1, trailing fellow 6th District Congressman Joe Barton, also with 14%, by 8,600 votes.

The People: Pop. 1990: 566,572; 35% rural; 7% age 65+; 85% White; 5% Black; 2% Asian; 3% Other; 7% Hispanic origin. Voting age pop.: 408,402; 5% Black; 6% Hispanic origin. Households: 64% married couple families; 35% married couple fams. w. children; 58% college educ.; median household income: $35,454; per capita income: $15,998; median gross rent: $439; median house value: $78,200.

1992 Presidential Vote			1988 Presidential Vote		
Bush (R)	134,184	(55%)	Bush (R)	134,412	(73%)
Clinton (D)	55,917	(23%)	Dukakis (D)	49,815	(27%)
Perot (I)	55,199	(23%)			

Rep. Jack M. Fields, Jr. (R)

Elected 1980; b. Feb. 3, 1952, Humble; home, Humble; Baylor U., B.A. 1974, J.D. 1977; Baptist; married (Lynn).

Career: Practicing atty., 1977–80; Vice Pres., Rosewood Memorial Funeral Home, 1977–80.

Offices: 2228 RHOB 20515, 202-225-4901. Also 111 E. University Dr., #216, College Station 77480, 409-846-6068; 300 W. Davis, #507, Conroe 77301, 409-756-8044; and 9810 FM1960 Bypass W., #165, Deerbrook Plz., Humble 77338, 409-540-8000.

Committees: *Energy and Commerce* (3d of 17 R): Telecommunications and Finance (RMM); Transportation and Hazardous Materials. *Merchant Marine and Fisheries* (RMM of 19 R).

Group Ratings

	ADA	ACLU	COPE	CDF	CFA	LCV	ACU	NTLC	NSI	COC	CEI
1992	5	5	25	0	13	0	96	100	90	75	84
1991	0	—	8	20	28	0	100	—	—	100	86

National Journal Ratings

	1991 LIB — 1991 CONS		1992 LIB — 1992 CONS	
Economic	4% —	90%	0% —	91%
Social	0% —	84%	0% —	85%
Foreign	0% —	88%	0% —	82%

Key Votes of the 102d Congress

1. Ban Striker Replace	AGN	5. Handgun Wait/7-Day	AGN	9. Use Force in Gulf	FOR
2. $ for Homeownership	FOR	6. Overseas Mil. Abortion	AGN	10. US Mil. Abroad $ Cut	AGN
3. Tax Rich/Cut Mid Cls.	AGN	7. Obscn. Art NEA $ Ban	FOR	11. Limit SDI Funds	AGN
4. FY93/$15B Def. Cut	AGN	8. Death Pen. from Jury	FOR	12. Cuba Trade Embargo	FOR

Key Votes of the 103d Congress

1. Family Leave	AGN	2. Deficit Reduction	AGN	3. Stimulus Plan	AGN

Election Results

1992 general	Jack M. Fields, Jr. (R)	179,349	(77%)	($746,361)
	Charles (Chas.) Robinson (D).	53,473	(23%)	
1992 primary	Jack M. Fields, Jr. (R), unopposed			
1990 general	Jack M. Fields, Jr. (R), unopposed			($420,288)

NINTH DISTRICT

From Spindletop park in Beaumont, where Texas's oil industry began, to the Lyndon B. Johnson Space Center south of Houston, where America's probes into space are planned, stretches the 9th Congressional District of Texas. About half its population is around Beaumont and Port Arthur, near the border of Cajun Louisiana, an area laced with the intricate metalwork of refineries, petrochemical plants and oil tank farms. For years this was one corner of Texas where labor unions had some strength, but since the collapse of oil prices in the 1980s there has been little growth here. The other half of the 9th's population lives around Galveston Bay. The city of Galveston, built on a sand spit and rebuilt after 6,000 people died in the devastating hurricane of 1900, was once the great entry port of Texas and is now the site of a Dickensian Christmas celebration (!) each year. After the hurricane, development centered on Houston, but the Houston metro area has long since expanded to the Bay—to the Space Center, brought here by Vice President Lyndon Johnson and longtime Houston Congressman Albert Thomas, and Texas City, where more than 500 perished in a huge liquefied natural gas tanker explosion in 1947. The 9th District was redrawn slightly for 1992, subtracting some Harris County precincts around the Space Center and adding some blue-collar ones around Baytown and northeast of Houston.

The congressman from the 9th District is Jack Brooks, second most senior member of the House, chairman of the Judiciary Committee, one of the toughest and smartest members of Congress. Brooks worked his way through school as a reporter, was a Marine in the Pacific in World War II, was elected to the state legislature from the Beaumont area at age 23, winning his crucial primary three months before Bill Clinton was born. He politicked astutely enough to chair the Banks and Banking Committee in his mid-20s and was elected to Congress in 1952, just before turning 30. With a deep accent and craggy appearance, Brooks is profane and witty, an old-fashioned man's man who likes to hunt and fish and smoke cigars (though his doctor has told him to stop); but he is also a collector of antique clocks. He is smart and shrewd, able to figure out how to get things done—and to see that they are done his way. Brooks is also fearless: representing a district that reached far into rural east Texas in the 1950s and early 1960s, he had a liberal voting record and voted without hesitation for the Civil Rights Act of 1964, when that took real guts.

As chairman of Government Operations for 14 years, Brooks was known as an aggressive investigator of agencies and a stickler on government procurement issues—the telephone contract, for example. On Judiciary, he was called "the executioner" by Richard Nixon for his aggressive questioning of administration officials. Chairman of Judiciary since 1989, he has been active on the committee's jurisdictional fights with Energy and Commerce Chairman John Dingell—a true battle of the giants. Brooks claims bills because of legal and copyright provisions, Dingell because they regulate communications or commerce. Brooks opposed Dingell's approach on cable reregulation, because it failed to phase out the compulsory copyright license, but Dingell controlled the conference committee and fashioned the one bill that passed over President Bush's veto. Brooks has a bill imposing new legal hurdles that would thwart the Baby Bells from entering new businesses such as manufacturing telecommunications equipment and providing long distance services and information services. A key provision imposing strict waiting periods on the Bells to enter new businesses was struck down, but the bill is generally favored by newspaper publishers and others who are vehemently opposed to the Bells providing information services. Brooks pushed his bill through Judiciary in 1992, but the issue will be revisited in the 103d Congress, most likely under the regulatory auspices of Dingell's Commerce Committee. The bitterest battles on Capitol Hill, it is said, are between lobbyists for competing economic interests; Brooks and Dingell are in the thick of them. "We are the ants and fleas," one lobbyist says. "They are tyrannosaurus rex. They can squash us."

On other Judiciary issues, Brooks has mostly but not always taken liberal positions. He opposes the balanced budget amendment ("filled with soft and fuzzy feel-good words") and favors the Freedom of Choice Act. He favors a new independent counsel law and wanted a counsel appointed for the Iraqgate scandal (although, as his 1992 opponent pointed out, he sent a letter to Agriculture Secretary Clayton Yeutter in May 1990 questioning delays in financing for rice shipments to Iraq from east Texas). He has favored various civil rights bills but has criticized the Civil Rights Commission for "divisive rhetoric." He has backed crime bills but opposed the Brady bill for a waiting period for gun purchases. He favors capital punishment but has referred such issues to the subcommittee headed by death penalty opponent Don Edwards. He is not an antitrust purist: he wants to modify the McCarran-Ferguson antitrust exemption for insurance companies to allow sharing of rate information and to allow joint venture manufacturing agreements. He gave crucial support to the 1990 immigration law. He called for a tribunal for war crimes prosecutions after the Gulf war, to "ensure that aggressive behavior that went beyond the bounds of international law would not be allowed to stand."

Brooks works to bring in pork to his district—the Trinity Marine floating drydock in Beaumont yards, a child care facility at Fort Point in Galveston, removing a hazardous railroad swing bridge over Clear Creek Channel, a new federal prison near Beaumont. But he is not afraid of high-risk politics and has had some close races—a 50%–43% primary in 1980, 58% in the 1990 general. In 1992, Republican Steve Stockman campaigned pointedly for term limits, while Brooks, in his 40th year in Congress, joked, "I don't want to make a career of this." His percentage went down to 54%, and he lost the Harris County portion of the district. But nothing is likely to scare Jack Brooks.

The People: Pop. 1990: 566,154; 13% rural; 11% age 65+; 67% White; 22% Black; 2% Asian; 3% Other; 9% Hispanic origin. Voting age pop.: 410,542; 20% Black; 8% Hispanic origin. Households: 56% married couple families; 27% married couple fams. w. children; 47% college educ.; median household income: $29,420; per capita income: $13,745; median gross rent: $398; median house value: $52,700.

1992 Presidential Vote

Clinton (D) 98,959 (44%)
Bush (R) 80,813 (36%)
Perot (I). 47,418 (21%)

1988 Presidential Vote

Dukakis (D). 104,860 (54%)
Bush (R) 90,445 (46%)

Rep. Jack Brooks (D)

Elected 1952; b. Dec. 18, 1922, Crowley, LA; home, Beaumont; Lamar Col., 1939–41, U. of TX, B.J. 1943, J.D. 1949; United Methodist; married (Charlotte).

Career: Marine Corps, 1942–46 (WWII), Marine Corps Reserves, 1946–72; TX House of Reps., 1946–50; Practicing atty., 1949–52.

Offices: 2449 RHOB 20515, 202-225-6565. Also 201 Jack Brooks Fed. Bldg., Beaumont 77701, 409-839-2508; and 601 25th St., Galveston 77550, 409-766-3608.

Committees: *Judiciary* (Chmn. of 21 D): Economic and Commercial Law (Chmn.).

Group Ratings

	ADA	ACLU	COPE	CDF	CFA	LCV	ACU	NTLC	NSI	COC	CEI
1992	75	82	83	80	80	31	23	17	70	33	12
1991	55	—	92	90	72	38	17	—	—	30	8

National Journal Ratings

	1991 LIB — 1991 CONS	1992 LIB — 1992 CONS
Economic	84% — 12%	69% — 31%
Social	69% — 31%	57% — 41%
Foreign	48% — 51%	44% — 56%

Key Votes of the 102d Congress

1. Ban Striker Replace	FOR	5. Handgun Wait/7-Day AGN	9. Use Force in Gulf	FOR
2. $ for Homeownership	AGN	6. Overseas Mil. Abortion FOR	10. US Mil. Abroad $ Cut FOR
3. Tax Rich/Cut Mid Cls.	FOR	7. Obscn. Art NEA $ Ban FOR	11. Limit SDI Funds	FOR
4. FY93/$15B Def. Cut	FOR	8. Death Pen. from Jury AGN	12. Cuba Trade Embargo FOR

Key Votes of the 103d Congress

1. Family Leave   FOR   2. Deficit Reduction   FOR   3. Stimulus Plan   FOR

Election Results

1992 general	Jack Brooks (D)	118,690	(54%)	($471,285)
	Steve Stockman (R)	92,270	(44%)	($98,622)
	Other.	6,401	(3%)	
1992 primary	Jack Brooks (D), unopposed			
1990 general	Jack Brooks (D)	79,786	(58%)	($885,090)
	Maury Meyers (R)	58,399	(42%)	($447,974)

TENTH DISTRICT

Austin, the southernmost state capital in the continental 48 states, was not so long ago a small, quirky city. But over the last dozen years it has become one of America's boom cities, a major center of high-tech innovation and economic growth. That's ironic, for through most of its history Austin has had little interest in commerce: its skies have been almost totally untainted with the smoke of industry, its ground unpocked with pumping oil rigs, its main street lined not with business offices but with buildings holding a few lobbyists and the antique Driskill Hotel. Not even state government has been a major employer during most of Austin's history: the dome on the rosy Capitol is a tad higher than its counterpart in Washington, but Texas has mostly believed in minimalist government. The real secret behind Austin's growth and vitality, the public sector sparkplug that has produced the private sector combustion, is the University of Texas. Endowed with thousands of west Texas acres that turned out to sit on top of oil, the nation's largest single university campus is here in Austin; with some 50,000 students, it has a tower at its symbolic center that looms high over the campus, and houses the exemplary LBJ Presidential Library with its 35 million documents.

The university, with its laid-back yet intellectual atmosphere, was the catalyst of Austin's high-tech boom, but helping was Austin's selection in 1983 as the site of the Microelectronics and Computer Technology Corporation research consortium. Home also to some 200 software companies and computer chip manufacturers, *Fortune* describes Austin as "something of an alternative Silicon Valley." The result has been a metropolitan area which grew 46% in the 1980s, even though the Texas boom imploded in mid-decade—the fastest pace of growth of any similar-sized or larger metro area outside of Florida and Las Vegas. The Austin city limits have expanded, and vast new tracts of houses have been built north of the old town, far beyond the Capitol and the University, and south of the Colorado River; soon-to-be-closed Bergstrom Air Force Base has been suggested as the site for a larger, much needed new airport. Much of Austin now looks like part of metro Houston or the Dallas-Fort Worth Metroplex, with new subdivisions, newly minted shopping centers at every major intersection and condominium developments where recently there was only scrub.

Historically Democratic, Austin trended Republican in the 1980s largely because affluent new neighborhoods were spreading over the countryside. Austin's old Democratic voting habits appear to have come back in the 1990s, however: in 1990 Travis County voted for its former county commissioner Ann Richards, a longtime Austin resident, over rancher and oil man Clayton Williams, an A&M graduate, and it was one of the few counties to vote against Senator Phil Gramm. In 1992, Travis voted for Bill Clinton over George Bush by a 47%–32% margin. The new affluent techie residents have built a bigger Republican base than in the old Austin; but as in other high-tech areas, Research Triangle and Silicon Valley, the cultural politics of the 1990s has driven voters back to the Democrats.

Congressional politics here remains in the traditional LBJ mode. Since Lyndon Johnson's victory in a 1937 special election, the district has been represented by moderate-to-liberal Democrats in Johnson's personal circle and of his generation, all born between 1908 and 1913—Johnson, Homer Thornberry whom Johnson tried to appoint to the Supreme Court, and current incumbent Jake Pickle. Pickle, who turns 80 in 1993, remains conscientious, hard-working, kindly, politically adept but also principled. He is the third ranking Democrat on the Ways and Means Committee. As chairman of the Social Security subcommittee in the 1980s, when other Democrats were demagoging the issue, Pickle pointed out its problems; he was the architect of the Social Security rescue of 1983, when taxes were raised and benefits cut by raising the retirement age to 67 in the 21st Century. In the 1990s, he has also been looking ahead, to the potential problems of government sponsored enterprises like Fannie Mae, Freddie Mac and Sallie Mae. They are not in trouble now, but Pickle worries that if they default on their obligations the government would suddenly have liabilities even greater than in the S&L crisis.

1234 TEXAS

He wants the Pension Benefit Guaranty Corporation to require collateralization of 90% of current benefits before plans can offer more. Pickle is a "convert" to a five cent gas tax increase, but objected to the coal tax on independent operators to bail out the United Mine Workers health funds: "It is as if we are a street gang, mugging an innocent passerby, and justifying it by saying that our friends and family are hungry."

Austin grew so much in the 1980s that the 10th Congressional District lost the Hill Country counties it has had for years—LBJ country—and is now made up of nearly all of Travis County. In 1992 Pickle calmed doubts about his health (he was treated for prostate cancer) and, campaigning by handing out squeaking plastic pickles, won easily; he still seems to have the vigor and motivation he did in 1986, when Republicans mounted a serious challenge and he raised over $1 million and won 72% of the vote.

The People: Pop. 1990: 566,357; 8% rural; 7% age 65+; 65% White; 11% Black; 3% Asian; 13% Other; 21% Hispanic origin. Voting age pop.: 430,048; 10% Black; 18% Hispanic origin. Households: 45% married couple families; 23% married couple fams. w. children; 64% college educ.; median household income: $27,280; per capita income: $14,978; median gross rent: $415; median house value: $76,700.

1992 Presidential Vote			1988 Presidential Vote		
Clinton (D)	128,813	(48%)	Dukakis (D)	126,311	(55%)
Bush (R)	84,560	(32%)	Bush (R)	102,287	(45%)
Perot (I)	54,304	(20%)			

Rep. J. J. (Jake) Pickle (D)

Elected Dec. 17, 1963; b. Oct. 11, 1913, Roscoe; home, Austin; U. of TX, B.A. 1938; United Methodist; married (Beryl).

Career: Navy, 1941–45 (WWII); Area Dir., Natl. Youth Admin., 1938–41; Co-organizer, KVET Radio, Austin; Ad. & P.R. business; Dir., TX Dem. Exec. Cmte., 1957–60; TX Employment Commission, 1961–63.

Offices: 242 CHOB 20515, 202-225-4865. Also 763 Fed. Bldg., Austin 78701, 512-482-5921.

Committees: *Joint Committee on Taxation* (3d of 5). *Ways and Means* (3d of 24 D): Oversight (Chmn.); Social Security.

Group Ratings

	ADA	ACLU	COPE	CDF	CFA	LCV	ACU	NTLC	NSI	COC	CEI
1992	65	65	64	70	73	38	33	26	80	63	21
1991	45	—	55	90	72	38	16	—	—	56	17

National Journal Ratings

	1991 LIB — 1991 CONS			1992 LIB — 1992 CONS		
Economic	43%	—	56%	50%	—	50%
Social	66%	—	33%	56%	—	43%
Foreign	51%	—	46%	38%	—	56%

Key Votes of the 102d Congress

1. Ban Striker Replace AGN	5. Handgun Wait/7-Day FOR	9. Use Force in Gulf AGN
2. $ for Homeownership FOR	6. Overseas Mil. Abortion FOR	10. US Mil. Abroad $ Cut AGN
3. Tax Rich/Cut Mid Cls. FOR	7. Obscn. Art NEA $ Ban FOR	11. Limit SDI Funds AGN
4. FY93/$15B Def. Cut FOR	8. Death Pen. from Jury AGN	12. Cuba Trade Embargo FOR

Key Votes of the 103d Congress

1. Family Leave FOR	2. Deficit Reduction FOR	3. Stimulus Plan FOR

Election Results

1992 general	J.J. (Jake) Pickle (D)	177,233	(68%)	($363,561)
	Herbert Spiro (R)	68,646	(26%)	($117,934)
	Four Others	16,013	(6%)	
1992 primary	J. J. (Jake) Pickle (D)	55,703	(82%)	
	John Longsworth (D)	12,034	(18%)	
1990 general	J. J. (Jake) Pickle (D)	152,784	(65%)	($562,967)
	David Beilharz (R)	73,766	(31%)	($261,528)
	Jeff Davis (LIB)	8,905	(4%)	

ELEVENTH DISTRICT

The heart of Texas, its center of traditional rural culture, was at the center of the nation's attention starting in February 1993 when agents of the Bureau of Alcohol, Tobacco and Firearms moved in on the Branch Davidian compound, Ranch Apocalypse, in Waco, Texas. For 51 days, all of America got to watch, thanks to the hordes of media that set up camp outside the compound (they even got regular Federal Express and postal service at their camps), the standoff between federal agents and cult members, until its tragic and fiery end in April. The area around Waco is a part of Texas where farm fields and small towns recall the state as it was years ago, before the growth of the oil industry transformed Texas from a rural backwater into one of the centers of western capitalism. Mostly white and characteristically Texan, the area has grown continually over the past several decades. One reason is Fort Hood, the Army's second largest installation, which occupies much of next-door Bell and Coryell Counties and employs just under 50,000 military personnel and civilians. Another is the "awl bidness." A third is Baylor University, the oldest college in Texas and the largest Baptist university in the world. Still another is the spread of high-tech growth up and down I-35 from Austin and the Dallas-Fort Worth Metroplex.

Waco, the Fort Hood area and the still mostly rural counties around it make up Texas's 11th Congressional District. The politics here is ancestrally Democratic, and loyalty to Lyndon Johnson was strong enough for Hubert Humphrey to carry the 11th over George Wallace and Richard Nixon in 1968. Support for national Democrats has waned since: Governor Ann Richards, a native of Waco, won with just 51% here, and Bill Clinton trailed George Bush 36%–41%. But in congressional politics the 11th has remained Democratic, thanks to strong Democratic candidates—Marvin Leath, who won the seat after 42-year incumbent Bob Poage retired in 1978, and Chet Edwards, who was elected to succeed Leath in 1990.

Edwards is typical of the Democrats' political wunderkinder. In 1978, after three years as a staffer to Congressman Olin Teague, he ran at age 27 for the 6th District House seat Teague was vacating. In the first Democratic primary, Edwards wound up in third place, just 115 votes behind his former Texas A&M economics professor Phil Gramm, who went on to win the seat; if Edwards had won just 116 more votes, a lot of Texas and national political history would be different. Then Edwards went off to Harvard and got an M.B.A. He returned and moved to Duncanville in southwest Dallas County, and at age 31 ran for the state Senate in 1982 and won. There he made a fairly liberal record, helping to incorporate Texas into the Super Tuesday

1236   TEXAS

primary and to attract the Supercollider, bucking the unions and trial lawyers on workmen's compensation reform.

In 1990, when Leath retired, Edwards dropped his race for lieutenant governor, moved his residence to Waco (the Senate district overlapped), and ran for the 11th District seat and was unopposed in the Democratic primary. In the Republican primary, Bell County legislator Hugh Shine beat two former mayors of Waco despite being a party-switcher who was a Mondale delegate in San Francisco in 1984. In the general, Shine emphasized his military experience and attacked Edwards for attending a gay and lesbian fundraiser in Houston, a copy of a tactic that worked for Gramm in the 1984 Senate race. But Edwards got a promise of an Armed Services Committee slot from Speaker Foley and strong campaigning support from Leath. Shine carried Bell County and the suburban fringe outside Austin, but Edwards got 56% in Waco's McLennan County and carried all the rural counties.

In the House, Edwards got the promised seat on Armed Services and one on Veterans' Affairs, and immediately bucked the Democratic leadership and voted for the Gulf war resolution. He was also one of the Democratic "Gang of Six" who launched an effort for the balanced budget amendment and initiated the idea of having 1992 freshmen propose specific reforms at their first caucus—more rebel moves. But he was a skillful enough maneuverer to pass within two months of taking office a Veterans' Medical Research Act, reportedly the quickest any freshman has passed a bill. On Armed Services, he worked to bring a second division and $100 million in construction to Fort Hood. Edwards also left unspent $231,000 in official allowances and used only 31% of his franking budget. It is hardly surprising that a politician of this acumen was reelected in 1992 with 67% of the vote—only surprising that he was not seriously considered for the U.S. Senate seat left vacant by Lloyd Bentsen.

The People: Pop. 1990: 566,280; 29% rural; 13% age 65+; 70% White; 16% Black; 2% Asian; 6% Other; 12% Hispanic origin. Voting age pop.: 413,467; 15% Black; 10% Hispanic origin. Households: 60% married couple families; 30% married couple fams. w. children; 43% college educ.; median household income: $22,283; per capita income: $10,630; median gross rent: $362; median house value: $49,700.

1992 Presidential Vote			1988 Presidential Vote		
Bush (R)	75,545	(41%)	Bush (R)	97,765	(58%)
Clinton (D)	66,440	(36%)	Dukakis (D)	70,916	(42%)
Perot (I)	42,305	(23%)			

Rep. Chet Edwards (D)

Elected 1990; b. Nov. 24, 1951, Corpus Christi; home, Waco; TX A&M U., B.A. 1974, Harvard, M.B.A. 1981; Methodist; married (Lea Ann).

Career: Legis. and Dist. Dir., U.S. Rep. Olin Teague, 1975–77; Marketing rep., Trammell Crow Co., 1981–85; TX Senate, 1982–90; Pres., Edwards Communications, 1985–90.

Offices: 328 CHOB 20515, 202-225-6105. Also 710 University Tower, 700 S. University Parks Dr., Waco 76706, 817-752-9600.

Committees: *Armed Services* (22d of 34 D): Military Installations and Facilities; Oversight and Investigations; Research and Technology. *Veterans' Affairs* (11th of 21 D): Compensation, Pension and Insurance; Hospitals and Health Care.

Group Ratings

	ADA	ACLU	COPE	CDF	CFA	LCV	ACU	NTLC	NSI	COC	CEI
1992	55	52	75	40	60	25	40	16	100	63	27
1991	40	—	75	80	72	38	35	—	—	50	15

National Journal Ratings

	1991 LIB — 1991 CONS		1992 LIB — 1992 CONS	
Economic	48% —	51%	53% —	46%
Social	54% —	44%	38% —	60%
Foreign	46% —	53%	30% —	64%

Key Votes of the 102d Congress

1. Ban Striker Replace	FOR	5. Handgun Wait/7-Day	AGN	9. Use Force in Gulf	FOR
2. $ for Homeownership	AGN	6. Overseas Mil. Abortion	FOR	10. US Mil. Abroad $ Cut	AGN
3. Tax Rich/Cut Mid Cls.	FOR	7. Obscn. Art NEA $ Ban	FOR	11. Limit SDI Funds	AGN
4. FY93/$15B Def. Cut	AGN	8. Death Pen. from Jury	AGN	12. Cuba Trade Embargo	FOR

Key Votes of the 103d Congress

1. Family Leave	FOR	2. Deficit Reduction	AGN	3. Stimulus Plan	FOR

Election Results

1992 general	Chet Edwards (D)...................	119,999	(67%)	($420,880)
	James W. Boyles (R).................	58,033	(33%)	($17,150)
1992 primary	Chet Edwards (D), unopposed			
1990 general	Chet Edwards (D)...................	73,810	(53%)	($668,936)
	Hugh Shine (R)	64,269	(47%)	($842,226)

TWELFTH DISTRICT

Fort Worth, Texas, has a fair claim to being the quintessential mid-American city: halfway across the continent, midway between the oceans, just west of the Balcones Escarpment that divides the dry treeless grazing lands of west Texas from the humid green croplands of the east. It is southern in heritage and northern in its advanced post-industrial economy. It has the nation's biggest row of Western wear shops and the nation's richest family, the Basses, whose steel-sheen skyscrapers dominate the skyline from hills miles away. This is where the West begins, Fort Worth boosters say, adding, as Will Rogers said, that Dallas is "where the East peters out."

Today, Fort Worth has a high-tech economy, with big employers like Texas Instruments and Tandy Radio Shack. Yet it also has been hard hit by defense cuts. The big General Dynamics plant that produced so many U.S. bombers has been sold to Lockheed; scheduled to be closed is Carswell Air Force Base next door, where an eight-engine B-52 bomber rolled off the runway and, circling lazily in the wide empty sky, broke the United States out of the SALT II treaty in 1986. And the lines at Bell Helicopter's nearby plant were kept going only when the Texas delegation and others overruled the cancellation of the V-22 Osprey. Fort Worth also has some of the nation's premier small museums, the Amon Carter Museum of Western Art, Louis Kahn's gem The Kimbell Museum and the Will Rogers Coliseum with exhibits of Texas history. Fort Worth for years was a defensive rival looking over its shoulder at Dallas; now it stands on its own. Other cities have their claims, but the visitor from abroad who wants to see what is quintessentially American would be well advised to head to Fort Worth.

Fort Worth's political heritage is Democratic, and for 34 years it was represented by Jim Wright, speaker of the House from 1987 until he was forced to leave office for ethical violations in 1989. Wright was first elected to Congress in 1954 after a primary victory over an anti-labor

Democrat in this still dusty blue-collar town, in contrast to white-collar Dallas, which was electing its first Republican congressman the same year. Now Fort Worth is more diverse, with extensive rich as well as poor neighborhoods, and not as solidly Democratic; Tarrant County, with the population boom in Arlington between Fort Worth and Dallas, has become as Republican as Dallas County if not more so. The September 1989 special election to succeed Wright was seriously contested, and about as close as could be. It was a contest in effect between Senators Lloyd Bentsen and Phil Gramm. Bentsen's man was Democrat Pete Geren, a well-off attorney who had worked on the Bentsen staff for two years and in 1986 had run and won 44% in the 6th District against Republican Joe Barton. Geren, pro-capital gains tax cut, was opposed by Democrat Jim Lane, who was backed by labor. Gramm backed Bob Lanier, a pediatric allergist known as "Dr. Bob" for his Dallas-Forth Worth Metroplex TV appearance on *60 Second Housecall*. The split Democratic vote enabled Lanier to lead Geren in the August 1989 first election, 39%–32%. But Geren capitalized on Lanier's mistakes—he hadn't voted in 1988 and couldn't identify the Second Amendment as granting the right to bear arms while backing some limits on gun-owning—and won the runoff by just 51%–49%; he would have lost but for carrying the absentee votes—a sign of Bentsen-style organization.

Geren has made a conservative record in office, fiscally cautious and as pro-defense as any member of the House. He was the unofficial leader of the "Gang of Six" Democrats backing the balanced budget constitutional amendment. As a former small businessman, an investor in a restaurant chain, he looks askance at government regulations and paperwork requirements. Wright's departure was followed by cuts in defense programs he had been able to protect, like the V-22 Osprey canceled by Defense Secretary Dick Cheney and the Carswell base closing. Geren worked with Pennsylvania Republican Curt Weldon to turn around the decision on the Osprey—for at least a year. He also worked to fund the F-16 (made in Fort Worth) after it was cut back and successfully pushed for lifting the ban on sales of F-16s to Taiwan.

The 1991 redistricting changed the 12th's profile not entirely to Geren's advantage. The district still includes most of Fort Worth and Tarrant County; high-income southwest Fort Worth is still in the Republican 6th District, and Republican-leaning Arlington is entirely outside the 12th. But Geren lost the black areas in southeast Fort Worth to the 24th District of master redistricter Martin Frost. In return, the 12th extends south and westward in a whorl around Fort Worth, taking in much of rural Johnson and Parker Counties, including Weatherford, where Jim Wright got his start in politics. Geren was reelected with 63% in 1992, a solid showing and an indication that his conservative record on so many issues has propelled him ahead of the Democratic base in a district that is no longer reliably Democratic.

The People: Pop. 1990: 565,988; 13% rural; 12% age 65+; 74% White; 8% Black; 1% Amer. Indian; 2% Asian; 9% Other; 16% Hispanic origin. Voting age pop.: 412,521; 7% Black; 14% Hispanic origin. Households: 57% married couple families; 28% married couple fams. w. children; 43% college educ.; median household income: $27,366; per capita income: $12,641; median gross rent: $402; median house value: $57,200.

1992 Presidential Vote

Clinton (D)	76,637	(38%)
Bush (R)	70,522	(35%)
Perot (I)	55,951	(28%)

1988 Presidential Vote

Bush (R)	102,339	(56%)
Dukakis (D)	80,239	(44%)

Rep. Pete Geren (D)

Elected Sept. 1989; b. Jan. 29, 1952, Ft. Worth; home, Ft. Worth; U. of TX, B.A. 1974, J.D. 1978; Baptist; married (Beckie).

Career: Practicing atty., 1979–84, 1985–89; Exec. asst., U.S. Sen. Lloyd Bentsen, 1984–85; Restaurant owner, 1986–91.

Offices: 1730 LHOB 20515, 202-225-5071. Also 100 E. 15th St., #500, Ft. Worth 76102, 817-338-0909.

Committees: *Armed Services* (32d of 34 D): Military Acquisition. *Public Works and Transportation* (17th of 39 D): Aviation; Water Resources and Environment. *Science, Space and Technology* (13th of 33 D): Space; Technology, Environment and Aviation.

Group Ratings

	ADA	ACLU	COPE	CDF	CFA	LCV	ACU	NTLC	NSI	COC	CEI
1992	45	43	55	20	33	13	60	55	90	88	54
1991	15	—	50	60	56	31	60	—	—	70	39

National Journal Ratings

	1991 LIB	—	1991 CONS	1992 LIB	—	1992 CONS
Economic	36%	—	63%	35%	—	65%
Social	37%	—	61%	38%	—	62%
Foreign	36%	—	62%	0%	—	82%

Key Votes of the 102d Congress

1. Ban Striker Replace	AGN	5. Handgun Wait/7-Day	AGN	9. Use Force in Gulf	FOR
2. $ for Homeownership	AGN	6. Overseas Mil. Abortion	FOR	10. US Mil. Abroad $ Cut	AGN
3. Tax Rich/Cut Mid Cls.	AGN	7. Obscn. Art NEA $ Ban	FOR	11. Limit SDI Funds	AGN
4. FY93/$15B Def. Cut	AGN	8. Death Pen. from Jury	FOR	12. Cuba Trade Embargo	FOR

Key Votes of the 103d Congress

1. Family Leave   AGN   2. Deficit Reduction   AGN   3. Stimulus Plan   AGN

Election Results

1992 general	Pete Geren (D)	125,492	(63%)	($812,234)
	David Hobbs (R)	74,432	(37%)	($384,635)
1992 primary	Pete Geren (D)	37,722	(100%)	
1990 general	Pete Geren (D)	98,026	(71%)	($495,937)
	Mike McGinn (R)	39,438	(29%)	($22,695)

THIRTEENTH DISTRICT

Heading west in Texas, the population thins out, the land becomes browner, until you can travel through a whole county where only a few hundred people—plus quite a few more head of cattle—live. And then the land rises nearly 1,000 feet in elevation, up steep gullies that surround the rivers which for most of the year are just tiny trickles, to the tilted tableland that is the High Plains of west Texas. The winds here sweep down from the Rockies, the land is barren except where irrigated, often with the now dangerously depleted waters of the Ogallala Aquifer. But here and there in this demanding environment—sticky-hot in the summer, swept by north winds from Canada in winter—comfortable cities have been built to house the people and businesses that bring forth oil, natural gas, helium and other elements from the earth.

The 13th Congressional District of Texas spans much of this territory. Population declined here in the 1980s, in some rural counties by as much as 30%, with only small gains in and around two of the three biggest cities, Wichita Falls and Amarillo. Around Wichita Falls, in the eastern part of the district, is the agricultural land of the Red River Valley—dusty land with empty skylines, like Archer City, the boyhood home of novelist Larry McMurtry, chronicled in *The Last Picture Show* and *Texasville* and where he lives now in the biggest mansion in town. This is white Anglo Texas: few blacks got this far west and few Mexican-Americans go this far north. Up on the High Plains, the economy is different: it is based on minerals. The largest city here is Amarillo, the home of former oilman and later corporate raider T. Boone Pickens, and contrary to popular thought, Amarillo—not Chicago—is the windiest city in America. Just outside town is the Pantex factory that made thousands of nuclear warheads—the epicenter of American defense in the Cold War, and its 16,000 acres are now scheduled (pending lawsuits) to be used to store the disarmed weapons. The political traditions here differ. The Red River Valley, settled by Confederate veterans, still remains Democratic; the High Plains, settled overland from Kansas wheatlands, is more Republican. The lines were changed for the 1990s: not all of Amarillo is in the 13th any more, and black portions of Lubbock have been added. The purpose was to subtract Republicans and add Democrats, and bolster the fortunes of Congressman Bill Sarpalius.

Sarpalius is the latest beneficiary of the bifurcated 13th's ability to switch parties, as it did in 1984 and 1988. Sarpalius has a gripping personal history: he came to the High Plains as a child, was stricken with polio, abandoned by his father, and sent with his brothers by his alcoholic mother to Cal Farley's Boys Ranch near Amarillo. He went to Texas Tech, taught agriculture, went into the farm business and then ran for the state Senate. In Austin, he was a crusader against drunk driving; back home he broke his back while driving an all-terrain vehicle in 1986, and was later beaten and had his jaw broken in an Amarillo bar in January 1988, but in neither case was he drinking. Interestingly, he is one of the few members of Congress of Lithuanian descent and has been a strong supporter of the democratic movement there.

In the House, Sarpalius got a seat on the Agriculture Committee. He has a conservative record on many issues: he was one of two Democrats who voted to expel Barney Frank, one of three Democrats to urge President Bush to restrict NEA grants; he backed the balanced budget amendment. He has sought funding for Red River chloride control, for clean water projects in the High Plains and for flood control projects. He moved to stop EPA's pesticide fees after 1997. With timely help from Health Subcommittee Chairman Henry Waxman, he stopped the Health Care Financing Administration from reducing federal matching funds for Medicaid programs.

Sarpalius first won in 1988 when 13th District Republican Beau Boulter ran against Senator Lloyd Bentsen and lost. (Bentsen dismissed him thus: "My opponent is simply not qualified.") Winning 62% in the Red River Valley, Sarpalius was elected with 52% district-wide. In 1990, Republican legislator Dick Waterfield ran a well-financed campaign here, was aided by Senator Phil Gramm, and had much the same result—except that this time Sarpalius carried the High Plains too and won 57% overall. In 1992, Boulter tried to regain this House seat but Sarpalius touted his own support from the NRA and Texas Farm Bureau and hit Boulter for his former attendance record in the House. Redistricting helped Sarpalius in 1992 and, although Bill Clinton won only about one-third of the vote, Sarpalius took 60%, carrying all but four of the district's 38 counties. In the 1990s' volatile political climate, that doesn't guarantee him continued victories, but it is a sign he has been gaining strength.

The People: Pop. 1990: 566,682; 27% rural; 14% age 65+; 71% White; 8% Black; 1% Amer. Indian; 1% Asian; 11% Other; 19% Hispanic origin. Voting age pop.: 409,705; 7% Black; 15% Hispanic origin. Households: 58% married couple families; 28% married couple fams. w. children; 37% college educ.; median household income: $20,907; per capita income: $10,344; median gross rent: $334; median house value: $38,100.

1992 Presidential Vote

Bush (R) 87,492 (43%)
Clinton (D) 73,454 (36%)
Perot (I). 41,187 (20%)

1988 Presidential Vote

Bush (R) 106,620 (57%)
Dukakis (D). 81,789 (43%)

Rep. Bill Sarpalius (D)

Elected 1988; b. Jan. 10, 1948, Los Angeles, CA; home, Amarillo; Clarendon Col., A.S. 1970, TX Tech. U., B.A. 1972, West TX St. U., M.A. 1978; Methodist; divorced.

Career: Agribusiness; Teacher, Cal Farley's Boys Ranch, 1972–77; TX Senate, 1980–88.

Offices: 126 CHOB 20515, 202-225-3706. Also 801 S. Fillmore, #400, Amarillo 79101, 806-371-8844; and 1000 Lamar, #208, Wichita Falls 76301, 817-767-0541.

Committees: *Agriculture* (10th of 28 D): Department Operations and Nutrition; Environment, Credit and Rural Development; General Farm Commodities. *Small Business* (11th of 27 D): Development of Rural Enterprises, Exports and the Environment (Chmn).

Group Ratings

	ADA	ACLU	COPE	CDF	CFA	LCV	ACU	NTLC	NSI	COC	CEI
1992	40	30	50	40	47	6	64	55	90	75	47
1991	25	—	42	60	50	23	70	—	—	60	33

National Journal Ratings

	1991 LIB — 1991 CONS	1992 LIB — 1992 CONS
Economic	36% — 63%	43% — 56%
Social	22% — 77%	19% — 81%
Foreign	49% — 50%	44% — 50%

Key Votes of the 102d Congress

1. Ban Striker Replace	FOR	5. Handgun Wait/7-Day AGN	9. Use Force in Gulf	FOR
2. $ for Homeownership	AGN	6. Overseas Mil. AbortionAGN	10. US Mil. Abroad $ CutAGN
3. Tax Rich/Cut Mid Cls.AGN	7. Obscn. Art NEA $ Ban FOR	11. Limit SDI Funds	FOR
4. FY93/$15B Def. Cut	FOR	8. Death Pen. from Jury FOR	12. Cuba Trade Embargo AGN

Key Votes of the 103d Congress

1. Family Leave   AGN   2. Deficit Reduction   AGN   3. Stimulus Plan   FOR

Election Results

1992 general	Bill Sarpalius (D) 117,892	(60%)	($521,328)
	Beau Boulter (R). 77,514	(40%)	($370,582)
1992 primary	Bill Sarpalius (D), unopposed		
1990 general	Bill Sarpalius (D) 81,815	(57%)	($668,020)
	Dick Waterfield (R) 63,045	(44%)	($679,117)

FOURTEENTH DISTRICT

Retreating east from the Alamo, the ragtag army led by Sam Houston passed over what would become, after their bloody and conclusive victory at San Jacinto, some of the prime cropland in the new Republic and later the state of Texas. The hilly and river-crossed land between Houston and Austin, both named after Texas's first leaders, was settled early; the flat coastal plains, steamy and humid so much of the year, were settled later when the railroads came in. The Gulf of Mexico coastline, though it has plenty of inlets, never had any important ports in the stretch between Houston and Corpus Christi until the discovery of oil here made it worthwhile to build channels to ship the oil out.

This is the land of the 14th Congressional District of Texas. Made up of rural countrysides, small towns and a couple of small cities, it runs along the Gulf coast and inland toward the old Texas German country. Its eastern and northern edges bring it within metropolitan range of Houston, Austin and San Antonio; more than one-third of its population is in this metropolitan fringe. Redistricting changed its shape somewhat, adding Blanco County, in the Hill Country west of Austin, the birthplace and first political base of Lyndon B. Johnson. About one-quarter of the people here are Hispanic, and one-tenth black—figures not far off from Texas as a whole. This country is ancestrally Democratic except for a couple of counties settled by Texas Germans, who were pro-Union in the Civil War and have remained Republican ever since. But it voted Republican in the 1980s and favored George Bush over Bill Clinton.

The congressman from the 14th District is Greg Laughlin, who won the seat after a series of improbable elections and odd incumbents; Laughlin beat a Republican in 1988 who had lied about his resume, his opponent and his mostly nonexistent legislative record. Laughlin was a lawyer from Brazoria County, a former intelligence officer in the Pentagon and the National Security Agency, and a former prosecutor in Houston who had run for the seat and lost two years earlier. Once in office, he worked hard to get in touch with all corners of this large district. A member of the Public Works Committee, he has labored to stop the erosion of Sargent Beach with a seawall which would also protect the Gulf Intracoastal Waterway; he supports construction of a new U.S. 87 between Austin and Victoria. He compares the Gulf of Mexico with the Great Lakes and Chesapeake Bay—much smaller bodies of water on which the government spends much more money (though of course most of the Gulf doesn't belong to the U.S.)—and calls for more funding to reduce erosion and pollution and wants to establish a Gulf of Mexico board within the EPA. He has promoted trading American crops for Russian oil, an interesting reversal of history.

Laughlin has served in the Army since he graduated from Texas A&M, and as a lieutenant colonel in the Army Reserve volunteered for two weeks of duty in the Persian Gulf in 1991. His record on military, as on economic and cultural, issues is fairly but not completely conservative. Working the district hard has obviously paid off for him. After winning with 53% in 1988 and 54% in 1990, he won 68%–27% in 1992, running some 30% ahead of Bill Clinton.

The People: Pop. 1990: 566,008; 51% rural; 13% age 65+; 65% White; 11% Black; 1% Asian; 11% Other; 23% Hispanic origin. Voting age pop.: 407,091; 10% Black; 20% Hispanic origin. Households: 61% married couple families; 30% married couple fams. w. children; 37% college educ.; median household income: $23,812; per capita income: $11,127; median gross rent: $344; median house value: $52,300.

1992 Presidential Vote

Bush (R)	86,225	(41%)
Clinton (D)	78,706	(37%)
Perot (I)	47,119	(22%)

1988 Presidential Vote

Bush (R)	103,065	(53%)
Dukakis (D)	92,141	(47%)

Rep. Greg Laughlin (D)

Elected 1988; b. Jan. 21, 1942, Bay City; home, West Columbia; TX A&M U., B.A. 1964, U. of TX, LL.B. 1967; Methodist; married (Ginger).

Career: Army, 1964–69, 1991 (Persian Gulf), Army Reserves, 1969–present; Asst. Dist. Atty., Harris Cnty., 1970–74; Practicing atty., 1974–88.

Offices: 236 CHOB 20515, 202-225-2831. Also 312 S. Main St., Victoria 77901, 512-576-1231; and 221 E. Main St., #203, Round Rock 78664, 512-244-3765.

Committees: *Intelligence (Permanent Select)* (10th of 12 D): Legislation; Program and Budget Authorization. *Merchant Marine and Fisheries* (11th of 29 D): Coast Guard and Navigation; Environment and Natural Resources; Oceanography, Gulf of Mexico and the Outer Continental Shelf. *Post Office and Civil Service* (12th of 15 D): Oversight and Investigations. *Public Works and Transportation* (16th of 39 D): Aviation; Surface Transportation.

Group Ratings

	ADA	ACLU	COPE	CDF	CFA	LCV	ACU	NTLC	NSI	COC	CEI
1992	45	41	50	30	53	19	52	40	100	63	34
1991	10	—	67	50	50	15	55	—	—	60	36

National Journal Ratings

	1991 LIB — 1991 CONS	1992 LIB — 1992 CONS
Economic	39% — 60%	48% — 52%
Social	37% — 61%	34% — 66%
Foreign	36% — 62%	37% — 63%

Key Votes of the 102d Congress

1. Ban Striker Replace	FOR	5. Handgun Wait/7-Day	AGN	9. Use Force in Gulf	FOR
2. $ for Homeownership	AGN	6. Overseas Mil. Abortion	AGN	10. US Mil. Abroad $ Cut	AGN
3. Tax Rich/Cut Mid Cls.	FOR	7. Obscn. Art NEA $ Ban	FOR	11. Limit SDI Funds	FOR
4. FY93/$15B Def. Cut	AGN	8. Death Pen. from Jury	AGN	12. Cuba Trade Embargo	AGN

Key Votes of the 103d Congress

1. Family Leave   AGN   2. Deficit Reduction   AGN   3. Stimulus Plan   FOR

Election Results

1992 general	Greg Laughlin (D)	135,930	(68%)	($540,139)
	Huberto J. (Bert) Garza (R)	54,412	(27%)	($13,550)
	Vic Vreeland (I)	9,329	(5%)	
1992 primary	Greg Laughlin (D), unopposed			
1990 general	Greg Laughlin (D)	89,251	(54%)	($851,294)
	Joe Dial (R)	75,098	(46%)	($450,095)

FIFTEENTH DISTRICT

The Lower Rio Grande Valley of south Texas is one of America's 20th Century frontiers. A century ago, there was little here but desert wilderness; only a handful of people lived anywhere near the shallow, sluggish Rio Grande; there was no Border patrol, because in this desert land no one bothered to cross it. Then in the early days of this century came pioneers like Lloyd Bentsen, Sr., father of the Treasury secretary and former senator, who arrived after World War I with five dollars in his pocket and became one of the biggest Valley landowners, remaining active in his business until he died in an auto accident in 1989 at age 95. Bentsen and others cleared the land and dug canals, hired Mexican and Mexican-American workers, planted citrus groves and cornfields and palm windbreaks, ran cattle and drilled for oil and gas. Along U.S. 83 north of the Rio Grande these pioneers built a string of towns with American names and storefronts. But most of the people here were Latino in culture and language. Wage levels higher than in Mexico (though low by U.S. standards) brought more Mexicans over the border. But if wages are low, so is the cost-of-living—which makes this a haven for low-income "winter Texan" retirees, coming down from the North in their RVs. The days are past when ranchers and oil men wielded absolute political power here; there is instead a robust mostly Hispanic politics, often with big Democratic majorities but with genuine two-party competition on occasion.

The 15th Congressional District of Texas is one of three districts dividing up the Lower Rio Grande Valley. Some two-thirds of its residents and 58% of its voters live in Hidalgo County in or near the string of towns from Mercedes through McAllen (where Bill Clinton made an election eve appearance in 1992) to Los Ebanos, just north of the river. The 15th then moves north taking in a narrow corridor of land between Corpus Christi and San Antonio to meet the population requirement, including Goliad, where 352 captured Texans were massacred by Santa Ana's troops in 1836, and Beeville, the big town nearby where George Bush goes for barbecue after shooting quail at year's end. The 15th's population is 75% Hispanic and solidly Democratic. This is the descendant of a district that in 1948, 1950 and 1952 elected Lloyd Bentsen, Jr., to the House, before he went to Houston to make his fortune.

The current congressman from the 15th District is Eligio (Kika) de la Garza. He came up from poverty, though his family was given part of the 18th Century Santa Gertrudis de la Garza Spanish land grant, worked as a shoeshine boy on the streets of McAllen, then went to law school at St. Mary's in San Antonio (which has educated many outstanding Texas Hispanics). De la Garza served 12 years in the legislature, where he was a favorite of big landowners and was sometimes attacked by Austin-based liberals. His voting record for years was rather conservative; he is somewhat liberal on economic issues and has always supported civil rights, but is more moderate on foreign policy and cultural matters. But this meshes well with the pro-military and culturally traditional views of Mexican-American voters. De la Garza is an earnest, pleasant man, who takes the trouble to learn new languages and to surprise foreign visitors by speaking to them in their native tongue; but he is capable of a little more guile than is first apparent.

That is seen in his stewardship of the House Agriculture Committee since 1981, a post he has now held for a longer uninterrupted period than anyone else in history. As chairman, de la Garza has superintended three major farm bills, in 1981, 1985 and 1990, with varying results. The 1981 farm bill boosted program costs enormously, by setting target prices above world levels and stimulating vast overproduction, while discouraging exports and letting farm land prices decline. In response, the 1985 bill cut subsidies sharply. In the years after, he did craftsmanlike work on the 1988 drought relief bill and a 1988 pesticide bill which, characteristically, did not include provisions sought by lobbies on any extreme. In 1990, de la Garza's task was to protect farm programs against further cuts, opposing a modest proposal to cut two cents out of the sugar subsidy (which stimulates totally uneconomic U.S. production and is disastrous for our Caribbean neighbors) and beating the Armey-Schumer move to ban subsidies for farmers with adjusted gross incomes of $100,000 or more a year. De la Garza shrewdly marshalled environmentalists, unions (who were against cargo preference) and the textile industry (who wanted support for textile import quotas), and prevailed.

Though he favors NAFTA, he sought 15-year phaseouts of tariffs of fruits and vegetables, and a pesticide use commission, and promises to monitor Mexican environmental standards and practices closely. He wants an import fee to pay for border area infrastructure and environmental improvements. With no major farm bill to pass, he kept the Commodity Futures Trading Commission from being merged with securities agencies. He has tried to mend the tattered farm credit system by making it easier for new farmers to get FmHA loans, and has pushed research to help get rid of the citrus blackfly and the sweet potato whitefly—big problems in south Texas. His next big projects on Agriculture are a pesticide reauthorization bill and a debt-for-nature plan which would grant more favorable payment terms to Latin American and Caribbean countries if they agree to steer the savings toward environmental projects.

De la Garza, with 284 overdrafts on the House bank, had more vigorous opposition in 1992 than he had for years in radio preacher Thomas Haughey, and was held to 60% of the vote; he actually lost two counties in the northern end of the district.

The People: Pop. 1990: 566,805; 29% rural; 11% age 65+; 24% White; 1% Black; 23% Other; 74% Hispanic origin. Voting age pop.: 369,686; 1% Black; 69% Hispanic origin. Households: 66% married couple families; 38% married couple fams. w. children; 29% college educ.; median household income: $17,866; per capita income: $7,407; median gross rent: $290; median house value: $36,900.

1992 Presidential Vote			1988 Presidential Vote		
Clinton (D)	80,135	(53%)	Dukakis (D)	87,323	(59%)
Bush (R)	52,102	(34%)	Bush (R)	59,541	(41%)
Perot (I)	19,995	(13%)			

Rep. E. (Kika) de la Garza (D)

Elected 1964; b. Sep. 22, 1927, Mercedes; home, Mission; Edinburg Jr. Col., St. Mary's U., LL.B. 1952; Catholic; married (Lucille).

Career: Navy, 1945–46; Army, 1951–52 (Korea); Practicing atty., 1952–64; TX House of Reps., 1952–64.

Offices: 1401 LHOB 20515, 202-225-2531. Also 1418 Beech St., McAllen 78501, 210-682-5545; and Alice Fed. Bldg., #210, 401 E. 2d St., Alice 78332, 512-664-2215.

Committees: *Agriculture* (Chmn. of 28 D).

Group Ratings

	ADA	ACLU	COPE	CDF	CFA	LCV	ACU	NTLC	NSI	COC	CEI
1992	70	61	75	90	80	31	19	11	70	43	11
1991	45	—	58	90	78	31	32	—	—	40	12

National Journal Ratings

	1991 LIB — 1991 CONS		1992 LIB — 1992 CONS	
Economic	51% —	48%	60% —	39%
Social	65% —	34%	44% —	56%
Foreign	58% —	42%	38% —	62%

1246   TEXAS

Key Votes of the 102d Congress

1. Ban Striker Replace	FOR	5. Handgun Wait/7-Day	AGN	9. Use Force in Gulf	FOR
2. $ for Homeownership	AGN	6. Overseas Mil. Abortion	AGN	10. US Mil. Abroad $ Cut	AGN
3. Tax Rich/Cut Mid Cls.	*	7. Obscn. Art NEA $ Ban	*	11. Limit SDI Funds	AGN
4. FY93/$15B Def. Cut	FOR	8. Death Pen. from Jury	AGN	12. Cuba Trade Embargo	FOR

Key Votes of the 103d Congress

1. Family Leave	FOR	2. Deficit Reduction	FOR	3. Stimulus Plan	FOR

Election Results

1992 general	E. (Kika) de la Garza (D)...............	86,351	(60%)	($267,600)
	Tom Haughey (R)......................	56,549	(40%)	($13,452)
1992 primary	E. (Kika) de la Garza (D), unopposed			
1990 general	E. (Kika) de la Garza (D), unopposed			($121,145)

SIXTEENTH DISTRICT

Spread out below the face of Comanche Peak, the bright green of its trees contrasting with the rough brown of the mountains, surrounded by hundreds of miles of some of the most desolate landscape in the country, 400 miles from Phoenix and 600 from Dallas-Fort Worth, is one of North America's and the world's largest border cities, known as El Paso in Texas and Juarez in Mexico. This is an area with history: Texas claims the first Thanksgiving took place in San Elizario near El Paso in 1598. But 50 years ago, there were still only 140,000 people here; now there are more than 1.5 million on both sides of the border. This is a bilingual, bicultural city, where most of the people have a Mexican heritage; the thrust of growth is from Spanish-speaking people and an English-speaking economy.

A huge metro area has grown up here, living off labor that is very low-wage by U.S. standards but was for years high-wage for Mexico, and which is now poised for rapid takeoff. Government has put some money into El Paso—there are big military bases here—but taking away government controls and restrictions will do even more. Just as Juarez's *maquiladora* plants grew and provided good wages for Mexico when U.S. law permitted certain products assembled in Mexico to be sold duty-free in the U.S., so the North American Free Trade Agreement's elimination of more barriers will increase U.S. purchases of Mexican-made goods; and even more importantly, boost Mexican purchases of U.S. goods and services. Already in place in El Paso-Juarez is a critical mass of infrastructure, distribution and know-how needed to take advantage of these opportunities.

The 16th Congressional District of Texas once went far out into the desert. Now, after redistricting, it is made up of only part of El Paso County, including most of the city of El Paso and communities up and down the Rio Grande, and giant Fort Bliss to the north. For years politics here was divided on ethnic lines, with most Anglos voting Republican in contested races and most Mexican-Americans—more numerous, but many not citizens—Democratic.

Ron Coleman, the congressman from the 16th District, is a Texas political type: the tough-guy liberal, practical and unprincipled (as readers of *Hill Rat*, a not at all flattering book by a former Coleman staffer, will know), a guy who has made a good but always a risky political career by backing labor unions and trial lawyers and getting support from them in return. Coleman was the lawyer for strikers in the big Farah slacks company strike of the 1970s, and in his 10 years in the legislature often tangled with the conservative House speaker. When a conservative incumbent retired in 1982, Coleman ran for Congress and had to win a tough primary against a Mexican-American and a tough general against a Republican. Once in the House, things seemed to go swimmingly for Coleman. From the Armed Services Committee and then the Appropriations Military Construction Subcommittee he has funneled money to Fort Bliss. He commended President Carlos Salinas's Mexico for its market-oriented economic reforms and strongly backed a free trade agreement as it was being negotiated, although he has also kept an eye on local air quality and urged tougher Mexican environmental rules and enforcement, and has called for $1 billion for border infrastructure to handle the new commerce.

Easy reelection seemed endlessly in the offing until it was revealed in early 1992 that an El Paso area businessman assumed $65,000 in debts for Coleman and, weeks later, that he had 673 overdrafts on the House bank, totalling $275,000; he was overdrawn 927 days of 39 months the records were examined, one of the worst offenders in the scandal. Suddenly Republicans were off and running: former Democrat Pat O'Rourke and newscaster Chip Taberski, with Taberski winning the Republican runoff with 76%. Taberski hit hard on the check-bouncing issue, with one ad showing a jail door swinging shut. Coleman was "either stupid or a liar," the *El Paso Herald Post* wrote. "Coleman's behavior—his deceit and the unbelievable arrogance of that deceit—cannot be countenanced." Some summer polls showed Coleman way behind.

But Coleman responded with characteristic feistiness. He ran a TV spot apologizing and then another, with an out of focus shot of Taberski, accusing him of being ignorant of Hispanic concerns and hitting him for supporting the English language only movement. Taberski also said he would replace Medicare and Medicaid, without saying how, and admitted he'd opposed minimum wage increases—this in a district with lots of Medicaid eligibles and minimum wage earners. Coleman vastly outspent Taberski, and wound up winning 52%–48%—an unambiguous victory, but not insurance against tough opposition, either in the primary or the general, in 1994.

The People: Pop. 1990: 566,238; 2% rural; 8% age 65+; 25% White; 4% Black; 1% Asian; 18% Other; 70% Hispanic origin. Voting age pop.: 383,578; 4% Black; 66% Hispanic origin. Households: 61% married couple families; 36% married couple fams. w. children; 41% college educ.; median household income: $22,632; per capita income: $9,195; median gross rent: $345; median house value: $57,000.

1992 Presidential Vote			1988 Presidential Vote		
Clinton (D)	65,614	(51%)	Dukakis (D)	61,247	(53%)
Bush (R)	45,367	(35%)	Bush (R)	53,619	(47%)
Perot (I)	18,779	(14%)			

Rep. Ronald D. Coleman (D)

Elected 1982; b. Nov. 19, 1941, El Paso; home, El Paso; U. of TX, B.A. 1963, J.D. 1967; Presbyterian; married (Amy).

Career: Army, 1967–69; Teacher, El Paso public schls., TX School for Deaf; Legis. Asst., TX House and Senate, 1965–67; Asst. El Paso Cnty. Atty., 1969; Practicing atty., 1969–82; 1st Asst. El Paso Cnty. Atty., 1971; TX House of Reps., 1973–82.

Offices: 440 CHOB 20515, 202-225-4831. Also Fed. Bldg., 700 E. San Antonio St., #723, El Paso 79901, 915-534-6200; and P.O. Bldg., #304, Pecos 79772, 915-445-6218.

Committees: *Appropriations* (18th of 37 D): Interior; Military Construction; Transportation. *Intelligence (Permanent Select)* (6th of 12 D): Legislation (Chmn.); Oversight and Evaluation.

Group Ratings

	ADA	ACLU	COPE	CDF	CFA	LCV	ACU	NTLC	NSI	COC	CEI
1992	85	83	83	90	80	69	13	0	50	29	9
1991	60	—	92	90	78	62	10	—	—	40	10

National Journal Ratings

	1991 LIB — 1991 CONS		1992 LIB — 1992 CONS	
Economic	72% —	23%	61% —	38%
Social	69% —	30%	59% —	41%
Foreign	58% —	42%	38% —	56%

Key Votes of the 102d Congress

1. Ban Striker Replace	FOR	5. Handgun Wait/7-Day	AGN	9. Use Force in Gulf	AGN
2. $ for Homeownership	AGN	6. Overseas Mil. Abortion	FOR	10. US Mil. Abroad $ Cut	AGN
3. Tax Rich/Cut Mid Cls.	FOR	7. Obscn. Art NEA $ Ban	FOR	11. Limit SDI Funds	AGN
4. FY93/$15B Def. Cut	AGN	8. Death Pen. from Jury	AGN	12. Cuba Trade Embargo	FOR

Key Votes of the 103d Congress

1. Family Leave	FOR	2. Deficit Reduction	FOR	3. Stimulus Plan	FOR

Election Results

1992 general	Ronald D. Coleman (D)	66,731	(52%)	($780,038)
	Chip Taberski (R)	61,870	(48%)	($209,271)
1992 primary	Ronald D. Coleman (D)	27,562	(64%)	
	Charles Ponzio, Jr. (D)	11,104	(26%)	
	R. K. Jones (D)	2,704	(6%)	
	Jorge Artalejo (D)	1,856	(4%)	
1990 general	Ronald D. Coleman (D)	62,455	(96%)	($286,407)
	Other	2,854	(4%)	

SEVENTEENTH DISTRICT

From Fort Worth west, stretching miles beyond the horizon are the west Texas plains, thousands and thousands of acres of rolling grazing land punctuated occasionally by oases of irrigated farmland (often in circles that show the reach of the sprinklers). This is primarily cattle country, although there is some oil here, and cotton and grain. On the interstate straight west of Fort Worth, the largest town is Abilene, with a high concentration of bankers, lawyers and professionals. Settled by Confederate veterans suspicious of eastern bankers and Yankee businessmen, never much concerned about civil rights one way or the other (for there are very few blacks this far west), this was one of the Democratic heartlands of America up through the 1970s. Now, the 31 and a half mostly sparsely populated counties west of Fort Worth that make up Texas's 17th Congressional District are fought-over political territory: still Democratic in local and congressional elections (thanks to the popularity of Congressman Charles Stenholm), and Republican in presidential contests and statewide races.

Stenholm is one of several conservative Texas Democrats first elected in 1978 who have made their mark in different ways, and the only one who is still a Democrat and still in the House. He is a farmer from a small town settled by Swedes near Abilene, a natural politician who went to Congress after running the Rolling Plains Cotton Growers Association in Stamford (the home town also of Democratic super-lobbyist Robert Strauss). He has brought to Washington his West Texas common sense rule—"how much sense would this idea make to the guys gathered down at the Sweetwater coffee shop?" He has been complaining for years about the Democratic liberal leadership and policies. In 1981, Stenholm, with Gramm and their fellow 1978 Texas Democrat Kent Hance, became known as the "Boll Weevils," for supporting the Reagan budget and tax cuts. They formed the Conservative Democratic Forum, which Stenholm still coordinates. He threatened momentarily to run against Speaker O'Neill in 1985, then desisted; there was talk in 1992 that he might be elected speaker by a Republican-conservative Democrat coalition, but he never encouraged the idea. "My opinion was that Foley was very vulnerable," he said. "I was wrong." He voted for Bush Administration stands more than any other House Democrat in 1992, yet he is not much resented by most House liberals. He is one of 15 deputy whips: technically a member of the House leadership, actually an independent whom leaders can use to round up votes once they have got his word.

Stenholm has been an active legislator on the Agriculture Committee, and not a free market purist. He has worked on farm credit, disaster relief and animal product safety as chair of the former Livestock, Dairy and Poultry Subcommittee. He opposes efforts to put a cap on subsidies. He sponsored the 1992 law to protect farm and research animal facilities against animal rights terrorism. He passed an amendment to let pesticide makers sue EPA for capricious bans of their products. He objected to applying the farm bill's definition of 'organic' to livestock. As co-chairman of the Rural Health Care Coalition, he has passed several bills for better rural health care and said that he was in substantial agreement with Clinton on the issue, against pay-or-play and favoring a managed competition mechanism.

Stenholm pushes with the fervor of a true believer for deficit reduction and for that reason voted against Clinton's stimulus package in early 1993. Nevertheless, he has mostly stayed aligned with Clinton, and the Boll Weevil alliances made with Republicans during the Reagan years does not seem apparent now. Stenholm seeks spending cuts as well as tax increases to battle the deficit, and he was one of the major boosters of the almost successful balanced budget amendment; he got the issue to the floor by gathering 218 signatures to bypass the Rules Committee, and then came an agonizing nine votes within winning the necessary two-thirds during a vote on the House floor. In 1992, he also helped move key votes to maintain the budget walls between defense and domestic spending which Democratic leaders wanted to knock down. He also voted in 1991 for the Brady bill waiting period to buy handguns vociferously opposed by the National Rifle Association, and against the flag-burning amendment. His Stenholm-Shaw child care proposal, aimed at enhancing parent choice, though defeated, helped make the case against the also unsuccessful ABC proposal.

Why does Stenholm stay a Democrat? One reason is that he does not entirely believe in a free market economics; some government intervention is acceptable to him. Another is that he is a legislative activist, and there are more opportunities for action on the majority side. A third reason may just be stubbornness: he started off this way, he keeps trying to move the party his way, and danged if he's going to give up on it. And some might suggest it's good politics back home. A Republican congressman in rural Texas would have vigorous general election opponents. Stenholm was unopposed in the general elections of 1980 through 1990, and he beat his one Democratic primary opponent, in 1984, by an 88%–12% margin. In 1992, he did face a serious opponent in Republican Jeannie Sadowski, and with the additional burden of 88 overdrafts on the House bank. But he still carried every county and won 66%–34%.

The People: Pop. 1990: 566,255; 38% rural; 16% age 65+; 79% White; 4% Black; 1% Asian; 10% Other; 17% Hispanic origin. Voting age pop.: 412,115; 3% Black; 14% Hispanic origin. Households: 62% married couple families; 29% married couple fams. w. children; 36% college educ.; median household income: $21,532; per capita income: $10,642; median gross rent: $329; median house value: $38,400.

1992 Presidential Vote

Bush (R) 86,490 (40%)
Clinton (D) 73,388 (34%)
Perot (I).................... 55,834 (26%)

1988 Presidential Vote

Bush (R) 116,567 (58%)
Dukakis (D)................ 84,865 (42%)

Rep. Charles W. Stenholm (D)

Elected 1978; b. Oct. 26, 1938, Stamford; home, Avoca; TX Tech. U., B.S. 1961; M.S. 1962; Lutheran; married (Cynthia).

Career: Farmer; Vocational educ. teacher, 1962–65; Exec. V.P., Rolling Plains Cotton Growers, 1965–68; Mgr., Stamford Electric Coop., 1968–76.

Offices: 1211 LHOB 20515, 202-225-6605. Also 903 E. Hamilton St., Stamford 79553, 915-773-3623; and 341 Pine St., Abilene 79604, 915-673-7221.

Committees: *Agriculture* (6th of 28 D): Department Operations and Nutrition (Chmn.); Foreign Agriculture and Hunger; General Farm Commodities; Livestock; Specialty Crops and Natural Resources. *Budget* (8th of 26 D).

Group Ratings

	ADA	ACLU	COPE	CDF	CFA	LCV	ACU	NTLC	NSI	COC	CEI
1992	30	9	25	50	40	0	72	60	100	57	61
1991	5	—	17	30	44	8	70	—	—	90	56

National Journal Ratings

	1991 LIB — 1991 CONS	1992 LIB — 1992 CONS
Economic	31% — 69%	40% — 60%
Social	16% — 81%	0% — 85%
Foreign	36% — 62%	44% — 50%

Key Votes of the 102d Congress

1. Ban Striker Replace	AGN	5. Handgun Wait/7-Day	FOR	9. Use Force in Gulf	FOR
2. $ for Homeownership	FOR	6. Overseas Mil. Abortion	AGN	10. US Mil. Abroad $ Cut	FOR
3. Tax Rich/Cut Mid Cls.	FOR	7. Obscn. Art NEA $ Ban	FOR	11. Limit SDI Funds	AGN
4. FY93/$15B Def. Cut	FOR	8. Death Pen. from Jury	FOR	12. Cuba Trade Embargo	AGN

Key Votes of the 103d Congress

1. Family Leave	AGN	2. Deficit Reduction	FOR	3. Stimulus Plan	AGN

Election Results

1992 general	Charles W. Stenholm (D)	136,213	(66%)	($377,949)
	Jeannie Sadowski (R)	69,958	(34%)	($17,791)
1992 primary	Charles W. Stenholm (D), unopposed			
1990 general	Charles W. Stenholm (D), unopposed			($311,378)

EIGHTEENTH DISTRICT

Of all major American cities, few come close to having such wide disparities of income and wealth, such vivid contrasts between rich and poor, as Houston. This is not accidental: in the last dozen years, Houston has seen rapid economic growth, huge flows of immigration, lack of centralized planning and the cultural diversity of a large Third World city; and such rapid growth does not pull everybody up at the same rate. The contrast is glaringly apparent at the edge of Houston's gleaming downtown with its keynote Pennzoil, Heritage Plaza and NationsBank buildings and the few blocks of Freedman's Village. Yet a few streets away are the slums where blacks and Mexican-Americans live in unpainted frame houses full of cracks wide enough to let in Houston's humid, smoggy air. When the great builders of Houston like Jesse Jones, millionaire cotton broker, newspaper publisher and distributor of government capital as Franklin Roosevelt's head of the Reconstruction Finance Corporation, started erecting downtown skyscrapers, they were operating in a town with a Third World economy, a low-skill producer of basic commodities. Today, Houston is much more than that, a high-tech mecca as well as the petroleum-servicing center of the world, a sophisticated patron of the arts, the host of the 1990 G-7 Economic Summit and the 1992 Republican National Convention. And much of that growth is now filtering down: many of Houston's blacks and Hispanics are moving up economically and moving out geographically, fleeing the horrifyingly high crime rates and disorganization in what were once stable if poor inner city neighborhoods.

The 18th Congressional District of Texas, a black-majority unit first created for the 1972 election and represented then by Barbara Jordan, has moved out too. Its 1990s configuration, designed to produce a 51% black majority but leave heavily Hispanic blocks for the Hispanic-majority 29th District next door, is incredibly complex. It goes in and out of Loop 610, all the way out to include Intercontinental Airport on the north and well past the Astrodome to include Hobby Airport in the south; it tracks east along the Houston Ship Channel and west out past Memorial Park. Politically, it is by far the most Democratic district in Texas.

The congressman from the 18th District is Craig Washington, a legislator representing black districts in Houston since 1972, an intellectually scrupulous politician with a disorderly personal life. Washington won the seat in a December 1989 special election to replace Mickey Leland, who was killed in a plane crash while investigating hunger in Ethiopia; Washington, supported by Leland's widow, beat Councilman Anthony Hall, Leland's chief rival when he first won the seat in 1978. In his 10 years in the Texas House and seven in the Texas Senate, Washington was named to the *Texas Monthly*'s list of best legislators and its list of the worst. As he was sworn in to congress, he was sentenced to 30 days in jail for leaving a legal client "in the lurch" and not appearing in court, though he managed not to serve time; in January 1991, he filed for personal bankruptcy, saying he owed $205,000 in federal taxes and $65,000 in various unpaid local taxes—the state Republican chairman called for garnishing his salary. On official matters, he can be so principled as to cause himself political trouble. Determined that money should be spent on nothing except basic needs until poverty in areas like central Houston is alleviated, Washington voted against the Supercollider and the Space Station, big Texas projects; he voted against a celebration to express thanks to U.S. military personnel for their work in Operation Desert Storm. He declined to vote on a crime bill because of his doubts about the death penalty; he voted with Republicans on Henry Hyde's antiabortion amendment because of personal conviction.

Washington's foibles and prickliness elicited a spirited challenge from pro-choice Republican Edward Blum in 1992. Blum cited Washington's personal problems and his votes against Texas projects and the Gulf war and advanced his own national service proposal. Both Houston papers endorsed Blum, but Washington still won 65%–33%. In December 1992, however, Washington lost the race to chair the Congressional Black Caucus to Kweisi Mfume by a 27–9 margin, though he picked up a spot on the Energy and Commerce Committee.

The People: Pop. 1990: 564,708; 1% rural; 9% age 65+; 31% White; 51% Black; 3% Asian; 8% Other; 15% Hispanic origin. Voting age pop.: 413,519; 49% Black; 13% Hispanic origin. Households: 40% married couple families; 19% married couple fams. w. children; 40% college educ.; median household income: $22,531; per capita income: $11,091; median gross rent: $375; median house value: $46,400.

1992 Presidential Vote

Clinton (D) 118,493 (66%)
Bush (R) 40,208 (22%)
Perot (I). 20,416 (11%)

1988 Presidential Vote

Dukakis (D). 115,057 (70%)
Bush (R) 50,107 (30%)

Rep. Craig Washington (D)

Elected Dec., 1989; b. Oct. 12, 1941, Longview; home, Houston; Prairie View A&M U., B.S. 1966, TX Southern U., J.D. 1969; Episcopalian; separated.

Career: TX House of Reps., 1972–82; TX Senate, 1982–89.

Offices: 1711 LHOB 20515, 202-225-3816. Also 1919 Smith St., Houston 77002, 713-739-7339.

Committees: *Energy and Commerce* (22d of 27 D): Energy and Power; Health and the Environment. *Government Operations* (20th of 25 D): Environment, Energy and Natural Resources; Human Resources and Intergovernmental Relations. *Judiciary* (15th of 21 D): Civil and Constitutional Rights; Crime and Criminal Justice.

Group Ratings

	ADA	ACLU	COPE	CDF	CFA	LCV	ACU	NTLC	NSI	COC	CEI
1992	90	100	83	90	80	88	0	0	10	13	11
1991	95	—	100	90	72	69	0	—	—	11	10

National Journal Ratings

	1991 LIB — 1991 CONS	1992 LIB — 1992 CONS
Economic	78% — 21%	91% — 0%
Social	88% — 0%	80% — 20%
Foreign	92% — 0%	90% — 0%

Key Votes of the 102d Congress

1. Ban Striker Replace	FOR	5. Handgun Wait/7-Day	FOR	9. Use Force in Gulf	AGN
2. $ for Homeownership	AGN	6. Overseas Mil. Abortion	FOR	10. US Mil. Abroad $ Cut	FOR
3. Tax Rich/Cut Mid Cls.	FOR	7. Obscn. Art NEA $ Ban	AGN	11. Limit SDI Funds	FOR
4. FY93/$15B Def. Cut	FOR	8. Death Pen. from Jury	AGN	12. Cuba Trade Embargo	*

Key Votes of the 103d Congress

1. Family Leave	FOR	2. Deficit Reduction	FOR	3. Stimulus Plan	FOR

Election Results

1992 general	Craig Washington (D)	111,422	(65%)	($184,742)
	Edward Blum (R)	56,080	(33%)	($209,453)
	Other	4,706	(3%)	
1992 primary	Craig Washington (D), unopposed			
1990 general	Craig Washington (D), unopposed			($157,053)

NINETEENTH DISTRICT

Up on the High Plains of Texas, separated from the dusty cattlelands further east by rising gullies astride wide river courses, is some of the most productive cotton and wheat land in the United States, centered around the city of Lubbock. This fertility is a triumphant work of man: for this is irrigated land, which gets its water from the giant Ogallala Aquifer that undergirds so much of the western Great Plains, making this part of Texas a sort of green island in a vast brown sea of arid grazing land. The area was settled relatively late, with most growth after World War II; Lubbock grew from 31,000 in 1940 to 128,000 in 1960 and 186,000 in 1990. But the 1980s were tough on the High Plains. The aquifer seemed to be going dry, populations declined in almost every rural county, hospitals were closed in small towns. But Lubbock, with an economy that includes Texas Tech University as well as agri-business, has continued to grow, and evidently to be pleased with the policies of the 1980s. Once Democratic enough to have produced George Mahon, chairman of the House Appropriations Committee from 1964 to 1979, Lubbock has indeed become heavily Republican, and Lubbock County voted 60% for Bush and only 23% for Bill Clinton in 1992. Alas for Bush, Lubbock turned out to be anything but a bellwether of the rest of the country.

The 19th Congressional District of Texas covers the western edge of the High Plains of Texas, from the northern edge of the Panhandle south to the Permian Basin. Tantalizingly, it includes only part of each of its four widely separated major cities. The Democratic legislature took the black area of Lubbock and the lower income areas of Amarillo and put them in the 13th District to help Democrat Bill Sarpalius; the Permian Basin oil towns of Midland and Odessa, where George and Barbara Bush moved in the pre-air conditioning days of 1948, were split so their Hispanic portions would help 23d District Democrat Albert Bustamante (they didn't). The Bush's oldest son, George W., grew up in Midland, and went into the oil business there; in 1978, he lost the race to replace Mahon to Kent Hance, then a Lubbock Democrat. But young George may make another run in 1994—this time as a candidate for governor.

The partisan redistricting irritated, but politically helped, Congressman Larry Combest, a Republican first elected in 1984; this is now by most measures one of the dozen or two most Republican congressional districts in the United States. An electronics distributor in Lubbock, Combest has always specialized in farm issues, working on them for seven years on Senator John Tower's staff; he is now ranking Republican on Agriculture's Environment, Credit and Rural Development Subcommittee. In the House, Combest serves on the Agriculture Committee. He has an almost perfectly conservative record on other issues, but opposed cutting target prices and ending subsidies called for in the 1990 farm bill. He has worked to reform FmHA lending programs and to fund Texas Tech Plant Stress Lab research. He is also looking ahead to complete the I-27 highway that Mahon obtained between Amarillo and Lubbock, south to I-20 in the Permian Basin. In 1993, Combest became ranking Republican on the Intelligence Committee. He believes strongly that 1970s cutbacks in intelligence spending severely damaged the interests of the U.S. and has vowed to be cautious about any future cuts. With new Chairman Dan Glickman, Combest will have unusual leverage for a relatively junior member.

After a tough primary, runoff and general election in 1984, Combest has been reelected without difficulty. In 1992 he won with 77%.

The People: Pop. 1990: 565,925; 18% rural; 10% age 65+; 77% White; 2% Black; 1% Amer. Indian; 1% Asian; 10% Other; 19% Hispanic origin. Voting age pop.: 402,873; 2% Black; 16% Hispanic origin. Households: 62% married couple families; 32% married couple fams. w. children; 50% college educ.; median household income: $27,267; per capita income: $13,184; median gross rent: $366; median house value: $55,000.

1992 Presidential Vote

Bush (R) 130,639 (60%)
Clinton (D) 50,815 (23%)
Perot (I) 36,068 (17%)

1988 Presidential Vote

Bush (R) 147,596 (74%)
Dukakis (D). 51,195 (26%)

Rep. Larry Combest (R)

Elected 1984; b. Mar. 20, 1945, Memphis; home, Lubbock; W. TX St. U., B.B.A. 1969; United Methodist; married (Sharon).

Career: Farmer; Teacher, 1970–71; Dir., U.S. Agric. Stabilization and Conservation Svc., Graham TX, 1971; Aide, U.S. Sen. John Tower, 1971–78; Founder & Pres., Combest Distrib. Co., 1978–1985.

Offices: 1511 LHOB 20515, 202-225-4005. Also 1205 Texas Ave., #613, Lubbock 79401, 806-763-1611; 5809 S. Western, #205, Amarillo 79110, 806-353-3945; 511 W. Ohio, #114, Midland 79701, 915-687-0926; and 3800 E. 42d St., #205, Odessa 79762, 915-362-2631.

Committees: *Agriculture* (6th of 19 R): Environment, Credit and Rural Development (RMM); General Farm Commodities. *Intelligence (Permanent Select)* (RMM of 7 R): Program and Budget Authorization (RMM). *Small Business* (2d of 18 R): Regulation, Business Opportunities and Technology (RMM).

Group Ratings

	ADA	ACLU	COPE	CDF	CFA	LCV	ACU	NTLC	NSI	COC	CEI
1992	10	0	33	0	20	0	100	80	100	88	82
1991	0	—	8	20	44	0	95	—	—	90	75

National Journal Ratings

	1991 LIB — 1991 CONS	1992 LIB — 1992 CONS
Economic	14% — 83%	16% — 80%
Social	19% — 78%	16% — 82%
Foreign	12% — 85%	18% — 74%

Key Votes of the 102d Congress

1. Ban Striker Replace	AGN	5. Handgun Wait/7-Day	AGN	9. Use Force in Gulf	FOR
2. $ for Homeownership	FOR	6. Overseas Mil. Abortion	AGN	10. US Mil. Abroad $ Cut	AGN
3. Tax Rich/Cut Mid Cls.	AGN	7. Obscn. Art NEA $ Ban	FOR	11. Limit SDI Funds	AGN
4. FY93/$15B Def. Cut	AGN	8. Death Pen. from Jury	FOR	12. Cuba Trade Embargo	FOR

Key Votes of the 103d Congress

1. Family Leave	AGN	2. Deficit Reduction	AGN	3. Stimulus Plan	AGN

Election Results

1992 general	Larry Combest (R)	162,057	(77%)	($197,657)
	Terry Lee Moser (D)	47,325	(23%)	($5,198)
1992 primary	Larry Combest (R), unopposed			
1990 general	Larry Combest (R), unopposed			($106,265)

TWENTIETH DISTRICT

San Antonio, with its antique past and theme park future, its Hispanic heritage, its military superstructure and its high-tech hopes, is unlike any other city in the United States. Here on a plaza is the Alamo, where Davy Crockett, Jim Bowie and 184 others were wiped out in 1836 (Crockett was a Tennessee congressman for three terms; if he had not lost his bid for reelection in 1835, he never would have left Tennessee for Texas). The Spanish architecture, recalling San Antonio's days as the most important town in Texas when the state was part of Mexico, contrasts with the 31-story Tower Life Building; the stark terrain contrasts with the lushness of the Paseo, the 1970s-redeveloped Riverwalk along the tiny San Antonio River. The city also includes old neighborhoods redolent of the Texas Germans who were its chief Anglo citizens for many years. For most of this century, San Antonio's economy has been built on the military: this is the home of four Air Force bases and the Brooks Army Medical Center at Fort Sam Houston, contributing some $3 billion to the local economy; San Antonio also has 30,000 military retirees, second highest in the country. Behind them as a local employer is the medical complex centered on the Health Science Center. And San Antonio is also becoming a tourist center: for generations Texas schoolchildren have made pilgrimages to the Alamo, and in recent decades, they stop at the nearby HemisFair, preserved from the 1968 World's Fair, and the Riverwalk. Now they also may spend days at Sea World and Fiesta Texas, a musical theme park similar to the Grand Ole Opry in Nashville.

San Antonio had 936,000 people in the 1990 Census and is the third largest city in Texas, though its metro area is barely more than one third the size of metro Houston or the Dallas-Fort Worth Metroplex. San Antonio is also notable as the only Hispanic-majority major city in the country, and it has the low education and income levels one might expect from a city whose economy is affected by the proximity of the border. Yet it has avoided the polarized politics and ethnic anger that was manifested in the urban black-white tensions of the 1960s, and has made a notable progress as a kind of low-wage, high-tech center, making some linkage with nearby Austin. Much of the credit is due Henry Cisneros, mayor from 1981 to 1989, educated at Texas A&M and Harvard, who sparked high-tech and tourism growth but who dropped out of politics in 1989 over bad publicity from an extramarital affair, and is now Bill Clinton's secretary of housing and urban development.

It was quite a different San Antonio that first elected Henry B. Gonzalez to the House in 1961. Then Texas's 20th District included all of Bexar County and it seemed unthinkable to Anglos in comfortable north side neighborhoods that a Mexican-American could represent them. Today, the 20th District includes just central San Antonio, roughly the part of the city within the I-410 loop, which has a large Hispanic majority and is solidly Democratic. It is hard now to imagine the prejudice against Mexican-Americans that existed in Texas decades ago, or how it affected Gonzalez, who learned to speak English by reading Carlyle and Stevenson. He began serving on the San Antonio Council in 1953 and was elected to the Texas Senate in 1956—and had the nerve to run for governor in 1958 and in the special election (against John Tower and Jim Wright, among others) for the Senate in 1961. Gonzalez ran poorly in those races, but later in 1961, when Congressman Paul Kilday, part of a long-successful San Antonio machine, was appointed to a federal judgeship, he got into the race for Congress—and won. In his early days in Congress, Gonzalez was the patron saint of Texas liberalism, as he compiled a record of support for the administration and civil rights. Later, in the late 1960s and early 1970s, he alienated some liberals because he did not share their scorn for American foreign policy and heartily disagreed with the efforts of some Hispanics to set up a separate La Raza Unida party—views which have been thoroughly vindicated now. Always, Gonzalez has brought a determination to do right and an indifference to what others may think. He is not afraid to show his temper: in 1963, he took a swing at Texas Republican Congressman Ed Foreman who accused him of being a Communist; in 1986, he punched a 40-year-old man in a San Antonio restaurant for the same offense—one which must particularly rankle a man who has served his country loyally for many years. And he is not afraid to go out on a limb: in 1991 he called for the impeachment of President Bush for his actions in the Gulf war against Iraq.

For years, Gonzalez toiled on the Banking Committee mainly on housing issues, but with the defeat in 1988 of Fernand St Germain, one of the architects of the S&L disaster, Gonzalez suddenly became chairman. His first major task was construction of the S&L bailout bill. Working in his usual independent style, but with support from the Bush Administration and regulators, Gonzalez proceeded in a workmanlike manner to hammer out a law which may have cracked down too hard on the S&Ls (some think it contributed to the 1990–91 recession) but which also enabled regulators to wind up most of their work by 1993. Next he held hearings on Charles Keating's affairs, which prompted the resignation of chief S&L regulator Danny Wall, whose job had been protected in the bailout bill by Senate conferees; Gonzalez was also a force for keeping FDIC head William Seidman. In 1990, Gonzalez also worked on his first love, housing, and after some highly charged negotiations with HUD Secretary Jack Kemp, passed a housing bill that included his National Housing Trust. But Gonzalez's go-it-alone style prompted some resentment: in December 1990, Bruce Vento mounted a last-minute challenge to his chairmanship, charging that Gonzalez was erratic and lacked a partisan edge (Gonzalez had cut a campaign TV spot defending ranking Republican Chalmers Wylie against charges he was responsible for the S&L mess); but Gonzalez won in the Democratic Caucus 163–89.

In his second term as chairman, Gonzalez had a harder time assembling majorities. On the 1991 banking bill, he was faced with jurisdictional challenges from John Dingell of Energy and Commerce, who claimed authority over insurance and financial services; Gonzalez went along with Dingell on many substantive provisions but retained management of the bill. The result was opposed on all sides and defeated in the House in November 1991 by 324–89. The next month Gonzalez passed a narrower bill which provided more money for deposit insurance claims and closer regulation. Again in April 1992, an RTC funding bill backed by Gonzalez and ranking Republican Chalmers Wylie was voted down, and in September Gonzalez attacked Dingell for bringing forward a bill regulating government securities offerings. Much of Gonzalez's attention at this time was going into his investigation of Iraqgate; he uncovered evidence that the Bush Administration knew or should have known that federal farm product guarantees were being used by Iraq and the Atlanta branch of Banca Nazionale del Lavoro to generate cash to pay for weapons before the Gulf war—a genuine scandal either way. But in May 1992, Attorney General William Barr cut Gonzalez off from receiving additional classified documents on the grounds that he would not promise their "unauthorized disclosure." Republicans tried to initiate an Ethics Committee investigation of Gonzalez, but their efforts were defeated.

After the 1992 election, Gonzalez was not challenged as chairman. But as in the past, many committee members sought other assignments, and he ended up with a committee of nearly half freshmen. He promised to work for a law centralizing certain functions of bank regulation in one agency, and may focus specifically on the role of the Federal Reserve, but he will have to show better majority-assembling skills than he did in 1991 to succeed. And he will surely continue his sometimes lonely crusades for what he thinks is right.

For all his fisticuffs and feuds, Gonzalez appears to be cherished at home in San Antonio. His 20th District changed shape in redistricting and gained some Anglo neighborhoods, but he was still unopposed in 1992.

The People: Pop. 1990: 564,865; 3% rural; 10% age 65+; 32% White; 6% Black; 1% Asian; 21% Other; 60% Hispanic origin. Voting age pop.: 398,058; 6% Black; 56% Hispanic origin. Households: 51% married couple families; 28% married couple fams. w. children; 44% college educ.; median household income: $22,372; per capita income: $9,672; median gross rent: $362; median house value: $48,500.

1992 Presidential Vote			1988 Presidential Vote		
Clinton (D)	81,381	(48%)	Dukakis (D)	80,307	(57%)
Bush (R)	57,977	(34%)	Bush (R)	61,599	(43%)
Perot (I)	28,968	(17%)			

Rep. Henry B. Gonzalez (D)

Elected Nov. 1961; b. May 3, 1916, San Antonio; home, San Antonio; San Antonio Jr. Col., A.A. 1937, U. of TX, St. Mary's U., LL.B., J.D. 1943; Roman Catholic; married (Bertha).

Career: Military Intelligence, 1941–44; Bexar Cnty. Chief Probation Officer, 1946; Dpty. Dir., San Antonio Housing Authority, 1950–51; San Antonio City Cncl., 1953–56, San Antonio Mayor Pro Tem, 1955–56; TX Senate, 1956–61.

Offices: 2413 RHOB 20515, 202-225-3236. Also #B-124 Fed. Bldg., 727 E. Durango St., San Antonio 78206, 512-229-6195.

Committees: *Banking, Finance and Urban Affairs* (Chmn. of 30 D): Consumer Credit and Insurance; Housing and Community Development (Chmn.); International Development, Finance, Trade and Monetary Policy.

Group Ratings

	ADA	ACLU	COPE	CDF	CFA	LCV	ACU	NTLC	NSI	COC	CEI
1992	80	91	92	100	87	63	4	0	30	38	9
1991	75	—	100	100	78	54	0	—	—	10	6

National Journal Ratings

	1991 LIB — 1991 CONS		1992 LIB — 1992 CONS	
Economic	72% —	23%	83% —	13%
Social	84% —	12%	72% —	24%
Foreign	78% —	19%	61% —	39%

Key Votes of the 102d Congress

1. Ban Striker Replace	FOR	5. Handgun Wait/7-Day	FOR	9. Use Force in Gulf	AGN
2. $ for Homeownership	AGN	6. Overseas Mil. Abortion	FOR	10. US Mil. Abroad $ Cut	AGN
3. Tax Rich/Cut Mid Cls.	FOR	7. Obscn. Art NEA $ Ban	AGN	11. Limit SDI Funds	AGN
4. FY93/$15B Def. Cut	FOR	8. Death Pen. from Jury	AGN	12. Cuba Trade Embargo	AGN

Key Votes of the 103d Congress

1. Family Leave	FOR	2. Deficit Reduction	FOR	3. Stimulus Plan	FOR

Election Results

1992 general	Henry B. Gonzalez (D), unopposed	($43,147)
1992 primary	Henry B. Gonzalez (D), unopposed	
1990 general	Henry B. Gonzalez (D), unopposed	($112,901)

TWENTY-FIRST DISTRICT

The Texas German country, on the gently rolling plains between San Antonio and Austin and west into the Hill Country, is one of this nation's lesser known ethnic enclaves. First settled by refugees from the failed democratic revolutions of 1848, the German country has always been a set of orderly communities in riproaring Texas, economically prosperous in a state that considered itself poor until it struck oil; antislavery and politically Republican in a state whose enthusiasm for the Democratic party had roots in Confederate loyalties and populist rebellions. The Texas Germans come into political history entwined with the career of Lyndon Johnson: the death of Republican Congressman Harry Wurzbach of Guadalupe County enabled the Democrats to elect John Nance Garner of Uvalde speaker in 1931, while Wurzbach's replacement in the House, Democrat Richard Kleberg (of the King ranch family) hired the then 23-year-old Johnson to his first Washington job. And, though Johnson never emphasized this, his LBJ Ranch was not in Blanco County or near poor Johnson City, where he grew up, but west in Gillespie County near the prosperous town of Fredericksburg, historically Texas German and heavily Republican.

The 21st Congressional District has its demographic center in the old Texas German country. But, as with so many Texas districts after the 1991 redistricting, its boundaries are quite complex; and this is now a metropolitan district, with most of its population technically in the San Antonio or Austin metropolitan areas. About 40% is on the north side of San Antonio and Bexar County (pronounced like a drawn-out *bear*), mostly Anglo neighborhoods around Alamo Heights and out Interstate 35, and in Guadalupe and Comal Counties just beyond—Texas German country now classified as part of metro San Antonio; all this is heavily Republican. Another 20% is in Williamson County, just north of Austin—suburban overspill subdivisions full of high-tech and white-collar workers who are much more Republican than the liberals who live in older neighborhoods near downtown Austin and UT. These two areas are connected by sparsely populated Hill Country and Texas German counties, including Fredericksburg and the LBJ Ranch, the almost mountainous country around Kerrville, sheep and goat ranching country reaching west to San Angelo, the mohair capital of America, all the way to Midland, headquarters of the high-income, oil-rich Permian Basin, where George Bush lived from 1949 to 1960; both these small cities are split with next door districts. Although some of the small counties are ancestrally Democratic, this is a heavily Republican district—from its Texas German heritage, from its affluent Anglos' free market conservatism, to its cultural conservatism and hawkishness.

The congressman from the 21st District is Lamar Smith, a Republican first elected in 1986, who is from an old San Antonio and south Texas ranching family and served both in the legislature and on the Bexar County Commission. Smith has combined a conservative record on all but a few cultural issues with a penchant for original initiatives, and a persistence which has resulted in some unexpected successes. In his first term, Smith pushed to passage a bill adding 100,000 acres to the Big Bend National Park in the western part of the district. In his second, he sponsored the administration's government-wide ethics act. In his third term, while serving as ranking Republican on Judiciary's Immigration Subcommittee, he worked long and hard on the 1990 immigration bill to hold down quotas and grants of refugee status, mostly with little success against an Irish-Hispanic-Asian alliance. One success, however, was a provision preventing illegal aliens from using Legal Service Corporation lawyers except in employment, housing or transportation cases.

More recently, Smith has specialized in spending cut amendments to appropriations bills, taking on the "College of Cardinals" (Appropriations subcommittee chairmen) one by one, and winning cuts in five different areas, for a total of $143 million. His goal was to squeeze tight on government overhead costs, especially year-end travel. But he was frustrated when the Democratic leadership refused to allow a vote on amending Congress's own budget. His overall goal is even more ambitious; reducing federal government's $340 billion overhead costs by 10% and then holding increases to the rate of inflation. Smith received a spot on Budget in 1993 and is certain to continue his crusade against wasteful government spending; he also had a hand in early 1993 in the development of John Kasich's GOP budget alternative.

Smith first won this seat in 1986, when the district boundaries ranged far wider and included more acreage than Ohio, by beating two other San Antonio-based candidates in the primary 31%–25%–20%, and then winning the runoff, with help from Senator Phil Gramm, against a religious right conservative. In the general, against an 18-year state senator from Midland, he got big margins in Bexar County and the Texas German country for a 61% win. He has won easily since. Redistricting vastly cut the acreage of the 21st but didn't change the political balance much; Smith won in 1992 with 72%.

The People: Pop. 1990: 566,105; 29% rural; 13% age 65+; 82% White; 3% Black; 1% Asian; 5% Other; 14% Hispanic origin. Voting age pop.: 420,543; 2% Black; 12% Hispanic origin. Households: 63% married couple families; 29% married couple fams. w. children; 59% college educ.; median household income: $32,103; per capita income: $16,086; median gross rent: $434; median house value: $79,400.

1992 Presidential Vote			1988 Presidential Vote		
Bush (R)	144,073	(52%)	Bush (R)	169,319	(70%)
Clinton (D)	70,677	(25%)	Dukakis (D)	71,647	(30%)
Perot (I)	63,454	(23%)			

Rep. Lamar S. Smith (R)

Elected 1986; b. Nov. 19, 1947, San Antonio; home, San Antonio; Yale, B.A. 1969, Southern Methodist U., J.D. 1975; Christian Scientist; married (Beth).

Career: U.S. Small Business Admin., 1969–70; Business writer, *Christian Science Monitor*, 1970–72; Practicing atty., 1975–76; TX House of Reps., 1981–82; Bexar Cnty. Commissioner, 1982–85.

Offices: 2443 RHOB 20515, 202-225-4236. Also 1st Federal Bldg., 1100 NE Loop 410, #640, San Antonio 78209, 210-821-5024; 201 W. Wall St., #104, Midland 79701, 915-687-5232; 1006 Junction Hwy., Kerrville 78028, 512-895-1414; 221 E. Main, #318, Round Rock 78664, 512-218-4221; and 33 E. Twohig, #302, San Angelo 76903, 915-653-3971.

Committees: *Budget* (8th of 17 R). *Judiciary* (8th of 14 R): Crime and Criminal Justice; Intl. Law, Immigration and Refugees.

Group Ratings

	ADA	ACLU	COPE	CDF	CFA	LCV	ACU	NTLC	NSI	COC	CEI
1992	20	18	36	30	33	13	88	75	100	88	73
1991	5	—	25	30	33	23	84	—	—	70	79

National Journal Ratings

	1991 LIB — 1991 CONS		1992 LIB — 1992 CONS	
Economic	18% —	79%	0% —	91%
Social	19% —	78%	34% —	66%
Foreign	0% —	88%	0% —	82%

Key Votes of the 102d Congress

1. Ban Striker Replace	AGN	5. Handgun Wait/7-Day	AGN	9. Use Force in Gulf	FOR
2. $ for Homeownership	FOR	6. Overseas Mil. Abortion	AGN	10. US Mil. Abroad $ Cut	AGN
3. Tax Rich/Cut Mid Cls.	AGN	7. Obscn. Art NEA $ Ban	FOR	11. Limit SDI Funds	AGN
4. FY93/$15B Def. Cut	AGN	8. Death Pen. from Jury	FOR	12. Cuba Trade Embargo	FOR

Key Votes of the 103d Congress

1. Family Leave	FOR	2. Deficit Reduction	AGN	3. Stimulus Plan	AGN

Election Results

1992 general	Lamar S. Smith (R)	190,979	(72%)	($476,501)
	James M. Gaddy (D)	62,827	(24%)	($5,694)
	William E. Grisham (LIB)	10,847	(4%)	
1992 primary	Lamar S. Smith (R), unopposed			
1990 general	Lamar S. Smith (R)	144,570	(75%)	($399,008)
	Kirby J. Roberts (D)..................	48,585	(25%)	($15,732)

TWENTY-SECOND DISTRICT

Spreading out in all directions from its historic center at Allen's Landing on Buffalo Bayou, Houston has become one of the great metropolises of North America. A half century ago, the steaming flatlands south of Houston running down to the Gulf of Mexico did not seem a likely site of one of the world's most advanced civilizations. But they are today. On Clear Lake, not far from the sluggish and oily shores of Galveston Bay, is the Johnson Space Center, where NASA's top engineers plan space flights. Farther south, where the narrow Brazos River enters the Gulf of Mexico, is the Brazosport complex of towns, with some of the biggest oil refinery and petrochemical operations anywhere—an example of the petroleum engineering expertise that makes greater Houston an oil capital even though less and less oil is actually drilled in these parts. Back up Route 288 are the outlying parts of central Houston—the Texas Medical Center and Rice University, the art museum complex and the 30- and 60-story high-rises that tower over the Southwest Freeway, where all manner of business genius is being employed. The success and sophistication is testimony to human—and Texas—creativity, and to the triumph of air conditioning: for who supposed that all these people would move here if they had to sweat through Houston's steamy five-month summer?

Put all these areas together, roughly, and you have the 22d Congressional District of Texas. First established in the 1950s, when it included all the south side of Houston, it has moved farther out each decade. In the 1991 redistricting, only 45% of its people live in Houston's Harris County—most in a jagged corridor running along the Southwest Freeway, where many of Houston's business and creative leaders live, and in a separate corridor around the Space Center and Galveston Bay. The 22d also includes most of Fort Bend County just southwest of Houston—starting with Sugar Land, a series of suburbs growing in what was once farming country. The 22d finally moves directly south to include most of Brazoria County, including land along 288 not yet filled in with suburbs, and most of the Brazosport area.

The 22d is a heavily Republican district: you will be hard put to find many national Democrats among the people who have come from other parts of Texas and the nation, and live now in these new, mostly affluent subdivisions. Even in local elections the historic Democratic leanings of the rural areas are usually overwhelmed by the strong Republican allegiance of the newcomers. It was a marginal district up through 1980, when it was centered farther into Houston and represented by Ron Paul, the Libertarian Party candidate for president in 1988; redistricting made it even more Republican, to give Democratic precincts to needy incumbents in Democratic districts next door.

The congressman here is Tom DeLay, an aggressive conservative Republican—and since December 1992, part of his party's leadership as secretary of the Republican Conference. DeLay is an interesting amalgam of practical politico and intellectual ideologue. He was born in the border town of Laredo and spent much of his childhood in Venezuela, where his father drilled oil wells. Settling in Sugar Land, Delay built a pest control business—environmentalists may bristle at that, but in the Houston area people want to control bugs not preserve them—and was elected to the state legislature in 1978, the first Republican from Fort Bend County. DeLay easily won the 1984 Republican primary and the general election for this seat. His voting record is almost purely conservative, but he sought posts that usually appeal to the practical pols. In his first term, he was the freshman representative on the Republican Committee on Committees; in his second term he got a seat on the Appropriations Committee, where he has been known to seek money for his district. He worked early on for funds for a bus system to alleviate the traffic-choked Southwest Freeway. But he opposed former Mayor Kathy Whitmire's $1.2 billion monorail (which surely would never pay its way) and took on Senators Lloyd Bentsen and Phil Gramm in 1991 when they sought $30 million for it, and got a provision postponing spending until there was a "consensus" on the type of transit system to build. DeLay is an ardent booster of the space program and worked to save the Space Station from demise; he has joined forces with Mike Andrews and Jack Brooks to fund a wider road, NASA Road 1, into the Johnson Space Center. DeLay was an ardent backer of Vice President Dan Quayle's Competitiveness Council and an outspoken opponent of regulators. With Senator Malcolm Wallop, he had a bill in 1991–92 to lower taxes; he wants the Social Security payroll tax down to 10.6% and capital gains down to 15%. He bristles at wetlands regulators and called provisions in the California Desert Protection Act "an outrageous land grab." He is a solid supporter of NAFTA and market-based healthcare reform.

When Newt Gingrich became Republican whip after Dick Cheney became secretary of defense in March 1989, DeLay didn't move up in rank. He resumed the role of critic, urging the Wallop-DeLay tax cut and opposing family and medical leave and the 1990 budget summit tax increase. In December 1992, he ran against Ohio's Bill Gradison for the post of Republican Conference Secretary and won by the strong margin of 95–71—a signal of conservative dominance in the Conference, though he was supported by some moderates like New York's Susan Molinari. His attitude toward the Clinton Administration was hard-right from the start. "Screaming and shouting is useful in educating the American public," he began, and was one of the first to harshly criticize the Clinton plan to drop the ban on gays in the military—in line with DeLay's earlier move to stop funding of the District of Columbia's domestic partnership law. DeLay can be expected to be a voluble and aggressive member of the Republican leadership, vying perhaps with Newt Gingrich and Dick Armey; and he could be a powerful leader if Republicans gain many seats or win a majority.

The People: Pop. 1990: 567,852; 14% rural; 6% age 65+; 69% White; 8% Black; 7% Asian; 8% Other; 16% Hispanic origin. Voting age pop.: 407,903; 7% Black; 14% Hispanic origin. Households: 63% married couple families; 35% married couple fams. w. children; 63% college educ.; median household income: $40,654; per capita income: $17,608; median gross rent: $453; median house value: $75,100.

1992 Presidential Vote

Bush (R) 116,557 (51%)
Clinton (D) 63,092 (27%)
Perot (I) 50,705 (22%)

1988 Presidential Vote

Bush (R) 123,211 (69%)
Dukakis (D)................ 54,775 (31%)

Rep. Tom DeLay (R)

Elected 1984; b. Apr. 8, 1947, Laredo; home, Sugar Land; U. of Houston, B.S. 1970; Baptist; married (Christine).

Career: Owner, Albo Pest Control, 1973–84; TX House of Reps., 1978–84.

Offices: 407 CHOB 20515, 202-225-5951. Also 12603 Southwest Frwy., #285, Stafford 77477, 713-240-3700.

Committees: *Appropriations* (11th of 23 R): Transportation; VA, HUD and Independent Agencies.

Group Ratings

	ADA	ACLU	COPE	CDF	CFA	LCV	ACU	NTLC	NSI	COC	CEI
1992	5	0	8	0	13	0	100	100	100	71	86
1991	5	—	9	10	17	8	100	—	—	90	87

National Journal Ratings

	1991 LIB — 1991 CONS	1992 LIB — 1992 CONS
Economic	12% — 86%	0% — 91%
Social	0% — 84%	0% — 85%
Foreign	0% — 88%	18% — 74%

Key Votes of the 102d Congress

1. Ban Striker Replace AGN	5. Handgun Wait/7-Day AGN	9. Use Force in Gulf FOR
2. $ for Homeownership FOR	6. Overseas Mil. AbortionAGN	10. US Mil. Abroad $ CutAGN
3. Tax Rich/Cut Mid Cls.AGN	7. Obscn. Art NEA $ Ban FOR	11. Limit SDI Funds AGN
4. FY93/$15B Def. Cut AGN	8. Death Pen. from Jury FOR	12. Cuba Trade Embargo FOR

Key Votes of the 103d Congress

1. Family Leave AGN	2. Deficit Reduction AGN	3. Stimulus Plan AGN

Election Results

1992 general	Tom DeLay (R).....................	150,221	(69%)	($371,362)
	Richard Konrad (D)..................	67,812	(31%)	($39,836)
1992 primary	Tom DeLay (R), unopposed			
1990 general	Tom DeLay (R).....................	93,425	(71%)	($297,153)
	Bruce Director (D)	37,721	(29%)	

TWENTY-THIRD DISTRICT

The border country of Texas is a zone all its own. This is a part of the United States whose culture and economy is not entirely Yanqui or Latino, partaking of both cultures and economies with varying mixes. For a time in the 1960s and 1970s it seemed that Mexico was moving north: incomes were exceedingly low along the Texas border, the population increasingly Hispanic; "brown power" political movements arose in small counties where white landholders had run things for years and where chicano militants wanted an economy and polity as in Mexico, where union and party apparatchiks were in charge. But those attempts fizzled, and now it seems that the United States, influenced by Mexican culture (fajitas are on McDonald's menu), is moving south. Incomes have been rising fast on both sides of the border, manufacturing plants have been springing up and the North American Free Trade Agreement promises to stimulate many more. Mexico has privatized government companies, reduced the powers of local political and labor bosses and opened up to U.S. imports—making itself over more like the U.S., or Texas, image.

The 23d Congressional District of Texas includes the longest portion of the 2,500-mile U.S.-Mexico border, following the Rio Grande almost from El Paso south to Laredo. It begins in the Anglo neighborhoods on the north side of San Antonio and goes all the way to the Big Bend territory, where 7,000-foot peaks tower over stony desert. It covers miles of arid hills and rugged desert, of cattle grazing, sheep ranching and oil well country, yet most of its people live in a few widely scattered metropolitan areas, about one-third in or near San Antonio, with others in Laredo, Midland and Odessa, and the fringes of El Paso. Politically, the border counties around Laredo and Eagle Pass are heavily Democratic, while many of the grazing counties inland are Republican. The Democratic legislature tried to help incumbent Democrat Albert Bustamante by adding mainly Mexican-American parts of Midland and Odessa. But he was hurt when almost all the heavily Democratic Hispanic precincts in San Antonio and Bexar County went to veteran Henry B. Gonzalez's 20th District and state Senator Frank Tejeda's new 28th, leaving Bustamante with heavily Anglo and Republican northwest San Antonio and suburbs. Some 63% of the new 23d's residents were Hispanic, but less than 50% of its registered voters, and the seat only went narrowly for Dukakis in 1988.

This is the one Texas district that saw an incumbent defeated in 1992. Bustamante's first problem arose in December 1990, when the *San Antonio Light* reported on an FBI investigation of Bustamante and a friend, local bingo operator Eddie Garcia, as part of a probe into a bingo parlor deal with the Kickapoo Indians in Eagle Pass. Bustamante charged the FBI with taking revenge on him for his 1986 support of a discrimination suit brought against the FBI by Hispanic agents. Then the *Light* sent a reporter to take pictures of Bustamante's new $618,000 house in an enclave with private guards, outside his old district but included in the new one; Bustamante's lawyer threatened legal action, and the paper ran pictures of the house and the lawyer's letter. This came on top of criticism for Bustamante's junkets to Europe and Asia, his 30 overdrafts at the House bank, and stories about connections with a law firm which received delinquent tax collection contracts and had at one time employed his wife.

Meanwhile *los Republicanos*, as some put it, were making a real effort to win. They elected Roy Barrera, Jr., a judge who was nearly elected Texas attorney general in 1990, as Bexar County chairman. To run against Bustamante, they got Henry Bonilla, public affairs producer at a local CBS affiliate. In that capacity, Bonilla was involved in all kinds of civic activities and also appeared regularly on the air; and it didn't hurt that his wife, Deborah Knapp Bonilla, was an anchor at the same station. Bonilla got support for opposing two new hazardous waste dumps near Del Rio, hit Bustamante for preventing a visiting Mexican legislator from attending an event at which Bonilla was scheduled to sign a joint anti-toxic waste pledge. Bonilla backed tax and environmental policies more favorable to the oil industry positions and sided with water users over the allegedly endangered fountain darter fish in a dispute over Comal Springs. He called for term limits, the line-item veto and a congressional ethics committee made up of private citizens, and attacked the incumbent for ducking debates. Bustamante bragged of bringing in defense contracts from his seat on the Armed Services Committee and called Bonilla "a eunuch for the plantation owners" for opposing a minimum wage bill, all the while keeping his fingers crossed for a big turnout in the counties around Laredo.

Bonilla won by a whopping 59%–38%, and three months later Bustamante and his wife were indicted on bribery and racketeering charges. Bustamante had carried the Laredo area by less than he had hoped and lost the other border counties narrowly and the interior counties by a solid margin. But in San Antonio and Bexar County, which cast 29% of the 23d's votes, Bonilla led by 81%–16%, for 31,000 of his 34,000-vote margin. Republicans, ecstatic at electing their first Mexican-American representative in Texas, gave Bonilla a seat on the Appropriations Committee, something no freshman has accomplished since 1967. Bonilla is not guaranteed reelection, but he looks to be in a strong position to win, and to improve his party's image in south Texas.

The People: Pop. 1990: 566,736; 25% rural; 9% age 65+; 34% White; 3% Black; 1% Asian; 22% Other; 62% Hispanic origin. Voting age pop.: 375,375; 3% Black; 58% Hispanic origin. Households: 66% married couple families; 38% married couple fams. w. children; 39% college educ.; median household income: $21,555; per capita income: $9,764; median gross rent: $322; median house value: $47,900.

1992 Presidential Vote			1988 Presidential Vote		
Clinton (D)	72,452	(42%)	Dukakis (D)	78,900	(51%)
Bush (R)	70,576	(41%)	Bush (R)	76,884	(49%)
Perot (I)	28,846	(17%)			

Rep. Henry Bonilla (R)

Elected 1992; b. Jan. 2, 1954, San Antonio; home, San Antonio; U. of TX, B.A. 1976; Baptist; married (Deborah).

Career: TV reporter, 1976–80; Asst. Press Secy., PA Gov. Thornburg, 1981; Writer/producer, WABC, New York, 1982–85; Asst. News Dir., WATF-TV, Philadelphia, 1985–86; KENS-TV, San Antonio, Exec. News Producer, 1986–89, Public Affairs, 1989–92.

Offices: 1529 LHOB 20515, 202-225-4511. Also 11120 Wurzbach, #300, San Antonio 78230, 210-697-9055; 1300 Matamoros St., #113B, Laredo 78040, 210-726-4682; 100 E. Broadway, #101, Del Rio 78840, 210-774-6547; 4400 N. Big Spring, #211, Midland 79705, 915-686-8833.

Committees: *Appropriations* (23d of 23 R): District of Columbia; Labor, Health and Human Services, and Education.

Group Ratings and 102d Congress Votes: Newly Elected

Key Votes of the 103d Congress

1. Family Leave	AGN	2. Deficit Reduction	AGN	3. Stimulus Plan	AGN

Election Results

1992 general	Henry Bonilla (R)	98,259	(59%)	($594,032)
	Albert G. Bustamante (D)	63,797	(38%)	($758,453)
	Other	4,291	(3%)	
1992 primary	Henry Bonilla (R)	9,013	(63%)	
	Dick Bowen (R)	5,216	(37%)	
1990 general	Albert G. Bustamante (D)	71,052	(64%)	($236,046)
	Jerome L. Gonzalez (R)	40,856	(37%)	($22,428)

TWENTY-FOURTH DISTRICT

In between Dallas and Fort Worth, the geographical heart of the Metroplex as it is locally known, was open country as late as the 1950s, when the Dallas-Fort Worth Turnpike was built to link the two downtowns. In the following decades, the bottomlands of the West Fork of the Trinity River and the barren hills overlooking them filled up. Grand Prairie and Irving in Dallas County and Arlington in Tarrant County became cities with more than 100,000 people, and with their own institutions—Turnpike Stadium, Texas Stadium, the original Six Flags Over Texas, the University of Texas at Arlington and of course the Dallas-Fort Worth Regional Airport. By the 1970s, this area was large enough to have its own congressional district, the Texas 24th; now, depending on where you draw the lines, it is big enough for two. For drawing the lines has become an art, and no one today is better at it than the 24th District's congressman since 1978, Martin Frost.

Frost is a Democrat whose tenure was threatened more than anyone else's by the interpretation of the 1982 amendments to the Voting Rights Act requiring a maximum number of black-majority districts. His problem was that there were enough blacks to create a black-majority district in the Dallas area, and a great many of them were in his district—providing key votes to put the seat out of reach of Republicans. The old 24th in 1990 was 29% black and 21% Hispanic; it included most of the Oak Cliff area of Dallas, just across the Trinity River from downtown, as well as most of Irving and Grand Prairie. Moreover, the chairman of the state Senate redistricting committee, Eddie Bernice Johnson, a black woman from Dallas, wanted to create a new black-majority district for herself. Expanding the 24th directly outward would bring in Republican areas of Arlington, Carrollton or Grapevine—or perhaps Waxahachie, where Frost was threatened with facing Republican incumbent Joe Barton. It would be an embarrassment for Frost to lose out in redistricting, as he headed the Democrats' IMPAC 2000 redistricting group; it would be a disaster for a man who first ran for Congress in 1974 at 32 and, except for a few years in school and stint as a public broadcasting commentator and a lawyer, has spent all his adult life in Congress.

Frost responded with breathtaking creativity. He and staffer Bob Mansker drew up a plan not just for the Metroplex but for the whole state which seemed to protect every Democratic incumbent (except for one, Bustamante, who lost through problems of his own), and which gave Texas's three new seats to Democrats and minorities while creating a 24th District he could easily win. Describing these boundaries could take until the next census. Frost's new 24th takes in low-income white neighborhoods near Dallas's Love Field, includes the non-black parts of Oak Cliff (including some fine old Victorian gingerbread houses, Mexican-American neighborhoods and million dollar homes in Kessler Park). It proceeds west through a corridor of Grand Prairie to take in the more Democratic half of Arlington, then runs southeast to open country, through Ellis County south to rural and Democratic Navarro County, while excluding Barton's base in Waxahachie and Ennis, then through a narrow salient coming north to include southeast Fort Worth—a heavily black part of the Metroplex beyond the possible reach of Eddie Bernice Johnson. This last inclusion was a stroke of genius, since in November 1992, against a little-known Republican, Frost got only 53% in the Dallas County portion of the district; he was rescued by his 68% in Fort Worth, Arlington and other parts of Tarrant County, none of which he has run in since 1980 and some of which he has never represented. His overall percentage was 60%, a pretty clear indication that he can count on another decade in the House.

After Frost first won the seat by beating incumbent Dale Milford in the 1978 primary, he got a seat on the Rules Committee, only the second freshman Democrat in the 20th Century to do so, thanks to then Majority Leader Jim Wright of neighboring Fort Worth. Ever since, Frost has been a solid supporter of the Democratic leadership. He works hard on local issues: keeping funding for the V-22 Osprey and the B-2 bomber, pushing defense conversion legislation and promoting the Supercollider. He strongly backed Jim Wright when he got into trouble in 1989, and he worked in tandem with Wright on banking and S&L legislation, helping to kill measures that would have tightened lending and investment requirements for S&Ls and would have increased capital requirements. In this case, he was innocently helping Texas S&L operators—some who turned out to be crooks—and opening up the taxpayers to some $500 billion of liability. Frost has had some setbacks: he backed off a bid to chair the Budget Committee after the 1984 election when it became apparent Bill Gray had the votes, and after Wright's resignation, Frost lost a bid to be Democratic Caucus vice chairman to Vic Fazio by 147–74. But Frost perseveres. Frost spent more on his 1992 campaign, $1.5 million, than any other Texas incumbent, receiving more than half of that amount from PACs. With a seat on House Administration, he will play a role on campaign finance reform, presumably looking after his Democratic colleagues as well as he did on Texas redistricting.

1266   TEXAS

The People: Pop. 1990: 565,779; 9% rural; 9% age 65+; 57% White; 19% Black; 1% Amer. Indian; 2% Asian; 14% Other; 21% Hispanic origin. Voting age pop.: 395,763; 18% Black; 18% Hispanic origin. Households: 57% married couple families; 31% married couple fams. w. children; 41% college educ.; median household income: $27,535; per capita income: $11,534; median gross rent: $417; median house value: $58,800.

1992 Presidential Vote			1988 Presidential Vote		
Clinton (D)	73,635	(41%)	Bush (R)	82,082	(52%)
Bush (R)	59,372	(33%)	Dukakis (D)	77,167	(48%)
Perot (I)	46,571	(26%)			

Rep. Martin Frost (D)

Elected 1978; b. Jan. 1, 1942, Glendale, CA; home, Dallas; U. of MO, B.A., 1964, Georgetown U., J.D. 1970; Jewish; married (Valerie).

Career: Army Reserves, 1966–72; Legal commentator, KERA-TV, Dallas, 1971–72; Practicing atty., 1972–78.

Offices: 2459 RHOB 20515, 202-225-3605. Also 3020 S.E. Loop 820, Ft. Worth 76140, 817-293-9231; 400 S. Zang Blvd., #1319, Dallas 75208, 214-948-3401; and 318 W. Main St., #102, Arlington 76010, 817-795-3291.

Committees: *House Administration* (5th of 12 D): Accounts (Chmn.); Elections; Libraries and Memorials; Office Systems. *Rules* (4th of 9 D): The Legislative Process. *Joint Committee on the Library* (2d of 5).

Group Ratings

	ADA	ACLU	COPE	CDF	CFA	LCV	ACU	NTLC	NSI	COC	CEI
1992	75	77	73	90	60	56	25	0	90	57	12
1991	65	—	100	90	72	54	20	—	—	20	8

National Journal Ratings

	1991 LIB — 1991 CONS		1992 LIB — 1992 CONS	
Economic	69%	— 29%	71%	— 27%
Social	72%	— 27%	57%	— 43%
Foreign	45%	— 55%	44%	— 50%

Key Votes of the 102d Congress

1. Ban Striker Replace	FOR	5. Handgun Wait/7-Day	FOR	9. Use Force in Gulf	FOR
2. $ for Homeownership	AGN	6. Overseas Mil. Abortion	FOR	10. US Mil. Abroad $ Cut	FOR
3. Tax Rich/Cut Mid Cls.	FOR	7. Obscn. Art NEA $ Ban	FOR	11. Limit SDI Funds	AGN
4. FY93/$15B Def. Cut	FOR	8. Death Pen. from Jury	FOR	12. Cuba Trade Embargo	FOR

Key Votes of the 103d Congress

1. Family Leave	FOR	2. Deficit Reduction	FOR	3. Stimulus Plan	FOR

Election Results

1992 general	Martin Frost (D)	104,174	(60%)	($1,549,556)
	Steve Masterson (R)	70,042	(40%)	($109,306)
1992 primary	Martin Frost (D), unopposed			
1990 general	Martin Frost (D), unopposed			($597,310)

TWENTY-FIFTH DISTRICT

Working-class Houston—it sounds like a contradiction in terms to those who think of elderly blue-collar ethnics in three-deckers in Boston or closely packed houses lined up and down the hills of Pittsburgh. But Houston is, among other things, a blue-collar town: the Ship Channel which made it a great city is lined with petrochemical plants and refineries and surrounded by port facilities, factories, truck terminals and railroad offloading platforms. And many of the neighborhoods that have sprouted up in and around Houston's wide city limits in the last three decades, with their plain, contemporary houses and commercial strip highways, could be called working class.

These neighborhoods, on the margins between the highly affluent and heavily Republican subdivisions on the west and south sides and the heavily black and Hispanic low-income neighborhoods in the central corridor of Houston, make up most of Texas's 25th Congressional District. On the map the 25th forms a curlicue around central Houston. It includes blue-collar neighborhoods on both sides of the Houston Ship Channel, Highlands and Channelview on the north, Deer Park and Pasadena on the south. It includes a strip of southern Houston from Hobby Airport west toward the Astrodome and beyond, with a salient reaching north to the more affluent, and in some cases Jewish, neighborhoods near Rice University and the giant Texas Medical Center. The 25th also proceeds south into Missouri City and Fort Bend County, to make up for heavily black and Hispanic precincts lost to the 18th and 29th Districts in redistricting. The boundaries seem erose, but were carefully crafted to make this a Democratic area and the Democratic percentage as measured by the 1988 election fell only 1%.

All this is testimony to the political strength of Democratic Congressman Mike Andrews, and not the first such testimony entered into the record. Andrews first ran for Congress in 1980, in the old 22d District, spending $750,000 and winning 49% against a Republican incumbent in a Republican year. For 1982, the new 25th District seemed tailor-made for him, and he spent $647,000 and won the primary and general with 58% and 60%, showing he could both raise money from business interests and win support from liberal groups. In the House, Andrews won a seat on the Ways and Means Committee, where he got credit for repeal of the oil windfall profit tax and for a $500 million cut in the 1987 welfare reform bill; he also pushed for mandatory withholding of delinquent child support from wages. In 1989, he was one of the "Gang of Six" Ways and Means Democrats who supported a capital gains tax cut and got it through the committee and the House. In 1992, with an eye to Houston's still low real estate prices, he had a bill to equalize passive loss deductions. He pushed successfully for tax credits for nonconventional fuels development, including drilling tight sand formations of natural gas. He voted for the Gulf war resolution and reversed his course as a longtime NRA supporter by voting for the Brady bill. Near afield and far: he worked to preserve the Manassas, Virginia, Battlefield and to solve the Sims Bayou flood controversy in Houston.

Andrews had a tough 1992. He had 121 overdrafts on the House bank totalling $103,000 and an energetic opponent in Dolly Madison McKenna, an investment banker and former Nixon aide who spent $200,000 to win the Republican primary. When Andrews sent a camera crew to tape McKenna moving into the district, she turned the situation around by issuing an invitation, drawn by her eight-year-old, to a housewarming-press conference-barbecue. McKenna attacked Andrews as a creature of Houston business interests and touted her pro-choice stance. But Andrews raised far more money, got some lukewarm endorsements from the two papers and won with his lowest margin yet, 56%–41%.

In December 1992, he was considered as a possible appointee to Lloyd Bentsen's Senate seat, but was opposed by some liberals. He is one Ways and Means member who may fill the vacuum if Chairman Dan Rostenkowski gets in trouble, especially regarding health care. He favors managed competition and using market forces to encourage HMOs to cut costs and opposes single payer plans. On energy issues, he wants to lift the tax for the Strategic Petroleum Reserve and give incentives for vehicles with clean-burning fuels; he staunchly opposed the five cent gas tax increase. Andrews also won a seat on the Budget Committee, where again he is likely to be a fulcrum point vote. Andrews is a member who excels at politics but also revels in legislative work and surely must be happy that the anti-incumbent mood of 1992 did not derail what could turn out to be a long congressional career.

The People: Pop. 1990: 565,202; 1% rural; 7% age 65+; 53% White; 27% Black; 4% Asian; 8% Other; 16% Hispanic origin. Voting age pop.: 404,772; 25% Black; 15% Hispanic origin. Households: 52% married couple families; 28% married couple fams. w. children; 52% college educ.; median household income: $30,614; per capita income: $14,269; median gross rent: $403; median house value: $57,000.

1992 Presidential Vote			1988 Presidential Vote		
Clinton (D)	85,412	(47%)	Bush (R)	78,504	(51%)
Bush (R)	64,962	(36%)	Dukakis (D)	76,478	(49%)
Perot (I)	32,515	(18%)			

Rep. Michael A. Andrews (D)

Elected 1982; b. Feb. 4, 1944, Houston; home, Houston; U. of TX, B.A. 1967, Southern Methodist U., J.D. 1970; Episcopalian; married (Ann).

Career: Law clerk, U.S. Dist. Judge, Houston, 1970–72; Asst. Dist. Atty., Harris Cnty., 1972–76; Practicing atty., 1976–82.

Offices: 303 CHOB 20515, 202-225-7508. Also 1001 E. Southmore, #810, Pasadena 77503, 713-473-4334; and Fed. Bldg., 515 Rusk, Houston 77002, 713-229-2244.

Committees: *Budget* (15th of 26 D). *Ways and Means* (11th of 24 D): Health. *Joint Economic Committee* (6th of 10).

Group Ratings

	ADA	ACLU	COPE	CDF	CFA	LCV	ACU	NTLC	NSI	COC	CEI
1992	70	55	55	70	80	38	38	20	100	63	32
1991	30	—	58	90	67	69	35	—	—	50	33

National Journal Ratings

	1991 LIB — 1991 CONS		1992 LIB — 1992 CONS	
Economic	50% —	49%	51% —	48%
Social	44% —	55%	50% —	49%
Foreign	36% —	62%	18% —	74%

Key Votes of the 102d Congress

1. Ban Striker Replace	FOR	5. Handgun Wait/7-Day	FOR	9. Use Force in Gulf	FOR
2. $ for Homeownership	AGN	6. Overseas Mil. Abortion	FOR	10. US Mil. Abroad $ Cut	AGN
3. Tax Rich/Cut Mid Cls.	FOR	7. Obscn. Art NEA $ Ban	FOR	11. Limit SDI Funds	AGN
4. FY93/$15B Def. Cut	FOR	8. Death Pen. from Jury	FOR	12. Cuba Trade Embargo	FOR

Key Votes of the 103d Congress

1. Family Leave	FOR	2. Deficit Reduction	FOR	3. Stimulus Plan	FOR

Election Results

1992 general	Michael A. Andrews (D)	98,975	(56%)	($1,397,469)
	Dolly Madison McKenna (R)	73,192	(41%)	($585,616)
	Other	4,710	(3%)	
1992 primary	Michael A. Andrews (D)	25,291	(82%)	
	Mary Robb Whipple (D)	5,371	(18%)	
1990 general	Michael A. Andrews (D), unopposed			($294,340)

TWENTY-SIXTH DISTRICT

On the northern edge of the Dallas-Fort Worth Metroplex, one of America's most affluent and fastest-growing metropolitan areas heads out into hardscrabble countryside. Here is a clash of cultures, and not least politically. North of the line of advancing subdivisions is the old Red River Valley of Sam Rayburn, where farmers for 125 years have eked out meager livings. Far west of the great centers of capital and trade, more than a day's journey for many years even from Dallas and Fort Worth, farmers here felt beset by some of the continent's harshest weather and at the mercy of market forces they had no chance of controlling. This was one of the centers of populism in the United States, and one of the hotbeds of the Democratic Party: counties in or near the Red River Valley gave the country three Democratic speakers of the House: Sam Rayburn, Jim Wright and Carl Albert (who was from the Oklahoma side).

An entirely different spirit is apparent in the advancing Metroplex. Here is optimism and promise of advance, as symbolized by the huge Dallas-Fort Worth Regional Airport, opened in 1972 with hopes of knitting the Dallas-Fort Worth area together and stimulating growth. Those hopes have mostly been realized, though as always in the process of economic growth some fall by the wayside (example: Braniff Airways, once DFW's biggest airline). DFW, the home of American Airlines, is the center of a complex of hotels, offices, apartments and shopping malls archetypical of late 20th Century America. Other enterprises too have stimulated growth here, so that subdivisions have moved far north of the Dallas and Tarrant County lines, reaching the county seats of McKinney in Collin County and Denton in Denton County. These new subdivisions are full of people whose talents and skills have made the Dallas-Fort Worth Metroplex a ranking high-tech and defense industry center; they are progressive, with clean new streets and commodious public services; they seem safe and secure against the urban ills that afflict many neighborhoods. These are overwhelmingly Republican areas, receptive to the message of free enterprise and respectful of traditional moral values; it seems difficult, in this pleasant, hard-working America, to understand that there are other parts of the country—indeed very large parts as the 1992 election suggested—which disagree.

The 26th Congressional District of Texas occupies much of the northern marchland of the Metroplex. About half its people are in Dallas County, not far from DFW Airport, and in or near Irving, a suburb that was mostly barren ground 20 years ago, and now boasts the Dallas Cowboys' Texas Stadium and the lavish but only partially occupied Las Colinas office-and-apartment mini-city. The other half are in the Metrocrest suburbs north of Dallas—Carrollton, Farmers Branch, Richardson, Coppell. The 26th also includes about one-quarter of fast-growing Collin County just north of Dallas, and to the west most of Denton County—Lewisville, Flower Mound and a portion of Denton. This represents a paring away of much of the 1980s 26th District, but that was necessary since its population rose from 526,000 in 1980 to 895,000 in 1990, making it the second most populous district in the country before redistricting.

The congressman from the 26th, Dick Armey, has had a career only possible in the last decade. In 1984, as Ronald Reagan was about to be renominated in Dallas, Armey was an economics professor at North Texas State University in Denton, a free market economist in a Keynesian department, a North Dakota-born academic in the Red River Valley of Texas: not a candidate for anything. But as he was watching the House sessions on C-SPAN the thought occurred to him that he could do just as well, or better; amazingly enough, he has proceeded to do just that. For he is now the chairman of the House Republican Conference, the number three position in the Republican leadership, an intellectual and political force to be reckoned with, and one of the dozen or so members of the House with a serious chance to be minority leader or even speaker some time in the next decade.

Armey's political beginning was inauspicious. He got the Republican nomination in the 26th in 1984 unopposed, because no one thought incumbent Tom Vandergriff, the longtime mayor of Arlington, could be unseated. After Armey won in an upset, he came to Washington in such modest circumstances that he saved money on personal expenses by sleeping first in the House gym and, when forced to stop, on his office couch. Unpretentious and cheerful, Armey also has fine political instincts and an appreciation of how to sell his principles to his colleagues.

His first major achievement was the military base closing bill. In 1987, Armey proposed an apolitical base closing commission, but neither Congress nor then-Defense Secretary Caspar Weinberger were ready to delegate such power. After a long debate, Armey worked with the Pentagon, the Joint Chiefs and then-Armed Services Chairman Les Aspin to create a commission that in 1989 approved the first base closings in 12 years. The Pentagon went on to use a similar procedure in closing even more bases in the early 1990s.

Armey's next big target was farm subsidies. He argued that subsidies are no more needed to maintain supplies of the six subsidized crops than they are for the hundreds of crops which manage to be produced without subsidies. Working with Brooklyn Democrat Charles Schumer, he drew up an amendment that, had it passed, would have denied subsidies to farmers with adjusted gross incomes of $100,000 or more a year. He likened the dairy price support system as "straight out of the Great Depression." While mostly unsuccessful in his efforts, the arguments are strong and savings are large, and Armey will continue sniping at farm bills.

Armey was, predictably, not very successful on the liberal-dominated Education and Labor Committee (where his school choice amendment lost 7–31) and the party-line Budget Committee (where his proposal to give the minority party a budget ombudsman went nowhere). He argued against a $264,000 budget increase for one of his own committees. He called Education Chairman William Ford "self-indulgent, autocratic, heavy-handed." Ford's reply: "He's just a kind of pain in the ass." Nor is he afraid to rile some constituents: he opposed the parental leave bill as "yuppie welfare," and voiced some doubts about Texas's Supercollider. But he has turned out to be suited to his district: his ebullience matches its mood and his faith in market economics reflects its settled convictions, and he wins reelection by overwhelming margins.

With a new resident in the White House, Armey is turning out to be suited to many House Republicans as well. Although he failed to win ranking spots on either Budget or Rules, he did get the top House Republican spot on the Joint Economic Committee, where he charged that Bill Clinton's "putting people first" program would cost the nation two million jobs in its first year. In 1992, he decided to take on Jerry Lewis, the Republican conference chairman who had supported George Bush's budget summit agreements, but refused to support Bush's school choice plan. Armey won 88–84, apparently winning the lion's share of the 47 freshman Republicans and breaking into Lewis's California delegation as well; he now has a staff budget of some $1.5 million. It is widely assumed that Minority Leader Robert Michel will step down or be challenged by Whip Newt Gingrich in 1994. In that case, Armey would probably run for whip. Whatever happens, his potential is great: he has Gingrich's incisive ideas plus Michel's political antennae, and a district that will reelect him without difficulty.

The People: Pop. 1990: 566,722; 5% rural; 5% age 65+; 82% White; 4% Black; 1% Amer. Indian; 4% Asian; 4% Other; 9% Hispanic origin. Voting age pop.: 422,805; 4% Black; 8% Hispanic origin. Households: 57% married couple families; 30% married couple fams. w. children; 68% college educ.; median household income: $40,533; per capita income: $20,675; median gross rent: $509; median house value: $99,000.

1992 Presidential Vote

Bush (R) 118,519 (47%)
Perot (I). 81,424 (32%)
Clinton (D) 52,727 (21%)

1988 Presidential Vote

Bush (R) 138,883 (73%)
Dukakis (D). 50,703 (27%)

Rep. Richard K. (Dick) Armey (R)

Elected 1984; b. July 7, 1940, Cando, ND; home, Cooper Canyon; Jamestown Col., B.A. 1963, U. of ND, M.A. 1964, U. of OK, Ph.D. 1969; Presbyterian; married (Susan).

Career: Prof., West TX St. U., 1967–68, Austin Col., 1968–72, North TX St. U., 1972–77, Chmn., Dept. of Economics, 1977–83.

Offices: 301 CHOB 20515, 202-225-7772. Also 1301 S. Bowen Rd., #422, Arlington 76013, 817-461-2555; and 250 S. Stemmons, #210, Lewisville 75067, 214-221-4527.

Committees: *Education and Labor* (5th of 15 R): Labor-Management Relations; Postsecondary Education and Training. *Joint Economic Committee* (7th of 10).

Group Ratings

	ADA	ACLU	COPE	CDF	CFA	LCV	ACU	NTLC	NSI	COC	CEI
1992	0	0	8	0	7	0	100	100	100	75	97
1991	0	—	0	10	11	0	100	—	—	100	99

National Journal Ratings

	1991 LIB — 1991 CONS		1992 LIB — 1992 CONS	
Economic	0% —	96%	0% —	91%
Social	0% —	84%	0% —	85%
Foreign	0% —	88%	0% —	82%

Key Votes of the 102d Congress

1. Ban Striker Replace	AGN	5. Handgun Wait/7-Day	AGN	9. Use Force in Gulf	FOR
2. $ for Homeownership	FOR	6. Overseas Mil. Abortion	AGN	10. US Mil. Abroad $ Cut	AGN
3. Tax Rich/Cut Mid Cls.	AGN	7. Obscn. Art NEA $ Ban	FOR	11. Limit SDI Funds	AGN
4. FY93/$15B Def. Cut	AGN	8. Death Pen. from Jury	FOR	12. Cuba Trade Embargo	FOR

Key Votes of the 103d Congress

1. Family Leave	AGN	2. Deficit Reduction	AGN	3. Stimulus Plan	AGN

Election Results

1992 general	Richard K. (Dick) Armey (R) 150,209	(73%)	($475,756)
	John Wayne Caton (D). 55,237	(27%)	($9,589)
1992 primary	Richard K. (Dick) Armey (R), unopposed		
1990 general	Richard K. (Dick) Armey (R) 147,856	(70%)	($198,305)
	John Wayne Caton (D). 62,158	(30%)	($14,303)

TWENTY-SEVENTH DISTRICT

Along the Gulf of Mexico, from the port and industrial city of Corpus Christi, down past the King Ranch and along Padre Island to the Mexican border is the 27th Congressional District of Texas. This part of south Texas, between the Nueces and the Rio Grande, was the land in contention in the Mexican-American War, and 150 years later is still inhabited mostly by people of Mexican ancestry. There is, however, plenty of variety here. Corpus Christi is an oil port, the most important one south of Houston, with big petrochemical plants and a causeway to the beach. About half its citizens are Mexican-American, but they are less segregated than was once the case. Half the 27th's people live in and around Corpus (as it is called locally); almost all the other half live some 150 miles south in the Lower Rio Grande Valley around Brownsville and Harlingen. Most citizens and politicians here back a Mexico-U.S. free trade agreement: they know that the economies are already interlinked, that this is a once-in-a-century opportunity to bring Mexico and the two-country zone along the border much closer to North American economic standards.

In between these two nodes are Texan versions of dreamland. Fronting the Gulf is the sandspit of Padre Island, for most of its length a national seashore, at the southern tip a high-rise resort to which college students throng for Spring break. Remains of a 1554 Spanish shipwreck have been found here, and it is here that Portuguese settlers began cattle ranching. Now, inland from the Laguna Madre, are the vast grazing and oil lands of the 825,000-acre (that's 1,289 square miles, partner) King Ranch. With a 66% Hispanic majority, the 27th is a Democratic district, though not quite so Democratic as some may suspect, since many Hispanics here are not citizens and those who are by no means vote solidly Democratic.

The congressman from the 27th, since its creation following the 1982 redistricting, has been Solomon Ortiz. He effectively won the seat in the 1982 primary, in which his tough law enforcer reputation as sheriff of Corpus Christi's Nueces County helped him win 26% in the first primary; then, facing a Corpus legislator, he made a propitious alliance in the Brownsville area and won the runoff. Ortiz's voting record is somewhat liberal on economics—though he voted against big labor's high-profile strikebreaker ban—moderate on cultural and military issues. He is a member of the Merchant Marine and Fisheries and the Armed Services Committees, a subcommittee chairman now on the former and a member of the pro-military majority on the latter. His successful legislation includes funding for the Palo Alto Battlefield and the Lower Rio Grande wildlife range. He has fought to ensure that the four military bases in his district remain open and is pushing for establishment of a new Veterans' hospital in south Texas. As chair of the Congressional Hispanic Caucus in 1991–1992, he led efforts to expand use of bilingual ballots and other election materials.

Ortiz, reelected easily for years, had a closer call than he might have expected in 1992. Redistricting cost him some heavily Democratic precincts in the Lower Rio Grande Valley, and he won only 51% in Nueces County, which with its relatively high turnout cast 62% of the district's votes. Overall he won only 56% against Republican Jay Kimbrough, who had to move from outside the district in Beeville where he'd been active in keeping a naval airfield open, and a Libertarian candidate angry at his treatment by Social Security employees unresponsive to his plight after he was shot and paralyzed in a burglary. Such a showing is not a sign of great strength.

The People: Pop. 1990: 565,992; 14% rural; 10% age 65+; 31% White; 2% Black; 1% Asian; 18% Other; 66% Hispanic origin. Voting age pop.: 380,498; 2% Black; 61% Hispanic origin. Households: 61% married couple families; 34% married couple fams. w. children; 38% college educ.; median household income: $21,552; per capita income: $9,366; median gross rent: $343; median house value: $47,000.

1992 Presidential Vote

Clinton (D) 78,441 (48%)
Bush (R) 58,780 (36%)
Perot (I). 27,468 (17%)

1988 Presidential Vote

Dukakis (D). 83,007 (53%)
Bush (R) 72,507 (47%)

Rep. Solomon P. Ortiz (D)

Elected 1982; b. June 3, 1937, Robstown; home, Corpus Christi; Del Mar Col., Natl. Sheriffs Training Inst., 1977; Methodist; divorced.

Career: Army, 1960–62; Nueces Cnty. Constable, 1965–68, Commissioner, 1969–76, Sheriff, 1977–82.

Offices: 2136 RHOB 20515, 202-225-7742. Also 3649 Leopard St., #510, Corpus Christi 78408, 512-883-5868; and 3505 Boca Chica Blvd., Brownsville 78521, 512-541-1242.

Committees: *Armed Services* (11th of 34 D): Military Installations and Facilities; Readiness. *Merchant Marine and Fisheries* (6th of 29 D): Environment and Natural Resources; Oceanography, Gulf of Mexico and the Outer Continental Shelf (Chmn.).

Group Ratings

	ADA	ACLU	COPE	CDF	CFA	LCV	ACU	NTLC	NSI	COC	CEI
1992	60	57	83	60	87	19	40	10	80	38	11
1991	30	—	64	80	72	23	26	—	—	56	14

National Journal Ratings

	1991 LIB — 1991 CONS	1992 LIB — 1992 CONS
Economic	52% — 46%	58% — 42%
Social	54% — 44%	38% — 62%
Foreign	43% — 55%	30% — 64%

Key Votes of the 102d Congress

1. Ban Striker Replace	AGN	5. Handgun Wait/7-Day AGN	9. Use Force in Gulf FOR
2. $ for Homeownership	AGN	6. Overseas Mil. Abortion AGN	10. US Mil. Abroad $ Cut AGN
3. Tax Rich/Cut Mid Cls.	FOR	7. Obscn. Art NEA $ Ban FOR	11. Limit SDI Funds AGN
4. FY93/$15B Def. Cut	*	8. Death Pen. from Jury AGN	12. Cuba Trade Embargo FOR

Key Votes of the 103d Congress

1. Family Leave   FOR   2. Deficit Reduction   FOR   3. Stimulus Plan   FOR

Election Results

1992 general	Solomon P. Ortiz (D).	87,022	(56%)	($343,904)
	Jay Kimbrough (R).	66,853	(43%)	($57,832)
	Other.	2,969	(2%)	
1992 primary	Solomon P. Ortiz (D), unopposed			
1990 general	Solomon P. Ortiz (D), unopposed			($140,756)

TWENTY-EIGHTH DISTRICT

The Mexican-American tradition in south Texas is connected with two institutions which might surprise some Washington liberals who assume that Hispanic politicians will be reliable left-wingers. One is the Roman Catholic Church and the other is the United States military. Both are a particular presence in San Antonio, which for many years had the largest Mexican-American population of any American city, a place just 150 miles north of the border where Spanish was widely spoken and political refugees from Mexico's revolution could be sure of freedom. The church in San Antonio was led for years by liberal bishops who also ran St. Mary's University, which educated many Hispanic politicians and leaders, including two chairmen of U.S. House committees, Henry B. Gonzalez and Kika de la Garza. Just as visible a presence in San Antonio are the Army and Air Force, with huge Fort Sam Houston, Lackland Air Force Base, Kelly Air Force Base, Randolph Air Force Base, the Brooks Air Medical Center all in or near the city limits. Mexican-Americans have long volunteered for military service in numbers far higher than most ethnic groups, and for many years Mexican-Americans in San Antonio (HUD Secretary and former Mayor Henry Cisneros's father is one) worked in civilian jobs for the military service—Uncle Sam was long an equal opportunity employer. San Antonio's Mexican-American community has produced many politicians who are liberal on economic issues and on civil rights and civil liberties. But it has not produced many who are hostile to the military or to traditional religious values.

The newest congressman from San Antonio, Frank Tejeda, is a good example. Tejeda left school at 17, volunteered for the Marine Corps and was sent to Vietnam. "I was a grunt, and proud of it. I wouldn't have it any other way," he told Roll Call. Two weeks before his tour was up, in 1966, he was hit with shrapnel and was later awarded a Bronze Star. Tejeda went back to San Antonio and graduated from St. Mary's, and then embarked on graduate law study at Berkeley and Yale and graduate school at Harvard even while building a political base in San Antonio. He was elected to the state House in 1976 and to the state Senate in 1986. As a Democrat he was part of the majority, but not a reliable liberal. He is antiabortion, and in the legislature opposed legalized parimutuel betting in the early 1980s and later opposed a state lottery. He voted against trial lawyers and with businesses on workmen's compensation. He attracted much attention investigating a state House committee chairman and two state Supreme Court justices who were later disciplined.

By 1991, Tejeda's clout was such that he was able to draw the new Hispanic-majority 28th District. Some 63% of its people are in San Antonio and Bexar County, on the south and east sides of the city. It has a salient north to Hispanic precincts in Guadalupe County and also heads south, through thinly settled ranch and oil well country, to the Lower Rio Grande. There it includes Starr County, home of many blatant and wealthy drug smugglers, and, not far north, Duval County, often the most Democratic county in the United States, whose then-boss George Parr provided the key votes Lyndon Johnson needed for his 87-vote victory in the 1948 Democratic Senate runoff. This new 28th was 60% Hispanic and solidly Democratic. Tejeda's popularity allowed him to win the Democratic primary with no opposition and the general with 87% against a Libertarian. He also won some chits for himself: when Bill Clinton was attacked for evading the draft and lying about it, Tejeda formed a Veterans for Clinton movement. Tejeda is one of nine Hispanic freshman and 17 Hispanics in the House. He won seats on the Armed Services and Veterans Affairs Committee, obvious choices given his record and his district. He is likely to have a somewhat conservative record on many issues.

The People: Pop. 1990: 566,447; 21% rural; 11% age 65+; 30% White; 9% Black; 1% Asian; 22% Other; 60% Hispanic origin. Voting age pop.: 382,367; 9% Black; 56% Hispanic origin. Households: 61% married couple families; 34% married couple fams. w. children; 30% college educ.; median household income: $20,276; per capita income: $8,050; median gross rent: $328; median house value: $39,900.

1992 Presidential Vote

Clinton (D) 94,113 (55%)
Bush (R) 51,292 (30%)
Perot (I). 27,202 (16%)

1988 Presidential Vote

Dukakis (D). 96,149 (57%)
Bush (R) 71,583 (43%)

Rep. Frank M. Tejeda (D)

Elected 1992; b. Oct. 2, 1945, San Antonio; home, San Antonio; St. Mary's U., B.A. 1970, U. of CA at Berkeley, J.D. 1974, Harvard, M.P.A. 1980, Yale, LL.M., 1989; Catholic; divorced.

Career: Marines Corps, 1963–67 (Vietnam), Marine Reserves, 1967-present; Practicing atty., 1974–1992; TX House of Reps., 1976–86; TX Senate, 1986–92.

Offices: 323 CHOB 20515, 202-225-1640. Also 1313 SE Military Dr., #115, San Antonio 78214, 210-924-7383.

Committees: *Armed Services* (24th of 34 D): Military Installations and Facilities; Oversight and Investigations; Research and Technology. *Veterans' Affairs* (15th of 21 D): Compensation, Pension and Insurance; Hospitals and Health Care.

Group Ratings and 102d Congress Votes: Newly Elected

Key Votes of the 103d Congress

1. Family Leave	FOR	2. Deficit Reduction	FOR	3. Stimulus Plan	FOR

Election Results

1992 general	Frank M. Tejeda (D).	122,457	(87%)	($304,286)
	David C. Slatter (LIB)	18,128	(13%)	($1,401)
1992 primary	Frank M. Tejeda (D), unopposed			
1990 election	Newly created district.			

TWENTY-NINTH DISTRICT

"What built Houston," wrote John Gunther in *Inside U.S.A.*, "was a combination of cotton, oil, and the ship canal." The cotton and oil were gifts of nature, though they require much human effort and ingenuity to produce in commercial quantities; the ship canal was almost totally man's creation. After the sand-spit port of Galveston was destroyed by a hurricane and tidal wave in 1900, Houston's town fathers decided to dredge out Buffalo Bayou and make their inland city a seaport, and they succeeded. And so a sluggish creek became a harbor and this small city built on a swamp became a major port by the 1940s and a world-class metropolis of 3.7 million people by 1990. On the west side of town Houston seems entirely a white-collar, office-bound city; but on the east and north, around the turning basin in the port and through the maze of refinery towers and tubing, Houston is plainly blue collar, with blacks, Mexican-Americans and large numbers of whites from the rural South and even Michigan and California, who came here to move up in the world.

The 29th Congressional District of Texas, newly created in the 1991 redistricting, is designed to be the new Hispanic district thought to be required in metro Houston by the 1982 amendments to the Voting Rights Act, though, as it turns out, less than a majority of its registered voters are Hispanic and it did not elect a Hispanic representative. For Hispanics in Houston—mainly Mexican-Americans, though there are migrants here from Central and South

America as well—do not live in the geographically cohesive neighborhoods and in the politically conscious state of mind which the framers of the Voting Rights Act, familiar with urban blacks, assumed. Instead, they are geographically dispersed and culturally apolitical, working overtime or even at two jobs. Their dispersion means that the boundaries of the 29th District, interlaced with the black-majority 18th, are grotesque. Paul Burka's description in the *Texas Monthly* cannot be improved on: "The 29th District looks like a sacred Mayan bird, with its body running eastward along the Ship Channel from downtown Houston until the tail terminates in Baytown. Spindly legs reach south to Hobby Airport, while the plumed head rises northward almost to Intercontinental. In the western extremity of the district, an open beak appears to be searching for worms in Spring Branch. Here and there, ruffled feathers jut out at odd angles." This can scarcely be regarded as a geographic unit. It is more in the nature of a mailing list with a lot of Spanish surnames on it. A lot of whom, it needs to be added, aren't citizens or voters.

The creation of the 29th sparked a picturesque primary. For the crucial Democratic primary in this heavily Democratic district of 566,000 people, all of 30,989 voters showed up. The most colorful candidate was Houston Councilman Ben Reyes, a Mexican-American politico since the 1960s, fresh from pleading no contest to a misdemeanor theft charge: to protest official inaction, he and friends demolished a crack house, after which they carted off a magnolia tree from its front yard and planted it on Reyes property. Reyes had also been charged with steering city business to relatives (should he have steered it to strangers?) and filed personal bankruptcy in 1990. Other Hispanics running were Sylvia Garcia, an appointee of former Mayor Kathy Whitmire, and legislator Al Luna, former Reyes ally and later foe. Also running was state Senator Gene Green. He had spent 18 years in the legislature supporting labor, teachers' union and trial lawyer positions; *Texas Monthly* named him one of the 10 worst legislators after he introduced a bill to allow citizens to carry concealed handguns, and a month before the primary he switched from antiabortion to pro-choice. But in the March primary, Green won 28%, ahead of Garcia's 21% and Luna's 15%, and not far behind Reyes's 34%.

In the April runoff, Green ran ads showing Reyes's face with "GUILTY" pasted over it; Reyes attacked Green for his hamhanded switch on abortion. Green came out ahead by 180 votes out of 31,508 cast. Then Reyes went to court and charged that Republican voters had illegally crossed over and voted in the runoff. That got him a July re-runoff, but to no avail. This time Green won with 52%, by 1,132 votes out of 36,722 cast. There was a spirited general election as well. Republican Clark Kent Ervin, a black lawyer and Rhodes Scholar who worked on the 1,000 Points of Light program in the Bush White House, ran an active campaign and got Reyes's angry endorsement. But Green won with 65%.

Green's election in a district expected to produce a Hispanic congressman made things a little awkward for everyone. Green promised to reach out to his constituency, though in fact he had already won; Bill Richardson of the Congressional Hispanic Caucus, offered a tepid welcome: "[I hope] he has a good term in Congress." Green can probably expect another challenge in 1994. But there is no reason he cannot win again.

The People: Pop. 1990: 566,937; 7% age 65+; 28% White; 10% Black; 2% Asian; 34% Other; 60% Hispanic origin. Voting age pop.: 377,824; 10% Black; 54% Hispanic origin. Households: 54% married couple families; 33% married couple fams. w. children; 22% college educ.; median household income: $20,612; per capita income: $7,898; median gross rent: $339; median house value: $38,000.

1992 Presidential Vote			1988 Presidential Vote		
Clinton (D)	54,344	(52%)	Dukakis (D)	67,793	(58%)
Bush (R)	31,839	(30%)	Bush (R)	48,971	(42%)
Perot (I)	18,427	(18%)			

Rep. Gene Green (D)

Elected 1992; b. Oct. 17, 1947, Houston; home, Houston; U. of Houston, B.A., 1971, Bates College of Law at U. of Houston, 1973–77; Methodist; married (Helen).

Career: TX House of Reps., 1972–84; Practicing atty., 1977–92; TX Senate, 1984–92.

Offices: 1004 LHOB 20515, 202-225-1688. Also 5502 Lawndale, Houston 77023, 713-923-9961.

Committees: *Education and Labor* (19th of 28 D): Elementary, Secondary and Vocational Education; Labor-Management Relations; Postsecondary Education and Training. *Merchant Marine and Fisheries* (19th of 29 D): Merchant Marine; Oceanography, Gulf of Mexico and the Outer Continental Shelf.

Group Ratings and 102d Congress Votes: Newly Elected

Key Votes of the 103d Congress

1. Family Leave	FOR	2. Deficit Reduction	FOR	3. Stimulus Plan	FOR

Election Results

1992 general	Gene Green (D)	64,064	(65%)	($691,275)
	Clark Kent Ervin (R)	34,609	(35%)	($509,818)
1992 rerunoff	Gene Green (D)	18,927	(52%)	
	Ben Reyes (D)	17,795	(48%)	
1992 runoff	Gene Green (D)	15,844	(50%)	
	Ben Reyes (D)	15,664	(50%)	
1992 primary	Ben Reyes (D)	10,504	(34%)	
	Gene Green (D)	8,533	(28%)	
	Sylvia R. Garcia (D)	6,487	(21%)	
	Albert E. (Al) Luna (D)	4,661	(15%)	
	Other	804	(3%)	
1990 election	Newly created district.			

THIRTIETH DISTRICT

Dallas is, among other things, the westernmost city of the Deep South. Cotton was the major crop originally in this part of Texas, and many of Dallas's first enterprising businessmen, when the railroad reached the Trinity River here in the 1870s, were cotton brokers. Geographically, Dallas is directly west of the Black Belt of Alabama and the Delta of Mississippi, both heavily cotton-producing areas in the days before the boll weevil. Many blacks and whites came west on U.S. 80 and now Interstate 20 to this metropolis, which is now larger than any in the Deep South, including Atlanta. Dallas has never had nearly as big a Mexican-American population as Houston, much less San Antonio; but it has always had a larger percentage of blacks than those cities. Indeed, south Dallas, south and west of the Trinity River, is predominately black, and black neighborhoods are scattered through other parts of the city and suburbs as well.

To see where, just look at a map of Texas's new 30th Congressional District: attached to the central body in south and east Dallas are tentacles that look as complex and attenuated as a series of DNA molecules. The 30th is one of those majority-black districts whose creations were required by the 1982 amendments to the Voting Rights Act; and in case that was doubted, its creation was insisted upon by Eddie Bernice Johnson, in 1991 chairman of the state Senate committee on redistricting, now congresswoman from the 30th District. Ten years before, Texas Democrats had split Dallas's blacks between John Bryant's 5th District and Martin Frost's 24th, while Republicans had tried to create a black-majority and a Republican district. Not so this time. Frost and his chief aide had to come up with an ingenious plan that stretched the 5th and 24th outward from urban bases safely past Republican suburbia into rural Democratic territory to concede Johnson her 30th district. Geographically, it covers south Dallas (except for white portions of Oak Cliff) down to Lancaster and DeSoto, includes land alongside the Dallas-Fort Worth Turnpike and the North Central Freeway, curves around Irving and takes in neighborhoods behind the Dallas-Fort Worth Regional Airport, and then curves around north Dallas out to black neighborhoods in Plano. In 1992, it was 50% black and 17% Hispanic, one of two majority-black seats in Texas.

Eddie Bernice Johnson was the first black woman elected to anything in Dallas when she won a seat in the state House in 1972; she became a regional HEW director in the Carter Administration and then was elected to the state Senate in 1986. She has worked for more minority contracts and wants to be involved in health and education issues. Johnson is a registered nurse and is said to be the first RN elected to Congress; she also has a degree in public administration. A person of strikingly elegant appearance, she is a formidable politician. In the primary, she had one nuisance opponent and won 92%; in the general she won 72%. Johnson has vowed to fight the proposed closing of Dallas's Naval Air Station in her district, the only Texas base targeted for closure in March 1993.

The People: Pop. 1990: 566,977; 8% age 65+; 31% White; 50% Black; 2% Asian; 10% Other; 17% Hispanic origin. Voting age pop.: 408,030; 47% Black; 15% Hispanic origin. Households: 39% married couple families; 20% married couple fams. w. children; 42% college educ.; median household income: $23,144; per capita income: $11,416; median gross rent: $402; median house value: $59,300.

1992 Presidential Vote			1988 Presidential Vote		
Clinton (D)	98,103	(62%)	Dukakis (D)	105,903	(63%)
Bush (R)	33,764	(21%)	Bush (R)	61,007	(37%)
Perot (I)	25,192	(16%)			

Rep. Eddie Bernice Johnson (D)

Elected 1992; b. Dec. 3, 1935, Waco; home, Dallas; St. Mary's at Notre Dame, B.A. 1955, Texas Christian U., B.S. 1967, Southern Methodist U., M.B.A. 1976; Baptist; divorced.

Career: TX House of Reps., 1972–1977; Regional Dir., U.S. Dept. of HEW, 1977–81; Mgmt. consultant, Sammons Corp., 1979–1981; Owner, Eddie Bernice Johnson & Assoc., 1981–present; TX Senate, 1986–92.

Offices: 1721 LHOB 20515, 202-225-8885. Also 2525 McKinney Ave., #1565, Dallas 75201, 214-922-8885.

Committees: . *Public Works and Transportation* (38th of 39 D): Investigations and Oversight; Public Buildings and Grounds; Surface Transportation. *Science, Space and Technology* (27th of 33 D): Science; Technology, Environment and Aviation.

Group Ratings and 102d Congress Votes: Newly Elected

Key Votes of the 103d Congress

1. Family Leave	FOR	2. Deficit Reduction	FOR	3. Stimulus Plan	FOR

Election Results

1992 general	Eddie Bernice Johnson (D).	107,831	(72%)	($282,734)
	Lucy Cain (R).	37,853	(25%)	($1,754)
	Other.	5,063	(3%)	
1992 primary	Eddie Bernice Johnson (D).	41,587	(92%)	
	Adolph Hauntz (D).	3,794	(8%)	
1990 election	Newly created district.			

UTAH

Utah is a triumph of man over nature, the creation of a productive and orderly civilization in a remote expanse of desert and mountain, arrayed around a desolate salt sea. Today's Utah and Mormonism have their roots in a very different landscape of more than 150 years ago, when a wave of religious enthusiasm, prophecy and utopianism swept across the "burnt-over district" of Upstate New York in the 1820s and 1830s. There Joseph Smith, a young farmer, experienced a vision in which the angel Moroni appeared and told him where to unearth several golden tablets inscribed with hieroglyphic writings. With the aid of special spectacles, Smith translated the tablets and published them as the Book of Mormon in 1831. He later declared himself a prophet and founded the Church of Jesus Christ of Latter-day Saints. The Mormons, as they were called, attracted thousands of converts and created their own communities; persecuted for their beliefs, they moved west to Ohio, Missouri and then Illinois. In 1844, the Mormon colony at Nauvoo, Illinois, had some 15,000 members living under the strict theocratic rule of Joseph Smith. It was here that Smith received a revelation sanctioning the practice of polygamy, which led to his death at the hands of a mob in 1844. After the murder, the new church president Brigham Young, decided to move the faithful, "the saints," farther west into territory that was still part of Mexico and far beyond white settlement. Young led a well-organized march across the Great Plains and into the Rocky Mountains. In 1847, they stopped on the western slope of the Wasatch Range and, as Brigham Young gazed over the valley of the Great Salt Lake spread out below, he uttered the now famous words, "This is the place."

The place was Utah. Young was governor of the territory for many years, and it is the only state that largely continues to live by the teachings of a church. The early pioneers laid out towns foursquare to the points of the compass, with huge city blocks, built sturdy houses and planted dozens of trees. Throughout the 19th Century and even today, this "Zion" has attracted thousands of converts from the Midwest, the north of England and Scandinavia. The object of religious fear and prejudice, Utah was not granted statehood until 1896, after the church renounced polygamy. Utah has grown steadily since then, and remains heavily Mormon, its basic character is stamped on the desert, mountain-shadowed, often surrealistic landscape which would have been, without the Mormons, mostly unpopulated.

The Church remains distinctive in many ways. It cares deeply about its past: in caves in the mountains of Utah, the Church preserves America's most complete genealogical records. It tries to spread the faith: many young Mormons spend missionary years abroad, and their experiences in turn give Utah the biggest inventory of people with knowledge of obscure foreign languages of any state in the union, a nice commercial advantage. It prohibits the consumption of tobacco, alcohol and caffeine; it encourages hard work and large families, and Utah has by far the nation's highest birth rates; its members are healthier than the average American, better educated, more likely to live in families and in affluent households. And while American mainline denominations are losing members, the Mormon Church is growing, with more members than either the Presbyterian or Episcopalian churches. There were 2.9 million Mormon in 1970 and 7.7 million in 1990: 4.3 million in the United States and 3.4 million abroad.

The Church's influence in Utah is great—it owns one of the two leading Salt Lake City newspapers and a TV station, it has holdings in an insurance company, several banks, real estate and owns ZCMI, the largest department store in Salt Lake City—and it is sometimes resented. The conservative hold that the Church has over the state can appear in political issues. In 1991 Utah passed the strictest abortion law of any state, banning abortion except in cases of rape and incest, or if the mother's life is endangered. Also in 1990, it became the first state to ban the sale of vending machine cigarettes; although earlier in the year it became the last state to abolish the provision which stated that hard liquor could not be served in public. And the Church itself, financed by the tradition of tithing, runs its own high-quality welfare programs: this is a society that favors market economics and free enterprise, but also has a lively tradition of communal effort and responsibility. Utah's state workfare program, started in 1983, requires one adult in a welfare family to spend 32 hours a week in community service or training, plus job search, and benefits are paid only after performance; social workers here seem to strengthen middle-class values rather than lead rebellions against them.

But if the moral underpinnings of life in Utah have not changed in 50 years, Utah's view of its place in the nation has. Before World War II, Utah saw itself as a colonial victim of East Coast bankers and financiers and Mormons saw themselves as suffering religious discrimination and bigotry—all with some cause. Its income levels were well below the national average, its cost of living higher, the prices paid for the things it produced seemed to be controlled elsewhere. Politically, this perspective translated into a Democratic allegiance: in 1940, Utah was represented by staunch New Dealers in Congress and cast 62% of its votes for Franklin Roosevelt. Today, Utah is more likely to see itself as a busy generator of wealth, with a raft of successful businesses and a knack for high-tech innovation. It has the youngest and highest-productivity work force of any in the nation, leading the nation in job creation in 1992 with 3.2% growth. Its information technology jobs doubled to 63,000 from 1986 to 1992, and it is home to such big software firms as Novell and WordPerfect; the state government has a Centers of Excellence program to fund small high-tech startups. Utah believes in the coexistence of high-tech and traditional values.

Politically, this perspective translates into a strong Republican preference; Utah was pretty solidly Republican by the middle 1960s. In the last 20 years, as traditional values thriving in Utah have come under attack elsewhere, it has become the most Republican of states—standing out in national statistics politically just as it does demographically. In 1960, Richard Nixon carried Utah with 55% of the vote; by 1972, he won with 72%. Ronald Reagan won 73% and 75% of Utah's votes; George Bush won 66% here in 1988: for four presidential elections in a row, Utah was the nation's most Republican state. In 1992, it was not, but not because of Bill Clinton, who finished third here with 25%: Ross Perot won 27% of the vote and George Bush fell to 43%. Democrats are competitive in other races, but only if they show themselves to be consistent with Utah values and attitudes; new residents may be occasionally more liberal, and Utah is less heavily Mormon than it was, but the basic character of the state has not changed.

Governor. Mike Leavitt, elected governor in 1992, promised voters more of the same for Utah: he had managed the campaigns of, and was endorsed by, two-term Governor Norman Bangerter and retiring Senator Jake Garn. Bangerter had passed a tax increase in 1987 but, after nearly losing in 1988, cut taxes in his second term and signed Utah's strict antiabortion bill. In the Republican convention and primary, Leavitt was opposed by Richard Eyre, author of *Utah in the Year 2000* and 20 other books, who backed a $1,200 school choice voucher; Leavitt helped author a Strategic Plan for Education reform plan and was backed by the teachers' union, opposed private school vouchers while calling for "world class education." Leavitt won the primary 56%–44%. Among Democrats, the winner was former Judge Stewart Hanson, who opposed the antiabortion law and who called for improved healthcare access, protecting the

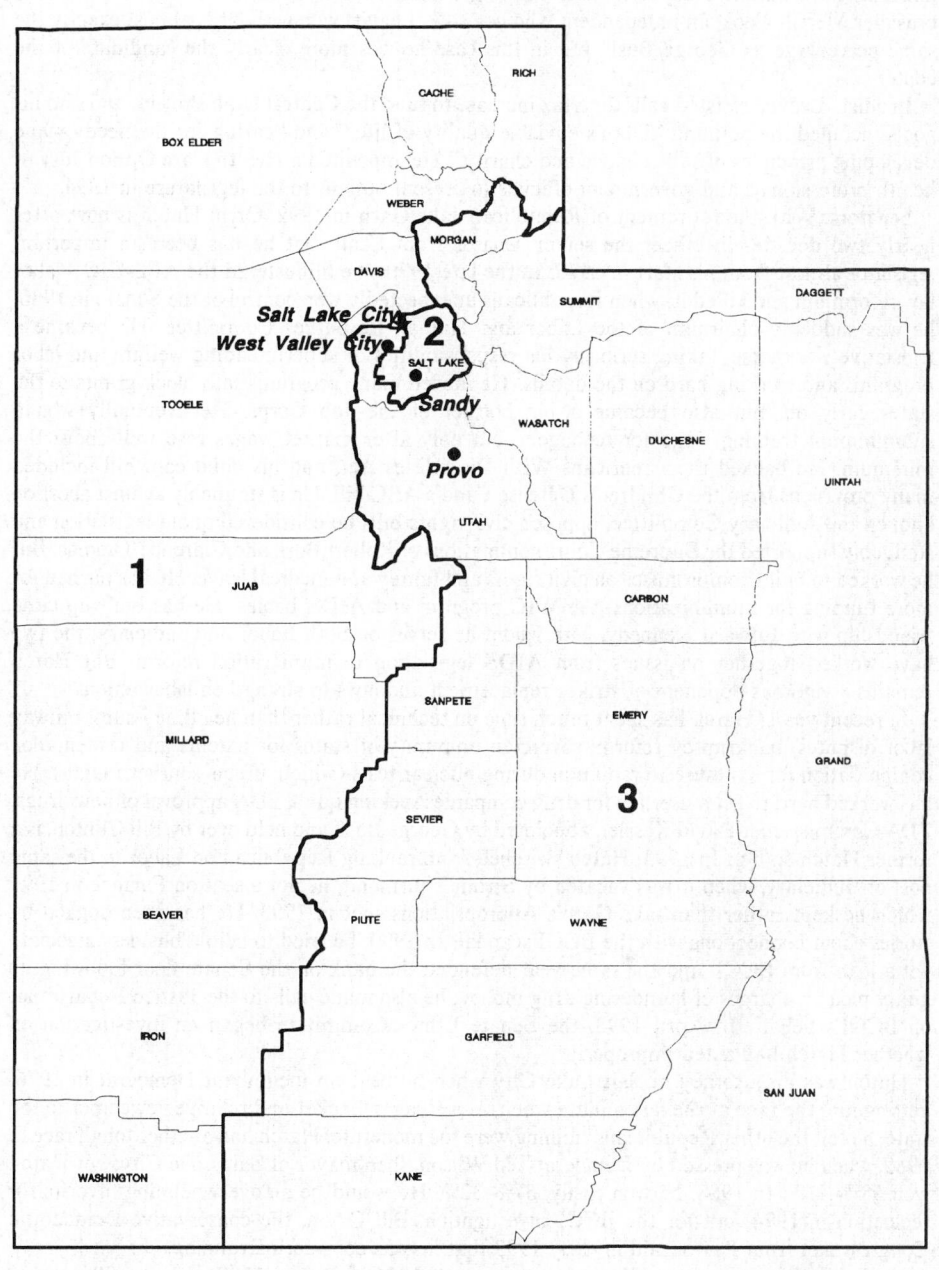

RICH

CACHE

BOX ELDER

WEBER

MORGAN

DAVIS

Salt Lake City   2

West Valley City   SALT LAKE

SUMMIT

DAGGETT

TOOELE

Sandy

WASATCH

DUCHESNE

Provo

UINTAH

UTAH

1

JUAB

CARBON

SANPETE

EMERY

MILLARD

GRAND

3

SEVIER

BEAVER

PIUTE

WAYNE

IRON

GARFIELD

SAN JUAN

WASHINGTON

KANE

Miles

0 10 20 30 40

environment and tax fairness—a liberal platform in Utah; he beat former state Chairman Pat Shea, who was against abortion, 57%–43%. In the general, Hanson got only 23% of the vote, finishing third almost everywhere and running behind explosives manufacturer and anti-tax crusader Merrill Cook, an independent who got 34%. Leavitt won with 42%, almost exactly the same percentage as George Bush, but in this case he was more clearly the candidate of the center.

In office, Leavitt resisted calls for a tax increase to fund the Central Utah Project, and said his goals included maintaining "Utah's enviable quality of life," and "caring for the needy while developing principles of self-reliance and charity." He appointed a Health Care Option Jury of health professionals and government officials to present options to the legislature in 1994.

Senators. With the retirement of Republican Jake Garn in 1992, Orrin Hatch is now, after nearly two decades in office, the senior senator from Utah, but he has been an important legislator almost from his start in 1976. In the late 1970s, he filibustered the AFL-CIO's labor law reform bill and killed it; when Republicans unexpectedly won control of the Senate in 1980, he was suddenly chairman of the Labor and Human Resources Committee. He became a legislative workhorse, taking seriously his responsibilities of superintending welfare and labor programs and working hard on the details. He moved many programs into block grants to the states early on, but also became a big booster of the Job Corps. He eventually won a subminimum training wage for teenagers, but only after market wages rose well above the minimum. He backed the Americans With Disabilities Act, and his child care bill included many provisions from the Children's Defense Fund's ABC bill. He is staunchly against abortion and, on the Judiciary Committee, opposed civil rights bills he considered quota legislation and staunchly supported the Supreme Court nominations of Robert Bork and Clarence Thomas. But he worked to build compromises on civil rights and family and medical leave. He has pushed for more funding for immunizations, the WIC program and AIDS babies. He has built up close friendship with Edward Kennedy, with whom he serves on both Labor and Judiciary; the two have worked together on issues from AIDS legislation to immigration reform. But Hatch remains a vigorous opponent of striker replacement and laws to strengthen labor unions.

In recent years, Hatch has spent much time on technical rather than headline issues: railway labor disputes, bankruptcy reform, sovereign immunity of states for patents and trademarks, compensation for exposure to radiation during nuclear tests (which affects southern Utah). He has worked hard to get a user fee for drug companies seeking quick FDA approval of new drugs; FDA Commissioner David Kessler, appointed by George Bush and held over by Bill Clinton, is a former Hatch staffer. In 1993, Hatch switched from ranking Republican on Labor to the same post on Judiciary, when it was vacated by Strom Thurmond; he got a seat on Finance in 1991 which he kept rather than take Garn's Appropriations spot in 1993. He has been dogged by stories about connections with the BCCI scandal. In 1990, he tried to help a business associate get a loan from BCCI, and the same year defended the bank on the Senate floor following its guilty plea on charges of laundering drug money; he also made calls to the Justice Department on BCCI's behalf. In April 1993, the Senate Ethics Committee began an investigation on whether Hatch had acted improperly.

Hatch was an attorney in Salt Lake City when he beat an incumbent Democrat in 1976, getting into the race at the last minute when, as a Reagan backer and relative newcomer to the state, he felt the other Republicans running were too moderate. Hatch had another tough race in 1982, when he was pressed by Democrat Ted Wilson, then mayor of Salt Lake City; but Hatch won 58%–41%. In 1988, he won easily, 67%–32%. He would be an overwhelming favorite for reelection in 1994, but for the BCCI investigation. Bill Orton, the conservative Democratic Congressman from Provo, said in early 1993 that he was considering running.

Utah has had two Republican senators since 1976, but the 1992 race to fill retiring Republican Senator Jake Garn's seat was fiercely contested in both the primary and the general. Utah's new senator is Bob Bennett, but he is scarcely a stranger to the Senate; his father served there from 1951 to 1974, and Bob Bennett was a congressional staffer and the Transportation

Department's chief lobbyist during the Nixon Administration; he also headed the public relations firm (and CIA front) that employed Watergate burglar Howard Hunt, but was involved in no wrongdoing himself and author Bob Woodward has denied that Bennett was his "Deep Throat" source. Back in Utah, he headed Microsonics Corporation, which makes audio disks for talking toys, for three years and then became head of Franklin Quest, which produces the Franklin day planners and organizers; he increased it from four to 700 employees and sales of $80 million; he sold his interest in 1991 for a reported $25 million.

Bennett headed the commission that produced Utah's Strategic Plan for Education and wrote *Gaining Control*, a book on the forces that control daily life. And Bennett was not the only millionaire in the 1992 Senate race. The initial favorite was Republican Joseph Cannon, who had taken over the old Geneva Steel plant and made it profitable; he is a great-grandson of Utah's first territorial delegate, George Q. Cannon, who "had five wives and a lot of progeny." Cannon spent $5 million of his own money on an expensive media campaign, but was hurt by late attacks on Geneva's environmental record and by ads for Bennett, who spent $1.4 million of his own money, with Bennett saying that business and not government makes jobs. Bennett won 51%–49%, with all of his margin and more in Salt Lake County. Meanwhile, Democratic businessman Doug Anderson was spending more than $1 million of his own money, largely on attacks on Congressman Wayne Owens, the one non-millionaire in the race. But Owens, a familiar figure since winning an upset victory in a 1972 House race, won 61%–39%.

The general election provided a clear contrast. Owens, a staffer for Edward Kennedy in the 1960s, is an environmentalist, and liberal on many issues; on the House Judiciary Committee, he voted to impeach Richard Nixon. He lost the 1974 Senate race to Jake Garn, and was called to head the Latter-day Saint Church Mission in Montreal for three years. In 1984, Owens ran for governor and lost; in 1986, he was elected to the House and won two more terms. Bennett campaigned as an outsider, despite his Washington experience; it helped that Owens had 87 overdrafts on the House bank. Bennett again spent his own money, and continually led in polls. He won on election day 55%–40%, with exit polls showing Owens carrying only the elderly—not a good omen for Utah Democrats. In the Senate Bennett serves on the Banking and Energy Committees, and can be counted on as a solid conservative vote.

Presidential politics. One state to Utah's east, Colorado saw intensive campaigning and barrages of ads in 1992 because it was a competitive state; Utah, heavily Republican, got no attention at all. For the national conventions, its relatively few delegates are chosen in caucuses. The Democratic caucus in March preferred Paul Tsongas and Jerry Brown to Bill Clinton.

Congressional districting. The Republican legislature drew new lines for Utah's three congressional districts for 1992. Salt Lake County, the most Democratic part of the state now, had to be split between districts, and the legislature gave some of the less Republican portions to the 1st and 3d Districts.

The People: Est. Pop. 1992: 1,813,000; Pop. 1990: 1,722,850, up 5.0% 1990–1992. 0.7% of U.S. total, 35th largest; 13% rural. Median age: 26.2 years. 8.7% 65 years and over. 93.8% White, 4.9% Hispanic Origin, 1.9% Asian, 1.4% American Indian, 2.1% Other. Households: 64.8% married couple families; 38% married couple fams. w. children; 58% college educ.; median household income: $29,470; per capita income: $11,029; 68.1% owner occupied housing; median house value: $68,900 median monthly rent: $300. 4.9% Unemployment. Voting age pop.(1980): 1,095,406. Registered voters (1992): 965,211; no party registration.

Political Lineup: Governor, Michael O. Leavitt (R); Lt. Gov., Olene S. Walker (R); Atty. Gen., Jan Graham (D); Treasurer, Edward T. Alter (R); Auditor, Tom L. Allen (R). State Senate, 29 (18 R and 11 D); State House of Representatives, 75 (49 R and 26 D). Senators, Orrin G. Hatch (R) and Robert F. Bennett (R). Representatives, 3 (2 D and 1 R).

1992 Presidential Vote

Bush (R)	322,632	(43%)
Perot (I)	203,400	(27%)
Clinton (D)	183,429	(25%)
Other	34,607	(5%)

1992 Democratic Presidential Primary

Tsongas	10,582	(33%)
Brown	8,971	(28%)
Clinton	5,780	(18%)
Kerrey	3,447	(11%)
Harkin	1,274	(4%)
Other, Uncommitted	1,584	(5%)

1988 Presidential Vote

Bush (R)	428,442	(66%)
Dukakis (D)	207,343	(32%)

GOVERNOR

Gov. Michael O. Leavitt (R)

Elected 1992, term expires Jan. 1996; b. Feb. 11, 1951, Cedar City; home, Salt Lake City; S. UT U., B.A. 1976; Mormon; married (Jacalyn).

Career: Army Natl. Guard, 1969–78; Pres. & CEO, Leavitt Group Insurance Co., 1984–92; Chmn., S. UT U. Bd. of Trustees, 1985–89; UT Board of Regents, 1989–92.

Office: 210 State Capitol, Salt Lake City 84114, 801-538-1000.

Election Results

1992 gen.	Michael O. Leavitt (R)	321,713	(42%)
	Merrill Cook (I)	255,733	(34%)
	Stewart Hanson(D)	177,181	(23%)
1992 prim.	Michael O. Leavitt (R)	143,647	(56%)
	Richard Eyre (R)	112,881	(44%)
1988 gen.	Norman H. Bangerter (R)	260,462	(40%)
	Ted Wilson (D)	249,321	(38%)
	Merrill Cook (I)	136,651	(21%)

SENATORS

Sen. Orrin G. Hatch (R)

Elected 1976, seat up 1994; b. Mar. 22, 1934, Pittsburgh, PA; home, Salt Lake City; Brigham Young U., B.S. 1959, U. of Pittsburgh, J.D. 1962; Mormon; married (Elaine).

Career: Practicing atty., 1962–76.

Offices: 135 RSOB 20510, 202-224-5251. Also 8402 Fed. Bldg., Salt Lake City 84138, 801-524-4380; 109 Fed. Bldg., 88 W. 100 N., Provo 84601, 801-375-7881; 1410 Fed. Bldg., 325 25th St., Ogden 84401, 801-625-5672; and 10 N. Main, P.O. Box 99, Cedar City 84720, 801-586-8435.

Committees: *Finance* (8th of 9 R): Energy and Agricultural Taxation (RMM); International Trade; Medicare and Long-Term Care. *Judiciary* (RMM of 8 R): Antitrust, Monopolies and Business Rights; Constitution; Patents, Copyrights and Trademarks (RMM). *Labor and Human Resources* (6th of 7 R): Disability Policy; Education, Arts and Humanities; Employment and Productivity; Labor (RMM).

Group Ratings

	ADA	ACLU	CDF	COPE	CFA	LCV	ACU	NTLC	NSI	COC	CEI
1992	5	5	50	17	33	0	96	94	100	100	73
1991	10	—	27	25	6	13	86	—	—	90	74

National Journal Ratings

	1991 LIB — 1991 CONS		1992 LIB — 1992 CONS	
Economic	0%	— 91%	25%	— 73%
Social	25%	— 74%	11%	— 86%
Foreign	0%	— 87%	0%	— 90%

Key Votes of the 102d Senate

1. $ for Homeownership FOR	5. Clarence Thomas Nom. FOR	9. Use Force in Gulf FOR
2. Have Cap Gains Debate FOR	6. Lmt Death Row Appeal FOR	10. Keep Salavador Aid FOR
3. Remove Budget Walls AGN	7. Handgun Wait/5-Day AGN	11. Cut $1B from SDI AGN
4. Ban Striker Replace AGN	8. Abortion Gag Rule FOR	12. Override China MFN AGN

Key Votes of the 103d Congress

1. Family Leave AGN	2. HIV Immigrants AGN	3. Clinton Budget AGN

Election Results

1988 general	Orrin G. Hatch (R).................	430,089	(67%)	($3,706,381)
	Brian H. Moss (D)	203,364	(32%)	($153,475)
1988 primary	Orrin G. Hatch (R), unopposed			
1982 general	Orrin G. Hatch (R).................	309,547	(58%)	($3,838,335)
	Ted Wilson (D).....................	218,895	(41%)	($1,703,170)

Sen. Robert F. Bennett (R)

Elected 1992, seat up 1998; b. Sept. 18, 1933, Salt Lake City; home, Salt Lake City; U. of UT, B.S. 1957; Mormon; married (Joyce).

Career: Chaplain, Army Natl. Guard, 1957–60; Cong. Liaison, U.S. Dept. of Transportation, 1969–70; Pres., Robert Mullen P.R., 1970–74; P.R. Dir., Summa Corp., 1974–78; Pres., Osmond Communications, 1978–79; Chmn., American Computers Corp., 1979–81; Pres., Microsonics Corp., 1981–84; Chmn., UT Educ. Strategic Plng. Comm., 1988; C.E.O., Franklin Quest Co., 1984–91.

Offices: 241 DSOB 20510, 202-224-5444. Also 4225 Wallace F. Bennett Fed. Bldg., Salt Lake City 84138, 801-524-5933; 51 S. University Ave., #310, Provo 84601, 801-379-2525; 324 24th St., #1410, Ogden 84401, 801-625-5676; and Fed. Bldg., 196-E Tabernacle St., #22, St. George 84770, 801-628-5514.

Committees: *Banking, Housing and Urban Affairs* (6th of 8 R): Economic Stabilization and Rural Development; International Finance and Monetary Policy. *Energy and Natural Resources* (7th of 9 R): Mineral Resources Development and Production; Public Lands, National Parks and Forests; Water and Power (RMM). *Small Business* (8th of 9 R): Export Expansion and Agricultural Development; Innovation, Manufacturing and Technology. *Joint Economic Committee* (10th of 10).

Group Ratings and 102d Congress Votes: Newly Elected

Key Votes of the 103d Congress

1. Family Leave	AGN	2. HIV Immigrants	AGN	3. Clinton Budget	AGN

Election Results

1992 general	Robert F. Bennett (R)	420,069	(55%)	($3,339,325)
	Wayne Owens (D)	301,228	(40%)	($1,904,750)
	Three Others	37,182	(5%)	
1992 primary	Robert F. Bennett (R)	135,514	(51%)	
	Joe Cannon (R)	128,125	(49%)	
1986 general	Edwin Jacob (Jake) Garn (R)	314,608	(72%)	($752,944)
	Craig S. Oliver (D)	115,523	(27%)	($24,508)

FIRST DISTRICT

In May 1869, a motley crowd of Irish and Chinese laborers, teamsters, engineers, train crews, officials and guests from California and Salt Lake City gathered in Promontory Point, Utah, to watch the opening of the transcontinental railroad. The Union Pacific train was late and Leland Stanford raised his hammer and totally missed the golden spike, but an alert telegrapher mimicked the sound over the wire and a photographer recorded the scene for posterity: united at last were the civilized East and the mostly untamed West. Here, beyond sight of the snow-capped mountains crossed by the Mormon pioneers, the salt flats still stretch out endlessly; the rail lines now pass north of here, and Promontory Point lies on uninhabited flat land beside the rising Great Salt Lake. The lake kept rising into the middle 1980s, despite state legislation forbidding it from going above a certain level. The local county commissioners called for a day of prayer for drought in May 1986, the lake finally obeyed the law, and the state didn't have to pump water through canals which would have formed a vast new lake in the salt flats to the west.

The 1st Congressional District of Utah includes the western half of the state, from Promontory Point down to the Arizona and Nevada borders near Las Vegas, where the Colorado

River flows south through Glen Canyon into Arizona; Zion National Park is in the south, there is mining country in the center and the desert lies west of the lake. But 75% of the people in this district live along the Wasatch Front, a thin strip of land on the east side of the Lake between the salt flats and the Wasatch Mountains. It takes in Brigham City and Logan near the Idaho border, goes south through Ogden, an old working-class town on the Union Pacific line and the nearest station stop to Promontory Point, and then proceeds through a strip of suburbs to the salt flats northwest of downtown Salt Lake City near the airport. The rest of the 1st's voters live in small communities, many entirely Mormon, in central and southern Utah.

The congressman from this district is James Hansen, a Republican with as solidly conservative a record as anyone in the House. He is on the Armed Services and Natural Resources Committees and ranking Republican of a subcommittee on each. On Natural Resources, he successfully got authorization for completing the Central Utah Project to bring Colorado River water to the Wasatch Front in 1992; he also cooperated with Chairman George Miller in cracking down on cheap water rates for users in the Central Valley of California. On Armed Services, he looked after Hill Air Force Base and in 1993 stoutly defended the Tooele Army Depot against threatened closure. He wants to amend education funding formulas that hurt Utah, which has many schoolchildren. But much of his time and energy seems to go into his work as ranking Republican on the Ethics Committee. Hansen is a stickler for ethics and often an advocate of stern punishment. He recognized early that the House bank and members' overdrafts had "awesome" political ramifications. He worked with Democrat Matthew McHugh on disclosing names of the most egregious offenders first and then—which took time, because the records were messy—of all offenders; he pressed Minority Leader Robert Michel not to resist special investigator Malcolm Wilkey's subpoena of House bank records. Hansen also superintended the investigation of the House post office.

Hansen has not held this ordinarily very Republican seat without some serious challenge; indeed, he won it from a Democrat, Gunn McKay, in 1980. McKay held him to 52% in a 1986 rematch, as did Kenley Brunsdale, former staffer for 2d District Democrat Wayne Owens in 1990. But in 1992, Hansen won 65%–28%.

The People: Pop. 1990: 574,205; 16% rural; 9% age 65+; 92% White; 1% Black; 1% Amer. Indian; 2% Asian; 2% Other; 5% Hispanic origin. Voting age pop.: 360,724; 1% Black; 4% Hispanic origin. Households: 69% married couple families; 40% married couple fams. w. children; 57% college educ.; median household income: $30,563; per capita income: $10,856; median gross rent: $364; median house value: $68,800.

1992 Presidential Vote

Bush (R)	115,627	(47%)
Perot (I)	68,884	(28%)
Clinton (D)	50,622	(20%)
Other	12,989	(5%)

1988 Presidential Vote

Bush (R)	156,533	(73%)
Dukakis (D)	59,228	(27%)

Rep. James V. Hansen (R)

Elected 1980; b. Aug. 14, 1932, Salt Lake City; home, Farmington; U. of UT, B.A. 1960; Mormon; married (Ann).

Career: Navy, 1951–55; Farmington City Cncl., 1962–72; UT House of Reps., 1972–80, Speaker, 1978–80.

Offices: 2466 RHOB 20515, 202-225-0453. Also 1017 Fed. Bldg., 324 25th St., Ogden 84401, 801-625-5677; and 435 E. Tabernacle, #301, St. George 84770, 801-628-1071.

Committees: *Armed Services* (6th of 22 R): Oversight and Investigations (RMM); Research and Technology. *Intelligence (Permanent Select)* (6th of 7 R): Legislation; Oversight and Evaluation. *Natural Resources* (2d of 15 R): National Parks, Forests and Public Lands (RMM); Oversight and Investigations.

Group Ratings

	ADA	ACLU	COPE	CDF	CFA	LCV	ACU	NTLC	NSI	COC	CEI
1992	5	5	18	0	13	6	100	100	100	88	82
1991	0	—	0	20	17	0	100	—	—	100	79

National Journal Ratings

	1991 LIB — 1991 CONS	1992 LIB — 1992 CONS
Economic	4% — 90%	0% — 91%
Social	0% — 84%	0% — 85%
Foreign	0% — 88%	0% — 82%

Key Votes of the 102d Congress

1. Ban Striker Replace	AGN	5. Handgun Wait/7-Day	AGN	9. Use Force in Gulf	FOR
2. $ for Homeownership	FOR	6. Overseas Mil. Abortion	AGN	10. US Mil. Abroad $ Cut	AGN
3. Tax Rich/Cut Mid Cls.	AGN	7. Obscn. Art NEA $ Ban	FOR	11. Limit SDI Funds	AGN
4. FY93/$15B Def. Cut	AGN	8. Death Pen. from Jury	FOR	12. Cuba Trade Embargo	FOR

Key Votes of the 103d Congress

1. Family Leave	AGN	2. Deficit Reduction	AGN	3. Stimulus Plan	AGN

Election Results

1992 general	James V. Hansen (R)	160,037	(65%)	($240,969)
	Ron Holt (D)........................	68,712	(28%)	($64,451)
	William J. Lawrence (I)	16,505	(7%)	
1992 primary	James V. Hansen (R), unopposed			
1990 general	James V. Hansen (R)	82,746	(52%)	($237,357)
	Kenley Brunsdale (D)	69,491	(44%)	($133,084)
	Reva Marx Wadsworth (AM)...........	6,429	(4%)	

SECOND DISTRICT

The center of Utah and of the Mormon Church is Temple Square, illuminated by 300,000 lights during Christmas week, and nestled beneath the towering, snow-capped mountains that flank Salt Lake City. Here you can find the Mormon Tabernacle, home of the famous choir, and the Temple itself, which is entered only by Church members. Two long blocks north is the state Capitol, four blocks south is City Hall and all around are Salt Lake City's impressive skyscrapers. Ironically, Salt Lake City is the least Mormon and most cosmopolitan part of Utah, with the state university and businesses bringing in outsiders. Some think it now has a non-Mormon majority, but most likely it doesn't; it grew nearly 18% in the 1980s, and the metro area has 1.1 million people now, but that growth is in large part internally generated by Utah's large Mormon families.

Utah's 2d Congressional District, which includes most of Salt Lake County, has somewhat fewer families and children than the other two Utah districts. Its boundaries exclude the western suburbs on the flats out toward the Great Salt Lake, which lean toward the Democrats—an attempt by the Republican legislature to help Republican chances. The 2d has most of Utah's affluent people, living in Salt Lake City and suburbs like East Millcreek, Holladay and Cottonwood, right next to the Wasatch Mountains which rise at that point to 9,000 feet. It's just a 20-minute drive—well, 30—from offices to ski slopes, as Utah boosters like to tell prospective new residents. The district also includes a string of suburbs south of Salt Lake City—West Jordan, South Jordan, Murray, Sandy, Draper, Riverton, Bluffdale. By national standards, this is a Republican district, though one which did not give George Bush a large margin over Bill Clinton in 1992. But by Utah standards, this is the most Democratic of the state's three House seats, and in fact has been seriously contested in 10 of the last 12 elections.

The new congresswoman from the 2d District is Democrat Karen Shepherd, elected in 1992. She grew up in small towns in Utah, the daughter of a U.S. Department of Agriculture employee, married, and became a high school and college English teacher. Active in the Democratic Party, in 1978 she started *network*, a magazine "for Utah women who were moving toward living and working in a more equal society," which she sold in 1988. Then she became community relations director for the University of Utah business school, and in 1990 was elected to the state Senate. In 1992, she ran for Congress when Wayne Owens, congressman here since 1986 and also from 1972 to 1974, ran for the Senate. The Republicans had a primary between Enid Greene, a top aide to Governor Norman Bangerter, and James Bartelson, former head of a conservative think tank. Greene won the primary nearly 2–1, and campaigned against the congressional pay raise and against abortion. Shepherd took liberal positions on health care, backing government caps on cost and tighter regulation of insurers, and called for New Deal-style training programs for defense conversion. But she also backed term limits and the balanced budget amendment, and her campaign was not shy in family-friendly Utah about pointing out that she was a wife and mother while Greene was single. Shepherd got an 'A' rating from Ross Perot's United We Stand Utah branch, while Greene got a 'C+'. And Shepherd, with national Democratic feminist connections, had more money to spend than Greene. In the end, Shepherd won 51%–47%.

In the House, Shepherd has seats on the Natural Resources and Public Works Committees, where she wants to work on defense conversion and funding for a light rail line in Salt Lake County. She was co-chair of the freshman Democrats' task force on rules, which declined to recommend major changes like limiting the terms of chairmen (though Republican freshmen pushed for and got an analogous rule on their side of the aisle) but introduced legislation to restrain outgoing members from buying up all their office furniture and equipment at drastically reduced prices.

The People: Pop. 1990: 574,412; 9% age 65+; 92% White; 1% Black; 1% Amer. Indian; 2% Asian; 2% Other; 5% Hispanic origin. Voting age pop.: 378,723; 1% Black; 4% Hispanic origin. Households: 60% married couple families; 34% married couple fams. w. children; 62% college educ.; median household income: $30,960; per capita income: $12,971; median gross rent: $379; median house value: $76,700.

1992 Presidential Vote

Bush (R) 101,169 (38%)
Clinton (D) 81,233 (31%)
Perot (I) 75,921 (29%)

1988 Presidential Vote

Bush (R) 138,467 (62%)
Dukakis (D) 85,967 (38%)

Rep. Karen F. Shepherd (D)

Elected 1992; b. July 5, 1940, Silver City, NM; home, Salt Lake City; U. of UT., B.A. 1962, Brigham Young U., M.A. 1963; Protestant; married (Vincent).

Career: High Schl. teacher, 1963; Instructor, Olympic Col., 1963–65; Instructor, American U., Cairo Egypt, 1965–67; Instructor, Brigham Young U., 1968–74; Dir., Salt Lake City Social Svcs., 1975–77; Dir., Continuing Educ., Westminster Col., 1975–80; Pres., Webster Publishing Co., 1979–88; Dir., Devel. & Commun. Relations, U. of UT, 1988–92; UT Senate, 1990–92.

Offices: 414 CHOB 20515, 202-225-3011. Also Bennett Fed. Bldg., 125 S. State St., #2311, Salt Lake City 84138, 801-524-4394.

Committees: *Natural Resources* (20th of 28 D): National Parks, Forests and Public Lands; Oversight and Investigations. *Public Works and Transportation* (29th of 39 D): Aviation; Economic Development; Water Resources and Environment.

Group Ratings and 102d Congress Votes: Newly Elected

Key Votes of the 103d Congress

1. Family Leave	FOR	2. Deficit Reduction	FOR	3. Stimulus Plan	FOR

Election Results

1992 general	Karen F. Shepherd (D)	127,738	(51%)	($617,594)
	Enid Greene (R)	118,307	(47%)	($446,334)
	Two Others	6,924	(3%)	
1992 primary	Karen F. Shepherd (D), unopposed			
1990 general	Wayne Owens (D)	85,167	(58%)	($1,087,829)
	Genevieve Atwood (R)	58,869	(40%)	($490,726)
	Two Others	3,835	(2%)	

THIRD DISTRICT

The heartland of the Mormon Church in America is in a geographically isolated valley between 11,000-foot peaks of the Wasatch Range and the shores of Utah Lake. Here is Provo, the home of Brigham Young University, an institution long known for the rigorously conservative views of its faculty, the old-fashioned moral standards it encourages and its welcoming of technological innovation. The Mormon commonwealth, after all, started off with a terrific shortage of both labor and water and was eager to use technology to make up for this and prosper in this fearsome terrain. Today this is one of America's high-tech centers, the home of WordPerfect and Novell and hundreds of other firms, some fleeing California's high taxes and regulations.

The 3d Congressional District of Utah includes Provo and Utah County and most of the west side of Salt Lake City and its suburb of West Valley, connected by a strip of desert along the Great Salt Lake. These two urban areas cast more than two-thirds of the district's votes; the rest are cast in towns scattered amid huge mountains, florid rock formations and deep canyons from Wyoming down to the Arizona border. Its northernmost point is in the Wasatch Range, and it includes the depressed uranium country in eastern Utah around Moab and the surreal rock formations of Canyonlands and Capitol Reef National Parks. Utah County is one of the most heavily Republican areas in the United States, and the 3d District was the number one Republican district in the 1980 presidential election. Republican redistricters for 1992, however, added the Democratic west side of Salt Lake County to make the 2d District more

Republican, which of course had the effect of strengthening the Democrats in the 3d.

That matters, since against considerable odds the 3d District has a Democratic Congressman, Bill Orton, a tax lawyer and former Internal Revenue Service agent, who won the seat in 1990 when the incumbent retired. Orton was helped by a fractious Republican primary, by Republican nominee Karl Snow's business ties to a convicted stock manipulator, and by a Snow newspaper ad that juxtaposed a picture of Snow and his family with a picture of Orton, who is single, labeled "Bill Orton and his family." Even in the Mormon heartland of large families, this was thought to be dirty pool. Orton won a stunning 58%–36% victory, carrying every county but one tiny rural enclave. In the House, Orton has had a voting record about as conservative as any non-southern Democrat, supporting the Gulf war resolution and voting against the Brady bill. He worked for the Central Utah Project, defended ranchers' grazing rights on federal lands and supported mandatory alcohol label warnings. He drew up his own version of a balanced budget amendment, which won the praise of Utah Republican colleague James Hansen among others. He passed a "Veteran Teacher Corps" bill to provide teaching opportunities for retiring military personnel; and this horse owner and resident of Sundance drew up his own Utah wilderness bill.

Republican efforts to oppose Orton turned farcical. Provo Chamber of Commerce head Steve Densley started running in 1991, attacking Orton as "single and socialist," arguing that his voting record supposedly resembled that of Vermont's Bernie Sanders, which it doesn't. In January 1992, Lieutenant Governor Val Oveson entered the race and Densley withdrew; in February, Oveson withdrew and Densley reentered; in April, Densley withdrew a second time, leaving Republican nominee Richard Harrington looking like a last resort. Harrington called for major slashes in federal spending, but couldn't deny Orton's rather conservative voting record and workaholic ways, and Orton vastly outspent him. In Utah County, which cast almost half the votes, Orton won by only 50%–46%. But he carried the Salt Lake County portion added by the Republican legislature 70%–24% and the smaller counties 64%–31% for a 59%–37% victory. His particular talents, and the blunders of his opponents, have clearly made a strong impression, and in early 1993 he was strongly considering running for Orrin Hatch's Senate seat in 1994.

The People: Pop. 1990: 574,233; 23% rural; 8% age 65+; 90% White; 3% Amer. Indian; 2% Asian; 2% Other; 5% Hispanic origin. Voting age pop.: 355,475; 5% Hispanic origin. Households: 68% married couple families; 41% married couple fams. w. children; 54% college educ.; median household income: $26,570; per capita income: $9,259; median gross rent: $358; median house value: $59,800.

1992 Presidential Vote

Bush (R)	105,836	(46%)
Perot (I)	58,595	(25%)
Clinton (D)	51,574	(22%)
Other	14,245	(6%)

1988 Presidential Vote

Bush (R)	133,442	(68%)
Dukakis (D)	62,148	(32%)

Rep. William H. Orton (D)

Elected 1990; b. Sept. 22, 1948, North Ogden; home, Provo; Brigham Young U., B.S. 1973, J.D. 1979; Mormon; single.

Career: Tax auditor, Internal Revenue Svc., 1976–77; Adjunct prof., Portland St. U., Portland Commun. Col., 1974–76, Brigham Young U., 1984–85; Practicing atty., 1980–90.

Offices: 1122 LHOB 20515, 202-225-7751. Also 51 S. University Ave., #317, Provo 84601, 801-379-2500; and 3540 S. 40th St., #410, West Valley City 84119, 801-964-5828.

Committees: *Banking, Finance and Urban Affairs* (13th of 30 D): Economic Growth and Credit Formation; Financial Institutions Supervision, Regulation and Deposit Insurance; International Development, Finance, Trade and Monetary Policy. *Budget* (22d of 26 D).

Group Ratings

	ADA	ACLU	COPE	CDF	CFA	LCV	ACU	NTLC	NSI	COC	CEI
1992	55	26	42	30	40	25	56	67	80	63	65
1991	25	—	33	30	39	15	63	—	—	60	47

National Journal Ratings

	1991 LIB — 1991 CONS		1992 LIB — 1992 CONS	
Economic	35%	—	64%	39%	—	61%
Social	29%	—	70%	26%	—	72%
Foreign	58%	—	41%	62%	—	35%

Key Votes of the 102d Congress

1. Ban Striker Replace	FOR	5. Handgun Wait/7-Day	AGN	9. Use Force in Gulf	FOR
2. $ for Homeownership	AGN	6. Overseas Mil. Abortion	AGN	10. US Mil. Abroad $ Cut	FOR
3. Tax Rich/Cut Mid Cls.	FOR	7. Obscn. Art NEA $ Ban	FOR	11. Limit SDI Funds	FOR
4. FY93/$15B Def. Cut	AGN	8. Death Pen. from Jury	AGN	12. Cuba Trade Embargo	FOR

Key Votes of the 103d Congress

1. Family Leave	AGN	2. Deficit Reduction	AGN	3. Stimulus Plan	AGN

Election Results

1992 general	William H. Orton (D)	135,029	(59%)	($241,403)
	Richard R. Harrington (R)	84,019	(37%)	($71,074)
	Four Others	10,013	(4%)	
1992 primary	William H. Orton (D), unopposed			
1990 general	William H. Orton (D)	79,163	(58%)	($88,234)
	Karl Snow (R)	49,452	(36%)	($290,439)
	Two Others	7,061	(5%)	

VERMONT

It is an antique state, summed up best in the Shelburne Museum, with its barn and jail, railroad station and blacksmith shop and covered bridge, 37 buildings of folk art, carefully preserved by rich New Yorkers in better-than-ever condition. Vermont, wrote Vermonter Dorothy Canfield Fisher half a century ago, "represents the past, is a piece of the past in the midst of the present and future." Today, reverence for that past has made Vermont, for many Americans approaching the 21st Century, a guide to a congenial future. Vermont's closeness to nature, the intimacy of its small communities, its lack of unattractive accoutrements of early 20th Century industrialism have all made it a kind of promised land for urban expatriates: the state that missed out on U.S. Steel now produces Ben & Jerry's Ice Cream. By the 1980s, for the first time in nearly 200 years, Vermont became a growth area: in an era when Americans are increasingly ill-served by the rigidities of big organizations and repelled by big-city congestion, small businesses and computers enable more and more Americans to make their livings where they want, which often means Vermont.

Vermont began as an agricultural state, a target of America's northward and eastward migration (as important, for a while, as westward movement), a place where starting in the 1790s, second sons and daughters from small New England farms went to scratch out livings from the rocky soil. Agriculture has remained important, especially dairy farming, but Vermont has commerce as well. With its legendary thriftiness, it has accumulated capital that, invested wisely, was used to build the solid stone office buildings and courthouses, the thick-timbered houses and gold-topped state Capitol that have remained long after ramshackle wooden buildings of the 1880s have crumbled into dust. But Vermont never developed labor-intensive industry, and so over the years it exported people, and aged. Today, millions of Americans have Vermont blood—far more than the half million who live here now, many of whom have no Vermont roots at all. Two presidents were born here, but both made their careers elsewhere: Chester Arthur in New York, Calvin Coolidge in Massachusetts. As a result of continuous outmigration, Vermont's population hovered between 300,000 and 400,000 from 1850 to 1960.

Since then—perhaps the key date was 1963, when people started outnumbering cows—Vermont has changed rapidly. Its economy has boomed, led by the leisure-time industries—ski resorts, summer homes—and IBM, with several big high-tech facilities around the Burlington area on the mostly undeveloped shores of glorious Lake Champlain. Vermont's tradition of cottage industries continues, with knitters seeking to overturn union-inspired federal bans on home production. Home-grown firms started by erstwhile Baby Boom rebels—Ben & Jerry's Ice Cream is the archetype—have flourished. The population rose from 390,000 in 1960 to 444,000 in 1970, 511,000 in 1980 and 562,000 in 1990, and it hasn't been random settlement. While next-door New Hampshire, trumpeting its low taxes and aversion to government, has attracted right-leaning migrants from Boston and other parts of the East willing to put up with ticky-tack development to maintain the low taxes, Vermont, proclaiming its love of the environment and desire to protect it, has attracted left-leaning migrants from New York and elsewhere, willing to pay higher taxes for the privilege of living in a seemingly pristine setting.

Another key point may have been in 1970, when Republican Governor Deane Davis, facing a primary challenge, pushed through a sweeping land use law (Act 250) that helped give Vermont its environmental reputation. Housing developments and new ski resorts were required to meet ten environmental criteria and get the approval of a state commission. Davis also raised more money for education, authorized higher fines for water polluters and liberalized divorce laws. Since then, Vermont has passed its own Clean Air Act that levies a tax on new cars that get less than 20 miles per gallon and is proud that it has no EPA-cited air pollution areas. With its

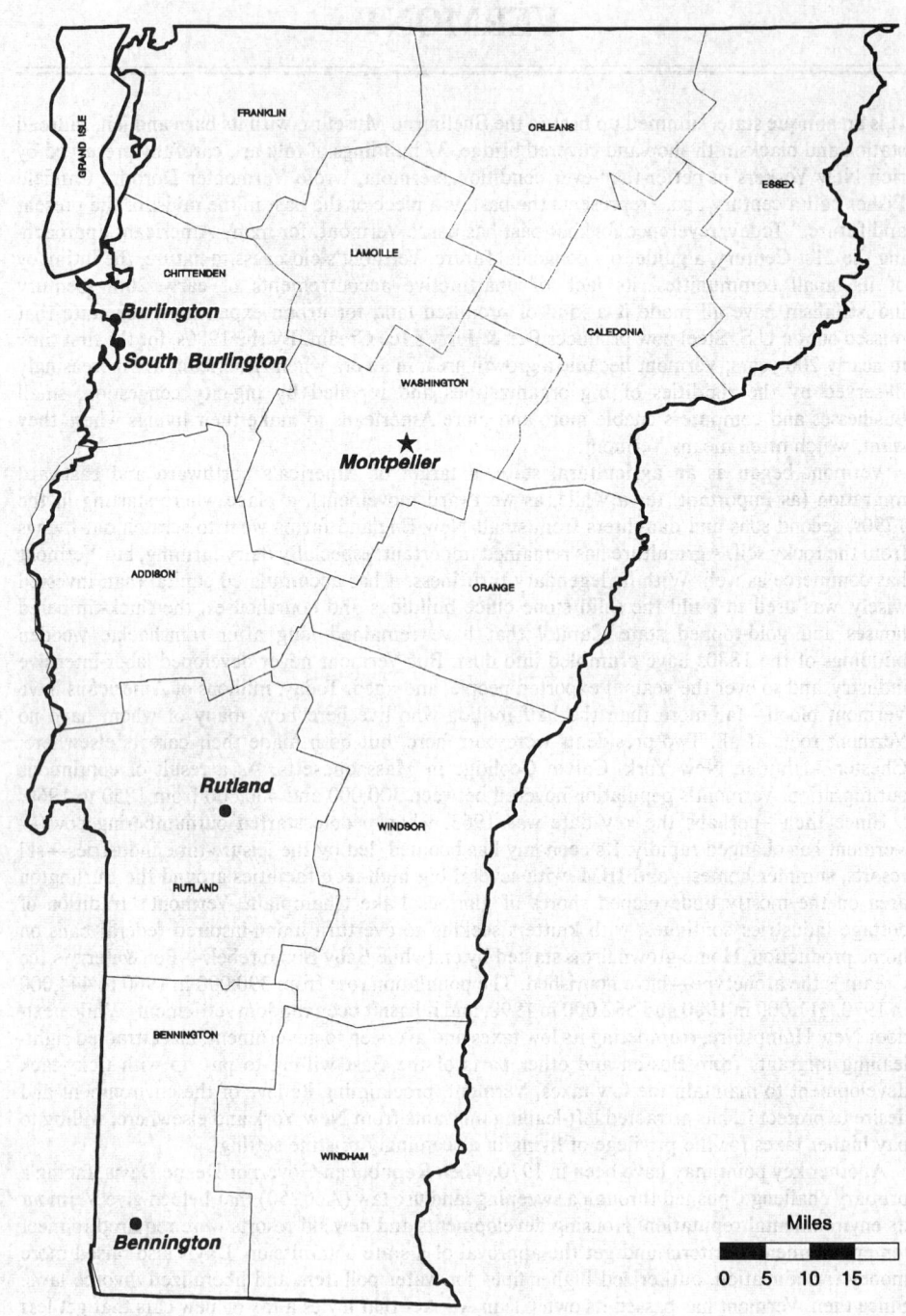

GRAND ISLE

FRANKLIN

ORLEANS

ESSEX

LAMOILLE

CHITTENDEN

CALEDONIA

Burlington

South Burlington

WASHINGTON

ADDISON

★ **Montpelier**

ORANGE

Rutland

WINDSOR

RUTLAND

BENNINGTON

WINDHAM

Bennington

Miles

0   5   10   15

Yankee heritage, it was the most Republican state in the nation in the 19th Century; in 1936 Vermont and Maine were the only states to resist Franklin Roosevelt's landslide. While its population stagnated, its Yankee Protestant Republicans always outnumbered its French Canadian and Irish Catholic Democrats. But now, with more growth in the last 30 years than in the preceding 110, it is liberal, especially on cultural issues, giving Bill Clinton one of his biggest percentage margins in the country (exceeded only in Massachusetts, Rhode Island, Arkansas and New York) and reelecting its Socialist congressman to a second term in 1992.

Governor. Vermont, together with New Hampshire, are the last states to cling to a two-year gubernatorial term. The governor, Howard Dean, came to office unexpectedly; he was lieutenant governor when Richard Snelling, elected in 1990 after holding the office from 1976 to 1984, died suddenly in August 1991. Snelling was a Republican and Dean a Democrat, but that does not seem to have made much difference. What distinguishes Dean is health care. He is a physician, as is his wife, an internist from Burlington elected to the legislature in 1982 and lieutenant governor in 1986. Dean pushed Snelling's budget plans, then in April passed his own healthcare reform, moving Vermont toward universal access by 1995; a state agency was set up to bargain with insurance companies and study whether to rely on them or have state government insurance. He also passed family leave legislation, pushed a bill to reduce phosphorus in lakes and streams, and created a $14 million small business fund. But he angered some liberals by backing workfare and a controversial Hydro Quebec contract. Dean was opposed in the 1992 election by state Senator John McClaughry, a genial free market advocate who criticized Act 250, but didn't make a dent: Dean won 75%–23%. Barbara Snelling, the late governor's widow, ran for lieutenant governor and won 53%–43%, and could possibly be Dean's 1994 opponent.

Senators. Patrick Leahy has held public office for most of his adult life. In 1966, two years after returning to Burlington from law school, he was elected Chittenden County State's Attorney and after eight years in that post—and few public officials are scrutinized as closely as a local prosecutor—he was elected to the U.S. Senate at 34, the first and only Democratic senator elected in Vermont history. Now he is finishing his second decade in the Senate, is chairman of the Agriculture Committee, and plays a pivotal role on some foreign issues and judicial appointments.

Leahy has chaired Agriculture since 1987. Unlike most committee Democrats, he has no subsidy program to defend except dairy, which is *sui generis* and which has far fewer farmers in Vermont or anywhere than even a decade ago. With ranking Republican Richard Lugar of Indiana, he has worked to pare back farm programs from unsustainable levels, first in the 1990 farm bill, more recently in moves to reduce its 110,000 Agriculture employees in 15,000 department locations. Leahy also moved to increase regulation of futures exchanges and increase the margins required of speculators. Leahy did much technical work on farm credit and drought bills in the 1980s; in the 1990s the committee's jurisdiction has taken him farther afield. Aid to Russia, for example: from Agriculture and his chairmanship of the Foreign Operations Appropriations subcommittee, Leahy argued in early 1993 that government-backed loans for food purchases helped neither Russia nor the U.S.; he called instead for $1 billion in direct aid and other grants to Russia and cuts in aid to Egypt and Israel to compensate. He expressed skepticism about Israel's use of foreign aid monies to build housing on the West Bank for new immigrants from Russia and elsewhere. In 1992, Leahy was involved in the investigation of "Iraqgate," the use of agricultural credits by Saddam Hussein to buy weapons materials. Leahy backs a "circle of poison" law banning export of pesticides forbidden from use in this country.

Leahy also serves on Judiciary, where he generally votes with the liberal bloc; he was the first senator to announce his opposition to Supreme Court nominee Clarence Thomas. On Appropriations, Leahy has not been afraid to oppose Chairman Robert Byrd (as on Byrd's coal miner compensation amendment, which lost by one vote). A Leahy-Dodd amendment, passed by a wide margin in 1990, cut military aid to El Salvador by 50% and conditioned future aid on human rights improvements and Salvadoran government effort to negotiate with the rebels. He resisted sending additional aid to Panama after the ouster of Manuel Noriega, but lost 48–51 on the amendment. And he was one of the leaders in cutting funding of the B-2 Stealth bomber. Leahy served as vice chairman of the Intelligence Committee in 1985–86, but voluntarily resigned from the committee in January 1987 after it was revealed he had shown a reporter an unclassified Iran-contra staff report.

To his generally liberal record, Leahy brings the parsimoniousness consonant with Vermont tradition, and a quiet, thoughtful temperament. But he also has a zest for life and a puckish sense of humor, part of the Yankee heritage of Vermont, though his Irish and Italian ethnic origin is certainly not Yankee. His standing in Vermont has been strong over the years: he survived the Republican sweep in 1980 and beat popular Governor Richard Snelling 63%–35% in 1986. During the 1992 campaign, Leahy seemed to be running well ahead, but Republican Jim Douglas, secretary of state since 1980, campaigned against special interest money and, somewhat contradictorily, accused Leahy of not doing enough for dairy farmers or getting enough federal money for Vermont. In May 1992, Leahy decided to stop taking PAC money and put his PAC contributions in escrow; he championed Governor Howard Dean's healthcare plan and cited his own achievements. In late October, a Republican flier hit Leahy for voting for the congressional pay raise and for the loss of dairy jobs; Leahy attacked this as "sleazeball negative campaigning," and Douglas said it was the state GOP that sent out the flier, not himself. Leahy won with 54% of the vote—a decisive margin, but less than a landslide.

Vermont's junior senator is Jim Jeffords, known since he was first elected to the House in 1974 for having one of the most liberal records of all Republicans. Jeffords returned from law school to his home town of Shrewsbury, was elected state Senator at 32 in 1966 and then state attorney general in 1968 and 1970. He often votes more with Democrats than with Republicans—against the 1981 Reagan tax cuts as Vermont's at-large congressman and, more recently as senator, against Clarence Thomas, for the Brady bill waiting period for handgun sales, for cable TV reregulation, and against the B-2 and SDI. He voted with the Clinton Administration on five of eight early budget votes in 1993, more than any other Republican, was one of two Republicans supporting motor voter registration and was a co-sponsor of family and medical leave. But he has stuck with Republicans on some tough issues. He backed President Bush on most favored nation status for China and, despite pleas from President Clinton, opposed the fiscal stimulus package. Jeffords's overall economic record is more conservative than that of many Democratic senators; it is on foreign and especially cultural issues that he is more liberal.

Other Jeffords causes include his "MediCore" a state-based, single payer medical insurance system, which he emphasizes would help finance Vermont's new plan, and raising grazing fees on public lands (of which there are very few in Vermont). He serves on Foreign Relations, where he has become interested in problems in Eastern Europe and the former Soviet republics. He was ranking member of the Senate subcommittee investigating the so-called October surprise, which found nothing to this exotic conspiracy theory. A Civil War buff interested in a Vermont regiment's critical role in the Shenandoah Valley Battle of Cedar Creek, and inspired by murals in the Vermont Capitol, he has a bill to catalogue and study unprotected Civil War sites to avoid repeating the imbroglio over Virginia's Manassas battlefield, in which Congress paid millions to save part of the battle site from becoming a shopping center.

Jeffords won this seat in 1988 when Senator Robert Stafford retired. His real hurdle was the Republican primary, in which he was attacked fiercely by conservative Mike Griffes on gun control, abortion, and church and family issues, as well as for accepting $5,000 from the Teamsters' PAC after asking the Justice Department not to take over the union; Jeffords won by a 61%–39% margin—not terribly impressive for a popular representative. In the general, he did better, winning with 70%; any threat to his incumbency in 1994 will likely come in the primary.

Representative-At-Large. At a time when the whole world seems to be rejecting socialism, Vermont, the state most solidly opposed to Franklin Roosevelt's New Deal, has now elected a Socialist to Congress twice in a row. But Bernie Sanders is not just a Socialist, but also very much a modern Vermonter: the son of a Flatbush paint salesman, he came here as part of the hippie invasion of 1968; his rumpled, tieless, sincere persona helped him win election as mayor of Burlington in 1981 by 10 votes, after losing four statewide races. There he governed ably for eight years, using the city's prosperity to start a municipal day care center, expand low- and moderate-income housing, put a pollution control facility on Lake Champlain and switch the tax base from property to hotel and restaurant fees and a utility tax on companies using certain public facilities. In 1990, he ran for Congress and reversed his defeat by Republican Peter Smith two years before, by capitalizing on Smith's support of the 1990 budget summit agreement and his vote for the ban on semiautomatic weapons. The National Rifle Association came out against Smith, with bumper stickers reading, "Smith & Wesson, Yes. Peter Smith, No." Gun control probably made the most difference: in ancestrally Republican Vermont, Sanders carried 227 of Vermont's 251 cities and towns, and three gores and one grant.

In his first months in the House, Sanders voted true to form, opposing both the Gulf war resolution and the Brady bill. As only the third Socialist elected to the House—the others were Victor Berger of Milwaukee (1911–13, 1923–29) and Meyer London of Manhattan's Lower East Side (1915–23)—he said he found it incomprehensible that the whole country wasn't turning left. Democrats have accommodated him, so far, on committees and seniority: he was given committee seats his first term, was given seniority as if he were the lowest-ranking Democrat elected in 1990 in his second term, and may be allowed subcommittee chairmanships in time. He moved without success to require on-budget, cash payoff of S&L and possible bank bailouts, to be funded by progressive taxes: Vermont thrift and Fabian socialism, all in one breath. He has sponsored a Canadian-style national health plan and passed a Cancer Registries law in 1992. He favors higher dairy prices and a ban on bovine growth hormone. Sanders has obviously struck a chord in Vermont, and won reelection 58%–31% over the Republican candidate.

Presidential politics. James A. Farley had a good laugh on Vermont in 1936 when he updated an adage to say "As goes Maine, so goes Vermont." But today's Vermont, liberal on cultural and foreign issues, not tremendously conservative on economics, has little use for conservative Republicans. That was apparent back in 1980, when Ronald Reagan got his seventh lowest percentage here and John Anderson, with 15%, his best; in 1984 and 1988 Vermont was more Democratic than the nation, and in 1992 it gave Bill Clinton one of his largest margins.

In May 1991, Vermont axed its presidential primary to save money; coming after New Hampshire, it never got much attention anyway. The state's caucuses went 80% for George Bush among Republicans and 46% for Jerry Brown among Democrats.

The People: Est. Pop. 1992: 570,000; Pop. 1990: 562,758, up 1.3% 1990–1992. 0.2% of U.S. total, 49th largest; 68% rural. Median age: 33.0 years. 11.8% 65 years and older. 98.6% White. Households: 56.4% married couple families; 28% married couple fams. w. children; 46% college educ.; median household income: $29,792; per capita income: $13,527; 69.0% owner occupied housing; median house value: $95,500; median monthly rent: $378. 6.6% Unemployment. Voting age pop.: 419,675. Registered voters (1992): 383,371; no party registration.

Political Lineup: Governor, Howard Dean (D); Lt. Gov., Barbara W. Snelling (R); Secy. of State, Don Hooper (D); Atty. Gen., Jeffrey L. Amestoy (R); Treasurer, Paul W. Ruse Jr. (D); Auditor, Edward S. Flanangan (D). State Senate, 30 (16 R and 14 D); State House of Representatives, 150 (87 D, 57 R, 4 I, and 2 Progressive Coalition). Senators, Patrick J. Leahy (D) and James M. Jeffords (R). Representative, 1 I at large.

1992 Presidential Vote

Clinton (D) 133,592 (46%)
Bush (R) 88,122 (30%)
Perot (I). 65,991 (23%)

1988 Presidential Vote

Bush (R) 124,331 (51%)
Dukakis (D). 115,775 (48%)

GOVERNOR

Gov. Howard Dean (D)

Assumed office, Aug. 1991, term expires Jan. 1995; b. Nov. 17, 1948, New York, NY; home, Burlington; Yale., B.A. 1977, Albert Einstein Col. of Medicine, M.D. 1978; Congregationalist; married (Judith).

Career: Practicing physician, 1981–91; VT House of Reps, 1983–86; VT Lt. Gov., 1987–91.

Offices: Pavilion State Office Bldg., 109 State St., Montpelier 05609, 802-828-3333.

Election Results

1992 gen.	Howard Dean (D)	213,523	(75%)
	Richard McClaughry (R)	105,191	(23%)
1990 prim.	Howard Dean (D), unopposed		
1990 gen.	Richard A. Snelling (R)	106,274	(52%)
	Peter Welch (D)	93,725	(46%)
	Two Others	4,063	(2%)

SENATORS

Sen. Patrick J. Leahy (D)

Elected 1974, seat up 1998; b. Mar. 31, 1940, Montpelier; home, Burlington; St. Michael's Col., B.A. 1961, Georgetown U., J.D. 1964; Catholic; married (Marcelle).

Career: Practicing atty., 1964–74; St. Atty., Chittenden Cnty., 1966–74.

Offices: 433 RSOB 20510, 202-224-4242. Also 199 Main St., Burlington 05401, 802-863-2525; and Fed. Bldg., Box 933, Montpelier 05602, 802-229-0569.

Committees: *Agriculture, Nutrition and Forestry* (Chmn. of 10 D). *Appropriations* (5th of 16 D): Defense; Foreign Operations (Chmn.); Interior; VA, HUD and Independent Agencies. *Judiciary* (5th of 10 D): Patents, Copyrights and Trademarks. Technology and the Law (Chmn.).

Group Ratings

	ADA	ACLU	CDF	COPE	CFA	LCV	ACU	NTLC	NSI	COC	CEI
1992	100	95	90	100	100	100	0	11	40	10	14
1991	95	—	82	92	94	100	5	—	—	20	18

National Journal Ratings

	1991 LIB — 1991 CONS			1992 LIB — 1992 CONS		
Economic	90%	—	3%	95%	—	0%
Social	84%	—	13%	79%	—	16%
Foreign	73%	—	26%	78%	—	14%

Key Votes of the 102d Congress

1. $ for Homeownership	AGN	5. Clarence Thomas Nom.	AGN	9. Use Force in Gulf	AGN
2. Have Cap Gains Debate	AGN	6. Lmt Death Row Appeal	AGN	10. Keep Salvador Aid	AGN
3. Remove Budget Walls	FOR	7. Handgun Wait/5-Day	AGN	11. Cut $1B from SDI	FOR
4. Ban Striker Replace	FOR	8. Abortion Gag Rule	AGN	12. Override China MFN	FOR

Key Votes of the 103d Congress

1. Family Leave	FOR	2. HIV Immigrants	FOR	3. Clinton Budget	FOR

Election Results

1992 general	Patrick J. Leahy (D).................	154,762	(54%)	($1,202,445)
	James H. Douglas (R)................	123,854	(43%)	($195,737)
	Other..................................	7,123	(2%)	
1992 primary	Patrick J. Leahy (D), unopposed			
1986 general	Patrick J. Leahy (D).................	124,123	(63%)	($1,705,099)
	Richard Snelling (R).................	67,798	(35%)	($1,502,304)

Sen. James M. Jeffords (R)

Elected 1988, seat up 1994; b. May 11, 1934, Rutland; home, Shrewsbury; Yale, B.S. 1956, Harvard, LL.B. 1962; Congregationalist; married (Elizabeth Daley).

Career: Navy, 1956–59, Naval Reserves, 1959–90; Law clerk, 1962–63; Practicing atty., 1963–69, 1973–75; Shrewsbury Repub. Chmn., 1963–74, Town Agent, Grand Juror, 1964; VT Senate, 1966–68; VT Atty. Gen., 1968–72; U.S. House of Reps. 1974–1988.

Offices: 513 HSOB 20515, 202-224-5141. Also P.O. Box 676, 138 Main St., Montpelier 05601, 802-223-5273; 95 St. Paul St., #100, Burlington 05401, 802-658-6001; and P.O. Box 397, 2 S. Main St., Rutland 05702, 802-773-3875.

Committees: *Aging (Special)* (5th of 10 R). *Foreign Relations* (7th of 8 R): African Affairs (RMM); International Economic Policy, Trade, Oceans and Environment; Near Eastern and South Asian Affairs. *Labor and Human Resources* (2d of 7 R): Children, Family, Drugs and Alcoholism; Disability Policy; Education, Arts and Humanities (RMM); Labor. *Veterans' Affairs* (5th of 5 R).

Group Ratings

	ADA	ACLU	CDF	COPE	CFA	LCV	ACU	NTLC	NSI	COC	CEI
1992	65	86	60	56	75	75	27	18	60	60	39
1991	65	—	91	50	61	87	10	—	—	22	27

National Journal Ratings

	1991 LIB — 1991 CONS		1992 LIB — 1992 CONS	
Economic	45% —	54%	37% —	61%
Social	68% —	30%	78% —	21%
Foreign	63% —	33%	59% —	40%

Key Votes of the 102d Congress

1. $ for Homeownership AGN	5. Clarence Thomas Nom. AGN	9. Use Force in Gulf FOR
2. Have Cap Gains Debate AGN	6. Lmt Death Row Appeal FOR	10. Keep Salvador Aid AGN
3. Remove Budget Walls AGN	7. Handgun Wait/5-Day FOR	11. Cut $1B from SDI FOR
4. Ban Striker Replace AGN	8. Abortion Gag Rule AGN	12. Override China MFN AGN

Key Votes of the 103d Congress

1. Family Leave FOR	2. HIV Immigrants FOR	3. Clinton Budget AGN

Election Results

1988 general	James M. Jeffords (R)	163,183	(70%)	($876,877)
	Bill Gray (D).......................	71,460	(30%)	($549,908)
1988 primary	James M. Jeffords (R)	30,555	(61%)	
	Mike Griffes (R).....................	19,593	(39%)	
1982 general	Robert T. Stafford (R)	82,259	(51%)	($407,340)
	James A. Guest (D)	78,447	(48%)	($282,600)

REPRESENTATIVE

Rep. Bernard Sanders (I)

Elected 1990; b. Sept. 8, 1941, New York, NY; home, Burlington; U. of Chicago, B.A. 1964; Jewish; married (Jane).

Career: Writer; Dir., Amer. People's History Soc.; Burlington Mayor, 1981–89; Lecturer, Harvard, 1989; Prof., Hamilton Col., 1989–90.

Offices: 213 CHOB 20515, 202-225-4115. Also 1 Church St., Burlington 05401, 802-862-0697.

Committees: *Banking, Finance and Urban Affairs* (1st of 1 I): Consumer Credit and Insurance; Housing and Community Development; International Development, Finance, Trade and Monetary Policy. *Government Operations* (1st of 1 I): Environment, Energy and Natural Resources; Human Resources and Intergovernmental Relations.

Group Ratings

	ADA	ACLU	COPE	CDF	CFA	LCV	ACU	NTLC	NSI	COC	CEI
1992	95	100	100	90	100	100	0	15	10	13	19
1991	95	—	100	90	89	85	15	—	—	10	11

National Journal Ratings

	1991 LIB — 1991 CONS		1992 LIB — 1992 CONS	
Economic	72% —	23%	64% —	35%
Social	88% —	12%	92% —	0%
Foreign	87% —	8%	90% —	0%

Key Votes of the 102d Congress

1. Ban Striker Replace FOR	5. Handgun Wait/7-Day AGN	9. Use Force in Gulf AGN
2. $ for Homeownership AGN	6. Overseas Mil. Abortion FOR	10. US Mil. Abroad $ Cut FOR
3. Tax Rich/Cut Mid Cls. FOR	7. Obscn. Art NEA $ Ban AGN	11. Limit SDI Funds FOR
4. FY93/$15B Def. Cut AGN	8. Death Pen. from Jury AGN	12. Cuba Trade Embargo AGN

Key Votes of the 103d Congress

1. Family Leave	FOR	2. Deficit Reduction FOR	3. Stimulus Plan FOR

Election Results

1992 general	Bernard Sanders (I)	162,724	(58%)	($575,791)
	Tim Philbin (R)......................	86,901	(31%)	($72,958)
	Lewis Young (D).....................	22,729	(8%)	
	Other...............................	9,799	(3%)	
1992 primary	Bernard Sanders (I), unopposed			
1990 general	Bernard Sanders (I)	117,522	(56%)	($569,772)
	Peter Smith (R)	82,938	(40%)	($688,907)
	Other...............................	9,396	(5%)	

VIRGINIA

Virginia's traditions endure. Through nearly 400 years of history, Virginians have honored, and sometimes been fixated by, traditions going back to its founding. Virginia has been growing lustily: it has the nation's first elected black governor, yet it still hews to a course close to its roots. For Virginia's recent growth, unlike that in the years after World War II, came less from an expanding government than from a vibrant private sector. The first Virginia was a Commonwealth ruled by a landed gentry which was, in the words of historian David Hackett Fischer, "elitist and libertarian." From the tobacco-growing counties emerged in the 1770s a group of leaders—George Washington, Patrick Henry, Thomas Jefferson, Richard Henry Lee, James Madison, James Monroe—who in learning, wisdom and strength of character, equal any such group from any similarly-sized polity since Periclean Athens: slaveholders who insisted on liberty, armed men living on the marchland of civilization who insisted on the rule of law, racists who propounded principles of equality to form the basis of an nonracist society. The Virginia they led into the American Revolution was not only the most populous and richest of the 13 colonies, it was also the indispensable creator of the Republic and the Constitution that has held together the world's greatest nation.

After the Revolution, gentry control continued even as Virginia was eclipsed in population and wealth by Pennsylvania and New York and, its tobacco fields exhausted, became a breeding ground for slaves. But Virginia had two more great heroes, Robert E. Lee and Stonewall Jackson, both of whom reluctantly and brilliantly fought for their state rather than their country; the state's leadership class was impoverished and embittered by the Civil War, so much of which was fought on Virginia soil. Industrialization was haphazard: railroads were constructed to ship cotton up from the South and coal east to the seaports; textile mills were built in Southside towns and tobacco factories in Richmond; the giant Newport News Shipbuilding & Drydock Company was built by railroad magnate Collis Huntington.

But most of Virginia remained agricultural, sunk in a low-wage economy and ruled by a small local class of landowning gentry which had become a small class of landowners, bankers and lawyers worshipping their Revolutionary past. They were pessimists, looking not for economic growth but for stability, bent on maintaining Virginia's segregation and content with its second-class economy, determined that the poor masses did not use government to pillage the rich as Yankee troops once had. These elite county courthouse organizations became the political machine of Harry Byrd, who ran the state from 1925, when he was elected governor, until 1965, when he retired from the Senate.

Nationally, the machine lost political battles more often than Lee lost military battles, and less gallantly. But it succeeded in keeping most vestiges of the welfare state and racial equality out of Virginia, to the point of closing public schools in the late 1950s rather than obey federal court integration orders. But this "massive resistance" collapsed in the late 1950s, and Governor Mills Godwin, a Byrd loyalist, accepted integration and upgraded state government in the late 1960s. Meanwhile, demographics changed the Old Dominion. As the 20th Century progressed, the peripheral parts of the state grew: the coal-mining counties of the southwest, the Tidewater area around the Navy bases in Norfolk and the shipbuilding yards in Newport News, and the government employee-filled suburbs across the Potomac from Washington, D.C. Courthouse politicians no longer carried the vote for the Byrd machine by the middle 1960s: Harry Byrd Jr., appointed to his father's Senate seat, was nearly beaten in the 1966 Senate primary, and 20-year Senate veteran A. Willis Robertson—and father of 1988 presidential candidate Pat Robertson—was beaten in his primary. In 1969, Linwood Holton, a believer in integration, was elected the first Republican governor of Virginia. But over the next decade, most victories were won by conservatives, some of them Byrd stalwarts turned Republican (like Mills Godwin, who returned to the governorship in 1973), some the sons of former insurgent Republicans (like John Dalton, elected governor in 1977) or Republicans with no deep local roots (like John Warner, elected Senator in 1978).

Then suddenly in the early 1980s, things began going the other way. The Democrats won the governorship in 1981 after a 16-year political drought and proceeded not only to hold on to it in 1985, but to elect a black lieutenant governor and a woman attorney general. These Democrats had strong black support, and carried the Washington suburbs, the Tidewater and the far western mountains; more important, they carried or ran even in the Richmond area and the rural counties that geographically and historically are the heart of the state. Democrats Charles Robb, Gerald Baliles and Douglas Wilder won the statehouse in 1981, 1985 and 1989 not because they no longer represented an attempt to impose a labor-liberal agenda on an unwilling Virginia, but because they argued they could use government effectively to improve education and build Virginia's economy. Wilder's election was in some sense a national breakthrough, an attempt by a black politician to campaign and govern on equal terms; he won largely because of his margins in the Tidewater and Northern Virginia, where his pro-choice stand on abortion clearly helped, but he also ran solidly across the state. His fiscal conservatism, which resulted in sharp spending cuts in the early 1990s, like his elegant manners and thick Richmond accent, echoed Virginia's elitist and libertarian tradition.

There has also been a certain amount of tumult and personal discord among these successful Democrats—not unheard of in Virginia history. Senator Robb's staff obtained a tape of a Wilder car phone conversation in which Wilder gloated over charges of misconduct by Robb in Virginia Beach vacations while he was governor; Robb staffers ultimately plea bargained with federal prosecutors, but a grand jury in January 1993 after long deliberations voted not to indict Robb. These developments improved neither man's standing with voters. Wilder is ineligible to run for a second term as governor in November 1993, and Robb's Senate seat comes up in November 1994; in June 1993 Wilder announced he would challenge Robb in the 1994 primary. These races give Republicans an opening in a state which George Bush carried even in 1992. Yet Democratic Attorney General Mary Sue Terry in early 1993 was running well ahead in the race for governor, and the best known Republican for the Senate seat was Oliver North, whose Iran-contra conviction was overturned only on the grounds some of the evidence used against him was inadmissible, a gravely flawed candidate if there ever was one. But one Virginia tradition, forgotten sometimes in its Williamsburg elegance, is turbulent politics.

Governor. Douglas Wilder leaves the governorship—Virginia is now the last state to limit its governor to a single term—with a record of accomplishment and acrimony. He entered politics as a state senator elected in 1969 attacking the state song "Carry Me Back to Old Virginny"; as governor, this Silver Star veteran of Korea instituted a Martin Luther King Holiday as part of a joint remembrance of Virginia's Confederate heroes, whose statues punctuate Richmond's well-

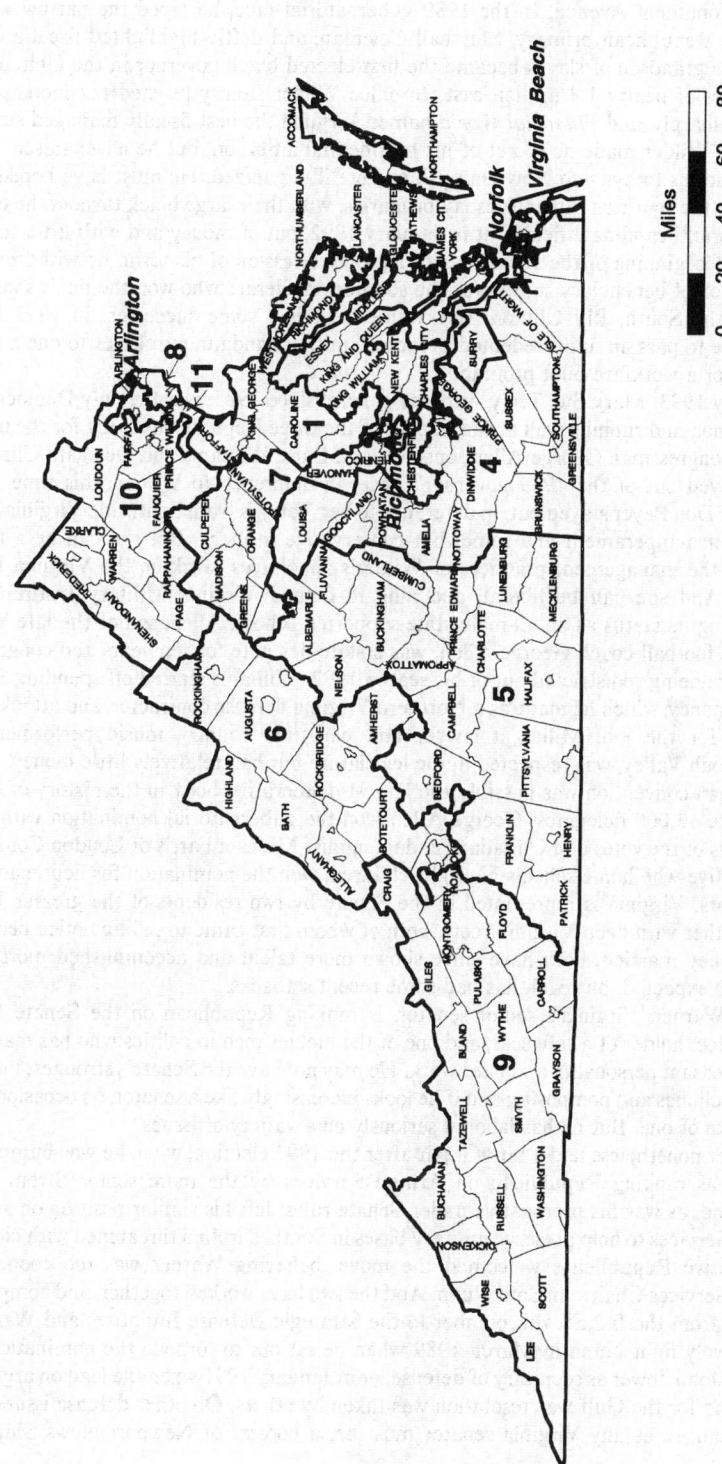

named Monument Avenue. In the 1989 gubernatorial race, he faced the narrow winner of a three-way Republican primary, Marshall Coleman, and deftly highlighted fiscal and abortion issues; this grandson of slaves became the first elected black governor in the United States by 6,741 votes of nearly 1.8 million cast. In office Wilder stoutly resisted tax increases and cut spending sharply, and *Financial World* named Virginia the best fiscally managed state in 1992 and 1993. Wilder made no secret of his presidential ambition, but he never raised substantial money, and his forays into New Hampshire were ill-organized. He must have hoped that if he made it to the southern Super Tuesday primaries, with their large black turnout, he could finish first in a multi-candidate field. But in January 1992, out of money and with little support, and facing the beginning of the second major legislative session of his term, he withdrew from the race; the chief beneficiary surely was the southern moderate who won the lion's share of black votes in the South, Bill Clinton. But Wilder still had some successes: in 1993 he got the legislature to pass an unprecedented proposal limiting handgun purchases to one a month and another for a workfare pilot program.

In early 1993, Mary Sue Terry, attorney general since 1985, was the only Democrat running for governor, and running well ahead in polls of the three Republicans vying for the nomination: former Congressman George Allen, businessman Earle Williams and Delegate Clinton Miller. Terry stayed out of the 1989 governor's race, in deference to Wilder; this time Lieutenant Governor Don Beyer stayed out, in deference to her. Terry is from Southside Virginia, and seems cautious in temperament and somewhat conservative in ideas. But she can be a fighter; she attacked the management practices of Wilder's appointees' work on the Virginia Retirement System. And she can be liberal, declining to defend Virginia Military Institute in a suit challenging its status as an all-male state-supported school. Allen, son of the late Washington Redskins football coach George Allen, was a state delegate for ten years and congressman for one before being redistricted out of his seat in 1992. Williams started off spending $600,000 of his own money, which he made as a Northern Virginia defense contractor, and attacked Allen as unready for the job. Miller, a lawyer and part-time country music performer from the Shenandoah Valley, was respected in the legislature but had relatively little money. The June 5 Republican convention was possibly the largest deliberative body in the history of democracy, with some 13,000 delegates. George Allen won the gubernatorial nomination with just under two-thirds of the votes and Christian fundamentalist Michael Farris of Loudon County, an arch conservative who home-schools his eight children, won the nomination for lieutenant governor.

Senators. Virginia is represented in the Senate by two residents of the greater Washington area, neither with deep Virginia roots, both of whom first came to public notice because of the women they married; both have since shown more talent and accomplished more than most observers expected, but each has had some recent setbacks.

John Warner, Virginia's senior senator, is ranking Republican on the Senate Intelligence Committee, holder of a safe seat, and one of the luckier men in politics who has made his mark with a pleasant personality and hard work. He may not have the Senate's strongest intellect; he is prone to cliches and pomposity; and if he looks increasingly like a senator, on occasion he seems a caricature of one. But he has labored seriously on a variety of issues.

Warner nonetheless had a bit of a jolt after the 1992 election, when he was bumped from his position as ranking Republican on Armed Services by the more senior Strom Thurmond. Thurmond, as was his prerogative under Senate rules, left his similar position on Judiciary for Armed Services to help preserve military bases in South Carolina threatened with closure. Some conservative Republicans welcomed the move, believing Warner was too cooperative with Armed Services Chairman Sam Nunn. And the two have worked together, and compromised, on projects from the B-2 Stealth bomber to the Strategic Defense Initiative; and Warner did not aggressively fight Nunn in March 1989 when he set out to torpedo the nomination of former Senator John Tower as secretary of defense, or in January 1991 when the lead on arguing against Nunn and for the Gulf war resolution was taken by others. On other defense issues, Warner, a Navy man, is, as any Virginia senator must be, a booster of Newport News Shipbuilding &

Drydock as the nation's chief submarine builder. He believes in extending American military force abroad and is cautious about defense reductions; on the first major issue of 1993, however, Warner was cautious about U.S. intervention in Bosnia, in sharp contrast to Republicans like Richard Lugar. For credibility in defending Virginia bases, he made a point of opposing NASA's space station, though it employs hundreds of Northern Virginians. Warner now also exerts influence from the Intelligence Committee. Momentarily, his position there as ranking Republican was threatened when Arlen Specter invoked a 1990 promise that he could return to the committee and have that post in 1993. But Warner protested vigorously, and prevailed with Republican Leader Bob Dole.

What does Warner believe in? A kind of well-intentioned Republican conservatism, influenced by the old eastern establishment. He is pro-choice on abortion, but favors parental consent laws; he voted against the nomination of Robert Bork in 1987. Representing a state which still has a large number of public employees (though the proportion is dropping), he favors higher federal pay and repeal of the Hatch Act. He seems to understand he is fortunate to be where he is. He ran for the Senate with few political assets other than his then-wife, Elizabeth Taylor. Finishing second at the huge Republican state convention, he graciously supported the winner; then, when the nominee died in a plane crash, Republican leaders reluctantly named Warner to fill his place. Warner won the general over Democrat Andrew Miller by a 4,721-vote margin. He has made few enemies, and was easily reelected over a liberal Democrat in 1984 and with no serious opposition in 1990.

Charles Robb has had a roller coaster of a career, in the spotlight in Virginia and nationally off and on for more than a quarter-century, the biggest Senate election vote-getter in Virginia history and the southern senator with the lowest job rating and vote-to-reelect numbers a few years later. Chuck Robb first came to national attention in 1967, when he married Lynda Bird Johnson in the White House, where he had been one of the Marine guards; he then served a year of combat duty in Vietnam. He began his political career in 1977 when, working in Washington and living across the river in McLean, he ran for lieutenant governor and won, while Republicans were carrying other offices; in 1981, he ran for governor and beat Marshall Coleman 54%–46%. As governor, he was widely popular and was given credit for much of Virginia's dynamic growth; he added $1 billion to the education budget, worked to boost Virginia's coal export industry and appointed blacks and women to top posts in large numbers. Out of office, Robb was a national figure as head of the Democratic Leadership Council. He was easily elected to the Senate in 1988: incumbent Paul Trible decided to retire at age 42 and Robb's only opponent was a hapless Republican black minister.

Trouble had already surfaced in August 1988, when newspaper stories reported that Robb, while governor, was present at parties in Virginia Beach where cocaine was used; that, plus charges of a sexual encounter with a former Miss Virginia were aired by NBC in April 1991. That same month, Robb aides played for reporters a tape, which initially they said they had received anonymously, of Governor Douglas Wilder in a car phone conversation gloating over Robb's problems; in July 1991, three Robb aides resigned by "mutual consent," and later plead guilty to charges of conspiracy. In May 1992, Robb was notified he was the object of a grand jury investigation of the incident, but despite wide speculation, the grand jury voted in January 1993 not to indict him. He immediately announced that he would run for reelection in 1994, and his ratings in the polls rose, but Wilder continued to attack him and the undisputed facts about this episode place Robb in anything but an appealing light. But Robb has shown a certain coolness under political fire which might not be so surprising in a man who has experienced wartime combat.

In the midst of all this controversy, Robb kept up his Senate duties. He chaired the Democratic Senatorial Campaign Committee, increasing its fundraising; the Democrats ended up losing a net of one seat in 1992, but could have done far worse. Robb managed this task despite voting for the Gulf war resolution and for the nomination of Clarence Thomas—two stands fervently opposed by most of the candidates for whom he was working. He was odd

1306   VIRGINIA

Democrat out on the Budget Committee, literally: Chairman Jim Sasser in January 1991 reduced the size of the committee to remove Robb, who favored bigger domestic cuts and more defense spending than Sasser and most other Democrats; Robb backs the Nunn-Domenici deficit reduction proposal and came out for entitlement caps in 1992 and 1993. He came out for lifting the ban on gays in the military, but urged President Clinton to approach the issue "pretty cautiously."

Robb will surely have to fight for his seat in 1994, quite possibly against two well-known competitors. One is Douglas Wilder, long at odds with Robb—in 1982 he forced Robb to back down when Robb picked conservative Democrat Owen Pickett as Senate nominee—and who considers himself the victim of Robb's wrongdoing. Wilder will take him on in a primary, where black voters and Robb detractors might add up to a majority, but he may also run as an Independent candidate in the general, should he lose to Robb in the primary. Wilder has attacked Robb for his support of Clarence Thomas, but his opposition goes beyond issues to character: Robb, he says, is "a Senator not worthy of representing Virginia" and "not fit to hold public office." The Republicans may have a well-known, though terribly flawed, candidate in Oliver North, who as a Marine lieutenant colonel assigned to the National Security Council put together the illegal sale of arms to Iran with proceeds going to the Nicaraguan contras. North made an attractive witness at the July 1990 Iran-contra hearings and by early 1993 was speaking around the state and had spent $500,000 on an undeclared campaign; he can surely raise much more, and indeed has been raising money for Republicans nationally for five years. But by his own account, North is a man who lied about gravely important matters, and whose policies lacked both sanction in law and a modicum of common sense. Republicans with worthier records may also run: Jim Miller, a free market economist who as OMB Director from 1986 to 1988 helped cut the federal budget deficit, to its lowest point since 1981; and Jay Stephens, the former U.S. attorney for the District of Columbia.

Presidential politics. Virginia's fast-growing areas may vote Democratic for the likes of Charles Robb and Douglas Wilder, but they lean Republican for president. Bill Clinton edged George Bush by some 1,700 votes in Fairfax County, but for the most part, the other fast-growing parts of the Washington metro area see growth generated more by the private sector and less by government. The heavy military presence in Tidewater also works against the national Democrats who are seen as too dovish on foreign policy. As a result, this is one of the most Republican states presidentially in the South.

Congressional districting. For all its genteel traditions, Virginia has one of the most partisan— in this case, Democratic—redistricting plans of the 1990s, a rival of Texas and North Carolina in this regard. A new district was created in fast-growing Northern Virginia, which picked a Democrat, though only narrowly; a new black-majority district was created linking Richmond and the Tidewater; two central Virginia Republican districts were collapsed into one. The lines are grotesque, but leave room for some serious contests, particularly when, as in the 6th District in 1992, a popular incumbent retires.

The People: Est. Pop. 1992: 6,377,000; Pop. 1990: 6,187,358, up 3.0% 1990–1992. 2.5% of U.S. total, 12th largest; 31% rural. Median age: 32.6 years. 10.7% 65 years and over. 77.4% White, 18.8% Black, 2.6% Hispanic origin, 2.6% Asian. Households: 56.8% married couple families; 27% married couple fams. w. children; 49% college educ.; median household income: $33,328; per capita income: $15,713; 66.3% owner occupied housing; median house value: $91,000; median monthly rent: $411. 6.4% Unemployment. Voting age pop.: 4,682,620. Registered voters (1992): 3,055,486; no party registration.

Political Lineup: Governor, L. Douglas Wilder (D); Lt. Gov., Donald S. Beyer, Jr. (D); Secy. of Commonwealth, Scott D. Bates (D); Atty. Gen., Steven Rosenthal (D); Treasurer, Eddie N. Moore, Jr. (D); Comptroller, William E. Landsidle (D). State Senate, 40 (22 D and 18 R); State House of Delegates, 100 (58 D, 41 R, and 1 I). Senators, John W. Warner (R) and Charles S. Robb (D). Representatives, 11 (7 D and 4 R).

1992 Presidential Vote

Bush (R) 1,150,517 (45%)
Clinton (D) 1,038,650 (41%)
Perot (I). 348,639 (14%)

1988 Presidential Vote

Bush (R) 1,309,162 (60%)
Dukakis (D). 859,799 (39%)

GOVERNOR

Gov. L. Douglas Wilder (D)

Elected 1989, term expires Jan. 1994; b. Jan. 17, 1931, Richmond; home, Richmond; VA Union U., B.S. 1951, Howard U., J.D. 1959; Baptist; divorced.

Career: Army, 1952–53 (Korea); Practicing atty., 1959–89; VA Senate, 1969–85; VA Lt. Gov., 1985–89.

Office: State Capitol, Richmond 23219, 804-786-2211.

Election Results

1989 gen.	L. Douglas Wilder (D)	896,936	(50%)
	J. Marshall Coleman (R)	890,195	(50%)
1989 prim.	L. Douglas Wilder (D), nominated by convention		
1985 gen.	Gerald L. (Jerry) Baliles (D) . . .	741,438	(55%)
	Wyatt B. Durette, Jr. (R)	601,652	(44%)

SENATORS

Sen. John W. Warner (R)

Elected 1978, seat up 1996; b. Feb. 18, 1927, Washington, D.C.; home, Middleburg; Washington and Lee U., B.S., 1949, U. of VA, LL.B. 1953; Episcopalian; divorced.

Career: Navy, 1944–46 (WWII), Marine Corps, 1950–52 (Korea); Law Clerk, U.S. Court of Appeals Chief Judge Barrett Prettyman, 1953–54; Practicing atty., 1954–56, 1960–69; Asst. U.S. Atty., 1956–60; Undersecy. of the U.S. Navy, 1969–72, Secy., 1972–74; Dir., Amer. Rev. Bicentennial Comm., 1974–76.

Offices: 225 RSOB 20510, 202-224-2023. Also 1100 E. Main St., Richmond 23219, 804-771-2579; 805 Fed. Bldg., 490 World Trade Ctr., Norfolk 23510, 804-441-3079; 235 Fed. Bldg., 180 W. Main St., Abingdon 24210, 703-628-8158; and 1003 Dominion Bank Bldg., 213 S. Jefferson St., Roanoke 24011, 703-832-4676.

Committees: *Armed Services* (2d of 9 R): Coalition Defense and Reinforcing Forces (RMM); Nuclear Deterrence, Arms Control and Defense Intelligence; Regional Defense and Contingency Forces. *Environment and Public Works* (4th of 7 R): Superfund, Recycling and Solid Waste Management; Toxic Substances, Research and Development; Water Resources, Transportation, Public Buildings and Economic Development (RMM). *Intelligence (Select)* (Vice Chmn. of 8 R). *Rules and Administration* (4th of 7 R).

Group Ratings

	ADA	ACLU	CDF	COPE	CFA	LCV	ACU	NTLC	NSI	COC	CEI
1992	20	27	30	17	25	8	74	83	90	100	71
1991	20	—	55	25	28	27	76	—	—	80	60

National Journal Ratings

	1991 LIB	—	1991 CONS	1992 LIB	—	1992 CONS
Economic	23%	—	76%	15%	—	80%
Social	31%	—	66%	30%	—	69%
Foreign	13%	—	77%	10%	—	80%

Key Votes of the 102d Congress

1. $ for Homeownership	FOR	5. Clarence Thomas Nom. FOR	9. Use Force in Gulf FOR
2. Have Cap Gains Debate	FOR	6. Lmt Death Row Appeal FOR	10. Keep Salvador Aid FOR
3. Remove Budget Walls	AGN	7. Handgun Wait/5-Day FOR	11. Cut $1B from SDI AGN
4. Ban Striker Replace	AGN	8. Abortion Gag Rule AGN	12. Override China MFN AGN

Key Votes of the 103d Congress

1. Family Leave　　　AGN　　2. HIV Immigrants　　AGN　　3. Clinton Budget　　AGN

Election Results

1990 general	John W. Warner (R)	876,782	(81%)	($1,219,726)
	Nancy B. Spannaus (I)...............	196,755	(18%)	
	Other...............................	10,153	(1%)	
1990 primary	John W. Warner (R), nominated by convention			
1984 general	John W. Warner (R)	1,406,194	(70%)	($2,974,498)
	Edythe C. Harrison (D)	601,142	(30%)	($492,201)

Sen. Charles S. Robb (D)

Elected 1988, seat up 1994; b. June 26, 1939, Phoenix, AZ; home, McLean; U. of WI, B.B.A. 1961, U. of VA, J.D. 1973; Episcopalian; married (Lynda).

Career: Marine Corps, 1961–1970 (Vietnam), Marine Corps Reserves, 1970–91; Law Clerk, Judge John Butzner, U.S. Court of Appeals, 1973–74; Practicing atty., 1974–77, 1986–88; VA Lt. Gov., 1978–82; VA Gov., 1982–86.

Offices: 493 RSOB, 20515, 202-224-4024. Also 1001 E. Broad St., Richmond 23219, 804-771-2221; 310 1st St., SW, #102, Roanoke 24011, 703-985-0103; Signet Bank Bldg., 530 Main St., Danville 24541, 804-791-0330; Dominion Towers, 999 Waterside Dr., Norfolk 23510, 804-441-3124; 1 Court Sq., #340, Harrisonburg 22801, 703-432-1551; and Dominion Bank Bldg., Main St., Clintwood 24288, 703-926-4104.

Committees: *Armed Services* (10th of 11 D): Defense Technology, Acquisition and Industrial Base; Military Readiness and Defense Infrastructure; Regional Defense and Contingency Forces. *Commerce, Science and Transportation* (9th of 11 D): Communications; Science, Technology and Space; Surface Transportation. *Foreign Relations* (8th of 11 D): East Asian and Pacific Affairs (Chmn.); Near Eastern and South Asian Affairs; Western Hemisphere and Peace Corps Affairs. *Joint Economic Committee* (5th of 10).

Group Ratings

	ADA	ACLU	CDF	COPE	CFA	LCV	ACU	NTLC	NSI	COC	CEI
1992	60	82	50	75	92	67	30	17	100	30	29
1991	60	—	73	67	78	80	43	—	—	10	24

National Journal Ratings

	1991 LIB — 1991 CONS			1992 LIB — 1992 CONS		
Economic	66%	—	31%	47%	—	52%
Social	62%	—	37%	69%	—	26%
Foreign	45%	—	54%	37%	—	60%

Key Votes of the 102d Congress

1. $ for Homeownership	AGN	5. Clarence Thomas Nom.	FOR	9. Use Force in Gulf	FOR
2. Have Cap Gains Debate	AGN	6. Lmt Death Row Appeal	AGN	10. Keep Salvador Aid	FOR
3. Remove Budget Walls	AGN	7. Handgun Wait/5-Day	FOR	11. Cut $1B from SDI	AGN
4. Ban Striker Replace	FOR	8. Abortion Gag Rule	AGN	12. Override China MFN	FOR

Key Votes of the 103d Congress

1. Family Leave	FOR	2. HIV Immigrants	FOR	3. Clinton Budget	FOR

Election Results

1988 general	Charles S. Robb (D)................. 1,474,086	(71%)	($2,881,666)
	Maurice A. Dawkins (R) 593,652	(29%)	($282,229)
1988 primary	Charles S. Robb (D), nominated by convention		
1982 general	Paul S. Trible, Jr. (R)................ 724,571	(51%)	($2,170,961)
	Richard J. Davis (D)................. 690,839	(49%)	($1,192,203)

FIRST DISTRICT

When the first British settlers sailed up the estuaries that flow into the Chesapeake Bay, they were searching for gold, hoping to sail back soon with fortunes. But they couldn't help noticing that the spot where the James River feeds into the Bay, now Hampton Roads, was a fine natural harbor, with calm, deep water and good anchorages. There they established a civilization whose elegance is recalled in the craftsmanship of restored Williamsburg and whose coarseness and brutality is brought to life by the story of Jamestown and the other beleaguered settlements. Tidewater Virginia brought slavery to America and tobacco to the world, and slave-raised tobacco was the center of its economy in the colonial era and in the years afterward, when its most talented sons left its depleted soil for better opportunities elsewhere.

Now the economy and tone of life in Tidewater Virginia are set by the American military. Fifty years ago, as America was on the brink of world war, the Navy base at Norfolk and the Newport News Shipbuilding and Drydock Company across Hampton Roads became the center of American naval might in the Atlantic. Just before World War II, there were some 369,000 people living on both sides of Hampton Roads. Today there are 1.4 million—a population collected not just from the local rural hinterland but from all over the country, making this a metropolitan area that is not so much southern in atmosphere as it is, in the manner of military bases abroad, national. But you can still see this area's origins in the Shipbuilding and Drydock Company that lies over the flat neighborhoods lining the baysides, with its ships looming larger than life, their turrets and superstructures bristling with armored might. This is, among other things, the biggest private employer in Virginia. At the height of 1980s naval expansion, 30,000 people worked here, and the Defense Department spent $1.2 billion a year in this area.

Virginia's 1st Congressional District contains much of this territory. Its boundaries are convoluted in order to accommodate the black-majority 3d District. About 45% of the district's residents live on the Peninsula, in and around Newport News, Williamsburg and other Hampton Roads area towns. It also includes the southern tip of the Delmarva Peninsula—Virginia's Eastern Shore, site of the annual roundup of wild Chincoteague ponies, and much of the Northern Neck between the Rappahannock and Potomac Rivers, where Robert "King" Carter, one of the great landowners of colonial Virginia, reigned, and where George Washington and

1310 VIRGINIA

Robert E. Lee were born; the Northern Neck is now growing again for the first time in two centuries. The 1st also dips south to the Hanover County suburbs outside of Richmond. Ancestrally, most of this area is Democratic, but with black precincts shorn away, the 1st now is pretty clearly Republican, voting 49%–34% for George Bush over Bill Clinton in 1992.

The congressman from the 1st District is Herb Bateman, who has deep roots in the area— deeper indeed than many Hampton Roads area locals, who were brought here by the military. Bateman was a sometime opponent, sometime ally of Byrd Democrats, and represented Newport News in the Virginia Senate for 15 years. He switched parties and became a Republican in 1976. He was outmaneuvered for the congressional nomination here in 1976 and for the lieutenant governor nomination in 1981, but when the district became open again in 1982 he easily won the nomination and then won the seat over a substitute after the first Democratic opponent withdrew. Bateman has a conservative record on economic and defense issues, but can be moderate on cultural matters at times. He has served on the Armed Services Committee since 1985, backing higher defense spending in the middle 1980s and warning after the end of the Cold War that America must "maintain a flexible military capability that can quickly respond to a crisis anywhere in the world." He led the effort to build two new Nimitz-class aircraft carriers at Newport News. He supports more pay for military personnel and pushes for NASA research at the Langley space center in Hampton. He has sought money for dredging in Hampton and cleanup of the Chesapeake Bay. He has also worked to set aside funds for the nation's only Continuing Electron Beam Accelerator Facility, which is being built in Newport News. Bateman, when not securing district pork, has called for cuts in spending generally and decried the Democrats' "manufactured budget crisis."

Bateman has had to face some serious challenges. In 1986, Robert Scott, then state senator and now congressman from the 3d District, held him to 56%. In 1990, former area TV anchorman Andy Fox held Bateman to 51%. Fox, energetic and effervescent, ran again, while Bateman underwent radiation treatment for prostate cancer in summer 1992. But the new district lines deprived Fox of many Democratic votes, and this time it was Bateman who carried the Peninsula handily, winning 58%–39% overall. That result suggests that Bateman now has a pretty safe seat.

The People: Pop. 1990: 563,126; 44% rural; 11% age 65+; 79% White; 18% Black; 1% Asian; 2% Hispanic origin. Voting age pop.: 419,128; 17% Black; 1% Hispanic origin. Households: 63% married couple families; 30% married couple fams. w. children; 47% college educ.; median household income: $33,285; per capita income: $14,675; median gross rent: $491; median house value: $92,700.

1992 Presidential Vote

Bush (R) 120,131 (49%)
Clinton (D) 81,826 (34%)
Perot (I). 39,307 (16%)

1988 Presidential Vote

Bush (R) 133,877 (68%)
Dukakis (D). 63,738 (32%)

Rep. Herbert H. Bateman (R)

Elected 1982; b. Aug. 7, 1928, Elizabeth City, NC; home, Newport News; William and Mary, B.A. 1949, Georgetown U., LL.B. 1956; Protestant; married (Laura).

Career: Air Force, 1951–53; Teacher, Hampton Schl., 1949–51; Law Clerk, Judge Bastian, 1956–57; Practicing atty., 1957–82; VA Senate, 1968–82.

Offices: 2350 RHOB 20515, 202-225-4261. Also 739 Thimble Shoals Blvd., Newport News 23606, 804-873-1132; 4712 Southpoint Pkwy., Fredericksburg 22407, 703-898-2975; and P.O. Box 447, Accomac 23301, 804-787-7836.

Committees: *Armed Services* (5th of 22 R): Military Acquisition; Readiness. *Merchant Marine and Fisheries* (3d of 19 R): Coast Guard and Navigation; Merchant Marine (RMM).

Group Ratings

	ADA	ACLU	COPE	CDF	CFA	LCV	ACU	NTLC	NSI	COC	CEI
1992	10	4	17	40	33	6	84	95	100	88	52
1991	10	—	17	20	17	8	80	—	—	100	56

National Journal Ratings

	1991 LIB — 1991 CONS	1992 LIB — 1992 CONS
Economic	18% — 79%	21% — 76%
Social	32% — 67%	0% — 85%
Foreign	15% — 84%	18% — 74%

Key Votes of the 102d Congress

1. Ban Striker Replace	AGN	5. Handgun Wait/7-Day FOR	9. Use Force in Gulf FOR
2. $ for Homeownership	FOR	6. Overseas Mil. Abortion AGN	10. US Mil. Abroad $ Cut AGN
3. Tax Rich/Cut Mid Cls.	AGN	7. Obscn. Art NEA $ Ban FOR	11. Limit SDI Funds AGN
4. FY93/$15B Def. Cut	AGN	8. Death Pen. from Jury FOR	12. Cuba Trade Embargo FOR

Key Votes of the 103d Congress

1. Family Leave   AGN   2. Deficit Reduction   AGN   3. Stimulus Plan   AGN

Election Results

1992 general	Herbert H. Bateman (R)	133,537	(58%)	($764,820)
	Andrew H. (Andy) Fox (D)	89,814	(39%)	($419,878)
	Donald J. MacLeay, Jr. (I)	8,677	(4%)	($7,755)
1992 primary	Herbert H. Bateman (R), nominated by convention			
1990 general	Herbert H. Bateman (R)	72,000	(51%)	($549,818)
	Andrew H. (Andy) Fox (D)	69,194	(49%)	($102,092)

SECOND DISTRICT

The United States Navy Atlantic fleet berthed in its home port of Norfolk is one of the great awe-inspiring sights in America, or anywhere. The aggregation of destructive power, in the line of towering gray ships, is probably greater than in any other single port in history—over 100 ships are based here, with some 100,000 sailors and Marines, some $2 billion in annual spending. Norfolk has been a Navy port since 1801, and has long been recognized as one of the best natural harbors on the East Coast, one that never freezes and is within 750 miles of three-quarters of

U.S. manufacturing activity. But this was just a small city until World War II, when the Navy, and Norfolk, grew vastly in size.

Now Norfolk is the center of a metropolitan area on both sides of Hampton Roads with over 1.4 million people—fourfold growth since Pearl Harbor, double the national growth rate in the 1980s. One-fourth of the jobs here are with the military, but with its skilled labor force and lack of unions the Hampton Roads area has also attracted a lot of private employment; the port has taken a great deal of business away from the labor-torn port of Baltimore. To the Hampton Roads area, this growth over the last 45 years has brought a wider cross-section of people than is usually found in the South. There is no heavy accent here: the brothy Tidewater accent is heard more often farther up the rivers, toward Richmond. And Norfolk preserves its antique past more carefully now, developing cultural institutions and commercial amenities appropriate to a major metro area. Older parts of Norfolk have the look and feel of a working-class town, with shipyard workers and many blacks (35% of the total), but most of it is white middle-class suburbia, except perhaps for Virginia Beach's string of oceanfront motels.

The 2d Congressional District of Virginia is made up of most of Norfolk and most of Virginia Beach, with boundaries carefully drawn to put heavily black neighborhoods in the black-majority 3d District. The politics here has changed as the area has become more heavily suburban, and the Democrats more associated with defense policy critics. In 1968, the 2d District voted for Hubert Humphrey, as Norfolk cast 65,000 votes and Virginia Beach 37,000. In 1992 the 2d District voted 48%–35% for George Bush, as its portion of Norfolk cast 45,000 votes and Virginia Beach 134,000.

The congressman from the 2d District is Owen Pickett, a conservative Democrat first elected in 1986. An accountant and lawyer with little personal magnetism, a legislator since 1972, he was known as a fiscal conservative and for his hard work restructuring the state retirement system. He was Democratic state chairman in 1981, when Charles Robb won the governorship beginning a string of Democratic victories. Pickett had a setback in 1982, when he was Robb's choice for the Senate but withdrew after Governor Douglas Wilder, then state senator, threatened to run as an independent against him. But by the time he ran for Congress in 1986, the quiet and methodical Pickett had Wilder's support and that of Jesse Jackson's Norfolk coordinator. He also had a Republican opponent plagued by close relationships with tawdry business associates. Pickett carried Norfolk heavily, lost Virginia Beach narrowly, and won 49%–42%.

In the House, Pickett showed his political acumen by getting a new seat created for him on the Armed Services Committee and getting a seat on Merchant Marine as well—two crucial committees for any Norfolk congressman. He stands on issues generally at about the mid-point of the House. He voted for the Gulf war resolution and against family and medical leave; he voted against the Clinton stimulus package and deficit reduction plan in 1993. He objected in early 1993 when the Base Closure Commission put the Norfolk Naval Aviation Depot on its list; he praised Bush's decision to open Hampton Roads ports to ships of the former Soviet Union.

In 1992, after winning reelection twice by wide margins, Pickett was opposed by Republican Jim Chapman, whose battle cry was "Change Congress." Chapman called for broad spending cuts, said Pickett was "soft on crime" and attacked him for voting to raise congressional pay. With the 2d shorn of many black precincts, it was about 7% more Republican, and Chapman held Pickett to a 56%–44% win—solid, but not overwhelming, and perhaps inviting another challenge in 1994.

The People: Pop. 1990: 562,789; 1% rural; 7% age 65+; 77% White; 17% Black; 4% Asian; 1% Other; 3% Hispanic origin. Voting age pop.: 420,036; 15% Black; 3% Hispanic origin. Households: 60% married couple families; 31% married couple fams. w. children; 55% college educ.; median household income: $32,576; per capita income: $14,492; median gross rent: $528; median house value: $92,500.

1992 Presidential Vote

Bush (R)	85,773	(48%)
Clinton (D)	62,946	(35%)
Perot (I)	30,587	(17%)

1988 Presidential Vote

Bush (R)	99,266	(66%)
Dukakis (D)	51,918	(34%)

Rep. Owen Pickett (D)

Elected 1986; b. Aug. 31, 1930, Richmond; home, Virginia Beach; VA Polytechnic Inst., B.S. 1952, U. of Richmond, LL.B. 1955; Baptist; married (Sybil).

Career: Accountant; Practicing atty., 1955–86; VA House of Delegates, 1972–86; Chmn., VA Dem. Party, 1980–82.

Offices: 2430 RHOB 20515, 202-225-4215. Also 112 E. Little Creek Rd., Norfolk 23505, 804-583-5892; and 2710 VA Beach Blvd., Virginia Beach 23452, 804-486-3710.

Committees: *Armed Services* (13th of 34 D): Military Forces and Personnel; Readiness; Research and Technology. *Merchant Marine and Fisheries* (8th of 29 D): Coast Guard and Navigation; Merchant Marine.

Group Ratings

	ADA	ACLU	COPE	CDF	CFA	LCV	ACU	NTLC	NSI	COC	CEI
1992	35	43	25	40	33	19	52	55	100	88	40
1991	25	—	58	70	28	38	35	—	—	60	29

National Journal Ratings

	1991 LIB	—	1991 CONS	1992 LIB	—	1992 CONS
Economic	40%	—	59%	36%	—	63%
Social	50%	—	48%	47%	—	53%
Foreign	46%	—	53%	38%	—	56%

Key Votes of the 102d Congress

1. Ban Striker Replace	AGN	5. Handgun Wait/7-Day	AGN	9. Use Force in Gulf	FOR
2. $ for Homeownership	AGN	6. Overseas Mil. Abortion	FOR	10. US Mil. Abroad $ Cut	AGN
3. Tax Rich/Cut Mid Cls.	AGN	7. Obscn. Art NEA $ Ban	*	11. Limit SDI Funds	AGN
4. FY93/$15B Def. Cut	AGN	8. Death Pen. from Jury	AGN	12. Cuba Trade Embargo	AGN

Key Votes of the 103d Congress

1. Family Leave	AGN	2. Deficit Reduction	AGN	3. Stimulus Plan	AGN

Election Results

1992 general	Owen Pickett (D)	99,253	(56%)	($373,047)
	J. L. (Jim) Chapman (R)	77,797	(44%)	($190,447)
1992 primary	Owen Pickett (D), nominated by convention			
1990 general	Owen Pickett (D)	55,179	(75%)	($82,828)
	Harry G. Broskie (I)	15,915	(22%)	
	Other	2,524	(3%)	

THIRD DISTRICT

The James River was one of the great water highways to America's interior. The first English colonists in 1607 sailed up the broad James and chose one of the marshiest, least healthy spots to establish their settlement at Jamestown. Only a dozen years later, after these settlers almost died out from disease and famine, the first slave ship sailed up the James and offloaded its human cargo: and so began the history of African-American slavery, and of the biracial black-and-white society which grew up in so much of the American South. Nowhere were its effects more visible than along the tidal expanse of the James from the falls at Richmond to where it empties into Hampton Roads and the Atlantic Ocean. Here are great plantation houses along the river, entire communities adorned by the highest architecture and learning of the day but also attended by hundreds of slaves. Charles City County, the site of William Byrd II's Westover, Benjamin Harrison III's Berkeley, John Carter's Shirley, was also the birthplace of two successive presidents, William Henry Harrison and John Tyler. Its population today is heavily black—the demography of the plantation remains.

The 3d Congressional District of Virginia is the state's new black-majority district, stringing together black precincts and communities along the James River from Norfolk and Newport News upriver on the Peninsula and past Jamestown and Charles City County, with spindly extensions into black neighborhoods of Richmond and Petersburg and their suburban fringe. It also includes several rural counties to the north with high black percentages. Great landmarks of Virginia are within its bounds: the James River mansions and Thomas Jefferson's chaste yet subtle Capitol in Richmond, plus Civil War battlefield sites.

Politically, this 3d District has been overwhelmingly Democratic—it voted 65% for Michael Dukakis in 1988—and it was obvious that its congressman would be chosen in the Democratic primary. It turned out to be not much of a contest. Two candidates from Richmond ran and one, state Senator Bobby Scott, from Newport News on the Peninsula, ran as well. Some 63% of the votes were cast in the Norfolk-Peninsula area, and Scott won 83% of those. He won 40% outside the peninsula, for a 67% overall vote. His general election victory was anticlimactic.

Scott grew up in Newport News and went to Harvard and Boston College Law School; he served in the National Guard and Army Reserves and returned home to practice law in 1973. In 1977, he was elected to the House of Delegates and in 1982 to the state Senate, representing a multiracial district in a community where, because of the military tradition of integration, biracial politics comes more naturally than in many parts of the country. Scott first ran for Congress in 1986 and won 44% of the vote against 1st District incumbent Herb Bateman, a good showing. In the legislature, Scott focused on job training, children in low-income families, and infant mortality. He passed a law giving tax incentives to businesses which donate to food banks, soup kitchens and other projects in low-income areas. He is a supporter of abortion rights and an opponent of capital punishment. In the House, he serves on the Judiciary, Education and Labor and Science Committees, and can be expected to have a solid liberal voting record.

The People: Pop. 1990: 560,640; 11% rural; 12% age 65+; 33% White; 64% Black; 1% Asian; 1% Other; 1% Hispanic origin. Voting age pop.: 413,025; 61% Black; 1% Hispanic origin. Households: 42% married couple families; 19% married couple fams. w. children; 36% college educ.; median household income: $22,556; per capita income: $10,558; median gross rent: $398; median house value: $61,700.

1992 Presidential Vote

Clinton (D)	124,857	(65%)
Bush (R)	48,843	(25%)
Perot (I)	16,779	(9%)

1988 Presidential Vote

Dukakis (D)	114,002	(65%)
Bush (R)	62,435	(35%)

Rep. Robert C. (Bobby) Scott (D)

Elected 1992; b. Apr. 30, 1947, Washington, D.C.; home, Newport News; Harvard, B.A. 1969, Boston Col. Law Schl., J.D. 1973; Episcopalian; divorced.

Career: Army Natl. Guard, 1970–73; Army Reserves, 1973–76; Practicing atty., 1973–91; VA House of Delegates, 1977–82; VA Senate, 1983–92.

Offices: 501 CHOB 20515, 202-225-8351. Also 2700 Washington Ave., Newport News 23607, 804-380-1000.

Committees: *Education and Labor* (18th of 28 D): Human Resources; Postsecondary Education and Training; Select Education and Civil Rights. *Judiciary* (18th of 21 D): Economic and Commercial Law. *Science, Space and Technology* (30th of 33 D): Energy.

Group Ratings and 102d Congress Votes: Newly Elected

Key Votes of the 103d Congress

1. Family Leave	FOR	2. Deficit Reduction	FOR	3. Stimulus Plan	FOR

Election Results

1992 general	Robert C. (Bobby) Scott (D)	132,432	(79%)	($500,359)
	Daniel (Dan) Jenkins (R)	35,780	(21%)	($16,318)
1992 primary	Robert C. (Bobby) Scott (D)	23,381	(67%)	
	Jean Wooden Cunningham (D).	7,520	(22%)	
	Jacqueline G. Epps (D).	4,003	(11%)	
1990 general	Newly created district.			

FOURTH DISTRICT

It took English settlers the better part of a century to explore, clear and cultivate Tidewater Virginia, the eastern part of the state where the riversides are lapped by the rise and fall of the tides. This was a water-oriented colony, where planters kept their houses and farm buildings on the river and sent their tobacco and produce on boats headed straight for London or Bristol. This was the scene of the first permanent English settlement, at Jamestown, and of its first revolution, Bacon's Rebellion, in 1676. It was the scene of bitter fighting almost 200 years later in the Civil War, as Union troops invested the battlements of the small industrial city of Petersburg, 25 miles south of Richmond. In between Tidewater and Petersburg are the flat lands of Southside Virginia fanning south from the James River—tobacco lands when the English first settled them; today they also produce Virginia's peanut crop and its Smithfield hams.

The 4th Congressional District of Virginia includes much of the Tidewater area. Nearly half its people are in the Hampton Roads area, in Portsmouth, a Navy port and industrial town with a charming old town section, and the suburban expanse of Chesapeake and Suffolk Counties. It takes in the peanut fields south of the James River, much of the area around Petersburg and Hopewell, with its Allied Chemical plant facing 18th Century plantations, and juts to lightly populated rural counties north and west of Richmond. Politically, this is a Democratic area, or would be if most of the black precincts had not been placed in the new black-majority 3d District; in its current boundaries, the 4th District voted for George Bush in 1988 and 1992.

The congressman from the 4th District is Norman Sisisky. He started off with a small Pepsi bottling company in Petersburg and built it into one of the largest soft drink bottling operations in the South, accumulating a multi-million dollar fortune. In 1982, he ran for Congress, with enough money to finance a solid campaign and an appeal for black voters, then 39% of the district. In the House, he immediately got a seat on the Armed Services Committee; the Hampton Roads area has the nation's largest accumulation of Navy bases, and a big Army base near Petersburg. Sisisky's voting record on economic and cultural issues is moderate; on foreign and defense policy, he's more conservative, supporting the defense buildups of the 1980s and resisting some of the builddown—cuts in the Navy's F-14 fighter jet and Marine Corps' Osprey helicopter, for example—in the 1990s. In 1993 he became chairman of the Armed Services Oversight and Investigations Subcommittee, and soon launched a probe of the troubled C-17 transport. On domestic issues, he has worked to save peanut and tobacco subsidies and has tried to prohibit deceptive television "infomercials." He was one of 22 House Democrats to vote against the Clinton stimulus package in March 1993. Redistricting reduced the Democratic percentage in the 4th District by at least 5%. But it is still 32% black, the second highest in Virginia, and Sisisky was reelected by a wide margin in 1992.

The People: Pop. 1990: 563,206; 37% rural; 12% age 65+; 66% White; 32% Black; 1% Asian; 1% Hispanic origin. Voting age pop.: 415,363; 31% Black; 1% Hispanic origin. Households: 61% married couple families; 29% married couple fams. w. children; 38% college educ.; median household income: $30,425; per capita income: $12,887; median gross rent: $424; median house value: $72,900.

1992 Presidential Vote			1988 Presidential Vote		
Bush (R)	106,392	(46%)	Bush (R)	118,408	(60%)
Clinton (D)	90,641	(39%)	Dukakis (D)	77,544	(40%)
Perot (I)	31,467	(14%)			

Rep. Norman Sisisky (D)

Elected 1982; b. June 9, 1927, Baltimore, MD; home, Petersburg; VA Commonwealth U., B.A. 1949; Jewish; married (Rhoda).

Career: Navy, 1945–46; Pres., Pepsi-Cola Bottling Co. of Petersburg, 1949–82; VA House of Delegates, 1973–82.

Offices: 2352 RHOB 20515, 202-225-6365. Also Emporia Exec. Ctr., 425-H S. Main St., Emporia 23847, 804-634-5575; 43 Rives Rd., Petersburg 23805, 804-732-2544; and 309 County St., #204, Portsmouth 23704, 804-393-2068.

Committees: *Armed Services* (8th of 34 D): Military Acquisition; Oversight and Investigations (Chmn.). *Small Business* (6th of 27 D): Procurement, Taxation and Tourism; Regulation, Business Opportunities and Technology.

Group Ratings

	ADA	ACLU	COPE	CDF	CFA	LCV	ACU	NTLC	NSI	COC	CEI
1992	55	45	55	40	47	13	48	44	100	88	34
1991	30	—	73	40	39	38	39	—	—	67	33

National Journal Ratings

	1991 LIB — 1991 CONS		1992 LIB — 1992 CONS	
Economic	41%	— 59%	44%	— 55%
Social	58%	— 42%	50%	— 49%
Foreign	48%	— 51%	18%	— 74%

Key Votes of the 102d Congress

1. Ban Striker Replace	AGN	5. Handgun Wait/7-Day	AGN	9. Use Force in Gulf	FOR
2. $ for Homeownership	FOR	6. Overseas Mil. Abortion	FOR	10. US Mil. Abroad $ Cut	AGN
3. Tax Rich/Cut Mid Cls.	FOR	7. Obscn. Art NEA $ Ban	FOR	11. Limit SDI Funds	AGN
4. FY93/$15B Def. Cut	AGN	8. Death Pen. from Jury	AGN	12. Cuba Trade Embargo	FOR

Key Votes of the 103d Congress

1. Family Leave	AGN	2. Deficit Reduction	FOR	3. Stimulus Plan	AGN

Election Results

1992 general	Norman Sisisky (D)	147,649	(68%)	($466,010)
	A. J. (Tony) Zevgolis (R)	68,286	(32%)	($82,068)
1992 primary	Norman Sisisky (D), nominated by convention			
1990 general	Norman Sisisky (D)	71,051	(78%)	($275,502)
	Don L. McReynolds (I)	12,295	(14%)	($19,883)
	Loretta F. Chandler (I)	7,102	(8%)	

FIFTH DISTRICT

Southside Virginia is a geographic name which for years was shorthand for a state of mind. Here is Appomattox Court House, where Robert E. Lee surrendered to his onetime subordinate Ulysses S. Grant; here also is Prince Edward County, where Harry Byrd's massive resistance shut down public schools in 1957 rather than obey a federal court desegregation order. This land north of the dividing line Colonel William Byrd surveyed in 1728 has some variety. Its eastern counties are flat and humid—frontier in the late colonial period, plantation country by 1800, now peanut fields and pine forests. To the west, into the Piedmont, the land gradually gets hillier. Here are textile mill towns and furniture manufacturing centers—Danville, Martinsville and a dozen smaller towns. Westward, nearer to the mountains, is more livestock and less tobacco, and the thick syrupy tones of the Southside Virginia accent turn to mountain twangs.

The 5th Congressional District consists of much of Southside Virginia, west of metropolitan Richmond and at some points up to the Blue Ridge. It includes Charlottesville and much of surrounding Albemarle County, but skirts around Lynchburg. Historically, politics here was Democratic, segregationist and conservative, run by chain-smoking local bankers and court-house lawyers, personified by the late House of Delegates Speaker A. L. Philpott. But that has changed. The 5th District contains the childhood homes of both Gerald Baliles, the distinctly urbane and moderate governor elected in 1985, and Mary Sue Terry, attorney general since then and the 1993 Democratic candidate for governor. Another change occurred with the death in 1988 of Congressman Dan Daniel, the last Virginia member to have been endorsed by the Byrd machine in its prime.

The congressman now is Lewis F. Payne, a middle-of-the-road Democrat, developer of the Wintergreen ski resort, which by 1988 accounted for half the payrolls in rural Nelson County. Payne won the seat in a June 1988 special election over Republican Linda Arey, a Reagan appointee who had returned home to run. "Before you ask someone what they will do, ask them what they have done," Payne argued, and financed much of his own campaign. Payne won the special election with 59% of the votes; Arey, in a huff, resigned the nomination for the November election and moved back to Washington. Payne won again in November by a narrower margin, was unopposed in 1990, and won solidly in 1992. Payne started off on Public Works and supported the Intermodal Surface Transportation Act of 1991. He said he wanted to "increase the economic pie not redistribute it" and supports the balanced budget amendment.

1318   VIRGINIA

Payne spent much of 1992 working and holding hearings on health care, and with Jim Cooper of Tennessee, introduced a bill proposing managed competition; in 1993, he won a seat on the Ways and Means Committee, where he may have some chance of putting it into effect.

The People: Pop. 1990: 562,273; 67% rural; 14% age 65+; 74% White; 25% Black; 1% Asian; 1% Hispanic origin. Voting age pop.: 432,813; 23% Black. Households: 58% married couple families; 24% married couple fams. w. children; 32% college educ.; median household income: $24,807; per capita income: $11,675; median gross rent: $325; median house value: $55,400.

1992 Presidential Vote			1988 Presidential Vote		
Bush (R)	104,236	(46%)	Bush (R)	118,464	(61%)
Clinton (D)	90,769	(40%)	Dukakis (D)	77,130	(39%)
Perot (I)	26,978	(12%)			

Rep. L. F. Payne (D)

Elected June 1988; b. July 9, 1945, Amherst; home, Nellysford; VA Military Inst., B.S. 1967, U. of VA, M.B.A. 1973; Presbyterian; married (Susan).

Career: Army Corps of Engineers, 1967–69; Engineering Assoc., C&P Telephone, 1970–71; Mgr., Wintergreen Development Inc., 1973–75, Pres., 1976–85, Chmn. 1985–88.

Offices: 1119 LHOB 20515, 202-225-4711. Also 301 P.O. Bldg., 700 Main St., Danville 24541, 804-792-1280; Abbitt Fed. Bldg., 103 S. Main St., Farmville 23901, 804-392-8331; and 103 E. Water St., #302, Charlottesville 22902, 804-295-6372.

Committees: *Ways and Means* (17th of 24 D): Select Revenue Measures; Trade.

Group Ratings

	ADA	ACLU	COPE	CDF	CFA	LCV	ACU	NTLC	NSI	COC	CEI
1992	65	43	50	60	60	38	32	30	100	63	33
1991	35	—	58	50	44	69	50	—	—	70	42

National Journal Ratings

	1991 LIB — 1991 CONS		1992 LIB — 1992 CONS	
Economic	39% —	60%	48% —	50%
Social	44% —	55%	47% —	53%
Foreign	51% —	46%	30% —	64%

Key Votes of the 102d Congress

1. Ban Striker Replace	AGN	5. Handgun Wait/7-Day	AGN	9. Use Force in Gulf	FOR
2. $ for Homeownership	FOR	6. Overseas Mil. Abortion	FOR	10. US Mil. Abroad $ Cut	AGN
3. Tax Rich/Cut Mid Cls.	FOR	7. Obscn. Art NEA $ Ban	FOR	11. Limit SDI Funds	FOR
4. FY93/$15B Def. Cut	FOR	8. Death Pen. from Jury	AGN	12. Cuba Trade Embargo	FOR

Key Votes of the 103d Congress

1. Family Leave	AGN	2. Deficit Reduction	FOR	3. Stimulus Plan	FOR

Election Results

1992 general	L. F. Payne (D)	133,031	(69%)	($414,696)
	W. A. (Bill) Hurlburt (R)	60,030	(31%)	($54,705)
1992 primary	L. F. Payne (D), nominated by convention			
1990 general	L. F. Payne (D)	66,532	(99%)	($317,271)
	Other	373	(1%)	

SIXTH DISTRICT

Starting before the Revolutionary War, down the Valley of Virginia west of the Blue Ridge on the great Wagon Road from Pennsylvania, came settlers: Englishmen and Scots, German Protestants and Mennonites and Moravians—members of religious communities and fiercely independent farmers, but almost no plantation slave-owners. This was not tobacco land, like the farms with exhausted soil to the east, but land planted in wheat, corn and hay, crops which could be rotated and which an individual farmer and his family could handle. Higher education and industry flourished here more than in most of Virginia east of the Blue Ridge. In Lexington alone are Washington and Lee University and the Virginia Military Institute; Robert E. Lee headed the former and Stonewall Jackson taught at the latter. Roanoke, farther south in the Valley, grew as the headquarters and chief junction of the Norfolk and Southern Railroad. Politically, election returns over the years recall the old Wagon Road, for the Valley has long had its own brand of Republicanism, an insurgent faith, a credo hospitable to economic assistance for the little guy, and Valley Republicans ran brave campaigns against Harry Byrd's Democrats from time to time.

The 6th Congressional District of Virginia covers the heart of the Valley of Virginia, from Harrisonburg south to Roanoke. It crosses over the Blue Ridge to take in Lynchburg. A solidly Republican area in most elections, it even gave George Bush a big margin in 1992. For 10 years, it was represented by a moderate Democratic Congressman, Jim Olin, a retired General Electric vice president active in civic affairs. When he retired in 1992, it fell again into Republican hands. It was the Democrats who had a struggle for the nomination, with a multi-ballot district convention in which the three candidates' backers wore T-shirts of different colors: the teal team of Vinton insurance agency executive Steve Musselwhite prevailed over the red team of Roanoke lawyer John Fishwick when some labor delegates went Musselwhite's way despite his opposition to the striker replacement bill. Musselwhite ran a vigorous campaign, outspending the Republican and putting the first ads on the air.

The new congressman, however, is Bob Goodlatte, a Republican who fresh out of law school went to work for Congressman Caldwell Butler's Roanoke office and has been active in Republican politics and running campaigns ever since. Goodlatte campaigned for the line-item veto, a tax credit for first-time homebuyers and promised to get legislation to speed up construction of the U.S. 29 bypass. Both candidates opposed national health insurance and backed workfare, but disagreed on some important details. Goodlatte favored medical IRAs and vouchers for the uninsured, and tax credits and incentives for businesses to hire people on welfare; Musselwhite came out for more government regulation of health care and job creation. Musselwhite was thrown on the defensive by charges that he wrote a letter to a judge seeking leniency for a close friend convicted of tax evasion. But the real story here seemed to be pure party preference. George Bush carried the 6th District by 12%; Goodlatte won by 20%, 60%–40%.

In the House, Goodlatte is a member of the Judiciary and Agriculture Committees. He is one of the Republican freshmen who pushed successfully for committee term limits on ranking minority members.

The People: Pop. 1990: 562,426; 34% rural; 15% age 65+; 87% White; 11% Black; 1% Asian; 1% Hispanic origin. Voting age pop.: 437,645; 11% Black; 1% Hispanic origin. Households: 57% married couple families; 24% married couple fams. w. children; 39% college educ.; median household income: $27,155; per capita income: $13,017; median gross rent: $358; median house value: $64,600.

1992 Presidential Vote			1988 Presidential Vote		
Bush (R)	111,405	(49%)	Bush (R)	122,874	(62%)
Clinton (D)	84,037	(37%)	Dukakis (D)	74,994	(38%)
Perot (I)	29,207	(13%)			

Rep. Bob Goodlatte (R)

Elected 1992; b. Sept. 22, 1952, Holyoke, MA; home, Roanoke; Bates Col., B.A. 1974, Washington and Lee Law Schl., J.D. 1977; Christian Scientist; married (Maryellen).

Career: Dist. Dir., U.S. Rep. Caldwell Butler, 1977–79; Practicing atty., 1979–92.

Offices: 214 CHOB 20515, 202-225-5431. Also 540 Crestar Plz., 10 Franklin Rd., SE, Roanoke 24011, 703-982-4672; 114 N. Central Ave., Staunton 24401, 703-885-3861; 2 S. Main St., #A, Harrisonburg 22801, 703-432-2391; and 916 Main St., #300 Lynchburg 24504, 804-845-8306.

Committees: *Agriculture* (14th of 19 R): Livestock; Specialty Crops and Natural Resources. *Judiciary* (14th of 14 R): Administrative Law and Governmental Relations; Economic and Commercial Law.

Group Ratings and 102d Congress Votes: Newly Elected

Key Votes of the 103d Congress

1. Family Leave	AGN	2. Deficit Reduction	AGN	3. Stimulus Plan	AGN

Election Results

1992 general	Bob Goodlatte (R)	127,309	(60%)	($452,048)
	Stephen Alan Musselwhite (D)	84,618	(40%)	($597,020)
1992 primary	Bob Goodlatte (R), nominated by convention			
1990 general	James R. Olin (D)	92,968	(83%)	($199,904)
	Gerald E. (Laser) Berg (I)	18,148	(16%)	
	Other	2,261	(1%)	

SEVENTH DISTRICT

In the center of Virginia, on a hill in downtown Richmond above the James River, is Thomas Jefferson's Capitol, one of the first classical-style buildings in North America, chaste and simple in the Jefferson style. Monument Avenue, Richmond's grand 140-foot wide boulevard, is punctuated by circles, each with a statue of a Confederate hero—Robert E. Lee (62 feet tall, dedicated Memorial Day 1890), Jeb Stuart, Jefferson Davis, Stonewall Jackson, Matthew Fountain Maury, "the Pathfinder of the Sea." On the grid streets of Church Hill, on the other side of the Capitol, Douglas Wilder grew up in a segregated neighborhood, working as a waiter in a hotel he could not check into, looking up the downtown streets at office buildings he could only dream of working in, staring at the Capitol where it was assumed he could never hold an office. It is not surprising that there eventually was a clash between the whites who occupied the leading places in Richmond's great institutions—the Virginia Electric and Power Company, the big Main Street banks and the big law firms, the Philip Morris tobacco company and the

Richmond newspapers—and the blacks who have become a majority within the Richmond city limits. When blacks first won a majority on the Richmond council in the 1970s, the outgoing administration feared the newcomers would tear down the statue of Lee, and so deeded it to the state. Now the state's governor is a black, and the Martin Luther King holiday law pays homage to Confederate heroes as well as to the civil rights leader. But there remains a gulf between these two separate cultures, in some ways connected but still not unified.

That gulf is now reflected in the Richmond metropolitan area congressional districts. Most black precincts, including downtown Richmond and the Capitol, are collected in the black-majority 3d District, which extends downriver along the James to Newport News and Norfolk. The mostly white precincts on the west side of Richmond, most of suburban Henrico, Chesterfield and Hanover Counties are in the 7th District, which extends north past James Madison's home at Montpelier to Culpeper County and the Blue Ridge Mountains. But much of the 7th's population is in metro Richmond. Demographically, the 7th District is only 10% black; politically, it is overwhelmingly Republican, 73% for George Bush in 1988, for Bush over Clinton 54%–30% in 1992.

The congressman from the 7th District is Thomas Bliley, who started off in politics as a conservative Democrat and was mayor of Richmond from 1970 to 1977. In 1980, he was elected to this seat as a Republican by a 53%–33% margin, and has been reelected easily every two years. He got a seat on the Energy and Commerce Committee, and became ranking Republican on John Dingell's Oversight Committee; in 1993, he switched to ranking Republican on Henry Waxman's Health Subcommittee. He has worked with Democrats on issues like rewriting the Public Utilities Holding Company Reform Act to open up the electric grid, modifying Medicaid formulas, trying to provide home medical services to create shorter hospital stays under Medicare and getting drug discounts for veterans' hospitals. He opposes restrictions on tobacco and cigarettes (the Philip Morris plant on the south side of the James River is one of the largest in the world). He favors free broadcasting time for qualified political candidates and wants to make carjacking a federal crime. He sought to require that those performing abortions under Title X for girls under 18 be required to send parental notification or seek a judicial bypass. He successfully passed an amendment to bar immigrants with the HIV virus from entering the country. He has been co-chairman of the Congressional Adoption Caucus. In 1991, Bliley became ranking Republican on the District of Columbia Committee, and worked with incoming Mayor Sharon Pratt Kelly and Delegate Eleanor Holmes Norton on Washington, D.C. affairs, starting with a $300 million increase in federal funds.

Redistricting not only changed Bliley's district, but brought into it another Republican incumbent, one-year Congressman George Allen, elected in November 1991 to replace D. French Slaughter, Jr., a conservative Republican who resigned for health reasons. But Allen considered running in the redrawn 10th, which contained much of his old district, not in the 7th, where as an unknown he would have stood little chance against Bliley; after a bit of analysis, Allen decided to leave the House and run for Governor of Virginia, and in June 1993, became the party's nominee. So Bliley won without major party opposition, (and has the satisfaction of representing the same area represented in the 1st Congress 204 years ago by James Madison.)

The People: Pop. 1990: 562,729; 26% rural; 11% age 65+; 87% White; 10% Black; 2% Asian; 1% Hispanic origin. Voting age pop.: 424,682; 9% Black; 1% Hispanic origin. Households: 59% married couple families; 29% married couple fams. w. children; 56% college educ.; median household income: $38,865; per capita income: $18,360; median gross rent: $520; median house value: $91,300.

1992 Presidential Vote			1988 Presidential Vote		
Bush (R)	154,575	(54%)	Bush (R)	164,525	(73%)
Clinton (D)	85,357	(30%)	Dukakis (D)	61,268	(27%)
Perot (I)	42,724	(15%)			

Rep. Thomas J. Bliley, Jr. (R)

Elected 1980; b. Jan. 28, 1932, Chesterfield Cnty.; home, Richmond; Georgetown U., B.A. 1952; Catholic; married (Mary Virginia).

Career: Navy, 1952–55; Funeral home Dir., 1955–80; Richmond City Cncl. 1968–77, Vice Mayor 1968–70, Mayor, 1970–77.

Offices: 2241 RHOB 20515, 202-225-2815. Also 4914 Fitzhugh Ave., #101, Richmond 23230, 804-771-2809.

Committees: *District of Columbia* (RMM of 4 R). *Energy and Commerce* (2d of 17 R): Health and the Environment (RMM); Telecommunications and Finance.

Group Ratings

	ADA	ACLU	COPE	CDF	CFA	LCV	ACU	NTLC	NSI	COC	CEI
1992	15	0	25	10	13	0	96	89	100	86	77
1991	0	—	17	10	11	0	95	—	—	100	73

National Journal Ratings

	1991 LIB — 1991 CONS		1992 LIB — 1992 CONS	
Economic	4%	— 90%	0%	— 91%
Social	19%	— 78%	22%	— 78%
Foreign	0%	— 88%	0%	— 82%

Key Votes of the 102d Congress

1. Ban Striker Replace	AGN	5. Handgun Wait/7-Day AGN	9. Use Force in Gulf FOR
2. $ for Homeownership	FOR	6. Overseas Mil. AbortionAGN	10. US Mil. Abroad $ CutAGN
3. Tax Rich/Cut Mid Cls.AGN		7. Obscn. Art NEA $ Ban FOR	11. Limit SDI Funds AGN
4. FY93/$15B Def. Cut	AGN	8. Death Pen. from Jury FOR	12. Cuba Trade Embargo FOR

Key Votes of the 103d Congress

1. Family Leave   AGN   2. Deficit Reduction   AGN   3. Stimulus Plan   AGN

Election Results

1992 general	Thomas J. Bliley, Jr. (R)	211,618	(83%)	($698,964)
	Gerald E. (Jerry) Berg (I)	43,267	(17%)	
1992 primary	Thomas J. Bliley, Jr. (R), nominated by convention			
1990 general	Thomas J. Bliley, Jr. (R)	77,125	(65%)	($710,739)
(VA 3)	James A. Starke, Jr. (D)	36,253	(31%)	($57,909)
	Other	4,776	(4%)	

EIGHTH DISTRICT

Two hundred years ago, when George Washington trod the brick sidewalks of Alexandria, Virginia, on his way to market or court or church, this was the largest city in northern Virginia, and dwarfed Georgetown, Maryland, just up the Potomac River; what is now Capitol Hill and downtown Washington were just hills above the river's mud flats. As Washington grew, Northern Virginia seemed left behind. The District of Columbia retroceded its land south of the Potomac—now Alexandria and Arlington—to Virginia in 1846 because it seemed obvious that the federal government would never need it, and it was 97 years before the first federal building was built on the Virginia side—the Pentagon; Franklin Roosevelt wondered out loud what they would do with all that space after the war. When the Pentagon was built, Alexandria and the rural countryside of Northern Virginia were represented in Congress by Judge Howard W. Smith, a Byrd Democrat, who saw as his mission the maintenance of the standards of George Washington, Thomas Jefferson and Robert E. Lee. Yet by the 1960s, even as Judge Smith kept his law offices in Old Town, Alexandria, the area was changing around him. New subdivision-dwellers with white-collar jobs and lots of children wanted schools with good academic programs—not the segregated schoolhouses Judge Smith's friends were willing to finance. They wanted freeways and traffic lights, planning instituted to regulate development, parks, playgrounds and recreation facilities. Smith's district was moved farther out into the countryside, two-party politics came to the suburbs, and local governments got to work. The congressional seat here, though often bitterly contested, was held from 1952 to 1974 by Republican Joel Broyhill, a real estate developer who ran a fine constituency service operation in a district more than one-third of whose residents were federal employees. But Democrats won many legislative and local offices .

Now the onetime suburbs of Arlington and Alexandria have become central cities of a sort—or edge cities, in Joel Garreau's term—themselves. Giant office developments sprang up from rail yards in Crystal City and from used car lots in Rosslyn. Vietnamese and other Asian-Americans have moved into these neighborhoods, and one of America's biggest Vietnamese commercial districts is in Clarendon, about a mile from Arlington National Cemetery and Fort Myer. Politically, this once hotly-contested territory is now solidly Democratic; in the three-way 1992 presidential race Bill Clinton carried Arlington and Alexandria with 57% of the vote.

The 8th Congressional District of Virginia consists of Arlington County and the Cities of Alexandria and Falls Church. It also takes in two separate parts of Fairfax County—the portion of high-income McLean inside the Capital Beltway and several areas south of Alexandria's Old Town: the gentle landscapes of Mount Vernon, lower-income Groveton along the old U.S. 1, suburban Springfield and the more rural areas around Lorton prison and Fort Belvoir. This is a newly shaped district for the 1990s, designed by a Democratic legislature and governor to be solidly Democratic; formerly there were two marginal Northern Virginia districts, now there is the safely Democratic 8th, the safely Republican 10th and the toss-up (currently Democratic) 11th.

The congressman from the 8th District is Jim Moran, an oft-embattled Alexandria politician with traces in his accent of his Massachusetts roots. He was elected to the Alexandria Council in 1979 and vice mayor in 1982; unable to afford a lawyer, in 1984 he pleaded no contest to a conflict of interest charge and resigned from the Council. The charges were eventually dropped (the law he supposedly violated was even changed), and a year later Moran was elected mayor. In 1990, he ran for Congress in what had become one of the most populous districts in the country, stretching from Alexandria south almost to Fredericksburg; the incumbent was Stanford Parris, an old battler himself, elected congressman in 1972 and then again throughout the 1980s, candidate for governor of Virginia in 1989. It was one of the nastiest-tempered races of 1990: Parris said Moran was a supporter of Saddam Hussein; Moran said he wanted to "break [Parris's] nose," and called him "a deceitful, fatuous jerk." The major substantive issue was abortion, on which Moran ran a pro-choice ad portraying Lady Liberty behind bars. With a big margin in Alexandria, Moran won 52%–45%.

In the House, Moran was freshman class whip, but flip-flopped pitifully on his first big vote, the Gulf war resolution, which he ultimately voted against. One of his legislative causes on the Banking Committee was an amendment to grant passive loss deductions for real estate investments, securitization of commercial loans and elimination of mark-to-market liquidation appraisals on performing loans—attempts to loosen up bank credit. He fought to stop the Navy from moving out of offices in Crystal City, opposed a landfill in Lorton and loudly opposed the deal concocted by Washington Redskins owner Jack Kent Cooke and Governor Douglas Wilder to build a new football stadium in Potomac Yards in Alexandria. In 1992, he was greatly strengthened by redistricting, but three Republicans still ran against him. The 54% primary winner, Kyle McSlarrow, was strongly against abortion, causing Moran's consultants to resurrect the Lady Liberty ad. The two candidates called each other liars, and Moran, angered in debate, dredged up McSlarrow's teenage drug experience, at the price of having to confess his own while in his 20s. Moran won 56%–42%, a solid margin, but not overwhelming; indeed, it was the same 14% by which Bill Clinton edged George Bush in the 8th, 51%–37%.

The Clinton economic plan presented Moran with his first great challenge in 1993. Its one-year pay freeze on federal employees struck hard in a district where 21% of workers are federal employees, the second highest in the country (although it was much higher in this area, over 30%, 20 years ago). Moran said he would probably swallow hard and vote for the economic package, but obviously had qualms. "My political career," he told *The Washington Post*, "will be largely shaped by how I deal with this economic plan. If I don't work hard enough and smart enough to make it fair to federal employees, I don't deserve to be in Congress and I don't expect I will be." This is probably pretty good prognostication; the 1992 results suggest this is a straight-ticket district, and Moran's fate will depend on Clinton's.

The People: Pop. 1990: 562,808; 9% age 65+; 71% White; 13% Black; 7% Asian; 4% Other; 9% Hispanic origin. Voting age pop.: 454,220; 13% Black; 8% Hispanic origin. Households: 48% married couple families; 21% married couple fams. w. children; 71% college educ.; median household income: $48,839; per capita income: $24,799; median gross rent: $729; median house value: $210,200.

1992 Presidential Vote			1988 Presidential Vote		
Clinton (D)	133,183	(51%)	Bush (R)	120,173	(53%)
Bush (R)	96,799	(37%)	Dukakis (D)	108,658	(47%)
Perot (I)	28,967	(11%)			

Rep. James P. Moran, Jr. (D)

Elected 1990; b. May 16, 1945, Buffalo, NY; home, Alexandria; Col. of Holy Cross, B.A. 1967, City U. of NY, 1968, U. of Pittsburgh, M.P.A. 1970; Catholic; married (Mary).

Career: Budget analyst, auditor, U.S. Dept. of H.E.W., 1968–74; Fiscal policy spec., Library of Congress, 1974–76; Staff, U.S. Senate Approp. Cmte., 1976–80; Alexandria City Cncl., 1979–82; Alexandria Vice Mayor, 1982–84, Alexandria Mayor, 1984–90; Investment broker, 1980–88.

Offices: 430 CHOB 20515, 202-225-4376. Also 5115 Franconia Rd., #B, Alexandria 22310, 703-971-4700.

Committees: *Appropriations* (33d of 37 D): Commerce, Justice, State and Judiciary; Legislative.

Group Ratings

	ADA	ACLU	COPE	CDF	CFA	LCV	ACU	NTLC	NSI	COC	CEI
1992	80	68	73	90	73	63	13	5	60	50	14
1991	70	—	83	90	56	54	10	—	—	40	19

National Journal Ratings

	1991 LIB — 1991 CONS		1992 LIB — 1992 CONS	
Economic	61%	— 36%	50%	— 49%
Social	73%	— 26%	70%	— 30%
Foreign	62%	— 36%	55%	— 44%

Key Votes of the 102d Congress

1. Ban Striker Replace FOR	5. Handgun Wait/7-Day FOR	9. Use Force in Gulf AGN
2. $ for Homeownership FOR	6. Overseas Mil. Abortion FOR	10. US Mil. Abroad $ Cut FOR
3. Tax Rich/Cut Mid Cls. FOR	7. Obscn. Art NEA $ Ban AGN	11. Limit SDI Funds FOR
4. FY93/$15B Def. Cut FOR	8. Death Pen. from Jury AGN	12. Cuba Trade Embargo FOR

Key Votes of the 103d Congress

1. Family Leave FOR	2. Deficit Reduction FOR	3. Stimulus Plan FOR

Election Results

1992 general	James P. Moran, Jr. (D) 138,542	(56%)	($923,999)
	Kyle E. McSlarrow (R). 102,717	(42%)	($424,895)
	Other............................ 5,867	(2%)	
1992 primary	James P. Moran, Jr. (D), nominated by convention		
1990 general	James P. Moran, Jr. (D) 88,475	(52%)	($883,216)
	Stanford E. Parris (R)................. 76,367	(45%)	($982,157)
	Other............................ 6,279	(4%)	

NINTH DISTRICT

One of the earliest probes of settlement from the seacoast to the great American interior came in what is now southwest Virginia; there, as early as 1765, the first settlements were being built in the great Valley of Virginia as it bends westward and south toward Tennessee and the Cumberland Gap. Most of the settlers were Scots-Irish rather than English, who came through the northern colonies rather than Virginia; and the mountainous region where they settled has been a region apart in Virginia since that time. Economically, it has depended on coal mines and heavy industry, like neighboring West Virginia; politically, it was antislavery, skeptical about, if not hostile to, the Confederacy. Split between secessionists and unionists, southwest Virginia developed a vigorous two-party politics after the Civil War, with both parties resembling their national counterparts more closely than in the rest of Virginia.

The 9th Congressional District of Virginia covers all of southwest Virginia west of Roanoke. Over the years, it became known as the "Fighting Ninth," because of its taste for raucous, noisy politics, both conservative and populist. It is getting somewhat more like the rest of Virginia now, with development moving down Interstate 81 to, and even past, Blacksburg, home of Virginia Tech. But the mountain counties farther west have been losing population and otherwise not changing much. There was a bitter coal strike here in 1989 and 1990; replacement workers were hired and there was some violence.

The current congressman, Rick Boucher, was elected in 1982, beating a Republican incumbent. Boucher, like other Fighting Ninth Democrats, has a record on issues not far out of line with national Democrats. He is, however, not likely to get way out of line with his district; he is as quick to oppose gun control as he is to champion coal interests. In the House, he has seats on Energy and Commerce and Judiciary, and chairs the Science Subcommittee of the Science and Technology Committee. He has been an active legislator on many issues. He worked on acid rain provisions in the Clean Air Act, to increase markets for Virginia's low-sulfur coal, and pushed for cable reregulation, a hot cause in these valleys. He has spent much time trying to rewrite the RICO statute whose overbroad definition of "racketeering" has caused an overload of flimsy court cases. His bill for stronger federal regulation of financial planners passed the House in 1992 and he hopes it can be passed in both houses by 1994. He was chief sponsor of the 1992 law for fire safety in new federal buildings. He wants to let local governments, not just states, veto deposit of out-of-state solid waste. He is pushing for federal protection of caves as worthy natural ecosystems. He was the lead sponsor of three bills, which he says taken together will stimulate the deployment of the "information superhighway." He wants to allow telephone companies to offer cable service through separate subsidiaries, and for them to participate in planning a national telecommunications network with "seamless interoperability."

Since first elected in 1982, Boucher has had a close race only in 1984, when he won with 52% of the vote. In 1992, he ran for the first time in a presidential year when the Democratic candidate carried the district, although not by much. There was talk that he might run for the Senate in 1988, but that ended when Charles Robb got into the race and, unknown outside the Fighting Ninth, Boucher seems committed to a career in the House.

The People: Pop. 1990: 562,508; 71% rural; 13% age 65+; 96% White; 2% Black; 1% Asian. Voting age pop.: 434,028; 2% Black. Households: 62% married couple families; 28% married couple fams. w. children; 30% college educ.; median household income: $20,857; per capita income: $10,097; median gross rent: $315; median house value: $49,100.

1992 Presidential Vote			1988 Presidential Vote		
Clinton (D)	99,099	(45%)	Bush (R)	108,448	(55%)
Bush (R)	93,673	(42%)	Dukakis (D)	88,263	(45%)
Perot (I)	26,676	(12%)			

Rep. Rick Boucher (D)

Elected 1982; b. Aug. 1, 1946, Abingdon; home, Abingdon; Roanoke Col., B.A. 1968, U. of VA, J.D. 1971; United Methodist; single.

Career: Practicing atty., 1971–83; VA Senate, 1975–1983.

Offices: 2245 RHOB 20515, 202-225-3861. Also 188 E. Main St., Abingdon 24210, 703-628-1145; 311 Shawnee Ave., Big Stone Gap 24219, 703-523-5450; and 112 N. Washington Ave., Pulaski 24301, 703-980-4310.

Committees: *Energy and Commerce* (14th of 27 D): Energy and Power; Telecommunications and Finance; Transportation and Hazardous Materials. *Judiciary* (12th of 21 D): Economic and Commercial Law. *Science, Space and Technology* (9th of 33 D): Science (Chmn.).

Group Ratings

	ADA	ACLU	COPE	CDF	CFA	LCV	ACU	NTLC	NSI	COC	CEI
1992	90	86	82	90	87	44	8	0	30	38	10
1991	65	—	75	80	72	62	10	—	—	40	12

National Journal Ratings

	1991 LIB — 1991 CONS			1992 LIB — 1992 CONS		
Economic	69%	—	31%	71%	—	27%
Social	62%	—	37%	59%	—	41%
Foreign	77%	—	23%	69%	—	30%

Key Votes of the 102d Congress

1. Ban Striker Replace	FOR	5. Handgun Wait/7-Day	AGN	9. Use Force in Gulf	AGN
2. $ for Homeownership	FOR	6. Overseas Mil. Abortion	FOR	10. US Mil. Abroad $ Cut	FOR
3. Tax Rich/Cut Mid Cls.	FOR	7. Obscn. Art NEA $ Ban	FOR	11. Limit SDI Funds	FOR
4. FY93/$15B Def. Cut	FOR	8. Death Pen. from Jury	AGN	12. Cuba Trade Embargo	AGN

Key Votes of the 103d Congress

1. Family Leave	FOR	2. Deficit Reduction	FOR	3. Stimulus Plan	FOR

Election Results

1992 general	Rick Boucher (D)	133,284	(63%)	($660,452)
	L. Garrett (Gary) Weddle (R)	77,985	(37%)	($100,089)
1992 primary	Rick Boucher (D), nominated by convention			
1990 general	Rick Boucher (D)	67,215	(97%)	($252,685)
	Other.............................	2,015	(3%)	

TENTH DISTRICT

Even as the Constitution was being hammered out in Philadelphia, the rolling green Piedmont of northern Virginia and the fertile mountain-bound lands of the Shenandoah Valley were buzzing with new settlers. They came up the rivers that flow into the Chesapeake, into the Valley from the great Wagon Road south from Pennsylvania, moving onto lands speculated by George Washington and his peers. During the Civil War, this was some of the most heavily contested land on the continent; afterwards, the surge of movement having propelled new settlers much farther west, this part of Virginia was well-settled and became prime fox hunting country. Subdivisions are sprouting up on fields, and the horse farms of the Piedmont, long first or second homes of some of the richest people in America, are attracting a growing population of Washington, D.C. commuters and weekend residents. What looked like marginal farmlands to the settlers of the early 19th Century now looks like heaven for city-dwellers: rolling green hills with views of the Blue Ridge and other mountains, antique houses and tiny crossroads communities. There is still an old-fashioned air in the narrow streets of the old county seat towns, but a McDonald's culture has developed on the bypass roads on their outskirts.

The 10th Congressional District of Virginia covers much of this territory. This district has expanded as people have moved outward from the Washington metropolitan area; today it is entirely, in the familiar phrase, outside the Beltway. About one-third of its people live in suburban Fairfax County, which is by some measures the most affluent county in the United States: 61% of its households had incomes over $50,000 in 1989, number one in the country, though it was only number seven in percentage of over $100,000 households. Also, 49% of its adults over 25 were college graduates, more than double the national figure. Fairfax, and especially the 10th's portion of it—affluent and woodsy Great Falls and parts of McLean, the new subdivisions around the old crossroads of Centreville and the upscale Fair Oaks Mall area— is full of high-salaried, two-earner families, young and well-educated, employed more often by the private sector than by government, frazzled with commuting on clogged roads. Beyond Fairfax, another one-third of 10th District residents live in Loudoun and parts of Prince William County, once rural—the Manassas battlefield is here—but now heavily settled, although not as high-income or well-educated as Fairfax nor as culturally liberal. The last third of the 10th's residents are in smaller, still rural-appearing Fauquier and Rappahannock Counties and west of the Blue Ridge in the Shenandoah Valley. Politically, this is a very Republican district. The Shenandoah tradition of Harry Byrd Democrats switched seamlessly to Republicanism, as indeed many local politicians switched parties themselves; the new suburbanites are if anything more determinedly Republican.

The congressman from the 10th District is Frank Wolf, a Republican first elected in 1980 from a district most of which was inside the Beltway, an earnest hard-working politician. His overall voting record is very conservative. He started off tending to local issues, but has broadened his focus. He still maintains a crackerjack constituency service operation and has supported federal employee causes, writing legislation that has enabled federal agencies to provide space for 100 child care centers. But he has taken risks (federal workers are still 9% of

1328   VIRGINIA

the work force in the 10th) opposing repeal of the Hatch Act in 1993 saying it would politicize the federal work force. It was an easier choice for him to oppose the Clinton economic package, whose tax increases he opposes and whose limits on federal pay raises are unpopular here. He has used his Appropriations seat to fund the Washington area Metro mass transit system and has backed a Gridlock Relief for Interstates bill. He worked to put child care centers near Metro subway stations.

But Wolf has also gone afield, to Romania and China, to back human rights, and has sought to increase penalties on businesses who knowingly import prison-made goods from such countries and to withdraw most favored nation status from Serbia and Montenegro. He is the prime sponsor of the move to increase the personal tax exemption for children under 18 from $2,050 to $3,500, with a goal of $6,000 by 2000. This would move the deduction back toward the value it had in real dollars following World War II, when it was the functional equivalent of a children's allowance and helped stimulate the postwar baby boom, with the family stability and economic growth many Americans would like to see again.

The Democrats have run respectable, though not always politically experienced, candidates against Wolf every two years, and he has won with more than 60% each time. In 1992, even in this vastly expanded district, he carried every county and city and won 64%–33%.

The People: Pop. 1990: 562,257; 44% rural; 7% age 65+; 89% White; 6% Black; 3% Asian; 1% Other; 2% Hispanic origin. Voting age pop.: 411,700; 6% Black; 2% Hispanic origin. Households: 67% married couple families; 35% married couple fams. w. children; 55% college educ.; median household income: $46,205; per capita income: $20,065; median gross rent: $657; median house value: $155,000.

1992 Presidential Vote			1988 Presidential Vote		
Bush (R)	124,783	(50%)	Bush (R)	132,359	(69%)
Clinton (D)	83,214	(33%)	Dukakis (D)	59,465	(31%)
Perot (I)	41,228	(16%)			

Rep. Frank R. Wolf (R)

Elected 1980; b. Jan. 30, 1939, Philadelphia, PA; home, Vienna; PA St. U., B.A. 1961; Georgetown, LL.B. 1965; Presbyterian; married (Carolyn).

Career: Army, 1962–63, Army Reserves 1963–67; Legis. Asst., U.S. Rep. Edward Biester, 1968–71; Asst., U.S. Interior Secy. Rogers Morton, 1971–74; Dep. Asst. Secy., U.S. Dept. of Interior, 1974–75; Practicing atty., 1975–80.

Offices: 104 CHOB 20515, 202-225-5136. Also 1651 Old Meadow Rd., #115, McLean 22102, 703-734-1500; and 19 E. Market St., #4B, Leesburg 22075, 703-777-4422.

Committees: *Appropriations* (10th of 23 R): Transportation (RMM); Treasury, Postal Service, and General Government.

Group Ratings

	ADA	ACLU	COPE	CDF	CFA	LCV	ACU	NTLC	NSI	COC	CEI
1992	20	4	42	20	33	13	84	95	100	88	61
1991	15	—	17	30	28	15	80	—	—	80	59

National Journal Ratings

	1991 LIB — 1991 CONS		1992 LIB — 1992 CONS	
Economic	14% —	83%	9% —	88%
Social	27% —	71%	0% —	85%
Foreign	23% —	75%	18% —	74%

Key Votes of the 102d Congress

1. Ban Striker Replace	AGN	5. Handgun Wait/7-Day FOR	9. Use Force in Gulf FOR
2. $ for Homeownership	FOR	6. Overseas Mil. Abortion AGN	10. US Mil. Abroad $ Cut AGN
3. Tax Rich/Cut Mid Cls.	AGN	7. Obscn. Art NEA $ Ban FOR	11. Limit SDI Funds AGN
4. FY93/$15B Def. Cut	AGN	8. Death Pen. from Jury FOR	12. Cuba Trade Embargo FOR

Key Votes of the 103d Congress

1. Family Leave   AGN   2. Deficit Reduction   AGN   3. Stimulus Plan   AGN

Election Results

1992 general	Frank R. Wolf (R)	144,471	(64%)	($431,829)
	Raymond E. (Ray) Vickery, Jr. (D)	75,775	(33%)	($191,260)
	Other..............................	6,945	(3%)	
1992 primary	Frank R. Wolf (R), nominated by convention			
1990 general	Frank R. Wolf (R)	103,761	(62%)	($511,853)
	N. MacKenzie Canter III (D)	57,249	(34%)	($93,659)
	Two Other..........................	7,566	(4%)	

ELEVENTH DISTRICT

The biggest center of office space between downtown Washington and Atlanta—or, for that matter, beyond downtown Atlanta—is not in Richmond or one of North Carolina's Piedmont cities, but in the cluster of office buildings around Tysons Corner, Virginia. Rising on a hill west of Washington and Arlington, Tysons Corner was a back country intersection 50 years ago and a junction of several suburban roads 25 years ago; none of Washington's cadre of metropolitan experts nor the designers of its Metro system expected office development here. They assumed that office work would still be centralized, and that if Washington's robust downtown needed to be supplemented it would happen in Crystal City near the Pentagon, or Rosslyn just across the river from Georgetown, both in Arlington County. It did, but Crystal City and Rosslyn together are overshadowed by Tysons Corner.

This emergence of "edge cities," as *The Nine Nations of North America* author Joel Garreau calls them, is a new chapter in the history of the Northern Virginia's counties. Fifty years ago, the atmosphere in Fairfax County, which includes all of Tysons Corner, was rural. Then in the years after World War II, at first a trickle and then a rush of young marrieds with large families, and whites avoiding the increasingly high-crime District of Columbia moved to Northern Virginia, first into Arlington and Alexandria, then farther out into Fairfax. With rising government salaries and local economic growth, they began to live in affluence that many had never anticipated. Fairfax County today has the nation's highest median household income, $59,284 in 1990, and highest percentage of over $50,000 households, 61% in 1989. These people in turn have prompted the growth of Tysons and other edge cities: employers want to be where high-skill workers are. Gradually, but with great force, Fairfax has been transformed from a suburban county where people commute to Washington generally to government jobs, to a 21st Century urban county where people work somewhere around the Beltway and mostly for private sector employers.

The 11th Congressional District of Virginia, the new seat gained by this fast-growing state in the 1990 Census, went to fast-growing Fairfax County and its somewhat lower income neighbor just to the south, Prince William. The 11th sits on both sides of the Capital Beltway. Inside it includes older but still affluent areas like Annandale, with its increasing Asian-American population; outside are Tysons Corner and the heavy office corridor out the Dulles Access Road, to Dulles Airport which, 30 years after its opening, is finally meeting its planners expectations. Near the Beltway are the new headquarters of Mobil and General Dynamics, moved here from New York and St. Louis. The 11th runs south through new subdivision areas like Burke and covers the somewhat lower-income Woodbridge and Dale City areas of Prince William. Politically, this area has a robust two-party politics. In the 1980s, it voted Republican for president, but alternated in hotly contested races for the County Board of Supervisors; it has Democratic and Republican state legislators; and in 1992, it had a hotly contested race for the House.

The new representative is Leslie Byrne, a Democrat who, dismayed by local Republicans' views, ran for and won a seat in the Virginia House of Delegates in 1985 and moved so unhesitatingly into the race for the 11th District when its boundaries were drawn that no other Democrat challenged her for the nomination. She was known as a skillful legislator, a "crafty strategist skilled at backroom deals and floor debates," as *The Washington Post* put it, who wanted to make repeatedly blocking access to an abortion clinic a felony and thwarted the trucking lobby with an amendment requiring truckers to cover their loads for safety reasons. Five candidates ran for the Republican nomination. One was former Michigan Congressman Mark Siljander, a strongly religious conservative who lost his seat in a 1986 primary after urging supporters to "break the back of Satan." Another was Andy Schlafly, a son of conservative activist and columnist Phyllis Schlafly. Also running were Delegate Jack Rollison III, high-tech entrepreneur Jay Khim and George Mason University law professor Henry Butler, whose father Caldwell Butler represented Virginia's 6th District for 10 years. The primary vote was distributed seemingly at random. Siljander and Schlafly split the strong conservative vote, with 22% and 11%, Rollison had 19% and Khim 16%, and Butler won with 32%. Byrne and Butler contrasted sharply on issues. Butler was for term limits and the balanced budget amendment, against all tax increases, for tax credits and vouchers for health care and education. Byrne was for higher taxes on the rich, targeted tax incentives to companies that create jobs, statewide health insurance pools, and family and medical leave, and against school vouchers; she also backed a balanced budget amendment and a line-item veto. She pounced on Butler's statements opposing federal funding for abortion, painting him as a right-wing pro-lifer. Byrne expressed unbridled disdain and contempt for Butler in joint campaign appearances, and described him as an "extremist," while expressing confidence that she had solutions to national economic problems.

This was a big-spending race: Butler spent $844,000, Byrne $773,000. Byrne won by a 50%–45% margin in a district George Bush was carrying over Bill Clinton 43%–42%. She agreed after her election that her political fortunes were tied to Bill Clinton's, and was obviously ill at ease when Clinton's first economic program contained a pay freeze for federal workers, who make up 17% of employed persons in this district. But in May 1993, Byrne spearheaded a petition calling for the ouster of House subcommittee chairmen who voted against Clinton's budget package. With more than 80 co-signers, including nine full-committee chairmen, she forced a Democratic Caucus meeting to confront the issue of party discipline. Speaker Foley convinced Byrne not to seek a formal vote, but did agree to convene the Steering and Policy Committee to discuss the matter. No action was taken against the subcommittee chairmen, but Byrne said she had accomplished her goal of reminding the leadership to lead. She may be a member to watch, but the 11th is likely to be a seriously contested district again in 1994.

The People: Pop. 1990: 562,596; 2% rural; 6% age 65+; 76% White; 8% Black; 8% Asian; 3% Other; 7% Hispanic origin. Voting age pop.: 420,391; 7% Black; 7% Hispanic origin. Households: 62% married couple families; 33% married couple fams. w. children; 71% college educ.; median household income: $54,369; per capita income: $22,202; median gross rent: $797; median house value: $190,400.

1992 Presidential Vote

Bush (R) 103,907 (43%)
Clinton (D) 102,721 (42%)
Perot (I)................. 34,719   (14%)

1988 Presidential Vote

Bush (R) 128,333 (61%)
Dukakis (D)............... 82,819   (39%)

Rep. Leslie L. Byrne (D)

Elected 1992; b. Oct. 27, 1946, Salt Lake City, UT; home, Falls Church; U. of UT, 1964–65; Catholic; married (Larry).

Career: Pres., Fairfax League of Women Voters, 1982–83; Co-founder, Quintech Assoc. consulting firm, 1985–92; VA House of Delegates, 1985–92.

Offices: 1609 LHOB 20515, 202-225-1492. Also 7620 Little River Tnpk., #203, Annandale 22003, 703-750-1992.

Committees: *Post Office and Civil Service* (9th of 15 D): Compensation and Employee Benefits. *Public Works and Transportation* (26th of 39 D): Investigations and Oversight; Surface Transportation; Water Resources and Environment.

Group Ratings and 102d Congress Votes: Newly Elected

Key Votes of the 103d Congress

1. Family Leave   FOR   2. Deficit Reduction   FOR   3. Stimulus Plan   FOR

Election Results

1992 general	Leslie L. Byrne (D).................	114,172	(50%)	($773,128)
	Henry N. Butler (R).................	103,119	(45%)	($844,695)
	Others.............................	10,981	(5%)	
1992 primary	Leslie L. Byrne (D), nominated by convention			
1990 election	Newly created district.			

WASHINGTON

All of a sudden the state of Washington, at the far northwest corner of the continental United States, seems to be the national trend-setter. Coffee and espresso bars have spread outward from Seattle, where the rich brew nourishes in the cold misty air, south to California and even to the East Coast. Grunge clothes, an exaltation of natural adolescent sloppiness, for a moment became the style to imitate, even for those long past their teens. Microsoft, founded by the usually tieless and tousle-haired Bill Gates and based in Redmond, Washington, became one of America's great success stories as its software business boomed, while the hardware business soured and IBM, with its white shirts and plain ties, laid off thousands; Boeing, though laying off workers as airlines remain in financial trouble, has proved again its excellence as the world's leading airframe manufacturer. With its flannel shirts and umbrellas, its blue-collar types working off a hangover as if in a Raymond Carver story and its professionals relaxing on woodsy acreage, Washington has set a tone for the 1990s, a style plainly Middle American but with attitude, an ordinariness that is so apt it is no longer ordinary.

All this comes to a state barely a century old, which in the two decades after statehood in 1889 built a new civilization, as transcontinental railroads reached the great ports of Puget Sound, the wheat-processing city of Spokane inland, orchard towns and fishing ports and lumber settlements. Shielded from the heavy rains and storms of the Pacific by the Olympic Mountains and the Sound, Seattle quickly became a serious American city, a lusty town full of lumbermen and railroad workers. When gold was struck in the Klondike and Alaska, it became a metropolis of miners, prospectors and get-rich-quick operators, the site of the original "Skid Road" (skid row is a corruption propagated by a 1937 magazine article), where logs were rolled downhill to the port; today it's the center of the restored Pioneer Square area. This booming, young Seattle had a turbulent class-warfare politics in the years before World War I, pitting the Industrial Workers of the World (the IWW, or Wobblies) against city business and civic leaders; the businessmen, brutally, prevailed. Adding to the area's distinctiveness was its large numbers of Scandinavian immigrants, more favorable to cooperative enterprises and government ownership than other Americans.

Over time, Washington was transformed by a series of national decisions which set the course of its development for decades. One was government development of hydroelectric power. The Columbia River and its tributary, the Snake, falling thousands of feet in a relatively short distance, had far greater hydroelectric potential than any other American river system, and Franklin Roosevelt was always interested in these river valley projects. In 1937, Bonneville Dam was completed on the lower Columbia; in 1940, Grand Coulee Dam, the largest man-made structure in the world at the time, was opened where the Columbia cuts through the arid, surrealistically contoured plains of eastern Washington. Washington proved hospitable to the industrial union movement of the 1930s and became one of the nation's most heavily unionized states. When war came, Washington's hydroelectric power—the cheapest electricity in the country—made it the natural site for huge aluminum production plants, which require vast amounts of electricity, and the Seattle area became the home not only of shipbuilders, but of the biggest aircraft manufacturer in the country, Boeing. After the war, the Hanford plant on the Columbia was one of the government's main nuclear weapons manufacturing sites. Cheap power, aluminum, aircraft, nuclear weapons and high unionized wages: these became Washington's economic foundations in the post-World War II years.

Today, Washington is a commonwealth of more than five million, economically booming, pleased to the point of smugness with its physical environment. But it has problems: it remains uncomfortably dependent on Boeing and the highly cyclical airframe business; its Washington payrolls topped 100,000 in 1988, but by late 1992 were falling, bringing back memories of how Boeing pared its payroll from 100,000 to 38,000 between 1967 and 1971. The Columbia basin's hydroelectric capacity has been used up, and electricity rates are now above national levels. The Hanford Works for years leaked radioactive waste, which must now be cleaned up at the cost of billions, while new underground storage procedures have been criticized as unsafe. Then there is the spotted owl. After a federal judge in Seattle ruled that old growth forests must be left uncut to preserve the apparently endangered spotted owl, thousands of logging jobs have been lost and whole communities left idle; President Clinton's April 1993 timber summit in Portland may produce a compromise, but in the meantime this once vital industry has shriveled.

Yet these are footnotes to what is mainly the story of success. Look at a map that shows elevation of mountains and density of population. On both sides of the Pacific, vast numbers of people are squeezed into small margins of level land between steeply rising volcanic mountains and the sea, or tucked into valleys. These islands of settlement are surrounded by vast wildernesses—desert and mountains, open sea and Arctic lands. Yet the inhabitants of these pockets of the Pacific Rim have, over the past two or three decades, produced more economic

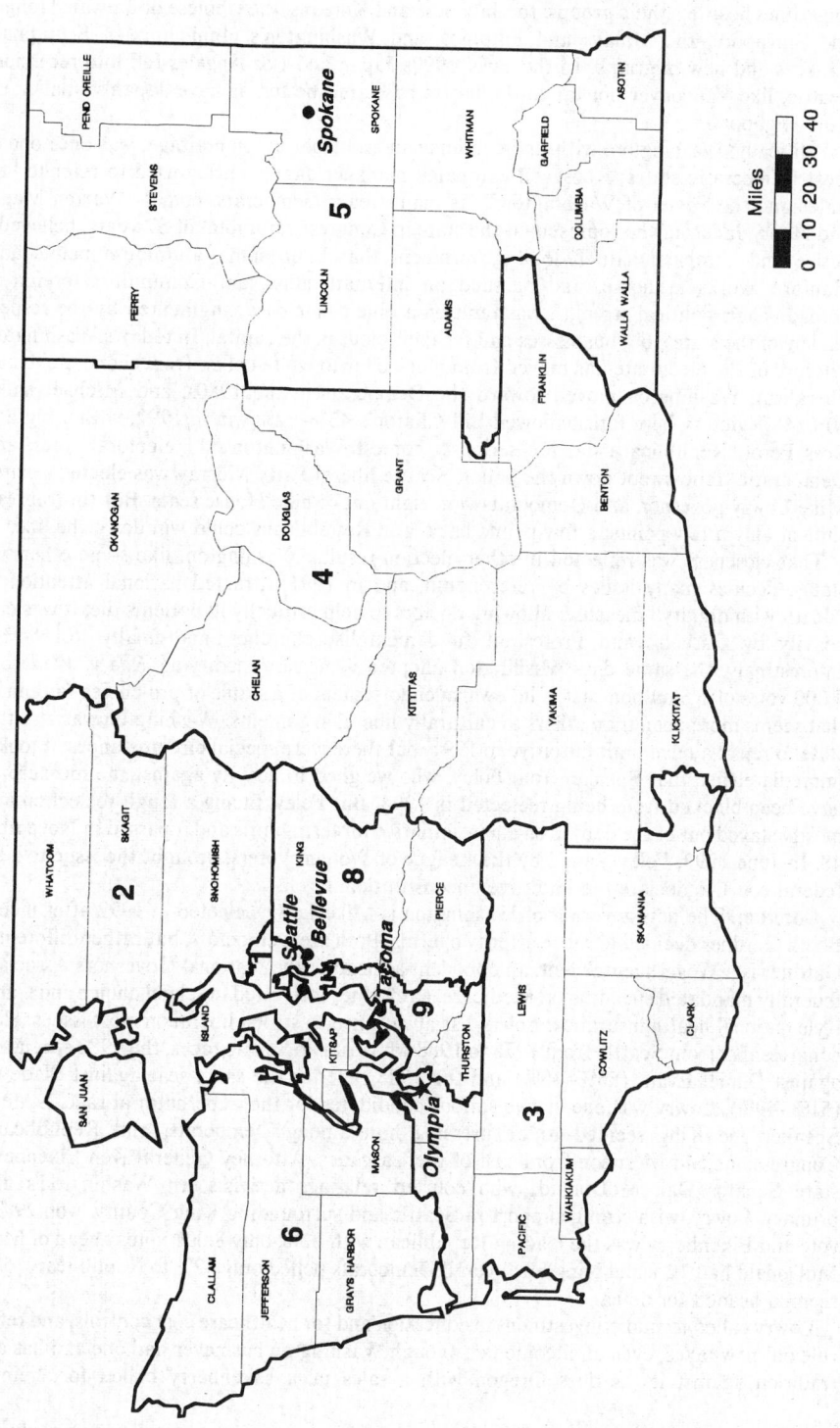

growth than anywhere else in the world. This has happened despite the widely diverse, sometimes hostile, ethnic groups: the Japanese and Koreans, the Chinese of Taiwan, Hong Kong and Singapore, the Malays and Filipinos; and Washington's ethnic mix of Scandinavians, Yankees and new migrants. In the early 1990s Japan and Los Angeles fell into recession, but Seattle, like Vancouver not far to the north, has fared better, as have Japan's smaller Pacific Rim neighbors.

Politically, Washington, with its Scandinavian and labor union heritage, was once one of the most Democratic states: Roosevelt campaign manager James Farley used to refer to "the 47 states and the Soviet of Washington." Its mainstream Democrats, notably Warren Magnuson and Henry Jackson who represented the state in Congress for a total of 87 years, believed in an active and compassionate federal government that built dams, aluminum plants and the Hanford Works at home, and pursued an internationalist, anti-Communist foreign policy abroad. Their political strength was built on a blue-collar base, augmented by the respect the leaders of the state's big businesses had for their clout in the capital. In today's Washington, the fulcrum of the electorate has moved from blue-collar to white-collar, from economic to cultural liberalism. Washington moved toward the Democrats in the 1980s, and Michael Dukakis's 50%–48% victory here foreshadowed Bill Clinton's 43%–32% win in 1992, with a big 24% for Ross Perot. Republicans did not seriously contest Washington's 11 electoral votes, and the Democratic trend swept down the ballot: Seattle liberal Patty Murray was elected senator and Mike Lowry governor, and Democrats won eight out of nine House seats. But this represents a shift of only a few points; a few points back, and Republicans could win down the line.

That closeness was reflected in other election results. Washington, like some other western states, decides many issues by referendum, and in 1991 attracted national attention for its "death with dignity" measure, allowing doctors to help critically ill patients die; it was opposed heavily by Catholic and Protestant fundamentalist churches, and finally lost 54%–46%. Interestingly, the same day, Washington adopted a measure codifying *Roe v. Wade* by only 4,000 votes of 1.5 million cast, a lukewarm endorsement of a staple of pro-choice faith in a state that seems more open than others to culturally liberal arguments. Washington was also the only state to reject a term limit initiative in 1991, but there were special circumstances: it took effect immediately, so that Speaker Tom Foley, who weighed in heavily against the measure, would have been blocked from being reelected in 1994. But Foley, facing a tough reelection in 1992, mostly stayed out of the debate on a new initiative for term limits and it passed in November 52–48. In June 1993, Foley, joined by the League of Women Voters, brought the issue to a Seattle federal court to declare the initiative unconstitutional.

Governor. The new governor of Washington is Mike Lowry, elected in 1992 after incumbent Booth Gardner decided to retire after two terms. Both are Democrats, but rather different kinds. Gardner is a Weyerhaeuser heir, an opponent as head of the National Governors Association of federally mandated spending on Medicare, a reformer interested in school choice and Canadian-style national health insurance. Lowry has always been a strong liberal on most issues. He was a congressman from Seattle from 1978 to 1988 who lost two Senate races, the 1983 special contest against Daniel Evans (55%–45%) and the 1988 race for the same seat against Slade Gorton (51%–49%). Lowry was one of five serious candidates for the gubernatorial race. State House Speaker Joe King seemed to be pressing him among Democrats, and Republicans had Congressman Sid Morrison from east of the Cascades, Attorney General Ken Eikenberry and state Senator Dan McDonald, who courted religious activists. In Washington's all-party primary, Lowry, with strong support in Seattle and surrounding King County, won 29% of the vote and Eikenberry was the leading Republican with 22%, only 8,000 votes ahead of Morrison. McDonald had 12% and King 8%; overall Democrats polled only 42% to Republicans' 58% and seemed headed for defeat.

Lowry called for more investment in education and for healthcare cost controls, and refused to rule out new taxes, even an income tax, though Washington has never had one and has a strong tradition against it (as does Oregon with a sales tax). Eikenberry called for "reinventing government" and pledged no new taxes. Lowry was pro-choice, Eikenberry took stands on parental notification. The race was close in most of the state, with Lowry leading 60%–40% in Seattle and King County and Eikenberry leading 56%–44% east of the Cascades; overall, Lowry won 52%–48%.

Once in office, he proposed removing the sales tax exemption on professional services (but not on some lawyers or doctors) to cover a $1.8 billion projected deficit; he pushed for healthcare reform with cost controls—a plan which Hillary Rodham Clinton called and congratulated him on—and came out against education spending cuts. With a Democratic legislature, he has a splendid chance to make Washington a laboratory of liberal reform, and will likely be held accountable for the results, plus or minus, in 1996.

Senators. Since the defeat of Warren Magnuson in 1980 and the death of Henry Jackson in 1983, Washington has been represented by freshmen senators—quite a contrast from the seniority clout of Scoop and Maggie. Slade Gorton is now the senior senator, with more than 20 years in statewide office: he was elected Attorney General in 1968 and served until he beat Magnuson in 1980, 54%–46%; he was known then as one of Washington's liberal Republicans. After six years, Gorton lost to Brock Adams in 1986; but, when Republican Daniel Evans surprised everyone by retiring in 1988, Gorton entered the race to succeed him and won. His Democratic opponent was Mike Lowry, now governor, and Gorton relied heavily on rural areas, losing Seattle and the Puget Sound metro counties, but carrying the traditionally Democratic logging counties and Washington east of the Cascades as well. He showed sympathy for loggers whose jobs were endangered by environmental rules and called for conversion of the Hanford nuclear power plant to an environmental clean-up facility.

Cerebral and deliberate, he has been more committed to listening to voters since his defeat. He supports some increased regulation—CAFE standards for higher gas mileage for autos and requiring airbags, cable reregulation, banning trucks from carrying toxic materials on one trip and foodstuffs the next. On the Endangered Species Act, he favors a balancing approach. He worked to keep the Mariners baseball team in Seattle. With West Virginia's Jay Rockefeller he introduced a law, strongly opposed by trial lawyers, to reform product liability litigation. He served on the Ethics Committee for two years, but recused himself from judging the sexual harassment charges against Brock Adams, saying that he was convinced Adams was guilty. Gorton's voting record tends to be conservative on most issues, but he is not part of the conservative bloc of Republican senators. When he ran for Republican Whip in November 1992, he did not receive the conservative support that prevailed in most other leadership races, and lost to incumbent Whip Alan Simpson 25–14.

It is generally assumed that Gorton will run for reelection in 1994, when he turns 66. He will again seek support in rural areas and the outer suburbs, now that Seattle seems so heavily Democratic. Some speculate that Booth Gardner, widely popular when he left the governorship in 1992, will run, and he certainly would be the favorite if he did; but he declined to run for an open Senate seat in 1992 and may not be interested in going back east. Other possible candidates include Seattle Mayor Norm Rice, who is black (blacks are a small minority in this city), state Treasurer Dan Grimm, and Seattle state Senator Phil Talmadge.

Washington's junior senator is Patty Murray, one of those 1992 winners who would have seemed an unlikely victor in any previous year, but was an unstoppable force in what many called "the year of the woman." A dozen years earlier, when she was in Olympia trying to save a parent education class she was teaching at Shoreline Community College from being cut from the budget, a state legislator told her gruffly, "You're just a mom in tennis shoes; you can't make a difference." But, like many committed public employees, she won her fight; then she ran for the school board, lost, was appointed and then elected, and served as president. In 1988, she challenged a Republican state senator, knocked on 17,000 doors, and won the seat. Her first great cause there was extending a family leave bill to include leave for a parent whose child is sick or dying; she threatened to put the issue on the ballot, and won; she worked on school bus safety, "negative option" mail orders, accidental pesticide exposure—the warp and woof of everyday life. Then in late 1991, she decided to run against U.S. Senator Brock Adams. On paper, there was no comparison in their credentials: Adams had been U.S. attorney in Seattle 30 years before, was elected to Congress in 1964 and became chairman of the House Budget Committee, was Jimmy Carter's first secretary of Transportation, and was elected to the Senate in 1986. But Adams was under a terrible cloud for charges that in 1987 he had drugged and fondled a young woman who was an old family friend; his job rating plummeted, and several Republicans—Congressman Rod Chandler, former POW war hero Leo Thorsness, King County Executive Tim Hill—were running against him. Then in March 1992, the *Seattle Times* wrote that eight more women, all remaining anonymous, were accusing Adams of sexual molestation and, in one case, rape. The Ethics Committee declined to investigate the matter when none of the women would come forward. Adams bowed out of the race, but refused to resign.

Suddenly Murray was, if not a favorite, in a position of visibility in what was starting to look like a Democratic year. She was joined in the primary by former Congressman Don Bonker, who had run behind Mike Lowry in the 1988 all-party primary, 32%–26%; he brought a record on trade and a home base in the logging country in western Washington. The Republicans distinguished themselves in different ways. Chandler, a booming voiced former TV reporter and 10-year congressman, had a moderate image and backing in Washington, D.C. Thorsness, who nearly beat Senator George McGovern in 1974 when he lived in South Dakota, was also in the Washington Senate, where he turned back his pay raise. Hill, a Seattle moderate, brought a record on local issues and defiance of pro-life delegates at the state party convention. But it was Murray, with her flat accent and her "mom in tennis shoes" line who attracted voters' attention, even while she captured union endorsements. In the September primary, she had 28% of the vote to 19% for Bonker; on the Republican side, Chandler's 20% edged Thorsness's 16% and Hill's 11%. Murray sprinted to a big lead in polls, but she performed poorly in initial debates, and Chandler started to catch up. But not enough: in November Murray won 54%–46%, carrying 60% in King County and winning Puget Sound and the west. Her margins over Chandler were similar to Bill Clinton's over George Bush, except in eastern Washington, which Clinton nearly carried but where Murray ran 10% behind.

Murray is likely to have a solidly liberal record. She called, as have other senators, for a more "family-friendly" legislative schedule and for action against sexual harassment in Congress. Quite astonishingly, she selected a U.S. attorney for Alaska—a prerogative enjoyed by the party in the White House. But Alaska has an entirely Republican delegation so Murray made the selection "because she's a Democrat from the neighborhood," a staffer explained. She serves on the Appropriations, Banking and Budget Committees.

Presidential politics. Washington is one of the most contrarian of states in presidential elections. It voted for Richard Nixon in 1960, Hubert Humphrey in 1968, Gerald Ford in 1976 and Michael Dukakis in 1988. It was also a better than average Perot state in 1992, especially in the outer edges of metro Seattle, where young voters with few roots in local institutions responded to his appeal.

Washington switched from a caucus system to primaries after 1988, when Pat Robertson won among Republicans and Jesse Jackson finished a solid second among Democrats. In the May 1992 primary, held the same day as Oregon's, George Bush overwhelmed Pat Buchanan 67%–10% (but the primary was non-binding) and Bill Clinton beat Jerry Brown 51%–29%. But there were plenty of write-ins for Ross Perot. Counting the results as they would be in Washington's all-party primary for state office, Bush had 43% of the votes to Clinton's 31% and Perot's 27%; this was not a good forecast of Clinton's eventual 43%–32% victory, but may have reflected opinion accurately at that time, when Clinton was running third in national polls.

Congressional districting. Washington gained a seat in each of the last two censuses, and both new districts went to the fast-growing suburban area east and south of Seattle. A nonpartisan commission drew the district lines for the 1990s, which are more regular than those of the 1980s. Democrats won eight of the nine districts, but only one is overwhelmingly Democratic, Seattle's 7th; the rest could vote for either party on any given election day.

The People: Est. Pop. 1992: 5,136,000; Pop. 1990: 4,866,692, up 5.2% 1990–1992. 2.0% of U.S. total, 18th largest; 24% rural. Median age: 33.1 years. 11.8% 65 years and over. 88.5% White, 4.4% Hispanic origin, 4.3% Asian, 3.1% Black, 1.7% American Indian, 2.4% Other. Households: 55.0% married couple families; 26% married couple fams. w. children; 56% college educ.; median household income: $31,183; per capita income: $14,923; 62.6% owner occupied housing; median house value: $93,400; median monthly rent: $383. 7.5% Unemployment. Voting age pop.: 3,605,305. Registered voters (1992): 2,814,680; no party registration.

Political Lineup: Governor, Michael Lowry (D); Lt. Gov., Joel Pritchard (R); Secy. of State, Ralph Munro (R); Atty. Gen., Christine Gregoire (D); Treasurer, Dan Grimm (D); Auditor, Brian Sonntag (D). State Senate, 49 (28 D and 21 R); State House of Representatives, 98 (65 D and 33 R). Senators, Slade Gorton (R) and Patty Murray (D). Representatives, 9 (8 D and 1 R).

1992 Presidential Vote

Clinton (D)	993,037	(43%)
Bush (R)	731,234	(32%)
Perot (I)	541,780	(24%)

1992 Democratic Presidential Primary

Clinton	62,171	(42%)
Brown	34,111	(23%)
Write-In (Perot)	28,311	(19%)
Tsongas	18,981	(13%)

1988 Presidential Vote

Dukakis (D)	933,516	(50%)
Bush (R)	903,835	(48%)

1992 Republican Presidential Primary

Bush	86,839	(67%)
Write-In (Perot)	25,423	(20%)
Buchanan	13,273	(10%)

GOVERNOR

Gov. Michael Lowry (D)

Elected 1992, term expires Jan. 1997; b. Mar. 8, 1939, St. John; home, Olympia; WA St. U., B.A. 1961; Baptist; married (Mary).

Career: Staff Dir., WA Senate Ways & Means Cmte., 1969–74; PR Dir., Group Health Coop. of Puget Sound, 1974–75; King Cnty. Cncl., 1975–78, Chmn., 1977–78; U.S. House of Reps., 1978–88; Prof., Seattle U. Inst. for Public Svc., 1989–92.

Offices: Office of the Governor, P.O. Box 40002, Olympia 98504, 206-753-6780.

Election Results

1992 gen.	Michael Lowry (D)	1,184,315	(52%)
	Ken Eikenberry (R)	1,086,216	(48%)
1992 prim.	Michael Lowry (D)	337,783	(29%)
	Ken Eikenberry (R)	258,553	(22%)
	Sid Morrison (R)	250,418	(22%)
	Dan McDonald (R)	144,050	(12%)
	Joe King (D)	96,480	(8%)
	Six Others	68,321	(8%)
1988 gen.	William Booth Gardner (D)	1,166,448	(62%)
	Bob Williams (R)	708,481	(38%)

1338   WASHINGTON

SENATORS

Sen. Slade Gorton (R)

Elected 1988, seat up 1994; b. Jan. 8, 1928, Chicago, IL; home, Seattle; Dartmouth, A.B. 1950, Columbia U., LL.B. 1953; Episcopalian; married (Sally).

Career: Army, 1946–47, Air Force Reserves, 1953–56; WA House of Reps., 1959–69, Majority Ldr., 1967–69; WA Atty. Gen., 1969–80; Pres., Natl. Assn. of Attys. Gen., 1976–78; U.S. Senator, 1980–86.

Offices: 730 HSOB 20510, 202-224-3441; 1350 Grandridge Blvd., #212, Kennewick 99336, 509-783-0640; 15600 Redmond Wy., #300, Redmond 98052, 206-883-6072; and 402 E. Yakima Ave., Box 4083, Yakima 98901, 509-248-8084.

Committees: *Appropriations* (10th of 13 R): Agriculture, Rural Development and Related Agencies; Energy and Water Development; Interior; Labor, Health and Human Services, Education; Military Construction (RMM). *Budget* (8th of 9 D). *Commerce, Science and Transportation* (7th of 9 R): Aviation; Communications; Consumer (RMM). *Indian Affairs* (4th of 8 R). *Intelligence (Select)* (4th of 8 R).

Group Ratings

	ADA	ACLU	CDF	COPE	CFA	LCV	ACU	NTLC	NSI	COC	CEI
1992	25	43	30	36	33	17	72	72	90	90	63
1991	30	—	55	17	33	40	67	—	—	80	56

National Journal Ratings

	1991 LIB — 1991 CONS			1992 LIB — 1992 CONS		
Economic	25%	—	73%	22%	—	76%
Social	47%	—	52%	34%	—	65%
Foreign	27%	—	67%	10%	—	80%

Key Votes of the 102d Congress

1. $ for Homeownership	FOR	5. Clarence Thomas Nom. FOR	9. Use Force in Gulf	FOR
2. Have Cap Gains Debate FOR	6. Lmt Death Row Appeal FOR	10. Keep Salvador Aid	FOR
3. Remove Budget Walls AGN	7. Handgun Wait/5-Day FOR	11. Cut $1B from SDI	AGN
4. Ban Striker Replace AGN	8. Abortion Gag Rule AGN	12. Override China MFN AGN

Key Votes of the 103d Congress

1. Family Leave	AGN	2. HIV Immigrants	AGN	3. Clinton Budget	AGN

Election Results

1988 general	Slade Gorton (R)	944,359	(51%)	($2,851,591)
	Michael Lowry (D)	904,183	(49%)	($2,191,187)
1988 primary	Slade Gorton (R)	335,846	(36%)	
	Michael Lowry (D)	297,399	(32%)	
	Don Bonker (D)	241,170	(26%)	
	Three Others	61,048	(6%)	
1983 special	Daniel J. Evans (R)	672,326	(55%)	($1,792,038)
	Michael Lowry (D)	540,981	(45%)	($1,007,973)

Sen. Patty Murray (D)

Elected 1992, seat up 1998; b. Oct. 11, 1950, Seattle; home, Seattle; WA St. U., B.A. 1972; Catholic; married (Rob).

Career: Shoreline Schl. Bd., 1985–89, Pres., 1985–86; WA Senate, 1988–92.

Offices: 302 HSOB 20510, 202-224-2621. Also 2988 Jackson Fed. Bldg., 915 2nd Ave., Seattle 98174, 206-553-5545; 601 1st Ave., Spokane 99201, 509-624-9515; and 140 Fed. Bldg., 500 W. 12th St., Vancouver 98660, 206-696-7797.

Committees: *Appropriations* (15th of 16 D): District of Columbia; Interior; Labor, Health and Human Services, Education; Legislative Branch. *Banking, Housing and Urban Affairs* (11th of 11 D): International Finance and Monetary Policy; Securities. *Budget* (12th of 12 D).

Group Ratings and 102d Congress Votes: Newly Elected

Key Votes of the 103d Congress

1. Family Leave   FOR   2. HIV Immigrants   FOR   3. Clinton Budget   FOR

Election Results

1992 general	Patty Murray (D)	1,197,973	(54%)	($1,342,038)
	Rod Chandler (R)	1,020,829	(46%)	($2,504,777)
1992 primary	Patty Murray (D)	318,455	(28%)	
	Rod Chandler (R)	228,083	(20%)	
	Don Bonker (D)	208,321	(19%)	
	Leo K. Thorsness (R)	185,498	(16%)	
	Tim Hill (R)	128,232	(11%)	
	Six Others	56,042	(5%)	
1986 general	Brock Adams (D)	677,471	(51%)	($1,912,307)
	Slade Gorton (R)	650,937	(49%)	($3,290,072)

FIRST DISTRICT

To the north and east metropolitan Seattle has spread out over the years, slowly in the early 1970s and rapidly in the late 1980s, reflecting the pace of the local economy. In growing, Seattle has lost some of its distinctiveness: the fishy odor of its docks does not permeate the new subdivisions built on what were once vegetable fields or vineyards; the Scandinavian heritage of old neighborhoods like Ballard has been mixed into a Pacific Northwest blend; the hoboes and day laborers that used to hang around Yesler Way, the original "Skid Road," with its cast iron buildings and its street clocks, aren't allowed in the shopping mall parking lots off I-5 or I-405. Yet there is a Seattle aura which most people appreciate and want to preserve, the evergreen smell of a well-watered land, the terrain with a beauty both breathtaking and subtle, cultural patterns that are plainly American yet geographically distant from most of the nation.

The 1st Congressional District of Washington includes much of the northern and eastern suburbs of Seattle, crossing Puget Sound and Lake Washington and taking in Bainbridge Island (where you can commute by ferry to downtown Seattle each day and then return home to what looks like the perfect American small town). There are comfortable suburbs north of Seattle along the Sound and inland off the main commuting roads. East of Lake Washington, in the Overlake towns of Bellevue (a part of which is in the district) and Redmond are the headquarters of some of America's most creative and rapidly growing corporations: Microsoft, in its campus of offices in pine-shaded, low-rise, turquoise buildings; northern-wear retailer Eddie Bauer and computer game inventor Nintendo; Sundstrand Data Control and SpaceLabs. The natural environmental beauty, the trendiness of the Seattle area and the welcoming business climate of the suburbs highlight the point that, as author Joel Garreau says, "If anywhere people would see the future of Edge Cities as the Machine in the Garden, it would be here." Politically, this is an area torn by forces of roughly equal strength between the two parties. The spectacular success of market economics is impossible not to notice, yet the yearning for a pristine and regulated environment tugs the other way.

The congresswoman from the 1st District is Maria Cantwell, a Democrat elected in 1992 when the incumbent Republican, John Miller, after four expensive campaigns in which he won no more than 56% of the votes, retired. This was a district held for 40 years by Republicans, though often tenuously, and was made a little more Republican by redistricting; but nothing stopped Cantwell from winning. She is one of those natural political operators of whom the Democrats have so many and the Republicans so few; she came to Washington from Indiana in 1983 to work for Alan Cranston's presidential campaign, and though that soon collapsed, she stayed, started a public relations business, and in 1986 was elected to the legislature. There she made a record as a self-proclaimed "pro-business Democrat," balancing environment and growth in a 1990 Growth Management Act, pushing for incentives for the biotech industry and chairing the Trade and Economic Development Committee. Her only misstep was operating her PR business out of her home without renewing her home-occupation license with the state in 1990.

Cantwell was running for the seat even before Miller dropped out in January 1992, and she soon had support from women's groups and labor. Her chief opponent was state Senator Gary Nelson, an engineer and 20-year legislator who was conservative on most issues, and was well known for sponsoring a Sexual Predator Act inspired by a horrible local crime. Cantwell attacked Nelson's antiabortion stand while calling for healthcare reform "without breaking the bank or building new bureaucracies"; she supported the line-item veto and huge defense cuts and said she was closer to Paul Tsongas or even Ross Perot than to Bill Clinton. "I've never seen anybody so pre-packaged in my life," Nelson said, but Cantwell was evidently persuasive when she said, "Voters are tired of elected officials who have lost touch with the reality of what it's like to get up every morning, fight traffic, earn a living, make a payroll." And Cantwell raised $287,000 from PACs and spent $621,000 total, to $114,000 for Nelson; Speaker Tom Foley came in and assured her of the seat she wanted on Public Works. Cantwell won 52% in the all-party primary in September to Nelson's 25% and another Republican's 14%; that was a good enough forecast of the general, which Cantwell won 55%–42%.

In the House, Cantwell got her promised seat on Public Works, plus Foreign Affairs and Merchant Marine, and put her skills to work on issues. She seems as admirably fitted for this district as a Democrat could be but, as she said, recalling her large promises, "The bottom line is that there are no excuses any more."

The People: Pop. 1990: 540,315; 10% rural; 9% age 65+; 90% White; 1% Black; 1% Amer. Indian; 5% Asian; 1% Other; 2% Hispanic origin. Voting age pop.: 400,376; 1% Black; 2% Hispanic origin. Households: 60% married couple families; 29% married couple fams. w. children; 67% college educ.; median household income: $40,390; per capita income: $18,687; median gross rent: $587; median house value: $147,900.

1992 Presidential Vote

Clinton (D)	118,386	(42%)
Bush (R)	90,537	(32%)
Perot (I)	70,340	(25%)

1988 Presidential Vote

Bush (R)	124,695	(52%)
Dukakis (D)	113,237	(48%)

Rep. Maria Cantwell (D)

Elected 1992; b. Oct. 13, 1958, Beach Grove, IN; home, Mountlake Terrace; Miami U. of OH, B.A. 1981; Catholic; single.

Career: Owner, Cantwell & Assoc. PR firm, 1985–91; WA House of Reps., 1986–92.

Offices: 1520 LHOB 20515, 202-225-6311. Also 21905 64th Ave., #101, Mountlake Terrace, 98043, 206-640-0233; and P.O. Box 185, Poulsbo 98370, 206-697-3112.

Committees: *Foreign Affairs* (19th of 27 D): Economic Policy, Trade and Environment. *Merchant Marine and Fisheries* (26th of 29 D): Fisheries Management. *Public Works and Transportation* (27th of 39 D): Aviation; Surface Transportation.

Group Ratings and 102d Congress Votes: Newly Elected

Key Votes of the 103d Congress

1. Family Leave	FOR	2. Deficit Reduction	FOR	3. Stimulus Plan	FOR

Election Results

1992 general	Maria Cantwell (D)	148,844	(55%)	($621,961)
	Gary Nelson (R)	113,897	(42%)	($114,546)
	Two Others	8,533	(3%)	
1992 primary	Maria Cantwell (D)	67,727	(52%)	
	Gary Nelson (R)	32,384	(25%)	
	Mark Gardner (R)	17,698	(14%)	
	John K. Dahl (R)	6,885	(5%)	
	Two Others	4,333	(3%)	
1990 general	John R. Miller (R)	100,339	(52%)	($912,969)
	Cynthia Sullivan (D)	92,447	(48%)	($351,660)

SECOND DISTRICT

The 172 San Juan Islands, in the waters of Puget Sound at the far northwest corner of Washington, were the last part of the continental United States to be turned over to this country; this was once a whaling area, and not until 1860 did the British relinquish the islands. Today, ferry boats ply the waters of the Sound, connecting the islands to mainland Washington, and to British Columbia directly to the west. This is some of the most beautiful land and water of North America, the steely blue Sound with green forested hills rising behind; it is wet country, shielded from the full force of Pacific rains by the Olympic Mountains but still seldom dry. The little towns have the look of pristine New England villages or Midwestern historic towns, but are better preserved than the original; the stores are full of fresh produce and local seafood. Here the Seattle metropolitan area has marched north along the shore of Puget Sound, to the old port and railroad terminus of Everett, with its huge Boeing 747 plant, and beyond.

The 2d Congressional District of Washington includes the San Juan Islands, Whidbey Island and most of Puget Sound from Everett north, plus the margin of mainland along the Sound and the huge mountains, topped by snow-capped Mount Baker, behind. The political tradition in most of the lumbering and fishing areas here is Democratic, while the agricultural areas are more Republican; overall, this is a pretty evenly balanced district which tends to vote as the state does.

The congressman here is Al Swift, a Democrat in a line of Democratic congressmen that goes back, with one Republican interruption, to Henry Jackson who was first elected here in 1940 and represented the district until he was elected to the Senate in 1952. Swift was first elected in 1978 after working for his predecessor Lloyd Meeds and as public affairs director for a Bellingham TV station. Swift got a seat on the Energy and Commerce Committee, and has been legislatively active since his first days in the House. His first big assignment was to frame the Northwest Power Act during the impending Washington Public Power Supply System (WPPSS) bankruptcy and as the Pacific Northwest was losing its historically low power rates. After the 1980 election, Swift attacked the television network news divisions for early projections of presidential elections; he pushed a uniform poll closing law through the House three times, but it never passed the Senate. Since 1984, Swift has chaired the House Administration Subcommittee on Elections, a frustrating assignment since it deals with the most partisan of issues. He was more successful with his motor voter bill, blocked by veto threats until 1992, but passed and signed into law after Bill Clinton became president in 1993.

In 1991, Swift became chairman of the Transportation and Hazardous Materials subcommittee of Energy and Commerce. He worked quickly to produce legislation to end the April 1991 rail strike, and he has been a champion of Amtrak and high speed rail. His major challenge now is reauthorization of RCRA, which covers solid waste disposal. In November 1991, Swift moved to set national standards for municipal disposal of solid waste, with special provisions for paper; he opposed a ban but allowed a ten-times-normal fee for disposal of out-of-state waste. His bill passed in committee in July 1992, but was attacked by industry and environmentalists, and stalled afterwards. Swift is likely to revisit RCRA again, but his main priority in the 103d Congress is to seek Superfund reauthorization. But not the 104th. In 1991, when Washington voters were considering a term limits initiative that would bar current members from running in 1994, Swift attacked it strongly and to underline his sincerity announced that he would retire in 1994 in any case. Many in both Washingtons expressed regret, as Swift is a hard-working, knowledgeable legislator.

In his last campaign, Swift was opposed by state Senator Jack Metcalf, a term limits advocate who ran for the U.S. Senate in 1968 and 1974—no limits on running for him. Swift, reelected 51%–41% in 1990, won 52%–42% in 1992: not overwhelming, but surely sufficient. Without Swift, the 2d District should be seriously contested in the general and quite possibly in the primary in 1994. Possible Democratic candidates include former Everett Mayor Bob Anderson, state Representative Rob Johnson, and Swift's own district director, Jill McKinnie. And Jack Metcalf could be back again for the Republicans.

The People: Pop. 1990: 540,861; 42% rural; 12% age 65+; 92% White; 1% Black; 2% Amer. Indian; 2% Asian; 1% Other; 3% Hispanic origin. Voting age pop.: 396,615; 1% Black; 2% Hispanic origin. Households: 60% married couple families; 28% married couple fams. w. children; 52% college educ.; median household income: $31,305; per capita income: $14,419; median gross rent: $468; median house value: $100,100.

1992 Presidential Vote

Clinton (D)	103,405	(39%)
Bush (R)	85,876	(33%)
Perot (I)	71,794	(27%)

1988 Presidential Vote

Bush (R)	93,159	(51%)
Dukakis (D)	88,525	(49%)

Rep. Al Swift (D)

Elected 1978; b. Sept. 12, 1935, Tacoma; home, Bellingham; Whitman Col., 1953–55, Central WA St. Col., B.A. 1957; Unitarian; married (Paula).

Career: Broadcaster, Pub. Affairs Dir., KVOS-TV, Bellingham, 1957–64, 1969–77; A.A., U.S. Rep. Lloyd Meeds, 1965–69, 1977.

Offices: 1502 LHOB 20515, 202-225-2605. Also Fed. Bldg., #201, 3002 Colby, Everett 98201, 206-252-3188; and Fed. Bldg., #308, 104 W. Magnolia, Bellingham 98225, 206-733-4500.

Committees: *Energy and Commerce* (5th of 27 D): Energy and Power; Transportation and Hazardous Materials (Chmn.). *House Administration* (2d of 12 D): Accounts; Elections (Chmn.). *Joint Committee on the Organization of Congress* (3d of 12).

Group Ratings

	ADA	ACLU	COPE	CDF	CFA	LCV	ACU	NTLC	NSI	COC	CEI
1992	90	96	75	100	87	31	4	0	40	25	10
1991	90	—	83	100	83	46	0	—	—	30	10

National Journal Ratings

	1991 LIB	—	1991 CONS	1992 LIB	—	1992 CONS
Economic	72%	—	23%	74%	—	25%
Social	84%	—	12%	72%	—	24%
Foreign	83%	—	15%	71%	—	26%

Key Votes of the 102d Congress

1. Ban Striker Replace	FOR	5. Handgun Wait/7-Day	FOR	9. Use Force in Gulf	AGN
2. $ for Homeownership	AGN	6. Overseas Mil. Abortion	FOR	10. US Mil. Abroad $ Cut	FOR
3. Tax Rich/Cut Mid Cls.	FOR	7. Obscn. Art NEA $ Ban	AGN	11. Limit SDI Funds	FOR
4. FY93/$15B Def. Cut	FOR	8. Death Pen. from Jury	AGN	12. Cuba Trade Embargo	FOR

Key Votes of the 103d Congress

1. Family Leave	FOR	2. Deficit Reduction	FOR	3. Stimulus Plan	FOR

Election Results

1992 general	Al Swift (D)	133,207	(52%)	($1,060,650)
	Jack Metcalf (R)	107,365	(42%)	($201,029)
	Two Others	15,348	(6%)	
1992 primary	Al Swift (D)	56,290	(43%)	
	Jack Metcalf (R)	31,661	(24%)	
	Tim Erwin (R)	13,114	(10%)	
	Doug Smith (R)	9,856	(8%)	
	Frank D. Sadowski (D)	6,344	(5%)	
	David Montgomery (R)	5,123	(4%)	
	Three Others	7,063	(6%)	
1990 general	Al Swift (D)	92,837	(51%)	($465,249)
	Doug Smith (R)	75,669	(41%)	($11,373)
	William L. McCord (LIB)	15,165	(8%)	

THIRD DISTRICT

From the Pacific Ocean to the majestic row of active and inactive volcanoes, from Mount Rainier to Mount St. Helens to Oregon's Mount Hood, this is one of America's most productive lumber areas. The moist air and almost constant rains blown in from the Pacific keep the trees on the coast growing rapidly; in the valleys just past the Coast Range, there is still plenty of precipitation and fast-growing forest. Then come the high mountains: the Cascades are a genuine divide, wrenching almost all the precipitation out of the air, so that the climate eastward for a thousand miles is arid. Americans were reminded of the force of the volcanoes when Mount St. Helens, dormant for 123 years, erupted in 1980, killing 65 people, pouring lava and mud down the rivers, damming lakes and flooding 160,000 acres, ruining the land in its path. The land and mountain reconfigured, nature has repaired itself, as it must have done dozens of times before.

The 3d Congressional District of Washington covers the land between the Ocean and the Cascades, from the state capital of Olympia on an inlet of Puget Sound, south to Vancouver, site of the Hudson Bay company headquarters in the 19th Century and now an industrial suburb across the Columbia River from Portland, Oregon. Despite its lumberjack, flannel shirt look, this is one of America's great international trading districts, with big exports of fish and, in the port of Portland, offloading of imported cars. But lumber has always been the biggest industry here, and one that has constantly roiled its politics. In the 1970s and 1980s, there were ferocious demands to stop the export of unprocessed timber to East Asia; local sawmills wanted the work. In the last half-decade, the raging issue has been the spotted owl, or rather the court decision closing off old-forest logging to save the spotted owl's habitat. These are elusive birds, not much different from other owls, that require vast territory and which range over much of the Pacific Coast forests: the Endangered Species Act here can mean not just endangering, but eradicating thousands of jobs. But the issue may have burned its brightest already: by the time President Clinton held his timber summit in Portland in April 1993, thousands of loggers were already looking for other work, and logging companies were moving their operations elsewhere. The initial political fallout worked against Democrats, who are identified with environmentalists here. But Bill Clinton carried this area handily, and the political atmosphere again has gone back to the tradition springing from the turn of the century.

The congresswoman from the 3d District, Jolene Unsoeld, brings a terrific determination to her work, which has enabled her to compile one of the most liberal records in the House and hold one of the most furiously contested seats in the country. Her bounce back from personal tragedy won her the admiration of many constituents and colleagues. Unsoeld is a mountain climber who lived in Nepal in the 1960s and was the first woman to climb the North Face of Mount Teton; her daughter Devi died in 1976 while climbing Nanda Devi, the highest peak in India, after which she had been named; her husband Willi died in 1979 in an avalanche on Mount Rainier. As an "unpaid independent citizen lobbyist," she published two books detailing contributions to Washington state legislators, triggering some lobbying spending reforms, and was elected to the legislature herself in 1984. In 1988, when incumbent Democrat Don Bonker ran for the Senate (and lost the primary), Unsoeld ran for the 3d District seat, winning 40% in the all-party primary and beating a career military officer, recently returned to the district, in the general by 618 votes, with big margins in Olympia and on the coast.

In the House, she promptly antagonized thousands of district voters by coming out for protecting the spotted owl even at the cost of logging jobs; her calls for balanced use of timber lands were met with jeers, but also won her some admiration for her guts. With Speaker Thomas Foley's help, she raised more than $1 million, about half of it from PACs, and in the all-party primary in 1990, she had 52% to 38% for an evangelical-minded Republican. Then late in the campaign, she got publicity for her amendment to permit U.S. companies to manufacture semiautomatic guns, a position supported by the National Rifle Association and a source of hefty PAC contributions. In the general election, she won 54%.

Unsoeld has worked hard on many local issues, from the North Bonneville dam site to forest management experimentation to driftnet fishing; she called for federal jobs programs for displaced forest workers; she convened meetings of environmentalists and loggers. She objected to disclosure of House bank records, citing separation of powers and individual rights, which showed her with one overdraft of 38 cents. Redistricting treated her kindly, and she won 52% again in the all-party primary and prevailed in the general by 56%–44%. It is risky to call safe a district so rocked by economic change, but Unsoeld has shown great vote-winning capacity here.

The People: Pop. 1990: 540,658; 38% rural; 13% age 65+; 93% White; 1% Black; 1% Amer. Indian; 2% Asian; 1% Other; 2% Hispanic origin. Voting age pop.: 392,660; 1% Black; 2% Hispanic origin. Households: 59% married couple families; 28% married couple fams. w. children; 50% college educ.; median household income: $29,154; per capita income: $13,328; median gross rent: $414; median house value: $70,300.

1992 Presidential Vote			1988 Presidential Vote		
Clinton (D)	104,682	(42%)	Dukakis (D)	101,683	(52%)
Bush (R)	82,648	(33%)	Bush (R)	93,833	(48%)
Perot (I)	61,609	(25%)			

Rep. Jolene Unsoeld (D)

Elected 1988; b. Dec. 3, 1931, Corvallis, OR; home, Olympia; U. of OR; no religious affiliation; widowed.

Career: Dir., English Language Inst., Nepal, 1965–67; Lobbyist, consultant, 1971–84; Author; WA House of Reps., 1984–88.

Offices: 1527 LHOB 20515, 202-225-3536. Also 1110 Capitol Way., #404, Olympia 98501, 206-753-9528; and 601 Main St., #205, Vancouver 98660, 206-696-7942.

Committees: *Education and Labor* (11th of 28 D): Elementary, Secondary and Vocational Education; Labor-Management Relations; Postsecondary Education and Training. *Merchant Marine and Fisheries* (12th of 29 D): Environment and Natural Resources; Fisheries Management.

Group Ratings

	ADA	ACLU	COPE	CDF	CFA	LCV	ACU	NTLC	NSI	COC	CEI
1992	90	96	100	90	87	81	0	10	30	38	10
1991	90	—	100	80	83	85	5	—	—	10	8

National Journal Ratings

	1991 LIB — 1991 CONS			1992 LIB — 1992 CONS		
Economic	88%	—	0%	88%	—	11%
Social	77%	—	22%	92%	—	0%
Foreign	92%	—	0%	90%	—	0%

Key Votes of the 102d Congress

1. Ban Striker Replace	FOR	5. Handgun Wait/7-Day	AGN	9. Use Force in Gulf	AGN
2. $ for Homeownership	AGN	6. Overseas Mil. Abortion	FOR	10. US Mil. Abroad $ Cut	FOR
3. Tax Rich/Cut Mid Cls.	FOR	7. Obscn. Art NEA $ Ban	AGN	11. Limit SDI Funds	FOR
4. FY93/$15B Def. Cut	FOR	8. Death Pen. from Jury	AGN	12. Cuba Trade Embargo	AGN

Key Votes of the 103d Congress

1. Family Leave	FOR	2. Deficit Reduction	FOR	3. Stimulus Plan	FOR

Election Results

1992 general	Jolene Unsoeld (D)	138,043	(56%)	($619,947)
	Pat Fiske (R)	108,583	(44%)	($212,192)
1992 primary	Jolene Unsoeld (D)	59,510	(52%)	
	Pat Fiske (R)	22,848	(20%)	
	Bill Hughes (R)	16,737	(15%)	
	Chuck O'Reilly (D)	10,495	(9%)	
	Gary Snell (R)	5,575	(5%)	
1990 general	Jolene Unsoeld (D)	95,645	(54%)	($1,298,593)
	Bob Williams (R)	82,269	(46%)	($817,944)

FOURTH DISTRICT

Washington's Cascade Mountains are a stark climactic divide. West of the Cascades, Washington is moist, green, full of watery inlets; to the east, it is barren and brown, except where the waters of the Columbia are fed by irrigation ditches into thirsty valleys, or where mountaintop waters fall east, as they do to water the apple orchards in the Yakima Valley. Into this forbidding, often surreal, landscape, the federal government left its impress half a century ago. Above the Columbia is the nation's only giant bust of Franklin Roosevelt, looking out over 550-foot-high Grand Coulee Dam, one of his favorite projects, where he was wheeled out to survey the world's largest structure, that he had initiated. Downriver are other dams, all the way to Bonneville, not far east of Portland, where the Columbia breaks through the Cascades; the dams generated the cheap power needed to make aluminum, from which Boeing began making airplanes in World War II.

Between these dams, near the Tri-Cities of Richland, Kennewick and Pasco, in a bleak landscape with temperatures as high as 110 in summer and 27 below zero in winter, is the Hanford Works. Built originally during World War II by the DuPont company as part of the Manhattan Project, it housed the first nuclear reactors; here today is one of the nation's major nuclear manufacturing facilities, threatened now with shutdowns because of hazardous leaks and contaminated waste. For all the controversy over whether to shut down all or part of the operation, it is still the area's largest private employer and the federal government's role here is highly resented.

The 4th Congressional District of Washington covers the western half of this east-of-the-Cascades, from Grand Coulee through the Hanford Works down to The Dalles Dam. Dependent on government development, the 4th remains sour on its intervention, and with some reason. The Yakima Valley is angry that the apparently groundless Alar scare hurt the sale of Washington apples. Lumber towns in the Cascades are furious that those who want to preserve the spotted owl from extinction may shut down their logging businesses. And everyone is angry because, after the WPPSS bungled a huge nuclear plant construction program and the Columbia's hydroelectric capacity was used up, electricity rates here are no longer so low. In the Tri-Cities around the Hanford Works, people are unhappy about the toxic wastes that have seeped out over the past 50 years—and unhappy with those who they see as overly concerned and trying to shut nuclear power down.

The congressman from the 4th District is Jay Inslee, one of three freshman Democrats from Washington and perhaps the biggest surprise winner. Inslee grew up in Seattle, the son of a school athletic administrator, and is an accomplished athlete himself. After law school in 1976, he settled in Selah, in Yakima County, and practiced law. In 1988, he was elected to the state House over a former Yakima mayor; in 1990, he beat a well known businessman who outspent him with 62% of the vote. In 1992, when Republican Congressman Sid Morrison ran for governor (and lost the primary), several candidates started running for the seat. Inslee did not enter the race until April and had competition from Tri-Cities Democratic legislator Jim Jesernig, who outspent him; Jesernig carried Tri-Cities 42%–9% in the all-party primary, but Inslee won Yakima 34%–8% and the northern counties as well, for a 23%–22% edge. But in first place with 24% was Republican Richard "Doc" Hastings, conservative and antiabortion, backed by the Christian Coalition, from Tri-Cities; he won there 57%–43% in the general, but Inslee won Yakima and the northern counties both with 54%–46%, for a 51%–49% district margin.

Like many freshman Democrats, Inslee promised to halve the federal budget deficit in five years and overhaul the healthcare system. In the House he was skeptical about the Clinton stimulus package, but voted for it: "I decided it was not the better part of wisdom to damage the quarterback so early in the game." But by 1994, voters may be asking whether he has scored according to promise.

The People: Pop. 1990: 540,701; 39% rural; 12% age 65+; 79% White; 1% Black; 3% Amer. Indian; 1% Asian; 12% Other; 16% Hispanic origin. Voting age pop.: 380,860; 1% Black; 12% Hispanic origin. Households: 59% married couple families; 29% married couple fams. w. children; 44% college educ.; median household income: $25,055; per capita income: $11,578; median gross rent: $333; median house value: $60,100.

1992 Presidential Vote			1988 Presidential Vote		
Bush (R)	87,995	(42%)	Bush (R)	105,894	(59%)
Clinton (D)	71,914	(35%)	Dukakis (D)	74,951	(41%)
Perot (I)	45,256	(22%)			

Rep. Jay Inslee (D)

Elected 1992; b. Feb. 9, 1951, Seattle; home, Selah; Stanford U., 1969–70; U. of WA, B.A. 1972, Willamette Law Schl., J.D. 1976; Protestant; married (Trudi).

Career: Selah City Prosecutor, 1976–84; Practicing atty., 1976–92; WA House of Reps., 1988–92.

Offices: 1431 LHOB 20515, 202-225-5816. Also 701 N. 1st St., #B, Yakima 98901, 509-452-3243; 112 N. Mission St., Wenatchee 98801, 509-662-4294; and 3311 W. Clearwater, #105, Kennewick 99336, 509-783-0310.

Committees: *Agriculture* (18th of 28 D): Department Operations and Nutrition; Environment, Credit and Rural Development; Specialty Crops and Natural Resources. *Science, Space and Technology* (26th of 33 D): Energy; Technology, Environment and Aviation.

Group Ratings and 102d Congress Votes: Newly Elected

Key Votes of the 103d Congress

1. Family Leave	FOR	2. Deficit Reduction	FOR	3. Stimulus Plan	FOR

Election Results

1992 general	Jay Inslee (D)	106,556	(51%)	($255,159)
	Richard "Doc" Hastings (R)	103,028	(49%)	($355,859)
1992 primary	Richard "Doc" Hastings (R)	28,952	(24%)	
	Jay Inslee (D)	27,429	(23%)	
	Jim Jesernig (D)	26,320	(22%)	
	Alex McLean (R)	13,605	(11%)	
	Jeffrey C. Sullivan (R)	12,074	(10%)	
	Bill Almon (R)	9,168	(8%)	
	Other	3,774	(3%)	
1990 general	Sid Morrison (R)	106,545	(71%)	($49,935)
	Ole H. Hougen (D)	44,241	(29%)	

FIFTH DISTRICT

Eastern Washington is a land of great rivers and bare parched land, where the Columbia, Spokane and Snake Rivers wind among vast plateaus, bringing water from the Rockies to the desert. Spokane grew up at the falls of the Spokane River when the railroads first came through, and became a major wheat, mining, electrical and railroad center early in this century, the center of the so-called "Inland Empire"; it celebrated with the 1974 World's Exposition on the downtown riverfront. Nearby are some of the most fascinating landscapes in the United States: surreally undulating yellow wheatfields, the ridges of the Palouse where the topsoil is 200 feet deep, the bare-rock coulees rising above dammed-up lakes and barren desert. It is remote, a spot of Middle America set off by itself. This is not hospitable land: the summers are blazing hot and winters bitter cold; the rivers run wildly. But it has been tamed by man, and the water from the Grand Coulee and other dams irrigates some of the richest farmland in the country.

The 5th Congressional District of Washington covers the easternmost segment of the state. Some two-thirds of the people here live in greater Spokane, a city whose voting habits are a fairly good proxy of the nation's. Its heritage leans toward the Republicans, but it is not nearly as Republican as most of the nearby Rocky Mountain states, though it veered toward them angrily at times in the 1970s and 1980s; but it is open to Democrats, and although Spokane County did not vote for Michael Dukakis in 1988 as Washington did, it gave Bill Clinton a smart margin in 1992. It helped that Clinton made a well-received campaign appearance in not very centrally located Spokane, but with good reason: Spokane and the 5th District are the home of Speaker of the House Thomas Foley, and Clinton, campaigning as an outsider and after keeping congressional leaders out of the spotlight at his convention, wanted to woo the man who would have much to do with his success or failure on Capitol Hill.

Tom Foley grew up in an affluent hillside neighborhood overlooking Spokane's downtown; he was the son of a judge, a Democrat who was widely respected in a community where most of the leading citizens were staunch Republicans. As a 35-year-old lawyer, after stints as a local prosecutor and on Senator Henry Jackson's staff in Washington, Foley filed on the last day to run for Congress in 1964; in the Johnson landslide that year, he beat a 22-year Republican incumbent. In the House, he advanced both through seniority and insurgency, a respectful young man working hard and rising in the ranks, and a principled reformer. He became chairman of the Democratic Study Group in 1972, when it was an upstart group dominated by Phillip Burton and supplanting Speaker Carl Albert's leadership by setting agendas, taking stands on issues, making head counts and whip calls. At the same time, Foley advanced quietly to second in seniority on the Agriculture Committee. Both forms of advance congealed in December 1974 when, under Burton's reform procedure, the Democratic Caucus voted out Agriculture Chairman Bob Poage, an elderly conservative, and voted in Foley. Characteristically, Foley supported Poage and deferred to him afterwards, while working steadily on farm bills.

Foley rose again after the 1980 electoral disaster for Democrats, as Whip John Brademas lost in Indiana and Dan Rostenkowski, who could have had the job, took the Ways and Means chairmanship instead. So Speaker Tip O'Neill and Majority Leader Jim Wright selected Foley for a post which was then, but is no longer, appointed. Foley's knowledge of parliamentary procedure and sense of fairness served him well. When O'Neill retired and Wright moved up, so did Foley: the last time the Democrats had chosen a majority leader, in 1976, there had been a bitter fight; in 1986 Foley won unopposed. When Speaker Jim Wright was under attack on ethics charges in spring 1989, Foley defended him loyally. When Wright resigned in June 1989, Foley's selection as speaker was automatic and was greeted with a sigh of relief.

As speaker, Foley retains the reputation for fairness and intellectual honesty that he has built up for 25 years. He has an elegant intellect that is apparent when he explains abstruse points of parliamentary procedure, and a droll appreciation of others that is apparent when he is telling anecdotes from the campaign trail in eastern Washington. Yet he is also at the head of a Democratic leadership that is aggressively partisan and keeps careful track of who supports its positions and who doesn't. Foley is a good listener and can be willing to accommodate others, but he does insist on doing things his own way. Underneath his pleasant, formal exterior there is a steely discipline: a lifelong hater of exercise inclined to overweight, he started lifting weights and lost 70 pounds when he became speaker.

Foley has a view of the speakership as being a bit above partisanship, and leaves much of the partisan heavy lifting to Majority Leader Dick Gephardt, of whose talents he seems not at all jealous and by whose ambitions he seems quite unthreatened. Foley has intervened with great force only when sees a threat to basic institutions, including Congress itself. In that spirit, he opposed the flag burning constitutional amendment in 1989 and 1990; in a similar spirit, he made a moving speech against the Gulf war resolution in January 1991. After the vote, Foley strongly supported the war effort and made clear his and other Democrats' personal commitment to American victory; he had handsome words of salute for Bush when he spoke to Congress in March 1991. In 1989, he managed to get a combined ethics package and pay increase through; in 1990 he supported the budget summit agreement package which he and Gephardt had pushed on the Bush Administration; here as on other occasions he takes the view that tax increases are needed to cut the federal budget deficit. To some House Democrats, Foley appeared insufficiently partisan for not advancing alternatives to Republican proposals more aggressively; to some House Republicans, he was harshly partisan because of increased restrictions on offering amendments, and for exerting pressure to change votes as he did successfully on the balanced budget amendment. His strategy has in fact been partisan; the question is how effective it has been politically. It has produced Democratic issues like higher taxes on the rich in October 1990 and family and medical leave in 1992, but it has also left Democrats taking positions on which the best that can be said politically is that they are not sure vote-losers. And his efforts to produce Democratic alternatives on healthcare reform and campaign finance reform in 1992 were unsuccessful.

In 1992, Foley dealt with another crisis and came out stronger. The fall 1991 revelations of overdrafts on the House bank and the spring 1992 handling of the disclosure process enraged many Democrats who felt that Foley should have abolished the antediluvian bank or he should have resisted demands for disclosure, or both. John Bryant of Texas said Foley should quit because "he refuses to be a political leader"; Committee Chairmen Charlie Rose and Dave McCurdy were openly critical, as were Bob Torricelli and Charles Stenholm; some members began talking about challenging him for speaker. Foley seemed dismayed, but kept his poise, and embarked on a disciplined process of conferring in person and at length with every Democratic member; he enlisted Sam Gejdenson as a campaign manager for his reelection as speaker; by August 1992 he had pledges from a majority of Democrats. After the November 1992 elections in which Democrats lost only 10 seats, far fewer than expected, Foley travelled the country to several meetings with newly elected Democrats, preventing them from coalescing as a rebellious force, as had the 1974 freshmen who had elected him Agriculture chairman, or from bonding with freshmen Republicans; and, in early 1993 these were leadership Democrats, even going along with such partisan proposals as the hamhanded attempt to give expanded voting rights to the delegates from the territories—something Foley had questioned as unconstitutional in the 1960s.

But was the new president a leadership Democrat? Foley had not been an early Bill Clinton supporter, and Clinton practically hid the Democratic congressional leadership at the New York convention. But after the Spokane visit, they cooperated in the campaign, and in the early months of the administration Foley gamely supported administration plans, and met the spirit of Clinton's White House staff cuts with a pledge to cut congressional staff by 1,300 by 1995. When Clinton proposals were plainly lacking a majority of Democrats, Foley communicated that to the White House, and negotiated change; but in the first months he mostly delivered—on the budget resolution, the stimulus package that was filibustered in the Senate, family and medical leave, the motor voter bill. Foley made a rare floor speech in May 1993, giving an impassioned plea for passage of Clinton's deficit reduction proposal which helped push it through 219–213. In return for all this, the administration negotiated with House Democratic grandees, watering down Clinton's line-item veto to something acceptable to Foley, negotiating education reform with Education and Labor Chairman William Ford, crafting campaign finance reform proposals to be palatable to Foley and Gephardt. In general it can be said that Foley has molded his Democrats into an effective governing majority. It can also be said that he is tying it firmly to the record of the Clinton Administration—and both are likely to rise and fall together in 1994 and 1996, as they did in 1992.

That tendency can be seen in the returns for Foley's own 1992 race. For years, he has run ahead of the Democratic ticket in the 5th District, winning in 1988 and 1990 with 76% and 69%. But in 1992, against free-spending doctor John Sonneland, who had run before and held him to 52% in 1980 and 64% in 1982, Foley won just 53% in the all-party primary and 55% in the general election; he carried Spokane solidly but lost four rural counties in November. Foley's seat is not necessarily in jeopardy should Clinton become unpopular, as many presidents have in their second years, for Foley certainly has many political assets beyond his association with Clinton. But it suggests that in such circumstances Foley may be tied down, as the House Republican leader was two years into Ronald Reagan's term, with defending himself in his district.

The People: Pop. 1990: 540,865; 29% rural; 13% age 65+; 92% White; 1% Black; 2% Amer. Indian; 2% Asian; 2% Other; 3% Hispanic origin. Voting age pop.: 398,951; 1% Black; 3% Hispanic origin. Households: 55% married couple families; 26% married couple fams. w. children; 54% college educ.; median household income: $25,107; per capita income: $12,177; median gross rent: $345; median house value: $57,400.

1992 Presidential Vote

Clinton (D) 99,676 (40%)
Bush (R) 90,294 (36%)
Perot (I)..................... 56,472 (23%)

1988 Presidential Vote

Bush (R) 105,489 (51%)
Dukakis (D). 99,555 (49%)

Rep. Thomas S. Foley (D)

Elected 1964; b. Mar. 6, 1929, Spokane; home, Spokane; U. of WA, B.A. 1951, LL.B. 1957; Catholic; married (Heather).

Career: Practicing atty., 1957; Spokane Cnty. Dep. Prosecuting Atty., 1958–60; Instructor, Gonzaga U. Law Sch., 1958–60; WA Asst. Atty. Gen., 1960–61; Asst. Chief Clerk and Special Cnsl., U.S. Senate Interior Cmte., 1961–63.

Offices: 1201 LHOB 20515, 202-225-2006. Also 601 1st Ave., #2-W, Spokane 99204, 509-353-2155; 12929 E. Sprague, Spokane 99216, 509-926-4434; and 28 W. Main, Walla Walla 99362, 509-522-6372.

Committees: *Speaker of the House.*

Group Ratings and Key Votes: Speaker does not usually vote.

Election Results

1992 general	Thomas S. Foley (D)	135,965	(55%)	($913,647)
	John Sonneland (R)	110,443	(45%)	($477,806)
1992 primary	Thomas S. Foley (D)	68,536	(53%)	
	John Sonneland (R)	27,384	(21%)	
	Duane Sommers (R)	20,110	(16%)	
	Marlyn A. Derby (R)	10,833	(8%)	
	Other	3,077	(2%)	
1990 general	Thomas S. Foley (D)	110,234	(69%)	($457,754)
	Marlyn A. Derby (R)	49,965	(31%)	($5,006)

SIXTH DISTRICT

The rainiest part of the continental United States is at its far northwest corner, where the Olympic Mountains of Washington thrust into the Pacific Ocean. The cold waters of the Pacific evaporate, condense and then mist or rain down on the hills and mountains that jut up from the ocean and Puget Sound. The mountains here are always green, the trees that line the inlets towering, and during heavy rainfalls the rivers can rise six feet a day. This has long been lumbering and fishing country, where men go out to work at 6 a.m. in air cold enough to see your breath year round, and where dependence on the vagaries of nature and the unpredictable requirements of environmentalists—like the ban on old-growth logging to protect the habitat of the spotted owl—have strengthened a traditional surly independence and suspicion of authority.

The inlets of Puget Sound, winding sinuously through the mountains, are among America's most picturesque waterways and strategically quite important. Here during World War II, shipyards built and sheltered much of the U.S. Navy's Pacific fleet, and here during the Cold War much of the nuclear submarine fleet anchored at the Bremerton Navy base, which today is home to great relics of those conflicts, the *U.S.S. Missouri* where the Japanese surrendered to General MacArthur in September 1945, and the *Turner Joy* which was the alleged object of attack in the Gulf of Tonkin incident in July 1965.

The 6th Congressional District of Washington contains the Olympic Peninsula, Bremerton and most of surrounding Kitsap County amid various inlets of Puget Sound and about half the city of Tacoma just to the east, over the bridge that replaced the Tacoma Straits suspension bridge that, in a scene preserved on newsreel, started vibrating on the wrong harmonic in high winds and collapsed in 1940. Politically, the Olympic Peninsula and Bremerton are working-class Democratic; Tacoma, a port and paper mill town, is traditionally Democratic, though the 6th's portion of it is the more white-collar side of town. On balance the 6th is, after the central Seattle 7th, Washington's most Democratic district.

The congressman from the 6th District is Norman Dicks, a onetime University of Washington football player who was on Senator Warren Magnuson's staff when it was one of the best staffs ever seen on Capitol Hill. Dicks returned home to Kitsap County to run for Congress in 1976, when the 6th District incumbent finally got the judgeship he had been hankering after for 12 years. Dicks was elected easily that year, and every year since except 1980, when Magnuson lost. In anti-incumbent 1990, Dicks won 58% in the all-party primary and 61% in the general; in 1992, after redistricting made the district slightly more Democratic, he had 58% in the primary and 64% in the general. Dicks passed up possible chances to run for the Senate in 1983, 1986 and 1988, and seems firmly committed to the House.

In the House, Dicks has shown an aggressiveness and political shrewdness that were hallmarks of the Magnuson staff in its golden days, plus an interest in defense and intelligence reminiscent of Magnuson's congressional colleague for 40 years, Henry Jackson. Dicks won a seat on the Appropriations Committee and is on both the Defense and Military Construction Subcommittees—vital posts for Kitsap County, where most workers depend on Pentagon payrolls, and for Washington generally, because of Boeing. He is now second in seniority on Defense, just behind Chairman John Murtha. In the early 1980s, Dicks took the lead on restoring Export-Import Bank loan authority—Boeing is America's biggest exporter and user of the loans—when the Reagan Administration wanted to cut it, and led a campaign that switched 80 House votes overnight. In the middle 1980s, working with Les Aspin, he helped keep the MX missile alive in return for arms control commitments from the Reagan Administration. More recently, he has helped to shape the downsizing of defense forces, while still looking after Washington interests; he has championed the yet unbuilt Everett Navy homeport, praised the F-117 Stealth aircraft for its role in the Gulf war and argued for the B-2 Stealth bomber; he pushed a critical amendment for advanced airborne reconnaissance; and of course looks after Bremerton's huge Navy facilities. He has also used his Appropriations seat to channel federal money to localities hurt by the ban on logging in old-growth forests and will push for funding of a Tacoma waterfront development from which visitors can gaze upon Mount Rainier.

Speaker Thomas Foley, who worked on Jackson's staff years ago, is obviously grooming Dicks to chair the House Intelligence Committee. Initially, Dicks seems to support CIA Director James Woolsey's arguments that cuts should be phased in deliberately. Foley appointed Dicks to the body in 1991 and in 1993 gave his newly appointed chairman, Dan Glickman, a single-year extension, which means his service will end in January 1995. At that point, assuming Foley and the Democrats hold their majority, Dicks is likely to begin a four-year period as Intelligence chairman.

The People: Pop. 1990: 540,836; 26% rural; 14% age 65+; 86% White; 5% Black; 2% Amer. Indian; 4% Asian; 1% Other; 3% Hispanic origin. Voting age pop.: 403,683; 5% Black; 2% Hispanic origin. Households: 55% married couple families; 24% married couple fams. w. children; 51% college educ.; median household income: $27,882; per capita income: $13,403; median gross rent: $415; median house value: $74,400.

1992 Presidential Vote

Clinton (D) 106,370 (43%)
Bush (R) 77,539 (31%)
Perot (I). 60,582 (25%)

1988 Presidential Vote

Dukakis (D). 100,901 (52%)
Bush (R) 92,431 (48%)

Rep. Norm Dicks (D)

Elected 1976; b. Dec. 16, 1940, Bremerton; home, Bremerton; U. of WA, B.A. 1963, J.D. 1968; Lutheran; married (Suzanne).

Career: Legis. Asst., U.S. Sen. Warren Magnuson, 1968–73, A.A., 1973–76.

Offices: 2467 RHOB 20515, 202-225-5916. Also 1717 Pacific Ave., #2244, Tacoma 98402, 206-593-6536; and 500 Pacific Ave., #301, Bremerton 98310, 206-479-4011.

Committees: *Appropriations* (10th of 37 D): Defense; Interior; Military Construction. *Intelligence (Permanent Select)* (3d of 12 D): Legislation; Oversight and Evaluation (Chmn.).

Group Ratings

	ADA	ACLU	COPE	CDF	CFA	LCV	ACU	NTLC	NSI	COC	CEI
1992	80	86	73	90	93	44	8	10	60	25	14
1991	70	—	82	90	72	54	5	—	—	38	9

National Journal Ratings

	1991 LIB	—	1991 CONS	1992 LIB	—	1992 CONS
Economic	68%	—	31%	66%	—	31%
Social	74%	—	23%	66%	—	34%
Foreign	59%	—	39%	38%	—	56%

Key Votes of the 102d Congress

1. Ban Striker Replace	FOR	5. Handgun Wait/7-Day FOR	9. Use Force in Gulf AGN
2. $ for Homeownership	AGN	6. Overseas Mil. Abortion FOR	10. US Mil. Abroad $ Cut AGN
3. Tax Rich/Cut Mid Cls.	FOR	7. Obscn. Art NEA $ Ban FOR	11. Limit SDI Funds AGN
4. FY93/$15B Def. Cut	FOR	8. Death Pen. from Jury AGN	12. Cuba Trade Embargo FOR

Key Votes of the 103d Congress

1. Family Leave   FOR   2. Deficit Reduction   FOR   3. Stimulus Plan   FOR

Election Results

1992 general	Norm Dicks (D)	152,933	(64%)	($617,460)
	Lauri J. Phillips (R)	66,664	(28%)	($6,438)
	Tom Donnelly (I)	14,490	(6%)	($15,810)
	Other	4,075	(2%)	
1992 primary	Norm Dicks (D)	73,832	(58%)	
	Lauri J. Phillips (R)	34,325	(27%)	
	Dennis Christiani (D)	10,306	(8%)	
	Tom Donnelly (I)	6,968	(5%)	
	Two Others	2,690	(2%)	
1990 general	Norm Dicks (D)	79,079	(61%)	($565,257)
	Norbert Mueller (R)	49,786	(39%)	($7,598)

SEVENTH DISTRICT

Seattle is no longer a secret. It zoomed into the national consciousness with the 1897 Klondike gold strike, has been a major American city since around 1910, had its own World's Fair in 1962, yet not until the late 1980s did it begin to make an impression as one of America's most booming cities, while remaining one of the most beautiful. Seattle rises from the Puget Sound harbor of Elliott Bay on steep hills, once covered with 300-foot-high Douglas firs; behind the hills and buildings you can see on a clear day, from almost anywhere, the nimbus of Mount Rainier. On the waterfront, below gleaming high-rises, is the Pike Place market, where you can get fresh salmon and Dungenesse crab; nearby is Pioneer Square, where stores and warehouses from the turn of the century have been restored and renovated; and Yesler Way, America's original "Skid Road," now has upscale shops but still some homeless too. Seattle's upper class, like San Francisco's, continues to be anchored downtown, which has a certain formality; but there is a high-tech Technology Corridor east of Lake Washington, and many comfortable old working-class neighborhoods of frame houses on steep hillsides. The old ethnic groups are not very distinctive to the untrained eye, because so many people are of Scandinavian ancestry; but Seattle is now getting an influx of Asians and Hispanics. Generally, blue-collar workers live on the south side of the city and in valleys, or midway between Puget Sound and Lake Washington; the factories, warehouses and railroad yards are concentrated in a flat plain near Puget Sound and south of downtown. The big Boeing factories are located farther south, and younger blue-collar workers have followed them into the suburban areas directly south of the city: Burien, Tukwila, Kent and Renton, which lie at the southern end of Lake Washington.

More affluent, white-collar workers and better-educated people tend to live on the hills and near the water, and are more likely to be found on the north side; here is Capitol Hill, though Seattle is not the state capital, and Queen Anne, with late Victorian and early prairie houses arrayed on grid streets with marvelous overlooks of the harbor, downtown and, on clear days, the Mountain. All this is knit together by infrastructure that was high-tech for its time: the pontoon bridge across Lake Washington, the Lake Washington Ship Canal, connecting the Sound and the Lake, whose Chittenden Locks are the second-largest locks in this hemisphere, behind Panama's. Seattle has been booming, and exporting its own institutions—Boeing airplanes have been the world's best sellers for many years; Nordstrom's department stores with their famously polite service, even in the New York area; Seattle espresso bars have been bringing caffe latte across America.

The 7th Congressional District of Washington includes almost all the city of Seattle, a little industrial suburban fringe to the south, plus rural-looking Vashon Island in Puget Sound. This is the Seattle area's minority district, 10% black and 12% Asian. The 7th has the highest education levels of any Washington district (37% of adults are college grads), but not at all the highest household income; it has the oldest housing and by far the highest percentage of householders living alone (39%) and the fewest households with families (49%). Central Seattle, in other words, shares more with central San Francisco than hills and scenery: it is heavily populated by singles and gays, young professionals and elderly pensioners. A generation ago, the city of Seattle was roughly split between the parties; today, it is heavily Democratic and liberal, proud of its black mayor, Norman Rice, and its vote rejecting an antibusing referendum.

The congressman from the 7th District is Jim McDermott, one of the most liberal members of the House and its only (credentialed) psychiatrist. McDermott was the first in his family to attend college, and went to conservative religious Wheaton College, though his views on issues reflect more the atmosphere of psychiatry. After service in the Navy, he came to the University of Washington Hospital in Seattle; almost immediately, he was elected to the state House in 1970 and state Senate in 1974, where he worked on issues from clean water to comparable worth to health care. He retired from the legislature in 1987 and went to Zaire as a medical officer in the Foreign Service. But when Congressman Mike Lowry ran for the Senate in 1988 (he lost, but in 1992 was elected governor), McDermott returned home and ran for the 7th District seat and easily won, beating Norm Rice 38%–29% in the primary and winning 76% in the general. He has been reelected without difficulty.

McDermott, from the Ways and Means seat he won in late 1990, is now the House's chief proponent of a single-payer, Canadian-type national health insurance program, on which he introduced a bill in March 1993. He got more than 60 co-sponsors, although Clintonites wanted members to hold off; Ways and Means colleague Pete Stark said McDermott's bill "defines the left edge of the scale." McDermott questions whether proposed managed competition plans would lead to a two-tiered standard of benefits and whether it would save any money. McDermott also serves on the Ethics Committee, and in February 1993 was named chairman—surely a thankless task, but one which he undertakes with the gravity and sense of duty he brings to all his work; he began the year by requesting a 12% cut in the committee budget.

The People: Pop. 1990: 541,202; 2% rural; 15% age 65+; 74% White; 10% Black; 1% Amer. Indian; 12% Asian; 1% Other; 3% Hispanic origin. Voting age pop.: 448,939; 8% Black; 3% Hispanic origin. Households: 38% married couple families; 14% married couple fams. w. children; 66% college educ.; median household income: $29,707; per capita income: $18,021; median gross rent: $462; median house value: $132,100.

1992 Presidential Vote			1988 Presidential Vote		
Clinton (D)	191,781	(65%)	Dukakis (D)	170,301	(70%)
Bush (R)	54,478	(18%)	Bush (R)	72,349	(30%)
Perot (I)	45,167	(15%)			

Rep. Jim McDermott (D)

Elected 1988; b. Dec. 28, 1936, Chicago, IL; home, Seattle; Wheaton Col., B.S. 1958; U. of IL, M.D. 1963; Episcopalian; divorced.

Career: U.S. Navy Medical Corps., 1968–70; Asst. Prof., U. of WA, Practicing psychiatrist, 1970–83; WA House of Reps., 1970–72; WA Senate, 1974–87; Medical Officer, U.S. Foreign Svc., Zaire, 1987–88.

Offices: 1707 LHOB 20515, 202-225-3106. Also 1212 Tower Bldg., 1809 7th Ave., Seattle 98101, 206-553-7170.

Committees: *District of Columbia* (4th of 8 D): Fiscal Affairs and Health (Chmn.); Judiciary and Education. *Standards of Official Conduct* (Chmn. of 7 D). *Ways and Means* (14th of 24 D): Health; Human Resources.

Group Ratings

	ADA	ACLU	COPE	CDF	CFA	LCV	ACU	NTLC	NSI	COC	CEI
1992	95	100	83	100	93	81	0	5	30	25	11
1991	95	—	83	100	83	85	0	—	—	20	9

National Journal Ratings

	1991 LIB — 1991 CONS			1992 LIB — 1992 CONS		
Economic	84%	—	12%	75%	—	24%
Social	88%	—	0%	92%	—	0%
Foreign	92%	—	0%	90%	—	0%

Key Votes of the 102d Congress

1. Ban Striker Replace	FOR	5. Handgun Wait/7-Day	FOR	9. Use Force in Gulf	AGN
2. $ for Homeownership	AGN	6. Overseas Mil. Abortion	FOR	10. US Mil. Abroad $ Cut	FOR
3. Tax Rich/Cut Mid Cls.	FOR	7. Obscn. Art NEA $ Ban	AGN	11. Limit SDI Funds	FOR
4. FY93/$15B Def. Cut	FOR	8. Death Pen. from Jury	AGN	12. Cuba Trade Embargo	AGN

Key Votes of the 103d Congress

1. Family Leave	FOR	2. Deficit Reduction	FOR	3. Stimulus Plan	FOR

Election Results

1992 general	Jim McDermott (D)	222,604	(78%)	($191,472)
	Glenn C. Hampson (R)	54,149	(19%)	($30,317)
	Other	7,197	(2%)	
1992 primary	Jim McDermott (D)	102,818	(73%)	
	Glenn C. Hampson (R)	26,042	(19%)	
	Ken Yeager (D)	8,741	(6%)	
	Other	3,288	(2%)	
1990 general	Jim McDermott (D)	106,761	(72%)	($211,961)
	Larry Penberthy (R)	35,511	(24%)	
	Robbie Scherr (SWP)	5,370	(4%)	

EIGHTH DISTRICT

East of Seattle's Lake Washington, across the pontoon bridge that was an engineering marvel in the 1940s and sunk during repairs in 1990 and had to be rebuilt, was vacant land half a century ago—orchards and vineyards, farms and pastureland. Today it is a suburban area with all the aspects of urbanness but high crime and unpleasant poverty. The focus here is not Seattle but Bellevue, now a suburb of more than 100,000, with enough office space to make it an edge city. While downtown Seattle specialized in banks and law firms and trading companies, Bellevue and other communities in the Overlake area specialized in high-tech startups. Not far away in what was once the farm town of Redmond is the headquarters of Microsoft, the software giant; but it is only one of dozens. Growth here was robust in the 1980s, and subdivisions have spread almost to the base of the Cascades, leaving not quite enough of the rural-looking land that attracted so many people here.

The 8th Congressional District of Washington includes most of this eastern edge of metro Seattle, plus much of the scarcely inhabited territory of the Cascades (*Twin Peaks* country, for those who remember). It includes almost all of Bellevue though not much of Redmond; it goes south to the suburban fringe east of Tacoma and includes Washington's great pride, Mount Rainier. This is the most affluent district in Washington, rivaled only by the 1st, market-oriented on economics, more liberal on the environment, tolerant on cultural issues; in partisan terms, it is one of the two most Republican districts in the state.

Currently, the 8th District is the only one in Washington represented by a Republican. She is Jennifer Dunn, for almost a dozen years the state Republican Party chairman, first elected in 1992 when Rod Chandler, the incumbent since the district was created in 1982, ran for the Senate and lost to Democrat Patty Murray. Dunn was once an IBM systems engineer, then worked as a lobbyist and public relations staffer in the King County Assessor's office. She was a Ronald Reagan supporter, and in a dozen years raised $13 million for her state party. Pro-choice on abortion, she otherwise seems aggressively conservative; she pledged to oppose any tax increase and backed the line-item veto, education choice vouchers, workfare, a tough stand on crime. Dunn's chief competition in the all-party primary was Republican state Senator Pam Roach, who campaigned as a solid opponent of abortion and said she was working class while Dunn was wealthy. Dunn got 32% of the vote, Roach 29%. That suggested, accurately, that there was little chance for Mercer Island businessman George Tamblyn, who started off running as a Republican, but switched parties when he found out the state Republican platform was against campaign spending limits and national health insurance. In the primary, he had 23% of the vote; in the general, 34%, to Dunn's 60%.

In the House, Dunn became something of a firebrand, although as the senior (and only) member of the minority party in her state, she accompanied Speaker Thomas Foley forward to take the oath of office. She called for a 25% cut in all House committee budgets, with one-third of investigative funds for Republicans; she asked Ross Perot to accompany her to a House Administration Accounts Subcommittee hearing, which he promised to do. She has seats on the Public Works, Science, and House Administration Committees, where she is already ranking Republican on the Personnel and Police Subcommittee. She was also the only freshman picked by Minority Leader Bob Michel to serve on the Joint Committee on the Organization of Congress.

The People: Pop. 1990: 540,735; 21% rural; 8% age 65+; 91% White; 2% Black; 1% Amer. Indian; 5% Asian; 1% Other; 2% Hispanic origin. Voting age pop.: 389,198; 1% Black; 2% Hispanic origin. Households: 65% married couple families; 33% married couple fams. w. children; 63% college educ.; median household income: $42,379; per capita income: $18,432; median gross rent: $550; median house value: $142,100.

1992 Presidential Vote			**1988 Presidential Vote**		
Clinton (D)	102,859	(38%)	Bush (R)	122,431	(56%)
Bush (R)	92,274	(34%)	Dukakis (D)	97,524	(44%)
Perot (I)	72,523	(27%)			

Rep. Jennifer B. Dunn (R)

Elected 1992; b. July 29, 1941, Seattle; home, Bellevue; U. of WA, 1960–62, Stanford, B.A. 1963; Episcopalian; divorced.

Career: Systems Engineer, IBM, 1964–69; P.R., King Cnty. Assessors Office, 1978–80; Delegate, U.N. Comm. on Status of Women, 1984, 1990; Chmn., WA St. Repub. Party, 1981–92.

Offices: 1641 LHOB 20515, 202-225-7761. Also 50-116th Ave., SE, Bellevue 98004, 206-460-0161.

Committees: *House Administration* (7th of 7 R): Accounts; Elections; Personnel and Police (RMM). *Public Works and Transportation* (12th of 24 R): Aviation; Economic Development; Surface Transportation. *Science, Space and Technology* (20th of 22 R): Space. *Joint Committee on the Organization of Congress.*

Group Ratings and 102d Congress Votes: Newly Elected

Key Votes of the 103d Congress

1. Family Leave	AGN	2. Deficit Reduction	AGN	3. Stimulus Plan	AGN

Election Results

1992 general	Jennifer B. Dunn (R)	155,874	(60%)	($704,674)
	George O. Tamblyn (D)	87,611	(34%)	($410,465)
	Bob Adams (I)	14,686	(6%)	($14,104)
1992 primary	Jennifer B. Dunn (R)	39,405	(32%)	
	Pam Roach (R)	35,387	(29%)	
	George O. Tamblyn (D)	28,213	(23%)	
	Roy A. Ferguson (R)	8,832	(7%)	
	Michael Campbell (R)	8,166	(7%)	
	Other	3,671	(3%)	
1990 general	Rod Chandler (R)	96,323	(56%)	($451,296)
	David Giles (D)	75,013	(44%)	($33,817)

NINTH DISTRICT

Along the misty shores of Puget Sound, south from Seattle, metropolitan growth has spread over the past several decades even beyond the industrial city of Tacoma, which once promoted itself as a rival to be the state's largest city. This is mixed suburban territory. The subdivisions along the Sound, with some of the loveliest views in America, tend to be high-income. But in the interstices between the ridges that run north and south inland is some of greater Seattle's prime industrial territory—the Boeing aircraft plants that have helped make that company America's number one exporter and the smaller factories near the rail lines that run from Minneapolis-St. Paul to Puget Sound.

The 9th Congressional District of Washington, the new seat created as a result of the 1990 Census and a June 1992 Supreme Court decision that upheld the counting of servicemen abroad in their state of residence (otherwise the seat would have remained in Massachusetts), covers much of this area. Its northern end is around Sea-Tac Airport and the industrial town of Renton at the south end of Lake Washington. Then it passes south past Kent, Auburn and Federal Way and reaches the docks of Tacoma to cover about half that city. It includes giant Fort Lewis and McChord Air Force Base and proceeds almost as far as the state capital of Olympia. Politically, this is a district balanced almost at equipoise. This area went narrowly for George Bush in 1988, and by a much wider margin for Bill Clinton in 1992. Industrial and affluent areas are balanced, leaving this open seat very much up for grabs in 1992.

The new congressman is Mike Kreidler, a member of the state House and Senate for eight years each. Kreidler is an optometrist, and has worked all that time for a group care cooperative in Puget Sound. As a state legislator, he specialized in health care, and helped draft the Washington state healthcare reform legislation, passed in 1993, which provided universal access, strict cost controls on the medical community, incentives for choosing care programs and calls for doubling state health spending. Kreidler is also a marathon runner and a lieutenant colonel in the Army Reserve; he was called to active duty in January 1991, and provided eye care at Fort Lewis, and his wife was appointed to fill his state Senate seat temporarily.

When the new district was created, Kreidler moved fast to run, though his residence was just outside its boundaries. He may have benefited from a bitter Republican battle between two legislators. Paul Barden had run in the then-new 8th District in 1982 and lost to Rod Chandler in the primary; he was strongly antipornography and antiabortion. Pete von Reichbauer, who, after seven years as a Democrat, switched parties in 1981 and turned over control of the state Senate to Republicans, called for fiscal tightness but hedged his position on abortion. Von Reichbauer beat Barden 26%–23% in the all-party primary; Kreidler also had 23%, and Democrats got fewer votes total than Republicans. Kreidler, though calling for major change on health care, took a Tsongas-like stand backing higher taxes if necessary and called for some defense spending cuts; von Reichbauer was hurt when a late campaign attack on Kreidler on a child protection law backfired. Kreidler won a decisive 52%–43% victory.

In the House, Kreidler has a seat on the Energy and Commerce Committee and its Health Subcommittee. He has a chance to play a central role on health care, and will be in a fine position to take credit if the result is popular, or to be held responsible if it is not.

The People: Pop. 1990: 540,519; 9% rural; 9% age 65+; 84% White; 5% Black; 2% Amer. Indian; 6% Asian; 1% Other; 4% Hispanic origin. Voting age pop.: 396,950; 5% Black; 3% Hispanic origin. Households: 57% married couple families; 27% married couple fams. w. children; 52% college educ.; median household income: $32,194; per capita income: $14,264; median gross rent: $478; median house value: $93,300.

1992 Presidential Vote			1988 Presidential Vote		
Clinton (D)	93,964	(42%)	Bush (R)	93,554	(52%)
Bush (R)	69,593	(31%)	Dukakis (D)	86,839	(48%)
Perot (I)	58,037	(26%)			

Rep. Mike Kreidler (D)

Elected 1992; b. Sept. 28, 1943, Takoma; home, Olympia; Pacific U., B.A. 1967, D.O. 1969; U. of CA at L.A., M.A., 1972; Protestant; married (Lela).

Career: Army, 1970–71, 1991, Army Reserves, 1969–present; Practicing optometrist, Group Health Coop. of Puget Sound, 1972–92; N. Thurston Schl. Bd., 1973–77; WA House of Reps., 1976–84; WA Senate, 1984–92.

Offices: 1535 LHOB 20515, 202-225-8901. Also 312 4th St., SE, Puyallup 98371, 206-840-5688; and 31919 1st Ave., #140, Federal Way 98003, 206-946-0553.

Committees: *Energy and Commerce* (25th of 27 D): Energy and Power; Health and the Environment. *Veterans' Affairs* (20th of 21 D): Hospitals and Health Care; Housing and Memorial Affairs; Oversight and Investigations.

Group Ratings and 102d Congress Votes: Newly Elected

Key Votes of the 103d Congress

1. Family Leave	FOR	2. Deficit Reduction	FOR	3. Stimulus Plan	FOR

Election Results

1992 general	Mike Kreidler (D)	110,902	(52%)	($430,476)
	Pete von Reichbauer (R)	91,910	(43%)	($414,594)
	Two Others	10,107	(5%)	
1992 primary	Pete von Reichbauer (R)	25,917	(26%)	
	Mike Kreidler (D)	23,687	(23%)	
	Paul Barden (R)	22,856	(23%)	
	Tim McDonnell (D)	14,387	(14%)	
	Dick Hill (D)	9,382	(9%)	
	Two Others	4,869	(5%)	
1990 election	Newly created district.			

WEST VIRGINIA

Things may be looking up for West Virginia. It's about time: this is a state that has had more than its share of tragedy and heartbreak, but whose people have never lost their sense of hope or their affection for the hills and mountains that make this the most unhorizontal state in the nation. West Virginia was born out of the tragedy of the Civil War, when 55 mountain counties with few slaves seceded from Virginia, and has made its living since mostly on that cruelest of commodities, coal. Coal kept the sons of large mountaineer families here for much of the 20th Century, men who would otherwise have left for big cities; coal brought immigrants in, a few from odd corners of Europe, but more from adjacent areas of the South where the local farming economies were stagnant when West Virginia's coal economy was booming. Coal helped bring the large concentration of chemical plants 50 years ago to the Kanawha Valley around Charleston; it built the steel mills in the panhandle and the Monongahela River valley, not far south of Pittsburgh.

But coal did not build a self-sustaining economy. When America was beleaguered abroad, demand for coal increased and energy prices rose, and West Virginia boomed, during World War II (the state reached its all-time population peak of 2 million in 1950) and the oil shocks of the 1970s. Coal changed West Virginia's politics too. West Virginia's heritage from the Civil War days was Republican, though some counties tilted toward the Confederacy and the Democrats. But after John L. Lewis's United Mine Workers organized most of the West Virginia mines in the 1930s, with the help of Franklin Roosevelt's Democrats, the coal country shifted toward the Democrats, and West Virginia for half a century has been one of the most Democratic states, deserting the ticket only in Republican landslide years (1956, 1972, 1984).

But neither Democratic administrations nor the pensions and medical benefits the UMW negotiated for retired miners have been able to provide the economic growth to keep thousands of West Virginians from leaving their mountains to find work elsewhere—now more often south on I-77 to the booming Carolinas than north to the Great Lakes industrial cities. As underground miners were replaced by strip-mining machines, coal tonnage has gone way up but coal mine employment dropped from 22% of the state's work force in 1950 to 10% in 1980 and 5% in 1990. The state's population, 1.95 million in 1980, fell to 1.8 million in 1990—the largest decrease, absolutely and in percentage terms, of any state. But West Virginians have a strong attachment to their unique state, where the accent sounds southern and the early 20th Century factories and houses look northern, where the landscape is rural and the economy industrial.

Now in the 1990s there are finally signs of a rebound, and without the energy price spurts that produced the 1970s booms. Population increased by 100,000 from 1990–92, and not just in the eastern panhandle counties now part of the Washington, D.C., metropolitan area. One reason, though probably overemphasized, is Senate Appropriations Chairman Robert Byrd's efforts to locate federal offices to the state; as West Virginians point out, there are good reasons for such relocations, which have induced private employers to move backoffice operations to low-wage, good-work-habits, electronically-accessible West Virginia. Another is that West Virginia has marketed itself as a tourist center. Within an easy drive of half a dozen major metro areas, West Virginia's hills have plenty of skiing, camping and river rafting; by some counts, tourism doubled between 1989 and 1992. There is reason to believe the state's economy is diversifying beyond coal and heavy industry. West Virginia's problems are by no means solved. There will always be a need for better roads in a place where people are scattered over constant hills and hollows. In the southern coal counties, wages are low, infant mortality is high and many jobs are controlled by some of America's most corrupt local politicians. West Virginia's unemployment was still the highest in the nation in late 1992, though it fell from 13% to under 10% during the year. But for

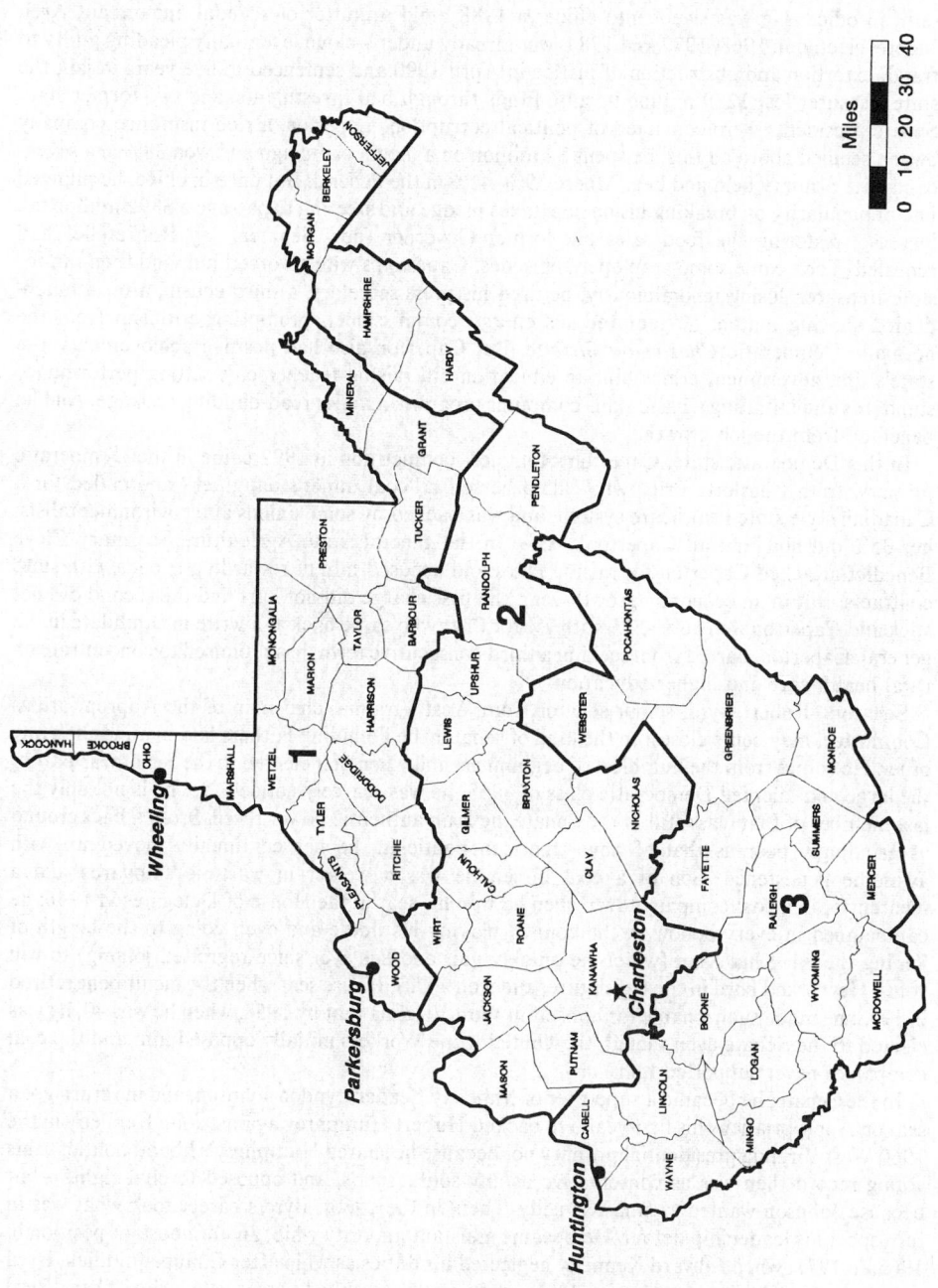

the first time in a dozen years, West Virginia seems on the rise.

Governor. Gaston Caperton had as wild a roller coaster ride as any state's governor in his first term in office. He was swept into office in 1988 amid a clutter of scandal: incumbent Arch Moore, elected in 1968, 1972 and 1984, was already under a cloud, eventually pleading guilty to fraud, extortion and obstruction of justice in April 1990 and sentenced to five years in jail; the state treasurer lost $279 million in state funds through bad investments, and two former state Senate presidents were convicted of political corruption. Caperton, a rich insurance company owner, seemed above all this; he spent $2 million on a media campaign and won 38% in a seven-candidate primary field and beat Moore 59%–41% in the general. But once in office, he plunged into unpopularity by breaking his no-new-taxes pledge and steering to passage a $392 million tax increase, restoring the food sales tax former Governor (now Senator) Jay Rockefeller had repealed. Then came some soap-opera episodes: Caperton's wife divorced him and then ran for state treasurer, losing ignominiously; he fired his press secretary, a third cousin, after a much-denied shoving match; he removed his energy commissioner, prompting criticism from the normally Democratic *Charleston Gazette*. But Caperton also had positive achievements: the state's first government ethics bill; an education bill raising teacher pay, setting performance standards and initiating a basic skills computer program; a major road-building package. And he benefited from the job growth.

In this Democratic state, Caperton's toughest competition in 1992 came in the Democratic primary, from Charlotte Pritt, who called herself a "coal miner's daughter" and called for a Canadian-style state healthcare system, and was backed by some unions and environmentalists; her 35% did not far trail Caperton's 43%. In the general, state Agriculture Secretary Cleve Benedict attacked Caperton for raising taxes and accused him of rewarding friends with state contracts. But in an economic growth year, the first charge did not hurt and the second did not stick and Caperton won 56%–37% with 7% for Pritt who came back as a write-in candidate in the general. Caperton, barred from seeking a third consecutive term, has promised to concentrate on rural health care and higher education.

Senators. Robert Byrd, senior senator from West Virginia, chairman of the Appropriations Committee, may come closest to the kind of senator the Founding Fathers had in mind than any other. He comes from the humblest of beginnings, and when first elected to the Senate, as part of the large and talented Democratic class of 1958, he was scarcely noticed. Yet he is not only the last member of that class still in the Senate, he is an authentic power there. From a background as grindingly poor as that of any American politician, he has continually moved up with awesome persistence. Son of a coal miner, he was a welder in wartime shipyards and a meatcutter in a coal company town when he won his seat in the House of Delegates in 1946; he campaigned in every hollow in the county, playing his fiddle and even going to the length of joining the Ku Klux Klan (which he quickly quit and has ever since regretted joining) to win votes. He worked hard in the legislature, and won a U.S. House seat when the incumbent retired in 1952; he made such a name for himself in West Virginia that by 1958, when he was 40, he was elected to the Senate even though the United Mine Workers initially opposed him and the coal companies never supported him.

In the Senate, he became a supporter of Majority Leader Lyndon Johnson, and in return got a seat on Appropriations his first year. He backed Hubert Humphrey against John Kennedy in the 1960 West Virginia presidential primary not because he shared Humphrey's liberal politics—his voting record then was as conservative as any southerner's, and opposed to civil rights—but because Johnson wanted to stop Kennedy. Then, in the 1960s, Byrd's career took what was in retrospect his leadership detour. He became assistant majority whip, an unimportant position in 1965; in 1971, when Edward Kennedy neglected his duties as whip after Chappaquiddick, Byrd quietly lined up support and, with Richard Russell's deathbed vote, ousted him. There Byrd performed ably, managing Senate business and accommodating colleagues' needs, and when Majority Leader Mike Mansfield retired in 1976, Byrd easily won the job. All the while Byrd was working hard to keep in touch with West Virginians, to the point that he won 78% of the vote in 1970, becoming the first candidate to carry all 55 counties.

Byrd was not a total success as leader. His manner is too formal for television, and he did not presume to speak for other Democrats on many issues; he felt strongly that he was working for other senators, and not vice versa. When Democrats lost control of the Senate in 1980 and failed to regain it in 1982 and 1984, there was naturally some restiveness; Byrd was challenged in 1984 and almost was in 1986. In 1987, as majority leader again, he had an agenda for a relatively united Democratic Caucus, and helped make way for the 1988 trade bill, with its plant-closing provision, and pushed hard for campaign finance reform. His own positions on issues have been somewhat more liberal since the early 1970s, when he led the opposition to Richard Nixon on some issues and his incisive questioning helped break open the Watergate scandal.

Byrd let it be known well ahead of time that he wasn't running for leader again in 1988 and would instead become chairman of Appropriations. In that position, he has been, if anything, more formidable. And he was anything but shy about one goal: "I want to be West Virginia's billion dollar industry," he announced in 1990. He met his pledge, bringing in $1 billion of projects to West Virginia in his first three years as chairman. In his first two years, he brought the FBI Identification Center to Clarksburg (2,600 jobs), the Treasury's Bureau of Public Debt (700) and an IRS processing center (300) to Parkersburg, a Fish and Wildlife Training Center in Harper's Ferry, the Coast Guard national Computer Operations Center and Bureau of Alcohol, Tobacco and Firearms to Martinsburg, a NASA Research center to Wheeling—the list goes on and on. West Virginia got almost none of the early 1980s defense buildup money; but in the late 1980s, when the Pentagon proposed $400,000 for military construction in the state, Byrd got $26,400,000. But Byrd does not always succeed: a GAO report helped defeat his attempt to build a $1.2 billion CIA facility in Jefferson County; and he lost by one vote, despite personally lobbying every senator, his amendment to compensate coal miners who lose their jobs because of the Clean Air Act. But Byrd usually wins. And, while he insists that he does not retaliate against those who oppose his projects, no one doubts he remembers how every senator voted.

It should be added that not all his initiatives are parochial and many are deeply rooted in his constitutional beliefs. He has targeted more money for biomedical research, education, drug initiatives and aid to Turkey and the Baltic states. In the 1990 budget summit agreement his obduracy, based on his sense of Congress's prerogative to appropriate money, kept in $12 billion in increases in domestic discretionary spending. For the same reason, he is a last ditch opponent of the line-item veto, which surely would increase Executive power in a way Byrd believes would violate the Constitution's scheme of government. These are not just makeweight arguments, as Byrd is a serious student of history. With the assistance of Senate historian Richard Baker, he wrote *The Senate 1789–1989*, which he delivered as a series of speeches; based on impressive research, gracefully written, full of arresting anecdotes and sound insights, it surpasses any previous work on the subject. Byrd, who earned his law degree while in the Senate and had his diploma presented to him by President Kennedy at the 1963 American University commencement where Kennedy delivered his most important foreign policy speech, has read the classics as well: Shakespeare, Thucydides, Cicero, Plutarch's Lives. He applies his learning to today's problems. His 1991 speech opposing the Gulf war resolution recalls Alcibiades's strategy in the Peloponnesian wars, and the fighting done by West Virginians in the War Between the States. In opposing the line-item veto in 1992, he reached back to Ethelred the Unready, William the Conqueror, the Magna Carta and the Constitutional Convention. At his best, he seems a contemporary of the founders and the ancients, a classical senator determinedly attentive to his mundane duties but guided by an expanding understanding of timeless principle.

In 1993, Byrd, who first won elective office the year Bill Clinton was born, emerged as a stalwart defender of the new president. He defended the economic stimulus package from modification by more fiscally conservative Democrats, though in the process he may have strengthened the hand of Bob Dole whose rock solid filibuster sunk the measure. And Byrd will have his own battles to fight in 1993: protecting his Appropriations turf from advocates of the line-item veto, and from bipartisan initiatives to eliminate the Appropriations Committee altogether. Byrd remains in this decade, as in the two previous, West Virginia's most popular politician, and can be reelected easily in 1994.

West Virginia's junior senator is Jay Rockefeller. His full name, John D. Rockefeller, IV, has a familiar ring to most older voters, who remember his great-grandfather as the oil billionaire who was America's richest man, and his grandfather as the heir who had more than enough money to build Rockefeller Center, restore Colonial Williamsburg and found the Museum of Modern Art in the Depression years. Jay Rockefeller's father and uncles were men of impressive achievement, each in a different field, and in two cases with political careers. His uncle Winthrop Rockefeller moved to an impoverished state in the southern hills—in his case Arkansas—ran for governor and lost, ran again and won two terms and ran an honest and reforming administration: the same could be said of Jay Rockefeller's career in West Virginia. There are interesting comparisons between the careers of Jay Rockefeller and his other governor-uncle: Nelson Rockefeller in his 30s became head of Franklin Roosevelt's Latin American policy program; Jay Rockefeller in his 30s studied for three years in Japan. Nelson Rockefeller became governor of the nation's biggest state and spent money expansively on generous welfare and gigantic monuments; Jay Rockefeller became governor of what turned out to be America's number one population-losing state of the 1980s, leaving behind a network of roads and highways and a progressive tax structure that removed the sales tax on food (since restored). Nelson Rockefeller was a Republican at a time when the party's Ivy League establishment believed it could soon resume its status as the majority party. Jay Rockefeller broke family tradition and became a Democrat at a time when the party's Ivy League ideologues believed it would always retain what seemed then its natural status as the majority party. Both Rockefellers were mentioned early on as presidential candidates: Nelson, never very shy about running, finally did so in 1964 at 56, and again in 1968; Jay for years avoided projecting his name forward, then almost decided to run in the summer of 1991 at 54, but now seems blocked by the Clinton-Gore team from running at least in 1996 and maybe for longer.

But the parallels stop here, for Jay Rockefeller lacks the aloof, imperial bearing of his uncle; he is affable, full of self-deprecating humor, tall enough so that he stoops to get through doorways, and uses hearing aids because of noise damage from frequent helicopters travel. He was careful to work his way up the political ladder. Originally coming to West Virginia as a VISTA volunteer, he was elected to the house of delegates in Kanawha County in 1966 and as secretary of state in 1968, and then had the chastening experience of losing to Governor Arch Moore in 1972. He served four years as president of West Virginia Wesleyan College in Buckhannon, and his politics became more practical: he dropped his opposition to strip mining, for example. He was not shy about spending his own millions and was elected governor in 1976 and, against Moore, in 1980, after which the state was plunged into deep recession. In 1984, he ran for the U.S. Senate and beat Republican businessman John Raese by just 52%–48% after spending $12 million. Every penny helped, especially the huge sums needed to air ads on Washington and Pittsburgh TV: in most counties in the state, Rockefeller ran between 1% and 7% ahead of Walter Mondale's 45% showing; in all but one of the dozen or so panhandle counties in these hugely expensive media markets, he ran 12% to 18% ahead of Mondale.

In his first term in the Senate, Rockefeller worked hard on West Virginia projects, and deferred carefully to Robert Byrd. His experience in East Asia made him less reflexively protectionist than most coal and steel representatives, but he did favor extension of the voluntary restraint agreements on steel. After four years he found his issue, and an important one indeed: health care. His ascent to a key institutional position was serendipitous: he got a seat on the Finance Committee in 1987 and then inherited the chair of the Medicare and Long-term Care Subcommittee in 1989; he got a seat on the Pepper Commission on long-term health care, a joint legislative-executive body, after George Mitchell became majority leader in January 1989, and then became chairman when Claude Pepper died six months later. But there has been nothing serendipitous about Rockefeller's work on health care since. He failed to win any unanimous consensus on the Pepper Commission in 1990 but did get an 11–4 vote for long-term care for all

Americans regardless of age and an 8–7 margin for universal medical insurance coverage, with a "pay or play" plan, including a tax on employers who don't offer the required coverage. Then the 1990 budget summit included $580 million for home care for elderly who would otherwise be hospitalized. In 1991 and 1992, health care became an even more visible issue, and Rockefeller became the chief Senate proponent of the "pay or play" approach; he also pushed home care for Alzheimer's and cancer patients. During his own out-loud thinking about running for president in spring and summer 1991, he talked more about health care, and more passionately and knowledgeably, than about any other issue. His specialization in health care was probably one reason he made the short list of Bill Clinton's possible running mates in July 1992.

In 1993 and beyond, Rockefeller will undoubtedly play a major role in healthcare reform. His political instinct is probably to be a team player with the Clinton Administration. He endorsed Clinton with an enthusiasm that seemed undimmed by regret that he had not run himself; he was fueled in part by an angry disdain for George Bush who had not, in his view, lived up to the patrician's obligation to be generous to those less fortunate (with taxpayers' money, critics might add). Rockefeller inherited the chair of the Veterans' Affairs Committee in 1993, where he must focus on what to do about the troubled system of veterans' hospitals. His biggest legislative achievement of 1992 was putting into the energy bill, over furious opposition from western coal states, a tax on non-union coal operators to bail out the United Mine Workers' healthcare trust funds. On most other issues, he has a rather conventional liberal Democratic record.

Rockefeller is in strong shape politically. He won reelection easily in 1990 with a (for him) bargain basement campaign costing $2.7 million; he prides himself now on raising money from others rather than spending his own, and even took on the job of finance chairman of the Democratic National Committee, capitalizing on those who relish the spectacle, as he seems to himself, of a Rockefeller asking for money.

Presidential politics. In national politics, West Virginia remains one of the most Democratic states, casting a big margin for Bill Clinton, solidly Democratic in the close elections of 1948, 1960, 1968, 1976 and 1988. West Virginia's presidential primary was important here only once, in 1960, when John Kennedy seized it as an opportunity to prove he could beat Hubert Humphrey in a virtually all-Protestant state, spending money freely and in ways that would not be legal today.

Congressional districting. West Virginia lost one of its four House seats for 1992, and so one of its four Democratic congressmen had to go. This game of musical chairs was played out lustily in the legislature, and the loser turned out to be Harley Staggers, whose 2d District was divided up among the other three, in all of which he would have been at a severe disadvantage; after some mulling, he ran against Alan Mollohan in the 1st District and lost.

The People: Est. Pop. 1992: 1,812,000; Pop. 1990: 1,793,477, up 1.0% 1990–1992. 0.7% of U.S. total, 34th largest; 64% rural. Median age: 35.4 years. 15.0% 65 years and over. 96.2% White, 3.1% Black. Households: 59.0% married couple families; 28% married couple fams. w. children; 29% college educ.; median household income: $20,795; per capita income: $10,520; 74.1% owner occupied housing; median house value: $47,900; median monthly rent: $221. 11.3% Unemployment. Voting age pop.: 1,349,900. Registered voters (1992): 956,172; 627,837 D (66%); 291,253 R (31%); 37,083 unaffiliated and minor parties (4%).

Political Lineup: Governor, Gaston Caperton (D); Secy. of State, Ken Hechler (D); Atty. Gen., Darrell V. McGraw, Jr. (D); Treasurer, Larrie Bailey (D); Auditor, Glen Gaynor (D). State Senate, 34 (32 D and 2 R); State House of Delegates, 100 (79 D and 21 R). Senators, Robert C. Byrd (D) and John D. (Jay) Rockefeller (D). Representatives, 3 D.

1992 Presidential Vote

Clinton (D)	331,001	(48%)
Bush (R)	241,974	(35%)
Perot (I)	108,829	(16%)

1988 Presidential Vote

Dukakis (D)	341,016	(52%)
Bush (R)	310,065	(48%)

1992 Democratic Presidential Primary

Clinton	227,815	(74%)
Brown	36,505	(12%)
Tsongas	21,271	(7%)
Other	21,275	(7%)

1992 Republican Presidential Primary

Bush	99,994	(81%)
Buchanan	18,067	(15%)
Fellure	6,096	(5%)

GOVERNOR

Gov. Gaston Caperton (D)

Elected 1988, term expires Jan. 1997; b. Feb. 21, 1940, Charleston; home, Charleston; U. of NC, B.A. 1963; Protestant; married (Rachael Worby).

Career: Pres., McDonough Caperton Ins. Group, 1963–88.

Office: State Capitol, Charleston 25305, 304-558-2000.

Election Results:

1992 gen.	Gaston Caperton (D)	368,302	(56%)
	Cleve Benedict (R)	240,390	(37%)
	Charlotte Jean Pritt (I)	48,501	(7%)
1992 prim.	Gaston Caperton (D)	142,261	(43%)
	Charlotte Jean Pritt (D)	115,498	(35%)
	Mario J. Palumbo (D)	66,984	(20%)
	Two Others	8,534	(3%)
1988 gen.	Gaston Caperton (D)	382,421	(59%)
	Arch A. Moore, Jr. (R)	267,172	(41%)

SENATORS

Sen. Robert C. Byrd (D)

Elected 1958, seat up 1994; b. Nov. 20, 1917, North Wilkesboro, NC; home, Sophia; American U., J.D. 1963; Baptist; married (Erma).

Career: WV House of Delegates, 1946–50; WV Senate, 1950–52; U.S. House of Reps., 1953–58; U.S. Senate Majority Whip, 1971–76, Minority Ldr., 1981–86, Majority Ldr. 1977–80, 1987–88.

Offices: 311 HSOB 20510, 202-224-3954. Also Fed. Bldg., 500 Quarrier St., #1006, Charleston 25305, 304-342-5855.

Committees: *President Pro-Tem. Appropriations* (Chmn. of 16 D): Defense; Energy and Water Development; Interior (Chmn.); Labor, Health and Human Services, Education; Transportation. *Armed Services* (8th of 11 D): Coalition Defense and Reinforcing Forces; Defense Technology, Acquisition and Industrial Base; Force Requirements and Personnel. *Rules and Administration* (3d of 9 D).

Group Ratings

	ADA	ACLU	CDF	COPE	CFA	LCV	ACU	NTLC	NSI	COC	CEI
1992	100	50	80	92	75	42	19	17	30	20	18
1991	65	—	82	83	72	33	33	—	—	10	28

National Journal Ratings

	1991 LIB — 1991 CONS		1992 LIB — 1992 CONS	
Economic	60%	35%	80%	17%
Social	44%	53%	39%	58%
Foreign	49%	46%	76%	22%

Key Votes of the 102d Congress

1. $ for Homeownership	AGN	5. Clarence Thomas Nom. AGN	9. Use Force in Gulf	AGN
2. Have Cap Gains Debate AGN	6. Lmt Death Row Appeal FOR	10. Keep Salvador Aid	AGN
3. Remove Budget Walls FOR	7. Handgun Wait/5-Day FOR	11. Cut $1B from SDI	AGN
4. Ban Striker Replace FOR	8. Abortion Gag Rule AGN	12. Override China MFN FOR

Key Votes of the 103d Congress

1. Family Leave FOR   2. HIV Immigrants AGN   3. Clinton Budget FOR

Election Results

1988 general	Robert C. Byrd (D)...............	410,983	(65%)	($1,282,746)
	M. Jay Wolfe (R)	223,564	(35%)	($115,284)
1988 primary	Robert C. Byrd (D)...............	252,767	(81%)	
	Bobby Myers (D)	60,186	(19%)	
1982 general	Robert C. Byrd (D)...............	387,170	(69%)	($1,792,573)
	Cleve Benedict (R)	173,910	(31%)	($1,098,218)

Sen. John D. (Jay) Rockefeller IV (D)

Elected 1984, seat up 1996; b. June 18, 1937, New York, NY; home, Charleston; Harvard, B.A. 1961, Intl. Christian U., Tokyo, Japan, 1957–60; Presbyterian; married (Sharon).

Career: Natl. Advisory Cncl., Peace Corps, 1961; Asst., Peace Corps Dir. Sargent Shriver, 1962–63; VISTA worker, 1964–66; WV House of Delegates, 1966–68; WV Secy. of State, 1968–72; Pres., WV Wesleyan Col., 1973–75; WV Gov., 1976–84.

Offices: 109 HSOB 20510, 202-224-6472. Also 405 Capitol St., #608, Charleston 25301, 304-347-5372; 115 S. Kanawha St., #1, Beckley 25801, 304-253-9704; and 200 Adams St., #A, Fairmont 26554, 304-367-0122.

Committees: *Commerce, Science and Transportation* (5th of 11 D): Communications; Foreign Commerce and Tourism; Science, Technology and Space (Chmn.); Surface Transportation. *Finance* (8th of 11 D): Health for Families and the Uninsured; International Trade; Medicare and Long-Term Care (Chmn.). *Veterans' Affairs* (Chmn. of 7 D).

Group Ratings

	ADA	ACLU	CDF	COPE	CFA	LCV	ACU	NTLC	NSI	COC	CEI
1992	100	90	90	91	75	75	7	0	40	20	15
1991	90	—	100	75	78	80	5	—	—	10	20

National Journal Ratings

	1991 LIB	—	1991 CONS	1992 LIB	—	1992 CONS
Economic	85%	—	11%	80%	—	7%
Social	70%	—	27%	79%	—	16%
Foreign	78%	—	14%	78%	—	14%

Key Votes of the 102d Congress

1. $ for Homeownership	AGN	5. Clarence Thomas Nom.	AGN	9. Use Force in Gulf	AGN
2. Have Cap Gains Debate	AGN	6. Lmt Death Row Appeal	AGN	10. Keep Salvador Aid	AGN
3. Remove Budget Walls	FOR	7. Handgun Wait/5-Day	FOR	11. Cut $1B from SDI	FOR
4. Ban Striker Replace	FOR	8. Abortion Gag Rule	AGN	12. Override China MFN	FOR

Key Votes of the 103d Congress

1. Family Leave	FOR	2. HIV Immigrants	*	3. Clinton Budget	FOR

Election Results

1990 general	John D. (Jay) Rockefeller IV (D)........	276,234	(68%)	($2,709,665)
	John Yoder (R)	128,071	(32%)	($22,904)
1990 primary	John D. (Jay) Rockefeller IV (D)........	200,161	(85%)	
	Ken Buchanon Thompson (D)	21,669	(9%)	
	Paul Nuchims (D).....................	14,467	(5%)	
1984 general	John D. (Jay) Rockefeller IV (D)........	374,233	(52%)	($12,055,043)
	John R. Raese (R)....................	344,680	(48%)	($1,147,123)

FIRST DISTRICT

The northern part of West Virginia is in many ways an extension of the Pittsburgh metropolitan area. People here are Steelers and Pirates fans, they drink Iron City and Rolling Rock beer, they watch Pittsburgh TV, they live in the crevasses between hills cut by the Monongahela and Ohio Rivers, on terrain that seems forbidding to industrial and urban development. Yet this has been an industrial area; for northern West Virginia was for many years a part of the same coal-and-steel economy that made Pittsburgh one of the nation's largest cities and filled the narrow bottomlands along the rivers with steel and glass factories, foundries and coal yards. In the 1980s and 1990s these have been declining industries, or rather industries becoming far less labor-intensive, shedding many jobs, leaving the fabric of everyday life badly frayed in these parts.

The 1st Congressional District of West Virginia includes the northern third of the state. On the panhandle along the Ohio River are the old steel towns of Wheeling, once one of the richest cities in the country with its steel company investors and executives, and Weirton, a steel company town and site of one of the most successful experiments with employee ownership, where steelworkers decided to cut their own pay in order to produce profits. South of Pittsburgh on the Monongahela are Morgantown, site of West Virginia University, and Clarksburg and Fairmont. Far to the west, the district includes Parkersburg and the surrounding hills on the Ohio River. To the east, it extends to the upper Potomac River opposite Cumberland, Maryland. Politically, most of this territory is solidly Democratic, except for some mountain countries never heavily industrialized which have remained Republican since the Civil War.

This 1st District was redrawn for the 1992 campaign, and included the homes of two incumbents, both sons of West Virginia congressmen, who both first won their seats in 1982. With the longer lineage was Harley Staggers, Jr., whose father held the 2d District from 1948 to 1980 and chaired the Commerce Committee for more than a decade. The current Staggers made his name as chief sponsor of the National Rifle Association-supported substitute for the Brady bill seven-day handgun purchase waiting period, to establish a computerized list of felons which gun sellers could check before sales; it lost on the House floor. Otherwise Staggers had a record liberal on economics and foreign policy, more conservative on cultural issues. But despite, or perhaps because of some lobbying, he was the victim of the 1991 redistricting. He tried to campaign as a political outsider and attacked incumbent Alan Mollohan for his 12 overdrafts on the House bank totalling $26,000. But only 20% of the 1992 Democratic primary vote here was cast by Staggers's old district, and although he carried it with 73%, that was not enough.

The winner was Alan Mollohan, whose father Robert Mollohan was elected in 1952 and 1954, ran for governor and lost in 1956, and then won the seat again when Arch Moore was elected governor in 1968 and kept it until he retired in 1982. Alan Mollohan, a Washington lawyer for Consolidation Coal among other clients, returned home in 1982 and won the seat. He has compiled a moderate record on economic and cultural issues but more conservative on foreign policy. He has used his seat on Appropriations to fund an a flight simulator for Fairmont State College and a defense procurement center in Parkersburg, and has helped form a West Virginia High Technology Consortium. With a base in the panhandle, Mollohan was in a stronger geographical position from redistricting. He claimed his seat on Appropriations would help the district and charged that Staggers spent too much time playing basketball in the House gym. He won 70% in his old district, for a 62%–38% overall victory.

That win gives him a chance to continue working for West Virginia pork on the Appropriations Committee; in effect, he is a kind of House partner of Senator Robert Byrd. He serves on the HUD-Independent Agencies Subcommittee which, among other things, superintends the space program, and there are three NASA projects in the 1st District, including the National Technology Transfer Center and the Classroom of the Future in Wheeling. Mollohan also won a seat on the Budget Committee in 1993, and rotated off Ethics.

The People: Pop. 1990: 598,056; 55% rural; 16% age 65+; 97% White; 2% Black; 1% Asian; 1% Hispanic origin. Voting age pop.: 456,485; 1% Black; 1% Hispanic origin. Households: 59% married couple families; 27% married couple fams. w. children; 32% college educ.; median household income: $21,903; per capita income: $10,920; median gross rent: $307; median house value: $46,400.

1992 Presidential Vote		
Clinton (D)	113,756	(46%)
Bush (R)	86,131	(35%)
Perot (I)	45,856	(19%)

1988 Presidential Vote		
Dukakis (D)	117,705	(50%)
Bush (R)	115,989	(49%)

Rep. Alan B. Mollohan (D)

Elected 1982; b. May 14, 1943, Fairmont; home, Fairmont; Col. of William and Mary, A.B. 1966, WV U., J.D. 1970; Baptist; married (Barbara).

Career: Army, 1970, Army Reserves, 1970–83; Practicing atty., 1970–82.

Offices: 2242 RHOB 20515, 202-225-4172. Also 213 Fed. Bldg., Morgantown 26505, 304-292-3019; 1117 Fed. Bldg., Parkersburg 26101, 304-428-0493; 316 Fed. Bldg., Wheeling 26003, 304-232-5390; and 209 P.O. Bldg., Clarksburg 26301, 304-623-4422.

Committees: *Appropriations* (19th of 37 D): Commerce, Justice, State and Judiciary; VA, HUD and Independent Agencies. *Budget* (16th of 26 D).

Group Ratings

	ADA	ACLU	COPE	CDF	CFA	LCV	ACU	NTLC	NSI	COC	CEI
1992	70	70	100	80	73	38	21	0	90	43	8
1991	50	—	92	90	72	38	30	—	—	20	13

National Journal Ratings

	1991 LIB — 1991 CONS		1992 LIB — 1992 CONS	
Economic	61%	36%	78%	22%
Social	50%	48%	48%	51%
Foreign	40%	58%	38%	56%

Key Votes of the 102d Congress

1. Ban Striker Replace	FOR	5. Handgun Wait/7-Day	AGN	9. Use Force in Gulf	FOR
2. $ for Homeownership	AGN	6. Overseas Mil. Abortion	AGN	10. US Mil. Abroad $ Cut	AGN
3. Tax Rich/Cut Mid Cls.	FOR	7. Obscn. Art NEA $ Ban	FOR	11. Limit SDI Funds	AGN
4. FY93/$15B Def. Cut	FOR	8. Death Pen. from Jury	AGN	12. Cuba Trade Embargo	FOR

Key Votes of the 103d Congress

1. Family Leave	FOR	2. Deficit Reduction	FOR	3. Stimulus Plan	FOR

Election Results

1992 general	Alan B. Mollohan (D), unopposed			($629,436)
1992 primary	Alan B. Mollohan (D)...............	57,568	(62%)	
	Harley O. Staggers (D)...............	36,038	(38%)	
1990 general	Alan B. Mollohan (D)...............	72,849	(67%)	($206,688)
	Howard K. Tuck (R)...............	35,657	(33%)	($34,077)

SECOND DISTRICT

Not all of West Virginia is coal country, not all of its valleys are industrial hollows choked with workingmen's homes and small factories, not all of its hills are scarred with strip mining wounds or piled with tailings. For miles you can see gentle hills and rugged mountains, stands of green trees and vistas stretching to far horizons. Yet over another hill you may find, amid scenery primeval and rural, sudden evidence of industrialization: a pulp mill or charcoal factory in a clearing scraped out of the forest; a small factory town, built close to a river in a cleft bordered with hills, its houses built in the same 1910s style as in the factory towns of Pittsburgh; the entrance to an underground coal mine or the exposed brown earth of a strip mine scar. Large parts of this naturally beautiful state look as verdant and unchanged as they must have when George Washington was speculating in land here and when the Civil War pitted brother against brother. The central part of West Virginia, in particular, has many such areas, between the industrial Monongahela of the north and the company town coal mining counties of the south.

The 2d Congressional District of West Virginia is the central part of the state, a belt of land from Berkeley Springs where George Washington used to take the waters and Harper's Ferry where John Brown raided the arsenal in 1859, all the way west to the Ohio River town of Point Pleasant where the Kanawha River (pronounced *kaNAW*) flows into the Ohio and Ravenswood. It could easily take a full day to drive through this district which, if flattened out, would probably spread across the country. The one major urban center here is Charleston, where on the banks of the Kanawha rises West Virginia's Capitol, built in 1932 and designed by Cass Gilbert with a dome higher than the U.S. Capitol and a chandelier with 10,000 pieces of cut glass. Charleston is the state capital, and, with its two partisan newspapers, the Democratic *Gazette* and the Republican *Daily Mail*, the center of the state's political culture. Charleston is also a major industrial center, with coal in the hills all around and, downriver from the Capitol, huge petrochemical plants that convert coal tar and other feedstocks into everyday products. This was a center of American high tech in the 1940s, when it produced all the nation's lucite, polyethylenes and nylon as well as much of its artificial rubber and antifreeze. More recently, these factories are seen as heavy polluters in a valley that has well above average rates of cancer. Yet Charleston is also West Virginia's white-collar and professional center, with a few downtown skyscrapers and some pleasant affluent residential districts.

The 2d is the least Democratic of West Virginia's three districts. Most of the mountain counties are Republican, and Charleston's Kanawha County sometimes goes Republican too; the 2d voted well under 50% for Bill Clinton in 1992 and gave George Bush a small margin in 1988. The congressman from the 2d District is Bob Wise, a Democrat from an affluent Charleston family, who returned home after law school to start a law practice geared to low- and middle-income clients and led a movement to force coal companies to pay higher taxes. A strong advocate of West Virginia culture—he is Congress's best clog dancer—he urges West Virginia students to make their careers, as he did, in their home state. But he is not a total traditionalist. In a state where past politicians got ahead by relying on ancestral loyalties and smoothing relations with big economic institutions, he has made his way by emphasizing issues on which he opposes the big interests. Wise was shrewd and popular enough to beat the state House majority leader and a former Kanawha County sheriff in the 1982 primary and then to beat the incumbent soundly in November. In the House, he started off as an insurgent, taking to the floor in 1983 to oppose a dam favored by the rest of the West Virginia delegation; he has supported local projects, but retains a national perspective.

Wise is one of the House's biggest boosters of alternative fuels, and has championed compressed natural gas as an auto fuel; he has had two CNG-powered cars (though one broke down on I-64 with transmission problems). He became the first West Virginian on the Budget Committee in 1989, where his concern about the deficit made him a convert to the balanced budget amendment. He has also championed a deficit reduction account which would put tax increase revenues in a fund for five years to generate money for physical capital and "infrastructure of the mind." His biggest legislative success was his 1990 amendment, adopted 274–146, to provide benefits for workers displaced by compliance with the Clean Air Act; this was similar to Senator Robert Byrd's amendment, which lost in the Senate by one vote, but Wise's amendment had a five-year spending cap of $250 million and was passed partly to forestall Byrd's. As chairman of the Democratic Study Group in 1992, he came up with a reform proposal designed to create a policy working group that would define a "core agenda" for each session of Congress—and which was quickly attacked by Energy and Commerce Chairman John Dingell.

Wise has been reelected easily and was able to maneuver out of redistricting problems in 1992; he had no primary opposition, his first Republican opponent dropped out of the race and his second won only 29% of the vote.

The People: Pop. 1990: 597,921; 62% rural; 14% age 65+; 96% White; 3% Black. Voting age pop.: 448,503; 3% Black. Households: 61% married couple families; 28% married couple fams. w. children; 30% college educ.; median household income: $22,253; per capita income: $11,083; median gross rent: $321; median house value: $55,200.

1992 Presidential Vote

Clinton (D)	104,257	(45%)
Bush (R)	90,375	(39%)
Perot (I)	36,813	(16%)

1988 Presidential Vote

Bush (R)	111,398	(51%)
Dukakis (D)	104,450	(48%)

Rep. Robert E. (Bob) Wise, Jr. (D)

Elected 1982; b. Jan. 6, 1948, Washington, D.C.; home, Clendenin; Duke U., B.A. 1970, Tulane U., J.D. 1975; Episcopalian; married (Sandy).

Career: Practicing atty., 1975–80; Dir., WV for Fair and Equitable Assessment of Taxes, 1977–80; WV Senate, 1980–82.

Offices: 2434 RHOB 20515, 202-225-2711. Also 107 Pennsylvania Ave., Charleston 25302, 304-342-7170; and 102 E. Martin St., Martinsburg 25401, 304-264-8810.

Committees: *Budget* (6th of 26 D). *Public Works and Transportation* (9th of 39 D): Economic Development (Chmn.); Investigations and Oversight; Water Resources and Environment.

Group Ratings

	ADA	ACLU	COPE	CDF	CFA	LCV	ACU	NTLC	NSI	COC	CEI
1992	80	96	92	70	93	44	17	0	40	38	10
1991	70	—	100	90	83	54	5	—	—	30	10

National Journal Ratings

	1991 LIB — 1991 CONS		1992 LIB — 1992 CONS	
Economic	72%	— 23%	71%	— 27%
Social	66%	— 33%	64%	— 35%
Foreign	69%	— 30%	56%	— 40%

Key Votes of the 102d Congress

1. Ban Striker Replace	FOR	5. Handgun Wait/7-Day	AGN	9. Use Force in Gulf	AGN
2. $ for Homeownership	AGN	6. Overseas Mil. Abortion	FOR	10. US Mil. Abroad $ Cut	FOR
3. Tax Rich/Cut Mid Cls.	FOR	7. Obscn. Art NEA $ Ban	FOR	11. Limit SDI Funds	FOR
4. FY93/$15B Def. Cut	FOR	8. Death Pen. from Jury	AGN	12. Cuba Trade Embargo	FOR

Key Votes of the 103d Congress

1. Family Leave	FOR	2. Deficit Reduction	FOR	3. Stimulus Plan	FOR

Election Results

1992 general	Robert E. (Bob) Wise, Jr. (D)............	143,988	(71%)	($330,052)
	Samuel A. Cravotta (R)................	59,102	(29%)	($36,405)
1992 primary	Robert E. (Bob) Wise, Jr. (D), unopposed			
1990 general	Robert E. (Bob) Wise, Jr. (D), unopposed			($53,137)
(WV 3)				

THIRD DISTRICT

Early in this century, the coalfields of southern West Virginia were one of America's boom areas. Into rural farmland and hollows, inhabited by the same families since they first arrived at these mountains 100 years before, came coal company lawyers with mineral rights' leases to sign, coal company engineers to design and sink the mineshafts, and men from other mountain counties, as well as Europe, to work the mines. Company houses were built, company stores stocked with goods as the company dictated and company paymasters kept close tabs on the finances of every employee. These conditions bred dull discontent, ignited into the fire of industrial unionism by the tongue of John L. Lewis, president of the United Mine Workers, who organized most of the mines in the 1930s. Lewis was not only a militant unionist, but an isolationist, and during and after World War II he called out his coal miners on strikes, to the fury of Franklin Roosevelt and Harry Truman. The entire national war effort and postwar economic recovery seemed gravely threatened by these labor stoppages involving perhaps 300,000 workers, centered in back corners of the country like southern West Virginia.

But that is history now. Coal is no longer central to our economy and there are only a few thousand coal miners left in southern West Virginia—and many are not UMW members anymore. In 1950, when coal area population peaked, there were 579,000 people in the eight counties that made up West Virginia's old 4th Congressional District. The population fell to 437,000 in 1970, then spurted up after energy prices were raised by the two oil shocks of the 1970s to 487,000 in 1980, but went down by 1990 to only 421,000. Most of the old underground mines have been abandoned, leaving behind mineshafts and piles of tailings—and lives that were snuffed out by cave-ins or simple carelessness in America's deadliest industry.

The new 3d Congressional District of West Virginia includes most of the coal country in the southern part of the state, the mountainous counties directly south of Charleston that are among America's most heavily Democratic—and in some cases most politically corrupt—jurisdictions: Mingo County, where in the 1980s a sheriff bought his job for $100,000 and other politicos bought votes for $2 or a half-pint of bourbon. But the coal mining counties are no longer populous enough for a full congressional district, and now make up about half the 3d District. About one-quarter is in and around the industrial city of Huntington on the Ohio River, and another quarter is to the east, in the farming uplands around the resort of White Sulphur Springs, where President John Tyler honeymooned in 1844, and the interstate junction at Beckley, which has become a popular whitewater rafting area. These two areas as a whole are much less Democratic than the coal counties.

This is still a Democratic House seat, though, and despite the particular problems of Congressman Nick Rahall. First elected in 1976 at age 27, with a personal fortune (his family owns radio and TV stations in Beckley and in St. Petersburg, Florida), and with high positions on committees important to the district, Rahall should be in no political trouble. But in 1984, he was sued by a Las Vegas casino for $60,000 in gambling debts and in 1988, he was plagued by a drunk-driving charge in California. In the 1990 primary, he was opposed by his predecessor, 75-year-old Secretary of State (and onetime Adlai Stevenson speechwriter) Ken Hechler, who called for a congressman "with high moral standards again," and won 43% of the vote; in the 1990 general election, Republican Marianne Brewster, though underfunded by her party, won 48%.

Rahall evidently took heed from this narrow escape. He used his senior position on Public Works to help West Virginia get $1.3 billion in highway projects in the 1991 transportation bill (Senator Robert Byrd helped, of course). He used his chairmanship of the Mining Subcommittee of Interior (now Natural Resources) to push for reform of the 1872 mining bill that allowed companies to cheaply purchase rights to mine federal land. With Senators Rockefeller and Byrd, he pushed for a tax on non-union coal operators to bail out the United Mine Workers healthcare funds. He worked on water and sewer projects, a trout hatchery in McDowell County, and protection against development of the New River. He introduced new black lung legislation, pressed for tamper-proof coal mine dust sampling devices, tried to create disincentives for U.S. companies to import coal from abroad.

Redistricting was perilous for Rahall, but he emerged from the legislature's musical chairs fight with a seat. Speaker Chuck Chambers worked to maintain a coal-country seat, perhaps to give coal representation, possibly so he could run himself some day. But in 1992, Rahall had no primary opposition. His Republican opponent, Ben Waldman, worked on Ronald Reagan's 1980s campaigns and for Pat Robertson in 1988, and moved to Monroe County in 1990. He raised some money but Rahall, with his family resources and committee position, raised far more, and won by an overwhelming margin. In the 103d Congress, Rahall took over the chair of the Public Works Subcommittee on Surface Transportation, one of the great pork barrel panels in the House, and at a time when freshmen were signing up for Public Works in record numbers to bring home bacon to their districts. Naturally, he will continue to work for coal and against other energy sources. On other issues, as a Lebanese-American, Rahall has taken an interest in Middle Eastern affairs; he is sympathetic to Palestinian claims and has voiced frustration on the amount spent overall on foreign aid.

The People: Pop. 1990: 597,500; 74% rural; 15% age 65+; 95% White; 4% Black. Voting age pop.: 444,283; 4% Black. Households: 60% married couple families; 29% married couple fams. w. children; 26% college educ.; median household income: $18,166; per capita income: $9,557; median gross rent: $284; median house value: $41,700.

1992 Presidential Vote			1988 Presidential Vote		
Clinton (D)	112,988	(55%)	Dukakis (D)	118,861	(59%)
Bush (R)	65,468	(32%)	Bush (R)	82,678	(41%)
Perot (I)	26,160	(13%)			

Rep. Nick J. Rahall (D)

Elected 1976; b. May 20, 1949, Beckley; home, Beckley; Duke U., A.B. 1971; Presbyterian; divorced.

Career: Civil Air Patrol, 1977–88; Staff Asst., U.S. Sen. Robert Byrd, 1971–74; Bd. of Dir., Rahall Communications Corp. 1974–76; Pres., Mountaineer Tour & Travel Agency, 1974–76; Pres., WV Broadcasting Corp. 1980–present.

Offices: 2269 RHOB 20515, 202-225-3452. Also 110½ Main St., Beckley 25801, 304-252-5000; 815 5th Ave., Huntington 25701, 304-522-6425; 1005 Fed. Bldg., Bluefield 24701, 304-325-6222; R.K. Bldg., 45 Washington Ave., Logan 25601, 304-752-4934; and P.O. Box 5, 101 N. Court St., Lewisburg 24901, 304-647-3228.

Committees: *Natural Resources* (5th of 28 D): Energy and Mineral Resources; National Parks, Forests and Public Lands. *Public Works and Transportation* (3d of 39 D): Surface Transportation (Chmn.); Water Resources and Environment; Economic Devel.

Group Ratings

	ADA	ACLU	COPE	CDF	CFA	LCV	ACU	NTLC	NSI	COC	CEI
1992	70	61	100	90	73	63	20	10	30	38	17
1991	65	—	100	90	78	54	21	—	—	11	10

National Journal Ratings

	1991 LIB — 1991 CONS		1992 LIB — 1992 CONS	
Economic	72% —	23%	61% —	38%
Social	58% —	40%	47% —	53%
Foreign	69% —	30%	76% —	19%

Key Votes of the 102d Congress

1. Ban Striker Replace	FOR	5. Handgun Wait/7-Day	AGN	9. Use Force in Gulf	FOR
2. $ for Homeownership	AGN	6. Overseas Mil. Abortion	AGN	10. US Mil. Abroad $ Cut	AGN
3. Tax Rich/Cut Mid Cls.	FOR	7. Obscn. Art NEA $ Ban	FOR	11. Limit SDI Funds	FOR
4. FY93/$15B Def. Cut	FOR	8. Death Pen. from Jury	AGN	12. Cuba Trade Embargo	AGN

Key Votes of the 103d Congress

1. Family Leave	FOR	2. Deficit Reduction	FOR	3. Stimulus Plan	FOR

Election Results

1992 general	Nick J. Rahall (D)	122,279	(66%)	($309,313)
	Ben Waldman (R).....................	64,012	(34%)	($150,822)
1992 primary	Nick J. Rahall (D), unopposed			
1990 general	Nick J. Rahall (D)	39,948	(52%)	($566,348)
	Marianne R. Brewster (R)	36,946	(48%)	($61,471)

WISCONSIN

Since the beginning of this century, Wisconsin has been one of the nation's premier "laboratories of reform," in Justice Louis Brandeis's phrase, a state that has originated new public policies, seen how they work and served as an example for others. Much of this is due to the state's unique history, to the German heritage of most of its citizens and to the political genius—and peculiarities—of Robert LaFollette and his sons. Just north of Chicago, west of the Great Lakes, Wisconsin is the first state of the Northwest—that vast stretch of the United States reaching all the way to the Pacific, settled more by immigrants from Germany and Scandinavia than by descendants of the Middle Atlantic and New England who populated the states just to the south. The German language is seldom heard now, the once plainly German beer brands now seem quintessentially American and few ties remained with the old country after two world wars. But in the late 19th and early 20th Centuries, Germans were among America's most numerous immigrants and until the 1880s probably the most distinctive. They established, on the rolling dairyland of Wisconsin and the orderly streets of Milwaukee, their separate religions, often keeping their language and maintaining old customs from country weddings to drinking beer—a source of friction in temperance-minded America—to eating bratwurst.

Politically, the Germans were not monolithic; their origins were diverse and they were spread too widely across the nation. But where they were concentrated, there was a distinctive politics, basically American, but with echoes of progressive ideas current in German-speaking countries in Europe. Nowhere was the politics of German-Americans more apparent than in Wisconsin. This is one of the two states that gave birth to the Republican Party in 1854, and German-Americans, then arriving in vast numbers, heavily favored it; they abhorred slavery and welcomed the free lands Republicans advocated in the Homestead Act, the free education promised by setting up land grant colleges and the transportation routes constructed by subsidizing railroad builders.

Then came Robert LaFollette and his Progressive movement, which can be dated conveniently from his election as governor in 1900. Up to that time a conventional Republican politician, LaFollette completely revamped the state government before going to the Senate in 1906. At a time when Germany was Europe's leader in graduate education and the application of science to government, LaFollette brought professors from the University of Wisconsin, just across town in Madison, to develop the state workmen's compensation system and income tax. The Progressive movement favored rational use of government to improve the lot of the ordinary citizen—an idea borrowed partly from German liberals and adopted by the New Dealers a generation later. LaFollette became a national figure; he tried to run for president in 1912 as a Progressive, but was shoved aside by Theodore Roosevelt; in 1924 LaFollette finally did run for president as a Progressive and won 18% of the nation's votes, the best third-party showing between 1912 and 1992. He was strongest in the northern tier from Wisconsin to Washington, along the West Coast, and in some hitherto Republican factory towns like Cleveland.

After the elder LaFollette's death in 1925, his sons maintained Wisconsin progressive tradition. Robert LaFollette, Jr., served in the Senate from 1925 to 1947, and was a leader of the liberal, pro-labor bloc. Philip LaFollette was elected governor of Wisconsin in 1930, 1934 and 1936, and in 1934 formed his own Progressive Party. The movement took on ominous tones later in the decade, with a Cross in Circle symbol his critics called a circumcised swastika, huge rally-like parades reminiscent of some in Europe at the time and a call for the governor to propose all legislation; his dream of forming a national party was never achieved. At home, he was beaten badly in 1938 and did not run for office again. Robert LaFollette, Jr., was reelected to the Senate in 1940 by only 45%–41% over a Republican; the Progressives won the governorship once more in 1942, but won only 6% in statewide contests in 1944 and voted to disband their party before the 1946 election. Senator LaFollette, who decided to run for reelection as a Republican but didn't campaign much because he was busy in Washington, was defeated in the 1946 primary by one Joseph McCarthy.

McCarthy's national prominence along with other Republican victories made Wisconsin seem like a Republican state in the 1950s. McCarthy's charges that Communists were influencing American foreign policy fed on the inarticulate convictions of many in Wisconsin and elsewhere that the U.S. should have been fighting Russia as well as Germany in World War II. Actually, McCarthy and other Republicans often won by narrow margins, and the energies of the old Progressive movement, centered in Madison somewhere between the State Capitol and the University of Wisconsin, were transferred largely to a Democratic Party led by the likes of William Proxmire and Gaylord Nelson. For two decades, liberal Democrats became the latest in a line of experimenters in the Wisconsin laboratory, as Wisconsin, a mostly Republican state in the mostly Democratic years from 1944 to 1964, became a mostly Democratic state in the mostly Republican years from 1968 to 1988. It was one of the most dovish states, as if many Wisconsin voters were hit by the same impulse that led so many West German voters in the early 1980s to fear the presence of nuclear weapons and to favor disarmament.

Now there are signs Wisconsin is turning in another direction. In 1986, it ousted liberal Democratic Governor Tony Earl for conservative Republican Tommy Thompson, who has become one of the nation's most popular governors. He has cut taxes, sponsored a school choice program championed by Milwaukee black activist Polly Williams, implemented a "learnfare" program which ties a parent's welfare grants to children's school attendance, passed a "bridefare" law paying welfare recipients more if they get married and less if they have more children and signed a law making parents or a guardian, rather than the state, responsible for supporting children of unmarried teenagers. He also signed what has been called the nation's most comprehensive recycling law. Wisconsin's high-skill, precision manufacturing economy—its biggest companies include Johnson Controls, Harnischfeger, Briggs & Stratton, Harley-Davidson—jumped into gear in the late 1980s, as its factories helped lead the nation's export boom; Wisconsin gained more jobs than other midwestern states and was hurt relatively little by the early 1990s recession. Some dismiss Thompson as a low-tax pragmatist; even if that is true, his policies mean a shift from the LaFollette era bureaucracies, which 80 years ago seemed the rational way to regulate a society whose economy was increasingly made up of big companies. Thompson has not swept all before him: in 1992 Wisconsin ousted Republican Senator Bob Kasten for one of Thompson's strongest critics, Russ Feingold. But Thompson does seem to have moved the fulcrum point of opinion. Feingold's campaign was almost devoid of issue content, while Republicans outpolled Democrats in House races and gained control of the state Senate for the first time in 18 years. Presidentially, Wisconsin, the number five state for George McGovern in 1972 and the number seven state for Michael Dukakis in 1988, was 27th for Bill Clinton in 1992.

Governor. From the small town of Elroy, 80 miles south to Madison, Wisconsin's Governor Tommy Thompson has been commuting most of his life, first as a student at the University of Wisconsin, then to the legislature when he was elected just after finishing law school, and now as governor. For years he was part of a minority in Madison; now he is the dominant political figure

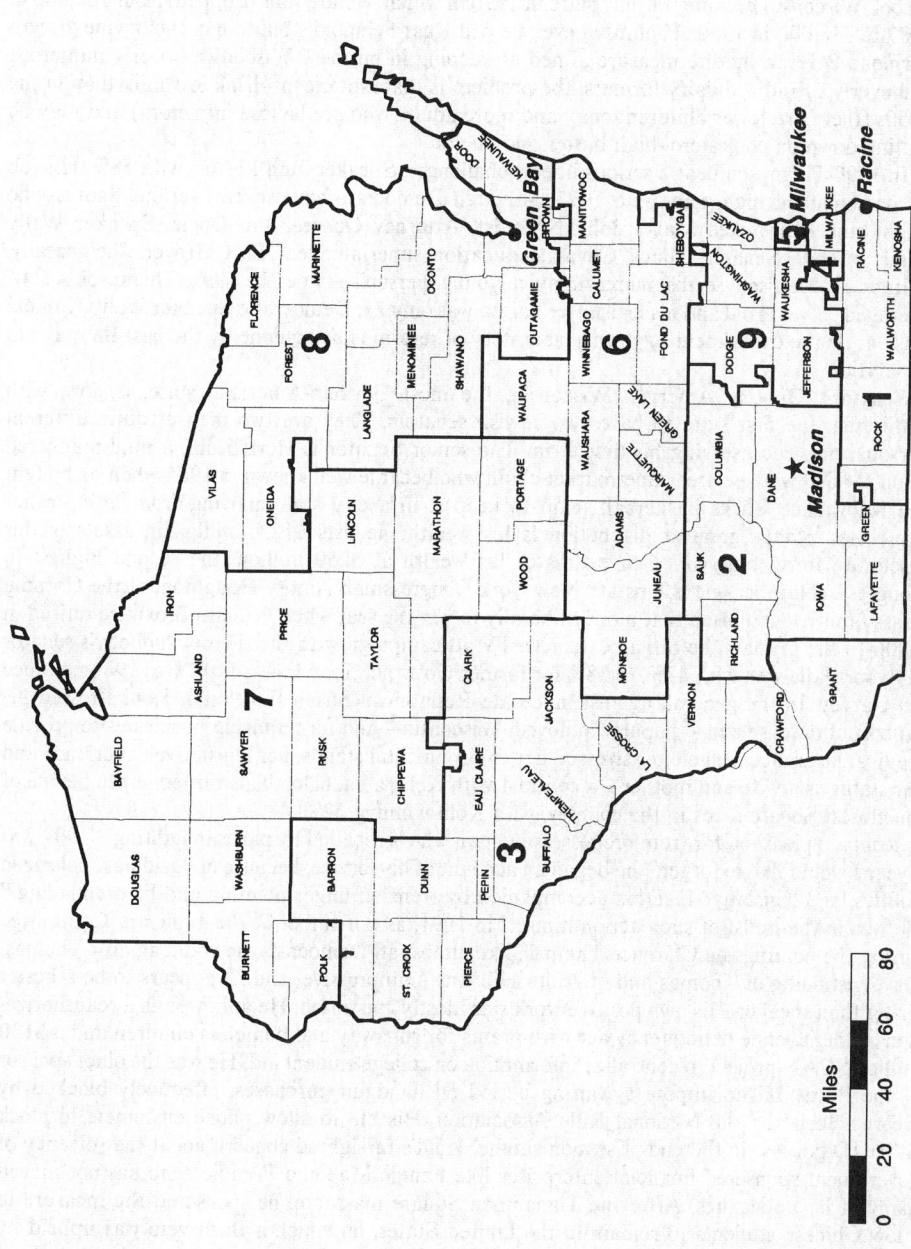

KEWAUNEE

DOOR

Green Bay

BROWN

MANITOWOC

KEWAUNEE

SHEBOYGAN

OZAUKEE

Milwaukee

Racine

MILWAUKEE

5

MARINETTE

FLORENCE

8

FOREST

OCONTO

MENOMINEE

SHAWANO

OUTAGAMIE

CALUMET

WINNEBAGO

6

FOND DU LAC

DODGE

9

WASHINGTON

WAUKESHA

4

RACINE

KENOSHA

WALWORTH

VILAS

ONEIDA

LINCOLN

LANGLADE

WAUPACA

PORTAGE

MARATHON

WAUSHARA

MARQUETTE

GREEN LAKE

ADAMS

COLUMBIA

JEFFERSON

ROCK

1

GREEN

DANE

★

Madison

IRON

PRICE

TAYLOR

WOOD

JUNEAU

SAUK

2

RICHLAND

IOWA

LAFAYETTE

ASHLAND

7

SAWYER

RUSK

CLARK

MONROE

VERNON

CRAWFORD

GRANT

BAYFIELD

JACKSON

LA CROSSE

DOUGLAS

WASHBURN

BARRON

CHIPPEWA

EAU CLAIRE

TREMPEALEAU

BUFFALO

3

BURNETT

POLK

ST CROIX

DUNN

PEPIN

PIERCE

Miles

0   20   40   60   80

in the state. He has used Wisconsin's extraordinary "partial veto" more than 1,200 times; he can strike not only lines from the budget, but words and numbers, enabling him to cut a program by 90% by dropping one zero or to restore his "bridefare" experiment by writing it back in. He cut the income and capital gains taxes and repealed the inheritance tax; he instituted and spotlighted school choice and "learnfare" to penalize welfare families whose children skip school. Wisconsin became the only state in 1990 in which welfare rolls dropped, from 300,000 in 1987 to 238,000 in 1990. Thompson even vetoed Russ Feingold's bill to ban the bovine growth hormone BGH, a luddite measure aimed at keeping in business Wisconsin's overly numerous and overly subsidized dairy farmers: the problem is that Americans drink less milk than in the 1950s (there are fewer children today and more adults who are lactose intolerant) and may be cutting down on cholesterol-high butter and cheese.

In 1990 Thompson beat a serious liberal challenger, Speaker Tom Loftus, with 58%. His job rating remained high going into 1993, although Democrats have several serious figures who might run: Milwaukee Mayor John Norquist, Attorney General Jim Doyle, Speaker Wally Kunicki, state Senator Chuck Chvala, education superintendent Bert Grover. Incidentally, politics in Madison seems increasingly a young person's game: in 1992 Thompson's staff averaged 31 years old and his legislative liaison was only 27; Democratic Speaker Wally Kunicki was 34. So the experimenting in this laboratory of reform is being done by the post-Baby Boom generation.

Senators. Only in America: Wisconsin, the most German-American state, is now, with California, the first state to have two Jewish senators. They are two men of quite different personalities, each serving his first term. The senior Senator is Herb Kohl, a mild-mannered scion of a Milwaukee area supermarket chain who became well known in 1985 when he bought the Milwaukee Bucks basketball team to keep it in a city still smarting from losing other franchises. Kohl's greatest distinction is his wealth; he lists $12.7 million in assets on his disclosure form, but *Roll Call* estimates his wealth at $250 million, the second highest in Congress. (Number one is Upstate New York Congressman Amory Houghton, of the Corning Glass family.) Kohl used that money liberally to win the seat when William Proxmire retired in 1988. In the primary, he ran an extensive TV ad campaign with the theme, "nobody's senator but yours"; he won with 47%, to 38% for former Governor Tony Earl and 10% to 1986 nominee Ed Garvey. In the general, against moderate Republican Susan Engeleiter, Kohl stressed his support of defense cuts—popular in dovish Wisconsin—and for requiring businesses to provide medical insurance; Engeleiter stressed her environmental stands, her legislative experience and her status as a wife and mother—a contrast with Kohl, a bachelor. This turned out to be one of the closest Senate races in the country, with Kohl winning 52%–48%.

Kohl is a pleasant, far from prepossessing man who is repelled by partisan fighting: "1992 was a year I would like to forget," he began an account of his service, because of "gridlock, polarized politics, and legislative inaction accompanied by frenzied finger pointing and blame placing." He was in the midst of such action himself in 1991, as a member of the Judiciary Committee during the hearings on Clarence Thomas; like almost all Democrats, he voted against Thomas. His questioning of Thomas and of Anita Hill was unimpressive, and he appears to be a better writer than speaker. His own positive work was mostly frustrated. He got through a reauthorization of the juvenile delinquency act with grants for runaway and homeless children and a $130 million SCAN project to centralize information on college student aid. He was the chief sponsor of the Brady bill to impose a waiting period on handgun purchases, effectively blocked by George Bush and the National Rifle Association. His bill to allow phone customers to block caller ID got lost in the end-of-session shuffle. Kohl's farsighted concern about the solvency of government sponsored financial enterprises like Fannie Mae and Freddie Mac has not moved many of his colleagues. After the Tiananmen Square massacre, he sponsored the measure to allow Chinese students to remain in the United States, on which a Bush veto was upheld by appeals to Republican partisanship. Kohl is usually dependably partisan but, worried about deficits, has been voting against enough spending bills to make him the National Taxpayer

Union's best-rated Senate Democrat.

Kohl has worked also on parochial Wisconsin causes. Chairing the Government Affairs Subcommittee on Government Information and Regulation, he stood stoutly against adjustment of the 1990 Census figures—a worthy stand against a measure that, as it happens, would have cost Wisconsin a congressional seat. He has worked on Great Lakes issues, from requiring that farm commodities be shipped from Great Lakes ports to preventing oil spills and eradicating the environmentally harmful zebra mussel. Additionally, he has worked for higher dairy prices, against a bill that would hurt the Cray supercomputer company of Chippewa Falls and for tough labor conditions on a local railroad merger.

Kohl's earnestness makes him an attractive—and his money makes him a formidable—candidate for 1994. Republican state Senator Bob Welch has announced he is a candidate for Kohl's seat, and Matt Gunderson, younger brother to Congressman Steve Gunderson, has said he may run. Governor Thompson seems uninterested in leaving Madison.

For its other Senate seat, Wisconsin saw one of the starkest ideological battles in the country—or would have seen, if both candidates had campaigned forthrightly. The winner was Russ Feingold, a 39-year-old state senator and Rhodes Scholar who had campaigned for the office for five years, during most of which time no one thought he had a chance. The loser was Bob Kasten, a conservative senator elected in this historically liberal state with 50% of the vote in 1980 and 51% in 1986. Kasten's lodestar has always been low taxes: he was the leading opponent of withholding from savings and brokerage accounts in 1983, the co-sponsor of the Republican alternative to the Bradley-Gephardt tax reform plan that helped produce the 1986 tax reform, and the prime sponsor of tort reform, the effort to set federal standards limiting product liability, strongly opposed by trial lawyers. He long favored a deep capital gains tax cut and a Social Security payroll tax cut. He gained a reputation for negative campaigning in his 1986 race against former National Football League players' attorney Ed Garvey, although arguably the nastiest stuff came from Garvey.

Democrats lined up to make the race: Feingold, Milwaukee Congressman Jim Moody and businessman Joseph Checota. Checota, self-financing his campaign, brought the most money to the race; Moody, from the Milwaukee area, the highest name identification; Feingold, after 10 years in the legislature, the most distinctive public record. Feingold had crusaded to ban the bovine growth hormone BGH and had also pushed to convert lottery profits to a property tax credit, and he opposed proposals to allow banking across state lines. He strongly opposed Thompson's welfare reforms and school choice, took pro-trial lawyer positions on legal reform issues and opposed capital punishment. For the Senate race, Feingold produced detailed position papers, including an 82-point plan for reducing the deficit, but of course many voters never got to the fine print. What they saw instead were a series of clever, humorous ads: one showing Elvis, alive and endorsing Feingold; another showing Feingold at home, opening up a closet and saying, "No skeletons"; another showing his three key pledges written out on his garage door. Meanwhile, Moody was leading in polls and Checota was spending heavily. But negative publicity about Checota's business—accusations of abuse of company funds, lawsuits, an angry press conference from Admiral Elmo Zumwalt—combined with attacks by Moody and Checota on each other created a negative atmosphere in contrast to Feingold's humor. Near primary day, Checota apologized for his ads and asked voters to vote for Feingold if they didn't vote for him. Feingold, already ahead in polls, zoomed to an astonishing 70% win in this three-way primary.

Feingold also zoomed way ahead of Kasten—23% in one public poll. He attacked Kasten for "disregard of decency in politics"—a form of negative campaigning effective because it didn't sound negative. He promised to hold "listening forums" in every one of the 72 counties each year, and to live primarily in Wisconsin. He said less about backing universal health care, upper bracket tax increases and targeted tax cuts to business and opposing the North American Free Trade Agreement: for all his issue papers, this was a campaign not of issues but of attitude. Kasten roared back with his own Elvis ad and attacked Feingold for wanting to raise taxes on the middle class, opposing capital punishment and a "life-for-life" anti-parole bill, and for being against the Gulf war resolution; Feingold responded by calling this deceptive campaigning, though the issues were legitimate and Kasten's charges were based on his stands. The race narrowed greatly, but in the end Feingold won 53%–46%, carrying Madison heavily and the Milwaukee area by his statewide percentage.

In the Senate, Feingold has seats on the Foreign Relations and Agriculture Committees. His skill at striking a humorous tone, making his stands seem non-political, and depicting attacks on his unpopular issue positions as illegitimate suggest that he has fine prospects for a more secure Senate career than his predecessor.

Presidential politics. Wisconsin was once one of the most influential states in presidential contests. Its presidential primary knocked Wendell Willkie out of the race in 1944 and helped John Kennedy establish his lead over Hubert Humphrey in 1960; Eugene McCarthy was all set to win heavily here in 1968 when Lyndon Johnson withdrew on the Sunday night before the election. Since then, it has attracted attention for synthetic reasons. In 1988, the press flew in after Jesse Jackson's surprise win in the Michigan caucuses, looking for the black-white blue-collar populist alliance so many reporters long to see. But as it turned out, almost all of Jackson's votes in Michigan, thanks to the caucus's peculiar rules, were cast by blacks, and his candidacy fizzled across Lake Michigan. In 1992, Wisconsin got less attention, since its primary was held the same day as New York's, and Gotham journalists had a psychic stake in portraying their contest as an ambush for Bill Clinton. But Clinton had essentially already clinched the nomination anyway and won New York handily, and beat Jerry Brown, 38%–35%, in Wisconsin. The national Democrats, incidentally, have allowed Wisconsin to continue its open primary, one of Bob LaFollette's reforms.

Wisconsin has been competitive in the last two presidential elections, and arguably in four of the last five; in fall 1992, George Bush made five Wisconsin visits and Bill Clinton four. When Democrats nominate a liberal from the northern tier of states, Wisconsin becomes one of the most Democratic states, as in 1972, 1984 and 1988; when Democrats nominate a southerner, it votes much like the national average, as in 1976, 1980 and 1992. The low Clinton percentage and the relatively small drop in George Bush's percentage (10% versus 16% nationally) may reflect the absence here of two phenomena which worked for Clinton and against Bush on the East and West Coasts: falling real estate prices and a large singles population. Wisconsin housing prices have held steady or risen, and the divorce rate here is one of the lowest in the country.

Congressional districting. Wisconsin did not lose a congressional district in the 1990 Census, and its population grew evenly enough that no major changes were needed in the current district lines to meet the equal-population standard. The Democratic legislature's plan, signed by Thompson, shifted a few dozen townships between districts.

The People: Est. Pop. 1992: 5,007,000; Pop. 1990: 4,891,769, up 2.3% 1990–1992. 2.0% of U.S. total, 16th largest; 34% rural. Median age: 32.9 years. 13.3% 65 years and over. 92.2% White, 5.0% Black, 1.9% Hispanic origin, 1.1% Asian. Households: 57.5% married couple families; 28% married couple fams. w. children; 42% college educ.; median household income: $29,442; per capita income: $13,276; 66.7% owner occupied housing; median house value: $62,500; median monthly rent: $331. 5.1% Unemployment. Voting age pop.: 3,602,787. No state voter registration.

Political Lineup: Governor, Tommy G. Thompson (R); Lt. Gov., Scott McCallum (R); Secy. of State, Douglas LaFollette (D); Atty. Gen., James Doyle (D); Treasurer, Cathy S. Zeuske (R). State Senate, 30 (16 R and 14 D). State Assembly, 99 (51 D, 45 R, and 3 vacancies). Senators, Herb Kohl (D) and Russell D. Feingold (D). Representatives, 9 (5 R and 4 D).

1992 Presidential Vote

Clinton (D)	1,041,066	(41%)
Bush (R)	930,855	(37%)
Perot (I)	544,479	(22%)

1992 Democratic Presidential Primary

Clinton	287,356	(38%)
Brown	266,207	(35%)
Tsongas	168,619	(22%)
Other	36,764	(5%)

1988 Presidential Vote

Dukakis (D)	1,126,794	(51%)
Bush (R)	1,047,499	(47%)

1992 Republican Presidential Primary

Bush	364,507	(78%)
Buchanan	78,516	(17%)
Other	17,699	(4%)

GOVERNOR

Gov. Tommy G. Thompson (R)

Elected 1986, term expires Jan. 1995; b. Nov. 19, 1941, Elroy; home, Elroy; U. of WI, B.A. 1963, J.D. 1966; Catholic; married (Sue Ann).

Career: Practicing atty; WI Assembly, 1966–86, Asst. Minority Ldr., 1973–81, Floor Ldr., 1981–86; Chmn., Repub. Govs. Assn., 1991–92.

Office: State Capitol, 115 E. State Capitol, Madison 53702, 608-266-1212.

Election Results

1990 gen.	Tommy G. Thompson (R)	802,321	(58%)
	Thomas Loftus (D)	546,280	(42%)
1990 prim.	Tommy G. Thompson (R)	201,467	(93%)
	Bennett A. Masel (R)	11,230	(5%)
	Three Others	4,673	(2%)
1986 gen.	Tommy G. Thompson (R)	805,090	(53%)
	Anthony S. Earl (D)	705,578	(46%)

SENATORS

Sen. Herb Kohl (D)

Elected 1988, seat up 1994; b. Feb. 7, 1935, Milwaukee; home, Milwaukee; U. of WI, B.A. 1956, Harvard, M.B.A. 1958; Jewish; single.

Career: Army Reserves, 1958–64; Businessman; Pres., Kohl Corp., 1970–79; Chmn., WI St. Dem. Party, 1975–77; Pres., Herbert Kohl Investments 1979–88; Owner, Milwaukee Bucks basketball team.

Offices: 330 HSOB 20510, 202-224-5653. Also 205 E. Wisconsin Ave., Milwaukee 53202, 414-297-4451; 14 W. Mifflin St., #312, Madison 53703, 608-264-5338; 402 Graham Ave., #206, Eau Claire 54701, 715-832-8424; 4321 W. College Ave., #235, Appleton 54914, 414-738-1640; and 625 52d St., #303, Kenosha 53140, 414-657-7719.

Committees:*Aging (Special)* (9th of 11 D). *Appropriations* (14th of 16 D): Agriculture, Rural Development and Related Agencies; District of Columbia (Chmn.); Labor, Health and Human Services, Education; Military Construction. *Judiciary* (8th of 10 D): Courts and Administrative Practice; Juvenile Justice (Chmn.); Technology and the Law. *Small Business* (11th of 12 D): Government Contracting and Paperwork Reduction; Rural Economy and Family Farming.

Group Ratings

	ADA	ACLU	CDF	COPE	CFA	LCV	ACU	NTLC	NSI	COC	CEI
1992	95	86	90	83	83	83	11	33	50	30	29
1991	90	—	82	58	72	73	24	—	—	20	42

National Journal Ratings

	1991 LIB — 1991 CONS		1992 LIB — 1992 CONS	
Economic	60%	— 35%	65%	— 33%
Social	64%	— 33%	69%	— 26%
Foreign	71%	— 27%	78%	— 14%

Key Votes of the 102d Congress

1. $ for Homeownership	AGN	5. Clarence Thomas Nom.	AGN	9. Use Force in Gulf	AGN
2. Have Cap Gains Debate	AGN	6. Lmt Death Row Appeal	AGN	10. Keep Salvador Aid	AGN
3. Remove Budget Walls	FOR	7. Handgun Wait/5-Day	FOR	11. Cut $1B from SDI	FOR
4. Ban Striker Replace	FOR	8. Abortion Gag Rule	AGN	12. Override China MFN	FOR

Key Votes of the 103d Congress

1. Family Leave	FOR	2. HIV Immigrants	FOR	3. Clinton Budget	FOR

Election Results

1988 general	Herb Kohl (D)	1,128,625	(52%)	($7,491,600)
	Susan Engeleiter (R)................	1,030,440	(48%)	($2,853,842)
1988 primary	Herb Kohl (D)	249,226	(47%)	
	Anthony S. Earl (D)..................	203,479	(38%)	
	Ed Garvey (D)	55,225	(10%)	
	Douglas J. LaFollette (D).............	19,819	(4%)	
1982 general	William Proxmire (D)................	983,311	(64%)	
	Scott McCallum (R).................	527,355	(34%)	($119,924)

Sen. Russell D. Feingold (D)

Elected 1992, seat up 1998; b. Mar. 2, 1953, Janesville; home, Middleton; U. of WI, B.A. 1975, Rhodes Scholar, Oxford U., 1977, Harvard Law Schl., J.D. 1979; Jewish; married (Mary).

Career: Practicing atty., 1979–83; WI Senate, 1983–92;

Offices: 502 HSOB 20510, 202-224-5323. Also 517 E. Wisconsin Ave., Milwaukee 53202, 414-276-7282; and 8383 Greenway Blvd., Middleton 53562, 608-828-1200.

Committees: *Aging (Special)* (10th of 11 D): *Agriculture, Nutrition and Forestry* (10th of 10 D): Agricultural Production and Stabilization of Prices; Domestic and Foreign Marketing and Product Promotion; Nutrition and Investigations. *Foreign Relations* (10th of 11 D): African Affairs; European Affairs; International Economic Policy, Trade, Oceans and Environment.

Group Ratings and 102d Congress Votes: Newly Elected

Key Votes of the 103d Congress

1. Family Leave	FOR	2. HIV Immigrants	FOR	3. Clinton Budget	FOR

Election Results

1992 general	Russell D. Feingold (D)	1,290,662	(53%)	($2,056,079)
	Robert W. Kasten, Jr. (R)	1,129,599	(46%)	($5,427,163)
	Other	34,863	(1%)	
1992 primary	Russell D. Feingold (D)	367,746	(70%)	
	Jim Moody (D)	74,472	(14%)	
	Joseph Checota (D).	71,570	(13%)	
	Other	14,056	(3%)	
1986 general	Robert W. Kasten, Jr. (R).	1,754,537	(51%)	($3,433,870)
	Edward Garvey (D)	1,702,963	(47%)	($1,702,963)

FIRST DISTRICT

Rolling dairy country, blanketed by snow during most of the winter, gloriously green under sunny blue skies in summer, the southern tier of Wisconsin from Lake Michigan inland to the Rock River valley is some of America's prime industrial country. Settled by Yankee and German farmers 150 years ago, it was once primarily dairyland. By the early 20th Century, the steady habits and high skills of the local dairy farmers provided a good labor pool for factories. Today, there are still major plants here: the operations center for Johnson Wax (and its Frank Lloyd Wright-designed tower and Wingspread center) in Racine; the old Nash plant, later run by American Motors and Chrysler but finally shut down, in Kenosha; and the Parker Pen operation in Janesville. In between on lakes are resorts, most notably Lake Geneva, a favorite of ric Illinois and squeaky-clean progressive politics of Wisconsin.

This is the land of the 1st District of Wisconsin, from Lake Michigan west to the Rock River and beyond, a politically marginal area in Wisconsin politics, a marginal district in congressih Chicagoans. To the untrained eye, this part of southern Wisconsin looks much the same as nearby northern Illinois; but politically there is a vast difference. The dotted line on the map is the boundary between the corruption-prone machine politics ofonal politics from 1958 to 1968, but from 1970 until 1993 the home base of Les Aspin, Pentagon whiz kid, Pentagon critic, chairman of the House Armed Services Committee and now secretary of defense: Aspin's career reads more like that of a British member of Parliament than of an American member of Congress. He went to Yale and Oxford, got a Ph.D. in economics from M.I.T., worked as a staffer for Senator William Proxmire, was part of Robert McNamara's whiz kid operation in the Pentagon when he served in the Army in the late 1960s, but was also detailed to manage Lyndon Johnson's hopeless campaign in the 1968 Wisconsin primary. After teaching at Marquette and moving to Racine, Aspin was elected to Congress in 1970, beating a LaFollette in the primary and a 10-year incumbent in the general; he had only minor difficulty winning reelection for 20 years. In the House, the road was rockier, as a rebel on Armed Services in the early 1970s; elected chairman to replace elderly incumbent Mel Price in 1984, Aspin was nearly ousted two years later by a combination of oldtimers miffed at his disrespect for seniority and doves furious at his apostasy on the MX missile and contra aid. But he worked hard and expertly pushed through always-controversial Pentagon authorizations, balancing a hawkish committee and a dovish caucus, a military cautious about committing to battle and civilian leadership deeply distrustful of Congress. His finest moment came in January 1991, when he not only backed the Gulf war resolution but predicted accurately the course of the battle, showing a greater knowledge of U.S. military capabilities and surer judgment than any other member of Congress, including Senate Armed Services chairman Sam Nunn. From that time on, his selection as secretary of defense by anything but the most stubbornly dovish of Democratic presidents was probably inevitable.

Aspin's appointment opened up the 1st District seat for the first time in more than two decades. History shows that parties in power often lose special elections early in a president's term, and this was the closest of the early 1993 special elections. Republican candidate Mark Neumann, a homebuilder who made a fortune by using computers to make quick and accurate estimates on custom-built houses, had held Aspin to an undistinguished 58%–41% margin in November 1992, in one of the nation's biggest spending contests (Neumann spent $941,000, mostly his own money, and Aspin spent $1.3 million, much of its from PACs). Neumann criticized the national debt and deficit spending, called for better education and advanced his own health plan (employers would pay $1,500 per employee for insurance with a $3,000 deductible and put $3,000 for each employee in a savings account). Pro-life on abortion, Neumann was supported by the Christian Coalition, which had Democrats muttering about the religious right.

Neumann ran again in the 1993 special, though not spending as much of his own money and minimizing connections with the Christian Coalition; he attacked the Clinton tax and spending programs sharply. Of the Democrats, former state party chairman Jeff Neubauer came the closest of any in the nation's special elections to defending the Clinton economic program. But this evidently had little positive impact: he won only 34% in the primary. The primary winner, with 49%, was Peter Barca, a state legislator with a solid base in Kenosha and strong labor union support. Barca said he would not vote for many of the new taxes proposed by Clinton, but backed healthcare and welfare reform, while labor unions conducted a heavy "negative persuasion" phone bank campaign against Neumann. Neumann stressed his opposition to the congressional pay raise and ways of doing business on Capitol Hill, but stumbled a bit by suggesting that some Social Security trust funds be invested in producing jobs. Barca seized on that, calling it a threat to Social Security. This charge made the difference, as Barca won 50%–49%.

Neumann, who lost by 675 votes, demanded a recount; Barca survived the recount, but the action delayed his swearing in to Congress until June 8. With a solid base, a district where labor unions are still important, a record as a hard-working and earnest legislator, Barca should be able to make this a safe seat, provided his party does not get into more trouble than it was in when he won it.

The People: Pop. 1990: 543,380; 29% rural; 12% age 65+; 90% White; 5% Black; 1% Asian; 2% Other; 3% Hispanic origin. Voting age pop.: 396,994; 4% Black; 2% Hispanic origin. Households: 60% married

couple families; 28% married couple fams. w. children; 39% college educ.; median household income: $31,431; per capita income: $13,567; median gross rent: $401; median house value: $61,200.

1992 Presidential Vote			1988 Presidential Vote		
Clinton (D)	109,790	(41%)	Dukakis (D)	115,873	(51%)
Bush (R)	94,712	(35%)	Bush (R)	109,474	(49%)
Perot (I)	62,465	(23%)			

Rep. Peter W. Barca (D)

Elected May 1993; b. Aug. 7, 1955, Kenosha; home, Kenosha; U. of WI, B.S. 1977, M.A. 1982; Catholic; married (Kathleen).

Career: Special Educ. teacher, 1977–80; Chmn., Kenosha Cnty. Dem. Party, 1980; Employment specialist for the developmentally disabled, 1982–83; WI Assembly, 1984–93.

Offices: 1719 LHOB 20515, 202-225-3031. Also 210 Dodge St., Janesville 53545, 608-752-9074; and 1661 Douglas Ave., Racine 53404, 414-632-4446.

Committees: *Public Works and Transportation* (40th of 40 D). *Science, Space and Technology* (32d of 33 D).

Group Ratings and Key Votes: Newly Elected

Election Results

1993 special	Peter W. Barca (D)	55,605	(50%)	($752,069)
	Mark Neumann (R)	54,930	(49%)	($716,570)
	Other	941	(1%)	
1993 primary	Peter W. Barca (D)	31,073	(49%)	
	Jeffrey Neubauer (D)	21,610	(34%)	
	Wayne W. Wood (D)	8,254	(13%)	
	Other	2,927	(4%)	
1992 general	Les Aspin (D)	147,495	(58%)	($1,355,737)
	Mark Neumann (R)	104,352	(41%)	($941,674)
	Other	4,433	(2%)	

SECOND DISTRICT

On a narrow isthmus between Lakes Mendota and Monona is the center of Madison and, in many ways, the center of Wisconsin. Here the state Capitol rises at the one end of State Street; at the other end of several commercial blocks is the main campus of the University of Wisconsin, on a beautiful, parklike, sometimes windswept setting above Lake Mendota. For most of this century, Wisconsin politics was dominated by the Madison-based LaFollettes and their liberal Democratic successors. And the traffic on State Street was two-way, with university faculty devoted to Bob LaFollette's "Wisconsin idea" of an enlightened, apolitical bureaucracy, his Wisconsin Tax Commission and workmen's compensation law—both firsts in the nation. The *Progressive* magazine is still published here, and the *Madison Capital-Times* continues to be one of the nation's most explicitly liberal newspapers, though its Republican rival, the *Wisconsin State Journal*, has a much larger circulation; they practice the kind of partisan journalism still seen in only a few major cities and state capitals (Nashville, Sacramento, Boston, Detroit).

Madison is the center of Wisconsin's 2d Congressional District, and with surrounding Dane County cast two-thirds of the district's votes. The rest are in several rural dairy counties which are more Republican and conservative; they include such picturesque Wisconsin scenes as Frank Lloyd Wright's home, "Taliesin," and the Swiss-settled town of New Glarus. Madison was LaFollette country for the first half of the century, and very liberal and Democratic for most of the second, enough so that despite the Republican leanings of the rural counties, the 2d District voted for George McGovern in 1972 and Walter Mondale in 1984. In 1990, these placid rural counties and the longtime liberal bastion of Madison combined to produce one of the most stunning upsets in recent House races, the defeat of Democrat Robert Kastenmeier after 32 years by Republican Scott Klug. It was a race which almost no one picked for an upset, in which the incumbent spent $372,000 to the challenger's $178,000, in which Klug conceded from the outset that "Bob Kastenmeier has served this district well and served it honorably and in many cases, frankly, I think he has done a very good job." This was respect earned over the long haul by one of Congress's most unflamboyant hard workers: Kastenmeier was even more cautious in demeanor than liberal in his voting record. Elected to Congress in 1958, he opposed the Vietnam war and defense buildups consistently (he was a soldier who saw the ruins of Hiroshima). On the House Judiciary Committee, his one moment in the spotlight was during impeachment hearings against Richard Nixon in 1974, where he insisted that each article of impeachment be voted on separately.

Yet this district is now represented by Republican Scott Klug, one of those rebels against the House Democratic leadership. His campaign against Kastenmeier was the numerals 32 with a line drawn through them, and he pledged to serve only 12 years if elected. Klug attacked the Democrat's opposition to troop deployment in the Persian Gulf as being "stuck in the '60s," an era which did not leave altogether good memories in Madison, where a graduate student was killed when a protester set off a bomb in a laboratory. Klug also built on his own background as an investigative reporter for Washington D.C.'s ABC affiliate WJLA for seven years and then as anchor on Madison's WKOW-TV. In not traditional Republican tones, during the campaign he called for better safety conditions on farms and early intervention programs for at-risk children. He said that social security should be subjected to means tests and possibly to cuts. Klug seemed to be speaking for a new generation of voters; he noted that a recent student government election at the University was won by a party organized by Republicans, and added that "as the system stands right now, it limits opportunities for my generation." Klug lost Madison's Dane County by only 52%–48% and won 63% in the smaller counties, for a 53%–47% victory, slightly ahead of Republican Governor Tommy Thompson's strong showing there.

In Congress, Klug compiled a moderate voting record on some issues but made waves as one of the freshman Republican "Gang of Seven" who insisted on full disclosure of House bank overdrafts, and managed to survive the embarrassment when he had three overdrafts himself. He joined the Porkbusters' Coalition identifying $1 billion in recommended cuts. He pushed to have Congress covered by the Freedom of Information Act. But he also did less confrontational things, working on details of federal dairy programs, trying to restrict cheese imports, boosting ethanol fuels and helping the University of Wisconsin, whose chancellor, Donna Shalala, he supported when Bill Clinton named her secretary of health and human services. He got a law changed so that U.S. soldiers killed by friendly fire can receive the Purple Heart. He strongly backs the WIC child nutrition program and a national child abuse prevention bill. In constituency service, Klug showed himself to be conscientious and knowledgeable.

Klug's 1992 opponent was expected to be state Senator David Clarenbach, at age 38 an 18-year Madison legislator; but in the year of the anti-incumbent and the woman, Clarenbach was defeated 60%–40% by Ada Deer, an American Indian (that term is her preference) who in the 1970s helped to reestablished the tribal status of her fellow Menominees. Deer said she would have voted against the Gulf war resolution and was not sure if she would have voted for declaring war against Germany and Japan in 1941; she held a fundraiser at an abortion clinic, with a basket full of condoms next to her basket of bumper stickers. But while Bill Clinton carried the district by a big margin, Klug's articulateness and moderate stands proved more attractive than Deer's enthusiasm and liberal stands. Klug carried Dane County with 60% of the vote and won

69% in the smaller counties, for a striking 63%–37% victory. Klug's success is an interesting precedent for the Republican Party, showing how a Republican hostile to higher taxes and nurturing of nationalism can win in one of the historic citadels of baby-boom liberalism. Klug says he is happy representing the 2d District, and said he would not run against Herb Kohl in 1994.

The People: Pop. 1990: 543,625; 36% rural; 11% age 65+; 95% White; 2% Black; 2% Asian; 1% Hispanic origin. Voting age pop.: 412,215; 2% Black; 1% Hispanic origin. Households: 55% married couple families; 26% married couple fams. w. children; 53% college educ.; median household income: $30,625; per capita income: $14,319; median gross rent: $441; median house value: $69,800.

1992 Presidential Vote			1988 Presidential Vote		
Clinton (D)	149,340	(50%)	Dukakis (D)	139,552	(56%)
Bush (R)	94,368	(32%)	Bush (R)	108,929	(44%)
Perot (I)	52,552	(18%)			

Rep. Scott Klug (R)

Elected 1990; b. Jan. 16, 1953, Milwaukee; home, Madison; Lawrence U., B.A. 1975, Northwestern U., M.S.J. 1976, U. of WI, M.B.A. 1990; Catholic; married (Theresa).

Career: Investigative reporter, WJLA-TV Washington, D.C., 1976–88; News anchor, WKOW-TV Madison, 1988–90.

Offices: 1224 LHOB 20515, 202-225-2906. Also 16 N. Carroll St., #600, Madison 53703, 608-257-9200.

Committees: *Energy and Commerce* (14th of 17 R): Energy and Power; Health and the Environment.

Group Ratings

	ADA	ACLU	COPE	CDF	CFA	LCV	ACU	NTLC	NSI	COC	CEI
1992	40	61	33	50	47	50	56	80	80	63	73
1991	35	—	33	60	50	31	55	—	—	80	63

National Journal Ratings

	1991 LIB — 1991 CONS		1992 LIB — 1992 CONS	
Economic	30% —	69%	16% —	80%
Social	46% —	53%	48% —	51%
Foreign	35% —	64%	52% —	46%

Key Votes of the 102d Congress

1. Ban Striker Replace	AGN	5. Handgun Wait/7-Day	FOR	9. Use Force in Gulf	FOR
2. $ for Homeownership	FOR	6. Overseas Mil. Abortion	FOR	10. US Mil. Abroad $ Cut	FOR
3. Tax Rich/Cut Mid Cls.	AGN	7. Obscn. Art NEA $ Ban	FOR	11. Limit SDI Funds	FOR
4. FY93/$15B Def. Cut	AGN	8. Death Pen. from Jury	AGN	12. Cuba Trade Embargo	FOR

Key Votes of the 103d Congress

1. Family Leave	FOR	2. Deficit Reduction	AGN	3. Stimulus Plan	AGN

1388   WISCONSIN

THIRD DISTRICT

On the rolling land of western Wisconsin, in the knobby hills just east of the Mississippi River, on beautiful river landscape, is the site where Laura Ingalls Wilder's "little house in the big woods" was built in the 1870s, before the first railroad came steaming up the narrow floodplain alongside the Mississippi River. Today, it is hard to imagine the big woods: the trees have long since been cut down and the hillsides are covered with grass grazed on by placid dairy cattle. Where pioneers tried to scratch out diversified crops, farmers today in western Wisconsin have made this the premier dairying region in America, producing good milk, butter and especially cheese. In fact, most of these lands along the Mississippi, except those within driving range of the St. Paul-Minneapolis metro area, have been in demographic decline. The dairy industry is in trouble: cows are more productive, while demand has decreased because there are fewer children in America today than in the 1950s, and fewer Americans are descended exclusively from the northern European stock that carries the genes for the enzymes adults need to digest milk. The railroads and riverboats need fewer workers, and Milwaukee's boom in export manufacturing and the Twin Cities' boom in services and high tech have not reached this far into Wisconsin.

The 3d Congressional District of Wisconsin follows the Mississippi and St. Croix River counties from the southern border of the state almost all the way to Lake Superior, and here and there reaches a county or two east. This is probably the nation's number one dairy district. It was settled largely by German and Scandinavian immigrants (Laura's Yankee family moved away as Swedes were moving into the area), and it used to vote for LaFollette progressives. More recently, it has been sharply contested partisan territory, Democratic in the Watergate years, Republican in the years around 1980, Democratic again recently, even as much of Wisconsin was trending Republican in state races; the 3d voted for Michael Dukakis in 1988 and Bill Clinton in 1992.

The congressman from the 3d District is Steve Gunderson, a Republican who has held the seat since he beat an incumbent in 1980 at age 29. Gunderson is a natural political operator who has specialized in dairy programs. He is now ranking Republican on the Livestock Subcommittee, and has tried to prop up supports and prices and hold down cheese and other dairy imports, as well as to manipulate other minutiae of agricultural law to benefit western Wisconsin farmers. In the 1990 farm bill, he got a provision imposing assessments on dairy farmers who overproduce milkfat, an attempt at supply control; he also got elimination of a higher support price for California, and moves toward eliminating a formula that prices all milk as if it is shipped from Eau Claire, in the 3d District, a policy that works against Midwest dairy farmers. He has worked to expand eligibility for student aid programs and for improved rural health care. Gunderson has other causes as well. He sponsored a bill to equip House offices with telecommunications for the deaf, introducing it with sign language, which he has learned through a deaf cousin; he has served on the Gallaudet University board. He is proud of the Environmental Management System he is sponsoring for the upper Mississippi, one of the nation's most beautiful river valleys.

But there has been tension in Gunderson's career. In March 1989, he was named one of two chief deputy Republican whips, but his moderate stands on cultural issues and his district's trend toward the Democrats left him uncomfortable and it probably cost him some votes. In

1992, Democratic nominee Paul Sacia, a former farm lobbyist, sounded protectionist notes and backed farm supply management. Gunderson's percentage, down in 1990, went down even farther in 1992, as he won by a 56%–42% margin, decisive but not entirely comfortable. In January 1993, after cooperationist Jerry Lewis lost a leadership post to confrontationist Dick Armey, Gunderson took the unusual step of resigning his leadership position, which was then abolished. "I do not believe our present leadership represents mainstream Republicans in this country or even in the Congress," he said, adding that he became unhappy with the party's "growing image of intolerance" as seen at the 1992 Republican National Convention.

The People: Pop. 1990: 543,447; 56% rural; 14% age 65+; 98% White; 1% Asian. Voting age pop.: 398,244. Households: 60% married couple families; 30% married couple fams. w. children; 39% college educ.; median household income: $25,758; per capita income: $11,505; median gross rent: $336; median house value: $52,400.

1992 Presidential Vote

Clinton (D)	119,721	(43%)
Bush (R)	90,813	(33%)
Perot (I)	67,134	(24%)

1988 Presidential Vote

Dukakis (D)	125,756	(53%)
Bush (R)	111,583	(47%)

Rep. Steve Gunderson (R)

Elected 1980; b. May 10, 1951, Eau Claire; home, Osseo; U. of WI, B.A. 1973, Brown Schl. of Broadcasting, 1974; Lutheran; single.

Career: WI Assembly, 1974–79.

Offices: 2235 RHOB 20515, 202-225-5506. Also P.O. Box 247, 622 E. State Hwy. 54, Black River Falls 54615, 715-284-7431.

Committees: *Agriculture* (3d of 19 R): Department Operations and Nutrition; Environment, Credit and Rural Development; Livestock (RMM). *Education and Labor* (4th of 15 R): Elementary, Secondary and Vocational Education; Labor-Management Relations; Postsecondary Education and Training.

Group Ratings

	ADA	ACLU	COPE	CDF	CFA	LCV	ACU	NTLC	NSI	COC	CEI
1992	40	30	50	30	40	25	64	55	100	88	58
1991	20	—	33	40	39	23	80	—	—	100	53

National Journal Ratings

	1991 LIB — 1991 CONS			1992 LIB — 1992 CONS		
Economic	30%	—	69%	21%	—	76%
Social	34%	—	65%	29%	—	70%
Foreign	12%	—	85%	44%	—	50%

Key Votes of the 102d Congress

1. Ban Striker Replace	AGN	5. Handgun Wait/7-Day	AGN	9. Use Force in Gulf	FOR
2. $ for Homeownership	FOR	6. Overseas Mil. Abortion	FOR	10. US Mil. Abroad $ Cut	FOR
3. Tax Rich/Cut Mid Cls.	AGN	7. Obscn. Art NEA $ Ban	FOR	11. Limit SDI Funds	AGN
4. FY93/$15B Def. Cut	AGN	8. Death Pen. from Jury	FOR	12. Cuba Trade Embargo	FOR

Key Votes of the 103d Congress

1. Family Leave	AGN	2. Deficit Reduction	AGN	3. Stimulus Plan	AGN

Election Results

1992 general	Steve Gunderson (R)	146,903	(56%)	($458,846)
	Paul Sacia (D)	108,664	(42%)	($33,109)
	Other	4,768	(2%)	
1992 primary	Steve Gunderson (R), unopposed			
1990 general	Steve Gunderson (R)	94,509	(61%)	($341,458)
	James L. Ziegeweid (D)	60,409	(39%)	($57,576)

FOURTH DISTRICT

The world's largest clock faces outward from all sides of the tower on the Allen-Bradley factory, looking out over the manufacturing city of Milwaukee. It is an apt symbol, a piece of precision engineering, in this high-skill manufacturing town, with its skyline of smokestacks and church steeples, the closest thing in America to the factory cities of the Germany whence so many Milwaukeeans' ancestors came. Chicago, just 90 miles away, provides much of the banking, advertising, insurance, accounting and legal services Milwaukee businesses need, and the retail and entertainment base as well, and Madison has the big research university. Milwaukee leads the nation in industrial control equipment, mining gear, cranes and independent foundries. The work force, with German, Polish, Mitteleuropan work habits, is highly skilled and hard-working; the Germans made Milwaukee the nation's major beer brewer for years, though brewing employs fewer than 4,000 here today. Milwaukee lost 60,000 manufacturing jobs in the 1979–82 recession years, but it stuck to its high-skill manufacturing strength and prospered. Since that recession, Allen-Bradley has spent millions on improvements and new facilities, Rockwell International doubled sales to $1.5 billion, Harnischfeger spent $39 million on machine tools for its mining shovels and papermaking machinery after nearly going bankrupt in 1983. Milwaukee was responsible for much of the nation's late 1980s export boom and weathered the early 1990s recession better than many American cities.

Prospering quietly from this growth, for this is still a union, high-wage town, are the residents of Milwaukee's traditionally blue-collar south side. Here, in neighborhoods with sturdy houses that withstand northern winters and streets lined with bars emblazoned with beer signs, are Milwaukee's prototypical Polish neighborhoods and its even larger number of German-Americans. The 4th Congressional District of Wisconsin, which has been the south-side district since 1892, has spread out with the population into the suburbs. Now, 100 years later, one-third of its voters are in Milwaukee, another 40% in the Milwaukee County suburbs and one-quarter farther west in suburban Waukesha County. Historically this was the only securely Democratic part of Wisconsin, and still is, though the Waukesha portion is Republican.

Gerald Kleczka, congressman from the 4th District, is one of the state's three highly skilled Democratic congressmen who have spent almost all their adult lives as legislators in Madison and Washington. He is a product of the south side, the sort of man who has remodeled his house from top to bottom and maintains the best lawn in the neighborhood. But he is also, says the *Milwaukee Sentinel*, "the sort of guy you wouldn't want on the other side in a tavern brawl," with a temper known to flare up even in the halls of Congress. He was elected to the Wisconsin assembly in 1968 at age 24, to the state Senate in 1974 where he was co-chairman of the Joint Committee on Finance from 1979 to 1984, and to the House in April 1984, after the death of Clement Zablocki, who had represented the district for 35 years and chaired the Foreign Affairs Committee. On the Banking Committee, Kleczka fought for higher capital requirements in the 1989 S&L bill and in 1992 passed into law a bill allowing housing authorities to maintain elderly-only and disabled-only units to prevent the high crime caused in some projects by mixing them, a popular measure that helped pass the entire housing bill. He maintains an interest in Eastern Europe and early on urged government insurance of investments in Poland after it threw off Communist control. After the 1992 election, Kleczka won a seat on Ways and Means, in effect the one left by the north side of Milwaukee's Jim Moody when he ran for the Senate, and got a seat on the Health Subcommittee, quite likely a hot spot in 1993 and 1994.

Kleczka essentially won the seat against a formidable field in the April 1984 primary, beating the Milwaukee County district attorney, a former Zablocki aide, and a state senator who had run against Zablocki in 1982. He seems uninterested in any other office and entirely capable of holding this seat for many years.

The People: Pop. 1990: 543,482; 2% rural; 13% age 65+; 91% White; 1% Black; 1% Amer. Indian; 1% Asian; 3% Other; 6% Hispanic origin. Voting age pop.: 410,091; 1% Black; 5% Hispanic origin. Households: 56% married couple families; 25% married couple fams. w. children; 43% college educ.; median household income: $32,260; per capita income: $14,177; median gross rent: $448; median house value: $71,400.

1992 Presidential Vote

Clinton (D)	116,048	(41%)
Bush (R)	108,761	(38%)
Perot (I)	59,263	(21%)

1988 Presidential Vote

Dukakis (D)	140,615	(56%)
Bush (R)	111,335	(44%)

Rep. Gerald D. Kleczka (D)

Elected Apr. 1984; b. Nov. 26, 1943, Milwaukee; home, Milwaukee; U. of WI; Catholic; married (Bonnie).

Career: Air Natl. Guard, 1963–69; Accountant; Milwaukee Cnty. Cncl., 1965–68; WI Assembly, 1968–74; WI Senate, 1974–84, Asst. Majority Ldr., 1977–82.

Offices: 2301 RHOB 20515, 202-225-4572. Also 5032 W. Forest Home Ave., Milwaukee 53219, 414-297-1140; and 414 W. Moreland Blvd., #105, Waukesha 53188, 414-549-6360.

Committees: *House Administration* (8th of 12 D): Elections; Office Systems; Personnel and Police. *Ways and Means* (15th of 24 D): Health; Oversight. *Joint Committee on Printing* (3d of 5).

Group Ratings

	ADA	ACLU	COPE	CDF	CFA	LCV	ACU	NTLC	NSI	COC	CEI
1992	80	91	82	100	93	38	4	0	10	25	14
1991	85	—	91	100	89	69	0	—	—	11	13

National Journal Ratings

	1991 LIB — 1991 CONS		1992 LIB — 1992 CONS	
Economic	88%	— 0%	78%	— 18%
Social	74%	— 23%	70%	— 29%
Foreign	83%	— 15%	65%	— 35%

Key Votes of the 102d Congress

1. Ban Striker Replace	*	5. Handgun Wait/7-Day FOR	9. Use Force in Gulf AGN
2. $ for Homeownership AGN		6. Overseas Mil. Abortion AGN	10. US Mil. Abroad $ Cut AGN
3. Tax Rich/Cut Mid Cls. FOR		7. Obscn. Art NEA $ Ban FOR	11. Limit SDI Funds FOR
4. FY93/$15B Def. Cut FOR		8. Death Pen. from Jury AGN	12. Cuba Trade Embargo FOR

Key Votes of the 103d Congress

1. Family Leave	FOR	2. Deficit Reduction	FOR	3. Stimulus Plan	FOR

Election Results

1992 general	Gerald D. Kleczka (D)	173,482	(66%)	($309,036)
	Joseph L. Cook (R)	84,872	(32%)	($67,267)
	Other	5,449	(2%)	
1992 primary	Gerald D. Kleczka (D)	52,479	(99%)	
	Other	371	(1%)	
1990 general	Gerald D. Kleczka (D)	96,981	(69%)	($393,562)
	Joseph L. Cook (R)	43,001	(31%)	($27,986)

FIFTH DISTRICT

Milwaukee is America's most German city, with an ethnic heritage noticeable not just in the names of its beers and its old German restaurants but in the solidness of its houses and the orderliness of its streets. Until the World Wars made this German character seem un-American, German was spoken on the streets and read in newspapers, German beer was brewed in dozens of breweries and German cultural traditions breathed in churches, union halls and parlors. There was a German-type politics, with a Socialist mayor and an efficient, honest city government. Wisconsin's 5th Congressional District, which since 1892 has included the north side of Milwaukee, elected Socialist Victor Berger to Congress in 1910 and again from 1918 through 1926, even though he was denied his House seat after the 1918 and 1920 elections because of his opposition to World War I; in 1919, he was sentenced to 20 years in prison for writing antiwar articles.

Though some ghetto neighborhoods here are beset by crime and drug use, exposed in the horrifying crimes of Jeffrey Dahmer, most of Milwaukee is solid and upstanding, and some of it—Brewers Hill near the old Schlitz brewery—is gentrifying. There is an Oktoberfest (as well as an Irish Fest, summerfest, etc.), and there are large and efficiently run factories that pay high wages to highly-skilled and well-disciplined workers. This is also the place where state legislator Polly Williams, a Jesse Jackson backer in 1988, joined forces with Republican Governor Tommy Thompson to oppose the Democratic education bureaucracy and institute an educational choice system, to give young blacks better opportunities for schooling. The 5th District, once Socialist and then LaFollette Progressive, is now the most heavily Democratic district in Wisconsin, giving both Dukakis and Clinton a 26% margin over Bush. For 28 years it was represented by Henry Reuss, who eventually chaired the Banking and Joint Economic Committees; for 10 years, it was represented by Jim Moody, who ran for the Senate in 1992 and lost to Russ Feingold in the primary.

That left a major contest for 1992 in the 5th District, which redistricting expanded to include the rich lakefront suburbs of Whitefish Bay and Fox Point, but which remained heavily Democratic. County Supervisor Terrance Pitts ran a campaign based in the north side black wards, and won 30% in Milwaukee and 23% districtwide. Former Circuit Judge Fred Kessler, who had run twice before, spent $200,000 of his own money and ran ads proclaiming his strong liberal views; he got 19% of the vote. Marc Marotta, a lawyer and former Marquette basketball star, raised a fair amount of money and ran as an anti-politician; he got 16%.

The winner, with 38% in the city and 41% districtwide, was state Senator Tom Barrett. Like so many House Democrats, he seems to be one of those young men with a flair for politics whose main vocation is running for and holding public office. He was elected to the state House in 1984 at age 30; four years later he won a huge margin in a primary and was elected to the state Senate in a district that conveniently was one of only two entirely within the 5th District. In the legislature, Barrett wrote a law bringing 911 emergency service to Milwaukee and sponsored a state version of the Brady bill to require background checks and a waiting period before handgun purchases. In 1992, Barrett talked of broader issues like the economy and health care, presenting detailed position papers and relating his stands to local situations. He wants national health insurance to cover the uninsured with a broad revenue base, federally regulated health care standards and federally set spending levels. He also backs large defense cutbacks, a national police corps and federal encouragement of direct investment in "microenterprises" in depressed city neighborhoods—all aimed at sprucing up neighborhoods like some in north Milwaukee. Barrett won the general election by a 69%–30% margin and should have no difficulty holding this seat.

The People: Pop. 1990: 543,607; 13% age 65+; 60% White; 35% Black; 1% Amer. Indian; 2% Asian; 1% Other; 2% Hispanic origin. Voting age pop.: 395,627; 29% Black; 2% Hispanic origin. Households: 41% married couple families; 18% married couple fams. w. children; 49% college educ.; median household income: $26,267; per capita income: $13,277; median gross rent: $435; median house value: $62,400.

1992 Presidential Vote			1988 Presidential Vote		
Clinton (D)	142,047	(56%)	Dukakis (D)	152,975	(63%)
Bush (R)	76,935	(30%)	Bush (R)	89,509	(37%)
Perot (I)	32,138	(13%)			

Rep. Thomas M. Barrett (D)

Elected 1992; b. Dec. 8, 1953, Milwaukee; home, Milwaukee; U. of WI, B.A. 1976, J.D., 1980; Catholic; married (Kristine).

Career: FDIC bank examiner, 1977; Law Clerk, Fed. Dist. Judge Robert Warren 1980–82; Practicing atty., 1982–84; WI Assembly, 1984–88; WI Senate, 1988–92.

Offices: 313 CHOB 20515, 202-225-3571. Also 135 W. Wells St., #618, Milwaukee 53203, 414-297-1331.

Committees: *Banking, Finance and Urban Affairs* (21st of 30 D): Consumer Credit and Insurance; Financial Institutions Supervision, Regulation and Deposit Insurance; Housing and Community Development. *Government Operations* (16th of 25 D): Human Resources and Intergovernmental Relations. *Natural Resources* (28th of 28 D): Oversight and Investigations.

Group Ratings and 102d Congress Votes: Newly Elected

Key Votes of the 103d Congress

1. Family Leave	FOR	2. Deficit Reduction	FOR	3. Stimulus Plan	FOR

Election Results

1992 general	Thomas M. Barrett (D)	162,344	(69%)	($387,469)
	Donalda A. Hammersmith (R)	71,085	(30%)	($98,338)
1992 primary	Thomas M. Barrett (D)	34,301	(41%)	
	Terrance L. Pitts (D)	18,928	(23%)	
	Frederick P. Kessler (D)	15,729	(19%)	
	Marc J. Marotta (D)	13,411	(16%)	
	Other	1,213	(2%)	
1990 general	Jim Moody (D)	77,557	(68%)	($515,159)
	Donalda A. Hammersmith (R)	31,255	(27%)	($21,348)
	Nathaniel J. Stampley (I)	4,968	(4%)	

SIXTH DISTRICT

Central Wisconsin is solid country, a producer of basic commodities—milk, butter and cheese, paper and paper products, Oshkosh overalls and machinery and other factory products. Settled first by Yankee Protestants, it was one of the birthplaces of the Republican Party in 1854, when a group of Whigs, Free Soilers and Democrats met in a small white schoolhouse in Ripon, Wisconsin, and proclaimed themselves Republicans; Jackson, Michigan, also claims to be the birthplace of the party. But whichever is right, the party's growth was phenomenal: Republicans won a near-majority of seats in the House in the congressional elections of 1854 and nominated their first presidential ticket in 1856. But Republican roots here are not just Yankee. The 1850s brought the first surge of German migration into the United States, and central Wisconsin was a favorite German destination. Here they built the dairy farms and factory towns that seemed steadfastly prosperous 50 years ago, though they have not grown as fast as the nation, and dairy farming has become heavily subsidized.

The 6th Congressional District of Wisconsin, which cuts a swath across the state from Manitowoc on Lake Michigan through Oshkosh and Ripon west almost to the Mississippi River, includes country which has voted Republican almost without interruption since that first meeting in Ripon. It has also elected Republican congressmen who have come up with thoughtful and original solutions to problems. One was William Steiger, first elected in 1966, whose chief monuments are the all-volunteer military and the 1978 Steiger amendment cutting capital gains tax rates—considerable accomplishments for a member of the minority party, and for one who died at age 40 in 1978. Another is Thomas Petri, who won the 1979 special election to succeed Steiger by a narrow margin and has also specialized in original proposals which cut across ideological and party lines.

Petri's major success has been reform of the Earned Income Tax Credit. This operates something like a negative income tax, except that it goes only to the employed, targeting aid to needy family heads far better than a higher minimum wage, most of whose beneficiaries are teenagers and young adults who are not heads of families. Petri pushed the EITC for four years, then picked up support from moderate Democrats like Charles Stenholm, Dave McCurdy and Tim Penny, from the Progressive Policy Institute, and from Ways and Means Chairman Dan Rostenkowski. The result was an increased EITC adjusted for family size. Petri's sequel is an initiative he calls IDEA, Income Dependent Education Assistance Act, to guarantee student loans to be repaid at rates based on incomes after school. He proposes to reform federal deposit insurance, to privatize insurance with risk-related rates. He wants to encourage multi-employer health insurance bills.

Petri has one of Congress's strongest records of opposing spending bills. He fought to scale back Washington, D.C.'s proposed International Cultural Trade Center and joined a lawsuit against the congressional pay raise. He lobbied successfully for a federal highway spending formula more favorable to Wisconsin.

Petri, usually reelected easily, was close to being defeated in 1992. The main problem was his 77 overdrafts on the House bank, which seemed out of character for a congressman who has given all his honoraria and pay increases to charity. That attracted serious competition from Democrat Peg Lautenschlager, Winnebago County District Attorney from 1985 to 1988, who moved back to Fond du Lac County and was elected to the assembly in 1988 and 1990; this made her a familiar figure to nearly half the 6th District. Juggling family and legislative duties with supermom zest, she campaigned as an "ordinary citizen," although she tended to back state employees and bureaucracies against Governor Tommy Thompson's reforms. Lautenschlager carried Manitowoc and Petri had big margins in the western counties. The key was in Fond du Lac and Winnebago Counties, which Petri carried with 52% and 53%, for a 53%–47% victory. Will he have such serious competition again? Probably not, unless successes of the Clinton Administration and Democratic House raise Democrats' strength.

The People: Pop. 1990: 543,531; 47% rural; 15% age 65+; 98% White; 1% Asian; 1% Hispanic origin. Voting age pop.: 399,900; 1% Hispanic origin. Households: 63% married couple families; 29% married couple fams. w. children; 34% college educ.; median household income: $28,038; per capita income: $12,400; median gross rent: $349; median house value: $54,800.

1992 Presidential Vote			1988 Presidential Vote		
Bush (R)	114,517	(41%)	Bush (R)	127,016	(54%)
Clinton (D)	97,121	(34%)	Dukakis (D)	106,937	(46%)
Perot (I)	69,339	(25%)			

Rep. Tom Petri (R)

Elected Apr. 1979; b. May 28, 1940, Marinette; home, Fond du Lac; Harvard, B.A. 1962, J.D. 1965; Lutheran; married (Anne).

Career: Peace Corps, Somalia, 1966–67; Law Clerk, Fed. Judge James Doyle, 1965–66; White House aide, 1969; Practicing atty., 1970–79; WI Senate, 1972–79.

Offices: 2262 RHOB 20515, 202-225-2476. Also 14 Western Ave., Fond du Lac 54935, 414-922-1180; and 105 Washington Ave., Oshkosh 54901, 414-231-6333.

Committees: *Education and Labor* (2d of 15 R): Elementary, Secondary and Vocational Education; Postsecondary Education and Training (RMM). *Public Works and Transportation* (3d of 24 R): Public Buildings and Grounds; Surface Transportation (RMM); Water Resources and Environment. *Post Office and Civil Service* (7th of 9 R): Census Statistics and Postal Personnel (RMM).

Group Ratings

	ADA	ACLU	COPE	CDF	CFA	LCV	ACU	NTLC	NSI	COC	CEI
1992	25	13	25	30	53	44	76	95	80	63	73
1991	10	—	8	20	39	38	85	—	—	90	82

National Journal Ratings

	1991 LIB — 1991 CONS		1992 LIB — 1992 CONS	
Economic	14%	— 83%	31%	— 68%
Social	25%	— 73%	0%	— 85%
Foreign	38%	— 61%	44%	— 50%

Key Votes of the 102d Congress

1. Ban Striker Replace	AGN	5. Handgun Wait/7-Day	AGN	9. Use Force in Gulf	FOR
2. $ for Homeownership	FOR	6. Overseas Mil. Abortion	AGN	10. US Mil. Abroad $ Cut	AGN
3. Tax Rich/Cut Mid Cls.	AGN	7. Obscn. Art NEA $ Ban	FOR	11. Limit SDI Funds	AGN
4. FY93/$15B Def. Cut	AGN	8. Death Pen. from Jury	FOR	12. Cuba Trade Embargo	FOR

Key Votes of the 103d Congress

1. Family Leave	FOR	2. Deficit Reduction	AGN	3. Stimulus Plan	AGN

Election Results

1992 general	Tom Petri (R)	143,875	(53%)	($775,594)
	Peggy A. Lautenschlager (D)	128,232	(47%)	($319,363)
1992 primary	Tom Petri (R), unopposed			
1990 general	Tom Petri (R), unopposed			($131,156)

SEVENTH DISTRICT

In the late 19th Century, on the rail lines radiating northwest from Chicago and Milwaukee, came thousands of migrants whose descendents have made the northern reaches of Wisconsin the most thickly settled land this far north in the United States east of the Mississippi. What brought people up so far was not farmland—there are no industrial-sized wheat farms as in the Red River Valley of Minnesota and North Dakota—but trees and iron and cows. This was one of America's largest virgin timberlands, and the river towns are still dotted with paper mills. Farther north, iron brought Finns and Italians to the port of Superior, Wisconsin, right next to Duluth, Minnesota, and to smaller towns on the chilly lake. Then, on the cleared forestlands, came dairy farms: dairy cattle, properly cared for, thrive in these northern uplands, and the sons of Wisconsin dairymen, many of them immigrants from Germany and Norway, moved their dairy herds even farther north. On this base, small cities grew, some with big enterprises. The town of Wausau, for example, is home to the Wausau insurance company, while the entrepreneur who designed the Cray supercomputers for years lived and worked in Chippewa Falls.

All these places are in Wisconsin's 7th Congressional District, which stretches from a point not far from Green Bay and Madison in the south up to Lake Superior in the north. The politics of northern Wisconsin and the 7th District has a rough-hewn quality, a certain lumberjack populist flavor; ancestrally Republican, this area favored the progressivism of the LaFollettes. Today Superior and Stevens Point are heavily Democratic, while much of the country in between leans Republican.

The representative from the 7th District is David Obey, one of the most accomplished and effective legislators in the House. He is chairman of the Joint Economic Committee and is almost certain—"if God doesn't play funny surprises," he has said—to become chairman of the House Appropriations Committee some time soon; he currently ranks fifth on the committee now but is two or three decades younger than the more senior members. He started his career young, a natural politician who was first elected to the legislature at 24, in 1962. He was elected to the U.S. House in an upset in a 1969 special election to replace Defense Secretary Melvin Laird. In 1972, when Obey was placed in the same district as a 30-year incumbent liberal Republican, he won with 63% of the vote. Obey is reelected every two years by wide margins.

In the House, Obey has not always been popular but has almost always been highly respected. He has a prickly personality and a vigorous temper and does not suffer fools or knaves gladly. He has integrity and an iron determination to stick with what he believes is right. A few colleagues still have not forgotten that in 1977–78 he chaired a special committee on ethics, pushing through a new ethics code requiring detailed disclosure of personal finances and limiting outside income to a percentage of the congressional salary. Even Tip O'Neill thought that may have cost him the Budget Committee chair or the chairmanship of the Democratic Caucus in 1984. Obey has also, starting in 1979, been a lead sponsor of campaign finance legislation to that would limit PAC contributions, reduce individual donations and provide public financing. Yet he has made himself a leading—sometimes *the* leading—power in the Democratic Caucus. When Jim Wright and Tony Coelho were under attack for alleged ethics violations in June 1989, Obey pushed Dick Gephardt to run for majority leader, even though in 1984 Gephardt had won the caucus chair Obey had wanted. In the December 1990 caucus, he led the campaign to oust S&L favorite Frank Annunzio from the chair of House Administration, which superintends campaign finance reform, and pushed through a rules change requiring that Ways and Means subcommittee chairmen be picked by the whole Caucus rather than just by Ways and Means members—an attack on capital gains cutter Andy Jacobs, but also on Ways and Means Chairman Dan Rostenkowski. For 1993, Obey was appointed to the Joint Committee on the Organization of Congress.

Obey remains a true believer in traditional liberalism, that government should provide economic security, create jobs and build infrastructure through public investment, that it should control healthcare costs and guarantee coverage with choice of physician for everyone. He has used the Joint Economic Committee bully pulpit to argue that in the Reagan-Bush years ordinary citizens' incomes went down and that government should counterbalance that trend. He bucked the leadership in that cause, opposing the first budget summit package in October 1990 on the ground it didn't shift enough spending from defense to domestic; most Democrats voted with him, not their leadership. In 1991, Obey supported the Gore-Downey plan to raise top bracket taxes to 35%. In 1992, he voted against the final tax bill, which passed by only 208–202. He is not a team player when he believes the team is not headed in the right direction.

On Appropriations, Obey, who turns 56 in 1994, now ranks behind Chairman William Natcher, who turns 85, ousted Chairman Jamie Whitten, who turns 84, Iowa's Neal Smith, who turns 74, and Illinois's Sid Yates, who turns 85. The chair is in sight, and obviously there is much he could do with it; back in 1988, thinking of that and also of what Les Aspin, then at Armed Services, could do, he said, "I salivate at what we could legally steal for Wisconsin." For the moment, much of his work comes from chairing the Foreign Operations Subcommittee, as he has since 1985, a frustrating job that often makes him the House's most powerful voice on foreign policy. One frustration is that he has no sympathy for the structure of foreign aid produced by the Camp David agreement, with huge percentages of aid going to Israel and Egypt; in general, he would like to see more money for humanitarian assistance, such as the Peace Corps, UNICEF and the vitamin A deficiency program. Obey is not beholden to or beloved by the Israel lobby, and worked hard to prevent the United States from assuming any liability on loan guarantees for Israel. But Obey has also argued that no additional foreign aid should go to the Middle East unless the Arab countries recognize Israel and unless Israel recognizes a Palestinian right to a homeland on a major portion of the West Bank and Gaza Strip. In the 1980s, he opposed aid to El Salvador; in 1991, he opposed the Gulf war resolution; in 1992, he suspended aid to Indonesia because of its brutal human rights violations in East Timor: his instincts on such issues are in line with those of the Vietnam doves he generally voted with in his first years in Congress. But in late 1992, he supported the dispatch of U.S. troops to Somalia and said there may have to be "UN trusteeships in several areas of the world, including Somalia."

Fervently, he has backed measures to cut defense spending and—though it's his own empire—foreign aid, and to increase spending on domestic policies from health care to infrastructure. Bill Clinton's victory made him "feel like a 1,000-pound weight has been lifted from my shoulders"; he advised the new president to "think long term," as he has done so himself and through what, for him, were the dark days of the 1980s. Yet Obey must also tend to local matters. He was proud in the 102d Congress to get an agreement improving the highway spending formula for Wisconsin. In 1993, he was looking forward to spending much of his time on Chippewa Indian fishing rights, a hot issue in northern Wisconsin. He was bedeviled by the House bank scandal, being, in typical forthright fashion, the first member to confess to overdrafts—an incident so out of line with his straight arrow reputation as to have caused him little trouble. Obey is reelected every two years without difficulty, with 64% in anti-incumbent 1992. As the Appropriations chair draws nearer, his seat should become even safer.

The People: Pop. 1990: 543,569; 59% rural; 15% age 65+; 97% White; 2% Amer. Indian; 1% Asian. Voting age pop.: 395,664. Households: 62% married couple families; 29% married couple fams. w. children; 34% college educ.; median household income: $25,277; per capita income: $11,427; median gross rent: $327; median house value: $48,400.

1992 Presidential Vote			1988 Presidential Vote		
Clinton (D)	117,203	(42%)	Dukakis (D)	132,110	(54%)
Bush (R)	93,156	(33%)	Bush (R)	111,206	(46%)
Perot (I)	67,558	(24%)			

Rep. David R. Obey (D)

Elected Apr. 1969; b. Oct. 3, 1938, Okmulgee, OK; home, Wausau; U. of WI, B.S. 1960, M.A., 1962; Catholic; married (Joan).

Career: Real estate broker; Owner, family supper club and motel; WI Assembly, 1962–69.

Offices: 2462 RHOB 20515, 202-225-3365. Also Fed. Bldg., 317 First St., Wausau 54401, 715-842-5606.

Committees: *Appropriations* (5th of 37 D): Foreign Operations, Export Financing and Related Programs (Chmn.); Labor, Health and Human Services, and Education; Legislative. *Joint Committee on the Organization of Congress* (2d of 12). *Joint Economic Committee* (Chmn. of 10).

Group Ratings

	ADA	ACLU	COPE	CDF	CFA	LCV	ACU	NTLC	NSI	COC	CEI
1992	100	100	92	90	87	73	0	0	30	38	11
1991	85	—	92	90	83	58	15	—	—	20	13

National Journal Ratings

	1991 LIB — 1991 CONS		1992 LIB — 1992 CONS	
Economic	79%	— 18%	71%	— 27%
Social	65%	— 34%	80%	— 19%
Foreign	78%	— 19%	86%	— 10%

Key Votes of the 102d Congress

1. Ban Striker Replace	FOR	5. Handgun Wait/7-Day	AGN	9. Use Force in Gulf	AGN
2. $ for Homeownership	AGN	6. Overseas Mil. Abortion	FOR	10. US Mil. Abroad $ Cut	FOR
3. Tax Rich/Cut Mid Cls.	AGN	7. Obscn. Art NEA $ Ban	*	11. Limit SDI Funds	FOR
4. FY93/$15B Def. Cut	FOR	8. Death Pen. from Jury	AGN	12. Cuba Trade Embargo	AGN

Key Votes of the 103d Congress

1. Family Leave   FOR   2. Deficit Reduction   FOR   3. Stimulus Plan   FOR

Election Results

1992 general	David R. Obey (D)	166,200	(64%)	($524,574)
	Dale R. Vannes (R)	91,772	(36%)	($20,327)
1992 primary	David R. Obey (D), unopposed			
1990 general	David R. Obey (D)	100,069	(62%)	($467,346)
	John L. McEwen (R)	60,961	(38%)	($10,683)

EIGHTH DISTRICT

In 1673, the French explorer and priest Father Marquette sailed from the open waters of Lake Michigan into what is now Green Bay, Wisconsin. He had hoped to come upon the Northwest Passage to the Pacific; actually, what he found was the Fox River, which leads to Lake Winnebago and, after a not-too-difficult portage, the Wisconsin River that flows into the Mississippi. Green Bay and the Fox River Valley remained mostly wilderness and Indian country for more than 150 years. But once settled by Europeans, they became, as Father Marquette would have liked, one of the most heavily Catholic parts of the United States (he might be surprised, however, to see that disputes over Chippewa Indians spearfishing rights were a media circus for 17 years). Economically, Green Bay and the towns clustered around Appleton at the head of Lake Winnebago live off paper mills and high-skill manufacturing; psychically, they live for the triumphs of the Green Bay Packers, America's only municipally-owned National Football League franchise.

Green Bay and the Fox River Valley make up most of the 8th Congressional District of Wisconsin. It also includes several north woods and dairy counties inland, plus the Door County peninsula that juts out into Lake Michigan, a favorite summer vacation spot for Chicago and Milwaukee families. Politically, this has often been malleable country. Democrats, especially Catholics, can win here: John Kennedy carried the Fox River Valley in the primary and general election in 1960, and the most recent Democratic congressman was Robert Cornell, a priest elected in 1974 and 1976. But the 8th District can turn almost ferociously Republican: Appleton was the home of Senator Joseph McCarthy, who did much to tar the good names of politics, Congress, conservatism and the Republican Party in the early 1950s.

The congressman from the 8th district today is Toby Roth, a Republican whose first victory in 1978 was a little noticed precursor of the conservative tide that swept the country in 1980. Roth has played a major role on export control legislation, insisting before the end of the Cold War on tough restrictions on exports of strategic products to Communist countries; more recently he questioned sale of U.S. military trucks to the Saudi Arabia and other countries. As much as any member of Congress, he seems mistrustful of foreigners and the closest thing in Congress to an isolationist on the right. He had qualms about U.S. military intervention in Lebanon in 1983 and was opposed to intervention in Bosnia in 1993; he wants to bring home troops from Europe and station them to patrol the U.S.-Mexico border. He says Congress should consider abolishing the Agency for International Development. He strongly backs declaring English as the official language. Solidly conservative on economics, he hailed the repeal of the luxury boat tax; but he sometimes breaks partisan ranks, as he did on an RTC bill, until he was lobbied by the Bush Administration. Locally, he is proud of bringing a veterans clinic to Grand Chute.

Roth has had a couple of serious challenges, and was held to 57% of the vote in 1982 and 54% in 1990, when state Senator Jerome Van Sistine carried his Green Bay base. But Roth did splendidly in anti-incumbent 1992, running far ahead of George Bush and winning with 70%.

The People: Pop. 1990: 543,526; 44% rural; 14% age 65+; 96% White; 3% Amer. Indian; 1% Asian; 1% Hispanic origin. Voting age pop.: 396,416. Households: 62% married couple families; 30% married couple fams. w. children; 37% college educ.; median household income: $28,169; per capita income: $12,628; median gross rent: $357; median house value: $57,800.

1992 Presidential Vote

Bush (R)	115,128	(40%)
Clinton (D)	101,493	(35%)
Perot (I)	69,373	(24%)

1988 Presidential Vote

Bush (R)	129,440	(53%)
Dukakis (D)	113,361	(47%)

Rep. Toby Roth (R)

Elected 1978; b. Oct. 10, 1938, Strasburg, ND; home, Appleton; Marquette U., B.A. 1961; Catholic; married (Barbara).

Career: Army Reserves, 1962–69; Realtor; WI Assembly, 1972–78.

Offices: 2234 RHOB 20515, 202-225-5665. Also 2301 S. Oneida St., Green Bay 54304, 414-433-3931; and 126 N. Oneida St., Appleton 54911, 414-739-4167.

Committees: *Banking, Finance and Urban Affairs* (6th of 20 R): Economic Growth and Credit Formation; General Oversight, Investigations, and the Resolution of Failed Financial Institutions (RMM). *Foreign Affairs* (4th of 18 R): Asia and the Pacific; Economic Policy, Trade and Environment (RMM).

Group Ratings

	ADA	ACLU	COPE	CDF	CFA	LCV	ACU	NTLC	NSI	COC	CEI
1992	15	9	8	20	27	13	83	80	70	75	76
1991	20	—	8	30	22	23	100	—	—	80	76

National Journal Ratings

	1991 LIB — 1991 CONS	1992 LIB — 1992 CONS
Economic	14% — 83%	21% — 76%
Social	19% — 78%	0% — 85%
Foreign	26% — 70%	52% — 46%

Key Votes of the 102d Congress

1. Ban Striker Replace	AGN	5. Handgun Wait/7-Day	AGN	9. Use Force in Gulf	FOR
2. $ for Homeownership	FOR	6. Overseas Mil. Abortion	AGN	10. US Mil. Abroad $ Cut	FOR
3. Tax Rich/Cut Mid Cls.	AGN	7. Obscn. Art NEA $ Ban	FOR	11. Limit SDI Funds	FOR
4. FY93/$15B Def. Cut	AGN	8. Death Pen. from Jury	FOR	12. Cuba Trade Embargo	FOR

Key Votes of the 103d Congress

1. Family Leave	AGN	2. Deficit Reduction	AGN	3. Stimulus Plan	AGN

Election Results

1992 general	Toby Roth (R)	191,704	(70%)	($444,548)
	Catherine L. Helms (D)	81,792	(30%)	($42,827)
1992 primary	Toby Roth (R), unopposed			
1990 general	Toby Roth (R)	95,902	(54%)	($499,968)
	Jerome Van Sistine (D)	83,199	(46%)	($274,112)

NINTH DISTRICT

For decades, the orderly, heavily German-American factory city of Milwaukee has been spreading slowly, mostly west and north, into Wisconsin dairy country. There has never been the explosive growth here of some metro areas, nor has it been characterized by the problems of many urban centers; only the most affluent are moving out in disproportionate numbers. And the close-in subdivisions and garden apartments of Mequon and Brookfield, of Germantown and Menomonee Falls and Pewaukee and Oconomowoc, are by no means entirely elite, though they are heavily Republican. The 9th Congressional District of Wisconsin includes most of the western, northwestern and northern suburbs of Milwaukee and spreads out into rich farm country and to smaller factory towns like Sheboygan, home of the Kohler plumbing company and America's bratwurst capital, and West Bend, home of West Bend appliances. This is usually the most Republican district in the state; in 1992 it voted solidly for George Bush over Bill Clinton.

The 9th District's congressman, Republican James Sensenbrenner, first elected in 1978, is now one of the senior Republicans in the House. His Wisconsin roots are strong—his great-grandfather was a top executive at Kimberly-Clark—and Sensenbrenner is one of the richest members of Congress and the most scrupulous (he discloses a complete list of his investments). He is conservative on most issues, gamely undertaking the Sisyphean task of opposing the Democratic majority in the House and on the liberal Judiciary Committee, with occasional success. He was the lead Republican, for example, arguing against racial quotas, which he felt were encouraged by the civil rights bill pending in 1990 and 1991; it promised to be a strong electoral issue for Republicans, until George Bush compromised on the bill and gave the issue away. Sensenbrenner argued for imposing on Congress the same civil rights and employee protection laws Congress imposes on the rest of the country. He opposes race-based standards in crime bills. As ranking member of the Science and Technology Space Subcommittee, he worked strongly for NASA's space station when it was imperiled, though it's not a Wisconsin project. On some issues, Sensenbrenner finds himself allied with liberals: he was a major backer of the Brady bill seven-day waiting period for handgun purchases, reflecting the views of many suburbanites appalled by central city crime. He is also against the hugely expensive Texas-based Superconducting Supercollider. He can be a successful stickler, insisting on impeachment action against federal Judges Walter Nixon and Harry Claiborne after they were convicted of crimes.

Sensenbrenner's only tough race was the 1978 primary, in which he beat Susan Engeleiter, a moderate who nearly won the Senate race against Herb Kohl in 1988. He is routinely reelected by overwhelming margins.

The People: Pop. 1990: 543,602; 36% rural; 12% age 65+; 96% White; 1% Asian; 1% Hispanic origin. Voting age pop.: 395,884; 1% Hispanic origin. Households: 69% married couple families; 33% married couple fams. w. children; 46% college educ.; median household income: $37,579; per capita income: $16,187; median gross rent: $430; median house value: $82,500.

1992 Presidential Vote

Bush (R) 142,465 (48%)
Clinton (D) 88,303 (30%)
Perot (I). 64,657 (22%)

1988 Presidential Vote

Bush (R) 149,007 (60%)
Dukakis (D). 99,615 (40%)

Rep. F. James Sensenbrenner, Jr. (R)

Elected 1978; b. June 14, 1943, Chicago, IL; home, Menomonee Falls; Stanford U., B.A. 1965, U. of WI, J.D. 1968; Episcopalian; married (Cheryl).

Career: Practicing atty., 1968–69; Staff asst., U.S. Rep. Arthur Younger, 1965; WI Assembly, 1968–74; WI Senate, 1974–78.

Offices: 2332 RHOB 20515, 202-225-5101. Also 120 Bishops Way, #154, Brookfield 53005, 414-784-1111.

Committees: *Judiciary* (4th of 14 R): Crime and Criminal Justice (RMM); Intellectual Property and Judicial Administration. *Science, Space and Technology* (2d of 22 R): Space (RMM).

Group Ratings

	ADA	ACLU	COPE	CDF	CFA	LCV	ACU	NTLC	NSI	COC	CEI
1992	15	9	17	0	13	25	92	95	90	88	88
1991	20	—	17	10	28	23	90	—	—	100	93

National Journal Ratings

	1991 LIB — 1991 CONS	1992 LIB — 1992 CONS
Economic	4% — 90%	0% — 91%
Social	23% — 76%	0% — 85%
Foreign	36% — 62%	52% — 46%

Key Votes of the 102d Congress

1. Ban Striker Replace	AGN	5. Handgun Wait/7-Day FOR	9. Use Force in Gulf FOR
2. $ for Homeownership	FOR	6. Overseas Mil. Abortion AGN	10. US Mil. Abroad $ Cut FOR
3. Tax Rich/Cut Mid Cls.	AGN	7. Obscn. Art NEA $ Ban FOR	11. Limit SDI Funds FOR
4. FY93/$15B Def. Cut	AGN	8. Death Pen. from Jury FOR	12. Cuba Trade Embargo FOR

Key Votes of the 103d Congress

1. Family Leave   AGN   2. Deficit Reduction   AGN   3. Stimulus Plan   AGN

Election Results

1992 general	F. James Sensenbrenner, Jr. (R) 192,898	(70%)	($457,292)
	Ingrid K. Buxton (D) 77,362	(28%)	($27,125)
	Other 6,527	(2%)	
1992 primary	F. James Sensenbrenner, Jr. (R), unopposed		
1990 general	F. James Sensenbrenner, Jr. (R), unopposed		($98,609)

WYOMING

"The land of the cowboy" the *WPA Guide* called Wyoming 50 years ago. "Its mountains, plains, and valleys are essentially livestock country. A cowboy astride a bucking bronco greets the visitor from enameled license plates, from newspapers, magazines and painted signs." The cowboy is still on the license plates, and Wyoming remains the most western of states in spirit—largely unsettled, the least populous state, a thin veneer of civilization stretched over a forbidding and beautiful land. "Wyoming seems to be the doing of a mad architect," writes Gretel Ehrlich, who moved there from California, "tumbled and twisted, ribboned with faded, deathbed colors, thrust up and pulled down as if the place had been startled out of a deep sleep and thrown into a pure light." Wyoming "has a 'lean-to' look," says Ehrlich. "Instead of big, roomy barns and Victorian houses, there are dugouts, low sheds, log cabins, sheep camps and fence lines that look like driftwood blown haphazardly into place. People here still feel pride because they live in such a harsh place, part of the glamorous cowboy past."

But this same Wyoming seems headed toward a high-tech future, while managing to preserve its cowboy past. The mining bust of the 1980s has been succeeded by new mining growth, with job growth in the 1990s after the job and population losses of the 1980s, new processing plants coming on line, and there are new demands for Wyoming's low-sulfur coal. Wyoming has also had glamour growth, notably around Jackson Hole, site of the 1989 summit between Secretary of State James Baker and then-Soviet Foreign Minister Eduard Shevardnadze, and now a possible presidential launching pad as Baker's vacation home and the home base of former Wyoming Congressman and Defense Secretary Dick Cheney.

And vestiges of Wyoming's pre-cowboy environment endure. In September 1992, a Worland hunter shot an animal he thought was a coyote, a predator whose killing is encouraged by state law, but which federal officials thought was a wolf, protected by the Endangered Species Act. A DNA test was performed which concluded that the animal was neither a hybrid dog-wolf nor coyote-wolf, but could not determine whether it was a pure coyote or wolf. As the ruckus started, it was asserted that wolves had been wiped out in Wyoming years ago; then the Wildlife Service said it had 101 reports of wolf sightings in Wyoming over the past dozen years. Wyoming may be growing and generating new mines and resorts, but in some important ways it is going back to nature—the cowboy state going back to the wolf.

This interplay between new technology and age-old nature is a continuing theme in Wyoming's history. After the open-range era, cattle ranches here were made possible only by the barbed wire that could fence in roaming herds, and the steam locomotives that could carry cattle to market back east. This 19th Century high tech was brought to Wyoming by large capitalist operators, some of them onetime Texas cowhands or second sons of English landed gentry, who started the first big operations and consolidated their power in the Johnson County land war of 1890. The 1970s energy boom brought in big operators again: Amoco and other major oil companies planted drilling rigs in the Overthrust belt near Evanston, while coal companies mined great quantities of surface coal up north. The result is not always a pretty picture: workers who flocked here lived in grimy trailers, linked only precariously to civilization's utilities and unprotected against the winds and snows that come out of the enormous sky; these communities have a mining-camp atmosphere, with prostitution, gambling and violent crime, redolent of 19th Century Virginia City, Nevada, or Deadwood, South Dakota. Wyoming was until recently one of the few states that has always had more men than women—a sure sign that it never got far from a frontier atmosphere, and also the reason it was the first part of the United States, when it was a territory in 1869, to give women the vote.

But there is a settled part of Wyoming as well, in the medium-sized towns that are the state's

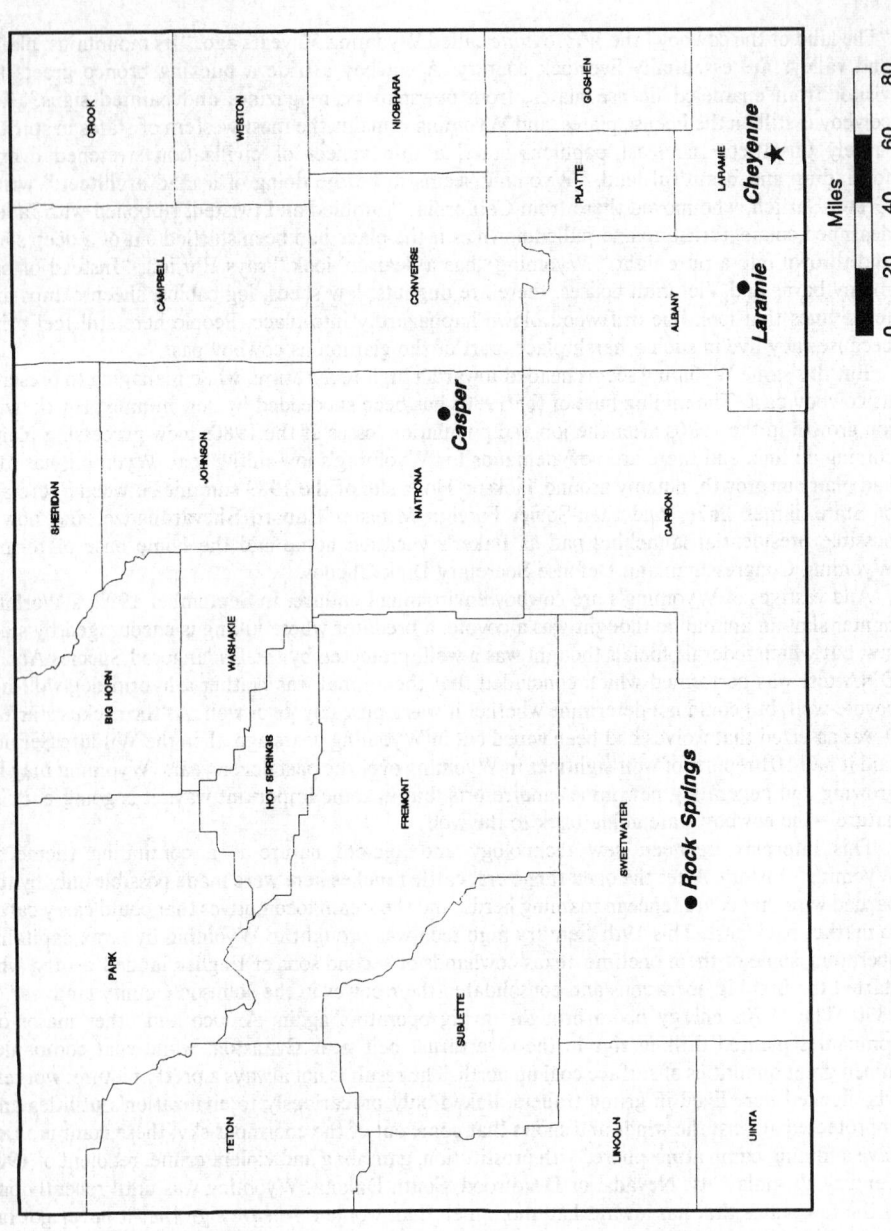

largest cities, and among sheep and cattle ranches, sugar beet farmers and denizens of tiny settlements. This is a small state, a single community really, where people remember who played what position, when and how well, for what high-school football team; where because all locals know who your father's cousins married, you mostly live pretty straight. Yet there is a sharp economic and regional split in Wyoming traditionally reflected in partisan politics. The big economic interests—cattle ranchers, organized in the Wyoming Stock Growers' Association, and the Union Pacific Railroad always favored the Republicans, as do the wildcatters, independent producers and oil company geologists, who want their industry liberated from government controls. The northern two-thirds of Wyoming voted 42% for George Bush, and Ross Perot's 27% here almost topped Bill Clinton's 31%. The mainstay for the Democrats was the Union Pacific railroad workers who built the first transcontinental line across southern Wyoming in the 1860s and have maintained it ever since; the southern tier of counties, from Cheyenne through Laramie to Evanston, usually votes Democratic, and voted 40%–36% for Bill Clinton.

Historically, the Republicans have been more numerous, though the state was closely contested from the New Deal days through the 1960s, and by the 1980s this was one of the nation's most Republican states. But there is an independence here—look at the Perot numbers—and personal campaigning is always important. There aren't many people—not even half a million, less than the size of an average congressional district, in 1990—and Wyoming voters expect to talk person-to-person with their governors, senators and congressmen every few years. There is a general agreement that Wyoming needs to build a more diverse economy, and that government should play some role in that. But state government is small and its powers limited; while the federal government, distant, domineering, insensitive to the feel of daily life here, is mistrusted. Wyomingites, with their high-tech sophistication in their vast, empty lands, will have to rely mostly on themselves for solutions, as usual.

Governor. Wyoming is one of those Rocky Mountain states which votes Republican for president and elects, it seems, only Democratic governors: the last time a Republican won the governorship was in 1970. The current governor, Mike Sullivan, extended the Democratic string by campaigning in a trademark Stetson with a hole in it, and beating Pete Simpson, Senator Al's brother, in 1986 and Mary Mead, daughter of former Governor and Senator Clifford Hansen, in 1990. In office, he seemed the least pompous or pampered of governors—he has no bodyguard and answers his own phone. He wants to diversify Wyoming's economy and reform education, and boasted of job increases since the late 1980s; he reorganized state government, proposed a work requirement for welfare, and managed to cut spending over his first five years, but he is not averse to new mining taxes. He was an early backer of Bill Clinton, campaigning for him in New Hampshire, which should not hurt Wyoming's relations with the federal government. Sullivan will probably be a favorite for a third term, if he runs; if not, another possibility is Democratic Secretary of State Kathy Karpan.

Senators. The senior member of Wyoming's congressional delegation is Malcolm Wallop, first elected in 1976, and reelected in 1982 and by the narrowest of margins in 1988. Wallop is descended from one of those 19th Century English toffs who came to Wyoming to ranch and breed horses that were used by the British Cavalry in the Boer War. In both physical appearance and attitude, he resembles the 19th Century imperial adventurers who penetrated remote corners of the world. Like one of Britain's imperial proconsuls, he is proud of having roughed it for many years and he is used to taking responsibility for worldwide issues; he takes some interest in local problems, but has directed most of his psychic energy to affecting foreign and defense policy, with varying results.

In many respects, Wallop's judgment has been vindicated. He came to the Senate in 1977 convinced that the Soviet Union was dangerous and evil, and that most arms control agreements only hobbled U.S. efforts at maintaining military superiority or parity, while legitimizing a regime it should be our intention to bring down. Widely derided in the early 1980s, and as late as 1987 when Wallop wrote *The Arms Control Delusion*, these views were substantiated by the end of the decade when Communism collapsed. Wallop opposed Ronald Reagan's INF Treaty as well as Jimmy Carter's SALT II; he is perhaps the Senate's strongest backer of the Strategic Defense Initiative, criticized both by congressional liberals and Pentagon service bureaucrats, despite the success, much pointed to by Wallop, of the Patriot missile in the Gulf war. Wallop rotated off the Armed Services Committee in 1992 and is now on Intelligence.

Wallop is as strong a tax-cutter as he is a defense builder. In early 1990, when Pat Moynihan called for cutting the Social Security payroll tax, Wallop and Texas Congressman Tom DeLay countered with a bill to cut that tax and capital gains too. In late 1990, Wallop led a Senate conservatives' revolt against the budget summit agreement, infuriating Minority Leader Bob Dole, but holding up the legislation and establishing conservatives as a group to be propitiated. That is more important after January 1993 than before, since Senate rules give a small number of Republicans leverage in a Washington otherwise controlled by Democrats. In 1991, Wallop became ranking Republican on the Energy and Natural Resources Committee, which handles Interior Department matters of so much practical importance to Wyoming. He played a significant role on the 1992 energy bill, holding it up to stop Jay Rockefeller's tax on independent coal operators which would have taxed Wyoming's low-sulfur coal to bail out the United Mine Workers' healthcare trust fund. He also sponsored the Wallop-Breaux sport fishing restoration program, which taxes motorboat fuel, fishing equipment and imported pleasure boats to fund fish maintenance programs, also important to Wyoming. In general, he is vehemently opposed to government regulation—of grazing lands, of banks, of OSHA regulations on small businesses which require warnings against toxic effects of gravel, sawdust and dishwashing liquid.

Wallop's vehemence and confidence and his interest in international issues have not always gone over well with Wyoming voters. In 1976, he upset three-term Democrat Gale McGee by portraying himself as a rancher concerned about Wyoming's environment and about federal overregulation; in 1982, he won comfortably. But in 1988, when state Senator John Vinich, a restaurateur and barkeeper from the rough-and-ready town of Hudson, argued that Wallop was out of touch, Wallop won by only a 50.4%–49.6% margin. Wallop lost not only the Union Pacific counties, but the Wind River country and Casper, where the Casper *Star-Tribune*, the state's largest paper, delights in baiting him. That result suggests Wallop may be serving his last term. But it came at the nadir of Wyoming's economic bust, and Wallop has been spending more time on Wyoming issues, and the state's Republican preference held even in 1992. One strong Democratic opponent would be Mike Sullivan, though not since 1948 has a Wyoming Democratic governor been elected to the Senate. Should Wallop retire, one obvious Republican candidate would be Dick Cheney; another, should he decline, would be Lynne Cheney, his wife, who served ably as chairman of the National Endowment for the Humanities.

Alan Simpson, Wyoming's junior senator, is well-known nationally, not always conservative according to the rating groups, but often partisan and sometimes bitingly controversial. Simpson has deep roots in Wyoming: he is the son of former Governor and Senator Milward Simpson, worked as a trial lawyer and raised his family in Cody and served in the legislature, then was elected to the Senate in 1978; Milward Simpson died in 1993 at age 95. He has long been a fixture in Washington, known for his gangly height (6'7", taller than Bill Bradley or Jay Rockefeller) and his droll delivery of a repertoire of jokes (including some that will not find their way into a proper volume like this). He is the Senate Republican whip, was considered at least briefly for the vice presidential nomination in 1988, has passed major legislation and taken a lead role in many debates; but he may be known best, to his chagrin, for his performance in the Clarence Thomas-Anita Hill hearings that were as contentious as any the Senate has held in decades.

Simpson initially made his reputation on immigration, after being unexpectedly saddled with Judiciary's Immigration Subcommittee chair in 1981. He fashioned bills to discourage illegal immigration by imposing sanctions on employers who hire illegal immigrants and to legitimize migrants already here for some years; he pushed this through the Senate three times and finally got agreement with the House in the end of the 1986 session. Since then, he has lost leverage, as subcommittee Chairman Ted Kennedy, largely at the behest of Irish groups, moved to increase immigration limits in 1990. More recently, Simpson played a major role on the 1990 Clean Air Act. He tried to exempt rock and coal mine dust from air quality measurements, backed state preemption of federal clean air laws and successfully fought Ron Wyden's amendment to ban any change in air quality in national parks; he voted for passage of the final bill. Simpson championed the use of nuclear power, and fought the Endangered Species Act because it prevents Wyoming ranchers from protecting their animals against grizzly bears and other predators. As a high ranking Republican on Veterans' Affairs, he has played a constructive role on veterans' laws, risking at times the ire of veterans' groups and Agent Orange critics.

Simpson's sarcasm and humor were widely admired in liberal Washington circles when he was using them to attack Jesse Helms or to champion his pro-choice position on abortion (the reason he was stricken from the list of 1988 VP nominees). They were not at all appreciated in that quarter when he attacked CNN correspondent Peter Arnett, who was broadcasting from Baghdad during the Gulf war in 1991, or when Simpson, in backing Clarence Thomas, said that he had more derogatory information about Anita Hill. In both cases, Simpson did go a bit far, as he himself granted later. He was right to point out that CNN's failure to indicate continuously that Arnett was broadcasting under the supervision of Iraqi censors; if it did not mislead many Americans, it might mislead others, notably the "Arab street." But Simpson was wrong to suggest that Arnett's patriotism was in doubt because of his relatives by marriage. Simpson was surely wrong also in suggesting the existence of serious charges against Hill without backing them up. But his other remarks during those hearings were well within the ambit of fair comment for a senator who disbelieved one witness and believed a nominee; and Simpson's imprecations against the press on this matter, while perhaps rash, had similarly strong foundation.

Simpson came in for more attack than he might have because his Washington admirers may not have understood that he has been, all along, a strong Republican partisan, against government intervention in the economy and private life and for an aggressive foreign policy. He remains the Senate Republican whip, beating back a challenge by Slade Gorton in 1992, although more consistent conservatives have been elected to lower leadership posts. In the meantime, Simpson continues to tend Wyoming interests, blasting Mexican beef and cattle tariffs, passing a "small towns" provision on the Federal Facilities Act, and superintending uranium miners compensation.

Simpson's standing in Wyoming remains very strong. He jumped from the state House of Representatives to the U.S. Senate in 1978 with wonderfully little competition when Senator Clifford Hansen retired. He was reelected with 78% in 1984 and 64% in 1990 against a 32-year-old antiabortion Democrat and political unknown.

Representative-At-Large. Wyoming's only congressman, since Dick Cheney resigned in 1989 to become secretary of Defense, has been Craig Thomas. But even in this Republican state, this Republican had to win a rough-and-tumble contest, as is often the case with special elections early in a president's term in districts long held by his party. Democrat John Vinich just a few months before had nearly beaten Malcolm Wallop. When Republican campaign committee honchos said they couldn't afford to lose Wyoming after dropping seats in Indiana and Alabama, Vinich sounded a powerful Wyoming theme—don't let outsiders make decisions for Wyoming. But Thomas rallied and won. His campaign attacked Vinich's heavy labor funding, unpopular in this right-to-work state, and a TV ad suggesting that Thomas had voted against an anti-crime measure which was denounced by the *Casper Star-Tribune*. Thomas won the 1989 special election with 53% of the vote.

Thomas is a Main Street Republican who grew up in Cody with Al Simpson; he worked for the Farm Bureau and the Wyoming Rural Electric Association, organizations with conservative political leanings that kept him in touch with hundreds of people active in their communities; he served five years in the state legislature. His voting record has been one of the more conservative in the House. As a junior member of the minority, he has concentrated on Wyoming issues: working for Wyoming nuclear radiation victims' compensation, cleaning up uranium tailings, opposing reintroducing wolves in Yellowstone Park, backing reclamation programs, and limiting federal land acquisition. He has spent considerable time on rural healthcare legislation. He has Cheney's old seat on the Natural Resources Committee.

Thomas has had Democratic opponents with serious credentials and has beaten them with rising margins. In 1990, he beat law professor Pete Maxfield 55%–45%. In 1992, he faced eye doctor Jon Herschler, who had the same surname as former (1974–86) Governor Ed Herschler though they are not related, and won 58%–39%.

Presidential politics. Despite its geographic remoteness and low population, Wyoming has come out pretty well in presidential politics. Its emergence as one of the most Republican states in the 1970s left it on the winners' side in 1980, 1984 and 1988. Then the early support of Bill Clinton by Governor Mike Sullivan and Secretary of State Kathy Karpan gave Wyoming some chits in Clinton's Washington. The high Perot vote here and disenchantment with Bush made Wyoming competitive in some 1992 polls, and Clinton actually made a stop here on October 24—the first time Wyoming has seen a presidential nominee in the stretch in a long time.

Wyoming's Democrats held a caucus March 7, just before Super Tuesday; Clinton emerged the marginal winner over Jerry Brown and Paul Tsongas; its winner four years before was Albert Gore. The Republicans met later and routinely backed George Bush.

The People: Est. Pop. 1992: 466,000; Pop. 1990: 453,588, up 2.7% 1990–1992. 0.2% of U.S. total, 51st largest; 35% rural. Median age: 32.0 years. 10.4% 65 years and over. 94.2% White, 5.7% Hispanic origin, 2.1% American Indian, 2.3% Other. Households: 59.7% married couple families; 31% married couple fams. w. children; 50% college educ.; median household income: $27,096; per capita income: $12,311; 67.8% owner occupied housing; median house value: $61,600; median monthly rent: $270. 5.6% Unemployment. Voting age pop.: 318,063. Registered voters (1992): 234,260; 83,091 D (36%), 125,363 R (54%), 25,806 unaffiliated and minor parties (11%).

Political Lineup: Governor, Michael J. (Mike) Sullivan (D); Secy. of State, Kathy Karpan (D); Atty. Gen., Joseph B. Meyer (R); Treasurer, Stanford Smith (R); Auditor, David Ferrari (R). State Senate, 30 (20 R and 10 D), State House of Representatives, 60 (41 R and 19 D). Senators, Malcolm Wallop (R) and Alan K. Simpson (R). Representative, 1 R at large.

1992 Presidential Vote			1988 Presidential Vote		
Bush (R)	79,347	(40%)	Bush (R)	106,867	(61%)
Clinton (D)	68,160	(34%)	Dukakis (D)	67,113	(38%)
Perot (I)	51,263	(26%)			

GOVERNOR

Gov. Michael J. (Mike) **Sullivan (D)**

Elected 1986, term expires Jan. 1995; b. Sept. 22, 1939, Omaha, NE; home, Casper; U. of WY, B.S. 1961, J.D. 1964; Catholic; married (Jane).

Career: Practicing atty, 1964–86.

Office: State Capitol Bldg., #124, Cheyenne 82002, 307-777-7434.

Election Results

1990 gen.	Michael J. (Mike) Sullivan (D)	104,638	(65%)
	Mary Mead (R)	55,471	(35%)
1990 prim.	Michael J. (Mike) Sullivan (D)	38,447	(88%)
	Ron (Suds) Clingman (D)	5,026	(12%)
1986 gen.	Michael J. (Mike) Sullivan (D)	88,879	(54%)
	Pete Simpson (R)	75,841	(46%)

SENATORS

Sen. Malcolm Wallop (R)

Elected 1976, seat up 1994; b. Feb. 27, 1933, New York, NY; home, Big Horn; Yale, B.A. 1954; Episcopalian; married (French).

Career: Army, 1955–57; Rancher, businessman; WY House of Reps., 1968–72; WY Senate, 1972–76.

Offices: 237 RSOB 20510, 202-224-6441. Also 2201 Fed. Bldg., Casper 82601, 307-261-5098; 2009 Fed. Ctr., Cheyenne 82001, 307-634-0626; P.O. Box 1014, Lander 82520, 307-332-2293; 2515 Foothill Blvd., Rock Springs 82901, 307-382-5127; and 40 S. Main, Sheridan 82801, 307-672-6456.

Committees: *Energy and Natural Resources* (RMM of 9 R). *Finance* (9th of 9 R): Deficits, Debt Management and Long-Term Economic Growth (RMM); Energy and Agricultural Taxation; International Trade. *Intelligence (Select)* (8th of 8 R). *Small Business* (2d of 9 R): Government Contracting and Paperwork Reduction; Rural Economy and Family Farming.

Group Ratings

	ADA	ACLU	CDF	COPE	CFA	LCV	ACU	NTLC	NSI	COC	CEI
1992	10	5	0	25	8	0	100	88	70	100	91
1991	5	—	9	25	17	7	95	—	—	90	88

National Journal Ratings

	1991 LIB — 1991 CONS			1992 LIB — 1992 CONS		
Economic	0%	—	91%	0%	—	89%
Social	14%	—	77%	0%	—	89%
Foreign	23%	—	75%	21%	—	72%

Key Votes of the 102d Congress

1. $ for Homeownership FOR	5. Clarence Thomas Nom. FOR	9. Use Force in Gulf FOR
2. Have Cap Gains Debate FOR	6. Lmt Death Row Appeal FOR	10. Keep Salvador Aid FOR
3. Remove Budget Walls AGN	7. Handgun Wait/5-Day AGN	11. Cut $1B from SDI AGN
4. Ban Striker Replace AGN	8. Abortion Gag Rule FOR	12. Override China MFN FOR

Key Votes of the 103d Congress

1. Family Leave *	2. HIV Immigrants AGN	3. Clinton Budget AGN

Election Results

1988 general	Malcolm Wallop (R).................	91,143	(50%)	($1,344,185)
	John P. Vinich (D).....................	89,821	(50%)	($490,230)
1988 primary	Malcolm Wallop (R).................	55,752	(83%)	
	Nora Marie Lewis (R)	3,933	(6%)	
	Brad Kinney (R)......................	3,716	(6%)	
	Two Others	3,600	(5%)	
1982 general	Malcolm Wallop (R).................	94,690	(57%)	($1,139,082)
	Rodger McDaniel (D)................	72,453	(43%)	($389,511)

Sen. Alan K. Simpson (R)

Elected 1978, seat up 1996; b. Sept. 2, 1931, Denver, CO; home, Cody; U. of WY, B.S. 1954, J.D. 1958; Episcopalian; married (Ann).

Career: Army, 1954–56; Practicing atty., 1959–78; WY Asst. Atty. Gen., 1959; Cody City Atty., 1959–69; WY House of Reps., 1964–77, Majority Floor Ldr. 1975–76, Speaker Pro-Tem, 1977.

Offices: 261 DSOB 20510, 202-224-3424. Also P.O. Box 430, Cody 82414, 307-527-7121; Fed. Ctr., #3201, Casper 82601, 307-261-5172; Fed. Ctr., #2007, Cheyenne 82001, 307-772-2477; 2201 S. Douglas Hwy., P.O. Box 3155, Gillette 82716, 307-682-7091; 2020 Grand Ave., #411, Laramie 82070, 307-745-5303; 2515 Foothills Blvd., #220, Rock Springs 82901, 307-382-5097; and 1731 Sheridan Ave., Cody 82414, 307-527-7121.

Committees: *Minority Whip. Aging (Special)* (4th of 10 R). *Environment and Public Works* (2d of 7 R): Clean Air and Nuclear Regulation (RMM); Superfund, Recycling and Solid Waste Management; Toxic Substances, Research and Development. *Judiciary* (3d of 8 R): Immigration and Refugee Affairs (RMM); Patents, Copyrights and Trademarks. *Veterans' Affairs* (3d of 5 R).

Group Ratings

	ADA	ACLU	CDF	COPE	CFA	LCV	ACU	NTLC	NSI	COC	CEI
1992	15	21	30	17	42	0	89	72	100	90	73
1991	10	—	45	17	28	13	80	—	—	80	66

National Journal Ratings

	1991 LIB — 1991 CONS		1992 LIB — 1992 CONS	
Economic	9% —	87%	12% —	86%
Social	34% —	65%	20% —	78%
Foreign	0% —	87%	0% —	90%

Key Votes of the 102d Congress

1. $ for Homeownership FOR	5. Clarence Thomas Nom. FOR	9. Use Force in Gulf FOR
2. Have Cap Gains Debate FOR	6. Lmt Death Row Appeal FOR	10. Keep Salvador Aid FOR
3. Remove Budget Walls AGN	7. Handgun Wait/5-Day AGN	11. Cut $1B from SDI AGN
4. Ban Striker Replace AGN	8. Abortion Gag Rule AGN	12. Override China MFN AGN

Key Votes of the 103d Congress

1. Family Leave AGN	2. HIV Immigrants AGN	3. Clinton Budget AGN

Election Results

1990 general	Alan K. Simpson (R)	100,784	(64%)	($1,435,814)
	Kathy Helling (D).....................	56,848	(36%)	($6,243)
1990 primary	Alan K. Simpson (R)	69,142	(84%)	
	Douglas W. Crook (R)	6,201	(8%)	
	Nora Marie Lewis.....................	6,577	(8%)	
1984 general	Alan K. Simpson (R)	146,373	(78%)	($862,039)
	Victor A. Ryan (D)..................	40,525	(22%)	

REPRESENTATIVE

Rep. Craig Thomas (R)

Elected Apr. 1989; b. Feb. 17, 1933, Cody; home, Casper; U. of WY, B.S. 1954; Methodist; married (Susan).

Career: Marine Corps, 1955–59; V.P., WY Farm Bureau, 1959–66; Legis. staff, Amer. Farm Bureau, 1966–75; Gen. Mgr., WY Rural Electric Assn., 1975–89; WY House of Reps., 1984–89.

Offices: 1019 LHOB 20515, 202-225-2311. Also 2015 Fed. Bldg., Cheyenne 82001, 307-772-2451; 4003 Fed. Bldg., Casper 82601, 307-261-5413; and 2632 Foothills Blvd., #101, Rock Springs 82901, 307-362-5012.

Committees: *Banking, Finance and Urban Affairs* (10th of 20 R): Consumer Credit and Insurance; Financial Institutions Supervision, Regulation and Deposit Insurance; Housing and Community Development. *Government Operations* (8th of 17 R): Information, Justice, Transportation and Agriculture (RMM). *Natural Resources* (6th of 15 R): Energy and Mineral Resources; National Parks, Forests and Public Lands; Native American Affairs (RMM).

Group Ratings

	ADA	ACLU	COPE	CDF	CFA	LCV	ACU	NTLC	NSI	COC	CEI
1992	20	17	45	0	20	0	79	95	100	88	77
1991	0	—	0	10	22	0	95	—	—	100	83

National Journal Ratings

	1991 LIB — 1991 CONS		1992 LIB — 1992 CONS	
Economic	4%	— 90%	16%	— 80%
Social	0%	— 84%	18%	— 81%
Foreign	16%	— 83%	30%	— 64%

Key Votes of the 102d Congress

1. Ban Striker Replace AGN	5. Handgun Wait/7-Day AGN	9. Use Force in Gulf FOR
2. $ for Homeownership FOR	6. Overseas Mil. Abortion AGN	10. US Mil. Abroad $ Cut AGN
3. Tax Rich/Cut Mid Cls. AGN	7. Obscn. Art NEA $ Ban FOR	11. Limit SDI Funds FOR
4. FY93/$15B Def. Cut AGN	8. Death Pen. from Jury FOR	12. Cuba Trade Embargo FOR

Key Votes of the 103d Congress

1. Family Leave FOR	2. Deficit Reduction AGN	3. Stimulus Plan AGN

Election Results

1992 general	Craig Thomas (R)	113,882	(58%)	($459,523)
	Jon Herschler (D)	77,418	(39%)	($348,361)
	Other	5,677	(3%)	
1992 primary	Craig Thomas (R), unopposed			
1990 general	Craig Thomas (R)	87,078	(55%)	($437,772)
	Pete Maxfield (D)	70,977	(45%)	($239,116)

PUERTO RICO, VIRGIN ISLANDS, GUAM, AMERICAN SAMOA

Four American insular territories are represented in Congress by elected delegates who, like the District of Columbia's representative, have floor privileges, votes on committees and—an initiative of the House Democrats in January 1993 that half-misfired and then was challenged in court—have votes in the committee of the whole proceedings (which is the way many bills are handled) except when their votes make the difference in the outcome. They are Puerto Rico, the Virgin Islands, Guam and American Samoa.

PUERTO RICO

Puerto Rico has a unique history. For four centuries, from Columbus's landing here in 1493 until the Spanish-American War of 1898, Puerto Rico was a Spanish colony and the port of San Juan the gathering place for its annual convoy of gold and silver from the Americas to Spain. Today, with 3.6 million people, it is the largest American territory—about the same population as South Carolina or Arizona (with perhaps an additional two million Puerto Ricans on the mainland). Fifty years ago, it was "the poorhouse of the Caribbean," heavily populated, devoted almost entirely to sugar cultivation. Then in the 1940s, 1950s and early 1960s, Puerto Rico was transformed by Governor Luis Munoz Marin and his Popular Democratic Party. Munoz initiated "Operation Bootstrap" to lure businesses to Puerto Rico with promises of low-wage labor and government assistance. Munoz also developed Puerto Rico's commonwealth form of government—better understood in Spanish, Estado Libre Asociado (ELA): Free Associated State—which became effective in 1952. Under commonwealth, Puerto Rico is part of the United States for purposes of international trade, foreign policy and war, but has its own separate laws, taxes and representative government, and is not subject to federal income taxes. Puerto Rico has also developed its own political parties: Munoz's Popular Democrats, the New Progressives who favor statehood, and two Independence parties.

But Munoz's solution, by its own terms, was regarded as open to amendment; and ever since his voluntary retirement in 1964, the central issue in Puerto Rico's politics has been status:

should this island continue or modify ELA, should it seek statehood, should it seek independence? In a referendum in 1967, voters gave solid though not overwhelming margins to ELA over statehood, with less than 1% for independence. Nor were there many pro-independence abstentions, for voter turnout in the enthusiastic politics of Puerto Rico is the highest under the American flag, higher than in even the most affluent, long-settled suburbs of the mainland. The status issue was raised again in 1989, when George Bush, fulfilling a promise he had made to win Puerto Rico's delegates to the national convention, called for statehood, and both the Popular Democrats and the New Progressives called on Congress to authorize a referendum on status. But both parties sought to frame the choice in terms that favored their side, and Congress was wary of promising to support any outcome when the votes were uncertain: for Congress clearly would not admit a Puerto Rico that insisted on Spanish as its only official language, and would be reluctant to admit a Puerto Rico that clung to its tax advantages while seeking eligibility for welfare and other benefits for which many Puerto Ricans would immediately qualify. Popular Democratic Governor Rafael Hernandez Colon, elected in 1972, defeated in 1976 and 1980, elected again in 1984 and 1988, tried to move Puerto Rico from the existing terms of ELA to something more like autonomy: in 1991, Spanish was declared the only official language, and in December 1991 a plebiscite was held on a referendum reaffirming certain Puerto Rican rights; one provision would keep Spanish as the only official language, regardless of any future change in status. The New Progressives, who want Puerto Rico to move in the direction of becoming more like the United States, charged that this would jeopardize U.S. citizenship and current benefits, and the referendum was beaten 53%–45%. That prompted Hernandez Colon to retire, and the gubernatorial election was fought out between two new but not totally unknown figures.

The new governor is Pedro Rossello, a New Progressive and statehood supporter. He is a physician and in the 1980s was director of the Health Department in San Juan (the big cities, with their modern middle classes, are the strongholds of the New Progressives; the countryside and farmlands, strongholds of the Popular Democrats). His 1992 opponent was probably better known: Senator Victoria "Melo" Munoz is the daughter of Luis Munoz Marin. But Rossello won 50%–46% and with Puerto Rico's straight ticket voting swept his party to large majorities in both the Senate (20–8) and House (36–16). Rossello moved to add English as Puerto Rico's second official language, and seemed to lean toward statehood. But in March 1993 he became preoccupied with another issue, when the Clinton Administration moved to revise Section 936, the provision that shelters earnings of some Puerto Rico manufacturing from federal taxation and allows their products into the U.S. duty-free. The Clinton Administration wants to raise $7 billion in revenues from the changes in 936, but in mid-1993 the Senate Finance Committee had scaled that back to $3.6 billion. As tax policy, 936 can hardly be justified. Yet it is the cornerstone of Munoz Marin's ELA, and remains responsible, boosters say, for some 300,000 Puerto Rican jobs, a great many in the pharmaceutical industry. Puerto Rico's unemployment remains high and its economic growth has been disappointingly sluggish since the 1970s; more than half the population here is eligible for U.S. food stamps, and the norm is Latin American-style bureaucratic regulations, systematically underenforced while choking off small business growth. Hernandez Colon shrewdly lobbied to preserve 936 when it was threatened in the 1986 tax reform; Rossello will try to save it in 1993. But Hernandez Colon may have contributed more to economic growth by cutting the higher-than-mainland Puerto Rico income tax rates in 1987, and Rossello may be able to hack away at Puerto Rico's taxes and regulations to stimulate growth regardless of what happens to 936.

Rossello's great problem could come if 936 is quickly repealed, and Puerto Ricans respond by quickly seeking what has always been Rossello's party's goal, statehood. The governor is expected to call for a November 1993 plebiscite with three basic choices: Independence, Commonwealth or Statehood. Puerto Ricans are proud of their American citizenship, proud that Puerto Ricans have volunteered for U.S. military service in large numbers. So proud, in fact, that they have long spurned the independence which articulate opinion elsewhere in Latin America sees as a *sine qua non* of existence. It comes naturally to Puerto Ricans to suppose that if they apply for statehood, they will be readily accepted. But sudden changes by an Executive Branch and Congress for whom Puerto Rico is only a peripheral issue could result in a painful rupture of relations between the mainland and the 3.6 million Americans living and working in Puerto Rico.

Carlos Romero-Barcelo, elected governor in 1976 and 1980, defeated in 1984, was in 1992 elected resident commissioner, Puerto Rico's (sometimes) non-voting member of the House of Representatives, and the only member of Congress with a four-year term. Romero-Barcelo, a longtime rival of Hernandez Colon, beat Antonio Colorado, Hernandez Colon's appointee to replace retiring Jaime Fuster in early 1992, by a narrow margin; but this was more straight ticket than personal politics. While most New Progressives have been affiliated with the mainland Republican Party over the years, Romero-Barcelo has always been affiliated with the Democrats. He was a backer of Jimmy Carter in the 1976 and 1980 primaries here, which paid off well for him, and his support of the Democrats gives him a voice in the majority caucus in years when important issues for Puerto Rico could be summarily decided by the administration and Congress.

Puerto Rico does not vote for president in November, but it does choose delegates to the parties' national conventions. It elects only a few Republicans, but its Democratic delegation is larger than that of 25 states and is invariably made up of backers of a single person, it casts a bigger margin for its candidate than all but a few large states. The Democratic delegation naturally belonged to Rafael Hernandez Colon in 1988 and 1992; now that he is out of politics, the likelihood is that the 1996 Popular Democratic candidate for governor will control the delegation—unless she or he is challenged by Romero-Barcelo.

Rep. Carlos A. Romero-Barcelo (D)

Elected 1992; b. Sept. 4, 1932, San Juan; home, San Juan; Yale, B.A. 1951, U. of PR Law Schl., LL.B. 1956; Catholic; married (Kathleen).

Career: Practicing atty., 1956–68, 1985–92; San Juan Mayor, 1968–76; PR Gov., 1976–84; Pres., New Progressive Party, 1989–91.

Offices: 1517 LHOB 20515, 202-225-2615. Also P.O. Box 4751, San Juan 00902, 809-723-6333; and P.O. Box 946, Ponce 00733, 809-841-3300.

Committees: *Education and Labor* (21st of 28 D): Elementary, Secondary and Vocational Education; Human Resources; Labor-Management Relations. *Natural Resources* (18th of 28 D): Insular and International Affairs; National Parks, Forests and Public Lands.

VIRGIN ISLANDS

The United States' other insular area in the Caribbean is the Virgin Islands, a very different sort of place than Puerto Rico. It is much smaller than Puerto Rico, with a resident population of 101,000, mainly on three separate islands, St. Thomas, St. John and St. Croix. Puerto Rico is multiracial and not self-conscious about it; most Virgin Islanders are black, with a clear divide between the races much resented by the blacks. While Puerto Rico has attracted all kinds of light industry, the Virgin Islands live off tourism and refineries, industries that have produced higher income levels for its few citizens but have not provided the basis for a mature economy. For years, the governor of the Virgin Islands was appointed by the president; some more recent contests have had some nasty racial overtones. The current governor is Alexander Farrelly,

Democrat first elected in 1986.

The delegate from the Virgin Islands is Democrat Ron de Lugo. He got his start in radio, inventing a character called Mango Jones on the first Virgin Island radio station in 1950; in 1952, he revived the Virgin Islands' traditional Eastertime clebration, Carnival. First elected to Congress in 1968, he lost a race for governor in 1978, but returned to Washington in 1980: he is now the senior member from the territories. He serves on the Natural Resources Committee (formerly Interior and Insular Affairs), Education and Labor, and Public Works and Transportation; importantly, he chairs the Natural Resources Subcommittee on Insular and International Affairs. In that capacity, he works on other insular matters, like Puerto Rico's status referendum, the Palau Compact of Free Association, and Guam's commonwealth proposal. De Lugo helped steer federal aid to the Virgin Islands after Hurricane Hugo in September 1989; more recently, he has been urging removal of the Virgin Islands and other U.S. territories from the jurisdiction of the Interior Department and creating a White House level office to consider the territories needs. He claims credit for getting federal money to extend the notoriously short airport runway in St. Thomas, and has worked to protect Virgin Island industries, notably rum, from competition with Mexico.

Rep. Ron de Lugo (D)

Elected 1980; b. Aug. 2, 1930, Englewood, NJ; home, St. Thomas; Col. San Jose, PR; Catholic; married (Sheila).

Career: Army, 1948–50; Radio broadcaster, 1950–56; VI Senate, 1956–66; VI Rep., Washington, DC, 1968–73; U.S. House of Reps., 1972–78.

Offices: 2427 RHOB 20515, 202-225-1790. Also Sunny Isle Box 5998, Christiansted, St. Croix, VI 00823, 809-778-5900.

Committees: *Education and Labor* (25th of 28 D). *Natural Resources* (8th of 28 D): Insular and International Affairs (Chmn.). *Public Works and Transportation* (5th of 39 D): Aviation (Vice Chmn.); Surface Transportation.

GUAM

Some 3,700 miles west of Hawaii, 19 hours of flying time to Washington, D.C., is Guam, the place where, as viewers of political conventions for years have been informed, America's day begins. Guam lies just west of the International Date Line, and it is indeed the early hours of Tuesday there when the rest of us are just trying to get through Monday afternoon. Geographically in the center of the Mariana Islands, Guam is judicially separate; an integral territory of the United States, while the Marianas and other nearby islands were for years United Nations territories administered by the United States, Marianas became a commonwealth in 1978 though Guam remained a territory. With a population of about 140,000, Guam is a more advanced society than the Marianas, but economically it is not yet self-supporting. Many of the workers are employed by the Guamanian or federal government (there are big defense bases here). The people are of mixed ethnic stock (Spanish and Pacific Islander), their religion is almost always Catholic, and they speak English, Spanish and the local language, Chamorro.

Guam's delegate in Congress is Robert Underwood, former academic vice president of the University of Guam, known for his efforts in promoting and preserving Chamorro culture. A Democrat, in 1992 he beat Republican incumbent Ben Blaz, a former Marine General. But the governor here, Joseph Ada, is still a Republican; on an island of 140,000 people, party labels clearly matter less than personal reputations and business alliances.

The major issue for Guamanian politicians is status. Governor Ada has been seeking greater self-government for Guam through commonwealth status. Beginning in 1982, Guamanians voted in two referenda for commonwealth, one of which, The Guam Commonwealth Act drafted by the Commission on Self Determination, was submitted by Underwood as a bill that would allow Guam's government to control its own immigration (preventing the Chamorros from becoming a minority), require Guam's consent for the application of federal laws, would allow for self determination by indigenous people only (Chamorros), and would require the U.S. to consult with Guam over treaties that affect it. The Bush Administration did not look kindly on this, and in 1993, Ada and others were looking to the Clinton Administration, warning that Chamarros and others, if rebuffed, might seek independence instead. The implied threat is to the military bases which, now that U.S. forces have left the Philippines, are a key part of the American presence in the western Pacific. Indeed, Ada and other Guam politicians have been trying to close Agana Naval Air Station for some years, and made some headway in 1993 by getting it on the list of possible U.S. base closures.

Guam attracted national attention in 1990 when it passed a strong antiabortion law allowing abortions only in life-threatening cases and upon approval of two independent doctors. That law was challenged and the ban overturned by a federal appeals court in April 1992, as clearly contrary to *Roe v. Wade*; the Supreme Court by a 6–3 vote in November 1992 declined to hear an appeal, thus avoiding the only case in which the heart of *Roe* was clearly challenged.

Rep. Robert A. Underwood (D)

Elected 1992; b. July 13, 1948, Tamuning; home, Baza Gardens; CA St. U., B.A. 1969, M.A. 1971, U. of S. CA, Ed.D. 1987; Catholic; married (Lorraine Aguilar).

Career: Teacher, Admin., Guam Public Schls., 1972–76; Prof., U. of Guam, 1976–88, Dean, 1988–90, Academic V.P., 1990–92.

Offices: 507 CHOB 20515, 202-225-1188. Also 190 Hernan Cortez St., Agana 96910, 671-477-2587.

Committees: *Armed Services* (28th of 34 D): Military Forces and Personnel; Military Installations and Facilities; Readiness. *Education and Labor* (28th of 28 D). *Natural Resources* (23d of 28 D): Insular and International Affairs; National Parks, Forests and Public Lands.

AMERICAN SAMOA

American Samoa obtained representation in Congress for the first time in 1980. That has not been an entirely happy experience for this Southern Pacific island which, unlike Guam, has been little influenced by western settlers and remains almost as Polynesian as it was when the United States took possession in 1900. Three-term Delegate Fofo I.F. Sunia pleaded guilty in August 1988 to $130,000 in payroll fraud, resigned from Congress in September, and his administrative assistant was sent to jail. Elected to succeed him in the November 22, 1988, runoff was Democratic Lieutenant Governor Eni F. H. Faleomavaega, who beat former Lieutenant Governor Tufele Li'a. Faleomavaega advanced one of the truly bad ideas of recent years, a proposal that American Indians be given four non-voting delegates to the House; he has concentrated on issues affecting Samoa on the Natural Resources, Foreign Affairs and

Education and Labor Committees.

American Samoa stages a Democratic presidential primary, but in 1988 only 36 people actually voted. Not surprisingly, none of the candidates campaigned in person here.

Rep. Eni F. H. Faleomavaega (D)

Elected 1988; b. Aug. 15, 1943, Vailoatai; home, Pago Pago; Brigham Young U., B.A. 1972, U. of CA, LL.M. 1973; Mormon; married (Hinanui).

Career: Army, 1966–69; A.A., U.S. Rep. from AS, 1973–75; Cnsl., U.S. House Interior Cmte., 1975–81; AS Dep. Atty. Gen., 1981–84; AS Lt. Gov., 1984–89.

Offices: 109 CHOB 20515, 202-225-8577. Also P.O. Drawer X, Pago Pago, AS 96799, 684-633-1372.

Committees: *Education and Labor* (26th of 28 D): Labor Standards, Occupational Health and Safety. *Foreign Affairs* (9th of 27 D): Asia and the Pacific; International Operations. *Natural Resources* (13th of 28 D): Insular and International Affairs; Native American Affairs.

SENATE COMMITTEES

This committee section includes all Standing, Special and Select committees of the U.S. Senate in alphabetical order.

AGING (Special)   G-31 Dirksen, 202-224-5364

Majority (11 D): Pryor (AR), Chmn.; Glenn (OH), Bradley (NJ), Johnston (LA), Breaux (LA), Shelby (AL), Reid (NV), Graham (FL), Kohl (WI), Feingold (WI), one vacancy.
Minority (10 R): Cohen (ME), Pressler (SD), Grassley (IA), Simpson (WY), Jeffords (VT), McCain (AZ), Durenberger (MN), Craig (ID), Burns (MT), Specter (PA).

NO SUBCOMMITTEES

AGRICULTURE, NUTRITION AND FORESTRY   328-A Russell
                                                 202-224-2035

Majority (10 D): Leahy (VT), Chmn.; Pryor (AR), Boren (OK), Heflin (AL), Harkin (IA), Conrad (ND), Daschle (SD), Baucus (MT), Kerrey (NE), Feingold (WI).
Minority (8 R): Lugar (IN), Dole (KS), Helms (NC), Cochran (MS), McConnell (KY), Craig (ID), Coverdell (GA), Grassley (IA).

SUBCOMMITTEES

AGRICULTURAL CREDIT
Majority (4 D): Conrad, Chmn.; Daschle, Boren, Baucus.
Minority (3 R): Grassley, Craig, Coverdell.

AGRICULTURAL PRODUCTION AND STABILIZATION OF PRICES
Majority (7 D): Pryor, Chmn.; Baucus, Kerrey, Feingold, Boren, Heflin, Harkin.
Minority (6 R): Helms, Dole, Cochran, McConnell, Craig, Grassley.

AGRICULTURAL RESEARCH, CONSERVATION, FORESTRY, AND GENERAL LEGISLATION
Majority (3 D): Daschle, Chmn.; Kerrey, Harkin.
Minority (2 R): Craig, Cochran.

DOMESTIC AND FOREIGN MARKETING AND PRODUCT PROMOTION
Majority (6 D): Boren, Chmn., Pryor, Conrad, Baucus, Feingold, Heflin.
Minority (5 R): Cochran, Helms, Coverdell, McConnell, Grassley.

NUTRITION AND INVESTIGATIONS
Majority (4 D): Harkin, Chmn.; Pryor, Kerrey, Feingold.
Minority (3 R): McConnell, Dole, Helms.

RURAL DEVELOPMENT AND RURAL ELECTRIFICATION

Majority (3 D): Heflin, Chmn.; Conrad, Daschle.
Minority (2 R): Coverdell, Dole.

APPROPRIATIONS   S-128 The Capitol, 202-224-3471

Majority (16 D): Byrd (WV) Chmn.; Inouye (HI), Hollings (SC), Johnston (LA), Leahy (VT), Sasser (TN), DeConcini (AZ), Bumpers (AR), Lautenberg (NJ), Harkin (IA), Mikulski (MD), Reid (NV), Kerrey (NE), Kohl (WI), Murray (WA), Feinstein (CA).
Minority (13 R): Hatfield (OR); Stevens (AK), Cochran (MS), D'Amato (NY), Specter (PA), Domenici (NM), Nickles (OK), Gramm (TX), Bond (MO), Gorton (WA), McConnell (KY), Mack (FL), Burns (MT).

SUBCOMMITTEES

AGRICULTURE, RURAL DEVELOPMENT AND RELATED AGENCIES

Majority (6 D): Bumpers, Chmn.; Harkin, Kerrey, Johnston, Kohl, Feinstein.
Minority (5 R): Cochran, Specter, Bond, Gramm, Gorton.

COMMERCE, JUSTICE, STATE AND JUDICIARY

Majority (6 D): Hollings, Chmn.; Inouye, Bumpers, Lautenberg, Sasser, Kerrey.
Minority (5 R): Domenici, Stevens, Hatfield, Gramm, McConnell.

DEFENSE

Majority (10 D): Inouye, Chmn., Hollings, Johnston, Byrd, Leahy, Sasser, DeConcini, Bumpers, Lautenberg, Harkin.
Minority (8 R): Stevens, D'Amato, Cochran, Specter, Domenici, Nickles, Gramm, Bond.

DISTRICT OF COLUMBIA

Majority (3 D): Kohl, Chmn.; Murray, Feinstein.
Minority (2 R): Burns, Mack.

ENERGY AND WATER DEVELOPMENT

Majority (7 D): Johnston, Chmn.; Byrd, Hollings, Sasser, DeConcini, Reid, Kerrey.
Minority (6 R): Hatfield, Cochran, Domenici, Nickles, Gorton, McConnell.

FOREIGN OPERATIONS

Majority (7 D): Leahy, Chmn.; Inouye, DeConcini, Lautenberg, Harkin, Mikulski, Feinstein.
Minority (6 R): McConnell, D'Amato, Specter, Nickles, Mack, Gramm.

INTERIOR & RELATED AGENCIES

Majority (8 D): Byrd, Chmn.; Johnston, Leahy, DeConcini, Bumpers, Hollings, Reid, Murray.
Minority (7 R): Nickles, Stevens, Cochran, Domenici, Gorton, Hatfield, Burns.

LABOR, HEALTH AND HUMAN SERVICES, AND EDUCATION

Majority (8 D): Harkin, Chmn.; Byrd, Hollings, Inouye, Bumpers, Reid, Kohl, Murray.
Minority (7 R): Specter, Hatfield, Stevens, Cochran, Gorton, Mack, Bond.

LEGISLATIVE BRANCH

Majority (3 D): Reid, Chmn.; Mikulski, Murray.
Minority (2 R): Mack, Burns.

MILITARY CONSTRUCTION

Majority (4 D): Sasser, Chmn.; Inouye, Reid, Kohl.
Minority (3 R): Gorton, Stevens, McConnell.

TRANSPORTATION

Majority (5 D): Lautenberg, Chmn.; Byrd, Harkin, Sasser, Mikulski.
Minority (4 R): D'Amato, Domenici, Hatfield, Specter.

TREASURY, POSTAL SERVICE AND GENERAL GOVERNMENT

Majority (3 D): DeConcini, Chmn.; Mikulski, Kerrey.
Minority (2 R): Bond, D'Amato.

VA, HUD AND INDEPENDENT AGENCIES

Majority (6 D): Mikulski, Chmn.; Leahy, Johnston, Lautenberg, Kerrey, Feinstein.
Minority (5 R): Gramm, D'Amato, Nickles, Bond, Burns.

ARMED SERVICES   228 Russell, 202-224-3871

Majority (11 D): Nunn (GA), Chmn.; Exon (NE), Levin (MI), Kennedy (MA), Bingaman
(NM), Glenn (OH), Shelby (AL), Byrd (WV), Graham (FL), Robb (VA), Lieberman (CT).
Minority (10 R): Thurmond (SC), Warner (VA), Cohen (ME), McCain (AZ), Lott (MS), Coats
(IN), Smith (NH), Kempthorne (ID), Faircloth (NC), Hutchison (TX).

SUBCOMMITTEES

COALITION DEFENSE AND REINFORCING FORCES

Majority (6 D): Levin, Chmn.; Exon, Glenn, Shelby, Byrd, Graham.
Minority (5 R): Warner, Cohen, Coats, Smith, Kempthorne.

DEFENSE TECHNOLOGY, ACQUISITION, AND INDUSTRIAL BASE

Majority (7 D): Bingaman, Chmn.; Levin, Kennedy, Byrd, Graham, Robb, Lieberman.
Minority (6 R): Smith, Cohen, Lott, Coats, Kempthorne, Faircloth.

FORCE REQUIREMENTS AND PERSONNEL

Majority (4 D): Shelby, Chmn.; Kennedy, Byrd, Lieberman.
Minority (3 R): Coats, McCain, Faircloth.

MILITARY READINESS AND DEFENSE INFRASTRUCTURE

Majority (4 D): Glenn, Chmn.; Bingaman, Shelby, Robb.
Minority (3 R): McCain, Smith, Faircloth.

NUCLEAR DETERRENCE, ARMS CONTROL AND DEFENSE INTELLIGENCE

Majority (4 D): Exon, Chmn.; Levin, Bingaman, Glenn.
Minority (3 R): Lott, Warner, Kempthorne.

REGIONAL DEFENSE AND CONTINGENCY FORCES

Majority (5 D): Kennedy, Chmn.; Exon, Graham, Robb, Lieberman.
Minority (4 R): Cohen, Warner, McCain, Lott.

BANKING, HOUSING AND URBAN AFFAIRS 534 Dirksen, 202-224-7391

Majority (11 D): Riegle (MI), Chmn.; Sarbanes (MD), Dodd (CT), Sasser (TN), Shelby (AL),
Kerry (MA), Bryan (NV), Boxer (CA), Campbell (CO), Moseley-Braun (IL), Murray (WA).
Minority (8 R): D'Amato (NY), Gramm (TX), Bond (MO), Mack (FL), Faircloth (NC),
Bennett (UT), Roth (DE), Domenici (NM).

SUBCOMMITTEES

ECONOMIC STABILIZATION AND RURAL DEVELOPMENT
Majority (5 D): Shelby, Chmn.; Campbell, Dodd, Kerry, Bryan.
Minority (4 R): Faircloth, Bennett, Gramm, Mack.

HOUSING AND URBAN AFFAIRS
Majority (6 D): Sarbanes, Chmn.; Kerry, Bryan, Boxer, Moseley-Braun, Dodd.
Minority (5 R): Bond, Domenici, Mack, Faircloth, Roth.

INTERNATIONAL FINANCE AND MONETARY POLICY
Majority (6 D): Sasser, Chmn.; Murray, Sarbanes, Kerry, Boxer, Campbell.
Minority (5 R): Mack, Gramm, Bennett, Roth, Bond.

SECURITIES
Majority (6 D): Dodd, Chmn.; Sasser, Shelby, Bryan, Moseley-Braun, Murray.
Minority (5 R): Gramm, Roth, Bond, Faircloth, Domenici.

BUDGET   621 Dirksen, 202-224-0642

Majority (12 D): Sasser (TN), Chmn.; Hollings (SC), Johnston (LA), Riegle (MI), Exon (NE),
    Lautenberg (NJ), Simon (IL), Conrad (ND), Dodd (CT), Sarbanes (MD), Boxer (CA),
    Murray (WA).
Minority (9 R): Domenici (NM), Grassley (IA), Nickles (OK), Gramm (TX), Bond (MO), Lott
    (MS), Brown (CO), Gorton (WA), Gregg (NH).

NO SUBCOMMITTEES

COMMERCE, SCIENCE AND TRANSPORTATION   508 Dirksen
                                                      202-224-5115

Majority (11 D): Hollings (SC), Chmn.; Inouye (HI), Ford (KY), Exon (NE), Rockefeller
    (WV), Kerry (MA), Breaux (LA), Bryan (NV), Robb (VA), Dorgan (ND), one vacancy.
Minority (9 R): Danforth (MO), Packwood (OR), Pressler (SD), Stevens (AK), McCain (AZ),
    Burns (MT), Gorton (WA), Lott (MS), Hutchison (TX).

SUBCOMMITTEES

AVIATION
Majority (5 D): Ford, Chmn.; Exon, Inouye, Kerry, Bryan.
Minority (4 R): Pressler, McCain, Stevens, Gorton.

COMMUNICATIONS
Majority (8 D): Inouye, Chmn.; Hollings, Ford, Exon, Kerry, Breaux, Rockefeller, Robb.
Minority (6 R): Packwood, Pressler, Stevens, McCain, Burns, Gorton.

CONSUMER
Majority (4 D): Bryan, Chmn.; Ford, Dorgan, one vacancy.
Minority (3 R): Gorton, McCain, Burns.

FOREIGN COMMERCE AND TOURISM

Majority (5 D): Kerry, Chmn.; Hollings, Rockefeller, Bryan, Dorgan.
Minority (3 R): Packwood, Pressler, one vacancy.

MERCHANT MARINE

Majority (3 D): Breaux, Chmn.; Inouye, one vacancy.
Minority (2 R): Lott, Stevens.

SCIENCE, TECHNOLOGY AND SPACE

Majority (6 D): Rockefeller, Chmn.; Hollings, Kerry, Bryan, Robb, one vacancy.
Minority (4 R): Burns, Pressler, Lott, one vacancy.

SURFACE TRANSPORTATION

Majority (7 D): Exon, Chmn.; Rockefeller, Inouye, Breaux, Robb, Dorgan, one vacancy.
Minority (5 R): McCain, Packwood, Burns, Lott, one vacancy.

ENERGY AND NATURAL RESOURCES   304 Dirksen, 202-224-4971

Majority (11 D): Johnston (LA), Chmn.; Bumpers (AR), Ford (KY), Bradley (NJ), Bingaman (NM), Akaka (HI), Shelby (AL), Wellstone (MN), Campbell (CO), Mathews (TN), one vacancy.
Minority (9 R): Wallop (WY), Hatfield (OR), Domenici (NM), Murkowski (AK), Nickles (OK), Craig (ID), Bennett (UT), Specter (PA), Lott (MS).

SUBCOMMITTEES

ENERGY RESEARCH AND DEVELOPMENT

Majority (7 D): Ford, Chmn.; Shelby, Vice Chmn.; Bumpers, Bingaman, Wellstone, Mathews, one vacancy.
Minority (5 R): Domenici, Specter, Nickles, Craig, Lott.

MINERAL RESOURCES DEVELOPMENT AND PRODUCTION

Majority (5 D): Akaka, Chmn.; Mathews, Vice Chmn.; Bumpers, Ford, Campbell.
Minority (4 R): Craig, Murkowski, Nickles, Bennett.

PUBLIC LANDS, NATIONAL PARKS AND FORESTS

Majority (8 D): Bumpers, Chmn.; Campbell, Vice Chmn.; Bradley, Bingaman, Akaka, Shelby, Wellstone, one vacancy.
Minority (7 R): Murkowski, Hatfield, Lott, Domenici, Bennett, Craig, Specter.

RENEWABLE ENERGY, ENERGY EFFICIENCY, AND COMPETITIVENESS

Majority (7 D): Bingaman, Chmn.; Wellstone, Vice Chmn.; Bradley, Akaka, Shelby, Mathews, one vacancy.
Minority (6 R): Nickles, Specter, Lott, Hatfield, Domenici, Murkowski.

WATER AND POWER

Majority (3 D): Bradley, Chmn.; Ford, Campbell.
Minority (2 R): Bennett, Hatfield.

1424   SENATE COMMITTEES

ENVIRONMENT AND PUBLIC WORKS   458 Dirksen, 202-224-6176

Majority (10 D): Baucus (MT), Chmn.; Moynihan (NY), Mitchell (ME), Lautenberg (NJ), Reid (NV), Graham (FL), Lieberman (CT), Metzenbaum (OH), Wofford (PA), Boxer (CA).
Minority (7 R): Chafee (RI), Simpson (WY), Durenberger (MN), Warner (VA), Smith (NH), Faircloth (NC), Kempthorne (ID).

SUBCOMMITTEES

CLEAN AIR AND NUCLEAR REGULATION
Majority (4 D): Lieberman, Chmn.; Moynihan, Graham, Metzenbaum.
Minority (3 R): Simpson, Faircloth, Kempthorne.

CLEAN WATER, FISHERIES AND WILDLIFE
Majority (6 D): Graham, Chmn.; Mitchell, Lautenberg, Reid, Lieberman, Wofford.
Minority (4 R): Chafee, Durenberger, Faircloth, Kempthorne.

SUPERFUND, RECYCLING AND SOLID WASTE MANAGEMENT
Majority (6 D): Lautenberg, Chmn.; Moynihan, Graham, Metzenbaum, Wofford, Boxer.
Minority (4 R): Durenberger, Simpson, Smith, Warner.

TOXIC SUBSTANCES, RESEARCH AND DEVELOPMENT
Majority (5 D): Reid, Chmn.; Lautenberg, Lieberman, Wofford, Boxer.
Minority (4 R): Smith, Warner, Simpson, Faircloth.

WATER RESOURCES, TRANSPORTATION, PUBLIC BUILDINGS AND ECONOMIC DEVELOPMENT
Majority (5 D): Moynihan, Chmn.; Mitchell, Reid, Metzenbaum, Boxer.
Minority (4 R): Warner, Durenberger, Smith, Kempthorne.

ETHICS (Select)   220 Hart, 202-224-2981

Majority (3 D): Bryan (NV), Chmn.; Mikulski (MD), Daschle (SD).
Minority (3 R): McConnell (KY), Vice Chmn.; Smith (NH), Craig (ID).

NO SUBCOMMITTEES

FINANCE   205 Dirksen, 202-224-4515

Majority (11 D): Moynihan (NY), Chmn.; Baucus (MT), Boren (OK), Bradley (NJ), Mitchell (ME), Pryor (AR), Riegle (MI), Rockefeller (WV), Daschle (SD), Breaux (LA), Conrad (ND).
Minority (9 R): Packwood (OR), Dole (KS), Roth (DE), Danforth (MO), Chafee (RI), Durenberger (MN), Grassley (IA), Hatch (UT), Wallop (WY).

SUBCOMMITTEES

DEFICITS, DEBT MANAGEMENT AND LONG-TERM ECONOMIC GROWTH
Majority (2 D): Bradley, Chmn.; Riegle.
Minority (1 R): Wallop.

ENERGY AND AGRICULTURAL TAXATION
Majority (3 D): Daschle, Chmn.; Boren, Breaux.
Minority (3 R): Hatch, Dole, Wallop.

HEALTH FOR FAMILIES AND THE UNINSURED
Majority (4 D): Riegle, Chmn.; Bradley, Mitchell, Rockefeller.
Minority (4 R): Chafee, Roth, Durenberger, Danforth.

INTERNATIONAL TRADE
Majority (10 D): Baucus, Chmn.; Moynihan, Boren, Bradley, Mitchell, Riegle, Rockefeller, Daschle, Breaux, Conrad.
Minority (7 R): Danforth, Packwood, Roth, Chafee, Grassley, Hatch, Wallop.

MEDICARE AND LONG-TERM CARE
Majority (6 D): Rockefeller, Chmn.; Baucus, Mitchell, Pryor, Daschle, Conrad.
Minority (6 R): Durenberger, Packwood, Dole, Chafee, Grassley, Hatch.

PRIVATE RETIREMENT PLANS AND OVERSIGHT OF THE INTERNAL REVENUE SERVICE
Majority (2 D): Pryor, Chmn.; Moynihan.
Minority (1 R): Grassley.

SOCIAL SECURITY AND FAMILY POLICY
Majority (2 D): Breaux, Chmn.; Moynihan.
Minority (2 R): Dole, Durenberger.

TAXATION
Majority (4 D): Boren, Chmn.; Baucus, Pryor, Conrad.
Minority (3 R): Roth, Packwood, Danforth.

FOREIGN RELATIONS   446 Dirksen, 202-224-4651
Majority (11 D): Pell (RI), Chmn.; Biden (DE), Sarbanes (MD), Dodd (CT), Kerry (MA), Simon (IL), Moynihan (NY), Robb (VA), Wofford (PA), Feingold (WI), Mathews (TN).
Minority (9 R): Helms (NC), Lugar (IN), Kassebaum (KS), Pressler (SD), Murkowski (AK), Brown (CO), Jeffords (VT), Coverdell (GA), Gregg (NH).

SUBCOMMITTEES

AFRICAN AFFAIRS
Majority (3 D): Simon, Chmn.; Moynihan, Feingold.
Minority (2 R): Jeffords, Kassebaum.

EAST ASIAN AND PACIFIC AFFAIRS
Majority (4 D): Robb, Chmn.; Biden, Kerry, Mathews.
Minority (3 R): Murkowski, Lugar, Pressler.

EUROPEAN AFFAIRS
Majority (4 D): Biden, Chmn.; Sarbanes, Simon, Feingold.
Minority (4 R): Lugar, Kassebaum, Brown, Gregg.

INTERNATIONAL ECONOMIC POLICY, TRADE, OCEANS AND ENVIRONMENT
Majority (6 D): Sarbanes, Chmn.; Biden, Dodd, Kerry, Wofford, Feingold.
Minority (5 R): Kassebaum, Helms, Murkowski, Brown, Jeffords.

NEAR EASTERN AND SOUTH ASIAN AFFAIRS

Majority (5 D): Moynihan, Chmn.; Sarbanes, Robb, Wofford, Mathews.
Minority (5 R): Brown, Pressler, Jeffords, Coverdell, Gregg.

TERRORISM, NARCOTICS AND INTERNATIONAL OPERATIONS

Majority (5 D): Kerry, Chmn.; Pell, Dodd, Simon, Moynihan.
Minority (4 R): Pressler, Helms, Murkowski, Coverdell.

WESTERN HEMISPHERE AND PEACE CORPS AFFAIRS

Majority (4 D): Dodd, Chmn.; Robb, Wofford, Mathews.
Minority (3 R): Coverdell, Helms, Lugar.

GOVERNMENTAL AFFAIRS   340 Dirksen, 202-224-4751

Majority (8 D): Glenn (OH), Chmn.; Nunn (GA), Levin (MI), Sasser (TN), Pryor (AK), Lieberman (CT), Akaka (HI), Dorgan (ND).
Minority (5 R): Roth (DE), Stevens (AK), Cohen (ME), Cochran (MS), McCain (AZ).

SUBCOMMITTEES

FEDERAL SERVICES, POST OFFICE, AND CIVIL SERVICE

Majority (3 D): Pryor, Chmn.; Sasser, Akaka.
Minority (2 R): Stevens, Cochran.

GENERAL SERVICES, FEDERALISM AND THE DISTRICT OF COLUMBIA

Majority (3 D): Sasser, Chmn.; Lieberman, Akaka.
Minority (2 R): McCain, Stevens.

OVERSIGHT OF GOVERNMENT MANAGEMENT

Majority (6 D): Levin, Chmn.; Pryor, Lieberman, Akaka, Nunn, Dorgan.
Minority (4 R): Cohen, Stevens, Cochran, McCain.

REGULATION AND GOVERNMENT INFORMATION

Majority (4 D): Lieberman, Chmn.; Nunn, Levin, Dorgan.
Minority (3 R): Cochran, Cohen, McCain.

PERMANENT SUBCOMMITTEE ON INVESTIGATIONS

Majority (7 D): Nunn, Chmn.; Glenn, Vice Chmn.; Levin, Sasser, Pryor, Lieberman, Dorgan.
Minority (5 R): Roth, Stevens, Cohen, Cochran, McCain.

INDIAN AFFAIRS   838 Hart, 202-224-2251

Majority (10 D): Inouye (HI), Chmn.; DeConcini (AZ), Daschle (SD), Conrad (ND), Reid (NV), Simon (IL), Akaka (HI), Wellstone (MN), Dorgan (ND), Campbell (CO).
Minority (8 R): McCain (AZ), Vice Chmn.; Murkowski (AK), Cochran (MS), Gorton (WA), Domenici (NM), Kassebaum (KS), Nickles (OK), Hatfield (OR).

NO SUBCOMMITTEES

INTELLIGENCE (Select)   211 Hart, 202-224-1700

Majority (9 D): DeConcini (AZ), Chmn.; Metzenbaum (OH), Glenn (OH), Kerrey (NE), Bryan (NV), Graham (FL), Kerry (MA), Baucus (MT), Johnston (LA).
Minority (8 R): Warner (VA), Vice Chmn.; D'Amato (NY), Danforth (MO), Gorton (WA), Chafee (RI), Stevens (AK), Lugar (IN), Wallop (WY).

NO SUBCOMMITTEES

JUDICIARY   224 Dirksen, 202-224-5225

Majority (10 D): Biden (DE), Chmn.; Kennedy (MA), Metzenbaum (OH), DeConcini (AZ), Leahy (VT), Heflin (AL), Simon (IL), Kohl (WI), Feinstein (CA), Moseley-Braun (IL).
Minority (8 R): Hatch (UT), Thurmond (SC), Simpson (WY), Grassley (IA), Specter (PA), Brown (CO), Cohen (ME), Pressler (SD).

SUBCOMMITTEES

ANTITRUST, MONOPOLIES AND BUSINESS RIGHTS
Majority (4 D): Metzenbaum, Chmn.; DeConcini, Heflin, Simon.
Minority (3 R): Thurmond, Specter, Hatch.

CONSTITUTION
Majority (4 D): Simon, Chmn.; Metzenbaum, DeConcini, Kennedy.
Minority (2 R): Brown, Hatch.

COURTS AND ADMINISTRATIVE PRACTICE
Majority (4 D): Heflin, Chmn.; Metzenbaum, Kohl, Moseley-Braun.
Minority (3 R): Grassley, Thurmond, Cohen.

IMMIGRATION AND REFUGEE AFFAIRS
Majority (2 D): Kennedy, Chmn.; Simon.
Minority (1 R): Simpson.

JUVENILE JUSTICE
Majority (3 D): Kohl, Chmn.; Biden, Moseley-Braun.
Minority (2 R): Cohen, Pressler.

PATENTS, COPYRIGHTS AND TRADEMARKS
Majority (5 D): DeConcini, Chmn.; Kennedy, Leahy, Heflin, Feinstein.
Minority (4 R): Hatch, Simpson, Grassley, Brown.

TECHNOLOGY AND THE LAW
Majority (3 D): Leahy, Chmn.; Kohl, Feinstein.
Minority (2 R): Specter, Pressler.

LABOR AND HUMAN RESOURCES   428 Dirksen, 202-224-5375

Majority (10 D): Kennedy (MA), Chmn.; Pell (RI), Metzenbaum (OH), Dodd (CT), Simon (IL), Harkin (IA), Mikulski (MD), Bingaman (NM), Wellstone (MN), Wofford (PA).
Minority (7 R): Kassebaum (KS), Jeffords (VT), Coats (IN), Gregg (NH), Thurmond (SC), Hatch (UT), Durenberger (MN).

SUBCOMMITTEES

AGING

Majority (5 D): Mikulski, Chmn.; Pell, Metzenbaum, Dodd, Wofford.
Minority (3 R): Gregg, Coats, Durenberger.

CHILDREN, FAMILY, DRUGS AND ALCOHOLISM

Majority (7 D): Dodd, Chmn.; Pell, Mikulski, Bingaman, Kennedy, Wellstone, Wofford.
Minority (6 R): Coats, Kassebaum, Jeffords, Gregg, Thurmond, Durenberger.

DISABILITY POLICY

Majority (4 D): Harkin, Chmn.; Metzenbaum, Simon, Bingaman.
Minority (3 R): Durenberger, Jeffords, Hatch.

EDUCATION, ARTS AND HUMANITIES

Majority (10 D): Pell, Chmn.; Metzenbaum, Dodd, Simon, Mikulski, Bingaman, Kennedy, Wellstone, Wofford, Harkin.
Minority (7 R): Jeffords, Kassebaum, Coats, Gregg, Thurmond, Hatch, Durenberger.

EMPLOYMENT AND PRODUCTIVITY

Majority (5 D): Simon, Chmn.; Harkin, Mikulski, Bingaman, Wofford.
Minority (4 R): Thurmond, Coats, Gregg, Hatch.

LABOR

Majority (5 D): Metzenbaum, Chmn.; Harkin, Dodd, Kennedy, Wellstone.
Minority (4 R): Hatch, Kassebaum, Jeffords, Thurmond.

RULES AND ADMINISTRATION   305 Russell, 202-224-6352

Majority (9 D): Ford (KY), Chmn.; Pell (RI), Byrd (WV), Inouye (HI), DeConcini (AZ), Moynihan (NY), Dodd (CT), Feinstein (CA), Mathews (TN).
Minority (7 R): Stevens (AK), Hatfield (OR), Helms (NC), Warner (VA), Dole (KS), McConnell (KY), Cochran (MS).

NO SUBCOMMITTEES

SMALL BUSINESS   428-A Russell, 202-224-5175

Majority (12 D): Bumpers (AR), Chmn.; Nunn (GA), Levin (MI), Harkin (IA), Kerry (MA), Lieberman (CT), Wellstone (MN), Wofford (PA), Heflin (AL), Lautenberg (NJ), Kohl (WI), Moseley-Braun (IL).
Minority (10 R): Pressler (SD), Wallop (WY), Bond (MO), Burns (MT), Mack (FL), Coverdell (GA), Kempthorne (ID), Bennett (UT), Chafee (RI), Hutchison (TX).

SUBCOMMITTEES

COMPETITIVENESS, CAPITAL FORMATION AND ECONOMIC OPPORTUNITY

Majority (3 D): Lieberman, Chmn.; Harkin, Lautenberg.
Minority (2 R): Mack, Bond.

EXPORT EXPANSION AND AGRICULTURAL DEVELOPMENT

Majority (5 D): Wofford, Chmn.; Harkin, Bumpers, Lautenberg, Moseley-Braun.
Minority (4 R): Coverdell, Pressler, Bennett, Chafee.

GOVERNMENT CONTRACTING AND PAPERWORK REDUCTION
Majority (4 D): Nunn, Chmn.; Lieberman, Harkin, Kohl.
Minority (2 R): Bond, Wallop.

INNOVATION, MANUFACTURING AND TECHNOLOGY
Majority (4 D): Levin, Chmn.; Kerry, Bumpers, Heflin.
Minority (3 R): Burns, Kempthorne, Bennett.

RURAL ECONOMY AND FAMILY FARMING
Majority (6 D): Wellstone, Chmn.; Nunn, Levin, Bumpers, Heflin, Kohl.
Minority (5 R): Pressler, Wallop, Burns, Coverdell, Kempthorne.

URBAN AND MINORITY-OWNED BUSINESS DEVELOPMENT
Majority (5 D): Kerry, Chmn.; Nunn, Wellstone, Wofford, Moseley-Braun.
Minority (3 R): Chafee, Mack, Pressler.

VETERANS' AFFAIRS   414 Russell, 202-224-9126

Majority (7 D): Rockefeller (WV), Chmn.; DeConcini (AZ), Mitchell (ME), Graham (FL), Akaka (HI), Daschle (SD), Campbell (CO).
Minority (5 R): Murkowski (AK), Thurmond (SC), Simpson (WY), Specter (PA), Jeffords (VT).

NO SUBCOMMITTEES

HOUSE COMMITTEES

This committee section includes all Standing and Select committees of the U.S. House in alphabetical order.

AGRICULTURE   1301 Longworth, 202-225-2171

Majority (29 D): de la Garza (TX), Chmn.; Brown (CA), Rose (NC), English (OK), Glickman (KS), Stenholm (TX), Volkmer (MO), Penny (MN), Johnson (SD), Sarpalius (TX), Long (IN), Condit (CA), Peterson (MN), Dooley (CA), Clayton (NC), Minge (MN), Hilliard (AL), Inslee (WA), Barlow (KY), Pomeroy (ND), Holden (PA), McKinney (GA), Baesler (KY), Thurman (FL), Bishop (GA), Thompson (MS), Williams (MT), Lambert (AR), Farr (CA).
Minority (19 R): Roberts (KS), Emerson (MO), Gunderson (WI), Lewis (FL), Smith (OR), Combest (TX), Allard (CO), Barrett (NE), Nussle (IA), Boehner (OH), Ewing (IL), Doolittle (CA), Kingston (GA), Goodlatte (VA), Dickey (AR), Pombo (CA), Canady (FL), Smith (MI), Everett (AL).

SUBCOMMITTEES

DEPARTMENT OPERATIONS AND NUTRITION

Majority (14 D): Stenholm, Chmn.; Brown, Sarpalius, Dooley, Inslee, English, Glickman, McKinney, Bishop, Volkmer, Clayton, Holden, Rose, Lambert.
Minority (8 R): Smith (OR), Emerson, Gunderson, Allard, Barrett, Ewing, Kingston, Canady.

ENVIRONMENT, CREDIT AND RURAL DEVELOPMENT

Majority (16 D): English, Chmn.; Johnson, Long, Clayton, Minge, Barlow, Pomeroy, Holden, McKinney, Thurman, Penny, Sarpalius, Peterson, Hilliard, Inslee, Baesler.
Minority (9 R): Combest, Gunderson, Allard, Barrett, Nussle, Ewing, Dickey, Pombo, Smith (MI).

FOREIGN AGRICULTURE AND HUNGER

Majority (8 D): Penny, Chmn.; Rose, Barlow, McKinney, Baesler, Thurman, Pomeroy, Stenholm.
Minority (5 R): Allard, Lewis, Doolittle, Canady, Everett.

GENERAL FARM COMMODITIES

Majority (17 D): Johnson, Chmn.; Glickman, Peterson, Volkmer, Long, Dooley, Minge, Pomeroy, Rose, English, Stenholm, Sarpalius, Condit, Barlow, Bishop, Williams, Thompson.
Minority (10 R): Emerson, Smith (OR), Combest, Barrett, Nussle, Boehner, Ewing, Doolittle, Dickey, Smith (MI).

LIVESTOCK

Majority (10 D): Volkmer, Chmn.; Condit, Hilliard, Stenholm, Holden, Long, Peterson, Rose, Dooley, Thurman.
Minority (6 R): Gunderson, Lewis, Smith (OR), Boehner, Goodlatte, Pombo.

SPECIALTY CROPS AND NATURAL RESOURCES

Majority (13 D): Rose, Chmn.; Baesler, Bishop, Brown, Condit, Clayton, Thurman, Minge, Inslee, Pomeroy, English, Stenholm, Peterson.
Minority (8 R): Lewis, Emerson, Doolittle, Kingston, Goodlatte, Dickey, Pombo, Everett.

APPROPRIATIONS　　　　　　H-218 The Capitol, 202-225-2771

Majority (37 D): Natcher (KY), Chmn.; Whitten (MS), Vice Chmn.; Smith (IA), Yates (IL), Obey (WI), Stokes (OH), Bevill (AL), Murtha (PA), Wilson (TX), Dicks (WA), Sabo (MN), Dixon (CA), Fazio (CA), Hefner (NC), Hoyer (MD), Carr (MI), Durbin (IL), Coleman (TX), Mollohan (WV), Chapman (TX), Kaptur (OH), Skaggs (CO), Price (NC), Pelosi (CA), Visclosky (IN), Foglietta (PA), Torres (CA), Darden (GA), Lowey (NY), Thornton (AR), Serrano (NY), DeLauro (CT), Moran (VA), Peterson (FL), Olver (MA), Pastor (AZ), Meek (FL).
Minority (23 R): McDade (PA), Myers (IN), Young (FL), Regula (OH), Livingston (LA), Lewis (CA), Porter (IL), Rogers (KY), Skeen (NM), Wolf (VA), DeLay (TX), Kolbe (AZ), Gallo (NJ), Vucanovich (NV), Lightfoot (IA), Packard (CA), Callahan (AL), Bentley (MD), Walsh (NY), Taylor (NC), Hobson (OH), Istook (OK), Bonilla (TX).

SUBCOMMITTEES

AGRICULTURE, RURAL DEVELOPMENT, FOOD AND DRUG ADMINISTRATION AND RELATED AGENCIES

Majority (9 D): Durbin, Chmn.; Whitten, Natcher, Kaptur, Thornton, DeLauro, Peterson, Pastor, Smith.
Minority (4 R): Skeen, Myers, Vucanovich, Walsh.

COMMERCE, JUSTICE, STATE AND JUDICIARY

Majority (7 D): Smith, Chmn.; Carr, Mollohan, Natcher, Moran, Skaggs, Price.
Minority (3 R): Rogers, Kolbe, Taylor.

DEFENSE

Majority (9 D): Murtha, Chmn.; Dicks, Wilson, Hefner, Sabo, Dixon, Natcher, Visclosky, Darden.
Minority (5 R): McDade, Young, Livingston, Lewis, Skeen.

DISTRICT OF COLUMBIA

Majority (7 D): Dixon, Chmn.; Natcher, Stokes, Durbin, Kaptur, Skaggs, Pelosi.
Minority (3 R): Walsh, Istook, Bonilla.

ENERGY AND WATER DEVELOPMENT

Majority (7 D): Bevill, Chmn.; Fazio, Chapman, Natcher, Peterson, Pastor, Meek.
Minority (3 R): Myers, Gallo, Rogers.

FOREIGN OPERATIONS, EXPORT FINANCING AND RELATED PROGRAMS

Majority (9 D): Obey, Chmn.; Yates, Wilson, Natcher, Olver, Pelosi, Torres, Lowey, Serrano.
Minority (4 R): Livingston, Porter, Lightfoot, Callahan.

INTERIOR

Majority (7 D): Yates, Chmn.; Murtha, Dicks, Bevill, Natcher, Skaggs, Coleman.
Minority (4 R): Regula, McDade, Kolbe, Packard.

LABOR, HEALTH AND HUMAN SERVICES, AND EDUCATION

Majority (9 D): Natcher, Chmn.; Smith, Obey, Stokes, Hoyer, Pelosi, Lowey, Serrano, DeLauro.
Minority (4 R): Porter, Young, Bentley, Bonilla.

LEGISLATIVE

Majority (7 D): Fazio, Chmn.; Moran, Obey, Murtha, Natcher, Carr, Chapman.
Minority (3 R): Young, Packard, Taylor.

MILITARY CONSTRUCTION

Majority (9 D): Hefner, Chmn.; Foglietta, Meek, Dicks, Dixon, Fazio, Hoyer, Natcher, Coleman.
Minority (4 R): Vucanovich, Callahan, Bentley, Hobson.

TRANSPORTATION

Majority (7 D): Carr, Chmn.; Durbin, Sabo, Price, Coleman, Natcher, Foglietta.
Minority (3 R): Wolf, DeLay, Regula.

TREASURY, POSTAL SERVICE, AND GENERAL GOVERNMENT

Majority (7 D): Hoyer, Chmn.; Visclosky, Natcher, Darden, Olver, Bevill, Sabo.
Minority (3 R): Lightfoot, Wolf, Istook.

VA, HUD, AND INDEPENDENT AGENCIES

Majority (7 D): Stokes, Chmn.; Mollohan, Chapman, Kaptur, Natcher, Torres, Thornton.
Minority (3 R): Lewis, DeLay, Gallo.

ARMED SERVICES   2120 Rayburn, 202-225-4151

Majority (34 D): Dellums (CA), Chmn.; Montgomery (MS), Schroeder (CO), Hutto (FL),
Skelton (MO), McCurdy (OK), Lloyd (TN), Sisisky (VA), Spratt (SC), McCloskey (IN),
Ortiz (TX), Hochbrueckner (NY), Pickett (VA), Lancaster (NC), Evans (IL), Bilbray (NV),
Tanner (TN), Browder (AL), Taylor (MS), Abercrombie (HI), Andrews (ME), Edwards
(TX), Johnson (GA), Tejeda (TX), Mann (OH), Stupak (MI), Meehan (MA), Underwood
(GU), Harman (CA), McHale (PA), Holden (PA), Geren (TX), Furse (OR), one vacancy.
Minority (22 R): Spence (SC), Stump (AZ), Hunter (CA), Kasich (OH), Bateman (VA),
Hansen (UT), Weldon (PA), Kyl (AZ), Ravenel (SC), Dornan (CA), Hefley (CO), Machtley
(RI), Saxton (NJ), Cunningham (CA), Inhofe (OK), Buyer (IN), Torkildsen (MA), Fowler
(FL), McHugh (NY), Talent (MO), Everett (AL), Bartlett (MD).

SUBCOMMITTEES

MILITARY ACQUISITION

Majority (15 D): Dellums, Chmn.; Lloyd, Spratt, McCloskey, Evans, Tanner, Taylor, Aber-
crombie, Andrews, Mann, Stupak, McHale, Holden, Geren, Sisisky.
Minority (10 R): Spence, Bateman, Weldon, Ravenel, Dornan, Hefley, Machtley, Saxton,
Cunningham, Inhofe.

MILITARY FORCES AND PERSONNEL

Majority (11 D): Skelton, Chmn.; Montgomery, Pickett, Lancaster, Bilbray, Stupak, Meehan,
Underwood, Harman, two vacancies.
Minority (6 R): Kyl, Ravenel, Buyer, Fowler, Talent, Bartlett.

MILITARY INSTALLATIONS AND FACILITIES

Majority (13 D): McCurdy, Chmn.; Montgomery, McCloskey, Ortiz, Hochbrueckner, Bilbray,
Browder, Taylor, Abercrombie, Edwards, Johnson, Tejeda, Underwood.
Minority (8 R): Hunter, Fowler, McHugh, Everett, Stump, Machtley, Saxton, Torkildsen.

OVERSIGHT AND INVESTIGATIONS

Majority (10 D): Sisisky, Chmn.; Spratt, Tanner, Browder, Edwards, Johnson, Tejeda, Mann,
Harman, Holden.
Minority (6 R): Hansen, Kyl, Hefley, McHugh, Everett, Dornan.

READINESS

Majority (10 D): Hutto, Chmn.; Ortiz, Pickett, Lancaster, Evans, Browder, Meehan, Underwood, McHale, McCurdy.
Minority (6 R): Kasich, Bateman, Weldon, Dornan, Cunningham, Inhofe.

RESEARCH AND TECHNOLOGY

Majority (13 D): Schroeder, Chmn.; Hochbrueckner, Pickett, Lancaster, Bilbray, Edwards,
Johnson, Tejeda, Meehan, Harman, Furse, Hutto, McCurdy.
Minority (8 R): Stump, Buyer, Torkildsen, Talent, Bartlett, Hunter, Kasich, Hansen.

BANKING, FINANCE AND URBAN AFFAIRS

2129 Rayburn
202-225-4247

Majority (30 D): Gonzalez (TX), Chmn.; Neal (NC), LaFalce (NY), Vento (MN), Schumer (NY), Frank (MA), Kanjorski (PA), Kennedy (MA), Flake (NY), Mfume (MD), Waters (CA), LaRocco (ID), Orton (UT), Bacchus (FL), Klein (NJ), Maloney (NY), Deutsch (FL), Gutierrez (IL), Rush (IL), Roybal-Allard (CA), Barrett (WI), Furse (OR), Velazquez (NY), Wynn (MD), Fields (LA), Watt (NC), Hinchey (NY), Dooley (CA), Klink (PA), Fingerhut (OH).

Minority (20 R): Leach (IA), McCollum (FL), Roukema (NJ), Bereuter (NE), Ridge (PA), Roth (WI), McCandless (CA), Baker (LA), Nussle (IA), Thomas (WY), Johnson (TX), Pryce (OH), Linder (GA), Knollenberg (MI), Lazio (NY), Grams (MN), Bachus (AL), Huffington (CA), Castle, (DE), King, (NY).

Independent (1): Sanders (VT).

SUBCOMMITTEES

CONSUMER CREDIT AND INSURANCE

Majority (18 D): Kennedy, Chmn.; Gonzalez, LaRocco, Gutierrez, Rush, Roybal-Allard, Barrett, Furse, Velazquez, Wynn, Fields, Watt, Hinchey, Kanjorski, Flake, Waters, Maloney, Deutsch.

Minority (12 R): McCandless, Castle, King, Pryce, Linder, Knollenberg, Bereuter, Thomas, Lazio, Grams, Bachus, Baker.

Independent (1): Sanders (VT).

ECONOMIC GROWTH AND CREDIT FORMATION

Majority (9 D): Kanjorski, Chmn.; Neal, LaFalce, Orton, Klein, Velazquez, Dooley, Klink, Fingerhut.

Minority (6 R): Ridge, McCollum, Roth, Nussle, Roukema, King.

FINANCIAL INSTITUTIONS SUPERVISION, REGULATION AND DEPOSIT INSURANCE

Majority (18 D): Neal, Chmn.; LaFalce, Vento, Schumer, Frank, Kanjorski, Kennedy, Flake, Mfume, LaRocco, Orton, Bacchus, Waters, Klein, Maloney, Deutsch, Barrett, Hinchey.

Minority (12 R): McCollum, Leach, Baker, Nussle, Thomas, Johnson, Pryce, Linder, Lazio, Grams, Bachus, Huffington.

GENERAL OVERSIGHT, INVESTIGATIONS, AND THE RESOLUTION OF FAILED FINANCIAL INSTITUTIONS

Majority (4 D): Flake, Chmn.; Neal, Velazquez, Hinchey.

Minority (2 R): Roth, Ridge.

HOUSING AND COMMUNITY DEVELOPMENT

Majority (18 D): Gonzalez, Chmn.; Vento, Schumer, Mfume, LaFalce, Waters, Klein, Maloney, Deutsch, Gutierrez, Rush, Roybal-Allard, Barrett, Furse, Velazquez, Wynn, Fields, Watt.

Minority (12 R): Roukema, Bereuter, Ridge, Baker, Thomas, Johnson, Knollenberg, Lazio, Grams, Bachus, Castle, Pryce.

Independent (1): Sanders (VT).

INTERNATIONAL DEVELOPMENT, FINANCE, TRADE AND MONETARY POLICY

Majority (15 D): Frank, Chmn.; Neal, LaFalce, Kennedy, Waters, LaRocco, Orton, Bacchus, Gonzalez, Kanjorski, Rush, Furse, Fields, Watt, Fingerhut.

Minority (10 R): Bereuter, McCandless, McCollum, Roukema, Johnson, Huffington, King, Baker, Nussle, Castle.

Independent (1): Sanders (VT).

BUDGET   214 O'Neill, 202-226-7200

Majority (26 D): Sabo (NM), Chmn.; Gephardt (MO), Kildee (MI), Beilenson (CA), Berman (CA), Wise (WV), Bryant (TX), Stenholm (TX), Frank (MA), Cooper (TN), Slaughter (NY), Parker (MS), Coyne (PA), Kennelly (CT), Andrews (TX), Mollohan (WV), Gordon (TN), Price (NC), Costello (IL), Johnston (FL), Mink (HI), Orton (UT), Blackwell (PA), Pomeroy (ND), Browder (AL), Woolsey (CA).

Minority (17 R): Kasich (OH), McMillan (NC), Kolbe (AZ), Shays (CT), Snowe (ME), Herger (CA), Bunning (KY), Smith (TX), Cox (CA), Allard (CO), Hobson (OH), Miller (FL), Lazio (NY), Franks (NJ), Smith (MI), Inglis (SC), Hoke (OH).

NO SUBCOMMITTEES

DISTRICT OF COLUMBIA   1310 Longworth, 202-225-4457

Majority (8 D): Stark (CA) Chmn.; Dellums (CA) Vice Chmn., Wheat (MO), McDermott (WA), Norton (DC), Lewis (GA), Jefferson (LA), one vacancy.

Minority (4 R): Bliley (VA), Rohrabacher (CA), Saxton (NJ), Ballenger (NC).

SUBCOMMITTEES

FISCAL AFFAIRS AND HEALTH

Majority (5 D): McDermott, Chmn.; Dellums, Jefferson, Wheat, Norton.
Minority (2 R): Ballenger, Saxton.

GOVERNMENT OPERATIONS AND METROPOLITAN AFFAIRS

Majority (4 D): Wheat, Chmn.; Stark, Lewis, Jefferson.
Minority (2 R): Saxton, Rohrabacher.

JUDICIARY AND EDUCATION

Majority (5 D): Norton, Chmn.; Lewis, Stark, Dellums, McDermott.
Minority (2 R): Rohrabacher, Ballenger.

EDUCATION AND LABOR   2181 Rayburn, 202-225-4527

Majority (28 D): Ford (MI), Chmn.; Clay (MO), Miller (CA), Murphy (PA), Kildee (MI), Williams (MT), Martinez (CA), Owens (NY), Sawyer (OH), Payne (NJ), Unsoeld (WA), Mink (HI), Andrews (NJ), Reed (RI), Roemer (IN), Engel (NY), Becerra (CA), Scott (VA), Green (TX), Woolsey (CA), Romero-Barcelo (PR), Klink (PA), English (AZ), Strickland (OH), de Lugo (VI), Faleomavaega (AS), Baesler (KY), Underwood (GU).

Minority (15 R): Goodling (PA), Petri (WI), Roukema (NJ), Gunderson (WI), Armey (TX), Fawell (IL), Henry (MI), Ballenger (NC), Molinari (NY), Barrett (NE), Boehner (OH), Cunningham (CA), Hoekstra (MI), McKeon (CA), Miller (FL).

SUBCOMMITTEES

ELEMENTARY, SECONDARY AND VOCATIONAL EDUCATION

Majority (16 D): Kildee, Chmn.; Miller (CA), Sawyer, Owens, Unsoeld, Reed, Roemer, Mink, Engel, Becerra, Green, Woolsey, English, Strickland, Payne, Romero-Barcelo.
Minority (9 R): Goodling, Gunderson, McKeon, Petri, Molinari, Cunningham, Miller (FL), Roukema, Boehner.

HUMAN RESOURCES

Majority (8 D): Martinez, Chmn.; Kildee, Andrews, Scott, Woolsey, Romero-Barcelo, Owens, Baesler.
Minority (4 R): Henry, Molinari, Barrett, Miller (FL).

LABOR–MANAGEMENT RELATIONS

Majority (16 D): Williams, Chmn.; Clay, Kildee, Miller (CA), Owens, Martinez, Payne, Unsoeld, Mink, Klink, Murphy, Engel, Becerra, Green, Woolsey, Romero-Barcelo.
Minority (9 R): Roukema, Gunderson, Armey, Barrett, Boehner, Fawell, Ballenger, Hoekstra, McKeon.

LABOR STANDARDS, OCCUPATIONAL HEALTH AND SAFETY

Majority (6 D): Murphy, Chmn.; Clay, Andrews, Miller (CA), Strickland, Faleomavaega.
Minority (3 R): Fawell, Ballenger, Hoekstra.

POSTSECONDARY EDUCATION AND TRAINING

Majority (15 D): Ford, Chmn.; Williams, Sawyer, Unsoeld, Mink, Andrews, Reed, Roemer, Kildee, Scott, Klink, English, Strickland, Becerra, Green.
Minority (9 R): Petri, Gunderson, Cunningham, Miller (FL), Roukema, Henry, Hoekstra, McKeon, Armey.

SELECT EDUCATION AND CIVIL RIGHTS

Majority (6 D): Owens, Chmn.; Payne, Scott, Sawyer, two vacancies.
Minority (3 R): Ballenger, Barrett, Fawell.

ENERGY AND COMMERCE   2125 Rayburn, 202-225-2927

Majority (27 D): Dingell (MI), Chmn.; Waxman (CA), Sharp (IN), Markey (MA), Swift (WA), Collins (IL), Synar (OK), Tauzin (LA), Wyden (OR), Hall (TX), Richardson (NM), Slattery (KS), Bryant (TX), Boucher (VA), Cooper (TN), Rowland (GA), Manton (NY), Towns (NY), Studds (MA), Lehman (CA), Pallone (NJ), Washington (TX), Schenk (CA), Brown (OH), Kreidler (WA), Margolies-Mezvinsky (PA), Lambert (AR).
Minority (17 R): Moorhead (CA), Bliley (VA), Fields (TX), Oxley (OH), Bilirakis (FL), Schaefer (CO), Barton (TX), McMillan (NC), Hastert (IL), Upton (MI), Stearns (FL), Paxon (NY), Gillmor (OH), Klug (WI), Franks (CT), Greenwood (PA), Crapo (ID).

SUBCOMMITTEES

COMMERCE, CONSUMER PROTECTION AND COMPETITIVENESS

Majority (7 D): Collins, Chmn.; Towns, Slattery, Rowland, Manton, Lehman, Pallone.
Minority (4 R): Stearns, McMillan, Paxon, Greenwood.

ENERGY AND POWER

Majority (12 D): Sharp, Chmn.; Markey, Lehman, Washington, Kreidler, Lambert, Swift, Synar, Tauzin, Hall, Boucher, Cooper.
Minority (7 R): Bilirakis, Barton, Hastert, Stearns, Klug, Franks, Crapo.

HEALTH AND THE ENVIRONMENT

Majority (15 D): Waxman, Chmn.; Synar, Wyden, Hall, Richardson, Bryant, Rowland, Towns, Studds, Slattery, Cooper, Pallone, Washington, Brown, Kreidler.
Minority (9 R): Bliley, Bilirakis, McMillan, Hastert, Upton, Paxon, Klug, Franks, Greenwood.

OVERSIGHT AND INVESTIGATIONS

Majority (7 D): Dingell, Chmn.; Brown, Margolies-Mesvinsky, Waxman, Collins, Wyden, Bryant.
Minority (4 R): Schaefer, Moorhead, Upton, Gillmor.

TELECOMMUNICATIONS AND FINANCE

Majority (14 D): Markey, Chmn.; Tauzin, Boucher, Manton, Lehman, Schenk, Margolies-Mezvinsky, Synar, Wyden, Hall, Richardson, Slattery, Bryant, Cooper.
Minority (8 R): Fields, Bliley, Oxley, Schaefer, Barton, McMillan, Hastert, Gillmor.

TRANSPORTATION AND HAZARDOUS MATERIALS

Majority (12 D): Swift, Chmn.; Lambert, Tauzin, Boucher, Rowland, Manton, Studds, Pallone, Schenk, Sharp, Markey, Richardson.
Minority (7 R): Oxley, Fields, Schaefer, Upton, Paxon, Gillmor, Crapo.

FOREIGN AFFAIRS   2170 Rayburn, 202-225-5021

Majority (27 D): Hamilton (IN), Chmn.; Gejdenson (CT), Lantos (CA), Torricelli (NJ), Berman (CA), Ackerman (NY), Johnston (FL), Engel (NY), Faleomavaega (AS), Oberstar (MN), Schumer (NY), Martinez (CA), Borski (PA), Payne, (NJ), Andrews (NJ), Menendez (NJ), Brown (OH) McKinney (GA), Cantwell, (WA), Hastings, (FL), Fingerhut (OH), Deutsch (FL), Wynn (MD), Edwards (CA), McCloskey (IN), Sawyer (OH), one vacancy.
Minority (18 R): Gilman (NY), Goodling (PA), Leach (IA), Roth (WI), Snowe (ME), Hyde (IL), Bereuter (NE), Smith (NJ), Burton (IN), Meyers (KS), Gallegly (CA), Ros-Lehtinen (FL), Ballenger (NC), Rohrabacher (CA), Levy (NY), Diaz-Balart (FL), Manzullo (IL), Royce (CA).

SUBCOMMITTEES

AFRICA

Majority (6 D): Johnston, Chmn.; Payne, Hastings, Torricelli, Edwards, Engel.
Minority (4 R): Burton, Diaz-Balart, Royce, one vacancy.

ASIA AND THE PACIFIC

Majority (6 D): Ackerman, Chmn.; Faleomavaega, Martinez, Torricelli, Brown, Fingerhut.
Minority (4 R): Leach, Rohrabacher, Royce, Roth.

ECONOMIC POLICY, TRADE AND ENVIRONMENT

Majority (9 D): Gejdenson, Chmn.; Oberstar, McKinney, Cantwell, Fingerhut, Wynn, Johnston, Engel, Schumer.
Minority (5 R): Roth, Manzullo, Bereuter, Meyers, Ballenger, Rohrbacher.

EUROPE AND THE MIDDLE EAST

Majority (9 D): Hamilton, Chmn.; Engel, Schumer, Borski, Andrews, Brown, Hastings, Deutsch, Lantos.
Minority (6 R): Gilman, Goodling, Meyers, Gallegly, Levy, Leach.

INTERNATIONAL OPERATIONS

Majority (8 D): Berman, Chmn.; Faleomavaega, Martinez, Andrews, Menendez, Lantos, Johnston, Edwards.
Minority (5 R): Snowe, Hyde, Diaz-Balart, Levy, Manzullo.

INTERNATIONAL SECURITY, INTERNATIONAL ORGANIZATIONS AND HUMAN RIGHTS

Majority (6 D): Lantos, Chmn.; Berman, Ackerman, Martinez, McCloskey, Sawyer.
Minority (4 R): Bereuter, Snowe, Smith, Burton.

WESTERN HEMISPHERE AFFAIRS

Majority (6 D): Torricelli, Chmn.; Menendez, Oberstar, McKinney, Deutsch, Wynn.
Minority (4 R): Smith, Ros-Lehtinen, Ballenger, Gallegly.

GOVERNMENT OPERATIONS   2157 Rayburn, 202-225-5051

Majority (25 D): Conyers (MI), Chmn.; Collins (IL), English (OK), Waxman (CA), Synar (OK), Neal (NC), Lantos (CA), Owens (NY), Towns (NY), Spratt (SC), Condit (CA), Peterson (MN), Thurman (FL), Rush (IL), Maloney (NY), Barrett (WI), Payne (NJ), Flake (NY), Hayes (LA), Washington (TX), Collins (MI), Brown (FL), Margolies-Mezvinsky (PA), Woolsey (CA), one vacancy.
Minority (17 R): Clinger (PA), McCandless (CA), Hastert (IL), Kyl (AZ), Shays (CT), Schiff (NM), Cox (CA), Thomas (WY), Ros-Lehtinen (FL), Machtley (RI), Zimmer (NJ), Zeliff (NH), McHugh (NY), Horn (CA), Pryce (OH), Mica (FL), Portman (OH).
Independent (1): Sanders (VT).

SUBCOMMITTEES

COMMERCE, CONSUMER, AND MONETARY AFFAIRS

Majority (5 D): Spratt, Chmn.; Rush, Margolies-Mezvinsky, Collins (MI), one vacancy.
Minority (3 R): Cox, Shays, Zeliff.

EMPLOYMENT, HOUSING AND AVIATION

Majority (6 D): Peterson, Chmn.; Lantos, Rush, Flake, Thurman, Collins (MI).
Minority (3 R): Machtley, Shays, McHugh.

ENVIRONMENT, ENERGY AND NATURAL RESOURCES

Majority (6 D): Synar, Chmn.; Thurman, Maloney, Hayes, Washington, Towns.
Minority (4 R): Hastert, McHugh, Pryce, Mica.
Independent (1): Sanders (VT).

HUMAN RESOURCES AND INTERGOVERNMENTAL RELATIONS

Majority (5 D): Towns, Chmn.; Waxman, Barrett, Payne, Washington.
Minority (3 R): Schiff, Horn, Mica.
Independent (1): Sanders (VT).

INFORMATION, JUSTICE, TRANSPORTATION AND AGRICULTURE

Majority (5 D): Condit, Chmn.; Owens, Thurman, Woolsey, one vacancy.
Minority (3 R): Thomas, Ros-Lehtinen, Horn.

LEGISLATION AND NATIONAL SECURITY

Majority (7 D): Conyers, Chmn.; Collins (IL), English, Neal, Maloney, Lantos, Brown.
Minority (4 R): McCandless, Clinger, Kyl, Zimmer.

HOUSE ADMINISTRATION   H-326 The Capitol, 202-225-2061

Majority (12 D): Rose (NC), Chmn.; Swift (WA), Clay (MO), Gejdenson (CT), Frost (TX), Manton (NY), Hoyer (MD), Kleczka (WI), Kildee (MI), Derrick (SC), Kennelly (CT), Cardin (MD).
Minority (7 R): Thomas (CA), Gingrich (GA), Roberts (KS), Livingston (LA), Barrett (NE), Boehner (OH), Dunn (WA).

SUBCOMMITTEES

ACCOUNTS

Majority (7 D): Frost, Chmn.; Swift, Gejdenson, Hoyer, Kildee, Kennelly, Cardin.
Minority (4 R): Roberts, Gingrich, Boehner, Dunn.

ADMINISTRATIVE OVERSIGHT

Majority (2 D): Rose, Chmn.; Clay.
Minority (2 R): Thomas, Barrett.

ELECTIONS

Majority (5 D): Swift, Chmn.; Frost, Hoyer, Kleczka, Cardin.
Minority (3 R): Livingston, Roberts, Dunn.

LIBRARIES AND MEMORIALS

Majority (4 D): Clay, Chmn.; Frost, Derrick, Kennelly.
Minority (2 R): Barrett, Roberts.

OFFICE SYSTEMS

Majority (4 D): Gejdenson, Chmn.; Frost, Kleczka, Kennelly.
Minority (2 R): Boehner, Barrett.

PERSONNEL AND POLICE

Majority (4 D): Manton, Chmn.; Clay, Kleczka, Derrick.
Minority (2 R): Dunn, Livingston.

INTELLIGENCE (Permanent Select)   H-405 The Capitol, 202-225-4121

Majority (12 D): Glickman (KS), Chmn.; Richardson (NM), Dicks (WA), Dixon (CA), Torricelli (NJ), Coleman (TX), Skaggs (CO), Bilbray (NV), Pelosi (CA), Laughlin (TX), Cramer (AL), Reed (RI).
Minority (7 R): Combest (TX), Bereuter (NE), Dornan (CA), Young (FL), Gekas (PA), Hansen (UT), Lewis (CA).

SUBCOMMITTEES

LEGISLATION

Majority (6 D): Coleman, Chmn.; Dicks, Bilbray, Pelosi, Laughlin, Cramer.
Minority (3 R): Gekas, Hansen, Lewis.

OVERSIGHT AND EVALUATION

Majority (6 D): Dicks, Chmn.; Pelosi, Reed, Torricelli, Coleman, Skaggs.
Minority (3 R): Young, Hansen, Bereuter.

PROGRAM AND BUDGET AUTHORIZATION

Majority (8 D): Glickman, Chmn.; Richardson, Dixon, Torricelli, Skaggs, Bilbray, Laughlin, Cramer.
Minority (4 R): Combest, Bereuter, Dornan, Lewis.

JUDICIARY   2138 Rayburn, 202-225-3951

Majority (21 D): Brooks (TX), Chmn.; Edwards (CA), Conyers (MI), Mazzoli (KY), Hughes (NJ), Synar (OK), Schroeder (CO), Glickman (KS), Frank (MA), Schumer (NY), Berman (CA), Boucher (VA), Bryant (TX), Sangmeister (IL), Washington (TX), Reed (RI), Nadler (NY), Scott (VA), Mann (OH), Watt (NC), Becerra (CA).
Minority (14 R): Fish (NY), Moorhead (CA), Hyde (IL), Sensenbrenner (WI), McCollum (FL), Gekas (PA), Coble (NC), Smith (TX), Schiff (NM), Ramstad (MN), Gallegly (CA), Canady (FL), Inglis (SC), Goodlatte (VA).

SUBCOMMITTEES

ADMINISTRATIVE LAW AND GOVERNMENTAL RELATIONS

Majority (6 D): Bryant, Chmn.; Glickman, Frank, Berman, Mann, Watt.
Minority (4 R): Gekas, Ramstad, Inglis, Goodlatte.

CIVIL AND CONSTITUTIONAL RIGHTS

Majority (5 D): Edwards, Chmn.; Schroeder, Frank, Washington, Nadler.
Minority (3 R): Hyde, Coble, Canady.

CRIME AND CRIMINAL JUSTICE

Majority (8 D): Schumer, Chmn.; Edwards, Conyers, Mazzoli, Glickman, Sangmeister, Washington, Mann.
Minority (5 R): Sensenbrenner, Smith, Schiff, Ramstad, Gekas.

ECONOMIC AND COMMERCIAL LAW

Majority (10 D): Brooks, Chmn.; Conyers, Synar, Schroeder, Glickman, Berman, Boucher, Scott, Mann, Watt.
Minority (6 R): Fish, Gallegly, Canady, Inglis, Goodlatte, Moorhead.

INTELLECTUAL PROPERTY AND JUDICIAL ADMINISTRATION

Majority (9 D): Hughes, Chmn.; Edwards, Conyers, Mazzoli, Synar, Frank, Berman, Reed, Becerra.
Minority (6 R): Moorhead, Coble, Fish, Sensenbrenner, McCollum, Schiff.

INTERNATIONAL LAW, IMMIGRATION AND REFUGEES

Majority (6 D): Mazzoli, Chmn.; Schumer, Bryant, Sangmeister, Nadler, Becerra.
Minority (4 R): McCollum, Smith, Gallegly, Canady.

MERCHANT MARINE AND FISHERIES   1334 Longworth, 202-225-4047

Majority (29 D): Studds (MA), Chmn.; Hughes (NJ), Hutto (FL), Tauzin (LA), Lipinski (IL), Ortiz (TX), Manton (NY), Pickett (VA), Hochbrueckner (NY), Pallone (NJ), Laughlin (TX), Unsoeld (WA), Taylor (MS), Reed (RI), Lancaster (NC), Andrews (ME), Furse (OR), Schenk (CA), Green (TX), Hastings (FL), Hamburg (CA), Lambert (AR), Eshoo (CA), Barlow (KY), Stupak (MI), Thompson (MS), Cantwell (CA), Deutsch (FL), Ackerman (NY).

Minority (19 R): Fields (TX), Young (AK), Bateman (VA), Saxton (NJ), Coble (NC), Weldon (PA), Inhofe (OK), Ravenel (SC), Gilchrest (MD), Cunningham (CA), Kingston (GA), Fowler (FL), Castle (DE), King (NY), Diaz-Balart (FL), Pombo (CA), Bentley (MD), Taylor (NC), Torkildsen (MA).

SUBCOMMITTEES

COAST GUARD AND NAVIGATION

Majority (15 D): Tauzin, Chmn.; Hughes, Hutto, Lancaster, Barlow, Stupak, Lipinski, Pickett, Hockbruechner, Pallone, Laughlin, Schenk, Hastings, Lambert, Taylor (MS).
Minority (9 R): Coble, Bateman, Gilchrest, Fowler, Castle, King, Diaz-Balart, Inhofe, Pombo.

ENVIRONMENT AND NATURAL RESOURCES

Majority (14 D): Studds, Chmn.; Hockbrueckner, Pallone, Laughlin, Unsoeld, Reed, Furse, Hamburg, Lambert, Eshoo, Hutto, Tauzin, Ortiz, Thompson.
Minority (8 R): Saxton, Young, Weldon, Ravenel, Gilchrest, Cunningham, Castle, Taylor (NC).

FISHERIES MANAGEMENT

Majority (8 D): Manton, Chmn.; Hughes, Unsoeld, Taylor (MS), Lancaster, Hamburg, Cantwell, Hutto.
Minority (4 R): Young, Coble, Ravenel, Kingston.

MERCHANT MARINE

Majority (13 D): Lipinski, Chmn.; Pickett, Taylor (MS), Andrews, Schenk, Green, Hastings, Reed, Furse, Stupak, Manton, Ackerman, Thompson.
Minority (8 R): Bateman, Inhofe, Cunningham, Kingston, Fowler, King, Diaz-Balart, Bentley.

OCEANOGRAPHY, GULF OF MEXICO AND THE OUTER CONTINENTAL SHELF

Majority (5 D): Ortiz, Chmn.; Green, Eshoo, Laughlin, Schenk.
Minority (2 R): Weldon, Saxton.

NATURAL RESOURCES   1324 Longworth, 202-225-2761

Majority (28 D): Miller (CA), Chmn.: Sharp (IN), Markey (MA), Murphy (PA), Rahall (WV), Vento (MN), Williams (MT), de Lugo (VI), Gejdenson (CT), Lehman (CA), Richardson (NM), DeFazio (OR), Faleomavaega (AS), Johnson (SD), LaRocco (ID), Abercrombie (HI), Dooley (CA), Romero-Barcelo (PR), English (AZ), Shepherd (UT), Deal (GA), Hinchey (NY), Underwood (GU), Mink (HI), Evans (IL), Barlow (KY), Barrett (WI), Farr (CA).

Minority (15 R): Young (AK), Hansen (UT), Vucanovich (NV), Gallegly (CA), Smith (OR), Thomas (WY), Duncan (TN), Hefley (CO), Doolittle (CA), Allard (CO), Baker (LA), Calvert (CA), McInnis (CO), Pombo (CA), Dickey (AR).

SUBCOMMITTEES

ENERGY AND MINERAL RESOURCES

Majority (9 D): Lehman, Chmn.; Sharp, Murphy, Markey, Rahall, LaRocco, Deal, DeFazio, Barlow.
Minority (6 R): Vucanovich, Thomas, Doolittle, Allard, McInnis, Pombo.

INSULAR AND INTERNATIONAL AFFAIRS

Majority (7 D): de Lugo, Chmn.; Faleomavaega, Romero-Barcelo, Underwood, Murphy, Miller, one vacancy.
Minority (2 R): Gallegly, Vucanovich.

NATIONAL PARKS, FORESTS AND PUBLIC LANDS

Majority (16 D): Vento, Chmn.; Markey, Rahall, Williams, DeFazio, Johnson, LaRocco, Abercrombie, Romero-Barcelo, English, Shepherd, Hinchey, Underwood, Murphy, Richardson, Mink.
Minority (9 R): Hansen, Smith, Thomas, Duncan, Hefley, Doolittle, Baker, Calvert, Dickey.

NATIVE AMERICAN AFFAIRS

Majority (7 D): Richardson, Chmn.; Williams, Gejdenson, Faleomavaega, Johnson, Abercrombie, English.
Minority (4 R): Thomas, Young, Baker, Calvert.

OVERSIGHT AND INVESTIGATIONS

Majority (14 D): Miller, Chmn.; Gejdenson, Dooley, Deal, Sharp, Vento, Lehman, DeFazio, English, Shepherd, Hinchey, Abercrombie, Evans, Barrett.
Minority (9 R): Smith, Hansen, Vucanovich, Duncan, Doolittle, Allard, Calvert, Pombo, Dickey.

POST OFFICE AND CIVIL SERVICE   309 Cannon, 202-225-4054

Majority (15 D): Clay (MO), Chmn.; Schroeder (CO), McCloskey (IN), Ackerman (NY) Sawyer (OH), Kanjorski (PA), Norton (DC), Collins (MI), Byrne (VA), Watt (NC), Wynn (MD), Laughlin (TX), Bishop (GA), Brown (OH), Hastings (FL).
Minority (9 R): Myers (IN), Gilman (NY), Young (AK), Burton (IN), Morella (MD), Ridge (PA), Petri (WI), Boehlert (NY), Saxton (NJ).

SUBCOMMITTEES

CENSUS STATISTICS AND POSTAL PERSONNEL

Majority (3 D): Sawyer, Chmn.; McCloskey, Wynn.
Minority (2 R): Petri, Ridge.

CIVIL SERVICE

Majority (3 D): McCloskey, Chmn.; Schroeder, Kanjorski.
Minority (2 R): Burton, Morella.

COMPENSATION AND EMPLOYEE BENEFITS

Majority (3 D): Norton, Chmn.; Ackerman, Byrne.
Minority (2 R): Morella, Young.

OVERSIGHT AND INVESTIGATIONS

Majority (3 D): Clay, Chmn.; Hastings, Laughlin.
Minority (2 R): Boehlert, Saxton.

POSTAL OPERATIONS AND SERVICES

Majority (3 D): Collins, Chmn.; Watt, Bishop.
Minority (2 R): Young, Gilman.

PUBLIC WORKS AND TRANSPORTATION   2165 Rayburn, 202-225-4472

Majority (40 D): Mineta (CA), Chmn.; Oberstar (MN), Rahall (WV), Applegate (OH), de Lugo (VI), Borski (PA), Valentine (NC), Lipinski (IL), Wise (WV), Traficant (OH), DeFazio (OR), Hayes (LA), Clement (TN), Costello (IL), Parker (MS), Laughlin (TX), Geren (TX), Sangmeister (IL), Poshard (IL), Swett (NH), Cramer (AL), Collins (MI), Norton (DC), Blackwell (PA), Nadler (NY), Coppersmith (AZ), Byrne (VA), Cantwell (WA), Danner (MO), Shepherd (UT), Menendez (NJ), Clyburn (SC), Brown (FL), Deal (GA), Barcia (MI), Hamburg (CA), Filner (CA), Tucker (CA), Johnson (TX), Barca (WI).
Minority (24 R): Shuster (PA), Chmn.; Clinger (PA), Petri (WI), Boehlert (NY), Inhofe (OK), Emerson (MO), Duncan (TN), Molinari (NY), Zeliff (NH), Ewing (IL), Gilchrest (MD), Dunn (WA), Hutchinson (AR), Baker (CA), Collins (GA), Kim (CA), Levy (NY), Horn (CA), Franks (NJ), Blute (MA), McKeon (CA), Mica (FL), Hoekstra (MI), Quinn (NY).

SUBCOMMITTEES

AVIATION

Majority (22 D): Oberstar, Chmn.; de Lugo, Vice Chmn.; Lipinski, Geren, Sangmeister, Collins (MI), Coppersmith, Borski, Valentine, DeFazio, Hayes, Clement, Costello, Parker, Laughlin, Swett, Cramer, Blackwell, Cantwell, Danner, Shepherd, Brown.
Minority (13 R): Clinger, Boehlert, Inhofe, Duncan, Ewing, Gilchrest, Dunn, Collins (GA), Kim, Levy, Horn, McKeon, Mica.

ECONOMIC DEVELOPMENT

Majority (21 D): Wise, Chmn.; Blackwell, Vice Chmn.; Coppersmith, Clyburn, Deal, Barcia, Filner, Oberstar, Lipinski, Traficant, Clement, Costello, Parker, Swett, Nadler, Danner, Shepherd, Menendez, Brown, Hamburg.
Minority (13 R): Molinari, Boehlert, Ewing, Dunn, Hutchinson, Baker, Collins (GA), Kim, Franks, Blute, Mica, Hoekstra, Quinn.

INVESTIGATIONS AND OVERSIGHT

Majority (10 D): Borski, Chmn.; Collins (MI), Vice Chmn.; Wise, Blackwell, Byrne, Barcia, Filner, Johnson, two vacancies.
Minority (6 R): Inhofe, Duncan, Molinari, Zeliff, Gilchrest, Baker.

PUBLIC BUILDINGS AND GROUNDS

Majority (6 D): Traficant, Chmn.; Norton, Vice Chmn.; Johnson, Applegate, Clyburn, Tucker.
Minority (3 R): Duncan, Petri, Emerson.

SURFACE TRANSPORTATION

Majority (22 D): Rahall, Chmn.; Valentine, Vice Chmn.; Clement, Costello, Laughlin, Poshard, Swett, Cramer, DeFazio, Nadler, Byrne, Cantwell, Danner, Menendez, Clyburn, Hamburg, Tucker, Johnson, Applegate, de Lugo, Lipinski, Traficant.

Minority (13 R): Petri, Clinger, Emerson, Zeliff, Dunn, Hutchinson, Baker, Collins (GA), Kim, Levy, Franks, Blute, McKeon.

WATER RESOURCES AND ENVIRONMENT

Majority (22 D): Applegate, Chmn.; Hayes, Vice Chmn.; Parker, Shepherd, Brown, Deal, Barcia, Filner, Oberstar, Rahall, Wise, Geren, Sangmeister, Poshard, Norton, Nadler, Byrne, Menendez, Hamburg, Tucker, Borski, Valentine.

Minority (13 R): Boehlert, Clinger, Petri, Inhofe, Emerson, Molinari, Zeliff, Ewing, Gilchrest, Hutchinson, Horn, Hoekstra, Quinn.

RULES   H-312 The Capitol, 202-225-9486

Majority (9 D): Moakley (MA), Chmn.; Derrick (SC), Beilenson (CA), Frost (TX), Bonior (MI), Hall (OH), Wheat (MO), Gordon (TN), Slaughter (NY).

Minority (4 R): Solomon (NY), Quillen (TN), Dreier (CA), Goss (FL).

SUBCOMMITTEES

THE LEGISLATIVE PROCESS

Majority (5 D): Derrick, Chmn.; Frost, Wheat, Gordon, Moakley.

Minority (2 R): Quillen, Goss.

RULES OF THE HOUSE

Majority (5 D): Beilenson, Chmn.; Bonior, Hall, Slaughter, Moakley.

Minority (2 R): Dreier, Solomon.

SCIENCE, SPACE AND TECHNOLOGY   2320 Rayburn, 202-225-6371

Majority (33 D): Brown (CA), Chmn.; Lloyd (TN), Glickman (KS), Volkmer (MO), Hall (TX), McCurdy (OK), Valentine (NC), Torricelli (NJ), Boucher (VA), Traficant (OH), Hayes (LA), Tanner (TN), Geren (TX), Bacchus (FL), Roemer (IN), Cramer (AL), Swett (NH), Barcia (MI), Klein (NJ), Fingerhut (OH), McHale (PA), Harman (CA), Johnson (GA), Coppersmith (AZ), Eshoo (CA), Inslee (WA), E. Johnson (TX), Minge (MN), Deal (GA), Scott (VA), Becerra (CA), Barca (WI), one vacancy.

Minority (22 R): Walker (PA), Sensenbrenner (WI), Boehlert (NY), Lewis (FL), Henry (MI), Fawell (IL), Morella (MD), Rohrabacher (CA), Schiff (NM), Barton (TX), Zimmer (NJ), S. Johnson (TX), Calvert (CA), Hoke (OH), Smith (MI), Royce (CA), Grams (MN), Linder (GA), Blute (MA), Dunn (WA), Baker (CA), Bartlett (MD).

SUBCOMMITTEES

ENERGY

Majority (10 D): Lloyd, Chmn.; Scott, Cramer, Swett, Klein, McHale, Coppersmith, Inslee, Roemer, McCurdy.

Minority (5 R): Fawell, Schiff, Baker, Grams, Bartlett.

INVESTIGATIONS AND OVERSIGHT

Majority (6 D): Hayes, Chmn.; Tanner, Lloyd, Johnson (GA), Coppersmith, one vacancy.
Minority (3 R): Henry, Morella, Barton.

SCIENCE

Majority (9 D): Boucher, Chmn.; Hall, Valentine, Barcia, Eshoo, E. Johnson (TX), Minge, two vacancies.
Minority (5 R): Boehlert, Barton, S. Johnson (TX), Smith, Blute.

SPACE

Majority (16 D): Hall, Chmn.; Volkmer, Torricelli, Traficant, Bacchus, Cramer, Barcia, Fingerhut, Hayes, Tanner, Geren, Roemer, Harman, Eshoo, McCurdy, one vacancy.
Minority (9 R): Sensenbrenner, Rohrabacher, Zimmer, S. Johnson (TX), Hoke, Royce, Dunn, Schiff, Calvert.

TECHNOLOGY, ENVIRONMENT AND AVIATION

Majority (19 D): Valentine, Chmn.; Glickman, Geren, Roemer, Swett, Klein, McHale, Harman, Johnson (GA), Coppersmith, Eshoo, Inslee, E. Johnson (TX), Minge, Deal, Becerra, Torricelli, Bacchus, one vacancy.
Minority (12 R): Lewis, Morella, Calvert, Smith, Grams, Linder, Blute, Bartlett, Rohrabacher, Zimmer, Hoke, Royce.

SMALL BUSINESS　　　　　　　　　　2361 Rayburn, 202-225-5821

Majority (27 D): LaFalce (NY), Chmn.; Smith (IA), Skelton (MO), Mazzoli (KY), Wyden (OR), Sisisky (VA), Conyers (MI), Bilbray (NV), Mfume (MD), Flake (NY), Sarpalius (TX), Poshard (IL), Clayton (NC), Meehan (MA), Danner (MO), Strickland (OH), Velazquez (NY), Fields (LA), Margolies-Mezvinsky (PA), Tucker (CA), Klink (PA), Roybal-Allard (CA), Hilliard (AL), Lancaster (NC), Andrews (ME), Waters (CA), Thompson (MS).
Minority (18 R): Meyers (KS), Combest (TX), Baker (LA), Hefley (CO), Machtley (RI), Ramstad (MI), Johnson (TX), Zeliff (NH), Collins (GA), McInnis (CO), Huffington (CA), Talent (MO), Knollenberg (MI), Dickey (AR), Kim (CA), Manzullo (IL), Torkildsen (MA), Portman (OH).

SUBCOMMITTEES

DEVELOPMENT OF RURAL ENTERPRISES, EXPORTS AND THE ENVIRONMENT

Majority (6 D): Sarpalius, Chmn.; Clayton, Danner, Poshard, Strickland, Hilliard.
Minority (4 R): Hefley, Ramstad, Manzullo, Collins.

MINORITY ENTERPRISE, FINANCE AND URBAN DEVELOPMENT

Majority (8 D): Mfume, Chmn.; Conyers, Flake, Velazquez, Tucker, Fields, Roybal-Allard, Hilliard.
Minority (5 R): Machtley, Talent, Knollenberg, Dickey, one vacancy.

PROCUREMENT, TAXATION AND TOURISM

Majority (6 D): Bilbray, Chmn.; Sisisky, Hilliard, Mfume, Clayton, Klink.
Minority (4 R): Baker, Knollenberg, Portman, one vacancy.

REGULATION, BUSINESS OPPORTUNITIES AND TECHNOLOGY

Majority (8 D): Wyden, Chmn.; Skelton, Strickland, Andrews, Sisisky, Bilbray, Meehan, Tucker.
Minority (6 R): Combest, Johnson, Dickey, Kim, Torkildsen, Huffington.

SBA LEGISLATION AND THE GENERAL ECONOMY

Majority (9 D): LaFalce, Chmn.; Smith, Mazzoli, Poshard, Meehan, Fields, Margolies-Mezvinsky, Klink, Roybal-Allard.
Minority (6 R): Meyers, Zeliff, Collins, Huffington, Talent, Ramstad.

STANDARDS OF OFFICIAL CONDUCT   HT-2 The Capitol, 202-225-7103

Majority (7 D): McDermott (WA), Chmn.; Darden (GA), Cardin (MD), Pelosi (CA), Mfume (MD), Borski (PA), Sawyer (OH).
Minority (7 R): Grandy (IA), Johnson (CT), Bunning (KY), Kyl (AZ), Goss (FL), Hobson (OH), Schiff (NM).

NO SUBCOMMITTEES

VETERANS' AFFAIRS   335 Cannon, 202-225-3527

Majority (21 D): Montgomery (MS), Chmn.; Edwards (CA), Applegate (OH), Evans (IL), Penny (MN), Rowland (GA), Slattery (KS), Kennedy (MA), Sangmeister (IL), Long (IN), Edwards (TX), Waters (CA), Clement (TN), Filner (CA), Tejeda (TX), Gutierrez (IL), Baesler (KY), Bishop (CA), Clyburn (SC), Kreidler (WA), Brown (FL).
Minority (14 R): Stump (AR), Smith (NJ), Burton (IN), Bilirakis (FL), Ridge (PA), Spence (SC), Hutchinson (AR), Everett (AL), Buyer (IN), Quinn (NY), Bachus (AL), Linder (GA), Stearns (FL), King (NY).

SUBCOMMITTEES

COMPENSATION, PENSION AND INSURANCE

Majority (6 D): Slattery, Chmn.; Applegate, Evans, Sangmeister, Edwards (TX), Tejeda.
Minority (4 R): Bilirakis, Everett, Stearns, King.

EDUCATION, TRAINING AND EMPLOYMENT

Majority (6 D): Montgomery, Chmn.; Penny, Clyburn, Rowland, Slattery, Clement.
Minority (4 R): Hutchinson, Stump, Ridge, Quinn.

HOSPITALS AND HEALTH CARE

Majority (13 D): Rowland, Chmn.; Applegate, Kennedy, Long, Edwards (TX), Clement, Filner, Tejeda, Gutierrez, Baesler, Bishop, Kreidler, Brown.
Minority (8 R): Smith, Stump, Burton, Bilirakis, Hutchinson, Everett, Buyer, Linder.

HOUSING AND MEMORIAL AFFAIRS

Majority (4 D): Sangemeister, Chmn.; Bishop, Brown, Kreidler.
Minority (3 R): Burton, Spence, Buyer.

OVERSIGHT AND INVESTIGATIONS

Majority (6 D): Evans, Chmn.; Waters, Filner, Gutierrez, Clyburn, Kreidler.
Minority (4 R): Ridge, Bachus, Everett, Quinn.

WAYS AND MEANS   1102 Longworth, 202-225-3625

Majority (24 D): Rostenkowski (IL), Chmn.; Gibbons (FL), Pickle (TX), Rangel (NY), Stark (CA), Jacobs (IN), Ford (TN), Matsui (CA), Kennelly (CT), Coyne (PA), Andrews (TX), Levin (MI), Cardin (MD), McDermott (WA), Kleczka (WI), Lewis (GA), Payne (VA), Neal (MA), Hoagland (NE), McNulty (NY), Kopetski (OR), Jefferson (LA), Brewster (OK), Reynolds (IL).

Minority (14 R): Archer (TX), Crane (IL), Thomas (CA), Shaw (FL), Sundquist (TN), Johnson (CT), Bunning (KY), Grandy (IA), Houghton (NY), Herger (CA), McCrery (LA), Hancock (MO), Santorum (PA), Camp (MI).

SUBCOMMITTEES

HEALTH

Majority (7 D): Stark, Chmn.; Levin, Cardin, Andrews, McDermott, Kleczka, Lewis.
Minority (4 R): Thomas, Johnson, Grandy, McCrery.

HUMAN RESOURCES

Majority (7 D): Ford, Chmn.; Matsui, Actg. Chmn.; McDermott, Levin, Kopetski, Reynolds, Cardin.
Minority (4 R): Santorum, Shaw, Grandy, Camp.

OVERSIGHT

Majority (7 D): Pickle, Chmn.; Ford, Rangel, Jefferson, Brewster, Kleczka, Lewis.
Minority (4 R): Houghton, Herger, Hancock, Santorum.

SELECT REVENUE MEASURES

Majority (7 D): Rangel, Chmn.; Payne, Neal, Hoagland, McNulty, Kopetski, Jacobs.
Minority (4 R): Hancock, Sundquist, McCrery, Camp.

SOCIAL SECURITY

Majority (5 D): Jacobs, Chmn.; Pickle, Jefferson, Brewster, Reynolds.
Minority (3 R): Bunning, Crane, Houghton.

TRADE

Majority (9 D): Gibbons, Chmn.; Rostenkowski, Matsui, Kennelly, Coyne, Payne, Neal, Hoagland, McNulty.
Minority (5 R): Crane, Thomas, Shaw, Sundquist, Johnson.

JOINT COMMITTEES

JOINT ECONOMIC COMMITTEE   G-01 Dirksen, 202-224-5171

Senate (10): Sarbanes (MD), Vice Chmn.; Kennedy (MA), Bingaman (NM), Bryan (NV), Robb (VA), Dorgan (ND), Roth (DE), Mack (FL), Craig (ID), Bennett (UT).
House (10): Obey (WI), Chmn.; Hamilton (IN), Stark (CA), Mfume (MD), Wyden (OR), Andrews (TX), Armey (TX), Saxton (NJ), Cox (CA), Ramstad (NM).

JOINT COMMITTEE ON THE LIBRARY   305 Russell, 202-226-7633

Senate (5): Pell (RI), Vice Chmn.; DeConcini (AZ), Moynihan (NY), Hatfield (OR), Stevens (AK).
House (5): Rose (NC), Chmn.; Frost (TX), Manton (NY), Barrett (NE), Roberts (KS).

NO SUBCOMMITTEES

JOINT COMMITTEE ON THE ORGANIZATION OF CONGRESS
175-C Ford, 202-226-0650

Senate (12): Boren (OK), Co-Chmn.; Domenici (NM) Co-Vice Chmn., Sasser (TN), Ford (KY), Reid (NV), Sarbanes (MD), Pryor (AR), Kassebaum (KS), Lott (MS), Stevens (AK), Cohen (ME), Lugar (IN).
House (12): Hamilton (IN), Co-Chmn.; Dreier (CA) Co-Vice Chmn., Obey (WI), Swift (WA), Gejdenson (CT), Spratt (SC), Norton (DC), Walker (PA), Solomon (NY), Emerson (MO), Allard (CO), Dunn (WA).

NO SUBCOMMITTEES

JOINT COMMITTEE ON PRINTING   818 Hart, 202-224-5241

Senate (5): Ford (KY), Chmn.; DeConcini (AZ), Mathews (TN), Stevens (AK), Hatfield (OR).
House (5): Rose (NC), Vice Chmn.; Gejdenson (CT), Kleczka (WI), Roberts (KS), Gingrich (GA).

NO SUBCOMMITTEES

JOINT COMMITTEE ON TAXATION   1015 Longworth, 202-225-3621

Senate (5): Moynihan (NY), Vice Chmn.; Baucus (MT), Boren (OK), Packwood (OR), Dole (KS).
House (5): Rostenkowski (IL), Chmn.; Gibbons (FL), Pickle (TX), Archer (TX), Crane (IL).

NO SUBCOMMITTEES

CAMPAIGN FINANCE BY MEMBER

ALABAMA

Sen. Howell T. Heflin (D)

Receipts	$3,988,563	PACS	$1,496,155	Out of St.	$814,540	C-P-V		$4.79
Expend.	$3,437,073	Cand.	$0	Sm. Indiv.	$303,219	Spnd. Edge	$1,571,451
C-O-H	$1,036,023	Party	$19,200	Lg. Indiv.	$1,750,959	Debts		$0

Sen. Richard C. Shelby (D)

Receipts	$3,778,582	PACS	$1,694,944	Out of St.	$493,215	C-P-V		$2.75
Expend.	$2,807,764	Cand.	$0	Sm. Indiv.	$190,825	Spnd. Edge	$2,658,186
C-O-H	$1,112,139	Party	$21,250	Lg. Indiv.	$1,533,915	Debts		$0

1st District, Rep. H. L. (Sonny) Callahan (R)

Receipts	$376,087	PACS	$214,808	Out of St.	$10,900	C-P-V		$2.98
Expend.	$383,760	Cand.	$0	Sm. Indiv.	$24,235	Spnd. Edge	$370,463
C-O-H	$228,837	Party	$19	Lg. Indiv.	$116,950	Debt		$0

2d District, Rep. Terry Everett (R)

Receipts	$1,070,472	PACS	$0	Out of St.	$24,900	C-P-V		$9.23
Expend.	$1,042,083	Cand.	$66,717	Sm. Indiv.	$16,878	Spnd. Edge	$404,310
C-O-H	$28,389	Party	$0	Lg. Indiv.	$92,757	Debt		$10,000

3d District, Rep. Glen Browder (D)

Receipts	$231,325	PACS	$105,550	Out of St.	$1,100	C-P-V		$0.91
Expend.	$108,814	Cand.	$0	Sm. Indiv.	$49,534	Spnd. Edge	$86,654
C-O-H	$242,422	Party	$2,350	Lg. Indiv.	$60,913	Debt		$0

4th District, Rep. Tom Bevill (D)

Receipts	$318,198	PACS	$110,675	Out of St.	$9,063	C-P-V		$3.29
Expend.	$519,416	Cand.	$0	Sm. Indiv.	$49,044	Spnd. Edge	$499,299
C-O-H	$365,281	Party	$500	Lg. Indiv.	$83,310	Debt		$0

5th District, Rep. Robert E. (Bud) Cramer (D)

Receipts	$400,693	PACS	$223,075	Out of St.	$2,600	C-P-V		$2.43
Expend.	$389,349	Cand.	$0	Sm. Indiv.	$62,411	Spnd. Edge	$361,124
C-O-H	$32,112	Party	$3,371	Lg. Indiv.	$102,498	Debt		$0

6th District, Rep. Spencer Bachus (R)

Receipts	$527,406	PACS	$150,307	Out of St.	$9,200	C-P-V		$3.43
Expend.	$502,793	Cand.	$0	Sm. Indiv.	$23,317	Spnd. Edge	($512,938)
C-O-H	$15,660	Party	$18,699	Lg. Indiv.	$306,377	Debt		$30,727

7th District, Rep. Earl F. Hilliard (D)

Receipts	$362,942	PACS	$118,000	Out of St.	$12,450	C-P-V		$2.44
Expend.	$352,237	Cand.	$54,581	Sm. Indiv.	$26,233	Spnd. Edge	$336,883
C-O-H	$10,603	Party	$0	Lg. Indiv.	$112,996	Debt		$36,421

ALASKA

Sen. Ted Stevens (R)

Receipts	$1,658,927	PACS	$914,956	Out of St.	$312,537	C-P-V	$12.86
Expend.	$1,618,098	Cand.	$0	Sm. Indiv.	$53,905	Spnd. Edge	$1,617,098
C-O-H	$233,321	Party	$17,367	Lg. Indiv.	$553,117	Debts	$0

Sen. Frank H. Murkowski (R)

Receipts	$1,872,991	PACS	$778,841	Out of St.	$505,104	C-P-V	$15.03
Expend.	$1,910,759	Cand.	$1,425	Sm. Indiv.	$185,516	Spnd. Edge	$1,000,621
C-O-H	$31,081	Party	$41,924	Lg. Indiv.	$713,368	Debts	$0

At-Large, Rep. Don Young (R)

Receipts	$867,848	PACS	$377,335	Out of St.	$109,900	C-P-V	$7.81
Expend.	$873,486	Cand.	$0	Sm. Indiv.	$130,102	Spnd. Edge	$403,748
C-O-H	$0	Party	$19,283	Lg. Indiv.	$318,392	Debt	$92,474

ARIZONA

Sen. Dennis DeConcini (D)

Receipts	$3,251,984	PACS	$1,064,221	Out of St.	$537,932	C-P-V	$4.31
Expend.	$2,765,485	Cand.	$0	Sm. Indiv.	$607,878	Spnd. Edge	$2,525,489
C-O-H	$486,498	Party	$0	Lg. Indiv.	$1,328,555	Debts	$23,951

Sen. John McCain (R)

Receipts	$3,623,397	PACS	$1,276,444	Out of St.	$387,063	C-P-V	$4.88
Expend.	$3,766,588	Cand.	$3,000	Sm. Indiv.	$915,466	Spnd. Edge	$3,478,906
C-O-H	$5,927	Party	$17,765	Lg. Indiv.	$1,096,381	Debts	$59,891

1st District, Rep. Sam Coppersmith (D)

Receipts	$247,608	PACS	$66,183	Out of St.	$36,815	C-P-V	$1.87
Expend.	$244,633	Cand.	$1,019	Sm. Indiv.	$44,269	Spnd. Edge	($92,135)
C-O-H	$2,974	Party	$5,150	Lg. Indiv.	$98,424	Debt	$39,000

2d District, Rep. Ed Pastor (D)

Receipts	$281,008	PACS	$137,122	Out of St.	$14,300	C-P-V	$2.94
Expend.	$266,660	Cand.	$0	Sm. Indiv.	$51,280	Spnd. Edge	$239,400
C-O-H	$33,661	Party	$1,400	Lg. Indiv.	$83,497	Debt	$0

3d District, Rep. Bob Stump (R)

Receipts	$233,476	PACS	$136,092	Out of St.	$7,950	C-P-V	$1.91
Expend.	$303,208	Cand.	$0	Sm. Indiv.	$26,712	Spnd. Edge	$204,075
C-O-H	$43,638	Party	$5,394	Lg. Indiv.	$52,450	Debt	$0

4th District, Rep. Jon Kyl (R)

Receipts	$616,410	PACS	$163,168	Out of St.	$12,045	C-P-V	$2.93
Expend.	$458,358	Cand.	$355	Sm. Indiv.	$76,345	Spnd. Edge	$458,358
C-O-H	$493,753	Party	$1,259	Lg. Indiv.	$323,960	Debt	$2,958

5th District, Rep. Jim Kolbe (R)

Receipts	$409,883	PACS	$143,400	Out of St.	$11,450	C-P-V	$2.71
Expend.	$469,053	Cand.	$0	Sm. Indiv.	$113,976	Spnd. Edge	$365,464
C-O-H	$21,918	Party	$7,029	Lg. Indiv.	$134,393	Debt	$0

6th District, Rep. Karan English (D)

Receipts	$394,253	PACS	$135,087	Out of St.	$13,487	C-P-V		$3.15
Expend.	$391,015	Cand.	$242	Sm. Indiv.	$189,843	Spnd. Edge		($276,945)
C-O-H	$3,238	Party	$0	Lg. Indiv.	$32,039	Debt		$88,029

ARKANSAS

Sen. Dale Bumpers (D)

Receipts	$2,063,717	PACS	$723,585	Out of St.	$235,319	C-P-V		$3.64
Expend.	$2,016,112	Cand.	$0	Sm. Indiv.	$180,645	Spnd. Edge		$1,105,900
C-O-H	$172,582	Party	$24,173	Lg. Indiv.	$1,039,738	Debts		$0

Sen. David Pryor (D)

Receipts	$1,449,981	PACS	$589,850	Out of St.	$194,313	C-P-V		$1.26
Expend.	$622,479	Cand.	$0	Sm. Indiv.	$18,225	Spnd.	Edge	$0
C-O-H	$1,001,203	Party	($28,450)	Lg. Indiv.	$677,672	Debts		$0

1st District, Rep. Blanche M. Lambert (D)

Receipts	$439,343	PACS	$176,400	Out of St.	$38,172	C-P-V		$2.19
Expend.	$327,100	Cand.	$4,000	Sm. Indiv.	$120,905	Spnd. Edge		$296,529
C-O-H	$112,243	Party	$8,300	Lg. Indiv.	$126,144	Debt		$0

2d District, Rep. Ray Thornton (D)

Receipts	$303,430	PACS	$141,550	Out of St.	$7,000	C-P-V		$1.33
Expend.	$206,328	Cand.	$0	Sm. Indiv.	$13,722	Spnd. Edge		$200,116
C-O-H	$115,739	Party	$600	Lg. Indiv.	$139,975	Debt		$0

3d District, Rep. Tim Hutchinson (R)

Receipts	$344,017	PACS	$93,805	Out of St.	$1,900	C-P-V		$2.71
Expend.	$339,772	Cand.	$0	Sm. Indiv.	$90,647	Spnd. Edge		($150,061)
C-O-H	$4,246	Party	$12,170	Lg. Indiv.	$149,308	Debt		$0

4th District, Rep. Jay Dickey (R)

Receipts	$412,465	PACS	$250	Out of St.	$19,050	C-P-V		$3.52
Expend.	$397,841	Cand.	$0	Sm. Indiv.	$92,563	Spnd. Edge		$39,930
C-O-H	$14,621	Party	$25,760	Lg. Indiv.	$141,600	Debt		$137,797

CALIFORNIA

Sen. Dianne Feinstein (D)

Receipts	$8,114,867	PACS	$941,048	Out of St.	$846,924	C-P-V		$1.38
Expend.	$8,054,222	Cand.	$77,695	Sm. Indiv.	$2,545,142	Spnd. Edge		$1,204,417
C-O-H	$60,645	Party	$17,500	Lg. Indiv.	$4,195,648	Debts		$57,680

Sen. Barbara Boxer (D)

Receipts	$10,431,140	PACS	$908,655	Out of St.	$1,372,404	C-P-V		$2.01
Expend.	$10,415,811	Cand.	$1,000	Sm. Indiv.	$4,453,685	Spnd. Edge		$2,766,739
C-O-H	$11,397	Party	$17,600	Lg. Indiv.	$4,333,979	Debts		$150,160

1st District, Rep. Dan Hamburg (D)

Receipts	$652,592	PACS	$185,507	Out of St.	$15,573	C-P-V		$5.41
Expend.	$647,532	Cand.	$0	Sm. Indiv.	$344,022	Spnd. Edge		($68,869)
C-O-H	$5,057	Party	$5,000	Lg. Indiv.	$61,399	Debt		$103,176

2d District, Rep. Wally Herger (R)

Receipts	$644,763	PACS	$225,289	Out of St.	$4,000	C-P-V		$3.19
Expend.	$533,861	Cand.	$0	Sm. Indiv.	$204,519	Spnd. Edge		$528,914
C-O-H	$225,763	Party	$966	Lg. Indiv.	$184,664	Debt		$0

3d District, Rep. Vic Fazio (D)

Receipts	$1,994,284	PACS	$1,148,438	Out of St.	$150,800	C-P-V	$15.61
Expend.	$1,906,584	Cand.	$0	Sm. Indiv.	$352,829	Spnd. Edge	$1,052,854
C-O-H	$282,634	Party	$1,425	Lg. Indiv.	$424,289	Debt	$10,549

4th District, Rep. John T. Doolittle (R)

Receipts	$610,104	PACS	$249,095	Out of St.	$7,755	C-P-V	$4.41
Expend.	$622,071	Cand.	$0	Sm. Indiv.	$144,872	Spnd. Edge	$245,881
C-O-H	$217	Party	$5,106	Lg. Indiv.	$200,854	Debt	$24,230

5th District, Rep. Robert T. Matsui (D)

Receipts	$656,875	PACS	$365,100	Out of St.	$50,250	C-P-V	$8.98
Expend.	$1,421,123	Cand.	$0	Sm. Indiv.	$88,410	Spnd. Edge	$1,388,297
C-O-H	$384,523	Party	$849	Lg. Indiv.	$81,800	Debt	$741

6th District, Rep. Lynn C. Woolsey (D)

Receipts	$598,664	PACS	$186,853	Out of St.	$5,350	C-P-V	$3.07
Expend.	$584,913	Cand.	$9,500	Sm. Indiv.	$258,084	Spnd. Edge	$148,161
C-O-H	$13,751	Party	$5,200	Lg. Indiv.	$55,503	Debt	$85,938

7th District, Rep. George Miller (D)

Receipts	$542,532	PACS	$261,790	Out of St.	$67,550	C-P-V	$4.25
Expend.	$651,360	Cand.	$0	Sm. Indiv.	$81,251	Spnd. Edge	$589,313
C-O-H	$328,659	Party	$0	Lg. Indiv.	$137,299	Debt	$0

8th District, Rep. Nancy Pelosi (D)

Receipts	$417,254	PACS	$204,689	Out of St.	$26,500	C-P-V	$2.31
Expend.	$443,238	Cand.	$0	Sm. Indiv.	$10,333	Spnd. Edge	$393,672
C-O-H	$71,704	Party	$0	Lg. Indiv.	$183,200	Debt	$0

9th District, Rep. Ronald V. Dellums (D)

Receipts	$854,478	PACS	$78,437	Out of St.	$41,351	C-P-V	$5.61
Expend.	$921,771	Cand.	$0	Sm. Indiv.	$528,968	Spnd. Edge	$848,112
C-O-H	$15,335	Party	$350	Lg. Indiv.	$105,771	Debt	$0

10th District, Rep. Bill Baker (R)

Receipts	$699,687	PACS	$178,550	Out of St.	$7,050	C-P-V	$4.79
Expend.	$697,982	Cand.	$0	Sm. Indiv.	$240,729	Spnd. Edge	$459,076
C-O-H	$1,704	Party	$7,650	Lg. Indiv.	$212,520	Debt	$127,474

11th District, Rep. Richard W. Pombo (R)

Receipts	$532,902	PACS	$152,486	Out of St.	$27,300	C-P-V	$5.60
Expend.	$528,989	Cand.	$0	Sm. Indiv.	$144,295	Spnd. Edge	($335,422)
C-O-H	$3,911	Party	$18,061	Lg. Indiv.	$216,414	Debt	$55,381

12th District, Rep. Tom Lantos (D)

Receipts	$499,867	PACS	$112,850	Out of St.	$38,900	C-P-V	$3.82
Expend.	$600,656	Cand.	$19,678	Sm. Indiv.	$228,451	Spnd. Edge	$595,102
C-O-H	$536,945	Party	$475	Lg. Indiv.	$106,080	Debt	$0

13th District, Rep. Fortney H. (Pete) Stark (D)

Receipts	$634,994	PACS	$349,444	Out of St.	$91,500	C-P-V	$4.76
Expend.	$589,500	Cand.	$0	Sm. Indiv.	$68,956	Spnd. Edge	$546,065
C-O-H	$401,292	Party	$0	Lg. Indiv.	$109,800	Debt	$0

14th District, Rep. Anna G. Eshoo (D)

Receipts	$917,346	PACS	$296,322	Out of St.	$62,150	C-P-V	$6.19
Expend.	$909,604	Cand.	$762	Sm. Indiv.	$291,211	Spnd. Edge	$239,327
C-O-H	$7,774	Party	$5,000	Lg. Indiv.	$319,727	Debt	$146,303

15th District, Rep. Norman Y. Mineta (D)

Receipts	$967,049	PACS	$546,295	Out of St.	$104,453	C-P-V	$6.60
Expend.	$1,112,414	Cand.	$0	Sm. Indiv.	$170,306	Spnd. Edge	$1,049,453
C-O-H	$197,336	Party	$0	Lg. Indiv.	$220,393	Debt	$0

16th District, Rep. Don Edwards (D)

Receipts	$249,478	PACS	$182,700	Out of St.	$16,210	C-P-V	$3.01
Expend.	$291,251	Cand.	$0	Sm. Indiv.	$21,721	Spnd. Edge	$290,746
C-O-H	$13,687	Party	$150	Lg. Indiv.	$39,910	Debt	$0

17th District, Rep. Sam Farr (D)
(Elected June 8, 1993; campaign finance figures not available)

18th District, Rep. Gary A. Condit (D)

Receipts	$362,490	PACS	$155,645	Out of St.	$6,000	C-P-V	$2.23
Expend.	$311,000	Cand.	$0	Sm. Indiv.	$116,265	Spnd. Edge	$311,000
C-O-H	$66,029	Party	$150	Lg. Indiv.	$76,338	Debt	$25,489

19th District, Rep. Richard H. Lehman (D)

Receipts	$826,532	PACS	$526,845	Out of St.	$44,643	C-P-V	$9.01
Expend.	$915,504	Cand.	$0	Sm. Indiv.	$66,506	Spnd. Edge	$761,720
C-O-H	$7,171	Party	$700	Lg. Indiv.	$217,418	Debt	$53,025

20th District, Rep. Calvin Dooley (D)

Receipts	$496,485	PACS	$242,583	Out of St.	$6,400	C-P-V	$6.94
Expend.	$504,352	Cand.	$0	Sm. Indiv.	$95,655	Spnd. Edge	$330,608
C-O-H	$1,544	Party	$4,050	Lg. Indiv.	$145,584	Debt	$70,003

21st District, Rep. William M. Thomas (R)

Receipts	$598,669	PACS	$277,436	Out of St.	$23,300	C-P-V	$4.82
Expend.	$615,587	Cand.	$0	Sm. Indiv.	$56,872	Spnd. Edge	$587,100
C-O-H	$90,932	Party	$5,963	Lg. Indiv.	$195,289	Debt	$0

22d District, Rep. Michael Huffington (R)

Receipts	$5,443,247	PACS	$0	Out of St.	$61,350	C-P-V	$41.41
Expend.	$5,435,177	Cand.	$5,191,728	Sm. Indiv.	$69,450	Spnd. Edge	$4,772,150
C-O-H	$8,071	Party	$0	Lg. Indiv.	$173,660	Debt	$0

23d District, Rep. Elton Gallegly (R)

Receipts	$679,886	PACS	$195,705	Out of St.	$7,900	C-P-V	$7.46
Expend.	$862,061	Cand.	$8,000	Sm. Indiv.	$216,081	Spnd. Edge	$318,945
C-O-H	$49,095	Party	$15,688	Lg. Indiv.	$205,176	Debt	$12,858

24th District, Rep. Anthony C. Beilenson (D)

Receipts	$753,415	PACS	$0	Out of St.	$20,600	C-P-V	$5.55
Expend.	$786,463	Cand.	$0	Sm. Indiv.	$206,997	Spnd. Edge	$316,749
C-O-H	$12,478	Party	$0	Lg. Indiv.	$475,409	Debt	$50,000

25th District, Rep. Howard P. (Buck) McKeon (R)

Receipts	$457,650	PACS	$96,775	Out of St.	$2,000	C-P-V	$3.99
Expend.	$452,792	Cand.	$0	Sm. Indiv.	$65,908	Spnd. Edge	$284,473
C-O-H	$4,858	Party	$2,140	Lg. Indiv.	$164,589	Debt	$201,101

26th District, Rep. Howard L. Berman (D)

Receipts	$548,212	PACS	$216,350	Out of St.	$19,900	C-P-V	$9.79
Expend.	$722,606	Cand.	$0	Sm. Indiv.	$13,995	Spnd. Edge	$645,939
C-O-H	$26,077	Party	$0	Lg. Indiv.	$284,648	Debt	$0

27th District, Rep. Carlos J. Moorhead (R)

Receipts	$448,791	PACS	$260,025	Out of St.	$10,000	C-P-V	$6.69
Expend.	$705,814	Cand.	$0	Sm. Indiv.	$57,266	Spnd. Edge	$537,916
C-O-H	$409,659	Party	$100	Lg. Indiv.	$37,050	Debt	$0

28th District, Rep. David Dreier (R)

Receipts	$646,323	PACS	$131,350	Out of St.	$17,250	C-P-V	$2.37
Expend.	$290,128	Cand.	$0	Sm. Indiv.	$41,585	Spnd. Edge	$264,867
C-O-H	$2,026,109	Party	$0	Lg. Indiv.	$219,170	Debt	$0

29th District, Rep. Henry A. Waxman (D)

Receipts	$682,214	PACS	$402,915	Out of St.	$65,350	C-P-V	$4.48
Expend.	$718,695	Cand.	$0	Sm. Indiv.	$36,537	Spnd. Edge	$570,421
C-O-H	$432,414	Party	$0	Lg. Indiv.	$190,691	Debt	$0

30th District, Rep. Xavier Becerra (D)

Receipts	$387,385	PACS	$97,450	Out of St.	$5,100	C-P-V	$7.65
Expend.	$373,551	Cand.	$0	Sm. Indiv.	$91,096	Spnd. Edge	$316,488
C-O-H	$13,833	Party	$5,050	Lg. Indiv.	$96,900	Debt	$64,658

31st District, Rep. Matthew G. (Marty) Martinez (D)

Receipts	$119,807	PACS	$77,450	Out of St.	$9,300	C-P-V	$2.19
Expend.	$149,441	Cand.	$0	Sm. Indiv.	$5,991	Spnd. Edge	$94,624
C-O-H	$13,570	Party	$0	Lg. Indiv.	$35,573	Debt	$6,000

32d District, Rep. Julian C. Dixon (D)

Receipts	$83,583	PACS	$54,750	Out of St.	$3,000	C-P-V	$0.93
Expend.	$140,461	Cand.	$0	Sm. Indiv.	$1,683	Spnd. Edge	$140,461
C-O-H	$80,101	Party	$0	Lg. Indiv.	$27,150	Debt	$0

33d District, Rep. Lucille Roybal-Allard (D)

Receipts	$283,770	PACS	$133,587	Out of St.	$13,250	C-P-V	$8.27
Expend.	$264,755	Cand.	$0	Sm. Indiv.	$68,374	Spnd. Edge	$96,740
C-O-H	$19,015	Party	$1,000	Lg. Indiv.	$73,206	Debt	$0

34th District, Rep. Esteban E. Torres (D)

Receipts	$169,451	PACS	$49,300	Out of St.	$19,650	C-P-V	$2.77
Expend.	$254,092	Cand.	$0	Sm. Indiv.	$21,846	Spnd. Edge	$122,821
C-O-H	$63,139	Party	$0	Lg. Indiv.	$77,703	Debt	$0

35th District, Rep. Maxine Waters (D)

Receipts	$191,510	PACS	$91,890	Out of St.	$22,731	C-P-V	$2.02
Expend.	$207,954	Cand.	$0	Sm. Indiv.	$15,183	Spnd. Edge	$200,811
C-O-H	$11,274	Party	$0	Lg. Indiv.	$78,606	Debt	$0

36th District, Rep. Jane Harman (D)

Receipts	$2,301,376	PACS	$199,208	Out of St.	$257,101	C-P-V	$18.32
Expend.	$2,285,356	Cand.	$773,000	Sm. Indiv.	$149,566	Spnd. Edge	$1,473,764
C-O-H	$16,019	Party	$5,000	Lg. Indiv.	$448,610	Debt	$214,694

37th District, Rep. Walter R. Tucker (D)

Receipts	$283,230	PACS	$65,100	Out of St.	$5,750	C-P-V	$2.86
Expend.	$277,586	Cand.	$32,250	Sm. Indiv.	$52,356	Spnd. Edge	$273,457
C-O-H	$5,644	Party	$0	Lg. Indiv.	$128,990	Debt	$13,216

38th District, Rep. Stephen Horn (R)

Receipts	$441,693	PACS	$3,000	Out of St.	$23,135	C-P-V	$4.79
Expend.	$441,198	Cand.	$5,000	Sm. Indiv.	$88,080	Spnd. Edge	($73,183)
C-O-H	$493	Party	$10,000	Lg. Indiv.	$273,767	Debt	$105,526

39th District, Rep. Edward R. Royce (R)

Receipts	$499,264	PACS	$200,562	Out of St.	$8,725	C-P-V	$4.33
Expend.	$530,196	Cand.	$0	Sm. Indiv.	$70,079	Spnd. Edge	$437,686
C-O-H	$6,772	Party	$8,029	Lg. Indiv.	$192,136	Debt	$132,381

40th District, Rep. Jerry Lewis (R)

Receipts	$471,956	PACS	$358,045	Out of St.	$24,700	C-P-V	$4.22
Expend.	$546,541	Cand.	$0	Sm. Indiv.	$14,349	Spnd. Edge	$524,986
C-O-H	$264,213	Party	$400	Lg. Indiv.	$74,250	Debt	$0

41st District, Rep. Jay Kim (R)

Receipts	$791,483	PACS	$91,900	Out of St.	$18,150	C-P-V	$7.52
Expend.	$764,895	Cand.	$550	Sm. Indiv.	$223,252	Spnd. Edge	$764,895
C-O-H	$28,312	Party	$11,000	Lg. Indiv.	$288,562	Debt	$113,000

42d District, Rep. George E. Brown, Jr. (D)

Receipts	$908,348	PACS	$506,920	Out of St.	$74,300	C-P-V	$11.37
Expend.	$907,227	Cand.	$0	Sm. Indiv.	$210,622	Spnd. Edge	$463,955
C-O-H	$5,564	Party	$5,000	Lg. Indiv.	$168,930	Debt	$17,294

43d District, Rep. Ken Calvert (R)

Receipts	$423,001	PACS	$138,485	Out of St.	$11,000	C-P-V	$4.75
Expend.	$422,717	Cand.	$0	Sm. Indiv.	$38,627	Spnd. Edge	$169,038
C-O-H	$934	Party	$15,313	Lg. Indiv.	$221,223	Debt	$92,406

44th District, Rep. Alfred A. (Al) McCandless (R)

Receipts	$318,312	PACS	$195,137	Out of St.	$6,550	C-P-V	$2.53
Expend.	$278,880	Cand.	$0	Sm. Indiv.	$43,208	Spnd. Edge	$273,132
C-O-H	$45,027	Party	$0	Lg. Indiv.	$77,426	Debt	$0

45th District, Rep. Dana Rohrabacher (R)

Receipts	$323,608	PACS	$108,926	Out of St.	$23,626	C-P-V	$2.60
Expend.	$321,912	Cand.	$0	Sm. Indiv.	$28,646	Spnd. Edge	$289,439
C-O-H	$52,281	Party	$0	Lg. Indiv.	$170,721	Debt	$1,600

46th District, Rep. Robert K. (Bob) Dornan (R)

Receipts	$1,443,564	PACS	$75,978	Out of St.	$81,484	C-P-V	$28.41
Expend.	$1,581,503	Cand.	$0	Sm. Indiv.	$1,188,786	Spnd. Edge	$1,581,503
C-O-H	$47,448	Party	$7,375	Lg. Indiv.	$143,158	Debt	$17,000

47th District, Rep. Christopher Cox (R)

Receipts	$515,754	PACS	$155,500	Out of St.	$21,200	C-P-V	$2.44
Expend.	$402,198	Cand.	$0	Sm. Indiv.	$28,769	Spnd. Edge	$402,198
C-O-H	$118,668	Party	$1,842	Lg. Indiv.	$317,930	Debt	$0

48th District, Rep. Ron Packard (R)

Receipts	$292,021	PACS	$191,832	Out of St.	$18,000	C-P-V	$2.58
Expend.	$363,341	Cand.	$0	Sm. Indiv.	$39,641	Spnd. Edge	$297,397
C-O-H	$105,268	Party	$237	Lg. Indiv.	$32,950	Debt	$0

49th District, Rep. Lynn Schenk (D)

Receipts	$1,154,531	PACS	$300,129	Out of St.	$132,800	C-P-V	$8.89
Expend.	$1,131,021	Cand.	$0	Sm. Indiv.	$172,483	Spnd. Edge	$697,372
C-O-H	$23,509	Party	$6,440	Lg. Indiv.	$480,621	Debt	$181,000

50th District, Rep. Bob Filner (D)

Receipts	$856,869	PACS	$267,797	Out of St.	$23,650	C-P-V	$11.08
Expend.	$856,046	Cand.	$0	Sm. Indiv.	$17,972	Spnd. Edge	$786,110
C-O-H	$822	Party	$10,350	Lg. Indiv.	$249,825	Debt	$155,000

51st District, Rep. Randy (Duke) Cunningham (R)

Receipts	$967,013	PACS	$283,367	Out of St.	$52,355	C-P-V	$6.85
Expend.	$972,606	Cand.	$0	Sm. Indiv.	$409,280	Spnd. Edge	$949,291
C-O-H	$19,196	Party	$370	Lg. Indiv.	$238,877	Debt	$13,595

52d District, Rep. Duncan Hunter (R)

Receipts	$561,203	PACS	$201,107	Out of St.	$47,600	C-P-V	$4.96
Expend.	$559,970	Cand.	$0	Sm. Indiv.	$44,435	Spnd. Edge	$395,490
C-O-H	$7,460	Party	$6,546	Lg. Indiv.	$204,158	Debt	$0

COLORADO

Sen. Hank Brown (R)

Receipts	$4,139,855	PACS	$1,384,698	Out of St.	$459,415	C-P-V	$6.47
Expend.	$3,684,020	Cand.	$0	Sm. Indiv.	$586,597	Spnd. Edge	$1,740,592
C-O-H	$545,576	Party	$47,500	Lg. Indiv.	$1,551,382	Debts	$0

Sen. Ben Nighthorse Campbell (D)

Receipts	$1,594,544	PACS	$741,686	Out of St.	$332,377	C-P-V	$1.94
Expend.	$1,561,347	Cand.	$539	Sm. Indiv.	$218,179	Spnd. Edge	($654,444)
C-O-H	$46,741	Party	$17,500	Lg. Indiv.	$612,463	Debts	$168,925

1st District, Rep. Patricia Schroeder (D)

Receipts	$361,845	PACS	$134,147	Out of St.	$110,753	C-P-V	$2.55
Expend.	$398,749	Cand.	$0	Sm. Indiv.	$20,844	Spnd. Edge	$398,749
C-O-H	$612,243	Party	$2,100	Lg. Indiv.	$144,608	Debt	$0

2d District, Rep. David E. Skaggs (D)

Receipts	$659,719	PACS	$316,637	Out of St.	$21,663	C-P-V	$4.09
Expend.	$673,887	Cand.	$1,728	Sm. Indiv.	$176,422	Spnd. Edge	$580,310
C-O-H	$17,460	Party	$5,000	Lg. Indiv.	$149,112	Debt	$21,336

3d District, Rep. Scott McInnis (R)

Receipts	$438,090	PACS	$144,614	Out of St.	$13,400	C-P-V	$3.03
Expend.	$434,449	Cand.	$0	Sm. Indiv.	$19,415	Spnd. Edge	$108,264
C-O-H	$3,638	Party	$12,725	Lg. Indiv.	$250,890	Debt	$0

4th District, Rep. Wayne Allard (R)

Receipts	$565,311	PACS	$266,115	Out of St.	$7,450	C-P-V	$3.94
Expend.	$551,110	Cand.	$0	Sm. Indiv.	$79,693	Spnd. Edge	$172,455
C-O-H	$6,808	Party	$19,115	Lg. Indiv.	$136,201	Debt	$0

5th District, Rep. Joel Hefley (R)

Receipts	$137,757	PACS	$99,515	Out of St.	$2,200	C-P-V	$0.94
Expend.	$162,718	Cand.	$0	Sm. Indiv.	$13,996	Spnd. Edge	$148,105
C-O-H	$60,257	Party	$723	Lg. Indiv.	$13,200	Debt	$0

6th District, Rep. Dan Schaefer (R)

Receipts	$357,020	PACS	$269,984	Out of St.	$7,250	C-P-V	$2.34
Expend.	$332,317	Cand.	$0	Sm. Indiv.	$31,905	Spnd. Edge	$322,523
C-O-H	$147,114	Party	$20	Lg. Indiv.	$37,155	Debt	$0

CONNECTICUT

Sen. Christopher J. Dodd (D)

Receipts	$4,342,880	PACS	$1,544,084	Out of St.	$1,143,659	C-P-V	$5.16
Expend.	$4,553,792	Cand.	$0	Sm. Indiv.	$504,041	Spnd. Edge	$2,158,530
C-O-H	$62,777	Party	$27,215	Lg. Indiv.	$2,085,235	Debts	$0

Sen. Joseph I. Lieberman (D)

Receipts	$2,626,557	PACS	$176,564	Out of St.	$775,324	C-P-V	$3.70
Expend.	$2,546,733	Cand.	$0	Sm. Indiv.	$512,481	Spnd. Edge ($93,617)
C-O-H	$79,825	Party	$29,966	Lg. Indiv.	$1,774,668	Debts $100,638

1st District, Rep. Barbara B. Kennelly (D)

Receipts	$523,025	PACS	$336,281	Out of St.	$29,855	C-P-V	$3.48
Expend.	$572,841	Cand.	$0	Sm. Indiv.	$59,567	Spnd. Edge $569,229
C-O-H	$127,166	Party	$1,277	Lg. Indiv.	$101,905	Debt $0

2d District, Rep. Samuel Gejdenson (D)

Receipts	$1,024,091	PACS	$336,601	Out of St.	$124,058	C-P-V	$8.27
Expend.	$1,019,417	Cand.	$0	Sm. Indiv.	$220,712	Spnd. Edge $879,278
C-O-H	$11,333	Party	$1,965	Lg. Indiv.	$250,961	Debt $85,000

3d District, Rep. Rosa L. DeLauro (D)

Receipts	$1,026,034	PACS	$494,781	Out of St.	$131,043	C-P-V	$6.29
Expend.	$1,022,131	Cand.	$0	Sm. Indiv.	$194,726	Spnd. Edge $802,345
C-O-H	$19,545	Party	$7,577	Lg. Indiv.	$319,674	Debt $65,385

4th District, Rep. Christopher Shays (R)

Receipts	$402,100	PACS	$56,800	Out of St.	$11,800	C-P-V	$2.59
Expend.	$383,207	Cand.	$0	Sm. Indiv.	$164,086	Spnd. Edge $354,045
C-O-H	$94,049	Party	$1,500	Lg. Indiv.	$164,088	Debt $0

5th District, Rep. Gary A. Franks (R)

Receipts	$644,632	PACS	$293,259	Out of St.	$75,450	C-P-V	$6.02
Expend.	$631,851	Cand.	$2,685	Sm. Indiv.	$78,109	Spnd. Edge $286,687
C-O-H	$18,140	Party	$30,360	Lg. Indiv.	$217,222	Debt $40,103

6th District, Rep. Nancy L. Johnson (R)

Receipts	$596,412	PACS	$339,312	Out of St.	$20,150	C-P-V	$3.41
Expend.	$570,046	Cand.	$0	Sm. Indiv.	$137,753	Spnd. Edge $531,078
C-O-H	$144,036	Party	$3,950	Lg. Indiv.	$104,984	Debt $0

DELAWARE

Sen. William V. Roth, Jr. (R)

Receipts	$2,016,200	PACS	$876,044	Out of St.	$556,560	C-P-V	$13.07
Expend.	$1,975,188	Cand.	$0	Sm. Indiv.	$89,018	Spnd. Edge ($231,924)
C-O-H	$89,302	Party	$15,400	Lg. Indiv.	$970,110	Debts $0

Sen. Joseph R. Biden, Jr. (D)

Receipts	$2,742,990	PACS	$699,466	Out of St.	$1,340,255	C-P-V	$22.58
Expend.	$2,550,061	Cand.	$0	Sm. Indiv.	$385,669	Spnd. Edge $2,309,388
C-O-H	$192,929	Party	$32	Lg. Indiv.	$1,452,141	Debts $49,000

At-Large, Rep. Michael N. Castle (R)

Receipts	$708,671	PACS	$206,868	Out of St.	$128,750	C-P-V	$4.51
Expend.	$690,740	Cand.	$0	Sm. Indiv.	$101,399	Spnd. Edge ($326,858)
C-O-H	$17,929	Party	$16,520	Lg. Indiv.	$371,370	Debt $0

FLORIDA

Sen. Bob Graham (D)

Receipts	$3,696,833	PACS	$1,247,448	Out of St.	$623,492	C-P-V	$1.02
Expend.	$3,318,473	Cand.	$0	Sm. Indiv.	$302,908	Spnd. Edge $3,076,222
C-O-H	$354,763	Party	$17,500	Lg. Indiv.	$1,888,921	Debts $0

Sen. Connie Mack III (R)

Receipts	$5,192,409	PACS	$1,017,047	Out of St.	$1,051,585	C-P-V	$2.51
Expend.	$5,149,988	Cand.	$0	Sm. Indiv.	$1,321,717	Spnd. Edge	$1,440,915
C-O-H	$42,421	Party	$22,181	Lg. Indiv.	$2,671,446	Debts	$388,612

1st District, Rep. Earl Hutto (D)

Receipts	$298,700	PACS	$144,704	Out of St.	$5,250	C-P-V	$2.60
Expend.	$308,621	Cand.	$0	Sm. Indiv.	$80,653	Spnd. Edge	$141,859
C-O-H	$94,485	Party	$9,950	Lg. Indiv.	$45,380	Debt	$0

2d District, Rep. Douglas (Pete) Peterson (D)

Receipts	$400,867	PACS	$282,350	Out of St.	$5,950	C-P-V	$2.25
Expend.	$376,786	Cand.	$0	Sm. Indiv.	$53,677	Spnd. Edge	$351,062
C-O-H	$25,352	Party	$1,901	Lg. Indiv.	$58,330	Debt	$0

3d District, Rep. Corrine Brown (D)

Receipts	$289,260	PACS	$147,363	Out of St.	$6,770	C-P-V	$3.00
Expend.	$275,705	Cand.	$0	Sm. Indiv.	$92,348	Spnd. Edge	$17,311
C-O-H	$13,552	Party	$300	Lg. Indiv.	$30,773	Debt	$16,308

4th District, Rep. Tillie K. Fowler (R)

Receipts	$524,951	PACS	$115,350	Out of St.	$16,900	C-P-V	$3.77
Expend.	$512,267	Cand.	$2,040	Sm. Indiv.	$78,004	Spnd. Edge	$84,787
C-O-H	$13,139	Party	$18,609	Lg. Indiv.	$308,378	Debt	$0

5th District, Rep. Karen L. Thurman (D)

Receipts	$360,160	PACS	$206,401	Out of St.	$7,762	C-P-V	$2.72
Expend.	$352,607	Cand.	$0	Sm. Indiv.	$75,838	Spnd. Edge	$207,994
C-O-H	$7,552	Party	$17,572	Lg. Indiv.	$47,963	Debt	$23,612

6th District, Rep. Clifford B. Stearns (R)

Receipts	$374,016	PACS	$171,239	Out of St.	$2,500	C-P-V	$2.15
Expend.	$309,532	Cand.	$0	Sm. Indiv.	$67,410	Spnd. Edge	$307,199
C-O-H	$112,117	Party	$616	Lg. Indiv.	$90,795	Debt	$20,848

7th District, Rep. John L. Mica (R)

Receipts	$465,407	PACS	$145,700	Out of St.	$25,049	C-P-V	$3.65
Expend.	$459,135	Cand.	$0	Sm. Indiv.	$59,307	Spnd. Edge	$151,278
C-O-H	$4,305	Party	$8,475	Lg. Indiv.	$94,949	Debt	$135,000

8th District, Rep. Bill McCollum (R)

Receipts	$642,785	PACS	$301,830	Out of St.	$24,250	C-P-V	$4.76
Expend.	$675,211	Cand.	$0	Sm. Indiv.	$83,966	Spnd. Edge	$500,271
C-O-H	$68,837	Party	$57	Lg. Indiv.	$212,175	Debt	$0

9th District, Rep. Michael Bilirakis (R)

Receipts	$779,124	PACS	$313,210	Out of St.	$38,399	C-P-V	$4.94
Expend.	$779,818	Cand.	$0	Sm. Indiv.	$286,059	Spnd. Edge	$510,201
C-O-H	$1,923	Party	$11,503	Lg. Indiv.	$164,084	Debt	$3,702

10th District, Rep. C.W. (Bill) Young (R)

Receipts	$274,122	PACS	$165,250	Out of St.	$9,850	C-P-V	$3.08
Expend.	$459,861	Cand.	$0	Sm. Indiv.	$32,799	Spnd. Edge	$257,861
C-O-H	$156,032	Party	$7,400	Lg. Indiv.	$30,650	Debt	$0

11th District, Rep. Sam M. Gibbons (D)

Receipts	$722,678	PACS	$427,161	Out of St.	$61,300	C-P-V	$9.51
Expend.	$960,511	Cand.	$0	Sm. Indiv.	$72,841	Spnd. Edge	$909,118
C-O-H	$41,127	Party	$0	Lg. Indiv.	$176,624	Debt	$0

12th District, Rep. Charles T. Canady (R)

Receipts	$158,777	PACS	$53,311	Out of St.	$0	C-P-V	$1.56
Expend.	$156,984	Cand.	$0	Sm. Indiv.	$47,183	Spnd. Edge	($192,911)
C-O-H	$1,792	Party	$9,533	Lg. Indiv.	$47,574	Debt	$0

13th District, Rep. Dan Miller (R)

Receipts	$453,193	PACS	$70,400	Out of St.	$14,448	C-P-V	$2.83
Expend.	$449,212	Cand.	$0	Sm. Indiv.	$100,216	Spnd. Edge	$150,903
C-O-H	$3,980	Party	$1,000	Lg. Indiv.	$156,931	Debt	$122,500

14th District, Rep. Porter Johnston Goss (R)

Receipts	$419,508	PACS	$41,900	Out of St.	$18,435	C-P-V	$1.88
Expend.	$414,185	Cand.	$0	Sm. Indiv.	$195,763	Spnd. Edge	$395,875
C-O-H	$106,397	Party	$3,144	Lg. Indiv.	$176,149	Debt	$0

15th District, Rep. James L. Bacchus (D)

Receipts	$841,298	PACS	$460,597	Out of St.	$19,600	C-P-V	$6.20
Expend.	$820,388	Cand.	$0	Sm. Indiv.	$78,088	Spnd. Edge	$604,850
C-O-H	$23,014	Party	$3,590	Lg. Indiv.	$276,435	Debt	$0

16th District, Rep. Tom Lewis (R)

Receipts	$296,405	PACS	$129,015	Out of St.	$2,250	C-P-V	$2.31
Expend.	$363,795	Cand.	$0	Sm. Indiv.	$66,967	Spnd. Edge	$265,924
C-O-H	$53,970	Party	$2,556	Lg. Indiv.	$79,642	Debt	$0

17th District, Rep. Carrie P. Meek (D)

Receipts	$574,719	PACS	$158,615	Out of St.	$28,100	C-P-V	$4.49
Expend.	$461,115	Cand.	$0	Sm. Indiv.	$225,718	Spnd. Edge	(unopp.)
C-O-H	$113,605	Party	$1,000	Lg. Indiv.	$188,734	Debt	$0

18th District, Rep. Ileana Ros-Lehtinen (R)

Receipts	$662,069	PACS	$149,344	Out of St.	$43,711	C-P-V	$6.52
Expend.	$669,350	Cand.	$0	Sm. Indiv.	$148,755	Spnd. Edge	$333,942
C-O-H	$7,076	Party	$250	Lg. Indiv.	$339,172	Debt	$0

19th District, Rep. Harry A. Johnston (D)

Receipts	$348,039	PACS	$180,300	Out of St.	$8,500	C-P-V	$1.33
Expend.	$235,412	Cand.	$0	Sm. Indiv.	$31,796	Spnd. Edge	$172,212
C-O-H	$154,908	Party	$2,850	Lg. Indiv.	$121,846	Debt	$0

20th District, Rep. Peter Deutsch (D)

Receipts	$856,210	PACS	$162,599	Out of St.	$99,150	C-P-V	$6.49
Expend.	$849,785	Cand.	$0	Sm. Indiv.	$20,611	Spnd. Edge	$760,974
C-O-H	$423	Party	$0	Lg. Indiv.	$303,160	Debt	$343,240

21st District, Rep. Lincoln Diaz-Balart (R)

Receipts	$279,773	PACS	$83,800	Out of St.	$18,720	C-P-V	N/A
Expend.	$279,481	Cand.	$0	Sm. Indiv.	$49,308	Spnd. Edge	(unopp.)
C-O-H	$292	Party	$3,595	Lg. Indiv.	$141,170	Debt	$9,226

22d District, Rep. E. Clay Shaw, Jr. (R)

Receipts	$948,514	PACS	$441,663	Out of St.	$41,000	C-P-V	$8.87
Expend.	$1,138,425	Cand.	$0	Sm. Indiv.	$118,298	Spnd. Edge	$201,465
C-O-H	$116,312	Party	$11,324	Lg. Indiv.	$333,980	Debt	$0

23d District, Rep. Alcee L. Hastings (D)

Receipts	$417,158	PACS	$98,200	Out of St.	$46,600	C-P-V	$5.08
Expend.	$427,931	Cand.	$0	Sm. Indiv.	$72,145	Spnd. Edge	$412,309
C-O-H	$7,211	Party	$5,100	Lg. Indiv.	$201,561	Debt	$0

GEORGIA

Sen. Sam Nunn (D)

Receipts	$2,088,554	PACS	$622,751	Out of St.	$346,360	C-P-V	$1.18
Expend.	$1,214,695	Cand.	$0	Sm. Indiv.	$83,685	Spnd. Edge	(unopp.)
C-O-H	$1,550,059	Party	$0	Lg. Indiv.	$1,062,682	Debts	$0

Sen. Paul Coverdell (R)

Receipts	$3,281,002	PACS	$585,557	Out of St.	$454,748	C-P-V	$5.03
Expend.	$3,193,774	Cand.	$5,518	Sm. Indiv.	$544,019	S. Edge	($2,343,936)
C-O-H	$113,792	Party	$121,959	Lg. Indiv.	$2,009,451	Debts	$0

1st District, Rep. Jack Kingston (R)

Receipts	$439,846	PACS	$113,985	Out of St.	$5,500	C-P-V	$4.03
Expend.	$418,883	Cand.	$0	Sm. Indiv.	$101,547	Spnd. Edge	$86,564
C-O-H	$20,963	Party	$20,020	Lg. Indiv.	$202,393	Debt	$18,282

2d District, Rep. Sanford D. Bishop, Jr. (D)

Receipts	$353,162	PACS	$142,100	Out of St.	$12,100	C-P-V	$3.70
Expend.	$353,973	Cand.	$0	Sm. Indiv.	$64,885	Spnd. Edge	$131,167
C-O-H	$3,737	Party	$0	Lg. Indiv.	$96,177	Debt	$80,630

3d District, Rep. Mac Collins (R)

Receipts	$255,683	PACS	$50,272	Out of St.	$5,100	C-P-V	$2.16
Expend.	$246,007	Cand.	$1,675	Sm. Indiv.	$48,321	Spnd. Edge	($882,545)
C-O-H	$9,676	Party	$17,775	Lg. Indiv.	$85,188	Debt	$44,202

4th District, Rep. John Linder (R)

Receipts	$543,357	PACS	$187,978	Out of St.	13,760	C-P-V	$4.29
Expend.	$542,137	Cand.	$2,000	Sm. Indiv.	$115,410	Spnd. Edge	($61,262)
C-O-H	$1,219	Party	$5,000	Lg. Indiv.	$163,752	Debt	$61,643

5th District, Rep. John Lewis (D)

Receipts	$300,865	PACS	$225,195	Out of St.	$15,650	C-P-V	$1.67
Expend.	$246,913	Cand.	$0	Sm. Indiv.	$22,242	Spnd. Edge	$188,301
C-O-H	$324,123	Party	$0	Lg. Indiv.	$51,150	Debt	$0

6th District, Rep. Newt Gingrich (R)

Receipts	$1,962,935	PACS	$653,712	Out of St.	$349,191	C-P-V	$12.37
Expend.	$1,963,810	Cand.	$0	Sm. Indiv.	$544,761	Spnd. Edge	$1,553,003
C-O-H	$16,625	Party	$40,167	Lg. Indiv.	$769,602	Debt	$109,380

7th District, Rep. George (Buddy) Darden (D)

Receipts	$410,958	PACS	$226,940	Out of St.	$12,675	C-P-V	$4.58
Expend.	$510,547	Cand.	$0	Sm. Indiv.	$69,355	Spnd. Edge	$469,769
C-O-H	$650	Party	$8,616	Lg. Indiv.	$92,185	Debt	$0

8th District, Rep. J. Roy Rowland (D)

Receipts	$454,319	PACS	$286,099	Out of St.	$7,248	C-P-V	$5.02
Expend.	$544,898	Cand.	$0	Sm. Indiv.	$59,731	Spnd. Edge	$334,665
C-O-H	$120,061	Party	$1,200	Lg. Indiv.	$54,033	Debt	$0

9th District, Rep. Nathan Deal (D)

Receipts	$543,942	PACS	$136,250	Out of St.	$2,650	C-P-V	$4.80
Expend.	$542,479	Cand.	$250	Sm. Indiv.	$96,536	Spnd. Edge	$381,419
C-O-H	$1,461	Party	$0	Lg. Indiv.	$132,281	Debt	$124,305

10th District, Rep. Don Johnson (D)

Receipts	$629,607	PACS	$161,235	Out of St.	$8,950	C-P-V	$5.74
Expend.	$622,590	Cand.	$4,395	Sm. Indiv.	$164,882	Spnd. Edge	$439,953
C-O-H	$7,016	Party	$9,000	Lg. Indiv.	$184,402	Debt	$74,153

11th District, Rep. Cynthia A. McKinney (D)

Receipts	$311,365	PACS	$166,642	Out of St.	$8,950	C-P-V	$2.55
Expend.	$306,978	Cand.	$2,809	Sm. Indiv.	$63,426	Spnd. Edge	$280,257
C-O-H	$4,386	Party	$3,750	Lg. Indiv.	$74,588	Debt	$41,540

HAWAII

Sen. Daniel K. Inouye (D)

Receipts	$2,929,237	PACS	$852,465	Out of St.	$1,246,637	C-P-V	$16.88
Expend.	$3,515,722	Cand.	$0	Sm. Indiv.	$232,229	Spnd. Edge	$3,076,871
C-O-H	$11,907	Party	$17,500	Lg. Indiv.	$1,641,237	Debts	$23,117

Sen. Daniel K. Akaka (D)

Receipts	$1,727,943	PACS	$830,064	Out of St.	$218,330	C-P-V	$8.95
Expend.	$1,691,384	Cand.	$0	Sm. Indiv.	$229,755	Spnd. Edge	($649,196)
C-O-H	$161,134	Party	$0	Lg. Indiv.	$628,562	Debts	$253,197

1st District, Rep. Neil Abercrombie (D)

Receipts	$359,336	PACS	$176,568	Out of St.	$15,200	C-P-V	$2.78
Expend.	$359,681	Cand.	$0	Sm. Indiv.	$69,991	Spnd. Edge	$343,578
C-O-H	$33,907	Party	$0	Lg. Indiv.	$49,203	Debt	$0

2d District, Rep. Patsy T. Mink (D)

Receipts	$336,089	PACS	$113,425	Out of St.	$3,400	C-P-V	$2.18
Expend.	$287,017	Cand.	$3,208	Sm. Indiv.	$149,405	Spnd. Edge	$286,245
C-O-H	$49,359	Party	$0	Lg. Indiv.	$56,482	Debt	$136,590

IDAHO

Sen. Larry Craig (R)

Receipts	$1,700,917	PACS	$801,704	Out of St.	$321,367	C-P-V	$8.37
Expend.	$1,620,304	Cand.	$0	Sm. Indiv.	$308,254	Spnd. Edge	$1,076,432
C-O-H	$91,834	Party	$45,801	Lg. Indiv.	$500,594	Debts	$0

Sen. Dirk Kempthorne (R)

Receipts	$1,351,127	PACS	$599,151	Out of St.	$118,970	C-P-V	$4.83
Expend.	$1,305,338	Cand.	$0	Sm. Indiv.	$313,579	Spnd. Edge	$83,116
C-O-H	$45,789	Party	$45,235	Lg. Indiv.	$387,733	Debts	$191,933

1st District, Rep. Larry LaRocco (D)

Receipts	$623,847	PACS	$408,955	Out of St.	$40,151	C-P-V	$4.42
Expend.	$623,327	Cand.	$0	Sm. Indiv.	$108,502	Spnd. Edge	$400,723
C-O-H	$2,042	Party	$3,355	Lg. Indiv.	$67,993	Debt	$52,637

2d District, Rep. Michael Crapo (R)

Receipts	$554,691	PACS	$234,599	Out of St.	$15,035	C-P-V	$4.10
Expend.	$572,532	Cand.	$0	Sm. Indiv.	$121,202	Spnd. Edge	$326,578
C-O-H	$2,568	Party	$18,775	Lg. Indiv.	$149,746	Debt	$52,345

ILLINOIS

Sen. Paul Simon (D)

Receipts	$9,504,736	PACS	$1,679,743	Out of St.	$1,754,436	C-P-V	$4.10
Expend.	$8,665,789	Cand.	$0	Sm. Indiv.	$3,967,229	Spnd. Edge	$3,769,341
C-O-H	$843,732	Party	$30,789	Lg. Indiv.	$3,523,046	Debts	$0

Sen. Carol Moseley-Braun (D)

Receipts	$6,770,711	PACS	$716,567	Out of St.	$849,800	C-P-V	$2.55
Expend.	$6,699,942	Cand.	$0	Sm. Indiv.	$3,806,624	Spnd. Edge	$4,874,696
C-O-H	$30,144	Party	$139,111	Lg. Indiv.	$1,932,594	Debts	$543,871

1st District, Rep. Bobby Rush (D)

Receipts	$257,455	PACS	$132,300	Out of St.	$14,550	C-P-V	$1.24
Expend.	$260,389	Cand.	$0	Sm. Indiv.	$30,255	Spnd. Edge	$246,649
C-O-H	$112	Party	$0	Lg. Indiv.	$94,900	Debt	$29,407

2d District, Rep. Mel Reynolds (D)

Receipts	$532,031	PACS	$195,772	Out of St.	$69,235	C-P-V	$2.97
Expend.	$542,911	Cand.	$10,000	Sm. Indiv.	$144,898	Spnd. Edge	$507,063
C-O-H	$6,032	Party	$2,500	Lg. Indiv.	$178,260	Debt	$30,506

3d District, Rep. William O. Lipinski (D)

Receipts	$561,335	PACS	$316,350	Out of St.	$30,350	C-P-V	$3.43
Expend.	$556,847	Cand.	$0	Sm. Indiv.	$69,096	Spnd. Edge	$489,856
C-O-H	$23,597	Party	$0	Lg. Indiv.	$162,650	Debt	$0

4th District, Rep. Luis V. Gutierrez (D)

Receipts	$438,253	PACS	$187,945	Out of St.	$18,600	C-P-V	$4.65
Expend.	$420,227	Cand.	$0	Sm. Indiv.	$50,982	Spnd. Edge	$416,653
C-O-H	$18,024	Party	$6,600	Lg. Indiv.	$191,899	Debt	$1,749

5th District, Rep. Dan Rostenkowski (D)

Receipts	$1,587,108	PACS	$962,937	Out of St.	$152,081	C-P-V	$10.95
Expend.	$1,455,455	Cand.	$0	Sm. Indiv.	$12,503	Spnd. Edge	$1,372,162
C-O-H	$1,245,721	Party	$150	Lg. Indiv.	$359,131	Debt	$0

6th District, Rep. Henry J. Hyde (R)

Receipts	$355,851	PACS	$170,882	Out of St.	$10,900	C-P-V	$2.48
Expend.	$408,987	Cand.	$0	Sm. Indiv.	$48,574	Spnd. Edge	$346,564
C-O-H	$134,632	Party	$0	Lg. Indiv.	$114,850	Debt	$0

7th District, Rep. Cardiss Collins (D)

Receipts	$344,933	PACS	$285,067	Out of St.	$9,026	C-P-V	$2.14
Expend.	$390,942	Cand.	$423	Sm. Indiv.	$1,336	Spnd. Edge	$383,964
C-O-H	$49,167	Party	$300	Lg. Indiv.	$25,126	Debt	$0

8th District, Rep. Philip M. Crane (R)

Receipts	$477,110	PACS	$0	Out of St.	$62,953	C-P-V	$3.98
Expend.	$528,818	Cand.	$0	Sm. Indiv.	$311,384	Spnd. Edge	$389,897
C-O-H	$64,211	Party	$5,050	Lg. Indiv.	$138,804	Debt	$0

9th District, Rep. Sidney R. Yates (D)

Receipts	$227,671	PACS	$34,350	Out of St.	$132,100	C-P-V	$1.40
Expend.	$228,812	Cand.	$0	Sm. Indiv.	$33,248	Spnd. Edge	$216,213
C-O-H	$52,684	Party	$150	Lg. Indiv.	$157,050	Debt	$0

1462 CAMPAIGN FINANCE BY MEMBER

10th District, Rep. John E. Porter (R)

Receipts	$453,794	PACS	$160,649	Out of St.	$14,703	C-P-V	$3.13
Expend.	$485,778	Cand.	$0	Sm. Indiv.	$104,078	Spnd. Edge	$450,830
C-O-H	$40,011	Party	$600	Lg. Indiv.	$181,180	Debt	$0

11th District, Rep. George E. Sangmeister (D)

Receipts	$339,478	PACS	$252,210	Out of St.	$5,300	C-P-V	$2.55
Expend.	$344,786	Cand.	$0	Sm. Indiv.	$37,880	Spnd. Edge	$63,543
C-O-H	$17,831	Party	$11,015	Lg. Indiv.	$28,426	Debt	$0

12th District, Rep. Jerry F. Costello (D)

Receipts	$503,778	PACS	$145,175	Out of St.	$25,050	C-P-V	$3.59
Expend.	$606,383	Cand.	$0	Sm. Indiv.	$68,373	Spnd. Edge	$585,359
C-O-H	$171,227	Party	$11,765	Lg. Indiv.	$258,850	Debt	$0

13th District, Rep. Harris W. Fawell (R)

Receipts	$563,194	PACS	$216,917	Out of St.	$4,450	C-P-V	$3.67
Expend.	$657,908	Cand.	$0	Sm. Indiv.	$103,662	Spnd. Edge	$653,581
C-O-H	$30,674	Party	$259	Lg. Indiv.	$227,434	Debt	$0

14th District, Rep. Dennis Hastert (R)

Receipts	$601,812	PACS	$317,656	Out of St.	$3,650	C-P-V	$3.96
Expend.	$615,535	Cand.	$5	Sm. Indiv.	$135,020	Spnd. Edge	$615,535
C-O-H	$177,247	Party	$3,600	Lg. Indiv.	$116,808	Debt	$0

15th District, Rep. Thomas W. Ewing (R)

Receipts	$381,502	PACS	$171,658	Out of St.	$1,777	C-P-V	$2.17
Expend.	$309,131	Cand.	$3,569	Sm. Indiv.	$146,475	Spnd. Edge	$302,803
C-O-H	$123,473	Party	$1,777	Lg. Indiv.	$54,396	Debt	$16,713

16th District, Rep. Donald Manzullo (R)

Receipts	$440,379	PACS	$123,598	Out of St.	$4,250	C-P-V	$3.06
Expend.	$435,468	Cand.	$0	Sm. Indiv.	$110,655	Spnd. Edge	($55,534)
C-O-H	$5,908	Party	$5,193	Lg. Indiv.	$148,776	Debt	$83,915

17th District, Rep. Lane Evans (D)

Receipts	$370,096	PACS	$188,260	Out of St.	$0	C-P-V	$2.40
Expend.	$374,415	Cand.	$0	Sm. Indiv.	$136,868	Spnd. Edge	$256,791
C-O-H	$25,957	Party	$5,469	Lg. Indiv.	$34,533	Debt	$0

18th District, Rep. Robert H. Michel (R)

Receipts	$646,637	PACS	$404,027	Out of St.	$37,650	C-P-V	$4.07
Expend.	$636,430	Cand.	$0	Sm. Indiv.	$100,327	Spnd. Edge	$636,430
C-O-H	$252,205	Party	$3,018	Lg. Indiv.	$115,085	Debt	$0

19th District, Rep. Glenn Poshard (D)

Receipts	$317,043	PACS	$0	Out of St.	$6,175	C-P-V	$1.67
Expend.	$312,530	Cand.	$0	Sm. Indiv.	$247,442	Spnd. Edge	$287,227
C-O-H	$6,650	Party	$6,514	Lg. Indiv.	$43,224	Debt	$5,000

20th District, Rep. Richard J. Durbin (D)

Receipts	$666,110	PACS	$420,402	Out of St.	$36,650	C-P-V	$5.95
Expend.	$921,659	Cand.	$0	Sm. Indiv.	$123,160	Spnd. Edge	$643,302
C-O-H	$51,822	Party	$5,430	Lg. Indiv.	$79,255	Debt	$0

INDIANA

Sen. Richard G. Lugar (R)

Receipts	$3,607,947	PACS	$833,549	Out of St.	$262,942	C-P-V	$2.27
Expend.	$3,244,452	Cand.	$0	Sm. Indiv.	$1,765,779	Spnd. Edge	$2,930,214
C-O-H	$417,310	Party	$22,359	Lg. Indiv.	$802,296	Debts	$0

Sen. Daniel R. Coats (R)

Receipts	$3,642,012	PACS	$1,135,005	Out of St.	$399,800	C-P-V	$3.00
Expend.	$3,802,077	Cand.	$0	Sm. Indiv.	$533,629	Spnd. Edge	$2,217,904
C-O-H	$183,495	Party	$18,225	Lg. Indiv.	$1,679,994	Debts	$0

1st District, Rep. Peter J. Visclosky (D)

Receipts	$275,278	PACS	$175,715	Out of St.	$8,060	C-P-V	$1.83
Expend.	$268,786	Cand.	$0	Sm. Indiv.	$41,695	Spnd. Edge	$268,786
C-O-H	$50,439	Party	$1,000	Lg. Indiv.	$40,725	Debt	$0

2d District, Rep. Philip R. Sharp (D)

Receipts	$624,265	PACS	$449,549	Out of St.	$34,800	C-P-V	$4.76
Expend.	$623,400	Cand.	$0	Sm. Indiv.	$90,535	Spnd. Edge	$447,366
C-O-H	$30,810	Party	$6,150	Lg. Indiv.	$63,250	Debt	$0

3d District, Rep. Tim Roemer (D)

Receipts	$467,094	PACS	$320,249	Out of St.	$41,050	C-P-V	$3.43
Expend.	$416,196	Cand.	$0	Sm. Indiv.	$24,710	Spnd. Edge	$170,696
C-O-H	$73,596	Party	$7,610	Lg. Indiv.	$105,027	Debt	$0

4th District, Rep. Jill Long (D)

Receipts	$366,814	PACS	$263,182	Out of St.	$3,200	C-P-V	$2.63
Expend.	$346,011	Cand.	$0	Sm. Indiv.	$63,544	Spnd. Edge	$339,522
C-O-H	$13,772	Party	$1,450	Lg. Indiv.	$29,556	Debt	$0

5th District, Rep. Steve Buyer (R)

Receipts	$395,825	PACS	$135,834	Out of St.	$32,517	C-P-V	$3.54
Expend.	$392,922	Cand.	$30,626	Sm. Indiv.	$94,260	Spnd. Edge	($190,107)
C-O-H	$2,902	Party	$22,381	Lg. Indiv.	$107,140	Debt	$986

6th District, Rep. Dan Burton (R)

Receipts	$629,390	PACS	$213,385	Out of St.	$135,252	C-P-V	$2.18
Expend.	$407,055	Cand.	$0	Sm. Indiv.	$113,927	Spnd. Edge	$374,902
C-O-H	$622,881	Party	$6,244	Lg. Indiv.	$236,477	Debt	$0

7th District, Rep. John T. Myers (R)

Receipts	$329,387	PACS	$199,784	Out of St.	$18,550	C-P-V	$2.86
Expend.	$369,882	Cand.	$0	Sm. Indiv.	$60,048	Spnd. Edge	$318,637
C-O-H	$62,387	Party	$12,350	Lg. Indiv.	$28,609	Debt	$0

8th District, Rep. Francis X. (Frank) McCloskey (D)

Receipts	$498,192	PACS	$329,569	Out of St.	$16,594	C-P-V	$4.09
Expend.	$512,852	Cand.	$0	Sm. Indiv.	$117,002	Spnd. Edge	$264,700
C-O-H	$8,622	Party	$10,750	Lg. Indiv.	$27,624	Debt	$2,500

9th District, Rep. Lee H. Hamilton (D)

Receipts	$484,849	PACS	$199,150	Out of St.	$99,950	C-P-V	$2.97
Expend.	$477,591	Cand.	$0	Sm. Indiv.	$155,844	Spnd. Edge	$302,578
C-O-H	$66,788	Party	$5,400	Lg. Indiv.	$115,800	Debt	$0

10th District, Rep. Andy Jacobs, Jr. (D)

Receipts	$15,690	PACS	$0	Out of St.	$0	C-P-V	$0.12
Expend.	$14,373	Cand.	$0	Sm. Indiv.	$9,726	Spnd. Edge	($52,354)
C-O-H	$33,505	Party	$0	Lg. Indiv.	$3,050	Debt	$0

IOWA

Sen. Charles E. Grassley (R)

Receipts	$2,833,083	PACS	$1,077,564	Out of St.	$284,433	C-P-V	$2.76
Expend.	$2,486,030	Cand.	$0	Sm. Indiv.	$742,260	Spnd. Edge	$2,075,136
C-O-H	$821,030	Party	$24,272	Lg. Indiv.	$636,267	Debts	$0

Sen. Tom Harkin (D)

Receipts	$5,682,912	PACS	$1,814,599	Out of St.	$1,554,637	C-P-V	$10.50
Expend.	$5,628,242	Cand.	$0	Sm. Indiv.	$1,696,612	Spnd. Edge	$582,008
C-O-H	$59,728	Party	$31,667	Lg. Indiv.	$2,025,077	Debts	$48,515

1st District, Rep. James A. Leach (R)

Receipts	$213,649	PACS	$0	Out of St.	$3,550	C-P-V	$1.46
Expend.	$259,804	Cand.	$0	Sm. Indiv.	$136,509	Spnd. Edge	$259,804
C-O-H	$759	Party	$300	Lg. Indiv.	$58,583	Debt	$10,000

2d District, Rep. Jim Nussle (R)

Receipts	$867,359	PACS	$350,565	Out of St.	$25,065	C-P-V	$6.44
Expend.	$865,838	Cand.	$0	Sm. Indiv.	$268,279	Spnd. Edge	$12,201
C-O-H	$5,194	Party	$35,412	Lg. Indiv.	$203,253	Debt	$23,600

3d District, Rep. Jim Ross Lightfoot (R)

Receipts	$623,098	PACS	$260,302	Out of St.	$12,892	C-P-V	$6.00
Expend.	$755,552	Cand.	$0	Sm. Indiv.	$233,030	Spnd. Edge	$110,210
C-O-H	$8,356	Party	$29,517	Lg. Indiv.	$83,505	Debt	$0

4th District, Rep. Neal Smith (D)

Receipts	$324,231	PACS	$210,300	Out of St.	$24,950	C-P-V	$1.24
Expend.	$197,159	Cand.	$0	Sm. Indiv.	$5,287	Spnd. Edge	$185,981
C-O-H	$502,580	Party	$2,150	Lg. Indiv.	$54,493	Debt	$0

5th District, Rep. Fred Grandy (R)

Receipts	$382,626	PACS	$296,149	Out of St.	$17,450	C-P-V	$1.49
Expend.	$292,752	Cand.	$0	Sm. Indiv.	$17,496	Spnd. Edge	$292,752
C-O-H	$174,722	Party	$2,048	Lg. Indiv.	$55,960	Debt	$43,772

KANSAS

Sen. Robert Dole (R)

Receipts	$3,143,115	PACS	$1,600,855	Out of St.	$765,230	C-P-V	$5.02
Expend.	$3,542,989	Cand.	$42	Sm. Indiv.	$91,688	Spnd. Edge	$3,293,630
C-O-H	$1,756,483	Party	$17,720	Lg. Indiv.	$961,529	Debts	$0

Sen. Nancy Landon Kassebaum (R)

Receipts	$520,471	PACS	$179,109	Out of St.	$40,000	C-P-V	$0.90
Expend.	$521,140	Cand.	$0	Sm. Indiv.	$66,599	Spnd. Edge	$504,510
C-O-H	$217,136	Party	$26,547	Lg. Indiv.	$176,695	Debts	$0

1st District, Rep. Pat Roberts (R)

Receipts	$313,020	PACS	$185,085	Out of St.	$14,337	C-P-V	$6.39
Expend.	$601,655	Cand.	$0	Sm. Indiv.	$43,718	Spnd. Edge	$536,805
C-O-H	$110,891	Party	$961	Lg. Indiv.	$38,337	Debt	$0

2d District, Rep. Jim Slattery (D)

Receipts	$701,965	PACS	$439,021	Out of St.	$50,050	C-P-V	$4.91
Expend.	$742,215	Cand.	$0	Sm. Indiv.	$80,518	Spnd. Edge	$705,511
C-O-H	$12,748	Party	$300	Lg. Indiv.	$171,445	Debt	$0

3d District, Rep. Jan Meyers (R)

Receipts	$431,501	PACS	$209,895	Out of St.	$6,400	C-P-V	$2.54
Expend.	$430,833	Cand.	$1,295	Sm. Indiv.	$140,322	Spnd. Edge	$430,833
C-O-H	$2,748	Party	$10,000	Lg. Indiv.	$60,290	Debt	$25,593

4th District, Rep. Dan Glickman (D)

Receipts	$873,194	PACS	$421,726	Out of St.	$169,939	C-P-V	$7.29
Expend.	$1,046,769	Cand.	$0	Sm. Indiv.	$94,730	Spnd. Edge	$650,515
C-O-H	$18,743	Party	$18,530	Lg. Indiv.	$312,126	Debt	$0

KENTUCKY

Sen. Wendell H. Ford (D)

Receipts	$2,406,052	PACS	$1,343,378	Out of St.	$290,150	C-P-V	$2.77
Expend.	$2,321,131	Cand.	$0	Sm. Indiv.	$116,746	Spnd. Edge	$1,985,827
C-O-H	$438,224	Party	$23,189	Lg. Indiv.	$695,717	Debts	$0

Sen. Mitch McConnell (R)

Receipts	$5,419,669	PACS	$1,184,129	Out of St.	$892,901	C-P-V	$10.94
Expend.	$5,229,296	Cand.	$0	Sm. Indiv.	$716,466	Spnd. Edge	$2,219,385
C-O-H	$190,373	Party	$23,151	Lg. Indiv.	$2,911,471	Debts	$0

1st District, Rep. Thomas J. Barlow, III (D)

Receipts	$218,358	PACS	$104,825	Out of St.	$3,900	C-P-V	$1.63
Expend.	$209,090	Cand.	$538	Sm. Indiv.	$21,118	Spnd. Edge	$142,385
C-O-H	$6,864	Party	$11,540	Lg. Indiv.	$22,360	Debt	$35,516

2d District, Rep. William H. Natcher (D)

Receipts	$6,624	PACS	$0	Out of St.	$0	C-P-V	$0.05
Expend.	$6,624	Cand.	$6,624	Sm. Indiv.	$0	Spnd. Edge	$5,499
C-O-H	$0	Party	$0	Lg. Indiv.	$0	Debt	$0

3d District, Rep. Romano L. Mazzoli (D)

Receipts	$223,091	PACS	$0	Out of St.	$0	C-P-V	$1.46
Expend.	$216,638	Cand.	$0	Sm. Indiv.	$202,157	Spnd. Edge	($148,021)
C-O-H	$6,743	Party	$0	Lg. Indiv.	$14,900	Debt	$0

4th District, Rep. Jim Bunning (R)

Receipts	$946,781	PACS	$439,491	Out of St.	$52,450	C-P-V	$7.05
Expend.	$984,180	Cand.	$0	Sm. Indiv.	$174,021	Spnd. Edge	$673,059
C-O-H	$59,618	Party	$16,165	Lg. Indiv.	$280,770	Debt	$0

5th District, Rep. Harold D. Rogers (R)

Receipts	$651,821	PACS	$233,890	Out of St.	$24,500	C-P-V	$7.69
Expend.	$885,966	Cand.	$0	Sm. Indiv.	$89,709	Spnd. Edge	$611,213
C-O-H	$32,933	Party	$11,694	Lg. Indiv.	$281,292	Debt	$0

6th District, Rep. Scotty Baesler (D)

Receipts	$301,557	PACS	$0	Out of St.	$750	C-P-V	$2.02
Expend.	$273,727	Cand.	$0	Sm. Indiv.	$157,244	Spnd. Edge	$208,084
C-O-H	$27,830	Party	$0	Lg. Indiv.	$138,719	Debt	$0

LOUISIANA

Sen. J. Bennett Johnston (D)

Receipts	$4,776,658	PACS	$1,444,715	Out of St.	$774,298	C-P-V	$7.19
Expend.	$5,389,624	Cand.	$0	Sm. Indiv.	$896,046	Spnd. Edge	$2,809,421
C-O-H	$945,372	Party	$5,000	Lg. Indiv.	$1,388,931	Debts	$0

Sen. John B. Breaux (D)

Receipts	$3,481,494	PACS	$1,697,455	Out of St.	$594,845	C-P-V	$3.26
Expend.	$2,007,675	Cand.	$0	Sm. Indiv.	$481,992	Spnd. Edge	$1,912,755
C-O-H	$1,522,344	Party	$17,500	Lg. Indiv.	$1,076,298	Debts	$0

1st District, Rep. Robert L. (Bob) Livingston (R)

Receipts	$337,316	PACS	$133,247	Out of St.	$19,500	C-P-V	$3.84
Expend.	$321,487	Cand.	$0	Sm. Indiv.	$69,924	Spnd. Edge	$321,487
C-O-H	$295,908	Party	$80	Lg. Indiv.	$100,500	Debt	$0

2d District, Rep. William J. Jefferson (D)

Receipts	$376,227	PACS	$223,735	Out of St.	$25,450	C-P-V	$5.25
Expend.	$352,058	Cand.	$0	Sm. Indiv.	$16,556	Spnd. Edge	$328,418
C-O-H	$25,522	Party	$150	Lg. Indiv.	$123,425	Debt	$110,255

3d District, Rep. W. J. (Billy) Tauzin (D)

Receipts	$590,179	PACS	$442,559	Out of St.	$38,650	C-P-V	$3.79
Expend.	$311,112	Cand.	$0	Sm. Indiv.	$22,655	Spnd. Edge	$311,112
C-O-H	$327,478	Party	$0	Lg. Indiv.	$107,150	Debt	$0

4th District, Rep. Cleo Fields (D)

Receipts	$304,719	PACS	$49,020	Out of St.	$19,550	C-P-V	$2.12
Expend.	$305,336	Cand.	$0	Sm. Indiv.	$13,973	Spnd. Edge	$151,796
C-O-H	$1,044	Party	$0	Lg. Indiv.	$194,550	Debt	$52,319

5th District, Rep. Jim McCrery (R)

Receipts	$768,933	PACS	$225,593	Out of St.	$22,850	C-P-V	$4.84
Expend.	$743,254	Cand.	$500	Sm. Indiv.	$168,382	Spnd. Edge	($49,064)
C-O-H	$63,367	Party	$27,244	Lg. Indiv.	$337,404	Debt	$0

6th District, Rep. Richard H. Baker (R)

Receipts	$711,147	PACS	$268,350	Out of St.	$16,750	C-P-V	$6.21
Expend.	$770,203	Cand.	$0	Sm. Indiv.	$113,844	Spnd. Edge	$345,333
C-O-H	$7,999	Party	$1,633	Lg. Indiv.	$314,696	Debt	$45,158

7th District, Rep. James A. (Jimmy) Hayes (D)

Receipts	$429,546	PACS	$240,552	Out of St.	$28,550	C-P-V	$5.19
Expend.	$436,331	Cand.	$0	Sm. Indiv.	$41,050	Spnd. Edge	$417,656
C-O-H	$42,064	Party	$15,000	Lg. Indiv.	$81,450	Debt	$148,396

MAINE

Sen. William S. Cohen (R)

Receipts	$1,506,228	PACS	$553,945	Out of St.	$423,675	C-P-V	$5.10
Expend.	$1,628,292	Cand.	$0	Sm. Indiv.	$205,528	Spnd. Edge	($305)
C-O-H	$17,907	Party	$25,220	Lg. Indiv.	$616,870	Debts	$0

Sen. George J. Mitchell (D)

Receipts	$1,938,946	PACS	$805,171	Out of St.	$508,564	C-P-V	$3.24
Expend.	$1,466,742	Cand.	$0	Sm. Indiv.	$307,412	Spnd. Edge	$1,319,029
C-O-H	$480,729	Party	$8,010	Lg. Indiv.	$688,133	Debts	$638

1st District, Rep. Thomas H. Andrews (D)

Receipts	$861,564	PACS	$392,357	Out of St.	$95,300	C-P-V	$3.65
Expend.	$850,122	Cand.	$0	Sm. Indiv.	$224,705	Spnd. Edge	($614,598)
C-O-H	$15,877	Party	$1,220	Lg. Indiv.	$231,290	Debt	$24,518

2d District, Rep. Olympia J. Snowe (R)

Receipts	$746,628	PACS	$246,095	Out of St.	$118,868	C-P-V	$4.88
Expend.	$746,611	Cand.	$0	Sm. Indiv.	$257,438	Spnd. Edge	$364,201
C-O-H	$3,353	Party	$16,359	Lg. Indiv.	$208,243	Debt	$0

MARYLAND

Sen. Paul S. Sarbanes (D)

Receipts	$1,584,034	PACS	$618,518	Out of St.	$403,690	C-P-V	$1.58
Expend.	$1,576,777	Cand.	$0	Sm. Indiv.	$285,194	Spnd. Edge	$913,982
C-O-H	$11,395	Party	$24,000	Lg. Indiv.	$596,335	Debts	$24,279

Sen. Barbara A. Mikulski (D)

Receipts	$3,789,523	PACS	$1,072,697	Out of St.	$533,866	C-P-V	$2.77
Expend.	$3,623,974	Cand.	$0	Sm. Indiv.	$1,350,792	Spnd. Edge	$2,448,292
C-O-H	$269,145	Party	$17,500	Lg. Indiv.	$1,081,678	Debts	$0

1st District, Rep. Wayne T. Gilchrest (R)

Receipts	$394,794	PACS	$94,529	Out of St.	$7,500	C-P-V	$3.29
Expend.	$395,104	Cand.	$0	Sm. Indiv.	$154,306	S. Edge	($1,158,745)
C-O-H	$2,582	Party	$40,099	Lg. Indiv.	$95,767	Debt	$19,695

2d District, Rep. Helen Delich Bentley (R)

Receipts	$959,100	PACS	$240,620	Out of St.	$126,540	C-P-V	$5.78
Expend.	$956,821	Cand.	$0	Sm. Indiv.	$275,391	Spnd. Edge	$907,980
C-O-H	$134,117	Party	$4,010	Lg. Indiv.	$425,596	Debt	$4,152

3d District, Rep. Benjamin L. Cardin (D)

Receipts	$591,234	PACS	$292,553	Out of St.	$22,750	C-P-V	$3.96
Expend.	$646,863	Cand.	$0	Sm. Indiv.	$45,183	Spnd. Edge	$638,031
C-O-H	$195,084	Party	$0	Lg. Indiv.	$175,558	Debt	$0

4th District, Rep. Albert R. Wynn (D)

Receipts	$571,408	PACS	$238,477	Out of St.	$21,100	C-P-V	$2.82
Expend.	$386,186	Cand.	$0	Sm. Indiv.	$58,845	Spnd. Edge	$250,241
C-O-H	$59,317	Party	$0	Lg. Indiv.	$122,736	Debt	$20,000

5th District, Rep. Steny H. Hoyer (D)

Receipts	$1,304,867	PACS	$711,367	Out of St.	$142,602	C-P-V	$13.39
Expend.	$1,584,271	Cand.	$0	Sm. Indiv.	$157,580	Spnd. Edge	$1,319,206
C-O-H	$41,000	Party	$300	Lg. Indiv.	$378,415	Debt	$0

6th District, Rep. Roscoe G. Bartlett (R)

Receipts	$311,819	PACS	$90,500	Out of St.	$22,199	C-P-V	$2.45
Expend.	$307,885	Cand.	$6,052	Sm. Indiv.	$53,652	Spnd. Edge	($288,166)
C-O-H	$3,933	Party	$8,420	Lg. Indiv.	$47,089	Debt	$97,731

7th District, Rep. Kweisi Mfume (D)

Receipts	$255,269	PACS	$131,687	Out of St.	$10,900	C-P-V	$1.42
Expend.	$216,518	Cand.	$0	Sm. Indiv.	$50,715	Spnd. Edge	$216,518
C-O-H	$123,136	Party	$450	Lg. Indiv.	$62,954	Debt	$0

8th District, Rep. Constance A. Morella (R)

Receipts	$430,301	PACS	$184,373	Out of St.	$10,136	C-P-V	$1.62
Expend.	$328,516	Cand.	$0	Sm. Indiv.	$126,156	Spnd. Edge	$254,062
C-O-H	$303,167	Party	$0	Lg. Indiv.	$101,196	Debt	$0

MASSACHUSETTS

Sen. Edward M. Kennedy (D)

Receipts	$3,587,319	PACS	$342,743	Out of St.	$1,682,562	C-P-V	$1.77
Expend.	$2,991,247	Cand.	$0	Sm. Indiv.	$730,164	Spnd. Edge	$2,403,920
C-O-H	$735,351	Party	$17,875	Lg. Indiv.	$2,347,287	Debts	$0

Sen. John F. Kerry (D)

Receipts	$8,016,051	PACS	$17,477	Out of St.	$1,857,922	C-P-V	$6.08
Expend.	$8,040,970	Cand.	$0	Sm. Indiv.	$3,179,406	Spnd. Edge	$2,863,178
C-O-H	$12,055	Party	$21,312	Lg. Indiv.	$4,282,444	Debts	$92,765

1st District, Rep. John Olver (D)

Receipts	$705,906	PACS	$296,780	Out of St.	$13,950	C-P-V	$5.21
Expend.	$704,238	Cand.	$0	Sm. Indiv.	$165,713	Spnd. Edge	$319,613
C-O-H	$3,502	Party	$3,803	Lg. Indiv.	$120,581	Debt	$103,516

2d District, Rep. Richard E. Neal (D)

Receipts	$384,741	PACS	$208,395	Out of St.	$8,250	C-P-V	$2.71
Expend.	$355,367	Cand.	$0	Sm. Indiv.	$108,182	Spnd. Edge	$253,188
C-O-H	$41,868	Party	$0	Lg. Indiv.	$62,719	Debt	$8,000

3d District, Rep. Peter Blute (R)

Receipts	$438,994	PACS	$43,900	Out of St.	$25,500	C-P-V	$3.32
Expend.	$435,911	Cand.	$1,400	Sm. Indiv.	$202,687	Spnd. Edge	($488,473)
C-O-H	$3,081	Party	$5,254	Lg. Indiv.	$185,752	Debt	$51,413

4th District, Rep. Barney Frank (D)

Receipts	$498,997	PACS	$185,360	Out of St.	$33,818	C-P-V	$2.06
Expend.	$376,829	Cand.	$0	Sm. Indiv.	$184,093	Spnd. Edge	$325,479
C-O-H	$175,056	Party	$265	Lg. Indiv.	$116,668	Debt	$4,068

5th District, Rep. Martin T. (Marty) Meehan (D)

Receipts	$832,266	PACS	$0	Out of St.	$42,750	C-P-V	$6.21
Expend.	$831,544	Cand.	$6,804	Sm. Indiv.	$190,559	Spnd. Edge	$279,648
C-O-H	$721	Party	$15,880	Lg. Indiv.	$438,145	Debt	$185,465

6th District, Rep. Peter G. Torkildsen (R)

Receipts	$463,007	PACS	$0	Out of St.	$11,825	C-P-V	$2.90
Expend.	$460,934	Cand.	$1,000	Sm. Indiv.	$180,351	Spnd. Edge	($209,176)
C-O-H	$2,072	Party	$16,115	Lg. Indiv.	$241,428	Debt	$57,738

7th District, Rep. Edward J. Markey (D)

Receipts	$450,926	PACS	$0	Out of St.	$169,975	C-P-V	$5.31
Expend.	$928,883	Cand.	$0	Sm. Indiv.	$60,004	Spnd. Edge	$602,690
C-O-H	$131,578	Party	$0	Lg. Indiv.	$334,175	Debt	$0

8th District, Rep. Joseph P. Kennedy, II (D)

Receipts	$769,635	PACS	$146,030	Out of St.	$171,820	C-P-V	$5.12
Expend.	$767,161	Cand.	$0	Sm. Indiv.	$132,653	Spnd. Edge	$767,161
C-O-H	$229,759	Party	$0	Lg. Indiv.	$456,146	Debt	$0

9th District, Rep. John Joseph (Joe) Moakley (D)

Receipts	$855,533	PACS	$430,075	Out of St.	$59,850	C-P-V	$6.02
Expend.	$1,056,446	Cand.	$0	Sm. Indiv.	$156,557	Spnd. Edge	$1,043,830
C-O-H	$288,902	Party	$450	Lg. Indiv.	$221,800	Debt	$0

10th District, Rep. Gerry E. Studds (D)

Receipts	$1,438,264	PACS	$413,068	Out of St.	$188,176	C-P-V	$7.61
Expend.	$1,440,376	Cand.	$0	Sm. Indiv.	$666,026	Spnd. Edge	$1,201,637
C-O-H	$19,799	Party	$3,949	Lg. Indiv.	$342,845	Debt	$83,952

MICHIGAN

Sen. Donald W. Riegle, Jr. (D)

Receipts	$4,019,665	PACS	$1,522,929	Out of St.	$1,380,606	C-P-V	$1.64
Expend.	$3,479,293	Cand.	$0	Sm. Indiv.	$229,260	Spnd. Edge	$3,036,597
C-O-H	$855,659	Party	$23,038	Lg. Indiv.	$1,778,891	Debts	$0

Sen. Carl Levin (D)

Receipts	$7,213,583	PACS	$1,405,560	Out of St.	$1,832,216	C-P-V	$4.80
Expend.	$7,066,832	Cand.	$0	Sm. Indiv.	$2,192,554	Spnd. Edge	$4,654,509
C-O-H	$201,967	Party	$48,192	Lg. Indiv.	$3,134,084	Debts	$106,157

1st District, Rep. Bart Stupak (D)

Receipts	$225,699	PACS	$104,950	Out of St.	$3,500	C-P-V	$1.56
Expend.	$225,572	Cand.	$0	Sm. Indiv.	$47,727	Spnd. Edge	($223,892)
C-O-H	$125	Party	$16,250	Lg. Indiv.	$41,575	Debt	$50,999

2d District, Rep. Peter Hoekstra (R)

Receipts	$104,861	PACS	$0	Out of St.	$300	C-P-V	$0.64
Expend.	$100,278	Cand.	$0	Sm. Indiv.	$37,656	Spnd. Edge	$79,760
C-O-H	$4,582	Party	$7,475	Lg. Indiv.	$26,430	Debt	$26,800

3d District, Rep. Paul B. Henry (R)

Receipts	$349,444	PACS	$72,650	Out of St.	$500	C-P-V	$1.74
Expend.	$282,472	Cand.	$0	Sm. Indiv.	$137,509	Spnd. Edge	$237,606
C-O-H	$342,492	Party	$10	Lg. Indiv.	$112,875	Debt	$0

4th District, Rep. Dave Camp (R)

Receipts	$507,855	PACS	$204,537	Out of St.	$15,850	C-P-V	$3.29
Expend.	$518,118	Cand.	$3,058	Sm. Indiv.	$119,339	Spnd. Edge	$502,468
C-O-H	$1,284	Party	$9,250	Lg. Indiv.	$164,076	Debt	$10,651

5th District, Rep. James A. Barcia (D)

Receipts	$289,443	PACS	$138,251	Out of St.	$2,200	C-P-V	$1.96
Expend.	$288,755	Cand.	$1,292	Sm. Indiv.	$43,242	Spnd. Edge	$195,198
C-O-H	$689	Party	$7,750	Lg. Indiv.	$66,784	Debt	$11,400

6th District, Rep. Fred Upton (R)

Receipts	$432,851	PACS	$149,585	Out of St.	$4,250	C-P-V	$2.55
Expend.	$367,596	Cand.	$0	Sm. Indiv.	$96,324	Spnd. Edge	$324,827
C-O-H	$107,399	Party	$1,399	Lg. Indiv.	$179,341	Debt	$0

7th District, Rep. Nick Smith (R)

Receipts	$242,908	PACS	$0	Out of St.	$3,500	C-P-V	$1.72
Expend.	$231,043	Cand.	$0	Sm. Indiv.	$49,634	Spnd. Edge	$231,043
C-O-H	$11,862	Party	$1,025	Lg. Indiv.	$78,192	Debt	$97,500

8th District, Rep. Bob Carr (D)

Receipts	$1,107,973	PACS	$568,003	Out of St.	$200,743	C-P-V	$10.00
Expend.	$1,355,199	Cand.	$0	Sm. Indiv.	$142,999	Spnd. Edge	($407,567)
C-O-H	$9,399	Party	$12,850	Lg. Indiv.	$336,128	Debt	$0

9th District, Rep. Dale E. Kildee (D)

Receipts	$762,758	PACS	$464,970	Out of St.	$23,041	C-P-V	$5.94
Expend.	$795,484	Cand.	$0	Sm. Indiv.	$137,638	Spnd. Edge	$665,644
C-O-H	$5,315	Party	$10,809	Lg. Indiv.	$100,973	Debt	$116,614

10th District, Rep. David E. Bonior (D)

Receipts	$1,295,553	PACS	$934,613	Out of St.	$74,462	C-P-V	$9.73
Expend.	$1,345,011	Cand.	$0	Sm. Indiv.	$124,667	Spnd. Edge	$1,086,954
C-O-H	$40,391	Party	$51,355	Lg. Indiv.	$157,242	Debt	$0

11th District, Rep. Joe Knollenberg (R)

Receipts	$496,036	PACS	$116,436	Out of St.	$9,750	C-P-V	$2.91
Expend.	$490,926	Cand.	$1,951	Sm. Indiv.	$140,695	Spnd. Edge	$218,504
C-O-H	$5,110	Party	$3,033	Lg. Indiv.	$184,146	Debt	$27,559

12th District, Rep. Sander M. Levin (D)

Receipts	$1,028,481	PACS	$504,521	Out of St.	$150,100	C-P-V	$8.62
Expend.	$1,185,400	Cand.	$0	Sm. Indiv.	$162,890	Spnd. Edge	$995,197
C-O-H	$98,288	Party	$12,790	Lg. Indiv.	$291,220	Debt	$0

13th District, Rep. William D. Ford (D)

Receipts	$681,981	PACS	$520,850	Out of St.	$55,700	C-P-V	$6.83
Expend.	$872,349	Cand.	$0	Sm. Indiv.	$48,754	Spnd. Edge	$684,211
C-O-H	$6,768	Party	$10,000	Lg. Indiv.	$75,450	Debt	$55,889

14th District, Rep. John Conyers, Jr. (D)

Receipts	$309,396	PACS	$215,008	Out of St.	$35,268	C-P-V	$2.01
Expend.	$332,818	Cand.	$0	Sm. Indiv.	$64,665	Spnd. Edge	$332,818
C-O-H	$35,601	Party	$375	Lg. Indiv.	$60,843	Debt	$0

15th District, Rep. Barbara-Rose Collins (D)

Receipts	$278,723	PACS	$121,721	Out of St.	$8,900	C-P-V	$1.91
Expend.	$284,049	Cand.	$0	Sm. Indiv.	$49,544	Spnd. Edge	$189,789
C-O-H	$55,717	Party	$500	Lg. Indiv.	$60,225	Debt	$0

16th District, Rep. John D. Dingell (D)

Receipts	$1,112,141	PACS	$767,931	Out of St.	$105,450	C-P-V	$6.92
Expend.	$1,086,152	Cand.	$0	Sm. Indiv.	$53,788	Spnd. Edge	$1,080,751
C-O-H	$523,361	Party	$5,018	Lg. Indiv.	$227,524	Debt	$0

MINNESOTA

Sen. Dave Durenberger (IR)

Receipts	$6,777,759	PACS	$1,770,786	Out of St.	$1,231,471	C-P-V	$5.82
Expend.	$6,840,128	Cand.	$0	Sm. Indiv.	$2,755,986	Spnd. Edge	$4,375,496
C-O-H	$27,478	Party	$23,085	Lg. Indiv.	$1,926,088	Debts	$113,553

Sen. Paul David Wellstone (DFL)

Receipts	$1,400,782	PACS	$294,523	Out of St.	$93,892	C-P-V	$1.47
Expend.	$1,338,283	Cand.	$0	Sm. Indiv.	$765,393	Spnd. Ed.	($6,386,405)
C-O-H	$62,500	Party	$30,835	Lg. Indiv.	$304,255	Debts	$117,514

1st District, Rep. Timothy J. Penny (DFL)

Receipts	$244,518	PACS	$92,743	Out of St.	$7,000	C-P-V	$1.42
Expend.	$292,920	Cand.	$0	Sm. Indiv.	$106,196	Spnd. Edge	$199,300
C-O-H	$207,789	Party	$1,725	Lg. Indiv.	$11,450	Debt	$0

2d District, Rep. David Minge (DFL)

Receipts	$365,394	PACS	$159,958	Out of St.	$5,350	C-P-V	$2.69
Expend.	$355,400	Cand.	$0	Sm. Indiv.	$90,281	Spnd. Edge	($73,700)
C-O-H	$9,799	Party	$16,719	Lg. Indiv.	$58,210	Debt	$32,658

3d District, Rep. Jim Ramstad (IR)

Receipts	$1,010,791	PACS	$260,016	Out of St.	$40,800	C-P-V	$3.47
Expend.	$695,521	Cand.	$0	Sm. Indiv.	$270,772	Spnd. Edge	$677,357
C-O-H	$317,719	Party	$3,735	Lg. Indiv.	$468,967	Debt	$21,792

4th District, Rep. Bruce F. Vento (DFL)

Receipts	$280,123	PACS	$207,495	Out of St.	$16,750	C-P-V	$2.18
Expend.	$348,920	Cand.	$0	Sm. Indiv.	$31,553	Spnd. Edge	$266,357
C-O-H	$86,382	Party	$550	Lg. Indiv.	$20,820	Debt	$0

5th District, Rep. Martin Olav Sabo (DFL)

Receipts	$408,981	PACS	$247,703	Out of St.	$29,488	C-P-V	$3.36
Expend.	$585,831	Cand.	$0	Sm. Indiv.	$63,557	Spnd. Edge	$569,050
C-O-H	$39,370	Party	$0	Lg. Indiv.	$48,705	Debt	$0

6th District, Rep. Rod Grams (IR)

Receipts	$464,693	PACS	$138,784	Out of St.	$7,250	C-P-V	$3.29
Expend.	$439,718	Cand.	$0	Sm. Indiv.	$168,450	Spnd. Edge	($778,114)
C-O-H	$24,973	Party	$15,230	Lg. Indiv.	$130,594	Debt	$54,185

7th District, Rep. Collin C. Peterson (DFL)

Receipts	$488,844	PACS	$321,507	Out of St.	$4,900	C-P-V	$3.70
Expend.	$495,882	Cand.	$0	Sm. Indiv.	$99,063	Spnd. Edge	$276,931
C-O-H	$2,281	Party	$17,411	Lg. Indiv.	$22,050	Debt	$15,079

8th District, Rep. James L. Oberstar (DFL)

Receipts	$340,642	PACS	$202,005	Out of St.	$22,650	C-P-V	$2.31
Expend.	$386,646	Cand.	$0	Sm. Indiv.	$27,187	Spnd. Edge	$354,230
C-O-H	$347,548	Party	$100	Lg. Indiv.	$45,600	Debt	$0

MISSISSIPPI

Sen. Thad Cochran (R)

Receipts	$1,461,838	PACS	$558,888	Out of St.	$258,675	C-P-V	$2.52
Expend.	$691,865	Cand.	$0	Sm. Indiv.	$135,872	Spnd. Edge	(unopp.)
C-O-H	$908,834	Party	$18,361	Lg. Indiv.	$560,905	Debts	$0

Sen. Trent Lott (R)

Receipts	$3,595,034	PACS	$1,113,113	Out of St.	$749,263	C-P-V	$6.66
Expend.	$3,397,795	Cand.	$0	Sm. Indiv.	$476,456	Spnd. Edge	$1,054,133
C-O-H	$197,239	Party	$25,710	Lg. Indiv.	$1,512,770	Debts	$0

1st District, Rep. Jamie L. Whitten (D)

Receipts	$82,667	PACS	$30,700	Out of St.	$0	C-P-V	$2.20
Expend.	$267,223	Cand.	$0	Sm. Indiv.	$5,387	Spnd. Edge	$38,219
C-O-H	$251,170	Party	$0	Lg. Indiv.	$550	Debt	$0

2d District, Rep. Bennie G. Thompson (D)
(Elected March 30, 1993; campaign finance figures not available)

3d District, Rep. G.V. (Sonny) Montgomery (D)

Receipts	$172,603	PACS	$97,600	Out of St.	$2,100	C-P-V		$1.07
Expend.	$174,165	Cand.	$0	Sm. Indiv.	$17,020	Spnd. Edge	$174,165
C-O-H	$170,345	Party	$0	Lg. Indiv.	$43,743	Debt		$0

4th District, Rep. Mike Parker (D)

Receipts	$416,677	PACS	$240,200	Out of St.	$50,750	C-P-V		$1.20
Expend.	$156,969	Cand.	$0	Sm. Indiv.	$27,236	Spnd. Edge	$156,969
C-O-H	$307,872	Party	$150	Lg. Indiv.	$103,286	Debt		$0

5th District, Rep. Gene Taylor (D)

Receipts	$340,357	PACS	$158,535	Out of St.	$21,350	C-P-V		$2.82
Expend.	$340,311	Cand.	$0	Sm. Indiv.	$66,539	Spnd. Edge	$104,171
C-O-H	$2,211	Party	$0	Lg. Indiv.	$99,502	Debt		$4,001

MISSOURI

Sen. John C. Danforth (R)

Receipts	$4,775,393	PACS	$1,380,461	Out of St.	$1,155,604	C-P-V		$2.94
Expend.	$4,132,748	Cand.	$0	Sm. Indiv.	$660,597	Spnd. Edge	$3,256,459
C-O-H	$645,785	Party	$16,850	Lg. Indiv.	$2,439,087	Debts		$0

Sen. Christopher S. (Kit) Bond (R)

Receipts	$5,087,184	PACS	$1,721,235	Out of St.	$562,382	C-P-V		$4.13
Expend.	$5,048,333	Cand.	$386	Sm. Indiv.	$727,133	Spnd. Edge	$3,936,146
C-O-H	$106,621	Party	$31,925	Lg. Indiv.	$2,319,911	Debts		$18,251

1st District, Rep. William (Bill) Clay (D)

Receipts	$300,187	PACS	$251,680	Out of St.	$13,100	C-P-V		$1.88
Expend.	$297,635	Cand.	$0	Sm. Indiv.	$20,421	Spnd. Edge	$275,773
C-O-H	$121,000	Party	$0	Lg. Indiv.	$20,260	Debt		$0

2d District, Rep. Jim Talent (R)

Receipts	$920,895	PACS	$213,472	Out of St.	$15,850	C-P-V		$5.78
Expend.	$910,893	Cand.	$0	Sm. Indiv.	$249,920	Spnd. Edge	$78,080
C-O-H	$10,004	Party	$9,715	Lg. Indiv.	$389,138	Debt		$21,446

3d District, Rep. Richard A. Gephardt (D)

Receipts	$3,237,531	PACS	$1,240,597	Out of St.	$1,237,598	C-P-V		$19.06
Expend.	$3,316,784	Cand.	$0	Sm. Indiv.	$241,881	Spnd. Edge	$2,890,818
C-O-H	$114,236	Party	$11,625	Lg. Indiv.	$1,620,483	Debt		$0

4th District, Rep. Ike Skelton (D)

Receipts	$310,017	PACS	$211,391	Out of St.	$4,000	C-P-V		$2.41
Expend.	$426,867	Cand.	$0	Sm. Indiv.	$65,990	Spnd. Edge	$422,239
C-O-H	$194,795	Party	$120	Lg. Indiv.	$30,939	Debt		$0

5th District, Rep. Alan Wheat (D)

Receipts	$488,439	PACS	$344,588	Out of St.	$31,720	C-P-V		$4.46
Expend.	$673,086	Cand.	$0	Sm. Indiv.	$44,546	Spnd. Edge	$615,686
C-O-H	$76,049	Party	$0	Lg. Indiv.	$71,818	Debt		$1,000

6th District, Rep. Pat Danner (D)

Receipts	$486,277	PACS	$183,992	Out of St.	$8,250	C-P-V		$3.24
Expend.	$482,984	Cand.	$0	Sm. Indiv.	$46,152	Spnd. Edge	($50,321)
C-O-H	$3,291	Party	$8,921	Lg. Indiv.	$103,386	Debt		$69,800

7th District, Rep. Mel Hancock (R)

Receipts	$393,638	PACS	$164,430	Out of St.	$11,350	C-P-V	$2.66
Expend.	$426,525	Cand.	$0	Sm. Indiv.	$78,681	Spnd. Edge	$115,867
C-O-H	$96,147	Party	$8,416	Lg. Indiv.	$120,804	Debt	$0

8th District, Rep. Bill Emerson (R)

Receipts	$518,998	PACS	$299,188	Out of St.	$20,440	C-P-V	$3.32
Expend.	$488,949	Cand.	$0	Sm. Indiv.	$117,638	Spnd. Edge	$476,975
C-O-H	$37,332	Party	$3,184	Lg. Indiv.	$95,815	Debt	$0

9th District, Rep. Harold L. Volkmer (D)

Receipts	$354,612	PACS	$247,010	Out of St.	$5,550	C-P-V	$4.10
Expend.	$511,550	Cand.	$0	Sm. Indiv.	$58,124	Spnd. Edge	$371,690
C-O-H	$2,883	Party	$1,447	Lg. Indiv.	$23,850	Debt	$5,500

MONTANA

Sen. Max Baucus (D)

Receipts	$3,037,932	PACS	$1,663,321	Out of St.	$686,368	C-P-V	$11.81
Expend.	$2,568,899	Cand.	$0	Sm. Indiv.	$333,490	Spnd. Edge	$1,822,362
C-O-H	$514,679	Party	$2,052	Lg. Indiv.	$889,453	Debts	$0

Sen. Conrad Burns (R)

Receipts	$1,098,751	PACS	$315,389	Out of St.	$257,351	C-P-V	$5.67
Expend.	$1,074,884	Cand.	$0	Sm. Indiv.	$221,891	Spnd. Edge	($391,174)
C-O-H	$23,866	Party	$40,131	Lg. Indiv.	$317,851	Debts	$38,922

At-Large, Rep. Pat Williams (D)

Receipts	$1,190,716	PACS	$501,505	Out of St.	$128,420	C-P-V	$6.56
Expend.	$1,336,673	Cand.	$0	Sm. Indiv.	$386,439	Spnd. Edge	$44,090
C-O-H	$68,395	Party	$14,905	Lg. Indiv.	$245,890	Debt	$24,102

NEBRASKA

Sen. J. James Exon (D)

Receipts	$2,629,180	PACS	$1,519,498	Out of St.	$314,870	C-P-V	$6.89
Expend.	$2,410,097	Cand.	$0	Sm. Indiv.	$447,707	Spnd. Edge	$960,183
C-O-H	$270,574	Party	$19,687	Lg. Indiv.	$566,849	Debts	$0

Sen. Robert Kerrey (D)

Receipts	$3,474,697	PACS	$791,483	Out of St.	$1,047,429	C-P-V	$9.10
Expend.	$3,446,992	Cand.	$2,500	Sm. Indiv.	$1,071,787	Spnd. Edge	$39,195
C-O-H	$27,705	Party	$27,595	Lg. Indiv.	$1,435,982	Debts	$116,193

1st District, Rep. Doug Bereuter (R)

Receipts	$315,824	PACS	$194,482	Out of St.	$5,700	C-P-V	$2.56
Expend.	$365,386	Cand.	$0	Sm. Indiv.	$82,866	Spnd. Edge	$280,853
C-O-H	$5,167	Party	$2,217	Lg. Indiv.	$29,577	Debt	$0

2d District, Rep. Peter Hoagland (D)

Receipts	$701,282	PACS	$457,190	Out of St.	$60,300	C-P-V	$5.85
Expend.	$699,387	Cand.	$0	Sm. Indiv.	$77,533	Spnd. Edge	$320,666
C-O-H	$13,744	Party	$2,299	Lg. Indiv.	$147,750	Debt	$142,649

3d District, Rep. William (Bill) Barrett (R)

Receipts	$485,326	PACS	$197,875	Out of St.	$7,400	C-P-V	$2.86
Expend.	$487,992	Cand.	$25,737	Sm. Indiv.	$137,042	Spnd. Edge	$396,822
C-O-H	$17,315	Party	$3,888	Lg. Indiv.	$105,330	Debt	$0

NEVADA

Sen. Harry Reid (D)

Receipts	$3,371,146	PACS	$1,105,739	Out of St.	$601,688	C-P-V	$12.88
Expend.	$3,259,802	Cand.	$0	Sm. Indiv.	$108,519	Spnd. Edge	$2,788,431
C-O-H	$144,835	Party	$2,000	Lg. Indiv.	$1,820,445	Debts	$0

Sen. Richard H. Bryan (D)

Receipts	$2,984,605	PACS	$802,795	Out of St.	$709,875	C-P-V	$16.83
Expend.	$2,953,642	Cand.	$0	Sm. Indiv.	$152,911	Spnd. Edge	($102,231)
C-O-H	$30,963	Party	$18,000	Lg. Indiv.	$1,861,351	Debts	$50,135

1st District, Rep. James H. Bilbray (D)

Receipts	$698,431	PACS	$228,534	Out of St.	$25,150	C-P-V	$5.20
Expend.	$667,018	Cand.	$0	Sm. Indiv.	$10,611	Spnd. Edge	$553,242
C-O-H	$32,519	Party	$1,443	Lg. Indiv.	$186,055	Debt	$40,000

2d District, Rep. Barbara F. Vucanovich (R)

Receipts	$686,022	PACS	$256,119	Out of St.	$31,283	C-P-V	$5.31
Expend.	$688,379	Cand.	$0	Sm. Indiv.	$145,488	Spnd. Edge	$485,491
C-O-H	$3,849	Party	$11,184	Lg. Indiv.	$211,703	Debt	$98,127

NEW HAMPSHIRE

Sen. Bob Smith (R)

Receipts	$1,508,246	PACS	$663,151	Out of St.	$297,340	C-P-V	$7.48
Expend.	$1,419,127	Cand.	$0	Sm. Indiv.	$200,975	Spnd. Edge	$1,104,618
C-O-H	$89,118	Party	$30,107	Lg. Indiv.	$575,046	Debts	$0

Sen. Judd Gregg (R)

Receipts	$990,836	PACS	$367,605	Out of St.	$150,091	C-P-V	$3.51
Expend.	$875,675	Cand.	$0	Sm. Indiv.	$152,446	Spnd. Edge	$41,708
C-O-H	$115,162	Party	$17,500	Lg. Indiv.	$423,680	Debts	$0

1st District, Rep. William H. Zeliff, Jr. (R)

Receipts	$776,283	PACS	$325,915	Out of St.	$86,599	C-P-V	$5.75
Expend.	$778,358	Cand.	$4,000	Sm. Indiv.	$102,995	Spnd. Edge	$603,793
C-O-H	$2,691	Party	$15,917	Lg. Indiv.	$309,837	Debt	$505,853

2d District, Rep. Dick Swett (D)

Receipts	$872,187	PACS	$403,900	Out of St.	$317,968	C-P-V	$4.99
Expend.	$785,452	Cand.	$0	Sm. Indiv.	$71,360	Spnd. Edge	$552,835
C-O-H	$91,820	Party	$5,000	Lg. Indiv.	$373,142	Debt	$0

NEW JERSEY

Sen. Bill Bradley (D)

Receipts	$12,842,957	PACS	$1,393,047	Out of St.	$6,698,994	C-P-V	$12.73
Expend.	$12,444,283	Cand.	$411	Sm. Indiv.	$1,023,868	Spnd. Ed.	$11,649,270
C-O-H	$775,770	Party	$0	Lg. Indiv.	$9,620,193	Debts	$83,000

Sen. Frank R. Lautenberg (D)

Receipts	$8,030,679	PACS	$1,641,065	Out of St.	$2,811,488	C-P-V	$5.03
Expend.	$8,046,705	Cand.	$0	Sm. Indiv.	$1,205,057	Spnd. Edge	$458,077
C-O-H	$40,147	Party	$2,945	Lg. Indiv.	$4,547,912	Debts	$3,759,000

1st District, Rep. Robert E. Andrews (D)

Receipts	$758,301	PACS	$345,800	Out of St.	$26,725	C-P-V	$4.97
Expend.	$762,588	Cand.	$0	Sm. Indiv.	$188,207	Spnd. Edge	$586,002
C-O-H	$1,284	Party	$3,250	Lg. Indiv.	$135,625	Debt	$73,727

2d District, Rep. William J. Hughes (D)

Receipts	$513,720	PACS	$223,125	Out of St.	$36,900	C-P-V	$4.59
Expend.	$608,150	Cand.	$0	Sm. Indiv.	$108,059	Spnd. Edge	$323,377
C-O-H	$116,489	Party	$4,650	Lg. Indiv.	$147,988	Debt	$0

3d District, Rep. H. James Saxton (R)

Receipts	$647,329	PACS	$278,875	Out of St.	$22,550	C-P-V	$2.75
Expend.	$416,807	Cand.	$0	Sm. Indiv.	$185,295	Spnd. Edge	$386,792
C-O-H	$279,382	Party	$3,324	Lg. Indiv.	$158,683	Debt	$0

4th District, Rep. Christopher H. Smith (R)

Receipts	$369,949	PACS	$110,958	Out of St.	$13,300	C-P-V	$2.77
Expend.	$413,493	Cand.	$0	Sm. Indiv.	$169,063	Spnd. Edge	$249,455
C-O-H	$20,850	Party	$16,755	Lg. Indiv.	$56,548	Debt	$11,768

5th District, Rep. Marge Roukema (R)

Receipts	$439,150	PACS	$224,598	Out of St.	$11,060	C-P-V	$2.57
Expend.	$504,596	Cand.	$0	Sm. Indiv.	$76,799	Spnd. Edge	$502,479
C-O-H	$32,842	Party	$80	Lg. Indiv.	$122,800	Debt	$47,161

6th District, Rep. Frank Pallone, Jr. (D)

Receipts	$932,079	PACS	$531,079	Out of St.	$38,920	C-P-V	$7.86
Expend.	$929,541	Cand.	$0	Sm. Indiv.	$150,810	Spnd. Edge	$526,388
C-O-H	$3,297	Party	$0	Lg. Indiv.	$224,855	Debt	$29,831

7th District, Rep. Bob Franks (R)

Receipts	$460,998	PACS	$131,032	Out of St.	$37,800	C-P-V	$3.43
Expend.	$453,991	Cand.	$0	Sm. Indiv.	$44,372	Spnd. Edge	$230,287
C-O-H	$7,007	Party	$16,610	Lg. Indiv.	$260,204	Debt	$20,120

8th District, Rep. Herb Klein (D)

Receipts	$1,291,518	PACS	$173,920	Out of St.	$22,250	C-P-V	$12.91
Expend.	$1,249,023	Cand.	$0	Sm. Indiv.	$187,017	Spnd. Edge	$816,239
C-O-H	$56,646	Party	$5,000	Lg. Indiv.	$236,117	Debt	$580,000

9th District, Rep. Robert G. Torricelli (D)

Receipts	$1,190,045	PACS	$350,495	Out of St.	$252,650	C-P-V	$7.19
Expend.	$1,001,343	Cand.	$0	Sm. Indiv.	$90,826	Spnd. Edge	$828,397
C-O-H	$1,035,163	Party	$1,199	Lg. Indiv.	$607,499	Debt	$0

10th District, Rep. Donald M. Payne (D)

Receipts	$358,688	PACS	$183,606	Out of St.	$8,536	C-P-V	$2.43
Expend.	$285,455	Cand.	$0	Sm. Indiv.	$60,664	Spnd. Edge	$259,179
C-O-H	$339,836	Party	$2,010	Lg. Indiv.	$82,086	Debt	$0

11th District, Rep. Dean A. Gallo (R)

Receipts	$567,280	PACS	$187,284	Out of St.	$20,450	C-P-V	$3.29
Expend.	$618,448	Cand.	$0	Sm. Indiv.	$130,385	Spnd. Edge	$485,928
C-O-H	$20,723	Party	$28	Lg. Indiv.	$243,730	Debt	$0

12th District, Rep. Dick Zimmer (R)

Receipts	$943,548	PACS	$214,214	Out of St.	$68,600	C-P-V	$5.23
Expend.	$911,638	Cand.	$0	Sm. Indiv.	$91,605	Spnd. Edge	$848,701
C-O-H	$35,026	Party	$19,223	Lg. Indiv.	$532,792	Debt	$96,243

13th District, Rep. Robert Menendez (D)

Receipts	$668,659	PACS	$226,497	Out of St.	$47,550	C-P-V	$6.89
Expend.	$645,640	Cand.	$0	Sm. Indiv.	$114,287	Spnd. Edge	$638,141
C-O-H	$23,018	Party	$0	Lg. Indiv.	$319,621	Debt	$25,000

NEW MEXICO

Sen. Pete V. Domenici (R)

Receipts	$2,431,983	PACS	$905,136	Out of St.	$550,945	C-P-V	$7.58
Expend.	$2,250,086	Cand.	$0	Sm. Indiv.	$436,184	Spnd. Edge	$2,211,576
C-O-H	$218,514	Party	$21,513	Lg. Indiv.	$913,775	Debts	$0

Sen. Jeff Bingaman (D)

Receipts	$4,160,449	PACS	$1,420,537	Out of St.	$966,323	C-P-V	$12.48
Expend.	$4,017,852	Cand.	$0	Sm. Indiv.	$943,438	Spnd. Edge	$3,358,599
C-O-H	$163,316	Party	$20,448	Lg. Indiv.	$1,314,721	Debts	$3,681

1st District, Rep. Steven H. Schiff (R)

Receipts	$573,884	PACS	$186,910	Out of St.	$4,055	C-P-V	$4.59
Expend.	$589,743	Cand.	$0	Sm. Indiv.	$270,747	Spnd. Edge	$508,202
C-O-H	$4,682	Party	$1,500	Lg. Indiv.	$109,949	Debt	$10,542

2d District, Rep. Joe Skeen (R)

Receipts	$387,893	PACS	$160,125	Out of St.	$20,800	C-P-V	$5.20
Expend.	$493,406	Cand.	$0	Sm. Indiv.	$109,788	Spnd. Edge	$452,433
C-O-H	$91,369	Party	$5,609	Lg. Indiv.	$84,663	Debt	$1,764

3d District, Rep. Bill Richardson (D)

Receipts	$680,154	PACS	$387,551	Out of St.	$72,650	C-P-V	$4.89
Expend.	$600,683	Cand.	$0	Sm. Indiv.	$93,627	Spnd. Edge	$552,619
C-O-H	$409,373	Party	$1,450	Lg. Indiv.	$141,828	Debt	$0

NEW YORK

Sen. Daniel Patrick Moynihan (D)

Receipts	$5,798,312	PACS	$1,220,625	Out of St.	$868,359	C-P-V	$1.35
Expend.	$5,454,883	Cand.	$0	Sm. Indiv.	$2,055,396	Spnd. Edge	$4,926,552
C-O-H	$460,076	Party	$17,500	Lg. Indiv.	$2,290,615	Debts	$0

Sen. Alfonse M. D'Amato (R)

Receipts	$11,239,373	PACS	$1,361,231	Out of St.	$1,087,128	C-P-V	$3.65
Expend.	$11,550,958	Cand.	$0	Sm. Indiv.	$2,248,612	Spnd. Edge	$5,141,977
C-O-H	$144,716	Party	$24,500	Lg. Indiv.	$6,388,212	Debts	$349,155

1st District, Rep. George Hochbrueckner (D)

Receipts	$628,248	PACS	$296,600	Out of St.	$10,850	C-P-V	$5.14
Expend.	$606,190	Cand.	$0	Sm. Indiv.	$163,260	Spnd. Edge	$379,907
C-O-H	$1,850	Party	$15,979	Lg. Indiv.	$85,325	Debt	$29,969

2d District, Rep. Rick A. Lazio (R)

Receipts	$276,487	PACS	$43,663	Out of St.	$6,740	C-P-V	$2.52
Expend.	$276,191	Cand.	$1,000	Sm. Indiv.	$108,396	S. Edge	($1,170,720)
C-O-H	$223	Party	$15,000	Lg. Indiv.	$89,477	Debt	$19,629

3d District, Rep. Peter T. King (R)

Receipts	$244,526	PACS	$117,550	Out of St.	$15,300	C-P-V	$2.11
Expend.	$263,345	Cand.	$0	Sm. Indiv.	$42,901	Spnd. Edge	($863,894)
C-O-H	$8,079	Party	$3,457	Lg. Indiv.	$78,401	Debt	$0

4th District, Rep. David A. Levy (R)

Receipts	$217,319	PACS	$60,880	Out of St.	$6,583	C-P-V	$1.89
Expend.	$209,225	Cand.	$395	Sm. Indiv.	$57,728	Spnd. Edge	($293,288)
C-O-H	$15,896	Party	$10,924	Lg. Indiv.	$80,908	Debt	$20,938

5th District, Rep. Gary L. Ackerman (D)

Receipts	$674,901	PACS	$342,775	Out of St.	$60,400	C-P-V	$8.30
Expend.	$917,483	Cand.	$0	Sm. Indiv.	$49,616	Spnd. Edge	$794,277
C-O-H	$42,779	Party	$9,800	Lg. Indiv.	$209,625	Debt	$20,000

6th District, Rep. Floyd H. Flake (D)

Receipts	$272,263	PACS	$142,490	Out of St.	$13,350	C-P-V	$2.90
Expend.	$281,172	Cand.	$0	Sm. Indiv.	$47,062	Spnd. Edge	$236,157
C-O-H	$39,483	Party	$9,975	Lg. Indiv.	$28,420	Debt	$39,044

7th District, Rep. Thomas J. Manton (D)

Receipts	$643,780	PACS	$427,492	Out of St.	$16,249	C-P-V	$14.02
Expend.	$1,013,635	Cand.	$0	Sm. Indiv.	$52,584	Spnd. Edge	$830,898
C-O-H	$108,919	Party	$3,200	Lg. Indiv.	$92,324	Debt	$0

8th District, Rep. Jerrold Nadler (D)

Receipts	$49,685	PACS	$37,750	Out of St.	$583	C-P-V	$0.33
Expend.	$45,505	Cand.	$0	Sm. Indiv.	$785	Spnd. Edge	$43,355
C-O-H	$9,178	Party	$0	Lg. Indiv.	$7,250	Debt	$12,799

9th District, Rep. Charles E. Schumer (D)

Receipts	$923,272	PACS	$187,114	Out of St.	$63,000	C-P-V	$3.32
Expend.	$387,059	Cand.	$0	Sm. Indiv.	$49,796	Spnd. Edge	$387,059
C-O-H	$2,116,689	Party	$450	Lg. Indiv.	$487,550	Debt	$0

10th District, Rep. Edolphus Towns (D)

Receipts	$560,977	PACS	$241,165	Out of St.	$67,875	C-P-V	$7.17
Expend.	$699,589	Cand.	$0	Sm. Indiv.	$91,315	Spnd. Edge	$699,589
C-O-H	$3,803	Party	$16,395	Lg. Indiv.	$168,746	Debt	$20,381

11th District, Rep. Major R. Owens (D)

Receipts	$173,365	PACS	$89,972	Out of St.	$6,445	C-P-V	$2.21
Expend.	$177,235	Cand.	$0	Sm. Indiv.	$51,965	Spnd. Edge	$177,235
C-O-H	$4,201	Party	$5,525	Lg. Indiv.	$19,545	Debt	$37,361

12th District, Rep. Nydia M. Velazquez (D)

Receipts	$480,174	PACS	$155,000	Out of St.	$36,400	C-P-V	$8.26
Expend.	$461,749	Cand.	$0	Sm. Indiv.	$114,859	Spnd. Edge	$456,359
C-O-H	$14,698	Party	$0	Lg. Indiv.	$90,295	Debt	$279,078

13th District, Rep. Susan Molinari (R)

Receipts	$523,755	PACS	$195,775	Out of St.	$37,950	C-P-V	$4.71
Expend.	$507,962	Cand.	$0	Sm. Indiv.	$107,254	Spnd. Edge	$260,223
C-O-H	$31,803	Party	$3,034	Lg. Indiv.	$172,630	Debt	$0

14th District, Rep. Carolyn B. Maloney (D)

Receipts	$283,909	PACS	$73,935	Out of St.	$41,600	C-P-V	$2.73
Expend.	$277,223	Cand.	$1,000	Sm. Indiv.	$34,756	Spnd. Edge	($864,247)
C-O-H	$6,685	Party	$4,750	Lg. Indiv.	$149,468	Debt	$73,749

15th District, Rep. Charles B. Rangel (D)

Receipts	$539,183	PACS	$325,850	Out of St.	$111,214	C-P-V	$6.37
Expend.	$669,095	Cand.	$0	Sm. Indiv.	$51,679	Spnd. Edge	$669,095
C-O-H	$174,093	Party	$0	Lg. Indiv.	$151,364	Debt	$0

16th District, Rep. Jose E. Serrano (D)

Receipts	$112,982	PACS	$93,350	Out of St.	$5,550	C-P-V	$1.13
Expend.	$96,339	Cand.	$0	Sm. Indiv.	$3,140	Spnd. Edge	$96,339
C-O-H	$41,830	Party	$0	Lg. Indiv.	$16,050	Debt	$0

17th District, Rep. Eliot L. Engel (D)

Receipts	$465,735	PACS	$285,450	Out of St.	$34,900	C-P-V	$4.78
Expend.	$469,220	Cand.	$0	Sm. Indiv.	$66,617	Spnd. Edge	$469,220
C-O-H	$8,107	Party	$7,615	Lg. Indiv.	$79,730	Debt	$67,364

18th District, Rep. Nita M. Lowey (D)

Receipts	$1,153,696	PACS	$307,977	Out of St.	$42,800	C-P-V	$11.03
Expend.	$1,277,433	Cand.	$500	Sm. Indiv.	$239,242	Spnd. Edge	$693,528
C-O-H	$215,816	Party	$500	Lg. Indiv.	$527,680	Debt	$162,192

19th District, Rep. Hamilton Fish, Jr. (R)

Receipts	$489,831	PACS	$229,000	Out of St.	$26,600	C-P-V	$4.43
Expend.	$617,832	Cand.	$0	Sm. Indiv.	$65,560	Spnd. Edge	$485,553
C-O-H	$6,830	Party	$6,588	Lg. Indiv.	$122,250	Debt	$0

20th District, Rep. Benjamin A. Gilman (R)

Receipts	$566,773	PACS	$212,397	Out of St.	$39,800	C-P-V	$3.84
Expend.	$576,538	Cand.	$0	Sm. Indiv.	$146,836	Spnd. Edge	$548,705
C-O-H	$58,491	Party	$4,360	Lg. Indiv.	$192,281	Debt	$0

21st District, Rep. Michael R. McNulty (D)

Receipts	$220,997	PACS	$126,386	Out of St.	$1,000	C-P-V	$1.52
Expend.	$252,821	Cand.	$0	Sm. Indiv.	$65,695	Spnd. Edge	$252,821
C-O-H	$68,572	Party	$5,030	Lg. Indiv.	$13,701	Debt	$0

22d District, Rep. Gerald B. H. Solomon (R)

Receipts	$382,251	PACS	$283,180	Out of St.	$16,800	C-P-V	$1.74
Expend.	$286,286	Cand.	$0	Sm. Indiv.	$54,641	Spnd. Edge	$254,097
C-O-H	$209,627	Party	$1,520	Lg. Indiv.	$33,960	Debt	$0

23d District, Rep. Sherwood Boehlert (R)

Receipts	$368,179	PACS	$197,496	Out of St.	$7,000	C-P-V	$2.66
Expend.	$372,109	Cand.	$0	Sm. Indiv.	$49,760	Spnd. Edge	$308,889
C-O-H	$185,722	Party	$1,595	Lg. Indiv.	$92,800	Debt	$0

24th District, Rep. John M. McHugh (R)

Receipts	$177,033	PACS	$96,351	Out of St.	$1,300	C-P-V	$1.40
Expend.	$170,749	Cand.	$0	Sm. Indiv.	$28,337	Spnd. Edge	$170,749
C-O-H	$6,282	Party	$8,950	Lg. Indiv.	$21,873	Debt	$0

25th District, Rep. James T. Walsh (R)

Receipts	$284,162	PACS	$82,495	Out of St.	$700	C-P-V	$2.18
Expend.	$294,850	Cand.	$0	Sm. Indiv.	$142,336	Spnd. Edge	$198,767
C-O-H	$30,264	Party	$7,040	Lg. Indiv.	$48,400	Debt	$0

26th District, Rep. Maurice D. Hinchey (D)

Receipts	$374,264	PACS	$145,258	Out of St.	$19,350	C-P-V	$3.08
Expend.	$368,777	Cand.	$0	Sm. Indiv.	$90,051	Spnd. Edge	$165,503
C-O-H	$5,484	Party	$3,400	Lg. Indiv.	$111,992	Debt	$13,698

27th District, Rep. Bill Paxon (R)

Receipts	$845,163	PACS	$329,412	Out of St.	$16,700	C-P-V	$6.50
Expend.	$1,017,327	Cand.	$0	Sm. Indiv.	$180,484	Spnd. Edge	$945,957
C-O-H	$5,784	Party	$11,735	Lg. Indiv.	$292,351	Debt	$0

28th District, Rep. Louise M. Slaughter (D)

Receipts	$473,871	PACS	$297,050	Out of St.	$3,700	C-P-V	$3.74
Expend.	$526,345	Cand.	$0	Sm. Indiv.	$91,119	Spnd. Edge	$280,819
C-O-H	$76,805	Party	$585	Lg. Indiv.	$65,621	Debt	$9,711

29th District, Rep. John J. LaFalce (D)

Receipts	$588,616	PACS	$312,570	Out of St.	$46,050	C-P-V	$3.65
Expend.	$467,841	Cand.	$0	Sm. Indiv.	$27,983	Spnd. Edge	$384,731
C-O-H	$765,913	Party	$450	Lg. Indiv.	$169,317	Debt	$0

30th District, Rep. Jack Quinn (R)

Receipts	$205,843	PACS	$10,665	Out of St.	$4,850	C-P-V	$1.58
Expend.	$199,257	Cand.	$1,000	Sm. Indiv.	$58,276	Spnd. Edge	($260,092)
C-O-H	$6,583	Party	$11,315	Lg. Indiv.	$123,950	Debt	$2,000

31st District, Rep. Amo Houghton (R)

Receipts	$359,995	PACS	$117,060	Out of St.	$80,450	C-P-V	$2.95
Expend.	$444,296	Cand.	$0	Sm. Indiv.	$37,468	Spnd. Edge	$438,446
C-O-H	$222,478	Party	$2,903	Lg. Indiv.	$180,298	Debt	$0

NORTH CAROLINA

Sen. Jesse A. Helms (R)

Receipts	$17,751,029	PACS	$1,001,336	Out of St.	$2,544,863	C-P-V	$16.32
Expend.	$17,761,579	Cand.	$0	Sm. Indiv.	$8,950,409	Spnd. Edge	$9,950,059
C-O-H	$12,326	Party	$1,850	Lg. Indiv.	$5,611,349	Debts	$914,288

Sen. Lauch Faircloth (R)

Receipts	$2,961,865	PACS	$365,783	Out of St.	$281,484	C-P-V	$2.27
Expend.	$2,952,102	Cand.	$30	Sm. Indiv.	$661,293	S. Edge	($1,711,096)
C-O-H	$9,763	Party	$17,500	Lg. Indiv.	$1,144,743	Debts	$1,199,569

1st District, Rep. Eva M. Clayton (D)

Receipts	$551,491	PACS	$281,665	Out of St.	$27,270	C-P-V	$4.75
Expend.	$551,028	Cand.	$1,021	Sm. Indiv.	$137,712	Spnd. Edge	$544,897
C-O-H	$258	Party	$17,905	Lg. Indiv.	$63,621	Debt	$45,196

2d District, Rep. Tim Valentine (D)

Receipts	$443,499	PACS	$237,040	Out of St.	$6,400	C-P-V	$4.03
Expend.	$457,958	Cand.	$0	Sm. Indiv.	$71,477	Spnd. Edge	$367,474
C-O-H	$5,853	Party	$5,000	Lg. Indiv.	$100,120	Debt	$27,500

3d District, Rep. H. Martin Lancaster (D)

Receipts	$588,664	PACS	$300,165	Out of St.	$83,200	C-P-V	$5.39
Expend.	$548,584	Cand.	$0	Sm. Indiv.	$96,279	Spnd. Edge	$312,351
C-O-H	$60,660	Party	$7,105	Lg. Indiv.	$175,303	Debt	$0

4th District, Rep. David E. Price (D)

Receipts	$480,758	PACS	$275,211	Out of St.	$12,450	C-P-V	$2.59
Expend.	$444,259	Cand.	$0	Sm. Indiv.	$138,928	Spnd. Edge	$431,989
C-O-H	$56,753	Party	$350	Lg. Indiv.	$45,385	Debt	$37,160

5th District, Rep. Stephen L. Neal (D)

Receipts	$493,627	PACS	$339,570	Out of St.	$10,000	C-P-V	$4.39
Expend.	$517,594	Cand.	$0	Sm. Indiv.	$56,214	Spnd. Edge	$329,464
C-O-H	$3,697	Party	$7,250	Lg. Indiv.	$83,600	Debt	$455

6th District, Rep. Howard Coble (R)

Receipts	$504,213	PACS	$207,135	Out of St.	$7,850	C-P-V	$2.67
Expend.	$435,093	Cand.	$0	Sm. Indiv.	$178,415	Spnd. Edge	$407,271
C-O-H	$84,967	Party	$10,179	Lg. Indiv.	$99,821	Debt	$0

7th District, Rep. Charlie Rose (D)

Receipts	$395,280	PACS	$251,535	Out of St.	$47,650	C-P-V	$2.75
Expend.	$254,579	Cand.	$0	Sm. Indiv.	$19,783	Spnd. Edge	$237,205
C-O-H	$681,533	Party	$0	Lg. Indiv.	$61,650	Debt	$0

8th District, Rep. W. G. (Bill) Hefner (D)

Receipts	$566,530	PACS	$356,179	Out of St.	$46,594	C-P-V	$5.25
Expend.	$594,617	Cand.	$0	Sm. Indiv.	$60,424	Spnd. Edge	$486,285
C-O-H	$83,385	Party	$5,350	Lg. Indiv.	$111,844	Debt	$0

9th District, Rep. Alex McMillan (R)

Receipts	$345,961	PACS	$268,000	Out of St.	$3,750	C-P-V	$1.54
Expend.	$236,315	Cand.	$0	Sm. Indiv.	$28,644	Spnd. Edge	$205,401
C-O-H	$212,977	Party	$0	Lg. Indiv.	$30,800	Debt	$0

10th District, Rep. Cass Ballenger (R)

Receipts	$277,122	PACS	$167,925	Out of St.	$38,000	C-P-V	$1.87
Expend.	$278,963	Cand.	$0	Sm. Indiv.	$10,437	Spnd. Edge	$255,862
C-O-H	$19,700	Party	$5,823	Lg. Indiv.	$88,650	Debt	$0

11th District, Rep. Charles H. Taylor (R)

Receipts	$1,216,256	PACS	$298,425	Out of St.	$17,400	C-P-V	$9.32
Expend.	$1,212,765	Cand.	$0	Sm. Indiv.	$231,855	Spnd. Edge	$781,043
C-O-H	$4,035	Party	$28,454	Lg. Indiv.	$165,661	Debt	$230,471

12th District, Rep. Melvin L. Watt (D)

Receipts	$483,601	PACS	$208,732	Out of St.	$35,950	C-P-V	$3.78
Expend.	$480,713	Cand.	$0	Sm. Indiv.	$92,199	Spnd. Edge	$457,952
C-O-H	$2,887	Party	$0	Lg. Indiv.	$134,590	Debt	$78,015

NORTH DAKOTA

Sen. Kent Conrad (D)

Receipts	$2,524,425	PACS	$1,708,368	Out of St.	$430,811	C-P-V	$24.01
Expend.	$2,479,021	Cand.	$1,000	Sm. Indiv.	$116,535	Spnd. Edge	$2,201,915
C-O-H	$132,101	Party	$37,558	Lg. Indiv.	$459,040	Debts	$0

Sen. Byron L. Dorgan (D)

Receipts	$1,054,618	PACS	$785,943	Out of St.	$78,493	C-P-V	$6.27
Expend.	$1,124,512	Cand.	$0	Sm. Indiv.	$113,649	Spnd. Edge	$626,405
C-O-H	$167,115	Party	$22,054	Lg. Indiv.	$99,293	Debts	$0

At-Large, Rep. Earl Pomeroy (D)

Receipts	$431,979	PACS	$296,260	Out of St.	$54,827	C-P-V	$2.54
Expend.	$430,228	Cand.	$0	Sm. Indiv.	$57,967	Spnd. Edge	$279,589
C-O-H	$1,750	Party	$14,515	Lg. Indiv.	$61,904	Debt	$30,045

OHIO

Sen. John H. Glenn Jr. (D)

Receipts	$4,245,138	PACS	$1,261,221	Out of St.	$752,278	C-P-V	$2.03
Expend.	$4,974,109	Cand.	$703,188	Sm. Indiv.	$506,067	Spnd. Edge	$1,920,953
C-O-H	$109,668	Party	$33,940	Lg. Indiv.	$1,565,493	Debts	$0

Sen. Howard M. Metzenbaum (D)

Receipts	$8,049,991	PACS	$1,131,985	Out of St.	$2,637,269	C-P-V	$3.55
Expend.	$8,798,731	Cand.	$0	Sm. Indiv.	$2,434,991	Spnd. Edge	$531,438
C-O-H	$221,751	Party	$40,598	Lg. Indiv.	$3,745,182	Debts	$9,798

1st District, Rep. David Mann (D)

Receipts	$281,158	PACS	$107,550	Out of St.	$28,100	C-P-V	$2.32
Expend.	$278,294	Cand.	$0	Sm. Indiv.	$62,430	Spnd. Edge	$195,256
C-O-H	$2,863	Party	$6,100	Lg. Indiv.	$102,618	Debt	$11,750

2d District, Rep. Rob Portman (R)
(Elected May 4, 1993; campaign finance figures not available)

3d District, Rep. Tony P. Hall (D)

Receipts	$342,116	PACS	$235,200	Out of St.	$9,250	C-P-V	$4.08
Expend.	$596,272	Cand.	$0	Sm. Indiv.	$39,695	Spnd. Edge	$422,214
C-O-H	$58,479	Party	$150	Lg. Indiv.	$30,242	Debt	$0

4th District, Rep. Michael G. Oxley (R)

Receipts	$491,631	PACS	$281,775	Out of St.	$16,210	C-P-V	$4.40
Expend.	$648,337	Cand.	$0	Sm. Indiv.	$81,524	Spnd. Edge	$580,013
C-O-H	$32,084	Party	$2,424	Lg. Indiv.	$106,020	Debt	$0

5th District, Rep. Paul E. Gillmor (R)

Receipts	$244,817	PACS	$160,137	Out of St.	$1,742	C-P-V	$1.36
Expend.	$254,988	Cand.	$0	Sm. Indiv.	$27,009	Spnd. Edge	(unopp.)
C-O-H	$72,967	Party	$812	Lg. Indiv.	$45,895	Debt	$0

6th District, Rep. Ted Strickland (D)

Receipts	$240,391	PACS	$112,457	Out of St.	$5,189	C-P-V	$1.93
Expend.	$237,082	Cand.	$0	Sm. Indiv.	$73,039	Spnd. Edge	($479,590)
C-O-H	$3,308	Party	$13,940	Lg. Indiv.	$20,025	Debt	$40,756

7th District, Rep. David L. Hobson (R)

Receipts	$380,267	PACS	$196,975	Out of St.	$3,100	C-P-V	$1.82
Expend.	$298,896	Cand.	$0	Sm. Indiv.	$97,757	Spnd. Edge	$298,896
C-O-H	$81,974	Party	$1,070	Lg. Indiv.	$53,870	Debt	$0

8th District, Rep. John A. Boehner (R)

Receipts	$557,539	PACS	$238,854	Out of St.	$1,700	C-P-V	$3.01
Expend.	$530,835	Cand.	$2,400	Sm. Indiv.	$200,786	Spnd. Edge	$524,105
C-O-H	$31,376	Party	$3,414	Lg. Indiv.	$107,699	Debt	$66,000

9th District, Rep. Marcy Kaptur (D)

Receipts	$290,940	PACS	$208,305	Out of St.	$2,850	C-P-V	$1.87
Expend.	$335,095	Cand.	$0	Sm. Indiv.	$55,010	Spnd. Edge	$291,165
C-O-H	$13,974	Party	$400	Lg. Indiv.	$19,740	Debt	$0

10th District, Rep. Martin R. Hoke (R)

Receipts	$684,560	PACS	$0	Out of St.	$25,015	C-P-V		$5.00
Expend.	$682,166	Cand.	$10,000	Sm. Indiv.	$114,162	Spnd. Edge	($610,120)
C-O-H	$3,391	Party	$14,050	Lg. Indiv.	$291,096	Debt		$271,291

11th District, Rep. Louis Stokes (D)

Receipts	$391,172	PACS	$149,293	Out of St.	$33,800	C-P-V		$2.90
Expend.	$449,248	Cand.	$0	Sm. Indiv.	$18,933	Spnd. Edge	$370,016
C-O-H	$183,789	Party	$150	Lg. Indiv.	$122,512	Debt		$0

12th District, Rep. John R. Kasich (R)

Receipts	$279,301	PACS	$116,470	Out of St.	$700	C-P-V		$1.42
Expend.	$242,096	Cand.	$0	Sm. Indiv.	$13,821	Spnd. Edge	$197,437
C-O-H	$130,431	Party	$0	Lg. Indiv.	$147,375	Debt		$0

13th District, Rep. Sherrod Brown (D)

Receipts	$495,275	PACS	$263,816	Out of St.	$23,050	C-P-V		$3.62
Expend.	$486,354	Cand.	$327	Sm. Indiv.	$72,417	Spnd. Edge	($377,984)
C-O-H	$8,920	Party	$2,835	Lg. Indiv.	$152,229	Debt		$61,657

14th District, Rep. Tom Sawyer (D)

Receipts	$195,200	PACS	$148,625	Out of St.	$1,500	C-P-V		$1.27
Expend.	$209,155	Cand.	$0	Sm. Indiv.	$22,031	Spnd. Edge	$209,155
C-O-H	$34,362	Party	$1,352	Lg. Indiv.	$17,832	Debt		$2,500

15th District, Rep. Deborah Pryce (R)

Receipts	$558,617	PACS	$211,227	Out of St.	$5,200	C-P-V		$5.04
Expend.	$556,741	Cand.	$0	Sm. Indiv.	$117,607	Spnd. Edge	$278,114
C-O-H	$1,874	Party	$24,579	Lg. Indiv.	$199,610	Debt		$37,786

16th District, Rep. Ralph S. Regula (R)

Receipts	$168,665	PACS	$0	Out of St.	$10,400	C-P-V		$1.32
Expend.	$209,305	Cand.	$0	Sm. Indiv.	$82,477	Spnd. Edge	$104,012
C-O-H	$12,012	Party	$9,182	Lg. Indiv.	$69,113	Debt		$0

17th District, Rep. James A. Traficant, Jr. (D)

Receipts	$155,474	PACS	$85,120	Out of St.	$5,100	C-P-V		$0.46
Expend.	$98,740	Cand.	$0	Sm. Indiv.	$38,382	Spnd. Edge	$95,252
C-O-H	$132,898	Party	$2,822	Lg. Indiv.	$28,400	Debt		$0

18th District, Rep. Douglas Applegate (D)

Receipts	$117,262	PACS	$88,170	Out of St.	$0	C-P-V		$0.62
Expend.	$102,335	Cand.	$0	Sm. Indiv.	$6,275	Spnd. Edge	$75,525
C-O-H	$176,449	Party	$0	Lg. Indiv.	$1,250	Debt		$0

19th District, Rep. Eric D. Fingerhut (D)

Receipts	$617,946	PACS	$210,017	Out of St.	$27,905	C-P-V		$4.42
Expend.	$611,478	Cand.	$1,000	Sm. Indiv.	$139,154	Spnd. Edge	$161,361
C-O-H	$6,465	Party	$0	Lg. Indiv.	$256,367	Debt		$99,607

OKLAHOMA

Sen. David Lyle Boren (D)

Receipts	$1,697,951	PACS	$0	Out of St.	$608,371	C-P-V		$2.16
Expend.	$1,591,093	Cand.	$1,500	Sm. Indiv.	$196,288	Spnd. Edge	$1,450,179
C-O-H	$158,133	Party	$300	Lg. Indiv.	$1,398,629	Debts		$0

Sen. Don Nickles (R)

Receipts	$3,686,883	PACS	$1,191,903	Out of St.	$419,178	C-P-V	$4.61
Expend.	$3,492,603	Cand.	$0	Sm. Indiv.	$443,710	Spnd. Edge	$2,036,755
C-O-H	$569,953	Party	$18,475	Lg. Indiv.	$1,613,117	Debts	$0

1st District, Rep. James M. Inhofe (R)

Receipts	$425,361	PACS	$227,931	Out of St.	$17,600	C-P-V	$3.51
Expend.	$418,928	Cand.	$0	Sm. Indiv.	$58,323	Spnd. Edge	$89,968
C-O-H	$7,551	Party	$14,569	Lg. Indiv.	$117,950	Debt	$18,212

2d District, Rep. Michael L. (Mike) Synar (D)

Receipts	$1,191,392	PACS	$0	Out of St.	$453,914	C-P-V	$10.04
Expend.	$1,190,197	Cand.	$0	Sm. Indiv.	$308,554	Spnd. Edge	$1,159,885
C-O-H	$26,075	Party	$7,155	Lg. Indiv.	$861,707	Debt	$0

3d District, Rep. Bill Brewster (D)

Receipts	$423,953	PACS	$266,973	Out of St.	$19,133	C-P-V	$2.48
Expend.	$386,144	Cand.	$0	Sm. Indiv.	$43,394	Spnd. Edge	$379,806
C-O-H	$39,867	Party	$150	Lg. Indiv.	$104,783	Debt	$0

4th District, Rep. Dave McCurdy (D)

Receipts	$556,174	PACS	$270,250	Out of St.	$115,950	C-P-V	$4.15
Expend.	$584,409	Cand.	$0	Sm. Indiv.	$59,650	Spnd. Edge	$584,409
C-O-H	$53,387	Party	$1,700	Lg. Indiv.	$209,650	Debt	$0

5th District, Rep. Ernest J. Istook, Jr. (R)

Receipts	$365,630	PACS	$72,277	Out of St.	$2,775	C-P-V	$2.96
Expend.	$364,915	Cand.	$1,544	Sm. Indiv.	$86,723	Spnd. Edge	$28,497
C-O-H	$914	Party	$11,200	Lg. Indiv.	$75,705	Debt	$41,892

6th District, Rep. Glenn English (D)

Receipts	$379,380	PACS	$203,400	Out of St.	$15,768	C-P-V	$4.11
Expend.	$553,316	Cand.	$0	Sm. Indiv.	$91,465	Spnd. Edge	$177,522
C-O-H	$150,105	Party	$1,700	Lg. Indiv.	$56,850	Debt	$0

OREGON

Sen. Mark O. Hatfield (R)

Receipts	$2,475,480	PACS	$1,066,257	Out of St.	$505,868	C-P-V	$4.60
Expend.	$2,714,661	Cand.	$0	Sm. Indiv.	$236,551	Spnd. Edge	$1,224,541
C-O-H	$4,333	Party	$63,243	Lg. Indiv.	$1,001,330	Debts	$25,224

Sen. Bob Packwood (R)

Receipts	$8,228,212	PACS	$1,275,358	Out of St.	$1,994,646	C-P-V	$11.20
Expend.	$8,034,249	Cand.	$0	Sm. Indiv.	$3,728,299	Spnd. Edge	$5,404,852
C-O-H	$890,256	Party	$17,500	Lg. Indiv.	$2,512,999	Debts	$0

1st District, Rep. Elizabeth Furse (D)

Receipts	$785,545	PACS	$186,049	Out of St.	$76,908	C-P-V	$5.09
Expend.	$778,290	Cand.	$4,294	Sm. Indiv.	$354,313	Spnd. Edge	$58,679
C-O-H	$7,255	Party	$0	Lg. Indiv.	$234,081	Debt	$36,431

2d District, Rep. Robert F. (Bob) Smith (R)

Receipts	$462,680	PACS	$165,725	Out of St.	$14,350	C-P-V	$2.18
Expend.	$401,670	Cand.	$0	Sm. Indiv.	$169,575	Spnd. Edge	$314,309
C-O-H	$240,746	Party	$2,016	Lg. Indiv.	$99,262	Debt	$0

3d District, Rep. Ron Wyden (D)

Receipts	$229,749	PACS	$123,675	Out of St.	$6,150	C-P-V		$1.72
Expend.	$357,402	Cand.	$0	Sm. Indiv.	$48,960	Spnd. Edge	$354,366
C-O-H	$328,099	Party	$550	Lg. Indiv.	$17,900	Debt		$0

4th District, Rep. Peter A. DeFazio (D)

Receipts	$248,887	PACS	$173,500	Out of St.	$4,527	C-P-V		$1.51
Expend.	$301,116	Cand.	$0	Sm. Indiv.	$49,565	Spnd. Edge	$294,768
C-O-H	$43,563	Party	$200	Lg. Indiv.	$11,777	Debt		$0

5th District, Rep. Mike Kopetski (D)

Receipts	$338,338	PACS	$241,832	Out of St.	$11,750	C-P-V		$1.87
Expend.	$325,620	Cand.	$0	Sm. Indiv.	$53,842	Spnd. Edge	$286,008
C-O-H	$40,351	Party	$450	Lg. Indiv.	$35,700	Debt		$51,937

PENNSYLVANIA

Sen. Arlen Specter (R)

Receipts	$10,451,746	PACS	$2,017,041	Out of St.	$2,080,136	C-P-V		$4.43
Expend.	$10,454,793	Cand.	$0	Sm. Indiv.	$1,607,563	Spnd. Edge	$5,426,124
C-O-H	$38,963	Party	$55,320	Lg. Indiv.	$6,275,632	Debts		$150,000

Sen. Harris Wofford (D)

Receipts	$3,334,768	PACS	$956,416	Out of St.	$1,080,327	C-P-V		$1.74
Expend.	$3,241,556	Cand.	$2,000	Sm. Indiv.	$424,028	Spnd. Edge	($599,439)
C-O-H	$93,212	Party	$29,050	Lg. Indiv.	$1,915,883	Debts		$28,289

1st District, Rep. Thomas M. Foglietta (D)

Receipts	$387,584	PACS	$168,450	Out of St.	$33,000	C-P-V		$2.44
Expend.	$366,203	Cand.	$0	Sm. Indiv.	$8,040	Spnd. Edge	$324,993
C-O-H	$383,478	Party	$0	Lg. Indiv.	$134,736	Debt		$0

2d District, Rep. Lucien E. Blackwell (D)

Receipts	$236,129	PACS	$133,010	Out of St.	$22,172	C-P-V		$1.39
Expend.	$228,229	Cand.	$0	Sm. Indiv.	$21,395	Spnd. Edge	$58,222
C-O-H	$16,359	Party	$150	Lg. Indiv.	$78,353	Debt		$0

3d District, Rep. Robert A. Borski (D)

Receipts	$512,477	PACS	$275,319	Out of St.	$29,534	C-P-V		$5.08
Expend.	$664,231	Cand.	$0	Sm. Indiv.	$54,650	Spnd. Edge	$448,910
C-O-H	$3,481	Party	$0	Lg. Indiv.	$155,783	Debt		$25,861

4th District, Rep. Ron Klink (D)

Receipts	$264,293	PACS	$18,150	Out of St.	$5,875	C-P-V		$1.29
Expend.	$240,419	Cand.	$0	Sm. Indiv.	$118,197	Spnd. Edge	$226,426
C-O-H	$2,497	Party	$1,000	Lg. Indiv.	$29,590	Debt		$103,929

5th District, Rep. William F. (Bill) Clinger, Jr. (R)

Receipts	$286,477	PACS	$142,894	Out of St.	$5,900	C-P-V		$1.41
Expend.	$266,090	Cand.	$0	Sm. Indiv.	$101,846	Spnd. Edge	(unopp.)
C-O-H	$96,640	Party	$1,421	Lg. Indiv.	$28,750	Debt		$11,000

6th District, Rep. Tim Holden (D)

Receipts	$293,468	PACS	$99,400	Out of St.	$1,700	C-P-V		$2.63
Expend.	$284,349	Cand.	$1,000	Sm. Indiv.	$100,488	Spnd. Edge	($157,709)
C-O-H	$9,118	Party	$15,300	Lg. Indiv.	$63,227	Debt		$40,500

7th District, Rep. Curt Weldon (R)

Receipts	$465,223	PACS	$185,187	Out of St.	$14,175	C-P-V	$6.13
Expend.	$565,974	Cand.	$0	Sm. Indiv.	$157,742	Spnd. Edge	$392,109
C-O-H	$34,613	Party	$3,870	Lg. Indiv.	$99,701	Debt	$0

8th District, Rep. Jim Greenwood (R)

Receipts	$721,654	PACS	$179,742	Out of St.	$33,680	C-P-V	$5.53
Expend.	$717,249	Cand.	$0	Sm. Indiv.	$149,071	Spnd. Edge	($525,106)
C-O-H	$4,403	Party	$10,000	Lg. Indiv.	$378,694	Debt	$5,640

9th District, Rep. E. G. (Bud) Shuster (R)

Receipts	$557,315	PACS	$187,250	Out of St.	$190,229	C-P-V	$3.05
Expend.	$556,385	Cand.	$0	Sm. Indiv.	$9,174	Spnd. Edge	(unopp.)
C-O-H	$103,032	Party	$1,138	Lg. Indiv.	$334,229	Debt	$0

10th District, Rep. Joseph M. McDade (R)

Receipts	$375,429	PACS	$242,172	Out of St.	$62,150	C-P-V	$1.82
Expend.	$343,892	Cand.	$0	Sm. Indiv.	$7,060	Spnd. Edge	$343,892
C-O-H	$367,412	Party	$736	Lg. Indiv.	$91,600	Debt	$0

11th District, Rep. Paul E. Kanjorski (D)

Receipts	$311,016	PACS	$235,360	Out of St.	$6,300	C-P-V	$2.46
Expend.	$342,314	Cand.	$0	Sm. Indiv.	$35,400	Spnd. Edge	$287,590
C-O-H	$63,183	Party	$1,750	Lg. Indiv.	$27,552	Debt	$0

12th District, Rep. John P. Murtha (D)

Receipts	$935,459	PACS	$540,060	Out of St.	$171,800	C-P-V	$4.76
Expend.	$794,097	Cand.	$0	Sm. Indiv.	$42,576	Spnd. Edge	(unopp.)
C-O-H	$174,483	Party	$0	Lg. Indiv.	$342,033	Debt	$236

13th District, Rep. Marjorie Margolies-Mezvinsky (D)

Receipts	$568,961	PACS	$172,273	Out of St.	$72,219	C-P-V	$4.38
Expend.	$559,060	Cand.	$0	Sm. Indiv.	$162,986	Spnd. Edge	($160,558)
C-O-H	$9,901	Party	$0	Lg. Indiv.	$233,429	Debt	$70,237

14th District, Rep. William J. Coyne (D)

Receipts	$264,042	PACS	$172,007	Out of St.	$18,375	C-P-V	$1.96
Expend.	$323,937	Cand.	$0	Sm. Indiv.	$9,410	Spnd. Edge	$250,001
C-O-H	$167,604	Party	$0	Lg. Indiv.	$69,125	Debt	$0

15th District, Rep. Paul McHale (D)

Receipts	$223,578	PACS	$109,450	Out of St.	$2,650	C-P-V	$1.98
Expend.	$221,935	Cand.	$0	Sm. Indiv.	$43,059	Spnd. Edge	($644,039)
C-O-H	$1,642	Party	$16,326	Lg. Indiv.	$43,965	Debt	$97,777

16th District, Rep. Robert S. Walker (R)

Receipts	$134,434	PACS	$58,350	Out of St.	$2,200	C-P-V	$1.15
Expend.	$158,564	Cand.	$345	Sm. Indiv.	$24,901	Spnd. Edge	$148,057
C-O-H	$11,278	Party	$426	Lg. Indiv.	$46,266	Debt	$0

17th District, Rep. George W. Gekas (R)

Receipts	$112,141	PACS	$68,435	Out of St.	$1,450	C-P-V	$1.27
Expend.	$190,885	Cand.	$0	Sm. Indiv.	$15,870	Spnd. Edge	$143,668
C-O-H	$62,800	Party	$2,059	Lg. Indiv.	$10,830	Debt	$0

18th District, Rep. Rick Santorum (R)

Receipts	$654,854	PACS	$267,454	Out of St.	$13,400	C-P-V	$4.07
Expend.	$626,793	Cand.	$0	Sm. Indiv.	$111,866	Spnd. Edge	$342,036
C-O-H	$34,355	Party	$18,723	Lg. Indiv.	$244,455	Debt	$0

19th District, Rep. Bill Goodling (R)

Receipts	$200,014	PACS	$12,950	Out of St.	$10,750	C-P-V		$2.05
Expend.	$201,951	Cand.	$0	Sm. Indiv.	$88,179	Spnd. Edge	($36,395)
C-O-H	$4,312	Party	$6,712	Lg. Indiv.	$90,479	Debt		$0

20th District, Rep. Austin J. Murphy (D)

Receipts	$235,296	PACS	$174,750	Out of St.	$2,750	C-P-V		$2.69
Expend.	$309,425	Cand.	$0	Sm. Indiv.	$34,201	Spnd. Edge	$257,650
C-O-H	$37,124	Party	$300	Lg. Indiv.	$11,100	Debt		$0

21st District, Rep. Tom Ridge (R)

Receipts	$530,372	PACS	$299,785	Out of St.	$8,800	C-P-V		$4.68
Expend.	$705,861	Cand.	$0	Sm. Indiv.	$139,240	Spnd. Edge	$690,061
C-O-H	$51,230	Party	$2,297	Lg. Indiv.	$70,650	Debt		$0

RHODE ISLAND

Sen. Claiborne Pell (D)

Receipts	$2,242,156	PACS	$882,584	Out of St.	$686,958	C-P-V		$10.50
Expend.	$2,363,904	Cand.	$0	Sm. Indiv.	$216,039	Spnd. Edge	$301,991
C-O-H	$216,257	Party	$17,750	Lg. Indiv.	$895,775	Debts		$0

Sen. John H. Chafee (R)

Receipts	$3,000,745	PACS	$1,180,104	Out of St.	$983,608	C-P-V		$13.83
Expend.	$3,004,072	Cand.	$0	Sm. Indiv.	$359,014	Spnd. Edge	$127,478
C-O-H	$50,361	Party	$15,972	Lg. Indiv.	$1,258,278	Debts		$0

1st District, Rep. Ronald K. Machtley (R)

Receipts	$608,563	PACS	$223,144	Out of St.	$18,867	C-P-V		$4.15
Expend.	$564,588	Cand.	$0	Sm. Indiv.	$232,550	Spnd. Edge	$474,129
C-O-H	$54,332	Party	$5,662	Lg. Indiv.	$136,951	Debt		$0

2d District, Rep. Jack Reed (D)

Receipts	$816,308	PACS	$416,190	Out of St.	$45,275	C-P-V		$5.65
Expend.	$815,622	Cand.	$2,500	Sm. Indiv.	$157,985	Spnd. Edge	$776,362
C-O-H	$6,837	Party	$2,400	Lg. Indiv.	$164,252	Debt		$180,225

SOUTH CAROLINA

Sen. Strom Thurmond (R)

Receipts	$2,190,097	PACS	$632,596	Out of St.	$458,701	C-P-V		$4.84
Expend.	$2,333,689	Cand.	$0	Sm. Indiv.	$668,079	Spnd. Edge	$2,327,456
C-O-H	$221,093	Party	$16,176	Lg. Indiv.	$783,401	Debts		$0

Sen. Ernest F. (Fritz) Hollings (D)

Receipts	$4,016,311	PACS	$1,620,274	Out of St.	$1,294,963	C-P-V		$7.09
Expend.	$4,188,829	Cand.	$0	Sm. Indiv.	$247,957	Spnd. Edge	$3,302,013
C-O-H	$25,336	Party	$17,500	Lg. Indiv.	$1,903,522	Debts		$15,000

1st District, Rep. Arthur Ravenel, Jr. (R)

Receipts	$282,816	PACS	$127,076	Out of St.	$5,350	C-P-V		$4.61
Expend.	$561,793	Cand.	$0	Sm. Indiv.	$56,336	Spnd. Edge	$504,891
C-O-H	$0	Party	$0	Lg. Indiv.	$57,900	Debt		$0

2d District, Rep. Floyd D. Spence (R)

Receipts	$169,036	PACS	$108,900	Out of St.	$2,400	C-P-V		$1.21
Expend.	$179,539	Cand.	$0	Sm. Indiv.	$44,269	Spnd. Edge	$179,539
C-O-H	$51,688	Party	$0	Lg. Indiv.	$7,650	Debt		$0

3d District, Rep. Butler C. Derrick (D)

Receipts	$681,632	PACS	$469,870	Out of St.	$33,050	C-P-V	$5.66
Expend.	$673,677	Cand.	$0	Sm. Indiv.	$59,096	Spnd. Edge	$656,338
C-O-H	$114,145	Party	$150	Lg. Indiv.	$114,312	Debt	$0

4th District, Rep. Bob Inglis (R)

Receipts	$226,577	PACS	$1,450	Out of St.	$10,875	C-P-V	$2.16
Expend.	$215,364	Cand.	$10,000	Sm. Indiv.	$67,491	Spnd. Edge	($133,164)
C-O-H	$11,214	Party	$17,250	Lg. Indiv.	$129,312	Debt	$0

5th District, Rep. John M. Spratt, Jr. (D)

Receipts	$281,855	PACS	$146,775	Out of St.	$48,250	C-P-V	$3.41
Expend.	$381,942	Cand.	$0	Sm. Indiv.	$28,536	Spnd. Edge	$279,214
C-O-H	$52,937	Party	$1,250	Lg. Indiv.	$87,050	Debt	$64,000

6th District, Rep. James E. Clyburn (D)

Receipts	$321,121	PACS	$101,210	Out of St.	$19,390	C-P-V	$2.69
Expend.	$324,379	Cand.	$215	Sm. Indiv.	$62,327	Spnd. Edge	$210,090
C-O-H	$795	Party	$15,100	Lg. Indiv.	$93,268	Debt	$136,560

SOUTH DAKOTA

Sen. Larry Pressler (R)

Receipts	$2,355,725	PACS	$963,390	Out of St.	$897,604	C-P-V	$15.66
Expend.	$2,124,359	Cand.	$0	Sm. Indiv.	$149,593	Spnd. Edge	$800,586
C-O-H	$556,585	Party	$20,260	Lg. Indiv.	$1,001,654	Debts	$0

Sen. Thomas A. Daschle (D)

Receipts	$4,122,119	PACS	$1,848,680	Out of St.	$1,216,765	C-P-V	$18.34
Expend.	$3,981,548	Cand.	$0	Sm. Indiv.	$650,844	Spnd. Edge	$3,503,127
C-O-H	$192,096	Party	$19,285	Lg. Indiv.	$1,391,257	Debts	$0

At-Large, Rep. Tim Johnson (D)

Receipts	$452,528	PACS	$221,653	Out of St.	$7,250	C-P-V	$1.64
Expend.	$376,741	Cand.	$0	Sm. Indiv.	$151,568	Spnd. Edge	$206,598
C-O-H	$180,431	Party	$3,225	Lg. Indiv.	$53,850	Debt	$0

TENNESSEE

Sen. James R. (Jim) Sasser (D)

Receipts	$3,687,745	PACS	$1,629,516	Out of St.	$634,791	C-P-V	$3.36
Expend.	$3,423,915	Cand.	$0	Sm. Indiv.	$441,202	Spnd. Edge	$2,816,589
C-O-H	$328,990	Party	$25,814	Lg. Indiv.	$1,426,810	Debts	$0

Sen. Harlan Mathews (D)
(Appointed January 1993)

1st District, Rep. James H. (Jimmy) Quillen (R)

Receipts	$455,846	PACS	$267,050	Out of St.	$26,505	C-P-V	$2.83
Expend.	$325,383	Cand.	$0	Sm. Indiv.	$7,450	Spnd. Edge	$325,383
C-O-H	$1,174,716	Party	$0	Lg. Indiv.	$72,805	Debt	$0

2d District, Rep. John J. Duncan, Jr. (R)

Receipts	$258,496	PACS	$162,509	Out of St.	$5,200	C-P-V	$1.15
Expend.	$170,836	Cand.	$0	Sm. Indiv.	$43,685	Spnd. Edge	$164,365
C-O-H	$225,372	Party	$578	Lg. Indiv.	$43,816	Debt	$0

3d District, Rep. Marilyn Lloyd (D)

Receipts	$463,643	PACS	$272,250	Out of St.	$7,800	C-P-V	$6.03
Expend.	$637,790	Cand.	$0	Sm. Indiv.	$67,455	Spnd. Edge	$369,946
C-O-H	$10,471	Party	$9,760	Lg. Indiv.	$86,222	Debt	$5,792

4th District, Rep. Jim Cooper (D)

Receipts	$164,092	PACS	$16,750	Out of St.	$6,050	C-P-V	$1.97
Expend.	$195,279	Cand.	$0	Sm. Indiv.	$68,145	Spnd. Edge	$195,279
C-O-H	$174,426	Party	$1,627	Lg. Indiv.	$60,275	Debt	$0

5th District, Rep. Bob Clement (D)

Receipts	$557,480	PACS	$288,762	Out of St.	$14,250	C-P-V	$4.79
Expend.	$600,244	Cand.	$0	Sm. Indiv.	$69,530	Spnd. Edge	$589,654
C-O-H	$121,256	Party	$2,900	Lg. Indiv.	$178,441	Debt	$0

6th District, Rep. Bart Gordon (D)

Receipts	$662,234	PACS	$388,590	Out of St.	$3,500	C-P-V	$8.19
Expend.	$988,920	Cand.	$0	Sm. Indiv.	$146,606	Spnd. Edge	$807,405
C-O-H	$208,386	Party	$950	Lg. Indiv.	$13,850	Debt	$0

7th District, Rep. Don Sundquist (R)

Receipts	$819,006	PACS	$359,884	Out of St.	$23,300	C-P-V	$8.00
Expend.	$1,001,217	Cand.	$0	Sm. Indiv.	$149,778	Spnd. Edge	$894,443
C-O-H	$289,691	Party	$581	Lg. Indiv.	$238,180	Debt	$0

8th District, Rep. John Tanner (D)

Receipts	$258,798	PACS	$164,739	Out of St.	$6,750	C-P-V	$1.23
Expend.	$167,669	Cand.	$0	Sm. Indiv.	$29,107	Spnd. Edge	$156,935
C-O-H	$319,398	Party	$2,700	Lg. Indiv.	$32,300	Debt	$0

9th District, Rep. Harold E. Ford (D)

Receipts	$202,187	PACS	$118,450	Out of St.	$16,450	C-P-V	$1.58
Expend.	$194,631	Cand.	$0	Sm. Indiv.	$8,503	Spnd. Edge	$194,631
C-O-H	$4,640	Party	$2,800	Lg. Indiv.	$71,250	Debt	$13,052

TEXAS

Sen. Phil Gramm (R)

Receipts	$16,142,848	PACS	$1,796,974	Out of St.	$2,217,770	C-P-V	$5.36
Expend.	$12,349,397	Cand.	$0	Sm. Indiv.	$4,513,211	Spnd. Ed.	$10,676,456
C-O-H	$4,147,379	Party	$14,601	Lg. Indiv.	$8,528,962	Debts	$0

Sen. Kay Bailey Hutchison (R)
(Elected June 5, 1993; campaign finance figures unavailable)

1st District, Rep. Jim Chapman, Jr. (D)

Receipts	$342,246	PACS	$212,577	Out of St.	$6,250	C-P-V	$1.37
Expend.	$208,815	Cand.	$0	Sm. Indiv.	$71,861	Spnd. Edge	(unopp.)
C-O-H	$286,303	Party	$0	Lg. Indiv.	$36,795	Debt	$44,900

2d District, Rep. Charles Wilson (D)

Receipts	$1,217,912	PACS	$638,825	Out of St.	$244,000	C-P-V	$10.06
Expend.	$1,193,599	Cand.	$0	Sm. Indiv.	$36,324	Spnd. Edge	$849,534
C-O-H	$25,181	Party	$5,476	Lg. Indiv.	$478,033	Debt	$106,911

3d District, Rep. Sam Johnson (R)

Receipts	$466,977	PACS	$213,475	Out of St.	$2,045	C-P-V	$2.39
Expend.	$481,802	Cand.	$0	Sm. Indiv.	$61,985	Spnd. Edge	$481,802
C-O-H	$13,717	Party	$0	Lg. Indiv.	$170,900	Debt	$0

4th District, Rep. Ralph M. Hall (D)

Receipts	$520,216	PACS	$349,840	Out of St.	$8,500	C-P-V	$5.78
Expend.	$739,979	Cand.	$0	Sm. Indiv.	$42,882	Spnd. Edge	$705,567
C-O-H	$38,176	Party	$1,550	Lg. Indiv.	$97,874	Debt	$0

5th District, Rep. John Bryant (D)

Receipts	$622,709	PACS	$353,633	Out of St.	$24,600	C-P-V	$8.07
Expend.	$795,462	Cand.	$0	Sm. Indiv.	$86,237	Spnd. Edge	$750,920
C-O-H	$85,087	Party	$0	Lg. Indiv.	$162,416	Debt	$0

6th District, Rep. Joe L. Barton (R)

Receipts	$1,018,595	PACS	$374,046	Out of St.	$26,550	C-P-V	$7.53
Expend.	$1,423,644	Cand.	$0	Sm. Indiv.	$211,372	Spnd. Edge	$1,409,893
C-O-H	$7,022	Party	$74	Lg. Indiv.	$303,722	Debt	$6,184

7th District, Rep. Bill Archer (R)

Receipts	$121,947	PACS	$0	Out of St.	$25,200	C-P-V	$0.72
Expend.	$121,751	Cand.	$0	Sm. Indiv.	$3,567	Spnd. Edge	(unopp.)
C-O-H	$671,097	Party	$225	Lg. Indiv.	$45,375	Debt	$0

8th District, Rep. Jack M. Fields, Jr. (R)

Receipts	$757,980	PACS	$453,076	Out of St.	$28,500	C-P-V	$4.16
Expend.	$746,361	Cand.	$0	Sm. Indiv.	$47,129	Spnd. Edge	$746,361
C-O-H	$46,066	Party	$840	Lg. Indiv.	$245,550	Debt	$0

9th District, Rep. Jack Brooks (D)

Receipts	$606,190	PACS	$456,357	Out of St.	$58,276	C-P-V	$3.97
Expend.	$471,285	Cand.	$0	Sm. Indiv.	$10,305	Spnd. Edge	$372,663
C-O-H	$465,327	Party	$300	Lg. Indiv.	$92,126	Debt	$0

10th District, Rep. J.J. (Jake) Pickle (D)

Receipts	$421,708	PACS	$263,432	Out of St.	$22,402	C-P-V	$2.05
Expend.	$363,561	Cand.	$0	Sm. Indiv.	$50,742	Spnd. Edge	$245,627
C-O-H	$124,589	Party	$0	Lg. Indiv.	$95,161	Debt	$0

11th District, Rep. Chet Edwards (D)

Receipts	$465,342	PACS	$321,575	Out of St.	$5,600	C-P-V	$3.51
Expend.	$420,880	Cand.	$0	Sm. Indiv.	$33,923	Spnd. Edge	$403,730
C-O-H	$47,902	Party	$2,618	Lg. Indiv.	$105,939	Debt	$0

12th District, Rep. Pete Geren (D)

Receipts	$809,664	PACS	$356,168	Out of St.	$15,950	C-P-V	$6.47
Expend.	$812,234	Cand.	$0	Sm. Indiv.	$62,583	Spnd. Edge	$427,599
C-O-H	$15,548	Party	$0	Lg. Indiv.	$371,112	Debt	$360,381

13th District, Rep. Bill Sarpalius (D)

Receipts	$521,447	PACS	$320,769	Out of St.	$7,150	C-P-V	$4.42
Expend.	$521,328	Cand.	$0	Sm. Indiv.	$46,994	Spnd. Edge	$150,746
C-O-H	$17,659	Party	$9,664	Lg. Indiv.	$123,517	Debt	$20,236

14th District, Rep. Greg Laughlin (D)

Receipts	$618,011	PACS	$353,940	Out of St.	$15,850	C-P-V	$3.97
Expend.	$540,139	Cand.	$0	Sm. Indiv.	$58,573	Spnd. Edge	$526,589
C-O-H	$79,691	Party	$0	Lg. Indiv.	$189,674	Debt	$57,277

15th District, Rep. E. (Kika) de la Garza (D)

Receipts	$248,430	PACS	$184,825	Out of St.	$11,890	C-P-V	$3.10
Expend.	$267,600	Cand.	$742	Sm. Indiv.	$27,545	Spnd. Edge	$254,148
C-O-H	$118,307	Party	$86	Lg. Indiv.	$34,037	Debt	$0

16th District, Rep. Ronald D. Coleman (D)

Receipts	$777,219	PACS	$486,544	Out of St.	$15,800	C-P-V	$11.69
Expend.	$780,038	Cand.	$0	Sm. Indiv.	$70,882	Spnd. Edge	$570,767
C-O-H	$6,719	Party	$5,000	Lg. Indiv.	$132,991	Debt	$101,186

17th District, Rep. Charles W. Stenholm (D)

Receipts	$412,834	PACS	$274,726	Out of St.	$17,884	C-P-V	$2.77
Expend.	$377,949	Cand.	$0	Sm. Indiv.	$70,702	Spnd. Edge	$360,158
C-O-H	$121,621	Party	$150	Lg. Indiv.	$56,984	Debt	$0

18th District, Rep. Craig Washington (D)

Receipts	$185,635	PACS	$121,250	Out of St.	$2,250	C-P-V	$1.66
Expend.	$184,742	Cand.	$0	Sm. Indiv.	$9,449	Spnd. Edge	($24,710)
C-O-H	$6,996	Party	$0	Lg. Indiv.	$42,300	Debt	$6,569

19th District, Rep. Larry Combest (R)

Receipts	$241,559	PACS	$125,675	Out of St.	$850	C-P-V	$1.22
Expend.	$197,657	Cand.	$0	Sm. Indiv.	$48,812	Spnd. Edge	$192,459
C-O-H	$173,124	Party	$1,138	Lg. Indiv.	$48,554	Debt	$0

20th District, Rep. Henry B. Gonzalez (D)

Receipts	$45,040	PACS	$11,525	Out of St.	$1,500	C-P-V	$0.42
Expend.	$43,147	Cand.	$0	Sm. Indiv.	$13,615	Spnd. Edge	$0
C-O-H	$18,039	Party	$0	Lg. Indiv.	$17,900	Debt	$0

21st District, Rep. Lamar S. Smith (R)

Receipts	$544,187	PACS	$134,839	Out of St.	$6,200	C-P-V	$2.50
Expend.	$476,501	Cand.	$0	Sm. Indiv.	$144,663	Spnd. Edge	$470,807
C-O-H	$420,613	Party	$3,219	Lg. Indiv.	$197,677	Debt	$0

22d District, Rep. Tom DeLay (R)

Receipts	$341,516	PACS	$226,178	Out of St.	$11,500	C-P-V	$2.47
Expend.	$371,362	Cand.	$0	Sm. Indiv.	$22,423	Spnd. Edge	$331,526
C-O-H	$46,466	Party	$0	Lg. Indiv.	$87,365	Debt	$0

23d District, Rep. Henry Bonilla (R)

Receipts	$588,673	PACS	$109,888	Out of St.	$6,250	C-P-V	$6.05
Expend.	$594,032	Cand.	$0	Sm. Indiv.	$76,412	Spnd. Edge	($164,421)
C-O-H	($5,359)	Party	$20,500	Lg. Indiv.	$294,176	Debt	$17,790

24th District, Rep. Martin Frost (D)

Receipts	$1,241,725	PACS	$667,804	Out of St.	$53,400	C-P-V	$14.87
Expend.	$1,549,556	Cand.	$0	Sm. Indiv.	$125,335	Spnd. Edge	$1,440,250
C-O-H	$8,276	Party	$0	Lg. Indiv.	$406,900	Debt	$0

25th District, Rep. Michael A. Andrews (D)

Receipts	$974,838	PACS	$527,931	Out of St.	$45,610	C-P-V	$14.12
Expend.	$1,397,469	Cand.	$0	Sm. Indiv.	$62,494	Spnd. Edge	$811,853
C-O-H	$388,519	Party	$200	Lg. Indiv.	$256,559	Debt	$0

26th District, Rep. Richard K. (Dick) Armey (R)

Receipts	$482,973	PACS	$195,110	Out of St.	$8,700	C-P-V	$3.17
Expend.	$475,756	Cand.	$0	Sm. Indiv.	$120,362	Spnd. Edge	$466,167
C-O-H	$369,528	Party	$70	Lg. Indiv.	$101,668	Debt	$0

27th District, Rep. Solomon P. Ortiz (D)

Receipts	$274,610	PACS	$99,518	Out of St.	$18,550	C-P-V	$3.95
Expend.	$343,904	Cand.	$0	Sm. Indiv.	$13,134	Spnd. Edge	$286,072
C-O-H	$149,788	Party	$150	Lg. Indiv.	$132,734	Debt	$0

28th District, Rep. Frank M. Tejeda (D)

Receipts	$305,673	PACS	$131,725	Out of St.	$1,500	C-P-V	$2.48
Expend.	$304,286	Cand.	$0	Sm. Indiv.	$14,648	Spnd. Edge	$302,885
C-O-H	$1,384	Party	$0	Lg. Indiv.	$142,924	Debt	$65,081

29th District, Rep. Gene Green (D)

Receipts	$702,330	PACS	$402,350	Out of St.	$6,290	C-P-V	$10.79
Expend.	$691,275	Cand.	$796	Sm. Indiv.	$50,211	Spnd. Edge	$181,457
C-O-H	$11,051	Party	$0	Lg. Indiv.	$176,620	Debt	$55,062

30th District, Rep. Eddie Bernice Johnson (D)

Receipts	$283,350	PACS	$114,176	Out of St.	$23,010	C-P-V	$2.62
Expend.	$282,734	Cand.	$0	Sm. Indiv.	$65,551	Spnd. Edge	$280,980
C-O-H	$2,696	Party	$1,015	Lg. Indiv.	$84,210	Debt	$16,000

UTAH

Sen. Orrin G. Hatch (R)

Receipts	$4,554,073	PACS	$1,252,397	Out of St.	$1,298,564	C-P-V	$9.78
Expend.	$4,206,995	Cand.	$0	Sm. Indiv.	$1,302,163	Spnd. Edge	$4,053,520
C-O-H	$443,171	Party	$65,390	Lg. Indiv.	$1,404,064	Debts	$176,188

Sen. Robert F. Bennett (R)

Receipts	$3,524,942	PACS	$342,310	Out of St.	$57,275	C-P-V	$7.95
Expend.	$3,339,325	Cand.	$1,792,718	Sm. Indiv.	$81,386	Spnd. Edge	$1,434,575
C-O-H	$131,617	Party	$19,617	Lg. Indiv.	$187,481	Debts	$298,167

1st District, Rep. James V. Hansen (R)

Receipts	$221,781	PACS	$147,351	Out of St.	$11,700	C-P-V	$1.51
Expend.	$240,969	Cand.	$0	Sm. Indiv.	$22,226	Spnd. Edge	$176,518
C-O-H	$22,756	Party	$3,154	Lg. Indiv.	$46,285	Debt	$0

2d District, Rep. Karen F. Shepherd (D)

Receipts	$640,031	PACS	$201,601	Out of St.	$82,131	C-P-V	$4.83
Expend.	$617,594	Cand.	$914	Sm. Indiv.	$260,128	Spnd. Edge	$171,260
C-O-H	$22,437	Party	$5,450	Lg. Indiv.	$164,732	Debt	$0

3d District, Rep. William H. Orton (D)

Receipts	$257,559	PACS	$190,995	Out of St.	$11,050	C-P-V	$1.79
Expend.	$241,403	Cand.	$0	Sm. Indiv.	$21,308	Spnd. Edge	$170,329
C-O-H	$18,398	Party	$15,110	Lg. Indiv.	$27,000	Debt	$21,690

VERMONT

Sen. Patrick J. Leahy (D)

Receipts	$1,144,189	PACS	$373,215	Out of St.	$412,991	C-P-V	$7.77
Expend.	$1,202,445	Cand.	$0	Sm. Indiv.	$111,800	Spnd. Edge	$1,006,708
C-O-H	$269,610	Party	$19,120	Lg. Indiv.	$459,290	Debts	$50,000

Sen. James M. Jeffords (R)

Receipts	$974,718	PACS	$679,396	Out of St.	$90,008	C-P-V	$5.36
Expend.	$875,144	Cand.	$0	Sm. Indiv.	$108,604	Spnd. Edge	$324,724
C-O-H	$312,249	Party	$15,742	Lg. Indiv.	$118,080	Debts	$0

At-Large, Rep. Bernard Sanders (I)

Receipts	$591,543	PACS	$147,057	Out of St.	$39,875	C-P-V	$3.54
Expend.	$575,791	Cand.	$5,311	Sm. Indiv.	$376,952	Spnd. Edge	$502,833
C-O-H	$19,231	Party	$0	Lg. Indiv.	$50,986	Debt	$2,498

VIRGINIA

Sen. John W. Warner (R)

Receipts	$1,812,542	PACS	$621,950	Out of St.	$363,804	C-P-V	$1.39
Expend.	$1,219,726	Cand.	$0	Sm. Indiv.	$244,055	Spnd. Edge	$1,086,462
C-O-H	$592,770	Party	$15,625	Lg. Indiv.	$866,624	Debts	$0

Sen. Charles S. Robb (D)

Receipts	$3,166,000	PACS	$911,765	Out of St.	$765,867	C-P-V	$1.93
Expend.	$2,849,037	Cand.	$0	Sm. Indiv.	$197,861	Spnd. Edge	$2,568,829
C-O-H	$316,963	Party	$22,403	Lg. Indiv.	$1,974,312	Debts	$0

1st District, Rep. Herbert H. Bateman (R)

Receipts	$766,895	PACS	$294,121	Out of St.	$12,550	C-P-V	$5.73
Expend.	$764,820	Cand.	$100	Sm. Indiv.	$227,900	Spnd. Edge	$344,942
C-O-H	$16,992	Party	$14,075	Lg. Indiv.	$220,610	Debt	$0

2d District, Rep. Owen Pickett (D)

Receipts	$281,279	PACS	$128,450	Out of St.	$1,650	C-P-V	$3.76
Expend.	$373,047	Cand.	$0	Sm. Indiv.	$37,650	Spnd. Edge	$182,600
C-O-H	$94,085	Party	$3,550	Lg. Indiv.	$94,535	Debt	$0

3d District, Rep. Robert C. (Bobby) Scott (D)

Receipts	$519,276	PACS	$185,250	Out of St.	$12,350	C-P-V	$3.78
Expend.	$500,359	Cand.	$0	Sm. Indiv.	$132,991	Spnd. Edge	$484,041
C-O-H	$18,915	Party	$4,675	Lg. Indiv.	$129,053	Debt	$108,791

4th District, Rep. Norman Sisisky (D)

Receipts	$257,047	PACS	$160,750	Out of St.	$3,750	C-P-V	$3.16
Expend.	$466,010	Cand.	$0	Sm. Indiv.	$26,574	Spnd. Edge	$383,942
C-O-H	$72,679	Party	$3,350	Lg. Indiv.	$44,984	Debt	$349,183

5th District, Rep. L. F. Payne (D)

Receipts	$418,643	PACS	$219,044	Out of St.	$8,100	C-P-V	$3.12
Expend.	$414,696	Cand.	$0	Sm. Indiv.	$62,055	Spnd. Edge	$359,991
C-O-H	$13,540	Party	$825	Lg. Indiv.	$136,320	Debt	$85,000

6th District, Rep. Bob Goodlatte (R)

Receipts	$464,535	PACS	$120,492	Out of St.	$7,650	C-P-V	$3.55
Expend.	$452,048	Cand.	$17,951	Sm. Indiv.	$121,992	Spnd. Edge	($144,972)
C-O-H	$12,486	Party	$15,125	Lg. Indiv.	$149,154	Debt	$40,000

7th District, Rep. Thomas J. Bliley, Jr. (R)

Receipts	$721,526	PACS	$441,292	Out of St.	$29,948	C-P-V	$3.30
Expend.	$698,964	Cand.	$0	Sm. Indiv.	$160,223	Spnd. Edge	$698,964
C-O-H	$52,852	Party	$453	Lg. Indiv.	$116,443	Debt	$0

8th District, Rep. James P. Moran, Jr. (D)

Receipts	$925,436	PACS	$436,121	Out of St.	$90,355	C-P-V	$6.67
Expend.	$923,999	Cand.	$0	Sm. Indiv.	$186,582	Spnd. Edge	$499,104
C-O-H	$1,455	Party	$14,738	Lg. Indiv.	$280,690	Debt	$48,098

9th District, Rep. Rick Boucher (D)

Receipts	$639,537	PACS	$404,579	Out of St.	$14,150	C-P-V	$4.96
Expend.	$660,452	Cand.	$0	Sm. Indiv.	$82,124	Spnd. Edge	$560,363
C-O-H	$380,922	Party	$4,685	Lg. Indiv.	$71,925	Debt	$0

10th District, Rep. Frank R. Wolf (R)

Receipts	$452,307	PACS	$180,401	Out of St.	$14,612	C-P-V	$2.99
Expend.	$431,829	Cand.	$0	Sm. Indiv.	$123,339	Spnd. Edge	$240,569
C-O-H	$79,889	Party	$300	Lg. Indiv.	$133,872	Debt	$0

11th District, Rep. Leslie L. Byrne (D)

Receipts	$793,566	PACS	$309,330	Out of St.	$30,748	C-P-V	$6.77
Expend.	$773,128	Cand.	$0	Sm. Indiv.	$290,912	Spnd. Edge	($71,567)
C-O-H	$20,439	Party	$17,122	Lg. Indiv.	$126,952	Debt	$56,677

WASHINGTON

Sen. Slade Gorton (R)

Receipts	$2,731,555	PACS	$937,408	Out of St.	$386,075	C-P-V	$3.01
Expend.	$2,847,045	Cand.	$0	Sm. Indiv.	$620,766	Spnd. Edge	$658,676
C-O-H	$45,959	Party	$34,502	Lg. Indiv.	$1,008,384	Debts	$114,209

Sen. Patty Murray (D)

Receipts	$1,496,204	PACS	$439,766	Out of St.	$255,625	C-P-V	$1.12
Expend.	$1,342,038	Cand.	$8,377	Sm. Indiv.	$545,687	S. Edge	($1,160,164)
C-O-H	$154,166	Party	$22,555	Lg. Indiv.	$448,696	Debts	$0

1st District, Rep. Maria Cantwell (D)

Receipts	$625,170	PACS	$287,103	Out of St.	$27,050	C-P-V	$4.18
Expend.	$621,961	Cand.	$0	Sm. Indiv.	$184,384	Spnd. Edge	$507,415
C-O-H	$3,209	Party	$1,477	Lg. Indiv.	$140,767	Debt	$63,536

2d District, Rep. Al Swift (D)

Receipts	$914,905	PACS	$649,844	Out of St.	$83,586	C-P-V	$7.96
Expend.	$1,060,650	Cand.	$0	Sm. Indiv.	$80,553	Spnd. Edge	$859,621
C-O-H	$22,730	Party	$623	Lg. Indiv.	$141,344	Debt	$0

3d District, Rep. Jolene Unsoeld (D)

Receipts	$664,308	PACS	$365,370	Out of St.	$56,700	C-P-V	$4.50
Expend.	$619,947	Cand.	$0	Sm. Indiv.	$168,711	Spnd. Edge	$407,749
C-O-H	$49,967	Party	$3,950	Lg. Indiv.	$114,778	Debt	$0

4th District, Rep. Jay Inslee (D)

Receipts	$257,153	PACS	$98,886	Out of St.	$3,232	C-P-V	$2.39
Expend.	$255,159	Cand.	$0	Sm. Indiv.	$63,653	Spnd. Edge	($100,700)
C-O-H	$3,551	Party	$0	Lg. Indiv.	$38,366	Debt	$52,800

5th District, Rep. Thomas S. Foley (D)

Receipts	$561,826	PACS	$406,490	Out of St.	$24,450	C-P-V	$6.72
Expend.	$913,647	Cand.	$0	Sm. Indiv.	$15,559	Spnd. Edge	$435,841
C-O-H	$244,887	Party	$3,025	Lg. Indiv.	$68,500	Debt	$0

6th District, Rep. Norm Dicks (D)

Receipts	$546,865	PACS	$310,818	Out of St.	$37,775	C-P-V	$4.04
Expend.	$617,460	Cand.	$0	Sm. Indiv.	$64,045	Spnd. Edge	$611,022
C-O-H	$55,882	Party	$1,530	Lg. Indiv.	$148,848	Debt	$0

7th District, Rep. Jim McDermott (D)

Receipts	$222,346	PACS	$169,015	Out of St.	$5,400	C-P-V		$0.86
Expend.	$191,472	Cand.	$0	Sm. Indiv.	$29,656	Spnd. Edge		$161,155
C-O-H	$68,692	Party	$0	Lg. Indiv.	$23,050	Debt		$0

8th District, Rep. Jennifer B. Dunn (R)

Receipts	$709,207	PACS	$168,373	Out of St.	$31,600	C-P-V		$4.52
Expend.	$704,674	Cand.	$0	Sm. Indiv.	$273,502	Spnd. Edge		$294,209
C-O-H	$4,533	Party	$20,000	Lg. Indiv.	$218,942	Debt		$18,467

9th District, Rep. Mike Kreidler (D)

Receipts	$430,480	PACS	$165,387	Out of St.	$7,825	C-P-V		$3.88
Expend.	$430,476	Cand.	$0	Sm. Indiv.	$178,962	Spnd. Edge		$15,882
C-O-H	$2	Party	$11,000	Lg. Indiv.	$43,726	Debt		$61,000

WEST VIRGINIA

Sen. Robert C. Byrd (D)

Receipts	$1,516,700	PACS	$981,221	Out of St.	$203,400	C-P-V		$3.07
Expend.	$1,260,154	Cand.	$0	Sm. Indiv.	$83,750	Spnd. Edge		$1,144,867
C-O-H	$482,690	Party	$0	Lg. Indiv.	$274,622	Debts		$0

Sen. John D. (Jay) Rockefeller IV (D)

Receipts	$3,575,358	PACS	$1,472,533	Out of St.	$1,183,457	C-P-V		$9.81
Expend.	$2,709,665	Cand.	$0	Sm. Indiv.	$300,559	Spnd. Edge		$2,687,959
C-O-H	$902,199	Party	$17,500	Lg. Indiv.	$1,677,943	Debts		$0

1st District, Rep. Alan B. Mollohan (D)

Receipts	$494,159	PACS	$242,669	Out of St.	$47,850	C-P-V		$3.64
Expend.	$629,436	Cand.	$0	Sm. Indiv.	$50,581	Spnd. Edge		(unopp.)
C-O-H	$1,176	Party	$3,700	Lg. Indiv.	$151,100	Debt		$72,516

2d District, Rep. Robert E. (Bob) Wise, Jr. (D)

Receipts	$295,894	PACS	$170,755	Out of St.	$17,950	C-P-V		$2.29
Expend.	$330,052	Cand.	$0	Sm. Indiv.	$54,418	Spnd. Edge		$330,052
C-O-H	$145,069	Party	$1,000	Lg. Indiv.	$50,600	Debt		$0

3d District, Rep. Nick J. Rahall (D)

Receipts	$444,624	PACS	$247,758	Out of St.	$71,500	C-P-V		$2.53
Expend.	$309,313	Cand.	$0	Sm. Indiv.	$42,728	Spnd. Edge		$158,491
C-O-H	$500,823	Party	$750	Lg. Indiv.	$83,650	Debt		$0

WISCONSIN

Sen. Herb Kohl (D)

Receipts	$7,576,152	PACS	$0	Out of St.	$287,244	C-P-V		$6.64
Expend.	$7,491,213	Cand.	$6,135,071	Sm. Indiv.	$158,599	Spnd. Edge		$4,639,767
C-O-H	$84,939	Party	$0	Lg. Indiv.	$483,940	Debts		$881,095

Sen. Russell D. Feingold (D)

Receipts	$2,094,575	PACS	$467,463	Out of St.	$310,591	C-P-V		$1.59
Expend.	$2,056,079	Cand.	$150	Sm. Indiv.	$794,091	S. Edge		($3,939,258)
C-O-H	$38,996	Party	$30,637	Lg. Indiv.	$768,719	Debts		$43,285

1st District, Rep. Peter W. Barca (D)
(Elected May 4, 1993; campaign finance figures unavailable)

2d District, Rep. Scott Klug (R)

Receipts	$879,091	PACS	$226,266	Out of St.	$20,650	C-P-V	$4.52
Expend.	$829,378	Cand.	$0	Sm. Indiv.	$311,971	Spnd. Edge	$306,422
C-O-H	$57,373	Party	$30,984	Lg. Indiv.	$300,096	Debt	$0

3d District, Rep. Steve Gunderson (R)

Receipts	$427,112	PACS	$222,462	Out of St.	$11,325	C-P-V	$3.12
Expend.	$458,846	Cand.	$0	Sm. Indiv.	$94,815	Spnd. Edge	$425,737
C-O-H	$66,434	Party	$2,466	Lg. Indiv.	$96,926	Debt	$0

4th District, Rep. Gerald D. Kleczka (D)

Receipts	$260,726	PACS	$156,407	Out of St.	$21,800	C-P-V	$1.78
Expend.	$309,036	Cand.	$0	Sm. Indiv.	$30,473	Spnd. Edge	$241,769
C-O-H	$76,093	Party	$450	Lg. Indiv.	$51,033	Debt	$0

5th District, Rep. Thomas M. Barrett (D)

Receipts	$356,052	PACS	$154,526	Out of St.	$6,220	C-P-V	$2.39
Expend.	$387,469	Cand.	$0	Sm. Indiv.	$123,776	Spnd. Edge	$289,131
C-O-H	$39,212	Party	$200	Lg. Indiv.	$65,428	Debt	$57,166

6th District, Rep. Tom Petri (R)

Receipts	$433,702	PACS	$204,000	Out of St.	$12,173	C-P-V	$5.39
Expend.	$775,594	Cand.	$720	Sm. Indiv.	$137,479	Spnd. Edge	$456,231
C-O-H	$55,773	Party	$14,501	Lg. Indiv.	$36,848	Debt	$0

7th District, Rep. David R. Obey (D)

Receipts	$497,123	PACS	$267,575	Out of St.	$70,255	C-P-V	$3.16
Expend.	$524,574	Cand.	$0	Sm. Indiv.	$109,704	Spnd. Edge	$504,247
C-O-H	$307,113	Party	$0	Lg. Indiv.	$72,105	Debt	$0

8th District, Rep. Toby Roth (R)

Receipts	$589,778	PACS	$292,200	Out of St.	$24,800	C-P-V	$2.32
Expend.	$444,548	Cand.	$0	Sm. Indiv.	$156,673	Spnd. Edge	$401,721
C-O-H	$239,081	Party	$7,376	Lg. Indiv.	$109,135	Debt	$5,200

9th District, Rep. F. James Sensenbrenner, Jr. (R)

Receipts	$283,602	PACS	$75,709	Out of St.	$1,750	C-P-V	$2.37
Expend.	$457,292	Cand.	$0	Sm. Indiv.	$110,901	Spnd. Edge	$430,167
C-O-H	$138,787	Party	$0	Lg. Indiv.	$55,995	Debt	$0

WYOMING

Sen. Malcolm Wallop (R)

Receipts	$1,596,500	PACS	$920,717	Out of St.	$432,010	C-P-V	$15.90
Expend.	$1,449,219	Cand.	$0	Sm. Indiv.	$96,825	Spnd. Edge	$963,986
C-O-H	$166,345	Party	$18,271	Lg. Indiv.	$516,447	Debts	$0

Sen. Alan K. Simpson (R)

Receipts	$1,663,444	PACS	$799,674	Out of St.	$408,960	C-P-V	$14.25
Expend.	$1,435,814	Cand.	$0	Sm. Indiv.	$74,040	Spnd. Edge	$1,429,569
C-O-H	$433,246	Party	$2,650	Lg. Indiv.	$533,053	Debts	$7,919

At-Large, Rep. Craig Thomas (R)

Receipts	$479,523	PACS	$222,403	Out of St.	$9,500	C-P-V	$4.04
Expend.	$459,523	Cand.	$0	Sm. Indiv.	$143,016	Spnd. Edge	$111,162
C-O-H	$24,529	Party	$12,300	Lg. Indiv.	$96,425	Debt	$0

CAMPAIGN FINANCE CHARTS

All data are derived from candidate and party reports as well as other official studies available from the Federal Election Commission (FEC) located at 999 E Street, N.W., Washington, DC 20463. Telephone 202-219-4140 (or toll-free 800-424-9530).

Chart I shows contributions from Political Action Committees (PACs), total receipts, expenditures and cash-on-hand (unspent) for all 1991–92 congressional candidates.

Chart I

1991–92 Total Senate Financial Activity: Winners/Losers

	No. of Cand.	Total PAC Contrib.	Total Receipts	Total Expenditures	Latest Cash-on-Hand
Senate	363	$51,853,075	$262,887,958	$271,610,245	$12,331,456
Democrats	122	30,145,487	142,790,537	146,684,049	6,771,833
Incumbents	17	17,771,009	45,466,949	48,230,520	5,020,050
Challengers	76	6,485,029	62,787,348	62,788,380	787,475
Open Seats	29	5,889,449	34,636,240	35,665,149	964,308
Republicans	125	21,698,088	118,822,568	123,656,367	5,539,573
Incumbents	12	14,113,419	51,895,144	57,369,627	4,614,394
Challengers	82	2,432,469	27,619,230	27,375,841	314,355
Open Seats	31	5,152,200	39,308,194	39,910,899	610,824
Others	116	9,500	1,274,853	1,269,829	20,050
Challenger	90	1,500	1,091,537	1,081,031	8,238
Open	26	8,000	183,316	188,798	11,812

1991–92 Total House Financial Activity: Winners/Losers

	No. of Cand.	Total PAC Contrib.	Total Receipts	Total Expenditures	Latest Cash-on-Hand
House	2593	$128,633,430	$395,672,442	$406,727,607	$48,059,889
Democrats	1058	85,770,662	217,275,727	227,837,746	29,373,659
Incumbents	227	64,442,459	126,564,286	138,735,203	27,589,484
Challengers	513	7,593,679	34,696,983	34,047,780	756,557
Open Seats	318	13,734,524	56,014,458	55,054,763	1,027,618
Republicans	991	42,539,125	174,406,657	174,974,009	18,595,799
Incumbents	143	30,258,469	75,887,858	77,649,754	17,305,452
Challengers	578	4,690,580	53,926,972	53,217,844	687,813
Open Seats	270	7,590,076	44,591,827	44,106,411	602,534
Others	544	323,643	3,990,058	3,915,852	90,431
Incumbent	1	147,057	591,543	575,791	19,231
Challenger	435	162,375	2,716,266	2,664,156	64,192
Open	108	14,211	682,249	675,905	7,008
Total Senate/House	2956	$180,486,505	$658,560,400	$678,337,852	$60,391,345

Chart II shows the total financial activity for Senate and House winners since 1981.

Chart II

1991–92 Senate/House Winners: Financial Activity
(in millions)

Senate	1991–92	1989–90	1987–88	1985–86	1983–84	1981–82
Receipts	$119.0	$121.5	$121.7	$106.8	$100.9	$70.7
Expend.	124.3	115.4	123.6	104.3	97.5	68.2
PAC Contrib.	31.8	31.1	31.8	28.4	20.0	15.6

House	1991–92	1989–90	1987–88	1985–86	1983–84	1981–82
Receipts	$232.9	$197.6	$191.0	$172.7	$144.8	$123.1
Expend.	239.8	178.4	171.0	154.9	127.0	114.7
PAC Contrib.	97.2	91.6	86.4	72.8	59.5	42.7

Chart III illustrates the Democratic and Republican Party financial activity for the 1991–92 election cycle.

Chart III

1991–92 Party Financial Activity: Democratic/Republican

Democratic	Net Receipts	Net Expenditures	C.O.H. (12-31-92)	Debt Owed By	Contrib. To Cand.	Coordinated Expenditures
DNC Services	$65,790,724	$65,018,428	$2,844,664	$ 450,018	$ 19,255	$11,368,560
Senatorial	25,450,835	25,494,157	5,878	1,914,441	745,000	11,377,607
Congressional	12,815,844	12,654,762	181,105	2,069,008	847,983	4,231,002
Totals	**$104,057,403**	**$103,167,347**	**$3,031,647**	**$4,433,467**	**$1,612,238**	**$26,977,169**

Republican	Net Receipts	Net Expenditures	C.O.H. (12-31-92)	Debt Owed By	Contrib. To Cand.	Coordinated Expenditures
RNC	$ 85,447,469	$ 81,919,094	$2,256,421	$ 0	$ 825,445	$11,230,638
Senatorial	72,309,085	71,760,867	299,675	6,397,295	920,951	16,477,217
Congressional	34,366,963	33,514,250	1,036,106	7,900,700	728,690	5,191,114
Totals	**$192,123,517**	**$187,194,211**	**$3,592,202**	**$14,297,995**	**$2,475,086**	**$32,898,969**
Grand Total	**$293,935,183**	**$306,284,681**	**$5,641,193**	**$13,904,400**	**$4,339,648**	**$19,285,300**

U.S. SENATE

The following charts show the top ten Senate members elected in 1992 in terms of the highest total net receipts, net expenditures, political action committee (PAC) contributions, out of state contributions, cash on hand and cost per vote during the 1986–92 election cycle.

1992 Senate: Top Ten Raisers

1.	Alfonse M. D'Amato (R-NY)	$11,239,373
2.	Arlen Specter (R-PA)	10,451,746
3.	Barbara Boxer (D-CA)	10,431,140
4.	Bob Packwood (R-OR)	8,228,212
5.	Dianne Feinstein (D-CA)	8,114,867
6.	Carol Moseley-Braun (D-IL)	6,770,711
7.	Christopher S. Bond (R-MO)	5,087,184
8.	Christopher J. Dodd (D-CT)	4,342,880
9.	John H. Glenn, Jr. (D-OH)	4,245,138
10.	Thomas A. Daschle (D-SD)	4,122,119

1992 Senate: Top Ten Spenders

1.	Alfonse M. D'Amato (R-NY)	$11,550,958
2.	Arlen Specter (R-PA)	10,454,793
3.	Barbara Boxer (D-CA)	10,415,811
4.	Dianne Feinstein (D-CA)	8,054,222
5.	Bob Packwood (R-OR)	8,034,249
6.	Carol Moseley-Braun (D-IL)	6,699,942
7.	Christopher S. Bond (R-MO)	5,048,333
8.	John H. Glenn, Jr. (D-OH)	4,974,109
9.	Christopher J. Dodd (D-CT)	4,553,792
10.	Ernest F. (Fritz) Hollings (D-SC)	4,188,829

1992 Senate: Top PAC Recipients

1.	Arlen Specter (R-PA)	$2,017,041
2.	Thomas A. Daschle (D-SD)	1,848,680
3.	Christopher S. Bond (R-MO)	1,721,235
4.	Kent Conrad (D-ND)	1,708,368
5.	John B. Breaux (D-LA)	1,697,455
6.	Richard C. Shelby (D-AL)	1,694,944
7.	Ernest F. (Fritz) Hollings (D-SC)	1,620,274
8.	Robert Dole (R-KS)	1,600,855
9.	Christopher J. Dodd (D-CT)	1,544,084
10.	Alfonse M. D'Amato (R-NY)	1,361,231

1992 Senate: Top Out of State Contributions

1.	Arlen Specter (R-PA)	$2,080,136
2.	Bob Packwood (R-OR)	1,994,646
3.	Barbara Boxer (D-CA)	1,372,404
4.	Ernest F. (Fritz) Hollings (D-SC)	1,294,963
5.	Daniel K. Inouye (D-HI)	1,246,637
6.	Thomas A. Daschle (D-SD)	1,216,765
7.	Christopher J. Dodd (D-CT)	1,143,659
8.	Alfonse M. D'Amato (R-NY)	1,087,128
9.	Harris Wofford (D-PA)	1,080,327
10.	Carol Moseley-Braun (D-IL)	849,800

1992 Senate: Top Cash-on-Hand

1.	Robert Dole (R-KS)	$1,756,483
2.	John B. Breaux (D-LA)	1,522,344
3.	Richard C. Shelby (D-AL)	1,112,139
4.	Bob Packwood (R-OR)	890,256
5.	Charles E. Grassley (R-IA)	821,030
6.	Don Nickles (R-OK)	569,953
7.	Wendell H. Ford (D-KY)	438,224
8.	Bob Graham (D-FL)	354,763
9.	Patrick J. Leahy (D-VT)	269,610
10.	Barbara A. Mikulski (D-MD)	269,145

1992 Senate: Top Cost Per Vote

1.	Kent Conrad (D-ND)	$24.01
2.	Thomas A. Daschle (D-SD)	18.34
3.	Daniel K. Inouye (D-HI)	16.88
4.	Frank H. Murkowski (R-AK)	15.03
5.	Harry Reid (D-NV)	12.88
6.	Bob Packwood (R-OR)	11.20
7.	Robert Bennett (R-UT)	7.95
8.	Patrick J. Leahy (D-VT)	7.77
9.	Ernest F. (Fritz) Hollings (D-SC)	7.09
10.	Byron L. Dorgan (D-ND)	6.27

U.S. HOUSE OF REPRESENTATIVES

The following charts show the top twenty House members elected in 1992 in terms of the highest total net receipts, net expenditures, political action committee (PAC) contributions, out of state contributions, cash on hand and cost per vote during the 1990–92 election cycle.

1992 House: Top Raisers

1.	Michael Huffington (R-CA)	$5,443,247
2.	Richard A. Gephardt (D-MO)	3,237,531
3.	Jane Harman (D-CA)	2,301,376
4.	Vic Fazio (D-CA)	1,994,284
5.	Newt Gingrich (R-GA)	1,962,935
6.	Dan Rostenkowski (D-IL)	1,587,108
7.	Robert K. (Bob) Dornan (R-CA)	1,443,564
8.	Gerry E. Studds (D-MA)	1,438,264
9.	Les Aspin (D-WI)	1,359,476
10.	Steny H. Hoyer (D-MD)	1,304,867
11.	David E. Bonior (D-MI)	1,295,553
12.	Herbert C. Klein (D-NJ)	1,291,518
13.	Martin Frost (D-TX)	1,241,725
14.	Charles Wilson (D-TX)	1,217,912
15.	Charles H. Taylor (R-NC)	1,216,256
16.	Michael L. (Mike) Synar (D-OK)	1,191,392
17.	Pat Williams (D-MT)	1,190,716
18.	Robert G. Torricelli (D-NJ)	1,190,045
19.	Lynn A. Schenk (D-CA)	1,154,531
20.	Nita M. Lowey (D-NY)	1,153,696

1992 House: Top Spenders

1.	Michael Huffington (R-CA)	$5,435,177
2.	Richard A. Gephardt (D-MO)	3,316,784
3.	Jane Harman (D-CA)	2,285,356
4.	Newt Gingrich (R-GA)	1,963,810
5.	Vic Fazio (D-CA)	1,906,584
6.	Steny H. Hoyer (D-MD)	1,584,271
7.	Robert K. (Bob) Dornan (R-CA)	1,581,503
8.	Martin Frost (D-TX)	1,549,556
9.	Dan Rostenkowski (D-IL)	1,455,455
10.	Gerry E. Studds (D-MD)	1,440,376
11.	Joe L. Barton (D-WV)	1,423,644
12.	Robert T. Matsui (D-CA)	1,421,123
13.	Michael A. Andrews (D-TX)	1,397,469
14.	Les Aspin (D-WI)	1,355,737
15.	Bob Carr (D-MI)	1,355,199
16.	David E. Bonior (D-MI)	1,345,011
17.	Pat Williams (D-MT)	1,336,673
18.	Nita M. Lowey (D-NY)	1,277,433
19.	Herbert C. Klein (D-NJ)	1,249,023
20.	Charles H. Taylor (R-NC)	1,212,765

1992 House: Top PAC Recipients

1.	Richard A. Gephardt (D-MO)	$1,240,597
2.	Vic Fazio (D-CA)	1,148,438
3.	Dan Rostenkowski (D-IL)	962,937
4.	David E. Bonior (D-MI)	934,613
5.	John D. Dingell (D-MI)	767,931
6.	Steny H. Hoyer (D-MD)	711,367
7.	Martin Frost (D-TX)	667,804
8.	Newt Gingrich (R-GA)	653,712
9.	Al Swift (D-WA)	649,844
10.	Charles Wilson (D-TX)	838,825
11.	Bob Carr (D-MI)	568,003
12.	Norman Y. Mineta (D-CA)	546,295
13.	John P. Murtha (D-PA)	540,060
14.	Les Aspin (D-WI)	536,425
15.	Frank Pallone, Jr. (D-NJ)	531,079
16.	Michael A. Andrews (D-TX)	527,931
17.	Richard H. Lehman (D-CA)	526,845
18.	William D. Ford (D-MI)	520,850
19.	George E. Brown, Jr. (D-CA)	506,920
20.	Sander M. Levin (D-MI)	504,521

1992 House: Top Out of State Contributions

1.	Richard A. Gephardt (D-MO)	$1,237,598
2.	Michael L. (Mike) Synar (D-OK)	453,914
3.	Newt Gingrich (R-GA)	349,191
4.	Dick Swett (D-NH)	317,968
5.	Jane Harman (D-CA)	257,101
6.	Robert G. Torricelli (D-NJ)	252,650
7.	Charles Wilson (D-TX)	244,000
8.	Les Aspin (D-WI)	201,200
9.	Bob Carr (D-MI)	200,743
10.	E.G. (Bud) Shuster (R-PA)	190,229
11.	Gerry E. Studds (D-MA)	188,176
12.	Joseph P. Kennedy II (D-MA)	171,820
13.	John P. Murtha (D-PA)	171,800
14.	Edward J. Markey (D-MA)	169,975
15.	Dan Glickman (D-KS)	169,939
16.	Dan Rostenkowski (D-IL)	152,081
17.	Vic Fazio (D-CA)	150,800
18.	Sander M. Levin (D-MI)	150,100
19.	Steny M. Hoyer (D-MD)	142,602
20.	Dan Burton (R-IN)	135,252

1992 House: Top Cash-on-Hand	
1. Charles E. Schumer (D-NY)	$2,116,689
2. David Dreier (R-CA)	2,026,109
3. Dan Rostenkowski (D-IL)	1,245,721
4. James H. Quillen (R-TN)	1,174,716
5. Robert G. Torricelli (D-NJ)	1,035,163
6. John J. LaFalce (D-NY)	765,913
7. Charlie Rose (D-NC)	681,533
8. Bill Archer (R-TX)	671,097
9. Dan Burton (R-IN)	622,881
10. Patricia Schroeder (D-CO)	612,243
11. Tom Lantos (D-CA)	536,945
12. John D. Dingell (D-MI)	523,361
13. Neal Smith (D-IA)	502,580
14. Nick J. Rahall (D-WV)	500,823
15. Jon Kyl (R-AZ)	493,753
16. Jack Brooks (D-TX)	465,327
17. Willis D. (Bill) Gradison (R-OH)	458,452
18. Henry A. Waxman (D-CA)	432,414
19. Lamar S. Smith (R-TX)	420,613
20. Carlos J. Moorhead (R-CA)	409,659

1992 House: Top Cost Per Vote	
1. Michael Huffington (R-CA)	$41.41
2. Robert K. (Bob) Dornan (R-CA)	28.41
3. Richard A. Gephardt (D-MO)	19.06
4. Jane Harman (D-CA)	18.32
5. Vic Fazio (D-CA)	15.61
6. Martin Frost (D-TX)	14.87
7. Michael A. Andrews (D-PA)	14.12
8. Thomas J. Manton (D-NY)	14.02
9. Steny H. Hoyer (D-MD)	13.39
10. Herbert C. Klein (D-NJ)	12.91
11. Newt Gingrich (R-GA)	12.37
12. Ronald D. Coleman (D-TX)	11.69
13. George E. Brown, Jr. (D-CA)	11.37
14. Bob Filner (D-CA)	11.08
15. Nita M. Lowey (D-NY)	11.03
16. Dan Rostenkowski (D-IL)	10.95
17. Gene Green (D-TX)	10.79
18. Charles Wilson (D-TX)	10.06
19. Michael L. (Mike) Synar (D-OK)	10.04
20. Bob Carr (D-MI)	10.00

DEMOGRAPHICS CHARTS

Population. All population figures are from the Bureau of the Census, U.S. Department of Commerce, Washington, D.C. 20233, 301-763-4040. Figures for 1970 and 1980 are final Census Bureau population counts as of April 1 of those years; 1990 figures are final as of April 1, 1990, but are subject to adjustment for undercount or overcount by the Census Bureau. (The District of Columbia is included as a state in all the following charts.)

Voting Age Population. This figure indicates all persons at least 18 years of age who are eligible to vote, including the Armed Forces, aliens and institutional members.

Chart I shows the total U.S. population and total U.S. voting age population for 1990, 1980 and 1970.

Chart I

Total U.S. Population		Total U.S. Voting Age Population	
July 1, 1992 (est.)	254,922,000	July 1, 1992(est.)	188,759,000
April 1, 1990	248,709,873	April 1, 1990	185,105,441
April 1, 1980	226,545,805	April 1, 1980	163,997,000
April 1, 1970	203,302,031	April 1, 1970	135,290,000

Chart II indicates the range of highest and lowest state population changes in percentage growth and absolute change for 1980–90.

Chart II

1980–90 Population Change
(National Avg.: up 9.8%)

State	Highest		State	Lowest	
Nevada	50.1%	401,340	West Virginia	−8.0%	−156,167
Alaska	36.9	148,192	District of Columbia	−4.9	−31,433
Arizona	34.8	947,013	Iowa	−4.7	−137,053
Florida	32.7	3,191,602	Wyoming	−3.4	−15,969
California	25.7	6,092,119	North Dakota	−2.1	−13,917

Chart III shows the ten highest and the ten lowest state populations.

Chart III

1990 U.S. Population: Ten Highest and Lowest States

State	Highest	State	Lowest
California	29,760,021	Wyoming	453,588
New York	17,990,455	Alaska	550,043
Texas	16,986,510	Vermont	562,758
Florida	12,937,926	District of Columbia	606,900
Pennsylvania	11,881,643	North Dakota	638,800
Illinois	11,430,602	Delaware	666,168
Ohio	10,847,115	South Dakota	696,004
Michigan	9,295,297	Montana	799,065
New Jersey	7,730,188	Rhode Island	1,003,464
North Carolina	6,628,637	Idaho	1,006,749

Chart IV lists the states with the highest and lowest median age.

Chart IV

Median Age
(National Avg.: 32.8 years)

State	Highest	State	Lowest
Florida	36.4 years	Utah	26.2 years
West Virginia	35.4	Alaska	29.4
Pennsylvania	35.0	Texas	30.8
New Jersey, Oregon	34.5	Louisiana	31.0
Connecticut	34.4	Mississippi	31.2

Chart V illustrates the states with the highest and lowest average percentages of married-couple family households.

Chart V

Married-Couple Family Households
(National Avg.: 55.9%)

State	Highest	State	Lowest
Utah	64.8%	District of Columbia	25.3%
Idaho	62.2	New York	49.9
Wyoming, New Hampshire	59.7	Nevada	51.4
Arkansas, Iowa, Kentucky	59.2	Massachusetts	52.1
North Dakota	59.1	California	52.7

Chart VI illustrates the states with the highest and lowest average percentages of population over 65 years of age.

Chart VI

Population Over 65 Years of Age
(National Avg.: 12.5%)

State	Highest	State	Lowest
Florida	18.3%	Alaska	4.1%
Pennsylvania	15.4	Utah	8.7
Iowa	15.3	Colorado	10.0
W. Virginia, Iowa	15.0	Texas, Georgia	10.1
Arkansas	14.9	Wyoming	10.4

Chart VII illustrates the states with the highest and lowest average percentages of Owner Occupied Housing.

Chart VII

Owner Occupied Housing
(National Avg.: 65.4%)

State	Highest	State	Lowest
West Virginia	74.1%	District of Columbia	38.9%
Minnesota	71.8	New York	52.2
Mississippi	71.5	Hawaii	53.9
Michigan	71.0	Nevada	54.8
Pennsylvania	70.6	California	55.6

Chart VIII illustrates the states with the highest and lowest median house value.

Chart VIII

Median House Value
(National Avg.: $84,209)

State	Highest	State	Lowest
Hawaii	$245,300	South Dakota	$45,200
California	195,500	Mississippi	45,600
Connecticut	177,800	Iowa	45,900
Massachusetts	162,800	Arkansas	46,300
New Jersey	162,300	West Virginia	47,900

Chart IX illustrates the states with the highest and lowest median monthly rent.

Chart IX

Median Monthly Rent
(National Avg.: $350)

State	Highest	State	Lowest
Hawaii	$599	Mississippi	$215
California	561	West Virginia	221
New Jersey	521	Alabama	229
Connecticut	510	Arkansas	230
Massachusetts	506	South Dakota	242

Chart X shows the states with the highest and lowest per capita income.

Chart X

1990 Per Capita Income
(National Avg.: $18,685)

State	Highest	State	Lowest
Connecticut	$25,358	Mississippi	$12,735
New Jersey	24,968	West Virginia	13,747
District of Columbia	23,491	Utah	14,083
Massachusetts	22,642	Arkansas	14,218
New York	21,975	New Mexico	14,228
Maryland	21,864	Louisiana	14,391
Alaska	21,761	Alabama	14,826
California	20,795	Kentucky	14,929
New Hampshire	20,789	S. Carolina	15,099
Illinois	20,303	Montana	15,110

Chart XI shows the states with the highest and lowest average unemployment rates for 1990. These figures are from the U.S. Department of Labor, Bureau of Labor Statistics, and were compiled independently of the Census Bureau figures.

Chart XI

1990 Average Unemployment Rate
(National Avg: 5.4%)

Highest		Lowest	
West Virginia	8.3%	Nebraska	2.2%
Mississippi	7.5	Hawaii	2.8
Michigan	7.5	South Dakota	3.7
Arkansas	6.9	North Dakota	3.9
Alaska	6.9	North Carolina	4.1
Alabama	6.8	Iowa	4.2
Rhode Island	6.7	Virginia	4.3
District of Columbia	6.6	Utah	4.3
New Mexico	6.3	Kansas	4.4
Texas	6.2	Wisconsin	4.4

Ethnic Breakdown. The racial and ethnic breakdowns illustrate the potential ethnic vote as opposed to the overall population. The concepts of race and ethnicity as defined by the Census Bureau reflect self-identification and not clear-cut biological definitions.

Chart XII lists voting age and total state population figures for the fourteen states with black populations well above the national average of 12.1% in 1990. Black ethnic classification refers to those persons who indicated their race as Black on the Census questionnaire.

Chart XII

1990 Black Population: Total State Population

State	% of voting age pop.	% of total state pop.	State	% of voting age pop.	% of total state pop.
District of Columbia	62.4%	65.8%	North Carolina	20.1%	22.0%
Mississippi	31.6	35.6	Virginia	17.6	18.8
Louisiana	27.9	30.8	Delaware	15.3	16.9
South Carolina	26.9	29.8	Tennessee	14.4	16.0
Georgia	24.6	27.0	New York	14.7	15.9
Alabama	22.7	25.3	Arkansas	13.7	15.9
Maryland	23.5	24.9	Illinois	13.4	14.8

Chart XIII illustrates the voting age and total population figures for the fourteen states with American Indian concentrations well above the national average of 0.8% in 1990. The American Indian classification includes persons who classified themselves as American Indian, Eskimo, or Aleut.

Chart XIII

1990 American Indian: Total State and Voting Age Population

State	% of voting age pop.	% of total state pop.	State	% of voting age pop.	% of total state pop.
Alaska	13.5%	15.6%	Wyoming	1.8%	2.1%
New Mexico	7.5	8.9	Washington	1.4	1.7
Oklahoma	6.9	8.0	Nevada	1.5	1.6
South Dakota	5.4	7.3	Utah	1.2	1.4
Montana	4.8	6.0	Oregon	1.2	1.4
Arizona	4.4	5.6	Idaho	1.2	1.4
North Dakota	3.1	4.1	North Carolina	1.1	1.2

1506   DEMOGRAPHICS CHARTS

Chart XIV illustrates the voting age and total state population figures for the eight states with Asian concentrations at or above the national average of 2.9% in 1990. The Asian classification includes persons who classified themselves as Asian or Pacific Islander.

Chart XIV

1990 Asian Origin: Total State and Voting Age Population

State	% of voting age pop.	% of total state pop.	State	% of voting age pop.	% of total state pop.
Hawaii	61.3%	61.8%	Alaska	3.6%	3.6%
California	9.2	9.6	New Jersey	3.2	3.5
Washington	4.1	4.3	Nevada	3.1	3.2
New York	3.8	3.9	Maryland	2.8	2.9

Chart XV illustrates voting age and total state population figures for the eight states with Hispanic origin concentrations well above the national average of 9.0% in 1990. The Hispanic origin classification includes three specific categories—Mexican, Puerto Rican and Cuban—as well as those who indicated that they were of other Spanish or Hispanic origin (origin can be viewed as ancestry, nationality group, lineage or country of birth of the person or the person's parents or ancestors prior to their arrival in the United States). Persons of Hispanic origin may be of any race.

Chart XV

1990 Hispanic Origin: Total State and Voting Age Population

State	% of voting age pop.	% of total state pop.	State	% of voting age pop.	% of total state pop.
New Mexico	33.0%	38.2%	Colorado	11.2%	12.9%
California	22.5	25.8	New York	11.2	12.3
Texas	22.4	25.5	Florida	11.7	12.2
Arizona	15.8	18.8	Nevada	9.1	10.4

INDEX

The names of Governors, Senators and Representatives appear in boldface type. The number of the page that includes their corresponding biographical, voting and campaign finance information also appears in bold.

1512   INDEX

1534   INDEX

THE AUTHORS

MICHAEL BARONE is a graduate of Harvard College and Yale Law School. He has been affiliated with the polling group of Peter D. Hart Research Associates, Inc. and has been an editorial writer and columnist for *The Washington Post*. Barone is currently senior writer for *U.S. News and World Report*. He lives with his daughter Sarah in Washington, DC.

GRANT UJIFUSA is a senior editor at *Reader's Digest* magazine in Pleasantville, New York. Ujifusa, a native of Worland, Wyoming and a graduate of Harvard College, lives with his wife Amy and sons Steven and Andrew in Chappaqua, New York. He is also the Strategy Chair for a group associated with the Japanese American Citizens League.

THE PUBLISHER

66The nation's most respected nonpartisan source of information about how Washington policymaking machinery really works.99

That's how *Newsweek* described *National Journal*. For more than 20 years, *National Journal* has reached subscribers with an award-winning weekly magazine noted for its dedication to "facts only" reporting. *National Journal* speaks to people who make it their business to know what's going on in the world's largest business—the United States Government.

Only *National Journal* is exclusively devoted to the coverage and analysis of what the government is doing today, what it's going to do tomorrow, and how its actions affect every facet of our lives.

This 1994 edition of *The Almanac of American Politics* marks the sixth volume to be published by National Journal Inc. In addition to the *Almanac* and *National Journal*, National Journal Inc. publishes the monthly *Government Executive* magazine; *CongressDaily*, a daily fax newsletter covering Congress; the semi-annual directory, *The Capital Source*; and the *National Journal Convention Daily*, in conjunction with the Democratic and Republican Conventions.

National Journal Inc. is a wholly-owned subsidiary of the Los Angeles-based Times Mirror Company.

1730 M Street, NW, Washington, DC 20036 Telephone (202) 857-1400